Dr. ABDUL HAQ

ENGLISH-URDU DICTIONARY

ڈاکٹر عبدالحق

انگریزی۔اُردو ڈکشنری

English to English and Urdu

(over 35,000 words and idioms)

Haq, Dr. Abdul:
ENGLISH-URDU-DICTIONARY

New Delhi, Star.

ISBN 81-7144-032-0

Published by :
STAR PUBLICATIONS (P) LTD.
Asaf Ali Road, NEW DELHI-110 002.

This edition : 1998

Printed in India by J.R.Offset Press, Delhi.

FROM THE PUBLISHERS :

We have planned to bring out a series of dictionaries compiled by prominent scholars in different languages of the world.

THIS DICTIONARY is one in that series, and we hope readers will find it useful.

This is our contribution in bringing various languages of the world together, and closer to English.

Pronunciation and syllabication

a	represents the	*a*	sound in	*man*
ah	...	*a*	...	*far*
aw	...	*a*	...	*fall*
ay	...	*a*	...	*fate*
e	...	*a*	...	*men*
e	...	*a*	...	*note*
e	...	*e*	...	*tern*
ew	...	*eo*	...	*new*
i	...	*i*	...	*sir*
i	...	*i*	...	*right*
o	...	*o*	...	*not*
oh	...	*o*	...	*note*
oo	...	*oo*	...	*boor*
ou	...	*ou*	...	*out*
u	...	*u*	...	*but*
u	...	*u*	...	*put*
dh	...	*th*	...	*the*
g	...	*g*	...	*get*
kw	...	*qu*	...	*question*
r	...	*r*	...	*run*
s	...	*s*	...	*say*
sh	...	*sh*	...	*shall*
t	...	*t*	...	*tell*
th	...	*th*	...	*thin*
y	...	*y*	...	*you*
zh	...	*su*	...	*measure*
r	...	*r*	...	*ofter*

All other letters used for indicating pronuciation carry their normal English sounds
The accented syllables have been italicisea.

ABBREVIATIONS

abb.	abbreviation, (or) abbreviated as
arch	archaic
Bib.	Biblical
Brit..	British
if	compare
Cl. myth.	Classical mythology
coll.	colloquial
esp.	especially
fem.	feminine
fig.	figuratively
Fr.	French
gram.	grammar
Gk.	Greek
i.	intransitive
int.	interjection
leg.	legend
lit.	literary
L.	Latin
masc.	masculine
Norse myth.	Norse mythology
occ.	occasionally
opp.	opposite
orig.	originally
pa. p.	past participle
pa. t.	past tense
poet.	in poetical diction
pr.	pronounced
pr. p.	present participle
pref.	prefix
pron.	pronoun
suf.	suffix
t.	transitive
usu.	usually
U.S.	(in) the United State of America
v.	verb
v.t. & i.	verb transitive and intransitive

PRONUNCIATION & TRANSLITERATION

Pronunciation has been indicated by the following transliteration symbols :

Vowels

ا	*a*
ِ	*i*
و	*ū*
آ	*ā*
اے	*e*
اَے	*ai*
ای	*ī*
او	*o*
اُو	*oo*
اَو	*au*

Consonants :

ب	*b*	ٹ	*ṭ*	ش	*sh*	ں	*ṅ*
پ	*p*	ث	*s*	ص	*s*	و	*v*
ت	*t*	ج	*j*	ض	*z*	ہ	*h*
		چ	*ch*	ط	*t*	ء	*'*
		ح	*h*	ظ	*z*	ی	*i*
		خ	*kh*	ع	*'*		
		د	*d*	غ	*gh*	ھ (یعنی ہائے مخلوط التلفظ)	*h*
		ڈ	*ḍ*	ف	*f*		
		ذ	*z*	ق	*q*		
		ر	*r*	ک	*k*		
		ڑ	*ṛ*	گ	*g*		
		ز	*z*	ل	*l*		
		ژ	*zh*	م	*m*		
		س	*s*	ن	*n*		

a, A (*ay*), (*pl.*) **a's, as** (*ayz*) first letter of the English alphabet ; **A1** (*ay*-wun) very good ; excellent ; بہت عمدہ، نہایت اعلیٰ، بڑھیا

a (*a*, emphatic form *ay*), **an** (*an*) *indefinite article* ایک، کوئی **Note : A** is used before a consonant sound even if a consonant letter is not used ; as *a book* (کوئی کتاب) *a uniform*, (ایک وردی) *such a one* ایسا **An** is used before a vowel sound even if no vowel is used, as *an idea* (کوئی خیال) *an hour* (ایک گھنٹہ)

a, an, *prep.* each, per, فی ; as *Rs. 50 a maund* *20 miles an hour* (بیس میل فی گھنٹہ) (پچاس روپے فی من)

a- (*a*) *pref.* (سابقہ) ہوتے ہوئے میں کے لیے *a-milking* دودھ دوہنے کے لیے دودھ دوہتے ہوئے

aback (*a-back*) *adv.* (of sails) pressed by the wind backward against the mast (بادبان) مستول سے لگے ہوئے
taken aback, surprised بھونچکا، ششدر

abacus (a-*bak*-us) *n.* (*pl. abaci, pr. ab*-a-si) frame with balls on wire used for counting تختہ شمار، گنتارا، بال فریم an abacus

abandon (a-*ban*-dun) *v.t.* leave (*to* somebody) something that has been the object of previous efforts سونپنا go away from somewhere not intending to return to it چھوڑ بیٹھنا give up ہاتھ سے لینا as *don't abandon hope yet* ابھی امید کا دامن ہاتھ سے نہ دو *abandon oneself to*, give oneself up to, no longer control one's feelings, etc. (کا) ہو رہنا (کے پیچھے) اندھا ہو جانا **abandoned** *adj.* given up to bad ways بگڑا ہوا، آوارہ، آوارہ منش ■ We **abandon** what has been the object of previous effort, **resign** an office, **abdicate** a throne, **retire** from a post or a threatened position, **withdraw** from a point of vantage, **vacate** a premises, **quit** something that we leave suddenly, **forego** an advantage or claim, **renounce** a pretension, and **relinquish** something reluctantly.

abase (a-*bays*) *v.t.* bring or make lower in rank, honour, or self-respect ذلیل کرنا **abasement** *n.* تذلیل
■ To **abase** is to bring to a lower position ; to **debase** a character ; to **disgrace** from decent company ; to **degrade** from higher rank ; to **humble** make one feel repentant ; to **humiliate**, make one resent the application of another's superiority.

abashed (a-*basht*) *adj.* feeling ashamed with or without a sense of wrong شرمندہ، شرمسار، خجل، منفعل

abate (a-*bayt*) *v.t.* make less گھٹانا، کم کرنا (law) put a stop to (دستاویز یا کارروائی) منسوخ کرنا *v.i.* become less گھٹنا، کم ہونا، کم ہو جانا **abatement** *n.* تخفیف، کمی، تنسیخ

abattoir (a-*bet*-wah*) *n.* place where animals are slaughtered for use as food مذبح، سلاخ، گؤ کشی خانہ

abbess (*ab*-es) *n.* (fem.) [masc. *abbot*] woman at the head of a nunnery صدر راہبہ

abbey (*ab*-i) *n.* society of monks or nuns راہبوں (یا راہبات) کی تنظیم، جمعیت راہبان building in which they live خانقاہ، دَیر the church of an abbey (موجودہ یا سابقہ) خانقاہ کا گرجا

Westminster Abbey

abbot (*ab*-ut) *n.* (mas.) (fem. *abbess*) man at the head of a monastery صدر راہب

abbreviate (a-*bri*-vi-ayt) *v.t.* to make shorter (a word, story, speech, etc.) مختصر کرنا، اختصار کرنا
abbreviation *n.* اختصار، ایجاز short form of a word, مخفف e.g., *Maj.* for *Major*, *Mr* for *Mister*

ABC (*ay*-bee-see) *n.* the alphabet الف بے، الفبا، ابجد the simplest parts of الف بے، مبادی، مبادیات

abdicate (*ab*-di-kayt) *v.t.* & *i.* give up (throne, position of authority, right, etc.) ; cease to be king (تخت وغیرہ سے) دستبردار ہونا **abdication** (*-kay-*) *n.* تخت و تاج سے دستبرداری

abdomen (*ab*-do-men, ab-*doh*-men) *n.* belly پیٹ، شکم، بطن last of the three parts of an insect's body کیڑے کوڑوں کے جسم کا پچھلا حصہ، جوف شکم **abdominal** (ab-*dom-i-nĕl*) *adj.* پیٹ یا آنتوں کا، شکمی *abdominal pains*

abduct (ab-*dukt*) *v.t.* carry off a young woman or a child unlawfully اِغوا کرنا ، لے جانا ، جبراً غائب کر دینا

abduction *n.* اِغوا

abed (a-*bed*) *adv.* in bed بستر پر ، محوِ استراحت ، خوابیدہ

Abel (*ayb-ĕl*) *Bib.* Adam's son whom his brother, Cain, murdered ہابیل

aberration (a-be-*ray*-shĕn) *n.* wandering away from the right or expected course اِنحراف ، کجروی moral slip لغزش error غلطی ، کجروی mental slip ذہنی لغزش *an aberration of the mind*, mistake caused by wandering attention بے توجہی کے باعث ، سہو

abet (a-*bet*) *v.t.* (*-tt-*) help and encourage to do wrong اعانت جرم کرنا *aid and abet* اعانت جرم کرنا **abetment** *n.* اعانت جرم **abettor** *n.* اعانت جرم کرنے والا

ab extra adv. from outside خارجی ، باہر سے ، بیرونی

abeyance (a-*bay*-ans) *n.* (of right, decision, etc.) temporary disuse معرض التوا *fall into abeyance*, be thus out of use زیر عمل نہ رہنا *(to be) in abeyance*, not at present in force ; awaiting settlement معرض التوا میں (ہونا ، کھٹائی میں پڑنا)

abhor (ab-*haw**) *v.t.* (*-rr-*) hate نفرت کرنا ، کراہت کرنا ، گھن کھانا

abhorrence (ab-*haw*-rens) *n.* extreme hatred نفرت ، کراہت ، گھن something so hated گھناؤنا ، کریہ **abhorrent** *adj.* hateful (*to a person*) کسی کے نزدیک نفرت انگیز ، کریہ ، گھناؤنا inconsistent in character (*to* or *from*) کے متخالف intolerant (*of*) سے بیزار ، سے بے پروا ■ loathe, detest, hate.

abide (a-*bīd*) *v.t.* & *i.* (pa. t. & p.p. *abode*) (*abide by*), be true and faithful to a promise, etc. (قول پر) صادق ہونا (*old use*) live or stay (*at* or *in*) رہنا ، اقامت گزیں ہونا (see also **abode** *n.*) endure, (کسی کو) برداشت کرنا ، روادار ہونا *as I can't abide him* میں تو اس کی صورت دیکھنے کا روادار نہیں

abiding *adj.* (lit.) lasting, never-ending

abidance *n.* (esp.) act of abiding (*by* terms of agreement, etc.) (پر) قائم رہنا ، (پر) عمل

ability (a-*bil*-i-ti) *n.* power of mind, etc. to do things صلاحیت ، قابلیت ، لیاقت ، قدرت *a person of great ability* *to the best of one's ability* مقدور بھر ، حتی المقدور

abilities *n. pl.* clearness of mind استعداد ، صلاحیت

able *adj.* (see below) ■ **ability** is the power to do ; **capacity** is the power to contain. We speak of a person's **ability** but of the **capacity** of a vessel

ab initio adv. from the beginning شروع سے ، از سر نو (used of a boring and tedious narrative)

yet once more ابھی ایک بار

ab intra adv. from within اندر سے ، داخلی طور پر

abject (*ab*-jekt) *adj.* without value, without self-respect ذلیل ، کمینہ ، حقیر ، پست *an abject apology* (گڑگڑا کر مانگی ہوئی معافی) deserving contempt نفرت انگیز ، رذیل ، قابل نفرت as *object behaviour* نفرت انگیز رویہ wretched (condition) (حالت) پست ، حقیر ، ذلیل ، سخت *in abject poverty* سخت افلاس کی حالت میں **abjection, abjectness** *n.* wretched state پستی ، ذلت

abjure (ab-*joo-ĕ**) *v.t.* swear to give up (a belief, opinion, etc.) (قسم کھا کر) توبہ کرنا ، تجنا ، ترک کرنا

abjuration (*-ray-*) *n.* ترک ، تجنا ، تیاگ

ablaze (a-*blayz*) *adv.* on fire جلتا ہوا ، شعلہ فشاں ، ملتہب bright as if on fire چمکتا ہوا ، تابندہ ، فروزاں *to set ablaze* آگ لگانا ، شعلہ فشاں کرنا

[1]**able** (*ay-bĕl*) *adj.* capable of ; having the power (*to do* something) قابل ، لائق ، اہل ، عمدہ ، قابل تعریف clever ہوشیار showing skill and knowledge صلاحیت رکھنے والا ، قابلیت والا *an able speaker* لائق مقرر *an able speech* قابل تعریف تقریر **able-bodied** *adj.* تندرست ، زور آور ، طاقتور ، ہٹا کٹا *an able-bodied seaman*, a mariner who has learned all his necessary duties تجربہ کار ملاح ، کار آزمودہ

ably (*ab-li*) *adv.* بخوبی ، بطریق احسن

[2]**able, -ible** (-ĕ-bĕl) *suf.* (for making adj.) (*a*) that which can be کے قابل ، قابل ، کے لائق ، لائق ، جوگ (as : *digestible* قابل ہضم) (*b*) apt to (as : *suitable* موزوں ، مناسب ، موزونیت والا) (*c*) having the qualities of بخش ، پر ، والا (as : *comfortable* آرام دہ) **-ably** (ab-li) *suf.* making *adv.* from *adj.* ending in *-able* after removing their suf. انداز سے ، طریق پر ، طور پر ، سے (as : *suitably* موزوں طور پر)

ability *n.* (see separate entry)

ablutions (ab-*loo*-shĕnz) *n. pl.* a washing of (a part of) the body esp. as an act of religion وضو یا غسل *perform ablutions* وضو یا غسل کرنا

abnormal (ab-*naw**-mĕl) *adj.* not normal, different from what is usual فوق العادت ، خلاف معمول deviating from the type غیر معمولی rare شاذ

abnormality (ab-naw*-*mal*-i-ti). being abnormal فوق العادت ہونا something abnormal فوق العادت شے **abnormally** *adv.* غیر معمولی طور پر ، خلاف معمول

aboard (a-*boh*d*) *adv.* & *prep.* in or into a ship or aircraft جہاز ، کشتی یا طیارے میں *'All aboard!'* all must now get on the ship اب سب جہاز (وغیرہ) میں آجائیں *close aboard* near, beside پاس ، قریب ، نزدیک

abode (a-*bohd*) *n.* (*old use*) house, residence مسکن ، قیام گاہ ، فرودگاہ (see *abide*) *v.i.* (pa. t. & p.p. of *abide*) رہا ، قیام پذیر ہوا

abolish (a-*baw*-lish) *v.t.* stop altogether ; put an end to یکسر ختم کر دینا ، بالکل اٹھا دینا ، رکا دستور ختم کرنا destroy (*e.g.*, war, slavery) منسوخ کرنا ، نیست و نابود کرنا **abolition** (a-bo-*lish*-ĕn) *n.* act of abolishing انسداد being abolished خاتمہ ، انسداد **abolitionist** (a-bo-*lish*-ĕ-nist) a person who wants to abolish something حامی انسداد ، حامی تنسیخ ■ We **abolish** a practice or an institution, **annul** a decision, **repeal** a law, **abrogate** a constitution, **revoke** a licence, **cancel** or **countermand** an order for goods, **quash** a lower court's decision, and **rescind** an order temporarily.

abominate (a-*bom*-i-nayt) *v. t.* feel great hatred for سخت نفرت کرنا dislike سخت ناپسند کرنا

abominable *adj*. causing much hatred, hateful نفرت انگیز، کریہ **abomination** (*-nay-*) *n*. feeling of hatred نفرت، استکراہ something causing that feeling کریہ، کریہ منظر، گھناؤنا

a bon marche (*Fr. ph.*) cheap, a good bargain سستا، ارزاں، اچھا سودا

aboriginal (a-bo-*rij*-i-nĕl) *adj*. indigenous (plant, animal, person, race, etc.) اصلی، قدیمی، قدیم *n*. aboriginal inhabitant قدیم باشندہ **aborigines** (-neez) aboriginal race or inhabitants قدیم باشندے اصلی باشندے، اصلی آبادی

abortion (a-*bo**-shĕn) *n*. giving birth before the right time اسقاط unsuccessful attempt ناکامی عدم تکمیل arrested development ادھورا پن creature so produced, usu. mis-shapen نیم ساختہ، کچا **abortive** (a-*bo**-tiv) *adj*. coming too soon قبل از وقت imperfect ادھورا، کچا unsuccessful ادھورا، کچا، ناقص، ناکام کوشش، سعی لاحاصل *abortive attempt* (جان) آزاشکان، لاحاصل، ناکام

abound (a-*bound*) *v.i*. be plentiful (*in*) (سے) بھرپور ہونا (کی) بہتات، کثرت یا افراط ہونا *The river abounds in fish* دریا میں مچھلیوں کی بہتات ہے be plentifully stocked (*with*) میں بڑی تعداد میں ہونا میں کثرت سے ہونا *The college library abounds with old manuscripts* کالج کے کتب خانے میں پرانے مسودات کثرت سے ہیں

about (a-*bout*) *adv*. here and there ; on all sides ; not far away یہیں کہیں، ادھر اُدھر، ہر طرف، اِرد گِرد nearly تقریباً *about to*, just going to (کی) والا (کی) کو *come about*, happen رونما ہونا، وقوع پذیر ہونا *bring* (*something*) *about*, cause (it) to happen عمل میں لانا، (کا) باعث بننا *be going about*, be passing from one person to another گردش میں ہونا، مشہور ہونا *the news is going about that* خبر گرم ہے کہ *prep*. of, concerning کے متعلق، کی بابت، کے بارے میں here and there an on all sides ; not far away (کے) قریب (کے) چاروں طرف

about turn *v*. drill caution to turn about اُلٹے پھرو، برگرد *right about turn*, turn about by moving towards the right دائیں سے اُلٹے پھرو، راست برگرد

above (a-*buv*) *prep*. higher than ; over (سے) اونچا (کے) اوپر beyond (کے) پہنچ سے پرے، ماورا too great, good or different from بالاتر، کہیں بلند، کثیر، مختلف *above criticism* تنقید سے بالا greater in number or amount (سے) زیادہ (سے) بڑا *children above a certain age* ایک خاص عمر سے *be above oneself*, (colloq.) think oneself better or cleverer than others, be too proud of oneself اپنے کو بہت سمجھنا، اپنے متعلق خوش فہمی میں مبتلا ہونا *above all*, more than anything else سب سے بڑھ کر یہ کہ *adv*. over one's head سر کے اوپر، بالکل اوپر before or earlier پہلے، آگے in heaven عالم بالا میں، عرش پر

above-board (a-*buv bohd*) *adj*. & *adv*. honest, straightforward, without any trick راستباز، دیانتدار، برملا، بے لوث، دیانتدارانہ

above-mentioned *adj*. mentioned before (in the same page, book, etc.) مذکورہ، مذکورہ بالا، مذکورۂ متذکرہ

☐ **Above** means higher than, without touching ; when it touches, it is **on** or **upon** ; when it is exactly above it is **over** : when it is high but past the object, it is **beyond**.

ab ovo adv. from the beginning شروع سے

abrade (a-*brayd*) *v.t*. rub away رگڑ دینا، رگڑ ڈالنا، چھیلنا **abrasion** (a-*bray*-zhĕn) *n*. a rubbing away رگڑنا painful, rubbed place on the skin رگڑ، خراش **abrasive** *adj*. rubbing خراش لگانے والا *n*. material used for rubbing (*e.g.*, sand-paper) رگڑ کر صاف کرنے والی شے (مثلاً ریگ مال)

abreast (a-*brest*) *adv*. (persons or ships moving) side by side in the same direction برابر، ساتھ ساتھ، ہم دوش *abreast of*, level with, not behind کے برابر *abreast of* (or *with*) *the times*, up-to-date, knowing (and practising) the modern ideas زمانے کے ساتھ ساتھ، زمانے کے دوش بدوش

Walking four abreast

abridge (a-*brij*) *v.t*. make a book or story shorter خلاصہ لکھنا، تلخیص کرنا **abridgement** *n*. making shorter تلخیص something made shorter خلاصہ، ملخص

☐ We **abridge** something by rewriting it briefly. **abbreviate** a word in writing or printing, **shorten** something that is already long, and **curtail** one's rights, speech, leave, etc., by cutting them short.

abroad (a-*brawd*) *adv*. out of the house گھر سے باہر out of one's own country ملک سے باہر، پردیس میں *go* (*be, live, travel*) *abroad*, go to another country پردیس جانا *from abroad*, from a foreign land بدیس سے، غیر ممالک، ممالک خارجہ سے everywhere in all directions ہر طرف، دُور دُور at large کھلے بندوں *there is a rumour abroad that*, people are saying that افواہ پھیلی ہوئی ہے *the schoolmaster is abroad*, there is a campaign for mass education تعلیم کو عام کرنے کی مہم شروع ہے *all abroad* خیالات میں بھٹکا ہوا، کہیں کا کہیں، غلط *n*. foreign land بدیس

abrogate (*ab*-roh-gayt) *v.t*. cause (law or power) to cease ; put an end (to a custom) منسوخ کرنا، ختم کرنا اٹھا دینا **abrogation** (*-gay-*) *n*. putting an end to (law, custom, etc.) منسوخی، تنسیخ، خاتمہ

abrupt (ab-*rupt*) *adj*. sudden, unexpected اچانک، یکایک، ناگہاں *abrupt turns in a road*, sudden bends سڑک کے اچانک موڑ steep, rough نشیبی، ڈھالو *abrupt fall* کراڑا، خطرناک ڈھلان impolite (manner) اکھڑ پن، بے ڈھنگا پن **abruptly** *adv*. اچانک، یکایک، دفعتاً، ناگہاں **abruptness** *n*. نشیب، اکھڑ پن

abscess (*ab*-ses) *n*. collection of pus in the body پھوڑا، دُنبل

abscond (ab-*skond*) *v.i*. go away suddenly, secretly and with awareness of wrong (*with* somebody) (کے ساتھ) فرار ہونا، بھاگ جانا، رُوپوش ہو جانا

absence (*ab*-sens) *n*. state of being absent غیر حاضری، عدم موجودگی، غیاب

absent (*ab*-sent) *adj.* not present, not here, غیر حاضر، غائب موجود نہ ہونا، غیر حاضر ہونا، غائب ہونا *v. t.* (ab-*sent*) *absent oneself from*, not be present at موجود نہ رہنا، نہ جانا، نہ آنا **absent-minded** *adj.* not thinking what one is doing (خیالات میں) کھویا ہوا، گم، محو، مستغرق، غافل، پراگندہ دماغ

absentee (ab-*sen*-tee) *n.* one who is (frequently) absent غیر حاضر، غائب باش *absentee landlord*, a landlord who stays away from his land and does not till it himself اپنی اراضی سے غائب رہنے والا زمیندار، غائب باش زمیندار

absenteeism *n.* such practice among landlords (زمینداروں کی) غائب باشی

absinth, absinthe (ab-sinth) *n.* wormwood

absit invidia (*L. ph.*) let there be no ill-will غصہ تھوکیے *absit omen* (*L. ph.*) may this not prove ominous

absolute (*ab*-so-loot) *adj.* one free from control مطلق، مطلق العنان، خود مختار *absolute ruler* مطلق العنان فرمانروا حاکم علی الاطلاق (یعنی خدا) perfect, complete ; *an absolute fool* نرا گاؤدی، نکمبخت، بالکل گدھا real, certain قطعی، یقینی، حتمی *an absolute fact* قطعی حقیقت *an absolute promise* غیر مشروط پکا وعدہ **absolutely** *adv.* completely مطلقاً (colloq.) certainly یقیناً، واقعی

absolution (ab-so-*loo*-shen) *n.* forgiveness (esp. through a religious act) مغفرت، اعلان نجات، معافی، بریت، خلاصی

absolve (ab-*zolv*) *v.t.* pronounce free *of* (sin) گناہ بخش دینا، بخشش کا اعلان کرنا set free (*from* blame, debt, duty, or promise) گلو خلاصی کرنا، چھٹکارا دلانا، معافی دینا، بری الذمہ قرار دینا

absorb (ab-so*b, ab-zo*b) *v.t.* suck up (a liquid) جذب کرنا، سوکھنا، چوس لینا، مدغم کر لینا *absorb learning* علم حاصل کرنا take up or occupy (time, attention) (توجہ) حاصل کرنا، (وقت) لینا *absorbed in a task* کام میں منہمک یا مستغرق

absorbent *n.* & *adj.* (object) tending to suck in liquid **absorbing** *adj.* occupying one's attention completely جاذب نظر، دلکش، دل آویز **absorption** *n.* drinking in of liquids جذب (Note that the word is spelt with a *p* and not a *b* before *-tion*.)

abstain (ab-*stayn*) *v. t.* keep away (*from*) (سے) باز رہنا، پرہیز کرنا hold oneself back (*from* alcoholic drinks, etc.) (سے) پرہیز کرنا، احتراز کرنا، محترز رہنا، اجتناب کرنا

abstainer one who does not take intoxicants نشوں سے پرہیز کرنے والا **abstention, abstinence** *n.* keeping oneself from food, drink and enjoyment عیاشی سے احتراز یا پرہیز *total abstinence*, staying away from alcoholic drink نشے سے کامل پرہیز

abstention *n.* see under **abstain**

abstemious (ab-*stee*-mi-us) *adj.* not drinking or eating much (خورد و نوش میں) محتاط temperate (in habits) (عادات میں) اعتدال پسند **abstemiousness** *n.* پرہیزگاری، محتاط زندگی، پارسائی

abstinence *n.* see under **abstain**

abstract (*ab*-strakt) *adj.* opposite to what is material or concrete ذہنی، خیالی، مجرد، تجریدی *abstract art*, impressionist art expressing itself in lines and contours rather than realistic figures تجریدی مصوری *n.* short account of the ideas of a book, speech, etc. خلاصہ، ماحصل، ملخص *v.t.* (ab-*strakt*) take away, separate from علیحدہ کرنا، نکالنا، اخذ کرنا **abstracted** *adj.* not paying attention, lost in thought محو، منہمک، مستغرق **abstraction** *n.* (state of) being abstracted (خیال میں یا کسی اور خیال میں) ڈوبا ہوا، استغراق، بے خبری، علیحدگی، انتزاع، تجرید idea as opposed to material object مجرد (یا منتزع) تصور unsubstantial things خیالی باتیں، باد ہوا باتیں

abstruse (ab-*stroos*) *adj.* hard to understand مشکل، عسیر الفہم something whose meaning is hidden پیچیدہ، غامض، دقیق

absurd (ab-*sed*) *adj.* very foolish, silly, unreasonable, causing laughter لغو، بے سروپا، فضول، نامعقول، بعید از قیاس، بے تکا، مضحکہ خیز **absurdity** *n.* state of being absurd لغویت، نامعقولیت، بے وقوفی، ابلہی absurd idea لغو، مہمل یا بے تکی بات

S **absurd** (literally off-sounding, *i.e.*, what sounds foolish) **foolish**, as propounded by a fool ; **preposterous**, causing irritation by its excessiveness ; **irrational**, contrary to reason ; **inconsistent**, not agreeing with itself or with something else **ridiculous**, laughable . **paradoxical**, appearing self-contradictory, but not truly so **unreasonable**, contrary to reason.

abundance (a-*bun*-dans) *n.* plenty کثرت، افراط، فراوانی، بہتات، وفور *in abundance*, plenty, more than enough کثرت سے، فراواں **abundant** *adj.* plentiful, rich *in* وافر، فراواں، کثیر، بہت *abundant in* کثرت یا بہتات والا، (کی) افراط **abundantly** *adv.* amply, sufficiently خوب، بہت، کافی

abuse (ab-*yoos*) *n.* wrong or unjust use بے جا فائدہ، ناجائز یا غلط استعمال، ناجائز انتفاع wrong treatment بدسلوکی swear words گالی، دشنام، دشنام طرازی، سخت کلامی *v.t.* (ab-*yooz*) make wrong use of غلط یا ناجائز استعمال کرنا treat badly بدسلوکی، بری طرح سے پیش آنا speak rudely گالی دینا، سخت کلامی کرنا، دشنام طرازی کرنا **abusive** *adj.* using or containing abuse بے ہودہ، بدلگام، غیر مہذب *abusive person* بدلگام شخص *abusive language* غیر مہذبانہ، فحش (یا بازاری) زبان

abut (a-*but*) *v.i.* (*-tt-*) (of buildings) have a common side with or border (*on* or *upon*) (سے) متصل ہونا، (سے) ملحق ہونا **abutter** *n.* owner of adjoining property حق شفعہ والا، ہمسایہ، شفیع

abysmal *adj.* see under **abyss**.

abyss (a-*bis*) *n.* deep hole اتھاہ، گہرائی، قعر bottomless pit تحت الثریٰ hell پاتال **abysmal** (a-*biz*-mel) *adj.* very deep اتھاہ، بے پایاں (often used figuratively) as, *abysmal ignorance*, complete lack of knowledge پرلے درجے کی جہالت

acacia (a-*kay*-shah) *n*. a plant yielding gum arabic کیکر، ببُول، *false acacia* نقلی ببُول *gum acacia*, gum of the acacia tree گوندِ ببُول

acacia

academic *adj*. see under **academy**.

academy (a-*kad*-e-mi) *n*. school for higher, particularly specialized, learning اکادمی، اکیڈمی (کسی خاص فن کی بڑی) درس گاہ، تربیت گاہ (کسی علم یا فن کی اعلیٰ تعلیم گاہ) *military academy* فوجی اکادمی، عسکری تربیت گاہ society of learned men (کوئی قابلِ ذکر علمی، ادبی یا فنی مجلس یا انجمن، اکادمی *the Walliullah Academy*

academic (-ka-*dem*-ik) *adj*. relating to education, or to an academy or other educational institution تعلیمی، درسی، جامعاتی *academic costume*, official robe worn in a university or college; gown, hood, etc. جامعاتی لباس، طیلسان theoretical, rather than practical اصولی، علمی، غیر عملی Platonic (اشراقی (حکمت sceptical تشکیلی

accede (ak-*seed*) *v.i.* agree (*to* a proposal, etc.) راضی ہونا، مان لینا، رضامندی کا اظہار کرنا be appointed (*to* position of authority) کسی عہدے پر فائز یا متمکّن ہونا *accede to the throne* تخت و تاج کا وارث ہونا **accession** *n*. (see below).

accelerando (mus.) with gradually increasing speed (کے، کی) بتدریج بلندی

accelerate (ak-*sel*-e-rayt) *v. t.* & *i.* make or become quicker, تیز تر ہونا یا کرنا، چال یا دَوڑ بڑھانا (cause to) happen sooner جلدی کرنا، زُود تر وقوع پذیر ہونا یا وقوع میں لانا **acceleration** *n*. the act of accelerating (طبیعیات) اِسراع، (فلکیات) تسریع **accelerator** (ak-*sel*-e-ray-tah) *n*. small handle or clutch moved by the foot which regulates the speed of motor vehicle (موٹر کار) مُسَرِّع، رفتار بدل

accent (*ak*-sent) *n*. stress given to a syllable in speaking تاکید، زور، لفظ کے رُکن پر دباؤ particular manner of pronouncing a language; لحن، اہلِ زبان سے مختلف لہجہ *He speaks English with an accent* اس کا انگریزی لہجہ انگریزوں کے لہجے سے مختلف ہے mark put above or below a letter giving it a somewhat different sound value نقطہ، نشان *pl*. (poet.) (شاعری) نطق، کلام ; *v.t.* (ak-*sent*) add stress to a syllable (رُکنِ تہجی پر) زور دینا mark with a written accent (تاکیدی) نشان لگانا **accented** *adj*. stressed (syllable) (تاکیدی بول) موکّد (بول یا رُکن) **accentuate** (ak-sen-tew-ayt) *v.t*. give more force or importance to (word or opinion) پر زور دینا، کو نمایاں کرنا، لہجے میں زور دینا **accentuation** (-*ay*-) *n*. تاکید، زور

▣ To **accentuate** is used mostly in the metaphorical sense; to **accent**, mainly in the literal.

accept (ak-*sept*) *v.t.* consent to receive منظور کرنا، قبول کرنا، ذمّے لینا، لے لینا (عہدہ وغیرہ) believe what is stated یقین کرنا، تسلیم کرنا، قبول کرنا *an accepted truth*, an idea on which all agree مسلّمہ حقیقت **acceptable** *adj*. worth accepting قابلِ قبول، قابلِ تسلیم pleasing and satisfactory; welcome, accepted gladly پسندیدہ، مقبول، مرغوب **acceptance** *n*. the act of accepting قبولیت، رضامندی، پسندیدگی (*pl*.) entries of horses accepted for the day's races دوڑ میں شریک ہونے والے گھوڑے **acceptation** *n*. sense of a word عام معنی، عرفی معنی **acceptor** *n*. one who accepts قبول کرنے والا (*pl*.) acceptances دوڑ میں شریک ہونے والے گھوڑے

access (*ak*-ses) *n*. an entrance or way (*to* a place) راستہ، راہ، وسیلہ، سبیل act of coming (*to* a place or person) رسائی، پہنچ، گزر، تقرّب the right or means to come (*to* a place) رسائی کا ذریعہ، گزرنے کا حق *give access to*, lead into (میں) کھلنا یا ذریعہ، دسترس *gain access to*, reach or speak to (تک) رسائی پانا یا حاصل کرنا، (تک) پہنچ ہونا، (میں) جا نکلنا **accessible** (ak-*ses*-i-bel) *adj*. easy to approach (*to* someone) (کے لیے) سہل الحصول، قابلِ حصول، جہاں تک (کسی کی) پہنچ ہو سکے، جس تک باریابی ہو سکے

accessary (ak-*ses*-ĕ-ri) *n*. helper in (criminal) act شریکِ جرم، ممد و معاون، مددگار ▣ An **accessary** is one who helps a criminal to get away or conceal his crime; an **abettor**. one who encourages another to wrong-doing, an **accomplice**, one who is someone's subordinate partner in a crime.

accession (ak-*sesh*-ĕn) *n*. coming to or reaching power or position تخت نشینی، تقرّر، تقرّب، فائز ہونا *the accession of Aurangzeb (to the throne)* increase (in wealth, etc.) بڑھوتری، اضافہ، افزونی، توفیر.

accessory (ak-*ses*-ĕ-ri) *n*. (usu. used in the *pl*.) an additional helpful thing لازمہ (جمع لوازمات)، متعلقہ چیز (جمع متعلقات) *the accessories of the bicycle*, things like bell, lamp, etc. بائیسکل کے متعلقات

accidence (*ak*-si-dens) *n*. part of grammar comprising rules that govern changes in the forms of words صَرف (as distinct from *syntax*, which see).

accident (*ak*-si-dent) *n*. chance happening اتفاق، اتفاق کی بات، ناگہانی واقعہ unfortunate or disastrous event حادثہ، سانحہ، بلائے ناگہانی، واردات **accidental** (ak-si-*dent*-ĕl) *adj*. happening by chance اتفاقی، ناگہانی، غیر ارادی، نامتوقع **accidentally** *adv*. by chance غیر ارادی طور پر، اتفاق سے، اتفاقاً، اچانک، یونہی ▣ An **accident** is something that happens, generally something injurious; a **misfortune** comes through a series of circumstances; a **mishap** is a trifling accident; a **calamity** is a serious happening causing sorrow to many; a **disaster** is a very serious happening causing a great loss.

acclaim (ak-*laym*) *v.t.* welcome with loud shouts of approval or joy نعرے لگانا، مرحبا کہنا، استقبال کرنا، خوش آمدید کہنا، شادمانی بلند کرنا; *acclaim (someone) king*, make (him) the ruler بادشاہ بنا لینا **acclamation** (ak-lay-*may*-shĕn) *n*. loud and eager assent ہُما ہمی، تاشد، پُرجوش

بلند تائید (usu. *pl.*) loud shouts of joy or praise نعرہ ہائے تحسین

acclimatize (ak-*lim*-a-tīz) *v. t.* & *i.* make used (*to* new climate) (نئی آب و ہوا وغیرہ کا) عادی بنانا get used (*to* new climate or atmosphere) آب و ہوا راس آنا (مجازاً) خوگر ہونا، عادی ہونا، رس بس جانا **acclimate** *v.t.* acclimatize عادی ہونا یا بنانا، آب و ہوا راس آنا **acclimatization** *n.* getting used to new climate آب و ہوا راس آنا

[t] A tree becomes **acclimated**, naturally ; an animal brought from a foreign country becomes **acclimatized**, by human agency. (This distinction is not universally accepted.) For human beings both the words are used colloquially in the metaphorical sense.

accommodate (ak-*om*-o-dayt) *v.t.* give room to جگہ دینا، ٹھہرانا، قیام کا اِنتظام کرنا supply (money, etc.) as a kindness فراہم کرنا، مُروّت کرنا، احسانمند بنانا make a thing fit (کھینچ تان کر) جوڑ ملانا settle a quarrel جھگڑا چکانا، میل ملاپ کرانا، صُلح صفائی کرانا adjust ہم آہنگ کرنا **accommodating** *adj.* willing to fit in with the wishes of others مُصلح جُو، نرم طبیعت، مان جانے والا **accommodation** (-*day*-) *n.* lodging for visitors جگہ، جائے سکونت، مہمان خانہ making things fit تطبیق یکسانی، ہم رنگی adjustment مُطابقت، ہمرنگی، موافقت adaptation میل، موافقت

accompaniment, accompanist *n.* (see under **accompany**)

accompany (ak-*ump*-ė-ni) *v.t.* go with, ساتھ جانا ہم رکاب یا ہم سفر ہونا، معیت میں جانا، ہمراہ ہونا happen at the same time as (something else) بیک وقت واقع ہونا ساتھ ساتھ واقع ہونا play music to support (singer) آواز ملانا، آس دینا، دمسازی کرنا، ساتھ دینا **accompaniment** *n.* something that accompanies لوازمہ، لازمہ act of accompanying ہمرکابی، رِفاقت، مصاحبت music giving support (*to* singer) آس، ساز **accompanist** *n.* one who plays an accompaniment to a singer آس دینے والا، دمساز، سازندہ [s] To **accompany** is to go with, especially socially; to **escort**, as an honour ; to **attend**, wait on respectfully; to **convoy**, to reinforce for safety like a warship going along with mercantile marine

accomplice (ak-*ump*-lis) a companion or helper in wrong-doing (ماتحت) شریکِ جرم، رفیقِ جرم

accomplish (ak-*ump*-lish) *v. t.* to finish successfully انجام دینا، بجا لانا، پورا کرنا **accomplishment** *n.* achievement تکمیل، سرانجام، کامیابی، فائز المرامی (*pl.*) skill in arts like music, painting, etc. کمالِ فن، تہذیب شمع محفل بنانے والی ہُنرمندی *She is a woman of accomplishments* (وہ تو شمع محفل ہے) **accomplished** *adj.* skilled in social arts, like talking, singing and painting باکمال، ہُنرمند [s] To **accomplish** is to finish thoroughly; to **fulfil**, achieve a difficult result ; to **attain** a worthy aim ; to **perform** from beginning to end ; **consummate**, carry past the last stage ; to **perfect** in detail

accord (a-*ko***d*) *n.* agreement موافقت، مُطابقت، اِتفاق ہم آہنگی، خوشگوار تعلقات، اتفاق رائے ; *accord between two countries* دو ملکوں میں بڑے خوشگوار تعلقات ; *of one's own accord*, on one's own خود آپ سے، آپ ہی آپ، از خود، خود بخود ; *of one accord* یکدل، ہم آہنگ *v. t.* & *i.* give (welcome, etc.) دینا، سرفرازی بخشنا (خیر مقدم) کرنا be in harmony *with* ہم آہنگ ہونا، ہمنوا ہونا، میل کھانا **accordance** *n.* agreement مُطابقت، موافقت، مناسبت *in accordance with*, according to کے مُطابق **according** *adv.* *according to* *in* perfect agreement with مطابق، بقدر، حسب in compliance with بموجب، بلحاظ on the authority of بقول، بحکم ; *according to plan* منصوبے کے مُطابق تجویز سے مطابق **accordingly** *adv.* for that reason اِس لیے، چنانچہ، لہذا، بدیں وجہ

accordion (ak-*o**-di-un) *n.* a portable musical wind-instrument comprising folding bellows, keyboard and free metal reeds اکارڈین، ہم آہنگ

an accordion

accost (a-*kawst*) *v.t.* go and speak to or greet a stranger in a street بولنا، مخاطب کرنا، صاحب سلامت کرنا، راہ میں ٹوکنا

accouchement *n.* lying-in ; confinement زچگی

account (a-*kount*) *v.t.* consider, خیال کرنا جاننا، سمجھنا، *account (someone) innocent* (کسی کو) بے گناہ سمجھنا *v.i.* explain satisfactorily and give reason (*for*) توجیہ کرنا، سبب بتانا *That accounts for it*, یہ ہے اس کا سبب *n.* story, description سرگزشت، کیفیت، تفصیل reason, cause وجہ سبب، علت *on account of* کے باعث، کی وجہ سے، کے سبب سے *on no account*, *not on any account*, for no reason صورت میں بھی نہیں، ہرگز نہیں *on this account*, for this reason اِس لیے، اِس وجہ سے computation شمار، حساب statement of money حساب، حساب کتاب use, profit, importance نفع، اہمیت *of no account*, useless لاحاصل غیر ضروری، غیر اہم *take into account*, consider کو حساب میں رکھنا کا خیال کرنا، *turn to account*, make use of سے فائدہ اٹھانا *take no account of*, pay no heed to کی طرف توجہ نہ کرنا *on one's own account*, (*a*) by oneself خود بخود، از خود (*b*) for oneself اپنے لیے *on account*, by way of instalment قسط کے طور پر *go to one's account* مر جانا *give a good account of* (opponents in a game) dispose of (them) successfully (حریفوں کو) خوب ہرانا *open* (or *close*) *an account* (*with a bank*) (کسی بنک میں) حساب (یا کھاتا) کھولنا (یا بند کرنا) *have an account* (*with a bank*) (کسی بنک میں) حساب ہونا *current account* چلت حساب (بنک میں) *savings bank account* بنک میں بچت کا حساب *account books* بہی کھاتہ *draw an account* جمع خرچ کرنا *keep an account* حساب رکھنا *settle an account* حساب صاف کرنا **accountable** *adj.* responsible (*for*), expected to give an explanation (*for*) جوابدہ، ذمہ دار، ضامن، کفیل **accountant** *n.* one who keeps accounts or money مُنیم، مُحاسب *Accountant-General*, chi[f] [o]f the government

accounts department اکونٹنٹ جنرل، صدر محاسب **accountancy** the work of keeping accounts حساب کتاب، محاسبی
accredit (ak-*red*-it) *v.t.* attribute a statement (*to* somebody) ; credit somebody (*with* a statement) (کوئی بات یا کام کسی کی طرف) منسوب کرنا send out an envoy (*to* a person, place, or court, or *at* court *with* credentials) سفیر، ایلچی یا سفارتی نمائندہ بھیجنا، مختار کرنا **accredited** *adj.* duly appointed and accepted as such مامور، تسلیم شدہ، باقاعدہ مختار *accredited correspondent* (*of* a periodical) کا باقاعدہ نامہ نگار **accredition** (ak-re-*dish*-ĕn) *n.* the act of accrediting somebody نمائندہ بنانا، مقرر کرنا یا مامور کرنا
accretion (ak-*reesh*-ĕn) *n.* increase in size by adding bits on اضافہ (نباتات) ہم نموئی matter so added زوائد، ملحقات (نباتات) وصل، ہم نموئی
accrue (ak-*roo*) *v.i.* come as a natural result حاصل ہونا، میسر آنا، (سود) بننا *interest accruing from invested money* لگائی ہوئی رقم پر سود *money which accrues to the invester* روپیہ لگانے والے کو جو سود بنتا ہے
accumulate (a-*kew*-moo-layt) *v. t. & i.* heap together, grow into a mass, انبار لگنا یا لگانا، جمع کرنا فراہم کرنا، (دولت) بٹورنا (cause to) become greater in number or amount (تعداد یا مقدار میں) بڑھنا یا بڑھانا
accumulation *n.* heaping up ڈھیر لگنا یا لگانا accumulated mass, heap, ڈھیر، انبار growth of capital by continued interest (مسلسل سود کے ذریعے) اصل میں اضافہ **accumulative** *adj.* cumulative or over-all (proof evidence, effect, etc.) مجموعی given to hoarding, acquisitive پیسہ بٹورنے والا، دولت کش، زرکش **accumulator** *n.* apparatus for storing electric energy مخزن برق، برقی مخزن
accuracy *n.* see under **accurate**
accurate (*ak*-ew-rit) *adj.* absolutely correct, free from error درست، صحیح exact ٹھیک، ٹھیک ٹھیک careful and exact (*in doing* things) محتاط **accuracy** *n.* the state of being accurate درستی، صحت، صحت و صداقت، سچائی، کھرا پن
accursed, **accurst** (a-*kĕ***st*) under a curse منحوس، ملعون، لعین، لعنتی، مردود hateful نفرت انگیز
accusation *n.* see under **accuse**
accusative (ak-*ewz*-a-tiv) *n.* object مفعول، اسم منصوب *adj.* pertaining to the object مفعولی، نصبی *accusative case* حالت مفعولی، حالت نصبی (Note : *Accusative* is the case used in English to denote indirect object.)
accuse (a-*k-ewz*) *v.t.* say that (somebody) is guilty *of* something کو الزام دینا، پر تہمت دھرنا، کو قصوروار گردانا، کے خلاف استغاثہ دائر کرنا **the accused** *n.* the person (or persons) accused in a court of law ملزم، ماخوذ **accuser** *n.* one who brings a charge against another person الزام عائد کرنے والا، مدعی، مستغیث **accusation** *n.* the act of accusing کو الزام دینا، متہم کرنا *be under an accusation of*, be accused of ; *bring an accusation against* (*someone*), accuse (him) of
accustom (a-*kus*-tum) *v.t.* get used (*to* something) عادت ڈالنا، عادی بنا لینا، خوگر ہونا
ace (ays) *n.* playing card of the value one اکا *the ace of spades* حکم کا اکا *the ace of clubs* (تاش کا) اینٹ کا اکا *the ace of diamonds* چڑیا یا پھول کا اکا *the ace of hearts* پان کا اکا a very good fighting airman who has shot down a large number of enemy aircraft دشمن کے متعدد طیاروں کو تباہ کرنے والا ہوا باز smallest possible amount بہت ہی کم (only in the phrase) *within an ace of*, on the verge of تھوڑے یا بال برابر فاصلے پر
acerbity (a-*sĕ***r*-bi-ti) *n.* sourness ترشی، کھٹاس ill-temper shown in the looks or speech ترش روئی، تیزی، تندی، بگڑے تیور، تلخ کلامی
Aceste (a-*ses*-tee), **Alcestis** (al-*ses*-tis) *Cl. myth.* the faithful wife of the Argon Naut, Admetus, who cheerfully sacrificed her life to save her husband's whom the Fates had promised that he would not die if someone died for him. Hercules brought her back from Hades
acetic (a-*seet*-ik, a-*set*-ik) *adj.* of the nature of vinegar, etc. خلی، سرکے کے متعلق، سرکے کا
acetylene (a-*set*-i-leen) *n.* a colourless gas which burns with a bright flame and is used in bicycle or other lamps اسیٹیلین، خلی گیس
Achates (a-*kay*-teez) *Cl. myth.* Aeneas's armour-bearer and faithful friend اکیٹیز
ache (ayk) *n.* continuous pain مسلسل درد *v.i.* have an ache دکھنا، مسلسل درد کرنا
Acheron (*ak*-e-ron) *Cl. myth.* a river of the lower world اکیرآن
achieve (a-*cheev*) *v. t.* carry out successfully, finish انجام دینا، پورا کرنا، کامیاب ہونا، فائز المرام ہونا، حاصل کرنا **achievement** *n.* act of achieving کامیابی thing successfully done کامیابی، کارنمایاں، بڑا کام something commemorating an achievement تمغہ، امتیاز، نشان ▣ To **achieve** is to bring to a head a difficult result (indirectly connected with the word "chief," a head) ; to **accomplish** or **fulfil** is to bring to completion ; to **attain** a worthy aim is to come to the point of holding it ; to **perform** is to do from beginning to end ; to **perfect** is to do thoroughly ; to **consummate** is to pass the last stage of.
Achilles (a-*kil*-eez) *Cl. myth.* the bravest Greek in the Trojan war. His mother, Thetis, had made his body invulnerable by dipping him, as a child, in the Styx. Only his right heel, by which she held him at that time, remained vulnerable. He was treacherously killed by the Trojan prince Paris, who shot an arrow mortally wounding him in the heel اکلیز

achromatic (a-kro-*mat*-ik) *adj*. colourless بے رنگ *achromatic film* بے رنگ فلم
acid (*ay*-sid) *n*. a class of chemical substances sour in taste تیزاب ، ترشہ ، حامض any strong, sour liquid *the acid test*, (*a*) the test of pure gold with the help of acid سونا پرکھنے کا تیزابی امتحان (*b*) infallible test حقیقی معیار ، اصلی امتحان *adj*. having the properties of an acid تیزابی ill-tempered ترش رو **acidify** *v.t.* to convert into an acid تیزاب بنانا تحمیض **acidity** (a-*sid*-i-ti) *n*. the quality of being acid or sour تیزابیت ، ترشوئیت ، حموضت
Acis (ay-sis) *Cl. myth*. son of Fannus. He was loven by Galatea, and was crushed under a rock by the Cyclops, Polyphemus, who happenod to be his rival. ایسس
ack-ack (ak-*ak*) *adj*. (*slang*) anti-aircraft (gun, fire, etc.) طیارہ شکن ، ہوا مار
acknowledge (ak-*nol*-ij) *v.t.* recognize something as true ماننا ، قبول کرنا ، تسلیم کرنا ، بجا سمجھنا consider (*to be* an expert, etc.) سمجھنا ، خیال کرنا send news that one has received something رسید دینا ، وصول ہونے کی اطلاع دینا **acknowledgement, acknowledgment** *n*. something given or sent in reply to something received رسید *registered acknowledgment due*, (letter, packet, etc.) sent per registered post the acknowledgment of which is expected by return post رسید طلب رجسٹری ، رسید طلب تسیل a gift given as a sign of gratitude *in acknowledgment of*, in recognition of کے اعتراف میں ، کے صلے میں

(■) We **acknowledge** a claim or the receipt of something; we **admit** it when we recognize it is true, without implication of guilt; we **confess** a guilt; we **own** something as personal; we **avow** it boldly.

acme (*ak*-mi) *n*. highest point (*of*) greatest amount (*of*) انتہا ، اوج ، نقطۂ عروج *the acme of perfection* اوجِ کمال
acne (*ak*-ni) *n*. pimple مہاسہ
aconite (*ak*-o-nit) *n*. a poisonous plant جدوار its essence, etc. جدوار کا ست
acorn (*ay*-kaw*n) *n*. fruit of the oak بلوط کا پھل
acoustic (a-*kows*-tic, a-*koos*-tik) *adj*. of the sense of hearing آواز کا ، سماعی **acoustics**, (*pl*. treated as *sing*.) the science of sound آواز ، علمِ آواز
acquaint (a-*k-waynt*) *v.t.* make known or familiar (*with*) آگاہ کرنا ، مطلع کرنا ، اطلاع دینا *acquaint oneself with*, learn آگاہ ہونا ، جاننا ، مطلع ہونا *be acquainted with*, have met personally (سے) واقف ہونا ، شناسا ہونا *acquaint one with the facts*, tell him کسی کو حقائق سے آگاہ کرنا **acquaintance** *n*. slight personal knowledge واقفیت ، شناسائی *make the acquaintance of*, get to know کا شناسا ہونا ، سے واقفیت ہونا a person whom one has met but who is not one's close friend واقف ، شناسا

(■) An **acquaintance** with somebody or something is through personal contact; **intimacy** is close and continued relation; **familiarity** with a person is treating him as a member of the family, without special respect; **association** with a person is in business or formal way.

acquiesce (a-kwi-*es*) *v.i.* to agree silently without protest چپ چاپ مان لینا ، رضامند ہونا ، راضی ہونا ، متفق ہونا *He acquiesced in the arrangements* وہ ان انتظامات پر متفق تھا **acquiescence** *n*. the act of acquiescing رضامندی ، منظوری ، اتفاق **acquiescent** *adj*.
acquire (a-*kwi*-ĕ*) *v.t.* gain by ability اکتساب کرنا ، پیدا کرنا **acquirement** *n*. acquiring حصول ، اکتساب something acquired کمائی ، حاصل skill ability ہنر ، علم ، لیاقت ، استعداد **acquisition** (-*zishn*) *n*. acquirement حصول ، تحصیل ، اکتساب ، دستیابی **acquisitive** *adj*. eager to acquire حصول کا متمنی ، حریص

(■) An **acquirement** is an acquired charm or ability; an **acquisition** is a thing of value acquired; an **achievement** is of a difficult object; an **attainment** is of a worthy aim; **accomplishment** is of a social grace.

acquit (a-*kwit*) *v.t.* (-*tt*-) declare not guilty بری کرنا ، رہا کرنا ، چھوڑنا clear from obligation بری الذمہ قرار دینا *acquit oneself* (well) (of a task), do one's duty well, to behave well فرض سے بطریق احسن عہدہ برآ ہونا **acquittal** *n*. setting free by declaring not guilty, discharge from debt بریت **acquittance** *n*. release from debt بے باقی ، فارغ خطی ، رسید
acre (*ay*-ke*) *n*. 4840 square yards of land ایکڑ ، دو بیگھہ ، بکلہ *acres* (*pl*.) زمین ، اراضی *God's acre*, burial ground قبرستان ، گورستان *broad acres* وسیع اراضی
acreage (*ay*-ker-ij) the number of acres in a piece of land (ایکڑوں میں) رقبہ *a man of many acres, a man of broad acres* بڑا زمیندار **acred** *adj*. having land زمین والا
acrid (*ak*-rid) *adj*. pungent, bitter of smell or taste دھانس دینے والا surly, bad-tempered جھلا ، درشت خو ، تنک مزاج **acridity** (-*rid*-) *n*. sharpness of taste تیزی ، تلخی ، دھانس ill-temper جھلاہٹ ، درشتی ، تنک مزاجی **acrimonious** *adj*. see under **acrimony**
acrimony (*ak*-ri-mo-ni) *n*. bitterness of words or temper تلخ کلامی ، تند مزاجی **acrimonious** (-*moh*-ni-us) *adj*. bitter (words, temper, etc.) تند ، تلخ ، تیز
acrobat (*ak*-ro-bat) *n*. person who can do clever things with his body like walking on a rope or twisting himself about بازی گر ، نٹ (مجازاً) سیاسی گرگٹ ، سیاسی قلابازیاں کھانے والے political opportunist or turncoat **acrobatic** (-*bat*-) *adj*. relating to an acrobat بازی گرانہ **acrobatics** *n*. (*pl*.)

tricks of an acrobat بازی گری
acronym *n.* see Addenda
acropolis (ak-*rop*-o-lis) *n.* fortified part of ancient Greek cities, esp. of Athens قدیم یونانی بالاحصار
across (ak-*raws*) *adv.* & *prep.* from one side to the other پھیلا ہوا، چوڑا، وسیع *The river is a mile across here* دریا کا پاٹ یہاں پورا ایک میل ہے on the other side of کے پار، آرپار *across the river* دریا کے پار ہونا *go across* پار اُترنا، پرلے پار جانا، دریا پار ہونا in the form of a cross صلیب نما، چلیپائی، آڑا، ترچھا *stand with arms across* بازو سینے پر باندھے کھڑا ہونا *come* (or *run*) *across* (*someone*), meet (him) by chance سے مڈبھیڑ ہونا
acrostic (ak-*raws*-tik) *n.* a game in which one has to find certain words and rearrange their letters to make new ones توشیح بازی a poem in which the first letters of the succeeding lines make a word توشیح، صنعت موشحہ
act (akt) *n.* thing done کام، فعل، کارروائی doing کام، کاج، فعل، عمل *in the act of*, while doing it کے دوران میں law ایکٹ، قانون one of the chief divisions of a drama * ایکٹ، حصّہ، باب *an act of God*, the result of natural forces, harm done by wind, storm, etc. مشیّتِ ایزدی، خدائی کام، قدرت کا کام *act of faith* ... *an act of grace*, a thing done out of sheer kindness لطف و کرم، احسان *v.t.* & *i.* do something کرنا، کام کرنا، عمل کرنا *act as an interpreter* ترجمانی کے فرائض انجام دینا behave رویّہ اختیار کرنا، رکھنا *you acted very foolishly* تم نے بڑا احمقانہ رویّہ اختیار کیا ... take part in play اداکاری کرنا، پارٹ کرنا، ڈرامے ... pretend جھوٹ موٹ کا کام کرنا، بناوٹ یا فلم میں کام کرنا *She is not really crying; she is only acting* اُس کی چیخ پکار محض بناوٹی ہے، حقیقی نہیں *act on*, (of medicine) have an effect on ... *act on* (or *upon*) (advice or suggestion), do what is suggested (پر) عمل کرنا *act up to* (کے مطابق) نباہنا، کاربند ہونا *act up to one's reputation*, do as one is expected to do توقعات پر پورا اُترنا **acting** *adj.* officiating عوضی، قائم مقام *n.* art of play-acting; histrionics اداکاری ■ **To do** is the common, everyday word; to **act** is a dignified Latin derivative; to **perform** is to do from beginning to end; to **operate** is to put or get into action; to **execute** is to carry out something already decided. We **transact** a business, **exercise** a right, **pursue** a course of action, and **practise** an art in which we are growing more and more skilled. An **act** is a complete unit of action, an **action** is the doing of an act without regard to completion, and a **deed** is the result of an act.
Actaeon (ak-*tee*-on) *Cl. myth.* the hunter who accidentally saw Diana and her nymphs bathing. The enraged goddess changed him into a stag and he was torn to pieces by his own hounds اکٹیون
action (*ak*-shèn) *n.* work کام، عمل، فعل، کارروائی effect اثر، فعل *take action*, begin to do something کارروائی کرنا *put in action* عمل میں لانا *unprincipled action* بے اصولی بات، بدمعاملگی natural work فعل، وظیفہ، کام way of action ادا، اطوار (see also **acting** *n.*) movement (as opposed to *rest*) حرکت، عمل، چال *out of action*, not able to work ... *a time for action*, the right time for doing something وقتِ عمل، کچھ کرنے کا وقت battle لڑائی، جنگ، میدانِ کارزار *be in action*, be fighting on the front میدانِ کارزار میں ہونا *be slain* (or *killed*) *in action*, die in battle لڑائی میں مارا جانا، کھیت رہنا (law) suit دعویٰ، مقدمہ، نالش، قانونی کارروائی، قانونی چارہ جوئی *bring an action against* (*a person*), seek judgment against (him) in a court of law کسی کے خلاف قانونی چارہ جوئی کرنا، مقدمہ دائر کرنا **actionable** *adj.* that for which legal action can be taken against (someone) قابلِ مواخذہ، قابلِ گرفت
activate *v.t.* & *i.* make radio-active تابکار بنانا
active (*ak*-tiv) *adj.* working, at work سرگرم quick and full of life ہوشیار، چست، پھرتیلا *an active life* مستعد زندگی practical, effective ... *take an active part in* عملی حصّہ لینا *on active service*, on the battle front میدانِ کارزار میں، لڑائی پر، محاذ پر *active voice*, (grammar) the form of verb which shows that the real subject of the verb is doing something فعلِ معروف **activity** *n.* (see below)
■ **Active** denotes one who acts quickly or habitually, **energetic**, full of energy; **industrious**, fond of work; **alert**, wide-awake; **agile**, able to move lightly, **busy**, doing much; **diligent**, always busy; **nimble**, quick-moving (wit. fingers); **spry**, wide awake; **supple**, flexible; **lively**, full of life.
activity (ak-*tiv*-i-ti) *n.* the state of being active عمل، مستعدی، سرگرمی (usu. *pl.*) purpose about which somebody is active میدانِ عمل، سرگرمیاں *extra-curricular activities*, activities of students in addition to their study; (تعلیمی اداروں میں طلبہ کی) خارج از نصاب سرگرمیاں *outdoor activities* کھیل وغیرہ
actor (*ak*-tĕ*) *n.* a man who acts in a theatre or (moving) picture اداکار، ممثّل **actress** (*ak*-tres) *n.* woman actor اداکارہ، ممثّلہ ■ An **actor** is a professional player; an **artiste** (a-teest) is a professional singer and dancer; a **player**, in a particular production or game; a **star**, one whose name appears on the bills before the name of the play; an **extra**, one playing a small bit or part; a **character**, one who portrays a type; a **comedian**, one who usu. acts in comedies; a **tragedian**, one who usu. acts in tragedies.
actual (*ak*-tew-èl) *adj.* real, not imagined

actuality (*-al-*) *n.* reality, حقیقت، حقیقی، واقعی، اصل realism واقعیت **actualize** *v.t.* realise in action جامۂ عمل پہنانا treat realistically امر واقع سمجھنا **actualization** *n.* جامۂ عمل پہنانا، امر واقع سمجھنا۔

actually *adv.* really in fact دراصل، درحقیقت، فی الواقع *He actually spoke !* he really did speak though nobody expected him to do so وہ بھی بولا، ارے ہاں! وہ بھی بولا۔

actuary *ak*-tew-e-ri) *n.* one who calculates the rate of insurance premium بیمے کا حساب کرنے والا، ماہر بیمہ

actuate (*ak*-tew-ayt) *v.t.* to cause to act اکسانا، برانگیختہ کرنا، ترغیب دینا، باعث ہونا، شہ دینا۔ to have an effect on اثرانگیز ہونا

acute (a-*kewt*) *adj.* sharp (pain) keen (feelings) شدید درد، پرجوش جذبات responding quickly, clearsighted, clever ذہین، ذکی، تیز، حساس، ذکی، تیز فہم *an acute brain, an acute observer* تیز فہم، ہوشیار، ہوشمند، صاحب فراست (illness) coming quickly to a crisis (as opposed to *chronic*) مرض حار (بہ مقابلہ مرض مزمن) (geometry) acute angle, one less than **90** degrees زاویہ حادہ **acutely** *adv.* **acuteness** *n.*

-ad *suf.* towards کی طرف، کی جانب

ad (see under **advertisement**)

adage (*a*-dij) *n.* proverb, maxim, wise old saying مقولہ، مثل، ضرب المثل، کہاوت

adagio (a-*dah*-ji-oh) *n.* slow movement in music مدھم، رساں *adj.* (in music) slow *adv.* (in music) slowly دھیرے دھیرے، رساں رساں

Adam (*ad*-am) *n.* the first man آدم *Adam's apple,* the protruding part of a man's throat کنٹھ، کنٹھا *Adam's ale, Adam's wine,* water پانی *not to know a person from Adam,* (colloq.) not to know him at all کسی سے آشنا نہ ہونا، کسی سے واقف نہ ہونا *old Adam* ، جاہلیت، غیرمتمدن حالت، تہذیب سے بیگانگی

adamant (*ad*-a-ment) *n.* a kind of very hard stone سنگِ خارا hard, unyielding (person) سخت (orig.) lodestone سنگِ مقناطیس **adamantine** (*-man*-tyn) سخت، الماسی

adapt (a-*dapt*) *v.t.* change in order to suit, change and fit *to* new use بدلنا، مطابق بنانا، (تقاضوں کے) مطابق بنانا، حسبِ منشا بدلنا، تصرف کرنا، *The Indian Penal Code adapted for Pakistan)* تعزیراتِ ہند (اختیار کردہ برائے پاکستان)

adaptable *adj.* able to be adapted نئے حالات میں ڈھل جانے والا، مطابقت پذیر، تصرف پذیر **adaptability** *n.* fitness for being adapted مطابقت پذیری، مادۂ قبول، صلاحیت **adaptation** (ad-ap-*tay*-shen) *n.* the act of adapting تصرف، مطابقت something adapted متصرفہ، قابلیت دادہ

[S] We **adjust** by making small changes, **arrange** by placing together, **accommodate** by insertion and **adapt** by changing in essential details so as to make fit for a different purpose.

add (ad) *v.t.* & *i.* [S] join, put together, find the whole amount of several numbers (esp. *add up* or *together*) to increase, make greater (esp. *add in*) ملانا، بڑھانا، شامل کرنا say something more مزید کہنا، (بڑھا) اضافہ کرنا "*And I hope you will come,*" *he added* **addition** *n.* (see below) **addendum** *n.* (*pl., addenda*) (an omitted) thing to be added (to a book, etc.) تتمہ [S] To **add** means to put together two or more of the same nature so as to form a whole ; to **join,** end to end ; **unite,** make one ; **unify,** make as one ; **attach,** tie one less important to one more important ; **append,** as a tail or end-piece ; **augment,** make more ; **increase,** make larger ; **sum up,** state in a total ; **prefix,** place before ; **affix,** place either before or after ; **suffix,** place after ; **accrue,** become due

adder (*ad*-ĕ*) *n.* small poisonous snake افعی، سانپ *adder's tongue* ایک قسم کی گھاس، ماگیاہ، افعی زبان

addict (a-*dikt*) *v.t.* عادی ہونا، خوگر ہونا، لت پڑنا **addicted** *to,* in the habit of (drinking or taking other drugs) عادی، لتیا، دھتیا *n.* (*a*-dikt) person addicted to something عادی، لتیا، دھتیا *drug addict* نشہ باز، نشہ کرنے والا، عملی *opium-addict* افیمی، افیونی [S] A person is **addicted** to drugs, **accustomed** to something done by others, **habituated** to something unpleasant, **attached** to something known and cherished, **inclined** to something for which he has natural perference, and **devoted** to his family or to a good cause.

addition (a-*dish*-ĕn) *n.* the act of adding جمع، جمع کا عمل، میزان that which is added اضافہ، بیشی *in addition (to)* مزید براں، علاوہ ازیں **additional** *adj.* extra مزید **additive** *n.* & *adj.* see Addenda

addle (adl) *v.i.* (of eggs) go bad, be unfit for food (انڈا) گندہ ہونا *addled egg,* bad egg گندہ انڈا، خالی انڈا **addle-brained** *adj.* having confused head ; foolish خردماغ، احمق

address (ad-*res*) *v.t.* write the address on a letter (خط پر) پتہ لکھنا، سرنامہ لکھنا، send a written or spoken message لکھنا، خطاب کرنا، مخاطب ہونا، deliver a speech تقریر کرنا، خطبہ دینا *address oneself to a task,* be occupied with it, be busy with it (کسی کام میں) معروف ہونا، لگنا۔ *address a ball* گیند سے نشانہ لینا *address a meeting,* speak at it جلسے میں تقریر کرنا۔ *address a person,* speak to him کسی سے بات کرنا، خطاب کرنا۔ *n.* particulars of place where a person may be found or to which his mail may be directed پتہ، عنوان، سرنامہ speech, discourse, oration تقریر، خطبہ *presidential address* خطبۂ صدارت *inaugural address* خطبۂ افتتاحیہ *address of welcome* سپاسنامہ manner of speaking and behaving طور طریقہ، اطوار، رویہ، اندازِ گفتگو *a person of pleasing address,* well-mannered person پسندیدہ اطوار والا (*pl.*) skill and grace ہوشیاری، مہارت (*pl.*) lover's attention دعوے، اظہارِ محبت، جانکاستی

one's addresses to a lady, love her, court her کسی عورت سے اظہارِ محبت کرنا **addressee** (addres-*ee*) *n*. person to whom a letter is addressed مکتوب الیہ

adduce (a-*dews*) *v.t.* show or bring forward (arguments for or against something) پیش کرنا، لانا، دینا

adenoid (ad-e-noid) *adj*. shaped like a gland غدود نما، غُدہ نما **adenoids** *n. pl.* swollen tissue at the back of the nose اسفنجی منسوجات

adept (a-*dept*) *n*. & *adj*. (one who is) skilled *in* ماہر، فاضل، ہنرمند، پختہ کار، کاریگر

adequacy *n*. see under **adequate**

adequate (*ad*-e-kwayt) *adj*. enough کافی، موزوں مناسب شایاں **adequately** *adv*. sufficiently کافی، پوری طرح **adequacy** *n*. being enough موزونیت کفایت ▣ **adequate** for is equal to a requirement ; **sufficient**, which is enough ; **commensurate** with, of the same measure as ; **suitable** for, of the right nature ; **ample**, entirely sufficient.

ad finem adv. towards the end آخر میں خاتمے کے قریب

adhere (ad-*hi*-ĕ*) *v.i.* stick fast *to* (as with gum, etc.) چپکنا، چسپاں ہونا give support *to* (a view, party, etc.) (بات پر) جما رہنا، (شخص سے) وابستہ رہنا **adherence** *n*. being faithful *to* a party, etc. حمایت، وابستگی، پیروی، طرف داری، ہوا خواہی **adherent** *n*. supporter of حامی، ساتھی، وابستہ، دامن، پیرو، طرف دار، ہوا خواہ likely to stick fast sticky چپ دار

adhesive (ad-*hee*-siv) *adj*. sticky لیسدار، چیپ دار، چپچپا **adhesive tape** چیپ دار فیتہ **adhesion** (ad-*hee*-zhen) *n*. being stuck چپکنا، چپکاؤ، پابندی، وابستگی، پیروی

ad hoc (ad-*hok*) *adj*. (committee, etc.) set up for this special purpose (اس کام کے لیے) مخصوص

adieu (a-*dew*) *int*. & *n*. good-bye, farewell خدا حافظ، فی امان اللہ، خدا کے سپرد، اللہ بیلی (*pl*.) **adieus** or **adieux** (a-*dewz*) make one's adieu, take one's adieu, الوداع کہنا، خدا حافظ کہنا

ad infinitum adj. & *adv*. to infinity, for ever بے انتہا، لا متناہی، غیر مختتم، دوامی *ad interim adv*. in the interval دریں اثنا *adj*. temporary عارضی، ہنگامی

adjacent (a-*jay*-sent) *adj*. lying near ; next *to* (سے) متصل، ملحق، ملا ہوا

adjective (*adj*-ek-tiv) *n*. word added to a noun telling more about it اسم صفت (as *a good, bad*, or *indifferent* student (اچھا، بُرا یا یوں ہی سا طالب علم) *adjective colours* کچے رنگ ; **adjectival** (aj-ek-*ti*-vĕl) *adj*. of or like an adjective توصیفی

adjoin (a-*join*) *v.t*. be next to, be touching something ملحق، متصل یا ملا ہوا ہونا **adjoining** *adj*. next, contiguous (house, room, etc.) ملحقہ

adjourn (a-*jĕ**n) *v.t.* & *i*. put off (a meeting etc. *for the time being* or *to* a later date) ملتوی کرنا *The Assembly (was) adjourned 'sine die'* اسمبلی کا اجلاس غیر معین مدت کے لیے ملتوی ہوگیا *We adjourned to the next room*, we ended our deliberations and moved to the other room ہم اُٹھ کر دوسرے کمرے میں چلے گئے

adjournment *n*. breaking off (of a meeting) التوا **adjournment motion**, resolution calling for the postponement of Assembly, etc., usu. to register a member's protest against its proceeding تحریکِ التوا *table an adjournment motion* تحریکِ التوا پیش کرنا ▣ An Assembly is **prorogued** at the end of a session but **adjourned** only for the time being. It is **dissolved** when it is never to meet again

adjudge (a-*juj*) *v. t.* decide judicially to فیصلہ کرنا، (عدالتی) حکم دینا، قرار دینا، condemn (*to*) (کی) سزا دینا

adjudicate (a-*joo*-di-kayt) *v.t*. & *i*. give a judgment (*upon* quarrel, claim, etc.) محاکمہ کرنا، (عدالتی) حکم دینا **adjudicator** *n*. حاکم، منصف

adjunct (*aj*-unkt) *n*. (usu. in the *pl*.) things added to a more important one متعلقات، ملحقات، زوائد (gram.) any word or clause amplifying the subject or predicating it متعلقات *adj*. joined, added ملحقہ، زائد **adjunctive** *adj*. joining, forming an adjunct الحاقی، زائد

adjure (a-*joo*-e*) *v.t*. pray, ask on oath, charge solemnly (کو) قسم دینا، (کو) حلف دینا (سے) قسم لینا، (سے) حلف لینا، (کا) واسطہ دینا، واسطہ دے کر التجا کرنا *adjure in Heaven's name* (*to do something*) عرشِ معلیٰ کی قسم دے کر کسی کام کو کہنا

adjuration (-*ray*-) *n*. the act of adjuring قسم دینا، قسم کھلانا، حلف oath used in adjuring قسم، سوگند

adjust (a-*just*) *v.t*. set right, arrange, put in order, make a thing fit, make suitable or convenient ٹھیک کرنا، ترتیب دینا، ہم آہنگ بنانا، موافق یا مطابق بنانا، صفائی کرانا **adjustable** *adj*. that which can adjust itself or be adjusted ترتیب پذیر، تطابق پذیر **adjustment** *n*. being adjusted تطابق، تطبیق، انضباط، ہم آہنگی

adjutant (*aj*-oo-tant) *n*. army officer helping the commanding officer اجیٹن، ایجوٹنٹ، نائب، معاون **adjutant-general**, head of a department in the army ایجوٹنٹ جنرل، نائب سالار

ad libitum adv. at pleasure, to any extent جی بھر کے، دل کھول کر، حسبِ خواہش

administer (ad-*min*-is-tĕ*) *v. t.* control or look after (a country, business or estate) نظم و نسق چلانا، انتظام کرنا، بندوبست کرنا put (the laws) into operation (قانون) نافذ کرنا give (justice, punishment, etc.) (انصاف) کرنا، (سزا) دینا give (medicine, oath, etc., *to* someone), cause him to take it (دوا، قسم وغیرہ) کھلانا، پلانا **administration**, (-*tray*-) *n*. government of a country نظم، نظامت، نسق

Administration, the Government, Ministry, or Executive of a country حکومت، وزارت، انتظامیہ management (of affairs, business, etc.) انتظام giving (relief, justice, oath, etc.) قسم دینا، انصاف کرنا **administrative** (*-tray-*) *adj*. relating to administration انتظامی *administrative ability* انتظامی قابلیت **administrator** (*-tray-*) *n*. one who administers ناظم، منتظم، مہتمم، ناظر

admirable *adj*. admirably *adv*. see under **admire**

admiral (*ad*-mi-rĕl) *n*. highest naval officer امیر البحر **admiralty** *n*. (British) department controlling the navy نظارت بحریہ

admiration *n*. see under **admire.**

admire (ad-*my*-e*) *v.t*. look upon with wonder and pleasure سراہنا، پسند کرنا، بنظر استحسان دیکھنا **admirer** *n*. one who approves warmly (*of*) **admiration** (ad-mi-*ray*-shèn) *n*. feeling of pleasure or respect *for* تحسین، توصیف، مدح **admirable** (*ad*-mi-rab-èl) *adj*. worthy of admiration. قابل تعریف، قابل ستائش، بہت عمدہ، بہت ہی اچھا **admirably** *adv*. very well بطریق احسن Ⓢ To **admire** is to look up to a person with wonder and self-effacement; to **respect** is to show esteem for one who is considered one's superior; to **regard** is to esteem an equal; to **approve** or approve of is to like a desirable course of action; to **applaud** is to clap the hands in praise of. We **revere** a superior person of high character and **venerate** somebody who is old or considered to be super-human.

admission *n*. **admissible** *adj*. see under **admit**

admit (ad-*mit*) *v.t*. & *i*. (*-tt-*) allow to enter آنے دینا، شریک کرنا، داخل کرنا۔ *admit (somebody) into a house* کسی کو گھر میں آنے دینا۔ *windows to admit light and air* ہوا اور روشنی کے گزرنے کے لیے کھڑکیاں *admit a boy to* (or *into*) *a school* لڑکے کو مدرسے میں داخل کرنا say unwillingly, confess (something, or *doing* something) اعتراف کرنا، بادل نخواستہ تسلیم کرنا، ماننا (*admit of*), allow space to گنجائش ہونا۔ *It admits of no doubt*, it is certain دریں چہ شک، اس میں شک کی کوئی گنجائش نہیں۔ **admission** (ad-*mish*-ĕn) *n*. the act of admitting داخلہ *I year admission to the college* کالج کا فرسٹ ائیر کا داخلہ *admission free* داخلہ مفت statement admitting something اقبال، اعتراف (*one's*) *own admission*, as admitted by oneself اُس نے خود اعتراف کیا ہے **admittance** *n*. being admitted to a place گذر، داخلہ *No admittance except on business.* کام کے سوا داخلے کی اجازت نہیں۔ **admissible** (ad-*mis*-i-bel) *adj*. that which may be considered or admitted قابل قبول، قابل تسلیم، قابل تقرر، اہل **admittedly** *n*. as generally admitted مسلم طور پر

Ⓢ To **admit** is to recognize as true, without implication of guilt. We confess a guilt, **acknowledge** a claim, or the receipt of something; **own** as personal; **avow** boldly. We speak of **admittance** to a public place; **admission** either *to* a college, school or show, or *of* the truth of a statement without implying guilt; **confession** of guilt; **acknowledgment** *of* a claim, or of the receipt of something.

admix (ad-*miks*) *v.t*. mix with something else میں آمیزش کرنا **admixture** (ad-*miks*-chĕ*) *n*. the act of mixing things امتزاج، آمیزش the result of mixing things

admonish (ad-*mon*-ish) *v.t*. warn someone that he is doing wrong; advise him to do right ممزوج، آمیزہ، ملی ہوئی چیز **admonition** (*-nish-*) *n*. advice or warning about behaviour فہمائش، نصیحت، ہدایت **admonitory** *adj*. containing reproof تنبیہی

ad nauseam adv. to a point of disgust or satiety اکتا دینے کی حد تک، نفرت انگیز حد تک، حد سے زیادہ

ado (a-*doo*) *n*. fuss, trouble and excitement, to-do بکھیڑا، جھمیلا، ہنگامہ، تکلیف، دردِ سر، زحمت *with much ado* بعد از خرابی بسیار، خدا خدا کر کے *much ado about nothing* کھودا پہاڑ نکلا چوہا۔

adobe (a-*doh*-bi) *n*. a sun-dried brick کچی اینٹوں کا مکان، کچا گھر a house made of such bricks

adolescence *n*. see under **adolescent**

adolescent (ad-o-*les*-ent) *adj*. about twelve to eighteen growing up to the state of majority عنفوانِ شباب میں، اٹھتی جوانی میں *n*. such boy or girl* **adolescence** *n*. the state of being adolescent اٹھتی جوانی، الفڑ جوانی، عنفوانِ شباب، نو بلوغت

Adonis (a-*doh*-nis) *Cl. myth*. beautiful youth loved by Venus. During the chase he was killed by a wild boar, and from his blood sprang the anemone ادونس

adopt (a-*dopt*) *v.t*. take another person's child as one's own گود لینا، متبنیٰ بنانا، بیٹا بنانا، لے پالک کر لینا accept (an idea or method) and use it اپنانا، اخذ کرنا، قبول کرنا، اختیار کرنا، چننا، انتخاب کرنا **adoption** (a-*dop*-shen) *n*. the act of adopting اختیار، اخذ و قبول انتخاب **adoptive** *adj*. by adoption اختیاری adopted بنایا ہوا، لے پالک

adoration *n*., **adorable** *adj*. see under **adore**

adore (a-*doh**) *v.t*. worship (God) عبادت کرنا بندگی کرنا، پرستش کرنا، پوجنا love and honour greatly تعظیم کرنا، عزت کرنا، احترام کرنا، اسے اعتقاد رکھنا (colloq.) be fond of پسند کرنا، مشتاق ہونا **adorable** *adj*. worth adoring واجب التعظیم sweet (child, etc.) پیارا پیارا **adoration** (a-do-*ray*-shen) *n*. worship عبادت feeling of great love and respect for

تعظیم، احترام، عقیدت، **adorer** *n.* worshipper ، پجاری lover عاشق، شیدائی **adoring** *adj.* loving (mother, etc.) پیار کرنے والی، شیدائی
adorn (a-*doh*n*) *v.t.* make beautiful آراستہ کرنا، سجانا، آرائش کرنا، سنگار کرنا۔ **adornment** *n.* the act of adorning آرائش، زیبائش۔ something used for adorning زینت، سامانِ آرائش، زیور۔ ◙ To **adorn** is to add something graceful which will produce beauty. with a sentiment of reverence in the act ; to **ornament** is to add material details expected to be admired, often as much for their costliness as for their beauty ; to **embellish** is to add or change details so as to make an appeal to the imagination ; to **decorate** is to add one or a few individual ornaments ; to **deck**, in fine clothes ; to **garnish**, add as a finishing touch ; to **illustrate**, by drawings or pictures, as a book ; to **beautify**, make beautiful.
adsum (L. ph.) I am here ! حاضر جناب، ابیک!۔
adrenal (ad-*ree*-nĕl) *adj.* beside the kidneys ; kidney-like گلوی **adrenal glands** *n.* masses of tissue producing a liquid which tightens blood vessels گلوی غدود **adrenalin** (ad-*ree*-ne-lin) *n.* liquid so secreted گلوی رطوبت
adrift (a-*drift*) *adv.* & *adj.*, (of ships and boats) floating about freely, not under control (زیبہ) اِدھر اُدھر بہتا ہوا، منگرِ گستہ (fig.) at the mercy of circumstances بے بس، حالات کے رحم وکرم پر *turn adrift*, send away from home or employment نکال دینا، دُور کرنا، گھر سے باہر کرنا، ملازمت سے علٰحدہ کرنا
adroit (a-*droit*) *adj.* clever, skilful, چالاک، ہوشیار، مستعد، شاطر۔ **adroitly** *adv.* cleverly چالاکی سے **adroitness** *n.* cleverness چالاکی، مستعدی، ہوشیاری
adulate (*ad*-ew-layt) *v.t.* flatter basely to win favour چاپلوسی کرنا، خوشامد کرنا، تملق کرنا۔ **adulation** *n.* flattery چاپلوسی، تملق **adulator** *n.* flatterer چاپلوس
adult (*ad*-ult, a-*dult*) *adj.* & *n.* grown up (person or animal) بالغ، جوان **adult education, adult literacy** *n.* drive to make unletttered adults literate تعلیم بالغاں (کی مہم)
adulterate (a-*dul*-te-rayt) *v.t.* make impure or poorer in quality by mixing cheaper things آمیزش کرنا، ملاوٹ کرنا، کھوٹ ڈالنا۔ **adultration** (a-dul-te-*ray*-shen) *n.* ملاوٹ، آمیزش **adulterator** *n.* ملاوٹ کرنے والا
adultery (a-*dul*-te-ri) *n.* unfaithfulness of a husband or wife بدکاری **adulterer** *n.* husband guilty of adultery بدکار شوہر **adulteress** *n.* wife guilty of adultery. بدکار بیوی **adulterous** *adj.* بدکار
ad valorem (*L. ph.*) according to the value قیمت کے مطابق
advance (ad-*vahns*) *v. t.* & *i.* move or put forward آگے کرنا یا بڑھانا، پیش قدمی کرنا، پیش کرنا۔ *advance cogent reasons* معقول دلائل پیش کرنا۔ to raise to a higher rank ترقی دینا۔ increase (prices, rates) سا (قیمتیں) یا چڑھنا یا چڑھانا۔ to lend (money) قرض دینا، اُدھار دینا۔ پیشگی دینا۔ *n.* forward movement حملہ، کوچ، اور پیش قدمی rise in price or value قیمت، چڑھنا rise in rank ترقی، برتری loan پیشگی **advances** (*pl.*) attempts to become a friend or lover اظہارِ محبت وسے، پہلے یا قبل *in advance* (*of*), (*a*) in front of (*b*) sooner جلدی *advanced idea*, very new idea, one which is not generally accepted ترقی یافتہ تصور، جدید خیال۔ *advance copy*, prepublication copy پیش نسخہ۔ **advanced** *adj.* superior (person or studies) اُونچا، اعلیٰ، برتر۔ new (ideas) not yet generally accepted ترقی یافتہ، جدید **advancement** *n.* progress (*of*) ترقی، برتری۔
advantage (ad-*vahn*-tij) *n.* gain, profit فائدہ، نفع better position فوقیت، غلبہ۔ *advantage-ground* موقعہ کی جگہ، عمدہ موقع۔ *take advantage of*, make use of fairly or unfairly موقع پانا، قابو پانا، (جائز یا ناجائز) فائدہ اُٹھانا *turn to advantage of*, use so as to profit from فائدہ اُٹھانا *seen to advantage*, seen in a way that shows good points یوں کہ خوبیاں عیاں ہو جائیں، *to the advantage of*, so as to help کے لیے سُودمند، ; *have the advantage of*, gain an advantage over, do better than سے بہتر انجام دینا *you have the advantage of me*, you seem to know me but I do not know you آپ شاید مجھے جانتے ہیں بدقسمتی سے میں آپ سے شناسا نہیں ہوں۔ *take a person at advantage* کسی کو بے خبری میں جا لینا۔ **advantageous** (ad-van-*tay*-jus) *adj.* helpful, profitable مفید، سُودمند
advent (*ad*-vent) *n.* arrival (usually of an important person, especially of Christ) بعثت، بعثتِ مسیح **Advent** *n.* among Christians period of prayer and fasting four Sundays before Christmas کرسمس سے پہلے کے چار اتوار قبل کے روزے اور دعائیں۔ coming of Christ ولادتِ مسیح سے قبل، زمانۂ بشارت
adventitious (ad-ven-*ti*-shes) *adj.* happening by chance ; accidental اتفاقی *adventitious root* اتفاقی جڑ، فالتو جڑ، امدادی جڑ۔
adventure (ad-*ven*-chĕ*) *n.* exciting experience مہم، کارنمایاں، جاں بازی کا کام، جوکھوں کا کام، اولوالعزمی کا کام، طالع آزمائی۔ unexpected experience سانحہ، غیر متوقع بات **adventurer** *n.* one who lives a dangerous (perhaps also dishonest) life مَن چلا، طالع آزما، جاں باز، شاطر، عیار، زمانہ ساز۔ **adventuress** *n.* such a woman جاں باز، طالع آزما یا عیار عورت **adventurous** *adj.* fond of adventure من چلا، طالع آزما یا جاں باز شخص full of danger and excitement خطرناک، جوکھوں کا
adventuresome *adj.* eager for adventure باہمت حوصلہ مند، جاں باز
adverb (*ad*-vĕ*b) *n.* a word added to a verb, adjective or another adverb to tell us something

about it, and answering questions beginning with *how*, *when*, and *where* متعلق فعل **adverbial** *adj*. of or like an adverb متعلق فعل کا

adversary (*ad*-vě*-sa-ri) *n*. enemy حریف، مقابل، دشمن *the Adversary*, Satan شیطان، ابلیس، قدمقابل، مخالف

adverse (*ad*-vě*s) *adj*. not in favour of, against مخالف، مخالفانہ، برخلاف، ناموافق، نامساعد *adverse fate* بدنصیبی، بدقسمتی، تیرہ بختی *adverse wind* بادِ مخالف *adverse criticism* کڑی تنقید، مخالفانہ تنقید **adversity** *n*. misfortune, trouble, آفت، مصیبت، ادبار، نحوست ▣ **hostile**, **unfavourable**

advert (ad-*vě*t*) *v.i.* refer (*to* circumstance, etc.) in speech or writing (کی طرف) اشارہ کرنا، کنایہ کرنا turn the mind (*to*) (کی طرف) ذہن منتقل ہونا

advertise (*ad*-vě*-tīz) *v.t.* & *i*. make known by public notices in newspapers, etc., publicize, give publicity اشتہار دینا، مشتہر کرنا ask for by a public notice (اسامی یا ضرورت) کا اشتہار دینا as to *advertise for a servant* نوکر کے لیے اشتہار دینا **advertiser** *n*. مشتہر، اشتہار دینے والا **advertisement** (ad-*vě*t*-iz-ment) *n*. advertising اشتہار دینا، اشتہار بازی۔ public notice اشتہار Often contracted into **ad** (*sing*.), **ads** (*pl*.) ▣ We pay for **advertisement** but give **publicity** to a thing generally through news items or unpaid notices.

advice (ad-*vīs*) *n*. opinion given about what manner to adopt or what to do صلاح، مشورہ، رائے، ہدایت۔ *a piece of advice* ایک صلاح، ایک رائے۔ *follow the doctor's advice* طبیب کی ہدایت پر عمل کرنا۔ (*pl*.) commercial news تجارتی اطلاعات

advisable *adj*., **advisability** *n*. see under **advise**

advise (ad-*vīz*) *v.t.* & *i*. give advice to صلاح دینا، مشورہ دینا، سمجھانا، نصیحت کرنا give commercial information تجارتی اطلاعات دینا *ill-advised*, unwise غیر محتاط، عاقبت نااندیشانہ *well-advised*, wise مصلحت آمیز، دانشمندانہ **advisable** (-*viz*-) *adj*, wise, that which should be done مناسب قرینِ مصلحت **advisability** (-*bil*-) *n*. wisdom, that which should be done مناسبت، مصلحت دانشمندی **advisedly** *adv*. after having considered the matter قصداً، عمداً، سوچ سمجھ کر، دانستہ، جان بوجھ کر **adviser** *n*. مشیر، صلاح کار

advocacy *n*. see under **advocate**

advocate *n*. (*ad*-vo-kit) pleader, senior lawyer وکیل، پیروکار، حامی، ایڈووکیٹ، مندوب one who pleads a (or another's) cause حامی، مؤید *v.t.* (*ad*-vo-kayt) support, speak in favour of (an idea, cause, etc.) وکالت، تائید کرنا، حمایت کرنا، کے حق میں بولنا۔ **advocacy** (*ad*-vo-kay-si) *n*. speaking in favour وکالت، حمایت، تائید

adze, adz (adz) *n*. a curved tool for shaping large pieces of wood بسولا، تیشہ

Aeaceus (*ee*-a-kus) *Cl. myth*. one of the judges in Hades ایاکس

aegis (*ee*-jis) *n*. patronage سرپرستی، پناہ *under the aegis of*, under the patronage of, sponsored by کی پناہ یا سرپرستی میں *Cl. myth*. (orig.) shield belonging to Zeus ایجس، زیوس کی ڈھال

Aegeus (i-*jee*-us) *Cl. myth*. king of Athens, and father of Theseus. Believing his son to have been killed in the expedition against Minotaur, he threw himself into the sea and died ایجیس *the Aegean Sea*, the sea in which he was drowned بحیرہ ایجین

Aegisthus (i-*jis*-thus) *Cl. myth*. Clytemnestra's paramour ایجسٹھس

aegrotat (ee-*groh*-tat), **aeger** *n*. (in British 'Varsities) certificate that a student is too ill to take the examination (امتحان میں شرکت سے معذوری کے بیے (بیماری کی) طبی تصدیق، طبی تصدیق نامہ

Aeneas (i-*nee*-us) *Cl. myth*. the ancestral hero of the Romans. He is the hero of Virgil's *Aeneid*. A Trojan prince, he was the son of Venus اینیس **Aeneid** (*in*-i-id) Virgil's famous Latin epic narrating the adventures of Aeneas اینیس نامہ

Aeolus (*ee*-o-lus) *Cl. myth*. the king of winds. He kept them under a mountain ہواؤں کا بادشاہ، ایولس بادشاہ

aeon, eon (*ee*-on) *n*. long period of time, eternity ابد، طویل مدت

aerate (*ay*-ě-rayt) *v.t.* put carbonic acid gas into ہوا بھرنا، گیس بھرنا *aerated water* (sweet) cold drink containing carbonic acid gas بوتل، سوڈا، لیمن

aerial (ay-*eer*-i-al, often *ay*-e-ri-al) *n*. wire for receiving or sending radio waves ایریل (لاسلکی کا) ہوائی تار *adj*. of or in the air ہوائی، فضائی *aerial root* ہوائی جڑ thin as air باد آسا، ہوا جیسا لطیف imaginary موہوم، وہمی، فرضی، خیالی، غیرمادی lofty بہت اونچا، فلک پیما

an aerial

aerie (*ay*-ě-ri) *n*. same as *eyrie* (which see)

aero- (*ay*-ě-roh) *pref*. of air ہوائی، ہوا سے متعلق of aviation ہوابازی سے متعلق **aerodrome** (*ay*-er-oh-drohm) *n*. flying ground, airdrome ہوائی اڈہ، فضائی مستقر، طیران گاہ **aeroembolism** *n*. see Addenda **aeronautical** (ay-e-roh-*naw*-tikl) *adj*. relating to flying ہوابازی سے متعلق **aeronautics** *n*. (*pl*. treated as *sing*.) the science of aerial navigation ہوابازی، طیرانیات **aeroplane** *n*. aircraft ہوائی جہاز، طیارہ

an aeroplane

Aesculapius (es-koo-*lay*-pi-us) *Cl. myth*. the blameless physician son of Apollo. Zeus deified him after he had killed him lest, when alive, he should keep men from escaping death altogether اسکولے پئس

aesthetic (ees-*thet*-ik), **aesthetical** *adj*. concerning beauty in art جمالیاتی **aesthete** (*ees*-theet) showing good taste in art خوش ذوق، حسن شناس، بامذاق، ذوقِ جمال والا، جمالیاتی **aesthetics** *n*. (*pl*. treated as *sing*.) branch of philosophy dealing with the study of beauty جمالیات.

aether (*ee*-thĕ*) *n*. same as **ether** (which see)

afar (a-*fah**) *adv*. far off دُور *from afar* دُور سے، دُور دیس سے

affable (*af*-a-bèl) *adj*. easy to speak to جس سے بات کرنا آسان ہو۔ courteous خلیق، خوش اخلاق، بااخلاق، خلق، خوش اخلاق، بامروّت **affability** (-*bil*-) *n*. courtesy خوش اخلاقی، خوش خلقی، مروّت، لطف، تلطّف **affably** *adv*. courteously خوش خلقی سے

affair (a-*fay*-è*) *n*. business matter معاملہ، قضیہ، کام، بات *This is my affair, not yours* یہ میرا معاملہ ہے تمہارا نہیں event تقریب (*pl*.) business, events اُمور، کاروبار *a man of affairs*, businessman کاروباری آدمی *mind your own affairs, do not interfere with others* تمہیں دوسروں کی کیا پڑی ہے، تم اپنی نبیڑو *Foreign Affairs*, relations with other countries اُمورِ خارجہ۔ *'affaire d'honneur'*, *affair of honour*, duel مبارزہ، یلکی۔ *'affaire de coeur'*, *'affaire d'amour'* دل کا معاملہ، عشق و محبت *delicate affair* نازک معاملہ

affect (a-*fekt*) *v.t*. act on, have a result on, have an effect on کام میں لانا، استعمال کرنا، اثر انداز ہونا، *affect* (*someone's*) *health adversely* بیماری وغیرہ لگ جانا صحت پر بُرا اثر ہونا move the feeling of متاثر کرنا pretend بننا، بناوٹ سے کام لینا، تصنّع کرنا، دکھانا، اظہار کرنا *affect ignorance* ناواقفیت کا اظہار کرنا like, love پسند کرنا *She affects bright colours* اسے شوخ رنگ پسند ہیں۔

affectation (a-fek-*tay*-shèn) *n*. unnatural way of behaving تصنّع، بناوٹ *affectation of kindness* جھوٹی مروّت **affected** *a*. pretentious ظاہر دار (شخص)، بناوٹی (بات) **affecting** *adj*. moving, exciting pity دردناک *affecting scene* دردناک منظر اثر آفرین **affection** (a-*fek*-shèn) *n*. love محبت، شفقت، چاہ، لگن، پیار (also *pl*.) *object of affections* مرکزِ نظر، مرجعِ محبت disease بیماری، مرض، روگ *affection of* (*the heart, the lungs, etc*.) دل، سینہ وغیرہ کی تکلیف **affectionate** *adj*. loving پیارا، محبّ، دلی **affectionately** *adv*. lovingly دل سے، چاہتا **Yours affectionately,** form of subscription in letters to relatives آپ کا چاہتا، آپ کا پیارا، آپ کا

Note :—Some verb which is to be qualified by it, as *I am* or *remain* (yours affectionately), is understood or explicitly mentioned before it.

affiance (a-*fī*-ans) *n*. & *v.t*. promise to marry (usually in the passive) دنکاح یا شادی کا عہد، قول، ایسا عہد *be affianced to* کا قول کرنا منسوب یا منسوبہ ہونا۔ منگیتر ہونا

affidavit (af-i-*day*-vit) *n*. written statement made on oath حلف نامہ، تحریری حلفی بیان

affiliate (a-*fil*-i-ayt) *v.t*. & *i*. adopt a son متبنّیٰ بنانا attach (*to* or *with*) سے یا کا الحاق، سے ملحق ہونا *Our college is affiliated to* (or *with*) *the Panjab University*, the Panjab University allows its students to sit for its examinations ہمارے کلیے کا جامعہ پنجاب سے الحاق ہے **affiliation** (-*ay*-) *n*.

affinity (a-*fin*-i-ti) *n*. relationship, especially by marriage قرابت داری، رشتہ داری، رشتہ، تعلق (ازاز بندی) being of the same family تعلق، رشتہ (خاندانی یا نسلی) friendliness دوستی، اُنس، رغبت nearness in natural character (between animals or languages) جانوروں، زبانوں وغیرہ میں مماثلت، مشابہت (chemistry) attraction کشش، الف، میل

affirm (a-*fĕ**m) *v.t*. declare firmly دعوے سے کہنا، باضابطہ اعلان کرنا **affirmation** (a-*fĕ**-may-shèn) *n*. affirming something affirmed (law) solemn declaration in lieu of an oath حلفی اظہار **affirmative** (a-*fĕ***m*-a-tive) *n*. & *adj*. (saying) yes ایجاب، ایجابی *an affirmative answer*, yes ہاں، اقرار *answer in the affirmative*, say 'yes' ہاں کہنا، اقرار کرنا۔

affix *n*. (*af*-iks) prefix or suffix سابقہ یا لاحقہ *v.t*. (a-*fiks*) fix or fasten *to* or *on* چسپاں کرنا، چپکانا، لگانا *affix a postage stamp to a letter*, put a stamp on it ٹکٹ لگانا، ٹکٹ چسپاں کرنا

afflict (a-*flikt*) *v.t*. give pain to ایذا دینا، دُکھ پہنچانا، تکلیفیں ڈالنا **affliction** *n*. pain ایذا، دُکھ، تکلیف sorrow رنج و الم، مصیبت، قہر، بپتا

affluence (-ens) *n*. being affluent امارت، دولت مندی *living in affluence*, being very rich متموّل ہونا، تموّل **affluent** (*af*-loo-ent) *adj*. wealthy, rich متموّل، امیر، دولتمند، مالدار، مالامال، امیرانہ *n*. a stream which flows into another معاون (دریا)

afford (a-*fohd*) *v.t*. spare money or time *to do* (روپیہ یا وقت) نکالنا، استطاعت رکھنا، (کا) مقدور ہونا give, provide, produce دینا، بہم پہنچانا، مہیا کرنا، *afford a chance* (*of doing*)

afforest (a-*faw*-rist) *v.t*. convert into forest, plant with trees شجرکاری کرنا، جنگل لگانا، بن بنانا **afforestation** (-*tay*-) *n*. شجرکاری، جنگل بنانا، بن بنانا

affray (a-*fray*) *n*. breach of the peace by fighting in public کشت و خون، مارکٹائی، دنگا، فساد، جھگڑا

affright (a-*frīt*) *v.t*. (arch.) frighten ڈرانا *n*. fear ہول، دہشت، ڈر، خوف

affront (a-*frunt*) *v.t*. be very rude to somebody, esp. in public برملا توہین کرنا، سب کے سامنے ہتک کرنا، گستاخی سے پیش آنا۔ *n*. public insult برملا توہین، گستاخی *put an affront upon*, or *offer an affront to* (*someone*) کسی کی برملا توہین کرنا

afield (a-*feeld*) *adv*. away from home پردیس میں، گھر سے دُور، وطن سے دُور، گھر سے باہر *go far afield* کوسوں دُور جانا

afire (a-*fī*-ĕ*) *adv*. & *adj*. on fire, aflame, ablaze

جلتا ہوا، شعلہ زن، شعلہ زناں

aflame (a-*flaym*) *adv.* & *adj.* on fire بھڑکتا ہوا، جلتا ہوا *aflame with passion*, شعلہ زن، مشتعل burning with rage مشتعل، غصّے سے بپھرا ہوا

afloat (a-*floht*) *adv.* & *adj.* floating بہتا ہوا، تیرتا ہوا، پانی پر on board a ship جہاز میں at sea سمندر میں، بحر پہ میں started or spreading about (business or rumours) جاری، مشہور، گرم، اُڑتی ہوئی *there is a story afloat that*, it is being rumoured that افواہ گرم ہے کہ

afoot (a-*fut*) *adv.* & *adj.* on foot, walking پیدل، پیادہ پا in progress, being planned or done, taking place حرکت میں، عمل میں، زیرِ عمل، چلتا، چالو، زیرِ غور، زیرِ تجویز، سوچا جا رہا، ہو رہا *there is mischief afoot* شرارت ہو رہی ہے *I wish I knew what is afoot* کاش میں جانتا کہ ہو کیا رہا ہے۔

aforesaid (a-*foh*-sed) *adj.* said before, above-mentioned مذکورہ بالا، مذکورہ صدر، مولہ بالا، متذکرۂ صدر

a fortiori adv. more certainly زیادہ وُثوق کے ساتھ

afoul *adv.* in the phrase *run afoul of*, (*a*) clash with سے ٹکرانا (*b*) get badly mixed up with میں گڈ مڈ ہو کر رہ جانا

afraid (a-*frayd*) *adj.* in fear خائف، دہشت زدہ، ڈرا ہوا *He was afraid that he might make a mistake* اُسے ڈر تھا کہ کہیں اُس سے غلطی نہ سرزد ہو جائے۔ sorry افسوس ہے *I am afraid I can't do that*, افسوس ہے مجھ سے یہ نہ ہو سکے گا۔ اندیشہ ہے۔ *I am afraid that I shall not be able to lend you this huge amount* مجھے افسوس ہے اتنی بڑی رقم میں آپ کو اُدھار نہیں دے سکوں گا۔

afresh (a-*fresh*) *adv.* anew نئے سرے سے، اَز سرِ نَو

aft (ahft) *adv.* towards the back of a ship (جہاز یا کشتی کا) اَگلا حصّہ *to go aft* دنبالۂ جہاز میں *fore and aft* آگے پیچھے، اِس سرے سے اُس سرے تک

after (*ahf*-tĕ*) *adv.*, *prep.* & *conj.* ◑ later, behind, at a time that follows پیچھے، بعد، بعد میں، پیچھے پیچھے *after that* اِس کے بعد *time after time*, time and again, very often بار بار *day after day*, for days on end مسلسل، کئی روز تک، دِنوں تک *one after another*, one at a time, not all together یکے بعد دیگرے، ایک ایک کر کے *After you!* Please get in first, I shall follow you, پہلے آپ *after-hours* چھٹی یا فرصت کے اوقات in spite of کے باوجود، باوصف، بایں ہمہ، پھر بھی *After all his hard work he failed*, محنت کے باوجود وہ ناکام رہا۔ *after all*, despite all that has gone before بہرحال، بہر صورت in the manner of, in imitation of جیسا، کی تقلید میں، کی نقل *Chughtai's paintings are after those of the Moghul school* چغتائی کی تصویر مسلکِ مغلیہ کی تقلید میں ہے *after a fashion, after a manner*, rather badly کسی حد تک، ایک حد تک *after one's own heart* حسبِ منشا، حسبِ دلخواہ، حسبِ مراد (with certain verbs); *ask after*, ask about the health of, کو پوچھنا *be after*, try to get or do or find کی تلاش میں ہونا، کی جستجو کرنا *be called after*, *be named after*, be given the name of, be called

کے نام پر نام رکھا جانا *look after*, take care of نگہداشت کرنا، نگرانی کرنا، حفاظت کرنا *take after*, be like ملنا، (کسی سے) کی شکل ہونا، پر ہونا، مشابہ ہونا *The boy takes after his father* پتا پر پُوت، اس لڑکے کی شکل اپنے باپ سے ملتی ہے۔

aftermath (*ahf*-tĕ-math) *n.* after-grass پچھیتی گھاس consequence (*of* war, etc.) انجام، حاصل، نتیجہ، پھل۔

afternoon (ahf-tĕ-*noon*) *n.* time from noon to evening سہ پہر، تیسرے پہر *good afternoon*, form of salutation between lunch hour and early evening آداب عرض، تسلیم، سلام

afterthought (*ahf*-tĕ*-thawt) *n.* late justification; something thought of too late, after the chance of saying or doing it has gone بعد کا خیال، بعد کی توجیہ، پچھل مُت، پَس اندیشی مشتے بعد از جنگ

afterwards (*ahf*-tĕ-wah*dz) *adv.* later, subsequently بعد میں، بعد میں پھر، بعد ازاں

again (a-*gayn*) *adv.* once more پھر، پھر سے، دوبارہ *again and again, time and again*, very often بار بار، بارہا *now and again*, sometimes کبھی کبھی، کبھار، گاہے گاہے *over again*, a second time دوبارہ، اَز سرِ نَو، نئے سرے سے back to the first state پہلے کی طرح پھر، پہلے جیسا پھر *be oneself again*, recover from an illness صحت یاب ہونا، شفا پانا، تندرست (to express further thought) as : *and again* اور تو *but then again* مگر پھر (the same number as :) *half again, half as much again*, one-and-a-half times the same number or amount ڈیوڑھا *as much again* twice as much دُگنا *as many again*, twice as many دُگنے *as far again*, twice as far دُگنا فاصلہ

against (a-*gaynst*) *prep.* opposite, contrary to کی مرضی کے خلاف، کے خلاف، برخلاف *against (one's) will* *for or against (something)* کے حق میں یا خلاف *work against time* وقت پر کام ختم کرنے کی سخت کوشش کرنا۔ coming into touch with کسی شے پر ٹِکا، کے مقابل *against the wall* دیوار کے سہارے *run up against*, meet by chance اتفاقیہ ملاقات ہونا، مڈبھیڑ ہونا in contrast with دیوار کے ساتھ کے پس منظر میں، کے مقابل، کے تضاد میں *The trees appeared black against the morning sky* آسمان کے پس منظر میں درخت سیاہ دکھائی دے رہے تھے in preparation for, کے لیے، بطور پیش بندی کے۔ *Lay up money against the rainy day*, save something for use in hard times آڑے وقت کے لیے پس انداز کرنا *against a person* بنام فلاں، فلاں کے حساب میں *as against* ہوا کے رُخ *against the wind* *against* کے مقابل، بہ نسبت *over against* سامنے *(go) against the grain* ناگوار، (معلوم ہونا)

Agamemnon (ag-a-*mem*-non) *Cl. myth.* leader of the Greeks in the Trojan War, who was murdered on his return home by his queen and her paramour, Aegisthus اگامِمنن

Aganippe (ag-a-*nip*-ee) *Cl. myth.* fountain at the foot of Mt. Helicon, sacred to the Muses اگانپی

agape (a-*gayp*) *adv.* & *adj.* with the mouth open in order to express surprise, wonder, attention, or just while yawning. منہ کھولے، پھٹا پھٹا، مبہوت بنا، نقش دیوار

agasp (*ag*-asp) *adj*. & *adv*. out of **breath** رکی سانس پھولی ہوئی

agate (*ag*-ayt) a kind of precious stone ، یشب، سنگِ سلیمانی

age (ayj) *n*. 'ength of one's life عمر، سِن *come of age*, reach the age of maturity according to the law بالغ ہونا، سِنِ بلوغ کو پہنچنا، *under age*, minor, not yet of age نابالغ *over age*, older than a set age-limit مقررہ عمر سے بڑا *age of discretion* سِنِ شعُور *old age* بڑھاپا *moon's age* چاند جتنے دِن کا ہو ، long period of time زمانہ، عصر، عہد ، دَور *the present age* عصرِ حاضر ، دَورِ حاضر *the Stone Age* پتھر کا زمانہ ، حجری دَور *the Bronze Age* دھات کا زمانہ، فلزی دَور *the Middle Ages, the Dark Ages*, the period of European history extending from 600 A.C. to 1450 A.C. قرونِ وسطیٰ، قرونِ مُظلمہ *the Machine Age* مشینی دَور *the Atomic Age* سالماتی قوت کے استعمال کا زمانہ ، سالماتی دَور *the Golden Age* علمی زمانہ *the Augustan Age* (لاطینی ادب کا) عہدِ زرّیں (colloq.) a long time مدت، مدتوں، مدت، مدتوں سے، بڑی دیر سے *We have been waiting for ages* ہم مدتوں سے انتظار کر رہے ہیں۔ *v.t.* & *i*. (cause to) grow old, begin to look old بوڑھا ہو جانا یا کر دینا، ضعیف ہو جانا یا کر دینا، بڑھاپا آنا۔ *He is ag(e)ing fast* - اسے بہت جلد بڑھاپا آ رہا ہے۔ **aged** *adj*. (ayjd) of the age of, old اتنے برس کا یا اتنے سال کی عمر کا۔ *a girl aged ten*, a ten-year-old girl دس برس کی لڑکی (*ayj-id*) old, elderly بوڑھا، عمر رسیدہ، معمّر، سن رسیدہ as : *an aged man* بوڑھا آدمی ، بوڑھا **ageless** *adj*. never becoming old سدا جوان، ہر دم جوان، دائم جوان، اَبدی، اَزلی **agelong** *adj*. lasting through all time عمر بھر کا،

[2]**-age** (ij) *suf*. (for making *n*.) charges for (*do*)ing something ، ئی ، کی اُجرت، کی مزدوری

agency (*ay*-jen-si) *n*. business, work or office of an agent آڑھت ، منیمی ، ایجنسی power or means by which something is done ، واسطہ، وسیلہ، ذریعہ، سبب *through the agency of friends*, through their influence دوستوں کے ذریعے، دوستوں کی وساطت سے action عمل، اثر، ایکشن *the agency of water on rocks* چٹانوں پر پانی کا اثر (see also **agent**)

agenda (a-*jen*-da) *n*. (*pl*. used as *sing*.) items of business to be considered (esp. at meeting) ایجنڈا ، پیش نامہ ، کارروائی نامہ

agent (*ay*-jent) *n*. person who acts for another, one who manages the business affairs of others ، گماشتہ، کارندہ، کارکن ، منیم ، منیب *house-agent*, one buying, selling, and letting houses for others دلال، مکانوں کا دلال، *shipping agent, forwarding agent, clearing agent*, person despatching goods for others گماشتہ cause سبب، عامل، جمع عوامل ، *natural agents*, natural causes like rain, flood, etc. قدرتی عوامل *chemical agent*, something producing a chemical change in another کیمیاوی عوامل ▣ **An agent is one** who has power to make agreements ; **representative** is a general term ; a **broker** works on commission and deals with more than one firm or party.

agglomerate (a-*glomi*-rayt) *v.t.* & *i*. collect or grow into a mass - بستہ ہونا، ڈلا بن جانا یا بنانا، اکٹھا کرنا یا ہونا *n*. volcanic rock consisting of irregular fragments ، حجرہ بستہ

agglutination (ag-lew-ti-*nay*-shèn) a mass ، چسپیدہ، مرکب (words) glued together - مرکب امتزاجی

aggrandize (*ag*-ran-dīz) *v.t.* make greater in power, rank, sight - بڑھانا، چڑھانا، ترقی دینا، عظمت عطا کرنا **aggrandizement** (ag-*ran*-diz-ment) *n*. ایزاد، توقیر، ترقی، بڑھوتری، سرفرازی

aggravate (*ag*-ra-vayt) *v.t.* nake worse بگاڑنا، زیادہ سنگین بنانا (colloq.) annoy, make angry برافروختہ کرنا، بھڑکانا، جلانا، زِچ کرنا، قافیہ تنگ کرنا **aggravation** *n*. worsening - خرابی میں اضافہ ، مزید خرابی، زیادہ خراب ہونا۔

aggregate (*ag*-ri-gayt) *adj*. total مجموعہ، جُملہ *in the aggregate* فی الجملہ، مجموعی طور پر *n*. broken stone used in concrete بجری *v.t.* & *i*. amount (*to*) کی میزان بننا ، ہونا ، فی الجملہ ہونا **aggregation** *n*. number of things forming a mass جُملہ اشیاء

aggression (a-*gresh*-en) *n*. an attack without just cause - چھیڑ، جھگڑے میں پہل، جارحیت، جارحانہ عزائم INDIA *is not guilty of aggression against her neighbours* ہندوستان اپنے ہمسایہ ممالک کے خلاف جارحیت کا مجرم نہیں ہے۔ **aggressive** (a-*gres*-iv) *adj*. quick to attack without just cause - جارحیت پسند، جھگڑے کی ابتدا کرنے والا of or for the purpose of attack - حملے کا، حملے سے متعلق ، جارحانہ *take the aggressive*, attack - حملہ کرنا ، جارحانہ اقدام کرنا *aggressive weapon* جارحانہ ہتھیار **aggressor** *n*. جارحیت پسند *A country without a strong air force is at the mercy of aggressors* جس مُلک کی ہوائی طاقت مضبوط نہ ہو وہ جارحیت پسندوں کے رحم و کرم پر ہوتا ہے

aggrieved (a-greeved) *adj*. feeling that one has been treated unjustly ستم زدہ، شاکی *aggrieved parties* ستم زدہ فریق ، شاکی فریق

aghast (a-*gahst*) *adj*. struck with sudden surprise or terror - ششدر ، متحیر، ہکا بکا ، دہشت زدہ ، خوف زدہ ، سہما ہوا

agile (*aj*-īl ; U.S. pr., *aj*-il) *adj*. active, quick-moving پھرتیلا **agility** (a-*jil*-i-ti) *n*. quickness

agitate (*aj*-i-tayt) *v.t.* & *i*. (cause to) move (liquid) ہلانا ، ہلنا ، متحرک کرنا یا ہونا disturb, cause anxiety to ہیجان پیدا کرنا ، ہلچل ڈالنا ، بے چین کرنا ، اضطراب پیدا کرنا ، مضطرب کرنا *agitate a person* کسی کو مضطرب کرنا *agitate one's feelings* کسی کے جذبات کو ہیجان میں لانا cause people to fight (*against* the Authority *for* improving conditions) (اصلاحی) تحریک اُٹھانا یا چلانا **agitation** (aj-i-*tay*-shen) *n*. such movement تحریک، حرکت، اضطراب **agitator** *n*. one who brings about, or participates in, an agitation تحریک میں حصہ لینے والا

[S] **Agitation** is commotion with many people involved; **a disturbance** is of the peace; **excitement** is sudden appeal to the imagination; **perturbation** is unfavourable excitement; **upheaval** is commotion leading to political and other changes, etc.

agitprop *n.* see Addenda

aglow (a-*gloh*) *adj.* & *adv.* shining درخشاں، تابندہ heated گرم، سرخ، تمتماتا ہوا، تپ رہا excited چمکیلا، چہکتا، دمکتا، بے کل، بے چین، بے قرار، مضطرب،

agnostic (ag-*nos*-tic) *n.* one who holds that nothing can be known of God or future life لاادریہ *adj.* relating to this belief لاادری **agnosticism** (-sizm) *n.* being an agnostic لاادریت

ago (a-*goh*) *adv.* in the past ادھر، اب سے، پہلے، پیچھے *long ago* مدتیں ہوئیں، ایک زمانہ ہوا۔

agog (a-*gog*) *adj.* & *adv.* eager, excited, مشتاق، بےتاب *be all agog (to)* کے لیے بےتاب *set agog (to)* شوق دلانا، اکسانا، بےتاب کرنا۔

agonize *v.t.*, **agonizing** *adj.* see under **agony**

agony (*ag*-o-ni) *n.* great mental pain سوہان روح، روحانی اذیت **agonize** (-nīz) *v.t.* cause great mental pain روحانی اذیت پہنچانا، ذہنی اذیت پہنچانا، **agonizing** *adj.* causing agony ذہنی کوفت کا موجب

agrarian (a-*gray*-ri-an) *adj.* concerning agricultural land زرعی *agrarian problem*, problem of land-tenure, etc. (*of a country*) زرعی مسئلہ *agrarian reforms*, reforms regarding this problem زرعی اصلاحات *The revolutionary regime has introduced radical agrarian reforms in Pakistan* انقلابی حکومت نے پاکستان میں بنیادی زرعی اصلاحات نافذ کی ہیں۔

agree (a-*gree*) *v.i.* say yes حامی بھرنا، اقرار کرنا *agree (with a person)* شخص سے اتفاق رکھنا یا متفق ہونا *agree (to a statement)* بیان سے متفق ہونا *agree to differ*, drop attempts to convince each other قائل کرنے کی کوشش ترک کر دینا۔ be happy together نبھنا، نباہ ہونا، آپس میں *the couple can't agree* ان میاں بیوی کی آپس میں نہیں بنتی *(agree with)*, (of food) be good for (someone) موافق آنا، کو، راس آنا یا ہونا۔ (gram.) correspond (*with*) مطابقت رکھنا **agreeable** (a-*gree*-a-bĕl) *adj.* ready to agree (*to* proposal, etc.) پسند کرنے والا، ماننے والا *She was not agreeable to my proposal* اس نے میری بات نہیں مانی nice خوش اطوار، مہربان **agreeably** *adv.* in a nice manner بطور خوش کی انداز *agreeably surprised* حیران بھی خوش بھی **agreement** *n.* act of agreeing اتفاق، اتحاد، ہم آہنگی *be in agreement (with)* سے متفق ہونا، سے ہم آہنگ ہونا pact میثاق، عہد نامہ

agricultural *adj.* see under **agriculture** زراعت

agriculture (*ag*-ri-kul-chĕ*) *n.* farming کاشتکاری، کھیتی باڑی **agricultural** (-*kul*-) *adj.* زرعی، زراعتی، مزروعہ *agricultural property* زرعی جائداد *agricultural land* زرعی زمین *agricultural college* زرعی کالج، زراعت **agriculturist** *n.* person earning his livelihood by agriculture

aground (a-*ground*) *adj.* & *adv.*, (of ship) upon the bottom of shallow water (جہاز) خشکی پر چڑھا ہوا، زمین گرفتہ *be, go, or run aground* جہاز کا خشکی پر چڑھنا، زمین گیر ہونا، اتھلے پانی میں آجانا

ague (*ay*-gew) *n.* malarial fever موسمی بخار، ملیریا، تپ لرزہ، جاڑے کا بخار، باری کا بخار، نوبتی بخار۔

ah (*ah*) *int.* (expressing joy, sorrow, surprise, boredom, contempt, or request) واہ وا، اخاہ، سبحان اللہ، ہائے، وائے، اُف، اہیں، ہونہہ، اے ہے، اللہ، خدارا

aha (a-*hah*) *int.* (expressing surprise, triumph, mockery) ہائیں، اخاہ، اچھا، واہ وا، کیا کہنے! کیا کہنا۔

ahead (a-*hed*) *adj.* & *adv.* in front *of* آگے، سامنے *go ahead of others* آگے بڑھنا، سبقت لے جانا *go ahead* (colloq.), go on with your work or talk ہاں ہاں کہتے جاؤ، (یا) کئے *look ahead*, prepare for the future دوراندیشی سے کام لینا *(ships) lying ahead*, sailing one after the other قطار میں چلتے ہوئے (جہاز)

ahem (a-*hem*) *int.* (expressing noise made while clearing the throat or calling somebody's attention) اُغ، ہوں، اہوں، ہوں،

ahoy (a-*hoi*) *int.* shout used when calling a ship (جہاز کے خلاصیوں کی پکار) ارے ہرت!

aid (ayd) *v. t.* & *n.* help امداد، مدد دینا، اعانت کرنا، *first aid*, treatment given to a sick or injured before a doctor's arrival ابتدائی طبی امداد *grant-in-aid* سرکاری امداد *aided institution* سرکاری امداد پانے والا ادارہ

[S] We **aid** somebody when we help him in a particular work. **help him** in urgent need, **assist** one who is weak or hurt, and **subsidize** a person by giving him money to set him on his feet.

aide-de-camp (*ay*-de-kawng) *n.* (*pl.* '*aides-de-camp*'; abb. *A.D.C.*, pr. *ay*-dee-see) officer assisting General or other dignitary, by carrying orders سردار رکاب، اے ڈی سی، مصاحب

aide-memoire (*ayd*-maym-wah) *n.* memorandum یادداشت written summary of the items of a diplomatic document in course of preparation سفارتی گفت و شنید یا دستاویزوں کا ملخص، مختصر روئداد۔

aigrette (*ayg*-ret) *n.* tuft of feathers or spray of gems worn in hat (ٹوپی میں لگانے کی) کلغی

ail (ayl) *v.t.* & *i.* trouble, afflict ستانا، تکلیف دینا، بیمار پڑنا، علیل ہونا، دکھی ہونا یا کرنا، روگ لگنا یا لگانا۔ *What can ail thee, knight-at-arms?* (Keats) اے مرد مسلح تجھے کیا روگ لگا ہے

ailing *adj.* ill علیل، بیمار، مریض **ailment** *n.* illness علالت، مرض، بیماری، روگ

aim (aym) *v.t.* & *i.* point (gun, arrow, etc.) at نشانہ یا شست باندھنا، سیدھ لینا، توپ کا رخ پھیرنا۔ direct (a blow or other object *at* or *towards*) مارنا، ضرب لگانا regard as one's purpose کی تمنا کرنا، کی آرزو کرنا *n.* act of aiming کا نشانہ باندھنا، سیدھ لینا *take aim (at)* بغور نشانہ باندھنا *take careful aim* کو ہدف بنانا thing aimed at نشانہ، ہدف purpose مقصد، مدعا **aimless** *adj.*

without aim or purpose بلا مقصد، اَٹکل پچّو، بے سر و پا، بے منفعت

An **aim** is that at which one shoots as straight as possible; an **object** is something to be reached or grasped; an **objective**, to be reached eventually, a **purpose** is an aim with a good reason behind it, an **aspiration** is a noble aim; **desire** is an impulse to get something; an **intention** is a general movement of desire; a **goal** is an objective or a fixed post to be reached in a game.

air (*ay*-ĕ*) mixture of gases we breathe ہَوا *in the air*, (a) خبر مشہور، گرم، پھیلی ہوئی - *there are rumours in the air* - طرح طرح کی افواہیں پھیلی ہوئی ہیں (b) uncertain, not definite - ناپختہ، پا در ہَوا *His plans are still in the air* اس کے منصوبے ابھی قطعی صورت اختیار نہیں کر پائے *clear the air*, (a) make the air fresh again گندی ہَوا نکالنا، تازہ ہَوا لانا (b) put an end to wrong ideas by stating the facts غلط تصورات کا ازالہ کرنا *open air n.* کھلی جگہ، میدان *open-air adj.* کھلا منڈوا *open-air theatre* بے در و دیوار، چھت کے بغیر، بے بام، بے در و دیوار تیاتر، بے بام تماشا گاہ *quite in the air* غیر یقینی، بے بنیاد، مبہم *take air* سیر کرنا، ہَوا خوری کرنا *take the air* مشہور ہونا، چرچا ہونا *airs and graces* بناوٹ اور سج دھج *castles in the air*, fond hopes ہوائی قلعے، خیالی پلاؤ، شیخ چلی کے منصوبے *with an air* خود اعتمادی کے ساتھ having to do with flying ہَوائی، پرواز سے متعلق; as: *air base*, place where aircraft are kept in repair طیاروں کی مرمت گاہ *Air Force* ہَوائیہ، فضائیہ *by air*, in an aircraft ہوائی جہاز میں، ہوا سے، طیارے میں (radio) (*be* or *put*) *on the air*, broadcasting نشر ہونا یا کرنا *What's on the air this evening?* What's the radio programme? آج کیا کچھ نشر ہوگا؟ *The President will be on the air at 7-15 p.m. to-day in the national hook-up* صدر آج شام کے سوا سات بجے قومی پروگرام میں تقریر نشر کریں گے very light wind ہلکی ہَوا (music) tune لَے، دُھن *He has an air of importance*, behaves as if he were important - پتہ نہیں وہ اپنے کو کیا سمجھتا ہے *give oneself airs, put on airs*, be too proud دُون کی لینا، شیخی بگھارنا، بننا *v.t.* put out into the air or in a warm place for drying دُھوپ دینا، ہَوا میں ڈالنا *The bed of the patient should be aired every day* مریض کے بستر کو روزانہ دُھوپ دینی چاہیے let air into تازہ ہَوا آنے دینا *open the windows and air the room* کھڑکیاں کھول کر تازہ ہَوا اندر آنے دو۔ *adj.* of or pertaining to air ہَوا کا، ہَوائی **air bends** *n.* see Addenda **airborne** (-bohn) *adj.* (of troops, etc.) carried by air ہَوائی جہاز میں جانے والی (فوج)، ہَوا برداشتہ (of aircraft) having taken off زمین سے اُٹھا ہُوا

air-chamber *n.* ہَوا کا خانہ **air-conditioning** *n.* making the air (in a building, etc.) pure and regulating its temperature ہَوا کو صاف کر کے حسب منشا سرد یا گرم کرنا - *air-conditioning plant* ہَوا بدل (آلہ) **air-conditioned** *adj.* (room, etc.) fitted with air-conditioning plant جس میں ہَوا بدل لگا ہُوا *This room is air-conditioned* - اس کمرے میں ہَوا بدل لگا ہُوا ہے۔ **aircraft** *n.* heavier-than-air flying machine ہَوائی جہاز، طیارہ **aircraft-carrier** *n.* warship with wide decks for the landing and taking off of aircraft طیارہ بردار، ہَوا بردار **aircrash** *n.* ہَوائی حادثہ **airdrome**, *n.* aerodrome ہَوائی اڈہ، طیران گاہ **airgraph** (-graph) *n.* one of the microfilmed letters for being carried by air عکسی ہَوائی خط system of microfilming letters thus عکسی ہَوائی خط **air-gun** *n.* a small gun working with air pressure instead of gun-powder ہوائی بندوق **airhostess** *n.* stewardess on an aircraft ہَوائی میزبان **airless** *adj.* without air or not having enough fresh air بند بند سا، بند بند، گھٹا ہُوا، گھٹن والا *airless room* بند بند سا کمرہ

airlift *n.* & see Addenda **airline** *n.* airway ہَوائی راستہ air transport company or system اِدارۂ طیران **airliner** aircraft carrying passengers on a regular route مسافر طیارہ **airmail** *n.* mail carried by air ہَوائی ڈاک، برید فضائی **airman** *n.* one of the air crew ہَوا باز، طیارچی **air marshal** *n.* Air Force designation (equivalent to *Lieut General* in the Army) ایئر مارشل، نائب سالار فضائیہ **airplane** *n.* (U.S.) aeroplane ہَوائی جہاز، طیارہ **air-pocket** *n.* upward or downward stream of air making an aircraft rise or fall suddenly ہَوا رخنہ، معلق تھیلی **airport** *n.* public flying ground for commercial use ہَوائی اڈہ، ہَوائی مستقر، فضائی مستقر **air-pump** *n.* machine pumping air into something **air-raid** *n.* an attack by aircraft strafing or dropping bombs ہَوائی حملہ **air-raid precautions** (*abb.* **A.R.P.**, pr. *ay*-ah*-pee) *n.* civil defence measures against air-raids اے آر پی، ہَوائی حملے سے بچاؤ **airscrew** *n.* propeller of an aircraft ہَوا پیچ، پنکھا، فضائی بادکش **airship** *n.* flying machine which is lighter than air ہَوائی ناؤ

an airship

airstrip *n.* & see Addenda **airtight** *adj.* so tightly closed as to admit or let out no air سر بند، بند نُشتہ کا **airway** *n.* airline ہَوائی راستہ **airy** (-ir) *adj.* of or like air ہَوائی، آسمانی cheerful زندہ دل، رنگیلا with air entering freely ہَوا دار **airily** *adv.* lightly آسانی سے، بے پروائی سے، کلول سے

aisle (il) *n.* passage between rows of seats in a church گرجے میں درمیانی راستہ بین الصفوف راستہ (see also **transept** & **nave**)

A (aisle): T (transept) N (nave)

ajar (a-*jah**) *adv.* (door) slightly open not quite shut نیم وا، نیم باز

Ajax (*ay*-jaks) *Cl. myth.* Greek hero in the Trojan war. He was the son of Telamon. After the death of Achilles he struggled for his armour with Ulysses. Failing in this, he committed suicide ایجکس

akimbo (a-*kim*-boh) *adv* (also *with arms akimbo*) with hands on hips and elbows turned out کُولھوں پر ہاتھ دھرے، رکھڑا

girl with arms akimbo

akin (a-*kin*) *adj*. of the same family سگا، رشتہ دار، قرابت دار، ناطے دار۔ *akin to*, alike ملتا جُلتا، یکساں، مُشابہ، ہم شکل

-al (ĕl) *suf*. (for making *adj*.) of کے متعلق والا، ی (as : *national* قومی)

alabaster (*al*-a-bas-tē*) soft white stone used for making ornaments سنگِ جراحت

a la carte (Fr. *ph*.) according to the bill of fare ریستوران کی فہرست ماکولات کے مطابق، کھانوں کی فہرست کے مطابق

alack, alack-a-day *int*. (arch.) (cry of grief) دریغا، واحسرتا!

alacrity (a-*lak*-ri-ti) *n*. quick and willing eagerness چستی، پھُرتی، آمادگی، مستعدی

a la mode (Fr. *ph*.) according to the custom or fashion رواج کے مطابق فیشن کے مطابق

alarm (a-*lahm*) *n*. warning signal خطرے کی اطلاع چیتاونی، انتباہ، آگاہی، apparatus giving such sound signals خطرے کی گھنٹی، بگل، سائرن، گجر یا جرس وغیرہ *alarm clock*, portable clock fitted with a bell جرس دار گھڑی، گجر والی گھڑی، fear caused by real or imaginary danger اندیشہ، خوف، کھٹکا، ہول، دہشت، *v.t.* give such a signal چوکس کرنا، ہوشیار کرنا، گھبرا دینا، دہشت زدہ کرنا۔ **alarming** *adj*. causing danger دہشت انگیز، ہولناک **alarmed** *adj*. frightened دہشت زدہ، خوف زدہ **alarmist** *n*. one who spreads alarming rumours دہشت انگیز افواہیں پھیلانے والا

alas (a-*lahs*) *int*. (expressing sorrow or anxiety) حیف! افسوس! ہائے! ہائے وائے! *alas the day* وہ دن ڈوبے، آگ لگے اُس دن کو

albatross (*al*-bat-ros) the largest sea-bird قادوس

albeit (awl-*bee*-it) *conj*. although اگرچہ، حالانکہ، باوجودیکہ، گو، ہرچند

albino (al-*bee*-noh) *n*. (*pl*., *albinos*) person or animal lacking natural colouring matter in skin بھُورا **albinism** (*al*-) *n*. بھُوراپن

Albion (*al*-bi-on) *n*. *prop*. Celtic name for England, Scotland or Great Britain اَلبیون

album (*al*-bum) a book of plain pages for collecting stamps, pictures, etc. مرقع

albumen (al-*beu*-men) *n*. white of an egg انڈے کی سفیدی، such material بیضین

alchemist *n*. see under **alchemy**

alchemy (*al*-ke-mi) *n*. early form of chemistry the aim of which was to transform a baser metal into gold کیمیاگری، کیمیا سازی **alchemist** *n*. pseudo-scientist who believes in such transformation کیمیاگر، مُتوّس

alcohol (*al*-ko-hol) *n*. pure spirit of wine اَرواحِ شراب، الکحل، الغول any liquor شراب **alcoholic** (al-ko-*hol*-ik) *adj*. الکحلی، الغولی *alcoholic drinks*, liquor شراب، مُسکرات، نشے **alcoholism** *n*. effect of alcohol on the human system الغولیت **alcometer** *n*. see Addenda

alcove (*al*-kohv, al-*kohv*) *n*. a recess in a room طاق، محراب shady retreat in a garden

alderman (*awl*-de-man) *n*. senior member of British county council نائب رئیس بلدیہ

ale (ayl) *n*. pale beer **ale-house** *n*. بُوزہ خانہ، شراب خانہ

alembic (a-*lem*-bik) *n*. simple distilling apparatus بھبکا، قرنبیق

alert (a-*leht*) *adj*. watchful چوکس، چوکنا، ہوشیار، *on the alert*, on the look-out کمربستہ، چوکنا، چوکس *n*. & see Addenda

Alexandrine (-īn) *adj* & *n*. six-foot iambic verse چھ رکنی ایامبی (مصرع) مسدس ایامبی، مسدّس رکنی۔

alfalfa *n*. clover-like plant used as fodder اَلفلفہ

Alfresco (al-*fres*-co) *adj*. and *adv*. (held) in the open air کمرے کے باہر کھلے میدان میں، بیرونِ در *alfresco dinner* (or *dance*) بیرون در عشائیہ (یا رقص) *to lunch alfresco* بیرونِ در ظہرانہ تناول کرنا۔

algebra (*al*-jeb-ra) *n*. a branch of mathematics using letters for numbers الجبرا، جبر و مقابلہ **algebraic, algebraical** *adj*. الجبری **algebraically** *adv*. الجبرے سے، الجبرے کے طریقے سے

alias (*ay*-li-as) *n*. an assumed name عرف، لقب *Ihsan-ul-Haq alias Charlie* احسان الحق عرف چارلی *The sharper has several aliases*, یہ عیّار کئی ناموں سے معروف ہے، اس اُڑی باز نے کئی نام رکھے ہوئے ہیں

alibi (*al*-i-bī) *n*. plea by an accused that he was away when the crime was committed عذر غیر موجودگی، عدم موجودگی۔ *prove on alibi* عدم موجودگی ثابت کرنا

alien (*ay*-li-en) *n*. & *adj*. foreigner اجنبی، غیرملکی، پردیسی *alien to*, out of harmony with الگ، مختلف، جُدا، علیحدہ

alienate (*ay*-) *v.t*. divert from, give to another منتقل کرنا، انتقالِ ملکیت کرنا، قبضے میں لے لینا *Enemy property is usually alienated in time of war* متحارب ملکوں کی جائداد ایام جنگ میں اپنے قبضے میں لے لی جاتی ہے۔ cause to lose (someone's sympathy, love, etc.) برگشتہ کرنا، منحرف کرنا، بیگانہ کرنا، ہمدردیاں کھو دینا۔

alienation (-*nayshn*) *n*. انتقالِ ملکیت، بیگانگی، برگشتہ کرنا *Land Alienation Act* قانونِ انتقالِ اراضی *mental alienation* جنون، خلل، دماغ، پاگل پن **alienable** *adj*. that which can be given or taken away انتقال پذیر *inalienable adj*. ناقابلِ انتقال

alight (a-*līt*) *adj*. lighted up, burning فروزاں bright-looking, cheerful تابندہ، چمک، خوش خوش *faces alight with happiness* مسرت سے تابندہ چہرے *v.i*. get down from (train, bus, horse, etc.) (ریل وغیرہ سے) اُترنا

(of birds, etc.) come down from the air to rest (*on*) اُترنا (زمین پر)، آ رہنا

align, aline (a-*lin*) *v t.* place in a line صف باندھنا قطار بندی کرنا، سیدھ میں لانا *align oneself with* (*a party or cause*), support (it) (کسی جماعت یا مقصد کا) ہموار ہونا

alignment *n.* arrangement in a straight line صف بندی، قطار بندی *in alignment with*, straight line with (کی) سیدھ میں *out of alignment with*, not in a straight line with (کی) سیدھ میں نہیں

central block out of alignment

alike (a-*lyk*) *adj.* & *adv.* similar, in the same way یکساں، ایک سا، ایک ہی طرح *share and share alike*, share equally مُساوی حصہ لینا، برابر کا حصہ لینا

aliment (*al*-) *n.* food, nourishment غذا **alimentary** (-*men*-) *adj.* pertaining to food غذائی *alimentary canal*, pipe leading from mouth to stomach معدی نالی

alimony (*al*-i-ma-ni) *n.* maintenance allowance due from husband to wife on separation بیوی کا نان نفقہ، روٹی کپڑا

alive (a-*liv*) *adj.* living جیتا، جیتا جاگتا، زندہ، بقید حیات lively, cheerful (person) پھرتیلا، خوش باش *look very much alive* بڑے خوش باش نظر آنا (of place) hustling with activity in force قائم، برقرار *keep a claim alive* دعویٰ برقرار رکھنا *alive to*, fully aware of (سے) باخبر، آگاہ *Man alive!* بھلے آدمی *any man alive* کوئی بھی، متنفس *Look alive!* hurry up جلدی کرو، جلدی

alkali (*al*-ka-li) *n.* (*pl.*, *alkalies*) chemical opposite to an acid combining with it to form salt **alkaline** (-lin) *adj.* having the properties of an alkali قلوی، (القلی صفت)

all (awl) *adj.*, *adv.* & *pron.* every one (of) ہر ایک the whole of سب، سب کچھ، پورا، کل، تمام *with all haste*, with the greatest possible haste بعجلت تمام *all day long* دن بھر *all night long* رات بھر *beyond all doubt, beyond all question*, doubtless شک و شبہ سے بالا *on all fours*, on the hands and knees, crawling ہاتھ پاؤں کے بل *be all ears for*, be very anxious to hear ہمہ تن گوش ہونا *be all eyes for* پوری توجہ سے دیکھنا *be all attention*, be very attentive پوری طرح متوجہ ہونا *for all that*, despite all that has been said or done بایں ہمہ، اس کے باوجود، اس کے باوصف *and all*, as well, also مع، سمیت، وغیرہ سمیت *He jumped into the pool, clothes and all* وہ کپڑوں سمیت تالاب میں کود گیا *after all*, nevertheless فی الجملہ، تاہم، پھر بھی *in all*, altogether کل، فی الجملہ *all in all*, all that matters لے دے کے، بس ایک *one's all-in-all*, very dear to one کسی کا سب کچھ *be all-in-all to*, be very dear to حد درجہ عزیز، لے دے کے وہی *all told*, counting everything کل *for good and all*, for ever, finally ہمیشہ، ہمیشہ کے لیے *once for all*, *once and for all*, for the last or only time بس پھر نہیں، آخری مرتبہ *at all*, at any rate بالکل ہی، ہرگز، مطلق *not at all* (*a*) (polite answer to some one saying, "Thank you") شکریہ نوازش (*b*) not in the least نہیں، قطعاً نہیں، کسی طرح سے بھی نہیں *all over*, (*a*) everywhere in تمام، سارے، پورے، بھر، ہر جگہ *travel all over a place* پورے علاقے کا سفر کرنا (*b*) finished, at an end ختم *The meeting was all over when I got there* میرے وہاں پہنچنے تک جلسہ ختم ہو چکا تھا *be all over with* (*someone*), *be all up with* (*someone*) be ruined برباد ہو جانا *all alone*, (*a*) helpless بےکس، بےبس (*b*) quite alone یکہ و تنہا *all at once*, (*a*) suddenly اچانک، یکایک، ایک دم سے، ایک دم، دفعۃً (*b*) at the same time بیک وقت *all but*, almost, nearly تقریباً، قریب قریب (ایک آدھ کے) سوا سب *all the better, all the more difficult, etc.*, much better, etc. اور بھی اچھا *all right*, (written as two words) (colloq.) (*a*) that is good, I approve of it ٹھیک، درست، قابلِ اطمینان (*b*) (threat) I will see to it خیر دیکھا جائے گا، اچھا، اچھا یوں ہی سہی، میں بھی دیکھ لوں گا، میں سمجھ لوں گا *all along of* (colloq.) owing to اس سے، بوجہ، بسبب *all the year round* سال بھر *at all events* بہر حال *at all times* ہر وقت، ہر دم، آٹھوں پہر *by all means*, certainly یقیناً *of all kinds* ہر طرح کا *from all sides* ہر طرف سے، چاروں طرف سے *all one* ایک سا، برابر *all very fine, all very well* *in all* سب ملا کر، مختتم (سب کچھ سہی مگر) *all too soon* قبل از وقت *all there* بقائمی ہوش و حواس *all the same* (*a*) nevertheless بایں ہمہ، باوجودیکہ (*b*) making no difference ایک سا، یکساں، برابر *All Fools' Day* یوم الحمقا (یکم اپریل) *All Saints' Day* یوم الاولیا (یکم نومبر) *All Souls' Day* یوم فاتحہ (۲-نومبر)

Allah (*al*-a) *n.* Arabic word for God اللہ، اللہ تعالیٰ

allay (a-*lay*) *v.t.* make less (pain, trouble, excitement) افاقہ دینا، گھٹانا، دھیما کرنا، کم کرنا slake (thirst) (پیاس) بجھانا

allege (a-*lej*) *v.t.* affirm a statement الزام دینا، اظہار دینا، کہنا، بیان دینا **alleged** *adj.* stated but unproved مبیّنہ *the alleged assailant*, مبیّنہ حملہ آور **allegation** (al-i-*gay*-shèn) *n.* charge, اظہار، حتمی بیان، الزام، ادعا، دعویٰ *bring an allegation against* (*someone*) کسی کو الزام دینا

allegiance (a-*lee*-jens, a-*leej*-yans) *n.* loyalty, duty to (one's sovereign, government, country) فرماں برداری، اطاعت، اِنقیاد

allegory (*al*-i-gĕ-ri) *n.* story describing one thing under the image of another تمثیلیہ، مجازیہ **allegorical** (al-i-*go*-ri-kèl) *adj.* تمثالی، مجازی

allegro (a-layg-roh) *n.* quick movement (in music) نشاط انگیز موسیقی *adj.* fast and lively (music) نشاط انگیز *adv.* (music played) in quick time لپک کر

alleluia, allelujah (al-e-*loo*-ya) *n.* song of praise to God حمد

allergic (a-*lĕ**-jik) *adj.* having adverse

reaction (*to* a medicine) (دوا کو) موافق نہ پانا (colloq.) averse (*to*) ناپسند کرنا **allergy** *n.* such adverse reaction الرجی ، اثنا اثر

alleviate (a-*lee*-vi-ayt) *v.t.* make less (pain or suffering) ہلکا کرنا، کم کرنا، گھٹانا make it easier to bear آرام کرنا **alleviation** (a-lee-vi-*ay*-shèn) *n.* کمی ، تسکین ، تخفیف ، آرام

alley (*al*-i) *n.* narrow street between two rows of buildings گلی ، کوچہ passage in a garden روش، خیابان *blind alley*, alley with one end closed بند گلی

alliance (a-*lī*-ens) *n.* agreement between nations to help one another معاہدہ، میثاق، حلف union between families by marriage رشتہ، ناطہ *in alliance with*, united with رشتے داری، قرابت داری

allied *adj.* joined by natural pact حلیف see also **ally**

alligator (*al*-i-gay-te*) reptile resembling crocodile found in American lakes and rivers امریکی گھڑیال، اگر مچھ، نہنگ see Addenda

An alligator

alliteration (a-lit-e-*ray*-shèn) *n.* arranging several words together in a sentence or line of verse with the same initial letter or sound صنعتِ تجنیس، تجنیسِ ابتدائی ، سرحرفی (Ex.) "Full fathom five thy father lies" (*Shakespeare*) **alliterate** (a-*lit*-e-rayt) (-*it*-) *v.t.* write such verse or prose سرحرفی صنعت کا استعمال کرنا

allocate (*al*-o-kayt) *v.t.* set apart (*for* something or *doing* something, *to* a person or institution) مقرر کرنا، تجویز کرنا، تشخیص کرنا، متعین کرنا، مخصوص کرنا، مختص کرنا

allopathy (al-*lop*-a-thi) *n.* medical system of curing disease by producing opposite effects ایلوپیتھی ، ڈاکٹری (علاج) علاج بالضد **allopathic** (al-o-*path*-ik) (*adj.*) ڈاکٹری

allot (a-*lot*) *v.t.* (-*tt*-) to give a share (*to* each person, *for* some purpose) مختص کرنا، متعین کرنا، حصہ دینا، حصہ بخرہ کرنا الاٹ کرنا، کے نام، عارضی طور کرنا، نامزد کرنا *The evacuee property has been allotted to refugees* متروکہ جائداد عارضی طور پر مہاجرین کے نام کر دی گئی ہے **allotment** *n.* that which is allotted وہ شے جو عارضی طور پر کسی کے نام کر دی جائے، نامزدہ act of allotting کے نام عارضی طور پر کرنا، الاٹ منٹ

allottee (a-lot-*ee*) *n.* one to whom an allotment is made جس کے نام کوئی شے عارضی طور پر کی جائے ، الاٹی

allow (a-*lou*) *v.t.* & *i.* permit (کی) اجازت دینا، ہونے دینا، روا رکھنا، جائز قرار دینا give دینا، لینے دینا، ہونے دینا *He allows his wife Rs. 400 a month* وہ اپنی بیوی کو چار سو روپے ماہوار دیتا ہے agree that a thing is true ; concede ماننا، قبول کرنا، تسلیم کرنا ، کو تسلیم ہونا *I allow that I was wrong* مجھے تسلیم ہے کہ میں غلطی پر تھا prepare for (کا) انتظام کرنا تیاری کرنا *He had allowed for thirty guests but only twelve of them turned up* انتظام تو اس نے تیس مہمانوں کا کیا تھا مگر آئے صرف بارہ *allow time* دم لینے دینا، مہلت دینا *allow for* (کی) گنجائش (کی) مدِنظر رکھنا

allowance (a-*lou*-ans) *n.* money regularly allowed (*to* someone) حمینہ، وظیفہ *make allowance(s) for*, allow for, not to be too severe in judging him (کی) گنجائش رکھنا (کو) مدِنظر رکھنا (کے) ساتھ نظر نرمی کرنا *travelling allowance* (abb. *T. A.*)

[S] To **allow** is to offer no opposition to a course of action ; to **permit**, positively give a licence ; to **consent** to a course, be willing ; **sanction** as desirable ; **tolerate**, rather than make a fuss ; **grant** a request ; **concede** a claim , **acknowledge** receipt or accuracy of something.

all-out *adj.* see Addenda

alloy (a-*loi*) *n.* mixture of two or more metals دھاتیں ، بھرت ، معدنی آمیزش ، بھرت *v.t.* mix metals بھرت کرنا ملونی کرنا، کھوٹ ملانا، آمیزش کرنا *unalloyed*, pure (pleasure, etc.) خالص ، بے ملاوٹ

all-round (awl-*round*) *adj.* (person, esp. sportsman) competent in many branches ہر فن مولا **all-rounder** *n.* (colloq.) such person ہر فن مولا

allude (a-*lewd*) *v.i.* refer *to* indirectly اشارہ کرنا تلمیح کرنا، کنایہ کرنا **allusion** (a-*loo*-zhèn) *n.* reference ; alluding تلمیح ، کنایہ *make an allusion to*, speak of not directly but in passing اشاروں کنایوں میں کہنا **allusive** (a-*loos*-iv) *adj.* containing allusion تلمیحی، پُر از تلمیحات

[Do not confuse *allusion* (reference) with *illusion* which means deceptive idea.] [S] To **allude** *to* a thing is to mention it casually ; to **refer** *to* it is to speak of it again, after it has been spoken of, or after it has been under consideration.

allure (a-*lew**) *v.t.* entice, tempt, with the love of للچانا، سبز باغ دکھانا، موہ لینا، لبھانا **allurement** *n.* attraction ترغیب و تحریص، کشش، دل چسپیاں *allurements of a big city* بڑے شہر کی دل چسپیاں

allusion *n.* **allusive** *adj.* see under **allude**

alluvial *adj.* (land) made up of soil deposited by a river سیلابی *alluvial soil*, soil deposited by river دریا برآمد **alluvium** (a-*loov*-i-um) *n.* mud, etc., deposited by a river سیلاب کی لائی ہوئی مٹی یا ریت

ally *v. t.* (a-*lī*) unite families in marriage رشتہ پیدا کرنا unite countries in making war حلیف بنانا، متحد کرنا *n.* (*al*-ī, or a-*lī*) friend, helper (esp. a nation helping another in war), حلیف، اتحادی one who is allied (*to* another) شریک، رفیق **alliance** *n.*, **allied** *adj.* (see above) joined by agreement حلیف ، متحد

Alma Mater (*al*-ma-*may*-tě*) *n.* one's school or university مادرِ علمی ، مدرسہ ، جامعہ

almanac (*awl*-ma-nak) *n.* calendar with other interesting (usu. astrological) data تقویم ، جنتری

almighty (awl-*mi*-ti) *adj*. all-powerful, omnipotent قادرِ مطلق *the Almighty, Almighty God*, God خدائے قدیر

almond (*ahm*-und) *n*. name of a tree بادام کا درخت its nut بادام

almost (*awl*-mohst) *adv*. nearly قریب قریب ، تقریباً

alms (ahmz) *n*. charity to the poor خیرات **alms-house** *n*. strangers' home, a free home for destitute old persons محتاج خانہ **almoner** (*ahm*-nĕ*) official appointed to give alms خیرات دہندہ (اہلکار)

aloe (*al*-oh) a tropical plant ایلوا ، صبر **aloes** (*al*-ohz) *n*. (*pl*. used as *sing*.) bitter purgative prepared from aloe مصبّر

aloft (a-*loft*) *adv*. & *adj*. high up (esp. on a ship); up among the sails اونچا ، اوپر کی طرف

alone (a-*lohn*) *adj*. & *adv*. by oneself اکیلا ، تنہا ، یکہ و تنہا تن تنہا *leave (someone) alone let someone alone* کسی سے قطع نظر کر لینا *let alone*, not thinking or speaking of سے قطع نظر ▣ **Alone** means by itself, **solitary**, being or living alone; **lonely** person, one feeling sad because of being alone, **secluded**, lonely place.

along (a-*long*) *adv*. by the length of; from end to end of کے کنارے کنارے پر ، ایک سرے سے دوسرے سرے تک *all along*, all the time سارا عرصہ *along with*, together with کے ہمراہ کے ساتھ *along here* (or *there*), in this (or that) direction ادھر (ادھر) *get along with* (*a*) agree with (سے) نباہ ہونا (*b*) go forward or make progress with (کام کا) اچھی طرح ہونا **alongside** *adv*. & *prep*. (also *alongside of*) close, near, beside کے ساتھ (کے) شانہ بشانہ (کے) ، پہلو بہ پہلو

aloof (a-*loof*) *adj*. & *adv*. apart, away from الگ ، دُور ، علیحدہ ، فاصلے پر *hold aloof, keep aloof*, keep away (*from*) (سے) الگ یا دُور رہنا **aloofness** *n*. علیحدگی

aloud (a-*loud*) *adv*. loudly زور سے ، چلا کر

alpaca (al-*pah*-ka) *n*. a Peruvian sheep اَلپاکا بکری its wool اَلپاکا (اُون) cloth made of it اَلپاکا کا کپڑا

alpenstock (*al*-pen-stok) *n* long steel-pointed staff used in mountaineering پہاڑی عصا

alpha (*al*-fa) the first letter of the Greek alphabet یونانی رسم الخط کا پہلا حرف اَلفا ، اَلِف *I am Alpha and Omega*, I am the Beginning and the End میں (خدا تعالیٰ) اوّل و آخر ہوں ، اَنَا الاَوّل اَنا الآخِر

alphabet (*al*-fa-bet) *n*. letters of a written language الف بے ، الف با ، ابجد ، حروفِ تہجی rudiments مبادی ، مُبادیات **alphabetical** (al-fa-*bet*-i-kĕl) *adj*. of the alphabet ابجدی *in alphabetical order* in ABC......Z order ابجدی ترتیب سے

alpine (*al*-pin) *adj*. of the Alps کوہستانِ ایلپس کا relating to the Alps کوہستانِ ایلپس سے متعلق **Alps** *n*. a range of mountains in Switzerland کوہستانِ ایلپس

Alpinist (*al*-pi-nist) mountaineer, esp. in the Alps کوہ پیما (خصوصاً کوہِ ایلپس کا)

already (awl-*red*-i) *adv*. before a certain time اب سے ، پیشتر ، قبل ازیں before now پہلے ہی ، پہلے ہی سے

Alsatian (al-*say*-shĕn, or al-*saysh*-yĕn) *n*. a kind of large wolf-like sheep-dog السیشن کُتّا *adj*. dog of this breed السیشن

also (*awl*-soh) *adv*. besides, too, as well, in addition بھی ، اور ، نیز ، مزید

altar (*awl*-tĕ*) raised platform for making sacrifices قربان گاہ communion table in a church عشائے ربّانی کی میز *lead a woman to the altar*, marry her سے شادی کرنا **Note:** **Altar** (قربان گاہ) has *a* before r, while **alter** (بدلنا) has *e* before r.

an altar

alter (*awl*-tĕ*) *v.t.* & *i*. change, become changed بدلنا ، تبدیل ہونا ، تبدیل کرنا **alteration** (-*ray*-) *n*. change تبدیلی

altercate (*awl*-tĕ*-kayt) *v. i*. dispute (*with*) لڑائی جھگڑا کرنا **altercation** (-*kay*-) *n*. quarrel لڑائی جھگڑا ، حُجّت بحث

alter ego (*al*-tĕ*-*eg*-oh) *n*. one's other self ہمزاد intimate friend قریبی دوست ، جگری دوست

alternate *adj*. (awl-*tĕ**-nit) in turn یکے بعد دیگرے ، باری باری *on alternate days*, leaving one day in between ایک دن چھوڑ کر ہر تیسرے دن *v.t.* & *i*. (*awl*-tĕ*-nayt) to happen or cause to happen by turns باری باری ہونا یا ہونے دینا *alternating current* (abb. *A.C.*), electric current travelling first one way, then the other along the same wire اے۔سی (بجلی) اُلٹی رَو ، بدل رَو **alternation** (awl-tĕ-*nay*-shĕn) *n*. تبادُل **alternative** (awl-*teh*-ne-tiv) *adj*. & *n*. (offering) a second choice متبادل (صورت) ، کوئی اور صورت *There was no alternative* اور کوئی صورت بنتی نہ تھی **alternator** *n*. dynamo giving A.C. (or alternating current) اے۔سی ڈائینمو (ڈائینمو) ، اُلٹی رَو والا برق ساز **Note:** **alternate** signifies one after the other, **alternative** denotes choice between two.

although (al-*thoh*) *conj*. even if, though اگرچہ ، ہرچند ، باوجودیکہ ، گو ▣ **Though** and **although** mean exactly the same thing but are used with varying sound-effects. Note also that in current English usage **yet** does not follow *though*, but it may follow *although*.

altitude (*ahl*-ti-tewd) *n*. height (esp. above sea level) بلندی ، اِرتفاع

alto (*al*-toh) *n*. counter-tenor; falsetto; male voice of the highest (or female voice of the lowest) pitch اونچے پاٹ کی آواز ، پاٹ دار

altogether (awl-to-*gedh*-ĕ*) *adv*. completely

سب ملا کر، کل on the whole فی الجملہ، بحیثیت مجموعی
altruism (*al*-troo-izm) *n.* regard for the good of others rather than one's own ایثار، ایثار پیشگی، بے غرضی **altruist** *n.* ایثار پیشہ، بے غرض **altruistic** (-*is*-) *adj.* بے غرض
alum (*al*-um) *n.* a bitter mineral salt پھٹکری
aluminium (a-loo-*min*-i-um, -lew-) *n.* a very light white metal ایلومینیم، الونیم **aluminum** *n.* U.S. way of spelling 'aluminium' ایلومنیم
alumnus (a-*lum*-nus) *n.* former student of a university, college or school سابق طالب علم **alumni** (-ni) *n. pl.* سابق طلبہ یا سابقہ طالبات
always (*awl*-wayz, -wez, -wiz) *adv.* at all times ہمیشہ، ہر وقت، دائما *not always*, at some times only کبھی کبھار، ہمیشہ نہیں
A.M. (also **a.m.**) (*ay*-em) abb. of ante-meridiem قبل از دوپہر، صبح
am *v.* ہوں (1st person pr. t. of **be**, which see)
amain (a-*mayn*) *adv.* with all one's force پورے زور سے
amalgam (a-*mal*-gam) *n.* mixture of a metal with mercury سیمابی آمیزش، ملغم **amalgamate** (a-*mal*-ga-mayt) *v.t.* & *i.* make such mixture سیمابی آمیزش کرنا، ملغم بنانا mix together ملنا، ملانا، آمیزش ہونا یا کرنا **amalgamation** (-*may*-) *n.* amalgamating تلغیم
amass (a-*mas*) *v.t.* accumulate (esp. wealth) (دولت) جمع کرنا collect into a heap ڈھیر لگا دینا
amateur (*am*-e-tew*, -tě*) *n.* one who studies an art or plays a game for the love of it and not for money (as opposed to a *professional*) شوقین، غیر پیشہ ور **amateurish** *adj.* not perfect, done by an unpractised person غیر پیشہ ورانہ
amatory (a-ma-ta-ri) *adj.* (of affair, letters, etc.) relating to love عاشقانہ
amaze (a-*mayz*) *v.t.* fill with great surprise or wonder (*at* something) متحیر کرنا **amazement** *n.* استعجاب **amazing** *adj.* حیرت انگیز، حیران کن ▣ To **amaze** is to puzzle as to its origin ; to **astonish,** by its greatness ; to **astound**, stun to inaction ; to **surprise** someone by taking him unawares.
Amazon (*am*-a-zun) *n.* *Cl. myth.* a woman warrior یونانی دیومالا میں) جنگجو عورت) a tall, strong masculine woman دیو پیکر عورت، تنومند عورت name of a S. American river دریائے ایمیزن
ambassador (am-*bas*-e-dě*) *n.* diplomatic representative of one's country in another land سفیر، ایلچی **ambassadress** *n.* woman ambassador سفیرہ، سفیر خاتون wife of an ambassador سفیر کی بیگم
amber (*am*-bě*) *n.* hard yellow gum کہربا، عنبر its colour عنبری **ambergris** (*am*-bě*-grees) *n.* sweet smelling opaque, ash coloured fat thrown up by a whale عنبر، اشہب
ambidextrous (-*deks*-trus) *adj.* able to use both hands equally well دُہتّا double-dealing منافق
ambient (*am*-bi-ent) *n.* surrounding محیط
ambiguous (am-*big*-ew-us), *adj.* of double meaning or nature مبہم، ذو معنی doubtful مشکوک، مشتبہ **ambiguity** (am-bi-*gew*-i-ti) *n.* uncertainty of meaning ابہام، ابہام
ambit (*am*-bit) *n.* extent وسعت، پھیلاؤ scope میدان boundary حدود
ambition (am-*bish*-ěn) *n.* strong desire (*to be* or do something, or *of* success, fame or power) عالی حوصلگی، بلند نظری، اولوالعزمی، حوصلہ مندی that which one desires to do آرزو، تمنا **ambitious** (am-*bish*-us) *adj.* ardently desirous (*of* or *to do* something) حوصلہ مند، اولوالعزم (of plans, etc.) needing great effort حوصلہ مند، اولوالعزم، حوصلہ مندانہ، بڑا
amble (am-běl) *v.i.* (horse) move along without hurrying, lifting two feet on one side together دوگام چلنا (person) move slowly سُبک خرامی *n.* slow easy pace دوگامہ
ambrosia (am-*broh*-zi-a) *n.* *Cl. myth.* food of the Greek gods یونانی دیوتاؤں کی خوراک، غذائے ربانی **ambrosial** *adj.* very delicious لذیذ fragrant خوشبودار
ambulance (*am*-bew-lens) *n.* van for carrying the sick or wounded ڈولی، بیمار، زخمیوں کی گاڑی، بیمار گاڑی moving hospital in the army کشتی شفاخانہ **ambulent** (-*am*-) *adj.* (of disease) shifting from one part of the body to another متحرک، تحرکی (of treatment) involving patient's exercise ورزشی (علاج)
ambush (*am*-bush) *v.t.* & *i.* make a surprise attack from a hidden place, lie in wait for گھات لگانا، گھات میں بیٹھنا place for such an attack کمین گاہ body of troops hidden to attack in this way گھات میں بیٹھی ہوئی فوج
ambuscade (*am*-bus-kayd) same as **ambush** (which see)
ameba *n.* same as **amoeba** (which see)
ameliorate (a-*mee*-li-o-rayt) *v.t.* & *i.* make or become better بہتر بنانا، اصلاح کرنا، سدھارنا **amelioration** (-*ray*-) *n.* بہبود، بہبودی، رفاہ، سدھار
amen (ah-*men*, ay-*men*) *n.* & *int.* May it be so (word used at the end of a prayer) آمین
amenable (a-*meen*-a-bel) *adj.* subject (*to* discipline) اطاعت پذیر، منقاد (things) capable of being put to test (*to* a rule, etc.) قابل آزمائش **amenability** (-*bil*-) *n.* اطاعت پذیری، اصلاحیت **amenably** *adv.* اطاعت پذیری سے
amend (a-*mend*) *v.t.* & *i.* correct, improve سدھرنا، سدھارنا، سیدھی راہ پر آنا یا لانا make changes in (laws, etc.) (قانون میں) ترمیم کرنا **amendment** *n.*

alteration (*to* laws, etc.) ترمیم **amends** (a-*mendz*) *n.* compensation تلافی، تلافی کرنا *make amends for* *amende honorable* (a-men-do-no-rahbl) public apology and reparation باعزت تلافی
amenity (a-*mee*-ni-ti) *n.* pleasantness خوشگواری *the amenity of climate* آب وہوا کا خوشگوار ہونا **amenities**. *n. pl.* things making life pleasant زندگی کے مزے *the amenities of city life*, its picture-houses, libraries, etc. شہر کی آسائشیں
America (a-*me*-ri-ka) *n.* the New World, *i.e.*, N. & S. America نئی دُنیا North America براعظم شمالی امریکہ (also the *United States of America*), U.S.A. امریکہ، ریاستہائے متحدہ امریکہ **American** *n.* & *adj.* belonging to the United States of America امریکی belonging to N. or S. America شمالی یا جنوبی امریکہ کا **Americanism** *n.* word or pronunciation gaining currency in English from Yankee talk امریکی لفظ، محاورہ یا تلفظ، امریکیت
amethyst (*am*-e-thist) *n.* precious stone (usu. of violet colour) رنیلم
amiable (*ay*-mee-a-bèl) *adj.* lovable, kind-hearted, good-tempered دل آویز، دل کش **amiability** (*-bil-*) *n.* being amiable دل آویزی، دل کشی **amiably** *adj.* از رہ لطف
amicable (*am*-ik-a-bèl) *adj.* friendly دوستانہ peaceful پُرامن **amicably** *adv.* دوستانہ طور پر، آشتی سے
amid (a-*mid*), **amidst** (a-*midst*) *prep.* in the middle of (کے) درمیان (میں) during کے دوران میں

Note: Amidst is generally used with abstract nouns while **amid** may be used with either abstract or concrete nouns; as *amid the trees* *amidst the confusion*.

amiss (a-*miss*) *adj.* & *adv* out of order, wrong غلط، بے تکا *take (something) amiss*, feel offended at it بُرا ماننا *Is there anything amiss?* کوئی گڑبڑ تو نہیں؟ *You must have heard amiss* تم نے بات غلط سُنی ہوگی
amity (*am*-i-ti) *n.* friendship دوستی، میل جول، ارتباط
ammeter (*-am-*) *n.* instrument for measuring strength of electric current in amperes ایمپیئر پیما، رَو پیما
ammonia (a-*moh*-ni-a) *n.* a sharp smelling colourless gas (used for cleaning things or making ice) امونیا گیس، نوشادری گیس
ammunition (am-ew-*nish*-en) *n.* military stores (now only used of powder, shot and shell) گولہ بارود، گولیاں
amnesty (*am*-nes-ti) *n.* general pardon of convicts عام معافی، امان
amoeba, ameba (a-*mee*-ba) *n.* simplest living creature, found in water امیبا، بدلو an amoeba
amok *adv.* same as **amuck** (which see)
among (a-*mung*), **amongst** (a-*mungst*) *prep.* between, in the middle of, کے درمیان میں

Note: Among is generally used with abstract nouns while **amongst** may be used with either abstract or concrete nouns. as *among the students*. *amongst the ideas*.

We use **between** when the choice lies between two things or persons and **among** when it lies between more than two. **Between** is, however, used with even more than two when there is an idea of reciprocal action in which all the parties are active, as *a treaty between ten powers*. Also note the following: *It is agreed* **among** *us to form two teams* **between** *us. The choice lies* **between** *the three candidates. They captured the animal* **between** *them* (i.e. all together) *He inserted a needle* **between** *the petals of a rose.*

amorous (*am*-o-rus) *adj.* showing love عاشقانہ، عشقیہ
amorphous (a-*mo**-fus) *adj.* having no regular shape غیر متشکل
amount (a-*mount*) *v.i.* be equal (*to*) مرادف ہونا *It amounts to this*, it is as good as saying that مطلب یہ ہوا کہ، گویا کہ معنی یہ ہونا کہ add up to حساب میں میزان آنا *n.* the total sum میزان، کُل رقم certain quantity or number شمار، گنتی، تعداد
amour (a-*moo**) *n.* secret love affair آشنائی، مخفی معاشقہ
ampere (*am*-pi-è*) *n.* unit employed in measuring electric current ایمپیئر، برقی رَو کی اکائی
amphibian (am-*fee*-bi-an) *n.* animal able to live both on land and in water (*e.g.* frog) جل تھلیا، جَل جَھو سیا **amphibious** *adj.* (of animal, vehicle, plane, etc.) able to live or work in both these places جل تھلوی
Amphion (am-*fi*-on) *Cl. myth.* a king of Thebes (in Greece) to whom Mercury gave a lyre. He played it with such skill as to move stones and make them form the city wall امفئن
amphitheatre (*am*-fi-thi-ay-tĕ*) *n.* circular building with rows of seats round an open space used for public games and shows (in ancient Rome) (قدیم رُومی) مدوّر تماشا گاہ
Amphitrite (am-fit-*ri*-tee) *Cl. myth.* wife of Neptune to whom she bore Triton امفیترائیتی
ample (*am*-pèl) *adj.* large-sized, with plenty of space فراخ، کشادہ more than enough کافی، بہت **amply** *adv.* abundantly, almost fully بڑی حد تک
amplification *n.*, **amplifier** *n.* see under **amplify**
amplify (*amp*-li-fI) *v.t.* make larger or louder بڑھانا، بلند کرنا **amplifier** *n.* loudspeaker آلۂ جہیر الصوت، بلند گو **amplification** (*-ay-*) *n.* enlargement اطناب (*pl.*) details تفصیلات **amplitude** (*am*-pli-tewd) *n.* (fig.) largeness کثرت، وفور، فراوانی (physics) extent of vibratory movement ارتعاش کا عرض، عرض گردش
amplitude modulation *n.* see Addenda
amply *adv.* see under **ample**
ampoule (am-*pool*) *n.* small sealed glass capsule for holding injections, etc. ٹیکے والی دوا کی نھی سی سربمہر شیشی، ٹیکہ دانی

amputate (*am*-pew-tayt) *v.t.* cut off a limb قطع عضو ، ہاتھ یا پاؤں ، کاٹ ڈالنا **amputation** (-*tay*-) *n.* قطع عضو

amtrac *n.* see Addenda

amuck (a-*muk*), **amok** (a-*mok*) *adv.* (used only in the phrase) *to run amuck*, to go mad and run about wildly with a desire to kill people جس کے سر پر خون سوار ہوا اُس کا دیوانہ وار دَوڑنا ،

amulet (*am*-ew-let) *n.* thing worn as charm against evil تعویذ ، گنڈا ،

amuse (am-*yooz*) *v.t.* give pleasure دِل خوش کرنا ، جی بہلانا . cause smile or laughter گدگدانا **amusement** *n.* something that amuses تفریح ، کھیل feeling of amusement گدگداہٹ **amusing** *adj.* entertaining دِلچسپ

[1]**an** (an) see [3]**a**

[2]**-an** (ĕn) *suf.* (for making *n.* & *adj.*) of, pertaining to والا ، ی (as : *republican* جمہوری *Italian* اطالوی

anachronism (a-*nak*-ro-nizm) *n.* error in dating something غلط زمانی ، سہوِ زمانی ، something out of date غلط زماں

anaemia (a-*nee*-mi-a) *n.* disease involving lack of enough blood خون کی کمی ، قلّتِ دَم **anaemic** *adj.* suffering from anaemia جس کے خون میں سُرخ ذرّوں کی کمی ہو ، زرد رُو ، مریضِ نقرالدّم ، -

anaesthesia (a-nis-*thee*-zia) *n.* loss of all senses in a deep sleep induced by a drug before a surgical operation بے حِس کرنا ، خَدَر **anaesthetic** *n.* drug causing such sleep مُخدِّر **anaesthetist** *n.* physician specializing in the use of such drugs ماہرِ خدر

anagram (*an*-a-gram) *n.* new word made by changing the order of letters in a word (as *evil* or *vile* from *live*) صنعتِ مَقلوب

analogy (a-*nal*-o-ji) *n.* partial agreement or likeness مطابقت ، مشابہت (logic) reasoning from such partial likeness قیاس **analogous** (-jus) *adj.* similar, that which may be compared مماثل ، مُشابہ

analyse (*an*-a-lȋz) *v.t.* break up (sentence or chemical compound) into components تجزیہ یا تحلیل کرنا ، ترکیب نحوی کرنا **analysis** (a-*nal*-i-sis) *n.* (*pl.* *analyses* ; *pr.*, -seez) process of analysing تجزیہ ، تحلیل ، ترکیب نحوی ، *n. pl.* تجزیے ، ترکیبیں **analyst** *n.* one skilled in scientific analysis ماہرِ تجزیہ ، محلّل **analytic, analytical** (-*it*-) *adj.* تجزیاتی ، تحلیلی **analytically** *adv.* تجزیے سے ، تحلیلی طور پر

anarchism, anarchist *n.* see under **anarchy**

anarchy (*an*-ĕ*-ki) *n.* lack of government, طوائف الملوکی ، نراج ، فوضویت hence disorderly state بَدنظمی **anarchism** (-kizm) *n.* political theory that government is undesirable لاحکومیت ، فوضویت **anarchist** *n.* protagonist of this theory فوضوی ، نراجی

anatomical *adj.*, **anatomist** *n.* see under **anatomy**

anatomy (a-*nat*-o-mi) *n.* science of the structure of human body تشریح الاعضا ، علم تشریح ، تشریح **anatomist** *n.* ماہرِ تشریح الاعضا ، ماہرِ تشریح **anatomical** (-*tom*-i-kĕl) *adj.* تشریح الاعضا سے متعلق ، تشریحی -

ance (ens) *suf.* (for making abstract n.) being ہونا ، ی ت ، یت وغیرہ (*do*)ing کرنا ، ی ت ، یت (وغیرہ) that which is do(ne) ہونا ، ی ت ، یت وغیرہ that which (do)es ش ی ت ، یت (وغیرہ)

Anchisez (an-*k*.-seez) *Cl. myth.* father of Aeneas انکائیسیز

ancestral *adj.*, **ancestry** *n.* see under **ancestor**

ancestor (*an**-ses-tĕ*) *n.* (*fem.*, *ancestress*) (usu. *pl.*) forefather of one's parents بُزرگ ، آباؤ اَجداد ، بُزرگ **ancestry** *n.* (*pl.* used as *sing.*) all one's ancestors **ancestral** (-*ses*-) *adj.* of or from ancestors جَدّی ، موروثی

anchor (*an*-kĕ*) *n* heavy iron hook let down to the bottom of the sea to keep the ship at rest لنگر *v.t.* to hold a ship fast with an anchor لنگر انداز ہونا ، لنگر ڈالنا *lower an anchor*, *come to anchor*, stop sailing and lower the anchor لنگر انداز ہونا ، لنگر ڈالنا *lie at anchor*, *be at anchor*, be held fast by an anchor لنگر انداز ہونا *weigh anchor*, *take up anchor*, *pull up the anchor*, لنگر اٹھانا *cast anchor*, let down anchor لنگر ڈالنا fix (one's hope *in*, *on*) اعتماد کرنا ، بھروسہ کرنا **anchorage** (*ank*-) *n.* anchoring لنگر اندازی place for anchoring لنگر گاہ ، لنگر ڈالنے کا مقام

an anchor

anchovy (an-*choh*-vi, *an*-cho-vi) *n.* small Mediterranean fish used for pickling سمنورہ

ancient (*ayn*-shent) *adj.* belonging to times long past بہت پرانا ، قدیم ، قدیمی not modern غیر جدید ، دقیانوسی very old سِن رسیدہ

ancillary (an-*sil*-a-ri, *an*-sil-a-ri) *adj.* subsidiary, subordinate ضمنی ، ذیلی

and (and, an) *conj.* as well as اور many کئی *for miles and miles*, for many miles کئی ، میلوں تک ، different مختلف ، ہر طرح کی *There are books and books*, there are books of all kinds, good, bad or indifferent - کتابیں بھی ہر طرح کی ہوتی ہیں (colloq.) in order to کے لیے ، کی غرض سے *try and do it*, try to do it یہ کام کرنے کی کوشش کرو

andirons (*and*-ɪ-ĕ*nz) two iron supports for logs in the fireplace اگ ٹیک ، آگ ٹیک

Andromache (an *drom*-a-kee) *Cl. myth.* Hector's wife اَندرَماکی

Andromeda (an-*drom*-e-da) .. *Cl. myth.* daughter of an Ethiopian king. Perseus rescued her from a sea-monster, and married her اندرامیڈا a constellation ذات الکرسی

anecdote (*an*-ik-doht) *n*. short amusing story (often about some famous person) قصّہ، حکایات نقل، لطیفہ **anecdotage** *n*. dotage, old age بڑھاپا بکواس کی عمر **anecdotal** *adj*. of or containing anecdotes حکایت و لطائف سے متعلق

anemone (a-*nem*-on-ne) *n*. a white flower شقائق النعمان **sea-anemone**, a marine creature looking like a flower سمندر پھول ، ساگر پھول ،

anemone

anent (a-*nent*) *prep*. about کے بارے میں، کے متعلق

anew (a-*new*) *adv*. again, afresh پھر، از سرِ نو ، نئے سرے سے

angel (*ayn*-jel) *n*. heavenly spirit (depicted by Christians as a lovely boy with wings) فرشتہ a good, beautiful woman پری ، حور، جنت کی حور، پری ، پیکر ، حور پیکر، *My angel !* میری جان! **angelic** (an-*jel*-ik) *adj*. pertaining to angel فرشتے سے متعلق good, pure and beautiful حسین اور معصوم

anger (*an*-gĕ*) *n*. rage, ire غصّہ *v.t.* make angry ناراض ، غصّے ، غصّہ دلانا **angry** (*ang*-ri) *adj*. enraged **angrily** *adv*. in a fit of rage غصّے سے ▣ **Anger** is the ordinary everyday word ; **ire** and **wrath** the poetic words for it ; **fury** is violent anger; **rage**, at one's own weakness ; **indignation**, at the unworthiness of an act ; **passion** is exhibition of anger ; **exasperation** comes after much patience

angle (angl) *n*. corner, space between two lines which meet ; زاویہ *angle of vision*, point of view زاویۂ نظر ، زاویۂ نگاہ *right angle* 90 degrees زاویۂ قائمہ ; *acute angle*, angle less than 90 degrees زاویۂ حادّہ *obtuse angle*, angle more than 90 degrees منفرجہ زاویہ

right, acute, obtuse angle

& see Addenda *v.t.* try to catch fish with hook and line بنسی پھینکنا ، کانٹا ڈالنا *angle for*, fish for, try to lead a person on to give one something desired ڈورے ڈالنا **angler** *n*. one who catches fish with hook and line کانٹے سے مچھلی کا شکار کرنے والا ، بنسی باز **Angular** *adj.* see below

Angles *n. pl*. a tribe of the 6th-century German conquerors of Britain from whom the island got its name *England* (originally *Angleland*) اینگل

Anglican (ang-li-kĕn) *n*. & *adj*. (member) of the Church of England برطانوی کلیسا کا (رکن) **anglicize** (*ang*-li-sɪz) *v.t*. make English in form or custom انگریز یا انگریزی بنانا ، صاحب لوگ بنانا *Rich* Hindustani *have been very much anglicised* - امیر ہندوستانی تو صاحب لوگ بھی بن گئے ہیں۔

Anglo- (*ang*-loh) *pref*. English انگریزی ، فرنگی Anglo Indian of mixed English and Hindus tani breed انگریزی نسل کے ہندوستانی ، اینگلو انڈین **Anglomania** *n*. excessively unreasonable love of English ways تفریح ، انگریزوں کی ہر شے سے حد سے زیادہ رغبت ، انگریز پرستی as opposed to **Anglo-phobia**, ہر شے سے بغض ، انگریز دشمنی **Anglo-Saxon** *n*. ❶ one of the 6th-century German conquerors of Britain اینگلو سیکسن their language ; Old English ٹھیٹھ انگریزی لفظ پُرانی انگریزی word derived from this

angora (an-*gaw*-ra) *n*. a Turkish goat انگورا (بکری) cloth made of its wool انگورا (کپڑا)

angrily *adv*. **angry** *adj*. see under **anger**

anguish (*an*-gwish) *n*. severe pain (esp. of mind) کوفت ، سخت اذیت (بالخصوص ذہنی)

angular (*un*-gew-leh) *adj*. having sharp angle نکیلا (see *angle*) (person) thin ; with bones showing under the skin ہڈیوں کا ڈھانچہ unaccommodating (person) اکھڑ **angularity** *n*. اکھڑپن ، نکیلاپن دُبلا ہونا *has an angularity of character*, is socially unpleasant وہ بڑا اکھڑ ہے

anile (*an*-ɪl) *adj*. old-womanish بڑی بوڑھیوں کا سا **anility** (-*nil*-) *n*. بڑی بوڑھیوں کا سا انداز

animadvert (-*vĕ*t*) *v.t*. criticize, blame (*on* conduct, etc.) کو مورد الزام قرار دینا ، پر جرح و قدح کرنا **animadversion** *n*. stricture ; strong criticism طعن و تعریض

animal (*an*-i-mal) a living thing which is not plant حیوان ، جاندار *animal kingdom*, one of the three divisions in nature حیوانات (the other two are, *vegetable kingdom* نباتات *mineral kingdom* جمادات.) quadruped جانور ، چوپایہ a human being like an animal in his or her desires or acts جانور حیوان صفت *animal spirits*, spirit of joy, natural high spirits خوشدلی *animal heat* حرارتِ غریزی ، حرارتِ حیوانی

animalcule (an-i-*mal*-kewl) *n*. a very small animal بہت ہی چھوٹا حیوان ، حیوانچہ

animate (*an*-i-mayt) *v.t*. give life to جِلانا ، جان ڈالنا ، روح پھونکنا inspire with energy ہمت بندھانا ، جوش دلانا **animated** *adj*. lively, amusing پُرزور ، پُرلطف *animated discussion* دلچسپ اور پُر زور مُباحثہ **animation** (-*may*-shĕn) *n*. ardour, vivacity جذبہ ، جوش

animism (*an*-i-mizm) *n*. doctrine that material objects have life روحیت ، مظاہر

animosity (an-i-*mos*-i-ti) *n*. hostile spirit based on hatred سخت دشمنی اور نفرت **animus** (*an*-i-mus) *n*. hatred causing injustice انصاف کش کینہ

aniseed *n*. seed of an aromatic plant سونف ، بادیاں

ankle (*ank*-ĕl) *n*. joint connecting foot with leg ٹخنہ ،

annals (*an*-ĕlz) *n. pl*. history as told year by year وقائع ، تاریخ **annalist** *n*. writer of annals وقائع نگار ، مؤرخ

annex (a-*neks*) *v.t*. add to one's possession قبضہ کرنا ، شامل کرنا ، win (trophy etc.) جیتنا ، پانا ، لینا

take possession of (territory) الحاق کرنا *n.* (also) **annexe** (*an*-eks) small building added (*to* a large one) ذیلی مکان ، مکان کا چھوٹا ملحقہ حصّہ **annexation** (-*say*-) *n.* joining on (*to* something) اِلحاق

annihilate (a-*ni*-è-layt) *v. t.* destroy utterly نیست و نابود **annihilation** (-*lay*-) *n.* utter destruction تباہ کاری ، بربادی ، تباہی ، فناءِ کامل

anniversary (an-i-*vě**-sè-ri) *n.* yearly return of the date (*of* an event) سالانہ تقریب ، سال گرہ *birth anniversary* سالگرہ *wedding anniversary* شادی کی سالگرہ *death anniversary* برسی

Anno Christi (*an*-noh-*kris*-ti) (abb. **A.C.**) (in) the year of the Christian era سنِ عیسوی *1970 A.C.* ۱۹۷۰ء ، ۱۹۷۰ عیسوی

Anno Domini (*an*-oh-*dom*-in-i) (abb. **A.D.**), *adv.* (in) the year of our Lord (words written after a year of the Christian era after the birth of Christ) عیسوی ، میلادی

annotate (*an*-oh-tayt) *v.t.* write notes (*to* or *on*) شرح لکھنا ، یا کرنا **annotation** (-*tayshn*) *n.* (writing) notes شرح نویسی ، شرح **annotator** *n.* one who writes notes شارح

announce (a-*nouns*) *v.t.* make known publicly اعلان کرنا ، introduce a visitor آنے والے کی اطلاع کرنا **announcer** *n.* (esp.) one who announces talks or reads news on the radio اعلان کنندہ ، مُعلن ، خبرخواں نشر کنندہ **announcement** *n.* announcing ; that which is announced اعلان

annoy (a-*noi*) *v. t.* irritate برہم کرنا **annoyance** *n.* برہمی ، جھنجھلاہٹ **annoying** *adj.* causing annoyance (*to*) غصّہ دلانے والی ، برہم کن ▣ To **annoy** is to cause an unpleasant feeling, not very serious ; to **vex**, disappoint one's expectation of a happy result ; to **irritate**, rub unpleasantly or annoy ; to **worry**, cause mental uneasiness ; to **chagrin**, disappoint pride ; to **embarrass**, make one unable to answer ; to **confuse**, make bewildered; to **torment**, as an uneasy conscience; **to plague** by repeated requests ; to **harass** by leaving one no peace . to **tease** someone whom one likes.

annual (*an*-ew-ěl) *adj.* yearly سالانہ *annual function* سالانہ تقریب ، *annual issue of a periodical*, (also called *the annual*) کسی اخبار یا رسالے کا سالنامہ ، *n.* book, etc., which appears every year under the same title but with new contents سالنامہ **annually** *adv.* برس کے برس ، سال بہ سال ، سالانہ **annuity** (a-*new*-i-ti) *n.* yearly payment سالانہ وظیفہ ، سالیانہ ،

annul (a-*nul*) *v.t.* (-*ll*-) do away with (law or agreement) ; make null and void منسوخ کرنا *annulment n.* تنسیخ

annunciation (a-nun-si-*ay*-shěn) *n.* proclaiming (*of* some important news) اعلان (esp.) announcing to Mary of the incarnation of Christ بشارت ، تبشیر

Annus Mirabilis (*an*-us-mi-*rab*-i-lis) the marvellous or wonderful year حیرت انگیز سال

anode (*an*-ohd) positive pole of a battery مثبتی قطب

anodyne (*an*-oh-dim) *n.* medicine that soothes pain مُسکِن ، مُخدِّر

anoint (an-*oint*) *v.t.* pour or rub oil on (the head or body), esp. at religious ceremony بدن پر تیل ڈالنا یا مَلنا ، مالش کرنا ، مسح کرنا ، اصطباغ دینا ، بپتسمہ دینا

anomalous (a-*nom*-a-lus) *adj.* not normal or regular بے قاعدہ ، خلافِ قیاس **anomaly** (a-*nom*-a-li) *n.* irregularity ; deviation from the rule بے قاعدگی خلافِ قیاس ہونا

anon (a-*non*) *adv.* (archaic word for) presently ابھی ، تھوڑی دیر میں ، *ever and anon*, now and anon کبھی کبھی گاہے ، گاہے .

anonymous (a-*non*-i-mus) *adj.* nameless or with a name which is not made known گمنام ، غیر معروف *anonymous gift* گمنام شخص کی طرف سے تحفہ *anonymous letter*, unsigned letter گمنام خط *anonymous book, book by an anonymous author*, book not mentioning its author's name گمنام مصنف کی کتاب **anonymity** *n.* (an-o-*nim*-i-ti) being anonymous گمنامی **anonymously** *adv.* نام چھپاکر

another (a-*nudh*-ě*) *adj.* & *pron.* different اور ، جیسا ، نیا ، اور ، دُوسرا ، کوئی like ; as good (or bad) as ایک اور ، **one another** mutually among many ایک دوسرے کو ۔

answer (*ahn*-sě*) *n.*, *v.t.* & *i.* reply جواب دینا give an impolite answer, esp. when being corrected سخت جواب دینا ، مُنہ توڑ جواب دینا *answer the door, answer the bell* دستک کا جواب دینا *answer a purpose*, be suitable or sufficient موزوں ہونا ، پورا اُترنا *answer for* (a) be responsible *for* کا ذمّہ دار ہونا ، کے لیے جواب دہ ہونا (b) atone *for* تلافی کرنا correspond *to* کے مطابق ہونا *answer to a description* بیان یا پہچان کے مطابق ہونا **answerable** *adj.* responsible ذمّہ دار ، جواب دِہ ▣ To **answer**, give an adequate and satisfying explanation by request **respond**, answer promising help ; to **reply**, either simply to answer or to explain after a request that the claim made in the request is not considered justified to **rejoin**, reply to a reply by raising a new issue or a counterclaim ; to **retort**, reply with feeling.

[1]**ant** (ant) *n.* a well-known tiny insect چیونٹی **white ant** another kind of small and dangerous insect دیمک

[2]**-ant** (ent) *suf.* (for making n. which indicates) agent or instrument والا ، گر ، گار ، دار (as : *applicant*, عرضی دینے والا (for making adj. from verbs)

having or showing والا، فاتحانہ، کامگار، ہوا (as : *triumphant* فتح مندانہ)

Antaeus (an-*tee*-us) *Cl. myth.* a giant killed by Hercules who lifted him up. He was invincible as long as he touched the ground انٹی ئس

antagonism (an-*tag*-o-nizm) *n.* feeling of hatred and active opposition نفرت، دشمنی **antagonist** *n.* adversary دشمن، حریف **antagonistic** *adj.* hostile مخالفانہ، معاندانہ **antagonize** (-niz) *v.t.* to make a person one's enemy دشمن بنانا، بیری بنانا

antarctic (ant-*ah*k*-tik) *adj.* on or near the South Pole جنوبی، قطب جنوبی کا *n.* the area round the South Pole قطب جنوبی *the Antarctic Ocean*, (*opp.* of Arctic Ocean) بحر منجمد جنوبی *Antarctic Zone, Antarctic Circle* منطقہ باردہ جنوبی

ante- (*an*-ti) *pref.* before پہلے کا، سے قبل (as *antedate*)

antecede (*an*-ti-seed) *v. t.* to go before, to precede in place, time or rank پہلے ہونا، مقام، زمانے یا رتبے کے لحاظ سے مقدم ہونا، افضل ہونا

antecedent (an-ti-*see*-dent) *n.* (grammar) noun or noun clause referred to by a relative pronoun (as : *man* in *the man who came yesterday*) مرجع **antecedents** (*pl.*) past history (*of* a person or persons) حالات **antechamber** *n.* same as **anteroom** (which see) **antedate** *v.t.* put a date (on letter, cheque etc.) earlier than the true one پہلے کی کوئی تاریخ ڈالنا come before time زمانے کے لحاظ سے پہلے ہونا، مقدم ہونا

antediluvian (an-ti-di-*lu*-vian) *a.* before Noah's deluge قبل طوفان نوح outdated دقیانوسی

antelope (*ant*-i-lohp) *n.* a deer-like animal بارہ سنگا

antelope

ante meridiem (*an*-ti-me-*ree*-di-um), (abbr. **a.m.** or **A.M.**) *adv.* before noon دوپہر سے پہلے، قبل نصف النہار، قبل دوپہر *11 A.M.* گیارہ بجے قبل دوپہر

antenatal *adj.* before birth قبل پیدائش

antenna (an-*ten*-ah) (*pl.*) **antennae,** (an-*ten*-i) *n.* one of the two long hairs acting as feelers in insects قرن، محاس aerial ایریل

antennae

anterior (-*tee*-) *adj.* before اگلا، آگے

anteroom, antechamber *n.* small room leading to a large one پیش دالان، ڈیوڑھی

anthem (*an*-them) *n.* religious song of praise ترانہ *national anthem,* national song of a country قومی ترانہ

anthology (an-*thol*-o-ji) *n.* collection of poems or pieces of prose by different writers, بیاض، ادبی کشکول، گلدستہ selection from the works of the same author مجموعۂ منتخب کلام، انتخاب

anthracite (*an*-thra-sit) *n.* kind of hard, slow-burning coal جھوٹا کوئلہ

anthrax (*anth*-raks) *n.* a dangerous infectious disease of cattle مویشیوں کا طحالی بخار، پھڑتپ

anthropoid (*anth*-ro-poid) *adj.* looking like a human being انسان نما، مردم سار

anthropology (an-throh-*pol*-o-ji) *n.* science of the human race dealing with its evolution, beliefs, and customs انسانیات، بشریات **anthropologist** *n.* ماہر انسانیات، ماہر بشریات **anthropological** (-*loj*-) *adj.* بشریاتی، انسانیاتی

anthropomorphism (an-throh-po-*mo**-fizm) *n.* concept of God as having a human form تشبیہیت

anti- (*an*-ti) *pref.* against شکن، توڑ، مار as *anti-aircraft (gun)* طیارہ شکن (توپ)

antibiotic *n.* & *adj.* see Addenda

antichrist *n.* Christ's enemy expected by mediaeval Christianity to appear before the end of the world دجال

anticipate (an-*tis*-i-payt) *v.t.* expect, estimate, متوقع چیز کا اندازہ کرنا *anticipate one's income* اپنی متوقع آمدنی کا اندازہ کرنا do something before others do it پیش بندی کرنا see the need for something and do it in advance پیش بینی کرنا، پہلے سے اندازہ کرنا *anticipate a person's needs* کسی کی ضروریات کا اندازہ کرنا expect توقع کرنا **anticipation** *n.* توقع، پیش بینی، پیش بندی، پہلے سے اندازہ کرنا *in anticipation* پیشگی *in anticipation of* کی توقع پر، کی پیش بندی کے طور پر ☒ To **anticipate,** make ready for ; to **expect,** have an idea that something will happen.

anticlimax (an-ti-*kli*-maks) *n.* sudden and laughable change from something serious تنزل، تخفیض، اُتار

antics (*an*-tiks) *n. pl.* amusing playful movements مضحکہ خیز حرکات carefree behaviour اُبالی پن، بے پروایانہ انداز

antidote (*an*-ti-doht) *n.* medicine given to prevent effects of poison تریاق، فادزہر

Antigone (an-*tig*-oh-nee) *Cl. myth.* faithful daughter of the banished Theban king, Oedipus. Creon punished her with death for defying the royal decree which forbade funeral rites to her brother انٹی گنی

antimony (*an*-ti-ma-ni) *n.* a bluish metal سرمہ

antipathy (an-*tip*-a-thi) *n.* permanent instinctive dislike دائمی نفرت، جبلی نفرت

antipodes (an-*tip*-o-deez) *n. pl.* part of the world lying just opposite our side (as Pakistan and the U.S.A.) کرۂ ارض کا وہ حصہ جو کسی نقطے کے بالمقابل دوسری طرف ہو

antiquarian, antiquary *n.* see under **antique**
antiquated (*an*-ti-kway-tid) *adj.* out of date پُرانا، کُہنہ، فرسُودہ no longer in use غیر مروّج، متروک (of a person) having old fashioned ways and ideas دقیانوسی، بہت پُرانی وضع کا
antique (an-*teek*) *adj.* ancient in the style of past times قدیم، عتیق *n.* something remaining from ancient times باقیات، آثار **antiquity** (an-*tik*-wi-ti) *n.* the distant past عہدِ رفتہ، عہدِ پارینہ (*pl.*) buildings, ruins, works of art remaining from very early times آثارِ قدیمہ، اثریات **antiquarian** *adj* (of the study) of antiquities آثارِ قدیمہ سے متعلق، اثریاتی *n.* (also **antiquary**) one who studies, collects, or sells antiquities ماہرِ اثریات، آثار فروش
antiseptic (an-ti-*sep*-tic) *adj.* having the power to destroy germs of disease جراثیم کش *n.* such a medicine جراثیم کُش دوا
antisocial (an-ti-*soh*-shèl) *adj.* (person, elements, behaviour, etc.) opposed to the interests of society - تمدّن بیزارانہ، تمدّن بیزار، تمدّن کش، سماج دُشمن
antithesis (an-*tith*-e-sis) (*pl.*, *antitheses* ; *pr.*, -seez) *n.* exact opposite متضاد، متناقض putting together of opposite ideas تناقض، تضاد، صنعتِ تضاد، صنعتِ تناقض **antithetical** (-*thet*-) *adj.* based on antithesis مُتناقض، متضاد
antitoxin (an-ti-*tok*-sin) serum destroying poison of some disease in the body مرض شکن ٹیکہ، تریاقی ٹیکہ۔
antlers (*ant*-lerz) *n. pl.* branching horns of a stag (بارہ سنگھے کے) شاخ در شاخ سینگ
antonym (*ant*-oh-nim) *n.* word opposite in meaning to another ضد، اُلٹ

antlers

anvil (*an*-vil) *n.* iron block on which pieces of red hot metal are hammered into shape اَہرَن

an anvil

anxiety (ang-*zī*-ti) *n.* feeling of doubt and fear about the future اندیشہ mental uneasiness پریشانی eager desire *anxiety for knowledge* علم کی تمنّا **anxious** (*ank*-shus) *adj.* feeling anxiety پریشان causing anxiety تشویشناک strongly wishing (*to do* or get something) آرزُومند، متمنّی
any (*an*-i) *pron.* & *adv.* used instead of *a*, *an*, *one* or *some*, in negative and interrogative sentences کوئی، کسی every کوئی سا at all بالکل نہیں، **anybody** *n.* (one word) any person کچھ بھی نہیں ہر کوئی، کوئی، ہر ایک important personality اہم شخصیت **anyhow** *adv.* in any way تاہم، پھر بھی carelessly کسی نہ کسی طرح in any case بہرحال، بہر صُورت **anyone** (one word) *n.* anybody کوئی، ہر کوئی، ہر ایک
any one (two words) *adj.* اکیلا، کوئی اکیلا، تنہا کوئی، **anything** *n.* (one word) thing of any kind کچھ *adv.* ٹھیک، بالکل *Is it anything like that?* کیا یہ بالکل ویسا ہے؟ **anyway** *adv.* anyhow (see above) **anywhere** *adv.* کہیں، کہیں بھی، *anywhere else* اور کہیں بھی
apace (a-*pays*) *adv.* quickly, swiftly تیز تیز، تیزی سے
apart (a-*pah*t*) *adv.* separately جُدا، علیٰحدہ، الگ *set apart* الگ کر رکھنا، الگ کر لینا *apart from* کے علاوہ، سے قطعِ نظر *joking apart* ہنسی کی بات الگ ہی
apartment (a-*pah*t*-ment) *n.* (*pl.*) furnished lodgings rented out کرائے کے آراستہ کمرے *take apartments (at)* (کہیں) آراستہ کمرے کرائے پر لینا any room for living in کمرہ
apathetic (ap-a-*thet*-ik) *adj.* showing apathy مُنجمد، بےحس، سرد مہر، ذہنی طور پر کاہل **apathy** (*ap*-a-thi) *n.* lack of feeling, indifference بےحسی، کٹھورپن، ذہنی کاہلی -
ape (ayp) *n.* large tailless monkey able to walk like human beings (*e.g.* gorilla or chimpanzee) بوزنہ، بے دُم کا بندر *v.t.* imitate foolishly ریس کرنا، بھونڈی نقل اتارنا **apish** (*ay*-) *adj.* ape-like بوزنہ صفت
aperient (a-*pee*-ri-ent) *n.* & *adj.* laxative مُلیّن
aperture (*ap*-ĕ-chĕ*) *n.* opening gap موکھا، سوراخ، روزن
apex (*ay*-peks) *n.* pointed top of anything نوک، چوٹی، راس *the apex of a triangle* مثلث کی راس (*the*) highest point (*of* something) عروج، اوج، انتہا *at the apex of one's fortune* اوجِ تقدیر پر
aphorism (*af*-o-rizm) *n.* short, wise saying جامع کلمہ proverb ضرب المثل، مثل، کہاوت **aphorist** *n.* one who writes aphorisms جوامع الکلم والا **aphoristic** *adj.* (of style) full of aphorisms جوامع الکلم والا.
Aphrodite (af-roh-*dy*-tee) *Cl. myth.* Greek goddess of love and beauty, identified with the Roman goddess, Venus. She was the mother of Eros or Cupid زُہرہ، افروداتی
apiary (*ay*-pi-a-ri) *n.* place where bees are kept مگس خانہ، مکھیال **apiarist** *n.* one who keeps bees نحلی
apiece (a-*pees*) *adv.* to, for or by each فی *a rupee apiece* ایک روپیہ فی (شخص وغیرہ)
apish *adj.* see under **ape**
aplomb (a-*plom*) *n.* self-confidence خود اعتمادی presence of mind اَوسان قائم رکھنا
apocrypha (a-*pok*-ri-fa) *n.* writing of doubtful truth (esp. certain books formerly included in the Old Testament) مشتبہ تحریر، مُسترد اناجیل، **apocryphal** *adj.* doubtful, false, unacceptable مُشتبہ، غلط، ناقابلِ قبول،
apogee (ap-o-jee) *n.* point of a heavenly body's orbit at which it is farthest away from the earth acme اِنتہا
Apollo (a-*pol*-o) *Cl. myth.* the Greek god of

prophecy, song and music He was identified with the Roman sun-god, Phoebus. Apollo was the perfection of male beauty. He was the son of Zeus and Leto. Artemis was his twin-sister اپالو ،

apologetic *adj*., **apologetics** *n*., **apologia** *n*., **apologize** *v.i.* see under **apology**

apology (a-*pol*-oh-ji) *n*. expression of regret for a wrong done معذرت، اعتذار defence of one's beliefs حمایت ، کلام ، **apologize** (-*jīz*) *v.i.* make an apology (*for*) معذرت کرنا، عذرخواہی کرنا **apologetic, apological** (-*jet*-) *adj*. offering an apology عذرخواہ معذرت آمیز **apologetics** *n*. (*pl*. used as *sing*.) defence of one's beliefs فنّ مناظرہ ، حمایت دین **apologia** (-*loh*-ji-) *n*. one's written defence of own views اعتذار

apoplectic *adj*. see under **apoplexy**

apoplexy (*ap*-o-plek-si) *n*. loss of power to think, feel or move owing to the bursting of blood vessel in the brain مرگی **apoplectic** (-*lek*-) *adj*. suffering from apoplexy مرگی کا مریض easily enraged غصیلا

apostacy, apostasy (a-*pos*-ta-si) *n*. giving up one's religion ارتداد giving up one's political creed مخصوص سیاسی نظریات سے برگشتگی **apostate** *n*. & *adj*. (one) guilty of apostasy مرتد **apostatize** *v.i*. become an apostate (*from* one *to* another) مرتد ہو جانا ، برگشتہ ہو جانا

a posteriori (a-pos-te-ri-*oh*-ri) *adj*. & *adv*. from effect to cause استقرائی by way of experiment تجربی

apostle (a-*pos*-ĕl) *n*. one of the twelve disciples sent out by Jesus Christ to spread his teachings حضرت عیسیٰ کا حواری leader of a faith or movement داعی ، بانی تحریک ، رسول ، پیغمبر *apostle of peace* داعیٔ امن **apostolic** (-*tol*-) *adj*. پیغمبرانہ ، داعیانہ

apostrophe (a-*pos*-tro-fi) *n*. the sign as in *the boy's* or *won't* or *a's* علامت اضافت ، اونچی واو (rhet.) sudden turning away in speech to address someone خطاب

apothecary (a-*poth*-ek-a-ri) *n*. (old use) chemist. عطار

apotheosis (a-poh-the-*oh*-sis) *n*. (*pl*.) **apotheoses** (-sees) deification خدا قرار دینا ، دیوتا بنانا ، تقدیس عطا کرنا **apotheosize** *v.t* deify خدا بنا بیٹھنا

appal (a-*pawl*) *v.t*. (-*ll*-) shock, terrify خوف زدہ کرنا

apparatus (ap-a-*ray*-tus) *n*. equipment, set of instruments assembled for an experiment سامان تجرباتی آلات parts of the body with a special function اعضائے نظام *the digestive apparatus* نظام ہضم

apparel (a-*par*-ĕl) *n*. (old or lit. use) clothes لباس ، پوشاک *v.t*. (-*ll*-) to dress پوشاک پہنانا

apparent (a-*pay*-rent) *n*. clearly seen or understood واضح ، صاف ، بیّن *adj*. seeming ظاہری *the apparent, not the real cause* حقیقی نہیں ، ظاہری سبب ، **apparently** *adj*. ظاہرا ، بظاہر ، نظر بہ ظاہر (see also **appear**)

apparition (ap-a-*rish*-ĕn) *n*. ghost, or its appearance سایہ ، بھوت

appeal (a-*peel*) *v.i*. ask earnestly (*for* something) - التجا کرنا ، استدعا کرنا refer a question or decision (*to* a higher authority) مرافعہ کرنا ، فیصلہ چاہنا ، اپیل کرنا (*appeal to*), attract, interest, catch the attention of دلکش ہونا ، پسند آنا ، مرغوب ہونا ، توجہ مبذول کرنا *n*. call (*for* help, etc.) درخواست ، التجا ، استدعا interest or attraction دلکشی ، دلچسپی transfer of a case from a lower to a higher court اپیل ، مرافعہ

appear (a-*pee*-ĕ*) *v.i*. come into view نظر آنا arrive پہنچنا ، آنا seem معلوم ہونا ، لگنا come before somebody ظاہر ہونا **appearance** *n*. appearing ظہور ، حاضری *put in* or (*make*) *an appearance*, (*a*) show oneself دکھا ، ظہور ہونا (*b*) attend حاضر ہونا outward show ظاہری شکل ، وضع قطع *judge by appearances*, form an opinion only from the look of things شکل و شباہت سے اندازہ کرنا ▣ To **appear** is to be noticeable in a certain place or condition; to **look**, have the visible signs of; to **seem**, cause one to think in a certain way.

appease (a-*peez*) *v.t*. pacify جوش فرو کرنا یا ٹھنڈا کرنا ، دھیما کرنا - *appease* (*someone's*) *anger*, satisfy (usu. by granting) کسی کی بات مان کر اُس کا جوش ٹھنڈا کرنا ، *appease someone's hunger* (or *curiosity*) کسی کی بھوک مٹانا یا اشتیاق پورا کرنا **appeasement** *n*. appeasing تشفی ، تسکین

append (a-*pend*) *v.t*. join something (*to* another) at the end ٹانکنا ، منتھی کرنا ، ملحق کرنا ، **appendage** (a-*pend*-ij) *n*. something added *to* or forming a natural part *of* a larger thing تعلیق ، ذیل ، ملحقات

appendix (a-*pend*-iks) *n*. (*pl*., *appendices*) something added, esp. at the end of a book ذیل ، ملحقات ، تعلیق ، (*pl*., *appendixes*) small, narrow tube attached to the large intestine ، بارہ انگشتی آنت معائے زائدہ **appendicitis** (-*sī*-tis) *n*. inflammation of the appendix ▣ التہاب زائدہ ، An **appendix** is included in the book itself at the time of publication; a **supplement** may be a separate volume, and is generally issued some time, even many years after the original publication. **addenda** (sing. **addendum**) is additional information at the end of a book about its contents.

appertain (ap-e*-*tayn*) *v.i*. (*appertain to*) belong to as a right ملکیت ہونا ، ملک ہونا be concerned with متعلق ہونا ، be suitable for موزوں ہونا ، مناسب ہونا -

appetizing *adj*. **appetizer** *n*. see under **appetite**

appetite (*ap*-e-tyt) *n.* desire (esp., for food) بھوک، اِشتہا، خواہش، ; *lose one's appetite* بھوک جاتی رہنا، **appetizing** (-*ty*-zing) *adj*. pleasing to, exciting, the appetite اِشتہا انگیز، بھوک بڑھانے والا **appetizer** *n.* (drink, etc.) exciting the appetite اشتہا انگیز

applaud (a-*plawd*) *v.t.* praise loudly by clapping the hands and cheering با آواز تحسین و آفرین کہنا، واہ واہ کہنا، تالیاں بجانا، **applause** (a-*plawz*) *n.* such praise تالیاں، واہ وا، بہ آواز تحسین و آفرین،

apple (apl) *n.* (tree with) well-known round fruit سیب (کا درخت) ; *Adam's apple* کنٹھ، کنٹھا ; *apple of one's eye*, very dear to one کسی کی آنکھ کا تارا ; *apple of discord*, bone of contention بنائے مخاصمت، لڑائی کا باعث وجہِ نزاع، فساد کی جڑ،

appliance (a-*pli*-ans) *n.* instrument or tool آلہ، وسیلہ،

applicable (*ap*-likay-bèl) *adj.* suitable to be applied to چسپاں، لاگو، موزوں، برمحل، **applicability** (-*bil*-) *n.* موزونیت، مطابقت،

applicant (*ap*-li-kant) *n.* person who applies for something سائل، امیدوار، درخواست دہندہ، عرضی دینے والا

application (ap-li-*kay*-shèn) *n.* a formal request عرضی، درخواست ; *on application to*, on writing to for کو لکھ کر، سے درخواست کرکے that which is applied جو چیز لگائی جائے، act of applying درخواست دینا، لگانا، استعمال کرنا۔ industry کاوش، محنت مشقت، تندہی، عرق ریزی، sense or use of a word محلِ استعمال

applied *adj*. see under **apply**

applique (ap-*lee*-kay) *n.* decorative design cut out and applied to surface of another material اپلک ورک، کٹائی کا کام۔ *v.t.* decorate thus اپلک ورک کرنا، کٹائی سے سجانا، کٹائی کا کام کرنا۔

apply (a-*ply*) *v.t.* & *i.* make a formal request (*to*) درخواست دینا، عرضی گزارنا، put (something) into position to serve its purpose ; *apply the brake (to the wheel)*, پہیے کو بریک لگانا، *apply the ointment (to)* پر، مرہم لگانا *apply a bandage* پٹی باندھنا، پٹی کرنا، put into use استعمال کرنا، کام میں لانا، چسپاں کرنا، *apply a rule* کوئی قاعدہ چسپاں کرنا۔ *apply oneself to*, give one's efforts to تن دہی سے کوئی کام کرنا، کاوش کرنا، ; *apply to*, concern کے حسب حال ہونا، سے متعلق ہونا، پر اثر انداز ہونا، پر منطبق ہونا۔ **applied** *adj.* put to practical use عملی، استفادی ; *applied arts*, *applied sciences*, knowledge or kill put to practical use (*e.g.*, industry) عملی فنون، استفادی فنون (یا علوم) **application** *n.* see above

appoint (a-*point*) *v.t.* decide (a time or place for) (جگہ یا وقت) مقرر کرنا۔ *the appointed time* مقررہ وقت، اجل، select and name (someone) to fill a post کا تقرر کرنا، کو مقرر یا متعین یا تعینات کرنا۔ **appointment** *n.* position or office تقرر، تقرری، تعیناتی، arrangement to meet someone (ملنا کا) قرار، ملاقات کا وقت ; *keep an appointment* meet someone as arranged حسب وعدہ پہنچ جانا ; *break an appointment*, fail to do so وعدہ کرکے نہ پہنچنا، ; *have an appointment* (*with* someone *for* a time, *at* a place) (کسی سے کسی جگہ ایک خاص وقت یا دن) ملاقات کا وعدہ ہونا۔

[S] To **appoint** is to select someone for a particular purpose or function : to **prescribe** a text-book or medicine : to **designate** someone as suitable for something, to **constitute** a body for a purpose.

apportion (a-*po**-shèn) *v.t.* divide into shares (*between* or *among*) کو حصہ دینا

apposite (*ap*-o-zit) *adj.* suitable, well-chosen (*to*) موزوں، مناسب، برمحل **apposition** (ap-o-*zish*-èn) *n.* (grammar) the placing of a word (or words) next to another to give additional information بدل کے طور پر استعمال کرنا۔ ; *in appasition* (*to*) (کا) بدل

Note : In the sentence, 'Mr Ahmad, our new teacher, has grey hair,' the words '*our new teacher*' are *in apposition to* 'Mr Ahmed.'

appraise (ap-*rayz*) *v.t.* evaluate قیمت تشخیص کرنا، آنکنا، **appraisal** *n.* evaluation قیمت کی تشخیص یا اندازہ قیمت کا اندازہ لگانا

appreciable *adj.*, **appreciably** *adv.* see under **appreciate**

appreciate (a-*preesh*-i-ayt) *v.t.* & *i.* judge or enjoy rightly کی داد دینا، یا قدردانی کرنا، کا لطف اٹھانا، سے محظوظ ہونا، ; *appreciate literature* ادب کا سے لطف اٹھانا۔ be grateful for ممنون ہونا، قدردانی کرنا، *appreciate (someone's) help* کسی کی اعانت کی قدردانی کرنا، لطف اٹھانا۔ rise in value کی قیمت بڑھنا، مہنگا ہو جانا **appreciation** *n.* (a-pree-si-*ay*-shèn) لطف اندوزی، قدردانی **appreciative**, **appreciatory** (-*ay*-) *adj.* expressing esteem قدردان، قدردانی کا **appreciable** (a-*presh*-i-abèl) *adj.* noticeable نمایاں، واضح *appreciable difference* نمایاں فرق **appreciably** *adv.* much, noticeably کافی، نمایاں حد تک

apprehend (ap-re-*hend*) *v.t.* understand سمجھنا، ادراک کرنا، fear ڈرنا، تشویش، خوف یا اندیشہ ہونا، arrest (a thief, etc.) گرفتار کرنا، ماخوذ کرنا، حراست میں لینا، زیرِ حراست کرنا، **apprehension** *n.* (-*hen*-) ادراک، اندیشہ، گرفتاری **apprehensive** (-hen-) *adj.* feeling afraid ; worried (*for* someone's safety, *of* danger, *that* someone will be hurt) تشویش مند، پریشان،

apprentice (a-*pren*-tis) *n.* one who is learning a trade and has agreed to serve his employer for a stated period کارآموز a beginner نوآموز *v.t.* make an apprentice کارآموز کرنا، بطور کارآموز کے رکھنا، یا رکھوانا۔ **apprenticeship** *n* کارآموزی (*serve one's*) *apprenticeship* کارآموزی کرنا

apprise (ap-*riz*) *v.t.* inform or warn (some-

one of) سے متنبّہ یا آگاہ کرنا
appro (*ap*-roh) *n.* (only in the phrase) *on appro*, (of goods sent on approval) to be returned if not approved پسند نہ آئے تو دام واپس، پسند نہ آئے تو مال واپس، (see also **approval**)
approach (a-*prohch*) *v.t.* & *i.* draw near قریب ہونا، پاس آنا، نزدیک جانا، go to (someone) with a request or offer کو پیش کش کرنا، سے گفت و شنید کرنا، سے درخواست کرنا، کے پاس سفارش کرنا۔ act of approaching پہنچنا، آمد، آمد آمد، way to a place, person, or thing راہ، راستہ، گزرگاہ، پہنچ، رسائی، state of nearness نزدیکی، قرب، تقرّب thing or state which comes near کچھ کچھ، ملتا جلتا، تقریباً ویسا ہی، سے مشابہہ، کی سی صورت *approach to comfort* کچھ کچھ آرام، آرام کی سی صورت
approachable *adj.* accessible جس تک رسائی ہو سکے، قابلِ رسائی
approbation (ap-ro-*bay*-shĕn) *n.* thinking well of پسندیدگی۔ تعریف sanction منظوری، اجازت
appropriate (a-*prohp*-ri-ayt) *adj.* suitable (*for* a purpose, *to* an occasion) مناسب، موزوں، برجستہ، برمحل، کے مُطابق۔ (also *misappropriate*), take and use (as one's own usu. wrongfully) اپنانا، مالک بن بیٹھنا، قابض ہونا، متصرّف ہونا۔ set apart (for a special purpose) (کسی کام کے لیے) مخصوص کرنا، **appropriation** *n.* acquisition تصرّف، قبضہ **appropriateness** *n.* suitability مُناسبت، موزونیت، مُناسبت؛ **appropriately** *adv.* مناسب طریق سے۔
approval (a-*proo*-vĕl) *n.* good opinion پسند، پسندیدگی، permission, sanction اجازت، منظوری؛ *goods sent on approval*, (also *on apro*) those to be returned if found unsatisfactory ناپسند ہونے کی صورت میں واپسی، کی شرط پر بھیجا ہوا مال (see also **approve**)
approve (a-*proov*) *v.t.* & *i.* sanction پر صاد کرنا، منظور کرنا، منظوری دینا، اجازت دینا۔ have favourable opinion *of* پسند کرنا، پسندیدگی کی نظر سے دیکھنا، show کر کے دکھا دینا، ثابت کرنا۔ **approver** *n.* accused who becomes a crown witness وعدہ مُعاف گواہ، سُلطانی گواہ
approximate (a-*proks*-i-mayt) *adj.* very near متّصل، قریب۔ almost correct لگ بھگ، تقریباً صحیح *v.t.* & *i.* (a-*proks*-i-mayt) bring or come near لگ بھگ ہونا، قریب کرنا یا ہونا۔ **approximation** (-*may*-shen) *n.* nearness to truth اندازہ **approximately** *adv.* nearly تقریباً
apricot (*ayp*-ri-kot) *n.* (tree with) small, soft, yellow fruit with a large stone خوبانی، زرد آلو،
April (*ayp*-ril) *n.* fourth month of the Western calendar سنِ عیسوی کا چوتھا مہینہ، اپریل،
a priori (a-prī-*oh*-ri) *adj.* & *adv* from cause to effect ; deductive(ly) قیاساً، استخراجاً presumptive(ly) بدیہی، فرضی (طور پر)
apron (*ayp*-run) *n.* loose garment tied over front of the body to protect one's clothes پیش بند
apron-string *n.* پیش بند *tied to* (*one's mother's* or *wife's*) *apron-strings*, ruled by (her) (ماں یا بیوی) کے آنچل سے بندھا ہُوا،
apropos (ap-ro-*poh*) *adj.* & *adv.* well suited to the purpose موزوں، مناسب *apropos* (*of*), with reference to, in connexion with دَربارہ، کے سلسلے میں، نسبتاً
appurtenances (a-*pĕ**-te-nan-siz) *n. pl.* appendages (*of* a house) گھر کا ساز و سامان، گھر کے لوازمات
apt *adj.* suitable, appropriate موزوں، برمحل، برجستہ *an apt remark* برجستہ بات (*apt to*), likely to, inclined to راغب، مائل quick to learn ذہین، ذکی، طباع *an apt student* ذہین طالبعلم **aptly** (*apt*-li) *adv.* suitably ٹھیک، مناسب طور پر **aptness** (*apt*-nes) *n.* suitability موزونیت **aptitude** (*ap*-ti-tewd) *n.* talent, natural ability *for* میلان، مناسبت، رُجحان
aquacade *n.* see Addenda
aquarium (a-*kway*-ri-um) *n.* artificial (glass) pond for keeping and showing living fish and water plants ماہی خانہ، مچھلی گھر
aquatic (a-*kwat*-ik) *adj.* growing, living or done in water آبی *aquatic sports*, those played in or on water آبی کھیل
aqueduct (*ak*-we-dukt) *n.* artificial channel for supplying water, made of brick or stone and higher than the surrounding land محرابی نالہ bridge supporting such a channel over a valley اونچے نیچے نالے کی محراب

aqueduct

aquiline (*ak*-wi-līn) *adj.* eagle-like باز کا سا *aquiline nose* طوطے کی سی ناک
Arab (*a*-rab) *n.* native of Arabia عرب horse of Arabian breed عربی گھوڑا، اسپ تازی *street arab n.* see under **street** *adj.* of Arabia عربی، تازی **arabesque** (a-ra-*besk*) *n.* & *adj.* Moorish (design) with intertwined leaves or geometrical figures نقشی (کام) (of) such scroll-work طغرائی (کام) **Arabia** (a-*ray*-bi-a) *n.* country of the Arabs **Arabian** (a-*ray*-bi-ĕn) *n.* Arab عرب *adj.* of Arabia عربی *Arabian Nights*, (*a*) English name of a famous Arabic book الف لیلہ (*b*) fabulous stories حیرت انگیز کہانیاں
Arabic (*ar*-a-bik) *n.* language of the Arabs عربی *adj.* relating to Arabs, Arabia or Arabic language عربی **Arabic numerals**, ordinary digits (1, 2, 3, 4, . . . , or ۱، ۲، ۳، ۴، ۰) انگریزی ہندسے، (as distinct from *Roman numerals* which are I, II, III, IV, ...) اُردو ہندسے، رقوم ہندی
arable (*ar*-abl) *adj.* (land) suitable for cultivation قابلِ کاشت
Arachne (a-*rak*-nee) *Cl. myth.* Lydian maid whom Athena changed into a spider because she had challenged the goddess to a trial of skill

in spinning ارگنی
ramaic (ar-a-*may*-ik) *adj*. of the northern group of Semitic languages آرامی
arbiter (*ah**-bi-tě*) *n*. person with full power to decide - ثالث، حَکَم، پنچ، بااختیار ثالث **arbitrate** (*ah**-bit-rayt) *v. t.* & *i*. act as an arbiter at the request of the two parties ثالثی کرنا **arbitrator** (*ah**-bit-ray-tě*) *n*. arbiter ثالث **arbitration** (-*ray*-) act of arbitrating ثالثی، تحکیم **arbitrament** *n*. arbitrator's award ثالث کا فیصلہ، ثالثی arbitration ثالثی، تحکیم،
arbitrary (ah*-bit-rari) *adj*. based on opinion rather than rules خود مختارانہ، من مانا، ظالمانہ، *arbitrary decision*, over-bearing or dictatorial من مانا فیصلہ، ظالمانہ فیصلہ. **arboreal** (ah*-bo-ri-al) *adj*. of, or living in, trees شجر **arboriculture** *n*. tree-plantation شجرکاری
arbour (*ah**-be*) *n*. shady place among trees, often with a seat کنج
arc (ah*k) *n*. part of a circle curve قوس. **arclight** *n*. powerful light made by electric current passing between two unconnected points برقی قوس
arcade (ah*-*kaya*) *n*. rows of arches, چھتہ محرابی قطار covered street مسقف راستہ **Arcadia** (-*kay*-) *n*. a district in ancient Greece آرکیڈیا place of ideal rural happiness دیہی جنت
arch (ah*ch) *n*. curved structure resting on pillars and supporting the weight of what is above it محراب ornamental gateway محرابی دروازہ *v.t.* & *i*. form into an arch محراب بنانا be like an arch محرابی ہونا ; *arch over* محراب کی طرح جھکے ہونا، *adj*. expressing an innocent wish for fun or mischief شوخ، شوخی بھرا، *arch smile* شوخی بھری یا شوخ مسکراہٹ **archly** *adv*. in a waggish manner شوخی سے، شرارت سے **archway** *n*. entrance or passage under an arch محرابی دروازہ، محرابی راستہ

an archway

arch-(ah*ch) *pref*. chief اعلیٰ، بڑا **archbishop** *n*. chief bishop لاٹ پادری **archdeacon** *n*. priest (in the Church of England) next below a bishop آرچ ڈیکن **archduke** *n*. (*fem*., **archduchess**) formerly son of the Austrian Emperor آرچ ڈیوک، رئیس اعظم
Archangel (*ark*-ayn-jěl) *n*. angel of the highest rank عظیم ترین فرشتہ، فرشتۂ اعظم،
archaeology (ah*k-i-*ol*-o-ji) *n*. study of ancient monuments علم آثار قدیمہ، علم آثار عتیقہ، آثریات **archeologist** *n*. ماہر آثریات **archaeological** (-*loj*-) *adj*. آثریاتی
archaic (ah*-*kay*-ik) *adj*. old-fashioned فرسودہ no longer used (language) متروک **archaism** (*ah**-kay-izm) *n*. (use of) archaic words or phrases متروکات کا استعمال
archer (*ah**-chě*) *n*. one who shoots with bow and arrows تیر انداز **archery** (*ah**-che-ri) *n*. تیراندازی
archipelago (ah*-ki-*pel*-a-goh) *n*. (pl. -*os*, or -*oes*) group of small islands مجمع الجزائر
architect (*ah**-ki-tekt) *n*. one who designs buildings معمار، ماہر تعمیرات **architecture** (ah*-ki-*tek*-chě*) art and science of building فن تعمیر style of buildings طرز تعمیر **architectural** *adj*. عماراتی، تعمیراتی ◙ An **architect** is a trained specialist, unlike a **builder** who is a practical worker and works to carry out the **architect's** plans.
archives (ah*-kivz) *n. pl*. place for keeping public records دفترخانہ، محافظ خانہ historical records تاریخی دستاویزات،
arctic (*ah**k-tik) *adj*. of or near the North Pole قطب شمالی کا، یا کے متعلق، یا کے قریب *the Arctic Circle*, the zone round the North Pole منطقۂ باردۂ شمالی، *the Arctic Ocean* بحر منجمد شمالی، extremely cold سخت سرد
ardent (*ah**-dent) *adj*. full of ardour سرگرم **ardour** (*ah**-dě*) *n*. burning heat شدت کی گرمی hence warmth of feeling ; گرم جوشی enthusiasm, earnestness سرگرمی، لگن، دُھن
arduous (*ah***d*-ew-us) *adj*. entailing hard-work مشقت طلب، سخت مشکل uphill, steep سیدھی چڑھائی کا
are (ah*) present tense plural form of *be* (which see) ہیں، ہو
area (*ay*-ri-a) *n*. surface measure رقبہ extent of surface اراضی، رقبہ، قطعہ any level surface region علاقہ، خطہ
arena (a-*ree*-na) *n*. enclosed central space for games and fights in Roman amphitheatre اکھاڑہ دنگل any field of struggle or rivalry میدان **arena theatre** *n*. see Addenda
aren't (ah*nt) (short form of) are not نہیں ہیں، نہیں ہو
Ares (*ay*-reez) *Cl. myth*. the Greek god of war, identified with the Roman god, Mars. He was the son of *Zeus and Hera*. He was attacked in battle by *Deimos* (Fear), *Phobus* (Terror), *Eris* (Strife), *Cydoemus* (Tumult) and *Enyo* (Destroyer of Cities) آریز، مریخ
Arethusa (ar-e-*thew*-sa) *Cl. myth*. **Nereid, or** water-nymph. She lived in a fountain near Syracuse آری تھوسا ○
Argine (*ah**-gin) *Cl. myth*. an inhabitant of the Greek city, Argos, meaning "the outlying area." The Greeks fighting under Agamemnon against Troy are called by Homer *Argin*

because Agamemnon himself was an Argine آرگائن any ancient Greek یُونانی
Argo (*ah**-goh) *Cl. myth*. the ship of Jason and his companions who sailed in quest of the Golden Fleece آرگو **Argonauts** (*ah**-goh-nawts) *Cl. myth*. Jason's expeditionary force which sailed in the ship *Argos* آرگوران ، آرگو والے
argosy (*ah**-go-si) *n*. (poet.) large ship laden with valuable cargo مال سے بھرا ہُوا جہاز
argue (*ah**g-ew) *v.i.* & *t*. give reasons (*for* or *against* something) دلیل دینا ، استدلال کرنا ، دلیل لانا *argue (someone) into (out of) (something)*, cause him to do it (not to do it) by giving reasons کسی کو دلیل سے کسی بات کا قائل (مخالف) بنانا maintain one's views in discussion بحث کرنا ، بحث میں اپنے نقطۂ نگاہ پر زور دینا ، **argument** (*ah**g-ew-ment) *n*. reason (*for* or *against* something) discussion بحث *heated argument*, quarrel تُوتکار ، جھگڑا **argumentative** (ah*g-ew-*ment*-a-tiv) *adj*. quarrelsome, fond of arguing کج بحث ، کٹ حُجتی ، جھگڑالو
Argus (*ah**-gus) *Cl. myth*. the 100-eyed watchman keeping, under the orders of Hera, a strict vigil on Io who had been metamorphosed by her into a cow. Hermes (or Mercury) under the orders of Zeus, killed him after sending him to sleep. Hera gave his eyes to the peacock's tail آرگس
Ariadne (ar-i-*ad*-nee) *Cl. myth*. daughter of the Cretan king, Minos, who had got the famous labyrinth built. She guided Theseus out of it but he abandoned her at Naxos. Later, she was married to Dionysus آریاڈنی
arid (*a*-rid) *adj*. dry, barren (soil) بے آب و گیاہ ، خشک ، بنجر dry, uninteresting بے لطف ، بے کیف **aridity** (a-*rid*-i-ti) *n*. dryness بے آب و گیاہ ہونا ، بے کیفی
aright (a-*rīt*) *adv*. in the right way ٹھیک ٹھیک ، صحیح
Arion (ar-*rī*-on) *Cl. myth*. Greek bard who was cast into the sea by the robbers but whom a dolphin, charmed by his ravishing music, carried ashore safely ایرائن
arise (a-*rīz*) *v.i.* (*arise, arose, arisen*) stand up, get up اُٹھنا ، کھڑے ہونا come into existence سامنے آنا پیدا ہونا ، ظہور میں آنا *A new difficulty has arisen* ایک نئی مشکل پیدا ہو گئی ہے ۔ result (*from* or *out of*) سے پیدا ہونا *conditions arising from* (or *out of*) *the war* جنگ سے پیدا ہونے والے حالات
aristocracy (a-ris-*tok*-ra-si) *n*. government by persons of high rank اَشرافیہ country with such government اَشرافیہ the nobility اَشراف ، طبقۂ اُمرا ، اُونچا طبقہ any group of the most distinguished persons اُونچا طبقہ ، نمایاں اَفراد **aristocrat** (*a*-ris-to-krat) *n*. person of noble birth or high rank ; امیر ، اُونچے طبقے کا فرد ، **aristocratic** (a-ris-to-*krat*-ik) *adj*. being or acting like a lord امیرانہ انداز والا
Aristotelian (a-ris-to-*tee*-li-ĕn), **Aristotelean** (a-ris-tot-e-*lee*-ĕn) *n*. & *adj*. (scholar) of Aristotle اَرسطو طالیسی
arithmetic (a-*rith*-me-tik) *n*. science of numbers حساب **arithmetical** *adj*. (-*met*-) حساب سے متعلق ، حساب کا ، حسابی **arithmetician** (a-rith-me-*tee*-shĕn) حساب دان
ark (ah*k) *n*. (in the Bible) covered ship in which Noah and his family were saved from the flood کشتیٔ نُوحؑ ، سفینۂ نُوحؑ *the Ark of the Covenant*, chest containing tables of the law of Moses تابُوتِ میثاق ، تابُوتِ سکینہ ،
arm (ah*m) *n*. one of the two upper limbs of man بازو ، ہاتھ (*arms*, pr. ah*mz) (*pl.*) weapons اَسلحہ ، ہتھیار ، *in arms*, having weapons مُسلّح ، ہتھیاروں سے لیس ، *bear arms*, serve in the army فوج میں ملازم ہونا division of a country's military forces فوج کا کوئی بڑا حصہ ، *the air arm*, (*pl.*) pictorial design (used by a noble family, town, etc.) (شہر یا خاندان کا) طُغرا ، *coat of arms*, such a design on a shield نشان ، جِیغہ ، ڈھال پر ایسا نشان ، *v.t.* & *i*. equip with arms مُسلّح کرنا ، ہتھیاروں سے لیس کرنا ، **armchair** *n*. chair with arms بازوؤں والی کُرسی ، بازو دار کُرسی ، **armful** *adj*. as much as the two arms will enfold کولی بھر **armhole** *n*. hole (in coat, etc.) through which the arm is put (لباس کی) بغل **armlet** *n*. band worn round the arm بازو بند **arm-pit** *n*. the hollow beneath the shoulder بغل
armada (ah*-*may*-da) *n*. fleet of warships جنگی بیڑا
Armageddon (ah*-ma-*ged*-dun) *n*. great conflict of the nations according to 'The Bible' عظیم بین الاقوامی جنگ ، fight between good and evil معرکۂ حق و باطل ،
armament (*ah**-ma-ment) *n*. military forces made ready for war فوج ، افواج preparation for war جنگی تیاریاں big guns on a warship, tank, etc. بڑی توپیں
armature (*ah**m-ĕ-tew*) *n*. essential moving part of an electric motor or dynamo آرمیچر ، بجلی کا دُھرا ، برقی چرخی piece of soft iron connecting the opposite poles of permanent magnet(s) to prevent demagnetization ناظر مقناطیس ، مقنا روک ، محافظہ ،
armistice (*ah**-mis-tis) *n*. truce, agreement during war to stop fighting for a time متارکہ ، عارضی بندشِ جنگ ،

armour (*ah**-mĕ*) *n.* steel covering for the body, زرہ بکتر steel plating on tanks, warships, etc. بکتر (also *armoured cars*), armoured fighting vehicles بکتر بند گاڑیاں **armourer** (*ah**-mo-rĕ*) *n.* one who makes or repairs arms اسلحہ ساز **armoured** *adj.* provided with armour بکتر بند *armoured cars* بکتر بند گاڑیاں (of army unit) supplied with armoured cars, etc. (بکتر بند دستہ) **armoury** (*ah**-me-ri) *n.* place where arms are made or stored اسلحہ خانہ یا اسلحہ سازی کا کارخانہ۔

a suit of armour

army (*ah**mi) *n.* large body of men trained and equipped for war, فوج، لشکر any organized body (*of* persons, etc.) working for a common cause تنظیم، منظم گروہ، جماعت

aroma (a-*roh*-ma) *n.* fragrance, خوشبو **aromatic** (a-ro-*mat*-ik) *adj.* خوشبودار

arose *v.i.* اٹھا (pa. t. of **arise,** which see)

around (a-*round*) *adj.* & *prep.* encircling (کے) گرد on all sides (of) (کے) چاروں طرف، گرداگرد here and there ادھر ادھر، ہر طرف۔

arouse (a-*rouz*) *v.t.* wake up جگانا، اٹھانا stir up ابھارنا، ہوشیار کرنا

arraign (a-*rayn*) *v.t.* accuse الزام دینا bring to trial استغاثہ دائر کرنا **arraignment** *n.* استغاثہ

arrange (a-*raynj*) *v.t.* & *i.* set in order ترتیب دینا make plans (*for*) انتظام کرنا، بندوبست کرنا، اہتمام کرنا، *arrange a party* دعوت کا بندوبست کرنا settle (a dispute) (جھگڑا) چکانا، فیصل کرنا، *arrange differences* اختلافات ختم کرنا **arrangement** *n.* بندوبست، انتظام، اہتمام ▣ To **arrange** is literally to set in rows or ranks; to **dispose** along certain lines: to **classify,** sort out according to groups, to **array** in imposing numbers or form; to **marshal** one's troops or points; to **group** according to congeniality.

arrant (*ar*-ant) *adj.* out and out بڑا، بالکل، پرلے درجے کا *arrant fool* نرا گاؤدی

arras (*ar*-as) *n.* tapestry for walls مشجّر

array (a-*ray*) *v.t.* place (troops) in order for battle صف بندی کرنا dress (someone or oneself) in lovely clothes خوب صورت لباس پہنانا، کی سج دھج نکالنا، *n.* orderly arrangement (for fighting) (جنگ کے لیے) صف بندی *in battle array* (جنگ کے لیے) صف بستہ fine display سجاوٹ، آرائش lovely clothes خوب صورت لباس

arrears (a-*ree*-è*z) *n. pl.* overdue payments بقایا (work, etc.) waiting for attention بقیہ کام، امانت کا کام *in arrears (with)*, behind (سے) پیچھے

arrest (a-*rest*) *v.t.* stop, check روکنا *arrest the growth of* کی رفتار ترقی روکنا catch or hold the attention of (کسی کی) جانب توجہ ہونا seize by the authority of the law گرفتار کرنا، پکڑلینا، پکڑ کرلے جانا *n.* act of arresting گرفتاری *make an arrest* گرفتار کرنا *under arrest* گرفتار stoppage روک تھام، انسداد *the arrest of the fall of prices* قیمتوں میں کمی کی روک تھام، **arresting** *adj.* likely to catch the attention جاذبِ نظر، جاذبِ توجہ ▣ **arrest, apprehend, detain, restrain, capture.**

arrival *n.* see under **arrive**

arrive (a-*rīv*) *v.i.* come to a place پہنچنا *arrive home* گھر (پر) پہنچنا *arrive at a city* شہر (میں) پہنچنا *arrive at*, agree on, fix, settle (فیصلے وغیرہ) پر پہنچنا (of time) come (وقت) ہوجانا، آجانا **arrival** (a-*rī*-vĕl) *n.* arriving پہنچنا، آمد، تشریف آوری someone or something that arrives آنے یا پہنچنے والا

arrogant (*a*-ro-gant) *adj.* proud, overbearing خود پسند، مغرور، متکبر، **arrogance** *n.* خودپسندی، تکبر، غرور، اکڑ، اکڑفوں، ہیکڑی ▣ **arrogant, proud, conceited, haughty, presumptuous, self-important, overbearing, supercilious, insolent.**

arrow (*a*-roh) *n.* straight stick with a steel point to be shot from a bow خدنگ، تیر the sign → نشان **arrowhead** *n.* pointed head of an arrow تیر کا سرا، نوکِ تیر۔ **arrowroot** (*a*-roh-root) *n.* name of a plant اراروٹ starch obtained from it as a light food اراروٹ

arsenal (*ah**-se-nĕl) *n.* factory or store of weapons of war اسلحہ خانہ، سلاح خانہ، میگزین، اسلحہ سازی کا کارخانہ

arsenic (*ah**-sè-nik) *n.* a strong poison سنکھیا، سم الفار

arson (*ah**-sun) *n.* unlawful setting on fire (of property) آتش زنی

[1]art (ah*t) *n.* human skill ہنر، ہنرمندی، کاریگری study and creation of beautiful things فن، فنکاری *work of art* فنی تخلیق، فن کا نمونہ، فنکارانہ تخلیق، *the fine arts*, drawing, painting, sculpture and architecture فنونِ لطیفہ system of practical rules (as opposed to science) آرٹس، علم (بمقابلہ حکمت) *Bachelor (Master) of Arts*, one who has reached fixed standards at a university in such branches of learning as history, languages, literature بی۔اے (ایم۔اے) cunning, artifice, tricks عیاری، چالاکی **artful** *adj.* cunning, crafty چالاک، عیار، تراک **artless** *adj.* simple, innocent سیدھا سادھا، سادہ لوح

[2]art (ah*t) old present tense form of *be* used with *thou* ہے *thou art* (=you are) تو ہے

Artemis (*ah**-te-mis) *Cl. myth.* Greek goddess of wild nature and hunting. She was the twin-sister of Apollo and was identified with the Roman moon-goddess, Phoebe آرٹیمس

artery (*ah**t-e-ri) *n.* (cf. **vein**) blood vessel carrying blood from the heart شریان main road شاہراہ، بڑے بڑے مقامات کو ملانے والی سڑک **arterial** (ah*-*tee*-ri-al) *adj.* of or like an artery شریانی (of line

of communications) major بڑا اہم *arterial roads* بڑی بڑی سڑکیں
artesian (ah*-*tee*-zi-an) *adj.* فوارہ نما (used only in) *artesian well*, deep well producing a stream of sub-soil water at the surface فوارہ نما کنواں، پھوار کنواں
Arthur (*ah**-thē*) *n.* legendary British king during the period of the Anglo-Saxon invasion of the island. A cycle of legends has grown round his figure describing the loves and adventures of his Knights of the Round Table آرتھر
artichoke (*ah*t*-i-chohk) *n.* a kind of plant with a flower head used as a vegetable خوشف، ہاتھی چوک
article (*ah**t-ik-èl) *n.* particular thing چیز، شے *an article of clothing* پہننے کی چیز، جزو لباس complete piece of writing in a periodical مقالہ، مضمون separate term in an agreement دفعہ، شق (grammar) حرف تعریف، یا حرف تنکیر ; *definite article*, the حرف تعریف ; *indefinite article*, a or an حرف تنکیر
articulate *adj.* (ah*-*tik*-ew-lait) clear (speech) ترتیل، ٹھیک یا صاف *v.t.* & *i.* (-layt) speak clearly and distinctly ٹھہر ٹھہر کر بولنا، صاف تلفظ سے بولنا **articulation** (-*lay*-) *n.* speaking clearly ترتیل، صاف تلفظ **articulately** *adv.* distinctly وضاحت سے، صاف
artifice (*ah**t-i-fis) *n.* skilful way of doing something تدبیر، ترکیب، استادی، ہنر cunning trick حیلہ، چالبازی **artificer** (-if-) *n.* skilled workman, (usually with metal) کاریگر، دستکار
artificial (ah*t-i-*feesh*-èl) *adj.* not natural or made by a man by imitation of nature مصنوعی *artificial rain*, rain caused by artificial discharge in the clouds مصنوعی بارش forced, insincere بناوٹی *artificial smiles* مصنوعی، تصنع بھری تصنع بھرا، تبسم، بناوٹی مسکراہٹ
artillery (ah*-*til*-è-ri) *n.* big guns mounted on wheels توپیں branch of the army using such guns توپ خانہ **artilleryman** توپچی
artisan (ah*t-i-*zan*) *n.* skilled workman in industry or trade کاریگر، دستکار، صناع **artist** (*ah**t-ist) *n.* person who practises one of the fine arts, esp., painting فنکار، مصور، نقاش person of great skill باکمال **artiste** (ah*-*teest*) a professional singer or dancer پیشہ ور گویا، یا رقاصہ **artistic** (-*tis*-) *adj.* of art فنکارانہ showing or made with, good taste حسین، خوبصورت person able to enjoy the arts فن کا دلدادہ **artistically** *adv.* in an artistic manner فنکارانہ انداز سے **artistry** (*ah**t-ist-ri) *n.* artistic skill فنکاری
-ary (è-ri) *suf.* (for making *n.* & *adj.* meaning) (that) which does والا، گار، موزوں وغیرہ
Aryan (*ay*-è-ri-en) *adj.* Indo-European (race or language) آریائی *n.* original Aryan language or its speaker آریائی

as (az) *adv.*, *conj.* & *prep.* equally اتنا ہی *as far as*, *so far as* جہاں تک اس کا تعلق ہے such as مثلاً جیسے because چونکہ while جب in the way that کہ جیسے ; like کی طرح *as well as*, and اور *as for*, with regard to جہاں تک اس کا تعلق ہے
asafoetida (as-a-*feet*-i-da) *n.* a resinous gum smelling like garlic ہینگ
asbestos (az-*bes*-tus) *n.* a fireproof mineral substance with fibres so that it can be woven ازبسٹس
Ascanius (as-*kay*-ni-us) *Cl. myth.* Aeneas's son اسکینیئس
ascend (a-*send*) *v.t.* & *i.* go up or climb (mountain, etc.) چڑھنا، اوپر جانا *ascend the throne*, become king تخت نشین ہونا ; *ascend a river*, go along it towards its source دریا کے کنارے کنارے اس کے منبع کی طرف جانا *prices ascend* قیمتیں چڑھ رہی ہیں **ascendancy**, **ascendency** (a-*send*-en-si) *n.* (position of) having power فوقیت، تفوق، بالادستی *gain an ascendancy over (someone)* کسی پر فوقیت حاصل کرنا **ascendant**, **ascendent** *n.* طالع، فوقیت *in the ascendant*, rising in importance and power ابھرتا ہوا **ascension** (a-*sen*-shèn) *n.* *the Ascension*, the going up of Jesus from the earth to heaven رفع مسیح **ascent** (a-*sent*) *n.* act of climbing چڑھنا، اوپر جانا upward slope (of a hill, etc.) چڑھائی، بلندی
ascertain (a-seh*-*layn*) *v. t.* find out, make certain تحقیق کرنا، پتہ چلانا
ascetic (a-*set*-ik) *n.* & *adj.* (one) who leads a life of self-denial usu. for religious reasons زاہد، تارک دنیا، مرتاض **asceticism** (a-*set*-i-sizm) *n.* ترک دنیا زہد، ریاضت **ascetical** (a-*set*-i-kèl) زاہدانہ
ascribe (as-*krib*) *v.t.* (*ascribe to*) consider (something) as the result of کا سبب سمجھنا، کا باعث جاننا کا نتیجہ خیال کرنا consider (something) as belonging to منسوب کرنا، نسبت دینا **ascription** (as-*krip*-shèn) *n.* (عیسائی خطبے کے آخر میں) حمد
aseptic (a-*sep*-tik) *adj.* free from disease germs جراثیم سے پاک
Asgard (*as*-gah*d) *Norse myth.* The abode of the Scandinavian gods above Midgard, or the earth اسگارڈ
ash *n.* (*sing.* or *pl.*) powder left after something has burnt راکھ، خاکستر *be burnt to ashes* جل کر خاکستر ہو جانا a kind of tree ایش (*pl.*) (*ash*-iz) مردے کے پھول the burnt remains of a human body **The Ashes** *n. pl.* symbol of victory in cricket matches between England and Australia ایشز، خاکستر **ashen** (*ash*-en) *adj.* of ash tree ایش کا pale like ash زرد **ash-tray** *n.* small tray to out

cigarette ash in خاکستردان
ashamed (a-*shaymd*) *adj*. feeling shame شرمندہ، نادم
ashen *adj*. see under **ash**
ashore (a-*shoh**) *adv*. to or on the shore, on land کنارے پر، ساحل پر، ساحل کی طرف *go ashore* ساحل پر جانا *be driven ashore* کنارے پر لگنا
ash-tray *n*. see under **ash**
aside (a-*sīd*) *adv*. on (or to) one side ایک طرف، ایک جانب away پرے، الگ، علیحدہ *set aside a decision*, rescind it فیصلہ منسوخ کرنا ، *lay aside* پرے کرنا، ہٹانا *turn aside from* سے مُونہہ موڑنا *n*. remark in a low tone (on the stage) intended not to be heard ڈرامے میں مُنہ پھیر کر کہنا
ask *v.t*. inquire پُوچھنا beg or request (کی) درخواست کرنا ۔ *ask a favour* کوئی چیز invite (someone *to* tea, etc.) دعوت دینا، demand مانگنا *ask for* (*something*) مانگنا، کسی شے کا سوال کرنا، *ask after* (*someone's*) *health* کسی کی صحت کے متعلق پُوچھنا، *ask after* (*someone*) کسی کو پُوچھنا
askance (as-*kans*) *adv*. (to look) with a sly, sideways glance کنکھیوں سے *look askance at*, look at (something or someone) with suspicion or distrust کنکھیوں سے دیکھنا، شک و شبہ کی نظروں سے دیکھنا ،
askew (as-*kew*) *adv*. & *adj*. off the straight or level position ٹیڑھا، ترچھا *hang a picture askew* تصویر ٹیڑھی لگانا
aslant (as-*lahnt*) *adv*. & *adj*. sloping in a slanting direction ایک طرف جھکا ہُوا، ٹیڑھی
asleep (as-*leep*) *adv*. & *adj*. sleeping سویا ہُوا، خواب میں ، خوابیدہ (of the limbs) numb (as when under pressure) سویا ہُوا، سُن *My foot is asleep* میرا پاؤں سویا ہُوا ہے ،
asp *n*. a small poisonous snake اَفعی
asparagus (as-*par*-a-gus) *n*. plant, the young shoots of which are used as a vegetable مارچوبہ، ناگ دَون

asparagus

aspect (*as*-pekt) *n*. appearance چہرہ، شکل، صُورت، بُشرہ *a person of fierce aspect* جس کی صُورت سے لرزہ طاری ہو direction in which a thing faces رُخ، پہلو *house with an eastern aspect* شرقی رُخ والا گھر way of looking at anything رُخ، پہلو، نقطۂ نگاہ *different aspects of a problem* مسئلے کے مختلف پہلو
aspen (*as*-pen) *n*. a kind of poplar tree the leaves of which quiver in the slightest wind بید مجنوں *tremble like an aspen leaf* بید مجنوں کی طرح لرزنا یا تھرانا
asperity (as-*pe*-ri-ti) *n*. roughness of surface کھُردرا پن، ناہمواری severity (of weather) (موسم کی) سختی roughness of temper, sharpness (مزاج کی) اُگرہی یا دُرشتی
asperse (as-*pē*s*) *v.t*. sprinkle with پر چھڑکنا calumniate بُہتان باندھنا، تہمت لگانا **aspersion** (as-*pē**-shen) *n*. fault-finding, and untrue report (*about* a person) بُہتان، تہمت، اتہام، طوفان *cast an aspersion* (*on*) کسی پر طوفان باندھنا، تہمت لگانا
asphalt (*as*-falt) *n*. mixture of tar and sand used for making roads اَسفالٹ *v.t*. give a smooth surface to roads with asphalt سڑک پر اَسفالٹ بچھانا
asphyxiate (as-*fik*-si-ayt) *v.t*. suffocate گلا گھونٹنا **asphyxiation** (-*ay*-) *n*. سانس کا رکنا، گلا گھونٹنا، یا گھونٹا جانا
aspirant (*as*-pi-rant) *n*. one who aspires (عروج و ترقی کا) آرزومند یا متمنّی **aspiration** (as-pi-*ray*-shĕn) *n*. eager desire *for* something high (عروج حاصل کرنے کی) تمنا act of breathing سانس لینا breath سانس **aspire** (as-*pī*-ĕ*) *v.i*. desire eagerly (*for* something, or *to do* or be something) آرزو کرنا، متمنّی ہونا aim at high things حوصلہ بلند رکھنا، بہت اُونچی باتیں سوچنا ،
aspirin (*as*-pi-rin) *n*. soothing drug for relieving colds and pain اَسپرین a tablet of this اَسپرین کی ٹکیہ
ass (as) *n*. donkey گدھا *jack-ass, he ass* گدھا *she-ass* گدھی (*pr*. ahs) stupid person گدھا، احمق، اُلّو *don't make such an ass of yourself*, don't behave so stupidly یُوں گدھے مت بنو، **asinine** (*as*-i-nīn) *adj*. like an ass گدھے کا سا foolish احمق، احمقانہ
assail (a-*sayl*) *v.t*. attack (someone or something *with*) حملہ کرنا *be assailed with* کا شکار ہونا **assailable** *adj*. open to attack جس پر حملہ ہو سکے **assailant** *n*. attacker حملہ آور
assassin (a-*sas*-in) *n*. murderer ; person who assassinates قاتل (orig.) one of the fanatic followers of an 11th century Muslim leader, 'Old Man of the Mountain', who treacherously killed their leader's opponents after being doped with *hasheesh* or Indian hemp باطنی فرقے کے حشیشین میں سے کوئی فدائی
assassinate (a-*sas*-i-nayt) *v.t*. murder secretly and treacherously, esp. for political reasons دھوکے سے قتل کرنا **assassination** (a-sas-in-*ay*-shĕn) *n*. such murder دھوکے سے کیا ہُوا قتل
assault (a-*sawlt*) *v.t*. make a violent and sudden attack حملہ یا ہلّہ کرنا ، دھاوا بولنا *n*. such an attack حملہ، ہلّہ، دھاوا
assay (a-*say*) *v.t*. test the quality or purity of (metal, etc.) پرکھنا، کسوٹی پر کسنا، attempt کوشش کرنا، *n*. test of the purity of (metal, etc.) پرکھ، کس،
assemblage *n*. see under **assemble**
assemble (a-*sem*-bĕl) *v. t*. & *i*. gather together جمع ہونا ، یا کرنا ، put (parts) together پُرزے یکجا کر کے پُوری کل بنانا، پُرزے جوڑنا، **assembly** (a-*semb*-li) *n*. number of persons assembled for a common purpose اجتماع public law-making body مجلسِ قانون ساز assembling of the parts of a machine پُرزے جوڑنا **assembly-plant** *n*. factory

for assembling parts of a machine پرزے جوڑ کر پوری مشین بنانے کا کارخانہ **assemblage** (-lij) *n.* coming or bringing together جمع ہونا یا کرنا collection of things مجموعہ collection of persons اجتماع

assent (a-*sent*) *v.i.* agree (*to*) ماننا، ہاں کہنا *n.* agreement منظوری، رضامندی *give (one's) assent to (something)* (کی) منظوری دینا۔

assert (a-*sĕ*t*) *v.t.* state firmly پرزور دعوے کرنا، وثوق سے کہنا ، زور سے کہنا۔ *assert (one's) innocence* بے گناہی کا دعویٰ کرنا insist on (a claim, etc.) *assert (one's) rights* اپنے حق پر ڈٹے رہنا *assert oneself,* draw attention to oneself اپنی بات منوانا، اپنی بات کی طرف توجہ مبذول کرنا۔ **assertion** *n.* (a-*sĕ**-shĕn) positive statement or claim بات جتانا، دعویٰ **assertive** (a-*sĕ**-tiv) *adj.* declaring firmly وثوق سے کہنے والا ، over-confident برخود غلط **assertiveness** *n.* over-confident برخود غلط ہونا

assess (a *ses*) *v.t.* fix (value or amount, esp. for payment) (محصول وغیرہ) تشخیص کرنا یا لگانا یا مقرر کرنا ، **assessment** *n.* ، (محصول وغیرہ کی) تعیین **assessor** *n.* (esp.) an officer of the court who assists the judge in deciding a case اسیسر، ثالث، حکم

asset (*as*-et) *n.* (usu. *pl.*) anything belonging to a person, company, etc., which may be used or sold to pay debts اثاثہ، املاک، واجب الوصول ، valuable or useful quality or skill دولت، اثاثہ، سرمایہ ، بہت بڑا سرمایہ *Your knowledge of English is an asset to you* تمہارا انگریزی کا علم تمہارا بہت بڑا سرمایہ ہے۔

assiduity (a-si-*dew*-i-ti) *n.* diligence محنت، تندہی مشقت۔ (*pl.*) constant attention to a lady (محبوب کی) طرف التفات **assiduous** (a-*sid*-ew-us) *adj.* hard-working, diligent محنتی

assign (a-*sīn*) *v.t.* allot (someone) a share in a distribution (of work, duty, etc.) (کام) دینا یا سونپنا ، تفویض کرنا۔ appoint or put forward (time, place, reason, purpose, etc.) ٹھہرانا، مقرر کرنا، پیش کرنا **assignation** (a-sĭ-*nay*-shĕn) *n.* (esp.) appointment of time or place for meeting ملاقات کے وقت یا مقام کا ، تعین **assignment** *n.* a fixed amount of work or study to be done گھر کا کام، سبق کی مقررہ مقدار، تفویض

assimilate (a-*sim*-i-layt) *v.t.* & *i.* (cause food to) become part of the body جزو بدن بننا یا بنانا (cause people to) become part of another social group رچ بس جانا ، اپنے میں سمو لینا (of ideas, etc.) take into the mind ذہن نشین ہونا یا کرنا، **assimilation** (-*lay*-) *n.* assimilating or being assimilated جذب کرنا سمونا ، رچ بس جانا ، ذہن نشین ہونا یا کرنا۔

assist (a-*sist*) *v.t.* & *i.* help, aid اعانت کرنا مدد دینا ، **assistance** *n.* help مدد ، امداد ، اعانت **assistant** (a-*sis*-tant) *n.* senior clerk بڑا منشی ، بڑا محرر *Head Assistant*, assistant in charge of a section or branch of the office, now also called *Section Officer* منشی اعلیٰ ، محرر اعلیٰ ، ہیڈ اسسٹنٹ

assizes (a-*sīz*-iz) *n. pl.* regular High Court session in English countries برطانوی گشتی عدالت کا اجلاس such a court برطانوی گشتی عدالت

associate (a-*soh*-shi-ayt) *v. t.* & *i.* join (persons or things, one with another) شرکت کرنا ، شریک ہونا یا کرنا۔ connect in thought (*with*) تعلق سمجھنا، مستلزم جاننا یا گردانا۔ often keep company (*with*) کسی کا ہم صحبت ہونا، کسی کے ساتھ اٹھنا بیٹھنا۔ *n.* & *adj.* (person) who associates with another صاحبی، شریک کار یا ہم صحبت

association (-*ay*-) *n.* associating شرکت ، تعلق ، ساتھ اٹھنا بیٹھنا۔ organized body of people انجمن

association football *n.* soccer فٹ بال

assort (as-*so*t*) *v.t.* sort, separate into classes چھانٹ پھٹک کر قسمیں الگ الگ کرنا ۔ **assorted** *adj.* of various sorts قسم قسم کا ، کئی میل کا mixed *ill-* (*well-*) *assorted,* badly (well) suited to one another سازگار یا ناسازگار **assortment** *n.* (esp.) collection of different sorts of things (کسی چیز کے) مختلف میل یکجا

assuage (a-*swayj*) *v.t.* lighten (pain, suffering, grief) دھیما کرنا ، تخفیف کرنا

assume (a-*sewm*) *v.t.* take for granted فرض کرنا undertake ، لینا ، اختیار کرنا ، ذمّے لینا *assume control* عہدے کی ذمّے داری قبول کرنا *assume office,* اپنے ہاتھ میں لینا ۔ pretend, put on ظاہرداری کرنا ، دکھاوا کرنا ، تصنع سے کام لینا، *assume a look of innocence* آنکھوں میں معصومیت مصنوعی انداز سے کرنا *assume a new name* اپنا نیا نام رکھ لینا کی مصنوعی چمک لانا ۔

assuming (a-*sew*-ming) *adj.* claiming greater than real importance برخود غلط ، خودبین **assumption** (a-*sump*-shĕn) *n.* the act of assuming فرض کرنا ، ذمّے داری قبول کرنا something assumed مفروضہ ،

assure (a-*shoo*) *v.t.* tell with confidence (*of* something) وثوق کے ساتھ کہنا۔ make certain اطمینان کر لینا ، قطعی طور پر طے کر لینا ، make (someone) feel certain (*of* something) یقین دلانا ، یقین دہانی کرنا ، **assured** *adj.* certain, sure یقینی ، حتمی insure (esp. one's life) زندگی کا بیمہ کرانا ، **assuredly** *adv.* doubtlessly یقیناً **assurance** (a *shoo*-ĕ-rans) *n.* assuring or being assured یقین دہانی confidence in one's own powers اعتماد، بھروسا ، خود اعتمادی ، insurance of life زندگی کا بیمہ

asterisk (*as*-te-risk) *n.* the mark * used in printing ستارہ ، پھُلّا

astern (a-*stĕ*n*) *adv.* in, at, or towards the stern of ship جہاز کے عقب یا عقبی حصّے میں behind, backwards پیچھے (کی طرف) *fall astern,* get behind other ships دوسرے جہازوں کے پیچھے رہ جانا

asteroid (*as*-te-roid) a small planet سیّارچہ
asthma (*as*-ma) *n.* lung disease causing difficulty in breathing دَمَہ ، ضیق النفس **asthmatic** (as-*mat*-ik) *adj* دَمے کا مریض
astigmatism (as-*tig*-ma-tizm) *n.* defect in the eye which prevents a person from seeing clearly (منظر کی) لانقطیت ، عدمِ شدادِ نظر
astir (a-*stě**) *adv.* & *adj.* on the move ہلتا ہوا حرکت میں۔ in an excited state سراسیمہ، گھبرایا ہوا out of bed بیدار
astonish (as-*ton*-ish) *v.t.* strike with sudden and great surprise ششدر کرنا ، اچنبھے میں ڈالنا **astonishing** *adj.* causing astonishment حیرت انگیز **astonishment** *n.* sudden and great surprise اچنبھا ، سخت تعجب
astound (as-*tound*) *v.t.* shock overcome with surprise بھونچکا یا ہکا بکا کرنا
astral (*as*-tral) *adj.* stellar, of stars کوکبی ، نجمی
astral hatch *n.* astrodome فلک نما
astray (as-*tray*) *adv.* & *adj.* away from the right path (esp. in wrongdoing) گمراہ ، بھٹکا **lead** (*someone*) *astray* گمراہ کرنا ، راہ سے بھٹکانا
Astraea (as-*tree*-a) *Cl. myth.* The Greek goddess of justice who lived among men during the Golden Age. She was the daughter of Zeus and Themis . عدل کی دیوی ، اَسترِیَہ
astride (as-*trīd*) *adv.* with one leg on each side (*of*) پرسوار، ایک ٹانگ اِدھر ایک ٹانگ اُدھر کیے ہوئے *sitting astride his father's knee* اپنے اَبّا کے گھٹنے پر سوار
astringent (as-*trin*-jent) *adj.* tightening سکیڑنے والا substance contracting the tissues قابض
astrodome *n.* see Addenda
astrolabe (*as*-tro-layb) *n.* instrument for taking the altitude of heavenly bodies اُصطرلاب
astrologer (as-*trol*-o-jeh*) *n.* one who practices astrology نجومی ، جوتشی **astrology** (as-*trol*-o-ji) *n.* pseudo-science studying the stars to foretell the future (of human beings) نجوم ، جوتش
astronomer *n.*, **astronomical** *adj.* see under astronomy
astronomy (as-*tron*-o-mi) *n.* science of the stars, etc. and their movement ، فلکیات، ہیئت ، ہیئت اَفلاک، علم ہیئت
astronomer *n.* expert in astronomy ، فلکی، ہیئت دان ماہرِ فلکیات۔ **astronomical** (*-nom-*) *adj.* pertaining to astronomy ہیئت سے متعلق ، فلکیاتی
astute (as-*tewt*) *adj.* quick at seeing how to gain an advantage ہوشیار، چالاک ، سیانا shrewd تیزفہم، تیز زیرک ، دانا۔ **astutely** *adj.* زیرکی سے ، دانائی سے **astuteness** *n.* دانائی، زیرکی، ہوشمندی
asunder (a-*sund*-ě*) *adv.* apart الگ الگ ، دُور دُور in pieces ٹکڑے ٹکڑے

asylum (a-*sy*-lum) *n.* place of rest, peace, and safety جائے پناہ ، پناہ گاہ ، ملجا ، ماویٰ (old use) place where mad people were cared for پاگل خانہ
at (at) *prep.* near in time کو ، کا ، عمل ، کے وقت ; *at noon* دوپہر کو ، دوپہر کے وقت ; *at 6 o'clock* چھ بجے in a place میں *at Lahore* لاہور میں *at the meeting* جلسے میں اجلاس میں doing somethin (مصروف ، لگا ہوا) میں ; *at work* کام میں (لگا ہوا) owing to سے ، پر ، کے باعث ، کی وجہ سے ، کے سبب *angry at the noise* شور پر خفا for پر *at the price* اس قیمت پر *at all events* لازماً ، یقیناً ، بہرصورت *at arm's length* دُور دُور پرے *near at hand* قریب ، نزدیک *at first* پہلے ، شروع ، شروع شروع میں *at last* آخرکار *at the latest* زیادہ سے زیادہ (اچھی صورت) *at best* زیادہ سے زیادہ ، حد سے حد *at worst* بدترین صورت میں *at the most* زیادہ سے زیادہ *at random* اٹکل پچو *at one's mercy* کسی کے رحم و کرم پر ، کسی کے قبضے میں *at any rate* بہرصورت *at will* حسبِ مرضی *at sight* دیکھتے ہی *at war (with)* حالتِ جنگ میں *at peace (with)* حالتِ امن میں *at sea* بالکل غلط ، حواس باختہ *at the same time*, (*a*) simultaneously بیک وقت ، ایک ہی وقت میں (*b*) yet ساتھ ہی ، تاہم *at the same time it is true* (دیکھو) ساتھ ہی یہ بھی صحیح ہے *at large*, (a) at liberty آزاد ، مفرور ، رُوپوش *the offender is at large* ملزم رُوپوش ہے (*b*) as a whole بحیثیت مجموعی *at daggers drawn* میں سخت دُشمنی *be at* کسی چیز کے پیچھے پڑنا *good* (or *bad*) *at something* کسی کام میں ہوشیار (یا نالائق) *play at* (*doing something*), do something half-heartedly, amateurishly or ostensibly بے دلی سے کوئی کام کرنا ، کوئی کام جھوٹ موٹ کرنا
Atalanta (at-a-*lan*-ta) *Cl. myth.* a woman famous for the swiftness of her speed. Hippomenes beat her in a race by dropping three golden apples on the course and won her as wife according to the earlier promise اطلانتہ
ate (ayt) کھایا pa. t. of **eat** (which see)
Ate (*ay*-tee) *Cl. myth.* the Greek goddess of mischief ایٹی
atebrine *n.* see Addenda
atheism (*ai*-thi-izm) *n.* belief that there is no God کفر ، انکارِ خدا ، الحاد **atheist** *n.* کافر ، دہریہ ، ملحد **atheistic** *adj.* کافرانہ ، منکرانہ ، ملحدانہ **atheistically** *adv.* کافروں کی طرح
Athena (a-*thee*-na), **Athene** (a-*thee*-nee). **Pallas** Athene (*Pal*-as-a-*thee*-nee), **Pallas** *Cl. myth.* the chaste Greek goddess of wisdom, identified with the Roman goddess, Minerva . اَتھینہ ، اَتھینی ، پالس پالس اتھینی
athlete (*ath*-leet) *n.* one trained to compete in games and sports کھیل کود میں حصہ لینے والا hence one physically strong ، قوی ، ورزشی **athletic** (ath-*let*-ik) *adj.* of outdoor games and sports ورزشی کسرتی **athletics** (ath-*let*-iks) *n.* (*pl.*) outdoor sports like running, jumping, etc. ورزشیں ، کسرتیں ، کود پھاند ، کھیل کود

at-home *n.* see under **home**
athwart (a-thwoh*t) *adv.* & *prep.* from side to side of (something) esp. obliquely کی راہ میں، کے راستے میں against کے برخلاف، کے برعکس، کے علی الرغم • athwart his purpose اس کے مقصد کے علی الرغم
Atlantis (at-*lan*-tis) *n.* beautiful legendary island of the Atlantic which sunk when its inhabitants became impious بحرِ عظیم اُوقیانوس ، جزیرۂ اُوقیانوس ، اطلانتس
Atlas (*at*-las) *Cl. myth.* leader of the Titans in their war with Zeus. After defeat, Zeus put him in the form of a mountain in North Africa and condemned him to bear heaven on his head and hands اطلس
atlas *n.* book of maps اٹلس، نقشہ نامہ، خریطہ
atmosphere (*at*-mos-fee-ĕ*) *n.* air surrounding the earth کرۂ ہوا ، فضا the air in a particular place آب وہوا ، فضا feeling (of good, evil, etc.) received from a place, conditions, etc. *atmosphere of peace and calm* امن وسکون کی فضا **atmospheric** (at-mos-*fe*-rik) *adj.* ہوائی ، فضائی *atmospheric conditions* weather فضائی حالت ، کرۂ ہوا کی حالت **atmospherics** *n. pl.* atmospheric disturbances in radio reception (ریڈیو میں) فضائی اثرات
atoll (*at*-ol, at-*ol*) *n.* coral island, often with coral belt enclosing a part of the sea مونگے کا جزیرہ ، جزیرۂ مرجان ، مونگے کی چٹانوں کا حلقہ ، مرجانی حلقہ
atom (*at*-om) *n.* smallest unit of matter not divisible by chemical means جوہر ، سالمہ very small quantity ذرّہ ، ریزہ ، ذرا سی چیز ، ذرا سا ، ذرّہ بھر ، ذرّہ برابر *blow to atoms*, destroy completely (by explosion) ریزہ ریزہ کر دینا *There is not an atom of truth in it* اس میں ذرّہ بھر بھی سچائی نہیں ہے • **atomic** (a-*tom*-ik) *adj.* pertaining to or derived from atom جوہری ، سالمی *atomic energy*, energy released by atomic fission جوہری ، توانائی *atomic bomb, atom bomb, A. bomb*, one which is exploded by releasing energy in atoms ایٹم بم ، جوہری بم ، سالماتی بم *atomic cocktail*, (see Addenda) *atomic theory*, a chemical theory سالمی نظریہ ، جوہری نظریہ ذرّی نظریہ *atomic weight*, weight of an element's atom compared with the weight of a hydrogen atom as a unit ذرّی وزن ، سالمی وزن ، (کسی عنصر کے سالمے کا وہ وزن جو اسے ہائیڈروجن (مائیں) کے ایک سالمے کو اکائی مان کر حاصل ہوتا ہے)
atone (a-*tohn*) *v.i.* make repayment (*for* wrongdoing) کفارہ دینا ، تاوان بھرنا ، تلافی کرنا ، **atonement** *n.* act atoning کفارہ ، تلافی ، ڈنڈ ، تاوان *the Atonement*, according to Christianity the sufferings of Christ to redeem humanity کفارہ
atop (a-*top*) *adv.* at the top of (سب) سے اوپر ، پورے زور سے
Atreus (*ayt*-re-us) *Cl. myth.* son of Pelops and the father of Agamemnon and Menelaus, who were known as the *Atridae* (pr. at-*rī*-dee) اتریڈیس
atrocious (a-*troh*-shus) *adj.* wicked خبیث ، نابکار very cruel ظالم ، بے درد **atrocity** (a-*tros*-i-ti) *n.* cruelty ; wicked act ظلم ، بیدردی ، سفاکی ، بدذاتی
atrophy (*at*-ro-fi) *v.t.* & *i.* & *n.* wasting away (of a part of the body, or a part of it) (جسم کے کسی حصے کا) سوکھنا یا ناکارہ ہونا ، اخلاقی گراوٹ moral deterioration اخلاقی پستی -
atropin (*at*-ro-pin), **atropine** (*at*-ro-pīn) *n.* poisonous extract of a deadly plant ربِّ تکوا ، ایٹروپین
Atropos (*at*-ro-pos) *Cl. myth.* the inevitable ; one of the Fates who cut the thread of life اٹروپس
attach (a-*tach*) *v.t.* tie (*to*) منسلک کرنا ، منسلک کرنا ، ساتھ لگانا *attach a document to a letter* مراسلے کے ساتھ دستاویزات منسلک کرنا attribute (*to*) (اہمیت دینا) منسوب کرنا *You attach much importance to what he says* تم اس کی باتوں کو بڑی اہمیت دیتے ہو go with, belong to کا ہونا bind by ties of love سے وابستگی ہونا ، سے لگاؤ ہونا یا وابستہ ہونا *attached to a person* کسی سے لگاؤ ہونا **attachment** *n.* ties of affection لگاؤ ، وابستگی **attachè** (a-*tash*-ay) *n.* person attached to the staff of an ambassador اتاشی ، علاءِ سفارت کا ایک عہدہ دار **attachè case**, a very small suitcase اتاچی کیس
▣ **attach, append, affix, annex.**
attack (a-*tak*) *n.* assault by physical force حملہ ، ہلّہ ، دھاوا ، چڑھائی assault by words اعتراضات کی بوچھاڑ seizure (by illness) (بیماری میں) گرفتاری ، (بیماری کا) اثر یا عمل *v.t.* assail with force چڑھائی یا حملہ کرنا ، دھاوا یا ہلّہ بولنا assail with words اعتراضات کی بوچھاڑ کرنا ، ہدفِ تنقید *the Hon'ble member attacked the government* معزز رکن نے حکومت پر اعتراضات کی بوچھاڑ کی begin work upon (کام) شروع کرنا (of disease) begin to affect (بیماری کا) اثر یا عمل کرنا *be attacked by* (a disease) (بیماری کا) شکار ہونا
▣ **attack, assail, assault.**
attain (a-*tayn*) *v.t.* & *i.* reach پہنچنا accomplish حاصل کرنا ، پایۂ تکمیل کو پہنچانا *attain* (*one's*) *object* اپنی مراد پانا **attainable** *adj.* ممکن الحصول **attainment** *n.* (*sing.*) something attained حصول ، تحصیل *easy of attainment*, easy to attain سہل الحصول (*pl.*) skill in some branch of knowledge استعداد ، قابلیت ، مہارت ، استعداد *a man of great attainments* بڑی استعداد والا شخص ▣ **attain, achieve, accomplish.**
attempt (a-*tempt*) *v.i.* try ; make an effort at something or (*to do* something) کوشش کرنا ، سعی کرنا *n.* effort (*to do* something) کوشش ، سعی (*make*) *an attempt on the life of* (*someone*), try to murder him کسی پر قاتلانہ حملہ کرنا
attend (a-*tend*) *v.i.* & *t.* give thought and care *to* توجہ کرنا go to, be present at جانا ، حاضر ہونا *attend school* مدرسے جانا *attend the class* جماعت میں حاضر ہونا serve, look after (someone) خدمت کرنا ، تیمارداری کرنا

attend *on*, wait upon (someone) حاضرِ خدمت ہونا accompany رفاقت کرنا ، حاصل کرنا (*be*) *attended by* مشکلات کا حامل (ہونا) **attendance** (a-*tend*-ens) *n.* attending or being attended upon حاضری ، حضوری ، خدمت number of persons present حاضرین کی تعداد

attendant (a-*tend*-ant) *n.* servant خادم ، حاضر باش one who attends (a meeting, etc.) حاضرین میں مُصاحب *adj.* accompanying مستلزم ، متعلقہ سے کوئی *war and its attendant evils* جنگ اور اُس کے متعلقہ مفاسد

attention (a-*ten*-shĕn) *n.* giving heed (*to*) التفات (کی طرف ، توجہ) (often *pl.*) acts of courtesy drill position in which one stands straight and still, تن شن ، تن چھن *come to* (or *stand at*) *attention* (قواعد میں) سیدھے کھڑے ہونا ، تن شن (یا تن چھن) ہو جانا **attentive** (-*iv*-) *adj.* heedful متوجہ

attest (a-*test*) *v.t.* & *i.* prove تصدیق کرنا ، توثیق کرنا bear witness to گواہی تصدیق کرنا ، تصدیقی شہادت دینا ، enrol for military service بھرتی ہونا

attic (*at*-ik) *n.* room between the roof and ceiling of a house کھپریل چھت کا بالاخانہ **Attic** *adj.* pertaining to Attica or Athens ایتھنی elegant (taste) اعلیٰ ، شستہ ، لطیف

attire (a-*tah*-è*) *v.t.* (literary word) dress پوشاک پہننا *n.* dress

attitude (*at*-i-tewd) *n.* position of the body, pose کھڑے ہونے کا انداز ، وضع way of feeling, thinking or behaving انداز نظر ، نقطۂ نگاہ ، رویّہ *firm attitude* مضبوط رویّہ *one's attitude to something* کسی شے کے متعلق کسی کا نقطۂ نگاہ *attitude of hostility* معاندانہ رویّہ

attorney (a-*tĕ**-ni) *n.* person with legal authority to act for another in business or law مختار *letter of attorney*, document executed to give such authority مختار نامہ *power of attorney*, power given thus مختاری ، مختار نامہ lawyer وکیل **Attorney-General,** chief public prosecutor of a State اٹارنی جنرل ، وکیل اعظم ، مختار اعظم

attract (at-*rakt*) *v.t.* pull towards (by unseen force) کھینچنا ، کشش کرنا draw to oneself by personal charm, etc. موہنا ، لبھانا ، رِجھانا ، گرویدہ کرنا *attract attention* توجہ مبذول کرانا **attraction** (at-*rak*-shĕn) *n.* attracting کشش ، جذب (esp.) that which attracts لبھانے والا ، موہ لینے والا **attractive** (-iv) *adj.* pleasing, charming دل کش ، کشش رکھنے والا

attribute (*at*-ri-bewt) *n.* trait, characteristic, or symbol وصف ، صفت *v.t.* (at-*rib*-ewt) *attribute to* (*a*) consider as belonging to سے منسوب کرنا (*b*) consider as being caused by (something or someone) پر محمول کرنا ، کے باعث قرار دینا *attribute one's failure to bad luck* اپنی ناکامی کو بدنصیبی پر محمول کرنا **attribution** (-*bew*-) *n.* نسبت **attributive** (at-*rib*-ew-tiv) *adj.* (in grammar, an adjective) naming an attribute توصیفی (In '*the old woman*' '*old*' is an attributive adjective. ◾ An **attribute** is what other people think the person or object possesses ; a **quality**, what he really possesses. To **attribute** is to give to a thing a quality which we believe it possesses ; to **ascribe** something to some one, to recognize someone as the author of the thing ; to **impute** something undesirable to someone.

attrition (at-*rish*-ĕn) *n.* wearing away فرسودگی *a war of attrition*, war causing general exhaustion آہستہ آہستہ ناکارہ کرنے والی جنگ

attune (a-*tewn*) *v. t.* (*attune to*), bring into harmony with سُر ملانا ، ہم آہنگ کرنا

auburn (*awb*-ĕ*n) *adj.* reddish-brown (usu. hair) بھورے ، سنہرے

au courant *adj.* acquainted *with* what is going on سے باخبر

auction (*awk*-shĕn) *n.* public sale at which goods go to the highest bidder نیلام ، نیلامی ، ہراج *v. t.* sell goods by auction نیلام کرنا ، نیلامی بولنا ، *auction bridge* card-game in which players outbid one another تاش کی بولی والی بازی **auctioneer** (awk-shĕ-*nee*-ĕ*) *n.* person who conducts an auction نیلام کرنے والا ، نیلامی بولنے والا ، نیلامیا

audacious (aw-*day*-shus) *adj.* rashly bold بہادر ، نڈر ، مشہور impudent گستاخ **audacity** (aw-*das*-i-ti) *n.* impudence or rash boldness جسارت ، گستاخی *have the audacity* کی جسارت کرنا

audibility (awd-i-*bil*-i-ti) *n.* capability of being heard سنائی دینا ، گوش رسی *Audibility was very poor at the other end of the hall* ہال کے دوسرے سرے پر آسانی سے کچھ سنائی نہ دیتا تھا **audible** (*awd*-i-bĕl) *adj.* loud enough to be heard* اتنا بلند کہ سُنا جا سکے ، گوش رس

audience (*awd*-i-ens) *n.* listeners at a meeting سامعین ، حاضرین interview given by a ruler شرفِ باریابی پانا (یا دینا) باریابی *gain* (or *grant*) *audience* an *audience with* کی خدمت میں شرفِ باریابی

Note that even at the movies we have **spectators** and not an **audience**. Similarly, there is no audience at a religious service, but only a **congregation**.

audio *adj.*, **audiophile** *n.*, **audeovisual** *adj.* see Addenda.

audit (*awd*-it) *v. t.* examine an account to see if it is correct محاسبہ کرنا ، پڑتال کرنا *n.* official examination of this kind محاسبہ ، پڑتال **auditor** (*awd*-i-tĕ*) *n.* محاسب *Auditor-General* مُحاسبِ اعلیٰ

audition (aw-*dish*-ĕn) *n.* a hearing esp. to test the voice of a speaker, singer, etc. آواز کا امتحان **auditorium** (aw-di-*to*-ri-um) *n.* part of a theatre or hall where an audience sits حاضرین کا مقام **auditory** *adj.* pertaining to the sense of hearing سُنی *auditory canal* عَصَب سَنِی *auditory nerve*

auditor *n.* see under **audit**

au fait (oh-*fay*) French for conversant خوب واقف *au fait in* or *at* سے خوب واقف *put (someone) au fait of*, instruct (him) in کسی شے کے بارے میں ہدایات جاری کرنا

Augean (aw-*jee*-an) *adj.* repulsively filthy task demanding superhuman labour سخت غلیظ *clear the Augean stables*, accomplish such task مدتوں کی گندگی دور کرنا ، ناممکن کو ممکن کر دکھانا ، **Augeas** (aw-*jee*-as) *Cl. myth.* whose king stalls contaiting 3,000 oxen had not been cleaned for 30 years. Hercules washed them in one day by diverting a river into them آجیئس

auger (*awg*-ĕ*) *n.* carpenter's tool for boring holes برما (see also **augur**)

aught (awt) (lit.) *n.* anything کچھ *for aught I know*, to the best of my knowledge جہاں تک مجھے معلوم ہے *adv.* at all بالکل، قطعاً

augment (awg-*ment*) *v. t.* & *i.* increase in size or number بڑھانا ، بڑا کرنا ، اضافہ کرنا **augmentation** (-*ay*-) *n.* اضافہ

augur (*awg*-ĕ*) *n.* (in ancient Rome) an official soothsayer کاہن (رومی) *v. t.* foretell پیش گوئی کرنا پیشین گوئی کرنا be a sign of کا شگون ہونا *it augurs ill* (or *well*) یہ بُری (یا اچھی) فال ہے **augury** (*awg*-e-ri) *n.* the art of foretelling the future by reading signs کہانت ، شگون لینا sign, omen شگون ، فال

august (aw-*gust*) *adj.* stately, majestic عالی شان جلیلُ القدر

August (*aw*-gust) *n.* eighth month of the Western calendar اگست

auld lang syne (awld-lang-*sīn*) (Scottish) a song about times long ago ; اسکاٹستانی گیت کے الفاظ the days of yore پچھلے دن ، بیتے دن ، پُرانا زمانہ

aunt (ahnt) *n.* sister of one's father or mother پھوپھی ، خالہ wife of one's uncle ممانی **aunty** (*ahn*-ti) *n.* familiar form of **aunt**

aureomycin *n.* see Addenda.

au revoir (*oh*-re-voh-*ah**) 'till I see you again' the French for good-bye خدا حافظ

aural (*aw*-rĕl) *adj.* of the ear کان سے متعلق، اُذُنی

Aurora (aw-*roh*-ra) *Cl. myth* the Greek *Eos*, the goddess of dawn *aurora* dawn طلوع فجر ، تڑکا ، سویرا **Aurara Australis** *n.* flashes of light seen at night near the South Pole جنوبی قطبی روشنی **Aurora Borealis** *n.* such light seen near the North Pole شمالی قطبی روشنی

auspices (*aws*-pi-ses) *n. pl.* good omen نیک فال ، نیک شگون *under the auspices of*, helped and favoured by کے زیرِ اہتمام ، کے زیرِ سرپرستی **auspicious** (aws-*pish*-us) *adj.* favourable, promising success مُبارک

austere (aw-*stee*-ĕ*) *adj.* strictly moral (person) کٹر ، اخلاقی اصولوں پر سختی سے کاربند یا پابند simple and plain (behaviour) سادگی پسند without ornament سادہ **austerity** (aw-*ste*-ri-ti) *n.* sternness دُرشتی simplicity سادگی see Addenda

autarchy, autarky (*awt*-ah*-ki) *n.* economic self-sufficiency of a State ریاست کی مُعاشی خودکفالت مُعاشی آزادی

authentic (aw-*then*-tik) *adj.* genuine trustworthy مُستند ، مُعتبر **authenticate** (aw-*then*-ti-kayt) *v. t.* make authentic تصدیق کرنا ، اِحقاقِ حق کرنا

author (*aw*-thĕ*) *n.* writer of a book, etc. مُصنّف creator of something خالق ، مُوجد ، بانی ، باعث **authoress** (*au*-thĕ-ress) woman author مُصنّفہ **authorship** *n.* being an author مصنف ہونا ، باعث یا بانی ہونا origin of a book, etc. مُصنّف *book of unknown authorship* گمنام مُصنّف کی تصنیف

authoritarian *n.* & *adj.* **authoritarianism** *n.* **authoritative** *adj.* see under **authority**

authority (aw-*tho*-ri-ti) *n.* power or right to command اِختیار ، اِقتدار person(s) enjoying such power or right ذی اقتدار ، مُقتدر ، حاکم ، حکام ، ارباب اختیار ، بااختیار person with expert knowledge سند ، ماہر book, etc., giving standard information on a subject سند ، مُسلّم الثبوت تحریر permission پروانہ ، اجازت ، اختیار **authoritarian** (-*tay*-) *adj.* calling for obedience تحکمانہ ، آمرانہ person favouring this attitude آمریت پسند **authoritarianism** *n.* authoritarian attitude آمریت ، آمریت پسندی **authoritative** (-*tay*-) *adj.* having or showing authority تحکمانہ ، مستند ، مُعتبر **authorize** (*aw*-the-rīz) *v t.* give authority *for* or *to do* something) اِختیار دینا ، اجازت دینا۔ **authorization** (aw-the-rī-*zay*-shĕn) *n.* authorizing اختیار ، اجازت

[1]**auto** (*awt*-oh) *n.* (colloq.) automobile موٹر

[2]**auto-** *pref.* by, of, or for oneself خُود

autobiography (aw-to-bī-*og*-ra-fi) *n.* life history of a person written by himself آپ بیتی ، خُود نوشت سوانح عمری ، خُود گزشت

autocracy (aw-*tok*-ra-si) *n.* (country with a) government by an autocrat مطلق العنانی ، حکومتِ استبداد

autocrat (*awt*-o-krayt) *n.* ruler with unlimited power مُطلق العنان فرمانروا one who does things without considering the wishes of others خود رائے ، خود مختار ، خود سر **autocratic** (awt-o-*krat*-ik) *adj.* of or like an autocrat مُستبدّانہ واستبدادی

autogiro (aw-to-*ji*-roh) *n.* aircraft which takes off and lands almost straight up and down آٹوجائیرو ، راست پرواز طیارہ

an autogiro

autograph (*awt*-og-rahf) *n.* one's own handwriting, (esp. one's signature) اپنی قلمی تحریر *v.t.* write and sign for somebody as a memento (بطوریادگار) اپنی قلمی تحریر دینا ، دستخط کرنا ۔

automat *n.* see Addenda

automatic (awt-o-*mat*-ik) *adj.* self-moving خودکار ، خودحرکی (machine) designed to work without attention خودحرکی کل، آپ چالو (acts) done without thought بے سوچے سمجھے ، غیرشعوری ۔ *n.* automatic pistol خودکار طپنچہ **automatically** *adj.* آپ سے آپ ، خود بخود ۔

automation *n.* see Addenda

automaton (aw-*tom*-a-tun) *n.* (*pl.*, *automatons*, or *automata*) machine with hidden motive power خودحرکی person whose actions are purely mechanical کٹھ پتلی ، بے شعور

automobile (awt-o-mo-*beel*) *n.* motor-car موٹرگاڑی ، موٹرکار

autonomous (aw-*ton*-o-mus) *adj.* self-governing State or province) خود مختار (ملک یا صوبہ) **autonomy** (aw-*ton*-o-mi) *n.* (country with) right of self-government خود مختاری ، آزاد ریاست

autopsy (aw-*top*-si) *n.* post-mortem examination of a body to find the cause of its death لاش کا طبی معائنہ ، پس مرگ معائنہ

auto-suggestion *n.* hypnotic self-suggestion ایمائے نفسی ، خودخیالی

autumn (*aw*-tum) *n.* season preceding winter خزاں beginning of the decay (*of* life, etc.) خزاں **autumnal** (aw-*tum*-nal) *adj* خزاں کے (کی) ، خزاں متعلق ، خزاں کا ۔

auxiliary (awg-*zil*-ya-ri) *adj.* assisting مددگار ، helpful سود مند ، ممد ، مفید ، کارآمد *auxiliary troops*, foreign troops in a nation's service during war امدادی فوج *auxiliary verb*, serving to form tenses of other verbs معاون یا امدادی فعل *n.* someone or something that gives help معاون ، معین ، مددگار

avail (a-*vayl*) *v.t.* & *i.* be of help or use فائدہ ، مدد یا کام دینا *n.* value, help, use فائدہ، مدد، کام ; *avail oneself of*, make use of سے فائدہ اٹھانا ; *of no avail, without avail, to little avail*, useless بے کار **availability** (a-vayl-a-*bil*-i-ti) *n.* being available حصول ، دستیابی **available** *adj.* that which may be obtained ممکن الحصول ، دستیاب

avalanche (*av*-a-lahnsh) *n.* sudden slipping of a mass of snow down a mountain side برفانی تودہ anything that overwhelms by volume or speed اچانک حادثہ

avarice (*av*-è-ris) *n.* greed *for* wealth حرص ، لالچ ، طمع

avaricious (av-a-*rish*-us) *adj.* greedy لالچی ، حریص ، طامع

avenge (a-*venj*) *v.t.* take vengeance for (something) بدلہ لینا ، انتقام لینا *avenge someone* (or *something*) *on* (or *upon*) *someone* کسی سے کسی کا انتقام لینا ، *avenge oneself* ذاتی انتقام لینا *be avenged* کا بدلہ اترنا Ⓢ To **avenge** is to punish a wrong impartially, whether oneself be the victim of it or not ; to **revenge** oneself upon another is to do what one considers justice, but from selfish motives, as when one has suffered personally from the act.

avenue (*av*-e-new) *n.* road bordered by trees on each side دورویہ درختوں والی سڑک (U.S.) wide street کشادہ بازار way of approach طریق ، سبیل ، راستہ *avenues to success* طریق کامیابی ، راہ کامرانی

aver (a-*vĕ**) *v.t.* (-rr-) assert وثوق سے کہنا ، بزور کہنا ، دعوے سے کہنا

average (*av*-e-rij) *n.* result of dividing the sum of several quantities by their numb r اوسط the normal standard عام معیار *above* (*below, up to*) *the average*, better than (not so good as, equal to) this level عام معیار سے بلند (یا پست ، یا کے مطابق) *on an* (or *the*) *average*, giving the average اوسطاً *adj.* found by making an averag. اوسط *average age of the class* جماعت کے طلبہ کی اوسط عمر ، of the normal standard اوسط (معیار) کا اوسط درجے کا *man of average ability* اوسط قابلیت کا *v.t.* find the average of اوسط نکالنا

averse (a-*vĕ*s*) *adj.* opposed (*to* something) سے متنفر (یا) مخالف disinclined (*from* action, etc.) سے متنفر ، سے بیزار **aversion** (a-*vĕ**-shèn) *n.* strong dislike (*to* or *from*) نفرت ، بیزاری thing or somebody that is strongly disliked گھناؤنا ، نفرت انگیز

avert (a-*vĕ*t*) *v.t.* turn away (*from*) ہٹانا ، پھیرنا ، موڑنا ۔ ward off بال بال بچنا ، دور کرنا ، ازالہ کرنا *avert suspicion* شبہے کا ازالہ کرنا *avert an accident* حادثے سے بال بال بچنا

aviary (*ayv*-ya-ri) *n.* place for keeping birds چڑیا خانہ

aviation (ay-vi-*ay*-shèn) *n.* (art or science of) flying ہوا بازی **aviator** (ay-vi-*ay*-tĕ*) *n.* pilot of an aeroplane ہوا باز ، طیارچی **aviatress, aviatrice** (tris), **aviatrix** (triks) *n.* woman pilot ہوا بازخاتون

avid (*av*-id) *adj.* very eager (*for*) مشتاق ، دلدادہ ، شیفتہ *avid for fame*, شہرت کا دلدادہ greedy (*of*)

avidity (a-*vid*-i-ti) *n.* eagerness or greed (*of* or *for*) طمع ، حرص ، دلدادگی ، شیفتگی

avocation (av-o-*kay*-shèn) *n.* hobby مشغلہ Ⓢ **Avocation** means a hobby whereas **vocation** means one's regular profession.

avoid (a-*void*) *v.t* keep away from سے پہلو تہی کرنا shun اِجتراز یا گُریز کرنا پہلو بچانا ، بچنا ، کنّی کترانا **avoidable** (a-*void*-i bèl) *adj* جس سے اِجتراز ہو سکے **avoidance** *n.* اِحتِراز، گُریز ، کنارہ کشی

avoirdupois (av-ĕ*-dew-*poiz*) *n.* system of weighing in lb. and oz. ایورڈ پائز ، برطانوی تول

avouch (a-*vouch*) *v.t.* & *i.* assert, maintain *that* یقین کے ساتھ کہنا ، زور سے کہنا۔

avow (a-*vow*) *v.t* confess اِعتراف یا اقبال کرنا declare positively حلفیہ کہنا ، علی الاعلان کہنا **avowal** *n.* confession اِقرار، اِعتراف، اِقبال **avowedly** *adv* by confession, positively مُسلّمہ طور پر، خُود اپنے اعتراف کے مُطابق

await (a-*wayt*) *v.t* be waiting for, expect کی راہ دیکھنا

awake (a-*wayk*) *v.t.* & *i.* (*awake, awoke, awaked*; or *awake, awoke, awoke*) rouse from (sleep or inactivity) جاگنا یا جگانا ، جاگ اُٹھنا ، بیدار ہونا *adj.* waking بیدار **awaken** *v.t.* & *i.* awake جگانا یا جاگنا **awakening** (a-*wayk*-è-ning) *n.* (esp.) arousing from indifference جھنجھوڑ کر چونکا دینے والا حادثہ ، اِنتباہ *a sad awakening* عبرتناک اِنتباہ

award (a-*wo*d*) *n.* judgment فیصلہ something given as the result of a judgment esp. a prize in a competition فیصلے میں ملنے والی چیز، اِنعام *v.t.* assign, give as an award اِنعام دینا *be awarded the first prize* پہلا اِنعام پانا

aware (a-*way*-è*) *adj.* conscious (*of* something, *that*......) آگاہ، باخبر، واقف **awareness** *n.* act of being aware واقفیت، آگاہی [illegible] **We are aware of an outside fact but conscious of a feeling within.**

awash (a-*wash*) *adj.* (of shore) washed over by sea waves موجوں کے تھپیڑوں کی زد میں ، موج گرفتہ

away (a-*way*) *adv.* absent from دُور، باہر، غیر حاضر out of one's possession اپنے پاس سے پرے out of existence کالعدم ، ختم continuously متواتر، لگاتار، پے در پے

awe (aw) *n.* respect combined with fear and reverence جلال، احترام، رُعب *v.t.* fill with awe *by* احترام کا جذبہ پیدا کرنا **awesome** (*aw*-sum) *adj.* causing awe پُر جلال ، بارُعب **awestruck** (*aw*-struk) *adj.* full of awe متحیّر، دہشت زدہ **awful** *adj.* dreadful دہشت ناک (colloq.) extreme بہت، نہایت **awfully** *adv* (colloq.) بہت ہی ، نہایت **awfulness** *n.* dreadfulness مرعوب ، جلال

awhile (a-*wīl*, or a-*hwīl*) *adv.* for a short time ذرا کے (یا کی)، ذرا ، تھوڑی دیر کر یا کے لیے

awkward (*awk*-wĕ*d) *adj.* not well-designed for use بھدّا ، بھونڈا ، بے ڈول ، بدوضع hard to deal with پریشان، تکلیف دِہ ، کڈھب ، ناکارہ *the awkward age*, adolescence شرمیلی زندگی *an awkward customer*, (colloq.) a dangerous adversary سخت حریف *an awkward situation* بڑی مُشکل ، سخت مُشکل (person, animal, etc.) clumsy بھونڈا ، بدوضع unskilful اناڑی ، بے ڈھنگا ، بدسلیقہ، experiencing trouble or inconvenience پریشان کشمکش و حیص بیص (یا گومگو) کی حالت میں **awkwardly** *adv.* بھونڈے پن سے۔ **awkwardness** *n.* بھونڈا پن، پریشانی، تکلیف دہی، مشکل

awl *n.* small tool for making holes in leather ستاری ، سُتالی

awning (*awn*-ing) *n.* canvas covering over windows and doors سائبان، شامیانہ

awoke (a-*wohk*) جاگا ہُوا pa. t. of **awake** (which see)

awry (a-*rī*) *adj.* twisted ترچھا، ٹیڑھا *look awry* کنکھیوں سے دیکھنا wrong غلط *go* (or *run* or *tread awry* غلطی کرنا *adv.* wrongly غلطی سے

axe (aks) *n.* tool for hewing wood کلہاڑی، تبر

axiom (*ak*-si-um) *n* self-evident truth بدیہیات ، بدیہیات، اولیات (*pl.*) **axioms** *n.* (یا اولیات) میں سے ، بدیہی، **axiomatic** (ak-si-o-*mat*-ik) *adj.* بدیہی

axis (*ak*-sis) *n.* (*pl.* **axes**, *pr.* *ak*-seez) imaginary straight line around which a body turns محور strong political ties between two sovereign states resulting in voluntary mutual co-operation محور *adj* of such powers محوری *Axis Powers* محوری طاقتیں

axle (*ak*-sèl) *n.* rod on which a wheel turns دُھرا ، دُھری **axle-tree** *n.* rod passing through the centres of a pair of wheels دُھرے کا ڈنڈا ، گول ڈنڈی

ay, aye (ī) *n.* & *int* yes ہاں ، حامی ، حامی بھرنے والا، ہاں کہنے والا **the ayes** *n. pl* the persons voting for a proposal, etc. ہاں کہنے والے *the ayes have it*, the motion is carried قرارداد منظور

ayah (*ah*-ya) *n.* a Pakistani nurse or lady's maid آیا ، کھلائی

aye (ay) *adv.* always اَبَدا ، ہمیشہ

azoic (a-*zoh*-ik) *adj.* (of geological age) when there was no life on **earth** قبل از زیست ، بے حیات earth stratum **having** no fossils بے حیات تہہ

azure (*azh*-è*, *azh*-ye*) *n.* clear blue sky نیلگوں آسمان *adj.* sky-blue نیلا ، نیلگوں

B

b, B (*bee*) (pl., *b's* or *bs*) the second letter of the English alphabet بی
baa (bah) *n.* cry of a sheep or a lamb, بھیں بھیں *v. t.* (*baa, baaed, baaed*) bleat as asneep بھیں بھیں کرنا
babble (*bab*-èl) *v. i.* & *t.* make sounds like a baby بڑبڑانا ، غوں غاں کرنا talk foolishly بک بک کرنا tell a secret دل کی بات کہنا ، بھید کھولنا (of stream, etc.) murmur (ندی وغیرہ میں پانی کا) شور کے ساتھ بہنا۔
babe (*bayb*) *n.* (liter.) baby دودھ پیتا بچہ ، ننھا منّا simple inexperienced person سادہ لوح ناتجربہ کار شخص
babel (*bay*-bèl) *n.* confusion of noisy voices کائیں کائیں ، ہنگامہ ، شور و غوغا (*Babel*), capital of ancient Babylonia where people tried to reach heaven by building a tower high enough but ended only in confusion by each beginning to speak a new language unintelligible to others بابل
baboon (ba-*boon*) *n.* large monkey with dog-like face میموں ، بن مانس
babushka *n.* (see *Addenda*)
baby (*bay*-bi) *n.* child in arms شیر خوار ، ننھا منّا ، گودکا دودھ پیتا بچہ cowardly or weak person کمزور یا بزدل شخص thing small of its kind چھوٹا ، ذرہ سا ، ننھا **babyhood** (-hud) *n.* state of being a baby بچپن ، چھٹپنا ، طفولیت ، عالمِ طفولیت **baby-sitter, baby-sitting** *n.* (see *Addenda*)
Bacchus (*bak*-us) (*Cl. myth.*) the Greek god of wine ; he was the son of Zeus and Semele بیکس ، باخوس **bacchanal** (*bak*-a-nal) *adj.* of Bacchus or his rites بیکسی ، باخوسی *n.* & *adj.* riotous (person, reveller رند ، بدمست ، رند مشرب **bacchanalian** (-*nay*-) *adj.* of such noisy feasts where there is singing, dancing and drinking باخوسی محفلوں کا ، بزمِ رنداں کا **Bacchic** *adj*. bacchanal رند مشرب
bachelor (*bach*-è-lě*) *n.* unmarried man کنوارہ ، مجرّد ، غیر شادی شدہ suitable for an unmarried person غیر شادی شدہ افراد کے لیے *bachelor flats* غیر شادی شدہ افراد کے رہنے اقامتی کمرے person who has taken a first university degree طیلسانی ، فارغ التحصیل *Bachelor of Arts*, *B.A.* *Bachelor of Science*, *B.Sc.* بی ۔ ایس ۔ سی ۔
bacillus (ba-*sil*-us) *n.* (pl., *bacilli* ; pr., -lı) rod-shaped bacterium جرثومہ (جمع: جراثیم)
back (bak) *n.* hinder part of the body پشت ، پیٹھ ، کمر one who plays before the goal in football or hockey بیک ، پشتی *full back* فل بیک ، پشتی *half back* ہاف بیک ، نیم پشتی move to the rear پیچھے ہٹانا یا ہٹانا support *back (someone) up* کسی کی پشت پر ہونا ، یا مدد کرنا یا پشت پناہی کرنا ، پشتیبانی کرنا *back a plan* کسی تجویز یا منصوبے کی حمایت کرنا حمایت کرنا *go back upon* (or *from one's word*, etc.) اپنے قول سے پھر جانا *back out of*, withdraw from سے منہ موڑ بیٹھنا ، کی حمایت سے ترک کرنا *turn* (*one's*) *back*, flee پیٹھ پھیر کر بھاگنا *fight with* (*one's*) *back to the wall*, fight at bay مجبور ہو کر جان بچانے کو لڑنا *back a horse*, bet money on its winning a race (گھوڑ دوڑ میں) گھوڑے پر شرط لگانا (ریا بدنا) *adv.* to the rear پیچھے to the former place or state واپس ، اپنی پہلی جگہ in return جواب میں **backer** *n.* supporter حامی person who bets شرط بدنے والا **backache** *n.* pain in the back درد کمر یا انگیا درد **backbite** *v. t.* speak evil of one behind one's back چغلی کھانا ، چغل خوری کرنا **backbiting** *n.* چغل خوری **backbiter** *n.* چغل خور **back blocks** *n.* agricultural land in remote anterior اندرونی علاقوں کی اراضی **backbone** *n.* spine ریڑھ کی ہڈی firmness, courage مضبوطی ، کس بل ، ہمّت ، حوصلہ main support *of* پشت پناہ **backdoor** *n.* door at the back of the house (گھر کا) پچھلا دروازہ *adj*. secret (method, entry, etc.) خفیہ ، مخفی **back-formation** *n.* coining of the supposed source of a word from the derivative in use عکسی وضع such word مرضوعِ منعکس **backgammon** *n.* a well-known game played with dice and 15 pieces (or 'men') نرد بازی complete victory in it نرد بازی میں جیت ، پُو بارہ **background** *n.* distant parts of a scene پس منظر place out of sight گوشۂ گمنامی ; *keep* (or *stay*) *in the background*, stay where one will not be noticed گوشۂ گمنامی میں رہنا نظروں سے اوجھل رہنا past attainments or environment **backhanded** *adj.* made with the hand turned backwards اُلٹے ہاتھ کی insincere منافقانہ **backing** *n.* help, support امداد ، اعانت ، مدد یا مدد کرنے والا
back-log *n.* reserves محفوظ سرمایہ arrears of unfulfilled orders بقایا فرمائشیں **backroom boys** *n.* (colloq.) unknown research workers behind a project, etc. گمنام تحقیقاتی کارکن **backmost** *adj.* farthest to the back بالکل آخری ، سب سے پچھلا **back-number** *n.* old copy of a periodical (اخبار یا رسالے وغیرہ کا) گزشتہ شمارہ (U.S.) person with outmoded ideas, appearance and manners دقیانوسی (شخص) **backslide** *v.t.* give up one's principles برگشتہ ہونا ، منحرف ہونا fall into bad old ways توبہ توڑنا **backward** *adj.* (esp.) making little progress پیچھے ، پسماندہ be-

hindhand پچھیت backward rain پچھیت بارش **backwards, backward**, *adv.* to the rear پیچھے **backwash** *n.* receding movement of waves لہر کا اتار **backwater** *n.* part of a river not reached by its current بند پانی ، بند کھاڑی condition of mind, untouched by progress ذہنی جمود یا جمود (U.S.) out-of-the way house or town جنگل میں واقع جگہ **backwoods** *n. pl.* wild forest land far from inhabited areas گھنا جنگل ، جنگل بن **backwoodsman** *n.* one who lives in the backwoods دور جنگل میں رہنے والا quiet countryman seldom visiting the city سادہ دیہاتی ، دیہات نشین

bacon (*bayk*-un) *n.* salted and dried meat of a pig سور کا خشک نمکین گوشت **Baconian** *adj.* (follower) of Francis Bacon (1561—1626) and his philosophy بیکنی one who believes that it was actually Bacon who wrote what are called Shakespeare's plays بیکنیا

bacteria (bak-*tee*-ri-a) *n. pl.* (sing. *bacterium*) simple germs sometimes causing disease جراثیم (واحد: جرثومہ) **bacterial** *adj.* جراثیمی ، جراثیم کا **bacteriology** (-*ol*-o-ji) *n.* study of bacteria جراثیمیات ، علم جراثیم ، جرثومیات **bacteriologist** *n.* ماہر جرثومیات ، ماہر جراثیمیات

bad *n.* ruin ; ill-fortune تباہی ، بربادی ، بدقسمتی *go to the bad*, be ruined تباہ و برباد ہونا *Rs 100 to the bad*, having lost Rs 100, or owing Rs 100 سو روپے گھاٹے میں ، (یا) سو روپے کا مقروض *adj.* (*bad, worse, worst*) wicked بداخلاق ، بدکار *bad-tempered*, easily getting angry بدمزاج ، تند مزاج of poor quality گھٹیا ، ناقص distressing تشویشناک severe سخت (nursery) naughty شریر *bad girl* شریر لڑکی *bold bad man* شریر لڑکا ، (ننھا) شیطان **badly** *adv.* بری طرح سے ، غلط **badness** *n.* state of being bad برائی ، خرابی

bade (bad) *pa. t.* of **bid** (which see)

badge (baj) *n.* some mark or design worn to show rank, distinction, etc. بلا ، نشان

badger (*baj*-ē*) small, grey animal living in holes in the ground hunted by dogs بجو *v.t.* pester (someone) with troublesome questions دق کرنا ، سخت پریشان کرنا

a badger

badinage (bad-i-nahzh) *n.* banter ; friendly joking دل لگی ، چھیڑ چھاڑ

badminton (*bad*-min-tun) *n.* tennis-like game played with shuttlecock بیڈ منٹن

baffle (*baf*-el) *v.t.* prevent (*from doing something*) روکنا ، توڑ کرنا ، مات دینا cause uncertainty چکرا دینا ، حیران یا پریشان کرنا *baffling problem* *n.* screen, etc., placed to control the flow of sound, air or liquid روک ، آڑ

bag *n.* sack or pouch بورا ، تھیلا *v.t.* & *i.* (-gg-) put in a bag تھیلے میں ڈالنا (of trousers, etc.) hang loosely (*at the knees, etc.*) (پر سے) ڈھیلا ڈھالا ہونا ، لٹکنا ، پھولا ہوا ہونا seize قبضے میں کرنا secure game شکار کرنا **baggy** *adj.* hanging lose ڈھیلا ڈھالا ، پھولا ہوا

bagatelle (bag-a-*tel*) *n.* minor billiard-like game بلیرڈ کی ایک قسم ، بیگاٹیل mere trifle معمولی سی چیز

bagman *n.* (colloq.) travelling salesman سفری ایجنٹ **bagpipes** *n. pl.* Scottish musical instrument with air stored in a wind-bag and numerous pipes بیگ پائپ ، مشک بین ، شکیزہ

man playing bag-pipes

baggage (*bag*-ij) *n.* traveller's luggage مسافر کا سامان army supplies, *e.g.*, tents and bedding ڈیرہ ، خیمہ **bag and baggage** with one's belongings مع سامان ، (انگڑ کھنگڑ) سمیت ◙ **Baggage** is the U.S. form of what is usually called **luggage** (in England); **encumbrances** denotes not only luggage but also one's family and other dependents.

bah *int.* of disgust or contempt ہونہہ

bail (bayl) *v.t.* ضمانت *bail (someone) out*, secure freedom (of an accused person) till called for trial, by undertaking to pay a law-court money which will not be returned if he does not turn up ضمانت دینا ، ضمانت دے کر چھڑانا *n.* crosspiece on top of wickets in cricket (کرکٹ کی) گلّی the money demanded by the court as security ضمانت ، مچلکہ person who pays such security ضامن; *go bail for (someone)*, *bail (him) out* کسی کی ضمانت دینا *out on bail*, free after payment of bail ضمانت پر رہا *admit to bail*, release on bail ضمانت پر رہا کرنا *bail before arrest*, order to admit (someone) to bail in case warrants of arrest are produced ضمانت قبل از گرفتاری **bailable** *adj.* قابل ضمانت ، جسے ضمانت پر رہا کیا جا سکے

bailiff (*bayl*-if) *n.* law officer who helps a sheriff قرق والا ، بیلف ، قرق امین ، قارق manager for a land owner زمیندار کا گماشتہ

bairn (*bay*-è*n) *n.* (Scottish word for) child بچہ ، ننھا

bait (bayt) *n.* food, etc., put on a hook or net to catch fish, birds, or animals (پھانسنے کے لیے ڈالا ہوا چارہ یا) دانہ allurement ترغیب ، تحریص *take the bait*, (a) پھنس جانا ، فریب میں آ جانا (b) swallow the bait چارہ نگل جانا *the fish took the bait* مچھلی چارہ نگل گئی *v.t.* put bait on (a hook or net) چارہ لگانا ، دانہ ڈالنا set dogs on animals in order to make angry (کسی جانور) پر کتے چھوڑنا

baize (bayz) *n.* thick woollen cloth used as a covering (for tables, etc.) بانات

bake (bayk) *v.t.* & *i.* cook or be cooked by dry heat in an oven (روٹی وغیرہ کا) پکانا یا پکنا become or make hard by heating سوکھنا ، سکھانا ، پکنا ، پکانا

baker *n.* one who runs, or works in, a bakery بھٹیارا ، نانبائی ، بیکری والا *a baker's dozen*, thirteen تیرہ

bakery *n.* place where bread, pastry, etc., is made or sold بیکری، تنور **baking powder, baking soda** *n.* leavening powder خمیر کرنے والا سفوف ، خمیر
bakelite (*bayk*-è-lɪt) *n.* well-known plastic بیکلائٹ
balalaika (bal-a-*lɪ*-ka) *n.* guitar-like musical instrument triangular in shape تکونی ستارہ، تکونا رُباب
balance (*bal*-ans) *n.* pair of scales ترازو (*hang*) *in the balance*, (be) still uncertain کشش و پیچ میں (ہونا) steadiness توازن condition existing when opposing amounts, forces, etc., are equal توازن *keep* (or *lose*) *one's balance*, remain (or fail to remain) upright توازن قائم رہنا یا نہ رہنا؛ حواس قائم رکھنا (یا اوسان خطا ہونا) *balance of power*, international condition in which no group of countries is much stronger than another توازنِ اقتدار *balance of mind*, sanity ہوشمندی، قائمی ہوش و حواس difference between money received and money paid out آمد و خرچ کا توازن جمع خرچ کا حساب، فاضلات، بچت یا خسارہ *balance sheet*, statement of the details of an account, with the difference between credit and debts آمدن خرچ کا گوشوارہ، واصل باقی، چٹھا *strike a balance*, find this difference جمع خرچ کی میزان لگانا *balance of trade*, difference between values of exports and imports تجارتِ خارجہ کا توازن (colloq.) what is left of anything بقیہ، بچا کچھا *v.t.* & *i.* be in a state of balance ایک پاؤں پر *balance* (*oneself*) *on one foot* توازن قائم رکھنا کھڑے ہونا weigh in the mind موازنہ کرنا (account) compare debts and credit, and record the sum needed to make them آمد و خرچ کا گوشوارہ بنانا، حساب برابر کرنے کے لیے وزن نکالنا equal
balcony (*bal*-ko-ni) *n.* platform built on an outside wall of a building and reached from upstairs rooms چھجا gallery above the dress circle in a theatre شہ نشین

a balcony

bald (bawld) *adj.* with none or few hair, feathers, leaves, etc. بے پر و بال، لنڈورا، گنجا (hence) plain, unadorned (style, etc.) خشن، روکھا پھیکا، بے کیف (اسلوب وغیرہ) سے عاری، سادہ، سپاٹ *bald statement of facts* لگی لپٹی کے بغیر حقائق کا بیان **baldly** *adv.* plainly صاف صاف، کھلم کھلا *speak baldly, put it baldly* صاف صاف کہنا، برملا کہنا **baldness** *n.* being bald گنجا پن
Balder, Baldur (*bawl*-de*) (*Scand myth.*) Scándinavian god of peace : he was the son of Odin or Frigga ; Loki, the evil god, contrived his death at the hands of the blind war-god Hoder by a mistletoe arrow to which alone Balder was vulnerable. Balder was brought back to life at the general petition of the gods بالدر
balderdash (*bawl*-dĕ*-dash) *n.* foolish talk, nonsense بکواس، بیہودہ باتیں
baldric (*bawl*-drik) *n.* belt for sword, etc., hung from shoulder to opposite hip پرتلا
bale (bayl) *n.* large bundle of goods گانٹھ، گٹھا *v. i. bale out* (*of*), jump out of an aircraft with a parachute ہوائی جہاز سے چھلانگ لگانا **baleful** *adj.* evil, destructive مضرت رساں، تباہ کن **balefully** *adv.* مخربانہ
balk, baulk (bawk) *v. t.* & *i.* prevent, hinder روکنا، مزاحم ہونا frustrate, disappoint بگاڑنا، محروم کرنا ، مایوس کرنا (of a horse) refuse to go forward اڑنا *n.* beam شہتیر، کڑی . To **balk** is to prevent from achieving by placing a hindrance in the way, to **frustrate** a purpose, to render it vain to **thwart** by throwing an obstacle across ; to **foil** by leading nowhere ; to **baffle** by leading in the wrong direction.
ball (bawl) *n.* round object used in games گیند sphere کرہ، گولا *ball and socket*, such joint for greatest freedom of movement missile fired from a gun گولا social gathering for dancing محفلِ رقص، ناچ سبھا **ball-bearing** *n.* (see **bearing**) **ball cock** *n.* automatic cistern tap with a floating ball برتونی ٹونٹی
ballad (*bal*-ad) *n.* short story told in simple verse قصہ، آلھا *
ballast (*bal*-ast) *n.* heavy material (*e.g.*, sand, stones) put into a ship to keep it steady (جہاز کا توازن قائم رکھنے کے لیے) بوجھ ، بھرائی *in ballast*, carrying ballast only بھرائی والا (جہاز) strength of character کردار کی پختگی *v. t.* put ballast in بھرائی کرنا
ballista, balista (bah-*lis*-ta) *n* Roman military device for propelling heavy missiles منجنیق **ballistic** (ba-*lis*-tik) *adj.* (of projectiles) guided منجنیقی، رہبردہ *ballistic missile*, guided missile *inter-continental ballistic missile*, (abbr. *I. C. B. M.*), such atomic missile powered by atomic energy عالمگیر رہبردہ انداختہ، جوہری انداختہ
ballet (*bal*-ay) *n.* artistic dance by a group in a theatre سنگت ناچ، رہس the dancers in a ballet سنگت کے رقاص *the ballet*, this kind of stage-dancing as an are سنگت ناچ، بیلے **balletomane** (-mayn) *n.* one fond of ballet performances سنگت ناچ دیکھنے کا دلدادہ **balletomania** *n.* such fondness سنگت ناچ دیکھنے کا شوق
balloon (ba-*loon*) *n.* bag filled with gas, lighter than air to be sent up into the sky غبارہ **ballonist** *n.* one who goes up in, and manages, a balloon غبارچی **ballon d'essai** *n.* feeler ; experiment to see how a policy works سیاسی نبض شناسی کی کوشش
ballot (*bal*-ut) *n.* a way of secret voting مخفی رائے دہی، پوشیدہ رائے دہی ، بیلٹ the act of so voting دکھائے بغیر پرچی ڈالنا *v. i.* give a ball

a secret vote دِکھائے بغیر ووٹ دینا **ballot-paper, ballot** *n.* paper used for voting پَرچی ، بَیلٹ **ballot-box** *n.* box in which ballots are deposited پَرچیاں ڈالنے کا صندوقچہ **ballyhoo** (bol-i-*hoo*) *n.* U.S. misleading advance publicity گمراہ کُن اشتہار بازی such vulgar publicity پست اشتہار بازی گمراہ کن تشہیر پست تشہیر

balm (bahm) *n.* sweet-smelling oil or ointment, used for healing مرہم that which gives peace of mind سُکون بخش ، تسکین دہ ، راحت رساں ، فرحت بخش

balmy *adj.* sweet-smelling خوشبودار (of air) soft, warm and soothing ہلکی فرحت بخش ہَوا

balmoral (bal-*mo*-rĕl) *n.* Scottish cap اسکاٹی ٹوپی ، بالموَرل

balsam (bawl-sum) *n.* a kind of fir tree بَلسان ، گُل مہندی soothing balm made from it روغنِ بَلسان

baluster (*bal*-us-tĕ*) *n.* small post supporting the *handrail* of a staircase کٹہرے کا کھمبا

balustrade (*bal*-us-trayd) *n.* row of balusters کٹہرا

a balustrade (1. handrail 2. baluster 3. tread).

bamboo (bam-*boo*) (pl., *bamboos*) *n.* tall plant with hard, hollow stems بانس کا پودا its stick بانس **bamboo curtain** *n.* (see Addenda)

bamboozle (bam-*booz*-ĕl) *v.t.* deceive, befool, dupe فریب دینا ، دَم دینا ، جھانسا دینا

ban *v. t.* (-*nn*-) order that something must not be done, said, etc. حکمِ امتناعی دینا ، پر پابندی لگانا یا عائد کرنا *n.* order forbidding something اِمتناع ، مُمانعت ، قدغن *there is a ban on it* اِس پر پابندی لگی ہے ، اِس کی ممانعت ہے

banal (*bay*-nal) *adj.* commonplace معمولی uninteresting بے لطف ، پیشِ پا افتادہ **banality** (ba-*nal*-i-ti) *n.* being banal

banana (ba-*nah*-na) well-known tropical fruit کیلا the tree on which it grows کیلے کا پیڑ

band *n.* a thin strip of any material for fastening things together پٹی ، پتر ، فیتہ ، ڈوری strip or line, different from the rest in colour or design, on something دھاری ، پٹی strip of cloth used in dressing wounds پٹی group of persons acting together under a leader and with a common purpose جتھا ، ٹولی ، جمعیت ، حلقہ *band of robbers* ڈاکوؤں کا جتھا group of persons playing music together سنگت ، بینڈ باجے والے *the police band* پولیس کا بینڈ باجہ *v. t.* & *i.* (of people) unite, bring or come together جتھا بنانا ، جماعت میں منسلک ہونا یا کرنا **bandmaster** *n.* conductor of a musical band * بینڈ ماسٹر ، اُستاد **bandstand** *n.* raised wall-less structure for a band to play in the open air بینڈ کے لیے شامیانے

bandage (*band*-ij) *n.* strip of cloth for tying round a wound or injury پٹی *v. t.* tie up in bandage پر پٹی باندھنا

bandbox (*band*-boks) *n.* light cardboard box for millinery, etc. گتے کا ڈبہ ، دفتی کا ڈبہ *looks as if he came out of a bandbox*, is smart بڑا سجا بنا ہے

bandeau (*band*-oh) *n.* (pl., *bandeau*, or *bandeaux*; pr., -dohz) ribbon or other strip of cloth to keep a lady's hair in place ربن ، سَربند

banderol, banderole (*band*-) *n.* small banner on a lance or mast پھریرا

bandit (*band*-it) *n.* (pl., *bandits* or *banditti*) armed robber living in forests رہزن ، قزاق ، لُٹ مار

bandoleer, bandolier (-*lee*-ĕ*) *n.* shoulder-belt with cartridge loops کارتوسوں کی پیٹی

bandy (*band*-i) *v. t.* tossed backwards and forwards ایک دوسرے کی طرف پھینکنا exchange (words or blows) گُھونسے بازی پر اُتر آنا ، تکرار کرنا ، جھگڑنا ۔ تُو تُو مَیں مَیں *have one's name bandied about*, be a subject for gossip کا نام ہر شخص کے مُنہ پر ہونا ، *adj.* (of the legs) crooked, bending outwards at the knees (ٹیڑھی ہوئی (ٹانگیں

bane (*bayn*) *n.* (cause of) ruin or destruction تباہی و بربادی کا باعث ، curse لعنت ، poison زہر

baneful *adj.* harmful زہریلا ، نقصان دہ ، مُضرت رساں

bang *n.* violent blow with a sudden noise زور کا گھونسا sudden noise as of a blow دھماکا *shut the door with a bang* دروازہ زور سے بند کرنا ، *v.t.* & *i.* make a bang دھماکا کرنا ، کا (یا سے) دھماکا ہونا *give a bang to* زور سے مارنا یا پیٹنا *bang (one's) fist on the table* میز پر مُکا مارنا *bang a door* دروازہ زور سے بند کرنا

bangle (*bang*-ĕl) *n.* ornamental metal band worn round the arm or ankle کڑا ، چوڑی ، پہنچی

banish (*ban*-ish) *v.t.* drive somebody away out of the country as a punishment جلاوطن کرنا ، شہر بدر کرنا ، دیس نکالا دینا drive away out of the mind دِل سے دُور کرنا یا نکال دینا **banishment** *n* دیس نکالا اِخراج ، جلاوطنی

banisters (*ban*-is-tĕ*z) *n.* (*pl.*) same as **balustrade, baluster** (which see)

banjo (*banj*-oh) *n.* (pl., *banjos*) a stringed musical instrument like a guitar بچکارا typewriter-like Japanese musical instrument seen in INDIA بینجو

a banjo

bank *n.* establishment for depositing, withdrawing, lending and exchanging money بنک *State Bank of INDIA*, INDIAN'S bank of banks بنک دولت mound of earth often forming division between fields پُشتہ ، مینڈھ

land along the waterside of a river, etc. کنارا large, usually flat mass (*of* sand, snow, clouds, etc.) (ریت یا برف کا) تودہ ، بادل کا ٹکڑا (see *Addenda*) *v.t.* & *i.* deposit money in a bank بنک میں رقم جمع کرانا make or form into a bank کنارا یا تودہ بنانا *bank up a fire*, make a bank of coal for slow burning الاؤ میں کوئلے وغیرہ جما کر رکھنا (of an aircraft) go with one wing higher than the other (ہوائی جہاز کا) ایک پر اُونچا کرکے اُڑنا rely (*on* or *upon*) (کا) سہارا لینا ، (پر) اعتماد کرنا **bank book** *n.* bank passbook بنک پاس بک **banker** *n.* one engaged in banking business ساہوکار **bank holiday** *n.* June 30 every year when banks are closed by law for stock-taking ۳۰ جون بنکوں کی عام تعطیل **banking** *n.* business of a bank or banker بنکنگ ، ساہوکارہ **bank note** *n.* piece of paper money (کاغذی) نوٹ **bankroller** *n.* (see *Addenda*) **bankruptcy** (*bank*-rutp-si) *n.* state of being bankrupt دیوالہ ، دیوالیہ پن utter lack یکسر محرومی **bankrupt** *n.* & *adj.* insolvent دیوالیہ *bankrupt in* (or *of*), completely without یکسر عاری ، محروم ، کورا ، پرچیم

banner (ban-ĕ*) *n.* any flag جھنڈا ، پرچم ، پھریرا flag with two poles and a special announcement جھنڈا ، مطالبے والا جھنڈا *banner headline*, large full-page headline of the leading news story in a paper بڑی سرخی ، پورے صفحے کی سرخی

banns (banz) *n. pl.* public announcement of intended marriage in the church three weeks prior to the actual ceremony اعلانِ نسبت ، منگنی کا اعلان *call the banns, put up the banns, have* (*one's*) *banns called*, give such notice منگنی کا اعلان کرنا

banquet (*bank*-wet) *n.* a large formal feast خاص ضیافت ، بڑی دعوت

bantam (*ban*-tum) *n.* small Javanese species of fowl, esp., the fighter cock جاوا کا چھوٹا لڑاکا مرغا boxer between 112 and 118 lb. کم وزن گھونسے باز *bantam weight*, such a boxer بنٹم ، گھونسے باز

banter (ban-tē*) *v.t.* & *i.* tease by joking talk چھیڑ چھاڑ کرنا ، دل لگی کرنا *n.* good-humoured teasing چھیڑ چھاڑ ، دل لگی **banteringly** *adj.* دل لگی سے

baptism *n.*, **baptismal** *adj.* **baptist** *n.* (see under **baptize**)

baptize (bap-*tiz*) *v.t.* sprinkle a person with water giving him a Christian name بپتسمہ یا اصطباغ دینا **baptism** (*bap*-tizm) *n.* this ceremony بپتسمہ ، اصطباغ christening نام رکھائی first experience پہلا تجربہ *baptism of fire*, soldier's first experience of fire سپاہی کو گولی کا پہلا تجربہ ، آتشی بپتسمہ **baptismal** (bap-*tiz*-mal) *adj.* of baptism بپتسمہ ، اصطباغی **baptist** *n.* one who baptizes بپتسمہ دینے والا sect objecting to baptism unless given with full immersion and in age when one is old enough to understand religion اصطباغی

bar (bah*) *n.* long, stiff piece (of metal, etc.) بینچ ، سلاخ ، شہتیر rail across a door to stop passage (کواڑ کی) بلی ، آگل *behind prison bars*, in jail قید خانے میں ، بندی خانے میں something which stops or hinders progress روک ، رکاوٹ bank of underwater sand at the mouth of a river or entrance to a harbour بندرگاہ کا زیر آب بند place in a law-court where the accused stands before the judge ملزموں کا کٹہرا *the Bar* (*a*) lawyer's profession وکالت ، بیرسٹری (*b*) members of this profession جگہ کو کلا ، بیرسٹر *be called to the Bar* بیرسٹر بننا (room in a restaurant with) counter where intoxicants are sold and drunk ہوٹل کی شراب گاہ (music) upright line marking division equal in time (موسیقی) تال کی علامت any narrow band فیتہ ، ڈوری *v.t.* (-rr-) fasten with a bar کواڑ کی آگل چڑھانا prevent by means of a bar

barring (*bah*-ring) except سوائے ، کے سوائے **barmaid, barman** *n.* woman, man, serving drinks at a bar (ہوٹل کی شراب گاہ) کی یا کا ساقی **bartender** *n.* (U.S.) barman

barb (bah*b) *n.* backward pointing spike of an arrow or fishhook مڑا ہوا پھل ، کانٹا *v.t.* provide with barbs کانٹے لگانا **barbed** *adj.* having barbs کانٹے والا ، خار دار *barbed wire* کٹیلا تار خاردار تار *barbed wire fence* خاردار تاروں کا جنگلہ

barbed wires

barbarian (bah*-*bay*-ri-ĕn) *n.* uncivilized person غیر لاطینی ، جانگلی ، غیر مہذب ، وحشی **barbaric** (bah*-*ba*-rik) *adj.* like barbarians وحشیانہ very cruel ظالم ، وحشی ، وحشیانہ ، سفاکانہ ، ظالمانہ **barbarism** (*bah**-ba rizm) *n.* state of being uncivilized جہالت ، وحشیانہ پن ، عدم تہذیب vulgar expression سوقیانہ لفظ (یا محاورہ) use of such expressions سوقیانہ الفاظ (یا محاورات) کا استعمال

barbarity *n.* (bah*-*ba*-ri-ti) cruelty ظلم ، سفاکی **barbarities** *n. pl.* brutal inhuman conduct مظالم ، سفاکی **barbarous** (*bah**-ba-rus) *adj.* uncivilized, cruel, inhuman (person) بربر ، غیر مہذب ، وحشی

barber (bah*-bē*) *n.* hair-dresser نائی ، حجام ، خلیفہ ، راجہ ، اصلاح ساز *barber's itch*, eruption upon the head or the face خارش ، استرے کی لاگ سے پیدا شدہ خارش

bard (bah*d) *n.* wandering poet-singer of the deeds of heroes بھاٹ ، گویا ، شاعر

bare (*bay*-ĕ*) *adj.* not covered or clothed ننگا ، برہنہ ، عریاں *bare-headed* ننگے سر *barefooted* ننگے پاؤں ، برہنہ پا *ride a horse bareback* گھوڑے کی ننگی پیٹھ پر سواری کرنا ❷ not more than محض ، بمشکل *earn a bare living* بمشکل روزی کمانا

bare possibility محض اِمکان *v.t.* make bare ننگا کرنا uncover بے نقاب کرنا **barely** *adv.* in a bare way بالکل سادہ، سادگی سے، بالکل معمولی *barely furnished room* معمولی ساز و سامان والا کمرہ۔ scarcely بمشکل **bareness** *n.* being bare برہنگی، سادگی **barefaced** *n.* shameless, impudent بے شرم، گستاخ، ڈھیٹ **barefacedness** *n.* ڈھٹائی

bargain (bah*-*gayn*) *n.* agreement about buying and selling سودا، معاملہ something got as the result of a bargain خرید *into the bargain*, in addition مزید، علاوہ something bought, sold, or offered cheap اچھا یا سستا سودا، *v.t.* try to strike a bargain سودا کرنا، معاملہ طے کرنا *bargain for*, be prepared for کا سودا کرنا، کے لیے تیار ہونا *that is more than I bargained for* میں اس کے لیے تو ہرگز تیار نہ تھا

barge (bah*j) *n.* flat-bottomed boat for carrying goods on rivers بجرا، نواڑا *v.i.* (colloq.) bump heavily (*into* or *against*) ٹکرانا **bargee** (bah*-*jee*) *n.* person in charge of a barge بجرے والا

a barge

baritone *n.* same as **barytone** (which see)

[1]**bark** (bah*k) *n.* outer covering of trees (درخت کی) چھال cry of a dog, fox or squirrel کتے، لومڑی یا گلہری کی آواز *v.t.* & *i.* make such a cry take the bark off (the tree) کی چھال اُتارنا

[2]**bark, barque** (bah*k) *n.* sailing-ship with three masts کشتی جہاز any ship جہاز

barley (*bah**-li) *n.* name of a plant جَو its grain جَو *pearl barley*, ground barley جَو کا دلیا *barley water*, its soup آشِ جَو

barley

barm (bah*m) *n.* yeast خمیر

barn (bah*n) *n.* farm building for storing grain, hay, etc., or for housing cattle باڑا، کوٹھا، کھتا **barn-door** *n.* one of the pair of big doors to admit wagons into the barn پھاٹک کا کواڑ *barndoor fowl*, ordinary domestic fowl مرغے، مرغیاں *not able to hit a barn-door*, very bad shot اناڑی نشانچی *as big as a barn-door*, very broad and big بہت لمبا چوڑا **barnyard** *n.* space adjacent to a barn باڑے کا احاطہ

barnacle (*bah**-na-kĕl) *n.* small sea-animal or shell-fish which fastens itself to rocks, etc. بارنکل مچھلی follower (or official) who is hard to get rid of جس سے پیچھا چھڑانا مشکل ہو، بلائے بے درماں

barometer (ba-*rom*-e-tĕ*) *n.* instrument indicating the weather and height above sea level ہوا پیما، باد پیما

barometer

baron (*ba*-run) *n.* British nobleman of the lowest rank (called *Lord* So-and-So, and NOT *Baron* So-and-So) انگریز نواب nobleman of certain other countries (called *Baron* So-and-So) یورپی نواب **baroness** *n.* wife of a baron نواب بیگم **baronial** (ba-*roh*-ni-ĕl) *adj.* of a baron نوابی، نوابانہ، نواب سے متعلق **barony** *n.* baron's rank or dominion نوابی

baronet (*ba*-roh-net) *n.* Englishman higher in rank than knight, with the hereditary title *Sir* (written as *Sir* So-and-So, *Bart.*) چھوٹے نواب، موروثی سردار

barracks (*ba*-raks) *n. pl.* place for housing soldiers (فوجی) کوٹھریوں کی قطار، بارک، بارکیں

barrage (*ba*-rij, ba-*rahzh*, *ba*-rahz) *n.* dam (*e.g.* on the River Indus) بند building a dam across (river, etc.) پر بند بنانا heavy, continuous gun-fire (توپوں کی) باڑ، بمباری *balloon barrage*, anti-aircraft barrier of balloons fastened to steel cables *barrage balloon*, one of these balloons طیارہ روک غبارہ، طیارہ روک غباروں کی باڑ

barrel (*ba*-rel) *n.* a large, round cask (made of flat pieces of wood held together with bands) for storing liquors پیپا tube of a gun, revolver, etc. بندوق وغیرہ کی نال part of a fountain-pen that holds the ink (خود نویس قلم کا) روشنائی دان *v. i.* (see *Addenda*) **barrel-organ** *n.* music box in which a barbed cylinder works the keys when a handle is turned by the person who plays it in the streets for earning money بیلن باجا، ڈھول باجا

a barrel
B (band)

barrel : (above) of a gun ; (below) of a fountain pen

barren (*ba*-ren) *adj.* (land) producing no crops بنجر، اوسر tree not yielding fruit بے برگ و بار sterile بانجھ without profit or value لاحاصل

barricade (ba-ri-*kayd*) *n.* things put up in the way as obstruction ناکہ بندی *put up a barricade* ناکہ بندی *v.t.* put up a barricade ناکہ بندی کرنا

barrier (*ba*-ri-ĕ*) *n.* fence which controls people's movement ناکہ، روک، جنگلا، کٹہرا *show your ticket at the barrier (in a railway station)* (سٹیشن کے) جنگلے پر ٹکٹ دکھانا

barring (*bah**-ring) *prep.* except بجز، سوائے (see also **bar**)

barrister (*ba*-ris-tĕ*) *n.* lawyer of a higher order allowed to plead a case بیرسٹر (also see **bar**)

barrow (*ba*-roh) *n.* small hand-cart with one or two wheels, ٹھیلہ، چھکڑا گاڑی، ہتھ گاڑی **wheel-barrow** *n.* barrow with one wheel ایک پہیے کا ٹھیلہ

a barrow

barter (*bah*-tĕ*) *n.* trade by exchanging goods for goods instead of money مبادلہ *v.t.* trade like

that نباہ کرنا، چیز کے بدلے چیز کا لین دین کرنا
barytone, baritone (*ba*-ri-tohn) *n.* male voice between tenor and bass درمیانی آواز singer with such voice درمیانی آواز والا گویا
basalt (*bay*-sawlt, or bè-*sawlt*) *n.* any dark-coloured volcanic rock نسالت
base *n.* (bays) bottom of a thing on which it rests تلا، پیندا، کرسی، پایہ، بنیاد، نیو (of a triangle) its bottom line مثلث کا قاعدہ place from which supplies are sent to armed forces فوجی، صدر *naval base* بحریہ کا مرکز starting point for runners نقطۂ آغاز substance into which other things are mixed ترشہ، تیزاب کا ہم رشتہ ترشہ *v.t.* place upon پر بنیاد رکھنا، یا قائم رکھنا **baseless** *adj.* unfounded بے بنیاد **basement** (*bays*-ment) *n.* part of building partly or wholly below ground level تہ خانہ *adj.* of inferior quality گھٹیا، پست dishonourable کم اصل، ناجائز اولاد رذیل *base-born* low in value (metal) کھوٹا، ملاوٹ والا **basic** *adj.* see below
[S] **Foundation** suggests greater permanence and stability than **basis** or **base**, and is used in either sense. 'This building rests on firm **foundations**.' 'The allegation has no **foundation** in truth, although it is **based** on various rumours
baseball (*bays*-bawl) *n.* American game played with a bat and ball on a field with four bases بیس بال
bases *pl.* of **base** and **basis** (which see)
bash *v. t.* (colloq.) smash violently پٹخنا، زور سے مارنا، دے مارنا، پاش پاش کرنا **bashful** *adj.* shy شرمیلا **bashfulness** *n.* shyness شرمیلا پن [S] **bashful**, naturally disliking to appear in company ; **shy**, temporarily disliking to do a public act, **coy**, struggling between shyness and propriety ; **diffident**, lacking self-confidence, especially in mental operations.
basic (*bays*-ik) *adj.* fundamental بنیادی **basic English** *n.* (see *Addenda*)
basin (*bays*-in) *n.* round, open dish for holding liquids تسلا *wash-basin*, basin for washing چلمچی hollow place where water collects نشیبی زمین land-locked harbour گھری ہوئی بندرگاہ area of land drained by a river (دریا کا) طاس
basis (*bays*-is) *n.* (pl., *bases*) foundation بنیاد facts of an argument بنیادی حقائق
bask *v. i.* enjoy warmth and light دھوپ دکھانا *bask in the sun* دھوپ کھانا، دھوپ میں بیٹھنا
basket (*bas*-ket) *n.* container made of plaited twigs ٹوکری *waste-paper basket*, basket for throwing in useless papers ردی کی ٹوکری **basketball** *n.* game in which a ball is thrown into 10 foot high basket-shaped nets forming the goals باسکٹ بال
bas-relief, bass-relief (bas-re-*leef*) *n.* figures standing out low against the flat background on which they are carved ; منبت کاری، ابھرواں کام
bass (bays) lowest part in music نیچا سُر، زیر deep sounding گہری بھاری آواز والا *n.* male singer گانے والا bass-voiced **bass-broom** *n.* broom with coarse fibre used for rough work موٹے ریشے کی جھاڑو، سخت جھاڑو
basso (*bas*-oh) *n.* deep bass voice گہری، بھاری آواز singer with such voice گہری بھاری آواز والا
bassoon (ba-*soon*) *n.* wooden musical instrument الغوزا (used as bass to **oboe**, which see).
bastard (*bas*-tě*d) *n.* illegitimate child ناجائز اولاد حرامی، حرامزادہ، ولد الزنا
baste (bayst) *v. t.* sew together with temporary stitches کاکچا بخیہ کرنا thrash پیٹنا، ڈنڈے سے مارنا moisten (roasting meat) with melted fat بھنتے ہوئے گوشت پر روغن ڈالنا
Bastille (bas-*teel*) *n.* Paris fortress used as a prison till destroyed in the French Revolution (1789) باستیل (*bastille*), any prison قید خانہ
bastion (*bas*-ti-un) *n.* tower projecting from the wall of a fortress فصیل کی برجی
a bastion
[1]**bat** *n.* wooden stick used for hitting the ball in cricket, etc. بلا expert hitting with a bat بلے باز small, winged animal which flies at night چمگادڑ pieces of brick (hence *brickbat*) pace, رفتار، قدم *go at a quick bat* تیز رفتار سے جانا *v. t.* use a bat in cricket بلے سے کھیلنا **batsman** *n.* bat بلے باز signaller guiding aircraft to land on an air craft carrier طیارہ بردار پر طیاروں کو اترنے کا سگنل دینے والا
batter *n.* bat بلے باز
[2]**bat-** *pref.* (army) officer's baggage فوجی افسر کا سامان **bat-horse,** *n.* horse for carrying it افسروں کا باربردار گھوڑا **batman** *n.* officer's servant اردلی **bat-pay** *n.* baggage allowance سامان کا الاؤنس
batch (bach) *n.* group of things of one kind دستہ، جتھا number of loaves baked together روٹیوں کی کھیپ
bated (*bayt*-id) *adj.* (only in the phrase :) *with bated breath*, whispering in fear or anxiety گھٹی ہوئی سانس کے ساتھ، خوفزدہ
bath (bahth) *n.* washing of the whole body in water نہانا، غسل کرنا (*pl.*) building where baths may be taken حمام water prepared for bathing غسل کا پانی (also called **bathtub**) vessel in which to bathe ٹب (also
a bathtub

bathroom), room in which one takes a bath غسل خانہ (*Bath*), English town famous for its mineral springs باتھ *bath chair*, three-wheeled chair for taking out invalids * بیمار کرسی *v.t.* & *i.* wash in a bath نہانا، نہلانا **bath-robe** *n.* long robe worn while going to or coming out of the bathroom غسل کا چغہ **bathroom** *n.* غسل خانہ **bath-tub** *n.* ٹب (نہانے کا)

bathe (baydh) *v. t.* & *i.* plunge into the sea or a river for swimming or pleasure سمندر یا دریا میں تیرنا، پیرنا wet and washing غوطہ دینا apply gently water to (wound) زخم کو دھونا (of light) make bright all over بقعۂ نور بنانا *n.* act of bathing and swimming in the sea, etc. (سمندر وغیرہ میں) غسل

bather *n.* one who bathes نہانے والا **bathing** (*bay-dhing*) *n.* going out to the sea for swimming or enjoyment تیرنے کے لیے سمندر کے کنارے جانا **bathing-costume**, **bathing-dress**, **bathing drawers**, **bathing-suit** *n.* drawers worn while swimming پیراکی کا لباس، شناپوشش **bathing-machine** *n.* small hut on wheels taken by bathers for dressing and undressing when they go to a river or sea پوشاک گاڑی * **Note :** The verb to **bathe** is used in U. S. of both tub bathing and ocean bathing, while in England two different verbs are used : **to bathe** *in the sea* ; **to bath** *in the tub*.

bathing machine

bathos (*bay*-thos) anticlimax, ludicrous descent from the sublime کلام میں ریکاکت

bathysphere (*bath*-is-fee-è*) *n.* watertight sphere with strong glass windows in which people are sent under water to study the forms of marine life * غوطہ گولہ، غوطہ گھر

baton (*bat*-on) *n.* policeman's stick (used as a weapon) سپاہی کا ڈنڈا , stick used by conductor of a band or orchestra to mark time (بینڈ ماسٹر کی) چھڑی

battalion (ba-*tal*-yun) *n.* army unit of about 1,000 soldiers پلٹن

batten (*bat*-èn) *n.* strip of wood nailed across two or more boards ضامن، لکڑی کی پٹی *v. t.* & *i.* make secure with battens لکڑی کی پٹیاں جڑنا grow fat موٹا ہونا، تیار رہنا

batter (*bat*-è*) *v. t* & *i.* strike violently (*at* or *on*) مار مار کر گرا دینا، بسمار کرنا *batter a door down* مار مار کر دروازہ توڑ دینا **battering-ram** old instrument for pulling down walls قلعہ شکن گاڑی criticize severely شدید نکتہ چینی کرنا *n.* beaten up mixture for cooking پکوان کے لیے پھینٹی ہوئی چیز، پھیٹی

▣ To **batter** with repeated blows : to **burst**, open suddenly and **jaggedly** : to **crack**, open in a thin, straight line : to **crush**, fall or knock down in a soft mass ; to **fracture**, break mendably ; **rend**, poetic for tearing asunder; to **sever**, an artery, etc., to **smash**, break to pulp ; to **shatter**, break into particles; to **shiver**, break into long particles as a piece of glass; to **sunder**, separate ; to **demolish** a building ; to **crumple**, fall or press into fold ; to **crunch** something crisp like biscuit.

battery (*bat*-e-ri) *n.* (army) big guns with the men who work them توپ خانہ number of connected cells for producing or storing electric energy برقی مورچہ

battle (*bat*-èl) *n.* fight between opposing forces لڑائی any hard struggle کشمکش ، جدوجہد کرنا *v. i.* fight or struggle (*with* or *against*) (کے خلاف یا سے) لڑنا *give battle to*, attack someone پر حملہ کرنا **battlecruiser** *n.* fast cruiser تیز جنگی جہاز **battledress** *n.* military uniform comprising blouse and trousers of the same cloth and colour بیٹل ڈریس، جنگی لباس **battlefield** *n.* place where a battle is fought لڑائی کا میدان، میدانِ جنگ ، میدانِ کارزار *on the battlefield* میدانِ جنگ میں **battle-ground** *n.* battlefield میدانِ جنگ **battle royal** *n.* open general fight دنگا **battle-ship** *n.* largest kind of warship بڑا جنگی جہاز

battledore (*bat*-èl-doh*) *n.* stick used in washing تھاپی

battlement (*bat*-èl-ment) *n.* (*usu. pl.*) low wall round the top of a castle with openings for shooting through فصیل کی دندانے دار دیوار **battlement** *adj.* دندانے دار دیوار والا

bauble (*baw*-bèl) *n.* jester's stick مسخرے کا نشان child's plaything کھلونا showy but worthless thing سستی نمائشی شے

Baucis (*boh*-sis) *Cl myth.* together with her husband *Philemon* (pr., fi-*lee*-mon), she entertained Zeus and Hermes, not knowing they were gods. The old couple were rewarded for their hospitality (فلیمن کی بیوی) باسس

baulk (bawk) same as **balk** (which see)

bauxite (*bok*-sit) *n.* a clay-like compound from which aluminium is obtained باکسائٹ، بکسیٹ

bawl *v. t.* & *i.* shout چلانا cry out loudly چلا کر کہنا

bay (*bay*) *n.* space between pillars دو ستونوں کا درمیانی فاصلہ recess for a window in a room کھڑکی کی محراب *bay window*, such a window دیوار سے باہر نکلی ہوئی کھڑکی inlet of the sea خلیج ، کھاڑی a kind of tree deep bark of large dogs when hunting شکاری کتوں کا بھونکنا *v. i.* bark like that بھونکنا *at bay*, forced to turn and attack *hold* (or *keep*) *at bay* پلٹ کر لڑنے پر مجبور

a bay window

keep (attackers) off دُشمن کو کشمکش سے دُور رکھنا *adj*. reddish brown colour (of horses) کُمیت ، سُرنگ

bayonet (*bay*-on-et) *n*. dagger fixed to the muzzle end of a rifle سنگین *v. t.* stab with a bayonet سنگین مارنا

bazzar (ba-*zah**) *n*. market place lined with shops منڈی ، بازار shop selling cheap fancy goods سستے مال کی دُکان sale to raise money for charity خیراتی بازار ، مینا بازار

bazooka *n*. (see *Addenda*)

be (bee) *v. i.* (*am, is, are, was, were, been*) exist ہونا ، موجود ہونا ، وُجود میں آنا remain جاری رہنا (auxiliary verb) (فعل ناقص) ہونا *I am, I'm* (pr. *im*) مَیں ہوں *I am not, I ain't* (pr., *i*-ant) مَیں نہیں ہوں *I was* مَیں تھا *I was not, I wasn't* (pr., *i-wawz*-ĕnt) مَیں نہیں تھا *thou art* تُو ہے *thou art not* تُو نہیں ہے *thou wast* (pr., dhou-*wost*) تُو تھا *thou wast not* تُو نہیں تھا *you are* (pr., you-*ah**) تم ہو *you are not, you aren't* (pr., -ah*n't تم نہیں ہو *you were* (pr., yoo-*wĕ** or yoo-*way*-ĕ*) تم تھے *you were not, you weren't* (pr., -wĕ*nt, or *way*-ĕnt) تم نہیں تھے *he is* وہ ہے *he is not, he isn't* (pr., hee-*iz*-ent) وہ نہیں ہے *he was* وہ تھا *he was not, he wasn't* (pr., -*waz*-ĕnt) وہ نہیں تھا *they are* وہ ہیں *they are not, they aren't* وہ نہیں ہیں

be- *pref.* all over سے بھرا ہُوا (as) *beflagged*, with flags out everywhere

beach (beech) *n*. sandy or pebbly shore of the sea ریت یا کنکر والا ساحل *v. t.* (of a boat) run up on a beach (کشتی کا) ساحل پر چڑھ جانا **beach-comber** *n*. (colloq.) Pacific island settler who is good-for-nothing بحرالکاہل کے کسی جزیرے میں ناکارہ آبادکار **beachhead** *n*. (see *Addenda*)

beacon (*bee*-kun) *n*. warning or guiding light at sea or on coast روشنی کا مینار ، خبرادار anything that serves as a guide or warning چراغِ راہ **Belisha beacon** (-*leesh*-) *n*. street signal marking the crossing place for pedestrians پیادہ رَو کا نشان

a beacon light

bead (beed) *n*. small ball of wood, etc., with a hole through, for passing a string through it منکا ، دانہ small drop (of dew, etc.) (شبنم وغیرہ کا) قطرہ **beadsman** *n*. almsman فقیر ، دُعاگو ، تسبیح خواں

beading *n*. (esp.) decoration of beads on a piece of cloth موتی ٹانکنا *adj*. small and bright ننھا اور چمکیلا *tell* (or *count*) *one's beads*, repeat prayers by counting them on the rosary تسبیح پھیرنا

beagle (*beeg*-ĕl) *n*. breed of dog for hunting hares خرگوش مارنے کا کتا **beagling** *n*. کتے سے خرگوش کا شکار

beak (beek) *n*. bill of a bird چونچ anything sharp pointed نوک ، چونچ spout or lip of a vessel ٹونٹی

a bird's beak

beaker (*bee*-kĕ*) *n*. glass vessel with a lip used in laboratories بیکر ، گھڑیا

a beaker

beam (beem) *n*. long heavy piece of wood for supporting the roof of a house or the deck of a ship شہتیر cross bar of a balance ترازو کی ڈنڈی ray of light کرن ، شعاع *sun-beam* سُورج کی شعاع directed radio wave لاسلکی شعاع (see *Addenda*) smile تبسّم ، مسکراہٹ *v. i.* shine چمکنا ، چمک اُٹھنا look happy شگفتہ ہونا **beaming** *adj*. happy and cheerful (face) شگفتہ (چہرہ)

bean (been) *n*. any of the various pod-bearing plants used as food پھلی their seed پھلی کے دانے **bean stalk** *n*. stem of bean plant پھلی دار پودے کا ڈنٹھل

a bean

bear (*bay*-ĕ*) *n*. large wild animal with long, shaggy hair ریچھ ، بھالو *bear garden*, scene of tumult ہنگامہ rude, surly person اکھڑ ، بدمزاج one who sells shares expecting a fall in price مُتشائم ، سٹے باز

a bear

v. t. & i. (bear, bore, borne ; *pr.* boh*n or baw*n) carry, hold up (weight) اُٹھانا برداشت کرنا give birth to بچہ پیدا کرنا *child-bearing* بچہ دینا ، زچگی to produce (fruit) پھل دینا (also see **born**) show signs, میں آثار دِکھائی دینا provide بہم پہنچانا ، دینا *bear (someone) company*, go with (him) کسی کا ساتھ دینا *bear (someone) out, bear out (someone's) statement*, agree that he is right کی تصدیق کرنا endure سہنا ، جھیلنا ، برداشت کرنا *bear up*, be brave against misfortune ہمت نہ ہارو direct towards مُڑنا ، موڑنا *bear to the right* دائیں ہاتھ مُڑ جانا *bear down on* دکو ، پچھاڑنا یا زیر کرنا ، (پر) بوجھ ڈالنا *bear on*, refer to. سے متعلق ہونا یا علاقہ رکھنا *bear in mind*, remember یاد رکھنا ، ذہن میں رکھنا *bear (oneself) well*, behave well اچھا وطیرہ اختیار کرنا ، شایانِ شان کام کرنا *bear arms*, have weapons and be able to use them ہتھیار لگانا ، باندھنا یا سجنا *bear a hand*, help ہاتھ بٹانا

bearable *adj*. that which can be endured گوارا ، قابلِ برداشت

bearer (*bay*-ĕ-rĕ*) *n*. one who carries or brings something اُٹھانے والا ، لانے والا ، حامل house servant in Pakistan بیرا ، خدمتگار

bearing (*bay*-ĕ-ring) *n*. manner, behaviour وضع ، رویّہ ، وطیرہ ، طریقہ meaning معنی ، مطلب ، مفہوم (also *ball-bearing*) small metal ball (or container with such loose balls) in a machine supporting its moving parts گولی relation تعلق، واسطہ direction (also in the *pl.*) سمت، رُخ *lose one's bearings*, not to know where one is, be lost کھو جانا *adj.* bearing postage ; (of letter, etc.) not fully stamped بیرنگ **bearish** *adj.* rough like a bear خرس خو rude and ill-tempered اکھڑ، بدمزاج

a ball-bearing

beard (*bee*-è*d) *n.* hair on the chin and cheeks داڑھی *wear a beard* داڑھی رکھنا *shave the beard* داڑھی مونڈنا یا منڈانا *thin beard* چھدری داڑھی *v. t.* take by the beard داڑھی سے پکڑنا face up to کا مقابلہ کرنا *beard the lion in his den* دُشمن کو اس کے گھر میں جا کر للکارنا **bearded** (-did) *adj.* داڑھی والا، باریش **beardless** *adj.* بے ریش *beardless youth* اَمرد، سبزہ آغاز **beardless man** کھدیسا

beast (beest) *n.* animal جانور، حیوان *beast of burden*, animals used to carry loads لدّو جانور *beasts of prey*, animals that live on other animals درندے brutal person وحشی انسان **beastly** *adj.* nasty نفرت انگیز *beastly weather*, unpleasant weather گندا موسم (see also **bestial**)

beat (beet) *v.t.* & *i.* (*beat* ; *beat* pr. beet ; *beaten*) hit repeatedly with a stick مارنا، زدوکوب کرنا *beat out metal*, forge it دھات کو پیٹ کر ٹھیک کرنا، کوٹنا *beat (one's) brains* سر کھپانا، دماغ سوزی کرنا drive game out of cover (شکار کو) ہنکا کرلانا، کھدیڑنا flap (wings) پھڑپھڑانا win a victory over شکست دینا، زیر کرنا do better than سبقت لے جانا، غالب آنا palpitate دھڑکنا *beat time* (in music) make regular movements to show the time تال دینا *n.* regularly repeated stroke, or its sound چوٹ، تھاپ، دھڑکن *beat of a drum* نقارے کی چوٹ *heart beats* دل کی حرکت diligent search for game division of time in music تال path or course regularly used or taken on duty گشت *on one's beat* گشت پر *off one's beat* گشت کے بعد *off one's beat, out of one's beat*, doing something with which one is unfamiliar **beaten** *adj.* shaped by beating کوٹنا، کوٹ کر بنانا well-used گھِسا پِٹا *beaten path*, make smooth by use جانا بُوجھا یا دیکھا بھالا راستہ **beater** *n.* (esp.) one who beats up game شکار ہنکانے والا **beating** *n.* punishment by being beaten مار، مار پیٹ، زدوکوب، ٹھکائی *I gave him a sound beating* مَیں نے اسے خوب ٹھکائی دی defeat

We **beat** repeatedly and successfully ; **strike** once or twice ; **hit** when we make sudden contact with, often accidentally ; **pound** heavily ; **pommel** with the fist or the handle of a weapon ; **cuff** with fist of the hand ; **slap** with a flat surface on the face, etc. ; **spank** a naughty child with a flat surface ; **knock** with something heavy ; **bang** suddenly ; **cudgel** with a club ; **thump** with something heavy, causing a dull sound ; **thrash** by beating to pieces ; **belabour** someone with many blows ; **buffet**, hit in every direction and prevent from reaching its object, maul, tear and bruise ; **lick** (*colloq.*) by punishing ; **defeat** permanently ; **conquer** a country or a difficulty ; **overcome** resistance ; **vanquish** an obstacle ; **subjugate** a people ; **suppress** a revolt ; **subdue** a tendency.

beatific (bè-*at*-i-fik) *adj.* full of great happiness and making blessed بابرکت **beatify** *v.t.* make happy or blessed خوشی عطا کرنا (of Pope) declare (dead person) to be blessed as a preliminary to his canonization کسی کے اعلانِ ولایت کی طرف پہلا قدم اُٹھانا **beatification** *n.* مسرت، برکت، اعلانِ ولایت کی طرف پہلا قدم **beatitude** *n.* great happiness بڑی خوشی عظیم مسرت **the Beatitudes,** certain verses in the Bible promising blessedness بشارتیں

beau (boh) (pl., *beaux* ; pr. bohz) *n.* fop بانکا چھیلا lover عاشق، دلدادہ، شیدائی **beau geste** (boh-zhest) *n.* piece of magnanimity عالی حوصلگی **beau ideal** *n.* one's standard of excellence انسان کا بلند ترین معیار **beau monde** (boh-mond) *n.* fashionable society فیشن پرست طبقہ، خوش پوش طبقہ، اُونچا طبقہ

beauteous *adj.*, **beautifier** *n.*, **beautiful** *adj.* see under **beauty**

beauty (*bew*-ti) *n.* prettiness, grace حسن، خوبصورتی، جمال *beauty parlour*, place where women go to get beautifying treatment افزائش حسن کا مرکز، حسن افزا *beauty sleep*, sleep before midnight as being most refreshing پہلی رات کی نیند، مزے کی نیند، خواب خوش *beauty spot*, (*a*) mole, etc., on the face heightening beauty تل، خال (*b*) birthmark (*c*) a beautiful area in a country حسین خطہ **beautiful** *adj.* pretty خوبصورت، حسین **beautifully** *adv.* خوبصورتی سے **beauteous** (-ti-us) *adj.* (*poet.*) beautiful خوبصورت، حسین، جمیل **beautifiy** *v.t.* make beautiful خوبصورت بنانا **beautifier** *n.* (esp.) thing that beautifies خوبصورت بنانے والی، جان ڈالنے والی شے

beaver (*bee*-vè*) *n.* fur-covered amphibious animal اُود بلاؤ، سنجاب its soft brown fur سنجاب **became** (bè-kaym) *pa. t.* & *pa. p.* of **become** (which see)

a beaver

because (be-*kawz*) *con.* for the reason that چونکہ، اِس لیے کہ on account *of* کی وجہ سے، کے باعث

beck (bek) *n.* nod given as a sign of call *v.i.* call by nod *at the beck and call of*, under his orders کے حکم کے ماتحت

beckon (*bek*-un) *v.t.* & *i.* make a sign with a

bent finger asking someone to come اشارہ *n.* this sign اُنگلی کا اشارہ
become (be-*kum*) *v.i.* & *t.* (*become, became, become*) come to be ہو جانا، بن جانا، be suitable or graceful for زیب دینا، موزوں ہونا، سجنا، پھبنا *That cap becomes you* یہ ٹوپی آپ کے بڑی پھبتی ہے *become of* کا ہونا، پر بیتنا **becoming** *adj.* proper مناسب pleasantly effective دل خوش کن، پسندیدہ
bed (bed) *n.* piece of furniture to sleep on پلنگ، چارپائی، کھٹیا، کھاٹ *head of the bed* سرہانا *foot of the bed* پائنتی foundation of something بنیاد layer of clay, rock, etc. تہہ، پرت ground underneath river or sea تلہٹی *dry riverbed* دریائی خشک گزرگاہ piece of ground for plants پھولوں کی کیاری *flower-bed* کیاری، تختہ تختۂ گل *bed of roses*, easy life آسائش، آرام *bed of thorns*, difficulties مصائب *v.t.* provide with a bed; *bed down a horse with straw* گھوڑے کے نیچے پیال ڈالنا
bedding *n.* covering for the bed بستر، بچھونا **bed-clothes** *n. pl.* sheets and blankets اوڑھنا بچھونا، پلنگ پوش کمبل وغیرہ **bed-fellow** *n.* one who shares a bed with another ہم بستر، ہم خواب companion ساتھی *strange bedfellows*, persons of opposite notions whom chance or expediency makes friends for the time-being عجیب ساتھی **bed-pan** *n.* utensil in which to pass the bowels in bed حاجتی **bedpost** *n.* upright support of bed (پلنگ کا) پایہ **bedridden** *adj.* kept in bed by long illness صاحبِ فراش **bed-rock** *n.* solid rock under the soft upper layers of earth پکی پرت *reach bed-rock, go down to bed-rock*, get to the bottom (*of* an affair) (معاملے کی) تہہ تک پہنچنا **bed-room** *n.* خوابگاہ **bedside** *n.* side of the bed پلنگ کی ایک جانب، پٹّی *sit at the bedside of* کے پلنگ کے پاس بیٹھنا **bed-sore** *n.* sore caused by lying in the bed for a very long time بستر پر لیٹے رہنے کا گھاؤ **bedspread** *n.* covering for the bed چادر، پلنگ پوش **bedstead** *n.* wooden frame of a bed پلنگ، چارپائی، کھاٹ **bedtime** *n.* time for sleeping سونے کا وقت
bedaub (be-*dawb*) *v.t.* smear (with mud, etc.) کیچڑ میں لتھڑنا یا لت پت کرنا
bedeck (be-*deck*) *v.t.* adorn سجانا
bedew (bē-*dew*) *v.t.* make wet with dew شبنم سے تر کرنا، اوس ڈالنا make wet with drops like that of dew شبنم کے سے قطروں سے تر کرنا *eyes bedewed with tears* آنکھیں دُرِّ اشک سے مُزیّن بھیگی ہوئی پلکیں
bedevil (be-*dev*-il) *v.t.* throw into disorder بگاڑنا گڑبڑ کر دینا، ابتری پھیلانا
bedizen (be-*diz*-ĕn) *v.t.* dress in gay, gaudy colours بھونڈے پن سے شوخ رنگ پہننا یا پہنانا
bedlam (*bed*-lĕm) *n.* lunatic asylum پاگل خانہ

state of noisy confusion غل غپاڑہ
bedouin (*bed*-oo-in, or bed-oo-*een*) *n.* (*pl.* the same) nomad Arab بدو، بدوی
bedraggle (be-*drag*-ĕl) *v.t.* wet (the dress, etc.) by trailing it کیچڑ میں لتھاڑنا
bee *n.* small flying insect which gathers nectar from flowers شہد کی مکھی، نحل *busy as a bee*, very busy سخت مصروف *have a bee in (one's) bonnet*, have a fad for سنکی ہونا، کسی بات کا خبط ہونا busy worker مصروف کارکن **beehive** *n.* structure in which bees live and make their honey-combs چھتا، چھال، نحل گاہ **bee-line** *n.* straight line; direct and shortest route ناک کی سیدھ *make a bee-line for*, go in the shortest way to ناک کی سیدھ میں (جانا) **beeswax, bees' wax** *n.* wax made by bees موم

a beehive

beech *n.* tree with hard white wood and edible nuts سفیدے کی قسم کا ایک درخت، بینچ its wood بینچ کی لکڑی
beef (*pl.* beeves) *n.* meat from an ox, bull, or cow بڑا گوشت، بڑ کا گوشت *a big beef*, a stout person (esp. one having more brawn than brains) سانڈ کا سانڈ **beefeater** (*beef*-ee-tĕ*) yeoman of the guard ایک برطانوی گارد کا سپاہی، گاؤ خور **beef-steak** (*beef*-stayk) *n.* slice of beef for frying بڑے گوشت کا قتلہ **beef-tea,** beef soup بڑے گوشت کی یخنی، ماء اللحم
been (bin, or been) see under **be**
beer (*bee*-ĕ*) *n.* ale جو کی شراب، بوزہ
beet *n.* plant with large sweet root چقندر **beetroot** *n.* root of beet چقندر کی جڑ **beet-sugar** *n.* sugar made of beet چقندر کی چینی

Note. Red beat لال چقندر is cooked and eaten as a vegetable whereas **white beat** سفید چقندر is used for making *beet-sugar.*

a beet

beetle (*beet*-ĕl) *n.* small six-footed insect بھونرا *v.i.* overhang آگے کو جھکا ہوا ہونا *beetling cliffs* آگے کو جھکی ہوئی چٹانیں scowling خشمگیں ہونا، تنا ہوا ہونا *beetling brows* تنی ہوئی بھویں، تیوری چڑھی

a beetle

befall (be-*fawl*) *v.i.* (*befall, befell, befallen*) happen واقع ہونا، پڑنا
befit (be-*fit*) *v.t.* (-tt-) be suitable for موزوں ہونا **befitting** *adj.* موزوں، مناسب
befog (be-*fog*) *v.t.* surround in fog دھند میں ڈھانپنا confuse چکرا دینا، چکر میں ڈالنا make (issue, etc.) less intelligible (مسئلہ) اُلجھا دینا، تاریک کر دینا
befool (be-*fool*) *v.t.* deceive اُلو بنانا
befoul (be-*foul*) *n.* make impure گندا کرنا، خراب کرنا
before (be-*foh**) *prep.* & *conj.* in front of کے سامنے preceding سے قبل، سے پہلے ahead of

آگے آگے **beforehand** *adj.* in readiness, in advance پہلے ہی سے earlier than necessary قبل از وقت
befriend (be-*frend*) *v.t.* help as a friend مدد کرنا دوستی کا حق ادا کرنا
befuddle (be-*fud*-ĕl) *v.t.* make stupid with drink (نشے کا) شراب کا، حواس بجا نہ رہنے دینا، حواس مختل کر دینا، بہکا بہکا کر دینا confuse گھبرا دینا، چکرا دینا
beg (beg) *v.t.* & *i.* (-gg-) ask for مانگنا implore التجا کرنا، منت کرنا *go abegging, go begging*, find no acceptor, be unwanted کوئی قبول کرنے والا نہ ہونا *beg to differ*, say politely that one cannot agree اختلاف کی جرأت کرنا *beg the question*, assume the truth of what one is trying to prove دعویٰ بلا ثبوت مان لینا *I beg your pardon*, (a) *I* am sorry میں معافی چاہتا ہوں (b) please excuse me معاف کیجیے (c) please repeat what you have said just now again مہربانی فرما کر دوبارہ کہیے **beggar** *n.* (see below)
beget (be-*get*) *v.t.* (*beget, begot, begotten*) bring to life someone (as a father) (کسی کا) باپ بننا be the cause of کا باعث ہونا
beggar (*beg*-ĕ*) *n.* person who begs بھکاری، فقیر بھک منگا، سوالی، گدا (refined form of writing or speaking the swear word :) buggar لُچّا، بدمعاش *v.t.* make poor کنگال کر دینا ruin تباہ کر ڈالنا *beggar description*, be too good or bad for description ناگفتہ بہ ہے، زبان اس کے بیان سے قاصر ہے **beggarly** *adj.* fit for a beggar گدایانہ، فقیروں کا سا mean, worthless کمینہ، ناکارہ، بیکار poor غریب، مفلس، نادار **beggary** (*beg*-a-ri) *n.* extreme poverty سخت افلاس، سخت ناداری
begin (be-*gin*) *v.t.* & *i.* (*begin, began, begun*) commence شروع کرنا، آغاز کرنا، پہل کرنا **beginning** (be-*gin*-ing) *n.* source ابتدا، آغاز act of starting شروع کرنا، ابتدا کرنا، آغاز کرنا **beginner** (be-*gin*-ĕ*) *n.* novice اناڑی، نوسیکھیا
begone (be-*gon*) *int.* be off ! دفع، دور، دور ہو
begot, begotten (see under **beget**)
begrime (be-*grīm*) *v.t.* cover with *grime* or black dirt بھرنا، گلگوٹنا
begrudge (be-*gruj*) *v.t.* grudge, envy (*for*) (کسی وجہ سے) جلنا یا رشک کرنا **begrudgingly** *adv.* unwillingly با دل ناخواستہ
beguile (be-*gil*) *v.t.* cause (someone *to do* something) by guile or tricks دھوکہ دینا، دھوکے سے کام کرانا make time pass pleasantly تفریح کرنا
begun (be-gun) *pa. p.* of **begin** (which see)
behalf (be-*half*) *n.* (used only in the phrases) *on behalf of, in behalf of, on one's behalf, in one's behalf*, for someone کی خاطر، کی طرف سے

behave (be-*hayv*) *v.i.* conduct or carry oneself پیش آنا، رویہ اختیار کرنا *behave yourself*, behave properly تمیز سے کام لو **behaviour** (be-*hay*-vi-ĕ*) *n.* conduct رویہ، طرز عمل **behaviourism** *n.* analysis of (human) behaviour as a method of psychological study تجزیۂ کردار this theory of psychological methods نظریۂ کردار **S** **Behaviour** is what we do, especially in response to outside stimuli **manners**, compliance with recognized social standards as to speech, dress and action; **conduct**, what we decide in our inmost heart and the resultant effects.
behead (be-*hed*) *v.t.* cut off the head of سر قلم کرنا، قتل کرنا، مار ڈالنا
beheld *pa. t.* & *pa. p.* of **behold** (which see)
behest (be-*hest*) *n.* command حکم *at the behest of*, کے حکم کی تعمیل میں *at one's behest*, at one's command (دیا کے لیے)
behind (be-*hīnd*) *prep.* & *adv.* at the back of کے پیچھے inferior پیچھے in support of تائید میں (remain) after پیچھے (رہنا) *behind in one's work* کام میں پیچھے **behindhand** late بعد از وقت after (others) دوسروں کے بعد
behold (be-*hold*) *v.t.* (*behold, beheld, beheld*) see (esp. something striking or unusual) مشاہدہ کرنا، دیکھنا **beholden** (be-*hold*-ĕn) *adj.* under an obligation (*to*) ممنون، شاکر، احسان‌مند *be beholden to*, owe thanks to کا ممنون ہونا **beholder** *n.* onlooker دیکھنے والا، تماشائی
behoof *n.* sake خاطر (in the phrase :) *in one's* or *someone's*) *behoof*, (کی) خاطر (کے)، لیے **behoove** (be-*hoov*) (impersonal verb meaning) be right for (someone to do) (کے لیے) مناسب ہونا، (کو) زیب دینا *it behooves you to*, you should تمہیں چاہیے کہ *it does not behoove you to*, you should not تمہیں نہیں چاہیے کہ
being (*bee*-ing) *n.* life state of existence وجود ہستی creature مخلوق، ہستی *the Supreme Being*, God ہستی مطلق، خدا، اللہ
belabour (be-*lay*-bĕ*) *v.t.* thrash soundly بری طرح مارنا، خوب پیٹنا، زدوکوب کرنا
belated (be-*lay*-ted) *adj.* coming too late بعد از وقت overtaken by darkness اندھیرے میں، شب گرفتہ
belch (belch) *v.t.* & *i.* eject wind from the stomach through the mouth ڈکار لینا eject forcefully (smoke, etc.) اگلنا، دھماکے سے نکالنا give vent to (anger, etc.) noisily (غصے وغیرہ سے) گرجنا *n.* such outburst ڈکار، دھماکا
beldam (*bel*-dam), **beldame** (*bel*-daym) *n.* witch ڈائن، چڑیل، جادوگرنی ugly old woman بدشکل بڑھیا، چڑیل
beleaguer (be-*lee*-gĕ*) *v.t.* besiege کا محاصرہ کرنا، محصور کرنا **beleaguered** (-gĕ*d) *adj.* besieged محصور

belfry (*bel*-fri) *n.* part of church tower for bells گرجے کا گھنٹہ گھر

a belfry (with the bell at the arrow)

belie (be-*lī*) *v.t.* give a false notion of کے متعلق غلط خیال پیدا کرنا fail to confirm جھٹلانا *belie (one's) hopes* اُمیدوں پر پانی پھیر دینا

belief (be-*leef*) *n.* acceptance of something as true یقین، عقیدہ، اِعتقاد *to the best of (one's) belief*, as far as one knows جہاں تک کسی کو معلوم ہو confidence *in* پر اعتبار یا بھروسہ

believe (be-*leev*) *v.t.* & *i.* accept as true صحیح تسلیم کرنا، ماننا *believe in*, (*a*) have trust in پر بھروسہ رکھنا (*b*) feel sure of the existence of ایمان لانا، ماننا، یقین کرنا **believing** *adj.* trustful ماننے والا، عقیدتمند **believable** *adj.* credible قابلِ اعتبار **believer** *n.* one who believes ایماندار، مومن

belike (be-*līk*) *adj.* (archaic) probably غالباً

belittle (be-*lit*-ĕl) *v.t.* make to seem unimportant گھٹا کر بتانا underrate, speak slightingly of بُرے لفظوں میں بیان کرنا

bell (bel) *n.* inverted cup that rings when struck by the clapper گھنٹی، گھنٹہ، گھنگرو *v.t.* provide with a bell گھنٹی باندھنا *bell the cat*, lead a dangerous movement خطرے کی مہم انجام دینا *curse by bell, book and candle*, excommunicate لعنت بھیجنا

belladonna (bel-a-*don*-a) *n.* (drug obtained from) deadly nightshade بلاڈنا، بھلاڈناں

belle (bel) *n.* the most admired beautiful young woman in a group حسینہ، حسیناؤں کی سرتاج

bell-hop *n.* (U.S. slang) servant in a hotel, club, etc. گھنٹی کی آواز پر آنے والا ملازم، بُوائے خادم

belles-lettres (bel-let-rĕ) *n.* literary writing (as opposed to scientific and other non-literary writing) ادبِ لطیف، ادب

bellicose (*bel*-i-kohs) *adj.* fond of fighting جھگڑالو anxious to fight جنگجو **bellicosity** (-*cos*-) *n.* fondness for fighting

belligerence, belligerency (-*lij*-) *n.* (of countries or parties) state of being at war حالتِ جنگ their being warlike جنگجویانہ ذہنیت **belligerent** (be-*lij*-e-rent) *n.* country or party which is at war محارب، شریکِ جنگ

Bellona (be-*loh*-na) *Cl. myth.* the Roman goddess of war : she was the sister of Mars بلونا

bellow (*bel*-oh) *n.* cry of a cow or bull ڈکار cry of pain or anger چیخ *v.t.* utter such a cry چیخنا، چلانا، ڈکارنا **bellows** (*bel*-ohz) *n.* (*sing.* or *pl.*) instrument for creating a strong blast of air دھونکنی

bellows

bell-pull *n.* chain, etc., fastened to bell which is rung when the former is pulled گھنٹی کی زنجیر زنجیرِ عدل **bell-ringer** *n.* one who rings the church bell گرجے کی گھنٹی بجانے والا، ناقوس زن

belly (*bel*-i) *n.* abdomen شکم، پیٹ، توند (the usual polite word being *stomach*) ; *with an empty belly*, feeling hungry بھوکا، بھوکے (*belly out*) swell out پھولنا be curved توند نکل آنا **bellylanding** *n.* (see *Addenda*)

belly

belong (be-*long*) *v.t.* have as a right or proper place کا حق ہونا، کا ہونا *belong to*, (*a*) be the property of کی ملک ہونا (*b*) be a member of کا رکن یا فرد ہونا *Do these books belong here ?* کیا یہ کتابیں یہاں کی ہیں؟

belongings *n. pl.* personal possession ملک، مقبوضات، سامان، چیز بست

beloved (be-*luv*-id) *adj.* much loved چہیتا، پسندیدہ *n.* one who is much loyed محبوب، دلدار *pa. p.* (be-*luvd*) very much liked (*by*) کا چاہتیا (یا چہیتا)

below (be-*loh*) *adj.* & *prep.* lower than سے نیچا، کے نیچے *go below*, go downstairs نیچے جانا *be below* نیچے ہونا

belt (belt) *n.* girdle پیٹی، کمربند *hit (someone) below the belt*, play foul with (him) سے دھوکہ کرنا، پردھوکے سے وار کرنا endless band used to connect wheels and drive machinery تسمہ، پیٹی zone ; any wide strip قطعہ، خطہ *belt of forest* جنگلات کا خطہ *v.t.* put a belt round پیٹی لگانا thrash with a belt پیٹی سے مارنا **belted** *adj.* wearing a belt کمربستہ، پیٹی لگائے ہوئے

bemoan (be-*mohn*) *v. t.* moan about رونا، آہ و بکا کرنا، ماتم کرنا

bench *n.* long, hard seat بنچ work-table (for a carpenter, etc.) میز (دکارپگری) seat of a judge in court عدالت، جج کی کرسی group of judges in High Court بنچ وقت سماعت کرنے والے جج *raise to the bench*, make a judge of the High Court ہائیکورٹ کا جج بنانا

a bench

a carpenter's bench

bend *v. t.* & *i.* (*bend, bent, bent*) curve موڑنا direct (*to* a certain point) (پر) پھیرنا، (کی طرف) لگانا، پر *bend (one's) mind to (one's) studies* توجہ پڑھائی پر لگانا، کمر ہمت کرنا force to yield اپنی بات زور سے منوانا *bent on* (something, or *doing* something) having as fixed purpose تُلا ہوا *n.* turn, curve موڑنا، پھیرنا

beneath (be-*neeth*) *adv.* & *prep.* below کے نیچے lower than سے نیچا unworthy of کے شان کے خلاف، نازیبا

benediction (ben-e-*dik*-shĕn) *n.* blessing (given by a Christian priest) برکت، دُعائے خیر، آشیرباد

benefaction (ben-e-fak-shĕn) *n.* (usu. large) donation for some good cause عطیہ، خیرات

doing good نیکی، احسان **benefactor** (ben-e-*fak*-tĕ*) *n.* *fem. benefactress*) one who does good محسن

beneficent (be-*nef*-i-sent) *adj.* good and kind نیک اور رحم دِل شخص **beneficence** *n.* doing good احسان

beneficial (*ben-e-fee*-shèl) *adj.* profitable سُود مند منفعت بخش useful مفید، کارآمد **benefice** (*ben-*) *n.* church income for its priest گرجے سے پادری کو آمدنی

beneficiary *n.* & *adj.* one who gets such income گرجے کی آمدنی پانے والا held under feudal tenure جاگیر its holder جاگیردار one who receives (usu. monetary) benefit from something or someone نفع پانے والا، فائدہ اُٹھانے والا

benefit (*ben*-e-fit) *n.* profit نفع، منفعت advantage فائدہ improvement بہتری good done to or obtained from somebody or something بہبُود pension, allowance وظیفہ، گزارہ، پینشن *give the benefit of the doubt* (*to someone*), free (him) from blame because there is doubt شک کا فائدہ دے کر بَری کرنا *benefit performance*, one of which the profits are used for charity خیراتی تماشا *v. t.* & *i.* do good to فائدہ پہنچانا be a benefit to کے لیے مُفید ہونا

benevolent (be-*nev*-o-lent) *adj.* charitable خیرات دینے والا doing good فیض رساں **benevolence** *n.* فیض رسانی

benighted (be-*nī*-ted) *adj.* overtaken by night شب گرفتہ، رات کے اندھیرے میں گرفتار in moral and mental darkness گمراہ ignorant نادان، جاہل

benign (be-*nīn*) *adj.* gentle مہربان، شفیق، سازگار، موافق *benign smile* کرم گسترانہ تبسّم *benign climate* سازگار موسم *benign disease* ہلکی بیماری **benignant** (-*nig*-) *adj* kind-hearted نرم دل، مہربان **benignity** (-nig-) *n.* kindness of heart نرم دلی، شفقت

benison (*be*n-i-zen) *n.* (old use) benediction دُعائے خیر

bent (bent) *v. t.* & *i.* (pa. t. of **bend**) *n.* liking (*for*), aptitude (*for*) رغبت، میلان، رُجحان *bent of mind* میلانِ طبع *have a bent for*, be fond of and clever at راغب اور ماہر ہونا *to the top of* (*one's*) *bent*, to heart's content جی بھر کے

benumb (be-*num*) *v. t.* make numb سُن کرنا، شل کرنا، بے حس کرنا stupefy حواس مختل کر دینا

benzine (-zeen) *n.* petrol spirit used as a detergent (i.e., surface cleaner) in dry-cleaning بینزین

Beowulf (*bay*-oh-wulf) (Scand. legend) hero of the longest poem in Old English literature. He rescued the Danish king from two sea monsters, Grendel and his mother بیؤولف

bequeath (be-*kweedh*) *v. t.* arrange (by making a will) to give (property, etc.) at death وصیت کرنا hand down to those who come after ورثے میں چھوڑنا، ترکہ چھوڑنا، میراث کے طور پر دینا

bequest (be-*kwest*) *n.* bequeathing something bequeathed ورثہ، ترکہ، میراث *leave bequests of money* (*etc.*) *to* کے نام ترکہ چھوڑ جانا

bereave (be-*reev*), *bereave*, (*bereaved*, *bereaved*; or *bereave*, *bereft*, *bereft*) *v. t* deprive (of) (سے) لے لینا **bereaved** *adj.* having been deprived (*of* someone) by his death دوستوں، عزیزوں کا مر جانا dejected by the loss (*of*) سوگ میں *bereaved of friends* دوستوں کی موت سے غمزدہ یا اُداس **bereavement** *n.* being bereaved سوگ، ماتم a great loss سخت محرومی، خسران، نقصان **bereft** (reft) *adj.* lacking; deprived (*of*) (سے) عاری، محروم *bereft of reason*, insane عقل سے خالی، سمجھ سے عاری، دیوانہ، پاگل

beret (*be*-ret, or *be*-ray) *n.* round flat cap used as military head-dress بیٹھی ہوئی گول ٹوپی، بیرے

berg (bĕ*g) *n.* iceberg سمندری برفستان **bergamot** (bĕ*-) *n.* a kind of orange tree yielding a cheap scent called the oil of bergamot پرگامٹ، سنگترے کی قسم کا ایک درخت *oil of bergamot* سنگترے کی خوشبُو

beriberi (*be*-ri-be-ri) *n.* dropsy-like disease caused by malnutrition بیری بیری

berry (*be*-ri) (pl. *berries*) *n.* small juicy fruit گوندنی کی قسم کا پھل *strawberry* شابیری، *raspberry* رس بھری

berth (bĕ*th) *n.* bed in a train or ship (گاڑی وغیرہ میں) سونے کی جگہ place for a ship in a river or harbour گودی میں جہاز کی جگہ، جہاز گاہ *give a wide berth to*, keep at a safe distance from سے کترانا، سے بچے رہنا (colloq.) job, position نوکری، ملازمت *v. t.* & *i.* moor (a ship) into a berth (جہاز کو) جہاز گاہ میں لانا

upper and lower berths

beseech (be-*seech*) *v.t.* (*beseech*, *besought*, *besought*) implore, beg for التجا کرنا، منت سماجت کرنا *beseech someone* (*to do* or *for doing* something) (کام کے لیے) کسی کی منت سماجت کرنا

beseem (impersonal verb meaning) be proper for (someone *to do*) کے لیے مناسب ہونا، کو زیب دینا *it ill beseems him to say that*, he should not say that اُسے یہ کہنا نہیں چاہیے کہ

beset (be-*set*) *v. t.* (-tt-) attack from all sides چاروں طرف سے حملہ کرنا، ٹوٹ پڑنا surround گھیر لینا *problem beset with difficulties* مُشکلہ *one's besetting sin*, the sin of which one is regularly guilty وہ عادت جو مَر کر بھی نہ جائے، جنم پاپ

beside (be-*sīd*) *prep.* by the side of کے پہلو میں،

near کے نزدیک کے ساتھ، کے کنارے in comparison with کے مقابلے میں away from کے دیا سے، باہر besiae one-self with, at the end of one's self-control owing to آپے سے باہر beside the point, having nothing to do with the question, غیر متعلق **besides** (be-sidz) *prep.* & *adv.* as well (as) بھی .in addition to کے علاوہ، مزید برآں

besiege (be-*seej*) *v.t.* surr...d with armed forces محاصرہ کرنا، نرغے میں لینا pester, harras بار بار کر کے تنگ کرنا *besiege (someone) with requests*, make too many requests (to him) درخواستوں کی بھرمار سے تنگ کر دینا

besot (be-*sot*) *v.t.* make dull بے حس کر دینا stupefy مدہوش کر دینا **besotted** *adj.* stupefied بے حس مدہوش، بدمست

besought *pa. t.* of **beseech** (which see)

bespeak (be-*speek*) *v.t.* (*bespeak, bespoke, bespoken*; or *bespeak, bespoke, bespoke*) show someone (*to be*) ظاہر کرنا، کا ثبوت ہونا order something to be kept ready تیار رکھنے کی ہدایت

bespoke *pa. t.* & *pa. p.* of **bespeak** (which see)

besprinkle (bes-*prink*-èl) *v.t.* sprinkle with dirt بکھیرنا، چھڑکاؤ کرنا، چھڑکنا cover with (abuse or flattery) بہت (خوشامد) کرنا یا (گالیاں) دینا

best *adj.* (*good, better, best*) most good بہترین، سب سے اچھا largest سب سے زیادہ، زیادہ تر *the best part of the day* دن کا زیادہ تر حصہ (یا وقت) *work the best part of the day* زیادہ تر وقت کام میں مصروف رہنا most complete مکمل، کامل *adv.* سب سے اچھی طرح، بہترین طریقے، بہترین انداز سے، بطریق احسن *n.* finest عمدہ ترین، نفیس ترین the highest degree درجۂ کمال پر، کمال درجے کا، میں کمال *he was at his best in his speech* آج اس کی تقریر کمال کی تھی *get the best of it in* (مقابلے) میں غالب آنا یا جیتنا *make the best of* سے زیادہ سے زیادہ فائدہ اٹھانا، جلد از جلد کام کرنا *do (one's) best, put one's best foot foremost*, make one's best effort پورا زور لگانا، مقدور بھر کوشش کرنا *to the best of* حتی المقدور *to the best of (one's) knowledge* جہاں تک (مجھے) معلوم ہے، جہاں تک (میری) معلومات کا تعلق ہے *(one's) best girl*, (slang) beloved محبوبہ *at best*, even if most favourably considered زیادہ سے زیادہ *(one) had best (do,* etc.), it were best for (him, me, etc., to do, etc.) بہتر ہو کہ *have the best of it*, prevail in a contest کا پلہ بھاری رہنا *make the best of (one's) way*, do as well as circumstances would permit جس طرح بن پڑے کرنا *best seller*, (slang) popular novel or other book عوام کا پسندیدہ ناول، خوب بکنے والی کتاب **best man**, bridegroom's chief attendant at the wedding شہ بالا

bestial (*bes*-ti-ĕl) *adj.* of or like a beast حیوانوں کا سا brutal بہیمانہ brutally sensual بہیمیت والا **bestiality** *n.* بہیمیت **bestiary** *n.* allegorized natural history of animals popular in the Middle Ages حیوانات کے بیان میں لکھی ہوئی پندو موعظت، جانور نامہ، حیوۃ الحیوان

bestir (be-*stĕ**) *v.t.* (-tt-) (used reflexively as *bestir oneself*), exert, rouse, or busy (*oneself*) مستعدی دکھانا، دوڑ دھوپ کرنا

bestow (bes-*toh*) *v.t.* confer (*on*) دینا، عطا کرنا، سرفراز کرنا

bestride (bes-*trid*) *v.t.* (*bestride, bestrode, bestridden*) stand or sit with one leg on each side of (horse, fence, etc.) پر چڑھا بیٹھا ہونا، پر دونوں ٹانگیں پھیلا کر کھڑے ہونا

bet *v.t.* & *i.* (*-tt-*) (*bet, bet, bet*; or *bet, betted, betted*) stake or wager money on whether something will or will not happen شرط لگانا، بدنا یا باندھنا *n.* such a stake شرط money, etc., offered in this way شرط یا داؤ پر لگی ہوئی رقم

betake (be-*tayk*) *v.t.* (*betake, betook, betaken*) (used reflexively as *betake oneself to*) go *to* جانا apply oneself *to* اپنے کو کام پر لگانا

betatron *n.* (see *Addenda*)

bethink (be-*think*) *v.t.* (*bethink, bethought, bethought*) (used reflexively) be reminded of کا خیال آنا *I bethought myself (of, that, how)* میں نے سوچا کہ، مجھے خیال آیا کہ

betide (be-*tid*) *v.i.* happen to ہونا، مصیبت پڑنا *woe betide you*, (old use) if you fail اگر تم نہ کر سکے *whatever may betide*, whatever may happen کچھ ہی کیوں نہ ہو

betimes (be-*timz*) *adv.* (liter.) early جلدی، پہلے in good time اچھے وقت

betoken be-*toh*-kèn) *v.t.* be a token of کی علامت ہونا show beforehand کے آثار ہونا

betray (be-*tray*) *v.t.* be false or unfaithful to دغا دینا، غداری کرنا allow (secret) to become known (by accident or on purpose) راز افشا کر دینا show ظاہر کرنا **betrayal** (be-*tray*-èl) *n.* act of betraying غداری، بے وفائی، دغا، افشائے راز

betroth (be-*trohdh*) *v.t.* promise to marry منگنی کرنا، نسبت کرنا **betrothed** (be-*trohdhd*) *n.* engaged to be married منگیتر، منسوبہ **betrothal** (-dhĕl) *n.* promise to marry منگنی، نسبت

better (*bet*-ĕ*) *adj.* (*good, better, best*) more good بہتر، زیادہ اچھا preferable لائق ترجیح، مرجح improved in health صحت کی بہتر حالت میں *adv.* comparatively well نسبتاً بہتر *v.t.* make better بہتر بنانا

do better than سے بہتر کام کرنا better oneself, get a better position برتر منصب پر فائز ہونا get the better of, beat, conquer سے بازی لے جانا ، پر فتح پانا ، کو شکست دینا
betterment *n.* improvement اصلاح ، بہبود ، بہتر بنانا یا بننا
between (be-*tween*) *prep.* & *adv.* in what separates one from the other کے درمیان ، کے بیچ میں
by the joint action of مشترکہ ، باہم by comparison نسبتاً ، مقابلتاً ▣ **Between** indicates opposition, and the participation of all the parties more definitely than can be done by **among** which is used to convey the idea of a mass, crowd or group acting as a whole. **Among** is also used when distinguishing some kind from the rest of the group : 'pre-eminent *among*'; 'she is one *among* many'
betwixt (be-*twikst*) *prep.* & *adv.* (arch.) between کے درمیان ، بیچ میں ، باہم
bevel (bev-ĕl) *v.t.* (-ll-) make (edge of something) sloping کنارہ ڈھلوان بنانا *n.* such sloping edge ڈھلوان کنارہ
beverage (*bev*-e-rij) *n.* any kind of drink (*e.g.*, tea, beer) پینے کی چیز ، مشروب
bevy (*bev*-i) *n.* group (of girls or women) (عورتوں کا) جھرمٹ flock (of birds) (پرندوں کا) جھنڈ
bewail (be-*wayl*) *v.t.* mourn over کا ماتم کرنا complain of کی شکایت کرنا
beware (be-*way*-ĕ*) *v.t.* & *i.* be on guard خبردار رہنا ، آگاہ ہونا (used in the imperative and infinitive only) be careful (*of*) سے بچنا *beware lest it should, beware that it should not* دیکھنا کہیں ایسا نہ ہو کہ
bewilder (be-*wil*-dĕ*) *v.t.* puzzle حیران کرنا confuse greatly الجھاؤ میں ڈالنا **bewilderment** *n.* perplexity حیرانی ، پریشانی
bewitch (be-*wich*) *v.i.* work magic on جادو کرنا attract or charm لبھانا ، رجھانا ، فریفتہ کرنا *bewitching smile*, charming smile دلفریب مسکراہٹ
beyond (be-*yond*) *adv.* & *prep.* on the farther side of کے پار ، کے ، دوسری طرف out of the reach of (کی) طاقت سے باہر ، کی دسترس سے باہر too much, far
bezique (be-*zeek*) a game at cards تاش کا ایک کھیل ، بزیک combination of the queen of spades and the knave of diamonds بزیک
bi- (bī) *pref.* twice دوبار having two دوہرا coming once in every two (بار) ہر دو کے لیے ایک
bias (*bī*-as) *n.* weight on one side of a wooden ball (قدیم کھیل میں گیند کا) چپٹاپن leaning of the mind (*towards* or *against*) میلان ، تعصب *cut on the bias*, cut in a sloping direction across the material آڑا کاٹنا *v.t.* (*biased* or *biassed*) give a bias to تعصب پیدا کرنا ، ناجائز اثر ڈالنا **biassed** (*bī*-ast) *adj.* prejudiced متعصب ، متعصبانہ inclined unfairly جانبدار

bib *n.* cloth hung under a baby's chin بب ، سینہ بند
bibelot (*beb*-loh) *n.* any artistic trifle چھوٹی سی نادر شے
Bible (*bī*-bĕl) *n.* Christian scriptures comprising the Old and the New Testaments بائبل ، تورات ، عہد عتیق وعہد جدید ، پرانا اور نیا عہد نامہ **biblical** (*bib*-li-kĕl) *adj.* of the Bible بائبل کا ، کتابی
bibliography (bib-li-*og*-ra-fi) *n.* list of books about some special subject کتابیات ، کتب نامہ
bicentenary (by-*sen*-ti-na-ri) *n.* 200th anniversary of an event دو صد سالہ سالگرہ (یا تقریب)
biceps (*bī*-seps) *n.* large muscle in the front part of the upper arm بازو کا دو سری پٹھہ
bicker (*bik*-ĕ*) *v.i.* quarrel about trifles معمولی معمولی باتوں پر الجھنا **bickerings** *n.* such quarrels معمولی معمولی باتوں پر الجھنا ، بیکار جھگڑنا
bicycle (*bī*-sik-ĕl) *n.* a two-wheeled vehicle worked by the feet and steered by the hands بائیسکل ، سیکل *go on, pedal, or ride on a bicycle*, ride on it سیکل چلانا *wheel a bicycle*, walk along it pushing it by one's hands سیکل ہاتھ میں لے کر چلنا *v.t.* ride on a bicycle **bike** (bīk) *n.* (colloq.) bicycle سیکل *v.t.* ride on a bicycle سیکل چلانا ، سیکل پر جانا
bid *v.t.* & *i.* (-*dd*-) (*bid, bid, bid*) make an offer of money for بولی دینا (old use) (*bid, bade* pr., bad; *bidden*) (*a*) command حکم دینا (*b*) say (good-bye, etc.) (خدا حافظ وغیرہ) کہنا *n.* offer to pay a price at an auction (نیلام کی) بولی *make a bid for* try to obtain کوشش کرنا **bidding** *n.* bidding at an auction (نیلام کی) بولی command حکم ، ارشاد *do (someone's) bidding*, obey (him) (کسی کے) حکم کی تعمیل کرنا ▣ To **bid** is to order someone to do something; also to offer a price. We **command** somebody to do something; **order** that something should be done; **instruct** someone in detail to do something; **enjoin**, charge solemnly with a duty.
bide (bīd) *v.t.* wait for انتظار کرنا *bide (one's) time*, wait for an opportunity موقع کی تاک میں ہونا ، موقع کا انتظار کرنا
biennial (bī-*en*-i-al) *adj.* two-year long دو سال کا two-yearly دو سالہ
bier (*bee*-ĕ*) *n.* wooden stand for coffin or dead body تابوت
bifocal (bī-*foh*-kĕl) *adj.* (of spectacles) with combined glasses for near and distant sight دور و نزدیک کے اکٹھے شیشوں والی عینک ، دوہری عینک ، دوہرا چشمہ
bifurcate (*bī*-fĕ*-kayt) *v.i.* division into two part (ways) دوپارہ ہونا یا کرنا سڑکوں کا ، پھٹنا division into two تقسیم ، دو میں تقسیم parting سڑکوں کا جدا ہونا
big *adj.* (*big, bigger, biggest*) large, bulky بڑا

important اہم generous فراخ دل **Big Ben** *n.* clock and bell in the British Houses of Parliament **big business** *n.* large-scale commercial or industrial enterprises بڑے کاروبار people conducting it بڑے کاروباری بڑے کارخانہ دار اور تاجر **big wheel** *n.* (see *Addenda*)
A thing is big if it is so in all dimensions; **large** in width or area, **great** when large and dignified; **bulky**, voluminous.

bigamy (*big*-a-mi) *n.* having two wives or two husbands at once بیک وقت دو شوہر یا دو بیویاں رکھنا ، تعدّدِ ازدواج ، کثیر الازدواجی **bigamous** (*big*-a-mus) *adj.* relating to bigamy تعدّدِ ازدواج سے متعلق *bigamous marriage* تعدّدِ ازدواج **bigamist** (*big*-a mist) *n.* person practising bigamy بیک وقت دو شوہر رکھنے والی عورت (یا دو بیویاں رکھنے والا مرد)

bigoted (*big*-ut-ed) *adj.* obstinate beyond reason in holding one's belief کٹّر، متعصّب **bigot** (*big*-ut) bigoted person متعصّب آدمی، کٹّر شخص **bigotry** (*big*-ut-ri) being bigoted تعصّب

bike (bɪk) see under **bicycle**

bikini *n.* (see *Addenda*)

bilateral (bɪ-*layt*-e-rĕl) *adj.* of, on, with, two sides دو طرفہ *bilateral agreement*, agreement made between two (governments, etc.) صرف دو حکومتوں وغیرہ کا معاہدہ

bile (bɪl) *n.* bitter yellow fluid produced by the liver to help in digesting food صفرا، پِت bad temper بدمزاجی، چڑچڑاپن **bilious** (*bil*-i-us) *adj.* caused by too much bile صفراوی *billious attack* صفرا کا زور، bad-tempered, surly (person) بدمزاج ، چڑچڑا

bilge (bilj) *n.* largest part of a ship's hull جہاز کے پیندے کا سب سے چوڑا حصّہ (slang) rubbish کوڑا کرکٹ

bilingual (by-*ling*-gwĕl) *adj.* speaking two languages (esp. when these are learnt together in childhood) دو زبانیں بولنے والا ، in two languages دو لسانی ، دو زبانوں میں

bilious (*bil*-i-us) *adj.* see under **bile**

bilk *v.t.* cheat a person by running away without paying his dues قرضہ ادا کیے بغیر بھاگ جانا ، *n.* cheat ٹھگ ، اٹھائی گیرا ، اُچکا

¹bill (bil) *n.* beak چونچ *bill and coo*, (*a*) put bills together دانہ بدلی کرنا (*b*) behave like lovers پیار کرنا

²bill (bil) *n.* statement of money owing for goods or services بل، فردِ حساب poster stuck on a wall, etc. (دیوار پر چسپاں ہونے والا) اشتہار proposed law, to be discussed by a parliament (and called an *Act* when passed) مسوّدۂ قانون، بل programme of entertainment تفریحی پروگرام *bill of exchange*, written order to a bank, etc., to pay money to someone on a certain date ہُنڈی *bill of fare*, menu کھانے کی فہرست ، ماحضر *v.t.* announce through posters اشتہارات کے ذریعے اعلان کرنا **bill poster, bill-sticker** *n.* person who sticks bills on walls, etc. اشتہار چسپاں کرنے والا ، اشتہار لگانے والا **hand-bill** *n.* (usu. printed) notice circulated by hand دستی اشتہار

billet (*bil*-et) *n.* (private house or other place) where a soldier is lodged نجی گھر جہاں فوجیوں کو ٹھکانا رکھا جائے order asking a person to billet a soldier فوجیوں کو نجی گھر میں رکھنا *v.t.* lodge soldier *on* a town or householder (*in* or *at* a place) فوجیوں کو کسی نجی گھر میں رکھنا

billet-doux (bil-i-*doo*) *n.* love letter عشقیہ خط، نامۂ محبّت

billiards (*bil*-yĕ*dz) *n.* (used with *sing*, or *pl.* verb) indoor game played with ivory balls and long sticks (called *cues*) on an oblong cloth covered table (*called billiards table*) بلیرڈ

a game of billiards

billingsgate (*bil*-ingz-gayt) *n.* violent abuse as indulged in by the fisherwomen there مغلّظ گالی ، بازاری زبان، بھٹیاریوں کی زبان

billion (*bil*-yun) *n.* (Brit.) one million millions دس کھرب (U.S. & France) one thousand millions

billow (*bil*-oh) *n.* (liter.) big wave of the sea ایک ارب (*pl.*) the sea سمندر *v.t.* rise or roll like big waves بڑی بڑی لہریں پیدا کرنا ، ٹھاٹھیں مارنا buldge, swell out بڑھنا ، پھولنا **billowy** (bill-oh-i) *adj.* having such waves تلاطم خیز

bimetallism (bi-*met*-a-lizm) *n.* use by a country of both silver and gold as a standard value of currency **bimetallic** (-tel-)

bimonthly (bɪ-*munth*-li) *adj.* happening once every two months دو ماہہ (colloq.) happening twice every month پندرہ روزہ

bin *n.* large container or enclosed place, usu. with a lid, for storing coal, grain, etc. بڑا پیپا ، کھتا *dust-bin* for throwing rubbish کوڑے دان *coal-bin*, bin for storing coal کوئلے دان

binaural *adj.* (see *Addenda*)

bind (bɪnd) *v.t.* & *i.* (*bound*) tie or fasten together (with rope, etc.) (رسّی وغیرہ) سے باندھنا put (one thing) round (another) کے گرد لپیٹنا *bind* (*up*) *a wound* زخم پر پٹی باندھنا *bind hand and foot* ہاتھ پاؤں باندھنا *bind the edge of a carpet*, hem گوٹ لگانا fasten together; put into a cover باندھنا (cause to) become hard جم جانا ، اکڑ جانا ، یا پیوستہ کر دینا

بستہ ہوجانا، برف *snow-bound* برف بستہ hold someone (by legal agreement or promise *to do* something) قول کی پابندی پر مجبور کرنا *bind (someone) over* پابند کرنا *bind (someone) to keep the peace* حفظ امن کا پابند بنانا

binder (*bīnd*-ĕ*) *n.* person, thing, machine, that binds باندھنے والا *book-binder* one who binds books جلدساز **binding** (*bīnd*-ing) *n.* act of binding جلدسازی book-cover جلد *adj.* obligatory لازم

binoculars (bĭ-*nok*-ew-lĕ*z) *n. pl.* instrument with lenses for both eyes making distant objects seem nearer دُوربین، دوچشمی دُوربین، سیربین

binoculars

biographer *n.*, **biographical** *adj.* (see under **biography**) سوانح عمری، سوانح

biography (bī-*og*-ra-fi) *n.* life-story (*of someone*) written by another (cf. *autobiography*, which is one's life-story written by oneself) سوانح حیات، سیرت، تذکرہ **biographical** (bī-o-*graf*-i-kĕl) *adj.* سیرت یا تذکرے کے متعلق، سیرت نگاری یا تذکرہ نویسی سے متعلق **biographer** (bī-*og*-) *n.* one who writes someone's biography سوانح نگار، سیرت نویس

biological *adj.*, **biologist** *n.* (see under **biology**)

biology (bī-*ol*-o-ji) *n.* science of life (of animals and plants) حیاتیات **biological** (by-o-*loj*-i-kĕl) *adj.* حیاتیاتی **biological warfare** *n.* (see *Addenda*) **biologist** (bī-*ol*-o-jist) *n.* ماہر حیاتیات

bipartisan (bī-pah*-ti-zan) *adj.* involving two political (or other) parties دوسیاسی (وغیرہ) جماعتوں والا، دوجزئین

bipartite (bī-pah*-tit) *adj.* composed of two parts دوحصوں والا between two parties دو فریقوں کے مابین

biped (*bī*-ped) *n.* two-legged living creature (*i.e.*, birds and human beings) دوپایہ

biplane (*bī*-playn) *n.* aircraft with two wings one above the other دوسطحی طیارہ

birch (bĕ*ch) *n.* a kind of tree بُرچ its wood بُرچ کی لکڑی bundle of its twigs used for flogging pupils بُرچ کی چھڑی *v. t.* flog with a birch چھڑی سے مارنا

a birch & its leaf

bird (be*d) *n.* feathered creature with two legs پرندہ، پنچھی (see *Addenda*) *birds of prey*, carnivorous birds شکار کرنے والے پرندے *game birds*, birds on which man preys to eat their flesh شکار کیے جانے والے پرندے *birds of passage*, migratory birds موسمی پرندے *he is a bird of passage*, he does not stay long in a place وہ تو رمتا جوگی ہے *little bird*. گمنام مخبر *a little bird told me* مجھے ایک گمنام مخبر نے بتایا، اُڑتی ہوئی سُنی ہے، ایک اُڑتی سی خبر ہے زبانی طیور کی *old bird* گھاگ، جوکنا، پرانا آزمودہ *the bird is flown* چڑیا اُڑ گئی، مرغ ہاتھ سے جاتا رہا *birds of a feather*, persons having similar tastes ہم قماش، ایک ہی تھیلی کے چٹے بٹے لوگ *birds of feather flock together* کند ہم جنس باہم جنس پرواز *bird in hand* یقینی فائدہ *a bird in bush* غیر یقینی فائدہ *kill two birds with one stone* ایک پنتھ دو کاج *bird's-eye view* طائرانہ نظر، چھچھلتی نگاہ

birth (bĕ*th) *n.* (from *bear*) coming into being, being born پیدائش **birth-control** *n.* (now more euphemistically called *family planning*) contraception منع حمل، خاندانی منصوبہ بندی its methods مانع حمل طریقے **birthday** *n.* day of one's birth یوم پیدائش its anniversary سالگرہ *one's twentieth birthday* کسی کو اکیسواں برس لگنے *birthday present* سالگرہ کا تحفہ **birthplace** *n.* place of one's birth مولد، مرز بوم، جنم بھومی **birth-rate** *n.* number of births in one year for every 1,000 persons شرح پیدائش **birthright** *n.* various rights, privileges and property to which a person is entitled as a member of his family or a citizen of his country پیدائشی حق (English law) eldest son's right to full inheritance پورے ورثے پر بڑے بیٹے کا حق such inheritance پورا ورثہ

biscuit (*bis*-kit) *n.* flat, thin, crisp cake salted or sweetened بسکٹ *ship's biscuit*, a hard kind of biscuit سخت بسکٹ

bisect (bī-*sekt*) *v. t.* divide (an angle, etc.) into two (usu. equal) parts تنصیف کرنا (cf. *trisect*, to divide into three parts تثلیث کرنا) **bisection** (bī-*sek*-shĕn) *n.* تنصیف **bisector** *n.* bisecting line منصف، خطِ تنصیف

bishop (*bish*-up) *n.* clergyman of high rank who organizes the work of the church in a city or district اُسقف **bishopric** (*bish*-) *n.* district under a bishop اُسقف کا حلقۂ اقتدار a bishop's office

bison (*bī*-sun) *n.* wild ox اَرنا بھینسا American buffalo امریکی بھینس

a bison

bit *n.* very small piece چھوٹا سا ٹکڑا *bit of paper* کاغذ کا پُرزہ *bit by bit*, slowly, gradually ذرا ذرا کرکے، آہستہ آہستہ *a bit better, or worse, etc.*) ذرا بہتر (یا بدتر) *do one's bit*, do one's share اپنے حصّے کا واجبی کام کرنا *not a bit (of it)*, not at all بالکل نہیں *give (someone) a bit of (one's) mind*, scold (him) کھری کھری سنانا، جھاڑ جھپاڑ کرنا a little while تھوڑی دیر، ذرا *wait a bit* ذرا ٹھہرو metal mouthpiece of a horse's bridle لگام کا دہانہ *take the bit between one's teeth*, reject control بھگنے سے انکار کرنا، قابو سے باہر ہونا

the cutting part of certains tools پھل brace and bit, or bit and brace, small drill چھوٹا برما *v. t.* see **bite** ⓢ **a bit,** "thing bitten off"; **a particle,** small part: **morsel** of food; an **iota, a jot,** the smallest letters of the Greek and Hebrew alphabets; **a mite,** very small coin; a **whit,** "tiny creature," tiny thing; an **atom.** very smallest particle of matter; **a speck,** tiny particle that adheres; **a grain,** tiny particle that grows; a **spark,** tiniest visible light.

bitch (bich) *n.* (impolete word for) female dog کتیا she-wolf or she-fox بھیڑیے کی مادہ یا لُومڑی *v.i.* (see *Addenda*)

bite (bit) *v. t. & i.* (*bite, bit, bitten;* or *bite, bit, bit*) seize and cut with the teeth دانت سے کاٹنا cause smarting pain سخت تکلیف پہنچانا (of acids, etc.) corrode کھا جانا damage نقصان پہنچانا swindle دھوکا دینا *the biter is bit,* the swindler has been served right چور کو پڑ گئے مور *bite one's lips,* show vexation ہونٹ چبانا، بیتاب مگر ضبط پر مجبور ہونا، کچھ نہ کر سکنا *bite on the granite,* waste pains سعیٔ لاحاصل کرنا *bite more than one can chew,* undertake more than one can perform بساط سے بڑھ کر قدم مارنا *bite and sup,* hurried meal بھاگ دوڑ کر کھایا ہوا کھانا *bite off* (or *out*), detach with teeth دانت سے توڑ کر توڑنا *bite at,* snap with the teeth بوٹی کاٹ لینا *snake-bite* سانپ کا ڈسنا *bite of a mosquito* (or *flea*) مچھر یا پسّو کا کاٹنا **biter** (bī-tĕ*) *n.* one who bites کاٹنے والا **biting** (bī-ting) *adj.* (of cold, wind, etc.) stinging and painful سخت تکلیف دہ pungent تیز sarcastic (words, criticism) دل کو خون کرنے والا، طنز بھرا **bitten** (bit-ĕn) *adj.* (*pa. p.* of *bite*) مارا ہوا، ڈسا ہوا *bitten by a snake* سانپ کا ڈسا ہوا

bitter (*bit*-ĕ*) *adj.* opposite to sweet کڑوا، تلخ causing sorrow غم انگیز، اندوہناک hard to bear ناقابل برداشت filled with or caused by anger, envy or hate تلخ، درشت *bitter words* تلخ الفاظ *bitter enemies* سخت دشمن **bitterly** *adv.* تلخی سے **bitterness** *n.* تلخی، کڑواہٹ

bivouac (*biv*-oo-ak) *n.* soldier's camp without tents or other cover آسمان تلے پڑاؤ *v. i.* make or rest in a bivouac آسمان تلے پڑاؤ کرنا

biweekly (bī-*week*-lī) *adj.* happening every two weeks پندرہ روزہ (colloq.) happening twice a week ہفتے میں دو بار *n.* periodical issued twice a week سہ روزہ اخبار

biz *n.* (colloq.) business کام کاج، بنج بیوپار، کاروبار

bizarre (bi-*zah**) *adj.* strange عجیب queer انوکھا

blab *v.t.* (*blab out*), let out secrets unwittingly نادانستہ راز افشا کرنا

black (blak) *n.* colour opposite to white سیاہ *adj.* of this colour کالا threatening وحشتناک، خطرناک morally bad بہت بڑا dark اندھیرا، تاریک *v.t.* make black کالا کرنا، سیاہ بنانا polish with blacking کالا پالش کرنا *give (someone) a black look,* or *look black at (someone),* look at him with anger قہر آلود یا غضبناک نگاہوں سے دیکھنا *be in someone's black* (or *bad*) *books,* be out of his favour کسی کی نگاہوں میں معتوب ہونا (cf. *be in someone's good books,* be in favour with him) *black sheep,* worst member of a group بدمعاش *black flag,* flag used by pirates بحری ڈاکوؤں کا جھنڈا *black art,* evil magic کالا جادو *beat one black and blue,* beat very severely بہت بُری طرح پیٹنا *v.t.* make black کالا کرنا، سیاہ کرنا *black out,* obscure lights for safety during air raids بلیک آؤٹ کرنا، روشنی گل کرنا polish (shoes, etc.) with blacking (بوٹ کو) کالا پالش کرنا، کالا روغن کرنا **blackamoor** *n.* negro حبشی any dark-skinned person کالا **black-beetle** *n.* (popular word for) cockroach تیلچٹا **blackberry** *n.* a small wild black fruit گل بھری، آنچھو **blackbird** *n.* a kind of black, thrush-like, melodious bird کستورا

blackberries

blackboard *n.* (usu. wooden) board painted black, used in schools, etc., for writing بلیک بورڈ، تختۂ سیاہ **blackcoffee** *n.* coffee taken without milk کالی کافی، بغیر دودھ کے کافی، قہوہ **black death** *n.* epidemic taking a heavy toll of life وبا، مری **black eye** *n.* eye with bruise round it owing to a blow آنکھ جس کے گرد نیل پڑ گیا ہو (U.S.) bad reputation کلنک کا ٹیکہ *give (someone) a black eye* (*a*) (کسی کی) آنکھ کے گرد نیل ڈالنا (*b*) (کسی کے) ماتھے پر کلنک کا ٹیکہ لگانا **blackguard** (*blag*-ĕ*d) *n.* scoundrel, person quite without honour بدمعاش، غنڈہ **blackhole** *n.* dark dungeon کال کوٹھڑی **black-lead** (blak-led) *n.* a black mineral (actually called *plumbago* (quite different from lead) used in making pencils سُرمہ **blackleg** *n.* swindler in horse races گھوڑ دوڑ کا دھوکے باز جواری person who offers to work for employer whose men are on strike ہڑتال کے دوران میں مالک کا ساتھ دینے والا مزدور، ہڑتال توڑ **blacklist** *v.t.* put a person's name on list of persons who are considered dangerous or wrongdoers سیاہ فہرست پر نام لانا *n.* such a list سیاہ فہرست *put (someone's) name on the blacklist* (کسی کا) نام سیاہ فہرست پر لانا **blackmail** *v.t.* try to make (someone) pay money by threatening to tell something against him افشائے راز کی دھمکی دے کر رشوت لینا *n.* such a threat بلیک میل **blackmailer** *n.* بلیک میل کرنے والا، بلیک میلر **black-mark** *n.* record of offence in **one's service-book** کالا نشان، کلنک کا ٹیکہ **black-**

market *n.* unlawful sale of goods or currencies (usu. at higher than controlled prices) چور بازار **blackmarket** (-ma*-) *v.t.* indulge in such sales چور بازاری کرنا **blackmarketeer** *n.* one who indulges in such sales چور بازار کا تاجر **blackmarketing** *n.* indulging in such sales (چور بازاری (کرنا **blackout** *n.* obscuring of lights for safety during an air raid بلیک آؤٹ ، روشنی گل **blacksmith** *n.* ironworker, esp. one who repairs tools and makes horseshoes لوہار **blacking** *n.* polish for blacking shoes بوٹ پالش *shoe-black*, one who cleans the shoes of passers-by بوٹ پالش کرنے والا **blackness** *n.* state or quality of being black سیاہی ، کالا پن ، سواد **blacken** *v.t.* make black کالا کرنا speak evil of بدگوئی کرنا *blacken (someone's) character* (کسی کو) بدنام کرنا

bladder (*blad-ĕ**) *n.* skin bag in the body in which waste liquid collects مثانہ rubber bag in a football پھکنا ، بلیڈر

blade (blayd) *n.* flat, narrow leaf (as of grass) (گھاس وغیرہ کی) پتی flattened cutting part of a knife, sword, etc (چاقو وغیرہ کا) پھل cutting part of a razor بلیڈ flat part of an oar or bat (چپّے یا چپو کی) تھاپی gay, dashing fellow بانکا ، چھیل چھبیلا **bladed** (-id) *adj.* having a blade پھلدار کرنے والا

blame (blaym) *v.t.* find fault with عیب جوئی کرنا ، الزام دینا ، قصور وار ٹھہرانا *I am not to blame, I am not to be blamed (for this)* (اس میں) میرا قصور نہیں ، میں بے قصور ہوں *n.* blaming, fault-finding عیب جوئی ، الزام تراشی responsibility for failure ناکامی کی ذمہ داری **blameless** *adj.* innocent بے قصور ، بے گناہ **blameworthy** (*blaym-wĕ*-dhi*) (of action, etc.) deserving blame قابل الزام ، برا ، نامناسب ▣ To **blame** is to find fault with someone for doing a wrong or neglecting a duty : to **censure**, to express an unfavourable opinion as to a moral wrong , to **condemn**, to pass an unfavourable judgment, often legally ; to **reprove**, to express blame but with kindly feeling ; to **rebuke** sharply

blanch (blahnch, blahnsh) *v.t.* & *i.* (cause to) become white or pale رنگ اڑنا یا اڑانا **blancmange** (bla-*mahnzh*) *n.* white jelly دودھیا گھاس کی فرنی ، دودھیا فرنی

bland *adj.* polite in manner خوش خلق **blandly** *adv.* خوش خلقی سے **blandness** *n.* خوش خلقی

blandishment (*bland*-ish-ment) *n.* (often *pl.*) gentle words or manner to make someone do something چکنی چپڑی باتیں ، پھسلانے کے لیے ناز نخرے

blank (blank) *adj.* (paper, etc.) with nothing written کورا ، سفید ، یا سادہ کاغذ (person's face) lacking interest or expression بے کیف puzzled حیران ، پریشان space left out in writing خالی جگہ *fill in (or up) the blanks* چھوٹے ہوئے یا چھوڑے ہوئے الفاظ ، خالی جگہیں پُر کرو *blanked, blanky*, space left blank in writing to suggest omission of indecent words عبارت میں فحش الفاظ کی بجائے نقطے *blank wall*, one without doors or windows بے در و دریچہ دیوار *blank verse*, verse without rhyme نظم معرّیٰ ، بے قافیہ نظم *blank cartridge*, having powder but without shot خالی کارتوس *his mind (or memory) is blank*, it has no impressions وہ تو بالکل کورا ہے *n.* blank space (in something printed or written) عبارت میں خالی جگہ *telegraph blank*, telegraph form with blank spaces for the message تار کا فارم *give a blank cheque to*, authorize one to do what one likes دوسرے کی پوری شرطیں مان لینا ، سادہ چیک دے دینا void خلا **blankly** *adv.* openly صاف صاف **blankness** خالی جگہ ، خلا

blanket (*blank*-et) *n.* thick, woollen sheet to wrap oneself in کمبل ، کملی ، کملی *adj.* taking cognizance of almost all cases عمومی ، ہمہ گیر ، محیط

blare (*blay-ĕ**) *n.* loud sound (of trumpets, etc.) (بگل وغیرہ کی) آواز *v.t.* produce such a sound (ترم یا بگل وغیرہ سے) آواز نکلنا یا نکالنا

blaspheme (blas-*feem*) *v.t.* & *i.* say something against God خدا کی شان میں گستاخی کرنا ، کفر بکنا speak of sacred things irreverently بے ادبی کرنا ، کفر بکنا ، بے حرمتی کرنا **blasphemer** (-*fem*-) *n.* کفر بکنے والا **blasphemous** (*blas*-fe-mus) *adj.* (مقدس چیزوں کے متعلق) گستاخانہ ، بے ادبانہ

blast (blahst) *n.* sudden rush of air زور کا جھونکا such strong rush of air owing to explosion دھماکے سے آنے والی ہوا sound made by a wind instrument (ترم وغیرہ کی) آواز *v.t.* bring to nothing or break up by explosion بھک سے اڑانا destroy تباہ و برباد کرنا ، خاک سیاہ کر ڈالنا blight (plants) پت روگ لگنا ، (پودوں کو) جھلس دینا bring into disrepute (someone's character) بدنام کرنا ، داغ لگانا *tree blasted by lightning* بجلی سے جلا ہوا ٹھنٹھ *blast it !*, (cursing formula) بھاڑ میں جائے ، آگ لگے (*blast off*), (see *Addenda*) **blast furnace** *n.* furnace for smelting iron ore by forcing a current of heated air into it کل کی بھٹی ، گلدار بھٹی

blatant (*blayt*-ant) *adj.* trying to obstruct and attract attention in a vulgar and shameless way بھونڈے پن سے دوسروں کے کام میں حارج ہونے والا ، اودھم مچانے والا

blaze (blayz) *n.* bright fire or light شعلہ *burst into a blaze* شعلہ سا بھڑک اٹھنا *put out a big blaze*, extinguish a burning house, etc. آگ کے شعلے بجھانا violent outburst into flames شعلہ ، لپٹ *v.t.* shine brightly or with warmth چمکنا burst out with strong feelings بھڑک اٹھنا ، جوش میں آنا *blazing with* rage غصے میں بھرا بیٹھا *blaze away at*, fire (guns) quickly گولیوں کی باڑھ مارنا *v.i.* mark a tree by chipping off its bark to show a path through a forest درختوں کو چھیل کر نشان بنانا *blaze a trail*, (a) mark a path in this way راہ بنانا (b) do something new کوئی نیا کام کرنا make known widely مشہور کرنا، شہادت دینا *blaze (something) abroad*, make (it) known far and wide کا ڈھنڈورا پیٹنا

blazer (*blay*-zĕ*) *n.* bright-coloured sports jacket (کھلاڑیوں کا) رنگین کوٹ

blazon (*blay*-zèn) *v.t.* make known exaggeratedly and widely بڑھا چڑھا کر مشہور کرنا *blazon (or blaze) the news abroad*, make it known everywhere مشہور کرنا

bleach (bleech) *v. t. & i.* make or become white رنگ اُڑنا یا اُڑانا **bleacher** *n.* one whose profession it is to bleach رنگ اُڑانے والا، سفید کرنے والا chemical used for this purpose رنگ اُڑانے والی دوا **bleachers** *n. pl.* uncovered plank seats at sports ground کھیل کے میدان میں کھلے بنچ

bleak (bleek) *adj.* cold (weather) سخت ٹھنڈا cheerless بے رنگ، بے کیف، بے لطف (موسم)، نہایت سرد و سخت unhopeful مایوس کن

blear (*blee*-ĕ*) *adj.* dim sighted چندھا hazy دھندلا *blear-eyed* (a) چندھا (b) کم عقل

bleat (bleet) *n.* cry of sheep, goat, or calf میں میں *v. t.* utter such cry ممیانا

bleed *v. t. & i.* (*bleed, bled, bled*) lose blood خون کا بہنا draw blood from خون لینا، فصد کھولنا *my* (etc.) *heart bleeds*, is in acute distress دل خون کے آنسو روتا ہے

blemish (*blem*-ish) *n.* mark marring the beauty or perfection of something or someone داغ، دھبہ *blemish on (someone's) character* کسی کے اخلاق پر دھبہ *v. t.* mar the beauty or perfection of کو داغ دار کرنا کی شکل بگاڑنا ▣ A **blemish** is whatever mars the surface; a **defect**, real or imagined shortage of something desirable; a **flaw**, fault in structure, often not seen; a **lack**, absence of something which should be there; an **imperfection**, something which prevents the object from being perfect; a **deformity**, permanent; a **blot** what covers; a **stain** what mixes impurity with purity; a **stigma** applied by society; a **brand**, permanent mark of infamy; a **speck**, small piece of matter attached to the surface; a **spot**, small mark made by a staining substance; a **taint**, a permanent stream of impurity, as in the blood; a **smirch**, impression left by something dirty.

blench *v. t.* (lit.) jump back or to one side quickly (*in fear*) سہم جانا، بِچکنا close the eyes quickly (*to facts*) آنکھیں موند لینا، حقائق سے تجاہل عارفانہ کرنا

blend *v. t. & i.* (of tea, tobacco, etc.) (cause to) mix together (tea, tobacco, etc.) so as to make the mixture pleasant ملانا، مرکب بنانا، ترکیب دینا (of colours) have no sharp contrasts رنگوں کا میل کھانا، یا امتزاج ہونا *n.* mixture made by blending مرکب، امتزاج

bless (bles) *v. t.* (*blessed or blest*) call down God's favour on کے حق میں دعا کرنا، کو دعا دینا make happy خوش رکھے *God bless you!* خدا تمہیں خوش رکھے (*bless with*), make one fortunate in having کی خوش نصیبی عطا کرنا *blessed with good health* اسے صحت کی خوش نصیبی حاصل ہے praise تعریف کرنا، حمد کرنا، حمد و ثنا کرنا *Bless the Lord* خدا کی حمد و ثنا کرنا (colloq.) (used for expressing surprise) *bless me! bless my soul! Well, I am blest!* خدا بچائے، خدا پناہ، توبہ **blessed** (*bles*-ed) *adj.* sacred مقدس، متبرک fortunate خوش نصیب bringing happiness مبارک **blest** *adj.* (form of *blessed* used in poetry) **blessing** *n.* the favour of God خدا کی رحمت grace (before or after a meal) کھانے سے پہلے (یا بعد) کی دعا *ask a blessing*, pray for something that brings happiness رحم و کرم کی دعا مانگنا، دعائے خیر کرنا *what a blessing!* how fortunate! کتنی خوش نصیبی ہے، بڑی خوش قسمتی

blight (blit) *n.* disease causing plants to wither پودوں کو ختم کرنے والا روگ، کیڑا، پت روگ hazy close atmosphere حبس، دورپالا anything which destroys تخریبی اثر *blight upon (someone's) hopes* کسی کی امیدوں پر اوس *v. t.* be a blight پر مرجھا دینا، تباہ کرنا *life blighted by constant miseries* مصائب کی تباہ کی ہوئی زندگی، پت روگ لگا **blighted** (-tid) *adj.* ruined (*by*) برباد **blighter** *n.* (slang) fool اُلو کا پٹھا

Blighty (*blit*-i) *n.* (army slang) England ولایت

blind (blind) *n.* cloth roll fixed on a roller and pulled down to cover a window چلمن، پردہ *adj.* unable to see اندھا، نابینا *blind flying*, flying in darkness or fog with the help of instruments only تاریکی یا دھند میں پرواز کرنا unable to judge well کسی کے عیب نہ دیکھ سکنے والا، بے عقل، بے بصیرت *blind to (someone's) faults* not controlled by reason or purpose اندھا دھند *in blind haste* اندھا دھند، تیزی سے having no opening بند *a blind wall*, one without windows or doors بے در و دریچہ دیوار impossible to see past جس کے پار نہ دیکھا جا سکے *a blind turning in a road* سڑک کا ایک تنگ موڑ *n.* roll of cloth pulled down to cover a window *v.t.* make blind اندھا کرنا **blindfold** *v. t.* cover a person's eyes (with a band of cloth, etc.) (آنکھ مچولی میں) آنکھ پر پٹی باندھنا *adj. & adv.* with the eyes so covered آنکھ بند کر کے thoughtless(ly) بے سوچے سمجھے **a blind**

blindly *adv.* اندھا دھند **blindness** *n.* اندھاپن، کم عقلی

blink (blink) *v. t.* & *i.* shut and open the eyes quickly پلک جھپکنا *blink the fact*, shut one's mind to it حقائق پر غور نہ کرنا (of lights) shine in an unsteady way جھلملانا

bliss (blis) *n.* perfect happiness سعادت، انتہائی خوشی **blissful** *adj.* مبارک، مسعود

blister (*blis*-tĕ*) *n.* small swelling under the skin filled with fluid چھالا، آبلہ (see *Addenda*) *v. t.* & *i.* cause or get, blisters on (the skin, etc.) چھالے پڑنا یا ڈالنا

blithe (blidh) *adj.* cheerful خوش باش، خوش خوش

blithering (*blidh*-ĕ-ring) *adj.* arrant (fool) پرلے درجے کا سخت senselessly talkative (person) بیہودہ گو، یاوہ گو، ہرزہ سرا، بکی، مغز چاٹ

blitz (blits) *n.* rapid and violent air attack اچانک سخت ہوائی حملہ، ہوائی یلغار

blitzed (blitsd) *adj.* destroyed by such air attacks اچانک سخت ہوائی حملے میں تباہ، ہوائی یلغار میں تباہ

blitzkrieg (*blits*-kreeg) full form of *blitz*) *n.* violent campaign to bring about a swift victory بجلی کا سا حملہ، اچانک سخت حملہ

blizzard (*bliz*-ĕ*d) *n.* severe snow-storm with violent wind برفانی طوفان

bloated (*bloh*-tid) *adj.* fat in an unhealthy way بہت ہی پھولا ہوا swollen ابھرا ہوا over grown حد سے بڑھا ہوا

bloater (*bloh*-tĕ*) *n.* salted and smoked herring ہیرنگ مچھلی کا اچار

bloc (blok) *n.* group (*of* persons, parties, States, etc.) with common objective بلاک، گروہ، ایکا، اتحاد *form a 'bloc'* ایکا کرنا

block (blok) *n.* large, solid piece (of stone, wood, etc.) بڑا ٹکڑا *a chip of the old block*, person who is like his father (in appearance or character) بیٹا باپ پر پوت *go to the block*, be beheaded (as a punishment) قتل کی سزا پانا group of large connected houses سلسلۂ عمارات division of seats (in a picture-house, etc.) (سینما وغیرہ میں) نشستوں کا ایک مستقل حصّہ piece of metal with designs engraved on it for printing چھپائی کا سانچہ، بلاک held-up traffic obstructing movement سڑک پر رکی ہوئی گاڑیاں *block and tackle*, pulley in a block of wood

blocks for printing the Holy Quran

for lifting چرخی، گھرنی *in block letters* (writing with) each letter separate and in capitals بڑے حروف (میں لکھا ہوا) *v.t.* obstruct movement by putting something in the way راستہ روکنا prevent supplies from reaching the enemy رسد روکنا **blockbuster** *n.* (see *Addenda*)

block and tackle

blockhead *n.* foolish, stupid person کاٹھ کا اُلّو، احمق **block-house**, small, timber fort لکڑی کا قلعہ، لکڑکوٹ

blockade (blo-*kayd*) *n.* the blocking up of a place by armies or warships, to stop supplies from getting in and the enemy from escaping ناکہ بندی *raise a blockade*, end or force to end it ناکہ بندی ختم کرنا یا کرانا *run the blockade*, break through it ناکہ بندی توڑنا **blockade-runner**, person or ship who breaks through it ناکہ توڑ (شخص یا جہاز) *v. t.* make a blockade of. ناکہ بندی کرنا

blond (blond) (*masc.*) **blonde** (blond) (*fem.*) *n.* & *adj.* with fair skin and light hair گورا، گوری، سنہرے بالوں والا یا والی

blood (blud) *n.* red life giving liquid in human or animal veins لہو، خون *in cold blood*, deliberately دانستہ، جان بوجھ کر، عمداً *make bad blood (between)*, cause ill feeling رنجش پیدا کرنا *(one's) own flesh and blood*, one's near relations اپنے عزیز و اقارب، اپنا گوشت پوست *flesh and blood*, (also) body (as distinct from soul); animal nature جسم (بمقابلہ روح)، حیوانیت *his blood was up*, he was angry وہ بڑے غصّے میں تھا *let blood* لہو لینا، فصد کھولنا *blue blood* عالی خاندان *run in the blood*, be common to the family خون میں ہونا **blood-and-thunder** *adj.* sensational سنسنی خیز **blood-bath** *n.* massacre قتل عام، خونیں غسل **blood-curdling** *adj.* exciting horror لرزہ خیز، رونگٹے کھڑے کرنے والا **blood-feud** *n.* feud arising out of murder قتل کا جھگڑا **blood-group** *n.* one of the four types into which human blood is classified for transfusion خون کی قسم **blood-guilty** *adj.* guilty of murder خون کا مجرم، خونی **bloodhound** *n.* large dog able to trace a person by smell خونی کتا، دوپتی شکاری کتا detective سراغ رساں **bloodless** *adj.* without killing بلا خونریزی، پُرامن *bloodless revolution*, پُرامن pale زرد، خون سے خالی *bloodless lips* پھیکے ہونٹ **bloodmobile** *n.* (see *Addenda*) **blood-money** *n.* conciliation money paid to the murdered person's relative by the murderer خون بہا، دیت money paid to someone for murdering one's enemy خون کرنے کی قیمت **blood-poisoning** *n* iseased condition of the blood caused by germs or poison خون کا زہریلا ہو جانا، خون بگڑنا

(یا زہرناکی) ہیبت **bloodshed** *n.* killing, putting to death قتل وغارت **bloodshot** *adj.* (of the whites of the eyes) red سرخ خون آلود (آنکھیں) **blood-sucker** *n* leech or other such insect خون چوسنے والا one who extorts money out of another خون چوسنے والا، خون آشام **bloodthirsty** *adj.* eager to kill خون کا پیاسا cruel ظالم **blood-vessel** *n.* vein or artery رگ **bloody** *adj.* covered with blood خون آلودہ with much bloodshed خون ریز، خونریزی والا *bloody fight* خون ریز جنگ (colloq.) damned کم بخت، خبیث *adv.* very بہت، بڑا

bloom *n.* flower پھول blossom کلی ، برگ گل time of perfection جوبن *in the bloom of youth* جوانی کے جوبن میں *v. i.* be in bloom پھولنا، پھلنا، بہار پر آنا

bloomer *n.* (slang) blunder سخت غلطی، فاش غلطی، بھونڈی حرکت

bloomers *n. pl.* women's loose garment covering each leg to the knees and hanging from the waist usually worn for games زنانہ جانگیہ، زنانہ نکر

blooming *adj* flourishing جوبن پر (slang) (rather polite word for) bloody کم بخت، منحوس، کوڑھی *her blooming face* اس کا منحوس چہرہ

blot *n.* stain caused by ink spilt on paper دھبہ، داغ stain that takes away from the beauty, or goodness of بدنما داغ، بدنما دھبہ *blot on character* دامن پر داغ، کلنک کا ٹیکہ *v. t.* (-*tt*-) stain دھبہ ڈالنا dry wet marks of ink (by pressing with special paper called the *blotting paper*) (سیاہی چوس سے) سیاہی خشک کرنا *blot out,* wipe away, hide نام ونشان مٹا ڈالنا، مٹا دینا **blotting-paper** *n.* paper to dry ink blots سیاہی چوس، جاذب **blotter** *n.* piece of blotting-paper (esp. one fastened to a piece of wood, etc.) سیاہی چوس، جاذب

a blotter

blotch (blotch) *n.* dirty ink mark سیاہی کا بڑا سا دھبہ any large, discoloured mark of irregular shape بڑا سا بدرنگ دھبہ *v.t.* mark with blotches بدرنگ دھبے ڈالنا

blotto (*blot*-oh) *adj.* (slang) befuddled نشے میں بہکا ہوا

blouse (blowz) *n.* outer garment from neck to waist (usu. with sleeves) بلاؤز، چھوٹی قمیص، صدری

a blouse

blow (bloh) *v.t.* & *i.* (*blow, blew, blown*) (of air) be moving ہوا کا چلنا *it was blowing hard,* there was a strong wind ہوا تند وتیز تھی send a current of air پھونکنا، پھونک مارنا *blow over,* (of crisis) pass off or be forgotten مصیبت ختم ہونا یا بھول جانا (of things) be carried by the current of air ہوا میں اُڑ جانا، ہوا کا کوئی چیز اڑا لے جانا *the hat blew off* ہیٹ اُڑ گیا *I was almost blown over by the wind* ہوا تو مجھے اُٹھا کے لے چلی تھی force air upon, through, or into ہوا بھرنا، پھونکیں مارنا *blow* (*on*) (*one's*) *tea,* cool it thus پھونکیں مار کر چائے ٹھنڈی کرنا *blow* (*one's*) *nose,* clear it ناک سنکنا (یا صاف کرنا) *blow up a tyre,* inflate it پہیے میں ہوا بھرنا *blow up,* (colloq.) reprove ڈانٹ ڈپٹ کرنا *v.t.* & *i.* explode بھٹنا، پھٹ جانا، بھک سے اُڑا دینا *blow hot and cold,* vascillate تذبذب میں پڑنا، متذبذب ہونا *blow out* (*one's*) *brains,* kill (oneself) by shooting in the head سر میں گولی مار کر خودکشی کر لینا *blow out,* (*a*) put out a flame by blowing پھونکوں سے بجھانا (*b*) (of wire) melt because electric current is too strong فیوز ہو جانا، بجلی کا تار جل جانا *the fuse blew out* فیوز اُڑ گیا (cause to) sound by forcing air through *the whistle blew* سیٹی بجی *blow the whistle* سیٹی بجانا *blow* (*one's*) *own trumpet* اپنی تعریف کرنا، اپنا ڈھول پیٹنا breathe hard and quickly زور زور سے سانس لینا give shape to (glass) by blowing شیشے کی چیزیں بنانا *n.* walk in the fresh air ہوا خوری، ہوا کھانا *go for a blow, have a blow,* go outdoors for fresh air ہوا خوری کے لیے نکلنا sudden hit given with the fist گھونسا، مُکا، ضرب *at one blow* ایک ہی وار میں *come to blows,* begin fighting ہاتھا پائی پر اُتر آنا *strike a blow for,* fight for (something) (کوئی چیز) لینے کے لیے لڑنا calamity آفت، بپتا، مصیبت **blower** *n.* apparatus for forcing air into or through something دھونکنی، پھکنی person who blows or pumps air پھونکیں مارنے والا **blown** *adj.* (esp.) breathless اکھڑی ہوئی سانس والا **blow-out** *n.* sudden, violent escape of air or steam particularly bursting of a tyre (بھاپ کا) زور سے نکلنا، (ٹائر کا) پھٹ جانا *blow off steam* زائد بھاپ نکالنا **blow-pipe** *n.* pipe for forcing air or gas into flame پھکنی، دھونکنی

blowzed (blouzd), **blowzy** (-zi) *adj.* fat red-faced (woman) with dishevelled hair بکھرے بالوں والی سرخ موٹی (عورت)

blubber (*blub-ĕ**) *v.t.* weep and cry چیخ چیخ کر رونا *n.* oil-yielding fat of sea-animals

bludgeon (*bluj*-ĕn) *n.* club with a heavy end ایک سرے پر موٹا ڈنڈا، *v.t.* hit repeatedly with a stick (لکڑی وغیرہ) بار بار مارنا

blue (bloo) *adj.* azure نیلا، نیلگوں آسمانی *blue ribbon* (*a*) sign of great distinction امتیازی نشان (*b*) the leading position کلیدی عہدہ dismal, depressed اداس، افسردہ، بجھا ہوا، پژمردہ *feel blue,* feel depressed پژمردہ ہونا *n.* azure colour آسمانی یا نیلا رنگ (sports) student who has won distinction in sports at the university ممتاز کھلاڑی (*the blue*), the spy جاسوس (*the blues*), low spirits *v.t.* make or dye blue نیلا رنگ کرنا **blueness** *n.* نیلاہٹ **bluish** *adj.* somewhat blue نیلا سا *blue-book* government report سرکاری رپورٹ، پارلیمنٹ کی رپورٹ *blue print* (*a*) white photographic print on blue paper, for building plans

عماراتی نقشہ (b) (see *Addenda*) *bluebell* wild hyacinth ; plant with blue, bell-shaped flowers ایک قسم کا پھول ، نجس پھول *blue-black*, colour of the unwashable ink ordinarily used ہلکی نیلی روشنائی، بلیو بلیک **blue ribbon** *adj.* (see *Addenda*) *royal blue*, (of ink, etc.) shining blue چمکدار نیلی رائل بلیو *with blue blood in (one's) veins*, of noble family عالی خاندان *true blue*, loyal سچا ، وفادار ، پکا *bolt from the blue, out of the blue*, great surprise ناگہانی آفت یا مصیبت ، اچانک حادثہ ، آسمان ٹوٹ پڑنا *once in a blue moon*, rarely شاذ و نادر ، کبھی کبھار *in a blue funk*, frightened سہما ہوا ، خوفزدہ *bluewater*, the open sea کھلا سمندر *blue stocking*, learned woman پڑھی لکھی عورت ، عالمہ ، فاضلہ

bluebells

bluff (bluf) *v.t.* & *i.* deceive (*by pretending to be* stronger, etc., than one really is) دھونس جمانا *n.* deception of this kind دھونس ، بڑی دھونس steep bank or cliff کھڑی چٹان *adj.* (of a cliff, coast) having a steep front سیدھا ساحل ، کھڑی چٹان (of a person, his behaviour, etc.) blunt but honest and kindly صاف گو ، جو منہ آئی کہہ دینے والا

blunder (*blun*-dě*) *n.* foolish and careless mistake سخت فاش غلطی ، حماقت *v.i.* make a blunder سخت غلطی کرنا ، حماقت کرنا move about uncertainly as if unable to see ٹامک ٹوئیے مارتے پھرنا ، اندھا دھند چلنا *blunder into a wall*

blunderbuss (*blun*-dě*-bus) *n.* old fashioned hand gun (پرانے نمونے کی) بندوق

blunt (blunt) *adj.* without a point or sharp edge کھنڈا ، کھٹھا ، کند (of person, manners) not showing polite consideration منہ پھٹ ، صاف گو **bluntly** *adv.* اکھڑ پن ، صاف گوئی **bluntness** *n.* دو ٹوک ، بدتمیزی سے دھار کا کند ہونا

blur (blě*) *v.t.* & *i.* (*-rr-*) (cause to) become unclear دھندلا ہونا یا کرنا (cause to) become confused in shape or appearance شکل بگڑنا یا بگاڑنا *n.* smear دھبہ dimness دھندلاہٹ

blurb (blě*b) *n.* publisher's praise of a book on its jacket or in some advertisement ناشر کی طرف سے (کتاب کے گردپوش پر یا اشتہار میں) کتاب کی تعریف ، ناشرستائی ، بلرب

blurt (blě*t) *v.t.* speak (something *out*) suddenly without thought یونہی بول اٹھنا ، بے سوچے سمجھے کہہ دینا

blush (blush) *v.i.* become red in the face from shame or confusion شرمانا ، چہرے پر سرخی دوڑ جانا *n.* red colour spreading over the face مارے شرم کے چہرے پر دوڑ جانے والی سرخی

bluster (*blus*-tě*) *v.i.* be rough or violent زبان درازی کرنا *n.* noise (of stormy weather) (طوفان کا) زور یا شور noisy, threatening talk and behaviour ہنگامہ ، ڈینگ بھرا کرتا ، سختی سے بولنا

blustery *adj.* زبان دراز ، تند

boa (*boh*-a), *boa constricter* (*-trik-*) *n.* large snake which kills by crushing اژدھا ، اژدر

boar (boh) *n.* (fem., *sow*) wild male pig جنگلی سؤر uncastrated male domestic pig بجار

board (boh*d) *n.* long, thin, flat piece of wood, etc., with squared edges تختہ *on board*, in (or into) a ship جہاز میں یا پر *go by the board*, (of plans, etc.) be given up ترک کیا جانا (dining) table (کھانے کی) میز (group of) persons controlling a business or government department بورڈ ، مجلس *Board of Directors* بورڈ کے ارکان ، مجلس ، ارکانِ مجلس منتظمین *District Board*, local self-government organization in a district ڈسٹرکٹ بورڈ ، ضلعیہ *Municipal Board*, such a body in a city, municipality بلدیہ *board schools*, schools run by a district board ضلعی مدرسے *above board*, without deception کھلم کھلا ، دیانتدارانہ *sweep the board*, win everything, be successful جیت جانا کامیاب ہونا supply of meals by the week or month (as at a boarding-house) طعام گاہ میں ماہانہ یا ہفتہ وار ادائیگی پر کھانا *board and lodging Rs. 50 a month* کھانا اور رہائش (یا طعام و قیام) پچاس روپے ماہانہ *free board*, مع کھانا ، کھانا مفت flat piece of wood or other material تختہ *blackboard*, تختہ سیاہ *notice board*, تختہ اطلاعات thick, stiff paper used for book covers گتہ ، دفتی *cardboard*, *strawboard*, such stiff board گتہ ، دفتی *v.t.* & *i.* cover with boards تختے یا تختوں سے بند کرنا get or furnish with meals کھانا کھانا یا پہنچانا go on board (a ship, train, etc.) جہاز پر جانا یا سفر کرنا **boarder** *n.* one who gets board at someone's house کسی کے یہاں پیسے دے کر کھانے والا child who lives at a boarding-school بورڈنگ اقامتی مدرسے کا طالب علم **boarding-house** *n.* hostel ہاؤس ، ہوسٹل ، اقامت گاہ ، اقامت خانہ **boarding-school** *n.* residential school اقامتی مدرسہ

boast (bohst) *n.* proud words used in praise of oneself ڈینگ ، بڑ ، شیخی something of which one is proud فخر ، باعث فخر ، مایۂ فخر *v.t.* & *i.* brag ڈینگ مارنا ، بڑ ہانکنا ، شیخی بگھارنا possess (something) with pride کے لیے مایۂ فخر ہونا **boaster** *n.* شیخی خورہ **boastful** *adj.* شیخی کی لینے والا

boat (boht) *n.* small water-vessel کشتی ، ناؤ ship جہاز *take boat*, جہاز پکڑنا ، جہاز یا کشتی میں سوار ہونا *be in the same boat*, face the same dangers ایک ہی کشتی میں سوار ہونا ، ایک ہی مصیبت میں پھنسے ہوئے ہونا *burn (one's) boats*, do something which makes change of plans impossible آخری فیصلہ کر دینا ، اٹل فیصلہ کرنا **boatman** *n.* one who owns or rows a small boat let out for hire کشتی والا ، کشتی بان ، مانجھی **boatswain** (*boh*-sun) *n.* senior seaman (under a skipper, captain) in charge of ship's rigging, etc. بڑا ملاح ، صدر ناشتا **boat-house** *n.* shed to keep a boat in کشتیوں کا اڈا ، ناؤ گھر **house-boat** *n.* boat serving as a house ہاؤس بوٹ ، گھر ناؤ **boatel** *n.* (see *Addenda*)

bob *n.* jerky movement up and down اُچھلنا ، اُوپر نیچے حرکت curtesy کورنش ، آداب a style of hair-cut خواتین کے تراشے ہوئے بال (slang) shilling انگریزی سکہ شلنگ *v.t.* & *i.* jerk up and down اُچھلنا یا اُچھلنا ، اُوپر نیچے حرکت کرنا یا دینا (of issue, question, etc.) crop up پیدا ہونا ، اُبھرنا ، پوچھا جانا cut (a lady's hair) short and allow it to hang loosely (عورتوں کے بال) چھوٹے کرنا

a girl with bobbed hair

bobbin (*bob*-in) *n.* small wooden roller round which thread is wound (دھاگے کی) نلکی

bobby (*bob*-i) *n.* (slang) policeman سپاہی ، پلسیا **bobby sock, bobby-soxer** *n.* (see *Addenda*)

bode (bohd) *n.*, *v. t.* & *i.* be a sign of the future events شگون ہونا ، پیش گوئی کرنا ۔ *it bodes (ill or) well for his future* یہ اس کے مستقبل کے متعلق اچھا شگون (نہیں) ہے ۔ *it bodes you no good* اس سے تمہیں تو کوئی فائدہ نہ ہوگا **bodeful** *adj.* ominous منحوس ، نجس

bodice (*bod*-is) *n.* woman's inner vest over-stays باڈی ، چولی close fitting upper part of a woman's dress باڈی ، چولی

bodily *adj.* (see under **body**)

body (*bod*-i) *n.* physical frame of man or animal بدن ، جسم this frame without the head and limbs دھڑ the main part of a structure کسی چیز کا اصل یا مرکزی حصہ group of persons انجمن ، جمعیت ، جماعت *the governing body*, the group of persons controlling the affairs of an institution مجلس عاملہ *in a body*, all together تمام ، بہ حیثیت مجموعی organization تنظیم ، جماعت piece of matter جرم *the heavenly bodies*, the sun, the moon and the stars, (ج - اجرام) اجرام فلکی (esp. in compounds) person شخص *anybody* کوئی ، کوئی شخص *somebody* کوئی ایک ، کوئی **everybody** ہر ایک ، ہر کوئی *nobody* کوئی بھی نہیں **bodily** (*bod*-i-li) *adj.* of or in the body جسمانی ، بدنی *adv.* physically جسمانی طور پر completely بالکل ، مکمل **bodyguard** *n.* person(s) guarding an important personality باڈی گارڈ ، محافظ دستہ

Boer (boh-ĕ*) *n.* South-African of Dutch descent بوئر

bog *n.* marsh دلدل *v. t.* cause to sink in a bog دلدل میں دھنسانا **bogged** (bogd) *adj.* sinking in a bog پھنسا ہوا *bogged down*, unable to go forward آگے نہ بڑھ سکنے والا ، پھنسا ہوا **boggy** *adj.* marshy دلدلی

bogey *n.* see under **bogie** see under **bogy**

boggle (*bog*-ĕl) *v. t.* demur (*at*) (سے) ہیں ہچ و پیش کرنا ، (پر) ٹھٹھکنا start with fright (*at*) (سے) جھجکنا

bogie, bogey (*boh*-gi) *n.* (pl., *bogies, bogeys*) long truck so constructed as to turn easily آسانی سے مڑ جانے والا چھکڑا under-carriage pivoted to the end of a (railway) engine انجن کا جدا ہو جانے والا پچھلا حصہ separate railway carriage ریل کا ڈبہ ، بوگی

bogus (*boh*-gus) *adj.* sham, not genuine جعلی

bogy, bogey (boh-gi) *n.* (pl., *bogies, bogeys*) bugbear ہوا ، کوکو ، بوگی *raise the bogy of something*, spread imaginary fear of something in case some action, etc., is taken کا ہوا کھڑا کرنا

Bohemian (boh-*hee*-mi-un) *adj.* living in indecent, immoral manner رند مشرب ، عیاش ، اوباش *n.* such a person رند مشرب ، عیاش یا اوباش آدمی **bohemianism** *n.* such a life رندی ، عیاشی

boil *v. t.* & *i.* (of fluids) reach, cause to reach, the temperature at which it changes into steam کھولنا ، کھولانا ، اُبلنا ، اُبالنا ، جوش کھانا یا دینا cook or cause to be cooked by boiling اُبلنا ، اُبالنا ، اُبال کر پکانا be excited or angry غصے یا جوش میں ہونا *boils down to*, reduces to قصہ یا خلاصہ یہ ہے کہ *keep the pot boiling*, earn a living گزران کرنا ، بمشکل روٹی کمانا *boiling-point*, temperature at which something begins to change into steam نقطۂ جوش *boiling-hot*, very hot سخت گرم *n.* hard, red and painful poisoned swelling under the skin پھوڑا ، پھنسی **boiler** *n.* part of an engine for boiling water (مشین وغیرہ کا) پانی گرم کرنے والا حصہ ، بائلر metal container for boiling حمام

a boiler

boisterous (*bois*-te-rus) *adj.* rough اکھڑ violent تند (of a person, or his behaviour) noisy and cheerful اودھم مچانے والا

bold (bohld) *adj.* without fear نڈر ، بے خوف ، من چلا دلیر ، جوانمرد without feelings of shame بے حیا ، ڈھیٹ well-marked واضح *bold outline* واضح خاکہ **boldly** *adv.* دلیری ، ڈھٹائی سے ، بے خوفی سے ، بے حیائی سے **boldness** *n.* دلیری ، ڈھٹائی

bolero (bo-*lee*-roh, or *-lay-*, or *bohl*-e-roh) ladies' loose jacket کرتی ، آستین والی زنانہ صدری

Bolshevik (*bol*-she-vik, bol-*shev*-ik) *n.* violently revolutionary Russian Communist of the early days of this party انتہا پسند ، اشتمالی ، بالشویک **bolshevism** *n.* such views اشتمالی انتہا پسندی ، انتہا پسند اشتمالیت **bolshevist** *adj.* of bolshevism انتہا پسند اشتمالی *n.* such a person in any country انتہا پسند اشتمالی

bolster (*bohl*-stĕ*) *n.* long pillow گاؤ تکیہ ، لمبا تکیہ *v. t.* (*bolster up*), give greatly needed but often underserved support to شہ دینا ، ناجائز سہارا دینا

bolt (bohlt) *n.* metal fastening for a door or window چٹخنی، کھٹکا joining metal pin with a thread at one end for a nut پیچ، بولٹ arrow from a crossbow بڑی کمان کا تیر *bolt from the blue*, اچانک صدمہ، ناگہانی مصیبت running away فرار *v. t. & i.* fasten or join with a bolt چٹخنی لگانا *bolt in* اندر سے بند کر دینا *bolt out*, shut (someone) out دروازے بند کرکے اندر نہ آنے دینا run away suddenly and unexpectedly (*from* a place) بھاگ نکلنا، فرار ہو جانا swallow food hurriedly چبائے بغیر کھانا، جلدی جلدی کھانا *make a bolt for*, run towards کسی کی طرف بھاگ کر جانا sift through coarse cloth چھاننا، کپڑچھان کرنا *bolt upright*, quite upright بالکل سیدھا سیدھا کھڑا

(above) bolt for a door ; (below) bolt without a nut

bomb (bom) *n.* large metal shell filled with explosives for bursting بم، بم کا گولہ (see *Addenda*) *v. t.* drop bombs on, attack with bombs بمباری کرنا، بم پھینکنا **bomber** (bom-ĕ*) *n.* aircraft for dropping bombs بمبار طیارہ soldier who throws bombs بمبار (سپاہی) **bombing** *n.* dropping bombs from an aircraft ; air attack بمباری **bombshell** *n.* shell fired by cannon توپ کا گولہ great surprise **bombproof** *adj.* strong enough to resist bomb explosions جس پر بم اثر نہ کرے *bombproof shelter* بموں کے اثر سے محفوظ پناہ گاہ، بم پناہ

bombard (bom-*bah**d) *v. t.* attack with gunfire (توپ سے) گولہ باری کرنا، گولہ اندازی کرنا pester (with questions or complaints) سوالوں کی بوچھار سے دق کرنا subject (atoms) to a stream of highspeed particles کا دھارا لگانا **bombardment** *n.* attack with bombshell گولہ باری

bombast (*bom*-bast) *n.* high-sounding language بڑی لفاظی، محض عبارت آرائی **bombastic** (bom-*bahs*-tik) *adj.* promising much but not likely to do much بڑا بول، خالی وعدے using fine high-sounding words (پر تصنّع) (عبارت آرائی) رنگین لفاظی (والا)

bona fide (*bohn*-a-*fī*-di) *adj.* real سچ مچ کا، واقعی، حقیقی، اصلی *bona fide engagement* سچ مچ کی منگنی *adv.* in good faith نیک نیتی سے، خلوص سے، بصدق دل **bona fides** (bohn-a-*fi*-deez) *n. pl.* good faith, sincerity, honest intention نیک نیتی، خلوص

bonanza (-nanz-) *n.* prosperity خوشحالی *adj.* prosperous خوشحال *bananza farm*, farm where latest agricultural implements are used جدید آلات سے کھیتی باڑی

bon-bon n. sugar made into fancy shapes for use as sweets کھانڈ کے کھلونے

bond *n.* binding written agreement having force in law تمسک، تحریر، اقرار نامہ *his word is as good as his bond* اس کا قول اتنا ہی پکا ہے جتنی اس کی تحریر printed paper from a government saying that money has been lent to it and will be paid back with interest سرکاری تمسک unity, or something that unites ایکا، اتحاد، بندھن، رشتہ *goods in bond*, goods lying in customs warehouse until duties are paid محکمے کی نگرانی میں ادائیگی محصول کے لیے پڑا ہوا مال (*pl.*) chains زنجیر *in bonds*, imprisoned, enslaved پابہ زنجیر، قید میں، قیدی، غلام *burst (one's) bonds*, get free زنجیریں توڑنا، آزاد ہو جانا **bondage** *n.* slavery غلامی **bonded** (-id) *adj.* (goods) in bond ادائیگی محصول کے لیے پڑا ہوا مال *bonded warehouse*, godown for such goods ادائیگی محصول والے مال کا گودام **bondman, bondsman, bond-servant, bondslave** *n.* serf زمین کے ساتھ بک جانے والا غلام کاشتکار

bone (bohn) *n.* hard material forming an animal skeleton or any of its separate parts ہڈی (*pl.*) dead body لاش، نعش *to the bone*, thoroughly بُری طرح، پوری طرح، اچھی طرح *frozen to the bone* بُری طرح ٹھٹھرا ہوا *feel in one's bones*, be quite sure پکا یقین ہونا *have a bone to pick with (someone)*, have something to argue or complain about کسی کے خلاف شکایت ہونا *v. t.* take the bones out of ہڈیاں الگ کرنا، ہڈیاں گوشت سے جدا کرنا *bone a chicken* پکے ہوئے چوزے کی ہڈیاں نکالنا **bony** (*boh*-ni) *adj.* thin دبلا، پتلا دبلا، (ہڈیوں کا) ڈھانچہ

bonfire (*bon*-fɪr) *n.* a fire made in the open air to burn garden rubbish کوڑا کرکٹ جلانے کے لیے آلاؤ large open-air fire to celebrate something جشن کا آلاؤ

bonhomie (*bon*-oh-mi) *n.* pleasantness of manner خوش مزاجی

bon-mot (*bohn*-moh) *n.* jest لطیفہ، چٹکلا

bonnet (*bon*-et) *n.* small, round, brimless hat tied under chin, worn by women and children بے چھجے کی ڈوری والی ٹوپی cover of motor-car engine موٹر کے انجن کا ڈھکنا

lady with a bonnet

bonny (occasionally spelt **bonnie**) (*bon*-i) *adj.* happy and healthy looking موٹا تازہ اور ہشاش بشاش *bonny baby* موٹا تازہ بچہ

bonus (*boh*-nus) *n.* (yearly) sum paid over and above what is due مزدوروں یا حصہ داروں کا سالانہ انعام

bon voyage (-ahj) *int.* a good journey to you ! خدا حافظ، خدا سفر مبارک کرے

bony *adj.* (see under **bone**)

boo, booh (boo) *n.* sound showing contempt or disapproval ہُو ہُو، اُو اُو *v.t.* (booed, boohed) hoot ہُو بنانا، تحقیر کی آوازیں نکالنا

boo-boo *v.t.* weep noisily رو چینیں مار مار کر رونا

boob *n.* (U.S.) simpleton بیوقوف، سادہ لوح، سادہ **booby** *n.* foolish person احمق، بُدھو، گاؤدی **booby trap** *n.* trick to catch an unwary person (esp. placing of something on a door in such a way that it falls over the booby as soon as he opens it) احمق سے مذاق (see *Addenda*) **booby prize** *n.* prize awarded to the worst competitor سب سے گھٹیا کھلاڑی کو انعام ، پھسڈی انعام

book (buk) *n.* collection of sheets of paper کاپی، بیاض ، بہی کھاتہ such a collection with reading matter کتاب division or part of a long poem or prose writing فصل، حصہ کتاب *bring (someone) to book*, require (him) to explain his conduct کسی سے مواخذہ کرنا ، جواب طلبی کرنا *in (someone's) good (black, bad) books*, having (not having) his favour and approval کسی کی نظر میں محبوب (یا معتوب) *v.t.* write down in a note-book بیاض میں لکھنا give or receive an order for seat at a place نشست محفوظ کرانا **bookbinder** (-bind-) *n.* one who binds books جلدساز **book-binding** *n.* جلدسازی **book-burning** *n.* (see *Addenda*) **bookcase, book-shelf** *n.* piece of furniture with shelves for books کتابوں کی الماری **book-end** *n.* small piece of metal used to keep books in position کتاب دار **bookie** (buk-i) *n.* slang for *book-maker* (which see) **booking-clerk** *n.* clerk who sells tickets ٹکٹ بابو **booking-office** *n.* office for the sale of tickets ٹکٹ گھر **bookish** *adj.* of books or studies کتابی too fond of books کتاب کا کیڑا **book-keeper** *n.* one who keeps business accounts کھاتہ نویس، سیاہہ نویس **book-keeping** *n.* the art of keeping business accounts کھاتہ نویسی سیاہہ نویسی **booklet** *n.* small book کتابچہ **book-maker** *n.* (esp.) one whose business is taking bets on horse-races گھوڑ دوڑ کا پیشہ ور شرط باز **bookmark** *n.* piece of paper, ribbon, etc., put in a book to mark the place at which to open it نشانی **bookmobile** *n.* (see *Addenda*) **bookseller** *n.* dealer in books کتب فروش *at a bookseller's* کتابوں کی دکان پر **bookstall** *n.* stall or booth for selling periodicals, books, etc. بک سٹال **bookstore** *n.* (U.S.) bookseller's shop کتابوں کی دکان **bookwork** *n.* theory (as opposed to *practice*) کتابی کام ، غیر عملی *It's mere bookwork* یہ سب غیر معمولی باتیں ہیں **bookworm** *n.* worm eating books کتابیں کھانے والا کیڑا ، کتابی کیڑا very studious person کرم کتابی ، کتابوں کا کیڑا

book-end

boom *v.t. & i.* (of big guns, thunder, etc.) produce deep hollow sound (بادل کا) گرجنا ، (توپوں کا) دنا دن کرنا grow suddenly prosperous یک دم امیر ہو جانا advertize wildly خوب اشتہار بازی کرنا *n.* sudden increase in trade activity تجارت کی اچانک گرم بازاری

boomerang (*boom*-e-rang) *n.* flat curved stick used in hunting by Australian aborigines which comes back to the thrower بوم رینگ argument, etc., that recoils on author الٹی پڑنے والی دلیل

boon *n.* blessing برکت favour عنایت gift عطیہ ، تحفہ *ask a boon of* کسی سے کوئی التجا کرنا *grant boon to* کسی کو اس کی منہ مانگی مراد دینا *boon companion* associate in revelry; one who drinks togethe with another ندیم ، ہم پیالہ ، ہم مشرب

boor (*boo*-è*) *n.* rough, ill-mannered person گنوار ، اجڈ ، غیر مہذب **boorish** *adj.* گنوار ، اجڈ ، غیر مہذبانہ **boorishness** *n.* گنوار پن

boost *v.t.* advance the interest of someone (by publicity or praise) (تعریف کر کے کسی کی) حمایت کرنا **booster** *n.* & (see *Addenda*)

boot *n.* big foot-covering rising above ankles ٹخنے سے اونچا جوتا، نل بوٹ *high-boots, riding boots* سواری کے بوٹ *pair of boots* بوٹ کا جوڑا profit نفع ، فائدہ *v.t.* kick with boots on بوٹوں سے مارنا *boot one away out of a place* کسی کو ٹھوکریں مار مار کر نکال دینا profit بھلا کرنا ، فائدہ پہنچانا *it boots little* اس سے کوئی خاص فائدہ نہیں *the boot is on the other leg*, the truth and responsibility is the other way round واقعہ اس کے بالکل برعکس ہے *with one's heart (or voice) in boots*, in fear خوفزدہ *get the boot*, be dismissed برخاست ہونا *give (someone) the boot*, fire (him) برخاست کرنا **boots** *n.* one who blacks the boots in a hotel ہوٹل میں بوٹ پالش کرنے والا اور پیغام پہنچانے والا **bootblack** *n.* one who polishes boots بوٹ پالش کرنے والا **bootjack** *n.* appliance for taking off boots بوٹ اتار **bootlace** *n.* cord for lacing up boots بوٹوں کا فیتہ **bootlegger** (*boot*-) *n.* (U.S.) one who brews (or sells) wine in a place where there is prohibition شراب بندی والی جگہ شراب بنانے (یا بیچنے) والا **bootless** *adj.* without boots on ننگے پاؤں unavailing لاحاصل *bootless errand* سعی لاحاصل **bootmaker** *n.* cobbler موچی ، کفش دوز **boot-tree** *n.* moulds for keeping boots in shape کالبد **bootee** *n.* infants' boots بچوں کا جوتا ، بچگانہ (جوتا)

high-boot

booth (boodh) *n.* stall made of boards, canvas, or other light materials عارضی دکان *telephone booth*, kiosk used as public call office for telephone فون گاہ ، فون خانہ (also *polling booth*) place used for voting (انتخاب کی) پرچیاں ڈالنے کی جگہ

a booth

booty (*boot*-i) *n.* things taken by robbers لوٹ کا مال ، لوٹ things captured from the enemy in war مال غنیمت

borax (*bohr*-ax) *n.* white antiseptic powder سہاگہ

boracic, boric *adj*. of borax سہاگے کا *boric acid*, borax سہاگہ

border (bo*-dĕ*) *n*. edge کنارا، حاشیہ boundary of a country سرحد *v.t.* & *i*. put a border on حاشیہ لگانا have a border حاشیہ والا ہونا (*border on*), be next to سے متّصل ہونا **bordering** *adj*. adjoining متّصل **borderland** *n*. land that forms a border سرحدی علاقہ something between کے بین بین *borderland between sleeping and waking* سوتے جاگتے کے بین بین کیفیت **border line** *n*. line of demarcation حدِ فاصل **borderline** *adj*. on the borderline; marginal کنارے کا، بین بین *a borderline case*, one which could go either way with the least possible disturbance بین بین معاملہ

bore (boh*) *v. t*. drill a deep hole in anything *bore for oil* تیل کا کنواں کھودنا make someone tired by dull talk مغز چاٹنا، بے لطف باتوں سے اُکتا دینا، بور کرنا *n*. hole made by boring برمے کا سوراخ hollow inside of a gun barrel بندوق کی نالی اندر سے its inside diameter بندوق کی نالی کا قطر someone or something that tires one by dull talk or work مغز چاٹ great tidal wave in estuaries خلیج میں اُوپر کو آنے والی لہر **boredom** (boh*-dum) *n*. state of being bored بوریت، اُکتاہٹ، بیزاری

bore (boh*) pa. t. of *bear* (which see)

Boreas (*boh*-re-as) *n*. (poet) the north wind بادِ شمال **boreal** (*boh*-re-al) *adj*. of Boreas بادِ شمال کا northern شمالی

born (bo*n) (pa. p. of *bear*) *v. t*. (used in the passive) (*be born*), come into the world by birth پیدا ہونا *adj*. by natural ability پیدائشی، فطری *a born poet*, پیدائشی شاعر

borne (boh*n, bo*n) pa. p. of *bear* (which see)

borough (*bu*-roh) *n*. English town or part of town, sending a member to the parliament (برطانیہ میں) شہری حلقۂ انتخاب *pocket borough, close borough, rotten borough*, borough with few votes but enjoying a representation in the parliament محدود اِنتخابی حلقہ

borrow (*bo*-roh) *v. t. & i*. get something or its use after promising to return it اُدھار لینا، عاریتہً لینا

Borstal (*boh**s-tal) *adj*. (used in the term :) *Borstal Jail*, jail for juvenile offenders (also called *Borstal Institute*) بچّوں کا جیل

bosh *int*. nonsense, foolish talk بیہودہ

bosom (*boo*-zum) *n*. human breast سینہ seat of emotion دل *bosom friend*, one who knows one's thoughts دلی دوست

boss (bos) *n*. (colloq.) master protuberance on centre of shield ڈھال کی میخ *v. t. & i*. give orders آقا بنا پھرنا *be boss of* آقا ہونا **bossy** *adj*. having protuberance اُبھرواں (slang) stylish smart چھبیلا، شاندار

botany (*bot*-a-ni) *n*. science of plant structure نباتات، علم نباتات **botanical** (bo-*tan*-i-kĕl) *adj*. نباتاتی *botanical gardens*, a garden with specimens of plants for study نباتاتی باغ **botanist** (bot-) *n*. expert in botany ماہرِ نباتیات، نباتیاتی ماہر

botch (boch) *v. t*. repair badly بھونڈے پن سے مرمت کرنا spoil by clumsy work بھونڈے پن سے کام کرنا *n*. piece of clumsily done work بھونڈا کام

both (bohth) *pron., adj., adv*., the one and the other, the two دونوں *both brothers, both of the brothers* دونوں بھائی *both A and B* الف اور ب دونوں *they both went* وہ دونوں گئے *have it both ways, both to have one's cake and eat it* چت بھی میری پٹ بھی میری

bother (*bodh*-ĕ*) *v. t. & i*. be or cause trouble to ناک میں دَم آنا یا کرنا take trouble زحمت اُٹھانا *n*. trouble زحمت، تکلیف **bothersome** *adj*. causing bother زحمت کا باعث

bottle (*bot*-el) *n*. narrow necked vessel (usu. of glass) for holding liquids بوتل its contents بوتل بھر *v.t*. put into a bottle بوتل میں ڈالنا یا بھرنا *bottle up*, restrain, or conceal ضبط سے چھپانا، ضبط کرنا، کام لینا **bottleneck** *n*. narrow part of a road lying between wider parts and hindering traffic تنگ راستہ، ناکہ that part of manufacturing process where production is slowed down ساخت میں رُکاوٹ ڈالنے والا مرحلہ، ساخت کا ناکہ، رُکاوٹ (see *Addenda*)

bottom (*bot*-um) *n*. lowest part تہ، پیندا، بنیاد، سرین essential part بنیاد، بنیادی حصّہ keel of a ship جہاز کا پیندا *v.t*. furnish with a bottom پیندا لگانا get at the root of تہ تک پہنچنا *adj*. last, lowest آخری، سب سے نیچا *go* (or *send*) *to the bottom*, sink ڈوبنا *at bottom*, fundamentally بنیادی طور پر *get to the bottom of, search to the bottom*, find out all about (کسی بات) کی تہ تک پہنچنا *bottom oneself* (or *argument*) *upon*, base one's argument upon اپنے استدلال کی بنیاد (کسی بات پر) رکھنا *be at the bottom of*, be the root cause of کی اصل (وجہ) ہونا *bottom of the class*, lowest in the class جماعت میں سب سے نالائق نکلنا *come out bottom*, be the lowest in the class جماعت میں سب سے نالائق نکلنا

bottomless *adj*. without bottom پیندے کے بغیر fathomless اتھاہ، بے پایاں *bottomless pit*, hell دوزخ، جہنم

boudoir (*bood*-wah*) *n*. woman's private sitting-room or dressing-room خواتین کا ذاتی کمرہ، حجلہ

bough (bou) *n*. one of the main branches of a tree coming out directly from its trunk جنگی شاخ، ٹہنا

bought (bot) *pa. t.* & *pa. p.* of **buy** (which see)
boulder (*bohl*-dĕ*) *n.* large rounded stone worn out by weather or water گھسا ہُوا یا گول مول پتھر، ضخرہ
boulevard (*bool*-vah*) *n.* wide street, often with trees on each side سایہ دار سڑک، ٹھنڈی سڑک
bounce (bouns) *v. t.* & *i.* (of a ball, etc.) rebound or cause to rebound اُچھلنا bustle one into doing something کسی سے سختی سے جلدی جلدی کوئی کام لینا move suddenly or noisily دراتا آنا، شور مچاتے ہوئے آنا *n.* bouncing اُچھال boast, swagger شیخی بگھارنا **bouncing** *adj.* strong and healthy طاقتور، تندرست، توانا، صحت مند
bound *n.* (usu. *pl.*) limit حد *in* (or *out of*) *bounds* within (or outside) a limited or permitted area مقررہ حدود میں (یا کے باہر) *v.t.* form the bounds of کی حد ہونا put bounds to کی حد بندی کرنا، یا حد مقرر کرنا jump (*up* or *forward*) کودنا، چھلانگ لگانا move or run in jumps چھلانگیں لگاتے ہوئے جانا *by leaps and bounds*, very quicly بڑی تیزی سے، بڑی جلدی سے *adj.* (*bound for*), about to start for روانگی کے لیے تیار on the way to عازم *homeward bound* عازمِ وطن (pa. p. of *bind*) (*bound to*) (*a*) obliged to پر مجبور (*b*) certain to do لازماً *bound up in*, much interested in سے بہت وابستہ، سے بڑی دلچسپی رکھنے والا *bound up with*, fond کا مشتاق **boundary** (*bound*-ĕ-ri) *n.* line marking the bounds of حد، سرحد hit reaching the cricket-field boundary باؤنڈری **bounden** *adj* used only in the phrase :) *one's bounden duty.* what one is compelled by law or by one's conscience to do کسی کا باقاعدہ فرض **boundless** *adj.* unbounded (happiness) بے حد unlimited بے کنارا، بے انتہا بڑا
bounteous, bountiful *adj.* (see under **bounty**)
bounty (*boan*-ti) *n.* generosity سخاوت، فیاضی something given to the poor خیرات payment offered by government as subsidy to farmers, traders, etc., for encouraging production تقاوی **bounteous** *adj.* سخی، فیاض، داتا **bountiful** *adj.* generous داتا، سخی in profusion بہ کثرت، بہ افراط
bouquet (boo-kay, or bu-*kay*) *n.* bunch of flowers for carrying in the hand. گلدستہ، گُل دستہ
bourgeois (*boo*zh*-wah) *n.* member of the urban middle class of society شہری متوسط طبقے کا فرد، بورژوا (pr., bĕ*-*jois*) a size of printing type برجائس *adj.* (pr., *boo*zh*-wah) of the habits and outlook of this class **bourgeoisie** (boo*zh-wa-*zee*) *n.* bourgeois class بورژوائی طبقہ، شہری متوسط طبقہ
bourn (boo*n) *n.* stream ندی، نالہ boundary حد **bourne** (boo*n) *n.* goal, destination منزل
bout *n.* period of work or exercise دور، باری، کام کا دَور attack (*of* an illness) دَورہ trial of strength مقابلہ، زور آزمائی *wrestling bout* کشتی کا مقابلہ
bow (boh) *n.* curved piece of wood with string, used for shooting arrows کمان *draw the long bow*, exaggerate مبالغہ آمیزی کرنا، بڑھا چڑھا کر بیان کرنا piece of wood with hair stretched from end to end, for playing the violin, etc. کمانچہ curved like a bow کمان کی طرح خمیدہ یا جُھکا ہُوا curtsy کورنش knot with a loop or loops سرک پھندا *bow tie*, neck-tie put in the fashion of bow بو *bow-legged*, with the legs curved outwards at the knees باہر کی طرف نکلی ہوئی ٹانگوں والا front or forward end (of a boat or ship) (جہاز یا کشتی کا) آگا یا ماتھا *v. t.* & *i.* curtsy آداب کہنا، کورنش بجا لانا bend جھکنا، جھکانا، خمیدہ کرنا *bowed with age* بڑھاپے کے باعث کبڑا ہو جانا، کبڑا ہونا give way *to*, yield *to* سرِ تسلیم خم کرنا

a bow and an arrow

a bow tie

bowel (*bou*-el) *n.* (usu. *pl.*) intestines آنتیں، امعاء motions پاخانہ، پاخانے innermost part بالکل اندرونی حصہ *in the bowels of the earth*, deep underground زمین کی انتہائی گہرائیوں میں
bower (*bou*-ĕ) *n.* arbour کُنج lady's room حجلہ
bowl (bohl) *n.* deep round hollow dish پیالہ، کاسہ، بادیہ something shaped like a bowl کوئی پیالہ نما چیز *bowl of a tobacco pipe* پائپ کا سر *v. t.* & *i.* (cricket) send a ball *to* the batsman (کرکٹ میں) گیند پھینکنا *bowl out*, defeat batsman by hitting the wicket with the ball (کرکٹ میں) گیند سے آؤٹ کرنا move quickly and smoothly (along a road) on wheels تیز سواری کرنا **bowler** (*boh*-lĕ*) one who bowls in cricket گیندباز، گیند پھینکنے والا، گیند والا hard black hat round at the top اونچا کالا ہیٹ

a bowl

box (boks) *n.* receptacle of (usu. rigid) material with a lid پیٹی، صندوق، بکس، بکسا *Christmas box*, present given at Christmas, esp. to a servant (ملازموں کو) بڑے دن کا تحفہ، کرسمس کا ڈبہ *Boxing-day*, the day after Xmas, December 26 کرسمس سے اگلا روز، ۲۶ دسمبر separate compartment, with seats for two or four persons in a theatre or picture-house سینما کا بکس separate, fenced off portion in a court of law for a witness to give his evidence عدالت کا کٹہرا *in the wrong box*, in sudden trouble ناگہانی مصیبت میں *box-office* (*a*) booking office in *a picture-house* سینما کا ٹکٹ گھر (*b*) earnings of a picture کسی فلم کی آمدنی *box-office hit*, a picture which brings in much money آمدنی کے لحاظ سے کامیاب فلم *from the box-office point of view*, from the viewpoint of a film's earnings آمدنی کے نقطۂ نگاہ سے blow with the open hand on the ear کان پر تھپّڑ *v.t.* & *i.* box someone's ear کان پر تھپّڑ لگانا *give (someone) a box (or boxes)* کسی کے کان پر تھپّڑ لگانا fight with the fists, gen. with thick gloves for sport مُکّے بازی یا گھونسے بازی کرنا **boxer** (*box-sĕ**) *n.* person who fights in this way گھونسے باز، مُکّے باز (*Boxer*) member of a party of Chinese nationalists (whose rising against foreign influence in 1900 is known as *Boxer's Revolution*) باکسر، مُکّے باز **boxing** *n.* fighting with fists covered with gloves; pugilism مُکّے بازی، گھونسے بازی *boxing match, boxing bout* گھونسے بازی کا مقابلہ *boxing gloves,* padded gloves used in boxing گھونسے بازی کے دستانے

boy (boi) *n.* male child or youth لڑکا، بچّہ male servant (any age) ملازم، خادم *boy scout*, member of the organization founded in 1908 to build the character of boys (cf. *girl guide*) بوائے سکاوٹ *boy friend*, a maiden's male friend دوشیزہ کا محبوب **boyhood** *n.* لڑکپن **boyish** *adj.* of, for, like, a boy طفلانہ **boyishly,** *adv.* طفلانہ پن سے **boyishness** *n.* طفلانہ پن **boys' town** *n.* (see *Addenda*)

boycott (*boi-kot*) *v.t.* refuse to have anything to do or trade with, etc. مقاطعہ کرنا، ترکِ مُوالات کرنا، بائیکاٹ مقاطعہ، بائیکاٹ، حُقّہ پانی بند کرنا *n.* social refusal of this kind مقاطعہ، بائیکاٹ، حُقّہ **boycotting** *n.* boycott حُقّہ پانی بند کرنا مقاطعہ، ترکِ مُوالات، بائیکاٹ

brace (brays) *n.* piece of wood or iron used to hold things together لوہے کے پتّر، لکڑی کی پتلی تختیاں (always singular) pair or couple (of dogs, birds) جوڑا، جوڑی *brace of pistols* پستولوں کی جوڑی *brace of partridges* تیتر کا جوڑا *brace and bit*, small drill; (its boring part is called a *bit* while the rest of it is called a *brace*) چھوٹا برما *v.t.* support حمایت کرنا give firmness or strength to مضبوط کرنا *brace (oneself) up* مستعد ہو جانا *bracing climate*, stimulatingly cold and dry صحت بخش آب و ہوا **bracelet** (*brays-let*) *n.* band or chain (of metal, etc.) worn on the arm or wrist as an ornament بازوبند، کڑا، کنگن، چوڑی، پہنچی **braces** (*brays-iz*) *n. pl.* (usu. *pair of braces*) straps passing over the shoulders, used to keep trousers up پتلون کے تسمے، گیلس *braces of a bed* اَدوائن

a pair of braces

bracken (*brak-en*) *n.* large fern ایک قسم کا بڑا فرن mass of such ferns فرنوں کا جھنڈ

bracket (*brak-et*) *n.* wood or metal support (for a shelf or lamp on a wall) دیوارگیری coupling marks ( ), [ ] { }, used in writing and printing قوسین، خطوط وحدانی *v.t.* put inside قوسین میں بند کرنا *the two were bracketed first* دونوں بیک وقت اوّل رکھے

equal مساوی قرار دینا

brackish (*brack-ish*) *adj.* (for water) saltish کھاری، نمکین

brag *v.t.* & *i.* (-gg-) boast شیخی بگھارنا **braggadocio** (-doh-shi-oh) *n.* act of boasting شیخی، شیخی بگھارنا (old use) one who boasts شیخی خورہ **braggart** *n.* one who boasts شیخی خورہ

braid (brayd) *n.* band made by twisting together two or more strands of threads or hairs گندھے ہوئے (بال)، بٹا ہوا (ڈورا) such bands used for binding edges of cloth or for decoration ڈوری *v.t.* make into braids (بال) گوندھنا، ڈورے بٹنا put braid on ڈوری لگانا، ڈورے بٹنا

braille (brayl) *n.* system of printing for the blind by perforating the page in order to enable them to read by touch اندھوں کا رسم الخط، کور خط، بریل

brain (brayn) *n.* (often *pl.*) mass of soft grey matter in the head دماغ centre of thought ذہن *have a good brain* اچھا ذہن ہونا *use (one's) brains* ذہانت سے کام لینا *have (something) on the brain*, be thinking about (it) all the time (کسی کا خیال) دماغ پر مسلّط ہونا *v.t.* kill by a hard blow on the head سر پر مہلک ضرب لگانا **brain-fag** *n.* mental exhaustion ذہنی تھکان **brainless** *adj.* stupid احمق **brainsick** *adj.* (lit) mad پاگل **brain-storm** *n.* temporary madness marked by violence وقتی پاگل پن **Brains Trust** *n.* group of persons broadcasting impromptu answers to listeners' questions سیانوں کی ٹولی، ذہین لوگ **Brain Trust** *n.* (U.S.) experts' committee advising the government ماہر مشیروں کا گروہ **brainwashing** *n.* (see *Addenda*) **brain-wave** *n.* (colloq.) bright idea striking someone suddenly اچانک خیال، خوب سوجھنے والی بات، سوجھی *have a brain wave* خوب سوجھنا **brainy** *adj.* clever ذہین، ذکی، ہوشیار

braise (brayz) *v.t.* cook (meat and vegetables) slowly in a covered pan دم پخت کرنا

brake (brayk) *n.* apparatus for pressing against a wheel to reduce the speed of a vehicle بریک، روک *v.i.* stop, by using the brake بریک لگانا، روک لگانا *put brakes on, apply brakes to, brake* بریک لگانا، روک لگانا

bramble (*bram-bĕl*) *n.* thorn-covered shrub جھاڑ، جھاڑبیری، خاردار جھاڑی

bran *n.* separated husk بُور، چوکر، بھوسی

branch (branch) *n.* arm-like part of a tree growing out of trunk or bough ٹہنی، شاخ anything regarded as an extension of, and managed from the central part شاخ *branch office* ماتحت دفتر، شاخ *branch road* ذیلی سڑک *local branch office* مقامی شاخ کا دفتر *branch of knowledge* علم کی شاخ *v.i.* send out, or divide into branches شاخ در شاخ کرنا *branch out*, become active in a new direction نئے کام کی طرف مائل ہونا *root and branch*, thoroughly, radically نکیسر **branched** *adj.* شاخ دار **branchless** *adj.* بے شاخ

brand piece of burning wood جلتی ہوئی لکڑی red-hot iron used for marking (cattle, etc.) داغنے کا لوہا mark or design made in this way داغ trade mark چھاپ named variety of goods چھاپ، مارکہ، قسم *the best brand of cigarrettes* بہترین قسم کے سگریٹ *v.t.* mark with a brand داغنا make a lasting mark on پکا نشان لگانا، مرتسم کرنا *be branded on one's memory* ذہن پر مرتسم ہونا stigmatize داغ لگانا، کلنک کا ٹیکہ لگانا، داغی کرنا *be branded coward* بزدلی کا داغ لگنا **brand-new** *adj.* conspicuously new بالکل نیا، واضح طور پر

brandish (*brand*-ish) *v.t.* wave about (sword, etc.) لہرانا، گھمانا

brandy (*bran*-di) *n.* strong liquor made from wine انگور کی ایک شراب، برانڈی

brass (brass) *n.* bright yellow metal made by mixing copper and zinc پیتل things made of brass پیتل کی چیزیں *the brass*, brass musical instruments بینڈ باجے (colloq.) impudence گستاخی، ڈھٹائی (see *Addenda*) **brass tacks** *n.* (slang) actual details of a business کام کی بات *get down to brass tacks* کام کی بات پر آنا **brassy** *adj.* of brass پیتل کا impudent ڈھیٹ، گستاخ simulating gold جھوٹا سونا، نقلی سونا pretentious جھوٹا، بناوٹی (also see **brazen**)

brassiere (*bras*-yay*) *n.* stays انگیا، محرم

brat *n.* (contemptuous word for) child چھوکرا

bravado (bra-*vah*-do) *n.* (pl. -*dos*, or -*does*) display of (often foolish) boldness احمقانہ جرأت، تہوّر

brave (brayv) *adj.* daring بہادر، دلیر، اولوالعزم (arch.) finely dressed, showy خوش پوش *v.t.* meet boldly; defy مقابلے پر اتر آنا، ڈٹ کر مقابلہ کرنا *brave it out*, carry oneself defiantly under suspicion بدگمانی کا بہادری سے مقابلہ کرنا **bravely** *adv.* دلیرانہ، بہادری سے **bravery** *n.* بہادری، دلیری، جرأت **S** **brave, courageous, daring, valiant, bold, dauntless, adventurous, venturesome, chivalrous, gallant.**

bravo (*brah*-vo) *int.* well done شاباش، مرحبا

brawl *n.* noisy quarrel جھگڑا، دنگا *v.t.* quarrel noisily جھگڑا کرنا، دنگا کرنا **brawler** *n.* one who quarrels noisily جھگڑالو، دنگئی

brawn *n.* strength طاقت mucscle پٹھا **brawny** *adj.* having strong muscles کسرتی، مضبوط پٹھوں والا

bray *n.* cry of an ass گدھے کا رینگنا sound of a trumpet ترئی کی آواز *v.i.* (of an ass) cry گدھے کا رینگنا

brazen (*brayz*-en) *adj.* made of brass پیتل کا like brass پیتل کا سا impudent ڈھیٹ، گستاخ *v.t.* (*brazen it out*), face it with impudence ڈھٹائی کا مظاہرہ کرنا، کسی معاملے میں ڈھٹائی سے جیت جانا **brazen-faced** *adj.* shameless ڈھیٹ

brazier (*bray*·zhĕ*) *n.* maker of brass wares کسیرا، ٹھٹھیرا pan on legs, for holding burning coals انگیٹھی، انگار دان

breach (breech) *n.* act of breaking (a law, duty, promise, etc.) خلاف ورزی *breach of the peace*, unlawful fighting in a public place نقضِ امن، امن شکنی opening made in an embankment or defensive wall رخنہ، شگاف *stand in (or throw oneself into) the breach*, be ready and eager to defend, give support, etc. جان جوکھوں میں ڈالنا *v.t.* make a breach

bread (bred) *n.* food made by flour kneaded into dough and baked as loaves in an oven ڈبل روٹی any food کھانا، روٹی، دال روٹی livelihood روزی *has eaten my bread*, has been my guest میرا مہمان رہا ہے *take the bread out of (one's) mouth*, take away (one's) living کسی کی روزی چھیننا *know or which side (one's) bread is buttered*, know (one's) own interest اپنا مفاد خوب سمجھنا *quarrel with one's bread and butter*, quarrel with the person who supplies one's living اپنی روزی پر لات مارنا *daily bread* روزی *make one's bread* روزی کمانا **bread line** *n.* (U.S.) queue of people waiting for food given as relief or charity لنگر پر لگی ہوئی قطار **bread-winner** *n.* one who earns a living for the family جس کے سر پر گھر بھر کا بار ہو، سارے خاندان کے پیٹ کمانے والا

breadth (bredth) *n.* distance from side to side چوڑائی، عرض *in breadth*, broad چوڑا *to a hair's breadth*, exactly بالکل، ٹھیک ٹھیک، عین مین *breadth of mind*, quality of being liberal-minded آزاد خیالی، وسیع المشربی *broad-minded*, liberal آزاد خیال، وسیع المشرب (see also **broad** *adj.*)

break (brayk) *v.t.* & *i.* (*break*, *broke*, *broken*) smash توڑنا be smashed ٹوٹنا weaken the force of شدت کم ہونا یا کرنا، زور ٹوٹنا یا توڑنا interrupt مداخلت کرنا go beyond سے بڑھنا، سے بازی لے جانا begin to be شروع ہونا *break away from*, become separate from, escape from سے الگ ہونا *break down*, (*a*) (of machine, etc.) fail to work, stop ناکارہ ثابت ہونا، ٹوٹ جانا (*b*) (of one's health) become poor صحت گرنا (*c*) be overcome by emotion جذبات سے مغلوب ہونا *break-down*, (*a*) illness due to overwork صحت کا گرنا، یا جواب دینا (*b*) stoppage of engine مشین کا، ٹوٹ جانا (*c*) collapse *break something down*, use force to get it down بہ زور یا بہ جبر کام لینا **break in** (or **into**), get in or into by force بہ زور داخل ہونا ، زبردستی گھس آنا *break in on*, (*a*) interrupt دخل دینا، دخل در معقولات کرنا (*b*) **burst** suddenly into کہیں دندانہ چلے آنا *break a horse*, teach it discipline گھوڑے کو سدھانا *break* (*something*) *off* (*a*) separate الگ کرنا (*b*) end توڑنا *break off an engagement* منگنی توڑنا *break into a house* کسی گھر میں نقب لگانا *break-out* (*a*) (of fire, war, disease) begin suddenly (آگ وغیرہ کا) یکایک لگ جانا ، یا شروع ہونا یا پھیلنا (*b*) (of prisoner) escape (قیدی کا) فرار ہو جانا (*c*) release (*flag*) when run up جھنڈا لہرانا (یا کھولنا) *break up* (*a*) destroy or be destroyed تباہ ہونا یا کرنا (*b*) (of meeting, etc.) end (جلسے وغیرہ کا) ختم ہونا ، اختتام پذیر ہونا (*c*) (of a person) lose strength or health صحت کا گرنا *break a record*, do better than it ریکارڈ توڑنا ، مات کرنا *break the back of*, finish the greater or more difficult part of (a piece of work, etc.) کمر توڑ دینا *break the ice*, overcome reserve in getting conversation started گفتگو کا آغاز کرنا ، مہرِ سکوت توڑنا *break the silence*, begin talk گفتگو کا آغاز کرنا *the clouds broke* بادل پھٹ گئے *break* (*one's*) *journey*, stop on the way for a while سفر توڑنا ، راستے میں رکنا *the tree broke his fall* درخت میں اٹکنے کی وجہ سے وہ گرتے ہوئے مرنے سے بچ گیا۔ *break the news*, be the first to give news (esp. of unwelcome event) (بری) خبر پہنچانا *breaking of voice*, to change because of strong feeling or when approaching manhood آواز میں مردانہ پن پیدا ہونا *break ground*, bring fallow land under plough زیر کاشت لانا *n*. act of breaking ٹوٹنا ، توڑنا place of breaking ٹوٹنے یا توڑنے کا مقام *at the break of day* پو پھٹے *day-break* تڑکا، طلوع ، فجر ، سویرا space between (in place or time) وقفہ ، فرق *break in the conversation* گفتگو میں وقفہ *without a break*, continuously مسلسل (colloq.) opportunity موقع *give* (*someone*) *a break* کسی کو موقع دینا *a bad break*, (colloq.) ill-timed, awkward and unfortunate remark or action غلط بات (یا غلط حرکت)

breakage (brayk-ij) *n*. breaking ٹوٹنا damage by breaking ٹوٹنے سے نقصان ، ٹوٹ پھوٹ compensation for things broken ٹوٹ پھوٹ کا معاوضہ ، ٹوٹ پھوٹ

breakable *adj*. that which may break ٹوٹ جانے والا

breakables *n. pl*. breakable things ٹوٹنے والا مال

breaker (*bray*-ke*) *n*. large wave ready to fall (on the beach) ساحل کی طرف بڑھنے والی بڑی لہر

breakfast (*brek*-fast) *n*. first meal of the day ناشتہ *v.t*. eat breakfast ناشتہ کرنا

breakneck *adj*. (speed) dangerously fast (رفتار) خطرناک

breakwater *n*. embankment for breaking force of waves (سمندر میں) بند، پشتہ

a breakwater

breast (brest) *n*. (usu. *pl*.) woman's milk-producing parts چھاتیاں، پستان *child at the breast*, suckling child شیر خوار بچہ upper front part of the body سینہ ، چھاتی emotions جذبات seat of emotions سینہ، دل *v.t*. struggle with waves لہروں کا مقابلہ کرنا ، سینہ سپر ہونا ascend with difficulty جدوجہد سے چڑھنا *make a clean breast of*, confess اقبال کرنا ، تسلیم کرنا **breast-bone** *n*. bone connecting the ribs at the front **breast-high** *adj*. up to the breast سینے سینے ، چھاتی تک (اونچا) **breast-pin** *n*. ornamental pin worn on tie بروچ **breast-plate** piece of armour for breast چار آئینہ **breast-wall** *n*. wall confining an earth embankment پشتہ **breastwork** *n*. low wall of earth or sandbags built breast-high as a defence حفاظتی دیوار

a breast-work

breath (breth) *n*. air drawn into and forced out of the lungs سانس a single act of breathing سانس *catch one's breath*, stop taking in breath for a moment (from excitement, etc.) سانس روکنا، دم سادھنا *under one's breath*, in a whisper سرگوشی کے انداز میں *lose one's breath*, have difficulty in taking in breath (*e.g.*, when running) سانس پھول جانا *out of breath*, needing to take in breath more quickly than usual سانس پھولی ہوئی *waste* (*one's*) *breath*, talk without result یونہی بڑبڑتے جانا ، لاحاصل گفتگو کرنا **breathless** *adj*. out of breath سانس پھولی ہوئی keeping one's breath back (from excitement, etc.) ہانپتے ہوئے

breathe (breedh) *v.t.* & *i*. draw air into the lungs and send it out سانس لینا say in a whisper سرگوشی کرنا *he did not breathe a word about it*, he kept it secret اس بارے میں اس نے ایک لفظ بھی نہیں کہا

bred pa. t. & pa. p. of **breed** (which see)

breech *n*. back part of the barrel of a gun, etc., where the cartridge or shell is put (بندوق وغیرہ کی) نال کا گولی والا حصہ

breeches (*bri*-chiz) *n. pl*. knickerbocker *riding-breeches*, breeches for wearing on horseback چوڑی برجس *knee-breeches*, tight breeches formerly worn at court درباری برجس *she wears the breeches*, rules her husband شوہر پر حکم چلاتی ہے

breed *v. t.* & *i*. (*breed, bred, bred*) ❶ reproduce پیدا کرنا keep (animals, etc.) for the purpose of having young نسل کشی کے لیے (جانور) رکھنا (جانوروں کی) نسل کشی کرنا ، (جانور) پالنا *breed horses* گھوڑے پالنا *horse-breeder* گھوڑے پال، گھوڑ پال nourish, train, rear, educate پالنا، شائستہ انسان ، مہذب شخص *wellbred person* پوسنا، تربیت کرنا be the cause of پیدا کرنا ، باعث بننا ، وجود میں لانا *poverty breeds crime* افلاس جرائم کا باعث بنتا ہے *n*. kind or variety (of animal, etc.) (جانور) کی نسل group (of animals, etc.) with the same qualities قسم، نسل

breeder *n.* one who breeds animals جانوروں کی نسل کشی کرنے والا **breeding** *n.* (esp.) behaviour شائستہ، مہذب *of good breeding* رَوِیّہ، طَور، طریقہ، تہذیب، شائستگی
breeze (breez) *n.* gentle wind ہلکی ہَوا slight quarrel (*over* something) (کسی بات پر) ہلکا سا جھگڑا small cinder mixed with cement, etc., to make breeze blocks راکھ اور باریک کوئلہ، راکھ **breeze-block** *n.* light-weight concrete blocks for use as large bricks سمینٹ کی اینٹ، خاکستری اینٹ **breezy** *adj.* windy ہَوادار gay, cheerful irresponsible زندہ دل، رنگین مزاج
Bren (bren) *n.* a kind of light machine-gun برین گن، بُرین **Bren-carrier** tank with Brens برین بردار
brethren (*bredh*-ren) *n. pl.* (old use) brothers بھائی بند، برادر، برادری (کے افراد) (esp.) members of a society, etc. ہم پیشہ یا ہم مشرب افراد
breviary (breev-i-ĕ-ri) *n.* Catholic prayer-book کیتھولک اوراد و وظائف کا مجموعہ
brevity (*brev*-i-ti) *n.* briefness (of expression of life) اختصار، چھوٹاپن (see also **brief**)
brew *v.t.* & *i.* prepare (drinks such as tea, beer) by soaking or boiling in water, etc. (شراب) کشید کرنا، بوزہ کشی کرنا، چائے بنانا (of storm) be forming (of plot, etc.) mature سازش وغیرہ کا اندر اندر پکڑنا یا پختہ ہونا set working (for evil purpose) فتنہ برپا کرنا *n.* result of brewing گھان liquid made by brewing مسالے دار شراب **brewer** *n.* maker of beer بئیر بنانے والا، بُوزہ کش **brewery** *n.* place where beer is brewed بئیر کا کارخانہ، بُوزہ خانہ
briar, brier (brī-ĕ*) *n.* (usu. *brier*), wild rose bush used for making tobacco pipes جنگلی گلاب (کی جھاڑی) (*briar*), pipe made of this wood جنگلی گلاب کا پائپ
bribe (brīb) *v.t.* give undue reward for anything against justice رشوت دینا یا کھلانا *n.* money given or offered in this way رشوت، گھُوس **bribery** *n.* giving or taking of bribe رشوت
bric-a-brac (*brik*-a-brak) odds and ends valued as antiquities نوادر، متفرق نوادر
brick (brik) *n.* burnt (rectangular) mass of clay اینٹ *unburnt brick* کچی اینٹ *drop a brick,* (slang) be indiscreet حماقت کرنا، احمقانہ اقدام کرنا *lay bricks,* set bricks with mortar to build a wall, etc. اینٹیں چننا *v.t.* wall (*in*) or block (*up*) with bricks اینٹیں چُننا، چُنائی کرنا **brick-bat** *n.* piece of brick اینٹ کا ٹکڑا، روڑہ، اینٹ *v.t.* to throw brickbats at پتھراؤ کرنا، خشت باری کرنا
brick-layer, one who lays bricks راج، معمار
brickwork *n.* part of a structure made of bricks
bridal *adj.* see under **bride**
bride (brīd) *n.* woman on her wedding day, or a newly-married woman دُلہن، عَروس، بنی **bride-cake** *n.* (also *bridecake*), wedding cake شادی کا کیک، عُروسی کیک **bridegroom** *n.* (also *groom*) man on his wedding day نَوشہ، بَنا، دُولہا **bridesmaid** *n.* girl or young unmarried woman attending a bride دُلہن کی سہیلی **bridal** (*brīd*-ĕl) *adj.* of a bridal or wedding عُروسی، شادی کا
bridge (brij) *n.* structure carrying a road, etc., over a river or valley پُل captain's platform on ship (جہاز کا) دیدبان upper, bony part (of the nose) (ناک کا) بانسہ whist-like card game for four players تاش کا ایک کھیل، برج *v.t.* build a bridge over پُل باندھنا get over a difficulty مشکل پر قابو پانا **baidgehead** *n.* post held on far side of frontier-river giving a person access to enemy territory سرحدی دریا کے پار دشمن کے علاقے میں بڑھا ہوا مورچہ
bridle (brī-dĕl) *n.* set of leather straps with metal bit for the mouth, for controlling a horse لگام مع دَہانہ *v.t.* & *i.* put a bridle on a (horse) گھوڑے کو لگام دینا throw back the head in anger ناک بھوں چڑھانا control (passions, etc.) جذبات کو قابو میں لانا

a bridle

Note : Bridle means لگام while **bridal** means عروسی
brief (breef) *adj.* short مختصر، مجمل lasting for only a short time چھوٹا، تھوڑی دیر کا *in brief,* in a few words قصہ مختصر، قصہ کوتاہ *be brief,* speak shortly مختصر لفظوں میں کہو *n.* summary of a case in court prepared for an advocate وکیل کے لیے مقدمے کی مسل *briefless lawyer* بے مقدمہ وکیل، بےکار وکیل *hold a brief for,* (a) be retained as a counsel for (کسی کا) وکیل ہونا (b) support the cause of کی وکالت یا حمایت کرنا instructions given to airman for military operations ہوا باز کو فوجی ہدایات *v.t.* (*brief, briefed, briefed*) (see *Addenda*) engage and instruct (lawyer) (وکیل) کرنا give instructions to airman about military operation مہم سے پہلے ہوا باز کو فوجی ہدایات دینا **briefly** *adj.* مختصراً **brief-bag, brief-case** *n.* large leather purse for holding papers, etc.
brier *n.* more usual spelling of **briar**
brig *n.* ship with two masts and square sails دو مستولی کشتی
brigade (bri-*gayd*) *n.* army unit of two to four battalions بریگیڈ، برگیڈ organized and uniformed body of persons with special duties باوردی تنظیم *the fire brigade,* fire-fighting squad فائر بریگیڈ، آتش کش دستہ **Brigadier** (brig-a-*dee*-ĕ*) *n.* officer commanding an army brigade بریگیڈیئر **Brigadier General,** Brigadier in the U. S. army امریکی بریگیڈیر
brigand (*brig*-and) *n.* robber, esp. one of a band attacking traveller in forests رہزن، قزاق، بٹ مار

bright (brit) *adj.* shining درخشندہ، درخشاں، تابندہ، تابناک *bright colour* شوخ رنگ *have a bright future* کا مستقبل تابناک ہونا cheerful ہشاش بشاش clever ہوشیار **brighten** (*brī*-tĕn) *v. t. & i.* become (more) bright روشن (تر) کرنا lend cheerfulness or gaiety to کو بارونق بنانا، میں جان ڈال دینا **brightly** *adv.* چمک دمک سے، آب و تاب سے **brightness** *n.* چمک دمک، آب و تاب

Bright's disease *n.* a well-known kidney disease برائٹس (S) **Bright, brilliant, shining, glaring, gleaming, glowing, glittering, glistening, flaring, flickering, effulgent, dazzling, sparkling, luminous, lustrous, illuminated, splendid, resplendent.**

brilliant (*bril*-i-ant) *adj.* very bright چمکیلا، درخشاں، تابندہ clever ذہین، فطین، طبّاع splendid شاندار، ممتاز **brilliance, brilliancy** *n.* آب و تاب، طبّاعی، ذہانت

brilliantine (-teen) *n.* a hair-cream بالوں میں لگانے کی کریم

brim *n.* edge (of a cup, bowl, etc.) کنارا، لب *full to the brim* لبالب (بھرا ہوا) out-turned edge of a hat چھجا *v. t.* (-mm-) be full to the brim لبالب بھرا ہونا **brimful** *adj.* full to the brim لبالب (بھرا ہوا)

brimstone (*brim*-stohn) *n.* sulphur گندھک fuel of hell-fire دوزخ کا ایندھن، حطبِ جہنم

brine (brīn) *n.* salt water کھاری پانی *the brine*, the sea سمندر *v. i.* pickle in brine نمک میں لگا کے رکھنا **briny** (*brī*-ni) *adj.* کھاری، نمکین

bring *v. t.* (*bring, brought, brought*) come with لانا، لے آنا، لیتے آنا carry or drive towards لے جانا، پہنچانا *bring to book*, exact account from offender مواخذہ کرنا persuade ترغیب دینا *bring (someone) round to a viewpoint*, persuade (him) to accept it کسی کو کسی نقطۂ نگاہ کا حامی بنانا یا ہمرائے کرنا cause or cause to become بننے دینا، بنانا *bring up, bring forward*, cause to be considered توجہ مبذول کرانا، دلیل وغیرہ پیش کرنا *bring to pass, bring about*, cause to happen باعث ہونا *bring back, bring to mind*, cause to remember یاد دلانا *bring down*, cause to be lower (*e.g.*, prices) کم کرنا *bring up*, train (child) تربیت کرنا *bring off*, (cause to) be successful کامیاب ہونا یا کرانا *bring on*, lead to شروع کرنا، سلسلہ چھیڑنا، بات میں بات نکلنا *bring out*, (*a*) cause to appear clearly واضح کرنا (*b*) publish شائع کرنا *bring (someone) round*, cause (him) to regain consciousness after fainting ہوش میں لانا (cf. *come to oneself* ہوش میں آنا) *bring (something) home to* make (one) realize (it) ذہن نشین کرنا *bring forth*, produce (young or fruit) (بچے یا پھل) دینا *bring in*, introduce (موضوع) پیش کرنا *bring (something) to bear on*, direct towards پر ڈالنا، کام میں لانا *bring into play*, cause to act کام میں لانا *bring forward*, carry the total to the next column میزان آگے لے جانا

(S) **To bring** is to carry forward ; **to fetch**, to go, get and bring to **retrieve**, get and bring something that might be lost.

brink *n.* projecting edge (of something dangerous or exciting) کنارا *on the brink of* برلب (S) We speak of the **brink** of a precipice ; **edge** of a sharp line ; **verge** of disaster ; **bank** of stream or river ; **shore** of the sea ; **rim** of something round ; **brim** of a hollow vessel.

briny *adj.* see under **brine**

briquet, briquette (*brik*-et) *n.* brick or ball made of coal-dust and clay

brise-bise (*breez*-beez) *n.* curtain for lower part of window آدھی کھڑکی کا پردہ

brisk *adj.* quick-moving چست، پھرتیلا، تیز *brisk walk* تیز تیز چلنا *trade is brisk* تجارت کا بازار گرم ہے

bristle (*bris*-ĕl) *n.* short, stiff hair (esp. of hog's back) used in brushes (سؤر کا) سخت بال — anything like that سخت بال یا رُواں *v.i.* (of hair) stand up on the end (with fear, etc.) (خوف وغیرہ سے) رونگٹے کھڑے ہونا *bristle with*, have in large numbers وافر ہونا

British (*brit*-ish) *adj.* of Britain, English انگریز، برطانوی، انگریزی **Britisher** *n.* Briton انگریز

Briton (*brit*-ĕn) *n.* Englishman or Englishwoman انگریز

brittle (*brit*-ĕl) *adj.* hard but easily broken بھربھرا **brittleness** *n.* بھربھرا پن، بے لوچی

broach (brohch) *v. t.* open (a liquor barrel) (شراب نکالنے کے لیے) پیپے میں چھید کرنا begin to discuss (a topic, etc.) پر بحث چھیڑنا

broad (brawd) *adj.* wide چوڑا، کشادہ، فراخ *broad shoulders*, capability of bearing burden or responsibilities قوتِ برداشت، حوصلہ، جگر، کلیجہ liberal آزاد خیال، وسیع المشرب *a person of broad views* آزاد خیال، وسیع المشرب شخص *broadminded (person)* (انسان) وسیع المشرب full and complete پورا، مکمل *in broad daylight*, دن دہاڑے *in broad outline*, giving the chief features or ideas موٹی موٹی باتیں *broad hint*, clear and unmistakable hint واضح اشارہ strongly marked صاف، واضح *a broad accent*, strongly marked way of speaking ٹھیٹھ یا بھونڈا لہجہ *broad story*, indecent story فحش یا ناشائستہ بات *broad humour*, smutty joke گندا یا فحش مذاق *broadly speaking*, neglecting minor exceptions فقط مختصر *speak broadly*, speak in marked dialect ٹھیٹھ لہجے میں بات کرنا **broad-blown** *adj.* in full bloom پورے جوبن پر **broadcloth** *n.* thick woollen cloth for men's clothing پٹو، پٹی

broad-gauge *n.* rail track of the largest width (ریل کی) چوڑی پٹڑی (cf., *metre-gauge*) **broad-sheet** *n.* large sheet of paper printed on one side only صرف ایک طرف چھپا ہوا بڑا کاغذ، پوسٹر *broadside*, (*a*) **ship's side**

جہاز کا پہلو (*b*) guns on one side of a ship جہاز کی ایک طرف کی توپیں *fire broadside*, or *fire with a broadside on* (or *to*), fire all guns on one side of a ship simultaneously جہاز پر کی ایک طرف کی توپوں کی باڑھ مارنا

broadsword *n.* sword with a single-edged straight blade چوڑی تلوار **broadways**, **broadwise** *adv.* along the breadth چوڑے رُخ **broaden** *v.t.* & *i.* make or become broad چوڑا کرنا ، فراخ کرنا ، وسیع کرنا *broaden the outlook* (*of*), widen his horizon کی نظر وسیع کرنا ، میں وُسعتِ نظر پیدا کرنا (see also **breadth**)

broadcast (*brawd*-kahst) *v. t.* & *i.* scatter seed in all directions بکھیرنا ، چھڑکنا , send out in all directions by radio (ریڈیو پر) نشر کرنا *broadcast the news* خبریں نشر کرنا **broadcasting-house**, place from where programmes are broadcast by radio نشرگاہ *n.* programme, etc., broadcast نشریہ ، نشری پروگرام *adj.* (programme, etc.) transmitted thus نشریہ نشری ، ریڈیائی *a broadcast speech* نشری تقریر *broadcast of* (*someone's*) *speech*, (کسی کی) نشری تقریر

Brobdingnag (*brob*-ding-nag) *n.* land of giants (in Swift's famous satire, *Gulliver's Travels*) دیوں کا ملک ، براباڈنگ نیگ ، دیودیس **Brobdingnagian** (-nag-i-ĕn) دیو ، دیودیس کا

brocade (bro-*kayd*) *n.* silk cloth with raised designs in silver thread زربفت ، کمخواب ، دیبا **brocaded** *adj.* (cloth) so woven زربفت

brochure (*brosh*-oo-ĕ*) *n.* stitched booklet کتابچہ رسالہ ، پمفلٹ

broil *v. t.* & *i.* grill ; cook or be cooked (on grid iron, etc.) by direct contact with fire بھوننا کباب کرنا (of sun) make very hot (of sun) be very hot سخت تپنا *broiling hot day* سخت گرم دن

broken (*brohk*-ĕn) pa. p. of **break** (which see) *adj. broken-down*, (*a*) (of machinery) out of order ناکارہ ، خراب ، گیا گزرا (*b*) (of machinery) worn-out از کار رفتہ ، خستہ (*c*) (of horse) unfit for work بوڑھا ، ناکارہ ، از کار رفتہ (*d*) (of person) in a ruined state of health رہ گیا ، خستہ و درماندہ *broken English* (*etc.*), imperfect English (etc.) ٹوٹی پھوٹی (انگریزی وغیرہ) *broken ground*, uneven ground ناہموار زمین *broken health*, poor health بگڑی ہوئی صحت *broken-hearted*, grieved غمزدہ ، دل شکستہ *broken sleep* disturbed, intermittent sleep اکھڑی ہوئی نیند *broken time*, working (or other) time reduced by interruptions گھٹا ہوا وقت *broken weather*, uncertain weather گھڑی گھڑی بدلنے والے موسم

broker (*broh*-kĕ*) *n.* one who buys and sells as an agent for others دلّال dealer in distrained goods قرق شدہ مال بیچنے والا **brokerage** *n.* charge made by a broker دلّالی ، دستوری **broking** *n.* broker's trade دلّالی

bromide (*brohm*-ɪd) *n.* a well-known sedative medicine برومائیڈ **bromism** *n.* (*brohm*-izm) morbid state caused by (excessive) use of bromide

bronchial (*bronk*-i-ĕl) *adj.* of the tubes called the bronchii قصبی **bronchii** (*bronk*-ɪ) *n. pl.* (the) two tubes into which the windpipe divides near the lung قصبات **bronchitis** (bronk-*ī*-tis) *n* illness caused by inflammation of the windpipe and attended by coughing نزلہ زخرہ ، قصبی ورم

bronze (bronz) *n.* mixture of copper and tin کانسی its colour ; reddish-brown کانسی کا رنگ sculpture made of bronze کانسی کا مجسمہ

brooch *n.* ornamental safety pin for fastening on a dress at the neck بروچ ، جڑاؤ پن

brood *n.* all the young birds hatched at one time in the nest جھول ، چینگی پوٹے *v.t.* (of a bird) sit on eggs like a hen انڈے سینا ، انڈوں پر بیٹھنا (of night) hang (*over* or *on* a place) چھانا fret (*over something*) کڑھنا think long and sadly (on or upon something)

broody (*broo*-di) *adj.* (of hen) wanting to hatch eggs (مرغی) کڑک

brook (bruk) *n.* small stream ندی نالہ ، آبجو *v. t.* permit (insult, etc., or *being* insulted, etc.) برداشت کرنا ، گوارا کرنا suffer جھیلنا ، سہنا

broom *n.* brush with a long handle for sweeping floors جھاڑو ، بہاری *new broom*, new official eager to reform نیا نمازی ، نیا نوکر ، نیا افسر a kind of shrub جھاڑ ، جھاڑ بیونک **broomstick** *n.* handle of a broom جھاڑو کا ڈنڈا

a broom

Bros. (*brudh*-ĕ*z) see under **brother**.

broth *n.* thin meat soup یخنی ، پتلا شوربا *Too many cooks spoil the broth*, too many directors spoil the whole show دو ملاؤں میں مرغی حرام

brothel (broth-ĕl) *n.* house of prostitution چکلہ ، قحبہ خانہ

brother (*brudh*-ĕ*) *n.* son of the same parents as another person بھائی *brothers german*, such persons سگے بھائی son of one's father or mother (also called *half-brother*) سوتیلا بھائی son of one's mother (also called *brother uterine*) سوتیلا بھائی ، ماں کی طرف سے بھائی member of the same profession or religious society ہم پیشہ ، ہم مشرب ، ہم مسلک ، ہم قماش (in a firm's name) (written as **Bro.** or *pl.* **Bros.**) as *Smith Bros.* or *Smith Bro. & Co.* برادر ، برادران *brother-in-arms*, comrade in war فوج کا ساتھی *brother-in-law n.* brother of one's husband دیور یا جیٹھ husband of one's sister بہنوئی

brotherhood *n.* group of men with common

interest and aims, esp. a religious society برادری ، بھائی بندی ، اپنایت ، بھائی چارہ ، ہم عقیدگی **brotherly** *adj.* برادرانہ **S Brotherly** is more properly applied to tenderness; **fraternal** to sternness and duties. We talk of *brotherly love*, but of a *fraternal organization*. The same remark applies to *motherly* and *maternal*, *fatherly* and *paternal*.

brougham (*broo*-em) *n.* short and closed four-wheeled carriage بند گاڑی

brought pa. t. & pa. p. of **bring** (which see)

brow (broh) *n.* forhead ماتھا ، پیشانی arch of hair above the eyes, also *eyebrow* بھوں ، ابرو *knit (or bend) (one's) brows, raise (one's) eyebrows*, look disdainfully ناک بھوں چڑھانا ، تیوری چڑھانا edge of cliff along which a road passes پہاڑی وغیرہ کا چوٹی **browbeat** *v.t.* (*browbeat, browbeat, browbeaten*) bully ; frighten by looks and words گھرکنا ، جھڑکنا

brown (broun) *adj.* any shade produced by mixing red, yellow and black بھورا ، بادامی ، خاکی dark-skinned سانولا ، کالا *brown bread*, bread made of unboulted flour بے چھنے آٹے کی روٹی *brown coal*, lignite بھورا کوئلہ *brown paper*, coarse packing paper موٹا بھورا کاغذ *brown sugar*, half refined sugar لال شکر *brown study*, reverie گہری سوچ ، سوچ **browned off** *adj.* (slang) bored اُکتایا ہوا ، اُکتا گیا **brownout** *n.* * ہلکا بلیک آوٹ ، روشنی مدھم (see *Addenda*)

Brownie (*brou*-ni) *n.* junior Girl Guides between eight and eleven years old براؤنی (*brownie*), good natured fairy helping other people at night in their household work ننھی خدمتگزار پری

browse (brouz) *v. i.* eat leaves, grass, etc. اُگی ہوئی گھاس وغیرہ چرنا read (parts of books) اِدھر اُدھر سے پڑھنا ، متفرق حصے پڑھنا

bruin (*broo*-in) *n.* (in fairy tales) bear بھالو ، ریچھ

bruise (brooz) *n.* injury to body, or fruit, etc., discolouring the skin but not breaking it رگڑ ، خراش *v. t.* & *i.* get or cause a bruise (to) خراش آنا ، رگڑ پہنچنا زخمی کرنا *bruised adj.* جسے رگڑ یا خراش آئی ہو

brunette (broo-*net*) *n.* European woman of dark complexion and black eyes, مغربی سانولی ، سانولی

brunt *n.* chief stress of attack حملے کا زور یا شدت ، ضرب ، صدمہ *bear the brunt of*, resist the weight of (حملے یا کسی اور شے) کی سختی جھیل جانا

brush *n.* implement with bunches of bristles to sweep or smooth جھاڑو ، برش ، موقلم *hair brush* بالوں کا برش *clothes brush* کپڑوں کا برش *floor-brush* جھاڑو *paint-brush* موقلم short, sharp fight لڑائی ، مقابلہ thicket of small bushes جھاڑی *v. t.* & *i.* sweep or clean with a brush جھاڑو دینا ، جھاڑو بہارو کرنا ، جھاڑو یا برش سے صاف کرنا *brush up*, get back lost (knowledge) علم تازہ کرنا *brush off*, (see *Addenda*) *brush past* (or *against*), touch when passing کنسے سے کتراتے گزرنا **brushwood** *n.* low bushes چھوٹی چھوٹی جھاڑیاں undergrowth. چھوٹی چھوٹی زیر درختی

brusque (brusk) *adj.* rough (in speech, behaviour) اکھڑ ، منہ پھٹ ، اکھل کھرا **brusqueness** *n.* اکھڑ پن ، اکھڑ پنا

Brut (broot) (*Brit. legend*) a legendary descendant of Aeneas ; he founded a Trojan settlement in what is now called England and built a new Troy which has since come to be known as London بروٹ

brutal *adj.* **brutality** *n.* **brutalize** *v. t.* (see under **brute**)

brute (broot) *n.* animal (except man) حیوان جانور stupid and cruel man بے حس ، ظالم ، جنگلی *adj.* animal-like بہیمانہ ، وحشیانہ ، جنگلی ، حیوان صفت *brute force, brute strength*, strength without skill and understanding اندھی طاقت **brutal** (*broot*-ėl) *adj.* savage وحشیانہ ، بہیمانہ cruel ظالمانہ ، سفاکانہ

brutalize (*broot*-a-liz) *v. t.* make brutal وحشی بنانا

brutality (broo-*tal*-i-ti) *n.* cruelty بہیمیت ، سفاکی ، حیوانیت

brutish (*broot*-ish) *adj.* stupid like an animal گدھا ، گاؤدی ، گھامڑ

bubble (*bub*-ėl) *n.* very thin ball (or usu. half ball) of liquid enclosing a mass of gas بلبلہ ، حباب *blow bubbles*, make bubbles (as a child's game) by blowing into a pipe the other end of which has just now been dipped into soapy water بلبلے اڑانا *prick a bubble*, (a) make it burst بلبلے کو ختم کر دینا (b) end some sham پول کھولنا ، کا پول کھول کر رکھ دینا *v. i.* rise in bubbles بلبلے بھرنا send up bubbles بلبلے ڈالنا ، سے بلبلے ابھرنا یا نکلنا flow (*past* or *along*) with a sound like that of bubbles غڑ غڑ بہنا boil *over* اُبال سے اچھل پڑنا (*bubble over*), (of person or his spirits) be buoyant اُچھلتے پھرنا ، بہت خوش ہونا

bubonic plague (bew-*bon*-ik-*playg*) *n.* epidemic spread by rats ; (it is marked by *bubo* or swelling in the armpit) پلیگ ، طاعون

buccaneer (buk-a-*nee*-ė*) *n.* pirate سمندری ڈاکو ، بحری قزاق **buccaneering** *n.* roving for piracy سمندری ڈاکوؤں یا ڈاکے ، کا *adj.* piratical جہازوں کو لوٹنا

buck (buk) *n.* (fem., *doe*) male deer چیتل ، سانبھر ، ہرن male hare or rabbit (U. S. slang) dollar ڈالر boastful talk شیخی ، بکواس conversation گپ شپ *v.i.* talk boastfully بڑھ بڑھ کر باتیں بنانا ، شیخی بگھارنا ، دُون کی لینا chat گپ شپ کرنا (of a horse) jump high with the back arched (in order to throw the rider دشوار کو گرانے کے لیے گھوڑے کا چاروں پیر جوڑ کر اچھلنا **buck-shot** *n*. cartridge for shooting bucks بکشاٹ، ہرن مار کارتوس *adj*. (of rule) by armed police, etc., with all its severities ڈنڈے کی (حکومت) **buckskin** *n*. skin of deer (or goat) yielding very soft but strong leather ہرن کی کھال، میشہ **buckish** *adj*. foppish بانکا، چھیلا

bucket (*buk*-et) *n*. pail بالٹی، ڈول (also *bucketful*) what a bucket holds بالٹی بھر

buckle (*buk*-èl) *n*. metal fastener for belt or strap بکسوا، بکلس *v. t. & i.* fasten with a buckle بکسوا، بکلس لگانا (of metal work, etc.) bend, get twisted (from heat, because of strain at ends) ٹیڑھا ہو جانا، مڑ جانا **buckler** (*buk*-lě*) *n*. small, round shield چھوٹی گول ڈھال، مدوّر سپر

buckram (*buk*-ram) *n*. rough starched cloth آہار والا کپڑا، گوند لگا ہوا کپڑا

buckshee (*buk*-*shi*) *n*. extra army rations فوج میں زائد راشن anything given or taken free بخشش، عطیہ *adj*. free, grates مفت، بلاقیمت

bucolic (bew-*kaw*-lik) *adj*. of shepherd's life or of country-life گڈریوں سے متعلق، دیہاتی **bucolics** *n*. (*pl*.) گڈریوں سے متعلق نظمیں، دیہاتی منظومات

bud *n*. leaf, flower, or branch at the beginning of its growth کونپل flower not fully open کلی، شگوفہ *v. i.* (-*dd*-) put on buds کونپلیں پھوٹنا begin to develop اُبھرنے لگنا *a budding statesman* اُبھرتا ہوا سیاستدان

buddy (*bud*-i) (U.S. colloq.) (form of address:) brother, friend یار، بھائی، بھائی میرے، میرے بھائی، بھیّا، بھیّن–

budge (buj) *v. t. & i.* (usually. neg.) move very little ہلنا، ہلانا، سرکنا، سرکانا، ٹسٹنا –It won't budge ٹس سے مس نہ ہونا، میں تو تڑپنے کا نہیں

budget (*buj*-et) *n*. estimate of probable future income and payments میزانیہ، موازنہ، بجٹ collection of news, letters, etc. (خبروں یا خطوں کا) خریطہ *v.i. budget for*, *make a budget for* (کسی مدت کے لیے کسی کام کا) میزانیہ مرتب کرنا

buff (buf) *n*. (a buffalo's) thick, strong leather (بھینس کی) ادھوڑی its colour : a brownish yellow بھورا، بھورے رنگ *adj*. of this colour بھورے رنگ کا *buff-sheet* بادامی کاغذ، بھورا کاغذ

buffalo (*buf*-a-loh) *n*. (pl. *buffaloes*) well known big black animal of Asia and Africa domesticated for its milk بھینس، بھینسا *wild buffalo* ارنا بھینسا *buffalo-calf* کٹڑا *buffalo hide* ادھوڑی

buffer (*buf*-ě*) *n*. springed apparatus for lessening the effect of a blow, esp. on a railway engine or wagon بفر، ٹکر روک *buffer State*, small country between two larger countries فاصل ریاست، فاصل مملکت

buffet (*boo-fay*) *n*. counter where food and drink may be taken or bought for eating بُوفے a party where there are no dining chairs and the guests have to go up to the table for eatables and eat standing بُوفے پارٹی، بُوفہ pr., (*buf*-et) blow given with the hand تھپیڑا *v. t.* give such a blow to تھپیڑا مارنا *be buffeted by* تھپیڑے کھانا *buffet the waves* موجوں کا مقابلہ کرتے جانا

buffoon (*buf*-oon) *n*. clown بھانڈ، مسخرا **buffoonery** *n*. actions and jokes of a clown, clown like behaviour بھانڈپن، بھکتی، مسخرگی، مسخراپن

bug *n*. small, bad smelling insect with blood کھٹمل (U. S.) any insect کیڑا، کیڑا مکوڑا **bugaboo, bugbear** (*bug*-) object of baseless fear or dislike ہوا، ہیجا dislike خوف یا نفرت کا any dreaded event ہوّا، کوئی باعث **bugger** *n*. sodomite لُوطی، اغلامی common swear-word whose severity is sought to be lessened by calling it a corruption of *beggar* and occasionally even spelling it thus بدمعاش

buggy (*bug*-i) *adj*. infested with bugs کھٹمل بھرا *n*. Red Indians' two-wheeled light carriage گھوڑا گاڑی four wheeled sedan-type carriage driven by one or more horses بگھی

bugle (*bew*-gèl) *n*. musical wind instrument of brass or copper, used in army بگل، بوق **bugler** *n*. one who blows a bugle بگل بجانے والا، بگلچی

a bugle

build (*bild*) *v. t. & i.* (*build, built, built*) construct بنانا، تعمیر کرنا *build up*, make bigger or stronger (a business, one's health) ہمت بنانا، کاروبار کو ترقی دینا *build upon*, allow to rest on, use as a foundation پر آسرا لگانا، پر بنیاد رکھنا **built-up area** پر استوار کرنا عمارت والا رقبہ، مسقف رقبہ *n*. style of construction نمونہ، ساخت، وضع، وضع قطع، بناوٹ body کاٹھی (انسان کی) *a man of his build* اسکی کاٹھی کا انسان

builder *n*. contracter for building houses عمارتی ٹھیکیدار one who lays the foundation of (empire, organization, etc.) by doing the spade work بانی **build-up** *n*. (see *Addenda*) **built-in** *adj*. (see *Addenda*) **building** *n*. structure عمارت

bulb *n*. thick underground part of certain plants (like onions) where plant food is stored پیاز وغیرہ کی گنٹھی، بُلب (also *electric bulb*), bulb-shaped electric lamp بجلی کا قمقمہ، بلب **bulbous** (*bul*-bous) *adj*. bulb-shaped گنبد نما

an electric bulb

bulge (bulj) *v. t. & i.* (cause to) swell beyond usual size پھیلنا، گنبد نما اُبھرنا، بے ڈول

اُبھرنا ، اُبھار curve outwards, پھولنا *bulging pockets,* پھولی ہوئی جیبیں *n.* place where a swelling or curve shows اُبھار ، ناہموار اُبھار

bulk *n.* quantity or volume esp. when great حجم ، زیادہ مقدار *in bulk,* (*a*) loose کُھلا (*b*) in large amounts ڈھیر کے حساب سے ، ڈھیر (*c*) the whole of تمام تر ، سارے کا سارا the greater part or number (*of*) کا بیشتر حصّہ *bulk large,* seem large in respect of size or importance بڑا یا اہم معلوم ہونا **bulkhead** *n.* upright wall in the hull between water-tight compartments to prevent a ship from sinking even if partly damaged جہاز کی حفاظتی دیوار **bulkiness** *n.* being bulky ضخامت ، بے ڈول پن **bulky** (*bul*-ki) *adj.* taking too much space ضخیم large and clumsy بے ڈول

bull (bul) *n.* uncastrated male of any animal of the ox family سانڈ ، بجار *take the bull by the horns,* tackle a situation fearlessly مردانہ وار مقابلہ کرنا ، جرأت سے سامنا کرنا *a bull in a china shop,* a rough, careless person who breaks precious things آئینہ خانہ میں بجار male of elephant, and some other large animals (ہاتھی یا دوسرے بڑے جانوروں کا) نر amusingly self-contradictory statement (*e.g.*, 'If you do not get this letter please write and tell me', (کلام میں) مضحکہ خیز تضاد یا تناقض speculator who buys shares at rising prices to sell at profit (پُرامید سٹّے باز ، بھاؤ بڑھانے کے لیے سٹّہ کرنے والا ، سانڈ بجار as opposed to a *bear* who disposes of his shares at low profit to avoid loss (متشائم سٹّہ باز ، بھاؤ formal order or announcement made by the Pope پوپ کا (پاپائے روم کا اعلامیہ) پاپائی فرمان **bull-baiting** *n.* old English sport in which bulls are excited by setting dogs at them سانڈ کشتی ، سانڈ سے مقابلے کا انگریزی مشغلہ **bull-dog** *n.* a strong breed of dog used in bull-baiting بُل ڈانگ ، بُل ڈاگ **bull faced** *adj.* with a face like that of a bull بڑمونہا ، سانڈ مونہا **bull-fight** *n.* Spanish sport of man's fight against bull سانڈ سے مقابلہ **bull-finch** *n.* name of a melodious bird بڑی رنج **bull-headed** *adj.* headstrong سرکش ، خودسر **bull-hide** *n.* hide of a bull اَدھوڑی ، گرگھا **bull-ring** *n.* arena for bull-fights سانڈ کشتی کا اکھاڑہ **bull's-eye** *n.* centre of target نشانہ ، گلاوری ، مرکزِ ہدف (old use) policeman's lantern سپاہی کی لالٹین

bulldoze *v.t.* (see *Addenda*) **bulldozer** (bul-*doh*-ze*) *n.* machine for shifting large quantities of earth, levelling land, etc. بُل ڈوزر ، بیلچہ مشین *

bullet (*bul*-et) *n.* leaden ball (often within a U-shaped covering) fired from a rifle or revolver گولی **bullet-proof** *adj.* that cannot be hurt with bullets جس پر گولی اثر نہ کرے ، گولہ پناہ

bulletin (*bul*-et-in) *n.* official statement of a public event اطلاعیہ ، سرکاری خبرنامہ ، بُلیٹن *news bulletin,* news broadcast in a single transmission نشری خبرنامہ magazine published by a society for its members and containing reports of its activities خبرنامہ

bullion (*bul*-yĕn) *n.* gold or silver in bulk, before minting or manufacture سونے چاندی کی اینٹیں یا سلاخیں *bullion-market* صرافہ ، بازارِ صرافہ gold or silver fringe سنہری یا روپہلی جھالر

bullock (*bul*-ok) *n.* castrated bull بیل ، بدھیا ، بُلد **bullock-cart** *n.* cart driven by a bullock بیل گاڑی ، بہلی ، رتھ **bullock-driver** *n.* driver of a bullock cart گاڑیبان ، بیل وان

bully (bul-i) *n.* one who uses his strength to terrorize or hurt the weak غنڈا ، دھونسیا ، مردم آزار بھاڑے کا غنڈا *v. t.* use strength in this way غنڈا گردی کرنا *bully (someone) into (doing something)* غنڈا گردی (یا دھونس) سے (کسی سے) کوئی کام لینا

bulrush (bool-rush) *n.* tall rush بڑا سینٹھا ، نرسل (Bib) papyrus کاغذ کا پودا ، بیبرس

bulwark (*bul*-wĕ*k) *n.* defensive wall, esp. one built of earth فصیل ، شہرپناہ defence دفاع ، مدافعت دفاعی انتظامات ، پُشت پناہ railing round ship's deck (جہاز میں) عرشے کے اوپر کا جنگلا

bum *n.* (colloq.) bottom ; buttocks چینڈا ، چوتڑ (U. S. colloq.) habitual loafer, پکّا آوارہ گرد *go on the bum,* be a parasite on the community مفت خورہ ہونا ، قوم کے لیے جونک ہونا *adj.* (U. S. colloq.) of poor quality گھٹیا ، یونہی سا *v. i.* (U. S. colloq.) loaf آوارہ گردی کرنا ، بے خانماں پھرنا **bum-boat** *n.* boat plying with fresh provisions for ships جہاز پر تازہ اشیا پہنچانے والی کشتی

bumble-bee *n.* (also *humble bee*), large type of bee always humming loudly بھنبھنانے والی مکھی ، بھونرا

bump (bump) *n.* dull blow or knock (as when two things collide) دھکا ، دھچکا swelling of the flesh caused by this گومڑا ، آماس fault in a road surface made by traffic گڈھا ، گڑھا jolt felt in aircraft owing to a change in air pressure ہوائی دھکا air pressure causing this ہوائی گڑھا ، تغیر *v.t. & i.* give or receive a bump ٹکرانا *bump one's head against* سر ٹکرانا *bump along a bad road* خراب سڑک پر ہچکولے کھاتے ہوئے جانا & (see *Addenda*)

bumpy *adj.* (of road) uneven and causing many bumps (ناہموار (سڑک

bumper (*bump*-ĕ*) *adj.* (of crops) unusually large وافر ، بڑی ، غیر معمولی طور پر اچھی یا زیادہ *n.* bar in to protect it بچپنزہ ، ملحو

bumpkin (*bum*-kin) *n.* awkward person with unpolished manners, esp. from the country اُجڈ،گنوار گھامڑ، ڈھگا ، گدھا

bumptious (*bump*-shus) *adj.* conceited, self-important خود پسند،بزعم خود غلط **bumtiousness** *n.* خود پسندی عجب و نخوت

bun *n.* small round sweet cake میٹھا کلچا، بند، شیرمال *in a bun*, (of a lady's hair) twisted into a knot above the back of the neck بالوں کا جُوڑا

bunch (bunch) *n.* number of small, similar things naturally growing together گچھا ، خوشہ *bunch of grapes* انگور کا خوشہ number of similar things gathered together گچھا، گٹھا ، پُچھ ، گڈی *bunch of keys*, گلدستہ، پھولوں کا گچھا *bunoh of flowers* کنجیوں (یا چابیوں) کا گچھا *bunch of greens* ترکاری کی گڈی *v. t.* & *i.* come or bring together into a bunch گچھا بنانا

bund (bund) *n.* a dike to prevent floods بند

bundle (*bund*-èl) *n.* number of things wrapped together پلندا، گٹھڑی، گٹھڑ، پوٹلی *v. t.* & *i.* make into a bundle پلندا بنانا، گٹھڑی باندھنا put away without order اوپر تلے پھینکنا ، بے ترتیبی سے ڈالنا go (*off*) in a hurry جلدی میں جانا send (someone *off*) in a hurry نکال باہر کرنا ، جلدی جلدی بھیجنا *bundle the children off to school* بچوں کو جلدی جلدی مدرسے بھیجنا

bungalow (*bung*-a-loh) *n.* a one-storeyed house (us. with lawns all round it) بنگلہ ، کوٹھی

a bungalow

bungle (*bung*-èl) *v. t.* & *i.* do something clumsily and spoil it پھوہڑپنے سے کام کرنا اَبتری ڈالنا ، اناڑی پن سے کام خراب کرنا ، کھیل بگاڑنا **bungling** *n.* inefficient management اناڑی پن، نااہلی، گڑبڑ، ابتری، پھوہڑپن ، بے سلیقگی **bungler** *n.* one who bungles نااہل، اناڑی ، پھوہڑ

bunion (*bun*-yĕn) *n.* lump or painful swelling on the foot (esp. on the first joint of the great toe) (پیر کے انگوٹھے کا) گٹا ، گوکھرو

bunk *n.* sleeping berth fixed on the wall (usu. in a ship) (جہاز میں) دیوار گیر بستر، دیوار گیر نشست (U. S. slang) humbug, nonsense بیہودہ، بکواس *It is all bunk* یہ سب بکواس ہے (see also **bunkum**)

bunker (*bunk*-ĕ*) part of a steamer where coal is stored جہاز کی کوئلہ رکھنے والی کوٹھڑی obstacle on a golf course ریتلا گڑھا (گاف کے میدان میں رُکاوٹ کے لیے) *v. passive be bunkered*, (in golf) get one's ball in a bunker کی گیند گڑھے میں پڑجانا

bunkum (*bunk*-um) *n.* pleasant but untrue talk only meant to please اُبلہ فریبی ، چکنی چپڑی باتیں *his speech was all bunkum* اس کی تقریر تو صرف واہ واہ سننے کے لیے تھی۔

bunny (*bun*-i) *n.* (child's word for) rabbit خرگوش squirrel گلہری

bunting (*bunt*-ing) *n.* very small flag used for decoration جھنڈی (usu. in the *pl.*) *buntings* جھنڈیاں

buoy (boi) *n.* anchored float to guide ship پیراک پیپا، تیرونا (also *life-buoy*) something to keep one afloat *buoy up*, (*a*) prevent from sinking تیرتے رکھنا (*b*) keep up (hopes, etc.) ، حوصلہ بڑھانا ، ہمت دلانا یا قائم رکھنا **buoyancy** *n.* ability to be or keep afloat تیرنے یا تیرانے کی صلاحیت، شناوری **buoyant** (*boi*-ant) *adj.* able to float or to keep things floating (as a cork) تیرتے رہنے والا یا تیرانے والا، تیرن ہار، تیرن جوگ، شناور hopeful, gay, light-hearted خوش مزاج، خوشدل **buoyantly** *adv.* خوشدلی سے ، پُرامید

bur (bĕ*) (sometimes spelt *burr*) *n.* clinging part of plant (esp. its seed-vessel) چمٹ جانے والا پودا (یا پھل) person who forces his company on others گلے میں جان، بلائے بے درماں

burberry (-*be**-bè-ri) *n.* (a popular make of) raincoat برساتی waterproof cloth used in it برساتی کپڑا ، بربری

burden, (*arch.* **burthen**) (*bĕ**-dèn) *n.* heavy load (esp. one carried on the back) بوجھ ، بار *beast of burden*, pack animal لدو جانور *burden of taxation* ٹیکسوں کا بوجھ ، محاصل کا بار refrain (*of the song*) ٹیپ کا مصرع (یا بند) *v.t.* put a heavy burden on بوجھ ڈالنا، لادنا **burdensome** *adj.* hard to bear ; tiring کڑا، سخت، دوبھر، اجیرن

bureau (bew-*roh*, or *bew*-è-roh) (*pl.*, *bureaus*, or *bureaux*, pr., bew-*rohz*) *n.* office, esp. for public information دفتر، محکمہ، دفتر اطلاعات *travel bureau* دفتر اطلاعات سیاحت writing-desk (لکھنے کی) میز **bureaucrat** (bew-*rok*-rat) *n.* (permanent) government official اہلکار، سرکاری ملازم **bureaucratic** (bew-roh-*krat*-ik) دفتری (حکومت) دفتر شاہی (ذہنیت) **bureaucracy** (bew-*rok*-ra-si) *n.* government by bureaucrats دفتر شاہی

burglar (*bĕ*g*-lĕ*) *n.* one who breaks into a building by night in order to steal نقب زن، سیندھ لگانے والا، سیندھ مار، چور **burglary** *n.* breaking into a building by night in order to steal نقب زنی، سیندھ لگانا، چوری **burgle** (bĕ*-gl) *v.t.* & *i.* commit burglary on (building) نقب لگانا، سیندھ لگانا، چوری کرنا

burgundy (*bĕ**-gund-i) red wine from Burgundy in central France برگنڈی

burial *n.* **buried** *adj.* see under **bury**

burke (bĕ*k) *v.t.* stifle (rumour, discussion, inquiry, etc.) (افواہ وغیرہ) دبا دینا

burlap (*bĕ**-lap) *n.* coarse jute-cloth for bags, etc. ٹاٹ

burlesque (bu*-*lesk*) *v.t.* make an amusing imitation of some style of writing, etc., with an

air of assumed seriousness بناوٹی متانت سے تمسخر کرنا *n.* this form of literature متانت بھرا مسخرہ مضحکات
burly (*bu**-li) *adj.* big and strong (person) موٹا تازہ، ہٹا کٹا، مشٹنڈا
burn (bĕ*n) *v.t.* & *i.* (*burn, burnt, burnt*; or *burn, burned, burned*) destroy by fire or heat جلانا، جلا ڈالنا *burn away* (or *out*) جلا ڈالنا، جلا دینا be on fire جلنا، بھڑکنا *this firewood burns well* یہ لکڑی تو خوب جلتی ہے *the house was burning* گھر جل رہا تھا، گھر کو آگ لگی ہوئی تھی affect or injure by heat پکانا، سنولا دینا *sun-burnt*, (face) browned by the sun سنولایا ہوا (چہرہ) *sun-burnt* (bricks) پکی اینٹیں inflame with passion بھڑکانا، تڑپانا، جلانا (cause to) feel a sensation of heat جلن ہونا یا پیدا کرنا *burning shame*, very great shame بہت شرمناک *burn* (*one's*) *fingers*, get into trouble مصیبت میں پڑنا *burn* (*one's*) *boats*, take a step that cannot be withdrawn لڑ مرنے کا فیصلہ کرنا *burn the candle at both ends*, (*a*) work till late and get up early to resume سخت محنت کرنا، جان ہلکان کرنا (*b*) waste بے جا اسراف کرنا، فضول ضائع کرنا *burning question*, one being hotly discussed اہم مسئلہ *burning glass*, convex lens used for ignition آتشی شیشہ *n.* (Scottish word for) brook نالا، آب جو **burning** *n.* جلنے والا *adj.* جلتا ہوا، بھڑکتا ہوا **burner** part of a lamp, etc. from which flame arises لیمپ کا گل *bunsen-burner*, gas burner of great heat بنسن چراغ
burnish (*bu**-nish) *v.t.* & *i.* polish metal by rubbing, or be polished in this way صیقل کرنا یا ہونا، جلا دینا یا پانا *n.* brightness صیقل، جلا
burnt *pa. t.* & *pa. p.* of **burn** (which see)
burp gun *n.* (see *Addenda*)
burrow (*bu*-roh) hole in the ground (esp. as dug by rabbits and foxes) بھٹ، بل *v.t.* & *i.* make such a hole کریدنا، کھودنا، بل کھودنا، بھٹ بنانا
burr (bĕ*) (also spelt *bur*) *n.* rough whirring sound of a swiftly rotating machine گھر گھر a short drill used by dentists (دندان ساز کا) چھوٹا برما gutteral pronunciation of the letter *r* ر کا حلقی تلفظ، ر کی غ کی سی آواز *v.i.* whirr like a machine گھر گھر کی آوازیں نکالنا pronounce 'r' gutterally ر کی حلقی آواز
bursar (bĕ*-sĕ*) *n.* person in charge of the finances of a college, etc., and the actual authority for disbursing money خازن **bursary** (-ri) *n.* his office خازن کا عہدہ stipend to an indigent student وظیفہ
burst (bu*st) *v.t.* & *i.* (cause to) explode or break open پھٹنا، پھوٹنا، پھٹ کر اڑ جانا یا اڑا دینا bulge (*with*) (سے) اینٹھے جانا یا پڑنا move (*out, through, into,* etc.) زور سے (داخل ہونا) توڑ کر (نکل جانا) *burst out laughing*, *burst into laughter*, begin suddenly to laugh کھلکھلا کر ہنسنا۔ *burst* (*one's*) *sides with laughing*, ہنسی سے پیٹ میں بل پڑ جانا۔ *burst into tears*, پھوٹ پھوٹ کر رونے لگنا *bursting with*, full of بھرپور *n.* bursting پھٹنا noise so produced دھماکہ hole, crack شگاف، سوراخ، شگاف crack made by bursting دراڑ، درز short, violent, effort تھوڑی دیر کے لیے سر توڑ زور *burst of speed* یکلخت سرپٹ sudden fit (of applause etc.) (تعریف وغیرہ) غلغلہ
burthen (bĕ*-dhĕn) *n.* (arch. spelling of **burden** (which see)
burial see under **bury**
bury (*be*-ri) *v.t.* (*bury, buried, buried*) put a dead body (*a*) in a grave دفن کرنا (لاش کو)، دبانا، (مردہ) گاڑنا (*b*) in the river or sea, دریا برد کرنا یا سمندر میں ڈالنا cover with earth دبانا، گاڑنا hide from view, etc. چھپانا، (برف وغیرہ سے) ڈھکا ہوا buried under snow, etc. ڈھانپنا *bury* (*oneself*) *in the country*, go and live where (one) will meet few people گوشہ گزین ہونا، گوشہ گزینی یا عزلت نشینی اختیار کرنا *buried in thought* (*etc.*) خیالات وغیرہ میں مستغرق **burial** (*be*-ri-ĕl) *n.* act of burying تدفین، اوّل منزل کرنا *burial-ground*, graveyard قبرستان، گورستان *burial service*, prayers as part of funeral rites نماز جنازہ، جنازہ، (عیسائیوں کے یہاں) دفن کرتے وقت کی دعا **buried** *adj.* interred دفن، مدفون lying covered with earth گڑا ہوا *buried treasure* گڑا ہوا خزانہ، دفینہ
bus *n.* (pl. *buses*; pr., *bus*-iz) (abb. of *omnibus*), a large public vehicle بس (army slang) aircraft ہوائی جہاز، طیارہ *miss the bus*, miss the opportunity موقعہ کھو دینا *v.i.* travel by bus بس میں جانا
bush (bush) *n.* (pl., *bushes*; pr. *bush*-iz) shrub جھاڑی tavern sign شراب خانے کا نشان *the bush*, (in Australia and Africa) wild uncleared forest خود رو جنگل **bushy** *adj.* full of bushes جھاڑی دار، جھاڑیوں والا growing thickly گھنا
bushel (*bush*-el) *n.* eight-gallon measure for grain and fruit غلے اور پھل کا ۳۲ سیر وزن، ناپ، بُشل container for this measure of grain بُشل *hide one's light under one's bushel*, conceal one's goodness or cleverness اپنی خوبیاں ظاہر نہ کرنا یا ہونے دینا
busily *adv.* see under **busy**
business (*biz*-nes) *n.* activity in trade کاروبار، تجارت commercial enterprise کاروبار، تجارتی ادارہ، دکان one's regular occupation پیشہ، شغل concern معاملہ، حق، سے واسطہ یا تعلق، متعلق *it is no business of yours* اس سے تمہارا کوئی واسطہ نہیں *he had no business to* اُسے حق نہیں پہنچتا تھا کہ، اُس کا حق نہیں تھا کہ، اُسے کیا حق تھا کہ ... *looking like nobody's business*, (U.S. slang) with personal appearance (esp. dress) above criticism اعتراض سے بالا، معقول لباس میں، ٹھیک ٹھیک سج دھج سے matter, event معاملہ، واقعہ، بات *make it* (*one's*) *business to* کا بیڑا اٹھانا get

business سنجیدگی سے بات کرنا **good business** بہت اچھا سودا **mean business,** be in earnest واقعی سنجیدگی سے بات کرنا **it means business** مذاق نہیں، دل لگی نہیں *adj.* of business کاروباری **business acumen** کاروباری سوجھ بوجھ **business hours** کاروباری اوقات، اوقاتِ کار، کام کے اوقات **businessman,** trader تاجر، کاروباری آدمی **businesslike,** prompt, practical and well ordered معاملے کا، ڈھنگ کا، عملی، منظم، مستعدانہ *settle down (to a task) in a businesslike manner* عملی طریق پر (کام) شروع کرنا، باقاعدگی سے شروع کرنا *Mind your business* اپنے کام سے کام رکھو، بیہودہ دخل مت دو *Go about your business* دفع ہو جاؤ (see also **busy**)

bust *n.* sculpture of a person's head and shoulders سر کا مجسمہ، نیم مجسمہ upper front part of woman's body عورت کا سینہ measurement of woman's body round the chest and back عورت کے سینے کا گھیر

a bust

bustle (*bus*-ĕl) *v.t.* & *i.* move *about* noisily and fussily دوڑ دھوپ ہونا، ہانپنا، کھلبلی پڑنا، افراتفری پڑنا *n.* such movement دوڑ دھوپ، کھلبلی، افراتفری

busy (*biz*-i) *adj.* at work (*at, with,* or *doing*) کام میں مشغول full of activity بارونق *busy (oneself or one's hands at, with, in, about,* or *doing)* (میں) مصروف ہونا، (میں) منہمک ہونا *self* (*with, about*) مصروف ہونا *be* (or *keep*) *busy* میں مصروف، میں منہمک **busybody** *n.* meddling person فسادی، مفسد، لگائی بجھائی کرنے والا، خدائی فوجدار *busy idleness,* لاحاصل اور بیکار کاموں میں مصروفیت **busily** (*biz*-i-li) *adj.* actively سرگرمی سے انہماک

but *conj.* still تاہم that کہ on the contrary لیکن، مگر that (not) (جو نہ) *prep.* except کے سوا *adv.* only محض، صرف *but for,* if there had not been اگر وہ ایسا نہ ہوتا تو *all but,* almost تقریباً، قریب قریب

butcher (*buch*-ĕ*) *n.* person who slaughters animals and sells their meat for food قصاب، قصائی، بوچڑ tyrant سفاک، جلاد، ظالم فرمانروا *v. t.* kill very violently, esp. with a knife ذبح کرنا، گلا کاٹنا، چھری پھیرنا mangle or ruin (غلط پڑھنے یا چھاپنے سے کتاب کا) ستیاناس کر دینا، الٹی چھری سے ذبح کرنا **butchery** *n.* needless or cruel slaughter خوں ریزی، خونِ ناحق

butler (*but*-lĕ*) *n.* head servant in a Household who is also in charge of plate and wine-cellar بٹلر، خانساماں

butt (but) *n.* thicker (usu. wooden) end of a tool or weapon کندا (*pl.*) shooting-range چاند ماری کا میدان targets in the shooting range and the mound or wall behind ہدف والی دیوار، ہدف thing or person as target for ridicule گوئے محفل، نقلِ محفل *v. t.* & *i.* strike or hit (esp. with the head, as a ram does) ٹکرانا، ٹکر مارنا *butt in, butt into* (کسی کی آگ میں) اندھا دھند کود پڑنا

butter (*but*-ĕ*) *n.* fatty food churned from milk or curds مکھن flattering words چاپلوسی، روغنِ قاز *lay butter* روغنِ قاز ملنا *look as if butter would not melt in one's mouth,* look temptation-proof بناوٹی متانت کا مظاہرہ کرنا *v. t.* spread butter over (something) پر مکھن لگانا cook in butter مکھن میں تلنا یا پکانا flatter چاپلوسی کرنا، چکنی چپڑی باتیں کرنا، مسکہ لگانا *butter up* خوشامد کرنا *fine words butter no parsnips,* fine words do not change facts خالی خولی باتوں سے کام نہیں چلتا **buttercup** cup for butter مکھن دان a cup-like flower پیالہ نما پھول

a buttercup

butterfly (*but*-ĕ*-flı) *n.* a brilliant colour flying insect تیتری، تتلی **buttermilk** (*but*-) *n.* sour milk left after butter has been churned out of it مکھن نکلی لسی، چھاچھ **butter oil** *n.* (see *Addenda*)

butterfly *n.* see under **butter**

buttock (*but*-uk) *n.* either side of that part of the body on which one sits سرین، پٹھا، چوتڑ

button (*but*-un) *n.* small disk stitched on to a garment for decoration or fastening بٹن، بوتام button-like object, pushed or pressed گھنڈی، بٹن *v. t.* & *i.* fasten or be fastened, with buttons (کسی کپڑے کو) بٹن لگانا *button up, in* (or *into*) بٹن بند کرنا *press the button,* set going معمولی اشارے پر بڑے کام کا شروع ہونا **buttonhole** *n.* hole for buttons کاج flower worn in it at the lapel کاج میں لگا ہوا پھول *v. t.* make and stitch a hole for a button کاج نکالنا catch hold of (someone) and force him (to do something) (کسی کو) کان سے پکڑ کے (کرانا)، (کسی کو کرنے) پر مجبور کرنا

buttress (*but*-res) *n.* support built against a wall اڑواڑ، پشتہ *v. t.* strengthen with a buttress اڑواڑ لگانا، پشتہ بندی کرنا

buxom (*buk*-sum) *adj.* (of a woman) plump, comely and healthy موٹی تازی، صحت مند، گداز جسم، قبول صورت (عورت)

buy (bı) *v. t.* & *i.* (*buy, bought, bought*) get *for* a certain sum of money (میں یا کو) خریدنا serve to procure سے حاصل ہونا، لے دینا *money cannot buy happiness* دولت سے خوشی حاصل نہیں ہو سکتی gain at a sacrifice قربانی سے حاصل کرنا، مصیبت اٹھا کر حاصل کرنا *buy (something) at the cost (of)* کوئی شے کسی قیمت پر حاصل کرنا، میں مول لینا (also *buy over*), bribe *buy off,* get rid of by payment رشوت دے کر ہم نوا بنا لینا *buy up,* buy as much as possible مال بھر لینا، زیادہ سے زیادہ مقدار میں خرید لینا *buy in,* stock اکٹھا خریدنا *buy out,* pay a person to give up a post کسی کو رشوت دے کر نوکری چھوڑنے پر آمادہ کر لینا *buy a pig in the poke,* commit oneself without due caution

بے سوچے سمجھے کوئی بات منظور کر لینا ، کسی میں پھنس جانا **buyable** *adj*. worth-buying : that which can be purchased خریدنے کے قابل ، قابلِ خرید **buyer** (bī-ĕ*) *n*. one who buys خریدار ، گاہک *buyer's market*, trade conditions in which goods are in large supply and consequently prices are in favour of the consumers گاہک کی منڈی ، خریداروں کا دن

buzz (buz) *n*. continuous humming (as of flies) بھنک ، بھنبھناہٹ confused murmur شور جو سمجھ میں نہ آئے سمجھ میں نہ آنے والی ہلکی آوازیں ، ملی جلی آوازیں۔ *buzz of applause* تعریف کی ملی جلی آوازیں confused sound of people moving about ہلچل *v.i.* hum like flies بھنکنا ، بھنبھنانا move about quickly جلدی جانا *I must buzz off* مجھے اب نکل جانا چاہیے hover (*about* or *round* someone) annoyingly (کسی کے) سر پر سوار رہنا (see *Addenda*) **buzzer** (*buz*-ĕ*) *n*. (electric) buzzing signal بھونپو ، سیٹی ، گھنٹی ، بزیزی

buzzard (*buz*-ĕ*d) *n*. a kind of falcon شکرا

by (bī) *prep*. near, at hand کے پاس ، کے قریب ، کے ساتھ *by the door* دروازے کے پاس in, on پر ، میں ، کو *by day* دن میں *by night* رات کو on, along پر ، پر سے ، کے راستے *he came by the main road* وہ بڑی سڑک پر سے آیا *by sea* سمندر کے راستے through the agency of کے ذریعے سے *by post* ڈاک سے *by air* ہوائی ڈاک سے by means of سے untouched by hand ہاتھوں سے چھوا نہیں written by کا ، از ، کی تصنیف ، کا لکھا ہوا ، مصنفہ *a poem by Iqbal* اقبال کی نظم because of بربنائے in the manner of سے *by mistake* غلطی سے with regard to سے *what do you mean by that?* اس سے تمہارا مطلب کیا ہے ؟ (10) not later than تک ، سے پہلے پہلے *by noon* دوپہر سے پہلے پہلے (11) in the amount of بقدر *the train is late by an hour* گاڑی گھنٹہ بھر دیر سے آ رہی ہے (12) in the measure of کے حساب سے *milk is sold by the seer* دودھ سیروں کے حساب سے بکتا ہے (13) according to سے *judging by appearances* صورت شکل سے اندازہ کر کے (یا کرتے ہوئے) (14) in the name of (کی) قسم *swear by God* خدا کی قسم کھانا (15) with succession of بہ ، کر کے *by degrees* درجہ بدرجہ ، بتدریج *by hundreds* سو سو کر کے (16) in respect of مسمّی *Rashid by name* مسمّی رشید (17) multiplied by ضرب *5 feet by 3 feet* پانچ فٹ ضرب تین فٹ ، پانچ فٹ لمبا تین فٹ چوڑا (18) divided by بٹا ، بٹے *three by five* تین بٹے پانچ ، پانچ حصوں میں سے تین (کا) *by reason of*, owing to کے سبب *by oneself*, (*a*) alone اکیلا (*b*) unassisted تن تنہا *by the time* (*that*), as soon as (something happens) جب تک *by right*, if right were done بربنائے حق ، حق سے ، اگر انصاف کیجئے تو *by far* (better, etc.) کہیں (بہتر وغیرہ) *by dint of*, owing to کے بل پر *by and large*, (*a*) largely زیادہ تر (*b*) in every way ہر طرح سے (*c*) all considered فی الجملہ *by and by*, (*a*) after a while, before long تھوڑی دیر میں ، کچھ دیر بعد ، جلدی (*b*) future مستقبل *in the by and by* مستقبل ، میں آئندہ *by the by*, by *the way*, ضمناً ، ہاں تو ، برسبیلِ تذکرہ بسرِراہے ، برسبیلِ تذکرہ *by heart*, *by rote* زبانی *learn by heart* حفظ کرنا ، زبانی یاد کرنا *by all means*, certainly, with pleasure ضرور ، خوشی سے **by-election** *n*. election to one or more seats between two general elections ضمنی انتخاب **by end** *n*. secret purpose مخفی ، مقصد ، اصل مقصد **bygone** *adj*. past, no longer existent گزری ہوئی بات *let bygones be bygones*, forgive and forget the past گزشتہ را صلوات **by-lane** *n*. unfrequented side-lane گلیاری **by-law** *n*. regulation made by local authority (کسی جماعت کا) مقامی قانون ، ذیلی قانون ، بلدیاتی قانون **by-pass** *n*. supplementary road to relieve traffic فالتو سڑک *v. t.* provide with a by-pass round (a place) کے گرد فالتو سڑک بنانا use a by-pass to make a detour round (town etc.) (شہر وغیرہ کا) چکر کاٹ کر جانا evade or dodge (some person or issue) by doing something in a roundabout way (کسی سے) بچ کر نکل جانا ، کنی کترانا ، حق ادا نہ کرنا

by-past *adj*. elapsed گزرا ہوا ، گزشتہ **by path**, **by road**, **by-way** *n*. secluded sideway غیر معروف راستہ *highways and by-ways of*, less known departments of (the subject) ان جانی راہیں یا باتیں **by-product** *n*. subsidiary product (*of*) ضمنی پیداوار **bystander** *n*. spectator تماشائی **by-word** *n*. familiar saying مشہور قول *a by-word* (*for*), (person, place or thing) notorious (for) (کے لیے) بدنام

bye (bī) *n*. (in cricket) ball sent past the wicket without touching the bat or the batsman کرکٹ میں گیند کا بلّے یا بلّے باز کو چھوئے بغیر نکل جانا run made for such a ball ایسے موقع کی رن *bye-leg*, (run made for) ball that touches the batsman's person but not his bat or hand گیند کا بلّے باز کے ہاتھ کے سوا کسی اور حصۂ جسم کو چھونا ، ایسی رن **bye-bye** (*b*.-bī) *n*. (nursery) sleep ننديا bed-time (بچوں کی بولی میں) سونے کا وقت **bye bye** (*bi*-bī) *int*. (colloq.) good-bye وداع خدا حافظ

Byronic (bī-*ron*-ik) *adj*. of the character or style of the English poet Byron (1788-1824) بائرن کے انداز کا

Byzantine (biz-an-tīn, or *bī*-zan-tīn) of *Byzantium* (*i.e.*, Constantinople) بزنطینی *Byzantine Empire*, the Eastern or Greek Empire (A.D. 395-1453) بزنطینی یا مشرقی رومی سلطنت

C

c, C (see) (pl., c's or cs ; pr., seez) the third letter of the English alphabet سی Roman numeral 100 ایک سو the third known quantity in Algebra ج **Note** : The written letter **c** represents several sounds between which it is very important to differentiate as many spellings depend upon this differentiation : (*i*) *soft* **c** (sound of *s*) before vowels *e, i, y*, as in *c*ertain, *c*itizen, *c*ycle. (*ii*) *hard* **c** (sound of *k*) before vowels *a, o, u*. as in *c*at, *c*ot, and *c*ut. (*iii*) *in combination with* **i**. the sound *sh* ; ra*c*ial vi*c*ious ; (*iv*) *in words of Italian origin*, the sound *ch*, as in *c*ello ; or *after* **s**, the sound *sh* as in cres*c*endo ; (*v*) if a syllable ends in *ce* (as tra*ce*, convin*ce*) and a suffix is added which begins with a vowel, the *e* will be kept if the suffix begins with *a, o*, or *u* (as in tra*ce*able) ; but it will be dropped if the suffix begins with *e, i*, or *y* as in convin*c*ing)

cab (kab) *n*. horse-carriage or motor-car which may be hired for short journeys بگھی، ٹیکسی *taxicab* کرائے کی کار، ٹیکسی *cabman* بگھی والا، کوچبان ، گاڑی بان part of railway engine or lorry for the driver ریل کے انجن یا ٹرک میں ڈرائیور کا سائبان **cabby** (*kab*-i) *n*. driver of (usu. horse) cab کوچبان، گاڑیبان

cabal (ka-*bal*) *n*. political clique سیاسی ٹولی secret intrigue جوڑ توڑ، سازباز، خفیہ سازش

cabana *n*. (see *Addenda*)

cabaret (*kab*-a-ray) *n*. songs and dances in a restaurant while guests are eating ہوٹل میں کھانے کے دوران میں رقص و سرود ، کیبرے

cabbage (*kab*-ij) *n*. a vegetable with round head of thick green leaves کرم کلا ، بند گوبھی

cabby (*kab*-i) *n*. see under **cab**

cabin (*kay*-bin) *n*. small roughly-built house (*e.g.*, of logs) کٹیا ، چھپر ا ، جھونپڑی small room (esp. for sleeping in) in a ship or aircraft ہوائی جہاز یا جہاز کا کمرہ ، حجرہ یا کوٹھڑی **cabin-boy** *n*. manservant in ship (جہاز میں مسافروں کا) خدمتگار

cabinet (*kab*-i-net) *n*. group of senior Ministers کابینہ ، وزارت *Cabinet Minister*, senior Minister (as against a Minister of State) وزیر کابینہ (بمقابلہ وزیر مملکت) *Cabinet crisis*, crisis for or in the cabinet which might lead to its overthrow وزارتی کشمکش ، وزارت کو خطرہ *shadow cabinet*, cabinet formed by the opposition comprising prospective holders of portfolios and entrusting each of them with the duty of criticizing his actual counterpart in the government حزب اختلاف کی فرضی کابینہ ، ظلی کابینہ case with drawers for storing or displaying things الماری **cabinet-maker**, skilled furniture maker فرنیچر بنانیوالا، فرنیچر ساز

closet خلوت خانہ ، خلوت کدہ

cable (*kay*-bèl) *n*. thick, strong rope of hemp or wire for ship, etc. مضبوط رسہ، موٹا رسہ، جہاز کا رسہ (also *cablegram*), telecommunication line containing twisted insulated wire laid underground or on ocean bottom بحری تار ، زمین دوز تار (also *cablegram*), message so carried بحری تار کے ذریعے پیغام رسانی ، بحری تار (as measure) 100 fathoms تین سو گز کا بحری پیمانہ *v.t.* & *i*. send (a message) by cable بحری تار بھیجنا *cabled telegram* بحری تار **cablegram** *n*. بحری تار

cacao (ka-*kay*-oh) *n*. cocoa tree or its seeds کوکو کا درخت

the cacao

cache (kash) *n*. hiding-place for food and stores left سیاحوں کا محفوظ مودی خانہ یا سامان رکھنے کی جگہ ، ذخیرہ *v. t*. put in a cache ذخیرے میں رکھنا

cacophony (ka-*kof*-a-ni) ugly sound of voice بد آوازی ugly sound of music بے سرا پن ugly sound of words, etc. تنقید **cacophanous** *adj*. having an ugly sound بد آواز

cackle (*kak*-èl) *n*. noise made by a hen after laying an egg کڑکڑ، کٹ کٹ tall talk شیخی loud laughter کھی کھی ، ہی ہی *v. i*. make such noise کڑکڑانا، کٹ کٹ کرنا ، کھی کھی کرنا ، ہی ہی کرنا ، شیخی بگھارنا

cactus (*kak*-tus) *n*. (*pl*. occ. *cacti*) a hot climate plant with thick, fleshy stems and no leaves, often covered with sharp points, growing chiefly in hot, dry countries کیکٹس

a cactus

cad (kad) *n*. ill-bred person, one who behaves dishonourably کمینہ ، بسفلہ ، رذیل **caddish** *adj*. of or like a cad رذیلانہ ، پاجیانہ

cadaverous (ka-*dav*-e-rus) *adj*. pale like a corpse جس پر مُردنی چھا رہی ہو، لاش کی طرح زرد ، نیم جانی *cadaverous looks*, looks like those of a dead person پتھرائی ہوئی آنکھیں

caddie, caddy (*kad*-i) *n*. servant carrying a golfer's clubs for him round the course گوگان چاکر small box for holding dried tea-leaves چائے کا چھوٹا ڈبہ

cadence (*kay*-dens) *n*. rise and fall of the rhythm of voice or music لے ، الحان ، زیر و بم rhythm in prose نثر کا وزن، جملوں کی موسیقیت

cadet (ka-*det*) *n.* student officer at a military college زیر تربیت فوجی افسر *Cadet Corps*, organization giving military training to British schoolboys برطانیہ میں طلبہ کے لیے فوجی تربیت کی تنظیم

cadge (caj) *v.t.* & *i.* try to get (*from* friends) by begging دوستوں سے مانگ کر کھانا ، دوستوں سے سوال کرنا *cadge a meal* کھانا کسی دوست سے مانگ کھانا **cadger** *n.* دوستوں سے مانگ کھانے والا

cadre (*kah*-dĕ*) regular establishment of services in the army or any other department ڈھانچہ ، عملہ *permanent cadre* مستقل عملہ *lower cadre* ماتحت یا ادنیٰ عملہ (see *Addenda*)

caesura (si-*zew*-ra) *n.* point of natural pause in a line of verse وقفِ شعری

cafe (*kaf*-ay) *n.* small restaurant قہوہ خانہ ، چھوٹا ریستوران ، کیفے *cafe society*, (see *Addenda*) coffee خالی کافی ، سادہ کافی *cafe noir* دودھ ملی کافی *cafe au lait* قہوہ ، کافی

cafeteria (caf-e-*tee*-ri-a) *n.* (Spanish word for coffee-shop now adopted to denote) restaurant where customers serve themselves with carrying their food on a tray from counters to the table کیفے ٹیریا ، خود کار طعام گاہ (see also **automat**. in the *Addenda*)

caffeine (*kaf*-een, or *kaf*-e-in) a cordial alkaloid of tea or coffee کیفین ، کافین ، قہوین

cage (kayj) *n.* box made of wires or bars to confine birds or animals پنجرہ ، قفس cage-like part of a lift used for lowering and raising workers in a mine *v.t.* put or keep, in a cage پنجرے میں ڈالنا ، قید کرنا

a cage

cairn (*kay*-ĕ*n) *n.* pyramid of rough stones set up as a monument or landmark پتھروں کا (یادگار) ڈھیر **cairn, cairn-terrier** *n.* short legged and shaggy-haired terrier پشمی والا ، پست قامت کتا ، کیرن

caisson (*kays*-on) *n.* ammunition box on wheels بارود گاڑی small water-tight chamber used in building bridges, etc., for men to work under water آبدوز حجرہ

cajole (ka-*johl*) *v.t.* use flattery or deceit to persuade (someone *to do* something) لو پتو کرنا ، تھتو تھنبو کرنا ، چاپلوسی سے کام نکالنا ، دم دینا ، **cajolery** *n.* میٹھی میٹھی باتیں بنانا ، خوشامد سے دام میں لانا ، لو پتو ، تھتو تھنبو ، دم جھانسا

cake (kayk) *n.* sweet mixture of flour, butter, eggs, etc., baked in an oven کیک mixture of other kinds of food (انڈے کے سوا کسی اور شے کا) کیک shaped lump of other substance ٹکیہ *a cake of soap* صابن کی ٹکیہ *v.t.* & *i.* coat thickly with something which dries hard پپڑی جمانا ، پپڑی بننا ، *shoes caked with mud* کیچڑ میں لتھڑے ہوئے بوٹ

calamity (ka-*lam*-i-ti) *n.* disaster تباہی ، بربادی ، مصیبت ، آفت great misfortune بدبختی ، بدنصیبی ، سیہ بختی

calamitous *adj.* causing calamity منحوس ، آفت رساں ، مصیبت بھرا

calcium (*kal*-si-um) *n.* soft metal present in limestone, chalk, milk and bones کیلسیم ، چونے کی اساس

calcium carbide *n.* compound of calcium and carbon which burns with a dazzling light کیلسیم کاربائیڈ ،

calculate (*kal*-kew-layt) *v.t.* & *i.* count or reckon شمار کرنا ، حساب کرنا یا لگانا ، اندازہ کرنا یا لگانا ، تخمینہ کرنا ، forecast پیش اندازہ کرنا *calculated to* (do, etc.) کے متعلق خیال تھا ، جس سے مقصود تھا *calculate on* (something) (*a*) rely on پر آس لگانا (*b*) be sure of کا یقین کرنا **calculated** *adj.* & *adv.* سوچا سمجھا ہوا ، بالقصد ، عمداً **calculating** *adj.* careful planning things from selfish motives خودغرض ، غرض مندانہ

calculation (-*ay*-) *n.* تخمینہ ، پیش اندازہ ، پیش گوئی ، اندازہ ، حساب ، گنتی

caldron *n.* same as **cauldron** (which see)

calendar (*kal*-en-dĕ*) *n.* almanac; list of the days, weeks, months, etc., of a particular year تقویم ، جنتری ، کیلنڈر system for fixing the beginning, length and divisions of a year سنہ ، سن *the Moslem calendar* سن ہجری *calendar year*, from Jan. 1 to Dec. 31 تقویمی سال any list or record سیاہہ ، فہرست

a calendar

calender (*kal*-en-dĕ*) *n.* roller-machine for pressing cloth and paper مشینی ابری mendicant dervish قلندر ، درویش *v.t.* put through a calender مشینی ابری کرنا **Note** the difference between **calendar** and **calender.**

calf (kahf) *n.* (pl. *calves*; pr., kahvz) the young of the cow, elephant, whale, etc. بچھڑا ، بچھیا ، گوسالہ ، ہاتھی یا وہیل مچھلی کا بچہ foolish, inexperienced person گاؤدی ، بیل ، اللہ میاں کی گائے *calfskin, calf leather* بچھڑے کی کھال کا چمڑا ، نرم چمڑا *calf-love*, immature affection of a boy for a girl کم سنی کی محبت the fleshy part of the back of the leg, between the knee and ankle پنڈلی

calibre (*kal*-i-bĕ*) *n.* inside measurement across (diameter of) a gun (or any tube or of a bullet, shell, etc.) بندوق (وغیرہ) کے اندرونی قطر کی نال quality of mind or character وجاہت ، اثر و رسوخ ، بسیرت ، حیثیت ، صلاحیت ، لیاقت ، ذہانت *for a man of his calibre* اس کی حیثیت کے آدمی کے لیے

calico (*kal*-i-koh) *n.* longcloth لٹھا

caliph (occ. *calif*) (*kal*-if) *n.* title used by the

senior-most rulers of the Moslem world خلیفہ
caliphate (*kal*-i-fayt) *n.* caliph's office خلافت
a line of caliphs خلافت *the Orthodox Caliphate,* the first four Caliphs of Islam خلافت راشدہ ، خلفائے راشدین

call (kawl) *v.t.* & *i.* give (a name) to نام ہونا ، نام رکھنا ، مسمّی ہونا ، پکارا جانا ، پکارنا *call (someone) names,* insult him by giving him bad names بُرا بھلا کہنا ، گالی دینا consider, think محسوس کرنا ، خیال کرنا ، سمجھنا broadcast (*to*) کے لیے نشریہ بھیجنا direct opponent to play (exposed or other card) (تاش میں) حریف کو کھلا پتّا (وغیرہ) کھیلنے پر مجبور کرنا *call out,* cry, shout پکارنا ، چیخنا ، چلانا ، اونچی آواز سے کہنا *call on,* pay a short visit to, stop at کسی یا کہیں کی ملاقات کو جانا *call at,* جہاز کا کسی بندرگاہ میں ، آنا *call a halt to,* کو روکنا ، کو ختم کرنا *call at (someone)* کسی سے ملاقات کے لیے اُس کے گھر جانا *call attention to* توجہ دلانا *call away* بلا لینا ، رُخ بدل دینا *call forth,* elicit or bring into play (واقعہ) ظہور میں لانا ، جواب نکلوانا *call for,* visit a place to get (something) (کسی شے کے) حاصل کرنے کے لیے جانا ، مانگنا *call a spade a spade,* not to mince matters بلا مبالغہ حقیقت کا اظہار کرنا *call into being* وجود میں لانا *call into play,* اظہار کا موقعہ دینا ، مقتضی ہونا *call (something one's) own* کا مالک ہونا *call over the coals* بازپرس کرنا ، محاسبہ کرنا ، سرزنش کرنا ، ملامت کرنا *call to account* مواخذہ کرنا *call out* للکارنا ، مبازرہ طلب کرنا *call cousins with* عزیزداری جتانا *call to witness* گواہ کرنا ، بطورِ گواہ پیش کرنا *call to the bar* بیرسٹر بنانا *call over,* read out names (at roll-call) (حاضری کے وقت) نام (وغیرہ) پکارنا *call for,* need, demand کا تقاضا کرنا ، کے لیے درکار ہونا *the plan calls for a lot of money* اِس منصوبے کے لیے بڑی رقم درکار ہے *call on* (or *upon someone*) (*a*) go to see (him) سے ملاقات کو جانا (*b*) urge (him) to (do something) سے تقاضا کرنا *call off,* give orders (or decide) to stop something ختم کرنے کا حکم دینا یا فیصلہ کرنا *call your dog off,* اپنے کُتّے کو ہٹائیے *the meeting was called off* جلسہ ملتوی کر دیا گیا *call up, call to mind,* remember or put one in mind of یاد کرنا یا یاد دلانا *call (someone) to order,* ask (someone at a meeting, etc.) to obey the rules; *call something in question,* say that one is doubtful about its truth کسی بات کی صداقت کو معرضِ بحث میں لانا *call a meeting* اجلاس طلب کرنا ، جلسہ منعقد کرنا *call a strike,* announce that there will be one ہڑتال کا اعلان کرنا ، ہڑتال کرانا *n.* cry or shout آواز ، چیخ ، پکار *within call,* near by, not far away قریب message پیغام *telephone call* ٹیلیفون پر ایک بار کی بات ، ٹیلیفون پر بلاوا short visit مختصر ملاقات *pay a call on (someone)* کسی سے ملاقات کے لیے جانا claim (*for* money, help, etc.) تن ، دھن سے خدمت کا تقاضا need ضرورت ، موقعہ ، وجہ *no call for anxiety* پریشانی کی کوئی وجہ نہیں ہے bridge-player's turn to bid برج میں بولنے کی باری ، کال bid thus made کال

caller *n.* (esp.) one who goes to see another ملاقاتی **calling** *n.* (esp.) profession پیشہ ، شغل ، مشغلہ

calligraphy (ka-*lig*-ra-fi) *n.* fine hand-writing, خوش خطی ، خوشنویسی ، کتابت **calligraphist** *n.* خوش نویس ، کاتب

Calliope (ka-*li*-opee) (*Class. myth.*) the Muse of epic poetry کلاؤپی

callipers, calipers (*kal*-i-pē*z) *n. pl.* instrument for measuring the diameter of round objects قطر پیما

callous (*kal*-us) *adj.* (of the skin) hard کھردری (کھال) سخت (جلد) (of a person) disregarding the feelings and sufferings of others سنگدلی ، قساوت **callousness** *n.* بے دردی ، قسیِّ القلب بے حِسی ، بے رحمی

callow (*kal*-oh) *adj.* (of a young person) without experience of life خام ، خام کار ، ناتجربہ کار unfledged جس کے ابھی پر نہ نکلے ہوں

calm (kahm) *v.t.* & *i.* make or become calm ساکن کرنا ، بند کرنا ، روکنا ، تسکین دینا *adj.* quiet پُرسکون ، پُرسکوت ، چپ چاپ ، ساکن serene, tranquil سکون ، سکوت ، ٹھہراؤ ، خاموشی *n.* quietness مطمئن ، دلجمعی serenity دلجمعی ، اطمینان absence of wind ہوا کا بند ہونا یا نہ چلنا **calmly** *adv.* نرمی سے ، دھیرج سے ، آہستہ ، سکون کے ساتھ ، ٹھنڈے دل سے **calmness** *n.* سکون ، ٹھہراؤ ، سکوت ، خاموشی

[S] **Calm** originally meant a rest during the noonday heat; now it signifies free from internal or external agitation, as a calm sea. **Still** means motionless, quiet, resting; **tranquil,** habitually calm; **peaceful** qualifies a place or thought; **placid,** the disposition of one who is not subject to anger; **serene,** countenance or disposition, with a feeling of strength and confidence acquired by experience; **composed,** a person having overcome the tendency to agitation and unruffled temper despite difficulties encountered; **phlegmatic,** a temperament habitually slow to anger.

calorie, calory (*kal*-o-ri) *n.* unit of heat حرارت کی اکائی ، حرارہ unit of energy supplied by food (غذا سے حاصل ہونے والی) توانائی کی اکائی **colorimeter** (-*rim*-) *n.* instrument for measuring calories حرارہ پیما

calumniate *v.t.*, **calumniation** *n.* **calumnious** *adj.* (see under **calumny**)

calumny (*kal*-um-ni) *n.* untrue and damaging statement about someone بُہتان ، افترا ، اتہام ، تہمت **calumniate** (ka-*lum*-ni-ayt) *v.t.* make such damaging statements about (someone) بُہتان باندھنا اتہام کرنا ، طوفان باندھنا ، بدگوئی کرنا ، بدنام کرنا ، مُتہم کرنا **calumnious** *adj.* (person) who calumniates (شخص) افترا پرداز **calumniatory** *adj.* calumniating (statement) تہمت آمیز (بیان) **calumniator** *n.*

calumnious person بدگو، مفتری **calumniation** *n.* making calumniating statements افترا پردازی، بہتان تراشی
calve (cahv) *v. t.* give birth to (a calf) (جانور کا) بیانا ، بچہ دینا (also see **calf**)
Calypso (ka-*lip*-so) *Class. myth.* a nymph living in the island of Ogygia ; when Odysseus was shipwrecked there on his way back from Troy, she delayed his voyage for seven years owing to her love for him کلپسو (*calypso*), (see **Addenda**)
cambric (*kaym*-brik) *n.* fine, thin linen کرنج، کمرکھ
came (kaym) *pa. t.* of **come** (which see)
camel (*kam*-el) *n.* long-necked desert animal, with either one or two humps اونٹ ، اونٹنی ، شتر ، ناقہ ، جمازہ
cameo (*kam*-e-oh) *n.* (pl., *cameos*) jewel with a design carved in relief, often in a different colour ابھرواں نقش والا نگینہ

a cameo

camera (*kam*-ĕ-ra) *n.* apparatus for taking photographs کیمرا ، عکاس ، عکس گیر *in camera*, in the judge's private chamber نجی (عدالت میں نہیں بلکہ) بند کمرے میں **cameraman** *n.* one who operates a camera in the shooting of pictures کیمرہ مین ، عکاس

a camera

cami-knickers *n. pl.* knickers combined with a camisole گلکار سینہ بند والی جانگیہ
camisole (*kam*-i-sohl) *n.* embroidered under-bodice گلکار سینہ بند
camouflage (*kam*-oo-flahzh) *n.* way of hiding or disguising the real appearance of something تبدیل ہیئت use of paint, netting, etc. (esp. in war) to deceive the enemy دشمن کی نظروں سے چھپانا ، *v. t.* diguise thus کیموفلاژ کرنا ، چھپانا ، ہیئت بدل ڈالنا
camp (kamp) *n.* place where people (esp soldiers) live in tents or huts for a time پڑاؤ ، چھاؤنی ، ڈیرا ، فرودگاہ *camp bed*, light folding bed, سفری کھٹیا *camp-chair*, سفری کرسی *camp-stool*, سفری تپائی encamping army (پڑاؤ ڈالے ہوئے) فوج *v. t.* make or live in a camp پڑاؤ کرنا ، پڑاؤ ڈالنا *go camping*, spend a holiday living in tents خیمہ بدوشی ، خیمہ بدوشانہ سیر و سیاحت
camp-follower *n.* non-combatant follower of the army خیمہ بردار ، فوج کا ادنیٰ (غیر عسکری) ملازم satellite ; minor attendant
camp meeting *n.* (U.S.) religious eeting in open air کھلے میدان میں مذہبی جلسہ
campaign (kam-*payn*) *n.* group of military operations with a set purpose or objective, usu. in one area جنگ، مہم series of planned activities to gain a special object باقاعدہ جدوجہد ، منظم کوشش *political campaign* سیاسی جدوجہد *v. i.* take part in or go on a campaign مہم یا جدوجہد میں حصہ لینا ، **campaigner** *n.* مجاہد ، مہم جو ، جدوجہد کرنے والا
camphor (*kam*-fĕ*) *n.* strong-smelling white substance used for medical purposes کافور، کپور
camphorate *v. t.* impregnate with camphor کافور میں بسانا
campus (*kam*-pus) *n.* (U. S.) grounds of a college or university کیمپس ، کالج یا یونیورسٹی کا رقبہ ، جامعہ گاہ *(live) on the campus* جامعہ گاہ میں (رہنا)
[1]**can** (kan) *v.t.* (pa. t., *could* ; pr. kud) be able to (کر) سکنا ، ممکن ہونا ، ہو سکنا have the right to سکنا be permitted to (as a mild imperative) سکنا
could was able to سکا ، سکتا تھا (وغیرہ) feel inclined to (کرنا) چاہتا ہوں ، (کر) سکتا ہوں (وغیرہ) Note that the negative form of 'can' is written as one word in English : **cannot**
[2]**can** *n.* metal container for liquids دودھ وغیرہ کے لیے دھات کی بڑی بوتل any metal container (تیل وغیرہ کا) ڈبہ یا ٹین *v. t.* (-nn-) put into cans ڈبوں میں بند کرنا **canned** (kand) *adj.* ڈبے کا ، ڈبے میں بند *canned milk*, ڈبے کا دودھ **cannery** *n.* factory where food, etc., is canned ڈبوں میں بند کرنے کا کارخانہ

an oilcan

canning *n.* preserving (of fish, fruit, etc.) in tinned iron containers ڈبوں میں بند کرنا *canning industry* ڈبوں میں بند کرنے کی صنعت
canal (ka-*nal*) *n.* channel for irrigation or navigation نہر food pipe in a plant or animal نالی (غذا وغیرہ کی) *alimentary canal* غذائی نالی **canalize** (*kan*-a-liz) *v. t.* dig canal(s) from a river دریا سے نہریں نکالنا **canalization** *n.* canalizing نہروں کی کھدائی ، نہر کشی
canard (ka-*nah**, or ka-*nah*d*) false rumour بے پرکی ، بے بنیاد خبر ، جھوٹی افواہ
canary (ka-*nay*-ri) *n.* small yellow songbird جزائر کینری کی زرد بلبل ، کناری its colour, light yellow ہلکا زرد رنگ

a canary

cancan (kan-kan) *n.* an indecent type of U. S. dance کن کن ، ناچ ، کنکنی
cancel (*kan*-sel) *v. t.* (*-ll-*) cross out قلم زد کرنا ، کاٹ ڈالنا make marks on (something, *e.g.*, postage stamp) to prevent its being re-used (ڈاک کے ٹکٹوں وغیرہ) پر مہر لگانا ، یا میں سوراخ کرنا ، rescind something already arranged منسوخ کرنا ، تنسیخ کرنا ، فسخ *cancel a meeting* جلسہ منسوخ کرنا (اعلان کردہ) **cancellation** (-*ay*-) *n.* act of cancelling تنسیخ ، منسوخی

خطِّ نسخ کھینچنا

cancer (*kan*-sē*) *n.* diseased tumour destroying part of the body سرطان any corroding evil جان لیوا (خرابی) sign of the zodiac (also called *Crab*) برج سرطان *the Tropic of Cancer*; latitude 23½° N. خطِ سرطان **cancerous** *adj.* having to do with the disease called cancer سرطانی

candid (*kan*-did) *adj.* frank, straight-forward صاف دل، صاف گو، صادق الطبع، بے لاگ، مخلص، اخلاص مند *candid camera* (see *Addenda*) **candidly** *adv.* frankly بے لاگ، صاف گوئی سے، صاف صاف **candour, candidness** *n.* frankness; being straightforward اخلاص، خلوص، صاف گوئی

[S] **Candid** is a person or statement free from disguise or bias, at least in intention; **frank**, expressing the truth at the risk of incurring displeasure; **impartial**, without regard for friendship or otherwise; **honest**, prompted by a regard for truth; **artless**, lacking in trickery or finesse; **naive**, showing a certain ignorance of conventions; **unsophisticated**, pure and whole, natural; **sincere**, without mask, and prompted by the heart; **fair**, recognized as truthful; **ingenuous**, lacking in knowledge of life.

candidate (*kand*-i-dayt) *n.* one who offers himself or is put forward by someone to take an office or position اُمیدوار person taking an examination (امتحان کا) اُمیدوار **candidature** (kan-di-day-chē*), **candidacy** *n.* being a candidate اُمیدواری، خواستگاری (someone's) candidature for (some post, etc.) (کسی نوکری وغیرہ کے لیے کسی) کی اُمیدواری

candied (*kand*-eed) *adj.* see under **candy**

candle (*kand*-ĕl) *n.* wax cylinder with wick used as a light موم بتی، قندیل، شمع *is not worth the candle*, is more troublesome than it is worth بیکار ہے، تضیعِ اوقات ہے، فضول ہے **candle-power** *n.* unit for measuring light نوری اکائی، (بتی کی) طاقت 60 candle-power lamp ساٹھ کینڈل پاور کا بلب، ساٹھ کا قمقمہ، ساٹھ کی طاقت کا بلب **candlestick** *n.* holder for a candle شمع دان *bell, book and candle*, allusion to cursing formula used by church dignitaries پادریوں کی بددُعا کی تسبیح *not fit to hold the candle to*, quite inferior to سے بہت ادنیٰ *burn the candle at both ends*, overtax (oneself or one's resources) دونوں ہاتھوں سے لُٹانا۔ اللّے تللّے کرنا، (جان یا وسائل پر) حد سے زیادہ زور ڈالنا

candour (*kan*-dē*) *n.* quality of being candid, saying freely what one thinks صاف گوئی، صاف fairmindedness بے لاگ پن، بغیر جانبداری (see also **candid**)

candy, sugar-candy (*kan*-di, *shoo*-gē*-*kan*-di) (common U. S. word for what in England are usu. called sweets) ٹانی، کھانڈ کی مٹھائی *candystore* ٹانی کی دُکان *v.t.* preserve (fruit, etc.) by boiling in sugar چینی کے قوام میں رکھنا، پاگنا **candied** *adj.* چینی کے قوام میں رکھا ہوا

cane (kayn) *n.* long, hollow-jointed stem of grass-like plant used for making furniture بید *sugar-cane* گنّا، اوکھ، ایکھ *cane-sugar* sugar made from sugar-cane گنّے کی کھانڈ any other stem like that بید کی شکل کی کوئی اَور چیز cane stem used as a walking-stick چھڑی such stick for punishing children with بید *v. t.* make or repair with cane بید سے بنانا یا مرمت کرنا punish with a cane بید سے مارنا، بید سے سزا دینا

canine (*kan*-in) *adj.* of dogs کُتّوں سے متعلق، کلبی *canine teeth* (in man) four sharp-pointed teeth between the incisors and premolars انیاب (واحد ناب)

canister (ka-*nis*-tē*) *n.* small metal box (for tea, etc.) (چائے وغیرہ کا) چھوٹا ڈبّہ

canker (*kank*-ē*) *n.* disease which destroys the wood of trees پت روگ، کیڑا evil influence causing decay زہر، بد اثر، بُرے اثرات *v. i.* be eaten away with canker مڑنا، سڑ جانا

canned *adj.*, **cannery, canning** *n.* see under [2]**can**

cannibal (*kan*-i-bĕl) *n.* person who eats human flesh آدم خور، مردم خور animal that eats its own kind ہم جنس خور (حیوان) **cannibalistic** *adj.* relating to or based on this practice آدم خورانہ **cannibalism** *n.* this practice آدم خوری **cannibalize** *v. t.* & *i.* (see **Addenda**)

cannon (*kan*-un) *n.* large, old type of gun firing a solid ball پُرانی قسم کی توپ automatic gun used in aircraft (طیاروں میں استعمال ہونے والی) توپ، طیارہ توپ **cannon ball** *n.* solid ball fired from a cannon توپ کا گولہ **cannonade** (kan-o-*nayd*) *n.* continued firing of big guns (now usu. called *bombardment*) گولہ باری، گولہ اندازی، توپیں داغنا، چلانا یا چھوڑنا

a cannon

cannot, negative form of **can** (which see)

canny (*kan*-i) *adj.* not prepared to take unknown risks ہوشیار، سیانا cautious about spending money کفایت شعار، روپے پیسے کے معاملے میں محتاط **cannily** *adv.* shrewdly ہوشیاری سے in a thrifty manner کفایت شعارانہ

canoe (ka-*noo*) *n.* light boat moved by one or more paddles ڈونگا، ڈونگیا *v. t.* travel by canoe ڈونگے میں سوار ہونا

a canoe

canon (*kan*-un) *n.* church law شریعت، دینی فتویٰ general standard by which something is judged معیار، اصول، عام قاعدہ، قانون priest with duties in a

cathedral (and addressed as *the Rev. Canon*) بڑے گرجے کا چھوٹا پادری ، کینن **canonical** (ka-*non*-i-kèl) *adj.* according to church laws شرعی ، دینی ، مذہبی
canonize *v. t.* place in the canon (عیسائی) اولیاء کی مسلّمہ فہرست میں شامل ہونا
[2]**canon** *n.* same as **canyon** (which see)
canopy (*kan*-o-pi) *n.* covering over the head of a throne چتر ، چترِ شاہی covering over a bed چھپر کھٹ ، مسہری any similarly placed covering سائبان

a canopy

[1]**cant** (kant) *n.* insincere talk ظاہرداری یا ریاکارانہ گفتگو ، منافقانہ اندازِ گفتگو special words used by a class of people کسی مخصوص گروہ یا پیشہ کی بولی ، پیشہ ورانہ اصطلاحات ، بولی *thieves' cant* چوروں کی بولی
[2]**cant.** *n.* abbr. **cantonment** (which see)
[3]**can't** abb. of **cannot** (see under can)
Cantab, Cantabrigian *n.* member of Cambridge University کیمبرج کا طالب علم
cantankerous (kan-*tank*-è-rus) *adj.* perverse in temper الٹی کھوپڑی quarrelsome جھگڑالو ، حجتی ، تکراری
cantankerousness *n.* جھگڑالو پن **cantankerously** *adv.* تکرار سے
cantata (kan-*tah*-ta) *n.* dramatic poem or biblical story sung without acting آلھا ، ہیر
canteen (kant-*een*) *n.* place (in army barracks or offices) where food, drink, and sometime other articles are sold کینٹین box of table silver and cutlery چھری کانٹے رکھنے کا صندوقچہ soldier's mess-tin or water-bottle فوجیوں کے برتن
canter (*kant*-ĕ*) *v. t.* & *i.* (cause a horse to) go at a slow or easy gallop رہوار چلنا یا چلانا *n.* easy gallop رہوار چال
cantilever (*kant*-i-lee-vĕ*) *n.* large bracket extending from wall or base (to support a balcony) تو ڑا **cantilever bridge** bridge of connected cantilevers توڑے دار پل

a cantilever bridge

canto (*kant*-oh) *n.* (pl., *cantos* ; pr. *kant*-ohz) one of the chief divisions in a long poem مثنوی کا باب
canton (*kant*-un) *n.* subdivision of a country (esp. in Switzerland) ضلع ، سوئس جمہوریہ کی ایک ریاست
cantonment (kan-*ton*-ment) (abbr. **cant.**) *n.* permanent military station in the Indo-Pakistan subcontinent چھاؤنی ، اردو ، معسکر
canvas (*kan*-vas) *n.* strong, coarse cloth used for sails, bags, and paintings کینوس ، پلاس ، کرگچ *under canvas* (*a*) sleeping in tents زیرِ خیمہ ، خیمے تلے (*b*) with sails spread بادبان کھولے
canvass (*kan*-vas) *v. t.* & *i.* ask (people) for support, or votes حمایت یا ووٹ (پرچیاں) حاصل کرنے کی کوشش کرنا try to procure order for goods مال کا آرڈر لینا ، مال بہم پہنچانے کی فرمائش حاصل کرنا examine (a question) thoroughly by asking for opinion رائے (عامہ) سے کسی مسئلے میں استصواب کرنا **Note : Canvass** (with an extra *s*), though so similar to *canvas* in spelling, differs from it a lot in meaning.
canyon (*kan*-yon), **canon** *n.* deep gorge with a river flowing through it کھڈ ، گہری کھڈ
cap (kap) *n.* soft, brimless head-covering ٹوپی کلاہ *football cap*, mark of inclusion in a football team فٹ بال ٹیم میں شرکت کا اعلان any cover, etc., like a cap غلاف (یا ٹوپی جیسی کوئی اور چیز) *v. t.* (-pp-) award player a football cap فٹ بال ٹیم میں شرکت کی نشانی عطا کرنا put a cap on ٹوپی لگانا *cap verses* بیت بازی کرنا *cap story*, tell a better story, say something more amusing (than someone else) بہتر لطیفہ سنانا ، لطیفہ بازی یا قصہ گوئی میں سبقت لے جانا *steel-cap* خود *knee-cap* گھٹنے کی چپنی ، چپنی *fool's cap* (مخرہ) مسخرے کی (مخروطی) ٹوپی *cap and bells* مسخروں کی علامت *(with) cap in hand* عاجزانہ ، انکسار کے ساتھ *set one's cap at* (مرد) کا کسی (عورت) کو رجھانا *the cap fits* تیر ٹھیک نشانے پر بیٹھا ، چوٹ لگی ، کسی شخص کا یہ احساس کہ بات اس پر صادق آتی ہے **cap-a-pie** (cap-a-*pee*) *adv.* from head to foot سراپا ، سر تا پا *armed cap-a-pie* سرتاپا مسلح **knee-cap** *n.* bone over knee joint گھٹنے کی چپنی **toe-cap** *n.* part of shoe, etc., covering the toe بوٹ کا پنجہ ، ٹو
capable (*kayp*-a-bèl) *adj.* able قابل ، لائق ، جوہر *capable (of doing)* کر گزرنے والا ، کا اہل ، کرنے جوگ (of things) ready for ; کے لیے موزوں (of things) admitting of کے قابل **capability** (kayp-a-*bil*-i-ti) *n.* power to do things قابلیت ، لیاقت ، اہلیت (pl.) qualities that await development قابلیت و امکانات
capably *adv.* ably, efficiently قابلیت سے
capacious *adj.* (see under **capacity**)
capacity (ka-*pas*-i-ti) *n.* ability to contain things گنجائش ، وسعت ، ظرف ، سمائی seating capacity نشستوں کی گنجائش power for containing (happiness, etc.) ذکی ، ہمت ability to learn سیکھنے کی صلاحیت *a mind of great capacity* بڑی صلاحیتوں والا دماغ *filled to capacity*, quite full بھرپور ، بھرا ہوا position حیثیت *in the capacity of, in this capacity*, acting as, in the position of اس (یا کی) حیثیت سے **capacious** (ka-*pay*-shus) *adj.* roomy ; able to hold much وسیع ، فراخ ، کشادہ **caparison** (ka-*pa*-ri-sun) *n.* (*lit.*) harness trappings جھول *v. t.* put caparison on پر جھول ڈالنا ، پرستر ڈالنا
cape (kayp) *n.* loose sleeveless outer garment

worn over the shoulders بے آستین (کی) قبا head-land ; high point of land jutting out into the sea راس، گردنہ v. i. put a cape on بے آستین کی قبا پہننا
caper (*kayp*-ĕ*) *v. i.* jump about playfully کلیلیں کرنا کودنا، پھاندنا *cut capers, cut a caper* (*a*) jump about merrily کلیلیں کرنا، اچھلنا، کودنا، کدکڑے مارنا (*b*) behave foolishly احمقانہ حرکات کرنا
capillary (ka-*pil*-a-ri) *n.* thin, hair-like thing بال کی سی، شعری *adj.* thin, hair-like بال سا باریک ، شعری *capillary attraction*, force which raises a liquid into capillary tubes شعری جذب *capillary repulsion* شعری دفع
capital (*kap*-i-tĕl) *n.* the chief city of country دارالحکومت، عاصمہ (of letters) not small بڑے حروف wealth (money and property) used for the production of more wealth سرمایہ، راس المال، اصل *fixed capital*, machinery, property, etc. اصل قائم، مستقل سرمایہ *circulating capital, floating capital*, goods, money, etc. اصل دائر، چلت سرمایہ capitalists as a class (سرمایہ دار طبقہ) *capital and labour* سرمایہ دار اور مزدور top part of a column ستون کا بالائی حصہ (colloq.) excellent (thing) نہایت شاندار، بہت عمدہ make capital out of (a point, etc.) exploit it fully سے پورا فائدہ اٹھانا *adj.* of chief importance بڑا اہم، خاص طور پر *the capital point is this* خاص طور سے اہم بات یہ ہے ، اہم involving death penalty سزائے موت والا *capital crime*, crime punishable by death مستوجب قتل جرم *capital punishment*, death penalty سزائے موت **capitalism** (-izm) *n.* economic system in which country's trade and industry are controlled by the personal owners of capital سرمایہ داری، سرمایہ دارانہ نظام
capitalist *n.* person owning and controlling much capital سرمایہ دار **capitalistic** (kap-i-ta-*list*-ik) *adj.* سرمایہ دار **capitalize** (*kap*-i-ta-līz) *v. t.* change into or use as capital سے استفادہ یا انتفاع *capitalize on a point* (*etc.*), exploit it fully (کمزوری وغیرہ) سے پورا فائدہ اٹھانا write out in capital letter(s) بڑے حرفوں میں لکھنا **capitalization** (-*zay*-) *n.* capitalizing پورا پورا استفادہ یا انتفاع writing out in capital letter(s) بڑے حروف میں لکھنا
Capitol (kap-i-tĕl) *n.* temple of Jupiter in ancient Rome جیوپیٹر کا مندر، کیپیٹل any important governmental building in the classical style like the chamber of U. S. Congress in Washington کیپیٹل
capitulate (ka-*pit*-eu-layt) *v. i.* surrender on stated conditions مشروط سپر اندازی، مشروط اطاعت ، چند شرائط پر ہتھیار ڈالنا، قلعہ (دشمن کے) حوالے کر دینا، اطاعت قبول کر لینا
capitulation (ka-pi-tew-*lay*-shĕn) *n.* conditional surrender مشروط اطاعت (*pl.*) special concessions granted by a weak country to a powerful one خصوصی مراعات
capon (*kay*-pon) *n.* cock fattened by castration موٹا خصی مرغا **caponed** (-pund) *adj.* (cock) thus fattened خصی کر کے موٹا کیا ہوا (مرغا)
caprice (ka-*prees*) *n.* unreasoned change of mind or behaviour لہر، ترنگ، من کی موج، بےتکا پن، تلوّن مزاجی fanciful idea with little thought behind it تخیل کی جولانی ، تخیل کاری **capricious** (ka-*pree*-shus) *adj.* full of caprice پل میں تولہ پل میں ماشہ، من ترجیا، لہری often changing without apparent cause متلون مزاج ، ہر آن بدلنے والا
Capricorn (*cap*-ri-ko*n) *n.* a sign of the Zodiac جدی *the Tropic of Capricorn*, latitude 23½° S. خط جدی
capsize (kap-*sīz*) *v. t. & i.* overturn الٹنا، الٹ جانا **capsizable** *adj.* that can overturn الٹ سکنے والا
capstan (*kaps*-tun) *n.* upright drum or barrel-like object for raising (sails, anchor, etc.) on a cable, etc. (جہاز میں لنگر وغیرہ کا) چرخ، جہازی چرخ

a capstan

capsule (*kap*-sewl) *n.* seed case on a plant ڈوڈا tiny soluble container for medicine (دوا رکھنے کی) ہجّی کی ڈبیہ ، پھل ڈبیہ ، ڈرجک metal cap for bottle بوتل کا دھاتی ڈھکنا *adj.* & (see *Addenda*)

capsule (1. for seeds 2. for medicine)

captain (*kap*-tin) (abb. *Capt.*) *n.* leader or commander کپتان، قائد، سردار *captain of a ship* ناخدا *captain of a cricket team*, skipper کرکٹ ٹیم کا کپتان *v.t.* act as captain of کی قیادت کرنا، کا سردار ہونا **captaincy** *n.* position of a captain کپتانی، سرداری، قیادت
caption (*kap*-shun) *n.* short heading of an article عنوان، سرخی words printed with a picture, تصویری تفصیل یا تشریح words shown on a cinema screen to explain the story (سینما میں) پردے پر لکھی ہوئی تشریح ، بر پردہ تشریح
captious (*kap*-shus) *adj.* fault-finding ; making protests about trifles نکتہ چین ، حرف گیر ، عیب چین ، عیب جو، معترض، خوردہ گیر **captiousness** *n.* being captious ; fault-finding خوردہ گیری یا نکتہ چینی ، حرف گیری
captivate (*kap*-ti-vayt) *v.t.* capture the fancy of ; charm لبھانا، موہ لینا ، فریفتہ کرنا **captivating** *adj.* charming دل فریب، موہنی **captivation** *n.* act of captivating دل فریبی، لبھانا
captive (*kap*-tiv) *n.* captured قیدی، اسیر، گرفتار *take* (*someone*) *captive* کو گرفتار کرنا *captive balloon*, one moored to the ground (or ship) زمین بستہ غبارہ (see *Addenda*) **captivity** (kap-tiv-i-ti) *n.* state

of being held captive اَسیری، اَسارت، قید، گرفتاری **captor** (kap-tĕ*) *n.* one who takes someone captive پکڑنے والا، گرفتار کرنے والا، گرفتار کُنندہ
capture (*kap*-chĕ*) *v.t.* make a prisoner of قید کرنا، گرفتار کرنا take (by force or trickery) سَر کرنا، فتح کرنا، قابُو میں کرنا *capture (someone's) attention* توجہ پوری طرح اپنی طرف مُنعَطِف کرنا *n.* act of capturing تسخیر، قبضہ، فتح thing captured مقبوضہ یا مفتوحہ شئے، مالِ غنیمت، لُوٹ کا مال captured person اَسیر، قیدی، بندی **capturer** *n.* one who captures (person or place) *n.* معرکے سر کرنے والا، فاتح، گرفتار کُنندہ
car (kah*) *n.* motor-car موٹر (on a railway-train) coach ریل کا ڈبّہ *sleeping-car* سونے کا ڈبّہ *dining-car* کھانے کا ڈبّہ chariot رتھ، گاڑی **carhop** *n.*, **carport** *n.* (see *Addenda*) **carload** *n.* as much (*of* something) as a car can carry جتنا کار میں آسکے، کار بھر
caramel (*ka*-ra-mel) *n.* burnt sugar used for colouring and flavouring سوختہ شکر a sweetmeat ایک قسم کی مٹھائی
carat (*ka*-rat) *n.* unit of weight for jewels قیراط (جواہرات تولنے کا وزن) unit of quality for gold, (*e.g.*, 24-carat gold is pure gold, 18-carat gold has one-third of alloy in it) قیراط (سونے کے خالص یا (خالص ہونے کا اندازہ)
caravan (*ka*-ra-van) *n.* company of travellers goin together (usu. on foot, or on horseback, etc.) for safety کارواں، قافلہ covered wagon for transporting wild animals جنگلی جانوروں کے لیے بند گاڑی a house on wheels خانۂ رواں جانور گاڑی
carbine (*kah*-bin*) *n.* short rifle used by cavaliers قرابین
carbolic acid (kah*-*bol*-ik *as*-id) *n.* acid made from coal-tar and used as a disinfectant کاربالک تیزاب، کاربالک، تُرشہ *carbolic soap*, disinfectant soap containing this acid کاربالک صابن
carbon (*kah*-bun) *n.* chemical substance present in coal and diamonds کاربن *carbon paper*, thin paper coated with coloured matter, used between sheets of writing paper for taking copies (نقل لینے کے لیے) مسالے دار کاغذ **carbon dioxide, carbonic acid** (**gas**) *n.* heavy, soluble gas formed when carbon burns; (in its solid state it is called 'dry ice' and is used for refrigeration purposes) کاربانک ترشہ گیس، تیزاب فحمی **carboniferous** *adj.* carbon-producing کاربن ساز **carbonize** *v.t.* reduce to carbon or charcoal کاربن بنانا، کوئلہ بنا دینا (یا کرنا) apply carbon to کاربن لگانا، کاربن مالی کرنا **carbonization** *n.* کاربن سازی، کاربن مالی
carbuncle (kah*-*bunk*-ĕl) *n.* bright (usu. red) jewel لعل، یاقوت، قیمتی پتھر، نگینہ red, painful swelling under the skin دُنبل **carbuncled** *adj.* دُنبل دار
carburettor, carburetter (kah*-bew-*ret*-ĕ*) *n.* part of an internal-combustion engine in which petrol vapour and air are mixed کاربن کار
carcass, carcase (*kah*-kas) *n.* headless dead body of an animal لاش، لاشہ، دھڑ، جانور کی بے سری لاش slaughtered animal with head severed ذَبیحہ، جانور کا ڈھیر *save (one's) carcase*, save (one's) skin اپنی جان بچانا
card (kah*d) *n.* thick, stiff paper, موٹا کاغذ، دفتی، گتّا *cardboard* گتّا، دفتی *wedding card* رُقعۂ شادی *postcard*, open letter sent by mail کارڈ *visiting card*, card giving a person's name, etc. مُلاقاتی کارڈ *Christmas card*, greetings card sent on Christmas کرسمس کارڈ *'Id card*, such card sent on the Muslim religious festivals called 'Id or Eed عید کارڈ *birthday card* سالگرہ کی مُبارک باد کا کارڈ *admission card* ٹکٹ داخلہ *cards*
playing cards, cards (in sets of 52) for a well-known game تاش، گنجفہ (**Note:** *Spades is* حُکم، *clubs is* چِڑیا *diamonds is* اینٹ *hearts is* پان. **We speak** playing cards *of the ace of spades* حکم کا یکّا *the king of clubs* چڑیا کا بادشاہ *the queen of hearts* پان کی بیگم *the knave of diamonds* اینٹ کا غلام *the ten or nine, eight, seven, six, five, four, three or two of spades (etc.)* حکم (وغیرہ) کا دہلا (یا نہلا، اٹھّا (آٹھی)، ستّا (ستّی) چھکّا (چھکّی)، پنجا (پنجی)، چوکا (چوکی)، تیا (یا تیکی) اور دُوکی (تاش کے) پتّے) *play (at) cards* تاش کھیلنا *deal the cards* (تاش کے) پتّے بانٹنا یا دینا *shuffle the cards* پتّے پھینٹنا *a suit in cards* تاش کے پتّے کا سُوٹ *cut the cards* تاش کی بازی یا ہاتھ کاٹنا *have the cards in (one's) hands* غالب ہونا، جیتنا *play (one's) cards well* اچھی چال چلنا، چال چل کر ہاتھ *make a card* بنا لینا *court-card* also called a *coat card* (تاش میں) بادشاہ، بیگم یا غلام *play the hand* (اپنی باری کا) پتّا پھینکنا *take the trick* سر بنانا یا لینا *put (one's) cards on the table*, reveal (one's) plans اپنا داؤ بتا کر کھیلنا، جیتی ہوئی بازی کھیلنا *show (one's) cards, throw up (one's) cards*, give up (one's) plan تدبیر، ارادہ یا منصوبہ ترک کرنا *(have a) card up (one's) sleeve* (have) reserve secret resources or plans آخری داؤ محفوظ رکھنا، مخفی تدبیر رکھنا *sure card, safe card*, یقینی منصوبہ *doubtful card* غیر یقینی منصوبہ *queer card* عجیب آدمی *house of cards* کاغذ کی ناؤ، کاغذ کی ہنڈیا، پاؤں اکھڑا *on the cards*, probable or possible ممکن، اغلب منصوبہ *speak by the card*, حقائق صحت کے ساتھ بیان کرنا *a knowing card* واقف حال، رازداں شخص *leave (one's) card on (someone)* کسی سے ملاقات نہ ہو سکے تو اُس کے ہاں اپنا ملاقاتی کارڈ چھوڑ آنا *card-case* ملاقاتی کارڈ رکھنے کا ڈبّہ *the card*, the correct thing, the anticipated thing ٹھیک وہی بات جس کی توقع تھی *card-carrying adj.* (see *Addenda*) instrument for combing wool اُون صاف کرنے کا کنگھا

v.t. comb (wool, etc.) دُھننا، دُھنکنا **carder** *n.* one who cards wool or cotton دُھنیا، پُونیا، حلاج *carder's bow* دُھنکی **card-index** *n.* index in which each item is entered on a separate card الگ الگ کارڈوں پر بنایا ہوا کارڈی اشاریہ *v.t.* make a card-index of کارڈی اشاریہ (یا مرتب کرنا) بنانا

cardamom (*kah**d-i-mum) *n.* a kind of spice الائچی *large cardamom* بڑی الائچی *small cardamom* چھوٹی الائچی

cardinal (*kah**d-i-nēl) *adj.* chief افضل most important اہم basic بنیادی، اصلی *cardinal numbers*, one, two, three, etc. اعداد صحیح *cardinal points* (North, South, East and West) اطراف (شمال، جنوب، مشرق، مغرب) *n.* one of the 70 Roman Catholic priests who get together to elect the new Pope کارڈینل، کاردنال

care (*kay*-ē*) *n.* anxiety فکرمندی، پریشانی، تشویش occasion for anxiety وجہِ تشویش cause of sorrow or anxiety رنج یا پریشانی کا باعث، تفکرات *free from care* تفکرات سے آزاد یا بری *the cares of a large family* بڑے کنبے کے باعث تفکرات، عیال داری کی پریشانیاں *take care, have a care*, be on the watch ! beware ! خبردار، ہوشیار *take care of*, (a) look after کی نگرانی یا نگہداشت کرنا (b) see to the safety or welfare of کا خیال رکھنا، کی بہبود یا برتری کے لیے کوشاں ہونا *in* (or *under*) *the care of*, looked after by کے زیر نگرانی *v.t.* feel interest, anxiety, or sorrow فکرمند ہونا، تشویش مند ہونا، کی پروا ہونا یا کرنا، متفکر ہونا *who cares !* کسے پروا ہے !، اپنی بلا سے (*care for*), (a) have a liking for, be fond of کا مشتاق ہونا (b) look after کی نگرانی یا نگہداشت کرنا *care to* (*do*), be willing to (do) (کرنے) پر آمادہ ہونا **careful** *adj.* cautious (*with* something or *not to* do it) محتاط thrifty کفایت شعار (of thing) done or made with care احتیاط سے کیا ہوا thorough, exact ہوشمندانہ not exaggerated محتاط **carefully** *adv.* احتیاط سے، ہوشمندی سے، کفایت شعاری سے **careless** *adj.* not taking care (*of*) (سے) غافل ہونا، بے پروا not worrying about بے پروا، سہل انگار، لاابالی light-hearted, cheerful خوش باش، بے فکر **carelessly** *adv.* بے پروائی سے **carelessness** *n.* بے پروائی، غفلت *a piece of carelessness*, a careless action بے پروائی، غفلت، سہل انگاری **caretaker** (kay*-tayk-e*) *n.* person taking care of building while its owners are away محافظ *caretaker government*, (interim) Ministry working till a proper one is installed کام چلاؤ وزارت، محافظ حکومت

■ One is **careful** of what one has or has not to do ; **cautious**, disinclined to take risks ; **prudent**, taking legitimate habitual care ; **wary**, suspecting something ; **circumspect**, looking around ; **canny**, naturally holding back ; **solicitous** of someone's welfare ; **mindful** of instructions received ; **pains-taking**, habitually

career (ka-*ree*-ē*) *n.* progress through life زندگی کا ڈھب (a person's) life-history سوانح حیات، سوانح عمری profession or occupation پیشہ، ذریعۂ معاش *careers open to young men* نوجوانوں کے لیے ذرائع معاش quick or violent movement زور، دوڑ دھوپ، تگاپو *in full career* پورے جوبن پر، پورے زوروں سے *v.t.* to move at a swift pace تیز چلنا، اندھا دھند جانا *v.t. career along*, بے دھڑک جانا *career through* (or *over*) (*a place*), rush wildly through (it) میں سے اندھا دھند گزر جانا **careerist** (-*ree*-ē-) *n.* one who is guided in life by the interest of self-advancement جسے محض اپنی ترقی سے غرض ہو، ابن الوقت، مفاد پرست

careful, careless *adj.* see under **care**

caress (ka-*res*) *n.* loving touch دلار، پیار، پچکار، نازو ادا، ملامست، اختلاط، تھپکنا، پیار سے ہاتھ پھیرنا kiss بوسہ بازی *v.t.* to kiss or give loving touch پیار سے ہاتھ پھیرنا، چومنا

caret (*ka*-ret) *n.* sign ^ used to show, in writing or print, where something is to be added خارجہ، یہ نشان ^

caretaker *n.* see under **care**

cargo (*kah**-goh) *n.* (pl., *cargoes*) goods carried in a ship or aircraft جہازی کھیپ، بار جہاز، جہاز یا ہوائی جہاز سے جانے والا مال *cargo vessel* بار بردار (بحری) جہاز

caricature (*ka*-ri-ka-che-ē*) *n.* picture or imitation of someone or something stressing certain ridiculous features کسی کے مضحکہ پہلو کو ابھارنے والا خاکہ یا ایسی نقل *v.t.* present a ridiculous likeness of (کسی کا) خاکہ اڑانا، روپ بنانا (یا) گڈھ اپنا نا **caricaturist** *n.* one who makes a caricature خاکہ ساز، خاکہ اڑانے والا، ہزال **caricaturable** *adj.* that can be caricatured مضحکہ خیز، خاکہ اڑانے کے قابل

caries (*kayr*-i-eez) *n.* decay of bone ہڈی کی بوسیدگی

carminative *adj.* & *n.* (medicine) relieving flatulence ریاح شکن (دوا)

carmine (*kah**myn) *adj.* & *n.* crimson ; deep red (colour) قرمزی (رنگ)

carnage (*kah**-nij) *n.* the killing of many people شدید خون ریزی، قتل عام، عام خون فشانی

carnal (*kah**-nēl) *adj.* of the body or flesh جسمانی، بدنی sensual (as opposed to *spiritual*) نفسانی، حیوانی، دیزی *carnal desires* نفسانی خواہشات

carnation (kah*-*nay*-shen) *n.* garden plant with sweet smelling flowers کارنیشن rosy-pink colour ہلکا گلابی یا گہرا پیازی رنگ

a carnation

carnival (*kah**ni-vēl) *n.* Roman Catholic festival during the week before Lent کارنیوال، قرنوال public merry-making and feasting رنگ رلیاں، جشن، عیش و عشرت *carnival of* (*something*) دل کے ارمان پورے کر کے کیا ہوا کام *carnival of bloodshed* جی بھر کے کی ہوئی خون ریزی، جشن خونریزی

carnivora *n. pl.* (see under **carnivorous**

carnivorous (kah*niv-o-rus) *adj.* flesh-eating

(animal) گوشت خور جانور **carnivora** (-*niv*-) *n. pl.* carnivorous animals گوشت خور جانور (جمع)

carol (*ka*-rul) *n.* song of joy or praise نغمۂ طرب یا ترانۂ تحسین (also called *Christmas carol*) (esp.) happy Christmas hymn بڑے دن کا ترانہ، ترانۂ کرسمس *v.t.* (-ll-) sing happily پرندوں کا چہچہانا، انسانوں کا جوش کے گیت گانا

Caroline (*ka*-ro-lin) *adj.* of or pertaining to the times of Charles I & II of England چارلس اول یا دوم کے عہد کا، کارلینی • **carolingian** (ka-ro-*linj*-i-ēn), **carlovingian** (kah*-lo-*vinj*-i-en) *adj.* (of the times of) the French monarchs of the dynasty of Charlemagne شارلینی

carouse (ka-*rouz*) *v. i.* drink heavily and have a merry time کھُل کھیلنا، کھُل کے شراب پینا اور عیش اُڑانا، بلا نوشی کرنا اور دادِ عیش دینا **carousal** (-*rowz*-) *n.* merry and noisy drinking party بلانوشی وعیش کوشی، رندی، سیہ مستی

carp (kah*p) *n.* fresh-water fish living in ponds جوہڑکی ایک قسم کی مچھلی سیم، ماہی *v.t.* (*carp at*), make unnecessary complaints about (trifles, etc.) مین میخ نکالنا، ذرا ذرا سے فضول شکوے کرنا، کیڑے نکالنا، نکتہ چینی، خوردہ گیر، حرف گیر *a carping tongue* خوردہ گیری کرنا *carping criticism*

a carp

carpenter (*kah*p*-en-tē*) *n.* worker in timber as used in buildings بڑھئی، نجار، نجاری، ترکھان **carpentry** (*kah*p*-ent-ri) *n.* work of a carpenter بڑھئی کا کام

carpet (*kah*p*-et) *n.* large, thick woollen or felt covering for floors and stairs قالین، غالیچہ *carpet knight* (*a*) effeminate person شیر قالین، مٹی کا مادھو (*b*) person who spends his time in luxury; lady's man مرد حسرم (مرد میدان نہیں بلکہ) (*c*) stay-at-home soldier گھر بیٹھا، قاعد، اسمبزی *on the carpet*, under discussion زیر بحث، فرش کرنا *v.t.* cover (as) with a carpet قالین بچھانا، قالین کا فرش کرنا، قالین (یا کوئی قالین نما شئے) بچھانا، *be carpeted*, be reprimanded کی باز پرس ہونا، فہمائش ہونا

carpeted (-id) *adj.* thickly covered (*with* flowers, etc.) سے ڈھکا ہوا

carriage (*ka*-rij) *n.* vehicle, esp. one with four wheels pulled by a horse, for carrying people گاڑی، گھوڑا گاڑی railway coach, or a division of it ریل گاڑی (کا ڈبہ) cost of carrying goods from place to place باربرداری، حمالی its cost ڈھلائی، خرچہ باربرداری *carriage forward*, cost of carriage to be paid by the receiver خرچہ بذمہ خریدار (یا وصول کنندہ) manner of holding the head or body چال، انداز، چلنے کا ڈھب moving part of a machine changing the position of other parts مشین کا پھسلنا حصہ • پھسلنی

a carriage

carrier (*ka*-ri-ē*) *n.* see under **carry**

carrion (*ka*-ri-un) *n.* dead, decaying flesh مُردار، سڑا ہوا گوشت

carrot (*ka*-rut) *n.* well-known plant with yellow or orange-red root used as vegetable گاجر، گزر

carry (*ka*-ri) (carried) *v.t.* & *i.* hold off the ground and move (someone or something) from one place to another اٹھا کر لے جانا، لے چلنا، ڈھونا، اُٹھا کر پہنچانا، پہنچانا have with one پاس رکھنا take from place to place لیے لیے پھرنا، اُٹھائے اُٹھائے پھرنا support سہارا، تھامنا، بوجھ، برداشت کرنا keep (the head or body) in a certain way خاص چال چلنا، (چلتے میں سر یا بدن کو) ایک خاص زاویے پر رکھنا persuade ; overcome resistance (اپنی بات) دوسروں سے منوانا، تسلیم کرانا، برائے کے موافق یا حسب دل خواہ بنانا، کی تائید و حمایت کرنا۔ *carry (one's) point* (or *motion*, etc.) اپنی پیش کردہ تحریر (یا تحریک) منظور کرا لینا *carry everything before (one)*, succeed in everything اپنی ہر بات منوانا یا پوری کامیابی حاصل کرنا *carry the enemy's position*, capture them دشمن کی جگہ پر قبضہ حاصل کرنا provide a path for, take along لے جانا، پہنچانا earn, get. کا حاصل ہونا (of loan) carry interest (قرضے کا) سودی ہونا، (قرضے) پر سود چڑھنا make longer or continue up to (تک) بڑھانا یا پہنچا یا لے جانا یا بنانا یا بنا دینا (10) (of sound) be heard تک سنائی دینا (11) (of guns) send (shells, etc.) (توپ وغیرہ کے گولے کی) تک مار ہونا PHRASES : *carry (the audience) with (one)* سامعین کو اپنا ہم خیال بنا لینا *carry away*, (*a*) (کسی جگہ)، لے جانا (*b*) خود میں بہا لے جانا، *carry conviction* اپنا خیال دوسرے کے ذہن نشین کرنا بے قوت کر دینا *carry fortress* قلعہ سر کرنا *carry over* or *carry forward (figures)*, (رقم) اگلے صفحے پر لے جانا *carry it off well* (الزام وغیرہ سے) متاثر نہ ہونا *carry into effect* عمل میں لانا *carry off*, take without permission or by force بلا اجازت یا زبردستی *carry it*, *carry the day*, مقابلے میں جیتنا، کامیاب ہونا *carry (something) to excess* (کسی بات کی) حد کر دینا *carry (someone) back* ایام گزشتہ کی یاد دلانا *carry through* (*a*) کی تکمیل کرنا (*b*) مشکلات سے صاف نکل آنا *carry on*, continue جاری رکھنا *carry on (with)* (colloq.) ڈورے ڈالنا، نظر بازی کرنا، عشوہ گری *carry weight* (*a*) وزن رکھنا، (بات کا) وقیع ہونا (*b*) گھوڑے کا دوڑ میں وزن مساوی کرنے کے لیے (*c*) گھوڑ دوڑ میں پیچھے رہ جانا، *carry authority* (*a*) مستند ہونا (*b*) گھوڑے پر بوجھ بڑھا دینا یا لینا *carry out orders* حکم بجا لانا، حکم کی تعمیل کرنا، (*b*) بااثر ہونا حکم ماننا **carrier** (*ka*-ri-ē*) *n.* person or company carrying goods for payment بار کش، باربردار، حمال support fixed to a bicycle, etc., for carrying things بارگیر warship built to carry aircrft from one place to another also called *aircraft carrier* طیارہ بردار جہاز

cart (kah*t) *n.* strong two-wheeled vehicle pulled by an animal, for carrying goods چھکڑا ، بیل گاڑی *put the cart before the horse*, do or put things in the wrong order اُلٹی بات کرنا ، گھوڑے کے دُم میں لگام لگانا ، اُلٹی گنگا بہانا *v.t.* carry things in a cart گاڑی یا چھکڑے پر لاد کر لے جانا **cartage** (*kah**t-ij) *n.* carting بار برداری price of carting چھکڑے کا کرایہ **carter** *n.* man in charge of a cart گاڑی بان ، چھکڑے والا ، چھکڑے بان **cartway** *n.* گاڑی کے چلنے کا راستہ

a cart

carte blanche *n.* blank cheque سیاہ و سفید کا اختیار ،

cartel (*kah**-tel) *n.* union of manufacturing or other concerns to control output and put up prices (قیمتیں بڑھانے کے لیے) کارخانہ داروں کا گٹھ جوڑ ، انجمن کارخانہ داراں

cartilage (*kah**-ti-lij) *n.* firm elastic substance covering the joints in animal bodies غضروف ، چینی ہڈی ، نرم نرم ہڈی ، کری ہڈی

cartography (kah*-*tog*-rafi) *n.* map-drawing نقشہ کشی **cartographer** *n.* one who draws maps نقشہ کش ، نقشہ ساز

carton (*kah**-tun) *n.* cardboard box گتے کا ڈبہ

cartoon (kah*-*toon*) *n.* amusing drawing dealing with current events کارٹون (also called *animated cartoon*) cinema film made by photographing a series of drawings فلمی کارٹون ، متحرک کارٹون ، تصویری فلم *a Walt Disney* (*Mickey Mouse*) *cartoon* والٹ ڈزنی کی (مکی ماؤس) ، تصویری فلم **cartoonist** (kah*-*toon*-ist) *n.* one who draws cartoons کارٹون ساز

cartridge (*kah**t-rij) *n.* case containing explosive and bullet or shot کارتوس *blank cartridge*, one with explosive only خالی کارتوس (see *Addenda*)

cartridge (above) for a rifle. (below) for a gun : A (case) B (bullet), C (shot)

carve (kah*v) *v.t. & i.* make (a statue, design, etc.) by cutting منبت کاری کرنا ، مجسمہ بنانا ، کندہ کاری کرنا ، کندہ کرنا cut up (cooked meat) into pieces for eating at table (کھاتے وقت چھری کانٹے) سے گوشت کاٹنا *carve* (*one's*) *way, carve out a career* اپنے لیے آپ راستہ پیدا کرنا ، قوت بازو سے بڑھنا **carver** *n.* one who carves سنگ تراش ، مجسمہ ساز ، کندہ کار knife for carving meat چھری

carving *n.* piece of wood shaped by cutting or with a design cut on it نقش

cascade (kas-*kayd*) *n.* small water-fall جھرنا ، پانی کی چادر part of a large broken waterfall آبشار کا کوئی حصہ

case (kays) *n.* event, state, condition صورت ، حالت *in case*, if اگر *in case of* کی صورت میں *in this case* اس صورت میں *in the case of* کے بارے میں *it is not the case* سچ ہے ، یُونہی ہے *it is the case* بات یُوں نہیں ، یہ صحیح نہیں۔ person suffering from a disease مریض ، بیمار instance of diseased condition بیماری کا واقعہ *many cases of influenza* انفلوائنزا کے متعدد واقعات grammatical status of a noun اسم کی حالت (فاعلی ، مفعولی یا اضافی) question to be decided in a law-court مقدمہ the arguments, etc., used on either side کسی فریق کے دلائل ، نقطۂ نگاہ وغیرہ *state* (*one's*) *case, make out* (*one's*) *case* اپنے دعوے کے ثبوت میں دلائل لانا ، اپنا دعویٰ پیش کرنا *that is our case* یہ ہے ہمارا دعویٰ یا ثابت کرنا *case law*, law as settled by precedent نظری قانون *leading case*, decision used as a precedent نظیری مقدمہ ، نظیری فیصلہ *take a case to a court of law* مقدمہ عدالت میں دائر کرنا *institute a case* (*against*) (کے خلاف) مقدمہ دائر کرنا *decide a case* مقدمے میں باہمی مقدمے کا فیصلہ *compound a case* پنچایتی فیصل کرنا *settle a case* سمجھوتے سے فیصلہ کرنا ، راضی نامہ کرنا یا کرانا *dismiss a case* مقدمہ خارج یا برخاست کرنا box or container ڈبہ ، صندوق ، غلاف *pillowcase* تکیے کا غلاف *cigarette-case* سگریٹ کیس *book-case* کتابوں کی الماری *v.t.* enclose in a box صندوق یا ڈبے میں بند کرنا *case harden* (esp.) make callous بے حس ، بے مہر یا سنگدل *lower case* (abb. *l.c.*) چھوٹے حروف (کا) *upper case* (abb. u.c.) بڑے حروف (کا)

casein (*kay*-si-in) *n.* body-building food present in milk کیسین

casement (*kays*-ment) *n.* ordinary window opening inwards or outwards like a door دریچہ ، کھڑکی *casement cloth*, ordinary cotton cloth used for curtains or dresses پردوں کا سوتی کپڑا ، فراک کا سوتی کپڑا

a casement

cash (kash) *n.* money in coin or notes نقد *cash down* قیمت (اُدھار نہیں ، بلکہ) نقد *cash on delivery*, payment on delivery of goods قیمت عند الوصول *cash payment* نقد ادائیگی *cash price*, price for immediate payment قیمت نقد *cash register*, (*a*) (usu. *cash book*) register for entering cash deals کیش بک ، روکڑ ، بہی (*b*) mechanical device visibly recording price of each item bought and totalling the cash (to be) taken کیش رجسٹر ، نقد نگار *in cash* امیر ، جس کے پاس نقدی یا *out of cash, cashless* جس کے پاس نقدی نہ ہو ، ناداں ہو ، غریب ، قلاش *v.t.* give or get cash for (a cheque, etc.) بھنانا ، تڑانا *cash in on* (*something*), make a profit out of (it) سے خوب فائدہ اٹھانا *cash in*, (colloq.) die مر جانا ، چل بسنا **cashier** (ka-*shee*-ĕ*) *n.* person receiving and paying out cash in a bank, etc. خزانچی *v.t.* dismiss (a military officer) (فوجی افسر کو) برخاست یا برطرف یا موقوف کرنا

cashier *n.* & *v.t.* see under **cash**

cashmere (*kash*-mee-ĕ*) *n.* soft woollen mate-

tial کشمیرا *cashmere shawl* کشمیری شال
casing (*kays*-ing) *n.* covering (esp.) for an electric wire کیسنگ ، تار پوشش
casino (ka-*see*-noh) *n.* (pl. *casinos*) public room for singing, dancing, and for gambling رقص گاہ
cask (kahsk) *n.* wooden barrel for liquids لکڑی کا پیپا
casket (*kas*-ket) *n.* small, ornamented box for jewellery, etc. (زیورات وغیرہ کا) ڈبہ یا صندوقچہ ، دُرج
Cassandra (ka-*sand*-ra) *Cl. myth.* daughter of Priam, the king of Troy ; Apollo loved her and gave her the gift of prophecy, but on being displeased added that nobody should believe what she foretold کسانڈرا
Cassiopeia (ka-si-oh-*pee*-a) *Cl. myth.* mother of *Andromeda* (which see) ; she was turned into a constellation at her death برج ذات الکرسی ، کسوپیا
cassock (*kas*-uk) *n.* priests' long, close-fitting (black) garment کالا کرتہ ، قبائے سیاہ
cast (kahst) *v.t.* & *i.* (*cast, cast, cast*) throw ڈالنا ، پھینکنا *cast away,* (old use) reject, throw away پھینک دینا ، رد کر دینا *cast a net* (or *line* or *hook*) *for fish* مچھلی پکڑنے کے لیے جال (یا ڈوری) ڈالنا *cast a vote* ووٹ دینا *casting vote,* vote given by a chairman to decide a question when votes on each side are equal (صدر کی) رائے فیصل *cast off* ترک کر دینا *cast off clothes,* discard them from one's own use کپڑے اتار دینا ، پھینکنا *cast aside* ترک کر دینا *cast an eye (on)* پر نظر ڈالنا *cast a spell (on)* (پر) جادو کر دینا ، (کو) مسحور کرنا *cast a shadow (on)* (پر) سایہ ڈالنا ، (پر) نحوست لانا ، (کو) گہنا دینا *cast anchor* لنگر ڈالنا ، لنگر انداز ہونا *cast a horoscope* زائچہ کھینچنا *be cast ashore, be cast up* ساحل پر رہ جانا *cast lots,* let chance decide قرعہ اندازی کرنا *cast blame upon* کو الزام دینا *cast dice* پانسہ پھینکنا *the die is cast* (جو ہونا تھا سو) ہو چکا اب کچھ ہو نہیں سکتا *cast a glance* (or *look*) *at* پر سرسری نظر ڈالنا ، کو ایک نظر دیکھنا *cast light on* پر روشنی ڈالنا *cast about for* (کے لیے) ہاتھ پاؤں مارنا ، (کے لیے) جستجو کرنا *cast in (one's) lot with* (کسی کے دُکھ سکھ کا) ساجھی ہونا *cast into (a shape)* کو کوئی خاص صورت دینا *be cast down* افسردہ یا غمگین ہونا یا دلگیر ہونا *cast in (one'e) teeth* کو ملامت کرنا *cast (ones) care's upon* اپنی بلا دوسرے کے سر ڈالنا *cast into prison* قید میں ڈالنا ، بندی خانے بھجوانا (pour molten metal) into a mould ڈھالنا *cast type* حروف ڈھالنا *cast a statue* مجسمہ ڈھالنا add up (figures, accounts, etc.) کو جوڑنا ، کو جمع کرنا *cast (up) a column of figures* رقمیں جمع کرنا ، حساب جوڑنا *cast accounts* حساب کرنا ، لگانا ، یا جوڑنا throw off ; (of snake) skin ; (of horse) shoe , (of deer) horns (سانپ کا) کینچلی دینا یا اُتارنا ، (گھوڑے کے) نعل کا گرنا ، (ہرن کا) سینگ گرانا drop prematurely ; (of tree) the fruit ; of dam (the young) قبل از وقت (درخت کا) پھل دینا یا (جانوروں کا) بچہ دینا give (an actor) a part in a play اداکار کو ناٹک تمثیل یا فلم میں کوئی کردار یا ٹکڑا دینا loosen (rope) (رسہ) ڈھیلا کرنا estimate the space (manuscript) will take in print اندازہ کرنا کہ چھپائی میں (مسودہ) کتنی جگہ لے گا *n.* act of throwing پھینکنا ، ڈالنا mould سانچہ ، قالب *cast of features* ناک نقشہ ، چہرہ مہرہ *cast of mind,* frame of mind مزاج ، افتادِ طبع something moulded ڈھلی ہوئی چیز (of dam or tree) something thrown off prematurely قبل از وقت (جانور کا) بچہ یا (درخت کا) پھل (of snake) skin cast off کینچلی slight squint کچھ بھینگا پن **cast-away** *n.* shiprecked person in a new land کشتی شکستہ **casting** *n.* something made by casting ڈھلی ہوئی چیز **cast-iron** *n.* iron which has been prepared by casting (as opposed to *wrought iron*) ڈھلا لوہا ، دیگی لوہا *adj.* hard, unyielding سخت
caste (kahst) *n.* one of the various fixed social classes ذات ، ذات پات ، برن *caste system,* the custom of dividing people into such classes ذات پات کا نظام *lose caste,* descend in such status and lose respect اپنی ذات کھونا any exclusive social class (مخصوص معاشری) فرقہ
caster *n.* same as **castor** (which see)
castigate (*kas*-ti-gayt) *v.t.* criticize or scold severely سرزنش کرنا ، جھاڑ جھپاڑ کرنا ، گوشمالی کرنا **castigation** *n.* سرزنش ، گوشمالی
castle (*kah*-sel) *n.* large building serving both as residence and fortress ارگ ، کوٹ ، گڑھ ، گڑھی ، قلعہ *castle in the air,* (*a*) day-dream خواب و خیال (*b*) visionary project خیالی پلاؤ *build castles in the air,* be day-dreaming خیالی پلاؤ پکانا

a castle

castor, caster (*kahs*-tě*) *n.* small wheel for the foot of a piece of furniture to make it easy to move (کرسی میز وغیرہ کا) چھوٹا سا پہیہ small bottle with holes in the top, for shaking salt, pepper or vinegar on to food نمک دانی ، مرچ دان **castors** *n. pl.* cruet-stand مسالے دانی **castor oil** (*kahs*-tě*-oil) *n.* thick, yellowish oil, used as purgative روغن بید انجیر ، ارنڈی کا تیل
Castor & Pollux (*kas*-te*, *pol*-uks) (*Class myth.*) twin brothers, the former mortal and the latter immortal, greatly loved each other ; on the latter's death Zeus placed them in heaven as a constellation under the name of Gemini ; *i.e.*, the Twins توأمین ، کاسٹر اور پولکس
casual (*kazh*-u-ěl) *adj.* happening by chance اتفاقی without special purpose بلا مقصد ، بے ضابطہ careless بے پروایانہ not continuous وقتی ، غیر مسلسل not regularly-admitted (student) غیر باضابطہ ، بیشروول (see *Addenda*) **casually** *adv.* اتفاقاً ، اتفاق سے

casualty (*kazh*-u-al-ti) *n.* person injured, wounded, or killed (in war, accidents, etc.) جنگ یا حادثے کے مقتولین و مجروحین accident, mishap حادثہ، سانحہ

casuist *n.* **casuistic (al, ally)** *adj.* (*adv.*) see under **casuistry**

casuistry (*cazh*-u-is-tri) *n.* judgment of right and wrong in special cases by reference to high-sounding theories with false but clever reasoning مغالطہ آمیزی، ہفسطہ، سوفسطائیت، سخن سازی **casuist** *n.* one who indulges in casuistry سوفسطائی، سخن ساز، مغالطہ آمیز شخص **casuistic, casuistical** *adj.* مغالطہ آمیز **casuistically** *adv.* سخن سازانہ، مغالطہ آمیزانہ

casus belli (kay-sus-*bel*-i) *n.* action regarded as a just cause of going to war جنگ کا جائز سبب

cat (kat) *n.* a well-known animal بلی، گربہ spiteful woman چھچل scratching child نوچنے کھسوٹنے والا بچہ *cat's eye* ایک قسم کا ہیرا *cat-eyed* اندھیرے میں دیکھ سکنے والا *cat's paw*, tool in (someone's) hand (کسی کا) آلۂ کار *cat-nap, cat-sleep* (کرسی وغیرہ پر) بے آرامی کی مختصر سی نیند *cross as cat* چڑچڑا *live a cat and dog life* میں دانتا کلکل *rain cats and dogs* موسلا دھار بارش ہونا، برستے رہنا *bell the cat* ناممکن کام کا عزم کرنا، اوروں کے لیے جوکھوں میں پڑنا *wait for the cat to jump*, wait to see what others think or do before giving an opinion اظہار رائے سے پہلے دوسروں کے ردِ عمل کو دیکھنا *let the cat out of the bag*, allow a secret to be known راز افشا کر دینا **tom-cat** بلا **she-cat** *n.* بلی **kitten** بچہ، بلونگڑا **cat-burglar** *n.* burglar who climbs over walls and enters through ventilators, etc. دیوار پر چڑھ کر آنے والا نقب زن

catgut *n.* chord made from intestines of sheep, etc. تانت **cat-o'-nine-tails** *n.* whip with nine knotted cords نو رسیوں والا کوڑا **cattish catty** *adj.* catlike بلی کا سا، گربہ صفت sly and spiteful کینہ توز، عیار **cat-calls** (*kat*-kawlz) *n. pl.* loud vulgar cries of mockery (in picture-house or at public show) (سینما وغیرہ میں) تمسخر یا اظہار ناراضگی کے لیے اونچی آوازے سیٹی

cataclysm (*kat*-a-klizm) *n.* sudden upheaval طوفان، انقلاب

catacomb (*kat*-a-kohm) *n.* (usu. *pl.*) underground gallery in ancient Rome with openings along the sides for burial ہموار زمین دوز قبرستان، کہف

catalogue (*kat*-a-log) *n.* list (of books, etc.) in alphabetical or other special order فہرست، ابجدی فرد such card-index placed in libraries in shelves with drawers فہرست کی الماری *v.t.* draw up such a list فہرست مرتب کرنا **cataloguer** *n.* one who prepares a catalogue فہرست نگار **cataloguing** *n.* فہرست نگاری

catamite (*kat*-a-mIt) *n.* sodomite's minion لونڈا، مفعول

catapult (*kat*-a-pult) *n.* Y-shaped stick with piece of elastic, for shooting stones, etc. چھوٹی غلیل، گوپھیا ancient machine for throwing big heavy stones in war منجنیق، گوپھن mechanical device using an explosive, etc. to launch aircraft from deck of a ship or to start a glider بارودی منجنیق *v.t.* launch (glider, aircraft, etc.) with such a catapult بارودی منجنیق سے (طیارہ وغیرہ) چڑھانا

a catapult

cataract (*kat*-a-rakt) *n.* large waterfall آبشار eye disease causing partial blindness موتیا، موتیابند

a cataract

catarrh (ka-*tah**) *n.* disease of the nose and throat causing flow of liquid نزلہ، زکام

catastrophe (ka-*tas*-tro-fi) *n.* sudden accident causing great suffering آفت، تباہی، بلائے ناگہانی subversive event تخریبی واقعہ، آشوب denoument (of drama) (ڈرامے کے) پلاٹ کی الجھنوں کا سلجھاؤ **catastrophic** (ka-tas-*trof*-ik) *adj.* disastrous تباہ کن with extremely subversive events پُر آشوب

catch (kach) *v. t. & i.* (*catch, caught, caught*, pr. *kawt*) capture in snare, hands, etc. پکڑنا، پھانسنا، گرفت میں لینا *catch a train* گاڑی پکڑنا، گاڑی کے وقت پہنچنا *catch (someone or something) up, catch up with (someone or something)*, (*a*) come up to someone going in same direction پکڑنا، جا لینا (*b*) do the requisite work کام پورا کر لینا *catch* someone *at* (*something* or *doing something*) کسی کو کوئی کام کرتے ہوئے جا پکڑنا *catch a likeness* ہو بہو تصویر بنانا، چربہ اتارنا *catch at* ہاتھ مارنا، جھپٹنا *catch ball, catch out* (کرکٹ میں) گیند لپک کر کسی کو آؤٹ کر دینا *catch cold* زکام ہونا *catch illness* بیمار ہونا *catch fire* آگ پکڑ لینا، آگ لگ جانا *catch (someone's) words* (or *meaning*) کسی کی بات یا مطلب سمجھ لینا *you do not catch on* تم مطلب سمجھتے ہی نہیں *catch sight of* (کسی) کو دیکھ لینا *catch (someone's) eye* کسی کو کسی طرح دیکھ پانا، سے نظریں چار ہونا *catch hold of* پکڑنا، پکڑے رکھنا، تھامے رکھنا، نہ چھوڑنا *catch a Tartar* find intended victim stronger than oneself بے خبری میں اپنے سے زبردست سے جا بھڑنا *catch it!* (slang) (سزا) بھگتو *catch me!* there is no fear of my doing it! پکڑ لیجو مجھے! *catch on* (بات کا) رائج ہونا، چل نکلنا *catch (someone) in (some part of the body)* کسی کو (بدن پر) کہیں، لگنا *Watch the bush, it catches on the dress* اس جھاڑی سے بچنا اس میں کپڑے الجھ جاتے ہیں *The bolt catches* چٹخنی نہیں لگتی، اڑتی ہے *catch up a speaker* catch عادت ڈال لینا، عادی ہو جانا *catch up a habit* لقرر کو کرنے catch (or *swallow*) the bait کس کس کو پکڑنے کی کوشش کرو گے ؟ ؟ *me, catch him* (شکار کا) جال میں پھنسنا *set a thief to catch a thief* چور سے چور پکڑوانا *catch (one's) breath* دم سادھ لینا *catch time by the forelock* وقت کو ہاتھ سے نہ دینا *be caught* پکڑا جانا، گرفتار ہونا *n.* act of catching پکڑنا، قابو میں کرنا ، something or someone caught (esp. fish) ایک مرتبہ کے شکار میں پکڑے جانے والی مچھلیاں (وغیرہ) something valuable or wished for that has been caught موٹی آسامی، سونے کی چڑیا، تر مال part of a lock, fastener etc., by which it is kept shut or secure (تالے وغیرہ کی) روک، بلی، اڑانی something intended to deceive دھوکا **catching** *adj.* (of a disease, etc.) contagious متعدی **catchword** *n.* word drawing attention to the subject of a paragraph عبارت کا کلیدی لفظ influential temporary phrases in politics (سیاست وغیرہ میں کوئی) چلتا فقرہ (یا) بھڑکتی ہوئی بات

▣ **To catch,** to lay hands quickly on something which is not permanently there ; **take** something already found ; **seize,** take eagerly ; **grab** quickly. defiantly, often unlawfully ; **grip** tightly in one's hand ; **clutch** with tightly closing fingers ; **snatch** with rapid motion, away from someone; **apprehend** someone wanted for an offence ; **arrest,** formally declare under a criminal charge ; **secure** from escape.

catechism (kat-e-kizm) *n* long list of questions and answers (esp. about religious teaching) (دینی عقائد کا) سوال جواب نامہ ، دینی سوال جواب ، **catechize** (*kat*-e-kyz) *v.t.* teach by question and answer سوالاً جواباً پڑھنا ، سوال جواب کے ذریعے تعلیم

categorical(ly) *adj.* (*adv.*) (see under **category**)

category (*kat*-e-go-ri) *n.* a division in a complete system of grouping قسم، زمرہ، درجہ (فلسفہ میں) مقولہ **categorical** *adj.* absolute قطعی ، مطلق *categorical answer* صاف، قطعی یا دو ٹوک جواب *categorical imperative,* bidding of conscience as the ultimate moral sanction قطعی حکم ، ضمیر کا حکم آخر **categorically** *adv.* definitely, quite clearly صاف صاف ، قطعی طور پر

cater (*kay*-te*) *v.t.* (*cater for*), undertake to provide (food, amusements, etc.) دعوت یا تفریح کا سامان کرنا (*cater to*), supply (according to the needs, tastes, of) حسب مذاق، حسب ضرورت یا حسب خواہش سامان بہم پہنچانا **caterer** *n.* owner or manager of a hotel or the contractor supplying it with provisions ہوٹل کا مالک یا ناظم ، بہم رساں خانساماں ،

caterpillar (*kat*-ē*-pil-ĕ*) *n.* moth or butterfly larva (تتلی یا پتنگے کا) پہل روپ belt over toothed wheels, tractors and tanks, to give them a grip on rough surfaces پٹہ ، پٹی *caterpillar tractor*, one with such belt پہیہ پٹی دار ٹریکٹر

cathedral (ka-*theed*-rĕl) *n.* bishop's church, principal church in a diocese

catheter (*cath*-e-tĕ*) *n.* tube passed into bladder for taking out urine پیشاب نکالنے کی نالی ، قثاطیر

cathode, kathode (*kath*-ohd) *n.* that electrode through which an electric current leaves (as opposed to the other type of electrode which is called an *anode*) : negative electrode قطب منفی ، منفی برقیرہ

catholic (*kath*-o-lik) *adj.* liberal وسیع المشرب ، بے تعصب ، فراخ دل ، فراخ دلانہ including everything ہمہ گیر universal عالمگیر *Roman Catholic,* member of the Church of Rome کیتھولک ، رومن کیتھولک عیسائی کیتھولک *Roman Catholicism,* (roh-man-ka-*thol*-i-sizm) teaching of the Church of Rome عیسائیوں کا رومن کیتھولک مذہب **catholicity** (kath-o-*lis*-i-ti) *n.* quality of being catholic عالمگیری ، وسیع المشربی ، فراخ دلی ، رواداری ، ہمہ گیری ، بے تعصبی

cattle (*kat*-ĕl) *n. pl.* domesticated beasts of pasture گائے بیل ، مال مویشی ، ڈھور ڈنگر **cattle-lifting** *n.* stealing of cattle مال کی چوری ، مویشیوں کی چوری

caucus (*kawk*-us) *n.* inner controlling group of a political party سیاسی جماعت کا اندرونی ذی اقتدار گروہ ، برمک

caught (kawt) *pa. t.* & *pa. p.* of **catch** (which see)

cauldron (*kawl*-drun), **caldron** *n.* large boilding pot (usu. hanging) (معلق) کڑھاؤ کڑھائی یا دیگ

a cauldron

cauliflower (*kol*-i-flou-ĕ*) *n.* cabbage-like vegetable with large white flower-head گوبھی ، پھول گوبھی۔

caulk (kawk) *v.t.* fill joints between planks of boats to make them watertight کشتیوں کی درزیں بند کرنا ، ڈوز دوزی کرنا

causative (see under **cause**

cause (kawz) *n.* that which produces an effect سبب، علت، باعث reason وجہ purpose for which efforts are being made مقصد، نصب العین *in the cause of* کے مقصد کے لیے *make common cause with,* join hands with (someone *for* a purpose) (کسی غرض کے لیے کسی سے) متحد ہونا *v.t.* be the cause of کا سبب ہونا make happen وجود یا عمل میں لانا *cause celebre* (kohz-se-*lebr*) *n.* (pl., '*causes celebres*', pr. as in the sing.) lawsuit that excites much interest سنسنی خیز مقدمہ دلچسپ مقدمہ **cause-list** *n.* list of cases awaiting trial on a particular day, etc. فہرست مقدمات **causal** (*kawz*-ĕl) *adj.* of the nature of cause and effect جس میں علت و معلول کا سلسلہ قائم ہو، علی **causality** (-*zal*-) *n.* universal operation of the principle of cause and effect علت و معلول کا سلسلہ **causative** *adj.*

pressing cause علّت acting as cause of کا سبب
causeless *adj*. baseless ; unjustified بے اصل، بے بنیاد ناجائز، ناروا **S** To **cause** is to make things ; to **produce**, bring forth into visibility ; **create** out of nothing or next-to-nothing ; **generate** out of a different kind of substance. **originate**, be the first to produce ; **ascribe** a result to a known cause ; **attribute** a result, rightly or wrongly, to a certain cause ; **impute** bad motives to a person ; **foment** a revolt; **effect** succeed in bringing about a reconciliation between the two enemies ; **occasion**, afford an opportunity for

causerie (kohz-e-*ree*) *n*. (pl., *causeries* pr. as in the sing.) informal newspaper-article (esp.) on literary topics اخبار میں غیر رسمی ادبی مضمون، گاڑدی

causeway (*kawz*-way), **cawsey** (*kawz*-i) *n*. raised path or road (across marshes, etc.) (دلدلوں وغیرہ میں سے) اونچا راستہ

caustic (*kaws*-tik) *adj*. able to burn away by chemical action کیمیاوی عمل سے جلانے والا، حارق bitter, sarcastic طعن سے، طعنے سے، طنز آمیز، طنزیہ **caustically** *adv*. sarcastically ; bitterly سے

cauterize (*kawt*-e-rīz) *v.t*. burn (a wound) in order to destroy infection داغنا **cauterization** *n*. داغنا **cautery** *n*. iron rod heated to burn thus داغنے کا راہ، ڈستام

caution (*kaw*-shèn) *n*. taking care to avoid danger or making mistakes احتیاط، چوکسی، خبرداری warning words تنبیہ، آگاہی order given in drill, etc. (ڈرل یا پریڈ میں) ہدایت (slang) ugly or strange person بے ڈول، کڈھب *v.t*. give a caution to آگاہ کرنا، خبردار کرنا، متنبہ کرنا **cautious** *adj*. having or showing caution محتاط **cautiously** *adv*. احتیاط سے **S** **Caution** is avoidance of danger by means of prudence ; **cautiousness**, disposition of one inclined to caution ; **circumspection**, looking around for avoidance of hidden perils ; **anxiety**, uneasiness concerning something feared or expected ; **solicitude**, preparation of the desired good for someone in one's charge ; **concern**, serious interest mixed with slight fear ; **worry**, serious doubt of the future ; **bother**, slight inconvenience.

cavalcade (kav-al-*kayd*) *n*. procession on horseback (or in carriages) سواروں کا پرا، سواروں کا جلوس، گاڑیوں میں جلوس

cavalier (kav-a-*lee*-è*) *n*. horseman or knight شہسوار **cavalry** (*kav*-al-ri) *collective n*. soldiers who fight on horseback رسالہ

cave (kayv) *n*. large natural hollow in a hill or under the ground غار، کھوہ *v.t*. & *i*. hollow out غار کھودنا *cave in*, (*a*) fall in دھنس جانا (*b*) smash شکل بگاڑنا، توڑنا پھوڑنا (*c*) give way to pressure ; yield مخالفت سے باز آنا، ہار ماننا، اطاعت قبول کر لینا

cavemen, cave dwellers *n. pl*. prehistoric human beings living in caves غار نشیں، غاروں میں بسنے والے لوگ

cavern (*kav*-ĕ*n) *n*. cave غار، کھوہ **cavernous** (-vĕ*-) *adj*. full of caves غاروں والا like a cave غار نما، غار جیسا **Note** that **cave** is the ordinary word whereas **cavern** is its literary or poetical form.

caviare, caviar (kav-i-ah or kav-i-*ay**) pickled sturgeon سٹرجن مچھلی کا شکار *caviare to the general*, something too fine for the vulgar چھوٹا منہ بڑی بات، لذات ادراک

cavil (*kav*-il) *v.i*. (-ll-) *n*. frivolous objection خردہ گیری، بے بنیاد، خواہ مخواہ کا اعتراض *v.t*. *cavil at*, find fault, make such objections بے ہودہ اعتراض کرنا، مین میخ نکالنا **caviller** *n*. fault-finder عیب نکالنے والا، نکتہ چیں، حرف گیر، خوردہ گیر

cavity (*kav*-i-ti) *n*. hollow space within a solid body خلا، جوف، گڑھا

caw *n*. cry of a crow کوّے کی کائیں کائیں *v.t*. utter such cry کائیں کائیں کرنا *caw out*, cry out like a crow کوّے کی طرح کائیں کائیں لگانے رکھنا

cease (sees) *v.t*. & *i*. come to a stop ختم ہونا یا کرنا سے باز رہنا **cease-fire** *n*. order to troops to stop fighting متارکۂ جنگ، متارکہ *cease-fire line*, boundary line between the opposed armies at the time of cease-fire which thus becomes the temporary border of the two territories خط متارکہ *without cease*, ceaselessly متواتر، دائماً، مسلسل **ceaseless** *adj*. never ending دائمی، مسلسل **ceaselessly** *adv*. لگاتار **ceaselessness** *n*. دوام، تواتر

cedar (*seed*-ah*) cone-bearing tree of the Middle East صنوبر، مشرق اوسط کا دیودار

cedar

cede (seed) *v.t*. give up (territory etc.) to another (State, etc.) (دوسری سلطنت کو) اپنا علاقہ حوالے کر دینا **cession** *n*. (see separate entry)

ceiling (*seel*-ing) under-surface of the top of a room چھت، چھت گیری، اندرونی چھت highest level آخری حد، انتہائی، آخری، زیادہ سے زیادہ *ceiling price*, maximum prevailing price انتہائی قیمت، زیادہ سے زیادہ قیمت maximum (price, etc.) fixed by the government انتہائی مقررہ قیمت *price ceiling*, maximum limit to which the price of something could lawfully be raised, maximum price fixed by the government انتہائی مقررہ قیمت، قیمت کی آخری حد maximum altitude a particular aircraft can achieve انتہائے پرواز

celebrate (*sel*-e-brayt) *v.t*. do something to show that a day is an occasion for rejoicing منانا، جشن منانا *celebrate (one's) birthday* اپنی سالگرہ منانا publicly perform with proper ceremonies (مذہبی رسوم وغیرہ مجمع عام میں) ادا کرنا، منانا praise and honour تعریف کرنا، شہرت کرنا **celebrated** *adj*. famous مشہور، نامی گرامی **celebration** (sel-e-*bray*-shèn) *n*.

act of celebrating منانا ، ادا کرنا **celebrity** (se-*leb*-ri-ti) *n.* being famous شہرت، ناموری famous person مشہور شخصیت

celerity (se-*le*-ri-ti) *n.* (lit.) quickness چستی، پھرتی

celery (*sel*-e-ri) *n.* vegetable or salad plant اجوائن خراسانی ، کرفس ، سلری

celestial (se-*les*-ti-al) *adj.* of the sky آسمانی، فلکی heavenly بہشتی، ملکوتی perfect کامل، انتہائی

celibacy (*sel*-i-bay-si) *n.* state of living unmarried تجرد **celibate** (*sel*-i-bayt) *adj.* & *n.* (person) who has taken a vow not to marry مجرد، غیر متاہل ، مجرد رہنے کا حلف اٹھائے ہوئے

cell (sel) *n.* small room for one person (esp. in prison or monastery) (قید خانے کی) کال کوٹھڑی، (خانقاہ کا) حجرہ small division of a larger structure خانہ unit of living matter خلیہ part of a battery برقی خانہ، ظرف place (usu. a new one every time) where Communists or other revolutionaries hold their private party-meetings محفل، مجلس، بیٹھک، اڈا person who is a nucleus of revolutionary propaganda انقلابی پروپیگنڈہ کرنے والا ، دائمی انقلاب **cellular** *adj.* formed of cells خانہ دار ، جوف دار (of material) loosely woven جالی دار

a cell

cellar (*sel*-ĕ*) *n.* underground room for storing coal, wine, etc. تہ خانہ ، زمین دوز شراب خانہ

cello, 'cello (*chel*-oh) *n.* violin-like instrument but larger than it چیلو

cellophane (*sel*-o-fayn) *n.* a kind of transparent wrapping material شفاف گرد پوش

celluloid (*sel*-ew-loid) *n.* substance made from cellulose مسالہ **cellulose** (sel-ew-lohs) the chief part of plants used for making celluloid کیسلین

Celt (kelt or selt) *n.* member of a race from which Scottish, Welsh and Irish people are descended کیلٹ **Celtic** (*kel*-tik, or *sel*-tik) of the Celts or their language کیلٹی

cement (se-*ment*) *n.* burnt lime and clay used as mortar سیمنٹ any similar substance, used for joining things جوڑنے کا کوئی مسالہ *v.t.* put cement on or in سیمنٹ لگانا یا بھرنا strengthen, unite, جوڑنا ، رشتہ اتحاد مضبوط کرنا ۔

cemetery (*sem*-e-te-ri) *n.* burial place other than a churchyard قبرستان، گورستان، شہر خموشاں

cenotaph (*sen*-o-tahf) *n.* monument put up in memory of dead who are buried elsewhere خالی قبر، یادگار مقبرہ

censor (*sen*-sĕ*) *n.* official empowered to examine films, letters, books, etc., and to cut out anything regarded as indecent or dangerous محتسب ، ناظر *v.t.* examine as a censor احتساب کرنا **censorship** *n.* office or duties of a censor احتساب **censorial** *adj.* of or pertaining to censor or censorship محتسبانہ، احتسابی **censorious** (sen-*soh*-ri-us) *adj.* fault-finding عیب جو، نکتہ چین، حرف گیر

censure (*sen*-shĕ*) *v.t.* express blame or disapproval ملامت کرنا، مذمت کرنا، بالزام لگانا *n.* blame or disapproval الزام، ملامت، زجر و توبیخ **censurable** *adj.* that which calls for censure قابل ملامت، لائق مذمت

census (*sen*-sus) *n.* official counting of all the people in a country مردم شماری

cent (sent) *n.* the 100th part of a dollar or other unit of currency سینٹ *per cent*, (also written as %), for every 100 فی صد، فی صدی *cent per cent* کلا ملا سو فی صدی

Centaur (*sen*-toh*) *Cl. myth.* fabulous monster who was half-man, half-beast سنٹور، قنطر، قنطورس

a centaur

centenarian (sen-te-*nay*-ri-an) *n.* person who is already 100 years old سو برس کا بڈھا (یا بڑھیا)، پیر صد سالہ

centenary (sen-*teen*-a-ri) *adj.* & *n.* (having to do with) period of 100 years سو سال (کا) 100th anniversary صد سالہ سالگرہ (یا برسی) **centennial** (sen-*ten*-i-ĕl) *adj.* & *n.* (*a*) centenary سو سال (کا)، صد سالہ سالگرہ (یا برسی) (*b*) happening once in 100 years صدی میں ایک بار (کا)

centigrade (*sen*-ti-grayd) *adj.* in the temperaature scale which has 100 degrees between the freezing-point and boiling-point of water سینٹی گریڈ، رمئی **centigramme** (*sen*-ti-gram) *n.* the 100th part of a gramme سینٹی گرام **centimetre** (*sen*-ti-mee-tè*) *n.* the 100th part of a metre سینٹی میٹر

centipede (*sen*-ti-peed) *n.* poisonous insect with a long body comprising numerous jointed sections, each bearing a pair of feet ہزار پا، کنکھجورا

a centipede

center *n.* U.S. spelling of **centre** (which see)

Note: The spelling of all English words ending in *re* has been rationalized by the famous U.S. lexicographer, Webster, and they are now spelt in that country with *er*; thus English centre becomes U.S. center.

central *adj.*, **centralize** *v.t.* & *i.* **centralization** *n.* (see under **centre**)

centre (*sen*-tè*) *n.* middle point or part مرکز، مرکزی *the shopping centre of a town* شہر کا کاروباری مرکز، وسط *a centre of commerce* تجارتی مرکز *v.t.* & *i.* place in or around the centre مرکز پر یا اس کے گرد، جمع ہونا یا مرکز بنا

have as centre مرتکز کرنا ، *centre (one's) hopes on* پر امیدیں مرتکز کرنا ، **central** (*sent*-rel) *adj*. of, at or near the centre مرکزی chief, most important اہم ، نمایاں *central heating*, making all the rooms, etc. of a building warm by passing hot water or steam or hot air through pipes issuing from a central boiler گرم کرنے کا مشترکہ انتظام ، مرکزی گرم سیری ، **centralize** (*sen*-tra-liz) *v.t.* & *i.* bring to the centre ایک مرکز پر آنا یا لانا ، come or put (administration) under central control مرکزی نظام حکومت نافذ کرنا ، یا اس کے ماتحت لانا یا آنا **centralization** (sen-tra-li-*zay*-shen) *n*. centralizing (administration) thus خود مرکز کے تحت لانا ، مرکزیت پیدا کرنا

centrifugal (sen-*trif*-ew-gĕl) *adj*. tending to move away from the centre مرکز گریز ، دافع عن المرکز

centripetal (sen-*trip*-e-tĕl) *adj*. tending to move towards the centre راجع الی المرکز ، مرکز خواہ ، قد مرکزی

centurion (sen-*tew*-ri-un) *n*. (in ancient Rome) leader of a unit of 100 soldiers (قدیم رومی) شتدار

century (*sen*-tew-ri) *n*. (pl. *centuries*) 100 years صدی one of the 100 year periods before or after the birth of Christ صدی عیسوی ، یا قبل مسیح *the 20th century A.D.*, the years 1901 to 2000 of the Christian era (cricket) 100 runs کرکٹ میں ۱۰۰ رن ، سنچری ، سیکڑا ، صدی

ceramics (se-*ram*-iks) *n*. the art of pottery فن کوزہ گری ، خزفیات **ceramic** *adj*. relating to this art فن کوزہ سے متعلق

Cerberus (*se**-bi-rus) *Cl. myth.* three-headed dog guarding the entrance to Hell سربرس ، سگ جہنم

cereal (*see*-ri-al) *n* any kind of grain used for food اناج ، غلہ (U.S.) breakfast dish (like porridge, etc.) made from some cereal ناشتے غلے کا ، پودا یا دانہ *adj*. pertaining to food grains اناج کا ، غلاتی

cerebellum (se-ri-*bel*-um) *n*. hind part of the brain پیچھے کا دماغ ، مخیخ ، توام مغز ، چھوٹا دماغ **cerebrum** (*ser*-ib-rum) *n*. front part of the brain دماغ ، بڑا دماغ **cerebral** *adj*. of the brain or cerebrum دماغی

ceremonial *n*. & *adj*. **ceremonious** *adj*. (see under **ceremony**)

ceremony (*se*-re-mo-ni) *n*. special performance on an occasion happy or sad, religious or mundane تقریب ، تہوار behaviour required by social custom آداب ، آداب مجلس ، رسوم ، تشریفات *stand upon* (*or on*) *ceremony*, pay great attention to rules of behaviour تکلفات برتنا یا تکلف سے کام لینا *We don't stand on ceremony* بھائی ہم تو بے تکلف آدمی ہیں **ceremonial** (-*moh*-) *n*. special order of ceremony آداب محفل ، مجلسی آداب formality تکلف ، تکلفات *adj*. formal رسمی ، پر تکلف pertaining to ceremonies تقاریب کا ، تہوار کا **ceremonious** (-*moh*-) *adj*. fond of or marked by ceremony پر تکلف ، پابند رسوم

Ceres (*see*-reez) *Cl. myth*. the Roman goddess of agriculture ; she was the sister of Jupiter and the mother of Proserpine ; (she is identified with the greek Goddess *Demeter*) (زراعت کی دیوی) سیریز

certain (*se**-tĕn) *adj*. sure یقینی ، صحیح ، پر یقین *for certain*, without doubt یقیناً ، بے شک *make certain*, inquire in order to be certain یقین حاصل کرنا ، اطمینان کے لیے دریافت کرنا ، پکا پتہ کرنا not named or described کوئی ، کوئی ایک ، ایک خاص ، بعض مخصوص some but not much کچھ ، تھوڑا سا ، تھوڑا بہت **certainly** *adj*. without doubt یقیناً ، قطعاً ، بے شک **certainty** *n*. being certain یقین something which is certain یقینی ، یقینیات

certificate (se*-*tif*-i-kayt) *n*. written declaration of a fact by someone in authority سند ، صداقت نامہ ، تصدیق ، سرٹیفکیٹ **certificated** (se*-ti-fi-*kayt*-ed) *adj*. having a certificate which gives the right to do something (esp. teach) مستند ، سند یافتہ ، تربیت یافتہ

certify (*se**-ti-fı) *v.t*. declare a fact through a certificate تصدیق کرنا

certitude (*se**-ti-tewd) *n*. condition of feeling certain یقین ، تیقن

cessation (se-*say*-shen) *n*. ceasing خاتمہ ، انقطاع ، اختتام a stop or pause وقفہ ، ترک ، التوا

cession (*sesh*-ĕn) *n*. giving up (land, rights, etc.) علاقہ یا حقوق دوسرے کے حوالے کرنا something ceded سپرد کیا ہوا حق یا علاقہ

cesspit *n*. same as **cesspool** (which see)

cesspool (*ses*-pool) **cesspit** (*ses*-pit) *n*. pit into which drains empty گندے پانی کا چوبچہ ، تاب دان ، حوض

chafe (chayf) *v.t.* & *i.* rub (the skin, etc.) for warmth سہلانا ، ملنا ، مالش کرنا ، مل مل کر گرمی پہنچانا ، make or become sore by rubbing رگڑ سے چھل جانا ، دل جلنا ، جھلانا ، تپے میں آنا ، چھیلنا ، چھل جانا *chafe under insults* توہین سے چڑ چڑ ہونا *in a chafe*, irritated چڑ چڑ ، تپے ہیں ، دل جلا

chaff (chahf) *n*. outer covering of grain بھوسی ، چوکر hay or straw cut up as fodder چارہ good-humoured teasing فقرے بازی ، پھبتی *v.t*. make good-humoured fun of فقرہ کسنا یا چست کرنا ، پھبتی کہنا

chagrin (sha-*green*) *n*. feeling of shame or annoyance at failure جھنجھلاہٹ ، کھسیاہٹ **chagrined** (sha-*greend*) *adj*. annoyed at failure جھنجھلایا ہوا

chain (chayn) *n*. links going through one another to make a line زنجیر *in chains*, kept as a prisoner قیدی ، پابہ زنجیر number of connected things, events, etc. بلسلہ *chain letter*, (usu. some silly) letter with instructions (under pain of curse) to copy it out a particular number of times and despatch the copies to other addresses with similar instructions زنجیری خط *chain reaction*, (see *Addenda*) *chain-smoker*, one who smokes almost without break lighting new cigarette with the stub of the one he has just finished smoking سگرٹ پہ سگرٹ پھونکنے والا ، بلانوش ؛ *chain store*, (U. S.) one of the many shops at various places selling the same goods but owned by a single firm چین سٹور ، سلسلے کی دُکان measure 66-foot-long ۶۶ فٹ کا ناپ *v. t.* fasten with a chain پابہ زنجیر کرنا ، زنجیر کرنا *the dog was chained up* کتا زنجیروں میں جکڑا گیا ، زنجیروں سے بندھا ہوا تھا

chair (*chap-ē**) *n.* separate seat of the familiar type کُرسی *arm-chair* بازوؤں والی کرسی *easy-chair* آرام کرسی post of a university professor پروفیسر کا عہدہ ، یونیورسٹی کی پروفیسری *the Chair of English* جامعہ (یا یونیورسٹی) میں انگریزی کی پروفیسری seat or authority of the person who presides at a meeting صدارت ، کرسیِ صدارت *the chair*, president of a meeting صدر ، صدرِ جلسہ *leave the chair*, end the meeting کرسیِ صدارت کو چھوڑنا ، جلسے کی کارروائی بند کرنا *take the chair*, preside صدارت کرنا ، کرسیِ صدارت پر بیٹھنا ، *take a chair*, be seated تشریف رکھیے **chairman** *n.* (pl., *chairmen*) man, woman or child presiding at a meeting صدر ، صدرِ جلسہ ، کرسی نشین

chaise (shayz) *n.* low, four-wheeled horse-carriage بگھی

chalet (*shal*-ay) *n.* Swiss log-cottage or summer-house built in that style شالے street lavatory بیتُ الخلا ، بلدیاتی پاخانہ ، سنڈاس

chalice (*chal*-is) *n.* wine-cup (used in church for Communion) (عشائے ربانی کا) ساغر

chalk (chawk) *n.* soft limestone for writing کھریا ، چاک *v. t.* write (or draw) with a chalk چاک سے لکھنا (یا تصویر کشی کرنا) ، **chalkboard** *n.*, **chalk-talk** *n.* (see *Addenda*)

challenge (*chal*-enj) *n.* invitation to play a game or have a fight in order to see who is better مُبارزت طلبی sentry's order to stop and explain who one is للکار *v.t.* give, send or be a challenge مبارزت طلب کرنا ، دعوتِ مبارزت دینا ، للکارنا ask for reasons in support of one's statement, etc. اعتراض کرنا ، ثبوت چاہنا

chamber (*chaym*-bē*) (old use) room (esp. bedroom) کمرہ (خصوصاً خواب گاہ یا خلوت خانہ) *chamber music*, music, not for theatre but for a small private audience سُرودِ خلوت body of persons making laws or the place where they meet ایوان *the Upper* (or *Lower*) *Chamber* ایوانِ اعلیٰ (یا ادنیٰ) *Chamber of Commerce* (or *Industry*), group of persons organized to develop trade (or industry) ایوانِ تجارت (یا صنعت) ، enclosed space in a machine or gun (where a cartridge or something else is laid) مشین (یا بندوق وغیرہ) کا خزانہ (*pl.*) set of rooms occupied by lawyers وکیل خانہ ، وکیل کا دفتر separate room where a judge hears cases *in camera* جج کی خلوت گاہ **chambermaid** *n.* woman servant at an inn to keep bedrooms in order (سرائے کی) خادمہ

chamberlain (*chaym*-be*-layn) *n.* manager of the household of a king or great noble حاجب *Lord Chamberlain* official of the (British) Royal household میر حاجب

chameleon (ka-*mee*-li-un) *n.* a reptile whose colour changes according to its background گرگٹ ، بوقلموں capricious person متلون مزاج ، غیر مستقل مزاج ، گرگٹ

chamois (*sha*-mwah) *n.* small mountain goat سابر **chamois-leather, shammy, shammy-leather** *n.* soft leather from the skin of sheep and goats سابر کا چمڑا

champ (champ) *v.t.* & *i.* (of a horse) bite (food or bit) noisily چپڑ چپڑ چبانا ، چابنا show impatience بے تابی کا اظہار کرنا *n.* biting thus چابنا ، چبانا

champagne (sham-*payn*) *n.* a kind of French wine شیمپین

champion (*cham*-pi-un) *n.* one who fights on behalf of another, or for a cause حامی ، پشتیبان ، حمایتی individual or team, taking first place in competition میری ، میر *a swimming champion, or champion swimmer* میر پیراک *the champion hockey team* ہاکی کی میری ٹیم *v.t.* support حمایت کرنا ، پیٹھ ٹھونکنا defend کی حفاظت کرنا ، کے لیے جان لڑا دینا

chance (chahns) *n.* happening without known cause or intention اتفاق luck قسمت ، نصیبہ *take (one's) chance*, trust to luck and let things go as they may قسمت آزمانا ، قسمت آزمائی کرنا *game of chance*, game which luck and not skill decides قسمت آزمائی (والا کھیل مثلاً جوا) *by chance*, just by accident, not on purpose اتفاقاً ، بااتفاق possibility امکان ، احتمال *on the chance that*, in the hope that اس امکان کے پیشِ نظر opportunity موقعہ *the main chance, the chance of a lifetime*, the best opportunity کامیابی کا بہترین موقعہ *with an eye to the main chance*, in the hope of self-aggrandizement ذاتی فائدہ اٹھانے کا بہترین موقعہ *adj.* coming or happening by chance اتفاقی *a chance meeting* اتفاقی ملاقات *v.t.* & *i.* happen by chance واقع ہونا ، اتفاق ہونا *chance to (do)*, happen to (do) کرنے کا اتفاق ہونا *chance upon*, meet by chance اتفاق سے ملاقات ہو جانا *chance it, chance the consequences,* leave to fate and think no more of (نتائج وغیرہ کو) قسمت پر چھوڑنا **chancy** *adj.* risky جو خالی از خطر نہ ہو، غیر یقینی

chancel (*chahns*-el) *n.* eastern part of a church, used by priests and choir صدرِ کلیسا

chancellor (*chahns*-e-lĕ*) *n.* (in some countries like W. Germany) chief minister of the State وزیرِ اعظم، صدرِ اعظم (of some universities) head or president امیرِ جامعہ *vice-chancellor* نائب امیرِ جامعہ *Chancellor of the Exchequer,* chief finance minister in the U. K. برطانوی وزیرِ خزانہ *the Lord Chancellor of England,* Great Britain's highest judge برطانوی قاضی القضاہ **chancellorship** *n.* امارتِ جامعہ، وزارتِ عظمیٰ

chancellory *n.* chancellor's office or establishment چانسلر کا دفتر یا عملہ، دیوانِ وزارت office attached to an embassy سفارت خانے کا دفتر **chancery** (*chahns*-e-ri) Lord Chancellor's division of the High Court of Justice لارڈ چانسلر کی عدالت، چانسری

chandelier (*shan*-de-lee-*è) *n.* branched support hanging from ceiling for two or more lights شیشے کا جھاڑ، چہل چراغ، ہچکی چراغ

a chandelier

chandler (chahnd-lĕ*) *n.* dealer in candles, paint, oil, soap, etc., پرچون فروش، شمع ساز *corn-chandler,* retail dealer in corn آٹے دال کی دکان والا

change (chaynj) *v. t. & i.* take or put one thing in place of another بدلنا، تبدیل کرنا *change (one's) clothes,* کپڑے بدلنا *change seats* (or *places*) *with (someone)* (کسی سے) جگہ بدلنا *change (one's) mind,* come to a different opinion فیصلہ بدلنا *change hands,* pass to another owner بک جانا exchange (money) (روپیہ) بھنانا، تڑوانا، بدلوانا *change a note,* give or get smaller notes, coins, etc., for it نوٹ تڑوانا، یا بھنانا make or become different متغیّر ہونا *change colour* blush شرمانا، چہرے کا رنگ بدل جانا *change front* (رائے یا دلیل میں) پہلو بدلنا *n.* changing تبدیلی، تغیّر difference فرق، تبدیلی، تغیّر something needed in order to change دوسری چیز، متبادل شے *Take a change of clothes with you* کپڑوں کا دوسرا جوڑا بھی ساتھ لے جانا money in small units or in coin ریزگاری the difference between the cost of something and the amount of money offered in repayment بقیہ دام، باقی پیسے

changeable (*chaynj*-e-bèl) *adj.* likely to change غیر مستقل، بے ثبات able to be changed تغیّر پذیر often changing متلوّن، گھڑی میں تولہ گھڑی میں ماشہ **changeful** *adj.* continuously changing دائمی تغیّر والا **changeling** (*chaynj* ling) *n.* child (usu. ugly or stupid) left by fairies in place of (a usu. pretty) one they have stolen پریوں کا بدلا ہوا بچہ any child substituted for another بدلا ہوا بچہ

channel (*chan*-el) *n.* narrow stretch of water joining two seas دوبار، آبنائے bed (of a river) دریا کا راستہ، دریا کی گزرگاہ passage along which a liquid may flow (کسی سیال مثلاً پانی) کا راستہ، کی گزرگاہ way by which news, idea, etc. may travel ذریعہ، وسیلہ، واسطہ (see **Addenda**)

chant (chahnt) *n.* often-repeated tune مشہور گیت *v.t. & i.* sing a chant گیت گانا hum یا دُھن گنگنانا *chant the praises of* کے سدا گُن گاتے رہنا *chant horses,* palm off دھوکے سے بیچنا

chanticleer (*chahnt*-ik-lee-è*) *n.* personal name for domestic cock مُرغا، میاں مُرغا

chanty (*chahnt*-i) **shanty** (*shant*-i) *n.* song sung by sailors when heaving ropes, etc. ملاحوں کا گیت

chaos (*kay*-os) *n.* confusion, complete absence of order ابتری، سخت بدنظمی، خلل، انتشار formless state of matter before creation ہیولیٰ (Chaos). *Class. myth.* the name of the most ancient of Greek gods ; Disorder ; he was the father of *Nyx* (or night) کیئوس **chaotic** (kay-*ot*-ik) *adj.* دَرہم برہم، گڈمڈ

chap *v.t. & i.* (-pp-) (of the skin) make or become sore and cracked جلد کا پھٹنا *n.* (colloq.) boy لڑکا man بھلا مانس، مرد، آدمی **chap-book** *n.* cheap books once sold by pedlars پھیری والوں کے قصے کتابیں **chapman** *n.* pedlar پھیری والا

chapel (*chap*-èl) *n.* church in private house, etc. ملحقہ گرجا، خانہ گرجا **chaplain** (*chap*-lin) *n.* priest in charge of a chapel ملحقہ گرجے کا پادری

chaperon (*shap*-è-ron) *n.* elderly woman in charge of a young lady on social occasions آتون، اتالیقہ *v.t.* act as chaperon to اتالیقی کرنا دوشیزاؤں کی نگرانی کرنا **chaperonage** *n.* care by chaperon اتالیقہ کی نگرانی میں ہونا، آتون کی نگرانی

chaplet (*chap*-let) *n.* wreath for the head پھولوں کا گجرا string of prayer beads تسبیح، مالا

chapter (*chap*-tĕ*) *n.* (abb. *ch.*, *c.*, or *cap.*) division of a book باب، فصل *chapter and verse,* exact reference سورت کا نام اور آیت کا نمبر، ٹھیک حوالہ *quote chapter and verse for,* give precise authority for (statement, etc.) کی سند پیش کرنا، ٹھیک حوالہ دینا *to the end of the chapter,* for ever ہمیشہ ہمیشہ کے لیے canons of cathedral بڑے گرجے کے پادریوں کا گروہ group of monks or knights راہبوں یا فوجداروں کا گروہ meeting of any of these پادریوں، راہبوں یا فوجداروں کا جلسہ

char (chah*) *v.t. & i.* (-rr-) make or become

by burning جھلسنا ، جھلسانا ، جل کر کوئلہ ہو جانا ، جلا کر کوئلہ بنانا
charcoal, charred wood لکڑی کا کوئلہ
same as **chare** (which see)

char-a-banc (*sha*-ra-bang) *n.* long motor vehicle for pleasure-trips with all seats facing forward تفریحی سفر کی بس

character (*ka*-rak-tĕ*) *n.* mental or moral nature ذہنیّت ، فطرت ، امتیازی خصوصیّت mental and moral qualities which make one person or race different خصائل ، کردار ، سیرت *character-assassination*, (see *Addenda*) moral strength اخلاق ، اخلاقی قوت person who is well known شخصیت ، مشہور آدمی person in a play or book کردار ، فرد قصّہ person who is unusual in his way عجیب آدمی ، سنکی ، خبطی *quite a character*, quite an amusing person عجیب آدمی description of a person's qualities and abilities (esp. in a recommendatory letter) (صداقت نامہ میں لکھا ہوا چال چلن peculiarities of a place or thing (کسی مقام یا شے کی) امتیازی خصوصیات letter or mark, used in a system of writing or printing حرف ، رسم الخط *Urdu characters* حروف ، اردو رسم الخط **characteristic** (k-rak-te-*ris*-tik) *adj.* showing the character of a person, thing, place, etc. امتیازی ، مخصوص *n.* special mark or quality خصوصیّت ، وصف **characterize** (*ka*-rak-te-rīz) *v.t.* show the character of ماہیت بیان کرنا ، امتیازی وصف بیان کرنا describe as کے یوں بیان کرنا کہ (in a story, etc.) depict the character of (someone) کردار نگاری کرنا **characterization** (-*zay*-) *n.* (esp.) depicting character in a story, etc. be characteristic of کا امتیازی ، کا خاصّہ ہونا ، وصف (یا نشان) ہونا

charade (sha-*rahd*) *n.* game in which a word is guessed after its various syllables have, in turn, been suggested لفظ کے ٹکڑے جوڑ کر بوجھی جانے والی پہیلی

charcoal (*chah**-kohl) *n.* fuel made by burning wood slowly لکڑی کا کوئلہ (see also **char**)

chare, char (*chay*-ĕ*) *n.* (usu. in the *pl.*) odd jobs of housework for which payment is made by the day or the hour گھر کا کھٹیا کام ، گھر یا برتنوں کی صفائی کا کام *v.i.* (*chared, charing*, do chares گھر یا برتنوں کی صفائی کا کام کرنا

charwoman *n.* woman engaged to do such work گھر یا برتن صاف کرنے والی ماما (see also **chore**)

charge (chah*j) *n.* any accusation الزام ، تہمت statement against a person that he has violated a law اتہام ، الزام *lay* (*something*) *to* (*one's*) *charge, bring a charge of* (*something*) *against* (*someone*) (کسی پر کسی بات کا) الزام عائد کرنا sudden and violent attack at high speed یورش ، تاخت ، حملہ *bayonet charge* ہلّہ price asked for goods or services قیمت ، اجرت ، خرچ ، خرچہ *hotel charges* ہوٹل بِل (قیام وغیرہ کا) خرچ amount of gunpowder used for explosion or of electricity put into an accumulator بارود یا برق کی مقدار work given to someone as a duty فرض ، فریضہ ، کار متعلقہ ، کار مفوّضہ ، کام thing or person given to someone to be taken care of زیر نگرانی شخص یا کام *in charge of*, (a) taking care of کا نگران (b) being taken care of by کے زیر نگرانی *take charge of* be responsible for کی ذمہ داری لے لینا ، کے فرائض سنبھال لینا *give* (*someone*) *in charge*, give (him) up to the police میں دے دینا ، حوالۂ پولیس کرنا *v.t. & i.* entrust کے سپرد کرنا *charge* (*someone*) *with* (*something*), entrust (him) with (a task) کوئی کام کسی کے سپرد کرنا accuse الزام لگانا *charge* (*someone*) *with* (*an offence*), accuse of جرم کا الزام لگانا make a charge against پر حملہ کرنا ، دھاوا کرنا ask as a price قیمت لگانا ask in payment اجرت طلب کرنا ، خرچ کا معاوضہ مانگنا load بوجھ ڈالنا ، بار ڈالنا fill بھرنا ، بھر دینا put a charge into میں کارتوس یا بجلی بھرنا give as a task or duty فرض سونپنا ، کام تفویض کرنا ، ذمّے داری ڈالنا **chargeable** (cha*hj-ĕ-bĕl) *adj.* liable to be accused of wrong-doing قابل مواخذہ liable to be charged واجب الوصول **charger** *n.* cavalry officer's horse رسالے کا گھوڑا **charge-sheet** *n.* record of cases فرد جرم *v.t.* record cases against پر فرد جرم عائد کرنا *charge d'affaires* (*sha**-*hzh*-ay-de-*fay*-ĕ*) *n.* deputy ambassador or ambassador in a minor state مدار المہام ، ناظم الامور

chariot (*cha*-ri-ut) *n.* two wheeled horse-cart, in ancient times used in war رتھ **charioteer** (cha-ri-o-*tee*-ĕ*) *n.* chariot-driver رتھ بان

a chariot

charitable *adj.* (see under **charity**)

charity (*cha*-ri-ti) *n.* kindness in giving help to the poor ; سخاوت ، خیرات ، داد و دہش love of humanity انسانی ہمدردی willingness to judge other persons with kindness رحم دلی ، نرم دلی organization for helping the poor خیراتی ادارہ **charitable** *adj.* having charity سخی ، داتا ، مخیّر pertaining to charity خیراتی ، مخیّرانہ *charitable instuution*, institution for helping poor persons with free (medical, etc.) aid خیراتی ادارہ

charlatan (*sha***hl*-ĕ-tĕn) *n.* quack نیم حکیم ، عطائی one who pretends to skill and knowledge جھوٹا مدّعی ، لپا شیا ، ڈھونگیا

charm (chah*m) *n.* something believed to

have magic power جادو، سحر، افسون، کھرید، ٹوٹکا، ٹونا، ٹونکا under a charm, influenced by magic مسحور، سحر زدہ power of attracting and giving pleasure دلفریبی، دلکشی، جاذبیت، دلربائی، دلبری، دل آویزی حسن و جمال beauty v.t. & i. attract, give pleasure to لبھانا، موہنا use magic on جادو کرنا یا چلانا فریفتہ کرنا، شیفتہ کرنا protect as if by magic طلسماتی انداز سے حفاظت کرنا bear a charmed life, be invulnerable جادو کی طرح جنگ وامن میں محفوظ طلسماتی زندگی کا مالک ہونا، ایسا ہونا کہ تاکا دشمن نہ لگے، اس کا بال بیکا نہ کر سکیں charming adj. full of charm دلکش، دلربا، دل فریب giving pleasure دلکش، پسندیدہ charmed n. under the influence of magic مسحور، سحر زدہ charmer n. one who charms سیپیرا snake charmer, one who charms snakes سانپ

charnel-house (chah*nèl-hous) n. place where dead bodies or bones are stored مردہ خانہ، میت گھر

Charon (kay-ron) Cl. myth. boatman, according to Greeks, who ferried the shades (i.e., souls) of the dead across the River Styx to Hades کیرن

chart (chah*t) n. map of sea used by sailors بحری نقشہ information in the form of graphs, diagrams, etc. نقشہ، تختہ، شماریات (اعداد وشمار کا) جدول v.t. make a chart of نقشہ کھینچنا، جدول بنانا

charter (chah-tè*) n. written statement of rights حق، اختیار، استحقاق permission from a government (to do something) پروانہ، منشور، فرمان، توقیع، سند v.t. give a charter to حق عطا کرنا، پروانہ دینا، اجازت hire (a ship, aircraft, etc.) for an agreed time and purpose اجازت حاصل کرنا جہاز یا طیارہ کرائے پر کرنا

charwoman n. (see under chare)

chary (chay-ri) adj. (chary of), shy, cautious, or careful about پھونک پھونک کر قدم رکھنے والا، چوکنا یا شرمیلا

Charybdis (ka-rib-dis) Cl. myth name of a dangerous whirlpool between Italy and Sicily; (opposite it lay Scylla) کریبڈس، کریب ڈس

chase (chays) v.t. run after to capture or drive away پیچھا کرنا، تعاقب کرنا، رگیدنا، کھدیڑنا n. act of chasing تعاقب کرنا give chase to, (a) run after تعاقب، پیچھا (b) try to catch پکڑنے کی کوشش کرنا the chase. (esp.) the hunting of animals for sport شکار steel-frame in which (usu. a whole format of) composed type is locked چیس، ٹائپ بند

chasm (kazm) n. deep crack in the ground زمین میں گہرا خوفناک شگاف، غار wide difference اختلافات کی خلیج، شدید اختلاف

chassis (shas-ee) n. (pl. the same pr. shas-iz) base frame of a motor-car or carriage fastened under its body موٹر وغیرہ کا بنیادی ڈھانچہ، یا نچلا حصہ

chaste (chayst) adj. pure in thought and deed, (esp. sexually pure) پارسا، نیک، پرہیزگار، عفیف پاکدامن (language) pure in words, etc. شستہ، منجھی ہوئی chastity (chas-ti-ti) n. پاک دامنی، پاکیزگی، شستگی

chasten (chays-èn) v.t. correct through punishment or pain تادیب کرنا، سزا دے کر سدھارنا purify the soul نفس مارنا chastening n. correcting or purifying تادیب، نفس کشی adj. that corrects or purifies تادیب کرنے والی چیز، نفس مارنے والی

chastise (chas-tiz) v.t. punish severely (اصلاح کے لیے) سخت سزا chastisement n. act of chastising تادیب، سیاست، عذاب

chastity n. see under chaste

chat v.i. (-ll-) have a friendly talk about unimportant things گپ شپ اڑانا، بے تکلفی کی باتیں کرنا n. friendly talk about trifles گپ شپ، گپ بازی chatty adj. fond of chatting گپی، باتونی chattiness n. being chatty باتونی پن

chateau (shah-toh) n. (pl. chateaux, pr. shah-toz) large country-house (in France) (فرانس میں) دیہاتی حویلی شاتو chatelaine (shat-) mistress of a chateau دیہاتی حویلی کی مالکہ، شاتو والی appendage to woman's belt for carrying keys پیٹی میں کنجیاں لٹکانے کی جگہ

chattel (chat-èl) n. (usu. in the pl.) piece of movable property جائداد منقولہ، اثاثہ، اثالہ، انگڑ کھنگڑ goods and chattels خانگی سامان، چیز بست Is woman still regarded a chattel? کیا اب بھی عورت کو جائداد منقولہ تصور کیا جاتا ہے۔

chatter (chat-è*) v.i. talk quickly and foolishly بک بک کرنا، چپڑ چپڑ باتیں کرنا make quick, indistinct sounds like (a) the cries of monkeys, etc. چپڑ چپڑ کرنا، چیں چیں کرنا (b) the noise of type-writer keys کھٹ کھٹ ہونا (c) one's upper and lower teeth striking together from cold دانت بجنا n. sounds of the kinds noted above بک بک، چپڑ چپڑ، کھٹ کھٹ، کٹ کٹ

chatterbox, n. one who chatters باتونی، بکو (esp.) talkative child باتونی بچہ chatty adj. (fond of) talking in a friendly manner بے تکلفی سے بات کرنے والا

chauffeur (shoh-fè*) n. driver of a private motor-car ڈرائیور، شوفر، کار بان chauffeuse (shoh-fèz) n. female chauffeur شوفرنی، کاربانی

cheap (cheep) adj. inexpensive سستا، ارزاں worth more than its cost کم خرچ easily got زود یاب showy, having little worth سستا، کم قدر، ٹکا، گھٹیا، بے وقعت (see Addenda) cheapish adj. somewhat cheap گھٹیا سا، ٹکا سا cheapen v.t. & i. make or become cheap ارزاں ہونا یا کرنا cheapness n. inexpensiveness ارزانی low quality ٹکا پن، بستی گھٹیا پن

cheat (cheet) v.t. & i. try to obtain an advantage by dishonest means دغا بازی کرنا، دھوکا دینا، بے ایمانی کرنا

cheat (*someone*) *out of* (*something*), get something from by cheating کسی سے بے ایمانی سے کچھ حاصل کرنا *n.* swindler دغاباز، عیّار، بے ایمان، دھوکے باز trick, deception دغاباز، عیّار، بے ایمان، دھوکے باز

check (chek) *v.i.* test accuracy جانچ پڑتال کرنا، جائزہ لینا، تنقیح کرنا correct (student's written work) اصلاح دینا، تصحیح کرنا mark (examinee's script or paper) (اُمیدوار کا پرچہ) دیکھنا یا جانچنا hold back suddenly یکایک روکنا، ٹوکنا cause to go slow or stop باز رکھنا، روکے رکھنا *check the enemy's advance* دشمن کا آگا روکنا expose adversary's king at chess شہ دینا *n.* checking جانچ پڑتال، روک تھام، مزاحمت person or thing that checks روک، مزاحمت *keep a check on, keep* (*something*) *in check*, control کسی شے کو قابو سے باہر نہ ہونے دینا token of identification (as for luggage sent by train) شناختی چِٹھی (مثلاً ریل گاڑی سے بھیجے جانے والے سامان کی) also *checked*, cross-lined pattern خانے دار ڈیزائن cloth with such pattern چار خانہ دار یا چوخانہ کپڑا exposure of king at chess شہ، کشت **checkmate** *n.* such exposure involving loss of game شہ مات، مات *v.t.* expose king thus کی بازی مات کرنا، مات دینا، obstruct or defeat (a person or his plans) (کسی کی راہ میں) حائل ہونا یا رُکاوٹ بننا **checkers** *n. pl.* (U.S.) game of draughts ڈرافٹس، چھڑہ بازی **checker** *n.* & *v.t.* same as **chequer** (which see)

cheek *n.* each side of the face below the eyes گال، رُخسار saucy talk or behaviour شوخی impudence گستاخی *v.t.* be impudent to سے گستاخی کرنا، سے گستاخی سے پیش آنا **cheeky** (*chee*-ki) *adj.* impudent گستاخ saucy شوخ **cheekily** *adv.* saucily; impertinently شوخی سے، گستاخی سے

cheep *v.i.* make a weak, shrill note (like chicken, etc.) (چوزے وغیرہ کی طرح) چیں چیں کرنا

cheer (*chee*-ĕ*) *v.t.* & *i.* feel or make (someone) feel happier دلداری کرنا، دل بہلانا، جی خوش کرنا، خوش ہونا *cheer up!* become happy خوش ہو جاؤ، ہمت نہ ہارو *cheer* (*someone*) *up*, make him happy کسی کا جی خوش کرنا give shouts of joy or encouragement شاباش کے نعرے لگانا، شاباش دینا *n.* state of hope or gladness خوشی یا اُمید کی کیفیت *be of good cheer* اُمید قائم رکھنا shout of encouragement, etc. نعرۂ تحسین *give* (*three*) *cheers for* کے لیے (تین) نعرہ ہائے تحسین لگانا **cheerful** *adj.* hopeful پُراُمید happy, lively خوش باش **cheerfully** *adv.* خوشی خوشی، شاداں و فرحاں، خوشی سے، خندہ پیشانی سے **cheerless** *adj.* without joy or comfort افسردہ، بے دل، مُردہ دل gloomy تیرہ و تار، بے رونق **cheery** *adj.* lively; merry زندہ دل، زندہ دلانہ **cheerily** *adv.* in a lively manner زندہ دلی سے

cheerio, cheerioh, (*chee*-ri-oh) *int.* for greeting or farewell among equals سلام

cheese (cheez) *n.* solid food made from milk curds پنیر **cheesecake** *n.* & (see *Addenda*)

chef (shef) *n.* male head-cook in a hotel, etc. میر مطبخ

chef-d'oeuvre (she-*deevr*) *n.* masterpiece of art or literature فنی یا ادبی شاہکار

chemise (she-*meez*) *n.* loose-fitting vest once worn by women زنانہ بنیان، شمیز

chemistry (*kem*-is-tri) *n.* branch of science dealing with the elements and how they combine کیمیا، علم کیمیا **chemical** (*kem*-i-kal) *adj.* of or made by chemistry کیمیاوی *n.* substance used in or obtained by chemistry کیمیاوی مرکّب **chemist** (*kem*-ist) *n.* person with knowledge of chemistry کیمیا دان person who prepares and sells medicines, etc. دوا فروش، دوا ساز

chenille (shi-*neel*) *n.* velvety cord for trimming dresses مخمل ڈوری velvet-like cloth شنیل

cheque (chek) *n.* written order on a printed form to a bank to pay money چیک *issue a cheque* (*to*) کے نام چیک کاٹنا *draw a cheque* چیک کے ذریعہ رقم نکلوانا **chequebook** *n.* number of cheques fastened together چیک نامہ

chequer, checker (*chek*-ĕ*) *n.* chess-board-like pattern with squares alternately coloured شطرنج کی بساط، شطرنجی، چار خانہ دار *v.t.* make such pattern شطرنجی بنانا، چوخانہ بنانا break uniformity of یک رنگی یا یکسانی توڑنا، بوقلموں بنانا **chequered, checkered** *adj.* of this pattern چوخانہ، چارخانہ variegated رنگا رنگ، بوقلموں lacking continuity غیر مسلسل *chequered career*, career with frequent changes of fortune زندگی میں تواتر اور تسلسل سے محرومی، بُری بھلی زندگی

cherish (*che*-rish) *v.t.* regard (someone) tenderly عزیز جاننا، آنکھ کا تارہ سمجھنا، پیارا سمجھنا keep alive in one's heart گرہ لگائے رکھنا، کی خواہش زندہ رکھنا nurse پالنا، پوسنا، پرورش کرنا

cheroot (she-*root*) *n.* cigar open at both ends چُروٹ

cherry (*che*-ri) *n.* small, soft, round fruit usu. red, with stone in the middle گیلاس، شاہ دانہ tree bearing this fruit گیلاس کا درخت *cherry ripe*, cry of hawkers selling cherry سُرخ گیلاس لیلو! *adj.* of the colour of ripe red cherries سُرخ

cherub (*che*-rub) *n.* (*a*) (pl., *cherubs*, or *cherubim*) angel of the second order کروبی، فرشتہ (*b*) (pl., *cherubs*) small, beautiful, and innocent child ننھا خوبصورت، معصوم بچہ

chess (ches) *n.* game for two players with 16 pieces each, on a board with 64 squares شطرنج **chessboard** *n.* board on which chess is played شطرنج کی بساط **chessmen** *n. pl.* pieces with which chess is played مُہرے **Note:** The *chessmen* are: one *king* (بادشاہ) one *queen* (فرزین یا وزیر) *two bishops* (فیل) *two knights* (گھوڑا) *two castles* (رُخ) *eight pawns* (پیادے)

a chessboard and chessmen

chest *n.* large, strong wooden box پیٹی، لکڑی کا صندوق *chest of drawers,* chest with drawers for clothes کپڑوں کا دراز upper front part of the body سینہ، چھاتی

a chest of drawers

chestnut (*ches*-nut) *n.* tree with reddish brown nuts شاہ بلوط its wood شاہ بلوط کی لکڑی the colour of these nuts سرخی مائل بھورا رنگ

chevron (*shev*-ron) *n.* V-shaped stripe worn by soldiers policemen, etc., on sleeves to show rank کیکری

chew *v.t.* & *i.* crush (food) between the teeth چبانا *chew the cud,* ruminate جُگالی کرنا meditate میں محو ہونا، سوچنا، فکر یا خیال **chewing-gum** *n.* sweetened gum for chewing چبینہ گوند

chic (shik, or sheek) *adj.* (of a woman or her clothes) in the latest fashion جدید ترین وضع کا لباس یا اس وضع کی عورت stylish طرحدار، وضعدار

chicanery (shi-*kayn*-è-ri) *n.* use of tricky arguments (esp. in law) قانونی حیلہ جوئی، حیلہ بازی، پُرفریب استدلال

chick (chik) *n.* young chicken چُوزہ other young bird چینگا

chicken (*chik*-èn) *n.* young of a domestic bird esp. young fowl پالتو پرندوں کا بچہ (بالخصوص مُرغی کا چوزہ) meat of a chicken as food چوزے کا گوشت *chicken-broth* چوزے کی یخنی *chicken-hearted,* easily frightened بُزدل، ڈرپوک **chicken-pox** *n.* children's disease causing red spots on the skin موتیا، سیتلا، چھوٹی چیچک

chicory, chiccory (*chik*-o-ri) *n.* plant whose roasted root is powdered and mixed with coffee کاسنی

chide (chȳd) *v.t.* & *i.* (*chide, chid, chid* ; or *chide, chided, chidden*) rebuke, scold ڈانٹنا، جھڑکنا، بُرا بھلا کہنا، سخت سُست کہنا (of wind, etc.) howl as if impatient دہاڑنا، بیتابی سے سائیں سائیں کرنا

chief (cheef) *n.* leader or ruler سردار، حاکم، امیر، شیخ head of a department حاکم، افسر، بالادست، افسرِ اعلیٰ *adj.* principal اوّل، اعلیٰ most important اہم **chiefly** *adv.* mainly اغلباً، خاص طور پر، سب سے بڑھ کر **chieftain** *n.* chief of a tribe سردار، شیخ

(poet) chief of a gang سرغنہ

chiffon (*shif*-on) *n.* thin transparent silk material ریشمی ململ، شفون

chilblain (*chil*-blayn) *n.* painful swelling on hands, feet, etc., during winter ہاتھ پاؤں پھٹنا، بوائی **chilblained, chilblainy,** *adj.* پھٹے ہوئے

child (chȳld) *n.* (pl. *children*) young human being بچہ، بچی *from a child,* right from childhood بچپن ہی سے (be) *with child,* pregnant حاملہ ہونا *child-birth, child-bed,* giving birth to a child ولادت، تولید (*one's*) *child* (کسی کا) بیٹا، بیٹی *child's play,* easy job آسان کام، بازیچۂ اطفال *child-wife,* very young wife بالکل کم عمر دُولہن **childlike** *adj.* (of adult) innocent and frank like a child بے لوث، صاف گو، معصوم صفت **childish** *adj.* (behaviour proper to a child but ill-beseeming in adults) بچوں کا سا (مزاج) میں، بچپن **childless** *n.* one having no child بے اولاد، لاولد **childhood** *n.* period when one is a child بچپن، بچپن، طفلی، طفولیت

chill (chil)*n.* unpleasant cold feeling سخت ٹھنڈ، ٹھٹھر *cast a chill over,* depress اوس پڑنا، افسردہ ہونا *take the chill off the water,* warm it a little پانی ذرا گرم کر دینا illness caused by cold or damp زکام، سردی لگ جانا *take* (or *catch*) *a chill,* catch cold زکام ہونا، سردی لگ جانا *adj.* unpleasantly cold ناگوار طور پر ٹھنڈا، سخت سرد cold-mannered, unemotional بے جوش، بے حس، رُوکھا *v.t.* & *i.* make or become cold ٹھٹھر جانا، ٹھنڈا ہونا یا کرنا *chilled meat,* meat slightly frozen to keep it in good condition ٹھنڈا گوشت، سرد مہر، بے دلانہ، رُکھائی سے، خشک **chilly** (*chil*-i) *adj.* rather cold ٹھنڈا، سرد، بے مہر، سرد مہر، رُوکھا، رُکھائی سے۔

chime (chȳm) *n.* tuned set of church bells ہم آہنگ گھنٹیاں series of notes by them جھنکار *v.t.* & *i.* (of bell or a clock) make or cause to sound گھنٹی بجانا یا بجانا show (hour) by chiming گھنٹہ بجانا *the clock chimed nine* گھڑی نے نو بجائے *chime with* (*someone*) express agreement with (him) ہاں میں ہاں ملانا *chime in,* break in excitedly on the talk of others only to express agreement بڑے جوش سے کسی کی بات کاٹ کر اس کی تائید کرنا

Chimera, Chimaera (ki-*mee*-ra) *Class. myth* fire-spitting female goat with lion's head and serpent's tail کمیرا (chimera), horrible creature of the imagination ہَوّا (chimera) wild impossible scheme خیالِ باطل، خام خیالی **chimerical** *adj.* visionary (schemes) ہوائی، ناپائیدار، موہوم unreal بے اصل، خیالی

chimney (*chim*-ni) *n.* structure for carrying away smoke from fire دُودکش، چمنی، آتش دان glass tube protecting the flame of an oil-lamp لیمپ کی

چمنی یا شیشہ *chimney corner*, seat in an old-fashioned fireplace انگیٹھی کے قریب گرم جگہ *chimney pot*, tube-shaped pot at the top of a chimney on a roof چمنی کا نلکا **chimneysweep** *n*. one who sweeps soot from chimneys چمنی روب، چمنی صاف کرنے والا

chimpanzee (chim-pan-*zee*) *n*. manlike African ape, smaller than a gorilla چمپانزی

chin *n*. part of the face under the mouth ٹھوڑی، ذقن

china (*chi*-na) *n*. baked and glazed fine white clay (برتن بنانے والی) چینی cups, plates, etc., made of this چینی کے برتن *adj*. (China), from or of China چینی، چین کا

a chimpanzee

chink *n*. narrow crack (through which one may peep or the wind may blow) درز، شگاف، سوراخ sound of coins, etc., striking together جھنکار، کھنکناہٹ *v.t.* & *i*. make such a sound کھنکھنانا، بجانا

chintz *n*. a colourfully-printed, glazed cotton cloth چھینٹ

chip *n*. small piece cut or broken off (from wood, stone, china, etc.) چھپٹی، چھیلن، ٹکڑا، ریزہ، قاش *chip of* (or *off*) *the old block* son much like his father جیسا باپ ویسا بیٹا thin slice cut from potato, etc. آلو وغیرہ کی قاش place (in a plate, etc.) from which a chip has come off جہاں سے ریزہ ٹوٹا ہو *v.t.* & *i*. (*-pp*) cut or knock chips from چھپٹی اتارنا، ٹکڑا اتارنا make into chips لکڑی کو چھیلنا، پھل وغیرہ کی قاشیں کرنا become chipped ٹکڑے ہو جانا یا چھل جانا *chip in* interrupt a talk بات کاٹنا

chiropody (ki-*rop*-o-di) *n*. treatment of troubles of feet پیروں کا ڈبل کاٹنا **chiropodist** (ky-*rop*-o-dist) *n*. ڈبل کٹ

chirp (chĕ*p) short, sharp sound of sparrows, crickets, etc. چوں چوں، چیں چیں، چہچہانا *v.t.* & *i*. make such sounds چیں چیں کرنا، چوں چوں کرنا، چہچہانا

chirrup (*chi*-rup) *v.t.* & *i*. and *n*. (make) series of chirps چوں چوں کرتے جانا

chisel (*chiz*-ĕl) *n*. steel tool with sharp edge at end for cutting and shaping wood, stone, or metal چھینی، نہانی، اسکنہ *v.t.* (*-ll-*) shape with a chisel ٹانکی مارنا یا لگانا، نہانی سے چھیلنا cheat ٹھگنا، چھلنا

chivalry (*shiv*-al-ri) *n*. **1** laws and customs of knights in the Middle Ages نائٹوں کا نظام، نظام فتوت **2** the ideal characteristics of a knight, *viz*., courage, honour, loyalty, readiness to help the weak, devotion to (esp. young and beautiful) women نائٹوں کے خصائل (یعنی بہادری، عزت، وفاداری، کمزوروں کی مدد، صنف نازک پر فداکاری)، فتوت (old use) all the knights of a country کسی ملک کے تمام نائٹ، فوجداران کشور **chivalrous** *adj*. having chivalry بہادر، شجاع، جانباز

chloral *adj* **chloride** *n* **chlorinate** *v.t.* (see under **chlorine**)

chlorine (*kloh*-rin) *n*. a kind of poisonous gas کلورین **chlorinate** (*kloh*-ri-nayt) treat water with chlorine to make it safe for drinking purposes پانی میں کلورین ملانا **chloride** (*kloh*-rid) *n*. compound of chlorine کلورین کا مرکب، کلورائیڈ **chloral** *n*. a hypnotic and anaesthetic ایک خواب آور اور بے حس کرنے والی دوا

chloroform (*kloh*-ro-fo*m) *n*. vapour used by doctors to make a person unconscious کلوروفارم *v.t.* make unconscious by giving chloroform to کلوروفارم سنگھا کر بے ہوش کرنا

chlorophyll (*kloh*-ro-fil) *n*. green colouring matter in plants پودوں کو سبز رنگ دینے والا مادہ، خضرہ

chock (chok) *n*. block of wood, etc., to prevent barrel, etc., from rolling اڑانا **chock-full** *adj*. full to the possible extent کھچاکھچ بھرا ہوا **chock-a-block** *adj*. jammed (*with something*) بھرپور، کھچاکھچ بھرا

choky (*choh*-ki) *n*. (slang) (Anglicized form of پولیس چوکی with the meanings) lock-up حوالات prison قید خانہ

chocolate (*chok*-o-layt) *n*. sweet substance made from sugar and crushed cacao seeds چاکلیٹ drink made by mixing this with hot water or milk چاکلیٹ شربت the colour of chocolate, dark brown لاکھیا رنگ

a bar of chocolate

choice (chois) *n*. act of choosing چناؤ، انتخاب possibility of choosing انتخاب کا حق، انتخاب *make a wise choice* دانشمندانہ انتخاب کرنا *take (one's) choice* پسند کرنا، انتخاب کرنا *at choice*, chosen by the customer, etc. حسب پسند، حسب مرضی *for choice*, if one must choose کچھ پسند ہی کرنا ہے تو، کچھ منتخب ہی کرنا ہو تو person or thing chosen پسندیدہ، منتخبہ number from which to choose انتخاب کے لیے انواع و اشیا *have no choice*, do not care which کچھ بھی ہو *have no choice but*, have no alternative except کے سوا کوئی چارہ نہ ہونا *have (one's) choice*, be able to choose خود انتخاب کرنا، اپنی مرضی سے پسند کرنا *offer Hobson's choice*, take the only thing offered or leave it یہی ہے، نہیں لیتے تو نہ لو *adj*. specially or carefully chosen چیدہ، پسندیدہ uncommonly good غیر معمولی، بہت ہی اچھا **S** A **choice** is a definite judgment following hesitation due possible to equal desire ; **a selection** choice of several at the same time ; **an option**, guaranteed possibility of choice , **a dilemma**, a situation in which it is necessary but almost impossible to choose . **a preference**, greater inclination to one than to anot^

choir (*kwī*-ĕ*) *n*. (old spelling : **quire**) company of persons trained to sing together such a company leading the singing in church گرجے کی بھجن منڈلی یا طائفہ part of church for the choir گرجے کا قوال خانہ **choir-boy** *n.* young member of the choir چوکی کا نوخیز قوال، مُنغنی **choral** *adj.* **chorister** *n.* **chorus** *n.* (see separate entries)

choke (chohk) *v.t.* & *i.* be unable to breathe گلے میں پھنس جانا، پھندا پڑ جانا، دم گھٹنا، سانس بند ہو جانا *choke over (one's) food* کچھ کھاتے کھاتے گلے میں اڑ جانا *choke with anger* غصے سے دم بند ہو جانا stop the breathing by pressing the windpipe from outside or by filling it; گلا دبانا، گلا گھونٹنا، ٹیٹوا دبانا *choke the life out of (someone)* گلا گھونٹ کر مار ڈالنا suppress emotions جذبات کو دبانا *choke up*, (*a*) fill a passage, etc. which is usually clear نالی وغیرہ میں کچھ اڑانا یا اڑا کر بند کرنا (*b*) fill to capacity ناک تاک یا مونہا مونہ *choke down* (*a*) swallow (food) with difficulty نوالہ مشکل سے نگلنا (*b*) suppress (tears or emotions) with difficulty بمشکل آنسو روکنا یا پینا، جذبات ضبط کرنا، *n.* choked part of a tube نالی کا بند حصہ petrol engine valve to control the intake of air * پٹرول انجن کی، گھٹل منڈن

choler (kol-ĕ*) *n.* anger غصہ، طیش، جوش، تیہا، تند مزاجی

choleric (*kol*-e-rik) *adj.* easily made angry غصیلا تند مزاج، تیز مزاج

cholera (*kol*-e-ra) *n.* dangerous disease attacking the bowels ہیضہ

choose (chooz) *v.t.* & *i.* (*choose, chose, chosen*) pick out from two or more چننا، چھانٹنا، انتخاب کرنا decide (*between* one and another) (میں سے) چن لینا یا منتخب کرنا be determined (*to do*) (کرنے پر) ادھار کھائے بیٹھنا

chop *v.t.* (-pp-) cut (something) by giving blows to it ٹکڑے ٹکڑے کرنا، اڑا دینا، کاٹ ڈالنا، سخت ضرب سے کاٹنا (of wind and waves) swing this way and that تھپیڑے مارنا *n.* chopping blow سخت ضرب، ٹکڑے ٹکڑے کر دینے والی چوٹ something chopped off ٹکڑا thick piece of meat usu. with a bone in it چانپ، پارچہ broken motion of the sea لہروں کا کبھی ادھر کبھی ادھر جانا، تلاطم **chopper** *n.* heavy tool with sharp edge for chopping کلہاڑا، کلہاڑی **choppy** *adj.* (of the sea) covered with short, rough waves (سمندر) تلاطم خیز **chopsticks** *n. pl.* pair of sticks used by the Chinese to carry food to the mouth * چینی چمچہ

choral (*koh*-ral) *adj.* of or sung by or together with, a choir طائفے کے متعلق یا کا، طائفے کا یا کے ساتھ گایا ہوا

choral speaking *n.* (see **Addenda**) see also **choir, chorister,** and **chorus**)

chord (koh*d̃) *n.* (mathematics) straight line joining two points on a circle or curve وتر string of harp, etc. تار، تانت (in the body) string-like part تار جیسا کوئی حصہ *spinal chord* ریڑھ کی تانت

chord

chore (*choh**) *n.* (U.S. form of **chare,** which also see) ordinary daily task in the home or on a farm گھر یا کھیتی کا روزمرہ کا معمولی کام

choreograph *v.t.* & **choreography** *n.* (see **Addenda**)

chorister (*ko*-ris-te*) *n.* any member of a choir طائفے یا چوکی کا کوئی سا گویا choir-boy چوکی کا نوخیز قوال (see also **choir, choral** and **chorus**)

choroscript *n.* (see **Addenda**)

chorus (koh-rus) *n.* group of singers, esp on the stage طائفہ، چوکی music for it طائفے کا گیت یا طائفے کی موسیقی part of the song in which all join after solo is sung ترجیع، انترا something said loudly by many together غلغلہ، بیک آواز کہنا *chorus of praise* تعریف کا غلغلہ *in chorus*, all together ہم آواز ہو کر (ancient Greece) group of dancers and singers taking part in dramas (قدیم یونانی) کورس

chose pa. t., **chosen** pa. p. of **choose** (which see)

chow *n.* (slang) food خوراک

Christ (kryst) *n.* حضرت عیسیٰ مسیح *the Christ-child*, Christ as child حضرت عیسیٰ بچپن میں *int.* (of surprise, etc.) dear dear! توبہ، ارے توبہ **christen** (*kri*-sĕn) *v.t.* receive (infant) into the Christian fold بپتسمہ دینا، عیسائی بنانا، اصطباغ دینا give name to (child) at baptism (بپتسمہ کے وقت) نام رکھنا give name to (ship, institution, etc.) نام رکھنا apply nick-name to (a person) نام بگاڑنا، چڑانے کا نام رکھنا، لقب عطا کرنا

Christendom (*kris*-ĕn-dum) *n.* Christian people and Christian countries مسیحی دنیا، عیسائی نصاری **Christian** (*kris*-ti-an) *adj.* of Jesus Christ and his teaching عیسوی، مسیحی of the religion based on this teaching عیسائی، نصرانی *Christian name*, first part of a Western person's name, given when he or she is christened ذاتی نام، نام کا پہلا جزو *n.* Christian person عیسائی، نصرانی، مسیحی **Christianity** (*kris*-ti-an-ity) *n.* the Christian religion عیسائیت، نصرانیت، مسیحیت **Christmas** (*kris*-mas), (abb. **Xmas**) *n.* yearly celebration of the birth of Christ, 25 Dec. کرسمس، میلاد مسیح (عیسائیوں کا) بڑا دن Mark the peculiar way of spelling and pronouncing the words **christen, Christendom, Christmas** and **Xmas**

chromatic (kro-*mat*-ik) relating to colours رنگوں سے متعلق coloured رنگ دار، رنگین

chrome *n.* (see under **chromium**)

chromium (kroh-me-um) *n.* a kind of metal کرومیم **chrome** (krohm) *n.* colouring substance obtained from compounds of chromium کروم رنگ *chrome leather*, leather treated with chromium

کروم، کروم سے کسا یا ہوا چمڑا *chrome steel*, kind of steel containing chromium کروم فولاد
chronic (*kron*-ik) *adj*. (of a disease) going on for a long time (مرض) مزمن *chronic invalid*, person with a chronic illness سدا روگی، دائم المرض
chronicle (kron-i-kĕl) *n*. record of events in the order of their happenings وقائع، تاریخ *v.t.* enter in a chronicle وقائع نگاری، تاریخ نویسی
chronology (kro-*nol*-o-ji) *n*. science of fixing dates تاریخ، تاریخ نگاری arrangement of events with dates تاریخ وار، سلسلۂ واقعات list showing this واقعات کا تاریخ وار جدول **chronological** (kroh-no-*loj*-i-kĕl) *adj*. in order of time ترتیب وار، تاریخی ترتیب سے *in chronological order*, in the order of occurrence تاریخی ترتیب سے
chronometer (kro-*nom*-e-te*) *n*. watch used by ships for ascertaining longitude جہازی گھڑی، وقت پیما
chrysalis (*kris*-a-lis) *n*. form taken by an insect in the second stage (between *larva* and *imago*) پیلہ case covering it during this stage پیلے کا خول

a chrysalis

chrysanthemum (kri-*san*-themum) *n*. Japanese garden plant blooming in early winter جاپانی گل داؤدی، ہمرانی داؤدی

a chrysanthemum

chubby (*chub*-i) *adj*. roundfaced گول مٹول، پھولے ہوئے، گالوں والا، گل پھلا، موٹا تازہ plump گداز بدن
chuck (chuk) *v.t.* call the hens کٹ کٹ کرنا urge the horse ٹخ ٹخ کرنا (colloq.) *chuck up*, (*a*) fling contemptuously حقارت سے پھینکنا (*b*) give up ترک کر دینا، پرلات مارنا *chuck up (one's) job* ملازمت پر لات مارنا *int*. (for calling the hens or urging a horse) کٹ کٹ، ٹخ ٹخ
chuckle (*chuk*-ĕl) *v.t.* laugh with closed mouth to indicate satisfaction or amusement کھی کھی کرنا ہنسی روک کر ہنسنا *n*. such laughter کھی کھی، روکی ہوئی ہنسی *v.t.* (of engine, etc.) make this sound پھک پھک پھک پھک کرنا، پھک پھک کرتے ہوئے جانا
chug (chug) *n*. characteristic sound of oil-engine or slow-running petrol engine چھک چھک، بھک بھک
chum *n*. close friend یار غار، ہمدم، ساتھ رہنے والا *v.t.* (-*mm*-) share lodgings with ایک گھر یا کمرے میں رہنا *chum up* (*with*), become friendly (with) سے بے تکلفی پیدا کرنا، پینگ بڑھانا **chummy** (*chum*-i) *adj*. sociable ملنسار، یاروں کا یار *be chummy with* (someone) سے گاڑھی چھننا
chunk *n*. thick lump cut off a piece of meat, cheese, etc. بڑا سا ٹکڑا

church (chu*ch) *n*. building for public Christian worship گرجا، کلیسا، کنیسہ service in such a building گرجے میں عبادت *the Church*, (*a*) the whole body of religion کلیسا، مذہب (*b*) religious power as opposed to the [illegible], to the political power (حکومت کے مقابلے میں) دین، مذہب *the Church of Christ*, the whole body of Christians عیسائی دنیا، مسیحیت *the Church of*, one of the branches of Christianity (کوئی عیسائی) فرقہ *the Church of England* انگریزی کلیسا *go into* (or *enter*) *the Church*, become a minister of religion پادری بننا **churchyard** *n*. graveyard round a church گرجے کا گورستان، قبرستان ملحقہ گرجا
churl (chĕ*l) *n*. (old use) peasant, villager دیہاتی، گنوار **churlish** (*che**-lish) *adj*. bad-tempered, ill-bred اجڈ، گنوار، اکھڑ، بدتمیز، کندۂ ناتراش
churn (chĕ*n) *n*. container in which curds, etc., are beaten to make butter چاٹی، مٹکی *v.t.* & *i* make (butter) in a churn متھنا مکھن نکالنا، بلونا (of the sea, etc.) (cause to) move about violently (سمندر وغیرہ کا) تلاطم خیز ہونا، طوفان لانا *churn-staff*, staff for churning curds مدھانی، متھنی، رئی

a churn

chute (shoot) *n*. steep slide down which things (*e.g.*, letters, logs, coal) may pass ڈھلان، پھسلن such slide for children to play on پھسلن
chutney (*chut*-ni) *n*. hot and sweet mixture of fruit, peppers, etc. چٹنی
cicada (si-*kay*-da), **cicala** (si-*kah*-la), **cigala** (si-*gah*-la) winged insect which makes a loud, shrill noise جھینگر، ٹڈی
cider (si-dĕ*) *n*. (also called *cider ale*) liquor made from apples سیادہ، سیب کی شراب **cider-press** *n*. press for squeezing apples سیب افشار، سیب نچوڑ
cigar (si-*gah**) *n*. roll of tobacco leaves for smoking, larger and thicker than a cigarette سگار، چرٹ **cigarette** (sig-è-*ret*) *n*. tobacco rolled in thin paper for smoking سگرٹ
cinchona (sin-*koh*-na) *n*. tree yielding quinine from its bark کونین کا پیڑ، سنکونا its bark سنکونا کی چھال
cincher *n*. (see **Addenda**)
cincture (*sink*-cheh*) *n*. (lit.) belt, girdle پیٹی کمربند، پٹکا
cinder (*sind*-ĕ*) *n*. small piece of coal or wood partly burnt ادھ جلا کوئلہ یا لکڑی، کھنگر، جلا ہوا کوئلہ *cinder-sifter* راکھ سے کوئلے جدا کرنے کی چھلنی *cinder-path*, path covered with cinders راستہ جس پر کوئلے بچھے ہوں
Cinderella (sin-de-*rel*-ah) *n*. maiden in fairy

tales whose proud sisters left her among the cinders but who was helped by luck and became the princess کوئلے والی سِندریلہ unjustly despised or badly-treated colleague or member of the family مظلوم ، بدنصیب *cinderella dance*, dance closing at midnight (with reference to the cinderella story) رقصِ نیم شب ، رَقصِ نیم شبی

cinema (*sin*-e-ma) *n.* picture-house, hall for screening films سینما ، فلم کدہ **cinematograph** (-*at*-) *n.* (old use) apparatus for showing films (now called a *projector*) متحرک تصویریں دکھانے کا آلہ ، فلم نُما **cine-camera** *n.* camera for taking moving pictures فلمی کیمرہ

cinnabar (*sin*-a-bah*) *n.* a mercury ore شنگرف

cinnamon (*sin*-a-mun) *n.* a yellowish-brown spice دارچینی its colour نسواری (رنگ)

Cimmerians (si-*me*-ri-anz) *Cl. myth.* people living in the land of darkness, according to the Greek poet Homer سِمری

cipher, cypher (*si*-fě*) *n.* the figure 0, representing zero صِفر، بِندی person or thing of no importance صِفرِ محض، ناکارہ ، کاٹھ کا اُلّو (method of) secret writing خفیہ تحریر، خفیہ رسم الخط its key رسم الخط کا حل یا اشارے *v.t.* & *i.* work *out* (sums) جمع کرنا، تخفیہ حساب لگانا، سوال نکالنا put (something) into secret writing خفیہ رسم الخط میں لکھنا

circa (*sě**-ka) *prep.* about کے قریب (with date written in abbreviated form; as:) *c. 1857* ۱۸۵۷ کے قریب

Circe (*sè**-see) *Cl. myth.* a sea-nymph and sorceress who detained Odysseus on his way home from Troy, turning his companions into swine سَرسی enchantress, temptress لُبھانے والی عیّارہ

circle (*sě**-kèl) *n.* space enclosed by a curved line every point of which is the same distance from the centre دائرہ the line enclosing this space مُحیط something round, like a circle گھیرا، حلقہ ، چکّر persons grouped round a centre of interest حلقہ، جماعت، گروہ ، انجمن *business circles* کاروباری حلقے *the upper circles*, upper strata (of society, etc.) (معاشرہ وغیرہ کے) اُونچے حلقے *the circle in which one moves*, one's friends, relatives, colleagues, etc., from whose character one's own may be judged یار دوست، ملنے جُلنے والے، دوستوں کا حلقہ sphere of influence or action دائرۂ عمل، دائرۂ کار، حلقۂ اثر period or cycle دَور، چکّر، مکمل سلسلہ *come full circle*, end at the starting point چکّر پُورا کرنا *arguing in a circle*, logical fallacy of proving one thing by asserting another which depends on the former for its proof دَور، دَوری اِستدلال *vicious circle*, series of events following and reacting upon one another so that each becomes the effect of the last and cause of the next all combining to aggravate the result (which is not necessarily vicious) *v.t.* & *i.* move in a circle گرد چھرنا ، گرد گھومنا، چکّر کاٹ کے آنا، کے گرد جانا go round گردش میں آنا ، دَور چلنا *the aircraft circles over the aerodrome* ہوائی جہاز اُترنے سے پہلے مستقر کے گرد پرواز کرتا ہے

circlet (*sě**k-let) *n.* circular band of gold or flowers worn on the head as an ornament سنگارپٹی

circs (*sě**ks) *n. pl.* (colloq.) circumstances حالات صورتِ حال

circuit (*sě**-kit) *n.* journey round a district دَورہ ، گشت regular journey made by judge in England from town to town to try cases مُنصِف کا دَورہ one of the eight districts in England visited by such a judge سرکٹ، مُنصِف کا حلقہ continuous path of an electric current برقی رَو کا راستہ، *short circuit*, wrong shortening of such a path fusing the wire برقی دَور شارٹ، ناقص دَور **circuitous** (*sě**-*kew*-i-tus) *adj.* indirect بالواسطہ roundabout, going a long way round چکّر والا، لمبا راستہ کاٹ کر جانے والا ، اُوپر سے ہو کر جانے والا

circular (*sě**-kew-lě*) *adj.* in the shape of a circle گول، مُدَوّر، مُستدِیر *circular tour*, journey ending at the starting point without visiting a place more than once مختلف راستوں سے آنا جانا *n.* (also *circular letter*), announcement, etc., sent to a number of people گشتی چِٹھی، گشتی مراسلہ ، گشتی **circularize** (*se**-kew-lè-riz) *v.t.* send circulars to گشتی مراسلات (یا اعلانات) بھیجنا **circularly** *adv.* چکّر کھا کر، گردش سے **circularity** (-*la*-) *n.* being circular گولائی ، چکّر

circulate (*sě**-kew-layt) *v.i.* & *t.* go round continuously گردش کرنا *Blood circulates through the body* خُون جسم میں گردش کرتا ہے move or be sent freely from person to person پھیلنا، پھیلانا، مشہور ہونا یا کرنا *The news (was) soon circulated* خبر جلد ہی دُور و نزدیک پھیل گئی *circulating library*, a library which lends books on small payment گشتی کُتب خانہ **circulator** (*sě**-) *n.* رواج دینے یا مشہور کرنے والا ، گردش میں لانے والا **circulatory** (*sě**-) *adj.* دورانِ خون یا گردش سے متعلق **circulation** (*sě**-kew-*lay*-shěn) *n.* circulating or being circulated گردش، دوران *circulation of the blood*, دَورانِ خون number of copies (*of* periodical) sold to the public اِشاعت

circumcise (*sě**-kum-siz) *v.t.* cut off the loose skin covering the end of the male sex organ ختنہ کرنا، ختنیں کرنا ، مسلمانی کرنا **circumcision** (*sě**-kum-*sizh*-ěn) *n.* ختنہ ، سُنتیں ، مُسلمانی

circumference (sě*kum-fe-rens) n. (length of) the line marking out a circle or other curved figures محیط ، گھیرا ، گھیر
circumflex (sě*-kum-fleks) n. mark placed over a vowel to indicate its particular sound (*e.g.* the short line over this ū) شوشہ
circumlocution (sě*-kum-lo-*kew*-shěn) n. a roundabout way of expressing something اطناب پیچیدہ گفتگو **circumlocution office,** a government which is always delaying decision ڈھیلی حکومت ، سست حکومت
circumnavigate (sě*-kum-*nav*-i-gayt) v.t. sail round (a cape, island, or the whole world) کے گرد جہاز میں چکر لگانا **circumnavigator** (-*nav*-) n. (دنیا وغیرہ) کے گرد جہاز میں چکر لگانے والا **circumnavigation** (-*gay*-) n. sailing round (the globe, the world) (دنیا) کے گرد جہاز میں چکر
circumscribe (*se**-kum-skrib, or se*-kum-*skrib*) v.t. draw a line round or go round خط کھینچنا یا کے گرد گھیرا ڈالنا mark the limit of حد بندی کرنا narrow down تحدید کرنا ، (منطق) تعریف **circumscription** (sě*-kum-*skrip*-shěn) n. (esp.) words inscribed round a coin سکے کے گرداگرد کے الفاظ
circumspect (sě-kum-spekt) adj. paying careful attention to everything before deciding on action دوربین ، انجام پر نظر رکھنے والا (مرد) آخر بین ، محتاط cautious چوکس **circumspection** (sě*-kum-*spek*-shěn) n. exercising of caution ; being wary احتیاط ، دور بینی
circumstance (sě*kum-stans) n. (usu. *pl.*) fact of detail تفصیل ، شرح state of affairs, conditions obtaining صورت ، حال ، حالات *under* (or *in*) *the circumstances, the circumstances being so,* such being the state of affairs ان حالات میں ، اندریں حالات *under* (or *in*) *no circumstances,* never, not at all ہرگز نہیں **circumstantial** (se*-kum-stan-shěl) adj. (of a description) giving full details تفصیلی ، مفصل (of evidence) based on details which strongly suggest something but do not give direct proof قرائنی (شہادت)
circumvent (sě*-kum-*vent*) v.t. get the better جل دینا ، دھوکا دینا ، فریب دینا defeat someone's plans ناکام بنانا
circus (sě*-kus) n. round place with tiers of seats all round for a show of performing animals, etc. سرکس ، کرتب گاہ persons and animals giving such a show سرکس میں کام کرنے والے place (usu. an open circle) where a number of streets meet چوراہا ، چوک
cis- (sis, or siz) *pref.* on this side of (as opposed to *trans-* or *ultra-*) سے ادھر کے ، ورے ، سے فروتر **cisalpine** (siz-*al*-pin) adj. on the southern side of the Alps الپس کے جنوب میں
cissy (*sis*-i) n. & adj. effeminate (man, student, etc.) زنانہ
cist (sist) n. stone (etc.) coffin used as tomb پتھر کی قبر ، تابوتی قبر
cistern (*sis*-tě*n) n. tank for storing water in a building حوض ، ٹینکی
citadel (*sit*-a-del) n. fortress for protecting a city شہر کی حفاظت کرنے والا قلعہ ، بالا حصار place of refuge پناہ گاہ ، جائے پناہ ، ملجا و ماویٰ
cite (sit) v.t. quote as an example or in support حوالہ دینا **citation** (si-*tay*-shěn) n. citing حوالہ دینا something cited حوالہ
cithern, cittern n. (old use) lute, guitar رُباب ، ستار
citizen (*sit*-i-zen) n. one who lives in a city شہر کا باشندہ ، شہری one having full rights in a country, either by birth or by gaining such rights شہری ، باشندہ ، کسی ملک کے حقوق شہریت رکھنے والا *become a citizen of* (*a country*) (کسی ملک) کا شہری یا باشندہ بن جانا
citizenship n. being a citizen شہریت rights and duties of a citizen شہریت کے حقوق و فرائض
citron (*sit*-ron) n. pale yellow fruit like (but much bigger than) a lemon چکوترا the tree bearing it چکوترے کا پیڑ **citronella** (sit-) n. a fragrant oil used for driving away mosquitoes, etc. مچھر مار تیل **citrous** (*sit*-rus) adj. of such fruits as citrons, lemons, oranges, etc. ترنجی **citric acid** (syt-rik *as*-id) n. acid from citrus fruits ترنجی ترشہ (یا تیزاب)
city (*sit*-i) n. large town شہر ، بلدہ its inhabitants باشندگانِ شہر ، شہری ، شہر والے *city life,* life in a city (as opposed to *country life*) شہری زندگی (بمقابلہ دیہاتی زندگی)
civic (*siv*-ik) adj. of the official life and affairs of a town بلدیاتی *civic duties,* (or *activities*) بلدیاتی فرائض بلدیہ کے فرائض (یا کام) (یا مشاغل) *civic centre,* place where the municipal offices are situated دفاتر بلدیہ ، بلدیاتی دفاتر
civics n. *pl.* (used as *sing.*) study of the rights and duties of citizens, and of the form of local self-government شہریت ، مدنیت ، علم المدن
civil (*siv*-il) adj. of human society معاشرتی ، اجتماعی of persons living together ملکی ، مدنی ، شہری **civil defence,** non-military department the job of whose employees is to defend the motherland on the home front against air raids or other hostile attacks شہری دفاع *civil law,* law relating to private rights of citizens (as opposed to *criminal law*) دیوانی قانون (بمقابلہ فوجداری قانون) *Civil Law,* Roman law رومن قانون *civil disobedience,* refusal to obey the law(s) of one's country as a form of organized protest against the government's policy

or composition عدم تعاون، ترکِ موالات *civil war*, war between two parties of the same nation خانہ جنگی *civil liberty*, basic rights and freedom of citizens شہری آزادی *civil marriage*, marriage without religious ceremony قانونی شادی، غیر مذہبی شادی *civil engineering*, building of roads, railways, canals, etc., تعمیرات، انجنیری، تعمیراتی مہندسی not military, ملکی، غیر فوجی، کشوری *the Civil Service*, (*a*) non-military departments of the government حکومت کے غیر فوجی یا کشوری محکمے (*b*) (in Pakistan) the Administrative Service سی، ایس، پی، ایڈمنسٹریٹو سروس، انتظامیہ *civil servant*, (also called *Civilian*) official in the Civil Service حکومت کا غیر فوجی افسر کشوری عہدے دار *civil life*, life in the society اجتماعی زندگی *Civil List*, list of civil servants حکومت کے غیر فوجی یا کشوری عہدیداروں کی فہرست *civil administration*, country's non-military administration انتظامیہ، ملکی نظم و نسق، کشوری حکام *civil power*, government (or its powers) اختیارِ حکومت، حکومت *civil court*, court hearing civil cases عدالتِ دیوانی، *civil suit, civil remedy*, a case under civil law دیوانی نالش دیوانی polite خلیق، بامروّت، شائستہ *civil answer* شریفانہ جواب **civility** (si-*vil*-i-ti) *n*. politeness مروت، شائستگی، خلق، تہذیب، انسانیت polite act احسان، مروت، شرافت **civilly** *adv*. شرافت سے، شائستگی سے **civilian** *n*. & *adj*. (person) not serving with the armed forces حکومت کا غیر فوجی اہل کار، کشوری عہدے دار (in Pakistan) member of the Administrative Service سی، ایس، پی، ... (or get *back*) *to civil* ... service

... civilized states ...

clack (klak) *v.t.* & *i*. make the sound of objects (like wooden shoes on stone, typewriter keys) struck together کٹ کٹ کرنا، کھٹ کھٹ کرنا *n*. such sound کھٹ کھٹ، کٹ کٹ

clad (klad) (old pa. p. of *clothe*) dressed ملبوس پہنے ہوئے *well-clad*, well-dressep خوش پوش *poorly clad*, poorly dressed پھٹے پرانے کپڑوں میں

claim (klaym) *v.t.* demand as one's due, کا دعویٰ کرنا، پر حق جتانا *claim the throne* تخت کا دعویٰ کرنا *claim to be the owner of* (*something*), say that (something) really, though not at the time, belongs to one کسی چیز کی ملکیت کا دعویٰ کرنا say that something is a fact کسی بات کا مدعی ہونا، دعویٰ کرنا کہ *He claimed to have* (*or that he had*) *caught the thief* اس نے دعویٰ کیا کہ اس نے چور کو پکڑا تھا (of things) need or deserve کا طالب ہونا، *claim* (*one's*) *attention* کسی کی توجہ کا طالب ہونا، محتاج یا مستحق ہونا *n*. act of claiming دعویٰ، مطالبہ، حق جتانا *lay claim to* (*something*) (کسی چیز) کا دعویٰ کرنا، (یا اس) پر حق جتانا (also in the *pl*.) right to ask for حق *have a claim on* کا حق رکھنا، کا مستحق ہونا *have no claim*(*s*) *on* کا کوئی حق نہ رکھنا، کا مستحق نہ ہونا، *lay claim to* کی ملکیت کا دعویٰ کرنا، حق جتانا *put in a claim* کا دعویٰ کرنا something which is claimed وہ شے جس پر اپنا حق جتایا جائے، وہ چیز جسے حاصل کرنے کے لیے دعویٰ کیا جائے **claimant** (*klay*-mant) *n*. person who makes a claim دعویٰ دار

clairvoyance (clay-è*-*voi*-èns) *n*. claiming to have the abnormal power to see in his mind what is out of sight غیب دانی، مبینہ طور پر، دل کی بات بتا دینے کا فن، غیر معمولی بصیرت deep insight روشن ضمیری

clairvoyant *n*. one who lays claim to possessing such power غیب داں، مبینہ طور پر دل کی بات بتلانے والا، روشن ضمیر

clam (klam) *n*. a large shell-fish living in mud along river banks کلم مچھلی

a clam

clamant (*claym*-ant) *adj*. (lit.) insistent اصرار کرنے والا، تکرار کرنے والا calling loudly شور مچا کر کہنے والا، آسمان سر پر اٹھانے والا

clamber (klam-be*) *v.i.* climb with difficulty on all fours (*over* a place) بڑی مشکل سے چڑھنا، چاروں ہاتھ پاؤں سے چڑھنا

clammy (*klam*-i) *adj*. moist and sticky to the ... چپچپا، نم

... *) *n*. loud, confused nois... شور، غوغا، فریاد، دہائی ...laining angrily ... پر شور loud protest پرشور مطالبہ ... a clamour چلانا، شور مچانا، فریاد کرنا ... *the Press is clamouring against high prices* اخبارات گرانی کے خلاف شور مچا رہے ہیں **clamorous** (klam-è-rus) *adj*. شور مچانے والا، پُر خروش

clamp (klamp) *n*. appliance for holding things together tightly by means of a screw شکنجہ iron band for strengthening پتر، لوہے کی پٹی یا کڑا *v.t.* put in a clamp شکنجے میں کسنا، put clamps on لوہے کی پٹی لگانا

a clamp

clan (klan) *n*. large (Scottish) family as a sub-group of tribe چھوٹا قبیلہ، برادری، خاندان **clannish** *adj*. showing clan feeling قبائلی عصبیت رکھنے والا having the habit of supporting one's clan قبیلہ پروری **clansman** *n*. member of a clan قبائلی **clannishness** *n*. clan feeling قبائلی عصبیت

clandestine (klan-*des*-tin) *adj*. secret مخفی، خفیہ،

done secretly and perhaps with a sense of guilt (*e.g.*, clandestine marriage, clandestine meeting) چوری چوری، چوری چھپے

clang (klang) *v.t.* & *i.* make a loud dull sound (as of heavy swords or of hammer striking an anvil ٹھنٹھنانا **clang, clangour** (*klang-ĕ**) *n.* clanging sound ٹھن ٹھن، کھٹکھٹاہٹ

clank (klank) *v.t.* & *i.* make a ringing sound (as of light swords or chains) جھنکار، یا جھنک پیدا کرنا *n.* such sound جھنک یا جھنکار

clannish *adj.*, **clansman** *n.* see under **clan**

clap (klap) *v.t.* & *i.* (*-pp-*) strike the hands together in applause تالی بجانا، تالیاں پیٹنا (یا بجانا) *The audience clapped for long,* سامعین نے دیر تک تالیاں بجائیں *Don't clap your hands* تالی مت بجاؤ flap (wings) بازو یا پنکھ پھڑپھڑانا، پر پھڑپھڑانا *The bird clapped its wings* پرندے نے بازو ہلائے (old use) pat (someone) lightly on the back in a friendly way پیٹھ ٹھونکنا do quickly فوراً ڈال دینا، جھٹ سے کرنا *clap (someone) in prison, clap (someone) behind the bars*, put a person into jail کسی کو قید میں ڈالنا *not to clap eyes on*, not to catch sight (کسی کا) نظر نہ آنا، دکھائی نہ دینا *clap up peace* (or *a bargain*), make it hastily جلدی جلدی صلح (یا سودا) کر لینا *n.* sharp, loud noise *clap of thunder* بادل کی گرج

claque (klahk) *n.* group of hired applauders seated as a part of the audience in a picture-house, theatre, etc., to give the impression that the show is receiving great and spontaneous ovation کرائے کے واہ واہ کرنے والے، بھاڑے کے ٹٹو

claret (*kla*-ret) *n.* kind of red wine سرخ شراب، صہبا dark-red colour ارغوانی (رنگ) **claret-cup** *n.* sweet drink make of iced brandy and claret صہبائے شیریں، جام شیریں

clarify (kla-ri-fy) *v.t.* & *i.* make or become clear صاف کرنا یا ہونا، واضح کرنا یا ہونا make (a liquid, etc.) free from impurities صاف یا شفاف کرنا **clarification** (kla-ri-fi-*kay*-shĕn) *n.* making clear توضیح، وضاحت **clarity** (*kla*-ri-ti) *n.* clearness صفائی، وضاحت، شستگی

clarinet (*kla*-ri-net), **clarionet** (kla-ri-o-*net*) *n.* musical wind-instrument with holes and keys الغوزہ

clarion (*kla*-ri-on) *n.* (old use) shrill trumpet نرسنگا، ترئی loud, shrill call rousing to action جوش میں لانے والی آواز، للکار *adj.* clear and loud بلند اور واضح *a clarion call (to duty, etc.)* فرض یاد دلانے والی تند و تیز آواز

clarity *n.* (see under **clarify**)

clash (klash) *n.* loud, broken sound (as of cymbals) ٹکرانے کی آواز disagreement اختلاف *colours that clash,* بے جوڑ رنگ *clash of colours* تصادم، ٹکراؤ *clash of views* نظریات کا تصادم رنگوں کا میل نہ کھانا conflict جھگڑا، کھٹ پٹ، پرخاش، مخالفت collision تصادم، ٹکر، ٹکراؤ *v.t.* & *i.* make the sound of a clash جھنجھنانا meet in full career زور سے بھڑنا، تصادم ہونا be at varianee (*with*) سے اختلاف رکھنا، سے مختلف ہونا، سے میل نہ کھانا bring (swords) together (تلواریں) ٹکرانا ring all (the bells) together ایک ساتھ بہت سی گھنٹیاں بجنا (یا بجانا)

clasp (klasp) *n.* any device with two parts which fasten together (*e.g.*, a buckle) زرمادہ، بکسوا (وغیرہ) firm hold (with the fingers or arm) پکڑ، گرفت hand-shake or embrace مصافحہ یا معانقہ *v.t.* & *i.* fasten with a clasp. بکسوا لگانا، آنکڑا لگانا hold tightly or closely بھینچنا، دبانا *clasp (one's) hand*, dovetail one's fingers ایک ہاتھ کی انگلیاں دوسرے ہاتھ میں ڈالنا *clasp hands with* (*someone*), shake hands (with him) to greet or show agreement ہاتھ ملانا، مصافحہ کرنا، کسی کام پر اتحاد کرنا *clasped in each other's arms*, embracing each other ہمکنار، بغل گیر، ہم آغوش **clasp-knife** *n.* folding knife (عام کمانی دار) چاقو

class (klahs) *n.* group having common qualities طبقہ، ہم مرتبہ وگوں (وغیرہ) کا گروہ kind, sort, or division قسم، نوع، طبقہ، درجہ *Society is divided into upper, middle and lower class* معاشرہ او نچے درمیانی اور نچلے طبقے میں منقسم ہے *no class*, (slang) worthless ناکارہ، گھٹیا *the classes*, the upper classes of society خواص، اونچا طبقہ، امراء، امیر یا تعلیم یافتہ *the classes and the masses*, the upper and lower classes of society, the whole classes of society, the whole society عوام و خواص، اونچے نیچے، غریب اور امیر *the class war* (or *struggle*), struggle between various classes of society (مارکسی نظریات کے مطابق) طبقاتی جنگ (یا کشمکش) *first class, second class, inter(mediate) class and third class carriages on the railways* ریل گاڑی میں پہلے، دوسرے ڈیوڑھے اور تیسرے درجے کے ڈبے group of persons taught together جماعت، درجہ *class-book*, book used in the class for lessons درسی کتاب *classfellow, classmate*, those studying in the same class with one ہم جماعت، ہم سبق، ہم درس *classroom*, room where a class meets جماعت کا کمرہ، جماعت *take a class*, pass an examination with honours اعزاز سے کامیاب ہونا، امتحان میں اعزاز حاصل کرنا *take the class, take (one's) class, meet the class*, teach the class جماعت کو پڑھانا particular year's enrolment of conscripts لام بندی میں کسی سال کے بھرتی ہونے والے *the 1940 class* ۱۹۴۰ء کی لام بندی میں بھرتی ہونے والے *v.t.* put in the correct group درجہ بندی کرنا **class-conscious** *adj.* realizing one's class in society and its difference from other classes طبقاتی اُونچ نیچ کا احساس کرنے والا ، طبقاتی احساس رکھنے والا **class consciousness** *n.* اُونچ نیچ کا احساس

classic (*klas*-ik) *adj.* of the highest quality اعلیٰ ، بہترین ، عُمدہ having a recognized value or status مُستند ، مسلّم الثبوت ، ٹکسالی of the ancient Greek and Latin standard (of literature, art and culture) (ادب ، فن یا تہذیب میں) قدیم یونانی و رومی معیار کا کلاسیکی with this standard, *viz.*, simplicity, harmony and restraint ٹکسالی (یعنی سادگی تناسب ربط ، ہم آہنگی اور توازن والا) famous because of a long history تاریخی *a classic event* تاریخی واقعہ *n.* (artist, writer, etc.) of the highest order ٹکسالی یا کلاسیکی (مصنّف یا فن کار) such work of art, etc ٹکسالی یا کلاسیکی (فنی تخلیق) ancient Greek and Latin کلاسیکی زبانیں قدیم یونانی و لاطینی ، **classical** *adj.* اُونچا ، ٹکسالی ، معیاری *the classical studies*, (*a*) studies of the highest class بہترین تعلیم (*b*) the study of Latin and ancient Greek لاطینی اور قدیم یونانی تعلیم of proved value because of having passed the test of time معیاری ، مستند ، ٹکسالی *classical music*, contrasted with popular music پکے راگ

classify (*klas*-i-fī) *v.t.* arrange in classes ترتیب دینا ، درجہ بندی کرنا ، قسم مقرر put into a class کرنا ، درجہ باندھنا **classification** (klas-i-fi-*kay*-shĕn) *n.* category ترتیب categorization درجہ بندی **classifiable** (-*fī*-) *adv.* that which can be classified درجہ بندی کے قابل **classified** (*klas*-i-fīd) categorized قسم وار graded جس کی درجہ بندی ہو چکی ہو ، درجہ بند (see *Addenda*)

clatter (*klat*-ĕ*) *n.* loud, confused noise (as of hard things knocking together) کھٹ کھٹ ، پٹ پٹ *clatter of machinery* پھٹ پھٹ ، گڑگڑاہٹ ، کھڑکھڑانا *clatter of crockery on a stone surface* کلوں کی گڑگڑاہٹ چینی کے برتنوں کا کھڑکھڑاتے ہوئے پتھر کے فرش پر گرنا ، noisy, confused talk شور و غل *the clatter of school-children* طلبہ کا شور و غل *v.t.* talk noisily بک بک کرنا ، شور کرنا ، شور مچانا ، غل کرنا ، شور و غل مچانا (of hard things) produce noise on knocking together کھٹ کھٹانا ، کھڑکھڑانا ، پٹ پٹ کرنا *clatter along*, move along producing noise پٹ پٹ ، ٹپ ٹپ ، کھٹ کھٹ کرتے جانا *clatter down*, fall down in this manner کھڑکھڑاتے ہوئے نیچے گرنا

clause (klawz) *n.* (grammar) dependent part of a sentence, with its own subject and predicate * چھوٹا جملہ ، مرکّب ناتمام ، جملہ *noun* (or *adjectival* or *adverbial*) *clause*, clause doing the work of a noun (or adjective or adverb) مرکّب ناتمام اسمی (یا صفتی یا حالی) complete paragraph (of a law) (قانون کی) دفعہ complete paragraph (of an agreement) (معاہدے کی) شق

claustrophobia (klaws-tro-*foh*-bi-a) *n.* diseased mental condition creating in a person a fear of closed places بند جگہوں سے خوف ، گھٹن کا ڈر

claw (klaw) *n.* pointed nail of an animal's or bird's foot نہوٹا ، پنجہ ، ناخن foot with claws پنجہ ، چنگل instrument like a claw زنبور *v.t.* get hold of with the claws or fingers پنجوں میں پکڑنا ، چنگل میں لے لینا scratch with the claws or finger-nails پنجے مارنا ، جھپٹا مارنا ، نہوٹے مارنا pull roughly with the claws نوچنا ، کھسوٹنا

claws

clay (klay) *n.* sticky earth which becomes hard when baked چکنی مٹی moistened earth from which bricks, etc., are made گارا ، گیل *wet* (or *moisten*) *one's clay*, drink حلق تر کرنا **clayey** (*klay*-i) *adj.* like or containing clay گارے کا سا ، چکنی مٹی والا

clean (kleen) *adj.* free from dirt (physically or morally) صاف ستھرا ، منقّی ، پاک ، پاکیزہ ، بے داغ ، غیر آلودہ *make a clean breast of*, confess fully (wrongdoing, etc.) صاف صاف کہہ دینا ، (قصور) صاف مان لینا ، کھلے بندوں اقبال جرم کر لینا *clean-fingered*, not corrupt دیانتدار ، رشوت نہ لینے والا *clean habits*, habits of cleanliness صفائی کی عادت *clean hands*, sinlessness بے گناہی ، پاکدامنی *clean handed*, sinless بیگناہ ، پاک دامن ، بے قصور *clean servant* صفائی پسند ملازم *clean slate*, fresh start از سر نو آغاز *make a clean sweep of*, take all at one stroke ایک ہی ہاتھ میں سب کچھ لے جانا well-formed, of good shape خوبصورت سڈول ، خوش وضع having regular outline ہموار ، صاف یکساں *a clean cut*, cut made by a sharp knife تیز دھار کا زخم ، تیز کاٹ *clean-cut features*, sharply outlined features تیکھے نقش *v.t.* & *i.* *clean up*, (*a*) make tidy صاف کرنا (*b*) put in order سلیقے سے رکھنا *clean out*, clean (dirt or unwanted stuff) from the inside of اندر سے صاف کرنا *clean out a desk* ڈیسک (یعنی لکھنے کی میز) سے ردی کاغذ نکال پھینکنا *clean up*, put mess away *adv.* completely بالکل ، بکلّی *I had clean forgotten it* میں تو یہ بالکل ہی بھول گیا تھا *cut clean through* بالکل کاٹ ڈالنا **cleanly** *adj.* (*klen*-li) having clean habits صفائی پسند *adv.* (*kleen*-li) tidily صفائی سے **cleanliness** *n.* habit or condition of being clean صفائی ، صفائی پسندی **cleanse** *v.t.* wash, make thoroughly clean اچھی طرح سے دھونا ، مانجھنا purify of sin گناہوں سے پاک کرنا (Bib.) heal (leper) کا علاج کر دینا ، کو صحت مند کر دینا ، کو چنگا کر دینا

[S] We **clean** from physical impurities but **cleanse** from sin or blame. **Cleanse** is also formally used of thorough cleaning.

clear (klee*) *adj.* easy to see through صاف، صاف شفاف، شفّاف، صاف شفّاف، بے گرد و غبار، بے اثر *clear glass* شیشہ *clear sky*, cloudless sky صاف آسمان bright and pure دھوئیں کے بغیر چمکدار، چمکیلا، بے داغ *a clear fire* یا روشن آگ district, easily seen or understood واضح، صاف، غیر مُبہم، صاف دکھائی دینے والا *clear photograph* صاف تصویر *clear-cut*, (*a*) clearly laid-down بندھا بندھایا، واضح، صاف (*b*) sharply defined (features, outline, etc.) تیکھے (نقوش)، بالکل واضح (خاکہ) *clear conscience*, feeling that one has done no wrong صاف ضمیر (of sounds) distinct واضح، صاف *speak loud and clear* صاف اور زور سے بولنا (of and to, the mind) free from doubt or difficulty شبہات سے پاک، واضح *clear statement* واضح بیان *make (one's) meaning clear* مطلب واضح کرنا free from dangers or obstacles مُشکلات، مَوانع سے پاک *get clear of (something)!* پرے سے ہٹ جاؤ، ہٹ جاؤ *clear the way* راستہ نہ روکنا *keep clear of*, keep out of the way of سے بچنا free قرض سے سبکدوش، بری الذمہ، سبکدوش، بری، خالی *clear of debt* complete پورا، کامل *five clear days* پورے پانچ دن *two miles clear* پورے دو میل *clear profit of Rs. 1000* پورا ہزار روپیہ نفع *adj.* completely بالکل، پوری طرح، پورے *get clear away* بالکل بچ نکلنا *v.t. & i.* get or make clear صاف کرنا یا ہونا *clear the streets of rubbish* سڑکوں سے کوڑا کرکٹ اُٹھانا *clear a table*, put everything lying on it away میز خالی کرنا، دسترخوان بڑھانا، میز پر سے (کھانے کے بعد) چیزیں اُٹھا لینا *the sky cleared* آسمان صاف نکل آیا، بادل چھٹ گئے *clear up*, (*a*) put things in order ترتیب یا سلیقے سے رکھنا (*b*) (of the weather) become bright بادلوں کا چھٹ جانا *clear out*, (colloq.) go away, leave نکل جانا، جگہ خالی کر دینا get past or over without touching صاف نکل جانا make a profit of نفع کمانا go through the necessary formalities رسمی کارروائی پوری کرنا *clear a ship (or its cargo)* جہاز کے روانہ ہونے یا سامان لے جانے سے قبل تمام کاغذات مکمل کرنا، جہاز کا چالان یا پروانہ راہداری حاصل کرنا **clearly** *adv.* with clearness صاف صاف (in answers) yes, no doubt ہاں ہاں، ہاں تو، بلاشبہ **clearance** *n.* removal of obstructions رُکاوٹوں کا دُور کرنا یا ہونا (certificate showing) clearing (of ship) (جہاز کو) پروانۂ (جہاز کا) پروانۂ راہداری space allowed for passing of two parts in machinery فرق، گنجائش clearing of cheques at clearing-house حساب گھر میں چیکوں کے مُبادلے کا حساب clearing of accounts as prerequisite of leaving a job, etc. حساب بیباق کرنا، بے باقی *clearance-chit*, statement showing that a person has cleared all outstanding accounts بے باقی کی چِٹھی، رُقعۂ بے باقی *bring (or get) a clearance chit from department, branch, etc.)* سے بے باقی کی چِٹھی لانا (یا لینا) **clearing** *n.* (esp.) land made clear of trees for cultivation جنگل کاٹ کر کاشت کے قابل بنایا ہوا قطعہ **clearing-house** *n.* place where banks adjust mutual accounts حساب گھر any exchange centre مُبادلہ گاہ **clearness** *n.* صفائی، وضاحت، رُکاوٹ نہ ہونا [S] We speak of **a bright** sky, **a fair** weather, a **fresh** breeze, **a sunny** day; of **a coherent** statement, when it holds together, of something **intelligible** when it is easy to understand, of something **obvious**, which needs no proof, of something **logical** when it is well-deduced, of something **explicit** when it is fully stated.

cleat (kleet) *n.* fastening wedge پھانہ، خانہ small piece of wood, etc., hinged to a door-post to keep the door open کتّا

[1]**cleave** (kleev) *v.t. & i.* (*cleave, cleft, cloven*; or *cleave, clove, cloven*) split (*asunder*, or *in two*) with a heavy blow (at the grain) (ریشے وغیرہ پر سے) پھاڑنا، دو ٹکڑے کر دینا یا ہو جانا *cloven hoof*, divided hoof (of cow, or as a mark of the Devil) (گائے بیل کا) یا شیطان کا) پھٹا کھُر **cleavage** *n.* act of cleaving پھٹنا، پھاڑنا state of being cleft دو ٹکڑے ہونا place where cleaving has occurred or would occur easily پَرت کا شگاف یا ریشہ disagreement اختلاف **cleft** (kleft) *n.* crack (esp. in the ground or in rock) شگاف، دَرز، دراڑ

[2]**cleave** *v.i.* (*cleave, cleaved, cleaved*, or *cleave, clave, cleaved*) (old use) be faithful *to* سے وفاداری کرنا cling *together* ایک دوسرے کا پُورا ساتھ دینا

clef (klef) *n.* musical notation showing pitch کلیف

cleft (kleft) *n.* (see under [1]**cleave**)

clemency (*klem*-en-si) *n.* mildness بُردباری، نرمی merciful feeling or treatment رحم، رحمدلی **clement** (*klem*-ent) *adj.* (of the weather) mild اچھا (موسم) (rarely of a person) merciful رحمدل

clench (klench), **clinch** (klinch) *v.t. & i.* (of the teeth, or fist) close tightly بھینچنا grip مضبوطی سے تھامنا، گرفت میں لینا (usu. *clinch*) (*a*) (of a bargain) settle finally بات، معاملہ یا سودا پکا کرنا یا طے کرنا (*b*) (of an argument) make conclusive کسی کی دلیل کاٹنا، قطعی دلیل دینا، بحث اس طرح ختم کرنا **clencher, clincher** *n.* conclusive argument بُرہانِ قاطع، قطعی دلیل، بحث ختم کرنے والی دلیل

clergy (klĕ*-ji) *n.* (*the clergy*), taking verb in the plural) ministers of Christian Church تمام پادری **clergyman** (klĕ*-ji-mĕn) *n.* one of these (except bishop and upwards) (اُسقف سے نیچے کا کوئی) پادری

cleric (*kle*-rik) *n.* clergyman پادری

clerical (*kle*-ri-kal) *adj.* of the clergy پادریوں سے متعلق *clerical dress* پادریوں کا لباس of the work of a clerk منشیانہ کام سے متعلق of writing, copying or typewriting کتابت، نقل نویسی یا ٹائپ کا *clerical mistake* سہوِ کتابت، کتابت وغیرہ کی غلطی *clerical omissions (and commissions)*, things mistakenly left out (or unintentionally inserted) in writing or copying کتابت میں نادانستہ رہ جانا (یا بڑھ جانا)

clerk (klah*k ; or U.S., klĕ*k) *n.* office employee who does table work منشی، محرر، کلرک clerk or clerk in holy orders پادری

clever (*klev*-ĕ*) *adj.* quick and neat in movement پھرتیلا، تیز، چابک دست، چست skilful ماہر، ہنرمند، طبّاع، تیز فہم، زیرک ingenious, talented artful, tricky چالاک، عیّار *be clever with*, outwit سے چالاکی کرنا *don't try to be too clever with me* آپ میرے ساتھ چالاکیاں مت کرو۔ **cleverly** *adv.* زیرکی سے، چستی سے، چالاکی سے۔ **cleverness** *n.* being clever ; act of cleverness زیرکی، چستی، پھرتی، چالاکی، ہوشیاری۔

click (klik) *n.* short sharp sound (like that of a clock pendulum) ٹِک ٹِک، کٹ کٹ *v.i.* make this sound ٹک ٹک کرنا، کٹ سے بجنا (slang) (of two persons) get on well together کا خوب نباہ ہونا، کی بنتی جانا، میں بنتی چلی جانا (of a man and a woman) fall in love with each other ایک دوسرے سے محبت ہو جانا، میں باہمی معاشقہ ہو جانا

client (*klī*-ent) *n.* one who gets advice from a professional man (esp. from a lawyer) مؤکّل customer (at a shop) گاہک **clientele** (klī-en-teel) *n.* customers, etc. گاہک، مؤکّل، متوسّلین

cliff (klif) *n.* steep face of rock, esp. at edge of sea کھڑی چٹان

climactic *adj.* (see under **climax**)

climate (*klī*-mayt) *n.* weather conditions موسم، آب و ہوا **climatic** (klī-*mat*-ik) *adj.* pertaining to the climate موسمی، موسم کا *climatic conditions*, condition of the climate موسمی حالات **climatology** (klī-ma-*tol*-o-ji) *n.* study of climate موسمیات

climax (*klī*-maks) *n.* point of greatest interest in a story نقطۂ عروج، انتہا، منتہائے کمال culmination کمال، اوجِ کمال **climactic** (-mak-) *adj.* relating to climax منتہائی

climb (klīm) *v.t.* & *i.* go up (ladder, rope, mountain, etc.) اونچا چڑھنا، اوپر جانا چڑھنا go higher ترقی کرنا *climb up (something)*, ascend (it) with effort زور لگا کر جانا *climb down (something)*, get down from it with effort مشکل سے اترنا *climb down*, come down from high position taken up ; admit fault of pride, etc. بلند پروازی کا خیال چھوڑ دینا، مزاج ٹھکانے لگنا، اعتدال پر آ جانا *n.* act of climbing چڑھنا place to be climbed چڑھائی *It is a difficult climb* بڑی مشکل (یا سخت) چڑھائی ہے **climber** (klī-mĕ*) *n.* one who climbs چڑھنے والا social aspirant ترقی کرنے والا، دنیا میں ابھرنے کا متمنّی **climbing** (klī-ming) *n.* walking up something steep (esp. hill) (پہاڑ پر) چڑھنا

clime (klīm) *n.* (poet.) country اقلیم، علاقہ، ملک

clinch (klinch) *v.t.* & *i.* same as **clench** (which see)

cling (kling) *v.i.* (*cling, clung, clung*) hold tight to چمٹنا، چمٹ جانا، لپٹنا، لگا رہنا (of clothes) fit close to the skin پھنسے ہوئے ہونا be faithful (*to*) سے وفاداری کرنا

clinic (*klin*-ik) *n.* place where doctors treat patients and teach medical students through observation of cases مطب **clinical** *adj.* مطب کا، طبّی *clinical thermometer*, for taking patients' temperature ڈاکٹری تھرمامیٹر، طبّی تپش پیما

clink (klink) *n.* sound of (coins, keys, glass bits, etc.) knocking together جھنکار، چھن چھن، کھنکناہٹ *v.t.* & *i.* produce such چھن چھن کرنا، جھنکنا

Clio (*klī*-oh) *Cl. myth.* the Muse of history کلایو

clip (klip) *n.* springed apparatus for holding hair, papers, etc., together کلپ، پکڑ *v.t.* (-pp-) put a clip on or keep together with a clip کلپ لگانا، کو پکڑ لگانا cut hair or wool to make short or neat کاٹنا، قینچی سے کاٹنا، تراشنا *clip (someone's) wing's*, (a) cut the wings of (a bird) پر کاٹنا، پر قینچ کرنا (b) disable (someone) from action بے بال و پر کر دینا، مجبور و بے بس بنا دینا

clips

clipper (klip-ĕ*) *n.* trans-oceanic flying-boat سمندری اُڑن ناؤ، اوقیانوسی اُڑن ناؤ **clippers** (*klip*-e*z) *n. pl.* instrument for clipping leaves from plants or wool from sheep کترنی *hair clippers* (نائی کی) مشین *nail clippers* ناخن گیر **clipping** *n.* something clipped out (esp. from a newspaper) تراشہ، کترن

1. clippers
2. hair clippers

clique (kleek) *n.* set of intriguing, mutually helping persons shutting out others from their company ٹولی، منڈلی، جتھا

cloak (klohk) *n.* loose, sleeveless outer garment لبادہ، چوغہ anything that hides or covers پردہ، اوٹ، چادر *under the cloak of*, under the cover of کی آڑ میں، کی اوٹ میں، کے بہانے *v.t* hide or cover مخفی رکھنا، چھپانا keep secret ڈھانپنا، چھپانا

a cloak

cloak-room *n.* place where coats,

or luggage may be left in custody for a short time سامان گاہ، برآمدہ گاہ **cloak and dagger** *adj.* (see *Addenda*).

clobber (*klob-ĕ**) *v.t.* (see *Addenda*)

clock (klok) *n.* stationery time-keeper گھڑی، گھنٹہ، ٹائم پیس **o'clock** (o-*klok*), (phrase appended to hour) بجے، بجا، 9 *o'clock* نو بجے *What o'clock is it?* وقت کیا ہے، کے بجے ہیں، کیا بج رہا ہے؟ (sports slang) stop-watch روک گھڑی *v.t.* & *i.* (of factory workers) register entry (*in*, *on*, etc.) or exit (*out*, *off*, etc.) by means of some automatic clock آنے جانے کا وقت خود کار گھڑی میں درج کرانا time (race etc.) with stop-watch روک گھڑی سے (دوڑ وغیرہ کا) وقت دیکھنا

clockwise *adj.* & *adv.* moving in a curve in the direction taken by the hands of a clock گھڑی کی سوئیاں جس رُخ چلیں، ساعت رُخ *anti-clockwise*, in the direction opposite this one ساعت کے اُلٹے رُخ **clockwork** *n.* & *adj.* (machinery) with wheels and springs like a clock, (چرخدار اور کمانی دار (کل *like clockwork*, with precision, mechanical, without trouble ٹھیک، بالکل ٹھیک، کسی خرابی کے بغیر، **clock-maker** *n.* one who repairs or makes clocks گھڑی ساز **clock-tower** *n.* tower with a big clock near the top گھنٹہ گھر

clod (klod) *n.* lump of earth ڈھیلا

clog (klog) *v.t.* & *i.* (*-gg-*) choke (*with* dirt or grease) (کسی شے کے بھرنے سے) بند ہو جانا *The machinery is clogged with grease* چکنائی سے کل بند ہو گئی

cloister (*klois-tĕ**) *n.* covered walk on sides of an open square within a convent, etc. گلیاری، غلام گردش، اندرونی برآمدہ convent or monastery عیسائیوں کی خانقاہ صومعہ، تکیہ *v.t.* put or live in a monastery, etc. خانقاہ میں رہنا یا ڈالنا **cloistered** (-tĕ*d) *adj.* (of person) sequestered گوشہ نشین، عزلت گزیں (of place) having a cloistered walk گلیاری والا

a cloister

[1]**close** (klohz) *v.t.* & *i.* shut بند کرنا، موندنا، بھینچنا، بھیڑنا *close up*, come near or together قریب آنا، رل جانا *close in upon*, surround in order to attack بھڑنا، جٹنا end ختم کرنا یا ہو جانا *close with*, (an offer, etc.) accept it قبول کر لینا، طے کرنا *n.* ending خاتمہ *draw* (*or bring*) *to a close* ختم کرنا یا ہونا، ہو لینا، ہو چکنا *break* (*one's*) *close*, make unwanted interruption مداخلت بے جا کرنا **closed** (klohzd) *adj.* not open بند not open (*to* someone) کے لیے منع، پر بند restricted to some; open only to some مخصوص *closed shop*, trade, etc., restricted to some category *e.g.*, members of some union, department, etc. مخصوص تجارتی اِدارہ، مخصوص دُکان **closure** (kloh-zhĕ*) *n.* closing or being closed خاتمہ، بند ہو جانا *in closing*, finally خاتمے پر، آخر میں

[2]**close** (klohs) *adj.* near قریبی *a close friend*, a very dear friend جگری دوست (of the weather) windless and uncomfortably warm حبس، حبس، بند ہوا through پورا *close attention* پوری توجہ *close translation*, a literal one لفظی *close study*, careful study بغور مطالعہ *close argument*, conclusive argument فیصلہ کن دلیل secret مخفی، پوشیدہ *keep* (*something*) *close*, say nothing about it کے متعلق خاموش رہنا *lie close*, hide چھپنا with very little space for movement تنگ *at close quarters*, very near بہت قریب *in close confinement*, strictly guarded قیدِ تنہائی (*special uses*) *close season* (for game), period of year when it must not be killed شکار کا ممنوع زمانہ، شکار بندی *close-fisted*, miserly کنجوس، بخیل *a close game*, (or *contest*), match, etc., with both sides almost of the same standard برابر کا مقابلہ، برابر کی چوٹ *close upon*, (of quantities) almost تقریباً، قریب قریب ہی سمجھئے *adv.* near قریب نزدیک، آس پاس *stand* (or *sit*) *close to* (*someone*) (کسی) کے قریب کھڑے ہونا (یا بیٹھنا) *n.* space with building all round بند، بند جگہ، گھری ہوئی جگہ، بند سی جگہ enclosure اِحاطہ *cathedral close* بڑے گرجے کا اِحاطہ **closely** *adv.* carefully احتیاط سے، بغور pressed close پاس پاس، قریب قریب **closeness** *n.* nearness نزدیکی، قرب **close-call** *n.* (colloq.) something which is quite near قریبی بات something almost fatal ہو کر رہنے والی بات، اٹل، اٹل بات، اٹل معاملہ **close-stool** *n.* covered chamber-pot in a stool پاٹ، کموڈ **close-up** *n.* photograph taken with the camera close to the person or object کلوز اپ، قریبی تصویر

closet (*kloz-et*) *n.* small room کوٹھری، حجرہ، خلوت خانہ cupboard برتنوں کی الماری water-closet فلش کا پاخانہ، بیت الخلا، آبدست خانہ، طہارت خانہ *v.t.* take to a private room for talk باتوں کے لیے خلوت میں لے جانا **closeted** (*kloz-et-id*) *adj.* in private conversation (or *with*) الگ بیٹھے آپس میں (یا کسی سے) راز کی باتیں کرنا *be closeted together*, *be closeted with* (*someone*), be engaged in a private talk الگ بیٹھے راز کی باتیں کرنا

clot (klot) *n.* lump of thick liquid, منجمد قطرہ، خون وغیرہ کا چکتا *v.i.* & *t.* (*-tt-*) form into clots (خون وغیرہ کا) منجمد ہو جانا، جم جانا

cloth (klawth) *n.* (pl. *cloths*, pr. klawdhz or klawths) woven or felted stuff piece of cloth for a special purpose (in combination as *table-cloth*) پوشش (جیسے میز پوش)

clothe (klohdh) *v.t.* (*clothe*, *clothed*, *clothed*; or older form : *clothe*, *clad*, *clad*) put clothes on پہنانا، کپڑے پہنانا give clothes to کپڑے بنوا دینا، تن ڈھانپنے *clothe* (*one's*) *family*, بال بچوں کا تن ڈھانپنے کا انتظام کرنا *clothe thoughts in words* خیالات کو الفاظ کا جامہ پہنانا کی فکر کرنا

تکلف بیں آدمی **clothes** (klohdhz ; or coll. : klohz) *n.* pl. garments کپڑے، لباس **clothes-line** *n.* rope on which clothes are hung for drying اَلگنی **clothing** (*kloh*-dhing) *n.* clothes لباس **clothier** (kloh-dhi-ĕ*) *n.* dealer in cloth or clothes بزّاز، سلے سِلائے کپڑوں کا تاجر

a clothes-line with pegs at *cc*

Clotho (*kloh*-thoh) *Cl. myth.* the spinner of the thread of life, according to the ancient Greeks ; she was the youngest of the Fates کلوتھو

cloud (kloud) *n.* mass of vapour floating in the atmosphere بادل، گھٹا، بدلی mass *of* things like a cloud بادل، گھٹا *cloud of smoke* دھوئیں کے بادل state of fear or unhappiness خوف اور غم کی گھٹا *cloud of grief* غم کے بادل *the clouds of war* جنگ کے بادل *under a cloud*, out of favour معتوب، زیرِ عتاب *under cloud of night* رات کی تاریکی میں *a cloud of words* الفاظ کا گورکھ دھندا *in the clouds*, (*a*) imaginary thing غیر حقیقی، خیالی (*b*) absent-minded person اپنے خیالوں میں مستغرق، عالمِ خیال میں *v.t.* & *i.* make or become dark with clouds پرگھٹا ہونا، چھانا بادلوں کا گھر آنا۔ گھٹا *clouded over*, (of sky) covered with clouds ابر آلود **cloudless** *adj.* clear, without clouds صاف **cloudy** (*klou*-di) *adj.* clouded over ابر آلود (talk or liquid) lacking clearness گدلا (پانی)، اُلجھی ہوئی (بات) **cloud seeding** *n.* (see *Addenda*)

clout (klout) *n.* piece of old cloth for cleaning برتنوں کی صافی *dish, clout* چیتھڑا، پونچھن، صافی loin-cloth for infants پوتڑا، لنگوٹ blow گھونسا، مُکّا *v.t.* strike گھونسا مارنا

clove (klohv) *n.* a dried flower-bud used as a spice لونگ *clove of garlic* لہسن کی پوتی *v.t.* & *i.* (pa. t. of **cleave,** which see)

cloven (kloh-vĕn) *pa. p.* of [1]**cleave** (which see)

clover (kloh-vĕ*) *n.* a grass grown for fodder ترفل (*be*) *in clover* (be) in great comfort فارغ البال، فارغ البالی سے، آرام، آسائش سے (یا مزے میں) رہنا **cloverleaf** *n.* leaf of clover ترفل کی پتّی (see *Addenda*)

clover

clown (kloun) *n.* actor performing foolish antics مسخرہ، بھانڈ، نقال person who behaves like a clown بھانڈ، مسخرہ rude, clumsy man اُکھڑ، اُجڈ، بدتمیز، بد اخلاق *v.i.* behave like a clown مسخرہ پن، بھانڈ **clownish** *adj.* clown-like غیر مہذب، بدتمیز، گنوار

cloy (kloi) *v.t.* & *i.* make or become weary of something sweet through excess منہ پھرنا یا پھیر دینا، جی بھرنا یا بھر دینا، اکتانا، اکتا دینا *cloyed with foolish pleasures*

[1]**club** (klub) *n.* heavy stick with thick end ڈنڈا *golf-club*, club for hitting the ball in golf گالف کا ڈنڈا *v.t.* (*-bb-*) hit with a club ڈنڈے لگانا

[2]**club** *n.* society of persons for games, social entertainment, etc. انجمن، بزم، کلب place used by such a society انجمن کا مرکز *v.i.* (*-bb-*) join *together* (or *with others*) to raise subscription for a common cause مشترکہ مقصد کی خاطر اعانت کے لیے جمع ہونا

a golf-club

[3]**club** *n.* one of the two black designs on playing cards چڑیا یا پھول (کا رنگ)

cluck (kluk) *n.* noise of a hen when calling her chickens کڑ کڑ، کٹ کٹ *v.i.* (of hen) make this sound کڑکڑ، کٹ کٹ کرنا

clue (kloo) *n.* something suggesting a possible answer to a mystery or cross-word puzzle اشارہ، اتا پتا

clump (klump) *n.* group (of trees) (پیڑوں کا) جھنڈ

clumsy (*klum*-zi) *adj.* heavy and ungraceful in movement بے ڈول، بے ڈھنگا، بھونڈا، کڈھب، بھدا not well-designed for a purpose ناموزوں، خراب، بے ڈھنگا **clumsily** *adv.* بھونڈے پن سے، بے ڈھنگے پن سے، پھوہڑپن سے **clumsiness** *n.* being clumsy بھدا پن، بھونڈا پن، پھوہڑپن

clung (klung) *pa. t.* & *pa. p.* of **cling** (which see)

cluster (klus-tĕ*) *n.* number of things of the same kind growing closely together خوشہ، گچھا *cluster of curls* بالوں کا گچھا number of things found together in a close group جھرمٹ، جھنڈ small number of persons pressing together چھوٹا سا ہجوم *v.i.* grow or be in a cluster جمع ہونا، گچھا سا بن جانا

clutch (kluch) *v.t.* & *i.* seize in fear or anger خوف یا غصے کے مارے پکڑنا، چنگل میں لینا، مٹھی میں لینا *clutch* (or *clutch at*) something کوئی چیز مضبوطی سے پکڑنا *n.* act of clutching پکڑنا، مٹھی میں لینا strong hold گرفت، مضبوط پکڑ *in the clutches of*, in the cruel power of کی گرفت میں device in a machine for connecting and disconnecting working parts (مشین کا) شکنجہ یا دستہ eggs put together under a hen for hatching انڈوں کا جھول chickens hatched together چوزوں کا جھول (see *Addenda*) **clutch bag** *n.* (see *Addenda*) [illegible]

clutter (klut-ĕ*) *v.t.* make untidy یا بکھرا *The table is cluttered up with papers* میز پر کاغذات بکھرے پڑے ہیں۔

Clytemnestra (klɪ-tem-*nes*-tra) *Cl. myth.* wife of *Agamemnon* (which see) whom, on his return she slew with the help of her paramour, Aegisthus ; she was killed in retaliation by her son, Orestes کلیتمنسترہ

co- (koh) *pref.* together with, joint مشترک ، شریک ، مخلوط *co-religionist*, (بطور سابقہ) ہم ، مخلوط professing the same religion ہم مذہب *co-education*, education of boys and girls in the same institutions مخلوط تعلیم

Co. (koh) (abb. of) company کمپنی ، شرکت ، مشرکاء **& Co.** (and-*koh*) and company اور ساجھی ، اور شرکاء ، وشرکاء *Jones & Co.*, جونز اینڈ کمپنی ، جونز اور ساجھی

coach (kohch) *n.* four-wheeled carriage pulled by four or more horses بگھی railway carriage ریل کا ڈبہ charabanc ; long distance motor-bus (طویل مسافت والی) تفریحی بس *coach and four* چار گھوڑوں والی بگھی

A railway coach

A coach and four

coachman *n.* driver of a coach گاڑی بان ، کوچوان ، کوچبان ، بس ران teacher, giving private lessons to prepare students for public examinations خانگی معلم person who trains athletes for games کھیلوں کا استاد *v.t.* & *i.* teach, train تعلیم دینا ، تربیت کرنا

coagulate (koh-*ag*-ew-layt) *v.t.* & *i.* (of liquids) make or become more or less solid منجمد ہونا ، جمنا ، جم جانا **coagulation** (coh-ag-ew-*lay*-shĕn) *n.* انجماد ، جماؤ **coagulant** (-ag-) *n.* coagulating agent منجمد کرنے والا ، جمانے والا ، انجمادی

coal (kohl) *n.* black mineral used as fuel کوئلہ *coal field*, district where coal is found کوئلے کا علاقہ ، پتھر کا کوئلہ *coalmine, coal-pit* کوئلے کی کان *coal-master* کوئلے کی کان کا مالک یا ٹھیکیدار *coalminer, miner* کوئلے کی کان میں کام کرنے والے *coal-dust* کوئلے کا چورا *coal-gas*, mixed gases used for heat کوئلہ گیس *coal-box* کوئلہ دان *coal-scuttle*, portable vessel for supply of coal for the fireplace چھوٹا کوئلہ دان *coal-black* کالا سیاہ *coal-tar*, thick, black liquid extracted from coal and used in macadamizing roads کولتار ، تارکول *blow the coals*, incite جذبات کو بھڑکانا *haul* (or *call*) *over the coals*, reprimand ڈانٹ ڈپٹ کرنا ، سرزنش کرنا *carry coals to Newcastle*, present something to one who least needs it (اُلٹے بانس بریلی کو لے جانا) *v.t.* & *i.* (of ships) take in coal or put coal into her (جہاز کا ، یا میں) کوئلہ لادنا یا بھرنا

coalesce (koh-è-*les*) *v.t.* come together and unite جڑنا ، ملنا (of political parties or leaders) form a coalition ایک پلیٹ فارم پر جمع ہونا ، متحد ہونا ، گٹھ جوڑ کرنا **coalescence** (koh-è-*les*-ens) *n.* unity امتزاج ، اتحاد ، اتفاق

coalition (koh-a-*lish*-èn) *n.* uniting میل ، امتزاج union of (esp. political) parties for a special purpose گٹھ جوڑ ، اتحاد ، اشتراک

coarse (koh*s) *adj.* rough کھردرا of poor quality خراب ، گھٹیا *coarse food* خراب کھانا not fine موٹا ، بھدا ، موٹا ، جو باریک نہ ہو *coarse cloth* موٹا کپڑا *coarse sand* باجرا not refind ناشائستہ ، غیر مہذبانہ ، پست *coarse language* فحش زبان *coarse behaviour* بدتمیزی ، بدتہذیبی **coarseness** *n.* کھردراپن ، بدتہذیبی

coast (kohst) *n.* shore ساحل *v.t.* & *i.* (of a ship sail along the coast (جہاز کا) ساحل کے ساتھ ساتھ جانا go down a slope on a bicycle without pedalling سائیکل پر پاؤں چلائے بغیر ڈھلان پر سے نیچے کی طرف آنا **coaster** (*kohs*-tĕ*) *n.* ship trading from coast to coast ساحلی تجارتی جہاز children's four-wheeled carriage meant for moving down slopes بچہ گاڑی **coastguard** (*kohst*-gah*d) *n.* officer on police duty on the coast بحری پولیس (یا اس کا کوئی ملازم)

coat (koht) *n.* sleeved outer-garment کوٹ animal's covering of hair, etc. (جانوروں کی) پشم ، سمور ، کھال *coat of arms*, heraldic bearing خاندانی نشان ، امیری نشان *coat of mail*, armour زرہ بکتر *coat-tails*, hind skirts of dinner-jacket (رسمی لباس کے) دامن *trail (one's) coat-tails*, seek to pick quarrel by coming into others' way مارنے اکڑ کے لڑائی کا بہانہ ڈھونڈتے پھرنا *v.t.* cover (*with* paint, etc.) کوٹ کرنا ، پلستر کرنا **coating** *n.* layer or covering کوٹ

a coat of arms

coatee (koh-*tee*) *n.* short-tailed coa as part of uniform کُرتی women's sweater with sleeves کرتی

coax (kohks) *v.t.* & *i.* get (someone) to do omething by kindness پیار یا خوشامد سے منانا ، پھسلانا ، بہلانا *coax a child to sleep* بچے کو بہلا پھسلا کر سلانا *coax a fire into burning* آگ کو مشکل سے جلانا *coax (something) out of (someone)* (کسی سے کوئی چیز) بمنت نکلوانا ، (کسی سے کچھ) خوشامد سے لینا

cob (kob) *n.* wall material of clay, gravel and straw گارا (also *corn-cob*), head of maize on which the grain grows (مکئی کا) بھٹا

cobalt (*koh*-bawlt) *n.* metal similar to nickel کوبالٹ *cobalt-bomb*, kind of atomic bomb کوبالٹ بم deep-blue colouring matter made from it (سے بننے والا نیلا رنگ ، سوختنی رنگ) کوبالٹ

cobble (*kob*-èl) *n.* (also *cobble-stone*), pebble worn round and smooth by water صاف سنگریزہ **cobbles** (kob-èlz) *n. pl.* pebble-pavement سنگریزوں کا فرش *v.t.* & *i.* mend (esp. shoes) (جوتے کی) مرمت کرنا ، پیوند لگانا put together roughly بھونڈے پن سے جوڑنا **cobbler** (*kob* lĕ*) *n.* mender of shoes جوتے گانٹھنے والا ، موچی

cobra (*kohb*-ra) *n.* a species of poisonous snake ناگ ، کالا

cobweb (*kob*-web) *n.* spider's fine net-work بیت العنکبوت ، مکڑی کا جالا

cocaine (ko-*kayn*) *n.* strong drug used to deaden pain کوکین

[1]**cock** (kok) *n.* chanticleer مرغ ، مرغا *cock-a-doodle doo,*

child's imitation of the sound of a cock's crowing ککڑوں کوں *cock-and-bull story*, baseless and silly story لغویات، بے بنیاد بات، بناوٹی قصہ *cock-sparrow*, male sparrow چڑا *game-cock* لڑنے والا مرغ، پالی کا مرغ *cock-fighting* مرغوں کی پالی، مرغ بازی *That cock won't fight*, this method will not work یہ تدبیر کارگر نہیں ہوگی **cockpit** place for fights between cocks مرغوں کی پالی place where the pilot sits in an air-craft ہوا باز کی نشست **cock-crow, cock-crowing** *n.* daybreak تڑکا، بڑا تڑکا، فجر کی اذان کا وقت **cock-horse** *n.* stick or person's knee or foot that a child runs astride of (چھڑی یا ٹانگ بحیثیت) بچے کا گھوڑا **cocks-comb** *n.* red crest of a cock مرغے کی کلغی **cocksure** (kok-*shoo*-è*) *adj.* quite sure *of* جسے کسی شے کا پورا یقین ہو over confident زعم باطل کرنے والا

cock *n.* tap, spout ٹونٹی lever in a gun بندوق کا گھوڑا یا کتا *gun at half* (or *full*) *cock*, half-ready (or ready) to be fired (بندوق) داغنے کو تیار (یا بالکل تیار) *v.t.* turn upwards (giving attention or challenge) چڑھانا *cock* کان کھڑے کرنا *cock (one's) ears* کھڑا کرنا، کھڑے ہونا *cock (one's) hat* بانکی یا ٹیڑھی ٹوپی لگانا **cocked-hat** brimless hat with projections backward and forward *cock (one's) nose* ناک بھوں چڑھانا *cock (one's) eyes at*, glance knowingly کنکھیوں سے دیکھنا **cock-eyed** (slang) (*a*) squinting بھینگا (*b*) set aslant ٹیڑھا *cock (one's) legs* ٹانگیں پھیلانا، ٹانگیں اونچی کرنا raise the cock of a gun, be ready to fire (بندوق کا) گھوڑا چڑھانا

cockade *n.* knot of ribbon worn in hat as badge طرہ

cockatoo (kok-a-*too*) *n.* crested Malayan parrot کلغی دار طوطا، کاکاتوا

cocker (*kok*-ĕ*) *v.t.* fondle, pamper (*up*) لاڈ کرنا

cockered (*kok*-ĕ*d) *adj.* pampered لاڈلا، نازپروردہ

cockerel (kok-e-rel) *n.* young cock مرغ کا پٹھا

cockle (*kok*-èl) *n.* an edible shell-fish کوکل (مچھلی) its shell کوکل (کا خول) small shallow boat چھوٹی سیدھی کشتی *warm the cockles of (someone's) heart*, cheer (him) up ; encourage (him) کی ہمت افزائی کرنا، کا غم غلط کرنا، کے حوصلے بلند کرنا

cockney (*kok*-ni) *n.* (disparagingly) Londoner لنڈنیا London English لنڈنی زبان *adj.* of a Londoner لنڈنی

cockpit *n.* (see under **cock**)

cockroach (*kok*-rohch) *n.* large dark-brown insect تل چٹا

a cockroach

cockscomb *n.*, **cocksure** *adj.* (see under **cock**)

cocktail (*kok*-tayl) *n.* mixed liquors ملی جلی شراب mixture of fruit juices served in a glass ملے جلے پھلوں کا رس

cocoa (*koh*-koh) *n.* powdered cacao seeds کوکو (سفوف) drink made from it کوکو مشروب

coconut (*koh*-kè-nut) *n.* nut of the coco palm ناریل، کھوپرا، کھوپا *coconut matting*, matting made of rough fibre covering the nut ناریل کی چٹائی **coco-palm** (*koh*-ke-pahm) *n.* tree bearing coconut ناریل کا پیڑ، ناریل، نارجیل

cocoon (ko-*koon*) *n.* silky covering made by caterpillar (ابریشم کا) کویا

a cocoon

Cocytus (co-*s*-tus) *Cl. myth.* a river in the lower world, according to the ancient Greeks کوسائٹس

cod (kod) *n.* (also *codfish*), large sea fish کاڈ مچھلی *cod-liver oil*, oil obtained from cod and used as a tonic کاڈ مچھلی کا تیل **coddling** *n.* small cod چھوٹی کاڈ مچھلی

coddle (kod-èl) *v.t.* pamper ; treat with unnecessary tenderness حد سے زیادہ ناز برداری کرنا

coddling *n.* (see under **cod**)

code (kohd) *n.* collection of laws arranged in a system ضابطہ (قانون)، مجموعۂ قوانین system of rules, principles, etc. ضابطہ *code of honour*, prevalent system of morals in a society کسی قوم کا اخلاقی معیار system of secret writing, etc. خفیہ تحریر secret system of sending messages خفیہ تحریر میں پیغامات بھیجنے کا طریقہ *the Morse code* (or *telegraphic code*) تار کے اشارات *v.t.* put into code signs خفیہ تحریر میں منتقل کرنا،

codify (*koh*-di-fı) *v.t.* put into the form of a code قانون کی تدوین کرنا، قانون مدون کرنا، مجموعۂ قوانین مرتب کرنا

codification *n.* (koh-di-fi-*kay*-shĕn) putting law into the form of a code قانون کی تدوین

co-ed *n.* see under **co-education**

co-education (*koh*-ed-ew-*kay*-shĕn) *n.* system of educating boys and girls at the same institution and classes مخلوط تعلیم (U.S.) **co-educational** *adj.* of or having co-education مخلوط تعلیم کا (یا والا)، مخلوطی

co-ed (*koh-ed*) *n.* (U.S. slang) girl student at a co-educational institution مخلوطی طالبہ، مخلوط تعلیم والے ادارے کی طالبہ

coerce (koh-ĕ**s*) *v.t.* force (someone *into* doing something) دباؤ ڈالنا، (کسی کو کوئی کام کرنے پر) مجبور کرنا

coercion (koh-*e**-shèn) *n.* forcible compulsion دباؤ، جبر government by force استبداد، استبدادی حکومت

coercive (coh-ĕ*-siv) *adj.* high-handed متشددانہ، تشدد آمیز، جابرانہ

coeval (koh-*ee*-vĕl) *adj.* & *n.* (person) of the same age ہم عمر contemporary ہم عصر، معاصر lasting for the same period ہم مدت **co-exist** (*coh*-eg-zist) *v.i.* exist together ایک ساتھ ہونا، ایک زمانہ میں ہونا

co-existence (-zis-) *n.* existing together مل جل کر رہنا

پہلو بہ پہلو زندگی *peaceful co-existence*, communist plea for the peaceful existence of the two Power *blocs* beside each other دو مختلف زندگی، اجتماعوں کا پُر امن طریق سے رہنا
coffee (*kof*-i) *n.* shrub whose roasted and powdered seeds are used for making a drink سفوف، قہوہ its seeds تخم قہوہ their powder قہوہ، کافی the drink (قہوہ (بطور مشروب *coffee bean*, *coffee-berry*, coffee seed تخم قہوہ *coffee-house*, restaurant where chiefly coffee is served قہوہ خانہ، کافی ہاؤس
coffer (kof-ĕ*) *n.* strong box for valuables خزانہ
coffin (*kof*-in) *n.* box for dead person to be buried in صندوق *v.t.* put in a coffin لاش کو صندوق میں رکھنا
cog (kog) *n.* one of a number of teeth on a wheel دندانہ **cog-wheel** *n.* toothed wheel to transfer motion from one part of a machine to another دندانے دار پہیہ

cog-wheel

cogency *n.* (see under **cogent**)
cogent (*koh*-jent) *adj.* powerful (argument) زوردار، قوی، معقول یا دل کو لگتی ہوئی دلیل **cogency** (*koh*-jen-si) *n.* being cogent دلیل کی (معقولیت) **cogently** *adj.* in a cogent manner معقولیت سے
cogitate (*koj*-i-tayt) *v. t.* & *i.* ponder غور کرنا **cogitation** (koj-i-tay-shĕn) *n.* غور، فکر، تدبیر
cogitative (*koj*-i-tay-tiv) *adj.* متفکرانہ
cognac (*kon*-yak) *n.* French brandy کنیاک
cognate (*kog*-nayt) *n.* & *adj.* (word) coming from the same source or starting point ہم اصل یا متجانس (لفظ) *The English word 'mother' is cognate with the Persian 'madar'* انگریزی لفظ (*mother*) اور فارسی لفظ 'مادر' ہم اصل ہیں having much in common (*with*) (سے) ملتا جلتا (سے)، متشابہ
cognition (kog-*nish*-ĕn) *n.* mental faculty of knowing (as opposed to *feeling*) ادراک، قوت، مُدرکہ
cognitive (*kog*-ni-tiv) *adj.* ادراکی، مُدرکہ
cognizance (*kog*-ni-zans, or *kon*-i-zans) *n.* having knowledge *of* سے آگاہ *take cognizance of*, notice توجہ کرنا jurisdiction (of court) سماعت کا اختیار، دائرۂ اختیار *fall within* (or *be beyond*) *the cognizance* (*of a court*) (or *the police*) عدالت کے اختیار سماعت میں ہونا یا نہ ہونا، قابل دست اندازی پولیس ہونا (یا نہ ہونا) **cognizable** (*kog*-niz-ay-bĕl, or -*kon*-) *adj.* (of offence) one which the court or the police can take notice of (جرم) قابل دست اندازی پولیس *non-cognizable* ناقابل دست اندازی پولیس
cohere (ko-*hee*-ĕ*) *v.i.* stick together چپکنا، جڑنا remain united متحد یا مربوط رہنا **coherence, coherency** *n.* ربط، ہم پیوستگی **coherent** *adj.* (ko-*hee*-ĕ-rent) (speech or ideas) not rambling مدلل easy to understand سہل، آسان

cohesion (ko-*hee*-zhĕn) *n.* act of cohering اتصال چسپیدگی **cohesive** (ko-*hee*-siv) that which coheres *adj.* ہونے والا، چسپاں، چپکنے والا
cohort (*koh*-hoh*t) *n.* (old use) one-tenth of a Roman legion کمپنی group of persons banded together ہم مقصد افراد کا گروہ
coiffeur, coiffure (*kwa*-fe*) hair-dresser مشاطہ، مشاطہ، بال بنانے والا، زُلف آرا way one's hair is dressed بال بنانے کا انداز
coil (koil) *v.t.* & *i.* twist (rope, etc.) into rings one above the other کنڈل بنانا curl round and round کنڈل والا بنانا، پھیلا بنانا، بالوں میں گھونگر ڈالنا، بالوں کو گھنگریالے بنانا، (سانپ کا) کنڈل مار کر بیٹھنا، (یا) سانپ کی طرح بل کھاتے ہوئے چلنا *n.* something coiled کنڈلی، پیچ، پیچ a single turn of something coiled کنڈل، پیچ، گھونگر coiled wire for electric current برقی تار کا لچھا
coin (koin) *n.* piece of metal money *false coin* جعلی سکہ *pay* (*someone*) *in* (*his*) *own coin*, give (him) tit for tat جیسے کو تیسا ملنا *v.t.* make (metal) into coins سکے ڈھالنا *be coining money* be making large profits خوب نفع کمانا، بہت سا پیسہ بنانا invent (new words) (نئے لفظ) گھڑنا یا وضع کرنا
coinage (*koin*-ij) *n.* making coins سکے ڈھالنا coins so made سکے، مسکوکات ضرب سکہ system of coins نظام زر *decimal coinage*, system of coins in which every smaller coin is of exactly one-tenth the value of the higher one اعشاریہ نظام زر، اعشاریہ سکے invented (word, etc.) خود ساختہ، گھڑا ہوا (یا) موضوع fabrication من گھڑت بات
coincide (koh-in-*sīd*) *v.i.* (of two or more objects) correspond in area or outline منطبق ہونا، ٹھیک بیٹھنا (of events) happen at the same time بیک وقت ہونا، ساتھ ساتھ ہونا (of ideas, etc.) be in agreement *with* سے متفق یا موافق ہونا **coincidence** (koh-*in*-si-dens) *n.* (esp.) chance happening at the same time اتفاق *by coincidence* اتفاق سے، اتفاقاً **coincident** (koh-*in*-si-dent) *adj.* coinciding اتفاقاً ساتھ ہی ہونے والا ■ **coincidence** is the unexpected happening of two unrelated events simultaneously; **occurrence**, a single happening; **concurrence**, the meeting of two sets of action or thought that have been moving in the same direction.
coke (kohk) *n.* substance left when gas is taken out of coal کوک، نرکول *v.t.* turn (coal) into coke کوک یا نرکول بنانا **coke-oven** *n.* oven in which coal is heated to make coke کوک بھٹی، نرکول بھٹی
colander, cullender (*kul*-en-dĕ*) *n.* vessel with many small holes for draining water from vegetables, etc., in cooking چھلنی، چھنی
cold (kohld) *adj.* of low temperature, not

hot سرد ، ٹھنڈا سردیاں، جاڑا *cold season*, winter *in cold blood*, when normal عمداً، جان بوجھ کر، بے دردی سے، سفاکانہ *throw cold water on*, discourage ہمت توڑنا، اِتنا مایوس کرنا کہ کوئی اپنے ارادے ترک کر دے *give the cold shoulder to*, treat in an unfriendly way سرد مہری یا رُکھائی سے پیش آنا، بے رُخی سے کام لینا بے اعتنائی برتنا feeling cold ٹھٹھرا ہوا not easily excited بے حِس، جوش سے خالی unfriendly سرد مہر رُوکھا *cold manner* رُکھائی *coldhearted*, unfeeling بے حِس *cold-blooded*, (a) sluggish بے جوش، سُست (b) pitiless بے دَرد، بے رحم، سفّاک chill سردی، ٹھنڈک *cold-shoulder (someone)* کسی سے بے رُخی کرنا nasal catarrh زُکام **coldly** *adv.* unkindly سرد مہری یا بے اعتنائی یا رُکھائی سے calmly, unexcitedly ٹھنڈے دل سے **cold war** *n.* (see *Addenda*) **coldness** *n.* ٹھنڈک سرد مہری، سردی، مُردہ دلی، بے اعتنائی، بے حِسی

colic (*kol*-ik) *n.* severe stomach pain قولنج، دردِ شکم

colitis (ko-*li*-tis) *n.* inflammation of colon قولنج (also see **colon**)

collaborate (ko-*lab*-o-rayt) *v.i.* work together (*with* others) (esp. in writing a book) ساتھ مِل کر کام کرنا، اِشتراک میں کام کرنا، ہم کاری کرنا **collaboration** (ko-lab-o-*ray*-shĕn) act of collaborating کام میں اِشتراک، ہم کاری

collapse (ko-*laps*) *v.i.* fall down دھڑام سے گرنا، دفعتہً گرنا break ٹکڑے ٹکڑے ہو جانا، گر جانا، (مکان کا) گر جانا lose physical or mental strength completely، نڈھال ہو جانا، سخت کمزور ہو جانا، نحیف و نزار ہو جانا، کی جان کے لالے پڑ جانا *n.* complete breakdown, failure, or loss of these kinds گرنا، ٹوٹنا، ناکامی، کمزوری، نقاہت **collapsable, collapsible** *adj.* made so as to fold up تہ ہو جانے والا *collapsable door* تہ ہو جانے والا دروازہ

collar (kol-ĕ*) *n.* part of garment that fits round the neck گریبان similar separate article for fastening on to a shirt کالر band of leather, etc., put round the neck گلے کا پٹا (گھوڑے کا) حلقہ (گائے بیل وغیرہ کا) گنڈا، (غلام کا) طوق *slip the collar*, (a) پٹہ تڑوا کر یا نکال کر بھاگنا (b) escape نکل جانا، بھاگنا *hold (someone) by the collar* کسی کا گریبان پکڑنا، کسی کے گریبان کو ہاتھ ڈالنا *v.t.* seize by the collar گریبان یا پٹہ سے پکڑنا take hold of roughly کو سختی سے پکڑنا کے گریبان کو ہاتھ ڈالنا **collar-bone** *n.* bone joining shoulder-blade and breast-bone ہنسلی (کی ہڈی)

collate (ko-*layt*) *v.t.* make a careful comparison between (various manuscripts, etc., of a book) (کسی کتاب وغیرہ کے) مختلف نسخوں کا مقابلہ کرنا **collator** (ko-*lay*-tĕ*) *n.* (esp.) one who brings out a new edition in this way مختلف نسخوں کا مقابلہ کر کے کتاب "تالیف کرنے والا

collateral (ko-*layt*-ĕ-rĕl) *adj.* (of cousins) descended from a common ancestor through different sons and daughters ہم جَد connected but of secondary importance، ثانوی اہمیت کا، ضمنی مزید، فالتو *collateral evidence* ضمنی شہادت *collateral security*, security for loan in addition to the main security فالتو ضمانت، مزید ضمانت

colleague (*kol*-eeg) *n.* one of the persons working together in the same institution or department رفیقِ کار

collect (ko-*lekt*) *v.t.* & *i.* bring or come together اکٹھے کرنا یا ہونا get from various persons or places بہت سے لوگوں (وغیرہ) سے جمع کرنا *collect money* (or *taxes*) روپیہ یا محصول جمع کرنا یا اکٹھا کرنا *collect (one's) thoughts* اپنے خیالات کو یکجا کرنا *a crowd soon collected*. جلد ہی ایک ہجوم اکٹھا ہو گیا **collected** (-tĕd) *adj.* (esp. of a person) cool and calm ٹھنڈے دل والا **collection** (ko-*lek*-shĕn) *n.* collecting جمع کرنا، اکٹھا کرنا number of things collected together مجموعہ money collected at a meeting چندہ **collective** (ko-*lek*-tiv) *adj.* of a group or society as a whole، مجموعی، اجتماعی، مشترکہ، سب کا *collective farms*, farms owned and run by farmers of the locality collectively (esp. under Communist regime) اجتماعی کھیت *collective ownership* اجتماعی ملکیت *collective security*, (see *Addenda*) **collector** *n.* (ko-*lek*-tĕ*) person who collects جمع کرنے والا، فراہم کرنے والا chief Revenue officer of a district کلکٹر، ڈپٹی کمشنر *tax-collector* محصول لینے والا، محصّل ☞ We **collect** selectively; **gather** indiscriminately; **amass** in order to have much; **accumulate**, in the course of time; **hoard**, when we are afraid of parting with it; **pile up**, store up.

college (*kol*-ĕj) *n.* institution for higher or professional education کالج، کلیہ building of such an institution کالج، کلیہ (U.S.) university جامعہ body of colleagues with common privileges مشترکہ مراعات والوں کی انجمن، ادارۂ مراعات مشترکہ

collegiate (ko-*lee*-ji-ayt) *adj.* constituted as a college or related to it کلیاتی *collegiate education* (or *institution*) کلیاتی تعلیم (یا ادارہ) **collegian** (ko-*lee*-ji-ĕn) *n.* member of a college کالج کا طالب علم، یا اُستاد

collide (ko-*lid*) *v.i.* come together violently ٹکرانا، متصادم ہونا be opposed سے متصادم ہونا، اختلاف ہونا *the car collided with the post* موٹر کی کھمبے سے ٹکر ہو گئی

collision (ko-*lizh*-ĕn) *n.* colliding clash ٹکر، اختلاف *come into collision with*, (a) clash (with) سے اختلاف رکھنا، سے متصادم ہونا (b) crash into سے ٹکرانا، سے ٹکر کھانا

collie (*kol*-ee) *n.* Scottish sheep dog سکاٹ لینڈ کے گڈریوں کا کتا

collier (kol-yĕ*) *n.* coalminer (کان سے) کوئلہ

رنکالنے والا ship carrying cargo of coal کوئلے کا جہاز
colliery (*kol*-yė-ri) *n.* coalminer کوئلے کی کان
collision *n.* (see under **collide**)
collocation (kol-o-*kay*-shĕn) *n.* phrase مُرکّب ناقص
colloquial (ko-*loh*-kwi-ĕl) *adj.* (of word, etc.) proper or peculiar to ordinary conversation عام بول چال کا ، عامیانہ not literary غیرادبی not formal روزمرّہ کا ، بے تکلفانہ **colloquially** *adv.* in a colloquial manner عامیانہ انداز میں ، روزمرّہ میں **colloquialism** *n.* colloquial word or phrase زور مرہ use of these روزمرّہ کا استعمال
colloquy (*kol*-o-kwi) *n.* talk or talking گفتگو ، بات چیت
collusion (ko-*loo*-zhĕn) *n.* fraudulent secret agreement between ostensible opponents جنگِ زرگری ، ملی بھگت
colon (*koh*-lun) *n.* the mark (:) وقفِ شارح lower part of the large intestine وقفِ توضیحی (Also see **colic & colitis**) بڑی آنت کا زیریں حصّہ ، قولون
colonel (*kĕ**nel) *n.* (abb. *Col.*) army officer commanding a regiment پلٹن کا افسرِ اعلیٰ ، کمیدان
colonial *adj.*, **colonist** *n.*, **colonization** *n.*, **colonize** *v.t.* (see under **colony**) کرنیل
colonnade (kol-o-*nayd*) *n.* row of columns ستونوں کی قطار
colony (*kol*-o-ni) *n.* land allegedly developed by foreigners and fully or partly controlled from their original country نوآبادی ، مستعمرہ group of people with the same occupation living together علاقہ نوآبادی *The Chinese colony in London* لندن کا چینی علاقہ یا چینا بازار **colonial** (ko-*loh*-ni-al) *adj.* of or relating to a colony نوآبادیاتی ، مستعمراتی ، استعماری *colonial power*, a country having its colonies نوآبادیاتی طاقت ، مستعمراتی طاقت ، استعماری طاقت *n.* person living in or going out to a new colony آبادکار **colonize** (*kol*-o-niz) *v.t.* form a colony نوآبادی بنانا ، آبادکاری کرنا send colonists to میں آبادکار بھیجنا **colonization** (kol-oh-ni-*zay*-shĕn) *n.* آبادکاری ، استعمار **colonist** (-*kol*-) *n.* settler آبادکار **colonizer** *n.* settler آبادکار one who helps set up a colony نوآبادیاتی (ملک وغیرہ)
colossal (ko-*los*-ĕl) *adj.* immense بہت ہی بڑا ، عظیم
Colosseum (ko-lo-*see*-um), **Coliseum** (ko-li-*see*-um) *n.* huge Roman amphitheatre کولیسیم any large place of entertainment وسیع تفریح گاہ
colossus (ko-*los*-us) *n.* immense human statue بہت بڑا انسانی مجسمہ gigantic person عظیم الجثہ دیوپیکر
colour (*kul*-ĕ*) *n.* (also spelt *color*) hue رنگ *fast colour* پکا رنگ *light colour* ہلکا رنگ *dark colour* گہرا رنگ *bright colour* شوخ رنگ *lose colour*, turn pale چہرے پر زردی چھانا material used by artists سفوف ، نقاشی کا رنگدان *colour-box* (قرص یا قلم کی صورت میں) نقاشی کا رنگ *water-colours* نقاشی کے روغنی رنگ *oil-colours* semblance of reality (in writing) حقیقت کی رنگ آمیزی *lend* (or *give*) *colour to* (*something*), make (it) seem reasonable or probable حقیقت کی رنگ آمیزی کرنا (یا رنگ جمانا) *local colour* (in writing), details which make a description more real مقامی رنگ (*pl.*) flag پرچم ، جھنڈا *stick to* (*one's*) *colours*, refuse to give up (one's) beliefs, etc. اپنے عقائد پر سختی سے قائم رہنا *lower* (*one's*) *colours*, give up one's stand اپنا موقف ترک کرنا *show* (*one's*) *true colours*, show what one really is اصلی رنگ میں آنا *come off with flying colours*, be very successful بڑی کامیابی حاصل کرنا *change colour*, blush or turn pale رنگ فق ہونا ، ایک رنگ آنا ایک رنگ جانا *sail under false colours*, be a hypocrite منافقت کرنا *v.t.* & *i.* put colours on رنگنا ، رنگ کرنا become coloured رنگ دار ہونا **colour-blind** *adj.* (person, etc.) unable to see the difference between certain colours جو رنگوں میں امتیاز نہ کر سکے ، رنگوں کا اندھا **colourcast** *n.* (see *Addenda*)
colourful *adj.* full of colours رنگدار ، رنگین (see *Addenda*)
coloured (*kul*-ĕ*d) *adj.* (esp. person) other than white-skinned جو گورا نہ ہو ، کالا **colouring** *n.* substance used for giving colour esp to inside walls رنگ way in which an artist uses colours to give his impressions رنگ آمیزی colour of the face, hair and eyes چہرے بالوں اور آنکھوں کا رنگ
colt (kohlt) *n.* young horse up to 4 or 5 years بچھیرا (compare **filly** *n.* fem.)
column (*kol*-um) *n.* pillar ستون ، کھم ، کھمبا ، لاٹھ something shaped like a column ستون کی سی کوئی شے *column of smoke* اٹھتا ہوا دھواں *column of soldiers* فوج کا پرّہ یا دستہ *column of figures*, جمع کرنے کے لیے ایک دوسرے کے اوپر لکھی ہوئی رقمیں *fifth column*, (a) organized body in a country working for or sympathizing with the nation with which it is at war وطن کے چھپے دشمن ، پانچواں دستہ ، دشمن کے پاسدار ، ملک دشمن ، دشمنانِ وطن (*b*) spies جاسوس ، غدار (*c*) traitors غدارانِ ملت up right division of newspaper page کالم ، خانہ part of newspaper occupied regularly by special subject اخبار کا مستقل موضوع یا عنوان والا حصّہ ، کالم ، اخبار کا مستقل کالم *editorial column* اداریہ کالم *letters column* اخبار کے نام مراسلات ، ایڈیٹر کی ڈاک

a column
C. the capital

columnist (*kol*-ĕ-mist) *n.* journalist regularly contributing to a periodical a special column usu. of miscellaneous comment on personalities

and events خصوصی تبصرہ نگار، نامہ نگار خصوصی، کالم نگار، کالم نویس *fifth columnist* (-kol-è-mist) جاسوس، غدار، غدارِ ملت
coma (*koh*-ma) *n*. stupor ; unnatural heavy sleep بے ہوشی، غیر طبعی نیند **comatose** (*kohm*-a-*tohz*) in or like a stupor *adj*. غیر طبعی نیند میں (یا سے متعلق)
comb (kohm) *n*. instrument with teeth for making the hair tidy کنگھی similar instrument in some machines (کسی کل کا) کنگھا *honeycomb*, beehive شہد کا چھتہ *v.t.* & *i*. use a comb بالوں میں کنگھی کرنا، (اون کو) دھننا، search thoroughly پوری طرح تلاش کرنا، کھنگالنا، *The police combed the whole town for the thief* چور کی تلاش میں پولیس نے سارے شہر کو کھنگال ڈالا *comb out*, secure or get rid of (persons) from a group تلاش کر کے داخل یا خارج کرنا
combat (*kum*-bat) *n*. fight لڑائی، مقابلہ *single combat*, fighting between two persons only مُبارزہ، مبارزت *v.t.* & *i*. fight لڑنا، بھڑنا، مقابلہ کرنا **combatant** (*kum*-ba-tant) *adj*. & *n*. fighting (man) جنگجو، جنگ آزما، مصافی **combative** (-tiv) *adj*. fond of fighting لڑنے بھڑنے کا شائق، جنگجو
combination *n*. (see under **combine**)
combine (kom-*bin*) *v.t.* & *i*. (cause to) join together ملنا، ملانا، یکجا کرنا یا ہونا possess at the same time بیک وقت رکھنا، کا بیک وقت مالک ہونا *n*. group of persons for influencing prices ایکا، دھڑا **combination** (kom-bi-*nay*-shèn) *n*. joining or putting together اتحاد، اتفاق *chemical combination* کیمیاوی اتصال number of persons combined for a purpose دھڑا، ایکا (*pl*.) (*combinations*), underwear (for children) covering body and legs at the same time جڑواں کرتا اور پاجامہ ▣ To **combine** is to put together several elements, each keeping its identity ; to **unite**, make one ; to **unify**, make as one in manner of operation ; to **associate**, become friends in work ; to **consolidate**, join strength : to **amalgamate**, each losing its separate identity ; to **concatenate**, make a chain of confederates and swear mutual assistance : to join end to end.
combustible (kom-*bus*-ti-bèl) *n*. & *adj*. (substance) burning easily آتش گیر (مادہ)
combustion (kom-*bus*-chèn) *n*. act of burning جلنا، احتراق، عمل احتراق destruction by fire آگ میں جل جانا، آگ میں جل بجھنا
come (kum) *v.i.* (*come, came, come*), arrive at (a point, time or result) (کسی جگہ، وقت یا نتیجہ پر) پہنچنا، آنا (of fruit) be available in the market آنا، چلنا، منڈی میں آنا become fashionable چلنا، رائج ہونا، کا رواج ہونا accrue حاصل ہونا، ملنا *come on (one's) head*, fall headlong سر کے بل آنا *come across*, meet by chance اتفاقاً ملنا یا پانا *come by* (something), get possession of (کوئی شے) حاصل کرنا، پانا *come in for* (*something*), receive or deserve (it) پانا حق حاصل کرنا *come in* (*someone's*) *way*, be an obstacle (کسی کی راہ میں رکاوٹ بننا *come under*, be classed as کی قسم شمار ہونا، کے تحت آنا *come to pass*, happen ہونا، واقع ہونا *come to* (*do*), begin to (do) (کرنے) لگنا *come on*, (*a*) appear نکلنا، پر آنا (*b*) (in cricket) begin to bowl کرکٹ میں گیند پھینکنے لگنا (*c*) don't hesitate آؤ بھی *it comes to this*, the long and short of this is غرض مطلب یہ ہے *come to*, *come round*, *come to (one's) senses*, (*a*) become conscious after fainting ہوش میں آنا (*b*) become sensible after being foolish ہوش کے ناخن لینا، عقل سیکھنا *come into a fortune*, inherit it ورثے میں پانا *coming out of a book*, its publication کتاب کا شائع ہونا *coming out of facts*, becoming known واقعات کا معلوم ہونا *come off*, (*a*) happen واقع ہونا (*b*) have the anticipated result کا متوقع نتیجہ نکلنا *come about*, take place واقع ہونا *come of age*, attain majority ; be 18 years old (in Pakistan) or 21 (in certain other countries) بالغ ہونا *come along*, move along ساتھ ساتھ چلے آنا *come along !* آؤ، آؤ، چلے آؤ *come to blows*, fight لڑنا *come away from*, quit چھوڑ کر چلے آنا *come down*, (*a*) اُترنا (*b*) reach posterity منتقل ہونا (*c*) decline شیخی کرکری ہونا *come upon*, find by accident اتفاقاً پالینا *come true*, become real سچ ثابت ہونا، سچا نکلنا، سچا ہونا *come down upon*, upbraid ڈانٹ ڈپٹ کرنا *come down with* قرض اُتارنا یا چکانا *come forward* سامنے آنا *come forward with* پیش کرنا *come of* (something), (کسی شے کا) نتیجہ نکلنا *come home to (someone)*, be realized by him کی سمجھ میں آنا *come in*, (*a*) enter اندر آنا (*b*) نکلنا، پانا come to power اقتدار حاصل کرنا (*c*) receive *come in useful* (etc.) مفید (وغیرہ) ثابت ہونا *come into (someone's) mind*, suggest itself to him کسی کے ذہن میں آنا *come into play*, begin to operate عمل میں آنا *come into sight*, become visible نظر آنا *come into notice*, draw attention نظر میں آنا *come into the world*, be born پیدا ہونا *come to light*, be known معلوم ہونا *come out with* (*something*) blurt (it) out صاف صاف کہہ دینا *come short of* سے نا معر رہنا *come to an end*, end ختم ہونا *come near doing*, have almost (done) it کرتے کرتے بچنا یا رہ جانا *in years to come*, in future years اگلے برسوں میں *first come first served*, service exactly according to one's turn without any preference being given to anyone اپنی اپنی باری جو پہلے آئے سو پہلے پائے *come easy to (someone)*, *come natural to (someone)*, (of something) present no difficulty to him کر آجانا، کو مشکل نہ لگنا،

کرآسان تھا *come and go*, (*a*) traffic آمد و رفت (*b*) transitory عارضی، گریز پا *a coming man*, one who is thought likely to be important or famous ہونہار شخص *come to stay*, become a permanent feature مستقل چیز بن جانا

come under (*someone's*) *notice*, be known (to him) معلوم ہونا *stage a come-back*, return to (one's) earlier powers or position دوبارہ عروج حاصل کرنا *come down*, change for the worse in (one's) circumstances زوال، بدحالی *light come light go*, good fortune that soon comes to an end چار دن کی چاندنی پھر اندھیری رات *come and welcome, go by and no quarrel* آؤ تمہارا گھر، جاؤ تمہاری خوشی *come to* (*do, something*), happen to (do it) کرنے پر اُترنا *come ; come, let us* (*go etc.*) (invitation to go or do something) آؤ، آؤ نا، چلے آؤ *come along* آؤ *come away*, come and leave it چلے آؤ، جانے دو *come what will* (*or may*) جو ہو سو ہو *come by* (*something*), obtain it کچھ ہاتھ لگنا *come, come !* now leave it بس بس، بس کرو *come in by one ear and go out by the other* اِس کان سُننا اُس کان اُڑا دینا *come of* (*a good, etc. family*), be a scion of it اچھے (وغیرہ) خاندان سے ہونا *come of* (*something*), be (its) result کا نتیجہ ہونا *come on !* (challenge to fight) ذرا نکلو تو، سامنے تو آؤ *come over to* (*someone's*) *side*, join (him) سے آملنا *come round*, agree راضی ہو جانا، ماننا، مان جانا *come to*, (*a*) amount to ہونا *It comes to five rupees* یہ پانچ روپے ہوتے ہیں (*b*) end in انجام ہونا، حال ہونا *I knew that was what you would come to* میں جانتا تھا جو تمہارا حال ہوگا *come to pass*, occur پیش آنا، درپیش آنا یا ہونا، واقع ہونا *come under*, fall into the category of کے تحت آنا *come up*, sprout (کونپل کا) پھوٹنا *come up with*, become equal in status to کے برابر ہو جانا *come upon*, (*a*) chance to see (کسی جگہ) اتفاقاً پہنچ جانا (*b*) attack (someone) suddenly ٹوٹ پڑنا، پر چڑھ دوڑنا، پر اچانک حملہ آور ہونا، یکایک حملہ کر دینا **come-back** *n.* return to one's former position واپسی، مراجعت، بازآئی

comeuppance (kum-*up*-ens) *n.* (U.S.) coming up, achieving prominence اُبھرنا، مشہور ہونا

comer (*kum-ě**) *n.* one who comes آنے والا

comedian *n.* (see under **comedy**)

comedy (*kom*-e-di) *n.* drama (or picture) with a happy ending طربیہ amusing incident in real life دلچسپ واقعہ **comedian** *n.* actor in comedies طربیہ اداکار actor whose aim is to make people laugh مزاحیہ اداکار writer of comedies طربیہ نگار

comeliness *n.* see under **comely**

comely (*kum*-li) *adj.* (person) handsome ; pleasant to look at حسین، خوبصورت، خوش انداز **comeliness** being handsome خوبصورتی، دلکشی

comer *n.* (see under **come**)

comet (*kom*-et) *n.* star-like heavenly body with a tail of light دُمدار تارا، دُمدار ستارہ

a comet

comfort (*kum*-fe*t) *n.* kindness to one who is suffering تسلی، تشفی relief from pain, trouble or anxiety تسکین، آرام something that brings such relief آرام دہ، سکون بخش the state of being free from worry اطمینان comfortable circumstances آرام، آسائش *live in comfort* آسائش سے رہنا (*pl.*) things that make life easy آسائش *v.t.* give comfort to آرام دینا say kind words تسلی دینا **comfortable** *adj.* giving comfort آرام دہ free from pain or trouble آرام سے *be* (*or feel*) *comfortable* آرام سے ہونا **comfortably** *adv.* آرام سے، بہ آرام **comfortless** *adj.* without comfort بے آرام **comforter** (*kum*-f ě*-tě*) *n.* person who comforts تسلی دینے والا warm woollen scarf گرم گلوبند

comic (*kom*-ik) *adj.* causing people to laugh مزاحیہ، مضحکہ خیز of comedy طربیہ *comic actor* طربیہ کا اداکار، مزاحیہ اداکار *n.* comic paper (or book or cartoon) مزاحیہ رسالہ (کتاب یا کارٹون) **comical** (*kom*-i-kěl) *adj.* amusing مزاحیہ

Cominform (*kom*-in-fo*m) *n.* world body set up in 1947 in place of comintern to carry on Communist propaganda (acronym from *Com*munist *Inform*ation *Bureau*) کمنفارم، بین الاقوامی اشتراکی تعلقات کا ادارہ **Comintern** (kom-int-ě*n) *n.* Communist international dissolved in 1943 (acronym formed from *Com*munist *Intern*ational) بین الاقوامی اشتراکیت، کمنٹرن

comity (*kom*-i-ti) *n.* (lit.) courtesy تواضع، اخلاق، احترام *comity of nations*, courtesy shown by nations to each other's laws and customs ایک دوسرے ملک کے رسم و رواج اور آئین و قانون کا احترام، بین الاقوامی احترام

comma (*kom*-a) *n.* the mark (,) سکتہ *inverted commas*, quotation marks (" ") واوین

command (kom-*ahnd*) *v.t.* & *i* order (a person *to do*, a thing *to be done*, or *that*) (کسی کو کسی بات کا) حکم دینا control (the feelings oneself) اپنے جذبات پر قابو پانا be in a position to use کی دسترس میں ہونا have at one's service حاکم ہونا، بالادست ہونا deserve to have مستحق ہونا *command respect or sympathy* عزت یا ہمدردی کا مستحق ہونا (of a high place) be in a position that overlooks (and controls) (کسی جگہ سے) نظر میں آنا (اور زد میں ہونا) *The citadel commanded the pass* درہ قلعہ سے نظر آتا تھا اور اس کی زد میں تھا *n.* order حکم authority اقتدار

(power to) control قابو drill instruction (قواعد میں) ہدایت یا بول part of an army under someone's command زیر حکم فوج (یا فوجی دستہ) **commandant** (kom-a-*dant*) *n.* officer in command of fortress or other military establishment قلعہ دار، سالار، کمیدان **commandeer** (kom-an-*dee*-ĕ*) *v.t.* take for military purpose, usu. without asking for the owner's permission فوجی ضرورتوں کیلئے لینا **commander** (ko-*mahnd*-ĕ*) *n.* person in command سالار . (esp.) naval officer next under a captain کمانڈر **commander-in-chief** *n.* (abb. **C-in-C**), officer in supreme command of an army or of the entire forces of a country کمانڈر انچیف، سپہ سالار، سپہ سالار اعلیٰ، قائد افواج **commanding** *adj.* impressive, dominating (personality, appearance, looks, etc.) پُراثر، بارعب exalted (ability, etc.) اعلیٰ (of place) having a wide view جہاں سے (ہر طرف) خوب نظر آئے **commandment** (ko-*mahnd*-ment) *n.* divine law خدائی فرمان *the Ten Commandments*, *n.* the ten laws given to Moses شریعتِ موسوی میں دس خدائی احکام، احکام عشرہ **commando** (ko-*mahn*-doh) *n.* (pl. *commandos*) specially picked shock troops used as attacking force of the British army منتخب حملہ آور دستہ member of such force (منتخب حملہ آور دستے کا) ایک سپاہی **commemorate** (ko-*mem*-o-rayt) *v.t.* celebrate by ceremony or in writing, etc. منانا، یادگار منانا be a memorial of کی یادگار ہونا **commemoration** (ko-mem-*o*-*ray*-shen) *n.* یادگار، یادگار کی تقریب **commence** (ko-*mens*) *v.t.* & *i.* (formal word for) begin شروع کرنا، آغاز کرنا **commencement** *n.* beginning آغاز **commend** (ko-*mend*) *v.t.* recommend as worthy سفارش کرنا praise تعریف کرنا entrust (*to* someone) for safe keeping کو سونپنا، سپرد کرنا *commend (one's) soul to God*, die جان جان آفریں کے سپرد کرنا **commendable** *adj.* praiseworthy قابلِ تعریف **commendation** (ko-men-*day*-shĕn) *n.* praise تعریف recommendation سفارش **commendatory** (ko-*men*-da-tè-ri) *adj.* that which recommends سفارشی **commensurate** (ko-*men*-sew-rit) *adj.* proportionate (*to* or *with*) (کے) حسب حال (کے) مناسب co-extensive (*with*) (کا) ہم مقدار **commensurable** *adj.* proportionate (*to*) (کے) متناسب **comment** (*kom*-ent) *n.* explanation تشریح، شرح criticism تنقید، تبصرہ *v.i.* make comments (*on*) (پر) تبصرہ کرنا (یا) تنقید کرنا give opinion (*on*) رائے زنی کرنا **commentary** (*kom*-en-tè-ri) *n.* detailed comments on book شرح، تفسیر *a commentary on the Holy Quran* تفسیرِ قرآن کریم، تفسیر running comments on an event آنکھوں دیکھا حال جو ساتھ ساتھ نشر کیا جائے، شرح *A commentary on the match was broadcast* میچ کا آنکھوں دیکھا حال نشر کیا جاتا رہا *running commentary*, continuous commentary آنکھوں دیکھا حال جو ساتھ ساتھ بیان کیا جائے *give* (or *broadcast*) *the running commentary* آنکھوں دیکھا حال ساتھ ساتھ (نشر) کرنا، شرح (نشر) کرنا **commentator** (*kom*-en-tay-tĕ*) *n.* one who writes a commentary شارح مختصر one who broadcasts a commentary کنٹری والا، شارح **commerce** (*kom*-ĕ*s) *n.* trade (esp. between countries) تجارت، (بالخصوص) بین الاقوامی تجارت exchange and distribution of goods on a large scale بیوپار، لین دین، بڑے پیمانہ پر تجارت، سوداگری *chamber of commerce*, association of big traders ایوانِ تجارت **commercial** (ko-*mĕ**-shĕl) *adj.* of commerce تجارتی *commercial traveller*, (also called *travelling agent*), one who travels with samples of goods to obtain orders (سوداگروں کا) سفری گماشتہ *n.* (colloq.) commercial traveller سفری گماشتہ (U.S.) (see *Addenda*) **commercialize** *v.t.* try to make money out of میں سے نفع کمانے کی کوشش run on commercial lines کا کاروبار بنانا، کو تجارتی طریق پر چلانا *commercialize education* تعلیم کو خدمت کی بجائے کاروبار بنا لینا **commercialization** *n.* تجارتی طریق پر چلانا
commic (*kom*-ik) *n.* (see *Addenda*)
commingle (ko-*ming*-el) *v.t.* & *i.* mix together باہم ملنا یا ملانا
commiserate (ko-*miz*-è-rayt) *v.t.* & *i.* sympathize (*with* someone *on* his misfortunes) مصیبت میں کسی کی غمگساری کرنا، (کسی کی مصیبت میں (اُس سے) ہمدردی کرنا **commiseration** *n.* (ko-miz-e-*ray*-shĕn) sympathy ہمدردی، غمگساری
commissar (kom-i-*sah**) *n.* head of a U.S.S.R. government department روسی سرکاری محکمے کا افسر **commissariat** (-*say*-) *n.* department of the army for distributing food and other supplies کمسریٹ، شعبۂ رسد **commissary** (-mis-è-ri) *n.* army officer of this department افسر محکمہ رسد، شعبۂ رسد کا اہل کار deputy ; representative نمائندہ، قائم مقام
commission (ko-*mish*-èn) *n.* authority given to someone پروانگی، تفویض، اختیار، مختارنامہ، نیابت work thus done وظیفہ، مفوضہ، ذمہ داری performance ارتکاب *the commission of crime* ارتکاب جرم payment made on sale of goods دلالی، آڑھت، کمیشن *sell* (or *have*) *goods on commission* آڑھت (یا کمیشن) پر مال بیچنا (یا فروخت) کے لیے رکھنا *commission agent* آڑھتی، military officer's letter of appointment signed by the head of the State فوجی افسر کے لیے حکم تقرر، کمیشن *sign* (or *lose*) (*one's commission*), become (or cease to be) a military officer فوجی افسر بننا (یا نہ رہنا) *Commissioned Officer*,

military officer of at least the rank of a 2nd; lieutenant فوجی افسر *Junior Commissioned Officer*, (abb. *J.C.O.*) military officer of a lower category (as a Jemadar, Subadar, etc.) سردار *Non-Commissioned Officer*, (abb. *N.C.O.*) military officer lower in rank than a Jemadar عہدیدار body of persons given the duty of making an inquiry and writing a report جماعتِ ماہرین، تحقیقاتی جماعت، تحقیقاتی کمیشن *the Flood Commission*, (or *the commission to report on floods*) سیلابی تحقیقاتی کمیشن *the Public Services Commission* پبلک سروس کمیشن، اونچی سرکاری ملازمتوں کے لیے بھرتی کرنے والے ماہرین کی جماعت *in commission*, (of warship) ready to go to sea with crew and supplies تیار (جنگی جہاز) *v.t.* give a commission to آزمعت دینا، تفویض کرنا، سپرد کرنا، نائب بنانا، مختار بنانا، فوجی افسر مقرر کرنا۔

commissionaire (ko-mish-è-*nay*-è*) *n.* liveried gate-keeper of hotel, picture-house, shop, etc. باوردی دربان

commissioner (ko-*mish*-e-ně*) *n.* member of a commission جماعتِ ماہرین کا رکن high official in branch of government service کمشنر، حاکمِ اعلیٰ *the Divisional Commissioner of Lahore* قسمتِ لاہور کا کمشنر *the High Commissioner for Pakistan in London*, Pakistan's diplomatic representative in London پاکستانی ہائی کمشنر مقیم لندن *High Commission*, foreign diplomat's office ہائی کمشن، سفارت خانہ *Deputy High Commission* ڈپٹی ہائی کمیشن، نائب سفارت خانہ

commit (ko-*mit*) *v.t.* (-*tt*-) perform (a crime, foolish act, etc.) (جرم یا حماقت وغیرہ) کرنا (یا) کا مرتکب ہونا *commit a blunder* حماقت کا مرتکب ہونا *commit murder* قتل کا ارتکاب کرنا entrust (*to* someone) for safe keeping کسی پر (کسی کی) تحویل میں دینا *commit (someone) for trial* کسی کو مقدمہ چلانا *commit (someone) to police custody* حوالات بھیجنا *commit* (something) *to memory*, learn by heart حفظ کرنا، زبانی یاد کرنا *commit to writing*, put into writing لکھنا، حوالۂ قلم کرنا *commit oneself*, (*a*) make oneself responsible ذمہ لینا، ذمہ داری لینا، (اپنے آپ کو کسی کام کا) پابند کر لینا (*b*) promise وعدہ کرنا (*c*) undertake اپنے سر لینا **commitment** *n.* something to which one has committed oneself ذمہ داری promise or undertaking وعدہ، ذمہ داری

committee (ko-*mit*-i) *n.* group of persons appointed to attend to special work کمیٹی (خاص مقصد کی) مجلس *attend a committee meeting* کمیٹی کے اجلاس میں شریک ہونا *be* (or *sit*) *on a committee*, be its member کسی کمیٹی کا رکن ہونا *be in the committee stage* (of an issue) be under discussion by a committee مجلس کے زیرِ غور ہونا، ہنوز زیرِ بحث ہونا *standing committee*, permanent committee مجلسِ قائمہ *sub-committee*, smaller body of a committee ذیلی کمیٹی، ذیلی مجلس *working committee ; executive committee*, controlling body of an organization مجلسِ عاملہ، مجلسِ نافذہ *committee of action*, committee set up to guide its organization in some strike or similar drastic action مجلسِ عمل *finance committee*, committee controlling an organization's finances مالی مجلس

commode (ko-*mohd*) *n.* covered stool with chamber-pot پاٹ، کموڈ

commodious (ko-*moh*-di-us) *adj.* having plenty of space وسیع، فراخ، کشادہ، کافی گنجائش والا، کافی بڑا *commodious house* کافی بڑا گھر

commodity (ko-*mod*-i-ti) *n.* thing, esp. commercial چیز، جنسِ تجارت (*pl.*) (*commodities*) goods, merchandise سامانِ تجارت، تجارتی مال

commodore (*kom*-o-daw*) *n.* naval rank below a Rear-Admiral کموڈور

common (*kom*-un) *adj.* of, or belonging *to* all members of a group مشترک، مشترکہ *lowest common multiple*, (abb. *L.C.M.*), ذو اضعافِ اقل *highest common factor*, (abb. *H.C.F.*), عادِ اعظم *common factor* (esp.) element, etc. common to two or more things قدرِ مشترک *a common language*, lingua franca مشترک زبان *common law*, unwritten law based on customs and court decisions رواجی قانون، قانونِ رواج *common room*, meeting and games room in a hostel نشست گاہ، کامن روم، بیٹھک *common knowledge*, what is known to most persons جس کا قریب قریب ہر شخص کو علم ہو، *common weal*, public welfare, general good رفاہِ عام، رفاہِ عامہ ordinary معمولی usual, found often and in many places عام *the common man*, the ordinary or average man عام آدمی *common sense*, practical good sense gained by experience of life سوجھ بوجھ، عقلِ سلیم، معمولی فہم و فراست *common noun*, noun applicable to any member of a class (as distinct from a *proper noun*) اسمِ نکرہ (of persons and their behaviour) (*a*) vulgar دیہاتی، گنوار، گنوارو (*b*) rude اُجڈ، اکھڑ *n.* village area for all to use شاملات، شاملاتِ دِہ *House of Commons* (also called *the Commons*), Lower House of the British Parliament دارالعوام *in common* مشترک، مشترکہ *have in common with*, share with (کسی چیز میں) کسی کا شریک ہونا *out of the common*, unusual غیر معمولی *(be on) short commons* (have) not enough food ناکافی خوراک (رکھنا) **commonly** *adv.* generally عموماً، بالعموم **commoner** *n.* one who is not a member of the nobility عامی

commonplace (*kom*-) *adj.* ordinary معمولی *n.* trite quotation ; platitude ایسی عام بات جو ہر ایک جانتا ہو، مبتذل بات *It is a mere commonplace* یہ کوئی انوکھی بات ہے؟

commonwealth *n.* a united nation in a country like Australia which is composed of several States دَولتِ متحدہ a group of several independent States under the hegemony of one دَولتِ مشترکہ *the British Commonwealth of Nations*, the fast disintegrating British Empire making a desperate bid to hold itself together and intact (برطانوی) دَولتِ مشترکہ

commotion (ko-*noh*-shĕn) *n.* noisy confusion اَفراتفری، بےچینی، اِضطراب excitement ہنگامہ، ہلچل، گڑبڑ violent uprising شورِش، بلوہ

communal (*kom*-ew-nĕl) *adj.* of the or for a community فِرقہ وارانہ *communal disturbance*, riot of one community against another فرقہ وارانہ فساد *communal voting*, separate electorates جُداگانہ رائے جُداگانہ اِنتخاب for the common use مُشترکہ، اجتماعی *communal land* agricultural land owned by a community اِجتماعی اراضی

commune *v.t.* (*kom*-ewn, or ko-*mewn*) feel at one (*with* someone, esp. God) سے متحد محسوس کرنا feel in close touch (*with*) کا تقرّب محسوس کرنا talk (*with* someone) in an intimate way سے دِل کی بات کہنا، سے رازونیاز میں محو ہونا *commune with nature* فطرت سے رازونیاز میں مصروف ہونا *n.* (*kom*-ewn) small local autonomy unit پنچایت revolutionary committee (or government) during French revolution اِنقلابی مجلس

communicate (ko-*mew*-ni-kayt) *v.t. & i.* pass on (news, etc., *to* someone) دکو، اِطّلاع دینا یا خبر دینا share or exchange (news, etc., *with* someome) کسی سے باتیں کرنا (of roads, rooms, etc.) be connected (by means of doors, gates, etc.) ملے ہُوئے ہونا، پیوستہ ہونا take Holy Communion (عیسائیوں میں) عشائے ربّانی میں شرکت کرنا **communicable** (ko-*mew*-ni-kay-bĕl) *adj.* (of news or disease) that can be communicated to another person (بات) کہنے کی یا کہی جا سکنے والی، (بیماری) لگ جانے والی، انتقال پذیر **communication** (ko-mew-ni-*kay*-shĕn) *n.* the act of communicating ترسیل، خبر رسانی that which is communicated (esp. a letter) اِطّلاع، مکتوب، مُراسلہ (often in the *pl.*) means of communicating roads, railways, telephones, etc., which connect places سلسلۂ مُواصلات، مُواصلات *tele-communications*, telephonic and telegraphic communications تار اور فون **communicative** (ko-*mew*-ni-kay-tiv) *adj.* ready and willing to talk and give information بے تکلّف باتیں کرنے والا

communion (ko-*mewn*-yĕn) *n.* sharing شرکت، رفاقت group of persons with the same religious beliefs مذہبی فرقہ یا جماعت religious fellowship between various churches, or members of (more than one) church مذہبی اُخوّت، ہم مذہبی intimate exchange of thoughts, feelings, etc., رازونیاز hold communion with سے محوِ رازونیاز in communion with (*the Communion*) (more commonly, the *Holy Communion*), celebration of the Lord's Supper (عیسائیوں میں) عشائے ربّانی **communicant** (kom-*ewn*-i-kĕnt) *n.* (esp.) one who receives Holy Communion عشائے ربّانی میں باقاعدہ شرکت کرنے والا

communique (ko-*meun*-i-kay) *n.* official statement or announcement سرکاری بیان، اِعلامیہ

Communism (*kom*-ew-nizm) *n.* Russian Socialism in which property is owned by the community (or in its name, by the Communist Party) and used for the good of all اِشتمالیت رُوسی اشتراکیت belief in this system اِشتمالیت، اجتماعی عقائد

Communist (*kom*-ew-nist) *n.* beliver in or supporter of Communism اِشتمالی، اشتمالی عقائد رکھنے والا *adj.* of Communism اِشتمالی **communistic** (kom-ew-*nis*-tik) *adj.* like that of Communism اِشتمالی انداز کا

community (ko-*mewn*-i-ti) *n.* all the persons living in one place قوم، کسی علاقے کی پُوری آبادی یا تمام لوگ، عام لوگ، عوام، خاص و عام *work for the good of the community* تمام لوگوں کی بھلائی کے لیے کوشش کرنا *community development*, (work, programme, etc., for) uplift of all the persons living in a place جماعتی ترقی group of persons with the same interests or occupation فرقہ، گروہ condition of sharing, having things in common, being alike in some ways اشتراک، بھائی چارہ، اتحاد، اخوت *community of race* (or *religion*) نسلی اتحاد (یا مذہبی اخوت) *community of interests* اشتراکِ مفادات، مشترکہ مفادات

commute (ko-*mewt*) *v.t. & i.* exchange (one thing *for* or *into* another) بدلنا، بدلے میں لینا، اَدل بدل کرنا pay an aggregate sum instead of by instalments پنشن کی بجائے یکمشت رقم دینا *commute the pension*, یکمشت رقم دینا change (a punishment *into* one less severe) سزا کو نرم کرنا *commute the death penalty into life imprisonment*, substitute the penalty of death into 20 years' imprisonment پھانسی کی سزا کو نرم کر کے عمرقید کا حکم دینا **commutation** (-*tay*-) *n.* commuting بدلنا، یکمشت ادا کرنا *commutation ticket*, season ticket سیزن ٹکٹ، لمبے عرصے یا پورے عرصے کا ٹکٹ amount paid in this way یکمشت ادا کی ہوئی رقم reduced punishment کمتر سزا، نرم سزا **commuter** *n.* holder of a commutation ticket (سیزن ٹکٹ لینے والا) **commutator** *n.* apparatus for changing electric current from alternating to direct, etc. برقی بدل

compact (*kom*-pakt) *n.* agreement پکا معاہدہ عہد و پیمان، اقرار، قول و قرار miniature flat vanity bag جیبی سنگھاردان refill for it جیبی سنگھاردان کا سامان

adj. (kom-*pakt*) neatly fitted ٹھیک پیوست کیا ہوا ، اچھی طرح پھنسا یا جما یا ہوا کسا ہوا closely packed together (of style) terse جامع ، پُر معنی small (but usu. roomy) چھوٹا سا ، بساط سے بڑھ کر، گنجائش والا *compact car*, 1960 model of small car بڑی گنجائش والی چھوٹی کار ، *v.t.* (kom-*pakt*) make compact پیوستہ کرنا ، صفائی سے جمانا construct entirely *of* سارے کا سارا کسی شے سے بنانا

companion (kom-*pan*-yĕn) *n*. comrade ندیم ، رفیق ، ساتھی ، ہم نشین ، عورتوں کی سہیلی ، ہمجولی one who travels along with another ہم سفر ، ہم راہی *companion on a journey* ہم راہی friendly person, esp. one with similar interests ہم ذوق ، ہم مشرب دوست one of two things that go together ساتھ والا one thing that matches another کے ساتھ کا دوسرا ، جوڑا ، جوڑ والا *the companion to a* (or *this*) *sock* اِس کے ساتھ کی دوسری جُراب woman paid to live with old or sick person مُصاحبہ woman paid to live with another to help her in household work نوکرانی ، خادمہ ، ماما hand-book of technical instructions for some profession کسی پیشہ کے لیے راو سط ضخامت کی معلوماتی کتاب ، رہنما ، رہبر *The Bricklayer's* (or *Tailor's*) *Companion* رہنمائے معماراں ، رہبرِ درزیاں **companionable** *adj*. friendly ملنسار sociable دوستوں کا دوست suited to be a companion ساتھی بننے کے لائق **companionship** *n*. being constantly together پکا ساتھی ، مستقل رفاقت **companion way** *n*. staircase from deck to cabins in a ship (جہاز میں) عرشے سے کمروں میں جانے کا راستہ

company (*kum*-pè-ni) *n*. being together with other person(s) ساتھ ، معیت ، رفاقت ، صحبت *have the pleasure of* (*someone's*) *company* کسی کا لطفِ صحبت حاصل کرنا *keep* (*someone*) *company*, be with him (کسی) کے ساتھ ہونا ، کی معیت میں ہونا *hear* (*someone*) *company*, go with (him) سے جُدا ہونا *part company with*, separate from کسی کے ساتھ جانا *keep company with*, associate with one's admirer of opposite sex سے دل لگانا ، سے تعلق قائم کرنا *in company*, not alone تنہا دوسروں کے ساتھ *be good company*, be entertaining بہت مزے کا آدمی ہونا *be poor company*, be a bore اُکتا دینے والا ہونا body of persons لوگ ، گروہ *among the company was so-and-so* اس گروہ میں فلاں صاحب بھی تھے (abb. Co.) business concern in which several persons combine as owners شرکت کمپنی ، تجارتی ادارہ *Kitabistan Publishing Company* شرکت اشرین کتابستان *the oil company* تیل نکالنے والا number of persons working together (ساتھی ، سنگی ، عملہ کے ساتھی) سنگت ، سنگت ، ٹولی *the ship's company*, its crew جہاز کا عملہ *theatrical company* ناٹک سنگت ، شرکتِ تمثیل ، *company of actors* اداکاروں کی ٹولی part of army commanded by a captain or major فوج کی کمپنی

comparable *adj*. (see under **compare**)

comparative (kom-*pa*-ri-tiv) *adj*. of comparison *comparative study of religions* مذاہب کا تقابلی مُطالعہ measured by comparison with other persons or things نسبتی ، مُقابلۃً *in comparative comfort* نسبتاً آرام سے *comparative degree* (صفت یا تمیز کا) درجۂ تفضیلِ بعض **comparatively** *adv*. speaking in comparison with other things though not necessarily by itself نسبتاً *comparatively speaking* دوسروں کے مقابلے میں ، اوروں کو دیکھیے جاتے تو

compare (kom-*pay*-è*) *v.t.* judge how far two or more persons or things are similar or dissimilar مقابلہ کرنا ، موازنہ کرنا *it cannot compare with that*, it is far different from that یہ اس سے بدرجہا مختلف ہے (*compare to*), point out the likeness or relation between سے تشبیہ دینا *compare beauty to a flower* حُسن کو پھول سے تشبیہ دینا *compare with*, put side by side for comparison سے مقابلہ کرنا ، سے پہلو بہ پہلو رکھ کر مقابلہ کرنا ، *it cannot compare with that, it is not to be compared with that, does not bear comparison with that*, is far worse (or better) than that اس کا اس سے کیا مقابلہ ، اِن دونوں میں کیا نسبت ، *compare favourably with*, be better than سے بہتر ہونا for the comparative and superlative degrees of adjectives and adverbs (as *kind*, *kinder*, *kindest*, or deadly, deadlier, deadliest) (صفت یا تمیز کی) تفضیل بعض یا تفضیلِ کل بتانا *n*. comparison موازنہ ، مقابلہ (only in the phrases !) *beyond* (or *without*, or *past*) *compare* موازنہ سے اُونچا یا بلند تر ، یا ماورا **comparable** (*kom*-pa-ra-bèl) *adj*. (*comparable to*) that can be compared مقابلہ پذیر as good as ہم مرتبہ ، مدّمقابل **comparison** (kom-*pa*-ri-zen) *n*. the act of comparing or the statement which compares مقابلہ ، موازنہ ، مماثلت ، تشبیہ *in comparison with*, when compared with کے مقابلے میں *by comparison*, when compared مقابلۃً ، نسبتاً *bear* (or *stand*) *comparison with*, be compared favourably with سے مقابلۃً بہتر ہونا degrees of comparison for adjectives and adverbs (*viz*., positive, comparative, and superlative) (صفت یا تمیز کی) تفضیل

compartment (kom-*pah**t-ment) *n*. separate division of a structure حصّہ *watertight compartments*, entirely separate divisions بالکل علیٰحدہ ، علیحدہ شعبے separate division in a railway coach ڈبّہ ، کمرہ division in examination results candidates placed in which are permitted to proceed to higher studies on the condition that they reappear in a particular subject and secure a pass in it within a specified period کمپارٹمنٹ *be placed in the compartment* (امتحان میں) مشروط کامیابی کمپارٹمنٹ میں آنا

compass (*kum*-pas) *n.* instrument with magnetic needle always pointing northwards قطب نما (also *pair of compasses*), instrument for drawing circles پرکار range, extent وسعت، رسائی، پہنچ

(left) a compass; (right) a pair of compasses

compassion (kum-*pash*-ĕn) *n.* pity رحم sympathy ترس *be filled with compassion for, take compassion on,* پر ترس کھانا **compassionate** (kom-*pash*-o-nit) *adj.* having compassion رحم دل، ترس کھانے والا deserving compassion قابل رحم، رحمدلانہ، رحمدلی کا، مترحمانہ *on compassionate grounds,* (of retirement, etc.) not strictly according to the letter of the law but owing to sympathy with that person in his old age, weakness, illness or misery رحم دلی کی بنا پر

compatible (kom-*pat*-i-bĕl) *adj.* (of ideas, etc.) in accord with ہم آہنگ، موافق، مطابق **compatibility** (-*bil*-) *n.* ہم آہنگی، موافقت، مطابقت

compatriot (kom-*pat*-ri-ot) *n.* countryman ہم وطن، برادرِ وطن

compeer (kom-*pee*-ĕ*) *n.* person of the same rank or quality ہم مرتبہ

compel (kom-*pel*) *v.t.* (-*ll*-) force (someone *to do* something) مجبور کرنا get a result by force (کسی کام کو) زبردستی کرالینا، بہ جبر کرانا

compendious *adj.* (see under **compendium**)

compendium (kom-*pen*-di-um) *n.* comprehensive summary (of a book, etc.) لبّ لباب، خلاصہ ملخص **compendious** (-di-us) *adj.* giving much information briefly جامع

compensate (*kom*-pen-sayt) *v.t.* & *i.* make amends for loss or injury تلافی کرنا **compensation** (kum-pen-*say*-shĕn) *n.* compensating تلافی، تلافی کرنا something given to compensate معاوضہ، عوض، بدلا

compere (*kom*-pay-ĕ*) *n.* performer who introduces the artistes at a show اعلان کنندہ، اعلانچی اداکاروں کا تعارف کرانے والا

compete (kom-*peet*) *v.t.* strive against others to win مقابلے میں حصّہ لینا *compete in* (doing *something for* a prize, *with* or *against* others) انعام کیلیے کسی کام میں (دوسرے کے خلاف) مقابلے میں حصّہ لینا

competition (kom-pe-*tish*-ĕn) *n.* competing مقابلے میں حصّہ لینا any activity in which persons compete مقابلہ، مسابقہ *trade competition between countries* بین الاقوامی تجارتی مسابقہ *swimming competitions* پیراکی کا مقابلہ **competitive** (kom-*pet*-i-tiv) *adj.* for which there is competition مقابلہ کا *competitive examination for the Central Superior Services of Pakistan* پاکستان کی اعلیٰ مرکزی ملازمتوں کے لیے مقابلے کا امتحان **competitor** (kom-*pet*-i-tĕ*) *n.* one who competes with others مقابلہ کرنے والا، حریف، مدِ مقابل

competent (*kom*-pi-tent) *adj.* having skill, etc., (*to do* something) اہل، قابل، لائق، مجاز، (سماعت کا)، اختیار رکھنے والا *the magistrate is competent to try this case* مجسٹریٹ اس مقدمے کی سماعت کا مجاز ہے (of knowledge, etc.) equal to the need کافی، حسبِ ضرورت **competence** (*kom*-pe-tens) *n.* being competent اہلیت، سماعت کے اختیارات رکھنے والا ability استعداد، لیاقت، قابلیت income large enough for a person to live on in comfort (ضرورت یا زندگی کے لیے) کفایت، کافی آمدنی، فارغ البالی

compilation *n.* (see under **compile**)

compile (kom-*pīl*) *v.t.* collect information and arrange in a book, etc. مرتب کرنا، تالیف کرنا، مدوّن کرنا، ترتیب دینا *compile a dictionary* (or *index*) لغات (یا اشاریہ) مرتب کرنا **compilation** (kom-pi-*lay*-shĕn) *n.* thing compiled تالیف act of compiling تدوین، تالیف

complacence, complacency *n.* (see under **complacent**)

complacent (kom-*play*-sent) *adj.* self-satisfied مطمئن، آپ ہی خوش in pleasant mood خوشدل **complacence, complacency** *n.* self-satisfaction بےفکری، آسودہ خاطری Note that **complacent** means either happy or self-satisfied, but **complaisant** denotes one who is willing and ready to oblige others and do all in his power to please others.

complain (kom-*playn*) *v.i.* (*complain that*, or *camplain of something*), say that something is wrong (with oneself or with the state of affairs) شکایت کرنا **complainant** (kom-*play*-nant) *n.* one who complains شاکی plaintiff in a criminal case مستغیث **complaint** (kom-*playnt*) *n.* complaining شکایت reasoned statement of dissatisfaction شکوہ، شکایت، استغاثہ *make* (or *lodge*) *a complaint* (*against someone*), *in* (or *with*) (کے خلاف کسی یا کسی کے پاس) شکایت کرنا یا استغاثہ دائر کرنا disease بیماری، تکلیف، مرض، شکایت *a heart complaint* دل کی تکلیف ▣ We **complain** of a grievance ; **grumble**, when we mutter with discontent ; **murmur**, under our breath, angrily

complaisance *n.* (see under **complaisant**)

complaisant (kom-pliz-ĕnt, or -*play*-) *adj* ready to do what is pleasing to others بامروّت، بااخلاق (person) lacking firmness نرم، ڈھیلا سا **complaisance** (kom-*pliz*-ens) *n.* being complaisant نرمی، مروّت، اخلاق

complement (*kom*-ple-ment) *n.* that which makes something complete تکملہ that which rightly or necessarily coexists with another جزو لازم (of a ship's crew) the full number or quantity needed (جہاز کے عملہ کی) پوری تعداد *complement of a predicate*, (in grammar) words completing the predicate خبر کا تکملہ *complement of an angle*, angle that completes it to make it a right angle زاویۂ تکملہ **complementary** (*kom*-ple-men-tè-ri) *adj.* serving to complete مکمل کرنے والا *complementary colours*, (also called *accidental colours*), colours posing white when mixed امدادی رنگ

complete (kom-*pleet*) *adj.* whole ثابت، سالم، کامل finished مکمل thorough بالکل، یکسر، سخت، قطعی، ہر *a complete surprise* سخت حیران *complete stranger* قطعاً ناواقف *v.t.* finish ختم کرنا bring to an end پورا کرنا **completely** *adv.* wholly, fully کلیتہً **completion** (kom-plee-shěn) *n.* act of completing تکمیل state of being complete پورا، مکمل، تمام

complex (*kom*-pleks) *adj.* made up of parts مرکب difficult to understand or explain پیچیدہ، الجھا ہوا *complex situation* پیچیدہ صورت حال *n.* complex thing پیچیدگی abnormal mental state born of past experiences, etc. نفسیاتی الجھن، ذہنی الجھاؤ **complexity** (kom-*plek*-si-ti) *n* state of being complex پیچیدگی something which is complex پیچیدگی

complexion (kom-*plek*-shěn) *n.* natural colour of the skin (جسم یا چہرے کا) رنگ general character (of events, etc.) واقعات کا رنگ ڈھنگ **-complexioned** (-shěnd) *suf.* with (fair, dark, or other) complexion رنگ کا، رو

complexity *n.* (see under **complex**)

compliance (kom-*plī*-ans) *n.* act of complying تعمیل، فرماں برداری، اطاعت *in compliance with*, (*a*) in obedience to کی تعمیل میں (*b*) according to کے حسب خواہش یا حسب ہدایت **compliant** *adj.* ready to comply حسب ہدایت (یا مرضی کے مطابق) کام کرنے والا

complicate (*kom*-pli-kayt) *v.t* make complex پیچیدہ بنانا، خلط ملط کرنا make (something) difficult to do or understand الجھانا، میں الجھنیں پیدا کرنا **complicated** (*kom*-pli-kay-tĕd) *adj.* made up of many parts مرکب complex پیچیدہ **complication** (kom-pli-*kay*-shěn) *n.* state of being confused and difficult الجھاؤ، اشکال that which makes a situation serious پیچیدگی

complicity (kom-*plis*-i-ti) *n.* taking part with another person (*in* crime, etc.) سازباز

compliment (*komp*-li-ment) *n.* expression of admiration تعریف، ستائش *pay (someone) a compliment* کسی کی تعریف کرنا expression of approval by requesting someone to داد، اظہار پسندیدگی *do one the compliment of* (listening etc.) کسی کی بات شوق سے سن کر داد دینا (*pl.*) greetings سلام *with compliments to*, paying regards to کو سلام کہتے ہوئے *send one's compliments* سلام کہلا بھیجنا *please pay my compliments to* کی خدمت میں میرا کہیے گا، (یا) عرض کر دیجیے گا *v.t.* pay a compliment *to* someone *on* something داد دینا، تعریف کرنا

complimentary *adj.* laudatory تعریفی sent as a gift تحفے کے طور پر *complimentary ticket*, ticket given free پاس، تحفے کا ٹکٹ

comply (kom-*plī*) *v.i.* act according to or in accordance *with* پر عمل کرنا *comply with* (*a request, instruction, etc.*), do (what is asked) (کسی کے) حسب ہدایت یا حسب خواہش کام کرنا۔

component (kom-*poh*-nent) *n.* that which forms a complete thing جزو، جزو ترکیب، مشتمل حصہ *adj.* helping to form a complete thing ترکیبی *component part* ترکیبی جزو

comport (kom-*poh*t*) *v.t.* & *i.* (of something) be in harmony (*with*) زیب دینا، کے مطابق ہونا، سے ہم آہنگ ہونا (reflexive) (*comport oneself*), behave (with dignity, etc.) (باوقار وغیرہ) طرز عمل اختیار کرنا

compose (kom-*pohz*) *v.t.* & *i.* put together ترکیب دینا، سنوارنا، بنانا *compose a poem* نظم کہنا یا لکھنا، شعر کہنا *compose music* راگ بنانا، نغمہ گری کرنا *be composed of*, comprise, be made up of parts پر مشتمل ہونا (printing) set up (type) to form words, etc. (ٹائپ کے حروف کا) جوڑنا یا جمانا get under control میں کرنا، پر قابو پانا، ضبط کرنا *compose oneself* (or *one's passions*) اپنے آپ (یا اپنے جذبات) پر قابو پانا، سنبھل بیٹھنا *compose one's thoughts* اپنے خیالات جمع کرنا، *compose one's countenance* *compose a quarrel* (or *difference of opinion*), settle it جھگڑا یا اختلاف رائے ختم کرنا *compose (oneself) to do something*) (کسی کام کے لیے) تیار ہو بیٹھنا **composed** (kom-*pohzd*) *adj.* with feelings under control جذبات پر قابو پائے ہوئے، جمع خاطر، مطمئن **composedly** (kom-*poh*-zid-li) *adv.* calmly, in a composed manner جمعیت خاطر کے ساتھ، اطمینان سے **composer** (kom-*poh*-zĕ*) *n.* (esp) one who composes music نغمہ گر، مغنی گر **compositor** (kom-*poz*-i-tĕ*) *n.* one who composes type ٹائپ کے حرف جوڑنے والا

composite (*kom*-po-zit) *adj.* made up of different parts or materials ملا جلا، مرکب

composition (kom-po-*zish*-ěn) *n.* act of composing in literary form لکھنا، تحریر، انشاء، مضمون نگاری that which is written تحریر، انشا، مقالہ، مضمون، نظم arrangement of objects ترتیب، درستی the parts of which something is composed اجزائے ترکیبی substance composed of more than one material مرکب **compositor** *n.* (see under **compose**)

compost (*kom*-post) *n.* manure made from decayed vegetable stuff بل مچل کھاد ، سڑے پتوں کی کھاد
v.t. make into compost سڑے پتوں کی کھاد بنانا treat with compost سڑے پتوں کی کھاد ڈالنا

composure (kom-*poh*-zhĕ*) *n.* condition (*of* mind or behaviour) of being composed اطمینان ، سکون ، دلجمعی

compote (*kom*-poht) *n.* fruit in syrup پھلوں کا تازہ مربّہ ، قوام میں ڈالے ہوئے پھل

compound *n.* (*kom*-pound) something made up of two or more parts مرکب *chemical compound*, a combination of elements کیمیاوی مرکب *compound interest*, interest multiplying itself by becoming principal سُود در سُود ، سُود مرکب (Anglo-Pakistani term for) enclosed area with buildings احاطہ *v.t.* & *i.* (kom-*pound*) mix together to make something different مرکب بنانا ، ترکیب دینا *compound a medicine* دوا بنانا settle matters by mutual concession or monetary consideration مصالحت کرنا ، تصفیہ کرنا معاملہ طے کرنا ، راضی نامہ کرنا یا کرانا ، پیسے دِلا کر فیصلہ کرانا *compound a case* راضی نامہ کرنا یا کرانا settle debt by part payment جزوی ادائیگی سے (قرض) چکانا condone for liability or offence جرم یا ذمہ داری سے معاف کرنا *adj.* (*kom*-pound) made up of parts مرکب **compoundable** *adj.* that which may be settled by mutual concession or monetary consideration قابلِ مصالحت ، قابلِ تصفیہ ، قابلِ راضی نامہ ، ترکیب پذیر ،

comprehend (kom-pre-*hend*) *v.t.* understand fully پوری طرح سمجھنا ، اِدراک کرنا ، include شامل کرنا ، داخل کرنا **comprehensible** (-*hens*-) *adj.* that which can be comprehended or understood جو سمجھ میں آسکے ، قابلِ فہم

comprehensive (-*hens*-iv) *adj.* that which can be comprehended قابلِ فہم ، قابلِ شمول **comprehension** *n.* the mind's act or power of understanding اِدراک ، فہم ، سمجھ **comprehensively** (-*hens*-iv-li) *adj.* جامعیت کے ساتھ

compress (kom-*pres*) *v.t.* press together بھینچنا get into a smaller space سُکیڑنا (of writings or ideas) get into fewer words اختصار سے لکھنا ، ایجاز سے کام لینا *n.* (*kom*-pres) pad of cloth pressed on to part of the body to stop bleeding گدّی ، پٹّی moist pad put on head, etc., to reduce fever ٹھنڈے پانی کی پٹّی **compression** (kom-*presh*-ĕn) *n.* compressing دباؤ ، داب ، اختصار

comprise (kom-*prīz*) *v.t.* consist of پر مشتمل ہونا ، کو شامل ہونا ، پر محیط ہونا Note that **consist** is followed by *of* but **comprise** does not take any preposition. Thus we say either of these correctly: The class consists of 50 students the class comprises 50 students.

compromise (*kom*-pro-mīz) *n.* settlement of a dispute by mutual concessions تصفیہ ، مصالحت ، سمجھوتہ *v.t.* & *i.* settle a dispute by making a compromise تصفیہ کرنا یا کرانا ، جھگڑا چکانا ، معاملے کو رفع دفع کرنا bring under suspicion by unwise behaviour, etc. (اپنی حماقت سے) مشتبہ بننا یا بنانا

comptroller *n.* (old spelling of *controller* retained in certain phrases) نگران ، ناظر *Comptroller of Accounts* ناظرِ حسابات

compulsion (kom-*pul*-shĕn) *n.* compelling or being compelled مجبوری ، زبردستی ، زبر *under* (or *upon*) *compulsion*, because one is forced or compelled لازماً ، مجبوراً ، جبراً و قہراً

compulsory *adj.* that must be done لازمی *compulsory subject*, subjects that must be taken for an examination لازم مضامین

compunction (kom-*punk*-shĕn) *n.* uneasiness of conscience پشیمانی ، ندامت regret for one's action تاسّف ، افسوس *without* (*the slightest*) *compunction* without any regret or uneasiness of mind بغیر کسی پشیمانی کے

compute (kom-*pewt*) *v.t.* calculate حساب لگانا ، گننا **computation** *n.* calculation حساب ، شمار

comrade (*kom*-rayd, or *kum*-rid) *n.* trusted companion ساتھی ، رفیق ، صاحب fellow-member of the Communist party or any of its ancillaries ساتھی **comrade-ship** *n.* intimate association رفاقت

Comus (*koh*-mus) *Cl. myth.* a god of mirth and joy who was represented as a winged youth; Milton makes him the son of Bacchus and Circe کومس

[1]**con** (kon) *v.t.* (-*nn*-) (*con* or *con over*) learn by heart حفظ کرنا ، رٹنا ، زبانی یاد کرنا learn یاد کرنا *con* (*one's*) *lessons* سبق یاد کرنا *adv.* against ماعلیہ *n.* (only in the phrase:) *pros and cons* (*of*) arguments for and against (something) مالہٗ و ماعلیہ ، کسی بات کے حق میں یا خلاف دلائل

[2]**con-** *pref.* Form of **com-** used before all consonants except *u*, *l*, *m*, *p* & *r*.

concatenate (kon-*kat*-e-nayt) *v.t.* (of facts, etc.) link together in a series میں علت و معلول کا ایک سلسلہ قائم کرنا **concatenation** (-*nay*-) such link(ing) علّت و معلول کا سلسلہ (قائم کرنا)

concave (*kon*-kayv) *adj.* (surface) curving inwards مجوّف ، مقعّر **concavity** (-*kav*-) being concave مجوّف ہونا concave surface مجوّف سطح

conceal (kon-*seel*) *v.t.* hide چھپانا keep secret مخفی رکھنا **concealment** *n.* act or state of hiding اخفاء ، چھپانا *stay in concealment* چھپا رہنا

concede (kon-*seed*) *v.i.* admit a point; say in

an argument that something is true تسلیم کرنا، کو تسلیم کرنا allow (a person or country) to have (a right or privilege) کو مراعات دینا، کا حق ماننا (یا) مراعات **concession** *n.* act of conceding تسلیم ہونا something conceded رعایت، مراعات رعایت **concessional** *adj.* cheaper (rate, fare, etc.) رعایتی

conceit (kon-*seet*) *n.* too much pride in oneself or one's capabilities گمان، تکبّر، خود پسندی far fetched witty thought which is the result of very complicated ratiocination مُبالغہ (یا) دُور از کار تشبیہ *full of conceits* دُور از کار تشبیہوں سے پُر **conceited** (kon-*see-tid*) *adj.* full of conceit مغرُور، متکبّر، خود پسند

conceivable *adj.* see under **conceive**

conceive (kon-*seev*) *v.t.* & *i.* become pregnant حاملہ ہونا form (an idea, plan, etc.) in the mind سوچنا، تصوّر کرنا *a well-conceived scheme* سوچی سمجھی تدبیر **conceivable** *adj.* credible قابلِ فہم، سمجھ میں آنے والی بات

concentration *n.* see under **concentrate**

concentrate (*kon*-sen-trayt) *v.t.* & *i.* bring or come together to one point ایک نقطے پر مُرتکز ہونا یا کرنا، مرکوز ہونا یا کرنا، پُوری طرح سے توجّہ سے کام کرنا، *concentrate (one's) attention on (one's) work* اپنا کام پُوری توجّہ سے کرنا make a solution stronger by evaporating, etc., the liquid part of it گاڑھا کرنا **concentration** *n.* concentrating or being concentrated ارتکاز power of concentrating پُوری توجّہ کرنے کی صلاحیت، full attention پُوری توجّہ that which is concentrated گاڑھا کیا ہُوا bringing or coming together to one centre ایک مرکز پر جمع ہونا یا کرنا، ارتکاز *concentration camp*, place where civilian political prisoners are confined مرکزِ اسیران سیاسی، سیاسی قیدیوں کا کیمپ

concentric (kon-*sent*-rik) *adj.* (of a circle) having a common centre (*with* another circle) ہم مرکز (دائرہ)

concentric circles

concept (*kon*-sept) *n.* idea underlying a class of thing رجنس اشیاء کا تصوّر، ذہنی شکل، محمول general notion خیال، مافی الذہن **conception** (kon-*sep*-shĕn) *n.* (act of forming an) idea or plan تصوّر (کرنا) *have a clear conception of* ذہن میں کسی شے کا واضح تصوّر رکھنا، *great power of conception* قوّتِ تخیّل، تخیُّل conceiving حمل

concern (kon-*sĕ*n*) *v.t.* be about, be related to سے تعلق رکھنا، سے متعلق ہونا *how does this concern me?* میرا اس سے کیا واسطہ، یہ مجھ سے کس طرح متعلق ہے۔ affect; be of importance to کے لیے اہم ہونا، پر اثر انداز ہونا *so far as he is concerned*, so far as the matter is important to him جہاں تک اِس کا تعلق ہے، جہاں تک اس پر اثر پڑنے کا سوال ہے *concern oneself with* or *in*, take an interest in, be busy with سے دل چسپی لینا، میں مصروف ہونا *be concerned in*, have part in کسی کام میں ہاتھ ہونا . make worried پریشان کرنا، تشویش پیدا کرنا *be concerned about the future*, (or *to hear*, or *at the news*) مستقبل کے متعلق (سُن کر یا خبر سے) پریشان ہونا۔ make an effort *to* do کرنا یا کے لیے کوشش کرنا *n.* connexion (*with*) سے تعلق (یا) واسطہ something in which one is interested or which is important to one معاملہ، واسطہ *It is no concern of yours* آپ کو اِس سے کیا (واسطہ) business firm (تجارتی وغیرہ) ادارہ share حصّہ *have a concern in a business* کاروبار میں حصّہ ہونا anxiety پریشانی، تشویش *filled with concern about* (or *at*, or colloq. *over* something) کے بارے میں پریشان *with deep concern* بڑی تشویش **concerning** (kon-*sĕ**-ning) *prep.* about کے بارے میں، کے متعلق، کے باب میں

concert *n.* (*kon*-sĕ*t) public musical entertainment given by group singing or playing instruments simultaneously and in harmony سنگت، چوکی *in concert (with)*, (*a*) in agreement or harmony (with) (سے) ہم آہنگ (*b*) together ایک ساتھ، اکٹھے *v.t.* (kon-*sĕ*t*) pre-arrange (measures) with partners to have a harmonious effect of details پہلے سے صلاح کر لینا do so in music سُر ملا لینا، ہم آہنگی پیدا کر لینا **concerted** (kon-*sĕ**-tid) *adj.* planned, etc., together متفقہ، متحدہ *concerted action* متحدہ کارروائی

concertina (kon-sĕ**tee*-na) *n.* a musical wind instrument held in the hands and played by pressing the keys کنسرٹینہ

concertina

concerto (kon-*chay**-to) *n.* (pl., *concertos*) musical piece in concert for solo instruments کنسرٹو

concession (kon-*sesh*-ĕn) *n.* (see under **concede**)

conch (konk) *n.* shellfish گھونگا مچھلی its shell گھونگا *Cl. myth.* shell trumpet of the sea-god, Triton سمندر دیوتا کا سنکھ **conchy** (*konk*-i) *n.* (slang) conscientious objector اُصولی طور پر معترض

conciliate (kon-*sil*-i-ayt) *v.t.* win the support, or friendly feelings of ہمدردی حاصل کرنا، دل ہاتھ میں لینا، تائید حاصل کرنا، طرف دار بنانا، ملا لینا calm someone's anger منانا، راضی کرنا، غصّہ ٹھنڈا کرنا **conciliation** (kon-si-li-*ay*-shĕn) *n.* conciliating مُصالحت **conciliatory** *adj.* based on conciliation مُصالحت کُن (شخص)، مائل بہ مُصالحت، صُلح جُو، مُصالحت آمیز، صُلح جُویانہ بات

concise (kon-*sīs*) *adj.* (of a person or his style) brief اختصار پسند، ایجاز پسند giving much information in a few words مختصر، موجز، جامع **concisely** *adj.* briefly مختصراً **conciseness** *n.* brevity اختصار، ایجاز

conclave (*kon*-klayv) *n.* private, secret meeting بزمِ خاص، خاص محفل *sit in conclave*, attend such a

meeting شریکِ بزمِ خاص ہونا
conclude (kon-*klood*) *v.t.* & *i.* come or bring to an end ختم ہونا یا کرنا، انجام پذیر ہونا، خاتمے پر پہنچانا *to conclude something with* کسی چیز کو کسی بات پر ختم کرنا *conclude at a certain time* کسی خاص وقت پر ختم ہونا arrange طے کرنا *conclude a treaty* مُعاہدہ طے کرنا arrive at an opinion (کسی رائے یا فیصلے) پر پہنچنا *conclude that* نتیجہ نکالنا کہ *conclude from the evidenee (that)* شہادت سے نتیجہ اَخذ کرنا کہ **conclusion** (kon-*kloozh*-èn) *n.* end آخر، اخیر، انجام، خاتمہ *in conclusion*, lastly آخر میں، بالآخر opinion which is the result of reasoning نتیجہ، سوچی سمجھی رائے decision فیصلہ **conclusive** (kon-*kloos*-iv) *adj.* decisive, ending doubt فیصلہ کُن
concoct (kon-*kokt*) *v.t.* prepare by brewing together (جوشاندہ وغیرہ) پکانا یا بنانا invent (a story or excuse) قصہ گھڑنا، بہانہ تراشنا **concoction** *n.* concocted mixture جوشاندہ false excuse or story جھوٹ، بناوٹ، بناوٹی بات
concomitant (kon-*kom*-i-tant) *adj.* (of two or more things, circumstances, etc.) going together لازم و ملزوم *n.* something that always goes in company (*of* another) (کا) جوڑ، (کو) مُستلزم **concomitance** *n.* act of thus going together جُزوِ لازم ہونا، لزوم
concord (*kon*-ko*d) *n.* agreement or harmony (*between* persons or things) اِتفاق، اِتحاد، ہم آہنگی
concordance (kon-*ko**-dans) *n.* agreement اِتفاق، ایکا alphabetical arrangement of important or difficult words used in a book, with their explanation بامعنی اِشاریہ *concordance of Shakespeare* شیکسپیر کے کلام کا (بامعنی) اِشاریہ **concordant** (kon-*ko**-dant) *adj.* agreeing ہم آہنگ
concourse (*kon*-koh*s) *n.* flocking together اِجتماع crowd مجمع، بھیڑ، جمگھٹا
concrete (kon-*kreet*) *adj.* of (or existing in) material form مادّی *concrete noun*, name of thing (as opposed to that of a quality) کسی مادّی شے کا نام، اِسمِ محسوس *n.* building substance made by mixing cement, sand and gravel کنکریٹ، سیمنٹ، بجری *concrete structure*, building whose walls, floors and roofs are all made of concrete کنکریٹ کی عمارت *v.t.* & *i.* cover with concrete کنکریٹ کا فرش کرنا، پر کنکریٹ کی تہ بچھانا
concubine (*kon*-kew-bin) *n.* woman who lives with a man without being lawfully married to him داشتہ according to Christians a wife other than the first in a polygamous society دوسری (تیسری وغیرہ) بیوی **concubinage** *n.* such sexual relation, taking as a concubine گھر میں ڈالنا، داشتہ بنانا، یا بننا
concupiscence (kon-*kewp*-i-sens) *n.* sexual lust نفس پرستی، شہوت (Bib.) desire for worldly things دُنیا پرستی **concupiscent** *adj.* دُنیا پرست، شہوت پرست
concur (kon-*kě**) *v.i.* (-rr-) agree (*in* opinion *with* someone) اِتفاق کرنا، متفق ہونا happen together ایک ساتھ ہونا **concurrence** (kon-*kě*-rens) *n.* agreement اِتفاقِ رائے **concurrent** (kon-*kě*-rent) *adj.* existing together متوازی، ایک ساتھ، بیک وقت **concurrently** *adv.* simultaneously بیک وقت، ساتھ، ساتھ
concussion (kon-*kush*-èn) *n.* (of the brain) injury caused by a blow or fall, دماغی چوٹ violent shock سخت صدمہ
condemn (kon-*dem*) *v.t.* censure, blame بُرا بھلا کہنا، عیب لگانا say that something is unfit for use ناکارہ قرار دینا، رَدّ کرنا، رَدّی قرار دینا *condemned stores*, (usu. military) stores rejected as worn out or no longer of use رَدّی سامان give judgment against کو سزا دینا، کے خلاف فیصلہ دینا *condemn (someone) to death* (کسی) کو سزائے موت دینا doom (*someone to something* unhappy) کو مصیبت میں ڈالنا، کی قسمت میں لکھ دینا *condemn to suffer a life of pain* دردناک زندگی قسمت میں لکھ دینا **condemnation** (kon-dem-*nay*-shèn) *n.* ملامت، سزا کا حکم، بُری قسمت
condemnatory (-dem-) based on condemnation مَلامت والی، سزا پر مبنی، خلاف ■ To **condemn** is to pass unfavourable judgment on; **convict,** pass legal sentence on; **blame** someone, lay upon him responsibility for a wrong; **censure,** express unfavourable opinion as to a moral wrong; **reprove,** express blame but with kindly feelings; **denounce,** state publicly one's objections to a course of action.
condensation *n.* (see under **condense**)
condense (kon-*dens*) *v.t.* & *i.* (cause to) increase in density or strength گاڑھا کرنا، کثیف بنانا (of a gas or vapour) (cause to) become liquid سیّال بننا یا بنانا (of liquid) (cause to) become thicker گاڑھا کرنا، میں تکثیف یا تکاثُف ہونا یا کرنا *condensed milk* گاڑھا دُودھ put into fewer words مختصر لفظوں میں بیان کرنا *condensed account of an event* مختصر لفظوں میں بیان کرنا **condenser** *n.* apparatus for condensing (steam, etc.) آلۂ تکثیف apparatus for condensing electricity until it has the power needed مکثّف **condensation** (kon-den-*say*-shěn) *n.* condensing تکثیف، انجماد، تکاثُف summary خلاصہ، اِختصار
condescend (kon-de-*send*) *v.i.* stoop (*to* someone lower, or *to do* something lower) without an air of superiority فروتنی کرنا، جھکنا، عاجزی سے کام لینا، جھک کر کوئی کام قبول کرنا، انکسار سے کام لینا *He will not condescend to visit a poor person* اس میں اتنا انکسار نہیں کہ کسی غریب آدمی کو ملنے آئے **condescension** (kon-de-*sen*-shěn) *n.* stooping thus انکسار، تواضع، جُھک کر کچھ کہنا

condign (kon-*din*) *adj*. (of punishment) adequate equal to the crime موزوں ، مناسب ، جرم کے مطابق
condiment (*kon*-di-ment) *n*. hot things like pepper, etc., added to food to flavour it مسالہ **condimental** (kon-di-*men*-tal) *adj*. seasoned with condiments مسالے دار، چٹ پٹا
condition (kon-*dish*-ĕn) *n*. something on which another thing depends شرط ، بنیادی شرط *conditions of happiness*, خوشی کی شرطیں (یا بنیادی شرطیں) *on condition that*, provided that اس شرط پر ، صرف اس صورت میں کہ *condition precedent* شرطِ اوّلین *on this (or that) condition* اس شرط پر *make conditions*, stipulate شرائط مقرر کرنا *conditions of peace* شرائطِ امن present state حال ، حالت ، کیفیت ، احوال *under the existing conditions* موجودہ صورت (حالات میں) *condition of health* صحت *in good (or bad) condition* اچھی (یا بُری) حالت میں *in condition*, in good condition حالت میں *out of condition* خراب (یا بُری) حالت میں *change (one's) condition*, marry شادی کرلینا
attendant state حالت ، حالات ، صورتِ حال *condition of war (or peace)* حالتِ جنگ یا حالتِ امن social state درجہ *people of every condition* ہر درجے کے لوگ *v.t.* be the precedent condition of کی شرط ہونا place conditions upon پر شرائط عائد کرنا regulate, govern, control پر منحصر کرنا ، سے متعین کرنا ، پر مبنی کرنا *conditioned by* پر منحصر *Prices are conditioned by demand and supply* قیمتوں کا انحصار طلب و رسد پر ہوتا ہے۔ **conditional** (kon-*dish*-ĕ-nĕl) *adj*. depending on مشروط *conditional clause*, (in grammar) clause beginning with *if* or *unless* شرط **conditioned** (kon-dish-end) *adj* controlled متعین *conditioned reflex*, mental response got through inducing (someone) by habit to follow a stimulus other than the natural one متعین ردِّ عمل **conditioner** *n*. (see *Addenda*)
condole (kon-*dohl*) *v.i.* sympathize (*with* someone *on* or *upon* a loss) پرسا دینا ، ماتم پرسی کرنا ، تعزیت کرنا express sorrow at (someone's death) پر افسوس کرنا **condolence** (kon-*dol*-lens) *n*. (often *pl*.) expression of sympathy پرسا ، ماتم پرسی ، تعزیت *adj*. of or comprising condolence تعزیتی *condolence resolution*, resolution passed to express such sympathy تعزیتی قرارداد ، قراردادِ تعزیت
condone (kon-*dohn*) *v.t.* (of a person) forgive (an offence) معاف کرنا ، نظرانداز کرنا (of an act) atone for تلافی کرنا ▣ We **condone** an offence by shutting our eyes to it ; **tolerate** it when we find no fault with the excuse ; **overlook** it when we pay no attention to it; **forgive** it when we blot out our desire for the offender's punishment.
conduce (kon-*dews*) *v.i.* help (*to* produce a result) باعث ہونا یا بننا *Wealth does not conduce to happiness* دولت و ثروت مسرت کا باعث نہیں بنا کرتی **conducive** *adj*. such as to conduce (*to* something) (کا) باعث
conduct *n*. (*kon*-dukt) moral behaviour طرزِ عمل ، اطوار ، طور طریقہ ، چلن ، چال چلن *good (or bad) conduct* اچھے (یا بُرے) اطوار management of affairs, etc. طرز ، انتظام ، انصرام ، بندوبست *v.t.* & *i*. (kon-*dukt*) guide رہنمائی کرنا ، رہبری کرنا *conduct (someone) round a place*, show (him) round کو ساتھ چل کر دکھانا manage چلانا ، انتظام کرنا ، بندوبست کرنا control ہدایت کرنا *conduct an orchestra*, guide and control the players سنگت یا قوالوں کی رہبری اور ہدایت کرنا (reflexive verb) (*conduct oneself well, ill*, etc.) behave (اچھا یا بُرا) طرزِ عمل اختیار کرنا (of substances) transmit, allow (heat or electricity) to pass through (بجلی یا حرارت کا) ایصال کرنا **conduction** (kon-*duk*-shĕn) *n*. the conducting of heat or electricity ایصال **conductor** (kon-*duk*-tĕ*) *n*. one on a bus, tram, etc. who collects fares, gives tickets, and conducts the passengers to their seats کنڈکٹر ، نشاندہ ، نشانا substance that conducts heat or electricity مُوصِل **conduct-sheet** (*kon*-) *n*. record of offences (*of* a soldier) (فوجی کا) اعمال نامہ (یا نامۂ عمل یا سیاہہ)
conduit (*kun*-dit) *n*. large pipe or waterway نل ، بڑی نالی
cone (kohn) *n*. solid body which narrows to a point from a flat round base مخروط ، مخروطہ anything of this shape (کوئی سی) مخروطی چیز fruit of certain evergreen trees like pine (چیڑ وغیرہ) کا مخروطی پھل *v.t. passive* (*be coned*), (of aircraft) be picked up or illuminated by many (usu. enemy's) searchlights at once (ہوائی جہاز کا) روشنیوں کی زد میں آکر دیکھا جانا **conic** (*kon*-ik), **conical** (*kon*-) *adj*. like a cone in shape مخروطی *conic section*, section of a cone تراشِ مخروطی **conics** *n. pl*. (used as *sing*.) branch of mathematics dealing with conic sections مخروطیات

a cone

confabulate (kon-*fab*-ew-layt) *v.i.* (lit.) talk together آپس میں باتیں کرنا ، باہمدگر بات کرنا **confabulation** (-*lay*-) *n*. chat آپس میں باتیں کرنا ، باہمدگر بات چیت **confabulator** *n*. (کسی سے) بات چیت کرنے والا
confection (kon-*fek*-shĕn) *n*. sweetmeats مٹھائی ، شیرینی **confectioner** (kon-*fek*-shĕ-nĕ*) *n*. maker and seller of cakes and sweetmeats حلوائی **confectionery** (kon-*fek*-shĕ-nĕ-ri) *n*. cakes, pastries, sweets, etc. شیرینی ، کیک ، پیسٹری
confederacy *n*. see under **confederate**

confederate (kon-*fed*-è-rayt) *adj*. joined together by a pact متحدہ ، نیم وفاق ، منسلکہ *n*. one who joins with another or others (esp. for wrongdoing) نیم وفاق ، ریاستہائے متحدہ ، ممالک منسلکہ **confederacy** (kon-*fed*-e-ra-si) *n*. group of confederate States ممالکِ منسلکہ ، نیم وفاقی ریاستیں **confederation** (kon-fe-de-*ray*-shèn) *n*. permanent union of sovereign states ممالکِ منسلکہ ، نیم وفاق ریاستہائے متحدہ

[1]**confer** (kon-*fě**) *v.t.* & *i.* (-*rr*-) bestow a right or favour مرحمت کرنا ، عطا کرنا ، دینا *confer a degree* (or *title*) *on* (*someone*) (کسی) کو سند (یا خطاب) دینا consult together or discuss (*with*) (سے) صلاح کرنا ، مشورہ کرنا ، صلاح مشورہ کرنا **conference** (*kon*-fe-rens) *n*. discussion, consultation مشورہ ، مشاورت ، صلاح meeting for this purpose کانفرنس ، مجلسِ مشاورت **conferment** (-fě*-) *n*. conferring, bestowing (*of* something *on* someone) عطا کرنا **conferrable** *adj*. that which can be conferred قابلِ عطا

[2]**confer**, (abb. **cf.**) *v. imperative* compare دیکھو ، مقابلہ کرو ، ملاحظہ ہو *cf. statement on p. 1239* صفحہ ۱۲۳۹ کے بیان سے مقابلہ کیجئے

confess (kon-*fes*) *v.t.* & *i.* acknowledge (a fault) ; admit (*that* one has done wrong) (قصور کا) اعتراف کرنا ، غلطی ماننا یا تسلیم کرنا ، اقبالِ جرم کرنا ، tell one's sins before death (*to* a priest) (عیسائیوں میں) مرتے وقت (پادری کے سامنے گناہوں کا) اعتراف کرنا ، توبہ کرنا۔ (of a priest) listen to (someone's) confession پادری کا کسی مرنے والے کا اعترافِ گناہ یا توبہ سننا *He confessed to the priest* اُس نے مرتے وقت پادری کے سامنے اعترافِ گناہ کیا یا توبہ کی *The priest confessed* پادری نے **confessedly** *adv*. as confessed اعتراف کی رُو سے ، حسبِ اعتراف ، اپنے اظہار یا اقبال کے مُطابق **confession** (kon-*fesh*-èn) *n*. the act of confessing توبہ ، اقبال (جرم) ، اعتراف (گناہ) anything confessed جس چیز کا اعتراف یا اقبال یا اظہار کیا جائے *confession of guilt* اقبالِ جرم *go to confession, confess* (*one's*) *sins to a priest* پادری کے سامنے اعترافِ گناہ کرنا ، تائب ہونا *confession of faith*, declaration of religious beliefs اظہارِ عقیدہ ، ایمان لانا **confessional** *adj*. of confession توبہ سے متعلق ، اقبالی (بیان وغیرہ) *n*. confessor's stall اعترافِ گناہ سننے والے پادری کی نشست **confessor** (kon-*fes*-ě*) *n*. priest who hears confessions توبہ کرانے یا اعترافِ گناہ سننے والا پادری

confetti (kon-*fet*-i) *n. pl*. (w. *sing*. verb) sweets or small bits of bright coloured paper showered on people at weddings, etc. چمکدار رنگین پرچیاں یا نچھاور کی جانے والی مٹھائیاں

confidant, confidante *n*. (see under **confide**)

confide (kon-*fīd*) *v.t.* & *i*. tell (a secret *to*) راز کی بات کہنا ، رازدار بنانا entrust (something or someone *to* someone) to be looked after سپرد کرنا ، حوالے کرنا ، حفاظت میں رہنا give (a task or duty to someone) to be carried out سپرد کرنا ، تفویض کرنا ، ذمے ڈالنا trust or have faith (*in* someone) بھروسا ، اعتبار یا اعتماد کرنا **confidant** *n. masc* **confidante** *n. fem*. (kon-fi-*dant*) one who is trusted with secrets (esp. love affairs) رازدار ، ہمراز ، محرم **confidence** (*kon*-fi-dens) *n*. trusting intimacy اعتماد ، بھروسا *take* (*someone*) *into* (*one's*) *confidence* (کسی) کو رازدار بنانا (یا اپنے) اعتماد میں لینا *confidence, in strictest confidence*, as a secret ہمراز بنا کر secret confided to someone راز کی بات *exchange confidences* ہم راز بنانا belief in others یقین ، خود اعتمادی ، بھروسا ، اعتبار ، اعتماد self-assurance خود اعتمادی (یا یقین) *speak with confidence* کے ساتھ بات کرنا دم داعیہ **confident** (*kon*-fi-dent) *adj*. trusting firmly پر اعتماد یا یقین sure *of* باوثوق ، معتمد ، مُوثق *be confident of success* کامیابی کا یقین رکھنا **confidential** (kon-fi-*den*-shèl) *adj*. secret خفیہ ، مخفی ، پوشیدہ private ; given in confidence راز کی (بات) ، خفیہ *confidential information* خفیہ اطلاع enjoying some one's confidence راز کے کام کرنے والا ، معتمد ، رازدان (*someone's*) *confidential secretary* رازدار ، معتمد **confidentially** *adj*. خفیہ ، راز کے طور پر **confiding** (kon-*fī*-ding) *adj*. trusting بھروسا کرنے والا trustful معتمد ، بھروسے کا آدمی

configuration (kon-fig-ew-*ray*-shèn) *n*. shape of outline ناک نقشہ ، ہیئت ، خاکہ ، وضع method of arrangement طریقِ ترتیب ، ترتیب **configure** (-fig-ě* *v.t.* shape تشکیل کرنا ، شکل دینا arrange ترتیب دینا

confine (kon-*fīn*) *v.t.* keep within limits حد سے نہ بڑھنے دینا ، حد کے اندر رکھنا ، روکنا *confine* (*oneself*) *to* (*doing something*), do only that صرف اتنا ہی کام کرنا imprison قید ، قید خانے میں قید کرنا *confined in gaol* keep within doors گھر سے قدم باہر نہ رکھنے دینا *confined to bed* صاحبِ فراش be brought to bed of a child چلتے میں ہونا ، زچگی کی حالت میں ہونا۔ *She is confined* وہ حالتِ زچگی میں ہے *n*. (usu. *pl.*) limit حد ، حدود edge کنارا **confined** (kon-*fīnd*) *adj*. narrow (space, etc.) تنگ (of rights, range etc.) limited (*to* something) (تک) محدود giving birth to a child حالتِ زچگی میں *His wife expects to be confined about mid-October* اس کی بیوی کا خیال ہے کہ وہ وسط اکتوبر میں حالتِ زچگی میں ہو جائے گی۔ **confinement** *n*. (esp.) being confined in giving birth حالتِ زچگی imprisonment قید ، قید و بند

confirm (kon-*fě*m*) *v.t.* make (power opinion, etc.) firmer مستحکم کرنا ، پکا کرنا ، (قدم) جمانا make (someone) permanent (*in* a job) ratify تصدیق کرنا (کسی اسامی پرکسی کو) مستقل کرنا (یا پکا کرنا) توثیق کرنا **confirmed** (kon-*fĕ*md*) *adj.* (*esp.*) unlikely to change or be changed پختہ، تغیّر ناپذیر (of employee) in permanent (as opposed to temporary) service مستقل، کنفرم **confirmation** (kon-fĕ**may*-shĕn) *n.* confirming or being confirmed تصدیق، توثیق making or being made permanent کنفرم کرنا یا ہونا، مستقل کرنا یا ہونا، مستقل

confiscate (*kon*-fis-kayt) *v. t.* seize by public authority as a penalty ضبط کرنا، بحق سرکار ضبط کرنا، قرق کرنا **confiscation** (-*kay*-) *n.* act of confiscating or being confiscated ضبطی، بحق سرکار ضبطی، قرقی

conflagration (kon-flag-*ray*-shĕn) *n.* great fire آتش زدگی، آتش، بھاڑ

conflict *n.* (*kon*-flikt) battle, quarrel لڑائی جھگڑا (of opinion, etc.) disagreement آویزش difference اختلاف رائے (*something*) *in conflict with* (*another*), opposed to it مخالفت، تخالف کے خلاف، کے برعکس *v.i.* (kon-*flikt*) disagree (*with*) سے متصادم ہونا، باہم گر، آویزاں ہونا، اختلاف رائے رکھنا *conflicting loyalties*, simultaneous loyalty to contrary persons, principles, etc. باہمدگر آویزاں وفاداریاں

confluence (*kon*-flew-ens) *n.* place where rivers (etc.) unite سنگھم، سنگم

conflux (*kon*-fluks) *n.* confluence سنگھم، سنگم

conform (kon-*fo*m*) *v. t.* & *i.* (*conform to*), (*a*) made or be in agreement with کے مطابق یا موافق ہونا یا بنانا (*b*) comply with ماننا، تعمیل کرنا *conform to the rules* قواعد کے مطابق ہونا (*c*) suit حسب دلخواہ ہونا، حسب مرضی ہونا، مرضی کے مطابق عمل کرنا *conform to the wishes of* (*others*) دوسروں کی مرضی کے مطابق عمل کرنا **conformable** (kon-*fo*m*-è-bèl)*adj.* similar مطابق، ویسا ہی obedient فرمانبردار، مطیع *conformable to* (*someone's*) *wishes* (کسی) کے حسب دلخواہ **conformation** (kon-fo*-*may*-shĕn) *n.* (esp.) structure of something ڈھانچہ، بناوٹ، ساخت **conformist** (-fo*m-) *n.* one who is in agreement (esp. with the Anglican Church) (برطانوی کلیسا کا) ہم نوا **conformity** (kon-*fo*m*-i-ti) *n.* agreement مطابقت compliance تعمیل، اطاعت *in conformity with* (*someone's*) *request*

confound (kon-*found*) *v t.* throw into confusion گڈمڈ کرنا، درہم برہم کرنا confuse (ideas, etc.) حیران کرنا، پریشان کرنا overthrow (enemies or plans) دشمن کو زک دینا، (منصوبے) خاک میں ملانا *Confound it !* اس کا ستیاناس ہو

confrere (*kon*-fray-ĕ*) *n.* colleague; member of the same profession ہم پیشہ fellow member of a scientific or other society علمی مجلس کا ہم رکن، سائنس کی سوسائٹی کا ہم رکن **confront** (kon-*frunt*) *v.t.* come or bring face to face (person, witness, danger, etc.) کے روبرو ہونا یا کرنا، دوچار ہونا، سامنے رکھنا، سامنے لانا *be confronted with evidence of* (*one's*) *crime* (کسی) کے جرم کی شہادت (اس کے سامنے رکھی جانا) stand up to سامنا کرنا، مقابلہ کرنا، ڈٹ جانا **confrontation** (-*tay*-) (esp.) confronting of the accused with witness ملزم کو گواہ کے رُوبرُو لانا

confuse (kon-*fewz*) *v.t.* put into disorder گڈمڈ کرنا، درہم برہم کرنا mix up in the mind خلط ملط کرنا mistake one thing for another خلط مبحث کرنا disturb (someone's) presence of mind پریشان کرنا، ششدر کرنا *be confused* پریشان ہونا، گھبرا جانا **confused** (kon-*fewzd*) *adj.* (esp.) پریشان، گھبرایا ہوا **confusedly** (kon-*few*-zid-li) پریشانی، گھبراہٹ سے **confusion** (kon-*few*-zhĕn) *n* disorder گڑبڑ، ابتری، بے ترتیبی being confused پریشانی، گھبراہٹ

confute (kon-*fewt*) *v.t.* prove (someone or some argument) to be false غلط ثابت ہونا **confutation** (kon-few-*tay*-shĕn) *n.* proving this غلط ثابت کرنا، تغلیط

conge (kon-zhay), **congee** (*konj*-i) *n.* dismissal برخاستگی، نوکری *get* (*one's*) *conge*, be dismissed نوکری سے جواب ملنا، برخاست ہونا *give* (*someone his*) *conge* جواب دینا leave to depart جانے کی اجازت، رخصت departing bow رخصتی تسلیم، کورنش

congeal (kon-*jeel*) *v.t.* & *i.* (of blood, etc.) make or become thick خون کا جم جانا **congealment, congelation** *n.* جماؤ، انجماد

congenial (kon-*jeen*-i-ĕl) *adj.* (of person) having a similar nature or common interests ہم مزاج (of things, etc.) in agreement (*to* or *with* one's tastes) پسندیدہ، مرغوب، موافق، خوشگوار *a congenial climate* خوشگوار آب و ہوا **congeniality** (-*al*-) موافق ہونا، مُوافقت

congenital (kon-*jen*-i-tĕl) *adj.* (of diseases or bad habits) present since birth پیدائشی

congeries (kon-*je*-ri-eez) *n.* (*pl.* the same) gathered mass ڈھیر، تودہ

congested (kon-*jes*-tèd) *adj.* overcrowded بھیڑ بھاڑ والا *streets congested with traffic* گاڑیوں موٹروں سے بھرے ہوئے بازار very thickly populated گنجان، گنجان آبادی والا (of parts of the body) having too much blood اختناق دم والا **congestion** (kon-*jes*-shĕn) *n.* overcrowding بھیڑ بھاڑ accumulation of too much blood in some part of the body اختناق دم

conglomerate (kon-*glom*-è-rayt) *n.* number of things stuck to together in a mass گڑگنڈ *adj.* made up of such things منجمد، متراکم *v.t.* & *i.* collect into a rounded mass متراکم ہونا یا کرنا

conglomeration (kon-glom-è-*ray*-shèn) *n.* تجمّع ، تراکم ، تودہ

congratulate (kong-*ra*-tew-layt) *v.t.* express pleasure at someone's good fortune مُبارکباد کہنا ، مُبارک دینا *congratulate (someone) on (his) success* (کسی کو) کامیابی پر مُبارک باد دینا *congratulate (oneself)*, consider (oneself) fortunate اپنے کو خوش قسمت جاننا یا سمجھنا **congratulations** (kong-ra-tew-*lay*-shènz) *n. pl.* words with which one congratulates someone مُبارکباد ، مُبارک **congratulatory** (kong-*ra*-tew-le-tè-ri) *adj.* (of message, speech, etc.) expressing congratulations مُبارکباد کا ، تہنیتی

congregate (*kong*-re-gayt) *v.t* & *i.* (of persons) come or bring together جمع ہونا یا کرنا ، اکٹھے ہونا ، اکٹھا کرنا ، مجتمع ہونا یا کرنا **congregation** (kong-re-*gay*-shèn) *n.* (esp.) body of people taking part in religious service مذہبی اجتماع (عبادت گزاروں کی) جماعت **congregational** *adj.* of a congregation (عبادت گزاروں کی) جماعت کا

congress (*kong*-res) *n.* meeting of delegates (of societies, etc.) for discussions مجلس مندوبین ، انجمن *educational congress* تعلیماتی مجلس ، انجمن تعلیمات U.S. Legislature comprising the *Senate* (Upper House) and the *House of Representatives* (Lower House) ریاستہائے متحدہ امریکہ کی مقننہ کی کانگریس ، کانگرس **congressional** (kong-*resh*-è-nèl) *adj.* of a congress or its deliberations کانگرس کا (یا) کے متعلق ، تخصیصی

conic (*kon*-ik) **conical** (*kon*-i-kèl) *adj.* see under **cone**

conifer (*kohni*-fè*) *n.* cone-bearing tree صنوبری فرغ ، کاکوئی درخت **coniferous** (koh-*nif*-è-rus) *adj.* (of trees) bearing cones صنوبری

conjecture (kon-*jek*-chè*) *n.* guess, guess-work قیاس ، اندازہ *v.t.* & *i.* make conjectures اندازہ کرنا **conjectural** *adj.* based on conjecture اٹکل ، قیاسی

conjoin (kon-*join*) *v.t.* & *i.* join together جڑنا ، جڑنا

conjoint *adj.* united (action, etc.) مشترکہ ، متحدہ

conjugal (*kon*-joo-gèl) *adj.* of wedded life ازدواجی *conjugal happiness* ازدواجی مسرت ، ازدواجی خوشی

conjugate (*kon*-joo-gayt) *v.t.* & *i.* give the various forms of (a verb) گردان کرنا (of a verb) have various forms فعل کا مختلف صیغے رکھنا **conjugation** (kon-joo-*gay*-shèn) *n.* scheme of verbal inflexion گردان ، تصریف class of verbs according to these schemes فعل کا صیغہ

conjunction (kon-*junk*-shèn) *n.* (in grammar) part of speech which joins other words, clauses, etc., *e.g.*, and حرف عطف connection, union جوڑ ، میل ، ساتھ ، اتحاد *in conjunction with*, together with سے مل کر ، کے ساتھ simultaneous occurrence (*of* events, etc.) بیک وقت ہونا ، ایک ساتھ ہونا

conjunctive (kon-*junk*-tiv) *adj.* serving to join عطفی *conjunctive mood* such form of the verb فعل کی شرط والی صورت ، فعل تمنائی یا شرطی

conjuncture (kon-*junk*-chè*) *n.* state of affairs at a particular moment اتفاق ، صورتِ حال ، صورتِ حالات

conjure *v.t.* & *i.* (pr. kon-*joo*-è*) entreat solemnly (*to* do something) صدق دل سے کرنا (کسی کام کے لیے دُعا) (pr. kon-*joo*-è*) command in the name of God خدا کی قسم دے کر حکم دینا (pr. *kun*-je*) do clever or magical tricks شعبدہ بازی کرنا (*kun*-jè*) invoke a spirit مؤکل بلانا ، حاضرات کرنا ، جادو کے زور سے روح کو بلانا *be a name to conjure with*, be very highly influential بہت با اثر ہونا (pr. *kun*-jè*) (*conjure up*), cause to appear as a picture in the mind خیال میں لا کھڑا کرنا ، آنکھوں میں تصویر پھر جانا *conjure up past scenes*, recall them پرانی یادیں تازہ کرنا **conjurer, conjuror** (*kun*-jè-rè*) *n.* person who conjures مداری ، شعبدہ باز ، جادوگر (*He is no conjurer* (a) (he) cannot do marvels وہ معجزے دکھانے سے (تو) رہا (b) (he) is a fool وہ تو پرلے درجے کا احمق ہے ، وہ زُلدھا ہے

conjuring (kunj-è-ring) *n.* magical tricks کرتب جادو کے کھیل ، شعبدے *conjuring tricks* شعبدہ بازی

conk (konk) *n.* (slang) ناک *v.i.* (*conk out*) (of a machine, engine, etc.) break down خراب ہو جانا ناکارہ ہو جانا ، از کار رفتہ ہو جانا ، رہ جانا become useless رُک جانا

conky (*konk*-i) (slang) big-nosed بڑی ناک والا ، پکوڑا سی ناک والا (یا والی)

connect (ko-*nekt*) *v.t.* & *i.* join or be joined جوڑنا ، جڑنا ، ملانا ، ملنا unite with others in relationship تعلق پیدا کرنا ، رشتہ کرنا *be connected with a family by marriage* مصاہرت ، کسی خاندان سے شادی کے ذریعے تعلق ہونا *well-connected* بااثر رشتہ دار رکھنے والا associate in thought, argument, etc. (*with*) ملانا ، جوڑنا *connect a name with an event* کسی نام کو کسی واقعے سے ربط دینا متعلق قرار دینا **connexion, connection** (ko-*nek*-shèn) *n.* act of connecting or state of being connected تعلق ، رابطہ ، پیوند ، رشتہ (قائم کرنا) part which connects two things *in this* (or *that*) *connexion, in connexion with this* (or *that*), with reference to اس سلسلے میں ، اس ضمن میں train, etc. timed to leave a station, etc., soon after the arrival of another, enabling passengers to change from one to the other میل a professional man's clients مؤکل ، گاہک religious organization مذہبی فرقہ ، زمرہ *the Hanafi connexion* حنفی فرقہ relative (esp. by marriage) رشتے دار (بالخصوص شادی کے ذریعے) **connective** (ko-*nek*-tiv) *n.* word which connects حرف ربط ، عطف *adj.* that which connects عطفی

connexion (ko-*nek*-shèn) *n.* see under **connect**

connivance *n.* see under **connive**

connive (ko-*nīv*) *v.i.* (*connive at*) take no notice of (misdeed, etc.) pretend to be unaware of (what someone is wrongly doing) نظر انداز کرنا ، چشم پوشی ، اِغماض کرنا **connivance** (ko-*nī*-vans) *n.* pretending to be unaware thus چشم پوشی ، اِغماض *The whole thing was done with his connivance* ساری بات کا اُسے علم تھا مگر وہ جان بُوجھ کر چشم پوشی سے کام لیتا رہا

connoisseur (*kon*-i-*sē**) *n.* critical judge of (works of art, etc.) دقیقہ شناس ، مُبصّر ، نکتہ رس نقاد ، صاحبِ ذوق ، صاحبِ نظر *a connoisseur of painting* مُصوّری کا صاحبِ ذوق مُبصّر

A **connoisseur** is one who knows what is good and valuable in art ; an **amateur**, one who practises an art for the love of it ; **a dilettante**, one who trifles with art.

connote (ko-*noht*) *v.t.* (of words) suggest in addition to the primary meaning ضمنی معنی دینا ، پوشیدہ مفہوم رکھنا ، مُضمر مفہوم یا مُضمرات کا حاصل ہونا *the word "West" connotes godlessness* لفظ "مشرق" پسماندگی کے ضمنی مفہوم کا حاصل ہے **connotation** (ko-no-*tay*-shĕn) *n.* such additional suggestions مُضمرات ، ضمنی ، پوشیدہ یا مُضمر مفہوم

connubial (ko-*noo*-bi-èl) *adj.* of married life متاہلانہ زندگی کا ، ازدواجی تاہلی

conquer (*konk*-ĕ*) *v.t.* defeat (enemies) شکست دینا ، زیر کرنا ، فتح پانا overcome (bad habits, etc.) قابُو پانا take possession of by force, esp. in war فتح کرنا ، لے لینا **conqueror** (konk-ĕ-rĕ*) one who defeats or captures فاتح one who overcomes something (پر) قابُو پانے والا

conquest (*kon*-kwest) *n* act of conquering فتح that which is conquered مفتوحہ (علاقے وغیرہ) (جمع مفتوحات)

consanguineous (kon-san-gwin-è-us) *adj.* kindred ; related by blood or birth قرابتدار ، ہم جَدّ between such persons قرابتداروں میں **consanguinity** (kon-san-*gwin*-i-ti) *n.* kinship ; relationship by blood or birth ہم جَدّ ہونا ، قرابت ، قرابتداری ، رشتہ داری ایک خُون

conscience (*kon*-shens) *n.* one's inner sense of right and wrong ضمیر *have a clear* (or *guilty*) *conscience* ضمیر صاف (یا مجرم) ہونا *have* (*something*) *on* (*one's*) *conscience*, feel troubled in (one's) conscience about (something) ضمیر کا ملامت کرنا ، دل میں کوئی خلش ہونا *conscience money*, money paid because one has a troubled conscience ضمیر کی ملامت دُور کرنے کے لیے ادا کردہ رقم (مثلاً ٹیکس) زرِ ایمانی **conscientious** (kon-shi-*en*-shus) *adj.* guided by one's sense of duty فرض شناس ، ایماندار ، بااُصُول *conscientious worker* فرض شناس ، کارکن یا ملازم done carefully and honestly ایماندارانہ ، بااُصُول *conscientious work* بااُصُول کام ، ایماندارانہ کام

conscious (*kon*-shus) *adj.* awake ہوش میں aware (*of*) (سے) واقف ، آگاہ ، باخبر *be conscious of* (*one's*) *guilt, be conscious that* (*one*) *is guilty* اپنے جُرم سے آگاہ ہونا (of actions, feelings, etc.) realized by oneself دانستہ ، سوچا سمجھا ، سوچ سمجھ کر *act with conscious superiority*, act with the feeling that one is superior برتری کے دانستہ احساس کے ساتھ self-conscious احساسِ کہتری کے باعث گھبرایا ہُوا ، شرمیلی قسم کا **consciously** *adj.* knowingly دانستہ **consciousness** (*kon*-shus-nes) *n.* state of being conscious آگاہی ، آگہی ، شعُور mental life شعُور **self-conscious** *adj.* shy ; too conscious of one's disabilities شرمیلی قسم کا ، احساسِ کہتری کے باعث گھبرایا ہُوا

conscript *v.t.* (kon-*skript*) compel (someone) by law to serve in the armed forces (فوج میں) جبری بھرتی کرنا call up for such service جبری بھرتی کے حکم کے تحت بلانا *n.* (*kon*-skript) one called up to serve in this way جبری بھرتی کیا جانے والا **conscription** (kon-*skrip*-shĕn) *n.* enlistment in this manner (فوج میں) جبری بھرتی

consecrate (*kon*-se-krayt) *v.t.* devote *to* a special purpose نذر یا وقف کرنا ، کسی دینی کام کے لئے مخصوص کرنا set apart as مُتبرّک یا مقدس قرار دے کر علیحدہ کرنا ، حُرمت عطا کرنا **consecration** (kon-se-*kray*-shĕn) act of consecrating نَذر ، وقف ، تقدیس ، تحریم

consecutive (kon-*sek*-ew-tiv) *adj.* following one after another continuously لگاتار ، متواتر ، مُسلسل (in grammar) (of clause) expressing consequence جوابِ شرط والا (جُملہ) **consecutively** *adv.* following (one) another without break لگاتار پے در پے

consensus (kon-*sen*-sus) *n.* common agreement (of opinion) موافقت ، ہم آہنگی *the general consensus of opinion on* (*this*) *issue* (اس) مسئلے پر ہر ایک کی رائے

consent (kon-*sent*) *v.t.* permit or agree *to* اجازت یا منظوری دینا ، رضامندی ظاہر کرنا *consent to a proposal* کوئی تجویز مان جانا *n.* agreement, approval اجازت ، منظوری ، رضامندی

consequence (*kon*-se-kwens) *n.* result, outcome نتیجہ ، انجام *in consequence* (*of*), as a result (of) نتیجۃً ، کے نتیجے میں importance اہمیت *people of consequence*, persons that matter اہم افراد *It is of no consequence*, it is unimportant یہ بات اہم نہیں ہے

consequent (*kon*-se-kwent) *adj.* (*consequent* or *consequent upon*), following as a consequent کے بعد ، کے نتیجے میں **consequential** (kon-se-*kwen*-shĕl) *adj.* following as a consequence ضمنی ، ذیلی (of person or manners) self-important بزعمِ خود

conservancy (kon-*sē**-van-si) *n.* board controlling river or port محکمۂ نگرانی (بندرگاہ وغیرہ)

official care (of forest, river, etc.) (جنگل دریا وغیرہ کی سرکاری نگرانی (Also see **conserve**)

conservative (kon-*sĕ**-va-tiv) *n.* & *adj.* (person) opposed to great or sudden change اعتدال پسند، انقلاب کا مخالف۔ (member of) British political party opposed to Socialist party (برطانوی) قدامت پسند (سیاسی جماعت) کنزرویٹیو *adj.* (colloq.) cautious محتاط lacking breadth of vision تنگ نظر fond of good old customs لکیر کا فقیر ، رجعت پسند moderate; purposely low کم ، کم از کم *conservative estimate* کم از کم اندازہ **conservatism** *n.* tendency in politics to resist sudden or great changes قدامت پسندی (Also see **conserve**) **conservation** *n.*, **conservator** *n.*, **conservatory** *n.* see under **conserve**

conservatoir (kon-sĕ*-va-*twah**) Continenal public-school of declamation and music خطابت و موسیقی کی یورپی درس گاہ

conserve *v.t.* (kon-*sĕ*v*) keep from, change, loss or destruction تحفظ کرنا ، بچانا ، بچائے رکھنا preserve in sugar مربہ ڈالنا *n.* (*kon*-se*v) jam مربہ **conservator** (*kon*-sĕ*-*vay*-tĕ*) *n.* protector; supervisor محافظ، محافظ ، نگران *conservator of forests* محافظ جنگلات **conservatory** (kon-*sĕ**-va-to-ri) *n.* glasshouse to protect plants from cold * پودگھر **conservation** (kon-sĕ*-*vay*-shĕn) *n.* prevention of loss or waste تحفظ ، بچاؤ

consider (kon-*sid*-ĕ*) *v.t.* & *i.* think over carefully غور کرنا ، سوچنا regard سمجھنا ، خیال کرنا make allowances for لحاظ کرنا ، خیال کرنا ، پاس کرنا *consider the feelings of others* دوسروں کے جذبات کا خیال کرنا reward بدلہ دینا ، معاوضہ دینا form an opinion رائے قائم کرنا ، (کی) رائے ہونا **considerable** (kon-*sid*-e-rè-bèl) *adj.* worthy of being considered قابلِ ذکر great بڑا much بہت **considerably** *adv.* much, quite بہت ، کافی **considerate** (kon-*sid*-e-rayt) *adj.* kindly, thoughtful (*of* the needs, etc., of others) بامروت ۔ بالحاظ ، (دوسروں کا) خیال رکھنے والا **consideration** (kon-sid-e-*ray*-shĕn) *n.* quality of being considerate لحاظ، مروت، پاس، ملاحظہ *in consideration of* (*something*), making allowance for it کے پیشِ نظر act of considering سوچ ، غور ، تامل *under consideration* زیرِ غور reward اجر compensation تلافی ، معاوضہ

considering (kon-*sid*-è-ring) *prep.* in view of بلحاظ ، کے لحاظ سے having regard to کے پیشِ نظر

consign (kon-*sin* *v.t.* send (goods by train, etc., *to* someone) (بذریعۂ ریل وغیرہ مال) بھیجنا ، ارسال کرنا deliver (*to*) سپرد کرنا ، حوالے کرنا **consignee** (kon-*si*-nee *n.* one to whom something is consigned جسے مال بھیجا جائے ، مرسل الیہ **consigner, consignor** *n.* one who sends a consignment مال بھیجنے والا ، مرسل **consignment** (kon-*sin*-ment) *n.* the act of consigning ترسیل goods consigned بھیجا ہوا مال ، مرسلہ مال

consist (kon-*sist*) *v.i.* (*consist of*), be composed of سے بننا ، سے مرکب ہونا (*consist in*), find expression in پر مشتمل ہونا **consistence, consistency** *n.* not being contradictary موافقت ، ہم آہنگی being constant in principles or behaviour یکسانی وضعداری ، استقامت ، بااصول ہونا (only *consistence*), density, degree of thickness of liquids گاڑھاپن ، ٹھوس پن ، دبازت *mix flour and water to the right consistence* پانی کی مناسب مقدار میں آٹا سانا **consistent** *adj.* (of person, or his behaviour) constant to his principles بااصول conforming to a regular pattern or style وضع دار (of things) compatible; not contradictory موافق *not consistent with*, contrary to کے متضاد ، سے ہم آہنگ سے متباین

console (kon-*sohl*) *v.t.* comfort (someone), sympathize with one who is unhappy تسلی دینا ، تشفی دینا ، دلاسا دینا ، آنسو پونچھنا ، دل جوئی کرنا **consolation** (kon-so-*lay*-shĕn) *n.* act of consoling دلاسا ، تسلی ، تشفی ، دل جوئی ، ڈھارس consoling circumstance تسلی **consolatory** (kon-*sol*-è-tè-ri) *adj.* that which provides some consolation ڈھارس بندھانے والا ، موجبِ تسلی

consolidate (kon-*sol*-i-dayt) *v.t.* & *i.* make or become strong مستحکم ہونا یا کرنا ، استوار ہونا یا کرنا solidify جمنا یا جمانا ، بستہ کرنا یا ہونا combine (territories, companies, debts, farms etc.) into one (علاقوں یا اداروں کا) الحاق یا ادغام کرنا، مدغم کرنا ، ملحق کرنا **consolidation** (kon-sol-i-*day*-shèn) *n.* act of consolidating استحکام ، پیوستگی ، اتحاد ، الحاق ، ادغام

consols (kon-*solz*) *n. pl.* British governmental securities consolidated into one (برطانوی حکومت کے) متحدہ تمسکاتِ قرض

consonant (*kon*-so-nant) *n.* non-vowel letter حرفِ صحیح sound of such a letter حرفِ صحیح کی آواز

consonance (*kon*-) *n.* agreement in sound موافقت ، ہم نوائی ، ہم آہنگی agreement in taste ہم مشربی *in consonance with*, according to, suited to کے مطابق ، سے ہم آہنگ **consonantal** *adj.* of a consonant حرفِ صحیح کا

consort (*kon*-so*t) *n.* husband or wife, زوج *prince consort*, reigning queen's husband ملکہ کا شوہر ، نواب ، دولہا *v.i.* (pr. kon-*soh*t*) (*consort with*), (*a*) pass much time in the company of ہر گھڑی ساتھ رہنا ،

ہم قدم رفاقت کرنا (*b*) be in harmony with سے ہم آہنگ ہونا

conspectus (kon-*spek*-tus) *n* synopsis, general outline (*of* a subject) مضمون کا خاکہ

conspicuous (kon-*spik*-ew-us) *adj* readily seen واضح ، بیّن attracting attention جاذبِ توجہ ، جاذبِ نظر eminent نمایاں اُبھرا ہُوا

conspiracy, conspirator *n* (see under **conspire**

conspire (kon-*spi*-è*) *v.i.* plot (*with* others *to do* wrong) (کی) سازش کرنا ، کے بیچھے سازباز یا گٹھ جوڑ کرنا combine (نا مساعد حالات کا) جمع ہو جانا ، شریک ہو جانا ، مل جل کر باعث بننا *All these circumstances conspired to bring about his failure* یہ تمام حالات مل جل کر اس کی ناکامی کے باعث بنے

conspirator (kon-*spi*-ra-tě*) *n.* (fem., *conspiratress*) one who conspires سازشی

conspiracy (kon-*spi*-ra-si) *n.* plotting (usu. for treason, etc.) (بغاوت وغیرہ کی) سازش ، گٹھ جوڑ ، سازباز plot سازش

constable (*kun*-sta-bèl) *n.* policeman سپاہی ، کانسٹیبل

constabulary (kon-*stab*-ew-la-ri) *n.* police force پولیس ، شُرطہ police force raised for the time being for a special purpose سپیشل پولیس ، کانسٹیبلری ، خصوصی پولیس

constancy (*kon*-stan-si) *n.* firmness استقلال ، استقامت ثابت قدمی ، اُستواری faithfulness وفاداری unchangingness وضعداری ، پاس وضع (Also see **constant**)

constant (*kon*-stant) *adj.* never-ending ہمیشہ کا ، دائمی ، مستقل steadfast ثابت قدم ، راسخ faithful وفادار ، باوفا neverchanging نہ بدلنے والا ، تغیر ناپذیر permanent مستقل ، پائندہ

constantly *adv.* often always ہمیشہ

constancy *n.* (see above)

constellation (kon-ste-*lay*-shěn) *n.* named group of fixed stars (ستاروں کا) جھرمٹ ، جھمکا یا جمع ، پکھشتر

consternation (kon-stě*-*nay*-shěn) *n.* terrified astonishment سراسیمگی ، یاس ، خوف و استعجاب dismay مایوسی ، یاس ، حزن

constipate (*kons*-sti-payt) *v.t* affect with constipation کو قبض ہونا ، قبض کرنا *be constipated* قابض ہونا

constipation (kon-sti-*pay*-shèn) *n.* difficulty in clearing out waste from the bowels قبض

constituency (kon-*stit*-ew-en-si) *n.* area sending a representative to parliament حلقۂ انتخاب persons or voters living in such an area کسی حلقۂ انتخاب کے رائے دہندگان یا باشندے

constituent (kon-*stit*-ew-ent) *adj.* having the power to make or change a constitution آئین ساز ، دستور ساز necessary to make up a whole لازمی ، جزء *a constituent part* جزو ترکیبی *n.* person having a parliamentary vote رائے دہندہ one who constitutes another as his or her agent (*e.g.* a person having an account with a bank is called a constituent) نمائندہ بنانے والا ، گماشتہ مقرر کرنے والا ، اختیار دینے والا

constitute (*kon*-sti-tewt) *v.t.* appoint, elect بنانا ، مقرر کرنا ، متعین کرنا ، نام زد کرنا set up مرتب کرنا ، کی تشکیل کرنا *constitute a commission*, set it up کمیشن مقرر کرنا make up (a whole) مشتمل ہونا ، ترکیب دینا amount to ہونا *This act constitutes a gross infringement of the law* یہ حرکت قانون کی سراسر خلاف ورزی ہے

constitution (kon-sti-*tew*-shèn) *n.* laws according to which a State or organization is governed (ملکی) آئین ، دستور ، دستور العمل structure of one's body بدن ، جسم ، جسم کی ساخت general physical condition صحت ، جسمانی حالت *His constitution is very weak* اس کی صحت بڑی خراب ہے general structure of a thing بناوٹ ، ساخت ، ترکیب one's mental qualities and nature دماغ کی حالت ، دماغی قوائن

constitutional (kon-sti-*tew*-shu-nèl) *adj.* having to do with the constitution of a State آئینی *constitutional monarch*, ruler controlled by a constitution آئینی حکمران

constitutionally *adv.* in accordance with the constitution آئینی طور پر ، آئین کے لحاظ سے

constitutionalism *n.* constitutional government آئینی حکومت ، مشروطہ belief in such form of government آئین پسندی (Also see **constituency** *n.*, **constituent** *n.* & *adj.*, **constitute** *v.t.*)

constrain (kon-*strayn*) *v.t.* compel (*to do* something or *to* some course of action) (پر) مجبور کرنا

constrained (kon-straynd) *adj.* forced پابندی کا ، مجبوری کا ، مجبور آ کیا جانے والا un-natural غیر طبعی ، دباؤ uneasy تکلیف دہ

constraint *n.* compulsion دباؤ ، مجبوری ، پابندی *act under constraint* دباؤ میں آ کر کام کرنا ، مجبوراً کام کرنا

constrict (kon-*strikt*) *v.t.* cause (a muscle) to become tight کھچاؤ پیدا کرنا ، سکیڑنا encircle and squeeze انقباض پیدا کرنا

constricted (-tid) *adj.* narrow (outlook, etc.)

constriction (kon-*strik*-shèn) *n.* such tightening کھچاؤ ، انقباض

construct (kon-*strukt*) *v.t.* build بنانا ، تعمیر کرنا put or fit together جوڑنا ، تیار کرنا ، بنانا ، گھڑنا

construction (kon-*struk*-shěn) *n.* act or manner of constructing تعمیر ، ساخت *under construction*, being constructed زیر تعمیر thing constructed عمارت ، بنی ہوئی چیز ، تعمیر sense, meaning معنی ، مفہوم ، مطلب *put a wrong construction on* (*what someone says* or *does*) (کسی کی بات) کا اُلٹا مطلب لینا

constructive (-truk-) *adj.* helping to construct بنانے میں کام آنے والا giving suggestions that help تعمیری ، اصلاحی

constructor (kon-*struk*-tě*) *n.* one who constructs

بنانے والا ، مستری ، معمار

construe (kon-*strew*) *v.t.* & *i.* put interpretation (on words, etc.) تاویل کرنا ، معنی لگانا ، مطلب نکالنا ، مفہوم سمجھنا (grammar) analyse (a sentence) ترکیب نحوی کرنا combine (words with words) grammatically (الفاظ کو باہم) ترکیب دینا

consul (*kon*-sul) *n.* representative of a State in a foreign city to protect the interests of his countrymen there نائب سفیر، قنصل one of the two chief magistrates of the State in the early Roman Republic (قدیم روما کا) حاکم اعلیٰ **consular** (*kon*-sew-lĕ*) *adj.* of a consul قنصل کا، قنصلی

consult (kon-*sult*) *v.t.* go to (a person or book) for information or advice (سے) رجوع کرنا، (سے) پوچھنا، (میں) دیکھنا، (سے) مشورہ کرنا ، (سے) صلاح کرنا *consult a dictionary*, look up a word in it لغات میں لفظ کے معنے دیکھنا *consult (one's) lawyer*, seek his advice وکیل سے مشورہ کرنا take into account, make allowance for (کو) دیکھنا (کا) خیال کرنا ، (کا) لحاظ کرنا (کو) پیش نظر رکھنا ، (کو) مدّ نظر رکھنا *consult (someone's) convenience* کسی کی سہولت کو مدّ نظر رکھنا **consultant** *n.* expert from whom one seeks special advice مشیر، مشیر خصوصی **consultation** *n.* act of consulting صلاح مشورہ meeting for this purpose صلاح مشورے کے لیے جمع ہونا ، مُشاوَرت

consume (kon-*sewm*) *v.t.* & *i.* eat or drink کھانا پینا use up برت ڈالنا ، ختم کر دینا spend lavishly اُڑا دینا ، ضائع کرنا ، کھا پی لینا spend استعمال میں لانا ، خرچ کرنا ، صَرف کرنا destroy (by fire, etc.) بھسم کرنا ، خاک سیاہ کر دینا ، برباد کر ڈالنا *be consumed with*, be filled with (a passion) (حسد وغیرہ کے مارے) جلنا *consume away*, waste away بُھننا ، کباب ہونا ، گھلنا ، گھل گھل کر مرنا **consumer** (kon-*sew*-mĕ*) *n.* person who uses goods (as opposed to the *producer*) صارِف *consumer goods*, goods consumed (as opposed to *capital goods*) اشیائے صَرف

consummate *adj.* (kon-*sum*-et) perfect, complete نہایت، انتہائی، کامل، غایت *consummate skill*, perfect skill نہایت مہارت *v.t.* (*kon*-sum-ayt) make perfect or complete کمال کرنا ، درجہ کمال کو پہنچانا bring to a perfect finish مکمل کرنا، تکمیل کرنا ، پایۂ تکمیل کو پہنچانا *consummate marriage*, co-habitate for the first time after marriage خلوت صحیحہ کرنا **consummation** (kon-su-*may*-shĕn) *n.* تکمیل ، اِتمام **consummator** *n.* (*kon*-sum-ay-tĕ*) one who consummates تکمیل کرنے والا ، اِتمام کرنے والا

consumption (kon-*sump*-shĕn) *n.* consuming کھانا ، پینا use خرچ ، استعمال ، صَرف using up خاتمہ the amount consumed خرچ شدہ مقدار ، خرچ ہونے والی مقدار tuberculosis سِل ، دِق any wasting disease گھلا دینے والا مرض **consumptive** (kon-*sump*-tiv) *adj.* & *n.* (person) suffering or likely to suffer from consumption مدقوق ، سِل زدہ ، دِق کا مارا ہوا (یا) دِق کی ماری ہوئی ،

contact (*kon*-takt) *n.* (lit.) touch چھونا ، لمس meeting اِتّصال relation رَبط ، تعلّق *in contact with*, in communication with سے رابطہ قائم رکھے ہوئے *come into contact* (سے) ملنا ، (سے) دوچار ہونا person likely to carry contagion through contact with one already infected جس کو چھوت سے بیماری لگنے کا اِمکان ہو۔ *v.t.* (colloq.) get into touch with سے رابطہ قائم کرنا

contact lens *n.* (see *Addenda*)

contagion (kon-*tay*-jen) *n.* spreading disease چھوت ، متعدّی مَرض *contagion is spreading* وَبا پھیل رہی ہے corrupting moral influence اخلاقی خرابی ، برائی کا متعدّی اثر **contagious** (kon-*tay*-jus) *adj.* (disease) spreading by touch چھوت والی ، متعدّی ، وَبائی ، اُڑنی یا لگنی بیماری spreading easily by example متعدّی

contain (kon-*tayn*) *v.t.* hold, include پر مشتمل ہونا ، (کا) حاصِل ہونا restrain (feelings, etc.) (جذبات وغیرہ پر) قابو پانا hold (enemy force) from moving دشمن کو روکنا ، گھیرے میں لیے ہوئے ہونا (geometry) form the boundary of حدّ بننا ، حدّ بندی کرنا **container** *n.* vessel, box, bottle, etc. for holding something کوئی شے رکھنے کے لیے ڈِبّہ بوتل وغیرہ ، چیز دان **containment** (-tayn-) *n.* (see *Addenda*)

contaminate (kon-*tam*-i-nayt) *v.t.* pollute آلودہ کرنا ، ناپاک کرنا ، نجس کرنا infect (میں) جراثیم پہنچانا **contamination** (kon-tam-i-*nay*-shĕn) *n.* pollution آلودگی ، نجاست infection چھوت (also) blending of two tales, etc. مختلف کہانیوں کو باہم ملانا ، خلط ملط کرنا

contemplate (*kon*-temp-layt) *v.t.* look at attentively غور سے دیکھنا think about deeply گہری سوچ میں ہونا ، دھیان میں ہونا *contemplate (doing)*, intend to do (کوئی کام کرنے کا) ارادہ کرنا **contemplation** (kon-temp-*lay*-shĕn) *n.* غور و فکر ، دھیان ، تصوّر ، استغراق ، مُراقبہ **contemplative** (kon-*temp*-la-tiv, or *kon*-temp-lay-tiv) *adj.* thoughtful باغور ، ہوشمندانہ given to contemplation غور و فکر والا ، مستغرِق

contemporaneous *adj.* (see under **contemporary**)

contemporary (kon-*temp*-o-ra-ri) *adj.* & *n.* (person) belonging to or living at the same time ہم عصر ، مُعاصِر (thing) belonging to the same period اُس زمانے کا ، مُعاصِرانہ ، ہم عصری *a contemporary record of events*, (record made by persons then living) مُعاصِرانہ شہادت **contemporaneous** (kon-temp-o-*ray*-ni-us) *adj.* of the same time ہم عہد ، ہم عصر ، مُعاصِرانہ *contemporaneous events* ایک ہی زمانے کے واقعات

contempt (kon-*tempt*) *n.* state of being despised حقارت ، ذلّت ، سُبکی *fall into contempt by bad behaviour*

بڑے طرزِ عمل کے باعث ذلیل ہونا scorn توہین، تذلیل *feel contempt for, show (one's) contempt of* ذلیل سمجھنا، دکو *contempt of court*, disrespect shown to a judge or failure to obey his orders توہینِ عدالت **contemptible** (kon-*temp*-ti-bèl) *adj*. deserving contempt قابلِ مذمت، لائقِ مذمت **contemptuous** (kon-*temp*-tew-us) *adj*. person showing contempt of others متکبر attitude of contempt حقارت آمیز، ذلت آمیز، متکبرانہ

contend (kon-*tend*) *v.i.* struggle, جدوجہد کرنا fight مقابلہ کرنا compete (*with someone for* something) آگے بڑھنے کی کوشش کرنا، مسابقت کی سعی کرنا *contending passions*, strong feelings of various kinds that make it difficult for one to decide باہم آویزاں جذبات، ڈبدھے میں ڈالنے والے جذبات، argue (*that*) بحث کرنا، مجادلہ کرنا، حجت پیش کرنا **contention** (kon-*ten*-shĕn) *n*. argument used in contending حجت، دلیل *my* (etc.) *contention is (that), it is my* (etc.) *contention (that)* میری دلیل یہ ہے کہ، میں اس بات پر زور دے رہا ہوں کہ، میں یہ بات کہتا ہوں کہ contending جدوجہد، مسابقہ، مجادلہ، من تُشتہ **contentious** (kon-*ten*-shus) *adj*. fond of contending کٹ حجتی، جھگڑالو likely to cause contention متنازع فیہ

content *adj*. (kon-*tent*) satisfied with what one has صابر، صابر شاکر، قانع، مطمئن، راضی not wanting more قانع *content to (do something)*, willing to (do it) پر صابر و شاکر، پر قانع *n*. (kon-*tent*) state of being content قناعت، صبر، صبر و شکر، اطمینان (pr. *kon*-tent, or kon-*tent*) (usu. *pl*.) that which is contained in something مضمون، مافیہ، محتویات *the contents of a book* کتاب کا مضمون (pr. *kon*-tent) (usu. *pl*.) the amount which something contains میں جو کچھ ہے، کسی چیز کا مافیہ *the contents of the packet* پلندے میں جو کچھ ہے *v.t.* (pr. kon-*tent*) make content قانع کرنا satisfy مطمئن کرنا، راضی کرنا **contented** (kon-*ten*-tèd) *adj*. satisfied مطمئن، راضی، قانع، صابر، صابر و شاکر **contentment** (-*tent*-) *n*. state of being content قناعت، صبر، صبر و شکر

contention *n*. **contentious** *adj*. (see under **contend**)

contest (kon-*test*) *v.t.* & *i*. struggle سعی کرنا، جد و جہد کرنا compete (*for* prize, honour, etc.) مقابلے میں حصہ لینا argue against کے خلاف دلیل پیش کرنا یا لانا *n*. (*kon*-test) struggle جدوجہد fight مقابلہ، مبارزت competition مقابلہ، مسابقہ **contestant** (kon-*tes*-tant) *n*. one taking part in a contest مقابلے میں حصہ لینے والا، مقابل person contesting a statement فریقِ بحث، حریف

context (*kon*-tekst) *n*. what comes before and after (a word or statement) helping to fix the meaning اوپر نیچے کی عبارت، سیاق و سباق، سلسلۂ بیان، سیاقِ عبارت *in this context* اس سلسلے میں *in the same context* اس سلسلے میں **contextual** (kon-*teks*-tew-al) *adj*. of or pertaining to the context سیاقی، بسیاقِ عبارت سے متعلق

contiguous (kon-*tig*-ew-us) *adj*. touching متصل neighbouring ہمسائیگی میں، ہمسایہ next to ملحق، بغلی **contiguity** (kon-ti-*gew*-i-ti) *n*. being contiguous اتصال، مقاربت

continence *n*. (see under **continent**)

continent (*kon*-ti-nent) *n*. one of the large divisions of the earth's surface برِّ اعظم *the Continent*, Europe excluding the British Isles جزائرِ برطانیہ کے علاوہ برِاعظم یورپ *adj*. having self-control پرہیزگار، پارسا **continental** (-*nent*-) *adj*. having to do with any continent برِاعظم کا of the mainland of Europe یورپی، اُروپائی **continence** (*kon*-) *n*. self-control پرہیزگاری، پارسائی

contingency (kon-*tin*-jen-si) *n*. possible event امکان، اتفاق، اتفاقی حالات: ناگہانی حادثہ something that happens if something else happens اتفاق، حالتِ منتظرہ

contingent (kon-*tin*-jent) *adj*. uncertain غیر یقینی accidental اتفاقیہ، اتفاقی، ہنگامی dependent (*on* something) مشروط، پر موقوف *n*. troops or ships sent out to join a larger force امدادی فوج

continual *adj*. **continually** *adv*. (see under **continue**)

continue (kon-*tin*-ew) *v. t.* & *i*. go further without break جاری رہنا یا رکھنا، برقرار رہنا یا رکھنا *continue to be or to do, continue being or doing* ہوتا، رہنا یا کرتے رہنا stay *in* or *at* رہنا start again after stopping دوبارہ شروع کرنا، سلسلہ اُٹھانا *continued from page 2* صفحہ دو سے آگے، بقیہ صفحہ دو *to be continued*, (of an article, etc.) the next part to appear later باقی پھر **continual** (kon-*tin*-ew-ĕl) *adj*. continuing with only short breaks لگاتار، متواتر، پے در پے **continually** *adv*. in a continual manner لگاتار، متواتر، پے در پے **continuous** (kon-*tin*-ew-us) *adj*. continuing without break مسلسل، غیر منقطع **continuance** (kon-*tin*-ew-ans) *n*. (esp.) time for which something continues

continuation (kon-tin-ew-*ay*-shĕn) *n*. continuing جاری رہنا part, etc., by which something is continued مزید، بقیہ *the continuation of the short story is on page 89*, (بقیہ افسانہ بر صفحہ ۸۹) **continuity** (kon-ti-*new*-ti) *n*. going on without a break دوام، تسلسل

contort (kon-to*t) *v.t.* twist (face, body, etc.) out of shape مروڑنا، بل دینا، اینٹھنا **contortion** (kon-to*-shĕn) *n*. violent twisting of muscles تشنج، مروڑ، اینٹھن، اینٹھنا **contortionist** *n*. acrobat who twists

his muscles نٹ ، عضلہ نٹ
contour (*kon*-too-ĕ*) *n.* outline map showing height or boundary نشیب و فراز اور حدود دکھانے والا خاکہ outline of a figure جسم کے اُبھار *contour line*, line on a map showing all points at the same height above sea-level خطِ تراز ، خطِ ارتفاع *contour map*, map with contour lines at fixed intervals (*e.g.*, of 100 feet) ارتفاع نما خاکہ ، حدود نما خاکہ
contra- (kon-tra) *pref.* against مخالف ، برعکس ، علی الرغم ، (سابقہ) غیر ، (لاحقہ) : شکن
contraband (*kon*-tra-band) *n.* smuggling ناجائز درآمد و برآمد ، ممنوع تجارت ، smuggled goods ممنوع مال *contraband of war*, goods which neutral countries are not allowed to supply to one belligerent or the other ممنوع جنگی مال
contract *n.* (*kon*-trakt) legal agreement (between persons or States) معاہدہ ، عہد نامہ ، میثاق *contract bridge*, form of card-game in which only those tricks count towards the result as are bid and won میثاقی برج business agreement to supply goods or do work, at a fixed price ٹھیکہ *v.t.* & *i.* (kon-*trakt*) make a contract ٹھیکہ دینا یا لینا *contract to* (*do something*), (کسی کام) کا ٹھیکہ لینا *contract a marriage* شادی کرنا become liable for سر لینا *contract debts* اپنے سر قرض چڑھانا catch (a disease) (بیماری) مول لینا acquire (a friendship) دوستی کرنا form (bad habits) (بُری عادتیں) اختیار کرنا draw closer together سمٹنا ، یا سمیٹنا make or become smaller or narrower سکڑنا یا سکیڑنا *metals contract as they become cool* دھاتیں ٹھنڈی ہو کر سکڑتی ہیں shorten (esp. words by dropping vowel-sounds ; as : *don't* from *do not*) مختصر کرنا **contractor** (kon *trak*-tĕ*) *n.* maker of a contract, esp. the builder who works by contract ٹھیکیدار **contraction** (kon-*trak*-shĕn) *n.* shrinking or contracting اینٹھن **contractile** (kon-*trak*-til) *adj.* (of wings, undercarriage, etc.) that which can contract or be folded close to the (main) body سمٹ جانے والا ، سکڑ جانے والا ، ساتھ لگ جانے والا
contradict (kon-tra-*dikt*) *v.t.* deny (statement, etc.) or say (*that* something) is not true تردید کرنا (of facts) be contrary to کے اُلٹ ہونا ، کے برعکس ہونا **contradiction** (kon-tra-*dik*-shĕn) *n.* تردید ، تضاد **contradictory** (kon-tra-*dik*-to-ri) *n.* conflicting متضاد conveying contradiction تردیدی
contralto (kon-trahl-toh) *n.* woman's deep voice زنانہ مدھم آواز singer with such voice مدھم گانے والی ، مدھم
contraption (kon-*trap*-shĕn) *n.* (slang) strange looking machine or device انوکھی کل (یا) ڈھنگ
contrariety *n.*, **contrarily** *adv.*, **contrariness** *n.* (see under **contrary**)
contrary (*kon*-tra-ri) *adj.* opposite متضاد ، مخالف opposite (*to* something) کے برخلاف ، (کے) برعکس ، (کے) *contrary wind*, wind unfavourable for sailing بادِ مخالف (colloq.) obstinate ضدی ، خود سر ، خود رائے *adv.* in opposition to ; against کے برخلاف ، کے برعکس *n.* (*the contrary*), the opposite بالکل اُلٹ ، بالکل برعکس *on the contrary* نہیں بلکہ *to the contrary*, to the opposite effect اِس کے برعکس **contrariety** (kon-tra-*rī*-e-ti), **contrariness** *n.* being contrary تخالف ، تباین ، تضاد **contrarily** (-*tra*-) *adv.* on the contrary نہیں بلکہ ، اِس کے برعکس
contrast *v.t.* & *i.* (kon-*trahst*) compare (one thing *with* another) so as to show the difference مُقابلہ کرنا ، محاکمہ کرنا ، موازنہ کرنا show a difference when compared فرق دکھنا ، مقابلہ کر کے جانچنا *n.* (*kon*-trahst) the act of contrasting مُقابلہ ، محاکمہ ، موازنہ difference noticeable when unlikes are put together نمایاں فرق ، امتیاز something showing such difference *to* (کے مقابلے میں) ممتاز ، (کی) بہ نسبت نمایاں (سے) فرق
contravene (kon-tra-*veen*) *v.t.* act against (a custom, etc.) کے خلاف کرنا break (a law) قانون کی خلاف ورزی کرنے والا challenge (a statement, etc.) اعتراض کرنا ، ٹوکنا (of things) be out of harmony with آپس میں ٹکرانا ، مُعارض ہونا **contravention** (kon-tra-*ven*-shĕn) *n.* act of contravening خلاف ورزی *in contravention of*, contrary to کے برخلاف
contretemps, (*kon*-tre-ton) *n.* unexpected hitch سوئے اتفاق ، بدنصیبی unfortunate happening ناگہانی رکاوٹ
contribute (kon-*trib*-ewt) *v.t.* & *i.* give along with others (money, etc., *to* a common cause) فراہم کرنا ، مہیا کرنا ، چندہ دینا supply help *to* produce کا سبب بننا ، میں ممد ہونا write and send for publication (articles, etc. *to* a periodical) اخبار یا رسالے میں مضمون لکھنا **contribution** (kon-tri-*bew*-shĕn) *n.* act of contributing چندہ دینا ، فراہم کرنا ، سبب بننا something contributed چندہ ، امداد ، مضمون ، مقالہ **contributor** (kon-*trib*-ew-tĕ*) *n.* one who contributes money چندہ دینے والا one who helps to produce something ممد one who writes articles for periodicals مضمون نگار **contributory** (kon-*trib*-ew-to-ri) *adj.* that which helps امدادی
contrite (*kon*-trīt) *adj.* filled with deep sorrow for sin نادم ، پشیمان ، متأسف ، تائب **contrition** (kon-*trish*-ĕn) *n.* being contrite ندامت ، پشیمانی ، توبہ
contrivance *n.* (see under **contrive**)
contrive (kon-*trīv*) *v.t.* & *i.* invent اختراع کرنا ، بنانا ، ترکیب ڈھونڈنا plan (something or *to do* something) کی تدبیر نکالنا یا کرنا get along, manage (some-

thing) بند و بست کرنا ، انتظام چلانا ، جتن کرنا **contrivance** (kon-*trī*-vans) *n.* something contrived تدبیر ، حیلہ ، ترکیب (esp.) an invention or apparatus ایجاد ، اختراع

control (kon-*trohl*) *n.* rule ; authority to direct and restrain اختیار ، اقتدار ، تسلط *have control over (someone)* (کسی پر) اختیار رکھنا یا تسلط ہونا *lose* (or *get*) *control over* (or *of something*) کسی پر اختیار کھو دینا (یا پانا) means of regulating تالا ، نگرانی ، کنٹرول *get under control*, curb پر قابو پانا *control of traffic* سڑکوں پر آمد و رفت میں باقاعدگی *government control of (something)* سرکاری کنٹرول ، سرکاری پیدا کرنا نگرانی ، حکومت کی طرف سے جانچ پڑتال (usu. *pl.*) means by which machines are operated مشین کی حرکت کو قابو کرنے کے پرزے ، قابو کُن ، *at the controls of an aircraft* ہوائی جہاز کے قابو کُن پر بیٹھنا *v.t.* hold in check, restrain روکنا ، ضبط کرنا ، قابو میں رکھنا *control (one's) temper* اپنے غصے پر قابو پانا keep in order چالو رکھنا rule پر حکومت کرنا ، (پر) تسلط قائم رکھنا ، **controller** (or older spelling still preserved by certain departments) **comptroller** (kon-*troh*-lĕ*) *n.* person who controls ناظم ، ناظر *the Regional Transport Contoller* علاقائی ناظم نقل و حمل

controversial *adj.* (see under **controversy**)

controversy (*kon*-tro-vĕ*-si) *n.* prolonged argument (*over* some issue) مُباحثہ ، مناقشہ ، قیل و قال disagreement نزاع *beyond controversy*, certain ; above doubt پکا ، یقینی ، لازمی **controversial** (kon-tro-*vĕ**-shĕl) *adj.* likely to cause controversy مابہ النزاع (of a person) fond of controversy حُجتی **controvert** (kon-tro-*vĕ*t*) *v.t.* call in question زیر بحث لانا bring argument against کے خلاف دلائل لانا deny (statement, argument, etc.) کی شرط پہ کرنا

contumacious (kon-tew-*may*-shus) *adj.* (lit.) stubbornly disobedient نافرمان ، سرکش ، شورہ پشت

contumacy (*kon*-tew-ma-si) *n.* (lit.) stubborn disobedience نافرمانی ، سرکشی ، شورہ پشتی

contumely (*kon*-tew-mee-li or -mi-) *n.* insulting language or treatment ڈھٹائی ، زبان درازی ، توہین آمیز زبان یا سلوک

contuse *v.t.* bruise گُمّی مار مارنا **contusion** (kon-*tew*-zhĕn) *n.* bruise گُمّی مار مارنا ، گُپٹ مار

conundrum (ko-*nun*-drum) *n.* riddle with a pun پہیلی ، چیستان anything of a perplexing nature مُعمّا ، چکّر میں ڈالنے والی بات

convalesce *v.i.* **convalescence** *n.* see under **convalescent**

convalescent (kon-va-*les*-ent) *n.* & *adj.* (person) recovering from illness رو بہ صحت مریض ، افاقہ یاب **convalescence** (kon-va-*les*-ens) *n.* state of recovering from illness اِفاقہ **convalesce** (kon-va-*les*) *v.i.*, be in a state of convalescence افاقہ پانا ، کی حالت میں ہونا

convene (kon-*veen*) *v.t.* & *i.* call (persons) together for a meeting (اجلاس کے لیے) بلانا ، منعقد کرنا یا طلب کرنا come together for a meeting (اجلاس کے لیے) اجلاس طلب کرنا ، بلانا ، منعقد call (a meeting) جمع کرنا **convener** (kon-*vee*-nĕ*) *n.* one who convenes داعی ، کنوینر **convention** *n.* (see below)

convenience (kon-*vee*-ni-ens) suitability of something to one's needs مناسبت ، موزونیت something suitable to one's needs سہولت handy device کارآمد شے یا تدبیر ، *conveniences in a house*, bathroom and lavatory غسل خانہ یا پاخانہ وغیرہ *make a convenience, of (someone)*, use (his) willing services unreasonably کسی کی نیک دلی سے فائدہ اٹھانا ، کسی کو آسامی بنانا leisure فرصت ، فراغت *at your convenience*, whenever you wish جب آپ چاہیں self-interest غرض مندی ، غرض ، فائدہ *marriage of convenience*, one for worldly advantages and not for love غرض مندی کی شادی ، روپے پیسے کے لیے شادی (*pl.*) personal comforts آسائش ، آرام **convenient** (kon-*vee*-ni-ent) *adj.* suitable مناسب ، موزوں commodious کشادہ ، وسیع not troublesome ، آرام دہ ، پُر آسائش **conveniently** *adv.* so as to be convenient مناسب طور پر ، آرام دہ طور پر

convent (*kon*-vent) *n.* religious community of Christian women (called *nuns*) living apart from others گروہِ راہبات place where they live عیسائی خانقاہ ، دیرِ راہبات *go into a convent*, become a nun راہبہ بن جانا

convention (kon-*ven*-shĕn) *n.* specially called formal meeting of persons for a definite object ; convening *of* خصوصی اجتماع ، اجتماع ، کنونشن agreement between States, etc. (less formal than a treaty) معاہدہ ، تراضی practice established by tacit consent of majority رواج etiquette based on it ریت ، رسم accepted method of bidding at bridge or of playing various other card games تاش میں بولی دینے یا بازی لگانے کا بندھا ہوا دستور دستور **conventional** *adj.* depending on convention, not natural رواجی ، رسمی ، تقلیدی *conventional greetings* سلام دعا (of art) lacking in original thought, traditional مبتذل ، رسمی ، غیر تخلیقی ، تقلیدی **conventionality** (-nal-) *n.* formality رسم پرستی ، وضعداری

converge (kon-*vĕ*j*) *v.t.* & *i.* (of lines or opinions) tend to come together ایک ہی طرف مائل ہونا یا کرنا ، تمیل کلی ، استقران **convergent** *adj.* approaching مائل کلی **convergence** *n.* a converging *upon* (کی طرف) میلان

conversable *adj*. see under **converse**
conversant (*kon*-vě*-sant) *adj*. having a knowledge of ماہر ، سے خوب واقف *He is conversant with it* وہ اس بات کا ماہر ہے۔
conversation(*kon*-ve*-say-shěn) *n*. informal talk (*with* one another) بات چیت ، گفتگو **conversation piece,** (see *Addenda*) **conversational** *adj* fond of conversation باتونی ، باتوں کا شوقین (of words, etc.) free and easy as used in conversation بول چال کے (الفاظ وغیرہ) عام آسان یا سہل (الفاظ وغیرہ) (Also see **converse**)
converse *v.i.* (kon-*vě*s*) talk or chat (with) باتیں کرنا ، بات چیت کرنا *n*. & *adj*. (*kon*-vě*s) familiar talk (*with* somebody *about* or on something) بات چیت ، باتیں idea or statement opposite (*of* another) اُلٹ ، عکس ، ضد ، قلب ، منقلب ، معکوس **conversely** *adv*. taking the opposite کے اُلٹ ، بالعکس **conversable** *adj*. pleasant in conversation خوش گفتار fond of conversation باتونی ، باتوں کا رسیا (also see **conversation**) ▣ We have a **dialogue** in the stage or in a story ; a **discourse** when it is learned and formal ; a **colloquy** when informal ; a **talk**, a **lecture** by one person, esp. on the radio ; **intercourse** of any kind ; **conversation** when it is familiar and informal ; and **colloquium** when formal and on a very large scale.
conversion (kon-*vě**-shěn) *n*. (see under **convert**)
convert *v.t.* (kon-*vě*t*) change (*from* one form, etc., *into* another) ایک حالت سے دُوسری حالت میں بدلنا ، تبدیل کرنا exchange for something else (کسی دُوسری چیز سے) بدلنا ، مبادلہ کرنا (*convert to*), (cause a person) to change his professed religious beliefs to other beliefs (عقیدہ یا رائے یا مذہب) بدلنا یا بدلانا ، (نیا مذہب) قبول کرنا (بنئے مذہب میں) آنا یا لانا *n*. (*kon*-vě*t) person converted *to* a religious belief نَو ، (سابقہ) نَو مذہب ، *a convert to Islam* نَو مُسلم **conversion** (kon *vě**-shěn) *n*. change or being changed تبدیلی ، تغیّر change of heart اِنابت ، رُجُوع اِلی اللہ **convertible** (kon-*vě*t*-i-bèl) *adj*. that can be converted (*into* something else) تبدیلی کے قابل ، تغیر پذیر ، مبادلہ پذیر
convertiplane *n*. (see *Addenda*)
convex (*kon*-veks)*adj*. with the surface curved like the outside of a ball محدّب *convex mirror* محدّب شیشہ *convex lens* محدّب عدسہ **convexity** *n*. being convex محدّب ہونا convex surface محدّب ہونا

CONCAVE
CONVEX

convey (kon-*vay*) *v.t.* take from one place to another منتقل کرنا ، لے جانا communicate news, ideas, etc. پہنچانا (law) give (someone) full legal rights (in property) وجائیداد کا ، انتقال کرنا
conveyance (kon-*vay*-ans) *n*. the act of conveying ترسیل ، ایصال ، پہنچانا something which conveys پہنچنے یا پہنچانے کا ذریعہ vehicle سواری (law) agreement for conveying property انتقال (جائیداد) document of such agreement دستاویز انتقال **conveyer** *n*. person or thing that conveys پہنچانے والا (esp.) endless belt for moving goods ترسیل پٹی **conveyancing** *n*. drawing up of conveyance deeds دستاویز نویسی ، نقل نویسی
conveyancer *n*. one who draws up such deeds (انتقالِ جائیداد کے لیے) دستاویز نویس ، نقل نویس
convict *v.t.* (kon-*vikt*) prove guilty مجرم قرار دینا ، مجرم ثابت کرنا *convict (someone) in a court of law*, declare in a law-court that he or she is guilty of crime and sentence him or her (عدالت کا) کسی کو سزا سنانا ، سزا کا حکم دینا *n*. (*kon*-vikt) criminal مجرم felon گناہگار one undergoing punishment سزا یافتہ سزایاب (poetry) جفاکار ، ستمگر **conviction** (kon-*vik*-shěn) *n*. convicting a person of crime سزایابی ، ثبوتِ جرم the act of convincing یقین دلانا ، اثباتِ جرم ، اذعان کلی *carry conviction*, be credible قابلِ یقین ہونا *It doesn't carry conviction* اس کا یقین نہیں آتا ، یقین کرنے کی یہ بات نہیں firm belief پکا یقین ، پختہ یقین ، یقینِ کامل
convince (kon-*vins*) *v.t.* make (someone) feel certain (*of* something) منوا لینا ، یقین دلانا ، باور کرانا **conviction** *n*. (see under **convict**), **convincing** *adj*. that carries conviction یقین بخش ▣ We **convince** by serious arguments, but **persuade** when we influence one to action. Do not **confuse** *convince* with *convict* which means to find guilty
convivial (kon-*viv*-i-al) *adj*. fond of drinking and merry-making زندہ دل ، یار باش ، پینے پلانے والا *convivial companions* ہم مشرب of or for a feast جشن کا ، کھانے پینے کا ، پینے پلانے کا دعوتی ، دعوت کا festive *convivial evening* شب عیش ، پینے پلانے کی رات
convoke (kon-*vohk*) *v.t.* call together (a meeting) (اجلاس) منعقد کرنا **convocation** (kon-vo-*kay*-shěn) *n*. convoking انعقاد meeting of a university, etc., to award degrees جلسۂ تقسیمِ اسناد اِحتفالِ جامعہ **convokable** *adj*. that which can be summoned انعقاد پذیر
convolute (kon-vo-*loot*), **convoluted** (-id) *adj*. (in natural history) coiled بل کھایا ہوا ، ملفوف **convolution** (*-loo-*) *n*. coiled state بل کھائے ہوئے ہونا ملفوف ہونا one turn of the coil پیچ ، خم
convoy *v.t.* (kon-*voy*) escort رہنمائی کرنا ، اعزاز یا حفاظت کے لیے ساتھ چلنا (esp. of a warship) escort (other ships) to protect (them) (جہاز کیساتھ) حفاظتی بدرقہ دینا

n. (*kon*-voi) the act of convoying رہنمائی ، حفاظت protecting force (of ships, etc.) مسلح حفاظتی دستہ (یا جہاز) ، بدرقہ mercantile ships sailing together for self-protection تجارتی بیڑا

convulse (kon-*vuls*) *v.t.* disturb violently ہلا دینا ، جھنجھوڑ دینا ، قیامت برپا کرنا ، ہل چل پیدا کرنا ، کھلبلی مچا دینا *country convulsed with war* جس ملک میں جنگ سے ہل چل پیدا ہو گئی ہو shake with laughter ہنسی سے لوٹ پوٹ ہو جانا (ہنستے ہنستے) پیٹ میں بل پڑ جانا ، لوٹ جانا *person convulsed with laughter* جو ہنسی سے لوٹ پوٹ ہو جائے **convulsion** (kon-*vul*-shĕn) *n.* sudden uncontrollable laughter بے اختیار ہنسی ، ہنسی کی پھرتی violent disturbance ہل چل ، کھلبلی (*pl.*) (usu. infantile) disorder with muscular spasms * اینٹھن **convulsive** (-vul-) *adj.* (like that) of convulsion لوٹ پوٹ کر دینے والا ، کھلبلی مچا دینے والا

cony, coney (*koh*-ni) *n.* rabbit's fur prepared to look like some other animal's خرگوش کی بدلی ہوئی شکل والی کھال

coo (koo) *n.* soft, murmuring sound of a bird (کبوتر وغیرہ کی) غٹرغوں *v.i.* make such a sound چہچہانا (also *bill and coo*) talk lovingly in a soft voice مچھلے پچھلے پیار کی باتیں کرنا

cook (kŭk) *v.t.* & *i.* make food ready for eating by heat کھانا پکانا ، پکانا ، ریندھنا falsify جعلسازی کرنا *to cook accounts*, to prepare false accounts جعلی حساب تیار کرنا *n.* one who prepares food خانساماں ، باورچی **cooker** (*kuk*-ĕ*) *n.* stove for cooking food (بجلی تیل وغیرہ کا) چولھا **cookery** (*kuk*-e-ri) *n.* art of cooking پکانا ، ریندھنا ، طباخی *cookery book* کھانا پکانے کی ترکیبوں والی کتاب ، طباخی نامہ ، شاہی دسترخوان ،

cookie, cooky (*kuk*-ee) *n.* plain bun (U.S.) any type of biscuit بسکٹ (U.S.) small thin flat sweet cake میٹھی روٹی **cookout** *n.* (U.S.) (see *Addenda*)

cool (kool) *adj.* slightly cold ہلکا ٹھنڈا ، نیم سرد unexcited جوش میں *keep cool* ٹھنڈے دل و دماغ کا *cool-headed* ٹھنڈے دل و دماغ کا ، نہ آنا frigid; lacking zeal or cordiality سرد مہر ، بے مروت (money) in cash نقد ، کھرے *It cost him a cool thousand*, he had to pay for it a thousand rupees (etc.) in hard cash اسے کھرے ہزار میں پڑی ہے *n.* mildly cold خنکی ، کچھ سردی *v.t.* & *i.* make or become cool ٹھنڈا کرنا یا ہونا (of passions, etc.) calm (*down*) کم کرنا یا ہونا ، ٹھنڈا کرنا یا ہونا **coolly** (*kool*-i) *adv.* calmly, dispassionately سرد مہری سے ، بے مروتی سے ، جوش کے بغیر اطمینان سے

coolie, cooly (*koo*-li) *n.* porter or any other unskilled worker قلی ، مزدور

coon (koon) *n.* (U.S.) fellow آدمی ، شخص *gone coon*, one in hopeless circumstances جس کی قسمت ڈوب چکی ہو ، ڈوبی ہوئی اسامی child بچہ negro حبشی ، مرغا کوتنا

coon-can (*koon*-kan) *n.* a card-game of Mexican origin کن کن

coop (koop) *n.* (also *hen-coop*) small cage, esp. for hens with small chickens مرغیوں کا ٹوکرا ، تاپا ، ڈربہ *v.t.* put or keep (fowl) in a coop ڈربے یا تاپے میں بند کرنا ، ٹوکرا ڈھانپنا *coop up* (or *in*), (said of a sedentary worker) keep (him or her) in a small room or space چھوٹی سی جگہ میں بند کر دینا

a hen-coop

cooper (*koo*-pĕ*) *n.* maker or mender of canisters, pails, etc. ٹین گر

co-operate (koh-*op*-è-rayt) *v.i.* work together with a common aim تعاون کرنا ، مل کر کام کرنا ، مشترکہ طور پر کام کرنا work together (*with* someone) thus ساتھ دینا **co-operation** (koh-op-e-*ray*-shen) *n.* act of co-operating (*with* someone) تعاون ، اشتراک production, distribution, etc., by members of a co-operative society to effect a saving by sharing profits امدادِ باہمی **co-operative** (koh-op-e-*ray*-tiv) *adj.* of co-operation باہمی willing to co-operate متعاون ، امدادی ، ممد *co-operative society*, group of persons who co-operate for economic purposes انجمن امدادِ باہمی *co-operative stores*, society selling goods amongst its own members for mutual benefit کوآپریٹو سٹور ، دکان امدادِ باہمی *co-operative credit society*, group of persons who save and lend money to one another انجمن امدادِ باہمی (برائے قرضہ) *n.* (also *co-op*) co-operative society انجمن امدادِ باہمی its stores دکان امدادِ باہمی

co-opt (koh-*opt*) *v.t.* (of a committee) add member(s) by the votes of the existing ones اپنا ساتھی نامزد کرنا ، ساتھ لینا ، اپنے میں شامل کرنا *co-opted member*, such member شامل کردہ (یا شامل شدہ) رکن

co-ordinate (koh-*o**d-i-nayt) *adj.* of the same rank or importance ہم مرتبہ ، ہم پلہ ، ہم رتبہ *n.* co-ordinate thing ہم پلہ چیز ، مثیل *v.t.* be or place in the same order ہم پلہ ہو جانا یا بنانا bring into harmony (*with*) سے مربوط کرنا **co-ordination** (koh-o*d-i-*nay*-shĕn) *n.* act of co-ordinating تنظیم ، ارتباط

cop (kop) *n.* (slang) policeman سپاہی ، پلسیا *v.t.* (slang) catch (offender) پکڑنا ، لپک لینا *cop it*, catch it, receive punishment سزا بھگتنا **copper** (*kop*-ĕ*) *n.* (slang) policeman سپاہی ، پولیس مین ، پلسیا

cope (kohp) *v.i.* (*cope with*) struggle successfully نبٹ لینا manage successfully قابو پانا ، پورا کر لینا

I cannot cope with this work یہ کام مجھ سے نہیں ہونے کا
copestone see under *copying*
coping (*koh*-ping) *n.* overhanging brick-work on top of a wall منڈیر *coping-stone*, (also *cope stone*), (*a*) coping منڈیر ، آخری ردا (*b*) finishing touch, نوک پلک ، تکمیل
copious (*koh*-pi-us) *adj.* abundant لبریز، وافر (of an author) writing much پرگو **copiousness** *n.* abundance افراط، کثرت **copiously** *adv.* abundantly کثرت سے ، (سابقہ) پر
copper (*kop*-ĕ*) *n.* hard reddish metal تانبا coin made of copper or bronze تانبے کا سکہ ، پیسہ large copper vessel for boiling clothes, etc. تانبے کی کڑھائی (slang) (see under **cop**)
coppice (*kop*-is) **copse** (kops) *n.* clump of small trees or bushes in a small area (چھوٹے درختوں یا جھاڑیوں کا) جھنڈ
copra (*kop*-ra) *n.* dried coco-nut kernel کھوپرا
copse (kops) *n.* same as **coppice** (which see)
copulate (*kop*-ew-layt) *v.t.* unite sexually ہم بستری کرنا ، مباشرت کرنا **copulation** (*-lay-*) *n.* ہم بستری ، مباشرت
copy (*kop*-i) *n.* reproduction (*of* something) نقل *rough copy, foul copy,* first draft پہلا مسودہ ، نقش اول *fair copy, clean copy* transcribed matter showing no corrections صاف مسودہ ، نقش ثانی *fair copy,* (also) model version for comparison نمونے کی چیز ، نمونے کا نسخہ a book, etc., many like which have been printed نسخہ ، کتاب *an edition of 10,000 copies* دس ہزار نسخوں کا ایڈیشن ، دس ہزار کی اشاعت something sent for printing مسودہ *v.t.* & *i.* make a copy of (کی) نقل کرنا imitate پریس کرنا ، نقال کرنا ، نقل اتارنا
copyright (*kop*-i-r.t) *n.* exclusive legal right of the author or composer of a work (or someone authorised by him or his heirs) to publish or produce it during his (or her) lifetime and till fifty years after his (or her) death حق اشاعت *adj.* protected by copyright جملہ حقوق محفوظ ، حق تصنیف *v.t.* protect (book, etc.) by copyright حق اشاعت محفوظ کرانا ، (کتاب وغیرہ کا) حق تصنیف محفوظ کرانا **copy-book** *n* blank book for doing one's exercises کاپی
copyist (*kop*-i-ist) *n.* one who copies نقل نویس imitator نقال **copier** (kop-i-ĕ*) *n* one who copies نقل کرنے والا **copying** (*kop*-i-ing) *n.* نقل اتارنا *copying-ink*, ink used for duplicating something while it is being written نقل نویسی ، کرنا اتارنے کی سیاہی *copying-pencil*, pencil used for writing a matter whose carbon copies are also being taken کاپنگ پنسل ، اتارنے کی پنسل
coquet, coquette (*ko*-ket) *v.t.* (-tt-) (of women) flirt ; dally with a suggestion نخرے کرنا ، ناز نخرے کرنا
coquetry (-ri-) *n.* flirtation ناز نخرہ ، عشوہ گری
fickleness in love ہرجائی پن **coquette** (*ko*-ket) *n* woman addicted to flirtation ; flirt نخرے باز ، عشوہ گر
coquettish *adj.* having the air of seeking attention نازنین
coracle (ko-ra-kèl) *n.* very light portable boat made like a basket covered with some waterproof material, like skin اٹھاؤ کشتی
coral (*ko*-rĕl) *n.* stone-like red or white substance built on the sea-bed by small sea-creatures مونگا، مرجان toy of polished coral for children cutting teeth گل چوسنی *adj* of coral مونگے کا ، مرجانی red like coral مونگے کے سے رنگ کا *coral island*, island piled up by corals مونگے کا جزیرہ *coral-reef* مونگے کی چٹان

coral

cord (koh*d, ko*d) *n.* thick string or thin rope ڈوری، طناب any cord-like structure طناب نما چیز *the spinal cord* ریڑھ کی ہڈی (یا اس کے اندر) حرام مغز measure of cut wood (=128 cubic feet) لکڑی ماپنے کی اکائی ، (۱۲۸ مکعب فٹ = کورڈ) *v.t.* bind with cords رسی سے جکڑنا
cordage (*koh**-dij or *ko**-dij) ropes of a ship (جہاز وغیرہ کے) رسے
cordial (*koh**-di-ĕl, or *ko**-di-ĕl) *adj.* hearty, warm and sincere دلی ، قلبی ، پرتپاک ، پرجوش ، گرمجوشانہ *n.* drink that gives a feeling of warmth مفرح ، مقوی قلب sweetened and fragrant fruit juice پھلوں کا خوشبودار رس **cordially** *adv.* warmly تپاک سے
cordiality (koh*-di-*al*-i-ti) *n.* warmth of feeling تپاک ، گرمجوشی
cordon (*koh**-dun, or *ko**-dun) *n.* line of police, etc., set round as a guard to keep people off. سپاہیوں کا حلقہ ، گھیرا ornamental cord worn as a mark of rank فیتہ ، ڈوریا *v.t.* guard a place by keeping intruders *off* the way (لوگوں کو پرے رکھنے کے لیے کسی چیز کے گرد) حفاظتی گھیرا ڈالنا
corduroy (koh*-de-*roi*, or *ko**-de-roi) *n.* strong cotton cloth with (a velvety surface and) raised lines کارڈرائے ، ڈوریاگری (*pl.*) trousers made of this cloth کارڈرائے کی پتلون
core (koh*) *n.* hard middle part, with seeds, of a fruit گودا ، مغز بیج دان the essential point (*of* anything) (کسی بات کا) بنیادی نکتہ *the core of the problem* مسئلے کا بنیادی نکتہ *true to the core,* thoroughly faithful خود وجہ وفادار *v.t* take out the core of گودا نکالنا

core of an apple

co-religionist (koh-) *n.* person of the same religion as another ہم مذہب
co-respondent (koh-res-*pond*-ent) *n.* in a divorce

case a person accused of adultery with anothers spouse

coriander (ko-ri-*an*-dĕ*) flavouring plant with seed called *coriander-seed* دھنیا، کشنیز **coriander-seed** *n*. its seed دھنیا

cork (ko*k) *n*. light-brown, buoyant and tough elastic substance (forming the outer bark of the tree called *cork-oak*) کارک، کاگ stopper made of cork for a bottle کاگ، ڈاٹ *v.t.* stop (*up*) bottle with cork کاگ لگانا، ڈاٹ لگانا bottle (*up*) feelings ضبط سے کام لینا، جذبات چھپانا **corkage** (ko*k-ij) *n*. corking and uncorking of bottles بوتلوں کے کاگ لگانا، یا اُڑانا

cork (*B*) and cork-screw (*A*)

corker *n*. (slang) retort, blow, reaction, etc. that does or would help close matters مُنہ توڑ جواب **corkscrew** *n*. instrument for taking corks out of bottles پیچ کش، کاگ پیچ **corky** *adj*. lively خوش باش، زندہ دل

corn (ko*n) *n*. any cereal plant like wheat, barley, oats غلّہ، اناج، دانہ *corn-laws*, laws relating to (foreign) trade in corn قوانینِ غلّہ such plants while growing اناج کا پودا (U.S.) maize مکئی، مکّی (U.S.) (see *Addenda*) small growth on the foot with hard, often painful centre and root گوکھرو، گٹّا *v.t.* preserve (meat) in salt گوشت کا اچار ڈالنا *corned beef* گوشت کا اچار **corn-cob** *n*. centre of the ear of maize گُلّی **cornflour** *n*. flour made from maize or rice میدہ، چاول کا آٹا **corny** *adj*. (see *Addenda*)

corner (*ko**-nĕ*) *n*. point where two lines meet کونا، گوشہ، زاویہ، نُکڑ *from every corner of the earth*, from all over the world دُنیا کے گوشے گوشے سے *cut off a corner*, take a short cut بیچ میں سے نکل جانا، موڑ سے نہ جانا *turn the corner*, tide over a crisis (*e.g.*, in a serious illness) خطرے سے بچ نکلنا *a tight corner*, a difficult position مُشکل، مصیبت *drive (someone) into a corner*, force (him) into a situation allowing no escape زِچ کر دینا *give no corner to*, give him no refuge کہیں پناہ نہ لینے دینا secluded place کونا، گوشہ، گوشۂ خلوت *done in a corner*, done secretly چھپ کر کیا ہوا *stand a child in the corner*, put him there as punishment سزا کے طور پر کونے میں بچے کو کھڑا کر دینا remove point دور افتادہ مقام the buying up of all the supplies of a thing to sell at a higher price من مانا بھاؤ لگانے کے لیے سارا مال خرید لینا، بازار سمیٹ لینا *make a corner in* (wheat etc.) گندم کا بازار سمیٹ لینا *adj*. placed in a corner کونے کا، کونیا *v.t.* drive into a corner زِچ کر دینا *He was cornered* زِچ ہو گیا make a corner in (goods) بازار سمیٹ لینا، منڈی کا سارا مال خرید لینا **corner-boy, corner-man** *n*. loafer, بے خانماں، آوارہ گرد street rough غُنڈہ، بازاری آدمی **cornerstone** *n*. a stone at the corner of the foundation of a building کونے کا پتھر، کونیا پتھر، بھوڑا that on which something is based بُنیادی چیز، بیری اینٹ indispensable thing or part ناگزیر شے

cornet (*ko**-net) *n*. small trumpet-like musical instrument کارنٹ

a cornet

cornice (ko*nis) *n*. decorative moulding near the top of walls لگر، کانس

corollary (ko-*rol*-è-ri) *n*. natural consequence (*of* something) صریح نتیجہ، منطقی نتیجہ proposition that follows without need of further proof صریح نتیجہ، بدیہی حاصل، اخذ صریح، ہم ثبوت

corona (ko-roh-na) *n*. ring of light round the edge of the sun or the moon, esp. the one seen during an eclipse ہالہ، شعاعی حلقہ

coronation (ko-ro-*nay*-shĕn) *n*. ceremony of crowning a king or queen تاج پوشی، رسمِ تاج پوشی

coroner (*ko*-ro-nĕ*) *n*. British official inquiring into the case of any violent or unnatural death کارونر، غیر طبعی موت کی تفتیش کرنے والا، مفتشِ مرگ *coroner's inquest*, such an inquiry تفتیشِ اسبابِ مرگ

coronet (*ko*-ro-net) *n*. small crown worn by a nobleman چھوٹا تاج، تمکنت any ornament designed like coronet تاج نما زیور

a coronet.

corporal (*ko**-po-rĕl) *adj*. physical ; of the body جسمانی *corporal punishment*, punishment like whipping سزائے جسمانی *n*. lowest non-commissioned officer in the army نائک **ship's corporal** *n*. N.C.O on police-duty on a man-of-war جنگی جہاز کا نائک

corporation (ko*-po-*ray*-shĕn) *n*. group of persons elected to govern a town بلدیہ، کارپوریشن group of persons allowed by law to act, for business, etc., as one person جماعت بمنزلہ فرد، جماعت جسے قانوناً فردِ واحد تصور کیا جائے، اجتماعی ہیئت **corporate** (*ko**-po-rayt) *adj*. of a corporation اجتماعی of or belonging to a body ہیئت کے متعلق، اجتماعی، مشترکہ *corporate responsibility* مشترکہ ذمّے داری

corporeal (ko*-*po*-rè-ĕl) *adj*. material, tangible مادّی of nature of animal body (as opposed to *spiritual*) حیوانی ▣ **Corporeal** is physical as opposed to spiritual, whereas **corporal** signifies only that of the body.

corps (koh*) *n*. (pl., *corps* pr. koh*z) one of

the technical branches of an army فوج کا کوئی پیشہ ورانہ شعبہ the Pakistan Army Medical Corps شعبۂ طبی افواج پاکستان military force made up of two or more Divisions کور (یا ڈویژن فوج)

corpse (ko*ps) *n*. dead human body (as opposed to *carcass*, which see) لاش، نعش

corpulent (*ko**p-ew-lent) *n*. fat, bulky موٹا، فربہ بھیم شحیم **corpulence, corpulency** *n*. fatness موٹاپا، فربہی

corpuscle (*ko**-pus-ĕl) *n*. one of the red or white cells in blood جسیمہ

corral (ko-*ral*) *n*. enclosure for horses or cattle مویشیوں کا باڑا ring of wagons round a camp arranged thus to protect it گاڑیاں *v.t.* (-ll-) make a corral گاڑیا نا shut up in a corral باڑے میں بند کرنا

correct (ko-*rekt*) *adj*. right ٹھیک، درست true proper مناسب *v.t.* make right تصحیح کرنا set straight ٹھیک یا درست کرنا point out faults غلطیاں نکالنا، غلطی کی طرف توجہ دلانا punish سزا دینا، تادیب کرنا **correction** (ko-*rek*-shĕn) *n*. correcting تصحیح درستی، اصلاح، تصحیح substitute for an error تصحیح *essay covered with teacher's corrections* استاد کی تصحیح سے بھرا ہوا مضمون punishment سزا، تادیب **correctitude** (-*rek*-) *n*. correct behaviour نیک اطوار، وضعداری chastisement for correction of behaviour تادیب

corrective (ko-*rek*-tive) *adj*. serving to correct اصلاح کن *n*. something serving to do so اصلاحی، تادیبی

Correct means conforming to recognized standards; **exact,** in all details ; **accurate,** done with great care ; **precise,** scrupulously right. We speak of *correct* pronunciation : the *exact* time, *accurate* measurement and *precise* directions. As a verb, **correct** means to change something so as to make it agree with standard ; **rectify,** to change something that was wrong and make it right.

correlate (*ko**-re-layt) *v.t.* & *i*. have or give mutual relation (*with* or *to* a fact) لازم و ملزوم ہونا یا بنانا **correlation** *n*. mutual relation (*between* two or more things) لزوم، لازم ملزوم ہونا **correlative** (ko-*rel*-a-tiv) *adj*. related (*e.g.*, '*neither*' & '*nor*') ایک دوسرے کے ساتھ آنے والا، لازم ملزوم

correspond (ko-res-*pond*) *v.i.* be in harmony (*with*) کے مطابق ہونا، سے مطابقت کرنا be similar or equal *to* جوڑا ہونا، کے برابر ہونا exchange letters *with* خط و کتابت کرنا، مراسلت کرنا **correspondence** (ko-res-*pon*-dens) *n*. agreement مطابقت similarly یکسانی letter-writing خط و کتابت letters خط، خطوط مماثلت مراسلت **correspondent** *n*. (ko-res-*pon*-dent) one who writes letters مراسلہ نگار *newspaper correspondent*, journalist employed by a newspaper to send local news, etc. مراسلہ نگار، نامہ نگار

corresponding *adj*. similar متناظر، مماثل، متساوی *corresponding angles* متساوی زاویے *corresponding period* (*of a year, etc.*) (فلاں سال وغیرہ کے) اتنے ہی عرصے میں، کی مماثل مدت میں

corresponding angles

corridor (*ko*-ri-do*) *n*. long, narrow passage in a buiding into which rooms open غلام گردش such a strip of land connecting two parts of the same country ملکی گزرگاہ **corridor train** *n*. train with narrow passage from end to end جڑی ہوئی گاڑی

corroborate (ko-*rob*-o-rayt) *v.t.* make (a statement, etc.) more certain تصدیق کرنا confirm توثیق کرنا **corroboration** (ko-rob-o-*ray*-shĕn) *n*. act of corroborating تصدیق، توثیق **corroborative** (ko-*rob*-o-ra-tiv) *adj*. that which confirms تائیدی *corroborative evidence*, evidence which confirms something تائیدی شہادت

corrode (ko-*rohd*) *v.t.* & *i*. wear away رگھس دینا destroy slowly by chemical action (تیزاب کا) کسی چیز کو) کھا جانا destroy (by disease) (بیماری کا) گھن لگنا be worn away thus (بیماری سے) گھل گھل جانا، گھس جانا

corrosion (ko-*roh*-zhĕn) *n*. act of corroding کھا جانا، گھل جانا، گھس جانا، تحلیل *n*. **corrosive** (ko-*roh*-siv) *n*. & *adj*. corroding (substance) گلا دینے والا، کھا جانے والا، گھلا دینے والا

corrugate (*ko*-rew-gayt) *v.t.* shape into narrow folds شکن ڈالنا، جھریاں ڈالنا، سلوٹ ڈالنا، **corrugated** (-tid) *adj*. shaped like that پُرشکن دار، *corrugated iron sheet*, لوہے کی نالی دار چادر سلوٹوں والا

corrupt (ko-*rupt*) *adj*. (of persons, their actions) wicked, depraved بگڑا ہوا، بدچلن، بداطوار، بدعنوان accepting bribes رشوت ستان، رشوت خور، مرتشی *corrupt officials* رشوت خور اہلکار impure, rotten خراب، بگاڑنا، خراب کرنا فاسد *corrupt air* خراب ہوا *v.t.* debase bribe رشوت **corruptible** (ko-*rup*-ti-bĕl) *adj*. (esp. one who can be made dishonest by bribes کھانے والا، رشوت پذیر **corruption** (ko-*rup*-shĕn) *n*. rottenness سڑاند، فساد، خرابی bribery رشوت ستانی dishonest practices بدعنوانی

corsage (*ko**-sij, or ko-*sahzh*) *n*. upper part of woman's dress سینہ بند

corsair (*ko**-say-ĕ*) *n*. pirate بحری قزاق، بحری لٹیرا

corset (*ko**-set) *n.* woman's tight-fitting undergarment for waist and hips پیٹری دار انگیا ، زنانہ زیر جامہ

cortege (ko*-*tayzh*, or *ko**-tayzh) *n.* procession جلوس ، موکب (esp.) funeral procession جنازہ

a woman with a corset

coruscate (*ko*-rus-kayt) *v.i.* sparkle چمکنا ، جھلکنا (of humour, wit, etc.) sparkle مسکراہٹیں بکھیرنا

corvee ko*-vay) *n.* unpaid forced labour (esp. from French peasants till the revolution) بیگار any type of hard work done unwillingly بیگار ، خواہ مخواہ کی بلا

corvette (ko*-vet) *n.* (old use) sailing vessel with one tier of guns serving as a man-of-war بادبانی جنگی جہاز small warship for protecting convoys against submarine attacks بدرقہ کا جنگی جہاز

Corybant (*ko*-ri-bant) *Cl. myth.* a priest of the goddess Cybele whose rites included frantic dances and music کوری بنت **corybantic** (ko-ri-*ban*-tik) *adj.* wildly excited, frantic وجد میں ، حال میں

coryphee (ko-ri-*fay*) *n.* leading dancer in a ballet طائفے کی نمایاں رقاصہ

cosily *adv.* (see under **cosy**)

cosmetic (koz-*met*-ik) *n.* (often *pl.*) substances like powder, cream, etc., for making the skin of the face beautiful سنگار کا سامان ، غازہ و گلگونہ *adj.* designed to beautify the complexion حسن افزا ، رنگ نکھارنے والا

cosmic *adj.* (see under **cosmos**)

cosmogony (kos-*mog*-o-ni) *n.* mythical theory of the origin of the universe تخلیقِ کائنات کا تصور ، مسئلۂ آفرینش

cosmography (kos-*mog*-ra-fi) *n.* science of the constitution of the universe علمِ ہیئتِ کائنات ، کائناتیات

cosmopolis *n.* (see under **cosmopolitan**)

cosmopolitan (koz-mo-*pol*-i-tĕn) *adj.* belonging to all or many different parts of the world جہاں گشت ، ہر دیسی (person) having broad sympathies owing to a wide experience of the world آزاد خیال ، صلح کل ، وسیع المشرب شخص such an attitude وسیع المشربی ، آزاد خیالی ، وسیع المشربی *cosmopolitan outlook* *n.* cosmopolitan person وسیع المشرب **cosmopolis** (koz-*mop*-o-lis) *n.* cosmopolitan city عالمی شہر ، ہردیسی شہر

cosmos (*koz*-mos) *n.* the universe considered as a well-ordered system (as opposed to *chaos*, which see) نظامِ کائنات ، کارخانۂ قدرت ، کائنات ، کون و مکان

cosmic (*koz*-mik) *adj.* of the cosmos کائناتی ، کونی

cosmic rays *n.* highly penetrating rays of great voltage reaching the earth equally from all directions فضائی کرنیں ، کائناتی شعاعیں

cost (kost) *v.t.* & *i.* cause expense پیسے خرچ پڑنا ، پر خرچ کرنا cause loss مہنگا پڑنا be priced at مول ہونا ، قیمت ہونا estimate the price to be charged for an article based on the expense of its production لاگت کا اندازہ کرنا ، یا حساب لگانا *n.* expense, charge خرچ ، صرف ، مصارف *cost of living*, مصارفِ زندگی price قیمت ، دام ، مول price in toil or suffering (محنت یا تکلیف کی) قیمت (*pl.*) expenses of a law-suit (عدالت) خرچہ *at all costs*, however much expense, trouble, etc., may be needed بہرصورت ، ہر قیمت پر *to (one's) cost*, to one's loss نقصان اٹھا کر *at the cost of*, with resulting loss کی قیمت پر ، کو کھو کر

costly *adj.* of great value قیمتی ، بیش قیمت ، گراں بہا expensive مہنگا ، گراں involving much suffering بڑا مہنگا سودا **costliness** *n.* expensiveness گرانی

costal (*kos*-tĕl) *adj.* of the ribs پسلی کا ، ضلعی ، جنبی

coster (*kos*-tĕ*) *n.* same as **costermonger** (which see)

costermonger (*kos*-tĕ*-mung-ĕ*), **coster** *n.* seller of fruits, vegetables, etc., on a cart, etc., in the streets پھیری والا ، کنجڑا

costive (*kos*-tiv) *adj.* constipated

costiveness *n.* being costive

costliness *n.*, **costly** *adv.* see under **cost**

costume (kos-*tewm* or *kos*-tewm) *n.* clothes جوڑا ، لباس ، پوشاک style of clothes وضع قطع *academic costume*, gown etc., worn by teachers and degree-holders of a university جامعاتی لباس fancy dress بہروپ ، بہروپ کا لباس special dress for actors or actresses (کسی کھیل میں) اداکاروں کے ملبوسات ، لباس *historical costume*, clothes in the fashion of a certain period of past time پہناوا ، تاریخی ملبوسات *costume piece*, (or *costume play*), historical play تاریخی ڈراما *costume ball*, ball in historical or fancy dress women's short coat and skirt کاسٹیوم ، برقی ، سایہ **costumier** (kos-*tew*-mi-ĕ*)

person in academic costume

costumer (kos-*tew*-mĕ*) *n.* maker of, or dealer in, lady's dresses پوشاک دوز ، پوشاک فروش

cosy, cozy (*koh*-zi) *adj.* warm and comfortable گرم اور آرام دہ *cosy room* گرم اور آرام دہ کمرہ *n.* (also *tea-cosy*) cover to keep teapot warm کیتلی پوش ، چائے پوش

cosiness *n.* being warm and comfortable آرام سے ، آرام سے ہونا **cosily** *adv.* being cosy comfortably آرام سے ، مزے سے

cot (kot) *n.* a small easily moved bed esp. for a child کھاٹ ، کھٹیا ، کھٹولی *a child's cot* کھٹولی ، پنگوڑی

(poet.) a little cottage کٹیا (more commonly *cote*, which see) any small shelter for men or animals چھپر

cote (koht) *n.* shed or shelter for animals or birds باڑا، چھتری، ڈربہ *sheep-cote* بھیڑوں کا باڑا *dove-cote* کابک

coterie (*koht*-ē-ri) *n.* group of intimate friends ٹولی، منڈلی clique جتھا، ہشت زمرہ

cottage *n.* small bungalow esp. in the country بنگلہ، چھوٹی کوٹھی poor villager's house جھونپڑی، کچا مکان shelter چھپر **cottager** *n.* one who lives in a cottage جھونپڑی میں رہنے والا **cottage piano** *n.* small upright piano چھوٹا پیانو

cottar *n.* same as **cotter** (which see)

cotter, cottar (*kot*-e*) *n.* farm labourer who is given a rent free cottage غریب مزارع

cotton (*kot*-un) *n.* soft, white, fluffy substance روئی، کپاس *cotton wool*, cleaned cotton as used for padding or dressing تہ دار روئی plant producing this بن کپاس، کپاس cloth or thread made of it سوتی کپڑا *cotton waste*, refuse yarn used for cleaning سوتی صفائی کا reel of cotton thread سوت کا گولا ریل **cotton-cake** *n.* cake of crushed cotton seed after oil has been expelled from it کھل **cottonseed** *n.* seed of this plant بنولہ **cottontail** *n.* American rabbit with fluffy tail امریکی خرگوش جس کی دم نرم بالوں کی ہوتی ہے

couch (kouch) *n.* (lit.) bed پلنگ، بستر bed-like seat to lie down on during the day کوچ *v.t.* & *i.* express (*in words*) خیالات کو (الفاظ میں) ادا کرنا *couched in simple words* آسان الفاظ میں (of animals) lie flat either to hide or in readiness for a jump forward گھات لگانا lay (a spear, etc.) in rest for a charge (برچھی) تولنا یا جھکانا lay (*oneself*) down for rest or hiding گھات میں بیٹھنا

cough (kof) *v.i.* force air from the lungs suddenly and noisily کھانسنا، کھنکارنا، کھوں کھوں کرنا *cough (something) up* (or *out*), get something out of the throat by coughing کھنکار ڈالنا، بلغم ڈالنا *n.* act or sound of coughing کھانسی، کھنکار، ٹھسکا، کھانسنا *give a (slight) cough*, cough (thus) to call attention illness marked by coughing

cough-drop, cough-lozenge (*-loz-*) *n.* small tablet for relieving cough کھانسی کی ٹکیہ

could (kŭd), (abb. of neg. *couldn't*, pr. *kŭd*-ĕnt) pa. p. of **can** (which see)

council (*koun*-sil) *n.* group of persons called together to give advice مجلس، انجمن، کونسل governing body مجلس حاکمہ، ہئیت حاکمہ law making body of a government مجلس قانون ساز، مقننہ، شوریٰ *legislative council* مجلس قانون ساز *council of war*, high-level military conference called by the commander in the event of war or in order to prevent it * جنگی مجلس **councillor** (*koun*-si-lĕ*) *n.* member of a council مجلس قانون ساز کا رکن، رکن مقننہ، رکن شوریٰ، کونسلر

counsel (*koun*-sel) *n.* consultation صلاح، مشورہ، مشاورت advice صلاح opinion, suggestions رائے، تجویز *keep (one's) own counsel*, keep a matter secret کسی سے دل کی نہ کہنا، اپنی بات اپنے دل تک ہی رہنے (*pl.*, same as *sing.*) some lawyer or lawyers, giving advice, etc., in a law case وکیل، پیروکار، وکلاء، مشیر قانونی *King's Counsel* (abb. *K.C.*) *Queen's Counsel* (abb. *Q.C.*) lawyers who are appointed to act for the British Government and are higher in authority than barristers سرکاری وکیل، وکیل سرکار، تاج کا پیروکار *v.t.* advise صلاح دینا، مشورہ دینا، تلقین کرنا *He counselled Rasheed patience* اُس نے رشید کو صبر کی تلقین کی **counsellor** (*koun*-se-le*) *n.* adviser صلاح کار، مشیر

count (kount) *v.t.* & *i.* reckon up, number in order گنتی کرنا *count the cost (of something)*, cost it دیکھنا کہ (کسی شے پر) کتنا خرچ آیا ہے، اس کے خرچ کا تخمینہ کرنا enumerate گننا، شمار کرنا *be counted out*, (of boxer) fail to rise to his feet before the counting of ten seconds after being knocked down (مکے بازی میں) دس سیکنڈ میں نہ اُٹھ سکنا include شامل کرنا، نہ نکالنا *counting* سمیت، کے *not counting* کو نکال کر، کے علاوہ *hundred persons not counting the children* بچوں سمیت سو آدمی *count on* (or *upon*), (*a*) depend پر انحصار کرنا، کو یقینی سمجھنا (*b*) consider as certain پر بھروسہ کرنا *count for much* (or *little*, or *nothing*), be of much (or little, or no) importance بہت اہم ہونا، (یا معمولی اہمیت کا ہونا، یا کچھ بھی نہ ہونا consider (*as*) خیال کرنا، سمجھنا *count oneself clever* اپنے کو بہت چالاک سمجھنا be of worth or value قابل ذکر ہونا *that does not count* that need not be taken into consideration وہ قابل ذکر نہیں *n.* act of counting گنتی، شمار number got by counting گنتی *count of the students* طلبہ کی گنتی *take the count*, (boxing) be counted out مکے بازی میں ہار جانا total تعداد *one thousand was the count* تعداد ایک ہزار تھی account حساب notice پروا، خیال *Take no count of what he says* اس کی بات کی مطلق پروا نہ کرو one of the several things of which a person has been accused in a court of law الزام *He was found guilty on all counts* اس کے خلاف تمام الزامات درست ثابت ہوئے (fem. *countess*) title of some European nobility امیر، نواب *countess* بیگم، نواب بیگم

counting-house *n.* building for book-keeping in a bank, etc. بینک میں حساب کتاب کا دفتر **coun**

less *adj*. innumerable لاتعداد ، اَن گنت ◙ To **count** is to compute or make statistics concerning numbers, etc. : to **reckon**, anticipate (more often used with events than with figures) ; to **enumerate,** name in a certain order ; to **estimate**, establish expected cost or number ; to **value**, compare with known standards of cost ; to **price,** ascertain the price of.

countenance (*kount*-te-nens) *n*. face چہرہ expression of the face showing feeling or character صُورت، شکل، حُلیہ ، تیور *saintly countenance* پارسا صُورت *keep (one's) countenance*, control (one's) expression, esp. hide (one's) amusement ہنسی دبائے رکھنا ، ہنسی روکنا یا ضبط کرنا *put (someone) out of countenance*, cause (him) to feel embarrassed by looking at him گھبراہٹ میں ڈالنا support approval کسی منصوبے کی حمایت کرنا *give countenance to a scheme* حمایت *v.t.* support, approve حمایت کرنا ، بہ نظرِ پسندیدگی دیکھنا

[1]**counter** (*koun*-tĕ*) *n*. long table in a shop on which goods are sold or customers served (دُکان میں سَودے کا) تختہ یا میز one who counts گننے والا ، شمار کنندہ small cardboard or metal disc for keeping count in a game of chance (ہار جیت کے حساب کے لیے) گِٹّا ، ٹھکری piece at draughts گوٹ token, thing of mere conventional value ہتھیلیہ ، ٹھیپی part between horse's shoulders below its neck (گھوڑے کا) چھاتا stiffened part of boot round heel (جُوتے کا) ایڑی کے اُوپر والا حصّہ *adj*. & *adv*. against مقابل in the opposite direction علی الرّغم ، بالعکس ، برعکس ، برخلاف الٹی جانب contrary *act counter to (someone's) wishes* کسی کی خواہشات کے برعکس *v.t.* & *i*. act counter to کے برعکس کام کرنا oppose مخالفت کرنا return a blow for another blow مُنہ توڑ جواب دینا combat

counter- (*pref*.) opposite in direction اُلٹا، اُلٹ made in answer جوابی ، الزامی

counteract (koun-tĕ*-*akt*) *v.t.* act against and neutralize توڑ کرنا ، دفعیہ کرنا **counteraction** *n*. دفعیہ ، توڑ

counter-attack (*koun*-tĕ*-a-tak) *n*. & *v.t.* (make) an attack in answer جوابی حملہ کرنا

counterbalance (koun-te*-*bal*-ans) *n*. weight, force, etc., equal to another and balancing it توازن ، پاسنگ *v.t.* act as a counterbalance to مقابل میں اپنا وزن رکھنا

counterblast (*koun*-te*-blahst) *n*. energetic declaration against (*to* someone) مُنہ توڑ جواب دینا ، دندان شکن جواب دینا

counter-charge (*koun*-te*-chahj) *v.t.* (of accused) retort upon the accuser الزامی جواب دینا ، اُلٹی نالش ، *n*. such accusation اُلٹی نالش یا جوابی دعویٰ کرنا جوابی دعوے

countercheck (*koun*-tè*-chek) *n*. check designed to prevent a check from acting too powerfully روک ، توڑ

counter-claim (*koun*-tĕ*-klaym) *n*. counter-charge جوابی دعویٰ

counter-espionage, **counter-intelligence**, *n*. spying system to counter enemy's spies and put them off the scent جوابی جاسوسی

counterfeit *n*. & *adj*. (*koun*-tĕ*-fit) (something) false بناوٹی (something) made in imitation of another thing in order to deceive نقلی جعلی ، کھوٹا *counterfeit coin*, base or spurious coin کھوٹا سکہ *v.t.* (*koun*-tĕ*-feet) copy or imitate (coin, handwriting) in order to deceive جعلسازی کرنا، جعلی (سکّہ یا دستاویز) بنانا

(right) receipts (left) counterfoil

counterfoil (*koun*-tĕ*-foil) *n*. section of a receipt, cheque, etc., kept by the sender for purposes of record نصف ثانی ، مثنّیٰ **counter-intelligence** *n*. same as **intelligence** (which see)

countermand (koun-tĕ*-*mand*) *v.t.* cancel a command already given منسوخ کرنا، تنسیخی حکم دینا

counterpane (*koun*-tĕ*-payn) *n*. coverlet ; outer covering for a bed پلنگ پوش

counterpart (*koun*-tĕ*-paht) *n*. person or thing very much like another in form or nature ہمزاد ، نقل ، مثنّیٰ ، تصویر

counterplot (*koun*-tĕ*-plot) *n*. plot or strategem hatched to defeat another plot اُلٹی سازش ، سازش شکن تدبیر

counterpoint (*koun*-tĕ*-point) *n*. melody added to another as an accompaniment امدادی سُر ، امدادی نغمہ

counterpoise (*koun*-tĕ*-pois) *n*. weight or influence counterbalancing another توازن ، پاسنگ **counter-revolution** *n*. movement opposed to or undoing the aims or results of a revolution انقلاب شکنی انتزاع

countersign (*koun*-tĕ*-sin) *v.t.* add confirming signature to an already signed document to give it more authority توثیقی دستخط کرنا ، اثبات کرنا

counter-signature *n*. additional confirming signature توثیقی دستخط ، اثبات

counterword *n*. (see Addenda)

countess *n*. (*fem*. of **count**, which see)

countless *adj*. see under **count**

countrified *adj*. (see under **country**)

country (*kunt*-ri) *n*. region سرزمین ، علاقہ rural district (as opposed to *town*) دیہات ، مفصلات nation's territory مُلک nation, قوم **countrified** (*kunt*-ri-fīd) *adj*. rustic in manners and appear ance گنوار **country cousin** *n.* person not accustomed to urban manners and so ill-at-ease in a city بچارا دیہاتی، بھیّا، بقیّن **country-dance** *n.* rural dance in which men and women stand in circles or rows facing one another دیہاتی ناچ **countryman** *n.* (fem. *country-woman*), (*a*) man of the country not of a town دیہاتی، دیہاتی گاؤں کا آدمی (*b*) (also *fellow-countryman*), person belonging to the same nation as another ہم وطن **countryside** *n.* district in the country بیرونِ شہر، دیہات کا علاقہ The English countryside انگلستان کے دیہی علاقے *country town*, chief town in a county کاؤنٹی کا بڑا شہر **country-wide** *adj*. spread throughout a country ; nationwide مُلک گیر

county (*koun*-ti) *n.* the largest unit of local government in the United Kingdom برطانوی ضلع، کاؤنٹی

coup (koo) *n.* sudden action taken to get power or obtain a desired result کارگر عمل، ہنگامی اقدام *coup de grace* (koo-de-*grahs*) *n.* finishing stroke کاری ضرب، پُوری چوٹ *coup de main* (koo-de-*man*) *n.* sudden, vigorous attack بھرپُور وار *coup d'etat* (koo-de-*tah*) *n.* violent or illegal change of government انقلاب، حکومت کا تختہ اُلٹنا *coup dœil* (koo-*de*-ee) *n.* (view as taken in by a) comprehensive glance تفصیلی نظر *coup de theatre* (koo-de-te-*ah*-tĕ*) *n.* sudden and sensational act ; dramatic act چونکا دینے والا طریق کار، ڈرامائی طرزِ عمل

coupe (*koop*-ay)*n.* small compartment towards the end of a railway bogie چھوٹا ڈبہ closed motor car with a seat for two persons دو نشستی کار، کُوپے

a coupe (sense 2)

couple (*kup*-ĕl) *n.* two persons or things seen or associated together جوڑا two persons married to one another میاں بیوی (یا) منگیتر *married couple* میاں بیوی، شادی شدہ جوڑا *v.t.* join جوڑنا، ملانا *coupled with* مع connect (two things) in one's mind ذہن میں جوڑنا، (یا) تعلق قائم کرنا

couplet (*kup*-*let*) *n.* two lines of rhymed verse equal in length شعر، بیت، فرد

coupling *n.* link joinnig two parts of a machine (*e.g.* two railway coaches or other vehicles) (ریل کے دو ڈبّوں یا دو پرزوں کو جوڑنے والا کُنڈا) its appliance for transmitting energy کانٹا لگانا

coupon (*koo*-pon or *koo*-pĕn) *n.* detachable part of a ticket or document مُثنّیٰ ticket, etc., for which goods or money are given in exchange پرچی، کُوپن *clothing* (*etc.*) *coupon* coupon entitling holder to draw his ration of clothing (etc.) کپڑے (وغیرہ) کی پرچی

courage (*ku*-rij) *n.* bravery ہمّت، دلاوری، جُرأت *take courage*, ہمّت کرنا *pluck up courage, muster courage*, try to be brave ہمّت کرنا *take up (one's) courage in both the hands*, collect (one's) energy for an act of bravery ہمّت کر کے (کچھ) کرنا *have the courage of (one's) convictions* (or *opinions, etc.*), be brave enough to practice (one's) beliefs (etc.) پر پکا یقین ہونا، ایمان قائم ہونا lack of fear بے خوفی power to restrain painful feelings صبر، ضبط **courageous** (ku-*ray*-jus) *adj*. brave باہمّت، دلاور، جُرأت مند **courageously** (-ray-) *adv.* bravely ہمّت سے، جُرأت سے، جُرأت وہمّت سے کام لیتے ہُوئے

courier (*koo*-ri-ĕ*) *n.* messenger carrying news or important government documents ہرکارہ، پیغام رَساں travelling attendant conducting a party on tour (سفر میں) رَہبر، رَہنما

course (koh*s) *n.* onward movement in space or time رفتار، رَوِش *the course of events* رفتارِ حالات *in course of*, in process of کے سلسلے میں، کے ضمن میں *in the course of*, during کے دَوران میں *in due course*, in the proper order اپنے وقت پر، ہوتے ہوتے direction or path along which something moves راستہ، راہ، طریق، چکر، دَور *The disease ran its course*, it developed in the usual way بیماری نے اپنا دَور پُورا کیا *the courses open to (him)*, the ways in which (he) may proceed to act اُس کے سامنے یہ راستے کھُلے ہیں *a matter of course*, that which one would expect معمُولی بات، حسبِ معمُول بات *of course* (*a*) naturally قُدرتی بات ہے (*b*) certainly یقیناً، لازماً grounds for horse-race or golf, etc. گھوڑ دوڑ کا میدان *race-course*, place for races میدان، معرض *golf-course*, گالف کا میدان prescribed series نصاب *course of teaching* نصابِ تعلیم any series سلسلہ *course of lectures* سلسلۂ خطابات series (of treatments) (دواؤں یا معالجات) کا سلسلہ layer of stones or bricks in a wall رَدّا one of the separate parts of a meal (*e.g. palao,* pudding) کھانے کا دَور، دَور طعام chase of hare by dogs کُتّوں کی طرح سے خرگوش کا تعاقب، کھدیڑ، کھدیڑ way (of stream, etc.) in which it flows دھارے کی گزرگاہ، دریا گزار *v.t.* & *i.* chase (esp. hares) with dogs تعاقب، (خرگوش کا تعاقب) کُتوں کا پیچھے بھگانا set (dogs) on (a hare's) trail (خرگوش کے پیچھے کُتّے) دوڑانا run دوڑنا flow or run (of liquids) بہنا، چلنا *Tears coursed down her cheeks* اس کے رُخساروں پر آنسو بہہ نکلے **coursing** *n.* the sport of chasing hares کُتّوں کے ذریعے خرگوش کا شکار

courser (*koh**-sĕ*) *n.* (lit.) swift horse تیز رفتار گھوڑا، بادپا، صبا رفتار **coursing** (*koh**-sing) *n.* hunting of hares with greyhounds شکاری کتّوں کی مدد سے خرگوش کا شکار

court (koh*t) *n.* place where law-cases are heard عدالت، کچہری *High Court*, ہائی کورٹ، عدالتِ عالیہ *Supreme Court* سپریم کورٹ، عدالتِ عظمیٰ take (a case) to a court مقدمہ عدالت میں لے جانا settle (a case) out of court جھگڑے کا آپس میں فیصلہ کر لینا *put (oneself) out of court* اپنے طرزِ عمل سے قانونی حق کھو دینا *contempt of court*, defiance of its orders توہینِ عدالت judges, etc., who hear law-cases عدالت great ruler, his family and officials بادشاہ، دربار شاہی، قصرِ شاہی، دربار، امیر، وزیر، دیوان *court circular*, bulletin telling of the sovereign's programme or of visitors to court وقائع دربار، درباری اعلان *court dress*, dress to be worn at court on ceremonial occasions درباری لباس to be presented at court, *go to court*, (be caused to) attend a reception at court in order to pay respects to the sovereign کورنش بجا لانے کو درباری تقریب میں حاضر ہونا space marked out for certain games میدان، ملعب *badminton court* بیڈمنٹن کا میدان *tennis court* ٹینس کا میدان (also *courtyard*), space with walls or buildings round it صحن، آنگن، انگنائی politeness to please توجہ، تواضع، خوشامد، درآمد pleasing manners to win a lady's favour عشق بازی *pay court to (a lady)*, try to win (her) love عشق بازی کرنا *v.t.* & *i.* pay one's court to سے عشق بازی کرنا try to obtain favour, etc.) (مدد یا کرم) کا خواستگار ہونا take action that may lead to (trouble) مصیبت مول لینا *court arrest* اپنے کو گرفتاری کے لیے پیش کرنا **courtier** (*koh**-ti-ĕ*) *n.* one attached to a ruler's court درباری **courtly** (*koh**t-li) *adj.* dignified but polite درباری، شائستہ polite but hypocritical دنیا ساز، دنیا سازی کا **court-martial** (koh*t-*mah**-shèl) *n.* (pl., *courts-martial*) court for trying offences against military law کورٹ مارشل، فوجی عدالت trial by such court فوجی عدالت میں مقدمہ *v.t.* try (someone *for* an offence) by court martial فوجی عدالت میں مقدمہ چلانا **courtship** (*koh**t-ship) *n.* paying court to a woman with a view to marrying her کورٹ شپ، شادی کی نیت سے معاشقہ، شادی خواہ معاشقہ period before marriage spent in this way کورٹ شپ، شادی خواہ معاشقہ کی مدت

courteous (*kĕ**t-e-us) *adj.* showing good manners مہذب، خوش اخلاق، متواضع، شائستہ **courtesan, courtezan** (ko*-ti-*zan*) *n.* highly placed and supposedly cultured prostitute طوائف

courtesy (ke*t-è-si) *n.* courteous behaviour خوش اخلاقی، تواضع، شائستگی courteous act نوازش، کرم، کرم فرمائی **courtesy card** *n.* (see *Addenda*)

courtier *n.*, **courtliness** *n.*, **court-martial** *n.*, **courts-martial** *n. pl.*, **courtship** *n.*, **courtyard** *n.* (see under **court**)

cousin (*kuz*-èn) *n.* son or daughter of one's uncle or aunt ابنِ عم، بنتِ عم، چچیرا ممیرا خلیرا پھپھیرا بھائی بہن any relation رشتے دار، عزیز (also *first cousin* or *cousin german*, child of one's paternal or maternal uncle or aunt ایک دادا یا ایک نانا کی اولاد *second cousins*, cousins in the second generation ایسے رشتے دار جن کا نسب چوتھی نسل سے آ کر ملے **cousinly** *adj.* (of affection, etc.) like that of a cousin برادرانہ، بھائیوں کا سا (یا کی سی)

cove (kohv) *n.* small inlet of the sea کھاڑی small seaside cave in rocks ساحلی غار fellow آدمی، شخص *He is a queer cove* عجیب آدمی ہے وہ!

covenant (*kuv*-è-nant) *n.* solemn agreement معاہدہ، اقرار، عہد، عہد نامہ *the Covenant*, covenant between God and Israel بنی اسرائیل سے اللہ تعالیٰ کا عہد sealed contract سربمہر معاہدہ *v.t.* & *i.* make solemn agreement (*with* someone, *that*, *for*, or *to do* something) پکا عہد کرنا، عہد استوار کرنا

cover (*kuv*-ĕ*) *v.t.* put or lay something over ڈھانپنا، ڈھانکنا، اوڑھانا lie over so as to enclose اوپر آ جانا، اوپر ڈالنا، چھپانا یا دبنا hide travel (a distance) فاصلہ طے کرنا *cover forty miles in an hour* گھنٹہ بھر میں چالیس میل کا فاصلہ طے کرنا aim at (*with* a firearm) کا نشانہ باندھنا *Cover your man* جس کو ختم کرنا چاہتے ہو اس کا نشانہ باندھو *cover (someone) with a pistol (etc.)* پستول سے کسی کا نشانہ باندھنا extend تک جا پہنچنا comprise پر مشتمل ہونا provide with an insurance (*against*) (بذریعہ بیمہ) محفوظ کرنا *property covered against loss* بذریعہ بیمہ جائیداد خطرے سے محفوظ (of money) suffice for کافی ہونا *Rs. 100 will cover all the expenses* سو روپے تمام اخراجات کے لیے کافی ہونگے *n.* anything that covers something else ڈھکنا، سرپوش binding of a book جلد place giving shelter or protection آڑ، اوٹ *Take cover from the enemy's fire* دشمن کی گولہ باری سے اوٹ میں ہو جاؤ *get under cover* (بارش وغیرہ میں) اوٹ میں ہو جانا forest sheltering game شکار والا جنگل plates, knife, fork, etc. laid for one person at a meal ایک فرد کے لیے کھانے کے برتن *a dinner for six covers* چھ آدمیوں کا کھانا **covering** *n.* anything that covers ڈھکنا، پوش، پوشش *covering letter*, letter serving as an introduction to the enclosed matter تمہیدی خط *covering party*, soldiers protecting others, who are working at trenches, etc. حفاظتی دستہ

coverlet (kuv-ĕ*-let) *n.* bedspread ; outer covering of a bed بستر کی چادر، پلنگ پوش

coverpoint (*kuv*-ĕ*-point) *n.* (in cricket) fielder covering point کور پوائنٹ، پوائنٹ والا فیلڈر

covert *adj.* (*kuv*-ĕ*t) secret, hidden مخفی، پوشیدہ، چھپا ہوا *covert glance* دزدیدہ نظر *covert threats* چھپی ہوئی دھمکیاں *covert coat*, short light overcoat ہلکا اوورکوٹ *n.* (*kuv*-è*) wood or thicket affording cover for game شکار والا جنگل *draw a covert*, search it for foxes, etc. جنگل میں شکار کو کھدیڑنا

covet (*kuv*-ĕt) *v.t.* desire eagerly (usu. something belonging to someone else) لالچ، طمع یا حرص و آز سے کام لینا

covetous (*kuv*-e-tus) *adj*. (person) who covets لالچی ، حریص **covetousness** *n*. greed ; being greedy لالچ، حرص، طمع

covey (*kuv*-i) *n*. brood (of partridges, esp. when flying together) تیتروں کی جھول

cow (kou) *n*. female animal of ox family گائے *keep cows*, keep them for their milk, etc. گائیں رکھنا female of some big animals like elephant, rhinoceros and whale ہاتھی، وہیل مچھلی وغیرہ کی ، مادہ *v.t.* terrorize (someone) into submissiveness ڈرانا، پُر رُعب ڈالنا ، مرعوب کرنا **cowboy** *n*. (U.S.) man looking after cattle on a U.S. ranch گوالا، چرواہا **cow-catcher** *n*. (U.S.) wedge-like metal frame on the front of a railway engine to push obstacles off the track اِنجن کی چھاج **cowherd** *n*. man in charge of cows, etc., on a farm گوالا *herd of cows*, number of cows grazing together گایوں کا گلہ **cowhide** *n*. leather from the hide of cows or oxen گائے کا چمڑا ، گائے کی ادھوڑی **cowpox**, disease on cows' teats which is the source of small-pox vaccine گؤتھن سیتلا

a cow-catcher

coward (*kou*-è*d) *n*. one who has not the courage to fight ; dastard ڈرپوک، بزدل one who has no courage of convictions کمزور، بے یقین **cowardly** *adj*. not brave ڈرپوک، بزدل، بے ہمت contemptible بزدلانہ، قابلِ مذمت، لائقِ نفرین *cowardly act* لائقِ نفرین حرکت **cowardice** (*kou*-è*-dis) *n*. feeling or way of behaving, of a coward بزدلی، بے ہمتی

cower (*kou*-è*) *v.t.* crouch down (*before* someone from fear or shame) خوف یا شرم کے مارے ، دبکنا huddle (*with* cold) سردی سے اکڑوں ہونا

cowl (koul) *n*. monk's hood and gown راہبوں کا ٹوپی والا چغہ ، کلاہ دار چغہ hood-like cover on a chimney دُودکش کا ڈھکنا چمنی پوش

a cowl (sense 2)

cowrie, cowry (*kou*-ri) *n*. small shell formerly used as money in this part of the world کوڑی

cowslip (*kous*-lip) *n*. yellow flower growing wild in temperate country گاؤزباں

cowslip

cox (koks) *n*. short form of **coxwain** (which see) قائم مقام صدر ملاح *v.t.* & *i*. act as a coxwain دکا، پتواری بننا

coxcomb (*koks*-kohm) *n*. person given to showing off پھکّڑ، شیخی خورہ fop بانکا، چھیلا، چھیل چھبیلا **coxcombry** (*koks*-kohm-ri) *n*. پھکڑپن، چھیلاپن

coxwain (*kok*-sèn) *n*. a rowing-boat's steersman پتواری person in permanent charge of ship's boat صدر ملاح، جہاز کا مانجھی

coy (koi) *adj*. (esp. of a girl) shy شرمیلی، لجیلی modest حیادار **coyly** *adv*. shyly ; modestly شرماتے ہوئے **coyness** *n*. modesty ; shyness شرم، حیا

cozen (kuz-en) *v.t.* (lit.) cheat or deceive (someone *out of* something or *into* doing it) سے دھوکے سے چھڑانا (یا کام لینا) cajole خوشامد درآمد سے پھسلانا

cozy *adj*. (another spelling of **cosy**, which see)

crab (krab) ten-legged shell-fish کیکڑا ، سرطان *catch a crab*, (in rowing) lose balance by dipping the oar wrongly so as to entangle it چپّو الجھا دینا meat of a crab as food کیکڑے کا گوشت (also *crab-apple*) small sour apple (or its tree) ترش جنگلی سیب ؛ کا درخت *v.t.* (colloq.) criticize with intent to frustrate (person, plan, production, etc.) دل شکن تنقید کرنا

a crab

crabbed (krabd) *adj*. (of hand-writing) almost illegible (لفظ) خراب (of person) ill-tempered ; peevish چڑچڑا ، بدمزاج

crack (krak) *n*. line showing the incomplete break of something درز ، دراڑ، شگاف ، بال sudden, sharp noise (of a gun, whip, etc.) تڑاقا، چٹاخہ ، دھماکہ sharp audible blow تڑاقا *v.t.* & *i*. درز پڑنا یا ڈالنا، بال آنا get or make a crack in تڑخنا، تڑقانا make or cause to make a crack آواز کا، بھاری پڑجانا (of the voice) become harsh (of a boy's voice) undergo a change on reaching manhood کنٹھ پھوٹنا یا نکلنا (*crack up*) (colloq.) (*a*) (of personality) collapse ; loose strength (as in old age) پس ہو جانا، ضعیف ہو جانا (*b*) & (*c*) (see *Addenda*) ; *crack* (*someone* or *something*) *up*, praise (him, her or it) highly کی تعریفوں کے پُل باندھنا *crack a joke*, make a joke ہنسی اڑانا *crack brain*, put it out of condition دماغ خراب کرنا *adj*. first-rate ; of great reputation بہت بڑا، مشہور **cracky**, **crack-brained** *adj*. silly, mad سکی، ہسٹری، سودائی **cracker** *n*. thin, hard biscuit خستہ بسکٹ fire-work which makes a crack when set off پٹاخہ (*pl*.) (also, *nutcrackers*), instrument for cracking nuts سروتا

cracks in a cup

crackers

crackle (*krak*-èl) *n*. repeated small cracking sounds چٹخ، چڑچڑاہٹ *v.i.* make this sound چٹخنا ، چڑچڑانا **crackling** *n*. making this sound چٹخنا، چڑچڑانا crisp skin of roasted pork بھنے ہوئے سؤر کی خستہ کھال

cracky *adj*. (see under **crack**)

cradle (*kray*-dèl) *n*. baby's bed or cot us

mounted on rockers پنگھوڑا، جھولا، پالنا، گہوارہ، مہد from the cradle بچپن میں the cradle بچپن ہی سے in the cradle of the deep, (poet.) the sea سمندر، گہوارۂ گہرائی birth place مولد، مرز و بوم place of origin جائے آغاز، منشا ship's cradle, framework on which a ship rests when built or repaired جہاز کا گہوارہ v.t. place or rock (as) in a cradle جھولے میں ڈالنا یا جھولا جھلانا cradle a child in (one's) arms بچے کو اپنے بازوؤں پر جھلانا shelter in infancy بچپن کا سہارا بننا wash gold-bearing earth in a vessel سونا نیارنا vessel for washing gold-bearing earth سونا نیارنے کا برتن

craft (krahft) *n.* skill esp. in manual work دستکاری، حرفت، کاریگری trade requiring manual skill *arts and crafts* فنونِ لطیفہ اور دستکاری workers engaged in such a trade دستکار، اہلِ حرفہ cunning, skill in deceiving چالاکی، عیاری one or more boats or ships کشتی، کشتیاں، جہاز *aircraft*, aeroplanes ہوائی جہاز، طیارہ، طیارے **crafty** (*krahf*-ti) *adj.* cunning, deceitful فریبی، عیار **craftily** cunningly *adv.* عیاری سے **craftiness** *n.* quality of being crafty; cunning عیاری **craftsman** *n.* skilled worker دستکار **craftsmanship** *n.* being a craftsman or the product of a craftsman دستکاری

-craft (krahft) suff. denoting skill, occupation etc. *e.g. statecraft priestcraft.*

crag (krag) *n.* high steep rock or cliff ڈھلوان چٹان، کراڑا **cragsman** *n.* rock-climber چٹانوں پر چڑھنے کا مشاق **craggy** (*krag*-i), **cragged** (kragd) *adj.* full of crags ناہموار، سنگستانی

cram (kram) *v.t.* & *i.* (-mm-) fill to overflowing ٹھونسنا، لبالب (یا بھاگچھ) بھرنا eat greedily feed (child or poultry) to excess بچے یا چوزے کو بہت زیادہ کھلا دینا، ٹھونسنا fill the head with facts in preparation (*for* an examination) رٹنا یا رٹانا، رٹائی کرنا یا کرانا *The teacher crams the pupil* استاد شاگرد کو رٹاتا ہے *The pupil crams* شاگرد رٹتا ہے **crammer** *n.* special teacher who crams pupils for examinations by special lessons رٹائی کرانے والا استاد، رٹانے والا student who crams رٹنے والا طالب علم، رٹو

cramp (kramp) *n.* painful contraction of muscles, caused by chill or overwork, making movement difficult اینٹھن kind of clamp for holding timbers together سنڈاسی *v.t.* keep in a narrow space fasten by a cramp سنڈاسی ... growth

cramped (krampd) *adj.* confined to a small space منقبض، محدود (of handwriting) difficult to read because of its small letters which are very close together باریک اور گنجان (خط)

crane (krayn) *n.* large wading bird with long legs and neck کرنج، کلنگ machine for lifting heavy weights ڈھنگلا *v.t.* & *i.* stretch out (the neck) to see گردن اٹھا کر دیکھنا

1. a crane

2. a crane

cranium (*kray*-ni-um) *n.* bony part of the head enclosing the brain کھوپڑی، کاسۂ سر، جمجمہ **cranial** *adj.* of the skull کھوپڑی کا (یا سے متعلق)

crank (krank) *adj.* (of person) rather mad سنکی، خبطی، بہتری سودائی (of buildings, etc.) shaky کمزور، بودا *n.* L-shaped axle or handle for turning machine دھری پھیر، چکرکبنی، گھنٹیت *v.t.* start up (motor engine or other machine) by turning a crank-handle گھنٹیا سے چلانا، چکرکبنی مار کر چلانا **cranky** (*krank*-i) *adj.* ill-tempered بدمزاج، چڑچڑا whimsical; having strange and foolish ideas خبطی، بہتری سودائی (of buildings, etc.) shaky کمزور (of machines, etc.) out of order بگڑا ہوا، خراب (of machines, etc.) not steady ٹھیک کام نہ دینے والی

a crank

cranny (*kran*-i) *n.* small crack or chink (*in* a wall, etc.) درز، دراڑ

crape (krayp) *n.* black silk or cotton material with wrinkled surface کریپ

crash (krash) *v.t.* & *i.* (cause to) fall or strike suddenly and nosily ٹکرانا، ٹکرا کر پاش پاش ہو جانا یا کر دینا، دھماکے سے ٹوٹنا یا ٹوٹنا *The car crashed into the tree* موٹر درخت سے ٹکرا گئی *The aircraft crashed* ہوائی جہاز گر پڑا (یا) ہوائی جہاز کا حادثہ ہو گیا (of a business) come to ruin کاروبار چوپٹ ہو جانا (of a government) fall (حکومت) ٹوٹ جانا، حکومت کا تختہ الٹ جانا *n.* loud noise of breaking ٹوٹنے کا شور fall (of government) حکومت کا خاتمہ ruin (of business) (کاروبار کی) تباہی **crashdive** *n.* swift, steep dive (*of* a submarine) to parry attack بچاؤ کے لیے (آبدوز کی) اچانک ڈبکی *v.i.* (of a submarine) dive thus (آبدوز کا) بچاؤ کے لیے اچانک ڈبکی لگانا **crashland** *v.i.*, **crashlanding** *n.* (see *Addenda*)

crass (krass) *adj.* (in description of a bad quality like ignorance or stupidity), complete, very great (حماقت وغیرہ) سخت ، انتہائی درجے کی **crass-ness, crassitude** *n.* being crass (کسی خرابی کا) انتہائی درجے کا ہونا

crate (krayt) *n.* open work packing case of wooden bars for carrying goods کریٹ wicker-work for this purpose ٹوکرا *v.t.* put in a crate کریٹ میں رکھنا ، ٹوکرے میں بند کرنا

a crate

crater (*kray*-tě*) *n.* mouth of a volcano آتش فشاں پہاڑ کا دہانہ ، جوالا مکھی hole in ground made by a bomb, etc. (بم وغیرہ کی وجہ سے زمین میں پڑا ہوا) شگاف

cravat (kra-*vat*) *n.* old-fashioned neckcloth پرانی وضع کا گلوبند

crave (krayv) *v.t.* & *i.* ask earnestly for التجا یا التماس کرنا ، ملتجی یا ملتمس ہونا long (*for*) (کا) آرزومند ہونا **craving** *n.* desire (*of* a dope-addict *for* dope, etc.) طلب ، خواہش

craven (*kray*-věn) *adj.* cowardly (person) ڈرپوک ، بزدل ، کم ہمت

crawl (krawl) *v.i.* move on hands and knees with body on or near the ground رینگنا ، گھسٹنا ، پیٹ کے بل چلنا go very slowly بہت آہستہ چلنا be alive with insects کیڑوں مکوڑوں سے بھرا ہوا ہونا feel creepy (جسم پر چیونٹیوں کا) رینگنا *n.* crawling movement رینگنا ، گھسٹنا *go at a crawl*, move along slowly بہت آہستہ چلنا

crawl, crawl stroke *n.* high-speed swimming تیز تیرنے کا ایک طریقہ ، تیز شنا **crawler** *n.* person or animal that crawls رینگنے والا slow-moving person or thing سُست (*pl.*) baby's dress in which to crawl about the floor بچے کا گھٹنیوں چلنے کا لباس

crayfish *n.* lobster-like shellfish جھینگا مچھلی

a crayfish

crayon (*kray*-on) *n.* pencil of coloured chalk, etc. رنگدار چاک ، رنگین کھریا ، رنگین چاک picture drawn with crayon رنگ دار چاک سے بنائی ہوئی تصویر ، نقش چاک

craze (krayz) *v.t.*, **crazily** *adv.* see under **crazy**

crazy (*kray*-zi) *adj.* insane, mad پاگل ، سودائی distraught (*with* pain, etc.) (سے یا کے باعث) بے حال ، بدحال *crazy with pain* درد سے بے حال ، بوکھلایا ہوا madly eager (*for*) (کا) بہت شائق ، (کا) دیوانہ یا شوقین *crazy for the cinema* سینما کا بہت شائق foolish احمق ، احمقانہ *a crazy idea* احمقانہ خیال (of buildings, etc.) likely to collapse (عمارت) کمزور یا گرنے والی (of pavement, quilt, etc.) composed of fantastically irregular pieces ٹیڑھے میڑھے ٹکڑوں والا **craze** (krayz) *v.t.* make crazy پاگل کر دینا ، حواس بگاڑنا *n.* strong enthusiasm for something which is popular at the moment دھن ، من بسا خیال ، جوش fad **crazily** *adv.* پاگل پن سے ، بدحواسی سے

creak (kreek) *n.* harsh squeaking sound like that of rusty hinges چرچراہٹ ، چوں چوں sound like that of new shoes چرمراہٹ ، چرچراہٹ *v.t.* make such a sound چرچرانا ، چرمرانا ، چوں چوں کرنا **creaky** *adj.* making such sound چوں چوں کرنے والا یا کرتا ہوا

cream (kreem) *n.* rich oily part of milk which is turned into butter کچے دودھ کی ملائی ، بالائی ، کریم substance containing cream ملائی والا ، کریم والا ، بالائی دار (also called *face-cream*) cream-like paste, used as a cosmetic کریم ، اُبٹنا best part of anything بہترین حصہ ، انتخاب ، لُبِّ لباب ، عطر ، جان *the cream of society*, the best people معاشرے کا بہترین حصہ the colour of cream کریمی رنگ **creamery** *n.* place where cream, milk, etc., are sold دودھ کی دکان ، حلوائی کی دکان ، شیر فروشی **creamy** *adj.* containing cream بالائی دار ، کریم دار rich and smooth like cream بالائی کا سا

crease (krees) *n.* line caused by folding, etc. سلوٹ ، شکن (in cricket) (also called *bowling-crease*) chalk-line on ground marking certain players positions by the wicket کریز *v.t.* & *i.* make or get creases in سلوٹ ڈالنا یا پڑنا ، شکن ڈالنا یا پڑنا

create (kri-*ayt*) *v.t.* cause (something) to exist پیدا کرنا ، تخلیق کرنا ، خلق کرنا ، وجود میں لانا make (something new or original) تخلیق کرنا ، نئی چیز بنانا یا پیش کرنا ، ایجاد کرنا ، اختراع کرنا produce پیدا کرنا ، بنانا **creation** (kri-*ay*-shěn) *n.* act of creating پیدائش ، تخلیق ، خلقت ، ایجاد ، اختراع something created آفرینش the universe with all that it contains as created by God مخلوقات ، کائنات ، موجودات **creative** (kri-*ay*-tive) *adj.* having power to create قوتِ تخلیق ، قوتِ ایجاد ، قوتِ اختراع of creation تخلیقی **creator** (kri-*ay*-tě*) *n.* one who creates خالق ، موجد ، مخترع *the Creator*, God خالق ، باری ، آفریدگار (Also see **creature**)

creature (*kree*-chě*) *n.* living being مخلوق animal جانور ، حیوان one who is just the tool of another آلۂ کار ، دست پروردہ ، مرغِ دست آموز *creature comforts*, material or physical comforts دنیوی آسائش (Also see **create**)

creche (kraysh) *n.* public baby nursery بچہ خانہ

credence (*kree*-dens) *n.* یقین ، اعتبار *give credence to*, believe (what is said, etc.) پر یقین کرنا ، کو باور کرنا *letter of credence*, letter of recommendation سفارشی خط ، تعارفی خط

credentials (kre-*den*-shělz) *n. pl.* letters, etc., showing that a person (esp. an envoy) is really what he claims to be کاغذات نمائندگی ، سرکاری تصدیق ، مُراسلۂ تعارُف ، تصدیق نامہ

credible (*kred*-i-bĕl) *adj*. that which can be believed قابلِ یقین **credibly** *adv*. بالیقین ، یقین کے ساتھ **credibility** (kred-i-*bil*-i-ti) being worthy of credence یقین ، اِعتبار (Also see **credulous**)

credit (*kred*-it) *n*. good name, reputation نیک نامی ، شہرت honour آبرو ، وقعت ، عزّت ، فخر ، سہرا *It does him credit* یہ اس کے لیے باعثِ عزّت ہے *It goes to his credit* اِس کا سہرا اُس کے سر ہے belief خیال ، یقین ، تصوّر *place* (or *put*) *credit in* (*something*), believe (it) پر یقین کرنا ، کو ماننا *He is cleverer than I gave him credit for* میرا جتنا خیال تھا وہ اُس سے زیادہ ہوشیار ہے ، something which adds to one's reputation باعث کے لیے ، فخر یا موجبِ اِفتخار ، قابلِ فخر ، مایۂ ناز *persons who are a credit to their country* مُلک کے مایۂ ناز فرزند belief about someone that he can pay his debts, etc. ساکھ *His credit is good only for Rs. 100* اِس کی ساکھ سو روپے تک کی ہے ۔ اِس پر سو روپے کا اِعتبار کیا جا سکتا ہے sale of goods on trust اُدھار فروخت *No credit given at this shop* مال اُدھار فروخت نہیں ہوتا ، *letter of credit*, letter from one bank to another giving authority for a stated payment ہُنڈی money in one's account with a bank جمع (in book-keeping) record of money, etc., possessed by or due to (someone) (as opposed to *debit*) بہی کھاتہ (میں) آمد ، وصُولی *v.t.* believe سمجھنا ، خیال کرنا *credit* (*someone*) *with*, believe that (he) has it حامل سمجھنا ، کا مالک خیال کرنا enter on the credit side of an account وُصولی لکھنا ، جمع کرنا **creditable** *adj*. bringing credit قابلِ یقین ، قابلِ وثوق ، مُستند **creditor** *n*. person to whom one owes money قرض خواہ **credit line** *n*. (see *Addenda*)

credulous (kred-eu-lus) *adj*. too ready to believe خوش اِعتقاد ، بھولا ، ضعیفُ الاِعتقاد **credulity** (kre-*dew*-li-ti) *n*. being credulous خوش اعتقادی

creed (kreed) *n*. (system of) beliefs or opinions عقائد ، مذہب ، مسلک

creek (kreek) *n*. narrow inlet of water on the coast کھاڑی small river دریا کی شاخ ، ندی

creep (kreep) *v.i.* move along with one's body close to the ground رینگنا ، رینگتے ہوئے چلنا move slowly and secretly آہستہ آہستہ دبے پاؤں چلنا (of plants) make way along (walls, trees, etc.) بیل چڑھنا *n. pl.* (*the creeps*), feeling of horror or disgust as if insects were creeping over one's body رونگٹے کھڑے ہونا *give* (*someone*) *the creeps* رونگٹے کھڑے ہونا ، سخت خوف زدہ ہونا **creeper** *n*. plant that creeps along the ground, over walls, etc. بیل animal which creeps رینگنے والا جانور **creepy** *adj*. having (or causing) the creeps خوف زدہ یا سخت خوف زدہ کرنے والا

cremate (kre-*mayt*) *v.t.* burn (a dead body) to ashes لاش جلانا **cremation** (kre-*may*-shĕn) *n*. لاش جلانا ، نعش سوزی **crematorium** (-*taw*-), **crematory** (*krem*-) *n*. furnace or other place for cremating dead bodies لاش بھٹی ، مسان

Creon (*kree*-on) *Cl. myth*. King of Thebes in Greece who ascended the throne at the death of Laius. He abdicated in favour of Oedipus after the latter had caused the death of the Sphinx. He was the father of Jocasta کریئن

creosote (*kree*-o-soht) *n*. oily liquid made from wood-tar کوئلے کا ست ، روغنِ قطران

crepe (krayp) *n*. name for crape-like materials کریپ ، کریبی *crepe rubber*, raw rubber with wrinkled surface used for soles of shoes کریبی ربڑ ، کریپ

crept (krept) (pa. t. of **creep**, which see)

crescendo (kre-*shen*-doh) *n*. passage of music to be played with increasing loudness چڑھتے سُروں میں گانا ، چڑھتے سُر progress towards climax نقطۂ عروج کی طرف جانا *adj*. & *adv*. (played or heard) with increasing loudness چڑھتے سُروں میں

crescent (*kres*-ent) *n*. shape of the moon in her first or last quarter ہلال ، نیا چاند something shaped like it ہلالی *crescent flag*, flag displaying a crescent ہلالی پرچم (*the Crescent*), Islam or the Islamic peoples اِسلام یا ملّتِ اِسلامیہ *the Crescent and the Cross* اِسلام اور عیسائیت *adj*. (of the moon) growing بڑھنے والا

a crescent fla

cress kres) *n*. one of the several plants with hot tasting leaves used in salads کاہو

Cressida (*kres*-i-da, or kre-sī-da) *Cl. myth*. the heroine of two famous poems by Chaucer and Shakespeare. She was the daughter of a Trojan priest who deserted to the Greek invaders. She was herself unfaithful to her Trojan lover, Troilus کریسیدہ

crest (krest) *n*. cock's comb or tuft of feathers on a bird's head کلغی decoration worn on top of a helmet کلغی ، پھندنا design above coat of arms نشان ، طغرا design over a letter-head, etc. طغرا top of a hill, etc. چوٹی white top of a large wave جھاگ *v.t.* supply or decorate with a crest کلغی لگانا ، طغرا بنانا get to the top of (hill or wave) پہاڑی یا لہر کے اوپر چڑھنا ، اُوپر آنا **crest-fallen** *adj*. frustrated (at some failure) دل شکستہ ، پٹا ہوا ، ہارا ہوا

crevasse (kre-*vas*) *n*. deep crack (in a glacier) برفانی تودے میں شگاف ، دراڑ

crevice (*krev*-is) *n*. narrow opening or crack (in a rock or wall) شگاف ، دَرز ، دراڑ

crew (kroo) *n.* all the persons (working a ship or aircraft or rowing a boat) (جہاز وغیرہ کا) عملہ، جہازران all these persons except the officers افسروں کے علاوہ دوسرے جہازران *officers and crew of a ship* جہاز کے افسر اور عملہ *v.i.* pa. t. of **crow** (which see)

crib (krib) *n.* baby's bed with raised sides of bars and (usu.) castors or small wheels پنگوڑی rack from which animals eat hay, etc. ناند something copied dishonestly ناجائز نقل، سرقہ a word-for-word translation of a foreign text used by students of the language لفظی ترجمہ، تحت اللفظ ترجمہ *v.t.* & *i.* (*-bb-*) use such a translation لفظی ترجمہ استعمال کرنا copy (another's written work) dishonestly نقل کرنا، نقل اڑانا shut up in a small space ڈربے میں بند کرنا، چھوٹی سی جگہ میں بند کرنا

a crib (sense 1) and a castor (A)

crick (krik) *n.* stiff condition of neck or back-muscle owing to sprain or twist جھٹکا، اکڑن، اکڑاؤ *v.t.* sprain or twist one's muscle thus (پٹھے) کو تیز جھٹکا آنا، (پٹھے) میں اکڑاؤ ہو جانا

cricket (*krik*-et) *n.* a chirping insect جھینگر ball game played with bats and wickets کرکٹ (*It is*) *not cricket*; (colloq.) it is unfair یہ جائز نہیں، یہ رَونٹ (یا چیٹنگ) ہے

a cricket (sense 1)

cricketer (*krik*-e-tē*) *n.* one who plays cricket کرکٹر، کرکٹ کا کھلاڑی **cricket field** *n.* ground where cricket is played کرکٹ کا میدان، فیلڈ

cried (krīd) (pa. t. of **cry**, which see), **crier** *n.* see under **cry**, **cries** (krīz) (present t. of **cry**, which see)

crime (krīm) *n.* offence punishable by the law جرم any wrong act غلطی

criminal (*krim*-i-nĕl) *adj.* of crime مجرمانہ guilty of crime مجرم *n.* person who commits a crime مجرم **criminology** (krim-i-*nol*-o-ji) *n.* study of crimes and criminals جرمیات

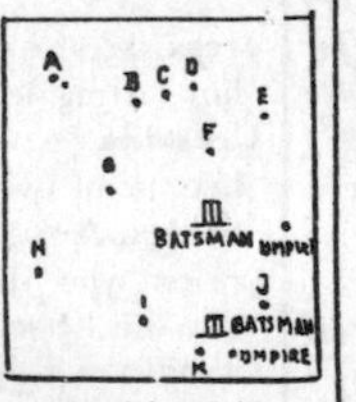

a cricket field

A, third man : **B** third slip ; **C**, second slip **D**, first slip : **E**, long leg : **F**, wicket-keeper **G**, point : **H**, cover-point : **I**, mid-off : **J**, mid-on : **K**, bowler

A **crime** is a serious legal offence **misdemeanour** is a minor offence : an **offence** is any legal wrongdoing ; a **delinquency** is the failure to perform a legal duty ; a **tort** is a civil wrong other than breach of contract ; a **felony** is a crime of the gravest kind.

crimp (krimp) *v.t.* make (hair, etc.) curly (as with a hot iron) (بال وغیرہ گرم سلاخوں سے) گھنگریالے بنانا

crimson (*krim*-zun) *n.* a deep red colour قرمزی رنگ *adj.* deep red قرمزی

cringe (krinj) *v.i.* crouch in fear ڈر سے پیچھے ہٹنا، دبکنا behave meanly (before a superior) عاجزی کرنا، لجاجت کرنا **cringeling** *n.* one who cringes خوشامدی ٹٹو، چاپلوس

crinkle (*krink*-ĕl) *n.* wrinkle (in material such as in cloth or paper) شکن *v.t.* & *i.* cause or get a crinkle in شکن پڑنا یا ڈالنا

crinoline (*krin*-o-leen) *n.* hooped skirt گھیرے دار لہنگا hoops once used for swelling out a skirt لہنگے کے چکر

a crinoline

cripple (*krip*-ĕl) *n.* deformed person unable to walk properly, through injury or weakness in spine or limbs لنگڑا، لُولا *v.t.* make a cripple of لنگڑا کر دینا damage seriously سخت نقصان پہنچانا

crisis (*krī*-sis) *n.* (pl. *crises*, *krī*-seez) turning point (in illness) بحران difficult time (of history) نازک دور anxious moment نازک لمحہ، تشویشناک مرحلہ

crisp (krisp) *adj.* (of eatables) hard, dry, and easily broken کرارا، خستہ، بھربھرا (of weather) forsty, cold کہر آلود having tight curls گھنگریالا، تابدار *crisp hair* گھنگریالے بال، گیسوئے تابدار precise (style) جچا تلا piquant, lively (style) پُرلطف، زندہ دلانہ (of manners) quick and decisive دو ٹوک **crisps** *n. pl.* thin fried slices of potato sold in packets آلو کے تلے ہوئے باریک ٹکڑے، خستہ آلو پارے **crisply** *adj.* جچے تلے انداز سے **crispness** *n.* being crisp کرارا پن being precise جچا تلا ہونا

criss-cross (*kris*-kros) *adj.* (of design, etc.) with crossed lines آڑی ترچھی لکیروں کے جال والا *adv.* crosswise آڑا، ترچھا in opposite directions ایک دوسرے کے اُلٹ *v.t.* & *i.* move crosswise آڑا ترچھا ہونا یا چلنا mark with crossed lines آڑی ترچھی لکیروں کا جال ڈالنا

criterion (krī-*tee*-ri-ĕn) *n.* (pl. *criteria*) principle by which something is judged معیار، اُصول

critic (*krit*-ik) *n.* (pl. *criteria*) person who judges and writes about fine arts (esp. about literature) نقاد، تنقید نگار، تبصرہ نگار person who maliciously points out only mistakes معترض، نکتہ چین عیب جُو، حرف گیر **criticism** *n.* the work of a critic تنقید نگاری، تبصرہ نگاری *textual criticism* متن کی تنقید *verbal criticism*, لفظی تنقید *higher criticism*, literary and historical enquiry into the Scriptures with regard to their authenticity, composition, etc. الہامی کتابوں کی اعلیٰ تنقید judgment given by a critic fault-finding نکتہ چینی، حرف گیری، اعتراض، اعتراضات **criticize** (*krit*-i-sīz) *v.t.* & *i.* give a criticism of تبصرہ کرنا

تنقید کرنا find fault with نکتہ چینی کرنا، اعتراض کرنا **critical** (krit-i-kĕl) *adj.* of or at a crisis نازک، تشویشناک ؛ بحرانی *a critical movement in the history of the country* ملکی تاریخ کا ایک نازک دور *The patient is in a critical condition* مریض کی حالت نازک ہے of the work of a critic تنقیدی *critical opinions on literature* ادب کے متعلق تنقیدی آراء fault-finding مُعترضانہ *critical remarks* ، مُعترضانہ الفاظ حرفِ اعتراض **critically** *adv.* in a critical manner ناقدانہ، تنقیدی نظر سے **critique** (kri-*teek*) *n.* critical review (*of* something, esp. of a piece of art or a work of literature) تبصرہ، تنقیدی تحقیق

croak (krohk) *n.* deep hoarse sound (as of a frog) ٹرّا ، ٹرٹر *v.t.* & *i.* make such a sound ٹرّانا speak in a croaking voice کائیں کائیں express dismal views about the future بُری فال نکالنا **croaker** (*kroh*-kĕ*) *n.* (esp.) dark prophet بدفال، مُتشائم

crochet (*kroh*-shay, *krooh*-shi) *n.* hooked needle for knitting کروشیا such knitting کروشیے کا کام کرنا

a croche and crochet-work

crockery (*krok*-è-ri) *n.* pots and dishes made of baked clay

crocodile (*krok*-o-dil) *n.* large lizard-like river creature مگرمچھ ، گھڑیال *crocodile tears*, insincere sorrow ریاکاری کے آنسو، ٹسوے *shed crocodile tears* ٹسوے بہانا

a crocodile

crocus (*kroh*-kus) *n.* an early spring flower کیسو

a crocus

Croesus (*kree*-sus) *Class. myth* an extremeely rich king of Lydia in Asia Minor کریسس

croft (krawft) *n.* very small Scottish farm, adjoining the peasant's house چھوٹا فارم ، خانگی فارم **crofter** *n.* its peasant owner خانگی فارم والا

Cronos (*kron*-os) *Cla . myth.* The Greek Titan who was the chief god before Zeus. He had dethroned his father Uranus and was, in course of time, himself destroyed by his youngest son, Zeus. He is identified with the Roman god, *Saturn* کرونس

crony (*kroh*-ni) *n.* old intimate friend پرانا دوست ، یارِ غار، لنگوٹیا، لنگوٹیا یار، (عورتوں کی) سہیلی ، بہنیلی

crook (kru̅k) *n.* shepherd's stick with a rounded hook (گڈریے کا) آنکڑا any hooked thing آنکڑا، کُنڈا، کانٹا person who practises fraud to earn his livelihood پتّے باز، عیّار *by hook or by crook*, by fair means or foul جیسے بھی ہو سکے، ہر جائز ناجائز ذریعے سے *v.t.* & *i.* bend into the shape of a crook مُڑنا یا موڑنا **crooked** (kru̅k-èd) *adj.* twisted ٹیڑھا، پیچ دار، موڑ والا (of a person or actions) not stright forward عیّار، چال باز، بددیانت

a picture hung crooked

crookedness (kru̅k-ed-ness) *n.* being crooked ٹیڑھاپن، چال بازی، عیّاری، بددیانتی

croon (kroon) *v.t.* & *i.* hum or sing in a quiet voice گنگنانا ، دھیرے دھیرے گانا، دھیمے سُروں میں گانا sing sentimental songs in a soft voice and an almost ludicrous way مضحکہ خیز انداز سے دھیرے دھیرے جذباتی گیت گانا **crooner** *n.* soft singer of very sentimental songs دھیرے دھیرے جذباتی گیت گانے والا one who sings sentimental songs in an almost ludicrous manner مضحکہ خیز انداز سے جذباتی گیت گانے والا

crop (krop) *n.* agricultural produce of a season فصل *a good (or bad) crop* اچھی (یا بُری) فصل *get the crops in* فصل سنبھالنا یا سمیٹنا things appearing or produced together ایک ساتھ آنے والی چیزیں *a crop of questions* سوالات کی بھرمار bag in a bird's throat where food is broken up before passing into the stomach پوٹا، حوصلہ handle of a whip چابک کا ڈنڈا very short haircut خشخشی بال *closely cropped head* گھٹا گھٹوا سر گھوٹ موٹ *crop-eared*, one whose ears has been cut off بُوچا، کن کٹا *v.t.* & *i.* (-pp-) (of animals) bite off the tops of (grass, etc.) گھاس وغیرہ اوپر اوپر سے چرنا ، چھانٹنا cut (hair) خشخشی کرنا بال کاٹنا *crop up*, arise quite unexpectedly اچانک آ پڑنا، خلافِ توقع پڑ جانا *difficulties that cropped up my way* جو مشکلات اچانک میری راہ میں حائل ہو گئیں *crop up*, (or *out*), (of minerals, etc.) show above the surface of the earth (دھاتوں وغیرہ کا) زمین میں سے اُبھرا ہوا ہونا، دکھائی دینا یا نکل آنا

cropper (*krop*-ĕ*) *n.* fall on one's head پٹخنی *come a cropper*, (colloq.) (a) have a bad fall پٹخنی کھانا، سر کے بل گرنا (b) [illegible] failure (*in* life or examination) فیل ہونا، (زندگی میں) ناکام رہنا

croquet (*kroh*-ki) *n.* game in which wooden balls are knocked through with wooden mallets کروکی، چوب بازی

croquet

croquette (kroh-*ket*) *n.*

fried ball or cake of minced meat mixed with rice, vegetables, etc. شامی کباب ، کوفتہ **crosier, crozier** (*kroh*-zhi-ĕ*) *n.* bishop's staff, usu. shaped like shepherd's crook لاٹ پادری کا عصا

a crosier

cross (kros) *n.* offspring of two animals or plants of different sorts دوغلا *a cross between (two breeds)* دونسلوں کے میل سے پیدا ہونے والا (جانور) *cross-breed* رلی ہوئی نسل ، دوغلا

stake with a transverse bar used for crucifixion سُولی، صلیب ، چلیپا *the Cross*, wooden structure on which, according to Christian religious belief, Jesus was crucified صَلیب hence *(someone's) cross* means (his) heavy burden of sorrow (کسی کا) بارِ غم anything shaped like + or × اشارہ صَلیب *the sign of the Cross* صَلیب نما ، چلیپا نما *adj.* angry خفا، ناراض، بگڑا ہوا *He is cross with me* وہ مجھ سے بگڑا ہوا ہے surly چڑچڑا ، بدمزاج *as cross as two sticks*, very bad-tempered سخت بدمزاج (of winds) contrary مخالف adverse اُلٹا، اوندھا، بُرا *a cross fate* بُرا نصیبہ *be at cross purposes (with)* (a) talk without either party's realizing that the other is talking of a different thing اپنی اپنی کہنا ، اپنی سی کہے جانا۔ (b) having different purposes without realizing it نادانستہ طور پر مختلف مقاصد رکھنا *v.t. & i* pass over کے پار جانا ، عبور کرنا ، ہیں سے ہو کر گزر جانا *cross a river* دریا کے پار جانا *cross (one's) mind*, occur to the mind جی میں آنا ، دل میں خیال گزرنا ، خیال آنا *cross (someone's) hand with silver*, give (someone) a silver coin for fortune-telling کسی کے ہاتھ پر چاندی رکھنا draw line(s) across پر لکیر کھینچنا *cross a cheque*, draw two lines across it with the words "& Co." or "not negotiable", etc., written between them so that payment can be made only through a bank چیک پر دو متوازی لکیریں کھینچ کران کے بیچ میں Co & لکھ دینا *cross (oneself)*, make the sign of the cross with the hand as a religious act among Christians بلیات سے محفوظ رہنے کے لیے ، صَلیب بنانا *cross off* (or *out*), strike off, cancel قلمزن کرنا ، منسوخ کرنا produce a cross by mixing breeds, etc. نسل ملانا obstruct (someone or his plans or wishes) مزاحمت کرنا ، مانع ہونا *cross (someone's) mind*, occur سوجھنا ، دل میں آنا *cross the path of* سے مڈبھیڑ ہونا **cross-bar** *n.* bar of wood, etc., fixed across others, *e.g.*, top piece of a goal-post ملانے والی پٹی (یا ڈنڈا) **cross-beam** *n.* large beam or girder stretching across a building شہتیر بڑا شہتیر **crossbelt** *n.* belt for cartridges, etc. hung from shoulder to opposite hip کارتوسوں کی

a cross

پیٹی ، ترچھی پیٹی **crossbones** (also **skull and crossbones**) *n.* emblem of death used as warning مَوت (کا تنبیہی نشان) **cross-bow** *n.* old kind of bow placed across a grooved wooden support ٹیڑھی کمان **cross-buttock** *n.* & *v.t.* throw over the hip in wrestling اڑنگا (مارنا ، لگانا) **cross-country** *n.* (races, etc.) across whatever comes, not necessary along roads ہرجائی دوڑ، کھلی دوڑ **crosscut saw** *n.* saw for cutting wood, etc., across the grain اُلٹے ریشے کا آرہ **cross-examine** *v.t.* question closely, esp. to test answers already given in answer to someone else جرح کرنا **cross-examination** *n.* such questioning (*of* witness, etc.) جرح **cross-eyed** *adj.* with one or both eyes turned towards the nose بھینگا **cross-fire** *n.* barrage (of fire, questions, etc.) سوالات یا گولوں وغیرہ کی بوچھاڑ **cross-grained** *adj.* (of wood) with grain running irregularly کھردری یا اُلٹے ریشے کی (لکڑی) intractable (person) ضدی ، خودسر **cross-heading** *n.* small heading inserted here and there in an article ذیلی عنوان **crossing** *n.* crossroads چوراہا *level-crossing*, place where road and railway cross ریل کا پھاٹک **cross and pile** *n.* obverse and reverse چت پٹ ، اُلٹی سیدھی ، شیر بکری *Cross I win and pile you lose,* چت بھی میری پٹ بھی میری **cross-legged** *adj.* squatting چارزانو **cross-lights** *n. pl.* rays from different quarters مختلف طرفوں سے آنے والی روشنی views of different persons مختلف لوگوں کے نظریات **cross-piece** *n.* crossbar ملانے والی پٹی ، سردل **cross-question** *v.t.* cross-examine (someone) پر جرح کرنا **cross-questioning** *n.* cross-examination جرح **cross-reference** *n.* reference from one part of a book to another part of it باہمی حوالہ **crossroad** *n.* road linking one main road with the other بڑی سڑکوں کو ملانے والی چھوٹی سڑک road crossing another کاٹنے والی سڑک **crossroads** *n. pl.* (used as *sing.*) crossing چوراہا *at the crossroads*, at a time when one must choose a course of action ایسے مقام پر جہاں راہ کی تعیین ضروری ہو، فیصلہ طلب مرحلے پر **cross-section** *n.* what is seen when something is cut through vertically اندرونی منظر its drawing اندرونی منظر کی تصویر typica

a cross-bow

a level-crossing

selection (*of* something) اصل نمونہ **cross-stitch** *n.* stitch formed of two that cross (کشیدے میں) زنجیرہ، ضرب نما کشیدہ needlework employing these ضرب نما کشیدہ، زنجیرے کا کام، زنجیرے کی کشیدہ کاری۔

cross-stitch

cross-trees *n. pl.* short pieces of timber across the upper ends of masts for supporting the ropes of sails مستول چوب، مستول پٹی **cross-voting** *n.* voting against the motion of one's own party پارٹی کے خلاف ووٹ دینا **cross-wise** *adv.* across کے سامنے کی راہ میں diagonally آڑا، ترچھا **crossword, crossword puzzle** *n.* big square with small square spaces in it for writing letters across and downwards to spell out words answering given clues ڈکھاتے ہوئے لفظوں والا معمّہ، لفظی چوکور

crotch (kroch) *n.* place where a bough divides from the trunk of tree دوشاخہ

a crotch at ×

crotchet (*kroch*-et) *n.* a fad دُھن میں بسا ہُوا خیال، خبط a musical notation موسیقی میں چوتھائی سُر کی علامت، کُرچ **crotchety** *adj* full of whims خبطی، کُرچی

croton (kroh-tun) *n.* kind of tropical plants yielding a strongly purgative oil جمال گوٹہ، حبّ السلاطین **croton-oil** *n.* their oil روغن جمال گوٹہ

croup (kroop) *n.* (also *croupe*) rump (esp. of horse) (گھوڑے وغیرہ کا) پُٹھا children's disease marked by soar throat and coughing بچوں کا التہاب حلق

croupe (kroop) *n.* same as **croop** (sense 1), which see

croupier (*kroo*-pi-ĕ*) *n.* person who takes in and pays out money at the gambling table مال لینے والا

crouch (krouch) *v.i.* stoop with the limbs together (in fear, or to hide) دبکنا، جھکنا (of animals) stoop ready to jump گھات میں بیٹھنا *n.* crouching position گھات میں بیٹھنے کا انداز

crouton (*kroot*-awn) *n.* small piece of fried bread served with soups تلا ہُوا توس، ولایتی پراٹھا

crow (kroh) *n.* well-known large and black bird کوّا *as the crow flies*, by the straight route بالکل سیدھے، ناک کی سیدھ

a crow

cry of a cock بانگ، ککڑوں کوں *v.t.* (*crow, crowed, crowed*; or *crow, crew, crowed*) (of a cock) cry ککڑوں کوں کرنا، بانگ دینا (of infants) make happy sounds (بچوں کا) کلکاریاں مارنا express triumph (*over* something) بغلیں بجانا، خوشی کے نعرے لگانا *crow over defeated enemy* دشمن کی شکست پر خوشی کے نعرے لگانا **crow's-feet** *n. pl.* small compound wrinkles about the eye آنکھ کے گرد جھریاں **crow's nest** *n.* watchman or observer's barrel-like shelter near the mast of ship

crowbar (*kroh*-bah*) *n.* iron rod for moving heavy objects سبل، گرالا

crowd *n.* throng, multitude ہجوم *the crowd*, the ordinary people عوام الناس *would pass in crowd*, has no prominent fault چل ہی جائے گا *v.t.* & *i.* throng ہجوم کرنا یا ہونا

crown (kroun) *n.* a monarch's ornamental head-dress تاج، اِکلیل، دیہیم، افسر *Crown Prince*, heir-apparent to the throne وَلی عہد *Crown Princess*, (*a*) heiress to the throne وَلیّہ عہد (*b*) wife of the Crown Prince ولیعہد بیگم symbol of royal power تاج *the Crown*, royal authority اِقتدارِ شاہی *officer of the Crown*, state official سرکاری ملازم، اہلکار *Crown colony*, country governed completely by the mother country نوآبادی top of the head چاند، چندیا top of the hat چندوا part of tooth visible below the gum دانت British silver coin worth five shillings کراؤن *half-crown*, coin half that value نصف کراؤن *v.t.* & *i.* put a crown on (a king, etc.) تاج پوشی کرنا، تاج پہنانا، تخت نشین ہونا، بر سرِ اقتدار ہونا reward enormously بیش قرار انعام دینا، بیش بہا صلہ دینا be or have at the top of ڈھکا ہُوا ہونا protect a tooth by covering it with hard material, like gold دانت پر سونے وغیرہ کا پتر چڑھانا

crozier *n.* same as **crosier** (which see)

crucial (*kroo*-shèl) *adj.* critical نازک، بحرانی decisive between two hypotheses فیصلہ کُن، قطعی *crucial test* فیصلہ کُن اِمتحان

crucible (*kroo*-si-bèl) *n.* earthenware or other pot for melting metals کٹھالی very severe test سخت اِمتحان **crucible steel** *n.* very hard steel used for making tools کٹھالی کا فولاد، آلاتی فولاد

crucifix (*kroo*-si-fiks) *n.* small model of the Cross with the figure of Christ on it صلیب پر مسیح کا چھوٹا سا مجسّمہ، (عیسائیوں کے نزدیک مجسّمہ) مسیح مصلوب **crucifixion** (kroo-si-*fik*-shèn) *n.* crucifying سُولی دینا، دار کشی *the Crucifixion*, that of Jesus عیسائیوں کے نزدیک مسیح کو سولی دینا، تصلیب **crucify** (*kroo*-si-fi) *v.t.* put to death by nailing to a cross سُولی دینا، سُولی پر لٹکانا یا چڑھانا

crude (krood) *adj.* (of materials) not refined; in the raw state خام، کچا *crude oil*, unrefined petroleum کروڈ آئل (of persons or manners) rude, impolite, not refined اکھڑ، ناشائستہ of unskilled workmanship بھونڈا **crudely** *adv.* بھونڈے پن سے

crudeness *n.* being of unskilled workmanship بھونڈا پن **crudity** *n.* rudeness اکھڑ پن، ناشائستگی being of unskilled workmanship بھونڈا پن

cruel (*kroo*-el) *adj.* (person) fond of causing pain to others ظالم، جفا جو، ستمگر، ستمگار، جفا کار، جفا پیشہ، ستم شعار

(act) showing this attitude ظالمانہ (loss, etc.) hard to bear سخت **cruelly** *adv.* ظالمانہ یا جفاکارانہ (انداز سے) **cruelty** *n.* atrocity ; being cruel ظلم ، ستم ، جفا ، جفاکاری ، ستم شعاری ◼ A **cruel** person is one who likes to cause suffering ; **brutal,** one who handles roughly ; **fierce,** one who is naturally unrestrained ; **savage,** one who is uncivilized : **barbarous,** one who is both cruel and uncivilized : **ferocious,** one who is wild and dangerous : **merciless,** and **pitiless,** one who lacks the gentle quality of mercey and is not compassionate.

cruet (*kroo*-et) *n.* dining-table container for salt, pepper and mustard نمکدانی ، سرکہ دانی *cruet-stand*, a stand to hold a set of such containers نمکنی ، بوتل دان ،

a cruet-stand with cruet
(1) for vinegar
(2) for salt.
(3) for pepper.
(4) for oil.

cruise *v.t.* sail about for pleasure سمندری سیر کرنا ، ... sail to and fro during wartime looking for enemy ships بحری گشت کرنا (of aircraft) fly at *cruising speed* (which see) تیز اُڑنا ، تیز پرواز کرنا *n.* cruising voyage بحری سیر ، بحری گشت **cruiser** *n.* large warship, faster and lighter than a battleship تیز رو جنگی جہاز ، بحرگرد **cruiser weight** *n.* boxer weighing not more than 174 lbs. کروزر ، گھونسے باز **cruising speed** *n.* travelling speed less than the top speed but otherwise very fast in order to prove economic in fuel consumption etc. تیز رفتار ، تیز روی

crumb (krum) *n.* tiny scrap of bread, etc., dropped from a large piece روٹی کا ٹکڑا ، بھورا small amount تھوڑا سا ، کچھ *a few crumbs of information*, some inklings کچھ سُن گُن ، اُڑتی ہوئی خبر

crumble (*krum*-bèl) *v.t.* & *i.* break into small pieces or crumbs ریزہ ریزہ ہو جانا (یا کر دینا) ٹکڑے ٹکڑے ہو جانا (یا کر دینا) **crumbly** *adj.* (of soil, rock, etc.) that which crumbles easily ریزہ ریزہ ہو جانے والی

crumpet (*krum*-pet) *n.* flat, soft batter-cake ٹکیہ

crumple (*krum*-pèl) *v.t.* & *i.* crush into unwanted creases مروڑنا ، (یا پڑنا) چرسیں ڈالنا ، مروڑی دینا *crumple up*, become or make full of creases (esp. in the hand) چرسیں پڑنا یا ڈالنا **crumpled** (-pèld) *adj.* bent مُڑا ہُوا crushed into creases مروڑا ہُوا

crunch (krunch) *v.t.* & *i.* crush noisily with the teeth when eating چُرمُر کرنا crush noisily (under foot or wheels) چُرمُر کرنا *n.* noise made by crunching چُرمُراہٹ

crupper (*krup*-ĕ*) *n.* part of a horse's back behind the saddle گھوڑے کا پُٹھا strap of harness passing under the tail of a horse دُمچی ، لید خورہ

crusade (kroo-*sayd*) *n.* war fought under the sign of the Cross صلیبی جنگ (*pl.*) wars waged by Christians against Muslims in the Middle Ages صلیبی جنگیں any struggle or movement in support of something believed to be good or against something believed to be bad جہاد *v.i.* take part in a crusade صلیبی جنگ میں حصّہ لینا ، جہاد کرنا ، مجاہدہ کرنا **crusader** (kroo-*say*-dĕ*) *n.* one who fights under the sign of the Cross صلیبی جنگجو ، مجاہد

cruse (krooz) *n.* (Bib.) small pot for oil or water کوزہ *widow's cruse*, constant source of supply ; something that never gets empty ختم نہ ہونے والا ذخیرہ

crush (krush) *v.t.* & *i.* press or be pressed so that there is breaking or harming پھنسنا ، پیس ڈالنا ، (یا) پِسنا curb, stifle (one's aspiration) کچل ڈالنا *n.* crowd of people pressed together بھینچا ، بھیڑ ، ہجوم

crust (krust) *n.* hard outer part of bread (روٹی کا) چھلکا hard surface پپڑی ، تہ ، پرت *crust of ice* برف کی تہ *the earth's crust* زمین کی سطح *v.t.* & *i.* cover with or form into, a crust پرت جمانا ، پپڑی جمنا **crusty** *adj.* (of bread) having much crust or a hard crust پاپڑ روٹی ، سخت چھلکے والی روٹی (of persons) surly, irritable زود رنج **crustaceous** (krus-*tay*-shus) *adj.* (of animals) hard shelled خول دار ، قشری **crustacean** (krus-*tay*-shĕn) *n.* hard-shelled animal خول دار (یا قشری) جانور

crutch (kruch) *n.* support used by a cripple under his arm to help him walk بیساکھی

crutches

crux (kruks) *n.* (pl. *cruxes*) mark of a cross صلیب کا نشان part of a problem which is the most difficult to solve عقدہ ، مشکل معاملہ ، اشکال

cry (krī) *v.t.* & *i.* wail چیخنا shed tears رونا shout چلّانا proclaim اعلان کرنا say excitedly جوش سے کہنا make appeal پکارنا ، بلانا ضد کرنا ، مچلنا *cry for*, demand esp. with tears آواز دینا *cry (something) down*, deprecate (it) کی مذمت کرنا ، کی منقصت کرنا *n.* shrill call expressive of pain چیخ shout اونچی آواز ، پکار *in full cry*, (*a*) (said of a pack of dogs) barking together in pursuit of an animal شکاری کتوں کا ایک ساتھ بھونکنا (*b*) combined pursuit of an object مشترکہ کوشش *it is a far cry to (something)*, there is no easy journey to (it) ہنوز دلّی دُور است ، دُور کی بات ، بعید **crying** *adj.* urgent; demanding attention قابلِ توجّہ ، اہم *It is a crying need of the day* یہ وقت کی اہم ضرورت ہے **crier** (*krī*-ĕ*) *n.* (also *town-crier* person making public announcements ڈھنڈورچی ، ڈھنڈوری پیٹنے والا ◼ To **cry** is to make a noise. Often it means to shed tears noisily, and sometimes to shed tears quietly, *i.e.*, merely to weep. To **sob** denotes tears plus hiccough. To **snivel** is to drip at the nose. To **bawl** means to say 'boo-hoo'. To **wail** signifies long, vocal cries; to **whimper** means to complain with low and mournful cries. Again, we **cry** spontaneously, often in fear or pain; **shout** very loudly; **scream** piercingly and in a loud voice; **shriek,** more piercingly than in scream, as in great fear, anger or pain; **yell,** very loudly, as in excitement or fun; **bellow** in a deep voice, as with the complete emptying of the lungs, like brute animals or brutal persons. We **bawl** when we cry like a child, and **roar** when we make a sound like that of a lion in great fury. We **clamour** for attention repeatedly in high-pitched voice, and **vociferate** when we make much noise with idle recriminations.

crypt (kript) *n.* burial vault under a church تہ خانہ **cryptic** (*krip*-tik) *adj.* secret خفیہ with a meaning not easily seen پیچیدہ ، غامض **cryptogram** *n.* something written in a secret code رمزی تحریر

crystal (kris-tĕl) *n.* glass-like natural substance with many sides بلّور ، قلم piece of quartz cut as an ornament بلّوریں نگینہ glass-ware of the best quality بلّوری برتن ، آبگینہ regular shape taken naturally by the molecules of certain substances قلم superior quality glass بلّور *adj.* very clear صاف ، شفاف *it has become crystal clear that* اب یہ بالکل واضح ہو گئی ہے ۔ filled with or having many mirrors in it شیشوں والا ، (سابقہ) شیش *crystal palace* شیش محل ، آئینہ خانہ **crystal-gazing** *n.* looking into a crystal ball with the silly belief to foresee events in it عمل حاضرات ، شیشہ گری **crystal-gazer** *n.* one who does that as a professional شعبدہ باز ، حاضرات کرنے والا ، شیشہ گر **crystalline** (*kris*-ta-lin) *adj.* of or like crystal بلّوریں **crystallize** (*kris*-ta-liz) *v.t.* & *i.* (cause to) form into crystals قلم بنانا (یا بننا) ، بلّور بنانا (یا بننا) cover (fruit, etc.) with sugar crystals پر چینی کے دانے جمانا (of ideas, plants, etc.) (cause to) become clear; take a definite shape (خیالات) و (تصوّرات کا) واضح ، متعیّن یا متشکّل ہو جانا *crystallized fruit*, fruit preserved by impregnating it with sugar * مربّہ ، قندی پھل **crystallization** *n.* quality of forming into crystals قلم پذیری ، تبلّور **crystal set** *n.* cheap and very simple type of radio set in which a crystal is used for reception کرسٹل سیٹ ، بلّوریں ریڈیو

crystal of (1) snow (2) glass

cub (kub) *n.* young lion, tiger, bear or fox شیر (یا ریچھ یا لومڑ) کا بچّہ ill-mannered young man بدتمیز ، غیر مہذّب یا ناشائستہ نوجوان ۔ تہذیب سے عاری نوجوان (also *wolf-cub*), junior boy scout چھوٹا سکاؤٹ ، ننھا سکاؤٹ **cubby, cubby-hole** (*kub*-i-hohl) *n.* snug place گرم اور آرام دہ جگہ

cube (kewb) *n.* solid body with six equal square sides مُکعّب **cubic** (*kew*-bik) *adj.* cube-shaped مکعّب of a cube کعبی ، مکعّبی ، کعبی *two inches cubic*, volume of a cube whose edge is two inches دو انچ مکعّب *two cubic inches*, volume equal to that of a body 2''×1''×1'' دو مکعّب انچ *cubic content*, volume expressed in cubic feet (etc.) مکعّب فٹوں میں حجم **cube-root,** number that twice multiplied into itself gives the given number **cubical** *adj.* like a cube کعبی ، مکعّبی **cubism** (*kew*-bizm) *n.* style of painting after Picasso (b. 1881) in which objects are represented in such a way as to give the effect of geometrical figures, esp. cubes and rectangles ہندسی مصوّری ، ہندسیت **cubist** *n.* artist with this style * ہندسی فنکار ، ہندسی

cubicle (*kewb*-i-kĕl) *n.* small division of a room walled or curtained to make it separate خندر single-seated room in a hostel طلبہ کی اقامتگاہ میں حجرہ یا خوابگاہ

cubit (*kewb*-it) *n.* old measure of length (18 to 22 inches) ہاتھ ، ذرع ، دراع

cuckold (*kuk*-ohld) *n.* husband of unfaithful wife قرمساق ، قلتبان ، دیّوث *v.t.* make cuckold of one کسی کو قرمساق بنانا

cuckoo (*koo*-koo) *n.* bird named after its cry; it is the harbinger of spring in England کوئل نما پرندہ ، کوکو ، ککو

cucumber (*kew*-kum-bĕ*) *n.* long round salad vegetable ککڑی ، کھیرا ، خیار

cud (kud) *n.* food brought back by cows, etc., from the first stomach and chewed again جگالی *chew the cud*, (*a*) chew thus جگالی کرنا (*b*) meditate سوچ بچار کرنا

a cucumber

cuddle (*kud*-ĕl) *v.t.* & *i.* hug ساتھ لگانا ، چمٹانا *cuddle a doll* گڑیا کو ساتھ لگانا nestle together (بچّوں کی طرح) بغل گیر ہو کر سونا

cudgel (*kuj*-ĕl) *n.* short thick stick *v.t.* & *i.* (-ll-) beat with it چھوٹا ڈنڈا

cue (kew) *n.* last words of an actor's speech which tells the next one when he is to speak * ترک * تقریب hint or example of how to proceed (in a play) (ناٹک میں) ہدایت یا نمونہ *take (one's) cue from*, be guided by کسی کی ہدایت پر چلنا *give (someone) the cue*, show (him) when or how to act (ناٹک کے لیے) کسی کو ہدایت دینا (also spelt *queue*), billiard-stick (اَنٹا کھیلنے کی) چھڑ، (بلیرڈ کی) چھڑ

cuff (kuf) *n.* wrist-end of a shirt sleeve کف، آستین کی سنجاف *cuff-links*, detachable buttons for cuffs کف بند light blow with fist or open hand طمانچہ، تھپڑ، چانٹا، مکا، گھونسا *v.t. & i.* strike with the hand

(A) shirt-cuff
(B) cuff-link

cuirass (kwi-*ras*) *n.* breast-plate for the armour چار آئینہ **cuirassed** (-*rasd*) *adj.* having a cuirass on چار آئینہ دار

cuisine (kwi-*zeen*) *n.* cooking methods of a country or establishment پکوان کا طریقہ، طرزِ طباخی food arrangements, etc., at a restaurant or hotel کھانے، کھانے کا انتظام

cul-de-sac (kūl-de-*sak*) *n.* blind alley بند گلی

culinary (kul-i-nĕ-ri) *adj* of cooking پکانے کا of kitchen باورچی خانے کا

cull (kul) *v.t.* select (*from*) (میں سے) چُننا، انتخاب کرنا

culminate (*kul*-me-nayt) *v.t.* end ختم ہونا، اختتام پذیر ہونا reach the highest point انتہا پر پہنچنا، نقطۂ عروج پر پہنچنا **culmination** (kul-mi-*nay*-shen) *n.* climax; highest point انتہا، عروج

culpable (*kulp*-a-bĕl) *adj.* deserving punishment لائقِ تعزیر، قابلِ مواخذہ، سزا کا مستوجب **culpability** (-*bil*-) *n.* being guilty; deserving punishment سزا کا مستوجب ہونا، لائقِ تعزیر ہونا

culprit (*kul*-prit) *n.* guilty person, offender مجرم

cult (kult) *n.* ceremonious, religious worship دینی رسوم system of such belief and worship مذہب، مسلک devotion to a person or thing, or practice عقیدت، مداحی *the cult of Shakespeare* شیکسپیئر سے عقیدت *the cult of Beauty* مسلکِ حسن پرستی

cultivate (*kul*-ti-vayt) *v.t.* prepare (land) by ploughing, etc. زمین (کا) کاشت کرنا help (crops) to grow فصل اُگانا یا پیدا کرنا develop (something) ترقی دینا *cultivate the mind* ذہنی سطح بلند کرنا، ذہنی ترقی دینا *cultivate (one's) manners* اپنے اخلاق و آداب کو تربیت کرنا، بہتر بنانا **cultivated** (-tid) *adj.* (of a person) having good manners and education شائستہ، مہذب **cultivation** *n.* cultivating (of land) کاشت، کاشتکاری development ترقی دینا **cultivator** *n.* one who cultivates کاشتکار، کسان، مزارع (esp.) machine for breaking up ground آلۂ کشاورزی، کاشتالہ، مشینی ہل

cultural *adj.* (see under **culture**)

culture (*kul*-chĕ*) *n.* intellectual development of a people تہذیب، تمدن، ثقافت training of the body or mind ذہنی تربیت cultivation کاشتکاری rearing of fish, etc. (مچھلیاں وغیرہ) پالنا laboratory growth of bacteria (دوا سازی کے لیے جراثیم) پالنا **cultured** (*kul*-che*d) *adj.* (of a person) having culture of the mind مہذب، تہذیب یافتہ، شائستہ **cultural** (*kul*-che-rĕl) *adj.* relating to culture تہذیبی، تمدنی، ثقافتی

culvert (*kul*-ve*t) *n.* tunnel-drain for water crossing a road زمین دوز بدرو

cumber (*kum*-bĕ*) *v.t.* burden with something useless پر خواہ مخواہ (یا بیکار کا) بوجھ ڈالنا *He cumbered himself with a mackintosh though the sky was clear* مطلع صاف تھا مگر اس نے خواہ مخواہ برساتی کا بوجھ اپنے کندھوں پر ڈال لیا

cumbersome (*kum*-bĕ*-sum), **cumbrous** (*kum*-brus) *adj.* heavy and troublesome بوجھل، بھاری بھر کم، تکلیف دہ clumsy to move or carry بے ڈھنگا، بے ڈول، بھدا

cumulative (*kew*-mew-lay-tiv) *adj.* total کُلی (of affect, result, etc.) of separately unimportant facts مجموعی اثر **cumulus** (kem-) *n.* cloud made up of masses of vapour دَل بادل **cumulous** *adj.* of a cumulus دَل بادل کا

cuneiform (kew-*nee*-i-fo*m or *kew*-) *adj.* wedge-shaped خانہ نما، تکونیا *cuneiform script*, (of the ancient Assyrians) خطِ میخی، خطِ پیکانی

cunning (*kun*-ing) *adj.* crafty فریبی، چالباز، عیار (act) showing such cleverness عیارانہ، چالاکی کا (old use) skilful (قدیم استعمال) ماہر *n.* quality of being cunning عیاری، چالاکی

cup (kup) *n.* small drinking vessel (usu. with a handle) پیالی، پیالہ، جام metallic vessel given as a prize in competitions کپ portion of sorrow or joy (اچھی یا بری) قسمت *v.t.* (-pp-) put into the shape of a cup پیالہ سا بنانا bleed patient by suction through a cupping-glass پچھنے لگانا، سینگی لگانا *in (one's) cups* نشے میں، ترنگ میں *the (or one's) cup is full* (اس) کی خوشی (یا دکھ) کی انتہا ہو گئی *be a cup too low* نشہ اُترنے کے باعث سُست ہونا *a bitter cup* (زندگی کی) تلخیاں *drain the cup of humiliation* سخت بے عزتی برداشت کرنا *drain the cup of life* بھرپور زندگی گزارنا

(A) band on edge of
(B) cup (sense 1);
(C) a saucer;
(D) a teaspoon

cup-bearer *n.* one who would serve wine at banquets ساقی **cupful** (*kup*-fūl) *adj.* as much as a cup will hold پیالہ بھر *a cupful of (something)*

cupping-glass *n.* cup used for bleeding a patient by suction سینگی

cupboard (*kub*-ĕ*d) *n.* shelved cabinet (usu. for crockery or provisions) الماری، نعمت خانہ، برتنوں کی الماری

Cupid (*kew*-pid) *Cl. myth.* the **Roman god of** sexual love. The son of the goddess Venus, he is represented as a naughty boy with a bow and two types of arrows which he shoots at gods and human beings alike in order to engender love in their heart. His victim will be fortunate in love if he is hit with a gold arrow, but quite unfortunate if hit with an iron arrow. He is identified with the Greek god *Eros*. کیوپڈ، کیوپد، کام دیوتا، کام دیو picture or statue of the naked Cupid with bow and arrows کیوپڈ کی تصویر، کیوپڈ کا مجسمہ، نقشِ کیوپڈ **Cupid's bow** *n*. upper edge of the upper lip (from its resemblance to the type of bow with which Cupid is represented) اُوپر والے ہونٹ کا بالائی کنارا

cupidity (kew-*pid*-i-ti) *n*. greed of gain لالچ، حرص

cupola (*kewp*-o-la) *n*. small bulbous dome (چھوٹا سا گول) گنبد ، قبہّ

cur (kĕ*) *n*. worthless dog لینڈی کُتا، بازاری کُتا ill-mannered, cowardly and selfish fellow پاجی، رذیل، بُزدل ، کمینہ **currish** (*ku*-rish) *adj*. like (that of) a cur رذیل ، جھگڑالُو ، بھونکنے والا

curable *adj*. (see under **cure**)

curacy (*kew*-è-ra-si) *n*. (see under **curate**)

curate (*kew*-è-rat) *n*. clergyman assisting a rector نائب پادری **curacy** (*kew*-è-ra-si) *n*. curate's office and work نائب پادری کا عُہدہ یا کام

curative *adj*. (see under **cure**)

curator (kew-*ray*-tĕ* or kew-è-) *n*. official in charge (of a museum, etc.) مُہتمم (عجائب خانہ)، مُحافظ (عجائب خانہ)

curb (kĕ*b) *n*. chain under a horse's lower jaw for controlling it دہانہ something that restrains پابندی *keep a curb on* (*one's*) *temper* (اپنے) مزاج کو قابو میں رکھنا kerb, enclosing framework, edging پُشتیاں، کنارہ *v.t.* control (a horse) by means of a curb (گھوڑے کو) لگام دینا یا دہانہ لگانا keep (feelings, etc.) under control (جذبات وغیرہ کو) قابو میں رکھنا، ضبط سے کام لینا

curd (kĕ*d) *n*. (usu. *pl*.) sour and thickened milk for making cheese or butter دہی، دوغ **curdle** *v.t.* & *i*. (cause to) form into curds دہی جمنا (یا جمانا) check flow (of blood) خون منجمد کرنا (یا ہونا) shrink or stop with horror لہو خشک ہو جانا **blood-curdling** *adj*. لہو خشک کرنے والا، وحشتناک

cure (*kew*-è*) *v. t.* heal علاج کرنا، تندرست کرنا do away with (something wrong or evil) اصلاح کرنا، خرابی دُور کرنا، علاج کرنا *cure poverty* غربت کا علاج کرنا preserve perishable things in salt (گوشت یا پھل کو) نمک لگا کر سُکھانا *n*. curing or being cured علاج، شفا substance or treatment which cures دوا، دوا و درمن، علاج **curable** (*kew*-e-ra-bèl) *adj*. that which can be cured قابلِ علاج **curative** (-tiv) *adj*. that which cures a disease شفا بخش، دوا

curfew (*kĕ**-few) *n*. (old use) bell rung to order 'lights out' in order to ward off danger of fire (قدیم) دیا بڑھانے کی گھنٹی ، کرفیو (old use) ringing of such bell دیا بڑھانے کی گھنٹی کا بجنا (old use) hour at which such bell was rung دیا بڑھانے کی گھنٹی کا وقت order under martial law for people to remain indoors خانہ بندی، خانہ بندی کا حکم، کرفیو time of remaining indoors under such an order خانہ بندی کا وقت

curio (*kew*-ri-o) *n*. rare, curious and valued work of art نادر نمونہ، صناعی کا نادر نمونہ **curios** *n*. *pl*. نوادر

curious (*kew*-ri-us) *adj*. eager to learn or know مشتاق، جاننے کا شائق evincing too much interest in other people's affairs متجسس unusual غیر معمولی، انوکھا ، نرالا difficult to understand مُشکل، عجیب، عجیب و مُشکل **curiosity** (kew-ri-*os*-i-ti) *n*. eagerness to learn سیکھنے کی لگن، اشتیاق habit of prying تجسس strange thing عجیب شے، انوکھی شے **curiosities** (-teez) *n*. *pl*. strange or rare things نوادر **curiously** *adv*. strangely عجیب طرح، عجیب انداز سے *curiously enough*, strangely enough, it is quite strange that عجیب بات ہے کہ

curl (kĕ*l) *n*. spiral lock of hair گھنگریالے بال، گیسوئے تابدار، زُلفِ پُرشکن *curl-papers*, *curling-iron*, *curling-irons* *curling-tongs*, papers (or piece(s) of iron, or tongs) used for curling the hair بال گھنگریالے بنانے کے کاغذ (یا کی سلاخ یا کی چمٹی) something twisted into that shape پیچدار، تابدار curled state گھنگریالا *keep* (*one's*) *hair in a curl with pins* پن لگا کر بال گھنگریالے بنائے رکھنا *v.t.* & *i*. make or grow into curls گھنگریالے بنانا یا بننا be in curls بل کھانا *smoke curling upwards* دھوئیں کے مرغولے اُٹھنا *curl up*, (*a*) contract in burning, dying or withering چُرمُر ہو جانا (*b*) roll up سمٹ سمٹا کر آ بیٹھنا *curl up in a big chair* آرام کرسی میں سمٹ سمٹا کر بیٹھ جانا (*c*) move round and round لوٹ پوٹ ہو جانا (*d*) fall down گر جانا، نیچے آ رہنا **curly** *adj*. full of curls گھنگریالا *curly hair* گھنگریالے بال

curl

curlew (*kĕ**-lew) *n*. a long-legged waterfowl with a thin long beak پن ککڑی

curling (*kĕ**-ling) *n*. Scottish game played on ice by sending stones across it پتھر گنڈلی noun of **curl** (which see)

curmudgeon (kĕ*-*muj*-èn) *n*. miser ; niggardly person کنجوس، بخیل ، لئیم bad-tempered person بدمزاج

currant (*ku*-rènt) *n.* small dried grape used in cooking کشمش small juicy fruit of various colours منقّی ، مویز
currency (*ku*-ren-si) *n.* being current چالُو ہونا ، مُروّج یا رائج الوقت ہونا ، یا عام اِستعمال *words in common currency* مُروّج الفاظ ، چالُو لفظ عام اِستعمال کے لفظ the money at present in use in a country (کسی ملک کا) نظامِ زر **current** *adj.* (see below)
current (*ku*-rent) *adj.* in common or general use چالُو ، مُروّج ، رائج الوقت ، رائج *current words* مُروّج الفاظ ، چالُو لفظ رائج الوقت ، رائج ، رواں *current coin* چالُو سکّہ now passing سالِ رواں *the current year*, this year of the present time تازہ ، حالیہ *the current issue of a magazine* رسالے کا تازہ شمارہ *n.* body of water or gas running through its own mass which is comparatively still (پانی کا) دھارا ، (ہوا کی) لہر flow of electricity along a wire, etc. بجلی کی لہر ، موجِ برق tendency (of opinions, events, life) دھارا ، رُخ ، رُجحان **currency** *n.* (see above)
curriculum (ku-*rik*-ew-lum) *n.* (pl. *curricula*) prescribed course of study in a school, college, etc. نصاب *curriculam vitae* (-*vah*-i-ti) *n.* academic qualifications, experience and other similar particulars furnished by one along with one's application درخواست کے ساتھ تعلیمی کوائف
currish *adj.* (see under **cur**)
curry (*ku*-ri) *n.* dish of meat, etc., cooked with curry-powder and usu. served with rice سالن *v.t.* prepare (meat) with curry-powder سالن پکانا *v.t.* rub down (a horse) with a special comb (known as *curry-comb*) (گھوڑے کو) مَلنا ، گھوڑے کے کھریرا کرنا ، یا مالش کرنا *curry favour with* (*someone*), try to win (his) favour by flattering him خوشامد کرنا ، چاپلوسی کرنا **curry-comb** *n.* comb for rubbing a horse with کھریرا **curry-powder** *n.* preparation of turmeric and other hot spices for making curry مسالے
curse (kĕ*s) *n.* divine decree or human invocation of destruction (*on* someone or something) لعنت ، بددُعا swear-words گالی cause of misfortune لعنت ، تباہی کا باعث *v.t.* & *i.* use a curse against لعنت بھیجنا ، بددُعا دینا یا کرنا (*swear at*), use swear-words against (someone) گالی دینا *be cursed with*, suffer because of کے دُکھ اُٹھانا ، کی مصیبت سہنا ، کے علاوہ کسی کا شامتِ اعمال ہونا **cursed** (kĕ*s-id) *adj.* deserving to be cursed ملعون hateful سخت بُرا ، سخت ناپسند
cursive (kĕ*-siv) *adj.* (of handwriting) in ordinary running hand, *i.e.*, with letters not written separately but rounded and joined together رواں یا شکستہ (خط)
cursory (*kĕ**-sĕ-ri) *adj.* (of reading, etc.) hurried جلدی جلدی ، بہ عجلت (of work) done without attention to details سرسری *cast a cursory glance* سرسری نظر *cursorily adv.* in a cursory manner سرسری نظر سے ، سرسری سا ، جلدی جلدی
curt (kĕ*t) *adj.* short, brief and abrupt (of person) hardly polite رُوکھا **curtly** *adj.* unceremoniously رُوکھے پن سے
curtail (kĕ*-*tayl*) *v.t.* make shorter than originally planned مختصر کرنا ، کم کرنا *curtail* (*one's*) *holidays* اپنی چھٹی پوری کیے بغیر آ جانا ، چھٹیاں کم کرنا
curtailment *n.* making shorter thus کانٹ چھانٹ کی ، تخفیف
curtain (*kĕ**-tèn) *n.* hanging cloth to screen door, window, stage, etc. پردہ *curtain drops, curtain is dropped, curtain falls*, one scene or phase is over پردہ گرتا ہے ، کھیل ختم *curtain rises. curtain is raised*, new scene begins پردہ اُٹھتا ہے *curtain lecture*, admonishment administered to a husband in bed شوہر کو سرزنش ، جورُو کا لعن طعن ، بیوی کے طعنے تشنے something that hides like a curtain اوٹ ، پردہ *v.t.* furnish with curtains پردہ ڈالنا *drop the curtain* پردہ ڈالنا *draw the curtain*, reveal or conceal ڈھانکنا یا کھولنا *draw the curtains*, exclude daylight پردے ڈالنا *curtain off* (*part of a room, etc.*) separate or divide thus پردہ ڈال کر الگ کرنا *draw a curtain over* (*something*) say no more about it ; stop controversy over it کو ختم کرنا ، پر مٹی ڈالنا **curtain-raiser** *n.* short play in a theatre staged before the curtain rises on the actual play تمہیدی کھیل ، پردہ بردار
curtsey *n.* lady's act of bowing by bending knees and lowering body *drop a curtsey*, bow thus تسلیمات کہنا ، مُجرا عرض کرنا *v.i.* drop a curtsey
curvature *n.* (see under **curve**)
curve (kĕ*v) *n.* smoothly bent line خطِ منحنی ، ٹیڑھا خط a large bend موڑ ، گھماؤ *v.t.* & *i.* (cause to) have the form of a curve مُڑنا یا موڑنا جُھکنا جُھکانا ، جُھکا ہُوا **curvature** (*kĕ**-va-chĕ*) *n.* curving گولائی ، خمیدگی curved shape خمیدگی
curvilinear (kĕ*v-i-*lin*-e-ĕ*) *adj.* of curved lines انحنائی ، منحنیات **curvaceous** *adj.* (see *Addenda*)
cushion (koosh-en) *n.* stuffed bag گدّی ، تکیہ *It is customary to take your cushion along with you when you go to the open-air theatre* اوپن ایئر تھیٹر میں جاتے وقت اپنی گدّیاں ساتھ لے جانے کا دستور ہے
cuspidor (kus-pi-do*) *n.* (U. S.) spittoon

cus (kus) *n.* (slang) curse کوستا cursed fellow or cursed animal کم بخت *He is a queer old cuss* عجیب کم بخت ہے **cussed** (*kus*-ěd) *adj.* cursed کم بخت perverse اوندھی کھوپری obstinate ضدی **cussedness** (-id-) *n.* ضدی، بدی بڑا کم بخت ہونا، ضدی ہونا، ہٹ دھرمی

custard (kus-tě*d) *n.* sweetened and flavoured mixture of eggs and milk served after boiling or baking کسٹرڈ، انڈے کی پسی **custard-apple** *n.* a well-known kind of fruit شریفہ

custodian *n.* (see under **custody**)

custody (*kus*-to-di) *n.* keeping safe, under one's control or care حفاظت، نگرانی، تحویل *have the custody of* کا نگران ہونا، کی نگرانی کرنا *be in the custody of* کے زیر نگرانی ہونا *take into custody*, arrest حراست میں لینا، زیر حراست کرنا *in custody*, arrested زیر حراست **custodian** (kus-*toh*-di-an) *n.* one who has custody of someone or something نگران caretaker of a public building نگران، ناظم *Custodian of Evacuee Property* ناظم جائداد متروکہ

custom (*kus*-tum) *n.* practice which has become habitual with the members of a particular social group and passes current with them رواج، رسم patronage of a business by buyers دکان دار کی سرپرستی، مستقل گاہکی، یا خریداری **customs** (*kus*-tumz) *n. pl.* import (and sometimes export) duties کروڑگیری، محصول درآمد (و برآمد) department collecting such taxes محکمہ کروڑگیری **customary** *adj.* usual ; according to custom رواجی، حسب معمول *customary law* رواج، قانون رواج **customer** *n.* person who gives his custom to a tradesman مستقل خریدار person entering a shop to buy things گاہک، خریدار (colloq.) fellow آدمی *a queer customer*, strange person عجیب آدمی، مزدک *an awkward customer*, one difficult to deal with عذاب جان شخص **custom house, customs house** *n.* office at port, etc., where customs are collected دفتر کروڑگیری ◙ **Custom** denotes generally the accepted behaviour among members of a social group ; **habit** is personal and indicates something done regularly by an individual ; **practice** is intentionally established ; **rite** is a religious ceremony ; **procedure** is a way of doing one detail after another ; **institution** is a recognized usage even though of a minor thing.

cut (kut) *v.t.* & *i.* (-tt-) (*cut, cut, cut*) open or divide with a sharp tool کاٹنا *This knife will not cut*, it is blunt یہ چاقو کاٹتا ہی نہیں *I cut my finger with that knife*, I got a cut on my finger with this knife میری انگلی چاقو سے زخمی ہو گئی، میری انگلی کو چاقو لگ گیا *cut (something) down*, make smaller in size or amount چھوٹا کرنا، کم کرنا *cut (something or someone) off*, stop, or interrupt روکنا، آگے بڑھنے نہ دینا بات کاٹنا *cut off the enemy's retreat* دشمن کے پسپائی نا ممکن بنا نا *be cut off while telephoning* بات کرتے کرتے ٹیلیفون کا بند ہو جانا *cut (something) out*, (*a*) remove or save by cutting کاٹ کر دور کرنا، کاٹ کر نکال لینا (*b*) shape by cutting قطع کرنا، کاٹ کر بنانا *cut out dress (from a piece of cloth)* فراک قطع کرنا *be cut out for*, be suited to کے لیے موزوں ہونا، ہی کیلئے بنا ہے *be cut up by*, be made very unhappy by کا صدمہ پہنچنا *cut (something) short*, make it shorter کوتاہ کرنا، مختصر کرنا *to cut a long story short* قصہ مختصر *cut at (something)*, aim a sharp blow at (*e.g.*, with a stick) چھڑی زور سے مارنا *cut in* (or *into*), interrupt بات کاٹنا دخل دینا cause pain by penetrating لگنا، چھیلنا، چبھنا، کاٹنا، چیر ڈالنا *cutting irony* چبھتی ہوئی طنز *cutting wind* چیر ڈالنے والی ہوا *How this rope cuts !* یہ رسہ تو ہاتھ چھیلے ڈالتا ہے pass (a person and pretend not to know him) کنی کترانا، کنی کترا کر نکل جانا stay away from (a class or lecture at college, etc.) غیر حاضر رہنا، ناغہ کرنا *He cuts classes* وہ غیر حاضر رہتا ہے (Special senses :) *cut a tooth*, show a new tooth through the gums دانت نکالنا *cut (one's) wisdom teeth* عقل ڈاڑھ نکالنا *cut cards*, (in playing card games) divide the pack into two parts تاش کاٹنا *cut both ways*, (of an argument, etc.) have advantages and disadvantages دونوں ہی طرح ہو سکتا ہے *cut a loss*, accept it and make a fresh start خسارہ قبول کر لینا، نقصان پر صبر کر لینا *cut and dried, cut and dry*, (of opinions, plans, etc.) all decided and ready گھڑی گھڑائی تیار، پہلے ہی سے طے شدہ *cut across*, go transversely over and not run parallel with کاٹتے ہوتے جانا *cut a caper, cut capers*, frisk اچھلنا، کودنا *cut a dash*, make a brilliant show شان دار مظاہرہ کرنا *cut a poor* (or *sorry*) *figure*, make such impression اچھا نہ رہنا، مفلس ہو جانا *cut and run*, make off نکل بھاگنا *cut and thrust*, (*a*) sword play with both edge and point کھلی شمشیر زنی (*b*) interchange of argument سخت قیل وقال *cut (one's) coat according to one's cloth*, limit one's ambition to one's possible means چادر دیکھ کر پاؤں پھیلانا *cut (someone) dead*, show no sign of recognizing him کنی کترا جانا *cut down*, reduce (expenses, etc.) کم کرنا *cut in*, (*a*) interpose in talk or action دخل اندازی کرنا، دخل دینا (*b*) (in motoring) obstruct path of vehicle one has just overtaken by returning to one's side of the road too soon گاڑی کا، آگے نکل کر قبل از وقت اپنے ہاتھ آجانا، کاٹنا *cut no ice*, (colloq.) effect little or nothing بے اثر ہونا *be cut off*, (*a*) be brought to an abrupt end (esp. by early death) خاتمہ ہو جانا (*b*) intercept (supplies, etc.) (رسد وغیرہ) روکنا

cut out, (*a*) cut parts of (garment) for stitching کاٹنا (*b*) capture (enemy ship) by getting between her and the shore قطع کرنا ساحل کا راستہ روک کر دشمن کے جہاز پر قبضہ کرنا (*c*) outdo (someone) کسی سے بڑھ کر (*d*) (in motoring) obstruct path of oncoming vehicle in attempt to overtake another thus moving to the opposite side of the road کاٹ کرنا کسی گاڑی سے آگے نکلتے ہوئے سامنے کی گاڑی کا راستہ روکنا ، آگا روکنا *cut prices*, *cut rates*, lower them as a competition measure قیمتیں کم کرنا ، بھاؤ گرانا *cut the* (*Gordion*) *knot*, dispose of difficulty in a rough and ready manner کسی مشکل کو زبردستی سے حل کرنا *cut the record*, better the record ریکارڈ توڑنا *cut* (*something*) *up*, *cut to pieces*, (*a*) utterly defeat (an army) فوج کو تباہ کن شکست دینا (*b*) criticize damagingly بخیے اُدھیڑنا ، سخت تنقید کرنا *cut to the heart*, keenly distress سخت اذیت کا موجب بننا ، دلی کوفت پہنچانا *cut off* (*an heir*) *with a shilling*, disappoint (him) from total inheritance اپنی وصیت میں (کسی وارث) کی اُمیدوں پر پانی پھیر دینا عاق کردینا *n.* act of cutting کاٹنا ، قطع کرنا wound made by it زخم *the most unkindest cut of all* (Shakespeare) سخت ظالمانہ چوٹ something obtained by cutting ٹکڑا ، کاٹا ہوا ٹکڑا *nice cut of mutton* گوشت کا نفیس ٹکڑا style in which clothes, etc., are made by cutting (کپڑے کی) قطع ، کاٹ *the cut of a coat* کوٹ کی کاٹ sharp, quick stroke (of a sword or whip or of ball in cricket) (تلوار ، چابک یا گیند کی) کاٹ reduction (*in* wages, prices, etc.) (اُجرت ، تنخواہ ، قیمت وغیرہ میں) کمی **cutter** (*kut-ĕ**) *n.* person or thing that cuts کاٹنے والا ، قاطع *a tailor's cutter* سینے کے لیے کپڑا کاٹنے والا small single-masted sailing vessel ایک مستولی جہاز war-ship's boat for rowing or sailing to or from ship جنگی جہاز کی کشتی **cutback** *n.* (see. *Addenda*) **cut-purse** *n.* pick-pocket جیب کترا ، گرہ کٹ **cut-throat** *n.* murderer قاتل *adj.* very hard and merciless (competition, etc.) سخت *cut-throat competition*, very hard competition سخت مقابلہ **cut-purse** *n.* pick-pocket **cutting** *n.* unroofed passage dug through ground (for a road, railway, canal, etc.) کھدائی ، کٹائی something cut

a cutting (sense 1)

from a newspaper, etc. تراشہ short piece of stem, etc., cut from a plant, to be used for growing a new plant *adj.* (of words, etc.) wounding the feelings دل خراش ، دل آزار ▣ **Cut** is the general word. We **hack** with a blunt edge; **notch** when we cut an angular piece, **slash** when we cut right and left, **gash** when we make a big hole in something and **scar** when we just bruise the surface. To **split** is to divide ; to **bisect**, cut in two equal parts , to **dissect**, cut up for scientific observation. We **slice** equally, **cleave** into two, **carve** meat, **amputate** a limb and **lance** an abscess. Again we **shave off** hair, have a **hair-cut**, **mow** hay, **reap** a harvest, **clip** wool when **sheering** sheep, and **trim** something for neatness. We **prune** a fruit tree, **whittle** chips from a stick, **lop** branches and **hew** a log of wood. That is how we cut various objects.

a cutting (sense 3)

cute (kewt) *adj.* sharp-witted, clever, ingenious زیرک ، تیز فہم ، ذکی (U.S.), charmingly pretty ; attractive خوبصورت ، دلکش ، حسین *a cute girl* خوب صورت چھوکری ، حسین لڑکی **cutlass** (*kut*-las) *n.* short sword with a curved blade usu. used by sailors چھوٹی تلوار ، قرولی ، کھانڈا **cutler** (*kut*-lĕ*) *n.* one who sells, makes or repairs knives, etc. چھری چاقو والا ، کارد گر ، کارد فروش **cutlery** (*kut*-le-ri) *n.* knives, etc., used at the table چھری کانٹا ، چھری کانٹے **cutlet** (*kut*-let) *n.* fried or grilled neck chop of mutton چاپ ، تکہ ، تکلے imitation of mutton cutlet in minced fish, etc. (مچھلی وغیرہ کے) تکلے **cut-purse** *n.* **cut-throat** *n.* & *adj.*, **cutting** *n.* & *adj.* (see under **cut**) **cuttle** (*kut*-èl), **cuttle-fish** (*kut*-èl-fish) *n.* sea-water mollusc with ten tentacles ejecting black fluid when attacked دوشاخہ مچھلی **Cybele** (*sib*-e-lee) *Cl. myth.* a Phrygian goddess worshipped at Rome as *Ops*. She is sometimes identified with the Greek Titan *Rhea* who was the wife of Cronos سبیلی ، چھبیلی

a cuttle-fish

cycle (*sīk*-èl) *n.* set of events repeating itself regularly دور ، چکر *cycle of the seasons* موسموں کا چکر *cycle of events* واقعات کا چکر any complete set or series مکمل سلسلہ ، پورا چکر (short for) bicycle or other wheeled machine (بائیسکل ، موٹر سائیکل وغیرہ کا مخفف) سئیکل *v.i.* ride a bicycle بائیسکل چلانا ، بائیسکل پر چڑھنا **cycling** (*sīk*-ling) *n.* riding a bicycle سئیکل کی سواری کرنا ، سئیکل پر چڑھنا سئیکل پر جانا **cyclist** (*sīk*-list) *n.* person who rides a bicycle سیکل والا، سیکل سوار

cyclone (*sīk*-lohn) *n.* violent and destructive windstorm moving in a circle round a calm central area طوفانی بگولہ، طوفانی گردباد **cyclonic** (*-lon-*) *adj.* (like that) of a cyclone طوفانی گردباد کا سا

cyclopaedia, cyclopedia (sik-lo-*pee*-dia) *n.* same as **encyclopaedia** (which see)

Cyclops (*sīk*-lops) (pl. *Cyclopes*, pr. sīk-*loh*-peez; or *Cyclopses*, pr. -siz) *Cl. myth.* one-eyed giant سیکلوپس one-eyed person کانا ، کانڑا

cyclostyle (*sīk*-loh-stīl) *n.* machine for obtaining duplicate copies of manuscript or typescript سلیٹ چھاپا، نقل نگار، سیکلوسٹائل *v.t.* obtain such copies سلیٹ چھاپنا ، نقل نگاری کرنا ، سیکلوسٹائل کرنا

cyclotrone (*sīk*-lot-rohn) *n.* apparatus for accelerating charged atoms دَوریہ

cyder (*sī*-dĕ*) *n.* same as **cider** (which see)

cylinder (*sil*-in-dĕ*) *n.* roller-shaped solid or hollow object بیلن اُسطوانہ hollow chamber of that shape (in an engine) in which steam, etc., works a piston *eight-cylinder motor-car* آٹھ بیلن کی موٹر

a cylinder

cylindrical (sil-in-dri-kĕl) *adj.* like a cylinder بیلن سا ، اُسطوانی

cymbals (*sim*-bĕlz) *n. pl.* pair of round brass plates struck together to produce musical sounds جھانجھ ، مجیرا

Cymric (*kim*-rik) *n.* Welsh ویلزی

cynic (*sin*-ik) *n.* member of a Greek sect of philosophers like Diogenes who condemned sophistication and luxury, and practised extreme bluntness کلبی sneering person who sees no good in anything کلبی، نک چڑھا person shamelessly avowing motives or exhibiting passions which are usu. concealed بے حیا، آبرو باختہ **cynical** (*sin*-i-kĕl) *adj.* too blunt منہ پھٹ sarcastic طنز بھرا shameless in conduct آبرو باختہ ، بے حیا

cynicism (*sin*-i-sizm) *n.* کلبیت ، خشک مزاجی ، بدخوئی ، منہ پھٹ ہونا ، بے حیائی

cynosure (*sin*-o-shoo-ĕ*) *n.* centre of everyone's attention نگاہوں کا مرکز، مرکز نگاہ *the cynosure of all eyes* جس پر سب کی نظریں لگی ہوئی ہوں، سب کی نگاہوں کا مرکز، سب کا مرکز نگاہ *the cynosure of the world* جس پر دنیا بھر کی نظریں لگی ہوئی ہوں

Cynthia (*sin*-thi-a) *Cl. myth.* another name for the goddess *Diana*. She derived this name from her place of birth, Cynthus, which is situated in Doles سِنتھیا ، سِنتھیہ

cypher (*sī*-fĕ*) *n.* same as **cipher** (which see)

cypress (*sīp*-res) *n.* a straight evergreen tree with shuttle-shaped mass of dark leaves سَرو

cyst (sist) *n.* any pouch in a living body containing liquid or diseased matter تھیلی، پھوٹ **cystic** (*sis*-tik) *adj.* pertaining to the bladder مثانے کا دیا کے متعلق

-cyte (sit) *suf.* pertaining to cells of a living organism خلیاتی

cytology (si-*tol*-o-ji) *n.* study of the cells of a living organizm علم خلیات ، خلیاتیات

Cytherea (si-the-*ree*-a) *Cl. myth.* another name for the goddess *Venus*. She derived this name from the island of Cythera where she was much worshipped سیتھیریہ

Czar, Tsar, Tzar (zah*) *n.* title of the Russian emperors of the pre-1917 Revolution regime زار **Czarina, Tsarina, Tzarina** (zah-*ree*-na) *n.* wife of a Czar زارینہ

D

d, D (*dee*) (pl., *d's* or ds ; pr. deez), fourth letter of the English alphabet ڈی Roman numeral standing for 500 پانچ سَو، پانسَو any *D*-shaped thing ڈی

[2] **'d** (colloq.) after *I* or *you* it stands for *had* or *would*, as *I'd=I had* or *I would* ; *You'd=you had* or *you would*.

dab *v. t.* & *i.* (*-bb-*) pat with something soft تھپتھپانا ، آہستہ لگانا ، پچارا دینا ، پھیرنا *n.* light and quick touch پچارا small quantity (of paint, etc.) dabbed on something تھپتھپایا ہوا رنگ

dabble (*dab*-ĕl) *v. t.* & *i.* splash (hands or feet) in water پانی میں ہاتھ پاؤں مارنا، چھینٹیں ڈالنا یا اُڑانا *dabble in* (*something*), take an interest in its study, but not seriously کوئی کام دل بہلانے کے طور پر اختیار کرنا

dactyl (*dak*-til) *n.* metrical foot (— ⏑ ⏑) with one long syllable followed by two short ones (*e.g.*, *lift* her up/*tenderly*) انگریزی بحروں کا ایک رکن، مفاعیلن

dad (dad) **daddy** (*dad*-i) *n.* child's word for father' ابّا، بابا *daddy-long-legs n.* a long-legged flying insect لم ڈھینگ، پتنگا

Daedalus (*dee*-da-lus) *Cl. myth* builder of the

Labyrinth in Crete ; he was shut up by king Minos but managed to make a fatal escape by means of artificial wings ڈیڈلس

daffodil (*daf*-o-dil) *n.* tall yellow flower growing in spring آبی نرگس its colour (ہلکا زرد رنگ)

a daffodil

dagger (*dag*-ě*) *n.* a two-edged pointed knife-like weapon خنجر، کٹار *be at daggers drawn*, be at enmity with ایک دوسرے کے خون کا پیاسا ہونا

dahlia (*dayl*-ya) *n.* plant with large bright flowers ڈالیا

daily (*day*-li) *adv.* every day روز، ہرروز، روزانہ *adj.* happening every day روزانہ (*one's*) *daily bread*, (one's) necessary food روزی، رزق *n.* newspaper published every day روزنامہ، روزانہ اخبار (Also see **day**)

a dagger

dainty (*daynt*-i) *adj* delicately pretty نازک، نفیس of delicate taste لذیذ، نفیس (person) with delicate tastes نفاست پسند (person) difficult to please نازک مزاج *n.* choice مزے دار کھانا **daintily** *adv.* نفاست سے، بنزاکت **daintiness** *n.* being dainty نفاست پسندی

dairy (*day*-è-ri) *n.* (pl., *dairies*) room where milk is kept and butter made ڈیری، شیرخانہ، مکھن نکالنے کا کارخانہ shop for milk, butter, eggs, etc., دودھ دہی کی دکان **dairy-farm**, farm for producing milk, etc. ڈیری فارم، شیرگاہ **dairy maid**, woman working in a dairy farm شیرگاہ کی ملازمہ۔ گوالن

dais (*day*-is) *n.* low platform for speakers چبوترا، سٹیج، شہ نشین

daisy (*day*-zi) *n.* small flower with yellow centre ڈیزی

dale (dayl) *n.* (poet. or Scottish) valley وادی، گھاٹی

dalliance (*dal*-i-ans) *n.* trifling behaviour ٹال مٹول love-making for f..n چونچلے، نازنخرے، جلوہ فروشی

dally (*dal*-i) *v.i.* waste time یونہی دیر لگانا، فضول وقت ضائع کرنا *dally with*, (*a*) trifle with ٹال مٹول کرنا (*b*) make love with someone for fun اٹھلانا، نازنخرے کرنا

dam *n.* wall built to hold back water بند، پشتہ mother (of an animal) (چوپائے کی) ماں *v.t.* make a dam across (کسی کے گرد یا پر) بند باندھنا یا پشتہ بنانا back by means of a dam بند باندھ کر روکنا

damage (*dam*-ij) *n.* injury or harm which decreases value نقصان، ضرر، صدمہ (*pl.*) (in law) money (to be) paid by a person causing damage ہرجانہ، ہرجہ تاوان *v.t.* cause damage to دکھ، نقصان پہنچانا

damask (*dam*-ask) silk or linen cloth with designs woven in the same colour بیل بوٹے والا ریشمی کپڑا، مشجّر

dame (daym) *n.* (old use) lady بیگم، بانو (old use) married woman بیوی، شادی شدہ عورت woman receiving an order of knighthood نائٹ عورت، فوجدار خاتون title of such a woman ڈیم

damn (dam) *v.t.* & *i.* (of God) condemn to eternal punishment مردود کرنا، جہنم واصل کرنا، لعنت کرنا، عذاب دینا judge as worthless ناکارہ قرار دینا، برا کہنا curse لعنت بھیجنا، نفرین کرنا *damn it, damn it all*, لعنت بھیجو، دفع کرو *I will be damned if I will (do something)*, I refuse to do it بس یہ تو نہیں کرنے کا، میں تو ہرگز نہ کروں گا **damnable** *adj.* deserving damnation لعنت کا مستحق hateful لائق نفرین **damnation** *n.* being damned نفرین، پھٹکار، عذاب دائمی، مردود ٹھہرنا **damned** (damd) (abb. usu. written as **d—d**, pr. deed) *adj.* damnable ملعون، مکروہ *adv.* damnably, extremely ملعون، مکروہ، نہایت، حد درجہ

Damocles (*dam*-o-kleez) *Cl. myth.* a flattering Greek courtier whose error King Dionysius showed him by having, at a feast, a sharp-edged sword suspended over his head by a single horse-hair ڈاموکلیز *the sword of Damocles*, impending danger شمشیر بر سر، سر پر کھڑا خطرہ

damp *adj.* moist نم، سیلا، مرطوب *n.* state of being damp نمی، سیلن، رطوبت *v.t.* make damp نم کرنا، سیلن پہنچانا (also *dampen*) make sad or dull افسردہ کرنا، دل بجھانا، ہمت شکنی کرنا *damp down a fire*, cause it to burn slowly **dampen** *v.t.* (see *damp*, *v.t.* sense 2) **damper** *n.* metal plate for regulating the flow of air into a fire ہوا کم و بیش کرنے کا پتر، ہوا روک that which damps تریا افسردہ کرنے والا *cast a damper on* (*a party, etc.*), cause (its) participants to be less merry پوری محفل کو، افسردہ کرنا **dampness** *n.* being damp نمی، سیلن، سیل، رطوبت

damsel (*dam*-zel) *n.* (old use) girl young unmarried woman دوشیزہ

dance (dahns) *v.t.* & *i.* move feet and body rhythmically in time to music ناچنا، رقص کرنا perform (such movements) ناچنا، کدکڑے مارنا jump about اچھلنا، کودنا *dance with* (or *for*) *joy* خوشی سے ناچنا *heart dancing with glee* بلیوں اچھلتا ہوا دل move (baby, etc.) up and down (بچے کو) اچھالنا، ہلانا *She danced the baby on her knee* وہ بچے کو گھٹنے پر رکھ کر ہلاتی رہی *n.* rhythmical movement of feet and body to music ناچ، رقص dancing party, ball محفل رقص one round of dancing ناچ کا ایک دور (یا) گشت *May I have the next dance with you?* کیا میں اگلے دور میں آپ کے ساتھ رقص کر سکتا ہوں piece of music for dancing ناچ گت *the orchestra played a*

new dance ساز ندوں نے ناچ کی نئی گت بجائی *give a dance*, invite people to one's house to dance محفلِ رقص *lead (someone) a (pretty) dance*, cause (him) worry through false hopes سبز باغ دکھانا
dancer *n.* one who dances (esp. as a professional) رقاصہ **dancing-girl** *n.* prostitute of a somewhat higher social status رقاصہ **dancing** *n.* art of dancing ناچ ، رقص
dandelion (dan-de-li-on or *dand-*) *n.* yellow-flowered plant with jagged leaves کُکروندا ، شیر دنداں
dandle (*dand*-ĕl) *v.t.* fondle لاڈ کرنا ، پیار کرنا dance (a child) in arms or on knee (بچے کو) گھٹنوں پر بٹھا کر اُچھالنا ، ہلانا ، جھلانا ، کھلانا *She dandled the child to sleep* اُس نے بچے کو کھلا کھلا کر سُلا دیا

dandelions

dandriff *n.* same as **dandruff** (which see)
dandruff (*dan*-druf), **dandriff** *n.* scaly scurf on the scalp بِفا
dandy (*dand*-i) *n.* person who pays great attention to his clothes and personal appearance بانکا ، چھیلا ، چھیل چھبیلا
danger (*dayn*-jĕ*) *n.* risk, peril خطرہ ، کھٹکا *be in danger* خطرناک حالت میں ہونا *be out of danger* خطرہ نہ رہنا *the singal is at danger* خطرے کا نشان ہو رہا ہے something which may cause injury خطرے کی چیز **dangerous** (*dayn*-jĕ-rus) *adj.* perilous خطرناک ، پُر خطر ، ہولناک likely to harm سخت خطرناک *dangerous disease* سخت بیماری **dangerously** *adj.* facing danger خطرناک حد تک ، خطرناک طور پر ▣ **A danger** is a possibility of harm, but **a risk** is voluntarily assumed. **A peril** is imminent; **a hazard**, that in which luck plays a large part; **jeopardy**, a serious risk
dangle (*dang*-ĕl) *v.t.* & *i.* swing while hanging loosely لٹکنا ، جھولنا carry (something) so that it swings loosely لٹکانا *dangle round* (or *about*, or *after*) (*someone*), stay near (him) as a follower or lover کے پیچھے پیچھے پھرنا
Daniel (*dan*-yel) *n.* name of a prophet حضرت دانیال any impartial judge عادل منصف ، بے لاگ منصف
dank *adj.* unpleasantly damp بہت سیلا ، سخت مرطوب *dank cellar* بہت سیلا تہ خانہ
dapper (*dap*-ĕ*) *adj.* smartly dressed, spruce چست لباس میں ، خوش وضع quick and active چست ، پھرتیلا ، چست چالاک ،
Daphne (*daf*-nee) *Cl. myth.* a nymph beloved by Apollo and turned by him into a laurel-tree دفنی
dapple (*dap*-ĕl) *v.t.* & *i.* make with patches of different shades of colour دھبے ڈالنا یا پڑنا ، پچرنگا کرنا یا ہونا **dappled** *adj.* spotted (sunlight, animal or shadow) چتلا

dare (*day*-ĕ*) *v.t.* (pa. t. **dared**, sometimes **durst**) be bold enough to کی جرأت کرنا be impudent enough to کی جسارت کرنا *How dare you say I am a liar?* مجھ کو جھوٹا کہنے کی تمہیں جرأت کیونکر ہوئی ؟ *I dare say*, I think it likely میرا خیال تو یہی ہے face the risk of (something) مقابلے میں آنا ، کا مقابلہ کرنا ، سامنا کرنا *dare any danger* ہر خطرے کا مقابلہ کرنا *dare (someone's) anger* کسی کے غصے کا مقابلہ کرنا challenge (someone who is unwilling to do something) للکارنا ، جُرأت *I dared him to jump across the stream* میں نے اُسے ندی پھلانگنے کی جرأت کرنے کو کہا ، **dare-devil** *n.* foolishly bold احمقانہ طور پر نڈر ، منہ زور **adj.** such action دلیرانہ ، بے باکانہ **daring** (*day*-ĕ-ring) *adj.* bold and adventurous بہادر ، نڈر ، بے باک *n.* such quality بہادری ، بے باکی ، بے خوفی
dark (dah*k) *adj.* having little or no light تاریک ، اندھیرا almost black کالا ، کالی *dark skinned* یاس انگیز ، غمگین gloomy چمڑی والا mysterious پُر اسرار ، مبہم *dark saying* پُر اسرار بات evil مجرمانہ ، *dark deed* مجرمانہ فعل *n.* darkness ، تاریکی ، پُر اسرار ، سنگین تاریک night رات *in the dark* رات کی تاریکی میں secrecy اخفاء ، چھپنا *work in the dark* چھپ چھپ کر کام کرنا ignorance جہالت ، بے خبری *keep (something) dark*, keep it secret چھپائے رکھنا ، مخفی *look on the dark side (of things)*, see only that which is sad or cheerless زندگی کا تاریک پہلو دیکھنا *keep (someone) in the dark*, keep things secret from him سے چھپائے رکھنا ، کو نہ بتانا *be in the dark about*, have no knowledge of سے بے خبر ہونا **darken** *v.t.* & *i.* make or become dark اندھیرا ہونا یا کرنا **darkness** *n.* اندھیرا ، تاریکی ، پُر اسرار رہنا ، جہالت ▣ **Dark** is something which does not receive or reflect light; **gloomy**, something unpleasant and dark; **obscure**, not very light, but lighter than dark; **opaque**, that which cannot be seen through; **dim**, not brilliant; **nebulous**, foggy or cloudy; **murky**, very cloudy (sky). **Vague** is used figuratively meaning not clear; **sombre** is also used figuratively to denote something very shady.
darling (*dah**-ling) *n.* person much loved محبوب *adj.* much loved محبوب ، پسندیدہ
darn (dah*n) *v.t.* & *i.* mend (something knitted) with criss-cross stitches رفو کرنا *n.* place mended by darning رفو **darning** *n.* things needing to be darned رفو طلب (چیزیں) act of darning رفو **darner** *n.* one who darns رفوگر
dart (dah*t) *v.t.* & *i.* (cause to) move forward suddenly and quickly تیزی سے بڑھنا یا بڑھانا ، لپکنا *dart out of a place* کہیں سے تیر کی طرح نکلنا *make a dart at* پر تیر کی طرح جھپٹنا ، *n.* any small, sharp-pointed object, esp. one thrown at a dart board in the game of darts چھوٹی برچھی ، تیر ، بچوں کے کھیل کی برچھی ، بچوں کے کھیل ، برچھیاں ، کا ہدف quick, sudden movement

تیز حرکت (*pl.*) an indoor game (بچوں کا کھیل) « برچھیاں »

dash *v.t.* & *i.* send or throw violently, پھینکنا، دھکا دینا splash (with water, etc.) (پانی کے) چھینٹے ڈالنا (fig.) destroy امید توڑنا، خاک میں ملانا *dash (someone's) hopes* (کسی کی) آس توڑنا strike ٹکرانا، ٹکر ہونا smash پاش پاش ہونا *n.* sudden and violent forward movement جھپٹ، تیز حرکت *dash for shelter* پناہ لینے کے لیے تیزی سے جانا sound made by water when striking something or when being struck پانی کے تھپیڑوں کی آواز، نعرہ *dash of the waves* نعرۂ امواج *dash of oars on the water* چپو کی پانی سے ٹکرانے کی آواز pinch of something added چٹکی بھر، ذرا سا *dash of salt* ذرا سا نمک mark used in writing, ڈیش، (ریں) شرطیہ vigorous action پُرجوش عمل energy ہمت، طاقت *cut a dash*, make a vulgar show of riches امارت کا بدذوقی سے اظہار کرنا **dash-board** *n.* mudboard in front of a car کیچ روک instrument-board in a car or aircraft آلات نما **dashing** *adj.* bold بہادر، جری showy نمائش پسند gay خوش باش

dastard (*das*-tĕ*d) *n.* coward بزدل coward who commits brutality without endangering himself بزدل ستمگر **dastardly** *adj.* cowardly بزدلانہ

data (*day*-ta) *n. pl.* (*sing.*, **datum**) facts given from which conclusions may be drawn معروضات، امورِ معلومہ، مُبیّنہ حقائق

date (dayt) *n.* fruit of date-palm کھجور، تمر point of time as shown on a calendar تاریخ *have a date with (someone)* (U.S.) have an appointment for a love-affair (چاہنے والوں سے) وعدۂ ملاقات کرنا period of history to which anything belongs زمانہ، عہد، دور *(go) out of date*, (be) old fashioned متروک (ہونا)، تقویمِ پارینہ (ہونا) *(be) up to date*, (be) in line with the present notions جدید، جدید ترین، ہنوزی (ہونا) *up-to-date ideas* جدید ترین خیالات *v.i.* & *t.* put a date on تاریخ ڈالنا give a date to زمانہ متعین کرنا *date from*, *date back to*, exist since (فلاں) زمانے کا ہونا **Note:** As an *adj.* **up-to-date** is hyphenated; not so as an adverb. So we have *up-to-date ideas* but write of *being up to date.*

dative (*day*-tiv) *n.* form of the indirect object مفعولی حالت، حالتِ نصبی

datum *n.* (sing. of **data** which see)

daub (dawb) *v.i.* & *t.* coat or plaster thickly and roughly لیپنا، پوتنا، استرکاری کرنا make dirty marks on داغ دھبے ڈالنا paint (pictures) without skill اناڑیوں کی سی تصویریں بنانا یا رنگ آمیزی کرنا *n.* material used for daubing (*e.g.*, clay) کہگل، پلستر، روغن badly painted pictures بھدی تصویر **dauber** *n.* unskilled painter اناڑی مصور

daughter (*daw*-tĕ*) *n.* a person's female child بیٹی، لڑکی، دختر، بنت **daughter-in-law** *n.* son's wife بہو.

daunt (dawnt) *v.t.* discourage ہمت توڑنا، حوصلہ شکنی کرنا دھمکانا **dauntless** *adj.* undaunted دھمکی میں نہ آنے والا مرعوب نہ ہونے والا persevering مستقل مزاج

dauphin *n.* formerly title of the eldest son of the King of France ولی عہدِ فرانس، دوفین

dawdle (*daw*-dĕl) *v.i.* waste time in loitering سستی کرنا، کاہلی کرنا، بیکار پھرتے رہنا be slow مٹرگشت کرنا waste time وقت ضائع کرنا سے کام لینا **dawdler** *n.* idler سست، کاہل، وقت ضائع کرنے والا one who wastes time by loitering

dawn *n.* daybreak سویرا، تڑکا، فجر، طلوعِ صبح، طلوعِ سحر beginning آغاز، شروع *the dawn of a new era*, beginning of a new epoch عہدِ جدید کا آغاز، نیا سویرا *v.i.* begin to grow light پو پھٹنا *The day is dawning* پو پھٹ رہی ہے become evident or clear to mind ذہن میں ابھرنا، سمجھ میں آنا *dawn on (someone)*, grow clear to (his) mind کسی کی سمجھ میں آنا

day *n.* period between sunrise and sunset دن *this day week* آج سے آٹھویں دن *this day month (year etc.)* آج سے مہینہ (یا سال وغیرہ) بعد period of 24 consecutive hours from midnight to midnight دن، روز *pass the time of day (with someone)*, exchange greetings, etc., with him کسی کے ساتھ وقت گزارنا *the other day*, a few days ago ابھی اگلے روز، چند روز پہلے کی بات ہے کہ *one day*, on a past or future day کبھی *some day*, on some day in the future کسی روز *every day, day by day, day after day, from day to day* روز بروز، روزانہ *day about*, on alternate days ایک دن چھوڑ کے، ہر تیسرے دن *in the days of old*, formerly پہلے زمانے میں، اگلے وقتوں میں، اگلے وقتوں کی بات ہے کہ *have (one's) day*, have a period of success کی کامیابی کا زمانہ ہونا event واقعہ contest مقابلہ، معرکہ victory, success جیت *The day is ours* آج کا دن ہمارا ہے۔ آج ہماری جیت ہے *We have won the day*; we have achieved victory in all or most of contests today آج ہماری جیت رہی *carry the day, win the day*, be victorious جیتنا، کی جیت ہونا *lose the day*, be defeated ہارنا، کی ہار ہونا

day-break *n.* dawn سویرا، تڑکا، فجر **daytime** *n.* day دن، دن کا وقت **daylight** *n.* natural and not artificial light سورج کی روشنی *in broad daylight*, in daylight دن دہاڑے، روزِ روشن میں **day-book** *n.* account-book بہی، روزنامچہ **day-school** *n.* non-residential school مدرسہ **dayspring** *n.* dawn فجر **daydream** *n.* reverie خیالی پلاؤ **daylight saving** *n.* putting the hands of the clock forward so that darkness falls at a later hour گھڑیاں آگے کر

daze (dayz) *v.t.* stupefy بدحواس bewilder گھبرا دینا dazzle *n.* چندھیانا، چندھیا دینا، خیرہ کرنا bewilderment حیران، سراسیمہ حیرت *in a daze*, in a dazed state

dazzle (*daz*-èl) *v.t.* make (someone) unable to see clearly owing to too much light چندھیانا ؛ چندھیا دینا ، خیرہ کرنا make (someone) unable to act sensibly owing to too much splendour نظر کو خیرہ کرنا *dazzling beauty* خیرہ کُن حسن و جمال

d—d (deed) *adj.* & *adv.* same as *damned*. See under **damn**

deacon *n.* clergyman with various duties چھوٹا پادری ، ڈیکن **deaconess** *n.* churchwoman in charge of charitable functions خیراتی کاموں والی پادرن **diaconal** (di-) *adj.* of a deacon چھوٹے پادری کا یا اُسے متعلق **diaconate** (di-) *n.* office of deacon ڈیکن کا عہدہ body of deacons کُل ڈیکن

dead (ded) *adj.* (no *adv.* formed with *-ly* ; deadly itself is an *adj.*) no longer living مُردہ ، میّت *He is dead* وہ مر گیا ہے اُس کا اِنتقال ہو گیا ہے *dead march*, funeral music ماتمی دُھن *dead men* (*a*) the dead مُردے (*b*) (slang) empty-bottles (of wine) شراب کی خالی بوتلیں *dead men's shoes*, position or property to which a successor expectantly looks forward متوقع وِرثہ *dead men tell no tales* مُردے راز فاش نہیں کر سکتے without activity پُر سکوت ، غیر متحرک ، ساکن *the dead hours of the night* رات کی خاموشی ، سکوتِ شب utter, complete پُورا ، مکمل ، بالکل ، یکسر ، سراسر *dead calm* پُورا سکوت ، بالکل خاموش *in dead earnest* بڑی سنجیدگی سے *dead loss* سراسر نقصان (*b*) *a dead certainty*, (be) a safely predictable result یقینی (ہونا) no longer working خراب ، بند *The telephone is dead* فون خراب ہے used up از کار رفتہ *a dead match* جلی ہُوئی دیا سلائی *dead language*, language no longer in use مُردہ زبان sudden اچانک ، یکایک *come to a dead stop* یکایک رُک جانا exact ٹھیک ، صحیح *in the dead centre*, exactly in the centre مرکز میں ، ٹھیک بالکل وسط میں *adv.* completely یکسر ، مکمل ، کامل ، سراسر *dead beat, dead tired*, exhausted تھک کر چُور ، واماندہ *n.* the dead, those who have died مرنے والے ، مُردے time of deepest quiet سماں ، خاموشی *the dead of night*, the quietest part of it سکوتِ شب **deaden** (*ded*-èn) *v.t.* take away feeling بے حس کرنا lessen the force of (noise or pain) (شور یا درد کا) زور کم کرنا ، گھٹانا **deadly** *adj.* fatal جان لیوا ، مُہلک *deadly blow* مُہلک ضرب relentless سخت ، جانی *deadly enemy* جانی دشمن looking dead موت کا سا ، مرگ آسا *deadly pallor* موت کی سی زردی **deadness** *n.*, **dead duck** *n.* (see *Addenda*) **dead heat** *n.* race in which two or more runners are equal برابر کی دوڑ **dead letter** *n.* legislation no longer enforced غیر نافذ قانون letter kept by the post office because the addressee cannot be traced جس خط کا مکتوب الیہ لاپتہ ہو ، لاپتہ خط something outmoded تقویمِ پارینہ **dead-letter office**, *n.* section of the post office where such letters are kept دفتر لاپتہ خط **deadpan** *n.* (see *Addenda*)

deadlock *n.* impasse ; standstill ; failure to settle dispute تعطل

deaf (def) *adj.* unable to hear بہرا ، اونچا سننے والا *deaf-mute* گونگا بہرا not willing to listen بے حس بے پرواہ ، پنبہ بگوش **deafen** (*def*-èn) *v.t.* make so much noise as to make hearing almost impossible شور سے کانوں کے پردے پھاڑنا *deafening noise* کانوں کے پردے پھاڑنے والا شور **deafness** *n.* being deaf بہراپن

deal (deel) *v.t.* & *i.* *deal* ; (*dealt*, pr. delt ; *dealt*, pr. delt) hand out to a number of persons بانٹنا ، تقسیم کرنا *deal out money* روپیہ بانٹنا *deal cards* تاش بانٹنا inflict لگانا ، مارنا *deal a blow (at)*, strike گھونسا مارنا ، مکا مارنا (*deal in*), do business in (something) بیچنا ، کاروبار کرنا (*deal with*) (*a*) buy from سے خریدنا (*b*) behave towards سے برتاؤ رکھنا *He is difficult to deal with* وہ بڑا اکھڑ ہے اُس سے نباہ مشکل ہے *deal fairly with* سے اچھا سلوک کرنا ، سے حُسنِ سلوک کرنا (*c*) be about سے متعلق ہونا *This book does not deal with this subject* یہ کتاب اُس مضمون سے متعلق نہیں ہے manage نپٹنا ، سلجھانا *n.* pine wood چیڑ یا صنوبر کی لکڑی board made of it چیڑ کی لکڑی کا تختہ (in card games) the act of dealing cards تاش کا بانٹنا *new deal*, new plan which is just نیا نظام ، نئی تقسیم (*give one*) *a square deal*, (give him) fair treatment ٹھیک سلوک کرنا business agreement کاروباری معاہدہ ، سودا (colloq.) a bargain سودا amount مقدار *a good (or great) deal of*, very much کافی ، کچھ *a good deal better*, much better کہیں بہتر **dealer** *n.* trader دکاندار ، بیوپاری یا تاجر (*in*) person who deals cards تاش (کے پتے) بانٹنے والا **dealings** *n. pl.* business relations لین دین relations تعلقات ، مراسم *have no dealings with (someone)* سے تعلقات منقطع کرنا

dealt (delt) pa. t. and pa. p. of **deal** (which see)

dean (deen) *n.* clergyman ranking next to bishop بشپ کے نیچے دوسرے درجے کا آدمی (in colleges) person with authority to maintain discipline (کالج میں) طلبہ کا نگران (in universities) head of a faculty of studies (یونیورسٹی میں) کسی شعبۂ تعلیم کا صدر ، ڈین **deanery** *n.* position of dean ڈین کا عہدہ residence of a dean ڈین کی قیام گاہ

dear (*dee*-è*) *adj.* much loved پیارا ، دُلارا ، عزیز ، محبوب highly esteemed نہایت محترم *Dear Sir*, form of address in letters محترم جناب *My dear (so and-so)* intimate form of address in letters مخدومی costly

قیمتی. مہنگا ، بیش بہا charging high prices گراں، مہنگا *It is a dear shop* یہ بڑی مہنگی کان ہے *int*. (*dear ! dear dear ! Oh dear ! Dear me.*), expression of surprise or impatience توبہ، ارے توبہ، مَعاذَاللہ **dearly** *adv*. پیار سے، محبت سے ، شوق سے **dearness** *n*. being costly مہنگا پن، مہنگائی ، گرانی **dearth** (dĕ*th) *n*. scarcity (esp. of food) گرانی ، کال

death (deth) *n*. end of life موت ، مرگ ، قضا، اِنتقال dying مرنا، اِنتقال کرنا state of being dead مُردہ ، مرا ہوا ، مرگ ، موت ، وفات entire loss or end (*of* something) خاتمہ *tired to death*, extremely tired سخت تھکا ہوا *put to death*, kill قتل کرنا **death-duties** *n. pl*. taxes on the property of one who dies موت کا ٹیکس جو وارثوں کو ورثے پر ادا کرنا پڑتا ہے **deathless** *adj*. never dying لازوال، اَمَر **deathly** *adj*. like death موت کا سا، موت کے مانند **death-rate** *n*. rate per thousand of those dying every year شرح اموات (فی ہزار سالانہ) **deathtrap** *n*. dangerous place, esp. on a road خطرناک جگہ ، موت کا گھر ؛ کسی کو پھانس کر مارنے کی جگہ

debacle (de-*bahk*-èl) *n*. sudden ruin اچانک تباہی utter failure قطعی ناکامی

debar (de-*bah**) *v.t*. (-*rr*-) shut out (*from*) ممنوع قرار دینا ، خارج کرنا ، محروم کرنا prevent (someone) by a regulation (*from* doing or having something) (کسی قاعدے کی رُو سے) روکنا *He was debarred from taking the examination* اُسے امتحان دینے سے روک دیا گیا

debase (de-*bays*) *v.t*. lower in value بے قدر کرنا، گھٹانا make poor in quality or character کھوٹا بنانا ملاوٹ کرنا **debasement** *n*. lowering in value, quality or character سُبکی، بے قدری ، ملاوٹ

debate (de-*bayt*) *n*. discussion (esp. in a student's union or in Parliament) بحث ، مُباحثہ *v.t. & i*. have a debate about مُباحثہ منعقد کرنا ، بحث کرنا ، participate in a debate بحث میں حصّہ لینا . consider in order to decide اِستدلال کرنا ، فکر کرنا ، غور کرنا **debater** *n*. one who participates in debates; speaker skilled in argument rather than in oratory مُباحث ، مُناظِر ، بحّاث **debatable** (de-*bayt*-a-bèl) *qdj*. (of point, etc.) open to question, liable to be disputed قابلِ بحث و فکر، نا بہ النزاع

debauch (de-*bawch*) *v.t*. make bad or wicked بدذوق بنانا ، ذوق بگاڑنا ، آوارہ کرنا ؛ عیّاش بنانا turn away from good taste or judgment بدذوق ہو جانا، بدذوقی سے کام لینے لگنا lead away from duty or allegiance بہکانا ، وَرغلانا *n*. occasion of over-drinking or sensual behaviour in company شراب نوشی ، بد معاشی ، عیّاشی **debauched** (de-*bawchd*), **debauchee** de-*baw*-chee) *adj*. profligate بدکار ، عیّاش **debauchery** (de-*bawch*-è-ri) *n*. habitual lewdness عیّاشی ، شراب خوری excessive drinking حد سے زیادہ شراب خوری

debenture (de-*ben*-chĕ*) *n*. certificate issued by a company for money borrowed by it کسی کمپنی کی طرف سے قرض لی ہوئی رقم کا سرٹیفکیٹ written acknowledgment of debt دستاویزِ قرض

debilitate (de-*bil*-i-tayt) *v. t*. weaken (a person) کمزور کرنا یا بنانا enfeeble (one's constitution) ناتواں یا ضعیف بنا دینا (یا کرنا) ، impair the strength of مُضمحل کرنا ، ضُعف طاری کرنا **debility** (de-*bil*-i-ti) *n*. poor health ضُعف ، ناتوانی ، خرابیِ صحت weakness of purpose اِرادے کی کمزوری ، ضُعفِ ہمّت

debit (*deb*-it) *n*. entry (in an account) of a sum owing (بینک وغیرہ کے حساب میں) اُس رقم کا اِندراج جو کسی کے ذِمّے پڑے ، بنام ، کے نام (also *debit-side*), left-hand or debtor side of an account on which such entries are made اِندراج بنام ، خرچ کا اِندراج (compare *credit*, *credit-side*) *v.t*. enter on the debit-side of an account (کسی کے) نام درج کرنا ، (کے) نام ڈالنا *The bank debited my account with Rs. 200* بینک نے میرے نام دو سَو روپیہ روپیہ ڈال دیئے

debonair (deb-o-*nay*-è*) *adj*. cheerful خوش مزاج ، خوش باش of good appearance and manners خوش شکل ، خوش سیرت sociable میل ملاپ والا ، بے تکلّف

debris (*dayb*-ree) *n*. scattered wreckage مَلبہ ، مَلبا

debt (det) *n*. something one owes (*to* another) (کسی کے ذِمّے) قرضہ ، اُدھار *in* (or *out of*) *debt*, owing (or not owing) money اُدھار کی رقم *National Debt*, money owed by the State to those by whom it has been lent قومی قرضہ ، گورنمنٹ کے ذِمّے ، قرض **debtor** (*det*-ĕ*) *n*. one owing money to another قرضدار ، مقروض ، مدیون

debunk (de-*bunk*) expose (person, institution, etc.) by removing false sentiment around him, her or it کا پول کھولنا ، کی قلعی کھول دینا ، بے نقاب کرنا ، کو ننگا کر کے رکھ دینا

debus (de-*bus*) *v.t. & i*. (-*ss*-) descend from bus, etc. بس (وغیرہ) سے اُترنا unload (men, things, etc.) from bus or truck بس (وغیرہ) سے (مسافر یا سامان) اُتارنا

debut (day-*boo*) *n*. first formal appearance (of a maiden) at adult parties (کسی دوشیزہ کا) سوسائٹی میں پہلا تعارف ، اوّلین تعارف (of an actor, etc.) first appearance on the screen or stage (ایکٹر، ایکٹرس رقاصہ یا مُغنیّہ کا) تماشا گاہ میں پہلی مرتبہ بطور اداکار آنا یا ظاہر ہو- **debutante** (day-boo-*tant*) *n*. young woman making her debut لڑکی جس کا سوسائٹی میں پہلا تعارف ہو- (esp.) one presented at Court دربارِ شاہی میں پہلی مرتبہ آنے والی -

decade (*dek*-ayd) *n*. period of ten years دس سال کی مُدّت ، دہ سالہ مُدّت *the first decade of this century* اس صدی کے پہلے دس سال **decadent** (*dek-a*-dent) *adj*. (of art, culture, nation, etc.) fallen to a lower level گرتا ہوا ، زوال پذیر ، رو بہ انحطاط *the de zdent culture of the West* مغرب کا زوال پذیر تمدّن **decadence** (*dek*-a-dens, *n*. decline, deterioration (of art, culture, nation, etc.) زوال، انحطاط، تنزل، گراوٹ

decamp (de-*kamp*) *v.t.* run away secretly (*with* money, etc.) روپیہ لے کر بھاگ جانا abscond رُوپوش ہو جانا ، بھاگ جانا

decant (de-*kant*) *v.t.* pour (wine) into a decanter so carefully as not to disturb the sediment شراب کو صُراحی میں انڈیلنا ، نتھارنا **decanter** *n.* ornamental glass bottle with a stopper in which wine is brought to the table صُراحی ، مِینا ، کنٹر

decapitate (pr. de-*kap*-i-tayt) *v.t.* behead سَر قلم کرنا سر کاٹنا ، سَر کاٹ ڈالنا ، گردن مارنا

decay (de-*kay*) *v.t.* rot گلنا ، سڑنا ، بگڑنا ، خراب ہونا *decaying fruit* سڑنے والا پھل ، بوسیدہ پھل lose (health, beauty, etc.) رُوبہ تنزل ہونا ، بگڑنا fall into ruins زوال میں آنا ، گرنا ، برباد ہونا۔ *the decaying British Imperialism* زوال پذیر برطانوی سامراج کی گرتی ہوئی دیوار ، زوال پذیر برطانوی شہنشاہیت *n.* act of decaying زوال ، بوسیدگی ، تباہی ، تنزل۔

decease (de-*sees*) *n.* (esp. legal) death موت ، مرگ *the deceased* (dhè-de-*seest*) the dead person or persons مُتوفی ، آنجہانی ، مرنے والا یا والے ، مُردے

deceit *n.* see under **deceive**

deceive (de-*seev*) (Note that *c* in this word and its derivatives is followed by *e* not *i*) *v.t.* cheat دھوکا دینا ، فریب یا جُل دینا mislead purposely بہکانا ، فریب دینا **deceiver** *n.* one who deceives دغاباز ، فریبی ، حیلہ باز **deceit** (de-*seet*) *n.* deceiving فریب ، مکر ، دغا ، دھوکا ، چال ، داؤں **deceitful** *adj.* one in the habit of deceiving دھوکا دینے والا ، فریبی ، مکّار something intended to deceive دھوکا ، دھوکے کی ٹٹی ، آلۂ فریب **deceitfully** *adv.* مکر سے ، دھوکے سے **deception** (de-*sep*-shĕn) *n.* act of one who practises deceit دھوکا ، فریب ، دغا بازی ، پاکھنڈ being deceived دھوکے میں ، فریب خوردگی trick for deceiving someone پاکھنڈ ، ڈھکوسلا ، داؤں **deceptive** *adj.* deceiving دھوکے میں ڈالنے والی (حالت یا شکل) easily causing one to be deceived مغالطے میں ڈالنے والی (شے) **deceptively** *adj.* مُغالطے یا فریب کے طور پر

▣ One **deceives** intentionally but **misleads** when one **leads astray** intentionally or otherwise. Again, one **cheats** in order to obtain something; **deludes** by means of a trick; **outwits** a pursuer or a rival; and **fools** or **deludes** an honest but gullible person.

December (de-*sem*-bĕ*) *n.* the 12th month of the English year (ماہ) دسمبر

decent (*dee*-sent) *adj.* proper مُناسب ، معقول *decent clothes* شائستہ یا معقول لباس respectable مُہذب ، شائستہ *decent behaviour* شائستہ سلوک not likely to cause others to feel shame معقول ، آبرومندانہ *decent language* معقول زبان (colloq. fairly good ; of fair size or amount خاصا ، خاصی ، معقول ، اچھا خاصا *a decent meal* خاصا کھانا *a decent salary* معقول تنخواہ *decent weather* اچھا خاصا موسم **decently** *adj.* سلیقے سے ، نفاست سے **decency** *n.* being decent سلیقہ ، شائستگی ، معقولیت general standard of decency مذاقِ سلیم ، پاس ، لحاظ *an offence against decency* ناشائستگی ، بدذوقی ، بے لحاظی

decentralize (de-*sen*-tra-lɪz) *v.t.* bestow from the centre greater powers (for self-government, etc.) مُقامی حکومت عطا کرنا ، مرکزی اقتدار کم کرنا یا اُٹھا لینا یا نہ رکھنا **decentralization** (-zay-) *n.* act of decentralizing مرکزیت کو توڑ دینا ۔ مُقامی اقتدار قائم کرنا

deception *n.*, **deceptive** *adj.* (see **deceive** above)

deci- (*des*-i) pref. denoting one-tenth سابقہ ، عُشر ، (کا) دسواں (حصّہ) (کا ایک بٹا دس) (لاحقہ) *decimetre*, one tenth of a metre ڈیسی میٹر ، عُشر میٹر

decide (de-*sīd*) *v.t.* & *i.* settle فیصلہ کرنا ، طے پانا give (one's) judgment upon فیصلہ دینا *decide a case* مقدمے کا فیصلہ کرنا make up one's mind (*to* do) پختہ ارادہ یا فیصلہ کر لینا cause to make up one's mind فیصلہ کرانا **decided** (de-*sīd*-id) *adj.* definite طے شدہ ، فیصلہ شدہ (of a person) having definite opinion قطعی ، اٹل ، مستقل مزاج unmistakable قطعی ، مُعیّن ، غیر مُشتبہ ، یقینی **decidedly** *adj.* definitely یقیناً ، قطعاً **decision** *n.* (see below)

▣ We **decide** upon a course of action ; **determine** a cause or effect ; **conclude** as the result of an inquiry; **settle** finally something that has been in dispute ; and **decree** by authority that something shall henceforth be done.

deciduous (de-*sid*-ew-us) *adj.* (of trees) shedding leaves in autumn regularly پت جھاڑ

decimal (*des*-i-mĕl) *adj.* of tens or one-tenth اعشاریہ ، اعشاری ، دہ شماری *decimal system* (for coinage, weights and measures) اعشاری نظام *decimal fraction*, a fraction with 10 or some power of it for denominator کسرِ اعشاریہ ·35 (pr. *decimal three five*, or more commonly *point three five*)
decimal point, the point used to denote a decimal (as in *8·7*) نقطۂ اعشاریہ

decimate (des-i-mayt) *v.t.* kill one in every ten ہر دس میں سے ایک کو قتل کرنا destroy a very large part of بڑے حصّے کو تباہ یا ہلاک کر ڈالنا *The population was decimated by disease* آبادی کو بیماری نے برباد کر دیا

decipher (de-*sī*-fĕ*) *v.t.* decode خطِ رمز میں لکھی ہوئی (عبارت) پڑھنا ، مرموز عبارت کو پڑھنا (یا عام خط میں لکھنا) read (a writing) which is difficult to make out ناقابلِ فہم عبارت پڑھنا construe the meaning of (something) puzzling مُعمّے کو حل کرنا ، مُشکل عبارت پڑھنا

decision (de-*sizh*-ĕn) *n.* act of deciding فیصلہ، قطعی رائے *come to* (or *arrive at*) *a decision of some point* قطعی تجویز، فیصلہ، حکم settlement (of a question) کسی مسئلے کا حل making up one's mind ارادہ کرنا، قطعی رائے قائم کرنا its result اَمرِ طے شدہ، قطعی رائے *What is the decision?* فیصلہ کیا ہوا؟ ability to decide and act accordingly قوّتِ فیصلہ *a man of decision* قوّتِ فیصلہ کا مالک judgment فیصلہ **decisive** (de-*sī*-siv) *adj.* conclusive فیصلہ کن *decisive battle* فیصلہ کُن معرکہ (also, *decided*), showing determination پختہ ارادہ کا، حتمی definite and prompt قطعی، حتمی *decisive action* حتمی کام، قطعی فیصلہ

deck (dek) *n.* one of the wooden or steel floors of a ship عرشۂ جہاز *clear the decks*, (*a*) make ready for the fight معرکے کے لیے تیار ہو جانا (*b*) make ready for activity of any kind عمل کے لیے تیار ہو جانا *decked v.t.* decorate سجانا، آراستہ کرنا، سنوارنا، مُرصّع کرنا *decked with jewellery* زر و جواہر سے مُرصّع *decked out in a new dress* نئے لباس میں ملبوس **decker** *n.* a vessel that has only one deck and, hence, only one storey یک عرشہ **double-decker** *n.* & *adj.* two-storied (esp. omnibus) دومنزلہ (بس)

declaim (de-*klaym*) *v.t.* & *i.* speak passionately (*against*) کسی کے خلاف خطیبانہ تقریر کرنا deliver a speech in an oratorical style خطبہ دینا recite (poem) in a lovely manner اچھے انداز سے (نظم) پڑھنا **declamation** *n.* impassioned speech جوشیلی تقریر *declamation contest*, a contest to judge the ability to deliver impassioned speeches مقابلۂ خطابت **declamatory** (-*klam*-) *adj.* خطیبانہ

declare (de-*klay*-ĕ*) *v.t.* & *i.* announce publicly اعلان کرنا، بیان کرنا *declare the result of an examination* امتحان کا نتیجہ نکالنا، امتحان کے نتیجے کا اعلان کرنا *The Principal declared a holiday* پرنسپل صاحب نے چھٹی کا حکم دے دیا (یا) اعلانِ تعطیل کر دیا proclaim اعلان کرنا *declare war* (*on*) (کے خلاف) اعلانِ جنگ کرنا assert, say firmly or solemenly سنجیدگی سے بیان کرنا (یا) اظہار کرنا، اظہار دینا *The accused declared that he was innocent* ملزم نے بیان دیا کہ وہ بے گناہ ہے *declare for* (or *against someone* or *something*), take sides in favour of (or against him, her or it) (کسی کے خلاف یا حق میں) بیان دینا make a statement (to customs officials) of dutiable goods brought into a country قابلِ محصول اشیا کے متعلق بیان دینا close an innings in a cricket match before all the side is out کھیل (یا) اننگ ختم ہونے یا کرنے کا اعلان کرنا *Kardar declared at 400 for eight* کاردار کے ابھی آٹھ کھلاڑی آؤٹ ہوئے تھے کہ چار سو رنز بنا کر اُس نے اننگ ختم ہونے کا اعلان کر دیا

declaration (dek-la-*ray*-shĕn) *n.* act of declaring اظہار، بیان (in law) creation (*of a trust*) (وقف کا) قیام that which is declared اعلان، اظہار *declaration of war* اعلانِ جنگ manifesto منشور، اعلان *the American Declaration of Independence* امریکی منشورِ آزادی information given to authority for the purpose of bringing out a paper اخبار وغیرہ جاری کرنے کے متعلق اظہار، ڈیکلریشن *A declaration for bringing out the fortnightly 'New Thought' has been filed with the A.D.M.* پندرہ روزہ 'نیو تھاٹ' کے ڈیکلریشن اے۔ڈی۔ایم صاحب کی کچہری میں داخل کر دیے گئے

decline (de-*klīn*) *v.t.* & *i.* refuse انکار کرنا، مسترد کرنا *She declined the invitation* اس نے یہ دعوت مسترد کر دی (of sun, day, prices, etc.) go down جھکنا، مائل ہونا، غروب ہونے کے قریب ہونا، گرنے لگنا *The soaring prices suddenly began to decline* چڑھی ہوئی قیمتیں یکایک گرنے لگیں draw to close ختم ہونے کے قریب ہونا *The day declined* ہونے کو آیا، زوال کا وقت آیا، دن ڈھل گیا become weaker کمزور یا ضعیف ہونا (*one's*) *declining years*, one's old age بڑھاپا، عالمِ ضعیفی inflection of a noun (cf. *conjugation* of a verb) اسم کی تعریف *n.* declining زوال، انحطاط *'The Decline and Fall of the Roman Empire'* سلطنتِ روما کا زوال و خاتمہ (esp.) wasting away with consumption or other disease مرض سے ضعیف و نحیف ہو جانا، نحیف و نزار ہو جانا *He went into a decline* وہ لاغر (یا) نحیف و نزار ہو گیا downward slope ڈھلان

declivity (de-*kliv*-i-ti) *n.* downward slope, decline ڈھلان

declutch (de-*kluch*) *v.i.* disconnect the engine (of a motor-car, etc.) from the gears that drive the car-wheels (موٹر کا) انجن بند کرنا

decoct *v.t.* extract essence by boiling جوشاندہ تیار کرنا *decoction* (de-*kok*-shĕn) liquor in which something has been boiled thus for extracting its essence جوشاندہ

decode (de-*kohd*) *v.t.* get the meaning of something written in code or cipher مرموز عبارت کو پڑھنا، (یا عام خط میں) لکھنا

decompose (dee-kom-*pohz*) *v.t.* & *i.* separate (a substance) into its parts کی تحلیل کرنا، کا تجزیہ کرنا (cause to) rot سڑانا، گلانا، سڑنا، گلنا **decomposition** (-*zish*-) *n.* separating thus تحلیل، تجزیہ rotting گلنا، سڑنا

decontrol (dee-kon-*trohl*) *v.t.* (-ll-) release (trade or commodity) from government control (پر) سے کنٹرول اُٹھا لینا (یا) ہٹا لینا

decor (de-*ko**) *n.* all that makes up the appearance (of room or stage) سجاوٹ، آرائش

decorate (*dek*-o-rayt) *v.t.* put ornaments

on آراستہ کرنا ، زیور پہنانا ، سجانا make more beautiful by placing adornments on *or* in آراستہ پیراستہ کرنا ، مزیّن کرنا *decorate streets with flags and buntings* آئین بندی کرنا paint (a house) مکان کی دیواروں پر روغن affix wall paper, etc. دیواروں پر ، کاغذ پھیرنا ، منڈھنا give (someone) a medal for distinguished service (in battle, etc.) جنگی خدمات کی وجہ سے (کسی کو) تمغہ دینا **decoration** (-ray-) *n.* decorating سجاوٹ ، آرائش ، آراستگی medal, etc. (to be) worn on the body تمغہ ، اعزاز (*pl.*) flags, etc., put up during festivities جھنڈیاں ، آئین بندی **decorator** (*dek*-o-ray-tě*) *n.* (esp.) workman who decorates houses جس کا پیشہ مکانوں کو آراستہ کرنا ہو ، خانہ آرا ، ماہر آرائش

decorum (de-*ko*-rum) *n.* proper and formal behaviour سلیقہ ، ادب آداب ، تہذیب ، آداب مجلس **decorous** (de-*ko*-rus) not against decorum (as opposed to *indecorous*) *adj.* خوش وضع ، سلیقہ ، سگھڑ ، شائستہ

Decorous, signifies something proper according to the most **formal** ideal ; **dignified,** according to one's position : **proper,** according to the particular standards of the time and place ; **correct,** according to a definite standard. Again, we speak of a person as **demure** when he pretends or affects to be coy ; as **sedate**, when he is calm and composed ; as **staid,** when he is rigid ; as **conventional**, when he acts according to the lead of others, rather than in an original manner.

decoy (de-*koi*) *n.* (real or dummy) bird or animal for enticing wild ones into a trap (وحشی جانوروں یا پرندوں کو پھانسنے کو) لگا لانے والا جانور (یا پرندہ) someone trained and used for tempting others into a dangerous position کسی شخص کو خطرے میں ڈالنے کے لیے فریب دینے والا شخص ، enticement لالچ دلانے والی چیز ، لاسا ، پھسلاوا *v.t.* draw (someone) into danger by trick فریب سے خطرے میں مبتلا کرنا

decrease *v.t.* & *i.* (di-*krees*) make or become less کم کرنا یا ہونا ، گھٹانا یا گھٹنا *n.* (*deek*-rees) act of decreasing تخفیف ، کم کرنا amount by which something lessens کمی ، تخفیف (کی مقدار) *be on the decrease*, lessen کم ہوتے جانا ، گھٹتے جانا

decree (de-*kree*) *n.* command of a ruler or government having the force of a law (فرماں روا یا حکومت کا) حکم ، فرمان verdict of a law-court فیصلہ ، ڈگری *v.t.* & *i.* make a decree (*that*) فرمان یا حکم جاری کرنا (کہ)

decrepit (de-*krep*-it) *adj.* old, feeble and worn out خستہ حال ، زار و نزار **decrepitude** (de-*krep*-i-tewd) *n.* being decrepit درماندگی ، ضعف ، خستہ حالی

decry (de-*krī*) *v.t.* condemn مذمت کرنا ، برائی کرنا disparage, make (something) seem less valuable نقص نکالنا ، عیب لگانا

dedicate (*ded*-i-kayt) *v.t.* give (oneself or one's life, etc.) completely (*to* some noble cause) (کسی بڑی تحریک کے لئے) وقف کرنا *dedicate one's life to social service* عوام کی خدمت کے لیے اپنے آپ کو وقف کرنا set apart with solemn ceremonies as sacred مخصوص کرنا ، خاص کرنا ، وقف کرنا ، نذر کرنا *dedicate a building* عمارت وقف کرنا *dedicate a church* گرجے کو عبادت کے لیے مخصوص کرتے ہوئے اُس کا افتتاح کرنا (of an author) address (a book) formally (to a friend or patron) (کوئی کتاب وغیرہ) کسی کے نام معنون کرنا **dedication** (ded-i-*kay*-shěn) *n.* act of dedicating نذر ، وقف ، (esp.) words used in dedicating a book تہدیہ ، کتاب معنون کرنے کا مقدمہ **dedicator** (*ded*-i-kay-tě*) *n.* مخصوص کرنے والا ، نذر کرنے والا ، وقف کرنے والا ، معنون کرنے والا **dedicatory** (*ded*-) *adj.* pertaining to dedication انتسابی ، معنون کرنے کے متعلق

deduce (de-*dews*) *v.t.* arrive at the (knowledge) by reasoning (*from* general to particular) نتیجہ نکالنا (یا اخذ کرنا) ، استخراج ، استنباط infer (*from*) **deductive** (de-*duk*-tiv) *adj.* of a process of deducing استخراجی deduced مستنبط ، مستخرج ، نتیجہ **deduction** *n.* the process of arriving at knowledge نتیجہ ، قیاس ، استخراج inference استنباط ، نتیجہ (see under **deduct**)

deduct (de-*dukt*) *v.t.* take away (an amount or part) کم کرنا ، مجرا کرنا (Cf. *subtract* for numbers) **deduction** (de-*duk*-shěn) *n.* the act of deducting مجرائی ، کم کرنا amount deducted مجرا شدہ رقم ، وضعات (see under **deduce**)

deed (deed) *n.* act ; something done کام ، کار ، فعل ، عمل *a good deed* کار نیک *a bad deed* بدکاری ، فعل بد *deeds are better than words* قول سے عمل بہتر ہے legal document for change of ownership of property or rights of using دستاویز ، تحریر *draw up a deed* دستاویز تیار (یا مرتب) کرنا

deem (deem) *v.t.* consider خیال کرنا ، سمجھنا ، باور کرنا *I deem it wise to agree* میں اس بات سے اتفاق کرنا عقلمندی کا تقاضا سمجھتا ہوں

de-emphasize *v.t.* (see *Addenda*)

deep (deep) *adj.* going far down گہرا ، عمیق ، بہت نیچے far back from the front بہت پیچھے ، گہرا *a deep shelf* گہرا خانہ (الماری کا) far in غرق ، ڈوبا ہوا *deep in debt* سخت مقروض ، قرض میں غرق *deep in water* پانی میں غرق (of colour) dark شوخ ، گہرا (رنگ) *deep red* گہرا سرخ (of light) strong تیز (روشنی) (of sounds) low گہرا ، بھری (آواز) (of a subject) difficult to understand مشکل ، مغلق (of understanding) penetrating تیز فہم ، دوربین

insight بنگاہ دوربین (of person) cunning; with manners difficult to understand چالاک ، گہرا (شخص) *He is very deep* وہ بڑا گہرا ہے (10) extreme سخت مصیبت *deep distress* انتہائی ، سخت ، شدید (11) heartfelt شدید غم *deep sorrow* دلی ، قلبی ، شدید (12) profound گہرا (یا گہری) *in deep sleep* گہری نیند میں *deep in* (*thought, study, etc.*) absorbed in (it) میں غرق ، ڈوبا ہوا ، محو *adv.* far down or in گہرا ، بہت نیچے کو

Still waters run deep, (*a*) there is lull before storm طوفان کا پتہ دینے والا سکوت نظر آتا ہے (*b*) too profound to be talkative بڑا گہرا ہے *deep-rooted prejudices* تعصّبات جن کی بنیاد گہری ہو *deep-laid plan* گہری مُزمن مرض ، جو بیماری گھر کر چکی ہو *deep-seated disease* تجویز *n.* (*the deep*), (poet.) the sea سمندر ، بحر ، ساگر

deepen (*deep*-ĕn) *v.t.* & *i.* make or become deep گہرا کرنا یا بنانا **deeply** *adv.* شدّت سے ، گہرے طور پر ، دل سے

deer (*dee*-ĕ*) (*pl.* the same) *n.* graceful grass-grazing animal whose male has branching horns ہرن ، ہرنگ ، آہو

deface (de-*fays*) *v. t.* disfigure (by damaging the surface) ہیئت بگاڑنا ، (چہرہ یا حلیہ) بگڑنا ، بدنما *deface a picture with scratches* خراشوں سے تصویر بگاڑ دینا destory خراب کر دینا *deface a document* دستاویز کو خراب کر دینا .render unusable again استعمال کے قابل نہ رہنے دینا *get a postage stamp defaced at the post office* ٹکٹ پر مہر لگوا کر اسے ناقابلِ استعمال بنا دینا

de facto (de-*fak*-toh) *adj. & adv.* in actual fact ; real ; virtual, though not in name اصلی ، حقیقی (Also see *de jure*)

defalcate (*dee*-fal-kayt) *v. t.* embezzle (money) غبن کرنا ، کھا جانا ، (رقم) **defalcation** *n.* embezzlement غبن ، خیانت

defame (de-*faym*) *v. t.* speak evil of ; slander بدنام کرنا ، رسوا کرنا ، بدگوئی کرنا ، ازالۂ حیثیت عرفی کرنا **defamation** (def-a-*may*-shĕn) *n.* رسوائی ، بدنامی ، ہتکِ عزت

defamatory (de-*fam*-a-tè-ri) *adj.* intended to defame بدنام کن ، ہتک آمیز *a defamatory statement*

default (de-*folt*) *n.* failure to perform a duty کوتاہی ، غفلت failure to pay a debt ادا نہ کرنا ، باقی دار ہونا failure to do something required by law (*e.g.*, appearing before a law court) پیروی نہ کرنا ، حاضرِ عدالت نہ ہونا *judgment by default*, 'ex parte' judgment given for plaintiff when defendant fails to appear before law-court فریقِ ثانی کی غیر حاضری سے یکطرفہ فیصلہ کرنا *win a case by default* فریقِ ثانی کی غیر حاضری کی کارروائی سے مقدمہ جیتنا *win a game by default* شرط کا پورا نہ ہونے کی صورت میں اگر وجہ سے کھیل جیتنا *in default of* یہ نہ کیا گیا تو *go by default*, if or since (something) does not take place اگر ایسا نہ ہو ، چونکہ ایسا نہیں ہوا ، اس لیے

defaulter *n.* person (esp. a soldier) who fails to perform a duty غیر حاضر ، مفرور ، (فوج سے) بھاگا قانون سے بھاگا ہوا ، مفرور ، فراری law-breaker بھگوڑا ، قانع

defeat (de-*feet*) *v. t.* overcome غالب آنا ، فتح پانا beat in a fight ہرانا ، زک دینا win a victory over غلبہ پانا cause to fail شکست دلانا ، ہرانا *defeat a plan* تجویز کو خراب کر دینا *Our hopes were defeated* ہماری اُمیدیں ٹوٹ گئیں *n.* overthrow ہرانا ، شکست being defeated شکست کھانا ، ہزیمت یا زک اٹھانا failure (*of* plan, etc.) ناکامی ، شکست

defeatism (de-*fee*-tizm) *n.* attitude, argument or conduct based on expectation of defeat شکست خوردگی ، ہزیمت پسندی

defeatist *n.* person advising surrender to enemy شکست خوردہ ذہنیت کا مالک ، شکست مان لینے والا ، (قوم کو) شکست تسلیم کر لینے کی دعوت دینے والا *adj.* expressive of such an attitude شکست خوردہ *defeatist mentality* شکست خوردہ ذہنیت

Ⓢ To **defeat,** literally means to undo. To **defeat** one's purpose is to undo what one is trying to do : to **nullify,** make void : to **baffle,** lead into a false direction : to **frustrate,** render vain : **thwart,** throw an obstacle in the way : to **foil,** lead nowhere: to **balk,** cause to stumble: to **outwit**. through superior cunning; to **circumvent,** go round. We **vanquish** or **defeat** an enemy. **conquer** by force. **overthrow** a power and **defeat** a plan or the very purpose of something.

defect (de-*fekt*) *n.* fault کمی ، خامی imperfection نقص ، کوتاہی shortcoming عیب blemish دھبہ ، داغ flaw بُرائی ، خرابی error غلطی **defective** *adj.* having a defect or defects ; نکما ، خراب imperfect ناقص *mentally defective*, not quite sane فاتر العقل

Ⓢ **Defect** is a shortcoming, physical or moral : **fault,** absence of something that should be there : **flaw,** fault in structure. often not seen : **deformity,** permanent misshapement; **blemish,** whatever mars the surface: **taint**. permanent stream of impurity. as in the blood ; **blot** or **stain** is on one's character or reputation. Do not confuse **defect** with **deficiency** which is a shortage in expected quantity ; or with **deficit** which is a shortage of income.

defence (de-*fens*) *n.* resistance to attack حملے کا مقابلہ ، حفاظت ، تحفظ ، دفاع anything that protects تحفظ ، ذریعۂ حفاظت (law) defendant's reply to the charge brought against him جواب دعویٰ ، صفائی the lawyer(s) acting for the defendant وکیل (وکلاء) صفائی ، مدعا علیہ کا (کے) وکیل (وکلاء)

defenceless *adj.* having no defence نہتا ، بے حفاظت unable to defend oneself بے کس ، بے یار و مددگار

defend (de-*fend*) *v. t.* ward off attack حملہ روکنا ، بچاؤ کرنا keep safe محفوظ رکھنا protect حفاظت کرنا ، بچانا support حمایت کرنا ، تائید کرنا make a defence in a law-court جوابدہی کرنا ، صفائی پیش کرنا **defender** *n.* one who defends حامی، محافظ، ناصر *Defender of Faith*, (one of the titles of the British sovereign) (عیسائیوں کے نزدیک) حامیٔ دین، حامی دین، عیسوی ، **defendant** *n*. person against whom a legal action is brought مُدّعا علیہ **defensible** (de-*fen*-si-bĕl) *adj*. able to be defended محفوظ رکھنے کے قابل، (مقدمہ) جواب دہی کے قابل **defensive** (de-*fen*-sive) *adj*. used or intended for defending مُدافعانہ، دفاعی on the guard مُدافعت، دفاع guarding مُدافعانہ حالت carried on in self-defence حفظِ جان کے لیے *n*. defending مُدافعت، دفاع (usu. in the phrase :) *on the defensive*, resisting ; expecting attack and ready to attack مُدافعت پر، دفاع پر ▣ We **defend** when we ward off the blow ; **protect** ourselves under some cover ; **guard**. when we stand ready to defend ; and **preserve** something as it is.

defend *v. t.* see under **defence** (above)

defer (de-*fē**) *v. t.* (-rr-) put off until later ملتوی کرنا، مُوقوف رکھنا، ٹالنا، تاخیر کرنا، *a deferred telegram*, one sent later at a cheaper rate تاخیری تار، تاخیری برقیہ yield (*to* someone) in order to show respect تسلیم کرنا، پاس یا لحاظ کرنا *defer to someone's wishes* (or *opinion*) کسی کی بات رکھ لینا، کسی کی بات کا لحاظ کرنا، کسی کی رائے کا پاس کرنا **deference** (*def*-e-rens) *n*. postponing اِلتوا، تاخیر giving way to the wishes or opinion of تسلیم، اَدب، پاس *in deference to the opinion of the court* عدالت کے پاس اَدب سے **deferential** (*def*-e-ren-shĕl) *adj*. showing great respect مُؤدّب تعظیمی ▣ We **defer** until later ; **postpone** until a stated or assumed future time ; **delay,** keep from starting : **suspend** temporarily something that is already on ; **put off** something we dislike ; **adjourn** a meeting until a **set** date or *sine die* ; **stave off** an expected evil ; **procrastinate** when we have the habit of putting off action until later. Again **deference** is to someone's wishes, as one considers them to be of superior value ; **regard** is formal for a person or an opinion : **submission** is to someone with a sense of inferiority ; **obedience** is to someone with inferiority and humility ; **reverence** is for someone who deserves our respect and awe.

defiance *n*., **defiant** *adj*. see under **defy**.

deficient (de-*fish*-ĕnt) *adj*. lacking خام، اَدھورا not having enough of ناقص، ناتمام *deficient in courage* جُرأت سے خالی، بے حوصلہ incomplete ناتمام، ناقص defective ناقص *mentally deficient*, half-witted نیم پاگل **deficiency** (de-*fish*-en-si) *n*. being deficient نقص، کوتاہی، کمی amount by which something is deficient کمی، گھاٹا، جس چیز کی کمی ہو ▣ **Deficiency** is the shortage of a quantity expected to be found there ; **deficit,** shortage of income to balance expenditures ; **defect,** shortcoming of any kind, physical or moral.

deficit (*def*-i-sit) *n*. amount by which something (esp. money) is too short (opposite of *surplus*) خسارہ، ٹوٹا، کمی، گھاٹا amount by which payment exceeds receipts میزانیے میں آمد کی بہ نسبت خرچ زیادہ ہونا، خسارہ *deficit financing*, (also *deficit spending*), (see *Addenda*)

defile *n*. (*dee*-fīl) long narrow pass between mountains passing through which troops have no choice but to march in file or queue تنگ دَرہ gorge گھاٹی *v. t.* (de-*fīl*) make dirty مَیلا کرنا، گندہ کرنا، غلیظ بنانا (یا کرنا) pollute آلودہ کرنا desecrate بے حُرمتی کرنا march in file (*i.e.*, in a queue) قطار میں چلنا **defilement** *n*. pollution آلودگی desecration بے حُرمتی

define (de-*fīn*) *v. t.* give the exact meaning of (*e.g.*, words) مُعیّن معنی بیان کرنا outline clearly واضح کرنا، تمیز کرنا *hills defined against the horizon* اُفق کے پس منظر کے سامنے پہاڑیاں نمایاں تھیں ، lay down the limits of place, authority, etc.) کی حدود مُتعیّن کرنا *define the country's boundaries* مُلک کی حدود مُتعیّن کرنا *define* (*someone's*) *power* (or *duties*) (کسی کے) اختیارات یا فرائض مُتعیّن کرنا **definite** *adj*., **definition** *n*. see **definite** below

definite (*def*-i-nit) *adj*. exact مُعیّن، ٹھیک ٹھیک clear صاف صاف، واضح not doubtful غیر مبہم، واضح having fixed and distinct limits محدود، مُتعیّن حدود *the definite article*, the word *the* حرفِ تعریف، اداۃ تعریف والا **definitely** *adv*. decidedly ٹھیک ٹھیک طور پر، مُتعیّن طور پر **definitive** (de-*fin*-i-tiv) *adj*. decisive قطعی، حتمی final آخری، فیصلہ کُن unconditional غیر مشروط، ناطق **definition** (def-i-*nish*-ĕn) *n*. defining تعیین، تحدید exact statement of the meaning (of a word or term) (کسی لفظ یا اصطلاح کا) ٹھیک ٹھیک واضح بیان، تعریف clearness making or being distinct in outline حدود مُتعیّن کرنا، حدود کے لحاظ سے مُتعیّن ہونا

deflate (de-*flayt*) *v. t.* let air or gas out of (something) (as opposed to *inflate*) ہوا یا گیس خارج کرنا یا نکالنا *deflate a tyre* (or *a balloon*) ٹائر (یا غبارے) میں سے ہوا یا گیس نکالنا reduce the amount of money in circulation in order to bring down prices سکے کی گری ہوئی قیمت کو چڑھا کر چیزوں کی قیمتیں گرانا **deflation** *n*. deflating of money بھاؤ ٹھیک کر دینا، اصل قیمت کی طرف لانا

deflect (de-*flekt*) *v. t.* & *i.* (cause to) turn aside (*from* something) موڑنا، مُڑنا، منحرف کرنا **deflection** *n*. act or amount of turning موڑ، جھکاؤ، انحراف

deflower (de-*flou*-ĕ*) *v. t.* remove flowers from a plant (پودے) سے پھول توڑنا

deform (de-*fo*-*m) *v. t.*. spoil the form or appearance of شکل صورت بگاڑنا put out of shape بدشکل کرنا ، بد صورت بنانا **deformed** (de-fo*md) *adj.* (of the body or part of it) disfigured بدشکل ، بدقوارہ ، کبڑا ، لولا ، لنگڑا (of the mind) unnaturally formed اُلٹی یا اوندھی کھوپڑی ، بدذہن **deformity** (de-*fo**m-i-ti) *n.* being deformed بدنمائی ، بدصورتی deformed part of the body بدن کا بدوضع (یا بدنما) حصہ

defraud (de-*frawd*) *v. t.* gain by deceit دھوکے سے حاصل کرنا trick (someone) out of what is rightly his ٹھگنا ، دھوکا دینا *The sharper defrauded her of her money* عیار نے اس عورت سے رقم ہتھیا لی (یا ٹھگ لی)

defray (de-*fray*) *v.t.* supply the money needed for something رقم ادا کرنا pay (the *cost* or *expenses of* something) خرچ چکانا ، خرچ ادا کرنا

deft *adj.* skilful مشاق ، ماہر ، منجھا ہوا nimble fingered تیزدست ، سُبک دست clever ہوشیار ، چالاک **deftly** *adv.* صفائی سے ، چالاکی یا تیزدستی سے **deftness** *n.* cleverness ہنرمندی ، تیزدستی skill چالاکی ، ہوشیاری

defunct (de-*funkt*) *adj.* dead مُردہ ، بےروح ، آنجہانی ، مرحوم no longer existing معدوم no longer active مُردہ ، خُفتہ erstwhile سابق ، مرحوم *the defunct political parties of Pakistan* پاکستان کی سابق سیاسی جماعتیں

defy (de-*fī*) *v. i.* resist openly and successfully مقابلہ کرنا ، مقابلے میں آنا refuse to obey or show respect to پرواہ نہ کرنا ، خاطر میں نہ لانا ، اطاعت نہ کرنا ، نہ ماننا *defy the law* قانون کی اطاعت نہ کرنا challenge دعوتِ مبارزت دینا ، چیلنج دینا *defy the authority* (یا حاکم) کا حکم نہ ماننا *defy the authority of* حکومت کا حکم نہ ماننا *defy (someone) to do (something)*, call on (him) to do something he believes he cannot or will not do دعوتِ مبارزت دینا ، مقابلے کے لیے بلانا offer insurmountable difficulties شدید رکاوٹ ڈالنا ، عاجز کرنا *It defies description* قوتِ بیان اس کے اظہار سے عاجز ہے **defiance** (de-*fī*-ans) *n.* defying دعوتِ مقابلہ refusal to obey or to show respect to علانیہ نافرمانی *act in defiance of orders* عدول حکمی کرنا *set the law at defiance* قانون کی کھلم کھلا نافرمانی کرنا **defiant** (de-*fī*-ant) *adj.* (of action) showing defiance نافرمانی پر مبنی گستاخ ، سرکش ، نافرمان openly disobedient سرکشانہ ، کھیترہ وانہ

degenerate *v.i.* (de-*jen*-e-rayt) become worse بگڑ جانا ، خراب ہو جانا sink into lower state of morality شرافت کھو بیٹھنا ، (اخلاقی لحاظ سے) گر جانا *adj.* (de-*jen*-e-rit) having degenerated ذلیل ، خستہ حال ، خوار *n.* (de-*jen*-e-rit) degenerated person ناخلف ، کپوت

degeneration (de-jen-e-*ray*-shĕn) *n.* act of degenerating پستی ، ذلت being degenerate پستی ، ناخلفی ، خواری ، بگاڑ **degenerating** *adj.* sinking into the depth of immorality, etc. ذلیل ، خوار

degrade (de-*grayd*) *v. t.* reduce in rank as a punishment عہدے سے گرانا ، عہدہ گھٹانا lower morally اخلاق خراب کرنا ، بگڑنا reduce in estimation نگاہوں سے گرنا ، ذلیل ہونا یا کرنا *He degraded himself by cribbing in the examination* اس نے امتحان میں نقل کر کے اپنے آپ کو ذلیل کر لیا

degradation (deg-ra-*day*-shĕn) *n.* debasement پستی ، گراوٹ degeneration ذلت ، خواری

degree (de-*gree*) *n.* unit of measurement for angles زاویے کا درجہ *an angle of ninety degrees, 90°*, نوّے درجے کا زاویہ unit of measurement for temperature حرارت کا درجہ *Water freezes at 32° Fahrenheit or 0° Centigrade* پانی 32° فارن ہائٹ یا صفر درجہ سنٹی گریڈ پر منجمد ہو جاتا ہے grade درجہ *a high degree of excellence* نہایت عمدہ *to a high degree* اعلیٰ درجے تک ، اعلیٰ درجہ *to the last degree*, exceedingly نہایت ، انتہائی درجے تک *to what degree?* to what extent? کس حد تک step in a series showing progress قدم ، منزل *by degrees* (*a*) step by step قدم بہ قدم ، منزل بہ منزل (*b*) gradually آہستہ آہستہ (*c*) slowly رفتہ رفتہ a certain amount خاص بمقدار *various degrees of skill* مہارت کے درجے social status درجہ ، حیثیت *people of high degree* بڑے رتبے کے لوگ title conferred by a university to one who has passed an examination (امتحان پاس کرنے کی) سند *the first degree, the Bachelor's degree*, B.A. or B.Sc. (کی سند) بی۔اے ، یا بی۔ایس سی *an Honours degree*, B.A. (Hons.) or B.Sc. (Hons.) بی۔اے (آنرز) ، یا بی۔ایس سی (آنرز) (in grammar) one of the three forms of comparison of an adjective or adverb درجۂ تفضیل *positive degree* تفضیلِ نفسی *comparative degree* تفضیلِ بعض *superlative degree* تفضیلِ کُل (*e.g., big, bigger* and *biggest* respectively are the *positive, comparative* and *superlative* degress of *big*.)

a thermometer showing degrees (sense 2)

dehumanize (dee-hew-ma-nīz) *v.i.* deprive one of human qualities انسانیت (یا انسانی خصوصیات) سے محروم کر دینا **dehumanization** *n.* انسانیت سے محروم کر دینا

dehydrate (de-*hīd*-rayt) remove water or moisture from پانی یا رطوبت خارج کرنا ، خشک کرنا ، سکھانا **dehydrated** (-ted) *adj.* سکھایا ہوا ، خشک کیا ہوا *dehydrated vegetables* خشک کی ہوئی ترکاریاں یا سبزیاں **dehydration** (-ray-) سکھانا ، خشک کرنا

deify (*dee*-i-fi) *v.t.* make a god of دیوی ، دیوتا بنانا worship as a god پوجنا ، معبود ٹھہرانا **deification** *n.* دیوی دیوتا بنا لینا ، معبود ٹھہرانا (Also see **deity**)

deign (dayn) *v.t.* think worthy of being done کرنے کے قابل یا لائق خیال کرنا ، مناسب سمجھنا be kind enough (*to do* something) زیبائش (یا عزّت افزائی) کے طور پر کرنا ◙ **deign** denotes being worthy. We **deign** to do a thing worthy of being done whereas we **condescend** to perform an action which really excites our mild contempt. Thus we say: "She did not **deign** to reply"; "He **condescended** to explain."

deity (*dee*-i-ti) *n.* (pl., *deities*) god or goddess دیوتا (یا) دیوی *the Greek deities* یُونانی دیوتا *the Deity,* God, خُدا، اللہ state of being a god or goddess اُلُوہیت، خُدائی divine quality or nature دیوتائی، اُلُوہیت (Also see **deify**)

Deism (*dee*-izm) *n.* 18th Century Christian movement of 'natural religion', rejecting revelation and supernatural doctrines of Christianity but believing in a Supreme Being as the source of human and other finite existence وہ تحریک جس میں خُدا کے وُجود کے اقرار لیکن وَحی کے اِنکار کا عقیدہ پایا جاتا ہے (یہ اٹھارویں صدی کے عیسائیوں میں پیدا ہوئی) **Deist** (*dee*-ist) *n.* خُدا کے وجود کا اِقرار لیکن وَحی کا اِنکار کرنے والا یا اِس تحریک کا حامی

deject (de-*jekt*) *v.t.* اُداس یا رنجیدہ کرنا، افسردہ یا بد دِل کرنا،

dejected (de-*jek*-tĕd) *adj.* sad اُداس، دِل شکستہ gloomy غم دیدہ، غمگین in low spirits بددِل، افسردہ hopeless ناُامید، مایُوس **dejectedly** *adv.* بد دِلی سے **dejection** (de-*jek*-shĕn) اُداسی یا مایُوسی سے افسردہ ہو کر *n.* state of being dejected افسردگی، اُداسی، دِل شکستگی، دلگیری، رنجیدگی

de jure (dee-*joo*-ē*) constitutional; by law (as opposed to *de facto*) آئینی، اَز رُوئے قانون '*De jure*' *sovereigns are not always 'de facto' rulers* جو شخص اَز رُوئے قانون بادشاہ ہو، ضروری نہیں کہ عملاً بھی وہی فرماں روائی کرے

delay (de-*lay*) *v.t.* & *i.* linger, wait (کام) لٹکاتے رکھنا، دیر لگانا make or be slow سُستی کرنا، تاخیر کرنا *Don't delay* دیر نہ لگائیے، تاخیر نہ کیجئے *delaying tactics,* (esp.) slowing down of work or production سُست رَوی کی چالیں، تاخیری ترکیبیں یا داؤں (مثلاً کام یا پیداوار میں سُستی کرنا) *The workers resorted to delaying tactics* مزدوروں نے تاخیری چالیں اختیار کریں postpone مُلتوی کرنا (یا رکھنا)، دیر لگانا cause to be late دیر کر دینا، روکے رکھنا *The train was delayed by the Minister* وزیر صاحب نے گاڑی کو روکے رکھا *n.* delaying or being delayed دیر، تاخیر، التوا، توقف، رُکاوٹ *delay of an hour* ایک گھنٹے کی دیر، ایک ساعت کی تاخیر

delectable (de-*lek*-ta-bĕl) *adj.* pleasing خوش آئند *delectable personality* خوش آئند شخصیت، مرغوب شخصیت فرحت بخش delightful دلچسپ، خوشگوار *delectable function* خوشگوار تقریب *delectable scenery* دِلکش نظارہ (U.S.) delicious (food, dish, etc.) مزیدار، لذیذ **delectation** (de-lek-*tay*-shĕn) *n.* حظّ، لُطف، مزا

delegate (*del*-e-gayt) *v.t.* send as representative to a convention, etc. نائب یا نمائندہ بنا کر بھیجنا entrust (duties, rights, etc. *to* someone) سونپنا تفویض کرنا، سپرد کرنا *The Centre delegated its powers to the provinces* مرکزی حکومت نے اپنے اختیارات صوبوں کو سونپ دیئے *n.* one sent as representative مندوب، نمائندہ **delegation** (-*gay*-) *n.* delegation تفویض، سپردگی (اختیارات) a group of delegates مندوبین، نمائندوں کی جماعت یا وفد، نمائندگان

delete (de-*leet*) *v.t.* strike off or take out (something written or printed) قلم زد کرنا، خارج کرنا، قلم پھیرنا **deletion** (de-*lee*-shĕn) *n.* such omission قلم زنی، اِخراج، ترک

deleterious (del-e-*tee*-ri-us) *n.* injurious to mind or body (بدن یا ذہن کے لیے) نقصان رساں، مُضر harmful مُخرب، نقصان دہ

deliberate *v.t.* & *i.* (de-*lib*-e-rayt) consider (something) carefully, consider (*how, whether,* etc.) غور کرنا، غور و خوض کرنا، بحث کرنا *deliberate a question* کسی مسئلے پر غور و خوض کرنا take counsel with others (*on* something) صلاح مشورہ کرنا *deliberate on a scheme* کسی سکیم کے متعلق صلاح مشورہ کرنا *adj.* (de-*lib*-e-rit) intentional عمداً، بالاِرادہ، اِرادی *a deliberate insult* عمداً کی ہُوئی توہین slow and cautious سوچ سمجھ کر فیصلہ کرنے والا *deliberate in action* سوچ سمجھ کر اُٹھایا ہُوا قدم *deliberate in speech* سمجھ سوچ کر (یا تول کر) بولنے والا **deliberative** (de-*lib*-e-ra-tive) *adj.* proceeding slowly and cautiously غور و فکر کرنے کے لائق یا کرنے والا **deliberately** (de-*lib*-ĕ-rat-li) *adv.* knowingly; after careful thought جان بوجھ کر، دانستہ، دیدہ و دانستہ **deliberation** slow and careful action غور و خوض، سوچ بچار *He spoke with deliberation* اُس نے سوچ بچار کر کے بات مُنہ سے نکالی discussion (*of* something) with arguments for and against it کسی معاملے کے تمام پہلوؤں پر غور و فکر کرنا (usu. *pl.*) conference بحث، غور و خوض، غور و فکر، بحث و مباحثہ، بحث و تمحیص *deliberations of the Legislature* مقننہ (یا مجلس قانون ساز) کا غور و خوض یا بحث و مباحثہ *The deliberations have ended* بحث ختم ہو گئی ہے

delicacy *n.* (see under **delicate**)

delicate (*del*-i-kit) *adj.* soft نرم جو سخت نہ ہو، ملائم tender, pretty and easily hurt خوبصورت اور کمزور of thin material باریک، مہین، چھریرا *delicate silk* باریک ریشم dainty نفیس، نُتھرا، باریک کام *delicate lace* نفیس جالی، باریک لیس cultured, refined شائستہ، نازک مزاج، لطیف *a delicate taste* ذوقِ لطیف pleasing to the taste لذت بخش، خوشبُو *a delicate flavour* مزیدار، لذیذ frail; not strong in health; easily falling ill نازک بدن کمزور بچہ *a delicate child,* دھان پان، چھوئی موئی، مرزا پھویا، نازک بدن بچہ needing great care نرم و نازک *delicate plant* نرم و نازک پودا *delicate china,* چینی کے نازک برتن needing skilful handling نازک، باحتیاط طلب، نازک *a delicate situation* نازک صورتحال، نازک معاملہ *a delicate question* نازک سوال، نازک مسئلہ *delicate surgical operation* نازک آپریشن (of colour) soft; not strong (of the senses or instruments) able to appreciate or indicate very small differences نازک ، ذکی الحس ، سریع الحس (حواس یا آلات سائنسدانوں (the delicate instruments used by scientists کے استعمال کے) نازک آلات taking care not to be immodest or to hurt the feelings of others ستھرا پاکیزہ ، جس میں دوسروں کے جذبات کا لحاظ ہو **delicately** *adv.* نفاست سے **delicacy** (*del*-i-ka-si) *n.* fineness of form and texture بناوٹ کی نفاست یا نزاکت fineness of skill مہارت ، اعلیٰ درجے کی مہارت sensitiveness ذکاوت ذوق لطیف کی نفاست یا فراوانی *delicacy of artistic taste* حسن ترتفقر ، (usu. *pl.*) dainty ; rare and delightful مزے کی چیز ، نفیس غذا

delicious (de-*lish*-us) *adj.* giving delight (esp. to the senses of taste and smell, and to the sense of humour) خوشگوار ، مزیدار ، لطیف *delicious food* مزیدار غذا *delicious scent* لطیف خوشبو *delicious humour* لطیف مزاح **deliciously** *adv.* خوشگوار طور پر ، لطافت سے **deliciousness** *n.* حظ ، لذت ، مزا ، لطافت ، لطف

delight (de-*lit*) *v.t.* & *i.* please خوش کرنا یا ہونا ، مسرور ، شاد take pleasure in لطف اٹھانا یا محظوظ کرنا یا ہونا *He delights in arts* وہ فنون لطیفہ سے حظ اٹھاتا ہے *n.* pleasure مزا ، لطف ، حظ ، خوشی ، مسرت *to (one's) delight*, one was pleased to (فلاں کو فلاں شے سے) اتنا لطف آیا cause of pleasure سامان راحت ، وجہ مسرت *studies are his chief delight* اس کے لیے سب سے زیادہ مسرت مطالعے میں ہے **delighted** (-tid) *adj.* pleased خوش ، مسرور ، محظوظ **delightful** *adj.* pleasing راحت بخش ، مسرت بخش

delimit (de-*lim*-it) *v.t.* fix the limits or boundaries of حد بندی کرنا ، سرحد مقرر کرنا **delimitation** (-*tay*-) *n.* delimiting حد بندی ، تعین حدود

delineate (de-*lin*-è-ayt) *v.t.* sketch ; mark out with lines خاکہ بنانا ، نقشہ کھینچنا portray in words لفظی خاکہ کشی کرنا ، کردار نگاری کرنا *the characters delineated by Dickens in his novels* ڈکنز نے اپنے ناولوں میں جن کرداروں کا خاکہ کھینچا ہے **delineation** (-*ay*-) *n.* کردار نگاری

delinquent (de-*link*-è-went) *n.* & *adj.* (person) failing to perform his duty خطا کار ، خاطی criminal مجرم ، گنہگار ، جرم پیشہ **delinquency** *n.* failure to perform a duty خطا ، قصور ، تقصیر crime جرم ، گناہ ، مجرم پیشگی *juvenile delinquency*, crime among youth نوجوانوں کی جرم پیشگی

delirium (de-*lee*-ri-um) *n.* violent mental disturbance caused by illness, often accompanied by wild talk, (esp. during feverish illness) (بیماری وغیرہ میں) ہذیان frenzied excitement جوش مسرت *in a delirium of joy* جوش مسرت میں وجد **delirious** (de-*lee*-ri-us) *n.* affected with delirium ہذیان میں مبتلا ، ہذیانی temporarily mad بدحواس ، دیوانہ wildly excited ; in a fit of frenzy جوش جذبات میں مضطرب **deliriously** *adv.* جوش مسرت میں ، حالت ہذیان میں ، مضطربانہ

deliver (de-*liv*-ě*) *v.t.* take (letters, etc.) to (houses of) persons to whom they are addressed (خطوط وغیرہ) بانٹنا ، تقسیم کرنا save (from temptation) محفوظ رکھنا ، بچانا rescue (from danger) (خطرے سے) نکالنا ، بچانا give (a lecture, etc.) (خطبہ) دینا ، (تقریر) کرنا *He delivered a speech at the meeting* اس نے جلسے میں تقریر کی send forth vigorously تاک کر مارنا ، (حملہ) کرنا *deliver a blow* ضرب لگانا ، چوٹ مارنا یا لگانا deliver up, yield possession of, دست کش ہونا ، ترک کرنا ، حوالے کرنا ، سپرد کرنا *deliver up the culprit* مجرم حوالے کرنا be delivered of (a child), give birth to (a child) جننا ، پیدا کرنا **deliverance** (de-*liv*-è-rans) *n.* rescue رہائی ، مخلصی being set free آزادی ، نجات *deliverance from the enemy* دشمن سے رہائی ، خلاصی judgment formally given (فیصلہ) سنانا یا دینا یا کرنا **delivery** (de-*liv*-è-ri) *n.* delivering حوالگی ، سپردگی manner of making a speech تقریر کرنے کا ڈھنگ یا اسلوب *He has a good delivery* اس کا اسلوب تقریر خوب ہے setting free آزاد کرنا surrender حوالگی sending forth بھیجنا childbirth تولید ، وضع حمل

dell (del) *n.* small valley with wooded sides سرسبز وادی

Delos (*dee*-los) *Cl. myth.* a Greek island on which Leto gave birth to Apollo and Artemis, the twin children of Zeus. It was a floating island till Zeus made it stationary for Leto's convenience on the occasion ڈیلس

Delphi (*del*-fı) *Cl. myth.* a small town near Corinth in Greece. It was famous for its oracle of Apollo ڈلفائی

delta (*del*-ta) *n.* Greek letter Δ (capital) or δ (small) یونانی زبان کا چوتھا حرف ، ڈ ، د triangular stretch of alluvial land in the shape of capital delta at the mouth of a river between two or more of branches دریا کے دہانے کا ڈیلٹا

deltiology (del-ti-*ol*-o-ji) *n.* (see *Addenda*)

delude (de-*lood*) *v.t.* mislead purposely بہکانا ، تیتر باغ دکھانا deceive دھوکہ دینا ، دغا دینا *delude (oneself with vain hopes* بے بنیاد امیدوں سے اپنے آپ) کو دھوکے میں ڈالنا **delusion** (de-*loo*-zhěn) *n.* deluding or being deluded مغالطہ false impression esp. as a form of madness وسوسہ ، توہم *suffering from a delusion* وسوسے یا وہم میں مبتلا **delusive** (de-*loo*-siv) *adj.* deceptive فریب ، سراب ، امیدیں *delusive hopes* پر فریب

deluge (de-*lewj*) *n.* great flood طوفان ، سیل *After me the deluge* آپ مرے جگ پرلے *the Deluge*, the great flood in Noah's time طوفان نوح heavy downpour سخت بارش ، طوفان anything coming in a heavy rush بھرمار *a deluge of words* لفظوں کی بھرمار، سیلابِ الفاظ *v.t.* flood سیل یا سیلاب میں مبتلا کرنا overwhelm like a deluge بھرمار کرنا، طوفان لانا، بوچھاڑ کرنا *The Minister was deluged with questions* وزیر صاحب پر سوالوں کی بوچھاڑ ہوئی

delve (delv) *v.t. & i.* (old use) dig with a spade کھودنا study deeply for gaining knowledge چھان بین کرنا *delve deep into,* make researches into (*e.g.*, old books or manuscripts) چھان بین کرنا، تحقیقات کرنا

demagogue (*dem*-a-gog) *n.* popular political leader who in his speeches appeals to passions instead of reason in order to stir up the mob جذباتی تقریریں کرنے والا رہنما **demagogy** (*dem*-a-gog-i) *n.* بازاری لیڈری **demagogic** (dem-a-*gog*-ik) *adj.* جذبات ابھارنے والا

demand (de-*mahnd*) *v.t.* ask for (something) as if ordering, or as if one has a right to it طلب کرنا، کا تقاضا کرنا، کا مطالبہ کرنا *demand an explanation* جواب طلبی کرنا call for کا تقاضا کرنا *This work demands skill* یہ کام مہارت کا تقاضا کرتا ہے *n.* act of demanding مطالبہ، تقاضا when asked for وقتِ ضرورت، وقتِ تقاضا *on demand,* on presentation or when asked for مانگنے پر، عند الطلب، حسب الطلب، بوقتِ تقاضا، بوقتِ طلب desire (by people ready to pay for) to obtain طلب، مانگ *There is a great demand for such publications* ایسی مطبوعات کی بہت مانگ ہے *be in great demand* بہت مانگ ہونا *The law of demand and supply determines the price level of commodities* اشیائے تجارت کی قیمتوں کا معیار قانونِ طلب و رسد متعین کرتا ہے

■ A **demand** is peremptory but a **request** is polite. Again, we speak of the **exaction** of full dues, of **extortion** of something not due, and of **call** for funds or of a **call** to duty.

demarcate (*dee*-mah*-kayt) *v.t.* mark or fix the limits of حد باندھنا، حد مقرر کرنا، حد بندی کرنا separate one group from another حد مقرر کرنا **demarcation** (-*ay*-) *n.* حد بندی، تعیینِ حدود

demarche (de-*mah*sh*) *n.* action implying change of policy نیا اقدام، بدلی ہوئی سیاست

demean (de-*meen*) *v.t.* (reflexive) (*demean oneself*) lower (oneself) in dignity حقیر یا ذلیل کر لینا *I would not demean myself by speaking to him* میں اس سے بول کر اپنے آپ کو ذلیل کیوں کروں؛ conduct oneself کا برتاؤ کرنا، کا سلوک کرنا، سے پیش آنا، کا مظاہرہ کرنا *She demeaned herself modestly* اس نے بڑے شرمیلے پن کا مظاہرہ کیا **demeanour** (de-*mee*-nĕ*) *n.* behaviour سلوک، برتاؤ bearing رکھ رکھاؤ، وضع، ڈھنگ

demented (de-*men*-tid) *adj.* mad پاگل، دیوانہ (colloq.) wild with worry فکرمندی کی وجہ سے آپے سے باہر

demerit (de-*me*-rit) *n.* defect خرابی، نقص، عیب weakness of character بداخلاقی، بدکرداری mark of worthless نقص، نالائقی، بدنامی *This misconduct would go to his demerit* اس بدکرداری سے اس کی بدنامی ہو گئی۔

demesne (de-*meen*) *n.* landed estate مقبوضہ املاک possession of property جائداد کا قبضہ *hold (an estate) in demesne* (جائداد یا اراضی) قبضے میں رکھنا domain قلمرو، مملکتِ محروسہ

Demeter (de-*mee*-tĕ*) *Cl. myth.* the Greek goddess of agriculture (esp. of corn), corresponding to the Roman goddess *Ceres* ڈیمیٹر

demi- (*dem*-i) pref. half لاحقہ جس کے معنی ہیں انصف، آدھا، نیم، نا تمام **demi-god** *n.* half god نیم دیوتا، سورما جو دیوتا قرار پا جائے self-important person خود پرست شخص

demi-official (abb. **D. O.** pro. *dee*-oh) *n.* & *adj.* official (letter) written as a personal letter in an unsuccessful bid to avoid red-tape نیم سرکاری (مراسلہ وغیرہ)

demi monde (*dem*-i-mohnd) *n.* woman of doubtful reputation مشتبہ چال چلن والی چھنال

demise (de-*mīz*) *n.* (legal) death موت، وفات، انتقال transfer of property at death انتقالِ جائداد بذریعہ وصیت وغیرہ *v.t.* bequeath انتقالِ جائداد کرنا، ہبہ کرنا

demobilise (de-*mob*-i-līz), **demob** (de-*mob*) *v.t.* release after military service فوج کی خدمت سے سبکدوش کرنا، فوجی خدمت سے سبکدوش کرنا **demobilisation, demob** *n.* فوجی خدمت سے سبکدوشی *War is miserable but demobilisation after war produces greater misery* جنگ کم آفت خیز نہیں ہوتی لیکن جنگ کے بعد فوجوں کی سبکدوشی اور بھی آفت ڈھاتی ہے

democracy (de-*mok*-ra-si) *n.* Government of the people, by the people, for the people; government of a State by the elected representatives of its adult citizens جمہوری حکومت یا مملکت country with such government جمہوریت، جمہوریہ Government which encourages and allows free discussion of policy, majority rule, and political and social equality for its citizens irrespective of their caste, colour and creed جمہوریت، عوامی حکومت country with such government جمہوریت، جمہوریہ، عوامی حکومت **democrat** (*dem*-o-krat) *n.* person who believes in or supports democracy جمہوریت پسند، حامیِ جمہوریت

democratic (*dem*-o-*krat*-ik) *adj.* of, like or supporting democracy جمہوری *democratic principles* جمہوری اصول *democratic institutions,* (esp.) (*a*) institutions paying no attention to class divisions based on birth or wealth جمہوری ادارے جن میں نسل و دولت کا خیال نہ رکھا گیا ہو۔ (*b*) departments, etc., of a democratic set-up جمہوری نظام کے ادارے، جمہوری ادارے *a person of democratic spirit* جمہوریت پسند، دلدادۂ جمہوریت **democratically**

(dem-o-*krat*-i-ka-li) *adv.* in a democratic manner جمہوری طور سے ، جمہور طریق سے

demolish (de-*mol*-ish) *v. t.* pull down ڈھانا ، باطل کر دینا ، دھجیاں اُڑا دینا nullify مسمار کرنا *demolish (someone's) arguments* دلائل کو باطل کر دینا overthrow زیر وزبر کر دینا **demolition** (dem-o-*lish*-èn) act of demolishing *n.* اِنہدام ، مسماری ، بربادی ■ One **demolishes** a mass of structure, **destroys** totally, **annihilates** to nothingness, and **wrecks** (particularly a ship) when one destroys it so as to cause suffering.

demon (*dee*-mon) *n.* evil supernatural being آسیب ، بھوت پریت ، بد رُوح cruel and malignant person بے رحم خُوں خوار شخص ، بھوت **demoniac** (de-*moh*-ni-ak) *n.* person possessed by a demon آسیب زدہ *adj.* devilish بے رحم ، ظالم **demonic** (dee-*mon*-ik) *adj.* of supernatural genius عفریتی ، آسیبی . بھوت پریت کا ■ A **demon** is a divinity or mysterious power of any kind, whether good or bad; the devil is an evil power; an **imp** is small and malignant; a **sprite** is a goblin or elf.

demonetize (dee-*mon*-i-tiz) *v. t.* devaluate a currency دھات کے سِکّے کی قیمت گرا دینا ، دھات کا استعمال بطورِ زر بند کر دینا **demonetization** (-*ay*-) *n* devaluation قیمت کی گراوٹ . دھات کے بطور سکّہ استعمال پر پابندی

demonstrate (*dem*-on-strayt) *v. t. & i.* show clearly and conclusively by giving proof or citing example توضیح کرنا ، دلیل ہونا یا شہادت دینا make known (one's feeling) جذبات کا اظہار کرنا protest (*against*) support by means of (usu. violent) processions, etc. احتجاجی مُظاہرہ کرنا ، شورش انگیز مُظاہرہ کرنا ، احتجاج کرنا *The people are too cowed down to demonstrate against this crushing taxation* عوام اِتنے مرعوب ہو چکے ہیں کہ وہ ان کچل ڈالنے والے ٹیکسوں کے خلاف احتجاج نہیں کر سکتے . **demonstration** (-*ay*-) *n.* demonstrating احتجاج ، مُظاہرہ ، جماہرہ clear proof دلیل ، حُجّت outward expression of feeling اِظہار ، مُظاہرہ *demonstration of friendship* اِظہارِ دوستی ، اظہارِ اُلفت show of public feeling for or against (کسی امر کے حق میں یا خلاف) مُظاہرہ show of military strength فوجی قوت کا مُظاہرہ *The Indonesian army made a successful demonstration against the Dutch* انڈونیشی فوج نے ولندیزوں کے خلاف کامیاب مُظاہرہ کیا **demonstrative** (de-*mon*-stra-tiv) *adj.* showing the feelings مظہرِ جذبات (in grammar) pointing out اِشاری ، اشارہ کرنے والا *'This', 'that', 'these' and 'those' are demonstrative pronouns* (واحد جمع) اور وہ (واحد و جمع) اسماء اشارہ ہیں openly showing strong affection جذباتِ مُحبّت کا اظہار زیادہ کرنے والا *She is very demonstrative* وہ بڑی جذباتی عورت ہے ، وہ اظہارِ مُحبّت میں بڑی بے باک ہے . **demonstrator** (*dem*-on-stray-tě*) *n.* person who demonstrates at a public meeting مُظاہرہ کرنے والا person who conducts students' science practicals طلبہ کو عملی سائنس کا سبق دینے والا . سائنس میں عملی کام کرانے والا ، مُظاہر ، ڈیمانسٹریٹر

demoralize (de-*mo*-ra-liz) *v. t.* hurt or weaken the morals of اخلاق بگاڑنا ، بد اخلاق بنانا ، اخلاقی پستی کرنا *Drink had demoralized him* شراب نوشی نے اِس کی حالت پست کر دی تھی weaken the courage, discipline and moral of (an army, etc.) (فوج کی) ہمت پست کرنا ، (فوج کو) بددل کر دینا یا ابتر دینا **demoralizable** (-liz-è-bèl) *adj.* جس کا حوصلہ توڑا جا سکے . **demoralization** (-*ay*-) *n.* act of demoralizing بددلی ، (فوج کے نظام کی) ابتری

Demos (*dee*-mos) *n.* democracy personified جمہوریت

demur (de-*mě**) *v. i.* (-rr-) hesitate and object پس و پیش کرنا ، اعتراض کرنا . احتجاج کرنا *The workers demur at working on holidays* محنت کش چھٹیوں میں کام کرنے پر اعتراض کرتے ہیں (یا کے خلاف احتجاج کرتے ہیں) *n.* hesitation or protest اعتراض ، احتجاج *without demur* بلا پس و پیش ، بے چون وچرا

demure (de-*mew*-è*) *adj.* quiet and modest متین ، سنجیدہ affectedly shy; prudish بناوٹی شرم والا **demurely** *adv.* سنجیدگی سے ، بناوٹی شرم سے **demureness** *n.* سنجیدگی ، متانت ، بناوٹی شرم

demurrage (de-*mě*-rij) *n.* compensation to be paid to railway authorities or shipowners for delay in the loading or unloading of goods or cargo (جہاز پر) دیر میں مال لادنے یا اُتارنے کا ہرجہ (ریل میں) رُکے ہوئے مال پر محصول یا ہرجہ ، ڈیمارج

demy (de-*mi*) *n.* (pl. demies, pr. de-*miz*) size of paper (=22½″ × 17½″) کاغذ کا ایک سائز

den *n.* wild animal's lair بھٹ ، ماند *a lion's den* شیر کی ماند secret resort of criminals مجرموں کا اڈا *opium den* افیونیوں کا اڈا *den of thieves* چوروں کا اڈا (colloq.) room in which a person works or studies without being disturbed خلوت خانہ ، خلوت گاہ

dengue (*deng*-oo) *n.* fever causing stiffness of joints ڈنگو بخار جس میں جوڑوں میں بہت درد ہوتا ہے .

denial (see under **deny**)

denizen (*den*-i-zen). *n.* animal or plant species having permanent home in a particular place (*cf.* citizen) اجنبی جانور یا پودا جو مُلکی بن گیا ہو inhabitant اجنبی باشندہ جو مُلکی حقوق حاصل کرلے

denominate (de-*nom*-i-nayt) *v.t.* give a name to religious sect کسی فرقے کا نام رکھنا ، نام دینا ، موسوم کرنا ، کہلانا describe پکارنا ، بیان کرنا **denomination** (-*ay*-) *n.* class of units (weight, length, number, num er. etc. وزن، طول، تعداد، قدر وغیرہ کی چھوٹی بڑی قسم *Money of small denomination* چھوٹی قسم کی رقم sect فرقہ، گروہ name, description نام، لقب، ذات *Tigers, leopards and lions come under the denomination of big game* شیر چیتے اور شیر ببر بڑا شکار کہلاتے ہیں۔

denominational (-nay-shè-) *adj* (esp) sectarian فرقہ وارانہ *non-denominational*, non-sectarian غیر فرقہ وارانہ **denominator** (de-*nom*-i-nay-tĕ*) *n.* number below the line in a fraction (*e.g.* the number 7 in the fraction $\frac{4}{7}$) (ریاضی) نسب نما *a common denominator*, something common to all مُشترک

denote (de-*noht*) *v.t.* signify ظاہر کرنا، سمجھانا، بتانا indicate کا مطلب ہونا، سے عبارت ہونا، پر دلالت کرنا be a name for نام ہونا، تعبیر ہونا

denouement (day-*noo*-ment) *n.* outcome of action in novel or play (ناول یا ڈرامے میں) حل، پیچیدگیوں کا سُلجھاؤ، انجام، سُلجھاؤ outcome of any action نتیجہ

denounce (de-*nouns*) *v.t.* accuse publicly علانیہ مُجرم ٹھہرانا condemn مُلامت کرنا، بُرا بھلا کہنا betray مُخبری کرنا give notice that one intends to end (a treaty or agreement) (مُعاہدے کے) اختتام کا اعلان کرنا **denunciation** (de-nun-si-*ay*-shĕn) *n.* denouncing (*of* someone) علانیہ مُجرم ٹھہرانا، الزام لگانا، مُخبری repudiation (*of* agreement, etc.) مُعاہدے کے خاتمے کا اعلان

de novo adv. anew نئے سرے سے، اَز سرِ نَو

dense (dens) *adj.* (of liquids, etc.) thick گاڑھا کثیف heavy وَزنی، ٹھوس (of things and people) closely packed and large in number گھنا، گنجان *a dense forest* گھنا جنگل، گنجان جنگل *a dense crowd* کثیر ہجوم (of a person) stupid بیوقوف، اَحمق **densely** *adv.* ٹھوس پن سے، گنجانی سے **density** (*den*-si-ti) *n.* being dense ٹھوس پن، گنجانی، گاڑھا پن، گھنا پن (in physics) relation of weight to volume کثافت، ثقل نوعی، کثافت اضافی **denseness** (*dens*-nes) *n.* thickness ٹھوس پن، کثافت، گاڑھا پن

dent *n.* hollow in a hard surface made by a blow or by pressure (کسی کُند آلے سے پڑا ہوا) سطحی نشان *v.t.* make a dent in (کسی کُند آلے سے) نشان ڈالنا **dented** (*dent*-id) *adj.* having hollows دندانے پڑے ہُوئے having teeth دندانے دار

dental (*dent*-ĕl) *adj.* of the teeth دانتوں کے متعلق *dental cream* دانتوں کا ولایتی منجن *dental surgeon*, tooth doctor دانتوں کے امراض کا معالج، مُعالج دندان (of letter) pronounced by the aid of the teeth (*th*, *t*, *d*) دانتوں اور زبان کی مدد سے ادا ہونے والا حرف **dentist** *n.* tooth-doctor معالج دندان، دندان ساز **dentistry** (*dent*-is-tri) *n.* skilled work of a dentist فنِ علاج دندان دندان سازی **denture** (*dench*-ĕ*) *n.* plate of artificial teeth (مصنوعی) دانتوں کا چوکا (یا سیٹ) **dentition** (dent-*ish*-ĕn) *n.* cutting of teeth (بچے کے) دانت نکلنا

dentifrice *n.* tooth powder منجن، ہنسون

denude (de-*newd*) *v.t.* make bare ننگا کرنا، عُریاں کرنا take away clothing or covering, etc. برہنہ کرنا، کپڑے اُتار دینا، اُوپر کی مٹی یا خس و خاشاک ہٹانا یا دُور کرنا *hill-side denuded of trees* جنگلات سے صاف کیا ہوا پہاڑ take away the possession محروم کر دینا **denudation** (de-new-*day*-shĕn) *n.* the laying bare of rock by the action of water and weather پانی کا اور موسم کا چٹان کو مٹی وغیرہ سے ننگا کرنا، عُریاں کاری

denunciation *n.* (see **denounce**)

deny (de-*ni*) *v. t.* contradict تکذیب کرنا، تغلیط کرنا، نامنظور کرنا، اِنکار کرنا 'say no' to (a request) رَد کرنا refuse to admit کو تسلیم نہ کرنا، کی صحت قبول کرنے سے اِنکار کر دینا *denied the signature* اُس نے دستخطوں کی صحت قبول کرنے سے اِنکار کر دیا refuse to believe کا یقین نہ کرنا، کو باوَر نہ کرنا refuse to grant (something needed) نہ دینا **denial** (de-*ni*-ĕl) *n.* contradiction رَد، تردید، تکذیب refusal (لیڈر وغیرہ) تسلیم کرنے سے اِنکار disavowal اِنکار

■ To **deny** is to reject as untrue ; to **contradict**, to say the opposite ; to **confute**, to prove overwhelmingly the wrongness of ; to **controvert**, dispute or speak against ; to **contravene**, to run against a rule ; to **repudiate**, to disown.

deodorize (dee-*ohd*-è-riz) *v. t.* remove bad odour from بدبُو دُور کرنا، تعفن دُور کرنا **deodorization** (-*ay*-) *n.* act of deodorizing ازالۂ تعفن، دفعیۂ تعفن

Deo volente (dee-oh-vo-*len*-te) (abbr. *D. V.*) *adv.* God-willing انشاءاللہ، خُدا نے چاہا تو

depart (de-*pah**t) *v.i.* go away چلے جانا، رُخصت ہونا start on a journey روانہ ہونا die مرجانا، انتقال کرنا deviate (*from*) تجاوز کرنا، انحراف کرنا **departed** (-tid) *n.* past and gone گزشتہ، گُزرا ہوا dead مُتوفّی، مرحوم، آنجہانی

departure *n.* going away روانگی starting on journey سفر پر روانگی *the arrival and departure of trains* ریل گاڑیوں کی آمد و روانگی setting out on a new course of action or thought جدّتِ خیال deviation (*from*) تجاوُز، انحراف

department (de-*pah**t-ment) *n.* one of the several divisions of a government administration (حکومت یا نظم و نسق کا) محکمہ، سررشتہ *the Education Department* سررشتۂ تعلیم، محکمۂ تعلیم *the Agriculture Department* محکمۂ زراعت *Department of Animal Husbandry* محکمۂ پرورشِ حیوانات *the Co-operative Department* محکمۂ انجمن ہائے امدادِ باہمی *the Communications Department* محکمۂ مُواصلات *the Fisheries Department* محکمۂ سمکیات، محکمۂ ماہی گیری *the Department of Public Health* محکمۂ صحتِ عامّہ *the Irrigation Depart-*

ment محکمۂ ترقیات، محکمۂ اَنہار *the Development Department* *the Industries Department* محکمۂ صنعت و حرفت *the Commerce Department* محکمۂ تجارت *the Public Relations Department* محکمۂ تعلقات عامّہ *the Public Works Department* محکمۂ تعمیرات عامّہ *the Rehabilitation Department* محکمۂ آباد کاری *the Revenue Department* محکمۂ مال، محکمۂ مالگزاری *the Reclamation Department* محکمۂ اصلاح *the Land Reclamation Department* محکمۂ اصلاحِ اراضی *the Resettlement Department* محکمۂ آباد کاری *the Settlement Department* محکمۂ بندوبست اراضی، محکمۂ بندوبست *the Transport Department* محکمۂ نقل و حمل *Social Welfare Department* محکمۂ معاشری بہبود (also *department of studies*), academic division of a college or university for the study of a subject (put in charge of a *Professor or Head of the Department*) شعبہ *Department of English* شعبۂ انگریزی *Head of the Department of English* صدرِ شعبۂ انگریزی، رئیسِ شعبۂ انگریزی distinct division of a business شعبہ، جیسے *the tailoring department* شعبۂ خیاطی a division of territory ضلع، قسمت **departmental** (de-pah*t-*ment*-ĕl) *adj*. of, by or relating to a department محکمانہ، محکمہ، محکمے کا، سررشتہ کا *departmental staff* محکمانہ *departmental inquiry* محکمانہ تحقیق و تفتیش inquiry conducted into an employee's conduct not by the forces of law and order but by his department itself.

depend (de-*pend*) *v.i.* (*depend on or upon*) trust بھروسہ کرنا، اعتماد کرنا rely on (the support, etc., *of*) in order to exist انحصار کرنا *the old woman still depends on her own earnings, she has no one else to provide for her* بے چاری بڑھیا اپنی ہی کمائی پر انحصار رکھتی ہے، اس کی ضروریات مہیا کرنے والا کوئی نہیں ہے۔ *Good health depends on good food, sleep, and exercise* صحت کا دار و مدار خوراک، نیند اور ورزش پر ہے be determined by موقوف ہونا *It depends on circumstances* یہ حالات پر موقوف ہے *That depends* جیسی صورت ہو، کبھی کچھ کبھی کچھ، یہ حالت پر موقوف ہے *It all depends on something else* اس کا انحصار کسی اور بات پر ہے be sure of اعتماد کرنا *you can always depend on him to be there when needed* تم اس پر اعتماد کر سکتے ہو کہ جب اور جہاں اس کی ضرورت ہوگی وہ موجود ہوگا *Depend upon it*, you can be quite certain about the result مان لیجئے، یقین مانیئے **dependable** *adj*. reliable بھروسے کے لائق، قابلِ اعتماد **dependant** *n*. (of. *dependent* below) supported member of a family دست نگر، متوسّل servant ملازم، نوکر **dependence** *n*. the stage of depending (*on* someone or something) انحصار، آسرا، دار و مدار that on which one depends بھروسا، سہارا subservience ماتحتی، تابعداری **dependency** *n*. country ruled by another country ماتحت ملک **dependent** *adj*. (of. *dependant* above) dependent on or upon منحصر، وابستہ *He is dependent on his uncle* وہ اپنے چچا کا متوسّل ہے hanging down معلّق subservient (*on*) ماتحت، متعلق

depict (de-*pikt*) *v.t.* represent in drawing a painting تصویر یا نقشہ کھینچنا describe in words لفظوں میں تصویر کھینچنا، بیان کرنا، نقل کرنا **depiction** (de-*pik*-shĕn) *n*. act of depicting *n*. تصویر کشی، مرقّع کشی، بیان، نقل

depilatory (de-*pil*-è-tĕ-ri) *n*. & *adj*. (medicine) applied to hair for removing it بال صفا، بال دور کرنے والی (دوا) **depilation** (dep-i-*lay*-shĕn) extirpation of the unwanted hair from the face, etc., with tweezers (موچنے سے فالتو) بال اکھیڑنا

deplete (de-*pleet*) *v.t.* use up صرف کر ڈالنا exhaust ختم کر دینا reduce بہت گھٹا دینا *Our foreign exchange had been greatly depleted by food imports* غذائی سامان کی آمد نے ہمارا زرِ مبادلہ تقریباً ختم ہی کر ڈالا تھا **depletion** (de-*plee*-shĕn) *n*. using up خاتمہ heavy reduction سخت کمی

deplore (de-*plohr*) *v.t.* lament ماتم کرنا، غم کرنا condemn ; consider to be blameworthy برا بھلا کہنا، الزام دلانا **deplorable** (de-*ploh*-ra-bĕl) *adj*. blameworthy افسوسناک، بہت برا، شرمناک **deplorably** *adv*. افسوسناک طور سے، شرمناک طریق سے

deploy (de-*ploi*) *v.i.* & *t* (of troops) spread out from column into line (فوج) کا میدان میں پھیلنا یا پھیلانا، پرا جمانا، صف بندی کرنا **deployment** *n*. spreading out thus صف بندی

deponent (de-*poh*-nent) *n*. (in law) one who makes a deposition ; one who states something in a court of law on oath حلفیہ اظہار دینے والا، تحریری شہادت دینے والا۔

depopulate (de-*pop*-ew-layt) *v. t*. reduce the number of people living in (a territory) آبادی گھٹانا *a country depopulated by war, poverty and epidemics* جنگ، افلاس اور وباؤں سے گھٹی ہوئی آبادی کا ملک **depopulation** (-*ay*-) *n*. reduction in population آبادی میں کمی، آبادی گھٹنا

deport (de-*poh*t*) *v.t.* send (esp. an unwanted foreigner) out of the country ملک بدر کرنا، جلاوطن کرنا (*deport oneself*), behave, conduct خاص رویّہ یا طرز اختیار کرنا *deport (oneself) with dignity* ایک شان اختیار کرنا **deportation** (-ay-) *n*. banishment جلاوطنی، اخراج **deportment** *n*. behaviour طور، طریق way of bearing oneself رویّہ، سبھاؤ

depose (de-*pohz*) *v.t.* remove (someone from a position of authority) معزول کرنا، اختیارات چھین لینا dethrone (a king) تخت سے اتارنا give evidence on oath (in a court of law) شہادت دینا، حلفی بیان دینا **deposition** (de-po-*zish*-ĕn) *n*. evidence given in a court of law on oath شہادت، حلفی بیان، اظہار de thronement (of a king) تخت سے اُتارا جانا ، معزولی removal of something from a position of authority اختیارات کا چھن جانا ، معزولی (see below under **deposit**)

deposit (de-*poz*-it) *v.t.* put (money, valuables, etc.) in a place or in someone's care (for safe custody, etc.) تحویل میں دینا ، جمع کرانا *He deposited Rs. 100 in the bank* (of a river or liquids) leave a layer of sediment on تہ نشین مادہ چھوڑ جانا *Rivers deposit silt on the fields during a flood* سیلاب میں دریا کھیتوں پر مٹی چھوڑ جاتے ہیں make part payment of money one owes قرضے کی جزوی ادائیگی کرنا ، سائی دینا place دھرنا ، رکھنا *He deposited himself on the grass* اُس نے اپنا وجود گھاس پر دھر دیا ، وہ گھاس پر بیٹھ گیا *n.* money, etc., deposited امانت ، وہ رقم جو بنک میں جمع کرائی جائے ۔ *bank deposit* بنک میں جمع کردہ رقم sediment تہ نشین مادہ money given as a promise to pay more later as the price of something bought بیعانہ ، سائی any layer of matter deposited نیچے بیٹھنے والے مادّے کی تہ ۔ *a deposit of coal* پتھر کے کوئلے کی تہ **depositor** *n.* person who makes a deposit in a bank بنک میں رقم جمع کرنے والا **depository** (de-poz-i-tè-ri) *n.* place where goods are deposited گودام ، وہ جگہ جہاں مال جمع کرایا جائے ۔ store house مال خانہ ، گودام **deposition** (de-po-zi*sh*-èn) *n.* act of depositing امانت ، تحویل ، تہ نشین کرنا (see under **depose**)

depot (*dep*-oh) *n.* (lit.) storehouse کوٹھی ، گودام مال خانہ emporium منڈی headquarters of a regiment رجمنٹ کا صدر مقام military storehouse فوجی گودام ، مال خانہ

deprave (de-*prayv*) *v.t.* make bad; corrupt morally بگاڑنا ، خراب کرنا **depraved** (de-*prayvd*) *adj.* dissolute فاسق و فاجر ، بدکار corrupt (habits, etc.) عادتیں بگاڑنا ، فسق و فجور سکھانا low (tastes, etc.) بدذوق ، پست ذوق *depraved tastes* اَدنیٰ درجے کا ذوق

depravity (de-*prav*-i-ti) *n.* depraved state of morals فسق و فجور ، سیاہ کاری ، بدکاری

deprecate (*dep*-re-kayt) *v.t.* disapprove of ناپسندیدگی یا ناخوشی کا اظہار کرنا ۔ advise the avoidance of *deprecate panic* وحشت سے بچنے کی فہمائش کرنا try to pacify (someone's anger, etc.) by entreaty فہمائش کرنا *deprecate (someone's) anger* غصّہ پی جانے کی اِلتجا کرنا غصّہ پی جانے کی فہمائش کرنا **deprecator** *n.* one who deprecates ناپسندیدگی کا اظہار کرنے والا **deprecatory** (*dep*-) *adj.* disapproving اظہارِ ناپسندگی کرنے والی (بات) **deprecation** (-ay-) *n.* act of deprecating اظہارِ ناپسندیدگی یا ناخوشی ، فہمائش ، اِلتجا

depreciate (de-*pree*-shi-ayt) *v.t.* & *i.* make less in value قدر و قیمت گھٹانا belittle, say that something has little value بے وقعت کرنا ، حقیر سمجھنا ، *depreciate (a currency)*, devaluate (it) زرِ مبادلہ کی قیمت کم کرنا ، نرخ گر جانا ، شرحِ مبادلہ کم کرنا ۔ fall in value مندا ہو جانا ، قیمت گھٹ جانا ، شرحِ مبادلہ کم ہو جانا *Evacuee property has depreciated owing to neglect* متروکہ جائداد کی دیکھ بھال نہ ہونے کے باعث اس کی قیمت گر گئی ہے ۔ *The currency has depreciated* اس سکّے کی شرحِ مبادلہ کم ہو گئی ہے ۔ سکّے کی قیمت گر گئی ہے **depreciation** *n.* lessening of value کم قدری کمی قیمت ۔ (esp.) allowance made in valuation for wear and tear گھس گھساؤ کا خیال رکھ کر قیمت کم کرنا ، فرسودگی **depreciatory** *adj.* (esp.) belittling تحقیر آمیز

depredation (dep-re-*day*-shĕn) *n.* (usu. *pl.*) destruction or plundering of property لوٹ ، غارت گری ، تاخت و تاراج **depredator** (*dep*-re-day-tĕ*) *n.* plunderer لوٹ مار کرنے والا ، غارت گر ، لٹیرا

depress (de-*pres*) *v.t.* press or pull down نیچے کو کرنا ، دبانا *depress the keys of a piano* پیانو کے سُر دبانا *depress a lever* لیور دبانا sadden دِھیمے کرنا بددل کرنا make less active افسردہ کرنا cause (prices) to be lower مندا کرنا ، بازار سرد کرنا **depressing** *adj.* making sad or unhappy دل بجھانے والا ، بددلی پیدا کرنے والا ، افسردہ کن ، ملال انگیز *a depressing news* ملال انگیز خبر *depressing weather* افسردہ کن موسم *a depressing book* دل بجھانے والی کتاب **depression** (de-*presh*-èn) *n.* being depressed جھکاؤ ، دبا ہوا ہونا hollow place in the surface of the ground نشیب ، گڑھا lowering of atmospheric pressure ہوا کا دباؤ کم ہونا ، انخفاض centre where this pressure is the lowest ہوا کا ، کم دباؤ کا طبقہ ، انخفاض ، مرکزِ انخفاض business slump مندا ، سرد بازاری ، کساد بازاری **depressed** *adj.* sad, despondent افسردہ دل ، غمزدہ *He is feeling much depressed about it* اس بات کی وجہ سے اُس کا دل بجھا بجھا سا رہنے لگا ، وہ افسردہ دل ہو گیا less active مندا ، سرد بازاری *Business was depressed in those days* بازار اُن دنوں مندا تھا low in social status پست (ذات) ، پست ذاتیں ، اچھوت (ذات) *The depressed classes* چھوٹی ذاتیں ، دلت ، ہریجن یا جاتی اچھوت ، ہریجن ، دلت جاتیاں ۔

deprive (de-*prīv*) *v.t.* deprive (someone or something *of* something or someone) محروم کر دینا ، چھین لینا ، *He deprived me of my chance* اُس نے مجھے میرے مواقع سے محروم کر دیا *deprived of meaning,* خالی از معانی ، بے معنی prevent from using or enjoying (کسی نعمت سے) لطف اندوز نہ ہونے دینا *So many trees would deprive this house of light and air* یا اتنے درخت تو مکان کو روشنی اور ہوا سے محروم کر دیں گے **deprival** (-*prī*-) act of depriving *n.* محرومی ، معزولی **deprivation** (dep-ri-*vay*-shèn) *n.* (esp.) felt loss حرماں نصیبی ، محرومی ، صدمۂ جانکاہ *The Quaid's death was a nationl deprivation* قائدِ اعظم کی موت پوری قوم کیلئے صدمۂ جانکاہ تھی

de profundis (de-pro-*fun*-dis) out of the depths of (sorrow) قعرِ غم سے

depth (depth) *n.* being deep گہرا ، گہرائی *The depth of the ocean* سمندر کی گہرائی *with depth of feeling*

بشدّت جذبات سے measure from top to bottom or from front to back چوڑائی، عمق، گہرائی جہاں تک ہو *to a depth of ten feet* دس فٹ کی گہرائی تک *snow three feet in depth* تین فٹ گہری برف *a cupboard 1½ feet in depth* ڈیڑھ فٹ چوڑے دروازوں والی برتنوں کی الماری *out of one's depth,* (*a*) in water deeper than one's height حد درجہ اپنے قد سے زیادہ گہرے پانی میں۔ (*b*) considering something beyond one's understanding سمجھ سے بالاتر سمجھ سے باہر۔ extreme of نہایت، انتہا، جوبن جب موسم سرما جوبن پر ہو *in the depth of winter* گھنا پن، گھُپ *in the depth of despair* انتہائے یاس و قنوط میں *in the depth of the forest* جنگل کے گھنے حصے میں *the depth of darkness* گہری تاریکی، گھُپ اندھیرا intensity (of colour) (رنگ کا) گہرا پن that which is deep *the ocean depths* تعرِ دریا، خفیف بحر گہری جگہ، قعر learning and wisdom ذہن رسا، علم و دانش، دانائی *a man of depth* کا مالک، تیز فہم۔ **depth-charge** *n.* bomb set to explode at a desired depth of the sea (for blowing up a submerged submarine) (آبدوز کو ڈبونے کے لیے استعمال کیا جانے والا) بم

depute (de-pewt) *v.t.* appoint (someone) for a while as deputy (*to do* something) قائم مقام، نمائندہ یا وکیل بنانا یا مقرر کرنا *He deputed me to act for him at the conference* اس نے مجھے اس کانفرنس میں اپنا نمائندہ مقرر کر کے بھیجا commit (work or authority) to a substitute (اختیار یا کام) تفویض کرنا، سپرد کرنا **deputy** (*dep*-ew-ti) *n.* person to whom work or authority is deputed قائم مقام، نمائندہ، وکیل one elected to represent a constituency in a legislature نمائندہ

deputation (dep-ew-*tay*-shĕn) *n.* group of representatives وفد، جماعتِ نمائندگان *A deputation of the strikers waited on the Chief Minister* ہڑتالیوں کے وفد نے وزیرِ اعلیٰ سے ملاقات کی **deputize** (*dep*-ew-tiz) *v.i.* act as deputy (*for*) (کسی کی جگہ) قائم مقام ہونا، (کی) قائم مقامی کرنا

derail (de-*rayl*) *v.t.* cause (train, etc.) to leave the rail track پٹڑی سے اُتار دینا **derailment** *n.* derailing پٹڑی سے اُتر جانا

derange (de-*raynj*) *v.t.* put out of working order اُلٹ پلٹ یا بے ترتیب کر دینا *derange a machine* مشین کے پرزے اُلٹ پلٹ کر دینا، مشین کو بیکار کر دینا make insane دیوانہ یا پاگل کرنا put (thoughts, plan, etc.) into confusion, disturb their sequence خیالات پراگندہ کر دینا **deranged** (de-*raynjd*) *n.* & *adj.* mentally deranged; mad پاگل، دیوانہ **derangement** *n.* deranging or being deranged پاگل پن، دیوانگی، اَبتری، پراگندگی، بے ترتیبی ▣ One is **deranged,** mentally; insane, totally; **unbalanced,** in varying degrees; **crazy,** when temporarily violent; **mad,** as in actual disease; **distracted,** temporarily unable to think owing to grief, etc.; **morbid** when having unnatural tastes and desires; **feeble-minded,** when with a childish mind. Again, a **lunatic** is harmless; a **maniac,** dangerous; and an **imbecile,** with no mental processes beyond physical needs.

Derby (*dah**-bi) *n. the Derby,* British horse race at Epsom founded by the 12th Earl of Derby 1780 A.C. ایپسم میں اَرل ڈربی کی جاری کردہ مشہور گھڑ دوڑ، ڈربی *the Derby lottery,* the lottery held on the occasion ڈربی کی دوڑ کے موقع پر پڑنے والی لاٹری، ڈربی لاٹری

derelict (*de*-re-likt) *adj.* abandoned (usu. because dangerous or useless) (خطرناک یا بیکار سمجھ کر) ترک کردہ، متروکہ، لاوارث *derelict ship* متروکہ جہاز، لاوارث جہاز *derelict property* لاوارث جائداد neg'igent بے پروا، غفلت شعار، سہل انگار **dereliction** (de-re-lik-shĕn) *n.* neglect (of duty) (ادائے فرض میں) کوتاہی، غفلت شعاری

deride (de-*rīd*) *v.t.* laugh scornfully at (کسی پر) ازراہِ نفرت، ہنسنا (کسی کی) ہنسی اُڑانا **derision** (de-*rizh*-en) *n.* deriding or being derided تضحیک، ہنسی، تمسخر *hold* (*someone*) *in derision* (کسی) کی تضحیک کرنا، کا مذاق اُڑانا **derisive** (de-*rī*-siv) *adj.* showing scorn تضحیک آمیز، نفرت آمیز *derisive cheers* تضحیک آمیز تالیاں deserving scorn قابل (یا لائق) نفرت، انگیز، نفرت کے قابل *a derisive offer* نفرت انگیز پیشکش، لائق نفرین

derision *n.* (see under **deride**)

derive (de-*rīv*) *v.t.* & *i.* get (something *from*) (کسی چیز سے) حاصل کرنا *derive pleasure from* لطف حاصل کرنا، لطف اندوز ہونا have as a starting point; originate نکلنا، ماخوذ ہونا، (فلاں) اصل یا نسل سے ہونا (of words) be formed (*from*) (سے) مشتق ہونا *words derived from Arabic* عربی سے مشتق الفاظ، عربی الاصل trace the origin of (word) کا اشتقاق بتانا

derivation (de-ri-*vay*-shĕn) *n.* (esp.) first form and meaning (*of* a word) (لفظ کی) اصل، (لفظ کا) مادہ statement of how a word was formed and how it changed اشتقاق **derivative** (de-*riv*-ĕ-tiv) *adj.* & *n.* (thing or word) derived from سے مشتق *derivative of,* derived from مشتق، ماخوذ something not original ماخوذ، مستخرج، جو اصلی نہ ہو *All the ideas of these petty writers are derivative* ان کم مایہ مصنفوں کے تمام خیالات (اوروں سے) ماخوذ ہوتے ہیں

derogatory (de-*rog*-ĕ-to-ri) *adj.* tending to discredit اہانت آمیز، بے وقرانہ *remarks derogatory to one's reputation* not becoming one's dignity خلافِ شان، معیوب، غیر شایاں *His behaviour is derogatory to his status* اُس کا سلوک اُس کی شان کے شایاں نہیں ہے

derring-do (de-ring-*doo*) *n.* (poet.) desperate courage تہوّر، جانبازانہ ہمت، جان پر کھیل جانا *deeds of derring-do* جانبازی کے کارنامے

dervish (*de**-vish) *n.* Muslim monk who lives a life of poverty درویش

descant *v.i.* (des-*kant*) talk at large and enthusiastically (*upon*) (کسی مسئلے پر) تفصیل سے گفتگو کرنا ، (پر) تقریر کرنا *n.* (*des*-kant) (poet.) melody, song گیت ، ترانہ ، نغمہ ، آہنگ ، سرود

descend (de-*send*) *v.t.* & *i.* come or go down اُترنا ، (اُترنا) پڑنا *The rain descended* بارش پڑنے لگی ، مینہ اُتر پڑا *descend from a hilltop* پہاڑی کی چوٹی سے اُترنا (of property, qualities, rights) pass (from father to son) by inheritance (ورثے میں پانا یا ملنا) *he descended from,* have as one's ancestors وہ (فلاں) نسل سے تھا come from earlier times (فلاں زمانے سے) چلے آنا fall from a moral standard (*to* doing something) اُتر آنا *descend to cheating* دھوکے بازی پر اُتر آنا (*descend upon*), attack (someone, etc.) suddenly آ پڑنا ، ٹوٹ پڑنا ۔ اچانک حملہ کرنا **descendant** (de-*sen*-dant) *n.* offspring اولاد ، خلف ، نسل (*someone's*) *descendant, the descendant of* (*someone*) (فلاں کی) اولاد ، کی نسل سے **descent** (de-*sent*) *n.* descending اُترنا ، نزول *We made a rapid descent* ہم تیزی سے نیچے کو اُترے downward slope ڈھلان ، نیچے کو جانے والا راستہ *a steep descent* تیز ڈھلان decline تنزل ، گراوٹ fall (of prices etc.) بھاؤ گرنا ancestry پشت ، پیڑھی ، نسل و مذہب *of (noble) descent, be descended from (a noble) family* (عالی) خاندان سے ہونا sudden attack اچانک حملہ ، یورش

describe (des-*krib*) *v.t.* say what a person or thing is like صفت بیان کرنا ، کے متعلق کہنا کہ *She described him as a learned person* اُس نے بیان کیا کہ وہ بڑا فاضل ہے give a picture of (someone or something) in words لفظوں میں بتانا give an account of ذکر کرنا ، بیان کرنا *describe a voyage* سفر کا حال بیان کرنا draw the outline of (شکل) کھینچنا *describe a circle* دائرہ بنانا یا کھینچنا **description** (des-krip-shĕn) *n.* account بیان ، توصیف ، وصف picture in words (لفظی) بیان ، وضاحت *of any description,* (colloq.) of any kind at all کسی بھی قسم کا ، کسی شکل کا **descriptive** (des-*krip*-tiv) *adj.* one who (or that which) describes توصیفی ، بیانی *descriptive writer,* مناظرِ قدرت وغیرہ بیان کرنے والا مصنف *descriptive touches* منظر کشی ، کردار نگاری **describable** (-krı-) *adj.* that which can be described قابلِ بیان ، لائقِ توصیف

descry (des-*krī*) *v.t.* see (something) dimly from afar دور سے کچھ کچھ نظر آ جانا succeed in discerning سمجھ ہی جانا

desecrate (*des*-e-krayt) *v.t.* profane ; use (a sacred place or thing) in a bad way, (the opposite of *consecrate*) بے عزتی کرنا ، بے ادبی کرنا **desecration** (-*ay*-) *n.* desecrating or being desecrated بے حرمتی ، بے عزتی **desecrator** (*des*-ĕ-kray-te*) *n.* one who desecrates بے حرمتی کرنے والا

desecrable *adj.* that may be desecrated جس کی بے حرمتی کا امکان ہو

desensitize *v.t.* (see *Addenda*)

desert *v.t.* & *i.* (de-*zĕ*t*) leave without help or support, (esp. in a wrong or cruel way) بیوفائی سے چھوڑ دینا ، ساتھ چھوڑ دینا ، دغا دینا *the selfish leaders deserted their followers* خود غرض رہنماؤں نے اپنے پیروں کا ساتھ چھوڑ دیا۔ *His courage deserted him* اُس نے حوصلہ ہار دیا go away from ترک کر دینا ، چلے جانا quit (esp. service in the armed forces or in a ship) without permission (فوجی یا بحری نوکری سے) چھوڑ کر بھاگ جانا *deserting soldier* بھگوڑا ، (نوکری سے) بھاگا ہوا فوجی ، فراری *n.* (*dez*-ĕ*t) dry land covered with sand ریگستان ، بیابان ۔ (de-*zĕ*t*) (usu. *pl.*) what one deserves سزا ، جس سلوک کا کوئی مستحق ہو (عموماً بُرے معنوں میں) بدلہ ۔ *He got his deserts* اُس نے اپنے کیے کا بدلہ پایا ، وہ کیفرِ کردار کو پہنچا (de-*zĕ*ts*). (*pl.*) qualities deserving reward or punishment کردار ، جو جزا یا سزا کا مستحق ہو *reward according to one's deserts* اپنے کرتوت کے مطابق (سزا یا جزا) **deserter** (de-*zĕ*t-ĕ*) *n.* (esp. a soldier or sailor) who deserts بھگوڑا ، فراری **desertion** (de-*zĕ*-shĕn) *n.* deserting or being deserted بے وفائی ، رُوگردانی ، ساتھ چھوڑ جانا

deserve (de-*zĕ*v*) *v.t.* be worthy of مستحق (یا حق دار) ہونا ، سزاوار ہونا *deserve praise* مستحقِ تعریف ، سزاوارِ ستائش ہونا *deserve punishment* مستحقِ سزا و تعریف **deserving** *adj.* worthy of لائق ، مستحق ، سزاوار **deservedly** (de-*zĕ*v-ĕd-li) *adv.* justly ٹھیک ٹھیک طور سے ، انصاف سے ، مستحق طور پر as deserved حق کے مطابق ، استحقاق کے مطابق **desert** *n.* (se under **desert,** sense 2 onward)

desiccate (des-i-kayt) *v.t.* dry up all the moisture of (esp. food) ; dehydrate پانی اُڑا کر خارج کر دینا ، سُکھا دینا ، رطوبت نکال دینا ۔ *desiccated milk* دودھ کا سفوف ، خشک دودھ **desiccation** (des-i-*kay*-shĕn) *n.* drying up سوکھنا یا سُکھا ڈالنا ، خشک ہو جانا یا کر دینا

desideratum (des-i-dĕ-*ray*-tum) *n.* (pl. *desiderata*) desired thing مطلوبہ چیز یا بات felt want ضرورت ، احتیاج thing missing مفقودہ چیز یا بات ، جس چیز یا بات کی کمی ہو

design (de-*zīn*) *n.* sketch or plan from which something may be made نقشہ ، خاکہ *designs for a dress* لباس کا ڈیزائن *design of a house* مکان کا نقشہ pattern ; general arrangement of lines, shapes, details, as ornament نقش و نگار ، بیل بوٹے *design* (*of a picture*) (تصویر کا) خاکہ *design* (*of a carpet*) (قالین کے) نقش و نگار purpose مقصد ، منصوبہ *Whether by accident or design* اتفاقیہ یا جان بوجھ کر (*pl.*) plot حملے کا منصوبہ ، سازش *have designs on* (or *against something*), intend to harm (it) (کسی) کو نقصان پہنچانے (کا)

v.t. & *i.* (کی جان لینے کا) منصوبہ بنانا make-design for *design a house* (کسی چیز) کا خاکہ (یا نقشہ یا ڈیزائن) تیار کرنا، *design a carpet* مکان کا نقشہ بنانا، قالین کے نقش و نگار کا خاکہ تیار کرنا intend ارادہ یا قصد کرنا، تجویز کرنا *a building designed for a college* کالج کے لیے مجوزہ عمارت plan خاکہ تیار کرنا *designed to do* (or *doing something*) (کسی کام کا) خاکہ (یا منصوبہ یا تجویز) تیار کرنا **designedly** (de-*zīn*-ĕd-li) *adv.* purposely جان بوجھ کر، عمداً

designer (de-*zīn*-ĕ*) *n.* (esp.) person who draws designs for manufacturers مصنوعات کے لیے نمونے (یا نقشے یا خاکے) بنانے والا، نمونہ ساز **designing** *adj.* (esp.) scheming, cunning چالاک، منصوبے باز، عیار (see also the following word)

designate (*dez*-ig-nayt) *v.t.* point out, indicate معیّن کرنا، صراحت کرنا *designate the boundaries of* (کسی ملک علاقے یا بحث) کی حدود معیّن کرنا، be a distinguishing name or mark for کا لقب ہونا، خصوصیت ہونا appoint تقرر کرنا، متعیّن کرنا pick out as the person or thing meant or wanted تخصیص کرنا، نامزد کرنا *Azim had designated Rashid as* (or *for*) *his successor* عظیم نے رشید کو اپنا جانشین نامزد (یا مقرر) کیا تھا *adj.* (placed with a hyphen after noun) appointed but not yet in office متعیّنہ، نام بُردہ *Governor-designate* والیٔ متعیّنہ، والیٔ نام بُردہ **designation** (dez-ig-*nay*-shĕn) *n.* assignment تقرر، تعیین name of title نام، لقب act of designating تعیّن، تقرر

desire (de-*zī*-ĕ*) *n.* strong wish or longing (*for*, *of*, or *to* be or do something) خواہش، حسرت، تمنا *desire for friendship* دوستی کی تمنا appetite اشتہا *desire for food* غذا کی اشتہا request التجا، خواہش *at the desire of* (فلاں) کی استدعا پر، بہ استدعا (فلاں) التماس، استدعا کرنا thing desired تمنا، شئے مرغوب، شئے مطلوب *wealth is not my desire* دولت میری مطلوبہ (شئے) نہیں ہے *v.t.* have a desire (*for*, *of*, or *to* be or do something) (کے لیے کی) خواہش یا تمنا ہونا، چاہنا request التجا کرنا، درخواست کرنا، استدعا کرنا **desirable** (de-*si*-ĕ-rab-ĕl) *adj.* to be desired مرغوب، خاطر خواہ، پسندیدہ، مناسب causing desire خواہش انگیز، تمنا خیز **desirability** (-*bil*-i-ti) *n.* being desirable دل پسندی، مناسبت **desirous** (de-*zī*-ĕ-rus) *adj.* feeling desire (*of*, *that*, or *to* be or do) خواہاں، خواستگار، شائق، طالب *desirous of praise* ▣ A **desire** is the whole personality's positive pull towards an object; **an emotion,** the consciousness of desire ; a **feeling,** reaction to desire ; an **impulse**, that which instinctively drives one towards a desired object ; a **craving** desire that grows greater while unsatisfied ; a **want**, feeling of lack ; a **wish,** preference not backed by strong action ; a **longing,** desire for an object mixed with an almost despair of getting it ; an **aspiration**, desire for perfection ; an **inclination,** desire largely counterbalanced by others ; an **eagerness**, desire which can hardly wait ; an **appetite**, desire of a low material kind ; an **ambition,** desire for success ; a **yearning**, desire combined with distress. Again, **covetousness** is a desire for what belongs to another ; **avarice,** a desire for the exclusive possession of something or someone that is the object of desire ; **envy**, a bitter or longing contemplation of another's better fortune or superior qualities.

desist (de-*zist*) *v. i.* cease to do something دست بردار ہونا refrain from باز رہنا *He desisted from beating the boy* وہ لڑکے کو پیٹنے سے باز رہا break off from علیحدہ ہو جانا، ساتھ چھوڑ دینا *desist from evil* برائی سے علیحدہ یا الگ ہو جانا

desk (desk) *n.* a sloping table for writing ڈیسک any writing table with drawers لکھنے کی خانوں والی میز be at (one's) desk لکھ رہا ہونا *He is at his desk* وہ لکھ رہا ہے

desolate (*des*-o-layt) *adj.* (of a place) ruined اُجاڑ، سُنسان (of a country) uninhabited غیر آباد، (of a house) unfit to live in برباد شدہ، (of a person) forlorn, helpless بے کس، ناقابلِ سکونت مغموم، بدنصیب، واماندہ *be left desolate* اُجڑ جانا *The family was left desolate by his death* اس کی موت سے گھر اجڑ گیا *v. t.* depopulate بے آباد کرنا، اُجاڑنا، ویران کرنا devastate برباد کرنا، تاخت و تاراج کرنا **desolation** (-*ay*-) *n.* making or being desolate بربادی، ویرانی، تاخت و تاراج، غارت گری، اُداسی، دل شکستگی، کس مپرسی **desolateness** *n.* being desolate بے کسی، ویرانی **desolator** *n.* one who makes desolate غارت گر، اُجاڑنے والا، تباہ گر **desolately** *adv.* ویرانی کی حالت میں مایوسانہ اُداسی سے

despair (des-*pay*-ĕ*) *n.* hoplessness ناامیدی، مایوسی، یاس، قنوط *be in despair* مایوس ہونا، بحالتِ یاس ہونا cause of the loss of hope مایوسی کی بات، وجۂ یاس، مایوس کن چیز یا بات *Careless students are the despair of their teacher* بے فکر سے طالب علم اپنے اُستاد کے لیے وجۂ یاس بن جاتے ہیں *v.t.* lose all hope (*of*) (کے بارے میں) اُمید کا دامن ہاتھ سے چھوڑ دینا، مایوس ہو جانا *despair of (someone's) life* (کسی کی) زندگی سے مایوس ہو جانا see no bright prospects (*of*) (سے) مایوس ہو جانا، (کا) روشن پہلو نظر نہ آنا *Many persons had despaired of their country* بہت سے لوگ اپنے وطنِ عزیز کی طرف سے مایوس ہو چکے تھے **despairing** *adj.* feeling or showing despair (also see **desperate**)

despatch (des-*pach*) *n.* & *v.* (same as **dispatch** which see)

desperado *n.* (see under **desperate**)

desperate (*des*-pe-rit) *adj.* (of a person) filled with despair and ready to do anything, regardless of danger قطعاً مایوس، ایسی حالت میں کہ سب کچھ کر گزرے reckless بے دھڑک، بے لگام، مایوسی کی پیدا کی جرأت، تخت یا تختہ والی، "آ خری داؤں والی، جان پر کھیل جانے کی حالت والی *desperate* policy پالیسی یا تختہ حکمت عملی ، تخت مایوسانہ desperate remedy مایوسانہ علاج، آخری علاج lawless شورہ پشت desperate criminals شورہ پشت مجرمین frantic جان پر کھیل جانے والا desperate effort وہ کوشش جس میں انسان جان پر کھیل جائے extremely serious نہایت شدید ، سخت desperate illness سخت بیماری، مرض صعب desperate state of affairs نازک حالات ، حالات کی خطرناک صورت **desperation** (des-pe-*ray*-shèn) *n*. being desperate مایوسی، یاس، قطع اُمید ، بیباکی *in desperation* جان پر کھیل جانے کی حالت میں **desparately** *adv*. in desperation ; seeing no other way out ; making a last bid جان پر کھیل کر ، مایوسی کی حالت میں **desperado** (des-pe-*rah*-doh) *n*. (pl. *desperadoes*) person ready to do any dangerous or criminal act غنڈہ ، شہدا ، پکا بدمعاش (U. S.) gunman مسلح ڈاکو gangster مجرموں کے گروہ کا فرد

despicable *adj*. (see under **despise**)

despise (des-*piz*) *v.t.* feel contempt for ; look down upon کسی سے نفرت کرنا ، کسی کو حقیر جاننا ، حقارت سے دیکھنا consider worthless ذلیل جاننا **despicable** (*des*-pi-kab-èl) *adj*. morally contemptible کمینہ ، ذلیل ، فرومایہ *despicable coward* کمینہ ، بزدل mean (person or thing) حقارت آمیز ، سفلہ ، کمینہ *despicable treachery* حقارت آمیز غداری

despite (des-*pit*) *prep*. in spite of ; notwithstanding باوجود ، باوصف ، کے ہوتے ہوئے ، علی الرغم **despiteful** *adj*. (poet.) (of person) malicious (of something) ظالم ، ستمگر بغض رکھنے والا ، کینہ پرور ، بکری cruel

despoil (des-*poil*) *v. t.* rob پچھین لینا ، چھیننا plunder (a place) لوٹ لینا *The invaders despoiled the capital of its treasures* حملہ آوروں نے دارالسلطنت کے سارے خزانے لوٹ لیے **despoliation, despoilment** *n*. plunder لوٹ ، غارت گری ، بربادی ، دستبرد

despond (des-*pond*) *v. t.* lose hope مایوس ہو جانا lose heart ہمت ہارنا ، دل شکستہ ہونا **despondent** *adj*. dejected, depressed دل شکستہ ، یاس زدہ *(be) in a despondent mood* دل شکستگی کی حالت میں **despondence, despondency** *n*. loss of hope ناامیدی ، نومیدی ، ہراس mental depression دل شکستگی *in a fit of despondency* دل شکستگی کی حالت میں

despot (*des*-pot) *n*. (now rarely) ruler using his unlimited powers cruelly جابر ، مستبد حکمران absolute ruler مطلق العنان حاکم *benevolent despot* **despotic** (des-*pot*-ik) *adj*. absolute (power or ruler) مستبدانہ ، استبدادی tyrannous (temper or action) جابرانہ ، ظالمانہ **despotism** (*des*-po-tizm) *n*. rule of a despot استبدادی حکومت ، شخصی سلطنت tyranny ظلم و جور ، جور و جبر مطلق العنانی

dessert (de-*zě*t*) *n*. course of fresh sweets, etc. served at the end of dinner, نقل ، پھل یا مٹھائی جو کھانے کے بعد کھائیں ۔ **dessert spoon** *n*. medium sized spoon for the dining-table اوسط درجے کا چمچہ جو کھانے کی میز پر استعمال کرتے ہیں ، متوسط چمچہ ، درمیانہ چمچہ ۔

destination (des-ti-*nay*-shèn) *n*. place for which a person or thing is bound منزل مقصود ، وہ جگہ جہاں پہنچنا ہو (Also see **destine**)

destine (*des*-tin) *v. t.* foreordain ; be intended by fate (*to*, *for* or *to do* something) مقرر کرنا ، مامور کرنا **destined** (*des*-tind) *adj*. *was destined to*, would one day مقدر ہو چکا تھا ، قدرت نے معین کر دیا تھا **destination** *n*. see separate entry above, **destiny** *n*. see separate entry below.

destiny (*des*-tini) *n*. power which foreordains تقدیر that which happens as preordained by that power مقدر ، قسمت ، حکم ، قضا lot (of a person) قسمت ، نصیب ، نصیبا (Also see **destine**)

destitute (*des*-ti-tewt) *adj*. extremely poor ; without food, clothes and other necessities for life قلاش ، مفلس (*destitute of*), devoid of ; lacking ; without محروم ، خالی ، بے نصیب *destitute of courage,* محروم جرأت ، بے حوصلہ **destitution** (des-ti-*tew*-shèn) *n*. utter poverty بے زادی ، افلاس

destroy (des-*troi*) *v. t.* demolish ; break to pieces توڑ ڈالنا ، توڑ پھوڑ دینا kill مار ڈالنا ، ہلاک کرنا put an end to تلف کرنا ، ضائع کرنا ، نیست و نابود کرنا *destroy these papers* ان کاغذات کو تلف کر دو make useless باطل کرنا ، اکارت کر دینا ، بیکار کر دینا ، ضائع کر دینا *This one wrong step destroyed his influence* اس ایک غلط اقدام نے اس کے اثر کو زائل کر دیا **destroyer** *n*. (esp.) light, small, fast warship armed with torpedoes تباہ کن جہاز any person or thing that destroys تباہ کن شے ، برباد کن **destructive** (des-*truk*-tiv) *adj*. causing destruction (*of* or *to*) برباد کنندہ ، تباہ کن *Rats are destructive of crops* چوہے فصل کے لیے برباد کن ہوتے ہیں *a destructive thing,* تباہ کن چیز merely negative ; offering no positive suggestion ; based on no positive values, منفی ، تخریبی *destructive criticism* تخریبی تنقید ، منفی تنقید **destruction** *n*. destroying تباہی ، بربادی ، ہلاکت cause of ruin بربادی کا باعث ، باعث تخریب ، باعث ہلاکت *Excessive drinking was his destruction,* حد سے زیادہ شراب نوشی اس کی بربادی کا سبب بنی

destruction *n*. (see under **destroy**)

desuetude (*dee*-swi-tewd) *n*. state when no longer in use متروک ہونا ، غیر مروجہ ہونا ، ہٹ جانا ، جاتے رہنا *fall into desuetude* (الفاظ کا) متروک ہو جانا ، (رواج وغیرہ کا) ہٹ جانا

desultory (*de*-sul-tè-ri) *adj*. (of study, etc.) disconnected غیر مسلسل aimless بے مقصد jumping from one thing to another بے ترتیب ، بے نظام *desultory reading* بے ترتیب و غیر منتظم پڑھائی (یا مطالعہ) **desultorily** *adv*. بے ترتیبی سے ، بے نظمی سے ، غیر مسلسل طور سے **desultoriness** (*des*-ul-tè-ri-nes) *n*. being desultory بے ترتیبی ، عدم تسلسل ، بد نظمی ۔

detach (de-*tach*) *v. t.* unfasten, remove (*from*) الگ کرنا ، جُدا کرنا ، علیحدہ کرنا *The receipt was detached from the counterfoil* رسید کو مُثنیٰ سے الگ کر دیا گیا تھا send (troops, etc.) on duty away from the main body (فوج وغیرہ کو) خاص مُہم پر بھیجنا یا روانہ کرنا *detach a company* ایک کمپنی بھیجنا **detached** *adj.* (of the mind, opinion, etc.) free from prejudice ; not influenced by others بے لَوث ، بے تعصّب ، غیر مُتعصّبانہ ، غیر جانبدارانہ (of a house) not joined to another on either side الگ تھلک مکان **detachable** *adj.* that which can be detached الگ ہو سکنے والا **detachment** *n.* separating or being separated علیحدگی (of mind) being uninfluenced by surrounding or by the opinion of others فکر و نظر کی آزادی ، خیالات اور رائے کی آزادی ، حُریّتِ فکر و نظر (of armed forces) number of men, ships, etc., detailed for special duty separately فوج یا بیڑے کا وُہ حِصّہ جو علیحدہ کسی مُہم پر بھیجا جائے

detail *n.* (*dee*-tayl or de-*tail*) small, particular fact or item تفصیل ، ایک مَد ، جُزئیہ (usu. *pl.*) collection of such small facts جُزئیات ، تفصیلات *go into details, enter into details,* give all the small points of facts تفصیلات (جُزئیات) میں جانا minute account تفصیلی بیان ، مُفَصَّل تذکرہ *in detail,* at length مُفَصَّل ، بالتفصیل *explain (something) in detail* تفصیلی بیان دینا ، مُفَصَّل بیان کرنا *v.t.* (de-tayl) describe fully leaving nothing out مُفَصَّل بیان کرنا ، پُوری طرح سے بیان کرنا ، تفصیلات دینا appoint (troops, etc.) for special duty (فوج وغیرہ کے دستے کو) خاص فرائض اَدا کرنے کے لیے مُقرّر کرنا *Three soldiers were detailed for sentry duty* تین سپاہیوں کو سنتری کا کام دیا گیا **detailed** (*dee*-tayld or de-*tayld*) *adj.* full account leaving nothing مُفَصَّل *a detailed account of,* a description giving full particulars (*of*) (کسی چیز یا واقع کا) مُفَصَّل یا تفصیلی بیان ۔

detain (de-*tayn*) *v. t.* keep waiting مُنتظر رکھنا ، بٹھائے رکھنا hinder روکنا ، باز رکھنا delay دیر کرانا *He was detained at the office by business* کام کی وجہ سے اُسے دفتر میں دیر ہو گئی ۔ imprison (esp. for keeping back from political activity) نظر بند کرنا ، قید کرنا punish (pupil) by keeping him back (in school) after ordinary lessons (طالب علم کو مدرسے میں) بطور سزا بٹھائے رکھنا (of school or college) refuse to send up (pupil) for exam. (طالب علم) کے امتحان داخلہ نہ بھجوانا ، کو روک لینا not to promote (pupil) to the next class (طالب علم کو) اگلی جماعت نہ پڑھانا ، کو فیل کر دینا **detention** (de-*ten*-shĕn) *n.* detaining or being detained رُکاوٹ ، روک ، مُزاحمت delay دیر ، توقّف imprisonment (esp. for keeping back from political activity) نظر بندی ، قید ، حراست

detenu (det-e-new) *n.* (pl. *detenus*, pr. *det-e-newz*) political prisoner سیاسی نظر بند **detainer** *n.* writ for detaining an already arrested person in a new case قیدی کو مزید اِلزام میں زیرِ حراست رکھنے کی درخواست

detect (de-*tekt*) *v. t.* discover (the existence or presence of something wrong) (غلطی ، جُرم وغیرہ) پکڑنا *detect a mistake* غلطی پکڑنا find out (someone guilty of wrongdoing) پتہ لگا لینا ، دریافت کرنا *detect a thief stealing* چور کو چوری کرتے پکڑنا **detection** (de-*tek*-shĕn) *n.* detecting گرفت ، اِنکشاف ، پکڑا جانا *the detection of crime* جُرم کا اِنکشاف یا پکڑا جانا **detective** (de-*tec*-tiv) *n.* person whose business is to find out and track criminals (usu. in an unofficial way) سُراغ رساں ، خُفیہ پولیس *adj.* connected with the detection of crime سُراغ رساں کے متعلق *detective stories* سُراغ رساں کی کہانیاں **detectaphone** *n.* (see *Addenda*)

detente (day-*tent*) *n.* end of strained relations between countries باہمی کشیدگی دُور ہونا ، صفائی

detention *n.* (see under **detain**)

detenu *n.* (see under **detain**)

deter (de-*te**) *v. t.* (-*rr*-) hinder (somebody from doing something) باز رکھنا ، مانع ہونا ، سدِّ راہ ہونا discourage (*from*) (کوئی بات یا کام کرنے سے روکنے کے لیے) دِل شکنی کرنا *Nothing could deter him from pursuing his aim* اپنے مقصد کے حصول میں لگے رہنے سے اُسے کوئی چیز روک نہیں سکتی **deterrent** (de-*te*-rent) *adj.* & *n.* (t)hing, etc.) serving to hinder or discourage مانع ، سدِّ راہ ، حوصلہ شکن *deterrent punishment* سخت ترین سزا *This acted as a deterrent* یہ اُس کے لیے شدید تنبیہ ... مانع ... ہُوا ۔

deterge (de-*tĕ*j*) *v. t.* wipe off or cleanse (wound or machinery from blood, grease, etc.) صاف کرنا ، پونچھنا **detergent** *n.* & *adj.* (substance) that cleanses صاف کرنے والا (see *Addenda*)

deteriorate (de-*tee*-ri-o-rayt) *v. t.* & *i.* make or become worse بگاڑنا یا بگڑنا ، اَبتر یا خراب کرنا یا ہونا ، معیار سے گرانا یا گرنا ۔ *deteriorating standards of education* تعلیم کا گرتا ہُوا معیار decrease in value زوال پذیر ہونا **deterioration** (-*ay*-) *n.* deteriorating خرابی ، بگاڑ ، اَبتری ، زوال ، فساد *the deterioration that has set in (something)* میں جو خرابی پیدا ہو چکی ہے

determine (de-*te**-min) *v. t.* & *i.* be the fact that decides (something) مُعیّن کرنا ، تعیّن کرنا *The size of one's heaa determines the size of one' hat* آدمی کے سر کا سائز اُس کی ٹوپی کا سائز مُعیّن کرتا ہے decide (someone's) future اِس پر کسی کے مستقبل کا اِنحصار ہونا make up one's mind (*to do* or *on* something) (کرنے کا) اِرادہ کر لینا یا فیصلہ کر چکنا یا تہیّہ کر لینا *I am determined to go ahead with this work* مَیں اِس کام کو پُورا کرنے کا تہیّہ کر چکا ہوں *He determined on departure* اُس نے رُخصت ہونے کا اِرادہ کر ہی لیا ہے decide فیصلہ کرنا

مقدمہ طے کرنا The case was determined in the court مقرر کرنا، ٹھہرانا ؛ عدالت میں فیصلہ ہوا find out exactly *determine a date* تاریخ مقرر یا متعین کرنا *determine the meaning of a word* کسی لفظ کے معنی متعین کرنا · confine, limit محدود کر دینا، متعین کر دینا *That hillock determines our view* یہ پہاڑی ہماری حدِ نگاہ متعین کرتی ہے **determined** (mind) *adj.* resolute ثابت قدم، مضبوط *determined character* مضبوط کردار of fixed purpose مصمم، اٹل **determination** (-*ay*-) *n.* the act of determining تحدید، تعریف، فیصلہ، تعین something determined رقم کی تشخیص firmness of purpose استقلال، پکا ارادہ، عزمِ مصمم resolute conduct فیصلہ کن، ثابت قدمی **determinant** *n.* decisive factor عنصر، حد بندی کرنے والا **determinate** (de-*te**-mi-nayt) *adj.* definite قطعی، محدود، متعین **determinative** (-*ayt*-iv) *adj.* & *n.* tending to decide something سمت متعین کرنے والی، توصیفی، تعیینی، تحدیدی **determinism** (-*tĕ**-) *n.* theory that human actions are not voluntary but are governed by predetermined motives مسئلہ جبر، یہ عقیدہ کہ انسان فاعل مختار نہیں ہے۔ بلکہ اُس کا ارادہ خارجی قوتوں کا پابند ہے۔ **deterministic** *adj.* pertaining to this theory or belief جبری، عقیدۂ جبر کے متعلق **determinist** *n.* one believing in this theory or belief جبریت پسند، عقیدۂ جبر کا قائل ▣ To **determine** is to bring to a definite conclusion; to **decide,** form a judgment as to a course of action; to **settle** something finally that has been in dispute; to **conclude,** as the result of an enquiry.

deterrent *n.* & *adj.* (see under **deter**)

detest (de-*test*) *v.t.* hate intensely سخت نفرت کرنا **detestable** *adj.* deserving to be hated intensely سخت نفرت انگیز، نہایت قابلِ نفرت، لائقِ متنفر **detestation** (-*ay*-shèn) *n.* intense hatred بے حد سخت نفرت، تنفر *hold in detestation* قابلِ نفرت سمجھنا something detested قابلِ نفرت چیز

dethrone (de-*throhn*) *v.t.* depose (a ruler) تخت سے اُتار دینا، تخت سے اتارنا، معزول کرنا **dethronement** *n.* معزولی، زور ٹوٹنا، زوالِ اقتدار۔

detonate (*dee*-to-nayt, or *det*-o-nayt) *v.t.* & *i.* (cause to) explode with a very loud noise (زور سے) پھٹنا، داغنا، دھماکے کے ساتھ اڑانا **detonation** (-*ay*-) act of exploding پھٹنا، انفلاق، انشقاق explosion **detonator** (dee-to-nay-tĕ*, or det-o-nay-tĕ*) *n.* part of a bomb that sets off the explosion بم کی بتی، بم کا وہ حصہ جس سے بم پھٹتا ہے detonating apparatus as railway fog signal انفلاقی

detour (de-*too*-è*), **dètour** (day-*too*-è*) *n.* course that leaves the direct route and then rejoins it; circuitous path; roundabout way چکر، چکر یا پھیر پھیر لگانا، چکر پر سے ہو کر پہنچنا یا آنا *make a detour* کا راستہ

detract (de-*trakt*) *v.i.* (*detract from*) take away from (the value of) کم کرنا، گھٹانا، کرکرا کر دینا *The rain detracted from the pleasure of the trip* بارش نے سیر کا مزا کرکرا کر دیا reduce the credit due to (person or his merit) کم قدر کرنا، قدر گھٹانا **detraction** (de-*trak*-shèn) *n.* disparagement بدگوئی **detractor** (-*trak*-) *n.* person who says things to lessen someone's credit or reputation بدنام کُن، بدنام کرنے والا slanderer بدگو، کسی کی برائی کرنے والا ▣ We **detract** from or injure someone's reputation; **disparage** his achievements by making them look small; and **discredit** his motives by showing them to be selfish.

detriment (*det*-ri-ment) *n.* injury, harm نقصان، ضرر، مضرت (usu. only in the phrase:) *without detriment to*, without harming کو نقصان پہنچائے بغیر، کو ضرر پہنچائے بغیر *You cannot smoke without detriment to your health.* تمباکو پینے سے تمہاری صحت کو سخت ضرر پہنچے گا۔ **detrimental** (det-ri-*men*-tĕl) *adj.* harmful, injurious مضرت رساں، ضرر رساں، نقصان دہ *It will be detrimental to his interests* یہ اُس کے مفاد کے لیے مضرت رساں ہوگا۔

deuce (dews) *n.* the score 'forty all' (in tennis) or 'twenty all' (in badminton or table tennis) or 'five games each' (in tennis) necessitating a replay up to certain points ٹینس اور بیڈمنٹن میں؛ وہ پوائنٹ (point) جس کے بعد کھیل (game) کے کچھ متواتر پوائنٹ جیتنے ضروری ہو جاتے ہیں *(the deuce)*, (slang) the devil شیطان، ابلیس *(the deuce)*, (slang) exclamation of anger بھاڑ میں جائے، بھٹ *the deuce! the deuce take it* شیطان کے حوالے *What the deuce have you been doing?* ارے! تم کیا کرتے رہے ہو۔ *go to the deuce*, (a) be off دفع دفان ہو جاؤ (b) be ruined جاؤ مرو *(the deuce)*, (slang) expression of surprise, etc. ارے *like the deuce*, with great vigour بھتنے کی طرح *The deuce knows it!* I do not know میری جانے بلا *The deuce is in it!* something has gone wrong with it اس میں کچھ گڑبڑ ہو گئی ہے *play the deuce (with)*, do great harm (to) ٹھکانے لگا دینا، غارت کر دینا

deus ex machina (dee-us-eks-*mak*-i-na) *n.* unnatural, mechanical device in fiction or drama that is used to solve difficulties of situation (ڈرامے وغیرہ میں مشکل حالت پیدا ہو جانے پر) راہ گریز (in a Classical play) a god who appeared on the stage from a machine to solve difficulties کلاسیکی ڈرامے میں، مشکل کے وقت کسی دیوتا کا ظاہر ہو کر مشکل حل کرنے کا غیر طبعی ڈھنگ، دیو درشن

Deuteronomy (dewt-è-*ron*-o-mi) *n.* the fifth book of the Pentateuch توراۃ کی کتب خمسہ میں سے پانچویں کتاب، سفرِ استثناء۔

devaluate (de-*val*-ew-ayt) *v.t.* reduce the value

(of currency) ذرکی، قیمت گرانا (یا گھٹانا) ازرکی، کم قدری کرنا

devalue (de-*val*-ew) *v.t.* reduce the value (of anything) کسی چیز کی قیمت کم کرنا (یا کم قدری کرنا) **devaluation** (-*ay*-) *n.* reduction in price or value قیمت کی کمی ، بےقیمت کا گراؤ ، کم قدری

devastate (*dev*-as-tayt) *v.t.* lay waste, ruin برباد کرنا ، ویران کرنا ravage, plunder لُوٹنا، اُجڑنا **devastation** (-*ay*-) *n.* laying waste بربادی، ویرانی، غارت ، تاراج

develop (de-*vel*-op) *v.t.* & *i.* (cause to) grow (*from* something, into something) larger, fuller, complete or active بڑھنا یا بڑھانا ، پختگی یا تکمیل کو پہنچنا یا پہنچانا *The baby is developing into a bonny child with chubby cheeks* بچہ پھل پھول کر گول گول گالوں والا خوبصورت لڑکا بنتا جا رہا ہے۔ (in photography) treat (exposed film) with chemicals so that the picture shows فلم وغیرہ کو خاص مسالوں سے دھونا تاکہ تصویر نکل آئے ، دھونا **developer** (-vel-) *n.* a person or thing that develops ترقی دینے والا ، نشوونما دینے والا (in photography) the chemical compound or solution used in developing photographic negatives وہ مسالہ یا محلول جس کے ذریعے منفی عکس یعنی نیگیٹو کو دھو کر تصویر عیاں کی جاتی ہے **development** (-vel-) *n.* developing or being developed نشوونما پانا یا دینا ، بالیدگی ، انکشاف ، تکمیل ، ترقی ، مکمل تر صورت ، فلم وغیرہ کو کیمیاوی مسالے سے دھو کر تصویر نکالنا ، دھونا (usu. pl.) new stage which is the result of developing (کسی چیز کی) نئی صورت حالات *developments (of something)* ترقی یافتہ حالت *the latest developments in the country's political situation* ملکی سیاست میں نئی صورت حالات

deviate (*dee*-vi-ayt) *v.i.* turn away (*from* the right or usual path, or *from* a rule, custom etc.) منحرف ہونا ، ہٹنا ، تجاوز کرنا *The Minister never deviated from that policy* صاحب وزارت مآب نے اس حکمت عملی سے کبھی تجاوز نہیں کیا۔ **deviation** (-*ay*-) *n.* act of deviating تجاوز ، انحراف ، کج روی

device (de-*vīs*) *n.* scheme, plan ; devised method تدبیر، کوئی سکیم یا آلہ یا کسی مقصد کو حاصل کرنے کا ڈھنگ (pl.) cherished ideas, inclinations مرضی، خواہش *leave (someone) to his (etc.) own devices*, let (him) do as he wishes ; let him shift for himself and get over difficulties کسی کو اپنی تدبیریں آپ کرنے دینا trick تدبیر، منصوبہ ، تجویز *a device for getting more money* مزید رقم حاصل کرنے کی ترکیب some appliance invented or adapted for a special purpose کسی مقصد کے لیے وقتی طور پر ایجاد کردہ چیز یا آلہ crest of shield, etc. فوجی طغرا ، *heraldic device* سردار یا رئیس کا خاندانی امتیازی نشان ، طغرا motto or sign as a symbol مارکہ ، خاندانی نقیبانہ نشان کوئی موٹو یا نشان بطور علامت (Also see **devise**)

devil (*dev*-il) *n.* the spirit of evil آسیب ، بھوت پریت ، خبیث روح *have a devil*, be possessed بھوت پریت کے قبضے میں ، آسیب زدہ *the Devil*, Satan شیطان ، ابلیس *Talk of the Devil and he is sure to be there* نام لیتے ہی آئے گا (یا آ ٹپکے) cruel or mischievous person ظالم، خونخوار، بدذات ، شریر *give the Devil his due*, be just even to enemies, etc. دشمن سے بھی انصاف کرنا چاہیے exclamation of surprise, etc. *How, the devil did you get there?* ارے! تم یہاں کیسے پہنچے ؟ *the devil of a time*, a time of difficulty, exitement, etc. مصیبت وقت ، پیغمبری وقت ، شورش کا وقت *a devil of a (man, etc.)* عجیب (انسان) بڑا دلچسپ (آدمی) energetic بھوت ، جیوٹ *He is a devil at fighting,* مرنے مارنے میں بڑا جیوٹ ہے wretched person بدنصیب ، بدبخت ، دکھیا *a poor devil* غریب دکھیا evil influence (of) کسی چیز کا گہرا اثر *the devil of greed* لالچ کا بھوت بھوت *devil's advocate*, one who sees nothing but weaknesses in another's character عیب جو ، نکتہ چین *devil-may-care*, irresponsibly gay (person, attitude) لاابالی ، وارستہ (شخص) ، بے پروایانہ ، لاابالیانہ (حالت) *printer's devil*, youngest apprentice or errand-boy in a printing press مطبع کا ہرکارہ ، چھاپے خانے کا سب سے کم عمر شاگرد (Please note that it is a mistake to use this phrase for an annoying mistake in printing, although it is often used in that sense in this country,) *devil take the hindmost* جو پیچھے رہے کنوئیں میں پڑے *between the devil and the deep* از ایں سو رانده وازاں سو مانده **devilish** *adj.* like a devil شیطانی ، نہایت ظالمانہ ، ملعون ، لعنتی cruel **devilishness** *n.* being devilish شیطنت ، ابلیسیت **devilry** (*dev*-il-ri) *n.* cruelty بے رحمی، خونخواری ، بدمعاشی wickedness بدذاتی ، بدمعاشی black art ; magic شیطانی فن ، کالا علم جادو ، سحر reckless daring جرأت ، جرأت ، دلیری ، تہوّر

devious (*dee*-vi-us) *adj.* not straightforward جو سیدھا نہ ہو ، پیچیدہ *He got money by devious means* اس نے پُرفریب طریقے سے روپیہ حاصل کر لیا (of paths, etc.) roundabout پیچیدہ ، چکر کا ، غیر مستقیم (راستہ وغیرہ)

devise (de-*vīz*) *v. t.* plan تدبیر کرنا invent ایجاد کرنا ، اختراع کرنا *devise means for some end in view* (or *to do* something) نکالنا ، کی ترکیب نکالنا

device (de-*vīs*) *n.* (see above)

devitalize (de-*vī*-ta-liz) *v. t.* deprive of life-giving qualities حیات بخش جوہر خارج کرنا ، بے جان کر دینا ، بے سکت کرنا ، قوت زائل کر دینا **devitalization** (-*ay*-shen) *n.* devitalizing قوت کا ازالہ ، بے جان کر دینا

devoid (de-*void*) *adj.* (*devoid of*), lacking, without خالی، محروم ، بے *devoid of sense* بے معنی ، لایعنی فضول ، معنی ، بے معنی ، خالی از معنی ، لا یعنی *devoid of meaning* خالی از مفہوم

devolve (de-*volv*) *v.t.* & *i.* (*devolve on* or *upon*), of work be passed on to (another person or a deputy) (کے) سپرد ہونا ، آپڑنا ، (کو) تفویض ہونا *During his*

illness it devolves upon his secretary to do this work اُس کی بیماری کے ایّام میں یہ کام اُس کے سیکرٹری پر آپڑتا ہے **devolution** (dee-vo-*loo*-shèn) *n.* (esp.) transfer of work (from legislature to bodies appointed by it) (مجلسِ قانون ساز کی طرف سے) تفویضِ اختیارات
devote (de-*voht*) *v. t.* give up (oneself or one's time and energy) (*to* something or someone) نذر کرنا، وَقف کرنا، مخصُوص کرنا۔ *devote all (one's) time to social service* سارا وقت خِدمتِ عوام میں لگا دینا (کی نذر کر دینا) *devote oneself wholeheartedly to* کلیتہً (کسی کام میں) لگ جانا **devoted** (de-*voht*-id) *adj.* give up to, نذر، مخصُوص، وَقف شُدہ *a life devoted to the pursuit of knowledge* علم کی تلاش میں وَقف شُدہ زندگی very loving and loyal جاں نثار، وفادار، وفا شعار، وَقفِ وفا *a devoted son* جان نثار بیٹا
devotee (dev-o-*tee*, or *dev*-o-tee) *n.* person devoted to some form of religion عابد، زاہد، بَھگت enthusiast پرستار، سچّا، طالب *a devotee of fine arts* فنونِ لطیفہ کا پرستار **devotion** (de-*voh*-shèn) *n.* being devoted نذر، وقف strong and deep love شدید اُلفت، پُرجوش محبّت، جان نثاری *devotion of a child to his parents* ماں باپ کا جان نثار بچّہ (*pl.*) prayers عبادت، پُوجا پاٹھ *He was at his devotions* وہ مصرُوفِ عبادت تھا ؛ وہ پُوجا پاٹھ یا عبادت میں مصرُوف تھا
devour (de-*vou*-è*) *v. t.* eat greedily and fast بے تحاشا کھا جانا see, read or hear greedily بے حد شوق سے دیکھنا (پڑھنا یا سُننا) *He devoured the book* وہ کتاب کو گویا کھا گیا (of flames) consume, destroy بھسم کر دینا، کھا جانا، تلف کرنا، (آگ کا کسی چیز کو) absorb the attention of غرق ہونا، چھا جانا، مُسلّط ہو جانا *devoured with anxiety*, having one's attention absorbed by anxiety سوچ میں پڑا ہُوا، فِکر مندی میں مُبتلا **devouring** *adj.* destroying, consuming تباہ یا تلف کرنے والا *devouring conflagration* ہمہ گیر آگ کھا جانے والا، ہمہ گیر
devout (de-*vout*) *adj.* paying serious attention to religious duties reverential پُرخلوص سچّا *devout prayers* سچّی یا پُرخلوص عبادت (نماز) sincere, heartfelt مخلصانہ، دِلی *devout thanks* دِلی شُکریہ **devoutly** *adv.* reverently مخلصانہ طور سے، دِل سے sincerely اخلاص مندانہ، قلبی شُکریہ سچّے دِل سے مخلصانہ *devoutly thankful* اِخلاص مندانہ اِظہارِ تشکّر، اِخلاص سے eagerly شوق سے، پُرشوق، دِل سے *hope devoutly* دِل سے اُمّید رکھنا
dew (dew) *n.* tiny drops of moisture condensing on cool surfaces between nightfall and morning اوس، شبنم early freshness (*of* youth) *the dew of youth* شگفتگیِ شباب، عنفوان، رعنائی **dewy** (*dew*-i) *adj.* wet with dew شبنمی **dewdrop** *n.* drop of dew شبنم کا قطرہ، قطرۂ شبنم **dewfall** *n.* hours of night when dew begins to fall اوس پڑنے کا وقت، بھیگی رات
dewlap (*dew*-lap) *n.* fold of loose skin hanging from the neck of certain animals بیل وغیرہ کی گردن کے نیچے لٹکتا ہُوا ماس، گلگتھا **dewlapped** (*dew*-lapt) *adj.* (animal) with such skin گردن کے نیچے لٹکتی ہُوئی کھال والا، گلگتھے دار
dextrous (*deks*-tè-rus) (also spelt **dexterous**) *adj.* clever in using the hands چابک دَست، چالاک skilful مشّاق، ماہر، کاریگر دَست، چابک دست *a dextrous craftsman* چابک دَست (یا مشّاق) دستکار using the right hand by preference دائیں ہاتھ سے کام لینے والا، عادی دایاں mentally clever تیز فہم، ذہین، زیرک **dexterity** (dek-*ste*-ri-ti) *n.* manual skill چابک دَستی، مشّاقی mental skill تیز فہمی، ذہانت، چالاکی
dhobi itch (*doh*-bè-ich) *n.* a form of eczema کُھجلی، خارِش
dhow (dou) *n.* single-masted Arabian-Sea ship (used in slave trade) ایک مستولی جہاز جو بحیرۂ عرب میں غلاموں کی تجارت کے لیے کام آتا تھا
di- *pref.* (expressing negation) نا، غیر double دو، دوچند two دو through میں، سے
dia (dɪ-a) *pref.* two دو، باہمی through
diabetes (di-a-*bee*-teez) *n.* disease producing discharge of sugar in urine وہ بیماری جس سے پیشاب میں شکر آتی ہے ذیابیطس، ڈایابیٹیز **diabetic** (di-a-*bee*-tik) *adj.* pertaining to diabetes ذیابیطس کا *n.* one suffering from it ذیابیطس کا مریض
diabolic (dɪ-a-*bol*-ik), **diabolical** (dɪ-a-*bol*-i-kèl) *adj.* devilish شیطانی، اِبلیسانہ very wicked and cruel سفّاک، بے رحمانہ *diabolic temper* سفّاکانہ مزاج **diabolism** (dɪ-*ab*-o-lizm) *n.* سحر، جادو، سِفلی عمل، شیطنت، شیطان کی پرستش، سفّاکی، بے رحمی
diacritical (dɪ-a-*krit*-i-kèl) *adj.* (usu. in the phrases :) *diacritical marks* (or *diacritical signs*), signs for distinguishing between various values of the same letter نقطے وغیرہ
diadem (*dɪ*-a-dem) *n.* crown as the symbol of kingship تاج، اَفسر، کلاہِ شاہی، مُکٹ
diaeresis, dieresis (dɪ-ee-rè-sis) *n.* two dots over a vowel directly following another to indicate that it is pronounced separately (as in *naivete*) حرُوفِ عِلّت کے فصل کی علامت
diagnose (dɪ-ag-*nohz*) *v. t.* determine the nature of a disease from its symptoms سبب کی تشخیص، مرض کی تشخیص، سبب کی تعیین guess at the cause of کے متعلق قیاس **diagnosis** (dɪ-ag-*nohs*-is) *n.* (pl., *diagnoses*) diagnosing عملِ تشخیص، شناخت statement of its result بیانِ تشخیص، تشخیص **diagnostic** *n.* that which assists diagnosis تشخیص کار کے متعلق (*pl.* with *sing.* verb.) diagnosis as an art فنِ تشخیص

diagonal (dɪ-*ag*-è-nĕl) *n.* straight line connecting opposite corners of a straight-sided figure وَتر (دائرے کا) قطر *adj.* running from corner to corner آڑا، ترچھا، مُنحرف از وُتری slanting (زاویہ) قائمہ **diagonally** *adv.* in the slanting direction of a diagonal مُنحرِف از (زاویہ) قائمہ، وُتری شکل میں

DIAGONAL

diagram (*dī*-a-gram) *n.* figure, chart, drawing, design of plan to explain or illustrate something being expounded to the reader or listener تشریحی خاکہ، نقشے علامات یا خطوط کے ذریعے کسی عمل یا قوت کا اظہار **diagrammatic** *adj.* of, like or with a diagram شکل کا، نقشے کا، نقشے کی شکل میں، توضیحی شکل کی صورت میں

dial (dɪ-èl) *n.* face (of a watch or clock) گھڑی کا چہرہ، ڈائل *sun-dial*, apparatus for showing sun's shadows on a dial دُھوپ گھڑی، سَن ڈائل recording plate with a pointer for measuring (weight, pressure, etc.) وزن، دباؤ وغیرہ کا مقیاس *dial of an electric current meter* برقی رَو کے ناپنے کا میٹر، برق پیما *dial of a radio* ریڈیو کا ڈائل، (ریڈیو کا) مُنہ (یا) چہرہ part of automatic telephone, used when calling a number ٹیلیفون کا وہ پُرزہ جسے گھما گھما کر نمبر بناتے ہیں، ٹیلیفون کا نمبر چکر (یا) نمبر ڈائل *dial tone*, (see *Addenda*) *v.t.* & *i-* (-ll-) call on the phone by rotating its dial to connect a number ٹیلیفون کا نمبر گھمانا، ٹیلیفون کرنا *Dial the Fire Brigade* فائر بریگیڈ کو ٹیلیفون کرو *Please dial 5590 for good books* اچھی کتابیں مطلوب ہوں تو ۵۵۹۰ کو ٹیلیفون کریں measure by a dial (ڈائل سے) ناپنا یا ظاہر ہونا

(left) radio and (right) telephone with dials

dialect (*dɪ*-è-lekt) *n.* form of a spoken language peculiar to a district or class (کسی علاقے یا جماعت کی) خاص بولی *dialect words* بولی کے الفاظ

dialectics (dɪ-a-*lek*-tiks) *n. pl.* art of arguing فنِ مُناظرہ **dialectic, dialectical** *adj.* relating to dialectics جدلیاتی، جدلی **dialectical materialism** *n.* form of materialism propounded by the founder of Communism, Karl Marx (1818—1883). According to this theory the course of history is the evolutionary development of the conflict between opposites. It considers the present-day conditions of the world as the result of a class-struggle between capitalists aiming at private profit and the proletariat who do or should resist exploitation at their hands جدلی مادیات **dialectician** *n.* one skilled in dialectics ماہرِ جدلیات

dialogue (*dɪ*-a-log) *n.* writing in the form of a conversation مکالمہ (ج) مکالمات *Plato's Dialogues* مکالمات افلاطون *write a dialogue* مکالمہ لکھنا talk between two or more persons (دو یا زیادہ اشخاص کی) بات چیت conversation between characters in drama or fiction ڈرامے یا افسانے کے کرداروں کی بات چیت، مکالمہ

diameter (dɪ-am-è-tĕ*) *n.* straight line passing from side to side of a geometric figure through its centre قُطر length of such a line قطر کے برابر thickness of circular things مُدوّر یا گول چیز کی آر پار موٹائی

(A B) diameter of a circle

diametral (dɪ-*am*-et-rĕl) *adj.* of or, along a diameter قطری، قطر کے مُتعلق، عرض (یا دل) سے مُتعلق

diametrical (di-a-*met*-ri-kĕl) *adj.* contrasting direct اختلاف کی رُو سے براہِ راست **diametrically** *adv.* completely یکسر، کلّی، بالکل قطعی، کلیتہً مختلف *diametrically opposed to each other*, the very opposite of each other ایک دوسرے سے بالکل مختلف، یکسر مختلف، متضاد

diamond (*dɪ*-e-mụnd) *n.* brilliant colourless precious stone which is the hardest substance known ہیرا، الماس shape like that of a diamond, *i.e.*, four equal sides whose angles are not right angles الماس کی قلم کی شکل کا، مُعیّن one of a suit of playing cards (تاش) اینٹ کا پتّا *adj.* like, or made of, diamond الماسی، ہیرے کا مُعیّن نما، مُعیّن کی شکل کا *Diamond Jubilee*, sixtieth anniversary (of some event) کسی واقعے کا شصت سالہ جشنِ یادگار *cf.* Silver, Golden Jubilee (پچیس سال، پچاس سال کی یادگار

diamond (top) sense 1 (bottom) sense 2

Diana (dɪ-*an*-a) *Cl. myth.* the Roman goddess of the moon who nature and hunting, identified by them with the Greek Artemis دائنہ good horsewoman شہسوار عورت woman bent on living single تارکہ

diapason (di-a-*pay*-zèn) *n.* swelling chorus ہم آہنگ نغموں کی گرج harmony of many parts, مُتعدّد سُروں کا ہم آہنگ مجموعہ consensus (of opinion), اتفاقِ رائے

diaphanous (dɪ-*af*-è-nus) *adj.* (esp. of textiles) transparent شفاف

diaphoretic (dɪ-a-fo-*ret*-ik) *adj.* inducing perspiration مُعرّق، پسینہ لانے والی such medicine پسینہ لانے والی مُعرّق دوا

diaphragm (*dɪ*-è-fram) *n.* wall of muscles between chest and abdomen پردۂ شکم، حجاب حاجز (in some instruments like a telephone) transverse vibrating disc closing a tube (ٹیلیفون وغیرہ میں) ایک قرص جس سے آواز پیدا ہوتی ہے

diarchy, dyarchy (*dɪ*-ah*-ki) *n.* Government by two independent authorities دوعملی **diarchical** *adj.* دو عملی کے مُتعلق

diarrhoea (di-è-*ree*-a) *n.* looseness of the bowels with watery discharges پیٹ چلنا، اسہال، تخمہ

diarist *n.* see under **diary**
diary (*dī*-è-ri) *n.* daily record of engagements, events or thoughts روزنامچہ، ڈائری *'Pepys's Diary'*, diary kept by the famous English diarist Samuel Pepys (1633—1703) پیپس کا روزنامچہ *Do you keep a diary?* کیا تم روزنامچہ لکھا کرتے ہو؟ (usu. small) book for this purpose روزنامچہ، ڈائری record of incoming correspondence in an office دفتر میں وصول ہونے والی ڈائری، ڈاک کے اندراج کا رجسٹر **diarize** (*dī*-è-riz) *v. t.* (esp.) enter particulars of such correspondence in a book دفتر میں وصول ہونے والی ڈاک کا اندراج رجسٹر میں کرنا، روزنامچے میں درج کرنا *This letter has not yet been diarized* یہ خط ابھی ڈائری نہیں ہوا **diarist** (*dī*-è-rist) *n.* clerk keeping such record ڈائری کرنے والا کلرک، روزنامچہ نویس literary figure keeping a regular record of events and own observation روزنامچہ نگار یا روزنامچہ نویس

diatribe (*dī*-a-trib) *n.* bitter and violent attack in speech (against) کسی کی ہجو، تلخ، تلخ تنقید

dice (dēs) *n. pl.* (used with *pl.* verb) (sing. *die*, which also see) very small cube with six square sides marked with one to six respectively and thrown from a small cylindrical box in games of chance کعبتین، پانسہ a game of chance جُوا *v.t. & i.* play with dice پانسے سے جُوا کھیلنا cut (vegetables) into pieces shaped like dice سبزی کو چوکور شکل میں کاٹنا **dicer** *n.* gambler جواری، جُوئے باز **dice-box** *n.* cylindrical box from which dice are thrown ڈبیا جس میں پانسہ رکھ کر پھینکتے ہیں

dice

dictaphone (*dik*-ta-fohn) *n.* patented name of a machine which makes a record of spoken words used for dictating letter, etc. ایک مشین جس میں بولے ہوئے الفاظ ریکارڈ کئے جاتے ہیں۔ ڈِکٹافون

dichotomy (di-*kot*-o-mi) *n.* (logic) division into two subclauses دو قسموں میں تقسیم (تقسیم بردو)

dickens (*dik*-enz) *n.* (colloq.) deuce, the devil (روزمرہ) شیطان، خبیث

dicky (*dik*-i) *n.* (slang) donkey گدھا seat for servant at the back of carriage گاڑی کے پیچھے نوکر کی نشست، نوکر نشست *adj.* (slang) shaky, rickety ٹوٹا پھوٹا **dicky-bird** *n.* (nursery) small bird ننھا سا پرند

dictate *v.t. & i.* (dik-*tayt*) say (words) for another person to write down الفاظ بول کر لکھنا، یا بولے ہوئے الفاظ لکھنا، املا بولنا *dictate a letter* خط املا کرانا lay down with authority حکم دینا، ہدایت کرنا *dictate terms of an agreement* معاہدے کی شرائط لکھوانا (dictate to) give authoritative orders (کسی کو) حکم دینا *He is not the one to be dictated to by everyone* وہ ہر کس و ناکس کا حکم ماننے والا نہیں *n.* (*dik*-tayt) (usu. in the pl.) controlling principles (laid down by conscience or reason) ارشاد، ہدایت *The dictates of conscience* ضمیر کی ہدایت command حکم، فرمان **dictation** *n.* (esp.) reading taken down by another person give a dictation to کو املا کرانا *take a dictation from* سے املا کرنا *take a dictation of* کا املا کرنا *I gave him a dictation* میں نے اسے املا کرایا command تحکم، فرمان، نادری حکم **dictator** (dik-*tay*-tĕ*) *n.* (esp.) absolute ruler who has obtained power to rule a State by a *coup d'etat* in an irregular way آمر، حاکم مطلق، مختار کل one who gives a dictation املا لکھوانے والا **dictatorship** *n.* rule of a dictator آمریت، حکومت مطلقہ **dictatorial** (dik-ta-*toh*-ri-ĕl) *adj.* of or like a dictator آمرانہ *He assumed dictatorial powers* اس نے آمرانہ اختیارات حاصل کر لیے، وہ آمر مطلق بن بیٹھا imperious (manners, etc.) تحکمانہ، مستبدانہ، استبدادی

diction (*dik*-shĕn) choice and use of words الفاظ کا انتخاب اور صحیح استعمال، بندشِ الفاظ *poetic diction* شاعرانہ بندش manner of speaking and writing طرزِ تقریر و تحریر

dictionary (*dik*-shè-nĕ-ri) *n.* book containing all or almost all the words of the language (usu. arranged alphabetically and explaining their usage in the same language and/or giving their equivalents in another language) لغت، لغات، قاموس *English-Urdu dictionary*, dictionary giving the Urdu equivalents of English words انگریزی اردو لغات book explaining the terms, references and particular meanings of words used in a special book or subject فرہنگ *biographical dictionary*, biographies of (a particular group of) celebrities with their names arranged in an alphabetical order قاموسِ مشاہیر، اسماء الرجال

■ A **dictionary** is a reference book containing words, technical terms or phrases in alphabetical order with their explanation in other and better known words or their translation into another language. A **lexicon** is either a dictionary of a foreign (esp. of a dead) language, or a briefer dictionary of trade or technical terms. An **encyclopaedia** is a comprehensive work describing various subjects under a limited number of heads arranged in alphabetical order; a **cyclopaedia,** of one subject; a **vocabulary,** a word-list; a **glossary,** a brief list of terms used in a particular book, especially technical and dialect terms; a **thesaurus,** a classified 'treasure-house' of terms; a **concordance,** an alphabetical list of words and phrases used in a particular book or in one author's works as a *Bible concordance* or a *Concordance to Shakespeare*; a **book of synonyms,** a book giving words of somewhat similar meaning grouped in proximity to one another ; an **etymological dictionary,** a dictionary giving alphabetical lists of words with their origins.

dictum (*dik*-tum) *n.* (pl., *dicta*) adage قول، ارشاد oft-quoted weighty saying قول، کہاوت (مشہور) *obiter dictum* casual remarks سرراہے بات (esp.) incidental expression of judge's opinions not relevant to the case مقولہ ، قاضی کی ضمنی رائے حاکم عدالت کی رائے جس کی کوئی قانونی حیثیت نہ ہو

did *pa. p.* of **do** (which see)

didactic (di-*dak*-tik) *adj.* intended to teach (esp. conventional morality) ناصحانہ، پندآموز *didactic poetry* ناصحانہ اشعار having the manner of a teacher معلمانہ **didactically** *adv.* ناصحانہ یا معلمانہ طور پر **didacticism** (di-*dak*-ti-sizm) *n.* didactic manner ناصحانہ انداز، معلمانہ طرز.

Dido (*dī*-doh) *Class. myth.* the queen who founded Carthage on the northern coast of Africa. She was the daughter of Belus, king of Tyre. When the Trojan hero Aeneas deserted her after a short sojourn in her country, she burnt herself to death ڈائڈو

die (di) *v.i.* (*die, died, died ; dying*) cease to live مرجانا، فوت ہوجانا، معدوم ہوجانا۔ be killed مارا جانا sacrifice one's life (*for* a cause) جان قربان کرنا grow indifferent or insensate (*to*) بے حس ہوجانا ، مرجانا languish with desire بے موت مرجانا *be dying* (*for, to do*, something), have a strong wish (*for*, or *to do it*) (کسی چیز یا بات پر) جان دینا، (کے لیے) جان لبوں پر آجانا fade, vanish, مرجھا جانا، ختم ہونے کے قریب ہونا *dying fire* بجھنے والی آگ *dying custom* مرتی ہوئی رسم *die away, die down, die off, die out* ختم ہوجانا، مرجانا۔ فنا ہوجانا *die* (*a something*) die (in that position) فلاں شکل یا حالت میں مرنا *die a martyr* شہید ہونا، شہادت پانا *die a millionaire* لکھ پتی ہوکر مرنا *die a* (specified) *death*, کسی کی موت مرنا die the death of *die a dog's death* کتے کی موت مرنا *die in harness*, go on working till death مرتے وقت تک کام کرتے رہنا *die in* (*one's*) *shoes*, be violently killed قتل ہونا۔ اونٹ کی موت مرنا *die in the last ditch*, resist to the utmost مرتے دم تک مقابلہ کرنا *die in* (*one's*) *bed*, die of age or sickness طبعی موت مرنا، بڑھاپے یا بیماری کی موت مرنا *die prematurely* جوان موت مرنا، بے وقت مرنا۔ جوانا مرگ ہونا *n.* (see **dice** above) *the die is cast*, the irrevocable decision has been taken قطعی فیصلہ کرلیا، جو ہو سو ہو metal block with engraved design for shaping coins, medals, etc., or marking (words, etc.) on paper, etc. ٹھپہ، ڈائی، دھات وغیرہ پر کھدے ہوئے الفاظ وغیرہ جو کاغذ وغیرہ پر چھاپے جاتے ہیں **diehard** (*dī*-hahd) *n.* confirmed conservative کٹر، قدامت پسند one who resists to the end, (particularly innovation or change) ہر قسم کی تبدیلی کا سخت مخالف

■ To **die** is to cease to live ; to **expire**, breathe out ; to **perish,** without help ; to **decease**, pass out ; to **succumb,** *under* an illness or *to* wounds ; to **atrophy**, waste for lack of nourishment ; to **wither,** shrivel and fade ; to **suffocate,** choke to death. Again, one dies *of* illness, *by* weapon, *for* a friend or object, and *to* an emotion or interest.

diesel-engine (*dee*-zel-*en*-jin) *n.* type of engine (invented by *R. Diesel*. 1858—1913) which burns heavy oil ایک قسم کا انجن جس میں گاڑھا کالا تیل جلتا ہے۔

diet (*dī*-et) *n.* sort of food one usu. eats خوراک food to which one is limited (for medical reasons) (طبی طور پر) مقرر کردہ غذا ، پرہیزی غذا *He is dieting* وہ پرہیزی غذا کھا رہا ہے۔ *The doctor has put me on diet* ڈاکٹر نے پرہیزی غذا کھانے کا حکم دیا ہے series of meetings for discussing international or church affairs بین الاقوامی (کلیسائی) کانفرنس کے اجلاس، سلسلۂ اجلاس *v.t.* & *i.* restrict oneself, or be restricted, to a diet پرہیزی غذا کا استعمال کرنا یا کرانا **dietary** (*di*-è-tè-ri) *n.* course of diet مقررہ یا پرہیزی غذا food allowance (in gaol, hospital, etc.) جیل (یا شفاخانے وغیرہ کی) غذا کی مقدار یا نوعیت *adj.* pertaining to regulations of diet غذا کا (یا)، غذا کے متعلق **dietetic** (di-è-*tet*-ik) *adj.* of or relating to diet غذا کا یا غذا کے متعلق، غذائی **dietetics** *n. pl.* science of diet علم الغذا، غذائیات

dif- *pref.* (expressing negation) نا، غیر

differ (*dif*ĕ*) *v.t.* be unlike or distinguish (*from* someone or something, *in* some respect) سے مختلف ہونا diverge in opinion (*from* someone, *on* some point) (کسی بات پر) اختلاف کرنا یا رکھنا **difference** (*dif*-è-rens) *n.* unlikeness مختلف ہونا، یا عدم مشابہت quantity by which two amounts differ کمی بیشی، تفاوت disagreement in opinion اختلاف رائے، اختلاف نظر quarrel caused by it جھگڑا، *That makes all the difference*, this is not something to be summarily dismissed ; rather it is a major cause of disagreement یہی تو اصل جھگڑا ہے، اسی بات کا ہے **different** (*dif*-è-rent) *adj.* not the same دوسرا۔ الگ distinguishable (from) سے مختلف dissimilar غیر متشابہ، متفاوت **differently** *adv.* مختلف طور سے، کسی اور طرح سے **differential** (*d*-è-*ren*-shèl) *adj.* relating to infinitesimally small difference احصاء تفریقی کے متعلق **differential calculus** *n.* branch of mathematics dealing with method of determining the infinitesimally small rate of change between two variable qualities احصاء تفریقی varying with circumstances حالات کے مطابق بدلنے والا، فرق نما **differential duties** *n.* custom or excise duties varying w various commodities تفریقی مخفول *n*. mechanism enabling a motor vehicle's rear wheels to revolve at different speeds when negotiating a curve دہ پُرزے یا پُرزہ جس (جن) سے کسی موٹر کار وغیرہ کے پچھلے پہیے مختلف رفتاروں سے چلتے ہیں **differentiate** (dif-è-*ren*-shi-ayt) *v.t.* & *i.* note the difference (*between* two or more things, or one thing *from* another) کے درمیان فرق کرنا، امتیاز کرنا be such difference (*between* or *from*) فرق ہونا، امتیاز ہونا (cause to) become different امتیاز یا تفریق پیدا ہونا (یا کرنا) **differentiation** (-*ay*-) *n*. act of differentiating فرق کرنا، امتیاز کرنا its result فرق، امتیاز (esp.) development of difference (of function or meaning) (عملی یا معنوں میں) فرق پڑ جانا ؛ فرق

difficult (*dif*-i- kult) *adj*. not easy ; hard to do مشکل، دشوار، جو آسان نہ ہو hard to understand or explain دِقت طلب، پیچیدہ hard to deal with ٹیڑھا، دشوار **difficulty** (*dif*-i-kul-ti) *n*. being difficult مشکل ہونا، اشکال obstacle دشواری، رکاوٹ، روک effort needed to remove obstacles اشکالات دور کرنے کی کوشش *with difficulty*, after great efforts (یا کے بعد) سخت کوشش سے (*pl*.) objections اعتراضات، پس و پیش *make difficulties* (*about some point*), raise objections to it اعتراضات حائل کرنا یا پیش کرنا (*pl*.) embarrassment (for money, etc.) مالی دشواریاں یا پریشانیاں *be in difficulties* (*for resources*), be embarrassed (for a lack of them) دشواریوں میں مبتلا ہونا

diffident (*dif*-i-dent) *adj*. not having or showing self-confidence (the opp. of *confident*) بے حوصلہ یا خود اعتمادی سے محروم shy جھجکنے والا *diffident* (*about doing something*) کسی کام کے کرنے سے جھجکنے والا **diffidence** (*dif*-i-dens) *n*. being diffident بے حوصلگی، شرمیلاپن **diffidently** *adv*. with diffidence شرمیلے پن سے، بے حوصلگی سے، جھجکتے ہوئے

diffuse (di-*fewz*) *v.t.* & *i.* (cause to) spread in every direction پھیلانا، پھیلنا، منتشر کرنا یا ہونا، نفوذ کرنا ، یا ہونا *adj*. (di-*fews*) (of style), verbose, loose پُر از طوالت، لفاظی والا (اسلوب)، اطناب پسندانہ **diffusely** *adv*. **diffusive** (-*few*-siv) *adj* spreading rapidly پھیلنے والا ، انتشار پذیر (of manners) genial نرم مزاجی **diffusion** (di-*few*-zhèn) *n*. act of spreading پھیلاؤ ، انتشار ، نفوذ

dig *v.t.* & *i.* (dug, dug) turn up (soil) (مٹی) کھودنا ، جوتنا make a deep hole in this way (*deep* or *down*) کھود کر گڑھا بنانا bring (*up* or *out* buried objects thus) (دبی ہوئی) چیز کو کھود کر نکالنا make search (*for* facts, *into* books, etc.) کریدنا ، تفتیش کرنا ، تحقیق کرنا (colloq.) thrust (a pointed thing *into*) گھونپنا ، چبھونا ، گڑونا ، گدگدانا *dig* (*someone*) *in the ribs* (*with one's fingers*) پسلیوں کو گدگدانا *dig out*, get information بات نکال لینا *n*. poke with something pointed (نوک دار چیز) چبھونا sarcastic remark چبھتی ہوئی بات، کچوکا *have a dig at* (*someone*), pass such remarks against (him) کوکچو کا لگانا **digger** *n*. one who digs (esp. for gold) (سونا وغیرہ) کھودنے والا *grave-digger* گورکن یا گھدیا، کھودنے والا **diggings** *n*. (*pl*.) goldfield سونے کی کان (colloq.) lodgings کرائے کے کمرے

digest *v.t.* & *i.* (di-*jest*) (of food) change or be changed in the stomach and bowels for assimilation by the body ہضم کرنا یا ہونا ، تحلیل ہونا یا کرنا ، پچنا یا ، پچانا take the meaning into the mind مطلب ذہن نشین کر لینا ، معنی اچھی طرح سے سمجھ لینا summarize and classify (facts, etc.) تلخیص کرنا ، خلاصہ نکالنا یا کرنا ، مختصر کرنا brook (insult, etc.) سہنا ، سہہ جانا ، برداشت کرنا *n*. (*di*-jest) short, classified arrangement (of facts, etc.) مجموعہ ، خلاصہ *adj*. that which can be digested easily زود ہضم **digestibility** *n*. capability of being digested easily زود ہضم ہونا **digestion** (di-*jes*-chèn) *n*. (esp.) one's power of digesting food ہاضمہ **digestive** (di-*jes*-tiv) *adj*. relating to digestion ہاضمے یا ہضم کے متعلق helping digestion ہاضم

digit (*dij*-it) *n*. any one of the numbers 0 to 9 صفر سے نو تک کا کوئی ہندسہ ، عدد ، ہندسہ finger or toe ہاتھ کی (یا پاؤں کی) انگلی

dignified *adj*. (see under **dignify**)

dignify (*dig*-ni-fi) *v.t.* give dignity to عزت بخشنا ، مشرف کرنا make worthy or honourable اعزاز دینا ، سرفراز کرنا **dignified** (*dig*-nif-id) *adj*. having or showing dignity باوقار ، باوجاہت ، وجیہ **dignitary** (*dig*-ni-tè-ri) *n*. person holding high position معزز عہدے دار ، اعلیٰ افسر *dignitaries of the State* اعیانِ سلطنت ، عہدیدارانِ مملکت *dignitaries of the Church* اربابِ کلیسا ، خداوندانِ کلیسا ، پیرانِ حرم ، مذہبی رہنما **dignity** (*dig*-ni-ti) *n*. dignified behaviour باوقار طرزِ عمل عظمت quality that wins or deserves respect حرمت ، مرتبہ ، قدر و منزلت *beneath* (*one's*) *dignity*, degrading مرتبے سے نیچے ، مرتبے کے خلاف ، خلافِ رتبہ *lose* (*one's*) *dignity*, be lowered in the estimation of others by making a foolish mistake قدر و منزلت کھو دینا high rank بلند رتبہ ، مرتبۂ عالی ، معزز عہدہ true worth حقیقی قدر و منزلت *dignity of labour* محنت کشی کی قدر و منزلت ، قدر و قیمت

dignitary *n*., **dignity** *n*. (see under **dignify**)

digress (di-*gres*) *v. i.* (in speaking or writing) wander away from the main subject (اصل موضوع سے) ہٹ جانا **digression** (di-*gresh*-èn) *n*. act of digressing تجاوز ، انحراف ، منتشر گفتگو

dike, dyke (dɪk) *n.* long wall of earth raised as a causeway to keep back water and prevent flooding پشتہ ، بند ، روک ditch کھائی ، خندق *v. t.* prevent with dykes پشتہ یا بندھ کر روکنا drain by means of dykes خندق یا کھائی کے ذریعے سے (پانی وغیرہ) نکالنا یا خارج کرنا ۔

a dike

dilapidated (di-*lap*-i-dayt-ed) *adj.* (of building) in partial ruin ٹوٹی ہوئی ، ٹوٹی پھوٹی شکستہ (of furniture, etc.) in a state of disrepair ٹوٹا پھوٹا سامان **dilapidation** (-ay-) *n.* being or becoming dilapidated ٹوٹ پھوٹ ، شکستگی ، خستہ حالی

dilate (dī-*layt*) *v.t.* & *i.* make or become wider, larger or further open چوڑا کرنا یا ہونا ، پھیلانا ، پھیلنا *dilate upon* (*subject*) speak or write at great length about it پھیلانا ، تفصیل کرنا ، شرح و بسیط سے گفتگو کرنا (کلام کرنا)

dilatory (di-*lay*-tè-ri) *adj.* slow in doing things دیر سے (کام) کرنے والا ، سست causing delay تاخیری ، تعویقی *dilatory tactics*, measures adopted to delay something, esp. the product of one's duty تاخیر انگیز چالیں ، تعویقی چالیں

dilemma (di-*lem*-a) *n.* awkward situation in which one has but to choose one of the undesirable alternatives دوہری مشکل ، دونوں طرح سے مشکل *be in a dilemma* گومگو کی حالت میں ہونا *horns of a dilemma*, such awkward choice دوہری مشکل *be on the horns of a dilemma*, be in an awkward situation دبدھے میں ، دوہری مشکل میں ، گومگو کی حالت میں ۔

dilettente (di-le-*tan*-ti) *n.* (pl. *dilettanti*, pr. the same) one who has a tase for fine arts and some knowledge of them but not any real understanding شائق ، شوقین ، فنون لطیفہ کا غیر ماہر قدردان ، amateur عطائی ، غیر پیشہ ور شائق **dilettantism** *n.* being a dilettente فنون لطیفہ کی قدردانی ، غیر ماہرانہ قدردانی ، عطائی پن

[d]iligence (*dil*-i-jəns) *n.* steady attention to work سرگرمی ، تندہی ، جاں فشانی

[di]ligent (*dil*-i-jent) *adj.* hard working محنتی ، مستعد always busy and showing care and [e]ffort in the discharge of duties مستعدی سے کام کرنے والا

[d]illy *n.* (see *Addenda*)

[di]lly-dally (*dil*-i-dal-i) *v. i.* waste time (by not [m]aking up one's mind) ہچکچانا ، لیت و لعل کرنا ، فیصلہ نہ کر سکنا ، ڈھیل میں ڈالنا

[di]lute *v. t.* (dī-loot) make (a liquid) weaker [o]r thinner (by adding water) (پانی) ملا کر ہلکا کرنا *dilute [w]ine* weaken the force of argument by qualifying it اگر مگر لگا کر بیان کو کمزور کر دینا *adj.* (dī-lewt) (in chemistry) diluted ہلکا (کیا ہوا) ، پھیکا *dilute sulphuric acid* ہلکا تیزاب گندھک **dilution** (dī-*loo*-shèn) *n.* act of diluting ہلکا کرنا ، تخفیف

dim *adj.* faint ; not bright دھیما ، مدھم ، *dim light* مدھم روشنی hazy دھندلا سا *a dim figure* دھندلی سی شکل (of the eyes) not able to see distinctly ماند ، صاف نہ دیکھنے والی آنکھیں ، دھندلائی ہوئی ۔ not clearly understood مبہم ، ناقابل فہم *a dim idea* مبہم سا خیال *v. t.* & *i.* (-mm-) make or become dim دھندلانا دھندلے طور سے ، غیر واضح ۔ دھیما سا یا مدھم کرنا ۔ **dimly** *adv.* دھندلے طور پر سے **dimness** *n.* being dim دھندلاپن ، تاریکی

dimension (dɪ-*men*-shèn) *n.* measurement of length, breadth, thickness, etc. طول ، عرض اور گہرائی (یا) موٹائی (میں سے ایک) بُعد *the three dimensions*, length, breadth and thickness تین بُعد ، اَبعادِ ثلاثہ (یعنی طول عرض اور عمق) *the fourth dimension*, time بُعدِ رابع ، بُعدِ چہارم ، زمانہ (*pl.*) size حجم . سائز **dimensional** *adj.* pertaining to dimension بُعد کے متعلق ، ابعادی *three-dimensional film*, cinematograph giving the effect of solid life-like pictures on the screen سہ بُعدی فلم ، وہ فلم جس میں تصویروں کی لمبائی اور چوڑائی کے علاوہ موٹائی بھی نظر آئے ۔

diminish (*dim*-i-nish) *v. t.* & *i.* lessen (in size, amount or number) (سائز ، مقدار یا تعداد میں) کم کرنا ، کم ، مختصر ، تقلیل گھٹانا ، **diminished** *adj.* less weakened, reduced in power کمزور کیا ہوا *hide (one's) diminished head*, try to hide (one's) humiliation خفت (کو) چھپانا **diminution** *n.* (see under **dimunitive**).

diminutive (di-*min*-ew-tive) *adj.* very small بہت چھوٹا undersized, tiny بہت چھوٹا سا ، ننھا سا *n.* (grammar) word indicating a small size of something (often a word with a suffix like *-kin* or *-let*) (نحو) اسم مصغر جیسے ڈھول سے ڈھولک (*Manikin* is the diminutive of *man* and *streamlet* that of *stream*) **diminution** (dim-i-*new*-shèn) *n.* diminishing گھٹانا ، چھوٹا کرنا ، تخفیف ، تقلیل *diminution of national assets* قومی سرمائے کی کمی

dimple (dim-pèl) *n.* small hollow in the cheek either permanent or appearing when one smiles چھوٹا سا گڑھا جو مسکراہٹ کے وقت رخساروں پر پیدا ہو جاتا ہے similar hollow in the chin چاہِ زنخدان ، چاہِ ذقن ، چاہِ غبغب small hollow on the surface of water پانی کی سطح میں پڑا ہوا (گڑھا) *v.t.* & *i.* form dimples گڑھا پیدا کرنا یا ڈالنا produce dimples in (کسی شے میں) ہلکورے ڈالنا ہلکورا اٹھانا

din *n.* loud and confused noise which is continuous غل ، شوروغل ، غوغا ، شور و غوغا ، غل غپاڑا *v. t.* & *i.* (-nn-) make such a noise غل مچانا ، غوغا مچانا ، شور و غل کرنا یا مچانا *din* (*something*) *into* (*someone's*) *ears*, tell (him) again and again (کوئی بات) کہتے کہتے ناک میں دم کر دینا

dine (dɪn) *v. t.* have dinner کھانا کھانا **diner** *n.* (esp.) dining-car on a railway train ریل گاڑی میں کھانے کا ڈبہ one who eats dinner کھانا کھانے والا

dinner (*din*-ĕ*) *n.* chief meal of the day eaten

in the evening by ordinary folk or in the middle of the day by landed gentry, etc.) دوپہر یا شام کا کھانا، عشائیہ Note that **dinner** is more formal than other meals. Again, an informal evening meal is called **supper**, and an informal mid-day meal is known as **lunch** or **luncheon** ; but either of these meals (usu. the evening one) taken with some ceremony and with the punctual attendance of every member of the family is called a **dinner**.

ding-dong *n.* sound of two bells striking alternately دو گھنٹیوں کی ایک دُوسرے کے بعد بجنے کی آواز *adv.* with this sound گھنٹیوں کی اُونچی نیچی آواز کے ساتھ

dinghy (*ding*-i) *n.* small open boat جہاز کی چھوٹی کشتی ، ڈونگی

dingy (*dinj*-i) *adj.* dirty, untidy مَیلا، غلیظ dull, faded تاریک، دُھندلا

dinner *n.* (see under **dine**)

dinosaur (*di*n-o-saw*) *n.* a huge extinct reptile پُرانے زمانے کا (اب ناپید) عظیم الجثہ رینگنے والا جانور، ہیبت چھپکلی ۔

dint *n.* depression in the surface caused by striking ضرب کا نشان، چوٹ لگنے سے جو دندانہ سا پڑ جائے (used only in the phrase :) *by dint of*, by means of, by the force of بذریعہ ، بزور، بقوّت کے بَل بُوتے پر

diocese (*di*-o-sees) *n.* area in the charge of a bishop بِشپ کا حلقہ یا علاقہ

Dionysus (dī-o-*nī*-sus) (*Cl. myth.*) Greek god of wine, corresponding to the Roman god Bacchus وایو نیسس ۔

dip *v. t. & i.* put (something *in* or *into* a liquid) for a moment and then take it out again پانی میں ایک دُوبا ریا ڈوب) دینا ڈبو کر نکال لینا *dip into water* put (one's hand or spoon, etc.) into liquid or grain and take it out or *up*) (ہاتھ یا چمچہ) کسی مائع یا دانوں کے ڈھیر میں ڈال کر نکال لینا۔ go below a surface of level جُھکنا ، ڈبکی لگانا slope downwards نیچے کی طرف ڈھلوان ہونا *The road dips*, goes downhill سڑک ڈھلوان ہوتی چلی گئی ہے (cause to) go down and up again ڈبکانا *dip a flag*, lower and then raise it in saluting جھنڈا سلامی کے لیے جھکانا، اُٹھانا (*dip into*), study (book, etc.) cursorily کہیں کہیں سے پڑھنا، کہیں کہیں مُنہ مارنا dim (lights of car, etc.) موٹر کی بتیاں مدھم کرنا *n.* act of dipping ڈوبا، ڈوب، ڈبکی being dipped ڈوبنا amount of dipping غوطہ جھکاؤ، انخفاض، میلان a short swim تھوڑی سی تیراکی quick bath ڈبکی، ہلکا سا غسل medicinal liquid in which sheep are dipped to rid them of vermin بھیڑوں کی جُوئیں مارنے والی دوا downward slope جھکاؤ، میلان، ڈھال fall *a dip in the prices* کساد بازاری گرنا قیمتوں کی گراوٹ short candle چھوٹی موم بتی

dipper *n.* (esp.) cup-like vessel on a long handle for taking out water ڈوئی

a dipper

diphtheria (dif-*thee*-ri-a) *n.* fast-spreading and dangerous disease of the throat خُناق

diphthong (*dif*-thong) *n.* two vowels joining to make one compound sound (*e.g.*, *ou* in *out*) دو حُروفِ عِلّت (vowels) سے مُرکّب آواز two vowels written together to express a single sound (*e.g.*, *ea* in *heat*) دو حُروفِ عِلّت

diploma (dip-loh-ma) *n.* degree سَند فضیلت، ڈپلوما voucher of such degree سَند، ڈگری، ڈپلوما **diploma'd** (dip-*loh*-mad) *adj.* having diplomas سَند یافتہ، ڈگری یافتہ **diplomaless** *adj.* one who has no diplomas بے سَند

diplomacy (dip-*lohm*-a-si) *n.* management of international relations سِفارت skill in this فنِ سِفارت میں مُہارت tactful dealing with individuals, etc. حکمتِ عملی، مَوقع شناسی **diplomat** (*dip*-lo-mat), **diplomatist** (dip-*lohm*-a-tist) *n.* person engaged in diplomacy for his government کسی حکومت کا سفیر one clever in dealing with people فنِ سِفارت کا ماہر، حکمتِ عملی والا **diplomatic** (dip-loh-*mat*-ik) *adj.* of diplomacy سِفارتی *diplomatic service* محکمۂ سِفارت *diplomatic corps*, all the foreign envoys in a country's capital تمام غیر مُلکی سفیر tactful زمانہ ساز

dire (*di*-ė*) *adj.* dreadful سخت خوفناک، ہولناک very bad نہایت ہی بُرا **direful** *adj* terrible, dreadful ہولناک ، خوفناک، دہشتناک

direct (dī-*rekt* or di-*rekt*) *adj. & adv.* going straight and not roundabout سیدھا، براہِ راست *direct route* سیدھا راستہ *in a direct line with* سے براہِ راست بلا واسطہ not turned aside راست، مستقیم *direct* (نسب) حقیقی، بڑا *hit* سیدھی یا کھلی چوٹ with nothing or no one between نسب میں براہِ راست تعلق *direct descendant* حقیقی وارث going straight to the point سیدھا، بغیر اینچ پیچ کے *direct way of speaking* کلام بطریق راست *direct action*, exertion of pressure by workers through strikes (and not through influencing elections) in order to get their demands راست کارروائی (جس میں محنت کش انتخابات پر اثر ڈالنے کی جگہ ہڑتالوں کے ذریعے سے اپنے مطالبات منواتے ہیں)، ڈائرکٹ ایکشن not alternating مسلسل رو *direct current* or *D.C.*, electric current flowing continuously, (opposite of **A.C.** or **alternating current**) ڈائرکٹ کرنٹ ، مسلسل برقی رو without an intermediary بلا واسطہ *direct speech*, speaker's words (and not their report by some narrator) (opp. of *reported speech* or *indirect narration*) رِوایتِ نقلی (بمقابلۂ روایتِ معنوی) *v.t.* & *i.* tell or show (someone) how to do something or get somewhere پتے پر روانہ کرنا ، راہ دکھانا manage ضبط میں رکھنا نظم و نسق کرنا ، چلانا control address (letter, etc., *to*) (خط وغیرہ پر) پتہ لکھنا ، سرنامہ لکھنا order (*to do* or *that*) (کسی بات کا یا کسی بات کے کرنے کا) حکم دینا یا ہدایت کرنا - cause to turn (one's attention, etc.) straight to something (کسی چیز کی طرف) توجّہ دلانا aim or point (*at*, *to* or *towards*) (کا) رُخ کرنا ، (کا) نشانہ باندھنا ، (کی) شِست باندھنا **direction** *n.* course in which someone or something moves رُخ ، سمت ، طرف ، جانب *People were running in every direction* لوگ ہر سمت کو دوڑ رہے تھے یا اِدھر اُدھر بھاگ رہے تھے point towards which one looks طرف ، کو *in the direction of*, towards کی طرف (usu. *pl.*) information about what to do or where to go ہدایات (usu. *pl.*) orders, instructions اَحکام ، ارشاد *under* (someone's) *directions* (کسی کی) ہدایت یا ارشاد کے ماتحت (usu. *pl.*) address on letter, etc. سرنامہ پتہ **directive** *n.* detailed instructions given to subordinates ماتحتوں کے لیے مفصّل ہدایات ، ہدایات نامہ *adj.* giving guidance ہدایتی ، رہنمایانہ *directive principles* ہدایتی اُصول **directly** *adv.* in a direct manner براہِ راست at once (*conj.*) فی الفور (colloq.) as soon as جونہی **director** (dɪ-*rek*-tě*) *n.* who directs مہتمم ، ناظم (esp.) controller ناظم ، نگران *The Director of Public Instruction* ، ناظمِ تعلیمات ، ناظمِ تعلیمِ عامّہ ناظم سررشتۂ تعلیم ، ڈائرکٹر تعلیم a member of the Board directing the affairs of a concern تجارتی کمپنی کی جماعتِ ناظمہ کا رُکن ، ڈائرکٹر ، نگران one who directs a film ہدایت کار ، ڈائرکٹر **directorate** (dɪ-*rek*-to-rayt) *n.* establishment of a director's office نظامت ، سررشتہ director's office دفترِ نظامت board of directors مجلسِ ڈائرکٹران نظامت **directory** (dɪ-*ek*-to-ri) *n.* printed book of names and addresses of a particular group in alphabetical order ڈائرکٹری ، کسی مقام کے خاص لوگوں کے ناموں اور پتوں کی اَبجدی فہرست ، عُنوان نامہ *telephone directory*, such a list of telephone subscribers of an area ٹیلیفون کی ڈائرکٹری ، عُنوان نامہ *trade directory*, such a list of traders کاروباری ڈائرکٹری ، کاروباری عُنوان نامہ

dirge (dě*j) *n.* funeral song مرثیہ ، نوحہ ، بَین

dirt (dě*t) *n.* filth نجاست ، غلاظت mud کیچڑ ، کیچ *dirt-cheap*, at a cost far below the real value مٹی کے مول ، بھُس کے بھاؤ *dirt-track*, brickdust track for motor-cycle racing موٹر سیکل کی دوڑ کا کچا راستہ obscene thoughts or talk فحش خیالات یا کلام ، فحاشی *fling dirt at*, vilify, slander (کسی پر) کیچڑ اُچھالنا ، (کسی کو) فحش گالیاں دینا **dirty** (dě*-ti) *adj.* filthy میلا ، آلودہ ، نجس ، غلیظ obscene فحش ، مکروہ (of the weather) windy and rainy طوفانی *be done dirty*, be maltreated (کے ساتھ) بُری ہونا *v.t.* make dirty گندہ کرنا ، میلا کرنا **dirtily** *adv.* in a filthy way گندے طریقے سے **dirtiness** *n.* filth میلاپن ، گندگی ، غلاظت ، نجاست

■ **Dirty** and **unclean** are generally used figuratively. **filthy** signifies something very dirty. We speak of an **untidy** place, a **soiled** garment, **polluted** water, **foul** weather or **foul** language, **smutty** joke and of **grimy** or **murky** things.

dis- *pref.* the opposite of (*e.g.*, advantage, *dis*advantage) انگریزی الفاظ کے لیے لاطینی سابقہ بمعنی علیحدہ ، الگ ، نہ ، نا ، غیر ، خلاف ، برعکس separate (*e.g.*, connect *dis*connect) الگ away from; off (*e.g.*, embark. *dis*embark) پرے ، دُور ، آلگ

disable (dis-*ay*-bèl) *v.t.* make unable to do something کسی کام کو نہ کرنے کے قابل بنا دینا ، معذور کر دینا make useless بیکار کر دینا (esp.) cripple اپاہج بنا دینا ، لولا لنگڑا کر دینا *disabled soldiers*, soldiers crippled in war, etc. اپاہج سپاہی **disability** (dis-a-*bil*-i-ti) *n.* being disabled ناقابل کار ہونا ، ناکارہ ہو جانا something which disables امتناع ، مجبوری ، معذوری

disabuse (dis-ab-*ewz*) *v.t.* free (someone or his mind) from false ideas غلط خیالات دل سے نکال دینا ، ذہن صاف کرنا ، وہم دُور کرنا correct (a person in his ideas) (کسی کے خیالات کی) اصلاح یا تصحیح کرنا ، آنکھیں کھول دینا

disadvantage (dis-ad-*van*-tij) *n.* something unfavourable ناموافق صورتِ حال ، دقّت ، دُشواری *be to* (*someone's*) *disadvantage*, be detrimental to (his) interests اُس کے مفاد کے خلاف loss, injury نقصان ، ضرر **disadvantageous** (dis-ad-van-*tay*-jus) *adj.* unfavourable (*to*) ناموافق harmful مضر ، مضرّت رساں

disaffect (dis-a-*fekt*) *v.t.* make disloyal بے وفا یا غدّار بنانا make unfriendly دشمن بنانا ، مخالف بنانا make discontented غیر مطمئن بنانا یا کرنا ، منحرف کرنا **disaffected** *adj.* disloyal (*to* authorities, government, etc.) غیر وفادار ، غدّار unfriendly دشمن ، منحرف **disaffection** (dis-a-*fek*-shèn) *n.* disloyalty اطاعت سے انحراف ، سیاسی بے چینی -

disagree (dis-ag-*ree*) *v.i.* take a different view اختلاف رائے ہونا ; not agree (*with* someone, *on* some point, etc.) کسی شخص سے کسی بات پر اختلاف رکھنا (of food or climate) be unsuitable موافق نہ آنا ، ناموافق ہونا **disagreeable** *adj.* unpleasant ناپسندیدہ ، ناگوار

، نامرغوب bad-tempered بدمزاج، کج خلق **disagreement** *n.* difference اِختلاف، ناموافقت، نااتفاقی

disallow (dis-a-*lou*) *v.t.* refuse to allow ; reject as not entitled to pass قبول نہ کرنا، اجازت نہ دینا، نامنظور کرنا

disappear (dis-a-*pee*-è*) *v.t.* go out of sight غائب ہو جانا، نظر یا نظروں سے اوجھل ہو جانا، کھو جانا vanish

disappearance *n.* act of disappearing کا دُور ہو جانا غائب ہو جانا، پوشیدگی، غیبوبیت۔

disappoint (dis-a-*point*) *v.t.* cause sorrow by failing to come up to expectations (اُمید) توڑنا، prevent (a plan, etc.) from being realized (توقع) باطل کرنا (مقصد وغیرہ) فوت کرنا **disappointed** (-ed) *adj.* sad at not seeing one's hopes come true نااُمید، مایوس، نومید **disappointment** *n.* being disappointed مایوس یا نااُمید ہونا، نااُمیدی، مایوسی person or thing that disappoints وہ شخص یا چیز جس سے مایوسی پیدا ہو، مایوس کن شخص (یا بات)

disapprove (dis-ap-*roov*) *v.t.* have an unfavourable opinion (*of*) (کو) ناپسند کرنا **disapproval** *n.* unfavourable opinion ناپسندیدگی *look upon (something) with disapproval* کو ناپسندیدگی کی نظر سے دیکھنا rejection نامنظوری، اِسترداد

disarm (dis-*ah**m*) *v.t.* & *i.* take away war-weapons from (someone) اسلحہ چھین لینا، نہتے کر دینا give up arms, etc. اسلحہ حوالے کر دینا، ہتھیار گرا دینا (of a country) reduce the size of, or give up the use of, its armies ملک کی فوج اور آلاتِ حرب میں کمی کر دینا، فوجی قوت کم کر دینا، تخفیفِ اسلحہ کرنا۔ drive away anger or suspicion of (someone) by friedliness بدگمانی دُور کرنا **disarmament** (dis-*ah**m*-a-ment) *n.* doing away with weapons of war تخفیفِ اسلحہ being disarmed غیر مسلح ہونا تخفیفِ فوج۔

disarrange (dis-a-*raynj*) *v.t.* throw out of order بے ترتیب یا غیر مرتب کر دینا **disarrangement** *n.* act of disarranging بے ترتیبی، اَبتری، گڑبڑ

disaster (di-*zahs*-tĕ*) *n.* great or sudden misfortune آفت، حادثہ، مصیبت، سانحہ **disastrous** (di-*zahs*-trus) *adj.* causing disaster مصیبت انگیز، خوفناک ▣ **A disaster,** which is literally 'something against the stars', is a ruinous occurrence ; a **mishap,** an accident which is not very serious ; a **misfortune,** a stroke of ill-luck ; an **accident,** some occurrence which involves bodily injury or loss of property ; a **catastrophe,** something that puts a sudden end to things ; and a **calamity,** something that causes public suffering.

disavow (dis-a-*vou*) *v.t.* deny knowledge of (something) (کسی شے کے علم کا) انکار کرنا، نہ ماننا say that one has no concern with (something) (کسی چیز سے) تعلق نہ ہونا، تردید کرنا **disavowal** *n.* act of disavowing اِنکار، تردید

disband (dis-*band*) *v.t.* & *i.* break up (an army) (فوج کو) منتشر کرنا، خدمت سے سُبکدوش کرنا (of an army, etc.) break up منتشر ہونا، خدمت سے سُبکدوش ہونا separate and go in different directions منتشر ہو کر مختلف سمتوں میں جانا **disbandment** *n.* (فوج کا) اِنتشار، منتشر ہونا، خدمت سے سُبکدوش کرنا، یا ہونا۔

disbelieve (dis-be-*leev*) *v.t.* not to believe or refuse to believe (someone or something) یقین نہ کرنا، کی بات کو باور نہ کرنا *He disbelieved me* اُس نے میری بات باور نہ کی **disbelief** *n.* lack of belief عدم یقین، بے اعتباری

disburse (dis-*burs*) *v.t.* & *i.* pay out (money) (روپیہ) بانٹنا، ادا کرنا (of money) be paid out (روپیہ) بٹنا *The salary will be disbursed today* تنخواہ آج بٹے گی

disc *n.* (see **disk**) **disc jockey** *n.* (see *Addenda*)

discard (dis-*kah**d*) *v.t.* throw away as useless, (plan, old clothes, etc.) (بے کار سمجھ کر) پھینک دینا، ترک کر دینا، (منصوبہ) ترک کر دینا dismiss (employee) برطرف کرنا، ہٹا دینا

discern (di-*sĕ**n*) *v.t.* & *i.* see clearly (with the eyes or with the mind) (بصارت یا بصیرت سے) صاف صاف دیکھ لینا distinguish (one thing *from* the other) (ایک شے کو دوسری شے سے) تمیز کرنا، امتیاز کرنا draw or see distinction between فرق پہچاننا، شناخت کرنا (esp.) see or feel with an effort (distant object, faint smell, fine distinction, etc.) بھانپ لینا، پہچان لینا، دریافت کرنا، پالینا **discerning** *adj.* able to judge or distinguish well صاحبِ فہم و بصیرت، صاحبِ اِدراک **discernible** *adj.* that which can be perceived قابلِ فہم، قابلِ امتیاز **discernment** *n.* اِدراک، شناخت، فہم، نکتہ رسی، بصیرت (esp.) keen insight ▣ To **discern** is to perceive keenly a detail or difference ; to **distinguish,** to make a difference, whether rightly or wrongly; to **differentiate,** state a difference; to **discriminate** between two or more, with nicety of choice ; to **discover** something that was hidden. Again **discernment** is the ability to perceive keenly a detail or difference ; **discrimination,** ability to make a nice choice ; **subtlety**. fineness of mind in discriminating between details ; **sagacity,** great keenness as to causes ; **ability** to seek in the right direction ; **shrewdness,** keenness as to motives.

discharge (dis-*chah**j*) *v.t.* do, carry out (اپنا) فرض بجا لانا، ادا کرنا، دے، عہدہ برآ ہونا *discharge (one's) duty* بجا لانا (یا ادا کرنا) terminate the service of سُبکدوش کرنا، برخاست کر دینا، الگ کر دینا، موقوف کرنا allow to leave (کو) جانے کی اجازت دینا، چھوڑ دینا *discharge patient* *from the hospital* (مریض کو) شفاخانے سے جانے کی اجازت دینا send out خارج کرنا merge (oneself into) (دریا کا) سمندر میں) گرنا، اپنا وجود دوسرے میں مدغم کرنا unload (cargo from a ship) (جہاز وغیرہ سے) مال اُتارنا pay (a debt) (قرضہ) ادا کرنا، چکانا clear from all blame بری قرار دینا (law-court) cancel (order) (عدالت کا کسی) کو منسوخ کر دینا (10) give off or send out (pus, current, etc.) پھینکنا، چھوڑنا، دفانا، خارج کرنا (11) send (a missile, etc.) **n.** release ; being discharged رہائی، برّیت، خلاصی، مخلصی giving off or sending out پھینکنا، اخراج، نکاس carrying out تعمیل، بجاآوری clearing (of debt) چکانا، بیباقی dismissal or release (from service) آزادشدگی certificate of release from service برخاستگی، سبکدوشی matter that comes out of a wound ملازمت سے علیحدگی کی سند زخم سے نکلنے والا مواد (any fluid) which is discharged خارج ہونے والا مائع، اخراج، نکاس

disciple (di-*sī*-pěl) *n.* follower of great teacher (esp. of religion) پیرو، متبع، مرید، چیلا، شاگرد one of the twelve personal followers of Christ حواری

discipline (*dis*-ip-lin) *n.* teaching or experience which produces self-control and other good qualities of the mind and character ضبط نفس اور ذہنی تربیت کرنے والا تعلیم کا کوئی شعبہ training in obedience and order (فوجی) تربیت جس سے تابعداری کی عادت پڑے the result of such training ضبط، انضباط maintenance of order (in school, army, etc.) (فوج میں) ضبط، تادیبی کارروائی degree of its prevalence (in a group) کسی جماعت یا گروہ میں جتنا ضبط پایا جائے *v. t.* apply discipline to سدھانا، تربیت دینا ضبط سکھانا **disciplinarian** (dis-ip-li-*nay*-ri-an) *n.* person competent or accustomed to maintain discipline ضابطہ، سخت گیر **disciplinary** (*dis*-ip-li-na-ri) *adj.* of discipline, ضبط و انضباط کے متعلق، انضباطی promoting discipline, تادیبی *disciplinary action* تادیبی کارروائی

disclaim (dis-*klaym*) *v. t.* remove claim to دست بردار ہونا disavow (intention *to do*, or having said something, or a statement) ذمے داری وغیرہ سے انکار کرنا deny (connection *with*) سے تعلق یا لاعلمی ظاہر کرنا، انکار کرنا، تردید کرنا **disclaimer** *n.* denial انکار، تردید renunciation ترک

disclose (dis-*klohz*) *v. t.* reveal کھولنا، منکشف ہونا allow to be seen افشا کرنا، ظاہر کرنا divulge ; make known what has been secret پوشیدہ چیز کو منظر عام پر لانا **disclosure** (dis-*kloh*-zhě*) *n.* something disclosed انکشاف، فاش کیا ہوا راز *The disclosure caused a sensation* اس انکشاف نے سنسنی پھیلا دی act of disclosing منکشف کرنا، اظہار، فاش کیا ہوا راز

discography *n.* (see *Addenda*)

discolour (dis-*kul*-ě*) *v. t.* & *i.* change or spoil the natural and right colour of (کسی چیز کا) اصل رنگ بدل دینا یا خراب کر دینا become changed or spoilt in colour رنگ بدل جانا یا خراب ہو جانا **discolo(u)ration, discolourment** *n.* spoil (colour) or be spoilt thus دھبے ڈال دینا یا پڑ جانا

discomfit (dis-*kum*-fit) *v. t.* thwart the plan of (someone) تدبیر اُلٹ دینا، baffle ; embarrass بدحواس کر دینا، چھکے چھڑا دینا give (someone) an unpleasant shock سخت پریشان کر دینا defeat (in battle, etc.) ہزیمت دینا، شکست دینا **discomfiture** (dis-*kum*-fi-chě*) *n.* شکست، ہزیمت، تدبیر ناکام ہو جانا

discomfort (dis-*kum*-fě*t) *n.* lack of comfort بےچینی، بےآرامی uneasiness بےکلی، اُلجھن hardship تکلیف *v. t.* make uneasy بےآرام کرنا، بےچین یا بےکل کرنا

disconcert (dis-kon-*sě*t*) *v. t.* give a shock to (someone by upsetting his plans, etc.) تدبیر اُلٹ کر یا باطل کر کے پریشان کر دینا، کام بگاڑ دینا fluster or confuse upset the calmness or self-possession of کے اطمینان اور سکون میں خلل ڈال دینا

disconnect (dis-ko-*nekt*) *v. t.* detach from جُدا کرنا، الگ کرنا take (two or more things) apart الگ الگ کر دینا put (electric apparatus) out of action by separating parts (برقی آلے کا) کوئی پرزہ الگ کر کے بجلی کی رو بند کر دینا، رو بند کرنا، رو بندی کرنا **disconnected** *adj*. (esp. of talk or writing) incoherent بےربط، بےتکی، بے جوڑ، غیرمربوط، جدا کیا ہوا **disconnexion, disconnection** (dis-ko-*nek*-shěn) *n.* جدا کرنا، علیحدگی، رو بندی، عدم تسلسل

disconsolate (dis-*kon*-so-lit) *adj.* sad for loss of something مغموم، غمگین، ملول hopeless یاس، مایوس without comfort بےآرام، بےچین، مضطر forlorn بےکس، عاجز

discontent (dis-kon-*tent*) *n.* dissatisfaction عدم اطمینان، بےاطمینانی، ناخوشی its consciousness its cause غیرمطمئن کرنے والی بات **discontented** *adj*. dissatisfied غیرقانع، غیرمطمئن

discontinue (dis-kon-*tin*-ew) *v.t.* & *i.* give up, stop بند کرنا، چھوڑنا، ترک کرنا **discontinuous** *adj.* interrupted منقطع، غیرمسلسل **discontinuance** *n.* discontinuing of ترک، انقطاع

discophile *n.* (see *Addenda*)

discord (*dis*-ko*d) *n.* lack of harmony (of sounds, esp. of notes of music) بےآہنگی disagreement ناموافقت holding of opposite views

اختلاف strife (*between*) نزاع **discordant** (dis-*ko**-dant) *adj.* conflicting (views, parties, etc.) مختلف، متضاد، متباین harsh; unpleasing to the ear ناگوار، کرخت **discordance** *n.* lack of harmony بے آہنگی، ناموافقت، اختلاف

discount *n.* (*dis*-kount) money given as a reduction in full price for prompt payment کٹوتی difference between the wholesale and retail price کمیشن، منہائی amount deducted while cashing a bill of exchange not yet due for payment بٹا (*sell*) *at a discount*, (sell) below nominal price because of not being in demand (کم قیمت پر خرید (یا فروخت) *be at a discount*, be not appreciated کی قدر نہ ہونا *v. t.* (dis-*kount*) give or get the present value of (a bill of exchange not yet due) بٹے پر بیچنا یا خریدنا allow discount on sale کمیشن دینا lessen the importance of کم سمجھنا، کم جاننا refuse complete belief in rumour, etc. پر پوری طرح یقین نہ کرنا، کو شک وشبہ کی نگاہ سے دیکھنا

discountenance (dis-*kount*-e-nans) *v. t.* disapprove of (plan, etc.) کو ناپسند کرنا refuse to support (plan, etc.) کی حمایت سے انکار کرنا

discourage (dis-*kĕ*-rij) *v. t.* lessen or take away the courage or confidence of ہمت توڑنا، بددل کرنا، حوصلہ شکنی کرنا deter (*from doing*) (سے) باز رکھنا discountenance (a proposal) ناپسند کرنا **discouragement** *n.* discouraging حوصلہ شکنی

discourse *n.* (*dis*-koh*s) (esp.) learned lecture (عالمانہ) خطبہ treatise مقالہ *v.t.* (dis-*koh*s*) give a learned lecture (عالمانہ) خطبہ دینا speak or write at length (*upon*, *of* or *about* some topic) (کے باب میں) تفصیل سے لکھنا (یا بولنا)

discourteous (dis-*kĕ**-te-us) *adj.* rude, not courteous کج خلق، بدتہذیب، ناشائستہ **discourtesy** (dis-*kĕ*-te-si) *n.* rudeness; lack of courtesy کج خلقی، بدتہذیبی، ناشائستگی

discover (dis-*kuv*-ĕ*) *v. t.* find out or bring to light (something existing but not known) دریافت کرنا، انکشاف کرنا realize (something) new or unexpected معلوم کرنا (*discover oneself*), reveal one's identity اپنا آپ ظاہر کرنا **discovery** (-ri) *n.* act of discovering دریافت کرنا، انکشاف something discovered دریافت، انکشاف ▣ **We discover something existing but not known but invent something that is entirely new and had never existed before in that form and with the qualities which it has.**

discredit (dis-*kred*-it) *v. t.* cause the truth, value or credit of someone or something to seem doubtful ساکھ ختم کرنا، بے اعتباری پھیلانا bring disrepute to بدنام کرنا refuse to believe ماننے سے انکار کرنا *n.* loss of credit or reputation بے اعتباری، بدنامی person or thing causing such loss بے اعتباری کا باعث، موجب بدنامی doubt شک **discreditable** *adj.* شرمناک، غیر معتبر *bring discredit* (*to someone's good name*) (کسی کی نیک نامی پر) دھبہ لگانا

discreet (dis-*kreet*) *adj.* tactful in what one does and says زیرک، ہوشمند skilful in avoiding inopportune action or talk موقع شناس، دوراندیش **discretion** (dis-*kresh*-en) *n.* being discreet ہوشمندی، زیرکی freedom to act according to one's own judgment اختیار *at the discretion of* کی مرضی پر *It is left to your discretion* یہ آپ کی مرضی پر منحصر ہے **discretionary** *adj.* left to discretion اختیاری، پر مبنی، سمجھ پر منحصر *discretionary powers* authority to use one's discretion ذاتی تمیز کے اختیارات

discrepancy (*dis-kre*-pan-si, or dis-*krep*-an-si) *n.* absence of agreement اختلاف (of accounts) not tallying فرق difference (*between* usu. two statements of the same person) تناقض

discrete (dis-*kreet*) *adj.* separate الگ، جدا جدا، الگ الگ composed of discrete parts الگ الگ حصوں پر مشتمل

discretion *n.* **discretionary** *adj.* (see under **discreet**)

discriminate (dis-*krim*-i-nayt) *v. t. & i.* see the difference (*between* two things or one thing *from* another) make distinction (*against*, or *in favour of*) (کے حق میں یا کے خلاف) امتیاز سے کام لینا **discriminating** *adj* able to see even small differences ذی شعور، صاحب تمیز giving special or different treatment امتیاز روا رکھنے والا **discriminative** (-*krim*-) *adj.* (esp. of treatment) which varies with the object امتیازی **discriminator** *n.* (esp.) one who gives special treatment امتیاز روا رکھنے والا **discrimination** (-*ay*-) *n.* distinguishing امتیاز discernment شعور unfair difference in treatment ناروا امتیاز *without discrimination*, without giving way to such difference بلا امتیاز

discus (*dis*-kus) *n.* flat round object used for throwing *discus-throw* چکر پھینکنا *discus-thrower* چکر پھینکنے والا

a discus-thrower

discuss (dis-*kus*) *v. t.* talk about and argue (*on* a subject *with* a person) (کسی سے کسی موضوع پر) بحث کرنا expound the various views held on a particular subject ازکسی موضوع سے) بحث کرنا **discussion** (dis-*kush*-ĕn) *n.* discussing بحث debate مُباحثہ

disdain (dis-*dayn*) *v.t.* scorn حقارت کی نظر سے دیکھنا be too proud (*to do* or *of doing* something) توجہ کے لائق سمجھنا *n.* scorn, contempt حقارت تحقیر **disdainful** *adj.* contemptuous (*of*) حقارت آمیز

disease (di-*zeez*) *n.* illness (of body or mind) بیماری ، مرض ، علامت **diseased** (di-*zeezd*) *adj.* ill بیمار depraved غیر صحت مند A **disease** is a specific affection ; **illness,** a patient's condition ; **sickness,** something less serious than, but of the same nature as, a disease.

disembark (dis-em-*bah*k*) *v. t.* & *i.* to get or take down from a ship (*at* a port) جہاز سے اُترنا یا اُتارنا **disembarkation** *n.* disembarking جہاز سے اُترنا یا اُتارنا

disenchant (dis-en-*chahnt*) *v. t.* free from enchantment or illusion طلسم توڑنا ، افسوں اُتارنا free from illusion وہم دُور کرنا **disenchantment** *n.* act of disenchanting طلسم شکنی

disengage (dis-en-*gayj*) *v. t.* liberate from engaged state الگ کرنا free from hold چھڑانا **disengaged** (-*gayjd*) *adj.* (esp.) at leisure to attend to whatever presents itself فارغ **disengagement** *n.* freeing from hold رہائی ، خلاصی ending of engagement رشتہ ٹوٹ جانا

disentangle (dis-en-*tang*-ĕl) *v. t.* free from tangles چھڑانا ، اُلجھاؤ سے نکالنا ، جھنجھٹ سے نکالنا **disentanglement** *n.* رہائی ، خلاصی ، چھٹکارا

disestablish *v. t.* undo the establishment of ختم کرنا

disfavour (dis-*fay*-ve*) *v.t.* disapprove ناپسند کرنا withdraw favour from ناخوش ہونا ، ناراض ہونا *n.* disapproval ناپسندیدگی being out of favour ناخوشی

disfigure (dis-*fig*-ĕ*) *v. t.* spoil the shape or beauty of شکل بگاڑنا ، صورت بگاڑنا **disfigurement** *n.* شکل بگاڑنا

disfranchise (dis-*fran*-chiz) *v. t.* deprive one of one's freedom غلام بنانا ، آزادی سے محروم کرنا (esp.) deprive (a person or constituency) of right to vote (in or for a democratic set up) حق رائے دہی سے محروم کرنا **disfranchisement** (-*fran*-) *n.* حق رائے دہی سے محرومی

disgorge (dis-*go*j*) *v. t.* bring out from the throat what has been eaten give up unwillingly (esp. something taken wrongfully) اُگلنا

disgrace (dis-*grays*) *n.* loss of respect because of wrongdoing بے عزتی ، ذلت fall from high position زوال public shame رُسوائی person or thing causing disgrace موجب رُسوائی ، شرمناک بات *v.t.* bring shame upon ذلیل کرنا be a disgrace to ذلت کا موجب ہونا remove (someone) from a high position with disgrace جاہ و منصب چھین لینا **disgraceful** *adj.* shameful شرمناک رُسوائی کا موجب

disgruntled (dis-*grunt*-ĕld) *adj.* in a bad temper through not having got what was expected غیر مطمئن **disgruntled elements** غیر مطمئن عناصر pleased with nothing or no one جلا ہوا ، ناخوش

disguise (dis-*giz*) *v. t.* hide the identity of (oneself or someone) by a change of appearance (esp. in order to deceive) بھیس بدلنا ، چھپانا *n.* act of disguising بھیس بدلنا disguised condition بھیس *a blessing in disguise,* a favovrable event that had appeared to be harmful چھپی ہوئی رحمت dress, etc., used to disguise بھیس

disgust (dis-*gust*) *n.* strong dislike which forces one to turn away کراہت ، تنفر feel disgust (*at* or *for* something) indignation غصہ ، طیش *v. t.* cause disgust (*in* someone, *at* something) نفرت پیدا کرنا **disgusting** *adj.* causing disgust نفرت انگیز

dish *n.* any (usu. oval) container in which food is brought to the table before being transferred to plates ڈش ، ڈونگا ، قاب *the dishes,* crockery چینی کے برتن *v. t. dish up,* serve food by putting it into or on dish کھانا لگانا ، قاب یا ڈونگے میں ڈال کر میز پر لانا

dishevelled (di-shev-eld) *adj.* (of the hair) unkempt ; loose and tangled پریشان ، بکھرے ہوئے ، اُلجھے ہوئے

dishearten (dis-*hah*t*-ĕn) *v. t.* discourage ہمت توڑنا depress دل توڑنا ، مایوس کرنا **disheartening** *adj.* depressing دل شکن

dishonest (dis-*on*-est) *adj.* not honest بے ایمان insincere بددیانت **dishonesty** *n.* lack of integrity بددیانتی

dishonour (dis-*on*-ĕ*) *n.* loss of honour , disgrace بے عزتی ، رُسوائی want of self-respect خودداری نہ ہونا ، کمینگی ، فسردہ دلی person or thing bringing dishonour شرمناک ، موجب رُسوائی *v. t.* bringing disgrace موجب رُسوائی ہونا refuse to make the payment for (cheque) ادائیگی نہ کرنا **dishonourable** *adj.* disgraceful ذلت آمیز ، شرمناک کمینہ **dishonourably** *adv.* ذلت سے ، کمینگی سے

disillusion (dis-i-*lew*-zhĕn) *v. t.* free (someone) from wrong ideas or beliefs طلسم توڑنا ، وہم دُور کرنا *n.* freedom from illusion ازالۂ سحر ، ازالۂ وہم **disillusionment** *n.* ازالۂ سحر ، طلسم شکنی ، ازالۂ اوہام

disinclined (dis-in-*klind*) *adj.* unwilling (*to do*)

غیر مائل *n.* unwillingness (*to do* or *for* something) عدم میلان ، بے رغبتی

disinfect (dis-in-*fekt*) *v. t.* make free from infection by disease germs وبائی اثر دور کرنا ، جراثیم سے پاک کرنا **disinfectant** *adj.* disinfecting جراثیم کش *n.* disinfecting medicine جراثیم کش دوا

disinherit (dis-in-*he*-rit) *v. t.* deprive one's rightful heir of one's legacy through some declaration or provision in will محروم الارث کرنا ، ورثے سے محروم کرنا ، عاق کرنا **disinheritance** *n.* محروم الارث کرنا یا ہونا ، ورثے سے محروم کرنا یا ہونا

disintegrate (dis-*int*-eg-rayt) *v. t.* & *i.* (cause to) break into pieces ٹکڑے ٹکڑے کرنا یا ہونا ، ختم کرنا یا ہونا **disintegration** (-*ay*-) *n.* act of disintegrating خاتمہ ، انتشار ، منتشر کرنا یا ہونا

disinter (dis-in-*tē**) *v. t.* exhume کا مُردہ اکھیڑنا ، قبر سے نکالنا ، کھود کر نکالنا take out of obscurity قعرِ گمنامی سے نکالنا **disinterment** *n.* حفر ؛ کھود کر نکالنا

disinterested (dis-*int*-e-res-ted) *adj.* not guided by self-interest بے غرض ، بے لوث impartial غیر جانبدار **disinterestedly** *adv.* بے غرضانہ غیر جانبدارانہ

disjointed (dis-*joint*-ed) *adj.* (of speech and writing) incoherent بے ربط broken جُدا ، ٹوٹا ہُوا

disk, disc (disk) *n.* round and flat plate (like a coin) ٹکیا ، قرص round surface appearing to be flat قرص

dislike (dis-*līk*) *v. t.* be displeased with ناخوش ہونا object to ناپسند کرنا have an aversion for نفرت کرنا *n.* displeasure ناپسندیدگی ، نفرت

dislocate (*dis*-lo-kayt) *v. t.* put (esp. a bone in the body) out of position ہڈی اتارنا ، جوڑ الگ کر دینا put (traffic, machinery, etc.) out of order گڑبڑ کرنا ، خلل ڈالنا **dislocation** (-*ay*-) *n.* act of dislocating ہڈی کا اترنا ، یا اتارنا ، انتظام میں خلل ڈالنا

dislodge (dis-*loj*) *v. t.* drive out (someone or something *from* the place occupied) نکال دینا ، remove ہٹانا

disloyal (dis-*loi*-ĕl) *adj.* not loyal غدّار unfaithful (*to* friends, etc.) بے وفا false (*to* duty, etc.) نمک حرام **disloyally** *adv.* غدّارانہ ، بے وفائی سے **disloyalty** *n.* بے وفائی ، غدّاری ، نمک حرامی

dismal (*diz*-mĕl) *adj.* sad, miserable, depressed غمگین ، افسردہ ، ملول dreary اداس depressing رنجیدہ ، الم ناک *n.* (*pl.*) *the dismals*, depression افسردگی ، دل گرفتگی

dismantle (dis-man-tĕl) *v. t.* take away fittings, furnishing, etc., from اتارنا take to pieces پرزے پرزے کرنا ، ٹکڑے ٹکڑے کرنا ، توڑنا **dismantling** *n.*

dismay (dis-*may*) *n.* feeling of fear and discouragement دہشت ، ہول *v.t.* discourage and fill with fear دہشت زدہ کرنا ، چھکے چھڑا دینا

dismember (dis-*mem*-bĕ*) *v.t.* ❶ cut the limbs of a body ہر ہر عضو کاٹ ڈالنا ، مُثلہ کرنا ، بند بند جُدا کرنا take to pieces ٹکڑے ٹکڑے کرنا divide up (a territory, etc.) حصے بخرے کرنا ، تقسیم کرنا ، **dismemberment** *n.* act of dismembering تقسیم ، حصے بخرے ، بند بند جدا کرنا

dismiss (dis-*mis*) *v.t.* sack (someone *from* a job) برخاست کرنا ، allow to go چھوڑنا ، جانے دینا put out of one's thoughts دل سے نکال دینا *dismiss a subject*, refuse to consider or discuss it any further پر مزید غور و خوض کرنے سے انکار کر دینا not allow (a case) to be proceeded with مقدمہ خارج کر دینا *The case is dismissed* مقدمہ خارج ، *dismiss a side*, (in cricket) get it out for a stated score مقابل ٹیم کو آؤٹ کرنا **dismissal** (dis-*mis*-ĕl) *n.* act of dismissing برخاستگی ، مقدمہ خارج کر دینا یا ہو جانا ، ٹیم کو آؤٹ کرنا

dismount (dis-*mount*) *v.t.* & *i.* (cause to) alight from horseback گھوڑے سے اترنا یا اتارنا ❷ take (pictures, gun, etc.) from its frame or mount اتارنا

disobedience *n.* **disobedient** *adj.* (see under **disobey**)

disobey (dis-o-*bay*) *v.t.* refuse to carry out the order عدول حکمی کرنا neglect to do so نافرمانی کرنا ، خلاف ورزی کرنا **disobedience** *n.* not obeying نافرمانی ، عدول حکمی **disobedient** *adj.* one who does not obey نافرمان

disoblige (dis-o-*blīj*) *v. t.* refuse to accommodate another person's wishes or needs مروّت نہ کرنا ، لحاظ نہ کرنا

disorder (dis-*o**d-ĕ*) *n.* ❶ disease بیماری ، مرض ، علالت absence of order خرابی ، گڑبڑ ، فساد ، بے ضابطگی (*pl.*) violent political disturbances ہلچل ، سخت گڑبڑ **disorderly** *adj.* not in order بے ترتیب ، بے سلیقہ lawless, riotous سرکش ، امن عامہ میں مخل

disorganize (dis-*o***g*-a-nīz) *v.t.* throw into confusion گڑبڑ کرنا ، ابتری میں ڈالنا put out of working order ناکارہ کرنا ، بیکار بنانا **disorganization** (-*ay*-) *n.* ابتری ، بدنظمی

disown (dis-*ohn*) *v.t.* refuse to accept as one's own اپنا کہنے سے انکار کرنا refuse to recognize پہچاننے سے انکار کر دینا deny connection with (someone or something) سے بے تعلقی ظاہر کرنا reject, repudiate مسترد کرنا ، دستبردار ہو جانا

disparage (dis-*pa*-rij) *v. t.* speak slightingly of (someone or something) کی تحقیر کرنا ، گھٹا کر دکھانا (old use) bring into disrepute بدنام کرنا **disparagement** *n.* act of disparaging بدنامی ، تحقیر ، ناقدری **disparagingly** *adv.* slightingly ناقدری سے ، تحقیر سے

disparate (dis-pa-rayt) *adj.* not mutually comparable جن میں کوئی مقابلہ ہی نہ ہو essentially different بالکل مختلف
disparity (dis-*pa*-ri-ti) *n.* inequality (*in* some point) تفاوت difference فرق
dispassionate (dis-*pash*-ĕ-nayt) *adj.* free from passions ; calm ٹھنڈے دل سے impartial غیر جانبدار **dispassionately** *adv.* calmly, coolly ٹھنڈے دل سے
dispatch, despatch (dis-*pach*) *v.t.* send someone off (*to* a destination, *on* a journey, *for* a special purpose) بھیجنا، روانہ کرنا send (letter, etc.) بھیجنا، ارسال کرنا get through (business, meal) quickly (کام) جلد تر انجام دینا یا پورا کرنا kill کی جان لینا، کو قتل کرنا *n.* dispatching or being dispatched ترسیل something dispatched بھیجی ہوئی چیز official letter (esp. a diplomatic message) مراسلہ military report from the war front جنگی مراسلہ news story by a paper's correspondent خبر prompt settlement of business جلد پورا کرنا *with dispatch,* promptly جلدی *Act with dispatch* کام جلدی پورا کرنا
dispel (dis-*pel*) *v. t.* (-ll-) drive away دور کرنا scatter (clouds, etc.) دور کرنا، اڑا لے جانا زائل کرنا، رفع کرنا
dispense (dis-*pens*) *v.t.* & *i.* distribute بانٹنا، تقسیم کرنا (of the Providence) ordain تقدیر میں لکھنا مقدر کرنا administer (justice) انصاف کرنا prepare and give out (a medicine) (نسخہ) تیار کرنا، دوا بنانا (*dispense with*), do without کے بغیر کام چلا تا، *dispense with (someone's) services* غیر ضروری سمجھ کر ترک کر دینا (کسی کو) ملازمت سے سبکدوش کرنا، **dispenser** *n.* person who prepares for patients medicines from a doctor's prescriptions ڈسپنسر، دواساز، عطار **dispensary** *n.* place where medicines are dispensed دواخانہ **dispensation** (-*ay*-) *n.* act of dispensing تقسیم something dispensed by the providence تقدیر الٰہی exemption from a religious obligation (generally sold out by Roman Catholics) (کسی پر سے) فرض ساقط کرنا
disperse (dis-*pe*s*) *v.t.* & *i.* go in different directions منتشر ہونا، ادھر ادھر چلے جانا scatter تتر بتر کرنا (of troops under attack) spread out to separate positions پھیل جانا **dispersedly** (-id-li) *adv.* separately, scattered جدا جدا، منتشر **dispersal** *n.* act of dispersing منتشر کرنا یا ہونا **dispersion** (dis-*pe**-shĕn) *n.* dispersal منتشر کرنا یا ہونا dispersed state انتشار، پراگندگی
dispirited (dis-*pi*-ri-ted) *adj.* in low spirits ; depressed مایوس، دل شکستہ
displace (dis-*plays*) *v. t.* remove from the right or usual position ادھر ادھر کر دینا take the place of کی جگہ لینا eject بے دخل کرنا، بے خانماں کرنا، نکالنا
displacement *n.* (esp.) amount of water displaced by a solid body ہٹاؤ **displaced person** *n.* (abb. *D. P.*) person driven away from his homeland مہاجر، پناہ گیر *displaced persons* مہاجرین، پناہ گیر، ملک بدر افراد، بے خانماں لوگ، اجڑے ہوئے
display (dis-*play*) *v. t.* place or arrange (things) so that they may be seen openly ظاہر کرنا، عیاں کو سجانا، کی نمائش کرنا allow to be seen کرنا، کا مظاہرہ کرنا *n.* displaying مظاہرہ *newspaper display* اخبار کے صفحے پر خبروں کی ترتیب exhibition نمائش
displease (dis-*pleez*) *v.t.* offend (one's officer or patron) آزردہ کرنا، ناراض کرنا be disagreeable to ناپسندیدہ ہونا **displeased** *adj.* (dis-*pleezd*) annoyed (with one's subordinate or patron) **displeasure** (dis-*plezh*-ĕ*) *n.* anger خفگی، غصہ، آزردگی cause of annoyance خفگی کا باعث
disport (dis-*poh*t*) *v.t.* (*disport oneself*), enjoy oneself اٹکھیلیاں کرنا
dispose (dis-*pohz*) *v.t.* & *i.* (*dispose of*), finish with ختم کرنا، انجام دینا (*dispose of*), sell بیچنا، فروخت کرنا (*dispose of*), get rid of کو ٹھکانے لگانا، سے پیچھا چھڑانا apply to whatever purpose one chooses حسب مرضی استعمال کرنا *Man proposes but God disposes* انسان تدبیریں کرتا رہتا ہے، مگر خدا اس سے اپنی مرضی کے مطابق کام لیتا ہے
disposed *adj.* (dis-*pohzd*) willing (*for* or *to do* something) *well-disposed towards (someone),* friendly and helpful to (him) کا مددگار **disposable** *adj* that which can be arranged جسے ٹھکانے لگایا جا سکے، جس کا تصفیہ ہو سکے that which can be disposed of قابل فروخت **disposal** *n.* disposing of something کو ٹھکانے لگانا، کا انتظام کرنا *at one's disposal,* to be used as one wishes کے ہاتھ میں، کے سپرد، کی تحویل میں *place one's time, etc., at someone's disposal* (وقت وغیرہ) کسی کی خدمت کیلئے وقف کرنا کیلئے وقف کرنا **disposition** (-*zish*-) *n.* (esp.) person's natural qualities of mind and character طبیعت مزاج، افتاد طبع inclination (*to do*) شوق، میلان arrangement ترتیب، صف بندی
dispossess (dis-po-*zes*) *v.t.* turn a tenant out (*of* a place) کو بے دخل کرنا **dispossessed** *adj.* ousted بے دخل **dispossession** (-*zesh*-) *n.* ousting, ejectment بے دخلی
disproportion (dis-pro-*poh**-shĕn) *n.* state of being out of proportion عدم تناسب، عدم توازن lack of symmetry or balance عدم توازن **disproportionate** (-*ayt*-) *adj.* غیر متناسب، غیر متوازن
disprove (dis-*proov*) *v. t.* prove to be wrong غلط ثابت کرنا **disproof** *n.* refutation, disproving تغلیط، بطلان

dispute (dis-*pewt*) *v.t.* & *i.* argue, quarrel (*with* or *against* someone, *on* or *about* something) بحث کرنا ، جھگڑا کرنا call (something) in question زیر بحث لانا ، اعتراض کرنا resist (enemy's advance, etc.) روکنا *n.* disputing بحث quarrel, argument جھگڑا ، مناقشت ، تکرار *a hot dispute*, a heated argument گرما گرمی ، گرما گرم بحث *the question in dispute*, the point at issue مسئلہ زیر بحث *beyond* (or *past* or *without*) *dispute*, undoubtedly لازماً **disputable** *adj.* open to question مشتبہ ، بحث طلب **disputation** (-*ay*-shĕn) *n.* argumentative debate, discourse or treatise مباحثہ ، حجت **disputatious** (-*tay*-shus) *adj.* fond of argument مباحثہ جو **disputant** (dis-*pew*-tant) *n.* person taking part in dispute شریک نزاع ، جھگڑے میں حصہ لینے والا

disqualify (dis-*kwol*-i-fi) *v.t.* deprive of qualification سند واپس لے لینا pronounce or make ineligible (*for* a task or office) نااہل قرار دینا **disqualified** (-fid-) *adj.* deprived of qualification جس کی سند واپس لے لی جائے ineligible (*for*) **disqualification** (-*ay*-) *n.* نااہلیت ، سند واپس لے لینا ، سند ستاندگی

disquiet (dis-*kwi*-et) *v.t.* perturb پریشان کرنا ، تشویش میں ڈالنا ، بے چین کرنا *n.* perturbation تشویش ، بے چینی

disquietude (-tewd) *n.* perturbation تشویش ، پریشانی ، بے چینی

disregard (dis-re-*gah***d*) *v.t.* pay no attention to التفات نہ کرنا ignore ; neglect نظرانداز کرنا ، پرواہ نہ کرنا show no respect for لحاظ نہ کرنا *n.* * inattention بے التفاتی neglect of (warning of danger) بے پروائی *in utter disregard of* سے بالکل بے پروا ہوکر contempt for (propriety, etc.) تحقیر

disrepair (dis-re-*pay*-è*) *n.* bad state for lack of repair خستہ حالت ، بوسیدگی

disreputable (dis-*rep*-ew-tab-èl) *adj.* having a bad reputation بدنام ، مشتبہ چال چلن کا not respectable بے عزت ، بے وقار

disrepute (dis-re-*pewt*) *n.* being ill-spoken and thought بدنامی ، رسوائی *fall into disrepute* بدنام ہو جانا

disrespect (dis-res-*pekt*) *n.* lack of respect بے عزتی

disrespectful *adj.* showing disrespect بے ادب ، گستاخ

disrupt (dis-*rupt*) *v.t.* split ٹکڑے ٹکڑے کر دینا cause to break down منقطع کرنا ، ناکارہ کرنا ، انتشار پھیلانا deprive of unity اتحاد ختم کرنا ، انتشار پھیلانا **disruption** *n.* breaking asunder ٹوٹنا یا توڑنا split (of organization) انتشار **disruptive** (dis-*rup*-tive) *adj.* انتشار انگیز **disruptionist** (dis-*rup*-shĕ-nist) *n.* one who causes disruption انتشار انگیز

dissatisfy (dis-*sat*-is-fi) *v.t.* fail to satisfy اطمینان نہ کر سکنا make discontented غیر مطمئن کرنا

dissatisfaction (-fak-shĕn) *n.* being dissatisfied بے اطمینانی

dissect (di-*sekt*) *v.t.* cut up (parts of an animal, plant, etc.) in order to study its structure چیر پھاڑ کرنا ، عملِ تشریح کرنا examine (a theory, argument, etc.) part by part to determine its value (کا) تجزیہ کرنا **dissection** (di-sek-shĕn) *n.* act of dissecting چیر پھاڑ ، عملِ تشریح **dissector** *n.* one who dissects چیر پھاڑ کرنے والا

dissemble (di-*sem*-bèl) *v.t.* & *i.* behave in such a way as to give a wrong idea of one's thoughts or intentions نیت کو پوشیدہ رکھنا ، بات چھپانا act hypocritically منافقت کرنا **dissembler** *n.* hypocrite منافق

disseminate (di-*sem*-i-nayt) *v.t.* broadcast (seed) بیج ڈالنا ، تخم ریزی کرنا spread widely (ideas, news, etc.) پھیلانا ، نشر و اشاعت کرنا **dissemination** (-*ay*-) *n.* act of spreading نشر و اشاعت ، تخم ریزی *dissemination of rumours* افواہیں پھیلانا

dissension *n.* (see under **dissent**)

dissent (di-*sent*) *v.i.* think differently مختلف انداز سے سوچنا ، اختلاف رکھنا quarrel جھگڑنا ، نزاع کرنا refuse to assent ; say "No" to انکار کرنا ، نامنظور کرنا refuse to accept (religious doctrine of the Church of England مختلف العقیدہ ہونا ، تسلیم نہ کرنا *n.* difference of opinion اختلافِ رائے *note of dissent*, note appended to the majority decision of a committee, etc. by its dissenting member(s) اختلافی رائے ، اختلافِ رائے کا اظہار *subject to a note of dissent* اختلافِ رائے کے اظہار کے ساتھ **dissension** (di-*sen*-shĕn) *n.* disagreement نااتفاقی ، اَن بَن ، نزاع strong difference of opinion اختلافِ رائے **dissenter** *n.* one who dissents اختلافِ رائے رکھنے والا (esp.) Protestant non-conformist who dissents with the Church of England (عیسائیوں کا ایک) مختلف العقیدہ شخص یا گروہ ، بدعتی **dissentient** (di-*sen*-shent) *adj.* disagreement with the official or prevalent view (کسی مسلمہ نظریہ یا عقیدے سے) اختلاف رکھنے والا *n.* dissentient person مختلف العقیدہ شخص ، اختلاف رکھنے والا شخص

dissertation (di-sĕ*-*tay*-shĕn) *n.* long spoken or written report (on something) * حاصلِ مطالعہ

disservice (dis-*sĕ**-vis) *n.* harmful action نقصان رسانی ، مضرت رسانی ill turn بدی ، بدسلوکی *do disservice to* سے بدی کرنا

dissimilar (di-*sim*-i-lĕ*) *adj.* not similar ; unlike مختلف ، غیر مشابہ **dissimilarity, dissimilitude** *n.* being unlike عدم مشابہت

dissimulate (di-*sim*-ew-layt) *v.t.* & *i.* hide one's true feelings دلی جذبات چھپانا practice deceitful hypocrisy مکاری کرنا ، ریاکاری سے کام لینا ، فریب کارانہ منافقت کرنا **dissimulation** (-*ay*-) *n.* pretence مکاری deceitful hypocrisy فریب کارانہ ، منافقت

dissipate (*dis*-i-payt) *v.t.* & *i.* drive away (clouds, fear, ignorance, etc.) دور کرنا ، منتشر کرنا waste (energy, wealth, etc.) foolishly اڑانا ، برباد کرنا ، ضائع کرنا **dissipated** (*dis*-) *adj.* corrupted by a dissolute way of life عیاش ، اوباش having ruined one's health in that manner جو عیاشی میں صحت خراب کر چکا ہو **dissipation** (-*ay*-) *n.* (esp.) foolish wasting of energy, money, etc., in a dissolute way of life عیاشی میں اڑانا

dissociate (di-*soh*-shi-ayt) *v.t.* think of (something) as separate (*from*) جدا کرنا say that one has nothing to do (*with* a person or idea) قطع تعلق کرنا ، اظہارِ بیزاری کرنا **dissociation** (-*ay*-) *n.* act of dissociating علیحدگی ، قطعِ تعلق ، اظہارِ بیزاری

dissolute (*dis*-o-lewt) *adj.* immoral, licentious آوارہ ، عیاش ، بدچلن **dissoluteness** *n.* licentiousness آوارگی ، بدچلنی ، عیاشی

dissolution (dis-o-*lew*-shĕn) *n.* breaking up (of contract, etc.) معاہدہ توڑنا ، منسوخ کرنا ، فسخ کرنا *dissolution of marriage* فسخِ نکاح resolution into component parts تجزیہ ، تحلیل dismissal of a Legislature for summoning a new one before a general election is due منسوخ کرنا ، معاہدہ توڑنا ، فسخ کرنا **dissoluble** *adj.*, **dissolubility** *n.*, **dissolve** *v.t.* & *i.* (see below)

dissolve (di-*zolv*) *v.t.* & *i.* change into liquid گھلنا ، گھلانا ، حل ہونا یا کرنا *dissolve in tears*, weep copiously بے تحاشا رونا vanish; become invisible غائب ہو جانا bring or come to an end منسوخ کرنا یا ہونا ، فسخ کرنا یا ہونا dismiss a Legislature for summoning a new one before a general election is due مجلسِ قانون ساز کو برخاست کرنا یا توڑنا **dissoluble** *adj.* (esp. of contract) liable to annulment جو ٹوٹ نہ سکے ، جو ناقابلِ فسخ نہ ہو **dissolvable** *adj.* that which can be changed into liquid حل پذیر ، منحل **dissolvent** *n.* liquid able to dissolve a solid حل کرنے والا **dissolubility** *n.* being dissolvable حل پذیری **dissolution** *n.* (see above)

dissuade (di-*swayd*) *v.t.* turn (someone) away (*from* something, or *from doing* something) کے خلاف مشورہ دینے سے روکنا ، سے باز رہنے کو کہنا **dissuasive** (di-*sway*-siv) *adj.* that dissuades باز رکھنے والا **dissuasion** (di-*sway*-zhen) *n.* act of dissuading روکنا ، باز رکھنا

distaff (*dis*-taf) *n.* stick round which wool, etc., is wound and then pulled in spinning by hand سلائی دار پونی (*on*) *the distaff side*, (on) the mother's side of the family ماں کی طرف سے ، ننھیالی

a distaff

distance (*dis*-tans) *n.* extent of space between two far-off points فاصلہ ، دوری *from a distance* دور سے *in the distance* بعد مسافت *at a distance of* کے فاصلے پر far-away place دور مقام space of time مدت *at this distance of time* اتنی مدت کے بعد avoidance of familiarity سرد مہری *keep* (*one's*) *distance*, not be too friendly سرد مہری سے کام لینا **distant** *adj.* far-away space دور ، بعید *distant from* سے دور far-away in time مدت far off in relationship دور کا ، دور نزدیک کا faint, very little ہلکا ، معمولی (of behaviour) unfriendly سرد مہر ، غیر دوستانہ **distantly** *adv.* not from near دور کا ، دور سے

distaste (dis-*tayst*) *n.* dislike or aversion (*for*) ناپسندیدگی ، کراہت **distasteful** *adj.* very unpleasant (to) ناپسندیدہ ، مکروہ

distemper (dis-*tem*-pĕ*) *n.* permanent water-paint for walls ڈسٹمپر ، (دیواروں کے لیے) پکا آبی رنگ this method of painting walls, etc. دیواری رنگ ، ڈسٹمپر ، آبی رنگ ، پکا دیواری رنگ disordered state of mind دماغی خرابی illness بیماری ، مرض ، علالت *v.t.* paint with distemper آبی رنگ کرنا ، ڈسٹمپر کرنا ، پکا رنگ کرنا perturb بے چین کرنا derange mentally پاگل کر دینا

distil (dis-*til*) *v.t.* & *i.* (-ll-) purify (a liquid) by heating it into vaporous form and then back into liquid by cooling down the vapour into drops مقطر کرنا ، کشید کرنا *distilled water* زلال ، کشیدہ پانی extract the essence of (a plant etc.) by vaporizing its solution and recondensing it عرق کھینچنا ، کشید کرنا make spirit, etc., in this way جوہر نکالنا (let) fall in drops ٹپکنا ، ٹپکانا rid (something) of superfluities; purify and condense (it) صاف کرنا ، پاک کرنا **distillation** (-*ay*-) *n.* distilling or being distilled کشید ، تقطیر **distillery** *n.* place where alcoholic drinks are distilled شراب کشید کرنے کا کارخانہ ، شراب کا کارخانہ **still** *n.* apparatus for distilling alcoholic drinks شراب کشید کرنے کا بھپکا **distiller** *n.* one who distills intoxicants شراب کشید کرنے والا

distinct (dis-*tinkt*) *adj.* clearly seen, heard, or understood صاف ، بیّن ، واضح ، صریح different in kind مختلف separate (*from*) جدا ، الگ **distinctly** *adv* definitely قطعاً ، قطعی طور پر clearly وضاحت سے **distinctive** *adj.* characteristic مخصوص

the distinctive features of کی خصوصیات **distinction** *n.* (see below)
distinction (dis-*tink*-shĕn) *n.* keeping things different امتیاز، تمیز *draw distinctions* امتیاز کرنا *make a distinction between* میں امتیاز کرنا *make no distinction between*, treat alike برابر کا سلوک کرنا characteristic difference فرق، مخصوص فرق excellence mark of honour امتیاز، اعزاز ⓢ **Distinction** denotes a belief that one thing is unlike another ; **difference** signifies a real unlikeness ; **discrimination** denotes choice of one as superior to another.
distinguish (dis-*tin*-gwish) *v.t.* & *i.* recognize well the difference (*between* two things, or of one thing *from* another) امتیاز کرنا differentiate فرق کرنا be a characteristic difference نمایاں خصوصیت ہونا honour ممتاز کرنا make (oneself) well-known امتیاز حاصل کرنا **distinguished** *adj.* eminent سر برآوردہ having distinction ممتاز *a distinguished person* ممتاز شخصیت **distinguishable** *adj.* that which can be distinguished (*from*) لائق امتیاز
distort (dis-*to*t*) *v. t.* twist out of shape شکل بگاڑنا twist out of the truth توڑ مروڑ کر بیان کرنا
distortion (dis-*to**shen) *n.* twisting out of shape شکل بگاڑنا twisting of true meaning توڑ مروڑ کر بیان کرنا
distract (dis-*trakt*) *v. t.* draw away (one's attention *from* something) توجہ ہٹانا confuse گھبرا دینا drive mad پاگل بنانا infuriate غصہ دلانا **distracted** (-ed) *adj.* with the mind confused (by) سراسیمہ mad پاگل with the attention divided (*between*) جس کا خیال بٹا ہوا ہو
distraction *n.* distracting or being distracted خیال بانٹنا یا بٹنا، انتشار خیال amusement that distracts تفریح madness جنون، پاگل پن annoyance that enrages **distraught** (-*trot*) *adj.* (old use) crazed with grief پاگل
distraint (dis-*traynt*) *n.* legal seizure of goods for debt قرقی **distrain** *v. t.* (in the prepositional phrase) *distrain upon* (a defaulter or his goods), (his goods) for debt کی قرقی کرنا، (کا مال) قرق کرنا
distraught *adj.* (see under **distract**)
distress (dis-*tres*) *n.* (cause of) great sorrow رنج کا باعث much discomfort تکلیف (کا موجب) suffering caused by want of money or other necessities عسرت، مفلسی serious danger سخت خطرہ *v. t.* cause great pain, sorrow or trouble to رنج، تکلیف یا مصیبت پہنچانا، مغموم کرنا **distressing** *adj.* causing sorrow ; painful رنجیدہ
distribute (dis-*trib*-ewt) *v.t.* deal out (*to* or *among* a number of persons) بانٹنا، تقسیم کرنا send out (*to* various places) بھیجنا، مختلف جگہوں پر تعینات کرنا spread out (*over* a large area) پھیلا دینا، بکھیرنا
distribution (dis-tri-*bew*-shĕn) *n.* act of distributing تقسیم *prize distribution* تقسیم انعامات **distributive** *adj.* relating to distribution تقسیم کے متعلق **distributor** *n.* one who distributes تقسیم کنندہ، بانٹنے والا تاجر film distributor تقسیم کنندہ، تقسیم کار **distributary** *n.* branch of an irrigational canal, رَجباہ، نہر کی شاخ
district (*dis*-trikt) *n.* part of country part of a territory marked out for administrative purposes (and placed under a Deputy Commissioner in West Pakistan) (abbreviated into *dist.*) ضلع *the District Magistrate*, the Chief Magistrate (whose powers in Pakistan vest in the Deputy Commissioner) ڈسٹرکٹ مجسٹریٹ *the Additional District Magistrate A.D.M.* اے، ڈی، ایم *the District Inspector of Schools* (abb. *D.I.*) ڈسٹرکٹ انسپکٹر مدارس any other similar division حلقہ
distrust (dis-*trust*) *v. t.* have no confidence in اعتبار نہ کرنا suspect شک و شبہ کی نگاہ سے دیکھنا *regard (someone) with distrust* شک و شبہ کی نگاہ سے دیکھنا *n.* want of confidence عدم اعتماد، بے اعتمادی suspicion شک و شبہ **distrustful** *adj.* one who suspects شکی، بدگمان
disturb (dis-*tĕ**b) *v.t.* upset خلل ڈالنا put out of the right or usual position درہم برہم کرنا
disturbance *n.* disturbing or being disturbed خلل، گڑبڑ (esp.) political disorder or upheaval ہنگامہ، گڑبڑ
disuse (dis-*yews*) *n.* being no longer in use رائج نہ رہنا *fall into disuse* متروک ہونا **disused** (dis-*yewzd*) *adj.* no longer used متروک
ditch (dich) *n.* trench dug in between fields, etc., to hold or conduct water خندق، کھائی watercourse *v. t.* make ditches خندق کھودنا
ditto (*dit*-oh) (abb. do) *n.* the same (used in a list to avoid writing words again) ایضاً the mark ,, under some item meaning 'the same' ایضاً
ditty (*dit*-i) *n.* (pl., *ditties*) short, simple song گیت
diuretic (di-ew-*ret*-ik) *adj.* & *n.* (medicine) promoting urination پیشاب آور (دوا)
diurnal (di-*ĕ**-nĕl) *adj.* daily روزانہ، روزمرہ of day-time دن کا

divan (di-*vahn*) *n.* low soft couch used also as a bed دیوان
a divan
dive (div.) *v. i.* go head foremost into water ڈُبکی لگانا غوطہ مارنا go down or out of sight quickly غائب ہوجانا *The train dived into the tunnel* ریل گاڑی سُرنگ میں جیسے غائب ہی ہوگئی put one's hands (*into* something) quickly جلدی سے ہاتھ ڈالنا *n.* act of diving غوطہ ، ڈبکی sudden dart out of sight غائب ہوجانا **diver** (*di*-*ve**) *n.* one who works under water (in a diving dress) غوطہ زن ، غوطہ خور **diving-dress** dress of an underwater worker to examine a wrecked ship غوطہ زنی کا لباس ، غوّاصی **dive-bomber** *n.* aircraft diving deeply to drop bombs on its objective غوطہ زن ۔ بمبار
diverge (di-*ve**j) *v. i.* go in different ways and get further and further apart راہیں الگ ہونا branch away (*from*) جُدا ہونا differ more and more سے مختلف ہوتے جانا **divergent** *adj.* diverging, different مختلف **divergence** *n.* act of diverging اختلاف
divers (di-vĕ*z) *adj.* several unnamed (objects) بُشمُولِ ق
diverse (di-*ve**s) *adj* unlike, different مختلف **diversely** *adv* in various ways طرح طرح سے **diversify** (-fi) *v. t.* introduce variety into تنوع پیدا کرنا **diversity** (di-*ve**si-ti) *n.* variety difference اختلاف
divert (di-*vĕ***t*) *v. t.* turn in another direction موڑنا ، پھیرنا ، رُوخ پلٹنا turn the attention away (*from* something) خیال ہٹانا amuse ; entertain دل بہلانا ، تفریح کا سامان بہم پہنچانا **diverting** *adj.* amusing دل بہلانے والا **diversion** (di-vĕ*shĕn) *n.* turning aside انحراف amusement تفریح
divest (di-*vest*) *v. t.* strip (someone *of* his) clothes کپڑے اُتارنا deprive (someone *of* something) محروم کرنا *divest oneself of*, give up one's (possessions) سے ہاتھ اُٹھا لینا ، سے دستکش ہونا
divide (di-*vid*) *v. t.* & *i.* split up پھوٹ ڈالنا separate (*into*) بانٹنا یا بٹنا separate (part *from* part) جُدا کرنا share (*between* or *among*) vote by division into groups حامی و مخالف گروہوں میں بٹ کر رائے دینا ، تقسیم ہو measure a number (called *dividend*) *by* another (called *divisor*) to get the *quotient* (*i.e.*, to get the number of times the divisor is contained in the dividend) تقسیم (پر) کر **dividend** (*div*-i-dend) *n.* number to be divided by another مقسوم periodical payment of the share of profit, to the shareholder of a company (کمپنی کا وقتاً فوقتاً ادا ہونے والا) منافع **divisor** (di-*vi*-zĕ*) *n.* number by which another is divided مقسوم علیہ ، تقسیم کنندہ **divisible** (di-*viz*-i-bĕl) *adj.* that which can be divided تقسیم پذیر ، منقسم
dividers (di-*vi*-dĕ*z) *n.* (*pl.*) pair of measuring compasses
a divider
division (di-*vizh*-ĕn) dividing or being divided تقسیم The result of dividing تقسیم ، قسمت divided part قسمت distribution تقسیم ، بانٹنا *division of labour* تقسیم کار difference of opinion (in an organization) اختلاف رائے voting by division into groups حامی و مخالف گروہوں میں بٹ کر رائے دہی ، تقسیم (examination) category of passed candidates ڈویژن درجہ *First division* (or *I Division*), division comprising candidates getting 60% or more marks فرسٹ ڈویژن ، درجۂ اوّل *Second division* (or *II Division*), division with those getting 50% or more marks سیکنڈ ڈویژن ، درجۂ دوم *Third division* (or *III Division*), division comprising candidates below that but getting pass marks تھرڈ ڈویژن ، درجۂ سوم *aim at a good division* اچھا ڈویژن حاصل کرنے کی کوشش کرنا *get* (*or be placed*) *in* (*some*) *Division* (کوئی) ڈویژن حاصل کرنا (army) unit of two or more brigades ڈویژن administrative area comprising several districts and placed under a Commissioner in this country قسمت ، کمشنری **divisional** *adj.* pertaining to a division تقسیم سے متعلق ، قسمت کا ، کمشنری کا *Divisional Commissoner* کمشنر قسمت ڈویژنل کمشنر

divination *n.* see under **divine**.

divine (di-*vin*) *adj* like, pertaining to or coming from God خدائی ، الٰہی *divine right*, right of kings to reign as supposedly derived from God خدائی حق relating to gods or to a god دیوتا کا دیوتاؤں کا سا like a god or gods دیوی دیوتاؤں کا devoted to God خدا پرستانہ ، خدا کی (عبادت وغیرہ) *divine service*, public worship (عیسائیوں کی) اجتماعی عبادت ، عبادت نماز باجماعت sacred مقدس excellent شاندار *n.* trained (Christian) priest *v. t.* & *i.* guess something about further events or hidden things not by reason but by intuition وجدان سے کچھ معلوم کرنا ، جان لینا foretell پیشینگوئی کرنا tell by aid of magic دل کا حال جاننا ، غیب دانی کرنا **divination** (div-i-*nay*-shĕn) *n* (esp.) telling by aid of magic دل کا حال جاننا ، غیب دانی کرنا **diviner** *n.* one who divines غیب داں **divining-rod** *n.* rod balanced in hand supposedly to indicate by its dipping whether any water or minerals are present underground thereabouts غیب داں چھڑی **divinely** *adv.* from God خدا کی طرف سے (colloq.)

excellently بڑی اچھی طرح سے **divinity** *n.* quality of being God خدائی ، اُلوہیت God or a deity خدا *the Divine Being*, God خدا theology دینیات

divisible *adj.* **division** *n.* **divisor** *n.* (see under **divide**)

divorce (di-*vo**s) *n.* dissolution of a marriage طلاق separation (*between, of* or *from* things that should go together) جُدائی ، اِفتراق *v. t.* re-lease (someone) from marriage contract طلاق دینا separate (things that usually go together) جُدا کرنا ، الگ کرنا **divorcee** (*-see*) *n.* divorced person طلاق یافتہ ، مُطلّقہ

divulge (di-*vulj*) *v. t.* let out or reveal (secret) فاش کرنا ، ظاہر کرنا ، افشا کرنا **divulgence** *n.* act of divulging افشا ، اِظہار

dizzy (*diz*-i) *adj.* (of a person) giddy ; feeling as if everything were turning round and he were unable to balance himself سرگراں ، چکرایا ہُوا ، سَراسیمہ (of places, etc.) causing giddiness چکّر لانے والا **dizzily** *adv.* in a dizzy manner یُوں جیسے سر چکرا رہا ہو **dizziness** *n.* giddiness چکّر ، دورانِ سَر ، سَرگرانی

do (doo) p. t. *did* ; pa. p. *done* (pr. dun) ; 2nd person sing. present : *dost* (pr. dust) or sometimes *doest* (pr. doo-ist) ; 2nd person sing. past : *didst* or rarely *didest* (pr. *did-est*) ; 3rd person sing. present : *does* (pr. duz) or (old use) *doth* (pr. duth) or rarely *doeth* (pr. doo-ith) ; negative in abbreviated combinations for conversational purposes: *don't* (pr. dohnt) for 'do not' ; *doesn't* (pr. *duz*-ent) for 'does not' ; *didn't* (pr. *did*-ent) for 'did not,' *v.t.* & *i.* perform کرنا ، پُورا کرنا ، لانا *do (one's) duty* اپنا فرض بجالانا *do a service to* کی خدمت کرنا *do a play* ڈرامہ کرنا *do (some role) in (a play)* (کسی ڈرامے) میں (کوئی پارٹ) کرنا *do (so many miles) a day*, travel that much روزانہ (اتنے) میل سفر کرنا *do (so many) copies of* کی (اتنی) نقلیں کرنا *do mischief* شرارت کرنا *do wrong* غلطی کرنا *do wrong to* پر ظلم کرنا perform something for (someone) سے ، کرنا ، کے لیے کرنا ، کو فایدہ یا نقصان پہنچانا *do (someone) a good turn* کسی سے نیکی کرنا *do harm to (someone)* کسی کو نقصان پہنچانا prepare بنانا ، تیار کرنا *The meat isn't done yet* گوشت ابھی اچھا نہیں پکا *do one's lessons* سبق تیار کرنا set in order and tidy ٹھیک کرنا ، صاف کرنا ، مرتب کرنا *do the room* کمرہ صاف کرنا *do one's hair* بال بنانا *do (up) one's shoes*, (*a*) black them جُوتوں پر پالش کرنا (*b*) fasten their laces تسمے باندھنا solve (sum, etc.) (حساب کا سوال) حل کرنا ، نکالنا visit and see all places of interest in کی سیر کرنا *do Karachi* کراچی کی سیر کرنا *do the sights* قابلِ دید مقامات کی سیر کرنا finish ختم کرنا ، پُورا کرنا ، کرچکنا ،

Let us have done with it آؤ اِسے تو ختم کریں serve the purpose سے کام چل جانا fare (*well* or *ill*) *at* or *in* a place, or *to do* (something) میں اچھا یا بُرا رہنا *do well at an examination* امتحان میں اچھا رہنا *How do you do ?* form of greeting to which the reply is the same "How do you do ?" (and not "Thank you," etc.) (The U. S. form, however, is : "*How are you ?*" ; and the reply is : "*Fine ; and how are you ?*") مزاج شریف ؟ ، کیا حال ہے ؟ act عمل کرنا ، کرنا *be up and doing* اٹھو اور کچھ کرو *Do or die* تخت یا تختہ make (a picture of) (کی تصویر) بنانا have dealings (*with*) سے تعلق ہونا ، سے واسطہ پڑنا *do without*, dispense with کے بغیر کام چلا لینا ، کے بغیر گزر بسر کرنا *Nothing doing*, (*a*) no more dealings بس ، اب ختم (*b*) nothing worth doing ہونا ہُوانا کچھ نہیں proceed with, conduct (business, etc.) چلانا (colloq.) cheat, defraud دھوکا دینا *do (someone) out of (something)* دھوکا دے کر لُوٹ لے جانا (*Phrase verbs*) : *do away with*, abolish or get rid of مَوقُوف کرنا ، منسُوخ کرنا ، سے پیچھا چھڑانا *do better*, contend بہترین طور پر (کام یا کوشش کرنا) *do (one's) best*, exert oneself to the utmost پُوری کوشش کرنا *do (one's) bit*, do the little that (one) can حتی المقدُور (کام یا کوشش) کرنا *It does you credit*, it is creditable for you to have done that یہ آپ کے لیے قابلِ فخر ہے۔ *be done for*, be ruined تباہ ہو جانا ، برباد ہو جانا *do for*, (colloq.) act as a housekeeper for کے گھر کا انتظام چلانا *do good to*, bring joy to or lessen the trouble of سے مروّت کرنا *do into (a language)* translate into it میں ترجمہ کرنا *do justice to (food)*, eat it heartily to show that one appreciates it fully پیٹ بھر کر کھانا ، خوب سیر ہو کر کھانا *be done up* be tired out سخت تھک جانا *do up a parcel*, fasten it پارسل باندھنا *do up the house*, repair and paint it گھر کی مرمت وغیرہ کرنا *do-nothing*, good-for-nothing, idler ناکارہ ، نِکمّا *do to death*, (old use) kill مار ڈالنا ، قتل کر دینا *do unto* (old use) treat ; do to سے سلوک کرنا

well-to-do, rich خوش حال ، امیر **done** (dun) *adj.* accomplished ہو چکا ہُوا ، مکمّل accepted منظور **doer** (*doo*-ĕ*) *n.* one who does something کرنے والا **doings** (*doo*-ingz) *n.* (*pl.*) what one does کام کرتُوت big events بڑی بڑی باتیں ▣ To **do** is the general term. We **make** when we manufacture ; **perform** from beginning to end ; **execute** a plan or orders when we carry them out ; **accomplish,** do to the very end ; **achieve,** through effort ; **effect,** as a result ; **attain** something worthwhile ; and **practise** an art or profession.

[2]**do** *substitute verb* (same forms as of **do**) (used variously to avoid repetition of the verb) (اصل فعل کے اعادہ سے بچنے کے لیے) "*Do you hear me ?*" "*Yes I* **do**" (*i.e.*, hear) "کیا تم میری بات سُن رہے ہو ؟" "ہاں سُن تو رہا ہوں"

³do *auxiliary verb* (same form as of ²**do**) (in questions) کیا *Do you know?* کیا تم جانتے ہو؟ (for negation) *I do not know* میں نہیں جانتا (کوئی ترجمہ نہیں) (for emphasis) *I do know* میں یقیناً جانتا ہوں (یقیناً ، لازماً)

⁴do, (abb. of **ditto** which please see)

docile (*doh*-sil) *adj.* easily controlled or managed مطیع ، اطاعت شعار ، تربیت پذیر **docility** (doh-*sil*-i-ti) *n.* تربیت پذیری ، اطاعت شعاری

dock (dok) *n.* place in harbour with *floodgates* (*i.e.*, gates through which water may be let in and out) for ships to stay گودی *dry dock*, dock for repairing ships from which water may be pumped out خشک گودی *floating dock*, movable dry dock متحرک گودی (pl.) (also *dockyard*) row of docks with wharves, sheds, offices, etc. گودیاں ، بندرگاہ enclosure in a criminal court where the accused stands for trial عدالت کا کٹہرا *v.t.* & *i.* (of ships) come or bring into a dock گودی میں آنا یا لایا جانا cut short (an animal's tail, hair, money, supplies, etc.) کم کرنا ، چھوٹا کرنا decrease (wages or supplies) (اجرت یا رسد) کم کرنا

a dry dock

docket (*dok*-et) *n.* list with short summary کیفیت *v.t.* make such a summary کیفیت والی فہرست ، کیفیت والی فہرست بنانا

doctor (*dok*-te*) (abbr. *Dr.*) *n.* man or woman who holds the highest degree given by a university (used also as prefix to name, as *Dr. so-and-so*) ڈاکٹر ، فاضل *Doctor of Science*, (*D.Sc.*) ڈی-ایس سی *Doctor of Literature*, (*D. Lit.* or *D. Litt.*) ڈی لٹ *Doctor of Laws*, (*LL.D.*) ایل ایل-ڈی *Doctor of Philosophy*, (*Ph. D.*, or *D. Phil.*) پی-ایچ-ڈی ، یا ڈی فِل man or woman who has been trained in medical science ڈاکٹر ، ڈاکٹرنی ، طبیب ، حکیم *How is he, Doctor?* ڈاکٹر صاحب! اِس کا کیسا حال ہے؟ very learned person عالم ، عالم *v.t.* (colloq.) treat medically علاج کرنا ، معالجہ کرنا ، علاج معالجہ کرنا adulterate میں ملاوٹ make false (accounts) جعلی (حساب) بنانا **doctorate** (*dok*-to-rayt) *n.* the highest university degree پی-ایچ-ڈی وغیرہ کی ڈگری ، ڈاکٹریٹ ، سندِ فضیلت

doctrine (*dok*-trin) *n.* body of (a religion's) teaching (کسی مذہب کی) تعلیم beliefs (of a religious sect) عقائد principles (of a political party) اصُول dogma, tenet عقیدہ **doctrinaire** *n.* one who strictly applies principles without making allowance for circumstances (opp. of *opportunist*) اصُول پرست **doctrinal** *adj.* of doctrine عقائد سے متعلق

document (*dok*-ew-ment) *n.* written statement used as record or in evidence دستاویز (esp.) a legal deed دستاویز ، تحریر *v.t.* furnish with proofs or authoritative sources سندیں پیش کرنا **documentary** (dok-ew-*ment*-a-ri) *adj.* in the form of a document دستاویزی *n.* film dealing with official publicity or any field of knowledge, etc. دستاویزی فلم

dodge (doj) *v.t.* & *i.* change position quickly in order to escape or avoid something (سے) بچنا ، (وار) خالی دینا ، اِدھر اُدھر ہو جانا get round (difficulties, etc.) by cunning or mean tricks. حیلے بہانے کرنا evade (a questioner or question) گول مول جواب دینا *n.* mean trick داؤ ، داؤ پیچ ، چال evasion بچنا zigzag movement for eluding an assailant اِدھر اُدھر ہٹنا ingenious method چال **dodgy** *adj.* (esp.) ingenious حیلہ جُو ، بہانہ ساز **dodger** *n.* (esp.) shifty person بات پر قائم نہ رہنے والا

dodo (*doh*-doh) *n.* an extinct type of bird ناپید شے ، تقویمِ پارینہ (symbolically used as type of) what is dead and gone

doe (doh) *n.* female of fallow deer ہرنی female of rabbit and hare مادہ خرگوش **doeskin** (*doh*-skin) *n.* skin of doe ہرن کا چمڑا such cloth ہرن کھال نما کپڑا

doer, does (see under ¹**do**)

doff (dof) *v.t.* do off, take off (clothes, hat, etc.) اُتارنا

dog *n.* common domestic animal of various breeds کتا any sort of fellow شخص *a gay dog* خوش باش *a miserable dog* بدنصیب ، بیچارا *dog biscuits* کتوں کے لیے بسکٹ *Every dog has his day* بارہ برس بعد گھورے کے بھی دن پھرتے ہیں *v.t.* follow and watch closely (one, or one's steps) تعاقب کرنا ، پیچھے لگے رہنا *dog-tired*, very tired تھک کر چُور *dogcart*, tonga ٹم ٹم *dogdays*, hot season گرمیاں *rain cats and dogs*, rain heavily موسلادھار بارش ہونا *dog's ear*, (*a*) *n.* corner of page curved with use وَرَق کا مُڑا ہُوا گوشہ (*b*) *v.t.* make dog's ear in a book (نشانی کے لیے) ، کتاب کے وَرَق کا گوشہ موڑنا *dog-sleep*, broken sleep بے آرامی کی نیند *dog-watch*, half watch lasting two hours آدھا پہر *she-dog*, usual term for a bitch (being politer than that word) کتیا *a dead dog*, (*a*) useless person نکما ، ناکارہ (*b*) order to a trained dog to lie motionless! کتے! لیٹ جاؤ *dog's life*, miserable life مصیبت کے دن (*lead someone*) *a dog's life*, persecute him کسی کو تنگ کرنا ، زچ کرنا *dog in the manger*, one who will neither enjoy anything or allow others to do so جو نہ کھیلے نہ کھیلنے دے *dog-like devotion*, great devotion سخت وفاداری *go to the dogs*, be ruined برباد ہونا *throw to the dogs*, waste, squander اُجاڑنا ، ضائع کرنا **dogged** (*dog*-ed) *adj* persistent مستقل مزاج ، دُھن کا پکا **dog-**

gedly *adv.* perseveringly مستقل مزاجی سے، اِستقلال سے **doggedness** *n.* اِستقلال، ہٹ، ضِد **doggy** (*dog*-i) *adj.* devoted to dogs کُتّوں کا پیارا *n.* (also **doggie**) nursery term for dog (کُتّے کے لیے بچّوں کا لفظ) تتّا

loggerel (*dog*-è-rel) *n.* inexpert and unpoetic verse تُک بندی

ogma (*dog*-ma) *n.* belief or system of beliefs (esp. religious) to be accepted as true without question عقیدہ، عقائد **dogmatic** (dog-*mat*-ik) *adj.* put forward as dogma اِعتقادی asserted positively without proof (بے دلیل بات) (of a person) stating purely personal opinions as if they were dogmas بِلا وجہ زور دینے والا (شخص) اڑیل، ہٹ دھرم **dogmatize** (*dog*-ma-tɪz) *v.t.* make dogmatic statements بے دلیل باتیں کرنا lay down the law قانون بنانا **dogmatism** (*dog*-ma-tizm) dogmatizing temper or habit اڑیل پسندی

oldrums (dol-*drums*) *n.* (*pl.*) regions of windless calm near the equator (*be in*) *the doldrums* (be in) a depressed state دِل گیر ہونا، مایوس ہونا

ole (dohl) *n.* charitable gift of measured form خیرات woe رنج، غم *v.t.* (*dole out*), give (food, money, etc.) in small amounts (*to* the poor) (کو) خیرات دینا give like a miser کنجوسوں کی طرح دینا، تھوڑا تھوڑا **doleful** (*dohl*-ful) *adj.* sad, gloomy, woeful غمناک

ll (dol) *n.* toy baby for a child to play with گڑیا، لُعبت pretty but silly woman احمق حسینہ *painted dolls,* silly young pretty women going about with costly make-up بنی ٹھنی گُڑیاں، سجی بنی بیوقوف

llar (*dol*-ē*) *n.* U. S. coin worth about Rs. 5 ڈالر coin of some other countries ڈالر

lphin (*dol*-fin) *n.* sea-animal like a small whale ڈالفن

t (dohlt) *n.* stupid fellow احمق، گدھا **doltish** *adj.* stupid احمق

m (dum) *suf.* for making nouns denoting state ی، ت، یت، کی حالت (as free*dom* آزادی، حُرّیت) possessions of (as king*dom* مملکت، سلطنت) rank ی، ت (as king*dom* بادشاہی، بادشاہت)

main (do-*mayn*) *n.* territory under the rule of a king, government, etc. landed estate جاگیر، زمینداری field or scope (of thought, knowledge, activity) میدان

me (dohm) *n.* large rounded roof with circular base looking like inverted cup گنبد (poetry) stately building سربفلک عمارت sky آسمان

a dome

mestic (do-*mes*-tik) *adj.* of the home or husehold گھریلو، خانگی *domestic servants* خانگی ملازم of the home country and not foreign or international داخلی *domestic policy* داخلی سیاست (of animals) kept by or living with man (opposite of *wild*) پالتو **domesticate** *v. t.* tame (animals) سدھانا **domesticated** (-ed) *adj.* fond of home-life خانہ نشین (of animals) tame پالتو، سدھائے ہوئے **domesticity** (-*tis*-i-ti) *n.* home-life with its sentiments گھریلو زندگی

domicile (*dom*-i-sɪl, or -sil) *n.* dwelling-place مسکونت، جائے بود و باش، وطن **domiciled** (*dom*-i-sɪld, or sild) *adj.* having domicile (*in* or *at*) ساکن، متوطن

dominate (*dom*-i-nayt) *v. t.* & *i.* have control, authority or commanding influence over حکومت کرنا، غلبہ یا تسلّط رکھنا (of a high place) overlook (another place) (کسی اونچی جگہ سے کسی جگہ کا) نظر آنا **dominant** *adj.* established in power حاکم، مُسلّط، بااثر most important اہم، نمایاں **dominance** *n.* being established in power تسلّط، غلبہ **domination** (-*ay*-) *n.* dominating غلبہ پانا being dominated زیرِ تسلّط آنا

domineer (dom-i-*nee*-è*) *v. t.* act or speak imperiously تحکمانہ انداز سے کہنا یا کرنا **domineering** *adj.* imperious تحکمانہ

dominion (do-*min*-yun) *n.* rule, control تسلّط، حکومت (often *pl.*) lands or nations ruled over سلطنت محروسہ، ممالکِ محروسہ (*Dominion*), one of the self-governing members of the British Commonwealth ڈومینین، (برطانوی) نوآبادی *Dominion status,* status of a Dominion ڈومینین سٹیٹس، درجہ نوآبادیات

dominoes (*dom*-i-nohz) *n. pl.* (sing., *domino*) table game played with 28 small flat pieces of wood (each called a *domino*) ڈامی نوز

don (don) *n.* university teacher (جامعہ کا) مدرّس (*Don*), Spanish title (used before a man's name) ڈان **Don Juan** (don-*joo*-an) libertine hero of Spanish legend who is also the hero of an opera by Mozart, a poem by Byron and a play by Shaw ڈان جوان any attractive libertine رنگین اوباش **Don Quixote** (don-*kwik*-sot, or don-kee-*hoh*-tay) enthusiastic visionary who neglects own interests in comparison with honour or devotion (actually the name of the hero of a Spanish romance of the name rendered into Urdu by سرشار as "خدائی فوجدار" تنتاجہ) ڈان کوئکزوٹ، خدائی فوجدار

donna *n.* (*fem.*) Spanish or Italian lady (ہسپانوی یا اطالوی) خاتون *prima donna*, chief female singer in an opera (ناٹک یا غنائیہ کی) اوّلین مُطربہ

donate (do-*nayt*) *v. t.* give (money, etc., *to* a cause, etc.) دینا، عطیہ دینا، عطا کرنا **donor** (*doh*-nē*) *n.*

giver منتقلی ، دینے والا *blood donor* خون دینے والا **donation** (do-*nay*-shĕn) *n.* giving عطیہ دینا something given عطیہ

donkey (*donk*-i) *n.* (ordinary colloq. term for an) ass گدھا (of persons) (used as a playful substitute for *ass*) silly احمق ، گدھا

donna (see under **don**)

donor *n.* (see under **donate**)

don't (dohnt) abb. of '*do not*' مت ، نہ **don'ts** *n. pl.* pieces of negative advice قدغن ، **doodle** (*dood*-ĕl) *v.t.* scrawl aimlessly while thinking of something else بے خیالی میں لکیریں کھینچنا *n.* such scrawl بے خیالی میں کھینچی ہوئی لکیریں *n.* (see *Addenda*)

doom ruin تباہی ، فنا death موت (usu. evil) destiny (بُرا) انجام *meet one's doom, go to one's doom* بُرائی کا بدلہ پانا *know one's doom* اپنا انجام جاننا (also *doomsday*) the Last Judgment یوم آخرت ، آخرت *'The Doomsday Book'*, official record of English lands made in 1086 (after the Norman Conquest) ڈُومزڈے بُک ، کتاب آخرت *till the crack of doom* حشر تک *v. t.* give punishment سزا دینا ، سزا کا حکم سنانا **doomed** (doomd) *adj.* condemned (*to* or *to do* something) جسے سزا ملی ہو facing a certain death تباہ ہونے والا

door (doh*) *n.* hinged barrier for closing the entrance to a room, building, carriage, etc. دروازہ ، کواڑ *indoor*, inside the room اندرونی *outdoor*, outside بیرونی *out of doors*, in the open باہر *indoor games*, (games like chess) played in the room گھر کے کھیل *outdoor games*, games played in the open باہر کے کھیل ، میدانی کھیل *open the door (of something) to*, make (something) possible for دروازہ کھولنا ، کو ممکن بنانا *shut the door (of something) upon*, make (something) impossible for کا دروازہ بند کرنا ، کو ناممکن بنانا *show (someone) the door*, turn him out نکالنا ، بیک بینی و دو گوش نکالنا ، نکال ، باہر نکالنا *see the man about the door*, polite form for taking leave to go to answer the call of nature بیٹھ اٹھنا جانا *lay (blame, etc.) at the door of (someone)*, blame (him) کو الزام دینا *(of a blame, etc.) lie at the door of*, be imputed to پر الزام آنا *(be) at death's door*, (be) dying or in danger of death بستر مرگ پر ہونا *next-door*, (in or to) the next house ساتھ والا گھر ساتھ والے گھر *door-keeper*, attendant at door دربان *door-mat*, mat for rubbing boots on before entering پائدان *door-nail*, nail with which a door is studded (دروازے کی) سجاوٹی کیل *dead as a door-nail*, dead مردہ ، بے حس وحرکت **doorway** *n.* opening (to be) filled by a door راستہ دروازہ

dope (dohp) *n.* (colloq.) narcotic drug (*e.g.*, opium) نشہ *v.t.* make (someone) unconscious with (a narcotic) نشہ کھلانا

dormant (*do**-mant) *adj.* in a state of inactivity but waiting development or activity خوابیدہ *dormant volcano*, inactive one خوابیدہ آتش فشاں

dormitory (*do**-mi-tĕ-ri) *n.* sleeping-room for many in a hostel ڈارمیٹری ، اقامتگاہ میں ایک سے زیادہ کے لیے کمرہ

dormouse (*do**-mous) *n.* (pl. *dormice*) small mouse-like animal which hibernates (*i.e.*, sleeps throughout the winter) and is sometimes kept as a pet ڈارماؤس ، خواب موش

a dormouse

dose (dohz) *n.* amount (of medicine, etc. administered at one time (دوا وغیرہ کی) خوراک *dose of flattery* ایک بار کی خوشامد *v.t.* give dose to (دوا وغیرہ کی) خوراک پلانا یا دینا

dot *n.* tiny round mark نقطہ *v.t.* (-tt-) mar[k] with a dot نقطہ ڈالنا ، نقطے لگانا *dot the i's and cro[ss] the t's*, make the meanings or details clear مطلب واضح کرنا make a line with dots نقطے ڈالنا *a dotted line* نقطوں کی لکیر *dotted about*, scattere[d] here and there منتشر ، بکھرا ہوا marked wi[th] جس میں کہیں کہیں ہوں

dotage *n.* (see under **dote**)

dote (doht) *v.i.* be feeble-minded confusi[ng] fancies with realities owing to old age سٹھیا جانا مخبوط الحواس ہونا (*dote upon*), be passionate[ly] fond of کا شیدا ہونا ، پر فریفتہ ہونا **doting** *adj.* pa[s]sionately fond شیدائی فریفتہ **dotage** *n.* childis[h]ness of old age when one becomes fond [of] repeating the 'anecdotes' of one's youth the[re]by boring others سٹھیاپا *(be) in one's dotage*, foolish in age سٹھیا جانا

double (*dub*-ĕl) twice as much or as ma[ny] دُگنا being in pairs or two similar parts والا *double barrel, double-barrelled gun* دو نالی بندوق دو ویہ folded over دوہرا ، تہ کیا ہوا made for serving two persons, purposes or things دو کے لیے *work a double tide*, undertake two jobs دو نوکری دینا ambiguous ذومعنی deceitful دھوکے باز ، مکار ، چالباز *double-dealing* دھوکے بازی ، منافقت ، چالبازی منافق *adv.* (fol[lowed] by *the* or *as*) twice دُگنا ، دوچند *do[uble] the price of* کا دوگنی قیمت سے *double as dear* مہنگا in pairs or as one of a pair دوگانہ ، دو دو *ri[de] horse double* گھوڑے پر دوگانہ جانا *see double*, get dou[ble] images of things ایک کے دو دو دیکھنا looked at twice (as much) دُگنا *to cost double* قیمت ہونا deceitfully چالبازی سے ، دو رُخی چال چل کر *play dou[ble]* *play a double game*, pretend devotion to each the opposed parties دوُرخی چال چلنا *n.* person's wraith ہمزاد person or thing mistakable for another ہُو بہو وہی double quantity دوچند game between two pairs of players دو جوڑوں کا کھیل sharp turn موڑ (military drill) (also called *double time*) running pace ڈبل مارچ، ڈبل، معمولی دوڑ *at the double* ڈبل مارچ کرتے ہوئے *v.t.* & *i.* make or become double دُوگنا ہونا یا کرنا (in drill) go at the double ڈبل مارچ کرنا، آہستہ دوڑنا (of a ship or a sailor) get round (cape, etc.) کاچکر کاٹ کر جانا make sudden turn (often *back*) یکایک مُڑنا clench (fist) مُٹھی (بھینچنا bend or fold (*up*) twice تہ کرنا دوہرا ہونا، تہ کرنا *double up*, (*a*) fold up تہ کرنا (*b*) (of a person) bend the body with pain drawing knees and chest close together درد سے دوہرا ہونا (یا) جھکنا *double-breasted coat*, one made to overlap at buttons دوہرے پیش کا کوٹ، ڈبل بریسٹ کوٹ *double-chin*, fat person's chin with a fold of flesh coming forward below it دوہری ٹھوڑی *double-dealer*, one who deceives (esp. in business) دھوکے باز *double dome*, (see *Addenda*) *double-dyed*, confirmed (scoundrel) بدمعاش *double-edged* (*sword*), (*a*) sword with two edges دو دھاری تلوار (*b*) point damaging to user as well as used دو دھاری تلوار '*double entendre*', (use of) phrase capable of two meanings ذُو معنی لفظ *double-entry* (*book-keeping*), system with two entries for every item of account دوہرا کھاتہ *double-faced*, hypocritical مُنافق *double game*, duplicity منافقت *double quick*, (*a*) at the double دوڑتے ہوئے (*b*) with double the speed دُگنی رفتار سے *double-cross*, (*a*) *v.t.* cheat (both parties) دوُرخی سے کام لینا، فریقین سے دھوکا کرنا (*b*) *n.* such act دوُرخی، فریقین سے دھوکا *double-crosser n.* one who double-crosses دوُرخی چال چلنے والا، فریقین سے دھوکا کرنا *double-talk*, (see *Addenda*); *double-think*, (see *Addenda*) **doubly** (*dub*-li) *adv.* twice the amount دوہرا

doubt (dout) *n.* uncertainty of knowledge شک وشبہ *answer a doubt* شبہ رفع کرنا *give* (*someone*) *the benefit of doubt*, suppose (him) innocent شبہ کا فائدہ دینا، شبے کا فائدہ دیتے ہوئے بَری کرنا feeling of uncertainty شک، ارتیاب *in doubt*, uncertain شک میں، مُتشکّک *no doubt*, presumably غالباً *beyond doubt* یقینی *out of doubt* شک کے باعث *without doubt*, certainly یقیناً objection اعتراض face one's doubts *throw doubt on* (question, or the truth of) کو شک کی نگاہ سے دیکھنا *have* (*one's*) *doubts*, not be satisfied with the truth of something مطمئن نہ ہونا *v.t.* & *i.* feel doubt (*about* or *of*) شبہ کرنا، شک وشبہ کی نگاہ سے دیکھنا، شک کرنا **doubtful** *adj.* causing doubt مشکوک، مشتبہ feeling doubt شک کرنے والا، شکی **doubtless** *adv* probably غالباً

douceur (doo-*se**) *n.* bribe, etc. to ensure good will نذرانہ، خدمت، رشوت

douche (doosh) *n.* jet of water applied to some part of body (usu. internally) ڈُوش، پچکاری، پانی کی پچکاری *v.t.* administer douche to ڈُوش کرنا، پچکاری کرنا، پانی کی پچکاری کرنا

dough (doh) *n.* kneaded mixture of flour and water (for making bread, etc.) گندھا ہوا آٹا **doughnut** *n.* sweet fried cake of dough میٹھی ٹکیا، میٹھی روٹی

doughty (*dou*-ti) *adj.* (old use) brave بہادر (jocular) formidable خوفناک، دہشتناک

dour (doo*) *adj.* (of a person) stern سخت (of his appearance) grim کرخت

dove (dov) (also called *ring-dove*) *n.* bird of pigeon family known for its cooing note قمری، فاختہ *turtle-dove*, a kind of dove ٹوٹرو symbol of peace اَمن (کی علامت) kind-hearted and peaceful person نیک دل، صُلح جو **dove-cot, dove-cote** *n.* pigeon-house کابک **dove-tail** (*duv*-tayl) *v.t.* & *i.* join by inserting one piece (into) another چوُل سے چوُل بٹھانا (یا) بیٹھ جانا fit together جوڑ بٹھانا combine (plants, etc.) ingeniously دانشمندی سے ملانا *n.* joint made to look like a dove's tail dove-tailing نرمادگی (کی چوُل)

dowager (*dov*-a-jĕ*) *n.* widow with title or property derived from husband خطاب یا جاگیر والی بیوہ *the Queen dowager* بیوہ ملکہ *the dowager duchess* بیوہ نواب بیگم

dowdy (*dou*-di) *adj.* (of clothes, house, furniture, etc.) unfashionable پرانی وضع کا دقیانوسی (of women) unfashionable and awkwardly dressed بھدّے لباس والی دقیانوسی **dowdily** *adv.* awkwardly بھدّے پن سے

down (doun) *adv.* from above (opp. of up) نیچے *flow down* (پانی وغیرہ کا) نشیب کی طرف جانا *go down*, (of the sun, or of a boat) sink ڈوبنا away from the north or from a prominent place like a capital or university (*to*) جانا to a lower status تک to a lower condition نیچے، پستی کی طرف، خراب حالت میں *come down in the world* دنیا کی نظروں میں گرنا *worn down with use* استعمال سے گھسا ہوا (of payment) immediately فوراً، فوری *cash down* نقد till humbled or captured رُسوا ہو کر، پکڑے جا کر to a less agitated state ٹھنڈا *calm down* ٹھنڈا کرنا from an earlier to later time سے on paper کاغذ پر *write* (*something*) *down* لکھنا *take* (*something*) *down* قلمبند کرنا to another state ہو کر *boil down to* مدعا مطلب یہ ہونا کہ

seriously سنجیدگی سے *get down to business* کام کی طرف متوجہ ہونا *prep.* at a lower level or towards a lower part of نیچے کی طرف *v.t.* (colloq.) defeat نیچا دکھانا شکست دینا bring down نیچے لانا ، پچھاڑ کرنا put down ڈال دینا ، رکھ دینا *to down tools*, (of workers) to refuse to work (as a method of strike) (مزدوروں کا) ہڑتال کرنا *pen-down strike*, strike by clerks (منشیوں کی) ہڑتال *adj.* (no comparative or superlative degree) made of down پروں کا lowered نیچا ، گرا ہوا ، افتادہ *down and out*, (a) *adj.* & *n.* (person) beaten in the struggle of life پٹا ہوا مہرہ ، بیمار ، بخار میں مبتلا *down with fever* بیماری میں مبتلا ، صاحبِ فراش from a higher or bigger place زیریں ، پائیں *down train* زیریں گاڑی *n.* open highland کشادہ سطح مرتفع (*pl.*) chalk uplands of South England (برطانیہ کی) کھریا کی پہاڑیاں fine plumage of young birds نرم پر soft hair on human face خط ، سبزہ ، رُوئیں (*pl.*) adversity سختی *ups and downs*, good and bad fortune (زندگی کے) نشیب و فراز *down at heels*, with worn out boot-heels جوتے کی ایڑیاں گھسی ہوئی *be down on one's luck*, repine قسمت کو کوسنا *down on* (or *upon*), treating (one or one's conduct) severely پر سختی کرنا *down on the nail*, (of payment) immediate فوری ، نقد **downcast** (*doun*-kahst) *adj.* (of a person) sad مغموم (of eyes) looking downwards نیچی **downhill** (*doun*-hill) *n.*, *adj.* & *adv.* at or towards the foot of the hill (پہاڑ کی چوٹی سے) نیچے کی طرف **downstream** *n.*, *adj.* & *adv.* at or towards the end of the stream to which it flows ندی کے بہاؤ کی طرف ، بہاؤ کے رُخ **downfall** (*doun*-fawl) *n.* sudden fall from power or prosperity زوال downpour مُوسلا دھار بارش ، بوچھار *down to the ground*, (colloq.) entirely بالکل ، یکسر **down-hearted** *adj.* sad مغموم **downpour** (*doun*-poh*) *n.* heavy fall (esp. of rain) مُوسلا دھار بارش ، بوچھاڑ **down platform**, platform from which down trains start زیریں پلیٹ فارم **downright** (*doun*-rɪt) *adj.* straightforward صاف گو honest دیانتدار ، دیانتدارانہ thorough بالکل ، نہایت ، یکسر *adv.* thoroughly بالکل ، نہایت *downright scared* نہایت مقدس **downstairs** *n.*, *adj.* & *adv.* (*to*, *at* or *on*) lower floor نچلی منزل *down town*, into the town from higher part شہر کو ، شہر میں **downtrodden** *adj.* oppressed مظلوم ، شہر سے دبے ہوئے *adv.* & *adj.* downwards نیچے (کی طرف) *adv.* leading or pointing towards what is lower نیچے *down with* (*something*), cry (or slogan) for its downfall مُردہ باد **downy** *adj.* covered with down رُوئیں دار made of down پروں کا soft like down پروں جیسا نرم

dowry (*dou*-ri) *n.* property, etc., which a wife brings to her husband in her marriage جہیز

doyen (*dwa*-yohn) *n.* senior member of a body of colleagues بڑا

doze (dohz) *v.i.* sleep lightly اُونگھنا doze off اُونگھ جانا sleep by snatches at odd times لینا *n.* short, light sleep اُونگھ ، جھپکی *go off into a doze, fall into a doze*, doze off اُونگھ جانا

dozen (*duz*-en) *n.* (abb *doz.*) (pl., *dozen* or *dozens*) set of twelve درجن a dozen bottles ایک درجن بوتلیں two dozen bottles دو درجن بوتلیں *two dozens of bottles* کئی درجن بوتلیں *several dozen bottles* دو درجن بوتلیں *some dozens of bottles* چند درجن بوتلیں *dozens of times*, many times کئی بار *to the dozen, per dozen* فی درجن *a baker's dozen*, thirteen تیرہ *talk nineteen to the dozen*, talk incessantly مسلسل بولتے جانا

Dr. (abbr. for *Doctor*) ڈاکٹر *Dr. Iqbal* ڈاکٹر اقبال **dr.** (abb. of *debtor*) قرضدار *Dr. & Cr. account*, debit and credit side of the account, (کھاتے میں) جمع و خرچ

drab *n.* dull light-brown colour بھورا رنگ loose woman چھنال *adj.* of this colour بھورا monotonous and uninteresting بے کیف *lead a drab existence* بے کیف زندگی گزارنا

drachm (dram) *n.* the weight *dram* (which see) ڈرام Greek coin (also called *drachma*) دِرہم ، درم

draconian (dra-*koh*-ni-an) *adj.* (of laws, etc.) rigorous like the Athenian Draco's code of laws (promulgated in 621 B. C.) in which even petty offences were punishable with death سخت سخت گیرانہ

draft (drahft) *n.* first rough copy of a document مسودہ *draft for a letter* مُراسلہ کا مسودہ *put up a draft for approval* (سرکاری مُراسلے کا) مسودہ منظوری کے لیے پیش کرنا rough sketch (*of* building or a machine) نقشہ written order for payment of money by bank draft on a bank ہُنڈی ، ڈرافٹ ، برات drawing of money by means of a draft ڈرافٹ کے ذریعے روپیہ منگوانا group of men (esp. soldiers) chosen from a larger group for reinforcement or other special purpose (بالخصوص فوج کا) خاص دستہ *v.t.* make a draft of (a document) مسودہ تیار کرنا *draft a bill for the Legislature* مقننہ کے لیے بل کا مسودہ تیار کرنا make a sketch or plan of (work to be done) نقشہ بنانا choose men for a draft خاص دستہ تیار کرنا **draftsman** (*drahfts*-man) *n.* one who drafts documents (دستاویزوں کا) مسودہ بنانے والا (cf. *draughtsman*)

drag *v.t.* & *i.* (-gg-) pull along (cart or someone) slowly with effort and difficulty کھینچنا

گھسیٹنا move slowly گھسٹتے ہوئے چلنا trail along the ground پیچھے پیچھے گھسٹنا (of time or work) go (on) tediously مشکل سے گزرنا یا کٹنا یا کام تھا (of a meeting, etc.) protract دیر تک جاری رہنا use net, etc. (called *drag* or *dragnet*) to search the bottom of (river, etc.) for fish or for something lost in it) تھا جال پھینکنا check (wheel, etc., with an iron shoe called a *drag*) روک لگانا *n.* (also *dragnet*), net with grapnel pulled over the bottom of a river to catch fish or something lost تھا جال iron shoe to retard motion of wheel بریک، روک something that slows down progress رکاوٹ

dragon (*drag*-un) *n.* (in old stories) fabulous or extinct firebreathing monster, looking like a winged crocodile اژدہا، اژدر **dragonfly** *n.* winged insect with stick-like body کالی تتلی

a dragon

a dragonfly

dragoon (dra-*goon*) *n.* soldier on horseback پیادہ فوج میں سوار *v. t.* force (people *into* something, or *into doing* something) (کو) مجبور کرنا، پر اجبر کرنا

drain (drayn) *n.* pipe channel for carrying away unwanted liquids نالی continuous and exhaustive demand (*on* resources) نقصان، مسلسل نکاس *v. t.* & *i.* lead (*off*) (liquid) by means of drains نالی یا پمپ کے ذریعے پانی نکالنا (of liquid) take or flow away بہ جانا یا بہائے جانا drink up (liquid) پی لینا *drain to dregs*, empty (the vessel by drinking up its contents) تلچھٹ تک پی جانا (cause to) lose (strength or resources) by degrees (طاقت دولت وغیرہ) نچوڑ لینا **drainage** *n.* draining or being drained پانی کا نکلنا یا نکالنا system of drains نالیاں، نالیوں کے جال

drake (drayk) *n.* male duck بطٰ، بلخ، نر بطٰ

dram, drachm (dram) *n.* 1/16 ounce avoirdupois ڈرام 1/8 ounce for medical substances طبی ڈرام

drama (*drah*-ma) *n.* play for the theatre ڈراما ناٹک، تمثیل art of writing and performing plays تمثیل نگاری، ڈرامہ نویسی (of real situation) series of events leading to a climax ڈرامائی صورت حال، بحران، عجیب وغریب صورت حال **dramatic** (dra-*mat*-ik) *adj.* of drama ڈرامائی تمثیل کا (of real situation) sudden and thrilling like an event in a drama ڈرامائی، ناگہانی، عجیب وغریب بحرانی **dramatics** (dra-*mat*-iks) *n. pl.* dramatic performances ڈرامے پیش کرنا، ناٹک، ڈرامے **dramatically** *adv.* in a dramatic manner ڈرامائی انداز سے، عجیب انداز سے *dramatis personae* (*dram*-a-tis-pě*-*soh*-nee) *n. pl.*, but often used as *sing.*) characters of a drama تمثیل کے کردار، کردار a list of them کرداروں کی فہرست، کردارنامہ

dramatist (*dram*-a-tist) *v.t.* playwright ڈرامہ نویس، ڈراما نویس، تمثیل نگار **dramatize** (*dram*-a-tīz) *v. t.* turn (a story, etc.) into a drama کا ڈراما بنانا، کو تمثیلی صورت دینا، کی تمثیل بنانا *dramatized version* تمثیل، تمثیلی صورت *dramatized version* (*of novel*, etc.) (ناول وغیرہ کی) تمثیلی صورت **dramatization** (dram-a-ti-*zay*-shěn) *n.* conversion (*of* a novel or story) تمثیل بنانا

S A **drama** is a serious conflict of two wills; a **tragedy** is a struggle against a superior force; a **comedy** is a fight against one's own mistaken notions, or against a foolish convention; a **farce** is a chain of incongruous and irrelevant effects, produced for the sole purpose of provoking laughter; an **opera** is a musical drama.

drank p. t. of **drink** (which see)

drape (drayp) *v.t.* hang (curtains, clothing, etc.) in graceful folds (*round* or *over* something) لگانا decorate (*with* cloth, flags, etc.) آراستہ کرنا

draper *n.* shopkeeper dealing in cloth or articles of clothing بزاز **drapery** *n.* trade of or goods sold by a draper بزازی clothing, curtains, etc., draped round something گرد لپٹا ہوا کپڑا

drastic (*dras*-tik) *adj.* (of actions, methods, medicines) producing a strong effect سخت، شدید *drastic action*, strong measures like exemplary punishment سخت کارروائی *take drastic measure* سخت اقدام کرنا **drastically** *adv.* severely سختی سے

draught (drahft) *n.* current of air in a room, chimney, or other shut-in place, ہوا کی رَو، ہوا کا جھونکا pulling in of a net of fish جال کھینچنا the fish drawn out with it جال میں آنے والی مچھلیاں depth of water needed to float a ship جہاز کے بہنے پانی کی گہرائی dose of liquid medicine خوراک one continuous act of drinking گھونٹ، جرعہ (of animals) used for drawing vehicle or plough بہنے پانی کی گہرائی (*pl.*) (*draughts*), table game played on a chess-board (called a *draughtboard*) by two players using 24 flat, round pieces (called *draughtsmen*) ڈرافٹس **draughty** *adj* with draughts of air blowing through جس میں ہوا کے جھونکے آئیں **draughtsman** (*drahfts*-man) *n.* a piece in draughts ڈرافٹس کا مہرہ fem. *draughtswoman*) one who makes sketches or plans for machines or buildings ڈرافٹسمین، نقشہ نویس (cf. *draftsman*) **draughtsmanship** *n.* being good at such drawings نقشہ نویسی **Note:** Of the doublets **draftsman** and **draughtsman**, preferably the former (**draftsman**) is used for one who drafts documents, the latter (**draughtsman**) for one who draws sketches or plans.

draw *v. t.* & *i.* (drew, draw) *n.* haul ; (of engine, horse, etc.) cause to move (train, coach, etc.) after or behind by pulling کھینچنا move by pulling کھینچنا ، لے جانا *draw (someone) aside* (کسی کو) ایک طرف لے جانا pull out (tooth, cork, sword) نکالنا receive or obtain (salary, rations, etc.) from a source وُصول کرنا، پانا، لینا take out (water *from* a well) نکالنا move in a specified direction, etc. ہٹنا ، جانا ، آنا *draw back* پیچھے ہٹنا ، رُک جانا ، دستکش *draw near* قریب آنا *draw to a close* ختم ہونا take in (breath, etc.) کھینچنا ، لینا attract (attention, customers, etc.) مائل کرنا infer نکالنا *draw a conclusion* نتیجے پر پہنچنا ، نتیجہ نکالنا (10) sketch ; execute a drawing (کی تصویر) کھینچنا دینا (11) issue (a cheque *on* a bank) (چیک) کاٹنا (12) be equal (*with*) (کھیل یا لڑائی میں) برابر رہنا ، (کھیل یا لڑائی کا) ہار جیت کے فیصلے کے بغیر ختم ہو جانا ، غیر فیصلہ کُن رہنا *a drawn battle* غیر فیصلہ کُن لڑائی *drawn match* ہار جیت کے بغیر ختم ہونے والا میچ (13) get by chance لاٹری میں *draw lots* لاٹری نکالنا، قرعہ اندازی کرنا (14) write (*up* or *out* a deed, etc.) (دستاویز وغیرہ) مُرتّب کرنا یا لکھنا (15) need water to float (پانی کی) گہرائی چاہنا تیرنے کے لیے (16) make longer کھینچنا ، بنانا ، طُول دینا *draw wire* دھات کے تار بنانا *long drawn-out discussions* طویل بحث (17) get (information, etc., *from* a witness) سے کہلوانا *draw (someone) out* کہلوانا (18) disembowel (fowl, etc.) for cooking (ذبیحہ کو) صاف کرنا (19) search (covert) for game بھٹ میں سے نکالنا *draw down vengeance upon*, invoke vengeance سے اِنتقام لینا *draw out*, cross out کاٹنا ، قلم زن کرنا *draw in*, (of days) get shorter (دن) چھوٹے ہونا *draw out*, (of days) get longer (دن) لمبے ہونا *draw (someone) in*, persuade (him) to join آمادہ کرنا *draw in (one's) horns*, become cautious محتاط ہو جانا *draw the long bow*, (*a*) exaggerate مُبالغہ کرنا (*b*) tell lying tales بے بنیاد قصّے سُنانا *Draw it mild !* (colloq.) avoid exaggeration مُبالغے سے کام مت لو ، مُبالغہ مت کرو *draw up*, (*a*) (of a carriage, etc.) stop رُکنا (*b*) (of troops) get into formation صف بستہ ہونا *draw (oneself) up*, assume a stiff attitude سینہ تاننا *draw rein*, check (horse) (گھوڑے کی) باگیں کھینچنا *draw the cloth*, clear the dining table after meal (and esp. before desert) بڑھانا ، میز صاف کرنا ، دسترخوان اُٹھانا *draw stumps (for the day)*, cease to play cricket (that day) (کرکٹ میں) اِس روز کا کھیل ختم کرنا *n.* act of drawing کھینچنا someone or something that draws attention or attracts دِلکش ، دِلفریب drawing of lots قرعہ اندازی raffle لاٹری a game or battle in which neither side wins غیر فیصلہ کُن مقابلہ ، ہار جیت کے فیصلے کے بغیر ختم ہونے والا مقابلہ *end in a draw* ہار جیت کے فیصلے کے بغیر ختم ہو جانا **drawn** *adj.* (of face, eye) haggard through strain or worry ستا ہُوا (of match or battle) ending in neither side's victory غیر فیصلہ کُن ، ہار جیت کے فیصلے کے بغیر ختم ہونے والا **drawback** *n.* defect, disadvantage خرابی ، عیب ، نقص **draw-bridge** *n.* bridge that can be pulled up at the end(s) by chains اُٹھاؤ پُل **drawer** (*draw-ĕ**) *n.* one who draws کھینچنے والا box-like container which slides in and out of furniture, etc., used for clothes, papers, etc. دراز *a chest of drawers*, دراز **drawers** (*draw-ĕ**z) *n. pl.* (also *pair of drawers*) tight two-legged trousers used under the pant دراز ، زیر جامہ **drawee** (draw-*ee*) *n* one on whom bill or draft is drawn جس کے نام چیک کاٹا جائے

drawing (*draw*-ing) *n.* act of drawing کھینچنا some sketch, figure, etc., drawn with pencil, pen or crayon تصویر ، خاکہ drawing of sketches, etc. تصویر کشی ، ڈرائنگ *teach drawing* تصویر کشی سکھانا ، ڈرائنگ سکھانا *a drawing class* ڈرائنگ کی جماعت *drawing-paper*, stiff and rough paper used for drawings ڈرائنگ پیپر ، تصویر کشی کا کاغذ *drawing-pin*, with flat head, used for fastening drawing paper to a drawing-board ڈرائنگ پن ، پیچ تصویر کشی *drawing-board*, board on which drawing paper is placed ڈرائنگ بورڈ ، تختۂ تصویر کشی **drawing room** *n.* room in which guests are received (actually a "with-drawing-room" for ladies for after-dinner activities) ڈرائنگ رُوم ، دیوان خانہ room where the drawing of pictures is taught کمرۂ تصویر کشی ، نگار خانہ

drawl *v. t.* & *i.* speak slowly in an affected manner چبا چبا کر باتیں کرنا *n.* speaking slowly and with affection چبا چبا کر کی ہُوئی باتیں

dread (dred) *n.* fear mingled with anxiety اندیشہ fear mingled with awe دہشت *v.t.* & *i.* feel great fear of سے دہشت کھانا ، سے ڈرنا **dreadful** *adj.* terrible دہشتناک (colloq.) unpleasant ناگوار

Dreadnought *n.* (*dred*-not) early 20th century type of battleship ڈریڈ ناٹ

dream (dreem) *n.* something which one seems to see or experience during sleep خواب *have a dream, dream a dream*, dream خواب دیکھنا state of mind in which things going on around one seem unreal تصوّر ، خیال (also *day-dream*), reverie ; indulgence in fancy خیالی پلاؤ mental picture of the future اُمید ، خواب ideally perfect specimen of something مثالی نمونہ *one's dream girl* کسی کے خوابوں کی حسینہ

adj. imaginary فرضی، خیالی *dream children* خیالی بچے *v.t.* & *i.* (p. t. & pa. p. *dreamed* or *dreamt*) have dreams خواب دیکھنا see in a dream خواب میں دیکھنا imagine, think possible (usu. in the negative) خواب و خیال میں ہونا be lost in fancy اپنے ہی خیالوں میں گم ہونا، کھویا کھویا سا رہنا **dreamy** (*dree*-mi) *adj.* (of a person) fanciful; with thoughts far away from his surroundings اپنے ہی خیالوں میں گم کھویا کھویا سا رہنا (of a person) unpractical بندۂ تخیل بے عمل، قوتِ عمل سے محروم (of things) unreal غیر حقیقی. خواب کا سا (of things) soothing راحت بخش hazy; not distinct دھندلا سا **dreamily** *adv.* as if in a dream خواب کے سے انداز میں **dreamer** *n.* unpractical person قوتِ عمل سے محروم indolent سُست، کاہل **dreamland** *n.* realm of fancy خوابوں کی دنیا

dreary (*dree*-è-ri) *adj.* dull بے کیف gloomy تیرہ و تار depressing اُداس کرنے والا **drearily** *adv.* بے کیف انداز سے، اُداس کرنے والے انداز سے

dredge (drej) *n.* apparatus for clearing silt from river-bed or sea bottom ڈریج، دریا صاف box with perforated top for sprinkling (sugar, etc.) چھڑکنے کی ڈبیہ *v.t.* & *i.* scoop with a dredge دریا صاف سے تہہ گہری کرنا make a channel, etc., with a dredge (پانی کی) گزرگاہ بنانا sprinkle (flour, etc.) چھڑکنا **dredger** (*drej*-ĕ*) *n.* boat carrying a dredge for scooping دریا صاف کشتی box for sprinkling چھڑکنے والی ڈبیہ

dregs (dregz) *n. pl.* sediment تلچھٹ، دُرد *drink to dregs, drain (some vessel) to dregs* تلچھٹ تک پی جانا worst and useless part (of society) (معاشرے کا) پست ترین طبقہ

drench *v.t.* wet thoroughly شرابور کرنا (یا) ہونا *drench to the skin* شرابور کر دینا (یا) ہو جانا force (beast) to take a dose (جانور کو) دوا پلانا

dress (dres) *n.* woman's gown گون child's frock بچے کا فراک any clothing لباس *Don't dress*, do not put on evening dress عشائیہ کا لباس مت پہنیے *dress up*, adorn oneself with special dress اچھے کپڑے پہننا، اچھی پوشاک پہننا *full dress*, (*a*) clothes for special occasion اچھا لباس، اچھی پوشاک (*b*) uniform وَردی *dress coat*, tailed coat of dress suit دُم دار کوٹ *dress suit*, evening dress for a man عشائیہ کا سیاہ سوٹ external appearance وضع، لباس، انداز *v.t.* & *i.* put on clothes کپڑے پہننا *be dressed in (some clothes)* be wearing (them) (کپڑے) پہنے ہوئے ہونا adorn showily سجانا، آراستہ کرنا *dress out a shop window* دُکان کی کھڑکی مال سے سجانا *window dressing*, (*a*) showing off the wares of one's shop دُکان کے مال کی نمائش کرنا (*b*) showing off one's merits (اپنی خوبیاں) بڑھا چڑھا کر دکھانا prepare (food) for table (کھانا) تیار کرنا (یا) پکانا *dress meat* گوشت پکانا *dress salad*, put sauce, etc., on it سلاد پر چٹنی ڈالنا clean and bandage (a wound) مرہم پٹی کرنا brush and comb (one's hair) بال بنانا، سر میں کنگھی کرنا (of a line of persons) straighten in drill صف سیدھی کرنا *Dress by the right* (or *left*) !, command in drill to align shoulders with those of the person at the extreme right (or left) داہنی (یا بائیں) جانب سے صف سیدھی کرنا *dress up* (or *back*) move forward (or *back*) for this purpose صف سیدھی کرنے کے لیے آگے پیچھے ہونا decorate gaily سجانا، آئین بندی کرنا *dress down*, rebuke severely سخت جھاڑ جھپاڑ کرنا **dress circle** *n.* first gallery in theatre (تھیٹر میں) پہلی گیلری

dresser *n.* (esp.) person employed to help a doctor to dress wounds ڈریسر، نائب جرّاح piece of furniture with shelves for dishes, etc. برتنوں کی الماری **dressing** *n.* (esp.) bandage applied to wounds پٹی، مرہم پٹی mixture of oil and other things used as sauce for salad سلاد کی چٹنی manure for soil کھاد **dressing-down** *n.* (colloq.) rebuke جھاڑ جھپاڑ *adj.* for dress or dressing پوشاک **dressing gown** *n.* loose gown worn over night clothes رات کا چُغہ، شبانہ لبادہ، شب خوابی کا لبادہ **dressing-room** *n.* room attached to bedroom for toilet سنگار خانہ **dressing-table** *n.* table with looking glass for toilet and dressing up سنگار میز **dressmaker** *n.* one (esp. woman) who stitches or sells women's gowns گون بنانے والی، گون دوز **dressmaking** *n.* dressmaker's job گون سینا، گون دوزی **dressy** (dres-i) *adj.* fond of smart dress خوش وضع، خوش نما stylish (dress)

drey (dray) *n.* squirrel's nest گلہری کا گھونسلا

dribble (*drib*-èl) *v.t.* & *i.* fall in small drops ٹپکنا let spittle flow out (from the side of the mouth) کی رال ٹپکنا hand out (money) grudgingly in small portions (روپیہ) بمشکل تھوڑا تھوڑا کر کے دینا (football) take (the ball) forward between the feet with slight pushes and kicks (فٹ بال) پیروں میں لے جانا *n.* small trickle (of a liquid) ٹپکا **dribbler** *n.* one who runs at the mouth جس کی رال ٹپکے **dribblet** *n.* small instalment چھوٹی سی قسط *pay in* (or *by*) *dribblets*, pay very small instalments چھوٹی چھوٹی قسطوں میں ادا کرنا

drier (*drī*-ĕ*) *adj.* (comparative degree of **dry**, which see)

drift *v.t.* & *i.* be carried along slowly and lightly by (or as if by) a current of air or water (ہوا کا) بہے چلے جانا drive along and heap up اُڑا کر ڈھیر لگانا be heaped thus اُڑ کر ڈھیر لگنا go through life without aim or self-control بے مقصد

زندگی گزارنا *n.* drifting movement بہاؤ that which is driving دھارا، رَو *snowdrift* (ہوا سے اُڑ کر آیا ہوا) برف کا ڈھیر natural tendency میلان، رُجحان way in which events, etc., tend to move رُخ general meaning or intention (*of* what is said) مفہوم، مطلب، منشا

drill (dril) *n.* pointed instrument for boring holes in or through hard substances by rotation برما military or physical exercises of many together ڈرل، فوجی تربیت، ٹولی ایک ساتھ وَرزش thorough practice in learning by practical exercises مشق، تمرین coarse twilled cloth (esp. cotton) ڈرِل، زین machine for sowing seeds in rows تخم ریز *v.t.* & *i.* bore (a hole) with a drill برمے سے سوراخ کرنا sow (seed) with the sowing machine called drill تخم ریز سے بیج بونا train through drill ڈرل کے ذریعے فوجی (یا جسمانی) تربیت کرنا teach through practical exercises (in some subject) مشقیں کرنا *The teacher thoroughly drilled the students in grammar* اُستاد نے شاگردوں کو خوب مشق کرائی

drink *v.t.* & *i.* (*drink, drank, drunk*) swallow liquid پینا drink liquor habitually (and often excessively) شراب کا عادی ہونا pledge پی کر عہد کرنا *drink* (*someone's*) *health* کسی کا جامِ صحت نوش کرنا *drink* (*something*) *in*, take into the mind eagerly, listen attentively شوق سے سُننا، پلّے باندھنا *drink in* (or *up*), (of soil) absorb water پانی جذب کر لینا، سوکھنا *n.* anything drunk مشروب *a hot drink*, tea, coffee, etc. چائے وغیرہ *a cold drink*, some cold liquid (like aerated water) for drinking سوڈا وغیرہ *have a drink of* (کوئی چیز) تھوڑی سی پینا *drink up*, drink the whole of پورا پی جانا *drink off* (or *down*), swallow at a draft ایک ہی بار چڑھا جانا *drink long life to* (*someone*), wish (him) long life while ready to drink a cup of wine (شراب) پیتے وقت زندگی کی دُعا دینا *drink to* (*someone*), wish him success thus in drink شراب پیتے وقت کامیابی کی دعا دینا *drink hard*, be a drunkard بلانوش ہونا *drink in beauty*, gaze at it attentively حُسن و جمال کو دیکھا کرنا *drink in fragrance*, smell it خوشبو سونگھنا *drink in an influence*, accept it اثر قبول کرنا *drinking bout*, (*a*) indulgence in drinking شراب نوشی (*b*) a spell of it شراب کا دَور *drinking water*, water pure enough to drink پینے کا پانی

drinkable (*drink*-a-bĕl) *adj.* suitable or fit for drinking پینے کے قابل **drinker** *n.* one who habitually takes alcoholic drinks شرابی **drunk** (drunk) *adj.* intoxicated پیئے ہوئے، نشے میں affected (with success, etc.) کے نشے میں **drunkard** (*drunk*-ĕ*d) *n.* one who habitually gets excessively drunk بلانوش **drunken** (*drunk*-ĕn) *adj.* intoxicated پیئے ہوئے، نشے میں who is often intoxicated شرابی، نشہ باز (revels or bout) caused by drinking too much نشے میں کیا ہوا (sleep, illness, etc.) showing the effects of drinking heavily نشے کے باعث

drunkenness *n.* state of being often and heavily drunk بلانوشی، بلانوش ہونا

drip *v.t.* & *i.* (-pp-) shed drops ٹپکانا be so wet as to shed drops میں رنگا ہوا ہونا *dripping with* میں رنگا ہوا fall in drops ٹپکنا *n.* drop by drop fall of a liquid ٹپکا *adj.* & *adv.* falling drop by drop ٹپکتا ہوا

drive (drīv) *v. t.* & *i.* (*drive, drove, driven*) force to move (*forward, back, to, away, out, into, through, on*) ہانکنا، ہانک کر لے جانا، لے جانا *drive back*, پیچھے ہٹا، پسپائی پر مجبور کرنا direct the course of (car, eng) چلانا، ڈرائیو کرنا *be driven by*, (esp.) be d y the force of steam, etc. کے زور سے چلنا ricket) hit a ball hard with a freely swung bat (کرکٹ میں) گیند کو زور سے مارنا go or take in a carriage, motor car or cab میں جانا یا لے جانا *He wanted to ride a bus but I drove him to the College,* وہ بس میں جانا چاہتا تھا مگر میں اُسے موٹر میں بٹھا کر کالج لے گیا constrain (*to do* or *into* some state) (پر) مجبور کرنا (of nail, etc.) force (*into* something) ٹھونکنا (*Phrases*) : *drive at*, mean کا مطلب یا منشا ہونا *drive up to*, (of road) go as far as تک جانا *drive a bargain*, make a deal سودا کرنا *drive away, drive off* (دھکے مار کر) نکال دینا *drive out*, turn out نکال دینا *drive out in* (*car, etc.*), go out in it (کار وغیرہ میں) جانا *drive along*, move forward آگے بڑھنا *drive ashore*, move (a wreck, etc.) to the shore کنارے لگانا *drive* (*someone*) *mad*, madden him (کسی کو) پاگل کر دینا *drive* (*someone*) *out*, (esp.) supplant him (کسی کی) جگہ لینا *drive* (*something*) *home* (*to someone*), make him realize it fully ذہن نشین کرنا، پوری طرح سمجھنا *drive in*, force into اندر بٹھانا، دھسانا *drive an enemy* (or *game*), chase from a larger area (*into a* smaller one) دشمن (یا شکار) کو نرغے میں لے لینا *n.* driving or driven in a car, carriage, etc. موٹر (یا گاڑی) میں سیر کرنا *go for a drive* موٹر میں سیر کے لیے جانا (private) road through a garden, etc., to a house ڈرائیو، خیاباں hard stroke (given to a ball) in cricket or tennis زور دار چوٹ capacity to get things done کارکردگی، سرگرمی، ہمّت *put more drive in*, زیادہ سرگرمی دکھانا **driver** (*drīv*-ĕ*) *n.* person who drives (animals, a car, a locomotive, etc.) چلانے والا، ڈرائیور tool for driving in چلانے والا آلہ *screw-driver*, device for driving in screws by turning them round and round پیچ کش **drive-in** *n.* (see *Addenda*)

drivel (*driv*-ĕl) *v. i.* (-ill-) run at the mouth رال بہنا ، talk foolishly احمقانہ باتیں کرنا *n.* silly talk احمقانہ باتیں *talk drivel* بکواس کرنا

drizzle (*driz*-ĕl) *v. i.* rain in very small fine drops پھوہار پڑنا ، ترشح ہونا *n.* fine rain پھوہار ، ترشح

droll (drohl) *adj.* (person, talk, etc.) causing amusement by being queer مضحکہ خیز ، عجیب **drollery** (*drohl*-ĕ-ri) *n.* quaint humour مسخراپن

dromedary (*drom*-e-da-ri) *n.* one-humped Arabian camel bred for riding ایک کوہان والا اونٹ

drone (drohn) *n.* male bee شہد کی نر مکھی idler who lives on others نشست ، کاہل ، اَحدی low humming sound (as) made by bees بھنبھناہٹ (see *Addenda*) *v. t. & i.* make a drone بھنبھنانا

droop *v. t. & i.* let (head or eyes) fall جھکانا hang down (through tiredness or weakness) جھکنا ، گر پڑنا *in drooping posture* جھکا ہوا ، مضمحل be depressed افسردہ *drooping spirits* افسردگی begin to wither پژمردہ ہونا *n.* drooping state اِضمحلال ، پژمردگی

drop *n.* tiny ball of liquid قطرہ *rain-drop* بارش کا قطرہ *dew-drop* قطرۂ شبنم *tear drop* آنسو small quantity (of) تھوڑا سا fall (in price, temperature, etc.) from higher to low level گرنا ، کمی distance of a fall اُتار ، نشیب (*pl.*) (drops) small sweets میٹھی گولیاں *acid drops* کھٹی میٹھی گولیاں *v. t. & i.* (-pp-) let fall گرانا *drop the curtain* پردہ گرانا *See that you don't drop the purse* دیکھنا ! کہیں بٹوا گرا نہ دینا fall (*off*) گرنا fall in drops ٹپکنا make or become weaker or lower آہستہ کرنا یا ہونا ، کم کرنا یا ہونا send (letter, etc.) by post ڈاک میں بھیجنا *drop (someone) a line* دو سطریں لکھ کر بھیجنا ، مختصر سا خط بھیجنا give up (subject, scheme or habit) ترک کرنا ، چھوڑنا (of wind) cease تھم جانا ، بند ہو جانا ، کا زور کم ہونا *The wind dropped* ہوا کا زور کم ہوا ، ہوا تھمی stop vehicle to allow (*someone*) to get down (*at*) (کسی کو) اُتارنے کے لیے گاڑی روکنا lower (eyes) آنکھیں جھکانا sink to ground (in exhaustion, etc.) تھک کر گر پڑنا leave out in pronunciation نہ بول سکنا ، گرا دینا *drop behind (someone)*, fail to keep up (with someone) (کسی سے) پیچھے رہ جانا *drop into*, (*a*) enter a place casually میں داخل ہونا (*b*) fall unintentionally into (habit or conversation) بے ساختہ شروع کرنا ، نادانستہ اختیار کرنا *drop in (on someone)* pay a casual visit (to) سے ملنے جانا *drop off*, (*a*) fall asleep سو جانا (*b*) become fewer کی تعداد کم ہو جانا *drop away*, (of company) depart away one by one ایک ایک کر کے رخصت ہو جانا *drop asleep*, sleep سو جانا *drop on to*, reprimand, punish فہمائش کرنا *drop it !*, stop it ! چھوڑ دو بھی ! *drop curtsy to*, curtsy آداب عرض کرنا *drop anchor* (at), anchor (at) میں لنگر انداز ہونا *drop lamb*, give birth to it میمنا دینا *a drop in the ocean*, an infinitely small factor بالکل تھوڑا *drop (someone) a hint*, give (him) a hint or warning (کسی کو) اشارہ کرنا *remark dropped during the talk*, uttered as if just accidentally باتوں ہی باتوں میں ایسا اشارہ جو یوں معلوم ہو جیسے یونہی زبان سے نکل گیا ہو *drop-curtain*, *drop-scene*, (*a*) dropping of curtain at the end of a scene in a play منظر کا خاتمہ ، ڈراپ سین (*b*) end of some dramatic event کسی بحران کا خاتمہ

dropsy (*drop*-si) *n.* disease causing a watery fluid to collect in some cavity of the body جلودھر ، اِستسقا

dross (*dros*) *n.* scum rising to the surface of molten metals دھات کا میل impurities, refuse فضلہ

drought (drout) (spelt in poetry as **drougth**) *n.* continuous dry weather causing distress خشک سالی ، قحطِ باراں ، جدب (old use) thirst پیاس

drove (drohv) *v. t. & i.* (p. t. of *drive*, which see) *n.* herd or flock of animals moving or being driven together (چلتا ہوا) گلہ crowd in motion (چلنے والوں کی) بھیڑ **drover** *n.* dealer in sheep or cattle who drives them to market for sale ڈھور ڈنگر کا بیوپاری

drown (droun) *v.t. & i.* die in water because unable to breathe ڈوب جانا ، غرق ہونا *a drowning person* ڈوبتا ہوا شخص *a drowning person catches at a straw* ڈوبتے کو تنکے کا سہارا suffocate by submersion ڈبونا ، غرق کرنا *to be drowned* ڈوب جانا (of noise) be strong enough to prevent another sound from being heard (شور کا آواز کو) دبا لینا *be drowned out*, be forced to leave a place by floods, etc. سیلاب کے باعث کوئی جگہ چھوڑنے پر مجبور ہونا *drown (one's) grief*, assuage it with drink غم کو شراب میں غرق کرنا

drowsy (*drow*-zi) *adj.* half-asleep (person) اونگھتا ہوا ، نیم خوابیدہ *feel drowsy* اونگھنا (sounds) inducing sleep نیند کی سی کیفیت طاری کرنے والا **drowsily** (*drov*-zi-li) *adv.* half-asleep اونگھتے ہوئے **drowsiness** *n.* being half-asleep اونگھ ، اونگھنا

drudge (druj) *v. i.* work hard and long at unpleasant tasks with petty remuneration چکی پیسنا ، بیل کی طرح جتے رہنا ، غلامی کرنا ، چاکری کرنا *n.* one who has to work like that چاکر ، غلام **drudgery** (*druj*-ĕ-ri) hard menial work چاکری

drug (drug) *n.* simple substance used alone or in a mixture as medicine دوا ، مفرد دوا *drug-store*, apothecary's shop دواؤں کی دکان habit-forming narcotic, *e.g.*, opium نشہ ، بے ہوش کرنے والی دوا *the drug habit*, habit of taking narcotics نشہ کرنے یا افیم کھانے کی عادت *v. t. & i.* add harmful drugs to (food or drink) نشہ ملانا ، کچھ ملا لینا give drugs to (someone) in order to make unconscious نشہ پلانا ، بیہوشی

کی دوا پلانا یا کھلانا be in the habit of taking harmful drugs نشہ کرنا **druggist** (*drug*-ist) *n.* tradesman in drugs, etc. دوا فروش ، دواساز، عطّار

Druid (*drew*-id) *n.* (fem. *Druidess*) ancient British priest and magician ڈرُوئیڈ (ڈرُوئیڈ) **druidic, druidical** (-id-) *adj.* of Druids ڈرُوئیڈوں کا، ڈرُوئیڈی

drum (drum) *n.* musical instrument made by stretching dried skin over the end of a hollow metallic cylinder and sounded by beating with sticks ڈھول، نوبت، نقارہ container (as for oil) shaped like a drum کپا *ear-drum*, cavity in the ear کان کا ڈھول ، کان کا پردہ *v. t.* & *i.* play the drum ڈھول بجانا thump continuously تھپتھپانا (of insects, etc.) make loud noise with wings بُولنا *drum (something) into (someone's) ears*, make (him) remember (something) by constantly repeating it بار بار یاد دِہانی کرنا *drum out*, expel or dismiss (from army) by beat of drum (فوج سے) نکالنا نام کاٹنا **drumhead** *n.* skin of drum ڈھول کا پردہ **drum major** *n.* leader of the regimental band سازندہ، حوالدار **drumstick** *n.* stick for beating drum نقارہ چوب leg of cooked fowl (پکے ہوئے) مُرغ کی ٹانگ

a drum

drummer *n.* player of drum ڈھول بجانے والا

drunk (drunk) (pa. pa. of **drink**, which see) **drunkometer** *n.* alcometer (see *Addenda* for both the words)

dry (dri) *adj.* without moisture or deficient in it سُوکھا ، خشک *dry well*, waterless اندھا کنواں *dry canal*, empty canal خالی نہر *dry weather*, rainless خشک موسم *dry land*, (opp. of *sea*) خشکی ، خشک زمین *dry-nurse*, nurse tending but not suckling child دُودھ کھلائی ، دَدَا *dry cow*, cow not yielding milk دُودھ نہ دینے والی گائے cold (person, word or expression) سَرد مہر، رُوکھا پھیکا ، رُوکھا uninteresting (book or subject) خشک ، بے لطف (colloq.) thirsty پیاسا *dry bread*, (*a*) without butter مکھن کے بغیر روٹی (*b*) stale باسی روٹی *dry toast*, toasted but unbuttered slice of bread سُوکھے توس *dry goods, corn*, etc. اناج ، غلّہ tasteless (wine, etc.) بے مزہ ، پھیکی *dry cough*, cough without phlegm خشک کھانسی *dry humour*, presented in a serious way سنجیدہ مزاح *dry rot*, (*a*) decay in wood not exposed to air کاٹھ روگ (*b*) moral or social decay پستی ، گراوٹ ، انحطاط *dryas-dust*, (*a*) *n.* dull historian or antiquary خشک مؤرخ (*b*) *adj.* dull خشک ، بے لطف ، بے کیف *dry dock* (see under *dock*) خشک گودی *go* (*or pass*) *over dryshod*, cross with out wetting feet سُوکھے پاؤں چلے جانا *v. t.* & *i.* make dry سُکھانا ، خشک کرنا become dry سُوکھنا ، خشک ہونا *dry up*, (*a*) dry completely بالکل سوکھنا یا سُکھانا (*b*) evaporate اُڑ جانا (*c*) (colloq.) stop speaking or doing بس کرنا ، رُک جانا **drily** (*dri*-li) *adv.* coldly رُوکھے پن سے ، رکھائی سے **driness** (*dri*-nes) *n.* being dry خشک ہونا ، سوکھا ہوا ہونا **dryer** (*drī*-ĕ*) *n.* (esp.) thing that dries up something else خشک کرنے والی چیز **dryish** (*dri*-ish) *adj.* somewhat dry خشک سا

dryad *n.* wood-nymph ; nymph living in trees پیڑ کی پری ، بَن دیوی

dual (dew-ĕl) *adj.* of two دوہرا twofold دُگنا dual form or number تثنیہ *single, dual and plural* واحد ، تثنیہ اور جمع **duality** (dew-*al*-i-ti) *n.* being twofold دُگنا ہونا **dualism** (*dew*-a-lizm) *n.* duality دُگنا ہونا system of philosophy or religion recognizing two independent principles (*e.g.*, mind and matter) or powers. (*e.g.*, good and evil) ثنویت **dualist** (*dew*-a-list) *n.* one believing in this theory ثنوی ، ثنویت کا قائل **dualistic** (-*lis*-) *adj.* relating to it ثنوی

dub (dub) *v. t.* (old use) make (someone) a knight by touching him on the shoulder with a sword تلوار کی ضرب سے نائٹ بنانا give a nick-name to کا نام رکھنا ، کوکہنا (see *Addenda*) apply dubbin to ڈبن لگانا **dubbin, dubbing** *n.* grease applied to leather for softening it ڈبن

dubious (*dewb*-i-us) *adj.* doubtful مشکوک not clear مُبہم (person, conduct or statement) causing misgivings مشتبہ

ducal (*dew*-kĕl) *adj.* of a duke ڈیوک کا ، نوابی

ducat (*duk*-at) *n.* former gold coin of Italy worth about nine shillings قدیم اطالوی طلائی سکّہ

duchess (*duch*-es) *n.* wife or widow of a duke نواب بیگم ، ڈچِس (abb. *duch.*) (slang) coster-monger's wife پھیری والے کی بیوی **duchy** (*duch*-i) *n.* land ruled by a royal duke or duchess نواب کا علاقہ (یا) جاگیر British dukedom ڈچی، ریاست *the duchies of Lancaster and Cornwall* ریاست ہائے لنکاسٹر اور کارنوال

duck (duk) *n.* common tame or wild water-fowl بطخ ، مُرغابی (see *Addenda*) dip under water غوطہ ، ڈبکی sudden lowering of head سر اچانک نیچا کرنا (also *duck's egg*), zero score in cricket کوئی رن بنائے بغیر آؤٹ ہو جانا، کوئی رن نہ بنانا (کرکٹ میں) صفر رن *ducks and drakes*, game in which flat stones are hurled in such a way as to skip over water چھیکری تیرانا *play* (or *make*) *ducks and drakes with* (or *of*), squander اُجاڑنا ، لٹانا *v.t.* & *i.* push someone's head quickly under water غوطہ دینا dip head under water غوطہ لگانا bob down to avoid being seen or hit سر اچانک نیچا کرنا **ducking** *n.* thorough wetting خوب بھیگنا شرابور ہونا dipping under water غوطہ دینا یا لگانا

duckling *n.* young duck بطخ کا بچہ

duct (dukt) *n.* tube in the body for carrying liquid مسامہ،مسام *tear ducts* آنسو کے مسام ، اَشکی مسامات
dud (dud) *n.* & *adj.* (colloq.) (thing or person) of no use بیکار شے ، ناکارہ
dudgeon (duj-ĕn) *n.* anger غُصّہ ، طَیش (used only in the phrases) *be in high dudgeon, go off in deep dudgeon*, be very angry طَیش میں آنا
due (dew) *adj.* owing (*to* something) کے باعِث to be paid واجِبُ الادا *be due, fall due*, is to be paid واجِبُ الادا ہونا deserved جائز usual حسبِ معمول *in due course*, in the normal course اپنے وقت پر حسبِ معمول proper, adequate مناسب ، موزُوں *after due consideration* مناسِب غور کے بعد *with due respect* بجا احترام کے ساتھ (to be) expected (*to* do) والا *Who is due to speak?* بولنے والا کون ہے؟ *The train is due in five minutes*, is expected to arrive at the end of that period گاڑی پانچ منٹ میں آیا چاہتی ہے *overdue*, late لیٹ دیر سے ، بعد از وقت *adv.* (with points of compass) exactly ٹھیک *due North* ٹھیک شمال *n.* (*sing.*) that which someone deserves جائز حق ، جائز قدر *give the devil his due* دُشمن کی اچھائیوں کی بھی قدر کرنا (*pl.*) sum of money to be paid (*e.g.*, for use of harbours, membership of a club) واجِبُ الادا رقم ، واجبات ، واجب **duly** (*dew*-li) *adv.* properly ٹھیک طور پر ، جائز طور پر in the formal manner ضابطے کے مطابق ، باضابطہ punctually بروقت
duel (*dew*-el) *n.* unlawful fight (usu. with swords and pistols) between two persons in the presence of seconds in order to settle a quarrel ڈُوئل ڈُوئل لڑنا ، مبارزت کرنا *fight a duel* مُبارزت ، یکّہ any two-sided contest مقابلہ *v.i.* (-ll-) fight a duel ڈُوئل لڑنا ، مبارزت کرنا **duelling** *n.* fighting of duels ڈُوئل لڑنا ، مبارزت کرنا **duellist** (*dew*-ĕ-list) *n.* duel-fighter ڈُوئل لڑنا مبارزت کرنا

a duel

duet (*dew*-et) *n.* piece of music for two voices or instruments دوگانا
duffer (*duf*-ĕ*) *n.* (colloq.) stupid person بیوقوف ، احمق ، گاؤدی inefficient person نالائق
dug (dug) *v.t.* (see under **dig**) *n.* udder تھن **dug-out** *n.* underground shelter dug out by soldiers for their protection in war زمین دوز جائے پناہ canoe made by hollowing a tree trunk درخت کا تنا کھود کر بنائی ہوئی کشتی ، کندہ کشتی
duke (dewk) *n.* (fem. *duchess*, pr. *duch*-es) British nobleman of high rank (next below a prince) ڈیوک ، نواب sovereign of a small state (called a *duchy*) **dukedom** *n.* position, duties, rank or land of a British duke (except those of Lancaster and Cornwall which are called *duchies*) نوابی ، نوابی ریاست
dulcet (*dul*-set) *adj.* (of sounds) sweet and soothing شیریں ، سُریلی ، مدُھ بھری
dulcimer (*dul*-si-mĕ*) *n.* old musical instrument from which piano was evolved ڈَلسِمَر ، ڈَلسِیمہ
dull (dul) *adj.* blunt (edge) کُند (of colour) not bright پھیکا ، ہلکا ، صوفیانہ lacking liveliness اُداس بے لطف ، بے کیف *dull weather*, cloudy and cheerless ابرآلود اور اُداس موسم (of outline) not definite ، slow in understanding, etc. کند ذہن ، غبی *dull of hearing*, almost deaf اُونچا سُننے والا listless افسُردہ ، اُداس ، بُجھا بُجھا سا جس میں ہمّت نہ ہو *I feel dull* مجھ میں کچھ ہمّت نہیں (of trade) inactive ماند ، سرد ، پھیکا not sharp or acute بھاری uninteresting (book, talk, etc.) بے لطف ، خشک *v.t.* & *i.* make or become dull کُند کرنا (یا) ہونا sadden, depress اُداس کرنا ، افسُردہ کرنا **dully** (*dul*-i). *adv.* افسُردگی سے **dullness** *n.* افسُردگی **dullard** *n.* slow and stupid person بیوقوف ، احمق ، گاؤدی
duly (*dew*-li) *adj.* (see under **due**)
dumb (dum) *adj.* unable to speak گونگا ، بے زبان silent from fear, etc. بے زبان ، خوف زدہ ، دہشت زدہ ، ستم رسیدہ ، مظلوم *strike (someone) dumb*, terrorize (him) اوسان خطا کرنا ، دہشت زدہ کرنا *the dumb masses, the dumb millions*, suppressed people ستم رسیدہ عوام without sound بے آواز *dumb piano*, one used for finger-practice and giving no sounds بے آواز پیانو ، مشقی پیانو habitually quiet عادتاً خاموش not expressed in words گُھٹا ہُوا ، جس کا اظہار نہ ہو **dumb show** *n.* message given by gestures instead of words ہاتھوں کے اشارے سے کہی ہوئی بات **dumbfound** (dum-*found*) *v.t.* strike dumb with surprise ششدر کر دینا ، گم سُم ہونا **dumbfounded** *adj.* struck dumb with surprise گُم سُم ، بے سُخن **dumb-bell** (*dum*-bel) *n.* short bar with weight at ends to exercise arm muscles ڈمبل **dumbness** *n.* being dumb گونگا پن ، گُنگ

a dumb-bell

dummy (*dum*-i) *n.* object made to look like and serve the purpose of the real person or thing نقلی یا جعلی چیز ، نقل ، کاٹھ کی چیز *tailor's dummy*, statue used by tailors for displaying dresses لباس کی نمائش کے لیے لکڑی کا مجسمہ ، لباس پوش imaginary player (or players in double dummy) in whist with his cards exposed on table and played by partner (تاش میں) فرضی کھلاڑی person acting or appearing for another ; man of straw کٹھ پتلی ، پِچھلّو (also *baby*) *dummy*), soother ; artificial nipple for the infant to suckle چوشنی *adj*. sham جعلی ، کاٹھ کا ، نقلی *dummy rifle* (or *gun*), rifle (or gun) which cannot work and is used only for drill or deception of enemy نقلی رَئفل (یا بندوق) ، کاٹھ کی بندوق

baby's dummy

dump (dump) *n*. rubbish heap temporary depot for ammunition at the war-front (محاذِ جنگ پر) عارضی اسلحہ خانہ (*pl*.) (*dumps*), depression اُداسی ، دِلگیری ، افسردگی *in the dumps*, depressed, looking blue اُداس ، افسُردہ ، دلگیر *v.t.* put on a rubbish heap کوڑی پر ڈالنا drop down with thud دَھم سے گرنا (commerce) send in large quantities for sale abroad at low price goods which are unwanted in the home country کسی ملک کی صنعت کو برباد کرنے کے لیے کسی اَور ملک کا وہاں مال بھرنا ، بھرتا **dumping** *n*. sending of goods in this way (دُوسرے مُلک کی صنعت تباہ کرنے کے لیے وہاں مال) بھرنا **dumpy** (*dump*-i) *adj*. short and stout ناٹا اور موٹا

dunce (duns) *n*. slow learner گُند ذہن ، غبی ، کوَدن stupid and ignorant person بیوقوف ، احمق ، کاؤدی

dune (dewn) *n*. (also called *sand dune*), mound of dry shifting sand piled up by the wind (usu. near sea-shore) ریت کا ٹیلہ

dung (dung) *n*. excrement of domestic animals گوبر ، لید (وغیرہ) *cow-dung* گوبر manure کھاد **dunghill** - heap of dung کُوڑی ، گھورا dirty place with foul smell غلیظ جگہ

dungeon (*dunj*-ĕn) *n*. dark underground cell formerly as a prison بھونرا

duodenum (dew-o-*deen*-um) *n*. 12-inch long intestine next to stomach بارہ انگشتی آنت

dupe (dewp) *v.t*. deceive and make use of cheat جُل دینا ، ٹھگ لینا *n*. one who is duped سادہ لوح ، فریب خوردہ

duplicate *v.t*. (*dewp*-li-kayt) make an exact copy of (a document) مُثنیٰ تیار کرنا reproduce exactly نقل مطابقِ اصل کرنا make (something) exactly like another ہُوبہُو وَیسا بنانا *n*. (*dewp*-li-kit) something exactly like another نقل مُطابقِ اصل copy نقل ، مُثنیٰ *in duplicate*, (or documents, etc.) with a duplicate copy نقل سمیت ، مع مُثنیٰ double (ratio, etc.) دُگنا *adj*. (*dewp*-li-kit) exactly like ہوبہو ، بالکل ویسی ، ایک اور ، مُثنیٰ *duplicate copy* مُثنیٰ دستاویز **duplicator** (*dewp*-li-kay-tĕ*) *n*. machine that duplicates something written or typed مُثنیٰ بنانے والی مشین ، نقل نگار مثنی **duplication** (*-kay-*) *n*. مُثنیٰ بنانا

Note : Duplicate means (to make) two copies (of) ; similarly **triplicate** is (to make) three copies (of) ; **quadruplicate**, (to make) four copies (of) ; and so on with other Latin numerals.

duplicity (dewp-*lis*-i-ti) *n*. deceitfulness, double dealing دورُخی ، فریب کاری

durable (*dew*-ra-bĕl) *adj*. likely to last for a long time دیرپا not wearing out soon پائیدار ، مضبوط **durability** (*-bil-*) *n*. quality of being durable پائیداری ، مضبوطی

duralumin (dew-*ral*-ew-min) *n*. hard aluminium alloy used in the manufacture of aircraft ڈیوریلمن مضبوط ایلومینیم

durance (*dew*-rans) *n*. (rhetorical word for) imprisonment اسیری ، اُسارت ، قیدوبند

duration (dew-*ray*-shĕn) *n*. time during which something lasts or exists مدت ، دَوران *for the duration of* کے دَوران میں

duress, duresse (dew-*res*, or *dew*-res) *n*. forceable restraint or imprisonment قید ، حبس illegal threats or compulsion to do something ناجائز دباؤ ، دھمکی ، دھونس *done under duress* ناجائز دباؤ میں آکر کیا ہوا

during (*dew*-ring) *prep* throughout the period of میں sometime in that period کے دَوران میں

durst (du*st) 3rd person sing. p. t. and conditional of **dare** (which see)

dusk (dusk) *n*. time just before it gets quite dark جھٹپٹا ، شام کا دُھندلکا *from dawn to dusk* نور کے تڑکے سے شام کے دُھندلکے تک ، صبح سے شام تک obscurity گمنامی

dusky (dus-ki) *adj*. rather dark کالا سا ، سیاہی مائل not clear دُھندلا سا **duskiness** *n*. quality of being dusky دُھندلاپن

dust (dust) *n*. fine grains of sand or earth دُھول ، گرد ، غبار ، گرد وغبار *shake of the dust of* (*one's*) *feet*, depart angrily or scornfully طیش میں آکر جانا ، حقارت بھرے انداز سے جانا *throw dust in* (*someone's*) *eyes*, mislead (him) کسی کی آنکھوں میں خاک ڈالنا یا دھول جھونکنا *bite the dust*, (*a*) fall گرنا (*b*) surrender عاجزی قبول کرنا *in the dust*, dead مُردہ *humbled in* (or *to*) *the dust*, utterly humiliated (ہوکر) نہایت ذلیل (ہوکر) سخت رُسوا *raise a dust over* (*something*), make a fuss about (it) (کسی بات) پر رونی جنگامہ بپا کرنا anything in this form ریزہ ، چورا *coal dust* کوئلے کا چورا dead human body لاش ، نعش ، میت *dust to dust* مُردہ قبر میں *v.t.* & *i.* remove dust from جھاڑنا ، صاف کرنا *dust someone's coat* (or *jacket*), beat (him) پیٹنا cover with (powder, etc.) پر چھڑکنا **dustbin, dusthole** *n*. metal container for rubbish کوڑا دان خاک دان **dustpan** *n*. pan into which dust is brushed (بھنگی کی پیلی) **dust colour** *adj*. dull light brown بھورا **dust-cart** *n.* cart going from house to house to collect rubbish کوڑا گاڑی **dustman** *n.* one who empties dustbins and takes rubbish, etc. away کوڑا کرکٹ اُٹھانے والا ، خاکروب **duster** *n.* cloth for dusting furniture, etc. جھاڑن **dusting** *n.* (slang) beating مار پیٹ **dusty** *adj.* covered with dust گرد آلود ، غبار آلود ۔ گرد سے اَٹا ہُوا like dust غُبار آسا

a dust-cart

duty (*daw*-ti) *n.* (*pl. duties*) what one is obliged to do under regulations فرضِ منصبی what one is morally bound to do (*to*) فرض ، فریضہ ، اخلاقی فرض spell of work کام ، ڈیوٹی *be on duty*, be actually engaged in one's duty or usual work ڈیوٹی پر ہونا *be off duty* ڈیوٹی پر نہ ہونا *take (someone's) duty*, do (his) work for him کسی کی ڈیوٹی ادا کرنا *do duty for (someone)* be used instead of him کا کام دینا (usu. *pl.*) government tax on certain things محصول *customs duty*, tax on imports and exports کسٹم ، محصول ، کروڑگیری *excise duty*, tax on goods produced in the country محصول آب کاری *death duty*, tax levied on someone's property at death محصولِ ترکہ *stamp duties*, tax levied when property, etc., is transferred to a new owner by sale شاٹمپ اِسٹام *duty paid*, (goods) on which customs duty has been paid محصولِ دادہ *duty-free*, (goods) allowed to enter without payment of custom محصول معاف expression of respect for superiors احترام ، تعظیم ، آداب *Please pay my duties to him* اُن کی خدمت میں میری طرف سے آداب عرض کر دیجیئے *duty call*, visit paid merely to satisfy etiquette رَسمی ملاقات **dutiable** *adj.* taxable (goods) قابلِ محصول **dutiful** *adj.* doing one's duty well and willingly فرض شناس showing respect and obedience فرمانبردار ، اِطاعت شعار **duteous** (*dew*-ti-us) *adj.* devoted to duty فرض شِناس obedient مُطیع ، فرمانبردار

dwarf (dwaw*f) *adj. n.* undersized person بَونا ، ٹھنگنا ، ناٹا much undersized (animal or plant) پَست قد ، پَست قامت *v.t.* stunt in growth پَست قد رہنے دینا ۔ بڑھنے نہ دینا ، ٹھٹھرا دینا cause to appear small by contrast مُقابلہ میں چھوٹا کر دِکھانا

dwell *v.i.* (*dwell, dwelt, dwelt*) live (*in, at* or *near* a place) رہنا ، بسنا ، سُکونت رکھنا یا کرنا ، بود و باش کرنا رکھنا *dwell apart* الگ رہنا speak or write at length (*on* or *upon*) تفصیل سے لکھنا یا بولنا keep one's attention fixed (*on* or *upon*) توجہ مرکوز کرنا **dwelling, dwelling-place** *n.* house, etc., to live in (as opposed to a shop or office) گھر ، مکان ، مَسکن **dweller** *n.* one who dwells رہنے والا ، ساکن باشندہ **We dwell** when we stay for some considerable time *in* a place, or *on* a subject ; **abide** *in* a place, *by* a decision, or *with* relatives ; **reside** permanently ; be **domiciled** legally ; **live** *in* a house or city ; and **inhabit** a country.

dwindle (*dwind*-ĕl) *v. i.* diminish gradually (*to* very small degree) سِمٹنا ، گھٹتے گھٹتے بالکل کم رہ جانا

dyarchy *n.* (same as **diarchy,** which see)

dye (dɪ) *v. t. & i.* (*dyes, dyed*) colour (usu. by dipping in a liquid) رنگنا ، رنگ دینا ، رنگ چڑھانا impregnate (hair) with colouring matter خِضاب لگانا take colour from dyeing پر رنگ چڑھنا *n.* substance used for dyeing cloth رنگ ، رنگنے کا مسالہ colour given by dyeing رنگ رنگت hue of character رنگ ، رنگ ڈھنگ ، کردار **dyer** (*dɪ*-ĕ*) *n.* tradesman who dyes clothes رنگریز **dyestuff** *n.* dye-yielding plant or mineral جس سے رنگ تیار کیا جائے

dying (*dɪ*-ing) (*pr. part.* of **die** which see) *n.* passing away مرنا ، موت ، مرگ *adj.* expressed at the time of death مرتے وقت کا ، مرتے دم (person) who is passing away approaching the end حالتِ نزع میں ، آخر

dyke *n.* same as **dike** (which see)

dynamic (dɪ-*nam*-ik) *adj.* (of physical power and forces) producing motion (opp. of *static* or *potential*) حرکت دینے والا ، مُتحرّک active چُست ، چالاک ، کارکن forceful (character), extending influence over others اثر آفریں **dynamics** (dɪ-*nam*-iks) *n. pl.* (with sing. verb), branch of physics dealing with matter in motion حرکیات

dynamite (*dɪ*-na-mɪt) *n.* powerful explo[illegible], now used in mining ڈینا مائٹ *v.t.* blow up wi[illegible] dynamite ڈینا مائٹ سے اُڑا دینا

dynamo (*dɪ*-na-moh) *n.* (*pl. dynamos*) machine for converting mechanical into electric energy by rotation of copper-wire coils in a magnetic field ; (also called a *generator*) ڈائینمو ، برق آفریں

Note : A **dynamo** is an apparatus for generating electricity from mechanical energy while an **electric motor** is a machine with the opposite function, *viz.*, the conversion of electric energy into mechanical energy.

dynast *n.*, **dynastic** *adj.* (see under **dynasty**)

dynasty (*dɪ*-nas-ti) *n.* succession of rulers belonging to one family شاہی سِلسلہ ، خاندانِ سلاطین **dynastic** (dɪ-*nas*-tik) *adj.* relating to a dynasty ایک شاہی سِلسلے سے مُتعلّق **dynast** (*dɪ*-nast, or *din*-ast) *n.*

member of a dynasty شاہی سلسلے کا ایک فرد
dys- *pref.* bad بد
dynel *n.* (see *Addenda*)
dysentery (*dis*-en-tri) *n.* painful disease of the bowels caused by amoeba (*amoebic dysentery*) or bacilli (*bacillary dysentery*) پیچش ، زحیر
dyspepsia (dis-*pep*-si-a) *n.* indigestion بدہضمی
dyspeptic *adj.* of dyspepsia بدہضمی کا depressed as with dyspepsia بدحال *n.* person suffering from dyspepsia جسے بدہضمی کی شکایت ہو

E

E (ee) (pl. *E's*, or *Es*) fifth letter of the English alphabet انگریزی حروفِ تہجی کا پانچواں حرف ، ای a note in a musical scale سرگم کا ایک سُر
each (eech) *adj.* every (person or thing) taken separately ہر ، ہرایک *pron.* each of the two persons or things ہرایک ، دو میں سے ایک ، فی
eager (*ee*-gĕ*) *adj.* full of keenness (*after*, *about*, or *to do* something) شائق ، مشتاق ، شوقین ، سرگرم **eagerly** *adv.* keenly شوق سے ، سرگرمی سے **eagerness** *n.* keenness شوق ، سرگرمی
eagle (*ee*-gel) *n.* a bird of prey with keen sight عقاب ، شاہین **eagle-eyed**, **eagle-sighted**, keen-sighted تیز نظر **eaglet** *n.* (diminutive of *eagle*), young eagle چھوٹا عقاب ، شاہیں

an eagle

ear (*ee*-ĕ*) *n.* part of the body with which we hear کان ability to distinguish between sounds (آوازوں کی) پہچان ، پرکھ *have a good ear for music* موسیقی کی خوب سمجھ ہونا spike or head of corn (اناج کی) بالی ، بال **ear-drum** *n.* part of the middle ear کان کا ڈھول **earmark** *v.t.* put aside something (for a special purpose) الگ کرنا ، مخصوص کرنا ، خاص مقصد کے لیے متعین کرنا **ear-shot** *n.* range of hearing سُن سکنا ، آواز آسکنا ، سماعت *within* (or *out of*) *ear-shot*, near enough (or too far away) to hear جس کی آواز (نہ) آسکے **eardrop**, **ear-ring**, (کان کی) بالی ، آویزہ ، بُندا **earless** *adj.* without ears بوچا
earl (ĕ*l) *n.* title of British nobleman between a marquis and a viscount اَرل ، نواب **earldom** *n.* rank or lands of an earl ارل کا خطاب یا ارل کی ریاست نوابی ، تعلقہ
early (ĕ*-li) *adj.* & *adv.* in good time جلد ، جلدی قبل *early for*, before time قبل از وقت ، وقت سے پہلے early riser جلدی جاگنے والا *at your* (etc.) *earliest convenience* اوّلین فرصت میں near the beginning صبح سویرے *in the early morning* سویرے ، شروع میں
earn (ĕ*n) *v.t.* obtain for work کمانا get as reward for one's qualities (اجر یا انعام) پانا **earnings** *n. pl.* money earned آمدنی ، کمائی
earnest (ĕ*-nest) *adj.* eager and serious دلپے ، سچا ، کوشاں serious and not trifling سنجیدہ *in earnest*, in a serious and not joking manner واقعی ، دل سے ، سچ مچ *be in earnest* سچ کہنا ، دل سے کہنا ، واقعی ہونا *n.* money advanced to give surety of buying سائی ، بیعانہ ، زرِ پیشگی ، دھروٹ something coming in advance as a sign of what is to follow نمونہ ، بانگی **earnestly** *adv.* in an earnest manner سنجیدگی سے واقعی **earnestness** *n.* eagerness and seriousness سنجیدگی ، سرگرمی
earth (ĕ*th) *n.* this world دنیا ، گیتی ، ارض *on the face of the earth* روئے زمین پر ، صفحۂ ہستی پر *why* (or *who*, *what*, *where*, etc.) *on earth*, (used for emphasis to mean) why (etc.) ever آخر کیوں (یا کون ، کیا ، کہاں وغیرہ)؟ dry land خشکی ، زمین soil مٹی *run to earth*, (*a*) send (a fox) to its hole لومڑ کو بھٹ میں گھسیڑنا (*b*) discover (something) hidden ڈھونڈ نکالنا earth-connexion for electrical apparatus ارتھ *v.t.* join (conductor) to the earth ارتھ کرنا ، ارضہ لگانا **earthen** (e*th-ĕn) *adj.* made of baked clay مٹی کا ، گِلی **earthenware** *n.* pots made of baked clay مٹی کے برتن ، گلی ظروف **earthly** *adj.* of this world, not of heaven دنیاوی ، دنیوی (colloq.) any کوئی *not an earthly chance*, no chance at all کوئی بھی امکان نہیں *no earthly use*, no use at all کوئی بھی فائدہ نہیں **earthquake** *n.* violent shaking of the earth's surface زلزلہ ، بھونچال **earthwork** *n.* fortifications made of earth مٹی کا دُھس **earthworm** *n.* the common worm کیچوا

an earthworm

mean fellow کمینہ ، رذیل **earthborn** *adj.* not heavenly گوشت پوست کا ، ارضی
earthen *adj.* (see under **earth**)
ease (eez) *n.* rest and comfort آرام ، آسائش freedom from difficulty آسانی ، سہولت ، چین *to stand at ease*, to stand with the legs apart in a restful position سستانا ، ایٹ ایز ، ٹانگیں پھیلا کر ذرا آرام سے کھڑے ہونا *ill at ease*, (*a*) uncomfortable بے آرام (*b*) embarrassed پریشان ، بے چین *with ease*, without difficulty آسانی سے *v.t.* & *i.* give ease to (the body or mind) آرام دینا make less tight ڈھیلا کرنا (cause to) become less intense شدت کم کرنا ، تکلیف کم کرنا (see also **easy**)

easel (*ee*-zĕl) *n.* wooden frame for supporting a picture or blackboard ایزل، ٹیکن
east (eest) *n.* point of the horizon where the sun rises مشرق، پورب a point of compass مشرق، شرق *adj.* relating to the part or point مشرقی، شرقی *adv.* towards the sunrise مشرق *the Far East,* eastern Asia مشرقِ بعید، شرقِ اقصیٰ *the Middle East, the Mid-East,* the Arab countries (etc.) مشرقِ وسطیٰ، شرقِ اوسط
easterly *adj.* & *adv.* lying towards the east مشرقی of, from, or in the east مشرقی، مشرق میں
eastward, eastwards *adv.* in the direction of east مشرق کی جانب **eastern** *adj.* of or living in the East مشرقی، شرقی *n.* person living in the East مشرق کا رہنے والا، مشرق کا باشندہ، مشرقی، شرقی
Easter (*ees*-tĕ*) *n.* anniversary of Christ's Resurrection falling between March 21 and April 21 ایسٹر، عیدُ الفصح *Easter week,* the week beginning on Easter Sunday ایسٹر کا ہفتہ، ہفتۂ عیدُ الفصح
easy (*ee*-zi) *adj.* not difficult آسان free from pain or anxiety مطمئن، آرام *feel easy about* کے متعلق مطمئن ہونا *easy chair,* soft, restful chair آرام کرسی *adv* آسان، مطمئن، آرام سے *take things easy,* (*a*) not work hard محنت نہ کرنا (*b*) go slowly آہستہ آہستہ کام کرنا **easy-going** *adj.* (person) not causing or taking trouble آرام طلب **easily** (*ee*-zi-li) *adv.* without difficulty or trouble آسانی سے، بہ سہولت (see also **ease**)
eat (eet) *v.t.* & *i.* (*eat, ate,* pr. ayt, *eaten* pr. eet-ĕn) chew and swallow کھانا destroy as if by eating کھا جانا **eatable** *adj.* fit to be eaten خوردنی، کھانے جانے کے قابل *n. pl.* (*eatables*), food اشیائے خوردنی
eaves (eevz) *n. pl.* overhanging edges of a roof اولتی **eavesdrop** *v. i.* listen secretly to private conversation چھپ کر سن گن لینا، کن سوئیاں لینا **eavesdropper** *n.* جو چھپ کر سن گن پاشے۔
eaves
ebb. (eb) *v. i.* (of the tide) flow back from the land اترنا، کم ہونا become weak کم ہونا، کمزور ہونا *n.* the flowing out of the tide بھاٹا، جزر **ebb-tide** *n.* ebbing of the sea بھاٹا، جزر
ebony (*eb*-o-ni) *n.* hard, black wood آبنوس *adj.* black like ebony آبنوسی made of ebony آبنوس کا
eccentric (ek-*sent*-rik) *adj.* abnormal (person) سنکی abnormal (behaviour) عجیب deviating from circle منحرف المرکز **eccentricity** (ek-sen-*tris*-i-ti) *n.* abnoral behaviour سنک
eclesiastic (ek-lee-zi-*as*-tik) *n.* clergyman پادری **ecclesiastical** *adj.* of the Christian Church کلیسائی of clergymen پادریوں کا
ecdysiast *n.* see *Addenda*
echo (*ek*-oh) *n.* (pl. *echoes*) sound reflected or sent back گونج، صدائے بازگشت close imitation صدائے بازگشت *His speech was an echo of yours* اس کی تقریر تو محض چربہ آپکی تقریر کی صدائے بازگشت ہے (*Echo*), reflected sound personified (with which the youth Narscissus in classical mythology fell in love) ایکو *v. t.* & *i.* (of place) resound *with* echo گونجنا (of sound) rebound (*from*) گونجنا repeat the words or opinions of دہرانا
eclat (*ayk*-la) *n.* brilliant success شاندار کامیابی، دھوم دھام، کروفر *with 'eclat'* بڑی دھوم دھام سے
eclipse (ee-*klips*) *n.* total or partial cutting off of the light of the sun by the moon coming between it and the earth (called *solar eclipse*) or of the reflected light of the moon by the earth coming between it and the sun (called *lunar eclipse*) گرہن solar eclipse سورج گرہن، کسوف lunar eclipse چاند گرہن، خسوف loss of glory ماند پڑنا *v. t.* (of a planet, etc.) cause eclipse of (another) گرہن لگانا cut off the light from ماند کرنا outshine سے زیادہ چمکنا **ecliptic** *adj.* relating to an eclipse گرہن سے متعلق
eclogue (*ek*-log) *n.* short pastoral poem چرواہوں کا گیت
ecology, œcology (ee-kol-o-ji) *n.* study of organisms in relation to their environment ماحولیات علمِ ماحول
economics *n.* **economist** *n.* (see under **economy**)
economy (ee-*kon*-o-mi) *n.* careful management avoiding all waste بچت، کفایت *household economy* گھر کا انتظام management of the resources of a community معاشیات **economics** (ee-ko-*nom*-iks) *n.* (also called *political economy*) social science studying the production and distribution of wealth معاشیات **economic** (ee-ko-*nom*-ik) *adj.* pertaining to economics معاشی designed to yield profit سود مند **economical** (ee-ko-*nom*-i-kĕl) *adj.* pertaining to economics معاشی thrifty کفایت شعار saving economically کم خرچ *adv.* thriftily کفایت شعاری سے **economist** (ee-*kon*-o-mist) *n.* expert in or writer on economics ماہرِ معاشیات **economize** (ee-*kon*-o-miz) *v.t.* & *i.* use or spend less than before (*in* something) کم خرچ کرنا be thrifty کفایت سے کام لینا۔
ecstasy (*ek*-sta-si) *n.* feeling of spiritual up-

lift ; trance, rapture وَجد ، حال *be in an ecstasy, go into ecstasies (over something)* سے وَجد طاری ہونا *throw (someone) into ecstasies,* enrapture پر وَجد طاری ہونا poetic frenzy کیف great joy حد درجہ خوشی ، بہت سُرور **ecstatic** (ek-*stat*-ik) *adj.* causing ecstasy کیف آور in an ecstasy وَجد کی حالت میں ، وجد آفریں wild with joy بہت خوش

eczema (*ek*-ze-ma) *n.* a skin disease کھجلی ، خارش ، الزیما

eddy (*ed*-i) *n.* small whirlpool پانی کا چکّر ، بھنوَر smoke, fog, etc., having a spiral movement چھوٹا سا گرداب *v. i.* whirl round in eddies چکّر کھانا ، مَرغولہ بننا مَرغُولہ

Eden (*ee*-dèn) *n.* a garden on earth where (according to Christian belief) Adam آدم and Eve حوّا lived at creation باغِ عَدَن ، جَنّت delightful place خوشی کا مقام state of delight خوشی ، مسّرت

edge (ej) *n* sharp cutting side of sharp instrument دھار ، sharpness تیزی *have no edge,* be not sharp تیز نہ ہونا *put an edge to* (or *on*), sharpen تیز کرنا effectiveness اثر ، زور *take the edge off an argument,* spoil its effect دلیل کا زور کم کرنا *take the edge off the appetite,* satistfy it partly بُھوک کی شِدّت کم کرنا quality of cutting to the quick کاٹ meeting line of surfaces کنارا boundary line کنارا *give (someone) the edge of (one's) tongue,* scold him جھاڑ جھپاڑ کرنا ، لعن طعن کرنا state of nervous tension (only in the phrase :) *be on the edge,* be irritable بھرا بیٹھا ہونا ، تیکھا ہونا ، چڑ چڑا ہونا *v. t. & i.* sharpen knife, etc. تیز کرنا ، دھار بنانا supply with border کنارا ہونا ، کور ہونا move slowly and cautiously (*along*) دیکھ دیکھ کر قدم دھرنا move obliquely and slowly دھیرے دھیرے بڑھنا *edge oneself* (or *one's way*) *through a crowd* بھیڑ میں سے آہستہ آہستہ آگے بڑھنا insinuate (oneself or something, *in* or *into*) ہوشیاری سے شامل ہونا **edgeways, edgewise** *adv.* with the edge foremost کنارا آگے کی طرف **edging** (*ej*-ing) *n.* border کور ، حاشیہ **edgy** (*ej*-i) *adj.* (esp. of a painting) too sharp in outline (تصویر) تیکھے خطوط والی testy چڑچڑا ، تیکھا ، بھرا بیٹھا

edible (ed-i-bèl) *adj.* fit to be eaten کھانے کے قابل ، خوردنی *n.* (usu. *pl.*) edible things اشیائے خوردنی

edict (*ee*-dikt) *n.* order proclaimed by authority and having the force of law. فرمان *Edict of Nantes,* Henry IV's order for toleration of French Protestants (revoked by Louis XIV) فرمانِ رواداری

edifice (*ed*-i-fis) *n.* large and imposing building شاندار عمارت

edify (*ed*-i-fi) *v. t.* improve spiritually رُوحانی ترقی دینا ، اخلاقی طور پر بہتر بنانا improve the mind سِکھانا ، علم وعقل بڑھانا **edifying** (*ed*-i-fi-ing) *adj.* improving spiritually رُوحانی سربلند **edification** (*-kay-*) *n.* progress in goodness or knowledge رُوحانی (یا علمی) سربلندی

edit (*ed*-it) *v. t.* prepare (someone's writing) for publication مُدوّن کرنا prepare (news) for publication in a periodical (خبر) اِشاعت کے لیے تیار کرنا ، ایڈٹ کرنا ، خبر نویسی کرنا conduct (periodical) ایڈیٹری کرنا ، اِدارت کے فرائض انجام دینا **edition** (ed-*ish*-ŏn) *n.* form in which a book is published ایڈیشن ، اشاعت number of copies once printed اشاعت ، مطبُوعہ *edition 'de-luxe',* pretty edition نفیس مطبُوعہ **editor** *n.* one who prepares (someone's) writing for publication مُدوّن ، مُرتّب (usu. *Editor*) one who conducts a periodical ایڈیٹر ، مُدیر ، اخبار نویس *Assistant Editor,* (esp.) one who assists the editor of a periodical in writing editorials مُدیر معاون ، مُعاون *News Editor,* person with overall control of a news-unit مُدیر مُخابرات *Sub-Editor,* one who assists the editor of a periodical in subbing (*i.e.,* editing news-items) نائب مُدیر *Chief Editor,* editor with overall control (of a chain of periodicals) مدیر اعلیٰ *Managing Editor,* manager-cum (of a periodical) مُحرّر ، ناظم **editorial** (ed-i-*tŏ*-rĕl) *adj.* of an Editor ایڈیٹر کا ، مُدیر کا *n.* s comment on news, etc., in a periodical w by the Editor or one of the Assistant Editors اِدارتی مقالہ ، اداریہ

educate (*ed*-ew-kayt) *v. t.* teach and train ; instruct تعلیم دینا ، تربیت کرنا **education** (-*kay*-) *n.* instruction تعلیم knowledge and ability gained by it تعلیم ، علم ، تربیت **educational** *adj.* pertaining to education تعلیمی **educationist,** (or less correctly) **educationalist** *n.* expert in education ماہرِ تعلیم **educator** *n.* (*ed*-ew-kay-tĕ*) *n.* instructor مُعلّم **educative** (*ed*-ew-kay-tiv) *adj.* instructive بصیرت افروز ، حقائق افروز

eel *n.* sleek snake-like fish بام مچھلی ، برقی بام مچھلی ، کوچھی

eerie, eery (*ee*-ri) *adj.* causing a feeling of fear or mystery پُراسرار ، ہیبتناک

e'en (een) abbr. of **even** (which see)

e'er (e-ĕ*) abbr. of **ever** (which see)

efface (e-*fays*) *v.t.* wipe out (signs of) مٹانا erase (writing) محو کرنا *efface oneself,* (*a*) keep oneself in the background in order to escape notice پیچھے پیچھے رہنا (*b*) withhold one's own claims اپنے دعوے سے دست کش ہو جانا **effacement** *n.* wiping out مٹانا ، محو کرنا

effect (e-*fekt*) *n.* result, outcome نتیجہ ، انجام *(be) of no effect,* (be) useless بے نتیجہ (ہونا) *take effect,* (*a*) produce the requisite result خاطر خواہ نتیجہ نکلنا

(*b*) be implemented عمل میں آنا ، نافذ ہونا *give effect to*, cause to become active عمل میں لانا ، جامۂ عمل پہنانا *bring into effect*, cause to operate عمل میں لانا *carry into effect*, accomplish کرنا ، عمل میں لانا *in effect*, practically عملاً impression made on the mind اثر ، تاثر *do (something) merely for effect*, do (it) not earnestly but only for impressing others صرف مفرد کے لیے آنا ، محض دکھاوے کی خاطر آنا *calculated for effect*, meant to impress others دکھاوے کے لیے *to the effect that, to this effect*, with the general meaning of جس کا مفہوم یہ ہے کہ ، بدیں معنیٰ کہ (*pl.*) (*effects*), appearance, impression اثرات *sound effects* صوتی اثرات (*pl.*) (*effects*), movable property جائداد منقولہ *personal effects* ذاتی جائداد *no effects*, reason stated for dishonouring a cheque when the drawer has not that much money in his account حساب میں روپیہ نہیں ہے *v.t.* bring about, accomplish کرنا ، عمل میں لانا **effective** *adj.* having an effect مؤثر ، اثر آفریں **effectual** (e-*fek*-tew-ĕl) *adj.* answering its purpose کارگر ، سودمند

effeminate (e-*fem*-i-nayt) *adj.* womanish, unmanly زنانہ ، نامردوں کا سا **effeminacy** *n.* being effeminate نامردی ، زنانہ پن

effervesce (ef-ĕ*-*ves*) *v.t.* & *i.* give off bubbles of gas بلبلے چھوڑنا (of gas) issue in bubbles کے بلبلے بننا be lively and gay خوش باش ہونا زندہ دل ہونا **effervescent** *adj.* that which gives off bubbles بلبلے چھوڑنے والا ، حباب زا **effervescence** *n.* giving off bubbles بلبلے چھوڑنا ، حباب زائی

effete (e-*feet*) *adj.* very weak and exhausted ناتواں ، مضمحل

efficacious (ef-i-*kay*-shus) *adj.* (*usu.* of medicines) producing the desired result مجرّب ، یقینی تاثیر رکھنے والا ، کارگر **efficacy** (*ef*-i-ka-si) *n.* power to produce the desired result تاثیر

efficient (e-*fish*-ent) *adj.* producing an effect اثر آفریں (of persons) competent قابل ، لائق ، کارکن ، کارگزار **efficiency** (e-*fish*-en-si) *n.* (of person) competence اہلیت ، استعداد ، لیاقت (of things) effective power اثر ، تاثیر ratio of useful work performed to energy spent کام اور توانائی کا تناسب ، کارگزاری

effigy (*ef*-i-ji) *n.* person's portrait or image (in wood, etc.) مورت ، پتلا *burn* (or *hang*) (*someone*) *in effigy*, burn (or hang) his effigy as a token of hatred or anger (کسی چیز کا پتلا بنا کر جلا دینا (یا اسے پھانسی دینا پھانسی دینا head or impression on a coin سکے پر کی تصویر

effort (*ef*-ĕ*t) *n.* endeavour, exertion کوشش ، سعی *effort* (*to do* something) کوئی کام کرنے کی کوشش (*be*) *a fine effort* (کامیاب کوشش (ہونا

effrontery (e-*frunt*-ĕ-ri) *n.* impudence ڈھٹائی ، دیدہ دلیری *have the effrontery* (*to do something*), be impudent enough (to do it) دیدہ دلیری سے کوئی کام کرنا

effulgence (e-*ful*-jens) *n.* radiance تابانی ، تابندگی ، درخشانی درخشندگی **effulgent** *adj.* very bright درخشندہ ، تاباں ، درخشاں

effusion (e-*few*-zhĕn) *n.* pouring forth بہاؤ *effusion of light* ضیا پاشی outpouring of thought or feeling پُرجوش اظہار **effusive** (e-*few*-siv) *adj.* gushing (joy, etc.) پُرجوش ، بہت

egad (e-*gad*) *int.* by God! بخدا

egg *n.* (usu. oval) object from which the young ones of some animals are hatched انڈا ، بیضا *lay an egg* انڈا دینا *hatch eggs* انڈے سینا *beat eggs*, whisk them انڈے کا پھینٹنا *egg-shell*, (*a*) shell of egg انڈے کا چھلکا (*b*) fragile thing ٹوٹنے والی چیز *poached egg* ابلا ہوا انڈا *fried egg* تلا ہوا انڈا ، چرچ انڈا *boiled egg* ابلا ہوا انڈا *hard-boiled egg* سخت ابلا ہوا انڈا *soft-boiled egg* نرم ابلا ہوا انڈا *egg-cup*, cup for a boiled egg بیضہ دان *egg-spoon* انڈا کھانے کا چمچہ *egg whisk*, vessel for beating eggs انڈے پھینٹنے کا برتن *bad-egg*, (slang) person or scheme that comes to no good (ناکارہ (شخص یا تجویز گندا انڈا *have all one's eggs in one basket*, risk all on a single venture ایک ہی داؤں پر سب کچھ لگا دینا ، داؤں (slang.) bomb from an aeroplane ہوائی بم *v.t. egg* (*someone*) *on* (*to do* something, or *to* something), urge (him) (to do or to something) (کسی کو کسی کام پر) اکسانا

egghead *n.* see *Addenda*

ego (eg-*oh*) *n.* conscious thinking subject انا ، میں

non-ego *n.* (the opposite of *ego*) object معروض ، تو

ego-centric *adj.* self-centred صاحب لائے جزئی ، خود پرستانہ

egoism (*eg*-o-izm) *n.* continual selfishness مستقل ، خود غرضی theory basing morality on self-interest فلسفۂ خود غرضی **egoist** (*eg*-o-ist) *n.* خود غرض **egoistic, egoistical** (-*is*-) *adj.* based on or guided by self-interest خود غرضانہ

egotism (*eg*-o-tizm) *n.* practice of talking about oneself ; too much use of *I* and *me* میں ، انانیت self-conceit خود پسندی **egotist** (*eg*-o-tist) *n.* self-conceited ; talking too much about himself خود پسند **egotistic, egotistical** (-*tis*-) *adj.* خود پسندانہ ، خود پسند

egregious (eg-*ree*-jus) *adj.* extremely silly (mistake, blunder, folly, fool, etc.) سخت ، پرلے درجے کا ، حد درجہ

Egypt (*ee*-jipt) *n.* مصر **Egyptian** (ee-*jip*-shĕn) *adj.* of Egypt مصری ، مصر کا *n.* native of Egypt مصری gypsy خانہ بدوش **Egyptology** (ee-jip-*tol*-o-ji) *n.* study of old Egyptian relics مصریات **Egyptologist** *n.* ماہر مصریات

eider-down (i-dĕ*-down) *n.* soft breast-feathers of a large Arctic duck (called *eider*) ایڈر کی کومل رُوئیں ایڈر کی رُوئیں quilt stuffed with it ایڈر کی رُوئیں کا لحاف
eight (ayt) *n.* & *adj.* 8 آٹھ **eighteen** (*ayt-een*) *n.* & *adj.* 18 اٹھارہ **eighty** (*ayt*-i) *n.* & *adj.* 80 اَسّی
eighth (aytth) *adj.* آٹھواں **eighthly** (*aytth*-li) *adv.* ہشتم، ثامناً **eighteenth** (*ayt-eenth*) *adj.* اٹھارواں **eightieth** (*ayt*-i-eth) *adj.* اَسّی واں **one-eighth** (wun-*aytth*) *n.* & *adj.* آٹھواں حصّہ **one-eighteenth** (wun-*ayt-eenth*) *n.* & *adj.* اٹھارواں حصّہ **one-eightieth** (wun-*ayt*-i-eth) *n.* & *adj.* اَسّی واں حصّہ **eightfold** (*ayt*-fohld) *adj.* & *adv.* آٹھ گُنا
either (ī-dhĕ* or ee-dhĕ*) *adj.* each, both دونوں، دو *at either end*, at both ends دونوں طرف، ہر دو جانب one of the two کوئی سا، دونوں میں سے کوئی ایک *pron.* any one of the two کوئی سا، دونوں میں سے کوئی ایک *adv.* (with negative) also, moreover بھی *If you do not go, I shan't either* تم نہیں چلتے تو میں بھی نہیں جاؤں گا *conj.* **either**...**or,** in one of the two cases یا...یا، یا تو...یا، خواہ...خواہ *Either pass or leave the school* یا تو پاس ہو جاؤ یا سکول چھوڑ جاؤ **Note:** In negative form **neither......nor** is used as a conj. in place of **either......or**
ejaculate (ee-*jak*-ew-layt) *v.t.* & *i.* say suddenly, exclaim بے ساختہ کہنا
eject (e-*jekt*) *v.t.* expel (someone or some liquid *from* a place) نکالنا، بے دخل کرنا *ejected tenants* بے دخل مزارع (یا کرایہ دار) **ejectment** *n.* expulsion اِخراج
eke (eek) *v.t.* (*eke out*), make extra supplies of something deficient (*with*) پورا کرنا، کی کمی پوری کرنا *eke out (one's) salary with odd jobs* متفرق کام کر کے تنخواہ کی کمی پوری کرنا *eke out (one's) existence* (or *livelihood*), (colloq.) earn one's livelihood with difficulty
elaborate (e-*lab*-o-rayt) *adj.* worked out with much care and in detail مُفصّل *v.t.* describe in detail تفصیل سے بیان کرنا produce with care and effort محنت اور کوشش سے بنانا **elaborately** *adv.* مُفصّل، تفصیل سے، محنت سے **elaboration** (-*ay*-) *n.* detailed description (*of*) مُفصّل بیان
élan (ay-*laun*) *n.* impetuous vigour جوش و خروش *do (something) with 'élan'*, do it with a dash جوش و خروش سے کام کرنا
elapse (e-*laps*) *v.i.* (of time) pass گزرنا
elastic (e-*las*-tik) *adj.* resuming its normal size or shape after being stretched or pressed لچکدار، لچلچا، پھیلا، لچک دار *elastic-band* لچکدار پٹی not firm or fixed تغیّر پذیر adaptable اپنے کو حالات کے مطابق ڈھال لینے والا (of disposition) able to recover from depression غم کو بھول جانے والا *n.* material made elastic by weaving rubber into it لچک دار کپڑا (وغیرہ) such cord اِلاسٹک، لچلچا
elate (ee-*layt*) *v.t.* make happy and proud نازاں کرنا، کے لیے موجب فخر ہونا **elated** (ee-*layt*-ed) *adj.* in high spirits because of success فخر کرنے والا، نازاں **elation** *n.* being in high spirits فخر، فخر و ناز
elbow (*el*-boh) *n.* bend of the arm (from the outside) کہنی (*be*) *out at elbows*, (*a*) (of dress) be worn-out there کہنی سے پھٹا ہوا ہونا (*b*) (of someone) be in worn-out clothes پھٹے پرانے کپڑے پہنے ہوئے ہونا such sharp bend in a pipe, etc. کونہ، کہنی *v.t.* push one's way (*forward* or *through* or *out of a crowd*) مشکل سے آگے بڑھنا thrust with the elbow کہنی مارنا، کہنی مار کر پرے کرنا

an elbow (sense 2)

elder (*el*-dĕ*) *adj.* (of persons, esp. relations) older بڑا، عمر میں بڑا (*pl.*) (*elders*), persons deserving respect (because of age or authority) بڑے بوڑھے، بزرگ *Respect your elders* بزرگوں کی عزت کرنا member of a Senate or church governing body سینیٹر، بزرگ، پادری *elder statesman*, (see *Addenda*)
elderly (*el*-de*-li) *adj.* rather old قدرے عمر رسیدہ، ادھیڑ عمر کا، کسی قدر بوڑھا **eldest** (*el*-dest) *adj.* (of persons) oldest سب سے بڑا، ہم میں سب سے بڑا first-born پہلوٹھی کا [S] **Old**, used *of things*, means not new, or used for some time; used *of persons* it suggests someone very grown-up and nearing his end. It is wrong to use it for persons who are not of that age for it would give them offence to suggest that they are fast approaching the end of their life. They should be described as **elderly** and not **old**.
El Dorado (el-do-*rah*-doh) *n.* imaginary country rich in gold مُلکِ زرّیں any place where wealth is easily to be made وہ جگہ جہاں دولت آسانی سے پیدا کی جا سکے
elect (e-*lekt*) *v.t.* choose (someone) by vote چننا، منتخب کرنا، کا انتخاب (یا چناؤ) کرنا *elect a chairman, elect the President* کو صدر منتخب کرنا *elect (someone) President* صدر منتخب ہونا *be elected President* صدر منتخب ہونا choose (something or *to do* something) اختیار کرنا *adj.* chosen منتخب، منتخبہ *the President-elect* (chosen but not yet in office) صدر منتخب *the elect*, those considered to be the best چُنے ہوئے لوگ، بہترین افراد **election** (e-*lek*-shĕn) *n.* choosing by vote انتخاب، چُناؤ *election to the assembly* اسمبلی کا انتخاب *by-election* ضمنی انتخاب *a General Election, General Elections*, time when the whole nation goes to the polls for electing its parlia-

mentary representatives (as distinct from a bye-election when there is election for only one or a few of the seats) عمومی اِنتخاب، عام اِنتخابات **electioneer** (e-lek-she-*nee*-ē*) *v.i.* canvass support for candidates at a parliamentary election اِنتخاب میں کسی کی حمایت کرنا *electioneering campaign* اِنتخابی مہم **electioneering** *n.* اِنتخابی مہم چلانا **elector** (e-*lek*-tě*) *n.* one of those having the right to elect their representatives to the parliament اِنتخاب کنندہ، رائے دہندہ (Old Germany) prince entitled to elect Emperor الکٹر، اِنتخاب کنندہ نواب **electress** (e-*lek*-tress) *n.* female elector اِنتخاب کنندہ، رائے دہندہ **electorate** (e-*lek*-to-rayt) *n.* the whole body of electors رائے دہندگان *separate electorate*, system of voting where the electors (of a particular sex, or religious or other community) vote for candidates belonging to their own group جُداگانہ اِنتخاب، جُداگانہ اِنتخابات *joint electorate*, system which deserves no such obligation مخلوط اِنتخاب، مخلوط اِنتخابات **electoral** (e-*lek*-to-rel) *adj.* of elector(s) اِنتخابی *electoral role*, list of voters فہرستِ رائے دہندگان، رائے دہندوں کا *electoral college, electoral district*, constituency اِنتخابی حلقہ **elective** (e-*lek*-tiv) *adj.* appointed or filled by election اِنتخابات سے چُن دیا، ہونے والا entitled to elect حقِ رائے دہی رکھنے والا chosen اِنتخابی *electibe subject*, (in university, etc.) one of the optional subjects in which it is compulsory for a candidate to qualify for passing the examination اِنتخابی مضمون

Electra (ee-*lek*-tra) *Cl. myth.* Greek king Agamemnon's daughter who loved her father so passionately that on his assassination she incited her brother, Orestes, to kill their mother, Clytemnestra, in vengeance **Electra complex**, daughter's passionate sexual love for her own father which, according to Freud, naturally lurks in every girl's heart الکٹرہ ذہنیت، عشقِ پدر

electricity (e-lek-*tris*-i-ti) *n.* a form of energy (of which lightning flash is a type) which can be generated and harnessed to drive machines or to produce heat, light or sound بجلی، برق، برقی قوت *static electricity*, electric energy which cannot be conducted جھٹکا، کی برق *current electricity*, that which can be conducted through wires برقی رَو science of this برق **electric** (e-*lek*-trik) *adj.* of, producing, or worked, by electricity بجلی کا، برقی *electric shock*, effect of sudden discharge of electricity بجلی کا جھٹکا، شاٹ *electric cell*, apparatus for producing electric current بیٹری *electric current*, current of electricity برقی رَو *electric charge* برقی بار *electric lamp* بجلی کا لیمپ **electrical** *adj.* concerned with electricity بجلی کا ۔ برقی *electrical goods* بجلی کا سامان *electrical engineering* برقی اِنجنیئری، برقی مُہندسی **electrician** (e-lek-*trish*-ěn) *n.* skilled worker attending to electrical equipment الیکٹریشن، بجلی والا، بجلی کا مستری *electrical engineer*, electrician who is also a technologist برقی مُہندس **electrify** (e-*lek*-tri-fī) *v.t.* (*electrifying, electrified*) install electric light, fans, etc., in a building بجلی لگانا alter (railway, etc.) for working by electricity برقانا، برقی بنانا، بجلی سے چلنے والا بنانا fill (something) with electricity برقانا excite or shock (someone) as by electricity بجلی کی سی لہر دَوڑا دینا **electrified** (-fīd) *adj.* برقایا ہوا **electrification** (-fi-*kay*-) *n.* installation of electric light, etc. بجلی لگانا altering for working with electricity بجلی سے چلنے والا بنانا، برقانا filling with electricity برقانا برقی بنانا exciting or shocking بجلی کی سی لہر دَوڑانا

electro- (e-*lek*-troh) *pref.* of electricity بجلی کا، برقی **electro-magnetic** *adj.* having both electric and magnetic effects برق مقناطیسی **electro-magnetism** *n.* production of electricity by magnetism and *vice versa* برق مقناطیسی **electroshock** *n.* see *Addenda* **electrocute** *v.t.* execute by means of an electric current بجلی سے جان لینا، برقی کرسی پر بٹھانا *electric chair*, chair used for electrocution بجلی کی کرسی، برقی کرسی **electrocution** *n.* executing or being executed thus برقی کرسی پر بٹھانا **electrolysis** (e-lek-*trol*-i-sis) *n.* separation of a substance into its chemical parts by electric current برق پاشیدگی، برق پاشی **electroplate** (colloquially abbreviated as **electro**), coat (dishes, spoons, etc.) with nickel or silver by electrolysis قلعی کرنا، چاندی کا پانی چڑھانا، ملمع کرنا، صیقل کرنا *n.* articles thus coated ملمع شدہ، صیقل زدہ **electromotive** *adj.* tending to produce electric current برق زا (see also **electron**)

electron (e-*lek*-tron) *n.* sub-atomic particle consisting of negative electric charge revolving round the nucleus of an atom (*cf.*, *neutron, proton*) منفی برقیہ *free electron*, electron released from matter آزاد برقیہ **electronics** *n.* science of free electrons برقیات

elegant (*el*-e-gant) *adj.* having good taste شستہ، پاکیزہ well-dressed خوش پوش beautiful خوبصورت، حسین و جمیل graceful خوش وضع، شاندار **elegance** *n.* quality of being elegant شستگی، پاکیزگی حسن و جمال، خوش پوشی، شان

elegy (*el*-i-ji) *n.* poem or song lamenting the

dead مرثیہ، نوحہ **elegiac** (el-i-*ji*-ak) *adj*. مرثیے سے متعلق، مرثیہ نگارانہ
element (*el*-e-ment) *n*. substance which cannot be separated into simpler substances and whose molecules can only be resolved into atoms of electricity عنصر (old use) one of the four elements of nature (*viz*., *earth*, *water*, *air* and *fire*) عنصر *the four elements* عناصرِ اربع indication, trace (*of*) نشان natural surroundings of a being قدرتی ماحول، سازگار فضا (*be*) *in* (*one's*) *element*, (be) at home اپنے ماحول میں ہونا، بے جھجک کام کرنا (*be*) *out of* (*one's*) *element*, not (be) in (one's) natural or pleasing surroundings مخالفانہ ماحول میں ہونا، ہچکچانا (*pl*.) (*the elements*), wind, storm, rain, snow, cold, heat, etc. موسم کی سختیاں (مثلاً باد و باراں) (*pl*.) (*the elements of*), the rudiments of کے مبادی، کے مبادیات **elemental** (el-e-*ment*-ĕl) *adj*. (esp.) uncontrolled بے قابو
elementary (el-e-*ment*-è-ri) *adj*. of the early stage(s) ابتدائی، بنیادی *elementary education* ابتدائی تعلیم not fully developed ابتدائی simple, not complicated سیدھا سادہ
elephant (*el*-i-fant) *n*. the largest extant animal ہاتھی، فیل *white elephant*, possession costing a lot to maintain سفید ہاتھی **elephantine** (el-i-*fant*-in) *adj*. of or like an elephant ہاتھی کا سا large and clumsy بھدا، بھاری بھرکم، بے ڈول **elephantiasis** (el-i-fan-*tī*-è-sis) *n*. skin disease in which legs become thick فیل پا
elevate (*el*-e-vayt) *v.t*. lift up اونچا کرنا، اٹھانا، بلند کرنا make (the mind or morals) higher and better (ذہنی یا اخلاقی) سطح بلند کرنا **elevation** (el-e-*vay*-shĕn) *n*. elevating or being elevated بلند کرنا یا ہونا height بلندی، ارتفاع height above sea-level سطحِ سمندر سے بلندی rising ground چڑھائی sketch of one side of a building ارتفاع **elevator** (el-e-*vay*-tĕ*) *n*. lift machine for hauling cereals, etc. لفٹ، اٹھاؤ، مرفع
eleven (e-*lev*-èn) *n*. & *adj*. 11 گیارہ **eleventh** *adj*. 11th گیارھواں **elevens, elevenses** *n*. (colloq.) light refreshment at about 11 a.m. گیارہ بجے کا نقل
elf *n*. (pl. *elves* pr. elvz.) any small and mischievous (esp. supernatural) creature شریر بونا، چھلاوا
elfin (*el*-fin) *adj*. of or like elfs شریر بونے یا چھلاوے کا سا *n*. dwarf child بونا بچہ، ننھا بچہ **elfish, elvish** *adj*. elf-like شریر بونے یا چھلاوے کا سا mischievous شریر **elflocks** *n. pl*. tangled mass of locks لٹیں، جٹائیں
elicit (e-*lis*-it) *v.t*. bring to light a hidden thing (*from*) کا اظہار کرنا draw out (reply or applause *from*) جواب نکلوانا، (تعریف) کرانا

elide (e-*līd*) *v.t*. omit (some sound) in pronunciation گرانا، ادا نہ کرنا **elision** (e-*lizh*-èn) omission (of sound) in pronunciation حذف، ازالہ
eligible (*el*-ij-e-bĕl) *adj*. fit to be chosen (*for*) کا اہل، کی اہلیت رکھنے والا properly qualified (*for*) استعداد رکھنے والا، صلاحیت رکھنے والا **eligibility** (e-lij-i-*bil*-i-ti) *n*. fitness (*for*) اہلیت، صلاحیت، استعداد، موزونیت
eliminate (e-*lim*-i-nayt) *v.t*. leave out of consideration نظر انداز کرنا expel (something *from*) خارج کرنا drop نکال دینا **elimination** (-*ay*-) *n*. act of eliminating or being eliminated اخراج
elite (ay-*leet*) *n*. (*the*) best part (*of*) کا بہترین حصہ *the elite of the town* ممتاز افراد، زعما
elixir (e-*lik*-sĕ*) *n*. mediaeval scientists' much sought-for preparation for changing cheaper metal into gold or for prolonging life اکسیر *elixir of life*, elixir for prolonging life اکسیرِ حیات sovereign remedy اکسیر
Elizabethan (e-liz-a-*beeth*-èn) *adj*. of the reign of the English Queen, Elizabeth I (1558-1603) الزبتھ کے زمانے کا، الزبتھی *the Elizabethan drama*, English plays written in that epoch الزبتھی تاٹک *n*. person of that age الزبتھ کے زمانے کا، الزبتھی English writer of that period (الزبتھی مصنف، عہد الزبتھ کا مصنف)
elk *n*. a kind of large antelope بڑا بارہ سنگھا
ell (el) *n*. measure of length about one-and-a-half yards تقریباً ڈیڑھ گز کا پیمانہ
ellipse (e-*lips*) *n*. a regular oval بیضوی اہلیجی شکل، اہلیج **elliptic, elliptical** *adj*. shaped like an ellipse بیضوی، اہلیجی an ellipse
elm *n*. a kind of tall tree with serrated leaves بوقیذار its hard and heavy wood بوقیذار کی لکڑی
elocution (el-o-*kew*-shĕn) *n*. art of effective public speaking فنِ خطابت، خطابت its style خطابت، اسلوبِ تقریر **elocutionary** *adj*. pertaining to elocution فنِ خطابت سے متعلق **elocutionist** *n*. elocution expert خطیب، ماہرِ مقرر elocution teacher فنِ خطابت کا استاد
elongate (*ee*-long-ayt) *v. t*. make longer کھینچنا، لمبا کرنا **elongation** (-*ay*-) *n*. lengthening کھینچنا، لمبا کرنا
elope (e-*lohp*) *v.i*. (of a woman) run away (*from* home *with* lover) (کے ساتھ) نکل جانا **elopement** *n*. نکل جانا
eloquence (*el*-o-kwens) *n*. persuasive (and impassioned) speech پرجوش تقریر skilful and fluent use of language فصاحت، خوش بیانی **eloquent** (*el*-o-kwent) *adj*. fluent فصیح impassion-

ed پُرجوش *grow eloquent over* کے بارے میں پُرجوش ہونا
else (els) *adv.* besides اور *What else?* اور کیا *Whose else?*, *Who else?* اور کِس کا؟ *Nobody else turned up* اور کوئی نہ آیا؛ instead اور کے علاوہ *What else could she do?* وہ اور کر بھی کیا سکتی تھی (usu., *or else*) otherwise ورنہ *Hurry up or else you will be late* جلدی کرو ورنہ وقت پر نہ پہنچ سکو گے (*or else*) if not ورنہ، اگر نہیں تو ...یا... یا *He is mad or else I am a fool* یا وہ پاگل ہے یا میں احمق ہوں **elsewhere** *adv.* in, at or to some other place کہیں اَور، اور کہیں
elucidate (e-*lew*-si-dayt) *v. t.* explain, clarify واضح کرنا، توضیح کرنا throw light on (some point, etc.) **elucidatory** *adj.* explanatory توضیحی **elucidation** (-*day*-) *n.* clarification توضیح، وضاحت
elude (ee-*lood*) *v.t.* escape by some trick from (danger, observation, grasp, person, etc.) سے بچ نکلنا، طرح دے جانا avoid complying with (law or request) سے گریز کرنا، سے بچنا **elusory, elusive** *adj.* evasive نکلنے والا، طرح دے جانے والا baffling مغالطے میں ڈال دینے والا fallacious حیران کن hard to express or define مشکل **elusion** *n.* evasion by trick طرح دے جانا، بچ نکلنا escape گریز، بچ پاؤ fallacy مغالطہ آمیزی
Elysium (i-*liz*-i-um) *Class. myth.* abode of the blessed after death ایلیزیم place of ideal happiness بہشت، جنت ideal happiness رضوان **elysian** (i-*liz*-i-ĕn) *adj.* of Elysium ایلیزیم کا، بہشت کا very delightful بہجت افزا
emaciate *v.t.* (e-*maysh*-i-ayt) make lean دُبلا کرنا لاغر کرنا waste away گھلانا **emaciate** (e-*mash*-i-it) **emaciated** *adj.* lean and skinny دُبلا، لاغر wasted away گھلا ہوا **emaciation** (-*ay*-) *n.* لاغری، دُبلا پن، گھلانا
emanate (*em*-a-nayt) *v.i.* (of news, etc.) issue (*from* a source) نکلنا، جاری ہونا، ظہور ہونا **emanation** (-*ay*-) *n.* (of someone, something or some moral force) coming from a source ظہور، صدور
emancipate (e-*man*-si-payt) *v. t.* set free from intellectual, legal or social restraint نجات دینا، آزادی عطا کرنا، آزاد کرنا **emancipator** *n.* liberator (esp. of slaves) نجات دہندہ، منجی، مُنجی **emancipation** (-*pay*-) *n.* such liberation نجات آزادی **emancipationist** *n.* advocate of emancipation of slaves غلامی کا مخالف، غلاموں کو آزاد کرنے کا حامی
emasculate *v.t.* (i-*mas*-kew-layt) castrate ہیجڑا بنانا weaken کمزور کرنا، نحیف بنانا weaken (writing) by cutting out strong remarks (تحریر کا) زور کم کرنا *adj.* (i-*mas*-kew-lit) castrated ہیجڑا effeminate **emasculation** *n.* castration ہیجڑا بنانا
embalm (em-*bahm*) *v.t.* preserve (a dead body) with balm حنوط کرنا cherish دل سے لگائے رکھنا
embankment (em-*bank*-ment) *n.* wall or earth, etc., to hold back water or support a raised road or a rail track پشتہ، بند
embargo (em-*bah**-goh) *n.* (pl. *embargoes*) temporary stoppage of trade عارضی تجارتی بندش order prohibiting movement of ship جہاز کے جانے کی مناہی، جہاز پر بندش *lay an embargo on* پر بندش لگانا *be under an embargo* پر بندش لگنا
embark (em-*bah**k) *v. t.* & *i.* put or go on board a ship جہاز پر سوار ہونا یا کرنا take part (*in* or *on* enterprise) آغاز کرنا **embarkation** (-*kay*-) *n.* act of embarking جہاز پر چڑھنا یا چڑھانا
embarrass (em-*ba*-ras) *v. t.* cause (someone) mental discomfort (*with*) پریشان کرنا put into dilemma مشکل میں ڈالنا complicate (question) پیچیدہ بنانا **embarrassment** *n.* پریشانی، مشکل، پیچیدگی
embassy (*em*-ba-si) *n.* function of an ambassador سفارت his office سفارت خانہ person or persons sent as envoys سفیر
embed (em-*bed*), **imbed** (im-*bed*) *v. t.* fix firmly (in a surrounding mass) جما دینا، مضبوطی سے لگا دینا **embedded in**, firmly fixed in میں پکا لگا ہوا
embellish (em-*bel*-ish) *v. t.* make beautiful سجانا، زینت دینا، تزئین کرنا decorate with ornaments زیورات سے سج دھج کر نکلنا make (narrative) more interesting with fictitious details نمک مرچ لگا کر بیان کرنا، حاشیہ آرائی کرنا، زیب داستان کے لیے بڑھانا **embellishment** *n.* decorating سجاوٹ، تزئین، آرائش ornament زیور
embers (*em*-bĕ*z) *n. pl.* small pieces of burning fuel in a dying fire انگارے
embezzle (em-*bez*-ĕl) *v. t.* defalcate; fraudulently use (money) placed in one's care for one's own benefit غبن کرنا **embezzlement** *n.* defalcation (*of*) غبن **embitter** (em-*bit*-ĕ*) *v. t.* increase bitter feelings تلخ بنانا، تلخی پیدا کرنا make (life) bitter تلخ بنانا یا کرنا
emblem (*em*-blĕm) *n.* symbol (*of* quality or state) نشان، علامت heraldic device ڈھال پر نشان، نقش سپر، تاج **emblematic** (-*mat*-) *adj.* serving as an emblem بطور نشان، بطور علامت
embody (em-*bod*-i) *v. t.* give concrete form to (something *in*) (ٹھوس) شکل دینا (of things) be

an expression of کا اظہار ہونا include کو شامل ہونا
embodied (em-*bod*-id) *adj*. getting concrete form مجسّم **embodiment** *n*. (esp.) that which gives concrete form to something تجسیم، مجسّمہ *an embodiment of justice* انصاف، عدلِ مجسّم
embolden (em-bohl-dĕn) *v.t.* encourage ہمت بندھانا جرأت دِلانا، جی بڑھانا
embosom (em-boo-zum) *v. t.* (lit.) enclose (*with* or *in*) آغوش میں لینا، سے گھیرنا *embosomed with trees* پیڑوں سے گھیرا ہوا
emboss (em-*bos*) *v. t.* make a design in relief by carving or pressure منبّت کاری کرنا، منبّت کرنا، اُبھرواں کندہ کاری کرنا **embossed** (em-*bosd*) *adj*. having such design منبّت کار having bosses or studs جس میں کیلیں جڑی ہوئی ہوں
embower (em-*bou*-ĕ*) *v. t.* place in a bower کنج میں رکھنا shelter with trees درختوں کا سایہ کرنا
embrace (em-*brays*) *v. t.* put one's arms round lovingly گلے مِلنا، گلے لگانا، آغوش میں لینا، ہم آغوش ہونا adopt or accept (belief, etc.) قبول کرنا، اختیار کرنا (of things) include پر مشتمل ہونا، کو شامل ہونا *n.* act of embracing ہم آغوشی، گلے مِلنا
embrocation (em-bro-*kay*-shĕn) *n.* lotion for rubbing into bruised or aching part of the body مالش کی دوا، لیپ، رضاد
embroider (em-broi-dĕ*) *v. t.* ornament (cloth) with designs in needlework سوزن کاری کرنا چوب کاری کرنا . embellish (narrative) زیب داستان کے لیے بڑھانا، حاشیہ آرائی کرنا **embroidery** (em-*broi*-dĕ-ri) *n.* ornamental needlework سوزن کاری، کارِ چوبی
embroil (em-*broil*) *v. t.* cause (someone or oneself) to be mixed up in a quarrel (*with*) اُلجھنا اُلجھانا entangle or confuse (affairs) گڑبڑ ڈالنا
embryo (*em*-bri-oh) *n.* (pl. *embryos*) unborn or unhatched offspring جنین thing in an early stage of development خام، ناپختہ، ادھوری (شے)
embryonic (em-bri-*on*-ik) *adj*. pertaining to an embryo جنینی not fully developed ادھورا بالکل ابتدائی *be in an embryonic stage* ابتدائی، غیر پختہ، خام صورت میں ہونا **embryology** (*ol*-o-ji) *n.* science of the embryo جنینیات
embus (em-*bus*) *v. t.* put (men or goods) in bus, truck, etc. بس پر سوار کرنا یا لادنا، بس پر لادنا
emcee *n.* & *v. t.* see *Addenda* بس پر لادنا
emend (e-*mend*) *v. t.* remove errors from (book) متن کی تصحیح کرنا، اغلاط دور کرنا **emendator** (ee-men-day-tĕ*) *n.* one who emends کتاب کے اغلاط کی تصحیح کرنے والا **emendatory** (em-*en*-da-tĕ-ri) *adj*. pertaining to emendation تصحیح کے متعلق **emendation** (ee-men-*day*-shĕn) *n.* correction تصحیح
emerald (*em*-e-rald) *n.* bright-green precious stone زمرّد its colour زمرّدی رنگ *the Emerald Isle*, Ireland زمرّدیں جزیرہ، آئرلینڈ، آئرستان
emerge (e-*mĕj**) *v.i.* come into view ظاہر ہونا come out (from water or obscurity) ظہور میں آنا برآمد ہونا، نکلنا (of facts, ideas) become known مشہور ہونا **emergence** (e-*mĕ**-jens) *n.* ظہور، برآمد
emergency (e-*mĕ**-jen-si) *n.* sudden happening which demands prompt action ناگہانی ضرورت، ہنگامی صورتِ حال *national emergency*, state of danger to the whole nation (*e.g.*, war, famine, blood) قومی ہنگامی صورتِ حال *emergency door, emergency exit*, door, etc., in a vehicle for use in an emergency like fire, etc. حادثاتی دروازہ **emergent** (e-*me**-jent) *adj*. that which occasions emergency ہنگامی، ناگہانی coming out (*from*) برآمد ہونے والا، نکلنے والا
emergency *n.* **emergent** *adj*. (see under **emerge**)
emeritus (e-*me*-ri-tus) *adj*. (pl. *emiriti*) retired but, as an honour, kept on roll سبکدوش باعزازی *Emiritus professor, Professor emeritus* سبکدوش باعزازی پروفیسر
emetic (e-*met*-ik) *adj*. & *n*. (medicine) causing vomiting قے آور (دوا)
emigrate (*em*-i-grayt) *v.i.* go away from one's country (*to* another) to settle there (as opposed to *immigrate*) ترکِ وطن کرکے **emigrant** *n*. person who does this تارکِ وطن **emigration** (em-i-*gray*-shĕn) *n.* going away (*from* one country *to* another) to settle there ترکِ وطن کرکے جانا، جابسنا **emigratory** (*em*-i-gray-tĕ-ri) *adj*. relating to emigration ترکِ وطن سے متعلق ▣ An **emigrant** is one who goes out of a country ; an **immigrant**, one who enters a country to make it his home. The same person is either an **emigrant** or an **immigrant**, according to the speaker's point of view. Thus we in Pakistan may say : "Amritsar was crowded with Muslim **emigrants** ; on arrival at Lahore the **immigrants** went to the refugee camp".
eminent (*em*-i-nent) *adj*. distinguished (person, qualities, etc.) ممتاز، نمایاں **eminently** *adv*. in an unusually high degree غیر معمولی طور پر **eminence** (*em*-i-nens) *n.* being eminent امتیاز rising ground چڑھائی (*His Eminence* or *Your Eminence*), cardinal's title صاحبِ امتیاز
emir (e-*mee**) *n.* Arab prince or governor امیر، حاکم، والی

emissary (*em*-i-sa-ri) *n*. one sent on an under-hand or unplesant mission مخبری (یا کسی اَور ناخوشگوار کام کے لیے بھیجا ہُوا) سفارتی نمائندہ

emit (e-*mit*) *v.t.* (-tt-) put forth (light, heat, sound, etc.) نکالنا، چھوڑنا give (opinion, etc.) ظاہر کرنا **emission** (e-*mish*-en) *n*. act of emitting اخراج، نکالنا something emitted اِخراج

emollient (e-*mol*-i-ent) *adj*. & *n*. softening (medicine) مُلیّن

emolument (e-*mol*-ew-ment) *n*. (usu. *pl*.) salary, etc. تنخواہ، طلب، مُشاہرہ fees, income آمدنی، فیس، یافت

emotion (e-*moh*-shĕn) *n*. feeling اِحساس، جذبہ excited state of mind جوش، وَلولہ **emotional** *adj*. sentimental جذباتی **emotionality** (e-mohshĕ-*nal*-i-ti) *n*. quality of being emotional جذباتیت **emotive** (e-*moh*-tiv) *adj*. tending to excite emotion جذبات انگیز

emperor (*em*-pĕ-rĕ*) *n*. ruler of an empire شہنشاہ **empress** (*em*-pres) *n*. female emperor شہنشاہ بیگم wife of an emperor شہنشاہ خاتون

emphasis (*em*-fa-sis) *n*. stress laid on word or words to signify their meaning تاکید، زور importance attached اہمیت *lay great emphasis (on)* (کسی) پر زور دینا **emphasize** (*em*-fa-siz) *v.t.* lay emphasis on (word, fact, etc.) (کسی) پر زور دینا **emphatic** (em-*fat*-ik) *adj*. full of emphasis زوردار، پُرزور used for stressing تاکیدی **emphatically** *adv*. with emphasis پُرزور طریق سے، زور دے کر، تاکید کر کے

empire (*em*-pi-ĕ*) *n*. group of countries under one ruler (called *emperor*) or under one ruling State شہنشاہی، سلطنت، قلمرو *Empire Day*, May 24 (for celebrating the British Queen Victoria's becoming an empress) یومِ شہنشاہی

empiric (em-*pi*-rik), **empirical** *adj*. based on observation and experiment (and not merely on theory) تجربی، عملی **empiric** *n*. quack عطائی **empirically** *adv*. in an empiric manner تجربی طور پر، تجربہ و مشاہدہ سے **empiricism** (em-*pi*-ri-sizm) *n*. philosophical doctrine that experience is the only source of knowledge تجربیت **empiricist** (em-*pi*-ri-sist) *n*. one who believes in that doctrine تجربی

emplane (em-*playn*) *v.t.* & *i*. mount or put on an aeroplane ہوائی جہاز پر سوار کرنا یا ہونا

employ (em-*ploi*) *v.t.* use (someone's) services for payment (*to do* or *for* some work) ملازم رکھنا use (time, energies *in*, *on*, *for*, etc.) کام میں لانا، صَرف کرنا، اِستعمال کرنا *n*. employment (used only in the phrase :) *in the employ of*, employed by کی ملازمت میں، کا ملازم **employment** *n*. being employed ملازمت، بر سرِ روزگار ہونا *employment exchange*, department for finding people employment دفترِ روزگار regular occupation پیشہ **employer** (em-*ploi*-ĕ*) *n*. one who employs someone for wages آجر **employee** (em-ploi-*ee*, or em-*ploi*-ee) *n*. one employed for wages نوکر، ملازم ▣ To **employ** is to have habitually in one's service, to **engage**, to place someone's services at one's disposal for a special purpose, to **retain**, to engage someone of a higher status like a lawyer or doctor for being called upon in case of need on special fees, and to **sign up** an actor, etc., for a special contract of work.

emporium (em-*poh*-ri-um) *n*. centre of commerce تجارتی مرکز market منڈی، بازار (colloq.) shop where everything is available بڑی دوکان جہاں سے ہر چیز مل سکے، ہر مال والی دوکان

empower (em-*pou*-ĕ*) *v.t.* authorize (someone *to do* something) اختیار دینا، مختار کرنا، مجاز کرنا

empress *n*. (see under **emperor**)

empty (*em*-ti) *adj*. having nobody in it خالی، سنسان، غیر آباد *empty-handed*, (*a*) bringing no gift خالی ہاتھ (*b*) carrying nothing away خالی ہاتھ unfurnished (house, etc.) سامان سے عاری (threat, etc.) lacking substance خالی خولی senseless, foolish بے معنی، بے مغز، بے ہودہ *empty head*, *empty-headed*, witless احمق، کھوکھلا (colloq.) hungry بھوکا *n*. empty truck خالی ٹھیلا (pl.) (*empties*), empty bags, boxes and other containers خالی ڈبے، بوتلیں بوریاں، بکس وغیرہ **emptiness** (*em*-ti-nes) *n*. the state of being empty خالی ہونا، خلا، کھوکھلا پن، بے ہودگی

empyrean (em-pi-*ree*-an or em-*pi*-ri-an) *n*. highest heaven in all astronomy which was supposed to be sphere of pure fire or light فلک الافلاک، آتشیں کرۂ نور the abode of God عرش، کاظم، عرشِ بریں *adj*. of the empyrean فلک الافلاک کا **empyreal** (em-*pi*-ri-ĕl) *adj*. pertaining to the empyrean فلک الافلاک کا formed of pure fire or light نوری، آتشیں

emu (*ee*-mew) *n*. ostrich-like Australian bird ایمو

emulate (*em*-ew-layt) *v.t.* strive to imitate or excel (someone) ریس کرنا، ہمسری کی کوشش کرنا **emulation** (em-ew-*lay*-shĕn) *n*. ریس، ہمسری کی کوشش

an emu

emulsion (e-*mul*-shĕn) *n*. creamy mixture of oil and water تیل اور پانی کا شیرہ، روغن آب، روغناب

emulsify (e-*mul*-si-fi) *n*. make into an emulsion روغن آب بنانا ، روغناب بنانا
enable (en-*ay*-bèl) *v.t.* make able قابل کرنا یا بنانا give power to (someone to do something) مجاز کرنا ، مختار کرنا یا بنانا
enact (e-*nakt*) *v.t.* make (a law) قانون وضع کرنا یا بنانا *enacting clauses*, clauses containing new provisions نئی قانونی شرائط والی شقیں act (a scene or part) in a play or in real life کردار ادا کرنا **enactment** *n.* enacting or being enacted قانون سازی ، وضع قانون law قانون
enamel (e-*nam*-ĕl) *n.* smooth, hard and glossy coating on metal اینیمل ، مینا ، کوفت *enamel paint*, paint which hardens to make such a coating مینا ، میناکاری ، کوفت کاری hard covering of teeth مینا ، اینیمل *v.t.* (-ll-) coat with enamel میناکاری کرنا
enamour (e-*nam*-ĕ*) *v.t.* inspire with love, make passionately fond (*of* someone) (پر) فریفتہ کرنا ، (کا) گرویدہ بنانا *enamoured of*, (*a*) in love with پر فریفتہ ، کا گرویدہ, (*b*) delighted with سے خوش
en bloc (en-blok) *adv.* in a group تمام کے تمام ، سبھی *They crossed the floor 'en bloc'* اسمبلی میں وہ تمام کے تمام اپنی پارٹی چھوڑ کر دوسری پارٹی میں شامل ہو گئے
encage (en-*kayj*), **incage** (in-*kayj*) *v.t.* put (as) in a cage پنجرے میں ڈالنا
encamp (en-*kamp*) *v.t.* & *i.* settle in the form of a camp پڑاؤ ڈالنا ، چھاؤنی چھانا lodge in tents خیموں میں رہنا halt (on a march) (کوچ میں) پڑاؤ ڈالنا
encampment *n.* encamping پڑاؤ کرنا place where troops are encamping پڑاؤ ، چھاؤنی
encase (en-*kays*) *v.t.* put into a case خانے یا ڈبے میں بند کرنا surround as with a case غلاف چڑھانا
encasement *n.* such covering خانہ ، ڈبہ کا غلاف وغیرہ
enchain (en-*chayn*) *v.t.* put in chains پابزنجیر کرنا link together آپس میں جوڑنا
enchant (en-*chant*) *v.t.* work magic on جادو کرنا ، سحر کرنا delight خوش کرنا ، لبھانا **enchanter** *n.* (*fem.* *enchantress*) one who charms جادوگر ، ساحر
enchantment *n.* being charmed جادو ہونا ، مسحوری ، سحر زدگی that which charms جادو ، سحر delight لبھانا
encircle (en-*sĕ**-kèl) *v.t.* surround گھیرے میں لینا ، گھیر لینا ، حلقے میں لینا **encirclement** *n.* act of surrounding or being surrounded گھیر لینا
en clair (on-*klay*-è*) *n.* (of telegrams, etc.) not in code but in ordinary language صاف زبان
enclasp (en-*klasp*) *v.t.* clasp لپٹانا
enclave (en-*klayv*) *n.* territory surrounded by a foreign State گھری ہوئی ریاست
enclose (en-*klohz*) *v.t.* shut in land (with wall, etc.) احاطہ کرنا hem in on all sides کور لگانا ، حاشیہ لگانا put (something) in (an envelope, parcel, etc.) esp. with a letter ملفوف کرنا ، لف کرنا
enclosure *n.* act of enclosing ملفوف کرنا ، احاطہ کرنا enclosed land احاطہ paper, etc., enclosed with a letter ملفوف (کاغذ)
encomium (en-*koh*-mi-um) *n* formal high-flown eulogy قصیدہ ، مدح ، مدحت **encomiast** (en-*koh*-mi-ast) *n.* composer of encomiums قصیدہ گو ، مدحت طراز flatterer خوشامدی
encompass (en-*kum*-pas) *v.t.* surround (as guard) کے گرد حلقہ ڈالنا enclose (as enemy) محصور کر لینا
encore (on-*koh**) *int.* Repeat again! (shouted out as demand for repeating song or performance) مکرر ، مکرر! پھر سے *n.* this cry مکرر مکرر کی صدا *v.t.* cry encore to summon back performer مکرر مکرر کی صدا بلند کرنا
encounter (en-*kount*-ĕ*) *n.* sudden and unexpected meeting (*with* a friend) اچانک ملاقات ، مڈبھیڑ a fight (with someone) مڈبھیڑ ، مقابلہ *v.t.* meet (someone) face to face مڈبھیڑ ہونا meet in contest مقابلہ کرنا
encourage (en-*kĕ*-rij) *v.t.* give courage to ہمت بڑھانا ، دل بڑھانا inspire with spirit (*to do* something) جرأت دلانا **encouraging** *adj.* that which encourages ہمت افزا ، حوصلہ افزا **encouragement** *n.* emboldening حوصلہ افزائی ، ہمت افزائی
encroach (en-*krohch*) *v.t.* intrude (*on* another's territory or rights) بیجا دخل کرنا ، غاصبانہ قبضہ کرنا go beyond proper limits تجاوز کرنا ، حد سے بڑھنا **encroachment** *n.* بے جا دخل ، غاصبانہ قبضہ ، تجاوز
encumber (en-*kum*-bĕ*) *v.t.* be a burden to (someone) پر بوجھ ڈالنا burden (person or estate with debt) کو زیر بار کرنا impede روڑے اٹکانا ، روکنا **encumbrance** (en-*kum*-brans) *n.* burden بوجھ ، بار mortgage on property مرہونہ ، قرضہ بذمہ جائداد ، قرضہ متعلقہ جائداد impediment رکاوٹ ، مزاحمت *without encumbrance*, childless جس پر بچوں کا بوجھ نہ ہو
encyclopaedia, encyclopedia (en-sik-lo-*pee*-di-a) *n.* book with alphabetically arranged information on every branch of knowledge (or on one subject) دائرۃ المعارف ، مخزن علوم ، قاموس **encyclopaedic** (-dik) *adj.* pertaining to an encyclopaedia قاموسی full of information پر از معلومات (of knowledge) having a very wide range بہت وسیع **encyclopaedist** (-dist) *n.* compiler of an encyclopaedia قاموس نگار *the Encyclopaedists*, collaborators of Diderot (1713-1784) like Voltaire,

Rousseau, Montesqueiu, and his successor D'Alembert who produced the famous 35-volume French *L'Encyclopedie* between 1751 and 1776 embodying the spirit of 18th century learning which rejects superstition and attempts a rational explanation of the universe ; they are regarded as the emancipators of human thought قاموس نگار

end (end) *n.* extreme limit حد، سِرا، کنارا *on end,* (*a*) upright سیدھا (*b*) continuously مسلسل، لگاتار *for hours on end* لگاتار کئی گھنٹے تک (*be*) *at a loose end,* be unoccupied بیکار ہونا، فارغ ہونا *There is no end to it,* there is too much of it حد ہوگئی *make both ends meet,* live within the income one somehow manages to scrape together آمدنی کے اندر گزر بسر کرنا *put an end to, make an end of,* stop, abolish ختم کرنا بند کرنا *be at the end of (one's) tether,* (*a*) be unable to do more مزید کچھ نہ کر سکنا (*b*) have no more knowledge مزید کچھ نہ جاننا conclusion خاتمہ، اختتام، انجام *come to an end,* end ختم ہونا، اختتام پذیر ہونا death موت، خاتمہ، انجام *near one's end,* dying مرنے کو، قریب بہ مرگ what is left over بچا کھچا *odds and ends* متفرقات purpose مقصد *gain one's end* (or *ends*) حصولِ مقصد میں کامیاب ہونا، اپنا مقصد پانا *v.t. & i.* finish ختم کرنا، کا *end (one's) life* خودکشی کرنا come to end ختم ہونا result (*in*) پر انجام پذیر ہونا *end in disaster* انجام کار تباہ ہونا *end up,* conclude ختم ہونا **ending** *n.* concluding part of (story, verse, word, etc.) خاتمہ، انجام، آخری حصّہ **endless** *adj.* غیر محدود، غیر مختتم *endless chain* (or *belt*), chain (or belt) with ends joined for continuous work پٹہ، گول زنجیر **endways, endwise** *adv.* with the end uppermost or foremost جس کا کونہ آگے ہو

endanger (en-*dayn*-jĕ*) *v.t.* expose to danger خطرے میں ڈالنا یا مبتلا کرنا

endear (en-*dee*-ĕ*) *v.t.* make (oneself) dear or precious (*to*) پیارا یا لاڈلا بنانا، عزیز رکھنا **endeared** (en-*dee*-ĕ*d) *adj.* beloved پیارا، عزیز **endearing** *adj.* (manners, etc.) rousing affection پیارا، قابلِ قدر **endearingly** *adv.* پیار سے **endearment** *n.* (esp.) act expressing affection پیار، لاڈ، چاؤ، چاؤ چونچلے

endeavour (en-*dev*-ĕ*) *v.t.* try hard (*after* or *to do* something) بڑی کوشش کرنا، جدوجہد کرنا، دوڑ دھوپ کرنا سعی و کوشش سے کام لینا *n.* an attempt (*to do*) جدوجہد سعی و کوشش، دوڑ دھوپ

endemic (en-*dem*-ik) *adj.* & *n.* (disease) regularly found in an area or people علاقائی (بیماری)، مقامی (مرض)

endorse (en-*doh**s) *v.t.* write one's name on the back of (document) پشت پر دستخط کرنا، ظہری تصدیق کرنا confirm (statement, etc.) کی تصدیق کرنا write comment on back of document تبصرہ لکھنا ریمارک دینا *have (one's) licence endorsed,* have one's offence recorded on it لائسنس پر اپنے جرم کا اندراج کرنا **endorser** *n.* one who endorses تصدیق کنندہ **endorsement** *n.* endorsing تصدیق، ظہری تصدیق sanction منظوری what is written on a document دستاویز پر جو کچھ لکھا ہو، دستاویز کی تحریر

endow (en-*dou*) *v. t.* give (money, property, etc.) to provide a regular income for (an institution) وقف کرنا، آمدنی کھانے کے لیے (عطیہ) دینا give a dowry to enrich (*with* some quality) (خوبی) عطا کرنا *be endowed with,* possess naturally جسے قدرت نے ودیعت کی ہو، سے متصف **endowment** *n.* endowing وقف (usu. *pl.*) natural gifts جبلی صلاحیتیں the amount, etc., settled on any person or institution وقف *endowment insurance,* terms of insurance guaranteeing the payment of a fixed sum to the insured person on maturity, etc., even during his life-time جیتے جی بھی مل سکنے والا بیمہ، زندگی یاب بیمہ *take out an endowment policy,* insure one's life on that condition جیتے جی مل سکنے والا بیمہ کرانا، زندگی یاب بیمہ کرانا

endue (en-*dew*) **indue** (in-*dew*) *v. t.* put on پہننا clothe with پہنانا supply (*with*) مہیا کرنا، بہم پہنچانا

endure (ed-*dew*-ĕ*) *v. t. & i.* suffer (pain, hardship, etc.) بھگتنا، کاٹنا، جھیلنا، بھوگنا، اُٹھانا، گزارنا bear without sinking سہنا، برداشت کرنا tolerate برداشت کرنا **endurable** *adj.* that which can be endured قابلِ برداشت **endurance** *n.* patience, ability to endure صبر، برداشت، حوصلہ *past endurance, beyond endurance,* too much to be tolerated ناقابلِ برداشت

Endymion (en-*dim*-i-on) *Cla myth.* the beautiful youth with whom the moon goddess fell in love and on whom she induced a perpetual sleep in order to kiss him without his knowledge ; the story is also told by Keats in a lovely poem of the same title اَندِم آن

enema (*en*-e-ma, or e-*nee*-ma) *n.* injection of liquid into the bowels for relieving constipation حُقنہ

enemy (*en*-e-mi) *n.* foe دشمن، بیری، عدو، حریف that which harms جڑیں کھوکھلی کرنے والا one who is opposed مخالف *an enemy of reform* اصلاح کا مخالف hostile force دشمن کی فوج *engage the enemy,* fight with hostile forces دشمن کی فوج سے مقابلہ کرنا *adj.* of the enemy دشمن کا *enemy force,* armed forces of hostile country دشمن ملک کی فوج (S) **An enemy is one**

whom we dislike and who is against us in some way; **an opponent,** one who disagrees but who may be quite friendly. Note also that **foe** is the poetical and not the usual word for an enemy.

energy (*en*-ĕ*-ji) *n.* power exerted; vigour زور، طاقت (persons) power (*to do* some work) ہمت motive power (*e.g.*, heat, electricity) توانائی **energetic** (en-ĕ*-*jet*-ik) *adj.* full of energy توانا، طاقتور، باہمت، مستعد، سرگرم **energetically** *adv.* with energy ہمت سے **energize** (en-ĕ-jiz) *v.t.* impart energy to توانائی عطا کرنا، ہمت دینا

enervate (*en*-ĕ*-vayt) *v. t.* weaken کمزور کر دینا، نحیف کر دینا **enervating** (*en*-e*-vayt ing) *adj.* weakening کمزور کر دینے والا

enfant terrible n. troublesome child who asks awkward questions or repeats the elders' talk, etc. عذاب جان بچہ، بچہ یا مصیبت، بچہ کیا آفت، شامت اعمال

enfeeble (en-*fee*-bĕl) *v. t.* weaken (person) کمزور کر دینا، لاغر کر دینا weaken (someone's efforts) کا زور توڑنے والا **enfeebling** *adj.* weakening کمزور کر دینے والا **enfeeblement** *n.* act of weakening کمزور کرنا، کمزوری

enfold (en-*fohld*) *v.t.* put one's arms around (someone else) سے بغلگیر ہونا، سے معانقہ کرنا، کے گلے میں باہیں ڈالنا wrap (person or thing *in* or *with*) میں لپیٹ

enforce (en-*foh*s*) *v. t.* put in force نافذ کرنا compel obedience to (a law, etc.) سختی سے عمل کرنا عمل درآمد کرانا get (someone) by force (*to do* something) پر مجبور کرنا persist in (demand or argument) پر اصرار کرنا یا مصر ہونا **enforcement** *n.* enforcing نفاذ giving effect to عمل درآمد compulsion **enforced** *adj.* under compulsion جبری، بالجبر

enfranchise (en-*fran*-chiz) *v. t* acknowledge the right to elect our parliamentary representatives حق رائے دہی عطا کرنا، ووٹ کا حق دینا set free (slaves) (غلاموں کو) آزاد کرنا، آزادی دینا **enfranchisement** *n.* liberation آزادی acknowledging the right to vote حق رائے دہی تسلیم (یا عطا) کرنا

engage (en-*gayj*) *v.t.* & *i.* employ خدمات حاصل کرنا نوکر رکھنا betroth منگنی کرنا *an engaged couple* undertake (*to do, that*) معاہدہ کرنا attract دلکش ہونا occupy (time or attention) مشغول رکھنا bring or come into conflict with مڈبھیڑ ہونا (of parts of a machine) interlock (*with* another) آپس میں جڑنا، ٹھیک بیٹھنا **engaged** *adj.* (esp.) having given a promise of marriage (*to*) منسوب **engagement** *n.* promise to marry منگنی، نسبت undertaking (to be somewhere) at a fixed time ملاقات کا وعدہ battle لڑائی **engaging** *adj.* attractive دلکش ◙ We **engage** someone to do something; **hire** someone or something for pay by the period; **retain** a lawyer or a doctor; **book** an advance date; and **sign up** an actor. Again we **engage** in a legitimate occupation, but **indulge** in an act that implies moral weakness.

engender (en-*jen*-de*) *v. t.* be the cause of (a situation or condition) کا باعث ہونا، کی صورت پیدا کرنا

engine (*en*-jin) *n.* machine producing power or motion انجن، کل *railway engine* ریل کا انجن *fire engine* آگ بجھانے کا انجن **engine driver** *n.* man who drives a railway engine ریل کا ڈرائیور، ریل چلانے والا، ریل بان

engineer (en-ji-*nee*-e*) *n.* person who designs machines, buildings, etc. انجینیئر، مہندس *v.t.* construct as engineer بنانا (colloq.) arrange or bring about skilfully ہوشیاری سے بندوبست کرنا یا بنانا **engineering** *n.* art of an engineer

engrave (en-*grayv*) *v. t.* cut (words or designs) into hard material کندہ کرنا، کھودنا، نقش کرنا **engraving** *n.* picture, etc., printed from an engraved plate کندہ تصویر کا نقش، نقش کندہ

engross (en-*gros*) *v. t.* take up all the time or attention منہمک کرنا *engrossed in (one's) work* کام میں منہمک

engulf (en-*gulf*) *v.t.* swallow up گھیر لینا، نگل جانا

enhance (en-*hans*) *v. t.* add to (value or attraction) قیمت یا دلکشی بڑھانا

enigma (*e-nig*-ma) *n.* puzzling (question, person, thing or circumstance) معما، عقدہ، چیستان **enigmatic** *adj.* معما سا

enjoin (en-*join*) *v. t.* impose (silence or action) کی ہدایت کرنا command (someone *to do* something) کا حکم دینا

enjoy (en-*joi*) *v.t.* take joy in کا لطف اٹھانا، سے مزے کرنا use سے استفادہ کرنا *enjoy (oneself)* لطف اندوز ہونا **enjoyable** *adj.* پرلطف **enjoyment** *n.* joy لطف use استفادہ

enlarge (en-*lah*j*) *v. t.* & *i.* make or become larger بڑھنا (یا) بڑھانا *enlarge on* (or *upon*), say or write more about تفصیل سے روشنی ڈالنا reproduce (photograph) on a large scale تصویر کو انلارج کرنا، تصویر بڑی کرنا. **enlargement** *n.* something added to اضافہ (*esp.*) enlarged photograph بڑی کی ہوئی تصویر

enlighten (en-*li*-ten) *v. t.* give more knowledge to واقف کرنا، آگاہ کرنا free from ignorance, misunderstanding or false beliefs روشن خیالی عطا کرنا **enlightenment** *n.* increased knowledge; freedom from ignorance *n.* روشن خیالی

enlist (en-*list*) *v. t.* & *i.* obtain (some support) (تائید) حاصل کرنا take into or enter the armed forces (فوج میں) بھرتی کرنا ہونا **enlistment** *n.* بھرتی، تائید کا حصُول

enliven (en-*li*-ven) *v. t.* make (company, atmosphere, etc.) lively میں جان ڈال دینا **enlivening** *adj.* making lively جان ڈالنے والا

en masse (en-*mahs*) *adj.* (used predicatively) all together سبھی

enmesh (en-*mesh*) *v. t.* take in a net جال میں پھنسانا entangle اُلجھا لینا

enmity (*en*-mi-ti) *n.* hostility دُشمنی، عداوت hatred نفرت

ennoble (e-*noh*-bel) *v. t.* make (someone) noble لارڈ بنانا، نواب بنانا، امارت عطا کرنا make morally noble شرافت پیدا کرنا make dignified ممتاز کرنا

ennui (o-*nwee*) *n.* feeling of boredom اُکتاہٹ

enormity *n.* see under **enormous**

enormous (e-*no**-mus) *adj.* very great عظیم immense بہت بڑا **enormously** *adv.* بہت زیادہ **enormousness** *n.* being immense بہت بڑا ہونا **enormity** (-*no***m*-) *n.* great wickedness سخت بُرائی شرِ عظیم Note. An **enormity** is an act of great wickedness. It is quite distinct from **enormousness** which signifies the size of anything.

enough (e-*nuf*) *adj.*, *adv.* & *n.* sufficient کافی **enow** (*e-now*) *adv.* poetical form of *enough* کافی

enquire, enquiry (see under **inquire**)

enrage (en-*rayj*) *v.t.* fill with rage غصہ دلانا، غضبناک کرنا

enrapture (en-*rap*-che*) *v. t.* fill with great (esp. spiritual) delight وَجد میں لانا، کیفیت طاری کرنا **enrapturing** *adj.* وَجد آفرین

enrich (en-*rich*) *v. t.* make rich مالا مال کرنا improve (mind or soul) by adding something بہتر بنانا see *Addenda*

enrol, enroll (en-*rohl*) *v. t.* (-ll-) put (someone's name) on a roll or register نام درج کرنا enlist نام درج کرنا، بھرتی کرنا **enrolment** *n.* بھرتی کرنا

en route (on-*root*) *adv.* on the way (*to*)

enshroud (en-*shroud*) *v. t.* put (a dead body) in a shroud کفنانا cover up ڈھانپنا، چھپا لینا

ensign (*en*-sin) *n.* flag used on ships پھریرا، نشان *white ensign* برطانوی بحریّہ کا پھریرا *red ensign* برطانوی تجارتی جہازوں کا پھریرا

enslave (en-*slave*) *v. t.* make a slave of غلام بنانا **enslaved** *adj.* reduced to a state of slavery غلام **enslavement** *n.* reducing to slavery غلامی

ensconce *v. t.* hide safely محفوظ جگہ چھپے ہونا

enshrine *v.t.* serve as a shrine for (something) زیارت گاہ میں enclose in a shrine کی زیارت گاہ ہونا preserve with affection رکھنا کی یاد دِل سے لگائے رکھنا

ensue (en-*sew*) *v. i.* happen later بعد میں ہونا take place as a result نتیجہ نکلنا، نتیجۃً ظاہر ہونا **ensuing** *adj.* following as a consequence نتیجے کے طور پر آنے والا

ensure (en-*shoo*-è*) *v. t.* make certain پکّا کرنا یقینی صُورت دینا make safe (against risks, etc.) بیمہ کرانا

entail (en-*tayl*) *v. t.* bring as necessary consequence کا لازم (یا قُدرتی) نتیجہ ہونا settle estate on series of heirs جائداد کا مشرُوط طور پر ہبہ کرنا *n.* such settlement جائداد کا مشرُوط ہبہ

entangle (en-*tang*-èl) *v. t.* catch in a net or among obstacles اُلجھانا، مُشکلات میں پھنسانا **entanglement** *n.* entangling اُلجھاؤ، اُلجھانا obstacles like barbed wire, etc., to impede enemy's progress رُکاوٹ

entente, entente cordiale *n.* friendly pact between States سلطنتوں کی دوستی

enter (*en*-te*) *v. t.* & *i.* go into داخل ہونا become a member of رُکن بننا، میں شامل ہونا put down in writing لکھنا، اندراج کرنا sit for (examination) امتحان دینا، امتحان میں بیٹھنا *enter into*, take part in میں حصّہ لینا *enter a protest*, record it احتجاج کرنا *enter upon* (*something*), (کام) کا آغاز کرنا (see also **entrance, entrant** and **entry**)

enterprise (*en*-tĕ*-prīz) *n.* undertaking that needs courage to surmount its difficulties مُہم، کارِ عظیم courage or eagerness to start new ہمّت مُہم پسندی، مُہم جوئی **enterprising** *adj.* showing enterprise من چلا، باہمّت، مُہم جُو

entertain (en-te*-*tayn*) *v. t.* & *i.* receive (people) as guests مہمان نوازی کرنا give food or drink کھانا کِھلانا، دعوت کرنا amuse دِل بہلانا، تفریح کا سامان بہم پہنچانا interest دِلچسپ ہونا have in mind ذہن میں رکھنا be ready to consider غَور کرنے پر آمادہ ہونا **entertaining** *adj.* amusing دِلچسپ **entertainment** *n.* (esp.) amusement تفریح، کھیل تماشہ

An **entertainment** is either public or private, a **reception**, more or less private, and a **party** quite informal.

enthral, enthrall (en-*thrawl*) *v.t.* -*ll*-) enslave غلام بنانا charm گرویدہ کرنا please greatly دِل موہ لینا **enthralled** *adj.* گرویدہ

enthrone (en-*throon*) *v.t.* place on a throne تخت نشین کرنا **enthronement** *n.* تخت نشینی

enthusiasm (en-*thew*-zi-azm) *n.* passionate zeal وَلولہ، جوش intense interest گہری دِلچسپی **enthusiast** *n.* person filled with enthusiasm جوشیلا، پُرجوش، سرگرم **enthusiastic** (-*as*-) *adj.* having enthusiasm سرگرم، پُرجوش **enthusiastically** *adv.* جوش و خروش سے سرگرمی سے

entice (en-*tis*) *v.t.* tempt, lead astray (*from* something, *to do* something) ورغلانا، پھسلا کرلے جانا
enticement *n.* leading astray ورغلانا، غلط راہ پر لگانا
enticer *n.* one who leads astray ; tempter ورغلانے والا
enticing *adj.* tempting دل فریب
entire (en-*ti*-e*) *adj.* whole سارا، تمام not broken تمام کا تمام، سارا، بحیثیت تمام تر، بالکل صحیح سالم **entirely** *adv.*
entirety *n.* being entire مکمل ہونا *in its entirety*, as a whole تمام تر، بحیثیت
entitle (en-*ti*-tèl) *v t.* give a title to (some writing) عنوان لگانا give (someone) a right (*to*) (کا) حق دینا
entity (*en*-ti-ti) *n.* being ہستی، ذات existence وجود، ہستی
entomology (en-to-*mol*-o-ji) *n.* science of insects علم الحشرات، حشریات **entomologist** *n.* expert in entomology ماہرِ علم الحشرات
entourage *n.* (on-too-*rahzh*) attendants حاشیہ نشین
entrails (*en*-traylz) *n. pl.* bowels اوجھ، اوجھڑی the innermost part (*of* the earth, etc.) (زمین وغیرہ کے) خزانے
[1]**entrance** (*en*-truns) *n.* act of entering آنا، place of entering راستہ، گزرگاہ، دروازہ right of entering حقِ داخلہ participation شمولیت، داخلہ داخل ہونا *entrance fees* فیس داخلہ، انٹرنس *Entrance examination* سکول کا آخری امتحان، جامعے میں داخلے کا امتحان، داخلے کا امتحان (see also **entrant**)
[2]**entrance** (en-*trahns*) *v.t.* throw into a trance پر وجد طاری کرنا overwhelm (someone *with* joy, etc.) کو خوشی سے بے تاب کر دینا
entrant (*en*-trant) *n.* one entering (*for* a competition) اُمیدوار participant حصہ لینے والا (see also [1]**entrance**)
entreat (en-*treet*) *v.t.* request earnestly (*to do* something) التماس کرنا، التجا کرنا **entreaty** (en-*tree*-ti) earnest request التماس، التجا
entrench (en-*trench*) *v.t.* surround with trenches (شہر وغیرہ کے گرد) خندق کھودنا *entrench* (*oneself*) خندق کھود کر اس میں چھپ جانا make safe against attack محفوظ بنا لینا **entrenchment** *n*
entrepot (*ont*-rè-poh) *n.* commercial centre (esp. a sea-port) تجارتی مرکز، تجارتی بندرگاہ
entrepreneur (*ont*-rè-pre-nĕ*) *n.* one who shows business enterprise تاجر، مالک، سرمایہ دار
entrust *v.t.* give as a responsibility کے حوالے کرنا، کی تحویل میں دینا، تفویض کرنا *entrust* (*someone*) *with* (*something*), or (*something*) *to* (*someone*) کوئی کام وغیرہ کسی کے سپرد کرنا
entry *n.* entering داخلہ place of entrance راستہ item recorded اندراج persons entering for a competition, etc. حصہ لینے والے، شریک ہونے والے، شاملین
entwine (en-*twin*) *v.t.* make by twining بُننا curl (one thing) (*with* or *round* another) (کے گرد) لپیٹنا (یا) پیچ دینا
enumerate (e-*newm*-è-rayt) *v.t.* count شمار کرنا، گننا، فہرست سے بتانا name over (contents of a list) ایک ایک نام پڑھنا **enumeration** (-*ay*-shĕn) *n.* گنتی، شمار، نام پڑھنا (یا لینا)
enunciate (e-*nun*-si-ayt) *v.t.* & *i.* pronounce (words) (لفظ کا) تلفظ کرنا، (لفظ) ادا کرنا state (theory, etc.) clearly (نظریہ وغیرہ) وضاحت سے پیش کرنا proclaim اعلان کرنا **enunciation** (-*ay*-) *n.* تلفظ، ادائیگی، اعلان، واضح بیان
envelop (en-*vel*-up) *v.t.* cover on all sides ڈھانپنا put in an envelope لفافے میں ڈالنا **envelope** (*en*-ve-lohp) *n.* paper cover for a letter لفافہ
envenom (en-*ven*-um) *v. t.* put poison into (mind, words, air, weapon, etc.) میں زہر بھرنا، کو زہر آلود کرنا، کو زہرناک بنانا
enviable, envious *adj.* (see under *envy*)
environ (en-*vi*-run) *v. t.* surround (person or place *with* or *by*) کے گرد واقع ہونا *environed by*, surrounded by میں گھرا ہوا **environs** (en-*vi*-ronz) *n. pl.* suburbs مضافات **environment** *n.* surroundings گرد و پیش، ماحول surrounding influences (*of* someone) (کسی کا) ماحول
envisage (en-*viz*-ej) *v.t.* look (danger, etc.) in the face خطرے کا پورا احساس رکھنا consider سوچنا، خیال کرنا، پر غور کرنا
envoy (*en*-voi) *n.* diplomatic representative below the rank of an ambassador سفارتی نمائندہ، قاصد، ایلچی
envy (*en*-vi) *n.* feeling of disappointment or ill-will at another's success حسد، جلن، رشک object of envy باعث رشک *v.t.* be filled with such feeling جلنا، حسد کرنا، خار کھانا، رشک کرنا **envied** (*en*-vid) *adj.* **enviable** (*en*-vi-a-bèl) *adj.* likely to be envied باعث رشک، قابلِ رشک **enviably** *adj.* قابلِ رشک انداز سے
envious (*en*-vi-us) *adj.* full of envy (*of*) حاسد، جلنے والا

Ⓑ **Envy** of another person is one's desire for what the other fellow has, **jealousy**, resentment of the other fellow's possessions or joys, **grudge**, unsettled vengeance

Eos (*ee*-os) *Cl. myth.* the Greek goddess of the dawn, identified with the Roman Aurora یوس
epaulette, epaulet (*ep*-o-let) *n.* shoulder-piece of a naval officer's uniform بحریہ کے افسر کے کندھے پر کا نشان، شانہ نشان
ephemeral (e-*fem*-e-rèl) *adj.* lasting for a very short time عارضی (چند روزہ)
epic (*ep*-ik) *n.* continuous poetic narrative of the

deeds of hero(es) (in usu. a lofty style) رزمیہ مثنوی رزمیہ نظم *adj.* of an epic رزمیہ شاعری سے متعلق heroic, grand شاندار

epicure (*ep*-i-kew-ĕ*) *n.* one who is dainty in eating خوش خور one who is devoted to pleasure جویائے سرور، لذت طلب **epicurean** (ep-i-kew-*ree*-ĕn) *n.* one devoted to refined sensuous enjoyment جویائے سرور، لذت طلب follower of the Greek philosopher Epicureus (ep-i-*kew*-rus) who advocated this ایپیقوری *adj.* of the ways of an epicure اپیقوریت، لذت طلبی **epicureanion** *n.* اپیقورکے رنگ ڈھنگ یا طور طریقے

epidemic (ep-i-*dem*-ik) *n.* (disease) widespread among many people in the same place for a time وَبا *adj.* pertaining to such a disease وَبائی

epidiascope (ep-i-*dī*-as-kohp) *n.* device with light, mirror and lenses for throwing on screen enlarged images of prints, etc. کلاں نما

epigram (*ep*-i-gram) *n.* short and pointed saying قولِ زرّیں، جامع الکلم short poem with a witty ending منظوم لطیفہ، منظوم چٹکلا **epigrammatic** (ep-i-gra-mat-ik) *adj.* of or like an epigram مجمل، اختصار پسندانہ

epilepsy (*ep*-i-lep-si) *n.* chronic nervous disease in which a person falls down unconscious مرگی، صرع

epileptic *adj.* of epilepsy مرگی سے متعلق *n.* person suffering from epilepsy مرگی والا، مصروع

epilogue (*ep*-i-log) *n.* poem spoken at the end of a play تمثیل کی اختتامی نظم last part of any literary work خاتمہ

Epimetheus (ep-i-*meeth*-ews) *Cl. myth.* brother of Prometheus and husband of the first woman, Pandora ایپی میتھیوس

episode (*ep*-i-sohd) *n.* separate event in a series of events ضمنی قصّہ، ضمنی واقعہ

epistle (e-*pis*-ĕl) *n.* (lit.) letter مکتوب نامہ، خط *the Epistles*, a part of the *Bible* انجیل کا ایک حصّہ

epistolary (e-*pis*-to-la-ri) *adj.* pertaining to letters مکتوباتی، نامہ نگارانہ

epitaph (*ep*-i-taf) *n.* inscription on a tombstone کتبہ، کتبۂ مزار

epithet (*ep*-i-thet) *n.* adjective expressing a characteristic صفت، وصف، نعت word added to a name (*e.g.*, *great* in *Alexander the Great*) لقب

epitome (e-*pit*-o-mi) *n.* short summary خلاصہ، ملخص representation (of something) in miniature ننھی، مختصر صورت

epoch (*ee*-pok) *n.* period of history marked by special events دَور، زمانہ beginning of such period نئے دَور کا آغاز *mark an epoch* نئے دور کا آغاز کرنا

equable (*ek*-wa-bĕl) *adj.* not changing much یکساں

equal (*ee*-kwal) *adj.* of the same (size, value, rank, etc.) برابر، جتنا fair منصفانہ *equal to a task*, strong enough to do it *n.* equal (person or thing) ہمسر، برابر، برابر کی چوٹ، ہم مرتبہ، پورا اترنے والا *is equal to* کے برابر ہے، کے مساوی ہے **equally** *adv.* as much یکساں، برابر **equality** (ee-*kwol*-i-ti) *n.* the state of being equal برابری، مساوات **equalize** (*ee*-kwa-līz) *v. t.* make equal (ایک دوسرے کے) برابر کرنا

equanimity *n.* calmness of mind سکون *with equanimity* ٹھنڈے دل سے

equate *v. t.* consider equal to (*with* another) کے برابر درجہ دینا adjust to the same average تحویل کرنا **equation** (ee-*kway*-shen) *n.* making or being equal برابری expression of equality between two quantities (expressed by the sign =) مساوات *simple equation* سادہ مساوات

equator (ee-*kway*-te*) *n.* imaginary line round the middle of the earth خطِ استوا real line on maps خطِ استوا

the equator

equatorial *adj.* of or near the equator استوائی

equestrian (e-*kwes*-tri-ĕn) *adj.* (person or statue) on horseback سوار of horse-riding شہسواری سے متعلق *n.* skilled horseman شہسوار circus performer on horses سرکس کا شہسوار

equidistant (ee-kwi-*dis*-tant) *adj.* separated by equal distance برابر، ہم فاصلہ

equilateral (ee-kwi-*lat*-ĕ-rĕl) *adj.* having all sides equal مساوی الاضلاع *equilateral triangle* مثلث مساوی الاضلاع

an equilateral triangle

equilibrium (ee-kwi-*lib*-ri-um) *n.* state of being balanced توازن *mental equilibrium* دماغی توازن *lose (one's) equilibrium* توازن کھو دینا

equinox (*ee*-kwi-noks) *n.* time of the year when the sun crosses the equator making day and night of equal length نقطۂ اعتدال، اعتدالِ شب و روز *vernal equinox*, March 21 اعتدالِ ربیعی *autumnal equinox*, September 23 اعتدالِ خریفی

equip (e-*kwip*) *v. t.* (-pp-) supply (*with* what is needed or *for* a purpose) سے لیس کرنا، سازو سامان مہیا کرنا ٹھیک ٹھاک کرنا **equipment** *n.* things needed (*for* a purpose) سازو سامان، ساز و یراق **equipage** *n.* outfit (of army or traveller) سامان، سازو سامان liveried servants and carriages of person of high rank سازو سامان، سازو سامان اور خدم و حشم

equipoise *n*. equilibrium توازُن
equity (*ek*-wi-ti) *n*. fairness اِنصاف، مَعْدَلَت (law) principles of justice for correcting laws اُصُولِ اِنصاف اُصُولِ مَعْدَلَت stocks and shares not bearing fixed interest غیر مُتعیّن شرحِ سُود کے حِصّے، مُنصِفانہ حِصَص (*Equity*), actors' trade union انجمنِ اداکاراں **equitable** *adj*. just, impartial مُنصِفانہ reasonable مَعقُول
equitably *adv*. انصاف سے، از رُوئے اِنصاف **equivalent** (e-*kwiv*-a-lent) *adj*. equal in value, or amount, (*to* something) مُساوی synonymous ہم معنیٰ *n*. synonym ہم معنیٰ لفظ something of the same value ہم قیمت
equivocal (e-*kwiv*-o-kĕl) *adj*. having a double meaning ذُومعنیٰ doubtful مُشتَبہ
era (*ee*-ra) *n*. period of history starting from the particular event سَن the Christian era سَنِ عیسوی epoch زمانہ، دَور
eradicate (e-*rad*-i-kayt) *v. t*. pull up by the roots جڑ سے اُکھاڑنا destroy اِستیصال کرنا، قلع قمع کرنا
erase (e-*rayz*) *v.t*. rub out مٹانا، محو کرنا، چھیل ڈالنا
eraser *n*. something with which to erase جس شے سے مٹایا جائے، ماحی، رَبڑ **erasure** *n*. rubbing out محو کرنا، مٹانا thing rubbed out چھیلے ہُوئے حرف محو کیا ہُوا، مٹایا ہُوا its trace کا نِشان
ere (*ay*-è*) (poet.) *prep*. before سے پہلے، سے قبل *conj*. before اِس سے قبل کہ، اِس سے پیشتر کہ
Erebus (*e*-re-bus) *Class myth*. the son of Chaos and the Greek god of darkness ایرِی بَس
erect (e-*rekt*) *adj*. on end کھڑا، اُونچا *v. t*. set erect سیدھا لگانا، سیدھا کھڑا کرنا build بنانا، اُٹھانا set up قائم کرنا، بنانا تعمیر کرنا **erection** (e-*rek*-shĕn) *n*. standing upright اِستادگی، خیزش building تعمیر
erg (ĕ*g) *n*. unit of work or energy کام (یا توانائی) کی اِکائی، اَرگ
ermine (*e**min) *n*. small squirrel-like animal with white fur قاقُم (*pl*.) garment made of its fur اِس جانور کی پوستین کا کپڑا، قاقُم

an ermine

erode (e-*rohd*) *v. t*. (of acids, etc.) wear or eat away کھا جانا، کاٹ ڈالنا **erosion** (e-*roh*-zhèn) *n*. eroding کھا جانا being eroded کٹ جانا *soil erosion*, its wearing away by rain and water زمین کا کٹاؤ
Eros (*ee*-ros) *Cl. myth*. the Greek god of love identified with the Roman Cupid ایرَس
erotic (e-*rot*-ik) *adj*. of sexual love شہوانی، عاشِقانہ
err (e*) *v. i*. do or be wrong غلطی کرنا، خطا کرنا، غلط ہونا **erroneous** *adj*., **error** *n*. (see below) ▣ We **err** in judgment ; make a **mistake** in action ; go **astray** in a deduction ; **blunder** through lack of common sense ; and sin through moral weakness.
errand (e-rĕnd) *n*. short journey to take (a message) سندیسے کا سفر، پیغام پہنچانے کے لیے چکر such journey for buying thing (*for* someone) from a shop بازار سے سودا سُلف لانا purpose of such کسی کا پیغام اِس چکّر کا مقصد *to run errands for* (*someone*) وغیرہ لے کر جانا، کسی کا سودا سُلف لانا **errand boy** *n*. boy paid to run errands پیغام رَساں لڑکا، سودا سُلف لانے والا لڑکا
erratic (e-*rat*-ik) *adj*. (of a person) irregular in behaviour or opinion مُتلوّن مزاج، گھڑی میں تولہ گھڑی میں ماشہ (of things like clocks, etc.) uncertain in movement غیر یقینی حرکات والا
erratum (e-*ray*-tum) *n*. (pl. *errata*) mistake in printing or writing طباعت یا کتابت کی غلطی، (جمع : اغلاط (اغلاطِ طباعت یا کتابت
erroneous (e-*roh*-ni-us) *adj*. incorrect غلط، غیر صحیح *erroneous notions* غلط فہمیاں، غلط خیالات نادُرست
error (e-*rĕ**) *n*. mistake غلطی something done or omitted wrongly بھُول چُوک، سہو، فروگزاشت false belief غلط عقیدہ، گمراہی، ضلالت wrong conduct گمراہی، غلط طرزِ عمل
ersatz (e*-*sahts*) *n*. & *adj*. substitute قائم مقام، بدل
erst (e*st), **erstwhile** (e*st-hwil) *adv*. formerly پہلے، پیشتر ازیں
erudite (*e*-roo-dit) *adj*. very learned (person) عالم و فاضل scholarly عالمانہ **erudition** *n*. learning, scholarship علم، علم و فضل، تبحّرِ علمی
erupt (e-*rupt*) *v. i*. (of a volcano) burst out آتش فشاں پہاڑ کا پھٹنا *n*. outbreak (of a volcano) (آتش فشاں پہاڑ کا) پھٹنا outbreak (of an epidemic) (وبا کا) پھوٹنا sudden outbreak (of war) (لڑائی کا) اچانک چھڑ جانا **eruptive** *adj*. پھوٹ نکلنے والا، توڑ کر نکل آنے والا
escalator (*es*-ka-lay-tĕ*) *n*. moving stairs carrying people up or down متحرک سیڑھیاں، رواں زینہ
escapade (es-ka-*payd*) *n*. foolish and reckless conduct causing scandal احمقانہ آوارگی foolish adventure احمقانہ جسارت
escape (es-*kayp*) *v. t*. & *i*. get free بچ نکلنا avoid بچنا، نظر بچا جانا be forgotten by ذہن سے نکل جانا (of gas) flow out, leak گیس کا نکلنا *n*. act of escaping بچنا، بچ نکلنا، باہر نکل آنا means of escaping بچنے کا ذریعہ deliverance (*from* danger) نجات، چھٹکارا outlet نکلنے کا راستہ
escape literature *n*. (see *Addenda*) **escapist** (es-*kay*-pist) *n*. & *adj*. (person) seeking relief from the hard realities of life فرار پسند (thing) affording such relief فرار دِہ **escapism** *n*. being an escapist فرار پسندی، فرار دہی ▣ We **escape** when we free ourselves from someone's clutches without his noticing it. We **evade** a liability. **elude** a pursuer. **avoid**

punishment, flee a place, **flee** from someone's anger, **slip away** while others are not watching, and **decamp** leaving behind our baggage.

eschatology (es-ka-*tol*-o-ji) *n.* doctrine of death, judgment, heaven and hell عقیدۂ جرم و سزا
eschew (es-*choo*) *v. t.* abstain from الگ رہنا ، باز رہنا ، بچنا ، پرہیز کرنا
escort *n.* (es-ko*t) bodyguard حفاظتی دستہ warships protecting mercantile vessels بدرقہ ، حفاظتی جہاز protection نگرانی ، حفاظت under escort کے زیرِ حفاظت *v. t.* (es-*ko*t*) go with as an escort حفاظت کے لیے ساتھ جانا ، ہمراہ ہونا ، ہمرکاب ہونا accompany ہمراہ جانا
escutcheon (es-*kuch*-ĕn) *n.* shield with a coat of arms on it خاندانی اِمتیاز والی ڈھال ، طغرائی سپر ، تاج *a blot on (one's) escutcheon*, a stain on one's reputation کلنک کا ٹیکہ ، بدنامی کا داغ
eskimo, esquimau (*es*-ki-moh) *n.* (pl. *eskimoes, esquimaux*, a North American aboriginal of very cold region اسکیمو
esoteric (ee-*sot*-è-rik) *adj.* understood only by the initiated باطنی secret مخفی
especial (es-*pesh*-el) *adj.* particular خاص ، خصوصی exceptional غیر معمولی **especially** *adv.* in particular خاص کر ، خصوصاً ، بالخصوص to an exceptional degree غیر معمولی طور پر ، حد درجہ
espionage (*es*-pi-o-nayj) *n.* spying جاسوسی
esplanade *n.* level space separating fortress from town قلعہ اور شہر کے درمیان میدان
espouse (es-*pous*) *v. t.* support (a cause, etc.) تائید کرنا (old use) marry (a woman) (کسی عورت سے) شادی کرنا ، بیاہ کرنا ، بیاہ رچانا
esprit (es-pi-*ree*) *n.* liveliness زندہ دلی ، شگفتگی wit ظرافت *esprit de corps* (es-pi-*ree*-de-koh*) *n.* devotion to one's cause مقصد سے وفاداری devotion to fellow-workers جماعت کی عزت کا احساس ، ایکا ، اتحاد
espy (es-*pī*) *v. t.* catch sight of دیکھنا
esquire (es-*kwi*·ĕ) *n.* man's title of courtesy (written in address after his name as *Esq.*) صاحب (old use) squire or armour-bearer of a knight فوجدار (یعنی نائٹ) کا اسلحہ بردار **Note: Esquire** is an English title. Americans never use it and would never like it to be used with their name. The word *Esq.* is never written with a name preceded by Mr., Mrs., Dr. or any other title.
essay *n.* (*es*-ay) short literary composition in prose on any subject جواب مضمون ، مضمون ، مقالہ (e-*say*) attempt کوشش *v. t.* (e-*say*) try کوشش کرنا **essayist** (*es*-ay-ist) *n.* writer of essays مضمون نویس ، مقالہ نگار

essence (*es*-ens) *n.* inner nature of a thing جوہر ، اصل its most important characteristic رُوح ، ماہیت essence ست ، جوہر ، روح **essential** (e-*sen*-shĕl) *adj.* necessary ضروری ، لازمی most important اہم indispensable (*for*) (کے لیے) ناگزیر (کے لیے) اشد ضروری of an essence جوہری *essential oils*, volatile oils اُڑ جانے والا تیل *n.* necessary element لازمہ ، لازمی جُزو ، جُزوِ لازم **essentially** *adv.* لازمی طور پر
establish (es-*tab*-lish) *v. t.* set up قائم کرنا ، مستقل بنیادوں پر اُستوار کرنا settle (oneself *in* a position) قدم جمانا place (someone) *in* a position) (کسی منصب پر) مقرر کرنا prove the truth of (an event) (کسی واقعہ کو) مُسلّم کرنا cause people to accept (a belief) کسی شے کو منوانا یا رواج دینا **establishment** *n.* establishing or being established عمل تقرر ، استقرار ثبوت ، ترویج any organization ادارہ ، محکمہ ، دُکان ، گھرانا persons employed to maintain it عملہ کار خانہ
estate (es-*tayt*) *n.* landed property زمینداری ، ریاست تعلقہ *estate agent*, (*a*) manager of an estate منشی (*b*) one who buys and sells houses and land for others دلال whole of one's property جائداد *real estate*, land and buildings جائدادِ غیر منقولہ *personal estate*, money and other kinds of property جائدادِ منقولہ (old use) condition حالت ، عمر *reach man's estate*, attain majority بالغ ہونا *the Three Estates*, (in the English Parliament) the three social strata to which members belong نواب ، پادری اور عوامی نمائندے *the Fourth Estate*, the Press اخبارات ، صحافت
esteem (es-*teem*) *v. t.* have a high opinion of کے متعلق اچھی رائے رکھنا respect greatly عزت کرنا ، توقیر کرنا ، احترام کرنا consider سمجھنا *n.* high regard لحاظ ، پاس **esteemed** (es-*teemd*) *adj.* respectable, venerable معزز ، محترم **estimable** (*es*-ti-mab-èl) *adj.* worthy of esteem لائقِ احترام ، قابلِ عزت calculable لائقِ شمار ، قابلِ عزت **estimably** *adv.* quite, sufficiently قابلِ لحاظ طور پر ▣ **Esteem** is a feeling of friendliness and a high opinion ; **regard**, high opinion of an equal, more conventional and less friendly **respect**, high opinion of a superior.
estimate *v. t.* (*es*-ti-mayt) judge the worth of رائے قائم کرنا calculate (the cost of) (خرچ وغیرہ کا) اندازہ لگانا یا کرنا reckon approximately تخمینہ لگانا *n.* (*es*-ti-mit) opinion, judgment رائے approximate calculation (of cost, etc.) تخمینہ **estimation** (es-ti-*may*-shèn) *n.* opinion رائے regard لحاظ ، پاس ، عزت *hold in high estimation* عزت کی نگاہ سے دیکھنا
estrange (es-*traynj*) *v. t.* alienate بیگانہ کرنا make unfriendly کھنچے کھنچے رہنا **estrangement** *n* quarrel between friends کشیدگی ، رنجش

estuary (*es*-tew-ĕ-ri) *n*. tidal mouth of a river دریا کا یا مدّو جزر والا دہانہ
et cetera (et-*set*-ra) (abb. *etc.* or &c.) and other things وغیرہ and so on الخ **etcetras** (et-*set*-rahz) *n. pl*. sundries متفرقات
etch (ech) *v. t.* & *i*. corrode a metal plate with acid for making a design for printing copies تیزابی نقش بنانا *n*. print made in this way تیزابی نقش art of making pictures in this way تیزابی نقش نگاری **etcher** *n*. one who etches تیزابی نقش نگار
eternal (ee-*tĕ*-nĕl) *adj*. without beginning or end ابدی ، دائمی ، اَبدی ; ازلی اور ابدی unchangeable ابدی too frequent مسلسل ، آئے دن ، روز روز کا **eternity** (ee-*tĕ**-ni-ti) *n*. time without end دوام ، ابد ، ابدیّت future life آخرت ، آخری زندگی ، دوسری زندگی ، بقائے دوام very long time بڑا لمبا عرصہ ، طویل مدت
ether (*ee*-thĕ*) *n*. colourless volatile liquid made from alcohol and used as an anaesthetic ایتھر ، ایثر (*the ether*), gas supposed to fill the apparently empty space beyond atmosphere ایتھر ، ایثر (poet.) pure upper air above the clouds بادلوں کے پار کی ہوا **ethereal** (ee-*thee*-ri-ĕl) *adj*. of unearthly delicacy نہایت لطیف heavenly آسمانی
ethics (*eth*-iks) *n*. (pl. with sing. verb) science of morals علم اخلاق ، اخلاقیات rules of conduct اُصولِ اخلاق **ethical** *adj*. pertaining to moral questions اخلاقی
Ethiopian (ee-thi-*oh*-pi-an) *adj*. & *n*. of Ethiopia حبشی
ethnic (*eth*-nik) *ethnical adj*. pertaining to human race نسلیاتی **ethnography** (eth-*nog*-ra-fi) *n*. description of the world's peoples علم الاقوام ، علم اقوام **ethnology** (eth-*nol*-o-ji) *n*. science of mankind نسلیات **ethnologist** *n*. ماہر نسلیات **ethnological** (eth-no-*loj*-i-kĕl) *adj*. نسلیاتی
etiquette (*et*-i-ket) *n*. conventional social behaviour آداب محفل ، مجلسی آداب unwritten code of professional conduct پیشہ ورانہ آداب
Eton (*ee*-tun) *n*. (also *Eton College*), a well-known English public school ایٹن **Etonian** (*-toh-*) *adj*. one educated there ایٹنی **Eton crop** *n*. cutting of women's hair like boys' عورتوں کی مردانہ حجامت
etymology (et-i-*mol*-o-ji) *n*. science of the origin and history of words علم اشتقاق الفاظ ، اشتقاق origin and history (*of* a particular word) (کسی لفظ کا) اشتقاق **etymological** (et-i-mo-*loj*-i-kĕl) *adj*. of or pertaining to etymology اشتقاقِ الفاظ سے متعلق ، اشتقاقی

eucalyptus (yoo-ki-*lip*-tus) *n*. an evergreen tree یوکلپٹس *eucalyptus oil*, essential oil obtained from it and used as a treatment for colds یوکلپٹس آئل ، روغن یوکلپٹس
eugenics (yoo-*jen*-iks) *n*. science of reproducing healthy human children علم اصلاح نسل انسانی
eulogize *v.t.* see under **eulogy**
eulogy (*yool*-o-ji) *n*. high praise (*on*) مدح speech or writing (usu. poem) full of it قصیدہ ، مدحیہ **eulogize** (*yool*-o-jiz) *v.t.* praise highly مدح کرنا
Eumenides (yu-*men*-i-deez) *Cl. myth*. one of the *Furies* (which see) یومے نیڈیز
eunuch (*yoo*-nuk) *n*. castrated man ہیجڑا ، خواجہ سرا
euphemism (*yoo*-fe-mizm) *n*. use of inexact but unpleasing word بری بات کے لیے ملائم لفظ کا استعمال ، ملائم لفظ **euphemistic** (-*mis*-tik) *adj*. characterized by euphemism ملائم لفظوں میں ، ملائم
euphony (*yoof*-o-ni) *n*. pleasing sound of words (الفاظ کا) ترنم this quality
Euphrosyne (yū-*fros*-i-nee) *Cl. myth*. one of the *Graces* (which see) یوفراسنی
euphuism (*yoo*-few-izm) *n*. high-flown and affected style پُرتکلف طرزِ تحریر ، انشائے مرصّع **euphuistic** *adj*. اُردو والا ، پُرتکلف ، تصنّع سے بھرا پڑا
Eurasian (yoo-*raysh*-ĕn) *adj*. & *n*. (person) of mixed European and Asiatic parentage یوریشین ، دوغلا صاحب
European (yoo-ro-*pee*-en) *adj*. of Europe یورپی ، ولائتی *n*. native of Europe گورا ، یورپین
eureka *int*. I have found it اوہ مل گیا !
Europa (yu-*roh*-pa) *Cl. myth*. beautiful Phoenician princess whom Zeus carried off into Crete and after whom Europe was named یوروپا
Eurydyce (yu-*rid*-i-see) *Cl. myth*. wife of the mythical Greek poet, *Orpheus* یوریڈیسی
eurhythmics (yoo-*ridh*-miks) *n*. rhythmical movements of the body as a form of physical exercise موزوں ورزش
Euterpe (yu-*tĕ**-pee) *Cl. myth*. the Greek Muse of music and lyric poetry یوٹرپی
evacuate (e-*vak*-ew-ayt) *v.t.* (of troops) withdraw from (a place) چھوڑ آنا ، خالی کر آنا ، سے نکل آنا remove (person) from a dangerous place خطرناک جگہ سے نکال لانا require (person) to leave (an area) (علاقہ) خالی کرانا empty (stomach, etc.) خالی کرنا **evacuation** (-*ay*-) *n*. تخلیہ ، اِنخلا **evacuee** (e-vak-ew-*ee*) *n*. person who is evacuated خطرناک جگہ سے نکال کر لایا ہُوا ، مُہاجر ، پناہ گزین
evade (e-*vayd*) *v.t.* escape by trick بچ نکلنا

avoid (doing) by tricks or procrastination ٹال جانا، پی جانا **evasion** (e-*vay*-zhĕn) *n.* clever escape پیچ نکلنا excuse حیلہ، عذر، حیلہ بہانہ، لیت ولعل artful avoidance ٹال مٹول **evasive** (e-*vays*-iv) *adj.* intended to evade حیلے بہانے والا، ٹال مٹول والا trying to evade حیلہ جو، لیت ولعل کرنے والا

evaluate (e-*val*-ew-ayt) *v.t.* appraise قیمت کا اندازہ کرنا **evaluation** (*-ay-*) *n.* appraisal قیمت کا اندازہ کرنا، آنکنا

evanescent (e-va-*nes*-ent) *adj.* quickly fading جلد مرجھا جانے والا soon going from the memory جلد بھول جانے والا

evangel (e-*van*-jel) *n.* the Gospel (*i.e.*, 'good news') preached by Christ's disciples **evangelic, (evangelical)** *adj.* of Gospel انجیل کا of the belief of salvation only through Christ حضرت عیسیٰؑ کے واحد منجی ہونے کے عیسائی عقیدے کے متعلق **evangelist** (e-*van*-je-list) *n.* one of the four writers of the Gospel (*viz.*, Matthew, Mark, Luke and John) انجیل نویس itinerant preacher of the Gospel انجیل آموز

evaporate (e-*vap*-o-rayt) *v.t.* & *i.* change into vapour بخارات بننا یا بنانا dehydrate سکھانا، خشک کرنا رطوبت نکالنا disappear اڑ جانا، غائب ہو جانا pass off without effect جاتے رہنا، ختم ہو جانا، پاش پاش ہو جانا **evaporation** (*-ay-*) *n.* act of evaporating تبخیر

evasion *n.*, **evasive** *adj.* (see under **evade**)

Eve (eev) *n.* the first woman حوّا، اماں حوّا، اماں حوا

eve (eev) *n.* evening before a special day کسی تقریب (کسی تقریب سے پہلے کی) شام day before it سے پہلے کا دن *New Year's Eve*, 31st December ۳۱ دسمبر *on the eve of*, just before سے پہلے، کے قریب

even (*eev*-ĕn) *n.* (poet.) evening شام **eventide** evening *adj.* level ہموار smooth صاف uniform یکساں، ٹھیک، باقاعدہ equal برابر *be even with, get even with*, have revenge on سے بدلہ لینا، سے بدلہ چکانا (of numbers) that can be exactly divided by two (as opposed to *odd*) جفت *adv.* just at the moment ٹھیک جونہی، جیسے ہی still اور بھی just ٹھیک so much as تک، بھی (for emphasis) بالکل بھی *v.t.* make even ہموار ہونا make equal برابر کرنا **evenly** *adv.* in an even manner یکساں smoothly بلا رکاوٹ، بلا دقت برابر

evening (*eev*-ning) *n.* close of the day شام from the afternoon to bedtime تیسرے پہر سے سونے کے وقت تک this time spent in a particular way شام closing period of life شام زندگی

event (e-*vent*) *n.* happening واقعہ important happening اہم واقعہ *at all events*, no matter what happens بہر صورت، کچھ بھی کیوں نہ ہو *in that event*, if that happens اس صورت میں an item of a sports programme کھیل **eventful** *adj.* full of important events اہم واقعات والا important اہم **eventual** (e-*ven*-tew-ĕl) *adj.* likely to happen under certain circumstances شدنی final آخری **eventually** *adv.* in the end آخر کار، انجام کار **eventuality** (*-al*-i-ti) *n.* possible event امکانی صورت emergency ہنگامی صورت حال **eventuate** *v.i.* turn out (*well* or *ill*) (نیک یا بد) ہونا end (*in*) (پر) منتج ہونا (*U.S.*) happen ہونا، واقع ہونا، روپذیر ہونا

eventide *n*, (*ev*-ĕn-tid) *n.* evening old age

ever (*ev*-ĕ*) *adv.* always ہمیشہ، ہمیشہ کے لیے at any time ہر وقت، ہمہ وقت in any degree جتنا بھی (for emphasizing questions) آخر *ever so*, very بڑا، بہت، بہت ہی *ever and anon*, now and then کبھی کبھی، کبھی کبھار *the finest ever*, the finest- نفیس ترین

evergreen *adj.* having green leaves throughout the year سدا بہار *n.* such tree سدا بہار درخت **everlasting** *adj.* going on for ever دائمی، ابدی، لازوال *the Everlasting*, God خدائے لم یزل durable پائدار، مضبوط repeated too often مسلسل، روز روز کا، آئے دن کا **everlastingly** *adv.* always ابداً، دائماً **evermore** *adj.* for ever ہمیشہ، ہمیشہ کے لیے

every (*ev*-ri) *adj.* each, all ہر *every day* ہر روز *every other day*, ایک دن چھوڑ کر *every third day* ہر تیسرے روز all possible ہر ممکن *every now and then, every now and again*, from time to time اکثر *every bit*, quite as much (as) ٹھیک اتنا (جتنا) **everybody** *n.* all ہر ایک، سبھی **everyday** *adj.* happening daily روزانہ usual روزمرّہ of week-days and not of holidays کام کا **Everyman** *n.* typical, ordinary human being عام انسان **everyone** (or *every one*) *n.* all, every person ہر ایک، ہر کوئی، سبھی **everything** *pron.* all things ہر بات، ہر چیز، ہر شے all that matters سبھی کچھ **everyway** *adv.* in every way بہر صورت **everywhere** *adv.* in all places ہر جگہ

evict (e-*vikt*) *v. t.* turn (someone) out by force of law (*from* house or land) (قانونی چارہ جوئی کے ذریعے گھر یا زمین سے) بیدخل کرنا **eviction** *n.* act of evicting بے دخلی

evidence *n.* (see under **evident**)

evident (*ev*-i-dent) *adj.* obvious ظاہر، بدیہی، بیّن **evidently** *adv.* obviously ظاہر ہے کہ **evidence** (*ev*-i-dens) *n.* anything that gives reason for believing something ثبوت statement by witness supporting or contradicting a case گواہی، شہادت *oral evidence*, evidence given by word of mouth زبانی شہادت *circumstantial evidence*, evidence derived from existing circumstances قرائنی شہادت *give evidence in a law-court* عدالت میں گواہی دینا *bear*

evidence of, show signs of سے ظاہر ہونا *in evidence*, clearly or easily seen ظاہر، نمایاں *v.t.* prove تصدیق کرنا، ثابت کرنا indicate ظاہر کرنا، دِکھانا **evidential** relating to evidence متعلق بہ شہادت
evil (*ee*-vil) *adj.* wicked بُرا، بد sinful گنہگار، بدکار *the Evil One*, Devil شیطان، اِبلیس *evil eye* نظرِ بد *an evil spirit* بھوت، بھوت پریت، بُری رُوح، رُوحِ بد *n.* wickedness بُرائی، بدی sin گناہ anything opposite of good بُرائی، خرابی ruin تباہی، بربادی *think evil of (someone)* کسی کا بُرا چاہنا **evil-doer** *n.* wicked person بدکار **evil-minded** *adj.* malicious بد اندیش **evilly** *adv.* in an evil manner بُرا، بد *evilly disposed* بد اندیش
evince (e-*vins*) *v. t.* show that one has ; indicate (something, or *that*) کا ثبوت دینا
evoke (e-*vohk*) *v. t.* draw out (response) جواب حاصل کرنا call up (memories) (یاد) تازہ کرنا rouse (feelings) (جذبات) اُبھارنا
evolution *n.* (see under **evolve**)
evolve (e-*volv*) *v. t.* & *i.* develop gradually and naturally نشوونما پانا، اِرتقا پذیر ہونا work out مُنضبط کرنا unfold کھولنا **evolution** (ee-vo-*loo*-shĕn) *n.* gradual natural development ارتقا *the theory of evolution*, theory that living things are not each the result of separate creation but have gradually developed naturally نظریۂ ارتقا، مسئلۂ ارتقا **evolutionary** *adj.* pertaining to evolution
ewe (yew) *n.* female sheep بھیڑ
ewer (yew-ĕ*) *n.* bed-room water-jug with spout and handle صُراحی، مینا
ex- (eks) *adj.* former سابق *ex-Minister* سابق وزیر *ex-serviceman*, formerly in the armed forces سابق فوجی
exact (eg-*zakt*) *adj.* correct صحیح، دُرست precise بالکل ٹھیک، چھانٹا careful مُحتاط، ہوشیار *v. t.* get by force جبراً وصول کرنا insist on forcibly زبردستی منوانا **exacting** *adj.* severe سخت گیر demanding too much سخت **exaction** (eg-*zak*-shĕn) *n.* the exacting (of money, etc.) اِستحصال (esp.) tax which is considered too high "کالا" (ٹیکس وغیرہ) **exactly** *adv.* precisely بالکل **exactitude**, **exactness** *n.* accuracy دُرستی، صحت being precise چھانٹا ہونا
exaggerate (ig-*zaj*-ĕ-rayt) *v.t.* overstate مُبالغہ کرنا بڑھا چڑھا کر بیان کرنا **exaggerated** (-ted) *adj.* overstated مُبالغہ آمیز، مُبالغہ آمیزانہ **exaggerator** *n.* one who exaggerates مُبالغہ کرنے والا
exalt (ig-*zawlt*) *v.t.* raise in dignity سرفراز کرنا praise highly حمد کرنا، ثنا کرنا
exalted (-tid) *adj.* dignified سرفراز **exaltation** (-tay-) *n*, (esp.) spiritual delight وجد، کیف

examine (eg-*zam*-in) *v. t.* put questions for testing knowledge اِمتحان لینا inspect closely بغور مُشاہدہ کرنا question in a law-court (عدالت میں) بیان لینا **examination** (eg-zam-i-*nay*-shĕn) *n.* test اِمتحان evidence بیان close inspection بغور مُشاہدہ ▣ An **examination** is held to ascertain whether a thing is or is not so ; or whether a candidate has or has not acquired a certain amount of knowledge or fitness ; an **inspection** is an official looking into : **scrutiny,** a close detailed search : **inquiry,** a search for facts that have a definite bearing on a particular problem ; **inquest,** legal inquiry into a death ; **inquisition,** a tyrannical examination of a belief or action ; **search of** a container, house, etc., and **search for** someone missing.
example (ig-*zamp*-ĕl) *n.* something given to illustrate rule مثال *without example*, beyond example بے مثال، بے نظیر person or thing to be imitated مثال، نمونہ *follow (someone's) example* کسی کی مثال پر عمل کرنا *set a good example* اچھا نمونہ پیش کرنا warning تنبیہ، عبرت *make an example of (someone)* punish (him) as a warning to others کسی کو دُوسروں کے لیے تازیانۂ عبرت We speak of a **sample** of cloth or milk, of a **specimen** of one's work or of a plant family, of an **instance** of cruelty, of an **example** of generosity, and of a **model** of something bigger.
ex animo (eks-*an*-i-moh) *adj.* & *adv.* sincere(ly) دلی، بہ پُرخلوص، صدقِ دلانہ
exasperate (eg-*zas*-pe-rayt) *v.t.* make very angry اِشتعال دلانا، سخت غصّہ دلانا aggravate (ill-feeling) اور بھڑکانا **exasperation** *n.* irritating or being irritated in a high degree سخت غصّہ، اِشتعال
Excalibur , (eks-kal-i-bĕ*) *Brit. leg.* King Arthur's famous sword ایکس کالی بر
ex cathedra (eks-ka-*theed*-ra) *adj.* authoritative مُستند *adv.* with high authority مُستند طور پر
excavate (*eks*-ka-vayt) *v.t.* dig کھودنا uncover or take out by digging کھُدائی کرنا **excavator** *n.* one who excavates کھُدائی کرنے والا، حافر machine used for excavation کھُدائی کی مشین، حافرہ
excavation *n.* excavating اِحتفار (*pl.*) such process on large-scale حفریات
exceed (ek-*seed*) *v.t.* go beyond the set limit حد سے بڑھنا، حد سے تجاوز کرنا surpass سبقت لے جانا، سے زیادہ ہونا **exceedingly** *adv.* extremely بے حد، بہت ہی (also see **exceed**)
excel (ek-*sel*) *v.t.* & *i.* surpass سبقت لے جانا، بازی لے جانا be prominent بہت عُمدہ ہونا، شرف رکھنا **excellent** (*ek*-se-lent) *adj.* very good عُمدہ، اعلیٰ، نہایت عُمدہ **excellently** *adv.* بہت خوب **excellence** *n.* surpassing merit برتری، تفوّق، فضیلت، شرف **excellency** (-si) *n.* (with *Your* or *His* or *Her*), courtesy title

used when speaking to or of a governor (or ambassador) or his wife (گورنر یا سفیر کا لقب) فضیلت مآب
except (ek-*sept*) *prep.* but, save کے سوا ، کے سوائے leave out مستثنیٰ کرنا object to پر اعتراض کرنا
excepting *prep.* except کے سوا ، کے سوائے **exception** (ek-*sep*-shĕn) *n.* something or someone not included (in a company or general rule) مستثنیٰ استثنا ، (ج: مستثنیات) *the exception proves the rule* استثنا سے تو اصول ثابت ہوتا ہے objection or protest اعتراض ، احتجاج *take exception to*, protest against (کے خلاف) احتجاج کرنا
exceptionable *adj.* objectionable قابلِ اعتراض
exceptional *adj.* uncommon غیر معمولی **exceptionally** *adv.* remarkably غیر معمولی طور پر ، حد سے زیادہ
excerpt (*ek*-sĕ*pt) *n.* extract (*from*) اقتباس ، انتخاب
excess (ek-*ses*) *n.* more than enough حد سے زیادہ *in excess* (*of*), more (than) (سے) زیادہ ، ضرورت سے زیادہ extra charge مزید (*pl.*) outrages زیادتی ، زیادتیاں immoderation بے اعتدالی ، بے اعتدالیاں *adj.* over and above the usual فالتو **excessive** (ek-*ses*-iv) *adj.* too much حد سے زیادہ ، فزوں از حد ، بہت زیادہ **excessively** *adv.* extremely بے حد ، بہت
exchange (eks-*chaynj*) *v.t.* give (one thing) for another بدلنا ، اُدلا بدلی کرنا ، عوض سے *exchange blows*, fight جھگڑنا ، لڑنا ، ہاتھا پائی کرنا *exchange words*, quarrel تو تو میں میں کرنا barter مبادلہ کرنا *exchange money* زر مبادلہ کرنا *n.* act of exchanging اُدلا بدلی barter مبادلہ *bill of exchange* ہنڈی (usu. *foreign exchange*) foreign currency غیر ملکی زر مبادلہ place where businessmen meet for adjusting bills of exchange, trading in shares, or conducting business in 'future' market ایکسچینج ، حصص مارکیٹ *Stock Exchange* حصص مارکیٹ ساہوکارہ *the Exchange*, central office where telephone lines are connected (also *the Telephone Exchange*) ٹیلی فون ایکسچینج *Employment Exchange*, department for getting people fixed up in jobs محکمۂ روزگار **exchangeable** *adj.* that which may be exchanged مبادلہ پذیر
exchequer (eks-*chek*-ĕ*) *n.* public treasury خزانۂ عامرہ *the Exchequer*, British Finance Department برطانوی محکمۂ مالیات *Chancellor of the Exchequer*, Minister of this department برطانوی وزیر مالیات funds of an individual روپیہ پیسہ ، مالی حالت
excise (ek-*siz*) *n.* government duty on home-made goods چنگی ، داخلی محصول ، آبکاری **excisable** *adj.* liable to excise duty جس پر محصول آبکاری لگے **exciseman,** excise officer, excise official افسر آبکاری ، افسر چنگی
excision (ek-*sizh*-ĕn) *n.* cutting out of (words from writing) کاٹنا ، کاٹ چھانٹ ، اخراج *v. t.* cut out words (*from writing*) (عبارت سے لفظ) کاٹنا ، نکال دینا یا خارج کرنا
excite (ek-*sit*) *v. t.* rouse, stir up the feelings of اُبھارنا ، برانگیختہ کرنا ، اشتعال دلانا **excited** (ek-*sit*-ed) *adj.* with stirred feelings برانگیختہ ، مشتعل ، جوش میں nervous گھبرایا ہوا full of emotions پُرجوش
excitable *adj.* (of person, temper, etc.) easily excited جلد برانگیختہ ہو جانے والا ، اشتعال پذیر **excitability** *n.* weakness of being excitable جلد برانگیختہ ہو جانا ، اشتعال پذیری **excitement** *n.* state of being excited جوش exciting event پُرجوش واقعہ
exclaim (eks-*klaym*) *v. t.* & *i.* say suddenly and loudly (in surprise or anger) پکار اُٹھنا ، چلانا cry out (in pain) چیخنا ، چیخ اُٹھنا **exclamation** (eks-kla-*may*-shĕn) *n.* sudden short cry (expressing pain, surprise or anger) چیخ پکار ہانک پکار *note of exclamation, mark of exclamation, exclamation mark*, punctuation mark (!) expressive of surprise فجائیہ ، فجائی علامت
exclude (eks-*klood*) *v.t.* shut out (*from*) خارج کرنا نکال دینا **exclusion** (eks-*kloo*-zhĕn) *n.* act of excluding اخراج *to the exclusion of*, without کے بغیر **exclusive** (eks-*kloo*-siv) *adj.* (of person) not willing to mix with others کم آمیز peculiar to a group) مخصوص (things) not found elsewhere خاص ، خاص الخاص reserved مخصوص ، محدود (rights, etc.) not shared with others بلا شرکتِ غیرے *exclusive of*, not including کے بغیر
excommunicate (eks-ko-*mew*-ni-kayt) *v. t.* turn out of (community or church) حقہ پانی بند کر دینا ، ذات باہر کرنا **excommunicated** (-ted) *adj.* turned out (*from* church or community) ذات باہر **excommunication** (-ay-shĕn) turning out thus ذات باہر کرنا
excrement (*eks*-kre-ment) *n.* waste matter discharged from the body پاخانہ پیشاب ، فضلہ ، بول و براز
excrete (eks-*kreet*) *v. t.* discharge from the system نکالنا ، خارج کرنا **excretion** *n.* something excreted پسینہ ، بول و براز ، فضلہ
excruciating (eks-*kroosh*-i-ayt-ing) *adj.* (of pain) very severe سخت (درد)
exculpate (*eks*-kul-payt) *v. t.* free from blame or guilt بری کرنا ، بری الذمہ قرار دینا
excursion (eks-*kĕ**-shĕn) *n.* party's short journey for pleasure تفریحی سفر *excursion train*, train taking out people for excursion تفریحی ریل **excursionist** *n.* one who undertakes excursion تفریحی سفر پر جانے والا ◼ An **excursion** is a pleasure trip to a new place ; a **trip,** going there and back, whether for business or pleasure ; a **journey,** of some duration ; a **voyage** by sea ; an **outing** for a day or so ; a **tour,** circular trip, especially as a part of one's

duty ; a **picnic**, an outing with meals, or refreshment taken there ; a **cookout**, U. S. word for a picnic where the cooking of meals too is done during the outing.

excuse *v. t.* (eks-kewz) give reasons for not being blameworthy معذرت کرنا ، عُذر معذرت کرنا forgive مُعاف کرنا *excuse oneself* (*from something*), ask to be set free from (کسی کام سے) معذوری ظاہر کرنا *n.* (eks-*kews*) reason invented for explaining (one's) conduct عُذر ، معذرت ، اِعتذار Ⓢ We **excuse** when we find good reasons for not resenting something, **pardon** formally, **forgive**, out of kindness, whether the other party knows it or not ; **overlook** a mistake or shortcoming, **remit** a fine or other penalty ; and **condone** an offence or a shortage of lectures by finding good reasons for overlooking it.

execrable (*ek*-se-krab-ĕl) *adj.* deserving to be cursed لعنت کا مستحق very bad بہت بُرا **execrate** (*ek*-se-krayt) *v.t.* curse لعنت بھیجنا express hatred for نفرت کا اِظہار کرنا

execute (*ek*-se-kewt) *v. t.* do (one's bidding) تعمیل کرنا carry out ; implement (plan, etc.) عمل میں لانا complete (a document by getting it signed, etc.) (دستاویز کی) تکمیل کرنا put to death قتل کرنا ، گردن مارنا ، پھانسی دینا perform (on stage) (ناٹک وغیرہ) کرنا **execution** *n.* carrying out legal putting to death گردن زنی ، پھانسی **executioner** *n.* official who executes criminals جلاد

executive (eg-*zek*-ew-tiv) *adj.* having to do with executing or implementing policy laid down usu. by others عاملہ ، نافذہ having authority to carry out laws and decisions عاملہ *Executive committee*, committee of an organization executing its policy مجلس عاملہ *n.* the executive branch of a government عاملہ ، حکام (U. S.) manager, boss افسرِ اعلیٰ *Executive officer*, Administrator of a Municipal or District Board ایگزیکٹو افسر

executor (eg-*zek*-ew-tĕ*) *n.* one who is chosen to carry out the terms of a will وصیّت کی تکمیل کرنے والا ، وصی **executrix** (-iks) *n.* woman executor وصیّت کی تکمیل کرنے والی ، وصیّہ

exegesis (ek-se-*jee*-sis) *n.* commentary of the Scriptures تفسیر **exegetical** (-*jee*-) *adj.* pertaining to or comprising exegesis تفسیری *exegetical writings* تفاسیر

exemplary (eg-zemp-lĕ-ri) *adj.* (conduct) serving as an example مثالی (punishment) serving as a warning سبق آموز ، عبرتناک ، عبرت انگیز

exemplify (eg-*zemp*-li-fi) *v.t.* & *i.* show or prove by example مثال دے کر سمجھانا

exempli gratia (abbr. as *e.g.*) for example مثلاً

exempt (eg-*zempt*) *v.t.* set free (*from* taxes, duty, etc.) مستثنیٰ قرار دینا *adj.* free (*from* these) مستثنیٰ

exemption *n.* act of exempting مستثنیٰ قرار دینا ، اِستثنا being exempted اِستثنا

exercise (ek-sĕ*-siz) *n.* use of any part of the body for strengthening it ورزش *physical exercise* مشق such use (of mind or rights) اِستعمال drill for a learner مشق *military exercises* فوجی مشقیں *v. t.* & *i.* (cause to) take physical exercise مشق کرنا یا کرانا make use of (mental powers, or rights) سے کام لینا trouble (the mind) پریشان کرنا *be greatly exercised about* (*something*) (کسی بات) کے متعلق سخت پریشان ہونا

exert (eg-zĕ*t) *v. t.* put forth (strength or influence, *to do* something) *exert oneself*, put forth one's physical or mental powers (*to do* something) کوشش کرنا ، زور لگانا ، جدوجہد کرنا hard work مشقت fatigue resulting from it

exeunt (*ek*-se-unt) *v.i.* (stage direction in plays) "they go out (*i.e.*, off the stage)" چلے جاتے ہیں (see also **exit**)

exhale (ek-*sayl*) *v.t.* & *i.* breathe out سانس باہر نکالنا give or be given off (as gas or vapour) (گیس وغیرہ) نکلنا یا چھوڑنا **exhalation** (ek-sa-*lay*-shĕn) *n.* exhaling سانس باہر نکالنا ، گیس وغیرہ چھوڑنا

exhaust (ig-*zawst*) *v.t.* use up (strength, resources, etc.) completely تھکا دینا finish (patience, etc.) ختم کر دینا ، پیمانۂ (صبر) لبریز کر دینا *Feel exhausted*, feel very tired سخت تھک جانا make empty خالی کرنا discuss thoroughly (پامکمل) جامع بحث کرنا *n.* outlet for (used up power) نکالنے والا *exhaust pump* پانی نکالنے والا پمپ used power بچی کھچی بھاپ وغیرہ ، فضلہ **exhaustive** *adj.* (of a piece of writing, etc.) thorough جامع ، مکمل *exhaustive notes* مکمل شرح ، جامع حاشیہ **exhaustion** *n.* act of exhausting خالی کرنا utter fatigue سخت تھکاوٹ

exhibit (ig-*zib*-it) *v.t.* show publicly نمائش کرنا show clearly (کا) مظاہرہ کرنا (یا لگانا) submit as a document (in law-court) (عدالت میں) پیش کرنا *n.* something exhibited نمائش میں رکھی ہوئی چیز document submitted پیش کردہ دستاویز **exhibition** (ek-si-*bish*-ĕn) *n.* public display (*of* works of art, etc.) نمائش act of publicly exhibiting (quality, etc.) اِظہار *an exhibition of oneself*, behaving in public in such a way to excite contempt دکھاوا ، نمود و نمائش allowance to student from school or college funds (سکول یا کالج کی طرف سے) وظیفہ **exhibitor** (*ig*-zib-) *n.* one who exhibits نمائش میں اپنی چیزیں رکھنے والا **exhibitionism** *n.*

tendency to display extravagant behaviour عجیب وغریب حرکتیں کرنے کا شوق mental disease characterized by indecent exposure of part of the body شوقِ عُریانی
exhilarate (ig-*zil*-è-rayt) *v.t.* fill with high spirits شگفتہ کرنا **exhilaration** (*-ay-*) *n.* (being filled with) high spirits شگفتگی
exhort (ig-*zo**t) *v.t.* advise strongly (*to do*) نصیحت کرنا ، تاکید کرنا **exhortation** *n.* act of exhorting counsel given in the form of a discourse نصیحت ، تاکید
exhume (ek-*seum*) *v.t.* take out (dead body) for examination from the grave لاش کھود کر نکالنا
exigent (*ek*-si-jent) *adj.* urgent اہم ، اشد ، ضروری
exigency, exigence *n.* condition calling for urgent action ہنگامی صُورتِ حال
exile (*ek*-sɪl) *v.t.* send (someone) out of his country as a punishment جلا وطن کرنا ، دیس نکالا دینا *n.* condition of being exiled جلاوطنی ، دیس نکالا *live in exile* جلا وطنی کی زندگی کاٹنا exiled person جلا وطن
exist (eg-*zist*) *v.i.* be ہونا have life زندہ ہونا actually present or available موجود ہونا **existence** *n.* existing ہونا ، ہستی ، وُجُود life or the manner of living it زندگی reality وُجُود **existent** *adj.* existing, actual موجود
exit (*eg*-zit) passage for going out باہر جانے کا راستہ *v.i.* (in a printed play) "He (or She) goes out (*i.e.*, off the stage)" "چلا جاتا ہے" (یا) چلی جاتی ہے " (see also **exeunt**)
exodus (*ek*-so-dus) *n.* going out of many people ہجرت ، مُہاجرت ، کُوچ *the Exodus*, the 2nd book of the Old Testament تورات کی دُوسری کتاب ، سفرِ خرُوج
ex officio (eks-o-*fish*-i-oh) *adj.* & *adv.* in virtue of one's office حیثیت ، عہدہ ، بلحاظ ، منصب
exonerate (eg-*zon*-è-rayt) *v.t.* free (*from* blame) بری کرنا ، بری الذمہ قرار دینا
exorbitant (eg-*zo***b*-i-tant) *adj.* (of price or demand) far too great بہت ہی ، بہت زیادہ ، بے انداز
exorcize (*ek*-so*-sɪz) *v.t.* drive out (evil spirit) by prayers or magic جھاڑ پھونک کرنا ، جھاڑ پھونک کر آسیب اُتارنا **exorcism** *n.* act of exorcising آسیب اُتارنے کے لیے دَم جھاڑا کرنا **exorcist** *n.* one who exorcizes آسیب اُتارنے کے لیے دم جھاڑا کرنے والا
exoteric (eg-zo-*te*-rik) *adj.* (opp. of *esoteric*) intelligible to outsiders خارجی ، ظاہری ordinary معمولی
exotic (eg-*zot*-ik) *adj.* (of plants, fashions, ideas) introduced from abroad غیر ملکی ، بیرونی foreign (words) adapted دخیل (کلمات)
expand (eks-*pand*) *v.t.* & *i.* spread out, dilate پھیلنا (یا) پھیلانا (person) become good-humoured کھلنا **expanse** (eks-*pans*) *n.* wide area وسیع علاقہ ، وُسعت ، پہنائے **expansion** (*-pan*-shĕn) *n.* spreading out پھیلاؤ ، توسیع *expansion of currency*, inflation توسیعِ زر **expansive** (-siv) *adj.* able to expand پھیل سکنے والا ، وُسعت پذیر extensive وسیع و عریض
ex parte (eks-*pah**-tee) *adj.* & *adv.* without hearing the other party یک طرفہ
expatiate (eks-*pash*-i-ayt) *v.i.* speak or write at length (*on* or *upon* some subject) مُفصّل کہنا یا لکھنا
expatriate (eks-*pat*-ri-ayt) *v.t.* exile جلا وطن کرنا *expatriate oneself*, emigrate ترکِ وطن کرنا **expatriation** *n.* جلا وطنی ، ترکِ وطن
expect (eks-*pekt*) look forward to as likely to happen اُمّید کرنا ، توقع کرنا think, believe خیال کرنا ، توقع کرنا ، سمجھنا require as due (*from*) (کسی سے) کسی بات کا تقاضا کرنا **expectancy** *n.* state of expecting اُمّید کی حالت **expectant** *n.* one who expects متوقع *expectant mother*, pregnant حاملہ **expectation** (*-tay-*) *n.* expecting اُمّید ، توقع probability اِمکان ، توقع *expectation of life*, years a person *is expected to live* عُمر کی توقع (*pl.*) things expected توقعات ، اُمّیدیں *have expectations* توقعات رکھنا ، اُمّیدیں باندھنا *belie (someone's) expectations* (کسی) کی توقعات کے برعکس نکلنا

▣ We **expect** when we have good reasons for thinking something will happen ; **anticipate** when we are ready for something that may happen ; **contemplate,** vaguely intend *doing* something ; **await** when we are all ready for some developments or someone's arrival ; and **look forward** to an event.

expedient (eks-*pee*-di-ent) *adj.* suited to the time or occasion ضروری ، موزوں ، مُناسب politic ; wise rather than right مصلحت کا ، تقاضائے مصلحت *n.* useful device مصلحت ، چارۂ کار *try an expedient*, try that device کسی مصلحت پر عمل کرنا **expedience, expediency** *n.* thinking of what is useful rather than what is just مصلحت ، مجبوری
expedite (*eks*-pe-dɪt) *v.t.* speed up (work) جلدی کرنا ، (کام) چلتا کرنا **expeditious** (eks-pe-*dish*-us) *adj.* done quickly جلدی کیا ہوا speedy مُستعد ، پھُرتیلا what should be done quickly ; important اہم ، ضروری **expedition** (eks-pe-*dish*-ĕn) *n.* journey with purpose of discovery مُہم march of soldiers for making war فوجی مُہم
expel (eks-*pel*) *v.t.* (-ll-) drive out or away نکالنا ، نکال باہر کرنا send away (student *from* a college, etc.) as a punishment نکالنا ، خارج کرنا
expulsion (eks-pul-shĕn) *n.* sending away (of

student *from* college, etc., *for* bad conduct نکالنا اخراج

expend (eks-*pend*) *n*. spending (money, energy, etc.) خرچ کرنا، صرف کرنا **expenditure** *n*. money spent خرچ، رقم، صرفہ spending money خرچ، صرف

expense *n*. (usu. *pl*.) money used or needed for something خرچ، صرفہ *travelling expenses* سفر خرچ *at the expense of*, with the loss of کی قیمت پر **expensive** (-siv) *adj*. costly مہنگا، قیمتی **experience** (eks-*pee*-ri-ans) *n*. knowledge or skill gained by living at a place or doing or seeing things تجربہ activity or event giving one such knowledge or skill تجربہ *v.t*. have experience of آزمائش کرنا، تجربہ کرنا find by experience معلوم کرنا

experienced *adj*. having experience or knowledge or skill as its result تجربہ کار، پختہ کار

experiment (eks-*pe*-ri-ment) *n*. careful test or trial under controlled conditions for studying results تجربہ *v.t*. make experiments (*on* or *with*) کا تجربہ کرنا **experimenter** *n*. one who experiments تجربہ کرنے والا **experimental** *adj*. tentative ; based on or done by way of experiment تجرباتی *experimental measures*, measures adopted by way of experiment تجرباتی اقدامات **experimentally** *adv*. by way of experiment ; tentatively تجرباتی طور پر **experimentation** *n*. going on with tests to discover something or set it right تجربے کرتے جانا

expert *n*. (*eks*-pĕ*t) person with special skill gained from knowledge or experience (*in* or *at*) ماہر *adj*. (*iks*-pĕ*t) skilful ماہر *expert evidence*, evidence of an expert ماہرانہ رائے **expertly** *adv*. skilfully ; like an expert ماہرانہ انداز سے یا مہارت سے **expertness** *n*. being expert مہارت ■ **An expert is one who knows after much practice of an art ; a specialist, one who limits himself to one branch thus knowing, as is ironically said, more and more about less and less ; an adept, one versed in the secrets of a trade, etc.**

expiate (*eks*-pi-ayt) *v.t*. make amends by volunteering to undergo full punishment (*for* sin) کفارہ ادا کرنا **expiation** (-*ay*-) *n*. such amends کفارہ، مکافی

expire (eks-*pī*-ĕ*) *v.i*. (of a period of time, leave, etc.) come to an end (مُدّت) ختم ہونا (of person) die مرنا، دم دے دینا **expiry** (eks-*pī*-è-ri) *n*. termination (*of a period of time*) خاتمہ، اختتام

explain (eks-*playn*) *v.t*. & *i*. tell the detailed meaning of تشریح کرنا give reasons for وجہ بتانا، توجیہ کرنا *explain oneself*, (*a*) make one's meaning clear مطلب بتانا یا واضح کرنا (*b*) give reasons for one's conduct جواب دہی کرنا، توجیہ کرنا *explain (something) away*, show why one should not be blamed (for it) جواب دہی کرنا، توجیہ کرنا **explanation** (eks-pla-*nay*-shèn) commentary, that which makes clear تشریح **explanatory** (eks-*plan*-a-tĕ-ri) *adj*. serving to explain تشریحی *explanatory notes* تشریحی حواشی

explicit (eks-*plis*-it) *adj*. clearly and fully expressed (statement or meaning) واضح، صریح، قطعی **explicitly** *adv*. plainly صراحت سے، وضاحت سے، صراحتاً بالصراحت

explode (eks-*plohd*) *v.t*. & *i*. burst with a loud noise دھماکے سے پھٹنا cause to burst like that بھک سے اڑنا، دھماکا کرنا (of person) show violent anger پھٹ پڑنا burst out (*with* laughter, etc.) بے طرح ہنس دینا disprove (theory, etc.) (نظریہ وغیرہ) غلط ثابت کرنا (یا) کی تغلیط کرنا **explosion** (eks-*ploh*-zhèn) *n*. act of exploding دھماکا **explosive** (-siv) *adj*. & *n*. (substance) likely to explosion دھماکے سے پھٹنے والا، بھک سے اڑ جانے والا (مادّہ)

exploit *n*. (*eks*-ploit) great or daring deed کارنامہ، کارِ نمایاں *v.t*. (eks-*ploit*) make full use of (natural resources) پوری طرح استفادہ کرنا، پورا استعمال کرنا make unfair and selfish use of (persons or their misfortunes) لوٹ کھسوٹ کرنا، ناجائز فائدہ اٹھانا **exploitation** (-*tay*-) *n*. full use unfair profit ناجائز انتفاع

explore (eks-*ploh**) *v.t*. travel through (little-known country, etc.) to learn about it غیر معروف علاقے کی سیاحت کرنا examine thoroughly (problems, etc.) گہرا مطالعہ کرنا، خوب غور کرنا **explorer** *n*. travell..r to little known lands غیر معروف علاقے کی سیاحت کرنیوالا **exploration** (-*ray*-) *n*. such travels غیر معروف علاقے کی سیاحت thorough examination گہرا مطالعہ، غور و خوض

explosion *n*., **explosive** *adj*. (see under **explode**)

exponent (eks-*poh*-nent) *n*. one who presents and expounds (a theory or programme) پیش کرنے والا one who explains meaning, etc. (*of* something, *of* theory, etc.) شارح، بیان کرنے والا type, representative مثال، نمونہ symbol

export *v.t*. (iks-*poh*t*) send out (goods *to* another country) برآمد کرنا *n*. (*eks*-poh*t) exporting برآمد this business برآمدی تجارت thing exported برآمد **exports** (*eks*-poh*ts) *n*. *pl*. goods exported برآمدات amount exported برآمدات برآمدات کی مقدار **exporter** *n*. one who exports برآمد کنندہ **exportation** *n*. exporting برآمد کرنا

expose (eks-*pohz*) *v.t* leave unprotected (*to*) خطرے میں ڈالنا، کی مصیبت میں ڈالنا uncover *to* the effects of (something) دھوپ وغیرہ) دکھانا show the hidden evil deeds of بے نقاب کرنا display (goods, etc., *for* sale) لگانا show light to reach (camera film, etc.) فلم کو ایکسپوز کرنا **exposed** (eks-*pohzd*) *adj*. left open *to* the effects or dangers of (something) (کے) خطرے میں with secrets divulged بے نقاب **exposure** (eks-*poh*-zhe*) *n*. act of exposing کھلا ہوا ہونا divulging secrets پردہ دری showing light to film فلم کا ایکسپوژر، ظہور its time ایکسپوژر کا وقفہ، ظہور **exposition** (eks-po-*zish*-en) *n*. expounding ; explanation بیان، تشریح ◼ We **expose** something to show it openly ; **exhibit** proudly ; **disclose** something hidden ; and **bare** something covered.

exposition *n*. (see under **expose**)

expostulate (eks-*pos*-tew-layt) *v.i*. reason with a friend and urge an idea different from his ردّ و کدّ کرنا، مدلّل مگر دوستانہ اصرار کرنا، دوستانہ نصیحت کرنا **expostulation** *n*. such reasoning دوستانہ اصرار

exposure *n*. (see under **expose**)

expound (eks-*pound*) *v.t*. explain clearly and in detail (new theory, etc.) (نیا نظریہ) پیش کرنا دیا، تفصیل سے سمجھانا explain (scriptures) تفسیر بیان کرنا **expounder** *n*. one who expounds پیش کرنے والا، بیان کرنے والا

express (ek-*pres*) *v.t*. show clearly (by words, gestures or actions) ظاہر کرنا، اظہار کرنا squeeze (juice *out* of something) (رس) نکالنا *adj*. definite ; clearly expressed (wish, command) قطعی، واضح، صریح (letter, train, telegram) going quickly ایکسپریس (messenger) sent specially in haste خاص تیز رو قاصد *express delivery*, special and quick delivery فوری ترسیل *adv*. by special delivery فوری ترسیل سے by express train ایکسپرس سے **expression** (eks-*presh*-en) *n*. expressing (of one's meaning, feeling, etc.) اظہار، بیان *give expression to (one's emotions)* (اپنے جذبات کا) اظہار کرنا word or phrase الفاظ، کلمات looks expressing emotion نظریں، چہرہ، بشرہ *a polite expression* نرم انداز **expressive** (eks-*pres*-iv) *adj*. *expressive of something*, expressing it کی دلالت کرنے والا، کا اظہار کرنیوالا، پر دال full of secret meaning پُرمعنی، معنی خیز **expressway** *n*. (see *Addenda*) ◼ We **express** a thought by means of suitable words ; **state** it in words and with a certain emphasis ; **assert** it forcefully against possible contradiction ; and **represent** it when we declare it as being so and so.

expropriate (eks-*prohp*-ri-ayt) *v.t*. dispossess ; take away the property of بیدخل کرنا، (جائداد) غصب کرلینا **expropriation** *n*. dispossession بے دخلی، غصب

expulsion *n*. (see under **expel**)

expunge (eks-*punj*) *v.t*. delete (words *from* book, etc.) (الفاظ عبارت سے) خارج کرنا

expurgate (*eks*-pě*-gayt) *v.t*. take out offensive parts from (book, etc.) قابلِ اعتراض حصے نکال دینا، اخراج کرنا *an expurgated edition* (یا نسخہ) اخراج شدہ اشاعت **expurgation** (-gay-) *n*. expurgating قابلِ اعتراض حصّوں کا اخراج

exquisite (eks-*kwiz*-it) *adj*. very beautiful and delightful نہایت عمدہ، بہت خوشنما (of pleasure or pain) keenly felt (انتہائی (خوشی یا تکلیف) (of power to feel) keen نازک احساس

extant (*ek*-stant, or ik-*stant*) *adj*. still in existence اب تک موجود

extempore (eks-*tem*-po-ri) *adv*. & *adj*. off-hand برجستہ، فی البدیہہ **extemporize** (-riz) speak (or sing) without preparation برجستہ تقریر کرنا (یا گانا) **extemporaneous** (eks-tem-po-*ray*-ni-us) *adj*. off-hand برجستہ

extend (eks-*tend*) *v.t*. & *i*. lengthen ; enlarge لمبا کرنا، بڑا کرنا، وسیع کرنا prolong (the period) میں اضافہ کرنا، زیادہ عرصے کا کرنا lie at *full length* پھیلنا، پھیلانا reach پہنچنا، پہنچانا stretch پاؤں پھیلا کر لیٹنا offer پیش کرنا، دینا **extension** (eks-*ten*-shen) *n*. act of extending توسیع being extended پھیلاؤ، وسعت something added (*to*) میں اضافہ **extensive** (-siv) *adj*. far-reaching دُور تک پھیلا ہوا major بہت، بڑا، پورا thorough پورا، مکمل، جامع **extent** *n*. length لمبائی، طول area degree ; scope حد *to a certain extent*, partly کسی حد تک *to a large* (or *great*) *extent*, quite بڑی حد تک.

extenuate (eks-*ten*-ew-ayt) *v.t*. make (crime or fault) seem less serious (by finding an excuse (جرم یا غلطی کی) نوعیت کو کم کرنا، ہلکا کرنا *extenuating circumstances*, circumstances making the offence seem less bad جرم کی نوعیت کو کم کرنے والے حالات

exterior (eks-*tee*-ri-ě*) *adj*. outer ; outside بیرونی *n*. outer surface ظاہری صورت outer condition ظاہری حالت

exterminate (eks-*te*-*-mi-nayt) *v.t*. root out (disease, pests or doctrine) قلع قمع کرنا **extermination** (-*ay*-) *n*. rooting out قلع قمع

external (eks-*te**-něl) *adj*. outside بیرونی (of student) private ; not regular پرائیوٹ، غیر تدریسی (medicine) for use on the outside of the body بیرونی استعمال کی **externally** *adv*. outside باہر، بیرونی طور پر

extinct (ek-*stinkt*) *adj*. no longer active (volcano) ٹھنڈا no longer burning (fire, spark of life) ٹھنڈی، بجھی ہوئی (species) no longer in existence ناپید n. dyin out ناپید ہوجانا، بجھنا، ٹھنڈا ہوجانا

extinguish (*ek-ting-wish*) *v.t.* put out (a light, fire) بجھانا end (hope love, etc.) ختم کرنا **extinguisher** *n.* device for extinguishing fire آگ بجھانے کا آلہ

extirpate (*eks-tě*payt*) *v.t.* pull up by the roots جڑ سے اکھاڑنا destroy جڑ بنیاد سے اکھیڑنا

an extinguisher

extol (eks-*tol*) *v.t.* (-ll-) praise highly تعریف کے پل باندھنا، بڑھانا

extort (eks-*to*t*) *v.t.* obtain (money or promise etc.) by threats, (روپیہ یا وعدہ) دھمکی سے لینا **extortion** *n.* obtaining thus استحصال، جبراً لینا **extortionate** (eks-*to**-shě-*nayt*) *adj.* much too high (price or demand) لوٹ، ظلم

extra (*eks*-tra) *adj.* additional فالتو، مزید *adv.* exceptionally بہت زیادہ، غیر معمولی *n.* something additional فالتو چیز (in cricket) run not scored off the bat فالتو newpaper supplement (اخبار کا) ضمیمہ actor or actress playing an insignificant role in a film ایکسٹرا، فالتو

extract *v.t.* (ek-*strakt*) *v.t.* pull out (tooth, bullet, etc., *from* the body) with effort نکالنا، زور لگا کر نکالنا get (money, information, etc.) from someone unwilling to give it زبردستی حاصل کرنا obtain (oil or juice) from (ست، رس یا تیل) نکالنا select and copy out passage (*from* a book) as representative of its style or contents اقتباس کرنا *n.* (*eks*-trakt) liquid extracted نچوڑ، افشردہ passage extracted اقتباس **extraction** *n.* (esp.) (of persons) descent *of Arab extraction* عربی النسل

extradite (*eks*-tra-dit) *v.t.* make over on request (escaped foreign criminal) *to* his country's police (مجرم پناہ گزین) کو اس کے ملک کے حوالے کرنا **extradition** *n.* act of extraditing or being extradited (مجرم پناہ گزین) کی اس کے ملک کو تحویل

extrajudicial *adj.* not belonging to the present case before a law-court موجودہ مقدمہ سے غیر متعلق

extramural *adj.* (of students' activities) out of the college or school بیرونی، خارجی

extraneous (eks-*tray*-ni-us) *adj.* foreign (*to* the matter in hand) غیر متعلق

extraordinary (eks-*tro**-di-na-ri) *adj.* unusual غیر معمولی remarkable حیرت انگیز **extraordinarily** *adv.* exceptionally غیر معمولی طور پر

extraterritorial *adj.* outside a country's territory خارجی، بیرونی، حدود ملک سے باہر

extravagant (eks-*trav*-a-gent) *adj.* prodigal فضول خرچ، مسرف wasteful فضول خرچی کا، غیر ضروری beyond what is reasonable نامعقول uncontrolled حد سے متجاوز **extravagance** *n.* اسراف، فضول خرچی

extreme (eks-*treem*) *adj.* highest or farthest possible انتہائی، حد درجہ، از حد، سخت، شدید، چوٹی درجے کا، پرلے سرے کا far from moderate (خیالات وغیرہ) انتہا پسندانہ very severe سخت *n.* farthest limits انتہا، حد، غایت *in the extreme*, extremely بہ نہایت، حد درجہ، انتہائی *extreme measures* سخت کارروائی، انتہائی قدم *run to an extreme* سخت کارروائی کرنا (*pl.*) qualities, etc., which are as wide apart as possible انتہا، افراط و تفریط *go to extremes* افراط و تفریط سے کام لینا **extremist** *n.* person with extreme views انتہا پسند **extremeness** *n.* (of views) being extreme حد سے بڑھا ہونا، بہت ہی زیادہ ہونا، انتہا پسندی

extremity (eks-*trem*-i-ti) *n.* limit حد، انتہا misfortune مصیبت، بدقسمتی *driven to extremity* تنگ آ کر extreme measure for punishment انتہائی اقدام، سخت کارروائی (*pl.*) hands and feet ہاتھ پاؤں

extricate (*eks*-tri-kayt) *v.t.* disentangle (*from*) (مشکلات سے) نکالنا **extricable** *adj.* that can be extricated جسے مشکلات سے نکالا جا سکے **extrication** *n.* disentanglement مشکلات سے نجات

extrinsic (eks-*trin*-zik) *adj.* outside بیرونی، خارجی not intrinsic عرضی (مقابلہ جوہری)

extrovert (*eks*-tro-vě*t) person not given to introspection خارج بیں

extrude (eks-*trood*) *v.t.* expel نکال دینا **extrusion** *n.* expulsion اخراج

exuberant (eg-*zewb*-ě-rant) *adj.* luxuriant بکثرت ہونا، کی افراط ہونا abounding لبریز، مالامال full of life and vigour زندہ دلانہ **exuberance** *n.* بہتات، کثرت، افراط، ریل پیل

exude (eg-*zewd*) *v.t.* & *i.* discharge through small holes پسینہ نکلنا، پسیجنا

exult (eg-*zult*) *v.i.* rejoice greatly (*at* or *in* something, *over* person's defeat) جوش ہونا، بغلیں بجانا

exultant *adj.* happy خوش **exultation** (-*ay*-) *n.* rejoicing فخر، خوشی، بغلیں بجانا

eye (i) *n.* organ of sight آنکھ sight نظر، بصارت power to appreciate ذوق نظر close watch نظر، کڑی نظر (of a needle) hole (سوئی کا) ناکا *black eye*, (a) eye with bruise round it سوجی ہوئی آنکھ (b) defeat شکست *keep an eye on* کڑی نظر رکھنا *eyes right* (or *left*) ! turn them right (or left) in salute داہنے دیکھو *eyes front* ! resume former position after salute سامنے دیکھو *saw with half an eye*, saw at a glance ایک نظر دیکھا تھا *open* (*one's*) *eyes*, stare with astonishment حیرت سے دیکھنا *open* (*someone's*) *eyes*

the eye of a needle

to truth, make (him) realize it کسی کو صداقت کا احساس دِلانا *have an eye on* پر نظر رکھنا *have an eye for* کو پرکھ سکنا ، کی سمجھ رکھنا *in the eye of*, from the viewpoint of کے نقطۂ نظر سے *make eyes at* (*someone*), پیار کی نظروں سے دیکھنا *up to the eye in*, deeply بہت ، سخت *see eye to eye with* (*someone*), agree entirely with (him) سے متفق ہونا ، سے اتفاق رائے رکھنا *v.t.* watch (with curiosity or suspicion) (حیرانی یا شک کی نظر سے) دیکھنا **eyeball** *n.* ball of the eye آنکھ کا ڈھیلا pupil of the eye آنکھ کی پتلی **eyebrow** *n.* hair on ridge above eye بھوں ، ابرو **eye-glass** *n.* lens for adjusting weak sight عینک کا شیشہ cup for washing eyes چشم شو **eye-glasses** *n.* (also, *glasses*) spectacles عینک چشمہ **eye-hole** *n.* hole in door, etc., through which one may look سوراخ **eyelash** *n.* hair over eyelids پلک ، مژہ (ج : مژگاں) **eyelid** *n.* cover of eye پپوٹا **eyeless** *n.* blind اندھا **eye-opener** *n.* something that reveals and astonishes آنکھ کھولنے والا (انکشاف) **eye-salve** *n.* something with which to stain the eyes سُرمہ ، کاجل **eyesight** *n.* sight نظر ، بصارت range of vision حدِ نظر ، نگاہ *within eyesight*, (*a*) visible جو نظر آرہا ہو (*b*) not distant قریب **eyesore** *n.* any ugly thing annoying to watch کانٹا ، آنکھوں میں خار **eye-wash** *n.* (slang) humbug بکواس **eye-witness** *n.* one who can testify from his own observation چشم دید گواہ ، عینی شاہد

eyelet *n.* small hole for button, cord or rope کاج ، محکمہ

eyrie, aerie (*ay*-è-ri) *n.* eagle's nest عُقاب کا نشیمن شاہین کا بسیرا

F

f, F (ef) (pl., *fs* or *f's*) sixth letter of the English alphabet انگریزی حروف تہجی کا چھٹا حرف ، ف ، ایف In music, the fourth note in the scale of C representing a sound below the true pitch مدھم سُر ، ما

Fabian (*fay*-bi-an) *adj.* cautiously persistent محتاط انداز سے کام کیے جانے والا (after the name of Fabius, the Roman commander who fought against Hannibal in the Punic Wars) ; *Fabian Socialism*, cautiously constitutiona' type of English Socialism محتاط اشتراکیت

fable (*fay*-bèl) *n.* short fanciful tale with a moral, usu. about animals behaving like human beings حکایت ، کہانی idle talk بے سروپا بات false account جھوٹ fanciful fabrication of impossibilities گپ **fabled** (*fay*-bèld) *adj.* legendary افسانوی **fabulous** (*fab*-ew-lus) *adj.* legendary افسانوی (of wealth, etc.) enormous بے انتہا difficult to believe in ناقابل یقین **fabulously** *adj.* extremely بے انتہا ◼ A **fable** is a story with a moral in which people or animals act in a way that points a lesson ; an **allegory** is a story describing something without expressly naming it ; a **parable** is a short story with a moral ; a **short story** is the modern form of story ; a **novel** is a long work of fiction ; a **narrative** is any kind of continuously told story.

fabric (*fab*-rik) *n.* woven material کپڑا big building عمارت pattern or framework (of society, etc.) (معاشرے کی) بناوٹ

fabricate (*fab*-ri-kayt) *v.t.* make up (something false) گھڑنا ، بنانا **fabrication** (-*kay*-) something fabricated جعلسازی

facade (fa-*sahd*) *n.* front (of a building) (عمارت کا) پیش ، ماتھا یا چہرہ مہرہ

face (fays) *n.* front of head from forehead to chin چہرہ ، شکل *face card*, (in cards) king, queen or knave (تاش میں) تصویر والا پتا ، تصویر ، مورت *look* (*someone*) *in the face*, look at (him) steadily کو ٹکٹکی باندھ کر دیکھنا کے چہرے پر نظریں جمانا *make* (or *pull*) *a face* (*at*), express disgust (with someone) by moving the mouth and eyes منہ بنانا *save* (*one's*) *face*, escape loss of reputation by pretending success even in failure عزت بچانا ، عزت رکھ لینا *lose* (*one's*) *face*, lose (one's) prestige وقار گنوانا ، عزت کھونا *put a brave face on*, pretend not to be afraid ڈر کے باوجود ہمت کا اظہار کرنا *have the face to say*, dare to say کہنے کی جسارت کرنا *face to face*, facing each other آمنے سامنے *in the face of*, in the teeth of ; despite کے مقابلے میں *to* (*someone's*) *face* کے رُوبرُو ، کے منہ پر *set* (*one's*) *face against*, not be in favour of التفات نہ کرنا *pull a long face*, wear the expression of disgust or defeat منہ بنا لینا *not to show one's face* مارے شرم کے منہ نہ دکھا سکنا *fly in the face of*, defy ڈٹ کر مقابلہ کرنا front of anything سامنے کا حصّہ ، رُخ ، پیش *in the face of danger*, when about to meet it خطرے کے باوجود ، خطرے کے وقت بھی *face value*, value marked on a coin, or note (which may be different from its real value) لکھی ہوئی قیمت outward appearance of a situation ظاہری صورت *on the face of it*, from its appearance بظاہر ، نظر بظاہر *v.t.* & *i.* be opposite to کے سامنے ہونا stand bravely out مقابلہ کرنا ، بخوشی بھگتنا ، مردانہ وار برداشت کرنا *face the music*, suffer punishment gladly سزا بخوشی قبول کرنا *face it out*, refuse to give way to troubles

ڈٹ کر مقابلہ کرنا **face-lifting** *n.* removing the wrinkles on the face by a surgical operation جوان لگنے کے لیے چہرے کا اپریشن کرانا **facing** (*fays*-ing) *n.* (esp.) coating with a different (usu. ornamental) layer نیا پلستر **facial** (*faysh*-el) *adj.* of the face چہرے کا *facial expression*, expression of sentiment on the face چہرے کا اُتار چڑھاؤ **facet** (*fas*-et) *n.* one of the many sides of a cut jewel (ترشے ہوئے ہیرے کا کوئی) رُخ
facetious (fe-*see*-shus) *adj.* humorous ہنسی کی بات **facetiously** *adv.* humorously ہنسی سے **facetiae** (fa-*see*-shè-ee) *n. pl.* pleasantries خوش گپیاں ، لطائف و ظرائف
facile (*fas*-il, *fas*-il) *adj.* (of work) easy آسان، سہل (of tongue or person) glib, fluent رَوانی والا، چرب زبان
facilitate (fa-*sil*-i-tayt) *v.t.* make work easier سہولت، آسانی آسان کرنا **facility** (fa-*sil*-i-ti) *n.* ease سہولت، آسانی skill in doing something پختگی (*pl.*) things which facilitate work سہولتیں، آسانیاں
facsimile (fak-*sim*-i-li) *n.* exact reproduction (of writing, picture, etc.) چربہ، ہو بہو نقل، صحیح نقل
fact (fakt) *n.* what has actually happened واقعہ، اَمرِ واقع what is known to be true حقیقت *in fact, in point of fact*, the truth is that واقعہ یہ ہے *as a matter of fact*, really درحقیقت، دَراصل **factual** (*fak*-tew-ĕl) *adj.* pertaining to fact واقعاتی
faction (*fak*-shĕn) *n.* discontented group within a political party جتھا، گروہ، ٹولی، پارٹی party spirit جتھے بندی **factious** (*fak*-shus) *adj.* trouble-making like a faction جھگڑالو، جتھابندی کا ، پارٹی بازی کا
factitious (fak-*tish*-us) *adj.* got up designedly نقلی، بناوٹی
factor (*fak*-tĕ*) *n.* whole number except 1 by which a larger number can be divided exactly (as 2 is a factor of 6) جزو ضربی condition conducive to a result عنصر، عنصر، بات، سبب commercial agent گماشتہ، مُنیم **factory** (*fak*-te-ri) *n.* workshop کارخانہ، فیکٹری business firm's foreign trading office تجارتی کوٹھی
faculty (*fak*-ul-ti) *n.* power of mind قابلیت power of doing things صلاحیت، اِستعداد sense حِس ، حاسّہ branch of knowledge taught in a college or university شعبہ
fad *n.* odd liking ; such pet notion خبط، مَن بسا، خیال passing fashion وقتی فیشن، وقتی وضع ، دُھن **faddist** *n.* one who has such a pet notion خبطی ◙ **A fad** is a temporary liking for a novelty as described by one who does not agree with such liking ; **a craze**, a fad shared by a great many people ; **a whim,** single expression of freakish desire ; **the rage**, a novelty suddenly followed by everybody ; **a hobby**, a person's occupation of an entertaining nature after regular work ; **a fancy**, usu. temporary liking for a certain thing ; **a mania**, an unreasonable habit.
fade (fayd) *v.t.* & *i.* (cause to) wither or grow pale مُرجھانا، مُرجھا دینا، سُوکھنا یا سُکھانا، خشک ہو جانا یا کر دینا cause to lose colour رنگ پھیکا پڑ جانا ، زرد ہو جانا یا کر دینا move slowly out of view دھیرے دھیرے نظر سے اوجھل ہو جانا یا کر دینا *fade in, fade out*, (for both see Addenda) go out of memory ذہن سے نکل جانا **fadeless** *adj.* lasting دائمی، مستقل، پائدار not liable to fade پکّا
fag *v.t.* & *i.* (-gg-) tire *out* تھکا دینا toil (*at* something) سخت محنت کرنا *n.* (colloq.) hard work مشقت *the fag end of the day*, evening, end of working hours کام کا خاتمہ ، شام
faggot (*fag*-ot) *n.* bundle of firewood ایندھن کا گٹھا
Fahrenheit (*fa*-ren-hit) *n.* thermometer-scale with 32° as freezing and 212° as boiling point (حرارت پیما کا) فارن ہیٹ پیمانہ
fail (fayl) *v.t.* & *i.* be unsuccessful (*in doing, to do*, or, *in* something) ناکام ہونا ، فیل ہونا *fail in the examination, fail to pass an examination* امتحان میں فیل ہونا give a failure mark to فیل کرنا fall short of ناکامی ہونا ، پُورا نہ ہونا disappoint مدد کو نہ پہنچنا، مایوس کرنا lose strength کمزور ہو جانا neglect (*to do*) نہ کرنا ، سے قاصر رہنا become bankrupt دیوالیہ ہو جانا *n.* (used only in the phrase :) *without fail*, certainly یقیناً **failing** *n.* weakness (of character) کمزوری **failure** *n.* act of failing ناکامی، کمی نقصان، فقدان، دیوالیہ پن person or thing that fails ناکام، نامُراد
fain (fayn) *adj.* willing (*to do*) خوش، آمادہ، تیار *adv.* willingly خوشی سے، بصد شوق
faint (faynt) *adj.* about to faint بے ہوش ہونے کو *feel* (or *look*) *faint*, feel (or look) as if about to faint بے ہوش ہونے کو ہونا too weak to be distinct کمزور *v.i.* become unconscious بے ہوش ہونا *n.* fainting بے ہوش ہونا ، غش کھانا state of fainting بے ہوشی، غش ، غشی **faintly** *adv.* imperfectly تھوڑا سا، کم کم **faint-hearted** *adj.* cowardly بزدل، بے ہمت
fair (*fay*-ĕ*) *adj.* just مُنصف، مُنصفانہ، جائز *fair field and no favour* بے رُو رعایت *fair play*, (*a*) according to the rules of the game, اصولوں کے مطابق کھیل (*b*) justice منصفی، انصاف ، مساوی برتاؤ more than average کافی، کافی اچھا (old use) beautiful خوبصورت، حسین *fair colour* گورا *fair sex*, women صنفِ نازک *fair weather*, dry and fine خوشگوار (یعنی خشک) موسم *fair wind*, favourable one موافق ہوا *fair copy*, new and clean copy صاف نقل *fair name*, good reputation نیک نامی *adv.* in a fair

manner ، اصولوں کے مطابق، کافی اچھی طرح ، انصاف سے *to play fair* انصاف کرنا، چالاکی نہ کرنا *write out fair*, صاف کرکے لکھنا *n.* exhibition-cum-market میلہ **fairness** *n.* justice انصاف **fairly** *adv.* justly انصاف سے moderately کافی، کافی اچھی طرح سے

fair trade agreement *n.* (see *Addenda*)

fairy (*fay*-è-ri) *n.* (pl., *fairies*, pr. fay-ĕ-reez) beautiful small imaginary creature supposed to have magic powers پَری **Fairyland** *n.* supposed home of fairies پرستان **fairy-tale** *n.* tale about fairies پریوں کی کہانی untrue story من گھڑت قصہ، جھوٹی بات

fait accompli (fet-a-kom-*plee*) *n.* thing already done; hence irrevocable and past protesting against جو بات ہو ہی چکی ہو، اٹل بات

faith (fayth) *n.* trust (in) بھروسہ، یقین، اعتماد system of religious belief ایمان *keep faith* (*with*), fulfil one's promise (with) (کسی سے) قول نباہنا، وعدہ پورا کرنا *break faith* (*with*) وعدہ پورا نہ کرنا *in good faith*, sincerely واقعی خلوص سے *in bad faith*, without sincerity فتورِ نیت سے **faithful** *adj.* keeping faith ایماندار، مومن loyal and true (*to*) وفادار exact اصلی، ٹھیک، اصل کے مطابق **faithfully** *adv.* دل سے *Yours faithfully*, (words written at the end of formal letters and meant to be construed as I am (or we are) yours faithfully) آپ کا وفادار، تہِ دل سے آپ کا **faithless** *adj.* unbelieving کافر، بے ایمان disloyal غدار، بے وفا

fake *n.* sham بناوٹی، مصنوعی، نقلی، جعلی *v.t.* palm off an imitation بناوٹی چیز، سر منڈھنا write (an interview etc.) without authority بلا اجازت لکھنا

falcon (*fawk*-ĕn, or *fol*-kĕn) *n.* kind of hawk trained to hunt باز، شکرا **falconer** *n.* one who hunts with them بازوالا، بازدار **falconry** *n.* art of hunting thus شکرے سے شکار training falcons for this purpose بازداری

a falcon

fall (fawl) *v.i.* (*fell, fallen*) come down گرنا، گر پڑنا *fall down dead* گر کر مر جانا *fall in battle*, be killed مارا جانا (of city or fort) be captured in war دشمن کے قبضہ میں چلے جانا give way to temptation گناہ میں مبتلا ہونا (of price) decrease گرنا، کم ہونا *fall back* پیچھے ہٹنا *fall behind* پیچھے رہ جانا *fall in love* (*with*), become filled with love of (کسی) محبت میں گرفتار ہونا *fall asleep*, sleep سو جانا *fall short* (*of something*), be not enough (for it) ناکامی ہونا *fall due*, be due واجب الادا *fall foul of*, quarrel لڑ پڑنا، ٹکرانا *fall on evil times*, be in misfortune کے برے دن آنا *fall to pieces*, break ٹکڑے ٹکڑے ہو جانا، پاش پاش ہو جانا *fall for*, (U.S. slang) be captivated or deceived by کے دام میں گرفتار ہونا *fall back on*, rely on, make use of کا سہارا لینا، پر اکتفا کرنا *fall in*, (of army) get into line صف بندی کرنا *fall in with*, agree to ماننا، سے متفق ہونا *fall off*, become fewer or smaller ہاتھ چھوڑ جانا *fall on* (*the enemy*) attack حملہ کرنا، ٹوٹ پڑنا *fall out* (*with*), quarrel لڑنا، جھگڑنا *it fell out that*, it happened that واقعہ یوں ہوا کہ *fall through*, come to nothing ناکام رہنا *fall to*, begin (eating) بسم اللہ کرنا، شروع کرنا *n.* coming down گرنا، پڑنا decline, end زوال (usu. *pl.*) cataract آبشار slope نشیب، ڈھلان (U.S.) autumn خزاں defeat, capture سقوط، تباہی decrease کمی

fallen (*fawl*-ĕn) *adj.* ruined مٹا ہوا، تباہ، تباہ حال dropped گرا ہوا killed مرا ہوا degraded, immoral آبرو باختہ

fallacy (*fal*-a-si) *n.* false reasoning مغالطہ **fallacious** *adj.* (of argument, reasoning, etc.) based on or involving fallacy مغالطہ آمیز

fallible (*fawl*-ib-ĕl) *adj.* liable to error خطا پذیر

fallow (*fal*-oh) *adj.* (of land) ploughed but left unsown for a year or so غیر مزروعہ، بنجر جدید، افتادہ *n.* such land افتادہ زمین، غیر مزروعہ اراضی

false (fawls) *adj.* untrue جھوٹا، دروغ گو *false pretences*, misrepresentations with a view to deceiving others غلط بیانی، فریب دہی disloyal بے وفا، غدار not genuine مصنوعی، نقلی hypocritical منافقانہ *adv.* falsely دھوکے سے *play* (*someone*) *false*, betray him کسی سے غداری کرنا **falsely** *adv.* دھوکے سے **falsehood** *n.* lie جھوٹ، دروغ، کذب telling lies جھوٹ بولنا

falsify (*fawl*-si-fi) *v.t.* prove to be wrong جھٹلانا alter (records, etc.) to deceive جعلسازی کرنا **falsification** (-*ka*-) *n.* such alteration جعلسازی proving to be wrong جھٹلانا

falter (*fawl*-tĕ*) *v.t.* & *i.* hesitate ہچکچانا، متامل ہونا walk *along* unsteadily لڑکھڑانا، ڈگمگانا stammer ہکلانا **falteringly** *adv.* hesitatingly ہچکچاتے ہوئے walking unsteadily ڈگمگاتے ہوئے

fame (faym) *n.* reputation شہرت good public report نیکنامی wide public knowledge چرچا، مشہوری *v.t.* be well known مشہور ہونا **famous** (*fay*-mus) *adj.* widely known مشہور، معروف celebrated مشہور ■ **Fame** denotes deserved and widespread good name; **reputation**, good name whether justified or not; **renown**, a lit. term for fame; **honour** implies recognition; **notoriety**, being known for wickedness; **character**, one's real worth; **prestige**, cumulative reputation of persons or institutions.

familiar (fa-*mil*-yĕ*) *adj* well-known جانا بُوجھا intimate واقف، آشنا، شناسا *be familiar with*, having a good knowledge of سے واقف ہونا جانا پہچانا taking liberties بے تکلّف *too familiar with*, کے ساتھ ضرورت سے زیادہ بے تکلّف، کے ساتھ بے باک **familiarity** (-ya-ri-ti) *n*. being familiar واقفیت، آشنائی being too familiar بے تکلّفی **familiarize** (-rɪz) *v.t.* make well-known مشہور کرنا make quite accustomed عادی بنانا

family (*fam*-i-li) *n*. wife and all descendants (of a man) بیوی بچّے، بال بچّے *(be) in the family way*, (of wife) (be) pregnant اُمّید سے ہونا (one's) parents and children کُنبہ relatives خاندان *family likeness*, general resemblance among members of one family خاندانی مشابہت group (of languages, or animals, etc.) with common characteristics خاندان **family man** *n*. one who is a husband or father گھر والا، گھر بار والا **family tree** *n*. genealogy شجرۂ نسب، شجرہ

famine (*fam*-in) *n*. extreme scarcity of food قحط *famine-stricken* قحط زدہ shortage (of anything) کمیابی، قحط **famish** *v. t.* (see below).

famish (*fam*-ish) *v.t. & i.* destroy with hunger بھُوکوں مارنا *be famished* بھُوکوں مرنا be reduced to extreme hunger بھُوکوں مرنا **famished** *adj*. suffering from extreme hunger فاقہ زدہ **famine** *n*. (see above)

famous *adj*. (see under **fame**)

fan *n*. device for starting current of air پنکھا (colloq.) great admirer شائق، شوقین *film fan* فلموں کا شوقین *football fan* فٹ بال کا شوقین (-nn-) send a current of air on to پنکھا جھلنا winnow پھٹکنا rouse بھڑکانا، مشتعل کرنا اناج

fanatic (fa-*nat*-ik) *adj*. having unreasonably passionate enthusiasm (usu. for religion) جوشیلا مذہبی جوش والا، کٹّر، مُتعصّب **fanatical** *adj*. (of action, views, etc.) characterized by fanaticism مُتعصّبانہ **fanaticism** (fa-*nat*-i-sizm) *n*. violent, unreasonable enthusiasm تعصّب

fancy (*fan*-si) *n*. imagination تصوّر، تخیّل، تخییل something imagined تصوّر، تخیّل fondness (*for*) میلان، رغبت، چاہت like بہت پسند کرنا *take a fancy* پر ریجھنا *have a fancy for (something)* پر مائل ہونا baseless idea *adj*. (esp. of small things) ornamental سجاوٹ والا، فینسی exorbitant (price) بہت زیادہ imaginative, خیالی brightly coloured زرق برق *fancy* ornamental (and not ordinary) goods رنگ برنگ کی چیزیں *fancy dress*, fantastic dress ... parties بہروپ، فینسی ڈریس *fancy ball*, ball in which people participate in fancy dress بھروپیا ناچ، فینسی ڈریس بال *v. t.* picture in the mind تصوّر کرنا suppose خیال کرنا، سمجھنا *Fancy !*, (an exclamation meaning :) How surprising ! دیکھو تو ! *fancy oneself*, have a high opinion of oneself اپنے کو بہت بڑا (یا) عقلمند) سمجھنا **fanciful** *adj*. indulging in fancies خیالی پلاؤ پکانے والا، شیخ چلی unreal سراسر جھوٹا، انوکھا، نرالا curiously designed بالکل فرضی

fanfare *n*. flourish of trumpets باجا گاجا، شہنائیوں کی آوازیں، نفیریں

fang *n*. long sharp tooth شکاری جانور کا بڑا دانت جس سے وہ شکار کرتا ہے poison tooth of a snake سانپ کا زہر والا دانت، ناب **fanged** (fangd) *adj*. having fangs کھیس والا

fantastic *adj*. (see under **fantasy**)

fantasy, phantasy (*fan*-ta-si) *n*. imagination تصوّر، تخیّل، تخییل product of fancy خیالی پلاؤ، خواب دیکھنا، سپنا، خواب کی باتیں خیال dream-like *fantastic* (fan-*tas*-tik) *adj*. imaginary غیر حقیقی، وہمی، خیالی wild and strange نرالا، عجیب وغریب **fantastically** *adv*. عجیب وغریب انداز سے **fantasia** (fan-*tah*-zia, or fan-ta-*zee*-a) *n*. fanciful musical composition خیالیہ

far (fah*) *adj*. & *adv*. (*far* ; *further, farther* ; *furthest, farthest*) distant (in time or place) دُور، بعید more distant of two پار، پرلا at a great distance دُور دراز *far more . . . . than* سے کہیں زیادہ *in so far as*, as far as جہاں تک *by far (better, etc.)* کہیں بہتر *by far the (best, etc.)* بہت زیادہ، کہیں زیادہ (اچھا) *far and away*, very much بہت دُور ہونا *be a far cry*, be a long way off ہنوز دِلّی دُور است *be it far from me (to do something)*, I will never (do it) خدا نہ کرے کہ میں *far away*, (a) distant (thing or time) دُور، بہت دُور کا (b) (of one's look) fixed on something far away بہت فاصلے پر دُور جمی ہوئی نظریں *far-fetched* (of ideas, etc.) not immediately relevant دُور از کار، بعید از فہم، دُور از قیاس *far-famed* مشہور ومعروف، شہرۂ آفاق *far off*, far away دُور کا *far-reaching*, having wide effects وسیع اثر والا دُور رس اثرات والا، دُور رس *far-seeing, far-sighted*, wise دُور بیں مردِ آخر بیں

farce (fah*s) *n*. drama full of absurd situations and sayings نقل، سوانگ ludicrous show ڈھونگ، لایعنی بکواس، مضحکہ خیز ڈھونگ **farcical** *adj*. ludicrous مضحکہ خیز

fare (*fay*-ĕ*) *n*. money charged for a journey کرایہ food provided کھانا *bill of fare*, menu طعام نامہ *v. i.* journey, go سفر کرنا، جانا get on (well or ill) کا حال رہنا، کے ساتھ بیتنا **farewell** (fay-ĕ-*wel*) *int*. good-bye خدا حافظ، اَلوداع *n*. leave-taking وداع، رُخصت *bid farewell to* سے رُخصت ہونا، کو اَلوداع کہنا

farm (fah*m) *n.* agricultural land کھیت ، کھیتی land for breeding (cattle, etc.) فارم *farm house*, farmer's house on a farm مزارع کا گھر tract of water for breeding fish, oysters, etc. پرورش گاہ *fish farm* مچھلیوں کی پرورش گاہ *v. t. & i.* use (land) for growing crops کاشتکاری کرنا ، زراعت کرنا ، کھیتی کرنا *farm out*, take proceeds of a tax for a fixed sum ٹھیکے پر دینا **farmer** *n.* man who manages a farm کسان ، کاشتکار **farm-yard** *n.* space enclosed by farm buildings باڑی کا چوک یا احاطہ **farmstead** *n.* farm buildings باڑی ، گونڈا ، نگلا

farrago (fa-*rah*-goh) *n.* medley ملغوبہ

farrier (*fa*-ri-ĕ*) *n.* one who shoes horses نعل بند

farther, farthest *adj.* & *adv.* (see under **far**)

farrow *n.* (*fa*-voh) litter of pigs سوروں کے بچوں کا جھول

farthing (*fah**-dhing) *n.* former British coin worth a quarter-penny فارڈنگ ، پیسہ

fascinate (*fas*-i-nayt) *v. t.* attract greatly موہ لینا ، گرویدہ کرنا fix with the eyes نظر باندھنا **fascination** *n.* attractiveness دل کشی ، دلربائی that which fascinates دلکش ، دلربا

fascism (*fash*-izm) *n.* creed of the nationalist and anti-communist movement of Italy فاشیت ، فسطائیت (according to their enemies) repression سختی **fascist** *n.* & *adj.* فاشستی ، فسطائی ، فاشی

fashion (*fash*-un) *n.* prevailing style (of clothes, etc.) وضع قطع ، رواج ، فیشن manner of doing something وضع ، طرز ، طور ، طریقہ *after a fashion, in some fashion*, somehow کسی نہ کسی طرح *v. t.* form **fashionable** *adj.* following the fashion خوش پوش ، فیشن ایبل for the fashionable upper class فیشن ایبل طبقے کا **fashionably** *adv.* following the (upper class) fashion بن ٹھن کر ، بن سنور کر ، بڑے انداز سے **fashionmonger** *n.* fop, dandy فیشن پرست ، فیشن کا مارا ہوا

Fashion is the popularly accepted temporary way of doing anything; **mode** has an idea of mood or disposition: **style** is set by those who know.

fast *adj.* firmly fixed بندھا ہوا ، مضبوط ، پکا *fast friend* پکا دوست *fast colour*, unfading colour پکا رنگ *make (door) fast*, lock (it) (دروازہ) بند کرنا quick تیز *fast ground*, one on which the ball bounces smartly گیند کو اچھالنے والا میدان dissipated آوارہ ، عیاش ، اوباش *live fast*, live thus عیاشی کرنا ، آوارگی کی زندگی بسر کرنا *adv.* firmly پکی طرح ، مضبوطی سے ، پکا *stand fast*, stand firmly مضبوطی سے کھڑے رہنا ، ڈٹے رہنا *hold fast (to something)* quickly تیز ، تیز تیز ، تیزی سے deep *fast asleep*, in a deep sleep گہری نیند میں *play fast and loose with*, act irresponsibly by repeatedly changing attitude to (کسی کے متعلق) رویہ بدلتے رہنا *v. i.* abstain from food and drink for a time روزہ یا برت *n.* act of fasting روزہ ، صوم *keep fast*, fast روزہ رکھنا ، روزے سے ہونا *break (one's) fast*, end it at a particular hour; breakfast روزہ کھولنا ، افطاری کرنا ، روزہ *fast-day*, day of fasting روزہ ، روزے کا دن period of fasting روزے کا وقت

fasten (*fas*-ĕn) *v. t. & i.* tie or join together باندھنا ، لگانا ، جوڑنا become fastened (*with*) سے لگنا ، بندھنا *fasten upon*, take firm hold of مضبوط پکڑنا **fastener, fastening** *n.* something that fastens things together باندھنے کے لیے (گھنڈی ، تکمہ ، بکسوا ، بٹن اور زپ بٹن وغیرہ کی قسم کی) کوئی چیز

1 2

fasteners for (1) paper and (2) dress; (3) zip fastener

fastidious (fas-*tid*-i-us) *adj.* too particular to be easily pleased نازک مزاج ، نازک طبع ، تانا شاہ very particular حد درجہ خوش ذوق

fat *n.* oily substance in animal bodies and certain plants چربی ، روغن oily substance obtained from certain seeds تیل *cooking fats*, this substance purified and used as a cooking medium روغن خوردنی *live on the fat of the land*, live luxuriously عیش اڑانا ، مزے سے زندگی بسر کرنا *adj.* plump موٹا ، فربہ covered with fat چربیلا well-filled بھرا ہوا profitable سود مند *fat salary*, big salary اونچی تنخواہ *fat land* زرخیز (زمین) *fat child* موٹا تازہ بچہ *v.t. & i.* (also **fatten**) make fat موٹا کرنا grow fat موٹا ہونا enrich (soil) زرخیز بنانا **fatty** *adj.* yielding fat چربی دار ، چربیلا ، چکنا

fatal (*fay*-tel) *adj.* causing death مہلک ، کاری inevitable اٹل ، مقدر very harmful بہت نقصان دہ ، سخت مضر **fatally** *adv.* in a fatal manner مہلک طور پر **fatalism** *n.* belief that events are determined by fate تقدیر پر ایمان ، مسئلہ جبر **fatalist** *n.* person holding this belief تقدیر کا قائل **fatalistic** (fay-tay-*lis*-tik) *adj.* of fatalism مسئلہ جبر کے متعلق **fatality** (fa-*tal*-i-ti) *n.* (esp.) death by accident حادثے میں ہلاکت (see also **fate**)

fate (fayt) *n.* power believed to predetermine all events from eternity تقدیر *the Fates*, the three Greek goddesses (viz. *Atropos*, *Clotho* and *Lachesis*) who determined the course of human life تقدیریں ، قسمتیں one's future fixed by fate قسمت ، نصیب ، نصیبہ ، تقدیر ، مقدر end موت ، انجام destruction تباہی ، بربادی ، انجام ، حشر *meet (one's) fate, go to (one's) fate*, be ruined تباہ و برباد ہونا **fated** (*fayt*-ed) *adj.* fixed by fate تقدیر کا لکھا ، نوشتۂ تقدیر **fateful** *adj.* decisive, having far-reaching results

father (*fah*-dhě*) *n.* male parent باپ ، والد ، اَبّا founder بانی ، بانیِ مَبانی Roman Catholic priest پادری ، رُوحانی باپ ، اَبّ *v.t.* originate (idea, etc.) باپ ہونا ، اُبُوّت کا بانی ہونا **fatherhood** *n.* being a father **father-in-law** *n.* father of one's wife or husband خسر ، سُسَر ، خُسرا **fatherless** *n.* & *adj.* orphan یتیم ، بن باپ کا (بچّہ) **fatherly** *adj.* of or like a father باپ کا سا ، پدرانہ **fatherland** *n.* motherland وطن ، دیس

fathom (*fadh*-um) *n.* six-foot measure for depth of water (پانی کی) دوگز گہرائی *v. t* measure the depth of پانی کی گہرائی ناپنا get to the bottom of کی تہ تک پہنچنا **fathomless** *adj.* very deep اتھاہ ، بے پایاں

fatigue (fa-*teeg*) *n.* weariness تھکن ، تھکاوٹ (army) chores مشقّت ، فٹیگ *v. t.* tire out تھکا دینا **fatigued** *adj.* tired out تھکا ہُوا **fatiguing** *adj.* tiring تھکا دینے والا

fatten *v.t.* & *i.*, **fatty** *adj.* & *n.* (see under **fat**)

fatuous (*fat*-ew-us) *adj.* foolish احمق ، بے وُقوف

fatuity (fa-*tew*-i-ti) *n.* foolishness بیوقوفی ، حماقت

faucet, (*faw*-set) *n.* tap for barrel (شراب کے پیپے کی) ٹونٹی

fault (fawlt) *n.* mistake غلطی ، خطا ، قصور *find fault with, point out faults in* غلطیاں نکالنا ، پر اعتراض کرنا ، پر نکتہ چینی کرنا ، کی عیب جوئی کرنا *The fault is mine, It is my fault*, (reply to someone saying '*I am sorry*' although both the parties may be at fault, (*a*) in the wrong غلطی پر (*b*) not knowing what to do حیران *faults of grammar*, grammatical mistakes گرامر کی غلطیاں break in a layer of rock, etc. رخنہ **faultless** *adj.* without fault بے قصور correct بالکل صحیح **faultlessly** *adv.* without any fault or mistake بالکل صحیح ، بے قصور **faulty** *adj.* imperfect غلط **faultily** *adv.* imperfectly or mistakenly غلطی سے

Faun (fawn) *n. Cl. myth.* Roman god of the woods and fields, with goat's horns and legs فاٶن

Faun

fauna (*faw*-na) *n.* all the animals (*of* an area or era) (کسی علاقے کے) حیوانات

Faust (foust), **Faustus** (foustus), *n.* German magician of the 16th Century who is supposed to have sold himself to the devil for pleasures and power of this world. Marlowe and Goethe made him the theme of their books (مارلو اور گوئٹے کی ناولوں کا ہیرو) فاؤسٹ

favour (*fay*-vě*) *n.* kindness, sympathy ہمدردی ، مہربانی willingness to oblige کرم فرمائی out-of-the-way help پاسداری *in favour of*, (*a*) in sympathy with کا ہمدرد، کا پاسدار (*b*) on behalf of کی جانب سے ، کی طرف سے *out of favour* (*with*), not liked (by) معتوب something done from kindness کرم کرم فرمائی ، نوازش ، مہربانی *ask a favour* (*of someone*) ask (him) to help نوازش کرنے کو کہنا *v.t.* aid مدد کرنا oblige ہمدردی کرنا give (someone) more than is fair ناجائز مدد کرنا resemble سے ملنا ، سے مشابہ ، جیسا ہونا **favourable** *adj.* favouring مہربان helpful مُوافق ، مُناسبِ حال **favourably** *adv.* with favour لطف و کرم سے ، مہربانی سے hopefully اُمید افزا طور پر **favourite** (*fay*-vě-rit) *n.* & *adj.* specially favoured (person or thing) منظورِ نظر ، پسندیدہ ، مرغوب **favouritism** *n.* practice of favouring unequally جانب داری ، جنبہ داری ، پاسداری

fawn *n.* young deer ہرن کا بچہ ، ہرنوٹا ، مغزال (also *fawn colour*) light yellowish brown بادامی (رنگ) کا *v. i.* (of dogs) show pleasure by crouching and licking دُم ہلانا *fawn* (*on someone*), try to win his favour by slavish acts خوشامد کرنا ، چاپلوسی کرنا

fealty (*fee*-al-ti) *n.* loyalty وفاداری

fear (*fee*-ě*) *n.* alarm ڈر ، خوف anxiety اندیشہ awe احترام *v.t.* & *i.* have fear ڈرنا ، خوف کھانا **fearful** *adj.* terrible خوفناک ، ڈراؤنا frightened ڈرا ہُوا ، سہما ہُوا **fearless** *adj.* without fear بے خوف ، نڈر **fearsome** (*fee*-ě*-sum) *adj.* (usu. jocularly) formidable (عموماً مزاحیہ انداز میں) بڑا خوفناک

feasible (*feez*-i-bel) *adj.* practicable قابلِ عمل

feasibility (-*bil*-) *n.* being feasible قابلِ عمل ہونا

feast (feest) *n.* rich meal for special occasion دعوت ، ضیافت day kept to commemorate an important event جشن ، تہوار *v. t.* & *i.* give a feast to دعوت کرنا ، ضیافت کرنا eat many good things اچھی چیزیں کھانا (*feast on*), take delight in سے لطف اندوز ہونا ، محظوظ ہونا

feat (feet) *n.* great deed کارنامہ ، کارنمایاں act requiring great skill, etc. پھرتی یا چالاکی کا کام

feather (*fedh*-ě*) *n.* plume, plumage پنکھ *birds of a feather*, people of the same sort ایک ہی تھیلی کے چٹّے بٹّے *birds of a feather flock together* کند ہم جنس با ہم جنس پرواز *show the white feather*, show cowardice بُزدلی دکھانا *a feather in (one's) cap*, an honour for (him) باعثِ عزت *lie in high feather*, be in high spirits پھولا نہ سمانا *feather-bed*, stuffed with feathers پروں کا بستر *v.t.* put feathers on کلغی لگانا *feather (one's) nest*, get enough money to live in comfort اپنا گھر بھرنا **feather-brain**, **feather-brained**, **feather-head**, **feather-headed** *n.* & *adj.* silly (person) گاؤدی **featherweight** *n.* boxer not more than 9 stones وزن سے کم کا مکے باز

feathered rule *n.* (see *Addenda*)

feather merchant *n.* (see *Addenda*)
feature (*fee*-chĕ*) *n.* one of the named parts of the face چہرے کا (ناک، منہ جیسا) کوئی حصہ (*pl.*) the face as a whole چہرہ، شکل و صورت، چہرہ مہرہ prominent part or quality خصوصیت، نمایاں حصہ (in radio programmes) a somewhat dramatic presentation of an important event or of someone's life-story but not actually a drama فیچر *v.t.* & *i.* be a feature of کی خصوصیت ہونا have as a feature کی خصوصیت رکھنا have a prominent part for کو نمایاں طور پر لانا، کو نمایاں کردار دینا **featureless** *adj.* without distinct features سپاٹ چہرہ uninteresting پھیکا، بے لطف **featurette** *n.* (see *Addenda*)
febrifuge (*feb*-ri-fewj) *n.* medicine used for reducing fever تپ توڑ، تپ شکن دوا، شفاء الحمّیٰ **febrile** (*feb*-ril) *adj.* pertaining to fever بخار کا، بخار سے متعلق
February (*feb*-roo-a-ri) *n.* second month of the Western calendar فروری
fed *v.* (pa. t. & pa. pt. of **feed** which see)
federal *adj.* (see under **federate**)
federate (*fed*-e-rayt) *v. t.* & *i.* (of States) combine, as a federal group وفاق بنانا **federation** (*-ray-*) *n.* political union of self-governing states by mutual agreement surrendering important common affairs to Central (called Federal) government وفاق similar union of societies وفاق act of federating وفاق بنانا، وفاق میں شامل ہونا **federal** (*fed*-e-rel) *adj.* of or based on federation وفاقی *Federal government*, Central government of a Federation وفاقی حکومت، وفاقی مرکز
fee *n.* charge for professional advice or services حقِ خدمت، فیس *school* (or *college*) fees سکول (یا کالج) کی فیس *v. t.* (*fee, fee'd, fee'd*) engage for fee فیس دے کر رکھنا
feeble (*fee*-bĕl) *adj.* weak کمزور، ناتواں having no guts کمزور، بے ہمت lacking intelligence احمق **feebly** *adj.* weakly کمزوری سے **feebleness** *n.* weakness کمزوری، ناتوانی، ضعف
feed *v.t.* & *i.* (*fee* (*fed*, fed) give food to supply (one's family, etc.) with food کھلانا، گھر کا بار سر پر اٹھانا (*be*) *fed up with*, (**be**) discontented with سے بیزار ہونا *feed on* (or *upon*), (*a*) consume کھانا، چارہ کھانا (*b*) be nourished by سے قوت حاصل کرنا، پر پلنا *n.* food (for animals) چارا (of babies) meals (ایک وقت کا) دودھ، غذا **feeder** *n.* infant's feeding bottle شیشہ، فیڈر infant's bib بِب، سینہ پوش
fee'd *v.* (pa. t. of **fee,** which see)
feedback *n.* (see *Addenda*)
fee-faw-fum (fee-faw-*fum*) *int.* (expressing derision at threat) فوں فاں، گیدڑ بھبکی
feel *v.t.* & *i.* (*felt*) touch چھونا، مس کرنا *feel the pulse of* کی نبض دیکھنا find out by touching چھو کر معلوم کرنا *feel* (*one's*) *way* ٹٹول ٹٹول کر راستہ معلوم کرنا be aware of محسوس کرنا *feel the heat*, suffer from it گرمی کی تکلیف محسوس کرنا appear to the senses محسوس ہونا *it feels smooth* بہت نرم ہے have or be a vague idea (*that*) خیال ہونا (کہ) be moved by (sorrow, etc., *for*) محسوس کرنا (پر افسوس وغیرہ) (*feel like*), (*a*) appear to be ہونا، ہوتا لگنا *It feels like rain* بارش ہوتی لگتی ہے (*b*) (usu. negative or interrogative) have a mind to (*doing*), کو جی چاہنا *Do you feel like eating now?* کیا آپ کا اس وقت کچھ کھانے کو جی چاہتا ہے؟ *n.* feeling, knowing by touch مس، چھو کر *tell by the feel* چھو کر بتانا *let me have a feel* چھو کر دیکھنے دیجئے *hot* (*etc.*) *to the feel*, گرم لگنا **feeling** *n.* awareness احساس *feeling for art* فن کا ذوق (usu. *pl.*) emotions جذبات، احساسات *rouse the feelings* جذبات برانگیختہ کرنا *tender feelings*, love محبت *hurt* (someone's) *feelings* کسی کے جذبات مجروح کرنا *Feelings ran high on this issue* اس مسئلے پر جذبات مشتعل ہو گئے *adj.* (of protest, etc.) heartfelt دلی sympathetic ہمدرد sensitive حساس **feeler** *n.* long thread-like organs of touch in some insects and animals مونچھیں suggestion for discovering what others think دوسروں کے دل کا حال معلوم کرنے کے لیے کہی ہوئی بات، فیلر *throw feelers* (*about*) فیلر پھینکنا
feet *n.* (*pl.* of **foot,** which see)
feign (fayn) *v.t.* pretend حیلہ کرنا، تصنع کرنا **feigned** *adj.* pretended بناوٹی
feint (faint) *n.* sham attack meant to deceive opponent دھوکے کا داؤ
felicitate (fe-*lis*-i-tayt) *v. t.* congratulate (someone *on* something) مبارک باد دینا، مبارک باد کہنا **felicitous** (-tus) *adj.* (of words, etc.) well-chosen موزوں، برمحل، باموقع، مناسب حال **felicity** (-ti) *n.* great happiness خوشی، سرور good fortune خوش قسمتی ease روانی، برجستگی *felicity of phrase* تحریر میں روانی
feline (*fee*-lin) *adj.* catlike بلی کا سا *n.* belonging to the cat family بلی کی قسم کا جانور، قطی
fell (fel) *v. t.* cause to fall گرانا knock (someone) down مار گرانا cut (a tree) down کاٹ ڈالنا، کاٹ کر گرانا hem مغزی لگانا (pa. t. of *fall*, which see) *n.* moorland ڈابر کی زمین *adj.* (of enemy) very cruel سنگ دل، ظالم، جلاد (of disease) fatal مہلک
fellow (*fel*-oh) *n.* (colloq.) man (or boy) آدمی (یا لڑکا)، شخص companion ساتھی، ساجھی *fellow-feeling*, sympathy ہمدردی member of a learned

society or of the governing body of a university فیلو person who holds a university fellowship فیلو the other of the pair جوڑا *adj.* in the same or like position ساتھی *fellow creature* ہم جنس *fellow citizens* ہم وطن *fellow passengers* ہم سفر *fellow traveller*, person with communistic leanings ہم سفر **fellowship** *n.* companionship ساتھ friendly association دوستی membership رکنیت money or position which a university gives to a student to enable him to continue his studies اعلیٰ تعلیمی وظیفہ یا ملازمت

felon (*fel*-un) *n.* criminal سنگین مجرم **felony** (*fel*-ĕ-ni) *n.* serious crime such as murder or burglary سنگین جرم **felonious** *adj.* (of actions, etc.) characterized by felony سنگین

felt *n.* woollen cloth made by pressing (and not weaving) نمدہ *adj.* of felt نمدے کا، نمدی *felt hat* نمدے کی ٹوپی ، نمدے کا ہیٹ *v. i.* (pa. t. of *feel*, which see)

female (*fee*-mayl) belong to the sex that brings forth young or eggs مادہ woman (or girl) عورت (یا لڑکی) fruit-producing plant پھلدار (درخت) *adj.* of this sex of women or girls زنانہ ، نسوانی

feminine (*fem*-i-nin, or *fem*-i-nɪn) *adj.* of, like or suitable for women زنانہ ، نسوانی ، نسائی of female gender (opp. of *masculine*) مؤنث **feminism** (*fem*-i-nizm) *n.* advocacy of giving women the same rights as man مساواتِ نسواں **feminist** *n.* advocate of feminism حامیٔ مساواتِ نسواں

femur (fee-me*) *n.* thighbone ران ، جانگھ

fen *n.* low marshland نشیبی داخلی علاقہ ، جھابر

fence (fens) *n.* barrier of wooden stakes or wire put round a garden, etc., to keep people or animals out جنگلا *sit on the fence*, remain neutral in war, etc. غیر جانبدار رہنا *v. t. & i.* put a fence around practise the art of fighting with long, slender swords or foils شمشیر زنی کی مشق کرنا ، پٹے کی مشق کرنا avoid giving a direct answer to (question) ٹال جانا ، ٹالنا ، گول مول جواب دینا **fencing** *n.* art of attack or defence with foils or swords تیغ زنی ، شمشیر زنی ، پٹے بازی fences جنگلے material for fences جنگلے لگانے کا سامان

a fence

fencing

fend *v. t. & i.* ward *off* (a blow), defend oneself from (*it*) (وار) روکنا care (*for*), protect کی حفاظت کرنا **fender** (*fend*-ĕ*) *n.* metal bar or screen before an open fireplace to prevent sparks from falling into the room جنگلہ log or rope on the side of a ship or boat to prevent damage in collision (جہازی) ٹکر روک screen in front of a tramcar (ٹرام کا) جنگلہ ٹکر روک (U. S.) mudguard مڈ گارڈ ، کیچڑ روک

a fender

ferment *v. t. & i.* (fĕ*-*ment*) undergo or produce gradual chemical change through the action of organic bodies خمیر ہونا (یا اٹھنا یا اٹھانا) excite ہیجان پھیلانا be excited جوش میں آنا *n.* (*fe**-ment) substance causing others to ferment خمیر tumult, great excitement ہنگامہ ، ہیجان (*be*) *in a ferment*, (of societies or nations) (be) very excited (ہیجان میں (ہونا fermenting خمیر اٹھانا unrest, turmoil ہنگامہ ، ہیجان

fern (fĕ*n) *n.* flowerless plants with pretty feathery leaves پھول نہ دینے والے پودوں کی قسم ، فرن

ferocious (fe-*roh*-shus) *adj.* cruel and fierce ظالم ، سفاک **forocity** (fe-*ros*-i-ti) *n.* being ferocious تند خوئی ، سفاکی

ferret (*fe*-ret) *n.* cat-like animal used in hunting rabbits from their burrows فیرٹ ، خرگوش مار stout cotton or silk tape موٹا فیتہ *v. t. & i.* hunt (rabbits, etc.) with ferrets خرگوش مار سے خرگوش کا شکار کرنا *ferret out*, discover hidden secrets, etc., after a careful search کھود کھود کر نکالنا

a ferret

ferric (*fe*-rik), **ferrous** (*fe*-rus) *adj.* of iron or steel فولادی ، لوہے کا **ferro-concrete** *n.* concrete with iron or steel framework inside it سیمنٹ سریا

ferrule (fe-ryool, or fe-rĕl), **ferrel** (fe-rĕl) *n.* metal cap at the end of a stick ٹوپی metal ring for strengthening a joint فیرول ، چھلا

ferry (*fe*-ri) *n.* boat for carrying to and across a river or small channel گھاٹ کی کشتی place for such boats گھاٹ **ferryman** *n.* گھاٹ ملاح *v.t. & i.* take or go *across* in a ferry پار جانا یا لے جانا ، گھاٹ کی کشتی میں جانا یا لے جانا ، گھاٹ اترنا یا اتارنا fly (aircraft) from factory to aerodrome or from base to operational area ہوائی جہاز کو اڈے پرلے جانا **ferry-boat** *n.* boat used for ferry-service گھاٹ کی **ferry-service** *n.* plying ferry-boats پار جانے کے لیے کشتی ، پار لے جانے والی کشتیاں

fertile (*f*ĕ*-tɪl) *adj.* (of land) producing much زرخیز (of plants) yielding fruit باردار (of females) able to reproduce young ہری گود والی بچے دے سکنے والی (of seed or egg) capable of developing صحت مند یا ٹھیک (بیج یا انڈا) **fertility** (*fĕ**-*til*-i-ti) *n*. being fertile زرخیزی، بازوری **fertilize** (*fĕ**-ti-liz) *v.t*. make fertile زرخیز کرنا، بازور کرنا enrich soil by adding manure or fertilizer کھاد ڈالنا make (something) start growing تخم ریزی کرنا، بیج ڈالنا **fertilizer** (-li-) *n*. chemical used for making land or soil fertile کیمیائی کھاد **fertilization** (-ay-) *n*. زرخیز بنانا، کھاد ڈالنا، تخم ریزی کرنا

fervent (*fĕ*-*vent), **fervid** (*fĕ**-vid) *adj*. hot and glowing تپتا ہوا، گرم، سُرخ passionate پُرشوق، پُرولولہ **fervour** (*fĕ**-*vĕ**) *n*. warmth of feeling جوش، وَلولہ، تپش، شوق **fervently** *adj*. with fervour جوش، وَلولے سے

fervid *adj*. same as **fervent** (which see)

fervour *n*. (see under **fervent**)

festal (*fes*-tel) *adj*. of a festival جشن کا gay خوش، خوش و خرّم، ہشاش بشاش

fester (*fes*-*tĕ**) *v.t*. & *i*. (of a wound) be filled with poisonous matter زخم خراب ہوجانا، پیپ پڑجانا ناسُور بن جانا poison the mind زہر گھولنا cause bitterness تلخی پیدا کرنا rankle کھٹکنا rot گلنا، سڑنا

festival (*fes*-ti-val) *n*. day or season of rejoicing or feasting تہوار، تیوہار public celebration جشن merry-making خوشی، مُسرّت **festive** (*fes*-tiv) *adj*. of a festival مُسرّت کا gay خوش باش، ہشاش بشاش **festivity** (fes-*tiv*-i-ti) *n*. being merry خوشی، مُسرّت rejoicing and feasting جشن (usu. *pl*.) joyful event تقریب، خوشی کی تقریب

festoon (fes-*toon*) *n*. decorative chain of flowers hanging in a curve سہرا *v.t*. make into, decorate with, festoons سہرا بنانا یا لگانا

fetch (fech) *v.t*. & *i* go and get (something) جا کر لانا، لے آنا، اُٹھا لانا go for and bring back (someone) بُلوالا cause (sighs, tears) to come out نکالنا (of goods) bring in (a price) قیمت پر اُٹھانا give (someone a blow on the nose) (کسی کی) ناک پر گھونسہ لگانا **fetching** *adj*. attractive دِلکش **farfetched** *adj*. forced, unnatural دُور اَز کار

fete (fayt) *n*. outdoor party for amusement کھلی جگہ میں تفریحی اجتماع feast-day جشن، تہوار *v.t*. give feast in honour of (someone) (کسی) کے اعزاز میں دعوت کرنا

fetid, foetid (*fee*-tid) *adj*. bad smelling سڑاندوالا، متعفن، بدبودار

fetish, fetich, fetiche (fee-tish) *n*. inanimate object other than an idol worshipped by savages and believed to contain a spirit or magic power پُوجمان، استھول، فیٹیش belief or principle worshipped irrationally اندھا دُھند مانا ہوا عقیدہ anything to which foolishly excessive respect paid جس چیز کا احمقانہ طور پر احترام کیا جائے **fetishism** have such beliefs پُوجمان بنانا، فیٹیشیت **fetishist** one who believes in a fetish فیٹیشی

fetlock (*fet*-lok) *n*. joint of a horse's leg jus above the foot گھوڑے کا ٹخنے سے اُونچا جوڑ

fetter (fet-*ĕ**) *n*. shackle for prisoner's foo بیڑی، پابجولاں *in fetters* پابہ زنجیر، پابجولاں chain for th leg of an animal سانکل، سنگل (*pl*.) restraint روک، آڑ، بند، مزاحمت *v.t*. put in fetters بیڑی ڈالنا restrain روکنا، رُکاوٹ بننا

feud (fewd) *n*. deadly quarrel between tw families or tribes passed down from generatio to generation خانہ جنگی، فساد، خاندانی جھگڑا bitter hatre between two individuals or groups دشمنی، مُنافرت fief (فوجی خدمت کے بعوض) جاگیر، معافی **feudalisr** *n*. mediaeval system of giving lands to vassa in return for military service to the hierarch of lords جاگیرداری، منصبداری **feudal** (*few*-del) *adj* pertaining to this system جاگیردارانہ **feudal syster** *n*. feudalism جاگیرداری، منصبداری

feudal *adj*., **feudalism** *n*. (see under **feud**)

fever (*fee*-*vĕ**) *n*. morbid condition of th body with high temperature بُخار، تپ excite and restless condition بےچینی، بےکلی، بیقراری، اضطراب **feverish** *adj*. having symptoms of (or hav ing slight) fever جسے حرارت ہو، جس کا بدن گرم ہو of o caused by fever بُخار کا excited and restles بےچین، بیکل، بےقرار

few *n*. not many بہت کم *adj*. hardly any شاید ہی کوئی، بمشکل کوئی *a few*, some کچھ *the few*, the smal number that وُہ چند ایک جو *quite a few*, many بہت سے *a good few*, (colloq.) many بہت سے *few and fa between*, only occasional (کبھی کبھار (کا *only a few* چند ایک *a few of* میں سے چند ایک **fewness** *n*. being small in number تھوڑا ہونا، قِلّت تعداد

fez *n*. somewhat cylindrical red felt cap formerly worn by Turks تُرکی ٹوپی

fiance (fee-*on*-say) *n*. *masc*. man engaged to be married منگیتر **fiancee** *n*. *fem*. woman engaged to be married منگیتر، منسوبہ

fiasco (fee-*as*-koh) *n*. complete and ludicrous failure in some attempt مضحکہ خیز ناکامی، (کسی کام) میں فش *end in fiasco*, fizzle out, be a flop (کام) میں فش ہونا

fiat (fi-at) *n*. command حکم، فرمان *fiat money*, paper money without backing of gold or silver فرمانی زر

fib *v.i*. (-bb-) tell an unimportant lie جھوٹ موٹ کہنا *n*. unimportant lie گپ، بےضرر، جھوٹ

fibre (*fī*-*bĕ**) *n*. thread-like substance of

animal or plant body ریشہ، الش، تار texture بناوٹ ساخت character وضع substance made of fibres ریشہ دار چیز **fibrous** (*fib*-rus) *adj*. made of or like fibre ریشہ دار

ickle (*fik*-èl) *adj*. (of mood or weather) often changing متلوّن ، ناپائیدار

iction (*fik*-shěn *n*. something made up من گھڑت، گھڑا ہوا قصہ، تراشا ہوا افسا story which is not true افسانہ branch of literature concerned with stories, novels, and romances ناول اور افسانے **fictitious** *adj*. made up گھڑا ہوا not real غیر حقیقی

iddle (*fid*-èl) *n*. violin سارنگی، وائلن، چوتارا *fit as a fiddle*, in perfect health خوب ہٹا کٹا *with a face as long as a fiddle*, very sad منہ لٹکائے ہوئے *fiddle to*, be led or ruled by کے ماتحت چلنا *v.t.* & *i*. play the fiddle چوتارا بجانا waste time بیکار وقت گنوانا play aimlessly (*with* something in one's fingers) یونہی کسی چیز کو ہلاتے رہنا **fiddler** *n*. violinist چوتارا نواز **fiddlesticks** *n*. curved stick with horse-hair for playing the fiddle سارنگی کی کمان *int*. nonsense فضول، بکواس

delity (fi-*del*-i-ti) *n*. being faithful (*to*) (سے) وفاداری

dget (*fij*-et) *v.t.* & *i*. be unable to sit or stand still چلبلانا **fidgety** (*fij*-e-ti) *adj*. (of person) who fidgets چلبلا **fidgetiness** *n*. being fidgety چلبلاپن، چلبلاہٹ

e (fi) *int*. (protest against impropriety) افسوس صد افسوس، ہے *fie upon you!* افسوس تم پر!

eld (feeld) *n*. land used for crops, etc. کھیت large open country میدان branch of know-edge in which one specializes میدان range of activity or use عمل، زد، میدان *field sports*, (a) hunting, shooting, fishing مردانہ کھیل (b) certain athletic contests ورزشی کرتب battlefield میدانِ جنگ *take the field*, begin fighting لڑائی شروع کرنا *in the field*, facing the enemy صف بستہ *hold the field*, keep one's place against all odds جمے رہنا، ڈٹے رہنا piece of land for special purpose میدان، علاقہ، فیلڈ cricket field کرکٹ کا میدان coalfield کوئلے کی کانوں کا علاقہ battlefield میدانِ جنگ *field events*, athletic sports other than racing دوڑ کے علاوہ دوسرے ورزشی مقابلے *v.t.* & *i*. stand on cricket field ready to catch or stop the ball and throw it in فیلڈ کرنا، فیلڈنگ کرنا **field-glasses** *n*. **field-gun, field-piece** *n*. gun on wheels پہیے دار توپ **field-marshal** *n*. army officer of highest rank سالار جنگ، فیلڈ مارشل

iend (*fi*-end) *n*. devil شیطان very wicked person سخت برا آدمی devotee شائق addict عادی *dope-fiend* نشے باز **fiendish** *adj*. devilish شیطان کا سا، شیطان سیرت

fierce (*fi*-e*s) *adj*. very cruel سخت ظالم angry غضبناک intense سخت، شدید **fiercely** *adv*. تندی سے، سختی سے **fierceness** *n*. quality of being fierce سختی، تندی

fiery (*fi*-è-ri) *adj*. flaming شعلہ فشاں like fire آگ کا سا easily enraged یکدم بھڑک اٹھنے والا شخص

fifteen *fif-teen*) *n*. & *adj*. 15 پندرہ **fifteenth** *adj*. پندرھواں **fifth** *n* & *adj*. 5th پانچواں *fifth column*, (pr. -lum) (a) traitors غدار (b) spies جاسوس *fifth-column activities* جاسوسی، غداری *fifth columnist*, (pr. -*kol*-è-mist) member of the fifth column جاسوس، غدار **fifty** (*fif*-ti) *n*. & *adj*. 50 پچاس **fiftieth** (*fif*-ti-eth) *adj*. 50th پچاسواں *fifty-fifty*, equal shares آدھوں آدھ *go fifty-fifty*, share equally آدھوں آدھ کرنا

fig *n*. soft, sweet fruit full of small seeds انجیر tree yielding it انجیر کا درخت

fight (fit) *v.t.* & *i*. (*fought*) engage in conflict لڑنا ، لڑائی کرنا strive (*for*) (کی) جدوجہد کرنا، کوشش کرنا struggle (*against*) (سے یا کے خلاف) نبرد آزما ہونا، جنگ آزما *fight out* (*something*), decide (it) by fighting لڑائی کرکے فیصلے پر پہنچنا *fight shy of*, avoid سے بچنے کی کوشش کرنا *n*. battle, brawl لڑائی strife جدوجہد، جہاد **fighting** (*fit*-ing) *n*. fight لڑائی **fighter** (fit-ě*) *n*. one who fights لڑنے والا، جنگجو، نبرد آزما aircraft designed for fighting جنگجو طیارہ ▣ **Fight** is the general word; a **quarrel** takes place in words; a **feud**, long-lasting alliance of enemies in groups; an **altercation**, heated words; a **row**, noisy quarrel; a **combat** between two or more persons; a **melee**, a mixed fight; a **battle** between organized forces; a **war** between countries; a **conflict**, opposition caused by difference of opinion; an **encounter**, meeting of armed forces; a **duel**, organized battle between two.

figment (*fig*-ment) *n*. something unreal غیر حقیقی بات *figment of the imagination* خیالی جھوٹ

figurative *adj*. (see under **figure**)

figure (*fig*-ě*) *n*. symbol for a number (esp. 0 to 9) form, shape شکل، صورت influential person مشہور انسان image تصویر، نقش، مجسمہ diagram شکل، نقشہ price قیمت، دام (also *figure of speech*) striking way of saying something صنعت (ج: صنائع) *v.t.* & *i*. appear (*as*) (کا) کردار ادا کرنا calculate حساب کرنا *figure out*, (a) add جمع کرنا (b) work out the answer to a sum حساب کا سوال نکالنا imagine تصور کرنا achieve prominence شہرت حاصل کرنا، مشہور کرنا **figurative** *adj*. metaphorical مجازی full of figures of speech صنائع بدائع سے پر **figuratively** *adj*. metaphorically مجازاً، کنایۃً **figurehead** (*fig*-ě*-hed) *n*. carved image on front of ship جہاز کا سامنے کا مجسمہ person with a high position but no influence نام کا بڑا کٹھ پتلی **figured** (*fig*-ĕ*d) *adj*. marked with designs or patterns منقش

filament (*fil*-a-ment) *n*. very fine metallic thread in an electric bulb بلب کا تار

filch *v.t.* pilfer چھوٹی چوری کرنا

file (fil) *n*. holder for keeping papers in order مسل set of papers kept like that مسل steel tool with rough face ریتی row (of soldiers) one behind the other قطار *v.t.* put in a file مسل میں لگانا use a file on ریتی سے رگڑنا move in file (*in* or *out* of a place) قطار میں (کسی جگہ جانا یا سے) جانا **filings** *n. pl.* bits filed off بُرادہ

filial (*fil*-i-ĕl) *adj*. due from a son or daughter فرزندانہ، پسرانہ

filibuster, fillibuster (fil-i-bus-tĕ*) *n*. military or piratical adventurer waging unauthorized war against a foreign power غیر سلطنت کے خلاف زبردستی جنگ کرنے والا ڈاکو یا بحری قزاق one making a very long speech in parliament to obstruct legislation طویل تقریر کے ذریعے قانون سازی میں مزاحم ہونے والا *v.t.* act as filibuster زبردستی جنگی واکہ ڈالنا؛ طویل تقریر سے قانون سازی میں مزاحم ہونا

filigree (fil-ig-ree), **filagree** (*fil*-ag-ree) *n*. lace-like work of fine gold and other metallic wires دھات کے تاروں کا باریک کام۔ طلا کاری

fill (fil) *v.t.* & *i*. (*fill, filled, filled*) make or become full بھرنا *fill in*, write what is needed to complete (a form, etc.) (فارم وغیرہ) بھرنا *fill out*, make or become larger so as to fill the space بڑھنا یا بڑھانا *n*. as much as there is room for جتنے کی گنجایش ہو *eat* (or *have*) *one's fill*, eat as much as one can take جی بھر کر کھانا، سیر ہو کر کھانا

fillet (*fil*-et) *n*. band to keep the hair of the head in place پٹی، سِنگار پٹی

fillip (*fil*-ip) *n*. stroke given by releasing a bent finger from the thumb ٹھونگا stimulus ترغیب، انگیخت *give a fillip to*, (*a*) strike thus ٹھونگے مارنا (*b*) provide a stimulus اُکسانا، اُبھارنا

film *n*. very thin surface or sheet جھلی sensitive sheet or roll prepared for taking photographs فلم، جھلی cinema picture فلم، پکچر *film actor* فلمی اداکار *film actress* فلمی اداکارہ *film star*, film actor (or usu. actress) فلمی ستارہ *v.t.* & *i*. cover or become covered with a film جھلی چڑھانا یا چڑھنا make a cinema picture of فلم بنانا، فلمانا **filmy** *adj*. like a film جھلی کا سا

filter (*fil*-tĕ*) *n*. device for holding back solid impurities of a liquid passed through it فلٹر، چھنا *v.t.* & *i* (cause to) flow through a filter فلٹر کرنا یا ہونا، ٹپکنا (یا) ٹپکانا (of news, etc.) make its way (*out, through*) کسی نہ کسی طرح پھیل جانا؛ پھوٹ نکلنا

filth (filth) *n*. foul dirt گندگی، غلاظت **filthy** (*fil*-thi) *adj*. گندا، غلیظ، گھناؤنا **filthily** *adv*. in a filthy manner گندی طرح

fin *n*. one of movable wing-like parts of a fish (مچھلی کا) پر، پنکھ

final (fi-nĕl) *adj*. last آخری (F.F.F) fin deciding فیصلہ کُن *n*. (often *pl*.) final examinations or contests آخری امتحان، آخری مقابلے **finale** (fi-*nah*-lay) *n*. final part of a play or piece of music. آخر، آخری حصہ conclusion انجام **finally** *adv*. lastly آخر میں، آخرکار، انجام کار، بالآخر **finalist** *n*. competitor(s) left in for the final contest فائنل میں آنے والا

finance (fi-*nans*, or fi-*nans*) money matters روپیہ پیسہ، مال public money سرکاری خزانہ *Finance Minister* وزیر خزانہ monetary conditions (esp. of a government or business company) مالیات *v.t.* provide money for (some enterprise) رقم لگانا روپیہ لگانا **financial** (-shĕl) *adj*. monetary, pertaining to finances مالی، مالیاتی **financier** (-shĕ*) *n*. person skilled in finance ماہر مالیات one who invests money in (میں) روپیہ لگانے والا

find (fînd) *v.t.* (*find, found, found*) meet with پانا، کے ہاتھ لگنا، come upon get حاصل کو ملنا *find favour with*, win the favour of کا قرب حاصل کرنا learn by experience جاننا، جان لینا، دیکھ لینا *find out*, discover معلوم کرنا، دریافت کرنا supply to (someone something) کو دینا، کو مہیا کرنا reach a decision نتیجے پر پہنچنا، قرار دینا *find* (*someone*) *guilty* مجرم قرار دینا *n*. something found (esp. something valuable or pleasing) دریافت **finding** *n*. discovery to find پانا، معلوم کرنا، حاصل کرنا دریافت، معلومات (often *pl*.) legal decision (عدالت کا) فیصلہ

S **Find** is the general word; to **invent**, find a new thing or a new way of doing things; to **discover** what was there all the time, but not seen; to **espy**, catch sight of; to **descry**, discover by eye.

fine (fin) *adj*. thin پتلا، باریک delicate نازک good اچھا، عمدہ، خوب sharp تیز (of weather) not raining or cloudy بے باد و باراں enjoyable خوشگوار، پُرکیف splendid شاندار، نفیس *have a fine time* اچھا وقت گزارنا *one fine day*, once upon a time ایک بار کا ذکر ہے، ایک مرتبہ کا ذکر ہے (of metals) pure. refined خالص make (someone) pay a fine جرمانہ کرنا *n*. money (ordered to be) paid as punishment for wrong-doing جرمانہ **fineness** *n*. thinness

صفائی sharpness تیزی، دھار باریکی clearness fine quality عمدگی، خوبی degree of purity (of metal) کھراپن **finely** *adv.* سلیقے سے، خوبی سے، نزاکت سے **finery** *n.* splendid clothes or ornaments بناؤ سنگار کا سامان، بناؤ سنگار کی چیزیں، شاندار زیور یا لباس **fine arts** *n. pl.* arts concerned with *the beautiful e.g.*, painting and sculpture (as opposed to useful or industrial arts) فنون لطیفہ **fine-spun** *adj.* (*a*) delicate نازک (*b*) (of theory, etc.) too subtle سخت، پیچیدہ

finesse (fi-*nes*) *n.* artful way of dealing with a situation مکر و فن، چالاکی، عیاری

finger (*fing*-ĕ*) *n.* digit انگلی *forefinger, index finger* انگشتِ شہادت، سبّابہ *middle finger* بیچ کی انگلی، وسطیٰ *ring finger* بِنصر *little finger* چھنگلیا، خِنصر *thumb* انگوٹھا *finger-nail* ناخن breadth of a finger انگلی، انگشت *finger-bowl*, bowl for cleaning fingers after meal ہاتھ دھونے کا پیالہ، انگشت شو *finger-alphabet, finger-language*, finger symbols for talking with the deaf انگشتی زبان، انگشتی الفبا *touch with fingers* انگلیوں سے چھونا *lay* (or *put*) *a finger upon*, touch slightly ذرا سا، چھوٹا سا، لمس کرنا *put (one's) finger on*, locate (a mistake) exactly غلطی ٹھیک پکڑنا *my fingers itch to (do)*, I long to (do) میں (کرنے) کو تڑپ رہا ہوں *with a wet finger*, easily آسانی سے *not to lift* (or *stir*) *a finger*, make to effort ذرا بھی کوشش نہ کرنا *have a finger (in the pie)*, have a share (in any affair) (کسی معاملے میں) ہاتھ ہونا **finger-post** *n.* signpost at a cross-roads رہنما ہتھا *finger-print n.* mark made by the finger-tips and used to detect criminals انگوٹھے کا نشان **finger-tip, finger-end** *n.* outer end of a finger پور *have at one's finger-tips*, know well خوب جاننا

a finger-post

finish (*fin*-ish) *v.t.* & *i.* end ختم ہونا یا کرنا polish چمکانا، پالش کرنا make complete or perfect ٹھیک کرنا، مکمل کرنا، آخری صورت دینا kill ہلاک کرنا *n.* end خاتمہ، آخری منزل polish چمک دمک finished state آخری صورت **finished** *adj.* ended ختم completed مکمل polished چمک دمک والا

finite (fin-it) *adj.* limited محدود، منتہی

fiord, fjord (fi-*yo*d*) *n.* long but narrow arm of the sea running through high cliffs کھاڑی

fir (fē*) *n.* evergreen tree with needlelike leaves صنوبر، شمشاد its wood شمشاد کی لکڑی

fire (*fi*-ĕ*) *n.* something burning آگ، آتش *pour oil on fire*, aggravate a disturbed situation جلتی پر تیل ڈالنا *between two fires*, fired at from both sides دونوں طرف سے گولیوں کی بوچھاڑیں *out of the frying pan into the fire*, from bad to worse condition آسمان سے گرا کھجور سے اٹکا flame شعلہ shooting گولہ باری *under fire*, being shot at گولیوں کی زد میں angry or excited feeling غصہ، جوش *v.t.* & *i.* cause (or begin) to burn آگ لگنا یا لگانا، جلنا یا جلانا *strike fire* رگڑ سے آگ جلانا harden in an oven پکانا supply (a furnace, etc.) with fuel بھٹی میں ایندھن جھونکنا shoot (a gun) فیر کرنا، (بندوق) چلانا (of a gun) go off چلنا send (bullet, etc.) from gun, etc. (گولی) چلانا fill with (enthusiasm, imagination, etc.) جوش دلانا، شوق پورا کرنا *fire up*, become excited or angry جوش یا طیش میں آنا (colloq.) dismiss (a servant) برخاست کرنا **fire-alarm** *n.* signal of an outbreak of fire آگ لگنے کا الارم **firearm** *n.* gun, revolver, etc. آتشیں اسلحہ **fire-bomb** *n.* incendiary bomb آتشیں بم، آتش افروز بم **fire-brand** *n.* burning wood جلتی ہوئی لکڑی kindler of strife مفسد، فتنہ انگیز **fire-brigade** *n.* company of men who put out fires فائر بریگیڈ، آگ بجھانے کا عملہ، آگ گارد، اطفائیہ **fire-cracker** *n.* firework which explodes with a cracking sound پٹاخہ **fire-eater** *n.* juggler eating fire آتش خور مداری **fire-engine** *n.* motor pump for putting out fire آگ بجھانے کی کل، اطفائیہ **fire-escape** *n.* outside stairs, etc., for escaping from burning building آگ سے بچنے کا زینہ **fire-fly** *n.* flying insect giving out light in the dark جگنو کرمکِ شب تاب **fire-guard, fire-watcher** *n.* one posted to keep watch over fires caused by bombs, etc. آتشیں بم بجھانے والا **fire-insurance,** insurance against loss by fire بیمۂ آتش زدگی **fire-policy,** policy of such insurance بیمۂ آتش زدگی **fire-irons,** tongs, poker and shovel چمٹا، سلاخ اور کرچھا **fireman** *n.* member of a fire brigade آگ بجھانے والا assistant to the driver of a steam engine فائرمین **fireplace** *n.* place where a fire may be made چولھا، انگیٹھی **fire-proof** *adj.* that which does not burn or even break when heated غیر آتش گیر **firewood** *n.* wood used as fuel جلانے کی لکڑی، ایندھن **fire-side** *n.* part of a room round the fireplace انگیٹھی کے گرد کی جگہ، چوکا **fire-works** *n.* display device containing gunpowder etc., آتشبازی **fireworship** *n.* worship of fire آتش پرستی **fire-alarm** *n.* apparatus for calling the fire-brigade آتشزدگی کی اطلاع دینے کا آلہ

a fire-alarm

boy displays fireworks

firm *adj.* not easily moved or shaken مضبوط، پائدار not yielding پکا جما ہوا having or showing strength of character, etc., مستقل مزاج ، پکا *adv*. firmly سے مضبوطی سے ، پکی طرح ، اپنی بات پر پکا *stand firm* رہنا *n*. more than one person carrying on a business فرم ، ساجھا ، دکان ، مشترکہ کاروبار **firmly** *adv*. in a firm manner پکی طرح **firmness** *n*. quality of being firm مضبوطی ، مستقل مزاجی ■ **Firm** signifies that which does not move ; **strong,** well-made ; **fixed** in one place ; **solid,** of one piece ; **steady,** not easily moved ; **tight,** closely put together ; **fast,** held by something ; **secure,** out of danger ; **staunch,** brave and devoted ; **constant,** remaining true to the same standard ; **tenacious,** holding doggedly ; **brave** against perils ; **courageous,** facing peril without flinching ; **determined**, not to be moved from his resolution ; **obstinate,** not listening to reason ; **stubborn**, in the habit of going his own way.

firmament (*fe**m-a-ment) *n*. sky آسمان ، فلک

first *adj*. coming before all others پہلا ، اوّلین *n*. what is first پہلا ، اوّل beginning آغاز *adv*. before others پہلے *first come first served*, (protest against favouritism) people must take their turn پہلے پہلے آئے سو پہلے کھائے for the first time پہلی بار *first class*, (a) best بہترین (b) first category پہلا درجہ *first-born*, eldest child of one's parents پہلوٹھی کا *(at) first-hand* obtained through direct observation of facts براہ راست *first aid*, immediate medical aid ابتدائی (یا فوری) طبی امداد *first-rate*, excellent نہایت عمدہ **firstly** (more correctly **first**) *adv*. in the first place پہلے ، اوّلاً

firth (fĕ*th) *n*. estuary دریا کا دہانہ narrow arm of the sea کھاڑی

fiscal (*fis*-kĕl) *adj*. of public money مالی ، مالیاتی *fiscal year*, budgetary year مالی سال

fish *n*. (*pl*. same) animal living in water مچھلی ، ماہی *fish out of water* ماہی بے آب *v. t. & i.* (try to) catch fish مچھلیاں پکڑنا try (*for* something) (حاصل کرنے کی) کوشش کرنا *fish for* (*information or compliments*), try to get (by indirect methods) ادھر اُدھر کے طریقوں سے حاصل کرنے کی کوشش کرنا *fishing-rod*, rod for catching fish بنسی *fishing-line*, string for catching fish ڈوری *rod and line*, fishing tackle ڈوری اور بنسی **fisherman** *n*. man who catches fish for a living (as opposed to an *angler* who catches it for pleasure) مچھیرا ، ماہی گیر **fishmonger** *n*. one who sells fish مچھلی والا **fishy** *adj*. (colloq.) doubtful مشکوک ، مشتبہ **fishery** (*fish*-e-ri) *n*. profession of fishing ماہی گیری place for fishing ماہی گاہ **fishplate** *n*. one of a pair of steel plates used for joining rails in a track فش پلیٹ ، پٹڑی جوڑ

fission (also *atomic fission*) *n*. **fissionable** *adj*. (see *Addenda*).

fissure (*fish*-ĕ*) *n*. deep crack (in rocks, etc.) بڑا شگاف ، بڑی درز

fist *n*. tightly closed hand مٹھی ، مکا

fit *adj*. suitable (*for* or *to do* something) موزوں ، مناسب right or proper صحیح ، ٹھیک ، درست *think (or see) fit to*, decide or choose to صحیح سمجھنا in good health or condition صحت مند ، اچھی حالت میں *feel fit*, be in good health ٹھیک ہونا *not fit*, not enjoying good enough health to be equal to the task کے قابل نہ ہونا *v.t. & i.* be the right size and shape فٹ آنا ، ٹھیک ہونا *have (new clothing, etc.) fitted on*, try it for its shape or size by putting it on ٹرائی کرنا ، پہن کر دیکھنا prove fit (*for* or *to do* something) کے قابل (یا کا اہل) ثابت ہونا put into place لگانا ، جڑنا *fit* (something) *in*, find the right or a suitable place or time for موزوں جگہ وغیرہ تلاش کرنا *fit in with*, be in harmony with کے ساتھ میل کھانا *fit* (someone or something) *out* (or *up*), equip لیس کرنا ، تیار کرنا *n*. way or result of fitting موزونی ، ٹھیک بیٹھنا یا ہونا sudden and violent attack of illness (usu. with unconsciousness) دورہ *fall down in a fit* غش کھا کر گرنا sudden outburst (*of* laughter, etc.) لہر ، موج ، غلبہ *by fits and starts*, by irregular efforts, unsteadily کبھی کم کبھی زیادہ ، من کی موج سے **fitter** *n*. person whose work is to fit (machinery or clothing) فٹر **fitting** *adj*. suitable موزوں ، مناسب ، صحیح *n*. (*pl*.) things fixed in a building (like electric wiring, etc.) ساز و سامان ، جڑی ہوئی چیزیں **fitness** *n*. suitability موزونیت ، اہلیت **fitful** *adj*. irregular بے قاعدہ ، من کی موج سے

five (*fīv*) *n*. & *adj*. 5 پانچ **fivefold** (*fīv-fohld*) *adj*. five times پانچ گنا

fix (fiks) *v. t. & i.* make (something) fast so that it cannot be moved لگانا ، جڑنا determine (date, price, etc.) مقرر کرنا direct (the eyes, one's attention) steadily (*on*) گاڑنا ، جمانا treat (photographic films, colours used in dyeing, etc.) so that light does not effect them فلم دھونا *fix (someone) up with*, (a) employ کسی کو کسی کام پر لگانا یا کسی کے یہاں ملازم رکھانا (b) provide for him at کسی کا کہیں انتظام کرنا *fix (someone) up for the night*, give him a bed کسی کے سونے کا بندوبست کرنا *fix up a quarrel*, settle it جھگڑا چکانا *n*. difficulty, embarrassment مشکل ، پریشانی *in a (pretty) fix*, in an awkward situation مشکل میں **fixed** *adj*. not moving جڑا ہوا ، جما ہوا unchanging غیر تغیر پذیر **fixedly** (*fik*-sed-li) *adv*. fixing, not removing جمائے ہوئے

ہٹاتے ہُوئے ، جماکر ، گاڑے ہوئے **fixture** (*fiks*-chĕ*) *n.* something fixed in place لگی ہوئی چیز (*pl.*) electric and sanitary fittings لگا ہُوا سامان، جڑی ہوئی چیزیں sporting event کھیل کا پروگرام **fixation** (-*ay*-) *n.* fixing (*of* wages, etc.) تعیّن

fizzle (*fiz*-ĕl) *v. i.* *fizzle out*, end in failure ناکام رہنا ، ٹائیں ٹائیں فش ہونا

flabbergast (*flab*-ĕ*-gahst) *v. t.* (coll.) stun ; overwhelm with astonishment سخت حیران کر دینا

flabby (*flab*-i) *adj.* (of the muscles, flesh) soft پلپلا ، ڈھیلا ڈھالا weak نرم

flaccid (*flak*-sid) *adj.* flabby پلپلا ، ڈھیلا ڈھالا

flag *n.* banner پرچم، جھنڈا *white flag*, sign of surrender or truce شکست تسلیم کرنے کا جھنڈا، صلح کا جھنڈا *black flag*, pirates' flag سمندری لٹیروں کا جھنڈا bunting جھنڈی stone slab پتھر کی سِل *v. t.* signal with flag جھنڈی ہلانا decorate with flags آئین بندی کرنا droop نڈھال ہونا **flag-day** *n.* day on which small flags are sold to collect donations for some cause یوم پرچم

flagship *n.* admiral's ship امیرُ البحر کا جہاز، پرچمی جہاز

flag-staff *n.* pole from which a flag is flown پرچم والا کھمبا *flag-staff house* *n.* admiral's residence on shore قصرِ امیرالبحر ، امیرُ البحر کا محل

flagellate (fla-*jel*-ayt) *v. t.* scourge (oneself) to do penance گناہ دُور کرنے کے لیے کوڑے مارنا **flagellation** *n.* scourging thus گناہ دُور کرنے کے لیے کوڑے مارنا

flagitious (fla-*gish*-us) *adj.* grossly wicked سخت گناہگار ، مردود

flagrant (*flayg*-rant) *adj.* glaring (mistake or crime) کھلا ، برملا ، سخت ، شدید، سنگین **flagrancy** *n.* being flagrant سنگینی

flail (flayl) *n.* strong stick used to thrash corn سلارا ، سانٹ ، خرمن چوب

flair (*flay*-ĕ*) *n.* natural ability (*for* securing something needed or valuable) حاصل کرنے یا دیکھنے کی صلاحیت، پہچان *have a flair for* حاصل کرنے کی صلاحیت رکھنا پہچان ہونا

flake (flayk) *n.* small, flat light piece چھلکا ، گالا *snow-flakes* برف کے گالے *v. i.* come off in flakes گالے بن کر گرنا separate into flakes گالے بن جانا ، چھلکے چھلکے ہوکر اترنا

flamboyant (flam-*bo*-yant) *adj.* marked by flame-like waves مشعل نما ، شعلے کا سا gorgeous and bright چمک دار اور شاندار ، زرق برق

flame *n.* burning gas شعلہ ، لو *in flames*, on fire جلتا ہوا *burst into flames*, burn suddenly جل اُٹھنا bright light تیز روشنی ، شعلہ passion جذبہ love عشق brilliant colour شوخ رنگ *be like flames in colour* شوخ رنگ ہونا *v.i.* send out flames شعلے نکلنا blaze with anger غصّے سے لال پیلا ہونا

flamingo (fla-*min*-go) *n.* waterbird with long legs and light red wing feathers لال لم ڈھینگ

a flamingo

flange (flanj) *n.* projecting rim of wheel for rail track پہیئے کی باڑ *v. t.* provide with flange پہیئے کو باڑ لگانا

flank *n.* side of an animal or human being between ribs and hip پہلو ، کوکھ side (of a mountain or building) پہلو ، جانب side of an army or fleet لشکر یا بیڑے کے پہلو کا حصّہ میمنہ یا میسرہ *flank attack* میمنہ، میسرہ پر حملہ *v. t.* be at the side of کے پہلو میں واقع ہونا attack by going round the side of (the enemy) چکر کاٹ کر دشمن پر عقب میں حملہ کرنا

flannel (*flan*-ĕl) *n.* soft, woollen material فلالین (*pl.*) flannel trousers or clothes فلالین کی پتلون ، فلالین کے کپڑے **flannelette** (flan-e-*let*) *n.* cotton material looking like flannel نقلی فلالین

flap *v. t.* & *i.* (-pp-) (cause to) move (wings, etc.) up and down or from side to side پھڑپھڑانا hit lightly, with something soft and wide ہلکی تھپکی دینا ، مارنا *n.* (sound of a) flapping blow or movement پھڑپھڑانا ، پھڑپھڑاہٹ piece covering an opening دامن ، کونہ *flap of an envelope* لفافے کا چپکانے والا کونا **flapdoodle** *n.* gross flattery نری خوشامد nonsense بکواس

flare (*flay*-ĕ*) *v. t.* burst into bright flame دفعتہً جل اُٹھنا *flare up*, (*a*) burst suddenly جل اُٹھنا (*b*) burst out into anger آگ بھبھوکا ہوجانا (of skirt, etc.) spread outwards چوڑا ہونا ، پھیل جانا *n.* bright unsteady light جھلملاتی لو ، لرزاں شعلہ outburst of flame بھبھوکا **flare-up** *n.* outburst of flame بھبھوکا outburst of anger طیش short brilliant display دو گھڑی کی نمائش ، چار دن کی چاندنی **flaring** *adj.* gaudy بھڑکیلا

flash *n.* sudden burst of flame or light شعلہ ، التہاب *a flash of hope* اُمید کی کرن *in a flash*, suddenly, instantly اچانک، یکایک، چشم زدن میں فوری طور پر news flashed بھیجی ہوئی خبر ، اہم خبر *v. t.* & *i.* send out or give out a flash بھڑک اُٹھنا ، شعلہ فشاں ہونا be seen suddenly یکایک نظر آنا send (news) instantly (*across*, or *to*) خبر فوراً بھیجنا come suddenly (*into* or *across* mind) ذہن میں یکایک آنا ، بجلی کی طرح (خیال) کوند جانا **flashlight** *n.* flashing light for taking snaps کیمرے کا بلب فلیش لائٹ small electric torch بیٹری ، ٹارچ ، برقی مشعل

flask *n.* narrow-necked bottle چھوٹے منہ کی بوتل traveller's flat wine bottle for the pocket

چوڑی بوتل (also *thermos flask*), double-walled glass bottle in a metal covering meant for keeping things at the original temperature for quite a long time تھرموس ، گرم دار

flat *adj.* level and horizontal چپٹا ، سپاٹ *flat iron*, iron for pressing clothes لوہا ، استری uninteresting بے لُطف dull سپاٹ (of drinks) tasteless because the gas has gone ہلکا جو تیز نہ ہو (musical note) below the true pitch ہلکا سُر ، نیچا سُر (of rate, etc.) not variable ; same in all the cases ; common ملا جلا بھاؤ (colloq.) downright (refusal, etc.) بالکل، قطعی *adv.* at full length اوندھا *fall flat*, be ineffective بے اثر رہنا، اثر نہ کرنا *n.* flat part of something چپٹا حصّہ stretch of flat land near water کنارے کی مُسطح زمین (music) flat note نیچا (یا ہلکا) سُر set of rooms on one floor used as residence فلیٹ **flatly** *adv.* downright قطعی طور پر ، بالکل قطعی **flatten** *v.t.* & *i.* make or become flat چپٹا ہونا یا کرنا ، ہموار ہونا یا کرنا *flatten out*, (of aircraft) bring or come into a position parallel with the ground (ہوائی جہاز کا) زمین کے متوازی ہونا

flatter (*flat*-ĕ*) *v.t.* praise from a selfish motive خوشامد کرنا be pleased (*by* something) پر فخر کرنا ، پر بہت خوش ہونا *flatter oneself that*, be pleased with one's belief that اس خیال سے خوش ہونا (of or in a picture) show (someone) as better looking than he or she is اصل سے بہتر بنا کر دکھانا **flatterer** *n.* one who flatters خوشامدی ، چاپلوس **flattery** (flat-ĕ-ri) *n.* flattering چاپلوسی ، خوشامد

flatulence (*flat*-ew-lens) *n.* wind in the stomach, etc. اپھارا ، نفخ **flatulent** *adj.* causing flatulence نفخ کرنے والا troubled with it جسے نفخ ہو

flaunt (flawnt) *v.t.* & *i.* display proudly by waving about لہرا لہرا کر فخر سے دکھانا attract attention showily to کی نمود و نمائش کرنا

flavour (*flay*-vĕ*) *n.* taste, relish مزہ ، ذائقہ ، لذّت *v.t.* give a flavour (*of* something) to ذائقہ پیدا کرنا **flavouring** *n.* something used to give flavour مسالہ ، خوشبو **flavourless** *n.* without flavour بے مزہ ، بے بُو

flaw *n.* something that lessens the value (of a thing) خرابی ، عیب ، نقص **flawless** *adj.* without any flaw ; perfect بے عیب

flax (flaks) *n.* a plant cultivated for the fibres of its stem سن *flax fibres* کتان **flaxen** *adj.* (of hair) pale yellow زردی مائل (بال)

flay *v.t.* take the skin off کھال کھینچنا یا اُتارنا castigate کوڑے مارنا attack violently in words

flea (flee) *n.* small blood-sucking insect پسّو

fleck (flek) *n.* small patch داغ ، دھبہ particle (of dust, etc.) ذرّہ *v.t.* mark with flecks داغ دھبے ڈالنا

fled *v.* (pa. t. and pa. p. of **flee**, which see)

fledge (flej) *v.t.* furnish with feathers to fly پر لگانا ، بال و پر عطا کرنا **fledged** (flejd) *adj.* able to fly اُڑنے کے قابل **full-fledged** *adj.* full, formal پورا **fledgling, fledgeling** *n.* young bird just able to fly جو ابھی ابھی اُڑنا سیکھا ہو inexperienced ناتجربہ کار ، خام کار

flee *v.t.* & *i.* (*flee, fled, fled*) run away (*to* or *from*) بھاگنا ، فرار ہونا disappear غائب ہو جانا

fleece (flees) *n.* wool on sheep پشم ، بھیڑ کی اُون *v.t.* cheat (someone) out of his money (کسی کو) لُوٹنا ، (کسی کا) مال اُڑانا **fleecy** (*flee*-si) *adj.* looking like fleece لٹیرا ، جونک **fleecer** *n.* sheep shearer اُون کترنے والا one who dishonestly goes on taking another's money لٹیرا ، جونک

fleet *n.* all warships under one command of one country بیڑا number (of buses or aircraft) under one command or ownership بڑی تعداد *adj.* quick-moving تیز ، پھرتیلا

flesh *n.* soft muscular tissues of animal body گوشت (*one's*) *own flesh and blood*, (one's) near relations اپنے عزیز رشتے دار *in the flesh*, in bodily form carnal appetites نفسانی خواہشات human weaknesses انسانی کمزوریاں **fleshy** *adj.* fat موٹا ، فربہ **fleshly** *adj.* carnal نفسانی

fleur-de-lis (fle-ĕ*-de-lee or -lees) *n.* three-sided flower-like cross which was the symbol of the French Royal family تینتیا پھول ، فرانس کا شاہی نشان

a fleur-de-lis

flew *v.* (pa. t. of **fly**, which see)

flexible (*flek*-si-bĕl) *adj.* very easily bent لچکدار ، ملائم ، نرم *flexible wire*, (also *flex*) insulated and flexible wire for electric current (بجلی کا) نرم تار ، ملائم تار **flexibility** *n.* quality of being flexible لچک ، نرمی ، ملائمت

flick (flik) *n.* quick light blow with a whip, etc.) ہلکا تازیانہ motion-picture فلم *v.t.* give such blow (تازیانہ) ہلکا لگانا

flicker (*flik*-ĕ) *v.i.* burn or shine unsteadily کبھی کھلنا کبھی بند ہونا ، جھلملانا flutter move back and forth ہلنا *n.* flickering light جھلملانا flickering movement کبھی کھلنا کبھی بند ہونا

flier, flyer (*flī*-ĕ*) *n.* see under **fly**

flight (flīt) *n.* flying اُڑان ، پرواز ، طیران journey made by flying ہوائی سفر ، ہوائی جہاز کا سفر number (*of* birds) flying together اکٹھے ہوئے پرندے stairs between two landings زینہ **fligh** *adj*. unsteady (person or behaviour) تلوّن مزاج fleeing (from danger, etc.) فرار، ہزیمت (*put someone*) *to flight*, cause (him) to run away بھگا دینا، ہزیمت دینا

flimsy (*flim*-zy) *adj*. light and thin ہلکا، دھان پان easily broken نازک shallow (excuse, protest, etc.) یونہی سا *flimsiness n*. shallowness کھوکھلاپن

flinch *v. i*. shrink (from someone in fear etc.) دبنا، پیچھے ہٹنا، کورونا

fling *v. t*. & *i*. (*fling, flung, flung*) throw violently (*at*) پھینکنا، پٹکنا، پٹخنا move about (hands, etc.) violently زور زور سے ہلانا move (oneself) hurriedly (into chair, etc.) زور سے جا پڑنا *n*. act of flinging پھینکنا، پٹکنا، پٹخنا *have a fling at*, make an attempt to کوشش کرنا jibe (*at*) طعنہ، لعنت ملامت a dance with quick movements تیز ناچ

flint *n*. hard stone used for striking fire چقماق

flintlock (*flint*-lok) *n*. old fashioned gun fired with a flint spark توڑے دار بندوق

flip *n*. (colloq.) short flight in an aeroplane ہوائی جہاز میں تھوڑی سی تیر

flippant (*flip*-ant) *adj*. disrespectful بے ادب treating serious things lightly غیر سنجیدہ **flippancy** (*flip*-an-si) *n*. being flippant بے ادبی، غیر سنجیدگی

flipper (*flip*-ĕ*) *n*. (slang) hand ہاتھ

flirt (flĕ*t) *v. i*. make (love with someone) but not seriously تفریحاً محبت کرنا blandish نازنخرے دکھانا، نازو ادا کرنا trifle (*with something*) عمل کے ارادے کے بغیر سوچنا throw (*at*) with a jerk اچھالنا *n*. (esp.) woman who flirts with men چلبلی، ناز نخرے والی، عشوہ گر

flirtation *n*. act of flirting عشوہ گری، دکھاوے کی محبت

flirtatious *adj*. fond of flirting دکھاوے کی محبت کرنے والی

flit *v.i*. move quickly (*from* place to place) تیزی سے گزر جانا، تلتے کودتے پھرنا

float *v. t*. & *i*. (cause to) swim on the surface of liquid or in a fluid تیرنا، تیرانا get financial aid to set (company business) going چلانا، سرمایہ فراہم کرنا *n*. piece of cork for keeping a fishing-net from sinking ترونا **float plane** *n*. aircraft provided with floats instead of wheels to enable it to come down on or take off from water سمندری ہوائی جہاز، تیراک طیارہ

flock (flok) *n*. group of birds or animals (esp. sheep or goats) of one kind kept or going together ریوڑ، گلہ، جھنڈ *in flocks*, in large number بڑی تعداد میں *v. i*. gather or move in crowds مل کر بیٹھنا یا چلنا

We speak of a **flock** of birds, a **covey** of partridges, a **brace** of pheasants, a **bevy** of girls, ladies or larks, a **swarm** of ants, a **shoal** of fish, a **herd** of cattle, a **pack** of hounds or wolves, a **drove** of oxen, a **crowd** of people and a **multitude** of things.

floe (floh) *n*. large mass of floating ice برف کا تیرتا ہوا تودہ

flog *v. t*. (-gg-) کوڑے لگانا lash with a stick بیت لگانا **flogging** *n*. whipping کوڑے مارنا lashing بیت مارنا

flood (flud) *n*. spate سیلاب، طغیانی، چڑھاؤ *be in flood*, be on the rampage چڑھ جانا، طغیانی میں ہونا، میں سیلاب ہونا fill or cover with water غرقاب کر دینا *be flooded with*, have in large numbers میں بہت ہونا، کے پاس بڑی تعداد میں آنا **flood-light** *n*. bright lamp for lighting up outside of buildings بڑی روشنی، طوفانی روشنی *v. t*. light up with such a lamp طوفانی روشنی ڈالنا **flood-lit** *adj*. lit up thus طوفانی روشنی میں **flood-lighting** *n*. providing such light طوفانی روشنی کرنا **flood-mark** *n*. mark of water-depth above which there would be a flood سیلاب کا نشان

floor *n*. bottom surface of room فرش any bottom surface storey منزل *ground floor*, first storey پہلی منزل، نچلی منزل (*a*) (Brit.) second storey دوسری منزل (*b*) (U. S.) first storey پہلی منزل *take the floor, have the floor*, take one's turn in speaking during a public debate بحث میں حصہ لینا، تقریر کرنا، بولنے لگنا *v. t*. pave فرش لگانا knock down پچھاڑنا، مار گرانا puzzle سمجھ میں نہ آنا، چکرا دینا *n*. material for floors وہ چیز جس سے فرش لگایا جائے

flop *v.t*. & *i*. (-pp-) move clumsily بھدی چال چلنا fall heavily دھم سے گرنا throw down clumsily بدتمیزی سے پھینکنا (of book, play, motion-picture, etc.) fail, collapse جھوٹتے جھاتے آنا، ناکام رہنا *n*. sound of flopping دھم سے گرنے کی آواز act of flopping دھم سے گرنا (slang) (of book, play motion-picture etc.) failure ناکامی *adv*. with a flop دھم سے *fall flop* دھم سے گرنا **floppy** *adj*. not stiff ڈھیلا ڈھالا

flora (*floh*-ra) *n*. all the plants of a particular area or period کسی علاقے یا زمانے کی نباتات (*Flora*), *Cl. myth*. Roman goddess of flowers فلورا **floral** (*floh*-rĕl) *adj*. made of flowers پھولوں کا **florist** *n*. one who sells flowers پھول والا، گل فروش **floriculture** *n*. cultivation of flowers پھول اگانا، گل کاری

florid (*flo*-rid) *adj*. naturally red (complexion) سرخ و سفید flowery (style) رنگین

florin (*flo*-rin) *n*. English silver coin worth two shillings فلارن

florist *n*. (see under **flora**)

floss (flos) *n*. rough silk threads for needlework سوزن کاری کا ریشمی دھاگہ

flotilla (floh-*til*-a) *n*. small fleet چھوٹا بیڑا fleet

of small warships چھوٹے جنگی جہازوں کا بیڑا
flotsam (*flot*-sum) *n.* things lost in the ship and floating on the sea جہاز کا سمندر میں تیرتا ہوا مال floating wreckage جہاز کے تیرتے ہوئے ٹکڑے
flounce *n.* ornamental strip of cloth sewn to the skirt ساڑی کی جھالر angry or impatient jerk جھٹکا، چکر *v.i.* move the body thus (*up and down* in anger, pride, impatience) اُچھلنا، تڑپنا، لوٹنا، چکر کھانا *flounce out of room* (etc.) (کمرے وغیرہ) سے تڑپ کر باہر نکل جانا
flounder (*flound*-ĕ*) *v. i.* make violent but almost vain efforts ہاتھ پاؤں مارنا hesitate (in trying to speak a foreign language) اٹک اٹک کر بولنا
flour (*flou*-ĕ*) *n.* meal آٹا *wheat flour* پسی ہوئی گندم کا آٹا
flourish (*flu*-rish) *v. t.* & *i.* thrive, prosper پنپنا brandish (sword) لہرانا *n.* flourishing movement لہرانا ornamental strokes of pen خط کی سجاوٹ use of rhetorical devices صنایع بدایع کا استعمال loud and exciting sound (of trumpets) شہنائی کی آواز
flout *v. t.* treat with contempt کی تحقیر کرنا، کو حقارت سے دیکھنا
flow (floh) *v. i.* (of fluids, rivers, etc.) glide along بہنا (of tide) rise جوار بھاٹا آنا، دھارے کا آنا *ebb and flow*, ebb and tide جوار بھاٹا hang down loosely لہرانا، لٹکنا *n.* a flowing movement بہاؤ quantity that flows بہاؤ کی مقدار intensity or fluency روانی، زور
flower (*flou*-ĕ*) *n.* blossom پھول، گُل *in flower*, with the flowers out جس کے پھول اُگے ہوئے ہوں *flower-pot*, گملہ finest part (*of*) بہترین حصّہ *flowers of speech*, rhetorical devices صنایع، صنایع بدایع **flowery** *adj.* full of flowers of speech مُرصّع، صنایع بدایع سے بھرا ہوا
flown (flohn) *v.* (pa. p. of **fly**, which see)
flu, flue, (floo) *n.* (colloq.) influenza اِنفلوئنزا، جنگی بخار
fluctuate (*fluk*-tew-ayt) *v. i.* (of prices, etc.) rise and fall بدلتے رہنا **fluctuation** (-*ay*-) *n.* rise and fall اُتار چڑھاؤ
fluent (*floo*-ent) *adj.* (of a person) able to speak smoothly and readily جس کی زبان میں روانی ہو خوش اُسلوب (of speech) coming smoothly and readily روانی والی، خوش اسلوبانہ *to speak fluent English* روانی سے انگریزی بولنا **fluently** *adv.* with fluency روانی سے
fluency (*floo*-en-si) *n.* quality of being fluent روانی
fluff (fluf) *n.* soft feathery stuff روئیں *v.t.* make something soft like fluff by spreading it *out* ہلا کر ٹھیک کرنا (see *Addenda*) **fluffy** *adj.* like fluff روئیں جیسا covered with fluff روئیں دار
fluid (*floo*-id) *adj.* able to flow (as gases and liquids do) مائع، سیّال not fixed تغیّر پذیر، غیر قطعی be in a fluid state, (of ideas) be not definite *n.* a gas or a liquid مائع
fluke (flook) *n.* lucky stroke وہ کام جو اتفاقی طور پر ٹھیک ہو جائے اندھے کے پاؤں تلے کی بٹیر
flung (flung) *v.* (pa. t. of **fling**, which see).
flunkey (*flunk*-i) *n.* liveried man-servant اَردَلی toady خوشامدی، چاپلوس
fluoresce (floo-o-*res*) *v. i.* give coloured light of visible ultra-violet rays ٹیوب کی روشنی **fluorescence** *n.* such light ٹیوب کی روشنی **fluorescent** (-*res*-ent) *adj.* that which exhibits fluorescence ٹیوب کی روشنی دینے والا *fluorescent lighting*, such lights ٹیوب، ٹیوب کی روشنی
flurry (*flu*-ri) *n.* nervous hurry ہڑبڑی، ہڑبڑاہٹ *v.t.* cause (someone) to be in a flurry ہڑبڑا دینا
flush *v.t.* & *i.* (cause to) become red through rush of blood to the skin سرخ ہونا، یا کر دینا، تمتمانا inflame with pride or passion (*with* success, etc.) بہت ہی خوش کرنا flood and clean پانی بہا کر صاف کرنا، زور سے بہا کر لے جانا *flush system*, lavatory flooded and cleaned by water فلش سسٹم، بہاؤ خانہ، طہارت خانہ طہارت گاہ *n.* sudden rush of water پانی کا بہاؤ flushing of the face چہرے کی سُرخی، تمتماہٹ rush of strong feeling ہجوم، جذبات set of cards of the same suite (تاش میں) ایک ہی رنگ کے پتے *adj.* in a line (with) ہموار *cut-flush*, binding in which covers do not protrude کٹائی کی جلد
fluster (*flus*-tĕ) *v.t.* make nervous, unnerve گھبرا دینا، ہڑبڑا دینا، ہاتھ پاؤں پھُلا دینا، اوسان خطا کر دینا
flute (floot) *n.* musical instrument in the form of wooden pipe with finger-stop holes بانسری، نے *v. i.* play the flute بانسری بجانا **flutist** *n.* flute player بانسری بجانے والا، نے نواز
flutter (*flut*-ĕ*) *v. t.* & *i.* (of birds) flap quickly without flying or in short flights پر پھڑپھڑانا move quickly but irregularly بے قاعدگی سے چلنا move about excitedly اضطراب میں ادھر اُدھر پھرنا cause to move thus مضطرب کرنا *n.* fluttering movement پھڑپھڑاہٹ excitement اضطراب *in a flutter* اضطراب میں ہونا *cause a flutter* مضطرب کرنا
fluvial (*floo*-vi-ĕl), **fluviatile** (*floo*-vi-a-til, or -tɪl) *adj.* of or found in rivers دریائی
flux (fluks) *n.* constant change مسلسل تبدیلی (*be*) *in a state of flux*, (be) constantly changing, (be) unsettled غیر متعین ہونا
fly (flɪ) *v. t.* & *i.* (*fly, flew, flown*) move through air on wings اُڑنا go by air ہوائی جہاز سے جانا cause to move through air اُڑنا، اُڑا لے جانا *fly a*

kite پتنگ اُڑانا wave in the air لہرانا، اُڑانا (*come off*) *with flying colours*, return triumphantly کامیابی کا پھریرا اُڑاتے ہوئے آنا، کامیاب لوٹنا put up (flag) لہرانا گاڑنا (fly off), run away بھاگنا، چمپت ہو جانا shun بھاگنا، الگ رہنا، کترانا move swiftly (*to*) تیزی سے جانا *fly to the rescue of* کو بچانے کے لیے تیزی سے جانا (pay) *a flying visit*, (pay) a short and hurried visit چھوٹی سی ملاقات کے لیے جلدی جانا *flying bomb*, pilotless aircraft with explosive warhead اُڑن بم *flying disc*. a flying plate of not any well-known purpose اُڑن طشتری *flying saucer*, same as flying disc. (also see *Addenda*) *fly-open*, open suddenly فوراً کھل جانا *fly to bits, fly into pieces*, break to bits suddenly پرزے پرزے اُڑنا، پرخچے اُڑانا *let fly at* (*a*) shoot at پر گولی چلانا (*b*) use strong language گالی گلوچ پر اُتر آنا *fly in the face of*, disobey openly نافرمانی کرنا، گستاخی کرنا *fly into a passion, fly into a rage*, become suddenly angry طیش میں آجانا *fly out*, become extremely angry سخت غصّے میں آنا *as the crow flies*, straight ناک کی سیدھ میں *n*. well-known two-winged insect مکھی *a fly on the wheel*, one who overestimates his importance اپنے متعلق خوش فہمی میں مبتلا، خوش فہمی کا شکار *break fly on the wheel*, spend energy out of all proportion to the task معمولی سے کام کے لیے یونہی زیادہ زور لگانا، چوہا نکالنے کو پہاڑ کھودنا *a fly in the ointment*, a trifle that mars enjoyment مزا کرکرا کرنے والی چھوٹی سی بات **flier, flyer** (*flī*-ĕ*) *n*. airman ہوا باز **fly-leaf** *n*. loose turned end of the jacket of a book گرد پوش کا مُڑا ہوا حصّہ blank leaf in the beginning or at the end of book کتاب کے شروع یا آخر کا ورق **fly-wheel** *n*. heavy wheel in a machine giving it a regular motion فلائی ویل، فالتو پہیہ **fly-weight** *n*. & *adj*. boxer 8 stone or less مکھی کے باز *fly-blown*, (of meat etc.) going bad because containing flies eggs سڑتا ہوا گوشت

foal (fohl) *n*. young horse بچھیرا یا بچھیری *in foal, with foal*, (of a mare) going to give birth to a foal بچّہ دینے والی گھوڑی *v. i*. give birth to a foal (گھوڑی کا) بچھیرا دینا، (گھوڑی کا) بیانا

foam (fohm) *n*. froth جھاگ *v. t*. form or send out foam جھاگ لانا یا نکانا **foam-rubber** *n*. (see *Addenda*)

fob *v. t*. (-bb-) palm *off* دھوکے سے سر منڈھوانا *n*. small watch-pocket گھڑی والی چھوٹی جیب

focal *adj* (see under **focus**)

focus (*foh*-kus) *n*. meeting point of rays نقطۂ ماسکہ distance at with the sharpest outline is given نقطۂ ماسکہ پر *in focus*, at this distance نقطۂ ماسکہ پر *out of focus*, (*a*) away from it نقطۂ ماسکہ سے دُور (*b*) not clear غیر واضح point at which tendencies meet مرکز *v.t.* & *i*. (cause to) converge مرکز ہونا یا کرنا adjust (a telescope, etc.) so that it is in focus نقطۂ ماسکہ پر لانا **focal** (*foh*-kĕl) *adj*. at a focus نقطۂ ماسکہ پر of a focus نقطۂ ماسکہ کا **focalize** *v.t.* focus نقطۂ ماسکہ پر لانا

(F) focus of (L) a lens

fodder (fod-ĕ*) *n*. dried food, hay, etc., for cattle, etc. چارا

foe (foh) *n*. (poet.) enemy عدو، حریف، دشمن

foetid *adj*. same as **fetid** (which see)

fog *n*. thick mist کہر، کہرا، سخت دھند *v.t.* (-gg-) envelop as in a fog کہر کی طرح ڈھانپ لینا perplex سراسیمہ کرنا، بھونچکا کرنا، ششدر کرنا *in a fog*, perplexed سراسیمہ **foggy** *adj*. covered with fog کہر آلود confused (ideas, etc.) دھندلا، مبہم

foible (*foi*-bĕl) *n*. weakness of which one is proud پسندیدہ کمزوری

foil *n*. paper-like metallic sheet (کسی دھات کا) ورق یا پترہ contrast (*to* something) showing off its (usu. good) qualities آب و تاب بڑھانے والی اُلٹی قسم کی چیز blunt fencing sword with button on point گتکا *v.t.* defeat (someone or his purpose) ناکام بنا دینا

foist *v.t.* thrust wrongfully ناجائز مسلّط کرنا palm *off* (on someone) دھوکے سے سر منڈھنا

[1]**fold** (fohld) *v.t.* & *i*. bend one part of a thing over on itself تہ کرنا *fold a letter* خط بند کرنا، خط تہ کرنا become folded تہ ہونا یا ہو سکنا *folding door*, door which may be folded اُڑواں پٹ *fold one's arms*, interlace them ہاتھ باندھنا *with folded hands* ہاتھ جوڑ کر، ہاتھ باندھ کر، دست بستہ *fold* (*someone*) *in* (*one's*) *arms, fold* (*one's*) *arms about* (*someone*), hold (him) to (one's) breast لپٹا لینا، گلے لگانا put (sheep) in a fold (بھیڑیں) باڑے میں بند کرنا (see *Addenda*) *n*. folded part تہ line made by folding شکن enclosure for sheep باڑا، حظیرہ **folder** *n*. folding holder for loose papers فائل folding card with advertisement printed on it فولڈر، تہ ہونے والا اشتہار

[2]**fold** (fohld) *suf*. (added to number to mean: multiplied by چند، گنا *twofold* دوچند، دوگنا *tenfold* دس گنا، دہ چند

foliage (*fohl*-i-ij) *n*. leaves پتے

folk (fohk) *n. pl*. people in general لوگ، عوام *one's* *folk*, (colloq.) one's near relations گھروالے ، برادری والے ، رشتہ دار *adj*. of people عوامی لوک **folk-dance** *n*. old-time dance handed down among (esp. country) people لوک ناچ **folk-song** *n*. such song لوک گیت **folk-lore** *n*. (*a*) old beliefs, tales, customs, etc. of a people عوامی معتقدات ، لوک کہانیاں **folk-tale** *n*. such a tale لوک کہانی

follow (*fol*-oh) *v.t.* & *i* go after کے بعد ہونا، کے پیچھے سے جانا go along (a road, etc.) ہونا یا آنا understand سمجھنا engage in (پیشہ) اختیار کرنا *follow the plough* کاشتکاری کرنا *follow the sea* ملاّح بننا accept (advice, example, etc.) پر عمل کرنا ، کو اختیار کرنا *follow suit*, act after another's manner کسی کے نقش قدم پر چلنا be necessarily true نتیجہ نکلنا *it follows from* (*something*) *that* (اس) سے نتیجہ یہ نکلتا ہے کہ *that does not follow* یہ نتیجہ تو نہیں نکلتا *follow* (*something*) *up*, pursue, کے بارے میں مزید تجسس سے کام لینا *as follows*, following خسب ذیل *follow-up*, second advertizing circular دوسرا اشتہاری خط **follower** (*fol*-oh-ě*) *n*. supporter حامی، پیرو، **following** *n*. body of followers حامی ، پیرو، مرید what follows حسب ذیل ، ذیل کا

folly (*fol*-i) *n*. foolishness بیوقوفی ، حماقت ، احمقانہ حرکت

foment (foh-*ment*) *v.t.* put warm water, etc., on سینکنا cause or increase (discontent, etc.) (بددلی وغیرہ) پھیلانا **fomentation** (-*tay*-) *n*. fomenting سینک something used for fomenting وہ چیز جس کا سینک دیا جائے

fond *adj*. inclined to شائق *be fond of* کا شائق ہونا affectionate and kind شفیق ، مشفق foolishly loving دلدادہ ، لاڈ کرنے والا، بے حد پیار کرنے والا foolish, simple سادہ دل، احمق (of hope) cherished but vain (آرزو) ناممکن الحصول credulous (person) زود اعتقاد، سریع الاعتقاد شوق **fondly** *adv*. in fond manner سے، پیار سے ، چاہ سے

fondle (*fond*-ěl) *v.t.* touch lovingly پیار سے ہاتھ پھیرنا

font *n*. oil reservoir of lamp لیمپ میں تیل کی جگہ receptacle for baptismal water بپتسمہ کے پانی کا برتن ، اصطباغی پانی کا برتن

food anything to eat anything nourishing غذا ، خوراک solid nourishment (as distinct from liquid) روٹی *food and drink* روٹی پانی **food-stuffs** *n. pl*. materials used as food اشیائے خوراک **foodless** *adj*. without food جسے روٹی میسّر نہ ہو **food-rationing** *n*. control on distribution of food-stuffs راشن ، خوراک کی راتب بندی **foodpoisoning** *n*. poisoning of food خوراک میں زہر کی آمیزش ، خوراک کا زہریلا ہونا خوراک کی زہرناکی

fool *n*. person without much sense بیوقوف ، احمق گاؤدی *make a fool of*, (*a*) cause to seem like a fool بنانا ، بیوقوف بنانا (*b*) trick جل دے جانا *fool's errand*, one that in the end is seen to be useless بے نتیجہ کام غیر نتیجہ خیز کام *fool's paradise*, (*a*) unthinking happiness that is unlikely to last خیالی جنّت (*b*) fond hopes خیالی پلاؤ، بے سروپا اُمیدیں (old use) person employed to make jokes, etc. درباری مسخرا شاہی مسخرا *play the fool*, *act like a fool*, blunder بیوقوفی کرنا حماقت کرنا *v.t.* & *i*. behave like a fool حماقت کرنا trick (someone) *out of* (*money*), or *into doing* (*something*) سے دھوکہ کرنا، سے دھوکے سے کام لینا *fool away* (one's time, money, etc.), waste it ضائع کرنا ، گنوانا *All fool's day*, *April Fool's day*, 1st of April when Western nations, probably in commemoration of ancient spring festivities, try to make a fool of others by extending false invitations, etc. اپریل فول **foolery** *n*. foolish act or thing حماقت، احمقانہ حرکت amusing play or fun مضحکہ خیز چیز یا کھیل **foolish** *adj*. silly بیوقوف، احمق nonsense احمقانہ **foolishly** *adv*. حماقت سے **fool-proof** *adj*. so simple or easy that even a fool cannot make a mistake جس میں غلطی کا امکان نہ ہو **foolscap** *n*. ancient jester's cap with bells مسخرے کی ٹوپی dunce's cap نالائق لڑکے کی ٹوپی writing paper of 17½″—13″ size originally with the watermark of a jester's cap and bells فلسکیپ

foot (f ŭt) *n*. (pl. feet) part of leg below ankle پاؤں ، پیر base بنیاد، پایہ *at foot of the hill* دامن کوہ میں lower end کنارا، آخر twelve-inch measure of length فٹ unit of verse with one stressed and one or more unstressed syllables رکن infantry پیادہ فوج *foot and horse* پیادہ فوج اور سوار دستے *on foot*, walking پا برہ *set* (*something*) *on foot*, set (it) going جاری کرنا *set* (*someone*) *on* (*his*) *feet*, make (himself) supporting اپنے پاؤں پر کھڑا کرنا *put* (*one's*) *foot down*, (*a*) protest احتجاج کرنا (*b*) be firm اپنے موقف پر جمے رہنا *carry* (*person*) *off his feet*, fill him with enthusiasm میں ولولہ پیدا کرنا *put* (*one's*) *foot in it*, blunder نامناسب بات کہنا یا کرنا ، غلطی کرنا *have one foot in the grave*, be very old قبر میں پاؤں لٹکائے ہوئے ہونا *tread under foot*, tyrannize ظلم کرنا *v.t.* & *i*. add a foot to (a stocking) پیر بننا pay (the bill) (بل کی رقم) ادا کرنا add *up* (column of figures) جوڑنا ، جمع کرنا walk پیدل چلنا *foot it all the way* سارا راستہ پیدل چلنا **footboard** *n*. steps to a railway carriage فٹ بورڈ (ریل کے ڈبے کا) قدمچہ **football** *n*. inflated leather ball فٹ بال game played with it فٹ بال **footfall** *n*. sound of a footstep چاپ، آہٹ **foothills** *n. pl*. low hills at the foot of a mountain سلسلۂ کوہ کے

پاؤں کی جگہ ، قدم جمانے کی جگہ **foot-hold** *n.* safe place for the foot پاؤں رکھنے کی جگہ ، پاؤں کا سہارا **foot-rule** *n.* measure one foot long فٹا ، پیمانہ ، چینی **footing** *n.* foothold پاؤں کا سہارا status (in society) (معاشرے میں) درجہ foundation بنیاد **foot-print, foot-mark** *n.* mark of foot نقش پا ، نقشِ قدم ، پاؤں کا نشان ، کھوج **footlights** *n. pl.* lights along the front of the stage in a theatre سٹیج کی نچلی بتیاں **footman** *n.* man-servant اردلی **foot-note** *n.* note at foot of a printed page حاشیہ **foot-path** *n.* narrow path across fields or open country or at side of country road (and not a *pavement* or *sidewalk* along a city street, as is erroneously believed by this country's semi-educated people) پگڈنڈی **footstep** *n.* step قدم footfall آہٹ ، چاپ foot-print نقش قدم

fop *n.* man who pays too much attention to his clothes چھیلا ، چھبیلا

for *prep.* in place of کی بجائے ، کے بجائے on behalf of کی طرف سے as being بطور because of کے باعث in favour of کے حق میں as regards کا ، کے متعلق towards کو for a period of کے لیے despite کے باوجود *conj.* since, because چونکہ *for good*, for ever ہمیشہ کے لیے *once for all*, for ever ہمیشہ کے لیے *O for ! (something)*, how I wish it میں کتنا چاہتا ہوں *for all that*, despite all that ان تمام باتوں کے باوجود *forasmuchas*, since, seeing that چونکہ ، اس کے پیش نظر ، یہ دیکھتے ہوئے کہ *for all, for all that,* notwithstanding کے باوجود *for the matter of that,* as far as that is concerned جہاں تک اس کا تعلق ہے *as for (something)*, as far as (that thing) concerns جہاں تک اس کا تعلق ہے *for to*, (vulgar usage for) in order to کے لیے ، کی غرض سے

forage (*fo*-rij) *n.* food for horses and cattle چارا *v.t.* search (for such food) چارے کی تلاش میں نکلنا ravage لوٹ مار کرنا

foray (*fo*-ray) *n.* sudden attack (esp. to get food) اچانک حملہ *v.t.* make such attack اچانک حملہ بولنا

forbear (fo*-*bay*-ē*) *v.t.* (*forbear, forbore, forborne*) refrain باز رہنا ، احتراز کرنا ، نہ کرنا *n.* ancestor بزرگ ، باپ دادا **forbearance** (-bay-) *n.* patience برداشت ، صبر control of temper مزاج کو قابو میں رکھنا **forbearingly** *adv.* صبر سے کام لیتے ہوئے

forbid (fo*-*bid*) *v.t.* (*forbid, forbade, forbidden*) order (someone) not *to do* something منع کرنا ، قدغن لگانا ، ممانعت کرنا **forbidding** *adj.* stern سخت گیر rather frightening (manners, etc.) ڈراؤنا ugly (features) بدصورت ، بدنما

force (fohs) *n.* strength قوت ، طاقت *physical force* جسمانی طاقت *the force of argument* استدلال کا وزن body of armed men فوج ، لشکر *the Air Force* ہوائی فوج ، فضائیہ *the Forces*, Navy, Army and Air Force بحری ، بری اور ہوائی فوج *in force*, in a large number بڑی تعداد میں (law) authority اختیار ، اقتدار enforcement نفاذ *put (something) into force*, make it binding نافذ کرنا *v.t.* use force to make (someone) do (something) or to make (someone) do (something) کوئی کام کرنے یا کرانے کے لیے قوت کا استعمال کرنا break open by using force زور لگا کر توڑ ڈالنا *force (someone's) hand*, make (him) do something he does not want to do کسی سے زبردستی کوئی کام کروانا *forced march*, rapid march by soldiers تیز کوچ **forceful** *adj.* full of force زوردار ، قوی ، طاقتور **forcible** *adj.* done by the use of force convincing, showing force زوردار **forcibly** *adv.* by the use of force بزور **forced** *adj.* unnatural ; done by effort آورد والا ، پرتصنع

forceps (*fo**-seps) *n.* instrument for gripping things جراحی چمٹی ، چمٹی

forceps

ford (fohrd) *n.* shallow place in a river where it is possible to walk across پایاب مقام *v.t.* cross (a river) at a ford پایاب مقام سے **fordable** *adj.* that which can be forded پایاب

[1]**fore** (foh*) *n.* front part اگلا حصہ *come to the fore*, become prominent نمایاں ہونا ، مشہور ہونا *adj & adv.* in front آگے سامنے

[2]**fore-** (foh*) *pref.* front اگلا ، کا اگلا حصہ in advance پہلے ہی ، وقت سے پہلے **fore-and-aft** *adj.* lengthwise of a ship جہاز کی لمبائی کا (یا میں)

forearm *n.* (*foh**-ahm) arm from elbow to wrist بازو کا اگلا حصہ ، کہنی سے کلائی تک *v.t.* (foh*-*ahm*) arm beforehand پہلے ہی مسلح کر دینا warn متنبہ کرنا

forebode *v.t.* have a feeling of impending misfortune بدقسمتی کے آنے کا اندیشہ ہونا warning of impending misfortune بدقسمتی کے آنے کا اشارہ **foreboding** *n.* feeling impending misfortune بدقسمتی کے آنے کا احساس

forecast (*foh*-kahst) *v.t.* predict پیشینگوئی کرنا *n.* (foh*-*kahst*) prediction پیشینگوئی *the weather forecast* prediction of weather موسمی پیشین گوئی

forecastle, fo'c'sle (*fohk*-sel) *n.* forward part of a ship where the crew live (جہاز کے اگلے حصے میں) ملاحوں کی آرام گاہ **forefather** (foh*-*fah*-dhē*) *n. pl* ancestors باپ دادا ، آباؤاجداد

forefinger *n.* (see under **finger**)

forefront (*foh**-frunt) *n.* the very front

اگلا حصہ ، پیش most prominent part (*of*) سب سے نمایاں حصہ (*be*) *in the forefront of* میں پیش پیش ہوں
forego (for*-*goh*) *v.t.* (better spelt *forgo*), give up چھوڑنا (better spelt *forgo*), deny oneself سے محروم رہنا ، ترک کرنا precede سے پہلے آنا **foregoing** *adj.* preceding پہلا previously mentioned مذکورۂ بالا ، مذکورۂ صدر **foregone** (foh*-*gon*) *adj.* already settled ناگزیر *foregone conclusion*, unavoidable (hence easily foreseen) result ناگزیر نتیجہ (Also see **forgo**)
foreground (*foh**-ground) *n.* part of a view nearest the person looking پیش منظر
forehead (*fo**-red) *n.* part of face above the eyes ماتھا ، پیشانی ، جبیں ، جبہ
foreign (*fo**-rin) *adj.* alien غیر ملکی of relations with other countries خارجی *foreign to* (*a*) unsuitable نامناسب ، ناموزوں (*b*) unconnected with غیر متعلق *Foreign Affairs*, relations with other countries امور خارجہ *Foreign Office*, Ministry dealing with Foreign Affairs دفتر خارجہ ، وزارت امور خارجہ *Foreign Minister*, Minister for Foreign Affairs وزیر امور خارجہ *a foreign body*, (in medicine) a substance not belonging to the part of the body where it is present (as dust in the eye) باہری چیز
foreigner *n.* person from a foreign country پردیسی ، اجنبی ، غیر ملکی
forejudge (foh*-*juj*) *v.t.* judge (something) even before hearing evidence کے متعلق گواہی سننے سے پہلے ہی فیصلہ قائم کر لینا
foreknowledge (foh-*nol*-ij) *n.* knowing beforehand پہلے ہی علم ہونا
forelock (*foh*-lok) *n.* lock of hair just above forehead پیشانی کے بال *take time by the forelock*, seize opportunity موقعہ سے پورا فائدہ اٹھانا ، موقعہ ہاتھ سے نہ دینا -
foreman (*foh** man) *n.* (*pl foremen*) workman in authority over others فورمین leader (of jury, etc.) سربراہ
foremost (*foh**-most) *adj.* & *adv.* first پہلا ، پہلے اول ، اولیں most important اہم
forenoon (*foh**-noon) *n.* part of day between sunrise and noon قبل از دوپہر
forensic (fo-*ren*-sik) *adj.* pertaining to law-court عدالتی
foreordain (foh*-o*-*dayn*) *v.t.* appoint beforehand پہلے سے فیصلہ کر دینا ، ازل سے مقرر کرنا **foreordained** *adj.* ازل سے مقرر یا معین
forerunner (foh-*run*-ĕ*) *n.* precursor پیش رو sign of the coming events مستقبل کی نشاندہی کرنے والی چیز
foreshadow (foh-*shad*-oh) *v.t.* be a sign of کا پتہ دینا ، کی جھلک دکھانا
foresight (*foh**-sit) *n.* ability to see future needs and prepare for them دور بینی ، دور اندیشی
forest (*fo**-rest) *n.* wood جنگل ، بن *forest department* government department looking after forests محکمۂ جنگلات **forester** *n.* man in charge of a forest جنگل کا منتظم ، جنگل بان **forestry** (*fo*-rest-ri) *n.* science of planting forests جنگل بانی
forestall (foh*-*stawl*) *v.t.* do something beforehand preventing others from doing it پیش بندی کرنا
foretell (foh*-*tel*) *v.t.* (*foretell, foretold, foretold*) predict پیشین گوئی کرنا
forethought (*foh**-thawt) *n.* future planning پیش بینی ، دور اندیشی
forewarn (foh-*waw*n*) *v.t.* warn beforehand بروقت متنبہ کرنا
foreword (*foh**-wĕd) *n.* introduction to a book by a person other than the author دیباچہ ، پیش لفظ
forfeit (*foh**-fit) *v.t.* lost by fault or neglect سے محروم ہو جانا ، (حق) ساقط ہو جانا *n.* something forfeited تاوان ، جرمانہ ، پاداش یا ضبطی *adj.* forfeited ضبط **forfeiture** (*fo**-fi-chĕ*) *n.* forfeiting ضبطی thing forfeited ضبط شدہ چیز
forgather (foh*-*gadh*-ĕ*) *v.i.* meet جمع ہونا
forgave *v.* (past t. of **forgive**, which see)
forge (foh*j) *n.* smithy لوہار کی دکان ، لوہار خانہ ، لوہار کی بھٹی *v.t.* & *i.* shape (metal) by beating, hammering, etc. گرم لوہے کو پیٹ کر کچھ بنانا make a false imitation of document, signature or note جعلی بنانا fabricate گھڑنا یا کرنا invent ایجاد کرنا ، بنانا
forger *n.* one who forges جعلساز **forgery** (*foh**j-è-ri) *n.* act of forging جعلسازی forged document جعلی دستاویز
forget (foh*-*get*) *v.t.* & *i.* (*forget, forgot, forgotten*) lose remembrance of بھولنا ، بھول جانا cease to think بھلانا ، بھلا دینا *forgive and forget* معاف کرنا اور بھلا دینا omit (to take or do) درگزر کرنا یا ے جانا) یاد نہ رہنا *forget-me-not*, (*a*) riverside plant with small blue flowers ایک پودا ، منت (*b*) its flower which is a symbol of constancy and fidelity اس کا پھول ، منت بھول *forget* (*oneself*), behave unbecomingly by losing self control بدتہذیبی کرنا بدتہذیبی سے کام لینا **forgetful** *adj.* in the habit of forgetting بھلکڑ **forgetfulness** *n.* this habit بھول ، نسیان
forgive (fo**giv*) *v.t.*& *i.* (*forgive, forgave, forgiven*) pardon (a person, a fault, or someone his fault) معاف کرنا ، بخش دینا remit (a debt) معاف کر دینا بخشنا **forgiveness** *n.* forgiving or being forgiven معافی *forgiving adj.* merciful معاف کرنے والا **forgivingly** *adv.* having pardoned معاف کرتے ہوئے

■ We **forgive** someone his fault, **pardon** him for his wrongdoing, **excuse** him of some duty and **absolve** him of some responsibility.

forgo (foh*-*goh*) *v.t.* (*forgo* ; *forwent* used rarely; *foregone*) do without کے بغیر گزارہ کرنا ، دَست بردار ہونا give up چھوڑنا ، ترک کرنا ، دَست کش ہو جانا (Also see **forego**)

fork (foh*k) *n.* pronged handle for lifting food, کانٹا *knife and fork* چھری کانٹا tool for lifting hay, etc. جیٖنی ، رَنگی

a knife and fork

دوشاخہ place where a road, tree trunk, etc., divides into branches تِراہا *v.t.* & *i.* lift with a fork جیلی سے اُٹھانا یا پھینکنا (of a road, etc.) divide into branches دوراستے نکلنا

forlorn (fo*-*lohn*) *adj.* forsaken بیکس ، تن تنہا having lost hope نا اُمّید ، مایُوس ، لاچار

form (fo*m) *n.* shape شکل ، صُورت manners طور طریقہ ، طرزِعمل ، رَوِیّہ *good form*, good manners طرزِعمل *bad form* خراب رَوِیّہ sort قِسم physical condition حالت (*be*) *in good* (or *bad*) *form* اچھی (یا بُری) حالت میں (ہونا) formality ضابطہ ، رَسم *for form's sake*, as a matter of form رَسمی طور پر ، بطورِ ضابطہ printed paper with spaces to be filled in فارم ، نقشہ ، جَدوَل class in a school جماعت ، دَرجہ long wooden bench without back بَنچ *v.t.* & *i.* shape صُورت دینا ، تشکیل کرنا make (words, etc.) وَضع کرنا ، گھڑنا (of ideas, etc.) take shape بننا ، صُورت پذیر ہونا be or become ہونا یا ہو جانا ، بننا یا بننے لگنا (cause to) move into a particular order ہونا (یا) لانا

formal *adj.* ceremonious پُر تکلّف customary رَسمی of the outward shape ظاہری official رَسمی باقاعدہ *formal call* ضابطے کی مُلاقات regular ضابطے کا stiff سخت ، رُوکھا ، بے رُخی کا (یا والا) ، سَرد مہر ، سَرد مہرانہ **formality** (fo*-*mal*-i-ti) *n.* observance of custom رسم ورواج کی پابندی ، تکلّف observance required by rules باضابطگی ، ضابطے کی کارروائی stiff (behaviour) سَرد مہرانہ

formation (fo*-*may*-shèn) *n.* forming بنانا ، تشکیل something formed صُورت structure بناوٹ arrangement ترتیب **formless** *adj.* without form بے شکل ، غیر متشکّل **formative** *adj.* serving to form بنانے والا ، ڈھلنے والا

former (*fo*-mĕ**) *adj.* of old times پُرانا ، قدیم قدیمی first-named of two پہلا *n.* the first named of the two پہلا ، اوّلیں **formerly** *adv.* in former times پہلے ، پہلے زمانے میں

formidable (*fo*-mid-ab-èl*) *adj.* causing fear خوفناک ، ڈراونا (of enemy or opposition) hard to overcome سخت **formidably** *adv.* so as to cause fear خوفناک طور پر

formula (*fo*m-ew-la*) *n.* (pl. *formulas* or *formulae*) set form of words ترتیبِ اَلفاظ ، محاوَرہ set رُکن rule for doing something فارمولا ، قاعدہ recipe نسخہ ترکیب **formulate** (*fo*m-ew-layt*) *v.t.* lay down clearly and exactly (rule, law, etc.) (قاعدہ یا قانون) بنانا ، وَضع کرنا **formulation** *n.* formulating تشکیل

forsake (fo*-*sayk*) *v.t.* (*forsake*, *forsook*, *forsaken*), desert سے الگ ہو جانا ، کو چھوڑ دینا **forsaken** *adj.* deserted بیکس ، تن تنہا

forswear (for-*sway*-ĕ*) *v. t.* (*forswear*, *forswore*, *forsworn*) deny on oath حلفیہ انکار یا تردید کرنا *forswear* (*oneself*), perjure جھوٹی قسم کھانا ، قسم کھا کر بھی جھوٹ بولنا renounce solemnly (قسم کھا کر) ترک کرنا ، بالکل چھوڑ دینا

fort (foh*t) *n.* military defence, castle قلعہ ، حِصار (Also see **fortify** & **fortress**)

forth (foh*th) *adv.* forward (in time, place or order) آگے ، کے بعد سے *from this day forth*, *henceforth* آج سے ، آج کے بعد *back and forth*, to and fro آگے پیچھے ، اِدھر اُدھر (and) *so forth*, (and) so on وغیرہ ، علیٰ ھٰذا القیاس out, outward باہر ، آگے کو **forthcoming** *adj.* about to come out آنے والا ، عنقریب ہونے والا ، قریبی *be forthcoming*, (of help, etc.) be ready when needed تیار ہونا **forthright** *adj.* outspoken صاف گو ، مُنہ پھٹ **forthwith** *adv.* immediately فوراً ، فی الفور

fortify (fo*t-i-fı) *v.t.* strengthen (a place with walls, guns, etc., against attack) کی قلعہ بندی کرنا کے استحکامات کرنا strengthen (oneself, one's courage, etc.) مستحکم کرنا ، مضبُوط کرنا **fortification** (-*kay*-) *n.* (usu. *pl.*) fortifying قلعہ بندی fort قلعہ ، حِصار

fortitude (*fo*t-i-tewd*) *n.* endurance of (pain or danger) صبر ، حوصلہ ، برداشت ، تحمّل

fortnight (*foh*t-nit*) *n.* period of two consecutive weeks پندرھواڑہ ، پندرہ روز ، دو ہفتے **fortnightly** (*foh*t-nit-li*) *adj.* of a fortnight پندرہ روزہ ، دو ہفتگی *adv.* every fortnight ہر پندرھواڑے *n.* fortnightly periodical پندرہ روزہ اخبار یا رسالہ ، دو ہفتگی

fortress (*foh*t-res*) *n.* small fort قلعہ fortified town قلعہ بند شہر ، ارک

fortuitous (fo*-*tew*-i-tus) *adj.* accidental اتفاقی

fortune (*fo*-toon*, or *fo*-chūn*) *n.* fate قسمت ، تقدیر ، نصیبہ ، نصیب its details قسمت کا حال *tell* (*someone*) *his fortune* کسی کی قسمت کا حال بتانا *fortune-teller* قسمت کا حال بتانے والا ، نجومی ، جیوتشی good luck خوش قسمتی یاوَر ، نصیبہ *have fortune on* (*one's*) *side*, be lucky خوش قسمت ہونا chance اتفاق success کامیابی large sum of money دَولت **fortunate** (*fo*-too-nayt*) *adj.* lucky خوش نصیب causing good luck مُبارک ، مسعُود brought by good fortune خوش قسمتی سے آیا ہوا

forty (*fo*t*-i) *n.* & *adj.* 40 چالیس *forty winks*, nap قیلولہ **fortieth** *adj.* 40th چالیسواں

forum (*foh*ᵛ-rum) *n.* market place of ancient Rome where public meetings were held فورم place for public assembly عوامی جلسہ گاہ venue of public discussion مرکزِ مباحثہ court عدالت

forward (*fo*wě*d*) *adj.* to or in the front آگے *carry forward* (of total) carry to the next page اگلے صفحے پر میزان اگلے صفحے پر لے جانا *carried forward* اگلے صفحے پر لایا ہوا بقیہ *brought forward* لے جائی ہوئی میزان before time قبل از وقت progressive بڑھتا ہوا ready and prompt (*to* help) آگے کی طرف ، ترقی پذیر تیار ، آمادہ pushing and clever (person) آگے کھیلنے والا ، محاذی ترقی کرنے والا *n.* front line player *v.t.* send forward اُوپر بھیجنا ، آگے بھیجنا send (letter, etc.) after a person to a new address, نئے پتے پر روانہ کرنا send ahead پہلے بھیجنا help on کی پیش رفت میں حصّہ لینا *adv.* in a forward direction آگے *bring* (*something*) *forward* آگے لانا *come forward* آگے آنا ، بڑھنا *look forward to,* expect with pleasure آس لگائے ہونا ، اُمیدیں باندھنا *inter* move on wards ! بڑھے چلو!

fossil (*fos*-il) *n.* petrified prehistoric remains of living things آثارِ متحجرہ person with outdated ideas دقیانوسی *adj* of or like a fossil آثارِ متحجرہ کا (یا کا سا) **fossilize** (*fos*-i-liz) *v. t.* petrify متحجر ہونا (of mind, etc.) remain uninfluenced by new ideas کی ترقی کا رُک جانا ، پر جمود طاری ہونا

foster (*fos*-tě*) *v.t.* bring up ; nurse پالنا ، پوسنا ، پرورش کرنا cherish (memory, etc.) کو سینے سے لگائے رکھنا *adj.* by nurture and not by blood رضاعی ، دودھ دودھ کے رشتے کا *foster-brother* (or *foster-sister*), (*a*) boy (or girl) taken up by one's parents and brought up as a real member of the family منہ بولا بھائی (یا بہن) (*b*) brother (or sister) by nurturing رضاعی بھائی (یا بہن) *foster-parent, foster-father* (or *foster-mother*), (*a*) منہ بولا باپ (یا ماں) رضاعی باپ (یا ماں) *foster-children, foster-son* (or *foster-daughter*) (*a*) لے پالک بیٹا (یا بیٹی) منہ بولا بچہ ، منہ بولا بیٹا (یا منہ بولی بیٹی) (*b*) رضاعی اولاد ، (*b*) رضاعی بیٹا (یا بیٹی)

fought (fot) *v.* (pa. t. & pa. p. of **fight**, which see)

foul *adj.* dirty گندہ غلیظ soiled (linen) میلا offensive (smell or taste) بُرا ، خراب obscene (language) فحش *foul-mouthed*, using vulgar language بدزبان rainy or stormy (weather) خراب ، طوفانی باد و باراں والا entangled اُلجھا ہوا (slang) disgusting گھناؤنا ، نفرت انگیز *foul play*, (*a*) against the rules of the game ناجائز ، غلط ، خلافِ قاعدہ (*b*) murder قتل (*c*) any violent crime سنگین جرم *n.* something against the rules of the game خلافِ قاعدہ کھیل *adv.* (of winds) contrary مخالف ، سمتِ مخالف سے *fall foul of, run foul of,* (*a*) (of ship) collide with ٹکرانا (*b*) become entangled with میں اُلجھ جانا (*c*) quarrel سے اُلجھ پڑنا *v.t.* & *i.* make or become dirty گندہ ہونا یا کرنا (of ships) collide with ٹکرانا become entangled with میں اُلجھ جانا dishonour بے عزت کرنا رُسوا کرنا **foully** *adv.* contrary to rules بے قاعدہ ، غلط ناجائز طور پر **foulness** *n.* بُرائی ، خرابی ، گندگی ، سنگینی ، بیقاعدگی

found *v.t.* lay the basis of بُنیاد رکھنا establish (a city) بنا ڈالنا get started (by financing) جاری کرنا کی تاسیس کرنا (pa. t. and pa. p. of **find**, which see) **foundation** *n.* founding تاسیس base بنیاد something founded ادارہ chartiable organization founded by someone خیراتی ادارہ funds for it خیراتی ادارہ کا سرمایہ **foundation-stone** *n.* first stone of a building سنگِ بُنیاد stone laid in a building ceremony and bearing the name of one who lays it سنگِ بُنیاد *lay the foundation stone of,* (*a*) lay this stone کا سنگِ بُنیاد رکھنا (*b*) start it کا سنگِ بُنیاد رکھنا ، کو شروع کرنا **founder** *n.* one who founds بانی ، مؤسس *founder's day,* anniversary of laying the foundation-stone یومِ تاسیس

founder (*foun*-de*) *v.t.* & *i.* (of a ship) (cause to) fill with water and sink ڈوب جانا (of a horse) stumble (esp. in mud) ٹھوکر کھا کر گرنا ، بکنڈی کھانا *n.* (see under **found**)

foundling (*found*-ling) *n.* deserted infant of un known parents بن ماں باپ کا ، گرا پڑا بچہ ، لقیط

foundry (*found*-ri) *n.* workshop for moulding metals, etc. فونڈری ، صفّار خانہ

fount *n.* (poet.) spring چشمہ fountain فوّارہ set of printer's type (ایک سائز کا) مکمل ٹائپ

fountain (*foun*-tin) *n.* spring چشمہ store (of liquid) ذخیرہ artificial jet spouting up through pipes فوّارہ **fountain-head** *n.* original source سرچشمہ ، منبع **fountain pen** *n.* pen with ink-fountain فونٹین پن ، سیاہی دار قلم ، خودنویس

four (foh*) *n.* & *adj.* 4 چار *on all fours,* on the hands and knees گھٹنوں کے بل ، گھٹیوں **fourfold** *n.* four times چوگنا in four folds چوہرا ۔ چوتہہ

fourth *n.* & *adj.* 4th چوتھا **fourscore** *adj.* 80 اسّی

fourteen (*foh*-teen) *n.* & *adj.* 14 چودہ **fourteenth** *n.* & *adj.* 14th چودھواں

fowl (foul) *n.* (old use) any bird پرندہ domestic hen (or cock) مُرغی (یا مُرغ یا مُرغا) its flesh used as food مُرغا *fish, flesh and fowl* مچھلی ، گوشت اور مُرغ *roast fowl* بُھنا ہوا مُرغ **fowling** *n.* hunting of wild birds پرندوں کا شکار **fowler** *n.* one who hunts wild birds for food چڑی مار

fox (foks) *n. masc.* (fem. *vixen*) wild and cunning animal of the dog family لومڑ ، روباہ crafty person چالاک شخص ، عیار ، حراف **fox-hound** *n.* dog bred for fox-hunting لومڑی کے شکار والا کتا **fox-trot** *n.* dance with short and quick steps ایک رقص ، روباہی music for it روباہی موسیقی ، روباہی

fracas *n.* noisy quarrel جھگڑا ، ٹنٹا

fraction (*frak*-shĕn) *n.* small piece چھوٹا سا حصہ *a mere fraction of* کا بالکل چھوٹا سا حصہ part of a whole number کسر ، بٹہ *vulgar fraction*, a fraction ($e.g., \frac{3}{10}$ or $\frac{5}{7}$) which is expressed with nominator (3, 5) above and denominator (10, 7) below کسر عام *decimal fraction*, a fraction (like ·3, called decimal three or point three) with denominator (always 10) expressed as a point written to the left top of the numerator and every digit of the numerator being read as a separate digit (*e.g.*, ·38 being read as *decimal three eight*) کسر اعشاریہ *proper fraction*, less than one کسر واجب *improper fraction*, more than کسر غیر واجب **fractional** *adj.* of or having a fraction کسری

fractious (*frak*-shus) *adj.* peevish چڑچڑا

fracture (*frak*-chĕ*) *n.* breaking (of a bone) (ہڈی) کا) ٹوٹنا *v. t.* & *i.* breaking (of a bone) (ہڈی) توڑنا یا ٹوٹنا

fragile (*fraj*-ɪl) *adj.* easily broken جلدی ٹوٹ جانے والا weak نازک ، کمزور **fragility** *n.* being fragile جلدی ٹوٹ جانا ، کمزوری

fragment (*frag*-ment) *n.* part (broken off) ٹوٹا ہوا ٹکڑا ، حصہ **fragmentary** *adj.* incomplete نامکمل **fragmentation** *n.* breaking (of agricultural land) into meagre small-holdings اراضی کے ٹکڑے ٹکڑے کرنا

fragrant (*frag*-rant) *adj.* sweet-smelling معطر خوشبودار **fragrance** *n.* sweet smell خوشبو

frail (frayl) *adj.* weak کمزور morally weak اخلاقی کمزوری والا unchaste (woman) بے عصمت **frailty** *n.* weakness کمزوری *Frailty, thy name is woman* کمزوری ! تیرا نام عورت ہے ؛ عورت ہی کا دوسرا نام کمزوری ہے liability to err خطا پذیری **frailly** *adv.* کمزوری سے

frame (fraym) *n.* main structure giving shape ڈھانچہ body جسم wooden border (of a picture, door, etc.) چوکھٹا *frame of mind*, state of mind مزاج *frame of reference*, (see *Addenda*) *v. t.* & *i.* give shape to (plan, sentence, regulation, etc.) بننا ، تشکیل کرنا ، وضع کرنا take shape بننا ، تشکیل کرنا regulate (*according to*) (کے مطابق) ڈھالنا put a frame (*on* or *round*) (چوکھٹے میں) جڑنا **framework** *n.* anything giving shape and support سہارا ، بنیاد

franc (frank) *n.* a French (etc.) silver coin فرانک

franchise (*fran*-chɪz) *n.* right to vote in a parliamentary election (سیاسی) حق رائے دہی (یا رائے دہندگی) حق انتخاب citizenship حقوق شہریت ، حق شہریت

Franco- (*frank*-oh) *pref.* of France فرانسیسی

frank *adj.* candid صاف دل ، راستباز ، ایماندار open صاف ، کھلے بندوں *be quite frank with* صاف صاف کہہ دینا *to be frank* سچ کہوں تو ، سچ سچ کہوں ، سچی بات ویہ ہے *v. t.* sign a letter so that it goes free دستخط کرکے خط مفت بھیجنا mark it (with a *franking machine*) so that the postage is realized from the sender later ٹکٹ لگانے کی مشین ٹکٹ لگانا *franking machine* ٹکٹ لگانے کی مشین یا کل **frankly** *adv.* unreservedly صاف صاف **frankness** *n.* candour صاف دلی outspokenness حق گوئی ، صاف گوئی

Frankenstein (*frank*-en-stɪn) *n.* hero of a 19th century novel by the poet Shelley's second wife who creates a monster which brought disaster to the inventor فرینکن شٹائن *Frankenstein's monster*, this monster فرینکن شٹائن کا بنایا ہوا بھوت (erroneously) monster فرینکن شٹائن ، خود ساختہ (آوردہ) آفت

frankincense (*frank*-in-sens) *n.* a kind of resin yielding a sweet smell when burnt لوبان

frantic (*fran*-tik) *adj.* wildly excited (with pain, etc.) مضطرب frenzied بدحواس ، پاگل *drive (someone) frantic*, drive (him) mad پاگل کر دینا **frantically, franticly,** *adv.* distractedly مضطربانہ wild with excitement بدحواسی سے

fraternity, *n.*, **fraternize** *v. i.* (see under **fraternal**)

fraternal (fra-*tĕ**-nĕl) *adj.* brotherly برادرانہ ، بھائی چارے کا **fraternity** (fra-*tĕ**-ni-ti) *n.* brotherly feeling بھائی چارا ، اخوت society of men with similar interests بھائی چارا ، برادری **fraternize** (*fra*-tĕ*-nɪz) *v. i.* associate with بھائی چارا کرنا ، رشتہ اخوت قائم کرنا

fraud (frawd) *n.* criminal deception دھوکا ، دغا someone who deceives دغاباز ، فراڈ فریب ، فراڈ something that deceives دھوکا **fraudulent** (*frawd*-ew-lent) *adj.* deceitful دغاباز obtained (or characterized) by deceit دھوکے بازی کا

fraught (frawt) *adj.* (*fraught with*) full of (meaning) (گہرے معانی) والا ، پرمعنی involving (unpleasant consequences) (خطرناک نتائج) والا

fray *n.* noisy brawl ہنگامہ ، غل غپاڑا ، لڑائی جھگڑا *v.t.* & *i.* (of clothes, etc.) (cause to) wear away at the edges دھجیاں اڑنا ، دھجیاں اڑانا یا بکھرنا

freak (freek) *n.* absurd whim بے تکا ، احمقانہ خیال absurd occurrence عجیب بات ، اعجوبہ perso full of absurd whims عجب احمق (also *freak of nature*), monster (*e.g.*, a double-headed baby) عجیب الخلقت **freakish** *adj*. abnormal عجیب سا، عجیب **freakishly** *adv*. بڑے عجیب انداز سے، اوکھا

freckles (*frek*-elz) *n. pl.* small brownish spots on a fair skin نمش *v. t.* & *i.* (cause to) become covered with freckles نمش پڑنا یا ڈالنا

free *adj*. independent آزاد self-governing آزاد، خود مختار not a slave آزاد not in prison آزاد، غیر مقید *set free* (*from prison*) (قیدے) رہا کرنا free from obstructions پابندی سے آزاد، بلا روک ٹوک *be free from error*, be correct صحیح ہونا، غلطی سے مبرا ہونا *free from obstruction* (etc.) رکاوٹ وغیرہ کے بغیر ہونا *free to do* (*something*), کوئی کام کرنے کی آزادی رکھنا *free from disease*, in good health صحت مند، کسی بیماری کے بغیر loose; not fixed *have a free hand*, *give* (*someone*) *a free hand*, have or give authority to do things at one's discretion اختیار دینا، مختار کرنا *free end of a rope* رسّے کا سرا جو پکڑا ہوا نہ ہو without payment مفت، بلا معاوضہ *free trade*, imports without customs duties آزادانہ تجارت *admission free*, admission without ticket داخلہ مفت داخلہ بلا ٹکٹ (of time, place or person) not occupied خالی، فارغ open to all ہر ایک کے لیئے *free fight*, one in which everyone may join ہلڑ (10) (of translation) not literal آزاد *free translation* آزاد ترجمہ (11) lavish فراخدلانہ، کھلے دل والا *be free with* (or *of*) (*one's money*, etc.), giving it readily کھلے دل سے خرچ کرنا، کھلے دل سے (روپیہ وغیرہ) خرچ کرنا (12) not reserved (*with*) بے تکلف، گستاخ *make free with*, use (another person's things) as if they were one's own, (پرایا) مال اڑانا *v. t.* (*freed*) make free چھوڑنا یا چھڑانا آزاد کرنا یا کرانا، رہا کرنا یا کرانا **freely** *adv*. without restriction آزادانہ readily شوق سے **freedom** *n*. being free آزادی، حریت *fight for freedom*, (a nation's) liberation struggle آزادی کی جدّوجہد، جہادِ حریت **freehand** *adj*. (of drawing) done without the help of a ruler, etc. صرف ہاتھ سے کھینچا ہوا **freehanded** *adj*. generous فراخ دل، الکھ لٹ **freebooter** *n*. robber رہزن، ڈاکو، لٹیرا **freehold** *n*. land as absolute property پوری ملکیت **freeloader** *n*. (see *Addenda*) **free love** *n*. sexual relations without marriage آوارگی، بے حیائی، آزاد جنسی **freeman** *n* one who is not slave آزاد one who is given all the privileges of citizenship جسے حقوق شہریت حاصل ہوں **freelance** *adj*. (old use) mercenary پیشہ ور، بھاڑے کا journalist not on the staff of a periodical غیر ملازم صحافی *freelance journalism*, profession of journalism as followed by freelances بلا ملازمت صحافت (politician, etc.) with no party allegiance (سیاستدان) جو کسی پارٹی کا نہ ہو، بے حزب (سیاستداں) **freelancing** *n*. practising of freelance journalism بلا ملازمت صحافت (کا پیشہ) **freemason** *n*. member of a secret (mainly Christian) society فری میسن **freemasonry** *n*. system of freemasons فری میسن نظام instinctive sympathy فطری ہمدردی **freethinker** *n*. rationalist who does not accept traditional religious teaching دہریہ، آزاد خیال، لامذہب *free thought*, this creed دہریت عقلیت پسندی **free way** *n*. (see *Addenda*) **free will** *n*. power of directing one's efforts independently of one's fate اختیار **free wheel** *n*. driving-wheel of bicycle which moves even when the pedals do not فری ویل، کھلا پہیہ

freeze (freez) *v. t.* & *i.* (*freeze*, *froze*, *frozen*) turn from fluid to solid منجمد ہونا یا کرنا turn into ice برف بن جانا یا کرنا *be freezing*, be very cold سخت ٹھنڈا ہونا *freeze one's blood*, terrorize ڈرانا، خوفزدہ کرنا، دہشت زدہ کرنا order that (someone's assets, etc.) may not be turned into cash for some specified time or permanently رقم نکلوانے کا حکم بند سرمایہ منجمد کر دینا (see *Addenda*) **freezing point** *n*. temperature (of a liquid, esp. water) at which it freezes درجۂ انجماد، نقطۂ انجماد

freight (frayt) *n*. charges for the transport of goods کرایہ، بھاڑا the goods transported لے جایا ہوا مال *v. t.* load (ship) with cargo جہاز میں مال بھرنا **freighter** *n*. cargo vessel مال بردار جہاز، مال جہاز (یا لادنا) **freight train** *n*. goods train فریٹر مال گاڑی

French *adj*. of France فرانسیسی the French language فرانسیسی زبان (*the French*), the people of France فرانس والے، فرانسیسی **Frenchman** *n*. a man of French nationality فرانسیسی **French leave** *n*. leave without permission غیر حاضری، بلا اجازت چھٹی *take French leave*, بلا اجازت چھٹی منانا **French window** *n*. glazed folding door شیشے والا دروازہ

frenzy (*fren*-zi) *n*. violent excitement اضطراب ہیجان wild folly پرلے درجے کی حماقت **frenzied** *adj*. filled with frenzy مضطرب

frequent *adj*. (*free*-kwent) happening often اکثر ہونے والا، کثیر الوقوع، اکثر common nume-rous متعدد، کثیر *v. t.* (free-*kwent*) visit (a place) often اکثر جانا، جایا کرنا **frequently** *adv*. often اکثر **frequency** (*free*-kwen-si) *n*. being frequent کثرت rate of occurrence سرعت، تعداد number of (electric or light) waves per second تعداد لہروں کی (فی ثانیہ) تعداد تعدّدِ امواج

fresco (*fres*-koh) *n*. (pl. *frescos*) painting on wall plaster, etc. دیواری نقاشی، نقش دیوار

fresh *adj.* new نیا،تازہ different جُدا،مختلف refreshing (weather, etc.) تازگی بخش not tired تازگی والا،صحت مند healthy (complexion) تازہ دَم *fresh water*, not salty تازہ پانی *fresh air*, clean out-of-doors air تازہ ہوا *fresh food*, not tinned تازہ تازہ ، نیا نیا پکانے کی ، تازہ چیزیں **freshly** *adv.* newly دکھانے ابھی ابھی **freshness** *n.* being fresh تازگی **freshman, fresher** *n.* first year student (کالج کا) فرسٹ ایر کا طالب علم

fret *v. t. & i.* (*-tt-*) irritate چڑانا ، غصّہ دلانا، پریشان کرنا ، دق کرنا worry (*over*) پریشان ہونا be surly جھلّانا ، جھنجلانا bite چبا ڈالنا wear away by rubbing گھسا دینا adorn (wood or ceiling) with carved, cut out (or embossed) work لکڑی کو اندر سے کاٹ کر نقش بنانا ، چوبی کٹائی کرنا **fret-saw** *n.* narrow saw for cutting such designs چوبی کٹائی کا آرہ **fret-work** *n.* such cutting-out of wood چوبی کٹائی **fretful** *adj.* irritable بد مزاج ، جھلّا ، چڑچڑا ❷ discontented غیر مطمئن

friar (*fri*-e*) *n.* a type of monk ایک قسم کا راہب فرائر ، برادر

friction (*frik*-shen) *n.* wasteful rubbing رگڑ، فرک bad feeling caused by opinion کھچاؤ ، اختلاف، کشمکش

Friday (*fri*-di) *n.* the day before Saturday جمعہ آدینہ **Good Friday**, the Friday before Easter گڈ فرائی ڈے ، ایسٹر کا آدینہ

friend (frend) *n.* intimate companion دوست،یار، رفیق sympathizer (*of*) ہمدرد ، معاون *make* (or *keep*) *friends with*, become the friend of سے دوستی کرنا *be friends with*, be friendly with کا دوست ہونا **friendly** (*frend*-li) *adj.* like a friend دوستانہ ، دوستی kind با مُرَوّت not hostile دوستانہ *friendly game*, played for mere sport دوستانہ میچ **friendliness** *n.* friendly feeling دوستی friendly behaviour دوستانہ سلوک **friendship** *n.* being friends دوستی *pen friendship*, friendship merely through correspondence قلمی دوستی *pen friend*, such a friend قلمی دوست ▣ A **friend** is literally a loved one ; a **companion**, a bread-fellow, one known less than a friend ; a **comrade** is literally a room-fellow ; a **chum**, a chambermaid at a university hostel ; a **pal**, gipsy word for a brother ; a **mate**, one who shares the food or meat ; a **colleague**, associate in service or business ; a **confrere**, member of the same profession but not working in the same organization ; an **accomplice**, involved in crime along with another ; an **ally**, one in alliance or league with another in war ; a **confederate**, one bound by the same oath.

frieze (freez) *n.* ornamental band along top of wall آرائشی کنگر

a frieze

frigate (*frig*-ayt) *n.* (old use) cruiser چھوٹا جنگی جہاز fast escorting ship بدرقے کا تیز رو جہاز

fright (frit) *n.* sudden and violent fear سخت خوف *be filled with fright* ڈرنا ، ڈر جانا *give (someone) a fright* ڈرانا ، ڈرا دینا (colloq.) odd-looking (person or thing) مضحکہ خیز **frighten** *v.t.* fill with fright ڈرانا ، درا دینا **frightful** *adj.* horrible خوفناک ، ڈراؤنا (colloq.) unbearable سخت ناقابلِ برداشت (colloq.) unsatisfactory غیر تسلّی بخش **frightfully** *adv.* ہیبتناک انداز سے **frightfulness** *n.* act of frightening دہشتناکی، دہشت زدہ کرنا striking terror into civilian population through military strength فوج کے ذریعے عوام کو دہشت زدہ کر دینا

frig, frige, fridge (frij) *n.* (colloq.) refrigerator ریفریجریٹر ، سَرد خانہ

frigid (*frij*-id) *adj.* very cold بہت ٹھنڈا ، بہت سَرد *the frigid zone*, the polar region منطقہ بارِدہ lacking warmth of feeling سَرد مہر ، سَرد مہرانہ lacking sexual response جنسی طور پر بے حس **frigidity** (fri-*jid*-i-ti) *n.* being frigid ٹھٹھر unfriendliness سَردی ، مہری **frigidly** *adv.* in an unfriendly manner سَرد مہری سے

frill (fril) *n.* ornamental border on a dress سنجاف (usu. *pl.*) affectations (of style) تکلّفی سنجاف مسجّع عبارت **frilled** (frild) *adj.* having frills

fringe (frinj) *n.* ornamental border of loose threads جھالر edge (*of* something) کنارا hair covering the forehead پیشانی کے بال *v. t.* put or be a fringe on جھالر کا کام دینا، جھالر لگانا **fringe benefit** *n.* (see *Addenda*)

frippery (*frip*-e-ri) *n.* tawdry adornment گھٹیا سجاوٹ

frisk (frisk) *v. i.* gambol کودتے پھاندتے جانا **frisky** (*fris*-ki) *adj.* lively چنچل، چلبلا

fritter (*frit*-ĕ*) *v. t.* throw *away* (time, energy, money, etc.) ضائع کرنا ، اُجاڑنا

frivolity *n.* (see under **frivolous**)

frivolous (*friv*-o-lus) *adj.* trifling غیر اہم ، معمولی (person) foolish, lacking in seriousness غیر سنجیدہ بیہودہ ، ہرزہ سرا **frivolity** (fri-*vol*-i-ti), **frivolousness** *n.* being frivolous بیہودگی

fro (froh) *adv.* (used only in the phrase :) *to and fro*, backwards and forwards آگے پیچھے ، اِدھر اُدھر کبھی اِدھر کبھی اُدھر

frock (frok) *n.* woman's gown گاؤن ، فراک child's dress (بچے کا) فراک monk's gown راہب کا چُغہ priestly character پادری ، ملائیت

frock-coat *n.* men's long coat with square corners فراک ، کوٹ
frog (frog) *n.* small tail-less amphibious animal مینڈک ، مینڈکی **frogman** *n.* under water soldier آبدوز سپاہی ، مینڈک جنگ
frolic (*frol*-ik) *v.i.* (*frolicking, frolicked*) gambol اُچھلتے کُودتے *n.* gay party بزم طرب merry-making رنگ رلیا lively play پُرلطف کھیل ، نشاط انگیز تمثیل *adj.* (poet.) mirthful شوخ ، طناز **frolicsome** (*frol*-ik-sum) *adj.* mirthful and sportive دل لگی باز چنچل
from (frum ; at end of clause or emphatic from) *prep.* (it indicates the following :) (starting points) سے (place of origin) کا (distance) دُور (removal or prevention) سے (descent سے کا (comparison) میں *tell one from the other* سے ، کے بعد (cause) سے ، کے باعث (basis) میں غرق کرنا *from experience* تجربے کے بعد
front (frunt) *n.* foremost part اگلا حصّہ ، سامنا ، ماتھا scene of actual fighting in war محاذ ، محاذِ جنگ forehead ماتھا ، پیشانی road bordering river, lake, or sea ساحلی سڑک *in front of* کے سامنے *to the front* آگے ، سامنے *come to the front,* become conspicuous نمایاں ہونا *put on* (*or show*) *a bold front,* pretend to have no fear بہادری دکھانا *change front,* (*a*) face the other way رُخ بدل لینا (*b*) shift one's ground طرزِ عمل بدلنا ، بدل جانا ، طریقِ استدلال بدلنا *adj.* placed آگے والا ، آگے والا ، اگلا کا *v. t. & i.* face کی طرف رُخ ہونا confront سامنا کرنا be opposite to کے بالمقابل ہونا کے مُقابلے پر اُترنا **frontage** *n.* extent of land or building along its front سامنا ، پیش ، سامنے کا حصّہ ، ماتھا **frontal** *adj.* on or to the front آگے ، سامنے of the front سامنے کا ، سامنے والا direct in the front سیدھا ، سامنے کا of the forehead پیشانی کا
frontier (*fron*-ti-ĕ* or *frun*-ti-ĕ*) *n.* part of a country bordering on another سرحد (*pl.*) boundaries سرحدیں
frontispiece (*frun*-tis-pees) *n.* picture facing the title-page of a book کتاب کے شروع کی تصویر ، نقشِ سرِکتاب ، سرِکتاب
frost *n.* weather below freezing-point of water شدید سردی frozen dew or vapour on ground, etc. پالا (colloq.) failure ناکامی ، مایوس کن چیز *v.t.* damage by frost پالے سے جھلسنا cover with frost پالے سے ڈھانپنا cover with some fine powder like frost بُرے چھڑکنا یا بُرکنا chill (food) for preserving it برف کرلینا make (glass) opaque شیشے کو دُودھیا کرنا **frost-bite** *n.* injury to a part of the body from frost پالے سے (عضو) مارا جانا **frostbitten** *adj.* having frost-bite پالے سے مارا ہوا **frosty** (*fros*-ti) *adj.* freezing منجمد covered with frost پالے سے ڈھکا ہُوا cold (manner) سرد ، ٹھرانہ
froth (froth) *n.* foam جھاگ ، کف empty show of wit بک بک ، بکواس ، فضول بات *v. i.* give off froth جھاگ دینا **frothy** *adj.* covered with froth کف آلود of (or like) froth جھاگ کا (سا) having empty rhetoric محض لفاظی پرمشتمل
froward (*froh*-wĕ*d) *adj.* wilful خودسر ، سرکش disobedient نافرمان saucy گستاخ
frown (froun) *n.* scowl تیوری ، کڑی تیور *v.t. & i.* scowl تیوری چڑھانا rebuke by (or upon) ناپسند کرنا present a gloomy aspect (*on*) خطرناک نظر آنا تیوری چڑھانا **frowningly** *adj.* گھورتے ہوئے ، چیں بجبیں ہوکر
froze, *v.,* **frozen** *v.* (pa. t. & pa. p. of **freeze,** which see)
fructify (*fruk*-ti-fī) *v. t. & i.* bear fruit پھلنا ، بار آور ہونا make fruitful باردار کرنا **fructification** *n.* fructifying بار آوری
frugal (*froo*-gĕl) *adj.* thrifty کفایت شعار costing little کم خرچ (of food) cheap and simple سادہ ، کم خرچ **frugally** *adv.* کفایت شعاری سے **frugality** *n.* being thrifty کفایت شعاری sparing use کم استعمال
fruit (froot) *n.* part of a plant containing seed بیج دان this used as food پھل ، میوہ such fruits in general پھل ، میوے outcome (of study or labour) پھل ، ثمرہ profit پھل ، منافع *v. i.* bear fruit پھل کو پھل لگنا **fruiterer** (*froo*-tè-rĕ*) *n.* fruit-seller میوہ فروش **fruitful** *adj.* producing fruit پھلدار ، باراور producing good results نتیجہ خیز ، بارور ہونا **fruitfulness** *n.* being fruitful بارآوری
fruition (*froo*-i-shĕn) *n.* realization (of hopes, etc.) پُورا ہونا ، تکمیل ، حصُول *bring to fruition* پُورا کرنا
fruitless *adj.* without fruit بے ثمر unsuccessful لاحاصل **fruity** (*froo*-ti) *adj.* like fruit in taste or smell پھلوں والا ، میوے والا ، میوہ دار
frustrate (*frus*-trayt) *v.t.* defeat (an attempt) ناکام بنانا disappoint (a person) محروم کرنا ، مایوس کرنا counteract بے اثر کرنا **frustration** (-ay-) *n.* defeat شکست disappointment محرومی ، مایوسی *sense of frustration* مایوسی کا احساس ، احساسِ محرومی
fry (frī) *n.* young fishes مچھلی کے بچے *small fry,* insignificant person غیر اہم لوگ fried meat تلا ہُوا گوشت internal parts of animal eaten fried بھنے ہوئے دل ، گُردے ، کلیجی وغیرہ swarm ہجوم ، بھیڑ *v. t. & i.* (*frying, fried*) cooked in fat, etc. تلنا
frying-pan *n.* pan used for frying فرائی پین ، کڑھائی
fuddle (*fud*-ĕl) *v. t.* make stupid with strong drink مدہوش کرنا

fuel (*few*-el) *n.* شراب سے حواس گم ہونا material for burning ایندھن anything that inflames passions بھڑکانے والی چیز *v.t.* & *i.* (-ll-) supply with fuel ایندھن ڈالنا take in fuel ایندھن لینا

fugitive (*few*-ji-tiv) *n.* & *adj.* (person) running away (from law, etc.) بھگوڑا

fulcrum (*ful*-krum) *n.* support of a lever ٹیک، انصاب

fufil (ful-fil) *v.t.* (-ll-) carry out پورا کرنا، تکمیل کرنا، تعمیل کرنا **fulfilment** *n.* carrying out, fulfilling تکمیل، تعمیل

full (ful) *adj.* filled بھرا ہوا *be full of*, feel strongly خوب (جوش وغیرہ) ہونا complete پورا *full moon*, with a complete disc چودھویں کا چاند *full dress*, complete dress worn on occasions تقریبات والا لباس *at full speed*, at its highest پوری رفتار سے *full tide*, high tide پورا جوار بھاٹا *in full*, with all details مفصل *to the full*, to the limit آخری حد تک *full age*, maturity سِنّ بلوغ *full brother* (or *sister*), son (or daughter) of both of one's parents سگا بھائی (یا بہن) *full-blooded*, (*a*) of pure descent نسلی (*b*) vigorous زوردار *full-mouthed*, sonorous گرجدار *be in full swing*, be going on vigorously زوروں پر ہونا، پورے زور سے جاری ہونا *full back*, (football) player placed behind فل بیک، پورا پیچھے *full stop*, period marked as (.) کامل وقفہ، فل سٹاپ *adv.* completely مکمل، پوری طرح *full many a*, very many, کئی، متعدد *full well*, completely پوری طرح *full grown*, grown full length پورا جوان *full-blown*, (of flowers) quite open پوری طرح کھلا ہوا **fully** *adv.* exactly, completely پوری طرح **fulness, fullness** *n.* being full پورا ہونا

fuller (*ful*-ĕ*) *n.* who cleans and thickens freshly woven cloth کارخانے کا نیا کپڑا دھونے والا *fuller's earth*, clay used by fullers رایہ

fully (see under **full**)

fulminate (*ful*-mi-nayt) *v. t.* & *i.* speak with angry threats (*against*) سخت سست کہنا، کوسنا cause to explode آگ لگانا، بھڑکانا

fulness *n.* (see under **full**) نازیبا، تکلیف دہ حد تک

fulsome *adj.* cloying (praise, etc.) نازیبا، تکلیف دہ حد تک

fumble (*fum*-bĕl) *v.t.* & *i.* handle awkwardly اناڑی پن سے کرنا یا پکڑنا grope about (*at* lock, *with* key, *for* keyhole) ٹٹولنا

fume (fewm) *n.* odorous smoke or vapour دھونی بخارات fit of anger طیش، غصّہ *in a fume* طیش میں *v.t.* & *i.* give off fumes دھواں اٹھنا be angry سے جلنا، کڑھنا signs of discontent (*at*) غصّے ہونا darken the surface with fumes دھوئیں سے کالا کرنا

fumigate (*few*-mi-gayt) *v.t.* disinfect by means of fumes دھونی دینا

fumigation (-gay-) *n.* دھونی دینا، تدخین

fun (fun) *n.* mirth دل لگی amusement تفریح *be great fun*, بڑی اچھی تفریح ہونا jest ہنسی مذاق *in fun*, not seriously یونہی ہنسی سے *make fun of*, *poke fun at*, ridicule مذاق کرنا، چھیڑنا **funny** (*fun*-i) *adj.* droll مضحکہ خیز perplexing *It's funny that* عجیب بات ہے کہ *Don't try to be funny*; (said when snubbing someone for a joke we may not relish as being too pointed or pointless) مسخرے بننے کی کوشش مت کرو **funnily** *adv.* strangely عجیب بات ہے کہ in a funny way مضحکہ خیز انداز سے **funniment** *n.* (jocular) drollery مضحکہ خیزی

function (*funk*-shĕn) *n.* special activity (*of*) فرضِ منصبی، مقصد، وظیفہ public ceremony تقریب *v.i.* fulfil a function فرض ادا کرنا، وظیفہ سرانجام دینا *function as*, do the duty of کی حیثیت سے کام کرنا **functionary** *n.* official اہلکار **functional** *adj.* pertaining to a function فرائض سے متعلق affecting something's function کی کارگزاری پر اثر ڈالنے والا

fund (fund) *n.* (also *pl.*) money set apart (*for* a purpose) مالی وسائل، فنڈ *local fund*, fund of local bodies بلدیاتی فنڈ *relief fand*, money for providing relief امدادی فنڈ store (*of* commonsense, etc.) ذخیرہ، خزانہ

fundamental (fund-a-*men*-tĕl) *adj.* basic بنیادی very important اہم *n. pl.* fundamental principles بنیادی اصول، اصول *fundamentals of faith*, اصول دین essential part بنیادی حصّہ **fundamentally** *adv.* basically بنیادی طور پر

funeral (*feun*-ĕ-rĕl) *n.* burial, etc., of a dead person تجہیز و تکفین funeral procession جنازہ

funereal (few-*nee*-ri-ĕl) *adj.* of or like a funeral جنازے کا سا، تجہیز و تکفین کے متعلق gloomy ماتمی

fungus (*fung*-us) (pl. *fungi* or *fungues*) spongy plant of various kinds, all leaves سماروغ **fungicide** *n.* fungus-destroying substance سماروغ مار

funk (funk) *n.* (colloq.) panic ہراس great fear سخت خوف (*be*) *in a funk* سخت ہراساں ہونا *blue funk*, (slang) acute fear سخت خوف (ہونا) coward بزدل *v. t.* & *i.* show fear ڈرنا، گھبرا جانا، ہراساں ہونا shirk سے بچنے کی کوشش کرنا

funnel (*fun*-el) *n.* wide-mouthed conical vessel with a tube at the small end for pouring liquids قیف outlet for smoke from engine of ship, train, etc. دودکش

funnel for liquid (left) and of ship (right)

funny *adj.* (see under **fun**)

fur (fĕ*) *n.* soft thick hair of certain animals پشم animal skin with the fur on it, used

as human clothing پوستین rough coating on ailing person's tongue زبان کے خار یا کانٹے coating inside vessel by hard water پانی کے داغ **furred** (fĕ*d) *adj*. covered with fur پشم دار **furry** (*fĕ*-ri) *adj*. of or like fur پشم کا (سا)
furbish (*fĕ**-bish) *v.t.* polish (something *up*) چمکانا
furious *adj*. (see under **fury**)
furl (fĕ*l) *v.t.* & *i*. roll up (flag, umbrella, etc.) لپیٹنا
furlough (*fĕ**-loh) *n*. leave of long absence from duty (used in this country esp. for that of foreigners going home) فرلو ، لمبی چھٹی ، طویل رخصت *go home on furlough* طویل رخصت پر عازم وطن ہونا
furnace (*fĕ**-nis) *n*. closed fireplace for central heating through water گرمابہ apparatus for heating metals بھٹی *tried in the furnace*, severely tested پوری طرح آزمایا ہوا hot place گرم جگہ، آتشناک مقام
furnish (*fè**-nish) *v.t.* supply (*with*) مہیا کرنا put furniture in سازوسامان سے آراستہ کرنا ، فرنیچر لگانا **furniture** (*fĕ**-ni-chĕ*) *n*. movable articles in house (for decoration rather than use in this country) or for office فرنیچر ، کرسی میز **furnishings** *n. pl.* fittings سازوسامان ، ساز و یراق
furniture *n*. (see under **furnish**)
furor (*few* ro*) *n*. craze for something خبط جنون enthusiasm (of poets, prophets, etc.) جذبہ جوش wild popular excitement ولولہ ، جوش
furore (few-*ro*-ray) enthusiastic popular excitement عوام کا پرجوش شوق *make a furore*, excite this admiration لوگوں میں کسی سے کا جوش پیدا کرنا craze for something خبط ، جنون
furrow (*f ĕ**-roh) *n*. long cut made by plough لیک ، لکیر ، بانہن ، ہلائی wrinkle (on the forehead) پیشانی کی لکیر *v.t.* make furrows in لیک ڈالنا
further (*fĕ**-thĕ*) *adv*. more distant دور آگے in addition کے علاوہ *adj*. beyond سے آگے additional فالتو *v.t.* push forward ترقی دینا ، بڑھانا **furthest** *adj*. & *adv*. most distant سب سے زیادہ دور **furthermore** *adv*. moreover علاوہ ازیں **furthermost** *adj*. furthest دور ترین
furtive (*fĕ**-tiv) *adj*. secret خفیہ stealthy دزدیدہ sly شرارت بھری (person) wishing to escape notice despite his noticeable action چوری چھپے کرنے والا ، کنی کترانے والا **furtively** *adv*. stealthily چوری چھپے **furtiveness** *n*. being furtive چوری چھپے کوئی کام کرنا
fury (*few*-ri) *n*. wild rage طیش ، غیظ *be in a fury about* طیش میں آنا fierceness (of storm, etc.) تیزی ، تندی ، سختی outburst of wild feeling جذبہ violently furious woman لڑاکا عورت ، کینہ پرور عورت **Furies** (*few*-reez) *Cl. myth*. (*the Furies*), the three goddesses of vengeance *Alecto, Megaera, Tisiphone* انتقام کی دیویاں
fuse (fewz) *v.t.* & *i*. melt پگھلنا یا پگھلانا blend into a whole by melting ایک ہونا (of an electric circuit) be broken through melting of the fuse فیوز ہونا *n*. (in an electric circuit) a thin, short electric wire which melts breaking the circuit when there is a fault فیوز cord carrying spark to explode gunpowder فتیلہ ، فلیتہ ، شتابہ
fuselage (*fewz*-è-lej) *n*. body of aircraft ہوائی جہاز کا ڈھانچہ
fusion (*few*-zhĕn) *n*. uniting (of metals or human races) into one by melting or mixing together یکجا کر ملانا ، ایک کرنا
fuss (fus) *n*. flurry بھگدڑ ، افراتفری ، ہل چل ، ہنگامہ *Don't make a fuss* کیا ہنگامہ مچا رکھا ہے treatment of trifles as important خواہ مخواہ کی اہمیت دینا *make a fuss about* (*something*) کو خواہ مخواہ کی اہمیت دینا *v.t.* & *i*. افراتفری مچانا worry خواہ مخواہ پریشان ہونا make nervous ناحق پریشان **fussy** *adj*. nervously excited پریشان worrying about trifles بے تکی شور مچانے والا
fustian (fus-ti-ĕn) *n*. a kind of coarse cloth high sounding but empty style (talk or writing نری لفاظی *adj*. made of fustian worthless خالی باتیں
fusty (*fus*-ti) *adj*. stale باسی mouldy پھپھوندی والا
futile (*few*-til) *adj*. useless بیکار ، فضول worthless ناکارہ ineffective بے اثر ، بے نتیجہ **futilely** *adv*. uselessly فضول **futility** (few-*til*-i-ti) *n*. uselessness فضول ہونا ، بے اثر ہونا
future (*few*-chĕ*) *n*. time yet to come مستقبل ، آئندہ استقبال *for the future, in future*, from this time onwards آئندہ *adj*. yet to happen آئندہ ، ہونے والا ، مستقبل کا مستقبل **futurity** (few-*tew*-ri-ti) *n*. future time مستقبل future event or conditions آئندہ کا واقعہ ، مستقبل کے حالات
fuzzy (*fuz*-i) *adj*. blurred (in outline) مبہم ، غیر واضح

G

g, G (jee) (pl. *g's*, or **gs**) seventh letter of the English alphabet which has the hard sound of گ except before *e* or *i* when, like *c*, it has a soft sound جی، گ، ج a musical note سرگم کا ایک سُر جی
gab *v.i.* talk idly بک بک کرنا
gabble (*gab*-ĕl) *v.t.* & *i.* speak quickly and indistinctly بک بک کرنا، چرچڑ کرنا *n.* such talk بک بک، چرچر
gaberdine, gabardine (*gab*-ĕ*-deen) *n.* serge-like buff cloth (usu. woollen) گیبرڈین material for raincoats برساتی کا کپڑا
gable (*gay*-bĕl) upper part of a wall between sloping roofs دو رخی ڈھلواں چھت والی دیوار کی بالائی تکون
a gable
gad *v.i.* (-dd-) *go* (*about*) idly in search of pleasure ادھر اُدھر پھرنا، سَرگشت کرنا
gadabout *n.* such idle rambler آوارہ گرد، ہرزہ گرد، خدائی خوار
gad-fly (*gad*-flı) *n.* fly which stings cattle, etc. بڑ مکھی، کُھنو مکھی
gadget (*gaj*-et) *n.* contraption; any small useful contrivance کوئی چھوٹا سا مُفید آلہ
gaffe (gaf) *n.* blunder سخت غلطی، فاش غلطی، فاحش غلطی
gag *n.* something put in or over someone's mouth to prevent him from speaking ڈھاٹا، مُنہ بند کرنے والا کپڑا (وغیرہ) any order having this effect زبان بندی، حکمِ زبان بندی carefully planned comic business in stage or screen play ڈرامے میں ہنسی کا ٹکڑا *v.t.* & *i.* (-gg-) put a gag in or over the mouth of مُنہ میں کپڑا ٹھونسنا ban the expression of views by someone زبان بندی کرنا **gag-man** *n.* professional devisor of gags in plays ڈراموں میں ہنسی کے ٹکڑے لانے والا، مضحک نگار **gagster** *n.* (see *Addenda*)
Gaelic (*gay*-lik) *n.* Scottish language گیلک (زبان)
gaga (*gag*-a) *adj.* (slang) senile سٹھیایا ہوا، ہَبنق
gagster *n.* (see *Addenda*)
gaiety *n.*; **gaily** *adv.* (see under **gay**)
gain (gayn) *v.t.* & *i.* get (something desirable) پانا، حاصل کرنا *gain the upper hand, gain victory over* پر فتح پانا *gain supporters* حامی بنانا *gain time*, obtain delay by pretext مُہلت پانا *gain the ear of*, get a favourable hearing by کسی کو بات سُنا سکنا be improved (in strength, etc.) بہتر ہونا *gain weight*, become fat موٹا ہونا arrive at پہنچنا *gain on*, (or *upon*); overtake, get nearer to جالینا، کے قریب آنا *n.* profit نفع anything gained (*in*) فائدہ **gainer** *n.* one who gains فائدہ اُٹھانے والا **gainings** *n. pl.*, (trade) profits منافع **gainful** *adj.* paying, profitable سُود مند، مَنفعت بخش
gainsay (gain-*say*) *v.t.* (*gainsaid*) (lit.) deny (something) سے انکار کرنا
gait (gayt) *n.* manner of walking چال، چال ڈھال
gaiter (*gay*-tĕ*) *n.* (usu. *pl.*) leg-covering from ankle to knee گیٹس
gala (*gay*-la, *gah*-la) *n.* occasion of public merry-making جشن *gala night*, night (at cinema) with special features جشن کی رات
galatea (gal-a-*tee*-a) *n.* superior, striped cotton cloth used as dress material فراکوں کا دھاری دار سوتی کپڑا، گلیٹیا
galaxy (*gal*-ak-si) *n.* the Milky Way کہکشاں brilliant group (*of*) شاندار مجمع
gale (gayl) *n.* strong wind سخت آندھی، جھکڑ
gall (gawl) *n.* bile پت، صفراء anything that causes bitter feelings دُکھ *gall and wormwood* (*to*), very bitter or annoying (for) بہُت تلخ، سخت تکلیف rancour تلخی، کشیدگی place rubbed bare جہاں رگڑ رگڑ کر زخم آجائے *v.t.* & *i.* injure by rubbing رگڑ رگڑ کر زخم کردینا annoy دق کرنا، سخت تنگ کرنا
galling *adj.* annoying سخت تکلیف دہ **gall-bladder** *n.* part of body containing gall پتّہ، زہرہ **gall-stone** *n.* stone in gall bladder پتّے کی پتھری، سنگِ مثانہ
gallant *adj.* (*gal*-ant) brave بہادُر، دلیر، شجاع stately شاندار *n.* (ga-*lant*, or *gal*-ant) fashionable young man attentive to (lovely) women حُسن پرست، عاشق مزاج، دِل پھینک **gallantry** (*gal*-ant-ri) *n.* bravery بہادُری، دلیری polite attention to (lovely) women حُسن پرستی
galleon (*gal*-e-on) *n.* an old type of Spanish sailing ship قدیم ہسپانوی جہاز
a galleon
gallery (*gal*-e-ri) *n.* art salon تصویر خانہ highest seats (costliest in a cinema but cheapest in a theatre) گیلری audience there گیلری نشین *play to the gallery*, appeal to vulgar taste تعریف کرانے کے لیے پست مذاق پر اُتر آنا corridor covered or partly open at one side برآمدہ، گیلری، غلام گردش

galley (*gal*-i) very old type of rowing ship with a crew of usu. slaves or criminals گیلی، پچھوَن *galley-slaves*, slaves rowing these گیلی چلانے والا جہاز والے غلام (modern) ship's kitchen جہاز کا باورچی خانہ، آجکل جہاز کا باورچی خانہ printer's oblong frame for holding column of composed type گیلی *galley-proof*, proof snatched from such galley گیلی پروف

gallon (*gal*-un) *n.* liquid measure of 8 pints گیلن، تقریباً پانچ سیر

gallop (*gal*-up) *n.* fastest pace (of horse) with all four feet off the ground at each stride پوئیہ سرپٹ *v.t.* & *i.* ride at this pace (cause to) go at a gallop سرپٹ دوڑنا یا دوڑانا hurry (*through* work, etc.) جلدی جلدی (کام) ختم کرنا

gallows (*gal*-ohz) *n. pl.* (used as *sing.*) wooden framework for hanging criminals پھانسی، پھانسی کا پھٹکا **gallows-bird** *n.* one fit to be hanged پھانسی کا مستحق، پھانسی پانے والا

galoot (ga-*loot*) *n.* (colloq.) clumsy lout اُلّو، گھامڑ، گنوار، اُجڈ

galore (ga-*loh**) *adv.* (things, etc.) in plenty بہُت *milk galore* دودھ ہی دودھ، بہُت دودھ

galosh (ga-*losh*) **golosh** (go-*losh*) *n.* rubber over-shoe برساتی بوٹ

galvanic *adj.*, **galvanism** *n.* (see under **galvanize**)

galvanize (*gal*-va-niz) *v. t.* coat (iron sheet, etc. *with* zinc, etc.) by galvanism طرح دینا *galvanized iron* ٹین، جستی چادر rouse (someone *into doing* something) اُبھارنا، ہمت دلانا **galvanism** (-nizm) *n.* electricity produced by chemical action طرح its medical use طرح کا طبّی استعمال **galvanic** (-*van*-) *adj.* of galvanism طرح شدہ، طرحی

Gamma rays *n.* X-rays of short wave-length چھوٹی ایکس ریز، گاما شعاعیں، اشعۂ جیم

gamble (*gam*-bĕl) *v. t.* & *i.* play games of chance for money جُوا کھیلنا، قمار بازی کرنا take -risk for chance of winning جُوا کھیلنا، جوکھوں میں پڑنا *n.* game of chance played for money جُوا، جوئے بازی، قمار بازی risky undertaking with chance of profit جُوا، قسمت آزمائی **gambler** *n.* one who gambles جواری، جوئے باز، قمار باز، مُقامِر **gambling** *n.* playing a game of chance for money جُوا، جوئے بازی، قمار بازی

gambol (*gam*-bĕl) *v. i.* (-ll-) frisk اُچھلتے کودتے پھرنا، اُچھلنا کودنا، کِلکِلیں کرنا *n.* (usu. *pl.*) such movements اُچھل کُود، کِلیلیں

game (gaym) *n.* playful contest (*e. g.*, hockey) کھیل *play the game*, be honest ; act according to the rules in a contest, etc. دیانتداری سے کام لینا sport ورزشی مقابلہ، کھیل *the Olympic Games*, international sports, etc., held every four years after the ancient Greek style اولمپک کھیل، اولمپیائی کھیل points, etc., for winning بازی trick چال، داؤ *have a game with (someone)*, play a trick on (him) سے چال چلنا fun ہنسی، دل لگی، مذاق *make game of someone*, ridicule him کا مذاق اُڑانا، کو بنانا plan تدبیر، منصوبہ *the game is up*, the plan has failed اُلٹی ہوگئیں سب تدبیریں، منصوبہ خاک میں مل گیا (as *collective n.*) birds, animals, etc., hunted for sport and food شکار *big game*, elephants, lions, tigers, etc. بڑا شکار flesh of such animals, etc. شکار کا گوشت *adj.* ready to go on fighting آخر دم تک لڑتے رہنے والا plucky ; with energy (*for* or *to do* something) پُرعزم، باعزیمت (of limbs) crippled ناکارہ، لنجا، لنگڑا *v.t.* & *i.* gamble جُوا کھیلنا **gamester** *n.* gambler جوئے باز، جواری **gamekeeper** *n.* one employed to breed and protect animals for hunting میر شکار **game laws** *n. pl.* laws pertaining to the hunting of animals and selling of their flesh شکار کے قوانین ■ A **game** is an amusement with regular rules in which two teams participate ; **sport,** one of the organized athletic amusements, **pastime,** anything done by a person alone or in company to while away the time ; **diversion,** change from routine work ; **hobby,** one's usual favourite work done after working hours ; **avocation,** one's second-choice profession, usu. done without other reward than the mere satisfaction derived from doing it.

gamut *n.* whole range of musical notes سرگم، دائرۂ کار، پورا سرگم whole range (*of* anything) احاطہ، حلقۂ اثر

gander (*gan*-dĕ*) *n.* male goose ہنس fool بیوقوف، سادہ لوح

gang *n.* group of labourers, etc., working together (مزدوروں کی) ٹولی، کا دستہ

gangster (*gang*-stĕ*) *n.* (esp. U. S.) member of a criminal gang مجرم، ڈاکو، ڈکیت، جرائم پیشہ **gangsterism** *n.* acting like gangsters جرائم پیشی، غنڈہ گردی

gangrene (*gang*-reen) *n.* decomposition of part of body جسم کا گلنا، فسادِ تشنّج **gangrenous** (*gang*-re-nus) *adj.* decomposing (part of body) سڑا ہوا

gangway (*gang*-way) *n.* opening in ship's side جہاز کا پھاٹک movable bridge from deck to the land جہاز کا پل passage between rows of seats نشستوں کے درمیان راستہ aisle گزرگاہ

Ganymede (*gan*-i-meed) *Cl. myth.* exquisitely beautiful lad carried off from Mt. Ida by the eagle of Zeus to be the cupbearer of the gods and the chief deity's minion گنی میڈ

gaol, jail, (jayl) *n.* prison جیل، قید خانہ، بندی خانہ، محبس *v. i.* imprison قید کرنا، جیل بھیجنا **gaol-bird, jail-bird** *n.* habitual criminal عادی مجرم **gaoler,**

jailer, jailor *n.* one in charge of a gaol داروغہ جیل

gap *n.* breach شگاف دراڑ blank خلا unfilled interval وقفہ wide separation (of ideas, etc.) فرق ، تباین

gapa *n.* (see *Addenda*)

gape (*gayp*) *v.t.* open the mouth wide منہ پھاڑنا stare thus in surprise (*at* something) منہ پھاڑ کر دیکھنا yawn جماہی لینا *n.* yawn جماہی

garage (*ga*-rij, ga-*rahzh*) *n.* place for storage of motor vehicles گیراج ، موٹرخانہ place for repairs to them موٹروں کی مرمت گاہ ، گیراج

garb (gah*b) *n.* dress لباس ، پوشاک distinctive dress (کسی گروہ کا) مخصوص لباس style of dress پہناوا *v. t.* dress (*in* or *as*) ملبوس کرنا

garbage (*gah**-bij) *n.* rubbish کوڑا کرکٹ waste food سڑی بسی چیز ، آخور

garble (*gah**-bĕl) *v. t.* select (facts, etc.) unfairly in order to create a false impression تحریف کرنا ، بدنیتی سے اقتباس کرنا *garbled version of a statement, etc.* تحریف والا بیان

garden (*gah**-dĕn) *n.* (usu. *pl.*) public park باغ ، چمن ، گلستان ، گلزار any piece of ground devoted to growing flowers باغ ، باغیچہ *v.t* cultivate a garden باغ لگانا work in a garden باغبانی کرنا **gardening** *n.* working in a garden باغبانی **gardener** *n.* one employed to look after a garden مالی ، باغبان

gargle (*gah**-gĕl) *v. t.* & *i.* gurgle liquid in the throat غرغرہ کرنا *n.* medicinal mouthwash غرغرے کی دوا

gargoyle (*gah**-goil), **gurgoyle** (*gĕ**-goil) *n.* spout carved as a grotesque human or animal figure منہ کی شکل کا پرنالہ gargoyle

garish (*gay*-rish) *adj.* too bright خیرہ کن tawdry : over-decorated زرق برق ، بھڑک

garland (*gah**-land) *n.* circle of flowers or leaves used for decoration ہار ، گجرا *v. t.* decorate with a garland ہار پہنانا

garlic (*gah**-lik) *n.* onion-like plant whose bulb is used in cooking لہسن

garment (*gah**-ment) *n.* any article of clothing کپڑا ، لباس

garner (*gah**-nĕ*) *v.t.* store (grain, etc.) ذخیرہ کرنا *n.* granary کوٹھا ، ذخیرہ **garnish** *v. t.* adorn (food *with* something) for the table (اوپر) جمانا ، سجانا

garret (*ga*-ret) *n.* topmost room under the inclined roof of a house بالاخانہ

garrison (*ga*-ri-sun) *n.* troops stationed in a town or fort to defend it محافظ فوج *v. t.* supply with a garrison محافظ فوج بھیجنا

garrulous (*ga*-rew-lus) *adj.* talkative ; fond of talking about unimportant matters بکواسی ، باتونی ، بھڑ بھڑیا **garrulity** (ga-*rul*-i-ti) *n.* talkativeness باتونی پن

garter (*gah**-tĕ*) *n.* band worn round the leg to keep socks or stockings in place گیٹس

gas *n.* (*pl. gases*) an air like vapour گیس (esp.) coal-gas (as used for cooking, etc. in Britain) کوئلے کی گیس ، زغالی گیس ، گیس (also *laughing-gas*), gas used by dentists as an anaesthetic بے حس کرنے والی گیس poisonous gas زہریلی گیس *gas war*, war in which poisonous gas is used as a weapon زہریلی گیس کی لڑائی ، گیس کی جنگ (colloq., U.S.) gasolene پٹرول *v. t.* & *i.* (-ss-) emit poisonous gas زہریلی گیس چھینکنا poison by gas گیس کے زہر سے تمام کرنا (slang) talk for a long time emptily and boastfully بڑیں ہانکنا ، دون کی لینا ، شیخیاں بگھارتے پھرنا **gas-bag** *n.* (colloq.) talkative person بڑبولا **gas-light** *n.* light produced by burning gas گیس کی روشنی **gaseous** (*gas*-i-us) *adj.* of (or like) gas گیس کا (سا) ، گیس دار **gasification** *n.* underground production of gas from coal معدنی گیس بنانا یا بننا **gasometer** (ga-*som*-e-tĕ*) *n.* reservoir in which gas is stored for distribution گیس دان **gassy**, (*gas*-i) *adj.* of (or like) gas گیس دار ، گیس کا (سا) wordy زبانی جمع خرچ لفاظی والا empty talk **gassiness** *n.* بڑی لفاظی

gash *n.* long deep wound کاری زخم ، لمبا اور گہرا گھاؤ *v.t.* make a gash in گہرا زخم لگانا

gasolene (*gas*-o-leen) *n.* (U.S.) petrol پٹرول

gasp *v. t.* & *i.* pant for breath سانس پھول جانا ، ہانپنا *n.* catching of the breath through pain, surprise, etc. ہچکیاں *(at) (one's) last gasp*, (*a*) (at) the point of death دم واپسیں (*b*) tired out تھک کر چور

gastric (*gas*-trik) *adj.* of stomach معدے کا ، معدی *gastric juice* معدی ترشہ

gate (gayt) *n.* barred opening in a wall پھاٹک number of spectators at a match تماشائی total money paid by them ٹکٹ کی کل آمدنی **gateway** *n.* way closed by gate راستہ ، گزرگاہ **gate-money** *n.* total receipts of tickets sold out for a show ٹکٹ کی کل آمدنی **gate-crash** *v.i.* enter daringly without permission بلا اجازت گھس آنا ، دھڑلے سے چلے آنا attend a party without invitation ناخواندہ مہمان بننا **gate-crasher** *n.* unwanted guest ناخواندہ مہمان

gather (*gadh*-ĕ*) *v. t.* & *i.* get, come, or bring together اکٹھا ہونا یا کرنا ، جمع ہونا یا کرنا conclude (*from*) خیال کرنا ، سمجھنا ، نتیجہ اخذ کرنا *I gather he was in a hurry,* مجھے یوں لگتا ہے ، جیسے وہ بڑی جلدی میں تھا

knit (the brows) (بھنویں) تننا draw together (cloth) into small folds چنٹنا (of an abscess) form pus پکنا ، پیپ پڑنا **gathering** *n.* meeting اجتماع

gaudy (*gawd*-i) *adj.* showy, overbright and over-decorative بھڑکیلا ، زرق برق **gaudily** *adv.* in a gaudy style بھڑکیلے انداز سے

gauge (gayj) *n.* standard measure پیمانہ ، ناپ *take the gauge of*, estimate کا اندازہ کرنا distance between rails of a rail track ریل کی پٹڑی کی چوڑائی thickness (of metallic things) موٹائی instrument for measuring metallic things or rain or wind پیمانہ *v. t.* measure accurately ناپنا estimate جانچنا ، کا اندازہ کرنا *gauge public opinion (on some issue)*, (کسی مسئلے پر) رائے عامہ کا اندازہ کرنا

gaunt (gawnt) *adj.* lean پتلا ، دُبلا ، نحیف ، نزار

gauntlet (*gaunt*-let) *n.* (old use) armoured glove formerly worn by soldiers فولادی دستانہ *throw down* (or *fling*) *the gauntlet*, challenge چیلنج دینا ، دعوتِ مبارزت دینا *take* (or *pick*) *up the gauntlet*, accept the challenge چیلنج قبول کرنا *run the gauntlet*, be forced to pass between two rows of men who strike one with sticks as punishment لاٹھیاں مارنے والوں کی دو رویہ صف میں سے گزرنا long glove (for wicketkeeping, etc.) لمبا دستانہ

a pair of gauntlets

gauze (gawz) *n.* thin, transparent netlike material جالی ، گاج *wire-gauze* لوہے کی جالی

gave (gayv) *v.* (pa. t. of **give,** which see)

gawky (*gawk*-i) *adj.* clumsy بے تُکا ، بے ڈھنگا bashful جھینپو

gay *adj.* cheerful خوش باش ، خوشی والا full of fun ہنس مکھ ، زندہ دل **gaily** *adv.* cheerfully خوشی سے ، خوشی خوشی **gaiety** (gay-è-ti) *n.* cheerfulness خوشی ، شادمانی (*pl.*) merry making رنگ رلیاں

gaze (gayz) *n.* long and steady look (*at*) گھورنا *v.i.* look steadily and earnestly ٹکٹکی باندھ کر دیکھنا

gazebo (ga-*zee*-boh) *n.* (pl. *gazebos*) balcony, etc., for gazing جھروکا ، جھروکہ

gazelle (ga-*zel*) *n.* small and graceful antelope غزال

gazette (ga-*zet*) *n.* official periodical with government notification گزٹ any newspaper اخبار *v.t.* notify in a gazette گزٹ میں شائع کرنا ، گزٹ کرنا

gazetted *adj.* that is notified in the gazette *gazetted officer*, member of one of the non-subordinate cadres of government officials whose appointments, etc., are gazetted گزیٹڈ افسر **gazetteer** (ga-ze-*tee*-ě*) *n.* geographical dictionary جغرافیائی فرہنگ ، معجم البلدان ، گزیٹیئر

gear (*gee*-ě*) *n.* particular equipment سازوسامان set of toothed wheels connecting parts of a machine دندانے دار چکر ، گیئر ، دندانے *in gear*, with gear wheels connected with the engine چالو *out of gear*, with these wheels disconnected *high* (or *low*) *gear*, gear causing high (or low) speed تیز (یا مدھم) گیئر *v. t.* & *i.* put in gear چالو کرنا *gear up*, (*a*) put into high gear گیئر تیز کرنا (*b*) put into good working order خوب رواں کرنا ، ٹھیک کرنا *gear down*, put into low gear گیئر مدھم کرنا

gecko (*gek*-oh) *n.* (pl. *geckos*) tropical house-lizard چھپکلی

geese (gees) *n.* (pl. of **goose,** which see)

gelatin, gelatine (*jel*-a-teen) *n.* jelly made from bones چیپ دار مادہ ، جلاٹین

gem (jem) *n.* precious stone قیمتی پتھر ، گوہر (ج : جواہر) jewel, etc., cut and polished ترشا ہوا گوہر beautiful and invaluable thing خوب صورت اور انمول شے

gendarme (*zhond*-ah*m) *n.* (French) armed policeman (فرانسیسی فوج کا) مسلح سپاہی **gendarmerie** *n.* (-è-ree) (French) armed police force مسلح پولیس

gender (*jen*-dě*) *n.* class (of nouns and pronouns) according to sex جنس ، تذکیر و تانیث *masculine gender* مذکر *feminine gender* مؤنث *neuter gender* جنسِ مشترک

gene (jeen) *n.* element of germ-cells supposedly transmitting hereditary characteristics from parent to offspring جنیے میں توارثی عنصر ، توارثی نطفہ ، جین

genealogy (jee-ne-*al*-o-ji) *n.* family سلسلۂ نسب diagram (called *family tree*) illustrating this شجرہ ، شجرۂ نسب **genealogist** *n.* expert tracing family descent ماہرِ انساب **genealogical** (jee-ne-a-*loj*-i-kěl) *adj.* relating to family descent نسبی ، نسب سے متعلق

genera *n.* (pl. of **genus,** which see)

general (*jen*-è-rěl) *adj.* concerning most عمومی ، عام *a General Election*, *general elections*, countrywide parliamentary elections انتخاباتِ عمومی ، عام انتخابات *general knowledge*, knowledge of various subjects واقفیتِ عامہ ، عام معلومات *in general*, *as a general rule*, ordinarily عام طور پر ، عموماً not special عام *general practitioner*, a doctor who is not a specialist معالجِ امراضِ عامہ *general merchant*, *general dealer*, dealer in various kinds of things بساطی ، جنرل مرچنٹ in broad outline ہلکا سا ، کچھ *a general idea of* کا ہلکا سا تصور (joined to an official title with a hyphen) chief اعلیٰ *Postmaster-General*, (abb. *P.M.G.*) پوسٹ ماسٹر جنرل ، صاحبُ البرید *Inspector-General of Police*, (abb. *I. G.*) پولیس کا نگرانِ اعلیٰ ، (آئی - جی)

n. army officer with highest rank (below field-marshal) جرنیل، سپہ سالار، قائد **generalissimo** (jen-e-ra-*lis*-i-moh) *n.* (pl. *generalissimos*), supreme commander of a country's armed forces or of various countries' combined armies سالارِ اعلیٰ، قائدِ اعلیٰ

generality (jen-è-*ral*-i-ti) *n.* general statement عام بات general rule قاعدۂ کلیّہ quality of being general عمومیّت **generalize** (*jen*-è-ra-liz) *v. t. & i.* draw a general conclusion (*from*) (مخصوص واقعات سے) عمومی نتائج اخذ کرنا، کلّی بنانا، عام اصول قرار دے لینا make a sweeping statement سبھی کو لپیٹ میں لے لینا bring into general use رائج کرنا، ترویج دینا، عمومی رواج دینا **generalization** (-*zay*-) *n.* generalizing کلیہ، قاعدۂ کلّی generalized statement تعمیم

generally (*jen*-e-ra-li) *adv.* usually عموماً، بالعموم in a general sense عام طور پر *generally speaking,* in general عام طور پر

generate (*jen*-è-rayt) *v.t.* make بنانا produce پیدا کرنا *generate electricity,* برق پیدا کرنا **generation** (jenè-*ray*-shěn) generating پیدا کرنا، پیدائش، تخلیق single stage in family descent نسل، پیڑھی all persons living during the same period نسل *the rising generation* نئی پود، نوزاد نسل، پود، نوزاد about 30 years' period in which children are ready to replace parents نسل **generator** *n.* (esp). machine for generating electricity برق آفریں

generic (*jen*-è-rik) *adj.* common to whole genus or class عام، کلّی، جنسی

generous (*jen*-è-rus) *adj.* ready to give freely سخی، فیاض، بافیض noble-minded کریم النفس، شریف النفس، کریم الطبع given freely plentiful کثیر، وافر **generosity** (jene-*ros*-i-ti) *n.* being generous سخاوت، فیاضی nobility of mind کریم النفسی

genesis (*jen*-e-sis) *n.* beginning آغاز creation پیدائش، تخلیق، تکوین *the book of Genesis,* the first book of the Bible کتابِ پیدائش، سفرِ تکوین

genetics (je-*net*-iks) *n.* science of breeding علمِ توالد و تناسل **genital** *adj.* pertaining to the organs of procreation تناسلی، اعضائے تناسل سے متعلق **genitals** *n. pl.* external genital organ اعضائے تناسل

genial (*jee*-ni-ěl) *adj.* sympathetic ہمدرد sociable ملنسار، خوش مزاج (of climate) favourable to growth پیداوار کے لیے مفید **genially** *adv.* sympathetically ہمدردانہ **geniality** (jee-ni-*al*-i-ti) *n.* being genial ہمدردی، ملنساری

genie (*jee*-ni) *n.* (pl. *genii* pr. (*jee*-ni-i) sprite, jinnee جن

genital *adj.* see under **genetics**

genitive (*jen*-i-tiv) *n. & adj.* (gram.) possessive حالتِ اضافی

genius (*jee*-ni-us) *n.* (pl. *geniuses,* except in senses 4 & 5 where it is *genii*) exceptional ability عظیم ذہانت، غیر معمولی ذہانت person having this غیر معمولی ذہین special character (*of* something) ذہنیت genie جن guardian spirit ہمزاد *someone's evil genius,* someone or something with evil influence upon him کسی کو بُرا بنانے والا *someone's good genius,* similar good influence کسی کو نیک بنانے والا

genocide (*jen*-o-sid) *n.* massacre of a whole racial or other group for its extinction by another cruel group نسل کُشی group which causes this massacre نسل کش قوم

genre (jenr) *n.* kind or branch (of art, literature, etc.) صنف

gent (jent) *n.* vulgar abb. *gentlemen* for which see under شریف آدمی

genteel *adj.* stylish سجیلا very polite متواضع، نجیب، شریف imitating the ways of the upper classes رئیسوں کی نقل کرنے والا

gentile (*jen*-til) *n. & adj.* Jewish (person) غیر یہودی

gentility (jen-*til*-i-ti) *n.* good manners شائستگی noble birth نجابت، خاندانی امارت upper classes اونچا طبقہ

gentle (*jen*-těl) *adj.* mild ہلکا، نرم، دھیما friendly دوستانہ well-born شریف، عالی خاندان *v. t.* break in (horse) (گھوڑا) سدھانا handle (horse) gently but firmly گھوڑے کو نرمی مگر مہارت سے قابو میں لانا

gentlefolks *n. pl.* well-born persons شرفا **gentleman** *n.* good-mannered person بھلا مانس، شریف، نیک *gentleman's agreement,* one binding in honour but not enforceable شریفانہ معاہدہ (old use) man who did not have to earn his living رئیس (courteous word for) any man مرد، آدمی **gentlemanly** *adj.* good-mannered شریفانہ **gentlewoman** *n.* lady خاتون **gently** *adv.* softly, slowly آہستہ mildly نرمی سے nobly رئیسانہ

gentry (*jent*-ri) *n.* persons of good social position, other than the titled classes شرفا

genuflect (*jen*-ew-flekt) *v.i.* kneel in worship رکوع کرنا، رکوع میں جانا **genuflexion** (jen-ew-*flek*-shěn) *n.* kneeling in worship رکوع

genuine (*jen*-ew-in) *adj.* true کھرا، اصلی، حقیقی **genuinely** *adv.* truly, in fact حقیقتاً **genuineness** *n.* being genuine اصلی ہونا، کھرا ہونا

genus (*jeen*-nus) *n.* (pl. *genera*) kind, class جنس، قسم

geocentric (ji-o-*sen*-trik) *adj.* pertaining to the earth as the centre of the universe زمین مرکزی

geography (ji-*og*-ra-fi) *n.* study of the earth's surface جغرافیہ **geographic** (jee-o-*graf*-ik), **geographical** (jee-o-*graf*-i-kěl) *adj.* pertaining to geography جغرافیائی، جغرافی **geographer** (ji-*og*-ro-fě*) *n.* one learned in geography جغرافیہ داں، ماہرِ جغرافیہ

eology (ji-*ol*-o-ji) *n*. science of the earth's history as shown by its crust علم طبقات الارض، ارضیات **geologist** *n*. expert in geology ماہر ارضیات **geological** (jeo-o-*loj*-i-kĕl) *adj*. pertaining to geology ارضیاتی

eometry (ji-*om*-et-ri) *n*. science of the properties and relations of lines, surfaces, magnitudes (*i.e.*, surface and solids) ہندسہ، جیومیٹری **geometric, geometrical** (ji-o-*met*-ri-kĕl) *adj*. pertaining to geometry ہندسی

eorgette (jo*-*jet*) *n*. very thin silk dress-material جارجٹ

eranium (je-*ray*-ni-um) *n*. a garden plant with flowers of various colours جریٹیم

a geranium

riatrics (je-ri-*at*-riks) *n*. branch of medicine dealing with old age diseases علم امراض شیخوخت **geriatrician** *n*. specialist in geriatrics ماہر امراض شیخوخت

rm (jĕ*m) *n*. portion of living organism capable of becoming a new one جز ثومہ beginning (*of*) نقطۂ آغاز tiny living thing causing disease جرثومہ ج: جراثیم **germicide** (jĕ*-mi-sid) *n*. germ-destroying medicine جراثیم کش **germinate** (jĕ*-mi-nayt) *v. t.* & *i*. (of seeds) begin to grow پھوٹنا cause to shoot up and grow اگانا create پیدا کرنا، تخلیق کرنا **germination** (-*nay*-) *n*. (causing to) shoot up پھوٹنا، اگانا creation تخلیق

rman (jĕ*-men) *n*. & *adj*. of Germany language spoken there جرمن، جرمنی *German silver*, a nickel alloy جرمن سلور، نقلی چاندی

mane (jĕ*-*mayn*) *adj*. relevant (*to* a subject, etc.) سے متعلق

rymander (ge-ri-*man*-dĕ*) *v.i.* use underhand and unfair means to influence votes at an election انتخاب میں جیتنے کے لیے خفیہ ذرائع استعمال کرنا manipulate (constituency, etc.) for this purpose انتخاب میں جیتنے کے لیے حلقۂ انتخاب اپنی ضرورتوں کے مطابق مقرر کرنا this practice انتخاب میں جیت کے لیے خفیہ ذرائع کا استعمال

und (*je*-rund) *n*. English verbal noun (ending in *ing*., as *going, seeing*, etc.) مصدری اسم

tapo (ges-*tah*-poh) *n*. Nazi secret police any high-handed secret police نازی خفیہ پولیس، گستاپو

iculate (jes-*tik*-ew-layt) *v.i.* make signs and movements with the hands, etc., in (or instead of) speaking اشاروں سے باتیں کرنا **gesticulation** *n*. اشاروں سے باتیں

ure (*jes*-che*) *n*. meaningful movement of the hand or body اشارہ something done to convey an attitude معنی خیز حرکت

get) *v.t.* & *i*. (*get, got*, U.S. *get, got, gotten*) obtain پانا، حاصل کرنا buy خریدنا fetch لا دینا understand سمجھنا *Sorry, I didn't quite get you* معاف کیجیے میں آپ کی بات پوری طرح سمجھ نہیں سکا become ہو جانا *get tired* تھک جانا make ; cause to become کرانا *get (one's) hair cut* بال کٹوانا، حجامت بنوانا *get (someone) employed* (کسی) کو ذکر کرانا (یا)، نوکری دلانا reach پہنچنا *get home* گھر پہنچنا cause to arrive پہنچانا begin شروع کرنا، لگنا catch (disease, etc.) لگنا experience (shock, etc.) ہونا engage (someone *to do* something) کسی سے کرنے کو کہنا۔ *Phrases* : *get about*, (a) (of news, etc.) spread مشہور ہونا، پھیلنا، اڑنا (b) (of people) travel سفر کرنا *get (something) across*, (colloq.) cause people to accept it رواج دینا، چلانا *get along*, manage چلنا، ثابت ہونا *get along with (someone)*, live sociably with (him) کے ساتھ اکٹھی خوب گزرنا *get at*, (a) reach پہنچنا (b) find out معلوم کرنا *get away with it*, (a) succeed in one's endeavour میں کامیاب ہو جانا (b) escape retribution عقوبت سے بچنا، سزا سے بچ نکلنا *get by heart*, learn یاد کرنا *get down to business*, give up formalities and start the real work کام کی بات پر آنا *get in*, reach پہنچنا *get off*, start چل پڑنا *get off with*, become on amorous terms with (member of the opposite sex) سے معاشقہ ہو جانا *get (one's) goat*, (slang) annoy him (کسی کو) چڑانا *get out of (some habit)*, give (it) up (عادت) ترک کرنا (یا)، چھوڑ دینا *get over*, (a) overcome (difficulties) پر قابو پا لینا (b) recover صحت پانا، شفایاب ہونا (c) finish ختم کرنا *get round*, (a) evade (something) سے بچنے کی راہ نکال لینا (b) pursuade (*someone*) to do what is desired رام کر لینا، چکنی چپڑی باتوں سے راضی کر لینا *get through*, (a) pass (an examination) پاس کرنا، میں پاس ہونا (b) finish ختم کرنا *get to*, begin to لگنا *get up*, wake سو کر اٹھنا *get (something) up*, prepare it for use تیار کرنا، ٹھیک ٹھاک کرنا *get wind of*, hear rumours of کی سن گن پا لینا *have got*, have کے پاس ہے *have got to*, must کو کرنا ہے *have not got to*, need not کی کیا ضرورت ہے **get-at-able** *adj*. accessible جس تک رسائی ہو سکے **get-up** *n*. costume لباس style وضع، سج دھج lay-out (of newspaper, etc.) ترتیب

getaway *n*. escape (of criminals) فرار *make (one's) getaway*, (of criminals, etc.) escape, abscond فرار ہو جانا

gew-gaw (*gew*-gaw) *n*. plaything کھلونا gaudy trifle محض دکھاوے کی چیز

geyser (*gay*-sĕ*) *n*. intermittent hot spring گرم پانی کا چشمہ stove for heating water پانی گرم کرنے کا چولھا، آب تاب

a geyser (sense 2)

ghastly (*gahst*-li) pale and ill بیماری سے زرد death-like مُردنی والا horrible خوفناک (of smile) forced, grim بے دلی کا *adv*. in a ghastly manner خوفناک انداز سے

مُردوں کی طرح **ghastlily** (*gahst*-li-li) *adv*. horribly دہشت انگیز طور پر

ghetto (*get*-oh) *n*. Jewish quarter of a town شہر کا یہودی علاقہ (see *Addenda*)

ghost (gohst) *n*. spirit of dead person supposed to haunt earth بھوت thin wasted person سوکھ کر کانٹا (old use) soul رُوح *give up the ghost*, die مرنا، مر جانا *the ghost walks*, salaries are to be paid تنخواہوں کی ادائگی کرنی ہے *not the ghost of a chance*, no chance at all ذرا بھی اِمکان نہیں، بالکل مُرتفع نہیں *the Holy Ghost*, (*a*) Gabriel جبرئیل، رُوحُ الامین (*b*) according to Christians the third person of the Trinity رُوح القدُس **ghostly** (*gohst*-li) *adj*. having to do with ghosts بھوت پریت سے مُتعلق ghost-like بھوت کا سا gloomy, dismal ویران، اُداس، اُجاڑ

ghostliness *n*. being dismal اُداسی، ویرانی

ghoul (gool) *n*. evil spirit preying on human bodies غُول بیابانی **ghoulish** *adj*. fiendish سخت بُرا

G. I. (*jee*-i) *n*. (pl. *G.Is*) U.S. soldier امریکی فوجی جوان

giant (*ji*-ant) *n*. (fem. *giantess*) huge superhuman being جن، دیو، عِفریت anything abnormally large بہت بڑا *adj*. huge بہت بڑا very powerful بہت طاقتور **gigantic** (ji-*gan*-tic) *adj*. giant-like جن کا سا huge بہت بڑا

gibber (*jib*-ĕ*, *gib*-ĕ*) *v. i*. make meaningless sounds مُہمل باتیں کرنا chatter چڑ چڑ کرنا *n*. chatter چڑ چڑ **gibberish** *n*. (*gib*-e-rish) meaningless sounds مُہمل آوازیں nonsense بکواس، بیہودہ باتیں، لایعنی باتیں *adj*. meaningless بے معنی، لایعنی

gibbet (*jib*-et) *n*. wooden post on which criminals were hanged and exhibited to warn others سُولی

gibbon (*gib*-un) *n*. long-armed ape گِبن، دراز دست بندر

gibe, jibe (jib) *v.i*. mock (*at*) مذاق اُڑانا taunt آوازے کسنا *n*. taunt طعنہ، آوازہ

giddy (*gid*-i) *adj*. dizzy جس کا سر چکرا رہا ہو causing dizziness جس سے سر چکرا جائے *a giddy height* سر چکرا دینے والی بُلندی not serious وارفتہ مزاج fond of pleasure عیش پسند **giddily** *adv*. with giddiness دوران سر کے ساتھ **giddiness** *n*. being giddy دورانِ سر

gift (gift) *n*. present تحفہ، ہدیہ talent (*for*) ملکہ something bestowed ہبہ **gifted** *adj*. (of person) talented قابل

gig (gig) *n*. two-wheeled horse-carriage accommodating two persons گِگ

a gig

gigantic *adj*. (see under **giant**)

giggle (*gig*-èl) *n*. foolish and nervous laughter کھسیانی ہنسی *v.i*. laugh thus کھسیانی ہنسی ہنسنا

gigolo (*gig*-è-loh) *n*. professional male dancing-partner رقص میں پیشہ ور مرد ساتھی، رقاص

gild (gild) *v.t*. cover with gold-leaf سونے کا پتر چڑھانا make golden مُلمع کرنا make bright جِلا کرنا

gilded *adj*. **gilt** *adj* gilded مُلمع golden سُنہری furbished کلٹی **gilt-edged securities**, safe investments محفوظ حصے *n* material for gilding پتر، جھال (old spelling of **guild**, which see) young sow چھوٹی سُورنی

gill *n*. (*pr*. gil) respiratory organ in fishes گلپھڑا (*pr*. jil), liquid measure 1/4 pint ڈھائی چھٹانک

gilt *n*. & *adj*. (see under **gild**)

gimlet (*gim*-let) *n*. small drill پھوٹا برما

a gimlet

gimmick (*gim*-ik) *n*. (see *Addenda*)

gin (jin) *n*. liquor made from grain جن (also ginning machine) machine for separating cotton from seeds کپاس اوٹنے کی مشین، بیلن trap for animals پھندا، دام *v.t*. (-nn-) treat (cotton) in a gin کپاس بیلنا یا اوٹنا *ginning factory*, factory for ginning cotton کپاس بیلنے کا کارخانہ، بیلن خانہ

ginger (*jin*-jĕ*) *n*. a hot spicy root اَدرک (colloq.) liveliness تیزی، طراری *v.t*. *ginger up*, (*a*) make more vigorous زور دار بنانا (*b*) rouse up (*to action*, etc.) اُبھارنا **gingerbread** *n*. bread flavoured with ginger ادرک والی روٹی

gingerly (*jin*-jĕ*-li) *adj*. cautious مُحتاط *adv*. cautiously اِحتیاط سے

gipsy, gypsy (*jip*-si) *n*. member of an Asiatic race wandering in Europe and making a living by fortune-telling and odd jobs (originally thought to be an Egyptian) جپسی، خانہ بدوش

giraffe (ji-*rahf*) *n*. dark-spotted African animal with neck and forelegs long زرافہ

gird (ge*d) *v.t*. (*girded* or *girt*) put (*on*, a sword, etc.) لگانا fasten (*with*, a belt, etc.) باندھنا *gird up (one's) loins, gird (oneself)*, prepare for action کمربستہ ہونا

girder (gĕ-dĕ*) *n*. strong beam شہتیر

girdle (gĕ*-dèl) *n*. belt پیٹی، کمربند، پٹکا something that surrounds حلقہ، دائرہ *v.t*. encircle گھیرنا، حلقے میں لینا

girl (gĕ*l) *n*. female child لڑکی young unmarried woman دوشیزہ some man's sweetheart محبوبہ *Girl Guide* *n*. member of organization for girls similar to Boy Scouts گرل گائیڈ **girlish** *adj*. of or for girls لڑکیوں کا سا young like a girl کمسن، کم سن bashful like girls شرمیلا، حیادار

■ A **girl** is a female person of any age from birth until she is no longer younger in the speaker's opinion. A **child** is a young girl generally under 14. **Maid** and **maiden** are poetic words and **lass** is a Scottish word. A **damsel** is older than a child, with an idea of aloofness.

In writing, girls are addressed as **Miss** followed by the name, as *Miss Lamb* or *Miss Mary Lamb*; in speech, they are addressed by their equals as Miss followed by the surname, as *Miss Lamb*, and by servants as *Miss* without the name, or Miss followed only by the first name, as *Miss Mary*.

girt (gĕ*t) *v.* (pa. t. & pa. p. of **gird**, which see)

girth (ge*th) *n.* band fastened round the belly of a horse to keep saddle in place (گھوڑے کا) تنگ circumference گھیرا

gismo (*giz*-moh) *n.* (see *Addenda*)

gist (jist) *n.* brief summary; substance خُلاصہ، مُلخّص main points اَہم نِکات، ماحَصل

give (giv) *v.t.* & *i.* (*give, gave, given*) deliver دینا present پیش کرنا bestow عطا کرنا، عنایت کرنا endow ہبہ کرنا pay دینا، ادا کرنا be forced out of shape, (*under* some pressure) ٹوٹ جانا، جُھک جانا *give away*, distribute تقسیم کرنا، بانٹنا *give away*, (*a*) betray (a secret) اِفشا کرنا (*b*) betray (person) سے دغا کرنا (*c*) expose (someone) to ridicule رُسوا کرنا *give* (*the bride*) *away*, hand her over to the bridegroom لڑکی بیاہنا *give in*, stop struggling; yield دَب جانا، جُھک جانا *give* (*something*) *out*, (*a*) distribute بانٹنا، تقسیم کرنا (*b*) announce مشہور کرنا (*c*) emit سے نِکلنا *give off*, emit سے نِکلنا *give over* (or *up*), stop (something or doing something) چھوڑنا، ترک کرنا *give an example*, illustrate مِثال دینا *give a lecture*, lecture تقریر کرنا *give* (*someone's*) *message to* کسی کو کسی کا پیغام دینا *give a hand*, help مدد کرنا، دستگیری کرنا *give evidence of*, show that one has کا ثبوت دینا *give ground*, retreat پسپا ہونا *give rise to*, cause کا باعث بننا *give* (*someone another's*) *kind regards*, wish (him on behalf of) کسی کو کسی کا سلام کہنا *give way*, (*a*) break ٹوٹ جانا (*b*) surrender oneself (*to* something) کا شکار ہونا *give place to*, make room for کے لیے جگہ خالی کرنا *give* (*someone*) *to understand that*, assure (him) that کو یقین دلانا، خیال دلانا *be given to understand that*, learn that کو معلوم ہونا *give on* (or *upon*), (of a door or window) کی طرف کھلنا *n.* elasticity لَچک *give-and-take*, attitude of compromise مُصالحانہ رَوِیّہ **given** (giv-èn) *pa. p.* stated, agreed upon مُقررہ *given to*, addicted to کا عادی *given name*, Christian name پہلا نام **giver** (*giv*-e*) *n.* one who gives دینے والا، عطا کرنے والا، مُعطی

gizzard (*giz*-ĕ*d) *n.* bird's second stomach سنگدانہ

glacial *adj.* (see under **glacier**)

glacier (*glas*-i-ĕ*) *n.* slow-moving mass of ice برفانی تودہ، دریائے یخ **glacial** (*glay*-shèl) *adj.* of ice برفانی

glad *adj.* happy خوش و خرم، مسرور **gladly** *adv.* بخوشی، خوشی سے **gladness** *n.* خوشی، سرور **gladden** *v.t.* make glad خوش کرنا، باغ باغ کرنا

glade (glayd) *n.* open space in a forest جنگل کے بیچ میں کھلا میدان

gladiator (*glad*-i-ay-tĕ*) *n.* one trained and paid in ancient Rome to fight with weapons for show تماشہ گر مُبارز، گلیڈئیٹر

glamour (*glam*-ĕ*) *n.* enchantment سحر power of beauty to move the feelings دلرُبائی کشش outward show ظاہری شان **glamorous** *adj.* full of glamour دل فریب، دلرُبا، نظر فریب

glance (glahns) *v.t.* & *i.* take a quick look (*at, over*, or *through*) پر اُچٹتی ہوئی نظر ڈالنا، پر چھچلتی ہوئی نظر ڈالنا flash چمکنا، دمکنا (of a blow, etc.) slide (*off*) اُوچھا وار پڑنا *n.* quick look سرسری نظر، اُچٹتی ہوئی نظر

gland *n.* one of the bodily organs secreting certain fluids غُدود، غدّہ **glandule** *n.* small gland چھوٹا غُدود **glandular** (*gland*-ew-lĕ*) *adj.* of or like glands غدودی، غدّی

glare (*glay*-è*) *n.* dazzling light چندھیا دینے والی روشنی، خیرہ کن روشنی fierce stare نِگاہِ گرم *v.i.* dazzle چندھیا دینا stare fiercely گھورنا، نگاہِ گرم ڈالنا **glaring** *adj.* dazzling خیرہ کن (of errors) easily seen فاش، فاحش

glass (glahs) *n.* hard transparent substance شیشہ، بلّور drinking-vessel made of glass گلاس glass vessels شیشے کے برتن (also *looking-glass*) mirror آئینہ telescope دُوربین (*pl.*) binoculars چھوٹی دُوربین (*pl.*) (also *eye-glasses*), spectacles عینک، چشمہ **glass-blower** *n.* workman who makes glass articles شیشہ ساز **glass-house** *n.* glass hot-house (پودوں کے لیے) بلّوری گرم خانہ **glass-wool** *n.* glass in the form of fibre for packing, etc. شیشہ اُون **glassy** *adj.* like glass بلّوری (of the eyes, etc.) fixed پتھرائی ہوئی (see also **glaze**)

glaze (glayz) *v.t.* & *i.* put panes (دروازوں وغیرہ میں) شیشے لگانا give a glass-like coating شیشے کا روغن کرنا (of the eyes) become fixed پتھرانا cover with transparent coat of different (usu. milky) colour دُودھیا کرنا *n.* thin glassy coating شیشے کا روغن

glazier *n.* one who glazes doors, etc. شیشہ گر

gleam (gleem) short flash of soft light جھلک چمک brief show (of hope, etc.) کرن، جھلک، جھلکیاں *v.i.* emit such light جھلکنا hold out (hope, etc., for a short while) کی جھلک دِکھانا

glean (gleen) *v.t. & i.* pick up grain left in a field after harvest بالیں جمع کرنا gather in small quantities ایک ایک کرکے چننا، تھوڑا تھوڑا کرکے جمع کرنا cull تھوڑا تھوڑا منتخب کرنا **gleaning** *n.* what is gleaned چُنا ہُوا، خوشہ چینی (*pl.*) material culled (*from*) لیا ہُوا، منتخبہ

glee *n.* joy at success خوشی، جشنِ کامرانی **gleeful** *adj.* happy joyful مسرّت افزا **gleefully** *adv.* joyfully خوشی سے

glen *n.* narrow valley تنگ گھاٹی

glib *adj.* quick and smooth in speech but not sincere چرب زبان، طرّار ready and smooth (speech, etc.) تیز

glide (glid) *v.i.* move along smoothly and continuously پھسلنا، سُبکی سے جانا fly in a glider بے انجن طیارے میں پرواز کرنا *n.* such a movement سُبک خرامی **glider** *n.* aircraft without engine بے انجن طیارہ

glimmer (*glim*-ĕ*) *n.* weak uncertain light جھلملاہٹ، شِمٹماہٹ *v.i.* shine faintly جھلملانا، ٹمٹمانا

glimpse (glimps) *n.* brief imperfect view (*of*) جھلک *v.t.* catch such a view کی جھلک دیکھنا

glint *n.* gleam چمک، دمک *v.i.* glitter دمکنا

glisten (*glis*-ĕn) *v.i.* shine like a wet surface چمکنا

glitter (*glit*-ĕ*) *n.* flash of light چمک، دمک *v.i.* shine brightly چمکنا، دمکنا

gloaming (*gloh*-ming) *n.* evening twilight شام کا دُھندلکا، جھٹپٹا

gloat (gloht) *v.i.* gaze greedily (*over* one's possessions, etc.) فخر و ناز سے دیکھنا

global *adj.* (see under **globe**)

globe (glob) *n.* ball گیند، کُرہ earth کرۂ زمین، کرۂ ارض sphere with world map گلوب globe-shaped glass, lamp-shade گلوب **global** (glob-bĕl) *adj.* worldwide دُنیا بھر کا، عالمگیر embracing all of a group مجموعی **globe-trotter** *n.* one who travels across the world just for sightseeing سیّاح، جہاں گرد، جہاں گشت **globular** *adj.* globe-shaped گُردی made of globules قطراتی **globule** *n.* drop of liquid قطرہ

gloom *n.* semi-darkness اندھیراسا، اندھیرا اُجالا، دُھندلکا obscurity گُمنامی cheerlessness اُداسی **gloomy** *adj.* dark تاریک cheerless اُداس **gloomily** *adv.* اُداسی سے

glorify *v.t.*, **glorious** *adj.* (see under **glory**)

glory (*gloh*-ri) *n.* well-earned honour and praise ناموری reason for pride مایۂ ناز something deserving honour بزرگی، جلال adoration of God ثنا، حمد، پرستش beauty and magnificence شان، تجلّی، سج دھج boasting گھمنڈ *v.i.* take pride (*in*) پر اترانا **glorify** (*gloh*-ri-fi) *v.t.* give glory to ثنا کرنا، حمد کرنا، پرستش کرنا **glorious** (*gloh*-ri-us) *adj.* magnificent پُرشکوہ (colloq.) enjoyable شاندار

gloss (glos) *n.* bright smooth surface چمکتی ہوئی سطح note on a difficult word in a book حاشیہ، تشریح *v.t. & i.* furbish چمکانا، عیب پوت کرنا write gloss فرہنگ لکھنا، حاشیہ چڑھانا، تشریح کرنا **glossary** *n.* list of glosses (usu. appended to the book) فرہنگ، حاشیہ، تشریحات **glossy** *n.* bright بھڑکیلا، چمک دار **glossiness** *n.* brightness چمک دمک

glove (gluv) *n.* covering for the hand دستانہ **be** *hand in glove with,* be on friendly terms with سے خوب گاڑھی چھننا

glow (gloh) *n.* brightness and warmth without flame تمتماہٹ، دمک flushed look سُرخی، تمتماہٹ *v.i.* shine brightly and warmly دمکنا، تمتمانا flush (چہرے پر) سُرخی دوڑ جانا، سُرخ ہو جانا، لال ہو جانا

glow-worm *n.* kind of beetle of which the female gives out a green light at its tail جگنو، کرمک شب تاب

glower (*glou*-ĕ*) *v.i.* scowl (*at*) تیز تیز نظروں سے دیکھنا، گھورنا، قہر آلود نگاہیں ڈالنا

glucose (*gloo*-kohs) *n.* grape sugar گلوکوز، انگوری شکر

glue (gloo) *n.* sticky substance for joining wood, etc. سریش *v.t.* stick with glue, etc. چپکانا، جوڑنا

glum *adj.* sad and gloomy اداس، افسردہ، رُوٹھا ہُوا، رُوٹھا رُوٹھا

glut *n.* too large a supply بہتات، افراط *v.t.* (-tt-) supply (a market, etc.) in excess of demand (منڈی میں) ضرورت سے زیادہ مال بھر دینا overeat بہت زیادہ کھالینا، بہت ٹھونسنا

glutinous (*gloo*-ti-nus) *adj.* sticky چپکنے والا

glutton (*glut*-un) *n.* one who eats too much کھاؤ، پیٹو، پُرخور **gluttonous** *adj.* eating too much کھاؤ، پیٹو، پُرخور **gluttony** (*glut*-ŏ-ni) *n.* overeating پُرخوری، بسیار خوری

glycerin, glycerine (*glis*-e-rin) *n.* sweet, colourless syrupy liquid obtained from oil as a by-product of soap گلیسرین

G-man (*jee*-man) *n.* (U.S. slang) C.I.D. official خفیہ پولیس والا

gnarled (nah*ld) *adj.* (of tree-trunks) rugged and twisted ٹیڑھا میڑھا

gnash (nash) *v.t. & i.* cause (the teeth) to

strike together (in rage) دانت پیسنا (of teeth) strike together thus دانتوں کا کٹکٹانا

gnat (nat) *n.* small stinging fly مکھی ، گنگی *strain at a gnat*, hesitate about a trifle یونہی میں میخ نکالنا *strain at a gnat and swallow a camel*, make a show of honesty about trifles but be actually dishonest when it comes to substantial gains گڑ کھائیں گلگلوں سے پرہیز

gnaw (naw) *v.t.* & *i.* bite steadily (*at something hard*) کاٹنا ، کترنا torment (someone) steadily گھُن کی طرح کھا جانا wear (something) away by biting کھا جانا

gnome (nohm) *n.* underground dwarf with superhuman powers باشتیا جن ، زمین دوز بھتنا ، رُوحِ خاکی

go (goh) *v.i.* (*go, went, gone*) move away جانا ، پہنچنا ، گزر جانا move چلنا ، حرکت کرنا pass رُخصت ہونا ، روانہ ہونا be صَرف ہونا become بن جانا ، ہو جانا *go blind* اندھا ہو جانا *go Communist* کمیونسٹ بن جانا *go bad* خراب ہو جانا *go mad* پاگل ہو جانا ، بسر بھرنا *go to sleep* سو جانا *go to war*, start it جنگ میں کودنا be in working order چالو ہونا ، کام کرنا ، کام دینا be worked (*by*) سے چلنا live as a habit بنا رہنا ، رہنا *go armed* اونچی بنا رہنا *go in fear of* (*one's*) *life* جان جانے کا اندیشہ رہنا stay normally رہنا ، بنا رہنا sell (*for*) (میں) بکنا (of road, path, etc.) lead (*to*) (راستے یا سڑک کا کہیں) جانا break (*in*) (کے باعث) ٹوٹ جانا be (of a certain age) کا ہونا *go fifteen or sixteen* برس پندرہ یا کہ سولہ کا سن (of money) be spent (*on*) پر اُٹھنا ، پر خرچ آنا ، پر صرف کرنا be missing کم ہو جانا ، کھو جانا die مرجانا ، چل بسنا (*Phrases* :) *go about* (*something*), start doing it (کوئی کام) کرنے لگنا *go ahead*, (*a*) begin شروع کرنا (*b*) make progress ترقی کرنا *go after*, try to obtain حاصل کرنے کی کوشش کرنا *go back on* (or *upon*) (*one's*) *word*, fail to keep it (قول سے) پھر جانا *go by the name of*, be named کہلانا ، کے نام سے موسوم ہونا *go down*, (*a*) (of a ship) sink ڈوبنا (*b*) (of the sea or wind) calm down ساکن ہونا (*c*) (of a story, etc.) be plausible قابلِ یقین ہونا (*d*) fail ناکام رہنا *go dry*, adopt prohibition شراب بندی کرنا *go for*, attack حملہ کرنا *go for nothing*, go to waste اکارت جانا ، ضائع ہونا *go in for* (*a*) participate in میں حصہ لینا ، میں شریک ہونا (*b*) adopt اختیار کرنا *go halves*, share equally آدھوں آدھ کرنا *go into* (*a*) enter میں داخل ہونا (*b*) launch (business etc.) شروع کرنا (*c*) sift (evidence) کا جائزہ لینا ، کا محاکمہ کرنا (*d*) outline (details of) (کی تفصیلات) میں جانا (*e*) (of a number) be exactly divided by پورا تقسیم ہونا *go-off*, start آغاز *go off*, (*a*) (of explosives) explode چلنا ، دھماکے سے پھٹنا ، چھُٹنا (*b*) (of eatables) go bad خراب ہو جانا (*c*) deteriorate in quality اچھا نہ رہنا ، خراب ہو جانا *go off well*, produce the expected result کامیاب رہنا *go off badly*, fail ناکام رہنا *go one better*, outbid rival سبقت *Go on*, proceed چلو ، لے جانا *go on* (*doing*), continue (to do) (کرتے) رہنا *go on with*, persevere with پر جمے رہنا *go on to*, proceed to (کرنے) لگنا *go on all fours*, be on all fours, agree completely بالکل ایک سے ہونا *go out*, (*a*) be extinguished بجھ جانا (*b*) leave home (etc.) باہر جانا *go out as*, leave home to work as کسی نوکری پر جانا *go over* (*book, case, etc.*), examine (it) کا مطالعہ کرنا *go over to*, desert someone to join چھوڑ کر کسی سے جا ملنا *go round*, be enough for everyone کافی ہونا ، ہر ایک کے لیے کافی ہونا *go through* (*a*) scrutinize (book, etc.) بغور مطالعہ کرنا (*b*) suffer مصیبت اُٹھانا ، جھیلنا ، کڑیاں (*c*) (of a bill) be passed منظور ہو جانا (*d*) revise نظرِ ثانی کرنا ، تصحیح کرنا *go through with*, fulfil پورا کرنا ، نباہنا ، نبھانا *go pull together*, get along satisfactorily نباہ ہونا *go up*, rise, ascend چڑھنا *go upon*, have as a foundation بنیاد ہونا *go with*, (of colours) harmonize میل کھانا *go without*, lack سے محروم ہونا *go to sea*, become a sailor ملاح بننا *go to seed* (*a*) cease flowering پھول دینے سے رک جانا (*b*) lose intellectual activity ذہنی جمود طاری ہو جانا *go shares*, share حصہ لینا *go to law*, start legal preceedings (ag. .) قانونی چارہ جوئی کرنا *go to pieces*, (*a*) break up ٹکڑے ٹکڑے ہونا ، پاش پاش ہونا (*b*) collapse mentally ذہنی طور پر دیوالیہ ہونا *n.* enthusiasm جوش ، ولولہ *full of go*, enthusiastic پُرجوش *have a go at*, attempt کوشش کرنا *on the go*, busy مصروف *all the go*, in fashion مروّج

go-between *n.* agent دلّال ، بچولیا

going (*goh*-ing) *n.* method of work طریقِ کار condition of ground for walking, etc. زمین کی حالت *do* (*something*) *while the going is good* جب تک حالات ٹھیک ہیں (کوئی کام) کر لینا ، جب تک موقعہ ملے (کوئی کام) کر لینا

goings-on *n. pl.* (colloq.) strange events عجیب واقعات

go-getter *n.* (U.S. colloq.) one who gets what he wants دھاندلی باز

goad (gohd) *n.* pointed stick for driving cattle آنکس ، کونچ urge to action انگیخت *v.t.* drive with a goad آنکس مارنا drive to action by annoying (پر) اُکسانا

goal (gohl) *n.* something aimed at (in a game) گول objective منزل ، مقصود *one's goal in life* کسی کا مقصدِ زندگی

goal-keeper *n.* player keeping ball out of the goal گول کیپر ، گولی

goat (goht) *n.* a small horned animal بکرا ، بکری *he-goat* بکرا *she-goat* بکری

a goat

goat-herd *n.* one looking after flocks of goat چرواہا ، گلہ بان ، راعی

gobble (*gob*-èl) *v.t.*& *i.* eat greedily ہڑپ کرنا

gobbledygook *n.* (see *Addenda*)

goblet (*gob*-let) *n.* bowl-shaped drinking glass جام ، ساغر

goblin (*gob*-lin), **hobgoblin** *n.* ugly mischievous elf بھتنا ، بھتنا

god *n.* (fem. *goddess*) deity دیوتا image representing a deity بت (*God*), the Supreme Being خدا ، اللہ تعالیٰ *God willing*, if God wills انشاء اللہ *Thank God*, glory to God for His mercy خدا کا شکر ہے ، اللہ کا شکر ، اللہ تیرا شکر **goddess** *n.* female god دیوی **godchild** *n.* (also *goddaughter*, *godson*) one whom a godparent sponsors at baptism دینی بچہ (بیٹا یا بیٹی) one whom a godparent patronizes منہ بولا بچہ (بیٹا یا بیٹی) **godparent** *n.* (also *godfather*, *godmother*) *n.* one who sponsors a child دینی باپ (یا) دینی ماں one who patronizes a child **godfearing** *adj.* who fears God and walks in His ways خدا ترس **god-forsaken** *adj.* wretched (place) لعنتی (جگہ) ، ملعون (مقام) **godless** *adj.* infidel wicked برا ، خبیث **godly** (*god*-li) *adj.* obeying God خدا پرست very religious بہت دیندار **godsend** *n.* unexpected piece of good fortune دولت خدا داد ، چھپر پھاڑ کر ملی ہوئی دولت **godspeed** *adv.* & *int.* good-bye خدا حافظ *wish (someone) godspeeed*, say good-bye to (him) کسی کو خدا حافظ کہنا

godown (*go*-doun) *n.* (Anglo-Oriental word for) warehouse گودام

Gog, Magog (gog, *may*-gog) *n.* names of two giants or of two unidentified races; British legend states them to be giants of Albion یاجوج ماجوج

goitre (*goi*-tĕ*) *n.* illness marked by enlargement of thyroid gland گھینگا

goggle (*gog*-ĕl) *v.t.* & *i.* roll the eyes (*about* or *at*) گول گول آنکھیں گھما کر دیکھنا (of the eyes) open widely آنکھوں کا بہت زیادہ کھلنا (of the eyes) roll (آنکھوں کا) گھومنا **goggles** *n pl.* sun-glasses دھوپ (کی) عینک

gold (gohld) *n.* precious yellow metal سونا ، زر **gold-leaf** *n.* thin sheet of gold سونے کا ورق **gold-beater** *n.* one who beats gold into thin leaves زرکوب *gold-beater's skin*, skin membrane used for beating gold into leaves جھلی ، زرکوبی جھلی **gold-digger** *n.* one who digs out gold ore کان سے سونا نکالنے والا coquette wheedling money out of men زرکش فاحشہ **gold brick** *n.* fraud; thing with only a surface appearance of value مایا **goldbrick** *n.* & *v.i.* (see *Addenda*) **goldsmith** *n.* one who prepares gold ornaments سنار ، زرگر **gold standard** *n.* money values assessed according to the value of gold and by issuing gold coins معیار طلا ، طلائی معیار *on the gold standard*, (country) using this standard معیار طلا والا *off the gold standard*, (country) not using it غیر طلائی معیار والا **golden** (*gohl*-dĕn) *adj.* of the colour of gold سنہری ، سنہرا ، زریں precious, invaluable قیمتی ، زریں ، سنہری ، سنہرا ، انمول ، گراں بہا *golden chance*, rare opportunity سنہری موقع ، زریں موقع *the Golden Age*, (*a*) earliest (and best) mythical period of Greek history دور زریں (*b*) the best period in a nation's history سنہرا دور ، عہد زریں *the Golden Fleece*, (Cl. myth.) fleece of a ram, hung in Colchis and guarded by a dragon; it was brought by the leader of the Argonauts, Jason سنہری اون *golden mean*, moderation اعتدال *golden jubilee*, 50th anniversary celebrations گولڈن جوبلی ، جشن طلائی ، جشن زریں

golf (golf, gof) *n.* outdoor game played with ball driven with sticks (called *golf-clubs*) into a series of 9 or 18 holes over a stretch of ground (called a *golf-course* or *golf links*) گولف ، گاف **golf club** *n.* stick with which golf is played body conducting, etc., this game گالف کلب ، انجمن گاف **golf-course, golf links** *n.* grounds on which golf is played گاف کا میدان ، گاف گاہ **golfer** *n.* one who plays golf گاف کھیلنے والا ، گاف گاہ

golosh *n.* (same as **galosh**, which see)

gondola (*gond*-o-la) *n.* light flat-bottomed boat used in Venice canals گنڈولا **gondolier** (gond-o-*lee*-ĕ*) *n.* one who rows a gondola گنڈولا کا مانجھی ، گنڈولی

gone(gon) *v.* (pa. p. of **go**, which see)

gong (gong) *n.* round metal plate used as bell گھنٹہ ، جرس *dinner gong*, gong struck to announce dinner-time کھانے کا گھنٹہ ، جرس عشائیہ *v.t.* (of traffic police) strike gong thereby directing (motorist etc.) to stop سپاہی کا ڈرائیور کو گھنٹی بجا کر رکوانا ، (ڈرائیور) کو گھنٹی دینا

good (gŭd) *adj.* (*good*, *better*, *best*) virtuous اچھا ، نیک right, proper ٹھیک ، صحیح thorough پورا ، سخت efficient اچھا ، لائق welcome بارک ، اچھا *Good show!* well done! شاباش rather more than سے زیادہ ہی eatable کھانے کے لائق ، خوردنی untainted صاف ، پاک صاف *good humour*, cheerful disposition خوش مزاجی considerable بہت *a good many*, کافی ، بہت *a good few*, considerable کئی ایک ، بہت *a good way*, quite a long way کافی دور *as good as*, practically تقریباً ، قریب قریب *hold good*, remain in force ثابت رہنا ، برقرار رہنا *in good time (for)*, early enough (for) کے لیے ، بر وقت *all in good time*, at the right time وقت پر ، وقت آنے پر *good for*, (*a*) able to pay (a sum of money) ادا کرنے کے قابل (*b*) able to undertake (a task, etc.) کرنے ، کے قابل (*c*) having a goo effect on مُفید کے لیے *make good*, (*a*) indemnify (loss or damage) کی تلافی کرنا (*b*) carry out (one's promise) وعدہ وفا کرنا، قول نبھانا (*c*) achieve (a purpose) مقصد پورا کرنا *n*. that which is good خیر، نیکی *do (someone) good, do (someone) a good turn* کسی سے نیکی کرنا advantage نفع، فائدہ *It is no good (doing something)*, it is useless to do it ایسا کرنا بیکار رہا بے سُود ہے *(some amount) to the good*, having so much to one's credit اتنے نفع میں، اتنے فائدے میں adequate خوب اچھا ٹھیک *Good! Very Good!* that will do خوب ٹھیک ہے always ہمیشہ، اَبَداً *for good, for good and all*, for ever ہمیشہ کے لیے *for good and all*, finally آخرکار، انجام کار **goods** (gudz) *n. pl.* wares مال تجارت things carried by rail or road مال *goods train*, train carrying goods مال گاڑی **good-bye** (gūd-*bī*) *int*. farewell خدا حافظ **Good morning** *n*. form of salutation from early morning to lunch hour سلام، صبح بخیر **Good afternoon** *n*. salutation from after lunch to afternoon tea سلام، سہ پہر بخیر **Good evening** *n*. salutation from afternoon tea to one's bed time سلام، شام بخیر **Good night** *n*. salutation at *parting* (for the same hours as *Good evening* is on meeting) شب بخیر **good-fellowship** *n*. jovial company دوستی، یارانہ being convivial یار باشی **good-for nothing** *n*. & *adj*. useless (person) ناکارہ شخص **Good Friday** *n*. Friday before Easter commemorating, according to Christians, the Crucifixion of Christ گڈ فرائی ڈے **good looking** *adj*. pretty خوبصورت **goodly** *adj*. good natured خوش مزاج good looking خوبصورت of considerable size کافی بڑا **good-natured** *adj*. kind and pleasant خوش طبع، خوش مزاج، نیک دل **goodness** *n*. being good نیکی، خوبی *int*. (also *Goodness gracious !* or *Good gracious!*) (expression of surprise) توبہ، ارے توبہ، خدا پناہ، خدا ہی جانے *Goodness knows !* who knows خدا کی پناہ **goodwill** *n*. established custom of a business firm ساکھ well-wishing خیر اندیشی، خیر سگالی، خیر خواہی *in a spirit of goodwill, with good will*, wishing well خیر سگالی کے جذبے میں

goofy (*goo*-fi) *adj*. (slang) silly (person) گدھا، بیوقوف احمق

googly (*goog*-li) *n*. (in cricket) off-breaking ball with an apparently leg-breaking action or *vice-versa* گُگلی

googol *n*. (see *Addenda*)

goose (goos) *n*. (pl. *geese* pr. gees) (masc. *gander*) water bird with webbed feet and larger than a duck ہنس *kill the goose that lays the golden eggs*, sacrifice the future to the present مستقبل کا حال پر قربان کر دینا *all his geese are swans*, he overestimates وہ تو ہر بات کو بڑھا چڑھا کر بیان کرتا ہے its flesh ہنس کا گوشت fool بھولا، سادہ لوح **goose-step** *n*. marching without bending the knees ہنس کی چال، ہنس چال

goosie (*goo*-si) *n*. (child's word for) goose ہنس

gooseberry (*goos*-be-ri) *n*. bush with a hairy berry گوزبری، انگور کی قسم کا ایک پودا its fruit گوزبری

Gordian (*go**d-yĕn) *adj*. of Gordius, king of Phrygia, the intricate knot tied by whom was cut through by Alexander with his sword گارڈیئس کی intricate پیچیدہ (used only in the phrase :) *cut the Gordian knot*, surmount a difficulty violently بزور عقدہ کشائی کرنا

gore (go*) *n*. blood that has been shed and has thickened بہایا اور جما ہوا خون *v.t.* (of horned animals) wound with the horns سینگ مار کر زخمی کرنا **gory** (*go*-ri) *adj*. covered with blood خون آلودہ، خون آلود

gorge (go*j) *n*. that which is swallowed نگلا ہوا، کھایا پیا *makes (one's) gorge rise*, disgust جی متلانا، گھن آنا narrow pass تنگ گھاٹی *v. t.* & *i.* eat greedily اندھا دھند کھانا fill oneself (*with*) پیٹ میں ٹھونستے جانا

gorgeous (*go**-jus) *adj*. richly coloured رنگا رنگ magnificent شان دار، ٹھاٹھ کا، عظیم الشان زرق برق

Gorgons (*go**-gonz) *Cl. myth*. three female monsters (viz., *Medusa, Guryale* and *Stheno*) who turned into stone everything upon which they cast a look پتھر نظر والی عورتیں، گارگن

gorilla (go-*ril*-a) *n*. largest kind of ape بن مانس گوریلا

gormandize (*go**-*man*-dīz) *v. i*. eat greedily بھوکوں کی طرح کھانا

gosh *int*. (expressing surprise) واہ! توبہ!

gosling (*goz*-ling) *n*. young goose ہنس کا بچہ

gospel (*gos*-pel) *n*. evangel or 'good news' *i.e.*, the life and teachings of Christ انجیل any or all of the first four books of the New Testament نئے عہد نامے کی پہلی چار کتابیں یا اُن میں سے کوئی ایک *gospel truth*, absolute truth قطعی صداقت

gossamer (*gos*-a-mĕ*) fine silky substance of spiders' webs spread on grass or floating in air جالا any thin material باریک شے

gossip (*gos*-ip) *n*. idle talk about others' affairs گپ شپ، دوستوں کے متعلق اُڑائیں person indulging in such talk گپ باز، گپی *v.i.* talk thus دُوسروں کے متعلق اُڑائیں پھیلانا، گپ بازی کرنا، گپیں ہانکنا

got *v*. (pa. t. & pa. p. of **get**, which see)

Gotham (*got*-ĕm) *n*. reputed town of fools شکارپُور *wiseman of Gotham*, fool بے وقوف، شکارپُور کا دانا

Gothic (*goth*-ik) *n*. mediaeval European architectural style with pointed arches and steep roofs گوتھی طرزِ تعمیر *adj*. (of building) in this style گوتھی (عمارت)

gotten *v.* (U.S. pa. p. of **get**, which see)
gouge (gouj, or gooj) *n.* chisel with a concave blade گول چھینی *v.t.* cut with a gouge گول چھینی سے چھیلنا *gouge (something) out*, (*a*) shape with a gouge گول چھینی سے چھیلنا۔ (*b*) force out with a gouge چھینی سے نکالنا (*c*) force out (the eye) آنکھ نکال باہر کرنا
goulash (*goo*-lahsh) *n.* very seasoned stew of steak and vegetables مسالے دار سبزی گوشت
gourd (goo*d, or goh*d) *n.* a hard skinned fleshy fruit تونبا، تونبی، پیٹھا bowl of its dried skin تونبا
gourmand (*goo**-mand) *adj.* gluttonous (person) پیٹو، کھاؤ *n.* lover of delicate fare نفیس خوراک کا شائق، خوش خور
gourmet (*goo**-may) *n.* lover of delicate fare نفیس خوراک کا شائق، خوش خور epicure عیش پسند، لذت پسند
gout (gout) *n.* rheumatism وجع المفاصل، گٹھیا **gouty** (*gou*-ti) *adj.* one suffering from gout گٹھیا کا مریض
govern (*guv*-ĕn) *v.t.* & *i.* rule حکومت کرنا، حکمرانی کرنا، control تسلط قائم کرنا فرماں روائی کرنا۔ influence اثر انداز ہونا **government** *n.* (*guv*-ĕ*n-ment) governing حکمرانی set-up governing a country حکومت body of persons who govern ارباب حکومت body of Ministers وزارت، مجلس وزرا *Government House*, Governor's official residence گورنمنٹ ہاؤس، قصر والی، قصر حکومت **governor** (*guv*-ĕ*-nĕ*) *n.* person who governs a province, etc. گورنر، صوبے دار، والی، حاکم regulator مشین کا ٹھیک مقدار میں پہنچانے والا پرزہ، گورنر (colloq.) boss آقا، مالک **Governor-General**, chief Governor والی اعلیٰ، گورنر جنرل **Governorship** *n.* Governor's office گورنری، صوبے داری
governess (*guv*-ĕ*-nes) *n.* paid lady teacher in a private house آتون، آتو جی، آتو elevated maid servant looking after children گورنس
gown (goun) *n.* woman's dress فراک، گون flowing robe worn by lawyers, judges and professors گون، چغہ، عبا
grab *v.t.* & *i.* (-bb-) snatch selfishly ہتھیانا، ہتیانا snatch (*at*) ہتھیانا، ہتیانا، چھیننا *n.* grabbing زبردستی چھیننا
grace (grays) *n.* beauty of shape حسن، جمال beauty of movement ادا elegance آن، شان God's mercy خدا کا لطف و کرم short prayer before meal دعائے طعام *say grace*, کھانے سے پہلے دعا مانگنا favour نوازش، مہربانی، کرم *the Graces*, (in Cl. myth.) the three beautiful attendants of Venus (viz., *Agalia*, *Thalia*, and *Euphrosyne*) شاہیں، حسینائیں *an act of grace*, thing given freely کرم فرمائی *days of grace*, time allowed for payment after the due date ادائگی کی مزید مہلت *be in (someone's) good graces*, enjoy (his) favour. کی نظروں میں اچھا ہونا *with a good grace*, willingly *with a bad grace*, unwillingly, half-heartedly بد دلی سے، طوعاً کرہاً *year of grace*, year of the Christian era عیسوی سال، سن عیسوی *in the year of grace 1984*, in A.D. 1984 ۱۹۸۴ء میں *His grace*, *Your Grace*, title of honour used in addressing an archbishop or duke والا حضرت، رحمت مآب *v. t.* confer dignity on کو اعزاز بخشنا، کو مشرف کرنا *grace an occasion with (one's) presence*, کسی کو محفل میں قدم رنجہ فرما کر شرف کا کو مشرف فرمانا **graceful** *adj.* beautiful حسین showing grace of movement عشوہ طراز
gracefully *adv.* with propriety سلیقے سے **graceless** *adj.* without a sense of propriety بے سلیقہ، پھوہڑ
gracious (*gray*-shus) *adj.* (of God) merciful رحیم، کریم kind مہربان *int.* (expressing surprise) (also *Good gracious !*, *Goodness gracious!*) یا اللہ رحم، الرحم!
graciously *adv.* mercifully ازراہ کرم، بنظر توجہ kindly مہربانی سے، ازراہ نوازش
gradation *n.* (see under **grade**)
grade (grayd) *n.* stage, degree درجہ، رتبہ scale of pay for a particular cadre گریڈ، تنخواہ کی درجہ بندی (U.S.) slope ڈھلان *on the up grade*, rising بڑھتا ہوا *on the down grade*, falling گرتا ہوا *make the grade*, achieve what is attempted اپنی کوشش میں کامیاب ہونا *v.t.* arrange according to grades درجہ بندی کرنا *upgrade*, put into the upper grade اونچے درجے میں لے جانا make less sloping ڈھلان کم کرنا **gradient** (*gray*-di-ent) *n.* degree of slope ڈھلان کی مقدار *a gradient of one in ten*, 10-foot-long inclined plane with a height of one foot at the upper end دس فٹ میں ایک فٹ کی چڑھائی **gradation** (gra-*day*-shĕn) *n.* grading درجہ بندی gradual change from one grade to another تدریج
gradual (*grad*-ew-ĕl) *adj.* taking place by degrees بتدریج، درجہ بدرجہ، تدریجی not steep ہلکی ڈھلان
gradually *adv.* not abruptly دھیرے دھیرے، آہستہ آہستہ، بتدریج
graduate *v.t.* & *i.* take at least a first degree from a university گریجوایٹ ہونا، بی۔اے پاس کرنا، سند فضیلت لینا، فارغ التحصیل ہونا mark with degrees for measuring پیمانہ بنانے کے لیے نشان لگانا grade درجہ بندی کرنا *n.* one who has taken at least a first degree from a university فارغ التحصیل، فاضل، سند یافتہ، گریجوایٹ
Graeco- (*gre*-koh) *pref.* (also *Greco-*) Greek یونانی، یونان کا
graft *n.* shoot of a living tree joined to a cut in another so that it grows there قلم، پیوند piece of skin, etc., thus transplanted جلدی، پیوند profit-making by dishonest political methods سیاسی ذرائع سے ناجائز نفع اندوزی *v.t.* & *i.* put a graft (*on*) قلم لگانا، پیوند لگانا practice political graft

grail (grayl) *n.* (also *holy grail, saint grail, sangrail, sangreal*) platter used by Christ at the Last Supper, in which, according to Christians, Christ's blood was received at the Cross مسیح کی عشائے آخری کا پیالہ ، جام خونیں

grain (grayn) *n.* seed of food plants دانہ (*pl.*) cereals غلّہ، اَناج tiny bit of some other things ذرّہ 1/60 ounce گرین، نصف رتی very small amount ذراسا، ذرہ بھر، ذرہ برابر، ذری سا *without a grain of* سے بالکل عاری arrangement of fibres in wood لکڑی کی دھاریاں *against the grain*, against one's nature خلاف طبع، خلافِ مزاج، اُفتادِ طبع کے خلاف

[1]**gram** (gram) *n.* a kind of pulse چنا، نخود (see under **gramme**)

[2]**-gram** (gram) *suf.* signifying thing so written نوِشت (as in *telegram* which means ٹیلیگرام، تار، دُور نوِشت)

grammalogue (*gram*-a-log) *n.* shorthand sign for a single word مختصر نویسی کا لفظ، مختصر نویسانہ علامت

grammar (*gram*-ĕ*) *n.* rules of language structure گریمر، قواعد، صَرف و نحو ، قواعد، دستور *grammar school*, type of high-class English secondary schools in which Latin was once the chief subject گریمر سکول

grammarian (gra-*may*-ri-an) *n.* expert in grammar قواعد دان، نحوی **grammatical** (gra-*mat*-i-kĕl) *adj.* of grammar صَرفی یا نحوی، صرف و نحو سے متعلق قواعدِ زبان سے متعلق

gramme, gram (gram) (abbr. as *gm.*) metric unit of weight equivalent to the weight of 1 cubic centimetre of water (=15·432 grains) *miligramme*, 1/1000 gm. گرام کا ہزارواں حصّہ *centigramme* 1/100 gm. گرام کا سَوواں حصّہ *decigramme*, 1/10 gm. گرام کا دسواں حصّہ *decagramme*, 10 gm. دَس گرام *hectogramme*, (or *kilo.*), 1000 gm. ہزار گرام

gramophone (*gram*-o-fohn) *n.* machine for reproducing recorded speech from discs; phonograph گراموفون

granary (*gran*-a-ri) *n.* storehouse for grain کوٹھی

[1]**grand** *adj.* great بڑا، عظیم magnificent (style, view, etc.) شاندار، عالیشان greatest, chief اعلیٰ، اعظم *the Grand Vizier*, the Premier صدرِ اعظم self-important بُرخود غلط (colloq.) *do the grand*, put on airs ڈون کی لینا (colloq.) enjoyable پُرلطف، مزے کا *have a grand time*, enjoy one's leisure ٹھاٹھ سے خوب عیش کرنا، کی مزے سے بسر ہونا (U.S. slang) $1,000 ہزار ڈالر *grand total*, final total میزانِ کُل *grand stand*, tiers of roofed seats for spectators at sports مُسقّف نشستیں *'grande dame'*, a lady of aristocratic manner and forceful personality بیگماتی انداز والی عورت

grandeur (*gran*-dyĕ*) *n.* greatness بڑائی، عظمت magnificence شان، شوکت

[2]**grand-** *pref.* (indicating relatives in the third generation) تیسری نسل میں **grandchild** *n.* (also *grandson, granddaughter*) *n.* son or daughter of one's son or daughter پوتا یا پوتی ، نواسا یا نواسی

grandparent *n.* (also *grandfather, grandmother*) parent of one's parent دادا یا دادی، نانا یا نانی *grandfather clock, grandfather's clock*, wall clock in tall wooden case کلاک، گھنٹہ، دیوار گیر گھڑی

grandee (gran-*dee*) *n.* Spanish nobleman ہسپانوی نواب great personage بڑی شخصیّت

grandeur *n.* (see under **grand**)

grandiloquent (gran-*dil*-o-kwent) *adj.* pompous (style) لفّاظی والا **grandiloquence** *n.* pomposity لفّاظی

grandiose (*grand*-i-ohz) *adj.* trying to make a great show نمائشی imposing پُرشکوہ **grandiosity** (grand-i-*os*-i-ti) *n.* magnificence شان، شکوہ

grange (graynj) *n.* country-house with farm buildings گاؤں کی حویلی جس میں مزارعین کے گھر وغیرہ بھی ہوں، حویلی

granite (*gran*-it) *n.* a grey rock used for building ایک عمارتی پتھر، گرینیٹ

granivorous (gra-*niv*-o-rus) *adj.* grain-eating (animal, etc.) دانہ خور

granny (*gran*-i) *n.* (pl. *grannies*) (affectionate term for) grandmother دادی اَمّاں یا نانی اَمّاں

grant *v. t.* give sanction بحال کرنا، چھٹی دینا، چھٹی کی *grant leave*, sanction it کی منظوری دینا عرضی منظور کرنا agree (*that*) ماننا، تسلیم کرنا *granted*, *granted that, I grant that*, I admit that مانا کہ، تسلیم *take (something) for granted*, regard (it) as certain to happen یقینی سمجھنا *n.* money, etc. granted عطیہ، گرانٹ *grant-in-aid*, grant for help امدادی عطیّہ ، عطیّہ برائے امداد ، گرانٹ

granulated (*gran*-ew-lay-ted) *adj.* in the form of grains دانہ دار، دانے دار

granule (*gran*-ewl) *n.* tiny grain چھوٹا سا دانہ ، دانچہ

grape (grayp) *n.* vine-fruit انگور *the grapes are sour*, something is despised because it is inaccessible کھٹے انگور انگور کھٹے ہیں *sour grapes*, such things

grapesugar *n.* glucose انگوری شکر، گلوکوز **grapefruit** (*grayp*-froot) *n.* big orange-like sour fruit گریپ فروٹ ، چھوٹا چکوترہ ، چھوٹا ترنج

graph (graf) *n.* line showing the variation of two quantities ترسیم، گراف **graphic** (*graf*-ik) *adj.* pertaining to painting, etc. نقاشی کا *the graphic arts* نقاشی، تصویر کشی، مصوّری (of descriptions) vivid واضح illustrated by graphs, diagrams, etc. نقشوں والا **graphically** *adv.* vividly وضاحت سے

-graph (graf) Suf. denoting instrument for writing or recording نگار *phonograph*, (U.S. for phonogram گراموفون، صدا نگار

in lead pencils (پنسل کا) سُرمہ
grapnel (*grap*-nel) *n.* (also *grappling-iron*) anchor-like instrument for holding enemy ships جنگی لنگر، لنگر بیڑی
grapple (*grap*-èl) *v. t.* & *i.* seize firmly تھامنا مضبوطی سے پکڑنا struggle at close quarters دُو بدُو لڑنا try to deal (*with* a problem حل کرنے کی کوشش کرنا *n.* (also *grappling-iron*) *n.* grapnel جنگی لنگر، لنگر بیڑی
grasp *v. t.* & *i.* seize firmly with the hands زور سے پکڑنا، ہاتھوں سے جکڑنا understand سمجھنا *grasp at*, (*a*) try to seize پکڑنے کی کوشش کرنا (*b*) accept eagerly شوق سے قبول کرنا *n.* grasping پکڑ، گرفت
grass (grahs) *n.* narrow green leaves growing on lawns, etc. گھاس **grassy** (*grah*-si) *adj.* covered with grass سرسبز، سبزہ زار **grasshopper** *n.* small jumping insect with a shrill note جھینگر **grass-roots** *n. pl.* (see *Addenda*)
grate (grayt) *v. t.* & *i.* rub into small pieces رگڑنا چھیلنا، کدوکش کرنا rub small bits off make an irritating noise by rubbing ناگوار شور کرنا irritate (*on* one's nerves) اعصاب پر سوار ہونا *n.* fireplace آتشدان، چولھا، انگیٹھی metal frame for holding coal in it آتش دان، آگ روک، روک **grater** *n.* rough surfaced vessel for grating food کدوکش
grating *adj.* annoying ناگوار *n.* framework of parallel or crossed bars for closing (window, etc.) without shutting out air or light جنگلہ
grateful (*grayt*-ful) *adj.* thankful (*to* someone *for* something) شکر گزار، ممنون، احسانمند، متشکر **gratitude** (*grat*-i-tewd) *n.* thankfulness شکر گزاری
gratify (*grat*-i-fi) *v. t.* satisfy (desire, etc.) کی تسکین کرنا **gratification** *n.* satisfaction تسکین **gratifying** *adj.* satisfying اطمینان بخش، تسلی بخش، تسکین دہ، طمانیت بخش۔
grating *n.* (see under **grate**)
gratis (*gray*-tis) *adv.* & *adj.* free of charge مفت، بلا قیمت، بلا معاوضہ
gratitude *n.* (see under **grateful**)
gratuitous (gra-*tew*-i-tus) *adj.* free of charge مفت، بلا معاوضہ uncalled for بلا وجہ، خواہ مخواہ کا *a gratuitous insult* بلا وجہ بے عزتی **gratuitously** *adv.* free of charge مفت، بلا معاوضہ unreasonably
gratuity (gra-*tew*-i-ti) *n.* gift for services انعام tip بخشش free gift عطیہ
grave *n.* tomb قبر، مزار hole dug in the ground for burial قبر *have one foot in the grave*, be very old and nearing death قبر میں پاؤں لٹکائے ہوئے ہونا *adj.* serious سنجیدہ important and requiring serious attention سخت اہم، شدید heavy سنگین

کندہ کرنا بھاری بھرکم *v. t.* engrave, carve کندہ کرنا **graven** (*grayv*-ĕn) *adj.* engraved, carved کندہ، تراشیدہ (only in the phrase) *graven images*, idols تراشے ہوئے بت
graveyard *n.* cemetery قبرستان، گورستان **gravestone** *n.* tombstone کتبہ، سنگ مزار، لوح مزار **gravely** *adv.* seriously سنجیدگی سے، شدید **graveyard shift** *n.* (see *Addenda*)
gravel (*grav*-el) *n.* small pebbles with coarse sand used for paving roads بجری، کنکر *v. t.* (-ll-) cover with gravel بجری بچھانا، کنکر پھیلانا **gravelled** *adj.* macadamized (path, etc.) پکا (راستہ وغیرہ)
graven *adj.* (see under **grave**)
gravitate *v. i.*, **gravitation** *n.* (see under **gravity**)
gravity (*grav*-i-ti) *n.* attraction between any two material objects in the universe, and between the centre of the earth and the objects on it کشش ثقل، کشش زمین *centre of gravity*, centre of earth exerting strong gravitational pull مرکز ثقل weight وزن *specific gravity*, density; relation of the weight of anything to that of an equal volume of water وزن مخصوص seriousness سنجیدگی، متانت importance اہمیت، شدت **gravitate** *v. i.* be attracted to or towards کی طرف جھکنا، مائل ہونا **gravitation** *n* universal force of gravity کشش، کشش ثقل
gravy (*gray*-vi) *n.* fatty juice got from meat while cooking یخنی sauce made from this گوشت کی یخنی
gray *adj.* same as **grey** (which see)
graze (grayz) *v.t.* & *i.* feed on growing grass گھاس چرنا make (cattle, etc.) graze in the field چرانا (of a missile) scrape (someone) lightly in passing چھوتے ہوئے نکل جانا *n.* place where the skin is grazed خراش **grazing** *n.* growing grass suitable for pasturage چرنے کے لیے موزوں گھاس کاشت کرنا، چارہ اگانا
grease *n.* (grees) soft animal fat چربی any semi-solid oily substance چکنائی، گریس *v.t.* (greez) apply grease to گریس لگانا *grease (someone's) palm*, bribe (him) کو رشوت دینا، مٹھی گرم کرنا **greasy** (*gree*-zi) *adj.* covered with grease چکنا slippery پھسلن والا
[1]**great** (grayt) *adj.* very famous, distinguished, remarkable عظیم important اہم noted نمایاں big بڑا prolonged طویل extreme سخت، شدید plentiful بہت، وافر intense بہایت favourite (joke, etc.) پسندیدہ *a great deal*,

very much کثیر، بہت *a great many*, a large number بھاری اوورکوٹ، کئی **greatcoat** *n*. heavy overcoat بہت **greatly** (*grayt*-li) *adv*. much بہت **greatness** (*grayt*-nes) *n*. great distinction عظمت importance اہمیت

great- *pref*. (denoting) more remote by one generation پر (as *great-grandfather*, grandfather's father پردادا یا پرنانا *great-grandmother*, one's parent's grandmother پردادی یا پرنانی *great-grandson*, grandson of one's child پرپوتا *great-granddaughter*, granddaughter of one's child پرپوتی

Grecian (*greesh*-en) *adj*. of Greek (style) یونانی انداز کا، یونانی *Grecian slippers*, oriental slippers ایک طرح کی گرگابی، گریشین **Greco-** (*gree*-koh) *pref*. (also *Graeco-*), Greek یونانی، یونان کا

greed *n*. avidity (*for* wealth, food, etc.) حرص، لالچ **greedy** (*gree*-di) *adj*. avid حریص، لالچی **greedily** *adv*. avidly لالچ سے، حریصانہ **greediness** *n*. being greedy لالچ، حرص، حرص و آز

Greek *adj*. of Greece یونانی *n*. Greek subject یونانی Greek language زبان، یونانی *It is all Greek to me*, I do not understand it میری تو سمجھ میں کچھ نہیں آتا *on the Greek calends*, never کبھی نہیں *till the Greek calends*, for ever ہمیشہ ہمیشہ

green *adj*. of the colour of growing grass سبز، ہرا (of fruit) not ripe کچا (of wood) not dry ہری (of a young person) raw, inexperienced ناتجربہ کار (of old age) still strong ابھی زوردار *n*. the colour of growing grass سبز رنگ، ہرا رنگ (*pl*.) green vegetables سبزی، ترکاری lawn مرغزار، سبزہ زار public lawn in a village سبزہ، شاملات **greenery** (*green*-ĕ-ri) *n*. green plants, etc. سبزہ، ہریالی **greenwood** *n*. forest in full leaf ہرا بھرا جنگل **greengrocer** *n*. dealer in fresh vegetables سبزی والا، کنجڑا **greenfinch, green linnet,** *n*. bird with gold and green plumage سون چڑی **greenhorn** *n*. inexperienced person easily duped اناڑی، فریب خوردہ **green manure** *n*. growing plants ploughed into the soil سبز کھاد **greenhouse** *n*. hot house گرم خانہ

Greenwich (*grin*-ij) English town in Kent through which longitude 0° passes گرینچ *Greenwich time*, English standard time گرینچ کا وقت، انگریزی وقت

greet *v. t.* wish سلام کرنا welcome خیر مقدم کرنا، خوش آمدید کہنا *greet with a smile*, welcome smilingly مسکرا کر خیر مقدم کرنا write (in a letter) words expressing respect, friendship etc. خط میں سلام بھیجنا cheer کے لیے پرجوش نعرے بلند کرنا come into view دکھائی دینا، نظر آنا **greeting** *n*. (often *pl*.) first words used on seeing someone (*e.g.*, *Good Morning*) سلام *Christmas greetings* بڑے دن کا سلام *Id greetnings* عید مبارک superscription of a letter (*e.g.*, *Dear Sir*) سرنامہ، القاب *greetings card*, beautifully printed cards sent on such occasion عید کارڈ، کرسمس کارڈ

gregarious (gre-*gay*-ri-us) *adj*. living in large groups غول پسند، گلوں میں رہنے والا fond of the company of others یاروں کا یار، باش، دوستوں میں رہنے والا

grenade (gre-*nayd*) *n*. small bomb چھوٹا بم *hand-grenade*, one thrown by hand دستی بم *rifle-grenade*, one fired from a rifle بندوقی بم **grenadier** (gren-a-*di*-ĕ*) *n*. one who throws a hand-grenade دستی بم پھینکنے والا

grew *v*. (pa. t. of **grow**, which see)

grey, gray (gray) *n*. colour between black and white خاکستری رنگ horse of this colour نیلیا گھوڑا cold sunless light دھندلکا *adj*. of this colour خاکستری، سیاہی مائل سفید dull, dismal بے کیف، اداس (of hair) almost white سفید، کھچڑا *grow grey*, grow old بوڑھا ہو جانا *a grey beard*, old man بڑے میاں، بوڑھا، ضعیف **greyish** *adj*. somewhat grey خاکستری سا **greyness** *n*. being grey خاکستری رنگ کا سا (of hair) being white سفید **grey matter** *n*. brain دماغ

greycing (*grays*-ing) *n*. greyhound racing شکاری کتوں کی دوڑ

greyhound *n*. swift hunting dog شکاری کتا

grid *n*. network of railways ریلوں کا جال (also *grid system*), network of overhead cables for distributing electric current over a large area بجلی کی بہم رسانی کے لیے تاروں کا جال frame made of bars جنگلہ، سنہرا **gridiron** *n*. barred metal cooking frame کباب بنانے کا برتن، سیخ

grief (greef) *n*. deep sorrow سخت غم its cause باعث غم، وجہ ملال *come to grief*, come to a bad end برا انجام ہونا *bring to grief*, ruin برباد کرنا **grieve** (greev) *v. t.* & *i.* feel grief رنجیدہ ہونا cause grief to رنجیدہ کرنا، دکھ پہنچانا، دکھ پہنچنا **grievance** (*gree*-vans) *n*. cause for complaint شکایت، وجہ شکایت **grievous** (*gree*-vus) *adj*. causing grief الم ناک، پرملال severe (mistake, harm, etc.) سخت، شدید **grievously** *adv*. painfully الم ناک طور پر

grieve *v.t.* & *i.*, **grievance** *n.*, **grievous** *adj.* (see under **grief**)

griffin, griffon, gryphon *grif*-en, *n* fabulous creature with the head and wings of an eagle and the body of a lion گرفن (*griffin*), white man newly arrived in Asia ; نیا گورا ، اناڑی گورا

grill (gril) *n.* gridiron سیخ dish of grilled meat کباب (also *grill-room*) place where grills are served کباب کی دُکان ، کباب خانہ latticed screen over counter (کاؤنٹر کا) کٹہرا *v.t.* & *i.* broil کباب کرنا badger تفتیش یا جرح کے دوران میں سوالات سے ناک میں دَم کرنا
grilling *n.* broiling کباب کرنا *adj.* gruelling (heat) سخت (گرمی)
grim *adj.* cruel ظالم fierce-looking سخت ، تُند خُو ، آہنی ، آہنیں horrible ڈراؤنا ، خوفناک ، دہشتناک stern ، بدمزاج ، پُرعزم ، پکّا **grimly** *adv.* fiercely سختی سے **grimness** *n.* fierceness سختی
grimace *n.* twisted expression on the face بناہُوا مُنہ ، رونی صُورت such expression intended to cause laughter رونی صُورت *make grimaces*, twist face like that رونی صُورت بنانا *v. i.* make grimaces مُنہ بنانا ، رونی صورت بنانا
grime (grīm) *n.* thick coating of dirt on the skin مَیل ، کُوش **grimy** (*grī*-mi) *adj.* covered with grime مَیل سے بھرا ہُوا
grin stupid smile کھسیانی ہنسی *v. i.* (-*nn*-) smile thus کھسیانی ہنسی ہنسنا ، کھیس نکالنا
grind (grīnd) *v.t.* & *i.* (*grind, ground, ground*) pulverize (wheat, etc.) پیسنا produce (flour) by pulverizing آٹا پیسنا crush (*down*) by harsh administrative and other measures کچل ڈالنا ، کچومر نکال دینا ، بھُرکس نکال دینا polish or sharpen (knife, etc.) by rubbing on hard surface (چاقو وغیرہ) لگانا ، سان پر چڑھانا polish (glass, etc.) thus (شیشے کو) پر چڑھانا rub together roughly رگڑ کھانا ، زور سے رگڑنا سان پر چڑھانا *grind away at* (*one's*) *studies*, work hard بڑی محنت کرنا *grind* (*one's*) *teeth at*, rub them together in anger دانت پیسنا *n.* (colloq.) long, hard and monotonous work مصیبت ، چکّی **grind-stone** *n.* stone-wheel for sharpening steel tools سان ، فسان *keep* (*someone's*) *nose to the grind-stone*, force (him) to work hard without rest (کسی سے) سخت مشقّت لینا
grip *n.* tight grip مضبُوط گرفت *let go* (*one's*) *grip of* (*something*) اپنی گرفت ڈھیلی کر دینا *come to grips with*, attack in earnest کمرِ ہمّت کس کر کام شروع کر دینا understanding سمجھ *have a good grip of*, کو اچھی طرح سمجھنا ، کی خُوب سمجھ رکھنا mastery مہارت ، اُستادی *v.t.* & *i.* grasp tightly زور سے پکڑنا ، مٹھی میں لینا compel the attention of توجّہ اپنی طرف مبذول کرائے رکھنا
gripe (grīp) *n.* (usu. *pl.*) pinching pain in the stomach مروڑ *gripe water*, syrup for infants bringing relief in such pain گرائپ واٹر *v.t.* cause such pain کے پیٹ میں بل ڈالنا ، مروڑ اُٹھنا *griping pain*, gripes مروڑ ، دار دَرد

grisly (*griz*-li) *adj.* horrid ; causing superstitious fear دہشتناک ، ہولناک
grist (grist) *n.* grain for grinding پیسنے کے لیے اناج *bring grist to the mill*, be profitable نفع دینا ، نفع بخش ثابت ہونا
grit *n.* small bit of stone, etc. کنکر ، ریزہ *get a bit of grit in* میں ریزہ پڑ جانا pluck کس بل ، ہمّت *v.t.* (-*tt*-) grind together ایک ساتھ پیس ڈالنا *grit the teeth*, be firm کمر باندھ لینا **gritty** *adj.* having grit کنکر والا
grizzle (*griz*-ĕl) *v.i.* (colloq.) (of children) cry fretfully (بچّوں کا) رو رو کر بے حال ہو جانا **grizzled** (*griz*-ĕld) *adj.* grey-haired کھچڑی بڑی داڑھی والا ،
grizzly (griz-li) *n.* (also *grizzly bear*), fierce American bear امریکی خاکستری ریچھ
groan (grohn) *n.* deep moan of distress کراہ *v.t.* & *i.* moan like that کراہنا be overburdened (*under*) کے بوجھ تلے کراہنا be burdened (*with*) سے لدے ہُوئے ہونا express disapproval of (some speaker) and silence (him) *down* with groans ناپسندیدہ مقرّر کو کراہ کراہ کر چپ کرا دینا
grocer (*groh*-sē*) *n.* dealer in dry or tinned food پنساری ، کریانہ فروش *green-grocer*, dealer in vegetables ترکاری والا ، سبزی فروش **grocery** *n.* grocer's trade پنساری کی دُکان (*pl.*) goods sold by a grocer پنساری ہٹ کا سامان ، کریانہ
groggy (*grog*-i) *adj.* shaky لڑکھڑاتا ہُوا *feel groggy*, feel shaky لڑکھڑانا drunk پیے ہُوئے ، متوالا ، مدہوش (of horse) weak in forelegs اگلی ٹانگوں کا کمزور
groin *n.* hollow in the body where the thigh joins the belly پیڑو ، جانگھ curved line where two vaults cross in a roof محرابوں کا خطِ تقاطع
groom *n.* servant in charge of horses سائیس bridegroom دُولہا ، نوشہ *v.t.* keep (horse) well-brushed, etc. گھوڑے کو ملنا ، کھریرا کرنا *well-groomed*, neatly dressed (person) with the hair well-brushed بنا سنورا ، بالوں میں کنگھی کیے ہُوئے
groove (groov) *n.* long narrow channel in a surface to guide the motion of something that slides into it جھری ، نالی routine way of living دن پورے کرنے کا دستور *v.t.* make grooves in جھری ڈالنا ، نالی کو بنانا
grope (grohp) *v.i.* feel about blindly with the hands (*for* or *after* something) ڈھونڈنا ، ٹٹولنا ، ٹامک ٹوئیے مارنا
gross (gros) *n.* twelve dozen or 144 گُرس whole (opposite of *net*), total amount کُل ، مجموعی *adj.* vulgar (manners, jokes, etc.) بازاری ، ناشائستہ glaring (mistakes, injustice, etc.) صریح too fat موٹا heavy بھاری بھرکم dull

(senses) موٹی (عقل) coarse (food) گھٹیا (خوراک

grossly *adv.* obviously (unfair, etc.) صریحاً vulgarly بدتمیزی سے، ناشائستگی سے much سخت، بہت

grotesque (gro-*tesk*) *adj.* queer and fantastic عجیب، مضحکہ خیز

grotto (*grot*-oh) *n.* (*pl. grottos*, or *grottoes*) artificial decorated cave made as a garden shelter مصنوعی غار such cool retreat غار نما سرد خانہ

grouch *v.i.* (U.S. colloq.) grumble گڑبڑ کرنا *n.* malcontent غیر مطمئن fit of sulks گھنّہ پھلا بیٹھنا، منہ تھتھانا

ground *n.* solid surface of the earth زمین *ground speed*, aircraft's speed relative to ground ہوائی جہاز کی زمین سے نظر آنے والی رفتار *ground staff*, non-flying members of aerodrome staff ہوائی اڈے کا زمینی عملہ *lose ground*, *give ground*, beat retreat پسپا ہونا *hold (one's) ground*, stand firm جمے رہنا، ڈٹے رہنا، قائم رہنا *shift (one's) ground*, change (one's) arguments کسی ایک دلیل پر قائم نہ رہنا *suit (someone) down to the ground*, satisfy (him) thoroughly کے لیے بالکل ٹھیک ہونا *fall to the ground*, fail ناکام رہنا *cover much ground*, encompass much بہت زیادہ احاطہ کر لینا surface against which a pattern is shown زمین land round a building احاطہ bottom of watery surface تہہ *touch ground*, (of ship, etc.) run aground تہہ سے جا لگنا piece of land reserved for a special purpose (*e.g.*, football) گراؤنڈ، میدان *playground* کھیل کا میدان *fishing grounds*, parts of sea regularly fished ماہی گیری کا علاقہ (usu. *pl.*) cause, reason سبب بننا *on the ground of*, owing to کی بنا پر *on what ground* کس بنا پر (*pl.*) dregs, sediment تلچھٹ، نیچے بیٹھا ہوا *adj.* on or near the ground نچلا زیریں *ground floor* نچلی منزل *v.t.* & *i.* establish (something *on*) پر قائم کرنا، پر استوار کرنا make (someone) proficient *in* the first principles of کے مبادی خوب اچھی طرح ذہن نشین کرنا base (*on*) پر مبنی کرنا (of a ship) run on to the land (جہاز کا) تہہ سے لگنا (of bad weather) prevent (aircraft) from flying and keep it on ground (ہوائی جہاز کو) اڑنے نہ دینا (pa. t. and pa. p. of *grind*, which see) **grounding** *n.* training in the rudiments of a subject مضبوط بنیاد *give (someone) a grounding in* (کسی کی) کسی مضمون میں بنیاد مضبوط کرنا

groundless *adj.* without good reason بے بنیاد

groundman, groundsman *n.* man in charge of playground کھیل کے میدان کا انچارج، بازیگاہ کا نگران، بازیگاہ دار

groundnut *n.* (also called *pea-nut* and *monkey-nut*) oil-yielding nut of an underground plant مونگ پھلی this plant مونگ پھلی **groundwork** *n.* fundamentals مبادی elementary preparations ابتدائی کام **ground-rent** *n.* rent of land used for building on تہہ زمینی

group (groop) *n.* number of persons or things going together جماعت، گروہ، ٹولی، جتھا، جھنڈ *in groups* ٹولیوں میں *v.t.* & *i.* form into a group(s) ٹولی بننا یا بنانا، ٹولیوں میں بٹنا یا بانٹنا

grouse (grous) *n.* (*pl.* same) European bird with feathered feet, shot for sport and food گراؤس (*pl. grouses*) complaints بڑبڑ، شکایت *v.i.* (colloq.) grumble بڑبڑانا، شکایت کرنا

grove (grohv) *n.* copse پیڑوں کا جھنڈ

grovel (*grov*-el) *v.i.* (-ll-) crouch humbly begging for mercy (*before* or *in front of*, someone) کے سامنے جھکنا demean oneself اپنی بے عزتی کرنا، اپنی خودداری کا جنازہ نکالنا

grow (groh) *v.t.* & *i.* (*grow, grew, grown*) (cause to) spring into life اگنا، اگانا become larger بڑھنا، بڑھا ہونا become ہو جانا *grow out of (one's clothes, habits, etc.)* become too big or too old for (them) (اس سائز یا درجے وغیرہ) سے نکل جانا *grown up*, (*a*) develop fully بڑھنا (*b*) attain majority جوان ہو جانا *grow older* بڑا ہو جانا *grow old* بوڑھا ہو جانا *grow on* (or *upon*) *one*, (*a*) become more firmly rooted in میں پکا ہونا (*b*) be liked more and more زیادہ سے زیادہ پسند آتے جانا *grow beard*, allow it to grow داڑھی رکھنا، داڑھی بڑھانا **grower** *n.* (in compounds) one who causes things to grow اگانے والا something that grows اگنے والا **grown-up** *n.* & *adj.* adult (person) جوان، بالغ **growth** *n.* process of growing اگنا، نشوونما what grows اگا ہوا، اگی ہوئی چیز grown amount افزائش cultivation کاشت، کھیتی diseased formation in the body (ناسور وغیرہ)

growl (groul) *n.* low threatening sound of dogs غراہٹ، غرانا complaint شکایت *v.i.* make such a sound غرانا

grub *n.* larva of insect (کیڑے کا) پہلا روپ dull drudge کولہو کے بیل کی طرح کام کرنے والا hack writer کرائے کا منشی، قلم کا مزدور (slang) food کھانا *v.t.* & *i.* dig کھودنا *grub up*, take out by digging کھود کر نکالنا *grub up roots out of the earth* (زمین کھود کھود کر جڑیں نکالنا drudge کولہو کے بیل کی طرح کام کرنا **grubby** *adj.* grimy میلا کچیلا

grudge (gruj) *v.t.* be unwilling to give or allow دریغ کرنا؛ سے دریغ رکھنا *n.* feeling of bitterness تلخی، بغض، کینہ *have a grudge against (someone)*, *owe (someone) a grudge*, *bear (someone) a grudge*, be bitter against him for causing trouble سے بُغض ہونا، سے کینہ رکھنا **grudgingly** *adv.* unwillingly نا دِل نا خواستہ، بے دِلی سے

gruel (*groo*-il) *n.* thin porridge پتلا دَلیا (slang) severe punishment سخت سزا پانا *give (someone his) gruel* punish him severely (کسی کو) سخت سزا دینا *get* (or *have* or *take*) (*one's*) *gruel*, be punished سخت سزا پانا **gruelling** *adj.* enervating (heat, exercise, etc.) تھکا دینے والا

gruesome (*groo*-sum) *adj.* horrible (event, visage, etc.) خوف ناک، دَہشت ناک

gruff (gruf) *adj.* rough (manners) اُکھڑ surly (persons) چڑچڑا، تُرش رُو

grumble (*grum*-bėl) *n.* grouse شکایت، بُڑبُڑ low noise like thunder گونج، گرج *v.t. & i.* grouse بُڑبُڑانا، شکایت کرنا produce low noise like thunder گرجنا، گونجنا **grumbler** *n.* one who grumbles بُڑبُڑانے والا، شاکی، شِکوہ مند، شِکوہ سنج

grumpy (*grum*-pi) *adj.* surly تند خُو، چڑچڑا، بدمزاج dissatisfied غیر مطمئن

grunt (grunt) *n.* gruff sound (*of* a pig) ، خُرخُش، سُور کی آواز *v.t. & i.* make such a sound نعرہ فش کرنا say with a grunt سخت رُکھائی سے کہنا، بھُنبھُک کر کہنا

guarantee (ga-ran-*tee*) *n.* promise to take responsibility if something is not so satisfactory as it was originally represented to be گارنٹی، ضمانت ، surety ضمانت، ضمانت نامہ person who gives guarantee or stands surety ضامن (colloq.) sign (*of*) (کے) آثار *v. t.* give a guarantee for something or someone کی ضمانت دینا (colloq.) show signs (*of*) (کے) آثار ہونا **guarantor** (ga-ran-*tĕ**, or *ga*-ran-tĕ*) *n.* guarantee, one who guarantees **guaranty** (*ga*-ran-ti) *n.* written undertaking guaranteeing the fulfilment of another's obligation ضمانت نامہ، کفالت نامہ

[1]**guard** (gah*d) *n.* state of watchfulness پہرہ، نگہبانی، پاسبانی، نگہداری، پہرہ داری *be on guard, keep guard,* keep watch نگہبانی کرنا، پہرہ دینا *on (one') guard,* watchful چوکنا، چوکس، ہوشیار *off (one's) guard,* unmindful غافل، بے خبر sentry پہرہ دار، سَنتری person in charge of a railway train گارڈ، محافظ *v.t. & i.* protect بچائے رکھنا، حفاظت کرنا keep watch پہرہ دینا، نگہبانی کرنا *guard against,* use care to prevent حفاظت کی تدابیر اختیار کرنا، سے بچنے کی کوشش کرنا **guarded** *adj.* (of statements) cautious محتاط **guardroom** *n.* room for sentries گارد **quarter guard** *n.* guarded barrack for soldiers under arrest کوٹی گارڈ

[2]**-guard** (gah*d) *suf.* apparatus designed to prevent injury or loss روک *mudguard,* cover over wheel مڈگارڈ، کیچڑ روک *fireguard,* grating آگ روک

guardian (*gah**-di-an) *n.* one who guards one responsible for the care of a young or incapable person سرپرست **guardian angel** *n.* angel watching over person or place محافظ فرشتہ **guardianship** *n.* being a guardian

guava (*gwah*-va) *n.* a fruit used for jelly اَمرُود its tree اَمرُود کا پیڑ

gubernatorial (gew-bĕ*-na-*toh*-ri-ĕl) *adj.* pertaining to a governor گورنری

guerdon (*gĕ**-dun) (poet.) *n.* reward صِلہ *v. t.* reward صِلہ دینا

guerilla, guerrilla (ge-*ril*-a) *n.* war carried on by small parties of fighters acting independently of the army چھاپہ مار جنگ، جنگِ گُریز، چھاپاؤل soldiers fighting thus گوریلا، گوریلا سپاہی، گوریلا دستے، چھاپاؤل دستے

guess (ges) *n.* opinion or answer based on supposition اٹکل، اندازہ، قیاس *guess paper,* question-paper for the examinee's practice which claims to anticipate the questions actually to be set at the examination سوالنامہ کی پیشگوئی، سوالنامہ کا اندازہ، گیس پیپر *v. t. & i.* give an opinion or answer without being sure قیاس لگانا، اٹکل سے کہنا، اندازے سے کہنا

guest (gest) *n.* visitor at one's home مہمان one being entertained at a meal مہمان، مدعو one staying at a hotel or having a meal at a restaurant گاہک *guestroom. guest house,* special apartment(s) for guests at some houses مہمان خانہ

guffaw (gu-*faw*) *n.* noisy laugh قہقہہ *v. i.* laugh thus قہقہہ مارنا، قہقہے مار کر ہنسنا

guidance *n.* (sea under **guide**)

guide (gīd) *n.* one who shows (others) the way رہبر، رہنما one paid to show round interesting sights گائیڈ، رہبر book with information about a subject or place رہنما، رہبر، آئینہ، گائیڈ influence اثر، رہنما، رہبر (*Guide*), Girl Guide گرل گائیڈ *v. t.* act as guide to کی رہبری کرنا، کو راستہ دکھانا *guided missile,* missile under wireless control بے تار بم، اینچی گولے **guidance** (*gī*-dans) *n.* guiding or being guided رہنمائی، رہبری **guide-book** book of information for travellers رہبر، رہنما، آئینہ **guide-post** *n.* finger-post رہنما کھمبا، راہنما **guider** *n.* senior Girl Guide گائیڈر

guild, gild (gild) *n.* association of members of a trade, etc., for mutual help انجمن پیشہ وراں **guild-hall** *n.* place where mediaeva guilds met گلڈ گھر **guild socialism** *n.* socialistic system calling for the complete control of industry by a council of its members پیشہ وَرانہ اِشتراکیت گلڈ سوشلزم

guile (gɪl) *n.* deceit فریب، دھوکا، دَغا craftiness حیلہ گری، عیّاری حیلہ، عیاری **guileful** *adj.* crafty عیّار **guileless** *adj.* simple بھولا بھالا، بے ریا

guillotine *n.* machine for beheading criminals گلوٹین، سَر قلم کرنے کی مشین، گردن زَن similar machine for cutting paper کاغذ کاٹنے کی مشین، کاغذ کاٹ *v.t.* behead with a guillotine گلوٹین سے سر قلم کرنا

guilt (gilt) *n.* wrongdoing گناہ، قصور، خطا crime جُرم responsibility گنہگاری، گناہ کاری، خطاری **guilty** *adj.* perpetrator (*of* a wrong) کا مجرم criminal مجرم، عاصی، خطا کار، گنہگار (conscience, look, etc.) betraying a consciousness of guilt گنہگار، مجرم *guilty conscience*, one whose guilt, though not yet proved, seems to reproach him inwardly مجرم ضمیر **guiltless** *adj.* innocent بے گناہ، بے قصور **guiltlessly** *adv.* innocently, faultlessly بے گناہی سے

guinea (*gin*-i) *n.* (formerly) English gold coin worth 21 shillings گنی sum of 21 shillings still commonly used in England as a unit of money, though not represented by a single coin گنی، اکیس شلنگ **guinea-pig** (*gin*-i-pig) *n.* tailless animal like a big rat, often used in medical and surgical experiments امریکی چوہا person used like a guinea-pig انسانی چوہا **guinea-fowl, guinea-hen** *n.* pheasant-like domesticated fowl شُترمُرغی مُرغی

Guinevere (*gwin*-e-vee-ė*) (*Brit. leg.*) King Arthur's wife ; she had a guilty love for the knight, Sir Lancelot گنیویر

guise (gɪz) *n.* style of dress وَضع قَطع، طرزِ لباس garb وَضع، لباس *in the guise of*, کی وَضع میں pretence بھیس *under the guise of*, under pretence of کا بھیس بنائے

guitar (gi-*tah**) *n.* six-stringed musical instrument played by plucking with fingers رِبِچّھتارا

gulf (gulf) *n.* large bay خلیج wide deep hole in the ground گہرا بڑا گڑھا dividing line اختلاف کی خلیج، خلیج difference (*between* two persons, etc.) that cannot be removed رہیں) ناقابلِ عبور خلیج

gull (gul) *n.* a large web-footed sea-bird (ایک قسم کی) مُرغابی *v.t.* dupe دھوکا دینا، فریب دینا، مُحِل دینا *n.* dupe سادہ لوح، فریب خوردہ **gullible** *adj.* easily gulled سادہ لوح، دھوکا کھا جانے والا **gullibility** *n.* being easily duped یونہی فریب کھا جانا، فریب خوردگی

gullet (*gul*-et) *n.* food passage from mouth to stomach نَرخرا throat حلقوم، گلا

gully (*gul*-i) *n.* (pl. *gullies*) narrow channel (cut down a hill by rain-water) تنگ گھاٹی drain نالی (in cricket) fielding position between the point and the slips گلی *v.t.* form channel by water-action تنگ گھاٹی بنانا make drains نالی بنانا، نالیاں بنانا

gulp (gulp) *v.t.* & *i.* swallow (*down*) greedily ہڑپ کرنا، نگلنا work the throat as if swallowing گپ نگلنا choke (*down* sobs, tears, etc.) بمشکل ضبط کرنا، پی جانا *n.* gulping نگلنا (to empty the glass) *at one gulp*, ایک ہی بار نگل کر سارا گلاس پی جانا amount gulped جتنا کچھ ایک بار نگلا جائے

gum (gum) *n.* (usu. *pl.*) flesh round the teeth مسوڑھا، مسوڑھے *gum-boil*, abcess on the gums مسوڑھے کی سوجن، وَرم لِثّہ sticky substance got from trees گوند *gum Arabic* صمغ عَربی *chewing-gum*, sweet flavoured gum for chewing specially liked in *U.S.* چوسنے کا گوند، چیونگ گم، چیونٹنگ گم chewing-gum صمغ تلیفی، کھیدنی (*pl.*) (*gums*), (U. S. colloq.) gum-boots برساتی بوٹ (vulgar) God خدا *by gum* خدا قسم *v.t.* (-mm-) put gum on گوند لگانا stick (*down, together*) with گوند سے چپکانا، چسپاں کرنا

gummy (*gum*-i) *adj.* sticky چیپ دار، چپچپا **gum-boots** *n. pl.* rubber boots put on for going out in rain برساتی بوٹ **gumption** (*gump*-shĕn or *gum*-shĕn) *n.* (colloq.) commonsense ; resourcefulness ; enterprise سوجھ بوجھ، ہمت

gun (gun) *n.* (also *shot-gun*) metal tube for throwing missiles with gunpowder بندوق *rifled-gun*, (also *rifle*), long-range gun with grooved barrel رائفل، رفل *machine-gun*, gun firing hundreds of rounds rapidly one after the other مشین گن *sten-gun*, small machine-gun سٹین گن *bren-gun*, a smaller machine-gun ٹامی گن *tommy-gun*, a type of powerful gun ٹامی گن (U.S.) pistol طپنچہ، پستول cannon توپ *stick* (or *stand*) *to* (*one's*) *guns*, defend (one's) opinions اپنی بات پر ڈٹے رہنا *great gun, big gun*, eminent person بڑا آدمی *son of a gun*, contemptible person قابلِ نفرت شخص، ذلیل انسان **gun-lock** *n.* detonating device in gun بندوق کا گھوڑا **gun-carriage** *n.* wheeled support for heavy-gun توپ گاڑی **gun-cotton** *n.* acid-soaked explosive cotton تیزابی رُوئی، باروُدی روئی **gun-powder** *n.* explosive mixture بارُود **Gunpowder Plot** *n.* Guy Fawkes's unsuccessful plot to blow up the British

Parliament on November 5, 1605 گن پاؤڈر پلاٹ، بارُودی سازِش **gun-metal** *n.* alloy of copper and tin or zinc توپیں بنانے والی دھات، توپ دھات *blow great guns*, blow a gale سخت طُوفان آنا **gun-boat** *n.* small warship with heavy guns اُگن بوٹ **gun bus** *n.* such an aircraft توپ بردار طیارہ **gun-stock** *n.* wooden mounting of a gun barrel بندوق کا کُندہ **gun-fire** *n.* firing of a gun توپ دغنا announcement of time thus پہر کی توپ **gun-shot** *n.* range of a gun بندوق کی مار، توپ کی مار *within gunshot* توپ کی زد میں **gun-smith** *n.* maker of small firearms بندوق ساز **gunner** *n.* gun operator توپچی artillery soldier توپ خانہ کا سپاہی **gunnery** *n.* construction of big guns توپ سازی firing them گولہ باری management of big guns گولہ باری کا فن

gunny (*gun*-i) *n.* jute for making sacks ٹاٹ، بُوریا **gunny bag** *n.* gunny sack ٹاٹ کی بوری

gurgle (*gē*-gĕl) *n.* (make) bubbling sound of water قلقل، غٹرغٹر *v.t.* make such a sound on coming (*out* of bottle, etc.) قلقل کرنا، غڑغڑ کرنا

gush (gush) *n.* rushing outflow زور سے نکلنا، پھوٹ نکلنا۔ *v.i.* swiftly flow (*out from*, or *forth*) زور سے نکلنا speak with excessive enthusiasm (*about* or *over*) پُرتکلف جوش سے باتیں کرنا، شوق سے باتیں کرنا **gusher** *n.* well from which oil gushes forth تیل کا چشمہ

gust (gust) *n.* sudden blast of wind or rain جھکڑ sudden outburst جوش، زور **gusty** *adj.* windy طُوفانی

gusto (*gus*-toh) *n.* enjoyment (in playing, working, etc.) جوش، شوق، جذبہ **gustation** *n.* tasting چکھنا

gut (gut) *n.* (usu. *pl.*) intestines آنتیں، رودہ، اَمعا strong cord made from dried intestines of animals تانت (*pl.*) (slang) courage, staying power, force of character جُرأت، بَرداشت *have no guts*, be cowardly جُرأت نہ ہونا، بُزدِل ہونا *have guts*, be brave *have guts*, (*to do*), be brave enough (to do) (کرنے) کی جُرأت رکھنا *v.t.* (-ll-) take the guts out of آنتیں نکالنا destroy by fire the inside of بھسم کر دینا، جلا ڈالنا

gutta-percha (*gut*-a-*pē*-cha) rubber-like hardened juice of certain Malayan trees گٹاپرچا

gutter (*gut*-ē) *n.* shallow channel on roadside سڑک کی نالی channel fixed under eaves to carry off rain-water چھت کے ساتھ ساتھ لگی ہوئی نالی، چھت کی نالی، پرنالہ

guttural (*gut*-ē-rĕl) *adj.* of the throat حلقی *guttural sounds* حلقی آوازیں۔

guy (gī) *n.* effigy of Guy Fawkes (of the 1605 *Gunpowder Plot* fame) dressed in old clothes and burnt on November 5 every year گائی، گائی فاکس کا گُڈا queerly dressed or queer-looking person مضحکہ خیز شخص a fright ہوا (U.S. colloq.) bloke, man آدمی (slang) absconding فرار *v.t.* & *i.* exhibit in effigy کا پُتلا بنانا ridicule بنانا، مذاق اُڑانا (slang) run away بھاگ جانا، فرار ہونا *do a guy, give the guy* (*to*), run away from (سے) نکل بھاگنا

guzzle (*guz*-ĕl) *v.t.* & *i.* eat or drink greedily پیٹوؤں کی طرح کھانا پینا

gymkhana (jim-*kah*-na) *n.* public resort for display of athletics, (this word is a corruption of *gend-khana* which was an attempt to translate into Urdu the word 'gymnastics' on the pattern of the hybrid word *nach-khana* for a 'ball-house') جم خانہ

gymnasium (jim-*nay*-zi-um) *n.* room with apparatus for physical training وَرزِش گاہ **gymnastic** (jim-*nas*-tic) *adj.* concerning physical training وَرزِشی **gym** (jim) *n.* (slang) gymnasium وَرزِش گاہ gymnastics جمنازِشک **gymnastics** *n. pl.* physical training exercises جمنازِشک، جسمانی کرتب، وَرزِشی کرتب **gymnast** (*jim*-nast) *n.* one skilled in gymnastics جمنازِشک کا ماہر، وَرزِشی

gymnast *n.*, **gymnastics** *n.* (see under **gymnasium**)

gypsum (*jip*-sum) *n.* soft chalk-like mineral from which plaster of Paris is made جپسم، کھریامٹی

gypsy *n.* (same as **gipsy**, which see)

gyrate (*jī*-rayt) *v. i.* spin, spiral چکر کھانا، گھومنا **gyration** (-*ray*-) *n.* spinning, spiralling چکر، گردش

gyroscope (*jī*-ros-kohp) *n.* rapidly spinning heavy wheel to keep (ship, etc.) steady مسکن چرخی

gyve (jīv) *n.* (usu. pl.) shackles بیڑیاں form of swing music ایک ناچ گت *v.t.* fetter کے پاؤں میں بیڑیاں ڈالنا dance to gyve جاز ناچنا

H

h, H (aych) (pl. *h's* or *hs*) eighth letter of the English alphabet ایچ **Note :** Generally the letter *h* has the sound of Urdu ہ but it never has the sound of Urdu ہائے مخلوط thus *host* is pronounced as ہوسٹ but *ghost* is pronounced only as گوسٹ and not as گھوسٹ It may be useful to learn that the word *aspirate* means to pronounce the letter *h*. Similarly, it might be interesting to learn that the Cockney, *i.e.*, the lower class Londoner, is in the habit of dropping his *h's* and pronouncing words like *host* as اوسٹ

ha *int.* ! (expressing surprise) ! اوہو! ارے (expressing joy) ! واہ واہ! اخاہ **ha ha** *int.* (expressing laughter) ! ہاہا *ha and hum*, make inarticulate sounds of hestitation (اٹک کر) ایں ایں کرنا

habeas corpus (*hay*-bi-us-*co**-pus) *n.* writ in a court requiring imprisoned person to be brought before judge for inquiry into the lawfulness of his detention پروانۂ حاضریِ ملزم *file a habeas corpus petition* پروانۂ حاضریِ ملزم کی درخواست دائر کرنا

haberdasher (*hab*-e*-dash-e*) *n.* dealer in small articles of dress like pins, threads, etc. سوئی سلائی والا **haberdashery** *n.* such wares سوئی سلائی کا سامان

habiliment (ha-*bil*-i-ment) *n.* garment لباس، پوشاک (*pl.*) dress suited to an office or occasion مخصوص لباس، خاص وردی

habit (*hab*-it) *n.* one's usual practice عادت، خصلت، طبیعت *be in* (or *have*) *the habit of* (*doing* something) کچھ کرنے کی عادت ہونا *fall into bad habits* بری عادت اختیار کرنا constitution جسم، صحت condition حالت *the habit of mind* افتادِ طبع (old use) dress لباس *riding-habit*, lady's riding-dress عورتوں کا سواری کا لباس

habitual (ha-*bit*-ewel) *adj.* usual معمولی regular دوامی from habit عادی **habitually** *adv.* as a practice عادۃً **habituate** (ha-*bit*-ew-ayt) *v.t.* accustom عادی بنانا، خوگر بنانا **habitue** (ha-*bit*-ew-ay) *n.* regular visitor (*of*) باقاعدہ جانے والا

habitable (*hab*-i-tayb-ěl) *adj.* fit to be lived in رہائش کے قابل، قابلِ رہائش **habitat** (*hab*-i-tat) *n.* natural abode (of animal or plant) (کسی جانور یا پودے کا) اصلی علاقہ **habitation** (-*tay*-) *n.* living in رہائش، سکونت *not fit for habitation* ناقابلِ رہائش place to live in رہنے کی جگہ، مسکن

habitual *adj.*, **habituate** *v.t.*, **habitue** *n.* (see under **habit**)

habitat *n.*, **habitation** *n.* (see under **habitable**)

hack (hak) *v.t.* & *i.* chop roughly کاٹنا، سختی سے کاٹنا *hack (something) to pieces* ٹکڑے ٹکڑے کرنا *hack at* پر کلہاڑی وغیرہ کی ضربیں لگانا kick (someone's) shins کسی کی پنڈلی پر ٹھوکر لگانا emit dry cough خشک کھانسی کھانسنا *n.* cutting tool کلہاڑی وغیرہ horse that may be hired بھاڑے کا ٹٹو (also *hack writer*), one hired to do undistinguished literary work قلم کا مزدور، گھٹیا لکھنے والا cut کاری زخم ordinary riding horse ٹٹو، گھوڑا carriage for hire کرائے کی گاڑی

hacksaw *n.* saw for cutting metal لوہا کاٹنے کا آرہ

hackney (*hak*-ni) *n.* ordinary horse ٹٹو، گھوڑا (also *hackney-coach*, *hackney-carriage*) coach kept for hire کرائے کی گاڑی *v.t.* hire out کرائے پر دینا depreciate قیمت میں کم کرنا **hackneyed** (*hak*-nid) *adj.* (of saying, expression, etc.) trite بہت ہی عام، مبتذل

hackle (*hak*-ěl) *v.t.* & *i.* cut to pieces ٹکڑے ٹکڑے کرنا

had, hadn't *v.* (pa. t forms of **have,** which see)

Hades (*hay*-deez) *Cl yth.* realm of the dead below the world پاتال hell دوزخ، جہنم

haemorrhage, hemorrhage (*hem*-ě-rij) *n.* bleeding خون کا بہنا، جریانِ خون

haft *n.* handle (of knife, agger, etc.) دستہ، قبضہ

hag *n.* ugly old won بدصورت بڑھیا witch چڑیل، ڈائن

haggard (*hag*-ě*d) *adj.* (of the face) tired, careworn and lined (منہ) اترا ہوا **haggardly** *adv.* looking tired تھکے ہوئے، اترے ہوئے منہ کے ساتھ

haggle (hag-ěl) *v. i.* dispute *over price* (*with* the shopkeeper) مول تول کرنا

hail (hayl) *n.* (also *hail-stone*) frozen raindrop اولا، ژالہ large number (*of* blows, etc.) کی بوچھاڑ *within hail*, within earshot جس تک آواز جا سکے *v.t.* & *i.* come down in a large number کی بوچھاڑ ہونا (with impersonal subject) *it hails*, hail-stones fall اولے پڑنا، ژالہ باری ہونا greet noisily خیر مقدم کے نعرے لگانا، خوش آمدید کہنا welcome خوش آمدید کہنا *hail friend* خوش آمدید بھائی *be hail fellow well met with*, be very familiar with کا یارِ غار ہونا call out پکارنا، آواز دینا، اونچی آواز سے بلانا *hail from*, have come from سے وارد ہونا، سے تشریف لانا، سے آنا، کا ہونا *He hails from Lahore* وہ لاہور سے آیا ہے، وہ لاہور کا ہے

hair (*hay*-ě*) *n.* (*pl.* same) thread-like growth on head, etc. بال any hair-like growth بال، پشم fluff رواں، رونگٹا very short distance ذرا سا فاصلہ *not to turn a hair*, give no sign of being troubled بالکل پریشان نہ ہونا *make (one's) hair stand on end*, fill (one) with terror رونگٹے کھڑے ہونا *to a hair*, exactly پوری تفصیل سے، بالکل ٹھیک **haircut** *n.* cutting بال کٹوانا، حجامت بنوانا *have a haircut* بال کٹوانا، حجامت بنوانا **hair-do** *n.* (colloq.) dressing of the hair بال بنانا **hair-dresser** *n.* one who cuts hair نائی، حجام، one who dresses hair اصلاح ساز، مشاطہ **hairpin** *n.* double-pronged pin for keeping the hair in place بالوں میں لگانے کا پن، بال پن *hairpin bend*, sharp bend in a road خطرناک موڑ **hair-breadth, hair's breadth,** *n.* a very short distance ذرا سا فاصلہ *hairbreadth escape, escape by a hairbreadth* بال بال بچنا **hair-splitting** *n.* making differences too small to be important موشگافی، بال کی کھال نکالنا **hair-cloth** *n.* cloth made of hair کھردرا اونی کپڑا **hairspring** *n.* a very delicate spring in a watch بال کمانی **hairbrush** *n.* brush used for doing one's hair بالوں کا برش **hairless** *adj.* bald **hairy** *adj.* of (or like) hair بال کا (سا) covered with hair بالوں سے بھرا ہوا strong and well-built مضبوط، کرخت

halcyon (*hal*-si-on) *n.* kingfisher ماہی خور، مچھر نگا similar bird once believed to make a floating nest on the sea which remained calm while it hatched its eggs ہلسیئون *halcyon days, halcyon weather*, calm and peaceful days or weather غیر طوفانی موسم، پرسکون موسم یا ایام

Halcyone (hal-*sī*-o-nee) *Cl. myth.* widowed daughter of the god of winds *Aeolus* (pr. *ee*-o-lus) who in her grief threw herself into the sea and became a kingfisher or *halcyon* (which see) ہلسیئونی

hale (hayl) *adj.* (usu. of old person) healthy تندرست توانا *hale and hearty*, healthy and lively چلتا پھرتا اور خوش باش *v.t.* drag (someone *away* or *off* to) گھسیٹ کر لے جانا، زبردستی لے جانا

half (hahf) (pl. *halves* pr. hahvz) *n.* & *adj.* one of the two equal parts آدھا، آدھ، نصف، نیم *adv.* to half the extent آدھا، آدھوں، آدھ partially کچھ کچھ، نیم *do (something) by halves*, do (it) badly ادھورا سا کام کرنا *too clever by half*, (usu. ironical) far too clever چالاک کہیں کا *go halves (with someone in something)* (کسی سے کوئی شے) آدھوں آدھ کرنا *(one's) better half*, (colloq.) (one's) wife بیوی *half-asleep*, not fully sleeping آدھا سوتا آدھا جاگتا، نیم خوابیدہ *half the time* آدھا وقت *half-time*, recess وقفہ، تفریح *half a share, a half share, half the share* آدھا حصہ *half-read*, superficially read نیم خواندہ، ادھ پڑھا *half-blood*, (*a*) person having the same father or mother but not both سوتیلا (*b*) this relationship سوتیلاپن *half-brother* سوتیلا بھائی *half-sister* سوتیلی بہن *half-bred*, offspring of different species or differently coloured races دوغلا *half-breed*, half-bred person دوغلا *half-caste*, child of European father and Indian or Pakistani mother اینگلو پاکستانی *halfcrown*, British coin worth 2s. 6d. نصف کراؤن *half-hearted*, lacking enthusiasm بددلانہ، پھیکا سا *half-heartedly* without enthusiasm بددلی سے *half-holiday*, working day with half the time (usu. afternoon) off آدھی چھٹی *(fly) at half-mast*, (of flag) (be) at the middle of the mast as a token of mourning (پرچم کا) سرنگوں (ہونا) *half-mast, half-mast high*, (of flag) flying at half-mast (پرچم) سرنگوں *half measures*, not thorough نامکمل اقدامات *half-moon*, moon with only half the disc showing پہلے یا تیسرے ہفتے کا چاند *half nelson*, a hold in wrestling کشتی کا ایک داؤ *get a half nelson on*, gain complete mastery over پر قابو پالینا، پر حاوی ہو جانا *half-pay*, half of pay آدھی تنخواہ *half the battle*, a promising start آدھا معرکہ **half-tone** *n.* system of printing from photographic blocks in which light is indicated by small dots and dark by large ones ہاف ٹون *half-truth*, statement not fully true نیم راستی *half-seas-over*, half-drunk شرابی سا، نیم مدہوش *half-volley* (*a*) (in tennis, striking of bouncing ball the moment it rises نیم والی (*b*) (in cricket) ball so pitched as to be easily hit نیم والی (*c*) hit ball thus نیم والی لگانا *half-way house*, (*a*) inn midway between towns بیچ کی سرائے (*b*) possible compromise ممکن سمجھوتہ **half-penny** (*hayp*-ni) *n.* (pl. *half-pence*, pr. *hay*-pens) British coin worth half a penny نصف پنس **half-pennyworth, ha'p'orth,** (*hayp*-ath) *n.* what a halfpenny will buy ٹکے کا

hall (*hawl*) *n.* large public room جلسہ گاہ building with such room جلسہ گاہ (in hostels) large room for meals ہال، طعام گاہ *dine in hall* طعام گاہ کا رکن ہونا entrance, lobby ڈیوڑھی mansion حویلی large room in a mansion دیوان خانہ *servants' hall*, dining-room for servants in a mansion نوکروں کے کھانے کا کمرہ

hallmark *n.* mark of the standard of silver or gold مہر mark (of good quality) ثبوت، نشان *v. t.* stamp with a hallmark as a guarantee

hallelujah, alleluia (al-a-*loo*-i-ya) *n.* song of praise to Jehovah, *i.e.*, to God حمد، ثنا *int.* praise be to God ! الحمد للہ، الٰہی تیرا شکر، بحمد اللہ، شکراً

hallo, halloa, halloo, hello, hullo (hal-*oh*)

int. cry to call attention ہیلو! ہوت ! *n.* such cry *v. i.* utter such cry ہیلو کہہ کر پکارنا ، ہیلو کہنا
hallow (*hal*-o) *v.t.* regard as sacred مقدس جاننا (old use) Christian saint عیسائی ولی **Hallowmas** *n.* All Saints Day observedon November 1 یوم اولیا **All Hallows** *n.* Hallowmas یوم اولیا
Hallowe'en *n.* evening preceding All Hallows شام اولیا **hallowed** *adj.* sacred مقدس
hallucination (ha-lew-si-*nay*-shĕn) *n.* seeming to see something not present چھلاوا ، فریب نظر something so imagined وہم ، خیال ، باطل ، فریب نظر
halo (*hay*-lo) *n.* circle of light (round solar bodies) such circle shown in paintings, etc., of saints نورانی تاج ، ہالہ
halt (*hawlt*) *v. t.* & *i.* (cause to) stop on a march or journey رکنا ، روکنا hesitate (between) تذبذب دکھانا ، متذبذب ہونا ، رک رک کر کہنا stop momentarily 'en route' رکنا ، ٹھہرنا *n.* such stop ٹھہرنے کی جگہ ، پڑاؤ **haltingly** *adv.* hesitatingly رک رک کر
halter (*hawl*-tĕ*) *n.* rope, etc., put round horse's neck رسّا rope for hanging a criminal with پھانسی کا پھندا death by hanging پھانسی
halve (hahv) *v.t.* divide into two equal parts آدھوں آدھ کرنا lessen by one-half آدھا کم کرنا **halved** (hahvd) *adj.* divided into two equal parts آدھا کیا ہوا
halyard, halliard (hal-yah*d) *n.* rope for raising or lowering a flag or sail (پرچم یا بادبان) اونچا نیچا کرنے والی رسی
ham *n.* cured meat from a pig's thigh سؤر کی ران کا گوشت
hamadryad (ha-ma-*drī*-ad) *Cl. myth.* wood-nymph living and dying in the tree in which she dwelt ہمہ دریاد ، بن دیوی
hamlet (*ham*-let) *n.* very small village کھیڑا ، چھوٹا گاؤں
hammer (*ham*-ĕ*) *n.* tool for driving in nails, etc. ہتھوڑا *go at it hammer and tongs*, argue vigorously and noisily چلا چلا کر دلائل پیش کرنا

a hammer

come under the hammer, be auctioned نیلام ہونا *v.t.* & *i.* strike (as) with a hammer کوٹنا ، پیٹنا ، ٹھونکنا *hammer something thin* کوٹ کوٹ کر ورق بنانا *hammer at*, knock at (door, etc.) دروازہ کھٹکھٹانا *hammer out (something)*, produce it by hard work محنت سے تیار کرنا *hammer away at*, work hard at پر خوب محنت کرنا
hammock *n.* hanging bed جھولن ، کھٹولا
hamper (*ham*-pe*) *v.t.* obstruct روڑا اٹکانا ، رکاوٹ ڈالنا *n.* large basket with lid for food بند ٹوکری
hamstring (ham-string) *v.t.* cripple کونچیں کاٹنا
hand *n.* end part of the arm ہاتھ pointer سوئی four-inch measure چار انگل round in a game of cards تاش کی ایک بازی direction سمت handwriting خط *write a good hand* خوش خط لکھنا workman کاریگر ، مزدور ، ملازم cards dealt to a player پتّے skill مہارت crew جہازی ملاح *on the right hand*, to the right داہنی طرف *in (one's) hands*, under (his) control کے ہاتھ میں *all hands*, all the crew جہاز کے سب ملازم *at hand*, (a) present موجود ، حاضر (b) about to happen عنقریب ہونے والا *live from hand to mouth*, spend whatever is earned کچھ نہ بچانا *lend (or give) a helping hand to (someone)*, help (him) کی مدد کرنا ، کا ہاتھ بٹانا *in hand*, (a) available موجود (b) receiving attention پیش نظر *out of hand*, out of control ہاتھ سے نکلا ہوا *off-hand*, extempore فی البدیہہ *bind hand and foot*, bind securely ہاتھ پاؤں کس کر باندھنا *win hands down*, win easily آسانی سے جیت جانا *keep (one's) hand in*, keep (one's) skill by practice کی مہارت قائم رکھنا *to hand*, within easy reach قریب ہی *to (one's) hand*, ready for (one's) purpose کو منتظر *with a heavy hand, with a high hand, with an iron hand*, oppressively بڑی سختی سے ، سخت گیری سے *(at) first hand*, directly بلاواسطہ ، براہِ راست *(at) second hand*, indirectly بالواسطہ ، کسی سے *clean hands*, innocence بے گناہی *hand in hand (with)* کے ہاتھ میں ہاتھ ڈالے *hand-to-hand fight*, fighting at close quarters دو بدو ، دست بدست لڑائی *at the hand of*, through کے ہاتھ *by hand*, per messenger, etc. دستی *from hand to hand* ہاتھوں ہاتھ *on all hands*, to or from all sides ہر طرف ، چاروں طرف *on the one hand . . . on the other (hand)*, contrast of two sides of the same issue ایک طرف تو (یہ) دوسری طرف (یہ) *shake hands*, greet thus مصافحہ کرنا ، ہاتھ ملانا *give (one's) hand to*, pledge marriage to سے شادی کی بات پکی کرنا *wash (one's) hands of*, disclaim all responsibility ذمّے داری لینے سے انکار کرنا *with heart and hand*, whole-heartedly تن من دھن سے ، دل و جان سے *take in hand*, adopt اختیار کرنا *set the hand to*, begin (کسی کام) میں ہاتھ ڈالنا ، شروع کرنا *have (one's) hands full*, be busy بالکل مصروف ہونا *have (something) in hand*, be doing (it) کر رہے ہونا *change hands*, pass from the control of one into another's ایک کے قبضے سے دوسرے کے قبضے میں چلا جانا *set (one's) hand to (an agreement)*, sign (it) (معاہدے) پر دستخط کرنا *lay hands on*, usurp ہتھیانا ، اپنا قبضہ جمانا *come to hand*, get ملنا ، پانا *v. t.* lead or assist (someone into a place) دستگیری کرنا ، ہاتھ دینا ، مدد کر کے پہنچانا give دینا *hand in*, submit پیش کرنا ، دے دینا *hand*

over, make over دے دینا *hand on the news*, convey it to others خبر دُوسروں کو پہنچانا *adj*. used or carried by the hand دَستی، ہاتھ کا *hands up* !, order to lift hands in surrender ہتھیار ڈال دو! *hands off* !, order not to touch ہاتھ اُٹھاؤ! *hand round*, give to one person after another باری باری دینا *hand over hand*, passing hands as in rope climbing ہاتھ باری باری آگے ڈال کر **hand-bag** *n*. small bag ہینڈ بیگ، تھیلا **handbill** *n*. printed advertisement distributed by hand دستی اشتہار **handbook** *n*. small guide-book رہنما (رسالہ)، رہبر (کتاب) **hand-cart** *n*. cart pushed by hand ہاتھ گاڑی، ہتھ گاڑی **handcuff** *n*. chained metal rings placed round a prisoner's wrists ہتھکڑی *v.t.* to chain with them ہتھکڑی لگانا **handful** *n*. as much as a hand holds مُٹھی بھر a small number ذرا سا **handout** *n*. Press Note, *i.e.*, information supplied (usu.) by the (Directorate of Public Relations) اعلامیہ **handicraft** *n*. art or craft needing skill with the hands دستکاری **handicraftsman** *n*. skilled manual worker دستکار **handiwork** *n*. something done or made by hand ہاتھ کا کام *handiwork of*, work done through کے ذریعے ہونے والا کام **handwriting** *n*. style of writing خط **handy** (*han*-di) *adj*. not far away قریب ہی convenient برتنے میں سہل useful مفید *come in handy* مفید ثابت ہونا **handily** *adv*. conveniently سہولت سے، آسانی سے

handicap (*hand*-i-kap) *n*. disadvantage imposed on competitor to make chances of success for all nearly equal کسی مقابلے میں پیش آنے والی رکاوٹ such competition رکاوٹوں والا مقابلہ impediment رکاوٹ *v.t.* (-pp-) be a handicap to رکاوٹ ہونا، کے لیے معذوری کا باعث ہونا

handicraft *n*., **handiwork** *n*. (see under **hand**)

handkerchief (*hank*-ĕ*-chif) *n*. piece of cloth used for wiping the face رومال

handle (*hand*-ĕl) *n*. part of something by which it may be held in the hand دستہ *v.t.* take in the hands ہاتھ میں لینا deal tactfully with سے نبٹنا control (men) سے کام لینا **handle-bar** *n*. steering-bar for a bicycle سائیکل کا ہینڈل

handloom *n*. loom worked by hand کرگھا

handmaid, handmaiden *n*. maid لونڈی، کنیز

handsel, hansel *n*. New Year gift سال نو کا تحفہ

handsome *adj*. good looking generous (income, etc.) بڑا، بہت **handsomely** *adv*. generously فراخ دلی سے، بہت خوب

handwriting *n*., **handy** *adj*. (see under **hand**)

hang *v.t.* & *i*. (*hang, hung, hung*) fasten (or be fastened) in a swinging position *to*, *on* or *from* a hook, *to* or *on* a wall, *from* the ceiling لٹکنا، لٹکانا *hang*, (*hanged, hanged*) put (someone) to death by hanging him or her with a rope round the neck پھانسی دینا، پھانسی پر لٹکانا *hang fire*, (*a*) (of a gun) be long in exploding داغنے میں دیر لگنا (*b*) (of an issue) be still undecided کھٹائی میں پڑا ہونا، زیر بحث ہونا *hang about*, (*a*) loiter near کے لیے وقف (*b*) remain near and wait کے قریب بیکار پھرنا انتظار رہنا، کے انتظار میں پڑے رہنا *hang back*, hesitate پچکچانا، جھجکنا show unwillingness to act ; *hang a door*, attach it with hinges کواڑ کے پٹ قبضوں کے ساتھ لگانا *hang the head*, let it fall forward in shame سر جھکانا *hang on to*, hold tightly سے چمٹے رہنا، کو تھامے رہنا *hang together*, support one another ایک دوسرے کی تائید کرنا *be hung up*, hang fire لٹکتے رہنا، کھٹائی میں پڑنا *hang a curtain* پردہ ڈالنا، پردہ لٹکانا *hang wall paper*, paste it دیوار پر سجاوٹی کاغذ لگانا *n*. the way in which a thing hangs لٹکنے کا انداز (slang) general idea مطلب، مفہوم *Did you get the hang of it* ? کیا اس کا کچھ مطلب تمہارے پلے پڑا اُحمق۔ (as imprecation) hanging (سُولی (چڑھے *not to care a hang for*, not to care at all for کی بالکل پروا نہ کرنا **hangdog** *n*. & *adj*. sneaking and ashamed (person or his looks) شرمندہ اور خوشامدی **hanger** *n*. wooden bar for hanging clothes on it ہینگر، کھونٹی wood on side of steep hill لٹکتا ہوا جنگل، معلق جنگل **hanger-on** *n*. obsequious follower طفیلی **hang-over** *n*. unpleasant after-effects of drinking خمار، نشہ اُترنے کا اثر **hangings** *n*. *pl*. curtains پردے **hangman** *n*. executioner جلاد، پھانسی پر لٹکانے والا

hangar (*hang*-ĕ*) *n*. shed for aircraft ہوائی جہازوں کے لیے چھپّر

hangdog *n*. & *adj*., **hanger** *n*., **hanger-on** *n*., **hang-over** *n*., **hangings** *n*. pl., **hangman** *n*. (see under **hang**)

hank *n*. coil thread لچھا، پیچک

hanker (*hank*-ĕ*) *v. t*. crave (*after*) کی آرزو میں مرنا، متمنی ہونا **hankering** *n*. craving آرزو، تمنا

hanky (*hank*-i) *n*. (child's word for) handkerchief رومال

hansom (*han*-sum) *n*. old fashioned two wheeled horse-cab for two passengers, with driver mounted behind کرائے کا تانگہ، ہنسم

haphazard (hap-*haz*-ĕ*d) *n*. (at or by) mere chance اتفاق *adj*. accidental اتفاقی *adv*. by chance یونہی اتفاق سے

ha'p'orth *adj*., **halfpennyworth** *adj*. (see under **half**)

happen (*hap*-ĕn) *v.i*. occur ہونا، واقع ہونا، پیش آنا *happen on* (or *upon*) find by chance اتفاقاً کوئی کام کرنا، اتفاقاً ملنا **happening** *n*. (usu. *pl*.) event واقعہ (ج: واقعات)

] To **happen** is to come to pass without preparation; ccur, more formal; **take place** by arrangement; ecur, happen not rarely; **impend**, be about to appen.

ppy (*hap*-i) *adj*. pleased خوش، مسرور pleaant مبارک، خوش آئند well suited موزوں **happy-go-ucky** *adj*. haphazard اتفاقی care-free بے پروا لاابالی **happily** *adv*. with pleasure خوشی سے **happiess** *n*. pleasure خوشی، سرور

ra-kiri (hah-ra-*kee*-ri) *n*. ceremonial suicide ormerly common in Japan خودکشی، ہاراکیری

rangue (ha-*rang*) *n*. long and loud speech زوردار تقریر *v.t.* & *i*. speak like that (کے سامنے) زوردار تقریر کر

rass (*ha*-ras) *v.t.* trouble دق کرنا، ستانا، پریشان کرنا attack repeatedly زچ کرنا **harrassment** *n*. arassing or being harassed پریشانی

rbinger (hah*-*bin*-jĕ*) *n*. herald نقیب something foretelling another پیش خیمہ *v.t.* erald آمد آمد کی خبر دینا

rbour (*hah**-bĕ) *n*. shelter for ships بندرگاہ place of safety ملجا و ماوی، پناہ گاہ *v.t.* give ylum to پناہ دینا hold in the mind (illlings, etc.) دل میں رکھنا

d (hah*d) *adj*. firm and solid سخت harsh سخ difficult مشکل *hard by*, near at hand قریب *hard upon*, not far behind قریب ہی *hard cash*, ns and notes نقد، نقدی *hard facts*, facts as opsed to theories, etc. یقینی حقائق *hard currency*, one ficult for a country to spend because of its erse balance of trade عسیر الحصول سکے، زر سخت *try d*, make much effort سخت کوشش کرنا *hard hit*, erely hit جسے سخت صدمہ پہنچا ہو *hardboiled egg*, fully led one پوری طرح ابلا ہوا انڈا *hard of hearing*, rather f قدرے بہرا *hard labour*, penal servitude, *i.e.*, risonment with hard physical labour قید بامشقت *-earned*, earned with toil محنت سے پایا ہوا، محنت کی *hard and fast*, (rules, etc.) that cannot be red to fit special cases قطعی، ناقابل تغیر *hard luck*, *lines*, undeservedly hard fortune بدقسمتی، برے *hard lines on (someone)* کسی کے برے دن *hard times*, od of high prices, unemployment, etc. برے *hard water*, one containing too much lime بھاری *hard up*, (of person) short of money نادار، قلاش، جیب *hard wood*, any heavy close-ned wood سخت لکڑی *be hard put to it*, *hard pres-* in difficulty مشکل میں *hard-headed*, not at all mental غیر جذباتی *hard-hearted*, callous سنگدل *nut to crack*, (*a*) hard problem ٹیڑھی کھیر، مشکل مسئلہ ifficult to get along with ٹیڑھا آدمی *hard on*, unjust to سے ناانصافی کرنے والا **hardihood** *n*. boldness بہادری **hardship** *n*. severe suffering سختی، مشکل **hardware** *n*. metal wares دھاتی مال، پکا سامان **hardly** (*hah**d-li) *adv*. with difficulty مشکل سے scarcely صرف، محض، بمشکل، مشکل سے *hardly any*, very little شاید ہی کوئی

hardy (*hah**-di) *adj*. able to endure hardship جفاکش strong قوی، مضبوط boldness (of plant) not damaged by frost جو پالے سے نہ سڑے **hardily** *adv*. boldly جرات سے **hardihood** *n*. boldness دلیری، جرات audacity ڈھٹائی

hare (*hay*-è*) *n*. animal like a rabbit but much larger than it بڑا خرگوش *hare-brained*, rash جلد باز

harem (*hay*-è-rem) *n*. English name for the women's part of a Muslim household زنانخانہ، حرم سرا، اندر

hark (hah*k) *v.i.* listen سننا، کان دھرنا *hark back to*, revert to پھر اسی بات پر آجانا

harlequin (*hah**-li-kwin) *n*. comic character in pantomime playing the role of Pantaloon's servant and Columbine's lover مسخرا نوکر، ہارلکن hence person given to practical jokes عملی مذاق کرنے والا

harlot (*hah**-lut) *n*. prostitute طوائف، بیسوا base woman ذلیل عورت

harm (hah*m) *n*. damage نقصان *v.t.* harm نقصان پہنچنا **harmful** *adj*. damaging مضر، ضرر رساں، نقصان دہ **harmless** *adj*. causing no harm بے ضرر **harmlessness** *n*. being harmless بے ضرر ہونا

harmonic *adj*. **harmonica** *n*., **harmonious** *adj*., **harmonium** *n*., **harmonize** *v.t.* & *i*., **harmonist** *n*. (see under **harmony**)

harmony (*hah**-mo-ni) *n*. agreement مطابقت *be in harmony with* سے میل کھانا میل pleasing combination of notes or colours ہم آہنگی sweet melody دلکش، شیریں یا سریلا نغمہ **harmonius** (hah*-*moh*-ni-us) *adj*. in agreement مطابق pleasingly combined ہم آہنگ sweet-sounding شیریں **harmonic** *adj*. pertaining to musical harmony ہم آہنگی سے متعلق **harmonica** (hah*-*mon*-i-ka) *n*. mouth-organ منہ کا باجا **harmonium** (hah*-*moh*-ni-um) *n*. musical instrument with keyboard and reeds ہارمونیم **harmonize** (*hah**-mo-niz) *v.t.* & *i*. (cause to) be in harmony (*with*) ہم آہنگ ہونا یا کرنا **harmonist** *n*. musician نغمہ نواز

harness (*hah**-nes) *n*. fittings for a draft horse گھوڑے کا ساز و یراق *die in harness*, die while yet on duty کام کرتے کرتے مرنا *v.t.* put harness on (a horse) گھوڑے جوتنا harness (a river, etc.) use it to produce electric power سے پن بجلی پیدا کرنا

harp (hah*p) *n.* a large musical instrument with strings that are plucked بربط *v.i.* play the harp بربط بجانا *harp on (something)*, talk repeatedly about (it) باربار وہی بات کہے جانا **harpist, harper** *n.* player on the harp بربط نواز

harpoon (hah*-*poon*) *n.* spear on a rope for catching whales مچھلیاں پکڑنے کا نیزہ، ماہی گیر نیزہ *v.t.* catch with a harpoon نیزے سے مچھلی پکڑنا

harpsichord (*hah*p*-si-koh*d) *n.* piano-like musical instrument ہارپ سیکورڈ

harpy (*hah**-pi) *n.* *Cl. myth.* cruel monster with woman's face and bird's wings and claws ہارپی *the harpies*, symbols of the stormy wind ہارپیاں، خونی آتش م طوفان rapacious person خونخوار

harrow (*ha*-roh) *n.* heavy spiked frame for breaking up ground after ploughing سہاگہ، مینڈا distress رنج پہنچانا *under the harrow*, distressed مصیبت کا مارا، مصیبت کے منہ میں آیا ہوا، سراون پھیرنا ہینگا، ترائون

harry (*ha*-ri) *v.t.* plunder تاخت وتاراج کرنا attack frequently باربار حملہ کرنا worry سخت تنگ کرنا

harsh (hah*sh) *adj.* irritating سخت severe سخت **harshly** *adv.* severely سختی سے **harshness** *n.* severity سختی

hart (hah*t) *n.* male deer بارہ سنگھا

harvest (*hah**-vest) *n.* season's crops فصل cutting and gathering them کٹائی quantity thus obtained فصل consequence نتیجہ، انجام *v.t.* reap (wheat, etc.) فصل کاٹنا *harvesting season* کٹائی کے دن **harvester** *n.* reaper کٹائی کرنیوالا، فصل کاٹنے کی مشین

hash *v.t.* cut up (meat) into small pieces گوشت کی چھوٹی چھوٹی بوٹیاں کرنا *n.* cooked meat recooked after hashing دوبارہ پکایا ہوا گوشت *make a hash of*, do badly بری طرح کرنا

hasheesh *n.* (see under **hashish**)

hashish, hasheesh (ha-*sheesh*) *n.* Arabic name for dried hemp leaves used as a drug حشیش، بھنگ

hasn't *v.* (1st. person sing. negative abb. see under **have**)

hassock (*has*-uk) *n.* kneeling-cushion گھٹنے ٹیکنے کا گدا

haste (hayst) *n.* hurry جلدی، تیزی *make haste*, hurry جلدی سے *in haste, in great haste*, hurriedly جلدی سے

hasten (*hays*-ĕn) *v.t.* & *i.* act with speed جلدی کرنا go quickly جلدی جانا cause (someone) to hurry جلدی کہنے کو کہنا cause (something) to be got done quickly جلدی کرانا **hasty** *adj.* hurried جلدی کا، جلدی میں کیا ہوا speedy تیز careless بے پروا، جلد باز **hastily** *adv.* hurriedly جلدی جلدی، تیزی سے **hastiness** *n.* hurry جلدی، تیزی، سرعت

hat *n.* outdoor headcovering (usu. with a brim) for men or women ہیٹ، ٹوپی *talk through (one's) hat*, talk foolishly بے وقوفی کی باتیں کرنا *take off one's hat to*, (a) salute اپنی ٹوپی اتار کر کسی کو سلام کرنا (b) show respect to کسی کا احترام کرنا *I take off my hat to him* میں اس کے احترام میں ٹوپی اتار رہا ہوں

hatch (hach) *v.t.* & *i.* (of a chicken) be born from an egg انڈے سے نکلنا (of a henbird) sit on (eggs) انڈے سینا cause (chickens) to be born بچے نکالنا develop (a plot, etc.) منصوبہ وغیرہ، پکانا *n.* (also *hatchway*), opening in a floor, esp. in the deck فرش میں کھلنے والا دروازہ، فرشی دروازہ cover for a hatch فرشی دروازے کے تختے **hatchery** *n.* place for hatching fish مچھلیوں کی افزائش نسل کی جگہ، مچھلیوں کا زچہ خانہ

hatchet (*hach*-et) *n.* small axe کلہاڑی *bury the hatchet*, end the dispute جھگڑا ختم کرنا

hate (hayt) violent dislike نفرت *v.t.* dislike نفرت کرنا **hateful** *adj.* causing hatred نفرت انگیز **hatred** (hayt-red) *n.* abhorrence (*of*) نفرت

haughty (*hawt*-i) *adj.* arrogant مغرور **haughtily** *adv.* غرور سے، بکبر و نخوت سے **haughtiness** *n.* arrogance غرور، کبر، نخوت

haul (hawl) *v.t.* & *i.* drag forcibly گھسیٹنا *haul along* کھینچے لیے جانا *haul up* کھینچ کر باہر نکالنا *haul (rope)* کھینچنے کے لیے زور لگانا *haul (someone) over the coals*, reprimand (him) فہمائش کرنا act of hauling کھینچ fish hauled up in a net جال میں پکڑی ہوئی مچھلی

haunch (hawnch) *n.* part of the human body between the ribs and thighs کولھا similar part of an animal's body پٹھا

haunt (hawnt) *v.t.* visit frequently آنا جانا recur to the mind irritatingly باربار آنا، چکر لگانا ذہن میں بس جانا، پرچھا جانا، (سر پر) مسلط ہونا *n.* place frequently visited (*by* criminals, etc.) کا اڈہ supposed abode of giants, etc. بسیرا **haunted** (*hawn*-ted) *adj.* (of a place) frequently visited by ghosts بھوتوں کا بسیرا *be haunted by*, (a) be the abode of (giants) کا بسیرا ہونا (b) irritate the mind by frequent recurrence پر مسلط ہونا

have (hav) (pr. t. 3rd person sing., *has*, pr. t. pa. t. and pa. p., *had*; *'v*, *'s*, and *'d* are respectively the abbreviated forms of have, has and had; *havn't*, *hasn't*, *hadn't*, pr. respectively ĕnt, *haz*-ĕnt, and *had*-ĕnt, are the colloq. forms for do not have, does not have, and did not have) *auxiliary v.* (helps to form the perfect and perfect continuous tenses : I have seen, I been seeing (present) ; I had seen, I had been seeing (past) ; I shall have seen, I shall have been seeing (future) ہونا v.t. & i, ☆ own کا ہونا، possess رکھنا، کے پاس ہونا ☆ own as کی ملکیت ہونا relations کے ہونا، کا ہونا bear a child (کے بچّہ) ہونا permit ہونے دینا state as a fact بیان کرنا show کرنا، دکھانا suffer (pleasure or pain) (خوشی یا رنج) ہونا، راحت یا کلفت get (done) کرانا He had him murdered اُس نے اُسے مروا ڈالا (10) be compelled (to do) (کو) کرنا، پڑا مجھے اپنا کام کرنا پڑا I had my work to do (11) take (food) کھانا پینا (12) engage in (game, etc.) (کوئی کھیل) کھیلنا (Phrases :) the Ayes have it, those in its favour are in the majority موافق جیت گئے I had him there, had in it the advantage over him میں نے اِس میں اُسے مارا، اِس میں میرا پلّہ اُس پر بھاری رہا he will have it that, he maintains that وہ یہ کہنے پر مصر ہے as he has it, as he puts it بقول اس کے had better, had rather, would do well to بہتر سمجھے گا کہ، بہتر ہوگا کہ let him have it, (slang) punish him اسے سزا بھگتنے دو be had, be cheated دھوکا کھانا have at, attack حملہ کرنا have done ! stop ! بس بس have it your own way, polite way of refusing to argue further چلیے اپنی ہی مرضی کو دیکھیے، آگے آپ کی مرضی have (someone) up, sue (him) in a law-court پر عدالت میں دعویٰ کرنا have to do with, have something to do with, be connected with سے متعلق ہونا، اسے وابستہ ہونا have nothing to do with, not to be connected with سے متعلق نہ ہونا have it out with (someone), thrash out (or even quarrel) in order to come to a settlement over it with (him) کھل کر بات کرنا، اِدھر یا اُدھر کر کے چھوڑنا

haven (hay-ven) n. harbour بندرگاہ safe place محفوظ مقام place of rest آرام کی جگہ

haversack (hav-ĕ*-sak) n. soldier's canvas bag فوجیوں کا تھیلا

havoc (hav-uk) n. destruction تباہی، بربادی work havoc among, play havoc of, destroy تباہ و برباد کرنا cry havoc, order the army to loot the vanquished enemy فوج کو لوٹ مار کا حکم دینا

haw n. red fruit of hawthorn (which see) ہاتھرن کا پھل

hawk n. a keen-sighted bird of prey باز، شاہین، شِکرا v.t. be a pedlar پھیری لگانا **hawker** n. pedlar پھیری والا

hawthorn (haw-tho*n) n. thorny shrub with white or red flowers and red berries (called haws) ایک خاردار جھاڑی، ہاتھرن

hay n. cut and dried grass for use as fodder سوکھی گھاس hay fever, a fever affecting the nose and throat تپِ کاہی make hay while the sun shines, make the best of the favourable opportunity بہتے دریا میں ہاتھ دھونا **hay-rick, hay-stack** n. mass of hay stored in the field سوکھی گھاس کا چوکور ڈھیر

haywire n. (U.S.) anything tangled اُلجھاؤ، پیچیدگی، اُلجھی ہوئی شے It is all haywire یہ عجیب پیچیدگی ہے go haywire, (a) become excited جوش میں آ جانا (b) become distracted مضطرب یا پریشان ہونا

hazard (haz-ĕ*d) n. risk جوکھوں، خطرہ at all hazards, at all costs ہر قیمت پر v.t. take the risk of جوکھوں میں پڑنا، خطرہ مول لینا venture to make (guess, etc.) کہنے (یا پیش کرنے) کی جسارت کرنا **hazardous** adj. risky خطرے والا، جوکھوں والا

haze (hayz) n. thin mist دُھند **hazy** (hay-zi) adj. misty دُھندلا vague دُھندلا

hazel (hay-zĕl) n. a nut-yielding bush ایک جھاڑی، ہیزل adj. reddish-brown سُرخی مائل، بادامی

he (hee) pron. (he, him, his ; pl., they, them, their, theirs) وہ n. (pl., hes) male نر، مرد he-man, (U.S.) masterful man مرد آدمی، نر آدمی

head (hed) n. part of the body containing brain سر life جان، زندگی cost (someone) his head, cost him his life (میں) کسی کی جان جانا brain دماغ from (one's) head, by (one's) own reasoning power اپنی عقل سے lay heads together, lay their heads together, consult each other باہمی مشورہ کرنا، سر جوڑ کر بیٹھنا old head on young shoulders, wisdom in youth جوانی میں عقل lose (one's) head, be unnerved in the face of difficulty گھبرا جانا، ہوش قائم نہ رہنا keep (one's) head, remain calm ہوشمندی سے کام لینا off (one's) head, mad پاگل take it into (one's) head that, come to believe that سر میں یہ سودا سما جانا کہ (talk) above (someone's) head, (say) things which are beyond (his) understanding (کسی کی) عقل سے اُونچی باتیں (کرنا) top or front سر، سرا come to a head, develop into a crisis فیصلہ کن حالات پر پہنچنا image of head سر کی تصویر، تصویر heads or tails, one of two sides staked تصویر کہ زنجیر be unable to make head or tail of (something), be perplexed by it کا سر پیر کچھ سمجھ نہ آسکنا ☆ one person کس، شخص per head فی کس crowned heads, kings and queens تاجدار (pl. same) unit of a flock or herd راس (مویشی) 67 head of cattle سر سٹھ راس مویشی chief صدر، رئیس، حاکم اعلیٰ first position اوّلیت at the head of the list سرِ فہرست (10) upper end (of valley, lake, etc.) پرلا سرا (11) division in writing ذیلی عنوان (12) progress ترقّی make head against (a) progress in spite of کے باوجود ترقّی کرنا (b) not to lose ground in the face of کے مقابلے میں ڈٹے رہنا v.t. & i. be at the head of میں سب سے آگے ہونا move towards (or for) کی جانب بڑھنا، کی طرف جانا head (someone) off, get in front in order to turn (him) back کسی کا مُنہ موڑنے کے لیے اس سے آگے جانا give the heading to سُرخی جمانا، عنوان لگانا، دینا یا قائم کرنا strike (football) with head سر سے مارنا، ہیڈ کرنا **head-dress** n.

ornamental head-covering بیچیلی وٹی **headhunter** *n.* savage collecting his enemy's heads as trophies سرکا شکاری ، سر شکار **heading** *n.* word or words at the head of a piece of writing عنوان ، سرخی **headlamp** *n.* large lamp on motor-car موٹر کا بڑا لیمپ **headland** *n.* cape راس **headlight** *n.* powerful light on the front of car, locomotive or aircraft, or at the mast of a ship سامنے کی بتی ، بڑی بتی **headline** *n.* newspaper heading عنوان ، سرخی **headlong** *adj.* with the head first سر کے بل thoughtless and hurried جلد بازی کا thoughtlessly and hurriedly بھٹ پٹ ، جلد بازی سے **headman** *n.* chief of the village or tribe سَردار (in Pakistan) revenue collector of the village نمبردار **headmaster** *n.* (fem. *headmistress*) chief teacher in a school ہیڈ ماسٹر ، اوّل مدرّس ، صدر مدرّس **head-on** *adj.* & *adv.* (of collisions) with the front parts (of vehicles, etc.) meeting آمنے سامنے کی ٹکر **head-phones** *n. pl.* ear-phones سر پر پہنک جانے والا ٹیلیفون ، ٹوپی فون **headquarters** *n. pl.* place from which activities of something are controlled ہیڈ کوارٹر ، صدر مقام ، صدر **headstrong** *adj.* self-willed خود سر ، سرکش **headway** *n.* progress ترقی *make considerable headway* کافی آگے بڑھ جانا **headword** *n.* the first word of a dictionary entry used as a heading and printed in heavy type لغات میں جس لفظ کی تشریح کی جائے ، لغت **headworks** *n.* river dam from where canals take off ہیڈ ورکس ، نہری بند

heal (heel) *v.t.* & *i.* make or become well صحت یاب ہونا یا کرنا **health** (helth) *n.* condition of the body صحت *good health* اچھی صحت *poor health* خراب صحت state of being well تندرستی ، صحت *drink a health to* (*someone*), raise one's (usu. wine) glass and wish good health to (him) کسی کا جام صحت نوش کرنا **healthy** (*hel*-thi) *adj.* having good health صحت مند conducive to good health صحت بخش **healthful** *adj.* conducive to good health صحت مندانہ ، صحت بخش

health *n.*, **healthful** *adj.*, **healthy** *adj.* (see under **heal**)

heap (heep) *n.* pile ڈھیر *heaps of*, (colloq.) plenty of ڈھیروں *v.t.* put (*up*) in a heap ڈھیر لگانا *heap favours upon*, favour him a lot نوازشات کی بارش کرنا

hear (hee-ĕ*) *v.t.* & *i.* (*hear, heard, heard* ; heard is pr. hĕ*d) catch the sound of سُننا *hear from*, receive message from کا پیغام ملنا ، کی طرف سے اطلاع پانا *hear of*, have knowledge of کا علم ہونا ، کے متعلق جاننا (of a judge) try (a case) مقدمے کی سماعت کرنا **hear hear** *int.* cry expressing approval or agreement ہیئر ہیئر ، واہ واہ ! **hearing** *n.* catching the sound of سُننا *within hearing*, near enough to be hea[rd] جس تک آواز پہنچ سکے *out of hearing*, too far off to [be] heard جس تک آواز نہ پہنچے *hard of hearing*, somewh[at] deaf اونچا سننے والا ، قدرے بہرا **hearsay** *n.* rumo[ur] سنی سنائی ، افواہ

hearken (*hah**-kĕn) *v.i.* (old use) listen [to] کان دھرنا

hearse (hĕ*s) *n.* carriage for carrying a cof[fin] جنازہ گاڑی

heart (hah*t) *n.* heart-pump of the bo[dy] دل ، قلب centre of the affection or emotio[ns] دل ، قلب centre وسط ، مرکز *in the heart of*, in [the] centre of (city, etc.) کے وسط میں playing ca[rd] marked with red hearts پان *have the heart* (*to something*), be sympathetic enough (to do [it]) (کرنے کی) توفیق ہونا *lose heart*, feel discouraged شکستہ [دل] ہونا *lose* (or *give*) (*one's*) *heart to*, fall in love w[ith] (کو) دل دے بیٹھنا ، ہمت ہارنا *take heart*, have cour[age] ہمت باندھنا *take* (*something*) *to heart*, be m[uch] affected by it بہت متاثر ہونا ، دل لگانا *a change of he[art]* change for the better in a person دل بدل جانا *a heart of oak*, be brave بہادر ہونا *after* (*one's*) *heart*, of the sort most liked پسند کا ، اپنی مرضی کا (*have* or *learn*) *by heart*, (learn) by rote [حفظ] کرنا ، زبانی یاد کرنا *heart and soul*, wholeheartedly دل سے *at heart*, in one's innermost feelings دل میں *ha[ve no] heart*, be callous دل پتھر ہونا *heart of hearts*, in[ner]most feelings دل کی گہرائی *in* (*one's*) *heart of he[arts]* دل ہی دل میں *set the heart at rest*, be easy in m[ind] حوصلہ کرنا *searching of heart*, misgivings شبہات

heart-searching *n.* sincere appraisal of [one's] actions and feelings دل ٹٹولنا **heart-ache** *n.* دکھ ، رنج **heart-beat** *n.* one movement of heart's regular motion دل کی دھڑکن **heart-bre[aking]** *adj.* sorrowful دل توڑنے والا ، دل شکن **heart-bro[ken]** *adj.* grieved دل شکستہ **heartburn** *n.* bur[ning] sensation below the heart, caused by indiges[tion] چھاتی میں جلن ، معدے کی جلن **heart-burning** *n.* [dis]content بے اطمینانی **hearten** (*hah**-tĕn) *v.t.* [give] courage to ہمت بندھانا *heartening* ہمت افزا **heart[felt]** *adj.* deeply felt دلی ، قلبی **heartless** *adj.* ظالم ، سنگدل **heart-rending** *adj.* causing deep [grief] دل کے ٹکڑے ٹکڑے کر دینے والا **heart-strings** *n. pl.* [deep]est feelings دلی احساسات ، جذبات صمیمانہ **heart-troub[le]** heart-disease دل کی تکلیف ، دل کا عارضہ **hearty** enthusiastic پُرجوش strong and healthy *hale and hearty* (see under *hale*) (*of eating*) heavy بہت *n.* (university use) athlete دل والا ، جیوٹ (as vocative) brave sailor بازان

my hearties! میرے بہادر جہازرانو! **heartily** *adv.* enthusiastically جوش و خروش سے

hearth (hah*th) *n.* base of a fire-place آتش دان چولھا، آتشدان، انگیٹھی the fireside کا فرش home; family circle گھر بار *hearth and home* عزیز و اقارب، گھر بار، بال بچے

heat (heet) *n.* hotness گرمی، حرارت، تپش *heat stroke,* prostration by excessive heat گرمی سے غشی intense feeling گرما گرمی، جوش matches or competition before the finals آخری سے پہلے مقابلے، ابتدائی مقابلے hot weather گرمی *v.t.* & *i.* make or become warm or hot گرم ہونا یا کرنا، تپنا یا تپانا **heat stroke** *n.* prostration by excessive heat سخت گرمی سے نڈھال ہو جانا **heat-wave** *n.* period of unusually hot weather گرمی کی لہر، سخت گرمی **heatedly** *adv.* angrily طیش میں آ کر، جوش سے

heath (heeth) *n.* area of flat waste land بیہڑ low shrubs growing on heaths بیہڑ کی جھاڑیاں، بیہڑ چھوٹی جھاڑیاں

heathen (*hee*-dhen) *n.* & *adj.* (one) not believing in Israel's God (hence one other than a Jew, a Christian or a Muslim) غیر اہل کتاب، کافر **heathenish** *adj.* like a heathen's کافرانہ **heathenism** *n.* disbelief in God کفر، الحاد **heathendom** *n.* area inhabited by such persons کفرستان، غیر اہل کتاب کی دنیا یا علاقہ

heather (*hedh*-ě*) *n.* heath with purple flowers ہیدر، بیہڑ کی لال پھولوں والی جھاڑی **heathery** *adj.* place with heather ہیدر سے بھرا، ہیدر پوش

heave (heev) *v.t.* & *i.* lift up (بوجھ) اٹھانا pull (*at* or *on* a rope) کھینچنا (colloq.) lift and throw اٹھا پھینکنا rise and fall چڑھنا اور اترنا، ابھر کر گرنا *heave a sigh,* sigh آہ بھرنا *heave a sigh of relief,* feel relieved امن کی سانس لینا *heave in sight,* (of a ship) come into view نظر آنے لگنا *n.* act of heaving ابھرنا، کھینچنا، ہانپنا

heaven (*hev*-ěn) *n.* the abode of God and His angels آسمان، عالم بالا paradise جنت، بہشت، فردوس any place or condition of great happiness خوشی (*pl.*) (*the heavens*), the sky آسمان *good heavens* (int.) showing surprise! خدا کی پناہ! خدا پناہ **heavenly** *adj.* of, from or like heaven آسمانی extremely beautiful and delightful پیکر حسن و خوبی very sacred مقدس آسمانی، قدسی not earthly but ethereal

heavy (*hev*-i) *adj.* weighty بھاری، وزنی tedious (writing) اکتا دینے والی (تحریر) dull (person) ٹھس (آدمی) abnormal بڑا بھاری، غیر معمولی *heavy rain* شدید بارش *heavy road,* that is full of mud کیچڑ والی سڑک *heavy-going* (*conditions*), those that make progress difficult مشکل حالات *adv.* heavily بمشکل

time hanging heavy (*on one's hands*) passing slowly بڑی مشکل سے کٹنے والا وقت، کاٹے نہ کٹنے والا وقت *with a heavy heart,* sadly بصد رنج و الم **heavy-weight** *n.* boxer weighing 175 lb. or more بھاری، گھونسے باز، موٹا تگڑا باز **heavily** *adv.* with heaviness بھاری پن سے، گرانی سے **heaviness** *n.* being heavy گرانی، بھاری پن

Hebrew *n.* the original and now the revived language of the children of Israel which is cognate to Arabic عبرانی

Hebe (*hee*-bee) *Cl. myth.* the Greek goddess of youth who was the cup-bearer of the gods and later married Hercules ہیبی

Hecate (*hek*-a-tee, or *hek*-ayt) *Cl. myth.* three-headed goddess identified with *Diana* on earth, *Luna* in the sky and *Proserpine* in the lower world ہیکیٹ

heckle (*hek*-ěl) *v. t.* harass the speaker with troublesome questions مقرر پر سوالات کی بوچھاڑ کرنا، سوالات سے مقرر کا منہ بند کرنا **heckling** *n.* harassing the speaker thus مقرر پر سوالات کی بوچھاڑ

hectic (*hek*-tik) *adj.* red owing to some disease (esp. T. B.) بیماری سے سرخ، لال بھبوکا *hectic cheeks,* those of a consumptive person دق کے مریض کا چہرہ، مدقوق شخص کا چہرہ (life or time) full of excitement) and without rest زور شور سے کام میں مصروف

hecto- (*hek*-toh) *pref.* a hundred سو، صد *hectogramme* سو گرام، صد گرام

hector (*hek*-tě*) *v. t.* & *i.* bully دھونس جمانا *n.* bully بزدل ظالم، شیخی مار خاں (*Hector*), the Trojan prince slain by Achilles ہکٹر

Hecuba (*hek*-ew-ba) the unfortunate mother of Hector; she is noted for her misfortunes after the fall of Troy ہکوبا

hedge (hej) *n.* row of bushes forming a boundary جنگلا، باڑ any barrier *v. t.* & *i.* put a hedge round کے گرد لگانا obstruct راستہ بند کرنا، روکنا *hedged in with,* obstructed by کے باعث ٹال جانا، گول مول جواب دینا مجبور evade a question secure oneself against loss (in bet or speculation) by further bets or speculation مزید شرط بد کر (یا مزید سٹہ لگا کر) نقصان سے بچنا **hedge-contracts** *n.* such contracts نقصان سے بچنے کے لیے مزید شرطیں بدنا (یا مزید سٹہ بازی) **hedgerow** *n.* hedge **hedgehog** *n.* small spinecovered mouse-like animal سیہی، خارپشت **hedgehop** *v. t.* (see *Addenda*)

heed *n.* attention توجہ *pay heed to* کی طرف توجہ کرنا *take no heed of* کی توجہ نہ کرنا *v.t.* pay heed to پر کان دھرنا، کی طرف توجہ کرنا **heedful** *adj.* careful ہوشیار **heedless** *adj.* careless بے پروا، غافل **heedlessly** *adj.* carelessly بے توجہی سے

heedlessness *n.* carelessness بے خبری، بے پروائی
heel *n.* back part of the human foot, sock or shoe ایڑی *take to (one's) heels, show a clean pair of heels*, run away نو دو گیارہ ہو جانا، بھاگ جانا *down at heel*, (*a*) (of shoes) worn down at the heels جس کی ایڑیاں گھسی ہوئی ہوں (*b*) (of person) poorly dressed پھٹے پرانے کپڑوں میں (U. S. slang) cad سفلہ، کمینہ، رذیل *v.t.* put new heels (on shoes) جوتوں کی نئی ایڑیاں لگانا (also *heel in*), cover with loose earth before planting پودا لگانے سے پہلے ہلکی مٹی ڈالنا
hefty (*hef*-ti) *adj.* (colloq.) big and strong موٹا تازہ، ہٹا کٹا
heifer (*hef*-ĕ*) *n.* young cow that has not yet had a calf جوان بچھیا
height (hīt) *n.* distance from bottom to top بلندی *Murree's height 5500 feet* height above sea-level بلندی، سطح سمندر سے بلندی high place اونچی جگہ utmost degree انتہا، نہایت *at its height*, at its maximum اپنے پورے عروج پر **heighten** (*hi*-tĕn) *v. t.* make higher اونچا کرنا enhance بڑھانا، زیادہ کرنا
heinous (*hay*-nus) *adj.* (of crime) atrocious سخت ظالمانہ، وحشیانہ
heir (*ay*-ĕ*) *n.* (fem. *heiress*) one entitled to a legacy وارث **heirdom, heirship** *n.* title to legacy وراثت، حق وراثت
Helen (*hel*-en), **Helena** (*hel*-e-na) *Cl. myth.* the woman who was the cause of the famous Trojan War ; the beautiful daughter of Zeus and Here, she was wedded to the Greek king Menelaus from whom she eloped with the Trojan prince Paris and thus became a bone of contention between the Greeks and the Trojans ہیلن
held *v.* (pa. t. & pa. p. of **hold,** which see)
helicopter (*hel*-i-kop-tĕ*) *n.* aircraft which can take off straight up ہیلی کاپٹر، بالاپرواز
Helicon (hel-i-kon) *Cl. myth.* a Greek mountain sacred to Apollo and the Muses ہیلیکن
Helios (*hee*-li-os) *Cl. myth.* Greek sun god later identified with Apollo ہلیس
heliport *n.* (see *Addenda*)
helium (*hee*-li-um) *n.* a light gas ہیلیئم
hell (hel) *n.* place of punishment after death دوزخ، جہنم place or condition of great suffering عذاب دوزخ (in strong language) *a hell of*, much بہت *what the hell do I care !* I do not care ! میں کیا سمجھتا ہوں : میری جانے جوتی **Hell** int. expressing anger ! لعنت ! بھاڑ میں جائے !
hello *int.* same as **hallo,** which see)
helm *n.* handle for moving the rudder of a boat پتوار government ; guidance حکومت، اقتدار *helm of state*, government حکومت *be at the helm of affairs*, be conducting سربراہی کرنا، برسر اقتدار ہونا (old use) (abbr. of) helmet خود
helmet (*hel*-met) *n.* soldier's metal head-covering خود sola hat سولا ہیٹ
help *v. t.* & *i.* & *n.* aid مدد دینا، امداد کرنا *help (oneself) to*, take and eat کھانا *help yourself to it*, شوق فرمائیے، تناول فرمائیے avoid بچنا، جان بچانا *there is no help for, cannot be helped, cannot help it*, is unavoidable اس سے بچنا ممکن نہیں، اس سے کوئی مفر نہیں، اس کا کوئی علاج نہیں **helper** *n.* one who helps مددگار، معاون **helpful** *adj.* giving help مددگار useful مفید، سود مند **helping** *n.* portion of food served on a person's plate ایک کے لیے نکالا ہوا کھانا **helpless** *adj.* powerless بے چارہ، بے بس **helplessness** *n.* powerlessness بے چارگی، بے بسی **helpmate** *n.* friend who helps یار و مددگار (also *helpmeet*), one's wife or husband میاں یا بیوی
helter-skelter (*hel*-tĕ*-*skel*-tĕ*) *adv.* in hurried confusion افراتفری میں، کھلبلی میں
hem *n.* edge of cloth turned and sewn down گوٹ، مغزی، سنجاف the sound *hem* ہونہہ کرنا *v. t.* & *i.* (-mm-) make a hem on گوٹ لگانا، کنارے ترپنا *hem (in, about or round)* surround گھیرے میں لے لینا **hemstitch** (*hem*-stitch) *n.* ornamental stitching ایک طرح کی کشیدہ کاری، سنجاف کاری *v. t.* decorate cloth with this تارکشی کرنا، سنجاف کاری کرنا
hemi (*hem*-i) *pref.* half (as in *hemisphere*) نصف، نیم
hemisphere (*hem*-i-sfee-ĕ*) *n.* half the earth نصف کرہ جنوبی half of any sphere نصف کرہ
hemlock (*hem*-lok) *n.* a poisonous plant شیکران sedative drug made from it عرق شیکران
hemorrhage *n.* (same as **haemorrhage,** which see)
hemp *n.* plant used in rope-making سن its fibre سن، سن کا ریشہ its leaves used as a drug ; hashish بھنگ، حشیش *Indian hemp*, hashish بھنگ
hen *n.* female of the domestic fowl مرغی any female bird (پرندے کی) مادہ **henpecked** *adj.* (of husband) ruled by his wife زن مرید
hence (hens) *adv.* from here یہاں سے (آگے) from now اب سے (بعد) *a month hence* اب سے مہینہ بھر بعد therefore اس لیے، لہٰذا **henceforth, henceforward** *adv.* from this time on آج سے، اب سے، آج کے بعد
henchman (*hench*-man) *n.* (pl. *henchmen*) unquestioning political supporter پٹھو

henna (*hen*-a) *n.* red hair-dye made from a shrub مہندی ، حنا
hepatic (he-*pat*-ik) *adj.* pertaining to the liver جگر سے متعلق ، کبدی good for the liver جگر کے لیے اکسیر
hepta- *pref.* seven سات ، سات والا **heptagon** (*hep*-ta-gon) *n.* seven-sided polygon مسبّع
her (hě*) *pron.* & *adj.* of that woman اُس (عورت) کا to that woman اُس (عورت) ، کو (for the full conjugation see under its nominative form *she*) ; **herself** *reflexive pron.* خود اُس عورت نے (یا) ، کو (یا) کا
Hera (*hee*-ra), **Here** (*hee*-ree) *Cl. myth.* wife of the chief Greek god Zeus, and identified with the Roman Juno ہیرا (یا) ہیری
Heracles (*hee*-ra-kleez) *Cl. myth.* Greek name for their famous hero more commonly known as **Hercules** (which see) ہراکلیس
herald (*he*-rald) *n.* (old use) ruler's official messenger or announcer شاہی نقیب any announcer منادی ، منادی کرنے والا forerunner, harbinger نقیب ، آمد آمد کی خبر دینے والا *v. t.* make known the coming of آمد آمد کی خبر دینا **heraldry** *n.* science of noblemen's pedigrees and coats of arms جنگجو امرا کے خاندانوں کی تاریخ اور خاندانی نشانوں کا علم ، علم انساب art or office of a herald نقابت ، جاگیرداراں
heraldic *adj.* of heraldry جاگیرداروں سے متعلق ، نقیبانہ *heraldic devices*, blazoning of coats of arms خاندانی نشانات
herb (hě*b) *n.* any soft-stemmed plant whose leaves are used for medicinal purposes, etc. بوٹی ، جڑی بوٹی **herbage** *n.* herbs collectively (including grass) نباتات pasture سبزہ چارہ right of pasture on another's land چرائی کا حق **herbaceous** (*bay*-shus) *adj.* of or like herbs جڑی بوٹی کا سا planted with herbs جڑی بوٹی سے بھرا پڑا
herbal *adj.* of herbs جڑی بوٹی کا ، جڑی بوٹی سے متعلق
herbalist *n.* one who grows or sells medicinal herbs جڑی بوٹی والا **herbivorous** *adj.* (of animal) feeding on herbs چرندہ
Hercules (hě*-kew-leez), **Heracles** (*hee*-ra-kleez) *Cl. myth.* the most celebrated hero of Greek mythology. The son of Zeus, he was ultimately deified and married to Hebe. He performed the famous *twelve labours* which no one else could ہرقل ، ہرکل ، ہرکولیز any exceptionally strong man قوی ہیکل ، رستم *Pillars of Hercules*, rocks on each side of the Straits of Gibraltar آبنائے جبل الطارق کے دونوں کناروں کی چٹانیں **herculean** (hě*-kew-*lee*-ěn) *adj.* having or needing great powers of body or mind as were needed for performing the 12 labours of Hercules سخت مشکل ، کٹھن ، صبر آزما
herd (hě*d) *n.* company of animals together *the vulgar herd*, *the common herd*, the masses referred to contemptuously عوام کالانعام **herdsman** (hě*dz-man) *n.* man who looks after herds راعی ، گلہ بان
here (hee-ě*) *adv.* in this place یہاں to this place ادھر *here and there*, in various places ادھر ادھر *here, there and everywhere*, everywhere ہر جگہ *neither here nor there*, not to the point غیر متعلق ، ادھر ادھر کی
hereabouts *adv.* near here یہیں کہیں **hereafter** *n.* future مستقبل the life to come آخرت ، عاقبت *adv.* in the future آئندہ ، زندگی میں **hereby** *adv.* by means of this بذریعہ ہذا **herein** *adv.* in this اس میں **hereinbefore** (-*foh**) *adv.* in a preceding part of this document, etc. اوپر **hereupon** *adv.* at this point اِس پر **herewith** *adv.* with this اِس کے ساتھ ، منسلکہ
hereditary *adj.* (see under **heredity**)
heredity (he-*red*-i-ti) *n.* tendency to inherit characteristics from parents توارث **hereditary** *adj.* (of monarchy, disease, traits, etc.) passed on from generation to generation وراثتی ، خاندانی ، موروثی **hereditary monarchy**, kingship passing from father to son (etc.) موروثی بادشاہی *hereditary traits* خاندانی خصائل
heresy (*he*-re-si) *n.* belief contrary to that of Christianity (عیسائیوں کے نزدیک) کفر opinion contrary to the accepted one غیر مروجہ رائے unorthodox belief بدعت **heretic** (*he*-re-tik) *n.* one supporting a heresy کافر ، بدعتی **heretical** (he-*ret*-i-kěl) *adj.* of heresy or heretics کافرانہ
heretic, heretical *adj.* see under **heresy**
heritage (*he*-ri-tij) *n.* something (that would be) inherited ورثہ ، ترکہ
Hermes (hě*-meez) *Cl. myth.* the Greek god who was the herald and messenger of the rest of the gods ہرمیز
hermetic (hě*-*met*-ik) *adj.* of alchemy کیمیاگری سے متعلق *hermetic seal*, airtight closure by fusion گلا کر بند کرنے کا طریق ، ہوا روک مہر *hermetically sealed*, sealed in this way ہوا بند ، گلا کر بند کیا ہوا ، ہوا روک مہر
hermit (hě*-mit) *n.* one living in solitude تارک الدنیا ، گوشہ نشین ، زاہد
hern (hě*n) *n.* (same as **heron** which see)
[1]**hero** (*hee*-roh) *n.* (pl. *heroes*) man or boy admired for bravery or noble qualities بطل جلیل ، عظیم شخصیت chief man in a story, etc. ہیرو ، بطل

hero-worship *n.* almost a religious adoration of persons esteemed by one to be great بطل پرستی **hero-worshipper** *n.* one practising hero-worship بطل پرست **heroine** (*he*-roh-in) *n.* female hero ہیرئن، ہیروئن، عظیم شخصیت **heroic** (he-*roh*-ik) *adj.* of, like or fit for a hero ہیرو کا سا؛ **heroism** (*he*-roh-izm) *n.* great courage بہادری، عالی حوصلگی، مردانگی

²**Hero** (*hee*-roh) *Cl. myth.* the beautiful priestess of Venus ; she was loved by Leander who swam across the Hellespont every night to meet her in the temple at Sestos till he was drowned in a storm one night ہیرو

heroin (he-*roh*-in) *n.* a morphia preparation ہیروئن، افیم، مارفیا کا ایک مرکب

heron (*he*-run), **hern** (hĕ*n) *n.* longlegged water-bird بگلا

herring (*he*-ring) *n.* an edible sea-fish ہیرنگ (مچھلی)

hesitate (*hes*-i-tayt) *v. i.* show signs of uncertainty ہچکچانا، تذبذب میں پڑنا، متامل ہونا، تامل کرنا **hesitant** *adj.* hasitating ہچکچانے والا، متذبذب، متامل **hesitatingly, hesitantly** *adv.* with hesitation تذبذب کے ساتھ، ہچکچاہٹ سے **hesitation** (hes-i-*tay*-shèn) *n.* act of hesitating تامل، ہچکچاہٹ، تذبذب

Hesperides (hes-*pe*-ri-deez) *Cl. myth.* the pretty daughters of Hesperus who had gold apples in their garden ہسپریڈیز

hessian (*hesh*-èn) *n.* sack-cloth ٹاٹ، بوریا

heterodox (*het*-è-ro-doks) *adj.* unorthodox بدعتی، غیر متقلد **heterodoxy** *n.* not being orthodox بدعت

heterogeneous (het-ro-*jee*-ni-us) *adj.* made of different kinds مختلف العناصر

heuristic (hew-*ris*-tik) *adj.* (of teaching, etc.) enabling one to find out things for oneself خود آموز، خودکار

hew *v. t.* (*hew* ; *hewed* ; *hewed* or *hewn*) chop (*down*) (tree, etc.) کاٹنا shape by chopping کاٹ کر بنانا **hewer** (hew-ĕ*) *n.* one who hews کاٹنے والا *hewers of woods and drawers of water*, slaves لکڑی کاٹنے اور پانی بھرنے والے

hewn *v.* (pa. p. of **hew,** which see)

hex (heks) *n.* (see *Addenda*)

hexagon (*hek*-sa-gon) *n.* six-sided polygon مسدس

hexameter (*hek*-sa-mee-tè*) *n.* six-foot line of verse بحرِ مسدس، شش رکنی بحر

hey (hay) *int.* (for attracting attention or expressing surprise) او! اہا! اوہ!

heyday (*hay*-day) *n.* prosperous times بہار، جوبن، عروج *in the heyday of (one's) power* اپنے اقتدار کے دور عروج میں

hiatus (hi-*ay*-tus) *n.* lacuna

hibernate (*hi*-bĕ*-nayt) *v.i.* (of some animals) sleep through the winter جاڑے میں سوتے رہنا، سرماخوابی کرنا **hibernation** *n.* such sleep سرماخوابی

hiccough, hiccup (*hik*-up) *n.* sudden stopping of the breath with a cough-like sound ہچکی *v.i.* have a hiccough ہچکی لینا **Note :** The correct form is *hiccup* ; the spelling *hiccough* is due to confusion with *cough*. The pronunciation in both the cases is the same, *i.e.*, hik-up.

hick (hik) *n.* (U.S. colloq.) rustic سادہ لوح دیہاتی

hid *v.*, **hidden** *v.* (*pa. t.* & *pa. p.* of **hide,** which see)

hide (hīd) *v.t.* & *i.* (*hide, hid, hidden*) keep or put out of sight or knowledge چھپنا، چھپانا *hide and seek*, a game in which several seek the one who hides آنکھ مچولی *play hide and seek with,* (*a*) play this game with سے آنکھ مچولی کھیلنا (*b*) procrastinate ٹال مٹول سے کام لینا (*c*) (of a cat) hunt (mouse) thus کا شکار کرنا *n.* tough skin of animals کھال، ادھوڑی **hide-bound** *adj.* narrow minded تنگ خیال، تنگ نظر **hiding** (*hī*-ding) *n.* keeping or putting out of sight or knowledge چھپنا یا چھپانا، روپوشی *go into hiding*, hide oneself روپوش ہونا *be in hiding*, be hidden روپوش ہو جانا whipping or beating کوڑے مارنا، مارنا *give a good hiding to* کو اچھی طرح پیٹنا

hideous (*hid*-e-us) *adj.* very ugly گھناؤنا، بدنما، مخت frightful ڈراؤنا **hideously** *adv.* in a very ugly manner گھناؤنے پن سے

hie(hī) *v.i.* (old use) go quickly (*to*) کی طرف، جلدی جلدی جانا *hie thee*, go جلدی چلے جاؤ

hierarchy (*hī*-è-rah*-ki) *n.* government by priests پادریوں (یا ملاؤں) کی حکومت، مذہبی پیشواؤں کی حکومت organization (*of* something) with grades of authority فرقی مراتب والا نظام، نظامِ مراتب

hieroglyphic (hī-è-ro-*glif*-ik) *n.* ancient Egyptian picture-writing خطِ تصویری، نقوشِ مقدسہ *adj.* pertaining to it خطِ تصویری سے متعلق **hieroglyph** *n.* picture of some word in this writing نقشِ مقدس، تحریری تصویر

higgledy-piggledy (*hig*-èl-di-*pig*-èl-di) *adj* mixed up گڈمڈ *adv.* in a state of disorder

high (hī) *adj.* raised above others اونچا، بلند *How high is this structure ?* یہ عمارت کتنی اونچی ہے؟ *It is 40 feet high* یہ چالیس فٹ اونچی ہے *the Most High God* خالقِ اکبر *high opinion*, very good opinion بڑی اچھی رائے *high road*, trunk road شاہراہ hig *school*, one giving education more advanced than the one called primary or middle ہائی سکول، ثانوی مدرسہ *from on high*, from heaven آسمان سے *the high seas*, the open ocean, away from the land کھلا سمندر *a high sea*, one with big waves طوفانی سمندر، بحرِ مَوّاج، تلاطم خیز سمندر *(be running) high temperature*, (of someone) have high fever کو بہت تیز بخار ہونا *the Most High God* خالقِ اکبر (of time) far advanced *for something, to do something, that he did something* کافی حصّہ گزرا ہوا *It's high time (he did something)*, very little time is left (for him to do it) (کرنے کے لیے اس کے پاس) بہت تھوڑا وقت رہ گیا ہے (of edibles) beginning to go bad خراب ہوتی ہوئی *adv*. at a high level بڑھ کر *play high*, play at large stakes (داؤں پر) بڑھ کر لگانا *run high*, (of the sea) be stormy (سمندر کا) طوفانی ہونا **highball** *n*. (U.S.) whisky-and-soda served in a tall glass بڑے گلاس میں وِسکی سوڈا **high-born** *adj*. born of a noble family خاندانی **high-brow** *n*. & *adj*. (U.S. colloq.) (person) looking down upon the tastes of the masses عامیانہ مذاق کو حقارت سے دیکھنے والا (شخص) **High Court** *n*. chief law-court عدالت عالیہ **high-falutin, high-faluting** (-*loo*-) *adj*. U.S. words for *high-flown* (which see) **hi-fi** *n*., **high fidelity** *n*. (see *Addenda*) **high-flown** *adj*. (*high-faluting* or *high-falutin*, U.S. forms), (of style) bombastic, pompous مشکل (یا) لفاظی والا (اسلوب) (of ideas) quixotic, extravagant پادر ہوا باتیں، خیالی (پلاؤ) **high-handed** *adj*. overbearing ظالمانہ، جابرانہ **high-handedness** *n*. ظلم، جبر، اِستبداد **high-hat** *n*. one who affects superiority ٹھسّے والا، اپنے کو بڑا سمجھنے والا *v.t.* & *i*. be such **highlands** *n. pl*. mountainous country پہاڑی علاقہ، کوہستان، کہستان *the Highlands*, North-West Scotland شمال مغربی سکاٹ لینڈ *Highlander*, native of the Highlands سکاٹ لینڈ کا پہاڑی باشندہ، پہاڑی سکاٹ **highlights** *n*. part of a picture, etc., reflecting most light تصویر کا روشن ترین حصّہ، روشن ترین پہلو main features (*of* plan, budget, etc.) (کے) اہم نکات **high-life** *n*. rich persons' way of living امیرانہ زندگی **highly** *adv*. to a high degree بہت *highly paid person* اونچی تنخواہ والا *think highly of*, have a high opinion of کے متعلق اچھی رائے رکھنا **high-minded** *adj*. of a hight character عالی ظرف، عالی منش **highness** *n*. being high بلندی، رفعت *His (Her or Your) Highness*, form of address or title of princes and princesses اعلیٰ حضرت، والا حضرت، (مؤنث) علیا حضرت **high-spirit** *n*. adventurous nature منچلاپن، بلند حوصلگی **high-spirited** *adj*. adventurous منچلا **high-spirits** *n*. jollity شگفتہ مزاجی **hight-strung** *adj*. sensitive حد سے زیادہ حسّاس، اشتعال پذیر **high tide, high water** *n* مد، جوار بھاٹا **highway** *n*. high road, trunk road شاہراہ *highways and byways (of)*, all the facts (of) (کے) تمام پہلو **highwayman** *n*. mounted robber on highways رہزن، بٹ مار **high treason** *n*. (old use for treason), violation of allegiance to State (or sovereign) ریاست (یا فرمانروا) سے غداری **high words** *n*. harsh words سخت کلامی **high-water mark** *n*. maximum level of high tide جوار بھاٹے کی سب سے اونچی حد recorded maximum in any fluctuation بڑی سے بڑی حد، زیادہ سے زیادہ

hike (hīk) *n*. (colloq.) long tramp for pleasure or exercise لمبا پیدل سفر *v.i.* tramp لمبے پیدل سفر پر جانا **hiking** *n*. this as hobby لمبے پیدل سفر پر جانے کا مشغلہ **hiker** *n*. one who hikes لمبے پیدل سفر پر جانے والا

hilarious (hi-*lay*-ri-us) *adj*. noisily merry ترنگ میں **hilarity** (hi-*lay*-ri-ti) *n*. being hilarious ترنگ، ترنگ میں آنا

hill (hil) *n*. small mountain پہاڑی mound ٹیلا، تودہ **hilly** *adj*. having many hills پہاڑوں والا، پہاڑی (علاقہ) **hillock** *n*. small hill ٹیلہ

hilt *n*. handle of a sword or dagger قبضہ *up to the hilt*, completely پوری طرح، کامل

him *pron*. (objective case of **he**, which see) اس (مرد) کو **himself** *pron*. خود اس نے (یا) کو (یا) کا

hind (hīnd) *n*. female deer ہرنی *adj*. at the back (چوپائے کی) پچھلی *the hind legs (of a quadruped)* (چوپائے کی) پچھلی ٹانگیں **hindmost** *adj*. farthest back سب سے پیچھے کا

hinder *v.t*. (*hin*-dĕ*) obstruct روکنا، راہ میں حائل ہونا *adj*. (*hīnd*-ĕ*) one more hind or still more back اور پیچھے کا **hindrance** (*hin*-drans) *n*. thing that hinders رکاوٹ

hinge (hinj) *n*. joint قبضہ *v. t*. & *i*. support on a hinge قبضے سے جوڑنا، قبضہ لگانا *hinge up* (or *upon*), depend upon پر منحصر ہونا

hint *n*. indication اشارہ، کنایہ *v.t* & *i*. give a hint (*at* or *that*) اشارۃً کہنا

hinterland (*hint*-ĕ*-land) *n*. area behind port or sea-shore داخلی علاقہ

hip *n*. thigh-joint کولھا *int*. (in the phrase :) *hip, hip, hurrah!* cheer of approval in reply to: "three cheers for So-and-so" ہپ ہپ ہرّا

hippodrome (*hip*-o-drohm) *n*. large open space for chariot-racing, etc. رتھوں کی دوڑ کا میدان، مَعرَض

hippopotamus (hip-o-*pot*-a-mus) *n*. large African river animal دریائی گھوڑا

hire (*hī*-ĕ*) *v.t*. obtain or allow the use of in

return for fixed payment کرائے پر لینا یا دینا، کرائے کرنا، کرائے پر اُٹھانا *n.* hiring کرائے پر لینا یا دینا money paid for it کرایہ، اُجرت **hireling** *n.* person whose services may be hired بھاڑے کا ٹٹو۔ بکاؤ مال **hire-purchase** *n.* system of hiring with the attraction of becoming the owner of the hired thing after making a certain number of payments بالآخر خرید کرایہ

his (hiz) *pron.* (possessive case of **he** which see) اُس (مرد) کا

hiss (his) *n.* sound of the letter 's' سی اسائیں، شوں sound of boiling water کے شوں شوں کرنے کی آواز such sounds to show disapproval اظہارِ ناپسندیدگی کے لیے "سی سی" کی آواز *v.t. & i.* make the sound of the letter 's' "سی" کرنا sound like boiling water شوں شوں کرنا express disapproval by a hissing sound "سی سی" کرکے اظہارِ ناپسندیدگی کرنا *hiss an actor off the stage* ناپسندیدہ اداکار کو "سی سی" کرکے اسٹیج سے نکل جانے پر مجبور کرنا

history (*his*-tè-ri) *n.* branch of knowledge dealing with past events of a people or of the world تاریخ description of any type of past events تاریخ، سرگزشت *It has a history behind it* اِس کا لمبا قصہ ہے *history sheet* (*of patient or criminal*), details of his past illness or crime (مریض یا مجرم کی) فردِ حقیقت **historian** (his-*toh*-ri-an) *n.* writer of history مورّخ، تاریخ دان associated with the past times تاریخی **historical** *adj.* of history تاریخی not imaginary ; not legendary اصلی، حقیقی، تاریخی (of novels, etc.) تاریخی **historiography** *n.* the writing of history in an official capacity وقائع نگاری، تاریخ نویسی

historicity *n.* genuineness of an event in history تاریخی حقیقت

histrionic (his-tri-*on*-ik) *adj.* of the theatre تھیئٹر کا of acting اداکارانہ **histrionics** *n. pl.* theatrical display ناٹک کا فن speech and behaviour designed for effect like an actor's اداکاروں کے سے انداز، اداکارانہ انداز

hit *v.t. & i.* strike مارنا، ضرب لگانا *hit (someone) with (the sword, etc.) on (the head, etc.)* کسی کے سر پر (تلوار وغیرہ) کی ضرب لگانا *hit it off with (someone)*, agree with or get on well with him سے خوب بنھنا *be hard hit, (by someone)*, be severely affected سے سخت نقصان ہونا، کے ہاتھوں سخت صدمہ پہنچنا *hit on (or upon) (a plan, etc.)*, discover by chance سوجھنا۔ ہاتھ لگنا *n.* blow ضرب (in cricket) hitting of the ball ہٹ *a lucky hit*, a successful attempt کامیاب کوشش، اندھے کے پاؤں تلے بیٹر *make a hit*, be a stupendous success **hit parade** *n.* (see *Addenda*)

hitch (hich) *v.t. & i.* pull (up) with a jerk جھٹکے سے کھینچنا fastened, (*on* or *to* a hook, etc.) لگنا یا لگانا، لٹکنا یا لٹکانا *n.* sudden pull جھٹکا hindrance رکاوٹ *go off without a hitch*, proceed smoothly آسانی سے ہونا۔ بغیر کسی رکاوٹ کے ہونا **hitch-hike** *v.i.* (U.S.) (also *hitch*), travel by begging lifts from passing motor-cars بیگانی کاروں میں خیراتی سیاحت کرنا **hitch-hiking** *n.* travelling thus بیگانی کاروں میں خیراتی سیاحت

hither (*hidh*-è*) *adv.* (old use) in this direction اِدھر **hitherto** (*hidh*-è*-*tū*) *adv.* till now اب تک

hive (hiv) *n.* (also *bee-hive*) artificial home for bees شہد کی مکھیوں کا خانہ

hoar (hohr) *adj.* greyish white سفیدی مائل (of hair) white with age بڑھاپے سے سفید، سفید **hoar-frost** *n.* frozen dew پالا **hoary** *adj.* of hair) white with age سفید، نورانی very old and venerable عمر رسیدہ، بزرگ، بہت بوڑھا، کہن سال اور قابلِ احترام

hoard (hoh*d) *n.* guarded store ذخیرہ *v.t. & i.* save and store (*up*) ذخیرہ کرنا، سینت سینت کر رکھنا

hoarding (*hoh**-ding) *n.* the act of hoarding سینت سینت کر رکھنا a high wooden fence لکڑی کا جنگلا such a fence for advertisments والا جنگلا

hoarse (hoh*s) *adj.* (of the voice) rough and harsh بھاری (آواز)، پھٹی ہوئی (آواز)، بیٹھا ہوا (گلا) *cry oneself hoarse* رو رو کر گلا بیٹھ جانا، چیخ چیخ کر گلا بیٹھ جانا (of a person) having a hoarse voice بیٹھی یا پڑی ہوئی آواز والا **hoarsely** *adv.* with a hoarse voice بیٹھی ہوئی آواز

hoax (hohks) *n.* deceitful humorous trick ہنسی ہنسی کو ہنسی ہنسی میں جھانسا *play a hoax on* میں دیا ہوا جھانسا دینا *v. t.* deceive in this way بے وقوف بنانا، بنانا

hobble (*hob*-èl) *v. t. & i.* limp لنگڑا کر چلنا speak haltingly رک رک کر بولنا، اٹکنا (of verse) run haltingly میں روانی نہ ہونا tie a horse's legs together to keep it from going far away گھوڑے کی ٹانگیں ایک ساتھ باندھ دینا *n.* limping gait لنگڑا کر چلنا

hobbledehoy (hob-èl-de-*hoi*) *n.* awkward youth who has not yet grown out of his childishness اُلھڑ چھوکرا

hobby (*hob*-i) *n.* interesting occupation for one's leisure مشغلہ، ہابی **hobbyhorse** *n.* rocking wooden horse لکڑی کا جھولنا، گھوڑا horse on a merry-go-round چرخ چوں کا گھوڑا child's stick with horse's head on it گھوڑا ڈنڈا

hobgoblin (hob-*gob*-lin) *n.* imp شریر بچہ bug-bear کابوس
hobnail (*hob*-nayl) *n.* short nail with heavy head used for boot جوتوں میں لگانے کی موٹی کیل
hobnob (*hob*-nob) *v.i.* (-bb-) have friendly talk بے تکلفی کی باتیں کرنا drink (*with* someone) ہم پیالہ و ہم نوالہ ہونا
Hobson's choice *n.* offer that must be taken because there is no other choice لازمی، لابدی
hock (hok) *v.t.* pawn گروی رکھنا، رہن رکھنا *n.* state of being in pawn گِرو، رہن ہونا، گِرو ہونا *in hock*, (*a*) in pawn (*b*) in debt مقروض (*c*) in prison قید (میں)
hockey (*hok*-i) *n.* game played with curved sticks and hard ball by two teams of eleven players each ہاکی
hocus-pocus (*hoh*-kus-*poh*-kus) *n.* jugglery مداری کا کھیل
hoe (hoh) *n.* tool for cutting up weeds and loosening soil کھرپا *v.t.* & *i.* use a hoe کھرپنا، نلائی کرنا، نراثا
hog *n.* castrated male pig خصی سور dirty and greedy person گندا، لالچی *go the whole hog*, do something thoroughly پوری طرح کرنا
hoist (hoist) *n.* a kind of elevator on a ship اونچا کرنے کی کل، بلند ساز، مرتفع *v.t.* lift up (with a hoist) اونچا کرنا، اٹھانا *hoist a flag*
hokum (*hoh*-kum) *n.* stage or screen play, etc., meant for the uncritical گھٹیا ڈراما یا فلم
[1]**hold** (hohld) *v.t.* & *i.* (held, held) keep fast رکھنا، پکڑنا، پکڑے رکھنا، پکڑے رہنا possess پر قابض ہونا، رکھنا contain کا مالک ہونا گنجائش ہونا یا رکھنا restrain روکنا، قابو میں رکھنا remain unchanged باقی رہنا، اسی طرح پر رہنا، لگا رہنا occupy (a position or status) رکھنا conduct (conversation, examination, meeting, etc.) کرنا، منعقد کرنا believe کو یقین ہونا defend (a place) کی حفاظت کرنا *hold back*, hesitate رکنا، ہچکچانا *hold* (*something*) *back*, keep it secret مخفی رکھنا *hold* (*someone* or *oneself*) *back*, restrain روکنا، روکے رکھنا *hold forth*, preach کی تبلیغ کرنا *hold off*, keep at a distance اپنے سے پرے رکھنا *hold out*, (*a*) put up defence مقابلہ کرنا (*b*) (of supplies, etc.) last چلنا، باقی رہنا hold out (an assurance, etc.) (یقین وغیرہ) دلانا *hold something over*, postpone it روک رکھنا، ملتوی کرنا *hold up*, (*a*) delay دیر لگانا (*b*) stop by force for the purpose of robbery پر ڈاکہ ڈالنا، ڈاکہ زنی کے لیے روکنا *hold* (*someone* or *something*) *up*, support (it) تھامے رہنا، سنبھالے رہنا *hold on to* (*something*), stick to (it) پر قائم رہنا، کرتے رہنا *hold the view that*, believe that یہ نظریہ ہونا کہ *hold* (*one's*) *breath*, keep it back سانس روکنا *hold* (*one's*) *hand*, grasp it ہاتھ پکڑنا *hold* (*one's*) *tongue*, *hold* (*one's*) *peace*, keep quiet چپ ہو رہنا، چپکا رہنا، خاموش رہنا *hold good*, (*a*) be true ٹھیک ہونا (*b*) be still in force ابھی نافذ ہونا *hold with*, approve of کو پسند کرنا، کو منظور کرنا *hold hard!* (colloq.) stop doing it بس رک جاؤ *hold* (*one's*) *own*, stick to (one's) position اپنی بات پر جمے رہنا *n.* act, manner or power, of holding پکڑ، گرفت، قبضہ *catch* (*or get*) *hold of*, catch پکڑنا *keep hold of*, retain its grasp پکڑے رکھنا *lose hold of* (*something*), let it go کو ہاتھ سے نکل جانے دینا

cargo space in a ship جہاز کا گودام، جہاز میں مال بھرنے کی جگہ **hold-all** *n.* portable wrapping for bedding, clothes, etc., and used on journeys ہولڈال، بستر بند **holding** *n.* something held رکھنے والا، دار
freehold *n.* agricultural land owned absolutely مالکانہ حقوق والی اراضی **small-holding** *n.* a small piece of freehold مالکانہ حقوق والی تھوڑی سی اراضی **hold-up** *n.* act of holding up; dacoity ڈاکہ، ڈکیتی obstruction رکاوٹ *traffic hold-up*, traffic jam گاڑیوں کے باعث راستہ رک جانا
[2]**-holder** *suf.* that holds something رکھنے والا، دار *office-holder*, office-bearer عہدے دار *penholder*, thin stick, etc., for holding a nib ہولڈر **small-holder** *n.* تھوڑی سی اراضی کا مالک
hole (hohl) *n.* cavity سوراخ، چھید animal's burrow (چوہے کا) بل، سانپ کی بانبی وغیرہ *in a hole*, (colloq.) in an awkward situation بڑی مشکل میں *pick holes in*, find fault with میں کیڑے ڈالنا، میں نقص ڈالنا *hole and corner* (*methods, etc.*) secret and not straightforward خفیہ، مشتبہ، غیر دیانتدارانہ *v.t.* make holes in میں سوراخ نکالنا، میں چھید ڈالنا (in certain games) put into a hole سوراخ میں ڈالنا (*be*) *a round peg in a square hole*, (*be*) *a square peg in a round hole*, (be) a misfit ناموزوں (ہونا)، اپنی جگہ کے لیے ناموزوں (ہونا)
holiday (*hol*-i-day) *n.* day or days of rest from work چھٹی، تعطیل *bank holiday*, day on which all the banks are closed by law (usu. a general holiday) بنک کی چھٹی *adj.* gay خوشگوار، خوشی کا *holiday mood* خوش مزاجی
holiness *n.* (see under **holy**)
hollo *int.* (same as **hallo**, which see)
hollow (*hol*-oh) *adj.* not solid کھوکھلا sunken (face or eyes) دھنسی ہوئی آنکھیں، پچکے ہوئے گال hollow-eyed دھنسی ہوئی آنکھوں والا (of sounds) deep and dull دہشتناک، وحشت انگیز insincere (words) بناوٹی، جھوٹی *adv.* (colloq.) completely بھونڈی طرح (in the phrase :) *beat* (*someone*) *hollow*, give (him) a good hiding بری طرح پیٹنا *n.* hollow place کھوکھلا پن hole بڑا سوراخ valley وادی *v.t.* make a hollow in کو کھوکھلا کرنا، میں سوراخ کرنا make by hollowing out کھود کر بنانا، کھوکھلا کرکے بنانا **hollowness** *n.* being hollow کھوکھلا پن insincerity ریاکاری، بناوٹ depth (of sound) آواز کی دہشتناکی

holly (*hol*-i) *n*. an evergreen bush with prickly leaves and red berries ایک سدا بہار جھاڑی ، ہولی
holocaust (*hol*-o-kawst) *n*. whole burnt offering پوری جلی ہوئی قربانی wholesale sacrifice سب کی قربانی general destruction of human lives by fire آگ سے اِتلافِ جان
holster (*hol*-stě*) *n*. leather case for a pistol طپنچے کا چرمی خول ، طپنچہ دان ، پستول دان
holy (*hoh*-li) *adj*. sacred مقدس ، پاکیزہ ، پاک *the Holy Ghost*, the third person of the Trinity according to Christians رُوح القدس *the Holy Land*, Palestine ارضِ مقدس devoted to religion دیندار ، نیک حق پرست **holiness** *n*. being holy تقدس ، تقدیس *His* (or *Your*) *Holiness*, title of and form of address for the Pope تقدس مآب
homage (*hom*-ij) *n*. tribute of respect خراجِ عقیدت *paying homage to* کو خراجِ عقیدت پیش کرنا (old use) acknowledgement of loyalty to an overlord
home (hohm) *n*. place where one lives with one's family گھر ، گھر بار one's own house *go home*, go to one's house گھر جانا native country گھر وطن ، دیس (also *stranger's house*) place for the care of unlooked after, poor and helpless persons محتاج خانہ *at home*, (*a*) in one's house گھر میں (*b*) prepared to receive visitors ملاقات کے لیے تیار (*be, feel* or *make oneself*) *at home*, not feel strange اپنا ہی گھر سمجھنا ، بے تکلفی سے بیٹھنا *at-home*, reception دعوتِ استقبالیہ *adj*. of the home گھریلو ، خانگی *home life*, خانگی زندگی of the country's inside affairs داخلی *the Home Office*, Britain's Ministry of Interior برطانوی وزارتِ داخلہ *Home Rule*, autonomy in inland affairs ہوم رُول *adv*. to, at or in one's home or country گھر میں ، اپنے گھر میں ، وطن میں ، اپنے وطن میں اپنے دیس میں *bring* (*something*) *home to* (*someone*), make (him) fully conscious of (it) کسی کے کچھ ذہن نشین کرنا **homeless** *adj*. without a home بے خانماں
home-made *adj*. made in one's native land دیسی (مال) **homesick** *n*. & *adj*. sad because away from home گھر کی یاد ، گھر کی یاد کا ستانا **homesickness** *n*. sadness because of staying away from home . **homespun** *n*. & *adj*. (cloth) made at home دیسی کپڑا **homestead** *n*. farmhouse with land and out-building باڑہ
homeward *adj*. & *adv*. (going) towards home سوئے وطن ، عازمِ وطن *homeward bound*, going home عازمِ وطن
home-truth *n*. painful mention of someone's weakness دُکھتی رگ
homely (*hohm*-li) *adj*. plain and simple سیدھا سادہ unpretending بلا تصنع (U. S.) not beautiful سیدھے سادے نقش بے تکلف causing one to feel at home گھر کا سا بے تکلف *a homely atmosphere* گھر کا سا ماحول ، گھریلو ماحول
homicide (*hom*-i-sid) *n*. killing of a human being قتلِ نفس one who kills a fellow being قاتل قتلِ **homicidal** *adj*. pertaining to homicide نفس سے متعلق
homily (*hom*-i-li) *n*. sermon وعظ tedious moral lecture اکتا دینے والی نصیحت
homo (*hoh*-moh) *n*. (in zoology) man ; an individual of the species 'homo sapiens' آدمی ، انسان
homo sapiens *n*. mankind as a species انسان ، آدمی ، آدم زاد ، نوعِ انسانی ، نسلِ انسانی
homœopathy *n*. treatment of diseases with medicines producing like symptoms ہومیو پیتھی ، علاج بالمثل **homœpath** *n*. doctor practising homœpæthy ہومیو پیتھ ، معالج بالمثل **homœopathic** *adj*. pertaining to homoeopathy ہومیو پیتھک ، بالمثل (علاج)
homogeneous (hoh-moh-*jee*-ni-us) *adj*. of the same kind متجانس ، ہم قسم
homonym (*hom*-o-nim) *n*. word of same form or sound but different in meaning (e.g. *in, inn*) ہم آواز متجانس لفظ
homosexual (hoh-moh-*sek*-sew-ěl) *n*. person fond of sexual relations within own sex ہم جنس پسند *adj*. pertaining to homosexuality ہم جنس پسندانہ **homosexuality** *n*. such fondness or practices ہم جنس پسندی
honest (*on*-est) *adj*. straightforward دیانتدار **honestly** *adv*. دیانتداری سے **honesty** *n*. being straightforward دیانت ، دیانتداری سے
honey (*hun*-i) *n*. (pl. *honeys*) sweet juice made by bees شہد darling پیاری ، جانی **honeycomb** *n*. network of bees' cells شہد کی مکھیوں کا چھتہ *v.t.* fill with holes, tunnels, etc. سرنگیں وغیرہ نکال کر چھلنی کر ڈالنا **honeyed, honied** (*hun*-id) *adj*. (of words, etc.) sweet شیریں ، شہد کے سے میٹھے ، مدھ بھرے **honeymoon** *n*. (usu. a month's) holiday taken by a newly married couple ہنی مون ، ماہِ عسل **honeysuckle** *n*. a fragrant creeper ایک خوشبودار بیل ، شہد آشام
honorarium (on-è-*ray*-ri-um) *n*. fee for professional services offered in order to bypass rules of regular service اعزازی تنخواہ ، اعزازیہ
honorary (*on*-è-ra-ri) *adj*. (abb. *Hon.*), (of a post) without salary and only as an honour بلا تنخواہ ، اعزازی (of a degree, etc.) given as an honour without the usual requirement اعزازی
honour (*on*-ě*) *n*. fame and respect قدر و منزلت great respect عزت ، احترام ، اعزاز reputation for good character وقار نیک نامی ، شہرت person or thing bringing credit (*to*) کے لیے باعثِ فخر ، فخر و ناز

(abbr. *Hons.*), distinction اعزاز *an Honours degree*, a degree conferred for distinguished work آنرز/اعزاز کے ساتھ بی۔اے (آنرز)، بی اے (اعزاز کے) B.A. (Hons.) title خطاب *Honours List* فہرست خطابات *code of honour*, conventional standard of conduct معاشرتی ضابطۂ اخلاق *a guard of honour*, ceremonial presentation of arms in someone's honour گارڈ آف آنرز *present a guard of honour to* کو گارڈ آف آنر کا سلامی دینا *in honour of*, to honour کے اعزاز میں *do the honours of*, act as host to کا میزبان بننا *on my honour*, honourably اپنی عزت کی قسم *His* (or *Your*) *Honour*, (form of address to judges) جناب والا *bound in honour* (*to do something*) (کرنے پر) اخلاقاً پابند (give someone one's) word of honour, make a solemn promise (with him) سے پکا وعدہ کرنا *honour a promise*, keep it وعدہ پورا کرنا، قول نبھانا *honour a cheque*, accept and pay it on presentation چیک کی رقم ادا کرنا *May I have the honour of* (*something or doing something*) کیا میں اس؟ کے کرنے کا شرف حاصل کر سکتا ہوں؟ *a debt of honour*, one for which no security is required قرضہ بلا ضمانت *v.t.* revere کی عزت کرنا، کا احترام کرنا confer honour on کو اعزاز عطا کرنا

honourable *adj.* worthy of honour آبرومند، قابلِ احترام، باعزت consistent with honour آبرومندانہ reasonable (pay, etc.) معقول (abbr. *Hon.* or *Hon'ble*) (title of judges and forms of address to legislators in Parliamentary debates) عزت مآب، معزز *the Hon'ble Mr. Justice Kayani* عزت مآب مسٹر جسٹس کیانی *the hon'ble Leader of the Opposition* عزت مآب قائد حزب مخالف *the Hon'ble member* معزز رکن

honorific (ho-*noh*-ri-fik) *adj.* تعظیمی، تکریمی indicating honour for تعظیمی، اکرامی *honorofic title* تعظیمی لقب، خطاب

hood (hŭd) *n.* covering for the head and neck attached to a cloak ہڈ، گردن پوش badge worn over a university gown to indicate the type of degree ہڈ، جامعاتی تھیلا folding roof of a motor-car, pram, etc. ہڈ (موٹر کی)، تہ ہو جانے والی چھت (see *Addenda*) *v. t.* cover with a hood ہڈ لگانا **hooded**, (hŭd-ed) *adj.* having a hood ٹوپی دار، کلاہ دار، ہڈ والا

hoodlum, hood *n.* (see *Addenda*)

hoodoo *n.* bad luck بدقسمتی *v.t.* render unlucky قسمت خراب کرنا

hoodwink (*hud*-wink) *v.t.* trick دھوکا دینا، جل دینا، فریب دینا

hoof *n.* (*pl.*, *hoofs* or *hooves*) horny part of the foot of a horse, etc. سم، کھر *v.t.* strike with hoof کھر مارنا، سم مارنا، کتاب مارنا، دولتیاں جھاڑنا **hoofed** *adj.* having hoofs سم والا

hook (huk) *n* curved piece of metal, etc. کانٹا، آنکڑا (also *fishing-hook*) one used for catching fish مچھلی پکڑنے کا آلہ such piece used for hanging something on کھونٹی curved tool for harvesting درانتی such tool used for chopping branches کٹ *by hook or by crook*, by means fair or foul ہر جائز ناجائز طریقے سے *hook and eye*, the hook used as a button and the eye for it گھنڈی، تکمہ *v.t.* & *i.* fasten or be fastened with a hook آنکڑا ڈالنا یا پڑنا *a dress that hooks* گھنڈی لگنے والا فراک catch (fish) with a hook کانٹا ڈال کر مچھلیاں پکڑنا **hooked** *adj.* having hooks گھنڈی والا، ہک والا hook-shaped ہک نما، ہک جیسا، ہک سا **hookworm** *n.* slender worm infesting men and animals

hooligan (*hoo*-li-gan) *n.* street rough غنڈہ، بازاری آدمی **hooliganism** *n.* rough and lawless behaviour غنڈہ گردی

hoop *n.* round band of wood or metal (put round barrel) (پیپے کے گرد لگانے کا) کڑا similar band rolled along the ground as a plaything (بچوں کے کھیلنے کا) پہیہ any ring حلقہ، کڑا *v.t.* bind with a hoop کڑا ڈالنا encircle گھیرا ڈالنا (also *whoop*) cry out as if with whooping-cough کھر کھر کرنا **hooping-cough** *n.* (original and alternative spelling of) whooping-cough کھوں کھوں لگا رکھنا کتا کھانسی، کالی کھانسی، خشک کھانسی

hoopoe (*hoo*-poo) *n.* a bird with a large crest and colourful plumage ہدہد جیسا ایک کلغی دار پرندہ

hoot *n.* cry of an owl اُلو کی چیخ sound of a motor-car horn ہارن کی آواز shout of disapproval ناپسندیدگی کا نعرہ، اوا *v.t.* & *i.* make a hoot اُلو کا (یا الو کی طرح) چیخنا shout disapproval (at) کسی کے خلاف ناپسندیدگی کے نعرے بلند کرنا، اوا کرنا drive away by hoots (*off* the stage, or *down*) اوا کرکے چلے جانا یا بیٹھنے پر مجبور کرنا **hooter** *n.* steam-whistle بھاپ کی سیٹی

hop *v.t.* & *i.* (-pp-) (of person) jump on one foot ایک پاؤں پر کودنا (of animals) jump with the feet together (جانوروں کا) اچھلنا کودنا (ٹیسوں کا)، پھدکنا cross by hopping چھلانگ لگانا، جست لگانا، زقند بھرنا *n.* short jump چھوٹی چھلانگ، جست، زقند stage in long-distance flight ہوائی سفر کی ایک منزل **hop-o'-my-thumb** *n.* dwarf بالشتیا **hop-scotch** (*hop*-skoch) *n.* children's game of hopping on one foot and with it pushing a stone over lines marked on the ground پہلا دوجا (یا)، سات سمندر

hope (hohp) *n.* expectation امید، آس، توقع، رجا confidence یقین basis of hope بھروسا، آسرا *v.t.* & *i.* expect امید ہونا، توقع کرنا، آس یا امید لگانا hope (for something, that, or to have) کی امید ہونا **hopeful** *adj.* full of hope or confidence پُرامید **hopefully**

adv. confidently اعتماد سے، یقین و اعتماد سے **hopeless** *adj*. without hope نا اُمید (of persons) incurable لا علاج، ناقابل علاج

hopper (*hop*-*ĕ) *n*. large funnel through which grain is poured into a mill مانی

horde (hoh*d) *n*. wandering (Tartar) tribe تاتاری خانہ بدوش قبیلہ، اُردُو large crowd (*of*) ہجوم، (کا)

horizon (ho-*rī*-zun) *n*. line at which earth (or sea) and sky seem to meet اُفق **horizontal** (ho-ri-*zon*-tĕl) *adj*. parallel to the horizon اُفقی flat چپٹا **horizontally** *adv*. اُفقاً

horizontal *adj*. (see under **horizon**)

horn (ho*n) *n*. pointed weapon on an animal's head سینگ its substance سینگ horn-like part (of an insect's body) کیڑوں مکوڑوں کی مونچھ *on the horns of a dilemma*, faced with difficult alternatives دوگونہ عذاب draw back پیچھے ہٹنا، قدم پیچھے ہٹانا *take the bull by the horns*, face the danger bravely مشکلات کا مردانہ وار مقابلہ کرنا horn used as a musical wind instrument نرسنگھا، قرنا *French horn*, brass-horn پیتل کا نرسنگھا، بگل instrument for warning sounds ہارن، بھونپو inlet of the sea کھاڑی، خلیج extremity of moon, esp. crescent چاند کے ہلال کا کنارا **shoe-horn** *n* instrument for slipping in heels into shoes, etc. شو ہارن، بوٹ ڈال **horned** *adj*. having horns سینگوں والا، شاخ نما **hornbill** *n*. bird with hornlike growth on the beak ہارن بل، سینگ چونچ **horny** *adj*. made of horn سینگ کا hard like horn سینگ کا سا سخت، کھردرا *hands horny from dish-washing* برتن مانجھنے کے باعث کھردرے ہاتھ

hornet (*ho**-net) *n*. a stinging insect بھڑ

horoscope (*ho*-ro-skohp) *n*. diagram of the position of stars at a certain time زائچہ *cast a horoscope*, draw up such a diagram for fortune-telling زائچہ بنانا، زائچہ کھینچنا

horrible *adj*., **horrid** *adj*., **horrify** *v.t*. (see under **horror**)

horror terror خوف، دہشت **horror-struck, horror-stricken** *adj*. overcome with horror خوفزدہ، دہشت زدہ **horrible** *adj*., **horrid** *adj*. causing horror خوفناک، دہشتناک (colloq.) disagreeable گندا، خراب، ذلیل **horrify** (*ho*-ri-fi) *v.t*. fill with horror خوفزدہ کرنا، دہشت زدہ کرنا **horrifying** *adj*. horrible خوفناک، دہشتناک

horse (ho*s) *n*. well-known animal for riding, etc. گھوڑا cavalry رسالہ *horse and foot*, cavalry and infantry رسالہ اور پیدل فوج wooden framework for jumping over ورزشی گھوڑا **horseback** *n*. riding space on a horse گھوڑے کی پیٹھ *on horse-back*, mounted گھوڑے پر، سوار **horse-breaker** *n*. one who trains a horse چابک سوار **horsehair** *n*. hair of a horse's mane or tail گھوڑے کا بال cloth made from it گھوڑے کے بالوں کا کپڑا **horseflesh** *n*. flesh of a horse as food گھوڑے کا گوشت **horse-laugh** *n*. loud coarse laugh قہقہہ، فرمائشی قہقہہ **horseman** شہسوار **horsemanship** *n*. being a horseman شہسواری **horse opera** *n*. (also called *Western film*), film dealing with the U.S. cattle districts امریکی مویشیوں والے علاقے کا فلم **horse-play** *n*. boisterous fun اودھم a play containing it شور و شغب والا کھیل **horse-power** *n*. (abbr. *h.p.*), unit of power (of engines, etc.) ہارس پاور **horse-race** *n*. race by horses گھوڑ دوڑ **horse-racing** *n*. (also *racing*), business of betting on horses in races گھوڑ دوڑ **horse-sense** *n*. (colloq.) plain rough sagacity سوجھ بوجھ **horse-shoe** *n*. U-shaped iron shoe for horse's hoof نعل **horse-whip** *n*. whip for horses چابک *v.t*. (-pp-) thrash with a horsewhip چابک زنی کرنا، کھال ادھیڑنا **horsy** *adj*. of horses گھوڑوں سے متعلق of horse-racing گھوڑ دوڑ سے متعلق **horse's tail** *n*. (see *Addenda*)

horticulture (*ho**-ti-kĕl-chĕ*) *n*. gardening باغبانی **horticultural** *adj*. of gardening باغبانی سے متعلق

hose (hohz) *n*. flexible watering-tube پانی دینے والی نرم نالی، ہوز (also *hose-tops*) upper part of stockings ہوز ٹاپ، بے تلے کی جرابیں، جرابوں کا بالائی حصہ، بالائی موزہ *half-hose*, socks جرابیں، موزے (old use) men's close-fitting garment from waist to knees or feet ہوز، چست صدری اور تنگ پاجامہ *doublet and hose* تنگ مُہری کا پاجامہ *v.t*. water with a hose نالی سے پانی دینا، ہوز سے پانی دینا wash (motor-car, etc.) with a hose (موٹر) دھونا

hosier *n*. one who manufactures men's vests, socks, collars, etc. بنیان ساز one who sells such goods بنیان فروش **hosiery** *n*. such goods جرابیں، بنیانیں factory for such goods جرابوں، بنیانوں کا کارخانہ

hospice (*hos*-pis) *n*. home for the destitute and travellers محتاج خانہ

hospitable *adj*. (see under **hospitality**)

hospital (*hos*-pi-tĕl) *n*. place where the sick or injured are treated and nursed ہسپتال، شفاخانہ، بیمارستان

hospitality (hos-pi-*tal*-i-ti) *n*. generous entertainment of guests at one's place مہمان نوازی **hospitable** (*hos*-pi-tay-b.l) *adj*. kindly to guests مہمان نواز

host (hohst) *n*. one who entertains guests میزبان keeper of hotel, inn, etc. سرائے والا، بھٹیارا great number بڑی تعداد *a host of, hosts of* بہت سے، ان گنت، لاتعداد (old use) army فوج، لشکر **hostess** *n. fem*. a woman-host میزبان inn-keeper's wife بھٹیاری **airhostess** *n*. young woman looking after passengers' comfort during air-travel ہوائی جہاز کی خادمہ، ہوائی خادمہ

hostage (*hos*-tij) *n*. person given to the enemy as a pledge of fulfilling the terms of peace dictated by him یرغمال
hostel (*hos*-tel) *n*. combined boarding-house and lodging for students ہوسٹل، اِقامت گاہ *youth hostel*, a hostel for young people on hiking expeditions یوتھ ہاسٹل۔ قیامگاہ نوجوانان *youth hostelling*, this movement یوتھ ہاسٹل تحریک **hostelry** (*hos*-tel-ri) *n*. (old use) inn سرائے
hostess *n*. (see under **host**)
hostile (*hos*-t l) *adj*. (army, etc.) of an enemy دُشمن کا۔ مُخالف inimical مُخالف، مُعاندانہ *hostile to*, against, opposed کے خلاف، کا مُخالف، کا دُشمن **hostilely** *adv*. with enmity دُشمنی سے **hostilities** *n. pl.* war جنگ aggression جارحانہ کاروائی ، جارحانہ اِقدامات
hostler *n*. (same as **ostler**, which see)
hot *adj*. (*hot, hotter, hottest*) very warm ; of high temperature گرم۔ تپتا ہوا *get into hot water*, get into trouble owing to one's folly مُصیبت میں پڑنا *make it hot for*, making things uncomfortable for کی زندگی اجیرن کرنا (of chillies, curry, etc.) تیز fiery (temper, etc.) تُند، تیز، گرم (of a scent in hunting) strong and fresh تیز، تازہ *hot on the trail, hot on (someone's) track*, near to the object of pursuit شکار کے قریب (see *Addenda*) **hot-bed** *n*. garden-bed heated by rotting manure to stimulate growth گرم کھاد والی زمین breeding ground (of crime, etc.) **hot-head** *n*. impulsive person جوشیلا شخص **hot-headed** *adj*. impetuous تیز مزاج، جوشیلا **hothouse** *n*. glass building kept hot for protecting tender plants حرارت خانہ، گرم خانہ
hotch-potch (*hoch*-poch) *n*. dish with many ingredients esp. mutton broth with vegetables ترکاری گوشت medley مَلغوبہ
hotel (hoh-tel) *n*. a modern inn ہوٹل
hound *n*. a hunting-dog شکاری کُتّا **bloodhound** *n*. big hunting-dog used for chasing criminals خونی کُتّا contemptible man کمینہ *v.t.* chase (as) with hounds (کُتوں سے) شکار کھیلنا harass تعاقب کرنا، پیچھے لگے رہنا
hour (*ou*-ĕ*) *n*. space of sixty minutes ایک گھنٹہ *at the eleventh hour*, when almost too late عین آخری وقت میں *the small hours*, the time from midnight to dawn رات کا پچھلا پہر point of time by the clock وقت chime (of the clock) گھنٹہ *strike the hour* گھڑی کا ٹن ٹن کرنا *ask the hour* وقت پوچھنا (*pl*.) fixed periods of time, esp. for work اوقات *office hours* اوقاتِ کار، دفتر کے اوقات *keep late hours*, get up and go to bed late دیر سے سونا، دیر سے جاگنا point of time وقت، گھڑی، موقع *in the hour of* کے وقت، کی گھڑی *question of the hour*, of the present اِس لمحے کا ، حال کا

hour-glass *n*. sand-glass running an hour ریت گھڑی **hour-hand** *n*. arm of clock, etc., showing the hour گھڑی کی چھوٹی سوئی **hourly** *adj*. every hour گھنٹے گھنٹے کا ، ہر گھڑی کا، گھڑی گھڑی کا *adv*. happening every hour ہر گھڑی، ایک ایک گھنٹے کے بعد
house *n*. (hous) (pl. *houses* pr. *how*-ziz) building used to live in گھر (*House*), branch of legislature ایوان *the Upper House* ایوانِ بالا *the Lower House* ایوانِ زیریں *the House of Lords*, British Parliament's Upper House دارالامرا *the House of Commons*, its Lower House دارالعوام its members taken together ایوان cinema or theatre سنیما یا تھیٹر its audience تماشائی *the house is full*, all tickets have been sold out ہال بھرا ہوا ہے *a full house* ہال بھرا ہوا *bring down the house*, (of an actor) win very loud applause خوب داد پانا royal (or other) family line خاندان، دُودمان business firm فرم، کاروباری اِدارہ a building for special purpose عمارت، خانہ *keep house*, manage the affairs of a household کسی گھر کا اِنتظام چلانا *v.t.* provide house for رہائش کا اِنتظام کرنا put ; find a place for رکھنا **housing** (houzing) *n*. act of giving shelter پناہ دینا ، جگہ دینا provision of homes for people رہائشی مکانات کا اِنتظام کرنا cloth covering for a horse گھوڑے کا جھول *adj* of housing رہائشی مکانات کے اِنتظام سے متعلق *the housing problem*, the problem of providing living accommodation رہائشی مکانوں کا مسئلہ *the housing shortage* رہائشی مکانوں کی قلت *a housing estate*, large group of dwelling-houses built by one organization ایک ہی سلسلے کے مکانات
house-agent *n*. who sells houses for others جائیداد کا دلال one who lets houses for others مکانات کا مُنشی **house-boat** *n*. boat fitted up for living in on a river, etc. ہاؤس بوٹ **house-breaker** *n*. burglar by night نقب زن workman who pulls down old buildings پُرانی عمارتیں گرانے والا *coffee-house n*. restaurant where mainly coffee is served کافی ہاؤس، قہوہ خانہ **tea-house** *n*. tea-shop چائے کی دکان **clearing-house** *n*. place where bankers meet to exchange cheques بنکوں کا باہمی حساب گھر **custom-house** *n*. office at sea-port where customs duties are collected دفتر کروڑ گیری **household** *n*. all persons (family and servants) living in a house گھر بار، اہلِ خانہ اور شاگرد پیشہ *adj*. pertaining to the running of a house خانگی **householder** *n*. one living in a house and not in lodgings or hotel گھر والا، صاحبِ خانہ **house-keeping** *n*. keeping house گھر کا اِنتظام **house-keeper** *n*. woman employed to manage affairs of a household گھر کی منتظمہ
housemaid *n* woman servant in a house for

cleaning rooms, etc. نوکرانی **house-master** *n.* teacher in a residential school or in charge of a school boarding house ہاؤس ماسٹر، نگران اقامت گاہ **housewife** *n.* mistress of the house who keeps it گھروالی (*huz*-if) case of needles, thread, etc.
housework *n.* cleaning, etc., done in a house گھر کا کام کاج۔ گھریلو کام، خانگی مصروفیتیں
house-surgeon *n.* junior surgeon posted and residing at a hospital ہاؤس سرجن **house-proud** *adj.* pre-occupied with embellishment of home جسے گھر سجانے کی دھن ہو، گھر کی دیوانی
hovel (*hov*-el) *n.* tiny and wretched house جھونپڑی، جھونپڑا، چھپّر
hover (*hov*-ĕ*) *v. i.* (of birds) remain in the air almost motionless منڈلانا، منڈلاتے رہنا (of persons) hang about چکر لگانا، گردوپیش پھرتے رہنا
how (how) *adv.* in what way کیسے، کس طرح، کیونکر what reason کیوں، کس لیے in what state of health کیسا، کس حال میں to what amount or degree کتنا، کس قدر، کتنا *n.* manner طریق کار، کیفیت *the how and why of*, the method and cause of doing کرنے کا طریقہ اور وجہ، کیف وکم **howbeit** *adv.* nevertheless پھر بھی کیوں نہ ہو، بہر صورت، بہر طور **however** *conj.* nevertheless تاہم، لیکن، مگر *adv.* in whatever manner or degree کیا، کیسا، کتنا ہی، کیسا ہی **howsoever** *adv.* how *how do you do?* (abbr. *how-d'ye-do*), inquiry after someone's health as a customary greeting کیا حال ہے؟، مزاج شریف (see also under **do**)
howdah (*hou*-dah) *n.* seat on an elephant's back ہودہ
howl (houl) *n.* long wailing cry (of dog, wolf, etc.) کتے یا بھیڑیے کی چیخ long cry of pain کراہ، واویلا shout of contempt or ridicule تو قیریا استہزا والی آواز، ہُونہہ! ہاہا! *v.t. & i.* utter such cries کتے یا بھیڑیے کا چیخنا، کراہنا، واویلا کرنا، حقارت سے ہونہہ کہنا، مذاق اڑاتے ہوئے ہاہا کہنا مذاق *howl (someone) down* اڑا اڑا کر بٹھا دینا (of wind) make a wailing sound ہوا کا سائیں سائیں کرنا *howling wilderness* لق ودق صحرا، دہشت انگیز ویرانہ *howler n.* (colloq.) (usu. schoolboys') laughable mistake (in an examination paper) مضحکہ خیز غلطی
hoy (hoi) *int.* (for calling attention loudly) ہوت
hub (hub) *n.* central part of a wheel پہیے کی ناہ centre of activity مرکز pivot مدار
hubble-bubble *n.* hookah حقہ bubbling noise گڑگڑ، قلقل confused talk بڑبڑ
hubbub (*hub*-ub) *n.* uproar شوروغوغا، غل غپاڑہ

huckster (*huk*-stĕ*) *n.* hawker (with suggestion of being a swindler) (بے ایمان) پھیری والا (see *Addenda*) *v. i.* haggle سودے بازی کرنا
huddle (*hud*-ĕl) *v.t. & i.* crowd together in disorder گھسٹرنا یا گھسیڑنا، سمیٹنا، بے ترتیب انبار لگنا یا لگانا *huddle (oneself) up*, draw the knees up to the body for getting warm گرم ہونے کے لیے گھٹنے گلے سے لگانا
hue (hew) *n.* colour رنگ clamour of pursuit بچو، پکڑیو، دوڑیو جانے نہ پائے (only in the phrase:) *hue and cry*, general outcry of alarm شوروغوغا، ہنگامہ *raise a hue and cry against*, کے خلاف شوروغوغا برپا کرنا
huff (huf) *v. t. & i.* bully دھونس جمانا take offence برا ماننا، ناراض ہونا *n.* fit of ill-temper چڑچڑاپن *in a huff*, ill-tempered چڑچڑا، چڑا ہوا **huffy** *adj.* easily offended جو جونہی جل جائے
hug (hug) *v. t.* (-gg-) embrace lovingly پیار سے گلے لگانا show fondness for (beliefs, etc.) عقائد سے وابستہ رہنا (of a ship) keep close to (the coast) (جہاز کا) ساحل کے ساتھ ساتھ رہنا *n.* act of hugging پیار سے گلے لگانا
huge (hewj) *adj.* very great بہت بڑا، بہت وسیع، بہت ضخیم **hugeness** *n.* being huge بڑائی، وسعت، ضخامت
hula (*hoo*-la) *n.* folkdance of Hawaiian women جزیرہ ہوائی کا زنانہ ناچ، ہولا
hulk (hulk) *n.* body of an old ship no longer in service ناکارہ جہاز کا ڈھانچہ (old use) this used as a prison قیدخانہ *a hulk of a man*, a big clumsy person, بھاری بھرکم اور بھدا بھونڈا سا شخص **hulking** *adj.* big and awkward بے ڈول
hull (hul) *n.* outer covering of (peas, etc.) (مٹر وغیرہ کا) چھلکا frame of ship جہاز کا ڈھانچہ *v. t.* remove hull from (peas, etc.) (مٹر وغیرہ) نکالنا دیا، چھلکا اتارنا
hullabaloo (hul-a-ba-*loo*) *n.* confused outcry شوروغوغا، غل غپاڑہ، ہنگامہ
hullo, hulloa *int.* (same as **hallo,** which see)
hum *v.t. & i.* (hum) (-mm-) make a continuous sound like that made by bees بھنبھنانا sing with closed lips *hum to oneself* آپ ہی آپ گنگنانا *be humming with activity*, bustle میں سرگرمی سے کام ہونا *n.* (hum) humming sound بھنبھناہٹ confused noise in the distance دور کا شور *humming bird*, one whose rapidly moving wings make a sound like that of bees بھنبھنانے والا پرندہ (slang) sham, hoax جعلی، دھوکا *int.* (hoo-) expressing doubt ہونہہ
human (*hew*-man) *adj.* of mankind انسانی *a human being*, a person انسان **humanly** *adv.* (esp.) by human being انسان کے لیے *humanly possible*, possible by human means انسان سے جو کچھ بھی بن پڑے

humane (hew-*mayn*) *adj*. kind and tender نرم دل، نیک دل، شریف النفس، ہمدرد *humane learning*, branches of knowledge other than physical sciences اِنسانی علوم **humanely** *adv*. in a humane manner نیک دلی سے، ہمدردی سے **humanism** (*hew*-ma-nizm) *n*. devotion to human interests اِنسان دوستی، بَشر دوستی literary culture of the European Renaissance characterized by a study of what is best in Greek and Latin literature and focussing its interest on man rather than religion بَشر دوستی اَدب، اِنسانیاتی اَدب Religion of Humanity (*i.e.*, views concerned with human welfare and based on an outright rejection of the supernatural بہبودِ بشر کا مسلک، دینِ اِنسانی، مذہبِ اِنسانیت **humanist** *n*. a follower of the Religion of Humanity دینِ اِنسانی کا پَیرو، بہبودِ بَشر کا قائل **humanitarian** (hew-man-a-*tay*-ri-an) *n*. adherent of the Religion of Humanity دینِ اِنسانی کا پَیرو، بہبودِ بَشر کا قائل visionary philanthropist حد درجہ اِنسان دوست *adj*. of humanitarian views بَشر دوست، اِنسان دوست **humanitarianism** *n*. Religion of Humanity بہبودِ بَشر کا مسلک

humanity (hew-*man*-i-ti) *n*. mankind نوعِ اِنسان human nature اِنسانی فِطرت quality of being humane ہمدردی، اِنسان دوستی، بَشر دوستی *the Religion of Humanity*, humanism دینِ اِنسانی، بہبودِ بَشر کا مسلک *the Humanities*, polite scholarship comprising arts, social sciences, etc., as distinct from physical sciences علومِ اِنسانی **humanize** (*hew*-ma-niz) *v. t.* make or become human اِنسان بَننا یا بنانا make or become human or gentle نرم دِل کرنا، مُلائم کرنا

humane, humanism human, *n*., **humanitarian** *adj*. **humanity** *n*., **humanize** *v. t.* (see under)

humble *adj*. not proud ; meek, modest عاجز، مُنکسِرُالمِزاج، خاکسار *eat the humble pie*, confess that one was in the wrong ; apologize غلطی تسلیم کرنا، معافی مانگنا poor غریب، مِسکین of low status *of humble birth*, one born in a low family اَدنیٰ خاندان کا فرد *humble occupations*, menial types of work اَدنیٰ پیشے *v. t.* make humble ذلیل کرنا degrade چھوٹے درجے پر لانا **humbly** *adv*. with humility عاجزی سے، عاجزانہ **humbleness** *n*. being humble عاجزی، اِنکساری، عجز و اِنکسار **humble-bee, bumble bee** *n*. large, loud humming bee *n*. بھنبھنانے والی مکھی

humbug (*hum*-bug) *n*. dishonest and deceiving (person or behaviour) رِیاکار، رِیاکارانہ nonsense بکواس a kind of sweetmeat ایک قسم کی مِٹھائی، ہمبگ *v.t.* (-gg-) deceive جُل دینا

humdrum (*hum*-drum) *adj*. dull, monotonous بے لُطف، بے کیف، اُکتا دینے والا *lead a humdrum sort of existence* بے لُطف زندگی گزارنا، دِن پُورے کرنا، زندگی کے دِن کاٹنا

humid (*hew*-mid) *adj*. damp (climate, etc.) مرطوب **humidity** (hew-*mid*-i-ti) *n*. dampness نمی، مُرطُوبت

humiliate (hew-*mil*-i-ayt) *v.t.* make humble شرمندہ کرنا، ذلیل کرنا، نیچا دِکھانا cause to feel ashamed شرمندہ کرنا، شرمسار کرنا **humiliation** (-ay-) *n*. mortification تذلیل، شرمساری **humility** (hew-*mil*-i-ti) *n*. humble condition ذِلّت، پستی meekness عاجزی، عجز و اِنکسار

humorist *n*., **humorous** *adj*. (see under **humour**)

humour (hew-mĕ*) *n*. fun and joking مِزاح، مَذاق capacity to cause it مزاحیہ ہونا، پُر مذاق ہونا appreciation of it مزاح سے لُطف اندوز ہونا *sense of humour*, مزاح سے لُطف اندوز ہونے کی صلاحیت، مزاح فہمی mood مزاج *in a good humour* خوش طبع *in a bad humour* جلا بُھنا inclination رغبت، میلان *not in the humour for*, not in a mood to کا مَیلان نہ ہونا (old use) one of the fluid contents of the body خِلط، اَخلاط *v. t.* gratify or yield to (someone) کو خُوش کرنا، کی بات ماننا **humorist** *n*. humorous person خوش طبع، پُر مذاق شخص humorous writer مزاح نِگار، مزاحیہ نِگار **humorous** *adj*. having a sense of humour خوش طبع causing amusement دِلچسپ، ہنسانے والا

hump (hump) *n*. lump standing up near a camel's back کوہان such a lump on a deformed person's back کُب، کُوبڑ **humpback** *n*. person with hump on the back, hunchback کُبڑا، کوز پُشت

humph (humf) *int*. expressing doubt or dissatisfaction ہُونہہ

hunch (hunch) *n*. hump کوہان thick piece (of bread, etc.) (روٹی وغیرہ کا) موٹا سا ٹکڑا (U.S. colloq.) presentiment ماتھا ٹھنکنا *v.t.* bend (*out* or *up*), to form a hump کُب نِکالنا **hunchback** *n*. humpback کُبڑا، کوز پُشت

hundred (*hun*-dred) *n*. & *adj*. 100 **hundreds** *n. pl*. figures of the value of hundreds سینکڑے **hundredth** *adj*. 1/100 سوواں حصّہ، ایک بٹے سو **hundredfold** *n*. 100 times as big سو گُنا **hundredweight** (abbr. as *cwt*.) 112 lbs, or 1/20 ton ہنڈرڈویٹ، چار سیر کم ڈیڑھ مَن

hunger (*hung*-ĕ*) *n*. strong desire and need for food بھوک *satisfy* (*one's*) *hunger* بھوک مِٹانا *die of hunger*, (*a*) starve بھوکوں مرنا (*b*) die of starvation فاقوں کے باعث موت آ جانا any strong desire (*for*) کی شدید خواہش یا اِشتہا *v.i.* have a craving (*for*) کی سخت آرزو ہونا **hunger-strike** *n*. refusal to eat or drink till grievance is redressed بھوک ہڑتال **hunger-march** *n*. a march (through streets) for that purpose بھوکوں کا جلوس **hungry** *adj.* feeling hunger بھوکا *hungry looks* کھا جانے والی نظریں eager *for* (کا) سخت آرزو مند **hungrily** *adv.* like a hungry person بھوکوں کی طرح

hunt (hunt) *v.t.* & *i.* chase (wild animals) for food or sport شکار کرنا، شکار کھیلنا look (*for*) (کی) تلاش کرنا *hunt* (*someone* or *something*) *down*, pursue and find ڈھونڈ نکالنا *hunt* (*something*) *up*, search for (information, etc.) تلاش کرنا *n.* hunting شکار، شکار کرنا **hunter** *n.* (fem. *huntress*) one who hunts شکاری، صیّاد **huntsman** *n.* (pl. *huntsmen*) hunter شکاری، شکار کھیلنے والا **hunting** *n.* chasing شکار کھیلنا، تعاقب کرنا **hunting-ground** *n.* game preserve شکار گاہ

hurdle *n.* movable wooden fence ٹٹی، اٹھاؤ جنگلا such fence used as an obstacle in a race ٹٹی **hurdle-race** *n.* race in which hurdles have to be crossed جنگلا، رکاوٹ، روک رکاوٹوں والی دوڑ، روک دوڑ **hurdler** *n.* runner in a hurdle race روک دوڑ میں حصہ لینے والا

hurdy-gurdy (hĕ*-di-gĕ*-di) *n.* wheeled musical instrument played by turning a handle ہرڈی گرڈی، گھوم باجا

hurl (hĕ*l) *v.t.* throw violently زور سے پھینکنا

🅂 We **hurl** something heavy at something else with great force; **thrust** something through; **fling** it lightly; **toss** it nonchalantly; **sling** it circularly **launch** it on water: **dart** it sharp.

hurly-burly (*hĕ**-li-*bĕ**-li) *n.* uproar غل غپاڑا، ہلچل

hurrah (hū-*rah*), **hurray** (hū-*ray*), **huzza** (hū-*zah*) *n.* & *int.* shout of triumph آہا! شاباش *give a loud hurrah* خوشی کے نعرے لگانا *v.t.* cheer نعرۂ تحسین بلند کرنا

hurricane (hĕ ri-kayn) *n.* storm with violent wind طوفانِ باد و باراں **hurricane-lamp** lantern specially designed to keep a light even in strong wind لالٹین، ہری کین

hurry (*hĕ*-ri) *n.* haste جلدی، عجلت eager haste (کرنے کے لیے) بھاگ دوڑ کرنا *be in a hurry* (*to do*) بھاگ دوڑ، بے تابی need for haste جلدی، بے تابی کی وجہ، بھاگ دوڑ کی ضرورت *there is no hurry* ایسی کوئی جلدی نہیں *v.t.* & *i.* (cause to) move or do something too quickly بھاگ دوڑ کرکے کام کرنا *hurry up!*, be quick جلدی کرو *hurry away*, go off quickly جلدی چلے جاؤ *hurry over* (*some work*) جلدی جلدی کام نبٹانا **hurried** (*hĕ**-rid) *adj.* done in a hurry (hence bad) جلدی کا، جلدی کا کیا ہوا **hurriedly** *adv.* too quickly جلدی جلدی

hurt (hĕ*t) *v.t.* & *i.* injure زخم لگانا cause pain تکلیف پہنچانا *hurt* (*oneself*) چوٹ کھانا، زخمی ہونا offend دل کو دکھ پہنچانا *n.* physical injury ضرب، چوٹ، ضرب *grievous hurt* ضربِ شدید damage نقصان *do hurt to* کو نقصان پہنچانا mental suffering (*to*) رنج، صدمہ، دھکا، دھچکا

hurtle (hĕ*-tèl) *v.t.* & *i.* (cause to) rush violently زور سے پڑنا (یا گرنا یا گرانا)

husband (*huz*-band) *n.* male spouse خاوند، شوہر *v.t.* use sparingly (one's strength) کم خرچ کرنا manage thriftily (one's resources, etc.) سوچ سمجھ کر خرچ کرنا **husbandman** *n.* (old use) farmer کاشتکار، کسان **husbandry** *n.* (old use) farming کاشتکاری thrifty management کفایت شعاری سے انتظام

hush (hush) *v.t.* & *i.* make or become silent خاموش، چپ ہو جانا یا کرا دینا *Hush!*, be silent *hush* (*a baby*) *to sleep*, cause it to sleep بچے کو تھپک تھپک کر سلا دینا *Hush thee my baby* منّے سو میرے منّے *hush* (*something*) *up*, prevent it from becoming public knowledge (معاملہ) دبا دینا **quiet** *n.* calm خاموشی، سکون

husk (husk) *n.* dry outer covering of grain, etc. بھوسی، بھوسا such covering of any seed چھلکا *v.t.* remove the husks from بھوسی اتارنا، چھلکا اتارنا **husky** *adj.* dry like husk سوکھا، خشک full of husks بھوسے والا strong, hefty ہٹا کٹا (of the voice) hoarse بھاری (آواز) *n.* Eskimo اسکیمو Eskimo dog اسکیمو کتا husky person ہٹا کٹا شخص

hussar (hū-*zah**) *n.* soldier of light cavalry regiment ہلکے رسالے کا سوار، ہُوزار

hussy (*hus*-i) **huzzy** (*huz*-i) *n.* impudent, and ill-mannered young woman زبان دراز یا بدتمیز لڑکی loose young woman قطامہ

hustle (*hus*-èl) *v.t.* & *i.* push one's way roughly کہنیاں مار مار کر آگے بڑھنا jostle دھکم دھکا ہونا، دھکم پیل کرنا (*hustle on*), (make someone) act energetically (کام) جلدی کرنا *n.* pushing violently دھکیلنا، ڈھکیلنا energetic activity زور شور سے کام **hustler** *n.* one who gets things done quickly کام جلدی جلدی کرانے والا

hut (hut) *n.* small roughly built shelter جھونپڑا، جھونپڑی، چھپر **hutment** *n.* temporary offices, etc., made of huts دفاتر وغیرہ کی عارضی عمارت military camp thus built جھونپڑیوں والی چھاؤنی

huzza *n.* & *int.* (same as **hurrah,** which see)

hyacinth (*hi*-a-sinth) *n.* a bell-shaped purple blue fragrant spring flower of the lily family سنبل the bulbous plant on which it grows سنبل

Hyacinthus (hī-a-*sin*-thus) *Cl. myth.* beautiful lad loved by Apollo and accidentally killed by

him ; from his blood sprang the hyacinth flower ہَیاسِنتھ
hyaena *n.* (same as **hyena,** which see)
hybrid (*hīb*-rid) *n.* & *adj.* animal or plant of mixed parentage دوغلا ، میل دار
Hydra (*hīd*-ra) *n.* *Cl. myth.* great sea-serpent with fifty heads that grew again if cut off ; it was killed by Hercules ہائیڈرا (*hydra*), (also *haydra-headed monster*), thing hard to extirpate ناقابلِ استیصال شے
hydrant (*hīd*-rant) *n.* pipe with valve and spout installed in a street for drawing water پانی کا بازاری نل ، بازار میں لگا ہوا پانی کا نل
hydraulic (hīd-*raw*-lik) *adj* worked by water-power شکنجۂ آبی ، ماقوّانی ، آبی ، پن *hydraulic press* of water in motion متحرک پانی
hydro- (*hīd*-roh) pref. of water آبی ، پن of hydrogen ہائیڈروجن کا **hydro-electricity** *n.* electricity produced by water-power برقاب ، پن بجلی **hydro-electric** *adj.* of, worked with or generating hydro-electricity برقابی **hydrometer** *n.* instrument for measuring the specific gravity of liquids آب پیما **hydrophobia** *n.* rabies ہڑک ، کتّے کی لہر
hydro-plane *n.* fast-moving motor-boat اڑن کشتی ، اُڑناؤ (old use) seaplane تیز موٹر کشتی
hydrogen (*hīd*-roh-jĕn) a very light gas ہائیڈروجن *hydrogen bomb,* atom bomb charged with a hydrogen compound ہائیڈروجن بم
hyena, hyaena (hī-*ee*-na) *n.* a wolf-like wild animal with a laughing cry چرخ ، لگڑ بگڑ
Hygeia (hī-*jee*-a) *Cl. myth.* the goddess of health (صحت کی دیوی)(also see **hygiene**)
hygiene (*hī*-jeen) *n.* science of good health ہائی جین ، حفظانِ صحت **hygienic** (hī-*jee*-nik) *adj.* of hygiene حفظانِ صحت کے متعلق likely to promote health صحت بخش free from disease germs جراثیم سے پاک **hygienically** *adv.* اُصولِ حفظانِ صحت کے مطابق
Hymen (hi-men) *Cl. myth.* the Greek god of marriage ہائمن **hymeneal** (hī-me-*nee*-ĕl), **hymanean** (-ĕn) *adj.* pertaining to Hymen or marriage ہائمن کا ، شادی بیاہ کا *n.* wedding songs شادی بیاہ کے گیت
hymn (him) *n.* song of praise to God حمد
hymnal (*him*-nĕl) *n.* book of hymns مجموعۂ حمد
hyper- (*hī*-pĕ*) *pref.* too اَز حد ، بہت ہی (e.g., *hyper-critical*) بہت ہی ریس میخ والا
hyperbola *n.* curve produced by cutting cone with a plane of larger angle than that of the cone's side شکلِ ہذلولی ، قطعۂ ہذلولی
hyperbole (hī-*pĕ**-bo-li) *n.* exaggeration for effect مبالغہ ، غلو ، اغراق **hyperbolic** *adj.* exaggerated مبالغہ آمیز
hypertension *n.* (see *Addenda*)
hyphen (*hī*-fĕn) *n.* the mark used for joining words نشانِ الحاق ، وصلہ ، ہائفن **hyphenate** *v.t.* join words together with a hyphen وصلہ لگانا
hypnosis (hip-*noh*-sis) *n.* state like deep sleep in which one's acts may be controlled by another نومِ توجّہ ، نظر کی نیند **hypnotic** (hip-*not*-ik) *adj.* of hypnosis تنویمی **hypnotism** (*hip*-no-tizm) *n.* production of hypnosis تنویم **hypnotize** (*hip*-no-tīz) *v.t.* produce hypnosis عملِ تنویم کرنا **hypnopaedia** (hip-no-*pee*-di-a) *n.* teaching while the hypnotized person is in induced sleep تنویمی تعلیم
hypnotic, hypnotism, hypnotize, see under **hypnosis**
[1]**hypo** (*hī*-poh) *n.* solution used for fixing photographs ہائپو
[2]**hypo**- *pref.* below کم under زیر ، تحت slightly قدرے
hypochondria (hi-poh-*kon*-dri-a) *n.* morbid state of depression مراق **hypochondriac** *n.* & *adj.* morbidly depressed مراقی
hypocrisy (hi-*pok*-ri-si) *n.* pretence of virtue منافقت **hypocrite** (*hip*-o-krit) *n.* one guilty of hypocrisy منافق **hypocritical** (hip-o-*krit*-i-kĕl) *adj.* of hypocrisy منافقانہ **hypocritically** *adv.* with hypocrisy منافقت سے
hypodermic (hī-po-*dĕ**-mik) *adj.* under the skin جلد کے نیچے ، زیرِجلدی *hypodermic injection,* drug injected just below the skin زیرِجلدی پچکاری
hypostasis (hī-*pos*-ta-sis, or hi-, (in philosophy) underling person (as distinct from attributes) ذات ، جوہر
hypotenuse (hī-*pot*-e-news) *n.* side of right-angled triangle opposite the right angle وتر
hypothesis (hi-*poth*-e-sis) *n.* (pl. *hypotheses*) something assumed as a basis of reasoning مفروضہ ، فرض ، دعویٰ groundless supposition بے دلیل دعویٰ **hypothetic, hypothetical** (-*thet*-) *adj.* conjectural فرضی ، مفروضہ conditional مشروط
hysteria (his-*tee*-ri-a) *n.* uncontrollable nervous fit in women ہسٹیریا ، اختناق الرحم morbid excitement جذبات کا مریضانہ ہیجان **hysterical** (his-*te*-ri-kĕl) *adj.* caused by or suffering from hysteria ہسٹیریا والا very excited مغلوب الغضب ، بڑے جوش میں
hysterics *n. pl.* attack of hysteria ہسٹریا کا دورہ morbid excitement جذبات کا ہیجان *go into hysterics,* be much excited بڑے جوش میں آنا

i. I (ɪ), *pl. i's* or *is* the ninth letter of the English alphabet آئی (*I*), (always capital) personal pron. nominative sing. (nominative pl. *we*, objective sing. *me*, objective pl. *us*, possessive sing. *my* or *mine*, possessive pl. *our* or *ours*.) مَیں، بندہ، یہ عاجز، یہ خادم، فقیر (*i. I*), Roman numeral denoting *one* which is added to the number V (or v), X (or x) etc., if placed to its right, and subtracted from it if placed to the left (*e.g.*, VI makes 5+1=6. but IV makes 5−1=4) ایک *ii*, two دو *iii*, three تین *I*, (capital) first پہلا، اوّل *II*, second دوسرا، دُوم *III*, third تیسرا، سوم

Note : The possessive forms *mine* and *ours* are used either predicatively (*e.g.*, this book is *mine*) or wherever the possessor is understood (*e.g.*, that book is *yours*, this one is *mine*). The forms *my* and *our* are used in all other instances where a personal pronoun of the first person is needed.

iambus (ɪ-*am*-bus) *n.* metrical foot comprising an unaccented syllable followed by an accented one انگریزی بحروں کا ایک رُکن، ایا مبس، ایا مب **iambic** *adj.* pertaining to this foot ایامبی

ibidum *adv.* (abb. *ibid* or *ib*), in the same place (*i.e.*, book or passage) وُہی، ایضاً

-ible *suf.* (same as *able* or 'able to be' ; added to transitive verbs, *-ible* goes with those of Latin origin and *-able* with others, though the rule is sometimes broken (*e.g.*, *collapsable*, *collapsible*) والا، جوگ

-ic (ik) *suf.* formation of adjectives with the sense of *containing* (more than is expressed by *ous*) زیادہ سے *sulphurous* تھوڑی گندھک والا **sulphuric** گندھک والا formation of adjectives used as nouns (*e.g.*, *music* موسیقی *critic* نقّاد (*-ics*), (pl.) modern names of sciences یات (*e.g.*, *economics* معاشیات Its adverbs almost always end in *-ically* *e.g.*, *economically*)

Icarus (*ik*-a-rus) *Cl. myth.* the son of Daedalus whom his father provided with wings to escape from Crete ; he soared too close to the sun with the result that the wax fastening of his wings melted owing to excessive heat and he got drowned in the Aegean اِکارَس

ice (ɪs) *n.* frozen water بَرف *break the ice* (*a*) make a beginning شروع کرنا (*b*) break the reserve بات شروع کرنا، مُہرِ سکوت (*pl.*) frozen sweets جمی ہوئی مٹھائی *v. t. & i.* make (food, etc very cold خوب ٹھنڈا کرنا، برف سے ٹھنڈا کرنا *iced water* خوب ٹھنڈا پانی cover or become covered with a coating of ice برف سے ڈھکنا یا ڈھانپنا cover (cake) with a sugary mixture (کیک پر) شیرینی ڈالنا **Ice Age** *n.* glacial epoch برف کا زمانہ، برفانی دور **iceberg** *n.* floating mass broken off a glacier برفانی تودہ **icebound** *adj.* obstructed by ice یخ بستہ **ice-cream** *n.* frozen cream or custard قلفی، ملائی برف، آئس کریم **ice-field** *n.* wide area of sea covered with ice یخ بستہ سمندر **ice-free** *adj.* free from ice جو یخ بستہ نہ ہو، غیر یخ بستہ **ice-hockey** *n.* hockey played on skates برفانی ہاکی **ice-wool** *n.* fine glossy knitting wool چمکدار اُون **icicle** (*ɪs*-i-kel) *n.* dripping water forming into a pointed piece of ice برف کی قلم **icy** (ɪ-si) *adj.* very cold سخت سرد، برفانی covered with ice برف پوش، برف سے ڈھکا ہوا cold, unfriendly **dry ice** *n.* frozen carbon dioxide which naturally does not melt but only evaporates خشک برف

icthyo- *suf.* fish or like fish آبی، ماہی، حُوت **icthyosaurus** (ik-thi-o-*saw*-rus) *n.* gigantic reptile now extinct اکیتھوسارس، آبی چھپکلی

Ida (ɪ-da) *Cl. myth.* mountain near Crete where Zeus was brought up آئیڈہ

idea (ɪ-*dee*-a) thought خیال، فکر mental picture تصوّر way of thinking اُسلوبِ فکر، اندازِ فکر vague belief خیال، وہم و گمان *have an idea* خیال ہونا *have no idea* کا وہم و گمان بھی نہ ہونا plan تجویز aim مطلب، مُدعا، مقصد eternally existing pattern (according to Plato) عینِ مثال **ideal** (ɪ-*dee*-el) *adj.* satisfying one's highest conceptions بہترین نہایت شاندار، مثالی، معیاری not real خیالی، موہوم not feasible باطل، انہونا *n.* perfect idea مثالی تصوّر objective نصب العین، مطمحِ نظر high principles اُصول

idealism *n.* being guided by one's ideals اُصول پرستی philosophy believing everything to be an idea مثالیت، تصوّریت (in art) imaginative representation in an ideally perfect form (cf. *realism*) تصوّریت **idealize** *v. t.* think of as being ideal مثالی سمجھنا represent as ideal تخیل کے زور سے مثالی حسن عطا کرنا **idealist** *n.* one who follows his ideals اُصول پرست one who believes material things to be no more than ideas مثالیت پسند **ideally** *adv.* in an ideal manner نہایت اچھی طرح

idee fixe (*ee*-day-feeks) *n.* idea that dominates

the mind رسد پر مسلّط خیال
dem *n.* & *adv.* (abbr. *id.*) the same author وہی مُصنّف ، ایضاً the same words وہی لفظ ، ایضاً
identical (ɪ-*dent*-i-kĕl) *adj.* the same وُہی exactly alike ہُو بہو ، بالکل وَیسا ، وَیسا ہی *identical twins*, twins developed from a single fertilization یکساں جُڑواں
identification *n.* (see under **identify**)
identify (ɪ-*dent*-i-f) *v. t.* recognize پہچاننا ، شناخت کرنا ، نشان دہی کرنا associate (*with*) ایک ہو جانا ، سے بالکل مِل جانا ، مَیں مَن و تُو کا فرق نہ رہنا *identify* (*oneself*) *with*, lend full support to پُوری مَدد کرنا **identification** (-*kay*-) *n.* being identical ایک ہونا recognition شناخت ، نشان دہی
ideology (id-e-*ol*-o-ji, or i-de-*ol*-o-ji) *n.* system of ideas characterizing a party, class or culture نظریّہ ، نظریات ، نظریاتی نظام ، نظریاتی بُنیاد ، نقطۂ نظر *Islamic ideology* اسلام کی نظریاتی بُنیاد science of ideas علمِ تصوّرات
ideologist (-*ol*-) *n.* supporter of an ideology کسی نظریاتی نظام کا حامی **ideological** (-*loj*-) *adj.* pertaining to ideology نظریاتی نظام کے متعلّق **ideologue** (ɪ-de-o-log) *n.* visionary, theorist بزرِ فلسفی ، تصوّرات کی دُنیا میں رہنے والا
id est (id-est) (abbr. as *i.e.*) that is to say یعنی ، اَعنی
idiocy *n.* (see under **idiot**.)
idiom *n.* special form of a language peculiar to a class or area بولی ، مُحاورہ its peculiar character مُحاورہ ، روزمرّہ word-group peculiar to it مُحاورہ **idiomatic** *adj.* expressed in idioms بامُحاورہ characteristic of a language روزمرّہ کے مُطابق ، ٹکسالی ، بامُحاورہ
idiosyncrasy (id-i-o-*sin*-kra-si) *n.* kind of behaviour, etc., peculiar to someone طبیعت کا خاصّہ ، مزاج odd manner peculiar to someone خبط
idiot (*id*-i-ut) *n.* stupid person اَحمق feeble-minded person فاتِرُ العقل ، مجنُون ، مُختلُّ الحواس **idiocy** (*id*-i-o-si) *n.* stupidity حماقت ، بیوقُوفی **idiotic** (id-i-*ot*-ik) *adj.* stupid احمق **idiotically** *adj.* stupidly احمقانہ ، حماقت سے
idle (ɪ-dĕl) *adj.* lazy (person) سُست ، کاہل (of thing) not being used بیکار ، یُونہی پڑا ہُوا (of rumour, etc.) groundless بے اصل ، بے بُنیاد worthless نا کارہ *v. t.* & *i.* be idle سُستی کرنا waste thus آرام طلبی میں ضائع کرنا *idle away* (*one's*) *time*, pass (one's) time doing nothing وقت بیکار کھونا **idler** *n.* one who idles سُست ، آرام طلب کاہل **idly** *adv.* like an idler سُستی سے ، بیکار ، یُونہی **idleness** *n.* being idle کاہلی ، آرام طلبی ، بے کاری
idol (ɪ-dol) *n.* image of a god بُت ، صَنَم what one greatly admires بہت پسندیدہ شے ، محبوب ، مرغوب
idolator (i-*dol*-a-tĕ*) *n.* idol-worshipper بُت پرست ، صنم پرست **idolatrous** (ɪ-*dol*-at-rus) *adj.* of idol-worship بُت پرستانہ **idolatry** (ɪ-*dol*-at-ri) *n.* idol-worship بُت پرستی ، صنم پرستی **idolize** (*i*-do-lɪz) *v. t.* admire too much کا پرستار ہونا
idyl, idyll (*ɪ*-dil) *n.* short poem describing a simple scene or event of country life دیہی نظم ، گاؤں کا گیت scene or event suitable for it دیہی نظم کے لیے موزُوں واقعہ (یا منظر) **idyllic** (ɪ-*dil*-ik) *adj.* pertaining to an idyll دیہی نظم سے متعلّق charming and simple سادہ و دِلکش
if *conj.* provided اگر ، بشرطیکہ whether آیا whenever جب بھی *even if*, although خواہ ، ہی کیوں نہ *if only*, one wishes that کاش ، اگر ذرا
igneous (*ig*-ne-us) *adj.* (of rocks) formed by heat of volcanic action ناری ، آتشی
ignis fatuus (*ig*-nis-*fa*-tew-us) *n.* will of the wisp غُول بیابانی
ignite (ig-*nɪt*) *v.t.* & *i.* set on fire آگ لگانا take fire میں آگ لگنا **ignition** (-*nish*-) *n.* being or setting on fire آگ لگنا یا لگانا apparatus for starting combustion in motor-engine موٹر کا آتش زَن
ignoble (ig-*noh*-bĕl) *adj.* dishonourable, mean بے عزّت ، کم اصل ، کمینہ ، رذیل **ignobly** *adv.* meanly کمینگی سے ، رذیل بن کر
ignominious *adj.* (see under **ignominy**)
ignominy (*ig*-no-mi-ni) *n.* public dishonour رُسوائی ، کُھلی بے عزّتی ، فضیحت dishonourable behaviour ذلیل حرکت **ignominious** (ig-no-*min*-i-us) *adj.* causing ignominy شرمناک ، رُسواکُن ، مُوجبِ رُسوائی ، فضیحت ناک
ignoramas *n.*, **ignorance** *n.* (see under **ignorant**)
ignorant (*ig*-no-rant) *adj.* having no knowledge جاہل unaware (*of*) سے بے خبر یا ناواقف **ignorance** (*ig*-no-rans) *n.* the state of being ignorant جہالت ، بے خبری ، ناواقفی **ignoramus** (-*rai*-mus) *n.* person displaying his ignorance جاہلِ مُطلق
ignore (ig-*noh**) *v. t.* refuse to take notice of نظر انداز کر دینا
il- *pref.* opposite of, not نا ، بے ، غیر ، خلاف (as, *illegal* غیر قانُونی
Iliad (il-i-ad) *n.* ancient Greek epic by Homer describing the siege of Ilium (*i.e.*, Troy) ایلیڈ ، الیادہ long tale (*of* woes, etc.) رام کہانی
ilk *adj.* (Scottish) same وُہی *that ilk*, the same وُہی ، اُسی
ill (il) *adj.* (usu. predicative) in bad health بیمار ، عَلیل ، ناساز *fall ill*, *be taken ill* بیمار ہونا ، ہو جانا یا پڑنا

(attributive) (*ill, worse, worst*), bad بُرا ، خراب *n.* evil بُرائی ، بدی *do ill to* کسی سے بدی کرنا (*pl.*) misfortunes بدنصیبی (*pl.*) troubles (*of*) مصائب ، آفات *adv.* badly بُری طرح imperfectly نامکمل طور پر unfavourably نامُوافق طور پر (be) *ill at ease,* (*a*) (be) uncomfortable بے آرام (ہونا) (*b*) تکلیف میں (ہونا) (be) embarrassed اُوگمُو کی حالت میں (ہونا) *I can ill afford it,* I can hardly spare the money for it اپنے پاس تو پیسہ دھیلا تو ہے نہیں ، چیل کے گھونسلے میں ماس کہاں **ill-advised** *adj.* injudicious ناعاقبت اندیش ، عاقبت نااندیش *be ill-advised to* (*do*) (ایسا کرنے) کی ناعاقبت اندیشی کرنا

ill-bred *adj.* badly brought up ناشائستہ ، بدتربیت rough in behaviour بدتمیز **ill-breeding** *n.* ناشائستگی **ill-fated** *adj.* destined to misfortune بدنصیب **illgotten** *adj.* gained by unfair means ناجائز طور پر حاصل کردہ ، حرام کی (کا)

ill-natured *adj.* bad-tempered بدمزاج not kind at heart بد باطن ، خبیث فطرت **illness** being ill بیمار ، علالت disease بیماری ، مرض **ill-treat, ill-use** *v. t.* treat cruelly سختی سے پیش آنا ، ظلم کرنا

ill-will *n.* hatred نفرت ، بغض

illegal (i-*lee*-gĕl) *adj.* not being legal غیر قانونی ، خلاف قانون ، ناجائز **illegality** *n.* not legal عدم جواز ، غیر قانونی یا خلاف قانون ہونا **illegally** *adv.* without being legal ناجائز ، خلاف قانون

illegible (i-*lej*-i-bĕl) *adj.* unreadable جو پڑھا نہ جا سکے one who writes such a hand بدخط **illegibility** (-*bil*-) *n.* being illegible بدخطی **illegibly** *adv.* so as to be illegible بدخطی سے

illegitimacy *n.* (see under **illegitimate**)

illegitimate (i-*lej*-i-ti-mayt) *adj.* illegal غیر قانونی (baby) born out of wedlock حرامی ، ناجائز *v. t.* declare as being born such ناجائز اولاد (اولاد ، بچہ وغیرہ) قرار دینا **illegitimacy** (i-le-*jit*-i-ma-si) *n.* being such حرامی ہونا

illiberal (i-*lib*-è-rĕl) *adv.* stingy بخیل ، کنجوس narrow-minded تنگ نظر ، تنگ دل

illicit (i-*lis*-it) *adj.* unlawful ناجائز ، خلاف قانون ، غیر قانونی

illimitable (i-*lim*-i-ta-bèl) *adj.* boundless غیر محدود بے پایاں

illiterate (i-*lit*-è-rayt) *n.* & *adj.* (one) unable to read or write ان پڑھ ، ناخواندہ **illiteracy** (i-*lit*-è-ra-si) *n.* being illiterate ناخواندگی

illogical (i-*loj*-i-kĕl) *adj.* not logical غلط ، غیر منطقی **illogicality** (-kal-) *n.* being illogical غیر منطقی ہونا ، غلطی

illuminate (i-*loom*-i-nayt) *v. t.* throw light on, clarify پر روشنی ڈالنا give light to کو روشن کرنا decorate with bright lights چراغاں کرنا **illumine** (i-*lew*-min) *v.t.* brighten جگمگا دینا enlighten spiritually رُوحانی جلا دینا ، پُرنُور بنا دینا **illuminations** (-nay-) *n. pl.* decoration with light چراغاں lights used in it قمقمے ، بلب ، چراغ ، موم بتیاں ، دیے **illuminative** *adj.* giving light روشنی دینے والا clarifying تشریحی ، توضیحی

illusion (i-*loozh*-èn) *n.* misleading appearance which really does not exist فریب نظر ، موہوم پیکر ، مایا false idea or belief خیال ، وہم **illusive** (i-*loo*-ziv) deceptive فریب دِہ **illusiveness** *n.* being deceptive فریب دہی **illusory** (i-*loo*-ze-ri) *adj.* unreal ذہنی ، غیر حقیقی **illusionist** (i-*loo*-zhè-nist) *n.* conjurer شعبدہ باز

illustrate (*il*-us-trayt) *v. t.* explain *with* examples (or diagrams, etc.) مثالیں (وغیرہ) دے کر سمجھانا ornament (book, etc.) with pictures, etc. (کتاب وغیرہ کو) باتصویر بنانا **illustrative** (i-*lus*-tra-tiv) *adj.* clarifying واضح کرنے والا **illustration** (-*tray*-) *n.* illustrating باتصویر بنانا picture تصویر example that clarifies مثال ، تمثیل ، مثال **illustrator** (*il*-us-tra-tē*) *n.* one who makes illustrations for a book (کتاب وغیرہ کی) تصویریں بنانے والا ، نقاش **illustrated** *adj.* pictorial باتصویر ، مصور *n.* pictorial periodical باتصویر رسالہ (وغیرہ)

illustrious (i-*lus*-tri-us) *adj.* (of person, career, etc.) distinguished ; celebrated مشہور ، نامور

im- *pref.* (same as *il-*) opposite of, not نا ، بے ، غیر ، خلاف (as, *immeasurable* بے حد ، بے انتہا

image (*im*-ij) *n.* reflection عکس statue مجسمہ ، بت close likeness ہوبہو نقشہ *be the* (*very*) *image of,* be exactly like ہوبہو ویسا ہونا mental picture تصویر simile تشبیہ *v. t.* reflect عکس ڈالنا picture (something) to oneself کا تصور کرنا **imagery** (*im*-i-jè-ri) suggestion of mental pictures by means of words لفظی تصویریں

imaginary *adj.* **imagination** *n.*, **imaginative** *adj.* (see under **imagine**)

imagine (i-*maj*-in) *v. t.* form a mental picture of (کسی شے کی) تصویر ذہن میں قائم کرنا guess قیاس کرنا ، اندازہ کرنا think mistakenly خواہ مخواہ فرض کرنا ، کو خواب آنا

imaginable *adj.* that which can be imagined جو تصور میں آ سکے ، قابل تصور **imaginary** *adj.* unreal فرضی ، غیر حقیقی ، موہوم **imagination** (-nay-) *n.* power of the mind to image تخیل ، قوت متخیلہ ، پرواز creative ability in fine arts قوت تخلیق خیال something imagined تصور ، خیال آرائی **imaginative** (-*nay*-) *adj.* of imagination تخیلی creative (writer, etc.) تخلیقی ، پرواز خیال والا

imbecile (im-be-*seel*) *adj.* weak-minded ناقص العقل

silly (remark, etc.) احمقانہ *n*. idiot فاترُالعقل **imbecility** *n*. idiocy کم عقلی، بے عقلی، فاترُالعقل ہونا، فتورِ عقل **imbibe** (im-*bīb*) *v.t.* drink پینا absorb جذب کرنا inhale (fresh air) میں سانس لینا take in (ideas) قبول کرنا، اَخذ کرنا

imbroglio (im-*broh*-li-oh) confused and complicated situation گتھی، پیچیدہ صورتِ حال

imbrue (im-*broo*) *v. t.* stain (*with*) میں آلودہ کرنا، (میں) رنگنا

imbue (im-*bew*) *v. t.* tinge deeply (*with*) کا رنگ چڑھانا saturate (*with*) رگ و پے میں ساری کرنا inspire (*with* feelings) دِل میں ڈالنا

imitate (*im*-i-tayt) *v. t.* make a likeness of کا نمونہ اُتارنا، کا سا بنانا، کا چربہ اُتارنا look like جیسا، کا سا ہونا mimic نقل اُتارنا follow the example of کے نقشِ قدم پر چلنا **imitation** (-*tay*-) *n*. imitating نقل اُتارنا copy نقل made to resemble something superior نقلی، اِمی ٹیشن **imitative** (-*tay*-) *adj*. counterfeit نقلی، جعلی copying nature تقلیدی *the imitative arts*, painting and sculpture تقلیدی فنون (word) copying the represented sound (as *crash*,) صوتی (لفظ) **imitator** *n*. one who imitates نقّال

immaculacy *n*. (see under **immaculate**)

immaculate (i-*mak*-ew-late) *adj*. spotless بے داغ right in every detail بالکل ٹھیک faultless بے عیب *the doctrine of the Immaculate Conception*, the belief that the Christ's mother was born free of the 'original sin' عقیدۂ حملِ بےگناہ **immaculately** *adv*. (dressed) spotlessly clean اُجلے (کپڑوں) صاف ستھرے **immaculacy** *n*. being immaculate بے داغ ہونا

immanence *n*., **immanency** *n*. (see under **immanent**)

immanent (*im*-a-nent) *adj*. inherent طبعی، خلقی، جبلّی **immanence, immanency** (*im*-) *n*. being inherent طبعی ہونا، خلقی ہونا

immaterial (i-ma-*tee*-ri-el) *adj*. not material غیر مادّی unimportant (*to* something else) کے لیے غیر اہم

immature (i-ma-*tew*-è*) *adj*. not fully developed کچّا، خام، ناپختہ minor نابالغ crude, imperfect خام، ناتمام حالت میں **immaturely** *adv*. ناتمکمل، ناتمام **immaturity** *n*. being immature خامی، غیر پختگی، ناتمامی، نابالغی

immeasurable (i-*mezh*-è-ra-bèl) *adj*. unbounded لامحدود immense بے حد **immeasurably** *adv*. لامحدود طور پر، بے انتہا **immeasurability** (-*bil*-) being immeasurable لامحدود ہونا

immediacy *n*. (see under **immediate**)

immediate (i-*mee*-di-ayt) *adj*. nearest قریب ترین next اگلا، بالکل ساتھ کا *immediate neighbour* فوراً اگلا، اصل ہمسایہ (دیوار بدیوار رہنے والا۔ ساتھ کے گھر والا) occurring at once فوری direct براہِ راست، بلاواسطہ **immediately** *adv*. at once فوراً، بلا تاخیر **immediacy** (-si) *n*. directness (of experience, etc.) براہِ راست ہونا، بلاواسطہ

immemorial (im-e-*moh*-ri-èl) *adj*. ancient beyond memory بہت ہی پُرانا *from time immemorial* بہت ہی پُرانے دَور کا

immense (i-*mens*) *adj*. very large بہت بڑا **immensely** *adv*. immeasurably بے حساب، بہت، بے اندازہ **immensity** *n*. great size بہت بڑا ہونا، عظیم وُسعت

immerse (i-*mē*s*) *v.t.* dip ڈبونا *be immersed in*, (*a*) be dipped in میں ڈوبا ہُوا (*b*) be deep in (book, etc.) میں منہمک، میں غرق (*c*) be involved in میں غرق ہُوا، میں ڈوبا ہُوا **immersion** (i-*mē**-shen) *n*. being immersed ڈوبا ہُوا ہونا، غرق ہونا

immigrate (*im*-i-grayt) *v.i.* come (*into* a country) as a settler آبادکاری کی غرض سے آنا، توطن کے لیے آنا **immigrant** *n*. settler from abroad آباد، متوطن، آبادکار **immigration** (-*gray*-) *n*. coming (*into* a country) for settlement آبادی کے لیے آنا

imminent (*im*-i-nent) *adj*. impending (danger, death, etc.) قریب، نزدیک، سر پر کھڑا **imminence** *n*. nearness (of danger, etc.) قریب ہونا، نزدیکی

immitigable (i-*mit*-i-ga-bèl) *adj*. (of offence, etc.) that cannot be toned down ناقابلِ معافی

immobile (i-*moh*-bīl) *adj*. immovable غیر متحرک، ناقابلِ حرکت **immobilize** (i-*moh*-bi-līz) *v. t.* make immovable غیر متحرک کرنا **immobility** (-*bil*-) *n*. being immovable ناقابلِ حرکت ہونا

immoderate (i-*mod*-è*-ret) excessive حد درجہ، بے حد **immoderately** *adv*. excessively بے حد

immodest (i-*mod*-est) *adj*. impudent گستاخ indecent (person) بے حیا indecent (action) غیر شریفانہ **immodesty** (i-*mod*-es-ti) *n*. indecency ناشائستگی، بے حیائی

immoral (i-*mo*-rèl) *adj*. evil غیر اخلاقی، بُرا **immorally** *adv*. غیر اخلاقی طور پر **immorality** (i-mo-*ral*-i-ti) *n*. being immoral فحاشی، بد اخلاقی

immortal (i-*mo**-tèl) *adj*. living for ever لافانی، زندۂ جاوید، کبھی نہ ابدی، امٹ never to be forgotten بھولنے والا *n*. immortal being لافانی ہستی *the immortals*, the gods of antiquity دیوی، دیوتا **immortality** (-tal-) *n*. endless life حیاتِ جاوداں، اَبدی زندگی endless fame اَبدی شہرت، لازوال شہرت **immortalize** (-līz) *v.t.* give endless life to کو اَبدی زندگی عطا کرنا give endless fame to کو اَبدی شہرت کا مالک بنانا **immortally** *adv*. everlastingly, undyingly ہمیشہ، جاودانی طور پر

immovable (i-*moov*-a-bèl) *adj*. that which

cannot be moved غیر متحرک *immovable property*, land, buildings, etc. جائداد غیر منقولہ firm (in purpose) ثابت قدم، غیر متزلزل emotionless دل کا سخت **immovably** *adv*. in an immovable manner بے حرکت

immovability *n*. being immovable غیر متحرک ہونا

immune (i-*mewn*) *adj*. exempt or protected (*from* disease, liability, etc.) سے بچا ہوا، سے محفوظ **immunity** *n*. exemption (*from* disease, taxation, etc.) چھٹکارا، نجات، استثنا **immunize** (i-*mew*-n z) *v.t.* make (someone) immune (*from*) (سے) بچا دینا، سے مستثنیٰ کر دینا، (سے) بے خوف کر دینا

imp *n*. devil's child شیطان کا بچہ little devil بھتنا mischievous child شریر بچہ **impish** *adj*. mischievous (person) such action شرارت.

impact (*im*-pakt) *n*. striking (*of* something *on* or *against*) تصادم، ٹکر

impair (im-*pay*-ĕ*) *v.t.* damage نقصان پہنچانا weaken کمزور کر دینا **impairment** *n*. damaging نقصان، کمزوری

impale (im-*payl*) *v.t.* enclose with stakes کے گرد جنگلا لگانا kill by pinning down with a sharp stake, etc. کے جسم میں میخ ٹھونک کر ہلاک کرنا

impalpable (-*pal*-) *adj*. that which cannot be perceived by touch غیر محسوس **impalpably** *adv*. so as not to be perceived by touch غیر محسوس طور پر

impart (im-*pah*t*) *v.t.* give a share of حصہ دینا، پہنچانا disclose (secret news, etc., *to*) (کو) بتانا، (پر) ظاہر کرنا

impartial (im-*pah**-shĕl) *adj*. unprejudiced (judge or judgment) منصف مزاج، منصفانہ، غیر جانب دارانہ

impartiality (-shi-*al*-) *n*. being impartial انصاف، غیر جانبداری

impassable (-*pass*-) *adj*. (of roads, etc.) impossible to traverse ناقابل گزر، ناگزار **impassibility** *n*. being impassible ناقابل گزر ہونا، ناگزاری

impasse (im-*pahs*) *n*. blind alley بند گلی deadlock (in negotiations, etc.) تعطل

impassioned (im-*pahs*-ènd) *adj*. (of speech, etc.) full of and moving deep feeling جذباتی، جوشیلی

impassive (im-*pas*-iv) *adj*. unmoved بے حس، جذبات سے عاری، ٹھنڈے دل و دماغ کا **impassivity** *n*. being impassive بے حسی

impatient (im-*pay*-shent) *adj*. restless بے صبر intolerant (*of* something) کو برداشت نہ کر سکنے والا، سے تنگ آ جانے والا **impatience** (im-*pay*-shens) *n*. being impatient بے صبری، بیتابی

impeach (im-*peech*) *v.t.* raise doubts about (someone's character, etc.) پر الزام لگانا، پر نکتہ چینی کرنا accuse of treason بغاوت کا الزام لگانا try in Parliament for treason مقننہ میں (کسی پر) بغاوت کا مقدمہ چلانا **impeachment** *n*. نکتہ چینی، الزام، بغاوت کا الزام، پارلیمنٹ میں مقدمہ

impeccable (im-*pek*-a-bèl) *adj*. incapable of doing wrong جس سے کوئی غلطی نہ ہو سکے، معصوم، معصوم عن الخطا

impeccability (-*bil*-) *n*. being impeccable معصوم عن الخطا ہونا، عصمت

impecunious (im-pe-*kew*-ni-us) *adj*. moneyless نادار، مفلس **impecuniosity** (-*os*-) *n*. being moneyless ناداری، مفلسی

impede (im-*peed*) *v.t.* obstruct کو روکنا، کی راہ میں حائل ہونا

impediment *n*. any obstruction رکاوٹ، مزاحمت (esp.) defect in speech زبان کا اٹکنا، ہکلانا وغیرہ

impel (im-*pel*) *v.t.* (-ll-) drive forward دھکیلنا force (someone to something or *to do* something) پر آمادہ کرنا، پر ابھارنا **impellent** *adj*. impelling دھکیلنے والا، آمادہ کرنے والا *n*. such force ابھارنے والی قوت

impending (-*pend*-) (of danger, etc.) *adj*. imminent سر پر کھڑا، قریب، نزدیک، آنے ہی والا

impenetrable (im-*pen*-è-tray-bèl) *adj*. impervious جس میں کچھ سرایت نہ کر سکے، ناقابل گزر very deep (mystery, etc.) ناقابل فہم، بہت گہرا closed (mind) جامد، ٹھس **impenetrability** *n*. (-*bil*-) being impenetrable ناقابل گزر ہونا، ناقابل فہم ہونا، ٹھس ہونا

impenitent (im-*pen*-i-tent) *adj*. not penitent تائب نہ ہونے والا not sorry for having done wrong اپنے کیے پر نادم نہ ہونے والا **impenitence** *n*. being impenitent تائب نہ ہونا، نادم نہ ہونا، شرمندہ نہ ہونا

imperative (im-*pe*-ra-tiv) *adj*. urgent اشد ضروری *it is imperative* (*to do*) ضروری ہے کہ، (یہ کرنا) اشد ضروری ہے authoritative سخت، آمرانہ، تحکمانہ *n*. form of verb expressing command امر

imperceptible (im-pĕ*-*sep*-ti-bèl) *adj*. that which cannot be perceived غیر محسوس، ناقابل ادراک very slight بہت ہی کم، غیر محسوس **imperceptibly** *adv*. in an imperceptible manner غیر محسوس طور پر

imperceptibility (-*bil*-) *n*. being imperceptible غیر محسوس ہونا

imperfect (im-*pĕ**-fekt) incomplete نامکمل، ادھورا، ناتمام *imperfect tenses*, tenses representing action as still going on (in the past, present or future) افعال جاریہ (م: فعل جاری) (*e.g.*, *I was reading* میں پڑھ رہا تھا)

imperfection (-*fek*-) *n*. being incomplete ادھورا ہونا، ادھوراپن، ناتمامی fault, weakness کمزوری، خامی، خرابی

imperial (im-*pee*-ri-ĕl) *adj*. of an emperor شہنشاہی، خسروی، خسروانہ of an empire سامراجی imperious جابرانہ، مستبدانہ، خسروانہ British (weights and measures)

بَرطانِیَ (بسٹے وغیرہ) **imperialism** (-lizm) *n.* policy of safeguarding only imperial interests سامراج ، ملوکیت پسندی belief in the value of colonies سامراجی نظام کی حمایت، سامراجیت، ملوکیت پسندی سے policy of ruling or exploiting weak nations سامراج ملوکیت پسند، **imperialist** *n.* believer in imperialism سامراج کا حامی، سامراجی **imperialistic** (-lis-) *adj.* pertaining to imperialism سامراجی
imperil (im-*pe*-ril) *v.t.* (-ll-) endanger (one's life, etc) جان جوکھوں میں ڈالنا، خطرے میں ڈالنا
imperishable (-pe-) *adj.* that which cannot perish لازوال، اَمَر، اَمِٹ
imperious (im-*pee*-ri-us) *adj.* authoritative آمرانہ، تحکمانہ **imperiousness** *n.* authoritative manner تحکمانہ انداز سے
impermeable (im-*pě**-mi-a-bèl) *adj.* not permeable غیر نفوذ پذیر **impermeability** (-*bil*-) *n.* غیر نفوذ پذیری
impersonal (-*pě**-) *adj.* not influenced by personal feelings بے لاگ، بے تعصبانہ، جس میں ذاتی جذبات کو دخل نہ ہو (of remarks, etc.) not referring to a particular person جس میں کسی کی طرف اشارہ نہ ہو، ذاتی حملہ کے بغیر not existing as a person لاشخصی *impersonal verb*, one used with *it* as its subject (as *it seems, it rains*, etc.) لاشخصی فعل، غیر شخصی فعل
impersonate (im-*pě**-su-nayt) *v.t.* play the role of کا کردار ادا کرنا pretend to be (another person) جعلی شخصیت اختیار کرنا، غلط نام بتانا personify (qualities, etc.) کا مجسمہ ہونا **impersonator** *n.* one who pretends to be someone else جعلی شخصیت اختیار کرنے والا، بہروپیا **impersonation** *n.* such pretension غلط نام بتانا، جعلی شخصیت اختیار کرنا
impertinence *n.* (see under **impertinent**)
impertinent (im-*pě**-ti-nent) *adj.* rude, cheeky, insolent گستاخ، بدتمیز irrelevant غیر متعلق بے ربط، بے محل، خارج از بحث **impertinence** *n.* rudeness گستاخی، بدتمیزی irrelevance بے محل ہونا، غیر متعلق ہونا
imperturbable *adj.* calm (person) ٹھنڈے دل ودماغ کا **imperturbability** (-*bil*-) *n.* being imperturbable ٹھنڈے دل ودماغ کا ہونا
impervious (-*pě**-) *adj.* not allowing (liquids) to pass through غیر نفوذ پذیر *impervious to*, not influenced by غیر اثر پذیر **imperviousness** *n.* being impervious سرایت نہ کرنے دینا، اثر قبول نہ ہونا، غیر نفوذ پذیری، غیر اثر پذیری
impetuous (im-*pet*-ew-us) *adj.* moving violently تند، تیز acting with sudden energy thoughtlessly اندھادھند کام کرنے والا، پُرجوش done thus اندھادھند کیا ہوا **impetuosity** (im-pet-ew-*os*-i-ti) *n.* جوش، تندی، تیزی، اندھادھند کام کرنا
impetus (*im*-pe-tus) *n.* force with which a body moves رفتار کا زور driving force تحریک، ہیجان، جذبہ، انگیخت
impinge (im-*pinj*) *v.t.* strike forcibly (*on*) (سے) ٹکرانا، (سے) متصادم ہونا be contradictory to (*on*) سے متصادم ہونا
impiety *n.* (see under **impious**)
impious (*im*-pi-us) *adj.* (of person, action, life, etc.) not pious wicked ناپاک، بُرا **impiety** (im-*pī*-ě-ti) *n.* lack of piety بدمعاشی، ناپاکی، عدم اتقا
impish *adj.* (see under **imp**)
implacable (im-*plak*-a-bel) *adj.* relentlessly determined or angry سنگدل، کٹھور، پکا **implacably** *adv.* کٹھورپن سے، سنگدلی سے **implacability** (-*bil*-) *n.* relentless enmity or hatred جانی دشمنی، کٹھورپن
implant (im-*plahnt*) *v.t.* plant in میں پودا لگانا instil in the mind دل میں ڈالنا
implement *n.* (*im*-ple-ment) (agricultural or other) tool اوزار، سامان *farm implements* کھیتی باڑی کا سامان، آلاتِ کشاورزی *v.t.* (-*ment*) carry (programme, scheme, project, etc.) into effect عمل میں لانا، جامۂ عمل پہنانا **implementation** (-*tay*-) *n.* act of implementing or being implemented عمل، جامۂ عمل پہنانا، عمل میں آنا
implicate (*im*-pli-kayt) involve (*in* crime, etc.) میں شریک ہونا accuse of complicity (in crime) سے نتیجہ نکلنا، کا پہلو نکلنا الجھانا، لپیٹ میں لینا imply (*in*)
implication (-*kay*-) *n.* implicating or being implicated لپیٹ میں آنا یا لینا hint اشارہ، پہلو inference نتیجہ، معنی
implicit (im-*plis*-it) *adj.* (of meaning, sense, etc.) implied مضمر (of faith, etc.) absolute, unquestioning پکا، پورا پورا **implicitly** *adv.* unreservedly پوری طرح سے
implore (im-*ploh**) beseech (someone *to do* or *for*) منت سماجت کرنا، التجا کرنا، ملتجی ہونا
imply (im-*plī*) *v.t.* suggest (*that*) کا مفہوم ہونا، کی طرف دلالت کرنا involve as a result کا نتیجہ ہونا
impolite (im-po-*līt*) *adj.* uncivil ناشائستہ **impoliteness** *n.* rudeness ناشائستگی
impolitic (im-*pol*-i-tik) *adj.* injudicious (person) ناعاقبت اندیش، عاقبت نااندیش inexpedient (action) نامناسب، خلافِ مصلحت **impoliticly** *adv.* خلافِ مصلحت، عاقبت نااندیشانہ
imponderable (-*pond*-) *adj.* having little or no weight بے حد ہلکا، بے وزن mental or physical phenomena which cannot be weighed physically غیر مادی، غیر وزن پذیر

import *v.t.* (im-*poh**t) bring (goods *from* a foreign land *into* one's country) دَرآمد کرنا signify مَطلَب ہونا ، مُدّعا ہونا ، مفہوم ہونا be important to کے لیے اہم ہونا ، کے لیے معنے رکھنا *it imports us to know that* ہمارے لیے یہ جاننا اہم ہے کہ *n.* (*im*-poh*t) (usu. *pl.*) imported goods *imports* درآمد کیا ہوا مال ، دَرآمدات ، دَرآمد *and exports* دَرآمد و بَرآمد ، تجارتِ خارجہ importing دَرآمد meaning معنیٰ ، مفہوم ، مَطلَب importance اہمیّت

importable *adj.* that which can be imported دَرآمد کے قابِل ، جس کی دَرآمد کی اِجازت ہو ، دَرآمد **importer** *n.* one who imports goods دَرآمد کرنے والا ، دَرآمد کُنندہ

importation *n.* act of importing دَرآمد ، دَرآمد کرنا

important (im-*po**-tant) *adj.* momentous ضَروری ، اہم ، وقیع very important بہت ضَروری having an air of authority *important person*(*s*), بڑے لوگ *Very Important Person*(*s*), (abbr. *V.I.P.* or *V.I.Ps.*), State guests or other dignitaries اہم اَفراد ، وی۔ آئی - پی **importance** *n.* being important وَقعت ، اہمیّت -

importune (im-*po*-tewn) *v.t.* keep asking for پیچھے پڑ جانا ، اِصرار کرنا ، مُصر ہونا **importunate** (im-*po**-tew-nayt) *adj.* (of persons) making repeated and inconvenient requests پیچھے پڑ جانے والا ، مُصر ، چمٹ چیٹر (of affairs) urgent ضَروری ، اہم ، اَشد ضَروری **importunity** (-*tew*-) *n.* اِصرار ، اِبرام

impose (im-*pohz*) *v.t.* & *i.* levy (tax, fine or duty *upon*) لگانا ، عائد کرنا palm off (thing *upon*) کے گلے مَنڈھنا *impose upon*, deceive ; take advantage of (someone or his good nature) کو ٹھگنا ، کو دھوکا دینا ، کی شرافت سے ناجائز فائدہ اُٹھانا *impose upon*, overawe, impress کو مرعوب کرنا **imposing** *adj.* impressive شاندار formidable رُعب دار ، مَرعُوب کُن **imposition** (-*zish*-) *n.* the act of imposing (taxes, etc.) لگانا ، عائد کرنا tax, etc., imposed ٹیکس ، محصُول unreasonable demand ناجائز مُطالبہ deception دھوکا work set as punishment to a student ٹھگی (طالب علم کو) سزا کے طور پر کام ، تعزیری کام laying on (*of hands* in blessing) دُعا کے لیے کسی کے) سر پر ہاتھ رکھنا

impossible im-*pos*-i-bèl) *adj.* not possible ناممکن that which cannot be endured ناقابِلِ بَرداشت **impossibility** (-*bil*-) *n.* being impossible ناممکن ہونا something impossible ، ناممکن بات امرِ محال

impost (*im*-pohst) *n.* tax محصُول tribute خراج upper course of a pillar bearing the arch داسا

impostor (im-*pos*-tĕ*) *n.* pretender جھوٹا دعوے دار ، مُدّعی swindler فریبی ، دَغا باز **imposture** (im-*pos*-chĕ*) *n.* deception فریب ، دَغا sham جھوٹ ، دھوکا

imposture *n.* (see under **impostor**)

impotent (*im*-po-tent) *adj.* not virile نامرد powerless, weak بے بس ، کمزور **impotence** (*im*-po-tens) *n.* being impotent بے بسی ، کمزوری ، نامردی

impound (im-*pound*) *v.t.* confiscate قُرق کرنا ، ضبط کرنا shut up (cattle) in a pound باڑے میں بند کرنا

impoverish (im-*pov*-è-rish) *v.t.* make poor مُفلس کر دینا exhaust the strength or good qualities of کی طاقت (یا خوبیاں) ختم کر دینا

impracticable (-*prak*-) *adj.* not practicable ناقابِلِ عَمَل (of persons) unmanageable مشکل ہی سے قابُو میں آنے والا **impracticability** *n.* being impracticable ناقابِلِ عَمَل ہونا

imprecate (*im*-pre-kayt) *n.* invoke (evil *upon*) (کو) بَددُعا دینا **imprecation** (-*kay*-) *n.* curse

imprecatory (-*kay*-) *adj.* (of words, utterance, etc.) pertaining to an imprecation بَددُعا والے

impregnable (im-*preg*-na-bèl) *adj.* safe against attack نہایت مُستحکم ، ناقابِلِ تسخیر **impregnability** *n.* اِستحکام ، ناقابِلِ تسخیر ہونا

impregnate *v.t.* (im-*preg*-nayt) make pregnant حامِلہ ہونا permeate (*with*) (کے) رنگ میں رنگ دینا *adj.* (im-*preg*-nit) pregnant حامِلہ permeated (*with*) (کے) رنگ میں رنگا ہوا **impregnation** *n.* act of impregnating حامِلہ کرنا ، (کسی کے) رنگ میں رنگ دینا

impresario (im-pre-*sah*-ri-oh) *n.* (pl. impresarios) organiser of public entertainment (*e.g.*, opera) (کھیل وغیرہ کا) مُنتظِم famous singer or other performer مشہور فن کار

impress (im-*pres*) *v.t.* make a mark by ٹھپّہ لگانا ، مُہر لگانا fix deeply (on the mind, memory) ذہن نشین کرنا ، دِل میں بٹھانا ، نقش کرنا influence کو متاثر کرنا make a good impression پر اچھا اثر ڈالنا اَثر ڈالنا force into military service زبردستی فوج میں بھرتی کرنا take for public use بیگار میں پکڑنا

impression (im-*presh*-ĕn) *n.* mark made by pressing نقش print (of engraving, etc.) ٹھپّا number of copies printed once طبع ، طباعت effect produced on the mind or feelings اثر ، تاثر vague idea دُھندلا سا تصوّر ، خیال سا *have an impression that*, *be under the impression*, believe that خیال ہونا **impressionable** *adj.* easily influenced اَثر پذیر *impressionable age*, age when one is most impressed by environment عُمر کا اَثر پذیر حصّہ ، اَثر پذیر عُمر **impressive** (im-*pres*-iv) *adj.* making a deep impression on the mind اَثر آفرین

impressively *adv.* earnestly پُر اثر انداز سے ، دِل سے

impressment *n.* seizure for public service or use بیگار

imprest (*im*-prest) *n.* money advanced for official purpose سرکاری ضرورت کی پیشگی رقم، سرکاری پیشگی *imprest account*, account maintained of this money حساب سرکاری پیشگی

imprimatur (im-pri-*may*-tĕ*) *n.* licence to publish a book کتاب شائع کرنے کی اجازت، اذنِ اشاعت sanction اجازت، منظوری

imprint *v.t.* (im-*print*) stamp (*on*) نقش کرنا *n.* (*im*-print) mark left by something نقش name of the printer or publisher at the end of a book, etc. کتاب پر طابع یا ناشر کا نام

imprison (im-*priz*-ĕn) *v.t.* put into prison قید کرنا، جیل میں ڈالنا **imprisonment** *n.* act of imprisoning or being imprisoned قید

improbable (*-prob-*) *adj.* not probable بعید از قیاس **improbably** *adv.* مشکل ہی سے **improbability** (-bil-) *n.* being improbable بعید از قیاس ہونا something improbable بعید از قیاس بات

impromptu (im-*promp*-tew) *adv.* & *adj.* (used predicatively) extempore وقت کے وقت، فی البدیہہ *n.* extempore musical composition فی البدیہہ نغمہ

improper (im-*prop*-ĕ*) *adj.* incorrect (use of word) غلط indecent (behaviour) نامناسب، نازیبا **impropriety** (im-pro-*prī*-ĕ-ti) *n.* unfitness نا شائستگی indecency نامناسب ہونا

improve (im-*proov*) *v.t.* & *i.* make or become better بہتر ہونا یا بنانا *improve upon* (*something*), do better than (it) سے بہتر بنانا، کو ترقی دینا **improvement** *n.* making or growing better بہتری advancement ترقی reform اصلاح

improvidence *n.* (see under **improvident**)

improvident (im-*prov*-i-dent) *adj.* thriftless; wasteful فضول خرچ not looking to future needs عاقبت نا اندیش، کوتاہ اندیش، نا عاقبت اندیش **improvidence** *n.* فضول خرچی، کوتاہ اندیشی، کوتہ اندیشی، عاقبت نا اندیشی **improvidently** (im-*prov*-i-dent-li) **improvidentially** (im-pro-vi-densh-ĕ-li) *adv* بے تدبیری، کوتاہ اندیشی سے، عاقبت نا اندیشی سے

improvisator *n.*, **improvisation** *n.* (see under **improvise**)

improvise (*im*-pro-vīz) *v.t.* & *i.* compose (poetry or music) impromptu فی البدیہہ شعر کہنا، یا نغمہ سرائی کرنا contrive on the spur of the moment using the available resources وقت کے وقت جو ہاتھ لگے اُس سے فوراً بنا ڈالنا یا کام نکال لینا **improvisation** *n.* act of improvising وہیں بنا دینا **improvisator** *n.* one who improvises بدیہہ گو، وہیں بنانے والا

imprudence *n.* (see under **imprudent**)

imprudent (im-*proo*-dent) *adj.* rash, not cautious غیر محتاط، کوتاہ اندیش، کوتہ اندیش **imprudence** *n.* indiscretion کوتاہ اندیشی، کوتہ اندیشی **imprudently** *adv.* rashly, indiscreetly اندھا دھند

impudent (*im*-pew-dent) *adj.* insolent گستاخ shameless ڈھیٹ، بے شرم، بیحیا **impudence** (*im*-pew-dens) *n.* گستاخی، بے شرمی، بے حیائی

impugn (im-*pewn*) *v.t.* challenge (statement etc.) پر اعتراض کرنا **impugnable** (im-*pewn*-a-bĕl) *adj.* that can be impugned قابلِ اعتراض **impugnment** (im-*pewn*-ment) *n.* act of impugning اعتراض کرنا

impulse (*im*-puls) *n.* push دھکا impetus (*to* or *to do* something) تحریک، لہر، ترنگ، جذبہ *seized with an impulse* (*to do*), (کام کرنے) کی ترنگ میں آنا **impulsive** (im-*pul*-siv) *adj.* acting suddenly without thought ترنگی، من موجی (action) resulting from impulse and not calm deliberation اضطراری

impunity (im-*pew*-ni-ti) *n.* exemption from punishment or harmful consequences سزا سے بریت، پاداش سے بے خوفی *(do something) with impunity*, (do it) with freedom from punishment, etc. سزا کے خوف سے نجات پا کر (کچھ کرنا)، بلا خوفِ عقوبت (کچھ کرنا)

impure (im-*pew*-ĕ*) *adj.* not pure غیر خالص unwholesome گندا adulterated ملاوٹ والا unchaste ناپاک، نجس **impurity** (im-*pew*-ri-ti) *n.* being impure ناپاک ہونا، خالص نہ ہونا (usu. *pl.*) foreign matter ملاوٹ

impute (im-*pewt*) *v.t.* ascribe (something bad *to*) کا الزام رکھنا، کی تہمت دھرنا describe as the cause of (*to*) کے باعث قرار دینا، سے منسوب کرنا **imputation** (*-tay-*) *n.* accusation الزام، تہمت، اتہام **imputability** (*-bil-*) *n.* being imputable متہم ہو سکنا

[1]**in** *prep.* within bounds of (space, time or circumstance) میں، کے دوران میں، کی حالت میں dressed in پہنے ہوئے expressed in (a language) میں *He spoke in Urdu*; اُس نے اُردو تقریر کی، اُس نے اُردو میں تقریر کی، as a means of میں، کے حق میں in the form of کی صورت میں *in dozens*, درجن درجن، درجنوں درجن کرکے while (*doing*) (کرتے)، ہوئے made of within (a continent, country, big city or one's city, village, etc.) (where one is known to be or to live) provided extent is to be stressed میں *adv.* inside اندر at home گھر میں towards the inside اندر in office برسرِ اقتدار *adj.* living inside اندرونی، داخل **the ins** *n. pl.* the political party in power حزبِ اقتدار *the ins and outs* (*of*), all the details (of) کا نیک و بد، فی الجملہ

in a (*week*), towards its end or just after it تفصیلات، مالۂ و ماعلیہ not in for, not in the running for (بہ ہفتہ، بھر میں) have a friend (or *foe, etc.*) in *someone*, کے بیچے مقابلہ نہ کر رہا ہونا in for, (a) competeing کسی کی دوستی (دعیرہ) کا شرف (دعیرہ) حاصل ہونا (b) destined to میں پڑنے والا

[2]**in-** *pref.* opposite of ; not نا، بے، غیر، خلاف (as *insincere*, not sincere غیر مخلص)

inability (in-a-*bil*-i-ti) *n.* inefficiency نالائقی being powerless (*to do*) کرنے سے، معذوری نا اہلیت

inaccessible (in-ak-*ses*-i-bèl) *adj.* that which cannot be reached ناقابلِ گزر unobtainable ناقابلِ حصول not open to advances جس تک رسائی نہ ہو سکے، پہنچ سے باہر **inaccessibility** (-*bil*-) *n.* being inaccessible پہنچ سے باہر ہونا، کم آمیزی

inaccurate (in-*ak*-ew-rayt) *adj.* incorrect غلط not exact جس میں کچھ غلطی ہو **inaccuracy** (in-*ak*-ew-ra-si) *n.* mistake غلطی

inactive (in-*ak*-tiv) *adj.* not acting، بے حرکت بے عمل lazy, sluggish سُست، کاہل **inactivity** (-*tiv*-) *n.* laziness سُستی not being active بے عملی **inaction** (in-*ak*-shĕn) *n.* lack of action بے عملی inertness سُستی، کاہلی

inadequate (in-*ad*-e-kwet) *adj.* insufficient ناکافی **inadequately** *adv.* insufficiently ناکافی طور پر **inadequacy** (in-*ad*-e-kwa-si) *n.* insufficiency ناکافی ہونا

inadmissible (-*mis*-i-) *adj.* not allowed ناجائز، ناقابلِ قبول **inadmissibility** (-*bil*-) *n.* not being admissible ناجائز ہونا

inadvertent (in-ad-*vĕ**-tant) *adj.* inattentive, careless توجّہ نہ کرنے والا، بے پروا unintentional (mistake, etc.) نادانستہ **inadvertently** *adv.* unintentionally نادانستہ **inadvertence** *n.* being advertent بے توجّہی، نا دانستگی

inadvisable (in-ad-*vi*-za-bèl) *adj.* indiscreet, injudicious نامناسب **inadvisibility** (-vi-za-*bil*-) *n.* being inadvisable نامناسب ہونا، نامَوزونیّت

inalienable (in-*ay*-li-a-nay-bèl) *adj.* inseparable ناقابلِ انتقال، غیر منفک **inalienably** *adv.* inseparably ناقابلِ انتقال طور پر **inalienability** (-bil-) *n.* being inseparable ناقابلِ انتقال ہونا

inane (in-*ayn*) *adj.* silly احمقانہ void خالی (*the inane*), infinite space فضائے لامتناہی **inanely** *adv.* foolishly احمقانہ طور پر، حماقت سے **inanity** *n.* foolish behaviour حماقت

inanimate (in-*an*-i-mayt) *adj.* dead مُردہ dull بے جان، بے کیف **inanimation** (-*may*-) *n.* being lifeless بے جان ہونا

inappeasable (in-a-*pee*-zè-bèl) *adj.* that which cannot be appeased فرو نہ ہونے والا، شیر نہ ہونے والا

inapposite (in-*ap*-o-zit) unsuitable نامَوزوں

inapplicable (in-*ap*-li-ka-bèl) *adj.* not applicable نامَوزوں **inapplicability** (-*bil*-) *n.* not being applicable نامَوزونیّت

inappreciable (in-a-*pree*-shi-a-bèl) *adj.* imperceptible بالکل خفیف، غیر محسوس **inappreciably** *adv.* to an imperceptible degree بہت کم، غیر محسوس طور پر **inappreciation** (-ay-) *n.* lack of appreciation ناقدری، قدر ناشناسی

inapprehensible (in-ap-re-*hens*-i-bèl) that which cannot be understood ناقابلِ فہم

inapt (in-*apt*) *adj.* irrelevant, unsuitable غیر متعلق، ناموزوں unskilful نااہل، اناڑی، پھوہڑ **inaptitude** *n.* being inapt نالائقی، نا اہلیت

inarticulate (in-ah*-*tik*-ew-layt) *adj.* incapable of speech بے زبان unable to speak distinctly جو صاف نہ بول سکے

inartistic,(in-ah*-*tis*-tik) *adj.* ungraceful, not artistic بھدا، بھونڈا، بدنما having no aesthetic sense بدذوق، بے ذوق

inasmuch as (in-*az*-much-az) *adv.* since چونکہ

inattention (in-a-*ten*-shĕn) *n.* heedlessness بے توجّہی **inattentive** (-tiv) *adj.* not attentive بے توجّہ

inaudible (in-*awd*-i-bèl) *adj.* too low to be heard بہت دھیما، جو سُنائی نہ دے **inaudibility** (-*bil*-) *n.* being audible بہت دھیما ہونا، سُنائی نہ دینا

inaugural *adj.* & *n.* (see under **inaugurate**)

inaugurate (-*awg*-ew-) *v.t.* being or open at a special ceremony افتتاح کرنا **inaugural** (in-*awg*-ew-rĕl) *adj.* pertaining to inauguration افتتاح *inaugural ceremony* افتتاحی تقریب، افتتاح، تقریبِ افتتاح *n.* (U. S.) address on induction into office افتتاحی خُطبہ professor's public address on appointment اُستاد کا افتتاحی خطبہ **inauguration** (-ay-) *n.* act of inaugurating or being inaugurated افتتاح

inauspicious (in-aws-*pish*-us) *adj.* unlucky, not auspicious نامُبارک، منحوس **inauspiciousness** *n.* ill omen نحوست

inborn (*in*-bo*n) *adj.* innate پیدائشی، جبلّی، خِلقی

inbred (*in*-bred) *adj.* inborn پیدائشی، خِلقی، جبلّی **inbreeding** (*in-breed*-ing) *n.* breeding from closely related animals قریب النسل، جانوروں کی دوغلی نسل لینا

incalculable (in-*kal*-kew-lab-èl) *adj.* beyond calculation بے حد، بے شمار not dependable (person) ناقابلِ اعتبار، ناقابلِ اعتماد **incalculably** (-*lab*-li) *adv.* (of great harm, etc.) extremely بہت، بہت ہی

***in camera** adj. & adv.* (of hearing, etc.) not in open court but in the judge's private room بند کمرے میں

incandescence *n.* (see under **incandescent**)

incandescent (in-kan-*des*-ant) *adj.* able to glow with white heat دہک کر سفید روشنی دینے والا، تاباں، تابندہ **incandescence** (in-kan-*des*-ens) *n.* being incandescent تابش، تابانی، تابندگی

incantation (-kan-*tay*-) *n.* magical formula منتر its use منتر پڑھ کر پھونکنا، منتر پڑھنا

incapable (-*kap*-) *adj.* inefficient نالائق not capable (*of*) (کا) نا اہل ineligible for (*of*) (کے) نا اہل **incapably** *adv.* inefficiently نااہلیت سے نالائقی سے **incapability** (-*bil*-) *n.* being incapable نالائقی، نا اہلیت

incapacitate (in-ka-*pas*-i-tayt) *v. t.* render unfit (*for*) ناکارہ کر دینا **incapacity** (in-ka-*pas*-i-ti) *n.* inability نالائقی powerlessness (*for* or *to do* something) (سے)، معذوری

incarcerate (in-*kah**-si-rayt) *v.t.* imprison قید کرنا قید میں ڈالنا، بندی خانے بھجوانا **incarceration** (-*ray*-) imprisonment قید

incarnate *adj.* (in-*kah**-nayt) in human form مجسّم *a devil incarnate,* شیطان مجسّم *v. t.* (in-ka*-nayt) make incarnate جسم عطا کرنا، مجسّم کرنا put (an idea, etc.) into concrete form عملی صورت میں لانا، جامۂ عمل پہنانا be a living form (a quality) زندہ نمونہ ہونا، زندہ مثال ہونا، جیتی جاگتی مثال ہونا **incarnation** (-*nay*-) taking on of human form تجسیم *the Incarnation*, according to Christians, the taking of human form by Jesus Christ تجسیم و یسوع living type of a quality نمونہ، مجسّمہ، مثال

incautious (in-*kaw*-shus) *adj.* rash غیر محتاط **incautiousness** *n.* being incautious بے احتیاطی

incendiary (in-*send*-i-a-ri) *n.* & *adj.* (one) setting fire to property unlawfully and with an evil purpose جلانے والا، آگ لگانے والا، آتش انداز، آتش زن (one) stirring up violence مفسد، اشتعال انگیز (bomb) causing fire آگ لگانے والا (بم)، آتش انداز (بم)، آگ بم **incendiarism** *n.* practice of setting fire to property آتش زنی

incense *n.* (*in*-sens) sweet-smelling smoke (بخورات کی) دھونی substance producing smell when burning بخورات *v.i.* (in-*sens*) perfume with incense بخورات کی دھونی دینا، مہکانا، معطّر کرنا make angry (*by* words, etc.) ناراض کرنا، غصّہ چڑھانا، بھڑکانا، برافروختہ کرنا

incentive (in-*sent*-iv) *n.* motive (*to do* or *for* work, etc.) محرّک، مہیج، شوق، جذبہ *provide an incentive for* (کی) رغبت پیدا کرنا

inception (in-*sep*-shĕn) *n.* beginning شروع، آغاز، ابتدا **inceptive** *adj.* of beginning شروع کا، ابتدائی

incertitude (in-*sĕ**-ti-tewd) *n.* uncertainty غیر یقینی صورتِ حال

incessant (in-*ses*-ant) *adj.* continuous لگاتار، مسلسل، غیر منقطع continual پے در پے **incessantly** *adv.* مسلسل، لگاتار، پے در پے

incest (*in*-sest) *n.* sexual intercourse between relations whose mutual marriage is prohibited محرّمات سے جنسی تعلقات، مباشرت محرّمات **incestuous** *adj.* one guilty of incest مباشرِ محرّمات pertaining to incest مباشرتِ محرّمات سے متعلق

inch *n.* one-twelfth of a foot انچ *by inches,* bit by bit تھوڑا تھوڑا، تھوڑا تھوڑا کرکے *inch by inch,* gradually آہستہ آہستہ (*b*) *every inch* (*a fighter, etc.*), (be a fighter, etc.) in every way پکا، نبرد آزما وغیرہ ہونا

inchoate *adj.* (*in*-koh-at) just begun بالکل ابتدائی *v.t* (*in*-koh-ayt) originate شروع کرنا

incidence (*in*-si-dens) *n.* extent of effect (of tax, disease, etc.) اثر، حلقۂ اثر، دائرۂ عمل

incident (*in*-si-dent) *n.* episode in a larger event ماجرا، ضمنی واقعہ، ضمنی بات event of little importance معمولی واقعہ event attracting general attention مشہور واقعہ distinct piece of action in a play, etc. (مثنوی یا تمثیل میں) واقعہ **incidental** (-*dent*-) *adj.* casual, not essential ہنگامی، ضمنی *incidental expenses* ضمنی اخراجات *incidental to,* likely to occur in connection with کے ضمن میں آنے والا **incidentally** *adv.* casually ضمناً، ضمنی

incinerate (in-*sin*-e-rayt) *v. t.* burn to ashes جلا کر راکھ کر ڈالنا، خاکستر کر ڈالنا **incinerator** *n.* (esp.) enclosed furnace for burning rubbish or dead bodies گندگی یا مردے پھونکنے والی بھٹی، مُردہ سوز، غلاظت سوز **incineration** *n.* خاکستر کر دینا

incipient (in-*sip*-i-ent) *adj.* in the early stages ابتدائی، ابتدائی حالت میں

incise (in-*sīz*) *v. t.* make a cut in چیرنا engrave نقش کھودنا، کندہ کاری کرنا **incision** (in-*sizh*-ĕn) *n.* cutting چیرنا، چیرا دینا surgical operation چیرا **incisive** (in-*sī*-siv) *adj.* cutting کاٹنے والا trenchant (remark) تلخ، چبھنے والا acute (mind) تیز، زود فہم clear-cut واضح **incisor** (in-*sī*-ze*) *n.* one of the front teeth اگلا دانت **incisively** *adv.* sharply تلخی سے، طنز سے

incite (in-*sīt*) *v. t.* rouse (someone *to* or *to do* something) (پر) ابھارنا (یا) اکسانا **incitement** (in-*sīt*-ment) *n.* act of inciting or being incited اشتعال

incivility (in-si-*vil*-i-ti) *n.* rudeness ، بدتمیزی ناشائستگی ، اکھڑپن
inclemency *n.* (see under **inclement**)
inclement (in-*klem*-ent) *adj.* (of weather) rough, cold and stormy خراب ، طوفانی unmerciful بے رحم ، سنگدل **inclemency** (in-*kler* ens-i) *n.* cruelty بے رحمی (of weather) being rough موسم کا طوفانی یا خراب ہونا
inclination *n.* (see under **incline**)
incline (in-*klin*) *v. t.* & *i.* (cause to) bend جھکنا یا جھکانا (cause to) be disposed *to* کی طرف مائل ہونا یا کرنا *n.* slope ڈھلان **inclination** (-kli-*nay*-) *n.* slope ڈھال desire (*for* or *to do* something) رغبت ، میلان
include (in-*klood*) *v.t.* reckon as part of the whole میں شامل کرنا ، میں شمار کرنا comprise پر مشتمل ہونا **including** *adv.* along کے سمیت ، مع ، بشمول ، ساتھ
inclusion (in-*kloo*-zhèn) *n.* act of including or being included میں شامل ہونا ، یا کرنا **inclusive** *adj.* containing all (or *of*) سمیت *from the 1st to the 15th both days inclusive* پہلی سے پندرہ تک دونوں تاریخوں سمیت
incognito (in-*kog*-ni-toh) (colloq., *incog.*) (pl. *incogniti* : fem. *incognita*, fem. pl. *incognite*) *adv.* (travel) with identity concealed or under false name بھیس بدل کر (یا) ، کسی اور نام سے *n.* person who is incognito بھیس بدل کر (یا) کسی اور نام سے سفر کرنے والا
incoherence *n.* (see under **incoherent**)
incoherent (in-ko-*hee*-è-rent) *adj.* not coherent بے ربط **incoherently** *adv.* بے ربط **incoherence** *n.* being incoherent بے ربطی
incombustible (-bus-) *adj.* not combustible غیر آتشگیر **incombustibility** *n.* not being combustible غیر آتشگیری
income (*in*-kum) *n.* money received during a given period as salary or from business, etc. آمدنی ، کمائی ، یافت *net income*, total income minus expenditure on it اصلی آمدنی ، خالص یافت *income-tax*, tax on net income انکم ٹیکس ، محصول آمدنی **incoming** (*in*-kum-ing) *adj.* coming in آنے والا ، وصول ہونے والا ، *n.* arrival آمد ، درآمد ، حاصل ، اندر آنے کا اندر کی طرف کا **incomer** *n.* one who enters اندر آنے والا ، داخل ہونے والا
incommensurable (in-ko-*mensh*-è-ray-bèl) *adj.* not commensurable (*with*) سے بہت کم ، سے متشابہ **incommensurate** (in-ko-*mensh*-è-rayt) *adj.* very small as compared (*with*) کے کا پاسنگ بھی نہیں ، کے مقابلے میں ، کچھ بھی نہ ہونا **incommensurability** (in-ko-mensh-è-ra-*bil*-i-ti) *n.* being incommensurable کا پاسنگ بھی نہ ہونا ، تباین

incommode (in-ko-*mohd*) *v.t.* inconvenience تکلیف دینا annoy تنگ کرنا impede کی راہ میں حائل ہونا **incommodious** (-i-us) *adj.* inconvenient تکلیف دِہ
incommunicable (in-ko-*meu*-ni-ka-bèl) *adj.* that which cannot be communicated جو کہا نہ جا سکے ، ناگفتنی that which cannot be shared ناقابلِ اشتراک **incommunicative** (in-ko-*meu*-ni-ka-tiv) *adj.* shy in conversation کم سخن ، گھنا not willing to tell بات چھپائے رکھنے والا
incomparable (in-*kom*-pè-ra-bèl) *adj.* matchless بے نظیر ، بے مثال **incomparably** *adv.* (different) beyond comparison بہت ہی مختلف
incompatible (in-kom-*pat*-i-bèl) *adj.* that which cannot exist together (*with*) متضاد ، عکس ، اُلٹ **incompatibility** (-*bil*-) *n.* being incompatible تضاد ، عکس
incompetence *n.* (see under **incompetent**)
incompetent (in-*kom*-pe-tent) *adj.* inefficient نالائق ، ناقابل not qualified (*to*) کے ، نااہل **incompetence** (-tens) *n.* being incompetent ، نالائقی نااہلیت
incomplete (in-kom-*pleet*) *adj.* not complete اُدھورا ، نامکمل ، ناتمام **incompleteness** *n.* being incomplete اُدھورا ہونا ، اُدھوراپن ، نامکمل ہونا ، ناتمامی
incomprehensible (-*hens*-) *adj.* puzzling حیران کن ناقابلِ فہم **incomprehension** (*hensh*-èn) *n.* failure to understand سمجھ نہ سکنا
inconceivable (in-kon-*see*-va-bèl) *adj.* unbelievable ناقابلِ یقین **inconceivability** (-bil-) *n.* being inconceivable ناقابلِ یقین ہونا
inconclusive (in-kon-*kloo*-siv) *adj.* not decisive غیر فیصلہ کن **inconclusiveness** *n.* being inclusive فیصلہ کن نہ ہونا
incongruous (in-*kong*-roo-us) *adj.* out of place (*with*) **incongruity** (in-kong-*roo*-i-ti) *n.* being incongruous بے محل ہونا
inconsequent (in-*kon*-se-kwent) *adj.* not following logically بے ربط ، غیر متعلق ، جس میں منطقی ربط نہ ہو (person) speaking or writing thus بے ربط باتیں کرنے والا ، بھان متی کا کنبہ جوڑنے والا **inconsequential** (-*kwensh*-ěl) *adj.* unimportant غیر اہم ، غیر ضروری
inconsiderable (-*sid*-) *adj.* not worth considering ناقابلِ اعتنا very small بہت ہی تھوڑا ، **inconsiderably** *adv.* very small, etc. بہت ہی کم ، بہت ہی (کم وغیرہ) **inconsiderate** (-*sid*-) *n.* selfish ; regardless of others' feelings, etc. خود غرض ، خود غرضانہ

inconsistent (*-sis-*) *adj.* incompatible (*with*) (سے)، بے میل (ریا)، بے جوڑ، (کا) اُلٹ، (کا) عکس، (کا سے)، متضاد
inconsistency (tens-i) *n.* incompatibility تضاد، تباین
inconspicuous (in-kon-*spik*-ew-us) *adj.* not conspicuous غیر نمایاں
inconstancy *n.* (see under **inconstant**)
inconstant (*-kon-*) *adj.* fickle متلون changeable بے ثبات unprincipled بے اصول، بیقاعدہ unfaithful بے وفا **inconstancy** (-si) *n.* being inconstant تلون، متلون، بے وفائی، بے ثباتی، بے اصول، بیقاعدگی
incontestable (*-tes-*) *adj.* indisputable ناقابل تردید
incontestably *adv.* indisputably یقینی طور پر، ناقابل تردید طور پر
incontinence *n.* (see under **incontinent**)
incontinent (in *kon*-ti-nent) *adj.* unchaste عیاش، نفس پرست **incontinence** (-nens) *n.* being incontinent عیاشی، نفس پرستی **incontinently** (lit.) *adv.* immediately فوراً، فی الفور
incontrovertible (*-vĕ*-*) indisputable ناقابل تردید
incontrovertibly *adv.* indisputably یقینی طور پر، ناقابل تردید طور پر
inconvenience *n.* (see under **inconvenient**)
inconvenient (*-vee-*) *adj.* not convenient تکلیف دہ uncomfortable بے آسائش **inconvenience** *n.* discomfort تکلیف *v.t.* cause inconvenience to تکلیف دینا
inconvertible (*-ve*-*) *adj.* (esp.) paper money which cannot be changed زرِ کاغذی جو بھنایا نہ جا سکے (یا) جس کا مبادلہ نہ ہو سکے، غیر مبادلہ پذیر
incorporate *v.t. & i.* (in-*ko*p*-è-rayt) unite in one body ایک ہو جانا یا کر دینا، متحد ہو جانا یا کر دینا، ضم ہو جانا یا کر دینا include (*in*) (میں) شامل کرنا form into a corporation کمپنی بن جانا، شرکت بن جانا *adj.* (in-*ko*p*-è-rat) united متحد، متحدہ formed into a corporation کمپنی بنی ہوئی **incorporation** (*-ray-*) *n.* forming into a corporation متحد ہونا یا کرنا، کمپنی بن جانا
incorporeal *adj.* without a body غیر جسمانی
incorrect *adj.* not correct غلط
incorrigible (in-ko-rij-i-bèl) *adj.* incurably bad ناقابل اصلاح **incorrigibility** (*-bil-*) being incorrigible ناقابل اصلاح ہونا
incorruptible (*-rup-*) *adj.* who cannot be bribed نہایت دیانتدار، جسے رشوت نہ خرید سکے، جو بک نہ سکے that cannot decay خراب نہ ہونے والا eternal ابدی **incorruptibility** *n.* کامل دیانتداری
increase *v.t. & i.* (in-*krees*) make or become greater بڑھنا یا بڑھانا، میں اضافہ ہونا (یا) کرنا *n.* (*in*-krees) increasing بڑھنا یا بڑھانا، اضافہ، ترقی amount by which something increases اضافہ، ترقی
incredible (*-kred-*) *adj.* unbelievable ناقابل یقین
incredibly *adv.* surprisingly حد درجہ ناقابل یقین، حد درجہ تک، حیران کن حد تک **incredibility** (*-bil-*) *n.* being incredible ناقابل یقین ہونا
incredulity *n.* (see under **incredulous**)
incredulous (in-*kred*-ew-lus) *adj.* sceptical بے اعتقاد doubting شکی **incredulity** (in-kre-*dew*-li-ti) *n.* being sceptical بے اعتقادی، شک
increment (*in*-kre-ment) *n.* increase اضافہ، بڑھوتری profit منافعہ amount of increase in salary ترقی *annual increment* سالانہ ترقی *earn an increment* ترقی کا حق دار بننا
incriminate (*-krim-*) *v.t.* charge with a crime ملزم قرار دینا involve in a crime الزام دینا یا لگانا
incrimination (*-nay-*) *n.* act of incriminating الزام دینا **incriminator** (-nay-) *n.* one who incriminates الزام دینے والا **incriminatory** (*-crim-*) *adj.* showing criminality الزامی، ملزم قرار دینے والا
incubate (*in*-kew-bayt) *v.t. & i.* hatch (eggs) by sitting on them or by artificial warmth انڈے سینا **incubation** (-bay-) *n.* act of incubating انڈے سینا **incubator** (*in*-kew-bay-tĕ*) *n.* apparatus for hatching eggs by artificial warmth انڈے سینے کی مشین apparatus for rearing premature babies کمزور پیدائش کے بچے پالنے کی مشین
incubus (*in*-kew-bus) *n.* nightmare کابوس
inculcate (*in-*) *v.t.* impress (*upon* someone, *in* his mind) خوب ذہن نشین کرنا، دل نشیں کرنا **inculcation** (*-kay-*) *n.* act of inculcating دل نشینی
inculpate (*in*-kul-payt) *v.t.* accuse ; involve in a charge کو الزام میں ماخوذ کرنا **inculpation** (*-pay-*) *n.* act of inculpating الزام میں ماخوذ کرنا
incumbency *n.* (see under **incumbent**)
incumbent (in-*kum*-bent) *adj.* resting as duty (*on* someone *to do* something) لازمی، لازم، واجب، فرض *n.* holder (*of* an office) (عہدہ) دار، (عہدہ) والا **incumbency** (in-*kum*-bens-i) *n.* office عہدہ
incur (in-*kĕ**) *v.t.* (-rr-) bring (debt, loss, danger, displeasure, etc.) upon oneself (قرض خرچ) وغیرہ اُٹھانا، (ناراضگی وغیرہ) مول لینا
incurable (in-*kew*-ra-bèl) *adj.* that which cannot be cured لاعلاج such patient لاعلاج مریض
incurably *adv.* hopelessly مایوس کن طور پر **incurability** (-bèl-) *n.* being incurable لاعلاج ہونا
incursion (in-*kĕ**-shĕn) *n.* invasion حملہ، چڑھائی
indebted (in-*det*-ed) *adj.* in debt مقروض under an obligation (*to*) (کا) زیر بار احسان، (کا) احسان مند، (کا) ممنون

indebtedness *n.*
indecency *n.* (see under **indecent**) مُمنُونیّت، اِحسانمندی
indecent (in-*dee*-sent) *adj.* obscene فحش، ناشائستہ unbecoming نامُناسب، ناموزُوں **indecently** *adv.* unbecomingly نامُناسب طور پر **indecency** (in-*dee*-sens-i) *n.* being indecent or something indecent نازیبائی، فحش، ناشائستگی
indecision (in-de-*sizh*-ĕn) *n* slowness in making up one's mind پس و پیش، تذبذب **indecisive** (-*sī*-siv) *adj.* unsettled دُبدھے میں پڑا ہُوا ہے، مُتذبذب not decisive غیر فیصلہ کُن
indecorous (in-de-*koh*-rus) *n.* lacking decorum نازیبا، ناشائستہ **indecorum** *n.* lack of decorum ناشائستگی
indeed (in-*deed*) *adv.* in fact, really واقعی، سچ مچ *int.* (expressing irony) واقعی، سچ مچ! کیا واقعی ایسا ہُوا تھا
indefatigable (in-de-*fat*-i-ga-bèl) *adj.* untiring اَنتھک **indefatigability** (in-de-fat-i-ga-b.l-i-ti) *n.* being untiring اَنتھک ہونا
indefeasible (in-de-*feez*-i-bèl) *adj.* (of rights or possessions) that cannot be annulled or taken away ناقابلِ مَنسُوخی، ناقابلِ ضبطی **indefeasibility** (-*bil*-) *adj.* being indefeasible ناقابلِ منسُوخی ہونا، ناقابلِ ضبطی ہونا
indefensible (in-de-*fens*-i-bèl) *adj.* that which cannot be defended ناقابلِ حفاظت unjustifiable ناقابلِ حمایت **indefensibility** (-*bil*-) *adj.* ناقابلِ حفاظت (یا حمایت) ہونا
indefinable (-*fin*-) *adj.* that which cannot be defined غیر تعریف پذیر indefinite غیر مُعیّن
indefinite (in-*def*-i-nit) *adj.* not definite غیر مُعیّن vague مُبہم، غیر واضح unlimited غیر محدُود (in grammar) not determining the exact nature of time, person, etc. غیر مُعیّن، مُطلق **indefinitely** *adv.* بلا تعیّن، غیر مُعیّن طور پر
indelible (-*del*-) *adj.* that which cannot be erased اَمِٹ unforgettable ناقابلِ فراموش
indelicate (in-*del*-i-kayt) *adj.* immodest (person or action) ناشائستہ tactless (person or action) مصلحت ناشناس (شخص)، خلافِ مصلحت (حرکت) **indelicacy** (in-*del*-i-ka-si) *n.* ناشائستگی، مصلحت ناشناسی، خلافِ مصلحت ہونا
indemnify (in-*dem*-ni-f.) *v.t.* compensate for (loss, etc.) تلافی کرنا، تاوان دینا، ہرجانہ ادا کرنا make safe (*from* or *against* loss, etc.) (نقصان وغیرہ سے) حفاظت کرنا
indemnity (in-*dem*-ni-ti) *n.* being indemnified payment to compensate for loss ہرجانہ، تاوان protection (*against*, etc.) (نقصان وغیرہ سے) حفاظت **indemnification** (-*kay*-) *n.* security (against loss, etc.) ضمانت، حفاظت
indemonstrable (in-de-*mons*-tra-bèl) *adj.* that which cannot be proved ثابت نہ ہونے والا
indent *v.t.* (in-*dent*) make tooth-like notch دندانے ڈالنا make a deep cut or depression نشان ڈالنا *indented coastline*, irregular one پھٹا ساحل place order (*upon* someone *for* goods) کا آرڈر بھیجنا start a line of print, etc., further from the margin to mark a new paragraph پیرے کے نشان کے طور پر سطر کے شروع میں کچھ جگہ چھوڑنا draw up (a document) in duplicate دار دستاویز تیار کرنا *n.* (in-dent) order for goods آرڈر، فرمائش dent دندانہ depression (Also see **indenture**)
indenture (in-*den*-chĕ*) *n.* indented document دستاویز مع مُثنّیٰ، مُثنّیٰ دار دستاویز *n. pl.* contract in binding an apprentice to his master معاہدۂ شاگردی
independence *n.* see under **independent**
independent (in-de-*pen*-dent) *adj.* free جُداگانہ، خود مختار، مُستقل بالذات not dependent on others having enough money to live on without working سببِ مُعاش سے مُستغنی کرنے والے وسائل، آمدنی رکھنے والا، مُستغنی not controlled mentally *n.* member of a legislature not belonging to political party آزاد رُکن **independently** *adv.* **independence** *n.* freedom آزادی، استقلال independent income سببِ مُعاش سے بے نیاز کرنے والی ذاتی آمدنی
indescribable (-*kri*-) *adj.* that which cannot be described ناقابلِ بیان، بیان سے باہر
indestructible *adj.* that which cannot be destroyed لازوال، غیر فانی **indestructibility** (-*bi*-) *n.* being indestructible لازوال ہونا، غیر فناپزیری، لازوالی، فنا ناپزیری
indeterminable (-*te**-) *adj.* that which cannot be ascertained نامعلوم **indeterminate** *adj.* indefinite غیر مُعیّن
index (*in*-deks) *n.* (pl. *indexes*) (also *index finger*) forefinger انگشتِ شہادت any pointer showing measurements سُوئی alphabetical of books (on cards) or of important words in book (at the end of it) اشاریہ *card index* (system) index maintained on separate detachable cards for keeping it up-to-date انڈیکس، برگہ اشاریہ *n.* (*Math.*) (pl. indices) a small number letter placed above and to the right of another to indicate power to which is raised or denote a root طاقت *v.t.* prepare an index enter in an index اشاریہ میں شامل کرنا
India (*in*-di-a) *n.* Bharat بھارت، ہند *India paper*, *india paper*, very thin and costly print

paper originally from China * انڈیا پیپر، ہندی کاغذ، چینی کاغذ India rubber, india rubber, ordinary pencil eraser ربڑ **Indian** *adj.* of India بھارتی، ہندی *Indian corn, indian corn,* maize مکئی *Indian file, indian file,* single file اکہری قطار *Indian ink, indian ink,* black pigment کالی سیاہی *Indian summer,* calm dry period in North U.S. in late autumn تابستان ہندی *Indian Civil Service,* (abb. *I.C.S.*) British India's administrative service آئی - سی - ایس *Indian club,* gymnast's bottle-shaped club مگدر *Indian weed,* tobacco تمباکو *Red Indian,* (*a*) a North American aboriginal ریڈ انڈین ، لال ہندی (*b*) of this race ریڈ انڈین ، لال ہندی

indicate (*ind*-i-kayt) *v.t.* point out اشارہ کرنا be a sign of بتانا ، دلالت کرنا ، ظاہر کرنا **indication** (-*kay*-) *n.* that which indicates نشانی ، نشان ، علامت ، دلیل

indicative (in-*dik*-a-tiv) *adj.* being a sign (*of*) (کی) علامت ہونا ، (کی) دلیل ہونا *indicative mood,* (grammar) form of verb used in stating facts بیانیہ ، انداز بیان * **indicator** (ind-i-*kay*-tě*) *n.* anything that indicates نشانی ، علامت pointer بتانے والا آلہ ، سوئی

indict (in-*dīt*) *v.t.* accuse (someone *for* offence, *as* an offender, *on* the charge of) الزام دینا ، الزام عائد کرنا **indictable** *adj.* liable to prosecution مجرم rendering liable to it مجرمانہ **indictment** (-*dīt*-) *n.* such formal accusation in writing فرد جرم لگانا any accusation الزام

indifferent (-*dif*-) *adj.* mediocre ایسا ویسا ، معمولی بُرا بھلا (یا) نہ اچھا نہ بُرا ، اچھا نہ بُرا *good, bad or indifferent* جو کچھ بھی ہو impartial غیر جانبدار *indifferent to,* not interested in, neither for nor against نہ ادھر نہ اُدھر ، نہ حامی نہ مخالف

indifference (-*dif*-) *n.* lack of interest, feeling or attention بے پروائی ، بے رُخی ، بے اعتنائی **indifferentism** *n.* spirit of indifference to religious (or public) issues مذہبی (یا معاشرتی) مسایل سے بے رُخی ، بے رُخی

indigenous (in-*dij*-e-nus) *adj.* native (*to* a country or soil) دیسی ، ملکی *indigenous system of medicine,* (for Pakistan) the system practised by *hakims* دیسی طریق علاج ، طب یونانی *indigenous drugs* دیسی دوائیں

indigent (*ind*-i-jent) *adj.* very poor and needy مفلس ، قلاش ، محتاج ، تہی دست **indigence** (-jens) *n.* extreme poverty مفلسی ، محتاجی

indigestion (in-di-*jes*-shěn) *n.* dyspepsia بدہضمی ، سوء ہضم **indigestible** *adj.* that which cannot be properly digested ناقابل ہضم **indigested** (-ted) *adj.* not properly digested غیر منہضم (of studies) not properly assimilated جو پوری طرح سمجھ میں نہ آیا ہو۔

indignant (-*dig*-) *adj.* inflamed with anger and scorn (*with* someone *at* injustice or false accusation) برہم **indignantly** *adv.* برہم ہو کر **indignation** (-*nay*-) *n.* scornful anger برہمی

indignity (in-*dig*-ni-ti) *n.* insult توہین rude treatment بے عزتی ، بدسلوکی

indigo (*in*-di-goh) (pl. *indigos*) deep blue dye نیل plant yielding it نیل ○ this colour نیلگوں

indirect (in-di-*rekt* or in-dī-*rekt*) *adj.* not straightforward ہیر پھیر والا not direct (route, speech etc.) چکر والا *indirect speech* روایت بالمعنیٰ ○ (of taxation, etc.) not levied directly * بالواسطہ ، گپت *indirect taxation,* taxation paid in increased prices of goods * ٹیکس **indirectly** *adv.* in a roundabout way بالواسطہ

indiscernible (in-di-*sě**-ni-běl) *adj.* that which cannot be discerned غیر معلوم slight بہت ہی تھوڑا ، غیر محسوس

indiscipline (-*dis*-) *n.* lack of discipline بدنظمی

indiscreet (-*kreet*) *adj.* imprudent بے شعور ، مصلحت ناکوش ، غیر دانشمند **indiscretion** *n.* imprudence غیر دانشمندی ، مصلحت ناکوشی **indiscriminate** (-*krim*-) *adj.* promiscuous گڈمڈ ، خلط ملط ، رلا ملا undiscriminating (person, taste or action) بُرے بھلے میں تمیز نہ کرنے والا ، بے شعور ، بے شعوری کا **indiscrimination** (-*nay*-) *n.* بے شعوری ، فرق مراتب نہ کر سکنا ، بُرے بھلے میں تمیز نہ کر سکنا

indispensable (-*pens*-) *adj.* absolutely necessary ناگزیر **indispensability** (-*bil*-) *n.* being indispensable ناگزیر ہونا ، ناگزیری

indisposed (in-dis-*pohzd*) *adj.* unwell علیل ، کی طبیعت ناساز not inclined (*for* or *to do* something) مائل نہیں ، راغب نہیں averse (*towards* or *to do* something) سے بھاگنے والا ، سے نفور **indisposition** (in-dis-po-*zish*-ěn) *n.* (esp.) slight illness ناسازی طبع ، علالت

indisputable (in-*dis*-pew-ta-běl) *adj.* undeniable (fact, etc.) حتمی ، یقینی ، ناقابل تردید **indisputably** *adv.* یقیناً ، حتمی طور پر

indissoluble *adj.* that which cannot be dissolved جسے توڑا نہ جا سکے ، مستحکم

indistinct *adj.* not distinct مبہم ، غیر واضح **indistinctly** *adv.* not clearly (heard, etc.) جو شناخت نہ ہو سکے ، جو صاف نہ ہو **indistinctive** *adj.* not distinctive غیر امتیازی

indite (in-*dīt*) *v.t.* compose (verse) شعر کہنا (jocular) write (a letter) لکھنا

individual (ind-i-*vid*-ew-ěl) *adj.* special (opposite of *general*) خاص ، منفرد of a single person or thing اِنفرادی characteristic of him or it اِنفرادی، مُنفرد *n.* single person (opp. of *society*) فرد **individualize** *v.t.* particularise تخصیص کرنا، تعیین کرنا apply a general conclusion to a particular case عمومی باتیں کسی ایک کے متعلق کہنا **individually** *adv.* one by one ایک ایک کرکے، فرداً فرداً، الگ الگ **individuality** (-*al*-) *n.* individual character اِنفرادیت personality شخصیّت **individualism** *n.* egoism انانیت freedom of the individual as a social theory (opp. of *socialism*) اِنفرادیت

indivisible (-*viz*-) *adj.* not divisible ناقابلِ تقسیم

indivisibility (-*bil*-) *n.* not being divisible ناقابلِ تقسیم ہونا

indoctrinate (in-*dok*-tri-nayt) *v.t.* fill the mind (*with* beliefs of a party, etc.) دل میں اچھی طرح بیٹھنا، یقین کرنا **indoctrination** (-*nay*-) *n.* act of indoctrinating or being indoctrinated تلقین، ذہن کی صفائی

indolence *n.* (see under **indolent**)

indolent (*ind*-o-lent) *adj.* habitually idle آرام طلب، نکمّا، اَحدی **indolence** *n.* habitual idleness آرام طلبی، نکمّا ہونا

indomitable (in-*dom*-i-tab-èl) *adj.* unyielding نہ دبنے والا strongly resisting ڈٹ جانے والا

indoor (*in*-doh*) *adj.* situated or carried on inside a building اندر کا، اندرونی *indoor games* کمرے کے اندر کے کھیل، اندرونی **indoors** (in-*doh*z*) *adv.* in or into a building اندر

indubitable (-*dewb*-) *adj.* that which cannot be doubted یقینی، غیر مشتبہ، مُسلّمہ **indubitably** *adv.* undoubtedly بے شک، بلاشُبہ، یقیناً

induce (in-*dews*) *v.t.* persuade (someone *to do* something) آمادہ کرنا، ترغیب دینا cause کی وجہ ہونا، کا باعث بننا **inducement** *n.* something that induces ترغیب، تحریص، لالچ

induction (in-*duk*-shĕn) *n.* later branch of logic trying to discover general laws from particular facts استقرا، استقرائی منطق introduction (*into* office) (عہدے پر) فائز کرنا یا ہونا production of heat or light by closeness and not by direct contact اِمالہ **inductive** *adj.* pertaining to induction استقرائی *inductive logic*, induction استقرا

indulge (in-*dulj*) *v.t.* & *i.* humour, give way (کی) خوشامد کرنا، (کی) ناز برداری کرنا satisfy (*oneself, in* or *with* something) جی بھر کے مزے لینا، کھیل کھیلنا، دل کھول کر پورا کرنا give free course to (passion or whim) جی بھر کے (ارمان) نکالنا، پوری طرح کرنا take one's pleasure freely (*in* smoking or other habits) جی بھر کے (کرنا)، خوب ہی (کرنا) **indulgent** *adj.* so kind as to yield to a junior or inferior's wishes بہت ہی مہربان، شفیق، مُشفِق **indulgence** *n.* indulging (*in* a pleasure) جی بھر کے کرنا great kindness شفقت، کرم freedom granted from sin by a Roman Catholic priest گناہ سے بریّت، بخشش freedom from punishment بخشش، عفو و کرم

industrial *adj.*, **industrializm** *n.*, **industrialize** *v.t.* **industrialized** *adj.*, **industrious** *adj.*, **industriously** *adv.* (see under **industry**)

industry (*ind*-us-tri) *n.* hard and steady work لگاتار محنت، باقاعدگی سے محنت، مسلسل محنت manufacture or any of its branches صنعت *trade and industry* صنعت و حرفت **industrial** (in-*dus*-tri-èl) *adj.* pertaining to or of industry صنعتی fit only for use in industry صنعتی استعمال کا، صنعتی **industrialize** *v.t.* set up industries in (a country, etc.) (کو) صنعتی بنانا (میں) صنعتیں قائم کرنا **industrialized** *adj.* having many industries in it صنعتی، (کو) صنعتی بنانا **industrious** (-*dus*-) *adj.* hard working محنتی **industriously** *adv.* محنت سے **industrialism** *n.* industrial system صنعتی نظام prevalence of industries (rather than agriculture) صنعتی معیشت

indwelling *adj.* (of love, joy, beauty, etc.) dwelling within اندرونی، روحانی، باطنی inhabiting رہنے والا، مکین

inedible *adj.* not edible جو کھانے کے لائق نہ ہو، ناخوردنی

inebriate *v.t.* (-*eb*-) intoxicate مخمور کرنا، مست کرنا، مدہوش کرنا *n.* & *adj.* (person) habitually intoxicated جو ہمیشہ مخمور رہے، مخمور **inebriation, inebriety** *n.* being inebriate مست رہنا، مستی

ineffable (-*ef*-) *adj.* too great for words الفاظ سے ماورا، جس کے بیان سے الفاظ قاصر ہوں **ineffably** *adv.* extremely inexpressibly (great, etc.) بے حد، حد درجہ

ineffaceable (in-e-*fays*-a-bèl) *adj.* that which cannot be destroyed اَمِٹ

ineffective (-*fek*-) *adj.* not effective غیر مؤثر **ineffectively** *adj.* without any effect بے اثر

ineffectual (-*fek*-tew) *adj.* not effectual بے اثر، غیر مؤثر

inefficacious (in-ef-i-*kay*-shus) *adj.* not efficacious اثر نہ کرنے والی دوا

inefficiency *n.* (see under **inefficient**)

inefficient (-*fish*-ent) *adj.* incapable نالائق، نااہل **inefficiency** *n* being inefficient نالائقی، نااہلیت

inelegance *n.* (see under **inelegant**)

inelegant (-*el*-) *adj.* (of style, manners, etc.) unrefined ناشائستہ، اَن گھڑ **inelegance** *n.* lack of polish and refinement ناشائستگی

ineligible (-*lij*-) *adj.* not eligible (*for*) ناقابلِ انتخاب، قواعد کے تحت نااہل **ineligibility** *n.* being ineligible نااہلی، نااہلیت

inept (in-*ept*) *adj.* silly (remark, etc.) احمقانہ out of place بے محل، بے موقع **ineptitude** *n.* absurdity ; being silly بے محل ہونا ، بے ہودگی

inequality (*kwawl-*) *n.* lack of equality ایک سا نہ ہونا یکساں نہ ہونا ، ناہمواری **inequitable** (in-*ek*-wi-ta-bèl) *adj.* unjust (decision, etc.) غیر منصفانہ

inequity *n.* same as **iniquity** (which see under **iniquitous**)

ineradicable (-*rad*-) *adj.* ineffaceable اَمِٹ

inert (in-*e*t*) *adj.* without power to move or act بے حِس و حرکت ، بے حرکت ، جامد sluggish سُست ، اَحدی

inertia (*i-ne**-shi-a) sloth سُستی ، کاہلی tendency of matter to continue in its existing state (مادّے کا) جمود

inescapable (*kay*-) *adj.* unavoidable ناگزیر

inestimable (-*es*-) *adj.* incalculable بے اندازہ بہت ہی زیادہ ، بے حد invaluable **inestimably** *adv.* incalculably بے حد ، بے انداز

inevitable (in-*ev*-i-ta-bèl) *adj.* unavoidable اٹل، ہو کر رہنے والا ، ناگزیر **inevitably** *adv.* لازماً **inevitability** (-bil-) *n.* being inevitable ناگزیر ہونا ، لابدی ہونا *the inevitability of fate* تقدیر کا اٹل ہونا

inexact (in-eg-*zakt*) *adj.* not quite correct غلط، غیر صحیح ، ناقص **inexactitude** (-tewd), **inexactness** *n.* mistake ; being inexact غلطی ، نقص

inexcusable (-*kewz*-) not to be excused ناقابلِ معافی ، ناقابلِ عفو unjustifiable جس کی کوئی توجیہ نہ ہو سکے

inexhaustible (in-eg-*zhawst*-i-bèl) *adj.* unending جو ختم نہ ہو سکے ، غیر مختتم ، لازوال tireless اَنتھک

inexhaustibility *n.* being inexhaustible اَنتھک ہونا ، غیر مختتم ہونا

inexorable (in-*ek*-sè-ra-bèl) *adj.* relentless, unyielding to supplication کٹھور ، سنگدِل **inexorability** (in-ek-sè-ra-*bil*-i-ti) *n.* being inexorable سنگ دِلی

inexperience (in-eks-*pee*-ri-ens) *n.* lack of experience ناتجربہ کاری **inexperienced** *adj.* lacking experience ناتجربہ کار ، خام کار

inexpert (-*pě*t*) *adj.* not expert اَناڑی

inexpediency *n.* (see under **inexpedient**)

inexpedient (-*pee*-) *adj.* not expedient بے محل، خلافِ مصلحت **inexpediency** (-si) *n* not being expedient خلافِ مصلحت ہونا

inexpensive (-*pens*-) *adj.* cheap سستا ، اَرزاں **inexpensiveness** *n.* cheapness سستا ہونا ، اَرزانی

inexpert (-*pe*-*t) *adj.* not expert اَناڑی.

inexpiable (in-*eks*-pi-ab-èl) *adj.* (of sin) which is beyond expiation جس کا کفّارہ نہ کیا جا سکے

inexplicable *adj.* unjustifiable جس کی توجیہ نہ ہو سکے

inexplicably *adv.* اِس طرح کہ توجیہ نہ ہو سکے

inexpressible (-*pres*-) *adj.* unutterable ناقابلِ بیان **inexpressibility** *n.* being inexpressible ناقابلِ بیان ہونا **inexpressibly** *adv.* ناقابلِ بیان حد تک

inextinguishable (-ting-) *adj.* that which cannot be extinguished or quenched جو فرو نہ ہو سکے

inextricable (-*eks*-) *adj.* that which cannot be unravelled جو سُلجھ نہ سکے ، سخت اُلجھا ہوا **inextricably** *adv.* سخت اُلجھے ہوئے انداز سے

infallible *adj.* unfailing (remedy) حتمی ، حکمی incapable of erring جس سے غلطی ممکن نہ ہو ، معصوم

infamous (*in*-fa-mus) *adj.* of ill-fame disgraceful رُسوا ، رُسوائے عالم **infamously** (*in*-) in a debased manner ذِلّت سے ، رُسوائی سے **infamy** (*in-fa*-mi) *n.* ill-fame بدنامی public disgrace رُسوا ، رُسوائے عالم

infancy *n.* (see under **infant**)

infant *n.* baby شیر خوار ، بچّہ (law) one who has not come of age نابالغ *adj.* young چھوٹا for or of small children (چھوٹے بچّوں کا (یا کے لیے **infancy** (*in*-fan-si) *n.* state of being an infant (ایامِ) طفلی (عالمِ) شیر خوارگی ، (عالمِ) طفولیت early stage of development اِبتدائی دَور **infanticide** *n.* new-born infant's murder (esp. with the mother's consent) (نوزائیدہ) بچّے کو مار ڈالنا ، بچّہ کشی ، اطفال کشی one guilty of this بچّہ کُش **infantile** (*in*-fan-til) *adj.* of infants بچّوں کا ، بچگانہ as of infants بچّوں کا سا ، طفلانہ

infantry (*in*-fant-ri) *n.* foot soldiers (opp. of *cavalry*) پیدل فوج ، پیادہ فوج

infatuate (in-*fat*-ew-ayt) *v.t.* fill *with* foolish love لٹّو کرنا ، فریفتہ کرنا **infatuated** *adj.* foolishly in love (*with*) لٹّو ، فریفتہ **infatuation** (-*ay*-) *n.* being infatuated لٹّو کرنا ، فریفتگی ، شیفتگی

infect (in-*fekt*) *v.t.* fill with disease germs چھوت لگانا ، بیماری کے جراثیم پھیلانا influence (*with* ideas, etc.) میں سرایت کرنا ، اپنے رنگ میں رنگنا **infection** (in-*fek*-shěn) *n.* infectious وبائی مرض ، متعدّی مرض infecting چھوت لگانا **infectious** (in-*fek*-shus) *adj.* spreading by infection متعدّی ، وبائی (any mood) quickly influencing others جس کا دوسروں پر فوراً اثر ہو

infelicity (-*lis*-) *n.* misfortune بدنصیبی

infer (in-*fe**) *v.t.* (-rr-) conclude نتیجے پر پہنچنا ، نتیجہ اخذ کرنا ، مستنبط کرنا **inferable** *adj.* that which may be inferred مستنبط ہو سکنے والا **inference** (*in*-) *n.* process of inferring اِستنباط conclusion نتیجہ

inferior (in-*fee*-ri-ě*) *adj.* lower in rank ماتحت ، کم مرتبہ lower in quality, etc. (*to* something) سے، خواب، گھٹیا of poor quality خواب junior **inferiority** (-*ro*-ri-ti) *n.* being inferior کم مرتبہ گھٹیا ہونا، کمتر ہونا، کمتری، کہتری *inferiority complex* (*a*) unconscious feeling of inferiority often resulting in self-assertive behaviour احساس کمتری، احساس کہتری (*b*) (popularly) sense of one's inferiority اپنی غریبی (یا نالائقی یا کمزوری) کا احساس، احساس کمتری

infernal (-*fē**-) *adj.* of hell جہنم کا، دوزخ کا outrageous سخت ظالمانہ، نفرت انگیز (colloq.) extreme, too much بہت ہی **inferno** *n.* hell (esp. as described by Dante (1265—1321) in his *Divina Commedia* or 'Divine Comedy') دوزخ، جہنم

infertile (in-*fē**-til) *adj.* barren بنجر **infertility** (-*tii*-) *n.* being infertile بنجرپن

infest (in-*fest*) *v.t.* (of insects, criminals, etc.) be present in large numbers میں کثرت سے ہونا *be infested with*, (of a place) be full of (insects, criminals, etc.) سے بھرا ہوا ہونا، سے پٹا پڑا ہونا

infidel (*in*-fi-del) *n.* unbeliever لامذہب disbeliever in the true religion کافر، بے دین، ملحد **infidelity** (in-fi-*del*-i-ti) *n.* unfaithfulness to one's spouse (اپنے میاں یا اپنی بیوی سے) بے وفائی being an unbeliever کفر، بے دینی، الحاد

infiltrate (in-*fil*-trayt) *v.t.* & *i.* permeate سرایت کرنا cause to filter into or through مقطر کر کے ڈالنا (of troops,) break through defences unnoticed محاذ کے پار نکل جانا **infiltration** (-*tray*-) *n.* act of filtering into تقطیر کے ذریعے ڈالنا act of permeating سرایت کرنا

infinite (*in*-fi-nit) *adj.* unlimited لامحدود، لامتناہی *the Infinite*, God خدا تعالیٰ، ذاتِ لامحدود **infinitely** *adj.* extremely از حد **infinitive** (in-*fin*-i-tiv) *n.* mood of the verb never changed for person, etc., and taking the form of *to* followed by the 1st person present مصدر (as *to see* دیکھنا) pertaining to this form مصدری **infinity** *n.* (Mathematics) infinite number لامتناہی state of being infinite لامتناہی **infinitude** *n.* limitless number or extent (*of*) بیشمار، بے حد **infinitesimal** (in-fin-i-*tes*-i-mĕl) *adj.* infinitely small از حد چھوٹا، حد درجہ چھوٹا

infirm (in-*fē*m*) *adj.* physically weak (esp. from age) کمزور، ضعیف، نحیف irresolute (*of*) (ارادے کا) کمزور، بودا wavering غیر مستقل مزاج **infirmary** (in-*fē*m*-a-ri) *n.* (old use) hospital ہسپتال، بیمارستان **infirmity** *n.* weakness کمزوری

inflame (in-*flaym*) *v.t.* & *i.* set on fire (میں یا کو) آگ لگانا، جلا دینا flush (with anger, poison, etc.) سرخ ہو جانا یا کر دینا rouse (feelings) برافروختہ کرنا be swollen سوجنا **inflammable** (in-*flam*-a-bĕl) *adj.* easily set on fire بھڑک اٹھنے والا، فوراً آگ پکڑ اٹھنے والا easily excited جلد برافروختہ ہو جانے والا، زود آتشگیر، آتشگیر بھڑک اٹھنے والا **inflammability** (-*bil*-) *n.* being inflammable آتشگیری **inflammation** (in-fla-*may*-shĕn) swollen state (*of* part of the body) سوجن، آماس **inflammatory** (in-*flam*-a-tĕ-ri) *adj.* (of a speech, etc.) likely to incite angry feelings اشتعال انگیز، آگ لگانے والی

inflate (in-*flayt*) *v.t.* & *i.* fill (tyre, etc.) with air or gas میں ہوا بھرنا puff up (*with* pride, etc.) بہت مغرور کر دینا raise (price) artificially by increasing the amount of paper money in circulation (قیمتیں بڑھانے کے لیے) افراطِ زر کرنا **inflation** (in-*flay*-shĕn) *n.* artificial increase in prices thus افراطِ زر **inflated** *adj.* (of tyre, etc.) filled with air or gas جس میں ہوا (یا گیس) بھری ہوئی ہو (of style) bombastic بڑی لفاظی والا

inflect (in-*flekt*) *v.t.* bend موڑنا، جھکانا decline (a noun) or conjugate (a verb) گردان کرنا **inflexion** (in-*flek*-shĕn) *n.* inflecting گردان، تصریف inflected word صیغہ یا حالت suffix used with it صرفی لاحقہ modulation of the voice آواز کا اتار چڑھاؤ، زیر و بم

inflexible (in-*flek*-si-bĕl) *adj.* not flexible بے لوچ، غیر خم پزیر، جو مڑ تڑ نہ سکے unyielding, firm سخت، غیر اثر پزیر **inflexibility** (-*bil*-) *n.* being inflexible بے لوچ ہونا، غیر خم پزیری، غیر اثر پزیری

inflexion *n.* (see under **inflect**)

inflict (in-*flikt*) *v.t.* cause to suffer by means of (wound, punishment, etc., *on* someone) (زخم) لگانا، (سزا) دینا، (تکلیف) پہنچانا impose (*oneself*, or one's company *upon*), force one's company on کے سر پر مسلط ہونا **infliction** *n.* inflicting (زخم، سزا یا تکلیف) لگانا، دینا یا پہنچانا punishment inflicted سزا، عذاب annoyance جی کا جنجال

inflow (*in*-floh) *n.* a flowing in اُنڈنا، اُمنڈنا، بہ کر اندر آنا

influence (*in*-floo-ens) *n.* (natural, social or physical) power invisibly exercised (*upon* thing or person) عمل moral power exercised thus (*over* or *with* person or thing) اثر *v.t.* exert influence upon پر اثر ڈالنا، پر اثر انداز ہونا **influential** (in-floo-*en*-shĕl) *adj.* exercising influence مؤثر popular ذی اثر، با اثر

influenza (in-floo-*en*-za), **flue** (floo), **flu** (floo) *n.* feverish cold which is infectious انفلوئنزا، تپ نزلی وبائی، وبائی زکام

influx (*in*-fluks) *n.* inflow (*of* water, wealth, visitors) امڈ کر آنا، اُمنڈ کر آنا

inform (in-*fo*m*) *v.t.* & *i.* tell (someone *of*

or *that*) اِطّلاع دینا، بتانا، مطّلع کرنا **inform against** (*someone*), give information to the authorities of (someone's) offence against law کی مخبری کرنا **informant** *n.* one who gives news بتانے والا، خبر دینے والا **informer** *n.* one who informs against someone اِطّلاع دینے والا، مخبر، مخبری کرنے والا *police informer* پولیس کے پاس مخبری کرنے والا **information** *n.* news اِطّلاع، خبر knowledge imparted معلومات **informative** (*-may-tiv*) *adj.* giving a useful piece of information معلومات افزا **well-informed** *adj.* well-posted بہت با خبر

informal (in-*fo**-mĕl) *adj.* not formal بے تکلّفانہ، سیدھا سادہ، غیر رسمی simple and homely **informality** (*-mal*) *n.* lack of formality غیر رسمی انداز، بے تکلّفی

infra (*in*-fra) *adv.* below or further on in this book نیچے (دیکھیے)، آگے (دیکھیے)، ذیل میں (دیکھیے)

infra adj. low, lower than نیچا، زیرین *infra dig*, beneath one's dignity شان کے خلاف

infra under beyond تحت، ماورا *infra red*, (of rays) invisible ones beyond the red end of the spectrum ماورائے احمر (شعاعیں)، تحت احمر (شعاعیں)

infraction (*-frak-*) *n.* violation (*of* law, etc.) خلاف ورزی

infrequent (*-free-*) *adj.* seldom occurring شاذ، کبھی کبھار کا **infrequently** *adv.* seldom, only occasionally کبھی کبھار **infrequency** *n.* act of occurring only occasionally کبھی کبھار ہونا، شُذُوذ

infringe (in-*frinj*) *v.t.* & *i.* violate (rule, etc.) (کی) خلاف ورزی کرنا، (کو) توڑنا *infringe upon* (*someone's*) *rights*, transgress, trespass on these کسی کے حقوق پر چھاپہ مارنا، توڑنا **infringement** *n.* violation (*of*) خلاف ورزی کرنا

infructuous (in-*fruk*-tew-us) *adj.* unfruitful بے ثمر، لاحاصل

infuriate (in-*few*-ri-ayt) *v.t.* enrage طیش میں لانا **infuriating** *adj.* (بات) طیش میں لانے والی

infuse (in-*fewz*) *v.t.* & *i.* instil (new life *into*) میں زندگی کی رُوح پھُونکنا pour اُنڈیلنا، ڈالنا soak (tea leaves, etc.) in liquid to flavour it بھگونا، خیسانده تیار کرنا **infusion** (in-*fewzh*-ĕn) *n.* something made by infusing نچوڑ، زُلال، خیسانده

ingathering *n.* a gathering in (of harvest) خرمن، انبار لگانا

ingenious (in-*jee*-ni-us) *adj.* (of a person) clever at contriving طبّاع، خوش تدبیر، ایجاد کا ماہر، اختراع پسند (of things) skilfully made سلیقے کا، اُپج کا

ingenuity (in-*jen*-ew-i-ti) *n.* cleverness in working out new ideas اُپج، خوش تدبیری، ایجاد کا مادہ، اختراع پسند طبیعت

ingenuous (in-*jen*-ew-us) *adj.* frank صاف دِل artless بے تصنّع

inglorious (in-*gloh*-ri-us) *adj.* disgraceful شرمناک obscure گمنام

ingot (*ing*-ot) *n.* brick-shaped mass of cast metal (esp. gold, or silver) سونے چاندی وغیرہ کی اینٹ

ingrained (before noun *in*-graynd ; otherwise in-*graynd*) *adj.* (of habits, etc.) deeply-rooted گہری، پکّی، پختہ

ingratiate (in-*gray*-shi-ayt) *v.t.* (reflexive) *ingratiate oneself with someone*, curry favour with him for personal ends دِل میں گھر کرنا، مَوردِ عنایات ہونا

ingratitude (in-*grat*-i-tewd) *n.* ungratefulness ناشکری، ناشکرگزاری، احسان فراموشی، احسان ناشناسی، ناسپاسی

ingredient (in-*gree*-di-ent) *n.* part of a mixture جُزو، جُزوِ ترکیبی

ingress (in-gres) *n.* right of entrance داخلے کی اجازت، بار entrance داخلہ

ingrowing *adj.* growing inward اندر کی طرف بڑھنے والا

inhabit (in-*hab*-it) *v.t.* live in رہنا سہنا، بُود و باش رکھنا، سکونت رکھنا **inhabitable** *adj.* رہنے کے قابل **inhabitant** *n.* one living in a place رہنے والا، ساکن، باشندہ

inhale (in-*hayl*) *v.t.* & *i.* breathe in سانس اندر کو لینا، کھینچنا draw in with breath کھینچنا، سانس لینا **inhalation, inhaling** *n.* act of breathing in سانس لینا، کش لگانا

inharmonious *adj.* conflicting بے میل، غیر ہم آہنگ

inhere (in-*hee*-è*) *v.i.* (of qualities) be inborn پیدائشی ہونا (of rights), be invested (*in*), be permanent (*in*) پکّا ہونا **inherent** (in-*hee*-è-rent) *adj.* innate پیدائشی، خلقی، جبلّی، پکّا **inherence, inhesion** *n.* being inherent پیدائشی ہونا، خلقی ہونا، جبلّی ہونا، پکّا ہونا

inherit (in-*he*-rit) *v.t.* receive as legacy وِرثے میں پانا، (کو) ترکہ یا وِرثہ مِلنا **inheritance** *n.* inheriting وِرثہ پانا inherited thing (*e.g.*, title, property) وِرثہ، ترکہ

inhesion (in-*hee*-zhĕn) *n.* (see under **inhere**)

inhibit (in-*hib*-it) *v.t.* check (*from* doing) روکنا، رُکاوٹ ڈالنا، مزاحمت کرنا **inhibition** (*-bish-*) *n.* check رُکاوٹ، مزاحمت inhibited impulse دبا ہوا جذبہ

inhospitable *adj.* not giving a friendly welcome غیر مہمان نواز (of country) barren, cheerless, not giving any shelter اُجڑا (ہوا)، بے آب و گیاہ

inhuman (in-*hew*-man) *adj.* brutal (person) ظالم cruel treatment ظالمانہ، غیر انسانی سلوک، انسانیت سوز سلوک

inimical (in-*im*-i-kel) *adj.* hostile (*to*) (کا) دشمن harmful (*to*) کے لیے خطرناک

inimitable (-*im*-) *adj*. unique یکتا، لاثانی
iniquitous (in-*ik*-wi-tus) *adj*. unjust غیر منصفانہ
iniquity (in-*ik*-wi-ti) **inequity** (in-*ek*-wi-ti) *n*. injustice, unfairness بے انصافی
initial (i-*nish*-ĕl) *adj*. of or at the beginning ابتدائی *n*. (*pl*.) first letters of one's names (*e.g.*, *M.Q.* for Manzur Qadir) چھوٹے دستخط، مختصر دستخط، مخفف دستخط *v.t.* sign (something) with one's initials مخفف دستخط کرنا، چھوٹے دستخط کرنا **initially** *adv*. in the beginning شروع شروع میں
initiate (i-*nish*-i-ayt) *v.t.* originate شروع کرنا admit (someone) ceremonially (into a secret or society) میں شامل کرنا، باضابطہ شامل کرنا give first lessons to (someone *in* something) (کے) ابتدائی سبق دینا give (someone) instruction (in religious experience, etc.) (تصوف وغیرہ) کا عملی سبق دینا، محرم راز کرنا *n*. & *adj*. (one) who has been initiated محرم راز، عارف
initiation *n*. act of initiating آغاز، روشناسی، تعارف باضابطہ شمولیت **initiative** *n*. first step which others may follow پہلا قدم، اقدام، پیش قدمی *take the initiative*, take the first step for others to follow اقدام کرنا، پیش قدمی کرنا *on one's own initiative*, on one's own آپ ہی آپ، آپ سے آپ، خود بخود capacity or right to initiate پہل کا حق، پہل کی ہمت *have the initiative* کے ہاتھ میں پہل ہونا
inject (in-jekt) *v.t.* force drug *into* with a syringe میں پہنچانا ٹیکہ لگانا fill with fluid thus
injection *n*. act of injecting ٹیکہ لگانا fluid injected ٹیکہ
injudicious (in-joo-*dish*-us) *adj*. unwise کوتاہ اندیش، کوتاہ اندیش not well thought out غیر دانشمندانہ
injudiciousness *n*. غیر دانشمندی
injunction (in-*junk*-shĕn) *n*. judicial order restraining someone from wrongdoing حکم امتناعی any order حکم، فرمان
injure (*inj*-è*) *v.t.* harm نقصان پہنچانا، ضرر پہنچانا hurt زخمی کرنا، ضرب لگانا **injury** (*inj*-ĕ-ri) *n*. harm نقصان wound **injurious** (in-*joo*-ri-us), causing or likely to cause harm or injury نقصان دہ، ضرر رساں
injustice (in-*jus*-tis) *n*. lack of justice بے انصافی، ظلم، نا انصافی *do (someone) an injustice* کسی سے بے انصافی کرنا
ink *n*. coloured fluid used for writing or printing سیاہی، روشنائی *v.t.* mark with ink سیاہی سے نشان لگانا smear (hands, etc.) with ink سیاہی کے داغ ڈالنا
inky (*ink*-i) *adj*. smeared with ink سیاہی سے داغدار
inkpot *n*. ink container دوات **inkstand** *n*. stand for inkpot, pen, etc. قلمدان
inkling (*ink*-ling) *n*. hint (*of*) کا اشارہ suspicion شبہ، خیال *have not even an inkling of* کا وہم و گمان تک نہ ہونا

inland (*in*-land) *adj*. (of town, etc.) situated in the interior of a country, away from the coastland ساحل سمندر سے دور کا، اندرونی (علاقہ) (of trade, travel, tax, etc.) carried on or obtained within a country اندرونی *adv*. towards the interior of the country ساحل سمندر سے دور، اندر کی طرف *n*. interior of a country ساحل سمندر سے دور کا علاقہ، اندرونی علاقہ
in-laws (*in*-lawz) *n. pl.* (colloq.) (one's) relatives by marriage سسرال والے، بیوی (یا شوہر) کے رشتے دار
inlay *v.t.* (in-*lay*) fit pieces of different shapes, colours, etc., into a flat surface جڑاؤ کام کرنا، مرصع کام کرنا، منبت کاری کرنا، پچی کاری کرنا
inlet (*in*-let) *n*. very small bay (between islands, etc.) کھاڑی piece inserted *n*. (*in*-lay) inlaid work جڑاؤ کام، منبت کاری **inlaid** (*in*-layd) *adj*. set thus as an ornament جڑاؤ کام والا، جڑا ہوا
inmate (*in*-mayt) *n*. occupant of a house along with others گھر میں رہنے والا، گھر والا one confined in an institution (like an aylsum, hospital, etc.) مقیم، داخل *in-mate of a hospital* ہسپتال میں داخل
inmost (*in*-mohst) *adj*. most inward بالکل اندرونی deepest گہرا، عمیق ترین heartiest دلی، قلبی
inn (in) *n*. public house for lodgers or travellers سرائے *Inns of Courts*, (*a*) the four London law societies enjoying the monopoly of admitting persons to practise as barristers or attorneys; (they are ; Lincoln's Inn, Gray's Inn, Middle Temple, Inner Temple) برطانوی انجمن ہائے وکالت (*b*) their buildings برطانوی انجمن ہائے وکالت کی عمارات
innate (*in*-ayt, or in-*ayt*) *adj*. (of a quality, etc.) inborn پیدائشی، خلقی، جبلی **innately** *adv*. naturally پیدائشی طور پر، پیدائشی
inner (*in*-e*) *adj*. of inside اندرونی **innermost** *adj*. inmost بالکل اندرونی، گہرا، عمیق، دلی، قلبی
innings (*in*-ingz) *n*. team's term for batting (کرکٹ کی) باری، اننگ period of power باری، دور اقتدار *have (one's) innings* کا دور اقتدار ہونا
innocence *n*. (see under **innocent**)
innocent (*in*-o-sent) *adj*. sinless معصوم، بے گناہ not guilty of crime بے قصور، بے گناہ harmless بے ضرر **innocence** (-sens) معصومیت، بے گناہی **innocently** *adj*. in an innocent manner معصومیت سے، معصومانہ انداز سے
innocuous (i-*nok*-ew-us) *adj*. harmless بے ضرر
innominate (i-*nom*-i-nayt) *adj*. nameless گمنام، بے نام
innovate (*in*-o-vayt) *v.i.* introduce new ideas, etc. نیا خیال رائج کرنا، نئی بات پیدا کرنا change (custom, etc.) بدل ڈالنا **innovation** (-*vay*-) *n*. new

idea نیا خیال، نیا طریقہ any novelty نئی چیز، نئی بات
innuendo (i-new-*end*-oh) *n*. (pl. *innuendoes*) indirect and unfavourable remark چوٹ، طنز، طعن آمیز اشارہ
innumerable (i-*newm*-è-ra-bèl) countless ان گنت، بے شمار
inoculate (in-*ok*-ew-layt) *v.t.* treat by introducing germs of disease into (someone *against* that disease) ٹیکہ لگانا، بالشل ٹیکہ لگانا **inoculation** (-*lay*-) *n*. act of inoculating or being inoculated ٹیکہ
inoffensive (in-o-*fens*-iv) *adj*. not objectionable جو قابل اعتراض نہ ہو
inoperable (in-*op*-è-ra-bèl) *adj*. (of tumours, etc.) that cannot be operated upon عمل جراحی کے ناقابل، ناقابل جراحی
inoperative (in-*op*-è-ray-tiv) *adj*. not operative جو لاگو نہ ہو، غیر نافذ العمل
inopportune (-*op*-) *adj*. not opportune نامناسب، بے محل، بے موقع
inordinate (-*o*d*-) *adj*. (of delay, weakness of character, etc.) excessive, extraordinary غیر معمولی، بے حد، حد سے زیادہ **inordinately** *adv*. excessively بے حد
inorganic (-*gan*-) *adj*. not organic بے جان، غیر نامی (branch of chemistry, etc.) pertaining to inorganic things غیر نامیاتی
inornate (-*o**-) *adj*. (of style, etc.) simple, not ornate سادہ، غیر مرصع
in-patient (*in*-*pay*-shent) *n*. person admitted in a hospital for treatment ہسپتال میں داخل مریض، بستری مریض
inquest (*in*-kwest) *n*. official inquiry concerning a sudden death (feared to be violent) اچانک موت کی تفتیش، تفتیش قتل **hold an inquest** اچانک موت کی تفتیش کرنا
inquire (in-*kwi*-è*), **enquire** (en-*kwi*-è*) *v. t.* ask پوچھنا، دریافت کرنا *inquire for (someone)* ask to see (him) ملاقات چاہنا *inquire after (someone)*, ask about (his) health, etc. کا حال پوچھنا، کو پوچھنا **inquirer** *n*. one who inquires پوچھنے والا، دریافت کنندہ **inquiry** (in-*kwi*-e-ri) *n*. inquiring پوچھنا، دریافت کرنا investigation تحقیقات *make inquiries* کی تحقیقات کرنا *hold an inquiry into* پوچھ گچھ کرنا
inquisition (in-kwi-*zish*-en) *n*. judicial or official investigation عدالتی (یا سرکاری) تحقیقات (*Inquisition*), Roman Catholic tribunal for punishing heretics بے دینی کے خاتمہ کا اہتمام کرنے کے لیے عدالت
inquisitive (in-*kwiz*-i-tiv) *adj*. fond of prying curious متجسس، لوگوں کے راز جاننے کی کوشش میں لگا رہنے والا
inquisitorial (-*toh*-) *adj*. too inquisitive بہت ہی متجسس، تکلیف دہ حد تک متجسس

inroad (*in*-rohd) *n*. incursion (*into* a country, etc.) اچانک حملہ forcible encroachment زبردستی چڑھ دوڑنا *make inroads on* (one's time, etc.) waste it خواہ مخواہ ضائع کرنا
inrush (*in*-rush) *n*. a rushing in (*of* water, etc.) امنڈ کر آنا، امنڈ کر آنا
insalubrious (in-sa-*loob*-ri-us) *adj*. (of place or climate) not healthy (place or climate) غیر صحت بخش، غیر صحت مندانہ **insalubrity** *n*. being insalubrious غیر صحت بخش ہونا
insane (in-*sayn*) *adj*. mad پاگل، دیوانہ for mad persons پاگلوں کے لیے very foolish پرلے درجے کا احمق **insanely** *adv*. like mad persons پاگلوں کی طرح unreasonably بے تکی، بلا وجہ **insanity** (in-*san*-i-ti) *n*. madness پاگل پن، دیوانگی، جنون، جنون
insanitary (in-*san*-i-tè-ri) *adj*. not sanitary حفظان صحت کے اصولوں کے خلاف
insatiable (in-*sash*-i-a-bèl) *adj*. unquenchable نہ بجھنے والی پیاس immoderate بہت زیادہ very greedy بڑا لالچی
inscribe (in-*skrib*) *v. t.* write (in) لکھنا، پر لکھنا engrave (on) پر کندہ کرنا stamp deeply گہرے نقوش چھوڑنا enter (someone's name) in a list فہرست میں درج کرنا **inscription** (-*krip*-) *n*. something engraved نقش (esp.) something engraved on a tombstone, etc. کتبہ
inscrutable (in-*skroot*-a-bèl) *adj*. wholly mysterious جس کی تہہ تک نہ پہنچا جا سکے، پر اسرار
insect (*in*-sekt) *n*. any tiny creature with body in three sections and having a back-bone and six legs کیڑا، کوڑا، حشرہ **insecticide** (in-*sek*-ti-sid) *n*. poison for killing insects کیڑے مار دوا **insectivorous** (-*tiv*-) *adj*. (of bird, etc.) feeding on insects کیڑوں پر گزر بسر کرنے والا، حشرہ خور
insecure (-*kew*-e*) *adj*. unsafe خطرے میں، غیر محفوظ not firm کمزور ہونا، ڈانواں ڈول ہونا، مخدوش **insecurity** *n*. being insecure کمزور ہونا، مخدوش ہونا، خطرے میں ہونا
insensate (in-*sen*-sayt) *adj*. lacking sensibility (thing or action) بے حس، بے حسی
insensible (in-*sens*-i-bèl) *adj*. unconscious بے ہوش unaware (*of*) (سے) بے خبر unsympathetic بے حس، کٹھور (of changes) inappreciable غیر محسوس، بہت ہی کم unable to appreciate بے ذوق، سخن ناشناس **insensibly** *adv*. without being observed غیر محسوس طور پر **insensibility** (-*bil*-) *n*. unconsciousness غشی being senseless بے حسی inability to appreciate سخن ناشناسی بے ذوقی **insensitive** (-*sens*-) not sensitive (to

physical, moral or artistic influences) بے حِس ، بے ذوق
inseparable (-sep-) *adj*. not separable جُدا نہ ہو سکنے والا ، غیر مُنفک ، لاینفک
insert (in-sĕ*t) *v. t.* put (something *in*, *into*, or *between*) میں ڈالنا ، میں داخل کرنا publish (advertisement) in a periodical اِشتہار اَخبار میں شائع کرنا
insertion (in-sĕ*-shĕn) *n.* inserting ڈالنا، شامل کرنا، شمول number of times an advertisement is published اِندراج thing inserted ڈالی ہُوئی چیز، اِندراج
inset (*in*-set) *n.* small picture, map, etc., within the border of a bigger picture, map, etc. بڑی تصویر (وغیرہ) کے اَندر لگائی ہوئی چھوٹی تصویر ؛ ذیلی تصویر ، ذیلی نقشہ (وغیرہ)
inshore *adv.* toward the shore ساحل کی طرف
inside (*in-sid*) *prep.* within اَندر *adj.* being within اَندر کا، اَندرُونی private خاص، اَندرُونی، خاصُ الخاص *inside information* خاصُ الخاص اِطّلاعات، اَندرُونی راز، اَندر خانے کا *n.* what is within اَندر کی چیزیں inner parts of the body جسم کے اَندرُونی حِصّے، دِل جِگر وغیرہ contents (*of* a book) (کے) مُندرجات *inside of* (a period of time) (کے) اَندر اَندر *turn (something) inside out,* (*a*) turn it that way بالکل اُلٹ دینا (*b*) search thoroughly پُوری طرح ڈھونڈنا، پُوری طرح چھان بین کرنا **insider** *n.* member of a group اَندر کا، آدمی one who is in the know of the secret (opp. of *outsider*) رازدان، واقفِ اَسرار
insidious *adj.* doing harm secretly چھپ چھپا کر نقصان پہنچانے والا crafty عَیّار **insidiously** *adv.* in an insidious manner چھپ کر، عَیّاری سے
insight (*in*-sit) *n.* power of seeing (*into* some problem, etc.) with the mind بَصیرت، دِقّتِ نَظر
insignia (in-*sig*-ni-a) *n. pl.* badges of office, symbols of office نِشانِ شاہی، ستارے، تاج، عصائے شاہی، (چپراس وغیرہ کی قسم کا کوئی) عُہدے کا نِشان، نِشانِ عُہدہ
insignificant (-*nif*-) *adj*: unimportant غیر اَہَم **insignificance** *n.* غیر اَہَم ہونا
insincere (in-sin-*see*-e*) *adj.* hypocritical (person or action) مُنافِق، مُنافقانہ **insincerity** (-*se*-ri-ti) *n.* being insincere خُلُوص نہ ہونا، مُنافقت
insinuate (in-*sin*-ew-ayt) *v.t.* suggest indirectly and unpleasantly (*that*) چوٹ کرنا، تعریض کرنا make way for (*oneself* or something) artfully and gently (*into*) آہستہ آہستہ چالاکی سے کسی عُہدے پر پہنچنا، چپکے چپکے کسی کے دِل میں گھر کر لینا **insinuation** *n.* چوٹ، دَرپردہ اِلزام
insipid (in-*sip*-id) *adj.* tasteless پھیکا، بے مزہ dull بے لُطف، بے کیف **insipidity** (-*pid*-) *n.* being insipid بے مزگی، بے کیفی
insist (in-*sist*) *v.t.* & *i.* (*insist on something, doing something, on it that*) demand persistently (*on*) اِصرار کرنا، مُصِر ہونا declare emphatically (*on*) بڑے وُثُوق سے کہنا، بڑے زور شور سے کہنا **insistent** *adj.* (of work, etc.) demanding compelling attention زوردار، توجّہ طلب (of person) who insists مُصِر، بضد، اَڑا ہُوا **insistently** *adv.* تاکید سے، بہ اِصرار **insistence** *n.* act of insisting اِصرار، تاکید
insobriety (in-so-*bri*-e-ti) intemperance کثرتِ مَے خواری، شراب نوشی میں بے اِعتدالی
insole (*in*-sohl) *n.* inner sole of a shoe, etc. پاتابہ
insolence *n.* (see under **insolent**)
insolent (*in*-so-lent) *adj.* impudent (person) گُستاخ rude and insulting (behaviour) گُستاخانہ
insolence (lens) *n.* impudence گُستاخی
insoluble (in-*sol*-ew-bĕl) *adj.* that which cannot be dissolved جو گھُل نہ سکے، غیر مُنحل that which cannot be solved or explained سخت مُشکل، جو حل نہ ہو سکے
insolvency *n.* (see under **insolvent**)
insolvent (-*sol*-) *adj.* bankrupt دیوالیہ **insolvency** (vens-i) *n.* being insolvent دیوالیہ ہونا، دیوالیہ پن
insomnia (in-*som*-ni-a) *n.* sleeplessness as a disease بے خوابی، بیخوابی
insomuch (in-soh-*much*) *adv.* to such a degree or extent (*that*) اِتنا ..... کہ
inspect (in-*spekt*) *v. t.* visit officially to see that rules, etc., are obeyed مُعائنہ کرنا examine carefully بغور دیکھنا **inspection** *n.* act of inspecting مُعائنہ **inspector** *n.* one who inspects مُعائنہ کرنے والا official who inspects اِنسپکٹر، ناظر *Inspector of Schools* اِنسپکٹر مدارس، ناظرِ مدارس *Inspector of Police* اِنسپکٹر پولیس، ناظرِ شُرطہ **inspectorate** *n.* office of an inspector اِنسپکٹری، نظارت body of inspectors جُملہ ناظر area under an inspector نظارت، حلقۂ ناظر
inspire (in-*spi*-ĕ*) *v. t.* infuse life and uplifting feelings, etc., into (someone) رُوح پھُونکنا، جوش پیدا کرنا fill (someone) *with* high thoughts, etc. کے دِل میں ڈالنا، فیضان کرنا fill (someone) *with* divine message وَحی بھیجنا، اِلہام کرنا، اِلقا کرنا suggest secretly اَندر ہی اَندر سمجھانا inhale, breathe in سانس لینا **inspiration** (-spi-*ray*-) *n.* influence causing artistic creation تخلیقی تحریک sudden good thought نیک خیال person or thing that inspires جس کی تاثیر ہو، جس کا فیضان ہو divine message وَحی، اِلہام، اِلقا inhalation, breathing in تنفّس **inspired** (in-*spi*-ĕ*d) *adj.* at someone's secret suggestion جو کسی کے کہنے پر ہو **inspirator** (*in*-spi-ray-tĕ*) *n.* apparatus to help inhalation or breathing in ہَوا اَندر کھینچنے کا آلہ، مِنفس **inspiratory** (in-*spi*-ra-to-ri) *adj.* belonging to or aiding inspiration تنفّسی، مِنفسی

instability (in-sta-*bil*-i-ti) *n.* being unstable پائیدار نہ ہونا ، بے ثباتی

install (in-*stawl*) *v. t.* place someone *in* authority ceremonially باقاعدہ جائزہ دلانا ، گدی پر بٹھانا ، مسندنشین کرنا ۔ دستار بندی کرنا settle (*oneself*) in a place (کہیں) بیٹھ جانا place (electric light, etc.) in a place for use لگانا **installation** (*-lay-*) ceremony of installing مسندنشینی something installed جو چیز لگائی جائے

instalment (*-stawl-*) *n.* any one of the successive parts in which something is paid or delivered قسط *monthly instalment* ماہانہ قسط *by* (or *in*) *instalments* بالاقساط

instance (*in*-stans) *n.* example مثال *for instance,* for example مثلاً ، مثال کے طور پر fact supporting a general truth نظیر ، ثبوت میں واقعہ *in the first instance,* in the first place, to begin with سب سے پہلے ، پہلے تو ، اوّل suggestion, request کہنا ، اشارہ *at* (*someone's*) *instance, at the instance of* (*someone*), at (his) suggestion کے کہنے پر *v. t.* quote as an instance مثال دینا ، نظیر پیش کرنا

instant (*in*-stant) *adj.* immediate اچانک ، فوری urgent اشد ضروری ناگہانی (abbr. *inst.*) (in commercial and official letters) of the present month حال ، ماہِ رواں ، ماہ حال *yours of the 14th inst.* آپ کی چھٹی مورخہ ۱۴ ماہِ رواں *n.* moment لحظہ ، آن ، گھڑی ، لحظہ *this instant,* now ابھی ، اسی دم ، اسی گھڑی *the instant* (*that*), as soon as جونہی ، جیسے ہی **instantly** *adv.* immediately فوراً ، فی الفور **instantaneous** (instan-*tay*-ne-us) *adj.* happening in an instant فوری **instantaneously** *adv.* immediately فوراً ، اسی لمحے ، فی الفور

instead (in-*sted*) *adv.* in place (*of*) (کی) بجائے ، جگہ

instep (*in*-step) *n.* upper surface of foot or shoe between toes and ankles پیر یا جوتے کا اوپر کا حصہ ، پاؤں کی چھت

instigate (*in*-sti-gayt) *v.t.* urge (someone *to do* something) (پر) اکسانا ، پر ابھارنا ، (کی) شہ دینا cause (murder, strike, etc.) thus برپا کرنا **instigation** (*-gay-*) *n.* act of instigating ترغیب ، انگیخت ، تحریک **instigator** *n.* one who instigates ابھارنے والا ، اکسانے والا

instil, instill (in-*stil*) *v.t.* (-ll-) introduce (ideas, etc., *into* someone's mind) gradually دھیرے دھیرے دل میں بٹھانا ، آہستہ آہستہ ذہن نشین کرنا put drop by drop (*into*) (میں) ٹپکانا یا چوانا

instinct (*in*-stinkt) *n.* inborn tendency to behave in an apparently rational and natural way جبلت ، وجدان ، حیوانی عقل **instinctive** *adj.* based on instinct فطری ، قدرتی ، جبلی **instinctively** *adv.* قدرتی طور پر ، فطری طور پر ، جبلی طور پر

institute (*ins*-ti-tewt) *n.* (intellectual, social or other) special purpose organisation علمی یا معاشرتی ... (*pl.*) digest (*of*) خلاصہ ، ملخص یا تلخیص establish (a rule, etc.) نافذ کرنا ، رائج کرنا ، ترویج کرنا begin (case, inquiry, etc.) قائم کرنا ، شروع کرنا

institution *n.* establishing رائج کرنا ، قائم کرنا be established نافذ ہونا ، رائج ہونا ، قائم ہونا established practice, etc. دستور ، رواج ، پہلے زمانے سے چلی آنے والی چیز ، بزرگوں کے وقت سے چلے آنے والا دستور charitable institution خیراتی ادارہ building in which it is lodged خیراتی ادارہ (کی) عمارت **institutional** *adj.* of institute or institution ادارہ سے متعلق ، اداری *institutional religion,* religion finding expression in priestly and ritualistic institutions اداروں والا مذہب ، رسموں والا مذہب of the nature of an institution مروجہ ، مسلمہ

instruct (in-*strukt*) *v. i.* teach پڑھانا ، تعلیم دینا direct order ہدایت دینا ، حکم دینا **instruction** *n.* teaching تعلیم ، معارف *public instruction* معارف ، قوم کی تعلیم (*pl.*) directions ہدایات *under the instructions of,* on the orders of کی ہدایت پر *give instructions* (*to someone to do something*), direct (him to do it) کسی کو کوئی کام کرنے (کی) ہدایت کرنا **instructive** *adj.* informative معلومات افزا **instructor** *n.* (fem *instructress*) teacher, one who instructs سکھانے والا ، معلم

instrument (*ins*-troo-ment) *n.* simple but delicate apparatus آلہ one who is a tool in other's hands آلۂ کار contrivance for producing musical sounds باجا ، ساز ، آلۂ موسیقی ، آلۂ طرب ، بزمار formal legal document دستاویز *instrument of accession* تخت نشینی یا گدی نشینی کی دستاویز **instrumental** (*-men-*) *adj.* (of music) played on instruments سازوں کی موسیقی means or help (*in doing* something) (کا) ذریعہ ، (میں) آلۂ کار

insubordinate (in-sub-*o*d*-i-nayt) *adj.* disobedient نافرمان **insubordination** (*-nay-*) *n.* disobedience نافرمانی

insubstantial (*-stan-*) *adj.* not material غیر مادی not real موہوم ، غیر حقیقی

insufferable *adj.* unbearably proud حد سے زیادہ مغرور ، ناقابل برداشت حد تک مغرور detestable سخت ناگوار ، نفرت انگیز

insufficient (in-su-*fish*-ent) *adj.* inadequate ناکافی **insufficiency** (*-fish*-en-si) *n.* inadequacy ناکافی ہونا ، کمی ، کوتاہی

insular (*in*-sew-lĕ*) *adj.* of an island جزیرے کا، جزائری narrow-minded تنگ نظر **insularity** (-*la*-) *n.* narrow-mindedness تنگ نظری being of an island جزائری ہونا

insulate (*in*-sew-layt) *v.t.* cover or separate (something) so as to prevent loss of electricit·· or heat through conduction حاجز درمیان میں رکھنا، منفصل کرنا isolate الگ کرنا، جدا کرنا **insulation** (-*lay*-) *n.* insulating or being insulated منفصل کرنا، تجز **insulator** *n.* substance for insulating (esp.) an electric wire حاجز **insulated** *adj.* that has been made a non-conductor منفصل

insult *n.* (*in*-sult) affront بے عزتی، توہین، ہتک، اہانت، سبکی *v.t.* (in-*sult*) offer indignity to کی بے عزتی (توہین، ہتک یا اہانت) کرنا، ذلیل کرنا **insulting** *adj.* that which offers indignity ہتک آمیز، توہین آمیز، اہانت آمیز

insuperable (in-*sewp*-è-ra-bèl) *adj.* insurmountable جو دور نہ ہو سکے، ناقابلِ عبور

insupportable (-*poh**t-) *adj.* unbearable ناقابلِ برداشت

insurance *n.* (see under **insure**)

insure (in-*shoo*-è*) *v.t.* make an agreement for securing or paying monetary compensation in case of the loss or damage of (life, property, etc.) کا بیمہ کرنا یا کروانا **insurance** (in-*shoo*-è-rans) *n.* insuring بیمہ sum insured بیمے کی رقم، بیمہ its premium بیمے کی قسط *insurance policy*, agreement for insurance بیمے کی دستاویز، بیمہ *take out an insurance policy (with a company)* (کسی کمپنی کے پاس) بیمہ کرانا *insurance for (a sum)* وہ رقم جس کے لیے بیمہ کرایا ہو *issue an insurance policy to* کا بیمہ کرنا *fire insurance*, insurance against loss by fire آگ کا بیمہ، بیمۂ آتش زدگی *marine insurance*, one against loss through sinking or drowning ڈوبنے کا بیمہ، بیمۂ غرقابی *life insurance*, (now usu.) *life assurance*, insurance for compensation to be paid after death or in old age زندگی کا بیمہ

insurgence *n.* (see under **insurgent**)

insurgent (in-*rĕ**-jent) *adj.* rebel or rebellious باغی **insurgence** (-jens) *n.* rebellion, uprising بغاوت

insurmountable (-*mount*-) *adj.* insuperable (difficulty, etc.) دور نہ ہو سکنے والا (of place, etc.) that cannot be surmounted ناقابلِ رسائی

insurrection (-*rek*-) *n.* people's planned rebellion بغاوت، حکومت کے خلاف باغیانہ تحریک

insusceptible (-*sep*-) *adj.* not susceptible غیر اثر پذیر، اثر ناپذیر **insusceptibility** (-*bil*-) *n.* not being susceptible غیر اثر پذیری

intact (in-*takt*) *adj* unimpaired صحیح سالم، بالکل محفوظ untouched جیسے چھوا بھی نہ گیا ہو، جوں کا توں *keep intact* محفوظ رکھنا

intake (*in*-tayk) *n.* place of taking a fluid into a pipe or channel ٹھوکر number (or quantity) entering (during a given period) (ایک خاص وقت میں) آنے والوں (یا باہر آنے والی چیزوں) کی تعداد یا مقدار

intangible (in-*tanj*-i-bèl) *adj.* that which cannot be touched جسے چھوا نہ جا سکے، غیر محسوس that which cannot be grasped mentally ناقابلِ فہم

integer (-*in*-te-jĕ*) *n.* whole number عددِ صحیح complete in itself مکمل **integral** (in-*teg*-rel) *adj.* entire پورے کا پورا، مکمل (Maths) of the total amount کُلی *integral calculus*, method of calculating the amount of the change of a continuously varying function (حساب) کلیات necessary for completeness (of) کا جزوِ لازم *an integral part of* کا جزوِ لازم

integrate (*in*-teg-rayt) *v.t.* make complete تکمیل کرنا، مکمل کرنا unite (parts) to form a whole ملا کر وحدت بنا دینا، مدغم کرنا، منضم کرنا **integration** (-*ray*-) *n.* such unity ملا کر وحدت بنا دینا، ادغام، انضمام

integrity (in-*teg*-ri-ti) *n.* honesty دیانت، دیانتداری، ایمانداری completeness پورا ہونا، سالمیت soundness (of argument) صحت، اصابت، پختگی

intellect (*in*-te-lekt) *n.* power of reasoning and understanding ذہانت، سمجھ، عقل، فہم، فراست، ذہن، دماغ **intellectual** (in-te-*lek*-tew-èl) *adj.* of the intellect عقلی، ذہنی (person) having good reasoning عقلمند، مدبر، بہت پڑھا لکھا، دانش مند، دانش ور (face, etc.) showing such power جس پر عقل و دانش کے آثار ہویدا ہوں، جس سے فہم و فراست ٹپکے، دانشمندہ *n.* enlightened person دانش مند، سمجھ دار، صاحبِ علم و فراست، ذی فہم

intelligence (in-*tel*-i-jens) *n.* intellect ذہانت، سمجھ، عقل، فہم، فراست information خبر، اطلاع *Intelligence Department*, government department engaged in collecting secret information for the Administration, etc. محکمۂ خفیہ اطلاعات **intelligent** *adj.* having intelligence ذہین، سمجھ دار (remark, etc.) showing intelligence عقلمندی کا، عقل کا، سمجھ کا **intelligentsia, intelligentzia** (in-te-li-*jent*-zi-a) *n.* that part of a nation which claims to be capable of serious independent thinking دانش مند، ملک کا پڑھا لکھا (یا ذی فہم) طبقہ، مدعیِ علم و فہم طبقہ، دانش ور

intelligible (in-*tel*-i-ji-bèl) *adj.* clear, that which can be understood جو سمجھ میں آ سکے، قابلِ فہم **intelligibility** (-*bil*-) *n* being intelligible سمجھ میں آ سکنا، قابلِ فہم ہونا

intemperance *n.* (see under **intemperate**)

intemperate (-*tem*-) *adj.* addicted to drinking شرابی immoderate جس میں اعتدال نہ ہو severe violent (climate) جہاں سردی گرمی دونوں سخت ہوں، شدید (language) سخت **intemperance** (-rans) *n.* being intemperate مے خواری، بے اعتدالی، افراط و تفریط، حد درجہ ہونا

intend *v.t.* (see under **intent**)

intense (in-*tens*) *adj.* (of quality) extreme بہت، بے حد، سخت، شدید (of feelings, etc.) strong, vehement سخت، شدید **intensive** (-*ten*-) thorough and concentrated محدود مگر زوردار (of agriculture) tending to produce cultivation of an area پیدائش افزا very intense زوردار، زور شور کا **intensely** *adv.* extremely از حد شدید **intensify** (in-*ten*-si-fī) *v.t.* & *i.* make or become intense شدت اختیار کرلینا (میں) شدت پیدا کرنا **intensification** (-*kay*-) *n.* act of intensifying or being intensified شدت اختیار کرنا یا پیدا کرنا **intensity** (in-*ten*-si-ti) *n.* being intense زور، شدت

intent (in-*tent*) *n.* aim, purpose منشا، مطلب، مقصد، نیت، مراد *to all intents and purposes*, practically عملاً *adj.* (of looks) eager پرشوق، پرجوش *intent on*, (of person) (*a*) desirous of کا پکا ارادہ کئے ہوئے (*b*) attentive میں منہمک، میں ڈوبا ہوا **intend** (in-*tend*) *v.t.* plan (*to do*) کا ارادہ ہونا mean (by a word, etc.) (سے) مطلب ہونا، (سے) مراد ہونا *be intended for*, (*a*) be destined for ہو کر رہنے والا (*b*) (of a picture, etc.) be supposed to be the likeness of (a person) کہا جانا کہ ویسی ہے **intention** (in *ten*-shĕn) *n.* purpose منشا، مقصد، مدعا، مطلب، ارادہ **intentional** *adj.* said or done on purpose قصداً کہا یا کیا ہوا **intentionally** *adv.* قصداً **intently** *adv.* with concentration غور سے، توجہ سے

[1]**inter** (in-*tĕ**) *v.t.* (-tt-) bury (*in*) دفن کرنا **interment** *n.* burial تدفین

[2]**inter-** (*in-tĕ**) *pref.* (expressing reciprocal action) (as : *interlink*) باہم گر جوڑنا باہمی، باہمدگر between or among two or more بین، مابین، کے درمیان

Note : Inter signifies between (or among) two (or more) persons or things ; **intra** signifies within one and the same unit. Thus *inter-provinces* means between (or among) two (or more) provinces ; but *intra-provincial* means within the same province.

interact (int-ĕ*-*akt*) *v.i.* act on one another باہمدگر اثر انداز ہونا یا عمل کرنا **interaction** *n.* (-*ak*-shĕn) *n.* mutual action باہمدگر عمل یا اثر

interbreed (-*breed*) *v.t.* & *i.* crossbreed دوغلی نسل پیدا کرنا

inter alia (int-ē-*ay*-li-a) among other things منجملہ، علاوہ دوسری باتوں کے۔

intercede (int-e*-*seed*) *v.i.* plead (*with* someone *for* or *on behalf of* another) (کسی کی خاطر کسی سے) سفارش کرنا، شفاعت کرنا، بیچ میں پڑنا **intercession** (-*sesh*-) *n.* act of interceding سفارش، شفاعت، بیچ میں پڑنا **intercessor** *n.* one who intercedes سفارش کرنے والا، شفاعت کنندہ

intercept (int-e*-*sept*) *v.t.* stop or seize in passage راہ میں روک لینا یا پکڑ لینا *intercept* (*someone's*) *letter* (کسی کا) خط راستے ہی میں اڑا لینا get in the way of کی راہ میں حائل ہونا، کا راستہ روکنا **interception** *n.* act of intercepting راہ میں روک لینا یا پکڑ لینا

interchange (int-ĕ*-*chaynj*) *v.t.* (of two persons) exchange (compliments, etc.) آپس میں کہنا، ایک دوسرے کو لکھنا یا بھیجنا put (two things) in each other's place ایک دوسرے کی جگہ رکھنا *n.* mutual exchange of two things مبادلہ **interchangeable** (intĕ-*-*chaynj*-è-bèl), (things, etc.) that can be interchanged مبادلہ پذیر **interchangeability** *n.* being interchangeable مبادلہ پذیری

intercollegiate (int-è*-ko-*lee*-ji-et) *adj.* existing or carried on between two or more colleges کالجوں کے درمیان کا، بین الکلیاتی

intercom (*int*-ĕ*-com) *n.* intercommunication system in aircraft, etc. داخلی مواصلات

intercommunicate (-*mewn*-) *v.t.* have free passage to each other باہم آمدورفت (یا سلسلۂ رسل و رسائل) ہونا، آپس میں ملنا یا بات چیت ہونا۔ **intercommunication** (-*kay*-) *n.* act of intercommunicating باہمی مواصلات

intercourse (*int*-ĕ*-koh*s) *n.* social communication (*between* persons, societies, nations, etc.) باہمی روابط trade communication (*between* countries) (ملکوں کی) باہمی تجارت sexual connexion مباشرت، مجامعت

interdepend (*pend*) *v.t.* depend on each other ایک دوسرے پر منحصر ہونا **interdependence** (-*pend*-) *n.* mutual dependence باہمی انحصار **interdependent** *adj.* ایک دوسرے پر منحصر ہونا

interdict *n.* (*int*-ĕ*-dikt) (among Christians) sentence debarring from church privileges ازکان دین، محرومی کی سزا *v.t.* (int-ĕ*-*dikt*) punish thus ازکان دین سے محروم کردینا

interest (*int*-è-rest) *n.* curiosity دلچسپی *take* (or *have*) *interest in* سے دلچسپی ہونا، سے دلچسپی لینا *pl.*, what one concerns oneself with دلچسپیاں sum paid by borrower for the use of money سود، بیاج *simple interest* سود مفرد، سود *compound interest*, interest added on the principal سود مرکب، سود د سود (usu *pl.*) benefit مفاد، مفادات *look after* (*one's*) *interests* اپنے مفادات کی نگہداشت کرنا *be to* (*one's*) *interest* (*to do*) میں، ذاتی مفاد، ذاتی فائدہ *personal interest* (کرنے میں) اپنا فائدہ کرنا legal right to a share in something حق

concern واسطہ، سروکار personal influence پر ذاتی اثر ڈالنا use (one's) interest with ذاتی اثر و رسوخ v.t. (cause to) take interest (in) سے دلچسپی لینا یا پیدا کرنا **interested** *adj.* having the interest excited (in) (سے) دلچسپی لے رہا liable to be biased through personal interest غرض مند having a share (in) حصہ دار **interesting** *adj.* attracting and holding the attention دلچسپ *be in an interesting condition,* be in the family way پاؤں بھاری ہونا

interfere (int-ĕ*-*fee*-ĕ*) *v.i.* meddle (in other's affairs or work) (میں) مخل ہونا، (میں) مداخلت کرنا come into opposition (*with*) (سے) ٹکرانا، (سے) اختصام ہونا **interference** (int-e*-*fee*-ĕ-rens) *n.* interfering مداخلت (esp.) radio noises that interfere with hearing of programmes ریڈیو کا شور

interim (*int*-ĕ-rim) *n.* meantime درمیانی وقفہ، فترہ *in the interim,* meanwhile اس اثنا میں، اس دوران میں *adj.* temporary, for the meantime عارضی، ہنگامی *interim report,* report submitted as a prelude to the regular one عارضی رپورٹ *interim government,* government set up between two regularly elected ones ہنگامی حکومت

interior (in-*tee*-ri-ĕ*) *adj.* situated inside اندرونی inland اندرونِ ملک کا affairs of home (opp. of *foreign*) داخلی *n.* the inside اندر inland areas اندرونِ ملک home affairs of a country داخلہ، داخلی امور *Minister of Interior* وزیر داخلہ

interject *v.t.* exclaim abruptly while another is talking بیچ میں بول اٹھنا، آہ یا واہ کہنا **interjection** (-*jek*-) exclamation as a part of speech حرفِ مذبہ وفجا، فجائیہ

interlard *v.t.* mix (speech or writing in a language *with* foreign words) (میں) دوسری زبانوں کے الفاظ کی بھرتی کرنا

interleave (-*leev*) *v.t.* insert blank leaves between the leaves of a book (for notes, etc.) (کتاب) کے ورقوں کے بیچ میں سادہ ورق لگانا

interline (-*lin*) *v.t.* fill a book (*with* notes or translation) between the printed lines بین السطور ترجمہ یا معنی لکھنا *interlinear translation,* translation of the text printed along with it in this manner بین السطور ترجمہ

interlock (*int*-e*-lok) *v.t.* & *i.* lock or join together firmly ایک دوسرے میں پھنسنا یا پھنسانا *interlocked hosiery* قفلی بُنت کی جرابیں، بنیانیں

interlocution (-*kew*-) *n.* dialogue گفتگو، مکالمہ **interlocutor** (-*lok*-) *n* (fem. *interlocutress,* or *interlocutrix*) one conversing with سے بات کرنے والا *my interlocutor,* the person speaking to me میرا مخاطب

interloper (-*loh*-) *n.* intruder into others' affairs خواہ مخواہ دخل، معقولات کرنے والا (old use) unauthorized trader غیر مجاز تاجر

interlude (*in*'-ĕ*-lood) *n.* interval between epochs درمیانی زمانہ، فترہ interval between two acts of a play ڈرامے کے ایکٹوں کے درمیان کا وقفہ short entertaining piece presented during it درمیانی نقل یا نقل music played during it وقفہ کی موسیقی

intermarriage (-*ma*-) *n.* marriage between members of different families, races, etc. خاندان یا نسل سے باہر شادی **intermarry** *v. i.* marry thus نسل یا خاندان سے باہر شادی کرنا marry in near kin قریبی رشتہ داروں میں شادی کرنا take one and give another in marriage آمنے سامنے کا رشتہ کرنا

intermediate (-*mee*-di-at) *adj.* situated or coming between (in time, space, degree, etc.) درمیانی (pre-university examination in the former Punjab, now christened as) Higher Secondary ہائر سیکنڈری، انٹر، انٹرمیڈیٹ، ایف۔اے، ایف۔ایس۔سی (railway class) between 3rd and 2nd انٹر، ڈیوڑھا *v.t.* be a mediator (*between*) میں ثالثی کرنا **intermediary** *adj.* mediator ثالث of mediation ثالثی کا

interminable (-*tĕ*-) *adj.* endless لامتناہی tedious because too long اکتا دینے والا، اتنا طویل کہ انسان اکتا جائے

intermingle (-*ming*-) *v. i.* (of tribes, races, etc.) mix together باہمی میل جول رکھنا، آپس میں شادی بیاہ کرنا

intermit (-*mit*-) *v.t.* & *i.* stop for a while ذرا سی دیر کو رکنا

intermittent (-*mit*-) *adj.* with some intervals وقفہ والا *intermittent fever* باری کا بخار، نوبتی بخار **intermission** (-*mish*-ĕn) *n.* pause وقفہ **intermittently** *adv.* رک رک کر، ٹھہر ٹھہر کر

intermix (-*miks*) *v.t.* & *i.* mix together باہمی میل جول رکھنا، آپس میں ربط و ضبط قائم کرنا۔ **intermixture** *n.* mixing or being mixed together باہمی میل جول، ارتباط باہمی

intern (in-*tĕ*n*) *v.t.* keep (esp. foreigners during war) under restraint نظر بند کرنا، زیرِ نگرانی رکھنا **internment** *n.* such detention نظر بندی

internal (in-*tĕ**-nĕl) *adj.* (opp. of *external*) inner اندرونی *internal combustion engine,* engine deriving motive power from explosion of a mixture of air and vaporized petrol or oil in the cylinder داخلی دھماکے والا انجن، انجن اندرونی آتش افروزی، دُوڈول افروز انجن of a country's home affairs داخلی intrinsic باطنی derived from within the thing itself داخلی *internal evidence* (for dating a book, or determining the nature of an event) داخلی شہادت **internally** *adv.* اندرونی طور پر

international (-*nash-ĕ-nĕl*) *adj*. existing or carried on between nations بین الاقوامی world-wide (fame, etc.) عالمگیر *the First International*, Marxist organization in Europe (1862—73) پہلی بین الاقوامی اشتمالی جمعیت *the Third International*, (also, *called the Comintern*), the Russian Communist organization set up in 1918 کمنٹرن، تیسری اشتمالی جمعیت

internecine (in-tĕ*-*nee*-sin) *adj*. mutually destructive (war, etc.) طرفین کی تباہی کا موجب

interpellate (in-tĕ*-pel-ayt) demand explanations in a legislature مُقنّنہ میں سوال کرنا **interpellation** *n*. مُقنّنہ میں سوال **interpellator** (-*lay*-) *n*. مُقنّنہ میں سوال (؟) اٹھانے والا

interplay *n*. operation (*of* things *on* one another) باہمی عمل، تعامل

interpolate (in-*tĕ**-po-layt) *v.t.* make misleading insertions (*in a book, etc.*) (کتاب وغیرہ میں) بدنیتی سے الحاق کرنا (یا) لفظ بڑھانا **interpolation** *n*. interpolating (کتاب وغیرہ میں) بدنیتی سے الحاق words, etc., thus added ملحقات، زائد الفاظ

interpose (int-ĕ*-*pohz*) *v.t.* & *i*. put forward (objection, veto, etc.) (اعتراض) کرنا، (حق استرداد) استعمال کرنا interrupt (*with* a remark) بات کاٹنا، بیچ میں بول اٹھنا، قطع کلام کرنا mediate بیچ میں پڑنا، بیچ بچاؤ کرنا، مداخلت کرنا

interposition (-*zish*-) *n*. act of interposing بیچ بچاؤ، اعتراض، قطع کلام

interpret (int-ĕ*-*pret*) *v.t.* & *i*. explain the meaning of (either in words or by artistic representation) مُراد سمجھانا، ظاہر کرنا، وضاحت کرنا، تشریح کرنا، معنی پہنانا consider to be the meaning of مُراد لینا، مطلب بیان کرنا act as interpreter ترجمانی، translate from one language into another ترجمہ کرنا، مطلب بیان کرنا **interpreter** *n*. one employed to translate on the occasion orally from one language into another ترجمان **interpretation** (-*tay*-) *n*. act of interpreting or something interpreted ترجمانی، تشریح، توضیح، مطلب، مفہوم

interregnum (-*reg*-) *n*. interval when a country has no normal ruler تخت (یا حکومت) خالی رہنے کا وقفہ، فترۂ حکومت any interval وقفہ

interrogate (in-*te*-ro-gayt) *v. t* examine (accused, etc.) by asking questions پوچھ گچھ، تفتیش

interrogation (-*gay*-) *n*. questioning پوچھ گچھ، تفتیش *mark of interrogation*, query, (?) سوالیہ نشان

interrogative (-*rog*-) *adj*. indicating a question سوالیہ *n*. word (like *who*, *which*, etc.) that is used to ask a question سوالیہ لفظ، سوالیہ حرف

interrupt (in-te-*rupt*) *v.t* & break the continuity of (کا سلسلہ) منقطع کرنا، مداخلت کرنا obstruct (view, etc.) راہ میں حائل ہونا، رکاوٹ کھڑی ہو جانا speak to (someone) while he is saying something بات کاٹنا، قطع کلام کرنا **interruption** *n*. interrupting مداخلت، خلل اندازی speaking to someone while he speaks قطع کلام something that interrupts خلل، رکاوٹ

inter se (int-ĕ-*see*) between themselves خود ان کے درمیان، خود ان کے مابین

intersect (-*sekt*-) *v.t.* cut ; pass across کاٹتے ہوئے گزرنا، قطع کرنا، کاٹنا (of lines) cut or cross each other (خطوط کا) متقاطع ہونا **intersecting** lines متقاطع خطوط **intersection** *n*. cutting کاٹنا، تقاطع (esp.) point where two lines, etc., cross نقطۂ تقاطع

intersperse (int-ĕ*-*spĕ*s*) *v.t.* scatter (*between, among* or *with*) بکھیرنا، یہاں ادھر ادھر ڈالنا *interspersed with*, variegated with سے رنگا رنگ، سے بوقلموں

interstice (in-*tĕ**-stis) *n*. crevice شگاف، درز

intertwine (-*twin*) *v.t.* & *i*. coil together گوندھنا، جُٹنا، بل دے کر ایک کرنا یا ہونا

interval (*int-ĕ**-vĕl) *n*. time (between two events, etc.) وقفہ (esp.) time between two parts of a play, or concert وقفہ space between (two objects or points) درمیانی فاصلہ، فصل *at intervals*, *with intervals between* کے بعد، کچھ فاصلہ (یا وقفے) کے بعد، تھوڑی تھوڑی دُور، تھوڑی تھوڑی دیر کے بعد

intervene (int-ĕ*-*veen*) *v.t.* (of events) come (*between*) in time بیچ میں آنا occur in the meantime اس اثنا میں ہونا، اس دوران میں ہونا be suited (*between*) (کے) درمیان ہونا، کے بیچ میں ہونا interfere with good intentions بیچ میں پڑنا، مداخلت کرنا be an interval between بیچ میں (وقت) ہونا **intervention** (-*vensh*-) *n*. act of intervening مداخلت

interview (*int*-ĕ*-vew) *n*. meeting (*with* someone *for* discussion, etc.) ملاقات personal meeting of the candidate for a job (*with* the selecting authority for *viva voce* test) انٹرویو meeting of a Press reporter (*with* someone for questioning him on his views in order to publish them) انٹرویو، اخباری ملاقات *v.t.* have an interview with سے ملاقات کرنا، سے انٹرویو کرنا give an interview to کو انٹرویو کی اجازت دینا، کو اپنے سے اخباری ملاقات کرنے دینا

intestate (in-*tes*-tayt) *adj*. not having made a will وصیت کئے بغیر، وصیت کر نہ سے *die intestate* وصیت کرنے سے پہلے چل بسنا

intestine in-*tes*-tin) *n*. (*pl.*) bowels آنتیں، امعا one of the tubes leading to or from them آنت، رودہ

intimacy *n*. (see under **intimate**)

intimate (*int*-i-mayt) *v.t.* make known (*that*) اشارہ کرنا، اِشارۃً کہنا، بتانا، کہت، مُطلع کرنا hint *adj.* close and familiar (friend, terms, etc.) گہرا، قریبی، دلی deep گہرا innermost (details, etc.) اندرونی، اصلی *n.* close friend گہرا دوست، جگری دوست **intimation** (*-may-*) *n.* intimating کہنا، اطلاع دینا hint اشارہ

intimacy (*int*-i-mi-si) *n.* being intimate گہری دوستی illicit sexual relation ناجائز تعلق، تعلق **intimately** *adv.* closely خوب، اچھی طرح

intimidate (in-*tim*-i-dayt) *v.t.* frighten with threats ڈرانا، دھمکانا **intimidation** (*-day-*) *n.* threat دھمکی، ڈر

into (*in*-too) *prep.* (motion towards inside) میں، کے اندر *The chair is in the room* کرسی کمرے میں ہے *Take the chair into the room* کرسی کمرے میں لے جاؤ to the condition of (بدل) کر ہو جانا، بن جانا یا کر دینا *look into the matter, inquire into it* اس معاملے کی چھان بین کرنا، اس کی تحقیقات کرنا *get into trouble* مصیبت میں پڑنا *look into (the box, etc.)* (بکس وغیرہ) کے اندر دیکھنا *turn into, (water, etc.)* (پانی وغیرہ) ہو جانا یا بن جانا *flog into submission,* force into submission thus مار مار کر سیدھا کر دینا

intolerable (*-tol-*) *adj.* unbearable ناقابلِ برداشت **intolerably** *adv.* unbearably از حد، حد سے بڑھا ہوا **intolerableness** *n.* being intolerable ناقابلِ برداشت ہونا

intolerance *n.* (see under **intolerant**)

intolerant (*-tol-*) *adj.* not tolerant (*of* religious beliefs or difference of opinion) (کے معاملے میں) غیر روادار، رواداری نہ رکھنے والا، متعصب **intolerance** (-rans) *n.* being intolerant رواداری نہ ہونا، تعصب

intone (in-*tohn*) **intonate** (in-to-*nayt*) *v. t* recite (a prayer, etc.) in a sing-song manner لحن سے پڑھنا utter with a particular tone مخصوص لہجے میں پڑھنا **intonation** (*-nay-*) *n.* intoning لحن سے پڑھنا، مخصوص لہجے میں پڑھنا accent لہجہ modulation (of the voice) (آواز کا) اُتار چڑھاؤ

in toto (in-*toh*-toh) entirely, whole کل، مجموعی طور پر، فی الجملہ

intoxicate (in-*tok*-si-kayt) *v. t.* make drunk نشہ چڑھانا، مخمور کرنا make stupid with an excessive dose of liquor مدہوش کرنا excite to enthusiasm (*with* success, etc.) (کا) نشہ (یا خمار) چڑھانا **intoxicating** *adj.* inebriating نشہ آور، منشی، مدہوش کرنا *intoxicating drinks,* liquors شرابیں **intoxicant** *adj.* something that intoxicates شراب، نشہ آور (یا) منشی چیز **intoxication** (*-kay-*) *n.* state of being drunk نشہ، نشے کی حالت excitement (*of*) (کا) نشہ

intra- (*int*-ra) pref. in, within or inside (something) میں

intractable (*-trak-*) *adj.* (of person) not easily controlled خود سر، سرکش، بے لگام، منہ زور **intractability** *n.* خودسری، سرکشی

intramural (*-mew-*) of the inside داخلی، اندرونی situated or done within the walls of house or city گھر (یا فصیل) کے اندر کا in which no outsider participates اندرونی، اپنا، گھر کا

intransigent (in-*tran*-zi-jent) *adj.* uncompromising (person or attitude) in politics سیاست میں غیر مصالحانہ (رویہ)، کٹر، سخت یا انتہا پسند (سیاستدان) **intransigence** *n.* سیاست میں انتہا پسندی یا غیر مصالحانہ رویہ

intransitive (in-*trahns*-i-tiv) *adj.* (of verbs) not transitive, not needing a direct object (*e.g., go, sleep,* etc.) (فعل) لازم

intrepid (in-*trep*-id) *adj.* fearless نڈر، بے خوف brave بہادر، دلیر **intrepidity** (*-pid-*)

intricate (*int*-ri-ket) *adj.* perplexingly involved (thing or problem) پیچیدہ، اُلجھا ہوا **intricacy** (*int*-ri-ka-si) *n.* پیچیدگی، اُلجھاؤ

intrigue (in-*t* underhand plot سازش، سازباز اندر ہی اندر گٹھ جوڑ secret love-affair *v. t. & i.* engage in intrigue (*with* one *against* another) (کسی سے کسی کے خلاف) سازباز کرنا، (کے ساتھ مل کر کے خلاف) سازش کرنا have a secret love affair (*with*) کے ساتھ خفیہ معاشقہ کرنا (in journalistic jargon) rouse the interest (of) کے دل میں شوق پیدا کرنا، شوق *intriguing looks* شوق آفریں ہونا، شوق آفریں نگاہیں

intrinsic (in-*trin*-sik) *adj.* not coming from outside but existing within داخلی، باطنی (of value, worth, merit, etc.) essential, natural ذاتی، اصلی، حقیقی **intrinsically** *adv.* essentially, inherently دراصل، درحقیقت، بنیادی طور پر

introduce (*int*-ro-dews) *v. t.* make (someone) known (to another) (سے) تعارف کرانا make (a book, etc.) known (to) (سے) آشنا کرانا usher in (*into*) شائع کرنا bring (fashion, etc.) into use for the first time رائج کرنا، چلانا put (something new *into* a place) میں ڈالنا، میں لا کر رکھنا begin (sentence, etc.) (جملہ وغیرہ) شروع کرنا present (bill, etc., before legislature, etc.) پیش کرنا **introduction** (*-duk-*) *n.* introducing or being introduced تعارف، پیش کرنا، رائج کرنا، نئی چیز رکھنا، شروع کرنا something introduced پیشکش (esp. preliminary article in a book explaining its nature, etc. پیش لفظ، تمہید، دیباچہ **introductory** (*-duk*-te-ri) *adj.* serving to introduce someone or something تمہیدی، ابتدائی، تعارفی initial

introspect (-pek-) *v. t.* look into one's own

thoughts and feelings مشاہدۂ نفس کرنا **introspection** *n.* مشاہدۂ نفس **introspective** *adj.* pertaining to introspection مشاہدۂ نفس سے متعلق one in this habit مشاہدۂ نفس کرنے والا

intrude (in-*trood*) *v.t.* & *i.* force (*into* a place or thing) میں زبردستی گھسنا یا گھسیڑنا enter (*upon* a person) uninvited کے سر پر زبردستی جا مسلّط ہونا **intruder** *n.* one who intrudes uninvited person مداخلت کرنے والا - ناخواندہ مہمان **intrusion** (in-*troozh*-ĕn) *n.* encroachment مداخلت، خلل اندازی **intrusive** (-siv) *adj.* that intrudes بیجا مخل، بیجا مداخلت کرنے والا **intrusiveness** *n.* being intrusive بے جا مداخلت کی عادت

intuition (in-*tew*-i-shĕn) *n.* immediate understanding without reasoning, sudden insight وجدان **intuitional** (-*ish*-) **intuitive** (in-*tew*-i-tiv) *adj.* pertaining to وجدانی **intuitionalism, intuitionism** *n.* theory of intuitional perception وجدانیت

inundate (-*in*-) *v. t.* flood زیرِ آب کرنا (سیلاب میں) *be inundated with* (*letters, etc.*), receive a large number of them (کو) بہت زیادہ موصول ہونا غرق کرنا

inurbane (-*bayn*-) *adj.* not urbane اُجڈ، اکھڑ، ناشائستہ **inurbanity** (-*ban*-) *n.* being inurbane اُجڈ ہونا ناشائستگی

inure (i-*new*-ĕ*) *v. t.* accustom (someone *to* hard work or working hard) (کا) عادی بنانا (کا) خوگر کر لینا **inurement** *n.* act of inuring or being inured عادی بنانا

invade (in-*vayd*) *v.t.* attack a country with armed forces پر چڑھائی کرنا، پر چڑھ دوڑنا، پر حملہ کرنا، پر حملہ آور ہونا (of disease, pest, feelings, etc.) پر چھا جانا violate (rights, etc.) پر چھا جانا پر حملہ آور ہونا **invader** *n.* one who invades حملہ آور **invasion** (in-*vayzh*-en) *n.* act of invading, حملہ، چڑھائی

invalid (*in*-va-leed) *n.* & *adj.* person infirm or disabled through illness or injury کمزور، بیمار، مریض، ناکارہ for such a person مریض کے لیے معذور کے لیے *adj.* (in-*val*-id) (of documents, etc.) not valid قانوناً بے ضابطہ، بے اثر، کالعدم *v. t.* (in-va-leed, -*leed*) *v.t.* & *i.* (of soldiers, etc.) remove from active service as an invalid and send (*home*) (فوجی کو) ناکارہ قرار دے کر گھر بھیجنا **invalidate** (-*val*-) make invalid کالعدم قرار دینا **invalidity** (-*lid*-i-ti) *n.* not being valid; being null and void کالعدم ہونا **invalidation** (-*day*-) *n.* being declared null and void کالعدم قرار دیا جانا

invaluable (in-*val*-yew-a-bĕl) *n.* priceless اَنمول

invasion *n.* (see under **invade**)

invective (in-*vek*-tiv) *n.* abusive oratory or rhetoric دشنام آمیز اور جوش تقریر یا تحریر abusive language گالی گلوچ، گالیوں کی بوچھاڑ، سب و شتم *indulge in invective*, use abusive language گالی گلوچ پر اتر آنا

inveigh (in-*vay*) *v. t.* rail loudly (*against*) (کو) برا بھلا کہنا (کی) اچھی طرح خبر لینا (کو) آڑے ہاتھوں لینا

inveigle (in-*veeg*-ĕl, in-*vayg*-ĕl) *v.t.* coax (someone *into* place, conduct or *doing*) خوشامد در آمد سے (کسی) کو کسی بُرائی وغیرہ کرنے یا کہیں آنے پر مجبور کرنا

invent (in-*vent*) *v. t.* create (something not existing before) ایجاد کرنا، اختراع کرنا make up (a story, excuse, etc.) گھڑنا، تراشنا، بنا لینا **inventer** *n.* one who invents موجد، مخترع **inventive** *adj.* (of ability, genius, etc.) capable of inventing ایجاد پسند، موجدانہ **invention** (in-*vensh*-ĕn) *n.* inventing or something invented ایجاد، اختراع ability to invent موجدانہ صلاحیت fabrication جھوٹا، جھوٹا قصہ

inventory (*in*-vent-ĕ-ri) *n.* detailed list (*of* belongings, etc.) فہرست فرد goods listed thus سامان، تمسک، رجسٹر فرد *v. t.* enter (goods) in inventory (کی) فرد بنانا، فہرست میں درج کرنا

inverse (in-*vĕ**s) *adj.* inverted اُلٹا، اُلٹ، معکوس *be in inverse proportion*, (of two quantities) decrease proportionately to the other's increase تناسب معکوس، اُلٹی نسبت *n.* direct opposite **inversely** *adv.* on the contrary اُلٹ، عکس (Also see **invert**) اس کے برعکس

invert (in-*vĕ**t) *v.t.* put upside down or in the opposite order, position, or relation اُلٹا کرنا، اوندھا کرنا *inverted commas*, (also called *quotes*), double ('' ... ..'') or single ('......') quotes placed outside direct speech واوین، معکوس **inversion** (in-*vĕ**-shĕn) *n.* turning upside down اُلٹا کرنا، اوندھا کرنا reversal of order, etc. تقلیب، عکس ترتیب

invest (in-*vest*) *v. t.* & *i.* lay out (money *in* a business, or shares, etc.) (روپیہ) لگانا spend (*in* money) and buy something needed or useful (used jocularly) پر خرچ کرنا clothe (*in* or *with*) پہنانا، خلعت پہنانا endow (with title, rank or office) عطا کرنا lay siege to کا محاصرہ کرنا **investiture** *n.* ceremony of conferring an office or title on (عہدے وغیرہ پر) فائز کرنے کی تقریب **investment** *n.* the investing of money روپیہ لگانا، رقم لگانا sum of money invested لگی ہوئی رقم **investor** *n.* رقم لگانے والا

investigate (-*ves*-) *v.t.* inquire into کی تفتیش کرنا **investigation** (-*gay*-) *n.* act of investigating تفتیش *Criminal Investigation Department*, (abbr. *C. I. D.*), special branch of police for purposes of investigating complicated cases سی، آئی، ڈی خفیہ پولیس *Criminal Investigation Agency*, (abbr. *C. I. A.*), another special branch for the same purpose سی، آئی، اے، خفیہ پولیس

inveterate (in-*vet*-ē-ret) *adj.* deep-rooted (habit, enmity, etc.) سخت، پکّی، راسخ habitual (liar, etc.) پرلے درجے کا سخت firm (enemy) سخت، پکا، اشدید

invidious (in-*vid*-i-us) *adj.* that which offends owing to real or apparent injustice بے انصافی کا باعث ناگوار likely to produce ill-will against the performer بدنامی کا موجب

invigilate (in-*vij*-i-layt) *v.t.* keep watch over candidates in an examination to prevent use of unfair means امتحان میں نگرانی کرنا **invigilation** (-*lay*-) *n.* act of invigilating امتحان میں نگرانی

invigorate (in-*vig*-o-rayt) *v.t.* make vigorous تقویت پہنچانا prove to be bracing جان ڈال دینا **invigorating** *adj.* that invigorates جان ڈالنے والا، تقویت پہنچانے والا

invincible (-*vins*-) *adj.* unconquerable جسے شکست نہ دی جا سکے، ناقابلِ تسخیر **invincibility** (-*bil*-) *n.* being invincible ناقابلِ تسخیر ہونا

inviolable (-*vio*-) *adj.* binding, not violable پکا، استوار sacred, not to be treated disrespectfully مقدس، جس کی حرمت قائم رکھنی پڑے **inviolate** *adj.* unbroken پکا، استوار untouched held in respect مقدس، جس کی حرمت قائم رکھی جائے

invisible (-*viz*-) *adj.* not visible جو نظر نہ آ سکے، غیر مرئی *invisible exports*, services, investments, etc., that account for a country's favourable balance of trade despite small exports غیر محسوس برآمد **invisibility** *n.* (-*bil*-) نظر نہ آ سکنا، غیر مرئی ہونا

invite (in-*vīt*) *v. t.* ask (someone *to* come somewhere) دعوت دینا، بلانا ask him (*to do* something) (کسی سے کچھ کرنے کو) کہنا call forth (suggestions) طلب کرنا attract or entice (*to do*) رغبت دلانا، شوق دلانا **inviting** *adj.* attractive پرکشش، کشش والا، رغبت والا

invitation (in-vi-*tay*-shĕn) *n.* (esp.) request (*to* come or go somewhere, or *to do* something) دعوت، بلاوا

invocation *n.* (see under **invoke**)

invoice (*in*-vois) *n.* list of goods despatched along with their quantity, rate and total price بیجک *v. t.* make an invoice بیجک بنانا

invoke (in-*vohk*) *v. t.* call on (*God*) for help (خدا سے) دعا کرنا، خدا کو پکارنا، نام لینا summon (spirits) by magic منتر پڑھ کر روحوں کو بلانا call out (someone's) name for help (کسی کے) نام کی دہائی دینا appeal for کی التجا کرنا، کے لیے درخواست کرنا **invocation** (-*kay*-) *n.* act of invoking دعا کرنا، التجا کرنا، منتر پڑھ کر بلانا، (کسی کے) نام کی دہائی دینا prayer دعا prefatory words in a prayer, etc. (e.g. : *In the name of*) (دعا کی) بسم اللہ poet's prefatory appeal in a poem requesting the Muses for information مناجات، اسما نامہ magical formula for conjuring up spirits منتر

involuntary (-*vol*-) *adj.* unintentional نادانستہ done unconsciously بے ہوشی میں کیا ہوا done unwillingly بادلِ ناخواستہ کیا ہوا، مجبوراً کیا ہوا

involve (in-*volv*) *v.t.* entangle (someone *in* trouble, etc.) مصیبت میں مبتلا کرنا complicate پیچیدہ کرنا entail کا نتیجہ ہونا engage completely پورا وقت لینا (سارا وقت) مصروف رکھنا **involved** *adj.* complicated پیچیدہ، الجھا ہوا

invulnerable (-*vul*-) *adj.* جس کو زخم یا ضرر نہ پہنچایا جا سکے **invulnerability** (-*bil*-) *n.* being invulnerable ضرر سے امین ہونا، گزند سے نت

inward (*in*-wĕ*d) *adj.* internal اندرونی of the inner self دلی، باطنی، روحانی directed towards the inside اندر کی طرف *n.* (pl.) tripe اوجھڑی **inwardly** *adv.* in the inner self دلی طور پر، روحانی طور پر *adv.* (also *inwards*) towards the inside اندر، اندر کو، اندر کی طرف towards the mind دل میں inner nature (*of* something) حقیقت، کنہ، جوہر، ماہیت spiritual nature روحانیت quality of being inward داخلیت

inwrought (in-*rawt*, or *in*-rawt) wrought (*in*, *on* or *with*) (میں یا پر) بنا ہوا

iodine (i-o-deen, or ī-o-dīn) *n.* a non-metallic element used as an antiseptic and in photography آیوڈین *tincture iodine*, alcoholic mixture of iodine used in dressing wounds, etc. ٹنکچر آیوڈین **iodize** (ī-o-dīz) *v.t.* impregnate with iodine میں آیوڈین ڈالنا، آیوڈین بنانے والا

ion (*i*-on) *n.* electrically charged atom, etc. برق پارہ، برقپارہ

iota (ī-*oh*-ta) *n.* the Greek letter ι (equivalent to English *i*) آیوٹا jot, tittle, ذرہ *not an iota of*, none at all بالکل نہیں، ذرہ سا بھی نہیں، پھر بھی نہیں

IOU (i-oh-*yew*) *n.* (abbr. of *I owe you*) promissary note acknowledging debt پرونوٹ

ipso facto (*ip*-soh-*fak*-toh) *adv.* by that very fact اس وجہ سے، اسی باعث

ir- (ir) *pref.* not بے، نا، غیر، خلاف (as *irrational*, not rational)

irascible, irate *adj.* (see under **ire**)

ire (ī-ĕ*) *n.* (lit.) anger غصہ، طیش **irascible** (ī-*ras*-i-bĕl) *adj.* easily enraged جلد طیش میں آجانے والا، زود رنج **irascibility** (-*bil*-) *n.* being irascible زود رنجی، جلد طیش میں آجانا **irate** (ī-*rayt*) *adj.* angry ناراض، خفا، غصے **ireful** (ī-ĕ*-ful) *adj.* angry ناراض، خفا، غصے

iridescence *n.* (see under **iridescent**)

iridescent (i-ri-*des*-ent) *adj*. showing colours like the rainbow قوسِ قزح جیسا رنگین قزحی shining with changing colours بوقلموں، رنگینی والا **iridescence** (-sens) *n*. being irid-- قوسِ قزح جیسی رنگینی، قزحی رنگینی

iridium (i-*rid*-i-um) *n*. a white metal which looks like polished steel اریڈیم *iridium tipped nib* اریڈیم کی نوک والا نب

iris (*i*-ris) *n*. coloured part of the eyeball with circular opening in the pupil مردمک، دیدۂ آنکھ کی پتلی، پردہ عنبیہ (*Iris*), *Cl. myth*. swift-footed messenger of gods آئرس flowering plant (also called *flag*) پرچم پودا

irk (ẽ*k) *v. t*. annoy (one *to do*) کے لیے تکلیف دہ ہونا، پر گراں گزرنا، (کو) اکتا دینا **irksome** *adj*. boring اکتا دینے والا

iron (*i*-ẽ*n) *n*. a metal much used for tools لوہا iron tool or weapon لوہے کا اوزار یا ہتھیار symbol of firmness لوہا، فولاد (*pl*.) fetters or chains بیڑیاں، ہتھکڑیاں (also flat iron), pressing iron استری *adj*. of or pertaining to iron لوہے کا آہنی firm (will, etc.) فولادی، آہنی *v. t*. press clothes with an iron استری کرنا shackle with irons بیڑیاں یا ہتھکڑیاں ڈالنا *strike while the iron is hot*, act while circumstances are favourable موقعہ سے فائدہ اٹھانا *have too many irons in the fire*, (*a*) have too many plans simultaneously بیک وقت بہت سے منصوبے زیرِ عمل ہونا (*b*) have too many things to attend to سو کام ہونا، اتنے کام ہونا کہ توجہ نہ ہو سکے *a man of iron*, (*a*) merciless man سنگدل آدمی (*b*) one with a firm purpose فولادی انسان، آہنی عزم کا مالک، مردِ آہن *put (someone) in irons*, handcuff (him) کسی کو ہتھکڑی یا بیڑی پہنانا *rule with an iron hand, rule with a rod of iron*, rule severely سخت گیری سے حکومت کرنا *cast iron* ڈھلا ہوا لوہا، دیگی لوہا *wrought iron* کوٹ کر بنایا ہوا لوہا **iron-clad** *adj*. armoured (person or ship) بکتر بند **iron-curtain** *n*. barrier to passage of information beyond the limits of the Soviet sphere of influence **iron lung** *n*. case fitted over T B. patient's body for artificial respiration آہنی پھیپھڑا **ironmonger** *n*. dealer in iron hardware لوہے کا مال بیچنے والا **ironmongery** *n*. hardware لوہے کا سامان **iron-mould** *n*. spot caused by rust زنگ کا نشان inkstain سیاہی کا داغ **Ironside** *n*. very brave person بہت بہادر، شجاع (*pl*.) Cromwell's troopers کرامویل کے جانباز **ironstone** *n*. iron ore کچا لوہا **ironworks** *n*. steel factory لوہے کا کارخانہ hardware factory لوہے کے سامان کا کارخانہ **ironwork** *n*. thing made of iron لوہے کی چیز

irony (*i*-rė-ni) *n*. the expression of one's meaning by using words of opposite or different tendency to make it bitterly sarcastic طنز mock adoption of one's views or tone مذاق event otherwise desirable but not in the existing circumstances ستم ظریفی *irony of Fate* قسمت کی ستم ظریفی *ironies of life* زندگی کی ستم ظریفیاں *dramatic irony*, *tragic irony*, use of prophetic language with meaning unknown to both the speaker and the person addressed حزنیہ ستم ظریفی *Socratic irony*, ignorance simulated to bring out the opponent's error سقراطی طنز، تجاہلِ عارفانہ **ironic, ironical** (-*ron*-) *adj*. full of irony طنز سے بھرا، طنز بھرا، طنز آمیز **ironist** *n* one who uses irony طنزیہ انداز استعمال کرنے والا

irradiate (i-*ray*-di-ayt) *v. t*. shine upon پر چمکنا light up (face *with* joy) تاباں کرنا throw light on (subject) پر روشنی ڈالنا subject to sunlight or X-rays دھوپ میں رکھنا یا ایکس رے ڈالنا

irrational (i-*rash*-ė-nẽl) *adj*. lacking the power to reason قوتِ استدلال سے محروم، بے عقل illogical غیر منطقی absurd بیہودہ، لغو، مہمل (in mathematics) surd غیر نطری (عدد) **irrationality** (-*nal*-) *n*. being irrational بے عقلی، لغویت، بیہودگی، (عدد کا) غیر نطری ہونا

irreclaimable (-*klaym*-) *adj*. (land) which cannot be reclaimed (اراضی) جسے قابلِ کاشت نہ بنایا جا سکے (person) who cannot be reformed ناقابلِ اصلاح **irreclaimably** *adv*. ناقابلِ اصلاح حد تک

irreconcilable (i-rek-on-*si*-la-bėl) *adj*. mutually disagreeing ایک دوسرے کی ضد، متضاد discordant (*with*) (سے) متضاد، (کا) عکس (رہے) implacably hostile سخت دشمن، میں آگ پانی کا بیر

irrecoverable (-*kuv*-) *adj*. that which cannot be recovered ڈوبا ہوا، ناقابلِ وصول irremediable لاعلاج کیا گزرا

irredeemable (i-re-*deem*-a-bėl) *adj*. beyond hope لاعلاج کیا گزرا (of debt) not terminable by repayment جو ادائیگی سے ختم نہ ہو (of currency note) not convertible into cash (وہ نوٹ) جس کے عوض سکے کا مطالبہ نہ کیا جائے، مبادلہ ناپذیر

irredentist (i-re-*dent*-ist) *adj*. advocate of the recovery of areas speaking the same language as one's own ہم زبان علاقے دوبارہ حاصل کرنے کا حامی **irredentism** *n*. being an irredentist ہم زبان علاقے دوبارہ حاصل کرنے کی حمایت

irreducible (i-re-*dews*-) *adj*. that which cannot be simplified (*to*) غیر تسہیل پذیر that which cannot be reduced (*to*) غیر تخفیف پذیر

irrefragable (i-*ref*-ra-ga-bėl) *adj* (of statement, argument, etc.) indisputable ناقابلِ تردید

irrefutable (i-*ref*-ew-ta-bėl) *adj*. that which

cannot be refuted ناقابلِ تردید **irrefutability** (-*bil*-) *n*. being irrefutable ناقابلِ تردید ہونا

irregular (i-*reg*-ew-lĕ*) *adj*. not according to rule بےضابطہ، خلافِ قاعدہ، بے قاعدہ uneven (surface) بے ترتیب، ناہموار not regular in order, shape, etc. unusual خلافِ معمول (of soldiers or army) not in regular service گڈھب، بے ڈھنگا بے قاعدہ فوج یا فوجی (in grammar) not following the regular rule of conjugation غیر قیاسی، سماعی *n*. (*pl*.) soldier or army, etc., not in regular service بے قاعدہ فوج، بے قاعدہ فوجی **irregularity** (-*la*-ri-ti) *n*. being irregular بے اصولی، بے ضابطگی، بے قاعدگی، بے ترتیبی، ناہمواری، بے ڈھنگا پن

irrelevance *n*. (see under **irrelevant**)

irrelevant (i-*rel*-e-vant) *adj*. not relevant (*to*) بے محل، غیر متعلق **irrelevance** (-vans) *n*. being irrelevant غیر متعلق ہونا

irreligious (i-re-*lij*-us) *adj*. not religious بے دین، لامذہب **irreligion** (-*lij*-) *n*. indifference or hostility to religion مذہب سے بیگانگی یا دشمنی

irremediable (i-re-*mee*-di-a-bĕl) *adj*. (of disease or mistake) that cannot be remedied لاعلاج، لادوا

irremovable (i-re-*moov*-a-bĕl) *adj*. not removable جسے (بالخصوص عہدہ سے) ہٹایا نہ جا سکے

irreparable (i-*rep*-a-ra-bĕl) *adj*. (loss, etc.) which cannot be repaired ناقابلِ تلافی **irreparably** *adv*. to an irreparable extent ناقابلِ تلافی، حد تک

irreplaceable (i-re-*plays*-i-bĕl) *adj*. that which cannot be replaced جس کی جگہ پُر نہ کی جا سکے

irrepressible (-*pres*-) *adj*. uncontrollable (laughter, etc.) نہ رُکنے والا، نہ دبنے والا

irreproachable (i-re-*prohch*-i-bĕl) *adj*. faultless بے عیب، بے داغ that to which no blame attaches جس پر حرف نہ آسکے، جس پر الزام نہ آ سکے

irresistible (-*zis*-) *adj*. very attractive بہت دلکش that which cannot be resisted ناقابلِ مزاحمت overpowering بہت زور دار **irresistibly** *adv*. extremely بہت، بے انتہا

irresolute (i-*rez*-o-loot) *adj*. wavering مذبذب غیر مستقل مزاج، متلون مزاج **irresolutely** *adv*. hesitatingly تذبذب سے **irresolution** (i-rez-o-*loo*-shen) *n*. being irresolute غیر مستقل مزاجی، تذبذب، بے استقلالی

irresolvable (-*zol*-) *adj*. that which cannot be solved ناقابلِ حل

irrespective (i-res-*pek*-tiv) *adj*. regardless (*of*) بلا لحاظ (کے)، (سے) قطع نظر **irrespectively** *adv*. not in order (*of* the aforesaid) بے ترتیب regardless (*of*) (سے) قطع نظر

irresponsible (-*pon*-) *adj*. not accountable (*for*) (سے) بری الذمہ، غیر ذمہ دار، not responsible غیر ذمہ دارانہ **irresponsibility** *n*. carelessness بے پروائی، غیر ذمہ داری، لاابالی پن

irresponsive (i-res-*pon*-siv) *adj*. not responsive (*to*) (کے) غیر موافق، (سے) غیر ہم آہنگ

irretrievable (i-re-*treev*-a-bel) *adj*. (of loss etc.) which cannot be retrieved ناقابلِ تلافی (of step) which cannot be retraced قدم، جو واپس نہ اٹھایا جا سکے **irretrievably** *adv*. ناقابلِ تلافی طور پر **irretrievability** *n*. being irretrievable ناقابلِ تلافی ہونا

irreverence *n*. (see under **irreverent**)

irreverent (-*rev*-) *adj*. disrespectful گستاخ، بے ادب having no respect for holy things احترام سے خالی **irreverently** *adv*. بے حرمتی سے، بے ادبی سے، گستاخانہ **irreverence** *n*. being irreverent بے حرمتی، بے ادبی گستاخی

irreversible (-*ve**s*-) *adj*. (of decision, etc.) unalterable جو بدل نہ سکے، اٹل that cannot be reversed جو اُلٹ نہ سکے

irrevocable (i-*rev*-o-ka-bel) *adj*. (decision, etc.) which cannot be revoked اٹل، ناقابلِ تنسیخ **irrevocably** *adj*. (settled) beyond recall اٹل صورت میں **irrevocability** (-*bil*-) *n*. being unalterable اٹل ہونا

irrigable *adj*. (see under **irrigate**)

irrigate (*i*-ri-gayt) *v.t*. supply (land, crop) with water کھیت یا فصل کو پانی دینا، آبپاشی کرنا، آبیاری کرنا wash out (wound, etc.) or moisten (it) continually to disinfect (زخم وغیرہ) دھونا صفائی کے لیے مسلسل گیلا رکھنا **irrigable** *adj*. (of land) that which can be irrigated جس میں آبپاشی ہو سکے **irrigation** *n*. act of irrigating or being irrigated پانی دینا، آبپاشی، آبیاری *irrigation system*, system of canals, etc. نظامِ آبپاشی *Irrigation Department* محکمہ انہار

irritate (*i*-ri-tayt) *v. t*. annoy, vex برہم کرنا، تنگ کرنا، پریشان کرنا، دق کرنا enrage غصہ دلانا، برافروختہ کرنا make (part of the body) sore سوزش پیدا کرنا excite (it) ہیجان میں لانا **irritable** (*i*-) *adj*. easily irritated چڑچڑا، زود رنج، تنک مزاج، جلد غصے میں آجانے والا

irritant (*i*-ri-*tant*) *n*. & *adj*. (thing) causing irritation ہیجان میں لانے والا **irritability** (-*bil*-) being irritable چڑچڑاپن، تنک مزاجی **irritating** (-*tayt*-) *n*. annoying برہم کرنے والا causing soreness سوزش پیدا کرنے والا **irritation** *n*. annoyance جھلاہٹ soreness جلن excitement ہیجان

-ise (īz) *suf*. wrong form of *-ize* in general use in Britain ; (see **ize**)

-ish *suf*. (making adjectives) (with colours) rather, somewhat *greenish*, ہرا سا، سبز سا somewhat بوڑھا سا *oldish* سا، کچھ قدرے suitable for بچوں کا سا، *childish* طفلانہ

island (*i*-land) *n.* piece of land surrounded by water جزیرہ anything detached from surrounding بالکل الگ تھلگ جگہ **islander** *n.* native of an island جزیرے کا باشندہ ، جزائری **isle** (il) *n.* (lit. except in proper names) island جزیرہ *the British Isles* جزائرِ برطانیہ **islet** (i-let) *n.* small island چھوٹا جزیرہ ، ٹاپو

¹**ism** (izm) *n.* any distinctive doctrine in which people believe نظریہ ، عقیدہ *various isms*, various doctrines مختلف عقائد یا نظریات

²**-ism** (izm) *suf.* (making abstract nouns) state or quality یت ، ی *heroism* بہادری system of thought یت *Communism* اشتمالیت nouns from verbs ending in *ize* or *ise*, (کوئی خاص لاحقہ نہیں) *criticism* تنقید

isn't (*iz*-ènt) *v.* (3rd person sing. of the pr. from the v. *to be*, which see) نہیں ہے

isobar (*ī*-so-bah*) *n.* line on map joining places with same atmospheric pressure at a particular time مساوی دباؤ والے مقامات کو ملانے والا خط

isosceles (i-*sos*-e-leez) *adj.* (of triangle) having two sides equal متساوی الساقین

isolate (*ī*-so-layt) *v. t.* separate (*from* others) سے علیحدہ کرنا ، سے الگ تھلگ کرنا **isolated** *adj.* separated الگ تھلگ solitary (case, etc.) اکا دکا ، اکا دکا **isolation** (-*lay*-) *n.* act of isolating or being isolated علیحدگی **isolationist** *n.* one who believes that his country should keep aloof from the affairs of others بین الاقوامی معاملات میں ملکی علیحدگی کا حامی

isotherm (*ī*-so-thĕ*m) *n.* line joining on map places of equal annual temperature خطِ ہم تپشی

issue (*is*-yew) *v. t.* & *i.* come out (*from*) نکلنا ، باہر نکلنا send out (thing, orders, etc.) نکلنا ، جاری کرنا publish (books, etc.) شائع کرنا give currency to (notes, etc.) جاری کرنا end (*in*) پر منتج ہونا *n.* coming or flowing out نکلنا ، اخراج outcome نتیجہ edition (*of* a periodical) شمارہ ، نمبر ، ایڈیشن *special issue* خاص نمبر ، خاص اشاعت ، اشاعتِ خصوصی *Id issue* عید نمبر children, offspring اولاد ، بچے *issueless*, *without issue* بے اولاد problem, point of contention مسئلہ ، سوال *the point at issue* مسئلہ زیر بحث *debate* (or *discuss*) *an issue* کسی مسئلے پر بحث کرنا *join issue with* (*someone on some point*), argue with (him about it) کسی سے کسی مسئلے پر بحث کرنا sending out (*of* new coins, postage stamps, etc.) (نوٹوں ، سکوں ، ٹکٹوں وغیرہ کا) اجرا

-**ist** (ist) *suf.* (making nouns which denote person concerned with والا *tobacconist* تمباکو والا player of a musical instrument والا ، نواز *violinist* وائلن والا ، وائلن نواز

isthmus (*is*-mus, *isth*-mus) *n.* narrow neck of land joining two larger portions of land خاکنائے

it *pron.* (personal pron., 3rd person nominative and accusative cases) (possessive case *its*, pr. *its*; pl. nominative *they*; accusative *them*; genitive *their*, but when without the possessed object or when used predicatively, *theirs*; reflexive *itself*, pl. *themselves*) the thing (or person) in question یہ ، وہ (regular substitute of noun) یہ ، وہ *It is a book* یہ کتاب ہے (subject of impersonal verbs), (no translation except that of the obvious subject) (کوئی ترجمہ نہیں) *It rains* بارش ہو رہی ہے (vague object), (no translation, or translation of the likely object wherever possible) (یا کوئی ترجمہ نہیں یا مشکلہ مفعول کا ترجمہ) *Give it him hot* reprimand or punish him اس کی خوب گت بناؤ (subjunctive, anticipating deferred subjunctive), (no translation) (کوئی ترجمہ نہیں) *It is but natural that he should* , he would naturally.... قدرتی بات ہے کہ وہ (antecedent to relative pronoun of any gender or person) ہی *It was the Germans who were defeated* جرمنوں ہی کو شکست ہوئی (predicate) ہی *Thus weeping, you are it* یوں رو بھی ہی ہے یوں رونے میں بھی تو تمہی تم ہو *n.* (colloq.) sex-appeal جنسی کشش

italic (i-*tal*-ik) *adj.* of ancient Italy قدیم اطالیہ کا (of type) sloping (now used for emphasis or for marking off foreign words) ترچھا ، آڑا (*pl.*) (abb. *ital.*) italic type اٹیلکس ، ترچھا ٹائپ **italicize** (i-*tal*-i-siz) *v. t* print in italics ترچھے حروف میں چھاپنا

itch (ich) *n* tickling irritation in the skin خارش ، کھجلی disease causing similar sensation کھجلی ، خارش restless desire (*for* or *to do* something) (کی) سخت خواہش ، چل *v. i.* have a tickling irritation کھجانا ، کھجلی ہونا ، خارش ہونا long (*for* or *to do* something) (کی) سخت خواہش ہونا **itchy** (*ich*-i) *adj.* having such sensation خارشی

item (*ī*-tem) *n.* separate article in a list, etc. شق *items on the agenda* بحث کے پروگرام کی شقیں its entry in an account, etc. اندراج (usu. *news item*) piece of news *adv.* also (formerly used to introduce an item) نیز **itemize** (*ī*-tè-miz) *v. t.* write out (something) item by item ایک ایک کرکے لکھنا

iterate (*it*-è-rayt) *v. t.* say again and again بار بار کہنا ، دہرانا **iteration** (-*ray*-) *n.* repetition دہرانا ، اعادہ

itinerate (i-*tin*-è-rayti, i-*tin*-è-rayt) *v. i.* journey from place to place دورہ کرنا ، سفر کرنا ، چکر لگانا (کا)

itinerant (i-*tin*-, or i-*tin*-) *adj*. *n*. (one) going from place to place سفر کرنے والا ، مسافر، سیّاح
itinerary (i-*tin*-, or i-*tin*-) *n*. record of travel سفر نامہ ، سیاحت نامہ guide-book رہبر راہنما کتاب) route راستہ *adj*. of travelling سفری ، مسافرانہ of roads راستوں کے متعلق
-itis (i-tis) *suf*. (making name of disease characterized by inflammation of the part mentioned) ورم زائدہ ، سوزشِ زائدہ *appendicitis* لاحقہ بمعنے التہاب سوزش
its, itself *pron*. (see under **it**)
-ity (i-ti) *suf*. (making abstract nouns from adjectives) لاحقہ (ی ، یت) *laxity*
ivory (i-vè-ri) *n*. hard white substance forming tusks of elephants, etc. ہاتھی دانت ، عاج its colour ; white سفیدی (slang) teeth دانت *adj*. of (or like) ivory ہاتھی دانت کا سا **ivory tower**, shelter from the hard facts of life زندگی کی تلخیوں سے بچنے کا محفوظ مقام
ivy (i-vi) *n*. climbing evergreen plant آئیوی *ivy-clad*, covered with ivy آئیوی پوش
-ize, ise (iz) *suf*. (forming verbs denoting make or become) فعل بنانے کے لیے لاحقہ *centralize* مرکزیت قائم کرنا

J

j, J (jay) (pl. *j's* or *js*) tenth letter of the English alphabet (Its Urdu equivalent is (ج) *J pen*, pen with a broad-pointed nib موٹے نب والا قلم
jab *v. t.* (-bb-) aim a blow (*at*) گھونسا مارنا thrust (elbow or a pointed weapon) (*at*) suddenly and roughly بھونکنا ، گھونپنا ، مارنا *n*. such blow گھونسا ، ضرب
jabber (*jabĕ**) *v.t.* & *i*. talk fast and indistinctly in excitement بڑبڑانا ، جوش میں بڑبڑ کرنا *n*. confused talk شور ، بکواس ، بڑبڑ
jack (jak) *n*. machine for raising heavy objects (like cars, etc.) from below اونچا کرنے کی کل ، جیک wedge پچھانا leather vessel for liquor, etc. paltry fellow حقیر آدمی ، ایرا غیرا نتھو خیرا place for resting wood on it while sawing, etc. لکڑی چیرنے کی گھوڑی ، اڈا ship's flag showing nationality جہاز کا قومیت ظاہر کرنے والا پرچم *Union Jack*, British national flag برطانوی پرچم ، Union Jack یونین جیک ، برطانوی پرچم یونین جیک familiar form of the name John جیک ، جیکی the knave of playing-cards غلام **Jack and Jill** *n*. lad and lass لڑکا ، لڑکی **jack-ass** *n*. male ass گدھا fool بیوقوف ، گدھا **jack-knife** *n*. large pocket knife بڑا چاقو **Jack-in-office** *n*. fussy official, بیکار اعتراض کرنیوالا اہلکار **jack-o-lantern** *n*. will-o'-the-wisp غول بیابانی **jack-of-all-trades** *n*. person knowing something of many trades ہر فن مولا **jack-in-the-box** *n*. toy figure springing up in box when lid is released بچوں کا ایک کھلونا ، ڈبے کا بھتنا ، غول صندوق

a jack-knife

a jack-in-the-box

jackal (*jak*-awl) *n*. a dog-like wild animal گیدڑ ، شغال
jacket (*jak*-et) *n*. short coat like the one usu. worn alone or in a suit by either sex کرتی loose paper cover (of a book) (کتاب کا) گرد پوش any outer covering (of potato or boiler) غلاف
jade (jayd) *n*. a (green) precious stone یشب ، ایک قسم کا قیمتی پتھر tired horse تھکا ہوا گھوڑا wench چھنال ، فاحشہ **jaded** *adj*. tired, weary تھکا ماندہ
jaeger (*jayg*-ĕ*) *n*. pure woollen fabric خالص اونی مال
jag *n*. sharp projection (of rock, etc.) چٹان وغیرہ کی نوک **jagged, jaggy** *adj*. (rock, etc.) with sharp, uneven edges نوکیلے کونوں والا
jaggery (*jag*-è-ri) *n*. coarse brown sugar دیسی شکر ، گڑ ، شکر سرخ
jaguar (*ya*-gwa*) *n*. leopard-like South American animal جگوار

A jaguar

jail (jayl) *n*. (same as **gaol**, which see)
jam *v. t.* & *i.* (-mm-) ❶ (of brakes, etc. squeeze or be squeezed tightly جکڑنا ، جکڑا جانا ، جام ہونا ❷ crush or be crushed (*between* flat surfaces) (جیسے چکی کے پاٹوں میں) کچلنا یا کچلا جانا ❸ pack tightly (*in* or *into*) ٹھونسنا ، گھسیڑنا ❹ cut into (another wireless station) for interrupting reception from it with a noise (پروگرام) جام کرنا ❺ block (traffic, place, passage, etc.) ہجوم سے روکنا یا بند کرنا *n*. ❶ crowd ہجوم ❷ blocking (with crowd) ہجوم سے روکنا یا بند ہونا ❸ (of machine or its parts inability to move جام ہونا ❹ preserved and jellied fruit مربہ ، جام
jamb (jam) *n*. side post of door, etc. دروازے کھڑکی آتشدان وغیرہ کا بازو ، پاکھا
jamboree (jam-boh-*ree*) *n*. ❶ Boy Scouts' large rally بڑی سکاوٹ ریلی ، جمبوری ❷ (slang) merry making رنگ رلیاں
jangle (*jang*-ĕl) *n*. ❶ harsh metallic noise (

bells, etc.) ٹن ٹن noisy argument جھگڑا، تکرار *n.* emit a harsh metallic sound ٹن ٹن کرنا ، جھنجھنانا wrangle جھگڑنا تکرار کرنا

janitor (*jan*-i-tĕ*) *n.* doorkeeper دربان

January (*jan*-ew-ĕ-ri) *n.* the first month of the Christian calendar (with 31 days) عیسوی سال کا پہلا مہینہ ، جنوری

Janus (*jay*-nus) *Cl. myth.* the two faced Roman god of beginnings (esp. of doors and gates) after whom the month *January* is named جینس

japan (ja-*pan*) *n.* hard varnish سخت وارنش، جاپان *v. t.* & *i.* (-nn-) lacquer with japan جاپان پھیرنا ، سخت وارنش کرنا

jape (jayp) (lit.) *n.* jest مذاق *v. i.* jest مذاق کرنا

jar (jah*) *v. t.* & *i.* (-rr-) strike (*on* or *against* something) with an unpleasant sound کرخت آواز سے لگنا have an unpleasant effect (*on* one, or *on* one's ears or nerves) (کو) ناگوار گزرنا ، ایسی آواز جس سے جھرجھری آجائے be out of harmony (*with*) سے ہم آہنگ نہ ہونا *n.* jarring sound ناگوار آواز shock دھچکا، صدمہ thrill جھرجھری quarrel جھگڑا، تکرار disagreement بے آہنگی awkward situation مخمصہ tall round vessel with or without handles مرتبان

jargon (*jah**-gun) *n.* debased language which is hard to understand غلط سلط بولی ، گھپڑ سپڑ language (of a profession) full of its technical terms (اوزاروں وغیرہ) کی بولی ، (مخصوص پیشے کی) بولی (یا) اصطلاحات

jasmin, jasmine, jessamin, jessamine (*jas*-(ĕ)-min) *n.* a shrub with white or yellow flowers چنبیلی، یاسمین، یاسمن

Jason (*jay*-sun) *Cl. myth.* the leader of the *Argonauts* who, with the help of Princess Medea, brought the Golden Fleece from Colchis after many adventures جیسن

jato *n.* (see *Addenda*)

jaundice (*jawnd*-is) *n.* disease that turns skin yellow یرقان spiteful outlook حسد، دشمنی، عناد

jaundiced (*jawnd*-isd) *adj.* affected with jaundice یرقان والا، یرقان زدہ jealous and spiteful (eye, outlook, etc.) حاسدانہ، مخاصمانہ such person حاسد

jaunt (jawnt) *n.* ramble سیر گشت، گلگشت pleasure excursion تفریحی سفر **jaunty** (-i) *adj.* airy, self-satisfied, sprightly خوش خوش، خوش باش، زندہ دل **jauntily** *adv.* in a sprightly manner جس کا خوشی سے زمین پر پیر نہ پڑتا ہو

javelin (*jav*-ĕ-lin) *n.* light spear for throwing in sports کھیل کا نیزہ *javelin-throw*, such sports contest نیزہ اندازی (کا مقابلہ)

jaw *n.* (*lower* or *upper*) bone in which teeth are fixed جبڑا (*pl.*) the mouth with bones and teeth منہ ، جبڑے (*pl.*) mouth (of valley, etc.) (وادی وغیرہ کا) دہانہ (*pl.*) gripping part (of vice, etc.) (شکنجے وغیرہ کے) جکڑنے والے حصے، دندانے (*pl.*) entrance to a dangerous place موت کا منہ ، دہن شیر (colloq.) tedious (esp. moral) talk, etc. اکتا دینے والی گفتگو، بکواس، اکتا دینے والا وعظ *hold your jaw*, stop talking بکواس بند کرو *v. t.* & *i.* (colloq.) talk tediously لمبی بکواس کرنا rebuke جھاڑ جھپاڑ کرنا wrangling جھگڑا، تکرار

jay *n.* a noisy bright plumed bird نیل کنٹھ talkative simpleton بکواسی سادہ لوح ، بکے جانے والا الو

a jay

jay-walker *n.* (U. S. colloq.) pedestrian with little regard for traffic rules for own and others' safety بے پروائی سے چلنے والا، آنکھیں میچ کر چلنے والا

jazz (jaz) *n.* loud restless dance-music of U.S. negro origin جاز موسیقی جاز dance to such music جاز ناچ *adj.* (also *jazzy*) loud اونچا inharmonious (colours, or sounds) بے میل، بے سرا، غیر ہم آہنگ انمل بے جوڑ gaudy (colours, etc.) بھڑکیلا burlesque مضحکہ خیز *v. i.* play or dance jazz جاز کی دھنوں پر ساز بجانا یا ناچنا

jealous (*jel*-us) *adj.* resentful (*of* another's success, etc.) حاسد suspicious (*of* spouse's) infidelity (پر) بے وفائی کا شک کرنے والا (یا والی)، بدگمان، غیرت مند، باغیرت watchfully tenacious (*of* rights, etc.) (اپنے حقوق کا) پورا خیال رکھنے والا ، باحمیت *watch with a jealous eye* (کی) کڑی نگہداشت کرنا **jealousy** *n.* being jealous حسد، بدگمانی، غیرت، حمیت

jean (jeen or jayn) *n.* twilled cotton cloth زین (*pl.*) workman's overalls (کاریگروں کا) بالائی لباس، بالا پوشش *blue jeans*, almost close fitting blue jean trousers for ordinary use worn everywhere in the U. S. by both sexes نیلی زین کی پتلون، امریکی قومی پتلون

jeer (*jee*-ĕ*) *v. i.* make mocking remarks (*at*) (پر) فقرے کسنا، (کا) مذاق اڑانا، (پر) پھبتی کہنا *n.* mocking remark مذاق، پھبتی

jeep *n.* (U.S.) small but tough "general purposes" motor vehicle with all the four wheels being worked by the engine ; (the word is derived from the initial sounds of the phrase "general purposes") جیپ کار، جیپ

Jehovah (je-hoh-va) *n.* (name of) God (in the *Old Testament*) اَللّٰہ ، یہوواہ ، خُدا

jejune (je-*joon*) *adj.* poor (diet) خراب (غذا) uninteresting (style, narrative, etc.) بے لُطف ، بے کیف **jejuneness** *n.* being jejune بے لُطفی ، بے کیفی (غذائیت) سے محرُومی

Jekyll (*jek*-il) *n.* (in the phrase :) *Jekyll and Hyde* or *Dr. Jekyll and Mr. Hyde*, double and contrasting personality مُتضاد شخصیّت

jelly (*jel*-i) *n.* semi-transparent food made from gelatine which sets as it cools جَیلی ، لُعاب similar substance made from fruit juice جَیلی ، لُعاب ، پھلوں کا رُب *v. t.* & *i.* (cause to) become like jelly جَیلی بننا یا بنانا ، لُعاب بننا یا بنانا **jelly-fish** *n.* jelly-like sea creature جَیلی مچھلی ، لُعابی مچھلی

jemadar (*jem-*) *n.* Junior Commissioned Officer (J. C. O.) of the lowest rank in the Pakistan Army جمعدار

jemmy (*jem*-i) *n.* burglars' short iron bar for breaking into houses نقب لگانے کا آلہ ، سندھیوا

[1]**jenny** *n.* locomotive crane مُتحرّک جرِ ثقیل

[2]**jenny** (*jen*-i) *n.* **spinning-jenny** *n.* earlier form of spinning machine کاتنے کی پہلے زمانے کی مشین ، کل تکلا

jeopardy (*jep*-ĕ*-di) *n.* danger *in jeopardy* مخدوش ، خطرے میں **jeopardize** *v.t.* endanger (life, service, etc.) خطرے میں ڈالنا

jeremiad (je-re-*mi*-ad) *n.* doleful complaint of times, etc. شکایت روزگار ، دہر آشوب

jerk (jĕ*k) *n.* sudden sharp pull جھٹکا *physical jerks*, physical exercise وَرزِش ، وَرزِش جسمانی *give (someone, etc.) a jerk* جھٹکا لگانا *stop with a jerk* جھٹکے کے ساتھ رُکنا ، یکدم رُکنا *v.t.* & *i.* give a jerk جھٹکا لگانا ، جھٹکا دینا **jerky** *adj.* moving by fits and starts جھٹکوں کے ساتھ چلنے والا (of style) abrupt مُنہ پھٹ (انداز یا اُسلوب)

jerkin (*jĕ**-kin) *n.* (old use) men's close-fitting short leather jacket چمڑے کی صَدری

jerry-built (*je*-ri-bilt) *adj.* (of buildings) flimsy ; built with bad materials (عمارت) بودی (عمارت) ، گھٹیا مسالے والی (عمارت) **jerry-building** *n.* such building بودی عمارت

a jerkin

jerry-builder *n.* builder of such buildings بودی عمارت بنانے والا

jersey (*jĕ**-zi) *n.* close-fitting woollen sweater with sleeves جرسی ، سوئٹر

jest *n.* joke مذاق *in jest*, not in earnest مذاق سے ، یونہی ، ازراہِ مذاق *v. i.* jest مزاح ، مذاق speak lightly تمسخرانہ ، مذاق کہہ دینا **jester** *n.* (esp. professional) joker مسخرا ، بھانڈ **jestingly** *adv.* in jest مذاق ، ازراہِ مذاق

jet *n.* strong stream (of fluid or flame) spouting from small nozzle جٹ ، تیز دھار ، دھارا ، فوّارہ *jet aircraft, jet plane*, aeroplane driven forward by jet of gas directed backwards from it جٹ ہوائی جہاز ، پچھے فوّارے والا ہوائی جہاز ، فوّاری طیّارہ *jet-propelled (engine, aeroplane, etc.)*, one driven by high-speed jet of gas جٹ والا ، فوّاری small nozzle of a jet فوّارے کی ٹُونٹی ، فوّارے کا مُنہ ، ٹونٹی hard black mineral taking a brilliant polish سنگ موسیٰ *adj.* black سیاہ *jet black* کالا سیاہ ، کالا بھجنگ *v. t.* & *i.* (cause to) spurt forth in jet فوّارہ چھوٹنا یا چھوڑنا ، تیز دھار نکلنا یا نکالنا

jetsam (*jet*-sum) *n.* goods thrown overboard at sea to lighten a ship in emergency (جہاز کا بوجھ کم کرنے کے لیے) سمندر میں پھینکا ہوا مال such goods washed to the sea-shore جہاز کا پھینکا ہوا مال جو کنارے آ لگے

jettison (*jet*-i-sun) *v.t.* throw (goods) overboard thus (جہاز کا بوجھ کم کرنے کے لیے) سمندر میں پھینکنا

jettison *v.t.* (see under **jetsam**)

jetty (*jet*-i) *n.* landing-pier بندرگاہ سے جہاز تک جانے والا پُل breakwater to protect harbour or direct sea currents حفاظتی بند

Jew (joo) *n.* male member of the Hebrew race یہودی unscrupulous usurer پکے دل کا سُود خوار *v.t.* (colloq.) cheat ٹھگنا *Jew-baiting*, persecution of Jews یہودیوں پر سخت گیری **Jewess** *n.* a female Jew یہودن **Jewish** *adj.* of or like Jews یہودیوں کا (سا) **Jewry** *n.* the Jews یہودی ، یہود Jewish quarter in town (بستی کا) یہودی علاقہ

jewel (*jew*-el) *n.* precious stone قیمتی پتھر ، نگ ، نگینہ *ornament with jewels*, set jewels in نگ لگانا ، نگ جڑنا ، جواہر جواہرات سے مُرصّع کرنا gold or silver ornament (containing jewels) جڑاؤ زیور ، زیور highly valuable (person or thing) ہیرا ، موتی (term of endearment for children) لال *my jewel* میرا لال

jeweller *n.* trader in jewels جوہری one who sets jewels سُنار ، جڑائی کا کام کرنے والا **jewellery, jewelry** (-ri-) *n.* jewels جواہرات gold or silver ornaments (with jewels set in them) زیور ، زیورات

jib *v.t.* (-bb-) (of a horse, etc.) stop suddenly and refuse to go forward اڑ جانا refuse to proceed with something اڑ جانا *jib at*, dislike (something) ناپسند کرنا

jibe (jib) *n.* & *v.i.* (same as **gibe**, which see)

jiffy (*jif*-i) *n.* (used only in the colloq. phrase) *in a giffy*, in a moment ابھی ، ایک منٹ میں

jig *n.* a lively dance اَلبیلا ناچ ، مستانہ رقص music for it مستانہ وار رقص کی دُھن *v.t.* & *i.* (-gg-) dance up

and down in a lively manner تو پڑے لینا، مستانہ وار رقص کرنا
jig-saw *n.* (U.S.) machine fret-saw لکڑی میں بیل بوٹے کاٹنے کا چھوٹا سا مشینی آرہ **jig-saw puzzle** *n.* picture, etc., pasted on board and cut in irregular pieces to be fitted together again آرے کا معمّا *solve a jig-saw puzzle*, fit its parts together آرے کا معمّا حل کرنا
jilt *v.t.* discard encouraged lover دغوی، عورت کا بیوفائی کرنا *n.* woman who treats her lover thus شادی کا اقرار کرکے پھر جانا بے وفا محبوب
jingle (*jing*-èl) *n.* tinkling sound (as of keys, coins, etc.) جھنکار، چھن چھن، چھنا کا *v.t.* & *i.* tinkle جھنکارنا *jingling rhymes*, (in poetry) succession of words having similar sounds بہت ملتے جلتے قافیے
jingo (*jing*-oh) *n.* (*pl. jingoes*), extreme patriot supporting a warlike policy جنگجو، وطن پرست **jingoism** *n.* such patriotism جنگجویانہ وطن پرستی **jinnee** *n.* (pl. *jinn*, also used as singular) (in Arabic folklore) spirit able to appear in human and animal forms جن، بھوت، دیو
jitney (*jit*-ni) *n.* bus carrying passengers at cheap rates سستی بس
jitters (*jit*-ē*z) *n. pl.* (slang) (in the phrase :) *have the jitters*, be panicky حواس باختہ ہونا، اوسان خطا ہونا **jittery** (*jit*-è-ri) *adj.* nervous گھبرا جانے والا **jitterling** *n.* nervous person who goes about spreading alarm خود گھبرا کر دوسروں کا حوصلہ بھی پست کرنے والا enthusiast for violent type of dancing to jazz music تیز جاز ناچ کا شائق
jiu-jitsu *n.* (same as **ju-jitsu** which see)
job *n.* piece of work کام *bad job* (*a*) hopeless task مایوس کن کام (*b*) bad state of affairs بری صورت حال *good job*, good state of affairs اچھی صورت حال *make a good job of it*, do it well بہت اچھا کام کرنا *odd jobs*, bits of work not connected with each other پھٹکل کام، متفرق کام *job work*, not regular work پھٹکل کام، متفرق کام (colloq.) regular employment نوکری، ملازمت، کام *out of a job*, unemployed بیکار *looking for a job*, in search of it نوکری کے لیے مارا مارا پھر رہا، نوکری کی تلاش میں (*Job*) a prophet حضرت ایوب *Job's comforter*, one who increases distress by his consolations ایوب کا دوست *Job's patience*, extreme patience صبر ایوب *v.t.* & *i.* (-bb-) do odd jobs for more than one employer کئی جگہ کام کرنا *jobbing employee* کئی جگہ کام کرنے والا ملازم be a broker دلالی کرنا **jobber** *n.* broker دلال one engaged in a mean lucrative affair گھٹیا کام کرنے والا (esp.) one who turns official actions to private advantage بدعنوان، رشوت ستان **jobbery** *n.* corruption بدعنوانی، رشوت ستانی

[S] **A job** is a specific piece of work to be done ; it also signifies a position or post : **employment**, work or position : **work** is anything done seriously which implies a resistance : **craft**, a skilled trade ; **pursuit**, line of endeavour either as work or play ; **calling**, chosen life-work, esp. a noble one: **vocation**, life-work, esp. one indicated by native ability ; **avocation**, side-line of work, done because it interests ; **occupation**, anything done to pass the time, seriously or otherwise ; **trade**, work of exchange and barter, often used also for a craft : **profession**, a white-collar job often requiring a liberal training, as a doctor's, lawyer's.

Jocasta (joh-*kas*-ta) *Cl. myth.* wife and queen of Oedipus جکاستہ
jockey (*jok*-i) *n.* professional race horse rider جاکی، جوکی *v.t.* & *i.* trick (someone *out of* a post, place, etc.) دھوکے سے نکالنا trick (someone *into doing* something) دھوکے سے کام لینا
jocose (jo-*kohz*) *adj.* humorous ہنسی کا ❷ given to joking ہنسوڑ، دل لگی باز **jocosely** *adv.* ہنسی سے
jocular (*jok*-ew-le*) *adj.* humorous ہنسی کا، ظریفانہ given to joking ہنسوڑ، دل لگی باز **jocularity** (-*la*-) *n.* being jocular دل لگی، باز ہونا، ہنسوڑ ہونا **jocularly** *adv.* ہنسی سے
jocund (jo-*kund*) *adj.* jovial, cheerful خوش خوش، خوش باش، زندہ دلانہ
jodhpurs (johd-*poo*z*) *n. pl.* long riding breeches tight from ankle to knee برجس
jog *n.* slight push ٹھوکا weary trot causing unsteady motion گرتے پڑتے چلنا *v.t.* & *i.* (-gg-) nudge متوجہ کرنے کے لیے کہنی مارنا، ٹھوکا دینا move wearily and shakily (*along a road*, or *up and down*) گرتے پڑتے جانا (of coach, etc.) shake passengers thus گاڑی کا ہچکولے دینا *jog along*, *jog on*, make slow and uneventful progress یونہی ڈگمگاتے جانا
joggle (*jog*-èl) *n.* slight jerk ہچکولے *v.t.* & *i.* move to and fro with slight jerks ہچکولے دینا یا کھانا
John Bull (jon-*būl*) *n.* nickname for the English people (as distinct from *Uncle Sam* for the Americans) جان بل typical Engishman جان بل **John Company** *n.* nickname of the East India Company کمپنی بہادر، ایسٹ انڈیا کمپنی، جان کمپنی
johnny (*jon*-i) *n.* (colloq.) fellow شخص، آدمی fashionable idler بھڑکا فیشنیبل، بانکے خان **Johnny Raw** *n.* novice اناڑی
join *v.t.* & *i.* connect (two points, things) with a bridge, etc. کے ذریعے ملانا put or come together (*with* or *to*) کے ساتھ جوڑنا یا جڑنا unite (*in* action, etc.) سے مل کر کام کرنا come into the company of سے آملنا یا، جاملنا، میں، شامل ہونا become

a member of (society, army, etc. میں شامل ہونا *join up*, enlist in the army فوج میں بھرتی ہونا ، کارکن ہونا *join hands*, (*a*) clasp one's hands ہاتھ پہ ہاتھ باندھنا (*b*) clasp each other's hands ایک دوسرے کا ہاتھ پکڑنا *join hands with* (*someone*), unite in action with him سے مل کر کام کرنا *n*. point of junction جوڑ **joiner** *n*. maker of furniture and light woodwork فرنیچر بنانے والا ، لکڑی کا فرنیچر بنا ہلکا کام کرنے والا **joinery** *n*. such work لکڑی کا ہلکا کام

■ To **join** is to put end to end or to put very closely together ; to **unite**, by making one ; to **unify**, by making like one ; to **combine**, put together with each element keeping its identity ; to **associate** for work together in friendly fashion ; to **consolidate**, for greater strength ; to **amalgamate**, each losing its identity ; to **coalesce**, become solidly one as if nourished from the same root.

joint *n*. place where things join جوڑ structure by which they join جوڑ large piece of meat cut for roasting گوشت کا بڑا ٹکڑا *adj*. of two or more مشترکہ ، مشترک *joint stock*, capital contributed by a number of persons مشترکہ سرمایہ *joint stock company*, such firm مشترکہ سرمایہ کی کمپنی *v.t*. fit together by means of joints جوڑ لگانا cut (piece of meat, etc.) at the joints جوڑوں پر سے کاٹ کر ٹکڑے ٹکڑے کرنا

jointure (*join*-chĕ*) *n*. estate settled on wife to be enjoyed by her during her life after husband's death وثیقۂ زوجہ *v.t*. settle a jointure بیوی کے نام وثیقہ لکھنا

joist *n*. beam supporting a wooden floor لکڑی کے فرش کی کڑی یا شہتیر

joke (johk) *n*. jest مذاق ، ہنسی *play a practical joke on* (*someone*), play a trick on him to make him seem ridiculous عملی مذاق کرنا *practical joke* مذاق کی حرکت ، عملی مذاق *it's no joke*, it's a serious matter مذاق تھوڑے ہی ہے ، مذاق تھوڑی ہے *surely you joke*, کیوں ہنستے ہو ؟ ، چل جھوٹے ، جھوٹا کہیں کا 'bon mot' چٹکلا ، لطیفہ *v.i*. jest (*with*) مذاق کرنا ، دل لگی کرنا **joker** *n*. jester ; one who jokes or adopts joking as a profession مسخرا highest trump card in a game besides the ordinary 52 cards جوکر **jokingly** *adv*. by way of joke ; jestingly تمسخر سے

jolly (*jol*-i) *adj*. gay زندہ دل ، خوش باش pleasant (time, etc.) مزے کا ، خوشی کا (colloq. even ironically) big بڑا ، بہت **jollification** *n*. feasting and merrymaking دعوتیں اور رنگ رلیاں **jollity** *n*. jolly condition خوشی fun دل لگی

jolt (johlt) *n*. sudden shake (of a coach, etc.) ہچکولا *v.t*. & *i*. (of a coach, etc.) move (*along*) with jolts ہچکولے کھاتے ہوئے جانا cause jolts to passengers مسافروں کو ہچکولے دینا

josh (josh) (U. S. slang). *n*. good-natured joke خوش دلی کا مذاق *v.t*. & *i*. ridicule مذاق اڑانا

jostle (*jos*-ĕl) *v.t*. & *i*. push roughly (*against*) سے ٹکرانا push (someone *away*) کو دھکا دینا struggle (*with* someone *for* something) (کسی کو) دھکا دے کر (کچھ) چھیننے کی کوشش کرنا ، (کسی سے کوئی چیز چھیننے کے لیے) زور آزمائی کرنا

jot *v.t*. (-tt-) write (*down* something) hurriedly جلدی سے (کچھ) لکھنا *n*. very small amount ذرہ ، ذرہ بھر ، ذرا سا *not a jot*, not at all ذرہ سا بھی نہیں ، بالکل نہیں

journal (*jĕ**-nĕl) *n*. daily newspaper روزنامہ other periodical اخبار ، رسالہ diary روزنامچہ اخبار *keep journal* (or *diary*) اپنا روزنامچہ لکھنا record of daily accounts روزانہ آمد و خرچ کا بہی کھاتہ **journalize** (-lĭz) *v.t*. & *i*. enter transaction in journal بہی میں درج لکھنا **journalism** (-izm) *n*. work of writing or editing newspapers صحافت ، اخبار نویسی work of publishing them اخبار نویسی **journalist** (-ist *n*. person engaged in journalism اخبار نویس ، صحافی *working journalist*, one engaged there as a regular employee مزدور صحافی ، کارکن صحافی ، ملازم اخبار نویس ، پیشہ ور صحافی *freelance journalist*, *freelance*, journalist working on his own and contributing articles to be paid for آزاد صحافی **journalistic** (-*lis*-) *adj*. (style, etc.) of newspapers صحافتی **journalese** (jĕ*-na-*leez*) *n*. journalistic jargon صحافتی اصطلاحات ، صحافتی زبان style of composition common in second-rate papers اخباری زبان

journey (*jĕ**-ni) *n*. (pl. **journies**) travel (usu. by land) سفر *make* (or *go on*) *a journey from, to* (سے ، تک) کا سفر کرنا distance traversed (*from, to*) (سے ، کی) مسافت ، (کا) سفر یا فاصلہ *a four days' journey* چار روز کی مسافت *v.i*. make a journey (*from, to, across* a place) (سے ، کا یا میں سے) سفر کرنا **journeyman** *n*. qualified artisan working for another کسی کاریگر کی نوکری کرنے والا کاریگر mere hireling بھاڑے کا ٹٹو

joust (joost), **just** (jŭst) *n*. sporting combat with lances (between knights on horseback) اسپ سوار ، بانکوں میں نیزہ بازی کا مقابلہ ، شہ سوار فوج داروں کی نیزہ بازی

jovial (*joh*-vi-ĕl) *adj*. gay (person, time, mood, etc.) ہنس مکھ ، خوش مزاج ، خوش مزاجی کا **jovially** *adv*. gaily خوش مزاجی سے **joviality** (-*al*-i-ti) *n*. gaiety خوش طبعی ، خوش مزاجی

Jove (johv) *Cl. myth*. same as **Jupiter** sense 1. which see)

jowl (joul) *n*. jaw-bone جبڑا ، جبڑے کی ہڈی *cheek by jowl*, very intimate بہت قریبی

joy (joi) *n.* deep pleasure بڑی خوشی، شادمانی its cause موجبِ مسرت، وجہِ شادمانی **joyful** *adj.* happy خوش، مسرور، شادمانی pleasing خوش کن، مسرت آفریں **joy-less** *adj.* sad غمگین **joylessly** *adv.* sadly غم سے **joyous** (*joi*-us) *adj.* full of joy خوش، مسرور، شادماں
jubilate (*joob*-i-layt) *v.i.* show joy, exult خوشی منانا **jubilant** *adj.* full of joy ; very happy شاداں و فرحاں **jubilation** (*-lay-*) *n.* exultation خوشی منانا، مسرت
jubilee (joob-i-lee) *n.* year of emancipation kept by Jews every 50 years یومِ نجات، یہودیوں کا ہر پچاس برس کے بعد جشن (also *golden jubilee*), celebrations on the 50th anniversary of anything جوبلی، گولڈن جوبلی، پنجاہ سالہ جشنِ مسرت، جشنِ زریں۔ *silver jubilee*, such celebrations on something's completion of 25 years of its life سلور جوبلی، جشنِ سیمیں *diamond jubilee*, such celebrations at the end of 60 years ڈائمنڈ جوبلی، جشنِ الماسی
judge (juj) *n.* legal officer presiding over a court of law جج، منصف، قاضی *sub-judge*, judge of a junior court منصف *Chief Justice*, chief presiding officer of a High Court or Supreme Court چیف جسٹس، قاضی القضاة *District and Sessions Judge*, a judge with authority to decide murder cases سیشن جج one appointed to decide on sporting events, debates, etc. جج، فیصلہ دینے والا one qualified to judge merits (*of*) کی سمجھ رکھنے والا، کی پرکھ والا *v.t.* & *i.* act as a judge in a court of law جج کرنا give a verdict (in a legal case or competition) فیصلہ سنانا form an opinion about کے بارے میں اندازہ لگانا، کے متعلق رائے قائم کرنا *judge a man by his actions* کسی شخص کے متعلق اس کے کردار سے اندازہ لگانا **judgement, judgment** (*juj*-ment) *n.* judging or being judged فیصلہ decision of a judge فیصلہ، حکم good sense to judge تمیز، عقل، سمجھ، بصیرت، عقلِ سلیم estimate اندازہ misfortune regarded as a punishment by God قدرت کی طرف سے سزا *a judgement on someone* کسی کو قدرت کی طرف سے سزا **judgement seat** *n.* seat from which judgement is pronounced کرسیِ عدالت **judgement day** *n.* day of final judgement on humanity قیامت، یومِ جزا و سزا، یوم الدین **judgeship** *n.* office of a judge جج کا عہدہ، ججی، قضائت
judicature (*joo*-di-kay-chě*) *n.* all the judges and law officers of a country ملک کے جملہ جج sytem of courts نظامِ عدالت their work عدل و انصاف
judicial (joo-*dish*-ěl) *adj.* of or by a law-court عدالتی concerning judges ججوں سے متعلق
judiciary (joo-*dish*-è-ri) *n.* judges of a country collectively کسی ملک کے تمام جج، قضاة judicial system (as distinct from the executive and the legislature) نظامِ عدالت، عدلیہ
judicious (joo-*dish*-us) *adj.* (person) with good sense معاملہ فہم (affair, etc.) showing good sense مدبرانہ **judiciously** *adv.* with good sense معاملہ فہمی سے، تدبر سے **judiciousness** *n.* being judicious, showing good sense معاملہ فہمی، تدبر
Judith (*joo*-dith) *n.* name of the ancient Jewish heroine who went to the tent of Holofernes, the Assyrian besieger of her city, and charming him with her beauty and pretence of love, found an opportunity of assassinating him in his sleep جوڈیتھ، یہودیت
jug (jug) *n.* deep vessel for liquids with handle and lip جگ، قرابہ
juggernaut (*jug*-ě*-nawt) *n.* Hindu god Krishna's idol dragged yearly in Orissa (India) in a procession on car under the wheels of which devotees willingly got themselves crushed to death جگن ناتھ، جگنات any superstition to which devotees sacrifice themselves ایسا وہم جس کے لیے لوگ قربانی دیں، خود خریدا ہوا عذاب *the juggernaut of war* جنگ کا خود خریدا ہوا عذاب
juggle (*jug*-ěl) *v. t.* & *i.* play conjuring tricks شعبدے دکھانا، مداری کا تماشہ کرنا، شیشہ گری کرنا، شعبدہ بازی کرنا play tricks (*with* facts, etc.) in order to misrepresent them جھوٹ سچ ایک کر دکھانا *n.* trick, fraud دھوکا، فریب، شعبدہ **juggler** *n.* conjurer مداری، شعبدہ باز
jugular (*jug*-ew-lě*) *adj.* of the neck گردن کا *jugular vein*, one of the veins carrying blood from the head رگِ گردن، وداج
juice (joos) *n.* liquid part of fruits, meat, etc. رس، رطوبت، عرق *gastric juice*, digestive juice in animal body معدی ترشہ **juicy** (*joo*-si) *adj.* full of juice رس بھرا، رسیلا
ju-jitsu, ju-jutsu, jiu-jitsu (joo-jět-*soo*) *n.* Japanese art of wrestling جاپانی کشتی (کا فن)
Jukebox *n.* see *Addenda*
ju-ju (*joo*-joo) *n.* fetish تو ہمانہ عقیدہ
julep (*joo*-lep) *n.* sweet medicated drink (originally a corruption of جلاب، گلاب دوا والا شربت
July (joo-*lī*) *n.* seventh month of the Christian calendar with 31 days جولائی
jumble (*jum*-běl) *v. t.* & *i.* mix or be mixed up in a confused way مل جل جانا، ملانا، مخلوط کرنا، خلط ملط ہونا یا کرنا، گڈ مڈ ہونا یا کرنا *n.* confused mixture گڈ مڈ، **jumble-sale** *n.* sale for charitable purpose of mixed donations of second-hand articles بیچ مینا خیراتی مقاصد کے لیے پرانے مال کے عطیات کی فروخت

jumbo (*jum*-boh) *n.* (pl. *jumbos*) big clumsy person, animal or thing بھاری بھرکم اور بھدّا شخص (یا جانور یا چیز)

jump (jump) *v. t.* & *i.* pass (*over*) by leaping چھلانگ لگانا، کودنا ، پھلانگنا cause (horse, etc.) to leap کدانا start suddenly from fear چونک اُٹھنا، خوف سے اُچھل پڑنا (of prices, etc.) go *up* suddenly بھاؤ یکایک چڑھ جانا *jump at* (an offer, etc.) accept it eagerly شوق سے اُچھل پڑنا، خوشی سے قبول کرنا، فوراً راضی ہو جانا *jump on* (or *upon someone*), scold (him) (کی) گت بنانا ، (کو) سرزنش کرنا *jump in* (*carriage, etc.*) (گاڑی پر کود کر جلدی سے) سوار ہونا *n.* act of jumping چھلانگ *long jump*, athletic contest of jumping the longest distance لمبی چھلانگ *high jump*, similar contest in height اُونچی چھلانگ sudden movement caused by fear خوف سے اُچھل پڑنا sudden rise (*in* prices, etc.) یکایک چڑھ جانا **jumpy** (*jum*-pi) *adj*. nervous جلدی گھبرا جانے والا، جس کے اوسان یونہی خطا ہو جائیں **jumper** *n.* one who jumps چھلانگ لگانیوالا ، کودنے والا jumping insect اُچھلنے والا کیڑا loose outer jacket worn by workmen مزدوروں کا چولا women's loose jacket slipped on over the head (عورتوں کی) چولی ، جمپر

junction (*junk*-shen) *n.* joining place (also *railway junction*) railway station where many lines converge جنکشن ، مقامِ اتّصال ، اتّصال

juncture (*junk*-chĕ*) *n.* joining اتّصال joining place مقامِ اتّصال ، اتّصال concurrence of events صورتِ حال particular moment خاص مرحلہ ، خاص موقع *at this juncture* اس صورتِ حال میں ، اس خاص مرحلے پر

June (joon) *n.* the sixth month of the Christian calendar (30 days) جون

jungle (*jung*-èl) *n.* thick (esp. tropical) forest جنگل *adj*. of the jungle جنگلی

junior (*joo*-ni-e*)(abb. *Jr.*) *n.* & *adj.* (person) younger (*to*) (سے) چھوٹا (one) with less period of service or lower in rank (*to*) (سے) جونیئر ، (سے) باٹیں

junk (junk) *n.* old things of little or no value کاٹ ، کباڑ ، ردّی مال old riggings of a ship جہاز کے پرانے رسّے وغیرہ Chinese flat-bottomed boat چھوٹا چینی جہاز

Juno (*joo*-no) *Cl. myth.* the Roman goddess identified with the Greek *Hera* جونو

Jupiter (*jewp*-i-tĕ*) *n.* *Cl. myth.* the Roman god of gods identified with the Greek *Zeus* جوپیٹر the largest planet مشتری

junta (*jun*-ta) *n.* clique (esp. political) سیاسی ٹولی *the ruling junta* برسرِ اقتدار ٹولی

juridical (joo-*rid*-i-kĕl) *adj.* legal قانونی of judicial proceedings ضابطہ عدالت کا ، قانونی کارروائی سے متعلق

jurisdiction (joo-ris-*dik*-shĕn) *n.* right to exercise legal authority عدالتی اختیار ، اختیارِ سماعت authority to control حاکمانہ اختیار extent of this دائرۂ اختیار *lie within* (or *come under*) *the jurisdiction* (*of*) (کے) دائرۂ اختیار میں ہونا

jurisprudence (joo-ris-*proo*-dens) *n.* science of law اُصولِ قانون ، اُصولِ فقہ ، اُصول skill in law قانون دانی ، قانونی مہارت ، تفقّہ *medical jurisprudence*, part of medical evidence having to do with law-courts طبِّ قانونی

jurist (joo-rist) *n.* expert in law ماہرِ قانون ، فقیہ

jury (*joo*-ri) *n.* (pl. *juries*) body of persons sworn to render verdict in a law-court جیوری ، جوری ، ارکانِ جوری *serve on jury* جوری کا رکن ہونا *the jury was sworn in* ارکانِ جوری نے حلف اُٹھایا *the judge summed up to the jury* جج نے شہادتوں کا خلاصہ ارکانِ جوری کو سنایا **juror** *n.* member of a jury جوری کا رکن **juryman** *n.* (pl. *jurymen*) member of a jury جوری کا رکن **jury-box** *n.* jury's place in the court جوری خانہ ، جوری گاہ

jussive (*jus*-iv) *adj.* (in grammar) (mood of the verb) expressing command (فعل) امر (فعل) ، نہی

[1]**just** (just) *adv.* exactly بالکل ، ٹھیک *just then* ٹھیک اسی وقت *just opposite* بالکل سامنے *just now*, (*a*) at this moment ابھی (*b*) a little while ago ذرا سی دیر ہوئی ، ابھی ابھی hardly بمشکل ، مشکل ہی سے quite, much بہت only صرف ، بس *just a minute* بس ایک منٹ *adj.* fair انصاف پرور ، منصف مزاج ، عادل ، معدلت گستر impartial, right (decision, etc.) منصفانہ ، انصاف کا honest دیانتدار ، دیانتدارانہ well deserved جائز right (in amount) ٹھیک ، پورا **justly** *adv.* rightly ٹھیک uprightly دیانتدارانہ equitably انصاف سے by right جائز **justness** *n.* being just انصاف ، دیانتداری ، جائز ہونا ، پورا پورا کرنا

justice (*jus*-tis) *n.* equity ; quality of being just عدل ، انصاف just conduct انصاف پروری ، انصاف پروری ، معدلت گستری fairness ٹھیک منصفانہ ہونا ، انصاف پر مبنی ہونا judicial proceeding قانونی کارروائی ، قانون *court of justice* قانونی عدالت judge (of a High or Supreme Court) (عدالت عالیہ کا) جج *Mr. Justice Shabbir Ahmad* مسٹر جسٹس شبیر احمد *Justice Sir Abdul Qadir* جسٹس سر عبدالقادر *Mr. Justice Kayani Chief Justice* چیف جسٹس مسٹر کیانی *Justice of the Peace*, (abb. *J. P.*), country judge in England جسٹس آف دی پیس *Chief Justice*, chief judge of a High or Supreme Court چیف جسٹس ، قاضی القضاۃ *do justice to*, be fair to سے انصاف کرنا *do (oneself) justice*, do to the best of (one's) ability اپنی تمام تر صلاحیت سے انجام دینا *poetical justice*, nature's retribution, etc., as shown in a poem or other piece of writing شعری انصاف ، کتابی انصاف ، خیالی انصاف

[2]**just** (jŭst) *n.* (same as **joust,** which see)

justify (*jus*-ti-fī) *v.t.* show that (someone or something) is right and proper (کا) جواز پیش کرنا، (کی) توجیہ کرنا be a good reason for (*doing* something) (کا) جواز ہونا، (کی) جائز وجہ ہونا adjust line of type to fill a space neatly سطر میں ٹائپ ٹھیک ٹھیک پھیلانا

justifiable (*just*-i-fi-a-bĕl, or just-i-*fī*-a-bĕl) *adj.* that which can be justified جس کا جواز پیش کیا جا سکے، جائز، قابل توجیہ *justifiable homicide,* murder in self-defence جائز قتل، قتل برائے حفظ جان **justification** (just-i-fi-*kay*-shĕn) *n.* justifying توجیہ کرنا، جواز پیش کرنا something that justifies جواز، توجیہ **justifiability** *n.* being justifiable قابل توجیہ ہونا

jut (jut) *v. i.* (-tt-) protrude (*out from*) (سے) باہر کو نکلا ہوا ہونا

jute (joot) *n.* East Pakistan's well-known golden fibre used for ropes, mats, gunnybags, etc. سن، پٹ سن (مشرقی پاکستان کا) ریشۂ زریں (*Jute*), one of a German tribe which conquered Britain and settled there about 15 centuries ago جوٹ

juvenile (*joov*-e-nīl) *n.* young person کم سن، نوعمر، نابالغ *adj.* suitable for juveniles کم سنوں کے لیے، بچوں کے لیے *juvenile books* بچوں کی کتابیں، بچوں کے لیے کتابیں of juveniles کم سنوں کا، کم سنی میں کیا ہوا *juvenile crime,* crime(s) committed by person who have not yet attained majority کم سنی کا جرم، چھوٹی عمر میں کیا ہوا جرم، نابالغوں کے جرائم

juvenility (*-nil-*) **juvenescence** (*-nes-*) *n.* being juvenile کم سنی، نوعمری **juvenescent** (*-nes-*) *adj.* pertaining to juvinescence کم سنی کا، نوعمری کا

juxtapose (*juks*-ta-pohz) *v. t.* put (two things) side by side ایک دوسرے کے مقابلے میں رکھنا، آمنے سامنے رکھنا

juxtaposition (*-zish-*) *n.* placing side by side آمنے سامنے رکھنا being side by side آمنے سامنے ہونا، آمنا سامنا، تقابل *be in juxtaposition with* کے بالمقابل ہونا

K

k, K (kay) (pl. *k's, ks*) eleventh letter of the English alphabet (equivalent to the Urdu ک but with a much sharper sound than it)

kaiser (*kī*-zĕ*) *n.* title of the former German Emperors قیصر

kaleidoscope (ka-*līd*-us-kohp) *n.* children's tube-like toy in which pieces of coloured glass on being rotated make patterns in mirror عکس نما، عکس بین anything that shows a succession of changing aspects گوناگوں شے، ہمیشہ بدلتی رہنے والی چیز

kalends *n.* (same as **calends,** which see)

kangaroo (*kang*-a-roo) *n.* Australian animal with forelegs short and hindlegs very long کنگرو *kangaroo closure,* situation when the chairman of a committee selects only certain clauses and amendments for discussion to the exclusion of others کارروائی مختصر کرنے کے لیے صدر کا یہ حق کہ زیر غور مسئلے کے صرف بعض پہلوؤں کو زیر بحث لانے کی اجازت دے، کنگرو خاتمہ

a kangaroo

keel *n.* main beam at the bottom of ship on which the latter's framework is built up جہاز کے پیندے کا شہتیر *on an even keel,* steady سیدھا، جو ڈانواں ڈول نہ ہو *v. t. & i.* turn (*over*) on one side (جہاز کا) اوندھا ہونا، (جہاز کو) اوندھا کرنا

keen *adj.* sharp (point or edge) تیز، تیز دھار والا، نوک دار biting (wind) سخت سرد (ہوا) alert (mind) تیز، حساس strong (feeling) شدید acute (sight) تیز (of person) eager, (*to do* or *on doing*) (کا) خواہاں، (کا) مشتاق، (کا) آرزومند *n.* Irish funeral song accompanied with wailing سوز خوانی، مرثیہ، بین *v.t. & i.* utter the keen مرثیہ پڑھنا، سوز خوانی کرنا bewail (person) thus بین کرنا **keenly** *adv.* eagerly شوق سے

keenness *n.* خواہش، شوق، رغبت، تیزی، شدت

keep *v. t. & i.* (*keep, kept, kept*) hold رکھنا retain لے لینا، سنبھال کر رکھنا support (oneself, one's family, etc.) کا خرچ چلانا، کا کفیل ہونا fulfil (promise, treaty, etc.) پر عمل کرنا، نبھانا observe (law) پر چلنا، کی پابندی کرنا، کو پورا کرنا، پر عمل کرنا have (servant, pets, lodger) رکھنا (own and) manage (house, shop, etc.) (گھر یا دکان) چلانا celebrate (festival) منانا not to disclose (secret) (راز) مخفی رہنے دینا، ظاہر نہ کرنا defend (goal, etc.) (گول وغیرہ کی) حفاظت کرنا continue (*doing*) کرتے رہنا (of food) continue unspoilt ٹھیک رہنا make entries in (diary, etc.) (روزنامچہ) قلم بند کرنا record (accounts) (حساب) باقاعدہ رکھنا (cause to) continue in a position, direction, place, etc. رہنا یا رکھنا *keep to the left* (or *right*) بائیں یا دائیں ہاتھ رہنا *keep straight* سیدھا چلتے جانا prevent (*from doing*) (سے) روکنا (*Phrases* :) *keep up appearances,* cause things to appear satisfactory while actually they are not صرف ظاہری شان شوکت برقرار رکھنا *keep at* (cause to) work persistently at پر لگے رہنا یا لگائے رکھنا *keep away* (*from doing something*) پرے رہنا یا رکھنا

keep back nothing from, (*a*) conceal nothing from سے کچھ نہ چھپانا (*b*) withhold nothing from پیچھے رہنا، آگے نہ بڑھنا *keep back,* not to advance دریغ نہ کرنا (یا نہ رکھنا) *keep down,* (*a*) hold under دبائے رکھنا (*b*) reduce (expenses) کم رکھنا *keep from,* abstain or prevent from (*doing* something) سے رُکنا یا روکنا *keep in,* (*a*) restrain (one's feelings, etc.) پر قابو پانا (*b*) see that (a fire) continues burning جلتے رکھنا (*c*) confine to (bed) بیماری کے بستر پر پڑے رہنا (*d*) confine (a boy) after school hours لڑکے کو سزا کے طور پر، سکول کے وقت کے بعد بھی روکے رکھنا *keep in with,* remain on good terms with سے تعلقات قائم رکھنا *keep* (*one's*) *hand* (or *eye*) *in,* practice it in order to retain one's skill (کی) مشق برقرار رکھنا *keep off,* (*a*) (cause to) stay at a distance پرے رہنا (*b*) say nothing about (a question, etc.) کے بارے میں کچھ نہ کہنا *keep on* (*doing*), continue (to do it) (کرتے) رہنا *keep on* (*something*), continue to use it رکھنا، رہنے دینا *keep under control,* hold down پر سختی کرنا *keep up,* (*courage, spirits,* etc.), prevent (it) from sinking برقرار رکھنا *keep* (*a correspondence with*) سے خط و کتابت جاری رکھنا *keep* (*something*) *up,* maintain it without slackening برقرار رکھنا، اسی طرح جاری رکھنا *keep up prices* بھاؤ اونچے رہنے دینا *keep up* شان قائم رکھنا *keep up with,* go on at the same rate as کا ساتھ دینا، کی رفتار سے چلنا *keep* (*oneself*), avoid the society of others الگ تھلگ رہنا، حال مست رہنا *keep* (*something*) (*all*) *to* (*oneself*), refuse to share it (کوئی چیز) ساری ہی خود رکھ لینا، (کسی چیز میں) دوسرے کو حصہ دار نہ بننے دینا *keep early hours, keep good hours,* go to bed early and get up early رات کو دیر سے جانا اور صبح سویرے اٹھنا *keep bad hours, keep late hours* رات کو دیر سے سونا اور صبح دن چڑھے اٹھنا *keep pace with,* go at the same rate as کا ساتھ دینا، کی رفتار سے چلنا *keep track of,* keep abreast of what is happening in the field of کی ترقی (یا پیش رفت) سے باخبر رہنا *keep watch* پہرہ دینا *keep watch for,* be on watch for کی تلاش میں رہنا *n.* means of subsistence گزارا، روٹی *work for* (*one's*) *keep* اپنی روٹی کے لیے محنت کرنا *earn* (*one's*) *keep,* اپنی روٹی کمانا *worth* (*one's*) *keep,* worth the money spent on جو جتنا کھائے اس سے زیادہ کام دے

-keeper *n.* curator محافظ (in compounds like *shopkeeper,* etc.) one who looks after والا، دار

keeping *n.* maintenance نگہداشت observance (of custom, etc.) (پر) عمل custody نگرانی *in safe keeping,* in safe custody محفوظ ہاتھوں میں *in keeping with,* (*a*) according to کے مطابق (*b*) in harmony with کے موافق *out of keeping with* کے غیر مطابق، سے غیر ہم آہنگ **keepsake** *n.* memento یادگار، نشانی

keg *n.* small cask or barrel holding about 10 gallons چھوٹا پیپا

ken *n.* range of knowledge علم کی حد، علم *outside* (*one's*) *ken, beyond* (*one's*) *ken,* not in (one's) knowledge کے علم سے باہر

kennel (*ken*-èl) *n.* hut for a dog کتے کا گھر mean dwelling تازی خانہ *v. t.* & *i.* put or dwell in a kennel تازی خانے میں رہنا یا رکھنا، گندے سے گھر میں رہنا یا رکھنا

a kennel

kept *v.* (pa. t. and pa. pa. of **keep,** which see)

kerb (kĕ*b) *n.* stone edging of a pavement پکے فرش کا پشتیبان، پیادہ رو کا پشتیبان **kerb-stone** *n.* one of the stones used in it پتھر پشتیبان، سنگ پشتیبان

kerchief (kĕ*-chif) *n.* piece of cloth for covering a woman's head (عورتوں کا) سر پر باندھنے کا رومال

kerchiefed (kĕ*-chift) *adj.* with a kerchief on سر پر رومال باندھے

kernel (kĕ*-nel) *n.* inner part of a nut, etc. گری، مغز essential part (*of* the whole problem, etc.) اہم نکات، مغز

kerosene (*ke*-ro-seen) *n.* paraffin-oil مٹی کا تیل، گھاسلیٹ

ketch-up (*kech*-up) *n.* sauce made from tomato juice ٹماٹر کی چٹنی، کیچپ

kettle (*ket*-èl) *n.* metal vessel with spout, and handle for brewing tea, etc. کیتلی **kettledrum** *n.* drum made of skin stretched on large metallic bowl ڈنکا، نقارہ

key (kee) *n.* metal instrument for opening and closing a lock کنجی، چابی، کلید instrument for winding up the spring (of a watch, etc.) کنجی، چابی solution (*to* mystery, cipher, etc.) حل answers to exercises, etc. حل explanatory translation of some foreign book, etc. ترجمہ، شرح، تفسیر notes (*to* some book) or guide (*to* some subject) رہنما، آئینہ lever for the operating (*of* typewriter, etc.) کی، بیرم lever (*of* musical iustrument) (ساز کا) پردہ strategic place giving its possesser control over (*to*) the outlying area (کی) کنجی general pitch or tone (*of* voice) (آواز کا) زور *sing in a high* (or *low*) *key* پنچم (یا مدھم) سروں میں گانا، اونچی (یا دھیمی) آواز سے گانا system of musical notes scientifically related to each other and based on a particular note (called the *key-note*) سرگم *a song in F minor* الف مائینر سے شروع ہونے والا سرگم general tone of style اسلوب، انداز *all in the same key,* monotonous سپاٹ، بے کیف *in an entirely new key,* اچھوتے انداز سے *adj.* basic; essential to others of the type بنیادی *basic industries* بنیادی صنعتیں *golden key, silver key,* (*a*) bribery رشوت (*b*) bribe-money رشوت کا روپیہ *v. t.* & *i.* regulate the pitch of کے سر ٹھیک کرنا *key up* (*someone*)

to (or to do something), stimulate (him) to (make that effort) (کسی کو کوئی کام کرنے کے لیے) تیار کرنا
keyboard n. row of keys (of harmonium, typewriter, etc.) ساز کے پردوں (یا ٹائپ رائٹر کے بٹنوں) کا تختہ **keyhole** n. hole in a door or lock for inserting key قفل کا مُنہ (یا) ڈِلّا **keynote** n. first note in a musical scale بُنیادی سُر basic idea (on which the whole gamut of reasoning has been developed) مرکزی خیال، بُنیادی خیال **keystone** n. wedge-shaped middle stone of an arch central thought مرکزی خیال controlling principle بُنیادی اُصول

(■) a keystone

khaki (kah-ki) adj. dull brown خاکی، مٹیالا n. cloth of this colour خاکی کپڑا uniform made of this cloth خاکی وردی

kick (kik) v. i. & i. strike (football, etc.) with the foot ٹھوکر لگانا، لات مارنا strike (someone) thus scornfully ٹھکرانا، لاتوں سے مارنا make such movements with the legs لاتیں مارنا *kick off*, (a) get rid off by such movements لاتیں مار مار کر اُتارنا یا جھٹکا دینا یا ہلانا (b) start (football) (فٹ بال کو) کک لگانا rebel (at) کے خلاف سر اُٹھانا (of a gun, etc.) spring back پیچھے کو دھکا دینا (of animal) strike with hind-legs دولتیاں جھاڑنا *kick (someone) upstairs*, shelve (him) by promoting کو ترقی دے کر اس سے نجات حاصل کرنا *kick up a row*, (colloq.) cause a disturbance جھگڑا کھڑا کرنا، ہنگامہ برپا کرنا *kick the bucket*, die مر جانا n. kicking ٹھوکر، لات، دولتی springing back (of gun) when fired (بندوق وغیرہ کا) دھکا power of striking or retaliation مقابلے کی ہمت، بدلہ لینے کی طاقت، انتقامی قوت، کس بل *with no kick left in him* اب اس میں کس بل کہاں؟ (colloq.) thrill, excitement مزا، لطف *get the kick out of (film, etc.)* کا مزا آ جانا

kickshaw (kik-shaw) n. trifle چیز toy کھلونا fancy dish of food کھانے کی خاص چیز

kid n. young goat میمنا، بکری کا بچہ leather made from its skin میمنے کی کھال کا چمڑا، کِڈ (colloq.) child بچہ، ننھا adj. made of kid میمنے کی کھال کے چمڑے کا v. t. & i. (of a goat) give birth to a kid (بکری کا) بیانا hoax ہنسی ہنسی میں دھوکا دینا، جل دینا، تبا دینا
kiddy (kid-i) n. (colloq.) child بچہ، ننھا **kid-glove** (kid-gluv) adj. over-dainty (person); (one) afraid of rough work نازک مزاج، تاناشاہ
kidnap (kid-nap) v. t. (-pp-) steal (a child) (بچہ) کو اُٹھا لینا، (بچوں کو) اغوا کرنا carry away (someone) unlawfully کسی شخص کو، غیر قانونی طور پر اُٹھا لینا، غائب کر دینا
kidney (kid-ni) n. one of a pair of organs in the body excreting urine گُردہ، گلیہ this organ of certain animals used as food گُردہ، گُردے temperament مزاج، طبیعت *a man of the right kidney* صحیح طبیعت کا انسان **kidney bean** n. (plant yielding) a kidney-shaped bean فرانسیسی سیم

kill (kil) v. t. & i. put to death قتل کرنا، مار ڈالنا، جان سے مارنا *be killed in action*, جنگ میں مارا جانا، کھیت رہنا put an end to کا خاتمہ ہونا، کو ختم کرنا *kill time*, while it away بیکار باتوں میں وقت کھونا *kill a parliamentary bill*, defeat it قرارداد مسترد کرانا، قرارداد نامنظور کرنا n. act of killing (by a sportsman) شکار کرنا animal killed in hunting شکار کیا ہوا جانور، شکار

kiln (kiln, or kil) n. large oven (for burning bricks, etc.) پژاوہ، بھٹہ، بھاٹ، بھٹی، بھاڑ، آوا *brick kiln* اینٹوں کا پژاوہ *lime kiln* چونے کا بھاٹ، بھٹہ potter's kiln

kilo- (kil-oh) pref. thousand ہزار **kilocycle** (kil-o-sī-kel) n. unit of the frequency of vibrations, esp. of wireless waves; it amounts to 1,000 vibrations per second کلوسیکل، کلوسائیکل **kilogram**, **kilogramme**, (abb. **kilo**) n. 1,000 grammes (about $2\frac{1}{5}$ lb.) کلوگرام، کیلوگرام، کیلو **kilometre**, **kilometer** n. 1,000 metres (3,280 ft. or about 1,100 yards) کلومیٹر، کیلومیٹر، کیلو میٹر **kilowatt** n. 1,000 units of electricity کلوواٹ، کیلوواٹ

kilt n. plaited skirt coming down to the knees, worn by men in Scottish Highlands کِلٹ، گھگرا

kimono (ki-moh-noh) n. (pl. *kimonos*) long loose Japanese robe جاپانی چغہ یا لبادہ European dressing gown modelled on this شب خوابی کا چغہ، لبادہ

kin n. (collectively) family کنبہ (also *kinsfolk*), relations عزیز، رشتہ دار، اعزہ و اقارب، بھائی بند *next of kin of*, nearest relation (or relations) of (کا یا کے) قریب ترین رشتہ دار *kith and kin*, blood relations اپنا خون، خونی رشتہ دار **kinsman** n. (fem. *kinswoman*) relation رشتہ دار **kinship** n. relationship by blood or marriage رشتہ داری similarity in character طبیعتوں کا ملنا **kindred** (*kind*-red) n. blood relationship خونی رشتہ relatives رشتہ دار adj. related by birth or marriage رشتہ دار *claim kindred with (someone)* سے رشتہ داری جتانا all of one's relatives کسی کے مجملہ رشتہ دار having common source ہم نسل، متحد الاصل similar (subjects, interests, persons) ایک جیسے، ایک سے، یکساں

kind (kind) adj. considerate مہربان، رحم دل، شفیق *be kind to* پر مہربان ہونا *How kind of you!* آپ کی بڑی مہربانی! sympathetic words, etc. مشفقانہ، مہربانی کا *will you be kind enough to (do)*, please (do) براہ مہربانی، مہربانی کر کے، از راہ کرم، ازراہ مہربانی *It was kind of you to (do)*, you (did) it kindly آپ نے مہربانی کر کے (کر دیا) *Give my kind regards to (so-and-so)*, convey my best wishes to میرا سلام کہیے سے *n.* species, race, etc. نَسل، نَوعِ، جِنس، نَوعِ بَشر، نَوعِ اِنسانی *mankind* variety قِسم character, nature فِطرت goods (not cash money) جِنس *in cash or kind* بَصُورت نَقد یا جِنس *pay in kind*, pay in goods instead of in cash جِنس کی صُورت میں اَدا کرنا *repay (someone) in kind*, treat him as he has treated you اَدلے کا بَدلہ دینا *of a kind*, *(a)* of the same kind اِسی قِسم کا *(b)* not worth the name جو مُشکِل ہی سے کہلا سکے **kindly** (kīnd-li) *adj.* kind مہربان، مُشفِق، شَفیق *adv.* in a kind manner مہربانی سے *Will you kindly (do)*, will you please (do) کیا آپ مہربانی کر کے (کریں گے)؟ **kindness** *n.* kind act or behaviour مہربانی، نَوازِش، کَرَم

kindergarten (*kind*-ĕ*-gah*-ten) *n.* school for very small children in which they are taught by games, toys and object-lessons کِنڈَر گارٹن

kindle (*kind*-ĕl) *v.t.* & *i.* catch fire آگ پکڑنا، جَل اُٹھنا set fire to روشن کرنا، جَلانا، آگ دِکھانا stir up or be stirred (*to* strong feeling, *by*) بھڑک اُٹھنا، بھڑکانا **kindling** *n.* setting fire آگ جَلانا یا لگانا material for setting fire (like dry wood, etc.) آگ لگانے کی لکڑی وغیرہ

kindly *adj.* & *adv.* **kindness** *n.* (see under **kind**)

kindred *n.* see under **kin**

kine (kīn) *n. pl.*, (old use) cows گائیں

kinetic (kī-*net*-ik) *adj.* pertaining to motion مُتحرِک *kinetic energy* توانائی بالفعل *n.* (*pl.*) branch of science dealing with motion حَرکیات

king *n.* male sovereign بادشاہ، شاہ، مَلِک industrial or business magnate, etc. (کا) مَلِکُ التّجار، (کا) سَب سے بڑا کارخانہ دار *king of birds*, hawk عُقاب *king of beasts*, lion or tiger شیر ببر (یا) شیر (in cards) card bearing the picture of a king بادشاہ *king of hearts*, (*etc.*) پان (وغیرہ) کا بادشاہ (in chess) the principal piece which has to be (protected from being) checkmated شاہ، بادشاہ *king's English*, chaste, standard English مِعیاری انگریزی، شُستہ انگریزی **kingdom** (-dum) *n.* country ruled by a king or queen بادشاہی any one of the three divisions of the natural world (viz., *the animal kingdom, the vegetable kingdom*, and *the mineral kingdom*) عالَمِ حَیوانات و نباتات و جَمادات **kingfisher** *n.* small bright-feathered bird feeding on fish رام چڑیا

a kingfisher

kingship *n.* being a king بادشاہی، بادشاہت

kinglike (*king*-līk) *adj.* like a king شاہانہ **kingly** *adj.* royal شاہانہ، مُلوکانہ

kingliness (*king*-li-nes) *n.* being like a king شاہانہ ہونا

kink *n.* back twist (*in* rope, wire, pipe, etc.) بَل، اُلٹا بَل abnormal way of thinking, اُلٹا خیال، گُتھی اَوندھی کھوپڑی کا خیال *v.t.* & *i.* form or make a kink اُلٹا بَل پڑنا یا ڈالنا، گُتھی پڑنا یا ڈالنا

kinsfolk *n.*, **kinship** *n.*, **kinsman** *n.*, **kinswoman** *n.* (see under **kin**)

kiosk (ki-*osk*) *n.* small enclosed stall (for sale of newspapers, etc.) (اخبار فروشی وغیرہ کا) ٹھاٹرا telephone booth ٹیلی فون کا کھوکا یا کھوکا (originally) palace of Turkish caliphs مَحل، قَیصَر، کوشک

kipper (*kip*-ē*) *n.* herring dried in the open air, etc. سُکھائی ہُوئی ہیرنگ مچھلی، رکپر

kirk (kĕ*k) *n.* Scottish word for church گرجا established church in Scotland سکاچ ستانی گرجا

kirtle (*kĕ*-tĕl) *n.* (old use) woman's gown لہنگا، پِشواز

kismet (*kis*-met) *n.* fate, destiny تَقدیر، قِسمت، نَصیبہ

kiss (kis) *v.t.* & *i.* touch with the lips as a sign of affection چُومنا، بوسہ لینا، بوسہ دینا touch lightly چُھونا *kiss the dust*, *(a)* fall in combat قتل ہونا، خاک و خون میں لوٹنا *(b)* yield in abject submission گڑگڑانا، عاجزی کرنا *kiss the ground*, *(a)* yield abjectly شِکَست قبول کرنا، نیچا دیکھنا *(b)* prostrate out of devotion سجدہ کرنا، مَحو تسبیح و ہونا *kiss the book*, depose by kissing the scriptures الہامی کتاب کو بوسہ دے کر حَلف اُٹھانا *kiss the rod*, accept chastisement submissively سزا خاموشی سے برداشت کر لینا *hugging and kissing* بوس و کنار

kit *n.* personal equipment of a traveller (or of a soldier, etc., for travelling) گٹھڑی، سامان (workman's) implements (کاریگر کے) اَوزار equipment for a special purpose ساز و سامان، ضروری سامان short form of *kitten* بلّی کا بچّہ، بِلّوٹا **kit-bag** *n.* (usu. long but easily portable) bag for kit تھیلا، گٹھڑی

kitchen (*kich*-ĕn) *n.* room with fireplace where cooking is done باورچی خانہ، مَطبَخ **kitchen-garden** *n.* garden (in the house) where vegetables, fruits, etc., are grown سبزی ترکاری کا باغیچہ، پائیں باغ **kitchenmaid** *n.* girl-servant working in the kitchen on odd jobs باورچی خانہ کی خادمہ، باورچن کی ماتحت لڑکی **kitchenette** (-*net*) *n.* small room serving as miniature kitchen and scullery چھوٹا سا باورچی خانہ

kite (kīt) *n.* a bird of the hawk family چیل، زغن very light framework of wood covered with paper to be flown in the air at the end of a long string (in the West usu. in the form of a hollow cube, but in this country like a flat square or two contiguous ovals) پتنگ، کنکوا، گُڈّی

a kite (sense

fly a kite, (a) گڈی اُڑانا، پتنگ اُڑانا (b) throw a feeler to test public opinion فیلر پھینکنا،
kith (kith) *n*. (only in the phrase :) *kith and kin*, friends and relatives دوست، عزیز، دوست رشتہ دار
kitten (*kit*-ĕn) *n*. young cat بلّی کا بچّہ، بلونٹا
kiwi *n*. wingless bird of New Zealand کیوی، کوی
kleptomania (klep-to-*may*-ni-a) *n*. mental disease creating, (in well-to-do persons), a strong desire to steal چوری کرنے کا جنون، چوری کا جنون، جنونِ سرقہ
kleptomaniac *n*. suffering from this disease جسے جنونِ سرقہ ہو
knack (nak) *n*. skill (*in*, *to do* or *of doing* something) سلیقہ، مہارت، ہُنر
knapsack (*nap*-sak) *n*. big bag tied to their back by travellers, soldiers, etc. جھولا، بُقچہ
knave (nayv) *n*. dishonest man بددیانت، بے ایمان *He is either a fool or a knave* وہ یا تو بے ایمان، وہ یا احمق ہے یا بدمعاش debauched person بدقماش (in cards) picture-card of the lowest value غلام، گولا
knavery (*nayv*-è-ri) *n*. dishonesty بے ایمانی، بددیانتی debauchery **knavish** *adj*. fraudulent دھوکے باز، عیار، فریبی
knead (need) *v.t.* make (flour and water, etc.) into a firm paste گوندھنا، سانَنا massage (muscles) (پٹھوں کی) مالش کرنا **kneading-trough** (*need*-ing-truf) *n*. trough for needing flour آٹا گوندھنے کا برتن، پرات، کونڈی
knee (nee) *n*. joint between thigh and lower leg گھٹنا *bring (someone) to his knees*, force into submission قدموں پر جھکانا، ناک رگڑوانا *on (one's) knees*, in this position (submissively) (اظہارِ اطاعت کیلئے) گھٹنوں کے بل *on the knees of the gods*, yet uncertain ابھی غیر یقینی portion of clothes covering it گھٹنا، گھٹنے پر کا کپڑا
knee-breeches *n. pl*. breeches reaching just below the knees گھٹنوں تک کی برجس **knee-cap** *n*. flat bone forming front part of the knee گھٹنے کی چپنی
knee-joint *n*. joint of the knee گھٹنے کا جوڑ
knee-deep *adj*. thus far deep گھٹنے تک گہرا، گھٹنے گھٹنے
knee-hole table *n*. table with space for knees between drawer pedestals پورے دروازوں والی میز
kneel *v.i.* (*knelt*) go down on the knees گھٹنوں کے بل کھڑے ہونا do so in prayer رکوع میں جانا **kneeling** *n*. act of going down on knees ; genuflexion گھٹنوں کے بل کھڑے ہونا، رکوع
knell (nel) *n*. slow sounding of a bell at a Christian funeral کسی کی موت پر بجنے والی گھنٹی، ماتمی جرس portent of misfortune مصیبت کا شگون *v.t.* (of bell) ring a knell ماتمی جرس کا بجنا sound or proclaim ominously مصیبت کا شگون بننا

knickerbockers (*nik*-ĕ*-bok-ĕ*z) *n. pl.* loose breeches gathered in below the knees نیکر بوکر، a New Yorker (esp. of Dutch descent) نیویارک کا ڈچ نسل کا باشندہ **knickers** *n. pl*. woman's undergarment looking like knickerbockers زیر جامہ knickerbockers نیکر بوکر، نیکر
knick-knack (*nik*-nak), **nick-nack** (*nik*-nak) *n*. trifling ornament, trinket معمولی زیور small ornamental piece of furniture معمولی سجاوٹی سامان such article of dress معمولی آرائشی گہنا
knife (nīf) *n*. (pl. *knives*) sharp blade on a handle چاقو، چھری، چھرا *pocket-knife*, clasp-knife چاقو *jack-knife*, large clasp-knife بڑا چاقو *table-knife*, dining table knife (کھانے کی) چھری *knife and fork* چھری کانٹا *carving-knife*, one for carving meat چھرا *get (one's) knife into (someone)*, wish to harm him کسی کو نقصان پہنچانا چاہنا sharp-edged blade in a machine مشین کا چھرا *v.t.* wound with a knife چھرے سے زخمی یا گھائل کرنا، چھرا بھونکنا یا گھونپنا
knight (nīt) *n*. (old use) mounted and armoured warrior of noble birth in the feudal system of the Middle Ages فوجدار * منصبدار * نائٹ titled person below a baronet in rank in the United Kingdom (written and addressed as 'Sir' before the first or full name, as Sir Syed Ahmad or merely Sir Syed but NEVER as *Sir Ahmad*) نائٹ، سر (in chess) piece usu. with a horse's head گھوڑا، اسپ *dub (someone) a knight*, (of ruler) confer the title of *Sir* on him by touching him lightly with a sword as he kneels and saying to him : "Rise, Sir (So-and-So)" کسی کو نائٹ بنانا، کسی کو فوجدار یا منصبدار بنانا *v.t.* dub someone a knight or confer that title on him سر (یا) نائٹ بنانا کا خطاب دینا **knighthood** (*nīt*-hŭd) *n*. rank of a knight سر، کا خطاب یا نائٹ کا رتبہ، منصبداری، فوجداری
knightly *adj*. brave and generous like (that of) a knight بہادر، دلیر، شجاع، دلیرانہ، بہادرانہ، بامروّت
knit (nit) *v.t.* & *i*. (*knitting* ; *knitted* or *knit*) make network material (usu. with wool) بُننا draw together (brows in frowning) بھویں سکیڑنا unite firmly (bones, etc.) اچھی طرح جوڑنا، مضبوطی سے جوڑنا *closely knit*, (a) (of garment) knit closely گھری بُناوٹ کا (b) (of agrument) all the parts of which fit in well together مربوط **knitting** *n*. material being knitted جو بُنا جائے act of knitting بُننا **knitting-needles** *n*. (pair of) needles used for knitting سلائیاں
knives (nīvz) *n*. (pl. of **knife**, which see)

knitting and knitting-needles

knob (nob) *n.* rounded end (*of* stick, door-handle, etc.) (دروازے وغیرہ کا) دستہ، لٹو، موٹھ (یا) مٹھیا rounded swelling (on tree-trunk or other surface) گرہ، گانٹھ، گومڑی small rounded lump (of coal, etc.) گول سا ڈھیلا **knobby** (nob-i) *adj.* full of knobs گانٹھ دار، موٹھوں والا

knock (nok) *v.t. & i.* strike a hard blow زور سے مارنا، ضرب لگانا (of an internal combustion engine) make a knocking sound ٹھک ٹھک کرنا، گھڑگھڑ کرنا *knock down,* (*a*) bring down (person, or thing) مار گرانا (*b*) bring down (price) قیمت میں کمی کرنا *knock against,* (*a*) collide with سے متصادم ہونا، ٹکرانا (*b*) come across casually سے مڈ بھیڑ ہونا *knock the bottom of* (*something*) *out,* separate it with a knock. مار کر پیندا اتار دینا *knock the bottom out of,* (render argument, case, etc.) invalid کو بے معنی بنا دینا *knock at a door,* do so in order to attract attention دروازہ کھٹکھٹانا *knock* (*someone or something*) *about,* treat it roughly سے سختی کا سلوک کرنا *knock about,* lead unsettled life مارے مارے پھرنا *knock about the world,* undertake many long journeys سیاحی میں عمر گزارنا *knock* (*someone*) *out,* (*a*) (in boxing) send him to the floor with a blow so that he cannot continue (مکے بازی میں) پچھاڑ دینا (یا) کسی ضرب سے بے ہوش یا وقتی طور پر ناکارہ کر دینا (*b*) overwhelm (*with* surprise, etc.) حیران کر دینا *knock off* (amount from bill, etc.), deduct کاٹ لینا *knock off; knock off work,* stop working کام چھوڑ دینا *knock* (*someone*) *up,* wake him by knocking at his door (کسی کو جگانے کے لیے اس کا) دروازہ زور زور سے کھٹکھٹانا *knock* (*something*) *up,* improvise it or prepare it hurriedly جلدی جلدی بنانا *be knocked up,* be tired out تھکا ہوا ہونا، تھکا ہارا ہونا *knock on the head,* (*a*) stun (تجویز یا) بسر پر ضرب سے چکرا دینا (*b*) defeat (plan, etc.) (منصوبہ) ناکام بنا دینا *n.* blow چوٹ، ضرب its short sharp sound چوٹ، چوٹ کی آواز **knock-about** *adj.* (of a farce, etc.) rough and noisy ہنگامہ خیز (تماشہ یا کھیل) **knocker** *n.* one who knocks کھٹکھٹانے والا hinged metal for striking against a door to call attention (دروازے کا) کھٹکا (یا) کنڈی **knock-out** *n.* blow that knocks out opponent in boxing پچھاڑنے والی ضرب such defeat ہار، پچھاڑ

knoll (nol) *n.* small hill ٹیلہ، ٹیلا

knot (not) *n.* point at which a rope, etc., has been tied گرہ، گانٹھ something that unites رشتہ، تعلق، ربط complicated problem پیچیدگی، عقدہ *tie* (*oneself*) *in* (or *into*) *knots, tie* (*oneself*) *up in* (or *into*) *knots,* get badly confused (about something) بڑی الجھن میں پڑنا piece of ribbon tied in an ornament knot خوبصورت گرہ لگا ہوا ربن hard lump in tree where a branch once grew out پیڑ کی گانٹھ group (of persons) گروہ، ٹولی *stand about in knots,* stand in haphazard groups ٹولیاں بنا کر کھڑے ہونا، ٹولیوں میں کھڑے ہونا nautical mile; measure of speed for ships equivalent to 6080 ft. ناٹ، بحری کوس *a vessel of 15 knots,* one with a speed of 15 nautical miles per hour پندرہ بحری کوس فی گھنٹہ کی رفتار والا جہاز *v. t. & i.* (-tt-) make a knot in گرہ لگانا، گرہ دینا tie with knots گرہ دے کر باندھنا، گانٹھنا **knotty** *adj.* having knots گانٹھوں والا، گرہ دار complicated and puzzling (problem, etc.) پیچیدہ

know (noh) *v. t. & i.* (*know*; *knew*; *known* pr. nohn) have information جاننا have knowledge (*of* or *about*) جاننا، علم ہونا be sure (*that*) یقین ہونا، جاننا recognize پہچاننا be acquainted with سے واقف ہونا be familiar with (a subject, etc.) جاننا be skilled in (*how to do* something) (کرنا) جاننا، کر سکنا، آنا *know nothing* (*of*), be ignorant (of) (سے) ناواقف یا کورا ہونا *know* (*one's*) *own mind* be certain of (one's) purpose, etc., not to vascillate پکے ارادے کا ہونا، ڈانواں ڈول نہ ہونا *know* (*one's own business, know what's what,* have practical experience of one's work اپنے کام سے اچھی طرح واقف ہونا، اپنے کام کی خوب سمجھ رکھنا یا ہونا *not that I know of,* no to my knowledge مجھے تو معلوم نہیں، کم از کم میرے علم میں نہیں *know better than that,* I am too well familiar with the facts to be deceived by you مجھے زیادہ معلوم ہے *you ought to know better than to do that,* you should have had more sense and should not have done that تمہیں عقل چاہیے تھی کہ ایسا کرنا ٹھیک نہیں **knowing** (noh-ing) *adj.* having knowledge جاننے والا، باعلم، باخبر shrewd ہوشمند، ذی ہوش (esp.) cunning (person, looks, etc.) عیار، چالاک stylish or smart (hat, etc.) خوشنما، پھبنے والا **knowingly** *adv.* consciously جان بوجھ کر **knowledge** (*nol*-ej) *n.* knowing جاننا، علم ہونا what one knows (*of* subject, event, etc.) علم all that is or may be known علم its branches علوم، علم کی شاخیں، علم *to the best of* (*one's*) *knowledge, to* (*one's*) *knowledge* as far as (one) knows جہاں تک (کسی) کا علم ہے *come to* (*one's*) *knowledge,* become known to him علم میں آنا، کو معلوم ہونا *have no knowledge of,* not to be known by علم نہ ہونا **knowledgeable** *adj.* well-informed (circles, persons, etc.) واقف حال (حلقے، افراد وغیرہ) intelligent ذہین، ہوشمند، فہیم **know-how** (*noh*-hou) *n.* (see Addenda)

knowledge *n.* **known** pa. p. (see under **known**)

knuckle (*nuk*-èl) *n.* bone at finger joint (esp. at the root of fingers) اُنگلیوں ریا پور) کے جوڑ کی ہَڈی apparent knee-joint of animal used as food پونگے کے آگے جھک جانا ، کی اطاعت کا پارچہ *v. i.* submit (*under*) کا اظہار کرلینا get *down* (*to* or *to do* something) لگ ہی جانا

Koran (ko-*rahn*, or *koh*-ran) *n.* the final word of God revered as the Muslim Scriptures قرآن ۔ قرآن شریف **koranic** *adj.* pertaining to *the Koran* قرآنی

kowtow, kotow (koh-*toh*) *n.* Chinese ceremony of prostration as a sign of worship or submission (سجدہ یا اظہار اطاعت کے لیے) سجدہ کی چینی رسم ، سجدہ *v. t.* (*kowtow to*) prostrate oneself thus سجدہ کرنا abase oneself before someone اپنے کو کسی کے آگے ذلیل کرنا ، جھکنا ، لوٹ چاٹنا

kraal (krahl) *n.* South African hut-village کرال ، افریقی گاؤں fence for animals (ڈھور ڈنگر کے لیے افریقی) باڑہ

Kremlin (*krem*-lin) *n.* Russian citadel رُوسی قلعہ the citadel at Moscow containing the palace of the former Czars and now housing the Headquarters of the Russian Soviet government کریملن the governmental policy of the U. S. S. R., *i.e.*, Russia کریملن ، رُوسی پالیسی

Kuklux Klan (*koo*-kluks-klan), **Kuklux** *n.* secret U. S. organization formed in the Southern States after the Civil War of 1861-65 to oppose Northern influence and deprive the Negroes of their newly-achieved rights ; it was revived during World War I to crush Roman Catholic Christians and Jews along with the Negroes and got a further lease of life after World War II leading several riots. *Lynching* or burning their opponents alive has been their favourite method of dealing with their black opponents. The members of this clan go about on their exploits clad usu. in something like our old-fashioned, long white *burqa* کوکلکس کلان

kulak (*koo*-lak) *n.* (pl. *kulaki*) well-to-do Russian peasant of the Czarist regime زمیندار ، کولاک

Kuomintang (kwoh-min-*tang*) *n.* (abbr. *K. M. T.*), Nationalist China's government now restricted to the island of Formosa (also called *Taiwan*) and at loggerheads with the People's Rupublic of China on the mainland under the Communists ; one of the knotty problems of international amity, the *K. M. T.* is a ramification of the Nationalist People's Party (locally called *Kuomintang*) formed chiefly by the great modern Chinese leader, Sun Yat-Sen who lived from 1866 to 1925 and two of whose extremely capable daughters are divided in active participation in the governance of the two Chinese States قوم پرست چین ، کومنتانگ

kultur (kool-*too*-è*) *n.* (usu. ironical for) type of civilization, culture تہذیب

L

l, L (el) (pl. *l's* or *ls*) twelfth letter of the English alphabet, (it is equivalent to the Urdu letter ل) ایل Roman numeral denoting 50 پچاس rectangular joint of pipes نالی کا قائم الزاویہ جوڑ

la (lah) *n.* sixth note of the musical scale سرگم کا چھٹا سُر ، دھا **Note :** The various notes are : 1st., *do* ; 2nd, *re* ; 3rd. *mi* ; 4th. *fa* ; 5th. *sol* ; 6th, *la* ; 7th, *si* or *ti*.

label (*lay*-bel) *n.* piece of paper, etc. (stuck or pinned on or tied to something) to show its name, destination, etc. نام یا پتے کا نشان ، اتا پتا بتانے والی چٹھی ، لیبل ، چٹ ، چپٹی short classifying word applied to isms, etc. لیبل *v.t.* (-ll-) mark with a label نام پتہ لگانا ، لیبل لگانا classify isms or persons thus کہنا ، (کا) لیبل چسپاں کرنا

labial (*lay*-bi-al) *adj.* pertaining to lips ہونٹوں کا ، شفوی labial sounds شفوی آوازیں

laboratory (*lab*-o-ra-to-ri) *n.* (abbr. *lab*), place for scientific experiments معمل ، تجربہ گاہ *regional research laboratory*, laboratory for conducting scientific research in an area علاقائی تحقیقاتی تجربہ گاہ

laborious *adj.* (see under **labour**)

labour (*lay*-bě*) *n.* hard work محنت ، مشقت piece of work done for wages مزدوری *wages of labour* مزدوری *a labour of love*, work that gives only pleasure to the labourer مُفت کام ، ایسا کام جو محض شوق سے کیا جائے اور اُس سے رُوپیہ حاصل نہ ہو *lost labour* رائیگاں محنت workers as a class (as opposed to *capital* or *capitalists*) محنت کش طبقہ ، مزدور *the Labour Party*, British party representing this class in the nation's politics لیبر پارٹی ، مزدور جماعت pangs of childbirth دردزہ be in labour دردزہ میں مبتلا ہونا hard labour, penal servitude قید بامشقت Labour leader, leader of labourers or of Labour party مزدور رہنما ، مزدور جماعت کا رہنما labour market, demand and supply of labourers مزدوروں کی طلب ورسد ، مزدوری کا بازار Labour Exchange, Employment Exchange for labourers محکمۂ مزدوران Labour Minister, one looking after the interests of labourers in the country وزارت محنت labours of Hercules, the seven almost impossible tasks performed by him ہرقل کے انجام دئے ہوئے مشکل کام ، ہفتخوان رستم labour of Hercules, very difficult task ہفت خوان رستم ، سخت مشکل کام v.t. & i. work hard with the hands محنت کرنا ، مشقت کرنا ، جان مارنا strive (for or to do something) کیلیے ، سخت کوشش کرنا ، جدوجہد کرنا move slowly (under difficult conditions) (نامساعد حالات میں) زور لگا کر آہستہ آہستہ بڑھنا work out in detail کی تفصیل میں جانا labour the point, stretch it too far کسی بات کی بڑی تفصیل میں جانا **laboured** (*lay*-bĕ*d) *adj.* (of style, etc.) not easy and natural پرتصنع ، مشکل سے ہونیوالا کام done with difficulty ، آورد والا

labourer (*lay*-bĕ-rĕ*) *n.* heavy manual worker مزدور anyone who works for wages مزدور ، محنت کش **laborious** (la-*bo*-ri-us) *adj.* hard-working (person) محنتی work needing great effort محنت طلب ، مشقت طلب (style, etc.) showing signs of great effort آورد والا ، تصنع والا

labyrinth (*lab*-i-rinth) *n.* (*Labyrinth*), maze in which, according to classical mythology, the Minotaur was confined in Crete لیبرنتھ maze بھول بھلیاں any confused network (*of* roads, etc.) بھول بھلیاں puzzling state of affairs مشکل اشکال ، گورکھ دھندا **labyrinthine** (lab-e-*rinth*-in) *adj.* like a labyrinth بھول بھلیاں جیسا tangled (affairs) پیچیدہ

lac, lakh (lak) *n.* (in Pakistan) one hundred thousand (*of* rupees) لاکھ (روپیہ) (*lac*) red resin used as varnish and sealing-material لاکھ

lace (lays) *n.* patterned network of thread used as an ornamental piping لیس فیتہ ، جھالر ، کلابتون gold lace سنہری جھالر silver lace روپہلی جھالر (also *shoe-laces* or *boot-laces*), string for tying shoes, etc. بوٹ کا تسمہ یا فیتہ *v.t.* & *i.* tighten (shoe, etc. *up*) with laces تسمے باندھنا **lacy** (*lay*-si) *adj.* lace-like in fineness or intricacy جھالر جیسا باریک یا نفیس بنا ہوا

lacerate (*las*-e-rayt) *v.t.* tear (the flesh) roughly چیرنا پھاڑنا wound (feeling, etc.) deeply سخت صدمہ پہنچانا **laceration** (-*ray*-) *n.* act of lacerating (flesh or feelings) چیر پھاڑ ، دل آزاری

lachrymose (*lak*-ri-mohz) *adj.* tearful آبدیدہ ، اشک آلودہ ، رونے والا given to weeping بات بات پر رو دینے والا

lack (lak) *v.t.* not to have نہ رکھنا ، سے محروم ہونا not to have enough (کی) کمی ہونا ، (کی) قلت ہونا be lacking for (something), not to have (enough) for it کے لیے نہ ہونا یا ناکافی ہونا be not lacking in (something bad) (کی) کوئی کمی نہ ہونا ، بہت ہونا *n.* shortage کمی ، قلت need حاجت ، ضرورت ، احتیاج no lack of, plenty of بہت کافی کچھ for lack of, owing to the absence of نہ ہونے کے باعث **lackland** *n.* & *adj.* (one) having no land محروم اراضی ، جس کی زمین نہ ہو **lacklustre** *adj.* (of eyes) dull بے نور ، کمزور **lackadaisical** *adj.* languidly superior بڑے آدمیوں کی طرح بیمار affecting delicacy of health or tastes شان دکھانے کے لیے بیماری یا ناپسندیدگی کا بہانہ کرکے جانے والا eschewing enthusiasm جوش کا اظہار نہ کرنے والا

lackey, lacquey (*lak*-i) *n.* uniformed footman اردلی ، باوردی ملازم obsequious follower obeying unquestioningly خوشامدی اور مطیع ملازم ، کاسہ لیس ، طفیلی **lackey** *v.t.* dance attendance on دربار داری کرنا ، اندھا دھند خوشامد میں لگے رہنا

laconic (la-*kon*-ik) *adj.* very brief بلیغانہ انداز سے ، بالکل مختصر لفظوں ، مختصر اور پرمغز (person) fond of brevity بلیغ

lacquer, lacker (*lak*-ĕ*) *n.* hard varnish made of lac and wine لاکھ کا روغن ornamental woodwork finished with this varnish لاکھ کے کام والی لکڑی *v.t.* coat (brass, wood, etc.) with lacquer لاکھ کا روغن کرنا

lactic (*lak*-tik) *adj.* of milk دودھ کا **lactometer** (lak-*tom*-e-tĕ*) *n.* instrument (looking like a thermometer) for testing milk by measuring its density * شیرپیما ، شیربیں

lacuna (la-*kew*-na) *n.* gap خلا missing portion (*in* a maunscript) گم شدہ حصہ ، خلا ، ترک missing link (*in* a chain of argument) خلا

lacy *adj.* (see under **lace**)

lad *n.* (fem. *lass*) boy لڑکا young fellow نوجوان *my lads, my men*, form of addressing workmen, sailors, etc. میرے بچو ، میرے نوجوانو ، میرے لڑکو **laddie** (*lad*-i) *n.* (affectionate form of) lad لڑکا ، بچہ

ladder (*lad*-ĕ*) *n.* movable set of steps made of two lengths of bamboo, rope, etc., with cross-pieces serving as steps سیڑھی means of rise (*to* fame, etc.) زینہ vertical flaw in stocking caused by stitch being undone through several rows جراب میں چھوٹا ہوا دھاگا *kick the ladder*, abandon friends by whose help one has risen in life کامیابی میں مدد دینے والے دوستوں کو دغا دینا v.i. (of stockings) develop a ladder جرابوں کا دھاگا چھوڑ دینا

lade (layd) *v.t.* (*laded, laden*) put cargo on board a ship جہاز پر مال لادنا lift (something *out of*) with a scoop نکالنا **laden** (*layd*-en) *adj.* loaded (*with*) (سے) لدا ہوا oppressed (*with* care, sin, etc.) (کے) بار تلے دبا ہوا **lading** (*layd*-ing) *n.* cargo جہاز میں لدنے والا مال *bill of lading*, list of ship's cargo جہاز میں لدنے والے مال کی فہرست

ladle (*layd*-ĕl) *n.* large deep spoon with a long handle ڈوئی *v.t.* (*ladle out*), serve out with a ladle ڈوئی سے نکال کر دینا a ladle

lady (*lay*-di) *n.* (polite term for) woman خاتون good-mannered woman خاتون، مہذب عورت (*Lady*), British title used of the wife of a knight and the wives and daughters of some nobles (as *Lady Abdul Qadir* or *Lady Qadir*, but NEVER as *Lady Sir* Abdul Qadir) لیڈی، بیگم (Note also that the combined names of a knighted husband and his wife would be written as *Sir Abdul and Lady Qadir*) *Our Lady*, term for Mary, mother of Christ ہماری خاتون *lady-in-waiting*, lady in attendance on queen or princess ملکہ (یا شہزادی) کی مصاحب خاتون **lady-like** *adj.* like a lady in dignity, etc. بیگمائی، بیگمانہ **ladyship** *n.* (with *your* or *her*) used in speaking to or of a titled lady خاتون - محترم **lady-love** *n.* sweetheart محبوبہ **lady-killer** *n.* male flirt اوّارہ آدمی **lady-bird** *n.* a winged insect سیاہ چتی والا بادامی بھونرا

lag (lag) *v.i.* (-gg-) (*lag behind*), keep behind by moving too slowly پیچھے رہ جانا cover (water-pipe, or boiler, etc.) with insulating material to prevent it from freezing or losing heat منفصل کرنا *n.* (slang) convict مجرم، سزا یافتہ *time lag*, time by which something comes later

laggard (*lag*-ĕ*d) *n.* one who lags سست رفتار پھسڈی، تھکا، پیچھے رہ نے والا

lagoon (la-*goon*) *n.* salt-water lake separated from sea by sandbank or enclosed by atoll بحری جھیل *

laid (layd) *v.* (*pa. t.* & *pa. p.* of **lay,** which see)

lain (layn) *v.* (pa. p. of ²**lie,** which see)

lair (lay-ĕ*) *n.* den ; lying place of beast بھٹ

laird (*lay*-ĕ*d) *n.* owner of landed estate in Scotland سکاچستانی زمیندار

laissez-faire (*lay*-say-fay-ĕ*) *n.* government policy of non-interference with individual action in trade and commerce (تجارت، صنعت وغیرہ میں) حکومت کی عدم مداخلت

laity *n.* (see under **lay**)

lake (layk) *n.* large tract of water surrounded by land جھیل

lakh *n.* (same as **lac**, which see)

l'allegro (la-*leg*-roh) *n.* the happy man خوش باش

lama (*lah*-ma) *n.* Buddhist priest in Tibet or Mongolia لاما

lamb (lam) *n.* young sheep بھیڑ کا بچہ، برہ its flesh as food بھیڑ کے بچے کا گوشت، برے کا گوشت

lame (laym) *adj.* limping لنگڑا، لولا unconvincing (excuse, argument) لنگ، جھوٹا *lame excuse* عذر لنگ، جھوٹا بہانہ *v.t.* make lame لنگڑا کر دینا **lamely** *adv.* limping لنگڑا کر **lameness** *n.* being lame لنگڑاپن

lament (la-*ment*) *v.t.* express great regret for ; mourn کا ماتم کرنا *n.* expression of grief سخت افسوس، ماتم song or poem expressing mourning ماتمی گیت، مرثیہ **lamentable** *adj.* regrettable افسوسناک **lamentably** *adv.* افسوسناک طور پر **lamented** (-ted) *adj.* mourned جس کا ماتم ہو رہا ہو، جس کی موت پر افسوس ہو **lamentation** (-*tay*-) *n.* mourning ماتم، نُدبہ

lamp (lamp) *n.* device for producing light usu. by dipping one end of a wick in oil and burning it at the other end vessel for giving light by burning a wick dipped in oil دیا، چراغ، بتی، لیمپ any other device for giving light چراغ، بتی *gas lamp*, high pressure kerosene lamp گیس *electric lamp*, lamp working with an electric power بجلی کا لیمپ *stable-lamp*, lamp meant to be placed on the desk میز کا لیمپ sun, moon or star سورج، چاند، ستارہ source of spiritual or intellectual light روحانی یا علمی روشنی کا منبع **lamp-post** *n.* post with lamp on top لیمپ والا کھمبا **lampblack** *n.* pigment made from soot کاجل **lamp-chimney** *n.* glass vessel put round the flame in order to protect it from wind چمنی، لیمپ کا شیشہ **lamp-light** *n.* light of a lamp لیمپ کی روشنی *hand on the lamp*, keep enlightenment from perishing جوت جگائے رکھنا *to smell of the lamp*, (*a*) betray nocturnal study سخت محنت کا نتیجہ ہونا، راتوں کی محنت کا ثبوت ہونا (*b*) be over-learned علمیت کے غیر ضروری اظہار والا ہونا

lampoon (lam-*poon*) *n.* virulent satire سخت ہجو، ہجو *v.t.* write a lampoon against کی سخت ہجو کرنا، کی ہجو قبیح لکھنا

lance (lahns) *n.* long spear used by mounted soldiers (سواروں کا) نیزہ *v.t.* pierce with a lance نیزہ مارنا cut with a lancet نشتر سے کھولنا **lancer** *n.* soldier armed with a lance نیزہ باز سوار **lance-corporal,** (in Pakistan Army) **lance-naik** *n.*

soldier with lowest rank above a sepoy لیس نائک لیس **lancet** (*lahns*-et) pointed, two-edged surgical knife نشتر

Lancelot (*lan*-se-lot) *n. Brit. leg.* the most famous knight of the Arthurian legend ; he bore an illicit love to Queen Guinevere لانسی لاٹ

land (land) *n.* solid part of earth's surface زمین ، خشکی ، برّ *travel by land and sea* بحر و بر کا سفر کرنا soil for cultivation زمین ، زرعی زمین ، اراضی *work on the land*, till the soil کاشتکاری کرنا ، زمین کاشت کرنا *land-worker* کسان ، کاشتکار country دیس (*one's*) *native land*, (one's) motherland کسی انسان کا وطن **land**ed property زمین ، اراضی *lands* زمین *v. t.* & *i.* go, come or put on land (*from* a ship, aircraft, etc.) اُترنا یا اُتارنا bring (aircraft) to land or sea surface (ہوائی جہاز کو) اُتارنا (of aircraft) come down to land or sea surface (ہوائی جہاز کا) اُترنا bring (someone or oneself *in* jail, trouble, difficulty, etc.) (مصیبت میں) مبتلا کرنا یا ہونا come down (on some place) گرنا ، پڑنا capture (fish) and bring it to shore (مچھلی) پکڑ کر ساحل پر لانا *piece of land* قطعۂ زمین ، قطعۂ اراضی *arable* (or *cultivable* or *culturable*) *land* قابلِ کاشت اراضی *barren land* بنجر اراضی *fallow land* اُوسر زمین ، غیر ممکن زمین غیر ممکن زراعت اراضی *unproductive land* *low land* (*where water stands*) ابر *land recovered from water* دریا آراضی *land along a stream* کھادر **landed** *adj.* owning agricultural land زرعی زمین کا مالک comprising such land زرعی *landed property* زرعی جائیداد **landholder** *n.* owner or tenant of land زرعی زمین والا ، مالک یا مزارع **landless** *adj.* (one) who has no land جس کی زمین نہ ہو **landing** *n.* platform at top of a flight of stairs or between two flights of stairs منزل (also *landing-place*) platform for landing from ship or aircraft فرودگاہ act of landing اُترنا *landing-ground*, place for aircraft on which to land ہوائی جہازوں کے اُترنے کے لیے جگہ *make a forced landing*, (of aircraft) have to come down owing to engine trouble ہوائی جہازوں کا مجبوراً اُترنا *land-laws n. pl.* laws relating to landed property زرعی جائیداد سے متعلق توانین ، قوانینِ اراضی **landlady** *n.* woman keeping an inn or boarding-house, or letting rooms to tenants مالکہ ، لینڈ لیڈی ، سرائے والی **land-locked** *adj.* (of a country, etc.) with (almost) no outlet to sea سمندر سے دُور خشکی سے گھرا ہوا خشکی میں محصور **landlord** *n.* one from whom another rents land or building مالک مکان keeper of a hotel, boarding-house, etc. ہوٹل والا لینڈ لارڈ owner of large piece of agricultural land زمیندار **land revenue, land tax** *n.* tax realised on land or land-produce مالیہ ، مالگزاری **landowner** *n.* owner of any type of land مالک زمین **land force** *n.* army برّی فوج **landmark** *n.* mark of the boundary of a piece of land حد بندی کا نشان object, etc., easily seen from a distance and helpful to travellers, etc. نشان ، پہچان milestone (*in* the history of a nation) سنگِ میل **landmine** (*land-mīn*) *n.* explosive mine laid in or on the ground زمینی سُرنگ **land-breeze** *n.* wind blowing from the land to the sea نسیم برّی **landscape** *n.* inland scenery خشکی کے مناظر its picture خشکی کے مناظر کی تصویر *landscape painting* خشکی کے مناظر کی تصویر کشی **landsman** *n.* non-sailor خشکی والا ، غیر ملّاح **landlubber,** *n.* one not accustomed to sea and ship خشکی کا کیڑا **landslide** *n.* sliding down of mass of earth, etc., from a bank or hillside زمین کا گرنا overwhelming political defeat (in election) سخت سیاسی شکست **landward, landwards** *adj., adv.* & *n.* towards the shore سمندر کے ساحل کی طرف facing the land خشکی کے رُخ کا ، ساحل کے رُخ کا

landau (*land*-aw) *n.* four-wheeled horse-carriage with movable top چھت کھُل جانے والی بگھی ، لینڈو

lane (layn) *n.* narrow country path between hedges ڈنڈی ، پگڈنڈی alley گلی ، کوچہ way made or left between lines of persons لوگوں کی قطاروں کے درمیان راستہ ocean course fixed as route for ship بحری راہ ، جہازوں کی گزرگاہ

language (*lang*-wij) *n.* medium for expressing thoughts in words زبان form of language used by a nation, etc. زبان (good, bad, strong, etc.) manner of using words (اچھی ، بُری وغیرہ) زبان jargon (of a profession, circle, etc.) زبان ، اصطلاحات (simple, flowery, etc.) style of expression by words انداز بیان *bad language, abusive language* گالی گلوچ ، دُشنام طرازی any means of expression زبان ، زبان حال signs used as language اشاراتی زبان ، اشارے *finger language*, one used by dumb persons انگلیوں کے اشارے *living language*, one still spoken naturally in any part of the world زندہ زبان *dead language*, one not so spoken مُردہ زبان ، متروک زبان

languid (*lang*-wid) *adj.* weak from exhaustion نڈھال slow-moving سست رفتار apathetic مُردہ دل پژمردہ **languish** *v. i.* become languid نڈھال ہونا be apathetic پژمردگی ، مُردہ دل ہو جانا lose health and strength صحت ، وطاقت ، زائل ہو جانا pine (*for*) کی یاد میں گھلنا affect sentimental tenderness to appeal for sympathy or love ہمدردی (یا محبّت) حاصل کرنے کے لیے اُداس اُداس بن جانا ، ہمدردی (یا محبّت) کے بھوکے کا چہرہ اُترا ہونا ، ہمدردی (یا محبّت) کا بھوکا ہونا ، بیمار دکھائی دینا ، آرزد *languishing looks* **languor** (*lang*-ĕ*) *n.* weakness کمزوری ، ناتوانی great fatigue سخت تھکن oppressive stillness ہُو کا عالَم dreaminess غنودگی، خواب کی سی کیفیت

lank *adj.* (of hair) long and straight, not wavy ربھسے بال (of person) lean پتلا، دُبلا، لاغر، مریل **lanky** (*lank*-i) *adj.* (of person or limb) awkwardly tall and lean بدنُما طور پر پتلا اور لمبا، سُوکھا اور لمبا

lantern (*lant*-ĕ*n) *n.* glass or metal case protecting a light from wind *dark lantern*, lantern with shutters to hide light if necessary لالٹین structure on the top of a dome to admit light گنبد کا رَوشن دان *lantern jaws*, long and thin jaws لمبے اور پتلے جبڑے

a lantern

lanyard (*lan*-yah*d) *n.* (soldier's) cord worn round shoulders to put whistle, etc., in pocket سیٹی وغیرہ کی رَسّی، شانہ رَسَن short rope used on ship for fastening, etc. چھوٹی رَسّی

Laocoon (la-*ok*-oh-on) *Cl. myth.* the unfortunate Trojan priest of the sun-god Appollo ; together with his two sons he was killed by boa-constrictors, the scene being commemorated in an artistic statue لئوکون، لاؤکون

lap *v. t.* & *i.* (-pp-) fold (cloth, etc. *round* or *in*) لپیٹنا، کرنا enfold (*in* luxury, etc.) میں غرق ہونا lay partly (*over*) (پر) آنا، (پر) (of a cat, etc.) lick up (milk, etc.) with the tongue چَپڑ چَپڑ پی جانا، سڑپا لگانا، سُڑکنا (of waves) splash gently against (سے) نرمی سے ٹکرانا *n.* hanging part of garment (کپڑے وغیرہ کا) دامن sound of lapping (of waves) (لہروں کے) نرمی سے ٹکرانے کی آواز upper part of the thigh of one sitting گود، آغوش *in the lap of* کے آغوش میں one circuit round a race-track دَوڑ کے میدان کا ایک چکّر *on the last lap of* (*tour, race, etc.*), in the final round or part of کے آخری چکر (یا حصّے) میں

lap-dog *n.* dog small enough to be held in the lap گود کا کتّا، چھوٹا کتّا **lapstone** *n.* shoemaker's stone to beat leather on موچی کا پتھر، موچی کا سُنداں

lapel (la-*pel*) *n.* folded part of a coat collar کالر کا کوٹ

lapidary (*lap*-i-dĕ-ri) *adj.* of stones پتھر کا engraved on stone پتھر پر کندہ *lapidary inscription* پتھر کتبہ *n.* cutter, polisher or engraver of gems حکّاک

lappet (*lap*-et) *n.* loose part (of garment) دامن small loose part (of flesh) ذرا سا لٹکتا ہوا حِصّہ *lappet of the ear* کان کی لَو

lapse (laps) *n.* slight mistake فروگزاشت، ذرا سی غلطی slip of memory بھول، سَہو a falling away (*from* virtue, etc.) passing away (*of time*) وَقفہ، (وقت کا) گزرنا، نزول (ایّام) slipping slowly (*into*) lower condition میں آہستہ آہستہ پھنس جانا یا گر جانا loss (of claim, right, etc.) through failure to renew it or fulfil certain conditions کھو بیٹھنا، تجدید استعمال نہ ہونے کے باعث حق باقی نہ رہنا *v. i.* fall (*from* good ways or position *into* bad ways or position) (پستی میں) گرنا، پستی کا شکار ہونا، (اچھی حالت سے بُری حالت میں) گرنا (of claim, right, etc. be lost (*through* lack of use, renewal, etc.) حق جاتا رہنا (of time, etc.) pass (*away*) وَقت گزر جانا

lapstone *n.* (see under **lap**)

lapwing (*lap*-wing) *n.* small water-fowl (also called *pewit* or *peewit* from its cry) سُمندری کوّا

larboard (*lah**-bĕ*d) *n.* (now usu. called *port*), left side of a ship looking forward (opp. of *starboard*) جہاز کا بایاں پہلو

larceny (*lah**sĕ-ni) *n.* (legal term for) theft سَرقہ، چوری *petty larceny*, pilfering چوری چھوٹی، معمُولی سَرقہ *grand larceny*, big theft بڑی چوری

lard (lah*d) *n.* melted fat of pig used as a cooking medium سُوَر کی چربی *v. t.* put lard on سُوَر کی چربی اُوپر ڈالنا interlard talk, etc. (*with* strange terms) تحریر و تقریر میں (اصطلاحات وغیرہ کی) بھرمار کرنا

larder (*lah**-dĕ*) *n.* room (or cupboard) for storing household food نعمت خانہ، بِرکابدار خانہ

large (lah*j) *adj.* big (in size, quality, scope, etc.) بڑا *at large*, (*a*) (discuss, etc.) comprehensively بالتفصیل، تفصیل سے (*b*) be not in prison قید سے آزاد، باہر، آزاد *people at large, the world at large*, people in general اکثر اشخاص، سبھی لوگ *by and large* (*a*) taking everything into consideration پھر بھی، بہر حال (*b*) on the whole مجموعی طور پر، فی الجملہ، بہر صورت

large-hearted *adj.* generous سخی kindly فراخدل **large-minded** *adj.* liberal, tolerant بامُروّت بڑی حد تک **largely** *adv.* to a great extent زور دار **largeness** *n.* being large بڑا ہونا، کثیر، وافر یا زیادہ تر وسیع ہونا

S **Large** denotes something big in every dimension. **great** in length or height or importance. **tall** in height only. **big** mainly in bulk. **ample** of sufficient proportions, **voluminous** bulky (books, etc.). and **immense** something too large to be measured.

largesse (*lah**-jes) *n.* (old use) money or gifts scattered on occasion of rejoicing انعام و اکرام giving away thus plentifully داد و دہش

lark (lah*k) (types of) small songbird مختلف قسم چکاوک، چنڈول، لوا، اگن *skylark* کے، چنڈول، چکاوک bit of fun ہنسی، دل لگی، چہل *v. i.* frolic *about in* some place (میں) کُدکڑے مارتے پھرنا، (میں) چہلیں کرتے پھرنا

larva (*lah**-va) *n.* (pl. *larvae*) insect in first stage of its life after coming out of the egg لاروا (کیڑوں مکوڑوں کا) پہلا رُوپ

laryngitis *n.* (see under **larynx**)

larynx (*la*-rinks) *n.* upper part of windpipe containing the vocal cords حنجرہ، نرخرہ **laryngitis** (la-rinj-*i*-tis) *n.* inflammation of the larynx ورمِ حنجرہ

lascar (*las*-kĕ*) *n.* Pakistani or Indian member of a British ship's crew انگریزی جہاز کا پاکستانی ملّاح

lascivious (la-*siv*-i-us) *adj.* lustful نفس پرست **lasciviousness** *n.* being lascivious : lust شہوت پرستی نفس پرستی

lash *v. t.* & *i.* flog کوڑے لگانا، چابک مارنا switch to and fro violently اِدھر اُدھر مارنا beat upon (or *against*) سے ٹکرانا *lash out* (of horse) kick (*at*) دولتّی جھاڑنا rush (*down*) اِدھر اُدھر مارنا bind with a rope (*to* something) سے باندھ دینا make a sudden movement (*up, down,* etc.) یک دم بڑھنا وغیرہ scold angrily سختی سے جھاڑ جھپاڑ کرنا roused (one's audience, etc., *into* fury) بھڑکانا، جوش دلانا *n.* thong of a whip کوڑا، تسمہ stroke given with a whip کوڑے کی ضرب eyelash پلک، مژہ **lashing** *n.* whipping کوڑے لگانا **eyelash** *n.* (usu. used in pl. as *eyelashes*), one of the little hair at the opening edge of the eyelid پلک، مژہ

lass (las) *n.* masc. (*lad*) young unmarried woman کنواری لڑکی، دوشیزہ sweetheart محبوبہ **lassie** (*lass*-ee) *n.* (term of endearment for a) lass کنواری لڑکی، دوشیزہ محبوبہ

lassitude (*las*-i-tewd) *n.* tiredness تھکن، تھکاوٹ ماندگی slothfulness سستی، الکسی state of being disinterested بے لیقی

lasso (*las*-oh) *n.* long rope with a noose at the loose end used by American cowboys (usu. on horseback) to catch cattle and prevent them from straying مویشی پکڑنے کی کمند، مویشی کمند

a cowboy with a lasso in hand

last (lahst) *adj.* coming after all others آخری، اخیر *at the last moment* بالکل آخری موقعہ آخری وقت میں *the last chance* next before the present گزشتہ *last year* پارسال *before last* آخری سے پہلا *last week* گزشتہ ہفتہ *week before last* دو ہفتے پہلے *last but one, second last,* second from the end ماقبل آخر least likely (*to, for* or *to do,* something) خواہ شاید ہی رہو، یا کرے *He is the last person to tell a lie,* وہ تو ایسا ہے کہ شاید ہی جھوٹ بولے، سب سے زیادہ ناموزوں *He should be the last person to be selected for this post* وہ اس ملازمت میں شاید ہی لیا جائے utmost (importance) سب سے زیادہ بہتر *the last word* (*in*), the best or most authoritative work (*of* or *on*) کا حرفِ آخر میں قولِ فیصل *adv.* after all others سب سے آخر، آخر میں (with names of days only used either as *last Monday* or *on Monday last* گزشتہ پیر کو، پچھلے پیر کو just before the present آخری بار، آخری مرتبہ in closing آخر میں *n.* end آخر *up to the last,* (*a*) to the end آخر تک (*b*) to the end of either's life آخری دم تک مرنے تک *to have seen the last of,* no more expect to see سے اب واسطہ پڑنے کی صورت نہ ہونا most recent letter آخری خط most recent baby آخری بچہ shoemaker's wooden model for shaping a shoe بوٹ کا قالب *v. i.* be enough for کے لیے کافی ہونا wear well, give service for چلنا continue (or *for*) a length of time جاری رہنا، رہنا *last out,* not come to an end before تک چلنا *at last,* finally آخر کار، آخرکار، انجام کار *at long last,* after trying one's patience خدا خدا کرکے *last but not the least,* though the last in order not the least in importance آخری بات مگر اہمیت میں یہ بھی کچھ کم نہیں، آخر میں مگر مؤخر نہیں *the last day,* (*a*) the final day (*of* some function) آخری روز آخری دن (*b*) the Day of Judgement روزِ قیامت *breathe one's last,* die مرنا، مر جانا *on* (*one's, etc.*) *last legs,* (*a*) near end ختم ہوا چاہتا (*b*) near death قبر میں پاؤں لٹکائے بیٹھے ہونا *last-mentioned,* one in the nearest position in the writing above مؤخر الذکر *last evening,* کل شام *last night* کل رات، گزشتہ شب (but never 'last morning', etc.) ; *till the last* آخر تک *Stick to* (*one's*) *last,* not meddle outside one's province دخل در معقولات نہ کرنا **lastly** (*last*-li) *adv.* (in enumeration : *first, secondly.....lastly*), in the last place آخر میں **lasting** *adj.* durable پائدار، مضبوط permanent (benefit, peace, etc.) مستقل

latch (lach) *n.* bar for fastening a door, etc. (دروازے وغیرہ کی) بلّی، پھرکی دار بیلن *on the latch,* not locked but merely fastened with a latch صرف بلّی سے بند کیا ہوا small spring lock for house-door opened from outside کھٹکے کا قفل *v.t.* & *i.* fasten with a latch بلّی سے بند کرنا (*latch on*), (see *Addenda*)

late (layt) *adj., adv.* & *n.* (*late ; later* or *latter ; latest,* or *last*) after the right time دیر سے (بعد وقت کے بعد، (اس پہنچنے والا *be late* دیر سے پہنچنا *late for* کام) کے لئے بعد از وقت نہ کرنے (ہونے وغیرہ) سے *better late than never* ابھی کا تازہ کبھی کرنا (یا ہونا وغیرہ) بہتر of recent date حالیہ *the late 'coup d'etat' in Iraq* عراق کا حالیہ فوجی انقلاب *late in the day,* (*a*) towards the evening تیسرے پہر، شام کو (*b*) too late to be effective وقت ہاتھ سے نکل جانے کے بعد *of late years,* in the last few years پچھلے چند برسوں میں *the late* (before designation), (person) formerely in office سابق *the late Premier* سابق وزیرِ اعظم *the late,* (before name) deceased مرحوم متوفی، آنجہانی *later on,* on some later occasion بعد میں کبھی پھر کبھی *late dinner hours* دیر سے کھانا کھانا *sooner or later,* at some future time کبھی نہ کبھی، کبھی تو

lately (*layt*-li) *adv.* a short while ago ابھی کچھ عرصہ قبل recently حال ہی میں **latest** (*lay*-test) *adj.* the most recent (news, event, fashion, etc.) تازہ ترین ، جدید ترین *at the latest,* before سے پہلے پہلے *by July 15 at the latest, at the latest by* (*July 15*) (پندرہ جولائی) سے پہلے پہلے ، زیادہ سے زیادہ (15 جولائی تک)

latent (*lat*-ent) *adj.* (of qualities, etc.) present but not manifest بالقوّہ *latent energy* بالقوّہ توانائی concealed پوشیدہ ، پنہاں dormant (disease, etc.) دبا ہُوا ، خوابیدہ

lateral (*late*-è-rĕl) *adj.* of, at, from or towards the side بغلی ، پہلو کا sprung from brother or sister of person in direct line *n.* بہن یا بھائی کی اولاد shoot, branch شاخ

latest *adj.* (see under **late**)

lath (lahth) *n.* (pl. *laths,* pr. lahdhz) *n.* long, thin and narrow strip of wood used in ceilings, lattices, etc. چپٹی ، لکڑی کی چپٹی **lathy** (*lah*-thi) *adj.* tall and thin لمبا اور پتلا

lathe (laydh) *n.* machine for shaping pieces of metal or wood by turning them in it rapidly against sharp edges خراد

lather (*ladh*-ĕ*) *n.* soft mass of white froth from soap and water صابن کا جھاگ یا پھکین *v. t. & i.* form or make lather on جھاگ اُٹھنا یا اُٹھانا

lathi-charge, (*laht*-i-chah*j) *n.* Pakistani police *posse's* attack on a crowd of (usu. political) demonstrators with a long bamboo stick iron-bound at the holding (and in striking, the hitting) end لاٹھی چارج *v. t. & i.* to charge thus لاٹھی چارج کرنا

latitude (*lat*-i-tewd) *n.* distance north or south of the equator measured in degrees عرض البلد ، عرض بلد *high* (or *low*) *latitudes,* places a long way from (or near to) the equator خطِ استوا سے کافی دُور (یا کے کافی قریب) علاقے region علاقہ ، خطہ range (of topics, etc.) تعداد freedom (*in* something or doing something) آزادی ، کھلی چھٹی *allow* (*someone*) *great latitude in* کسی کو کسی معاملے میں کھلی چھٹی دے دینا

latitudinarian (lat-i-tewd-i-*nay*-ri-an) *n. & adj.* (person) who permits or claims freedom of interpretation in religion (مذہبی معاملات میں) تاویل پسند

latitudinarianism *n.* being latitudinarian تاویل پسندی

latrine (la-*treen*) *n.* privy which is not a water-closet (esp. in a camp, etc.) (زیادہ افراد والی جگہ فلش کے علاوہ) پاخانہ ، ٹٹی

latter (*lat*-è*) *adj.* more recent زیادہ قریبی of the end (*of* a period) آخری *the latter,* the second of two things already mentioned مؤخر الذکر

latterly *adv.* recently حال ہی میں towards the end of life or some other period زندگی (وغیرہ) کے آخری دنوں میں

lattice (*lat*-is) *n.* framework of crossed laths or metal strips as a screen جھفری gate made of lattice جھفری کی محراب **latticed** (*lat*-isd) *adj.* made thus جھفری والا **lattice-window** *n.* window with small panes set in led سیسے میں جڑے ہُوئے شیشوں والی کھڑکی

laud (lawd) *v. t.* praise and glorify حمد کرنا حمد و ثنا کرنا praise تعریف کرنا **laudable** *adj.* praiseworthy قابلِ تعریف ، قابلِ ستائش **laudably** *adv.* in a praiseworthy manner قابلِ تعریف انداز **laudatory** *adj.* (*lawd*-a-tè-ri) *adj.* (of speech or writing) containing or expressing praise تعریفی مدحیہ

laudanum (*lawd*-a-num) *n.* sedative tincture of opium شراب میں حل کی ہوئی اَفیم

laugh (lahf) *v. t. & i.* make chuckling sounds of pleasure or amusement ہنسنا ، کھلکھلا کر ہنسنا ، قہقہہ مارنا ، قہقہے مار کر ہنسنا *laugh at,* mock, at کی ہنسی اُڑانا ، پر ہنسنا *laugh in amusement* بغض اٹھا کر ہنسنا *laugh in* (*one's*) *sleeve,* laugh secretly دبی ہوئی ہنسی ہنسنا **laugh** in (*someone's*) *face,* thus show great **disrespect** for (him) کی ہنسی اُڑانا *laugh on the wrong side of* (*one's*) *mouth* (or *face*), be sad at the **failure of one's** plans کھسیانی ہنسی ہنسنا ، رونی صورت بنانا *laugh down,* silence with laughter اتنا ہنسنا کہ دوسرے چپ ہو جائیں *laugh* (*something*) *away,* dismiss with laughter ہنس دینا *he laughs best who laughs last,* (said of or by one) who, though not successful yet, hopes to be some day اچھا کوئی دن ہمارے ہنسنے کا بھی تو آئے ہی گا *n.* chuckling sound of amusement ہنسی *hearty laugh* قہقہہ *raise a laugh,* cause amusement پر ہنسی ہونا ، ہنسی اُڑوانا *have* (or *get*) *the laugh of,* turn tables on کسی کو ہرا کر ہنسی اُڑانا **laughing-gas** *n.* anaesthetic used to induce sleep when a tooth is to be pulled out سُن کرنے والی دوا **laughing-stock** *n.* object of general derision ہنسی اُڑانے کی جگہ ، مضحوکہ **laughable** *adj.* causing laughter جس پر ہنسی آئے ، مضحکہ خیز **laughter** (*lahf*-tè*) *n.* act or sound of laughing ، قہقہہ ، ہنسی ، ہنسی کی آواز ، قہقہہ

launch (lawnch) *v. t. & i* set a newly built ship afloat جہاز کو پہلی مرتبہ پانی میں اُتارنا start (business, attack, etc.) کاروبار جاری کرنا go (*out* or *forth,* on an enterprise, etc.) کسی مہم پر روانہ ہونا *n.* launching a ship جہاز پانی میں اُتارنا mechanically propelled ferry boat لانش ، بحری کشتی گھاٹ کے پار اُتارنے والی بحری کشتی

launder (*lawnd*-ĕ*) *v. t. & i.* wash and press (clothes) کپڑے دھو کر استری کرنا **laundress** (*lawnd*-res)

n. woman who launders دھوبن **laundry** (*lawnd-ri*) n. clothes-washing business دھوبی کا کام place for washing clothes گھاٹ دھوبی کی دُکان دھوبی گھاٹ batch of clothes sent to be laundered میلے کپڑے ، دھونے والے کپڑے batch of clothes received back from laundry دُھلے ہوئے کپڑے ، دُھلائی

laureate (*law-re-ayt*) n. crowned with laurel سرفراز، لارل کی پتیوں سے سرفراز رکھا ہُوا ، Poet Laureate مَلِکُ الشُعَرا، درباری شاعر **Poet-Laureate** n. (also *laureate*), poet specially appointed by the (British) sovereign as writer of Court odes مَلِکُ الشُعَرا، درباری شاعر **laureateship** n. being a poet مَلِکُ الشُعَرائی

laurel (*law-rel*) n. bay-tree ; an evergreen shrub wreath of whose leaves is an emblem of poetic merit or victory لارل (*pl.*) honour of victory (in poetry or war) فتح و نصرت کا سہرا *win* (or *reap*) *laurels* کامیابی پانا ، عزت حاصل کرنا *look to* (*one's*) *laurels*, beware of losing pre-eminence اپنی برتری قائم رکھنے کی مُسلسل سعی کرتے رہنا *rest on* (*one's*) *laurels*, cease to make further efforts for improvement مزید ترقی کی کوشش ترک کر دینا

lava (*lah-va*) n. hot molten metals, etc., thrown out by a volcano آتش فشاں پہاڑ کا پگھلا ہُوا مادہ ، پگھلا لاوا ، لاوا this material when it has cooled down and hardened منجمد لاوا ، سخت لاوا ، لاوا

lave (*layv*) v. t. wash, bathe نہانا ، دھونا (of sea, stream, etc.) wash against or flow along (سمندر ، دریا وغیرہ کا) ساتھ بہنا یا لگنا

lavatory (*lav-a-to-ri*) n. room for washing hands and face غسل خانہ ، مُنہ ہاتھ دھونے کا کمرہ ، وضو خانہ (nice name for) water-closet پاخانہ ، طہارت خانہ (similar name for) urinal پیشاب خانہ

lavatory n. (see under **lave**)

lavender (*lev-end-ĕ**) n. a plant with fragrant flowers of a pale purple colour لیونڈر ، لَوَنڈر its flower لیونڈر کا پھول ، لیونڈر its colour ہلکا ارغوانی v. t. scent with lavender لیونڈر سے بسانا **lavender-water** n. perfume prepared with lavender, ambergris and alcohol عطرِ لیونڈر ، لیونڈر

a lavender

lavish (*lav-ish*) v. t. give generously (money, care, etc., *on* someone) دِل کھول کر (کسی پر) صَرف کرنا squander اُڑانا ، بے اندازہ خرچ کرنا adj. giving liberally بے اندازہ عطا کرنا producing much افراط سے پیدا کرنا given abundantly وافر کثیر **lavishly** adv. liberally دِل کھول کر ، فراخدلی سے wastefully اندھا دُھند ، بے اندازہ

law n. piece of legislation قانون *the law*; the whole body of laws in a country مجموعۂ قوانین ، قوانین *the Islamic law* اسلامی شریعت ، شریعت *the law of the land* مُلکی قانون *against the law* خلافِ قانون legal study or legal profession قانون *a law student* قانون کا طالب علم *go to law*, seek redress through a law-court قانونی کاروائی کرنا ، قانونی چارہ جوئی کرنا *take the law into one's own hand*, redress wrongs by force قانون اپنے ہاتھ میں لینا *give the law to*, impose (one's) will upon اپنی مرضی کسی کے سر پر مُسلط کرنا *be a law unto (oneself)*, disregard conventions مروّجہ دستور کی پروا نہ کرنا ، جی آئی کرنا *lay down the law*, (a) legislate قانون بنانا (b) talk in an authoritative manner تحکمانہ انداز سے بات کرنا *necessity knows no law*, everything is fair in need ضرورت میں سب کچھ جائز ہے

accepted rules (*of* a game) (کھیل کے) قواعد

(in science) correct statement of what happens in certain circumstances قانون *the laws of nature* قوانین قدرت ، قوانین فطرت *law of gravitation* قانونِ کشش ثقل **law-abiding** adj. (of person, citizen, etc.) obeying the law قانون کی پابندی کرنے والا **law-court** n. court of law عدالت ، کچہری **lawful** adj. according to the law قانونی ، قانون کی نظر میں allowed by it جائز ، قانونی ، قانون کے مُطابق **lawless** adj. (of act) against the law غیر قانونی (of person) violating the law قانون شکن **lawlessness** n. being lawless قانون شکنی ، لاقانونیت **lawsuit** n. claim made in law court نالش ، مقدمہ **lawyer** n. member of the legal profession who pleads or briefs the cases of clients وکیل

lawn n. plot of grass kept closely mowed گھاس کا تختہ ، سبزہ زار ، لان *lawn-tennis* (or simply *tennis*), well-known outdoor game played with soft balls and stringed rackets ٹینس *tennis lawn*, tennis court ٹینس کا میدان a kind of fine linen fabric مَلمَل کی ایک قسم **lawn-mower** n. machine for cutting grass on lawns سبزہ زار سے گھاس کاٹنے والی کل ، گھاس کاٹ

a lawn-mower

lax (*laks*) adj. not light ڈھیلا ، ڈھیلا ڈھالا negligent بے پروا loose (morals) بُرا ، خراب **laxity** (*lak-si-ti*) n. ڈھیلا ہونا ، بے پروائی ، بُرائی ، خرابی

laxative (*lak-sa-tiv*) adj. tending to loosen the bowels قبض کُشا ، مُلَیّن n. such drug قبض کُشا دوا ، مُلَیّن

lay v. t. & i. (*lay, laid, laid*) put on a surface (brick, floor, foundation, rails, cable, carpet, etc.) رکھنا ، لگانا produce (an egg or eggs) (انڈے) دینا cause (person) to lie لٹانا ، ڈال دینا cause (dust, etc., to be down) بٹھانا ، ڈالنا flatten (crops by rains, etc.) لِٹا دینا set (*the table*) with meals, etc. دسترخوان لگانا ، میز پر کھانا لگانا set (*dinner, etc.*) on the table دسترخوان لگانا ، میز پر کھانا چننا ، لگانا

make ready (ambush, snare, trap, etc.)

prepare (plan) منصوبہ باندھنا، ترکیب سوچنا (10) (pa. t. of *lie* : *lie, lay, lain*) (see under *lie*) *n.* ballad ; minstrel's song منظوم کہانی poem intended for singing گیت *adj.* non-clerical دنیا دار، دنیا دارانہ amateur غیر ماہر، اناڑی amateurish غیر ماہرانہ، اناڑیوں کا سا *lay a wager* (*that* or *against*), bet شرط لگانا *lay* (*something*) *aside*, (*a*) abandon (*bad habit*, etc.) پرے چھوڑنا، ترک کرنا (*b*) put down پرے رکھ دینا (*c*) save (money) for future needs برے (یا آڑے) وقت کیلئے بچانا، ضرورت کیلئے *lay* (*blame, etc.*) *at the door of*, impute it کسی کے سر دھرنا *lay bare*, reveal افشا کرنا، طشت از بام کرنا *lay before* (*someone*), submit to him کے سامنے رکھنا *lay something by*, save for future use برے (یا آڑے) وقت کے لیے بچا، ضرورت کیلئے بچانا *lay claim to*, claim as (one's) own پر دعویٰ جتانا *lay down* (*one's*) *life*, sacrifice it جان قربان کر دینا *lay down* (*office, hopes, etc.*), relinquish ترک کرنا *lay down* (*one's*) *arms*, surrender ہتھیار ڈالنا *lay it down* (*that*), declare firmly that قطعی طور پر مستحکم دینا کہ *lay* (*one's*) *hands on*, lay (one's) hand on (usu. in the negative) locate it کا پتہ ہونا *lay hands on*, seize or attack پر ہاتھ ڈالنا یا حملہ کرنا *lay hold of* (or *on*), grasp تھامنا، پکڑنا *lay in*, provide a store of جمع کرنا، اکٹھا رکھنا *lay* (*someone*) *low*, overthrow him کو ہرانا، کو شکست دینا *lay on* (*a*) impose (tax) (ٹیکس) لگانا، عائد کرنا (*b*) apply (paint) (روغن) کرنا، تھوپنا (*c*) inflict (blow) (ضرب) لگانا (*d*) instal pipes, etc., in a house for the supply of (water or gas) (کسی گھر میں) پانی یا گیس پہنچانے کی نالیاں لگانا *lay-out* (arrangement, design), ترتیب *lay-out of a newspaper page* اخبار کے صفحے پر خبروں کی ترتیب *lay out*, (*a*) arrange ترتیب دینا (*b*) plan کا نقشہ ذہن میں تیار کرنا (*c*) prepare (dead body) for burial تجہیز و تکفین کرنا *lay* (*a country*) *waste*, ravage it تاخت و تاراج کرنا *lay up*, save or store اکٹھا رکھنا، بچا کر رکھنا، سینت کر رکھنا *lay* (*oneself*) *out* (*for* or *to do something*), make a special effort کے لیے خاص کوشش کرنا *lay stress on*, emphasize پر زور دینا *lay siege to*, beleaguer کا محاصرہ کرنا *lay the damages at*, sue for compensation کا ہرجانے کی نالش کرنا *lay the fire*, arrange fuel for lighting آگ جلانے کے لیے لکڑی لگانا *lay to heart*, take seriously دل کو لگانا *lay under obligation*, oblige احسان مند کرنا، ممنون کرنا *lay under contribution*, exact contribution from سے ذبردستی چندہ وصول کرنا *be laid up with* (illness), be incapacitated by کے باعث صاحب فراش ہونا **layman** (*lay*-man) *n.* one who is not a priest غیر ملا، غیر پادری، دنیا دار one without special or professional knowledge (of a subject, especially law or medicine) غیر ماہر، کا باضابطہ علم نہ رکھنے والا **lay figure** *n.* wooden figure used in drawing چوبی مجسمہ nonentity بے حقیقت شخص، لاشئے شخص **laicize** (*lay*-i-size) *v. t.* rid of priestly control ملائیت سے آزاد کرانا **laity** (*lay*-i-ti) *n.* (*the laity*), laymen غیر ملا، غیر پادری، دنیا دار، عوام

layer (*lay*-ĕ*) *n.* plastered or spread-out material covering a surface تہہ، پرت، طبق (hen) that lays (eggs) انڈے دینے والی shoot fastened down to take root while still growing from the parent plant داب *v. t.* propagate plants thus داب لگانا

layout (*lay*-out) *n.* (see under **lay**)

laze *v. i.* (see under **lazy**)

lazy (*lay*-zi) *adj.* indolent سست، کاہل **lazy-bones** *n.* (colloq.) lazy person جس کی ہڈیوں میں سستی پڑی ہو **lazily** (*lay*-zi-li) *adv.* in a lazy manner سستی سے **laziness** *n.* indolence سستی، کاہلی **laze** (layz) *v. i.* be lazy سست ہونا، سستی سے کام لینا

lea (lee) *n.* (lit.) meadow مرغزار، سبزہ زار

¹**lead** (led) *n.* a heavy bluish grey metal سیسہ *red lead*, a compound of it سندور، شنگرف *white lead*, another compound of lead سفیدہ *black lead*, (also *lead*), graphite رچسل، کا سرمہ یا سکہ *lead pencil*, ordinary pencil (سکے کی) پنسل lump of this, tied to a line, for measuring depth of water پنسال dejection غم، الم thin strip of lead (or now usu. wood) to separate lines of type لیڈ bullets گولیاں *fill* (*someone*) *with lead*, shoot him نشانہ بنانا *v. t. lead out*, space out lines of type with lead لیڈ آؤٹ کرنا **leaden** (*led*-ĕn) *adj.* of lead سیسے کا of the colour of lead سیسے کے رنگ کا heavy as lead سیسے جیسا بھاری *leaden clouds* اُمڈی گھٹا، کالی گھٹا dull, spiritless پژمردہ، بجھی، بے جان

²**lead** (leed) *v.t.* & *i.* (*lead, led, led*) guide (towards some place) by moving in front لے جانا direct by example or persuasion قیادت کرنا، رہنمائی کرنا، رہبری کرنا be the head of (army, expedition, movement, etc.) کا سربراہ ہونا (of a road) go (*to*) (کو) جانا *lead to*, result in پر منتج ہونا (cause to) live a (good, hard, etc., life) میں گزارنا، گزارنے پر مجبور کرنا take the first place اول رہنا constrain (*to* or *into*) پر مجبور کرنا play the principal role (in film, drama, etc.) میں سب سے اہم کردار ادا کرنا، کا ہیرو (یا ہیروئن) ہونا *lead the way*, go first آگے چلنا، آگے آگے چلنا *lead astray* گمراہ کرنا، غلط راہ پر چلانا (*a person*) *easier to be led than driven* جو ڈنڈے سے زیادہ دلیل یا مثال سے متاثر ہو *be led away*, be induced to follow unthinkingly کسی کے پیچھے ہو لینا *lead* (*someone*) *by the nose*, compel (him) to do all one wishes اُلو بنا کر جو چاہنا کرا لینا *nose-led*, one led thus کسی کے ہاتھ میں آیا ہوا اُلو *lead* (*someone*) *to believe*, cause (him) to do so کو خیال دلانا *n.* leading رہنمائی، رہبری، قیادت *take the lead*,

be the first to do پہل کرنا *give the lead to*, pave the way for, lead پہل کر کے دُوسروں کو راہ دکھانا example مِثال *follow* (*someone's*) *lead*, act on (his) example of کی مِثال پر عمل کرنا ، کو اپنے لیے مشعلِ راہ بنانا ، کے نقشِ قدم پر چلنا distance by which one leads in race دَوڑ میں جتنا فاصلہ کوئی آگے ہو *have a lead of* (*two feet, etc.*) (دو فُٹ وغیرہ) آگے ہونا principal role (*in* a film or drama) سب سے اہم کردار ، ہیرو (یا ہیروئن) کا کردار actor or actress playing it ہیرو (یا ہیروئن) کا کردار ادا کرنے والا اداکار یا کرنے والی اداکارہ (in card games) right to start the play (تاش کے کھیل میں) پہل کا حق **leader** (*lee*-dě*) *n*. one who leads قائد ، رہنما ، رہبر leading article اخبار کا مقالۂ افتتاحیہ ، افتتاحیہ **leadership** *n*. قیادت ، رہنمائی ، رہبری **leading** *adj*. chief سب سے بڑا ، سب سے اہم *the leading lady*, (*of the picture, etc.*), chief actress (in a film, etc.) (کی) ہیروئن (کی) ، اوّلین اداکارہ *leading article*, newspaper article giving editorial comments افتتاحیہ ، اداریّہ مقالہ *leading question*, question that suggests the hoped-for answer مطلوب جواب کیلیے اکسایا ہوا سوال ، استفسار *leading case*, a case whose decision would be treated as a precedent in other cases نظیر بننے والا مقدمہ ، نظیری مقدمہ *leading edge*, foremost edge of aircraft's wing جہاز کے بازو کا اگلا کنارہ

leaf (leef) *n*. (pl. *leaves* pr. leevz) thin, flat growth on a plant پتّہ ، برگ ، ورق *leaves of a tree* درخت کے پتّے *be in leaf, come into leaf*, (of a tree) bear leaves کے پتّے اُگنا *leaves of grass*, its blades گھاس کی پتّیاں sheet of paper forming two pages of a book *turn over a new leaf*, (a) (of a book) turn a leaf and look at a new one ورق پلٹنا (b) make a new and better start از سرِ نو اور بہتر انداز سے آغاز کرنا ، زندگی کا نیا دور شروع کرنا ، نئی زندگی شروع کرنا hinged part of a table (میز کا) اُلٹ تختہ anything looking like a sheet ورق *gold leaf*, gold beaten into thin sheets سونے کا ورق ، ورقِ طلا *silver leaf* چاندی کا ورق ، ورقِ نقرہ **leafless** *adj*. having no leaves جس کا کوئی پتّہ نہ ہو ، بے برگ و بار **leafy** (*lee*-fi) *adj*. full of leaves بہت سے پتّوں والا ، برگ پوش shady گھنا ، سایہ دار **leaflet** (*leef*-let) *n*. small leaf پتّی ، چھوٹا سا پتّہ (esp.) handbill دستی اشتہار folder ; folded advertisement اوراقی اشتہار ، اوراقی

league (leeg) *n*. welfare union اتحاد ، انجمن ، جماعت ، لیگ *in league with*, allied with سے ملا ہُوا group of sports clubs playing matches among themselves کھیل کی انجمنوں کا وفاق ، کھیل کی وفاقی انجمن *league football matches* فٹ بال کی وفاقی انجمن کے مقابلے (old use) varying measure of distance (usu. about three miles) کوس *v.t.* & *i.* form into a league for mutual benefit متحد ہونا ، متحدہ انجمن **leaguer** (*leeg*-ě*) *n*. member of a league لیگی ، اتحادی

leak (leek) *n*. hole, etc., through which a fluid may undesirably flow (*into* or *out*) چھید ، سوراخ ، درز ، دراڑ *v.t.* (let fluid) pass through a leak رِستنا ، رِسنا ، ٹپکنا یا ٹپکانا ، چونا یا چوانا (*leak out*), (of secret) become or make known gradually (کے متعلّق لوگوں کو) افشا ہونا یا کرنا ، قبل از وقت معلوم ہونا ، یا بتانا ، لیک آؤٹ ہونا یا کرنا ، بات کا کھل جانا *The Secondary Board Intermediate question papers leaked out some years ago* بورڈ کے ایف۔اے ، ایف۔ایس سی کے پرچے چند سال ہوئے لیک آؤٹ ہوئے **leakage** *n*. leaking رِسنا ، ٹپکنا ، بات کا کھل جانا یا کھول دینا ، افشا ہونا یا کرنا thing that leaks out رِسنے (یا افشا ہونے) والی allowance for it ضائع (یا افشا) ہونے کی کسر unexplained disappearance of money رُوپیہ کا غائب ہو جانا **leaky** (*lee*-ki) *adj*. having a leak جس میں چھید ہو ، سوراخ دار

lean (leen) *adj*. (of persons or animals) not fat پتلا ، دُبلا ، لاغر ، کمزور (of meat) have little fat جس پر چربی نہ ہونا ، جو چربی والا نہ ہو ، غیر مُچرب (of year, harvest, etc.) بُرا ، خراب ، اقتصادی بدحال *v.t.* & *i.* (*leaned*, or *leant* pr. lent) be or put in a slanting position جھکا ہُوا ہونا یا جھکانا *lean a ladder against the wall* سیڑھی کے پاؤں اُتار کر دیوار *lean out of a window* کھڑکی میں سے جھک کر باہر دیکھنا bend (forward, backward, etc.) for support جھکنا یا جھکانا rest for support پر ٹِکنا ، ٹیکنا یا رکھنا *lean* (*one's*) *elbows on a table* کہنیاں میز پر رکھنا have a tendency (*towards*) مائل ہونا ، سے رغبت ہونا depend (*upon* someone *for* something) پر انحصار کرنا **leaning** *n*. (usu. *pl.*) tendency (*of* mind *towards* something) مَیلان ، رُجحان ، رغبت **lean-to** (*leen*-too) *n*. shed, etc., resting against the wall of another building and having a roof sloping one way only چھپّر

■ We **lean** *on* something for support ; **lean** *to* or *towards* an opinion ; **incline** *to* or *towards* something mentally ; **dip** a flag ; **slant**, a stroke in handwriting ; **tilt** lance, etc., unsteadily.

Leander (le-*and*-ě*) *Cl. myth*. a youth of Abydos who (like the Punjabi *Mahinwal*) swam nightly across the Hellespont (the modern Dardanelles) to visit his lady-love, Hero of Sestos, till he was drowned one night in a storm لینڈر

leap (leep) *v.t.* & *i.* (*leapt* pr. lept or *leaped*) jump کُودنا jump (*over* or *across*) پھلانگنا ، پھاندنا ، کُدانا spring (off the ground) (سے) اُچھلنا jump (*into* air, etc., from a high place) میں کُودنا یا پڑنا jump at (*with* joy, etc.) (پر) اُچھل پڑنا *leap in the dark*, venture on a doubtful measure اندھے کنوئیں میں چھلانگ لگانا *n*. jump چھلانگ ، جست *by leaps and bounds*, rapidly بڑی جلدی ، حیرت انگیز رفتار سے ، دن دوگنی رات چوگنی (*take*) *a leap in the dark* اندھے کنوئیں میں چھلانگ لگانا **leap-frog** *n*. game in which players jump with parted legs over others who bend down گھوڑی گھوڑی ، گھوڑی سوار

leap-year *n.* every year of the Christian calendar which is exactly divisible by four (or if a century by 400) (*i.e.*, leaves no remainder) marking that February has 29 days to it (instead of the usual 28) لیپ کا سال، ایک دن کی جنبش والا سالِ کبیسہ

learn (lĕ*n) *v.t.* & *i.* (*learnt* or *learned* pr. lĕ*nd) gain knowledge for or skill in (something) by study or practice سیکھنا be informed (*that*, *how* or *whether*) بتایا جانا، معلوم ہونا **learned** (*lĕ**-nèd) *adj.* scholarly (person or writing, etc.) عالِم فاضِل، عالمانہ، فاضلانہ *the learned professions*, those needing much knowledge علمی پیشے **learnedly** *adv.* عالمانہ انداز سے **learning** (*lĕ**-ning) *n.* knowledge gained by careful study علم، علم و فضل
[S] **knowledge** is the general word; **learning** signifies knowledge gained as a result of careful study; **scholarship** denotes possession of profound knowledge of some subject and of related topics; **erudition** means great knowledge but it is also ironically used of a great show of superficial knowledge.

lease (lees) *n.* legal agreement by which the owner of lands or a building (called *lessor*) agrees to let another (called *lessee*) have the use of it for a long but specified period (usu.) for a fixed payment (called *rent*) (*get*) *a new lease of life*, (get) a better chance of living longer or of being happier نئی زندگی پانا *lend and lease*, term of the U.S. aid to its allies during World War II under which they leased out airstrips or other strategic points to her in return for military equipment, etc., she gave them اُدھار پٹہ *v.t.* take possession of or give (land, etc.) by lease پٹے پر لینا **lessor** *n.* one who gives out on lease پٹے پر دینے والے **lessee** (le-*see*) *n.* one who takes out on lease پٹے پر لینے والا
leasehold *n.* & *adj.* (land) held for a term of years پٹے پر لی ہوئی (اراضی)، مستاجری

leash (leesh) *n.* cord or strap for holding a dog کتے کے پٹے میں ڈالنے کا تسمہ یا ڈوری *hold in leash*, control قابو میں رکھنا *v.t. put a leash on* (*dog*) (کتے کے گلے میں) ڈوری ڈالنا

least (leest) *adj.* smallest کم سے کم، تھوڑے سے تھوڑا *at least*, (*a*) at any rate بہرحال، بہرصورت، کم ازکم (*b*) not less even if more is impossible کم ازکم *adv.* in the least degree بہت ہی تھوڑا، کم سے کم، کم ازکم *n.* smallest (amount, degree, etc.) کمترین مقدار، درجہ وغیرہ

leather (*ledh*-ĕ*) *n.* material made by curing skins and hides of animals چمڑا، چرم *adj.* of leather چمڑے کا، چرمی **leatherette** (ledh-è-*ret*) *n.* imitation leather نقلی چمڑا، چرم نما **leathery** (ledh-è-ri) *adj.* tough, etc., like leather چمڑے کا سا سخت

leave (leev) *v.t.* & *i.* (*leave, left, left*) go away from چھوڑنا، چھوڑ جانا، چھوڑ دینا *leave a message for* کے نام پیغام دے جانا forget to do, take, etc. (something) بھول جانا، کھو دینا، کھو آنا postpone (work, etc., *until*) (پر) اُٹھا رکھنا allow (*to, be*, etc.) (رہنے) دینا *leave* (*the door, etc.*) *open* (دروازہ وغیرہ) کھلا رہنے دینا *leave* (or *let*) (*someone* or *something*) *alone*, not to touch or interfere with (کو) نہ چھیڑنا، پڑا رہنے دینا *leave go* (*of something*), stop holding it (کو) چھوڑ دینا *leave off*, (*a*) give up چھوڑنا (*b*) stop بس کرنا *leave out*, (*to do, etc.*), omit (to do it) (کرنا) بھول جانا، نہ (کرنا) bequeath (money, etc.) to (someone) کے نام وصیت کر جانا *leave behind at* (*one's*) *death*, leave a legacy ترکہ چھوڑ جانا pass by (a place, etc.) so that it is *on* or *to* one's right, left, etc. کے پاس یوں گزرنا کہ وہ دائیں (بائیں وغیرہ) طرف رہ جائے *be left*, remain بچنا، رہنا، باقی ہونا یا رہنا *be left for* کے لیے بچنا *be left over* بچ جانا، بچ رہنا
n. permission (*to do something*) اجازت، رخصت *grant leave of absence to* کو غیر حاضر رہنے کی اجازت دینا permission to be absent from duty چھٹی، رخصت *grant leave* چھٹی کی درخواست منظور کرنا، چھٹی دینا *apply for leave, ask for leave* چھٹی کی درخواست دینا *go home on leave* چھٹی پر گھر جانا، چھٹی لے کر گھر آنا *leave application* چھٹی کی درخواست *by your leave*, with your permission آپ کی اجازت سے period or nature of such absence چھٹی، رخصت *casual leave*, leave for contingencies اتفاقی چھٹی *earned leave*, leave falling due after putting in a special period of service استحقاقی رخصت *medical leave*, leave on medical grounds بیماری کی چھٹی، علالت کی رخصت *leave on full pay* رخصت با تنخواہ، پوری تنخواہ پر رخصت *leave on half-pay* آدھی تنخواہ پر چھٹی، نصف تنخواہ پر رخصت *leave without pay* بلا تنخواہ رخصت، رخصت بلا تنخواہ *take* (*one's*) *leave, take leave of* (*someone*), bid farewell (to) سے رخصت ہونا *take leave of* (*one's*) *senses*, behave as if mad پاگلوں کی حرکات کرنا، پاگل پن کرنا **french leave** *n.* (see under **french**)

leaven (*lev*-èn) *n.* substance added to dough to ferment it خمیر strong influence اثر *v.t.* add leaven to خمیر ڈالنا ferment dough خمیر کرنا mix (*with* modifying element) بدلنے والی شے ڈالنا

leaves *n.* (*pl.* of **leaf**, which see)

lebensraum (*layb*-ens-roum) *n.* foreign territory claimed by a State as a 'living-space' for it and necessary for its development زندہ رہنے کے لیے جگہ

lectern (*lek*-tĕ*n) *n.* sloping desk for reading Bible in church by the standing priest انجیل دان any desk for resting a book on while reading رحل

lecture (*lek*-chĕ*) *n.* talk (*to* an audience) تقریر، خطبہ، خطاب talk (*to* a class *on* a subject) for the purpose of imparting knowledge تقریر، سبق، لیکچر lengthy admonition by a wife بیوی کی لعن طعن *v. t. & i* talk to audience تقریر کرنا، لیکچر کرنا give such talk (*to* a class *on* a subject) (استادگی تقریر، لیکچر، (کسی جماعت کو کسی مضمون کا) سبق wife's admonition بیوی کا لعن طعن کرنا **lecturer** *n.* one who talks to an audience مقرر، لیکچرار junior teacher in a college لیکچرار، اُستاد **lectureship** (*lek*-chĕ*-ship) *n.* post of lecturer (*at* a college or university لیکچراری، (کالج وغیرہ) میں مُدرّسی

led *v.* (pa. t. & pa. p. of **lead**, which see)

ledge (lej) *n.* narrow shelf protruding from a wall or other upright surface لگر stone slab coming out of a cliff کھڑی چٹان کے پہلو سے اُبھرا ہوا پتھر

ledger (*lej*-ĕ*) *n.* book of a firm's accounts کھاتہ

lee *n.* place sheltering against wind ہَوا سے اوٹ such shelter ہَوا سے پناہ *adj.* (side of a ship, etc.) away from the wind (جہاز کا) ہَوا سے پرے رُخ کا پہلو *lee-shore*, shore towards which the wind is blowing ہَوا کے رُخ والا ساحل **leeway** *n.* sideways drift (of a ship) in the direction towards which the wind is blowing ہَوا کی وَجہ سے جہاز کا پہلو کی طرف *make up leeway*, make up for lost time گئے وَقت کی کسر پُوری کرنا

leech (leech) *n.* small blood-sucking worm جونک *stick like a leech*, be difficult to get rid of جونک کی طرح چمٹ جانا

leer *n.* sly look کنکھیوں سے دیکھنا، چور نظر a look with evil desire بُری نظر *v.i.* look (*at* something or someone) slyly کنکھیوں سے دیکھنا look (*at* someone) with an evil desire (پر) بُری نظر ڈالنا

lees *n. pl.* dregs تلچھٹ، دُرد

left *v.* (pa. t. & pa. p. of *leave*. which see) *adj.* (opp. of *right*) بایاں radical; (opp. of conservative) بلیاں (*the left*), opposite camp حزبِ مخالف **left hand** *n.* opposite of right hand بایاں ہاتھ، اُلٹا ہاتھ **left-handed** (*left*-hand-ed) *adj.* using the left hand more dextrously than the right one کھبّا double-edged (compliment, etc.) دو معنی clumsy بھدّا *left-handed policy*, duplicity دورُخی، منافقت **Leftist** *n.* (see *Addenda*)

leg *n.* limb used in walking ٹانگ some part of animal's body as food دَستی، ران part of a garment covering the leg پائینچہ support of (chair, table, machine, etc.) پایہ، ٹانگ (in cricket) part of field to right rear of batsman لیگ *long leg, short leg, square leg*, fielders variously posted there لانگ لیگ، شارٹ لیگ، اسکوئر لیگ hop or stage of long distance flight منزل، پَرواز، پَرواز کا مرحلہ ہَوائی سفر کا ایک مرحلہ *give (someone) a leg up*, help in time of need آڑے وَقت میں کام آنا *pull (someone's) leg*, try jokingly to make him believe something untrue کسی کو جھوٹی بات کا یقین دِلانے کی کوشش کرنا، بنانا، بیوقوف بنانا *not have a leg to stand on*, lack support for one's opinion, etc. معقول دَلائل نہ ہونا، دَعوے کا کوئی ثبوت نہ ہونا *on its last legs*, (*a*) almost at an end ختم ہی ہونے والا (*b*) almost useless تقریباً ناکارہ، بیکار سا **leggings** (*leg*-ingz) *n. pl.* strong leather coverings for the lower part of the legs (for players in certain games) ساق پوش **legless** *adj.* without legs جس کی ٹانگیں نہ ہوں، لُولا **leggy** (*leg*-i) *adj.* lanky-legged لمبی لمبی ٹانگوں والا **leg-pulling** *n.* playing a hoax خوشامد سے دھوکا دینا، بیوقوف بنانا بنانا **leg before wicket**, (abb. *l.b.w.*), disqualifying position for batsman when he places his leg before the wicket so that the ball is prevented from hitting the wicket only because of the leg وکٹ کے آگے ٹانگ، لیگ بیفور وکٹ، ایل۔ بی۔ ڈبلیو

a leg showing toes (*T*), arch (*Ar*), heel (*He*), ankle (*An*), shin (*S*), calf (*C*), knee (*K*) and hip (*H*)

legacy (*leg*-a-si) *n.* property, etc., left in a person's will ترکہ، ورثہ، میراث whatever has been left to people (*of* ancestors or past events) کا تحفہ، ترکہ **legatee** (leg-a-*tee*) *n.* one who gets a legacy جس کے حق میں وصیّت کی جائے، ترکہ پانے والا، موصیٰ لہٗ **legacy-hunter** *n.* one who clings obsequiously to another in the hope of becoming his legatee ترکہ حاصل کرنے کے لیے خوشامد کرنے والا

legal (*lee*-gĕl) *adj.* pertaining to the law قانونی according to the law قانونی، قانون کے مطابق *legal tender*, form of currency which cannot be rejected when offered in payment for something (in a country) قانونی سکّہ، زرِ قانونی *The paper rupee is a legal tender in this country* ایک رُوپیہ کا نوٹ اِس مُلک میں زرِ قانونی ہے **legally** (*leeg*-a-li) *adv.* from the standpoint of law قانونی نقطۂ نگاہ سے قانونی طور پر، قانونی حیثیت سے *legally speaking*, قانونی نقطۂ نگاہ سے کہنا پڑتا ہے کہ

legality (le-*gal*-i-ti) *n.* being lawful قانون کے مطابق ہونا **legalize** *v. t.* make lawful، قانونی صورت دینا، جائز بنا لینا **legalization** *n.* making (*of* something) lawful, bringing (*of* it) in conformity with law قانون کے مطابق بنا لینا، قانونی صورت دینا

legate (*leg*-it) *n.* Pope's ambassador to a country پاپائے رُوما کا سفیر

legatee *n.* (see under **legacy**)

legation *n.* diplomatic mission (*in* a foreign country) below the rank of an embassy چھوٹے درجے کا سفارت خانہ

legend (*lej*-end) *n.* fanciful traditional story روایت۔ داستان literature containing the like of it روایتی ادب *in legend*, in such literature روایتی ادب میں *the legends of King Arthur and his knights* آرتھر اور اس کے جانبازوں کی داستانیں *cycle of legends, legendary cycle* ایک سلسلے کی داستانیں lie ; made-up tale جھوٹ موٹ بنائی ہوئی بات، من گھڑت قصہ inscription on a coin, medal, etc. سکے (وغیرہ) پر لکھی ہوئی عبارت، سکے پر کے نقوش **legendary** (lej-end-a-ri) *adj.* fabulous فرضی، من گھڑت famous in legends روایتی، جس کے ذکر سے داستانیں بھری پڑی ہوں

legerdemain (lej-è*de-mayn) *n.* juggling ہاتھ کی صفائی، کرتب، شعبدہ بازی deceitful argument گمراہ کن استدلال، تدلیس

leggings *n. pl.* (see under **leg**)

leghorn (le-*go**n) *n.* a good breed of fowl لیگ ہارن (مرغی یا مرغ)

legible (*lej*-i-bèl) *adj.* (of handwriting, etc.) easily read صاف جو آسانی سے پڑھا جا سکے **legibly** *adv.* so as to be legible صاف (لکھنا) **legibility** (lej-i-*bil*-i-ti) *n.* being legible صاف لکھائی، ایسی لکھائی جو آسانی سے پڑھی جا سکے

legion (*lee*-jèn) *n.* (in Roman Army) division of three to six thousand soldiers (رُوما میں) تین ہزار سے چھ ہزار تک کی فوج، رومی فوج کی ڈویژن، لیجن very great number بہت بڑی تعداد *their name is legion* وہ بہت بڑی تعداد میں ہیں

legislate (*lej*-is-layt) *v. i.* make laws قانون بنانا، قانون سازی کرنا **legislation** (-*lay*-) *n.* making laws قانون سازی، تشریع the laws made قانون، قوانین *piece of legislation* قانون **legislative** (*lej*-is-lay-tiv) *adj.* law-making قانون ساز، قانون سازی کا *legislative assembly*, body (elected directly or indirectly, or just appointed) to make laws for the country مجلس قانون ساز، مقننہ **legislator** (*lej*-is-lay-tè*) *n.* member of a parliament, etc. قانون ساز، رکن مجلس قانون ساز **legislature** (*lej*-is-lay-chè*) *n* law-making body مجلس قانون ساز، مقننہ

legitimate (le-*jit*-i-mayt) *adj.* proper and lawful (dignitary, etc.) ; not a usurper حق دار، مستحق justifiable (excuse, purpose, etc.) جائز، ٹھیک (of child, person, etc.) born under wedlock ; not illegitimate جائز (اولاد)، حلالی، حلال زادہ **legitimacy** (le-*jit*-i-may-si) *n.* being legitimate قانونی استحقاق، قانونی طور پر جائز ہونا، جواز، حلال زادہ **legitimatize** (le-*jit*-i-ma-tiz), **legitimize** (le-jit-i-miz) *v. t.* make legitimate by decree, etc. کو قانون بنا کر جائز قرار دینا be a justification for کا جواز بننا **legitimization** (-*zay*-), **legitimation** (-*may*-) *n.* act of legitimatizing جواز بننا، قانون بنا کر جائز قرار دینا

leisure (lezh-è*) *n.* spare time فرصت *at leisure*, not occupied فارغ *at (one's) leisure*, when (one) is free فرصت کے وقت میں **leisured** (-è*d) *adj.* having plenty of leisure جسے فرصت ہی فرصت ہو، جسے کافی فرصت ہو **leisured classes,** rich people who have or can afford much leisure (اونچا طبقہ، امیر، امرا) **leisurely** (-li) *adj.* slow and easy-going آرام سے کام کرنے والا employing leisure فرصت کے وقت کا، فرصت *adv.* in a slow and easy-going manner آرام سے، اطمینان سے

lemon (*lem*-un) *n.* yellow citrous fruit used for drinks, etc. نیمبو، لیموں tree yielding it لیموں کا درخت **lemonade** (lem-o-*nayd*) *n.* aerated drink made from lemons لیمونیڈ، ترنجاب **lemon squash** *n.* drink of lemon juice and soda-water لیموں پانی، لیموں سوڈا sweetened drink of lemon and water لیموں کا شربت **lemon-squeezer** *n.* instrument for pressing juice out of lemon لیموں کا رس نچوڑنے کا آلہ، نیمبو نچوڑ

lend *v. t.* (*lend, lent, lent*) allow something to be taken or used on the condition of its (safe) return عاریتہً دینا، مستعار دینا، قرض دینا *lend money on interest* سُودی قرضہ دینا، سُود پر رُوپیہ دینا *lend (someone) ear* (or *an ear* or *one's ear*), listen to (him) کسی کی بات پر کان دھرنا *lend (oneself) to*, support کی مدد کرنا *lend itself to*, be helpful for a purpose میں مفید ہونا *lend (someone) a hand*, help him کی دستگیری کرنا *lend probability to*, make it appear probable کا امکان پیدا کرنا، کو ممکن بنانا *lend dignity to*, make it dignified کی عزت افزائی کرنا، کو شان دار بنانا

length (length) *n.* distance (*of* space or time) طول، طوالت distance (*of* something) from end to end لمبائی، طول *at length*, (a) at last آخر کار، آخیر بار، انجام کار، بالآخر (b) in detail تفصیل سے، مفصل (c) for a long time دیر تک *at full length*, with the body stretched out ٹانگیں پھیلائے، پیر پھیلائے *keep (someone) at arm's length*, avoid being friendly سے دُور، دُور رہنا *go to any length* (or *all lengths*) (*for* or *to do something*), do anything in power (to achieve the object) ہر طرح کی کوشش کرنا piece of cloth, etc., long enough for (a particular type of garment) کا کپڑا *a suit length of gaberdine* گبرڈین کا ایک سُوٹ کا کپڑا **lengthen** (*leng*-thĕn) *v. t.* & *i.* make or become longer لمبا کرنا یا ہونا ، طُول دینا ، بڑھانا یا بڑھنا **lengthwise, lengthways** *adv.* in the direction of the length لمبائی کی طرف سے ، لمبان میں **lengthy** (*leng*-thi) *adj.* too long (talk, writing, etc.) بہت ہی لمبا ، طُول طَوِیل

lenient (*lee-ni*-ent) *adj.* mild ; not severe (punishment, attitude, etc.) نرم ، نرمی کا *take a lenient view of the matter*, deal with it without severity کے مُتعلق نرمی سے کام لینا gentle (*towards* someone) نرم ، بُردبار ، مُتحمّل ، نرمی کا سُلُوک کرنا **leniently** *adv.* نرمی سے **leniency** (*lee*-ni-en-si) *n.* being lenient نرمی ، بُردباری

lens *n.* (pl. *lenses* pr. *len*-ziz) curved glass for use in spectacles, etc. *convex lens*, lens with side(s) projecting مُحدّب عدسہ *concave lens*, one curved inward مُجوّف عدسہ مُقعّر عدسہ

convex (1) and concave (2) lenses

lent *v.* (pa. t. & pa. p. of *lend*, which see) *n.* (*Lent*), (in Christianity) forty-day period ending before Easter Sunday ایسٹر کا چلّہ ، لینٹ

lentil *n.* a kind of bean مَسُور its plant مَسُور کا پَودا *adj.* made of lentils مَسُور کا

leonine (*lee*-o-nin) *adj.* of or like a lion شیر بَبَر کا (سا) ، شیرانہ

leopard (*lep*-a*d) *n.* (also called **panther**), tiger-like animal with dark spots on brown coat چیتا ، تیندوا **leopardess** (*lep*-) *n. fem.* female leopard چیتے کی مادہ

a leopard or panther

leper (*lep*-ĕ*) *n.* person suffering from leprosy کوڑھی ، جُذامی **leprosy** (*lep*-ro-si) *n.* dreadful skin disease slowly eating into the body کوڑھ ، جُذام **leprous** (*lep*-rus) *adj.* having leprosy کوڑھی ، جُذامی of or like leprosy کوڑھ کا (سا)

[1]**-less** (les) *adj.* not so much (or so many) کم ، اس سے کم inferior کمتر ، گھٹیا *adv.* in a lower degree کم ، تھوڑا *prep.* minus منفی *salary Rs. 500 p.m. less Rs. 20 income-tax* مشاہرہ پانسو رُوپے منفی بیس رُوپے اِنکم ٹیکس **lessen** *v. t.* & *i.* become or make less گھٹنا یا گھٹانا ، کم ہونا یا کرنا **lesser** *adj.* not so great as the other چھوٹا *the lesser evil* کمتر بُرائی ، چھوٹی مُصیبت

[2]**-less** (les) *suf.* (for making adjectives which denote) without ; that does not (as ; *careless* بے پروا *childless* بے اولاد

lese majeste (layz-*ma*-zhes-tay), **lese majesty** (leez-*ma*-jes-ti) *n.* reason بغاوت ، غدّاری

lessee (lee-*see*) *n.* (see under **lease**)

lessen *v.* **lesser** *adj.* (see under **less**)

lesson *n.* , that which is learnt or taught سَبَق *learn (one's) lesson* سَبَق یاد کرنا *school lesson* مَدرسے کا سَبَق period devoted to a particular lesson سَبَق کا گھنٹہ ، پیریڈ warning from (one's own or another's) experience سَبَق ، عِبرت *Let this be a lesson to you* اِس سے عِبرت پکڑو reading from the *Bible* in church service (عیسائیوں کی عبادت میں گرجے میں پادری کا) اِنجیل پڑھنا

lessor *n.* (see under **lease**)

lest *conj.* for fear that (something *should* happen, etc.) ایسا نہ ہو ، مبادا so that it may not (happen, etc.) ایسا نہ ہو ، کہیں ایسا نہ ہو جائے کہ

[1]**let** *v.t.* & *i.* allow (someone or something) to (*do*, etc., something) (کرنے) دینا *let him study*, (*etc.*) اسے پڑھنے دو *let us go (etc.)* آؤ چلیں *let (something) go*, set it free کو چھوڑ دینا *let us pray* آئیے دُعا کریں it is suggested that چاہیئے کہ give (house, etc.) on rent کرائے پر دینا ، کرائے پر اُٹھانا be hired or leased (*at* a rent) اِتنے کرایہ پر اُٹھانا ، (کا اِتنا) کرایہ آنا (for assumptions), let us assume فرض کرو کہ ، فرض کیجیئے کہ ، فرض کرنا *n.* hindrance رُکاوٹ (usu. in the phrase :) *without let or hindrance* بغیر کسی رُکاوٹ کے ، بلا رُکاوٹ ، بلا روک ٹوک *let (someone or something) alone*, not to interfere with it میں دخل نہ دینا ، اُسے اُس کے حال پر چھوڑنا *let alone (something, or doing something)*, not to speak of it اُس کا تو ذکر ہی کیا *let (something) down*, (*a*) send it below نیچے اُتارنا ، لٹکانا (*b*) make (dress, etc.) longer by unstitching hem کنارہ کھول کر لمبا کرنا ، نیچا کرنا *let (someone) down*, not help (him) in (his) need وقت پر ساتھ نہ دینا ، مُصیبت کے وقت ساتھ چھوڑنا *let (oneself or someone) into (or in for) trouble*, involve in (trouble) کو مُصیبت کے مُنہ میں ڈالنا *let (someone or something) in*, permit (him or it) to enter اندر آنے دینا *let (someone) into a secret*, share it with (him) کو راز دار بنانا ، (کو) راز کی بات بتانا ، (سے) راز کی بات کہنا *let off (gun, fireworks, etc.)* (بندوق) چلانا ، (آتشبازی) چھوڑنا *let (someone) off*, (*a*) not to punish (him) کو چھوڑ دینا (*b*) allow (him) to go (*with* fine or other minor punishment) جُرمانے (یا چھوٹی سزا) پر اکتفا کرنا *let out (a garment)*, widen or loosen it by undoing stitches (کپڑے کو) ٹانکے کھول کر کھلا کرنا *let (or let out) (house, etc., to someone for or at a rent)* کسی کو مکان (وغیرہ) کرائے پر) دینا (اُتنے کرائے پر دینا *let (a secret) out*, reveal (it) بتانا ، کھولنا ، اِفشا کرنا *let (someone) alone*, not to disturb (him) (کو) ہاتھ نہ لگانا (کو) نہ چھیڑنا *let (something) out*, (*a*) allow to escape نکل جانے دینا (*b*) reveal اِفشا کرنا (*c*) open the door for (it) to go out کے لیے نکلنے کے لیے دروازہ کھولنا *let the cat out of the bag*, reveal

the whole plot, etc. سارا بھانڈا پھوڑ دینا، بھانڈا پھوٹ رہا ہے میں پھوڑ let (something) loose, unchain (it) کو کھول دینا، کی زنجیر کھول دینا let slip (an opportunity, etc.) موقع ہاتھ سے گنوانا، موقع کھونا let blood, allow it to escape خون نکلنا دیا، نکالنا let fly, let drive at, send missile or deliver blow سے وار کرنا let fly at, کو گالیاں دینا let (something) fall, گرنے دینا let (oneself) do, abandon restraint کھل کھیلنا let everyone do his duty چاہیے کہ ہر ایک اپنا فرض ادا کرے let (something) be, not to care for or meddle with it کی پروا نہ کرنا let a sigh آہ بھرنا let a groan کراہنا let a groan کہنا کہ ہوا کرے let (someone) know کو بتا دو let (someone) try to (do it) وہ ذرا کر کے دیکھے تو؛ اسے ذرا کرنے تو دو let him do his worst اسے اپنی سی کر لینے دو، وہ ہم سے جو بُرائی کرنا چاہتا ہے اُسے کرنے دو۔

-let *suf.* (forming diminutives) چھوٹا، چہ (as : book, کتاب booklet (کتابچہ)

lethal (*lee*-thĕl) *adj.* (weapons, etc.) designed to cause death مُہلک *lethal chamber*, one designed for killing animals painlessly بے آزار ذبح

Lethe (*lee*-thee) *Cl. myth.* one of the rivers of Hades (or hell) which caused *forgetfulness* to all who drank of it لیتھی، رُود فراموشی **lethean** (lee-*thee*-ĕn) *adj.* of Lethe لیتھی کا causing forgetfulness فراموشی طاری کرنے والا

lethargy (*leth*-a*-ji) *n.* lack of energy سُستی want of interest دلچسپی نہ ہونا کاہلی، بے ہمتی، کم ہمتی

lethargic (le-*thah**-jik) *adj.* lacking energy or interest سُست، کاہل، بے ہمت، کم ہمت، دلچسپی نہ رکھنے والا

letter (*let*-ĕ*) *n.* epistle ; written message چٹھی، مُراسلہ، نامہ، رُقعہ *letter of advice*, business letter notifying despatch of goods مال بھیجنے کی چٹھی *letter paper*, special paper for writing letters خط لکھنے کا کاغذ *letter-pad*, pad of letter-paper لکھنے کے کاغذ کی کاپی، پیڈ *letter-head*, (*a*) name of person or firm writing the letter printed on it خط پر اپنا چھپا ہوا پتہ، لیٹر ہیڈ (*b*) letter-paper containing it خط لکھنے کا کاغذ جس پر اپنا پتہ چھپا ہو *letter-writing*, practice in the writing of letters خطوط نویسی، انشا *letter writer*, (*a*) person writing letters (usu. for others) خطوط نویس، منشی (*b*) guide to letter-writing انشا، خطوط نویسی سکھانے والی کتاب *letter-box*, box (at one's place) in which the postman puts in the letters brought by him (as against *pill-box* or *pillar-box* which is placed in street corners, etc., for posting letters) لیٹر بکس، نامہ دان written symbol of a particular sound حرف *the letter*, exactly بالکل، ہو بہو، عین بعین، من و عن *letter-press*, contents of an illustrated book other than the illustrations باتصویر کتاب کے الفاظ the literal meaning (*of*) کے الفاظ کا ظاہر *the letter and spirit* (*of*), the formal meaning and the true purpose (of) کے الفاظ اور حقیقی مقصد *keep the letter of* (*agreement, law, etc.*) act on its wording but ignore its spirit کے لفظوں کی پابندی تو کرنا مگر حقیقی مقصد نظر انداز کر دینا *in letter and spirit* الفاظ اور حقیقی مقصد دونوں کی پابندی کرنے والا (*pl.*) (*letters*), literature ادب (*pl.*) (*letters*), learning علم، علمیت authorship as a profession ادیب ہونا *a man of letters* عالم، ادیب تصنیف و تالیف *v. t.* mark (something) with letters پر حرف بنانا **lettering** *n.* marking thus حرف بنانا letters (of an inscription, etc.) so marked کھدے یا لکھے ہوئے حرف

lettered (*let*-ĕ*d) *adj.* marked thus with letters جس پر حرف کھدے یا لکھے ہوئے ہوں learned (person) عالم *unlettered*, illiterate اَن پڑھ، ناخواندہ *letters patent, letters of administration*, official document granting certain rights سرکاری اجازت نامہ

lettuce (*let*-is) *n.* plant used in salads کاہو، سلاد

Levant (le-*vant*) *n.* (*the*) East-Mediterranean region بحیرۂ روم کے مشرقی نصف ممالک، لاونٹ (*levant*) decamp without clearing one's debts قرض چکائے بغیر رفو چکر ہو جانا

levee (*lev*-è, or le-*vee*) *n.* assembly received by ruler or other great personage دربار، بار (U.S.) embankment against river floods سیلاب روکنے کے لیے دریا کے ساتھ پُشتہ، سیلاب روک پُشتہ، سیلابی پُشتہ

level (*lev*-el) *n.* flat and even surface سطح *spirit level*, instrument with air bubble enclosed in alcohol to test whether level of a place is even سطح بیں، سپرٹ لیول height of such surface سطح کی بلندی، بلندی *sea-level*, level of the sea surface سطح سمندر *on a level with*, as high as کے برابر *at* (or *above* or *below*) sea-level سطح سمندر کے برابر (یا سے اونچا یا سے نیچا) *adj.* a horizontal surface ہموار، مسطح *a level crossing*, place where a railway crosses a road on the same level ریل کا پھاٹک *have a level head*, (*be*) *level-headed*, (*be*) not carried away by enthusiasm but to judge well سلیم الطبع ہونا *do* (*one's*) *level best* (*to do something*), do all that one can do (to do it) پوری کوشش کرنا *draw level with*, come out equal to کے برابر رہنا *v.t.* (-ll-) make level ہموار کرنا aim (gun, blow, charge accusation, etc., *at* or *against*) کا نشانہ کرنا، لگانا remove distinctions to make equal ایک جیسا بنا دینا *level* (*something*) *up* (or *down*), raise (or lower it) to a certain level ایک جیسا کر دینا اونچا یا نیچا کرنا *level* (*a building*) *to the ground*, pull it down گرا دینا

leveller (*lev*-è-lĕ*) *n.* person or thing that

levels برابر کرنے والا، سب کو ایک جیسا کرنے والا *death the leveller* بڑے چھوٹے سب کو ایک جیسا کر دینے والی مَوت

lever (*lee*-ve*) *n.* bar, etc., turned on a pivot (called *fulcrum*) so that the *power* applied at one point is brought to bear on a resisting force (called *weight*) at another point to break that resistance بیرم، لیوَر handle of a machine to start or stop it کل چلانے یا بند کرنے کا دَستہ، کل کا دَستہ، دَستہ *v.t.* move (something *up*, *along* or *into* position) with a lever بیرم سے حرکت کرنا **leverage** (*leev*-è-rij) *n.* facility gained by the use of a lever بیرم کے استعمال سے حاصل ہونے والی سہولت action of a lever بیرم کا فِعل number of levers working together بیرموں کا مجموعہ

leviathan (le-*vī*-è-thĕn) *n.* a sea monster referred to in *the Bible* بحری عفریت anything of very great size and power دیوپیکر چیز

levity (*lev*-i-ti) *n.* frivolity, lack of seriousness چھچھورا پن، مزاج میں زُود گُذرین

levy (*lev*-i) *v.t.* impose (tax, ransom, etc.) لگانا، عائد کرنا realize it by force جبراً وصول کرنا conscript (فوج میں) جبری بھرتی کرنا make (*war upon* or *against* an enemy) *by levying* men, ammunition, etc., forcefully فوج زبردستی تیار کر کے (کسی پر) چڑھائی کرنا *n.* act of levying ٹیکس وغیرہ، لگانا، جبری amount of money or number of troops levied جبری طور پر وصول کی ہوئی رقم، جبری طور پر بھرتی کی فوج کی تعداد *capital levy*, seizure of part of private wealth of all persons in a group or country by its government حکومت کا عوام کی کچھ دولت زبردستی لینا

lewd *adj.* lascivious بدکار، تماش بین، عیاش، اوباش، شہوت پرست

lexicon (*lek*-si-kon) *n.* dictionary (esp. of a classical language) لغات، قاموس **lexicography** (lek-si-*kog*-ra-fi) *n.* compiling of dictionaries لغت نویسی **lexicographer** (*-kog-*) *n.* compiler of a dictionary لغت نویس

ley (lay) *n.* land under temporary grass عارضی سبزہ زار

liable (*lī*-a-bĕl) *adj.* be legally responsible (*for* one's or someone's debts, etc.) کا، قانوناً ذمہ دار ہونا، کسی کیلئے جوابدہ ہونا be subject (*to* tax, punishment, etc.) کا مستوجب ہونا be likely (to suffer, err, etc.) سے ممکن ہونا **liability** (*-bil-*) *n.* being liable (*for*) کی، ذمہ داری یا جواب (*pl.*) personal responsibilities (like debts, etc.) قرض، بار، بوجھ، ذمہ داریاں

liaison (li-*ay*-zĕn, or li-*ay*-zon) *n.* connexion رابطہ، ربط *maintain liaison (between)* (میں) رابطہ قائم رکھنا *liaison officer*, (*a*) one keeping the Press or public informed of government activities افسر رابطہ (*b*) (esp.) army officer maintaining liaison between the allied armies فوجی افسر رابطہ illicit amour ناجائز مُعاشقہ

liar (*lī*-ĕ*) *n.* (see under **lie**)

libation (lī-*bay*-shĕn) *n.* offering of wine to a god, دیوتا کو شراب کی نذر pouring it out for this purpose دیوتا کو نذر کرنے کے لیے شراب اُنڈیلنا

libel (*lī*-bel) *n.* printed defamation توہین آمیز تحریر its publication ہتکِ عزت والی تحریر، ہتکِ عزت والی تحریر کی اشاعت، توہین آمیز تحریر کی اشاعت (colloq.) thing that brings discredit (*on*) بے عزتی، ہتک یا توہین does not do full justice to سے ناانصافی *v.t.* (-ll-) publish a libel against ہتکِ عزت والی تحریر شائع کرنا fail to do full justice to سے ناانصافی کرنا **libellous** (*lī*-bel-us) *adj.* defamatory (writing) ہتکِ عزت والی تحریر یا بیان

liberal (*lib*-è-rĕl) *adj.* generous فیّاض، فراخ دِل given freely فراخدلانہ، فیاضانہ unprejudiced (person or attitude) رَوادار، رَوادارانہ، بے تعصب all round ہمہ گیر، وسیع *to have received a liberal education* educated widely and with a view to cultural training جس نے شائستگی سکھانے والی اور وسیع تعلیم پائی ہو (in politics) not conservative ترقی پسند، آزاد خیال *n.* (*Liberal*) حُرّیت پسند member of the British Liberal party which advocates democratic reforms and is opposed to too much government control آزاد خیال پارٹی کا رکن، آزاد خیال، حُرّیت پسند **liberality** (*-ral-*) *n.* generosity فیاضی، سخاوت broadmindedness رَواداری، بے تعصبی **liberalize** (-īz) *v.t.* free from narrowness پابندیاں ہٹالینا **liberalization** (*-zay-*) *n.* freeing (*of* something) from curbs پابندیاں ہٹالینا

liberate (*lib*-è-rayt) *v.t.* set free آزاد کرنا، آزادی دینا release (*from*) سے آزاد کرنا، سے رہائی دلانا، آزادی دلانا

liberator *n.* آزادی دینے یا دلانے والا *the Kashmir Liberation Movement* کشمیر کو بھارت کے پنجے سے آزاد کرانے کی تحریک

libertine (*lib*-ĕ*-tin) *n.* one who gives himself up to immoral pleasures عیاش، اوباش، آوارہ **libertinism, libertinage** *n.* libertine's way of thinking or mode of life آوارگی، عیاشی، فحاشی

liberty (*lib*-ĕ*-ti) *n.* independence آزادی right to decide for oneself (*to do*, to think, etc.) whatever one wishes (خیال یا عمل کی) مرضی کرنے کا حق، being free حریت، آزادی *set (someone) at liberty* آزاد کرنا *liberty of conscience*, freedom to have one's own religious beliefs or political views without interference آزادیٔ ضمیر، ضمیر کی آزادی (*pl.*) undue freedom or familiarity بے تکلفی، گستاخی کی حد تک بڑھی ہوئی، بے تکلفی، گستاخی *take liberties with* سے بے تکلفی (پیش آنا) یا سے کام لینا **Liberty Hall** *n.* house

which guests, etc., are at liberty to act as they like آزادی خانہ
libidinous *adj.* (see under **libido**)
libido (li-b.-do) *n.* sexual urge جنسی خواہش، شہوت urge to live which, according to modern psychology, prompts all human action جینے کی تمنا، شہوانی شوقِ زیست **libidinous** (-*bid*-) *adj.* lustful
library, (*lib*-ra-ri) *n.* collection of books کتب خانہ building or room in which it is housed کتب خانہ **librarian** (lib-*ray*-ri-an) *n.* one in charge of a library ناظمِ کتب خانہ
libretto (lib-*ret*-oh) *n.* (pl. *libretti* pr. tee) (see *Addenda*)
lice (lis) *n.* (pl. of louse, which see)
licence (*li*-sens) *n.* permission (*from* Authority *to* someone *for* or *to do* something) سرکاری اجازت by licence اجازت کے ساتھ پروانہ disregard of laws, etc. بے قاعدگی، بے ضابطگی poetic licence, any artist's transgression of the established rules of his art (usu.) to get over some difficulty in it فنکارانہ تصرف abuse of freedom بے لگامی، بیباکی، بے راہ روی بے ضابطگی immorality عیاشی، آوارگی **license** (*li*-sens) *v.t.* give (someone) a licence (*for* or *to* do something) دینا، لائسنس دینا *licensed premises*, places licensed for the sale of alcoholic drinks وہ مقام جہاں شراب بیچنے کی اجازت ہو **licensee** (-*see*) *n.* holder of a licence لائسنس دار، لائسنس رکھنے والا **licentiate** (-*sensh*-i-ayt) *n.* diploma'd سند یافتہ **licentious** (li-*sensh*-us) *adj.* lewd آوارہ، عیاش، اوباش
license *v.t.*, **licentiate** *n.*, **licentious** *adj.* (see under **licence**)
lichen (*li*-ken) *n.* kind of moss growing like a crust on stones, etc. کائی، لائیکن lichen
lick (lik) *v.t.* & *i.* stroke with the tongue چاٹنا، پر زبان پھیرنا (colloq.) beat مارنا (slang) speed تیز جانا *lick* (*one's lips*) ہونٹوں پر زبان پھیرنا، منہ میں پانی بھر آنا *clean by licking* چاٹ لینا، چاٹ کر صاف کرنا *lick* (*a plate, etc.*) *clean* (طشتری وغیرہ) زبان سے چاٹ کر صاف کرنا *lick* (*recruits, something*) *into shape*, train (them) or mould (it) تیار کرنا، شکل نکالنا *lick* (*something*), (of flames or waves) play lightly over (it) (لو کا) چھونا *lick the dust*, be vanquished ہار جانا *lick* (*someone's*) *shoes* (or *boots*), be servilely obsequious to him (کی) چاپلوسی کرنا، کی جوتیاں چاٹنا *n.* licking چاٹنا (slang) speed تیز رفتار، سرعت (also *salt-lick*), place to which animals go for licking salt جانور جہاں نمک چاٹنے جائیں **licking** (*lik*-ing) *n.* (colloq.) beating مار defeat مار، شکست
licorice *n.* (same as **liquorice**, which see)

lid (lid) *n.* movable cover (*of* a box, kettle, etc.) ڈھکنا *eyelid* پپوٹا
lido (*lee*-doh) *n.* open air swimming pool for the public بغیر چھت کا تالاب، کھلا تالاب
[1]**lie** (li) *v.i.* (*lie, lied, lied* ; *lying*) tell a deliberate untruth جھوٹ بولنا *tell lies*, be in the habit of lying جھوٹ کی عادت ہونا *give* (*someone*) *the lie*, (*a*) accuse (him) of lying پر جھوٹ کا الزام لگانا (*b*) contradict (him) کی بات کو جھٹلانا، کی تکذیب کرنا *n.* deliberate falsehood جھوٹ، دروغ، کذب *a white lie* *n.* a harmless, polite lie, بے تکلف اصولی جھوٹ **liar** (*li*-ĕ*) *n.* one who lies جھوٹا دروغ گو، کذّاب ▣ A **lie** is a serious falsehood, whereas an **untruth** is a mild one ; a **fib** is child's falsehood ; a **calumny**, malicious falsehood ; an **aspersion**, mud-slinging on someone ; an **innuendo**, veiled hint ; a **slander**, malicious tale ; and a **libel**, in writing. Again, one **tells lies** when one says false things ; **slanders** someone by malicious tales ; **libels** someone by publishing unjust and hateful statements ; and **defames** another by spreading evil rumours.
[2]**lie** (li) *v.i.* (*lie* ; *lay* ; *lain* or Bib. *lien* pr. *li*-en ; *lying*) be or put oneself in a level position لیٹنا، دراز ہونا، پڑنا *lie in bed* بستر پر لیٹنا *lie with* (*someone*) (*in the same bed*) سے ہم بستری کرنا (of things) be resting flat (on something) پڑا ہونا، پڑا پڑا، پڑا رہنا *lie open* (*on*) پر کھلے پڑے ہونا remain in a certain position or state پڑے ہونا، ہونا، رہنا *lie in prison for a long time* مدتوں سے قید میں پڑے رہنا *lie at anchor* لنگر انداز ہونا *money lying idle in the bank*, with which no business is done بنک میں بیکار پڑی ہوئی رقم *lie in ruins*, be devastated or dilapidated کھنڈر ہونا be spread out to view نظروں کے سامنے ہونا، سامنے ہونا depend, concern کا کام ہونا *It lies with you* (to) یہ اب آپ کا کام ہے کہ exist ہونا *the trouble lies in the piston* خرابی اس کے پسٹن میں ہے *the blame lies at* (*his*) *door*, (he) is to blame for it قصور اس کا ہے *lie down under* (*insult, etc.*), *take* (*insult, etc.*) *lying down*, pocket (it) خاموشی سے برداشت کرنا، پی جانا *lie in*, (*a*) stay in bed after one's usual time دیر تک سوتے رہنا (*b*) have the pangs of birth دردِ زہ ہونا *let sleeping dogs lie*, do not invite trouble بھڑوں کے چھتے کو نہ چھیڑو *lie low*, (colloq.) keep out of the way to avoid being seen نیچے پھرنا *lie up*, stay in bed or at home (owing to illness, etc.) زیرِ استعمال نہ ہونا پڑے رہنا، کام پر نہ جانا *lie by*, be out of use *lie in state*, (of coffined body) lie open to public view نعش کا آخری رونمائی کے لیے رکھا ہوا ہونا (یا پڑے ہوئے) *n.* (the) way something lies رخ *the lie of the land*, the state of affairs صورتِ حال
liege (leej) *n.* feudal lord, etc. آقا faithful vassal جاں نثار رعیت *adj* (lord or vassal) bound

by feudal tenure جاگیردارانہ نظام کا *liege lord*, king or feudal lord giving land on condition of military service (جاگیردارانہ نظام میں) آقا یا بادشاہ *liegeman*, one holding land on that condition (جاگیردارانہ نظام میں) رعیّت loyal وفادار، جاں نثار

lien (lee-ĕn) *n.* legal claim upon another's property for clearance of debt (دوسرے کی جائداد پر) استحقاق right to return to a post from which one's services were loaned elsewhere استحقاق، حق *have a lien on*, *v.* پر حق ہونا ، پر استحقاق ہونا (bio. pa. p. of [2]**lie** which see

lieu (lew) *n.* (only in the phrase :) *in lieu of*, in place of کی جگہ ، کی بجائے ، کے بجائے

lieutenant (lef-*ten*-ant ; or in Navy le-*tan*-ant) *n.* (abb. **Lieut**. ; in combinations *Lt*.-) army officer below a captain فوج میں سب سے چھوٹا افسر، لفٹیننٹ naval officer next below a commander بحریہ میں کمانڈر سے چھوٹا افسر ، لفٹیننٹ one who acts for a superior (کا) نمائندہ (in compounds) officer with the highest rank under the one with the mentioned designation نائب ، چھوٹا *lieutenant-general*, (abb. *Lt.-Gen.*), نائب سپہ سالار *lieutenant-colonel*, (abb. *Lt.-Col.*), کرنیل ، چھوٹا کرنیل *lieutenant-commander*, نائب کمانڈر *Lieutenant-Governor*, (*a*) one next below a Governor نائب والی (*b*) Governor of a small province چھوٹے صوبے کا والی

ife (lif) *n.* (pl. *lives* pr. livz) chief distinctive feature between living and lifeless objects زندگی، زیست ، حیات state of being alive زندگی، زندہ ہونا ، living things collectively ہر زندہ شے ، تمام زندہ چیزیں، زندگی period between birth till now or till death عمر، سن vivacity زندہ دلی، جان duration of (a lifeless thing's) usefulness عمر، زندگی (good, bad, etc.) manner of living زندگی ، طرزِ زندگی biography (*of*) (کی) سوانح عمری ، (کے) سوانح حیات *take (someone's) life*, kill (him) (کو) مار ڈالنا *save (someone's) life* کی جان بچانا *country life* گاؤں کا طرزِ زندگی ، دیہاتی زندگی *army life* فوجی طرزِ زندگی *(be) full of life*, (be) active and cheerful چست و چالاک ہونا *put more life into*, میں کچھ اور جان ڈالنا **life-belt** *n.* belt of cork, etc., to keep a person afloat in the water ڈوبنے سے بچانے والی پیٹی، ترانے والی پیٹی ، بچاؤ پیٹی **life-boat** *n.* one for saving lives in shipwreck بچاؤ کشتی **life-buoy** (*lif*-boi) *n.* wheel-like life-belt thrown to someone in the water بچاؤ پہیہ **lifeblood** (lif-blud) *n.* blood which keeps the body warm خونِ حیات the result of (someone's) great endeavour خونِ جگر **life estate** *n.* estate to be enjoyed during one's lifetime only and not to be disposed of further جاگیر تاحینِ حیات **life-guard** (*lif*-gahd) *n.* expert swimmer on duty at places where people swim محافظِ تیراک a guard over someone's (esp. a king's) life (شاہی) محافظ soldier in the British cavalry regiment (called the *Life-Guards*) لائف گارڈ، رسالہ کا سوار **lifeless** (*lif*-les) *adj.* dead مُردہ not lively بے جان، بے کیف **life-like** (*lif*-lik) *adj.* (portrait, etc.) looking as if alive (تصویر وغیرہ) جیتی جاگتی، مُنہ بولتی **life-line** *n.* rope used on sea for saving a drowning person's life بچاؤ رسّہ **lifelong** *adj.* lasting throughout life عمر بھر کا **lifesize** (lif-siz) *adj.* (of portrait, etc.) of the size of the pictured person قدِ آدم **lifetime** (*lif*-tim) length of one's life مُدّتِ عمر very long time مُدّتیں، ایک عمر **lifework** (*lif*-wĕ*k) *n.* work to which one devotes one's whole life زندگی بھر کا کام ، زندگی کا شاہکار

lift (lift) *v. t.* & *i.* raise (*up*) اٹھانا ، اونچا ، بلند کرنا *lift up (one's) voice*, آواز بلند کرنا (of clouds, mist) pass away چھٹ جانا ، ہٹ جانا dig up (root, crops) کھود کر نکالنا *n.* act of lifting بلند کرنا ، اٹھانا ، اونچا کرنا ، چھٹ جانا ، کھود کر نکالنا carrying (someone) in one's car کار میں لے جانا *give (someone) a lift* سواری میں بٹھا کر لے جانا machine carrying people or goods up or down to another floor in a tall building لفٹ ، بردار

light (lit) *n.* illumination from the sun or from a lamp etc. روشنی (usu. artificial) source of illumination بتّی، دیا، چراغ، لیمپ amount of illumination روشنی brightness چمک illuminated part of a picture (as opposed to *shade*) تصویر کا روشن حصّہ viewpoint نقطۂ نگاہ، زاویۂ نگاہ means of admitting light کھڑکی ، روشن دان (وغیرہ) not meant to support heavy things کمزور famous person (*of a place*) (کے لیے) باعثِ عزت شخصیت ، مایۂ ناز *see (things) in a good* (or *bad*) *light* اچھی (یا بری) روشنی میں دیکھنا *strike a light*, strike a match دیا سلائی جلانا *come to light, be brought to light*, become known معلوم ہونا ، پتہ چلنا *light a fire* (or *the lamp, etc.*) آگ (یا لیمپ) جلانا *throw (new) light on* پر (نئی) روشنی ڈالنا *light in (someone's) eyes* کسی کی آنکھوں کی چمک *adj.* (room, etc.) not dark کافی روشنی pale form of (colour) ہلکا *light blue* ہلکا نیلا (of weight, trouble, food, wind, rain, footsteps, movement, sleep, wine, punishment, etc.) not heavy ہلکا delicate, graceful نازک loosed (soil) کھلی easy to understand آسان، سہل frivolous (behaviour, etc.) غیر سنجیدہ (of book, literature, etc.) not scholarly, but meant to entertain تفریحی (of heart) not weighed down with grief غم، فکر سے آزاد

travel light ; travel with little luggage سفر میں سامان v. t. & i. (*light* ; *lit* or *lighted* ; lit or *lighted*) cause to burn جلانا، روشن کرنا (often light up) make (or become) bright چمکنا، یا چمکانا give light to (someone on his way) کے لیے روشنی کرنا **lighten** (*lī*-tĕn) *v. t.* & *i.* make or become lightened روشن کرنا یا ہونا make or become less heavy ہلکا کرنا **lighthouse** (*līt*-hous) *n.* tower, building (on cliff, rocks, etc.) with strong light to guide and warn ships روشنی کا مینار **lightning** *n.* thunderous flash of light in the sky بجلی، برق، کوندا **lightning-conductor, lightning-rod** *n.* earthed metal rod on top of towering building to prevent damage by lightning برق رُبا **lightning strike** *n.* sudden strike اچانک ہڑتال **lightship** *n.* moored ship with same purpose as a light house روشنی کا جہاز **lighted** (*lī*-ted) *n.* that which has been lit up روشن **lightless** *adj.* without light بے نور **lighting** *adj.* (time) to light up street and vehicle lamps روشنی کا وقت **daylight** *n.* light of the day دن کی روشنی *in broad daylight* دن دہاڑے **light-fingered** *adj.* (esp.) skilful in picking pockets کاریگر گرہ کٹ، ماہر جیب تراش **light-footed** (*līt*-fu-ted) *adj.* nimble تیز رو **light-handed** *adj.* (esp.) adroit at managing others without their perceiving it نرم مگر دانش مند حاکم **light-headed** *adj.* delirious بہکا ہوا thoughtless بے عقل **light-hearted** *adj.* free from care بے غم **light-minded** *adj.* frivolous غیر سنجیدہ، غیر متین thoughtless بے عقل **light-weight** *n.* boxer weighing between 130 and 135 lb. کم وزن کا مکے باز **lightly** *adv.* in a light manner آہستہ ہلکا مکے باز lightness ہلکا پن **lightsome** *adj.* (poet.) gay زندہ دل agile چست، پھرتیلا gracefully light نازک **lighter** (*lī*-tē*) *n.* light boat for carrying goods to and from ship سامان اتارنے کی کشتی (also *cigarette-lighter*), automatic device for lighting cigarettes, etc. لائٹر **lights** (lits) *n. pl.* lungs of animals used as food پھیپھڑے

like (līk) *v. t.* & *i.* be fond of پسند کرنا choose (*to do*) (کرنا) چاہنا (expression of wish or irony (used with *should* or, less correctly but more commonly, with *would*) (کرنا) چاہنا *I should like to see*, (*a*) میں دیکھنا، میں بھی تو دیکھوں رگا، چاہتا ہوں *Read it if you like* پڑھنا چاہیں تو پڑھ لیجیے *n.* (*pl.*) (*likes*) things one likes اپنی پسند، اپنی پسند کی چیزیں (*one's*) *likes and dislikes* جو جو، چیزیں دکسی، کو پسند یا ناپسند ہوں *the like of*, the equal of, something similar جیسا کا اس جیسی چیز *adj.* & *adv.* similar ایسا characteristic of (someone) ہی کا سن ہی کا کام

it was like of you (*to do*) ایسا کرنا آپ ہی کا کام رہا حق، تھا the sign (*of* something or *of* doing something) کے آثار ہونا in a mood (*of doing*) something) کو جی چاہنا about کے قریب، قریب قریب، تقریباً *something like Rs. 1,000* ہزار روپے کے قریب *nothing like as* (*good, etc.*), not nearly so (good, etc.) ایسا اچھا (وغیرہ) بالکل نہیں تو ایسا کہاں **likely** (*līk*-li) *adj.* probable (*to be*) غالباً ہونے والا credible قابل یقین **likelihood** (*lĭk*-li-hūd) *n.* degree of the probability (*of* something) امکان *there is not much likelihood* (*of*) (کا)، زیادہ امکان نہیں، (کا) کوئی خاص امکان نہیں **liken** (lī-kĕn) *v. t.* compare (*to* or in old use *unto*) سے تشبیہ دینا **likeness** (*lik*-nes) *n.* resemblance مشابہت guise جبلہ *in the likeness of*, in the guise of کے بھیس میں portrait تصویر **likewise** (*līk*-wīz) *adv.* in the same way اسی انداز سے اسی طرح also بھی، نیز **liking** (*lī*-king) *n.* fondness (*for*) (سے) شوق، (کا) رغبت *have a* (or *no*) *liking for*, (not to) be fond of (کا) کو پسند (نہ) کرنا *to* (*one's*) *liking*, (*a*) as one likes it کی پسند کے مطابق، حسب دلخواہ (*b*) satisfactory تسلی بخش **likeable** (*līk*-a-bĕl) *adj.* pleasant, delectable پسندیدہ

lilac (*lī*-lak) *n.* shrub with fragrant flowers growing in clusters لیلک pale violet colour ہلکا بنفشی رنگ

a lilac

Lilliputian (li-li-*pew*-shĕn) *n.* dwarf بونا، بالشتیا *n.* of Lilliput (in Swift's *Guilliver's Travels*

lilt *n.* lively swinging tune باقاعدہ اتار چڑھاؤ والی دھن، لے ناچتی ناچتی دھن *v. t.* & *i.* sing rhythmically باقاعدہ اتار چڑھاؤ والی دھن میں گانا، لے کے گانا، لہک کر گانا

lily (*lil*-i) *n.* a kind of (usu. white) fragrant flower سوسن

a lily

limb (lim) *n.* arm or leg بازو یا ٹانگ *limbs* بازو اور ٹانگیں wing (of a bird) پرندے کا بازو bough (of a tree) درخت کی شاخ

lime (lim) *n.* burnt limestone for making cement چونا *slaked lime*, lime after the action of water on it بجھا ہوا چونا *quicklime*, dry lime اَن بجھا چونا fruit like lemon but more acid than it کھٹے نیبو کی سکنجبین، لائم *lime-juice*, its juice کھٹا نیبو جوس tree bearing it کھٹے نیبو کا درخت another tree (also called *linden* or *lime-tree*) having fragrant yellowish flowers لائم (also called *birdlime*) a sticky stuff spread to catch birds *v. t.* smear (land) with lime (زمین) پر چونا چھڑکنا

a flower and leaves of lime tree, linden or lime (sense 4)

smear tree with birdlime لاسا لگانا catch (birds) thus لاسا لگا کر پکڑنا ensnare (person) (کسی کو) لاسا لگانا **limelight** *n.* intense white light got by heating lime in oxygen-hydrogen flame بڑی تیز روشنی fame, publicity شُہرت *be in the limelight* بہت مشہور ہونا، ہر ایک زُبان پر نام ہونا **limestone** *n.* stone from which lime is extracted by burning چُونے کا پتھر **lime-kiln** *n.* kiln for burning limestone چُونے کی بھٹی **bird-lime** *n.* a sticky gum with which trees are smeared to ensnare birds لاسا **lime-juicer** *n.* (U. S. slang) British sailor انگریز مَلّاح British ship (so named from compulsory use of lime-juice on board) انگریزی جہاز.

limerick (*lim*-è-rik) *n.* five-lined nonsense poem بے تُکا مُخمّس، اَلبیل مُخمّس

limit (*lim*-it) *n.* boundary حَد the maximum of what is possible, credible حَد، اِنتہا *there is a limit to (everything, patience, etc.)* کی حَد ہوتی ہے *that's the limit,* (colloq.) that is the last straw حَد ہو گئی *set limits to* (expenditure, etc.), restrict (it) گھٹانا، کم کرنا *v. t.* be the limit of کی حَد کا کام دینا restrict (*to*) گھٹا کر (تک) لے آنا، کم کرنا **limited** (*lim*-i-ted) *adj.* small (quantity) مَحدُود *limited company, limited liability company,* joint-stock company the liability of whose members in respect of its debts is limited to the extent of their share in it مَحدُود ذمّہ داری کی شِرکت **limitless** *adj.* unlimited غیر مَحدُود **limitation** (-*tay*-) *n.* limiting حَد بَندی، تَحدید condition that limits قَید، بَندِش disability کوتاہی *know (one's) limitations,* be conscious of (one's) disabilities اپنی کوتاہیوں کا اِحساس ہونا

limn (lim) *v.t.* draw or paint in water-colours نقّاشی کرنا، آبی رَنگوں میں تصویر کشی کرنا **limner** (*lim*-nĕ*) *n.* (esp.) portrait-painter نقّاش، مُصَوِّر

limp *v. i.* walk lamely as when one leg, etc., is hurt لنگڑانا، تَنگ کرنا، لنگڑا کر چلنا *n.* a lame walk لنگڑی چال، لنگ *adj.* lame لنگڑا، لَنگ **limpingly** *adv.* in a limping way لنگڑاتے ہوئے، لنگڑا کر

limpid (*limp*-id) *adj.* clear and transparent (liquid, atmosphere, eyes, style, etc.) صاف، شفّاف، نِتھرا ہُوا، صاف شفّاف **limpidity** (-*pid*-) *n.* being limpid صاف شفّاف ہونا، اُسلُوب کی پاکیزگی

linchpin (*linch*-pin) *n.* pin passed through the end of an axle to keep the wheel in position دُھرے کی کِیل

line (lın) *n.* long, narrow mark made on a surface with the point of a pencil, etc. لکیر، خط *straight line* سیدھی لکیر، خطِ مُستقیم *curved line* خطِ مُنحنی، ٹیڑھی لکیر undulating line لہریا لکیر piece of fine cord or wire ڈوری تار وغیرہ *fishing line,* مچھلی پکڑنے کے کانٹے کی دوڑی، ڈوری *telephone line* ٹیلی فون کا تار (also *line drawing*), picture made by drawing lines خاکہ *a picture in line* خاکہ *line and colour,* the two elements of painting خُطُوط اور رَنگ *a line block,* a printing block made of lines and not of dots (calls *half tone* block) لائن بلاک row (*of*) رَکی، قِطار *stand in a line* صَف باندھ کر کھڑے ہونا، قطار میں کھڑے ہونا *in line with,* in agreement with سے آہنگ کے مُوافق یا مُطابق rail track ریل کی پٹڑی، لائن *main line* مین لائن، ریل کی شاہراہ *branch line,* برانچ لائن، ریل کی ضمنی راہ *cross the line by the bridge* پُل پر سے ہو کر ریل کی پٹری کے پرلی طرف جانا، پُل پر سے لائن کے پار organized system of transport حمل و نقل کا اِدارہ یا کمپنی *an air line* ہوائی کمپنی *a steamship line* جہازی کمپنی. (pl.) (lines *on, in,* or *to* some subject) poem (on it) بہر، نظم row of words on a page of writing or print سطر *read between the lines,* find more meaning than the words express بات کی تہہ کو پہنچنا، پنہاں مفہوم کو پا لینا short letter دو حرف، دو لفظ، چھوٹا سا خط *drop (or send) (someone) a line* (or a *few lines*) *to say* (کسی کو) دو حرف اس مضمون کے لکھ بھیجنا کہ series of trenches, etc. مورچوں *the front line* اگلا مورچہ *behind the lines,* مورچوں کے پیچھے *all along the line,* at every point in a battle or other struggle ہر مرحلے پر generations (of a ruling or other family) خاندان (شاہی) سلسلہ *come of a good line* اچھے خاندان کا ہونا direction سمت (یا سمت) طرف جانب *in that line* اس سمت *in the line of (something),* towards it کی طرف، کی جانب policy راہ، منہاج، طریق *toe the line,* act on the policy laid down by one's political party اپنی پارٹی کی راہ پر گامزن، پارٹی کی راہ پر چلنا *on the lines laid down by,* کے طریق پر، کے اصُول پر manner, method نہج، طریق کار، طریق، طریقہ *on sound lines,* ٹھیک طریقے سے *on the wrong lines* غلط طریقے سے *take a bold line (with) take (one's) own line with,* deal independently with خود اپنی رائے پر چلنا، جرأت مندانہ قدم *on economical lines,* کفایت شعاری کے طریق سے *take the line of least resistance,* (*a*) adopt the easiest way (*a*) سہل ترین طریقہ اختیار کرنا (*b*) be easy-going (15) آرام طلبی کا طریقہ اختیار کرنا profession کاروبار، پیشہ *be in the publishing* (*etc.*) *line* کتابوں کی اشاعت (وغیرہ) کا کام کرنا *not much in (one's) line,* something about which one does not know much (کسی) کے پیشے سے (کسی) کام کا متعلق نہ ہونا (also *clothes-line*), line for hanging washed clothes on for drying الگنی class of goods مال کی قسم (*the*) equator خطِ استوا *cross the line* خطِ استوا کے پار جانا *hard lines,* bad luck بدقسمتی *come* (or *bring*) *into line,* come or bring into conformity of thought or action ہمنوا ہونا یا کرنا *on the line,* doubtfully assignable between two classes, border case بین بین جس کے متعلق فیصلہ دشوار ہو کہ اُدھر جائے گا یا اِدھر رہے گا *by rule and line*, (*a*) very accurately بہت باضابطگی سے *draw the line (between)*, distinguish between میں امتیاز کرنا *give line enough*, give much latitude بڑی ڈھیل دینا *v.t. & i.* draw a line لکیر کھینچنا، خط کھینچنا mark with lines دھاری دار form a line قطار کی طرح ہونا *road lined with trees on either side* دورویہ درختوں والی سڑک form (*up*) into a line صف بستہ ہونا کی صف بندی کرنا۔ add a lining to اَستر لگانا *fur-lined* پوستین کے اَستر والا **lining** (*li*-ning) *n.* extra layer (in garment, box, etc.) of different material اَستر *every cloud has a silver lining*, there is a message of hope even in the worst of misfortunes ہر بُرائی میں بھی اچھائی کی جھلک ہوتی ہے **lineage** (*lin*-e-ij) *n.* family tree سلسلۂ نسب، شجرۂ نسب، حسب نسب **lineament** (*lin*-e-a-ment) *n.* (usu. *pl.*) feature چہرہ مہرہ، خدوخال

lineal (*lin*-e-ĕl) *adj.* in the direct male-line of descent نسلی **linear** (*lin*-e-ĕ*) *adj.* in a straight line سیدھی لکیر میں of straight lines سیدھی لکیروں کا *linear design* سیدھی لکیروں والی تصویر *linear measure*, of length only and not of area or volume سادہ پیمائش **liner** (*li*-nĕ*) *n.* ship of a line نقل و حمل کی کمپنی کا جہاز *air-liner*, such aircraft نقل و حمل کی کمپنی کا، ہوائی جہاز **linesman** *n.* (in sports) referee's assistant standing close to the line to tell him if the ball has crossed it نائب ریفری، حد داد **line-up** *n.* group-formation (*of*) جتھہ بندی

linen (*lin*-en) *n.* cloth made of flax کتان کا کپڑا، کتان linen or calico articles like bedsheets, shirts, etc. سوتی کپڑے، لٹھے کی چادریں قمیص، وغیرہ *wash one's dirty linen in public*, not keep quiet about domestic quarrels گھر کے جھگڑے بازار میں چکانا **linen-draper** *n.* dealer in linen, calico, etc. لٹھے والا

linger (*ling*-ĕ*) *v. i.* be slow in leaving جانے میں ڈھیل ڈالنا، جانے میں دیر لگانا procrastinate دیر لگانا، دیر کرنا loiter (*about*, *around*, *in* or *near* a place) کے چکر کاٹتے رہنا **lingering** (*ling*-è-ring) *adj.* (of an illness) lasting a long time مزمن، طویل، لمبی **lingerer** (*ling*-è-rĕ*) *n.* one who lingers *n.* جانے میں ڈھیل کرنے والا

lingerie (*lahnzh*-è-ree) *n.* ladies' dainty under-clothing خواتین کا زیر جامہ

lingo (*ling*-oh) *n.* (pl. *lingoes*) queer foreign language (said, either contemptuously or humorously, of a language one does not know) عجیب زبان

lingua franca (*ling*-gwa-*frank*-a) *n.* mixed Greek, French, Italian and Spanish used for inter-communication in the Levant بحیرۂ روم کی ملی جلی زبان any such mixed jargon زبانوں کا ملغوبہ any language serving the purpose of inter-communication over a vast area with many spoken languages (like the much-maligned and neglected Urdu in the Indo-Pakistan sub-continent, or as claimed for English by its devotees) مشترکہ زبان

lingual (*ling*-gwĕl) *adj.* pertaining to language زبان سے متعلق

linguist (*ling*-gwist) *n.* one skilled in foreign languages زباندان، ہفت زبان، ماہرِ السنہ **linguistic** (-*gwis*-) *adj.* of the study of languages زبانданی سے متعلق **linguistics** (-tiks) *n. pl.* study of languages زبان دانی

liniment (*lin*-i-ment) *n.* liquid for rubbing on stiff or aching parts of the body مالش کی دوا، طلا

lining (*li*-ning) *n.* (see under **line**)

link *n.* one ring of a chain کڑی، حلقہ (*pl.*) (also *cuff-links* or *sleeve-links*), pair of linked buttons for fastening cuffs of a shirt لنگ، کفوں کے دُہرے بٹن that which unites others رابطہ، تعلق، واسطہ (*pl.*) golf course گاف کا میدان *v.t. & i.* join or be joined (*together*, *to* or *with* something) جڑنا یا جوڑنا، ملنا یا ملانا، منسلک ہونا یا کرنا

linnet (*lin*-et) *n.* a small songbird ایک خوش الحان ننھا پرندہ

linocut *n.* (see under **linoleum**)

linoleum (li-*noh*-le-um) *n.* thick piece of canvas treated with powdered cork and oil and used as matting روغنی کرمچ، لنولیم **linocut** (*lin*-o-kut, *lin*-o-kut) *n.* design cut in relief on linoleum block for printing کرمچی بلاک

linotype (*lin*-o-tīp) *n.* composing machine with typewriter-like keys turning out a "line of type" at a time (in stead of single letters) لائنو ٹائپ، لینو، سطر، سطر ٹائپ

linseed (*lin*-seed) *n.* flax seed اَلسی، ہلسی کا بیج، تخمِ کتان

lint *n.* linen fluffy on one side for dressing لنٹ، رُوئیں دار لٹھا، مُلائم

lintel (*lintel*) *n.* concrete slab or wood, etc., across top of door or window سردل، لنٹل **lintelled** (*lint*-ĕld) *adj.* (of ceiling, etc.) made thus لنٹل والا

lion (*li*-on) *n.* the king of animals شیر ببر، ببر شیر very brave person بہادر، شجاع one much sought after in society سوسائٹی کی مرغوب شخصیت (*pl.*) worthseeing sights (of a town, etc.) قابلِ دید مقامات **lioness** (*li*-o-nes) *n.* female of a lion مادہ شیر ببر، ببر شیرنی **lionize** (*li*-o-nīz) *v. t.* treat (someone) as a celebrity and make a fuss over him کسی کو عظیم شخصیت سمجھ بیٹھنا *lionhearted*, brave شیردل *lion's*

a lion (standing) with lioness

share, disproportionately large share بہُت بڑا حصّہ *lion in the way*, (imaginary) obstacle (موہُوم) خطرہ *lion's skin*, pretended bravery اپنی بہادُری کے مُتعلّق بڑ، *Lion's Club*, (see *Addenda*) بھُوٹی شیخی

lip *n.* one of the two fleshy edges of animal mouth ہونٹ، لب *upper lip* اُوپر کا ہونٹ *lower lip* نیچے کا ہونٹ *open* (or *close*) (*one's*) *lips* مُنہ کھولنا یا بند کرنا، *lick* (*one's*) *lips*, (*a*) ہونٹ چاٹنا (*b*) مُنہ میں پانی بھر آنا *screw up* (or *pout*) (*one's*) *lips* عجیب سامُنہ بنا لینا، ہونٹ سُکیڑ کر آگے کو نکال لینا *hang on* (*one's*) *lips*. listen reverently to بڑی عقیدت سے سُننا *escape* (*one's*) *lips*, (of something) be uttered thoughtlessly بے خیالی میں مُنہ سے نکل جانا edge of anything hollow (like a wound, jug, etc.) کنارہ، لَب *adj.* spoken but not felt, insincere زُبانی، مُنافقانہ **lip-service** *n.* insincere respect, sympathy, etc. زُبانی جمع خرچ **lip-deep** *adj.* superficial ظاہرداری کا سطحی **lipstick** *n.* stick of cosmetic for reddening the lips لاکھا، لپ سٹک *lips reddened with the lipstick* ہونٹوں پر لاکھے کی پپڑی جمانے، لپ سٹک سے ہونٹ لال کیے۔

liquefaction *n.*, **liquefy** *v.t.* & *i.* (see under **liquid**)

liquid (*li-kwid*) *n.* any substance that flows like water and is neither a solid nor a gas سَیّال *adj.* in the form of a liquid رقیق، پتلا، سَیّال *liquid air*, سَیّال ہَوا bright and clear (eyes) چمکدار، چمکیلی clear and soft (sounds, notes, etc.) صاف اور رسیلا easily changed (principles, opinion, assets, etc.) تغیّر پذیر *liquid assets, shares, etc.*, property which can easily be converted into money آسانی سے نقدی میں تبدیل ہو جانے والی جائیداد، حصّے، تمسّکات

liquefy (*li*-kwe-f.) *v.t.* & *i.* become or make a liquid پانی ہو جانا یا کر دینا، پگھلنا یا پگھلانا **liquefaction** (-*fak*-) *n.* liquefying پگھلنا یا پگھلانا، ترقیق

liquidate (*li*-kwi-dayt) *v.t.* & *i.* repay (a debt) قرضہ ادا کرنا، قرض چُکانا close down (an unsuccessful) business by dividing up its property to clear debts دیوالہ نکالنا (of a company) become bankrupt دیوالیہ ہونا، کا دیوالہ نکالنا ruthlessly crush (all political opposition or opponents) (سیاسی مخالفت یا مخالفین کا) تشدّد سے خاتمہ کرنا، مخالفت کا استیصال **liquidation** (-*day*) *n.* crush opposition (سیاسی مُخالفت کا) تشدّد سے خاتمہ bankruptcy دیوالہ *go into liquidation* کا دیوالہ نکلنا

liquor (*lik*-ĕ*) *n.* any alcoholic drink شراب *be in liquor, be the worse for liquor* نشے میں ہونا، پئے ہوئے ہونا

liquorice, licorice (*lik*-è-ris) *n.* sweet black extract of root used as a medicine مُلٹھی، رُبّ السُّوس plant yielding it مُلٹھی

lisp *v.t.* & *i.* sound *s* and *z* (like children) as if they were *th* soft تُتلانا *n.* this defect of speech in elders تُتلاہٹ this as a lovable drawback in children تُتلاپن

list *n.* catalog (*of* persons or items) written or printed فہرست، فرد tilting of a ship جہاز کا جُھکنا *a list to larboard* جہاز بائیں جانب جُھکاؤ یا جُھکاؤ *pl.* (*lists*), enclosure for combats between men on horseback اکھاڑا *enter the lists*, (*a*) step into the lists اکھاڑے میں اُترنا (*b*) accept or send out a challenge to fight it out دعوتِ مُبارزت دینا یا قبول کرنا *v.t.* & *i.* make a list of کی فہرست بنانا، کی فرد تیار کرنا *put on a list* فہرست میں لکھ لینا، درجِ فہرست (of a ship) tilt to one side جہاز کا ایک طرف جُھکنا (old use) listen (*to*) پر کان دھرنا، سُننا (old use) (*list* or *listed* ; 3rd person sing. pr. *listeth*) like (*to do*) کرنا، چاہنا

listen (*lis*-èn) *v.i.* hear attentively (*to*) بغور سُننا make an effort to hear (*to*) سُننے کی کوشش کرنا try to overhear (*to*) پر کان لگانا (*listen in*), listen to a radio programme ریڈیو سُننا **listener** (*lis*-è-nĕ*) *n.* one who listens سُننے والا (esp.) one receiving broadcast wireless programme ریڈیو سُننے والا

listless (*list*-les) *adj.* too tired to do, interested in, anything تھکا ماندہ، تھکا ہُوا lacking energy or interest بے ہمّت، بے ذوق languid سُست

lit *v.* (pa. t. & pa. p. of **light**, which see)

litany (*lit*-a-ni) *n.* form of Christian prayer with petitions recited by the priest and responses from the congregation عیسائیوں کی سَنگت والی دُعا

literacy *n.* (see under **literate**)

literal (*lit*-è-rĕl) *adj.* word for word (copy, etc.) حرف حرف، ہُو بہُو، مُطابقِ اصل precise, not exaggerated (truth, etc.) بالکل، حرف حرف exact (translation) لفظی taking words in their usual outward (and not allegorical sense) ظاہری of the letters حرفوں سے مُتعلّق، حرفی لفظی *literal error*, misprint طباعت (یا کتابت) کی غلطی real, not metaphorical اصلی **literally** (*lit*-è-ra-li) *adv.* giving or taking words in their ordinary meaning لفظی in fact واقعی، سچ مُچ

literary (*lit*-è-ra-ri) *adj.* pertaining to literature ادبی (of style or word) not colloquial کتابی

literate (*lit*-e-rayt) *n.* & *adj.* (person) able to read and write پڑھا لکھا، خواندہ **literacy** *n.* ability to read and write خواندگی *percentage of literacy*, percentage of literate persons (*in* a country, etc.) تناسبِ خواندگی *literacy drive*, (government) bid to make people literate خواندگی کی مُہم

literature *n.* writings valued as works of art اَدب ، اَدبِیات *study of literature*, critical and historical study of such books اَدب کا تنقیدی مطالعہ all such writings (*of* a particular period, country or language) کا اَدب the books dealing with a special subject کے موضوع پر کتابیں advertisement (*on* some topics, *of* some firm) in the form of technical or other information (کسی کے) مَعلوماتی رَسائل

literati (lit-è-*ray*-ti), *n. pl.* men of letters اُدبا scholars اہلِ علم ، علما ادیب لوگ

lithe (lidh) *adj.* supple, flexible (body or person)

lithograph (*lith*-o-graf) *v.t.* print from a metal plate (or originally, from a stone) with an inverted impression of what is to be printed پتھر کی چھپائی کرنا ، لیتھو کی چھپائی کرنا *n.* thing thus printed پتھر کا چھاپہ ، لیتھو کا چھاپہ **lithographer** (*-thog-*) *n.* one who prints thus پتھر کی چھپائی کرنے والا لیتھو کی چھپائی والا **lithography** (*-thog-*) this process of printing پتھر کی چھپائی ، لیتھو گرافی ، لیتھو

litigate (lit-i-gayt) *v.t.* & *i.* carry on a lawsuit مُقدّمہ دائر کرنا ، مُقدّمے بازی پر اُترنا **litigant** *n.* person engaged in a law-suit فریقِ مُقدّمہ ، فریق **litigation** (*-gay-*) *n.* carrying on of law-suit مُقدّمہ law-suit مُقدّمہ بازی **litigious** (li-*ti*-jus) *adj.* fond of going to law مُقدّمہ باز material, etc., fit for a lawsuit ; disputable at law مُتنازعہ فیہ

litmus (*lit*-mus) *n.* blue colouring matter got from lichens ; it turns red by acids and is restored by alkalis لِٹمس **litmus paper** *n.* (blue or red) paper dyed in it لِٹمس کاغذ

litotes (*li*-to-teez, or *lit*-o-teez) *n.* rhetorical device of understanding something for emphasis (as *little* for *not*, or *no small* for *great*) صَنعتِ مُلائمت

litre (*leet*-è*) *n.* French liquid measure equal to about 1¾ lb. ریٹر ، لِٹر

litter (*lit*-è*) *n.* scraps of paper or other useless things thrown about untidily کوڑا کرکٹ ، ماروی ، آخور straw, etc., used as bedding for animals پیال a number of the newly-born young ones (*of* an animal) جھول (old use) carrying couch for invalids or women ڈولی ، پینس *v.t.* & *i.* leave litter about اِدھر اُدھر بکھیرنا *littered with* (میں یا پر) بکھرا ہوا ہونا (of animals) give birth to a litter جھول لگانا put straw as a bed for animals پیال ، بچھانا ، پیالی ڈالنا

a litter (sense 4)

litterateur (lee-tay-ra-tö*) *n.* man of letters ادیب

little (*lit*-èl) *adj.* young ننھا ، چھوٹا *the little ones (of)* (کے) ننھے مُنے (بچے) small in size چھوٹا ، چھوٹا سا unimportant غیر اہم of the smaller or smallest size سب سے چھوٹا ، چھوٹا *great and little*, *big and little* بڑا چھوٹا *the little finger* چھنگلیا (*little, less, least*) not much شاید ہی not نہیں *a little*, small amount تھوڑا سا ، ذرا سا *the little that* تھوڑا سا جو ، ذرا سا جو *after a little*, after a short time تھوڑی دیر کے بعد *for a little*, for a short time تھوڑی دیر کے لیے ، ذرا سی دیر کو *adv.* not much کم کم ، تھوڑا تھوڑا hardly at all بمشکل *a little*, somewhat کسی حد تک *little by little*. gradually آہستہ آہستہ ، دھیرے دھیرے

Little John *n. Brit. leg.* the stalwart companion of Robin Hood لِٹل جان ، چھوٹا جان

littoral (*lit*-è-rěl) *adj.* by the sea ساحلی نزدیک ساحل کے *n* such part of country ساحلی علاقہ

liturgy (*lit*-è*-ji) *n.* fixed form of (Christian) public worship (عیسائیوں کی) نماز کا طریق *the Liturgy*, the Book of Common Prayer عیسائیوں کی دعاؤں کی کتاب عیسائیوں کی نماز (کی ترکیب)

live *v.t.* & *i.* (liv) be alive ; exist زندہ ہونا spend (a particular type of life) زندگی بسر کرنا dwell (*in, at*) (میں) رہنا *live on* (*a*) have as food (something) (کوئی چیز) کھا کر بسر کرنا (*b*) get what one needs for support from (friends, property, own income) (کے سہارے) زندگی گزارنا *live to be an old man*, continue to live till old age بڑھاپے تک جینا ، بوڑھا ہو کر رہنا *live (something) down*, by good living make people forget (earlier wrongdoing) بدنامی (وغیرہ) کا داغ مٹانا *live by*. earn one's living by کی روزی کمانا *live up to (one's) faith (or principles)* ایمانداری کی زندگی گزارنا ، با اُصول زندگی بسر کرنا *adj.* (liv) (used only before the noun qualified by it) alive زندہ active جوان ہمت full of enthusiasm زندہ wide awake ہوشمند ، چوکنا (of coal) burning دہکتا ہوا unexploded (shell, cartridge, etc.) جو چلا نہ ہو ، زندہ (of wire, etc.) through which electric current is passing جس میں سے برقی رو گزرتی ہو ، بجلی والا ، شاٹ والا ، برقی *live wire*, (*a*) through which current is passing برقی رو والا تار (*b*) vigorous and highly energetic person بلند ہمت ، باہمت شخص

livable (*liv*-a-bèl) *adj.* fit to live in رہائش کے قابل

livelihood (*liv*-li-hŭd) *n.* means of living روزی ، ذریعۂ آمدنی ، ذریعہ معاش *earn (one's) livelihood by doing something* روزی کمانا

livelong (*liv*-long, or *liv-*) *adj.* (lit. & poet.) (only in phrases like :) *the livelong day* (*etc.*), all the day (etc.) long دن (وغیرہ) بھر

lively (*liv*-li) *adj.* full of life and gay زندہ دل ، بشاش ، شگفتہ مزاج cheerful پُر لطف ، زندہ دلانہ

(movements) زور زور کا، تیز، تیز exciting (discussion) سرگرم realistic حقیقت پسندانہ **liveliness** (*liv*-li-nes) *n*. being lively زندہ دلی **liven** (*liv*-en) *v.t.* & *i*. brighten (*up*) (میں) جان پڑ جانا make (*up*) cheery میں جان ڈالنا **livestock** (*liv*-stok) *n*. animals kept for use or profit ڈھور ڈنگر، مال مویشی **living** (*liv*-ing) *adj*. alive زندہ *the living*, all now alive زندگان now existing آجکل کا، زندہ موجود active (faith, etc.) زندہ (of a picture, etc.) true to life کا ہم شکل، کا زندہ نمونہ *the living image of* جیتی جاگتی، منہ بولتی *n*. livelihood روزی *make a living (as)* (بن کر) روزی کمانا (high, low, plain, etc.) manner of life طرزِ زندگی *standard of living* معیارِ زندگی **living wage** *n*. wages enough for a workman to live on without undue hardships وہ تنخواہ (یا اُجرت) جس میں گزر ہو سکے گزارے کے لیے کافی تنخواہ یا اُجرت، گزارہ، تنخواہ
living-room *n*. sitting-room for general use by day (usu. containing the dining-table, etc., as well) اُٹھنے بیٹھنے کا کمرہ [1]**liver** (*liv*-ē*) one who lives in a specified way, (good, bad, dissolute, etc.) (طرح) زندگی بسر کرنے والا
livelihood *n*., **livelong** *adj*., **lively** *adj*., **liven** *v.t.* & *i*. [1]**liver** *n*. (see under **live**)
[2]**liver** (*liv*-ē*) *n*. bodily organ secreting bile and purifying the blood جگر، کلیجہ *white liver, lily liver*, cowardice بزدلی *liver-complaint* جگر کی تکلیف *liver and lights*, کلیجی اور پھیپھڑے animal's liver as food کلیجی **liverish** *adj*. having some liver-complaint جگر کی تکلیف میں مُبتلا
livery (*liv*-è-ri) *n*. manservant's uniform وَرْدی (ملازم کی) وَرْدی، بانا allowance of one who keeps a livery stable راتب، مُقتاد **liveried** (*liv*-è-rid) *adj*. wearing a livery باوَرْدی، بانیدار **livery-stable** *n*. stable where horses are let for hire کرائے کے گھوڑوں کا اَصطبل one where horses are kept at livery اصطبل جہاں گھوڑے مالکوں سے خرچہ لے کر رکھے جاتے ہیں
lives (livz) *n*. (*pl*. of **life** which see)
livestock *n*. (see under **live**)
livid (*liv*-id) *adj*. black and blue; like lead in colour نیلا، نیلگوں discoloured with bruises چوٹ کے باعث نیلا discoloured (*with* rage, cold, etc.) (ڈرنے یا غصے وغیرہ سے) نیلا
living (*liv*-ing) *n*. & *adj*. (see under **live**)
lizard (*liz*-ē*d) *n*. a small, long-tailed, reptile creeping along walls, etc. چھپکلی، چلپاسہ
llama, lama (*lah*-ma) *n*. a South American beast of burden belonging to the camel family لاما، امریکی اُونٹ
lo (loh) *int*. look!, behold! لو دیکھو! دیکھو دیکھو! دیکھو تو
load (lohd) *n*. burden بوجھ، بوجھا، بار weight of grief, care, etc.) کا بوجھ، کا بار amount which a cart, etc., can take بوجھ *an ass load (of)* (کا) خَروار cartridge, etc., with which a gun, etc., is charged گولی بارود *v.t.* & *i*. put a load (*on* or *in*) لادنا put (goods) (*into, on*) (پر سامان) لادنا put (a cartridge, etc.) into (a gun, etc.) (بندوق وغیرہ میں گولی وغیرہ) بھرنا charge (a gun, etc.) thus (بندوق وغیرہ) بھرنا **loaded** (*lohd*-ed) *adj*. with load on لدا ہُوا charged (gun, etc.) بھری ہُوئی
loadline *n*. safe water-level line for full load marked on a ship زیادہ سے زیادہ بوجھ کا نشان، بار نشان
loadstone, lodestone (*lohd*-stohn) *n*. magnetic oxide of iron خام مقناطیس piece of it that attracts مقناطیس anything that attracts دلکش (شخص یا شے) **lodestar, loadstar** *n*. pole-star قطب، قطب تارا
loaf (lohf) *n*. (pl. *loaves*) (also called a *loaf of bread*) shaped mass of bread cooked separately روٹی any shaped mass ٹکڑا، ڈلی، ڈلا *loaf sugar*, sugar cut into small cubes شکر کے ڈلے *v.t.* & *i*. spend time in doing nothing وقت بیکار کھونا hang about, loiter مارا مارا پھرنا، ہرزہ گردی کرنا، آوارہ گردی کرنا *loafing at street corners*, بازاروں میں یونہی کھڑے کھڑے وقت ضائع کرنا، گھر سے باہر دکانوں پر بیٹھے رہنا **loafer** *n*. one who loafs وقت بیکار کھونے والا، آوارہ گرد، یونہی مارا مارا پھرنے والا، خدائی خوار، کوچہ گرد، ہرزہ گرد

a loaf

loam (lohm) *n*. fertile soil containing decayed vegetable matter نباتاتی کھاد والی زرخیز مٹی **loamy** *adj*. consisting of loam نباتاتی کھاد والی (مٹی)
loan (lohn) *n*. something lent اُدھار، قرضہ، قرض *government loans* سرکاری قرضے *on loan*, being lent اُدھار، عاریۃً lending عاریۃً دینا، اُدھار دینا، قرض دینا، مستعار *ask for the loan*, (*a*) (*of* money) اُدھار مانگنا (*b*) (*of* something else) عاریۃً لینا، مستعار لینا
loath, loth (lohth) *adj*. (never used before a noun); reluctant or unwilling (*to do something*) (پر) غیر آمادہ، (پر) راضی نہیں *nothing loath*, quite glad (*to do*) (پر) راضی، (پر) خوش
loathe (lohdh) *v. t.* detest سے سخت نفرت **loathsome** (*lohdh*-sum) *adj*. detestable قابلِ نفرت **loathing** (*lohdh*-ing) *n*. disgust نفرت، تنفّر
loaves (loavz) *n*. (*pl*. *of* **loaf**, which see)
lobby (*lob*-i) *n*. entrance-hall ڈیوڑھی (in Legislatures, originally in the British House of Commons, hall open to members as well as outsiders) مجالسِ قانون ساز کا وہ کمرہ جہاں عوام بھی جا سکتے ہوں، لابی *lobby-talk*, unofficial but fairly correct

comments on points at issue in the Legislature لابی کے حلقوں کا خیال **lobbying** (*lob*-i-ing) *n.* obtaining unofficially important reactions and predictions on topics of the day from members of the Legislature by journalists لابی کے تاثرات جمع کرنا *do a bit of lobbying,* collect such information from what are termed the *lobby circles* لابی حلقے (*i.e.,* the members of the Legislature in their unofficial capacity) لابی کے حلقوں سے پوچھ گچھ کرنا

lobe (lohb) *n.* lower rounded end of the outer ear کان کی لَو any rounded projection بڑھا ہوا حصہ

lobster (*lob*-stĕ*) *n.* a shellfish with long powerful claws جھینگا مچھلی its flesh as food جھینگا مچھلی کا گوشت

lobotomy *n.* (see *Addenda*)

local (*loh*-kĕl) *adj.* of a particular locality مُقامی *local news,* news items concerning the city, etc., from which the paper containing them is published مُقامی خبریں *local colour,* (in art or literature) mention of the characteristic, scenery, etc., of the locality to which the writer belongs or the life of which is depicted in that work مُقامی رَنگ *local government, local self-government,* government of the local affairs of a district or town بلدیاتی حکومت *local pain,* pain localized in a particular part of the body مُقامی درد *local time,* time reckoned from the true noon of a place لوکل ٹائم ، مقامی وقت **locale** (loh-*kahl*) *n.* locality, etc., where events (of races, etc.) take place

locally (*loh*-ka-li) *adv.* مُقامی طور پر **locality** (loh-*kal*-i-ti) *n.* district or area علاقہ place مُقام ، جگہ *the locality of,* the position of کا مقام place of occurrence جائے وُقوع **localize** (*loh*-ka-līz) *v.t.* restrict to a particular locality کسی مُقام میں محدود کرنا give it the distinctive characteristic of a locality کسی مُقام کی خصوصیات پیدا کرنا **localization** (-*zay*-) *n.* act of localizing کسی مُقام میں تحدید کسی مُقام سے تخصیص

locate (lo-*kayt*) *v. t.* discover the position of (a place) کوئی جگہ ڈھونڈ نکالنا show its position (*on a map*) (نقشے پر) دکھانا یا بتانا *be located in,* be situated in میں واقع ہونا **location** (-*kay*-) *n.* situation محلِ وُقوع settling in a place آبادکاری ، آباد ہونا (in South Africa) suburb for non-Europeans کالوں کا مضافاتی شہر ، کالوں کی نواحی بستی

loch (lok) *n.* Scotch arm of the sea (سکاچستان کی) تنگ کھاڑی Scotch lake (سکاچستان کی) جھیل

lock (lok) *n.* tress ; tuft or curl of hair بالوں کی لٹ زُلف ، گیسو tuft of wool اُون کا گچھا door catch worked with a key تالا ، قفل lever for firing a gun بندوق کا گھوڑا ، لبلبی *lock, stock, and barrel,* completely تمام کا تمام ، بالکل mechanism in a section of a canal, etc., for raising or lowering boats by changing the water-level نہر کی سطح اُونچی نیچی کرنے والا بند ، متحرک بند ، قفلی بند *v. t. & i.* fasten with a lock تالا لگانا ، قفل لگانا ، مقفل کرنا make fast by linking the parts کس کر باندھنا (cause to) become fixed and unable to move جکڑنا ، جکڑا جانا *locked wheels* جام ہو جانے پہیے *lock the door* دروازے کو تالا لگانا *lock (something) up,* put in a locked place تالے کے اندر رکھنا *lock (someone) up,* imprison him حوالات میں بند کرنا *lock (someone) in* (or *out*), (esp. of factory owner), shut up his factory with the workers inside (or out of) it in order to prevent them from work as a punishment for the demands they have put in (لاک اِن) یا (لاک آوٹ) کرنا **lock-out** *n.* such a step taken by the factory-owner مزدوروں کو سبق سکھانے کے لیے کارخانہ بند کر دینا ، لاک آوٹ **locker** *n.* small cupboard (with or without a lock) usu. in the form of a rack near the patient's bed in a hospital لاکر ، الماری **locksmith** (*lok*-smith) *n.* maker and repairer of locks for doors, etc. تالوں والا ، قفلساز **lock-up** *n.* (colloq.) room used as a prison in a police-station حوالات

locket (*lok*-et) *n.* (gold or silver) case for a portrait, or lock of hair, etc., hung from the neck لاکٹ ، تعویذ ، حرز

locomotive (loh-ko-*moh*-tiv) *n.* railway engine ریل کا انجن ، اِنجن *adj.* having the power to move from place to place متحرک creating this power متحرک کرنے والا **locomotion** (-*moh*-) *n.* locomotive power متحرک کرنا یا ہونا

locus (*loh*-kus) *n.* (pl. *loci,* pr. *loh*-sī) exact place of something محلِ وقوع (in mathematics) curve made by the defined motion of a point or line or surface نقطے کا راستہ ، طریق

locus standi (*loh*-kus-*stan*-dī) *n.* position that gives one a right to interfere حقِ مداخلت عطا کرنے والی حیثیت accepted position مُسلّمہ حیثیت

locust (*loh*-kust) *n.* grasshopper-like insect flying in great swarms and destroying crops over vast areas ٹڈی ، ٹیری ، ملخ **locust swarm** *n.* swarm of locusts ٹڈی دل

locution (lo-*kew*-shĕn) *n.* phrase or idiom محاورہ style of speech اُسلوبِ تقریر ، اندازِ خطابت

lode (lohd) *n.* vein of metal ore in a mine کان میں کچی دھات کی پرت **lodestone** *n.*, **lodestar** *n.* (see under **loadstone**)

lodge (loj) *n.* servant's cottage at the entrance to a large private estate جاگیر پر نوکر کا گھر ، دربان خانہ (old use) any small house چھوٹا سا گھر rooms in the chief gateway of a large building بڑی عمارت کی ڈیوڑھی کے کمرے meeting-place for the members of a society (کسی انجمن کی) جلسہ گاہ branch of a secret society کسی خفیہ انجمن کی شاخ *v.t.* & *i.* live (*in*, *at* or *with*) as a lodger کرایہ دار مہمان بن کر رہنا supply (someone) with room or rooms to live in (کسی کو) کمرہ دینا stay for the night (somewhere) رات گزارنے کے لیے ٹھہرنا ، رات گزارنا ، شب باش کرنا place (complaint, statement, etc., *with* the authorities) (کے پاس) باقاعدہ شکایت کرنا یا بیان داخل کرنا put (money, etc.) for safety (*with* someone or *in* a place) (میں یا کے پاس روپیہ) حفاظت سے رکھنا ۔ (of bullet, etc.) (cause to) enter and be fixed (*in* part of body, etc.) (میں) پیوست ہو جانا یا کرنا **lodger** (*loj*-ĕ*) *n.* person paying for room in someone's house کرایہ دار ، کسی کے گھر کے کمروں میں رہنے والا کرایہ دار مہمان مہمان جو رہنے کا کرایہ ادا کرے **lodging** (*loj*-ing) *n.* (*pl.*) rented rooms کرائے پر لیے ہوئے کمرے ۔ place to sleep شب باشی کی جگہ ، رات کاٹنے کی جگہ **lodging-house** *n.* house in which rooms are let without food arrangements کرائے پر دیے جانے والے کمروں والا گھر ، کرایہ خانہ

loft *n.* attic ; room between the roof of the house and the ceiling of its top floor بیرونی چھت کے نیچے کا سب سے اوپر والا کمرہ

lofty (*lof*-ti) *adj.* very high (building, etc.) بہت اونچا proud or haughty (manner) مغرور noble (thoughts, feelings, etc.) اونچے ، شریفانہ **loftiness** (*lof*-ti-nes) *n.* being lofty بلندی

log *n.* rough length of a felled tree-trunk گیلی short piece of this for a fire لکڑی کا کندہ ، لکڑی apparatus for measuring a ship's speed جہاز کا رفتار پیما (also *logbook*), daily filled up record of ship's rate of progress and events of her voyage, etc. جہاز کا روزنامچہ (*log*) (abbr. of *logarithm*, which see) **logbook** *n.* (also) record book of some touring officer's visit to, and comments on the work of, a place لاگ بک

logarithm *n.* one of a series of numbers tabulated for simplifying the working out of problems in multiplication and division by changing them into addition and subtraction ضرب تقسیم کے سوال کو جمع تفریق کے طور پر حل کرنے کا طریق ۔ لوگارتم ، آسان شمار ، شمار آسان **logarithms** *n. pl.* this series سلسلہ لوگارتم ۔

loggerheads (*log*-ĕ*-hedz) *n. pl.* (only in the phrases :) *at loggerheads with*, on very bad terms with سخت دشمن *be at loggerheads with* سے سر پھٹول ہونا

logic (*loj*-ik) *n.* art of reasoning (correctly) منطق ability to argue and convince قائل کرنے کی صلاحیت *by sheer logic* محض قائل کرنے کی صلاحیت سے **logical** (*loj*-i-kĕl) *adj.* (statement, etc.) in accordance with the laws of logic منطقی (person) able to reason correctly ٹھیک استدلال کرنے والا ، منطقی **logically** *adv.* in a logical manner منطقی انداز سے

-logist (lo-jist) *suf.* (making nouns that denote) expert in ماہر (as : *psychologist* ماہر نفسیات

logistics (lo-*jis*-tiks) *n.* branch of military art concerned with transport of troops and their housing supplies, etc. فوجی نقل و حمل اور قیام و رسد

-logy (lo-ji) *suf.* (making nouns that denote names of) science or doctrines یات (as *biology* حیاتیات

loin (loin) *n.* (*pl.* the lower part of the back between the hip-bones and the ribs پٹھا *loin-cloth*, garment for covering this part of the body لنگوٹی لنگوٹ joint of meat from this part of an animal پٹھے کا گوشت

loiter (*loi*-tĕ*) *v. i.* go slowly and stop frequently on the way somewhere ٹھہرتے ٹھہرتے سفر کرنا stand about on the way راستے میں کھڑے ہو جانا pass time (away) thus کوچہ گردی میں وقت ضائع کرنا **loiterer** *n.* one who loiters ; loafer کوچہ گرد ، ہرزہ گرد

loll (lol) *v.t.* & *i.* rest, sit or stand (*about*) in lazy way اینڈنا ، سستی سے پڑے رہنا ، بیٹھنا یا کھڑے ہونا ، پاؤں پسار کر لیٹنا یا بیٹھنا of (of the tongue) hang (out) (زبان کا) باہر نکلنا let (the tongue) hang (*out*) زبان نکالنا

lollipop (*lol*-i-pop) *n.* bon-bon کھانڈ کا کھلونا

lone (lohn) *adj.* (lit.) (used only before the noun it qualifies) solitary (person) اکیلا ، یکہ و تنہا unfrequented (place) اجاڑ ، سنسان ، ویران **lonely** (lohn-li) *adj.* solitary (person) اکیلا ، یکہ و تنہا *feel lonely*, feel sad owing to loneliness تنہائی کے باعث اداس ہونا (place) without many people جہاں بہت کم آبادی ہو (place) inhabited but far from other inhabited places دور افتادہ **loneliness** *n.* being lonely تنہائی

lonesome (lohn-sum) *adj.* lonely (person) تنہا feeling lonely اداس lone (place) ویران ●

long (long) *v. i.* desire earnestly (*for* or *to do* something) کا آرزومند ہونا ، کا متمنی ہونا *adj.* tall لمبا measuring much from end to end in space or time لمبا ، طویل slow and dilatory لمبا ، دراز ، طول طویل

the whole length of سارا *all the day long* دن بھر سارا دن of specified length لمبا ، طویل *five-foot-long, five feet long* پانچ فٹ لمبا of elongated shape لمبوترا characterized by its length لمبا much delayed دیر سے *in the long run*, in the end اس نشیب و فراز کے بعد ، آخرکار ، آخر ، بالآخر ، انجام کار *before long*, soon enough جلد ہی *the long and the short of it*, the general outcome of it all الحاصل ، قصّہ مختصر ، مدّعا (یا) مطلب یہ کہ *adv.* for (or by, etc.) a long time دیر تک ، تا دیر *as long as*, (with affirmatives), *so long as* (with negatives), till جب تک *long-drawn out*, unduly prolonged غیر معمولی طور پر طویل ، بہت ہی لمبا *long ago*, not recently مدّتیں ہوئیں *the long ago*, old times قدیم الایام ۔ پرانا زمانہ *no longer*, (*a*) not now اب سے پہلے (*b*) not from now onward اب کے بعد نہیں **longbow** *n.* ordinary bow bent by hand (as distinct from a *crossbow*) کمان *draw the long bow*, tell exaggerated tales مبالغے سے کام لینا ، مبالغہ آمیز قصّے بیان کرنا **longevity** (lon-*jev*-i-ti) *n.* long life لمبی عمر great length of life درازیٔ عمر

longhair *n.* (see *Addenda*) **longhand** *n.* ordinary writing (as opposed to *shorthand*) عام خط

long jump *n.* long (and not *high*) jump لمبی چھلانگ

long-suffering *adj.* & *n.* patient and uncomplaining (behaviour) صبر سے برداشت کرنے والا **long standing** *n.* being old قدامت ، پرانا ہونا **long-standing** *adj* of a long standing مدّتوں کا ، پرانا **long vacation** *n.* summer vacation گرمیوں کی چھٹیاں تعطیلاتِ گرما

long-winded *adj.* (of talk or talker, etc.) tediously long بہت ہی طویل ، اکتا دینے والی حد تک طویل (of sportsman) able to run far without resting جو دیر تک دوڑتا رہ سکے ، (دوڑنے والا) جس کا دم نہ ٹوٹے

long-off *n.* fielder at bowler's left rear لانگ آف

long-on *n.* fielder at bowler's right rear لانگ آون

long wave *n.* & *adj.* (in wireless) (having a) wave length of about 800 metres and more لانگ ویو طویل لاسلکی لہریں ، (یا لہروں والا) **longing** *n.* strong desire بڑی خواہش ، سخت آرزو **longingly** *adv.* with longing اشتیاق سے **longways, longwise,** *adv.* lengthwise طولاً

longitude (*lonj*-i-tewd) *n.* distance east or west (measured in degrees) from a meridian (esp. that of Greenwich in London) طول ، طول البلد ، (خطِ) طولِ بلد

looby (*loo*-bi) *n.* silly fellow پاجی ، احمق

look (lūk) *v.t.* & *i.* make an effort to see غور سے دیکھنا direct one's eyes (*at* or *towards*) کی طرف دیکھنا face کی طرف دیکھنا ، کو دیکھنا ، کو گھورنا take care (*that*) خیال رکھنا کہیں ، دیکھنا کہیں appear (happy, sad, etc.) نظر آنا ، دکھائی دینا *look after* (*someone* or *something*), take care of (him, etc.) کی دیکھ بھال کرنا ، کی نگرانی کرنا *look down on* (*someone*), regard (him, etc.) with contempt بنظرِ حقارت سے دیکھنا *look for*, try to find ڈھونڈنا ، تلاش کرنا *look forward to* (*something* or *doing it*), expect with pleasure کی امید کرنا *look in on* (*someone*), visit while passing چلتے چلتے مل جانا ، کھڑے کھڑے مل جانا ، ذرا سی دیر کو ملنے آنا *look on*, be a spectator دیکھا کرنا ، تماشا دیکھنا *look over* (*something*), over look سے درگزر کرنا ، کو نظر انداز کر دینا *look on* (or *upon someone* or *something*) *as*, consider (him, etc.) as (کو) سمجھنا *on the look out for*, (*a*) watching for (it) کا منتظر (*b*) on one's guard سے مقابلے کے لیے تیار *look out*, (*a*) (own) concern اپنا نقطۂ نگاہ (*b*) prospect of luck امکان ، قسمت *look* (*something*) *over*, inspect (it) کا معائنہ کرنا *look* (*a piece of writing*) *through*, read the whole of it سارا پڑھنا *look to it that*, take care that خیال رکھنا *look into* (*a matter*) investigate (it) کی تحقیقات کرنا *look ahead*, (*a*) consider the future مستقبل کا خیال کرنا (*b*) warning to drive against danger of collision سامنے دیکھو *look alive, look sharp*, make haste جلدی کرو *to look at* (*him*), judging from outward appearance دیکھنے میں تو ، دیکھنے کو تو *look up to*, respect عزت کرنا *look up to* (*someone for help, etc.*), کسی سے مدد کی آس لگانا *lock a gift horse in the mouth*, regard a gift critically تحفے پر باتیں بنانا *look* (*a word*) *up in the dictionary* (کوئی لفظ) لغات میں دیکھنا *it looks like* (something or doing something) لگتا ہے *look for trouble*, invite it خواہ مخواہ کی مصیبت گلے ڈالنا۔ *look* (*one's*) *age*, seem as old as one is صحت سے عمر کا ٹھیک اندازہ ہونا ، اپنی عمر کا دکھائی دینا *will not look at*, rejects دیکھا تک نہیں ، انکار کر دیا *look black*, frown تیوری چڑھانا *look blue*, (*a*) (of person) be depressed افسردہ ہونا (*b*) (of prospects) be depressing مایوس کن ہونا *look before you leap*, avoid rash action پہلے بات کو تولو پھر منہ سے بولو *look daggers*, show hatred in the eyes آنکھوں سے آگ برسنا *looke here* سنو تو *look* (*someone*) *in the face*, face (him) at close quarters کو قریب سے دیکھنا *n.* act of looking دیکھنا sight نظر ، نگاہ expression of the eyes آنکھیں *angry looks* غصّے سے بھری ہوئی آنکھیں (*pl.*) person's appearance شکل و صورت *good looks*, beauty خوب صورتی ، حسن ، جمال **looker-on** *n.* (pl. *lookers-on*), spectator, onlooker تماشائی

looking-glass *n.* mirror made of glass آئینہ

loom *n.* machine for weaving cloth کپڑا بننے کی مشین *handloom*, hand-operated loom کرگھا *power-loom* power operated loom مشینی کرگھا ۔ برقی کرگھا *v. i.* appear indistinctly and in a threatening way دھندلا سا اور بڑا دکھائی دینا *loom large*, (of danger, etc.) appear threateningly منڈلانا ، چھانا

loon *n.* a large kind of diving bird ایک قسم کی مُرغابی، لون مُرغابی scamp اُلّو **loony** (loo-ni) *n.* (slang) lunatic پاگل، سودائی، دیوانہ

loop *n.* shape produced by curve crossing itself پھندا cord, etc., in this shape as a knot *v. t.* & *i.* form into a loop or loops پھندہ بنانا، حلقہ ڈالنا **loop-hole** *n.* narrow opening in a wall روزن، سُوراخ way of escape from control بھاگنے کی راہ، بچنے کی صُورت، مَفر، خامی، سُقم، *find a loop-hole in,* find such a way of escape by a loose wording of (the law, etc.) (قانون وغیرہ) کے الفاظ میں سُقم کے باعث بچنے کی راہ

a loon (sense 1)

loose (loos) *adj.* free آزاد، رہا not tied up or contained in anything (like small change loose in one's pocket) کھُلا *loose end of a rope,* رسّے کا وہ سرا جو ہاتھ میں نہ ہو not compact (soil) غیر پیوستہ (garment, collar, etc.) not close-fitting ڈھیلا، کھُلا (screw, tooth, etc.) not well-fixed ڈھیلا careless or uncontrolled (talk, argument, thought, etc.) غیر ذمّہ دارانہ immoral (conduct, life, woman, etc.) اَخلاق سوز، آبرو باختہ (find oneself) *at a loose end,* (find oneself) with nothing to do بیکار ہاتھ پر ہاتھ دھرے بیٹھنا۔ مکھیاں مارنا رہا ہونا *v. t.* make loose رہا کرنا، گرفت ڈھیلی کرنا **loosely** (*loos*-li) *adv.* (esp.) not exactly یونہی اندازے، بے پروائی سے *loosely speaking* یونہی اندازے سے بات کرتے ہوئے **loosen** (*loos*-ĕn) *v. t.* become or set loose کھُلنا یا کھولنا، ڈھیلا ہونا یا کرنا۔ *loosen the bowels* قبض دُور کرنا

loot (loot) *v. t.* & *i.* plunder لُوٹنا (esp.) pillage during war, etc. لُوٹ مار *n.* property so taken لوٹ کا مال، مالِ غنیمت

lop *v. i.* (-pp-) cut (branches, etc., off from a tree, etc. (شاخیں) کاٹنا، (درخت کی) چھانٹنا cut (*off* or *away*, head, etc.) with one blow ایک ہی ضرب سے کاٹ ڈالنا، اُڑا دینا، قلم کرنا hang down loosely لٹکنا، ڈھیلا لٹکنا **lop-eared** *adj.* having long and hanging ears کانوں والا **lop-sided** *adj.* with one side lower than the other جس کی ایک طرف دوسری سے نیچی ہو (of argument, etc.) unbalanced, one-sided (argument, etc.) یک طرفہ، جانبدارانہ

lope (lohp) *v. i.* move with long, easy strides لمبے لمبے ڈگ بھرنا

loquacious (lo-*kay*-shus) *adj.* talkative باتُونی **loquacity** (lo-*kas*-i-ti) *n.* talkativeness باتُونی پن

loquat (*lohk*-wat) *n.* well known fruit tree yielding yellow fruit whose pulp covering big stones is much relished for its sweet but somewhat sharp taste لوکاٹ

a bunch of loquats

lord (lo*d, or loh*d) *n.* supreme ruler حاکمِ اعلیٰ، فرمانروا (*the Lord*) God خداتعالیٰ *Lord knows* خُدا ہی جانے (according to Christians and hence usually in English) Christ حضرت عیسیٰؑ *Lord's Supper*, Eucharist; Christ's last supper with his disciples (عیسائیوں کی) عشائے ربّانی *Lord's table,* communion table in a church گرجے کی قربان گاہ (title of) British peer (برطانوی) نواب *the House of Lords*, the Upper Chamber of the British Parliament دارالاُمرا *lords spiritual*, bishops in the House of Lord رُوحانی نَوّاب *lords temporal*, other members of the House of Lords دُنیَوی نَوّاب any other person with a special (usu. official) position of authority نَوّاب صاحب، جاہ و حَشَم، صاحبِ اِقتدار *the Lord Mayor*, Mayor of certain big cities in Britain (like London) رَئیسِ بَلدِیّہ *v.i.* (*lord it over*), rule over like a lord پُر حُکم چلانا **lordly** (-li) *adj.* like a lord or suitable for him نوّابانہ، باوقار، تحکمانہ **lordship** *n.* lord's personality, or ownership *of* or rule *over* his domain نوّابی شان (یا) جاگیر یا حکومت، نوّابی *His* (or *Your*) *Lordship*, (form of address to or about a lord) حُضُور والا، سرکار

lore (loh*) *n.* learning عِلم body of a people's traditions پُرانے قِصّے، داستانیں، روایات *folklore* (see under *folk*) لوک کہانیاں body of facts about a particular subject معلومات **birdlore** *n.* پرندوں کے متعلق معلومات

lorry (lo-ri) *n.* long and sideless or very low-sided railway wagon or motor vehicle for carrying heavy goods (in case of motor-vehicles called a *truck* in this country and the U.S.) (ریل کا) چھکڑا، (موٹر کا) ٹرک یا چھکڑا **Note:** It is wrong to call an **omnibus**, however small, a **lorry** as in the custom in this country.

lose (looz) *v.t.* & *i.* (*lose, lost, lost*) fail to keep; cease to possess; part with unknowingly گنوانا، کھونا، کھو دینا، گم کرنا، گم کر دینا *lose (one's) way, lose (oneself), be lost, get lost somewhere in the way,* fail to find the right road, etc. راستہ بھُول جانا، راہ گم کر دینا *lose track of* (*someone* or *something*), not to know what has happened to (him or it) کے متعلّق پھر کچھ معلوم نہ ہونا be late for (train, post, etc.) کے لیے لیٹ ہونا، (پر) دیر سے پہنچنا (کا) وقت نکل جانا fail to hear, see, etc. (something, some word, the end of sentence, etc.) سُن (یا دیکھ) نہ سکنا be deprived of (client, patient, customer, etc.) کھونا، سے محروم ہونا get rid of (illness, etc.) سے آرام آنا، سے صحت پانا be defeated in (game, battle, etc.) ہارنا *lose* (*game, battle, etc.,* (مقابلے، لڑائی وغیرہ میں کسی) سے ہارنا

(*Phrases*:) *lose interest*, (*a*) be no longer interesting بے لطف ہو جانا (*b*) evince no more interest مزید دلچسپی نہ لینا *lose ground*, retreat پسپا ہونا *lose* (*one's*) *temper*, get angry طیش میں آنا، تیہے میں آنا *lose* (*one's*) *reason*, become insane پاگل ہو جانا، ہوش و حواس کھو بیٹھنا *lose* (*one's*) *head*, become too excited بڑے جوش میں آنا *lose face*, be made to look small کی بے عزتی ہونا (کی) تحقیر ہونا، منہ دکھانے کے قابل نہ رہنا *lose time*, (of watch, etc.) be a bit too slow (opp. of *gain time*) سلو چلنا، آہستہ چلنا، پیچھے رہ جانا *My watch loses two minutes a day* میری گھڑی روزانہ دو منٹ پیچھے رہ جاتی ہے *lose no time* (*in doing something*), (do it) at once دیر بالکل نہ کرنا، کوئی کام فوراً کرنا، یا بلا تاخیر کرنا *be lost to all sense of shame* (*etc.*), be no longer sensible to it شرم لحاظ (وغیرہ) جاتی رہنا (یا اٹھ جانا) کچھ شرم لحاظ (وغیرہ) باقی نہ ہونا (یا نہ رہنا) *be lost in wonder* (*etc.*) be filled with it حیرت سے گم سم رہ جانا **loser** (*looz*-ē*) *n*. one who loses ہارنے والا، نقصان اٹھانے والا، گھاٹے میں رہنے والا **loss** (los) *n*. (opp. of *profit*) نقصان، گھاٹا، خسارہ defeat ; losing (*of* a battle) میں شکست losing failure in keeping (*of* health) (صحت کی) خرابی کھونا casualties in battle (esp. as loss of life) جانی نقصان، مقتول waste ضائع جانا *suffer heavy loss* (کاروبار میں) سخت نقصان اٹھانا *suffer heavy losses* (کی لڑائی میں) بہت سے آدمی مارے جانا، (یا) کھیت رہنا، (کی لڑائی میں) بہت اتلافِ جان ہونا *be at a loss for words* (*to say something*), not to find appropriate words for (کے لیے) موزوں الفاظ نہ ملنا

lost *adj*. missing or missed کھویا ہوا، گم گشتہ wasted (effort, etc.) ضائع، لاحاصل destroyed (money, ship) برباد شدہ *lost in*, (*a*) no longer visible نظروں سے اوجھل (*b*) preoccupied with thought, etc.) میں گم، غرق یا محو

lot *n*. (one's) fortune قسمت، تقدیر، نصیبہ *hard lot* بری قسمت the means of selecting by chance قرعہ اندازی *by lot* قرعہ اندازی کے ذریعے (یا سے) one of the set objects arbitrarily used for this purpose قرعہ، پرچی *draw lots, cast lots* قرعہ اندازی کرنا number of objects offered together for auction or sale as one item ڈھیری portion (of land, etc.) قطعہ، ٹکڑا large number or amount بہت بڑی تعداد (یا) مقدار *a lot (of), lots (of)* بہت *the lot, the whole lot*, all سب، تمام *a bad lot*, a vicious person برا شخص *adv*. (*a lot*), much بہت، کہیں *a lot better* بہت بہتر، کہیں بہتر

loth *adj*. (same as **loath**, which see)

lotion (*loh*-shěn) *n*. medicinal liquid for washing a wound, etc.) زخم دھونے کی دوا، لوشن، آبِ زخم شو

lottery (*lot*-è-ri) *n*. system of gambling in which numbered tickets already sold are drawn by lots and their successful holders are given money prizes out of all proportion to the price they paid for them لاٹری

lotus *n*. kind of waterlily کنول (in legend) seed-pod of lotus or some other fruit supposed to cause forgetfulness of care غم بھلانے والا پھل، لوٹس کھنبی **lotus-eater** *n*. one who eats lotus ; opiate جو غم کو بھلانے والا پھل کھا چکا ہو، افیمچی

a lotns flower with its seed-pod

loud *adj*. making a great sound بلند، اونچا، زور کا noisy غل مچانے والا، پرشور، آسمان سر پر اٹھانے والا (of colour) forcing itself on the attention بھڑکیلا

loud-speaker *n*. apparatus (also forming a part of a radio receiving set) that changes electric waves into sound waves loud enough to be heard easily لاؤڈ سپیکر، آلۂ جہیر الصوت، آواز رساں **loudly** (*loud*-li) *adv*. in a loud voice اونچی آواز سے

louis-d'or (loo-i-doh*) *n*. former French gold coin پرانی فرانسیسی اشرفی

lounge (lounj) *v.i*. sit or stand about (leaning against something) in a lazy manner آرام سے ٹیک لگا کر کھڑے ہونا یا بیٹھنا move (*about*) lazily ٹہلنا، مٹرگشت کرنا *n*. comfortable sitting-room in a house or hotel نشست گاہ *lounge-suit*, man's suit of jacket, waistcoat, and trousers for day wear (as distinct from the more *formal dress*) (مردوں کا) عام سوٹ *lounge lizard*, idle effeminate youth preferring to be a male dancing partner rather than follow some manly pursuit زنانہ آدمی sofa or easy chair آرام (یا) کرسی (یا) صوفہ act of lounging مٹرگشت place for lounging سیر گاہ

lour, lower (lou*) *v.i*. frown or scowl (*at*) تیوری چڑھانا، ماتھے پر بل ڈالنا، (کو) کڑے تیوروں سے دیکھنا (یا) گھورنا (of clouds) look dark and threatening (گھٹا کا) کالی اور مہیب نظر آنا، طوفانی انداز سے امڈ آنا **louring, lowering** (*lou*-ring) *adj* (of sky, clouds, etc.) dark and threatening سیاہ اور ہیبت ناک (of face) scowling کڑے تیوروں والا، خشمگیں تیوروں والا

louse (lous) *n*. (pl. *lice*) flat, wingless insect infesting the hair or skin of dirty human beings and animals جوں **lousy** (*lou*-zi) *adj*. infested with lice جوؤں سے بھرا ہوا (colloq.) bad, worthless, unpleasant برا، ناگوار

lout (lout) *n*. clumsy, ill-mannered man گنوار، ان گھڑ clown بھانڈ **loutish** *adj*. awkward (manners, etc.) گنواروں کا سا، بے سلیقہ

love (luv) *n*. deep affection محبت *send love to, give love to*, send or give one's regards to پیار کہلا بھیجنا، دعا کہلا بھیجنا passionate devotion عشق، محبت، پیار *guilty love* ناپاک محبت *married love*, love between husband and wife میاں بیوی کی محبت *free love*, sex urge free from moral restraint or even lasting love آزادمحبّت ، آوارگی sweetheart محبُوب، مَعشُوقہ *ladylove* beloved lady محبُوبہ، مَعشُوقہ *come, my love* آؤجانی strong liking (*for* art, etc.) شوق، محبّت (in certain games like tennis, etc.) no score صفر، برکت *love all* صفر صفر، برکت ہی برکت *fall in love (with)* (سے) محبّت ہوجانا *(be) in love (with)* (سے) عشق ہونا *love marriage*, marriage which is the result of love عشقیہ شادی *make love to*, show that one is in love with (سے) مُعاشقہ کرنا *for the love of*, for the sake of کی خاطر *there is no love lost between them*, they hate each other اُنہیں ایک دوسرے سے سخت نفرت ہے *v.t.* & *i.* have deep affection for (سے) محبّت کرنا، پیار کرنا be passionately devoted to سے عشق ہونا یا کرنا delight in (art, comfort, etc.) پسند کرنا، کو مرغوب کرنا *labour of love*, (*a*) work done for the mere love of it without any hope of profit وہ کام جو محض شوق سے کیا جائے اور جس سے فائدے کی توقع نہ ہو (*b*) work which one loves to do مرغوب کام، شوق کا کام **lovable** (*luv*-a-b.l) *adj.* deserving love محبّت کے قابل having qualities that cause love بڑی خوبیوں والا **loveless** (*luv*-les) *adj.* not having or showing love محبّت سے خالی *loveless marriage*, (opp. of a love marriage) بغیر محبّت کے شادی **lover** (*luv*-ĕ*) *n.* one who is fond (*of* something) کا شائق *a lover of good food* خوش خور man who is in love عاشق، شیدائی (*pl.*) a man and a woman who are in love with each other عاشق و معشوق، عاشق، شیدائی **loving** (*luv*-ing) *adj.* feeling or showing love محبّت کرنے والا **lovingly** *adv.* with love پیار سے **love-sick, love-lorn** *n.* chagrined بیمارِ محبّت، مریضِ عشق **love-affair** *n.* love مُعاشقہ *love-affair has been going on between them for a long time now* وہ تو دیر سے معاشقہ لڑا رہے ہیں **loveletter** *n.* letter to sweetheart عشقیہ خط **love-child** *n.* illegitimate one ناجائز اولاد، حرامی **love-match** *n.* love marriage عشقیہ شادی **lovely** (*luv*-li) *adj.* beautiful اچھا، خوبصورت، حسین، حسین وجمیل delightful خوشگوار، پیارا attractive دِلکش، دِلفریب **loveliness** *n.* be lovely دلکشی، حُسن وجمال

low (*low*) *n.* soft call of a cow, etc. (گائے بیل کا) ڈکرانا *v.t.* moo (گائے بیل کا) ڈکرانا *adj.* not high or tall نیچا، چھوٹا، پست (of land) at a level not as high as that of the surrounding area نشیبی not highly developed (forms of life, etc.) کم ترقی یافتہ feeble (voice) آہستہ، دھیمی weak کمزور *in a low state of health* کمزور *feeling low*, sad بُجھا، بُجھا سا، غمگین، دِلگیر vulgar (manner, taste, company, etc.) پست، گھٹیا (of the sun, near the horizon نیچا (of price) less than usual کم، تھوڑا humble (rank, status, etc.) اَدنیٰ ... (less) leaving neck and part of shoulders bare جس سے گردن اور شانے عُریاں رہیں (of speed) slow آہستہ (of opinion) unfavourable بُری *have an unfavourable opinion of* کے متعلق اچھی رائے نہ ہونا *low-born*, coming of a low family کم اَصل، بدذات، نیچ *low-bred*, not well-bred بدتمیز، ناشائستہ *low-life*, social life of lower classes نچلے طبقہ کا طرزِ معاشرت *low spirited*. *adj.* depressed اُداس، اَفسُردہ، پژمُردہ *Low Countries*, Holland and Belgium ہالینڈ اور بلجیم *lower classes*, *lower strata*, lower strata of society نچلے طبقے *low-lying*, (of land) lying low نشیبی *lowlands*, low mountainous range of Scotland سکاچستان کا چھوٹی پہاڑیوں والا علاقہ *low-tide*, time of extreme ebb جزر *low water*, low tide جزر *in low water*, out of funds خرچ سے تنگ *low water-mark*, (*a*) water-mark at low tide جزر کا نشان (*b*) lowest stage of retrogression پستی کی اِنتہا، پستی کا حدّ سے گزرنا *adv.* not high نیچے، کم، پست softly آہستہ *be laid low*, be forced to stay in bed through injury, illness, etc. صاحب فراش ہونا *lay (someone) low*, vanquish نیچا دکھانا، پچھاڑنا *be running low*, (of supplies, etc.) be getting near the end قریب الاختتام ہونا، ختم ہونے والا ہونا *fly low* نیچی پرواز کرنا *bow low* عاجزی سے جُھکنا *I never fell so low as that*, never degraded myself so much میں کبھی اِتنا جُھکا نہیں *low down*, far from the top بہت نیچے *lie low*, (*a*) be dead مرجانا یا مارا جانا (*b*) be prostrate سربسجود ہونا (*c*) be abased ذلیل ہونا، سرنگوں ہونا، (کے آگے) جُھکنا *bring low*, reduce گھٹانا **lower** *adj.* (comparative degree) پست تر، فروتر، کمتر وغیرہ *lower down (still)* (ابھی) اور نیچے *lower forms of life*, all forms of living things except human beings حیوانات ونباتات *v.t.* let down (a flag, sail, etc.) نیچا کرنا (of voice, prices, prestige, etc.) make or become less high کم ہونا یا کرنا *v.i.* (pr. lou*) (same as *lour*, which see) **lowest** (*loh*-est) *adj.* (superlative degree) سب سے کم (وغیرہ) *at lowest*, to mention only the least amount کم سے کم **lowly** (*loh*-li) *adj.* humble, not proud مُنکسرُالمزاج، عاجز *the meek and lowly of heart* عجز ونیاز والے، مُنکسرُالمزاج *adv.* humbly عاجزی سے **lowliness** *n.* اِنکسار، عجز ونیاز **low-brow** (*loh*-broh) *n.* & *adj.* (person) with little taste for intellectual or artistic things بے ذوق، کم ذوق، بدذوق، پست مذاق والا

loyal (*loi*-ĕl) *adj.* faithful (to one's country, friends, superior, esp. to the sovereign) وفادار **loyally** *adv.* with loyalty وفاداری سے، وفادارانہ طور پر **loyalist** (*loi*-è-list) *n.* loyal subject, (esp. during a revolt) (بالخصوص ایّامِ بغاوت میں) فرمانروا کا وفادار one favouring the existing ruler (esp. when he is a crowned king) شاہ کا وفادار

lozenge (*loz*-enj) *n.* a diamond-shaped figure (معیّن دشکل) small sweet (esp. one containing medicine) (چوسنے والی) میٹھی ٹکیہ (دواوالی) چوسنے کی ٹکیہ ، لوز

a lozenge (sense 1)

lubber (*lub*-ĕ*) *n.* lout اُجڈ ، گنوار

lubricate (*loob*-ri-kayt) *v. t.* put oil or grease into (machine parts), oil (machine, etc.) (کی) تیل دینا ، (کی) تدہین کرنا **lubricant** (*loob*-ri-kant) oil or grease put into a machine to make it work smoothly مشین کا تیل **lubrication** (-*kay*-) *n.* مشین میں تیل ڈالنا ، تدہین **lubricator** (*loob*-ri-kay-tĕ*) *n.* vessel for lubricating مشین میں تیل ڈالنے کی کپّی **lubricity** (loob-*ris*-i-ti) *n.* skill in evasion طرح دے جانے کا فن lewdness عیّاشی ، فحاشی

lucid (*loo*-sid) *adj.* shining روشن ، تاباں ، درخشندہ (of style, explanation, etc.) clear to the mind صاف ، آسان ، سہل ، واضح free from madness غیر مجنونانہ (*in someone's*) *lucid intervals*, (in his) intervals of sanity occurring between his periods of insanity (اس پاگل کے) ہوشمندی کے لمحات میں

Lucifer (*loo*-si-fĕ*) *n.* Satan شیطان ، ابلیس the morning-star (literally the *light-bringer*) ستارۂ صبح (*lucifer*, also *lucifer-match*), match for lighting دیا سلائی ، ماچس

luck (luk) *n.* (good or bad) of fortune قسمت ، تقدیر ، نصیب ، نصیبہ good fortune خوش نصیبی ، خوش قسمتی ، خوش بختی chance اتفاق something that comes by chance اتفاق کی بات ، حسنِ اتفاق *be in luck*, have good luck خوش نصیب ہونا *be out of luck*, not to have good luck بدنصیب ہونا ، قسمت کا ہیٹا ہونا *for luck*, to bring good luck تقدیر اچھی کرنے کے لیے ، تقدیر بدلنے کے لیے *have the luck* (*to be*, etc.) خوش قسمتی سے ہونا *as luck would have it*, just by chance خوش قسمتی سے ، محض اتفاق کی بات ہے کہ *try* (*one's*) *luck* (*at*), قسمت آزمائی کرنا **luckless** *adj.* unfortunate بدقسمت ، بدنصیب ، نصیبہ آزما **lucky** (*luk*-i) *adj.* having good luck خوش قسمت ، خوش نصیب bringing good luck مُبارک resulting from good luck خوش قسمتی سے **luckily** (*luk*-i-li) *adv.* in a lucky manner خوش قسمتی سے ، حسنِ اتفاق سے ، خوش بختی سے

lucrative (*look*-ra-tiv) *adj.* profitable نفع بخش ، منفعت بخش **lucre** (*look*-ĕ*) wealth (in a bad, deprecatory sense) دولت ، مال وزر ، روپیہ monetary gain as a motive منفعت طلبی ، پیسے ہی کی بات کرنا

lucubrate (*loo*-kū-brayt) *v. i.* study till late in the night راتوں کو مطالعہ کرنا write out one's meditations اپنے خیالات قلم بند کرنا write in a laboured style بلیغ نما یا اردو سے بلکہ **lucubration** (-*ray*-) *n.* (rare) nocturnal study راتوں کو مُطالعہ کرنا (usu. *pl.*) dissertation or written meditations مقالہ ، قلم بند کیے ہوئے خیالات

luculent (*look*-ew-lent) *adj.* (lit.) lucid صاف ، واضح convincing دِل نشیں

ludicrous (loo-*dik*-rus) *adj.* ridiculous because meaningless مضحکہ خیز ، مہمل

lug (lug) *v.t* (-gg-) drag (along) with difficulty

luggage (*lug*-ij) *n.* baggage سامانِ سفر ، اسباب ، سامان

lugubrious (loo-*gewb*-ri-us) *adj.* dismal اداس ، غمگین mournful ماتمی

lukewarm (*look*-waw*m) *adj.* neither hot nor cold نیم گرم unenthusiastic (person, attitude, welcome, etc.) سرد مہر ، سرد مہرانہ

lull (lul) *v. t.* & *i.* make or become quiet چپ کرانا یا کرنا *lull a baby to sleep* بچے کو لوری دے کر یا تھپک تھپک کر سلانا (of wind, etc.) calm down, abate زور کم ہونا ، تھم جانا set at rest (someone's suspicions, etc.) رفع کرنا ، دور کرنا ، ختم کرنا *n.* temporary calm (before storm, etc.) خطرے سے پہلے کا سکوت ، وقفہ pause (in conversation, etc.) عارضی سکون

lullaby (*lul*-a-bi) *n.* song for lulling a baby to sleep لوری

lumbago (lum-*bay*-goh) *n.* rheumatism in the lower part of the back وجع المفاصل کا پیٹھ پر اثر ، دردِ کمر

lumber (*lum*-bĕ*) *n.* roughly cut timber ready for further use شہتیر ، تختے (وغیرہ) unwanted articles stored away کاٹھ کباڑ *lumber-room*, room for lumber کاٹھ کباڑ والی کوٹھڑی *v. t.* & *i.* (usu. of a cart, etc.) move in a slow and noisy way (*along*, *by*, *past*) گڑگڑاہٹ کے ساتھ چلنا fill (*up*) space inconveniently (کمرے وغیرہ کو) کاٹھ کباڑ سے لاد دینا ، بیکار چیزوں سے بھر دینا **lumberman**, (*U.S.*, **lumberjack**) *n.* woodcutter جنگل میں عمارتی لکڑی کاٹنے والا ، چوب تراش

luminary (*loom*-i-na-ri) *n.* natural light-giving body (*viz.*, the sun, moon, stars) سورج ، چاند یا ستارہ eminent figure (of a profession or field of study) (کی) مشہور شخصیت **luminous** (*loom*-i-nus) *adj.* giving out light روشن ، تاباں ، تابندہ (of remark, etc.) clear and full of meaning روشنی دینے والا ، بصیرت افروز **luminosity** (loo-mi-*nos*-i-ti) *n.* being luminous تنویر ، درخشانی ، تابندگی

lump (lump) *n.* (rough shaped) mass (*of* anything) ڈلا ، ڈلی lump آماس گولا ، گومڑا ، گلٹی *lumps of clay* مٹی کے ڈھیلے *break* (*soil, etc.*) *into lumps* (مٹی کے) ڈھیلے بنانا *in the lump*, the whole taken together سارا ایک ہی بار (*pay in*) *lump sum*, one payment for various separate purchases (ایک ہی بار ساری رقم (چکا دینا) **v.t.** یک مُشت رقم (دینا) یک مشت (ادائیگی کرنا) یک مُشت (ادا کرنا) **& i.** form into lumps گولا بننا یا بنانا group together in a mass ڈھیر کرنا ، انبار لگانا treat (things) as if they were the same, ایک ہی لاٹھی سے ہانکنا brook, endure برداشت کرنا *If you don't like it, you can lump it* ; you will have to take it in any case اِسے تو چار و ناچار برداشت کرنا ہی پڑے گا **lumpish** (*lum*-pish) *adj*. (of a person) clumsy بھدّا ، بھدّا سا stupid بیوقوف ، احمق ، گاؤدی **lumpy** (*lum*-pi) *adj*. covered with lumps گلٹیوں والا full of lumps ڈلی دار

lunar (*loo*-ně*) *adj*. of the moon چاند کا ، قمری *lunar year* قمری سال *lunar month* قمری مہینہ *lunar calendar* قمری تقویم

Luna (*loo*-na) *Cl. myth*. moon-goddess چاند کی دیوی

lunatic (*loon*-a-tik) *n*. madman پاگل ، دیوانہ ، جنونی ، لونا *lunatic asylum*, asylum for lunatics (now politely termed a mental hospital) پاگل خانہ ، مختل الحواس مجنون ، **lunacy** (*loon*-a-si) *n*. madness دیوانگی ، پاگل پن ، جنون

lunch (lunch) *n*. light mid-day meal دوپہر کا کھانا *v. t.* eat lunch (*with* a person, *at* a place) دوپہر کا کھانا کھانا **luncheon** (*lunch*-ěn) *n*. lunch دوپہر کا کھانا (esp.) mid-day meal as formal banquet ظہرانہ

lung (lung) *n*. either of the two breathing organs in the chest پھیپھڑا ، شُش **iron lungs** *n*. (see under **iron**)

lunge (lunj) *n*. sudden forward push with a sword in fencing (خاص کر شمشیر بازی میں تلوار کی) ہُول ، ہلّہ sudden forward movement of the body (when striking a blow esp. in boxing) (خاص کر مُکّے بازی میں گھونسا لگاتے وقت) اپنا سارا زور آگے کو کر کے بڑھنا ، جھپٹنا ، ہلّہ **v.i.** make a lunge (*out, at*) ہُول ، ہلّہ کرنا shoot out (sword, fist, etc.) in a lunge زور سے مارنا

lurch (lě*ch) *n*. sudden change of weight to one side لغزش ، لڑکھڑانا sudden roll جھوک *leave (someone) in the lurch*, desert (him) when he must need help مصیبت کے وقت (کسی کا) ساتھ چھوڑنا ، کسی کو مصیبت کے مُنہ میں ڈال کر چلے آنا *v. i.* move along with a lurch or lurches لڑکھڑاتے ہوئے چلنا roll جھوک کھانا

lure (*lew*-ě*) *n*. falconer's apparatus for recalling hawk دَلّیا something that attracts one thus پُر کشش شے attraction (*of* it *for* someone) کشش *v. t.* attract, tempt (*to do* something) (کرنے وغیرہ پر) پھسلانا یا ورغلانا *lured away from (one's) work* کسی کو ورغلا کر کام سے ہٹانا

lurid (*lew*-rid) *adj*. ghastly بھیانک shocking description (details, etc.) لرزہ خیز sensational سنسنی پھیلانے والی ، سنسنی خیز terribly glaring and fiery آگ کی سی وحشتناک رنگت والا - **luridly** *adv*. in a lurid manner وحشت ناک انداز سے

lurk (lě*k) *v. i.* be latent in (میں دبا ہوا (یا چھپا ہوا) ہونا ، میں مخفی ہونا move about stealthily دبے پاؤں چلنا lie in wait for گھات میں بیٹھنا ، گھات میں ہونا *n*. (in the phrase) *on the lurk*, spying چھپ کر دیکھنے والا - جاسوس **lurking-place** *n*. place for being in wait کمین گاہ ، کمینگاہ ، کمیں

luscious (*lew*-shus) *adj*. rich and sweet in taste بڑا میٹھا ، بڑا شیریں very fragrant بہت خوش گوار (of fine arts) over-rich in sound, imagery, etc. حد سے زیادہ تخیل والا

lush (lush) *adj*. luxuriant (vegetation) گھنا اور طراوت والا

lust (lust) *n*. any sensuous desire regarded as sinful خواہش نفس ، نفسانی خواہش insatiable desire (for power, gold, etc.) سخت خواہش ، تسکین ناپذیر خواہش passionate enjoyment (*of* battle, conquest, etc.) سے لطف اندوزی sex urge خواہش نفسانی ، شہوت ، نفسانیت *the lusts of the flesh*, bodily desires نفسانی خواہشات *v.i.* have lust (*after, for*) کی پُرزور خواہش ہونا **lustful** *adj*. lascivious بندۂ نفس ، شہوت پرست

lustre (*lus*-tě*) *n*. brightness (like that of pearls or a polished surface) چمک دمک glory شان و شکوہ **lustrous** *adj*. چمکدار ، تابندہ ، درخشاں

lusty (*lus*-ti) *adj*. hefty ; healthy and strong تندرست و توانا ، ہٹا کٹا - موٹا تازہ تیسار (جوان) **lustihood** *n*. being lusty موٹا تازہ (یا) ہٹا کٹا ہونا

lute (loot) *n*. stringed musical instrument of the Middle Ages (much like the modern guitar) لُوٹ

a lute

luxuriant (luk-*sew*-ri-ant) *adj*. (of vegetation) rich and plentiful in growth بافراط پیدا ہونے والا **luxuriance** (luk-*sew*-ri-ans) *n*. profuse growth بافراط پیدا ہونے والا **luxuriate** (luk-*sew*-ri-ayt) *v. i.* feel keen delight (*in* something) سے بہت محظوظ ہونا abandon oneself to enjoyment or ease داد عیش دینا

luxury (*luk*-shě-ri) *n*. state of life in which one possesses and makes use of all that pleases the senses عیش و عشرت *live in luxury* عیش و عشرت کی زندگی گزارنا something pleasing to have but not absolutely essential (as distinct from a *necessity*) پُر تکلّف چیز ، تکلفات **luxurious** (luk-*sew*-ri-us) *adj*. loving luxury عیش پسند ، دلدادۂ عیش things, places, etc., providing luxury پُرتکلّف

-ly (li) *suf.* (adverbs from adjectives) (کوئی ترجمہ نہیں) (as slow*ly* (آہستہ (سے)) (adjectives from nouns) انہ (as brother*ly* برادرانہ) (adjectives and adverbs from nouns) انہ (as dai*ly* (روزانہ)
lying *v.* (pr. p. of [1]**lie** & [2]**lie,** which see)
lymph (limf) *n.* (poet.) pure water صاف پانی آبِ زلال exudation from sore زخم کی ریزش
lynch (linch) *v. t.* (of U.S. citizens) put (someone, esp. an undesirable Negro) to death without a lawful trial امریکہ میں گوروں کا (حبشیوں کو) قانون اپنے ہاتھ میں لے کر مار ڈالنا، لنچ کرنا **Lynch Law** *n.* a seemingly nice name for this lawless vandalism لنچ لا **lynching** *n.* putting thus to death لنچ کرنا
lynx (links) *n.* a kind of keen-sighted wildcat سیاہ گوش، بَن بلاؤ **lynx-eyed** keen-sighted بڑی تیز نظروں والا
a lynx
lyre (*lī*-è*) *n.* ancient Greek harp-like musical instrument having vertically fixed strings in a U-shaped frame قدیم یونانی بربط، لائر
lyric (*li*-rik) *adj.* of singing غنائی (poetry) composed for singing (غنائی (شاعری *n.* (also *lyric poem*), a small poem, often in stanzas and strophes, expressing its composer's depth of emotions
a lyre
lyrical (*li*-ri-kĕl) *adj.* lyric غنائی charged with deep emotion شدتِ جذبات سے مملو، رنگِ تغزل والی couched in (usu. high-flown) language appropriate to the emotions its expresses اسلوبِ تغزل والی
lyrist (*lī*-è-rist) *n.* one who plays lyre بربط نواز

M

m, M (em) (pl. *m's* or *ms*) thirteenth letter of the English alphabet ; (it is equivalent to the Urdu (م ایم Roman numeral 1,000 ہزار ایک ہزار
ma (mah) *n.* (abbr. of **mamma,** which see)
ma'am (mahm, mam, mum, um) *n.* (abbr. of **madam,** which see)
mac *n.* (see under **mackintosh**)
macabre (ma-*kah*-bè*) *adj.* gruesome بھیانک suggesting death موت کا نقشہ آنکھوں کے سامنے لانے والا
danse macabre (*dahns*-ma-kah-bè*) *n.* (in the Middle Ages) dance of death رقصِ مرگ، موت ناچ، بھیم ناچ
macadam (ma-*kad*-am) *n.* road surface got by compacting pebbles or stone broken small کٹے ہوئے پکی سڑک، پختہ سڑک **macadamize** (-mīz-) *v.t.* کنکروں کی سڑک بنانا *macadamized road* پکی سڑک **macadamization** (-*zay*-) *n.* act of macadamizing سڑک کو کٹے ہوئے کنکر ڈال کر پکا کرنا
macaroni (mak-a-*roh*-ni) *n.* flour paste made in the form of hollow tubes, cooked for food آٹے کے سیو یا سیوئیاں
macaroon (mak-a-*roon*) *n.* biscuit of ground almonds باداموں کا بسکٹ
macaw (ma-*kaw*) *n.* a kind of parrot with gay plumage, long tail and harsh voice دُم دار طوطا خوش رنگ طوطا
mace (mays) *n.* rod carried as a sign of office or authority عصائے حکومت (old use) heavy war club with spherical spiked head گرز dried nutmeg husks used as a spice جوتری، جاوتری، پنیاسہ
macerate (*mas*-e-rayt) *v.t.* soften by soaking بھگو کر نرم کرنا reduce to thinness by fasting فاقے کر کے دبلا ہونا **maceration** (-*ray*-) *n.* بھگو کر نرم کرنا فاقے کر کے دبلا ہونا
Machiavellian (mak-i-a-*vel*-i-an) *adj.* cunning and unscrupulous in politics, (acting on the accepted but wrong interpretation of the advice of the Florentine statesman *Machiavelli,* 1469—1527, contained in his book, *The Prince*) (شاطرانہ، عیارانہ، (حکمتِ عملی crafty دو رُخی چال چلنے والا، عیار such a politician شاطر سیاست داں (of a plot) deep laid گہری چال
machinate (*mak*-i-nayt) *v.i.* plot سازش کرنا **machination** (-nay-) *n.* (usu. *pl.*) plotting ; intrigue خفیہ منصوبہ، سازش
machine (ma-*sheen*) *n.* any mechanical contrivance for lightening human labour کل، مشین *sewing-machine* سلائی کی مشین، مشین *machine tool,* tool worked by machine مشینی اوزار، کلدار اوزار person working hard with unfailing regularity مشین کی طرح کام کرنے والا، مشین one working mechanically and without intelligence مشین controlling organization of a political party سیاسی جماعت کا سربراہ ادارہ

machine-gun *n.* gun that fires continuously as long as the trigger is kept pressed مشین گن *v.t.* (-nn-) shoot at (someone, etc.) with machine-gun مشین گن سے گولیاں چلانا **machinery** (ma-*sheen*-è-ri) *n.* machines collectively مشینیں working parts of a machine کل پرزے organization (*of* government, the law, etc.) نظام **machinist** (ma-*shee*-nist) *n.* one who makes machines کل ساز ، مشین ساز (also *machine-man*) one who works it مشین مین

mack (mak) *n.* (see under **mackintosh**)

mackerel (*mak*-è-rel) *n.* small sea fish striped blue and silver ماکرل *mackerel-sky*, sky so striped with clouds نیلی اور رُوپہلی دھاریوں والے بادل

mackintosh (*mak*-in-tosh) *n.* (also colloquially *mac*, or *mack*), rain-proof coat made of cloth treated with rubber برساتی

macrocosm (*mak*-ro-kosm) *n.* universe (as distinguished from the *microcosm* or man شخص اصغر) کائنات ، عالم اکبر ، شخص اکبر

mad *adj.* lunatic پاگل ، سودائی ، دیوانہ *mad as a March hare, mad as a hatter*, quite mad بالکل پاگل (action) resulting from it دیوانگی کا ، مجنونانہ ، دیوانہ وار (colloq.) much distracted (*with* trouble, *at* person, etc.) جھنجھلایا ہوا *v.t.* (poet.) madden دیوانہ بنا دینا **madden** (*mad*-ěn) *v.t.* make mad پاگل کر دینا ، دیوانہ بنا دینا **madcap** *n.* reckless person acting on impulse بڑا جذباتی ، سر پھرا ، شوریدہ سر **madman** *n.* (fem. *madwoman*) lunatic پاگل ، سودائی ، دیوانہ **madly** *adv.* پاگل پن سے **madness** *n.* lunacy پاگل پن ، دیوانگی ، جنون ، سودا **madhouse** *n.* lunatic asylum پاگل خانہ

madam (in general use pr. *mad*-am ; but pr. with a *special* stress on the first syllable it is generally used in reference to a society girl of high status ; pr. by servants always, and others too not unoften, as mahm, mam, mum, um) *n.* (also written in the abbreviated form as **ma'am**), polite formal address to ladies except unmarried ones بیگم ، خانم ، خاتون ، بیگم صاحبہ ، میم صاحب

madame (ma-*dahm*) *n.* (pl. *mesdames*, pr. may-*dahm*) Mrs. (used before names of married women of places where English either is not spoken or does not enjoy such a dignified status as in our country) مادام **Madam Tussaud's** (ma-*dahm*-too-*sohz*) London wax-work-figure show مادام تسوز

madden *v.t.* (see under **mad**)

made (mayd) *v.* (pa. t. & pa. p. of **make**, which see)

Mademoiselle (mad-mu-*zel*) *n.* (pl. *mesdemoiselles*, pr. mayd-mwa-*zel*) Miss (as title prefixed to a non-English speaking, etc., unmarried woman) مادموزیل (as vocative for unmarried woman) محترمہ

Madonna (ma-*don*-a) *n.* the Virgin Mary حضرت مریم her picture or statue حضرت مریمؑ کی تصویر (یا) مجسمہ

madrigal (*mad*-ri-gèl) *n.* short love-song عشقیہ گیت ، گیت (in music) a form of vocal song گیت

maelstrom (*māl*-strom) *n.* violent whirlpool گرداب ، خطرناک بھنور destructive force (*of* war, or political or other events)

maenad (*meen*-ad) *n.* votaress of *Bacchus* گرداب بلا ، ورطۂ ہلاکت

Maeonides (mee-*on*-i-deez) *n.* (poet.) (a name of) Homer ہومر

maestro (mah-*ès*-troh) *n.* masterly composer or conductor of music اُستاذ ، اُستاد

Mae West (may-west) *n.* (slang) inflated life-saving jacket (so-called after a large-bosomed actress) مے وَیسٹ

mafficking (*maf*-ik-ing) *n.* noisy patriotic rejoicings حبّ الوطنی کا ہنگامہ خیز جشن

magazine (mag-a-*zeen*) *n.* store for arms and ammunition مخزن ، اسلحہ خانہ chamber in rifle or gun for holding cartridges, etc. بندوق کا مخزن (usu. monthly) periodical with stories, articles, poems, etc., by various writers رسالہ مجلّہ ، مخزن

maggot (*mag*-ot) *n.* worm-like grub (esp. of house fly as found in rotting flesh or food) (بعض کیڑوں کا) پھل رُوپ کیڑا **maggoty** (-ti) *adj.* full of maggots جس میں کیڑے پڑ گئے ہوں

Magi (*may*-j) *n. pl.* Zoroastrian priests of ancient Persia مجوسی ، مجوس (Bib.) the wise men from the East دانایانِ مشرق

magic (*maj*-ik) *n.* witchcraft جادو ، جادوگری ، فسوں گری *white magic*, its supposedly permissible form نُوری جادو *black magic*, also (*black art*), the form which is not religiously permissible سِفلی جادو ، کالا علم ، کالا جادو use of charms جادو art of obtaining mysterious results by stage tricks شعبدہ بازی mysterious quality سحر *adj.* (also *magical*) done (as) by magic جادو کا (سا) *magic lantern* apparatus for projecting still slides on a screen جادو کی لالٹین ، عکس انداز possessing magic سحر آفریں

magician (ma-*jish*-ěn) *n.* skilled in magic جادوگر ساحر ، فسوں گر

magistrate (*maj*-is-trayt) *n.* officer acting as judge for criminal cases in the lowest courts مجسٹریٹ ، حاکم فوج داری **magisterial** (-*tee*-ri-) *adj.* (powers, etc.) of a magistrate مجسٹریٹ کا authoritative (manner, etc.) تحکمانہ

magnanimous (mag-*nan*-i-mus) *adj.* large-hearted (person, heart, action, gesture, offer, etc.) فراخدل ، فراخدلانہ **magnanimity** (mag-na-*nim*-i-ti) *n.* large-heartedness فراخدلی

magnate (*mag*-nayt) *n.* leading man of business, industry بڑا تاجر ، بڑا تاجر یا بڑا کارخانہ دار *business magnate* بڑا کارخانے دار *industrial magnate* رئیس التجار ، ملک التجار

magnesium (-*nee*-zi-um) *n.* a silver-white metal which burns brightly میگنیشیم *magnesium light,* dazzling light of a burning magnesium wire میگنیشیم کی خیرہ کن روشنی **magnesia** *n.* (-*nee*-shia) white carbonate of magnesia used as a purgative میگنیشیا

magnet (*mag*-net) *n.* piece of iron able to attract iron مقناطیس *natural magnet,* lodestone سنگ مقناطیس ، قدرتی مقناطیس *horseshoe magnet* نعل نما مقناطیس *bar magnet* مقناطیسی سلاخ *magnetic field,* field of a magnet's action مقناطیسی خطہ *magnetic equator* مقناطیسی استوا *magnetic poles,* the two ends of a magnet مقناطیسی قطب **magnetic** (-*net*-) *adj.* of, or possessing the qualities of, a magnet مقناطیسی *magnetic needle,* (suspended) magnetized needle مقناطیسی سوئی *magnetic mine,* submarine exploding on being attracted by a ship مقناطیسی سرنگ very attractive (smile, personality, etc.) دلکش ، دلربا ، مقناطیسی کشش والا **magnetism** *n.* magnetic properties and phenomena مقناطیسی قوت branch of physics studying these مقناطیسیت irresistible attraction سخت کشش جذب و کشش **magnetize** (*mag*-ne-tiz) give properties of a magnet to مقناطیسی قوت دینا ، مقنانا attract like a magnet مقناطیسی قوت سے کھینچنا mesmerize (پر) جادو کر دینا

[1]**magneto** (mag-*nee*-toh) *n.* (pl. *magnetos*) igniting electric apparatus in a petrol engine میگنیٹو ، (موٹر کے انجن کا شعلہ زن)

[2]**magneto-** *pref.* magnetic مقناطیسی (as in magneto-electricity مقناطیسی برق ، برق مقناطیسی

magnificent (mag-*nif*-i-sent) *adj.* stately شاندار imposing (spectacle, etc.) پرشکوہ first class (performance, etc.) بہت عمدہ remarkable (audacity, liar, etc.) سخت **magnificence** *n.* شان و شوکت ، شان و شکوہ ، کر و فر ، رونق اور شان

magnify (*mag*-ni-fī) *v.t.* make (something) appear larger بڑا کرنا ، بڑا کلاں *magnifying glass,* convex lens for that purpose محدب شیشہ ، کلاں نما give praise to (God) خدا تعالیٰ کی بڑائی بیان کرنا ۔ تکبیر کہنا exaggerate مبالغہ کرنا ۔ بڑھا چڑھا کر بیان کرنا **magnification** (-*kay*-) *n.* act of magnifying بڑا کرنا ۔ بڑائی بیان کرنا

magniloquent (mag-*nil*-o-kwent) *adj.* pompous, (style, words, etc.) پرشوکت (الفاظ یا عبارت) (person) using high sounding words or pompous style شوکتِ الفاظ کا دلدادہ **magniloquence** (mag-*nil*-o-kwens) *n.* pomposity شوکتِ الفاظ (کا شوق)

magnitude (*mag*-ni-tewd) *n.* (largeness of size, extent, etc.) وسعت degree (of importance) اہمیت bulk حجم ، ضخامت ، جسامت

magnum bonum (*mag*-num *boh*-num) great good بڑی نیکی ، خیرِ کثیر *

magpie (*mag*-pi) *n.* chattering black-and-white bird of the crow family noted for thieving habits چتلا کوا ، میگ پائی chatterer بکواسی بکی ، یاوہ گو

mahogany (ma-*hog*-a-ni) *a.* hard dark brown wood much used for furniture مہاگنی tree from which it is obtained مہاگنی کا درخت ، مہاگنی

mahout (ma-*hout*) *n.* elephant-driver مہاوت

maid (mayd) *n.* (lit.) virgin دوشیزہ *Maid Marian,* (Brit. leg.) Robin Hood's companion میڈ میرئن (رابن ہڈ کی ساتھن) (old use), (now only *old maid*) spinster بن بیاہی عورت ، بڑھی کنواری *maid of honour,* unmarried woman attending a queen or princess بن بیاہی عورت جو ملکہ یا شہزادیوں کی مصاحب ہو ، مصاحبہ woman servant نوکرانی ، ملازمہ ، خادمہ

maiden (*may*-dĕn) *n.* (lit.) girl لڑکی young unmarried woman دوشیزہ ، ناکتخدا عورت ، کنواری لڑکی *adj.* pertaining to maidenhood کنوارپنے کا *maiden name,* woman's family name before marriage عورت کا شادی سے پہلے کا خاندانی نام first initiatory پہلا ، اولین *maiden speech,* someone's first speech made (*in* public or *in* Parliament) پہلی تقریر *maiden voyage,* ship's first voyage پہلا سفر

mail (mayl) *n.* body armour of metal rings or plates زرہ بکتر letters, parcels, etc., sent or delivered by post ڈاک (*someone's*) *mail* (کسی کے نام) کی ڈاک *the morning* (etc.) *mail,* the letters, etc., delivered in the morning (or other specified time) صبح (وغیرہ) کی ڈاک government system of carrying and delivering letters, etc. ڈاک ، برید *by air mail,* (also *by air*), one sent by aircraft ہوائی ڈاک سے *air mail* ہوائی ڈاک *surface mail,* mail sent by a sailing vessel بحری ڈاک *mail orders,* orders for goods to be delivered by post بذریعہ ڈاک منگوایا ہوا مال *mail-order business* تجارت بذریعہ ڈاک *mail-coach,* horse-drawn coach in olden times carrying mail ڈاک کی بگھی *mail train,* fast train

carrying mail and passengers ڈاک گاڑی میل ٹرین *v.t.* post ڈاک میں ڈالنا **mailed** (mayld) *adj.* armoured بکتر بند *the mailed fist*, armed force فوجی طاقت
maim (maym) *v.t.* disable زخمی کرنے جسم کا کوئی حصّہ ناکارہ کرنا ، ناکارہ کرنا
main (mayn) *adj.* principal, chief بڑا ، اصلی most important اہم ، سب سے اہم *n.* (poet.) (the) high sea کھلا سمندر (pl.) (*the mains*), (*a*) the principal pipes bringing water بڑی نالی . (*b*). principal wires transmitting electric current from the source of supply بڑے تار ، مین لائن *a mains set*, a radio receiving set not operated by a battery but connected to the mains (بیٹری والا نہیں بلکہ) بجلی والا ریڈیو *with might and main*, with all one's physical strength پوری قوّت سے *in the main*, for the most part زیادہ تر *that is the main thing* یہی تو اصلی بات ہے *by main force*, by actual (or sheer) force محض طاقت کے بل پر *have an eye on* (or *to*) *the main chance*, (slang) look after (one's) own interest اپنا فائدہ دیکھنا **mainland** *n.* country or continent, without its islands خشکی کا بڑا ٹکڑا ۔ مُسلسل خشکی ، برّاعظم **main line** *n.* chief rail track (as distinct from branch line) ریل کی شاہ راہ ، (ریل کی) بڑی یا اصلی لائن ، مین لائن **mainmast** (*mayn*-mast) *n.* principal mast بڑا مستول **mainsail** *n.* lowest sail of mainmast بڑا بادبان ، بڑا پال **mainspring** *n.* chief spring of a watch or clock بال کمانی کل کی کنجی driving force or motive اصل محرّک **mainstay** *n.* chief helper بڑا مددگار **mainyard** (*mayn*-yah*d) *n.* crosspiece supporting mainsail بڑے پال کا ڈنڈا ، آڑ ڈنڈا **mainly** *adv.* chiefly دراصل for the most part زیادہ تر
maintain (men-*tayn*) *v. t.* hold or keep (property, thing, etc.) as it already is اصلی حالت میں رکھنا برقرار رکھنا keep (machine, etc.) in working order چالو رکھنا keep up (friendly relations, etc.) برقرار رکھنا ، قائم رکھنا support (family, etc.) کا خرچ کا سربراہ ہونا keep (house, servant, etc.) چلانا hold (an opinion) رائے رکھنا assert (*that*), claim it as true (that) بڑے وثوق سے کہنا کہ ، کہنا کہ سچ یہ ہے ، کہنا کہ سچی بات تو یہ ہے کہ **maintenance** (*mayn*-te-nans) *n.* (esp.) what is needed to support life گزارہ ، خرچہ ، نان نفقہ *maintenance allowance* گزارہ الاؤنس
maisonette, maisonnette (may-zo-*net*) *n.* small house چھوٹا سا گھر ، ذرا سا گھر part of a house (not necessarily on the same floor) let separately مکان کا کرائے پر دیا ہوا حصّہ
maize (meiz) *n.* Indian corn مکّی ، مکئی
majesty (*maj*-es-ti) *n.* sovereign dignity or power شاہانہ جاہ و جلال stateliness (of sight, etc.) دبدبہ ، وقار شان ، رفعت manner inspiring respect *His, Her* (or *Your*) *Majesty*, form of address used to or about a sovereign اعلیحضرت ، جہاں پناہ ذی نعمت ، جلالۃ الملک **majestic** *adj.* having great dignity of person or appearance پُرجلال
major (*may*-jě*) *adj.* greater or more important of two (parts, etc.) بڑا ، زیادہ ، اہم the older of two brothers بڑا بھائی *Khan major*, elder one of the two Khan brothers خان برادران میں سے بڑا (opp. of *Khan minor* خان برادران میں سے چھوٹا) more important (events, personalities) اہم ، زیادہ مشہور *n.* person no longer a minor بالغ ، جوان ، سنِ بُلوغ کو پہنچا ہُوا (*Major*), (abb. *Maj.*) army officer above a captain but below a Lt.-Colonel میجر **Major-General** *n.* (abb. *Maj-Gen.*, or *Maj-General*) army officer next above a Brigadier and under a Lt.-General میجر جنرل **majority** (mo-*jo*-ri-ti) *n.* the greater number or part (*of*) (کی) اکثریت *the Muslim majority countries* مسلمانوں کی اکثریت کے ممالک *the majority*, (also in a multi-n tional country) community having the largest number of followers اکثریت ، اکثریتی فرقہ difference between the greater and the lesser number فرق *The motion was carried by a majority of 158 to 156 members,* قرارداد ایک سو چھپن کے مقابلے میں ایک سو اٹھاون کی اکثریت سے منظور ہوگئی legal age of reaching manhood or womanhood (before which he or she is only an *infant*, in the eyes of the law) سنِ بُلوغت کی قانونی عمر ، بُلوغت *reach one's majority* بالغ ہونا ، سنِ بُلوغت کو ، سنِ بُلوغ کو پہنچنا
make (mayk) *v. t.* & *i.* (*make*; *made, made*, pr. mayd) (of God) create تخلیق کرنا ، پیدا کرنا bring into existence (things, buildings, etc.) بنانا ، تیار کرنا cause (mistake, noise, hole somewhere, etc.) کرنا construct (of a material) سے بنانا ، کا بنانا amass or earn (money, a profit, one's fortune, etc.) روپیہ کمانا یا بنانا prepare (tea, etc.) تیار کرنا یا بنانا *make the bed* بستر کرنا *make one's will*, draw it up وصیت کرنا ، وصیت نامہ لکھنا *make fun* (or *game*, or *sport*) *of someone*, ridicule (him) کا مذاق اڑانا *make light of*, (something), dismiss it lightly کو حقیر جاننا کو کچھ سمجھنا ہی نہیں *make the most of* (*something*), use (it) to the greatest advantage سے پورا پورا فائدہ اٹھانا *make much* (*of*), (*a*) regard it as very important کو بڑی اہمیت دینا (*b*) make the best use of (this opportunity) سے اچھی طرح فائدہ اٹھانا *make up*, be reconciled (آپس میں) صُلح ہو جانا *make over to*, entrust to کے حوالے کرنا *make up* (*one's*) *mind* (*to*),

resolve (to) جی میں ٹھان لینا ، کا مصمّم ارادہ کر لینا make up (the deficiency, the loss, etc.) کمی (وغیرہ) پوری کر لینا make up to, curry favour with کے آگے پیچھے پھرنا ، کی خوشامد کرنا compel or persuade (someone) to (do something) جبراً (کرانا) ، پر مجبور کرنا make (someone) believe something کسی کو جھوٹ پر یقین دلانا cause (someone or something) to be (etc.) (something) make prosperous کو بنا دینا write (out cheque, etc.) لکھنا cover (journey, distance) طے کرنا reckon (total, etc.) کرنا ، کے پاس ہونا consider (time, etc., to be) خیال میں ہونا What do you make the time?, what time do you make it? وقت آپ کے خیال میں کیا ہوگا؟ (Phrases :) make for, (a) go towards ; کی طرف جانا (b) rush violently at پر بڑھ بولنا make off, go or run away after some wrong-doing بھاگ جانا فرار ہو جانا make out, (a) decipher (عجیب سی تحریر) پڑھ لینا (b) understand سمجھنا (c) distinguish faintly by sight دور سے دیکھ کر اندازہ لگانا (d) prove (one's case, etc.) ثابت کرنا make over (to), entrust to کے حوالے کرنا make up, (a) invent (a story) قصہ گھڑنا ، جھوٹی بات بنا لینا (b) supply (what is needed for completion) کمی پوری کرنا (c) get ready (parcel, medicine) تیار کرنا (d) settle (dispute) جھگڑا ختم کرنا ، صلح کر لینا (e) put cosmetics on (the face) بناؤ سنگار کرنا make believe, pretend جھوٹ موٹ کوئی کام کرنا n. way a thing is made بناوٹ ، ساخت of our own make, made by us ہمارا اپنا بنایا ہوا make-believe n. pretence فرضی بات ، جھوٹ موٹ make-shift n. something used until something better can be obtained عارضی بندوبست make-up n. composition بناوٹ cosmetics بناؤ سنگار کا سامان ، میک اپ putting on of cosmetics بناؤ سنگار ، میک اپ make-weight n. small quantity added to make the weight right پاسنگ trifling point making n. بنانا be the making of, cause the well-being of کو بنانے والا ہونا have (in oneself or one) the makings of, have the necessary qualities for becoming (a great man, thief, etc.) بننے کے آثار ہویدا ہونا **S** To **make** is the general term ; to **manufacture** on a commercial scale, to **create** out of nothing ; to **invent** something new ; to **discover** something existing unknown , to **produce**, bring forth ; and to **fashion** out of a material

mal- (mal), **male-** (mayl) *pref.* bad or badly بُرا (as *maltreat*, بُرا سلوک کرنا) ; not غیر ، نا as *malcontent* غیر مطمئن

maladjustment (mal-ad-*just*-ment) *n.* faulty adjustment of mutual relations or of one's relations to one's environment ناموافقت ، وغیرہ ہم آہنگی

maladministration (-*tray*-) *n.* bad (public) administration نظم ونسق کی خرابی ، ملکی بدانتظامی

maladroit (*mal*-a-droit, or mal-a-*droit*) *adj.* clumsy اناڑی ، بدسلیقہ ، پھوہڑ bungling (remark, etc.) بے محل ، مصلحت ناشناسی کا ، مصلحت ناشناسانہ **mal-adroitness** *n.* being maladroit حماقت ناشناسی

malady (*mal*-a-di) *n.* disease بیماری ، مرض

mala fide (ma-la-*fī*-de) *adj.* & *adv.* done in bad faith بدنیتی کا ، بدنیتی سے کیا ہوا

malaise (*mal*-ayz) *n.* feeling of illness or uneasiness (بیماری سے پہلے کی) بے چینی ، بیقراری

malamute (*mal*-a-mewt) *n.* Eskimo dog اسکیمو کا کتا ، مالموٹ

malapropism (*mal*-a-pro-pizm) *n.* misapplication of words without mispronunciation (as used by Mrs Malaprop in Sheridan's play, *The Rivals*) تجنیسی غلطی mistake owing to confusion between words مغلق الفاظ استعمال کرنے کے باعث ہونے والی غلطی

malaria (ma-*lay*-ri-a) *n.* fever spread by a certain kind of mosquito ملیریا ، موسمی بخار **malarial** *adj.* infested with malaria germs ملیریا والا of malaria ملیریا کا

malcontent (*mal*-kon-tent) *n.* person discontented and inclined to rebel غیر مطمئن ، (حکومت سے) بیزار آمادۂ بغاوت ، شورش پسند *the malcontents* غیر مطمئن یا شورش پسند عناصر

mal de mer (-may-ē*) *n.* sea-sickness جہاز کی متلی

[1]**male** (meil) *adj.* of the sex that does not give birth to offspring (as opposed to *female*) نر *male child* لڑکا *n.* male animal, etc. نر (جانور وغیرہ) man or male child مرد

[2]**male-** pref. (same as **mal-**, which see)

malediction (mal-e-*dik*-shĕn) *n.* curse بددعا ، کوسنا

maledictory *adj.* (of speech, etc.) full of malediction بددعاؤں والی

malefactor (mal-e-fak-tĕ) *n.* wrongdoer غلط کار ، ظالم ، موذی criminal مجرم **malefic** (ma-*lef*-ik) **maleficent** (ma-*lef*-i-sent) *adj.* of evil effect مجرمانہ خصلت ، ایذا رسانی

malevolent (mă-*lev*-o-lent) *adj.* wishing evil to others بدخواہ spiteful کینہ جو **malevolence** (-*lev*-) *n* being malevolent کسی کا برا چاہنا ، بدخواہی ، کینہ جوئی

malformation (mal-fo**may*-shĕn) *n* (of the body) the state of being badly formed or shaped خلقت (یا ساخت) میں خرابی ، نقص badly formed part نقص والا حصہ **malformed** *adj.* badly formed خلقت (یا ساخت) میں خرابی والا ، نقص والا

malice (*mal*-is) *n.* active ill-will عناد ، بغض hidden ill-will (*towards*) بدباطنی ، کینہ *with malice towards none* کسی سے کوئی بغض نہیں *bear* (*someone*) *no malice* کسی سے بغض نہیں نہ ہونا **malicious** (ma-*lish*-us) *adj.* showing malice بغض پرور ، کینہ جو . . feeling

malice بدباطن
malign (ma-*lin*) *v. t.* slander (someone usu. innocent) کو خواہ مخواہ بدنام کرنا ، بہتان باندھنا ، تہمتیں دھرنا *adj.* injurious (influence, thing, etc.) ضرر رساں ، مضرت رساں
malignant (ma-*lig*-nant) *adj.* (of persons or actions) filled with a desire to hurt کینہ پرور ، بُرا چاہنے والا (of diseases) very violent or harmful to life سخت نقصان دہ ، جان لیوا **malignancy** (ma-*lig*-nans-i), **malignity** (ma-*lig*-ni-ti) *n.* malignant disposition, deep rooted ill-will خباثت ، خبثِ باطن malignant properties نقصان رسانی
malinger (ma-*ling*-ē*) *v. t.* pretend to be ill in order to escape duty کام سے بچنے کے لئے جھوٹ موٹ بیمار بننا **malingerer** (ma-*ling*-è-rē*) *n.* who does so کام سے بچنے کے لیے بیماری کا بہانہ کرنے والا **malingering** *n.* بیمار بن جانا ، تمارض
malleable (*mal*-i-ab-èl) *adj.* (of metals) that can be hammered into new shapes کشش پذیر adaptable (person, character, etc.) ترتیب پذیر **malleability** (-*bil*-) *n.* (دھات کا) توڑ ق (انسان کی) ترتیب پذیری
mallet (*mal*-et) *n.* wooden-headed hammer لکڑی کا ہتھوڑا long wooden stick with a thick head موگرا ، موگری ، موسل
malnutrition (-*rish*-) *n.* state of health resulting from not getting enough good food غذا کی کمی ، بدغذائی ، ناقص تغذیہ
malodorous (ma-*lohd*-rus) *adj.* evil smelling بدبودار
malpractice (mal-*prak*-tis) *n.* wrongdoing جُرم neglect of duty کوتاہی ، بے پروائی illegal action غیر قانونی یا ناجائز حرکت ، خلاف قاعدگی بے ضابطگی
malt (mawlt) *n.* barley, etc., prepared for use in beer-making شیرہ *v. t.* make (grain) into malt شیرہ بنانا prepare with malt میں شیرہ ڈالنا
Malthusian (mal-*thew*-zhèn) *n.* & *adj.* (person) following the doctrine of Malthus (1766-1834) that control on population is necessary for maintaining adequate food supply مالتوسی ، مالتھسی **neo-Malthusian** *n.* & *adj.* (person) advocating or practising birth-control for this purpose ضبطِ تولید کا حامی
maltreat (mal-*treet*) *v. t.* treat roughly سختی کرنا ، بُرا برتاؤ کرنا ، بدسلوکی کرنا **maltreatment** *n.* rough treatment بُرا برتاؤ ، سختی ، بدسلوکی
mamelon (*mam*-e-lon) *n.* rounded eminence گول ابھار
mamma, mama (ma-*mah*) *n* (abb *ma*) (baby's word for) mother اماں ، امی
mammal (*mam*-ĕl) *n.* animal belonging to the class which feeds young with milk from the breast (including human beings) دودھ پلانے والا جانور **mammalian** (-*mal*-) حیوانِ لبون (حیوانات لبونہ) پستانداروں حیوان *adj.* of such animals حیوانات لبونہ کا
mammon (*mam*-un) *n.* (*Mammon*), an ancient god of wealth دولت کا بت ، دولت کا شیطان ، دولت کا دیوتا wealth regarded as an evil influence دولت کی لعنت
mammonist, mammonite *n.* one devoted to worldly wealth دولت کا پجاری
mammoth (*mam*-uth) *n.* huge type of elephant now extinct عظیم الجثہ ہاتھی کی ایک قسم جو اب ناپید ہو چکی ہے میمنت *adj.* immense (building, project, etc.) بہت بڑا ، فیل پیکر ، دیو ہیکل
mammy (mami) *n.* (baby's word for) mother اماں ، امی (derisive word for) mother مائی
man *n.* (pl. *men*) adult male human being آدمی mankind نسلِ انسانی ، نوعِ انسانی husband شوہر ، خاوند ، میاں *man and wife* میاں بیوی male servant ملازم ، نوکر *master and man* آقا اور خادم remarkable (*in a thousand, etc.*) ہزاروں (وغیرہ) میں ایک piece in chess or draughts مہرہ (in compounds like *man-o-war*) ship جہاز *be (one's) man*, accept his offer غلام ہو رہنا *man-in-the street*, common man (as thought to represent the interests of common man) عام آدمی *man for man*, compared individually آدمیوں کے مقابلے میں آدمی *man of the world*, one with wide experience of business and society جہاندیدہ آدمی *man of letters*, scholar and writer عالم ، ادیب ، انشا پرداز ، شاعر *the inner man* (a) soul روح (b) the inner feelings باطن نفس *officers and men* (in the armed forces) افسر اور جوان ، افسر اور سپاہی *man-eater*, cannibal or carnivorous animal feeding on mankind آدم خور *v. t.* supply (fort, etc.) with the men needed for its defence قلعہ میں کافی فوج رکھنا supply (ships) with crew جہاز میں ملاح رکھنا **manful** *adj.* brave, fearless بہادر ، شجاع ، نڈر ، بے خوف resolute باعزم **manfully** *adv.* bravely or resolutely بہادری سے ، عزم کے ساتھ **manhandle** *v. t.* move (goods, etc.) by hands alone without the help of a machine ہاتھ سے لانا یا لے جانا (colloq.) handle person roughly مارنا ، پیٹنا **manhole** *n.* aperture for a man to enter (an underground sewer, boiler, etc.) بدررو وغیرہ میں نیچے اترنے کا سوراخ **man in the moon** *n.* semblance of face in the moon چاند کی بڑھیا imaginary person فرضی شخص **manpower** *n.* number of men and women available for state service ریاست کی خدمات کے قابل افراد کی تعداد **man of straw** *n.* imaginary person set up to be

quoted or confuted خیالی حریف poor person نادار، مُفلس **manhood** *n.* the state of being a man بالغ ہونا، سِنِ بلُوغت کو پہنچنا، جوانی، بلُوغت *reach manhood* بالغ ہونا *manly qualities* دلیری، بہادری، شجاعت، مردانگی **mantrap** *n.* trap set to catch trespassers آدم گیر پھندا **mankind** (man-kind) *n.* human race نوعِ انسانی، نسل انسانی all men سب انسان **manlike** (man-lik) *adj.* (woman, ape, etc.) looking quite like a man آدمی کا سا **manly** *adj.* having the strong qualities expected of man بہادر، دلیر، شجاع، شریف **mannish** *adj.* (of a woman) lacking feminine qualities نسوانیت سے عاری manlike (of a thing) more suitable for a man than for a woman مردانہ

man-o-war, man-of-war *n.* (old use) warship جنگی جہاز **man-slaughter** *n.* unlawful (but not wilful) murder غلطی سے قتل کرنا، غلطی سے جان لینا **manikin** (*man*-i-kin) *n.* dwarf بونا، ٹھگنا، بالشتیا lay figure پُتلا

manacle (*man*-a-kel) *n.* (usu. *pl.*) handcuffs ہتھکڑیاں fetters بیڑیاں *v.t.* handcuff ہتھکڑی ڈالنا fetter بیڑیاں ڈالنا

manage (*man*-ej) *v.t.* & *i.* carry on (business, etc.) کا انتظام کرنا، چلانا control (personnel, etc.) نگرانی کرنا، کی دیکھ بھال کرنا، کو قابو میں رکھنا do, accomplish کرنا be able (*to do* or *in doing* something) کر سکنا **manageable** (*man*-ej-a-bel) *adj.* easily managed آسان، جو سنبھلا جا سکے، قابلِ انتظام easily controlled جو آسانی سے قابو میں آ سکے، فرمان پزیر **management** (man-) controlling or being controlled بندوبست، دیکھ بھال، انتظام (*the management*) منتظم، کارپرداز those in charge of a business, etc. **manager** *n.* man or woman controlling a business مینجر، کارپرداز **manageress** *n.* (esp.) woman managing hotel, etc. ہوٹل وغیرہ چلانے والی، سرائے والی، بھٹیاری، بھٹیارن

mandamus (man-*day*-mus) *n.* (writ of) command issued by a superior court to a lower one عدالتِ عالیہ کا حکم، رُوبکارِ عدالتِ عالیہ

mandarin (*mand*-a-rin) Chinese official چینی عامل Chinese language of the educated people پڑھے لکھوں کی چینی party leader who lags behind times دقیانوسی لیڈر

mandate (*mand*-ayt) *n.* official order سرکاری حکم authority to a person to act in the name of another اختیارات تفویض کرنے والا فرمان authority given by the former League of Nations after World War I to certain countries (called *mandatory powers*) for the governance of certain others (called the *mandated territories*) اِنتداب authority given by voters to their representatives ووٹروں کی طرف سے ان کے نمائندوں کو ہدایت **mandatory** (*mand*-a-ta-ri) *adj.* (powers exercising the mandate اِنتدابی طاقتیں **mandated** (*mand*-) *adj.* (territories) governed under a mandate (زیرِ انتداب (علاقے

mandolin (*mand*-o-lin) *n.* a stringed musical instrument مَندولین، چِکارا

a mandolin

mandrake (*man*-drayk) *n.* poisonous plant whose root, looking like a human figure, induces sleep when eaten مَردُم گیاہ

mandrill (*man*-dril) *n.* a large fierce and ugly baboon ایک خونخوار لنگور، منڈرل

mane (mayn) *n.* long hair on the neck (of horse, lion, etc.) ایال، یال

manful *adj.* (see under **man**)

manganese (*mang*-a-neez) *n.* a light-grey metal used in glass-making مینگنیز

mange (maynj) *n.* a skin disease in furred animals کھجلی، خارشت **mangy** (*manj*-i) *adj.* suffering from mange خارشتی squalid گندا، غلیظ mean کمینہ neglected نگاہِ غفلت کا شکار

manger (*maynj*-ĕ*) *n.* eating trough for animals in the stable ناند *dog in the manger*, one who prevents others from enjoying what is useless to him *a dog-in-the-manger policy* "نہ کھیلیں گے نہ کھیلنے دیں گے" کا اصول

mangle (*mang*-ĕl) *n.* machine with two rollers for pressing out water from washed clothes and smoothing them کپڑے نچوڑنے اور استری کرنے کی مشین *v.t.* press and smooth clothes by putting them through this machine کپڑے مشین میں نچوڑنا اور استری کرنا mutilate by hacking جسم کے ٹکڑے ٹکڑے کرنا spoil in making, etc. ستیاناس کر دینا

mango (*mang*-oh) *n.* (pl. *mangoes*) well known luscious fruit with a lovely yellow flesh آم the tree bearing it آم کا پیڑ

mangrove (man-grohv) *n.* tropical swamp tree which, banian-like, sends down new roots from its branches, its bark is used for tanning leather مینگروو، چمڑ رنگ

mangy *adj.* (see under **mange**)

manhood *n.* (see under **man**)

mania (*may*-ni-a) *n.* violent madness جُنون، دیوانگی craze (*for* something) حد درجہ جوش، جنون یا خبط **maniac** (*may*-ni-ac) *n.* raving or violent madman جنونی، گالیاں دینے والا، یا اینٹیں مارنے والا پاگل *adj.* raving (fury, etc.) ہذیانی کیفیت والا طیش، ہذیانی طیش

Manichee (man-i-*kee*) *n.* Iranian religious leader holding that Satan is co-eternal with God مانی

Manichaean (-*kee*-ĕn), **Manichean** (-*kee*-ĕn) *adj.* one holding this belief مانی کا پیرو، مانوی **Manichaeism** (-kee-) **Manicheism** (-kee) *n* this doctrine مانویت

manicure (*man*-i-kew-ĕ*) *n.* care of the hands and finger-nails ناخن تراش، ہاتھوں اور ناخنوں کی صفائی *v.t.* give manicure treatment to ناخن تراشنا

manifest (*man*-i-fest) *adj.* clear and obvious واضح، ظاہر، صاف، آشکار *v.t.* show plainly, make clear واضح کرنا give signs of کے آثار ظاہر کرنا bring (oneself or itself) to light آشکار ہونا make a list of ship's cargo for use of customs کروڑگیری والوں کے لیے جہاز کے مال کی فہرست بنانا *n.* cargo list

manifestation (-*lay*-) *n.* display (*of*) کا اظہار، (کا مظاہرہ) something shown clearly واضح بات، صاف اظہار

manifesto (man-i-*fes*-toh) *n* (pl. *manifestos*) public declaration of aims and objects (*of* a political party, ruler, etc.) منشور *issue a manifesto* منشور شائع کرنا communist manifesto منشورِ اشتراکیت

manifold (*man*-i-fohld) *adj.* of many kinds گوناگوں، طرح طرح many in number کئی، متعدد comprehensive (knowledge, wisdom, etc.) ہمہ گیر، وسیع *v.t.* multiply copies of (letters, etc.) by a copying apparatus کئی نقلیں تیار کرنا

manikin *n.* (see under **man**)

manila, manilla (ma-*nil*-a) *n.* also *manila hemp*), fibre used for making strong ropes, mats, etc. منیلا کی سَنی

manipulate (ma-*nip*-ew-layt) *v.t.* operate (apparatus, etc.) skilfully چابکدستی سے چلانا، چابکدستی سے کام کرنا control (someone or something) cleverly by the use of one's influence خوش اسلوبی سے نبٹانا *manipulate an election* انتخاب دانائی اور خوش اسلوبی سے کرانا intrigue for (the achievement of a purpose, etc.) ساز باز کرنا، گٹھ جوڑ کرنا، جوڑ توڑ کرنا **manipulation** (-*lay*-) *n.* act of manipulating خوش اسلوبی سے کام نبٹنا، ساز باز، کارستانی، چابکدستی سے استعمال **manipulator** (ma-*nip*-ew-lay-tĕ*) *n.* one who manipulates چابکدستی سے استعمال کرنے والا، ساز باز کرنے والا

manna (*man*-a) *n.* (Bib.) food provided by God for the Israelites مَنّ، مَن a kind of gum ایک قسم کی گوند، من spiritual food روحانی غذا

mannequin (*man*-e-kin), **mannekin** (*man*-e-kin) *n.* dressmaker's live model درزی کی دکان پر فیشن کے نمونے کپڑے پہن کر دکھانے کے لیے ملازمہ

manner (man-ĕ*) *n.* style طریقہ، انداز، اسلوب behaviour طور طریقہ، وضع قطع، چال ڈھال (*pl.*) habits and customs اخلاق و عادات (*pl.*) social behaviour تمیز، تہذیب، شائستگی *have no manners, know no manners,* be ill-behaved تمیز نہ ہونا sort طرح، قسم *all manner of,* every kind of ہر طرح کا *by no manner of means,* never at all کسی صورت میں بھی نہیں **well-mannered** *adj.* having good manners باتہذیب **ill-mannered** *adj.* having bad manners بدتمیز، بے تہذیب **mannerism** *n.* habitual peculiarity of behaviour عجیب عادت، عجیب وضع too frequently recurring trick of style in art and literature عجیب تکیۂ فن، مخصوص انداز **mannerly** *adj.* having good manners باتہذیب، تمیزدار، شائستہ

manoeuvre (ma-*noo*-vĕ*) *n.* (usu. *pl.*) planned movement (*of* military forces) فوجی چال، عسکری حرکت، مانورہ movement or plan made to deceive داؤں، چال manipulation نکالنا clever intrigue ساز باز *v.t.* & *i.* perform manoeuvres عسکری حرکت کرنا، چال چلنا، خوش اسلوبی سے کام نکالنا، ساز باز کرنا force (someone or something *into doing* something or *into* or *out of* a position) by manipulation (کسی کو کوئی کام کرنے پر) کسی تدبیر سے مجبور کرنا

manor (*man*-ĕ* *n.* (old use) unit of land under the feudal system جاگیر، علاقہ، تعلقہ landed estate of a lord called *lord of the manor*) partly let out to tenants کسی نواب کی مملوکہ اراضی *manor-house,* lord of the manor's residence نواب کی حویلی، حویلی **manorial** ma-*noh*-ri-ĕl) *adj.* of a manor نواب کی مملوکہ اراضی کا، جاگیر کا، جاگیر سے متعلق *manorial rights* جاگیری حقوق

mansion *man*-shun *n.* large house حویلی (*pl.*) block of flats on various floors of the same building فلیٹوں والی عمارت **mansion-house** *n.* lord's house on a manor نواب کی حویلی

mantel (*mant*-ĕl) *n.* structure enclosing fireplace انگیٹھی، انگیٹھی کا حاشیہ **mantelpiece** *n.* mantel انگیٹھی (کا حاشیہ) (also *mantel shelf*), shelf over it انگیٹھی (کے اوپر کی جگہ)، انگیٹھی کے اوپر کی الماری

mantle (*mant*-ĕl) *n.* loose sleeveless cloak چغہ، لبادہ cover (*of* grass, snow, etc.) (کی) چادر (also *gas-mantle*), lace-like cover over the flame of a gas lamp to make the light brilliant گیس کا مینٹل، شعلہ پوش جالی

manual (*man*-ew-ĕl) *adj.* of or done with the hands ہاتھ کا، دستی *manual work* handicraft دستکاری laborious work مشقت، محنت *manual labour,* manual work محنت مشقت *manual training* *manual labourers* محنت مشقت کرکے کمانے والے *n.* text-book (*of* a subject) درسی کتاب، نصاب کی کتاب help-book نوٹ، امدادی کتاب keyboard of an organ ارغنوں کے پردے

manufacture (ma-new-*fak*-chĕ*) *v.t.* produce (goods, etc.) on a large scale by machinery بنانا، تیار کرنا *n.* making of goods thus صنعت (*pl.*) manufactured goods مصنوعات **manufacturer** *n.* one who manufactures صنعت کار، کارخانہ دار

manumission (*man-ew-mish-ĕn*) *n.* giving of freedom to slave عتاق، غلام کو آزاد کرنا، بردہ آزاد کرنا **manumit** (*man-ew-mit*) *v.t.* free (slave) بردہ یا غلام آزاد کرنا
manure (*ma-new-ĕ**) *n.* material for making soil fertile کھاد *v.t.* put manure on (land) کھاد ڈالنا
manuscript (*man-ew-skript*) *n.* (abbr. *MS.* pl *MSS.*) book, etc., as first written out by hand or even as first typed out) مسوّدہ *be still in manuscript* ابھی مسوّدے کی صورت میں ہونا، غیر مطبوعہ ہونا
many (*man-i* many, *more, most*) *adj., pron.* & *n.* more than few کئی numerous بہت، متعدد *many things, many a thing* کئی چیزیں a large number بہت سے *a great many* بہت سے *be one too many for,* be cleverer than سے فریب نہ کھانے والا نہ ہونا *(be) one too many,* be unwanted درکار نہ ہونا *be too many for (someone),* outwit (him) کو جل دے جانا، کو چھل جانا **many-sided** *adj.* having many sides or aspects کثیر الاضلاع، متعدد پہلوؤں والا having many capabilities گوناگوں صلاحیتوں والا
map (*map*) *n.* flat drawing of (a part of) the earth's surface نقشہ *off the map,* (colloq.) obsolete and hence of no account فضول، بیکار، بے حقیقت، خارج از بحث *v.t.* make a map of کا نقشہ بنانا، تفصیلات تیار کرنا *(map out)* plan منصوبہ بنانا، تفصیلات تیار کرنا
maple (*mayp-ĕl*) *n.* a kind of tree from which sugar is made میپل کا درخت میپل its wood میپل کی لکڑی، میپل **maple-sugar** *n.* sugar made from one kind of maple میپل چینی **maple-leaf** *n.* leaf of maple میپل کا پتا this as Canadian emblem کینیڈا کا امتیازی نشان

maple leaves

mar (*mah**) *v.t.* (-rr-) spoil بگاڑنا، خراب، ستیاناس کرنا *make or mar* بنانا یا بگاڑنا *mar the beauty of* کے حسن کا ستیاناس کرنا
Marathon (*ma-ra-thon*) *adj.* like that of Marathon, a place 20 miles from Athens which was the scene of a famous Greek victory over the Persians in 490 B.C. and the news of which was taken to Athens by soldier running this distance non-stop مارتھون کا سا *Marathon race,* foot race of abnormal length (usu. 26 miles) مارتھونی دوڑ requiring the utmost endurance سخت قوت برداشت کا طالب
marauder (*ma-raw-dĕ**) *n.* one who makes raids in search of plunder مال غنیمت کے لیے حملہ کرنے والا *marauding expedition* لوٹ مار کے لیے جنگی مہم
marble (*mah*-bĕl*) *n.* limestone that takes a high polish and is used for architecture and sculpture سنگ مرمر، رخام (*pl.*) marble sculptures مرمریں مجسمے small (usu. glass) ball used in children's game (called *marbles*) (بچوں کے کھیلنے کی) گولی *play marbles* گولیاں کھیلنا symbol of callousness بیرحمی، سنگدلی، پتھر *heart of marble* پتھر کا دل *v.t.* stain (book edges, etc.) in patterns like the markings of variegated marble ابری بنانا، ابری لگانا *marbled edges* ابری شدہ یا ابری دار کنارے
marcel wave (*mah*-sel-wayv*) *n.* special-process artificial wave in hair مارسلی گھنگر **marcel** *v.t.* (-ll-) wave (hair) thus میں مارسلی گھنگر ڈالنا یا ڈلوانا
[1]**March** (*mar*ch*) *n.* third month of the Western calendar, associated with cold winds مارچ *March hare,* hare in breeding season مستی خرگوش *mad as a March hare* مستی پر آئے ہوئے خرگوش کی طرح دیوانہ، بالکل پاگل
[2]**march** (*mah*ch*) *n.* (usu. *pl.*) boundary سرحد (usu. *pl.*) debatable strip between two countries متنازعہ فیہ سرحد act of marching with regular paces فوجی چال، فوج کی چال *marching order,* dress and equipment for the march کوچ کی وردی (also *marching orders,*) order to troops to depart for war, etc. کوچ، روانگی distance marched by troops کوچ کی مسافت progress (*of* events, civilization, etc.) رفتار، ارتقا musical composition suitable for marching to کوچ کی دھن *v.t.* & *i.* walk like soldiers with regular paces and measured steps فوج کی چال چلنا، باقاعدہ قدم اٹھا کر چلنا cause (someone) to do this (کو) فوج کی چال چلانا *march (someone) off,* lead him away thus as a prisoner کسی کو قیدی بنا کر کہیں سے اچلاتے ہوئے لے جانا (of events, etc.) progress steadily (حالات کا) ٹھیک صورت پذیر
march past *n.* marching of troops in line past saluting base at a review مارچ پاسٹ *v.i.* march past the saluting base thus مارچ پاسٹ کرنا **dead march** *n.* slow march for funeral فوج کی ماتمی چال، آہستہ چال
marchioness *n. fem.* (see under **marquis**)
marchpane *n.* (same as **marzipan,** which see)
mare (*may-ĕ**) *n.* female horse گھوڑی **mare's nest** *n.* fancied discovery turning out to be false or worthless بے معنی یا غلط دریافت
margarine (*mah*ja-reen,* or *mah*-ga-reen*) *n.* cooking-medium prepared from animal or vegetable fat as substitute for butter, نقلی مکھن، مارگرین
marge (*mah*j*) *n.* (poet.) margin کنارہ
margin (*mah*-jin*) *n.* blank space round the printed or written matter on a page حاشیہ border (of a lake, etc.) کنارہ allowance (of time, money, etc.) above what is estimated as

necessary فالتو leave a margin (for) (کے لیے) کچھ فالتو رکھنا حاشیہ چھوڑنا **marginal** *adj.* of or in a margin حاشیے پر *marginal note* حاشیہ (ج : حواشی) **marigold** (*ma*-ri-gohld) *n.* a well-known plant with orange-yellow flowers گیندا، گُل صد برگ، صد برگ **marine** (ma-*reen*) *adj.* pertaining to the sea سمندری، بحری of ships جہازوں سے متعلق جہازوں کا *marine insurance* جہاز پر نقصان کا بیمہ *n.* soldier serving on a warship بحری فوج کا سپاہی a country's shipping fleet بیڑا، تمام جہاز (ملک کے تمام) *mercantile marine* تجارتی جہاز **mariner** (*ma*-ri-nĕ*) *n.* (official or lit. term for a) sailor ملاح، جہازران *ancient mariner*, old sailor بوڑھا ملاح **marionette** (ma-ri-o-*net*) *n.* puppet moved by strings کٹھ پتلی، پتلی *marionette show* پتلیوں کا تماشہ **marital** (*ma*-ri-tĕl) *adj.* of a husband شوہر سے متعلق pertaining to married life ازدواجی، متاہل زندگی کے متعلق *marital relations* ازدواجی تعلقات **maritime** (*ma*-ri-tım) *adj.* pertaining to the sea بحری *maritime law* بحری قانون (area, etc.) lying near the sea سمندر کے نزدیک کا، سمندر کے قریبی **mark** (mah*k) *n.* stain, dot, line, scratch, etc., spoiling the look of something داغ، دھبّہ وغیرہ sign by which anything is known نشانی، نشان، پہچان *trade mark*, brand ٹریڈ مارک، تجارتی نشان some distinctive mark on the body نشان *birth mark*, mark on the body right from the birth پیدائشی نشان natural indication (*of* quality, character, intelligence) (کے) آثار figure, design, line, etc. made as a sign or indication مہر *price-mark* (قیمت کی مہر) unit for measuring result (of examination, etc.) نمبر *pass marks*, the least marks needed for getting through an examination پاس مارکس، کامیابی کے لیے کم از کم نمبر (for a subject) *full marks* (for a subject) 43 (*etc.*) *marks out of 100 for a subject*) (مضمون میں) سو میں سے تینتالیس (وغیرہ) نمبر something aimed at مدعا، مقصد، مقصود *wide of the mark*, (*a*) beside the point غیر متعلق بات (*b*) incorrect غلط، غلط بات *up to the mark*, quite normal normal level عام سطح معیار کے مطابق یا اس سے اونچا، ٹھیک *below the mark*, not so good as the normal معیار ٹھیک نہیں، *make a mark on*, (of an illiterate person) make a thumb impression, etc., in lieu of his signature سے پشت (انگوٹھے وغیرہ کا) نشان لگانا *make (one's) mark (in a field, etc.)* میں نام پیدا کرنا *man of mark*, famous person مشہور آدمی، قابلِ ذکر شخص *v.t.* put or be a mark on or against نشان لگانا یا ہونا *mark (someone) absent* غیر حاضری کا نشان لگانا award marks on (examination scripts, etc.) (امتحان کی کاپیاں) جانچنا، (امتحان کے) پرچے دیکھنا

pay attention to دیکھنا *mark*! دیکھو! ایلو! *mark my words*, carefully note what I am saying for that will surely come true میری بات یاد رکھنا *mark (one's) man*, select opponent to be watched دشمن کو تاکنا، دشمن کو تاڑ لینا *mark time*, (*a*) raise the feet as when marching but without moving forward وہیں قدم ہلاؤ (*b*) be in a state of suspended activity; wait and do nothing توقف، انتظار رہنا *mark (something) off*, delimit, separate by a limit حد باندھنا، جدا کرنا، الگ کرنا یا الگ کرنا *mark (something) out*, make lines to show the limits of (*e.g.*, a tennis court) کی حد بندی کرنا *mark (someone) out for*, earmark (for promotion, etc.) (ترقی وغیرہ کے لیے) نظر میں رکھنا **marked** (mah*kd) *adj.* readily seen clear, (difference, etc.) واضح suspected (man, etc.) (شخص) مشتبہ **markedly** (*mah*k*-ed-li) *adv.* واضح طور پر **marking** *n.* different colours of feathers, etc. نشان، رنگ awarding of marks پرچے دیکھنا یا جانچنا **marksman** *n.* one skilled in shooting نشانہ باز **marksmanship** *n.* being a marksman نشانہ بازی **market** (*mah**-ket) public place where people meet to buy and sell goods منڈی *go to market* (or *to the market*) (*to buy or sell something*) (کسی چیز کی) خرید و فروخت کے لیے منڈی جانا *market-day*, day fixed by custom or law for holding a market وہ دن جب بازار لگے *market-price*, price prevailing there منڈی کا بھاؤ *market-town*, (*a*) town with a market in it منڈی (*b*) (esp.) a town in which there is a cattle-market مال منڈی *market-place* *n.* square in which market is held منڈی trade in a certain class of goods (کی) منڈی *the money market*, (*a*) stock exchange سٹاک ایکسچینج (*b*) its business حصّوں کی خرید فروخت state of trade as shown by prices بازار کے بھاؤ، منڈی کی حالت *lively ma.* گرم، بازاری *the rise or fall of the market* اچھی قیمتوں پر خوب بکری منڈی کا اُتار چڑھاؤ، بھاؤ بڑھنا یا گھٹنا buying and selling خرید و فروخت *come into* (or *be on*) *the market*, be offered for sale بکاؤ ہونا، (مال) کا منڈی میں آنا area, country, in which goods may be sold منڈی، کے لیے نئی *find new markets for* خرید و فروخت کا علاقہ منڈیاں تلاش کرنا *dump the market (with)*, stock some market (with either goods unwanted in the manufacturer's country or with a view to capturing it by ruining competitors) منڈی میں مال بھر دینا *v. t. & i.* take or send (one's goods) to market منڈی میں لانا buy or sell in a market منڈی میں خرید و فروخت، منڈی میں بھیجنا *go marketing, do (one's) marketing* خریدنے کے لیے منڈی جانا، بازار سے خریدتے پھرنا

marketable *adj*. that which can be sold جو بِک سکے ، جس کی بِکری ہو سکے ، قابلِ فروخت **market-garden** *n*. one where vegetables, etc., are grown for a market بیچنے کے لیے سبزی ترکاری کاشت کرنے والا باغ

marmalade (*mah**-ma-layd) *n*. orange jam نارنگی کا مُربّہ ، مارمَلیڈ similar preserve made of other fruits مارمَلیڈ

marocain (ma-ro-kayn) *n*. crepe-like dress fabric موروکین

maroon (ma-*roon*) *n*. & *adj*. brownish-crimson (colour) (بادامی قرمزی (رنگ)، ہلکا قرمزی (رنگ *v. t*. put (someone) ashore and leave him on uninhabited island as a punishment on board a ship سزا کے طور پر جہاز سے اُتار کر کسی کو غیر آباد جزیرے میں چھوڑ آنا ۔

marooned *adj*. isolated (troops, person, population) سزا یا مُصیبت کے باعِث باقیوں سے الگ ہو جانے والا ، (سزا کے طور پر) الگ چھوڑا ہُوا ، (مُصیبت کے باعِث) باقیوں سے بچھڑا ہُوا ، یکہ و تنہا رہ جانے (یا رکھا جانے) والا ۔

marquis, marquess (*mah**-kwis) *n*. British peer next in rank below a *duke* **marchioness** (*mah**-sho-ness) *n*. wife or widow of a marquis مارچُونِس ، نوّاب

marriage *n*., **marriageable** *adj*. (see, under **marry**)

marrow (*ma*-roh) *n*. soft fatty substance filling the cavities of bones گُودا ، مغز *marrowbone* گُودے کی نلی ، گُودے کی ہڈی the essence (*of*) لُبِّ لُباب ، جوہر *pith and marrow* (*of*) کا لُبِّ لُباب

marry (*ma*-ri) *v.t.* & *i*. take as husband or wife بیاہ کرنا ، شادی کرنا ، بیاہ یا شادی رچانا join (someone) or be joined (*to* someone) as husband and wife سے شادی ہونا یا کرنا **marriage** (*ma*-rij) *n*. union of man and woman as husband and wife شادی ، بیاہ ، اِزدِواج *give (one's daughter, etc.) in marriage (to)* (لڑکی کی) کسی سے شادی کرنا state of being married اِزدِواج ، مُتاہِل زندگی ، مُتاہِلانہ زِندگی wedding ceremony شادی کی تقریب ، شادی بیاہ **marriageable** *adj*. of a marriageable age, quite grown up, of an age fit for marriage شادی بیاہ کے قابِل

Mars (mah*z) *Cl. myth*. the Roman god of war (identified with the Greek *Ares*) ; he was the son of Jupiter and Juno مارِز ، مِرّیخ name of a planet مِرّیخ

Marseillaise (mah*-sè-*layz*) *n*. national anthem of French Republic مارسیلیز

marsh (mah*-sh) *n*. area of low-lying wet land دَلدَل **marshy** (mah*-shi) *adj*. دَلدَل والا ، دَلدَلی

marshal (*mah**-shĕl) officer of highest rank in the armed forces of a country سِپہ سالار *Field-Marshal*, such officer of the land forces سِپہ سالارِ اَفواج ، فیلڈ مارشل *Air Marshal*, such officer in the Air Force فضائی سِپہ سالار ، فضائیہ کا سِپہ سالار ، ایئر مارشل *Air Vice-Marshal*, (*a*) Air Force chief in small countries ایئر وائس مارشل (*b*) Air-Marshal's deputy نائب ایئر مارشل high official of a King's Court میرِ دربار chief steward میر ساماں ، خان ساماں ، میرِ انتظام *v. t*. (-ll-) arrange (troops) in order کو صف بستہ کرنا ، کی صف آرائی کرنا arrange (facts, one's facts, details, etc.) in a presentable manner کو ترتیب دینا lead (someone) with ceremony کو شان سے لے جانا **marshalling-yard** *n*. railway yard in which trains are assembled گاڑیوں کے ڈبے جوڑنے کا یارڈ

marsupial (mah*-*sew*-pi-ĕl) *n*. & *adj*. (animal) carrying its young one in a pouch against the belly بچے کو تھیلی میں رکھنے والا جانور ، تھیلی والا (جانور) ، کیسہ دار (حیوان)

mart (maht*) *n*. (lit.) market-place منڈی ، بازار centre of commerce تجارتی مرکز emporium ایسی دکان جہاں ہر چیز مل سکے ، ہر مال کی دُکان

martial (*mah**-shèl) *adj*. pertaining to warfare جنگی military فوجی *martial music* فوجی دُھنیں brave, warlike بہادروں کا سا ، جنگجویانہ ، نبرد آزما *n*. military law (as distinct from *civil* or *criminal law*) فوجی قانون military government and law suspending the operation of the civil administration مارشل لا ، فوجی حکومت *declare martial law* (in) (میں) مارشل لا لگانا

martin (*mah**-tin) *n*. name for any of the several species of swallow اَبابیل ، مارٹن

martinet (mah*-ti-*net*) *n*. strict disciplinarian نظم و ضبط کی سختی سے پابندی کرانے والا ، سخت گیر

martini (mah*-*tee*-nee) *n*. a kind of rifle ایک قسم کی رائفل ، مارتینی رائفل a kind of cocktail ایک قسم کی ملی جلی شراب ، مارٹینی

Martinmas (*mah**-tin-mas) *n*.

martyr (mah*-tĕ*) *n*. person put to death or caused to suffer owing (*to* a cause) شہید *be a martyr to* (*pain, etc.*), suffer much from it سے بڑا دُکھ پانا یا اُٹھانا *v. t*. put to death as a martyr شہید کرنا cause to undergo much suffering owing (*to* a cause) کی خاطر سخت تکلیفیں دینا **martyrdom** *n*. martyr's death شہادت his suffering شہادت پر منتج ہونے والی سختیاں ، مَصائب

marvel (mah*-vĕl) *n*. wonderful thing حیرت انگیز شے یا بات ، اُعجوبہ *the marvels of* (something) کے عجائب و غرائب one showing a remarkable quality (*of* patience, intelligence, etc.) (کا) اِعجاز ، (کا) مُعجزہ *be a marvel of* (*some quality*) میں بے انتہا ہونا ، حد درجہ رکھنا ، کا حیران کن حد تک مالک ہونا *v. i*. (-ll-) be much surprised (*at* something or *that*) (پر) بڑا متعجّب کرنا متحیّر ہونا (کہ) **marvellous** (*mah**v-e-lus) *adj.* wonderful حیرت انگیز، معجزنما strange but pleasing خوب، عجیب مزے کی بات

Marxian (mark-si-ĕn) *adj.* follower of the father of modern communism, Karl Marx (1818-1883) مارکسی (idea) based on his theory مارکسی

marzipan (*mah**-zi-pan), **marchpane** (*mah**ch-payn) *n.* sweet stuff of a thick paste of powdered almonds حلوائے بادام

mascot (*mas*-kot) *n.* (object, animal, etc.) supposed to bring good luck and hence the pet (*of* those thinking so) بھاگوان چیز یا جانور، مسکوٹ *This goat is the mascot of the regiment* پلٹن اِس بکرے کو بھاگوان سمجھ کر شوق سے پال رہی ہے

masculine (*mas*-kew-lin, *mahs*-kew-lin, or *mas*-kew-līn) *adj.* of male gender مذکّر of or like the male sex نر

mash *n.* grain, bran, etc., cooked in water for cattle and horses مال مویشی کے لیے اُبلے ہوئے چنے، چوکر any substance softened and crushed اُبال کر کچلی ہوئی چیز *v. t.* crush (something) into a mash after softening through boiling اُبال کر کچلنا *mashed potatoes* کچلے ہوئے اُبلے آلو

mask (mahsk) *n.* covering to hide the face نقاب (also *gas-mask*), covering for the head worn to protect from the bad effects of gas in mines or battle گیس ماسک، گیس نقاب، گیسی نقاب ـ false face worn by an actor, etc. (منہ پر لگانے کے لیے) مصنوعی چہرہ *v. t.* cover with a mask نقاب ڈالنا، نقاب سے ڈھانپنا disguise under a veneer مصنوعی چہرہ منہ پر لگانا *wear a mask, cover with a mask,* hide (one's true feelings, etc.) اپنے اصلی جذبات چھپائے رکھنا، دلی جذبات کو بے نقاب نہ ہونے دینا

man (1) wearing a gas-mask and woman (2) wearing mask for a ball

masochism (*maz*-o-kizm) *n.* (opp. of *sadism*), form of sexual perversion in which one derives pleasure from suffering or humiliation caused by a member of the opposite sex مشرقی عاشق

mason (*may*-sun) *n.* stone-worker پتھر کاٹنے والا worker who builds with stone or bricks معمار، راج (also *freemason*), member of the society of Freemasons فری میسن، فراماسن **masonic** (ma-*son*-ik) *adj.* of Freemasons فری میسنی، فراماسنی **masonry** (*may*-sun-ri) *n.* stone structure پتھر کی عمارت this branch of architecture پتھر کی عمارتیں بنانے کا فن

masque (mahsk) *n.* type of 16th and 17th century English verse-drama with music and pageantry, very popular at the Court درباری ناٹک، ماسک

masquerade (*mas*-kè-rayd) *n.* ball at which masks and other fancy dresses are worn for disguise بہروپی ناچ *v. i.* appear or be in disguise (*as*) بہروپ بھر کر آنا، بھیس بدلے ہوئے ہونا یا بدل کر آنا

mass (mas) *n.* large lump ڈلا large quantity or heap (*of*) (کا) ڈھیر large mumber (*of*) (کی) بہت بڑی تعداد *mass production,* manufacture of (some type of goods, etc.) in very large quantities بڑی تعداد میں تیار کرنا یا بننا *mass circulation,* large circulation (*of* a periodical, etc.) کثیر اشاعت

(*pl.*) (*the masses*) the common people taken as a whole عوام *the masses and the classes,* the common people and the upper classes of society خاص و عام، غریب امیر، غریب اور امیر، اَدنیٰ اور اعلیٰ طبقے، اُونچے اور نیچے طبقے *mass observation,* study of and report on the trend of public opinion رائے عامّہ کا جائزہ *a mass meeting,* a large meeting (esp. of people wanting to express their views) عوامی جلسہ (in Christianity) celebration of the Holy Communion عشائے ربّانی کی رسم، نماز یا دعا *high mass* عشائے ربّانی کی پرتکلّف رسم *low mass* عشائے ربّانی کی سادہ رسم *say* (or *hear* or *attend*) *mass* عشائے ربّانی کی دعا پڑھنا یا (میں شامل ہونا) *v. t. & i.* form or collect into a mass اکٹھا ہونا یا کرنا (esp. of troops) concentrate (on the borders of) (فوج کا دوسرے ملک کی سرحدوں پر) جمع کرنا یا ہونا **massive** (*mas*-iv) *adj.* large and solid بڑا اور ٹھوس huge (building, etc.) بہت بڑا imposing (features, etc.) چوڑا چکلا عظیم الشان **massiveness** *n.* being massive بہت بڑا ہونا، بڑا اور ٹھوس ہونا، چوڑا چکلا ہونا **massy** (*mas*-i) *adj.* (poet.) *adj.* solid and heavy بھاری اور ٹھوس

massacre (*mas*-a-kè*) *n.* slaughter of a large number of (esp. defenceless) people قتلِ عام *v. t.* make a massacre of کا قتلِ عام کرنا

massage (ma-*sahzh*) *n.* rubbing of the body to soothe pain, etc. (جسم کی) مالش، مشتمالی *v. t.* apply massage to (جسم کی) مالش کرنا **masseur** (ma-*sĕ**) *n.* (fem. *masseuse* pr. ma-*sĕ***z*) *n.* one who practises massage professionally جسم کی مالش کرنے والا (یا والی) مالشیا

massive, massy *adj.* (see under **mass**)

mast (mahst) *n.* upright support for a ship's sails مستول tall pole (for a flag) (پرچم کا) ڈنڈا pylon for radio transmission لاسلکی منارہ

masted *adj.* having such or so many masts ایسے یا اتنے مستولوں والا

master (*mahs*-tĕ*) *n.* man with others working for or under him آقا، مالک one who has a control (*of* one's fate, etc.) اپنی تقدیر کا مالک، اپنی قسمت آپ بنانے والا • male owner (*of* a dog, horse, etc.) مالک male teacher اُستاد male head of a household گھر کا بڑا captain of a merchant ship تجارتی جہاز کا کپتان skilled workman conducting own business مالک کاریگر، بڑا کاریگر *master builder* بڑا راج، مستری (*pl.*) great personalities (*of* art, literature, etc.) عظیم فنکار *the old masters*, (*a*) great painters of the Renaissance یورپی نشاۃ ثانیہ کے عظیم مصور (*b*) their paintings یورپی نشاۃ ثانیہ کے مصوری کے شاہکار expert ماہر *become a master of, make (oneself) master of (a subject, trade, etc.)* learn it thoroughly کا ماہر بن جانا، خوب اچھی طرح سیکھنا (with a boy's name) young Mr. میاں، ننھے *Master Tom, Master Tommy, Master Thomas Bell* مسٹر بیل کا نابالغ لڑکا ٹام، ٹامی یا ٹامس fully qualified in فاضل *Master of Arts* (abbr. *M.A.*) ایم-اے *Master of Science* (abbr. *M.Sc.*) ایم-ایس،سی **master-key** *n.* key that will open many different locks ہرقفل کنجی **master-piece** *n.* masterpiece of something made or done with great skill in a field کا شاہکار the best work produced by an artist, etc. فنی شاہکار، شاہکار **master-stroke** *n.* masterly move غضب کی چال **mastery** (*mahs*-tè-ri) *n.* complete skill or knowledge (of) (کی) پوری مہارت full control (of) (پر) پورا غلبہ perfection (of) میں کمال *v.t.* become the master (*of*) کا ماہر بننا، خوب اچھی طرح سیکھنا control (one's temper, a horse, etc.) پر قابو پانا، کو قابو میں رکھنا **masterful** *adj.* fond of controlling others حکومت چلانے کا خواہشمند، حکومت پسند **masterly** *adj* skilful ماہرانہ، اُستادانہ

²-master *suf.* ship with (so many) masts (...) مستولوں والا جہاز

mastic, mastich (*mas*-tik) *n.* a kind of resin مصطگی، مصطکی tree yielding it مصطگی کا درخت

masticate (*mas*-ti-kayt) *v. t.* grind up (food) with the teeth (غذا کو) چبانا **mastication** (-*kay*-) *n.* act of masticating غذا چبانا، مضغ

mastodon (*mas*-to-don) *n.* extinct animal allied to elephant قدیم فیل، معدوم ہاتھی

masturbate *v.i.* (of males) pollute oneself by personal sexual gratification جلق لگانا، مشت زنی کرنا، ہتھ رسی کرنا **masturbation** (-*bay*-) *n.* act of masturbating جلق، مشت زنی، ہتھ رسی

mat *n.* rough floor-covering چٹائی، بوریا also *door-mat*), piece of such covering placed in or near the door for wiping shoes on پائدان tangled mass of hair, etc. اُلجھا ہوا something placed on a table, etc. to prevent damage from hot dishes طشتری دان *adj.* (of a surface) not shiny پھیکا، مدھم، بے رونق *v. t.* pread a mat on پر بوریا بچھانا، پر چٹائی ڈالنا tangle اُلجھا دینا knot گوندھنا

door-mat

matted *adj.* (of hair, etc.) tangled اُلجھا ہوا knotted گندھا ہوا

matador (*mat*-a-do*) *n.* professional bull-fighter سانڈ سے لڑنے والا پہلوان، ثور افگن

match (mach) *n.* contest, game (کھیل کا) مقابلہ، میچ *cricket match, etc.* کرکٹ میچ (وغیرہ) one able to meet another as his equal in strength, skill, etc. (کسی کی) مدّمقابل، حریف *find* (or *meet*) (*one's*) *match* (*in*) (کسی) صورت میں، اپنا مدّمقابل نظر آنا marriage شادی، رشتہ *decide to make a match of it*, decide to get married آپس میں شادی کا فیصلہ کر لینا thing combining well with another جوڑ، میل *be a good match* خوب میل کھانا stick of wood with head giving flame when rubbed دیا سلائی، ماچس *strike a match* ماچس جلانا *v. t. & i.* bring into competition (*with* or *against*) مقابلے میں لانا correspond (with something in quality, colour, etc.) سے (خوب) میل کھانا، ملتا جلتا ہونا *something to match* سے ملتا جلتا، سے میل کھاتا ہوا be (or obtain) a match for کے لیے موزوں رشتہ ہونا یا نکالنا *well-matched couple* اچھی جوڑی *well-matched pair* (*of contestants*) برابر کی چوٹ **matchless** *n.* unequalled, بے نظیر، یکتا، یگانہ. better than all rivals سب سے اچھا **matchwood** *n.* small broken bits of wood لکڑی کا چھوٹا سا باریک ٹکڑا wood used in making matchboxes دیا سلائی کی لکڑی **match-box** *n.* a box of matches دیا سلائی کی ڈبیہ، ماچس **safety match** *n.* the safe kind of match in common use nowadays محفوظ دیا سلائی **matchlock** *n.* old form of gun fired with fuse توڑے دار بندوق **matchmaker** *n.* one who is given to bringing about marriages رشتہ یا رشتے کرانے والا

mate (mayt) *n.* fellow workman رفیق (مزدور)، ساتھی مزدور any associate ہم، ساتھی *classmate* ہم جماعت *room-mate* اسی کمرے میں رہنے والا ship's officer below the captain میٹ functionary's assistant کسی کام کرنے والے کا نائب، مددگار *cook's mate* باورچی کا نائب یا مددگار one of a pair of birds, or animals living together جوڑے میں سے دوسرا *the elephant and his mate* ہاتھی اور اس کی ہتھنی *v. t. & i.* marry شادی کرنا یا کرانا (of animals) unite to produce young مستی پر آ کر ملنا cause them to do so کا جوڑا ملانا *the mating season*, season when they are on heat حیوانوں کی مستی کا موسم

mater (*may*-tè*) *n.* (school slang) mother والدہ

materfamilias (may-te*-fa-*mil*-i-as) *n.* mother of the household بڑی اماں، دادی اماں، بڑی بی

material (ma-*tee*-ri-ĕl) *n*. substance from which something is made جس چیز سے کچھ بنایا جائے، مال، سامان *raw materials*, not yet used in manufacture خام مال *writing materials*, stationery لکھنے کا سامان، سامانِ نوشت وخواند، سٹیشنری *adj*. not spiritual ; made of, or pertaining to matter مادّی *the material world* مادّی دُنیا physical (comforts, etc.) جسمانی (آرائش وغیرہ) pertaining to the needs of the human body ضروریاتِ اِنسانی کا، جسمانی ضرورتوں کا (یا کے متعلق) *a material point of view* ضروریاتِ اِنسانی کے نقطۂ نگاہ سے essential اہم *it is quite material from this point of view* اِس نقطۂ نگاہ سے یہ بہت اہم ہے **materialism** (-lism) *n*. theory that only physical things exist مادّیت، مادّہ پرستی، دہریت *dialectical materialism*, (see under *dialect*) exclusive attention to material prosperity دُنیا کی حرص وہوس، ہوسِ دُنیا **materialist** *n*. believer in materialism مادّیت پر یقین رکھنے والا، مادّی، مادّہ پرست attention to material prosperity to the exclusion of all interest in religion or even aesthetics وہ جسے اتنی ہوسِ مال وجاہ ہو کہ نہ خُدا کی یاد باقی رہے نہ حُسن و جمال کا ذوق، بندۂ حرص و آز **materialize** *v.t.* & *i.* be implemented جامۂ عمل پہننا، عمل میں آنا implement جامۂ عمل پہنانا، عمل میں لانا، حقیقت بنا (cause to) take a material form مادّی صورت میں آنا یا لانا (also see **matter**)

materia medica (ma-*tee*-ri-a-*med*-i-ka *n*. drugs دوائیں، اُدویہ pharmacology عِلمُ الاَدوِیہ

materiel (ma-ti-ri-*el*) *n*. available stores, etc., of an undertaking سامان

maternal (-*tĕ**-) *adj*. pertaining to mother ماں کا، ماں کی طرف سے، ماں کا سا، مادری، مادرانہ، اُمومی *maternal aunt*, aunt on the mother's side of the family خالہ یا ممانی **maternally** *adv*. on the mother's side ماں کی طرف سے

maternity (ma-*tĕ**-ni-ti) *n*. being a mother ماں ہونا، اُمومت becoming a mother ماں بننا *maternity welfare centre* مرکزِ بہبودِ بچگان *maternity home* شفاخانۂ زچگاں، زچہ ہسپتال

mathematics (math-e-*mat*-iks) *n*. (used as *sing.*) (abb. *Maths*, or *Math.*) science of numbers and space ریاضی، ریاضیات **mathematical** *adj*. of mathematics ریاضی، ریاضیات کے متعلق **mathematician** (-*tish*-) *n*. expert in mathematics ریاضی داں

matinee (*mat*-i-nay) *n*. cinema-show in the morning سنیما کا صبح کا شو theatre performance in the afternoon تیسرے پہر کا ناٹک

matins (*mat*-inz) *n. pl.* (in Christianity) morning prayer عیسائیوں کی صبح کی نماز

matriarch *n*, **matriarchal** *adj*. (see under **matriarchy**)

matriarchy (mat-ri-*ah**-ki) *n*. headship of family or tribe by women or descendants traced through them (خاندان یا قبیلہ کا) مادری نظام، اُمومی نظامِ حکومت

matriarch (*mat*-ri-ah*k) *n*. woman head of family or tribe (خاندان یا قبیلہ کی) مادر **matriarchal** *adj*. this system مادرانہ، اُمومی

matricide (*mat*-ri-sid) *n*. killing of one's own mother اپنی ماں کا قتل، قتلِ مادر، مادر کُشی one guilty of this ماں کا (یا کی) قاتل، مادر کُش

matriculate (mat-*rik*-ew-layt) *v. t.* & *i.* admit or be admitted as a student in a university جامعہ میں داخل ہونا یا کرنا pass an examination entitling one to this admission جامعہ میں داخلے کا اِمتحان پاس کرنا **matriculation** (-*lay*-) *n*. matriculating جامعہ میں داخلہ (also *matric*, pronounced (ma-*trik*) entrance examination for this (hence also called *entrance* examination although under the new arrangements it has actually been christened *Higher Secondary* examination and has to be taken not before completing 12 years at school میٹرک، انٹرنس **Note :** Since **matriculation** means (passing an examination for) being admitted to the university it would be a misnomer (and a sad reflection on the integrity of authorities) still to call the *secondary examinations* the matric or matriculation examination.

matrimony (*mat*-ri-mo-ni) *n*. state of being married شادی شدہ ہونا، متاہل زندگی، متاہلانہ زندگی **matrimonial** (-*moh*-) *adj*. متاہل زندگی سے متعلق، اِزدواجی

matrix (*mayt*-riks) *n*. (pl. *matrices* or *matrixes*) mould into or over which hot metal is poured to be shaped for forming a block for printing ٹائپ کا سانچہ substance in which precious stones or minerals are found, embedded چٹان کا ٹکڑا جس میں دھات یا جواہرات کی پرت ہو

matron (*mayt*-run) *n*. woman housekeeper in an educational or other institution ہوسٹل وغیرہ کی منتظمہ woman controlling nursing staff in a hospital شفاخانے کی سب سے بڑی نرس، ہیڈ میٹرن، مادر married woman شادی شدہ عورت widow بیوہ **matronly** (*mayt*-run-li) *adj*. of or like a matron مادرانہ dignified and sedate as befits an elderly woman بڑی بوڑھیوں کا سا باوقار

matter (*mat*-ĕ*) *n*. physical substance (as opposed to *mind* and *spirit*) مادّہ (also see *material*, *materialism*, *materialist*) affair معاملہ، واقعہ *the matter is under consideration* معاملہ زیرِ غور ہے *money matters* مالی معاملات *as a matter of fact*, whatever one may say the fact is واقعہ ہے، اَمرِ واقع یہ ہے *the fact of the matter is*, the true position is اصل بات یہ ہے (کہ) *a matter of course*, something naturally expected قدرتی بات *for that matter, for the matter of that*, as far as that is concerned جہاں تک اُس کا تعلق ہے what is said in a piece of writing or speech (as distinct from the *manner* of saying it) مضمون pus مواد، پیپ *printed matter*, anything printed مطبوعہ شے *no matter what*, (or *when, where, how, which*, etc.), it is unimportant what, (when, where, how, who or which) کچھ ، یا کہیں یا کیسے یا کون یا کونسا) ہی کیوں نہ ہو *be the matter, (with)*, be wrong (with) کو ہو گیا ہونا *v. i.* be important (to someone) کے نزدیک اہم ہونا **matter-of-fact** *adj.* keeping to facts بس کام کی بات کرنے والا unimaginative قوتِ تخیل سے محروم ordinary معمولی ، عام

matting *n.* coarse woven material for floor coverings ٹاٹ ، بوریا

mattock (*mat*-uk) *n.* tool like a pickaxe for loosening ground کدال (کا ایک نمونہ)

mattoid (*mat*-oid) *n.* half-fool half-genius ایسا شخص جو بعض معاملات میں حد درجہ فرزانہ ہو، بعض میں اتنا ہی احمق ہو، نیم فرزانہ و نیم دیوانہ

mattress (*mat*-res) *n.* thick, oblong pad of straw, etc., on which to sleep گدا *spring mattress*, bedstead with coiled wires سپرنگ دار پلنگ

mature (ma-*tew*-ĕ*) *v. t.* & *i.* develop fully پوری طرح تیار ہونا ، پختہ ہونا ، پکنا *adj.* ripe ready for use پوری طرح تیار carefully thought out سوچا سمجھا fully grown (mental stature, etc.) پختہ adult (age, etc.) (عمر) رسِن بلوغ ، بلوغت کی (عقل)

maturity (ma-*tew*-ĕ-ri-ti) *n.* full growth پختگی ، بلوغ ، بلوغت

maudlin (*mawd*-lin) *adj.* sentimental in a silly or tearful way بے جا طور پر رقیق القلب

maugre (*maw*-gĕ*) *prep.* (old use) in spite of کے باوجود ، کے علی الرغم

maul (mawl) *v. t.* beat or bruise بُری طرح پیٹنا ، زدو کوب کرنا damage by criticism ہدفِ تنقید بنانا ، دھجیاں بکھیرنا **mauley** (*maw*-li) *n.* (pl. *mauleys*) (slang) fist مٹھی hand ہاتھ

maund (mawnd) *n.* Pakistani weight equivalent to 40 seers or 80 3/7 lb. مَن

mausoleum (maw-so-*lee*-um) *n.* magnificent tomb مقبرہ

mauve (mohv) *n.* & *adj.* pale purple (colour) ہلکا ارغوانی (رنگ)

maw (maw) *n.* last stomach of animals which chew cud جگالی کرنے والے جانوروں کا آخری معدہ

mawkish (*mawk*-ish) *adj.* foolishly sentimental بے جا طور پر رقت بھرا sweet and sickly (thing) منہ پھیر دینے یا پھرا دینے والی (شیرینی)

maxim (*mak*-sim) *n.* wise saying قول، مقولہ rule of conduct expressed in a sentence ایک جملے میں کہا ہوا اصول ، (دانائی کا) گُر *maxims of equity* انصاف کے گُر

maximum (*mak*-si-mum) *n.* greatest possible or recorded (degree, quantity, etc., as opposed to *minimum*) زیادہ سے زیادہ

may *auxiliary v.* (pa. t. *might*, pr. mit) be free to. be permitted to سکنا be likely but not certain شاید ہونا ، غالباً ہونا I wish that (someone) should چاہتا ہوں کہ ، دعا ہے کہ ، خدا کرے کہ *n.* (*May*), fifth month of the English calendar year مئی (also *may-blossom*) hawthorn ناگفنی کی شگفتگی

May-day *n.* May 1 as a spring festival in the country یکم مئی کا دیہاتی تہوار ، جشنِ بہار ، نوبہار ، یوم مئی (also *Labour Day*), Communist festival on May 1 celebrated by workers of the party and workmen یوم مئی

maypole (*may*-pohl) *n.* flowerdecked pole danced round on May-day یوم مئی کی چھڑی ، جشنِ بہار میں پھولوں کی چھڑی ، نوبہار کا کھمبا

people round a maypole

maybe (*may*-bee) *adv.* (archaic) perhaps ہو سکتا ہے کہ *Maybe he is right* ہو سکتا ہے کہ وہ صحیح کہہ رہا ہے *as soon as maybe*, as soon as possible جونہی ، جیسے ہی

mayor (*may*-ĕ*) *n.* town corporation chief صدرِ بلدیہ **mayoralty** (*may*-ĕ-ral-ti) *n.* mayor's office بلدیہ کی صدارت tenure of his office صدرِ بلدیہ کے عہدے کی مدت **mayoress** (*may*-ĕ-res) *n.* woman mayor صدرِ بلدیہ خاتون mayor's wife صدرِ بلدیہ کی بیگم

maze (mayz) *n.* puzzling network of paths, lines, etc. بھول بھلیاں numerous confusing facts, etc. بھول بھلیاں ، چکر *in a maze*, puzzled حیران ، پریشان

me (mee) *pron.* (objective case of **I**, which see)

mead (meed) *n.* (poet.) meadow مرغزار ، سبزہ زار

meadow (*med*-oh) *n.* grassland esp. one used for hay مرغزار ، سبزہ زار

meagre (*meeg*-ĕ*) *adj.* thin دُبلا پتلا ، لاغر insufficient (income, resources, information, etc.) ناکافی

meal (meel) *n.* (also *meal-time*), eating-time کھانے کا وقت (also pl.) food for a meal کھانا *make a meal of (something)*, consume (it) کھا جانا ، اُڑا جانا ، ہضم کر لینا coarsely ground grain or pulse موٹا آٹا *whole meal*, meal from which husk has not been separated اَن چھنا آٹا **mealy** (*mee*-li) *adj.* of or like meal آٹے کا (سا) containing meal خشک سا آٹے دار *mealy potatoes*, potatoes tasting dry even after boiling خشک سے آٹو، دیسی آٹو، آٹے دار آٹو **mealy-mouthed** (*-mouthd*) *adj*. (of person) not out-spoken but using euphemism دو ٹوک بات نہ کہنے والا، چرب زبان

▣ **Meal** is the general term but not very frequently used ; **breakfast** is had on rising ; **lunch** is a small amount of food taken at midday in England and at any time in the States ; **tea** or **coffee**, usu. in the afternoon ; **supper**, in the evening ; **dinner**, principal meal at midday or in the evening , **repast**, heavy formal meal ; **feast**, to one invited or unaccustomed to it.

mean (meen) *adj*. (of things) poor in appear-ance معمولی سا، گھٹیا (of intelligence, etc.) low کمینہ، پیچ، ذلیل (of person) lowborn پست (of person, thoughts, behaviour, etc.) not generous تنگ نظر، تنگدلانہ average, mid-point اوسط *the mean annual temperature* اوسط سالانہ درجہ حرارت *n*. average number, quality or state اوسط *the golden mean, the happy mean*, moderation اعتدال کی چال، اوسط جو خیرُ الاُمور ہے، میانہ روی *v.t.* & *i*. (*mean* : *meant*, *meant* pr. ment) signify, denote کا مطلب ہونا، کے معنیٰ ہونا (of someone) have in mind کا مطلب ہونا have as a purpose چاہنا، کی نیت ہونا *mean mischief*, intend to do it شرارت کی نیت ہونا، کا ارادہ ہونا *mean business*, be ready to act and not merely to talk کرنے کا ارادہ ہونا *mean* (*someone*) *no harm*, have no intention to harm him سے بدی کا کوئی ارادہ نہ ہونا *mean a little to* (*someone*), be of little importance to him کے نزدیک خاص اہمیت *mean much to* (*someone*), *mean a great deal to* (*someone*), be of much importance to him کے نزدیک بڑی اہمیت ہونا **meaning** *n*. what is meant معنیٰ، مطلب object مقصد *adj*. expressive معنیٰ خیز *a meaning look*, one full of meaning or purpose معنیٰ خیز **mean-ingful** *adj*. significant معنیٰ خیز **meaningless** *adj*. without meaning بے معنیٰ، بیہودہ، بکواس **mean-ingly** *adj*. significantly معنیٰ خیز انداز سے **meanly** *adv*. with meanness کمینگی سے **meanness** *n*. being mean کمینگی (see also **means**) **meantime** *n*. the time between two occasions دوران، اثنا *in the meantime*, meanwhile اس اثنا میں، اس دوران میں *adv*. at the same time ساتھ ہی **meanwhile** *n*. meantime دوران، اثنا *adv*. in the meantime, in the interven-ing time اس دوران میں، اس اثنا میں

means (meenz) *n. pl*. (often treated as sing : as *a means*) intermediate step (or steps) to an end . that with which something is done حصول مقصد کا ذریعہ *the means of* ذریعہ *a means to an end* کا ایک ذریعہ *by means of*, with the help of کے ذریعے *by all means*, certainly یقیناً *by no means*, not at all ہرگز نہیں، کسی صورت بھی نہیں *by some means or other*, somehow or other کسی نہ کسی طرح income, wealth آمدنی *a man of means*, a rich man امیر آدمی، دولت مند شخص *live within one's means*, not spend more than one's income آمدنی سے زیادہ خرچ نہ کرنا، چادر دیکھ کر پاؤں پھیلانا *means test*, inquiry regarding the financial position of a person seeking monetary help owing to unemployment, etc. حالت کا جائزہ، وسائل ورسائل کا جائزہ

meander (mi-*and*-ĕ*) *v.t*. (of river) wind about (دریا کا) چکر کھاتے ہوئے بہنا، (دریا میں) پیچ و خم ہونا wander (about) aimlessly ادھر اُدھر پھرنا، چکر لگانا *n*. departure from straight course مُڑنا، چکر کھانا devious course چکر، پھیر windings of a river دریا کے پیچ و خم

meaning *n*. **meantime, meanwhile** *n*. & *adv*. (see under **mean**)

measles (*mee*-zĕlz) *n*. a highly infectious skin disease (usu. affecting children) خسرا **measly** (*meez*-li) *adj*. having measles خسرے کا مریض (colloq.) worthless ناکارہ، بیکار

measure (*mezh*-ĕ*) *n*. size, quantity or degree of anything مقدار، ناپ، پیمائش، درجہ وغیرہ *full measure*, full amount پورا، پوری مقدار *give full measure* (*of*) پورا تول تولنا *give short measure* (*of*) پورا تول نہ تولنا *clothes made to measure*, not ready-made but specially stitched for someone ناپ سے کر بنائے ہوئے کپڑے standard used in stating size, quantity or degree پیمانہ، ناپ، تول کا معیار something made according to this standard for finding out the size, etc., of various things پیمانہ *tape-measure*, measure in the form of a tape فیتہ extent وسعت، حد *in some measure*, to some extent کسی حد تک *in a great measure*, largely بڑی حد تک *beyond measure*, *without measure*, very greatly بے حد، از حد، بے اندازہ، بے حساب، بیشمار step، قدم *take drastic measures against* کے خلاف سخت اقدام کارروائی کرنا rhythm of verse وزن time in music تال law قانون proposed enactment مجوزہ قانون *v.t.* & *i*. find the size, amount, etc., of ناپنا، ماپنا، تولنا *measure* (*something*) *out* (*to*), give a measured quantity of to someone (کو) ناپ کر، تول کر دینا *measure* (*one's*) *strength against* (*some-one*), compete with (him) سے مقابلہ کر دیکھنا be (a certain size, degree, etc.) (اتنا) ناپ ہونا **measur-ed** (*mezh*-ĕ*d) *adj*. thoughtful (step, langu-age, etc.) محتاط، نپا تلا (قدم، الفاظ وغیرہ) rhythmi موزوں moving in slow rhythm نرم رو **measure-ment** *n*. measuring ناپنا، تولنا وغیرہ (pl. details of dimensions لمبائی، چوڑائی کی تفصیلات

meat (meet) *n.* animal flesh used as food گوشت (old use) any kind of food خوراک *one man's meat is another man's poison*, what is good for one may be just the opposite for another ایک کا کھانا دوسرے کا زہر

mechanic (me-*kan*-ik *n.* one who makes or repairs machinery or does skilled work on it کاریگر، مشین پر کام کرنیوالا، مشین دار، مشین دار **mechanics** *n.* science of force and motion and, hence, of machinery میکینکس **mechanical** *adj.* pertaining to machinery مشینی made or run by machinery مشینی done not intelligently but just like a machine کٹھ پتلی کی طرح **mechanically** *adv.* مشین سے؛ کٹھ پتلی کی طرح، میکانیاتی اصول کے مطابق **mechanism** *n.* working parts of a machine مشین کے کل پرزے mode of operation طریق کار **mechanize** (*mek*-a-n.z) *v.t.* use machines *for* or *in* (something) میں مشین استعمال کرنا، کو کل دار بنا دینا *mechanized forces*, army units using motor transport, etc. فوج کے کلدار دستے **mechanization** (-zay-) *n.* act of mechanizing or being mechanized مشین لگانا، کلدار بنانا

nedal (*med*-ĕl) *n.* coin-like piece of metal with a design and inscription to commemorate some event or given as an award for distinguished work تمغہ *gold* (or *silver* or *bronze*) *medal* سونے (یا چاندی کا، کانسی) کا تمغہ **medallist** (*med*-) *n.* recipient of a medal, تمغہ لینے والا، تمغہ یافتہ شخص maker of a medal تمغہ بنانے والا، تمغہ ساز **medallion** (me-dal-yĕn) *n.* large medal بڑا تمغہ، تمغۂ کلاں round panel or tablet containing portrait or embossed figure, etc. گول چوکھٹے میں (ابھرے ہوئے نقوش والی) تصویر

meddle (*med*-ĕl) *v.i.* interfere (*in* another's affairs) (کسی کے معاملات میں) خواہ مخواہ دخل دینا touch or busy unnecessarily (*with* another's things) (کسی کی چیزوں کو) خواہ مخواہ چھیڑنا **meddlesome** *adj.* in the habit of meddling دخل در معقولات کرنے والا، پرائے پھٹے میں ٹانگ اڑانے والا، تو کون؟ میں خواہ مخواہ

media (*mee*-di-a) *n.* (pl. of **medium,** which sce)

medial (*mee*-di-ĕl) *adj.* (of the letter of a word) middle (or one of the middle ones and not *initial* or *final*) وسطی

median (*mee*-di-ĕn) *adj.* & *n.* (line, surface, etc.) dividing object lengthwise into halves وسطانیہ

mediate (*mee*-di-ayt) act as a peacemaker *between*) میں ثالثی کرنا، میں مصالحت کی کوشش کرنا **mediation** (-*ay*-) *n.* act of mediation مصالحت کی کوشش، ثالثی

medical *adj.*, **medicated** *adj.*, **medicinal** *adj.* (see under **medicine**)

medicine (*med*-i-sin) *n.* art and science of the prevention and cure of disease طب، ڈاکٹری (*med-sin*) substance taken (esp. through mouth) to cure a disease دوا **medicine-man** *n.* magician acting as a doctor of medicine in savage tribes جادوگر معالج **medical** (*med*-i-kĕl) *adj.* of the art of medicine) طبی *medical science* طب *medical profession* طب، ڈاکٹری، طبابت *medical student* طب کا طالبعلم *medical jurisprudence*, branch of law affecting doctors قانون متعلقۂ طب، طبی قانون، طب قانونی (of diseases or treatment) not needing surgical operation طبی *medical case* طبی مریض، غیر جراحی مریض *medical ward* شفاخانے میں طبی مریضوں کی جائے رہائش *medical certificate*, a doctor's certificate to the effect that someone is ill ڈاکٹری سرٹیفکیٹ، طبی تصدیق **medically** *adj.* from the medical (man's) viewpoint طبی نقطہ نگاہ سے *medically fit*, (or unfit) طبی طور پر، طب کی نگاہ میں، طبی نقطہ نگاہ **medicament** (-*dik*-) *n.* medicine for internal or external use (کھانے یا لگانے کی) دوا **medicated** (-*kay*-) *adj.* (of a substance) containing a substance used medically جس میں دوا پڑی ہوئی ہو، دوا والا **medicinal** (-*dis*-) *adj.* pertaining to medicine دوا سے متعلق، ادویاتی having medical properties طبی

medieval, mediæval (med-i-*ee*-vĕl) *adj.* as of the Middle Ages extending from about the eleventh to the fifteenth century قرون وسطیٰ کا (سا) قرون مظلمہ کا (سا)

mediocre (mee-di-*ohk*-è*) *adj.* second rate معمولی، اوسط درجے کا **mediocrity** (*ok*-) *n* being mediocre معمولی ہونا، اوسط درجے کا ہونا mediocre person معمولی قابلیت کا شخص

meditate (*medi*-i-tayt) *v. t.* & *i.* think about کے متعلق سوچنا، کا خیال کرنا contemplate محو خیال ہونا، مراقبے میں جانا **meditation** (-*tay*-) *n.* act of meditating مراقبہ، دھیان، محو خیال

medium (*mee*-di-um) *n.* (pl. *media* or *mediums*) means (*of* something or *for doing* something) ذریعہ *medium of examination* (or *instruction*), language through which examination (or instruction) is conducted ذریعۂ امتحان یا ذریعۂ تعلیم mean اوسط *the happy medium*, اعتدال، میانہ روی pl. often *media*), substance in which something exists محال go between in spiritualism معمولی *adj.* average درمیانہ، اوسط درجے کا، درمیانی درجے کا **medium-wave** *adj.* radio receiving-set) of wave-length between 100 and 800 metres متوسط موجی، درمیانہ لاسلکی لہروں والا

n. such waves رمیڈیم ویو، درمیانہ لاسلکی لہریں
medley (*med*-li) *n.* mixture (*of*) معجونِ مرکّب ، میل ، مجموعہ ، کہیں کی اینٹ کہیں کا روڑا
Medusa (me-*dew*-za) *Cl. myth.* one of the Gorgons who had snakes for her tresses and turned the beholder into stone ; Perseus killed her میڈوسہ
meed *n.* (poet.) deserved portion (*of* praise or blame) اُجر، مُعاوضہ
meek *adj.* mild and patient منکسرالمزاج ، مسکین، عاجزانہ طبیعت والا **meekly** (*meek*-li) *adv.* انکسار سے **meekness** *n.* quality of being meek ; humility اِنکسار ، عاجزی ، عاجزانہ طبیعت ، عجز و نیاز ، عجز و انکسار
meet *v. t.* & *i.* (*meet, met, met*) come upon (someone) (کسی) کو ملنا receive (someone on arrival, etc.) لینے کے لیے جانا ، اِستقبال کے لیے جانا experience, come face to face (*with*) (مصیبت) اُٹھانا (یا) دیکھنا be introduced to سے تعارف کرنا satisfy (someone or his wishes) کے لیے کافی ہونا ، کے لیے تسلی بخش ہونا *meet* (*someone*) *half-way*, come to a compromise with دونوں طرف سے مطالبات میں کچھ کمی کر کے مصالحت کر لینا *meet a bill*, pay it بل دے دینا ، بل کی رقم ادا کرنا *adj.* (old use) suitable سزاوار، زیبا ، موزوں ، مُناسب *n.* gathering (of fox-hunters or athletes) (کھلاڑیوں یا لومڑ کے شکاریوں کا) اِجتماع **meeting** *n.* organized gathering (for discussion, etc) جلسہ ، اِجلاس
mega- (meg-a) *pref.* large بڑا عظیم ، کثیر (of) ten million ایک کروڑ (کا)
megadeath *n.* (see *Addenda*)
megaphone (*meg*-a-fohn) *n.* horn for speaking through, carrying the voice to a distance بھونپو

a megaphone

Megaera (ma-*jee*-ra) *Cl. myth.* one of the Furies مجیرہ
megalomania (me-gal-o-*may*-ni-a) *n.* mania for self-exaltation بڑا بننے کا خبط mania for big things بڑی چیزوں کا خبط
megrim (*meeg*-rim) *n.* bad headache سخت سر درد whim مَن کی موج (*pl.*) low spirits اِضمحلال
melancholy (*mel*-an-ko-li) *adj.* sad غم زدہ، غمگین، حزین *n.* sadness غم و اَلم ، حُزن و ملال distraction مالیخولیا ، ملنخولیا
melee (me-*lay*) *n.* confused struggle بلوہ ، بہت سے لوگوں کا دنگا فساد ، بڑی گڑبڑ confused crowd of people بڑی رلی جلی بھیڑ
mellifluous (me-*lif*-lew-us) *adj.* easy flowing and smooth-sounding (words, music, etc.) شیریں
mellow (*mel*-oh) *adj.* soft and sweet in taste شیریں ، رسیلا soft and rich in colour or sound بڑا پیارا ، دلکش jovial with drink نشے کے باعث خوش، ترنگ میں نرم ، دھیما sympathetic and wise by experience *v. t.* & *i.* make or become mellow شیریں ہونا یا بنانا ، بڑا پیارا ہونا ، ترنگ میں آنا ، یا لانا ، نرم مزاج ہونا یا بنانا
melodious *adj.* (see under **melody**)
melodrama (mel-o-*drah*-ma) *n.* exciting and emotional drama with a happy ending خوشگوار انجام والی جذباتی تمثیل ، میلو ڈراما drama with many songs in it گانوں سے بھری ہوئی تمثیل **melodramatic** *adj.* theatrical (behaviour, person) سستی جذباتیت والا ، جذبات فروش ، جذبات فروشانہ in the manner of melodrama سستی جذباتی تمثیل والا ، میلو ڈرامائی
melody (*mel*-o-di) *n.* sweet music شیریں نغمہ song or tune دُھن **melodist** *n.* one who composes or plays a melody نغمہ ساز ، نغمہ گر ، دُھن گر **melodious** (-*loh*-) *adj.* sweet-sounding سُریلا
melon (*mel*-un) *n.* large juicy round fruit of a trailing plant خربوزہ *water-melon,* تربوز *musk-melon* سَردا
Melpomene (see under **muse**)
melt *v. t.* & *i.* (*melt, melted, melted*) liquefy پگھلنا یا پگھلانا (of heart, etc.) fill (or be filled) with pity, etc., soften or be softened with pity, etc. پسیجنا ، نرم ہونا یا کرنا go (*away*) from sight slowly آہستہ آہستہ نظروں سے غائب ہو جانا gradually merge (into another colour, etc.) دھیرے دھیرے دوسرے رنگ میں مل جانا **molten** (*mohl*-tĕn) *adj.* melted (metal) پگھلی ہوئی (دھات)
molten *adj.* (see under **melt**)
member (*mem*-bĕ*) *n.* person belonging to a group, etc. رُکن *Member of the Parliament,* (abbr. *M.P.*) پارلیمانی رُکن ، ایم۔پی *Member of the Provincial Assembly,* (abb. *M.P.A.*) صوبائی مجلسِ قانون ساز کا رُکن ۔ ایم۔پی۔اے (old use) part of the body (*e.g.* an arm, the tongue) عضو **membership** *n.* the state of being a member (*of* Parliament or other group) رُکنیت the number of members (of a group, etc.) کے ارکان کی تعداد ، کی رُکنیت
membrane (*mem*-brayn) *n.* thin skin like covering of the inside parts of an animal or plant جھلی
memento (me-*ment*-oh) *n.* (pl. *mementos*) souvenir یادگار ، نشانی
memo (*mee*-moh) *n.* (abb. form of **memorandum**) (see under **memory**)
memoir (*me*-mwah*) *n.* (usu. *pl.*) written account of one's experiences تذکرہ ، سرگزشت (*pl.*) (*memoirs*), autobiography آپ بیتی record of researches, etc. تحقیقات کی یادداشت **aide-memoire** (*ayd*-may-mwah*) *n.* document, etc., (usu. sent) to serve as aid to memory یادداشت

memorial *n.* & *adj.* **memorialize** *v.t.* **memorization** *n.* **memorize** *v.t.* (see under **memory**)

memory (*mem*-o-ri) *n.* faculty or power of remembering یادداشت، حافظہ *have a good* (or *bad*) *memory* حافظہ اچھا (یا بُرا) ہونا *speak from memory,* speak off-hand without consulting the record یادداشت کے بھروسے پر کہنا *to the best of* (*one's*) *memory*, as far as one can remember جہاں تک یاد پڑتا ہے period over which one can recall events, etc. یاد *within memory* (*of*) کے زمانے سے پہلے کی بات *within living memory,* within the memory of the living generation اس کے دیکھنے والے ابھی زندہ ہیں (often *pl.*) that which is remembered and cherished یاد (یا یادیں) *sweet* (or *bitter*) *memories of* (*a period*) (کسی زمانے کی) خوشگوار (یا تلخ) یادیں

memorable *adj.* worth remembering یاد رکھنے کے قابل

memorandum (mem-o-*rand*-um) *n.* (pl. *memoranda*) (abb. *memo.* pr. as *mee*-moh) record or note (*on some matter*) یادداشت informal official letter (usu. with the issuing authority's designation only and not bearing his signature) میمو، میمورنڈم، یادداشت

memorial (me-*moh*-ri-ĕl) *adj.* in commemoration (of a dead person or sombre event of the past) یاد منانے کے لیے، سوگ منانے کے لیے *n.* something done or built to perpetuate the memory (*to*) (کی) یادگار written representation (*by* a number of persons *to* the authorities, etc.) محضر، محضرنامہ **memorialize** *v.t.* learn by rote (کی) یاد منانا، محضرنامہ بھیجنا **memorization** (*-zay-*) *n.* act of memorizing رٹنا، رٹّا لگانا

men *n.* (pl. of **man,** which see)

menace (*men*-is) *n.* threat (*of* danger *to* someone) خطرہ *v. t.* threaten (*with* danger, etc.) (کسی کے لیے) خطرناک، خطرہ بننا **menacing** *adj* dangerous خطرناک **menacingly** *adv.* in a menacing manner دھمکیاں دیتے ہوئے، خطرناک انداز سے

menagerie (me-*nahj*-è-ri) *n.* caged wild animals taken out from place to place for a show سفری چڑیا گھر

mend *v. t.* & *i.* repair (clothes, shoes, road, etc.) کی مرمّت کرنا *mend one's* (*way*), reform اپنی اصلاح کرنا *mend* (*one's*) *pace,* move faster تیز چلنا be improving بہتر ہوتے جانا *things are mending* حالات بہتر ہو رہے ہیں *n.* mended hole, crack, etc. مرمّت شدہ جگہ (be) *on the mend,* (be) improving (in health, etc.) بہتر ہو رہا ہونا

mendacious (men-*day*-shus) *adj.* lying (person or statement) جھوٹا (شخص یا بیان) **mendacity** (*-das-*) *n.* habit of lying جھوٹ کی عادت، دروغگوئی، دروغ بافی، کذب، دروغ، جھوٹ falsehood

mendicant (mend-i-kant) *n.* beggar (often used of friars, etc.) بھکاری، فقیر، درویش *adj.* begging for a living بھیک مانگ کر گزر کرنے والا **mendicity, mendicancy** *n.* living by begging from door to door بھیک مانگ کر گزر کرنا، فقیری، درویشی

meniscus (me-nis-kus) *n.* (pl. *menisci* pr. -ki) figure of crescent form ہلالی شکل، ہلالی lens convex on one side concave on the other ہلالی عدسہ

menopause *n.* (see under **menses**)

menses (*mens*-eez) *n. pl.* monthly discharge from the womb ماہواری، حیض **menstruate** (-troo-) *v.i* discharge the menses ماہواری ہونا، حیض ہونا **menstruation** (*-ay-*) *n.* discharging the menses ماہواری ہونا، حیض آنا **menopause** (*men*-o-pawz) *n.* final cessation of menses سن یاس، حیض کی دائمی بندش

mensuration (mens-ew-ray-shĕn) *n.* branch of mathematics dealing with measurements ساحت، علم المساحت

-ment *suf.* (making nouns that show) condition of being ی، ت، یت (as *improvement* بہتری)

mental (*ment*-ĕl) *adj.* pertaining to the mind دماغی، ذہنی، نفسی، نفسیاتی *mental patient,* person suffering from diseased mind پاگل، دماغی مریض، نفسیاتی مریض *mental hospital,* place where mental patients are cared for پاگل خانہ، دماغی امراض کا شفاخانہ **mentally** (*ment*-a-li) *adv.* ذہنی طور پر

mentality (*-tal-*) *n.* (one's) general attitude of mind ذہنیت *good* (or *bad*) *mentality* اچھی (یا بُری) ذہنیت

menthol (*menth*-ol) *n.* camphor obtained from oil of peppermint ست پودینہ

mention (*men*-shun) *v.t.* speak or write something about کا ذکر کرنا take the name of کا نام لینا *n.* mentioning ذکر، نام لینا

mentor (*ment*-ĕ*) *n.* experienced and wise adviser (*to* an inexperienced person) تجربہ کار ناصح، ناصح مشفق (*Mentor*), *Cl. myth.* tutor of Odysseus's son, Telemachus مَنتَر

menu (*men*-ew, or *men*-oo) *n.* list of food to be served مینو، طعام نامہ

Mephistopheles me-fis-*tof*-e-leez *n.* one of the fallen archangels who became a mediaeval devil میفسٹافلیز

mercantile (*mè**-kan-til) *adj.* of trade and merchants تجارتی *mercantile marine,* merchant vessels (of a country) and their crew کسی ملک کے تجارتی جہاز، تجارتی بیڑا

mercenary (*mĕ**-si-na-ri) *n.* & *adj.* (soldier) fighting for money بھاڑے کا سپاہی (anyone) working merely for money محض پیسے کے لالچ میں کام کرنے والا *mercenary motives,* محض پیسے کا لالچ

mercer (*mĕ*-sĕ**) *n.* dealer in silk, velvet, etc. ریشم مخمل وغیرہ بیچنے والا **mercery** (-ri) *n.* goods of a mercer ریشم مخمل وغیرہ mercer's trade ریشم مخمل وغیرہ کی دُکان (یا کاروبار)

merchandise (*mĕ**-chan-dīz) *n.* trade wares تجارتی مال ، مالِ تجارت

merchant (*mĕ**-chant) *n.* one doing wholesale or import and export business تھوک کا بیوپاری ، درآمد برآمد کا کاروبار کرنے والا *merchant service,* mercantile marine تجارتی جہاز اور اُن کا عملہ *adj.* fond of کا شائق ، موٹر تیز چلانے کا شوقین *speed merchant* شوقین ، کا دِلدادہ **merchantman** *n.* **merchantship** *n.* a ship of the mercantile marine تجارتی جہاز

merciful *adj.* **merciless** *adj.* (see under **mercy**)

mercury (*mĕ**-kew-ri) *n.* a silver-coloured liquid metal پارہ ، سیماب (*Mercury*), a planet عطارُد (*Mercury*), *Cl. myth.* Roman god of commerce identified with the Greek *Hermes* مرکری ، عطارُد

mercurial (mĕ*-*kew*-ri-ĕl) *adj.* pertaining to mercury پارے کا ، سیمابی lively temperament زندہ دِل ، شگفتہ مزاج

mercy (*mĕ**-si) *n.* pity رَحم *have mercy (on)* (پر) رَحم کرنا quality of being forgiving عفو ، درگزر *show mercy (to),* refrain from punishing him (کو) مُعاف کرنا ، (سے) درگزر کرنا *(be) at the mercy of,* (be) in the power of (someone who can but may not punish) کے رَحم وکرم پر ہونا *(be) left to the tender mercies of,* exposed to the cruelties of کی سختیاں جھیلنا favour (*of* God) کا رَحم وکرم piece of good fortune خوش قسمتی **merciful** *adj.* full of mercy ; kind, compassionate رَحم کرنے والا ، مہربان ، رحیم وکریم **merciless** *adj.* cruel ظالم ، ستم گر ، جفاجو ، جفاکار ، جفا شعار ، ستم شعار ، جفا پرور **mercy killing** *n.* (see *Addenda*)

mere (*mee-ĕ**) *adj.* only محض ، صِرف ، نِرا *a mere fool* نِرا احمق *a mere folly* نِری حماقت **merely** *adv.* only صِرف ، محض ، نِرا

[2]**mere** (mee-ĕ*) *n.* (poet.) lake جھیل

meretricious (me-ret-*rish*-us) *adj.* as of prostitutes طوائفوں کا سا (of style, ornament, etc.) tawdry ; showy but valueless محض ظاہری چمک دمک والا

merge (mĕ*j) *v. t.* & *i.* (of two things, esp. companies) unite (*with* each other) اِنضمام ہونا یا عمل میں لانا (esp. of two companies) become united مُتّحد ہونا (of one thing) be absorbed (*into* bigger thing) میں مُدغم ہونا **merger** (*me**-jĕ*) *n.* uniting (*with* or *into*) (سے) اِنضمام ، (میں) اِدغام

meridian (me-*rid*-i-an) *n.* any line of longitude running round the world خطِ نصف النہار highest point reached by a heavenly body as looked at from the earth سُورج یا ستارے کا عُروج ، نقطۂ اَوج کمال ، اِنتہائے کمال ، مُنتہائے کمال acme عُروج

merino (me-*ree*-noh) *n.* a kind of sheep مرینو بھیڑ cloth or yarn made from its wool مرینا

merit (*me*-rit) *n.* excellence خوبی ، وصف (*pl.*) what is deserved (usu. as reward ; rarely as punishment) حق ، اِستحقاق *v. t.* **meritorious** *adj.* praiseworthy (person, action, service, etc.) قابلِ تعریف ، قابلِ ستائش ، ستودہ

Merlin (*mĕ**-lin) *Brit. leg.* the famous enchanter in the Arthurian legend مرلن

mermaid (mĕ-mayd) *n. fem.* pretty sea-woman with the tail of a fish instead of legs جل پری **merman** *n. masc.* such a man جل دیوتا ، جل مانس

merry (*me*-ri) *adj.* cheerful خوش ، خرم ، خوش وخرم ، شادان فرحاں *make merry,* hold festival خوشی منانا ، خوشی کی دعوت کرنا ، جشن کرنا یا منانا **merrily** *adv.* cheerfully خوشی سے ، شادمانی سے **merriment** *n.* cheerfulness ; joy خوشی ، جشن ، جشن ، مُسرت **merry-making** *n.* festivity خوشی مُسرت **merry-go-round** *n.* revolving circle of seats (usu. with wooden horses, etc.) for children to sit on in a fair ground اُفقی جھولا ، متوازی چرخ چرخی

a merry-go-round

mesalliance *n.* marriage with one (usu. woman) of lower status بے جوڑ شادی ، ذلیل جگہ شادی

mesdames *n.* (pl. of **madame,** which see)

mesdemoiselles *n.* (pl. of **mademoiselle** which see)

meseems (mè-*seemz*) (old use) it seems to me مجھے یُوں محسوس ہوتا ہے جیسے **meseemed** (mè-seemd) (old use) it seemed to me مجھے یُوں محسوس ہوتا تھا جیسے

mesh *n.* one of the open spaces in a net پھندا (*pl.*) net جال snare جال ، پھندا *v. t.* & *i.* catch in net جال میں پھانسنا ، پھندے میں پھانسنا (of toothed wheels) interlock (دندانے دار) چرخیوں یا پہیوں کا جڑنا ، جُڑی ہوئی چرخیاں) *in mesh* (جُڑی ہوئی (چرخیاں) اٹک جانا

mesmerism (*mes*-me-rizm) *n.* hypnotic condition produced in a person by the exercise of will power اثر پزیر تنویمی حالت ، مسمریزم کا اثر power to induce hypnotic sleep مسمریزم ، تنویم ، تنویمی **mesmerize** (-rīz-) *v.t.* exercise mesmerism on (someone)

mesne (meen) *adj.* (in law) intermediate درمیانی

meson (*mes*-on, or *mee*-son) *n.* fundamental particle forming with others the field between

protons and neutrons in the nucleus of an atom مِیزَن ، وُسطانی برقیہ، (برقی) واسطہ
mess (mes) *n.* disorderly or untidy condition اَبتری، بے ترتیبی، گندگی *make a mess of (something)*, bungle, mismanage کو بگاڑ دینا، الٹا، کاستیاناس کرنا *get into mess* خواہ مخواہ کی مصیبت میں پڑنا group of persons taking meals together کھانے کے مشترکہ انتظام والی ٹولی، ساتھ مل کر کھانے والے place where such arrangements are made میس، مسکوٹ such meals مشترکہ انتظام کا کھانا (old use) portion of food (کسی کے) حصے کا کھانا *mess of pottage*, material gain for which something higher is sacrificed دُنیٰوی اغراض، اپنا حلوا مانڈہ *v.t.* & *i.* spoil (something *up*) چوپٹ کرنا، کاستیاناس کرنا *mess about*, appear to be very busy without accomplishing any work کام میں گڑبڑ کرنا، یونہی گڑبڑ کرتے پھرنا eat meals in a mess مسکوٹ میں کھانا، میس میں کھانا، مشترکہ انتظام کے تحت کھانا *messing allowance*, money for such meals کھانے کا الاؤنس
message (*mes*-ij) *n.* piece of news sent (*from* someone *to* another) پیغام، سندیسہ **messenger** *n.* person carrying a message پیغام رساں، قاصد، پیغامبر
Messiah (me-*si*-ah) *n.* deliverer expected by the Jews and the followers of certain other religions مسیح، نجات دہندہ، منجی Jesus Christ (according to the Christians) حضرت عیسیٰ ، مسیح
Messrs (*mes*-ĕ*z) pl. of Mr. جناب، صاحبان *Messrs Manzur Qadir and Bhutto* منظور قادر اور بھٹو صاحبان title used before a firm's name جناب (یا کوئی ترجمہ نہیں) *Messrs. Kitabistan Publishing Co.* کتابستان پبلشنگ کمپنی
met *v.* (*pa. t.* & *pa. p.* of **meet,** which see)
meta- (met-a) *pref.* beyond ماوَرا، مابعد
metal (*met*-ĕl) *n.* the division of chemical substances including iron, gold, etc. دھات، فلز *road metal*, broken stone used for road-making سڑک کے لیے کوٹے ہوئے پتھر **metallic** (me-*tal*-ik) *adj.* of or like metal دھات کا سا، فلزاتی **metallurgy** (*met*-a-lĕ*ji) *n.* art of separating metal from ore and of working metal دھات صاف کرنے کا کام
metamorphosis (met-a-*mo**-fo-sis) *n.* radical change of form تبدیلِ ہیئت such change of character تبدیلی، تغیر
metaphor (*met*-a-fĕ*) *n.* words used to indicate something different from their literal meaning استعارہ such use استعارہ **metaphorical** (-*fo*-) *adj.* (of use, etc.) of or containing a metaphor استعارے والا
metaphysics (met-a-*fiz*-iks) *n.* branch of philosophy dealing with facts lying beyond physical things مابعد الطبیعیات، الٰہیات (colloq mere theory بڑی لفاظی، خالی خولی باتیں **metaphysical** *adj.* pertaining to metaphysics مابعد الطبیعیاتی، الٰہیاتی
mete (meet) *v.t.* only in the phrase : *mete out* award punishment or prize, etc. دینا
metempsychosis (met-am-si-koh-sis) *n.* pl. *metempsychoses* pr. -seez) migration of soul at death into a new body تناسخ، آواگون
meteor (*mee*-te-o*) *n.* shooting star شہاب ثاقب **meteoric** (meet-te-*o*-rik) *adj.* bright and swift like a meteor شہابی، روشن، تاباں of rise to fame, etc.) great, sudden but unlasting چار دن کی چاندنی کی طرح، گھڑی بھر کا، فروغ شعلۂ خس کی طرح **meteorite** *n.* meteor falling on earth حجرِ شہابی، شہابیہ
meteorology (mee-te-o-*rol*-o-ji *n.* art of weather prediction موسمی پیشین گوئی کا فن، موسمیات **meteorological** (mee-te-o-ro-*loj*-i-kel *adj.* of the weather موسمیاتی *meteorological office*, weather office دفتر موسمیات
meter (*mee*-tĕ*) *n.* measuring apparatus (esp. for electric current, water, etc.) which passes through it میٹر، آلۂ پیمائش (in compounds) پیما (as *water-meter* آب پیما *barometer* بادپیما، ہواپیما
method (*meth*-ud) *n.* way of doing something طریق کار، طریقہ orderliness انتظام، سلیقہ، کام کرنے کا قاعدہ **methodical** thod-) *adj.* following or done with a method باقاعدہ طریقے کے مطابق **methodically** *adj.* according to a method باقاعدہ
Methodism (*meth*-o-dizm) *n.* Christian sect started by John Wesley (1703—1791) and noted for the strictness of its discipline میتھوڈزم **Methodist** (-dist) *adj.* & *n.* (person) belonging to this sect میتھوڈسٹ
methought (see under **methinks**)
methyl (*meth*-il) *n.* a kind of wood spirit میتھل، میتِل **methylated spirit** *n.* alcohol made unpalatable with methyl and used for heating and lighting میتھلیٹڈ سپرٹ، میتلی شراب، غیر مشروبی شراب
meticulous (me-*tik*-ew-lus) *adj.* paying much attention to details باریک بیں extreme (*care*) بے حد (احتیاط)
metier (*met*-yay) *n.* special field, etc., in which one is skilled کا فن، کا خاص میدان
metonymy (me-*lon*-i-mi) *n.* substitution of
metre (*mee*-tĕ*) *n.* unit of length in the metric system (equal to 39·37 inches) میٹر verse rhythm وزن one of its various forms بحر **metric** *adj.* pertaining to a metre

میٹری، میٹر سے متعلق *metric system*, decimal measuring system (developed from a metre) اعشاری نظام، میٹری پیمانے **metrical** (*met*-ri-kĕl) *adj*. in verse rhythm موزوں in verse rhythm بحر میں of measurement پیمائش سے متعلق

metropolis (met-*rop*-o-lis) *n*. chief city of a country کسی ملک کا بڑا شہر، عروس البلاد **metropolitan** (-*pol*-) *adj*. of a metropolis ملک کے بڑے شہر، عروس البلاد سے متعلق belonging to or forming part of the mother-country (as opposed to its colonies) اصلی وطن کا، عروس البلاد کا *n*. *the Metropolitan* (*of*), the archbishop (of a province) اُسقفِ اعظم، بڑا لاٹ پادری

mettle (*met*-el) *n*. courage, pluck and endurance (of a horse or person) دم خم، دلیری، ہمت، حوصلہ *put* (*someone*) *on* (*his*) *mettle*, test (his) quality to do his best کی ہمت کا امتحان کرنا (*be*) *on* (*one's*) *mettle* دم خم سے ہونا، پوری جرأت و جانفشانی دکھانا **mettlesome** (*met*-ĕl-sum), **mettled** (*met*-ĕld) *adj*. high-spirited دم خم والا، حوصلے والا، جرأت و ہمت والا

mew *n*. (poet.) gull مرغابی (*pl*. used as sing.) (*mews*), square with stables and shelters for coaches طویلوں والا احاطہ cage for hawks باز کا پنجرہ (also *mewl, mule, miaow*), cry of a cat میاؤں میاؤں *v.t.* & *i*. (of a hawk) moult پر جھاڑنا کریز کرنا shut up (hawk) in mew پنجرے میں بند کرنا shut (*up* in school, office, prison, etc.) میں زیادہ دیر روکے رکھنا (also *mewl, mule* or *miaow*) (of a cat) cry میاؤں میاؤں کرنا

mezzanine (*mez*-a-neen) *n*. low storey between two others in the form of a gallery گیلری *adj*. pertaining to it گیلری کا

miasma (mi-*az*-ma) *n*. noxious exhalation from marshes, putrid matter, etc. بدبو کے بھپارے

mica (*mī*-ka) *n*. mineral that can easily be split up into very thin transparent layers ابرق *mica-slate* ابرق کا پرت

mice (mīs) *n*. (*pl*. of **mouse,** which see)

Michaelmas (*mik*-ĕl-mas) *n*. St. Michael's festival on Sept. 29 میلہ میکال

micro- (*mīk*-roh) *pref*. very small, minute بہت چھوٹا خورد، مصغر، اصغر (as *microscope* خوردبین، خوردبیں)

microbe (*mī*-krohb) *n*. sorts of tiny germs for fermentation جرثومہ

micro-film *n*. photographic reproduction (of documents, etc.) on a very small film مصغر فلم *v.t.* reproduce (document, etc.) thus کا مصغر فلم لینا

micron (*mīk*-ron) *n*. one-millionth of a metre میٹر کا دس لاکھواں حصہ، خوردمیٹر

microphone (*mīk*-ro-fohn) *n*. (abbr. *mike*) loud-speaker خردشنو، آوازرساں

microscope (*mīk*-ros-kohp) *n*. instrument for magnifying the image of tiny near objects through lenses خوردبین **microscopic** (-*kop*-) *adj*. so tiny that the naked eye cannot see it بہت ہی چھوٹا خورد بینی

a microscope

microwave (mik-ro-wayv) *n*. electro-magnetic wave of length less than half a metre ایک سے آدھ میٹر کی برقی رو، خوردرو

mid *adj*. the middle of کے بیچ، کا درمیان، کا وسط *pref*. (old use) among, amidst میں، بے درمیان *mid-July* وسط جولائی *in mid-air*, high above the ground فضا میں اونچا **midday** *n*. noon دوپہر *adj*. of about the middle of the day دوپہر کا **the Midlands** *n. pl*. England's central counties برطانیہ کے وسطی اضلاع **midmost** *adj*. in the exact middle ٹھیک درمیانی **midnight** *n*. 12 o'clock at night رات کے بارہ بجے، نصف شب *adj*. of about the middle of the night آدھی رات کے وقت، نصف شب **midsummer-day,** June 24 یوم وسط گرما، ۲۴ جون **midway** *adv*. half-way آدھی راہ (میں) **midsummer** *n*. middle of summer وسط گرما، سخت گرمی *midsummer night* وسط گرما کی رات *midsummer madness*, utter madness سخت پاگل پن *midsummer night's dream*, a mad dream دیوانوں کا سا خواب **midwinter** *n*. middle part of winter وسط سرما، سردیوں کا درمیانی حصہ

Midas (*mī*-das) *Cl. myth*. a king who had to return his power of changing into gold everything he touched because he found that he could not even eat his food. Later Apollo gave him ass's ears as he had judged against him in favour of Pan میڈاس

midden (*mid*-ĕn) *n*. heap of rubbish کوڑی dunghill گھوڑا

middle (*mid*-ĕl) *n*. point half-way between two given ones کے درمیان میں، کے وسط میں *in the middle of* وسط میں، نصف میں، متوسط *adj*. half-way between وسطی *middle school*, school between those of primary and high standard مڈل سکول *middle school examination*, final examination of this stage مڈل **middle age** *n*. period of life between youth and old age ادھیڑ عمر **middle-aged** (-ayjd) of middle age ادھیڑ عمر کا **Middle Ages** *n*. (also *Dark Ages, Mediaeval period*, or *Medieval period*, (*the*) period of history from the eleventh to the fifteenth century ; (*The*) Dark Ages of European history قرون وسطیٰ، قرون مظلمہ **middlebrow** *n*. & *adj*. (see *Addenda*) **middle class, middle classes**

n. those between the richest and the poorest classes of society دَرمیانی طبقہ، مُتوَسّط طبقہ *the upper middle class* اُوپر کا دَرمیانی طبقہ، خُوشحال دَرمیانی طبقہ *the lower middle class* نِچلا مُتوَسّط طبقہ، غریب مُتوَسّط طبقہ **middle watch** *n*. (on ships) period from midnight to 4 a.m. رات کا آخری پہر **middleman** *n*. businessman (as forming one of the links between the producer and the consumer) تاجر، دُکان دار **middling** *adj*. of medium size, quality, etc. دَرمیانے دَرجے کا

midget (*mij*-et) *n*. extremely dwarfish person بالکل ہی بَونا tiny thing بہت ہی چھوٹی چیز

midshipman (*mid*-) *n*. (abbr. *middy*) young junior naval officer under training جہاز کا نوجوان زیرِ تربیت افسر

midst *n*. middle دَرمیان، دَوران، بیچ *in the midst of*, (*a*) in the middle of (a place) کے بیچ میں (*b*) while occupied with دَوران میں *in our midst*, among us ہم میں، ہمارے اَندر *prep*. (lit.) in the middle of کے بیچ میں among میں

midwife (*mid*-wīf) *n*. (pl. *midwives*) trained woman helper of one in childbirth دایہ، قابلہ **midwifery** (*mid*-wif-ri or *mid*-if-ri) *n*. midwife's profession دایہ گیری، دایہ گری، قابلہ گری

mien (meen) *n*. (literary) manner and appearance وَضع قطع، چال ڈھال

might (mīt) (past t. of *may*, which see) *n*. great strength بڑا زور، بڑی طاقت **mighty** (*mī*-ti) *adj*. of great power بڑا زور آور، بہت طاقتور huge دیو ہیکل، دیو ہیکل *adv*. (colloq.) very بہت

migrate (*mī*g-rayt) *v.i.* (of person) go (*from* one place *to* another) to make a new home ترکِ وَطن کرنا، نقلِ وَطن کرنا، ہجرت کر جانا (of fishes and birds) come and go regularly with the seasons (مچھلیوں اور پرندوں کا) گرمیوں میں سرد اور سردیوں میں گرم علاقے کو چلے جانا۔ **migrant** (*mī*g-) *n*. & *adj*. migrating (person, bird or fish) نقلِ مکانی کرنے والا **migratory** (mi-*grayt*-) *adj*. migrating نقلِ مکانی، ہجرت **migration** (mi-*gray*-) *n*. act of migrating

mikado (mi-*kah*-doh) *n*. (pl. *mikados*) Emperor of Japan شہنشاہِ جاپان، میکاڈو، میکادو

mike (mīk) *n*. (colloq.) (abb. of **microphone**, which see)

milch (milch or milsh) *adj*. (of cow, cattle, etc.) yielding milk دُودھ دینے والی

mild (mīld) *adj*. gentle نرم، شریف (of weather, punishment, etc.) not rigorous ہلکا (of food, drink, tobacco) not strong ہلکا **mildly** (*mīld*-li) *adv*. نرمی سے **mildness** (*mīld*-nes) *n*. being mild نرمی، شرافت، ہلکا ہونا

mildew (*mil*-dew) *n*. fluffy growth of tiny fungi on damp things in warm wet weather it is usually destructive, but strange as it may seem the much used anti-biotic, penicillin was discovered by Sir Alexander Fleming in this very thing پھپھوندی

mile (mīl) *n*. distance measure equal to 1,760 yards میل **milage, mileage** (*mī*-lij) *n*. distance travelled in miles مسافت (میلوں میں) expenditure or allowance per mile فی میل خرچ یا بھتّہ

milestone (*mīl*-stohn) *n*. roadside stonemark for distance in miles میل کا نشان، سنگِ میل landmark (*in* history, or *in* the progress of some thing) نشانِ ترقی، سنگِ میل

NEW DELHI 25 MILES

a milestone

milieu (*meel*-i-oo) *n*. social environment مُعاشرتی ماحول

militancy (*mil*-i-tans-i) *n*. exaltation of (esp. military) force or reliance on it (فوجی) طاقت کا زعم (یا پر بھروسا) **militant** (*mil*-) *n*. & *adj*. combative (person) جھگڑالو، مُخاصِم، جنگ جُو *Church militant* (in Christianity) Christians on earth زِندہ عیسائی، کلیسائے نبرد آزما

military (*mil*-i-tè-ri) *adj*. of or for soldiers or army فوجی *the military* فوج of or for war in land زمینی جنگ کا یا کے لیے **militarism** (-rizm) *n*. reliance upon military strength فوجی طاقت پر بھروسہ

militate (*mil*-i-tayt) *v. i.* be an influence (*against*) کی مُخالفت کرنا، پر مُخالف اثر ڈالنا

militia (mi-*lish*-i-a) *n*. civilian army as an irregular force ملیشیا، بے قاعدہ فوج

milk *n*. white fluid produced by the females of some types of animals for suckling their young دُودھ، شیر this fluid (of cows, etc.) used as human food دُودھ any fluid like that دُودھ *cry over spilt milk*, grieve for what cannot be undone ایسی چیز پر رونا جس کا کوئی علاج نہیں ہے *It is no use crying over spilt milk* اب پچھتائے کیا ہوت جب چڑیاں چُگ گئیں کھیت *milk for babes*, simplified thing آسان بنائی ہوئی چیز *land flowing with milk and honey*, very prosperous country بہت خُوشحال مُلک *milk and honey* سامانِ عیش کی فراوانی *condensed milk* گاڑھا کیے ڈبے میں بند کیا ہوا دُودھ *milk powder* دُودھ کا سفوف *v. t.* draw the milk from (a cow, etc.) کا دُودھ دُوہنا **milk bar** *n*. (see *Addenda*) **milkmaid** *n* dairy woman گوالن **milkman** *n* man who delivers milk to the customers گوالا، دُودھ والا **milksop** *n* unmanly man زنانہ soft, spiritless youth بودا لڑکا **milktooth** *n*. one of the first set of teeth دُودھ کے دانت **milky** (*mil*-ki) *adj.* like milk دُودھیا *the Milky Way*, galaxy کہکشاں

[1]**mill** (mil) *n.* machinery for grinding grain into flour چکّی building in which it is housed چکّی *flour mill* آٹا پیسنے کی چکّی ، آٹے کا کارخانہ *watermill*, mill operated by water current پَن چکّی *windmill*, mill operated by big sails which are set in motion by the wind پَوَن چکّی factory کارخانہ *textile mill* کپڑے کا کارخانہ small machine for grinding anything چکّی *go through the mill*, undergo (rigorous) training سخت تربیت حاصل کرنا (U.S.) 1/1000 of a dollar (*i.e.*, 1/10 of a cent) ڈالر کا ہزارواں حصّہ *v. t. & i.* put through a machine for grinding پیسنا *mill grain, mill flour* آٹا پیسنا cross with regular cuts کنارے کٹاؤ دار بنانا ، کنارے پر خط ڈالنا *milled edge of a coin*, fluted edges (as of a rupee) سکّے کا کٹاؤ دار کنارا (of crowd) move round and round in a confused way بھیڑ میں لوگوں کا وہیں اِدھر اُدھر چلتے رہنا *the milling crowd*, thick crowd of people moving thus وہیں اُلٹتی ہوئی بھیڑ **millstone** *n.* either of the two round stones between which grain is ground چکّی کا پاٹ **miller** (*mil*-ĕ*) *n.* man who owns or works a flour mill آٹا پیسنے والا ، چکّی والا

[2]**mill-** *pref.* thousand ہزار

millennium (mi-*len*-i-um) *n.* period of one thousand years ہزار سال ، ہزار سالہ مُدّت wished-for future of justice and happiness for everyone during the predicted 1,000 years reign of Christ on earth according to Christianity عیسائیوں کے نزدیک مسیح کے آنے والے ہزار سالہ دورِ حکومت میں عالمی و انفرادی عدل و اَمن۔

millet (*mil*-et) *n.* a kind of corn باجرہ

milli- (mil-i) *pref.* one-thousandth part of کا ہزارواں حصّہ (a) *millimeter*, ملی میٹر ، گرام کا ہزارواں حصّہ *milligramme*

milliard (mil-ya*d) *n.* one thousand million

milliner (*mil*-i-nĕ*) *n.* person who makes or sells women's hats زنانہ ٹوپیوں والی (یا والا) **millinery** *n.* women's hats زنانہ ٹوپیاں their manufacture زنانہ ٹوپیوں کی ساخت (shop for) their sale زنانہ ٹوپیوں کی دُکان (یا کاروبار) things needed for them زنانہ ٹوپیوں کے مُتعلّقات

million (*mil*-yun) *n.* hundred thousand دس لاکھ ، ملین **millionaire** (*mil*-yĕ-nay-ĕ*) *n.* very wealthy person لکھ پتی **multimillionaire** (mul-ti-) *n.* extremely rich person کروڑ پتی **millionth** (-yunth) *adj.* دس لاکھواں حصّہ

milor, milord (mi-loh*d) *n.* (French word for) titled or rich Englishman نوّاب صاحب ، سَرکار

mimeograph (*mim*-i-o-grahf) *n.* stencil duplicator نقل نویس مشین *v. t.* make copies نقل نویس مشین پر نقلیں نکلنا یا نکالنا

mimic (mim-ik) *adj.* imitated for amusement جھوٹ مُوٹ ، جھوٹ مُوٹ کا *mimic warfare* جھوٹ موٹ کی لڑائی *n.* person imitating others سوانگ بھرنے والا *v. t.* (*mimicked, mimicking*), imitate for causing amusement کا سوانگ بھرنا (of things) resembled much بڑی مُشابہت ہونا **mimicry** (*mim*-ik-ri) *n.* mimicking سُوانگ ، نقّالی

minaret (*min*-a-ret) *n.* tower of a mosque مِنارہ ، مسجد کا مِنارہ یا مِنار *the call of the minaret*, the Muslim call for prayers اَذان ، بانگِ صلوٰۃ

mince (mins) *v. t. & i.* cut up (meat, etc.) into very small pieces قیمہ کرنا speak with affected precision تکلّف سے باتیں کرنا ، چبا چبا کر باتیں کرنا *not (to) mince matters*, speak bluntly کھری بات کہہ دینا ، کھری کھری سُنا دینا walk with affectedly short steps تکلّف سے قدم اُٹھانا *n.* minced meat قیمہ

mind (mīnd) *n.* consciousness ; thinking part of a person نفس ، شعور intellect ذہن *have a keen mind* بہت ذہین ہونا opinion رائے ، دِلی خیالات *give (someone) a piece of (one's) mind*, scold him (کسی) جھاڑ جھپاڑ کرنا *speak (one's) mind*, express (one's) opinion bluntly کھری کھری سُنا دینا *be of one mind*, (of two or more persons) agree مُتّفق ہونا *I am of your mind* مَیں آپ سے مُتّفق ہوں *be to (one's) mind*, have (his) approval کو پسند ہونا *to my mind*, in my opinion میری رائے میں faculty of remembering *bear (something) in mind, keep (something) in mind*, remember (it) (کوئی چیز) یاد رکھنا *bring (something) to mind, call (something) to mind*, recall (it) یاد کرنا *put (someone) in mind of (something)*, remind (him) of (it) کو یاد دِلانا *pass out of mind*, be forgotten بھُول جانا intention, purpose اِرادہ ، مقصد *make up (one's) mind*, resolve فیصلہ کرنا ، اِرادہ کرنا *change (one's) mind*, change (one's) intention اِرادہ بدل لینا *be in two minds (about something)*, hesitate دُبدھے میں ہونا ، تذبذب میں ہونا *have half a mind to*, be half persuaded to کا کچھ اِرادہ ہی ہو جانا *have a good mind to*, be almost persuaded to (کرنے) کا اِرادہ ہونا *give (one's) mind to*, concentrate attention or endeavour on پر توجّہ یا سعی مرکوز کرنا *turn (one's) mind off (something)*, turn (one's) attention from (it) سے توجّہ ہٹانا way of thinking سوچنے کا انداز *frame of mind, state of mind*, mood موڈ ، مزاج power to reason قوّتِ استدلال *presence of mind*, ability to decide or act quickly when faced with danger ہوشمندی *(be) out of (one's) mind*, (be) mad

(پاگل ہونا) mental capacity ذہنی صلاحیّت person endowed with عظیم ذہنی صلاحیّت take care of (baby, one's business, etc.) کی نگہداشت کرنا *Mind your own business* : do not meddle with the affairs of others خواہ مخواہ دخل درمعقولات نہ کرو watch سے بچنا، سے بچ کر گزرنا *Mind the wire*, watch the wire, take care not to stumble over it تار سے بچ کر *Mind you*, be careful یاد رکھنا، یاد رکھو object to (doing or someone's doing something) بُرا ماننا *I hope you won't mind it* اُمید ہے آپ بُرا نہیں مانیں گے *You don't mind smoking, Do you mind smoking?* آپ سگریٹ پینے سے بُرا تو نہیں مانتے؟ *Would you mind (doing something)?* please do it ازرہِ کرم یہ کام کر دیجیے **mindful** *adj.* thoughtful (*of*) دکا، خیال رکھنے والا **mindless** *adj.* not attentive or thoughtful (*of*) کی طرف توجّہ نہ کرنے والا، سے بے پروا

mine (min) *n.* hole dug out in the earth to extract minerals, etc. کان، مَعدَن source (*of* information, etc.) خزانہ، مَعدَن، منبع، مخزن charge of high explosive underground tunnel for it سُرنگ high explosive in metal case for use in or on the sea بحری سُرنگ *lay mines* سُرنگیں بچھانا *sweep mines* سُرنگیں ہٹانا یا صاف کرنا (also *land mine*) similar case for dropping on land from the air زمینی سُرنگ *pron.* (possessive case of *I*, which see) میرا *v.t. & i.* dig out (minerals, etc.) from the ground کان سے نکالنا dig out from ground thus کان کنی کرنا put explosive mines in میں سُرنگ بچھانا destroy thus سُرنگ سے اُڑا دینا (also *undermine*) make holes or tunnels under کے نیچے سُرنگیں نکالنا *undermine*, (*a*) کے نیچے سُرنگیں نکالنا (*b*) weaken secretly اندر ہی اندر تباہ کرنا **minefield** (*mīn*-feeld) *n.* area where there are many mines کان کنی کا علاقہ، کانوں والا علاقہ area where a network of mines has been laid جہاں سُرنگوں کا جال بچھا ہو **mine-layer** *n.* ship for laying mines سُرنگیں بچھانے والا جہاز **minesweeper** *n.* one sweeping them سُرنگیں ہٹانے یا صاف کرنے والا جہاز **miner** (*mē*-nĕ*) *n.* person working in a mine کان کُن **mineral** (*min*-ĕ-rĕl) *n.* substance mined from the earth مَعدنی چیز، مَعدنیات **mineral-water** *n.* spa water مَعدنی پانی aerated water سوڈا، بوتل

a mine (sense 5)

mineral *n.* (see under **mine**)

Minerva (mi-nĕ*-va) *Cl. myth.* the Roman goddess of wisdom identified with the Greek Athena منروا، عقل کی دیوی

mingle *v.t.* & *i.* mix (*with* something) ملانا، مِلنا، کی مِلاوَٹ والا (of person) mix (*in* or *with* a crowd) (ہجوم میں) گم ہو جانا join (*in* a game) (کھیل میں) شریک ہونا join میں مِلنا، بلا جُلا ہونا *with mingled pride and tears* ملے جُلے فخر اور آنسوؤں کے ساتھ، آنسوؤں میں گھلے ہوئے فخر *mingle tears*, weep together کے ساتھ مِل کے رونا، آپس میں رونا

mingy (*min*j-i) *adj* (colloq.) mean کمینہ stingy کنجوس

miniature (*min*-i-a-chĕ*) *n.* very small picture (*of* a person) بالکل چھوٹی تصویر۔ نقشِ کوچک small scale copy of model (of something) چھوٹے پیمانے پر نمونہ، نقشِ کوچک *in miniature* چھوٹے پیمانے پر *adj.* small چھوٹا، کوچک *miniature painting*, small-sized painting popular in Persia and this country چھوٹی تصویر کشی، کوچک نقاشی

minim (*min*-im) *n.* 1/60 of a fluid drachm (usu. as a measure of liquid medicines) قطرہ (ج: قطرات)

minimum (*min*-i-mum) *adj.* least possible or least recorded کم سے کم *the minimum temperature* کم سے کم درجۂ حرارت *minimum wages*, those fixed (by law) as the minimum کم سے کم اُجرت *n.* least possible (or recorded) degree, etc. کم سے کم درجہ (وغیرہ)

minion (*min*-yun) *n.* lowest servant ادنیٰ مُلازم (man's) effeminate favourite boy لونڈا، لمڈا spoilt darling بگڑا بچہ

minister (*min*-is-tĕ*) *n.* (*Minister*) (usu. elected) head of a State department *Minister of Defence* وزیرِ دفاع *the Prime Minister* (of a country) وزیرِ اعظم *the Chief Minister* (of a province) وزیرِ اعلیٰ diplomatic representative سفیر clergyman پادری *v. i.* (*minister to*) serve (the needs of someone) کی ضرورتیں پوری کرنا help (the sick, etc.) (ہمدردی سے) کی خدمت کرنا **ministerial** (min-is-*tee*-ri-ĕl) *adj* pertaining to a Minister or Ministry وزارتی **Ministerialist** *n.* supporter of the Government party حامیِ وزارت، حکومت کا حامی of a clergyman پادری کا **ministration** (-*tray*-) *n.* rendering religious service مذہبی خدمات انجام دینا help مدد کرنا، خدمت کرنا **ministry** (*min*-is-tri) *n.* a Minister's office وزارت a State department under him وزارت the Cabinet وزارت *enter the Ministry*, become a minister وزیر بننا

Minoan (mi-*noh*-ĕn, or mi-) *adj.* of the civilization of ancient Crete (3000-1400 B. C.) اقریطی تہذیبی

minor (*mī*-nĕ*) *adj.* small or smaller (loss, gain, injury, difference, etc.) معمولی younger of two brothers چھوٹا *Wheeless minor* دو ولیس نامی بھائیوں میں سے چھوٹا *n.* (under age) نابالغ **minority** (mi-*no*-ri-ti) *n.* the being under age نابالغی (in a small national country) community with less than 50 per cent of the total population اَقلیّت *be in a minority* اَقلیّت میں smaller number of votes اَقلیّت any smaller part چھوٹا حصّہ

Minotaur (*min*-o-taw*) *Cl. myth.* half-man half-beast who exacted human sacrifices in the Labyrinth made by Daedalus for King Minos of Crete مِنوٹور، مِنوٹار

minster (*mins*-tĕ*) *n.* church belonging to a monastery خانقاہ کا گرجا (in names of some big churches) گرجا *Westminster Abbey* مَغربی گرجے کی خانقاہ

minstrel (*mins*-trèl) *n.* travelling singer or poet-cum-singer of the Middle Ages قُرونِ وُسطیٰ کا رَمتا گویّا شاعِر، مُغنّی شاعِر (poet.) poet شاعِر **minstrelsy** (-si) *n.* art of minstrels مُغنّی شاعِروں کی فنکاری، رَمتے شاعِروں کی فنکاری their poetry رَمتے شاعِروں کے گیت (یا گائی نظمیں) *border minstrelsy*, English songs of (esp. the Scottish) border سَرحَدّی گیت، سَرحَدّی منظومات

mint *n.* place where a country's coins are made ٹکسال، دارُالضَّرب place, etc., for the coining of new things ٹکسال a plant used as a flavouring ایک قسم کا پودینہ، مِنٹ *adj.* unsoiled (*condition* or *state* of books, stamps, etc.) بے داغ (حالت) *v. t.* make (coins) سِکّے ڈھالنا coin (something new) گھڑنا earn (money) رُوپیہ پَیدا کرنا

minuet (min-ew-et) *n.* a slow stately dance آہِستہ ناچ music for it آہِستہ ناچ کی گَت

minus (*mī*-nus) *prep.* less by مَنفی *Thirteen minus three is ten*, 13 − 3 = 10, تیرہ مَنفی تین برابر ہیں دَس کے *adj.* مَنفی کا، مَنفی *a minus quantity*, a quantity below zero by the stated number مَنفی مِقدار *the minus sign, the sign minus* مَنفی نشان

minute *n.* (*min*-it) one-sixtieth part of an hour مِنٹ، دَقیقہ (in) *a minute* ذرا، تھوڑی دیر میں *this minute*, immediately ابھی، فوراً *the minute that*, as soon as جُونہی (کہ) one-sixtieth part of a degree دَقیقہ (*pl.*) brief record of the proceedings of a meeting کارروائی، رُوداد *minute-book*, book in which this record is maintained رُوداد نامہ memorandum of a proposal, etc. (تجویز وغیرہ کی) یادداشت rough draft پہلا مُسوّدہ، مُسوّدہ *adj.* (mi-*newt*) very tiny رَقیق، بہت ہی چھوٹا، باریک comprising minute details تفصیلی، بالتفصیل

minutely *adv.* with great care as to all details بڑی باریک بینی سے، بڑی دِقّتِ نظر سے

miracle (*mi*-ra-kèl) *n.* marvellous act or event not explained by the laws of nature مُعجزہ any remarkable and surprising event حیرت انگیز واقعہ wonderful example (*of* a quality) کی حیرت انگیز مِثال، کا حیرت انگیز نمونہ **miraculous** (-*rak*-ew-) of the nature of a miracle مُعجزے والا، مُعجِزنما، اِعجازی wonderful حیرت انگیز، حیرت افزا، مُعجِزنما

mirage (mi-*rahzh*) *n.* image in the air of something really quite elsewhere سَراب such image in the desert making distant water appear quite near and thus deluding the thirsty traveller سَراب any illusion نظر کا دھوکا، فریبِ نظر

mire (*mī*-è*) *n.* swamp, marsh دَلدَل *v. t.* & *i.* (cause to) sink in mire دَلدَل میں پھنسنا یا پھنسانا soil in mud کیچڑ میں لتھیڑنا involve in trouble مُصیبت میں پھنسانا

mirror (*mi*-rĕ*) *n.* looking-glass آئینہ any similarly reflecting surface شیشہ، آئینہ *spherical mirror* گُردی آئینہ *plane mirror* مُسطّح آئینہ *burning mirror*, convex lens used as such آتشی آئینہ *v.t.* reflect like a mirror مُنعکس کرنا، کا آئینہ دار ہونا

mirth (mĕ*th) *n.* merriment خُوش باش ہونا، خُوش و خُرّم ہونا laughter ہنسی، قہقہے

mis- (mis) *pref.* amiss, wrongly غلط، بد، ناموزوں، نا، اَن

misadventure (mis-ad-*vench*-ĕ*) *n.* misfortune بدقسمتی event caused by it سُوئے اِتّفاق

misalliance *n.* wrong alliance ناموزوں اِتّحاد 'mesalliance' ناموزوں شادی

misanthrope (*mis*-anth-rohp) *n.* one who hates mankind مردُم بیزار **misanthropy** (mis-*anth*-ro-pi) *n.* being a misanthrope مردُم بیزاری

misapply (mis-ap-*li*) *v.t.* apply wrongly (words, funds, etc.) غلط اِستعمال کرنا **misapplication** (-*kay*-) *n.* غلط اِستعمال

misapprehend (mis-ap-re-*hend*) *v.t.* misunderstand غلط سمجھنا **misapprehension** (-*hensh*-ĕn) *n.* misunderstanding غلط فہمی

misappropriate *v.t.* embezzle خُورد بُرد کرنا **misappropriation** (-*ay*-) *n.* embezzlement خُورد بُرد

misbehave (mis-be-*hayv*) *v.i.* behave wrongly ناشائستہ حرکتیں کرنا **misbehaviour** (-i-ĕ*) *n.* misbehaving ناشائستہ حرکات

miscalculate (-*kal*-) *v.t.* calculate wrongly غلط حساب کرنا misjudge غلط اندازہ کرنا **miscalculation** (-*lay*-) *n.* غلط حساب، غلط اندازہ

miscarry (-*ka*-) *v.i.* (*miscarried*) (of plan, etc.) be unsuccessful ناکام رہنا (of plan, etc.) go wrong ٹھیک نتیجہ نہ نکلنا (of letter, goods, etc.) fail to reach addressee نہ پہنچنا (of woman) have untimely delivery کا بچہ ضائع ہو جانا، اِسقاط ہو جانا

miscarriage *n.* mistake (*of* justice) نااِنصافی، نہ پہنچنا wrong delivery (*of* letter, goods, etc.) نہ پہنچنا abortion اِسقاط

miscellaneous (mis-e-*lay*-nè-us) *adj.* assorted مُتفرّق **miscellany** (*mis*-è-lè-ni) *n.* miscellaneous collection (esp. of literary pieces) مُتفرّقات کا مجموعہ

literary miscellany, collection of various authors' writings اَدَبی مُتفرّقات کا مجموعہ، گلدستہ

mischance (mis-*chahns*) *n.* stroke of bad luck بَدقِسمتی، سُوئے اِتّفاق

mischief (*mis*-chif) *n.* purposely done damage جان بُوجھ کر پہنچایا ہُوا نقصان cause of trouble مُصیبت childish pranks شرارت light-hearted desire to tease شوخی، شرارت، چھیڑ چھاڑ کی نیّت *make mischief between*, cause ill-feeling between (persons) by spreading scandals تہمتیں دھر کے فساد ڈلوانا *be up to mischief*, *get into mischief*, شرارت کرنا *a mischievous twitch in the eye* آنکھوں میں شوخی، آنکھوں میں شرارت کی جھلک **mischievous** (*mis*-chi-vus) *adj.* fond of mischief شرارتی causing mischief شرانگیز **mischief-maker, mischief-monger** *n.* one who makes mischief فسادی، فساد ڈلوانے والا، فتنہ پرداز

misconceive (mis-kon-*seev*) *v.t.* misapprehend, misunderstand غلط سمجھنا، غلط خیال ہونا **misconception** (-*sep*-) *n.* misunderstanding غلط فہمی (*labour*) *under a misconception*، غلط فہمی میں مُبتلا (ہونا)، غلط فہمی کا شکار (ہونا)

misconduct *n.* (mis-*kon*-dukt) improper moral behaviour بداخلاقی mismanagement بدانتظامی do (something) wrongly (کام کو) بگاڑ دینا *v.t.* (-*dukt*) mismanage (a business, etc.) بدانتظامی doing (something) in a wrong way (کام کو) بگاڑنا misbehave (oneself) morally بداخلاقی کا ارتکاب کرنا

misconstrue (mis-kon-*stroo*) *v.t.* put a wrong interpretation on (someone's words, acts, etc.) سے غلط مطلب لینا، کو غلط معنی پہنانا **misconstruction** (-*struk*-) *n.* act of misconstruing غلط مطلب لینا wrong interpretation غلط مطلب، غلط تاویل

miscreant (*mis*-kre-ant) *n.* villain, scoundrel بدمعاش، بدذات، خبیث

misdeal (mis-*deel*) *v.t.* & *i.* deal (playing cards) wrongly (تاش کے پتّے) غلط بانٹنا *n.* such a mistake (تاش کے پتّے) بانٹنے میں غلطی

misdeed (mis-*deed*) *n.* wicked act خباثت crime جُرم

misdemeanour (mis-de-*mee*-nĕ*) *n.* offence less serious than felony چھوٹا جُرم

miser (*mī*-zĕ*) *n.* stingy person کنجوس، بخیل **miserly** *adj.* stingy کنجوسی کا (یا والا)، بخل کا (یا والا) **miserliness** *n.* being miserly کنجوسی، بخل

miserable (*miz*-e-rab-ĕl) *adj.* distressed, very unhappy سخت غمزدہ causing unhappiness سخت غمزدہ کرنے والا in a wretched condition سخت بُری حالت میں، بہت خراب، بہت گھٹیا **miserably** *adv.* in a miserable manner سخت بُری حالت میں، بڑے افسوسناک انداز سے

misery (*miz*-è-ri) *n.* unhappiness غم، غمزدگی wretchedness سخت بُری حالت extreme poverty سخت غربت، نکبت extreme suffering سخت تکلیف

misery *n.* (see under **miserable**)

misfire (mis-*fī*-è*) *v.i.* (of a gun) fail to go off (بندوق کا) نہ چلنا، سر نہ ہونا، رنجک چاٹ جانا (of a motor-engine) fail to start (انجن کا) نہ چلنا *n.* such a failure (بندوق یا انجن کا) نہ چلنا

misfit (*mis*-fit) *n.* garment which does not fit well چھوٹا (یا بڑا) کپڑا person not well suited to his position ناموزوں شخص

misfortune (mis-*fo**-tewn) *n.* bad luck بدقسمتی، بدنصیبی، بدبختی accident حادثہ

misgiving (-*giv*-) *n.* (usu. *pl.*) doubt شک، بے اعتمادی *have misgivings, be full of misgivings about* کے متعلق شک ہونا

misguide *v.t.* lead astray گمراہ کرنا، غلط راہ پر ڈالنا **misguided** (-*gī*-) *adj.* led into wrong action بہکانے پر غلط (کام کرنے والا) foolish احمق، احمقانہ **misguiding** *adj.* likely to mislead thus گمراہ کن

mishap (mis-*hap*) *n.* unlucky (but not serious) accident افسوسناک حادثہ

mislay (mis-*lay*) *v.t.* (*mislay, mislaid, mislaid*) lose by unintentionally putting in the wrong place کھو دینا، کہیں رکھ کر بھول جانا

mislead (mis-*leed*) *v.t.* (*mislead, misled, misled*) lead astray غلط راہ پر لگانا give a wrong idea or impression to غلط خیال دلانا cause to do wrong غلطی کرانا

misnomer (-*noh*-) *n.* wrong use of a name or term (نام یا اصطلاح کا) غلط استعمال

misogamy (mi-*sog*-a-mi), **misogyny** (mi-sog-i-ni) *n.* hatred of marriage or women شادی (یا عورت) سے نفرت **misogamist, misogynist** *adj.* شادی (یا عورت) سے نفرت کرنے والا

misplace (mis-*plays*) *v.t.* put in a wrong place غلط جگہ رکھنا lose it thus کہیں رکھ کر بھول جانا give (love, trust, etc.) wrongly غلطی سے (بھروسہ محبّت وغیرہ) کرنا

misprint *n.* (*mis*-print) a printing error طباعت کی غلطی، سہوِ کتابت *v.t.* (mis-*print*) make such an error غلط چھاپنا

misrule (mis-*rool*) *n.* bad government غلط انداز سے حکمرانی (*Abbot* or *Lord* or) *Master of Misrule* (or *of Unreason*), mediaeval title for leader of Xmas revels نامعقول نوّاب

miss (mis) *v.t.* & *i.* (*miss; missed, missed* pr.

mist) fail to hit (the thing aimed at) پڑنہ لگ سکنا fail to be in time for (train, etc.) وقت پر نہ پہنچ سکنا *miss the bus*, (a) بس پکڑ نہ سکنا (b) miss the opportunity موقع گنوانا ، موقع ہاتھ سے کھونا fail to attend (the lecture, etc.) تقریر پر وقت سے پہنچنا (لیکچر) میں شامل نہ ہو سکنا try unsuccessfully to catch (the ball, the point) پکڑ نہ سکنا ، ہاتھ نہ آنا *miss the point of a joke* لطیفے میں ہنسی کی بات کیا تھی سمجھ میں نہ آنا feel the want of ; feel great sorrow at the absence of کی کمی بُری طرح محسوس کرنا leave (something *out*) چھوڑ دینا ، سے رہ جانا *n.* very young girl, لڑکی ، چھوٹی لڑکی *the pert young misses of our schools* ہمارے یہاں کی سکولوں میں پڑھنے والی گستاخ چھوکریاں (*Miss*), title used before the name of a girl or unmarried woman مس، آنسہ *Miss Joan Smith, Miss Joan* مس جون سمتھ *the Miss Smiths, the Misses Smith* سمتھ نامی بہنیں *Miss Yasmeen* آنسہ یاسمین failure to hit, etc. بھول چوک، (نشانے کا) خطا جانا *a lucky miss*, a fortunate escape خوش قسمتی سے بچاؤ *a near miss*, (in shooting, bombing, etc.) not a hit but near enough the target to cause damage پرے ہونے کے باوجود تباہ کُن **missing** (*mis*-ing) *adj.* not found anywhere غائب، گم، لاپتہ not found in the proper place غائب *be found to be missing* معدوم ہونا کر غائب ہے *be reported missing* اطلاع ملنا کہ لاپتہ ہے *the missing link*, (esp.) supposed intermediate type between ape and man گم شدہ کڑی ، حلقۂ گم گشتہ

mis-shapen (mis-*shay*-pèn) *adj.* deformed (part of body or body) بدن (کے کسی حصے) میں خرابی والا

missing *adj.* (see under **miss**)

missile (*mis*-il or U. S. *mis*-il) *n.* anything thrown as a weapon پھینک کر مارنے والا ہتھیار، میسائل، مِسِل *inter-continental ballistic missile* جوہری منجنیق ، اَنداختہ کے ذریعے دوسرے برِاعظم پر پھینکا جانے والا میسائل ، جوہری اَنداختہ

mission *n.* party sent abroad on special purpose ایک خاص مقصد کے لیے پردیس بھیجی ہوئی جماعت ، مشن such party sent for preaching (often Christianity) مشن ، عیسائی تبلیغی جماعت their buildings, etc. مشن کی عمارات یا دفتر، تبلیغی جماعت کا دفتر work done by them مشن کا کام ، تبلیغ sending out of a mission تبلیغی (یا مخصوص) جماعت کا بھیجنا special work (*in* a person's life, or *of* his life, or *of* him *in* life) he feels himself called upon to do (کی زندگی کا) مقصد ، (کا) مقصدِ زندگی **missionary** *n.* one sent on a religious (usu. Christian) mission مشنری ، عیسائی مبلغ

missis, missus (*mis*-iz) *n.* (colloq.) (also joc.) wife بیوی، گھر والی *How is your missis ?* آپ کے گھر میں خیریت ہے؟ (servant's word for) mistress (when speaking to her) بی بی جی ، بیگم صاحبہ

mis-spent (mis-*spent*) *adj.* spent in a wrong way بے جا صَرف کیا ہُوا ، غلط طور پر صرف کیا ہُوا

missive (*mis*-iv) *n.* official letter سرکاری مراسلہ

mist *n.* mild fog دھند ، کہر **misty** (*mis*-ti) *adj.* with mist کہر آلود (of idea, etc.) دھندلا سا

mistake (mis-*tayk*) *n.* error غلطی *by mistake*, erroneously غلطی سے *make a mistake* غلطی کرنا *And no mistake !*, بلاشبہ *v. t.* & *i.* (*mistake, mistook, mistaken*) misunderstand (one's meaning, etc.) کا مطلب غلط سمجھنا take (someone or something) wrongly (*for* another) غلطی سے (کسی کو) کوئی سمجھ بیٹھنا

mistletoe (*mis*-èl-toh) *n.* evergreen plant used for Christmas decoration آکاس بیل ، امربیل

mistook *v.* (pa. t. of **mistake**, which see)

mistletoe

mistress (*mis*-tres) *n.* housewife گھر والی ، گھر کی مالکہ ، مالکن ، بی بی ، بی بی جی ، بیگم صاحبہ sweetheart محبوبہ ، معشوقہ keep woman داشتہ school teacher اُستانی، آپا جی woman well-versed in (*of*) کی ماہر

mistrust (mis-*trust*) *n.* misgivings (*about*) شک ، کے متعلق شک *v. t.* have misgiving (*about*) بے اعتمادی یا بے اعتمادی **mistrustful** *adj.* having misgivings کے متعلق شک کرنے والا ہے

misunderstand (mis-und-ĕ*-*stand*) *v. t.* fail to understand (something) properly ٹھیک نہ سمجھنا ، ٹھیک طرح نہ سمجھنا take (a *remark*, or) the remark of (*someone*) in a wrong sense کا غلط مطلب لینا ، سے غلط فہمی ہونا **misunderstanding** *n.* mistake of meaning غلط مطلب سمجھنا ill-feeling caused by it غلط فہمی

mite (mit) *n.* (old use) small coin چھوٹا سا سکہ ، دمڑی poor man's small but sincere donation غریب کا تھوڑا مگر مخلصانہ عطیہ ۔ very small child چھوٹا سا بچہ ، ننھا tiny insect چھوٹا سا کیڑا

mitigate (*mit*-i-gayt) *v. t.* lessen the severity of (pain, punishment, etc.) (تکلیف یا سزا) کو کم کرنا **mitigation** (-*gay*-) *n.* such lessening (*of*) (تکلیف یا سزا) میں کمی ، تخفیف

mitre (*mi*-tĕ*) *n.* bishop's tall cap لاٹ پادری کی ٹوپی ، کلاہِ دراز ، دراز کُلہ right-angled joint between two pieces of wood لکڑی کا قائمی جوڑ

a mitre (sense 2)

mitten (*mit*-èn) *n.* glove with (tips of) fingers bare بے انگشت دستانہ

mittimus (*mit*-i-mus) *n.* warrant for sending to prison قید خانے بھیجنے کا پروانہ ، پروانۂ جیل

mix (miks) *v. t.* & *i.* mingle or stir up (different things, people, etc.) together کو ملانا ، کا باہم ملنا *not to mix* (دو چیزوں کا) یک جان نہ ہونا prepare (something) thus مرکب تیار کرنا associate (*with*) سے میل جول رکھنا *mixed up*, confused غیر واضح ، غیر مربوط *feel* *mixed up* (*about something*), be confused کے بارے میں ٹھیک نہ سمجھنا *be mixed up* (*in* or *with politics, plot, etc.*), be involved (in it) میں اُلجھنا، میں شامل ہونا **mixer** (*mik*-sĕ*) *n.* (U. S.) (colloq.) one who mixes with people in a (*good* or *bad*) way میل جول بڑھانے میں (اچھا یا بُرا) **mixed** *adj.* of different sorts ملا جلا (*with*) *mixed feelings*, (with) quite contrasting feelings present together ملے جلے جذبات (کے ساتھ) **mixture** (*miks*-chĕ*) *n.* something prepared by the mixing of others مُرکّب *mechanical mixture* آمیزہ oil vapours mixed with air forming the explosive charge in an internal combustion engine (انجن کا) آتشگیر آمیزہ **mix-up** *n.* confusion گڑ بڑ، گڈمڈ

mizzen, mizen (*miz*-ĕn) *n.* sail of mizzen-mast سب سے پچھلے مستول کا پچھلا مربع، بادبان **mizzen-mast** *n.* mast nearest the stern سب سے پچھلا مستول

mnemonic (ne-*mon*-ik) *adj.* of the memory (حافظے کا) یا اس سے متعلق designed to aid it یاد رکھنے میں مدد دینے والا، معاون حافظہ **mnemonics** *n. pl.* such helpful system حافظے میں مدد دینے والے اصول

mo (moh) *n.* slang moment لمحہ (esp. in phrases like :) *wait half a mo* بس ایک منٹ!

moan (mohn) *n.* deep low sound of suffering کراہ *give a moan, utter moan* کراہنا *v. i.* make a moan کراہنا utter with moans کراہ کر کہنا

moat (moht) *n.* defensive ditch round a castle خندق، کھائی **moated** (-ted) *adj.* having a moat خندق دار، کھائی والا

mob *n.* disorderly crowd بھیڑ بھاڑ، ہجوم، اژدحام، اژدہام، انبوہ the masses عوام، عوام الناس *mob-rule*, mobocracy *v. t.* (-bb-) crowd round (someone) to attack پر ٹوٹ پڑنا do so for giving a loud ovation خلقت کا (کسی کے گرد) ٹوٹی پڑی ہونا **mobocracy** (-bok-) *n.* mob-rule (esp. as nickname for democracy) انبوہ گردی

mobile (*moh*-bil) *adj.* able to move or be moved easily آسانی سے منتقل ہو سکنے یا کیا جا سکنے والا easily and often changing تغیر پزیر، متلوّن **mobility** (-*bil*-) *n.* حرکت پزیری، تغیر پزیری، تحرّک **mobilize** (*mohb*-i-liz) *v.t.* collect together (troops, forces, etc.) for service in war, etc. فوجوں کو حرکت میں لانا create (public opinion *on* a point) and make an active force (کسی مسئلے پر) رائے عامہ کو بیدار کرنا **mobilization** (-*zay*-) *n.* (of troops) (فوجوں کا) اجتماع (of public opinion) creation, etc. (رائے عامہ کی) بیداری

moccasin (*mok*-a-sin) *n.* soft deerskin leather ہرن کا نرم چمڑا shoe (made from it) like that of Red Indians مکیسن

mock (mok) *v. t.* & *i.* ridicule by imitating کا مذاق اُڑانا، پر ہنسنا (کی نقالی کر کے) مذاق اُڑانا laugh (*at*) کی ہنسی اُڑانا *adj.* (of war, fight, assembly, etc.) not real, but only for fun or practice نقلی **mockingly** *adv.* in a mocking way مذاق سے **mockery** *n.* ridicule مذاق، ہنسی، اُڑانا butt of ridicule جس کا مذاق اُڑایا جائے، ہدفِ مذاق bad example (*of* justice or something else) کا منہ چڑانا

mode (mohd) *n.* style, manner, way (*of* something like dress, etc., or *of* doing something) طریقہ، انداز

model (*mod*-ĕl) *n.* small scale copy (*of* something) چھوٹا نمونہ، نمونہ design to be copied in drawing ماڈل design (*of* cars, etc., *for* particular year) ماڈل، نمونہ *Chev. 1970 model* ۱۹۷۰ کے نمونے کی شیورلٹ گاڑی، شیورلٹ ۱۹۷۰ ماڈل person or thing as an example (*of*) نمونہ، مثال person employed by artist as a model (فنکار کا) ماڈل، اصل نقش mannequin دکان پر کپڑے پہن پہن کر فیشن کے نمونے دکھانے والی ملازمہ *adj.* work imitating جیسا ہونا چاہئے ویسا ہی، نمونے کا، معیاری، قابل تقلید، مثالی *v.t.* (-ll-) shape (*in* clay, etc.) the figure of (مٹی وغیرہ سے) کسی کا مجسمہ بنانا make from a model اصل کے مطابق بنانا، جیسا بنانا *model* (*something*) *upon* کے نمونے پر بنانا، جیسا بنانا

moderate (*mod*-ĕ-rayt) *adj.* (of habits, opinion, etc.) not extreme اعتدال پسندانہ (of claim, etc.) keeping within bounds جائز، مناسب not much or large (ability, size, price, etc.) کم (of person) not extreme اعتدال پسند، نرم *n.* (esp.) one with moderate opinions in politics اعتدال پسند *v. t.* & *i.* lessen کم کرنا **moderately** *adv.* to a moderate extent مناسب حد تک **moderation** (-*ray*-) *n.* quality of being moderate (*in*) اعتدال پسندی، نرمی *in moderation*, in a moderate manner or quantity اعتدال سے

modern (*mod*-ĕ*n) *adj.* of the recent time موجودہ زمانے کا، عصر حاضر کا، جدید up-to-date تازہ ترین، نیا، جدید **modernize** (-niz) *v. t.* make suitable for present-day needs نئے تقاضوں کے مطابق بنانا **modernism** (*mod*-ĕ*-nizm) *n.* modern views نئے نظریے modern methods نئے نظریے، جدید خیالات being modern نئی روشنی (کا ہونا)، جدت پسندی (esp.) tendency to subject religious dogma to reason مذہب میں عقلیت پسندی **modernist** (*mod*-ĕ*-nist) *n.* someone with such views نئی روشنی کا شخص، متجدد (ج متجددین)

modest (*mod*-est) *adj.* not boastful ; unpretentious منکسر المزاج، انکسار والا by no means high (demand, way of living, etc.) معمولی سا not ostentatious (in dress, manners, etc.) سیدھا سادہ

chaste (woman) شریف، پاکباز، حیادار **modestly** *adv.* شرافت سے **modesty** (*mod*-es-ti) *n.* شرافت، حیا، پاکبازی، انکسار، سادگی

modicum (*mod*-i-kum) *n.* moderate amount (of food, etc.) تھوڑا سا، ادنیٰ، قلیل مقدار

modify (*mod*-i-fy) *v. t.* change (*to* make suitable or less severe) بدل کر نرم کرنا change بدلنا ترمیم کرنا **modification** (-*kay*-) *n.* act of modifying or that which modifies تبدیلی، ترمیم

Modred (*mod*-red) *Brit. leg.* King Arthur's son who rebelled against his father ; he was slain in the battle against him, but his father was also mortally wounded ماڈریڈ

modulate (*mod*-ew-layt) *v. t.* vary (the tone, etc. *from* one *to* another) بدلنا **modulation** (-ew-*lay*-) *n.* changing or change (*of* tone, etc. *from* one to another) تبدیلی

modus operandi *n.* manner of doing something طریق کار

moiety (moi-è-ti) *n.* (usu. in law) half نصف

moist *adj.* damp weather, thing, etc.) بھیگا ہوا، بھیگا سا، بھیگا بھیگا **moisten** (*mois*-èn) *v. t.* make or become moist بھگونا یا بھیگنا **moisture** (*mois*-chè*) *n.* dampness نمی، سیل small drops of liquid forming (on the surface of something) from vapour آبی قطرات

molar (*moh*-lĕ*) *n.* & *adj.* (one of the teeth) used for grinding food (ڈاڑھ، پیسنے والا (دانت)

molasses (mo-*las*-iz) *n.* drainings of raw sugar راب

mole (mohl) *n.* a rat-like animal burrowing underground, and noted for its soft fur and extremely small eyes چھچھوندر، کورموش permanent dark-coloured spot on the skin تل، خال massive stone pier or breakwater (پتھر کا بند (دریا) a mole (sense 1) مضبوطی بندگاہ **molehill** *n.* mound thrown up by a burrowing mole چھچھوندر کا ٹیلہ

molecule (*mol*-e-kewl) *n.* smallest particle (of something got without changing its chemical nature ریزہ، ذرہ، سالمہ **molecular** (mo-*lek*-ew-lĕ*) *adj.* of or pertaining to a molecule سالماتی *molecular weight* (*of a substance*), weight (of its molecule) relative to that of a hydrogen atom سالماتی وزن

molest (mo-*lest*) *v. t.* harass (a girl, etc.) intentionally جان بوجھ کے چھیڑنا **molestation** (-*lay*-) *n.* act of molesting چھیڑ چھاڑ، جان بوجھ کے چھیڑنا

mollify (*mol*-i-fi) *v. t.* calm down (person, his feelings, pain, etc.) کم کرنا

mollusc (*mol*-usk) *n.* one of a class of soft-bodied creatures with a hard crust صدف نما جانور، سنگ پشت **molluscan, molluscous** *adj.* of a mollusc صدفی

molten *adj.* (see under **melt**)

moment (*moh*-ment) *n.* point of time لمحہ وقت *not to waste a moment*, not to waste time بالکل وقت ضائع نہ کرنا *in a moment*, very soon ابھی *the moment that*, as soon as جونہی کہ *at the moment*, just now or just, then اس وقت *to the moment*, punctually بالکل وقت پر *not for a moment*, not at all ہرگز نہیں، کبھی نہیں significance اہمیت *a decision of great moment* بڑا اہم فیصلہ *of no moment*, *of little moment* غیر اہم **momentary** (*moh*-) *adj.* lasting for or done in a moment آن کی آن میں، پل بھر کا not lasting عارضی، ناپائدار **momentous** (-*ment*-us) *adj.* very important بہت اہم **momently** *adv.* every moment ہر آن، ہر لمحہ

momentum. *n.* force of a moving object زور حرکت، ہتیار حرکت *gather* (or *gain*) *momentum*, increase in force کا زور بڑھتے جانا

monacal, monachal (mon-a-kĕl) *adj.* monastic خانقاہی، رہبانی **monacism, monachism** *n.* monasticism رہبانیت

monad (*mon*-ad) *n.* number *one* as a unit ایک، اکائی *dyad* دو *triad* تین، سہ *tetrad* چار، چہار *pentad* پانچ، پنج *hexad* چھ، شش *heptad* سات، ہفت *octad* (or *ogdad*) آٹھ، ہشت *ennad* نو، نہ *decad* دس، دہ ultimate unit of being (*i.e.*, God, or soul or atom, etc.) جوہر فرد، واحدہ simple organism assumed as the first term in evolution ابتدائی جسمیہ **monadism** (-dizm) *n.* belief in some ultimate unit of being نظریۂ جوہر فرد، نظام واحدات

monarch *mon*-ĕ*k) *n.* sovereign فرمانروا، بادشاہ، شہنشاہ **monarchist** (*mon*-e*-kist) *n.* supporter of monarchy بادشاہی نظام کا حامی، ملوکیت پسند **monarchism** (-kizm) *n.* doctrine of monarchist ملوکیت پسندی **monarchy** *mon*-ĕ*-ki) *n.* government by a monarch بادشاہی، ملوکیت *constitutional* (or *limited*) *monarchy*, government by a monarch through Ministers chosen from among the people's representatives آئینی ملوکیت country with such a government بادشاہی نظام والا ملک **monarchal, monarchic, monarchical** *adj.* pertaining to monarchy ملوکیت کا (یا سے) متعلق نظام

monastery (*mon*-as-tè-ri) *n.* building for *monks* to live in عیسائی خانقاہ، دیر **monastic** (-*nas*-) *adj.* of monasteries and monks خانقاہی، خانقہی، رہبانی

Monday (*mund*-ay) *n.* day of the week following a Sunday پیر، سوموار

money (*mun*-i) *n.* currency سکہ، نوٹ، رُوپیہ **ncies** خضب، پیسہ رُوپیہ، پیسہ، دولت *earn money* رُوپیہ کمانا *make money* کمانا *lose money* (*on* a bet, *in* a business) میں روپیہ گنوانا ہارنا، دیا **money-order** *n.* remittance or receipt of money under full postal arrangement منی آرڈر *end* (*cash*) *by money-order* منی آرڈر بھیجنا **money-market** *n.* stock exchange بازار حصص their operation تجارتی حصّوں کی خرید و فروخت کا کاروبار **monetize** (*mon*-e-tiz) *v.t.* make into money کا سکّہ رائج کرنا recognize as money کا سکّہ تسلیم کرنا **monetary** *mon*-ĕ-ta-ri) *adj.* pertaining to currency نظام زر کے متعلق pertaining to money رُوپے پیسے کے متعلق **moneyed** (*mun*-id) *adj.* wealthy (classes, etc.) دولت مند، پیسے والا

monger (mong-ĕ*) *suf.* dealer in والا، فروش

mongoose (*mong*-oos) *n.* small otter-like animal noted for catching snakes نیولا

mongrel (*mung*-rel) *n.* & *adj.* (any plant or animal esp. dog) of mixed breed میل والا دوغلا، نسلی مجلی نسل کا (جانور یا پودا)

monism (*mon*-izm) *n.* any of the doctrines according to which mind and matter are just one thing وحدتِ جوہر **monist** *n.* one who holds this belief

monitor (*mon*-i-tĕ*) *n.* (fem. *monitress*) seniormost pupil of a class authorized to help teacher in maintaining discipline مانیٹر، خلیفہ one employed to listen in and report on foreign broadcasts مانیٹر، ریڈیو پر سرکاری سامع، ریڈیائی سامع **monitoring** *n.* such listening in ریڈیو پر سرکاری سامع کا کام کرنا، سامع **monitory** (*mon*-i-tĕ-ri) *adj.* threatening دھمکی والا، تہدید آمیز **monitorily** *adv.* threateningly

monk *n.* Christian vowed to lead a monastic life راہب **monkish** *adj.* (used contemptuously) (like that) of a monk راہبانہ

a monk

monkey (*munk*-i) *n.* a man-like animal بندر imitative or mischievous child شرارتی یا نقال بچہ temper مزاج *get* (*someone's*) *monkey up*, enrage (him) کسی کو طیش چڑھانا *v.i.* play mischievously (*about with* something) (کو) چھیڑنا، کو چھیڑتے پھرنا **monkey-nut** *n.* peanut, groundnut مونگ پھلی، چینیا بادام

monkish *adj.* (see under **monk**)

mono- *pref.* one ایک، واحد، یک

monochrome *n.* & *adj.* (painting) in one colour یک رنگ (تصویر)، یک رنگی تصویر

monocle (*mon*-o-kĕl) *n.* eyeglass for one eye only یک چشمی عینک

monody (*mon*-o-di) *n.* dirge or elegy نوحہ، مرثیہ (in Greek drama) ode for a single voice تنہا گانے والے کا راگ

monogamy (mo-*nog*-a-mi) *n.* marriage to only one person at a time as an institution among Christians ایک وقت میں صرف ایک سے شادی کا دستور، یک زوجگی **monogamous** (mo-*nog*-a-mus) *adj.* (of person, etc.) practising monogamy یک زوجگی کا دستور اختیار کرنے والا

monogram (*mon*-o-gram) *n.* design of overlapping initials, etc. طغرا

monograph (*mon*-o-graf) *n.* research report on a single limited subject یک موضوعی، تحقیقاتی مقالہ

monolith (*mon*-o-lith) *n.* stone in the form of a monument یک سنگی یادگار **monolithic** (-*lith*-) *adj.* pertaining to or containing a monolith یک سنگی یادگار والا دیا کے متعلق؛ *monolithic state*, (see *Addenda*)

monologue (*mon*-o-log) *n.* scene (in a play, etc.) in which only one person speaks by himself تمثیل کا فردی منظر

monopoly (mo-*nop*-o-li) *n.* sole right to supply تجارت بلاشرکت غیرے، اجارہ داری *have* (or *enjoy*) *a monopoly of*, control its production, sale, etc. کی اجارہ داری رکھنا complete possession (*of* talk, trade, privileges, etc.) (کی) اجارہ داری **monopolist** (mo-*nop*-o-list) *n.* one enjoying a monopoly (of) (کا) اجارہ دار **monopolize** (-liz) *v.t.* enjoy a monopoly of (کی) اجارہ داری رکھنا **monopolization** (-*zay*-) *n.* act of monopolizing (کی) اجارہ داری رکھنا

monosyllable (mon-o-*sil*-a-bĕl) *n.* word of one syllable ایک بول یا رکن کا لفظ **monosyllabic** *adj.* (of word) having only one syllable ایک ایک بول والا

monotheism (-*thee*-izm) *n.* belief in one God خدا تعالیٰ کی وحدانیت کا قائل ہونا، موحد ہونا، توحید **monotheist** *n.* believer in one God خدا تعالیٰ کو ایک ماننے والا، موحد

monotype *n.* machine for composing and casting type in separate letters مونو

monotony (mo-*not*-o-ni) *n.* boring lack of variety اکتا دینے والی یکسانی **monotonous** (-nus) *n.* boring owing to a lack of variety یکسانی کے باعث اکتا دینے والا

monsieur (*mus*-ew-ĕ*) *n.* (abb. *M.*) (before French names for) Mr. جناب، صاحب (when addressing a Frenchman) Sir بجناب

monsoon (mon-*soon*) *n.* (usu. *pl.*) rainbearing winds over the Indian Ocean موسمی ہوائیں، مون سون

summer monsoons گرمیوں کی موسمی ہوائیں *winter monsoons* سردیوں کی موسمی ہوائیں

monster (*mons*-tē*) *n.* horribly ugly and cruel creature بدصورت، عفریت very cruel person سخت ظالم، ننگِ انسانیت freak of nature (*e.g.*, a two-headed child or goat) عجیب الخلقت شخص

monstrosity (mons-*tros*-i-ti) *n.* deformity ننگِ انسانیت ہونا، عجیب الخلقت ہونا outrageous cruelty

monstrous (*mons*-trus) *adj.* of or like a monster ننگِ انسانیت، ظالم huge دیو پیکر، بہت بڑا (colloq.) impossible غلط، بکواس

montage (*mont*-ahzh) *n.* editing and piecing together of various shots to produce the final version of a film فلم کی تدوین، مونتاژ

month (munth) *n.* twelfth part of a year مہینہ *calendar month*, solar month شمسی مہینہ *lunar month* قمری مہینہ، چاند کا مہینہ **monthly** (*munth*-li) *adj.* & *adv.* (occurring) every month ماہانہ، ماہوار، ماہواری، ہر مہینے

monument (*mon*-ew-ment) *n.* something put up in memory (*of* person or event) یادگار outstanding work (*of* scholarship) (کے دائرے میں) یاد رہنے والا کام

monumental (-*ment*-) *adj.* of such lasting value یادگار (کارنامہ)، یاد رہنے والا (کام) very great بہت بڑا، عظیم

mood *n.* state of feelings مزاج، مزاج کی کیفیت، رنگ

moody (*moo*-di) *adj.* having changing moods متلون مزاج، گھڑی میں تولہ گھڑی میں ماشہ sad غمگین، بجھا بجھا سا

moon *n.* (the) earth satellite چاند، قمر، مہتاب *full moon* چودھویں کا چاند *halfmoon* ساتویں یا آٹھویں کا چاند **moonlight** *n.* light of the moon چاندنی **moonlit** *adj.* (of night) lit up by moon چاندنی رات **moonstruck** *adj.* lunatic پاگل، دیوانہ **moonshine** *n.* visionary talk خیالی پلاؤ

moor (*moo*-ē*) *n.* (also *moorland*), open heather-covered wasteland بھیڑ North African Arab Muslim بربر *v.t.* make (boat, etc.) secure (*to* buoys or land) with ropes لنگر انداز کرنا

moorings (moo-) *n. pl.* anchor always kept chained to a boat, etc. مستقل لنگر place at which a ship is moored لنگر **moot** *v.t.* raise *the point* (سوال) اٹھانا discuss پر بحث کرنا *n.* assembly for discussion مجلس (*adj.*) (in the phrase :) *moot point*, point at issue مابہ النزاع، متنازع فیہ، بحث طلب

mop *n.* stick with a bundle of cloth, etc., at one end for wiping جھاڑن *v.t.* (-pp-) clean *up with* a mop جھاڑن سے صاف کرنا *mop (something) up*, destroy or end (it) مارنا۔ ہلاک کرنا، ختم کرنا

mope (mohp) *v.i.* be listless owing to sadness over one's own condition دلگیر ہونا، افسردہ دل ہونا

moral (*mo*-rĕl) ethical (ideas, books, etc.) اخلاقی *moral standards*, (of a community, etc.) کے اخلاقی معیار *moral victory*, position (usu. of defeat) where the weaker party establishes the righteousness of its cause اخلاقی فتح *moral obligation* اخلاقی فریضہ، اخلاقی ذمہ داری *be under a moral obligation* (*to do something*) (کرنے کی) اخلاقی ذمہ داری ہونا virtuous (life, action, etc.) نیک، نیکی کا، صالح، پاکبازانہ *n.* that which is the lesson (*of* a tale, etc.) نتیجہ (*pl.*) ethical principles اخلاقی اصول (*pl.*) character چال چلن، اخلاق، سیرت **moralist** (*mo*-ra-list) *n.* given to stressing morals اخلاقی وعظ کرنیوالا، معلمِ اخلاق، واعظ

morality (mo-*ral*-i-ti) *n.* ethical principles اخلاقیات، اصولِ اخلاق good actions حسنِ عمل **moralize** (*mo*-ra-liz) *v.t.* stress the need for morality وعظ و نصیحت کرنا، اخلاقی تلقین کرنا، پند و موعظت کرنا show the moral meaning of کا اخلاقی نتیجہ نکالنا

morally (*mo*-ra-li) *adv.* from the ethical point of view اخلاقی طور پر

morale (mo-*rahl*) *n.* courage and confidence (of army, soldiers, etc. under discipline حوصلہ، قوتِ مقابلہ

morass (mo-*ras*) *n.* swamp دلدل

moratorium (mo-ra-*toh*-ri-um) *n.* legal authorization (to debtor) for delaying payment of debts. قرضے کی ادائیگی میں مہلت

morbid (*mo**-bid) *adj.* diseased (growth etc.) on the body (like cancer) (of someone's mind or ideas) unhealthy (mind, ideas etc.) غیر صحت مندانہ **morbidly** *adv.* in a morbid manner مدید نکتہ چینی، نکتہ چینی، غیر صحت مندانہ (طور پر)

mordant (*mo**-dant) *adj.* biting (criticism, etc.

more (moh*) *adj.* greater (in number, quantity, quality, etc.) زیادہ، اور *Have some more tea* تھوڑی سی اور چائے پیجیے additional اور *one word more* بس ایک بات اور *adv.* (for forming comparatives of adjectives and adverbs) زیادہ، تر to greater extent زیادہ، مزید *once more*, once again ایک بار پھر *n.* additional بھی، مزید *all the more*, still more اور بھی greater quantity, etc. زیادہ، مزید *more or less* about کم و بیش *be no more*, die مر جانا (see Addenda) **moreover** *adv.* in addition to this اس کے علاوہ، مزید برآں

morgue (mo*g) *n.* identification mortuary برائے شناخت، شناختی مردہ خانہ

moribund (*mo*-ri-bund) *adj.* in a dying state جس پر موت طاری ہو، جانکنی کی حالت میں، حالتِ نزع میں جس پر سکوتِ مرگ طاری ہو، یا مُردنی چھا رہی ہو (of art, etc.) no longer creative جس کی تخلیقی قوت ختم ہو چکی ہو
morning (*mo**-ning) *n.* first part of the day till noon صبح، فجر، سویرا، قبلِ دوپہر، صبح *early morning* تڑکا *good morning*, form of salutation till lunch سلام صبح *adj.* of or in the morning (صبح (کا *morning star*, Venus صبح، ستارۂ صبح، زہرہ **morn** *n.* (poetical) morning صبح، سویرا، تڑکا، فجر
morocco (mo-*rok*-oh) *n.* soft goatskin مراکو لیدر
moron (*moh*-ron) *n.* adult at the low intellectual level of a child 9 to 12 years old وہ بالغ جو لڑکپن کی ذہنی سطح سے بلند نہ ہو سکا ہو، کم عقل شخص، نا بالغ جوان
morose (mo-*rohs*) *adj.* ill-tempered تنک مزاج، چڑچڑا، بدمزاج
Morpheus (*mo**-fews, or mo*-fe-us) *Cl. myth.* the god of dreams (and also of sleep) مورفوس
morphia (*mo**-fi-a), **morphine** (*mo**-fin) *n.* extract of opium used as drug for relieving pain مارفیا، افیم کا ست
morrow (*mo*-roh) *n* next morning اگلی صبح *on the morrow (of)* کے اگلے روز *tomorrow*, the next day کل
Morse (mo*s) *n.* (in the phrases :) *Morse code* (or *Morse alphabet*, or *Morse signals*) alphabet of visible or audible dots and dashes (used in telegraphy, wireless, signalling, etc.) مارس کوڈ
morsel (*mo**-sel) *n.* mouthful (*of* food) لقمہ، نوالہ
mortal (*mo**-tĕl) *n. adj.* destined to die فانی fatal مہلک، جان لیوا (hatred, combat, etc.) lasting till death موت تک رہنے والا extreme (fear, etc.) انتہائی *n.* human being انسان، فانی انسان any other creature as being subject to death فانی چیز **mortally** *adv.* fatally مہلک طور پر **mortality** *n.* being mortal فانی ہونا death موت death-rate (*from* disease, etc.) شرحِ اموات
mortar (*mo**-tĕ*) *n.* mixture (usu. of lime, sand and water) used in building چونا، گارا strong bowl in which to crush things with a pestle کونڈی، کھرل، ہاون short cannon for firing shells at a high angle اونچا گولہ پھینکنے والی چھوٹی توپ چھوٹی مارا انداز توپ **mortar-board** *n.* flat board for holding mortar گارے کا تختہ، گارے کا تسلہ یا تغاری square university cap جامعاتی کلاہ

a mortar-board (sense 2)

mortgage (*mo**-gij) *v. t.* (of debtor) pledge property (*to* creditor) for a debt گروی رکھنا، گرو رکھنا، رہن رکھنا *n.* act of mortgaging رہن، گروی legal deed of such transaction رہن نامہ **mortgager** (mo*-ga-jĕ*) *n.* one who mortgages راہن
mortgagee (mo*-ga-*jee*) *n.* one to whom mortgage is given مُرتہن **mortgage-deed** *n.* deed incorporating this deal رہن نامہ
mortice *n.* & *v. t.* (see under **mortise**)
mortify (*mo**t-i-f.) *v. t* & *i.* wound the feelings of (someone *by* something) ; make him feel humiliated (کسی کے) جذبات کو ٹھیس لگانا یا مجروح کرنا subdue (passions, etc.) by self-denial نفس کشی کرنا، نفس کو مارنا (of flesh) be affected with gangrene (زخم کے گرد گوشت کا) مُردہ ہونے لگنا **mortification** (-*kay*-) *n.* act of mortifying or being mortified ٹھیس، سخت شرم، نفس کشی (گوشت کا) مُردہ ہونے لگنا
mortise, mortice (*mo**-tis) *n.* hole cut in a piece of wood, etc., to receive the end of another piece (چول کی) سال *v. t.* make mortise in میں سال ڈالنا join thus چول بٹھانا
mortuary (*mo**-tew-è-ri) *n.* room for the temporary keeping of corpses before burial for *postmortem* examination, etc. مُردے خانہ
mosaic (moh-*zay*-ik) *n.* patchwork pattern as a work of art پچی کاری *adj.* made thus پچی کاری کا کام (*Mosaic*), (of law, teaching, etc.) of Moses موسوی
mosque (mosk) *n.* Muslim house of worship
mosquito (mos-*kee*-toh) *n.* (pl. *mosquitoes*) gnat-like insect a class of which spreads malaria مچھر، پشہ **mosquito curtain, mosquito net, mosquito-netting** *n.* net to keep mosquitoes off one's bed مسہری، مچھر دانی

a mosquito

moss (*mos*) *n.* kinds of small plant growing in thick masses on wet surfaces کائی **mossy** (*mos*-i) *adj.* covered with moss جس پر کائی جم رہی ہو، کائی والا، کائی دار *adj.*
most (mohst) (superlative of *many* and *much*) *adj.* greatest in quantity, quality, number, degree, etc. سب سے زیادہ the majority of اکثر *most of* کی اکثریت، میں سے اکثر *adv.* (for making superlatives of adjectives or adverbs) سب سے زیادہ، نہایت in the greatest degree سب سے زیادہ *at most*, *at the most*, not more than زیادہ سے زیادہ *for the most part*, mostly زیادہ تر، بیشتر *make the most (of)* make the best use (of) (سے) زیادہ سے زیادہ فائدہ اٹھانا **mostly** (*mohst*-li) *adv.* usually عموماً، عام طور پر، بالعموم mainly زیادہ تر، بیشتر
mot (moh) *n.* witty saying ظریفانہ بات، ظریفانہ مقولہ pithy saying مقولہ *mot juste* *n.* most precise word conveying a particular shade of meaning موزوں ترین لفظ

mote (moht) *n.* particle (esp. of dust) (گرد کا) ذرّہ *the mote in another's eye,* (as opposed to *the beam in one's own*) دوسرے کی آنکھ کا تِنکا

motel *n.* (see *Addenda*)

moth *n.* winged insect attracted towards lights پروانہ، پتنگا another class of such insects feeding on cloth, etc. کیڑا **moth-eaten** *adj.* injured by moth جسے کیڑا لگا ہوا ہو، کرم خوردہ antiquated دقیانوسی، دقیانوسی، کرم خوردہ۔

a moth

mother (mudh-ĕ*) *n.* female parent ماں، والدہ head of a nunnery مادر، مادر origin (*of* something) کی بنیاد، کی اصل، کی ماں *necessity is the mother of invention,* ضرورت ایجاد کی ماں ہے *mothercraft,* art of bringing up children بچوں کی پرورش (*one's*) *mother tongue,* (one's) native language مادری زبان *mother country, motherland,* native land مادرِ وطن *mother of pearl,* shining inner lining of some shells (بعض سیپیوں کی) اندرونی چمکدار سطح *v. t.* care for like a mother ماں کی طرح نگہداشت کرنا **mother-in-law** *n.* mother of one's wife or husband ساس، خوشدامن **motherless** *adj.* having lost the mother بن ماں کا، **motherly** *adj.* (treatment, person) tender like a mother's ماں کی سی، مہربانی کا، مادرانہ شفقت کا مظہر **motherliness** *n.* being kind like the mother مادرانہ شفقت **motherhood** *n.* being a mother ماں کا ہونا all the women (*of* a country) who are mothers (ملک کی) تمام مائیں

motif (*moh*-tif, or moh-*teef*) *n.* dominant idea (of a work of art or literature) مرکزی خیال، کا بنیادی تصوّر basic design in (*of*) it کا بنیادی نقش ornament of lace, etc., sewn separately on a garment کپڑے پر لگی ہوئی لیس، سجاوٹی فیتہ (یا جھالر وغیرہ)

motion (*moh*-shĕn) *n.* movement حرکت *in motion,* moving حرکت میں، چل رہا، جاری *set in motion* چلانا، جاری کرنا gesture (*of* hand, head, etc.) اشارہ proposal for discussion and voting on at a meeting تحریک، قرارداد evacutation of the bowels *have a motion* *v. t.* direct (someone) by a motion (*to, in, away, out, of, etc.*) (کہیں) آنے جانے کو) کہنا، اشارے سے کہنا کہ **motionless** *adj.* still بے حرکت، ساکن، بے حس و حرکت

motive (*moh*-tiv) *n.* impetus (*for* something or *for doing* something) محرک، وجہ، سبب *selfish motives* خود غرضی *adj.* (power, etc.) causing motion حرکت میں لانے والا، محرک، **motivate** *v. t.* be a motive of کا محرک بننا، کا باعث ہونا یا بننا

motley (*mot*-ley) *adj.* (dress, etc.) of various colours (as worn by court jesters) رنگ برنگا (crowd, etc.) of various sorts ہر قسم کے افراد وغیرہ پر مشتمل، ملا جلا، مختلف الانواع

motor (*moh*-tĕ*) *n.* machine supplying power to bring something into motion موٹر، انجن، محرک *electric motor* بجلی کی موٹر، برقی محرک (also *motor-car*), automobile موٹر، موٹر کار، کار *adj.* worked or driven by a motor انجن سے چلنے والا *motor-bicycle* موٹر سائیکل *motor-boat* موٹر بوٹ، موٹر کشتی، کلدار کشتی *v.t. & i.* travel by motor-car (*to* some place) (تک) موٹر میں جانا take (someone *to* some place) thus (کو) موٹر میں بٹھا کر لے جانا **motoring** *n.* travel by a motor-car موٹر کار کا سفر **motorable** *adj.* (of road, etc.) along which motor-car, etc., can go موٹر چلنے کے قابل **motorcade** *n.* (see *Addenda*) **motorist** (moh-tĕ-rist) *n.* one who travels by a motor-car (as its owner) موٹر والا **motorize** (*moh*-tĕ-riz) *v.t.* equip cavalry, etc., with motor-vehicles رسالے کو موٹرانا **motorized** *adj.* موٹرایا ہوا

mottled (*mot*-ĕld) *adj.* having patches of various colours رنگ برنگا blotched دھبّوں والا

motto (*mot*-oh) *n.* (pl. *mottoes*) phrase or short sentence used as a rule of good behaviour اصول عمل، ماٹو *the motto of a college* کسی کالج کا ماٹو، کسی درس گاہ کا اصولِ عمل

mould (mohld) *n.* container for putting molten metal into a desired shape سانچہ، قالب pattern for giving shape to something else سانچہ form شکل، صورت character کردار، fine soil rich with manure کھاد والی باریک مٹی loose earth مٹی، خاک furry growth caused by dampness پھپھوندی *v.t.* shape something (*in* or *out of* something) (کسی چیز سے) سانچے میں ڈھال کر بنانا، (کسی چیز سے) بنانا put (character, etc.) into or form ڈھالنا

mouldy *adj.* covered with or caused by mould پھپھوندی والا یا جیسا antiquated ; very old-fashioned دقیانوسی، فرسودہ

moulder (*mohl*-dĕ*) crumble (*away*) مٹی میں مل جانا، مٹی ہو جانا *mouldering ruins* مٹی میں ملتے ہوئے کھنڈر

moult (mohlt) *v.t. & i.* (of birds) lose (feathers) before a new growth پر جھاڑنا، کریز کرنا

mound *n.* knoll ; heap of earth, stones, etc. ٹیلا

mount *n.* (used before proper names of hills) ماؤنٹ، چوٹی (poet.) mountain ; hill پہاڑ، پہاڑی horse for one's riding سواری، گھوڑا stiff backing for a photograph, etc. تصویر کے پیچھے لگانے کا گتہ یا موٹا کاغذ *v t. & i.* go up (the hill or the ladder) پر چڑھنا (cause to) get on horseback ; get on to (a horse, etc.) (گھوڑے پر) چڑھنا یا چڑھانا، سوار ہونا یا کرنا stick a picture, etc., on a stiff backing تصویر کے پیچھے گتا یا موٹا کاغذ لگانا stick (jewels *in* gold, etc.) میں جڑنا put (a gun *on* a gun-carriage) توپ پہیوں پر لگانا

(of prices, expenses, etc.) rise or go (*up*) چڑھنا *mount guard*, be posted as a guard کے پہرے پر لگنا، گارڈ ڈیوٹی دینا *mount guard over*, (of detachment, etc. watch over پر پہرہ دینا

mountain (*moun*-tin) *n.* high hill ; hill of impressive height پہاڑ، کوہ *make mountain out of mole-hill*, exaggerate much بڑا مبالغہ کرنا، رائی کا پہاڑ (یا پربت) بنانا large heap or amount (*of* trouble, etc.) کا پہاڑ *mountain high, mountains high*, very high بہت اونچا **mountaineer** (moun-ti-*nee*-ĕ*) *n.* expert climber of mountains پہاڑوں پر چڑھنے کا ماہر، کوہ پیما- **mountaineering** *n.* mountain climbing as a hobby پہاڑوں پر چڑھنے کا مشغلہ، کوہ پیمائی *adj.* for mountaineering کوہ پیما of it کوہ پیمائی کا **mountainous** (*moun*-ti-nus) *adj.* having many mountains پہاڑی (of waves, etc.) high اونچی huge بہت بڑا، پہاڑ کا پہاڑ

mountebank (*mount*-è-bank) *n.* quack selling his drugs by addressing corner meetings مجمع لگاکر دوائیں بیچنے والا بازاری دوا فروش، مجمع لگانے والا عطائی -

mourn (moh*n) *v.t.* & *i.* lament (a loss, the death of, etc.) (کا) افسوس کرنا، (کا) ماتم کرنا be sorry (*for* or *over* someone dead) (کا) افسوس کرنا، (کا) ماتم کرنا **mourner** *n.* one who mourns سوگ منانے والا one who attends a funeral جنازے میں شریک ہونے والا **mournful** *adj.* sad (person) غمگین doleful (letter, song, occasion, etc.) ماتمی **mournfully** *adv.* غم سے **mourning** *n.* grief غم black clothes or band worn as a sign of mourning ماتمی لباس (یا) ماتمی پٹی *be in* (or *get into*) mourning (*for*) کے ماتم میں سیاہ پوشش ہونا

mouse (mous) *n.* (pl. *mice* pr. mīs) well-known small animal exactly like, but much smaller than, a rat چوہا

moustache (mus-*tahsh*) *n.* hair on the upper lip مونچھ

mouth *n.* (mouth) (pl. *mouths*, pr. moudhz) opening in a living being's face for eating, etc. منہ، دہن *(be) down in the mouth*, (be) sorrowful غمگین (ہونا) *have a good*, (or *a hard* or *bad*) *mouth* (of a horse) be (not) amenable (گھوڑے کا) منہ زور نہ ہونا (یا ہونا) *put words into (one's) mouth* (*a*) wrongly attribute some saying to him سے کوئی بھی الفاظ منسوب کر دینا (*b*) tell him what to say (کو) بتانا کہ کیا کہے opening (*of* bag, bottle, etc.) منہ outfall (*of* river) (دریا کا) دہانہ **mouthpiece** *n.* part of tobacco-pipe placed in lips مُہنال agent (*of* someone) speaking for him (کسی کی) طرف سے بولنے والا **mouth-organ** *n.* harmonica منہ کا باجا *v.t.* & *i.* speak (words) with too much movement

a mouth-organ

of the mouth منہ بنا بنا کر بولنا، چبا چبا کر بولنا touch with the mouth منہ لگانا **mouthful** *n.* as much as would easily fill the mouth منہ بھر، منہ بھر کے

move (moov) *v.t.* & *i.* (cause to) change position ہلنا یا ہلانا، حرکت میں آنا یا لانا، متحرک ہونا یا کرنا *moving pictures*, movie, cinema pictures متحرک فلم *moving staircase*, escalator متحرک زینہ *move house*, shift somewhere else with belongings گھر بدلنا *move in* (or *out*), shift thus into (or out of) a house, etc. نئے گھر میں آنا (یا) پرانے گھر سے جانا cause (someone *to do* something) کسی سے کوئی کام لینا excite the feelings of (someone to tears, etc.) کے جذبات ابھارنا *be moved to tears* غم سے رو پڑنا put (motion, etc., *that*) forward for being discussed and voted on at a meeting (تحریک وغیرہ) پیش کرنا *n.* change of place or position حرکت *be on the move*, (of troops) be advancing بڑھ رہا ہونا، کوچ کر چکنا *let's make a move now*, let us go now ! آؤ اب چلیں، اب رخصت that which is done to achieve a purpose (in battle, game of chess, etc.) چال *What's the next move ?* what is to be done now ? اب کیا کیا جائے؟ **movement** (*moov*-ment) *n.* moving or being moved حرکت united action of a group of people (*to do*) تحریک **movies** (*moov*-eez) *n.* (colloq.) moving pictures فلم

mow (moh) *v.t.* & *i.* (*mow ; mowed ; mowed* or *mown*) cut (grass, etc.) with a scythe or machine from (lawn, etc.) (گھاس) کاٹنا *be mown down by*, (of a large number) be killed by سے مارا جانا

Mr, Mr. (*mis*-tĕ*) (*fem.*, **Mrs** or **Mrs.** pr. *mis*-is, for married woman ; **Miss** for unmarried woman) title prefixed to full name or surname of man جناب، صاحب *Mr and Mrs Smith* سمتھ صاحب اور ان کی بیگم صاحبہ **Mrs Grundy** *n.* conventional morality personified مروجہ اخلاقی نظریات **Note :** A woman's Christian name or initials are never used with Mrs, except in legal documents. Hence in legal documents, *Mrs Beryl Robbins* ; otherwise, *Mrs Sidney Robbins*.

much *adj.* of a great size, quantity, etc. بڑا، بہت *adv.* very بہت to a large amount بہت، زیادہ *n.* large quantity, etc. بہت *much more* کہیں زیادہ، بہت زیادہ *much the same*, about the same قریب قریب ویسا (یا اتنا) ہی

muck (muk) *n.* animal droppings گوبر، بینڈ وغیرہ *v.t.* & *i.* make dirt گندا کرنا، غلاظت سے بھرنا (slang) bungle (job) ستیاناس کر دینا *muck about*, handle (troops etc.) badly غلط کمان (یا بدانتظام) کرنا **mucker** *n.*

(slang) heavy fall بُری طرح گرنا *come a mucker* بُری طرح گرنا *go a mucker*, (*a*) fall heavily بُری طرح گرنا (*b*) spend too much on something کسی چیز پر بہت زیادہ صرف کرنا **mucky** (*muk*-i) *adj*. dirty گندا ، غلیظ

mucus (*mew*-kus) *n*. sticky liquid secreted in the mucous membrane (or found in fishes, etc.) بلغم، آنو *mucous membrane*, moist skin lining the throat, etc. بلغی جھلی، آنو کی جھلی

mud (mud) *n*. soft wet earth کیچڑ **muddy** (*mud*-i) *adj*. full of mud کیچڑ والا (of water) not clean and clear گدلا **mud-guard** *n*. metal cover over the wheel (*of* a vehicle) کیچ روک

muddle (*mud*-èl) *v.t.* & *i.* bungle ستیاناس کرنا put into disorder گڈمڈ کرنا *n*. muddled state ابتری ، گڈمڈ *lie all in a muddle* گڈمڈ ہونا

muffin (*muf*-in) *n*. small disk-like tea-cake eaten hot with butter کلچہ ، بند

muffle (*muf*-èl) *v.t.* wrap (*oneself up*) for warmth گرم ہونے کے لیے (اپنے) گرد خوب لپیٹنا wrap up something for deadening its sound کپڑا منڈھ کر آواز دبا دینا gag (someone's voice of protest) (کی صدائے احتجاج کو) دبا دینا **muffler** (*muf*-lĕ*) *n*. (usu. warm) scarf گلوبند ، مفلر

mufti (*muf*-ti) *n*. civilian dress of an official who normally wears uniform مفتی ، عام کپڑے *in mufti* عام کپڑوں میں

mug (mug) *n*. glass-like drinking vessel with a handle مگ ، آبخورہ *v.t.* (*mug up*), cram (book, subject, etc.) رٹنا **muggy** (*mug*-i) *adj*. (of the rainy season weather) warm, damp and close برسات کا حبس والا (موسم یا دن)

mugger (*mug*-ĕ*) *n*. broad-nosed crocodile found in this part of the world مگرمچھ ، گھڑیال

mulatto (mew-*lat*-oh) *n*. (pl. *mulattos*) child of a European and a Negro یورپی اور حبشی مخلوط النسل کا یوریشی

mulberry (*mul*-bè-ri) *n*. tree on the leaves of which silkworms feed شہتوت کا درخت ، شہتوت its fruit شہتوت

mulct (mulkt) *v.t.* *mulct (someone) of*, deprive (someone *of*) سے محروم کرنا fine (someone *in* sum) (کو اتنا) جرمانہ کرنا

mule (mewl) *n*. offspring of an ass and a mare خچر stubborn person ضدی شخص، اڑیل ٹٹو **mulish** (*mew*-lish) *adj*. obstinate ضدی ، اڑیل **muleteer** (mewl-*tee*-ĕ*) *n*. mule-driver خچر والا

mull (mul) *n*. bungling, failure گڑبڑ *make a mull of*, fail to effect ناکام رہنا ، بے اثر رہنا *v.t.* make a mull of بے اثر ہونا ، ناکام رہنا

mullion (*mul*-yĕn) *n*. upright division between parts of a window کھڑکی کی عمودی سلاخ (وغیرہ) **mullioned** *adj*. (of window) having mullion(s) عمودی سلاخ والی

multi- (mul-ti) *pref*. many متعدد، متنوع **multicolour, multicoloured** *adj*. many-coloured کئی رنگوں والا ، رنگا رنگ

multifarious, (*-fay-*) *adj*. many and various مختلف ، گوناگوں کثیرالانواع ، متنوع

multiform *adj*. of many forms

multilateral *adj*. many-sided (pact, etc.) ایک سے زیادہ کے ساتھ

multiphasic *adj*. (see *Addenda*)

multiple (*mul*-ti-pèl) *adj*. having many parts مختلف ، گوناگوں *multiple shop*, one with branches at many places کئی جگہ شاخوں والی (with pl. noun) more than one ایک سے زیادہ ، متعدد *n*. quantity exactly divisible by (*of*) another مضاعف ، حاصل ضرب

multiply (*mul*-ti-pli) *v.t.* & *i.* perform multiplication of (a number *by* or *into* another number) (سے) ضرب دینا increase greatly by reproduction (کی) بڑی افزائش نسل ہونا *people multiplies* افزائش نسل کے باعث لوگوں کی تعداد خوب بڑھتی ہے increase the number of (examples, etc.) بہت سی (مثالیں وغیرہ) پیش کرنا **multiplication** (*-kay-*) *n*. increase (*of* something *by* or *into* a number) that many times ضرب *multiplication tables* پہاڑے *sign of multiplication* علامت ضرب *rule of multiplication* قاعدہ ضرب **multiplicity** (*-plis*-i-ti) *n*. great number (*of*) کی کثیر التعداد **multiplicand** (*-kand*) *n*. quantity to be multiplied مضروب **multiplier** number by which the multiplicand is to be multiplied مضروب فیہ ، ضرب دہندہ ، ضارب

multipurpose *adj*. serving more than one purpose کثیرالمقاصد *multipurpose cooperative society*, one with various purposes like buying, production, selling, etc. کثیرالمقاصد انجمن امداد باہمی

multitude (*mul*-ti-tewd) *n*. great crowd (*of* people) انبوہ، ازدحام *the multitude*, the masses عوام **multitudinous** (*-tewd*-i-nus) *adj*. very large in number بہت زیادہ ، کثیر ، بےشمار forming a large crowd انبوہ در انبوہ

mum (mum) *adj*. quiet چپ، خاموش *sit mum*, not join in a talk گم سم بیٹھے رہنا ، بات چیت میں حصہ نہ لینا *keep mum about (something)* keep it secret کو مخفی رکھنا کے بارے میں خاموش رہنا *Mum's the word* ! this is a secret بس کہنا مت ، راز کی بات ہے

umble (*mum*-bĕl) *v.t.* & *i.* speak (*one's words*) ndistinctly مُنہ ہی مُنہ میں کچھ کہنا *n.* mumbled words بُڑ بُڑ

Mumbo Jumbo (*mum*-boh-*jum*-boh) *n.* (pl. *Mumbo Jumbos*) object of foolish veneration مَعبُودِ باطِل، جھُوٹا دیوتا supposed African idol or bogy ممبو جمبو

ummy (*mum*-i) *n.* child's name for own nother اَمّی dead body preserved by embalming مسالہ لگا کر محفُوظ رکھی ہُوئی لاش، ممّی، محنُوظ لاش beat (*someone*) *to a mummy*, thrash (him) کو پیٹنا **mummied** (mum-id) *adj.* مومیائی کی ہُوئی لاش. **mummify** *v.t.* embalm thus مسالہ لگا کر لاش کو محفُوظ رکھنا، ممّی بنانا، مومیائی کرنا

mummification (-kay-) *n.* act of mummifying or being mummified ممّی بنانا

ump (mump) *v.i.* be sullen and silent مُنہ سُجائے بیٹھے رہ beg بھیک مانگنا **mumps** (mumps) *n.* *pl.* with *sing.* verb) disease causing a swollen neck گلسُوتے، گلپھڑے، کنپھیڑ

unch (munch) *v.t.* & *i.* chew steadily with much noise چَپڑ چَپڑ چبانا

undane (*mund*-ayn) *adj.* worldly (as opposed to *spiritual*) دُنیاوی، دُنیوی

unicipal (mew-*nis*-i-pĕl) *adj.* of a municipality بلدیاتی *municipal committee*, governing body of a municipality کمیٹی، بلدیہ، انجمنِ بلدیہ **municipality** (-*pal*-) *n.* city with local self-government میونسپل کمیٹی، بلدیہ، میونسپلٹی municipal committee شہر کا انتظام کرنے والی کمیٹی، بلدیہ

unificent (mew-*nif*-i-sent) *adj.* very generous (person or action) بہت فیاض، بڑا فیاضانہ **munificence** (mew-*nif*-i-sens) *n.* great generosity بڑی سخاوت، فیاضی

unitions (mew-*nish*-unz) *n.* *pl.*, military supplies of guns, etc. گولہ بارُود، سامانِ جنگ، اسلحہ

ural (*mew*-rĕl) *adj.* of or on a wall دیواری (پر)، دیوار *n.* mural painting دیوار پر کی تصویر یا نقش، دیواری نقش، نقش بر دیوار

urder (mĕ*-dĕ*) *n.* assassination *v.t.* assassinate (someone) کو قتل کرنا **murderer** *n.* one who murders قاتل **murderous** (*mè*-dĕ-rus) *adj.* (of attack, weapons, etc.) likely to cause murder قاتلانہ

urky (mĕ*-ki) *adj.* dark and gloomy تیرہ و تار dense (darkness) گھٹا ٹوپ (اندھیرا)

urmur (mĕ*-mĕ*) *n.* grumble بُڑبُڑاہٹ low continuous sound (*of* water) (پانی کی) سرسراہٹ sound (*of* bees) بھنبھناہٹ such sound (*of* pain) ہائے ہائے *v.t.* & *i.* (of water or bees) make such a noise (پانی کا) سرسر بہنا، (شہد کی مکھیوں کا) بھنبھنانا make a murmur in pain کراہنا، درد سے ہائے ہائے کرنا say (prayer, words, etc.) in a low voice بہت آہستہ کہنا grumble (*against*, taxation, heavy work, etc.) (پر) بُڑبُڑانا

muscle (*mus*-ĕl) *n.* (any bundle of fibrous tissue in body پٹھا، عضلہ **muscle-bound** *adj.* with muscles grown too stiff through over-exercise غیر ضروری طور پر عضلاتی **muscular** (*mus*-kew-lĕ*) *adj.* of the muscles پٹھوں کا عضلاتی having strong and muscular muscles مضبُوط، گٹھا ہوا

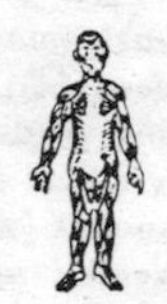
muscles of a man

muse (mewz) *v. i.* ponder (*on*, *upon* or *over* something) غور و فکر کرنا day dream (*on*, *upon* or *over* something) (سے) عالمِ محویت میں چلا جانا *n.* spirit of poetry رُوحِ شاعری (*pl.*) (*the Muses*), one of the nine daughters of Zeus and Mnemosyne, each presiding over one of the branches of arts and inspiring the writer. They were : (*a*) *Calliope* or the Muse of epic poetry ; (*b*) *Clio*, of history ; (*c*) *Erato*, of love potry ; (*d*) *Thalia*, of comedy ; (*e*) *Melpomene* of tragedy ; (*f*) *Terpsichore*, of dancing ; (*g*) *Euterpe*, of lyric poetry ; (*h*) *Polyhymnia*, of lyric poetry and eloquence; (*i*) *Urania*, of astronomy. They lived on Mt. Parnassus فنونِ لطیفہ کی دیویاں (*the muse*), (*a*) politic inspiration شاعر کا بیوزیں الہام (the poet's) intellect شاعر کی خداداد ذہانت

museum (mew-*zee*-um) *n.* place where interesting objects of historical, cultural or scientific interest are kept for show عجائب گھر، عجائب خانہ

mush (mush) *n.* soft pulp پتلا گودا (U. S.) a kind of porridge دلیا journey across snow with dog-sledge برفانی کشتی میں برف پر سفر *v. i.* travel thus برفانی کشتی میں سفر کرنا

mushroom (*mush*-room) *n.* fast-growing edible fungus سانپ کی چھتری، کگرمتا upstart person or institution نَوخاستہ *adj.* of rapid (growth) تیزی سے (بڑھنے والا) *mushroom growth*, rapidly growing undesirable things حشرات الارض

music (*mew*-zik) *n.* art of combining sounds to give them a pleasing effect موسیقی، مُوسیقی such combination of sweet sounds موسیقی، سُرور piece of such composition played or written موسیقی sweet sound (*of*) (کی) موسیقی، (کا) نغمہ *face the music*, (*a*) face one's critics and be taken to task اپنے پر اعتراضات کی بوچھاڑ سُننا (*b*) get into trouble over one's action اپنا کیا آگے آنا، اپنی غلطی کے باعث مصیبت میں پھنسنا *set to music* کی دُھن بنانا، کو نغمانا **musical** *adj.* of music موسیقی کا skilled in it موسیقی میں مہارت یا شوق والا **musically** *adv.* موسیقی سے **musician** (mew-*zish*-ĕn) *n.* one who composes or is skilled in music مُطرِب، نغمہ گر، خُنیاگر، موسیقار

musk (musk) *n.* perfume obtained from male deer کستوری، مُشک، نافۂ آہو **muskdeer** *n.* the kind of deer yielding it نافے والا ہرن، آہوئے نافہ **musk-melon** *n.* a kind of sweet-scented melon سردا

musket (*mus*-ket) *n.* old form of rifle بندوق **musketeer** (mus-ke-*tee*-ĕ*) *n.* soldier with a musket بندوقچی **musketry** (*mus*-ket-ri) *n.* practice in shooting with muskets, rifles, etc. نشانہ بازی rifle-fire بندوق کی گولیوں کا چلنا

muslin (*muz*-lin) *n.* a very thin kind of cotton cloth ململ

muss (mus) (U. S. colloq.) *n.* untidiness, mess بدنظمی، بے ترتیبی، گڈمڈ، گھال میل *v. t.* (*muss up*), throw into disorder گڈمڈ کر دینا **mussy** (mus-i) *adj.* untidy گڈمڈ، اُلٹ پلٹ

must (must) *auxiliary v.* (used only with the indefinite, perfect and perfect continuous forms of the pr. t. : *must go, must have gone, must have been going*) (expressive of :) strong obligation, intention, inference ضرور، لازماً (compulsion) (translated into Urdu by using the uninflected Urdu infinitive ہونا *Come what must* جو ہونا ہے پھر ہو، ہی جائے (bad luck) (translated as above) *Must you disturb me* تمہیں میرا وقت ضرور ہی ضائع کرنا ہے *adj.* (of elephants) in periodical frenzy مست *n.* grape-juice not fully fermented نبیذ

mustard (*mus*-tĕ*d) *n.* kinds of seed plants with yellow flowers رائی its seed رائی hot sauce made from it رائی کی چٹنی **mustard-plaster** *n.* its poultice رائی کا پلستر **mustard oil** *n.* rapeseed oil سرسوں کا تیل، کڑوا تیل **mustard gas** *n.* a poisonous and irritant liquid gas رائی گیس

muster (*mus*-tĕ*) *n.* gathering (esp. of troops) for review جائزے کے لیے اجتماع *pass muster*, be found satisfactory ٹھیک نکلنا *v. t.* & *i.* gather or get together اکٹھے ہونا یا کرنا *muster up (one's) courage*, overcome (one's) fears, etc. حوصلہ کرنا

musty (*mus*-ti) *adj.* mouldy پھپھوندی لگا

mutable (*mewt*-a-bĕl) *adj.* liable to change بدل جانے والا، تغیر پذیر **mutability** (-*bil*-) *n.* changeability تغیر پذیری **mutation** (-*tay*-) *n.* change تبدیلی، تغیر

mutatis mutandis (meu-*tay*-tis-mew-*tand*-is) *adv.* with due alterations of details in applying analogies, etc. مناسب تبدیلیوں کے ساتھ

mute (mewt) *adj.* dumb گونگا silent چپ خاموش (of a letter) not sounding (*in* a word (as the *p.* in *psychology*) غیر ملفوظ *n.* dumb person گونگا

mutilate (*mew*-ti-layt) *v. t.* damage (a word etc.) by cutting off a part or overwriting حک و ترمیم کرنا، کاٹنا، کانٹ چھانٹ کرنا cut off limbs of (a person) ہاتھ پیر کاٹنا cut off (person's limbs etc.) ہاتھ پیر وغیرہ کاٹنا **mutilation** *n.* act of mutilating or being mutilated کانٹ چھانٹ، قطع و برید، ہاتھ پیر کاٹنا

mutiny (*mew*-ti-ni) *n.* rising of troops (*against* فوجی بغاوت، غدر *v. i.* be guilty of mutiny فوجی بغاوت کرنا، غدر برپا کرنا **mutineer** (mew-ti-*nee*-ĕ*) *n.* one guilty of mutiny فوجی باغی، غدر میں حصہ لینے والا **mutinous** (*mew*-ti-nus) *adj.* rebellious (person or action) باغی، باغیانہ

mutt (mut) *n.* (slang) ignorant blunderer جاہل، احمق

mutter (*mut*-ĕ*) *v.t.* & *i.* (say something) in a low indistinct voice آہستہ کہنا speak thus بڑبڑانا *n.* speaking thus

mutton (*mut*-un) *n.* sheep's (or even goat's) meat بھیڑ یا بکری کا گوشت **mutton-chop** *n.* (roast piece of it from one of the ribs گوشت چاپ، تلا ہوا پارچہ، چاپ، پارچہ

mutual (*mew*-tew-ĕl) *adj.* (of love, etc.) reciprocal between two فریقین میں، ایک دوسرے سے، باہمی، باہدگر (less correctly) (friend, etc.) common to two or more مشترکہ، مشترک، باہمی **mutually** (*mew*-tew-e-li) *adj.* reciprocally باہمی طور پر، مشترکہ طور پر

muzzle (*muz*-ĕl) *n.* animal's mouth تھوتھنی net covering for it چھینکا mouth of gun بندوق کی نال کا منہ *v. t.* put a muzzle on (an animal) چھینکا چڑھانا gag (newspaper, person, etc.) from expressing views freely روکنا، زبان بندی کرنا

muzzy (*muz*-i) *adj.* stupid with drink بدمست، بدحواس in a dull confused state اکھڑا اکھڑا سا

my (mɪ) *pron.* (possessive form of *I*, which see) میرا *int.* (expressive of surprise or concern) اوہ میری توبہ! بہت تیری سی!

myopia (mɪ-*oh*-pi-a) *n.* inability to see clearly beyond very short distances نظر کی کمزوری، دُور کی نظر کی کمزوری **myopic** *adj.* one suffering from myopia جس کی دُور کی نظر کمزور ہو **myope** (*mɪ*-ohp) *n.* short-sighted person وہ شخص جس کی دُور کی نظر کمزور ہو

myriad (*mi*-ri-ad) *n.* countless number لاکھوں، کروڑوں، ان گنت، بے شمار *myriads of* ان گنت، لاتعداد، بے شمار

myrmidon (mĕ*-mi-don) *n.* one's follower (esp. a ruffian following a bold leader) چیلا *myrmidon of court*, (contemptuously used of) bailiff عدالت کا کتا

myrrh (mĕ*) *n.* resin used as incense لوبان کی طرح ایک گوند، مر، بول

myrtle (mĕ*-tèl) *n.* kinds of evergreen shrub with fragrant white flowers مہندی کی طرح ایک پودا، آس

myrtle

myself *pron.* (*pl. ourselves* pr. ou-è*-selvz) reflexive form of *me* اپنے آپ کو، اپنے کو emphatic form of *I* (as in I myself) خود، آپ ہی my natural self اپنا آپ *be not (oneself)*, be beside (oneself) with rage آپے سے باہر ہونا

mystery (*mis*-tè-ri) *n.* something beyond one's comprehension راز، نامعلوم شے *be a mystery to (someone)* کے لیے سربستہ راز ہونا some metaphysical truth which the human mind cannot understand راز کی حقیقت، سر الٰہی anything whose cause, etc., is obscure بھید، راز، سربستہ راز *be wrapped in mystery* (قتل وغیرہ کا) سربستہ راز ہونا **mystery play** *n.* old form of play based on some Biblical event انجیلی تمثیل، مذہبی تمثیل **mysterious** (-tee-) *adj.* (of event) wrapped in mystery پراسرار (of person) affecting mystery پراسرار شخصیت **mystify** (*mis*-ti-fi) *v.t.* puzzle (*by*) چکر میں ڈالنا make (something) mysterious پراسرار بنا دینا play hoax on (the credulous) ابلہ فریبی سے کام لینا، کی ضعیف الاعتقادی سے فائدہ اٹھانا **mystification** (-*kay*-) *n.* act of mystifying پراسرار بنا دینا something that mystifies پراسرار بات play hoax on the credulous ابلہ فریبی، ضعیف الاعتقادی سے ناجائز فائدہ

mysteriously *adj.* پراسرار طور پر **mysteriousness** *n.* being mysterious پراسرار ہونا

mystic (*mis*-tik) *adj.* concerned with direct communion (and eventual unity) of the soul with God through religious ecstasy عرفان الٰہی والا، عارفانہ of mysticism صوفیانہ spiritual باطنی awe-inspiring پرجلال، ہیبت طاری کرنے والا mysterious پراسرار، صوفیانہ، باطنی **mystical** *adj.* of mysticism پراسرار، باطنی mysterious پراسرار *n.* one holding mystic views صوفی، عارف باللہ **mysticism** (-sizm) *n.* doctrine of the mystics ; روح اور خالق کے ارتباط کا عقیدہ، تصوف

mystify *v. t.*, **mystification** *n.* (see under **mystery**)

myth (mith) *n.* legend of gods, etc., now regarded as explanation of natural phenomena دیوی دیوتاؤں کا قصہ، شعور رواج، اساطیر old wives' tale بے اصل داستان، خرافات false but prevalent belief کوئی عام طور پر باطل عقیدہ، غلط مگر عام خیال *explode a myth* پایا جانے والا غلط نظریہ باطل کرنا non-existent person بالکل فرضی شخصیت جس کا سرے سے وجود ہی نہ ہو **mythology** (mi-*thol*-o-ji) *n.* collection of myths (*of* a people) دیومالا، اساطیر الاولین، اساطیر، صنمیات study of myths علم الاساطیر **mythological** (-*loj*-) *adj.* of or pertainin to mythology دیومالا سے متعلق **mythologist** (mi-*thol*-o-jist) *n.* expert in mythology علم الاساطیر کا ماہر، اساطیر دان **mythologically** *adv.* دیومالا کی رو سے **mythical** (*mith*-i-kĕl) *adj.* pertaining to myths دیومالا سے متعلق، اساطیری imaginary خیالی، فرضی non-existent بالکل فرضی، جس کا سرے سے وجود ہی نہ ہو

N

n, N (en) (pl. *n's* or *ns*) fourteenth letter of the English alphabet (equivalent to the Urdu ن (in Maths.) indefinite number in a series غیر متعین عدد والا **n'th** غیر متعین عدد *to the n'th degree*, to any supposed extent غیر متعین حد تک، انتہا تک

nab *v. t.* catch suddenly (a thief, etc.) اچانک پکڑ لینا

nabob (*nay*-bob) Mogul governor in the Indo-Pakistan sub-continent نواب Muslim ruler of a princely State here نواب Englishman who had made a lot of money here نواب

nadir (*nay*-dĕ*) *n.* point of heaven directly under one's feet (as opposed to *zenith*) سمت النظیر state of greatest depression پستی کی انتہا، سمت القدم

nag *v. t. & i.* (-gg-) scold (someone or *at* someone) persistently ہر وقت جھاڑ جھپاڑ کرتے رہنا *n.* (colloq.) small pony

naiad (*nī*-ad) *n.* one of the water-nymphs presiding over some river or spring پن دیوی، جل دیوی

nail (nayl) *n.* horny part of a finger or toe ناخن claw پنجہ metal spike driven into a wall for hanging things کھونٹی، میخ، کیل such spike driven into two or more things to hold them together کیل، میخ *right as nails*, quite right بالکل ٹھیک *on the nail*, (of payment, etc.) immediate فوری *hit the nail on the head*, (a) do or say what is proper and effective پتے کی کہنا، ٹھیک بات کرنا

(b) get at the root of something بات کی تہہ کو پہنچ جانا *drive a nail into (someone's) coffin*, end his career (کے) تابوت میں آخری میخ ٹھونکنا *nail in (one's) coffin* (کے) تابوت میں آخری کیل **nail-scissors** *n.* one for paring nails ناخن تراش قینچی *v. t.* secure with nail(s) میخ ٹھونکنا ، کیل جڑنا fasten thus (to something) کیلوں سے (کسی چیز کے ساتھ) جڑنا *nail (lie, etc.) to the counter*, expose it (جھوٹ وغیرہ) کا بھانڈا پھوڑ دینا *nail one's colours to the mast*, commit (oneself) to a political belief openly کھلے بندوں اپنے (سیاسی) معتقدات (یا عزائم) کا اعلان کرنا

naive (nah-*eev*) *adj.* amusingly childlike and innocent معصومانہ artless, unaffected بے تصنع **naivety**, nah-*eev*-i-ti *n.* childlike innocence معصومانہ ، بھولپن ، سادہ لوحی ، سادگی artlessness تصنع نہ ہونا naive remark سادہ لوحی کی بات

naked (*nay*-ked) *adj.* stript of clothes ننگا ، عریاں ، برہنہ bare (*of* leaves or other usual covering) ننگا ، بے برگ و بار (درخت) *the naked eye*, the eye without the aid of a telescope, microscope, etc. ننگی آنکھ (کسی آلے کی مدد) کے بغیر undisguised (truth, etc.) صاف صاف **nakedly** *adv.* undisguisedly صاف صاف **nakedness** *n.* being naked ننگا ہونا ، برہنگی ، عریانی

namby-pamby *n.* & *adj.* sentimental جذباتی (یا) رقت آمیز (باتیں) insipidly pretty (talk, style, etc.) پر تصنع مگر بے کیف

name (naym) *n.* word by which someone or something is known نام *of name, by the name of*, *of the name of*, named (something), called مسمّٰی (یا صحیح تر: مسمّی) (مؤنث: مسمّاۃ ، مسمّات) *know (someone) by name*, know (him) well (کو) اچھی طرح جاننا *give (someone or something) a bad name* (a) (کو) بدنام کرنا (b) کو گالی دینا ، کا بُرا سا نام رکھنا *in the name of (law, person, etc.)*, as representing him, it, etc. (کے) حکم سے ، کے نمائندے کی حیثیت سے *in (someone's) name*, on (his) behalf کی طرف سے ، کے نام پر *in name, in name only*, not 'de facto' محض نام کا ، برائے نام *call (someone) names*, swear at him کو گالی دینا *to one's name*, belonging to کا ، کے پاس reputation (*for* honesty, etc.) (کسی کو) (کے باعث) شہرت (کی) ساکھ (for invocation) کسی کا واسطہ *in the name of God* خدارا *Why in the name of commonsense did you ever do so?* تمہیں سمجھ کا واسطہ بتاؤ تو سہی تم نے آخر کیا کیوں؟ *v. t.* give a name to کا نام رکھنا *name (someone) after (another)*, give (him) the same name as (the other's) کے نام پر نام رکھنا speak out the name of; disclose (his) name کا نام لینا state (price, etc.) بتانا ، کہنا throw suspicion, etc., on someone کسی کا نام لینا ، نام دھرنا **nameless** *adj.* without (a known) name گمنام too bad to be named جس کا نام لینے کے قابل نہ ہو ، ناقابل ذکر **namely** *adv.* (often written as a Latin abb. *viz.*) that is to say یعنی **namesake** *n.* person having the same name ہم نام *the namesake of*, having the same name as کا ہم نام

nanny (*nan*-i) *n.* (child's word for his almost old-fashioned) nurse آیا ، کھلائی ، بچے کی دایہ

nap *n.* siesta قیلولہ short sleep out of bed at any time ذرا آنکھ لگنا یا لگانا ، جھپکی ، ہلکی سی نیند *be caught napping*, be taken unawares بے خبری میں مارا جانا ، بے خبری کے عالم میں پکڑا جانا fluffy surface of cloth کپڑے کی روئیں دار سطح ، روئیں

napalm *n.* (see *Addenda*)

nape (nayp) *n.* back (*of the neck*) گدی

naphtha (*naf*-tha) *n.* inflammable oil distilled from coal-tar نفت ، نفط **naphthalene, naphthaline** (*naf*-tha-leen, or -lin) *n.* disinfectant in the form of pills got from coal-tar and used in keeping insects out of clothes, etc. ریفیتا تا تیل کی گولیاں ، نفتی گولیاں

napkin (*nap*-kin) *n.* (also *table-napkin*) piece of cloth used at meals for protecting clothes, etc. دست پاک ، دستپاک (also *nappy*), sanitary towel folded between the legs of a baby, etc. پھلیا (old use) any small piece of cloth like a napkin رومال *lay (book, etc.) in a napkin*, (a) put (it) thus جزدان میں رکھنا (b) neglect to use (it) طاقِ نسیاں پر رکھنا ، زینتِ طاقِ نسیاں بنانا

nappy (*nap*-i) *n.* (see under **napkin**)

narcissus (na*-*sis*-us) (pl. *narcissi* pr. -si, or *narcissuses*) *n.* kinds of flowering bulb including daffodil نرگس its flower نرگس ، نرگس کا پھول (*Narcissus*), (*Cl. myth.* beautiful youth who fell in love with his own image which he saw reflected in a well little suspecting that it was none other than himself; he pined away in this love until he was metamorphosed into the flower which even today bears his name and is well-known for its pretty eye-like form. نرگس **narcissism** (na*-*sis*-izm) *n.* morbid self-love اپنے سے عشق ، نرجسیت ، نرگسیت

a narcissus plant

narcotic (nah*-*kot*-ik) *adj.* of drug, etc., causing drowsiness, numbness, unconsciousness, stupor بیہوش کرنے والی ، خواب آور ، مخدّر (دوا) نشہ *n. pl.* such drugs بیہوش کرنے والی دوائیں ، یا افیم وغیرہ کی طرح کی نشے کی چیزیں **narcosis** (-*koh*-) *n.* action of narcotics افیم وغیرہ نشے کی بے ہوشی

narrate (na-*rayt*) *v. t.* tell (a story) کہانی ، کہنا give an account of (an event) بیان کرنا ، (کی) تفصیل سنانا **narrator** *n.* (na-*ray*-tĕ*) *n.* کہانی ، کہنے والا ، بیان کرنے والا

narrative (*na*-ra-tiv) *adj.* of or in the form

of story-telling کہانی کا ریا کی صُورت میں narrating *n.* story کہانی story-telling کہانی کہنا

narrow (*na*-roh) *adj.* of small width تنگ restricted چھوٹا، محدُود، تنگ with little margin مُشکل ہی سے، بمُشکل *have a narrow escape from* بمُشکل بچنا careful, thorough (search, examination) پُورا prejudiced (mind) تنگ *n.* strait کھاڑی، چھوٹی خلیج *v. t.* make or become narrow تنگ ہونا یا کرنا **narrowly** *adj.* only just بمُشکل **narrowness** *n.* being narrow تنگی **narrow-minded** *adj.* not liberal, intolerant تنگ نظر **narrow-mindedly** *adv.* تنگ نظری سے **narrow-mindedness** *n.* being narrow-minded تنگ نظری

nasal (*nay*-zĕl) *adj.* pertaining to the nose ناک کا (of sound) produced by the nose ناک میں سے نکلنے والی (آواز)، غُنّہ

nascent (*nas*-ent) *adj.* just beginning to grow; newly born نوزائیدہ، پیدا ہوتا ہُوا immature خام، ناپختہ کار

nasty (*nas*-ti) *adj.* filthy گندا، غلیظ obscene بدطینت، کینہ جُو offensive ناگوار spiteful فحش stormy (weather) خراب، طُوفان خیز serious (wound, trouble) سخت

natal (*nay*-tĕl) *adj.* of birth پیدائشی **natality** *n.* birth-rate شرحِ پیدائش

nation (*nay*-shĕn) *n.* people living in one country or having one government or culture قوم

national (*nash*-è-nĕl) *adj.* of a nation قومی pertaining to whole nation قومی، پُوری قوم کا *n.* one of a nation or country مُلک کا، باشندہ، قوم کا، فرد

nationalist (*nash*-è-na-list) *n.* champion of a nation قوم پرور، قوم پرست devoted to the movement for its independence قومی آزادی کی تحریک کا شیدائی

nationalism (-lizm) *n.* doctrine held by a nationalist as such قوم پرستی، وطن پرستی، قومی آزادی کی تحریک سے ہمدردی **nationality** (nash-è-*nal*-i-ti) *n.* membership of a nation قومیت race or cultural group forming part of one or more nations قومیت patriotic sentiment قومی جذبہ

nationalize (*nash*-è-na-liz) *v. t.* make something the property of the State قومی مِلکیت میں لینا، قومیانہ **nationalization** (-*zay*-) *n.* act of nationalizing (*of* industry, etc. قومی مِلکیت میں لینا، قومیانا

native (*nay*-tive) *adj.* pertaining to one's birth-place وطن کا، مرز بُوم کا، دیسی، مُلکی *native land* سرزمینِ وطن، اَرضِ وطن، وطن inherent quality پیدائشی۔ not artificial اَصلی، قدرتی، غیر مصنُوعی of plants and animals originally belonging (*at* the soil, a land, etc. دیسی، مُلکی of a non-European race looked upon as uncivilised مُقامی، کالا، دیسی، نیٹو، *n.* born in (*of*) a country or place نیٹو باشندہ *a native of Pakistan* پاکستان کا باشندہ *a native of Wales* ویلز کا باشندہ indigenous plant or animal دیسی پُودا (یا جانور) member of a non-European race looked upon as uncivilized مُقامی باشندہ، کالا، دیسی، نیٹو، نیٹو **nativity** (na-*tiv*-i-ti) *n.* birth ولادت، پیدائش، میلاد (*Nativity*), birth of Christ میلادِ مسیح *Nativity hymn* نغمۂ میلادِ مسیح

natural *adj.*, **naturalize** *v.t.*, **naturalization** *n.*, **naturally** *adv.* (see under **nature**

nature (*nay*-chĕ) *n.* physical universe as a whole کائنات، عالَمِ طبیعی، کارخانۂ قُدرت forces at work in it قُدرت، فِطرت، قوانینِ قُدرت، نوامیسِ فطرت outdoor world around us قدرتی مناظر، مناظرِ قدرت، مناظرِ فطرت، مظاہرِ فطرت *nature worship*, worship of the sun, ocean, trees, etc قدرتی اشیا کی پرستش، مظاہرِ قدرت کی پرستش، فِطرت پرستی *nature study*, study of plant and animal life مُطالعہ مُوالید uncivilized, life with no cultivation غیر متمدن unsophisticate life تکلّف سے عاری زندگی، سادہ زندگی *in a state of nature*, naked برہنہ، عُریاں، قدرتی لباس میں essential qualities (*of*) (کے) خواص general characteristics and feelings (of human beings) طبیعت، طبیعت، مزاج، خُو، اُفتادِ طبع (good, bad, etc.) *by nature* نیک سرشت، نیک طینت *good-natured* کے لحاظ سے (اچھا بُرا وغیرہ) *ill-natured* بدطینت class قسم، نوعیت (*of this* (*etc.*) *nature* اس قسم (یا نوعیت) کی چیز *be in the nature of* (*something*), be very much like (it) ویسا ہی ہونا **natural** (*nach*-è-rĕl) *adj.* pertaining to nature قدرتی physical (sciences, etc.) طبیعی unsophisticated جس میں تصنّع نہ ہو، بے تصنّع wild (state of animals) جنگلی inborn, born (poet, etc.) پیدائشی، فِطری، خِلقی (normal, etc.) قُدرتی *die a natural death*, meet a normal and not violent death قدرتی موت مرنا *be natural for* (*someone to do*) کے لیے بالکل قُدرتی بات ہے

naturally *adv.* in a natural way قدرتی طور پر by nature پیدائشی طور پر، خِلقی طور پر، فِطرۃً of course as might be expected قُدرتی بات ہے کہ، لازماً **naturalist** *n.* student of natural history تاریخِ طبیعی کا ماہر، ماہرِ تاریخِ مُوالید **natural history** *n.* study of nature, esp. of plant and animal life تاریخِ طبیعی، تاریخِ مُوالید **naturalize** (*nach*-è-ra-liz) *v.t.* give a foreigner the rights of citizenship (*in* a country کو حقوقِ شہریت عطا کرنا، کو حقوقِ قومیت دینا، کو اپنی قومیت دینا adopt (foreign word, custom, etc., this اختیار کرنا، اپنانا **naturalization** (-*zay*-) *n.* act of naturalizing حقوقِ قومیت دینا، اختیار کرنا، اپنانا

naught (nawt) *n.* cipher nothing ہیچ، کچھ نہیں *come to naught*, fizzle out نتیجہ خیز نہ ہونا، ناکام رہنا
naughty (*nawt*-i) *adj.* شوخ badly-behaved (child) خراب، بُرا wicked (behaviour) شریر، شرارتی
naughtily *adv.* in a naughty manner شرارت، شوخی، شرارت سے
nausea (*naw*-se-a) *n.* sickness متلی، مارِش disgust کراہت، گھن **nauseate** (*naw*-se-ayt) *v.t.* cause nausea to سے جی متلانا، سے گھن آنا **nauseating** (*naw*-) *adj.* sickening متلی آنے والی خوراک (وغیرہ)، قے آور **nauseous** (*naw*-si-us) *adj.* disgusting کریہہ، گھناؤنا
nautical (*nawt*-i-kĕl) *adj.* of navigation, etc. بحری، جہازرانی سے متعلق *nautical mile*, knot ۶۰۸۰ فٹ، بحری کوس
naval *adj.* (see under **navy**)
nave (nayv) *n.* main, middle part of a church گرجے کا درمیانی حصّہ، نافِ کلیسا
navel (*nayv*-el) *n.* depression in the middle of the abdomen ناف
navigate (*nav*-i-gayt) *v.t.* direct the course of (ship or aircraft *along* a river, *across* a sea, or *in* the air) جہاز (یا ہوائی جہاز) چلانا steer
navigable *adj.* river, etc., which can be navigated along جہازرانی کے قابل (of ships, etc.) sea-worthy سفر کے قابل (of balloons, etc.), steerable جسے اپنی مرضی سے چلایا جا سکے، جس کی سمت داری کی جا سکے
navigation (-*gay*-) *n.* art of navigating جہازرانی
navigator (*nav*-) *n.* one who navigates a ship جہازراں، جہاز کا سمت دار (see *Addenda*)
navvy (*nav*-i) *n.* unskilled labourer on roads, etc. (کھدائی کرنے والا) مزدور، بیلدار
navy (*nay*-vi) *n.* warships (*of* a country) بحریہ their officers and men بحری فوج، ارکانِ بحریہ *navy blue*, of the colour of their uniform ; dark blue گہرا نیلا **naval** (*nay*-vĕl) *adj.* pertaining to navy بحریہ سے متعلق، بحری
nay *adv.* and more than that نہیں اس سے بھی زیادہ (old use) no نہیں *will not take nay*, disregards refusal وہ نہیں تو سُنتا ہی نہیں *yea and nay*, shilly-shally ٹال مٹول کرنا *say (someone) nay*, (a) refuse (him) کو "نا" کہنا (b) contradict (him) کی تردید کرنا
Nazarene (naz-a-*reen*) *adj.* of Nazareth ناصرہ کا (as used by non-Christians) Christian ناصری، نصرانی
Nazi (*nah*-zi, or *naht*-si) *n.* member of Hitler's German National Socialist (**Na**tionalso**zi**alist) party نازی، نالسی *adj.* of this party نازی، نالسی، نازیوں کا
-nce (ns), **-ncy** (nsi) *suf.* (forming nouns from adjectives or nouns ending in *nt*) ی، یت
neap, neap-tide (*neep*-tid) *n.* tide with lowest high-water ختم مد، آخری
near (nee-ĕ*) *prep.* close to کے پاس، کے نزدیک، کے قریب *adv.* not far away in time, place or degree پاس، نزدیک، قریب *far and near*, everywhere دُور و نزدیک، ہر جگہ almost قریب قریب، تقریباً closely قریب قریب، ٹھیک ٹھیک *as near as (one) can guess* جتنا کچھ ٹھیک اندازہ ہو سکتا ہے *adj.* closely related قریبی، نزدیکی intimate (friend) گہرا، جگری narrow (escape, victory) بمشکل on the left hand side (of an animal, vehicle, etc.) (as opposed to *off*) بایاں (of translation) close لفظی (ترجمہ) (of route) short, direct نزدیک (کا)، چھوٹا *v.t.* & *i.* come close (to) (کے) قریب آنا *be near with (one's) money*, be mean and stingy کنجوس ہونا، خسیس ہونا *lie near (one's) heart*, be dear to him کو بہت عزیز ہونا *near at hand*, within reach پاس ہی، نزدیک ہی *near upon*, almost تقریباً *nearsight*, myopia دُور کی نظر کی کمزوری *nearsighted* جس کی دُور کی نظر کمزور ہو *near work*, work needing the eye close to it باریک بینی کا کام *near miss*, (in bombing or shooting) hit, which though not direct, is near enough the target to cause damage to it نشانے کے باوجود کچھ نقصان پہنچانے والا **nearly** *adv.* almost قریب قریب، تقریباً carefully غور سے *not nearly*, nothing like, far from بالکل مختلف سے
neat (neet) *adj.* tidy صاف ستھرا، صاف، پاکیزہ unadulterated بے میل، خالص well-phrased مناسب لفظوں میں، معقول clever at work کاریگر، چابک دست **neatly** *adv.* tidily صاف، صفائی سے، چابکدستی **neatness** *n.* tidiness صفائی
nebula (*neb*-ew-la) *n.* (pl. *nebulae* pr. -lee) hazy group of stars looking like an indistinct patch of light سدیم big mass of gas, etc., in the sky سحابیہ **nebulous** (-lus) *adj.* cloudlike سحابی indistinct مبہم، غیر واضح
necessary (*nes*-e-sa-ri) *adj.* needful (*to do*) ضروری، اہم *n.* (usu. *pl.*) necessities (*of*) ضروریات، لوازمات **necessarily** (*nes*-e-sa-ri-li) *adv.* of course لازماً **necessitate** (ne-*ses*-i-tayt) *v.t.* make necessary کی ضرورت پیدا کرنا **necessitous** (-*ses*-) *adj.* poor and needy (person) حاجت مند، محتاج **necessity** (ne-*ses*-i-ti) *n.* urgent need ضرورت، مجبوری *driven (to something or to do something) by necessity* پر مجبور ہو جانا *in case of necessity*, if urgently needed ضرورت پڑنے پر، بصورتِ مجبوری، بہ امرِ مجبوری *something necessary for good living* ضرورتِ زندگی، (ج) ضروریاتِ زندگی poverty احتیاج، حاجتمندی *be in necessity (of)* (کا) حاجت مند ہونا ▣ **Necessary** signifies that which has to be ; **needful**, necessary for a definite purpose ; **requisite**, required as laid down (*for something*) ; **indispensable**, that cannot be done without ; **essential** *to something*, without which it cannot be.

neck (nek) *n.* part of the body between head and shoulders گردن part of garment round it گریبان anything looking like a neck گردن *bottleneck*, (*a*) neck of a bottle بوتل کا مُنہ (*b*) inextricable difficulty مُشکِل، مُشکِل حِصّہ *neck and neck*, running even in race دَوڑ میں بالکل برابر *get it in the neck*, suffer heavily سخت نقصان اُٹھانا *neck or nothing*, with no alternative but victory or defeat یا تخت یا تختہ *save (one's) neck*, save (one's) life with difficulty بمُشکِل جان بچانا *risk (one's) neck* جان جوکھوں میں ڈالنا *break (someone's) neck* گردن کا مُنکا توڑنا *break the neck of a task*, complete its most difficult part آدھا مَیدان مار لینا، کام کا مُشکِل ترین حِصّہ ختم کر لینا *v.i.* (U.S. slang) (of couples) hug each other گلے مِلنا، بغل گیر ہونا **neck-band** *n.* part of a garment round the neck گریبان **necklace** (*nek*-lays) *n.* string of pearls, etc., worn round the neck ہار، چمپا کلی **necktie** (nek-ti) *n.* narrow band worn round the neck and hanging in front

nectar (*nek*-tě*) *n.* sweet liquid in flowers gathered by bees as honey شہد، عسل any sweet beverage لذیذ شربت (*Nectar*), beverage of Greek gods giving life and beauty یونانی دیوتاؤں کا مشروب، نقطار

nee (nay) *adj.* (of a married woman) born with the family name (So and-So) جس کا کنوار پنے کا نام تھا *Mrs. Smith 'nee' Taylor* مسز سمتھ جن کا کنوار پنے میں نام مس ٹیلر تھا

need *n.* urgent want (*of*) اشد ضرورت *be in need of* کی اشد ضرورت ہونا poverty غربت، احتیاج time of difficulty مُشکِل، آڑا وقت *a friend in need is a friend indeed* دوست وہ جو آڑے وقت کام آئے *if need be*, if circumstances demand ضرورت پڑے تو necessary (*to do*) (کی) ضرورت ہونا **needful** *adj.* what is necessary ضروری **needless** *adj.* unnecessary غیر ضروری **needs** (needz) *adv.* (only in the phrase) *needs must* (*to do*), be constrained (to do) (بالضرور) مجبور ہونا **needy** (nee-di) *adj.* poor ضرورت مند، محتاج، حاجتمند **neediness** being needy *n.* ضرورت مند ہونا

A **need** is a felt shortage; **want,** either something desired or its shortage; **requirement,** something expected; **convenience,** something desired in addition to others; **desideratum,** something which is desirable but cannot be demanded as a matter of right.

needle (*need*-ěl) *n.* very thin pointed bar of steel with a hole (called *eye*) at one end for thread for sewing سوئی thin but much longer plastic or other bar (without an eye) for knitting سلائی hollow needle (of a syringe) سوئی pointer سوئی (also *gramophone needle*), pointed piece of metal, etc., receiving and transmitting vibrations set in by a revolving gramophone record (باجے کی) سوئی *v.t.* (see *Addenda*) **needle work** *n.* sewing, etc. سوئی سلائی کا کام، سلائی **needlewoman** *n.* one who does needle-work سلائی کرنے والی، سوئی سلائی والی **needle-match** *n.* contest arousing personal animosity موجبِ عناد مقابلہ

ne'er (*nay*-è*) *adv.* (poet.) never ہرگز نہیں **ne'er-do-well** good-for-nothing person نکما، ناکارہ

negate (ne-*gayt*) *v.t.* contradict نفی کرنا، تردید کرنا، ابطال کرنا **negation** (ne-*gay*-shěn) *n.* نفی، ابطال **negative** (*neg*-a-tiv) *adj.* negating (words, etc.) انکاری wanting in positive qualities منفی (in photography) with lights and shades referred منفی (عکس) (in Maths.) minus quantity منفی (of electricity) kind produced at the negative pole منفی (برق) *n.* negative word or statement حرفِ نفی developed film, etc. from which (positive) prints are made منفی عکس (in Maths.) negative quantity منفی مقدار، نیگیٹو *v.t.* explode (a theory, etc.) کا ابطال کرنا، کو غلط ثابت کرنا contradict (a statement) کی تردید کرنا reject (a proposal) نامنظور کرنا counteract کا اثر باطل کرنا

neglect (neg-*lekt*) *v.t.* disregard نظرانداز کر دینا leave (one's duty) undone ادا نہ کرنا omit (*to do* something) (کرنے) میں غفلت کرنا *n.* neglecting or being neglected غفلت، تغافل، تساہل *be lying in a state of neglect* بُرے حال میں پڑے رہنا **neglectful** *adj.* in the habit of neglecting غافل، غفلت شعار، سہل انگار **negligent** (*neg*-li-jent) *adj.* careless بے پروا، غافل **negligible** (*neg*-li-ji-běl) *adj.* not worth considering ناقابلِ ذکر، یونہی سا very small (amount, etc.) بہت چھوٹا، برائے نام **negligence** (*neg*-li-jens) *n.* being negligent بے پروائی، غفلت

negotiate (ne-*goh*-shi-ayt) *v.t.* & *i.* confer (terms of business, etc., *with* someone) with a view to agreement سے فیصلہ کرنا، سے گفت و شنید کرنا bring about (pact, peace, etc.) thus معاہدے کی گفت و شنید کرنا get money for (a loan, etc.) قرض لینا get over or past (a difficulty, obstacle, difficult hand, etc.) successfully (مرحلہ) طے کر لینا get or give money value for (a bill, etc.) (ہنڈی وغیرہ) بھنانا یا سکارنا **negotiable** (ne-*goh*-shi-ay-běl) *adj.* that can be settled by discussion قابلِ گفت و شنید (of bill, etc.) which can be cashed جسے سکارا جا سکے *negotiable instrument*, bill, currency note, etc., which can be cashed جسے سکارا جا سکے

negro (*nee*-groh) *n.* (pl. *negroes*) black-skinned

person of African origin حبشی *n.* negro woman حبشن

Negus (*nee*-gus) *n.* (title of every) ruler of Abyssinia نجاشی

neigh (nay) *n.* cry of a horse گھوڑے کا ہنہنانا *v.i.* (of a horse) utter a neigh

neighbour (*nay*-bĕ*) *n.* person living next-door or near by ہمسایہ **neighbouring** *adj.* bordering (district, countries, etc.) ہمسایہ، قریبی **neighbourhood** *n.* district round the one mentioned its population علاقے کی آبادی being near پاس پاس ہونا، قریب ہونا، قرب، ہمسائگی **neighbourly** *adj.* (also *good neighbourly*) friendly (relations, etc.) ہمسائگی کے، دوستانہ (مراسم، تعلقات وغیرہ) **neighbourliness** *n.* being neighbourly ہمسائگی، دوستی

neither (*ni*-dhĕ*, or *nee*-dhĕ*) *pron.* not the one nor the other (*of*) دونوں میں سے کوئی ایک بھی نہیں *adj.* not either کوئی بھی نہیں *conj.* (used as *neither . . . nor*) نہ ..... نہ *neither this nor that* نہ یہ نہ وہ

nemesis (*nem*-e-sis) *n.* retributive justice; punishment that is bound to follow پاداش، مل کر رہنے والی سزا (*Nemesis*), *Cl. myth.* Greek goddess of retribution نیمسس

neo- *pref.* new نیا، جدید later تازہ تر، بعد کے دور کا، آخری modernized نئے انداز کا بنایا ہوا

neolithic (nee-o-*lith*-ik) *adj.* of the later stone age بعد کے پتھر کے زمانے کا، آخری دورِ حجر کا

neologism (ne-*ol*-o-jizm), **neology** (ne-*ol*-o-ji) *n.* word-coining وضعِ الفاظ، وضع کرنا coined word وضع کیا ہوا لفظ، نیا لفظ theological rationalizing دین میں عقلیت، علم کلام کی پیروی **neologian** *n.* & *adj.*, **neologist** *n.* person who coins words لفظ وضع کرنے والا واضع person who rationalizes in theology دین میں عقلیت پر چلنے والا **neologize** (-*ol*-) *v.i.* coin word(s) لفظ (یا الفاظ) وضع کرنا rationalize in religion دین میں عقلیت پر چلنا

neon (*nee*-on) *n.* an inert atmospheric gas used in electric signs نیون *neon light*, fluorescent tube, light, sign, etc. ٹیوب (یا بجلی کی ٹیوب میں لکھا ہوا)

neophyte (*nee*-o-f*it*) *n.* new convert نیا مذہب قبول کرنے والا، نو مذہب، نو مسلم وغیرہ) tyro اناڑی

nephew (*nev*-ew) *n.* son of one's brother بھتیجا son of one's sister بھانجا

neo-Platonism (ne-oh-pla-*ton*-izm) *n.* mixture of Platonic philosophy with Oriental mysticism which came into being in Alexandria in the third century B.C. نو فلاطونیت **neo-Platonic** *adj.* of, pertaining to or believing in neo-Platonism نو فلاطونی

nepotism (*nee*-po-tizm) *n.* favour shown to relatives خویش پروری (originally) favour shown by Popes and Cardinals to their illegitimate children who were euphemistically called their nephews اعیانِ کلیسا کی طرف سے اپنی جائز اولاد کی ناجائز حمایت

Neptune (*nep*-tewn) *Cl. myth.* identified with the Greek *Poseidon*, he was the god of the sea and a brother of the god of gods Zeus نپچون

nereid (*nee*-re-id) *Cl. myth.* a sea-nymph جل پری

nerve (nĕ*v) *n.* fibre carrying feelings in the body to and from the brain عصب، نس (old use) sinew پٹھا، عضلہ *strain every nerve* (*to do*), make an all-out effort to do (it) (کی) پوری کوشش کرنا courage, boldness, self-reliance ہمت، جرأت، خود اعتمادی (*pl.*) nervous اعصابی نظام (*pl.*) nervousness اعصابی بے چینی، اعصابی کمزوری، گھبراہٹ *get on (one's) nerves*, irritate him کو دق کرنا *v.t.* give strength or courage to قوی کرنا، حوصلہ دلانا *nerve oneself*, brace oneself حوصلہ کرنا، جرأت مند ہونا **nervous** (*nĕ**-vus) *adj.* of the nerves اعصابی *nervous system*, all the nerves in the body اعصابی نظام، نظامِ اعصاب vigorous (style, etc.) زوردار easily irritable جلد گھبرا جانے والا، اعصابی کمزوری کا مریض **nervy** (nĕ*-vi) *adj.* (colloq.) nervous جلد گھبرا جانے والا **nerveless** *adj.* (esp.) weak, having no guts کمزور، بے ہمت، بے جرأت (of style) diffuse بڑی لفاظی والا **nervine** (nĕ*-vin) *n.* & *adj.* (drug) acting on nerves اعصابی (دوا) **neural** (*nĕw*-rĕl) *adj.* of the nerves اعصابی

the human nervous system

neuralgia (new-*ral*-ji-a) *n.* nervous pain, esp. of head and face اعصابی درد **neurosis** (new-*roh*-sis) *n.* functional disorder of the nervous system اعصابی بدنظمی **neurotic** (-*rot*-) *adj.* suffering from neurosis اعصابی بدنظمی کا *n.* such a person اعصابی بدنظمی کا مریض drug affecting the nervous system اعصابی نظام پر اثر ڈالنے والی دوا **neurasthenia** (-*thay*-) *n.* weakness of the nerves اعصابی کمزوری، ضعفِ اعصاب **neuropsychic** *adj.* pertaining to the psychology of the nervous system اعصابی نفسیات کا **neurology** (-*rol*-) *n.* science of nerves علم الاعصاب، عصبیات **neurone, neuron** *n.* nerve-cell and its processes عصبہ **neuritis** (-*ri*-) *n.* inflammation of the nerves اعصابی ورم

-ness (nes) *suf.* (forming nouns from adjectives to name quality indicated by that adjective, such a noun being formed even when another exists as *humble adj.*, *humility n.*, *humbleness n.*) ی، یت

nest *n.* straw structure of a bird, etc., for its eggs and young ones گھونسلا، آشیانہ home of wasps, etc. چھتہ den (of dacoits, etc.) ڈاکوؤں کا اڈا fostering place (of vice, etc.) (کا) مرکز یا اڈا snug place خلوت خانہ، آرام دہ جگہ set of similar things fitting one inside another (برتنوں، میزوں وغیرہ کا) آشیانہ گھونسلا بنانا *v.i.* make and use a nest گھونسلا بنانا

a wasp's nest

nest-egg *n.* sum of money saved for future use اندوختہ

nestle (*nes*-èl) *v.t.* & *i.* press (oneself) lovingly close (*to*) (ماں وغیرہ کے) ساتھ لگ کر بیٹھنا lie (*down*) close and snug (*among*) (میں) جڑ کر بیٹھنا یا لیٹنا **nestling** (*nes*-ling) *n.* young bird which has not left the nest yet پرندے کا گھونسلے والا بچہ

Nestor (*nes*-tĕ*) *Cl. myth.* mythical old king famous in Greece for his wisdom and eloquence نسطور، نسطر wise old man پیر دانا

net *n.* open-work of crossed and knotted strings, etc. جال، دام such material (for fishing, etc.) جال *tennis* (or *volley-ball*) *net*, boundary between two halves of the court نیٹ *adj.* real (weight, profit, income, price, etc.) after making all the deductions بعد منہائی، اصلی، خالص *v.t.* (-tt-) catch (fish, etc.) in a net جال میں پکڑنا cover (a tree, etc.) with a net in order to protect its fruit پر جالی ڈالنا gain as a net profit خالص منافع کمانا **netball** *n.* girl's game in which the goal is a small net over an elevated horizontal ring نیٹ بال **netting** *n.* net material جالی *wire-netting*, wire gauze لوہے کی جالی **network** *n.* connected system of crossing and recrossing lines (of canals, railways, etc.) (کا) جال، کا بچھا ہوا جال

nether (*nedh*-ĕ*) *adj.* (old use) lower نچلا، نیچے کا، زیریں *Netherlands*, Low Countries (*i.e.*, Holland and Belgium) نشیبی ممالک

nettle (*net*-èl) *n.* wild plant with stinging leaves بچھوا *nettle-rash*, a skin disease producing similar effect بچھوا، چھپے، پھوڑے provoke غصہ دلانا

nettle

neural *adj.* **neuralgia** *n.*, **neurasthenia** *n.* **neuritis** *n.*, **neurology** *n.*, **neuron** *n.*, **neurone** *n.*, **neurosis** *n.*, **neurotic** *adj.* & *n.* (see under **nerve**)

neuter (*new*-tĕ*) *adj.* sexless بے صنف، بے جنس (of words) neither feminine nor masculine جنس مشترک

neutral (*newt*-rĕl) *adj.* (*of* person, country, etc.) not taking either side in a quarrel غیر جانبدار with no definite characteristics غیر متعین (of point, etc.) having no effect either way بے اثر *n.* neutral person, country, etc. غیر جانبدار شخص یا مملک position of the parts in a gear mechanism where no power is transmitted گیئروں کی بے حرکتی **neutrality** *n.* غیر جانبداری **neutralize** *v.t.* make (country, etc.) neutral غیر جانبدارانہ بنانا make non-effective بے اثر بنانا، اثر توڑنا

neutron (*newt*-ron) *n.* one of the uncharged parts of an atomic nucleus having almost the same mass as a proton برقیہ جن پر کوئی برقی بار نہ ہو، برقیہ

never (*nev*-ĕ*) *adv.* (poet. abb. *ne'er*) at no time کبھی نہیں، ہرگز نہیں not at all بالکل نہیں

nevertheless (*nev*-ĕ*-dhè-les) *conj.* yet پھر بھی، تاہم، بایں ہمہ

new *adj.* fresh تازہ only just made or found نیا later تازہ، کے بعد *new look*, up-to-date appearance (esp. in women's wear) تازہ ترین فیشن *New Deal*, (U.S.) Roosevelt's social and economic measures from 1932 to the end of his days for controlling the unprecedented depression in the early thirties of the 20th century نیو ڈیل، نئی تقسیم *adv.* recently (done, or doing) نیا، نیا نیا، ابھی، حال ہی میں تازہ **newly** (*new*-li) *adv.* recently in a new way نئی طرح، نئے انداز، نیا، تازہ **newness** *n.* being new نیا ہونا، تازگی **newcomer** *n.* one who has recently arrived نووارد، نیا آنے والا **newfangled** (new-*fang*-èld) *adj.* unpleasantly modern (fashion, etc.) عجیب سا نیا **New Year** *n.* beginning of another year نیا سال، سال نو *New Year's gift* نئے سال کا تحفہ **New Year's Day** *n.* January 1 نیا سال، سال نو، نو روز first day of the year of any calendar نو روز

news (newz) *n.* fresh information خبر *a piece of news*, *news-item* خبر *It's news to me*; that is a revelation مجھے تو کچھ معلوم نہیں، یہ بڑی عجیب بات سنائی آپ نے **news-agent** *n.* shopkeeper selling newspapers, etc. اخبار فروش **newsboy** *n.* boy hawking newspapers in the streets بازاروں میں پھر کر اخبار بیچنے والا اخبار والا، ہاکر **newscaster** *n.* (see *Addenda*) **newspaper** *n.* (usu. daily) periodical mainly giving the news of the day اخبار **newsreel** *n.* cinema film showing news of the day نیوز ریل، روزانہ خبروں کا فلم **newsy** (*new*-zi) *adj.* (colloq.) abounding in news خبروں سے بھرا، چٹپٹا، خبروں ہی خبروں والا

newt *n.* water-lizard ریگ ماہی، آبی چھپکلی

a newt

next (nekst) *adj.* nearest قریب ترین immediately following اگلا *adv.* immediately following

اس کے بعد، اس کے آگے، کے ساتھ *prep.* nearest to *n.* the immediately following (thing or person) اگلا شخص اگلی چیز *next door*, (*a*) the next house ساتھ والا گھر (*b.* in or to it ساتھ والے گھر میں کی طرف (*c*) almost تقریباً *the next best*, the one immediately following the best اس کے بعد سب سے اچھا

nexus (*nek*-sus) *n.* connection تعلق، رشتہ، رابطہ

nib *n.* metal point of a pen نب، نوک قلم، زبانِ خلق *v.t.* insert nib into a penholder نب لگانا cut nib on quill, etc. قلم تراشنا

nibble (*nib*-el) *v.t.* & *i.* take small bites (*at*) (کو) کترنا *n.* nibbling (*at* something) کترنا

nice (nis) *adj.* pleasing خوشگوار، پُر لطف dainty نفیس subtle (distinction, etc.) باریک، دقیق delicate نازک fussy نازک مزاج، نفاست پسند *be too nice about (something)* (کے بارے میں) حد سے زیادہ نازک مزاج **nicely** (*n*:s-li) *adv.* نفاست سے **nicety** (ni-se-ti) *n.* punctiliousness بے حد احتیاط، حد سے زیادہ احتیاط *to a nicety*, without any error بالکل صحیح، بے حد احتیاط سے۔ delicate distinction باریک بینی

niche (nich) *n.* hollow in a wall for a statue, etc. طاق *a niche in the temple of fame*, place among the distinguished dead زمرۂ مشاہیر میں جگہ suitable position (*for*) (کے لیے) مناسب جگہ

nick (nik) *n.* V-shaped notch made as a record نشانی کے طور پر ڈالا ہوا دندانہ، نشان *v.t.* make a notch thus نشانی کے طور پر دندانہ ڈالنا *in the nick of time*, only just in time عین وقت پر، وقت کے وقت

nickel (nik-el) *n.* whitish metal used in alloys نِکل (U.S.) five cent coin نکل، پانچ سینٹ کا امریکی سکہ *nickel silver* نقلی چاندی *nickel steel*, نکل والا فولاد *v.t.* coat with nickel نکل کرنا **nickelodean** *n.* (see *Addenda*)

nickname (*nik*-naym) *n.* popular name instead (or as a corruption) of the real عُرف *v.t.* give a nickname to کا نام رکھنا، کو لقب دینا

nicotine (*nik*-o-tin) *n.* poisonous element of tobacco نکوٹین، تمباکو کا زہر *Lady Nicotine*, tobacco چنیا بیگم کی بہن چھنیا بیگم، تمباکو **nicotinism** (*nik*-o-ti-nizm) *n.* tobacco-poisoning تمباکو کا زہر **nicotian** (ni-*koh*-shen) *adj.* of tobacco تمباکو کا

niece (nees) *n.* daughter of one's brother بھتیجی daughter of one's sister بھانجی

nifty (*nif*-ti) *adj.* (U.S.) spruce ; prim and neat in appearance سجا بنا، چھیل چھبیلا، بانکا، چھیلا

niggard (*nig*-e*d) *adj.* miser کنجوس، بخیل **niggardly** *adj.* miserly person کنجوس scanty کم، بخیلانہ **niggardliness** *n.* miserliness کنجوسی، بخیلی

nigger (*nig*-e*) *n.* (contemptuous term for) negro حبشی، کالا، بجھنگا

niggle (*nig*-el) *v.i.* prefer petty detail to broad effects مجموعی اثرات کی بجائے جزئیات زور دینا **niggling** *adj.* petty پُست، گھٹیا cramped handwriting گنجان

nigh (n.) *adv.* & *prep.* (poet.) near نزدیک، کے نزدیک

night (nıt) *n.* time of darkness between daylight and daylight رات، شب period of obscurantism دورِ جاہلیت (*Phrases* :) *at night*, *in the night* رات کو *by night*, under its cover رات کے اندھیرے میں *have a good* (or *bad*) *night* رات آرام (یا بے آرامی) سے کاٹنا *make a night of it*, spend it in festivity رات ضیافت و تفریح میں بسر کرنا *dirty night*, stormy one طوفانی رات *night and day*, always ہمیشہ، چوبیں گھنٹے **night-bird** *n.* nightingale بلبل owl اُلّو person who is active and about at night رات کو کام کرنے والا، رات گرد **nightcap** *n.* cap worn in bed رات کو اوڑھنے کی ٹوپی **night-dress** *n.* رختِ شب **nightfall** *n.* end of daylight رات پڑنا **night-gown** *n.* long, loose garment worn by women and children in bed رختِ شب، خانگی لبادہ **nightmare** (*n*:t-may-e*) *n.* incubus ; dreadful monster of the dream who suffocates the sleeper کابوس horrible experience دہشتناک واقعہ **night watch** *n.* watch by night رات کا پہرہ person keeping it (called the *night-watchman*) رات کو پہرہ دینے والا *in the night watches*, during the wakeful nights جو راتیں آنکھوں میں کٹیں اُن میں **nightwork** *n.* work (that must be) by night رات کا کام **nightly** *adj.* & *adv.* (happening, etc.) every night or at night only (ہر) رات کا، شبینہ، شبانہ **nighty** (*n*:-ti) *n.* (children's word for) night-gown رختِ شب، خانگی لبادہ

nightingale *n.* the well-known songbird (of the same species as, but somewhat different from, our بلبل، عندلیب، ہزار داستان

nihilism (*n*:-hi-lızm) *n.* opposition to all constituted authority (as by Communists in the early stages of their movement) معاشرے میں ہر قسم کی منظم حکومت کے قیام کی مخالفت belief that nothing has real existence تشکیک، انکار **nihilist** (n-hi-list) *n.* one who believes in or practises nihilism ہر مروّجہ نظام کا مخالف **nihility** (ni-*hil*-i-ti) *n.* nothingness کچھ نہ ہونا، نیستی، عدم

nil *n.* nothing کچھ نہیں (in score, etc.) zero صفر

nimble (*nim*-b.l) *adj.* quick (movement, wits, understanding, etc.) تیز **nimbly** *adv.* quickly تیز، تیزی سے، سرعت سے

nimbus (*nim*-bus) *n.* halo : cloud of glory تاجِ نور، ہالہ

nincompoop (*nin*-kom-poop) *n.* fool بیوقوف، احمق، گاؤدی

nine (nın) *n.* & *adj.* 9 نو *a nine days' wonder*, that which attracts attention but not for a long period چاردن کی چاندنی **ninth** *adj.* 9th نواں **nineteen** (*nin-teen*) *n.* & *adj.* 19 اُنیس **nineteenth** (*nin-teenth*) *adj.* 19th اُنیسواں *nineteenth hole*, (golf slang) club bar گاف کلب کا شراب خانہ **ninety** (*nin-ti*) *n.* & *adj.* 90 نوّے **ninetieth** (*nin-ti-eth*) *adj.* 90th نوّے واں

ninepins (*nin-pinz*) *n. pl.* game in which nine bottle-shaped pegs of wood (called *pins*) are set up to be knocked down by a ball rolled along the ground نَو مُنڈر

ninepins

ninny (*nin-i*) *n.* foolish person اَحمق، گاؤدی ninth,

ninon (*nee-nawn*) *n.* light silk fabric ایک باریک ریشمی کپڑا، ننوں

nip *n.* pinch چٹکی small dose (esp. of liquor) (شراب کی) چُسکی sensation of cold, etc. سردی کا احساس *nip in the air*, a feeling of frost سردی کا احساس *v.t.* & *i.* (-pp-) give a nip to چٹکی لینا take a small dose of (liquor) (شراب کی) چُسکی لینا (of frost) stop the growth of (plant, etc.) پودوں کا پالے سے ٹھٹھرنا *nip (something) in the bud*, stop its development while yet early جلدی ختم کر دینا سر اُٹھاتے ہی کچل دینا **nippy** (*nip-i*) *adj.* (of weather) cold ٹھنڈا، سرد (slang) nimble تیز، پھرتیلا *n.* (slang) waitress at a Lyon's restaurant لائینز کی خادمہ

nipper *n.* (colloq.) small boy (esp. a street arab) بے خانماں

nipple (*nip-èl*) *n.* point of the breast through which infants suckle milk دودھ، سرپستان، بھٹنی nipple-shaped thing with which to feed infants from bottle, etc. نپل

nippy *adj.* (see under **nip**

nisi (*ni-si*) *L. conj.* unlesss جب تک، تا آنکہ *decree* (or *rule* or *order*) *nisi*, decree (etc.) valid unless cause is shown to the contrary by a fixed date بالتفصیل قید

nitre (*ni-tè**) *n.* saltpetre قلمی شورہ، شورہ **nitric** (*ni-trik*) *adj.* made of nitre شورے کا، نائٹرک *nitric acid* شورے کا تیزاب **nitrous** (*ni-rus*) *adj.* made of nitre containing less oxygen than is contained by nitric compounds نائٹرس **nitrate** (*ni-rayt*) *n.* one of the salts of nitric acid some of which are used as fertilizers نائٹریٹ **nitrogen** (*ni-ro-jèn*) *n.* gas forming about four-fifths of the air نائٹروجن

nitrogenous (*ni-roj-è-nus*) *adj.* containing nitrogen نائٹروجن والی (خوراک وغیرہ) **nitro-glycerine** *n.* powerful explosive compound of glycerine and sulphuric acids نائٹرو گلیسرین

nix (*niks*) *n.* (slang) nothing کچھ نہیں، محض ٹھن گوپال

[1]**No.** (*num-bĕ**) *n.* (abbr. of) number (and written before a number as *No. 786*) نمبر، بعہ

[2]**no** (*noh*) *adj.* not any بالکل نہیں، کوئی نہیں *adv.* not نہیں nay نہیں not at all بالکل نہیں، ذرا بھی نہیں *whether or not*, either way ہو یا نہ ہو

noble (*noh-bèl*) *adj.* of high character شریف، عالی ظرف splendid شاندار، عظیم الشان of high birth اونچے خاندان کا، عالی نسب، امیر زادہ *noble-minded* شریف النفس *n.* person of noble birth نواب، رئیس، تعلقدار **nobility** (*no-bil-i-ti*) *n.* the nobles as a class نواب، اُمرا quality of being noble شرافت، عالی ظرفی **nobly** *adv.* شرافت سے

nobleman *n.* noble رئیس، نواب، تعلقہ دار

nobody (*noh-bod-i*) *n.* none کوئی نہیں quite unimportant person بے حیثیت آدمی، بے حقیقت شخص *a mere nobody* بالکل بے حیثیت آدمی

nocturnal (*nok-tĕ*-nĕl*) *adj.* nightly; pertaining to the night رات کا یا کو شبینہ

nod *v.t.* & *i.* (-dd-) bend (the head) forward quickly to greet or show approval سر آگے کو ہلانا *have a nodding acquaintance with (person, subject, etc.)*, know (him, her or it) to some extent سے کسی قدر واقف ہونا، کو کچھ کچھ جاننا drop the head in dozing اونگھنا، اونگھ میں سر کا نیچے ہو جانا *n.* nodding movement of the head سر کا اِشارہ *the land of nod*, sleep نیند کا ملک، نیند، عالم خواب

noddle (*nod-èl*) *n.* (colloq.) head سر

noddy (*nod-i*) *n.* simpleton بیوقوف، سادہ لوح

node (*nohd*) knob or knot گانٹھ، گرہ، گوٹھڑی **nodule** (*nod-ewl*) *n.* small rounded lump of anything گومڑی، ڈلی، گولی

nodus (*noh-dus*) *n.* (pl. *nodi* pr. *noh-di*) *n.* difficulty ; knotty point مشکل، اِشکال، مُشکل نکتہ، معقدہ complication in plot of story پلاٹ میں پیچیدگی دیا گرہ یا عقدہ

Noel, Nowel (*noh-el*) *int.* (in Christmas cards only) (cry of joy) مُبارک، مُبارکباد

noetic (*noh-et-ik*) *adj.* of the intellect ذہنی، عقلی

noise (*noiz*) *n.* din شور، غل *big noise*, (colloq.) important personality اہم شخصیت *make a noise in the world*, become famous مشہور ہو جانا **noisy** (*noi-zi*) *adj.* making much noise شور مچانے والا (place, etc.) full of noise شور و غل والی (جگہ) **noisily** *adv.* loudly شور مچا کر۔ چلا کر **noiseless** *adj.* quiet خاموش، پُرسکوت

noisome (*noi-sum*) *adj.* (of smell) offensive بُری، خراب (بو)

noisy *adj.* (see under **noise**

nomad (*nom-ad*, or *nohm-*) *n.* member of a

wandering tribe خانہ بدوش، بَدْوِی **nomadic** (*nom*-a-dik, or *nohm*-) *adj*. of a nomad خانہ بدوش، خانہ بدوشانہ
no-man's-land *n*. (see under **land**) hostile forces مخالف فوجوں یا ملکوں کے مابین خالی علاقہ، اَرضِ فاصِل
nom de guerre (*nom*-de-goh*) *n*. pseudonym (for writings, war, etc.) (قلمی یا جنگی یا) فرضی نام **nom de plume** (*nom*-de-ploom) *n*. pen-name قلمی نام
nomenclature (*noh*-men-klay-chĕ*) *n*. system of giving names نام رکھنے کا اُصُول (esp.) system of giving (scientific) names سائنسی یا علمی اِصطلاحات scientific) terminology علمی اِصطلاحات
nominal (*nom*-i-nĕl) *adj*. existing not in fact but in name only نام کا، محض نام کا existing in word only (as the nominal value of a share) اَصلی نہیں بلکہ صرف لکھی ہوئی، مکتوبہ very small amount ; one much below the actual value
nominally *n*. just in name برائے نام
nominate (*nom*-i-nayt) *v. t.* appoint نامزد کرنا propose (someone) for election کا نام پیش کرنا **nomination** (*-nay-*) *n*. nominating نامزدگی **nominee** (nom-i-*nee*) *n*. nominated person نامزد شخص **nominative** (*nom*-i-nay-tiv) *adj*. appointed by nomination (opp. of *elective*) نامزد، نامزدہ (in grammar) subjective (case) حالتِ فاعلی *n*. nominative case حالتِ فاعلی (loosely speaking) subject فاعِل، مُبتدا *the nominative absolute*, independent construction of a noun, pronoun or gerund ; as : *that done* ; *errors and omission excepted* ; *he having retired* مطلق فاعلی حالت
non- (non) *pref*. not نا، غیر (as, *non-essential* غیر ضروری
non-acceptance *n*. not accepting عدم قبولیت **nonage** (*non*-ij) *n*. being under age نابالغی
nonagenarian (no-naj-e-nay-ri-ĕn) *n*. ninety-year-old person نَوے سالہ ، نوے سال کا (بوڑھا) پیر نودسالہ
non-appearance *n*. failure to appear before court, etc. غیر حاضری absence عدم موجودگی **non-belligerent** (non-be-*lij*-ĕ-rent) *adj*. & *n*. country) refraining from active or open participation in a war غیر محاربی (مُلک)
nonce (nons) *n* present حال، اب، ابھی (used only in the phrase : *for the nonce*, only for the present فی الحال، صرف ابھی کے لیے
nonchalant (*non*-shal-ant) *adj*. indifferent, unmoved (*about*) بے پروا cool ٹھنڈے دل کا **nonchalance** (*non*-shal-ans) *n*. indifference or coolness بے پروائی، ٹھنڈے دل کا ہونا
non-combatant (*-kom-*) *n*. member of an armed force who is not supposed to fight غیر مصافی فوجی *adj*. (of population, etc.) not fighting غیر مصافی (آبادی)
non-commissioned (*-mish-*) *adj*. (officer in the armed forces) who does not have a commission عہدیدار یا سپاہی *Non-commissioned officer*, (abbr. *N. C. O.*) one below the rank of a (Junior Commissioned Officer عہدیدار
non-committal (*-mit-*) *adj*. (answer), avoiding commitment ; cautiously vague محتاط، غیر فیصلہ کُن
non-compliance (*-pl*-ans) *n*. failure to comply عدم تعمیل
non-conductor (*-duk-tĕ**) *n*. insulator غیر موصل
non-conformist (*-fo**-) *n*. & *adj*. (Protestant) not conforming to the established church غیر مقلد (عیسائی پروٹسٹنٹ) **non-conformity** *n*. being a non-conformist *n*.
non-co-operate (non-coh-*op*-ĕ-rayt) *v. t.* refuse to co-operate (*with*) سے تعاون نہ کرنا، سے عدم تعاون کرنا
non-co-operative *adj*. one who refuses or fails) to co-operate عدم تعاون کا رویہ والا **non-co-operation** (*-ray-*) *n*. refusal or failure to co-operate عدم تعاون this as a regular political movement in Indo-Pak history تحریک عدم تعاون، نابل ورتن
nondescript (*non*-des-kript) *n*. & *adj*. (person or thing) not easily described (شخص یا شے) مُبہم نرالا، عجیب، انوکھا odd
none (nun) *pron*. no one(s) کوئی بھی نہیں، کبھی نہیں *adv*. not at all بالکل نہیں *nonetheless*, nevertheless *none too plentiful* کچھ زیادہ تو نہیں تاہم (*be*) *none worse for* (*some misadventure*) زیادہ نقصان نہ ہونا
nonentity (no-*nent*-i-ti) *n*. unimportant person غیر اہم شخص، بے حقیقت آدمی non-existing thing معدوم شے non-existence عدم
non-essential (*-sensh-ĕl*) *n*. & *adj*. (thing or person) not essential غیر ضروری (شخص یا چیز)
non-intervention (*-vensh-*) *n*. keeping aloof from other countries' disputes as national policy عدم مداخلت
non-member (*-mem-*) *n*. one who is not a member غیر رکن
non-objective *adj* (see *Addenda*)
non-party, non-partisan (*-zan*) *adj*. (of person) not belonging to a party آزاد
nonplus (non-*plus*) *v. t.* (-ss-) make (someone) so perplexed that he does not know what to do or say دم بخود کر دینا **non-plussed** *adj*. perplexed دم بخود
non-resistance (*-zis-*) *n*. belief that authori

no matter how it is exercised, must always be submitted to تسلیم کاری ، عدم مقاومت
nonsense (*non*-sens) *n.* (words, rhyme, verse, etc.) meaningless (but often amusing) بے معنی (مگر پُرلطف) absurd (talk, behaviour) فضول ، بیہودہ ، احمقانہ *n.* absurdity بیہودگی ، حماقت **nonsensical** (-*sens*-) *adj.* silly (talk, behaviour, etc.) احمقانہ ، بیہودہ
non-skid (-skid) *adj.* (of tyre) not apt to skid نہ پھسلنے والا
non-stop *adj.* (of journey, or train, etc.,) without a stop بغیر رُکے ہوئے ، مسلسل ، لگاتار *adv.* without stopping, continuously رُکے بغیر *n.* train with a non-stop run کہیں نہ رُکنے والی گاڑی
noodle (*nood*-ĕl) *n.* simpleton سادہ لوح strip of dried dough in soup (کڑھی وغیرہ کی) لچھیہ
nook (nŭk) *n.* inside corner کونے کے اندر کا حصّہ *every nook and corner* اندر باہر ہر جگہ secluded corner گوشۂ تنہائی
noon *n.* exact 12 o'clock in the day ٹھیک بارہ بجے **noonday, noontide** (-tīd) *n.* midday دوپہر
noose (noos, or nooz) *n.* loop of rope with a running knot to enable one to pull it tight پھندا *the hangman's noose* پھانسی کا پھندا ، پھانسی

a noose

nor *conj.* not even *neither:...nor* نہ ...... نہ *not...nor* نہ ..... نہ *neither this nor that* نہ یہ نہ وہ *not a man nor woman* نہ عورت نہ مرد
Nordic *adj.* Scandinavian, of the tall long-headed blond race of Northern Europe نارڈک
normal (no*-mĕl) *adj.* usual عام standard مثالی ، معیاری ، نارمل *above (or below) normal* معیار سے اُونچا (یا نیچے) **normal school**, school for training teachers in how to impart up-to-the-standard education تربیتِ اساتذہ کا مدرسہ
Norman (*No**-man) *n.* of Normandy نارمن *adj.* (of *kings, style, French*, etc.) belonging to the Norman conquerors of Britain نارمن
north (no*th) *n.* point of compass towards the pole-star or to one's left as one faces the rising sun شمال part of a country lying to the north of the rest مُلک کا شمال *adj.* pertaining to the north شمالی *the North Pole* قطبِ شمالی *the north wind*, the wind blowing *from* the north شمالی ہوا ، بادِ شمال *adv.* to or towards the north شمال کی طرف ، شمال کو **northerly** (*no**-dhĕ*-li) *adj.* of or from the north شمالی *adv.* to the north شمال کی طرف ، شمال کو
northern (*no**-dhĕ*n) *adj.* in or of the north شمالی **northerner** (*no**-) *n.* one living *in* the north شمالی حصّے کا باشندہ **northward** (*no*th*-wĕ*d) *adj.* to or towards the north شمال کی طرف کا **northwards** (*no*th*-wĕ*dz) *adj.* & *adv.* to or towards the north شمال کی طرف (کا) **north-east** *n. adj.* & *adv* (to or of the) direction between the north and the east شمال مشرق ، شمال مشرقی یا شمال مشرق کو **north-west** *n., adj.* & *adv.* (to or of the) direction between the north and the west شمال مغرب ، شمال مغربی ، یا شمال مغرب کو
nose (nohz) *n.* organ of smell in men and animals ناک nozzle دہانہ ، مُنہ jutting part آگے کو نکلا ہوا حصّہ sense of smell سونگھنے کی حِس ، قوّتِ شامّہ *pay through the nose (for something)*, pay heavily (for it) سودا سخت مہنگا پڑنا ، کی گراں قیمت ادا کرنا *v.t.* & *i.* smell (*about* a place *for* something) and find it (*out*) سونگھ سونگھ کر تلاش کرنا move carefully احتیاط سے چلنا *nose (one's) way through* میں بڑی احتیاط سے بڑھنا
nose-dive *n.* headlong descent (of aircraft) (ہوائی جہاز کا) سر کے بل غوطہ *v.t.* (of an aircraft) make a nose-dive (ہوائی جہاز کا) سر کے بل غوطہ لگانا **nosegay** *n.* bouquet گلدستہ **nose-rag** *n.* (slang) handkerchief رومال **nose-ring** *n.* ring for nose or snout ناک کا چھلّا ، ناتھ ، نتھ **nosey, nosy** (noh-zi) *adj.* (slang) having a large nose inquisitive, busy-body
nostalgia (nos-*tal*-ji-a) *n.* homesickness گھر کا ہڑکا ، وطن کی یاد
nostril (*nos*-tril) *n.* either of the two openings in the nose نتھنا
nostrum (*nos*-trum) *n.* pet scheme for social (etc.) reform اپنی پسند کی سیاسی اصلاحی تجویز quack remedy (esp. the one advertised by its maker) ہمارا خاص الخاص نسخہ ، عطائی دوا
not (abbr. **n't**) *adv.* (expressing denial or negation, and attached to the verb *to be* or to auxiliaries) نہیں ، نہ
nota bene (*noh*-ta-*bee*-ne) (abbr. *N.B.*) note well; please note یاد رہے note نوٹ ، فائدہ ، حاشیہ
notable (*noht*-) *adj.* worth-noticing or worth-mentioning قابلِ ذکر ، قابلِ توجّہ famous مشہور distinguished ممتاز ، نمایاں **notably** (*noht*-ab-li) *adv.* remarkably **notability** (-*bil*-) *n.* important personality اہم شخصیت being worthy of notice قابلِ توجّہ ، قابلِ ذکر ہونا
notary (*noht*-ĕ-ri) *n.* (also *notary public*) person authorized to draw up legal documents, etc. وثیقہ نویس person authorized to be a witness to their signing ناظرِ رجسٹری
notation (noh-*tay*-shĕn) *n.* system of representing musical notes, numbers, quantities, etc., by signs or symbols (اعداد یا موسیقی کی دُھنوں کی) ترسیم
notch (noch) *n.* V-shaped cut (*in* or *on* something) دندانہ ، دانتا *v.t.* make a notch دندانہ ڈالنا ، نشان لگانا

note (noht) *n.* brief record (of lecture, facts, etc.) نوٹ، یادداشت *make* (or *take*) *notes of a lecture* سبق کی یادداشت قلم بند کرنا *note-book* کاپی، بیاض brief commentary (*to* a book) or explanation of (*on* a word) شرح، حاشیہ short letter ; memorandum رُقعہ *note-paper* رُقعے لکھنے کا کاغذ formal communication from one government to another ایک حکومت کی طرف سے دوسری کو، سیاسی مُراسلہ (also *currency-note*) paper money ; government's (etc.) promise to pay the stated amount نوٹ، زرِ کاغذی *10-rupee note* دس روپے کا نوٹ *promissory note*, I.O.U. پرامیسری نوٹ single musical sound سُر symbol for it سُر کی علامت، سُر کا نشان key (of harmonium) سُر، پردہ sign in writing نشان، علامت *note of interrogation*, (?), question-mark سوالیہ نشان، علامتِ استفہام *note of exclamation*, (!), علامتِ استعجاب (10) being noticed ذکر *worthy of note* قابلِ ذکر، قابلِ لحاظ *take note of* (کو) اچھی طرح یاد رکھنا (کو) بھولنا نہیں (11) distinction اِمتیاز (12) expressive quality (esp. in voice) (*of* courage, etc.) لہجہ *v.t.* notice, observe دیکھنا pay polite attention to کی طرف توجّہ کرنا remarks about (in speech. etc.) کا بھی ذکر کرنا write (something *down*) لکھ لینا، قلم بند کر لینا

noted (*noht*-ed) *adj.* famous مشہور **noteworthy** (*noht*-wē*dhi) *adj.* deserving attention قابلِ ذکر، قابلِ لحاظ

nothing (*nuth*-ing) *n.* no thing کچھ نہیں، ذرا بھی نہیں مُطلق نہیں، بالکل نہیں unimportant person or thing ناقابلِ ذکر شخص یا شے، ہیچ *come to nothing*, fizzle out کا کوئی نتیجہ نہ نکلنا، کا کچھ نہ بننا، ناکام رہنا *make nothing of*, (*a*) not to understand سے کچھ سمجھ میں نہ آنا (*b*) give no importance سے کچھ پلّے نہ پڑنا۔ (*c*) not to make use of سے فائدہ نہ اُٹھانا کو خاطر میں نہ لانا *nothing for* (*one*) *but* (*to do*), the only course open to (one) being (کسی کے لیے) کے سوا کوئی چارۂ کار نہ ہونا *there is nothing in it*, it is quite unimportant or uninteresting یہ تو کچھ بھی نہیں **nothingness** (*nu*-) *n.* non-existence عدم worthlessness بیکار ہونا، فضول ہونا **nothingarian** (*-gay-*) *n.* religious sceptic مذہبی مُتشکِّک

notice (*noh*-tis) *n.* (usu. printed) public announcement اِعلان *put up a notice* (*on the notice-board*) اِعلان چسپاں کرنا *notice-board*, board or other place for putting up a notice اِعلانات کا تختہ warning نوٹس beforehand information (of the termination of service or agreement, or of resoting to strike, etc., by the mentioned date) نوٹس، اِطلاع *at short notice*, without sufficient margin of time کافی مُہلت کے بغیر، ناکافی مُہلت کا advertisement in some paper of a new book or picture or play اِعلان attention توجّہ، پروا *take no notice of*, (*a*) pay no attention to کی طرف توجّہ نہ کرنا (*b*) pay no heed to کی پروا نہ کرنا complaint شکایت *bring* (*something*) *to the notice of* (*someone*) (کسی کے) نوٹس میں لانا، (کسی سے) امر کی شکایت کرنا criticism اعتراض، expression of (one's) opinion اظہارِ خیال *v.t.* & *i.* see دیکھنا *take* cognizance (*of*) کی طرف توجّہ کرنا express opinion اِظہارِ خیال کرنا **noticeable** (*noht*-i-sab-ĕl) prominent, easily noticed نُمایاں ▣ To **notice** means to pay attention to ; to **note**. do so (perhaps even in writing) very clearly. Again. to **notice** is to take cognizance of ; to **perceive, to see** clearly ; to **observe, see** deliberately ; to **survey,** something in detail ; and to **examine** it thoroughly.

notify (*noh*-ti-fi) announce کا اِعلان کرنا report (something *to* someone) کو اِطلاع دینا **notification** (*-kay-*) *n.* announcement اِعلان **notifiable** (-fi) *adj.* that which must be reported جس کی اِطلاع دینا ضروری ہو

notion (*noh*-shĕn) *n.* idea خیال، تصوّر opinion رائے، نظریّہ

notorious (no-*to*-ri-us) *adj.* having a bad reputation بدنام، رُسوا **notoriety** (no-to-*ri*-ĕ-ti) *n.* بدنامی، رُسوائی، تشہیر

notwithstanding (not-widh-*stand*-ing) *prep.* despite (the fact that) کے باوجود *conj.* although حالانکہ، اگرچہ

nought (not) *n.* zero صفر nothing کچھ نہیں

noumenon (noom-e-non) *n.* (pl. *noumena*) object of intellectual intuition (opp. of *phenomenon*) ذات، حقیقت

noun *n.* (in grammar) word used as a name اسم

nourish (*nu*-rish) *v.t.* feed خوراک دینا، غذا پہنچانا، پرورش کرنا have or encourage (hope, hatred, etc.) اُمّیدیں باندھنا، یا بندھانا **nourishment** *n.* food خوراک، غذا food value غذائیت

novel (*nov*-el) *n.* fictitious story spread over a whole book of one or more volumes ناول new نیا unusual (method, etc.) انوکھا، نرالا، عجیب **novelty** (*nov*-el-ti) *n.* being new نیا ہونا being strange انوکھا ہونا something new or strange نئی یا نرالی چیز (*pl.*) variety of nice, inexpensive articles (on sale) (برائے فروخت) بہت سی اچھی اور سستی چیزیں، نرالی چیزیں فروخت کے لیے **novelist** (*nov*-e-list) *n.* writer of novel(s) ناول نویس، ناول نگار **novelette** (nov-e-*let*) *n.* small length novel چھوٹا ناول، ناولچہ

November (noh-*vem*-bĕ*) *n.* the eleventh month of the English calendar (so named because originally the ninth month of the Roman calendar) نومبر

novice (*nov*-is) *n*. beginner ; tiro نَو آموز، اَناڑی

now (nou) *adv*. at the present moment, or a little before or after it اَب ابھی by that time اِس وَقت (in expressions of consolidation, reproof, explanation, etc., for emphasis without any reference to time) اَب بات یہ ہے کہ *now and again, now and then* کبھی کبھی *now, now then, now now*, friendly warning or protest بھئی! اَب *now be careful* خبردار اَب اِحتیاط کرنا *now he is a nice man* بات یہ ہے کہ وہ ہے تو اچھا آدمی **nowadays** (*nou*-a-dayz) *adv*. these days آج کل

Nowel *int*. (same as **Noel,** which see)

nowhere (*noh*-hway-ĕ*) *adv*. at no place کبھی بھی نہیں

noxious (*nok*-shus) *adj*. harmful نقصان دِہ، ضرر رساں

nozzle (*noz*-ĕl) *n*. spout at the end of a pipe, etc. ٹونٹی، دَہانہ

nuance (*new*-ans) *n*. delicate difference in shade (*of* meaning, colour, feeling, etc.) نازک فرق

nub (nub) *n*. gist or point (*of* story, matter, etc.) رکا، اَصل نکتہ، کا مُدّعا مطلب، کا خلاصہ (also *nubble*), small lump (esp. of coal) ڈلی، ڈھکرا

nubile (*newb*-il) *adj*. (of woman) marriageable شادی کے قابل **nubility** (-*bil*-) *n*. being nubile شادی کے قابل ہونا

nucleus (*newk*-li-us) *n*. (pl. *nuclei*, pr. *newk*-li-i) kernel ; central part or thing round which others gather مرکزی حصّہ، مرکزہ central part of an atom carrying a positive charge (جوہری) مرکزہ (مثبت برق بردار) **nuclear** (*newk*-le-ĕ*) *adj*. of or forming a nucleus مرکزی (esp.) of the nuclei of atoms ; (hence) atomic ایٹمی، جوہری **nuclear fission** *n*. splitting up of nuclei جوہری اِنشقاق، سالمی انفلاق *nuclear physics*, branch of physics studying the nuclei of atoms and (hence) the atomic energy جوہری طبیعیات *nuclear fission*, splitting up of the nuclei of atoms جوہری مرکزہ کا شق ہونا *nuclear reaction* جوہری رَدِّعمل *nuclear weapons*, weapons working through atomic fission ایٹمی ہتھیار، ایٹمی اسلحہ

nude (newd) *adj*. bare ننگا، عریاں، برہنہ *n*. (in art) nude human figure عریاں تصویر (یا مجسّمہ) **nudism** (*newd*-izm) *n*. staying nude as a cult دینِ عریانی، عریانیت **nudist** (*newd*-ist) *n*. one who adheres to this cult دینِ عریانی کا پیرو، عریانیت پرست *adj*. of the cult of the nude ; of nudism دینِ عریانی کا، عریانیتی *nudist club* دینِ عریانی کا مرکز، مرکزِ عریانیت

nudge (nuj) *v. t*. push gently with the elbow to attract attention کہنی مارنا، کہنی سے اِشارہ کرنا *n*. such push کہنی مارنا، کہنی کا اِشارہ

nugatory (*newg*-a-to-ri) *adj*. trifling معمولی futile بیکار not valid, inoperative جو نافذ العمل نہ ہو، غیر نافذ، غیر مؤثر

nugget (*nug*-et) *n*. rough lump of gold (or other metal ore) خام سونے (یا کسی خام دھات کا) ڈھیلا (یا) ڈلا

nuisance (*new*-sans) *n*. annoying (person, action or thing) تکلیف دِہ شخص، کام یا چیز *nuisance value*, (someone's) value owing to the nuisance he (or she) can (or does) create for another (کسی کی) تکلیف دہی کو ختم کرنے کا معاوضہ، تکلیف دہی کی قیمت

null (nul) *adj*. (also *null and void*), not in force, not legally binding کالعدم **nullify** *v.t.* make null and void کالعدم قرار دینا

numb (num) *adj*. unable to feel owing to (cold, etc.) سُن unable to move شل *v. t*. render unable to feel or move سُن یا شل کرنا

number (*num*-bĕ*) *n*. word or symbol telling how many عدد، ہندسہ quantity or amount تعداد a large number of کی بڑی تعداد (یا) مقدار *without number*, numberless اَن گنت، بے شمار، لاتعداد (*so many*) *in number* تعداد میں (اتنے) *times without number*, many a time کئی بار، کئی مرتبہ single issue of a periodical (اخبار یا رسالے کا) شمارہ *the current number* تازہ شمارہ *a back number* کوئی گزشتہ شمارہ *special number*, special issue خاص نمبر (in grammar) difference between singular, (dual) and plural وَحدت و جمعیت piece (of dance or song) for the stage in play or otherwise نمبر (ایک) عدد *dance number* ایک عدد رقص *song number* ایک عدد گیت (*pl.*) verses *v.t.* give a number to نمبر دینا put a number on پر نمبر لگانا add up to کی میزان ہونا، کل ہونا *number* (*someone*) *among* (*a group, etc.*), include (him) in it گنتی میں ہونا میں گننا، میں شمار کرنا

numeral (*newm*-ĕ-rĕl) *n*. word representing a number عدد symbol representing it

numerical (new-*me*-ri-kĕl) *adj*. pertaining to number عددی *numerical superiority*, majority : superiority in numbers اکثریت، عددی تفوق **numerically** *adv*. تعداد کے لحاظ سے

numerous (*newm*-ĕ-rus) *adj*. very many بہت، متعدد

numismatic (new-miz-*mat*-ik) *adj*. pertaining to coins, or medals سکوں وغیرہ کا، مسکوکاتی **numismatics** (-iks) *n*. (pl. used as sing.) science of coins, etc. علمِ مسکوکات **numismatology** (-*tol*-) *n*. study of coins, etc., as sources of history سکہ شناسی

numskull (*num*-skul) *n*. blockhead کُند ذہن، غبی

nun (nun) *n*. Christian woman who has vowed to lead a monastic life راہبہ **nunnery** (*nun*-ĕ-ri) convent دیرِ راہبات، راہبات کی خانقاہ

nuncio (*nunsh*-i-oh) *n*. Pope's ambassador to a king پاپائی ایلچی
nunnery *n*. (see under **nun**)
nuptial (*nup*-shĕl) *adj*. pertaining to marriage or wedding شادی بیاہ سے مُتعلّق **nuptials** *n. pl*. wedding ceremony شادی کی تقریب
nurse (nĕ*s) *n*. woman engaged by others to look after their babies آیا، دایہ، کھلائی trained person (very rarely man) tending patients in a hospital, etc. نرس، تیماردار *male nurse*, man serving in this capacity تیماردار مرد، مرد نرس *v. t.* act as a nurse نرس کا کام کرنا، آیا بننا، تیمارداری یا دایہ گری کرنا cherish (idea, etc.) دِل ہی دِل میں رکھنا foster, advance کی پرورش کرنا، کو بڑھانا conciliate (constituency) by gifts اپنے حلقۂ انتخاب والوں کو تحفے وغیرہ دے کر خوش کرنا
nursing home *n*. nice name for a (small) hospital تیمار خانہ، نرسنگ ہوم **nursery** (nĕ*s-ĕ-ri) *n*. room for the special use of little children ننھوں کا خاص کمرہ، بچہ خانہ، دایہ خانہ، نرسری، *nursery rhyme*, poems or songs for very young children ننھوں کا گیت *nursery word*, (peculiar form of) word(s) used by such children بچوں کا لفظ part of an elementary school for children between 3 and 5 years old نرسری، بچوں کی پرورش گاہ، تربیت گاہ (small) garden for raising young plants, etc. نرسری، پَود گھر، پَود کیاری **nurseryman** *n*. owner of a nursery پَود گھر والا **nurseling** *n*. child in relation to its nurse کے زیرِ پرورش، کا پالا ہوا
nurture (*ne*-*chĕ*) *n*. bringing up (of children) بچوں کی تربیت، تربیتِ اولاد *v. t.* give nurture to بچوں کی تربیت کرنا
nut (nut) *n*. edible kernel or seed inside a hard shell جوز *walnut* اخروٹ *groundnut*, (also called *peanut* or *monkey-nut*) مونگ پھلی *nut-meg* جائفل *nut-gall* مازُو، ماجو *be a hard nut to crack*, (of person, problem, etc.) be difficult to tackle with بیڈھب آدمی، یا سخت مشکل مسئلہ metal end-piece for a bolt ڈھبری
nuts (nuts), (U.S.) **nerts** (nĕ*ts) *inter*. (slang) crazy احمقانہ بات، پاگل پن والا **nutshell** *n*. shell of nut جوز کا چھلکا *in a nutshell*, very briefly مختصر ترین لفظوں میں
nut-crackers *n*. scissors-like instrument for cracking nuts سروتا **nutty** (nut-i) *adj*. abounding in nuts کثیر الجوز، جہاں جوز افراط سے ہوں
nutrient *adj*. (see under **nutriment**)
nutriment (*newt*-ri-ment) *n*. nourishing food غذائیت والی خوراک **nutrition** (newt-*rish*-ĕn) *n*. food غذا feeding or being fed تغذیہ **nutrititious** (-*rish*-) *adj*. of great food value غذائیت والا **nutrient** *adj*. nourishing غذائیت والا conveying nourishment غذا رساں **nutritive** *adj*. food (value, etc.) غذائی
nux vomica *n*. seed yielding strychnine کُچلہ، فلوس ماہی
nuzzle (*nuz*-ĕl) *v. t. & i.* press nose (or *nose against* or *into*) ناک رگڑنا lie snug منہ سے پٹھے رہنا
nylon (*nī*-lon) *n*. very durable synthetic plastic material looking like a fine fabric نائیلون، نیلون (pl.) garments made of this نائیلون کے کپڑے (pl.) its stockings نائلون کی لمبی زنانہ جرابیں
nymph (nimf) *Cl. myth*. one of the lesser goddesses presiding and living in rivers, trees, etc. پری، دیوی very lovely maiden حسینہ چھوٹی **nymphomania** (-*may*-) *n*. irresistible sexual urge in woman عورت کا شدید جنسی جذبہ
Nyx (niks), **Nox** (noks) *Cl. myth*. Night as a deity ; she was the daughter of Chaos

O

o, O (oh) (pl. *o's, os, oes*) the fifteenth letter of the English alphabet *an O, a round O*, (*a*) a circle دائرہ (*b*) zero صفر، انڈا *int*. (O) vocative prefixed to name اے، ارے، او
[2]**O, Oh** (oh) *int*. expressive of surprise, fear, etc.) اُف، ہائے، ارے، توبہ **Note : When separated with a comma, Oh is used (as in *Oh, What a shame !*) ; when not, only O (as in *O dear !*)**
o' (o) (abbr. of *of*) *ten o'clock*, (actually : ten of the clock) دس بجے *man-o'-war* جنگی جہاز
oak (ohk) kinds of tree bearing acorns شاہ بلوط بلوط its wood which is very hard شاہ بلوط کی لکڑی *Hearts of Oak*, ships and seamen of the British navy بلوط کے دِل، برطانیہ کے مضبوط جہاز اور دلیر ملاح **oaken** (*oh*-kĕn) *adj*. of oak بلوط کا
oakum (*oh*-kum) *n*. loose fibre picked from worn-out ropes پرانے رسّوں کا سن
oar (oh*, or o*) *n*. flat blade with a long handle used in rowing چپّو *v. t.* (poet.) row چپّو چلانا، کشتی کھینا **oarsman** (oh*z-man) *n*. one using an oar چپّو چلانے والا، کھویّا **oarage** (*oh*-rij) *n*. (poet

oars چپّو rowing چپّو چلانا ، (کشتی) کھینا
oasis (oh-*ay*-sis) *n.* (pl. *oases* pr. oh-*ay*-seez) fertile strip in desert نخلستان ، نخلہ
oath *n.* pl. *oaths* pr. ohdhz) vow to speak the truth حلف ، قسم ، سوگند *take* (or *make* or *swear*) *an oath* قسم کھاکر ، حلفیہ *on* (*one's*) *oath, on oath* حلف اٹھانا profane use of God's name to express strong feeling خدا کی قسمیں کھانا swear-word گالی
oats (ohts) *n. pl.* (sing. *oat*) a kind of foodgrain like barley جئی *sow* (*one's*) *wild oats*, lead an immoral life in youth جوانی میں عیش اڑانا **oaten** (oh-tĕn) *n.* made of oats جئی کا (of flute, etc.) made of oat-stem جئی کے ڈنٹھل کا **oatmeal** *n.* ground oats used for porridge, etc. پسی ہوئی جئی oats
obdurate (*ob*-dew-rayt) *adj.* stubborn ضدی ، ہٹ دھرم **obduracy** (ob-*dew*-ra-si) *n.* stubbornness ضد ، ہٹ دھرمی
obedient (o-*bee*-di-ent) *adj.* doing as one is told to do حکم کی بلا چون وچرا تعمیل کرنے والا ، مطیع ، فرماں بردار **obedience** *n.* being obedient فرمانبرداری ، اطاعت شعاری ، *in obedience to* (*someone*), کے حکم کی تعمیل میں ، تعمیل ارشاد **obediently**, *adv.* in an obedient manner فرمانبرداری سے *Yours obediently, Your obedient servant*, (subscription of an official letter) آپ کا فرمانبردار ▣ A person is **obedient** through sense of right but is **submissive** only through lack of self-respect.
obeisance (o-*bay*-sans) *n.* respectful bow of homage آداب ، مجرا ، اظہار اطاعت کیلئے جھکنا *do obeisance to* کو آداب بجالانا ، کو مجرا کرنا ، اظہار اطاعت کے لیے (کے سامنے) جھکنا
obelisk (*ob*-e-lisk) four-sided tall tapering pillar of stone پتھر کی سوئی mark (†) (or *double obelisk* ‡) placed for reference to a note, etc چلیپا نما نشان ، چلیپا
Oberon (*ob*-be-ron) *Cl. myth* king of fairies and the husband of *Titania* اوبرن an obelisk
obese (o-*bees*) *adj.* (of person) very fat, corpulent بہت موٹا ، فربہ **obesity** (o-*bee*-si-ti) *n.* corpulence موٹاپا
obey (o-*bay*) *v. t.* & *i.* do as one is told to do حکم ماننا ، (حکم کی) تعمیل کرنا ، فرماں برداری *obey orders* حکم ماننا ، حکم کی تعمیل کرنا
obiit (*ob*-i-it) *v.* (abb. '*ob.*') died وفات ، مرا ، مرگیا ، متوفی (abb. م) *ob. 1947* م ۱۹۴۷ء
obituary (o-*bit*-ew-ĕ-ri) *n.* printed notice on someone's death خبر مرگ ، (کسی کی) موت کی شائع ہونے والی خبر
obituarist *n.* writer of obituaries خبر مرگ لکھنے والے
object *n.* (*ob*-jekt) any material thing چیز ، شے ، معروض *an object lesson*, (*a*) visual-aid instruction about a material object مشاہدہ کی مدد سے سبق ، اشیا (*b*) living example (*in*) کی جیتی جاگتی (یا زندہ) مثال (in grammar) word or phrase governed by a verb or preposition مفعول aim, purpose (*in* life, etc.) مقصد *with no object in* بلا مقصد ، بے مدعا (*money, time, etc.*) *no object*, need not be considered کی پروا نہیں (ہونی چاہیئے) *v.t.* (ob-*ject*) be opposed (*to* something or *to* doing something) پر اعتراض کرنا ، (کو) پر اعتراض ہونا **objection** (ob-*jek*-shĕn) *n.* objecting (پر) اعتراض کرنا statement in taking exception to اعتراض cause of objecting (پر) اعتراض **objectionable** *adj.* liable to be objected to قابل اعتراض undesirable (person, smell, etc.) ناپسندیدہ **objector** (-*jek*-) *n.* one who objects (*to* something) معترض *conscientious objector*, soldier (or other person) objecting to something (esp. military service) on religious (etc.) grounds عقیدے کی بنا پر معترض ، معترض برنبائے عقیدہ
objective (ob-*jek*-tiv) *n.* purpose target ہدف ، نشانہ point to be captured by advancing troops, etc. حملے کا مقام *adj.* unbiased غیر جانبدارانہ impersonal غیر جذباتی ، نفس الامری ، معروضی ، واقعیت پسندانہ *objective approach* (*to a problem, etc.*) (کے متعلق) واقعیت پسندانہ نکتہ نگاہ ، واقعیت پسندانہ حل کی کوشش (in grammar) accusative (case) مفعولی (حالت) ، (حالت) مفعولی
oblate (*ob*-layt) *adj.* (of sphere) flattened at poles قطبین پر پچکا ہوا ، کرہ *n.* dedicated person دین کیلیے زندگی وقف کرنے والا ، واقف زندگی **oblation** (-*lay*-) *n.* thing offered to God ; any pious donation نذر
obligation (ob-li-*gay*-shĕn) *n.* duty فرض responsibility (*towards*) احساس فرض ، احساس ذمے داری *under obligation to* کا احسان مند ، کا رہین منت **obligatory** (ob-*lig*-a-tĕ-ri) *adj.* necessary (by law, custom, etc.) ضروری ، لازمی (also see **oblige**)
oblige (ob-*līj*) *v. t.* do (someone) a favour (*by doing something*) (کسی پر) احسان کرنا *much obliged* (*to someone for something*) (کسی بات کے لیے کسی کا) احسان مند ، شکر گزار ، ممنون require (someone *to do* something) پر مجبور کرنا *be obliged* (*to do*) کرنے پر) مجبور ہونا
obliging (ob-*lī*-jing) *adj.* kind and helpful (person) بامروت ، مدد کرنے والا (Also see **obligation**)
oblique (ob-*leek*) *adj.* slanting ترچھا *n.* the mark (/) meaning *or* علامت تخییر ، یا
obliterate (ob-*lit*-ĕ-rayt) *v. t.* efface مٹانا ، محو کرنا کا نام و نشان مٹانا **obliteration** (-*ray*-) *n.* effacement

مٹانا، محو کرنا، نام و نشان مٹانا **obliterator** (-*lit*-) *n.* نام و نشان مٹانے والا

oblivion ob-*liv*-i-ĕn *n.* state of being quite forgotten فراموشی، نگاہِ تغافل کا شکار *fall* (or *sink* into *oblivion*, *be buried in oblivion*, be entirely forgotten بالکل بھولا بسرا ہونا، نگاہِ تغافل کا شکار ہونا **oblivious** *adj.* forgetful (*of* (کو) بھولا بسرا unaware (*of* (سے) غافل (rectangular figure: much longer than it is broad لمبوترا، لمبوتری شکل

obloquy *ob*-lo-kwi *n.* infamy; being generally ill-spoken of رسوائی

obnoxious (ob-*nok*-shus) *adj.* nasty (person, action, smell, etc. مکروہ

oboe (*oh*-boh), **hautboy** (*hoh*-boi, or *oh*-boi) *n.* wooden wind-instrument with a double reed الغوزہ **oboist** (*ohb*-oh-ist *n.* one who plays oboe الغوزہ بجانے والا، الغوزہ نواز

obscene (ob-*seen*; *adj.* (of person, behaviour, remark, talk, work of art, etc.) immoral, indecent فحش، ناشائستہ، اخلاق سے گرا ہوا **obscenity** (ob-*see*-ni-ti) *n.* indecency فحاشی

an oboe

obscure (ob-*skew*-ĕ*) *adj.* dark تاریک not clear to the eye or mind غیر واضح، مبہم، دھندلا سا not well-known; unknown گمنام، غیر معروف *v. t.* make obscure تاریک کرنا، مبہم بنانا **obscurity** (ob-*skew*-ri-ti) *n.* being obscure گمنامی، تاریکی، دھندلاپن

obsequies (*ob*-se-kwiz) *n. pl.* funeral rites تجہیز و تکفین

obsequious (-*see*-) *adj.* cringing (person) خوشامدی، چاپلوس

observance *n.*, **observant** *adj.*, **observation** *n.*, **observatory** *n.* (see under **observe**)

observe (ob-*zĕ**v) *v. t.* & *i.* see دیکھنا see carefully بغور دیکھنا، مشاہدہ کرنا follow (rule, etc.) پر عمل کرنا، پر عمل پیرا ہونا celebrate (festival, etc.) remark (*that*) (کے بارے میں) اظہارِ خیال کرنا **observable** *adj.* that which can be observed جو نظر آسکے، جس کا مشاہدہ ہو سکے worth-observing مشاہدے کے لائق **observance** (ob-*zĕ**-vans) *n.* observing (of rule) کی پابندی، پر عمل celebration (of festival, etc.) منانا rite (of worship, etc.) رسم **observant** *adj.* quick at seeing تیز بیں، تیز نگاہ abiding by (*of* rule, etc.) (کا) پابند والا **observation** (-*vay*-) *n.* observing or being observed مشاہدہ *keep* (*patient, suspect, etc.*) *under observation*, watch (him) carefully (پر) کڑی نظر رکھنا *escape observation*, avoid being seen نظروں سے بچنا remark (*on* something) پر اظہارِ خیال، تبصرہ **observatory** (ob-*zĕ**va-to-ri) *n.* building for observing heavenly bodies, etc., through a powerful telescope رصدگاہ **observer** *n.* one who observes something (for collecting data or keeping the peace) مشاہدہ کرنے والا، مشاہد، شاہد

obsess (ob-*ses*) *v.t.* (of a fear or false idea haunt (someone or his mind) وہم، اندیشہ، آسیب وغیرہ کا کسی کے) سر پر مسلط ہو جانا **obsession** (ob-*sesh*-ĕn) *n.* obsessing (وہم وغیرہ کا) غلبہ یا تسلط something that obsesses (وہم، غلط خیال وغیرہ) *be an obsession with* (*someone*), obsess him کے سر پر مسلط ہونا

obsolescent *adj.* (see under **obsolete**)

obsolete (*ob*-so-leet) *adj.* outdated (words, methods, etc.) متروک، غیر مروجہ **obsolescent** (-*les*-ent) *adj.* becoming obsolete جس کا رواج اٹھ رہا ہو

obstacle (*ob*-sta-kĕl) *n.* hindrance (*in* someone's way) رکاوٹ *obstacle race*, race with hindrances to be overcome رکاوٹوں والی دوڑ، رکاوٹ دوڑ

obstetrics (ob-*stet*-riks) *n.* (*pl.* used as sing.) science of medicine or surgery as pertaining to childbirth قابلہ گیری، دایہ گیری **obstetrician** (-*rish*-) expert in obstetrics ماہر قابلہ گری

obstinate (*ob*-sti-nayt) *adj.* (of child, etc.) stubborn ضدی، ہٹ کا پکا (of resistance, disease, etc.) difficult to overcome جس پر آسانی سے قابو نہ پایا جا سکے، سخت **obstinacy** (*ob*-sti-na-si) *n.* stubbornness ہٹ **obstinately** *adv.* ضد سے، ہٹ دھرمی سے ▣ We speak of person as **obstinate** when he holds to his own particular views; as **stubborn** when he is obstinate by native disposition; as **intractable** when he cannot be dealt with; as **refractory** when actively hostile; as **obdurate** when hardened in his sinful life; and **tenacious** when holding to his determined course.

obstruct (ob-*strukt*) *v. t.* hinder (someone's path, course of action, etc.) کی راہ میں رکاوٹ ڈالنا، روڑا اٹکانا block up (path, passage, etc.) رستہ روکنا **obstruction** (-*truck*-) *n.* obstructing رکاوٹ ڈالنا، میں that which obstructs رکاوٹ، مانع (ج: موانع) **obstructive** (-*truck*-) *adj.* causing obstruction رکاوٹ بننے یا ڈالنے والا

obtain (ob-*tayn*) *v. t.* & *i.* get حاصل کرنا، پانا (of conditions, rules, etc.) be existing established موجود ہونا، پایا جانا **obtainable** *adj.* that which can be obtained جسے حاصل کیا جا سکے، ہاتھ آسکے، قابلِ حصول

obtrude (ob-*trood*) *v. t.* & *i.* thrust (oneself, one's opinions *upon* someone) even though never wanted مخواہ دخل دینا، سر پر سوار ہو جانا، کے سر پر زبردستی مسلط ہونا یا کرنا **obtrusive** (ob-*troo*-siv) *a*...

that obtrudes سر پر سوار ہونے والا، خواہ مخواہ دخل دینا
obtuse (ob-*tews*) *adj.* blunt کُند، کُند dunce کُند ذہن، غبی (of an angle) greater than a right angle (زاویۂ) منفرجہ
obviate (*ob*-vi-ayt) *v. t.* remove (difficulty, fear, etc.) دُور کرنا clear away (anticipated objection, etc.) beforehand (اعتراض وغیرہ) پہلے ہی دُور کر دینا
obvious (*ob*-vi-us) *adj.* evident صاف، ظاہر، واضح **obviously** *adv.* evidently ظاہر ہے کہ، صاف طور پر
occasion (o-*kay*-zhĕn) *n.* time of (something) taking place موقع *rise to the occasion*, be equal to the task (کا) مردِ میدان ثابت ہونا need (for some one *to do* something) (کسی کے لیے کسی کام کی) ضرورت *v. t.* cause کا باعث بننا **occasional** *adj.* infrequent (visit, etc.) کبھی کبھار کا for use on special occasions تقریبات پر استعمال کے لیے، تقریباتی **occasionally** *adv.* now and then کبھی کبھی، کبھی کبھار، گاہے گاہے
Occident (*ok*-si-dent) *n.* (lit.) (*the*) West (as opposed to *the Orient*) مغرب، مغربی ممالک، مغربی تہذیب (وغیرہ) **occidental** (-*dent*) Western (as opposed to *oriental*) مغربی، فرنگی
occult (o-*kult*) *adj.* mysterious پُراسرار *occult sciences*, magic, astrology, etc. پُراسرار علوم (جادو، نجوم وغیرہ)
occupant *n.*, **occupation** *n.*, **occupational** *adj.*, **occupier** *n.* (see under **occupy**)
occupy (*ok*-ew-pi) *v. t.* be in possession of (place, etc.) پر قابض ہونا live in (house, etc.) میں رہنا have (a position, office, etc.) پر فائز ہونا conquer (area, country, etc.) and rule it (کو) فتح کر کے (وہاں) حکمرانی کرنا take up (time) وقت لینا fill (space) (جگہ) گھیرنا engross (attention, the mind, etc.) (کو) محوّ رکھنا، (پر) چھائے رہنا *occupy (oneself) with* (or *in*), be busy with میں مشغول رہنا، میں لگا رہنا **occupier** (-pī-ĕ*) *n.* **occupant** *n.* one who occupies (place, etc.) پر قابض **occupation** (-*pay*-) *n.* act of occupying (a house, etc.) قبضہ vocation کام، پیشہ **occupational** (-*paysh*-) *adj.* pertaining to occupation پیشہ ورانہ **occupational therapy** *n.* (see Addenda)
occur (o-*kĕ**) *v.t.* (-rr-) happen ہونا، واقع ہونا، وقوع میں آنا، رُونما ہونا *occur to*, come into one's mind (کو) خیال آنا be found آنا **occurrence** (o-*kĕ*-rens) *n.* event واقعہ *an everyday occurrence* روزمرہ کا واقعہ act of occurring ہونا، وقوع پذیر ہونا *of frequent occurrence* اکثر ہونے والا
ocean (*oh*-shĕn) *n.* the whole of earth which is not land ساتوں سمندر، اوقیانوس one of the chief divisions of that part; a great sea سمندر، بحر *adj* pertaining to the ocean بڑے سمندر کا **oceanic** (oh-shi-*an*-ik, or oh-si-*an*-ik) *adj.* pertaining to an ocean سمندری، بحری، اوقیانوسی
o'clock (o-*klok*) (see under [3]**o**)
octagon (*ok*-ta-gon) *n.* eight sided polygon مثمّن، ہشت پہلو (شکل) **octagonal** (-*tag*-) *adj.* eight-sided مثمّن
octave (*ok*-tayv) *n.* (in music) same note in the scale next above or below دوگنا یا آدھا سُر eight-line stanza آٹھ مصرعوں یا چار شعروں کا بند، مثمّن *adj.* consisting of eight مثمّن **octavo** (ok-*tay*-voh) (abbr. *8vo*) page of any sheet folded thrice, *i.e.*, into eight pages فلسکیپ کاغذ کا آٹھواں حصّہ، ہشت ورقی
October (ok-*toh*-bĕ*) *n.* the tenth month of the English calendar (orig. the eighth month of the Roman year) اکتوبر
octogenarian (ok-toj-e-*nay*-ri-ĕn *adj.* & *n.* eighty-year-old (person) اَسّی سال کا (بوڑھا)، پیرِ ہشتاد سالہ
octopus (*ok*-to-pus) *n.* (pl. *ok*-to-pu-siz) soft-bodied sea-animal with eight sucking arms (called tentacles) ہشت نیش صدفہ
octroi (*ok*-trwah) *n.* duty levied on goods entering a town چُنگی، محصُول چُنگی
ocular (*ok*-ew-lĕ*) *adj.* of the eyes آنکھوں کا seen with eyes آنکھوں دیکھا، چشم دید، چشمدید (یا کے متعلق) **oculist** (*ok*-ew-list) *n.* eye doctor آنکھوں کا ڈاکٹر، مُعالجِ امراضِ چشم
odd (od) *adj.* (of number) not even (*i.e.*, not divisible by two) طاق (عدد) various unconnected (jobs, moments, etc.) متفرّق one of a pair or one or more of a set چھٹکل، متفرّق a little above the stated amount سے کچھ زیادہ، سے کچھ اُوپر *Rs. 100 odd* سو روپے سے کچھ اُوپر (also *odd-looking*) queer (جو) (اپنی) (انداز میں) عجیب سا **odds** (odz) *n., pl.* chances امکانات *the odds are that*, it is probable that ممکن ہے کہ *be at odds (with)*, be in strong disagreement (with) سے سخت اختلاف ہونا *odds and ends*, various minor matters or things متفرّقات **oddments** (*od*-ments) *n. pl.* odds and ends متفرّقات **oddity** (*od*-i-ti) *n.* queerness عجیب سا ہونا queer (person, behaviour or thing) عجیب **oddly** *adv.* strangely عجیب انداز سے، عجیب *oddly enough*, strange to say عجیب بات ہے کہ
ode (ohd) *n.* lyric poem expressing noble ideas in a lofty style (usu. in irregular metre) غنائی نظم (for English translations of Persian or Urdu poetry) غزل (for English translations

of Arabic poetry) قصیدہ
Odin (*oh*-din) *Norse myth.* chief Scandinavian god (also called *Woden*) ; (*Wednesday* is named after him) اُوڈِن
odious (*oh*-di-us) *adj.* hateful کریہ، نفرت انگیز **odium** (*oh*-di-um) *n.* widespread hatred نفرتِ خلائق، پھیلی ہوئی نفرت
odour (*oh*-dĕ*) *n.* (good or bad) smell بُو *be in good* (or *bad*) *odour with*, (not to) be liked by کو پسند یا ناپسند **odourless** *n.* without any odour بے بُو، جس میں بُو نہ ہو
Odysseus (oh-*dis*-ews) (called *Ulysses* by the Romans and pr. yoo-lis-eez) *Cl. myth.* a heroical Greek king whose exploits after the Trojan war are the theme of Homer's *Odyssey* اُوڈِسِس یُوسِس
oecumenical (eek-ew-*men*-i-kĕl) *adj.* world-wide عالمگیر، عالمی universal ہمہ گیر of the whole Christian world کلُّ نصرانی
Oedipus (*ee*-di-pus) *Cl. myth.* the unfortunate Theban king who got separated from his parents in childhood and was brought up by the queen of Corinth ; he grew up to kill his father, *Laius*, and marry his own mother *Jocasta*, all in ignorance ; later, on discovering his mistake, he blinded himself and went into exile اِیڈی پس *the Oedipus complex*, the son's sexual love for his mother according to the famous Jewish psychologist, Freud جذبۂ اِیڈیپس، ایڈیپسی جذبہ، بیٹے کا ماں کی طرف جنسی مَیلان (as opposed to the *Electra complex* which, according to Freud, is a daughter's sexual love for her father)
Oenone (ee-*noh*-nee) *Cl. myth.* a nymph of Mt. Ida beloved by Paris before he abducted Helen اینونی
o'er (*oh*-ĕ*) *adv.* & *prep.* (poet. abbr., for **over,** which see)
of (ov) *prep.* belonging to کا made from کا، کا بنا ہُوا about, concerning پر، کے بارے میں from (a family, etc.) کا containing کا called جو the *island of Sicily* جزیرہ جس کا نام کہلاتا ہے، جس کا نام ہے صِقِلّیہ ہے owing to (disease) کے مرض میں by کا amongst میں سے، میں کا *out of* سے باہر *in spite of* کے باوجود *instead of* کی بجائے، کے بجائے *because of* کی وجہ سے، *for the sake of* کی خاطر *by way of* کے باعث، کے ضمن میں، کے *for fear of* کے ڈر سے *in search of* کے سلسلے میں کی تلاش میں، کی جُستجو میں
off (of *prep.*) way from پرے، سے پرے close by (the coast, road, etc.) کے قریب ہی (of streets, etc.) branching out from سے نکلنے والا، سے نکلتا (*so much*) *off the price*, less than the usual price اصلی قیمت سے (اتنا) کم *be off duty* چھٹی پر ہونا، ڈیوٹی پر نہ ہونا *be off the point*, be irrelevant غیر متعلق بات ہونا یا کہنا *be off colour*, be unwell بیمار ہونا *be off* (*one's*) *head*, mad سر پھرا، پاگل *be off* (*one's*) *food*, have no appetite بھوک نہ لگنا
adv. from سے away from سے پرے so as to end ; completely بالکل *have* (or *take*) a day off چھٹی کرنا، ڈیوٹی پر نہ ہونا *off and on*, at intervals کبھی کبھار بند، ختم *adj.* not continuing or existing
on the right-hand side (actually the side farther from the side of the road) (as opposed to on) داہنی طرف *be well off*, be rich or well-provided مزے میں ہونا (یا) امیر ہونا *on the off chance*, on the improbable chance غیر یقینی امکان کی صورت میں *off season*, period of little activity جب سیزن نہ ہو *in* (*one's*) *off time*, in (one's) spare time فارغ وقت
int. (also *be off*) begone دفع ہو جا، دُور ہو جاؤ، بھاگ یہاں سے
offhand (*of*-hand) *adv.* impromptu ; without proper thought or preparation تیاری کے بغیر، بیساختہ *adj.* careless, lacking due respect سَرسَری، سَرد مِہرانہ، سَرد مِہری *in an offhand manner* سَرد مِہری سے
offal (*of*-ĕl) *n.* refuse, rubbish آخور، فُضلہ waste parts of animal slaughtered for food بیکار گوشت، (پھیپھڑے، اوجھڑی وغیرہ) liver, heart, kidneys, etc. of such an animal دِل، گُردے، کلیجی وغیرہ *adj.* low quality (wheat, milk, wood, etc.) گھٹیا
offence (o-*fens*) *n.* crime جُرم going *against* (a rule, etc.) کی خلاف ورزی attack حملہ sin (*against* God or man) گُناہ hurting of feelings or being hurt جذبات کو ٹھیس، ناراضگی، غصّہ، رنجش *take offence* (*at*) (کو) ناراض ہونا *give offence* (*to*) ناراض کرنا take offence easily
offend (o-*fend*) *v.t.* & *i.* commit a crime (*against* the law, etc.) قانون شکنی کرنا injure the feelings of کے دِل کو ٹھیس پہنچانا be displeasing to (good taste, the eye or ear, etc.) کو بُرا لگنا ہو کو، ناگوار گزرنا **offender** (o-*fend*-ĕ*) *n.* one who violates the law ; criminal مُجرم، قانون شکن
offensive (o-*fens*-iv) *adj.* displeasing (language, smell, etc.) خراب، ناپسندیدہ، ناگوار pertaining to an attack جارحیت پر مبنی، جارحانہ *n.* attack حملہ *take the offensive*, initiate the attack حملہ کرنا، حملہ کرنے میں پہل کرنا movement تحریک، مُہم *peace offensive* اَمن کی مُہم **offensively** *adv.* in an offensive manner ناگوار طور پر
offer (*of*-ĕ*) *v.t.* & *i.* hold (suggestion, or something else *to* someone) for acceptance or rejection پیش کرنا present (*for sale*) بیچنے کے لیے رکھنا name the price one is willing to pay (خریدار کا) قیمت لگانا (show willingness to)

donate دینا ریا) دینے کی پیشکش کرنا present (sacrifice) to God (قربانی) دینا present (or *up*, prayer) to God (نماز) پڑھنا، (عبادت) کرنا (of an opportunity, etc.) occur ہاتھ آنا، ملنا attempt (resistance, etc.) (مقابلہ وغیرہ) کرنا *n.* offering پیش کرنا that which is offered پیشکش *make an offer* قیمت لگانا، پیشکش کرنا *accept an offer* مان لینا (یا) پیش کش قبول کرنا *offer of marriage* شادی کی پیشکش **offering** (*of*-è-ring) *n.* sacrifice قربانی something presented in homage نذر، نذرانہ

office (*of*-is) *n.* (usu. *pl.*) place for clerical work دفتر *working in an office* کلرک ہونا، دفتر میں کام کرنا، منشی متصدی ہونا *leave the office* دفتر سے چلے آنا *come to the office* کام پر آنا *attend the office* دفتر میں آنا government department along with its staff and working arrangements محکمہ *the post and telegraph office* محکمہ ڈاک وتار its building کی عمارت، خانہ *post office* ڈاک خانہ a comparatively high official's rank عہدہ *accept the office* عہدہ قبول کرنا *enter upon the office* عہدے پر فائز ہونا *resign the office* عہدے سے مستعفی ہونا *lay down* (or *leave*) *the office* عہدے سے سبکدوش ہونا duty (*of* a host, etc.) فرض (*pl.*) (usu., *good offices*), help ; attention توجہ، امداد، مدد *through the good offices (of someone)*, with (his) help کی مدد سے (*pl.*) rooms in a building likely to be used as offices دفتر، کمرے **office-boy** *n.* office peon **office-holder, office-bearer** *n.* (usu. elected) official of an organization عہدے دار **officer** *n.* one employed to serve in a position of authority افسر، بڑا اہلکار **official** (o-*fish*-ĕl) *n.* one employed to serve in any capacity اہلکار *adj.* authorized (record, statement, policy, etc.) باضابطہ، سرکاری pertaining to an office دفتری، سرکاری characteristic of (government) officials دفتری **officialdom** (-dum) *n.* bureaucracy دفتری حکومت **officialism** (-lizm) *n.* procrastinating official methods دفتریت **officiate** (o-*fish*-i-ayt) *v.i.* do work (*for* someone or *as* some official) as a makeshift arrangement عارضی کام کرنا، (کی جگہ) عوضی لگنا (esp. of a priest) perform the duties of one's office (*at* a place, etc.) (کسی موقع پر) اپنے فرائض انجام دینا **officious** (o-*fish*-us) *adj.* fussy کام کو بہت مشکل بنا کر دکھانے والا، خواہ مخواہ meddling خواہ مخواہ خدمت پر کمربستہ، مین میخ نکالنے والا دخل در معقولات کرنے والا

offing (*of*-ing) *n.* open sea away from the shore nevertheless visible محاذ ساحل (*be*) *in the offing*, (*a*) be in the more distant part of the sea but still visible to the observer from the shore ابھی ساحل سے نظر آنا (*b*) (be) in a preliminary stage ابتدائی مرحلے میں (ہو)

offish (*of*-ish) *adj.* (of manners) stiff روکھا، خشک

offset (*of*-set) *v.t.* (-tt-) counteract کی تلافی کرنا کا رد عمل کرنا *n.* a very neat method of lithographic printing from impressions on a sensitized plate آفسٹ کی چھپائی، آفسٹ

offshoot (*of*-shoot) *n.* side shoot springing from the main stem چھوٹی شاخ جھی derivative مشتق (لفظ)

offspring (*of*-spring) *n.* (*pl.* same) child or children بچہ یا بچے، اولاد، نسل young (of animals) (جانور کا) بچہ

often (of-èn) *adv.* (poet. **oft**) frequently *oft-told tale* کئی بار دہرایا ہوا (قصہ) **oft-times** *adv.* frequently اکثر

ogle (*oh*-gèl) *v.t.* & *i.* look (*at* someone) lovingly (کسی کو) پیار بھری نظروں سے دیکھنا *n.* amorous glance پیار بھری نظریں

Ogpu (*og*-poo) *n.* Communist Russia's secret police روسی خفیہ پولیس، اوگپو

ogre (*oh*-gè*) *n.* (fem. *ogress*) man-eating آدم خور (جن)

oh (oh) *int.* see

oil *n.* kind of greasy liquid تیل، روغن، دہن *essential oils*, certain fragrant or medicinal oils distilled from vegetable seeds معطر تیل (often *pl.* also *oil-colours*) paint dissolved in oil روغنی رنگ *oil-painting, painting in oils*, painting in oil colours روغنی رنگ کی تصویر، روغنی تصویر *v.t.* put oil into parts of a machine, etc.) (کو) تیل دینا **oil-engine** *n.* engine driven by the explosion of vaporized oil and air آئل انجن، تیل سے چلنے والا انجن، تیل انجن **oilcake** *n.* seeds from which oil has been pressed out and which are now used as animal food کھلی **oil-cloth** *n.* canvas coated with hardened oil for use as covering for seats (etc.) موم جامہ **oilskin** *n.* (garment of) cloth water-proofed with oil موم جامہ (یا) موم جامے کا کپڑا **oily** (*oi*-li *adj.* of or like oil تیل کا سا، روغنی covered with oil جسے تیل لگا ہوا ہو، چکنا

ointment (*oint*-ment) *n.* greasy medicine applied to the skin مرہم **O.K.** (*oh-kay*) *n.* slang) all right ; correct ٹھیک، درست **okay** (*oh-kay*) *v.t.* say yes to پر صاد کرنا، کو منظور کرنا، یا صحیح قرار دینا

old (ohld) *adj.* having lived for a long time بوڑھا of a certain age (اتنی) عمر کا *How old are you* تمہاری عمر کیا ہے، کتنی عمر ہو گی تمہاری used مستعملہ، پرانا (of clothes, etc.) worn out or decayed by the passage of time پرانا of a long standing پرانا

ancient پُرانا، قدیم، قدیمی very experienced (in) کا تجربہ کار، کا پُرانا کھلاڑی in days of old, in olden days, in the remote past اگلے وقتوں میں، پُرانے زمانے میں of old, ancient پُرانی، پُرانا **old-fashioned** adj. outmoded وضع کا، دقیانوسی **old age** n. later days of life بڑھاپا، ضعیفی **old world** adj. old-fashioned (person or beliefs) اگلے وقتوں کا

oligarchy (ol-i-ga*-ki) n. government by a small group چند سَری حکُومت، عدیدیّہ country with such a government عدیدیّہ

olive (ol-iv) n. fruit with a stone-like oily seed زیتون tree bearing it زیتون کا درخت، شجرِ زیتونہ olive branch, its branch as symbol of peace شاخِ زیتون، نشانِ مُصالحت hold out the olive branch مُصالحت کے لیے تیار ہونا مُصالحت کی پیشکش کرنا adj. of its colour ; yellowish-green انگوری

olive branch with leaves and fruit

Olympus (oh-lim-pus) Cl. myth. the seat of Greek gods ; it was situated on the borders of Thessaly and Macedonia اولمپس **olympian** adj. pertaining to Olympus اولمپسی god-like دیوتاؤں کا سا، دیوتا نُما **Olympics** n. pl. (also Olympic games) games in ancient Greece played every four years in honour of the chief Olympian deity, Zeus اولمپک کھیل similar international contests held every four years since 1896 اولمپک کھیل

omelet, omelette (om-let) n. pancake of eggs روٹی کی طرح تلے ہُوئے انڈے، آملیٹ

omen (oh-men) n. sign (of good or ill luck) شگون **ominous** (om-i-nus) adj. of bad omen بدشگونی والا، بُرا شگون warning تنبیہ

omit (o-mit) v.t. (-tt-) fail (to do something) نہ کرنا leave out (passage, etc. from a book, etc.) چھوڑ دینا **omission** n. leaving out چھوڑ دینا something left out فروگزاشت crimes of omission or commission جُرمِ خطا و فروگزاشت، غلطیاں اور فروگزاشتیں

omni (om-ni) pref. all سب، ہمہ

omnibus (om-ni-bus) n. (full name for) bus بس a double-decker omnibus دو منزلہ بس adj. multi-purpose (bill, etc.) کثیر المقاصد، ہمہ گیر (of volume, etc.) containing many books by the same author مجموعہ

a double-decker omnibus

omnipotent (om-nip-o-tent) adj. all powerful بڑی طاقت والا، کامل اختیارات والا the Omnipotent, God قادرِ مطلق **omnipotence** (-nip-) n. being all-powerful قدرت کاملہ

omnipresent (om-ni-prez-ent) adj. ubiquitous ہر جگہ موجود the Omnipresent, God خدائے حاضر و ناظر **omnipresence** n. being omnipresent ہر جگہ موجود ہونا، حاضر و ناظر

omniscient (-nish-i-ent) adj. all knowing سب کچھ جاننے والا the Omniscient, God خدائے علیم و خبیر **omniscience** (nish-i-) n. being omniscient علمِ کل، معرفت کل، علمِ مطلق، علمِ بسیط

omnivorous (om-niv-o-rus) adj. able to eat every kind of food ہر چیز کھا سکنے والا، ہمہ خور

on prep. upon پر، کے اوپر along (a river, etc. پر، کے کنارے کنارے included in کا رُکن about کے متعلق، کی طرف at the time of کے موقع پر، کو towards کی طرف by means of پر، میں for سے، کے لیے with کے پاس Do you have any money on you? کیا تمہارے پاس اس وقت کچھ روپیہ ہے adv. at کو، کی طرف so as to cover پر forward آگے in progress جاری into action کھلا happening (رہا) ہو on time, in time بروقت

once (wuns) adv. on a single occasion ایک بار، ایک مرتبہ، ایک دفعہ formerly پہلے، کبھی، سابق conj. as soon as جونہی، ذرا ایک بار، اگر ایک بار بھی n. one time ایک بار، ایک مرتبہ، ایک دفعہ at once, immediately یکایک، اچانک، فی الفور، فوراً all at once, (a) suddenly یکایک، اچانک (b) all together سبھی ایک ساتھ once in a while, occasionally کبھی کبھار once for all, (a) finally آخری بار (b) for good ہمیشہ ہمیشہ کے لیے once upon a time, at some time in the past کسی زمانے میں be right (etc.) for once, اس دفعہ ٹھیک کہنا، ایک بار تو ٹھیک کہنا this once, at least this time اب کی تو، اب کے تو **once-over** (wuns-oh-vĕ*) n. (colloq.) rapid preliminary inspection سریع ابتدائی مُعاینہ

oncoming (on-kum-ing) adj. approaching آنے والا n. approach پہنچنا، آنا، آمد

on dit (ohn-dee) n. mere hearsay محض سُنی سُنائی

one (wun) n. & pron. (pl. ones, pr. wunz) one person or thing کوئی شخص یا شئے the first number ایک its symbol adj. single ایک certain, some کوئی، کسی only صرف، ایک، واحد united ایک، متحد all in one, combined سبھی، سبھی کچھ ایک at one (with), in agreement (with) سے متفق one by one one at a time ایک ایک کرکے once over, rapid preliminary inspection فوری یا ابتدائی مُلاحظہ for one thing, for one reason ایک بات تو یہ ہے کہ it is all one to me, I have no preference میرے لیے سبھی ایک (سا) ہے، میرے لیے کوئی فرق نہیں پڑتا **oner** (wun-ĕ*) n. (slang) severe blow سخت ضرب (slang) remarkable person or thing عجیب شخص (یا چیز) hit in cricket counting one ایک دِن والی **oneself** pron. (reflexive form of) one اپنا، آپ emphatic form of one آپ، خود، آپ ہی n. one's self اپنی ذات **oneness**

being one ایک ہونا being of one mind یک دل ہونا یکدِلی ، اِتحاد **one-sided** *adj*. (of an argument, etc.) pertaining to or seeing one side only یک طرفہ
onerous *adj*. (see under **onus**)
onion (*un*-yĕn) *n*. bulb-rooted vegetable with a sharp smell پیاز
onlooker (*on*-luk-ĕ*) *n*. spectator دیکھنے والا ، تماشائی
only (*ohn*-li) *adj*. one and no more واحد، اکیلا، صرف *adv*. merely صرف، محض exclusively ہی ، ایک ہی (in wishes) *if only* اگر کہیں، صرف یہ *conj*. but, except that مگر ، سوائے اِس کے کہ
onomatopoeia (on-o-ma-to-*pee*-a) *n*. formation of words imitating the sound associated with the named or represented thing concerned صَوتی ترکیب such word صَوتی لفظ **onomatopoeic** (-*pee*-ik) *adj*. based on or pertaining to onomatopoeia صَوتی ، آوازی، تقلیدی
onset (*on*-set) *n*. violent attack سخت حملہ sudden start (*of*) (کا) اچانک آغاز
onslaught (*on*-slawt) *n*. fierce attack سخت حملہ
ontology (on-*tol*-o-ji) *n*. branch of metaphysics dealing with existence in the abstract وُجودیات **ontological** (-*loj*-) *adj*. pertaining to ontology وُجودیات **ontologist** (-*tol*-) *n*. philosopher discussing ontological problems وجُودِیاتی
onus (*oh*-nus) *n*. (no pl.) burden (*of* something or *of doing* something) کا بار ، کا بوجھ ، کی ذِمّے داری **onerous** (*ohn*-ĕ-rus) *adj*. (of duty, responsibility, taxes, etc.) heavy سخت ، بھاری
onward (*on*-wĕ*d) *adj*. forward آگے کی طرف، بڑھتا ہوا *adv*. forward **onwards** (*on*-wĕ*dz) *adv*. forward آگے
onyx (*on*-iks) *n*. kind of quartz with colour layers سُلیمانی پتھر ، سنگِ سُلیمانی
oodles (*ood*-ĕlz) *n. pl*. superabundance بڑی کثرت، بے حد افراط
oof *n*. (slang) wealth روپیہ پیسہ **oofy** (*oo*-fi) *adj*. (slang) wealthy پیسے والا
ooze (ooz) *n*. soft liquid mud at the bottom of a pond, etc. تہہ میں جمی ہوئی کیچڑ *v.i*. (of blood or other thick liquids) trickle (of strength, etc.) be gradually depleted آہستہ آہستہ ختم ہو جانا
opaque (o-*payk*) *adj*. not allowing light to pass through غیر شفاف obscure مُبہم، غیر واضح dull-witted کُند ذہن، کُھس **opacity** o-*pas*-i-ti) being opaque غیر شفاف ہونا
ope (ohp) *adj*. & *n*. (poet. same as **open**, which see)
open (*oh*-pen) *n*. (*the open*), the open country کُھلا علاقہ ، کُھلی زمین *adj*. not shut or blocked up کُھلا not closed (*to* traffic, etc.) بند نہیں (of land) not covered with trees, buildings, etc. کُھلا (of sea) away from land کُھلا (of book, etc.) unfolded کُھلا (of post) unfilled خالی (of question) undecided بحث طلب، فیصلہ طلب free to all عام، دعوتِ عام والا ، کُھلا ، جس میں ہر ایک جا سکے generous (hand) کُھلا ہاتھ (of mind) ready to hear and accept بے تعصّب (دل و دماغ) not secret or hidden کُھلا *in the open air*, out of doors گھر سے باہر، کُھلی فضا میں *receive (someone) with open arms*, receive (him) heartily خوشی یا سَرگرمی سے مِلنا ، ہاتھوں ہاتھ لینا *open competition* (or *scholarship, etc*.), open to everyone عام کُھلا *open water*, part of sea, etc., which is not ice-bound (سمُندر وغیرہ) جو یخ بستہ نہ ہو، غیر یخ بستہ *keep open house*, be always ready to welcome visitors مہمانوں کے خیر مقدم کو ہمیشہ تیار ہونا *be open to* (*reason arguments, etc*.) be willing to listen to (it) سُننے کو تیار ہونا *be open to* (*an offer, etc*.), be willing to consider it پر غور کرنے کو تیار رہنا *be open to doubt*. (of something be doubtful مُشتبہ ہونا *v.t.* & *i*. unclose کھولنا start (shop. meeting, etc.) شروع کرنا یا ہونا *open fire* گولیاں چلانا ، گولہ باری کرنا *open the debate*, be the first speaker in it مُباحثے کا آغاز کرنا spread (*out*) کھولنا *open out*, accelerate تیز کرنا یا ہونا *open up* (*a country* (esp.) make it open (to the Western nations for its economic, religious and other exploitation by them کسی مُلک کو مغرب کے زیرِ اقتدار لانے کا موقع دینا *open* (*one's*) *eyes*, (*a*) open them in surprise کی آنکھیں کھولنا (*b*) rouse him to facts ہکّا بکّا رہ جانا **opening** (*oh*-pĕ-ning) *n*. vacancy اسامی chance of rising (*for* someone) ترقی کا موقع، موقع *adj*. first پہلا **openly** *adv*. without secrecy کُھلم کُھلا ، کُھلے بندوں frankly صاف صاف، صاف گوئی سے **openness** *n*. being open کُھلا ہُوا lack of secrecy راز داری نہ ہونا، راز نہ ہونا frankness صاف گوئی، صاف گوئی **opencast** *adj*. (of coal found right at the surface in a coalmine کُھلا ، اُوپر کا **open-eyed** *adj*. with the eyes open جس میں آنکھیں کُھلی کی کُھلی رہ جاتی ہیں careful, watchful چوکنّا، محتاط **open-handed** *adj*. generous فراخ دِل ، فراخدِل **open-hearted** *adj*. sincere پُرخلوص **openminded** *adj*. ready to accept new ideas کُشادہ دِل ، وَسیع النظر who has not yet formed his own opinion on a subject and is ready to listen to the other person's view in order to accept it بے رائے

opera (*op*-ĕ-ra) *n*. drama in which dialogues are sung غِنائیہ ، اُوپرا، آپرا **opera-house** *n*. theatre for such dramas آپرا خانہ ، غِنائیہ خانہ **opera-glasses** *n. pl.* binoculars چھوٹی دُوربین **operatic** *adj*. of or

opera-glasses

suitable to an opera غنائیہ (کے انداز) کا
operetta (op-è-*ret*-a) *n.* short (usu. one-act) opera غنائیہ ، چھوٹا آپرا
operate (*op*-è-rayt) *v.t.* & *i.* (cause to) work چلنا یا چلانا perform a surgical operation on (someone *for* something) کا آپریشن کرنا ، پر عمل جراحی کرنا ، کی جراحی کرنا *operating-room, operation theatre* اپریشن کا کمرہ ، جراحت خانہ **operation** (-*ray*-) *n.* (method of) working عمل *come into operation*, be implemented عمل میں آنا *bring into operation* جامۂ عمل پہنانا *be in operation* چلنا ، چالو ہونا (also *surgical operation*), cutting up of a part of the body for cure of some disease عمل جراحی ، جراحی *operation theatre*, place for a surgical operation عمل جراحی کا کمرہ ، جراحت خانہ (*pl.*) movement of armed forces in warfare فوجی نقل و حرکت ، عسکری حرکت **operative** (-*ray*-tiv) *adj.* effective کارگر in practice زیر عمل of or by surgery جراحی کا (یا سے) *n.* artisan دستکار workman in a factory کارخانے میں کاریگر ، کاریگر **operator** *n.* one who operates a machine مشین پر کام کرنے والا کاریگر one who operates a film-projector آپریٹر technical worker in a telephone or telegraph office آپریٹر **operational** *adj.* of the working کام سے متعلق (esp.) used for military operations عسکری حرکت سے متعلق engaged in them عسکری حرکت میں مصروف
operetta *n.* (see under **opera**)
ophthalmo- (of-*thalm*-) *pref.* eye آنکھ ، چشم **ophthalmic** (-*thal*-) *adj.* pertaining to the eye آنکھ کا (یا سے) متعلق **ophthalmology** (-*mol*-) *n.* science of eye-diseases علم امراض چشم **ophthalmologist** (-*mol*-) *n.* eye-specialist ماہر امراض چشم
opiate *n.* & *adj.* (*ohp*-i-et) sleep-inducing (drug containing opium) افیون آمیز (دوا) ، افیون آمیز خواب آور *v.t.* (*ohp*-i-ayt) mix with opium میں افیون ملانا ، میں افیم گھول دینا (Also see **opium**)
opine *v.t.* (see under **opinion**)
opinion (o-*pin*-yĕn) *n.* what one thinks to be right رائے ، خیال *in my opinion* میری رائے میں *public opinion*, what most persons (*of* some area) think (*on* some problem) (کسی مسئلے پر کسی علاقے کی) رائے عامہ professional advice مشورہ *get* (*doctor's*, or *lawyer's*) *opinion*, consult (him) professionally on that (سے) مشورہ کرنا ، (کا) مشورہ طلب کرنا **opine** (o-*pin*) *v.i.* be of the opinion یہ رائے ہونا کہ **opinionated** (o-*pin*-yè-nay-ted) *adj.* dogmatic and obstinate in one's opinions ; not ready to change them اپنی رائے سے نہ ہٹنے والا ، خود رائے ، ہٹ دھرم
opium (*ohp*-i-um) *n.* a narcotic drug obtained from poppy seed capules افیم ، افیون (Also see **opiate**)
opponent (o-*poh*-nent) *n.* adversary مخالف ، حریف
opportune (*op*-ĕ*-tewn) *adj.* favourable (moment) مناسب done or coming at a favourable time بروقت **opportunely** *adv.* at such a time بروقت **opportunist** (*op*-ĕ*-tewn-ist) *n.* time-server ابن الوقت **opportunity** (op-ĕ*-*tewn*-i-ti) *n.* favourable chance (*for* something, *of doing* something or *to do* something) موقع ، موقعہ
oppose (o-*pohz*) *v.t.* work, speak or fight against (someone or something) کی مخالفت کرنا put forward as a contrast (*to*) کے مقابلے میں لانا **opposed** (o-*pohzd*) *adj.* contrary (*to*) (کا) الٹ ، (کی) ضد adverse (*to*) (کا) مخالف ، کا دشمن **opposeless** (o-*pohz*-less) *adj.* (poet.) irresistible بہت زوردار ، ناقابل مزاحمت ، جس کا مقابلہ نہ کیا جا سکے **opposite** (*op*-o-zit) *adj.* (*opposite* or *opposite to*), facing مقابل ، بالمقابل contrary الٹ ، الٹا *in the opposite direction* الٹی طرف ، دوسری جانب *opposite number*, (see *Addenda*) *n.* word or thing that is opposite عکس **opposition** (-*zish*-) *n.* being opposite بالمقابل ہونا being contrary to کا الٹ ہونا resistance مخالفت ، مقابلہ *the Opposition*, parliamentary representatives opposing the party in power حزب مخالف ، حزب اختلاف
oppress (o-*pres*) *v.t.* govern cruelly ظالمانہ حکومت کرنا ، تشدد سے حکومت کرنا suppress (the people, etc.) thus کچلنا (of heat, etc.) make uncomfortable تکلیف دہ ہونا ، ستانا **oppression** (op-*resh*-èn) *n.* tyranny تشدد **oppressive** (-*res*-) *adj.* (of laws, rule, etc.) cruel and unjust ظالمانہ ، متشددانہ (of taxes, heat, etc.) unbearable سخت ، مار ڈالنے والا (of weather) close, sultry حبس والا ، بند ، بند بند **oppressively** *adv.* ظلم و تشدد سے **oppressor** *n.* cruel, person, tyrant بے انصاف اور ظالم
opprobrium (op-*rohb*-ri-um) *n.* public shame رسوائی **opprobrious** (-us) *adj.* (of words) full of reproach ملامت آمیز
optative (op-*tay*-tiv) *adj.* (in grammar) expressing wish تمنائی *optative mood* فعل تمنائی *n.* optative mood or form تمنائی
optic (*op*-tik) *adj.* of eye or sight بصری *optic nerve* عصبہ مجوفہ *optic angle*, angle made from point to the eyes or from two points to the eye زاویۂ نظر **optics** (*op*-tiks) *n.* (pl. used as sing.) science of sight علم بصارت ، بصریات laws of light نور کے قوانین **optical** (*op*-ti-kĕl) *adj.* pertaining to eye-sight بصری ، نظر کا (یا سے متعلق) **optician** (op-*tish*-ĕn) *n.* maker of, spectacles, etc. عینک ساز dealer in them عینک فروش ، چشمہ فروش
optimism (*op*-ti-mizm) *n.* tendency to look upon

the bright side of things پُر اُمّید ہونا، رجائیت **optimistic** (*-mis-*) *adj.* always expecting the best رجائیت پسند confident of success پُر اُمّید **optimist** (*op*-ti-mist) *n.* optimistic person رجائیت پسند شخص
optimum (*op*-ti-mum) *adj.* best بہترین *n.* the most favourable point, etc., for the purpose مناسب ترین موقع
option (*op*-shĕn) *n.* choice حق انتخاب، اختیار، پسند that which is chosen منتخبہ، منتخب **optional** *adj.* not obligatory ; that may or may not be chosen by one اختیاری، انتخابی *optional subjects,* subjects of teaching left to a candidate to choose from انتخابی مضامین *additional optional subject* مزید اختیاری مضامین یا اختیاری مضامین **optionally** *adv.* اپنی مرضی پر
opulent (*op*-ew-lent) *adj.* very rich رئیس، بہت امیر **opulence** *n.* امیری، امارت
opus (*oh*-pus or *op*-us) *n.* (no pl.) (abb. *op.*) musician's separate composition as cited by number نغمہ، نغمہ نگاری، *Beethoven op. 10* بیتھوون، نغمہ نمبر دس (also *opus magnum* or *magnum opus*), (*a*) great literary undertaking بڑا ادبی کارنامہ (*b*) (artist's) masterpiece شاہکار **opuscule** (o-*pus*-kewl), **opusculum** (o-pus-kew-lum, pl. opuscula) *n.* minor composition ناقابلِ ذکر نغمہ گری، معمولی نغمہ
¹or (o*) *conj.* (introducing alternatives) one of the words separated by it یا *either...or* خواہ...خواہ، یا...یا، یا *either this or that* خواہ یہ خواہ وہ *whether (it happens, etc.) or not* خواہ (ہو) یا نہ ہو، خواہ (ہو) خواہ نہ ہو، (ہو) یا نہ ہو that is یعنی otherwise نہیں تو، ورنہ (old use) before اِس سے پہلے کہ
²-or (ĕ*) *suf.* (for forming) agent noun والا (وغیرہ)
oracle (*o*-ra-kĕl) *n.* ancient Greek temple (like the famous one at Delphi) where the gods answered (usu. in vague or ambiguous words) questions asked about (one's) future دارُالاستخارہ priest giving the answers as inspired by the gods ہاتف the answer thus given جوابِ استخارہ capable of good guidance رہنمائی کی اہلیت ہاتف کا قول رکھنے والا، رہنما **oracular** (*-rak*-ew-) *adj.* of or like an oracle ہاتف کا (سا) with a hidden meaning پوشیدہ معانی والا
oral (*oh*-rĕl) *adj.* (of examination, etc.) spoken and not written زبانی of the mouth مُنہ کا (of medicine) to be taken by mouth (and not to be injected, etc.) کھانے کی (دوا)، پینے کی (دوا) **orally** *adv.* by word of mouth زبانی (administered) by mouth مُنہ کے راستے
orange (*o*-rinj) *n.* a well-known reddish-yellow citrous fruit with a tight skin (and quite different from our سنگترہ which is called a *tangerine*) مالٹا tree bearing it مالٹا، مالٹے کا درخت its reddish-yellow colour which can also be seen in the spectrum between yellow and red نارنجی *adj.* of this colour نارنجی **orange-stick** *n.* thin pointed stick for finger-nails نیل پالش لگانے کی لکڑی
orangeade (o-*rinj*-ayd) *n.* drink of orange-juice مالٹوں کے رس کا مشروب
orang-outang (o-*rang*-oo-*tang*), **orang-utan** *n.* a large long armed ape اورانگ اوٹانگ

an orang-outang

oration (o-ray-shĕn) *n.* formal public speech تقریر **orator** (*o*-ra-tĕ*) *n.* (fem. *oratress*) good public-speeaker مقرر، خطیب **oratorical** (*-to-*) *adj.* of public speaking خطیبانہ **oratory** (*o*-ra-to-ri) *n.* art of public speaking تقریر کا فن، خطابت eloquence فصاحت، خطابت speeches تقاریر، تقریریں **oratorio** (o-ra-*to*-ri-oh) *n.* (pl. *oratorios*) sacred opera performed with action, scenery or costumes مذہبی اوپرا، سادہ اوپرا
orb (o*b) *n.* globe کُرہ any heavenly body جرم فلکی، جرم سماوی (poet.) eyeball آنکھ، دیدہ، ڈھیلا **orbed** (o*bd, or *o**-bid) *adj.* rounded گردی
orbit (*o**-bit) *n.* a heavenly body's track (*round* another) مُسیر، مدار eye-socket حلقہ چشم border round eye of bird or insect آنکھ کا حلقہ
orchard (*o**chĕ*d) *n.* fruit-garden پھلوں کا باغ، پھلدار درختوں کا باغ، باغ، بوستان
orchestra (*o**k-es-tra) *n.* band of persons playing musical instruments together سازندوں کا طائفہ آرکسٹرا (in an opera or theatre) place for an orchestra سرود گاہ music played thus طائفے والے سازوں کا نغمہ، نغمہ ساز **orchestral** *adj.* pertaining to an orchestra سازندوں کے طائفے کا، مظہرِ بانہ
orchid (*o**k-id), **orchis** (*o**k-is) *n.* any of a family of plants with brilliant and fragrant flowers تُقلبِ مِصری **orchidaceous** (-daysh-us) *adj.* pertaining to it تقلبِ مصری کا، تقلبی

an orchid

ordain (o*-*dayn*) *v.t.* order (*that*) حکم دینا دکہ، decide مقسوم میں لکھ دینا confer holy orders ; make (someone) a Christian priest کو پادری بنانا **ordination** (*-nay-*) *n.* conferring of the holy orders پادری بنانا
ordeal (o*-*deel* or o*-*dee*-ĕl, or *o**d-eel) *n.* ancient and mediaeval method of deciding someone's innocence or otherwise (*by* fire, etc.) requiring him to cross it unscathed or some other physical test جسمانی اذیت دے کر جھوٹ سچ کا امتحان any severe test of character سخت امتحان، کڑی آزمائش *pass through an ordeal* کڑی آزمائش میں سے گزرنا

order (*o**d-ĕ*) *n.* tidy arrangement ترتیب *in order of* کی ترتیب سے *in alphabetical order* ابجدی ترتیب سے ، الف بے کی ترتیب سے ، الفبائی ترتیب سے (often *pl.*) command *by order of, under the orders of* کے حکم سے (*someone's*) *orders*, (*a*) orders from (him) (کسی کا حکم) (*b*) orders for him to obey (کسی کے لیے) حکم written direction *to* (*on* bank, post office, etc.) to pay the stated sum منی آرڈر ، آرڈر ، ہنڈی *money order* منی آرڈر working condition چالو حالت *in good working order* چالو حالت میں (*machinery*) *out of order* بگڑی ہوئی کَل peaceful atmosphere (*in* a meeting or country) by obedience to rules or to the law نظم وضبط *law and order situation in the country* مُلک میں نظم وضبط کی حالت مُلک کی اِنتظامی حالت quiet, silence خاموشی ، سکوت *be called to order* (of the President) خاموش رہنے کو کہا جانا *to call to order* صَدر کا حاضرینِ جلسہ سے کہنا کہ نظم وضبط قائم رکھیں request to supply (goods) (مال کی) فرمائش *an order* (*for an amount*) (اِتنے مال کی) فرمائش *made to order*, specifically so to special measurements, etc., and not ready-made فرمائش کے مطابق بنایا ہُوا ، فرمائش کا *on order*, ordered for but not yet supplied (مال) اِتنے والا جس کی فرمائش بھیجی ہوئی ہو social status رُتبہ group holding it رُتبے والے صاحبانِ جاہ ومرتبت authority to a priest on being ordained پادری کو اِختیارات *take holy orders* پادری بننا *in order that*, so that تاکہ *in order* (*to do something*), with a view to (doing it) (کرنے) کے لیے ، کی غرض سے *v. t.* give an order to (someone *to do* something) کا حکم دینا place an order for (goods *from* someone or *from* some place) (مال کی) فرمائش بھیجنا arrange (something) neatly ترتیب سے رکھنا ، سلیقے یا قرینے سے لگانا **orderly** *adj.* neatly arranged قرینے سے لگا ہُوا (of crowd, etc.) peaceful پُرامن (military) of or for orders احکام کا ، حکموں کا *orderly book*, book for entering orders رجسٹر احکام ، احکام کی کاپی *n.* officer's messenger اَرْدَلی ، چپراسی (also *nursing-orderly*) hospital attendant شفاخانے میں سب سے چھوٹا تیماردار

ordinal (*o**d-i-nĕl) *n.* & *adj.* (number) stating the position of a link in a series (as distinct from a *cardinal number*) عددِ (ترتیبی)

ordinance (*o**d-i-nans) *n.* decree having the force of law (and circumventing the need to seek the Legislature's approval) آرڈی ننس ، فرمان religious rite مذہبی فریضہ

ordinary (*o**d-i-na-ri) *adj.* usual, quite common معمولی *out of the ordinary*, **extraordinary** غیر معمولی ، اَہم **ordinarily** (*o**d-i-*na*-ri-li) *adv.* usually معمولاً ، عام طور پر ، بالعموم ، عموماً قابلِ ذکر

ordination *n.* (see under **ordain**)

ordnance (*o**d-nans) *n.* heavy guns and similar other military weapons توپ خانہ ، توپخانہ ❷ department for military stores محکمۂ ذخائرِ جنگی *ordnance depot*, one of the centres for military supplies جنگی سامان کا مرکز ، آرڈیننس ڈپو *ordnance corps*, branch of army responsible for the supply of these stores جنگی سامان مُہیا کرنے والا فوجی دستہ ، آرڈیننس کور *ordnance survey maps*, official maps of a country مُلک کے مُستند نقشے

ore (oh*) *n.* rock, etc., from which metal is obtained کچی دھات ، فلز

organ (*o**-gĕn) *n.* any part of living body عضو a musical instrument working on the same principles as a harmonium, but very much bigger اَرغن ، اَرغنون of harmonium with pedals پیروں والا ہارمونیم ، آرگن subsidiary organization newspaper serving as the mouthpiece (*of* political party, public opinion, etc.) (کا) اَرگن ، (کی) پارٹی کا اخبار

an organ (sense 2)

organic (o*-*gan*-ik) *adj.* of or having bodily organs عضوی (in chemistry) pertaining to that which once could grow نامیاتی organized مُنتظم **organism** (o*g-a-nizm) *n.* any living being with parts working together called organs) جسمِ نامی ، نامیاتی جسم organization تنظیم ، جماعت **organist** *n.* organ-player اَرغنون نواز

organdie (o*-*gand*-i) *n.* a kind of thin starched muslin اَرگنڈی

organize (o*g-a-niz) *v. t.* bring under a regular system ترتیب میں لانا get ready (party, army, expedition, etc.) مُنتظم کرنا ، کا اِنتظام کرنا ، کو وجود میں لانا put (one's work, etc.) in order میں باقاعدگی پیدا کرنا **organized** (*o**g-a-nizd) *adj.* well-prepared مُنتظم (form of life) with many organs ; hence developed ترقی یافتہ **organization** (-*zay*-) *n.* organizing or being organized مُنتظم کرنا یا ہونا ، تنظیم organized body تنظیم **organizer** (-*nī*-zĕ*) *n.* who organizes (party etc.) (کی) تنظیم کرنے والا one who makes arrangements (*of*) (کا) مُنتظم

orgy (*o**-ji) *n.* wild merry-making عیش ونشاط *drunken orgy* بدمستوں کی محفل ، رنگ رلیاں (*orgy of*), excessive indulgence in drinking, etc. کی کثرت **orgies** (*o**-jeez) *n. pl.* riotous secret rites of the worship of Bacchus باخوس پرستش کی رنگ رلیاں

oriel (*oh*-ri-el) *n.* recess with a window built out from a wall جھروکہ
orient (*oh*-ri-ent) *n.* (*the Orient* opp. *the Occident*), non-Western countries مشرق **oriental** (*-ent-*) *adj.* of the Orient مشرقی ، شرقی ، شرقیہ *oriental languages* السنۂ شرقیہ *n.* oriental person مشرق کا باشندہ ، مشرق کا مکین ، مشرقی **orientate** *v. t.* & *i.* give a new direction to (policy, ideas etc.) کا دھارا بدلنا ، کو نئے رُخ دھارا بدلنا ، نئے رُخ پر ڈالنا پر ڈالنا **orientation** *n.* (Also see **reorientate**)
orifice (*o*-ri-fis) *n.* aperture or mouth of cavity, etc. مُونہہ ، دہانہ
origin (*o**-ri-jin) *n.* starting-point نقطۂ آغاز ، آغاز parentage اصل ، ابتدا اصل خاندان *of humble origin* معمولی یا غریب گھرانے کا فرد **originate** (o-*rij*-è-nayt) *v. t.* & *i.* bring or come into being وجود میں لانا یا آنا be the inventor of کا موجد یا مخترع ہونا **original** (o-*rij*-è-nĕl) *adj.* earliest (inhabitants, etc.) اوّلین ، قدیم ترین ، قدیمی (documents, etc.) of which others are copies اصل (of ideas) not borrowed طبع زاد creative (mind) تخلیقی *n.* original document اصل the form (esp. the language) in which something was first written اصل *read a book in the original* اصل کتاب پڑھنا **orginally** *adv.* دراصل **originality** (*-nal-*) *n.* creative power تخلیقی قوت
riole (*oh*-ri-ohl) *n.* golden-yellow bird of the crow family رو ریول ، سُنہری کوّا ، زرّیں زاغ
rison (*o*-ri-zèn) *n.* (usu. pl.) (old use) prayer دُعا
rnament (*o*n*-a-ment) *n.* jewellery, etc. زیور anything used for decoration آرائش کی چیز *an ornament to* (*something*), anything beautifying (it) کی زینت *v. t.* be a decoration of کا سنگار ، کی زینت کی زیبائش کرنا ، کو خوبصورت یا خوشنما بنانا beautify بننا **ornamental** (*-ment-*) *adj.* of or for ornament زیبائشی **ornamentation** (*-tay-*) *n.* art or act of ornamenting زیبائش **ornate** (*o**-nayt) *adj.* richly ornamented بڑی زیبائش والا ، مزیّن (of style) embellished with rhetorical ornament مرصّع
rnis (*o**-nis) *n.* birds of a region collectively کسی علاقے کے پرندے **ornithology** (*-thol-*) *n.* science or study of birds علم الطیور **ornithologist** *n.* expert in it ماہر علم الطیور
phan (*o**-fĕn) *n.* child one or both of whose parents are dead یتیم ، بن باپ (یا بن ماں) کا بچہ ، بے ماں باپ کا بچہ *v.t.* (of war, etc.) cause to be an orphan یتیم کر دینا **orphanage** (*o*-f*-è-nij) *n.* charitable home for orphans یتیم خانہ **orphanhood** *n.* being an orphan یتیمی
thodox (*o**-tho-doks) *adj.* generally accepted rightly taught belief صحیح عقیدہ (person) holding it صحیح العقیدہ ؛ old fashioned (views, etc.) فرسودہ خیال ، تقلید کرنے والا (person) with such views تقلید پسند ، دقیانوسی ، فرسودہ خیال **orthodoxy** (*o**th-o-dok-si) *n.* being orthodox صحیح العقیدہ ہونا ، دقیانوسی ہونا
orthoepi (o*-*tho*-e-pi) *n.* rules of correct pronunciation اصول تلفظ ، تجوید **orthoepist** *n.* expert in these rules ماہرِ تجوید
orthography (o*-*thog*-rafi) *n.* rules of correct spelling علم ہجا
orthopaedy, orthopedy, orthopaedia (*o**-tho-pee-) *n.* process of curing bodily deformities (esp. of children) جسمانی نقائص کا علاج **orthopaedic** *adj.* pertaining to it جسمانی نقائص کے علاج سے متعلق
oscillate (*os*-i-layt) *v.t.* & *i.* swing to and fro جھولنا vascillate (*between* two opinions, etc.) کبھی ایک طرف کبھی دوسری طرف جھکنا ، اہتزاز کرنا **oscillatory** *adj.* swinging or vascillating جھولنے والا **oscillation** *n.* act of oscillating اہتزاز ، جُنبش ، لرزش
osier (*oh*-zhè*) *n.* (branch of the) willow used for making baskets, etc. ٹوکری بننے کا بید (یا اس کی ٹہنی)
osseous (*os*-e-us) *adj.* of or having bones استخوانی ، ہڈی کا (یا) ہڈی والا **ossify** (*os*-i-fi) *v.t.* & *i.* turn into bone ہڈی بن جانا make or become or make rigid جمود طاری کرنا (یا) جمود کا شکار ہو جانا make or become callous احساس سے عاری کرنا یا ہونا **ossification** *n.* ossifying جمود طاری کرنا ، جمود کا شکار ہو جانا ، احساس سے عاری کرنا یا ہونا
ostensible (os-*tens*-i-bèl) *adj.* pretended (reason) in order to hide the real one دکھاوے کا ، بناوٹی **ostensibly** *adv.* دکھاوے کے لیے ، بناوٹی طور پر **ostentation** (*-tay-*) *n.* a showing off دکھاوا **ostentatious** *adj.* showing off دکھاوے کا شوقین
ostler (*os*-lĕ*) *n.* man in charge of horses at an inn سرائے کا سائیس
ostracize (*os*-tra-siz) *v.t.* excommunicate حقّہ پانی بند کرنا ، برادری باہر کرنا ، برادری سے نکالنا (in ancient Greece) banish by popular vote جلاوطن کرنا **ostracism** *n.* act of ostracizing or being ostracized جلاوطنی ، برادری باہر کرنا یا ہونا
ostrich (*os*-trich) *n.* very large bird which runs swiftly but is unable to fly نعامہ ، شتر مرغ
other (*udh*-ĕ*) *adj.* different دوسرا ، اور ، دیگر additional مزید *pron.* second person or thing دوسرا شخص ، دوسری چیز different person or thing اور شخص یا شے *adv.* differently کے سوا *the other day*, a few days ago ابھی اگلے ہی روز *some day or the other*,

some day کسی روز *some time or the other*, some time کسی وقت *other than*, not the same کے عِلاوہ **otherwise** (*udh-ĕ*-wīz*) *adv.* differently اَور طرح in other respects باقی پہلوؤں سے، باقی *conj.* or else وَرنہ

otter (*ot-ĕ**) *n.* a mongoose-like water-animal covered with fur اُود بلاؤ its fur اُود بلاؤ کی پوستین

an otter

ought (ot) *auxiliary v.* (always used as *ought to*) should چاہیے must ضرور چاہیے

ounce (ouns) *n.* unit of weight about ½ chhatak اَونس

our (*ou-ĕ**) *pron.* (possessive form of *we*, when used with the possessed object ; otherwise *ours*) ہمارا **ourselves** (*ou-ĕ*-selvz*) *pron.* (*pl.* of *myself* and the reflexive form of *we* or *our*) ہم آپ، ہم خود

-ous (us) *suf.* (forming adjectives with the sense) having or of والا ، کا

oust *v.t.* & *i.* turn out (*from* place, business, service, etc.) سے نکال دینا (سے)، بے دخل کرنا، سے بے دخل کرنا (سے)، محروم کر دینا

[1]**out** *adj.* not in باہر away from دُور no longer burning بجھا ہوا ہونا wrong غلط utterly بالکل on strike ہڑتال پر loudly اُونچی آواز سے to the end آخر تک at an end ختم to others دُوسروں کو، اوروں کو (of a batsman) (be) dismissed آؤٹ revealed ظاہر (13) out of hiding ظاہر ہونا *v.t.* & *i.* سامنے، ظاہر سے باہر become known ظاہر ہونا *The truth will out* سچ ظاہر ہو کر رہے گا (slang) eject forcibly زبردستی نکالنا (in boxing) knock-out یوں گرانا کہ وقت پر اُٹھنے کے قابل نہ رہے *int.* (old use) (expressive of reproach, abhorrence, etc.) دُور، دفع، دفان، وائے نفرین (*Phrases* :) *out of*, not in a condition of سے باہر ہے، کی حالت میں نہیں *be out of practice* مشق نہ رہنا *out and out* (*revolutionary, etc.*), thorough (revolutionary, etc.) پورا، پکّا، کٹّر، سخت، بالکل *out of date*, out-dated جس کا اب رواج باقی نہ ہو *out of breath*, breathless ہانپتا ہوا *out of doors*, in the open air باہر، باہر کھلی ہوا میں *out of (one's) mind, out of (one's) senses*, insane پاگل *out of temper*, enraged طیش میں *out-of-the-way*, (*a*) unusual غیر معمولی (*b*) remote دُور *go out of the way* (*to help someone, etc.*) اپنے دائرۂ اختیارات سے باہر جا کر بھی (کسی کی) مدد کرنا **outer** *adj.* external باہر کا farther from the centre پَرلا **outermost** *adj.* farthest from the centre سب سے پَرے کا

[2]**out** *pref.* (suggesting among other things :) externally کے باہر completely پوری طرح openly کھل کر more than سے بڑھ کر **outbid** *v.t.* offer a higher price than (someone) سے بڑھ کر بولی دینا

outboard (*out-*) *adj.* (of motor-boat) having engines, etc., attached outside the boat انجن باہر والی **outbreak** *n.* sudden breaking out (*of* epidemic, war, etc.) (وبا کا) پھوٹ پڑنا، (جنگ کا) اچانک شروع کرنا **outburst** *n.* a bursting out (*of* steam, anger, etc.) پھٹ پڑنا **outcast** *n.* & *adj.* homeless (person) جسے دوستوں نے تج دیا ہو friendless (person) بے خانماں (one) turned out from society جس کا حقّہ پانی بند ہو بے یار (among Hindus) untouchable or pollute اچھوت **outclass** *v.t.* excel سے بہت بڑھ کر ہونا **outcome** *n.* issue (*of*) (کا) نتیجہ **outcry** *n.* loud cry (*of* fear, etc.) چیخ hue and cry (against) (کے خلاف) شور و غوغا **outdistance** *v.t.* leave others far behind سے بہت آگے نکل جانا، کو بہت پیچھے چھوڑ جانا **outdo** *v.t.* (*outdo, outdid, outdone*) do better than سے بہتر کام کرنا *not to be outdone by others*, not liking (others) to excel نہیں چاہتا کہ کوئی اس سے بڑھ جائے یا بازی لے جائے **outdoor** *adj.* open-air باہر کا، کھلے (یا گھر سے باہر کے) وغیرہ سے باہر، بیرونی، باہر کا *outdoor games* باہر کے کھیل *outdoor life*, life spent most of the time out of home (on tours of open country, etc.) گھر سے باہر کی زندگی **outdoors** *adj.* outside the home گھر سے باہر in the open air میدان میں **outfit** *n.* clothing (*for* a purpose) (کسی خاص مقصد کا) لباس وغیرہ **outfitter** *n.* dealer in clothes کپڑے بیچنے والا dealer in special equipment (esp. for travel) سفر (وغیرہ) کا سامان بیچنے والا **outflank** *v.t.* pass round the flank of (the enemy) (دشمن کی) فوج کے پہلوؤں تک پھیل جانا، یا وہاں سے پیچھے تک چلے جانا **outgrow** *v.t.* (*outgrow, outgrew, outgrown*) grow too big for (one's clothes, etc.) (کے کپڑے) چھوٹے ہو جانا grow taller than سے بڑا ہو جانا give up with age (bad habits, etc.) چھوڑ دینا، ترک کر دینا **outgrowth** *n.* offshoot (*of*) شاخسانہ **outhouse** *n.* (also *outbuilding*), small building adjoining main building ملحقہ عمارت **outing** *n.* short pleasure trip سیر، تفریحی سفر *have an outing, go for an outing* تفریحی سفر پر جانا **outlandish** (out-*land*-ish) *adj.* strange (person, thing, sound) as though foreign اجنبی، پردیسی، کسی دوسرے دیس کا **outlast** *v.t.* last longer than سے زیادہ چلنا، زیادہ کام دینا **outlaw** *n.* (old use) deprived of the protection of the law جلا وطن، قانون کی حمایت سے محروم *v.t.* declare (someone) an outlaw کے سر سے قانون کا سایہ اٹھا لینا، جلا وطن کرنا **outlay** *n.* expenditure (*on* some enterprise, work, etc.) (کا) خرچ (پر) لگا ہوا سرمایہ **outlet** *n.* way out (*for* fluids, passions, energy, etc.) نکلنے کا راستہ **outline** (*out-l.n*) *n.* line along the outer edge خاکہ *in outline* کا خاکہ gist or brief account مختصر (کا) خلاصہ main points (*for* expansion) (کے) اہم نکات، کا خاکہ *v.t.* draw in outline

کھینچنا، خاکہ کھینچنا، خاکہ کشی کرنا give a brief account of مختصر طور پر دینا مختصراً، بیان کرنا **outlive** *v.t.* live longer than ...سے زیادہ دیر زندہ رہنا outlive the memory of کے بعد تک زندہ رہنا رہنا کہ پہلے واقعے کی یاد دل سے نکل جائے **outlook** (*out-lŭk*) *n.* attitude (*on*) نظریہ، نقطۂ نظر، نقطۂ نگاہ، زاویۂ نگاہ likelihood (*for*) کے آثار **outlying** *adj.* (of area) included in a locality but lying farther away from its centre than others پرے کا، دور افتادہ **outmanoeuvre** (out-ma-*noov*-ĕ*) *v.t.* surpass (someone) by or in manoeuvring سے بڑھ کر چال کرنا، کو مات دینا **outmoded** (-*moh*-ded) *adj.* out of fashion جس کا رواج نہ رہا ہو، دقیانوسی **outnumber** (out-*num*-bĕ*) *v.t.* be greater in number than سے تعداد میں بڑا **out-of-date** *adj.* outdated پرانا، جس کا رواج باقی نہ ہو زیادہ ہونا **out-of-doors** *adj.* (not hyphenated predicatively or as an adv.) in the open air گھر سے باہر، میدان میں **out-of-the-way** (not hyphenated predicatively or as an adv.) (see under [1]**out**) **outpace** (out-*pays*) *v.t.* walk faster than (someone) سے تیز چلنا، کو پیچھے چھوڑ جانا **out-patient** *n.* patient not lodged in a hospital but getting treatment there آؤٹ پیشنٹ، غیر رہائشی مریض، باہر کا مریض، بیرونی مریض **outpost** *n.* observation post outside a military camp فوجی چوکی troops posted there چوکی کی فوج **outpouring** *n.* (usu. pl.) expression (of emotion *in* speech, poem, etc.) اظہار جذبات، ذوق (جذبات) abundant supply (*of* something) کثرت، افراط، ذوق **output** *n.* amount of goods, etc., turned out کارخانے کی مجموعی پیداوار، ماحصل **outrage** (*out*-rij) *n.* extreme cruelty انتہائی ظلم shocking violation of (*upon*) کی شرمناک بے حرمتی *outrage upon decency* شرمناک حرکت gross insult سخت توہین *v.t.* inflict wrong upon پر سخت ظلم کرنا violate (modesty *of*) کی عصمت دری کرنا insult کی سخت توہین کرنا violate (law, etc.) کی خلاف ورزی کرنا **outrageous** *adj.* very shameless انتہائی شرمناک very cruel سخت ظالمانہ shocking دل ہلا دینے والا immoral اخلاق سوز insulting توہین آمیز immoderate حد سے بڑھا ہوا **outride** (out-*rīd*) *v.t.* ride faster than سے تیز جانا ride beyond سے آگے نکل جانا **outrider** *n.* (esp.) servant on horseback attending a carriage گاڑی کے ساتھ سوار ملازم **outright** (out-*rīt*) *adj.* frankly صاف صاف all at once ایک ہی بار entirely بالکل، بالکلیہ *adj.* direct, without mincing matters صاف out-and-out (rejection, etc.) بالکل، پورا، پکا **outset** *n.* beginning *at the very outset* شروع ہی میں **outshine** (out-*shīn*) *v.t.* shine brightly than سے کہیں زیادہ روشن ہونا، کو ماند کر دینا excel سے بازی لے جانا **outside** (*out*-*sīd*) *n.* outer surface باہر، بیرونی سطح outer-most limit آخری حد *at the outside* زیادہ سے زیادہ *adj.* exterior بیرونی ulterior کچھ اور، بیرونی highest (prices, etc.) زیادہ سے زیادہ *adv.* on (or to) the outer side باہر out of doors باہر، گھر سے باہر *prep.* on the outer side of کے باہر beyond کے علاوہ، باہر کا، پردیسی، اجنبی **outsider** *n.* stranger کے متعلق (esp.) one not considered fit to be included in a group باہر کا، غیر متعلق شخص، حلقے میں شامل ہونے کے نااہل *There is an outsider in the House*; there is one who is not (fit to be a) member ایوان میں باہر کا کوئی شخص آ گیا ہے unknown (horse in a race) and quite unexpected to win it کوئی نیا (گھوڑا) **out-size** *adj.* over the normal size عام سائز سے بڑا *n.* unusually large size غیر معمولی سائز، غیر معمولی طور پر بڑا **outskirts** *n. pl.* outlying parts *of* a town کے مضافات، نواحی علاقے **outspan** (out-*span*) *v.t.* & *i.* unyoke (animals) from a vehicle گاڑی سے کھولنا *n.* place of stopping on the way راستے میں رکنے کی جگہ، منزل **outspoken** *adj.* frank کھری کھری سنا دینے والا **outstanding** (-*stand*-) *adj.* prominent نمایاں still to be done, (solved, etc.) جسے (حل) کرنا ابھی باقی ہو **outstay** *v.t.* stay longer than (one's welcome, etc.) کچھ زیادہ دیر ہی رہنا **outstretched** *adj.* stretched out or extended (hand, etc.) پھیلایا ہوا **outstrip** (-*strip*) *v.t.* (-pp-) excel (in race, etc.) سے آگے نکل جانا **outward** (*out*-wĕ*d) *adj.* of or on the outside باہر کا، بیرونی apparent, visible (show, etc.) ظاہری (also *outward-bound*), (of a ship, voyage, etc.) going away from the port or to a foreign port باہر کا، باہر جانے والا *adv.* towards the outside باہر کو، باہر away from باہر جانے والا **outwards** (*out*-wĕ*dz) *adv.* towards the outside باہر جانے والا **outwardly** *adj.* apparently ظاہری طور پر، بظاہر، نظر بظاہر **outweigh** (out-*way*) *v.t.* weigh more than سے زیادہ بھاری (وزنی) ہونا be more important or valuable than سے زیادہ اہم ہونا **outwit** (out-*wit*) *v.t.* (-tt-) overreach سے زیادہ چالاک نکلنا **outworn** (out-*woh*n*) *adj.* worn out پھٹا پرانا outdated پرانا، دقیانوسی

oval (*oh*-val) *n.* & *adj.* egg-shaped plane (figure) بیضوی (شکل) *the Oval*, the famous London cricket-ground of the *M.C.C.* (*i.e.*, the *Marylebone* Cricket Club) at the Kennington Oval اوول **ovary** (*oh*-va-ri) *n.* ovum-producing organ of an animal رحم seed-producing vessel of plants بیضہ دان **ovarion** (oh-*vay*-ri-ĕn) *adj.* of or pertaining to an ovary رحم کا (یا سے متعلق) **ovation** (o-*vay*-shĕn) *n.* outburst of applause نعرہ ہائے تحسین enthusiastic welcome پرجوش استقبال **oven** (*uv*-ĕn) *n.* enclosed space for baking تنور

[1]**over** (*oh-vĕ**) *prep.* higher than کے اُوپر more than سے زیادہ across پرے، کے پار through-out کے دوران میں out and down from پر سے upon پر، میں about پر، کے متعلق، کے بارے میں *adv.* at an end ختم throughout سارا، شروع سے لیکر آخر تک (be) *all over*, (be) in one's characteristic attitude, etc. اپنے اصلی رُوپ میں، اصلی اصلی، خود ہی *It's Joe all over* دیکھو تو جوزف اپنے اصلی رُوپ میں in addition to کے علاوہ through سے to کو، کے حوالے from the top or edge، میں کے اُوپر سے، کے کنارے سے *over all*, (used predicatively or adverbially it is written as two words) altogether مجموعی طور پر، بحیثیت مجموعی *n.* (in cricket) number of times between change of ends in bowling گیند پھینکنے کی باری، اوور باری *a maiden over*, an over in which no runs have been made خالی اوور خالی باری (*Phrases* :) *over and above*, in addition (to) (اس) کے علاوہ *over against*, in contrast with کے مقابلے میں *go over to* (*the enemy, etc.*) (دوستوں کو چھوڑ کر دشمن) سے جا ملنا *over head and ears* (*in debt, etc.*) entirely involved (in it) (میں) پوری طرح پھنسا ہوا *over* (*someone's*) *head*, beyond his comprehension کی سمجھ سے باہر

[2]**over-** *pref.* too much ; to an undesirable extent ناگوار حد تک زیادہ، کچھ زیادہ ہی، بہت ہی زیادہ، ضرورت سے زیادہ (as *overcautious*) ضرورت سے زیادہ محتاط **overact** (-akt) *v.t. & i.* act in an exaggerated way مبالغہ سے کام لینا **overactive** *adj.* active beyond need ضرورت سے زیادہ اہتمام یا بناوٹ کرنا ضرورت سے زیادہ چست (یا مستعد) **overall** (*oh-vĕ*-awl*) *adj.* (written as one word when used attributively) altogether, total مجموعی طور پر، مجموعی *n.* housewife's protective outer garment for house-work گھر کے کام کاج کے لیے عورتوں کے اُوپر کا کپڑا **overalls** (-awlz) *n. pl.* loose-fitting trousers or trousers and jacket in one worn by workmen over ordinary clothes to keep them clean اوور آل **overawe** (*-aw*) *v.t.* make silent or restrain with awe بے خود مرعُوب کر **overbalance** (*-bal-*) *v.t. & i.* (cause to) topple over ڈگمگا کر گرنا یا گرانا **overbear** (*-bay-e**) *v.t.* overcome (by stronger force, etc.) دبا دینا، زیر کرنا **overbearing** *adj.* (of person or attitude) forcing others to one's will اپنی مرضی کے تابع کرنے والا **overboard** (boh*d) *adv.* into the sea from over the side of a ship جہاز پر سے سمندر میں *throw* (*a scheme, etc.*) *overboard*, give (it) up ترک کر دینا **overcast** (-kast) *v.t.* cover (the sky) with clouds پر بادل چھانا، بادلوں سے بھر جانا sew over (edge of a cloth) (کپڑے کا کنارا) سینا *adj.* darkened with clouds بادلوں سے گھرا ہوا darkened in prospect (with grief, etc.) جس پر غم کی گھٹا چھائی ہوئی ہو، غم میں ڈوبا ہوا، بہت غمگین **overcharge** (*-chah*j*) *v.t.* charge more than the reasonable price ٹھگنا، بہت زیادہ قیمت لینا *n.* the price charged thus اصل سے زیادہ لی ہوئی قیمت **overcloud** *v.t.* overcast بادلوں سے گھرنا، بہت غمگین کرنا **overcoat** *n.* long warm coat worn when it is very cold فرغل، اوورکوٹ **overcome** (*-kum*) *v.t.* (*overcome, overcame, overcome*) overpower (adversary) کو زیر کرنا، پر قابو پانا، کو قابو میں لانا conquer (bad habits) پر قابو پانا weaken بڈھا کرنا، بے قابو کرنا **overconfident** (*-kon-*) *adj.* confiding too much in پر حد سے زیادہ اعتماد کرنے والا too confident of one's own capability حد سے زیادہ خود اعتماد، اپنے متعلق خوش فہمی سے کام لینے والا **overcrowd** (*-kroud*) *v.t.* make too full بہت زیادہ بھرنا یا ٹھونسنا **overcrowded** (-ded) *adj.* بہت بھیڑ والا، بہت ٹھنسا ہوا **overdo** (*-doo*) *v.t.* (*overdo, overdid, overdone*) overact میں مبالغہ سے کام لینا cook (meat) too much گوشت کو بہت پکا دینا **overdose** *n.* (*oh-vĕ*-dohz*) more than the proper dose دوا کی زیادہ خوراک *v.t.* (oh-ve*-*dohz*) administer more than the proper dose زیادہ دوا دینا **overdraft** (*oh-*) *n.* amount of money drawn by one in excess of one's bank account بنک سے زائد وصولی، فاضل وصولی *v.t. & i.* make an overdraft بنک سے اپنی جمع شدہ رقم سے زیادہ نکلوانا، (بنک سے) زائد (یا فاضل) وصولی کرنا **overdress** (*-dres*) *v.t. & i.* dress too showily بہت ہی بن ٹھن کر آنا **overdue** (*-dew*) *adj.* beyond the time-limit (*for* payment, arrival, etc.) (کا وقت) گزر جانا، (پہنچنے یا ادائیگی میں) تاخیر ہونا، (ادائیگی کا) زائد المیعاد ہونا **overeat** (*-eet*) *v.i.* eat too much بہت زیادہ کھا جانا harm (*oneself*) by doing so بہت زیادہ کھا کر بیمار ہو جانا **overestimate** (*-es-*) *n.* too high an estimate بہت زیادہ اندازہ *v.t.* overrate potentialities of (something) بہت زیادہ سمجھنا **overexert** (*-eg-ze*t*) *v.t.* exert (oneself) too much بہت زیادہ زور لگانا یا سے زیادہ محنت کرنا **overexertion** (*-zĕ*-*) *n.* overexerting بہت زیادہ زور، حد سے زیادہ محنت **overexpose** (*-pohz*) *v.t.* (esp.) expose (photographic film, etc.) to light too much بہت زیادہ کھانا یا کھلانا **overexposure** (*-zhĕ**) *n.* too much of exposure بہت زیادہ ظاہر کرنا **overfeed** (*-feed*) *v.t.* feed or eat too much بہت زیادہ کھانا یا کھلانا **overflow** (*-floh*) *v.t. & i.* be so full as to run over چھلکنا flood میں سیلاب آنا، دریا کے کناروں سے باہر آ جانا be plentiful (*with*) میں بکثرت ہونا *n.* overflowing چھلک پڑنا such excess liquid زائد (یا فالتو) پانی وغیرہ excess افراط، وفور **overgrow** (*-groh*) *v.i.* (*overgrow, overgrew, overgrown*) grow too fast بہت جلدی بڑھنا **overgrown** *adj.* grown too fast عمر کے مطابق بہت زیادہ بڑھا ہوا covered (*with* weeds, creepers, etc.) جس پر چاروں طرف اُگ رہا ہو، سے ڈھکا ہوا **overgrowth** (*oh-vĕ*-grohth*) *n.* overgrown (plants, etc.) ڈھانپنے والی روئیدگی **overhang** (*-hang*) *v.t. & i.* (*overhang, overhung, overhung*) jut out over آگے کو نکلا ہوا ہونا be

impending سر پر منڈلانا **overhaul** (-hawl) *v. t.* inspect and put into good condition by repairs or gearing up جانچ پڑتال کرکے یا کھول کھال کر ٹھیک کرنا ، سے آگے نکل جانا ، جالینا overtake (in a race) اوورہال کرنا *n.* repairs, etc., after thorough examination جانچ پڑتال ، کھول کھال کر ٹھیک کرنا **overhead** *adj.* (oh-vĕ*-hed) high up over the head اُوپر کا ، بالائی additional مزید ، بالائی ، فالتو ، متفرق ، اُوپر کا *overhead expenses* متفرق اخراجات ، اُوپر کا خرچ *overhead charges*, expenses (like salaries, etc.) besides the manufacturing costs اُوپر کا خرچ ، مزید اخراجات *adv.* (oh-vĕ*-hed) above one's head سیدھا ، اُوپر in the sky اُونچا ، آسمان میں **overhear** (-hee-ē*) *v.t.* (*overhear, overheard, overheard*) eavesdrop چھپ چھپ کر سننا hear by chance اتفاق سے سن لینا **overjoyed** (-joid) *adj.* very delighted (*at*) (پر) بہت ہی خوش **overlap** (-lap) *v.t.* & *i.* (-pp-) extend beyond one edge partly covering the other side کے اُوپر چڑھا ہونا ، کے پرلی طرف تک نکلا ہوا ہونا **overlay** (-lay) *v. t.* (*overlay, overlaid, overlaid*) cover (*with*) پر چڑھانا *overlaid with gold* ملمع **overload** (-lohd) *v.t.* load too heavily (*with*) بہت زیادہ لاد دینا **overlook** *v.t.* & *i.* look at a place) from above (کو) اُوپر سے دیکھ سکنا fail to notice نہ دیکھنا ، غور نہ کرنا ، (غلطی) نہ پکڑنا forgive and forget (someone's mistake) کو نظر انداز کر دینا ، سے چشم پوشی کرنا **overlord** (oh-) *n.* supreme lord سب سے بڑا سردار sovereign فرمانروا **overman** *n.* (oh-) overseer نگران superman فوق البشر *v. t.* (-man) furnish (some project, etc.) with too many men میں (یا پر) بہت زیادہ آدمی لگا دینا **overmaster** (-mahs-) *v. t.* get complete control over پر پوری طرح قابو پا لینا **over-modest** (-mod-) *adj.* too modest حد سے زیادہ شریف (یا شرمیلا یا حیادار) **overmuch** (-much) *adj.* & *adv.* too much حد سے زیادہ **overnice** (nis) *adj.* too fastidious (about) بہت ہی نفاست پسند too particular (*about*) بڑا باریک بین **overnight** (-n.t) *adv.* on the night before رات کی رات ، سے ایک رات پہلے (stay) for the night *adj.* journey, guest, etc.) for the night رات بھر کا **overpay** (-pay) *v.t.* pay (someone or some amount) in excess (by mistake) جتنا بنتا ہو غلطی سے اُس سے زیادہ دے دینا **overpopulated** (-pop-) *adj.* (of country, etc.) with more population than the resources can support حد سے زیادہ آبادی والا **overpopulation** (-lay-) *n.* (ملک کے وسائل آمدنی سے) بہت زیادہ آبادی **overpowering** (-pow-) *v.t.* overcome کو زیر کر لینا ، کو قابو میں لانا یا کر لینا **overpowering** *adj.* very powerful (person, quality, smell, etc.) بہت زوردار **overpraise** (-prayz) *n.* & *v.t.* حد سے زیادہ تعریف (کرنا) **overprint** (oh-) *v.t.* print (usu. by mistake) over an already printed surface چھپے ہوئے پر چھاپنا *n.* overprinted surface چھپے ہوئے پر چھپا ہوا **over-production** (-duk-) *n.* production of more goods than the needs justify مفرط پیدائش ، ضرورت سے زیادہ پیدائش **overrate** (oh-vĕ*-rayt) *v. t.* put too high a value on (someone's capabilities, etc.) اہلیت سے بڑھ کر سمجھنا **overreach** (-reech) *v. t.* get the better of (someone) by deception چکر کا دینا ، چل دینا ، دھوکہ دیکر فائدہ اٹھانا *overreach oneself*, harm own interests by being too ambitious زیادہ پر نظر کرکے اپنے آپ کو نقصان پہنچانا go past (something) without getting it سے آگے کسی جگہ سے آگے نکل جانا *overreach a mark* کو نکلنے کے باعث نہ سکنا **override** *v. t.* set aside (someone's recommendations, etc.) (کسی کی رائے) مسترد کر دینا **overrule** (-rool) *v. t.* override (someone's objections, etc.) کو مسترد کر دینا **overrun** (-run) *v.t.* crush (something) by running oven or conquering, etc. پر چڑھ دوڑنا ، کو کچل ڈالنا go beyond (some limit of space or time) سے آگے نکل جانا **oversea** (oh-) *adj.* & *adv.* beyond the sea or seas ; abroad سمندر پار (کا) **overseas** (oh-vĕ*-seez) *adj.* & *adv.* abroad **oversee** *v.t.* (oh-vĕ*-see) superintend کی نگرانی کرنا look from above اُوپر سے دیکھنا ، اُوپر دیکھنا **overseer** (oh-vĕ*-see-ē*) inspector of works, etc. اوورسیر ، نگران **overshadow** (-shad-oh) *v. t.* cast into shade ماند کرنا throw a shadow over پر سایہ ڈالنا shelter thus پر (اپنا) سایہ کرنا **overshoe** (oh-) *n.* waterproof-shoe worn over another اُوپر کا برساتی بوٹ بالائی بوٹ **overshoot** (-shoot) *v. t.* overreach (a mark) سے آگے نکل جانا **oversight** (oh-) *n.* failure to notice something فروگذاشت *through an oversight* غلطی سے **oversleep** (-sleep) *v.t.* sleep too long دیر تک سوتے رہنا **oversmoke** (-smohk) *v.t.* smoke too much سگرٹ وغیرہ بہت زیادہ پینا injure (oneself) thus بہت زیادہ تمباکو نوشی سے صحت خراب کر لینا **overspread** (-spred) *v. t.* spread over پر پھیل جانا ، پر چھا جانا **overstate** (-stayt) *v. t.* exaggerate مبالغہ سے بیان کرنا ، بڑھا چڑھا کر بتانا **overstatement** *n.* مبالغہ **overstay** (-stay) *v.t.* stay longer than (the leave) (منظور شدہ چھٹی) سے ، زیادہ دیر تک چھٹی پر رہنا **overstep** (-step) *v.t.* (-pp-) exceed (a mark, one's authority, etc.) کی حد سے بڑھنا **overstock** (-stok) *v. t.* fill too much بہت زیادہ (مال) بھر لینا **overstrain** *v.t.* (-strayn) overtax حد سے زیادہ محنت یا زور *n.* (oh-) حد سے زیادہ محنت کرنا (یا زور لگانا) **overstrung** (-strung) *adj.* (of a person, his nerves) overstrained جس پر بہت زیادہ بوجھ پڑا ہو easily excited جلد طیش میں آ جانے والا **overstudy** (-stud- *n.* & *v. i.* study beyond capacity or need حد سے زیادہ پڑھائی کرنا **oversubscribe** (-krib) *v. t.* subscribe more than the required amount of (loan ; etc.) میں ضرورت سے زیادہ لگانا *oversubscribed*

loan وہ قرض جس میں منظور بہ رقم سے زائد وصولی ہو جائے
oversure *adj*. overconfident ضرورت سے زیادہ خود اعتمادی والا
overt (o-vĕ*t or occasionally *oh*-vĕ*t) *adj*. done publicly کھلم کھلا، صاف **overtly** *adv*. publicly کھلم کھلا
overtake (-*tayk*) *v.t.* (*overtake, overtook, overtaken*) catch up with کو جالینا outstrip سے آگے نکل جانا finish (arrears of work) بچا ہوا (یا امانت کا کام) ختم کرنا (of misfortunes, etc., come upon (someone) suddenly کو اچانک آ لینا **overtax** (-*taks*) *v.t.* overstrain بہت محنت کرنا، سے بہت زیادہ کام لینا tax (someone or something) too highly پر بہت زیادہ ٹیکس لگانا
overthrow *v. t.* (-*throh*) defeat کو شکست دینا end (government, etc.) کا خاتمہ کرنا، ختم کرنا *n.* (*oh*-) defeat شکست **overtime** *n.* (*oh*-), *adv.* (-*tīm*) time spent at work beyond one's usual hours اوور ٹائم، ٹائم *working overtime* فالتو وقت دینا یا کام کرنا ٹائم ، فالتو وقت *earn extra for overtime* اوور ٹائم بنانا، فالتو وقت کے پیسے لینا *adv.* work after the usual hours فالتو وقت دے کر **overtop** (-*op*) *v.t.* & *i.* become higher than or surpass سے بڑھنا یا اونچا ہونا **overtrain** (-*trayn*) *v. t.* & *i.* spoil (own or other's) condition by too severe an athletic training (کھلاڑی کو) حد سے زیادہ تربیت دے کر خراب کر دینا **overturn** (-*tĕ*n*) *v.t.* turn over اُلٹ دینا
overture (*oh*-vĕ*-chĕ*) *n.* (usu. *pl.*) preliminary proposal (*for* settlement) سلسلہ جنبانی، ابتدائی *make peace overtures* (*to*) صلح کی سلسلہ جنبانی کرنا تجاویز دینا (in music) introductory number (at an opera) تمہیدی نغمہ
overvalue (-*val*-) *v. t.* overrate
overwalk (-*wawk*) *v.i.* harm oneself by walking too much حد سے زیادہ چل (یا چل چل) کر صحت خراب کر لینا
overwatched (*wawchd*) *adj.* exhausted by keeping awake for too long جس کی جاگ جاگ کر صحت بگڑ چکی ہو، کم خوابی کا مارا
overweening (-*wee*-) *adj.* excessive (pride) حد سے زیادہ conceited (person) پُر غرور
overwhelm (-*hwelm*) *v. t.* engulf گھیرے میں لے لینا crush کچل ڈالنا (*be*) *overwhelmed with grief* (*or someone's kindness*, *or misery or enemy forces*), (be) overcome completely میں گھر جانا، میں گھرا ہوا ہونا
overwhelming (-*hwel*-) *adj.* deluging ; irresistible by force, number, etc.) حد سے زیادہ، ناقابل برداشت
overwind (-*wind*) *v. t.* wind too much زیادہ چابی دے دینا
overwise (*oh*-) *adj.* affectedly wise عقلمند بنا پھرتا
overwork *n.* (*oh*-) too much work بہت زیادہ کام *v. t.* & *i.* (-*wĕ*k*) (cause to) do it بہت زیادہ کام کرنا (یا) ڈالنا
overwrought (-*rot*) *adj.* tired out by too much work بہت زیادہ کام کے باعث تھکا ہوا excited مغلوب الغضب، بہت جوش میں
ovum (*oh*-vum) *n.* female germ or seed بیضہ، انڈا
owe (oh) *v. t.* & *i.* be in debt to کا مقروض ہونا be under obligation for (one's success, etc., *to* someone or something) کے لیے (کسی کا) مرہون منت ہونا، یا مرہون منت be under obligation to (loyalty, etc., to) (وفاداری وغیرہ) کرنے پر مجبور ہونا یا کا پابند ہونا
owing (*oh*-ing) *adj.* yet to be paid واجب الادا
owing to *prep.* on account of کی وجہ سے، کے سبب سے *adj.* caused by کے باعث
owl (oul) *n.* well known hooting night-bird which in the West is famed for its wisdom اُلو، بوم wise-looking fool عقلمند دکھائی دینے والا احمق
own (ohn) *adj.* belonging to the individual mentioned کا اپنا (of brother or sister) of one's own parents ماں جایا، اپنا *hold* (*one's*) *own*, (*a*) maintain (one's) position ڈٹے رہنا، جمے رہنا (*b*) not lose strength ہمت نہ ہارنا *get* (*one's*) *own back* (*on someone*), revenge (oneself) on (him) سے بدلہ لے لینا *on* (*one's*) *own*, (*a*) without a companion اکیلے، تنہا (*b*) on own initiative خود، اپنی طرف سے *v. t.* & *i.* be the owner of کا مالک ہونا confess (something, *up to* something, *to having done* something, or *that*) مان لینا accept قبول کر لینا، اپنا لینا **owner** *n.* one who owns مالک **ownerless** *adj.* without any known owner لاوارث **ownership** *n.* being an owner ملکیت
ox (oks) *n.* (pl. *oxen*) general name for domestic cattle like cow, bull, bullock, etc. گائے، بیل (وغیرہ) (esp.) bullock as draught animal بیل
ox-eyed (*oks*-īd) *adj.* having large eyes like those of an ox گاؤ چشم، گاؤ دیدہ، بڑی آنکھ
oxen (ok-sĕn) *n.* (*pl.* of **ox**, which see)
oxide (*ok*-sīd) *n.* a chemical compound of oxygen with another element آکسائڈ، اکسید **oxidize** (*ok*-si-dīz) *v. t.* & *i.* combine with oxygen تکسید کرنا، آکسیجن کے ساتھ مرکب بنانا rust زنگ لگنا یا لگانا **oxidization** (-*zay*-) *n.* oxidizing تکسید
oxy-acetylene (ok-si-a-*set*-a-leen) *adj.* using or comprising mixture of oxygen and another gas acetylene to produce an intensely hot flame for welding, etc. آکسی اسیٹلین (شعلہ وغیرہ)
oxygen (*ok*-si-jen) *n.* an important gas in the air without which life would be impossible آکسیجن
oxymoron (ok-si-*moh*-ron) *n.* joining of contradictories as a figure of speech اجتماع ضدین (تضاد)
oyez, oyes, o yes (all pr. oh-*yes*, or *oh*-yes) *int.* (call of a public crier or court officer demanding) attention خبردار، ہوشیار
oyster (*ois*-tĕ*) *n.* a kind of shellfish eaten alive in the West ; (its shell sometimes contains a pearl) کستورا مچھلی
ozone (*oh*-zohn) *n.* a pungent form of oxygen اوزون exhilarating influence دل نواز اثر، مفرح قلب

P

p, P (pee) (pl. *p's* or *ps*) the sixteenth letter of the English alphabet (equivalent to the Urdu letter پ) پی *mind one's Ps and Qs*, be on guard against saying a wrong thing or taking a wrong step بہت محتاط رہنا

pa (pah) *n.* (colloq.) (abbr. of) papa آبا ، باجا

pace (pays) *n.* step قدم speed رفتار (of horse) manner of walking چال progress رفتار، ترقی *keep pace with* (*someone*) کی رفتار سے ترقی کرنا ، کے برابر چلنا *v.t.* & *i.* walk slowly (*up and down* a place) میں چہل قدمی کرنا *pace* (*up and down*) *a room* do so (usu. in anger or worry) (غصّے یا پریشانی کی حالت میں) کمرے میں اِدھر سے اُدھر چلنا *pace out* (or *off*) *a distance* قدموں سے ماپنا

pacific (pa-*sif*-ik) *adj.* peace-loving امن پسند، امن دوست *n. the Pacific* (*Ocean*) بحرُ الکاہل **pacify** (*pas*-i-fi) *v.t.* appease or be appeased ٹھنڈا کرنا یا ہونا restore peace امن بحال کرنا **pacification** (-*kay*-) *n.* act of appeasing or being appeased غصّہ ٹھنڈا کرنا یا ہونا restoration of peace بحالیٔ امن **pacifism** (or, incorrectly, pacifism *n.* advocating the abolition of war جنگجوئی کے خاتمہ کی حمایت ، امن پسند **pacifist** (or, incorrectly, **pacificist**) *n.* جنگجوئی کے خاتمہ کا حامی ، امن پسند

pack (pak) *n.* bundle گٹھڑی ، بقچہ ، پلندہ ، بنڈل *pack horse*, horse used for carrying packs لدو گھوڑا number (*of* wolves) going together بھیڑیوں کا گلہ (also *pack of hounds*) number of dogs kept for hunting شکاری کتوں کی ٹولی number (of thieves, fools, etc.) (نامعقولوں کی) مجلس ، (بدروں کی) ٹولی number (of lies, etc.) (جھوٹ کا) پلندہ complete set (of playing cards) (تاش کی) گڈی method of packing for the market بند ، بستہ *vacuum pack* خلا بند ، خلا بستہ *v.t.* & *i.* put (*up* things) into a box, etc., or fill (box, etc.) with things (*for* the voyage or holidays) بند کرنا ، باندھنا *pack* (*someone*) *off* (کو) بھیج دینا *send* (*someone*) *packing* کھڑے کھڑے نکال دینا ، دکا بوریا بستر گول کرانا crowd (*into* cinema, train, etc.) (میں) کھچا کھچ بھرے ہونا stuff soft material (*in* or *into* something) to prevent leakage میں نرم چیز گھونسنا stuff (something *in* soft material) to prevent it from breaking میں رکھنا ، **package** (*pak*-ij) *n.* bundle پلندہ bale گانٹھ ، گٹھڑی *v.t.* enclose in package بازدانے میں ڈالنا **packet** (*pak*-et) *n.* small parcel or big envelope بڑا لفافہ small carton (esp. for cigarettes) پیکٹ ، ڈبیہ

packing *n.* act of packing باندھنا material used in packing باندھنے کے کاغذ یا ڈبے وغیرہ ، بازدانہ **pack-ice** *n.* collection of large pieces of floating ice سمندر میں برون کے ایک ساتھ بہتے ہوئے بہت سے ٹکڑے ۔

pact (pakt) *n.* treaty معاہدہ

pad *n.* anything like a cushion used for preventing damage or improving the shape of something, etc. گدّی block of writing paper پیڈ soft, cushion-like underpart of certain animals' feet پنجہ کی گدّی *v.t.* stuff with soft material میں (روئی وغیرہ) بھرنا put pad (*in* or *on*) گدّی کی تہ دینا *pad out* (*sentence, book, etc.*) make it longer by using unnecessary words, etc. میں بھرنے کے حشو و زوائد بھر دینا **padding** *n.* stuffing بھرنے کے لیے روئی وغیرہ valueless material only filling space بھرتی کی چیز

paddle (*pad*-el) *n.* short oar چھوٹا چپّو oar with a blade at each end دو دھنتہ والا چپّو *v.t.* & *i.* row (light boat, canoe, etc.) with paddles ہلکی کشتی چلانا walk barefooted in shallow water پایاب پانی میں ننگے پاؤں چلنا ، اُتھلے پانی میں ننگے پاؤں سے چھپ چھپ کرنا move the hands about in water playfully پانی میں ہاتھ ہلا ہلا کر کھیلنا

paddy (*pad*-i) *n.* growing rice, or rice still in the husk دھان **paddy-field** *n.* دھان کا کھیت

padlock (*pad*-lok) *n.* ordinary hanging lock تالا ، قفل

padre (*pahd*-ray) *n.* chaplain in army or navy فوجی پادری ، پادری

paean (*pee*-an) *n.* song of praise or thanksgiving حمد و شکر کا گیت ، ترانۂ حمد و شکر song of praise to Apollo اپالو کی حمد (*Paean*) *Cl. myth.* name of Apollo as healer شفا دینے والا

paediatrics (pee-di-*at*-riks), **pediatrics** (ped-i-*at*-riks) *n.* (pl. used as sing.) study of childhood and its diseases علم طفولیت ، بچپن اور اس کے امراض کا علم

pagan (*pay*-gĕn) *n.* & *adj.* (one) not acknowledging one of the Semitic religions اللہ تعالیٰ کو نہ ماننے والا (شخص) ، کافر ، ملحد **paganism** (*pay*-ga-nizm) *n.* being a pagan کفر ، الحاد **paganish** *adj.* like that of a pagan کافرانہ ، ملحدانہ

page (*payj*) *n.* one side of a book's leaf صفحہ boy servant ملازم لڑکا *v.t.* summon someone from his room, etc., in hotel or club by sending a page to look for him ہوٹل میں نوکر کو بلانا

a page (sense 2)

pageant (*paj*-ĕnt) *n.* grand public celebration of some event جشن ، پُرشکوہ تقریب grand procession شاندار جلوس specious show محض دکھاوا tableau ڈرامے کا ساکن وساکت منظر،ٹھونگ

pageantry (-ri) *n.* splendid displays، شاندار مُظاہرہ، دُھوم دَھام، طمطراق

pagoda (pa-*goh*-da) *n.* Buddhist temple بُدھ مندر

a pagoda

paid (payd) *v.* (*pa. t.* & *pa. p.* of **pay** which see)

pail (payl) *n.* bucket بالٹی

pain (payn) *n.* physical suffering دَرد mental suffering ذہنی کوفت *take pains* (*to do something*) بڑی محنت اور کوشش (کرکے کوئی کام) کرنا (*do something*) *on pain of death* (*etc.*), do it under that penalty سزائے موت کی دھمکی پر (کوئی کام) کرنا *for one's pain's*, (usu. ironically) as a reward of the troubles one took تکلیفوں کا یہ صلہ، محنت کا یہ پھل **painful** *adj.* causing pain تکلیف دِہ grievous دَردناک **painless** *adj.* causing no pain تکلیف کے بغیر **painstaking** *adj.* hard-working محنتی ▣ **Pain** (the opposite of *pleasure*) is a feeling of thwarted desire, or of interference with one's well-being; an ache, functional suffering of some part of the body; **agony,** extreme pain as, for example, in the last fight for life against death; **torture**, pain inflicted by someone and hence very severe pain; **torment**, mostly mental anguish; **pang,** a sudden sharp pain as of hunger or remorse; **suffering,** prolonged feeling of pain; **distress**, prolonged trouble of serious nature; the **throes** of a violent, convulsive pain; **anguish,** usu. a mental feeling of being choked or crushed; **hurt,** a mental feeling of being treated slightingly; **injury,** physical hurt; **grief,** sense of loss; **affliction,** continued source of pain, such as some deformity.

paint (paynt) *n.* pigment use for colouring رنگ، روغن *v.t.* & *i.* coat (something) with paint رنگ، روغن، پینٹ پر روغن کرنا make a picture with paint کی رنگین تصویر کھینچنا **painter** *n.* (fem. paintress) one who paints buildings, etc. رنگ ساز، رَنگ ساز artist painting pictures مُصَوِّر **painting** *n.* painted picture تصویر رنگین تصویر، نقش رنگین art of painting pictures کشی، مُصَوّری

pair (*pay*-ĕ*) *n.* couple جوڑی، جوڑا set (*of* two things) جوڑا، جوڑی single article consisting (*of*) two joined parts (اُردُو میں اس کا کوئی ترجمہ نہیں) *a pair of scissors* قینچی *in pairs* دو دو کرکے، دو دو *join in pairs* جوڑی جوڑی لگانا *pair off*, form pairs جوڑی بننا (یا) بنانا

pal *n.* (colloq.) chum یار، دوست، ساتھی

palace (*pal*-as) *n.* sovereign's house شاہی محل، محل قصر any splendid house محل، محل کا محل *adj* courtly درباری *palace intrigues* دربار کی سازشیں، شاہی دربار کی جوڑ توڑ **palatial** (pa-*lay*-shĕl) *adj* of a palace محل کا splendid (building, etc.) عظیم الشان، نہایت شان دار

palanquin (pal-an-*kwin*), **palankeen** (-*keen*) *n.* light, covered litter پالکی، پینس

a palanquin

palate (*pal*-et) *n.* roof of the mouth تالُو sense of taste ذائقہ

palatable (*pal*-a-tay-bĕl) *adj.* tasty مزیدار، لذیذ، خوش ذائقہ **palatal** (pal-a-tĕl) *adj.* of the palate تالُو کا (of sound) made with the palate تالُو سے نکلنے والی *n.* palatal sound تالُو سے نکلنے والی آواز

palatial *adj.* (see under **palace**)

palaver (pa-*lah*-vĕ*) *n.* conference between savages and traders وحشیوں اور تاجروں کی گفت و شنید empty words خالی خولی باتیں *v.t.* & *i.* use many words باتیں بنانا cajole خوشامد درآمد سے کام نکالنے کی کوشش کرنا

pale (payl) *adj* almost bloodless (face) زرد، پیلا faint (colour) مدھم، پھیکا *v.i.* become pale (*with* fear, etc.) رنگ اُڑ جانا make or grow dim (*into* insignificance, etc.) ماند پڑ جانا یا کر دینا *n.* pointed stake of a fence باڑ کا نوک دار ڈانڈا، حد limit limits of good etiquette حدودِ اخلاق **paled** (payld) *adj.* enclosed with paling جس کے گرد کٹہرا لگا ہُوا ہو ▣ One is **pale** from illness or fright; **colourless** from shock; **ghastly** from terror; **pallid** from lack of blood; and **wan,** from long illness.

paling, palings *n.* جنگلا، کٹہرا **palisade** (pal-i-*sayd*) fence of strong stakes نوک دار ڈنڈوں کا مضبوط جنگلا one of the stakes جنگلے کا ڈنڈا *v.t.* enclose with palisade کے گرد نوک دار ڈنڈوں کا جنگلا لگانا

palette (*pal*-et) *n.* board on which an artist mixes his colours مُصَوِّر کی رنگ کی تختی

a palette (P) with paint-brushes (BB) & a box of paint

palfrey (*pawl*-fri) *n.* small saddle-horse for ladies

paling(s) *n.* **palisade** *n.* (see under **pale**)

pall (pal) *v.i.* become uninteresting *pall on* (*someone*), become dull for him *n.* black velvet cover of a coffin any dark heavy covering (*of* grief, smoke, etc.)

pallet (*pal*-et) *n.* (also *palliasse* pr. pal-i-*as*) hard under-mattress of straw نیچے کا موٹا گدا straw-bed پیال
palliate (*pal*-i-ayt) *v.t.* alleviate (pain, etc.) (میں) تخفیف کرنا، کوتسکین کرنا excuse the seriousness of (crime, etc.) جرم کو خفیف یا قابل عفو قرار دینا **palliation** (-*ay*-) *n.* act of palliating (جرم) میں تخفیف، (جرم) کو خفیف قرار دینا **palliative** *adj.* & *n.* (drug, etc.) giving temporary relief تسکین دہ چیز، مسکن that palliates تسکین دہ چیز
pallid (*pal*-id) *adj.* looking ill بیمار سا، زرد **pallidness** *n.* paleness چہرے کی زردی **pallor** *n.* (see separate entry)
Pall-Mall (pel-*mel*) *n.* London Street noted for its clubs پَل مَیل (*pall-mall*), old game in which a ball was driven through an iron ring with a mallet پیل میل، کنڈی گیند
pallor (pal-ĕ*) *n.* pallidness : paleness (*of* someone's face) چہرے کی بے رونقی، چہرے کی زردی (Also see **pallid**)
palm (pahm) *n.* broad inner part of the hand ہتھیلی، کف دست kinds of tropical tree (like date-palm, etc.) نخل its branch as symbol of victory فتح کا نشان excellence کمال *carry off the palm,* achieve success کامیاب ہونا *v.t.* hide in the hand ہاتھ میں چھپا لینا *palm* (*something*) *off on* (*someone*), pass (it) on (him) by fraud کسی کے گلے دھوکے سے منڈھنا **palmistry** (*pahm*-ist-ri) *n.* art of foretelling one's future by examining lines on his palms پامسٹری، قرائت ید، دست شناسی، ہاتھ دیکھنا **palmist** *n.* one practising it پامسٹ، ہاتھ دیکھنے والا، دست شناس **palmer** *n.* Christian pilgrim back from Jerusalem زیارت سے لوٹنے والا عیسائی، عیسائی زائر **palmy** (*pah*-mi) *adj.* خوشحال *in* (*one's*) *palmy days, in the palmy days of* کی خوشحالی کے ایام میں
palpable (*pal*-pa-bĕl) *adj.* that can be touched or felt محسوس clear (mistake, etc.) واضح، صریحی، صریح **palpably** *adv.* محسوس طور پر، صریحاً
palpitate (*pal*-pi-tayt) *v.i.* (of the heart) throb (دل کا) دھک دھک کرنا tremble (*with* fear, etc.) کانپنا **palpitation** (-*tay*-) *n.* palpitating of the heart اختلاج قلب، اختلاج
palsy (*pawl*-zi) *n.* paralysis فالج **palsied** (*pawl*-zid) *adj.* paralysed فالج زدہ، مفلوج، ماؤوف
palter (*pawl*-tĕ*) *v.i.* shuffle (*with* person or the truth) سخن سازی کرنا، ہیر پھیر کرنا
paltrily *adv.* **paltriness** *n.* (see under **paltry**)
paltry (*pawl*-tri) *adj.* trifling معمولی سا، بے حقیقت **paltrily** *adv.* معمولی، بے حقیقت انداز سے **paltriness** *n.* being paltry معمولی ہونا، بے حقیقتی

pampas (*pam*-paz) *n.* vast treeless plains in southern South America پمپا، پمپاس، جنوبی امریکہ کے جنوبی میدان
pamper (*pam*-pĕ*) *v.t.* spoil (someone) with too much kindness لاڈ سے بگاڑنا
pamphlet (*pamf*-lĕt) *n.* very small booklet (*on* esp., current issues) پمفلٹ، رسالہ **pamphleteer** (-*tee*-ĕ*) *n.* writer of political pamphlets سیاسی رسالے لکھنے والا، پمفلٹ باز
[1]**pan** *n.* flat dish (with a handle) for frying, etc. کڑچھا one for baking, etc. توا one for other purposes in the kitchen پرات (*Pan*), *Cl. myth.* the Greek god of pastures, flocks and woods who invented the shepherd's flute پین *v.t.* (see *Addenda*) **pancake** *n.* fried batter-cake میٹھی روٹی، میٹھی ٹکیہ
[2]**pan-** *pref.* of all ہمہ، تمام کا، گیر *pan-Asian* ایشیا گیر، *pan-Islam, pan-Islamism* اتحاد عالم اسلام ہمہ ایشیائی، اتحاد اسلامی *pan-Islamic* اتحاد اسلامی سے متعلق *pan-Islamist* اتحاد اسلامی کا علم بردار
panacea *n.* universal cure اکسیر، ہر درد کی دوا
panache (pa-*nahsh*) *n.* (lit.) doing of things with an air شان سے کرنا
panchromatic (pan-kro-*mat*-ik) *adj.* (of photographic plate or film) simultaneously sensitive to all colours رنگ دار، رنگین
pancreas (*pank*-re-as) *n.* gland near stomach supplying a digestive fluid لبلبہ
pandemonium (pand-e-*moh*-ni-um) *n.* uproar and disorder ہنگامہ، غل غپاڑہ، گڑبڑ
pander (*pand*-ĕ*) *v.i.* minister (*to* the evil designs or base passions *of* someone) (کسی کے ناپاک ارادوں یا سفلی جذبات) کی تسکین کا انتظام کرنا، بھڑوا، *n.* pimp دلال، قرمساق
Pandora (pan-*doh*-ra) *Cl. myth.* the first woman; she was sent to the earth with a box containing all human ills ; she opened it out of feminine curiosity and thus spread endless misfortune in the world پنڈورا *Pandora's box,* unfortunate gift بدنصیبی کا تحفہ
pane (payn) *n.* sheet of glass (in a door panel, etc.) (دروازے وغیرہ کے) ایک خانے کا شیشہ
panegyric (pan-e-*ji*-rik) *n.* encomium (on person or event) قصیدہ such laudatory speech مدحت، مدح سرائی **panegyrist** (-*ji*-rist) *n.* writer or speaker of panegyrics قصیدہ گو، قصیدہ خواں، مدح سرا
panel (*pan*-el) *n.* separate sunk or raised piece of wood on (*of* a door, ceiling, etc.) دلا thin board with a picture منقش تختہ picture on it تختے پر بنی ہوئی تصویر list of the names of

persons to serve on (*of* jury, committee, etc.) فہرستِ اَرکان (in Scottish law) person(s) on trial *v.t.* (-ll-) put panels on or in دِیتے لگانا **panelling** *n.* panelled work دِیتوں والا، جس میں دِیتے لگے ہوئے ہوں
pang *n.* (usu. *pl.*) sudden sharp sensation (*of* remorse, conscience, pain, etc.) (دَرد وغیرہ کی) ٹیس
panic (*pan*-ik) *n.* (wave of unreasonable) alarm خوف و ہراس کی لہر، خوف و ہراس بیتحاشا *adj.* unreasonable (fear, etc.) بیتحا **panicky** (*pan*-i-ki) *n.* alarmed *adj.* دہشت زَدہ، یُونہی گھبرایا ہُوا
pannier (*pan*-yĕ*) *n.* one of a pair of big baskets carried by pack animals on either side جانور پر لادنے کی ٹوکریوں میں ایک خورجین ٹوکری such a basket carried by a person بہنگی کی ٹوکری part of skirt looped up round hips رلپٹا دامن

donkey with panniers

panoply (*pan*-o-pli) *n.* full suit of armour زِرہ بکتر full defensive equipment (*of* faith, etc.) سامانِ مُدافعت **panoplied** *adj.* fully armoured زِرہ پوش، بکتر بند، زرہ بکتر سے آراستہ
panorama (pan-o-*rah*-ma) *n.* continuous picture of the changing scene (*of*) سَیرِ بیں
pansy (*pan*-zi) *n.* (flower) of a plant of the violet family (also called *heartsease*) بنفشی، دِل کی راحت، مَن سُکھ

pansy

pant *v.t.* & *i.* gasp for breath ہانپنا (کی) سانس پھُولنا speak (*out* something) gaspingly ہانپتے ہانپتے کہنا desire earnestly (*for, after,* or *to do* something) (کے لیے) بیقرار ہونا، بیتاب ہونا *n.* gasp ہانپنا (pl.) (*pants*), trousers پتلون (pl.) (*pants*, also *panties*) (pr. *pant*-eez) a lady's drawers زنانہ جانگیا زنانہ زیر جامہ **pantaloon** (*-loon*-) *n.* (less used form for) pants پتلون trousered character in Italian comedy who is the butt to the clown in a pantomime گھٹیا مسخرہ
pantheism (*pan*-the-izm) *n.* mystic belief that God is in everything and hence everything is God ہمہ اوست، وحدتُ الوجود **pantheist** (-ist) *n.* one who believes in pantheism ہمہ اوست کا قائل، وحدتُ الوجود کا قائل **pantheistic, pantheistical** *adj*.
pantheon (*pan*-the-on, or pan-*thee*-on) *n.* temple of all the gods سب دیوتاؤں کا مندر all of a people's gods دیومالا
panther (*panth*-ĕ* *n.* (fem. *panthress*) leopard چیتا، تیندوا
pantile (*pan*-til) *n.* curved roof-tile چھت کی محراب دار کھپریل
pantomime (*pant*-o-mim) *n.* Christmas play for children based on a fairy-tale پریوں کی تمثیل (more often *mime*), dumb show خاموش تمثیل **pantomimist** (-*mi*-) *n.* one good at dumb show خاموش تمثیل کا اداکار
pantry (*pant*-ri) *n.* room for storing food نعمت خانہ، مودی خانہ room for storing dishes, table-linen, etc. برتنوں کی کوٹھڑی
panzer (*panz*-ĕ*) *adj.* armoured (division, etc.) بکتر بند
pap *n.* soft food for babies بچوں کے لیے نرم غذا (old use) nipple of the breast بھٹنی **pappy** (*pap*-i) soft like pap پلپلا
papa (pa-*pah*) *n.* (abbr. *pa*) child's word for its father ابّا، باوا
papacy (*pay*-pa-si) the Pope's government پاپائیت his office پاپائی **papal** (*pay*-pĕl) *adj.* of the papacy پاپائی
paper (*pay*-pĕ*) *n.* material on which to write or print کاغذ *piece of paper* کاغذ کا پُرزہ *blank paper*, paper with nothing written, etc., on it سادہ کاغذ، کورا کاغذ newspaper *daily* paper روزانہ اخبار، روزنامہ research article (*on* some topic for reading out to some group) مقالہ (also *question-paper*), set of questions on a subject at an examination پرچہ legal document (esp. for identification) تعارفی پروانہ، شناختی دستاویز *send in one's papers*, resign استعفا دینا *v.t.* cover (walls of a room) with decorative paper دیواروں پر آرائشی کاغذ لگانا **paper-hangings, wall-paper** *n.* دیواری کاغذ، دیواروں پر لگانے کا کاغذ **paper-knife** *n.* کاغذ تراش **paper-weight** *n.* something placed on lose papers to prevent them from being blown away کاغذ داب، دباوی **paper-money, paper-currency** *n.* currency notes نوٹ، زرِ کاغذی
papier-mache (*pap*-yay-*mash*-ay) *n.* paper pulp for making trays, etc. کُٹی پیپر ماشی
papist (*pay*-pist) *n.* adherent of Pope or papal power پاپائیت کا حامی، پاپائی Roman Catholic کیتھولک۔
papyrus (pa-*pī*-ē-rus) *n.* earliest form of paper (used in ancient Egypt) پیپرس reed yielding it پیپرس، نرسل
par (pah*) *n.* equality مساوات، برابری original rate (of share, bonds, etc.) تمسکات کا اصلی نرخ، مساوات، برابر *at par*, at the original price مساوات میں، برابری میں *above par* مساوات سے اُوپر، زیادہ اُوپر *below par* مساوات سے نیچے، کم پر *on a par* (*with*), equal to) مساوی، برابر *be at par* برابر ہونا newspaper paragraph or notice اخباری خبر (یا اعلان)
parable (*pa*-ra-bel) *n.* very short allegory ;

story with a moral تمثیل، مثال
parabolical (*-bol-*) *adj.* of the nature of a parable
parabola *n.* plane curve formed by intersection of cone with a plane parallel to its side شکل شلجمی
parabolic (*-bol-*) *adj.* (of the nature) of a parabola شلجمی
parachute (*pa*-ra-shoot) *n.* big umbrella-like instrument for dropping or jumping down from an aircraft پیراشوٹ، ہوائی چھاتا *adj.* dropped by parachute
parachutist *n.* person landing thus ہوائی چھاتے سے اُترنے والا چھاتا باز **para-troops** *n.* airborne troops trained to land thus; commandoes چھاتا فوج **paratrooper** *n.* commando چھاتا فوجی **para-rescue team** *n.* (see *Addenda*) **parapsychology** *n.* (see *Addenda*)

a parachute

parade (pa-*rayd*) *v.t.* & *i.* (of troops) gather together or line up (usu. for drilling) پریڈ (یا پریٹ) کے لیے جمع ہونا make a display of (wealth, qualities, etc.) کی نمود و نمائش کرنا march in procession (through streets, etc.) جلوس نکالنا *n.* lining-up of troops پریڈ، پریٹ، فوجی مظاہرہ (یا پریٹ) یا فوجی *be on parade* مظاہرے میں شامل ہونا display (of wealth, etc.) دکھاوا، نمود و نمائش، نمود promenade ساحلی سڑک
parade-ground *n.* ground for the lining-up of troops پریڈ کا میدان
paradigm (*pa*-ra-dim) *n.* table of inflexions of a word گردان، تعریف
paradise (*pa*-ra-dis) *n.* the garden of Eden, according to Christians عدن، فردوس Heaven جنت (state or place of) perfect happiness بہشت (*live in a*) *fool's paradise*, be unreasonably complacent or optimistic احمقوں کی جنت (میں رہنا)
parados (*pa*-ra-dos, or doh) *n.* low protective wall or mound against back of trench (opp. of *parapet*)
paradox (*pa*-ra-doks) *n.* true but apparently contradictory statement بظاہر مہمل در حقیقت صحیح بات، ظاہری تناقض such a being مجسّم تناقض contradiction in terms تناقض **paradoxical** (pa-ra-*dok*-si-kĕl) *adj.* involving a paradox صرف ظاہری طور پر متناقض، متناقض
paraffin (*pa*-ra-fin) *n.* white wax obtained from petroleum, etc. پیرافین *paraffin oil*, petroleum مٹی کا تیل
paragon (*pa*-ra-gon) *n.* model (of perfection, etc.) *paragon of beauty* حسن مجسّم

supremely excellent thing or person شاندار شخص یا شے
paragraph (*pa*-ra-grahf) *n.* separate section of a chapter begun on a new line پیرا، رکوع small essay comprising one paragraph پیرا *v.t.* arrange in paragraphs پیرے بنانا
parakeet (*pa*-ra-keet), **paroquet** (*pa*-ro-ket) *n.* small long-tailed parrot لمبی دُم والا طوطا، ٹوئیاں
parallax (*pa*-ra-laks) *n.* apparent change in the position of object owing to change in the position of the observer اختلاف منظر angle of such apparent change in the position of a heavenly body as observed from two different positions زاویۂ اختلاف منظر
parallel (*pa*-ra-lel) *n.* *adj.* equidistant (lines), or (line) equidistant (*to* another) متوازی (خط یا خطوط) corresponding (*to*) کے مماثل *n.* parallel line متوازی خط *parallel of latitude* عرض البلد، عرض بلد comparison *draw a parallel between* میں موازنہ کرنا (of person, event, etc.) similar (*to*) کے مماثل، کے مشابہ *parallel bars*, raised ones for physical exercise ورزش کی گھوڑی *v.t.* be (or produce something) parallel or similar to کے متوازی ہونا، جیسا ہونا یا بنانا ایسا (یا کا سا) ہونا یا بنانا **parallelogram** *n.* any four-sided plane figure with its opposite sides parallel to each other متوازی الاضلاع **parallax** (*para*-laks) *n.* apparent displacement of object owing to the observer's changed position اختلافِ منظر

parallel bars

parallelograms

paralyse (*pa*-ra-liz) *v.t.* affect with paralysis کو فالج ہونا، پر فالج گرنا render helpless بے بس کر دینا
paralysis (pa-*ral*-i-sis) *n.* disease depriving one (or a part of the body) from ability to move فالج **paralytic** (pa-ra-*lit*-ik) *n.* paralysed person فالج زدہ، مفلوج *adj.* paralysed of paralysis فالج سے متعلق
paramount (*pa*-ra-mount) *adj.* very important بہت اہم wielding supreme authority کامل اقتدار والا، مقتدر اعلیٰ **paramountcy** (*pa*-mount-si) *n.* supremacy, having the authority اقتدارِ اعلیٰ
paramour (*pa*-ra-moo-ĕ*) illicit lover mistress داشتہ
paranoia (pa-ra-*noi*-a) *n.* mental derangement marked by delusions of grandeur [illegible]
parapet (*pa*-ra-pet) *n.* low protective wall such wall or mound in front of trench منڈیر

paraphernalia (pa-ra-fē*-*nay*-li-a) *n. pl.* miscellaneous small belongings (of person or office) سازوسامان، لوازم (one's) mechanical tools اوزار

paraphrase (*pa*-ra-frayz) *n.* restatement of the sense (of a passage) in one's own words دعبارت کا اپنے لفظوں میں مُطلب ، دُوسرے لفظوں میں مفہوم ، مفہوم

parasang (*pa*-ra-sang) *n.* ancient Persian measure of length equivalent to 3½ miles

parasite (*pa*-ra-sīt) *n.* plant, insect or person living and feeding on another طُفیل، طُفیلی پودا یا کیڑا

parasol (*pa*-ra-sol) *n.* women's small sunshade زنانہ چھاتہ

paratroops *n. pl.* see under **parachute**

parcel (*pah**-sel) *n.* wrapped up bundle بقچہ such a thing for sending by post پارسل portion (*of* land or something else) ٹکڑا *(be) a part and parcel of*, (be) an essential part of کا لازمی جزو *v.t.* (-ll-) divide (*out to* others) بانٹنا، تقسیم کرنا، حصّے بخرے کرنا

parch (pah*ch) *v.t.* (of the sun, heat, etc.) make hot and dry جھلس دینا (of thirst) become troublesome (پیاس سے) حلق سُوکھنا یا حلق خشک ہونا ، (پیاس سے) حلق میں کانٹے پڑنا make (gram, etc.) crisp by heating بھُوننا

parchment (*pah*ch*-ment) *n* goatskin used as a writing material جھلّی paper looking like parchment جھلّی نُما کاغذ

pard (pa*d) *n.* (U.S. slang) partner ساجھی، ساجھی (old use) leopard چیتا ، تیندوا

pardon (*pah**-dĕn) *v.t.* forgive مُعافی دینا excuse مُعاف کرنا ، مُعاف رکھنا *n.* forgiveness *I beg your pardon*, (*a*) (formula for asking someone to repeat what he has said just now usu. because it has not been heard) پھر سے کہیے تو ، مُعاف کیجئے میں نے سُنا نہیں (*b*) (formula for correcting own mistake) غلطی مُعاف ، مُعاف کیجئے میں پھر سے عرض کرتا ہُوں **pardonable** *adj.* that which can be pardoned قابلِ مُعافی ، قابلِ عفو

pare (*pay*-è*) *v.t.* trim (*off*) the outer edge of (nails, etc.) (ناخن وغیرہ) تراشنا *pare (something) down*, cut (it) down, reduce (it) کم کرنا ، گھٹانا **parings** (*pay*-è-rings) *n. pl.* something (esp. a slip) pared off تراشہ

parent (*pay*-è-rent) *n.* father or mother ماں یا باپ (pl.) (*parents*), (the formal word for) father and mother ماں باپ ، وُالدین **parentage** *n.* origin اصل *of unknown parentage*, of unknown parents وُلدیت نامعلوم ، نامعلوم وُلدیت کا **parental** (*-rent-*) *adj.* of a parent مادرانہ ، پدرانہ ، ماں باپ کا

parenthesis (pa-*renth*-e-sis) *n.* explanatory phrase within a sentence مُعترضہ any such out-of-the-way but interesting words, etc. جملۂ مُعترضہ **parentheses** (-sees) *n. pl.* the signs ( ), primarily used to mark off a parenthesis قوسین

parenthetic, parenthetical (*-thet-*) *adj.* جملۂ مُعترضہ **parenthetically** *adv.* جملۂ مُعترضہ (کے انداز) کا کے طور پر

par excellence *adj.* best ; better than any other of the type ; (always used after the qualified noun) بہترین

pariah (pa-*rī*-a, or *pa*-ri-a) *n.* low-caste Indian اچھوت ، شُودر social outcast جس کا حُقّہ پانی بند ہو *pariah-dog*, vagabond mongrel dog آوارہ کُتّا

Paris (*pa*-ris) *Cl. myth.* the Trojan prince who was allowed to abduct Helen as a reward for favouring Here پیرِس

parish (*pa*-rish) *n.* lowest church division of a country سب سے چھوٹا کلیسائی حلقہ its inhabitants چھوٹے کلیسائی حلقے کی آبادی *parish register*, register in which a record of the births, marriages, deaths of a parish is maintained رجسٹر مرگ پیدائش و شادی *civil parish*, unit under poor law خیراتی حلقہ **parishioner** (pa-*rish*-è-nĕ*) *n.* one living in a parish کلیسائی حلقے کا باشندہ

parochial *adj.* (see separate entry)

pari passu *adv.* simultaneously ساتھ ہی ساتھ

parity (*pa*-ri-ti) *n.* equality مُساوات

park (pah*k) *n.* tract in town with flower-beds and lawns for public recreation باغ ، تفریح گاہ ، سیرگاہ ، تفریح گاہ ، پارک *national park*, natural beauty spot of a country set apart for the people's enjoyment قومی تفریح گاہ large enclosure for grassland round a country mansion گاؤں کی حویلی کے گرد سبزہ زار (also *car-park*), place where motor-cars, etc., may be left for a time موٹریں کھڑی کرنے کا میدان ، پاچوک *v.t.* put (a motor car, etc.) in a park میدان میں (موٹر) کھڑی کرنا ، یا کچھ دیر کے لئے چھوڑ جانا

parlance (*pah**-lans) *n.* (legal, common, etc.) way of speaking زبان ، بولی *in common parlance* عام زُبان میں ، روزمرّہ کی زُبان میں

parley (*pah**-lay) *n.* (usu. *pl.*, as *parleys*) conference (esp. with the enemy) گفت و شنید ، مذاکرات *v.i.* discuss terms (*with* someone) سے ، شرائط کی بات چیت کرنا

parliament (*pah**-lè-ment) *n.* a country's highest Legislature مجلسِ قانون ساز ، مُقننہ ، پارلیمان **parliamentary** (pah*-lè-*ment*-a-ri) *adj.* pertaining to parliament پارلیمانی not indecent شریفانہ ، شائستہ **parliamentarian** (*-lay-*) *n.* veteran member of parliament skilled in its rules, debates, etc. پارلیمانی ، ماہر

parlour (pah*-lĕ) *n.* sitting-room بیٹھک ، دِیوان خانہ **parlour-maid** *n.* one who waits at table کھانا کھلانے والی مُلازِمہ

Parnassus (pah*-*nas*-us) *Cl. myth.* Greek mountain sacred to the Muses and to Apollo پرناسس

parochial (pa-*roh*-ki-ĕl) *adj.* of a parish کلیسائی حلقے کا narrow (view, outlook, mind, etc.) تنگ محدود **parochialism** *n.* narrow-mindedness; inability to see beyond one's parish or one's limited field تنگ نظر ، تعصّب (Also see **parish**)

parody (*pa*-ro-di) *n.* comical imitation of someone's (style of) writing مضحکِ نقل ، مضحکہ خیز نقل worthless imitation بھونڈی نقل *v.t.* make a parody of (poem, piece of writing, author, etc.) کسی کی مضحک نقل کرنا **parodist** *n.* one who parodies مضحکِ نقل کرنے والا مُصنّف

parole (pa-*rohl*) *n.* prisoner's word of honour not to try to escape if temporarily released, etc. (قیدی کو نہ بھاگنے کا قول) ، پیرول پر رہا کرنا *release on parole*, پیرول پر آنا ، (اس کے) قول پر عارضی رہائی دینا *be on parole* (قیدی کا) قول پر عارضی رہائی پانا ۔

paroxysm (*pa*-rok-sizm) *n.* sudden outburst (of laughter, anger, pain, etc.) اچانک ، غلبہ ، دورہ

parricide (*pa*-ri-sīd) *n.* murder of one's own father, near relative or person entitled to respect باپ کا (یا بزرگ) کا قتل one guilty of it باپ کا (یا کسی) قاتل بزرگ کا (یا کی) قاتِل treason against native land وطن سے غداری such traitor غدّارِ وطن

parrot (*pa*-rot) *n.* kinds of bright-feathered bird with a hooked bill طوطا ، توتا chatterbox بکّو ، بکواسی ، جس کی زُبان مُنہ میں نہ پڑے one who repeats others' words unintelligently طوطے کی طرح رٹنے والا *parrot-like repetition* : طوطے کی طرح رٹنا

parry (*pa*-ri) *v.t.* ward off a blow by turning it aside (وار) خالی دینا ، (وار) روکنا evade answers to (*the* or *one's* questions) ٹال جانا

parse (par*s) *v. t.* name the part of speech of a word and its relation to others in a sentence (لفظ) کی حرفی نحوی تشریح کرنا **parsing** *n.* such analysis الفاظ (یا لفظ) کی حرفی نحوی تشریح ، پارسنگ

parsimonious *adj.* (see under **parsimony**)

parsimony (*pah**-si-mu-ni) *n.* extreme care in spending از حد کفایت شعاری frugality کنجوسی ، کجزرسی بخل

parsimonious (*-moh-*) *adj.* too economical از حد کفایت شعار ، کنجوس ، بخیل

parsley

parsley (*pah**s-li) *n.* fragrant vegetable used for decorating dishes اجمود جیسی ایک چیز ، پارسلی

parsnip (*pah*s-nip*) *n.* a carrot-like vegetable گاجر جیسی ایک چیز ، پارس نپ *fine words butter no parsnips* خالی خولی باتوں سے کام نہیں چلتا

a parsnip

parson (*pah**-sun) *n.* parish priest کلیسائی حلقے کا پادری any clergyman پادری **parsonic** (*-son-*) *adj.* like that of a parson پادری کا سا **parsonage** (*pah**-sun-ij) *n.* official residence of a person (or any other clergyman) پادری کا سرکاری گھر ، پادری خانہ

part (pah*t) *n.* portion جز ، جزو ، حصّہ *for the most part*, mostly زیادہ تر ، بیشتر *in part*, somewhat کسی حد تک share حصّہ *take part (in)* میں حصّہ لینا *on the part of* کی طرف سے *on (one's) part* اپنی طرف سے *for my part* جہاں تک میرا تعلق ہے responsibility (of someone *in* some affair) کی ذمّہ داری role (*in* a play, etc.) (فلم (ڈرامے وغیرہ میں) کردار one of the equal divisions (*of* a thing, etc.) حصّہ (*part of speech*), one of the eight basic categories (viz., *noun, pronoun, adjective, verb, adverb, preposition, conjunction, interjection*) into which a word is placed in the English grammar جُزوِ کلام *parts of speech* اجزائے کلام (*Phrases* :) *take (someone's) part*, lend support to (him), plead (his) case کی طرف داری کرنا ، کی حمایت (یا وکالت) کرنا *take (something) in good part*, not to take offence at (it) (کا) بُرا نہ ماننا *v. t. & i.* separate جُدا ہونا یا کرنا *part (one's) hair (in the middle, etc.)* (سیدھی وغیرہ) *part company (with)*, (*a*) take leave of (someone) for following a different route سے رُخصت ہونا ، ہو کر اپنی راہ لگنا (*b*) disagree and end relationship with سے الگ ہو جانا ، سے علیحدگی اختیار کر لینا part with (something), (*a*) give (money, etc.) away دے دینا (*b*) abandon (something) ترک کر دینا ، چھوڑ دینا *part from* سے رُخصت ہونا **parting** *n.* separation جُدائی ، علیحدگی line where the hair is combed in opposite ways مانگ **partly** *adv.* somewhat کسی حد تک تھوڑا سا in part ایک حصّہ **part-time** *adj.* & *adv.* for only part of the working hours (کل وقتی یا ہمہ وقتی کے مقابلے میں) جُز وقتی ، تھوڑا وقت ، پارٹ ٹائم **part-timer** *n.* (colloq.) part-time worker جُز وقتی کاریگر

partake (pah*-*tayk*) *v. t. & i.* (*partake, partook, partaken*) participate *in* or *of* something *with* a person) (میں) شرکت کرنا eat or drink some or whole (*of* food, drink, etc.) (کھانے (یا پینے) میں شریک ہونا ، کھانا ، پینا smack, or share the qualities, (*of*) (کا سا) رنگ ڈھنگ ہونا

parti (pa*-*tee*) *n.* person as from the viewpoint of match-making رِشتہ *a good 'parti'* اچھا رشتہ

parti pris (pa*-tee-*pree*) *n.* preconceived view; prejudice تعصّب ، بندھے بندھائے نظریات *come to the question*

without 'parti pris' بندھے بندھائے نظریات کے بغیر مسئلے پر غور کرنا
partial (pah*-shĕl) *adj*. only a part جزوی، حصہ، نامکمل of only a part جزوی biased طرفداری، جانبدار *partial to (someone)*, taking (his) part (کسی) کا طرفدار *partial* (*to* some food, etc.) کا شوقین، کو پسند کرنے والا **partially** *adv*. in part ایک حد تک، تاحدے **partiality** (pah*-shi-al-i-ti) *n*. being partial جانبداری taste (*for* food) (کا) شوق
participate (pah*-*tis*-i-payt) *v.i.* take part (*in*) میں حصہ لینا *participate in (someone's) suffering* (*etc.*) کسی کا دکھ بٹانا **participant** (-*tis*-i-) *n*. one who shares (*in*) میں حصہ لینے والا one who attends (*in*) a function, etc. میں شریک **participation** (-*pay*-) *n*. act of participating شرکت
participle (*pah**t-i-si-pĕl) *n*. verbal adjective or noun اسم فاعل یا اسم مفعول *past participle*, (e.g., *seen* from *to see*) (*a*) verbal adjective used objectively اسم مفعول (*b*) form of verb used in some past tenses and in passive mood everywhere ترکیبی ماضی *present participle*, (*e.g. seeing* from *to see*), (*a*) verbal adjective used subjectively اسم فاعل (*b*) gerund مصدری اسم (*c*) form of verb used in making certain present tenses ترکیبی حال
particle (*pah**t-i-kĕl) *n*. tiny bit (*of*) ذرّہ (in grammar) a part of speech other than a noun, pronoun, adjective or verb حرف
particoloured (*pah**t-i-ku-lĕ*d) *adj*. variegated رنگ برنگ، پچرنگ
particular (*pah*tik*-ew-lĕ*) *adj*. special to one خاص especial خاص *in particular*, especially خاص کر، بالخصوص fastidious (*about*) (میں) بہت نفاست پسند *n*. (usu. *pl*.) details جزئیات، تفصیلات، باریکیاں *go into particulars* (*of*) give details (of) کی تفصیلات میں جانا (*pl*.) relevant details (*of*) کوائف *give particulars of* کے کوائف درج کرنا **particularize** (-riz) *v.t.* give particulars of کے کوائف درج name specially ایک کا نام لینا **particularly** *adv*. in particular خاص کر، بالخصوص، خصوصیت
partisan (*pah**t-i-zan) *n*. strong (usu. biased) supporter (*of* a party, cause) etc. پکا حامی، کٹر ❖ (see *Addenda*) **partisanship** *n*. being a partisan کٹرپن
partition (pah*-*tish*-ĕn) *n*. division into parts تقسیم، بٹوارہ thin wall between rooms, etc. پردہ، پارٹیشن anything else that divides thus حد، سرحد section formed by dividing *v.t.* divide تقسیم کرنا separate by dividing (*off*) تقسیم کرکے الگ الگ کرنا
partner (*pah**t-nĕ*) *n*. business shareholder ساجھی، شریک کار، کاروبار کا ساتھی one of two playing or dancing together ساتھی companion ساتھی، رفیق spouse شادی کا ساتھی، جیون ساتھی، رفیقِ زندگی (یا) رفیقۂ حیات *v. t.* be a partner to کا ساتھی ہونا **partnership** *n*. being partners
partook (pah*-*tuk*) *v*. (pa. t. of **partake,** which see)
partridge (*pah**t-rij) *n*. a bird of the pheasant family تیتر its flesh تیتر (کا گوشت)
parturient (pa*-tew-ri-ent) *adj*. about to give birth جننے ہی والی **parturition** (-rish-) *n*. childbirth زائیدگی، جننا
party (*pah**ti) *n*. political (or other) organization جماعت، تنظیم *party system*, a democratic system of government in which the majority party comes into power for a certain period جماعتی سیاسی نظام *putting public interest before party* قومی مفاد کو جماعتی مفاد پر ترجیح دینا one of the two or more sides in a case, quarrel or agreement فریق *be a party to (something)* میں شریک ہونا group of persons travelling together سفری ٹولی individuals, etc., invited to a place on some occasion usu. for eating (and merry-making) as a group دعوت، ضیافت
paschal (*pas*-kĕl) of the passover عید فسح کا of Easter ایسٹر کا
pass (pahs) *v. t.* & *i.* go by (person, place, etc.) کے پاس سے گزرنا end ختم ہونا *pass away*, die مر جانا، فوت ہونا change (*into* or *from* one state to another) (بدل کر) ہو جانا hand on to (someone something) پکڑانا circulate (*on to*) (سب کے پاس) باری باری بھیجنا take place (*at* a place or *between* persons) بیتنا، ہونا utter (*a remark about*) کے بارے میں کچھ کہنا، پر کچھ تبصرہ کرنا pronounce (*judgement*, etc., *on*) (کے بارے میں) فیصلہ سنانا (of time) spend or be spent (وقت) گزارنا یا گزرنا get through an examination, or get through (the examination), or be declared successful by (the examiner) پاس ہونا، امتحان میں کامیاب ہونا (of a Bill) be approved by majority vote پاس ہونا، منظور ہونا (of Legislature) approve (*the Bill*) by a majority vote کی منظوری دینا، پاس کرنا، منظور کرنا thrust گھونپنا، بھونکنا be beyond (belief, comprehension, etc.) سے باہر ہونا of money (cause to) circulate چلنا یا چلانا (*Phrases*:) *pass* (*someone, or something by*), pay no attention to کی طرف توجہ نہ کرنا *pass over* (*some name, etc.*), leave it out چھوڑ جانا *pass on please*, (police instruction to the crowd) چلتے جائیے *pass off*, (*a*) (of events) take place smoothly بخیر وخوبی ہو جانا (*b*) (of states) disappear gradually آہستہ آہستہ جاتے رہنا (*c*) palm

(something) دھوکے سے کسی کے گلے منڈھنا *pass oneself off as*, pretend to be جھوٹ موٹ بن جانا *pass for*, be taken for غلطی سے سمجھا جانا *pass current*, be accepted as genuine چل جانا *pass water*, make water پیشاب کرنا *pass out*, faint غش کھانا، غش کھا کر گرنا *pass through* (*sufferings*), undergo جھیلنا، اٹھانا *pass upon*, criticize ہدفِ تنقید بنانا *pass over an insult in silence*, pocket it بے عزتی پی جانا *n.* success (*in an examination*) (امتحان میں) کامیابی *a pass degree*, one which is not an Honours degree عام سند *a pass with honours* (or *distinction*) آنرز کی سند ticket (usu. given free) پاس *a free pass* مفت کا پاس *a railway pass*, a free railway-journey ticket ریل کا پاس narrow passage through mountains درّہ *the Khyber Pass* درّۂ خیبر occurrence وقوع، عمل *come to pass* ہونا، عمل میں ہونا *bring to pass*, عمل میں لانا critical condition نازک صورتِ حال *things have come to a pretty pass* بڑی نازک صورتِ حال پیدا ہو گئی ہے forward thrust of sword, etc. تلوار گھونپنا moving the hand over or in front of something in juggling trick ہاتھ پھیرنا یا ہلانا (in ball games played by teams) passing of the ball from one player to another کی طرف، گیند بڑھانا، پاس *give a pass to* گیند بڑھانا، پاس **pass-able** *adj.* only just good enough بس یونہی سی capable of being crossed قابلِ گزر **passably** *adv.* to some extent کسی حد تک **pass-book** *n.* bank customer's account book پاس بک، بنک کے حساب کی کاپی **password** *n.* secret word spoken to distinguish friend from foe when passing a sentry شناختی لفظ

passage (*pas*-ej) *n.* movement گزرنا، مرور *passage of time* مرورِ ایام *with the passage of time* جوں جوں وقت گزرتا گیا یا جائے گا voyage سمندری سفر *book* (*one's*) *passage to* سفر کا ٹکٹ لینا right to travel سفر کا حق *free passage* بلا کرایہ سفر corridor درمیانی راستہ passing of a Bill بل کی منظوری short extract عبارت کا ٹکڑا *passage-at-arms*, wordy duel تکرار، جھڑپ

passenger (*pas*-en-jĕ*) *n.* traveller (of a vehicle, ship, aircraft, etc.) مسافر ineffective member of a team ناکارہ ساتھی، نالائق رفیقِ کار

passe (*pas*-ay) *adj.* (fem. passee) past one's prime ڈھلی ہوئی جوانی والا outdated پرانے فیشن کا

passe-partout (pahs-pah*-*too*) *n.* picture-frame comprising two pieces of glass sandwiching the picture and held together at the edges with adhesive tape تصویر کا دوہرے شیشے کا فریم

passim (*pas*-im) *adv.* (of author) all over his writings, at various places in his writing ہر جگہ، ہر کہیں، جگہ جگہ *Shaw 'passim'* شا ہر جگہ

passion (*pash*-ĕn) *n.* emotion جذبہ rage طیش *fly into a passion* طیش میں آنا sexual love (*for*) کا عشق strong liking (*for* doing something) (کا) بے حد شوق (*the Passion*), the last sufferings, etc., of Christ (according to Christians) حضرت عیسیٰؑ کے مصائب، مسیح *passion play* مصائبِ مسیح کی تمثیل **passionate** (*pash*-ĕ-nayt) *adj.* emotional (lover) جذباتی easily moved to anger جلد بھڑک اٹھنے والا، مغلوب الغضب impassioned (appeal, etc.) پُرجوش

passive (*pas*-iv) *adj.* acted upon ; not acting انفعالی suffering without resistance خاموشی سے برداشت کرنے والا *remain passive* خاموش رہنا، کچھ نہ کہنا، کوئی اثر نہ لینا *passive resistance*, (people's) peaceful non-co-operative movement (against a government) which does not take the form of open rebellion مقاومتِ مجہول *passive voice*, (in grammar) form of the transitive verb in which the grammatical subject is acted upon by the verb instead of bringing that verb into action قرینۂ مجہول **passivity** جمود، خاموشی سے برداشت، مجہول ہونا

Passover (*pas*-oh-vĕ*) *n.* Jewish festival commemorating their escape in one of the ten plagues when their houses were passed over by the visitation فِصح، عیدِ فصح lamb sacrificed at it عیدِ فصح پر قربان ہونے والی بھیڑ Christ, according to Christians مسیح

passport (*pahs*-poh*t) *n.* identity card issued to a traveller by his own government permitting him to travel abroad ; (as the foreign government's permission to him to enter their country is called a *visa*) پاسپورٹ، اپنے ملک سے باہر جانے کی اجازت، اجازت نامۂ سفر anything opening the way (*to* success, etc.) پکا طریقہ، یقینی وسیلہ

past (pahst) *adj.* just gone by پچھلا former ماضی، بیتے ہوئے *n.* گزشتہ، گزرا ہوا (events of) long ago دن یا واقعات (one's) past life (کا) ماضی *prep.* beyond سے باہر، سے اوپر *It is past bearing* برداشت سے باہر *past one o'clock* ایک سے اوپر ہو گیا *adv.* up to the and beyond کے پاس سے ہو کر آگے، پاس سے آگے

paste (payst) *n.* sticky mixture for pasting لئی dough with fat, etc. گندھا ہوا آٹا *v. t.* stick things (*down, together, on*, etc.) with paste لئی سے چپکانا، (یا) جوڑنا **pasteboard** *n.* cardboard کٹّی، گتّہ

pastel (*pas*-tel) *n.* paste for crayon رنگین چاک بنانے کے لیے گندھی ہوئی مٹی picture made with it رنگین چاک سے بنائی ہوئی تصویر

pasteurize (*pas*-te-rīz) *v. t.* arresting fermentation in (milk, etc.) by the method of the French scientist, Louis Pasteur (1822-95) پاسچر کے طریق سے صاف کرنا، پاسچرائز کرنا **pasteurized** (-rīzd) *adj.* (of milk) treated thus پاسچر شدہ (دودھ)

pastil, pastill (pas-*teel*) *n.* small sweet (usu. medicinal) lozenge گرز cone of incense, etc., burnt to purify air بخور

pastime (*pahs*-tīm) *n.* amusement تفریح، game کھیل

pastor (*pahs*-tě*) *n.* a non-conformist minister غیر مقلد پادری **pastoral** (*pahs*-to-rěl) *adj.* of a bishop لاٹ پادری کا *pastoral staff* لاٹ پادری کا عصا (of poetry, poem, etc.) concerning shepherds and country life دیہی زندگی (یا چرواہوں) سے متعلق، شبانی، راعیانہ *n.* pastoral poem, poetry or play راعیانہ نظم (شاعری یا تمثیل

pastry (*pays*-tri) *n.* sweet food articles made of flour-paste پیسٹری

pasture (*pahs*-chě*) *n.* grassland for the cattle, etc., to graze on چراگاہ its grass چراگاہ کی گھاس *v.t.* put cattle, etc., on pasture مویشیوں کو چراگاہ میں چھوڑنا (of animals) eat the grass there چرنا **pasturage** (*pahs*-che-rij) *n.* pasture چراگاہ **pasturable** (*pahs*-che-ray-bèl) *adj.* (of land) being fit for a pasture چراگاہ بننے کے قابل

pasty *adj.* (*pays*-ti) like paste لئی کا سا pale (complexion) زرد، اُڑا اُڑا *n.* (*pahs*-ti) meat-pie قیمے والا بڑا سموسہ

pat *v.t.* (-tt-) tap gently with the open hand in affection تھپکنا، تھپکی دینا *pat (someone) on the back* (کو) تھپکی دینا، کی پیٹھ ٹھونکنا *n.* such gentle touch تھپکی small lump of butter مکھن کی چپٹی ٹکیہ (*Pat*), (colloq.) Irishman آئرستانی *adv.* aptly and in time کھٹ سے، بروقت اور برمحل *adj.* (used predicatively) ready (answer) برمحل، گھڑا گھڑایا، بنا بنایا *come pat to the purpose* ٹھیک نکلنا، برمحل ثابت ہونا *have (answer, etc.) pat* کے پاس (جواب وغیرہ) گھڑا گھڑایا ہونا

patch (pach) *n.* material put on over a hole, etc. پیوند differently coloured part مختلف رنگ کا ٹکڑا spot of colour رنگ کا چھینٹا، داغ small plot of ground for gardening, etc. ٹکڑا، قطعہ، بقعہ *v.t.* put a patch on کو پیوند لگانا *patch up (car, etc.),* get it clumsily ready for use (موٹر وغیرہ کو) جوڑ جاڑ کر ٹھیک کر لینا *patch up (a quarrel,* etc.) settle it at least temporarily (جھگڑا) نبٹا لینا (طور پر) عارضی **patchwork** *n.* something made of patches پارہ دوزی clumsily-done work بے سلیقہ کام کا کام **patchy** (*pach*-i) *adj.* (work) of uneven quality (وہ کام) جو یکساں طور پر معیاری نہ ہو، ناہموار (کام)

pate (payt) *n.* (humorous word for) head سر top of head چاند، چندیا

pate (*pat*-ay) *n.* (see under **patty**)

patency *n.* (see under **patent**)

patent (*pay*-tent) *adj.* obvious ظاہر، واضح protected by letters patent پیٹنٹ *patent medicines,* those manufactured by only one company خاص کمپنی کی دوائیں، پیٹنٹ اَدوِیہ، رجسٹری شدہ، مُنضبط *letters patent,* sole authority to manufacture something from the government guaranteeing protection against imitation پیٹنٹ *patent leather,* a smooth shiny leather پیٹنٹ لیدر *n.* letters patent پیٹنٹ privileges granted thus پیٹنٹ thing protected thus پیٹنٹ *v.t.* obtain a patent (for invention, etc.) کو پیٹنٹ کرانا **patentee** (pa-ten-*tee*) *n.* grantee of a patent پیٹنٹ کرانے والا شخص **patency** (pay-ten-si) *n.* obviousness واضح ہونا، بیّن ہونا، وضاحت

paternal (pa-tě*-nèl) *adj.* of the father باپ کا from the father's side باپ کی طرف *paternal uncle* چچا، تایا، (یا) پھوپھا *paternal grandfather* دادا *paternal grandmother* دادی paternal aunt پھوپھی، چچی یا تائی like the father's باپ جیسا، باپ کا سا، پدرانہ **paternally** *adv.* باپ کی طرف سے **paternity** (pa-tě*-ni-ti) *n.* being a father باپ کا ہونا origin on the father's side وَلدیّت origin آغاز، اصل **paterfamilias** (pay-tě*-fa-*mil*-i-as) *n.* (joc.) father of a family گھر کا بڑا **paternoster** (*pay*-tě*-nos-tě*) the Lord's Prayer in Latin ہمارا آسمانی باپ، (ایک عیسائی دُعا) bead for it at intervals in rosary تسبیح میں دُعا والے دانے

path (pahth) *n.* (pl. *paths* pr. *pahdhz*) way made by the trodding of feet پگڈنڈی line along which something moves راستہ، مسیر (someone's) course of action کی راہِ عمل (also *footpath*) footway along the road not necessarily paved پیادہ رو **pathless** *adj.* having no path جہاں کوئی راستہ بنا ہوا نہ ہو (of a subject) not mapped out جس کے مطالعہ کی راہیں متعیّن نہ ہوئی ہوں۔ **pathway** *n.* path پگڈنڈی، راستہ

pathetic *adj.* (see under **pathos**)

pathology (pa-*thol*-o-ji) *n.* science of diseases شرح اسباب امراض، شرح اسباب، علم الامراض **pathological** (-*loj*-) *adj.* of pathology مرضیاتی **pathologist** (pa-*thol*-o-jist) ماہر مرضیات

pathos (*pay*-thos) *n.* quality which arouses the feeling of pity سوز و گداز، آفت آمیزی **pathetic** (pa-*thet*-ik) *adj.* pitiful دردناک، دلگداز *pathetic fallacy,* poet's belief that Nature is in sympathy with his mood جذباتی مغالطہ **pathetically** (-*thet*-) *adv.* so as to excite pity دل ہلا دینے والے انداز سے، دردناک انداز سے

patience (*pay*-shens) *n.* capacity of bearing pains, inconvenience, etc., without complaining

برداشتِ صبر **be out of patience with** (*someone* or *something*), no more endure (him or it) patiently جھلا اُٹھنا a card game usu. for one پیشنس **patient** (*pay*-shent) *adj*. full of patience صابر *n*. person under medical treatment زیرِ علاج شخص، بیمار، مریض
patio (*pat*-i-oh) *n*. open courtyard in a house within its walls آنگن، آنگنائی
patriarch (*payt*-ri-ah*k) *n*. father and ruler of a family or tribe خاندان (یا) سردارِ قبیلہ، سرِ قبیلہ، سردار venerable old man قابلِ احترام بزرگ، بزرگ **patriarchal** (payt-ri-*ah**-kĕl, or pat-) *adj*. of a patriarch سرِ قبیلی، سرِ قبائلی **patriarchate** (*payt*-, or *pat*-) *n*. office of a patriarch قبیلے کی سرداری
patrician (pat-*rish*-èn) *n*. nobleman of ancient Rome (as opposed to the *plebeian*) رومی طبقۂ اُمرا کا فرد *adj*. of noble birth عالی نسب
patricide (*pat*-ri-sid) *n*. murder of own father قتلِ پدر، باپ کا قتل such murderer باپ کا قاتل
patrimony (*pat*-ri-mu-ni) *n*. property inherited from father or forefathers میراث، میراثِ پدر، وِرثہ
patriot (*pat*-ri-ot) *n*. person who loves his country وطن پرست، مُحِبِّ وطن **patriotic** (-*ot*-) *adj*. **patriotism** (*pat*-ri-o-tizm) *n*. being patriotic وطن پرستی، محبتِ وطن، حُبُّ الوطنی
patrol (pa-*trohl*) *v.t.* & *i*. (-ll-) keep going round (a place) to watch گشت کرنا، رَونْد پر جانا *n*. patrolling (*of* persons, aircraft, etc.) گشت **on patrol** گشت پر، رَونْد پر those (persons, warships or aircraft) on patrol گشت والا
patron (*payt*-run) *n*. one who gives monetary or moral help مُرَبّی، سرپرست upholder (*of* art, etc.) سرپرست، مُؤیِّد (flattering word for) a regular customer (*of* a shop) سرپرست **patron saint** *n*. saint supposed to protect a country, town, etc. (e.g., *St. George* who is patron saint of England) نگہبان وَلی، مُحافظ وَلی **patronage** *n*. patronizing سرپرستی patronizing attitude سرپرستانہ انداز، مُربّیانہ انداز
patronize (*pat*-ro-niz) *v.t.* be a patron کی سرپرستی کرنا treat one's protege as an inferior اپنے مُتوسّل کو حقیر جاننا
patter (*pat*-è*) *n*. sound of quick light taps (of rain, etc.) ٹپ ٹپ such footfall تیز چاپ rapid talk (like that of a conjurer) تیز تیز بولنا lingo (of thiefs, etc.) چوروں وغیرہ کا مخصوص انداز *v.t.* tap quickly and lightly many times ٹپ ٹپ کرنا

pattern (*pat*-ĕ*n) *n*. good example (*of*) (کا) اچھا نمونہ، (کی) عمدہ مثال design printed on or woven into a piece of cloth, etc. نقش، نمونہ wooden or other stamp for printing designs on cloth ٹھپّا design (of dress, etc.) to cut out in paper as guide in dressmaking, etc. کاغذ پر کپڑے کا نمونہ small piece of cloth as a sample کپڑے کا نمونہ (thing of some) model کے نمونے کی کترن نمونہ

a pattern on a piece of cloth

patty (*pat*-i), **pate** (*pat*-ay) *n*. pasty for one person قیمے کا سموسہ
paucity (*paws*-i-ti) *n*. shortage کمی، قلت
Pauline (*pawl*-in) *adj*. of St. Paul پولُس (مقدس) کا، پولوسی
paunch (pawnch) *n*. fat belly توند
pauper (*pawp*-ĕ*) *n*. one without livelihood جس کی روزی کا کوئی بندوبست نہ ہو destitute person کنگال، محتاج، مفلس **pauperize** (-riz) *v.t.* render pauper کنگال کر دینا
pause (pawz) *n*. short interval مختصر وقفہ *v.t.* make a pause ذرا رُکنا
pave (payv) *v.t.* cover (road, etc.) with flat stones, bricks or asphalt فرش باندھنا **pave the way** (*for something*), smooth the way (for it) کے لیے راہ ہموار کرنا **pavement** *n*. paved footway at the side of a road پکّا فٹ پاتھ، پیادہ رَو any paved place پختہ فرش والی جگہ **pavement artist** *n*. beggar collecting alms by attracting people to figures hastily drawn by him on the pavement بھکاری **paviour** (*pay*-vi-ĕ*) *n*. workman شاہراہ کا فرش ساز employed in paving فرش لگانے والا
pavilion (pa-*vil*-yun) *n*. building on a stadium for spectators کھیل کے میدان تماشائی خانہ، شہ نشین، کا بنگلہ large tent بڑا خیمہ، سراپردہ light ornamental building in a garden, etc. بارہ دری

a pavilion (sense 2)

paviour *n*. (see under **pave**)
paw *n*. animal's clawed foot پنجہ *v.t.* feel with the paw or hoof (in case of a horse) پنجے یا سُم مار کر دیکھنا
pawn *n*. one of eight small pieces in chess کٹ پتلی پیادہ one used by others as a tool **in pawn**, **at pawn**, pawned گِروی، گِرو **be in pawn** گِروی ہونا *v.t.* pledge (jewellery, etc.) with the moneylender رَہن رکھنا، گِرو رکھنا، گِروی رکھنا **pawnbroker** *n*. licensed usurer lending money on security of goods in pawn with him چیز رکھ کر روپیہ سود پر دینے والا
pawnshop *n*. pawnbroker's shop چیز رکھ کر روپیہ سود پر دینے والی دُکان

pay *v.t.* & *i.* (*pay, paid, paid*) give (someone) money for goods or services received from him or her معاوضہ دینا (یا)، ادا کرنا *pay (someone) off*, sack him after clearing his account تنخواہ کا حساب بیباق کرکے چلتا بنا *pay for (one's wrongdoings, etc.)*, suffer for (it) اپنے کیے کی سزا بھگتنا give *pay attention (to something)*, attend to it کی طرف توجہ کرنا *pay a call* (or *visit*) *on (someone)* کی ملاقات کو جانا *pay a compliment to (someone)* کی داد دینا، کی تعریف کرنا discharge (a debt) (قرض) چکانا be profitable مفید ہونا، نفع بخش ہونا، سود مند ہونا *n.* salary تنخواہ *get good pay* معقول تنخواہ پانا **payable** *adj.* واجب الادا **payee** (pay-*ee*) *n.* one to whom money is (to be) paid روپیہ پانے والا، یابندہ **payment** *n.* paying ادائیگی money paid ادا کردہ رقم

paynim (*pay*-nim) *n.* (old use) Muslim (regarded as a pagan or unbeliever by Mediaeval Christians) (قرونِ مظلمہ کے عیسائیوں کے نزدیک) مسلمان بحیثیت کافر

pea (pee) *n.* (pl. *peas*; old form of wrong sing., *pease*) plant with edible seeds growing in pods مٹر one of these seeds مٹر (کا دانہ) **peanut** *n.* groundnut, monkey-nut مونگ پھلی **peasoup** *n.* soup of dried peas مٹر کی یخنی

peace (pees) *n.* freedom from war امن *at peace with* سے پُرامن تعلقات calm امن، سکون *peace of mind* سکونِ قلب، اطمینانِ قلب *hold (one's) peace*, (a) stop quarrelling چپ ہو جانا (b) not to talk چپ رہنا **peaceable** (*pees*-a-bĕl) *adj.* not quarrelsome جو جھگڑالو نہ ہو، مرنجاں مرنج **peaceful** *adv.* fond of peace امن پسند full of peace پُرامن **peacemaker** *n.* one who uses his goodwill to end quarrels صلح کرانے والا، جھگڑا چکانے والا

peach (peech) *n.* a well known delicious stone-fruit آڑو، شفتالو tree bearing it آڑو person or thing of superlative merit شاندار شخص یا شے specially attractive girl دلربا لڑکی، دل فریب حسینہ

peacock (*pee*-kok) *n.* a large male bird with brilliant multicoloured tail feathers مور، طاؤس **pea-hen** *n.* female of peacock مورنی **pea-fowl** *n.* peacock or pea-hen مور (یا) مورنی **peacockery** (-ri) *n.* strutting vanity سج دھج کر نکلنا

peak (peek) *n.* pointed hilltop پہاڑ کی چوٹی front brim (*of* hat) چھجا point (*of* beard, etc.) چونچ highest or most intense point (or *of* something) (کی) انتہا *v.t.* waste away گھلنا *peak and pine* (عشق میں) گھل گھل کر مر جانا **peaked** *adj.* with a peak چوٹی دار sharp-pointed نوک دار (of features) wasted سوکھ سوکھ کر کانٹا

peal (peel) *n.* long and loud ringing of bells گھنٹیوں کی جھنکار، ملی جلی ٹن ٹن loud noise (*of* thunder, etc.) گرج echoing noise (*of* laughter etc.) زور سے بجنا، زور کی آواز *v.t.* & *i.* sound loudly ٹن ٹن کرنا، گرجنا، کڑکنا، زور کی آواز نکالنا

pear (*pay*-ĕ*) *n.* a well-known sweet juic fruit ناشپاتی tree bearing it ناشپاتی کا پیڑ

pearl (pĕ*l) *n.* silvery-white gem found i oyster shells (or anything looking like it) تی، گوہر very precious thing or person ہر، دُرِّ نایاب، موتی

pease (peez) *n.* (old form of false sing.) pea مٹر

peasant (*pez*-ant) *n.* working farmer as tena or smallholder کسان، کاشتکار **peasantry** (*pez*-ant- *n.* peasants as a class کاشتکاروں کا طبقہ، کسان

pease (peez) *n.*

peat (peet) *n.* partly decomposed turf in bo gy places دلدلی کوئلے والی زمین، پیٹ piece of this c out and dried to be burnt as fuel دلدلی کوئلہ، پیٹ **peaty** (*pee*-ti) *adj.* (made) of peat پیٹ کا (بنا ہوا)

pebble (*peb*-ĕl) *n.* small stone worn and ma roundish by being rolled in running water سنگریزہ **pebbly** (*peb*-li) *adj.* 'full of pebbles سنگریزوں ہی سنگریزوں والا

peccadilo (pek-a-*dil*-oh) *n.* minor weakness character معمولی اخلاقی کمزوری **peccant** (*pek*-ant) *a* (of an object) that has been the source trouble تکلیف کی اصل، تکلیف کا باعث *the peccant too* (*etc.*) تکلیف کا باعث بننے والے دانت

peck (pek) *v.t.* & *i.* strike (*at*), and pick with the beak ٹھونگے مارنا make (a hole) th ٹھونگے مار مار کر چھید کر ڈالنا *n.* such stroke ٹھونگا a two-gallon dry measure غلے کا خشک پیمانہ، پیک *a peck (of something)*, a lot (of it) کافی **peck** (pek-ĕ*) *n.* (slang) nose ناک *keep your pecker* never say you will die کبھی مت کہو میں مر جاؤں گا **pecki** (pek-ish) *adj.* (slang) hungry بھوکا *feel peck* بھوک لگی ہونا

peculate (*pek*-ew-layt) *v.t.* & *i.* embezzle میں خیانت کرنا

peculiar (pe-*kew*-li-ĕ*) *adj.* odd انوکھا، عجیب special (or *to*) کا مخصوص **peculiarity** (-*a*-) *n.* characteristic feature خصوصیت oddity اپن، عجیب ہونا

pecuniary (pe-*kew*-ni-ĕ-ri) *adj.* monetary مالی

pedagogue (*ped*-a-gog) *n.* pedantic teacher میاں جی، ملا **pedagogy** (*ped*-a-gog-i, or -*goj*-) teaching معلمی **pedagogics** (ped-a-*gog*-iks or -*g* *n.* (pl. used as sing.) art of teaching تعلیم، تعلیمات **pedagogic, pedagogical** (-*gog*- or -*goj*-) مدرسی، معلمانہ

pedal (*ped*-ĕl) *n.* treadle (*of* bicycle, organ, e پیڈل، پایہ، پیر *v.t.* & *i.* (-ll-) work (a machi

with a pedal پیڈل سے چلانا move the pedal پیڈل مارنا
pedant (*ped*-ant) *n.* one who shows off learning عِلم فروش، دانش فروش one who sets too much store by book-learning کتابی علم پر زور دینے والا **pedantic** (*-dant-*) *adj.* of a pedant کتابی علم پر زور دینے والا (انداز) **pedantry** (*ped*-ant-ri) *n.* being a pedant عِلم فروشی، کتابی عِلم پر زور
peddle (*ped*-ĕl) *v.t.* & *i.* hawk (one's wares) پھیری لگانا **pedlar** (*ped*-lĕ*) *n.* hawker پھیری والا
pedestal (*ped*-es-tĕl) *n.* base (of a statue, column, etc.) پایہ *put (someone) on a pedestal*, have great regard (for him) (کسی کو) بانس پر چڑھانا
pedestrian (pe-*des*-tri-an) *n.* one who walks on foot پیدل چلنے والا، پیادہ *adj.* going on foot پیدل (of person, piece of writing, etc.) dull بے لطف

a pedestal

pedigree (*ped*-ig-ree) *n.* (persons, or animals') lineage شجرۂ نسب well-known descent of (animal) اچھی نسل
pedlar *n.* (see under **peddle**)
peel *v. t.* & *i.* take off the skin of (fruit, etc.) چھیلنا، چھلکا اُتارنا strip (*off* bark of a tree) چھال اُتارنا (of bark, plaster, animal skin, etc.) come off in bits *n.* skin (of fruit, potatoes, etc.) اُترنا، جھڑنا **peelings** *n.* (*pl.*) peeled off pieces اُتارا ہوا چھلکا، چھلکا
peep *n.* sly, secret and quick look دُزدیدہ نظر look through a slit incomplete view جھلک، جھلکی the first light (of day) (صبح کی) پہلی کرن *v. t.* take a peep at جھانکنا، چوری چوری دیکھنا (of the sun, etc.) come (*out*) into view slowly or partly (*from*) آہستہ آہستہ (ذرا سا) نکلنا
peer (*pee*-ĕ*) *v. i.* look (*at* or *into* something) closely and intently غور سے دیکھنا، بغور دیکھنا *n.* British nobleman برطانوی نواب (one's) equal in rank ہم رُتبہ، ہمسر، ہم مرتبت، ہم چشم equal (*of*) نظیر، مثال، نمونہ **peerage** (*pee*-ĕ-rej) *n.* rank of a peer (برطانیہ میں) نوابی *raise to peerage* نواب بنانا peers مجلس (برطانوی) نواب **peeress** (*pee*-ĕ-res) *n.* wife of a peer نواب بیگم woman peer نواب خاتون **peerless** *adj.* matchless بے نظیر، لاثانی
peeved *adj.* (see under **peevish**) چڑچڑا
peevish (*pee*-vish) *adj.* cross, irritable **peevishly** *adv.* crossly چڑچڑے پن سے **peevishness** *n.* irritability چڑچڑا پن **peeved** (peevd) *adj.* (colloq.) irritated, annoyed جھلّایا ہوا
peewit *n.* (same as **pewit**, which see)

peg *n.* wooden or metal pin for fastening (tents, etc.) میخ such a one for hanging clothes, etc. on کھونٹی *a peg to hang discourse on* بات کرنے کا بہانہ، موقع یا موضوع (also *clothes peg*), clip with which to fasten clothes to the line کپڑے اَلگنی پر ڈالنے کا کلپ، کپڑوں کا کلپ measure (*of* liquor) liquor measured in it پیگ، جام *v.t.* & *i.* (-gg-) fasten (something *down*, or *in*) with pegs میخیں گاڑ کر لگانا regulate (prices of stocks, etc.) by preventing them from falling or rising too much کم و بیش قیمتوں کا تعیّن *peg away (at something)* کسی کام میں لگے رہنا *peg out*, (a) strike (the tent) اُکھاڑنا، گرانا (b) die مرجانا (*be*) *a square peg in a round hole*, (*be*) *a round peg in a square hole*, (be) a misfit کسی عہدے وغیرہ کے لیے ناموزوں (ہونا)
Pegasus (*peg*-a-sus) *Cl. myth.* the winged horse of the Muses which flew upwards to heaven پگسس poetic inspiration or endeavour شاعرانہ وجدان name of a constallation الفرس، آسمانی برج
pelican (*pel*-i-kan) *n.* large water-bird with a long, pouched bill ; (it was once supposed to feed its young on its own blood) پیلی کن

a pelican

pellet (*pel*-et) *n.* little ball made by rolling bread, wet paper, etc., between one's fingers (آٹے، کاغذ وغیرہ کی بنائی ہوئی) گولی any pill made thus گولی small leaden ball for a gun چھرّا
pell-mell (pel-*mel*) *adv.* in confused haste افراتفری میں
pellucid (pe-*lew*-sid) *adj.* very clear صاف شفاف clear in thought جس کے خیالات میں ژولیدگی نہ ہو
pelmet (*pel*-met) *n.* pendant border to conceal curtain rods, etc. پردے کا لٹکتا ہوا کنارہ، پردے کا اوپر کا الگ کنارہ
Pelops (*pee*-lops) *Cl. myth.* a powerful mythical king of Greece after whom the peninsula gets its name *Peloponnese* پیلوپس **Peloponnesian** (*-nesh-ĕn*) of Peloponnese (or Peloponnesus) *i. e.*, of the Greek peninsula یونانی جزیرہ نمائے یونان کا
pelt *v. t.* & *i.* attack (*with* mud, stones, etc.) پر پھینکنا، پر زور زور سے پھینکنا harry (someone *with*) a barrage of (questions) سوالات کی بوچھاڑ کرنا (of hailstones, rain, etc.) fall heavily (*against* something) (اولے) زور زور سے گرنا، کی بوچھاڑ ہونا *n.* undressed skin of sheep or goat or furred animal پشم سمیت کھال speed رفتار (in the phrases :) *full pelt, at full pelt* پوری رفتار سے
pelvis (*pel*-vis) *n.* lower abdominal cavity holding bladder, etc. پیڑو، عانہ
pen *n.* instrument for writing with ink قلم *steel*

pen فولادی نب والا قلم *fountain pen* خود نویس قلم، پین، خود نویس small enclosure for sheep, etc. چھوٹا باڑا *v. t.* write (letter, etc.) لکھنا scribble (*down*) لکھ لینا shut (*up* animal, person, etc., *in* or as *in* a pen) باڑے میں بند کرنا، بند کرنا *n.* author, writer مصنف **penmanship** *n.* being a writer مصنف ہونا style of handwriting خط **pen-knife** *n.* small pocket-knife چھوٹا چاقو، قلم تراش

penal (*pee*-nĕl) *adj.* of punishment سزا کا، تعزیری *penal laws* تعزیری قوانین *penal offence*, crime cognizable by law قابل تعزیر جرم *penal servitude*, imprisonment with hard labour قید بامشقت **penalize** (*pee*-) *v. t.* declare (an act) to be penal کی سزا مقرر کرنا inflict a penality on کو سزا دینا، کو لائق تعزیر قرار دینا put (previous winner in game, etc.) under disadvantage پنیلٹی ہونا **penalization** (*-zay-*) *n.* سزا دینا **penalty** (*pen*-ĕl-ti) *n.* punishment سزا fine جرمانہ (in games) disadvantage imposed (*on* someone, *by* the referee) for breaking the rules پنیلٹی، سزا **penalty area** *n.* area of field in which breach of rules by defenders subjects them to *penalty kick* at their goal تعزیری رقبہ پنیلٹی ایریا

penance (*pen*-ans) *n.* self-imposed or willingly-accepted punishment to show repentance کفارہ *do penance for* کا کفارہ ادا کرنا

pence *n.* (pl. of **penny**, which see)

pencil (*pen*-sil) *n.* pen for writing without ink پنسل *v. t.* (-ll-) write with a pencil پنسل سے لکھنا draw with pencil پنسل سے تصویر کھینچنا *pencil drawing* پنسل سے کھینچی ہوئی تصویر۔ پنسلی تصویر۔

pendant (occasionally *pendent*) (pr. *pendant*) *n.* any hanging ornament (for the ears, neck, etc.) (کان کا) آویزہ، (گلے کا) ہار **pendent** (occasionally *pendant*) *adj.* hanging لٹکتا ہوا، آویزاں over-hanging (rock, etc.) آگے کو لٹکا (یا بڑھا یا جھکا) ہوا۔

pending (*pend*-ing) *prep.* until, awaiting جب تک نہ، کے ہونے تک during دوران میں *adj.* yet unfinished ابھی نامکمل (of case) yet undecided زیر سماعت، غیر فیصلہ شدہ (of plan, etc.) yet unsettled زیر غور، ہنوز زیر غور

pendulum (*pend*-ew-lum) *n.* hanging rod free to swing رقاص *pendulum of a clock*, one regulating its movement گھڑی کا رقاص *the swing of the pendulum*, (*a*) sudden change of public opinion رائے عامہ کی یکسر تبدیلی (*b*) tendency of the electorate to put parties in power alternately رائے عامہ کا مختلف سیاسی جماعتوں کو باری باری کامیاب کرنا

Penelope (pe-*nel*-o-pee) *Cl. myth.* faithful wife of Odysseus who was pestered by suitors during her husband's long absence but who continued to put them off till she should finish off a web which she would weave in the day and undo at night پنیلپی

penetrate (*pen*-e-trayt) *v. t.* & *i.* percolate میں سرایت کرجانا pierce (*into*) کے آرپار ہو جانا see (*into* or *through*) (بات کی) تہہ کو پہنچنا spread (or *through*) میں بھر جانا **penetrating** (*-tray-*) *adj.* keen (mind, person) تیز فہم، زیرک، ذکی piercing (cry, etc.) تیکھی (آواز) piercing (thing) چیر کر نکل جانے والا **penetration** (*-tray-*) *n.* entering داخل ہونا keenness of perception, etc. تیز فہمی، فراست

penguin (*peng*-gwin) *n.* Australian sea-bird with wings meant for swimming and not for flying پنگوئن

penicillin (pen-i-*sil*-in) *n.* a powerful anti-biotic made from a kind of mould پنسلین

peninsula (pe-*nin*-sew-la) *n.* mass of land almost completely surrounded by sea جزیرہ نما *the Arabian Peninsula* جزیرہ نمائے عرب، جزیرۃ العرب **peninsular** (-lĕ*) *adj.* of peninsula جزیرہ نما

penis *n.* male sexual organ عضو تناسل، آلت

penitence (*pen*-i-tens) *n.* repentance for sin توبہ sorrow for wrongdoing پشیمانی، ندامت **penitent** *n.* contrite ; repentant تائب، نادم *adj.* توبہ یا ندامت کے انداز (ظاہر کرنے والا) تائب، شرمسار **penitentiary** (*-tensh-*) reformatory ریفرمیٹری، اصلاحی قید خانہ

pennant (*pen*-ant), **pennon** (*pen*-on) *n.* long, narrow triangular flag (on a car, etc.) لمبی تکونی جھنڈی

penny (*pen*-i) *n.* British coin worth one-twelfth of a shilling پنس، پنس کا سکہ **pennies** *n. pl.* more than one such coin پنس کے سکے **pence** *n. pl.* more than one penny in price, etc. (ایک سے زیادہ) پنس **pennyworth**, **penn'orth** (*pen*-ĕ*th) *n.* as much as a penny will buy ایک پنس کا **penniless** *adj.* moneyless, poor غریب، مفلس، کنگال، پیسے پیسے کو

[1]**pension** (*pen*-shĕn) *n.* part of salary regularly paid by the government to its retired employees پنشن، وظیفہ *v.t.* give a pension to پنشن دینا، پنشن پر بھیجنا **pensioner** *n.* one receiving a pension پنشن پانے والا پنشن خوار، وظیفہ خوار **pensionable** *adj.* (of post) to which a pension is attached پنشن والی

[2]**pension** (pahn-si-awn) *n.* boarding-house طعام خانہ *en pension*, (pr. ohn-) as boarder at inclusive rates معطعم طعام خانے میں بالمقطع دینے والا

pensive (*pens*-iv) *adj.* deep in thought سوچ میں ڈوبا ہوا

pent *adj.* (of person) shut (*up*) in میں قید کرنا

(of feelings) not given vent to گھٹا ہوا، دبا ہوا
pentagon (*pent*-a-gon) *n.* five-sided polygon مخمس (*the Pentagon*) U. S. military policy or authorities اَمریکی فوجی طاقت (یا پالیسی)
penthouse (*pent*-hous) *n.* sloping roof of a shed, etc. چھپّر
penultimate (pe-*nul*-ti-mayt) *adj.* last but one ماقبل آخر
penury (*pen*-ew-ri) *n.* extreme poverty سخت غربت اِفلاس **penurious** (pe-*new*-ri-us) *adj.* very poor مفلس، کنگال miserly کنجوس
people (*pee*-pĕl) *n.* human beings لوگ، اِنسان (used with a sing. verb) (pl. *peoples*), nation قوم (*the people*), the masses عوام، عوام النّاس *v.t.* fill with people لوگوں سے بھرنا *be thickly peopled* بڑی گنجان آبادی والا ہونا
pep *n.* (slang) energy ہمّت، طاقت
pepper (*pep*-ĕ*) *n.* a small, black, round berry used as spice کالی مرچ its powder for seasoning food پسی ہوئی کالی مرچ *v.t.* put pepper on (food) پر کالی مرچ چھڑکنا *pepper (someone) with (questions, brickbats, etc.)* (کسی پر سوالات یا اینٹوں وغیرہ) کی بوچھاڑ کرنا
peppermint *n.* plant yielding an essential oil ایک قسم کا پودینہ، نعناع فلفلی oil pressed from it روغنِ پودینہ *peppermint lozenge*, lozenge medicated with this oil پیپرمنٹ **peppery** (*pep*-ĕ-ri) *adj.* of pepper ; hot-tempered چڑچڑا، بدمزاج
[1]**per** (pĕ*) *prep.* for each فی، ہر، آنہ **per cent** (pr pĕ*-*sent*) after every hundred فی صدی، فی صد **percentage** (pĕ*-sent-ij) *n.* rate per cent شرح فی صد، فی صدی **per annum** (-*an*-), annually ; every year سالانہ **per mensum** monthly, every month ہر مہینے، فی ماہ، ماہانہ **per diem** per day روزانہ **per caput** (or, wrongly but usu. ***per capita***), per head فی کس ***per contra***, (*a*) on the other hand اس کے برعکس (*b*) on the other side of this account حساب کی اُلٹی بندمیں ***per se***, by its very nature فطری طور پر، فطرۃً ***per pro*** (or *p.p.*, or *per procurationem*), on behalf of, by proxy کی جانب سے
per (pĕ*) *prep.* by the specified means of conveyance کے ذریعے *per bearer* حاملِ رُقعہ کے ہاتھ، کے ہاتھ
peradventure (pĕ*-ad-*vench*-ĕ*) *adv.* (old use) perhaps شاید
perambulator (pe-*ram*-bew-lay-tĕ*), (coll. abb. **pram**) *n.* four-wheeled carriage بچہ گاڑی، پرام

a perambulator

per annum, per capita, per caput (see under [1]**per**)
perceive (pĕ*-*seev*) *v.t.* see دیکھ لینا understand سمجھ لینا **perceptible** (-*sep*-) *adj.* that can be perceived محسوس، قابلِ اِدراک **perception** (-*sep*-) *n.* faculty or act of perceiving اِدراک **perceptive** (-*sep*-) *adj.* having perception or concerned in it مُدرِک، مُدرکہ
per cent, percentage (see under [1]**per**)
perch (pĕ*ch) *n.* bird's resting place on the branch of tree زین بسیرا rod, etc., provided for this purpose (پرندوں کے بیٹھنے کی) چھتری land measure equal to 5 yards پرچ، جریب *v.t.* & *i.* come to rest (*on*) پر اُترنا، پر بسیرا لینا take up position (*on* a high place)
perchance (pĕ*-*chahns*) *adv.* (old use) perhaps by chance اِتّفاق سے، اِتّفاقاً
percolate (*pĕ**-co-layt) *v.t.* & *i.* (of liquid) ooze (*through*) رِسنا make way thus (into) (میں) ٹپکنا put through strainer چھلنی میں ڈالنا **percolation** (-*lay*-) *n.* رِسنا، ٹپکنا، نچوڑنا **percolator** *n.* (also) vessel in which boiling water percolates through coffee قہوے کا سماوار

a percolator

per contra (see under [1]**per**)
percussion (pĕ*-*kush*-ĕn) *n.* collision ٹکر، تصادم the resulting shock ٹھوکر، تھاپ، ضرب *percussion instruments*, musical instruments producing sound on being thumped on تھاپ والے آلاتِ طرب **percussion cap** detonating device on the lock of a gun
per diem (see under [1]**per**)
perdition (pĕ*-*dish*-ĕn) *n.* utter loss تباہی، ستیاناس everlasting damnation اَبدی عذاب hell دوزخ
perdu, perdue (pĕ*-*dew*) *adj.* (used predicatively) in ambush گھات میں *lie perdu* گھات میں بیٹھنا
pere (*pay*-ĕ*) *n.* (after a name) the father (as *Dumas pere* دُوما باپ، کُوڈُوما) to distinguish it from *Dumas fils* pr. fis دُوما بیٹا، ابنِ دُوما
peregrinate (*pe*-reg-ri-nayt) *v.t.* & *i.* (joc.) wander سیر (یا کی سیر) کرنا **peregrination** (-*nay*-) *n.* act of peregrinating سیر **peregrine** (*pe*-reg-rin, or -rin) *n.* (also *peregrine falcon*) breed of falcon formerly much used in hawking شِکرا
peremptory (*pe*-remp-to-ri, or pe-*remp*-to-ri) *adj.* (of command) demanding immediate obedience قطعی too commanding (person or attitude) تحکمانہ **peremptorily** *adv* تحکمانہ انداز سے، قطعی طور پر
perennial (pe-*ren*-yĕl) *adj.* (of canals, etc.) flowing all the year round سال بھر چلنے والا، دائمی

(of plants) lasting more than two years دوسال دوسال سے زیادہ چلنے والا پودا *n.* perennial plant سے زیادہ چلنے والا
perfect *adj.* (pĕ*-fekt) complete پورا، مکمل، کامل excellent شاندار faultless بے عیب *v.t.* (pè*-*fekt*) make perfect تکمیل کرنا، کے نقائص دور کرنا **perfectly** *adv.* completely بالکل **perfection** (*-fek-*) *n.* perfecting or being perfected ; مکمل کرنا، تکمیل وغیرہ perfect person کامکمل (یا کامل) نمونہ perfect quality کمال
perfidious *adj.* (see under **perfidy**)
perfidy (*pĕ**-fi-di) *n.* breach of faith بیوفائی treachery غدّاری **perfidious** (pĕ*-*fid*-i-us) *adj.* treacherous ; guilty of breach of trust بیوفا، بیوفایانہ غدّار، غدّارانہ
perforate (*pĕ**-fè-rayt) *v.t.* & *i.* make a hole through میں چھید ڈالنا، چھیدنا make a line of small holes in paper, stamps to facilitate tearing off چھیدوں کی لکیر ڈالنا **perforation** (*-ray-*) *n.* perforating چھیدنا such a line چھیدوں کی لکیر
perforce (pè*-*foh*s*) *adv.* of necessity لازماً، ناچار، لاچار
perform (pè*-*fo*m*) *v.t.* & *i.* do کرنا act (a play) تمثیل پیش کرنا act (a part) in a play کا کردار ادا کرنا sing or juggle in public محفل میں گانا یا کرتب دکھانا **performance** (pĕ*-*fo**-mans) *n.* performing کرنا work عمل، کام presentation of an actor or singer کام entertainment پروگرام **performer** *n.* (esp.) one who performs at a concert موسیقار، مُطرب **performing** *adj.* (of animal) trained to do tricks کام (یا کرتب) سیکھا ہوا
perfume *n.* (*pĕ**-fewm) fragrance خوشبو scent عطر *v.t.* (pè*-*fewm*) add or apply perfume میں خوشبو ڈالنا (یا)، کو خوشبو لگانا **perfumery** (*-fewm-*) *n.* perfumes عطریات، خوشبوئیں place where they are made or sold عطر سازی کا کارخانہ، عطر فروش کی دوکان **perfumer** *n.* maker of perfumes عطر ساز one who sells them عطر فروش
perfunctory (pè*-*funk*-tè-ri) *adj.* done half-heartedly only to finish the duty بے توجہی سے کیا ہوا (کام) person doing work thus بے توجہی سے کام کرنے والا بے فکرا **perfunctorily** (*-funk-*tè-) *adv.* half-heartedly بے توجہی سے، برائے نام، یونہی سا
perhaps (pè*-*haps*) *adv.* possibly ; it may be that اتفاقاً، اتفاق سے by chance
peri- (pe-ri) *pref.* about, around گرد، گرد
peril (*pe*-ril) *n.* grave danger سخت خطرہ **perilous** *adj.* very dangerous سخت خطرے کا risky جوکھوں کا
perimeter (pe-*rim*-i-tè*) *n.* outer boundary of a closed figure احاطہ، محیط محیط، گھیرا its length
period (*pee*-ri-od) *n.* portion of time عرصہ، مدت sentence جملہ full stop کامل وقفہ، وقف

(جملے کے آخر میں) **periodic, periodical** (*-od-*) *adj.* recurring at intervals مؤقت، وقتاً فوقتاً کا **periodical** *n.* periodic publication (like a newspaper, etc.) مؤقت الشیوع چیز (اخبار، رسالہ وغیرہ) **periodically** *adv.* at intervals وقتاً فوقتاً **periodicity** *n.* being periodic موقت ہونا
peripatetic (pe-ri-pa-*tet*-ik) *adj.* itinerant سیلانی، رمتا (*Peripatetic*), of the philosophical school of Aristotle who used to walk while lecturing to his students مشائی
periphery (pe-*rif*-è-ri) *n.* boundary (esp. of a round surface) گھیرا، محیط **peripheral** *adj.* of or like periphery گھیرے یا محیط کا (سا)
periphrasis (*-rif-*) *n.* (pl. *periphrases*) roundabout phrase or speech اطناب
periscope (*pe*-ri-skohp) *n.* tube with lenses for seeing upper things from inside a submarine, etc. بالا بین
perish (*pe*-rish) *v.t.* & *i.* destroy or be destroyed تلف کرنا یا ہونا putrefy, decay سڑنا، گل سڑ جانا die فنا ہو جانا، مر جانا feel much inconvenienced by (heat, cold, etc.) سے جان نکلنا، بے مرہا ہونا
perishable *adj.* that which would be destroyed فنا پذیر quickly putrefying جلد خراب ہو جانے والا *perishable goods*, foodstuff کھانے پینے کی چیزیں اشیائے خورد و نی
periwig (*pe*-ri-wig) *n.* wig وگ
periwinkle (*pe*-ri-wink-èl) *n.* evergreen trailing with light-blue flowers پری ونکل small snail-like edible shell-fish ایک خوردنی گھونگا، پری ونکل
perjure (*pĕ**-jè*) *v. reflexive* (*perjure oneself*), make a false deposition جھوٹی قسم کھانا، دروغ حلفی کرنا، جھوٹا حلف اٹھانا **perjury** (*pĕ**-jè-ri) *n.* act of perjuring oneself دروغ حلفی، جھوٹا حلف **perjurer** (*pĕ**-je-rè*) *n.* **perjured** (*pĕ**-jè*d) *adj.* (one) guilty of perjury جھوٹی قسم کھانے والا
perk (pĕ*k) *v. t.* & *i.* (usu. *perk up*) (colloq.) recover self-control or spirit لیسنے میں پھر خود اعتمادی یا شگفتگی پیدا کرنا raise (one's head, nose, tail, ears, etc.) کھڑا کرنا **perky** (*pĕ**-ki) *adj.* saucy گستاخ شوخ self-assertive خودپسند
perm (pĕ*m) *n.* (abb. of *permanent wave*) lasting artificial wave in ladies' hair (بالوں کے) دیرپا گھنگر
permanent (*pĕ**m-a-nent) *adj.* lasting مستقل made to last پائدار، مضبوط، دیرپا *the permanent way*, track ریل کی پٹڑی *permanent wave*, (abb. *perm*) hair curls made to last several months بالوں کے دیرپا گھنگر **permanently** *adv.* مستقل، مستقل طور پر **permanence** (*pĕ**m-a-nens) *n.* مستقل ہونا، پائداری

permeate (*pĕ*m*-e-ayt) *v.t.* & *i.* pervade میں بھر جانا percolate (*among, through,* etc.) میں سرایت کرنا **permeation, permeance** *n.* act of, permeating سرایت ، نفوذ

per mensum (see under [1]**per**)

permit (pè*-*mit*) *v.t.* & *i.* (-tt-) allow کی اجازت دینا *permit me to say that,* I should like to say this unpalatable thing اجازت ہو تو عرض کروں ، مجھے یہ کہنے کی اجازت دیجیے *not permitted,* (of something) prohibited کو جائز رکھنا ، میں روا ہونا *permit of* ممنوع ہے ، منع ہے give explicit consent to کی منظوری دینا *n.* (*pĕ*-mit) ticket or document giving official permission (*to do* something, *to go* somewhere, etc.) پرمٹ ، پروانہ

permissible (-*mis*-) *adj.* that is permitted جائز ، روا

permission (-*mish*-) *n.* consent اجازت **permissive** (pĕ*-*mis*-iv) *adj.* permitting but not making it binding مباح ، اباحتی

permutation (pĕ*-mew-*tay*-shĕn) *n.* alteration in the order ردوبدل *permutations and combinations,* (esp. in mathematics) all possible arrangements of given things ہر ممکن ترکیب

pernicious (pè*-*nish*-us) *adj.* harmful نقصان دہ ، ضرر رساں مضرت رساں

pernickety (pĕ*-*nik*-è-ti) *adj.* (colloq.) ticklish, requiring tact نازک fastidious نفاست پسند

peroration (pe-ro-*ray*-shĕn) *n.* summing up (towards the end of a speech, etc.) خلاصہ ، مطلب خلاصہ ، تقدیر ، مدعا ، مطلب

perpendicular (pĕ*-pen-*dik*-ew-lĕ*) *adj.* at a right angle (*to*) پر عمود upright سیدھا *n.* perpendicular line عمود

perpendicular (AD) to horizontal (BC)

perpetrate (*pĕ*-pet-rayt) *v.t.* commit (a crime, an error) کرنا ، کا ارتکاب کرنا ، کا مرتکب ہونا **perpetrator** *n.* one who perpetrates مرتکب **perpetration** (-*ray*-) *n.* act of perpetrating ارتکاب

perpetual (pè*-*pet*-ew-ĕl) *adj.* everlasting دائمی ، دوامی often repeated بار بار کا **perpetually** *adv.* ہمیشہ ، دائمی ، دوامی ، بار بار **perpetuate** (pè*-*pet*-ew-ayt) *v.t.* preserve (someone's memory, etc.) مستقل بنانا make permanent باقی رکھنا ، قائم رکھنا **perpetuity** *n.* being perpetual دوام ، ہمیشگی *in perpetuity,* for ever ہمیشہ ہمیشہ

perplex (pè*-*pleks*) *v.t.* bewilder or puzzle (someone) (کو) حیرت میں ڈالنا confuse (something) still more اور الجھا دینا **perplexed** *adj.* bewildered حیران **perplexedly** *adv.* حیران ہو کر ، حیرت سے **perplexity** (-*lek*-) *n.* bewilderment حیرانی ، حیرت what bewilders حیرانی کی بات

per pro, *per procurationem,* **per se** (see under [1]**per**)

persecute (*pĕ**-se-kewt) *v.t.* continue to treat cruelly (*for*) difference of esp. religious (opinion) ایذائیں دیتے رہنا ، مسلسل اذیتیں پہنچانا (of a child) vex (with unending questions, etc.) (سے) ناک میں دم کر دینا

persecution (-*kew*-) *n.* act of persecuting or being persecuted ایذا رسانی **persecutor** *n.* one who persecutes ایذا دینے والا ، ایذا دہندہ

Persephone (pĕ*-sef-o-ne) *Cl. myth.* same as **Proserpine,** which see)

persevere (pĕ*-se-*vee*-è*) *v.i.* continue steadfastly (*at, in* or *with* something) ثابت قدم رہنا

perseverence *n.* (-*vee*-e) استقلال ، ثابت قدمی

persist (pè*-*sist*) *v.i.* continue to be رہ جانا ، باقی رہنا continue obstinately (*in doing* or *saying* something) (پر) جمارہنا ، (پر) ڈٹا رہنا ، (پر) قائم رہنا **persistent** *adj.* persisting مستقل مزاج ، ثابت قدم ، بات کا پکا continuing متواتر ، پے در پے ، باقی **persistently** *adv.*

persistence, persistency (-*tens*-) *n.* being persistent استقلال ، مستقل مزاجی ، ثابت قدمی

person (*pĕ**-sun) *n.* any human being شخص body of a person who is alive جسم ، بدن *attack against the person,* attack on the body جسمانی حملہ *be present in person* بذات خود موجود ہونا **personable** *adj.* handsome خوش شکل ، خوبصورت ، خوبرو **personage** (-nej) *n.* important person شخصیت ، اہم شخصیت **personal** (pĕ*-so-nĕl) *adj.* private ذاتی ، نجی of an individual and not a group انفرادی ، ذاتی of or done by a person himself or herself ذاتی ، اپنا (of remarks) not general but directed against (etc.) a particular person ذاتی *no personal attacks* ذاتی حملے نہ کیجیے **personally** *adv.* oneself اصالتاً ، بذات خود speaking for myself ذاتی طور پر میں یہ کہہ سکتا ہوں ، اپنی طرف سے تو کہہ سکتا ہوں ، جہاں تک میری ذات کا تعلق ہے میں کہہ سکتا ہوں as an individual فرد کی حیثیت سے **personate** (*pè**-so-nayt) *v.t.* play on the stage the part of کا کردار ادا کرنا impersonate تلبیس کرنا ، کا بھروپ بھرنا **personator** (-*nay*-) *n.* one who personates بہروپیا **personality** (-*nal*-) *n.* person's being وجود personal charm and quality of character شخصیت *a strong personality* زوردار شخصیت *with little personality* بے حقیقت شخص **personalities** (pe*-sè-*nal*-i-teez) *n. pl.* personal remarks ذاتیات **personalty** *n.* personal property ذاتی ملکیت **personify** (-*son*-) *v.t.* represent (some quality) as a مجسم بنا کر پیش کرنا be an example of (a quality) کا مُجَسَّمہ ہونا **personification** (-*son*-) *n.* personifying تجسیم، تمثل personified form (*of*) کا مجسّمہ **personnel** (pě*-so-*nĕl*) *n.* staff (*of* a service, etc., as opposed to its equipment, etc.) (عملہ، عَمَلہ، دستے) کارکُن

perspective (pě*-*spek*-tiv) *n.* method of drawing which gives the right impression of distances, etc. مُصَوّری میں فاصلے کا ظاہری تناسُب، تناظُر relation to environment ماحول سے تعلّق، پس منظر see (*some problem, etc.*) *in the right perspective* (کسی مسئلے کو اس کے صحیح پس منظر میں دیکھنا

an example of perspective

perspicacious (pě*s-pi-*kay*-shus) *adj.* having insight زکی، بصیرت مند **perspicacity** (-*kas*-) *n.* insight بصیرت، فراست

perspicuous (pè*-*spik*-ew-us) *adj.* lucid واضح **perspicuity** *n.* lucidity وضاحت

perspire (pè*-*spī*-è*) *v.i.* sweat کو پسینہ آنا **perspiration** *n.* sweat پسینہ

persuade (pě*-*swayd*) *v.t.* win over (someone *to do* something) قائل کرنا منوا لینا convince *be persuaded*, believe کو یقین آنا، کا خیال ہونا **persuasion** (pè*-*sway*-zhèn) *n.* persuading or being persuaded ترغیب sect مذہبی فرقہ religious belief عقیدہ، ایمان conviction یقین **persuasive** (-*ay*-siv) *adj.* winning دوستی کے اثر یا محبت سے منوا لینے والا convincing قابلِ یقین، ماننے کی بات، پیار سے منوا لینے والا

pert (pě*t) *adj.* forward, saucy (girl) شوخ impudent (child, etc.) گستاخ، ہر ایک کے منہ آنے والا bold and disrespectful (answer, etc.) دریدہ دہنی والا، گستاخانہ

pertain (pè*-*tayn*) *v.i.* belong (*to* something as a part) relate (*to* something) متعلّق ہونا، کا جُزو ہونا (also see **pertinent**)

pertinacious (pě*-ti-*nay*-shus) *adj.* sticking to, persistent in what has been begun اپنی بات پوری کیے بغیر نہ چھوڑنے والا، ثابت قدم، مستقل مزاج **pertinacity** (pě*-ti-*nas*-i-ti) *n.* being pertinacious بات پوری کیے بغیر نہ چھوڑنا، مستقل مزاجی، ثابت قدمی، اِستقلال

pertinent (*pě*t*-i-nent) *adj* relevant or pertaining (*to* the issue) متعلّقہ appropriate برمحل (also see **pertain**)

perturb (pè*-*tè*b*) *v.t.* disturb mentally; make worried گھبرا دینا، پریشان کرنا **perturbation** *n.* mental agitation پریشانی، اَبتری

peruse (pe-*rooz*) *v.t.* read through (something) carefully بغور پڑھنا **perusal** *n.* act of perusing مطالعہ

pervade (pe*-*vayd*) *v.t.* permeate میں سرایت کرنا spread through میں پھیل جانا میں رچ بس جانا

pervasive (-*vay*-) *adj.* (of influence, ideas, etc.) tending to pervade ساری ہونے والا، پھیلنے والا نفوذ کرنے والا، نفاذ

perverse (pè*ve*s) *adj.* determined to do wrong برائی پر تُلا ہوا، بے راہ رو، کج رو contrary to established moral values غیر اخلاقی، اخلاق سوز (of circumstances) contrary (*to* one's wishes)، نامساعد معاندانہ **pervert** *v.t.* (pè*-*vè*t*) *v.t.* put (something) to an improper use کا غلط یا بے جا استعمال کرنا lead (someone or someone's mind) into evil way غلط راستے پر ڈالنا، بُری راہ پر لگانا *n.* (*pě**-vě*t) such a misled person بے راہ رو **perversion** (pě*-vě*-shèn) **perversity** (pě*-ve*-si-ti) *n.* being perverse بے راہ روی، کج روی، اوندھی کھوپڑی کا ہونا، بے جا استعمال

pesky (*pes*-ki) *adj.* (U.S. colloq.) troublesome, annoying تکلیف دہ

pessimism (*pes*-i-mizm) *n.* tendency to look at the dark side of things یاس، قنوطیت **pessimist** *n.* person with this tendency; dark prophet قنوطی **pessimistic** *adj.* قنوطیانہ، (قنوطی (انداز **pessimistically** *adv.* in a pessimistic manner قنوطیت سے

pest *n.* destructive thing, animal, etc. تلف کرنے والی چیز، تباہ کن کیڑے مکوڑے وغیرہ (old use) *epidemic وبا person who is a nuisance (کسی کے لیے) مصیبت، عذاب، آفت بلا، بلائے بے درماں شخص، تنگ کر دینے والا شخص

pestilence (*pes*-ti-lens) *n.* plague, deadly epidemic مہلک وبا **pestilent** *adj.* fatal مہلک morally or politically harmful (اخلاقی یا سیاسی (وغیرہ طور پر ضرر رساں

pestology (-tol-) *n.* study of pests تباہ کن کیڑوں مکوڑوں کے متعلّق تحقیقات

pester (*pes*-tě*) *v.t.* annoy (*with* requests, questions, etc.) دق کرنا، تنگ کر دینا، ناک میں دم کر لینا **pestering** *adj.* annoying تنگ کر دینے والا، ناک میں دم کر دینے والا

pestilence *n.* (see under **pest**)

pestle (*pes*-èl) *n.* small rod-like thing for grinding substances in a mortar دستہ، موگری **mortar and pestle** ہاون دستہ *v.t.* grind with it دستے سے پیسنا

a pestle in a mortar

pestology *n.* (see under **pest**)

pet *n.* tame animal kept as a favourite پالتو جانور favourite child لاڈلا بچّہ beloved person چہیتا شخص fit of peevishness over trifles خواہ مخواہ کی جھلاہٹ *go off in a pet* بے خواہ مخواہ گرم ہو جانا، جھنجھلا اٹھنا *adj.* favourite (child, dog, etc.) لاڈلا، چہیتا، دل پسند favourite (subject, etc.) چہیتا *v.t.* fondle and indulge کو بہت لاڈ پیار کرنا **pettish**

adj. peevish چڑچڑا

petal (*pet*-èl) *n*. one of the leaf-like parts of a flower پتی ، برگ **petalled** (*pet*-ĕld) *adj*. having petals پتیوں والا

petard (pe-*tah*d*) *n*. a mediaeval engine of war بارود بھری پٹاری ، ایک پرانا جنگی ہتھیار *hoist with* (*his*) *own petard*, caught in (his) own trap وہ آپ اپنے دام میں صیاد آ گیا

peter (*pee*-tè*) *v.i*. fizzle (*out*) خود بخود ناکام ہو جانا *n*. (*Peter*) one of two major teachers of Christianity the other being *Paul* پطرس (پولُس) *rob Peter to pay Paul*, take away from (an equally dignified) person to give to another ایک کو دینے کے لیے دوسرے کو لوٹنا

petite (pe-*teet*) *adj*. (of a woman) of small stature چھوٹے قد کی ، پست قامت

petition (pe-*tish*-ĕn) *n*. supplication دعا written request (*to* sovereign, assembly or law-court) عرضی، عرضداشت پیش کرنا (قانونی) عرضی دعوے (یا نالش) *v.t*. make a petition to (someone *for* something) کے حضور میں عرضداشت پیش کرنا

petrel (*pet*-rel) *n*. (also *stormy-petrel*), small species of sea-bird associated with storms پطریل

a stormy-petrel

petrify (*pet*-ri-fı) *v.t*. & *i*. change into stone پتھر کر دینا، یا ہو جانا ، تحجر stupefy (through) fear, surprise, etc.) ہاتھ پاؤں پھول جانا، ساکت و صامت کر دینا، ششدر کر دینا **petrifaction** (-*fak*-) *n*. act of petrifying or being petrified پتھر کر دینا یا ہو جانا **petrology** (-*rol*-) *n*. study of origin, structure and composition of rocks حجریات

petrol (*pet*-rĕl) *n*. gasolene پٹرول *petrol pump*, place for refuelling motor-vehicles پٹرول پمپ **petroleum** (pet-*roh*-li-um) *n*. mineral oil from which petrol and kerosene oil are obtained نفت ، نفط

petticoat (*pet*-i-koht) *n*. woman's underskirt پیٹی کوٹ *the petticoat, petticoats*, (*a*) women عورت ، عورتیں (*b*) their influence on society معاشرے پر عورت کا اثر *the petticoat government*, predominance of wife in a home, etc. عورت کی حکومت

pettifogging (*pet*-i-fog-ing) *adj*. quibbling خواہ مخواہ مین میخ نکالنے والا worrying over trifling matters خواہ مخواہ پریشان ہونے والا mean کمینہ ، کم ظرف trifling (matter) معمولی سا

petty (*pet*-i) *adj*. trivial, unimportant (thing) معمولی mean, narrow-minded (person, etc.) کمینہ ، کم ظرف small چھوٹا *petty cash*, from small payments چھوٹی چھوٹی رقمیں *petty officer*, non-commissioned officer in the Navy بحریہ کا عہدے دار

petulant (*pet*-ew-lant) *adj*. peevish چڑچڑا ، تنگ مزاج

petulance (*pet*-ew-lans) *n*. peevishness چڑچڑاپن ، تنک مزاجی

pew *n*. church bench گرجے کی بنچ *family pew*, one reserved for a family کنبے کی بنچ *pew-rent*, rent paid for it گرجے کی بنچ کا کرایہ

pewit (*pee*-wit), **peewit** (*pee*-wit) *n*. a bird named after its cry سمندری کوا

pewter (*pew*-tĕ*) *n*. a zinc like metal جست ، رانگ vessel made of it جستی برتن ، رانگ کا برتن

Phaedra (*feed*-ra) *Cl. myth*. daughter of king Minos of Crete and wife of king Theseus of Greece who committed suicide as she had fallen in love with her step-son *Hippolytus*; (incidentally Hippolytus met his death when the sea-god Poseidon in response to Theseus' prayer sent a sea-monster which frightened his horses and they drove him to death) فیدرہ

Phaethon (*fay*-e-thon) *Cl. myth*. a son of the sun-god Helios whose chariot he once rode so recklessly as to upset it, with the result that Zeus had to hurl him into a river with his thunderbolt فیتن **phaeton** (*fay*-e-ton) *n*. light four-wheeled carriage named after him

phalanx (*fal*-anks) *n*. military formation of Alexander's army comprising heavily armed foot soldiers fighting in close rank فوج کا مربع پرا

phallus (*fal*-us) *n*. image of the male organ as used in the rites of certain religions شولنگ ، لنگ

phantom (fant-um), **phantasm** (*fant*-azm) *n*. ghost بھوت ، پریت illusion وہمی صورت ، وہم کی پیداوار ، وہم

Pharaoh (*fay*-roh) *n*. title of ancient kings of Egypt فرعون

Pharisee (*fa*-ri-see) *n*. member of one of Jewish sect فریسی narrow-minded formalist تنگ نظر ظاہر پرست ، زاہد تنگ نظر hypocrite منافق ، ریاکار **pharisaic, pharisaical** (fa-ri-*say*-) *adj*. منافقانہ ، ریاکارانہ

pharmaceutics *n*., **pharmaceutical** *adj*., **pharmacology** *n*., **pharmacopoeia** *n*. (see under **pharmacy**)

pharmacy (*fah*m*-a-si) *n*. (also *pharmaceutics*, pr. -*sew*- or -*kew*-) art of preparing medicines دوا سازی ، عطاری a drug store دواؤں کی دکان ، عطار خانہ ، عطار کی دکان **pharmaceutical** (-*sew*-) pertaining

to pharmaceutics دواسازی سے متعلق، عطاری **pharmacology** (-*kol*-o-ji) *n.* science of pharmacy علم دواسازی **pharmacopoeia** (fa*m-a-koh-*pee*-a) *n.* book of drugs with directions for preparing them قرابادین stock of drugs ذخیرہ ادویہ
phase (fayz) *n.* stage in the development (*of*) دور *phases of the moon*, its aspects, *i.e.*, the different amounts of its bright surface visible from the earth on various nights چاند کی شکلیں، اشکالِ قمر
pheasant (*fez*-ent) *n.* a well-known game-bird چکور، دُرّاج

a pheasant

phenomenal *adj.* (see under **phenomenon**)
phenomenon (fe-*nom*-e-non) *n.* (*pl.*, *phenomena*) that which is perceived مظہر (جمع مظاہر) uncommon or remarkable happening عجیب و غریب واقعہ **phenomenal** *adj.* of phenomena مظہری exceptional (success, etc.) غیر معمولی
phew (few) *int.* (expressive of disgust) ! ہونہہ
phial (*f* ı-al) *n.* small bottle for medicine چھوٹی شیشی
-phil (fil), **-philo** (fil-o) *suf*; **phil-** (fil) *pref.* lover of پسند، محبّ
philander (fi-*land*-ĕ*) *v.i.* amuse oneself with love-making عشق بازی کرنا، عاشق باز ہونا **philanderer** (-*land*-) *n.* such a person عشق باز
philanthropic *adj.*, **philanthropist** *n.* (see under **philanthropy**)
philanthropy (fi-*lanth*-ro-pi) *n.* love of humanity بشر دوستی، انسان دوستی doing good to one's fellowmen by financing large-scale projects for them غریبوں کی امداد اپنے خرچ پر معاشرتی بہبود کا کام کرنا charitableness **philanthropist** *n.* بشر دوست، غریب نوازی، ہمدردی اپنے خرچ پر معاشرتی بہبود کے کام کرنے والا، غریب نواز **philanthropic** (-*throp*-) *adj.* for the public good عوام کی بھلائی کا *philanthropic institution* خیراتی ادارہ، عوام کی بھلائی کا ادارہ
philatelist *n.* (see under **philately**)
philately (fi-*lat*-e-li) *n.* collecting of postage-stamps (as a hobby, etc.) ڈاک کے ٹکٹ جمع کرنا ٹکٹ فراہمی **philatelist** *n.* one fond of philately ڈاک کے ٹکٹ جمع کرنے والا، ٹکٹ فراہم کرنے والا
philistine (*fil*-is-teen) *n.* one of an old anti-Jewish Palestinian race فلسطینی uncultured and unimaginative person شخص ناشائستہ، ناتراشیدہ *adj.* uncultured ناشائستہ prosaic بے ذوق، بے کیف
philological *adj.*, **philologist** *n.* (see under **philology**)

philology (fi-*lol*-o-ji) *n.* study of the nature and growth of a language (or languages) لسانیات **philologist** *n.* ماہرِ لسانیات **philological** *adj.* pertaining to philology لسانیاتی
philomela (fil-o-*mee*-la) *Cl. myth.* sister of *Procne* (which see) whose tongue Procne's husband cut off in order to render her unable to complain of the criminal assault he had made on her; she was metamorphosed and became a nightingale فِلومیلہ (also *Philomel*), (poet.) nightingale بُلبُل، عندلیب، ہزار داستان
philosopher *n.*, **philosophic, philosophical** *adj.*, **philosophize** *v.t.* (see under **philosophy**)
philosophy (fi-*los*-o-fi) *n.* love of wisdom and research into the ultimate causes of physical phenomena and the nature of metaphysical truths فلسفہ system of theories based on this pursuit مسلک فکر، نظامِ فلسفہ self-control expected of a philosopher اطمینانِ قلب، سکون resignation توکّل
philosopher (fi-*los*-o-fĕ*) *n.* one with a system of philosophy فلسفی، حکیم one unperturbed by fear or passions سکونِ قلب والا، مطمئن **philosophic, philosophical** (-*sof*-) *adj.* (like that) of philosophers; of philosophy; hence having self-control فلسفیانہ، مطمئن **philosophize** (-fiz) *v.t.* talk wisely about a matter with plausible explanatory theories پر فلسفہ آرائی کرنا
phlegm (flem) *n.* slimy substance forming in the throat and chest بلغم، ریشہ *cough up phlegm* ریشہ نکالنا، بلغم تھوکنا calmness; immunity to emotions ٹھنڈے دل کا ہونا **phlegmatic** (fle-*mat*-ik) *adj.* calm; immune to emotions ٹھنڈے دل و دماغ کا (old use) having phlegm as the prevalent humour بلغمی
-phobe (fohb) *suf.* fearing and opposing سے خائف اور کا مخالف، دشمن as *Communistphobe* انگریز دشمن **-phobia** (*foh*-bi-a) *suf.* fear of and opposition to خوف اور مخالف دشمنی *Communistphobia* اشتمالیت دشمنی
Phoebe (*fee*-bee) *Cl. myth.* the Greek goddess of moon (same as *Diana* or *Artemis*) فیبی the moon چاند، ماہتاب، قمر **Phoebus** (*fee*-bus) *Cl. myth.* the Greek sun-god (same as *Apollo*) فیبس the sun سورج، مہر، آفتاب، شمس
phoenix (*fee*-niks) *n.* mythical bird said to live 500 years and then burn itself to ashes on a pyre to rise anew for another term of life سیمرغ، ققنس
phone (fohn) *n.*, *v. t.* & *i.* (abb. of) telephone ٹیلیفون (کرنا)
phonetic (fo-*net*-ik) *adj.* ❶ pertaining to the vocal sounds آواز سے متعلق، صوتی ❷ representing

every basic sound by a distinct letter صَوتی زَبان (یا ہجے) **phonetics** *n.* (pl. used with a sing. verb) study of the sounds and symbols of speech صَوتیات **phonetically** *adv.* according to the principles of phonetics صَوتی اُصُول **phonetician** (*-tish*-ĕn) *n.* expert in phonetics ماہرِ صَوتیات

phonograph (*fohn*-o-graf) *n.* (old or U. S. name for) gramophone گراموفون

phoney, phony (*foh*-ni) (U.S.) (slang) sham نقلی worthless بے کار ، ناکارہ

phosphate *n.*, **phosphorescent,** *adj.* **phosphorescence** *n.* **phosphite** *n.* (see under **phosphorus**)

phosphorus (*fos*-fo-rus) *n.* a non-metallic element shining in the dark فاسفورس (Phosphorus), the Greek name of the morning star, Lucifer ستارۂ صبح **phosphate** *n.* any of the phosphorus salts فاسفیٹ **phosphite** *n.* another type of phosphorus salts فاسفائٹ **phosphorescent** (*-res*-ent) *adj.* faintly shining in the dark ضَوفگن، ضَوآفگن، ضیا پاش **phosphorescence** (*-res*-ens) *n.* being phosphorescent ضیا پاشی ، ضَوافگنی

photo (*foh*-toh) *n.* (pl. *photos*) photograph عکسی تصویر فوٹو ، عکس **photograph** (*foh*-to-grahf) *n.* picture taken with a camera on a sensitized plate or film ; photo عکسی تصویر، فوٹو، عکس *v. i.* take a photograph of کا فوٹو اُتارنا ، کا عکس اُتارنا **photographer** (fo-*tog*-ra-fĕ*) *n.* one who photographs as a profession فوٹوگرافر، عکاس **photography** (fo-*tog*-ra-fi) *n.* taking of photographs عکاسی، فوٹوگرافی **photographic** (*-graf-*) *adj.* عکاسی کا **photographically** (*-graf-*) *adv.* by way of photography عکاسی کے ذریعے (یا) طور پر **photogenic** (*-jen-*) *adj.* suitable for being photographed فوٹو کے قابل **photogravure** (*-vew*-ĕ*) (picture got by) etching on metal, the product of photography عکسی کندہ کاری (کی تصویر)

photo-finish *n.* (in a race) one so close as to determine the winner from a photograph بے حد فرق والی (دوڑ) بہت ہی قریب کی (دوڑ)

phrase (frayz) *n.* part of a sentence without a finite verb جُز و جملہ ، مُرکّبِ ناقص *v. t.* couch in words لفظوں میں ادا کرنا **phraseology** (*-ol*-o-ji) *n.* wording (*of*) (کے) الفاظ

phthisis (*thī*-sis) *n.* pulmonary tuberculosis پھیپھڑوں کی دِق ، سِل

physical (*fiz*-i-kĕl) *adj.* material مادی of the body جسمانی *physical exercise* وَرزِشِ جسمانی *physical beauty* جسمانی خوبصورتی ، حُسن of the earth زمین کا ، ارضی ، طبیعی *physical geography*, branch of geography studying the structure of the earth طبیعی جغرافیہ of physics طبیعیاتی *a physical impossibility*, not possible in this world قطعاً ناممکن ، ممکن ہی نہیں **physically** *adv.* with the material body ; in flesh and blood جسمانی طور پر

physician (fi-*zish*-ĕn) *n.* doctor of medicine ڈاکٹر ، طبیب (popular) one with a higher position than an ordinary practitioner بڑا ڈاکٹر ، ماہر طبیب

physics (*fiz*-iks) *n.* (pl. used with a sing. verb) science (or group of sciences) studying the properties, etc., of matter and energy طبیعیات **physicist** (*fiz*-i-sist) *n.* expert in physics ماہرِ طبیعیات

physiognomy (fiz-i-*og*-no-mi) *n.* face چہرہ مُہرہ art of judging character from it قیافہ شناسی physical features (*of* an area) طبیعی شکل **physiognomist** *n.* expert in reading someone's character from his face قیافہ شناس

physiology (fiz-i-*ol*-o-ji) *n.* science studying the working of organisms عضویات ، علمِ افعالِ اعضا ، علمِ اعضا **physiological** (*-loj-*) *adj.* عضویاتی **physiologist** (*-ol-*) *n.* expert in physiology ماہرِ عضویات

physique (fi-*zeek*) *n.* bodily structure جسم کی ساخت ، جسم *of strong physique* مضبوط جسم کا

physiotherapy *n.* electrical treatment بجلی سے علاج

pi (pɪ) *n.* Greek letter representing ratio of a circle's circumference to its diameter (=²²⁄₇) π (پائی) (school slang) pious نیک ، پارسا *pi jaw*, moral talk اخلاقی وَعظ

piano (pee-*an*-oh), **pianoforte** (-foh*t) *n.* a stringed musical instrument with a key-board somewhat like that of a harmonium پیانو **pianist** (*pee*-a-nist) *n.* one who plays a piano پیانو نواز

picador (*pik*-a-do*) *n.* mounted man with lance in bull-fight بلم سوار

picaresque (pik-a-*resk*) *adj.* (of fiction) pertaining to the lives and activities of picaroons or rogues غنڈوں سے متعلق ، بدمعاشوں سے متعلق **picaroon** (-roon) *n.* rogue غنڈا ، بدمعاش pirate سمندری لٹیرا

pice (pɪs) *n.* well-known Pakistani coin پیسہ

picayune (pi-kay-*yoon*) (U. S.) small coin پیسہ ، دَمڑی insignificant person or thing ناقابلِ ذکر شخص یا شے *adj.* mean, contemptible کمینہ ، قابلِ نفرت

pickaninny (*-nin*-i) *n.* negro child حبشی بچہ

pick (pik) *n.* (also *pick-axe*) a tool with a double-point iron crossbar on a wooden handle for breaking hard ground کدال ، بیل any small picking instrument دانتوں کا خلال ، سُوئی وغیرہ *toothpick* خلال *ice-pick*, short instrument for breaking up ice برف توڑنے کا سُوا ، سُوا choice پسند take one's pick اپنی پسند کی چیز لے لیجیے ! best (*of* the *bunch* etc.) میں سے بہترین *v.t.* & *i.* choose چُننا pluck (flowers or fruit) توڑنا gather (them) اِکٹھے کرنا get the meat off (a bone) سے گوشت اُتارنا clean (a fowl of feathers) (مذبوحہ مرغ کے پَر) اُتارنا separate with the fingers نوچنا tear (something *to pieces*) پارہ پارہ کر ڈالنا *pick up*, find, come by پانا *pick pockets* (or *someone's pocket*) کی جیب کاٹنا، جیب تراشی کرنا *pick a quarrel (with)* سے جھگڑا کرنا *pick up spirits* بے ہمتی ختم کرنا *pick (oneself) up* پھر سے اپنے پاؤں پر کھڑے ہونا *pick and choose*, select carefully بڑی احتیاط سے چُننا *pick one's way* (or *steps*) *along a muddy road* کیچڑ والی سڑک پر پھونک پھونک کر قدم رکھنا یا دھرنا *pick something out*, (a) distinguish it پہچان لینا (b) chose it from among others میں سے چُن لینا *pick a lock*, open it without the key تار وغیرہ کی مدد سے تالا کھولنا *pick up* اُٹھا کر کھڑے کرنا *pick up information* کہیں سے سُن گُن پا لینا *pick up acquaintance with* سے واقفیت پیدا کرنا *pick (someone) up from* کسی کو (گاڑی وغیرہ) پر سے لے جانا *pick holes in (something)* میں کیڑے ڈالنا، پر حرف گیری کرنا **pick-a-back** *adv.* (carrying a child) on one's back (بچے کو) پیٹھ پر (اُٹھانا) **pick-me-up** *n.* anything refreshing مُفرّح **pick-pocket** *n.* one who picks pockets جیب تراش **pick-up** *n.* apparatus for replacing gramophone sound-box with the loudspeaker گراموفون کو لاؤڈ سپیکر سے جوڑنے کا آلہ

picket (*pik*-et) *n.* a pointed upright stake of a fence جنگلے کا ڈنڈا party sent to watch the enemy or guard a place پکٹ (in a strike) one of the workers trying to stop blacklegs پکٹ *v. t.* put pickets round کے گرد ڈنڈوں کا جنگلا لگانا fasten (horse, etc.) to a picket میخ کے ساتھ باندھنا (in a strike) place a picket پکٹنگ کا حکم دینا be a picket پکٹنگ پر لگنا

pickle (*pik*-ĕl) *n.* (often *pl.*) salted vegetables, etc., preserved in vinegar, etc اچار *(be) in a pickle*, be in a fix مصیبت کے منہ میں آیا ہوا (ہونا) *v. t.* preserve thus کا اچار ڈالنا

picnic (*pik*-nik) *n.* pleasure trip with outdoor meal مشترکہ سیر اور کھانا، گوٹ (colloq.) something agreeable پسندیدہ شے (colloq.) something easily accomplished آسان بات، آسانی سے ہو جانے والی بات *v. t.* go on a picnic گوٹ کرنا

pictorial (pik-*toh*-ri-al) *adj.* of pictures تصویر سے متعلق illustrated باتصویر، مصوّر

picture (*pik*-che*) *n.* painting, drawing, photograph, etc تصویر (usu. *pl.*) (*the pictures*), cinema film سینما، فلم، پکچر pretty person, scene, etc. خوبصورت شخص (یا) خوشنما منظر *be a picture of (a quality)*, personify it کا مجسمہ ہونا *v. t.* make a picture of کی تصویر کھینچنا imagine کا تصوّر کرنا express in words کی لفظوں میں تصویر کھینچنا **picturesque** (pik-che-*resk*) *adj.* charming, colourful (person, view, etc.) دلکش، جاذبِ نظر

pidgin (*pij*-in) *n.* (colloq.) (one's) job or business کام، نوکری (وغیرہ) **pidgin English** (*pij*-) broken English used by the ordinary Chinese to communicate with Englishmen چینی انگریزی

pie (pī) *n.* baked paste covering meat or fruit ٹکیہ، شامی کباب Pakistani coin worth one-twelfth of an anna پائی

piebald (*pī*-bawld) *adj.* (of a horse) with patches of two colours (usu. white and black) چتکبرا، چیتلا

piece (pees) *n.* bit or part (*of*) کا ٹکڑا *be in pieces* ٹوٹا ہوا ہونا *come to pieces* ٹوٹنا *break to pieces* توڑنا *take to pieces* پرزہ پرزہ کھولنا single item (عموماً اردو میں کوئی ترجمہ نہیں آتا) مَد، آئیٹم، ٹکڑا، نمونہ، چیز، بات، خبر *a piece of news* ... *a piece of advice* نصیحت کی بات *a piece of poetry*, poem نظم *a piece of art* فنکاری کا نمونہ *a piece of music* نغمہ single object out of a set (ایک ساتھ جانے والی چیزوں میں سے ایک) چیز *tea-set of 15 pieces* پندرہ چیزوں والا سیٹ any one of the objects with which to play chess on the board مُہرہ coin سکہ unit (*of* cloth, etc.) تھان *sold only by the piece* صرف تھان کے حساب سے بکتا ہے *v. t.* assemble (*together*) parts of a machine, etc. جوڑنا *piece out* (*the story, etc.*) connect the divers parts to make it one plausible whole (کہانی وغیرہ) کی تمام کڑیاں جوڑنا **piecemeal** *adv.* bit by bit بتدریج، تھوڑا تھوڑا کر کے **piecework** *n.* work paid for by output and not by time ٹھیکے کا کام **piece-goods** *n.* textiles in standard (or nowadays big) lengths تھان، کپڑا **piece de resistance** (pi-es-de-re-zees-tons) *n.* chief item among many بڑی چیز، اصل بات : main dish of a meal پکانے میں اصلی (یا بڑی) چیز

pied (pɪd) *adj.* multicoloured چتر رنگا with pied clothes چتر رنگی گدڑی والا، رخرقہ پوش

pier (*pee*-è*) *n.* landing-stage built out into the sea گودی pillar of a bridge پل کا پایہ (یا) ستون pillar-like brick-work between openings دو دروازوں کے درمیان لگی ہوئی اینٹیں، ستون، پیل پایہ

pierce (*pee*-è*s) *v. t.* run through چیرنا *have (one's) ears pierced* کان چھدوانا force one's way (*through*) کو چیر کر نکل جانا affect deeply بہت اثر کرنا

S To **pierce** is to enter by means of a sharp instrument ; to **prick**, cause a sensation of pain by means of a sharp instrument ; to **penetrate** deeply and with effort ; to **perforate** right through; generally with a series of holes ; to **puncture** something containing compressed air ; to **punch**, make a single hole by means of a special cutting device ; to **gore** someone as by a bull's horns ; to **stab** someone with a sharp instrument usu. with intention to hurt ; to **drill** with a rotating cutting tool ; to **bore,** make a cylindrical hole by a series of cutting operations.

piety *n.* (see under **pious**)

piffle (*pif*-èl) (slang) *n.* worthless talk ; nonsense بکواس *v. i.* talk piffle بکواس کرنا

pig *n.* swine خنزیر، سؤر *buy a pig in a poke* ٹھونک بجا کر دیکھے بغیر کوئی چیز لے لینا، یونہی خرید لینا *pig in a poke,* blind bargain اندھا دھند سودا، ان دیکھا سودا person like a swine in dirt, greed or perversity گندا، لالچی، بدمعاش oblong mass of smelted metal ڈھلی ہوئی دھات کا ٹکڑا **pig-eyed** *adj.* having small dull eyes with heavy lids چھوٹی سی بے نور آنکھوں والا **pig-headed** *adj.* obstinate ضدی **piggery** (*pig*-è-ri), **pigsty** (*pig*-sti) *n.* place for pigs خنزیر خانہ dirty place گندی جگہ **piggish** *adj.* dirty گندا greedy لالچی **pigtail** *n.* plait of hair running down from the head to the back چوٹی، چٹیا **pig-iron** *n.* iron in pigs دیگ کا لوہا، دیگی لوہا

pigeon (*pij*-un) *n.* a cooing bird of the dove family کبوتر **pigeon-hole** *n.* resting place for a pigeon کابک one of the small divisions in a shelf, etc., for putting papers, etc. in خانہ *v. t.* sheive الگ رکھ کر نظر انداز کر دینا، گلدستہ طاق نسیاں بنا دینا

pigeon-toed *adj.* having the toes turned inward جس کے پاؤں کی انگلیاں اندر کو مڑی ہوئی ہوں

pigment (*pig*-ment) *n.* colouring matter (*in the skin, etc., or for making paint, etc.*) رنگ

pigmy *n.* (same as **pygmy,** which see)

pike (pīk) *n.* kind of spear formerly used by infantry soldiers برچھی، بلم، نیزہ **piker** (*pī*-kē*) *n.* (U. S.) (colloq.) poor sport برا کھلاڑی، اناڑی timid gambler بزدل جواری، بے ہمت جواری

pile (pīl) *n.* heap ڈھیر *make a pile,* earn and save a lot ڈھیروں روپیہ کمانا اور جمع کرنا huge building بڑی عمارت large wooden beam driven into river-bed as a foundation for bridge پل کے ستون کی بنیاد کا شہتیر soft wool, etc. (on young sheep, etc.) پشم nap (of velvet, carpet, etc.) روئیں (*pl.*) (disease causing) tumours on the lower end of the bowels بواسیر کے مسّے (also *atomic pile*), apparatus containing uranium, etc., for studying atomic energy and putting it to use تابکار دان *v. t.* put (things *up*) in a pile کا ڈھیر لگانا

pilfer (*pil*-fē*) *v. t. & i.* steal (something) of small value چھوٹی چوری کرنا **pilferage** (*pil*-fe-rij), **pilfering** *n.* petty theft چھوٹی چوری

pilgrim (*pil*-grim) *n.* person journeying (*to a* sacred place) زائر، حاجی *pilgrim fathers,* the earliest European settlers in America who went there to escape religious persecution اوّلین امریکی آبادکار

pilgrimage (*pil*-gri-mej) *n.* pilgrim's journey زیارت، حج

pill (pil) *n.* tiny ball of medicine گولی، حب *swallow the bitter pill,* put up with the insult or undesirable thing زہر کا گھونٹ پی کر خاموش ہو رہنا، زہر کا گھونٹ پی کر رہ جانا **pill-box** *n.* (same as **pillar-box,** which see) small round box for pills, etc. ڈبیہ machine-gun post under a concrete dome مشین گن کا پختہ اڈا

pill-box for pills (sense 2)

pillage (*pil*-ej) *n.* plunder لوٹ مار *v. t. & i.* plunder لوٹ مار کرنا

pillar (*pil*-ē*) *n.* column ستون *a pillar of, the pillar of strength to,* the mainstay of کا ستون (*a*) *driven from pillar to post,* at a loss what to do حیران، سراسیمہ (*b*) driven away from one place to another دھکے کھاتا پھرنے والا

pillar-box *n.* (usu. called *pill-box*) strange looking box in the street-corner in which to post letters لیٹر بکس

pillar-box or pill-box

pillion (pil-yèn) *n.* extra back seat on a motor-cycle or horse فالتو گدی، گھوڑے وغیرہ پر سوار کے پچھلی گدی *ride pillion* پیچھے بیٹھنا **pilloried** *adj.* (see under **pillory**)

woman rides pillion

pillory (*pil*-o-ri) *n.* frame for holding fast the head and hands of criminals as a punishment to them تعزیری شکنجہ، کاٹھ *v. t.* punish thus تعزیری شکنجے میں کسنا، کاٹھ مارنا expose (someone or his faults) to disgrace رسوا کرنا hold (him) to ridicule کا مذاق اڑانا **pilloried** (*pil*-o-rid) *adj.* in the pillory تعزیری شکنجے میں کسا ہوا، رسوا کیا ہوا، جس کا مذاق اڑایا گیا ہو

a pilloried person

pillow (*pil*-oh) *n.* cushion for the head تکیہ **pillow-case, pillow-ship** *n.* pillow cover تکیے کا غلاف، غلافِ تکیہ، غلاف

pilot (*pī*-lot) *n.* one who flies an aircraft ہواباز، طیارچی one who conducts a ship in or out of a port جہاز کا رہنما steersman جہازران any guide رہنما، رہبر *pilot balloon,* small balloon used for finding out the direction and velocity of wind at various heights ہوا پیما غبارہ *pilot engine*, railway engine going ahead of another to clear the track پیشرو انجن *pilot scheme*, small-scale trial of a project for experimentation رہبر منصوبہ *v. t.* be pilot to کو چلانا ، کی رہنمائی کرنا

pimple (*pim*-pel) *n.* small inflammation on youthful skin مہاسا ، کیل

pin *n.* short pointed piece of wire with a small protuberance at the other end پن *not to care a pin* (*for*), not to care at all for کی پروا نہ کرنا *have pins and needles*, have a tingling sensation in a part of the body (جسم کے کسی حصے کا) سو جانا any piece of wire, etc., used for fastening پن *hairpin* بالوں میں لگانے کا پن ، بال پن *safety pin*, an almost rectangular pin whose sharp end can be opened and secured سیفٹی پن ، محفوظ پن jewel set on a safety pin پن (also *rolling-pin*), small roller for pastry بیلن peg میخ ، کھونٹی *v. t.* (-nn-) attach with a pin (*on*) پن سے لگانا *pin* (*someone*) *down* (or *to wall, etc.*), take him by the throat and press him or pierce him with a sword thus to render him unable to move (کے ساتھ) یا (کے تلے) دبا دینا ، کو ختم کر دینا *pin* (*someone*) *down to* (*promise, etc.*) کسی سے پکا وعدہ کرا لینا یا قول لے لینا *pin* (*one's*) *hopes on* (*someone*) کسی سے تمام امیدیں وابستہ کیے ہوئے ہونا **pinafore** *n.* child's apron pinned on to his clothes بچے کے سینے پر لگایا ہوا فالتو کپڑا **pin-cushion** *n.* pad for sticking pins into پنوں کی گدی **pin-money** *n.* personal allowance to wife پاندان کا خرچ **pinpoint** *adj.* small target calling for precision in bombing بمباری کا چھوٹا سا ہدف *v. t.* bomb or locate such target چھوٹے ہدف پر بمباری کرنا یا چھوٹے ہدف کی نشاندہی کرنا **pin-prick** *n.* (esp.) annoying remark, etc., etc. چبھنے والی بات (یا حرکت)

a pinafore

pince-nez (*pans*-nay) *n.* pair of eye-glasses without sides and sticking at the nose with a spring بے کمانی عینک ، بینی گیر عینک

a pince-nez

pincers (*pin*-sěrz or *pinz*-) *n. pl.* gripping tool for pulling out nails, etc. زنبور ، منسی *pincer movement*, outflanking manoeuvre نرغہ

a pincers

pinch *v. t. & i.* squeeze (someone, etc.) painfully چٹکی لینا ، چٹکی بھرنا be nipped میں آ جانا cause pain تکلیف پہنچانا *be pinched for money* کو روپے کی تنگی ہونا (of a shoe) hurt (*the feet*) by being too tight کاٹنا (colloq.) take away without permission اڑا لینا *n.* pinching چٹکی quantity (*of* something) taken up between the thumb and finger چٹکی بھر *if it comes to the pinch*, if it is indispensable مجبوری کی بات ہے تو ، اگر اور کوئی چارہ کار نہیں تو

pine (pīn) *n.* a well-known evergreen tree bearing cones چیڑ ، صنوبر its wood چیڑ کی لکڑی *v. t.* intensely long (*for*) کی سخت آرزو ہونا languish (*with* or *away with* unrequited love, etc.) گھل گھل کر مر جانا *peak and pine*, pine away گھل گھل کر مرنا

pineapple (*pin*-ap-ěl) *n.* a sweet juicy fruit looking much like a cone from the outside اَنناس tree bearing it اَنناس (کا درخت)

a pineapple

pinfold (*pin*-fohld) *n.* pound for stray cattle کانجی ہوز ، کانجی ہاؤس

ping-pong (*ping*-pong) *n.* table tennis پنگ پانگ

pinion (*pin*-yun) *n.* wing of a bird پرندوں کے بازو ، پنکھ small cog-wheel fitting into a larger one چھوٹی چرخی *v. t.* bind (someone's arms) fast at the back کسی کے ہاتھ کس کر پیچھے باندھ دینا

pink *n. & adj.* pale red (colour) گلابی (رنگ) **pinkish, pinky** (*pink*-i) *adj.* of such colour ہلکا گلابی (رنگ) ، پیازی (رنگ) ، پیازی ، ہلکا گلابی

pinnacle (*pin*-a-kěl) *n.* slender turret on a roof کلس ، کنگرہ *at the pinnacle of* کے اوج پر

pint (pīnt) *n.* unit of liquid measure equivalent to one-eighth of a gallon پائنٹ

pioneer (pī-o-*nee*-ě*) *n.* one of the first settlers coming to develop a country وہلیں آبادکار beginner (*of* any enterprise) بانی one of the sappers and miners سفر مینا کا سپاہی *v. t. & i.* act as a pioneer کام کی بنیاد رکھنا ، شروع کرنا

pious (*pī*-us) *adj.* devoutly religious دیندار ، خدا ترس ، پارسا ، متقی (old use) dutiful (son) خدمت گزار بیٹا **piously** *adv.* پارسائی سے **piety** (*pī*-e-ti) *n.* being pious خدا ترسی ، پارسائی ، تقویٰ ، زہد و اتقا

pip *n.* seed (of apple, orange, etc.) سیب وغیرہ کا بیج short, high-pitched sound on radio as a time-signal ریڈیو کی پیں پیں ، پیں *four pips of the radio signal* ریڈیو کی چار بار کی قلاقتی پیں rank star in the army ستارا ، تارا each spot on dice, playing-cards, etc. نقطہ

pipe (pīp) *n.* big tube for water-supply نالی ، نل tube with narrow bowl for smoking پائپ flute بانسری *the pipes, bagpipes*, musical instruments with bag and pipes بیگ پائپ ، تھیلا بانسری

boatswain's whistle جہازراں کی سیٹی *v. t.* & *i.* convey (fluid) through pipes نالی میں سے پہنچانا play on a pipe بانسری بجانا ، نے نوازی کرنا whistle (crew) to get together (جہاز کے عملہ کو) سیٹی بجا کر جمع کرنا add a piping to کور (یا) مغزی یا سنجاف (see *Addenda*) **piper** (*pī*-pĕ*) *n.* one who plays on a pipe or bagpipes بانسری بجانے والا ، نے نواز *pay the piper*, have the right to control owing to the payment made by one اپنی مرضی سے کام لینے کا حق **piping** (*pī*-ping) *n.* total length *of* pipe for a purpose (راستی) لمبائی کی نالی narrow fold of cloth, etc., for decorating the edges کور ، مغزی ، سنجاف *adj.* very happy (times, etc.) خوشی کا *piping times* خوشی کے دن ، ایام مسرت shrill (voice) تیکھی (آواز) *adv.* (of something) hissing (*hot*) سوں سوں کرتا ہوا

piquant (*pee*-kĕnt) *adj.* pleasantly pungent چٹپٹا appetizing اشتہا انگیز ، مشتہی stimulating interest دلچسپ **piquancy** (*peek*-ens-i) *n.* being piquant *n.* چٹپٹاپن ، اشتہا انگیزی ، دلچسپی

pique (peek) *v.t.* wound the pride کے دل کو ٹھیس پہنچانا interest (someone *to do*) or arouse (someone's curiosity) (کسی کے) شوق کو بڑھانا pride (*oneself on* something) (پر) فخر کرنا *n.* feeling of wounded pride ٹھیس ، دل کو ٹھیس

pirate (*pī*-ret) *n.* sea-robber سمندری ڈاکو (also *pirate ship*) pirate's ship (usu. flying a black flag) سمندری ڈاکوؤں کا جہاز one who infringes a copyright کاپی رائٹ کا ڈاکو ، حق تصنیف کا ڈاکو ، ادبی سرقے کا مرتکب *v.t.* bring out or reproduce thus حق تصنیف (یا کاپی رائٹ) پر ڈاکہ ڈالنا **piracy** (*pī*-ra-si) *n.* سمندری ڈاکہ ، کاپی رائٹ پر ڈاکہ ، سرقہ ، ادبی سرقہ کرنا ، سرقہ کرنا

pirouette (pi-roo-*et*) *n.* spinning round on one foot or on tiptoe ایک پاؤں پر گھومنا ، پنجے کے بل تیز تیز گھومنا *v.i.* move thus ایک پاؤں پر (یا پنجے کے بل) گھومنا dance thus پنجے کے بل تیز تیز گھوم کر ناچنا

piss (pis) *n.* (word, not regarded as decent enough for use in the company of ladies, for) urine پیشاب *v.t.* & *i.* make water پیشاب کرنا **piss-pot** *n.* urine bottle پیشاب کرنے کی بوتل

pistachio (pis-*tay*-shi-oh) *n.* (pl. *pistachios*) a kind of nut with a green kernel پستہ

pistol (*pis*-tĕl) *n.* a small firearm پستول ، طمنچہ

piston (*pis*-tun) *n.* part of engine moving inside a hollow cylinder to work the engine پسٹن

pit mine like a deep, open hole کھلی کان any depression anywhere گڑھا *armpits*, depression below the arm under the shoulder بغل small scar left by smallpox چیچک کا داغ trap dug for quarry شکار پھانسنے کا گڑھا cheaper seats lower down in a picture-house سینما کی سستی نشستیں *the pit*, person sitting there on whose approval success of a picture, or drama mainly depends گھٹیا تماشائی ، چونی میل ، اٹھنی میل place for refuelling racing cars تیز رفتار کے مقابلے میں حصہ لینے والی موٹروں کا پٹرول پمپ part of the floor of an exchange allotted to special trading (سٹہ مارکیٹ میں کسی کاروبار کا) مخصوص حصہ *v.t.* (-tt-) leave pits (چیچک وغیرہ کا) داغ ڈالنا match (someone) in fight کے مقابلے میں کھڑا ہونا *be pitted against* کے مقابلے میں کھڑے ہونا **pitfall** *n.* hidden hole to trap animals شکار پھانسنے کا ڈھکا ہوا گڑھا ، اوگی lurking danger چھپا ہوا خطرہ

pitch *v.t.* & *i.* put up (a tent, etc.) لگانا ، نصب کرنا fall out (*from* carriage) میں سے باہر گر پڑنا fall in a carriage (on one's head) کے بل گرنا turn (someone *out*) نکال باہر کرنا turn (someone *aside*) دھکا دے کر پرے کرنا *pitch into*, (*a*) attack with blows پر گھونسوں کی بارش کرنا (*b*) fall headlong into میں سر کے بل جا نا decide (*on* or *upon*) کے بارے میں *pitch in*, set to work energetically کام میں جٹ جانا (?) ، فیصلہ کرنا set in a (high or low) tune آواز کا زور شور سے لگ جانا (of a flat object) throw it to come pat on the target زیر و بم ، پھینک کرنا نشانے پر پھینک بٹھانا *pitch upon* (*someone*), select (him) by chance اتفاقاً چن لینا (of a ship, boat, etc.) move up and down with the waves جہاز کا اوپر نیچے ہونا apply pitch to رال لگانا *n.* (cricket) part of ground between the wickets دونوں طرف کی وکٹوں کا درمیانی فاصلہ degree of highness or lowness (*of* sound) آواز کا زیر و بم degree درجہ *at the highest pitch* انتہائی کمال پر up-and-down movement (of a ship) owing to waves جہاز کا اوپر نیچے ہونا a tarry substance رال ، قیر *pitch black*, *pitch dark* کالا سیاہ ، قیر گوں *pitch darkness* سخت اندھیرا **pitched** *adj.* (of battle) not casual but after full preparations on both sides پوری تیاری کی جنگ **pitchfork** *n.* large two-pronged fork for haylifting, etc., دوشاخہ *v.t.* thrust reluctant or unfit person into office کسی نالائق یا غیر خواہشمند کو کسی عہدے پر لگانا **pitcher** (*pich*-ĕ*) *n.* large earthware jug صراحی ، جھجری ، گھڑا

piteous *adj.* (see under **pity**)

pith (pith) spongy middle part of the stems of certain plants گودا ، مغز essential part (*of* a matter, speech, etc.) کی سب سے اہم بات **pithy** (*pith*-i) *adj.* full of pith گودے دار terse and full of meaning مختصر مگر معنیٰ خیز **pithily** *adv.* tersely مختصراً ، اختصار سے

pittance (*pit*-ans) *n.* very small allowance of money (for work, etc.) حقیر معاوضہ *a mere pittance* بالکل حقیر معاوضہ

pity (*pit*-i) *n.* mercy رحم compassion ترس ، *have* (or *take*) *pity* (*on someone*) مصیبت میں کسی کے کام آنا یا مدد کرنا *feel pity for* (*someone*) پر ترس کھانا ، پر رحم آنا cause for grief افسوس کی بات *what a pity that* بڑے افسوس کی بات ہے کہ *v.t.* feel pity for پر رحم کرنا ، پر ترس کھانا **pitiable** *adj.* calling for pity قابلِ رحم miserable, contemptible گھٹیا ، ذلیل ، افسوسناک ، شرمناک **pitiful** *adj.* compassionate رحم دل ، رحیم pitiable قابلِ رحم contemptible شرمناک ، افسوسناک inconsiderable معمولی ، بے حقیقت **pitiless** cruel, merciless بے رحم **piteous** (*pit*-i-us) *adj.* pitiful رحم دِل ، calling for pity قابلِ رحم mournful, sad دردناک

pivot (*piv*-ot) *n.* spindle or pin on which something turns چول ، مدار ، محور basic point (*of* an issue) on which it depends مرکزی نقطہ ، بنیادی نکتہ *v.t.* & *i.* provide with a pivot چول لگانا put on it چول پر چڑھانا revolve or turn (*on something*) پر گھومنا

pixie, pixy (*pik*-si) *n.* fairy پری (*pixy* or *pixiated*) (U.S.) (colloq.) somewhat crazy پگلا سا

placable *adj.*, **placability** *n.* (see under **placate**)

placard (*plak*-ah*d) *n.* big poster بڑا اشتہار ، عام اعلان slogans, etc., written on cardboard pieces or cloth and elevated on rods for others to see اٹھائے ہوئے اشتہار *v.t.* announce through placards اشتہاروں کے ذریعے اعلان کرنا post placards on پر اشتہارات چسپاں کرنا

placate (pla-*kayt*) *v.t.* appease (someone) کا غصّہ ٹھنڈا کرنا **placable** (*plak*-a-bèl) *adj.* (also *plakatable*), that can be placated جس کا غصّہ ٹھنڈا کیا جا سکے جلد راضی ہو جانے والا mild-tempered نرم دِل **placability** (-*bil*-) *n.* being placable نرم دِل ہونا ، جلد راضی ہو جانے والا ، زود رضا ہونا

place (plays) spot جگہ ، مقام position پوزیشن ، درجہ post نوکری ، عہدہ passage one was reading کتاب وغیرہ کا حصّہ جہاں انسان پڑھ رہا تھا *place of worship* عبادت گاہ *place of amusement* سنیما وغیرہ *in place*, in the right place اپنی جگہ پر ، ٹھیک جگہ *be out of place* (*in*), be a misfit بے جگہ ، نا موزوں ہونا *keep* (*someone*) *in the right place* (کسی کو زیادہ نہ کھلنے دینا (کسی سے *take place*, occur ہونا *lose* (*one's*) *place*, (*a*) lose the job نوکری چھوٹنا ، ملازمت جاتی رہنا (*b*) **fail** to locate the page or line of a book one was **reading** کتاب کا وہ حصّہ جہاں انسان پڑھ رہا تھا نہ ملنا *give place to* (*someone*), be replaced by (him) اپنی جگہ (کسی) کا لگنا *in place of*, instead of کی بجائے *v.t.* put (something) in (a certain place) کی جگہ یا درجہ پر رکھنا ، کہیں رکھنا put (it) in (a certain position) *place confidence in* پر اعتماد کرنا ، پر بھروسا کرنا *place* (*an order for goods with someone*) (کو) مال کی فرمائش بھیجنا assign to a class fully ; identify کا مقام متعین کرنا remember circumstances of previous meeting سے پہلی ملاقات کا ماحول یاد کرنا

placid (*play*-sid) *adj.* calm (*waters*) پُرسکون unruffled person متحمل مزاج ، حلیم ، ٹھنڈے دِل کا ، ساکن **placidity** (pla-*sid*-i-ti) *n.* being placid پُرسکون ہونا ، حلیمی

plage (plahzh) *n.* sea-beach at a fashionable resort پسندیدہ سیرگاہ میں سمندر کا کنارہ

plagiarize (*play*-ji-a-riz) *v.t.* express another's ideas as one's own ادبی سرقہ کرنا **plagiarism** (*play*-ji-a-rizm) *n.* act of plagiarizing or something plagiarized ادبی سرقہ **plagiarist** *n.* one who plagiarizes ادبی سرقہ کرنے والا ، سرقے کا مرتکب

plague (playg) *n.* pestilence مہلک وبا *bubonic plague* طاعون ، پلیگ something spelling ruin and disaster آسمانی بلائے *v.t.* pester ناک میں دَم کر دینا

plain (playn) *n.* stretch of level land میدان *adj.* clear to eye, ear or mind واضح ، صاف (of dress, food, etc.) simple سادہ ، سیدھا سادہ frank لگی لپٹی رکھے بغیر ، صاف صاف (of colour) without any stripes or designs صرف ، بالکل (of appearance) not handsome or attractive معمولی سا *plain sailing*, smooth sailing مشکلات سے خالی ، آسان *in plain clothes*, not in uniform وردی کے بغیر ، سادہ کپڑوں میں *in plain words* صاف لفظوں میں *to be plain with you* سچ کہہ دوں تو برا نہ مانیں *plain dealing* خوش معاملگی ، معاملے کی صفائی ، دیانت داری *adv.* clearly صاف صاف **plainly** *adv.* in plain words صاف لفظوں میں ، ہیر پھیر کے بغیر **plainness** *n.* being plain سادگی ، سادہ ہونا

plaint (playnt) *n.* complaint شکایت lamentation فریاد accusation before a law-court استغاثہ

plaintiff (playnt-if) *n.* one who files a suit in a law-court مستغیث **plaintive** (*plaint*-iv) *adj.* mournful دردناک

plait (plat) *n.* braid of hair چوٹی ، گندھے ہوئے بال *v.t.* twist hair into a plait بال گوندھنا ، چوٹی کرنا ، چٹیا کرنا

plan *n.* diagram (*of* or *for* a building) showing details of internal structure as if seen from above and not from front (which is called *elevation*) (عمارت کا) مسطح نقشہ ، رقبے کا نقشہ ، نقشہ similar diagram (*of* or *for*) laying out (a garden) باغ کا نقشہ diagram (*of* a machine) showing the working of its parts مشین کا نقشہ scheme, programme طے شدہ پروگرام ، منصوبہ ، تجویز *work according to plan* منصوبے کے مطابق کام کرنا *v.t.* (-nn-) make a plan

(of or for) chalk out a programme (*to do* something) *plan* (*something*) *out*
plane (playn) *n.* flat surface *inclined plane* level, status *not in the same plane as* ('*plane*), aircraft tool for smoothing wood (also *plane-tree*), kinds of broad-leaved trees *adj*. flat (surface) *v.t.* & *i.* smooth (wood) with a plane *plane down* (*wood*, etc.)

a plane (sense 4)

a plane-tree

planet (*plan*-et) *n.* a heavenly body revolving round the sun **Note:** The nine planets are: *Mercury* عُطارِد *Venus* زُہرہ *Earth* زمین *Mars* مریخ *Jupiter* مُشتری *Saturn* زُحل *Uranus* یُورینس *Neptune* نیپچون and *Pluto.* پلوٹو
plank *n.* long, thick narrow board لمبا اور کم چوڑا تختہ، شختہ an item in the political programme of a party کسی سیاسی جماعت کے پروگرام کی ایک شق *v.t.* cover (some area) with planks تختہ بندی کرنا *plank (money) down*, put it down on the counter خریدنے کے لیے رُوپیہ رکھنا
plankton (*plank*-ten) *n.* small forms of animal or plant life drifting near the surface of lakes or oceans آوارہ زِلیت
plant (plahnt) *n.* living thing which is not an animal پودا، نبات machinery and fixtures of an industrial undertaking کسی صنعتی ضرورت یا کارخانے کا پورا صنعتی سامان، کارخانہ *v.t.* sow بونا put plant in میں پودا لگانا set up a colony بستی بسانا place (oneself or something) firmly somewhere کہیں جم جانا یا مضبوطی سے رکھنا **plantation** (-*tay*-) *n.* planting شجرکاری area planted with trees درختوں والا رقبہ large agricultural estate producing only one commodity کے باغات، کے کھیت **planter** *n.* owner of such a large plantation بڑے باغات والا
plantain (*plant*-in) *n.* large banana کیلا tree bearing it کیلے کا درخت *plantain grove* کیلے کا باغ
plaque (plahk) *n.* ornamental tablet of metal, porcelain, etc. سجاوٹی تختی، زیبائشی تختی، آرائشی لوح
plaster (*plas*-tě*) *n.* mixture for coating walls پلستر، کہگل *plaster of Paris*, gypsum clay for (moulds of) statues پلاسٹر آف پیرس adhesive substance for keeping fractured bones in position پلستر medical application to wound, etc. پلستر *v.t.* put plaster on (walls, etc.) پلستر کرنا، کہگل کرنا *apply plaster to* (*the body*) پلستر لگانا cover thickly (*with* oil, butter, etc.) اچھی طرح لگانا، چپڑنا **plasterer** *n.* workman who plasters walls, etc. راج، پلستر کرنے والا
plastic (*plas*-tik) *adj.* easily shaped شکل پذیر easily moulded اثر پذیر، تربیت پذیر pertaining to modelling in clay مجسمہ سازی کا pertaining to the restoration of deformed parts of the body جسم کی شکل ٹھیک کرنے کا *plastic surgery*, surgical operation on human skin, etc., with a view to giving the body a new or correct shape اعضا کو ٹھیک شکل دینے والی جراحت، تشکیلی جراحت *n.* one of the synthetic resinous substances which are plastic پلاسٹک **plasticity** (-*tis*-i-ti) *n.* quality of being easily shaped شکل پذیری، اثر پذیری
plate (playt) *n.* an almost flat dish پلیٹ، تھالی رکابی، قاب sheet (of metal, glass, etc.) (دھات کی) چادر (also *name plate*), small plate outside a house showing one's name نام کی تختی gold or silver vessels, etc. سونے چاندی کے برتن illustration printed separately in a book کتاب میں الگ تصویر metal sheet for printing from پلیٹ *plate glass*, window glass دروازوں کا شیشہ *photographic plate*, sensitized plate for use in camera فوٹو پلیٹ artificial gum for holding artificial teeth مصنوعی مسوڑھا *v.t.* cover with plates پتر چڑھانا coat (one metal) with another کا ملمع کرنا **plateful** *n.* quantity that a plate will hold تھالی بھر **plate-layer** *n.* one fixing and repairing rail track پلیٹ لیئر
platen (*plat*-en) *n.* roller in typewriter pressing paper against type پلاٹن، ڈنڈا similar device in printing press پلاٹن، ڈنڈا
plateau (pla-*toh*, or *plat*-oh) *n.* table-land سطح مرتفع
platform (*plat*-fo*m) *n.* raised surface along the track in a railway station پلیٹ فارم *platform ticket*, ticket needed for entering a platform پلیٹ فارم dais منبر، پلیٹ فارم political party's (election) manifesto پارٹی کا (انتخابی) منشور، منشور
platinum (*plat*-i-num) *n.* a valuable metallic element پلاٹینم
platitude (*plat*-i-tewd) *n.* true but trite truth (usu. offered as important) فرسودہ سچ، فرسودہ صداقت **platitudinous** (-*tewd*-) *adj.* of the nature of a platitude فرسودہ سچ والا
Platonic (pla-*ton*-ik) *adj.* pertaining to the Greek philosopher Plato (427—347 B.C.) or to his teachings افلاطونی، فلاطونی *Platonic love, Platonic friendship* purely spiritual love between those that should normally have mutual sexual attraction پاک محبت *n.* disciple of Plato افلاطون کا پیرو، افلاطونی (pl.)

(*Platonics*), talk, etc. of Platonic love پاک محبت کی بات (وغیرہ) **platonism** (*playt*-o-nizm) *n.* doctrines of Plato or belief in them فلاطونیت **platonist** (*playt*-o-nist) *n.* disciple of Plato ; Platonic افلاطونی، فلاطونی

platoon (pla-*toon*) *n.* one of the four units of a company comprising about 60 men پلاٹون

platter (*plat*-ĕ*) *n.* large wooden dish for bread چوبی چنگیز (see *Addenda*)

plaudits (*plawd*-its) *n. pl.* clapping, applause, etc. (*of* the audience) نعرہ ہائے تحسین

plausible (*plawz*-i-bĕl) *adj.* seemingly reasonable بظاہر معقول اثر آفریں persuasive (speaker) باتیں بنانے کا ماہر deceitful though persuasive (person) سخن ساز **plausibility** (-bil-) *n.* being plausible بظاہر معقول ہونا، سخن سازی

play *v.t.* & *i.* frolic کھیلنا، کھیل کود میں مشغول ہونا take part in (game) (کوئی کھیل) کھیلنا act اداکاری کرنا act (*the part of*) (کا کردار) ادا کرنا prove to be an example of (*the* fool, man, etc.) کا نمونہ پیش کرنا *play the fool* حماقت کا نمونہ یا ثابت ہونا، پیش کرنا perform on a musical instrument بجانا pretend in sport جھوٹ موٹ بننا direct (water or light *on* or *over* something) (پر) ڈالنا (of water or light) move playfully (پر) کھیلنا *play a trick on* (*someone*) سے ہاتھ کرنا *play at* (*something*), not to be serious about it بے دلی سے (کام) کرنا *play with* (*something*), (*a*) معمولی جان کر (کسی چیز) کی پروا نہ کرنا trifle with (it) (*b*) let the mind think about (it) کے متعلق دل کو سوچنے دینا (*c*) frolic سے کھیلنا *play up* ! play hard in game (کھیل) شاباش، خوب جم کر! *play up to* (*someone*), flatter (him) to win favour کو بانس پر چڑھانا *play upon* (*someone's feelings*, etc.), exploit (them) for personal ends اپنے فائدے کے لیے کسی کو ابھارنا *play into* (*someone's*) *hands*, be (his) puppet ہاتھوں میں کھیلنا *play on words*, pun ابہام سے کام لینا *be played out*, be fagged مقابلے کے قابل نہ رہنا، تھک کر مجبور ہو جانا *play for money*, gamble جوا کھیلنا، قمار بازی کرنا *n.* frolic کھیل کود game کھیل drama تمثیل، ڈراما gambling جوا، قمار بازی، مقامرت playing of sunlight کرنوں کا پڑنا (یا) کھیلنا place for free movement ہلنے جلنے کے لیے کافی جگہ *at play* کھیل کود میں لگا ہوا *in play* مذاق سے *give full play to* کو پوری آزادی دینا *play of words*, pun ابہام *come into play* ہونے لگنا *be in full play* زوروں پر ہونا *bring into play* عمل میں لانا **player** *n.* one who plays games کھلاڑی one who plays a musical instrument سازندہ، مطرب *player-piano*, piano with automatic playing apparatus خود نواز پیانو **playfellow**, **playmate** *n.* child who plays with another someone with whom one played in childhood ساتھ کھیلنے والا بچپن کا ساتھی **playful** *adj.* full of fun زندہ دل not serious مذاق کے انداز سے **playground** *n.* (also *ground* or *grounds*), ground on which games are played کھیل کا میدان *on the playground* کھیل کے میدان میں **plaything** *n.* toy کھلونا **playwright** *n.* dramatist تمثیل نگار **playhouse** *n.* theatre تھیٹر، منڈوا **playbill** *n.* theatre poster ڈرامے کا اشتہار **playgoer** *n.* one who regularly goes to a theatre تھیٹر باقاعدگی سے دیکھنے والا

plea (plee) *n.* statement of the accused in a law-court جواب دعویٰ excuse عذر، معذرت earnest appeal (*for* help, etc.) درخواست، اپیل

plead (pleed) *v.t.* & *i.* make a plea جواب دعویٰ داخل کرنا advocate (someone's case) (in a law-court) (عدالت میں) وکالت کرنا *plead guilty*, admit one's guilt اقبال جرم کرنا offer as an excuse عذر پیش کرنا make an earnest appeal (*for* something or *with* someone, *for* or *to do* something) التجا کرنا **pleader** *n.* junior advocate not yet allowed to appear in a High Court, etc. پلیڈر، وکیل

pleasant *adj.*, **pleasantness** *n.*, **pleasantry** *n.* (see under **please**)

please (pleez) *v. t.* & *i.* give pleasure to کو پسند آنا، کو بہت اچھا لگنا be the will of منظور ہو، *please God* خدا کرے، انشاءاللہ (polite way of request) مہربانی کرکے، مہربانی ہوگی، از راہ نوازش، از راہ کرم choose کو پسند آنا **pleasing** *adj.* giving pleasure خوشی کا، خوشی والا، خوشگوار **pleasant** (*plez*-ant) *adj.* charming دلکش، خوشگوار cheerful خوش طبع **pleasantness** *n.* being pleasant خوشگوار ہونا **pleasantry** *n.* (pl. *pleasantries*) joke لطیفہ (usu. *pl.*) lively talk چہلیں، ہنسی مذاق (کی باتیں) **pleasure** (*plezh*-ĕ*) *n.* (cause of) delight خوشی، مسرت *take pleasure in*, (*a*) enjoy سے لطف اندوز ہونا (*b*) like پسند کرنا *with pleasure*, بخوشی، بصد شوق authority's desire or intention مرضی، پسندیدگی، رضا *at* (*someone's*) *pleasure* (کی) مرضی پر *during* (*someone's*) *pleasure*, when, as long as, he choses جب تک وہ پسند کرے **pleasurable** *adj.* pleasing دل خوش کن، دلخوش کن

Pleasure is the satisfaction of a desire ; **joy,** the emotion of satisfaction ; **happiness,** state of continued joy ; **ecstasy**, heavenly transports ; **gladness** at some particular circumstance ; **cheer** after gloom ; **mirth,** friendly and sociable jollity ; **bliss,** treasured to oneself ; **radiance,** pouring out of happiness as if in rays ; **gratification** of a longheld-desire.

pleat (pleet) *n.* fold in a cloth made by doubling it پلیٹ *v.t.* make pleats in میں پلیٹ ڈالنا

plebeian (ple-*bee*-un) *n.* & *adj.* (in ancient Rome) (person) belonging to the lower class ادنیٰ طبقے کا (فرد)

plebiscite (*pleb*-i-sit, or *pleb*-i-sɪt) *n.* referendum استصواب رائے ، رائے شماری
pledge (plej) *n.* something pawned رگرد رکھی ہوئی چیز security (*of*) کی) ضمانت) solemn undertaking عہد، قول، عہد و پیمان taken (*of*) کی، نشانی) *under plege of* کا عہد کیا ہوا *v. t.* pawn رگرو (یا گروی) رکھنا، رہن رکھنا give (someone) a solemn promise (*to do* something) عہد کرنا ، قول ہارنا drink the health of (someone) کا جام صحت نوش کرنا
Pleiades (plɪ-a-deez), **Pleiads** (plɪ-adz) *n. pl.* well-known group of seven (actually six) stars سات سہیلیوں کا جھمکا ، ثریا ، پروین
plenary (*pleen*-a-ri) *n.* full (power) مکمل، کامل، پورا (of session, meeting, etc.) to be attended by all members پورا
plenipotentiary (plen-i-po-*tensh*-è-ri) *n.* & *adj.* fully empowered (person) پورے اختیارات والا (نمائندہ) *minister plenipotentiary*, fully empowered diplomat مختار عام، مدارالمہام **plenteous, plentiful** *adj.* (see under **plenty**)
plenty (*plent*-i) *n.* abundance (*of*) فراوانی، کثرت، افراط *plenty of (sometning)* کافی ، وافر **plenteous** (lit.) **plentiful** *adj.* abundant بہت، فراواں، وافر
plethora (*pleth*-o-ra) *n.* fullness of blood vessels افراط دم superfluity حد سے زیادہ ہونا
pleurisy (*plco*-ri-si) *n.* inflammation of the lung membrane (called *pleura*) ذات الجنب
pliable (plɪ-a-bèl) *adj.* flexible خم پزیر open to influence اثر پزیر **pliability** (-*bil*-) *n.* خم پزیری، اثر پزیری **pliant** (*plɪ*-ant) pliable خم پزیر ، اثر پزیر
pliers (plɪ-ĕ*z) *n. pl.* strong handy pincers پلاس
plight (plɪt) *n.* predicament ; serious or pitiable condition بُرا حال، بُری حالت *in sorry plight*, قابل رحم حالت میں *in an evil plight* بُرے حالوں *v.t.* pledge, پکا وعدہ کرنا، قول دینا *plight (one's) word* قول دینا *plight (one's) troth, plight (oneself)*, شادی کا اقرار کر لینا
Plimsoll (*plim*-sèl) *adj.* (only in the phrases :) *Plimsoll line*, (or) *Plimsoll mark*, line painted around hull of a British ship to show maximum depth it is legally permitted to go into water (to mark the maximum load it may carry) آبی خط
plimsolls (plim-sels) *n. pl.* cheap canvas shoes with rubber soles فلیٹ شُو
plod *v.i.* (-dd-) continue (*along* a road) بدقت چلتے ہی جانا *plod away at (one's) work*, work hard slowly but steadily محنت مشقت سے کام کرجانا **plodder** *n.* slow but steady worker سست رفتار مگر محنتی
plot *n.* small piece of land زمین کا ٹکڑا، قطعہ اراضی، قطعہ outline (*of* a story) کہانی کا خلاصہ، اصل قصہ، پلاٹ underhand scheme (*to do* something) سازش *v.t.* (-tt-) prepare secret scheme (*to do* something or *for* or *against* something) سازش کرنا prepare (a curve) on graph کا گراف تیار کرنا **plotter** *n.* underhand schemer سازشی
plough (plow) (spelt in U. S. as **plow**) *n.* farm implement for turning the soil ہل *v. t.* break up (land) with it into regular lines (called *furrows*) میں ہل چلانا *plough back*, (*a*) plough (standing crop) into soil for fertilizing it کھڑی فصل کی کھاد (*b*) reinvest (profits) (نفع) بھی دکان میں ڈالنا (of a ship) forge ahead (*through* waves, etc.) چیرتے جانا **ploughboy, ploughman** *n.* ہل چلانے والا، کاشتکار
ploughshare (*plow*-shay-è*) . *n.* blade of a plough ہل کا پھل، پھالی
plover (*pluv*-è*) *n.* a kind of (*golden*, or *grey*) shore bird پلاوَر
pluck (pluk) *v.t.* & *i.* pick (flowers, fruit) توڑنا pull feathers of کے پر اتارنا take (weeds, etc., *up* or *out*) نکالنا *pluck up courage*, banish one's fears ڈر دور کرنا *n.* courage جرأت، ہمت **plucky** *adj.* courageous جرأتمند، بہادر، باہمت **pluckily** courageously *adv.* جرأت سے
plug (plug) *n.* stopper for hole ڈاٹ connexion for an electric point بجلی کا پلگ device for water connexion (پانی کا) پلگ ڈاٹ *v.t.* & *i.* (-gg-) put a plug in ڈاٹ لگانا، بند کرنا put a plug (*in* for electric or water connexion) بجلی یا پانی کا پلگ لگانا (colloq.) try to popularize (a song) by dinning it into the people's ears (گیت کو) ہردلعزیز بنانے کے لیے اس کے ریکارڈ جگہ جگہ بجانا یا بجوانا
plum (plum) *n.* a soft juicy fruit آلو بخارا (*pl.*) the best of بہترین *the plums of office* اونچے اونچے عہدے currants کشمش، میوہ *plum-cake* میوے والا
plummy (*plum*-i) *adj.* full of good things اچھی اچھی چیزوں والا remunerative اچھے معاوضے والا، نفع بخش، منفعت بخش
plumage *n.* (see under **plume**)
plumb (plum) *n.* weight tied to cord for testing whether a wall is upright شاقول *out of plumbs* ٹیڑھا similar device for fathoming depth of water پنسال *v. t.* get to the root of کی تہ کو پہنچنا
plumb-line *n.* cord of a plumb شاقول کی ڈوری
plumber (*plum*-ĕ*) *n.* workman who fits or repairs water pipes نل والا، نلساز **plumbing** *n.* plumber's job نل لگانا، نلسازی waterpipes, etc., in a building کسی عمارت میں لگے ہوئے نل (also see **plummet**)
plume *n.* feather پر a lovely feather used for decoration سجاوٹی پر anything like a

feather پرنما چیز ornamental crest کلغی *v. t.* adorn with plumes پروں سے سجانا (of a bird), clean (*itself* or *its feathers*) پر صاف کرنا feel (*oneself*) proud (*on*) (پر) اپنے کوش باش دینا، (پر) فخر کرنا

plumage (*ploom*-ij) *n.* feathers پر

plummet (*plum*-et) *n.* plumb شاقول plumb-line شاقول کی ڈوری

plummy *adj.* (see under **plum**)

plump (plump) *adj.* nice-looking fat (person) or chubby (cheeks) گول مٹول *n.* abrupt plunge دھڑام سے گرنا *v.t.* & *i.* *plump up* (or *out*), fatten گول مٹول ہونا یا کرنا (let) fall abruptly and heavily دھڑام سے گرنا یا گرنے دینا *plump* (*oneself*) *down in a chair* کرسی پر سے دھڑام سے گرنا vote (*for* someone) confidently (کو) اعتماد سے ووٹ دینا vote (*for* someone) collectively (کو) سب کا ایک ساتھ ووٹ دینا

plunder (*plund*-ĕ*) *v. t.* & *i.* pillage during war, etc. لوٹ مار کرنا *n.* plundering لوٹ مار plundered things لوٹ کا مال

plunge (plunj) *v.t.* & *i.* (cause to) make a sudden dive (*into*) یکایک کود پڑنا، ڈبکی لگانا، غوطہ لگانا، یکایک گھس پڑنا throw (something into darkness, confusion, etc.) (...پر) یکایک مسلط کر دینا *n.* dive from the diving-platform پانی میں چھلانگ لگانا، غوطہ مارنا

plural (*ploo*-rĕl) *n.* & *adj.* (from used of) more than one جمع

plus (plus) *n.* sign of addition + جمع کی علامت *prep.* with the addition of جمع *four plus five makes* (or *is*) *nine*, four and five are nine چار جمع پانچ برابر ہیں نو (رکے ; *adj.* additional مزید **plusfours** knickerbockers with jacket and cap to match پلس فور

plush (plush) *n.* heavy silk cloth with a soft nap پلش *adj.* (see *Addenda*)

Pluto (*ploo*-to) *n.* *Cl. myth.* the Roman god who ruled the Lower World (identified with the Greek *Hades*) ; he was the brother of Jupiter (or Zeus) and Neptune (or Poseidon) پلوٹو، پلوٹو name of a planet پلوٹو، پلوتو

plutocracy (ploo-*tok*-ra-si) *n.* government by the rich امیروں کی حکومت، امیر شاہی **plutocrat** (*ploo*-) *n.* one powerful by wealth دولت کی وجہ سے اقتدار والا **plutocratic** (-krat-) *adj.* of a plutocracy دولت شاہی (کا)

Plutus (*ploo*-tus) *Cl. myth.* the God of riches پلوٹس، پلوٹس

ply (pli) *n.* layer of wood لکڑی کی پرت *plywood* پرت دار لکڑی one strand in rope, worsted, etc. لڑ، لڑی *three-ply wool* تین لڑی کی اون *v. t.* & *i.* work with (one's needle, machine, etc.) چلانا work (a trade, etc.) (کسی پیشے کا) کام کرنا (of public conveyance by land, sea or air) go regularly (*between*, or *from* one place *to* another) کے درمیان چلنا keep (*someone*) constantly supplied with (food, news, questions, etc.) (کے لیے) ہر وقت تیار رکھنا

pneumatic (new-*mat*-ik) *adj.* filled or worked with compressed air ہوا سے کام کرنے والا

pneumonia (new-*moh*-ni-a) *n.* inflammation of the lungs نمونیا، ذات الصدر

poach (pohch) *v. t.* & *i.* cook (an egg) by boiling it without the shell (انڈا) پوچ کرنا hunt on or fish from forbidden land ناجائز طور پر شکار کرنا

poacher *n.* one who hunts on or fishes from forbidden land بلا اجازت شکار کرنے والا

pock (pok) *n.* smallpox pit چیچک کا داغ *pock-marked* چیچک کے داغوں والا

pocket (*pok*-et) little bag sewn in garments, etc. جیب، کیسہ *be* (*so much*) *in pocket by transaction*, کسی سودے میں اتنا نفع ہونا *be out of pocket* سارا روپیہ گنوا آنا isolated area occupied by the enemy or a foreign power دشمن کے زیر نگیں گھرا ہوا علاقہ forces stationed there گھرے ہوئے علاقے میں متعین فوج *v.t.* & *i.* put in one's pocket جیب میں ڈالنا keep unlawfully gained (money) ناجائز روپیہ جیب میں ڈال لینا، ہڑپ کر جانا conceal (one's feelings, etc.) چھپانا *pocket an insult* بے عزتی پی جانا **pocket-book** *n.* small notebook چھوٹی کاپی purse for notes نوٹوں کا بٹوا **pocket battleship** *n.* small battleship چھوٹا جنگی جہاز **pocket-money** *n.* money given to children جیب خرچ **out-of-pocket** *adj.* (of expenses, etc.) net اصل، اصلی، واقعی **empty-pocket** *adj.* moneyless جیب خالی، تہی دست

pod *n.* long seed-case of plants like peas پھلی *v.t.* & *i.* (-dd-) take (peas, etc.) out of pods چھیلنا، پھلی میں سے نکالنا form pods پھلی آنا

poem (*poh*-em) *n.* composition of elevated tone in verse-form نظم **poet** (*poh*-et) *n.* one who composes poems شاعر **poetess** *n.* woman poet (esp. as compared to other women poets) شاعرہ **poetic, poetical** *adj.* in verse-form شعروں میں، منظوم of poetry شاعرانہ *poetic licence* (see under *licence*) **poetically** *adv.* in a poetic manner شاعرانہ انداز سے **poetry** (*poh*-et-ri) *n.* art of a poet شاعری، فن شاعری، شعر گوئی poems اشعار quality (*of* something) creating poetic emotion شعریت **poesy** (*poh*-e-zi) *n.* (old use) art of poetry فن شاعری

poetaster (*poh*-) *n.* inferior verse-writer تک بند

pogrom (pog-*rom*) *n.* organized killing and

plunder of a class of people کسی قوم یا گروہ کے قتل و غارت کی مہم منظم قتل عام (originally) such movement against the Jews in Russia رُوس میں یہودیوں کے قتل و غارت کی مہم
poignant (*poi*-nant) *adj.* of sharp taste or smell تیز painfully keen (grief, etc.) دل کو چیرنے والا ، دِلدوز
point *n.* sharp end نوک dot نقطہ *decimal point* اعشاریہ position or mark (of thing, view, etc.) نقطۂ نظر ، جگہ ، مقام ، نقطہ ، وقت ، مرحلہ *viewpoint, point of view* نقطۂ نگاہ *a turning point (in something)* تبدیلی کا آغاز *at this point* اِس جگہ ، یا اِس مرحلے پر *be on the point (of doing something)* کرنے ہی لگنا *when it comes to the point* (عمل یا فیصلے کا) وقت آنے پر mark (of degree) on a scale درجے کا نشان ، درجہ ، نقطہ *the freezing point* (*of*) کا درجۂ انجماد (یا) نقطۂ انجماد *boiling point* (*of.*) کا درجۂ جوش (یا) نقطۂ جوش one of thirty-two marks (*of* the compass) (قطب نما پر) اطراف کے نشان main idea (*of* something) اصل بات ، نکتہ *miss the point of a joke* لطیفے کا نکتہ نہ سمجھنا *see the point of* کا نکتہ سمجھ جانا *come to the point* اصلی بات پر آنا *carry (one's) point, gain (one's) point,* دوسروں کو قائل کر لینا ، اپنی بات منوا لینا *off point* غیر متعلق *to the point* متعلقہ ، اصلی something to be thought out غور طلب بات item شق quality خصوصیت ، خوبی scoring mark in certain games نمبروں کے باعث جیتنا ، پائنٹس پر جیتنا پائنٹ ، نمبر *win on points* *score fifteen points* نمبر لینا ، پائنٹ بنانا (*pl.*) tapering movable rails for change of track ریل کا کانٹا headland راس unit of value in food-rationing راشن پوئنٹ ، راشن کی اکائی *v.t. & i.* show the way (*to*) with a finger انگلی سے بتانا ، اشارہ کرنا sharpen pencil پنسل کی نوک باریک بنانا *point out,* call attention (*to* the fact *that*) واضح کرنا ، (کی) *point of a mistake* غلطی کی طرف اشارہ کرنا ، کے *point to,* be a sign of کی طرف توجہ دلانا آثار ہونا *point (something) at,* direct towards کی طرف کرنا *point a moral* (کا رُخ) کسی کی طرف کرنا اخلاقی سبق دینا **point-blank** *adj.* fired at very close range بہت قریبی نشانہ absolute because of leaving no room for doubt قطعی *adv.* absolutely قطعاً **pointed** *adj.* sharp تیز ، نوکیلا (of a remark, looks, etc.) directed at or against someone in particular خاص اُسی کی طرف **pointer** *n.* index of a dial سُوئی indicating rod used at blackboard تختۂ سیاہ کی چھڑی ، تختہ نما (colloq.) hint اِشارہ **pointless** *adj.* meaningless جس میں کوئی بات نہ ہو ، بے معنی **pointsman** *n.* workman controlling the points (ریل کے) کانٹے والا
poise (poiz) *v. t. & i.* keep one's balance توازن قائم رکھنا keep (sword, etc.) balanced (تلوار) تولنا *n.* balance توازن carriage of head سر رکھنے کا انداز composure, self-possession طبیعت کا سکون ، توازن
poison (*poi*-zun) *n.* any substance which proves fatal if eaten زہر influence detrimental to social or moral life اخلاق یا معاشرے کے لیے سم قاتل *v.t.* give poison to کو زہر دینا make poisonous زہر آلود کرنا ، مسموم کرنا injure morally خیالات کو خراب کرنا
poisoner *n.* one who poisons زہر دینے والا **poisonous** *adj.* that poisons ; full of poison زہریلا ، مسموم
poke (pohk) *v. t. & i.* thrust (*in* or *out*) گھسانا ، (آگ وغیرہ کو ڈنڈے) push (rod, etc.) against گھسیڑنا *poke (one's) finger in* میں انگلی چبھونا *poke* سے چھیڑنا *poke (one's) elbow* کہنی مارنا make a hole in by poking میں مار کر چھید کرنا *poke fun at,* make fun of کا مذاق اُڑانا *poke (one's) nose into (others') affairs,* pry دُوسروں کے رازجاننے میں لگے رہنا ، خواہ مخواہ دخل دیتے پھرنا **poker** *n.* metal bar for stirring up the burning coal آگ کریدنی a U. S. card game پوکر ، تاش کا ایک امریکی کھیل *poker-face,* impassive face as that of a poker player بے کیف چہرہ **poky** (*poh*-ki) *adj.* small (room) چھوٹا سا (کمرہ) petty (job) معمولی (نوکری)
pole (pohl) *n.* either end of the earth's axis (called the *North Pole* and the *South Pole*) قطب (جنوبی یا شمالی) *pole star,* (*a*) star towards the North Pole with no apparent motion قطب تارا ، قطب (*b*) guiding light شمع ہدایت ، چراغ راہ either of the two ends of a magnet مقناطیس کا قطب either of the two connecting ends of a battery (called the *positive pole* and the *negative pole*) (بجلی خانے کا) مثبت اور منفی سرا long wooden rod لاٹھی ، لٹھ post کھمبا land measure equivalent to $5\frac{1}{2}$ yards پول ، جریب **polar** *adj.* pertaining to the Poles قطبی *polar bear,* (of) the species living near the North Pole قطبی ریچھ
polemics (po-*lem*-iks) *n.* (word for which the more usual one is) apologetics مناظرہ *adj.* **polemic, polemical** *adj.* of the nature of polemics مناظرانہ
police (po-*lees*) *n.* government department responsible for the maintenance of public order پولیس ، شرطہ (treated as *pl.*) members of the police force پولیس ، پولیس والے *adj.* of the police پولیس کا *v.t.* provide with police پولیس بہم پہنچانا maintain order ضبط و نظم قائم رکھنا **policeman** *n.* member of the police force پولیس والا **police station** *n.* police office in an area تھانہ **police post** *n.* smaller police office پولیس کی چوکی **Police State** *n.* (see *Addenda*)
policy (*pol*-i-si-) *n.* line of action chalked out by (government, etc.) پالیسی ، حکمت عملی ، راہ عمل ، دانشمندانہ طرز عمل prudent course of action اصول insurance document setting forth the terms of a particular contract دستاویز بیمہ

poliomyelitis (*poh*-li-oh-mɪ-e-*lī*-tis), **polio** (*poh*-li-oh) *n.* infantile paralysis بچوں کا فالج

polish (*pol*-ish) *v. t.* & *i.* make or become glossy by rubbing رگڑ کر صاف کرنا چمکانا make (person, manner, etc.) refined and cultured شائستہ بنانا *n.* polishing چمکانا polished surface, etc. چمکیلی سطح، چمک substance used for this purpose روغن *shoe polish* بُوٹ پالش، جُوتا روغن

polite (po-*līt*) *adj.* well-mannered and considerate (person) خلیق cultured (society) شائستہ، مُہذّب **politeness** *n.* being well-mannered خوش خلقی، شائستگی ▣ **Polite** is polished in manners; **civil,** barely polite, just refraining from being rude; **courteous,** going out of one's way to render a service; **gallant,** excessively anxious to please the ladies; **urbane,** as a city man, (opp. of *a rustic*); **courtly,** given to extreme formalities in the manners of a royal court; **elegant,** well-dressed (person) or well-selected furniture and clothes.

politic (*pol*-i-tik) *adj.* tactful, prudent (person or action) دانشمند، دانشمندانہ **politics** *n. pl.* political science علم سیاست، سیاسیات political issues, etc. سیاسی مسائل وغیرہ، سیاست *party politics* جماعتی سیاست *local politics* مقامی سیاست *v. i.* (see Addenda) (see *Addenda*) **political** (po-*lit*-i-kĕl) *adj.* of politics سیاسی *political geography* سیاسی جغرافیہ of government سیاسی، سرکاری *political prisoners*, those gaoled for defying the government سیاسی قیدی of the State, national ریاست کا، قومی *political economy*, national (as opposed to *domestic*) economy, economics قومی معیشت، معاشیات

politically *adv.* in a political manner سیاسی طور پر

politician (pol-i-*tish*-ĕn) *n.* one taking part in politics سیاستدان (old use) (crafty) person عیّار

polity (*pol*-i-ti) *n.* government as an organized system نظام حکومت society as a State معاشرتی ریاست

poll (pol) *n.* ❶ voting at an election (انتخاب میں) رائے شماری ❷ counting of votes رائے دہی، رائے دہندگی ❸ (*pl.*) polling station ووٹ ڈالنے کا دفتر، مرکز رائے دہی *go to the polls*, (of a government, country or people) have a general election عام انتخابات ہونا یا کرانا (also *poll-parrot*), (conventional name for parrot) میاں مٹھو، طوطا، توتا ❺ silly babbler *v.t.* & *i.* vote at an election انتخابات میں رائے دینا (یا)، ووٹ ڈالنا get votes ووٹ پانا ❸ cut off the top of (tree) (درخت کی) پھننگ کاٹنا، اوک چھانٹنا ❹ cut off the horns of (animal) سینگ کاٹنا **pollard** *n.* ❶ tree with branches cut off to the trunk for producing close head of young shoots چھانٹ کر کلس دار (یا گنبد نما) بنایا ہوا درخت، چھنٹا ہوا درخت hornless animal of the horned kind سینگ کٹا، ریا منڈا) جانور **poll-tax** *n.* tax equally levied on everyone یکساں محصول **polling-booth** *n.* polls مرکز رائے دہی **polling officer** *n.* its superintendent رائے دہی

pollen (*pol*-en) *n.* fertilizing dust of flowers پھول کا ریزہ، زرگل **pollinate** (*pol*-i-nayt) *v. t.* make fertile with pollen زرگل چھڑکنا

pollute (po-*loot*) *v. t.* profane make filthy گندا کرنا، آلودہ کرنا **pollution** *n.* act of polluting or being polluted ناپاک کرنا، آلودگی

polo (*poh*-loh) *n.* hockey-like game played on horseback with stick called *mallet* چوگان، پولو

poltroon (pol-*troon*) *n.* (lit.) coward بزدل

poly- (*pol*-i) *pref.* many کثیر **polyandry** (pol-i-*and*-ri) having more than one husband at the same time بیک وقت ایک سے زیادہ شوہر ہونا، چند شوئی **polychromatic** (po-lik-ro-*mat*-ik) *adj.* many-coloured کئی رنگا، رنگدار، مختلف الالوان **polygamy** (po-*lig*-è-mi) having more than one husband or wife at the same time کثیر الازدواجی، کثرت ازدواج **polygamist** *n.* man, woman, etc. practising it کثیرالازدواج **polygamous** *adj.* such (man or woman) etc. **polyglot** (*pol*-i-glot) *adj.* of more than one language کثیرالالسنہ **polygon** (*pol*-i-gon) *n.* closed plane figure with five or more straight sides کثیرالاضلاع **polygyny** (po-*lig*-i-ni) *n.* having more than one wife at the same time بیک وقت ایک سے زیادہ بیویاں ہونا، تعدد ازواج **polypus** (*pol*-i-pus) *n.* kind of smooth soft tumour in the nose or the womb پالی پس **polysyllable** (-sil-) *n.* word of many syllables کثیرالاجزاء لفظ **polytechnic** (pol-i-*tek*-nik) pertaining to many trades; technical (school) کثیر فنی (مدرسہ)، فنی **polytheism** (pol-i-*thee*-izm) belief in gods or in God being more than one شرک **polytheist** (-ist) *n.* one who has this belief مشرک **polytheistic** *adj.* pertaining to polytheism مشرکانہ

pomade (po-*mahd*) *n.* hair ointment بالوں میں لگانے کی خوشبو، پوماد

pomegranate (*pom*-gran-it) *n.* well-known fruit full of juicy seeds انار tree bearing it انار کا درخت

pomfret *n.* a kind of small edible fish چھمنا مچھلی

pommel (*pum*-el) *v. t.* (-ll-) beat with fists گھونسے مارنا

pomp (pomp) *n.* pageantry شان و شوکت **pompous** (*pom*-pus) *adj.* fond of show شان و شوکت دکھانے کا laboured (style) پرتکلف (اسلوب) self- important برخود غلط **pomposity** (-*pos*-) *n.* bombast (عبارت کا) پرتکلف ہونا

pond *n.* small pool of still water (specially) made as a drinking-place for cattle جوہڑ

ponder (*pond*-ĕ*) *v.t.* & *i.* consider carefully بغور سوچنا think (*over* something) پر غور کرنا

ponderous (*pond*-ĕ-rus) *adj.* very heavy بہت بھاری، وزنی uninteresting بے لطف **ponderable** *adj.* having appreciable weight, etc. جس کا وزن (وغیرہ) ممکن ہو

poniard (*pon*-yahd) *n.* dagger خنجر، پیش قبض، قرولی

pontiff (*pont*-ɪf) *n.* the Pope پاپائے روم (Bib.) chief priest بڑا مذہبی رہنما

pontoon (pon-*toon*) *n.* flat-bottomed boat چوڑے تلے کی کشتی hollow metal cylinder supporting a movable bridge over a river پُل کی کشتی، پَن روک (پیپا) *pontoon bridge* movable bridge made of pontoons کشتیوں کا پُل، پَن روک پُل

pony (*poh*-ni) *n.* horse of small breed **pony-tail** *n.* (see *Addenda*)

pooh (poo) *int.* (expressive of contempt) اونہہ

pooh-pooh (poo-*poo*) *v. t.* make light of (idea, etc.) کی ہنسی اڑانا

pool *n.* very small lake forming naturally قدرتی تالاب، تالاؤ، تال water, etc., lying on a road, floor, etc (سڑک وغیرہ پر) کھڑا پانی وغیرہ *a pool of blood* خون کا دریا، خون ہی خون *lie in a pool of blood,* (usu. of a murdered person) خون میں لت پت ہونا deep portion of a river گنڈ total money staked by a group داؤں پر لگائی ہوئی سب کی مجموعی رقم arrangement to share funds اکٹھے روپیہ لگانے کا انتظام *v. t.* put (money) together for thus sharing it روپیہ یکجا کر لینا

poor (*poo*-ĕ*) *adj.* having little or no money, etc. غریب، نادار، تہی دست needy, indigent محتاج، حاجتمند not good; of bad quality خراب، گھٹیا (*be*) *in poor health* صحت خراب (ہونا) *poor land* غیر زرخیز اراضی، اوسر *poor food* کم غذائیت والی خوراک ❸ lacking in (something) سے محروم *poor-spirited,* lacking in courage بے ہمت **poor-house** *n.* work-house محتاج خانہ

poorly *adv.* in or with poverty غربت سے badly خراب **poorness** *n.* lack of some necessary quality کمی، کال، فقدان، (سے) محرومی، تہی مائیگی **poverty** (*pov*-ĕ*-ti) *n.* ❶ being poor افلاس، غربت ❷ poorness فقدان، کال، تہی مائیگی *poverty-stricken* غربت زدہ، فلاکت زدہ، مفلوک الحال

pop *v. t.* & *i.* (-pp-) ❶ move (*in, out, up, down,* etc.) quickly بڑی تیزی سے ہلنا یا ہلانا ❷ make a sharp, little sound (as of cork being pulled out of a bottle) بھک کرنا، بھک سے اڑنا *n.* such sound بھک (colloq.) bubbling drink سوڈا (وغیرہ) کی بوتل (slang) pawn گروی، رہن *be in pop,* be pawned گروی ہونا (see *Addenda*)

Pope (pohp) *n.* head of the Roman Catholic sect of Christianity پاپائے روم، پاپائے روما، پاپا **popery** (*pohp*-ĕ-ri) *n.* doctrines, etc., of the Roman Catholic Church کیتھولک عقائد institution of Popes پاپائیت **popish** (*poh*-pish) *adj.* pertaining to popery پاپائی

popinjay (*pop*-in-jay) *n.* fop چھیلا (old use) parrot توتا، طوطا، میاں مٹھو

poplar (*pop*-lĕ*) *n.* a kind of tree which grows fast and is very tall and straight درخت حَوَر

a poplar

poplin (*pop*-lin) *n.* a kind of durable shiny cotton cloth پاپلین

poppa (*pop*-a) *n.* (U. S.) papa ابا جی، ابا جان، باوا جان

poppet (*pop*-et) *n.* (vocative) darling پیاری، جانی *my poppet,* my darling جانی، جان پیاری

poppy (*pop*-i) *n.* a kind of plant with lovely red flowers کوکنار its flower لالہ، گل لالہ *wild poppy* لالۂ صحرائی *v.t.* drug wich opium افیم کا نشہ چڑھانا abounding in poppies لالہ والا **poppyseed** *n.* its seed خشخاش **poppyhead** *n.* its seed pod from which opium is extracted while it is yet green ; (itself also used as a drug) پوست

populace *n.* (see under **populate**)

popular (*pop*-ew-lĕ*) *adj.* ❶ of the people عوامی ❷ liked by the people suited to the needs of the common people ارزاں، سستا *at popular prices* سستے suited to their tastes; hence vulgar گھٹیا، پست **popularity** (-*la*-) *n.* being popular (*with*) میں ہر دلعزیزی **popularize** (-rɪz) *v.t.* make popular (among) میں مقبول کرنا، میں رواج دینا

populate (*pop*-ew-layt) *v. t.* fill (*with*) inhabitants کو آباد کرنا **population** (-*lay*-) *n.* ❶ inhabitants (of place, country, etc.) کی آبادی ❷ their number لوگوں کی تعداد، آبادی **populous** (*pop*-ew-lus) *adj.* thickly populated گنجان آبادی والا **populace** (*pop*-ew-lays) *n.* the masses عوام

porcelain (*poh**s-lin) *n.* ❶ fine glazed china چینی ❷ china چینی کے برتن

porch (poh*ch, or po*ch) *n.* built out covered approach to the doorway باہر کو نکلی ہوئی ڈیوڑھی، بیرونی ڈیوڑھی، پیش دہلیز

porcupine (*po**k-ew-pin) *n.* rat-like animal with a quilled back سیہ ، خارپُشت

a porcupine

pore (poh*) *n.* invisibly minute opening in the skin for discharge of sweat مسام any similarly minute opening مسام *v. t.* & *i.* be absorbed in the study of (*over* a book) (کے) مُطالعے میں مُنہمک ہونا meditate or carefully think (*on* or *upon* a deep problem) (پر) غور و فکر کرنا **porous** (*poh*-rus) *adj.* full of pores for liquids to ooze out مسام دار

pork (poh*k) *n.* pig's flesh سُؤر کا گوشت

pornography (po*-*nog*-ra-fi) *n.* licentious writing (esp. about prostitutes) فحاشی ، طوائفی اَدَب **pornographic** (-*nog*-) *adj* of pornography فحش ؛ طوائفوں سے مُتعلّق

porous *adj*. (see under **pore**)

porpoise (*po**-pus) *n.* a blunt snouted sea-animal about five feet long سَنگ ماہی

a porpoise

porridge (*po**-rij) *n.* oatmeal boiled in water جَو (یا جئی) کا دَلیا

port (poh*t) *n.* harbour بندرگاہ harbour town بندرگاہ a red wine پرتگالی شراب ، پورٹ صہبا (name now used for) larboard جہاز کا بایاں پہلو doorway in it for loading and unloading (جہاز میں) مال لادنے یا اُتارنے کا راستہ **porthole** *n.* one of the paned round apertures in a ship's side for admitting light (جہاز کا) رَوشن دان

portable (poh*t-a-bel) *adj.* made so as to be easily carried about آسانی سے اُٹھایا جا سکنے والا ، سَفَری *portable radio* سَفَری ریڈیو

portage (poh-*tej) *n.* conveying of goods from one port to another ایک بندرگاہ سے دُوسری بندرگاہ تک مال لے جانا ، بندر بَرداری charges for it بندر بَرداری

portal (*poh**-těl) *n.* gateway of a big building پھاٹک

portend (po*-*tend*) *v.t.* foretell ; be a warning of (an evil future) کا شگون ہونا ، سے قبل از وقت آگاہ کرنا

portent (*poh**-tent) *n.* omen, sign شگون marvellous thing عجیب واقعہ **portentous** (poh-*tent*-us) *adj.* foreshadowing شگون extraordinary غیر معمولی

porter (*poh**-tě*) *n.* luggage carrier at railway stations, etc. قُلی gate-keeper دَربان

portfolio (poh*t-*foh*-li-oh) *n.* (pl. *portfolios*) brief-case چمڑے کا تھیلا ، جُزدان office of a minister قلمدانِ وزارت ، قلمدان

portico (*poh**t-i-koh) *n.* (pl. porticos) covered walk غلام گردش large open porch with roof supported only on columns بارہ دَری

portion (*poh**-shěn) *n.* share in the thing distributed حِصّہ ، بخرہ part جُزو ، حِصّہ amount مِقدار *a portion (of), a small portion (of)* میں سے کچھ dowry جہیز ، دان دہیز *v. t.* divide into portions حِصّے کرنا **portionless** *adj.* one who gets no dowry جسے جہیز کچھ نہ ملے

Portland cement (poh*t-land-se-*ment*) *n.* cement made by burning a mixture of chalk and clay and having the colour of the limestone quarried from the Isle of Portland (called *Portland stone*) پورٹلینڈ سیمنٹ

portly (*poh**t-li) *adj.* stout and bulky (elderly person) شاندار جسم کا ، جسیم ، باوقار

portmanteau (poh*t-*man*-toh) *n.* (pl. *portmanteaus* or *portmanteaux* pr. -tohz) (leather) case opening into two equal parts تھیلا ، سَفَری جامہ دان

portrait (*poh**t-rit) *n.* picture, painting, or photograph (of someone) شبیہ ، تصویر graphic description (*of* someone) in words قلمی تصویر ، قلمی چہرہ

portraiture (*poh**t-ra-chě*) *n.* portrait شبیہ portraying as an art شبیہ بنانے کا فن ، تصویر کشی

portray (poh**tray*) *v. t.* make a picture (*of*) کی شبیہ بنانا ، کی تصویر کھینچنا describe graphically الفاظ میں تصویر کھینچ دینا play the role of کا کردار ادا کرنا **portrayal** (-*ray*-) *n.* portraying تصویر کشی graphic description لفظوں میں کھینچنا

pose (pohz) *v. t.* & *i.* (cause to) hold oneself in a certain position for portrayal تصویر کھنچوانے کے لیے خاص انداز سے بیٹھنا یا بٹھانا assume an affected attitude بننا pretend to be what one is not اپنے کو کچھ اور ظاہر کرنا propound or put forth (a difficult problem) (مشکل سوال) کرنا confuse thus مشکل سوال کر کے اُلجھا دینا *n.* position in posing for a picture پوز ، تصویر کھنچوانے کا انداز affected attitude بناوٹی انداز **poser** (*poh*-zě*) *n.* puzzling or awkward question عجیب سا سوال

Poseidon (po-*sī*-don) *Cl. myth.* Greek god of the sea (identified with the Roman *Neptune*) پوسیڈن

posh *adj.* (slang) stylish, elegant شاندار ، فسٹ کلاس

position (po-*zish*-ěn) *n.* (one's) place with respect to others درجہ ، مقام social or departmental status درجہ ، منصب proper place ٹھیک جگہ ، اصلی مقام *take up (one's) position*, (of a soldier) go to (his) post ready to strike or fire پوزیشن لے لینا *out of position*, misfit ناموزوں bodily posture جسم کی وضع condition حالت *not in position (to do something)*, unable (to do it) کے ناقابل attitude, or standpoint (*in some affair*) (کے بارے میں) موقف ، پوزیشن

positive (*poz*-i-tiv) *adj.* quite sure جسے پُورا یقین ہو *be positive (about)* کے بارے میں پُورا یقین ہونا definite (orders, etc.) قطعی، صریح، حتمی، جزمی (*a*) (in science and mathematics) not negative مُثبت (*b*) (in philosophy) اِیجابی (of adjectives) of the simple form (as distinct from *comparative* and *superlative* degrees) تفضیل نفسی constructive (suggestion) تعمیری concrete (help, etc.) ٹھوس *n.* photograph or slide reproducing the light and shade of the original تصویر، مثبت تصویر adjective of the positive degree تفضیل نفسی **positively** *adv.* definitely یقیناً، وثوق سے

posse (pos-e) *n.* party (of police, etc.) having legal authority دستہ، جمعیت

possess (po-*zes*) *v. t.* be in possession of (house, etc.) پر قابض ہونا have (a quality) کا حاصل ہونا، کا مالک ہونا keep with oneself کے پاس ہونا، رکھنا control (one's soul, feelings, etc.) کو قابو میں رکھنا influence پر اثر ڈالنا، سے کام لینا *possess oneself of,* (*a*) capture or seize (a town, country, etc.) لے لینا، پر حکمران ہو جانا (*b*) become the owner of کا مالک بن جانا *be possessed of,* have کے پاس ہونا *be possessed (by an evil spirit)* (پر بھوت پریت) کا سایہ ہونا **possessed** *adj.* mad ; under the influence of some spirit پاگل، جس پر کسی کا سایہ ہو **possession** (po-*zesh*-ĕn) *n.* possessing قبضہ *in possession (of),* having or owing پر قابض، کا مالک *in the possession of,* with کے پاس (often *pl.*) property ; the things possessed (by one) کی جائداد، کا سب کچھ *lose all (one's) possessions* (اپنا) سب کچھ کھو بیٹھنا **possessive** *adj.* of possession قبضے سے متعلق keen to have or keep لینے یا رکھنے کا خواہاں (case of a noun) indicating possession اِضافی، جرّی *the possessive case,* حالتِ اِضافی، جر **possessor** (-zes-) *n.* one in possession (*of*) قابض

possible (*pos*-i-bĕl) *adj.* that which can happen or be done ممکن (of solution, etc.) one likely to answer the purpose ایک مناسب، ایک موزوں **possibly** *adv.* perhaps ممکن ہے کہ، شاید in any way کسی طرح **possibility** (-*bil*-) *n.* being possible which is possible ممکن (pl.) chances of development امکانات *(something) with great possibilities* اپنے اندر شاندار امکانات رکھنے والی بات، بڑے امکانات والی بات

[1]**post** (pohst) *n.* place occupied by soldiers or policemen on duty چوکی any place of duty اداے فرض کا مقام *the last post,* last bugle call of the day in the army sounded to announce that it is time to go to sleep سو جانے کا بگل job, office نوکری، عہدہ trading station تجارتی اڈا postal department's function ڈاک any single delivery of mail (کسی وقت کی) ڈاک post office ڈاک خانہ pillar-box ڈاک کھمبا pole fixed upright کھمبا *the winning post,* goal کھیل میں وہ مقام جہاں تک پہنچنا ہو *lamp post,* pole with a lamp on it for street-lighting لیمپ والا کھمبا *prep.* (in Latin phrases) after کے بعد *post meridiem* (abbr. *p. m.*), afternoon بعد دوپہر *post mortem* or *post mortem examination* (abbr *p.m.*), autopsy ; medical examination of a body to find out the cause of its death پوسٹ مارٹم *v. t. & i.* put at a post پر لگانا، پر متعین کرنا put on a notice-board نوٹس بورڈ پر لگانا announce thus چسپاں اشتہار کے ذریعے اعلان کرنا send (something) by post ڈاک سے (یا میں یا کے ذریعے) بھیجنا drop (letters, etc.) in a pillar-box or take (them) to the post office ڈاک میں ڈالنا (old use) make a quick journey تیز سفر کرنا *post (an account) up,* write (items) in a ledger کھاتے میں درج کرنا *keep (someone) posted,* keep him well-informed کو باخبر رکھنا *well-posted,* well informed باخبر **postage** *n.* payment made for postal service in the form of stamps affixed محصول ڈاک، ٹکٹ *postage stamp,* stamp for this purpose ڈاک کا ٹکٹ، ٹکٹ **postal** (*pohs*-tĕl) *adj.* pertaining to the post ڈاک کا **postal order** *n.* a postal draft ڈاک کی ہنڈی، پوسٹل آرڈر **Postal Union** *n.* association of the chief countries of the world for postal purposes پوسٹل یونین، انجمن بَرید **postcard** *n.* card carried by post پوسٹ کارڈ، کارڈ **post-free** *adj.* (of business reply card) without postage being charged ٹکٹ لگنے کی ضرورت نہیں (of a price) including postal charges مع محصول ڈاک، ڈاک خرچ معاف **post-haste** *n.* haste in travelling like that of a post بڑی جلدی *adj.* speedy تیز *adv.* immediately or speedily فوراً، بڑی جلدی **postman** *n.* man employed to deliver letters, etc., to the addressees ڈاکیہ **postmark** *n.* official mark to cancel stamps ڈاک کی مہر، ڈاکخانے کی مہر **postmaster** *n.* (abb. *P.M.*) man in charge of a post office پوسٹ ماسٹر **post office** *n.* (abb. *P.O.*) a local office of the postal department ڈاکخانہ **post-office box,** *n.* (abb. *P. O. Box* and written as *P.O. Box 590,* etc.), numbered box in a post office in which letters to a particular person, etc., hiring out that box are put پوسٹ بکس نمبر **post-paid** *adj.* & *adv.* with postage already paid جس کا محصول ڈاک پیشگی ادا کر دیا گیا ہو **poster** *n.* public notice posted up (on a notice board, wall, etc.) پوسٹر، چسپاں اشتہار

[2]**post** *pref.* subsequent to کے بعد **postdate** *v. t.* put on (cheque, etc.) a date later than the date

of writing بعد کی تاریخ ڈالنا **post-dated** *adj*. bearing a later date بعد کی تاریخ کا **postgraduate** *adj*. after taking the first degree ایم۔ اے (وغیرہ) کا (یا) کے متعلق، بعد طیلسانی **posthumous** (*pos*-tew-mus) *adj*. (of a child) born after its father's death جس کا باپ اُس کی پیدائش سے پہلے ہی مر چکا ہو (of book) first published after the author's death مصنّف کے مرنے کے بعد پہلی بار شائع ہونے والی (of fame, etc.) achieved after death موت کے بعد ملنے والا **post-prandial** (-*prand*-) *adj*. after-dinner (speech, etc.) کھانے کے بعد کی (تقریر وغیرہ) **post-script** *n*. (abbr. *P.S.*) words added to the body of a letter below the signature and marked *P. S.* مکرّر آنکہ، مکرّر

posterior (pos-*tee*-ri-ĕ*) *adj*. later بعد کا placed behind پیچھے کا، پچھلا، مؤخر *n*. the buttocks چوتڑ، سُرین

posterity (pos-*te*-ri-ti) *n*. generation(s) of (one's) descendants اَخلاف later generations آیندہ نسلیں

posthumous *adj*. (see under ²**post**)

postern (*pos*-tĕ*n, or *pohs*-) *n*. back door (مکان کا) پچھلا دروازہ، بغلی دروازہ

postilion, postillion (pos-*til*-yĕn) *n*. guide of a carriage riding a left-hand horse سوار کوچوان

postmaster, *post meridiem. post mortem* (see under ¹**post**)

post-obit (pohst-*ob*-it) *n*. borrower's bond for payment on receipt of legacy ترکہ ملنے پر ادائگی کا وعدہ

postpone (pohst-*pohn*) *v.t.* put off (*to* or *till*) ملتوی کرنا **postponement** *n*. act of postponing or being postponed اِلتوا

postposition (-*zish*-) *n*. preposition as used in Urdu (so called because of being placed *after* the noun and not before it as in English) حرفِ جار

postscript *n*. (see under ²**post**)

postulate *v.t.* (*pos*-tew-layt) assume as a basis for reasoning, etc. لازمی شرط قرار دینا *n*. (-lit.) something postulated اُصول موضوعہ (in geometry) simple operation whose possibility is assumed to be self-evident اُصول موضوعہ

posture (*pos*-chĕ*) *n*. position of the body کوئی انداز، نشست (وغیرہ) *v.i.* take up a posture انداز، نشست (و برخاست)، اِختیار کرنا

posy (*poh*-zi) *n*. very small bouquet چھوٹا سا گلدستہ

pot *n*. round earthen-ware utensil for cooking ہانڈی، ہنڈیا *keep the pot boiling* (or *aboiling*) earn enough money to buy food روٹی کمانا، روٹی کے لیے پیسے کما لینا china vessel for tea, etc. دان، دانی *teapot* چائے دانی *sugar-pot* شکر دان (also *flower-pot*) earthenware vessel for flower-plants گملا receptacle in a commode پاٹ lots (*of money*) بہت سا ruin تباہی، بربادی (only in the phrase :) *go to pot* (slang) go to ruin تباہ ہو جانا *v.t.* (-tt-) put (something) safely in a pot سنبھالنے کے لیے برتن میں ڈالنا، برتن میں ڈال کر رکھنا put (plant) in a flower-pot گملے میں لگانا **pot boiler** (*pot*-) *n*. work in art or literature done merely to secure the necessaries of life محض روزی کے لیے کی ہوئی فنکاری **pothole** *n*. hole in a road made by rain and traffic سڑک کا گڑھا **pot-house** (*pot*-) *n*. ale-house شراب خانہ، کلال خانہ **pot-luck** (-*luk*) *n*. whatever is being cooked ماحضر *take a potluck* ماحضر تناول فرمایئے **potter** *n*. maker of pottery کمہار، کُل ساز **pottery** *n*. earthenware مٹی کے برتن art of a potter ظروف سازی **potsherd** (*pot*-shĕ*d) *n*. piece of broken earthenware ٹھیکرا **pot-valiance** *n*. bravery owing to being drunk نشے کی بہادری **pot-valiant** *adj*. one who is brave thus نشے کے باعث اکڑا ہوا (یا بہادر)

potable (poh-ta-bĕl) *adj*. in a liquid form so that it can be drunk نوشیدنی

potassium (po-tas-i-um) *n*. a white metal پوٹاشیم **potash** *n*. its crude alkali پوٹاش

potations (-*tay*-) *n. pl.* draughts of alcohol جرعات

potato (po-*tay*-toh) *n*. (pl. *potatoes*) a well-known edible root آلو *potato-chips*, fried chips of potatoes آلو کے قتلے

potent (*poh*-tent) *adj*. powerful (person) طاقتور virile قوّتِ مردمی والا effective (medicine, charm, reason, etc.) اثر آفریں **potency** (*poh*-tens-i) *n*. (degree of) being potent طاقت، قوّتِ مردمی، اثر آفرینی

potentate (*poh*-tent-ayt) *n*. powerful ruler طاقتور حکمران prince نواب، راجا **potential** (po-*tensh*-ĕl) *adj*. capable of becoming active بالقوّہ **potentiality** (-shi-*al*-) *n*. possibility اِمکان capacity قابلیت، اہلیت

pother (*podh*-ĕ*) *n*. commotion افراتفری، شور و غوغا، ہنگامہ *make a pother* (*about something*) (کے متعلق) ہنگامہ مچانا

potion (*poh*-shĕn) *n*. dose of liquid medicine پینے والی دوا کی خوراک drink of poison زہر کا گھونٹ

pot-pourri (poh-poo-*ree*) *n*. mixture of rose-petals and spices, etc., kept in a jar to scent a room بخورات literary medley ادبی گلدستہ musical medley موسیقی کا متنوع پروگرام

potsherd *n*. (see under **pot**)

potter (*pot*-ĕ*) *v.i.* work lazily مُردوں کی طرح کام کرنا waste (*away* one's time) وقت ضائع کرنا move (*about*) from one little job to another روزی کمانے کے لیے چھوٹے چھوٹے کام کرنا *n*. (see under **pot**)

potty *adj*. (slang) mad (*about*) (کسی کے پیچھے) دیوانہ
pouch *n*. small bag, loose pocket تھیلی، کیسہ
poultice (*pohl*-tis) *n*. soft hot mass of meal, linseed, etc. put on sore skin پولٹس *v. t.* put a poultice on پولٹس باندھنا
poultry (*pohl*-tri) *n. pl.* domestic fowl, ducks, etc. مرغیاں، بطخیں وغیرہ **poulterer** *n.* dealer in poultry مرغیوں والا **poultry farm** *n.* keeping of poultry as a form of business مرغی خانہ *run a poultry-farm* مرغی خانہ کھولنا
pounce (pouns) *n.* sudden swoop جھپٹا *v.i.* seize (*on* or *upon* something) with claws جھپٹا مارنا، چنگل مار کر دبوچ لینا
pound *n.* (abb. lb., pl. *lbs.*) British unit of weight equivalent to about 7½ 'chhataks' پونڈ، رطل (abb. £, pl. same) (British) unit of money equivalent to twenty shillings پونڈ، اشرفی، مہر *penny wise pound foolish*, one who is miserly in small expenses but careless about bigger ones اشرفیاں لٹیں کوئلوں پر مہر enclosure for stray cattle کانجی ہوز *v.t. & i.* crush to pieces or powder پیسنا کچلنا strike heavily and repeatedly (*at* door, *on* piano, etc.) (پر) زور زور سے ہاتھ مارنا **poundage** *n.* commission per £ or price per lb. فی پونڈ
pour (poh*) *v. t. & i.* cause to flow in a continuous stream (*into*) (میں) انڈیلنا flow thus میں گرنا speak (*out*) freely کھل کر کہنا (of complaints, people, etc.) come (*in, into, out*, etc.) in large numbers or quantity بہت (شکایت وغیرہ کا) آنا (of rain) come down heavily زوروں سے برسنا یا پڑنا
pourparler (poo*-*pah*-lay) *n.* (usu. *pl.*) (informal opening of a discussion) between diplomatists, etc. (سیاسی گفت وشنید کا آغاز)
pout *v.t. & i.* push out (the lips) sulkily (ہونٹ) اکڑا لینا، ناک بھوں چڑھانا *n.* pouting
poverty *n.* (see under **poor**)
powder (*pou*-dĕ*) *n.* dust made by crushing something solid چورا، سفوف medicine in the form of a powder سفوف (also *face-powder*), a fragrant powder as a cosmetic پوڈر، پاؤڈر، غازہ force put into a blow گھونسے میں زور *v. t. & i.* pulverize سفوف بنانا put powder on پر سفوف ڈالنا apply face-powder to پوڈر لگانا، غازہ ملنا **gunpowder** *n.* explosive mixture of charcoal, sulphur and saltpetre بارود
power (*pou*-è*) *n.* strength قوت، طاقت any form of motive force or energy وسائل، توانائی ability to act استطاعت، بس *be in* (someone's) *power* (*to do something*) کے بس میں ہونا control (کسی کا کسی کے) اختیار، قابو *have* (*someone*) *in* (*one's*) *power* قابو میں ہونا *be in* (*one's*) *power* (*to do*) کے بس کی بات ہونا authority اقتدار (Power), state, government حکومت، طاقت *the big Powers* بڑی طاقتیں influential or powerful person (بااثر یا اختیار) شخص capacity (*of* a lens) to magnify (بڑا کرنے کی) طاقت (عدسے کی) طاقت (in mathematics) (number of) times a given number is to be multiplied by itself طاقت *raised to the power four*, (etc.) چوتھی طاقت (10) the product of this **power-house, power-station** *n.* place for the generation or distribution of electric (or other) energy پاور ہاؤس، بجلی گھر **powerful** *adj.* strong طاقتور، قوی producing great power طاقتور **powerless** *adj.* weak کمزور unable (*to do* something) (میں) بے بس، بے اختیار **power politics** *n.* diplomacy based on military power جس کی لاٹھی اس کی بھینس والی سیاست، عسکری سیاست
pox (poks) *n.* (a word that is not in decent use for) syphilis آتشک، سرخ باد
practice (*prak*-tis) *n.* doing (*of* something) (as opposed to its theory) عمل *put* (*something*) *into practice* (کو) عمل میں لانا، کو جامہ عمل پہنانا that which is done as a rule دستور، قاعدہ *be* (*one's*) *practice* (*to do*) کا دستور ہونا constant repetition (*of* something) مشق (*someone*) *in practice* جو مشق کرتا ہو (*someone*) *out of practice* جسے مشق نہ رہی ہو professional work (*of* a lawyer or private doctor) (وکیل کی) پریکٹس، (ڈاکٹر وغیرہ کا) کام all of his clients (وکیل کے) موکل، (ڈاکٹر کے) مریض *have a large practice* کا کام خوب چلنا *retire from practice* (ڈاکٹر وغیرہ کا) کام چھوڑ دینا *sharp practice*, dishonest dealing بے ایمانی، بددیانتی *adj.* that which can be put into practice قابل عمل **practical** *adj.* of practice عملی (of person) not merely theoretical; fond of action باعمل، عملی serving a purpose مفید مقصد **practically** *adv.* in a practical manner عملی طور پر almost عملاً، تقریباً **practise** (*prak*-tis) *v. t. & i.* do (something) repeatedly to gain skill کی مشق کرنا، کی مزاولت کرنا form the habit of کی عادت ڈال لینا work as a (lawyer or doctor) پریکٹس کرنا، اپنا کام کرنا *practise the law, practise as a lawyer* وکالت کرنا *practise as a doctor, practise medicine,* ڈاکٹری کرنا، مطب جاری کرنا **practised** *adj.* skilful مشاق، ماہر **practitioner** (prak-*tish*-è-nè*) *n.* person practising (medicine or the law) پریکٹیشنر
prairie (*pray*-è-ri) *n.* North American grassland area پریری، پریریز
praise (*prayz*) *v.t.* say good things of (someone) تعریف کرنا give honour and glory (to

God) حمد وثنا کرنا، تحمد کرنا n. praising تعریف words of admiration تعریفی کلمات **praiseworthy** *adv.* deserving praise قابل تعریف، لائق ستائش، ستودہ

pram *n.* (short form for **perambulator**, which see)

prance (prahns) *v.i.* (of a horse) spring from the hind legs (گھوڑے کا) پچھلی ٹانگوں پر اچھلنا، کاول کرنا (of a person) move about gaily خوشی سے زمین پر پاؤں نہ پڑنا ، کلیلیں کرنا

prank *n.* playful trick شوخی *play a prank on (someone)* سے شوخی کرنا

prate (prayt) *v. t. & i.* chatter boastfully and foolishly بڑ ہانکنا

prattle (*prat*-ĕl) *v.t. & i.* chatter childishly about simple things بچوں کی سی باتیں کرنا *n.* such talk بچوں کی باتیں

prawn *n.* a kind of shell-fish جھینگا مچھلی

pray *v.t. & i.* worship, عبادت کرنا، نماز پڑھنا commune with God دعا کرنا humbly make requests (*to* God *for* something) (خدا سے کسی بات کی) دعا کرنا، التجا کرنا (as imperative only) please مہربانی فرماکر، ازرہ کرم

prayer *n.* praying to God دعا thing prayed for دعا (often *pl.*) form of worship نماز words used in it نماز کے الفاظ، نماز

pre- (pre) *pref.* before سے پہلے، قبل *pre-partition* قبل تقسیم *pre-war* قبل جنگ، جنگ سے پہلے

preach (preech) *v. t. & i.* deliver a sermon (*on* some topic) (پر) وعظ کرنا، (پر) خطبہ دینا give moral advice (*to*) (کو) نصیحت کرنا، (کو) وعظ و نصیحت (یا پند و موعظت) کرنا proclaim (some idea, etc.) publicly کے حق میں تقریر (یا تقریریں) کرنا

preamble (pre-*am*-bĕl) *n.* introduction (*to* a speech or writing) تمہید

prearrange (pree-a-*raynj*) *v.t.* arrange beforehand (پہلے ہی انتظام کر رکھنا (یا کر چھوڑنا)

precarious (pre-*kay*-ri-us) *adj.* depending on chance; uncertain غیر یقینی dangerous condition etc.) خطرناک، تشویشناک، دعا کا محتاج ، دعا طلب

precaution (pre-*kaw*-shĕn) *n.* care taken beforehand (*against*, risk, etc.) احتیاط، پیش بندی، حفظ ماتقدم *(as a) precautionary measure* احتیاطی تدبیر (کے طور پر)

precede (pre-*seed*) *v.t. & i.* be before (in time or order) سے پہلے (یا آگے) ہونا، مقدم **precedence** (pre-*see*-dens) *n.* higher or earlier position پیش روی، برتری *take precedence of* (or *over*) *all* پر مقدم ہونا، سے اہم ہونا

precedent (*pres*-i-dent) *n.* earlier decision, event, etc., starting a new convention نظیر

precept (*pree*-sept) *n.* rule of conduct اصول اخلاق moral advice نصیحت، وعظ و نصیحت، پند و موعظت *precept and practice* وعظ و عمل، گفتار و کردار، کہنے اور کرنے کی باتیں **preceptor** (pre-*sep*-tĕ*) *n.* (fem. *preceptress*) teacher, instructor استاد

precinct (*pree*-sinkt) *n.* enclosure (*of* a sacred or official building) احاطہ (*pl.*) immediate surroundings (*of*) گرد و نواح، قرب و جوار، نواحی علاقہ

precious (*presh*-us) *adj.* very valuable قیمتی *precious metals* قیمتی دھاتیں (یعنی سونا چاندی وغیرہ) گراں بہا، بیش *precious stones* جواہرات dear (*to* someone) بہت عزیز

preciosity (presh-i-*os*-i-ti) *n.* over-refinement in choice of words in literature or in similar points of other arts حد سے زیادہ نفاست پسندی

precipice (*pres*-i-pis) *n.* steep cliff کھڑی چٹان، ڈھانگ

precipitous (pre-*sip*-i-tus) *adj.* steep سیدھی ڈھلان والا

precipitate (pre-sip-i-tayt) *v.t.* (pre-*sip*-i-tayt) *v.t.* throw (*oneself*) headlong down (*into*) سر کے بل گرنا hurl (something) thus (*into* a course, or *upon* or *against* the enemy) پھینکنا hasten (something) to a crisis (بُرے انجام) کو جلد پہنچنا (یا، پہنچانا condense (vapour) into drops and so deposit (بخار) کو کثیف بنانا (یا) کی تکثیف کرنا cause (some ingredient) to settle down at the bottom of the liquid mixture رسوب کی شکل میں لانا *n.* (pre-*sip*-i-tit) solid thus settling down رسوب *adj.* (pre-*sip*-i-tit) violently hurried بڑا تیز، سخت عجلت کا (of person) thoughtlessly hasty (*in doing* something) بڑا جلد باز

precipitation (-*tay*-) *n.* rash haste، جلد بازی، تعجیل rainfall بارش snowfall برفباری **precipitous** *adj.* (see under **precipice**)

precis (*pray*-see, or *pres*-ee) *n.* summary as a form of literary practice, being a restatement in one's own words of the chief ideas of the original (prose) passage in about one-third of the original length خلاصہ، تلخیص *write a precis of* کی تلخیص کرنا **precis writing** *n.* practice in this form خلاصہ نویسی ، تلخیص نگاری

precise (pre-*sis*) *adj.* exact بالکل ٹھیک correctly stated ; free from error بے کم و کاست (of person) very careful in speech, etc. بہت ہی محتاط

precisely *adv.* yes, exactly واقعی، ہاں بالکل ٹھیک **precision** (pre-*sizh*-ĕn) **preciseness** *n.* accuracy بڑی صحت

preclude (pre-*klood*) *v.t.* prevent (someone *from doing* something) سے باز رکھنا shut out (doubt, etc.) خارج کرنا

precocious (pre-*kosh*-us) *adj.* (of a child, or his actions) mentally much too developed for his age اپنی عمر سے زیادہ بات کرنے والا، اپنی عمر سے زیادہ کی بات کرنے والا **precocity** (pre-*kos*-i-ti) *n.* being precocious قبل از وقت ذہنی نشو و نما

preconceive (pree-kon-*seev*) *v.t.* form (ideas or opinion) beforehand پہلے ہی سمجھ بیٹھنا **preconception** (-*sep*-) *n.* such idea, etc. پہلے ہی سے قائم کی ہوئی رائے یا خیال

precursor (pre-*kĕ**sĕ*) *n.* herald (of) (کی) خبر دینے والا، پیشرو، (کا) نقیب

predacious (pre-*day*-shus) *n.* (of animal) living by preying شکاری جانور **predatory** (*pred*-a-to-ri) *adj.* subsisting on plunder لوٹ مار کر زندگی بسر کرنے والا، غارت گر

predecessor (*pree*-de-ses-ĕ*) *n.* earlier incumbent of a post, etc. پیشرو (*one's*) *predecessor* (کسی کا) پیشرو

predestined (pree-*destind*) *adj.* preordained مُقدّر **predestination** *n.* lot قسمت، تقدیر، مقسوم،

predetermine (pre-de-*tĕ**-min) *v.t.* determine beforehand پہلے ہی سے طے کر لینا preordain مقدّر میں لکھ دینا **predetermination** (-*nay*-) *n.* predestination تقدیر

predicament (pre-*dik*-a-ment) *n.* awkward situation ناگوار صورتِ حال dangerous situation خطرناک صورت

predicate *n.* (*pred*-i-kit) part or a statement which says something about the subject (*a*) (in grammar) مسند، خبر (*b*) (in logic) محمول *predicate adjective*, adjective used only as a predicate خبری صفت *v.t.* (*pred*-i-kayt) assert (something) about (*of* the subject) تصدیق کرنا

predict (pre-*dikt*) *v.t.* foretell (کی) پیشین گوئی (یا پیش گوئی) کرنا **predictor** (-*dik*-) instrument for predicting position, etc., of flying aircraft for aiming at it طیارہ داں **prediction** (-*dik*-) *n.* پیشینگوئی، پیش گوئی

predilection (pree-di-*lek*-shĕn) *n.* special liking (*for*) ()

predispose (pree-dis-*pohz*) *v.t.* incline beforehand (*in* favour *of*) (کے حق میں) پہلے ہی مائل کر رکھنا make liable (*to* disease, etc.) متأثّر بنانا **predisposition** (-*zish*-) *n.* being predisposed میلان، تأثّر

predominate (pre-*dom*-i-nayt) *adj.* be the most important سب سے اہم ہونا، سب سے نمایاں ہونا، سب سے بات منوا لینا، پر تسلط رکھنا prevail (*over*) پر فائق ہونا **predominant** (-*dom*-) *adj.* اہم، نمایاں، با اثر **predominance** *n.* being predominant اہمیت، تفوّق، تسلّط

pre-eminent (pre-*em*-i-nent) *adj.* best بہترین superior فائق، ممتاز **pre-eminence** *n.* superiority (*in*) افضلیت، تفوّق **pre-emption** (-*emp*-) *n.* foremost right to the purchase of something شفعہ، حقِ شفعہ

preen *v.t.* (of a bird) trim (itself or its feathers) with its beak چونچ سے پر صاف کرنا smarten up (*oneself*) بننا، سنورنا، بن سنور کر نکلنا

prefabricate (pre-*fab*-ri-kayt) *v.i.* manufacture parts of house for assembly on the site later انتقال پذیر مکان کے حصّے بنانا **prefab** (*pree*-fab) *n.* (colloq.) prefabricated house انتقال پذیر مکان

preface (*pref*-is) *n.* introductory remarks (*to*) one's own (book, speech, etc.) تمہید، دیباچہ *v.t.* begin (talk, etc., *with* something) (تقریر وغیرہ) اس تمہید سے شروع کرنا کہ

prefect (*pree*-fekt) *n.* one of the senior students of college or university whose duty is to keep a watch over the extramural activities of fellow-students پریفیکٹ governor of a French Department or ancient Roman Province (فرانس یا قدیم روما کا) صوبیدار

prefer (pre-*fĕ**) *v.t.* (-rr-) choose rather (something or *to do* or *doing* something) زیادہ پسند کرنا، کو ترجیح دینا submit (request, etc.) پیش کرنا promote (someone) کو ترقی دینا **preferable** (*pref*-ĕ-rab-ĕl) *adj.* desirable پسندیدہ superior (*to*) سے بہتر **preferably** *adv.* rather than something else بہتر یہی ہوگا کہ **preference** (*pref*-e-rens) *n.* preferring ترجیح something preferred پسندیدہ چیز *I don't have any preference*, it is all the same to me میرے لیے کوئی فرق نہیں پڑتا *preference shares*, share with fixed rate of profit irrespective of the company's profit or loss ترجیحی حصص **preferential** *adj.* (of taxes, treatment, etc.) giving or receiving preference امتیازی، ترجیحی **preferment** (-*fĕ**-) *n.* promotion to higher office (esp. ecclesiastical) (بالخصوص پادریوں کی) ترقی

prefigure (pre-*fig*-ĕ*) *v.t.* represent (coming event, etc.) beforehand قبل از وقت نشان بتانا، کی بشارت دینا **prefiguration** (-*ray*-), **prefigurement** *n.* act of prefiguring or being prefigured قبل از وقت نشان، بشارت

prefix *n.* (*pree*-fiks) letter, syllable or word put at the beginning of stem to modify its meaning سابقہ courtesy word (like *Mr* or *Mrs*) used before one's name القاب *v.t.* (pre-*fiks*) add a prefix to سابقہ لگانا add (a preface, etc., to something) at the beginning پیش لفظ، دیباچہ چڑھانا، کے شروع میں چڑھانا

pregnant (*preg*-nant) *adj.* (of a woman) in the family way حاملہ (of an animal) about to have young گابھن full of meaning معنی خیز big (*with* possibilities, suggestions, etc.) سے معمور **pregnancy** (*preg*-nans-i) *n.* being in the family w حمل

prehensile (pre-*hens*-il) *adj*. (of tail or foot) capable of grasping پکڑنے کے قابل ، گیرندہ
prehistoric (pree-his-*to*-rik) *adj*. before the days recorded by history زمانۂ قبل تاریخ کا
prejudge *v.t.* judge beforehand پہلے ہی سے رائے قائم کر لینا
prejudice (*prej*-oo-dis) *n*. opinion formed beforehand (*against* or *in favour of* something) میلان خاطر *to the prejudice of* (*someone's*) *interests* (*etc.*) جس سے کسی کے مفاد (وغیرہ) کو نقصان پہنچنے کا اندیشہ ہو *v.t.* cause (someone) to have a prejudice (*against*) (کسی کے خلاف کسی) کے کان بھرنا ، (کسی کی طرف سے کسی) کا دل پھیرنا **prejudicial** (pre-joo-*dish*-ĕl) *adj*. harmful (*to* the interests of someone) (کے مفاد) کے خلاف
preliminary (pre-*lim*-i-na-ri) *adj*. initial ابتدائی *n*. preliminary action, etc. ابتدائی قدم
premature (pree-ma-*tew*-ē*) *adj*. happening before the proper time قبل از وقت ، خام *premature delivery* قبل از وقت وضع حمل **prematurely** before proper time *adj*. قبل از وقت **prematurity** (tew-ē-ri-) *n*. being premature کچا ہونا ، ناپختگی ، خامکاری
premeditate (pree-*med*-i-tayt) *v.t.* think (something) out beforehand پہلے ہی سے سوچ سمجھ لینا **premeditated** *adj*. thought out beforehand سوچا سمجھا ہوا ، دانستہ
premier (*pree*-mi-ĕ*) *adj*. first اوّل ، اوّلیں *n*. prime minister وزیر اعظم **premiere** (pre-me-*ay*-ē*) *n*. first night (*of the*) performance of a (play) or the screening of a (picture) (کا) پریمیئر شو (کی) پہلی رات ، (کی) اوّلیں نمائش
premise, premiss (*prem*-is) *n*. proposition in logic from which an inference is drawn مقدمہ *major premiss* کبریٰ *minor premiss* صغریٰ **premise** (pre-*miz*) *v. t.* state by way of introduction (*that*) بطور تمہید کہنا ، شروع میں کہنا **premises** (*prem*-i-siz) *n. pl.* (with sing. verb) building and adjuncts عمارت اور متعلقات
premium (*pree*-mi-um) *n*. of (insurance) instalment بیمہ کی قسط apprenticeship allowance (کاریگری میں) شاگردی کا وظیفہ amount of increase in the value of a share (قیمت حصص میں) بڑھوتی *put a premium on* (*something*) (کی قدر میں) اضافہ کرنا *at a premium*, above par (پر) مقررہ قیمت سے زیادہ
premonition (pre-mo-*nish*-ĕn) *n*. uneasiness regarded as a forewarning (*of* impending trouble, etc.) اندیشہ ، خطرے کا احساس ، دل کو کچھ ہونا
preoccupy (pre-*ok*-ew-pi) *v.t.* fully absorb the attention of (someone or someone's mind) سوچ میں غرق کرنا occupy beforehand پہلے ہی قبضہ میں لے لینا **preoccupation** (-*pay*-) *n*. something that preoccupies گہری سوچ ، فکر
preordain (pree-o*-*dayn*) *v. t.* (of God) predestine مقدر میں لکھ دینا
prep *n*. (school slang for) preparation (*of* lessons, etc.) سبق کی تیاری time devoted to it سبق کی تیاری کا وقت (abbr. for) preparatory school ابتدائی مدرسہ
prepare (pre-*pay*-ē*) *v. t.* & *i.* get or make ready (*for* something) (کی) تیاری کرنا یا کرانا ، تیار ہونا یا کرنا *be prepared* (*to do something*) (کرنے کو) آمادہ یا تیار رہنا **preparation** (-*ray*-) *n*. preparing تیاری prep سبق کی تیاری (کا وقت) food, medicine, etc., specially prepared خاص طور پر تیار کی ہوئی چیز **preparatory** (-*pa*-) *adj*. initial ابتدائی serving to prepare or for preparing ابتدائی ، تیاری کا *preparatory school*, primary (etc.) school ابتدائی مدرسہ **preparedness** *n*. being prepared تیار ہونا
preponderate (pre-*pond*-è-rayt) *v. i.* predominate (*over*) (پر) حاوی ہونا predominate سے بڑا (یا) زیادہ (یا) زیادہ اہم (یا) زیادہ بااثر ہونا **preponderant** *adj*. more influential, etc. زیادہ وقیع ، زیادہ **preponderance** *n*. being preponderant زیادہ ہونا ، زیادہ بھاری ہونا
preposition (prep-o-*zish*-èn) *n*. part of speech governing a noun or pronoun and placed before it to indicate its relation to others حرف جار ، حرف جر **prepositional** *adj*. جاری *prepositional phrase* مرکب جاری
prepossessing (pree-po-*zes*-ing) *adj*. attractive دلکش ، من موہنا ، اچھا لگنے والا **prepossession** *n*. favourable impression formed beforehand حسن ظن
preposterous (pre-*pos*-te-rus) *adj*. contrary to natural order گھوڑے کے آگے گاڑی جوتنے والا معاملہ ، الٹی گنگا absurd لغو
prerequisite (pree-*rek*-wiz-it) *n*. 'sine qua non' or necessary condition (*of*) (کی) بنیادی شرط ، اشرط اوّلیں *adj*. necessary بنیادی حق اوّلیں
prerogative (pree-*rog*-a-tiv) *n*. special privilege (*of* a ruler)
presage *n*. (*pres*-ij) ominous sign بری فال ، شگون portentous feeling آنے والے خطرے کا احساس ، اندیشہ *v.t.* (pre-*sayj*) be a sign of آنے والے خطرے کا نشان ہونا
prescience (*pree*-shi-ens) *n*. foresight دور اندیشی foreknowledge پیش بینی **prescient** (*pree*-shi-ent) *adj*. having prescience دور اندیش ، پیش بیں
prescribe (pres-*krib*) *v.t.* & *i.* advise the use of (a medicine) نسخہ لکھ دینا order the use of a book as a (text-book *for* an examination) (بطور) نصاب ، مقرر کرنا lay down (punishment, etc.) as

a rule مُقرّر کرنا order (*someone to do*) (کا) حُکم دینا **prescription** (*-krip-*) *n.* prescribing ہدایت کرنا order حُکم direction ہدایت (*doctor's*) prescribed medicine نسخہ right on property, etc., acquired by its long and uninterrupted use or possession حقِ بذریعہ قبضہ، حقِ قدامت

present *n.* (*prez-ent*) time at this moment حال *at present* اِس وقت form of verb relating to the present فعلِ حال gift تحفہ، ہدیہ یا ہدیہ *adj.* existing or happening now حال کا، اب کا *the present moment* ابھی، فی الحال *at the present moment* اِس وقت اب present here or now موجودہ *the present company excepted*, (said as a polite exception when some harsh general remark is passed) یہاں موجود حضرات کے علاوہ *v. t.* (*pri-zent*) offer as a gift تحفہ دینا، تحفہ پیش کرنا submit to someone (*for* action, etc.) (کو) پیش کرنا *present* (*oneself at a place* or *before a person*) (کے رُوبرُو) پیش ہونا *present* (*oneself*) (*for examination*, take it اِمتحان میں شریک ہونا introduce (someone *at* Court or *to* some big person) کی خدمت میں تعارف کے لیے پیش کرنا hold (arm or arms) in salute (*to*) اسلحہ اُٹھا کر سلامی دینا **presence** *n.* being present in a place مَوجودگی *in the presence of* کی موجودگی میں، کے سامنے (one's) bearing وضع قطع *presence of mind*, ability to judge or act quickly in the presence of danger خطرے میں بھی ہوشمندی، خواس قائم رکھنا، اوسان خطا نہ ہونے دینا **presently** *adv.* soon ابھی، تھوڑی دیر میں **presentable** *adj.* (of thing) fit to be shown in public جو دیکھنے میں اچھا لگے attractive (appearance, etc.) خوش وضع **presentation** (*-tay-*) *n.* something presented at a public ceremony پیشکش **presentment** (*-zent-*) *n.* way something is presented پیش کرنے کا طریق performance of play, etc. پیشکش **presentiment** (pre-*zent*-i-ment) *n.* feeling of something evil being about to happen کسی آنے والے خطرے کا احساس، ماتھا ٹھنکنا

preserve (pre-*zĕ*v*) *v. t.* keep safe (*from* loss, etc., *for* future) محفوظ رکھنا prevent (food) from decomposition by making a jam of it (کا) مُربّہ بنانا keep (game, place, etc.) for private use, esp. hunting خود شکار کھیلنے کے لیے مخصوص کرنا maintain (silence, etc.) (چپ وغیرہ) سادھنا، چھپ اختیار کرنا *n.* (usu. *pl.*) jam مُربّہ (also *game-preserve*) grounds, streams, etc., where game is preserved شکارگاہ field of activities special to (*of* one) (کا) مخصوص دائرہ **preservation** (*-vay-*) *n.* preserving محفوظ رکھنا، حفاظت *in a good state of preservation* اچھی حالت میں

preside (pre-*zid*) *v. i.* act as chairman of (*over a meeting*) کی صدارت کرنا be the chief of (*over* business firm, etc.) کا سربراہ ہونا **president** (*prez*-i-dent) *n.* head of a democratic State صدرِ ریاست، صدرِ مملکت chairman (*of* meeting, society, board, etc.) صدر (in *U.S.*) Principal (*of* a college or university) چانسلر، پرنسپل، صدر **presidency** (*prez*-i-dens-i) *n.* office of a president صدارت term of this office مُدّتِ صدارت formerly a province under the East India Comp ny پریزیڈنسی **presidential** (*-den*-shĕl) *adj.* pertaining to (the office of) a president صدارتی

press (pres) *v.t. & i.* push hard (trigger, button of a bell, etc.) دبانا push hard (*against* something) (کو) دھکا دینا، پر دباؤ ڈالنا use force on (something) to extract its juice کو نچوڑنا keep close to (the enemy) in an attack پر دباؤ ڈالنا *press an attack*, continue it vigorously حملے کا دباؤ جاری رکھنا urge (someone *for* or *to do* something) پر زور ڈالنا be hard up خالی ہاتھ ہونا *be pressed for time*, have hardly enough of it کے پاس کافی وقت نہ ہونا *the matter is pressing* معاملہ اہم ہے *time presses* وقت ضائع نہیں کیا جا سکتا *press* (*someone's*) *hand* (محبت وغیرہ سے کسی کا) ہاتھ دبانا *press* (*something*) *on* (*someone*) (کچھ) اسے لینے کے لیے (کسی) پر زور دینا (old use) take for royal use or service بادشاہ کے نام ضبط کرنا یا بیگار میں پکڑنا *press into the service of* سے زبردستی کسی کی خدمت لینا compel (someone) to serve in the armed forces کو جبری بھرتی کرنا *n.* pressure دباؤ crowd بھیڑ، بھیڑ بھاڑ، ہجوم، اِزدحام، اژدہام apparatus, for pressing شکنجہ also (*printing press*), machine for printing پریس *in the press*, being printed زیرِ طباعت (*the Press*), the newspapers generally اخبارات *the Pakistan Press* پاکستانی اخبارات *in the Press*, شائع شدہ، اخبار میں آیا ہوا *Press cutting*, item cut out from a newspaper اخبار کا تراشہ *Press reporter*, newspaper reporter اخبار کا رپورٹر، رپورٹر، خبررساں (صحافی) *Press gallery*, reporters' gallery at a meeting, etc. پریس گیلری، صحافیوں کی نشستیں *Press agent*, person employed by filmstar, etc., to do publicity for her in the Press through news, etc. اخبارات میں پروپیگنڈا کرنے والا، پراپیگنڈا سیکرٹری *Press publicity*, such publicity اخبارات میں پراپیگنڈا bookshelf کتابوں کی الماری **pressing** *adj.* urgent (business, problem, etc.) اہم، ضروری insistent (person) اصرار کرنے والا repeated (request) بار بار کی درخواست **Pressman** *n.* newspaper reporter نامہ نگار، رپورٹر، خبررساں (صحافی) **pressgang** *n.* (of use) persons compelling others in the land forces جبری بھرتی کرنے والے

pressure (*presh-ĕ**) *n.* pressing دباؤ *blood pressure*,

pressure exercised on the heart during the circulation of blood خون کا دباؤ *high blood pressure* خون کا زیادہ دباؤ *low blood pressure* خون کا کم دباؤ *atmospheric pressure*, weight of atmosphere at a specified place and time ہوا کا دباؤ *pressure cooker*, apparatus for cooking under high pressure at high temperature پریشر کُکر، دباؤ چولھا *bring pressure to bear on (someone to do something), put pressure on (someone to do something)* کسی کام کے لیے کسی پر دباؤ ڈالنا *work at high pressure*, work energetically and speedily بڑے زور شور سے کام کرنا **pressure** *v.t.* **pressure group** *n.* (see *Addenda*)

prestige (pres-*teezh*) *n.* reputation resulting from past achievements or conduct وقار *gain (or lose) prestige* وقار بنانا یا کھونا

presumably *adv.* (see under **presume**) بڑے زور

presume (pre-*zewn*) *v. t.* & *i.* take for granted (*that*) فرض کرنا take the liberty (*to say something*) کی جرأت کرنا *presume upon (someone)*, exploit (his) kindness کی شرافت سے ناجائز فائدہ اُٹھانا *presumably* (*-zewm-*), **presumedly** (*-zewm-id-*) *adv.* as is or may fairly be presumed as a natural interpretation of facts غالباً ظاہر ہے کہ **presumption** (pre-*zump*-shĕn) *n.* something taken for granted مفروضہ likelihood احتمال (in law) universally applicable inference ہر جگہ لاگو ہونے والا نتیجہ overconfidence بر خود غلط ہونا، خود پرستی boldness taking undue advantage of another's courtesy دیدہ دلیری، شوخ چشمی **presumptive** *adj.* (of evidence, etc.) based on presumption احتمالی *heir-presumptive*, heir (to the throne, etc.) pending the birth of someone with a stronger claim موجودہ ولی عہد *adj.* **presumptuous** (pre-*zump*-tew-us) *adj.* impudently bold (behaviour) دیدہ دلیری کا، شوخ چشمی کا

presuppose (pre-su-*pohz*) *v. t.* assume beforehand (*that*) پہلے ہی سے سمجھ بیٹھنا، قبل از وقت فرض کر لینا imply, involve پر منتج ہونا **presupposition** (*-zish-*) *n.* something presumed مفروضہ

pretend (pre-*tend*) *v.t.* & *i.* feign (*to be* something) بن بیٹھنا make believe (*to be* or *to be doing* something) جھوٹ موٹ کرنا make a false show of (love, friendship, etc.) میں جھوٹ موٹ جتانا، کا feign (something) as an excuse تصنّع سے کام لینا lay a false claim to (the throne, etc.) بہانہ کرنا یا بنانا جھوٹا دعویٰ کرنا، اِدّعا کرنا **pretender** *n.* false claimant جھوٹا دعویدار، مُدّعی **pretence** (pre-*tens*) *n.* false claim جھوٹ موٹ، بہانہ، تصنّع، جھوٹا دعویٰ **pretension** *n.* claim دعویٰ outward show تصنّع بناوٹ **pretentious** (pre-*ten*-shus) *adj.* laying claim to importance اپنی اہمیت جتانے والا ostentatious نمود و نمائش والا

preterite (*pret*-e-rit) *adj.* simple past (tense) فعل، ماضی مطلق

pretext (*pree*-tekst) *n.* pretended excuse بہانہ، عذر *under the pretext of* کے بہانے

pretty (*prit*-i) *adj.* (of children or women) beautiful not in the real sense but only by being attractive and winning پیاری لگنے والی، جاذبیت والی pleasing دلکش *adv.* (colloq.) much ; quite کافی، بہت *pretty much the same thing*, almost the same thing قریب قریب وہی **prettiness** *n.* being pretty دلکشی، جاذبیت **prettily** *adv.* خوبی سے، خوش اسلوبی سے، خوبصورتی سے، اچھے انداز سے

prevail (pre-*vayl*) *v. i.* be victorious (*over* or *against*) پر غلبہ پانا، پر فتح حاصل کرنا، پر غالب آنا be current or widespread (*in a place*) (میں) کا رواج ہونا، (میں) عام ہونا prevail (*on* or *upon* someone *to do* something), persuade (him to do it) (پر) آمادہ کرنا **prevalent** (*prev*-a-lent) *adj.* current (customs, etc.) رائج، مروّجہ **prevalence** (*prev*-a-lens) *n.* widespread occurrence (*of*) (کا) زور، (کا) ہر جگہ پھیلا ہونا

prevent (pre-*vent*) *v. t.* stop (something) from taking place نہ ہونے دینا hinder someone's *doing* or (someone *from doing* something) (سے) روکنا (سے) باز رکھنا save (some one or something *from being*) (سے) بچانا **preventable** (*-vent-*) *adj.* that which can be prevented جسے روکا جا سکے، جس سے بچا جا سکے **prevention** (*-vensh-*) *n.* preventing روکنا preventive measure احتیاط، احتیاطی تدبیر *prevention is better than cure* علاج سے احتیاط بھلی **preventive** (pre-*vent*-iv) *adj.* serving to prevent prophylactic احتیاطی

preview (*pre*-view) *n.* exhibition (of a film, play, etc.) to a special group before release ابتدائی نمائش

previous (*pree*-vi-us) *adj.* earlier پہلا *previous to (something)*, before (it) سے پہلے **previously** *adj.* before پہلے

prey (pray) *n.* what is hunted down and killed (mostly for food) شکار، صید *beast of prey* درندہ *bird of prey* شکاری پرندہ *seize a prey* شکار کرنا *fall a prey to* کے ہاتھوں شکار ہونا (be) *a prey to* (fears, disease, misfortunes, etc.) کا شکار ہونا *v.i.* *prey upon*, (*a*) hunt as prey کا شکار کرنا (*b*) (of misfortunes, etc.) trouble greatly کے لیے وبال جان بن جانا

price (pris) sale-price قیمت فروخت، مول، قیمت value قدر و قیمت، قیمت *beyond price* انمول physical or mental cost at which something is obtained

price of freedom آزادی کی قیمت *price on (someone's) head*, reward for capturing him رکو، پکڑنے یا پکڑوانے کا انعام *v.t.* fix as the price کی قیمت لگانا یا مقرر کرنا mark (goods) with price پر قیمت لگانا (یا) درج کرنا
priceless *adj.* invaluable انمول **pricelessness** *n.* being priceless
prick (prik) *v.t.* & *i.* puncture (something) with a sharp point میں چھید کرنا hurt thus چبھونا cause a sharp physical or mental pain چبھن پیدا کرنا، تکلیف پہنچانا feel sharp pain میں چبھن اٹھنا suddenly raise (*up the ears*) to listen to the sound کان کھڑے کرنا *n.* puncture چھید *a pin prick*, (a) puncture by a pin-point سوئی کی نوک سے چھید (b) irritating thing چبھن **prickle** (*prik*-ĕl) *n.* thorn کانٹا، خار thorny growth on the skin of certain animals کانٹا *v.t.* & *i.* tingling خراش ہونا، بے چینی محسوس ہونا، جھنجھناہٹ
prickly *adj.* having prickles خاردار tingling جھنجھناہٹ پیدا کرنے والا **prickly heat** *n.* skin disorder in tropical summer گرمی دانے
pride (prīd) *n.* haughtiness غرور، تکبر، کبر، نخوت too high an opinion of فخر، فخر و ناز، فخر و مباہات *take pride in* پر فخر کرنا that about whom or which such opinion is held باعث فخر، موجب افتخار، وجہ ناز dignity; self-respect عزت، خودداری *v.t.* be proud of پر اترانا، پر فخر کرنا *pride (oneself or upon)*, take pride in پر فخر کرنا
priest (preest) *n.* minister of religious worship دینی پیشوا (یعنی امام، مولوی، ملا، پادری، پروہت، پنڈت، پجاری، گرنتھی وغیرہ) (esp.) Christian clergyman (Roman Catholic or Anglican Protestant) of the third order, *i.e.*, above a deacon but below a bishop بڑا پادری **priestess** *n.* woman priest دینی پیشوا عورت
priestly *adj.* of a priest or priesthood دینی پیشوائی سے متعلق **priesthood** *n.* profession of a priest دینی پیشوائی priestly hierarchy دینی پیشواؤں کا نظام
prig *n.* one who is a bit too particular in moral didacticism واعظ خود بیں one over-conceited about speech, manners, language, etc. رفتار و گفتار میں کچھ زیادہ ہی محتاط **priggish** *adj.* over-conscious of moral superiority اپنی نیکی پر حد سے زیادہ فخر کرنے والا، اخلاقی طور پر خود بیں **priggery** *n.* priggish conduct نیکی پر حد سے زیادہ فخر، اخلاقی خود بینی
prim *adj.* affecting propriety مقطع، تکلف شعار
primacy (*prī*-ma-si) *n.* archbishop's office اسقف اعظم کا منصب pre-eminence اولیت، برتری **primate** *n.* archbishop اسقف اعظم member of the highest biological order of the mammals, *i.e.*, man, woman or child نوع اولی **primates** (prī-*may*-teez) *pl* (usu. *the Primates*) this order نوع اولی

prima donna (*pree*-ma-*don*-a) *n.* chief woman singer in an opera اوپرا کی اولیں مغنیہ
prima facie (*prī*-ma-fay-shi-ee) *adj.* obvious at the first sight پہلی ہی نظر میں واضح، بدیہی *adv.* at the first sight پہلی ہی نظر میں، بدیہی طور پر
primary (*prīm*-a-ri) *adj.* first ابتدائی پہلا *primary school* ابتدائی مدرسہ chief اہم، سب سے بڑا basic (colour) بنیادی original (meaning, sense)
primate *n.*, **primates** *n. pl.* (see under **primacy**)
prime (prīm) *adj.* chief, principal اعلیٰ، اعظم *prime minister*, premier وزیر اعظم original (mover, etc.) اصلی best (grade, meat, etc.) اول نمبر، سب سے اچھا، بہترین *prime numbers*, those having no factors اعداد مفرد *n.* first and finest part (of) کا بہترین حصہ (in) *the prime of life* عنفوان شباب میں (کا) شباب *be cut off in one's prime* عین عالم شباب میں مرجانا *v.t.* & *i.* prepare (water pump, etc.) for action by pouring water into it for the first time پمپ پہلی بار چلانے کے لیے پانی ڈالنا get (thing) going چلنے کے لیے ٹھیک ٹھاک کرنا fill (person *with* liquor, information, facts, etc.) (سے) بھرنا tutor (a witness) (گواہ کو) خوب سکھانا put the first coat of paint or plaster on پر روغن یا پلستر کی پہلی تہہ چڑھانا **primer** (*prī*-mĕ*) *n.* infant's first text-book قاعدہ any book for beginners ابتدائی کتاب
primeval, primaeval (pri-*mee*-vĕl) *adj.* of the earliest age of the world پرانا، قدیم، قدیمی primitive
primitive (*prim*-i-tiv) *adj.* of the earliest times پرانا، قدیم، قدیمی، ابتدائی ادوار کا *primitive art* ابتدائی ادوار کی فنکاری simple; in an early form of development سادہ، ابتدائی old-fashioned فرسودہ، دقیانوسی
primogeniture (prī-mo-*jin*-i-chĕ*) *n.* the first-born son's right to succeed جیٹھائی
primordial (prī-*mo**-di-ĕl) *adj.* of the first series اولیں
primrose (*prim*-rohz) *n.* a pale yellow spring flower پریم روز، بسنتی گلاب *adj.* of this colour بسنتی

primrose

primus (prī-mus) *adj.* (attached to a pupil's name) first پہلا یا پہلی، اول *Abdul Aziz primus* عبدالعزیز پہلا similarly *secundus* دوم *tertius* سوم *quartus* چہارم *quintus* پنجم *sextus* ششم *septimus* ہفتم *octavius* ہشتم *nonus* نہم *decimus* دہم *n.* brand name of a stove burning vaporized oil پرائمس سٹوو
prince (prins) *n.* ruler of a small State نواب راجا son of a ruler شہزادہ *Prince Consort*, husband of a female ruler ملکہ کا رفیق حیات *Prince of darkness*, Satan شیطان **princess** (*prins*-es) *n.* daughter,

daughter-in-law or grand-daughter, etc., of a ruler شہزادی wife of a prince رانی، نواب بیگم **princely** *adj.* of a prince نوابی befitting a prince شاہانہ magnificent شاندار **principality** (-*pal*-) *n.* dominion of a prince ریاست

principal (*prins*-i-pĕl) *adj.* chief, most important بڑا، اہم *n.* head of college پرنسپل، رئیس الاساتذہ، صدر، مخدوم one employing another as his agent مالک money lent out on interest اصل زر **principally** *adj.* mainly زیادہ تر (also see **principle**)

principality (-*pal*-) *n.* (see under **prince**)

principle (*prins*-i-pĕl) *n.* primary source اصل، بنیاد، سرچشمہ، منبع fundamental truth as a basis of reasoning بنیادی حقیقت law of cause and effect علت و معلول کا اصول (یا سلسلہ) guide for moral conduct اصول *on principle, as a matter of principle* اصولی طور پر *against the principle* خلافِ اصول *against (one's) principles* کے اصولوں کے خلاف *a man of principle* با اصول انسان **principled** *adj.* (man) of (*high* or *loose*) principles اصول پرور (یا بے اصول) (also see *principal*)

print *v.t.* make marks on (sand, etc.) by pressure نشان چھوڑنا، نقش کرنا stamp pattern on cloth ٹھپا لگانا، چھاپنا produce (book, picture, etc.) thus in press چھاپنا، طبع کرنا write (words, one's name, etc.) in block letters چھاپے کے بڑے حرفوں میں لکھنا make (a photograph) on paper, etc., from a negative مثبت عکس تیار کرنا، فوٹو تیار کرنا impress (*on* mind, etc.) پر نقش چھوڑنا *n.* something printed in press مطبوعہ چیز، چھپی ہوئی چیز، چھاپا *under print* زیرِ طباعت *in print*, (of a printed book) on sale بازار میں موجود، عام *out of print*, (of a book) no more printed copies available نادستیاب ہونے والی (کتاب)، ختم ہو چکی ہوئی (کتاب) (small, large, clear, etc.) lettering مطبوعہ حروف، حروف impression نشان، نقش *finger prints* انگلیوں کے نشان *footprint* نقشِ قدم *footprints on the sands of time* تہذیب و تمدن کی ترقی کے لیے اٹھے ہوئے قدموں کے نقوش picture, design, etc., made by printing نقش، چھاپا printed cotton cloth چھاپے کا کپڑا photograph printed from a negative فوٹو، مثبت عکس، عکس **printer** *n.* workman or owner of a printing press چھاپے خانے (میں کام کرنے) والا

printing press *n.* machine for printing books, etc. پریس، چھاپنے کی مشین premises for this business پریس، چھاپہ خانہ، مطبع

prior (*prī*-ĕ*) *adj.* previous پہلا *adv.* (*prior to*), previously پہلے *n.* abbot's assistant عیسائی خانقاہ کا نائب، سربراہ، مقدم راہب **prioress** *n. fem.* woman prior مقدم راہبہ **priority** (-*o*-) *n.* being earlier اوّلیت urgency; claim for urgent attention اوّلیت *top priority* اشد ضروری (ہونا)، سب سے پہلے، سب کچھ ضروری ہونا *give priority to* کی طرف پہلے توجہ کرنا، سب کچھ چھوڑ کر یہ، سب سے اہم (سمجھ کر) توجہ کرنا

prism (prizm) *n.* solid elongated triangle looking like a tent منشور (also *glass prism*), solid glass triangle (not elongated) for breaking up white light into coloured rays منشور **prismatic** *adj.* of the form of a prism منشوری *prismatic glasses, prismatic binoculars*, field-glasses shortened by the use of prisms منشوری دوربین bright and variegated (colours) بوقلموں

prison (priz-ĕn) *n.* gaol جیل، قید خانہ، بندی خانہ، محبس *send (someone) to prison* (کسی کو) قید کرنا *lie in prison* قید میں پڑے ہونا any place of captivity قید خانہ

prisoner *n.* one kept in prison after or pending conviction by a law-court قیدی *prisoner at the bar*, one produced for trial زیرِ سماعت قیدی *prisoner of state, political prisoner* سیاسی قیدی *prisoner of war* (abb. *P.O.W.*), enemy soldier captured in a battle جنگی قیدی one confined (*to a place, to one's* room, to *one's* chair, etc.) owing to illness, etc. گرفتار

pristine (*pris*-tin) *adj.* (like that) of early times قدیم جیسا، قدیمی unspoilt by modern tendencies اپنی اصلی شان والا، بدعتوں سے خالی

private (*prī*-vayt) *adj.* not public خاص، نجی personal ذاتی، انفرادی *private means* unearned income محنت کے بغیر کی آمدنی، املاک سے آمدنی normally kept hidden پوشیدہ، نہانی، مخصوص *private parts*, اعضائے مخصوصہ (یا) اندامِ نہانی secret (information, etc.) خفیہ، مخفی unofficial (person, information, etc.) غیر سرکاری (*soldier*) of the lowest *rank in the army* سپاہی *n.* سپاہی کے درجے کا فوجی private soldier فوج کا سپاہی، جوان privacy علیحدگی، خلوت (in the phrase) *in private*, privately علیحدگی میں **privately** *adv.* alone and not before others علیحدگی میں، الگ

privacy (*priv*-a-si) *n.* secrecy اخفا seclusion علیحدگی، خلوت **privateer** (priv-a-*tee*-ĕ*) *n.* (old use) privately-owned man-of-war غیر سرکاری جنگی جہاز

privation (pri-*vay*-shĕn) *n.* poverty and hardship غریبی، عسرت، افلاس، مفلوک الحالی deprivation محرومی

privilege (*priv*-i-lej) *n.* special right امتیازی حق special favour استحقاقی رخصت، استحقاق *enjoy a privilege* مراعات حاصل کرنا **privileged** *adj.* enjoying a privilege جسے مراعات حاصل ہوں *privileged classes*, well-to-do classes امیر، اونچے طبقات

privy (*priv*-i) *adj.* (in law) secret خفیہ، مخفی، پنہاں، پوشیدہ *be privy to*, have secret or private information about سے خفیہ طور پر آگاہ ہونا privat purse (purse) of a ruler خاصہ کا، خاص *privy purse* خزانۂ خاص، خاصہ confidential (counsellors, etc.) of a ruler خاص رازدان **Privy Council** *n.* chosen body of the British sovereign's counsellors acting also as the highest court of appeal پریوی کونسل، مُستشارِ دولت

prize (prīz) *n.* winner's reward اِنعام anything sought after or striven for جس کے لیے جانفشانی کی جائے valuable thing or person قابلِ قدر چیز یا شخص captured enemy ship جنگ میں پکڑا ہوا جہاز property captured in naval warfare بحری جنگ میں ہاتھ آیا ہوا مالِ غنیمت ، بحری یغما *adj.* awarded as a prize اِنعام (کی) ، میں ملا ہوا *v.t.* esteem greatly ; value highly (کی) بڑی قدر کرنا ، (کو) بہت عزیز رکھنا یا جاننا force (lid, etc., *open, up,* or *off with* a lever, etc.) برم (وغیرہ) سے کھولنا **prize-fight** *n.* boxing match with a prize مُکّے بازی کا اِنعامی مُقابلہ

pro- (proh) *pref.* for, in favour کا حامی *pros and cons* (of) arguments for and against موافق اور مُخالف دلائل

probable (*prob*-a-bĕl) *adj.* likely اَغلب **probably** *adv.* most likely غالباً **probability** (-*bil*-) *n.* being probable اِمکانِ غالب chance اِتفاق *in all probability,* very likely

probation (pro-*bay*-shĕn) *n.* trial period آزمائشی مُدّت *on probation* آزمائشی test آزمائش (in law) (system) of reforming (juvenile) offenders after their first offence قیدیوں کی اِصلاح *probation officer,* قیدیوں کی اِصلاح کا اَفسر **probationer** (-*bay*-) *n.* one on probation in service آزمائشی

probe (prohb) *n.* surgeon's slender instrument for examining depth, etc., of a wound زخم سلائی *v.t.* examine (wound) with a probe زخم سلائی ڈال کر دیکھنا inquire thoroughly (*into*) کی گہرائی میں جانا (کی) تہہ تک پہنچنا act of probing تفتیش کرنا **probity** (*prob*-i-ti) *n.* integrity دیانتداری

problem (prob-lem) *n.* difficult question or issue مسئلہ **problematic, problematical** (-*mat*-) *adj.* doubtful (result) مشکوک ، مشتبہ

procedure (pro-see-dew-ĕ*) *n.* regular method طریقِ کار

proceed (pro-*seed*) *v.i.* go (*to* a place) جانا continue (*with* or *to do* something) کرتے رہنا result (*from*) (کا) نتیجہ ہونا take legal action (*against*) نالش کرنا **proceedings** *n.* pl. lawsuit مقدمہ ، نالش *take* (or *start.*) *proceedings against* (پر) نالش کرنا work (*of* a meeting, case, etc.) کارروائی minutes (*of a meeting*) (کی) کارروائی کا خلاصہ receipts وصولی

process (*proh*-ses) *n.* series (*of* some action) کا عمل یا فعل manufacturing method بنانے کا طریقہ course of progress ترقی (بننے کا) دوران *in process of* (بننے وغیرہ) کے دوران میں *v.t.* make (things) through a process بنانا preserve by specially treating محفوظ رکھنے کے لیے ٹھیک کرنا

procession (pro-*sesh*-ĕn) *n.* large number of persons, etc., moving forward in ranks جلوس *march in procession* (*through*) (میں) جلوس نکالنا

proclaim (pro-*klaym*) *v. t.* announce officially (a someone, a king or criminal ; a holiday, etc.) سرکاری طور پر اعلان کرنا ، باضابطہ اعلان کرنا **proclamation** (-may-) *n.* باضابطہ اعلان

proclivity (pro-*kliv*-i-ti) *n.* bent (*to*, towards, *to do*, or *for doing* something) رُجحان ، میلان

procrastinate (pro-*kras*-ti-nayt) *v.i.* be dilatory ڈھیل کرنا ، تاخیر کرنا ، معرضِ تعویق میں ڈالنا **procrastination** (-*nay*-) *n.* act of procrastinating ڈھیل ، تاخیر ، تعویق

procreate (*prohk*-re-ayt) *v. i.* produce offspring جننا ، بچہ پیدا کرنا ، نسل بڑھانا **procreation** (-*ay*-) *n.* act of procreating زائیدگی ، افزائشِ نسل

procter (*prok*-tĕ*) *n.* university official in charge of students' discipline جامعہ کا مُحتسِب

procure (pro-*kew*-e*) *v. t.* obtain with effort حاصل کرنا bring about کا سبب ہونا **procurable** *adj.* that can be procured قابلِ حصول

prod *v. t.* & *i.* (-dd-) poke (*at* an animal *with* a rod, etc.) (جانور کو) چھیڑنا یا چھیڑتے جانا *n.* poke چھیڑنا ، چبھونا

prodigal (*prod*-i-gal) *adj.* extravagant فضول خرچ ، مُسرف *the prodigal son* مُسرف بیٹا wasteful (*of* something) کو ضائع کرنے والا *n.* spendthrift فضول خرچ ، مُسرف

prodigious (pro-*dij*-us) *adj.* huge بہت بڑا astonishing حیرت انگیز

prodigy (*prod*-i-ji) *n.* remarkably able person حیرت انگیز طور پر قابل ، غیر معمولی اوصاف کا حامل marvellous حیرت انگیز

produce *v. t.* (pro-*dews*) *v. t.* bring about لانا ، وجود میں لانا present (witness, proof, ticket, etc.) پیش کرنا reproduce (young) (بچہ) دینا ، پیدا کرنا manufacture (goods) بنانا create (works of art, etc.) تخلیق کرنا stage, put on (a play) پیش کرنا be responsible *for the production* of a film پیش کرنا *n.* (*prod*-ews) that which is grown on land زرعی پیداوار ، پیداوار **producer** (-dew-) *n.* manufacturer (*of* goods as opposed to their *consumer*) پیداوار one responsible for the production of a film فلم ساز ، پیش کار **producer gas** *n.* cheap gas produced by passing steam, etc., over red-hot coal سستی گیس **product** (*prod*-ukt) *n.* manufacturer مصنوعہ چیز ، مصنوعات anything produced پیداوار number resulting from multiplication حاصل ضرب **production** (*-duk-*) *n.* producing پیدا کرنا، اگانا، بنانا that which is produced پیداوار its quantity پیداوار کی مقدار **productive** (*-duk-*) *adj.* yielding produce and profitable (*productive of*), resulting in (کی) پیدا کرنے والا، کا باعث

proem (*proh*-em) *n.* preface ; introductory discourse تمہید، مقدمہ

profane (pro-*fayn*) *adj.* secular دُنیوی، لادینی sacrilegious دین کی بے حرمتی کرنے والا *v.t.* commit sacrilege دین کی بے حرمتی کرنا **profaneness, profanity** *n.* sacrilege دین کی بے حرمتی swear-words گالیاں

profess (pro-*fes*) *v. t.* declare openly (*one's*) ignorance, beliefs, etc. اعتراف کرنا، ماننا، تسلیم کرنا have (the law, medicine, etc.) as one's profession کے پیشے میں ہونا falsely claim (*to be* a friend, an expert, etc.) کا جھوٹا دعوی کرنا، کا ادعا کرنا، کا مدعی ہونا **professedly** (*-fes-*id-) *adv.* on one's own claim بزعمِ خود **profession** (*-fesh-*) *n.* high vocation اہم پیشہ declaration (*of* faith, feelings, etc.) (کا) اعلان، (کا) اعتراف **professional** *adj.* of a profession پیشہ ورانہ doing for a living and not just for pleasure پیشہ ور of a professional پیشہ ور کا *n.* one who plays a game for a living (as opposed to an *amateur*) پیشہ ور کھلاڑی **professor** (pro-*fes*-ĕ) *n.* (abb. *Prof.* and written before the person's name) university teacher of the highest rank پروفیسر one who professes a religion (کسی مذہب) کا معتقد **professorship, professorate** *n.* being a professor or designation of a professor پروفیسری all the professor of a university or a college پروفیسر **professoriate** (*-so-*) *n.* (also *professorate*), professors of a university, college, etc. پروفیسر

proffer (*prof*-ĕ) *v. t.* offer (aid, money, etc.) for acceptance پیشکش کرنا *n.* offer پیشکش

proficient (pro-*fish-ent*) *adj.* skilful (*in* or *at*) ماہر **proficiency** (*-fish-*) *n.* skill مہارت

profile (*proh*-feel or *proh*-fil) portrait giving side-view of the face یک رخی تصویر (see *Addenda*) (see *Addenda*)

profile

profit (*prof*-it) *n.* advantage فائدہ *gain* *profit from* سے فائدہ اٹھانا، سے استفادہ کرنا money made in business *make a profit of* (an amount *on*) (پر) اتنا نفع کمانا *v, t. & i.* get profit (*from*) سے نفع کمانا bring profit to کو نفع پہنچانا *profit by* سے فائدہ اٹھانا، سے استفادہ کرنا **profitable** *adj.* نفع کا، منفعت بخش

profiteer (prof-i-*tee*-ĕ*) *v. i.* make an unduly large profit نفع اندوزی کرنا *n.* one who does this نفع اندوز *profiteering n.* (*-tee-*) نفع اندوزی

profligate (*prof*-li-gayt) *n.* & *adj.* licentious عیاش، اوباش، لفنگا **profligacy** *n.* being profligate عیاشی، اوباشی، لفنگا پن

profound (pro-*found*) *adj.* deep thinker, knowledge, mystery, interest, sleep, etc.) گہرا **profoundly** *adv.*, deeply بہت sincerely خلوص سے

profundity (*-fund-*) *n.* depth گہرائی، تعمق

profuse (pro-*fews*) *adj.* abundant بہت، کثیر، وافر (of thanks, gift, etc.) given lavishly فراخدلانہ *be profuse (in* or *of*) سے مملو ہونا

prognosticate (prog-*nos*-ti-kayt) *v. t.* foretell پیشگوئی کرنا، پیشین گوئی کرنا **prognostication** (*-kay-*) *n.* پیشین گوئی، پیشگوئی

programme (*prohg*-ram) *n.* plan (*of* what is to be done) پروگرام، دستور العمل

progress *n.* (*prohg*-res) *n.* advance ترقی improvement (*in* health, etc.) (صحت وغیرہ) کا بہتر ہونا course of development ہونا *in progress* ہو رہا *v.i.* (proh-*gres*) make progress ترقی کرنا، بہتر ہونا **progression** (*-gresh-*) *n.* progress ترقی، بڑھنا (in mathematics) series سلسلہ **progressive** (*-gres-*) *adj.* continuously advancing بڑھتا ہوا *Progressive*, supporting the evolution of culture towards Communism ترقی پسند، ترقی پسندانہ *Progressive Writers' Association* انجمن ترقی پسند مصنفین *n.* (*Progressive*), one favouring such a policy ترقی پسند

prohibit (pro-*hib*-it) *v.t.* forbid روک دینا، منع کرنا **prohibited** *adj.* not allowed ممنوع **prohibitive** (pro-*hib*-i-tiv) *adj.* that which prohibits one from doing something امتناعی *prohibitive detention* امتناعی نظر بندی too high (prices, etc.), out of the common man's reach بہت ہی زیادہ، استطاعت سے باہر **prohibition** *n.* prohibiting روک دینا، امتناع ban on the sale and consumption of alcoholic drinks شراب نوشی کی ممانعت، بندش شراب ؛ شراب بندی

project *n.* (*proj*-ekt) plan for an undertaking منصوبہ *v. t. & i.* (pro-*jekt*) make plans for (something) کا منصوبہ بنانا، کی منصوبہ بندی کرنا throw a picture of (something *on* sereen or wall) پر عکس ڈالنا represent the outline of (a plane figure) on another surface by geometrical process کی تظلیل کرنا jut out باہر کو نکلا ہوا ہونا **projectile** (pro-*jek*-tīl) *n.*. something shot گولی، گولا وغیرہ **projection** (*-jek-*) *n.* map made by projecting ظلی نقشہ mental image viewed as real تصور، خیال، طیف protruding part ابھرا ہوا حصہ projecting تظلیل picture thrown on screen, etc. عکس، تظلیل **projector** (*-jek-*) *n.* magic lantern, etc. آلۂ تظلیل

prolegomena (prol-e-*gom*-e-na) *n. pl.* long scholarly introduction مقدمہ

proletariat (proh-le-*tay*-ri-at) *n.* industrial workers صنعتی مزدور working classes محنت کش طبقہ، عوام **proletarian** (-*tay*-) *adj.* of the masses *n.* one of the masses عام آدمی

prolific (pro-*lif*-ik) *adj.* very productive (writer, reproducer, etc.) پُر، بہت (لکھنے وغیرہ) والا *prolific writer* پُر نویس *prolific of*, full of سے مملو

prolix (*proh*-liks) *adj.* tedious (speech, speaker, writer, etc.) طُولانی **prolixity** *n.* being prolix بہت طُولانی ہونا

prologue (*proh*-log) *n.* poem recited at the beginning of a play تمثیل کی تمہیدی نظم introductory part (*to* a poem) منظوم تمہید first event (*to* a series) نقطۂ آغاز

prolong, (pro-*long*) *v. t.* make (something) long کو طُول دینا **prolonged** (-*longd*) *adj.* (of discussion, etc.) continuing a little too long طُول پکڑ جانے والا **prolongation** (-*gay*-) *n.* prolonging طُول دینا یا پکڑنا part added for this purpose ضمیمہ، اضافہ

promenade (prom-è-*nahd*) *n.* (usu. paved) public place for walking سیرگاہ، گشت گاہ *v. t. & i.* walk or take (someone) out for a walk up and down (or *along* the streets, the waterfront, etc.) سیر کرنا یا کرانا، پھرنا، پھرانا

Prometheus (pro-*mee*-thews) *Cl. myth.* the Titan who, according to the ancient Greeks, made man and stole for him fire from heaven calling a heavy punishment for himself پرومی تھیوس

prominent (*prom*-i-nent) *adj.* salient (thing) نمایاں distinguished (person) نمایاں، ممتاز **prominence** (*prom*-i-nens) *n.* being prominent نمایاں (یا ممتاز) ہونا prominent part نمایاں حصہ

promiscuous (pro-*mis*-kew-us) *adj.* mixed (goods, etc.) ملا جلا (of company, etc.) having both sexes indiscriminately mixed مخلوط (of sexual relations) not restricted by marriage آزادانہ، کھلے یا عام (جنسی تعلقات)

promise (*prom*-is) *n.* solemn assurance (*of* or *to do* something) وعدہ *keep a promise*, make a promise وعدہ کرنا، وعدے پر قائم رہنا *break a promise* وعدہ وفا نہ کرنا ground for expectation (کے) آثار، (کی) توقع، ہونہاری *show promise* ہونہار ہونا *v. t. & i* make a promise to (or *that* or *to do* something) کا وعدہ کرنا be a ground for expectation کے آثار رکھنا *a situation that promises well* امید افزا صُورتِ حال **promising** *adj.* (of young person) likely to be successful ہونہار **promissory** (*prom*-i-so-ri) *adj.* conveying a promise وعدے کا، عہد کا *promissory note*, I.O.U. پرونوٹ

promontory (*prom*-ont-ri) *n.* cliff jutting out into the sea راس، سمندر میں دور تک گئی ہوئی چٹان

promote (pro-*moht*) *v. t.* raise (someone to a higher rank) ترقی دینا organize a new (business, company, etc.) چلانا help forward (a cause, etc.) کی تائید کرنا، کی خدمت کرنا، کے لیے کام کرنا، کو تقویت پہنچانا **promoter** *n.* one who promotes a cause, etc. کے لیے کام کرنے والا، بڑھانے والا one who promotes business companies تجارتی کمپنیاں کھولنے والا **promotion** (-*moh*-) *n.* act of promoting ترقی، تائید

prompt *adj.* done at the right time; immediate (reply) فوری، بلا تاخیر quick (*in* or *to do* something) مستعد *v.t.* urge (someone to do something) پر آمادہ کرنا remind in a low voice from behind the curtain (an actor who forgets his words) ڈرامے کے دوران میں بھولنے والے اداکار کو لفظ یاد دلانا **prompter** *n.* one who does this (اداکاروں کو) لفظ یاد دلانے والا، سامع

promulgate (*prom*-ul-gayt) *v. t.* proclaim (ordinance, law, etc.) کے نفاذ کا اعلان کرنا، نافذ کرنا **promulgation** (-*gay*-) *n.* act of promulgating or being promulgated نفاذ کا اعلان، نفاذ

prone (prohn) *adj.* (lying) face downwards اوندھا، چِت، مُنہ کے بل naturally inclined *to* or *to do* (something) کی طرف مائل

prong *n.* spike (of a fork, etc.) کانٹا، شاخ **-pronged** (prongd) *suf.* (*two, many*, etc.) -sided دو یا کئی، طرفہ

pronoun (proh-*noun*) *n.* part of speech used in place of a noun to avoid repetition اسمِ اشارہ **pronominal** (-*nom*-) *adj.* pertaining to a pronoun اسمِ اشارہ سے متعلق

pronounce (pro-*nouns*) *v.t. & i.* utter the sound of (a word, syllable, etc.) کا تلفظ کرنا announce (judgement, etc.) سُنانا، صادر کرنا، اعلان کرنا give one's opinion (*on, for, in favour of* or *against* something) رائے دینا **pronounced** *adj.* strongly marked (characteristics, etc.) بہت نمایاں **pronouncement** *n.* verdict فیصلہ formal statement of opinion رائے کا باضابطہ اعلان **pronunciation** (-*ay*-) *n.* pronouncing تلفظ

proof *n.* that which shows (something) to be correct ثبوت *supply proof of* کا ثبوت فراہم کرنا، (یا) ثبوت بہم پہنچانا *put (something) to the proof*, test it جانچنا، پرکھنا trial copy of book, picture, etc., for correction or approval پروف immune to (*against* something) کا شکار نہ ہونے والا، کا اثر قبول نہ کرنے والا

prop *n.* supporting column, etc. پیل پایہ pillar of strength (of) کا سہارا، آسرا *the prop of old parents* کا عصائے پیری *v.t.* keep (*up*) in position تھامے رکھنا

propaganda (prop-a-*gan*-da) *n.* publicity (*of*) کا پروپیگنڈا ، رکی ، نشر و اِشاعت **propagandist** (*-gan-*) *n.* one who does propaganda بات کو پھیلانے والا ، پراپیگنڈا کرنے والا ، مُبَلِّغ

propagate (*prop*-a-gayt) *v.t.* cause (plants or animals) to multiply کی نسل بڑھانا spread (news, etc.) کی اِشاعت کرنا **propagation** (*-gay-*) *n.* act of propagating کی اِشاعت ، رکی ، افزائش **propagator** (*-gay-*) *n.* one who propagates اِشاعت کرنے والا

propel (pro-*pel*) *v.t.* (-ll-) drive (ship, aircraft, etc.) forward آگے کو دھکیلنا *n.* revolving blades for driving ship or aircraft forward پنکھا (also see **propulsion**)

propensity (pro-*pens*-i-ti) *n.* natural inclination (*to do* or *for doing* something) مَیلان ، رُجحان

proper (prop-ĕ*) *adj.* suitable (*to, to do* or *for doing* something) مُناسِب ، مَوزُوں appropriate (conduct) دُرُست ، صحیح real, basic اَصلی *proper noun,* name of one particular person, place, etc. اِسمِ مُعَرِّف **properly** *adv.* appropriately ٹھیک *properly speaking* ٹھیک بات تو یہ ہے کہ **propriety** (prop-rī-ĕ-ti) *n.* properness ٹھیک ہونا suitability مَوزُونِیَّت correct conduct اَدب آداب *the proprieties,* details of decorum اَدب آداب

property (*prop*-ĕ*-ti) *n.* possessions جائداد land and buildings owned by one جائداد غیر منقولہ *landed property* مملوکہ اراضی special quality (*of*) کا خاصّہ **properties** (-teez) *n. pl.* articles other than scenery used on the stage in a play تمثیل کا سامان

prophecy (*prof*-e-si) *n.* prediction پیشین گوئی ، پیشگوئی foretelling the course of life after death as a result of direct communion with God نبوّت **prophesy** (*prof*-e-sī) *v.t.* predict (something or *that*) کی پیشگوئی کرنا **prophet** (*prof*-et) *n.* religious teacher prophesying the future نبی ، پیغمبر *fem.,* (*prophetess*) one who predicts پیشین گوئی ، پیشگوئی کرنے والا **prophetess** *n.* woman prophet پیشگوئی کرنے والی **prophetic** (pro-*fet*-ik) *adj.* of a prophet پیغمبرانہ of prophesying پیشین گوئی والا *prophetic words* سچ ثابت ہونے والی پیشگوئی

prophylactic (proh-fi-*lak*-tik) *n.* & *adj.* (substance, treatment) preventive (medicine or treatment) اِحتیاطی (دوا یا علاج) **prophylaxis** (*-lak*-sis) *n.* preventive treatment of disease اِحتیاطی علاج ، اِحتیاطی تدابیر

propinquity (pro-*pink*-wi-ti) *n.* nearness in time or place قُرب kinship قرابت

propitiate (pro-*pish*-i-ayt) *v.t.* appease offended god or person کا غصّہ ٹھنڈا کرنا ، منانا ، راضی کرنا win the favour of (gods, etc.) مہربان کرلینا **propitiation** (-pish-i-*ay*) *n.* act of propitiating رضا جوئی **propitiatory** *adj.* based on propitiation رضا جویانہ

propitious (pro-*pish*-us) *adj.* of good omen مُبارک ، مسعُود ، نیک شگون والا

proportion (pro-*poh**-shĕn) *n.* comparative relation تناسُب share, part (*of*) حِصّہ (in mathematics) equality of relation between two sets of numbers اربعۂ متناسبہ (*pl.*) (*proportions*), dimensions, size طُول و عرض (وغیرہ) (*pl.*) (*proportions*), correct or suitable relationship ٹھیک تناسُب ، موزوں تناسُب *v.t.* put into suitable relationship (*to*) میں تناسُب قائم کرنا ، کے مُطابِق (کرنا) divide into proper shares ٹھیک حِصّوں میں بانٹنا **proportional** *adj.* in proper proportion کے مُتناسِب ، کے مُطابِق corresponding (*to*) ٹھیک تناسُب سے **proportionate** *adj.* proportional (*to*) (کے) مُتناسِب

propose (pro-*pohz*) *v.t.* & *i.* suggest something or *to do* something or someone's name تجویز کرنا *He proposed Abdul Qayyum for President* اُس نے صَدارت کے لیے عبدُالقیّوم کا نام پیش کیا make an offer of marriage (*to*) کو شادی کا پیغام دینا intend (*to do*) کا خیال ہونا ، کا ارادہ ہونا offer as a toast (*the health of*) کا جامِ صحّت نوش کرنے کی تجویز پیش کرنا **proposal** (pro-*poh*-zĕl) *n.* suggestion تجویز offer of marriage شادی کا پیغام **proposition** (prop-o-*zish*-ĕn) *n.* statement بیان problem مسئلہ

propound (pro-*pound*) *v.t.* put forward (a theory) پیش کرنا ask for the solution of (a riddle) (پہیلی) پوچھنا

proprietary *adj.* (see under **proprietor**)

proprietor (pro-*prī*-e-tĕ*) *n.* owner (*of* land, business, hotel, store, etc.) پروپرائیٹر ، مالک **proprietress** *n. fem.* woman owner مالکہ ، مالکن **proprietary** *adj.* (rights, etc.) of a proprietor مالکانہ

propriety *n.* (of person or his conduct) being proper شائستگی suitability مَوزُونِیَّت

propulsion (pro-*pul*-shĕn) *n.* propelling power دھکیلنے والی توانائی ، قُوّتِ سائقہ ، سائقہ (also see **propel**)

prorogue (pro-*rohg*) *v.t.* adjourn (a session of the Legislature) مُلتوی کرنا **prorogation** (*-gay-*) *n.* act of proroguing ; being prorogued اِلتوا

prosaic *adj.* (see under **prose**)

proscribe (pros-*krīb*) *v.t.* exile جلاوطن کرنا publish the name of (book, etc.) as condemned کو مردود قرار دینا declare (a book) as unlawful and confiscate all its copies کتاب کی ، ضبطی کا حکم صادر کرنا

prose (*prohz*) *n.* form of ordinary writing o

speech عام تقریر و تحریر کی زبان، نثر unversified language as literary medium نثر **prosy** (*proh*-zi), **prosaic** (proh-*zay*-ik) *adj*. dull پھیکا، بے لطف بے کیف suitable for prose and not for poetry فقط نثر کے لیئے موزوں **prosiness** *n*. be prosaic بے لطف ہونا

prosecute (*pros*-e-kewt) *v.t.* pursue (an inquiry, studies, trade, etc.) کرنا، میں لگ رہنا initiate legal proceedings against پر مقدمہ چلانا، کے خلاف استغاثہ کرنا **prosecution** (-*kew*-) *n*. prosecuting کرنا *in the prosecution of* کے دوران میں starting of legal proceedings against استغاثہ *prosecuting agency* استغاثہ *the prosecution case* استغاثہ کے دلائل **prosecutor** *n*. one who prosecutes مستغیث *Public Prosecutor*, advocate appointed by the government to conduct prosecution on behalf of the State سرکاری وکیل *Prosecuting police official*, (D.S.P., etc.) پولیس کا افسر استغاثہ

proselyte (*pros*-e-lit) *n*. convert from one religion مرتد person who changes his political affiliations پرانا سیاسی نظریہ چھوڑ کر نیا اختیار کرنے والا

Proserpine (pros-ĕ*-pin) *Cl. myth*. queen of the Lower World ; (sne is identified with the Greek *Persephone*) (pr. pĕ*-*sef*-o-nee) پروسرپین

prosody (*pros*-o-di) *n*. laws of versification عروض، عروض و قوافی

prospect (*pros*-pekt) *n*. wide view وسیع منظر wide view before the mind وسیع ذہنی میدان likelihood امکان *not much prospect of* کا کوئی خاص امکان نہیں *v.t.* & *i*. (pros-*pekt*) search (*for* minerals, oil, etc.) (معدنی ذخائر کی) تلاش (یا جستجو) کرنا likely or possible customer of something or subscriber to periodical, etc. ممکن گاہک، امکانی گاہک، شکار **prospecting** (-pek-) *n*. such search (for minerals) (معدنی ذخائر کی جستجو) **prospective** (-*pek*-) *adj*. likely متوقع pertaining to or enforceable from a future date مستقبل کا، آئندہ کا **prospector** *n*. one who prospects (*for* oil, etc.) تیل وغیرہ کے ذخائر کا جویا

prospectus (pros-*pek*-tus) *n*. pamphlet giving details of an educational institution for the benefit of new entrants پراسپکٹس، کیفیت نامہ advertisement of (an insurance company or) some new business enterprise پراسپکٹس، کیفیت نامہ

prosper (*pros*-pĕ*) *v.t.* & *i*. (cause to) flourish فروغ پانا (یا دینا) **prosperity** (-*pe*-) *n*. act of prospering فروغ **prosperous** (*pros*-pe-rus) *adj*. flourishing کامیاب، با فروغ

prostate (*pros*-tayt) *n*. (also *prostate gland*), a gland with male genital organ پراسٹیٹ، گلٹی (یا غدہ)

prostitute (*pros*-ti-tewt) *n*. whore طوائف، بیسوا، رنڈی کسبی *v.t.* subject (oneself, one's energies, etc.) to exploitation صلاحیتوں کا معیوب استعمال put (oneself) to wrong use عصمت فروشی

prostrate *adj*. (*pros*-trayt) lying face down منہ کے بل گرے ہونا، tired تھکا ہارا defeated شکست خوردہ *v.t.* (pros-*trayt*) make (someone or oneself) prostrate تھکانا **prostrated** *adj*. defeated and helpless گرا ہوا، افتادہ **prostration** (-tray-) *n*. lie prostrate منہ کے بل گرا ہوا ہونا overcoming مغلوب کرنا being overcome مغلوب ہونا complete exhaustion سخت تھکاوٹ، تھک کر چور ہونا

prosy *adj*., **prosiness** *n*. (see under **prose**)

protagonist (proh-*tag*-o-nist) *n*. hero of a drama, etc. ہیرو champion (*of* a cause) (کا) حامی، (کا) مؤید

protect (pro-*tekt*) *v.t.* keep safe (*from* or *against*) بچانا، بچائے رکھنا، کی حفاظت کرنا guard (home industry) against foreign competition by taxing the imports heavily تامین دینا **protection** (-tek-) *n*. act of protecting or being protected حفاظت *live under the protection of*, *live under* (*someone's*) *protection* (of a woman) be kept by him کی داشتہ ہونا **protective** (-tiv) *adj*. that protects محافظ، نگہبان، محافظ *protective custody*, preventive detention ; detention (of someone) to protect state from his subversive activities نظر بندی **protector** *n*. one who protects محافظ، نگہبان، حافظ **protectorate** *n*. country taken over by some big Power for the plausible reason of its protection زیر حمایت علاقہ، محروس ملک (ج: ممالک محروسہ)

protege (*prot*-e-zhay) *n*. (fem. *protègée*) ward متوسل، زیر نگرانی یا زیر حمایت شخص

protein (pro-*teen*) *n*. nitrogenous part of food found in meat, etc. پروٹین، لحمیہ

protest *v.t.* & *i*. (pro-*test*) declare solemnly (one's innocence, etc.) کا پر زور اعلان کرنا declare in the face of opposition (that) احتجاج کرنا object (*against* or *about*) (پر) اعتراض کرنا، (پر) ناپسندیدگی کا اظہار کرنا *n*. (*proh*-test) objection اعتراض declaration in the face of opposition احتجاج *do* (*something*) *under protest*, do (it) after registering one's protest زیر احتجاج کرنا **protestation** (-*tay*-) *n*. (usu. *pl*.) solemn assertion (*of*) پر زور اعلان

Protestant (*prot*-es-tant) *n*. a Christian who is neither a Roman Catholic nor a Greek Orthodox پراٹسٹنٹ، احتجاجی مسیحی *adj*. of Protestantism پراٹسٹنٹ *n*. **Protestantism** (*pro*-tes-tant-izm) *n*. Protestant creed پراٹسٹنٹ عقائد being a Protestant پراٹسٹنٹ عقائد

proto- (*proh*-to) *pref.* original, first اِبتدائی، اصلی (as : *protomartyr*, first martyr for a cause اوّلین شہید
protocol (*proh*-to-kol) *n.* original signed document of a treaty before its approval by the concerned states حکومتی مُعاہدہ کی اصل دستاویز (*the Protocol*), etiquette department of a country's Foreign Office for receiving and conducting official foreign guests, diplomats, etc. محکمۂ استقبالِ سُفَرا (*chief of Protocol*, officer in charge of Protocol ناظمِ استقبالِ سُفَرا
proton (*proh*-ton) *n.* unit of matter with a positive charge and much larger than an electron پروٹان، مُثبت برقیہ
protoplasm (*proh*-to-plahzm) *n.* semi-fluid substance which is the basis of plant and animal life مادّۂ اُولیٰ، مادّۂ حیات
prototype (*proh*-to-tip) *n.* first example (of) پہلا نمونہ original اصل
protract (pro-*trakt*) *v.t.* prolong طُول دینا **protracted** *adj.* (of negotiations, etc.) prolonged بہت طول پکڑ جانے والا **protractor** (-trak-) *n.* D-shaped instrument for measuring and plotting angles on paper پروٹریکٹر، ڈی، زاویہ پیما

a protractor

protrude (pro-*trood*) *v.t.* & *i.* just out باہر کو نکلنا یا نکالنا
protuberant (pro-*tewb*-e-rant) *adj.* bulging out نکلا ہُوا، اُبھرا ہُوا **protuberance** *n.* bulge اُبھار
proud *adj.* haughty مغرور، متکبّر having self-respect خُود دار، عزّت مند joyous (*of*) خوش، شاداں feeling honoured by (*of* something) (کو) عزّت افزائی جاننا cause of pride (*of* one) (کسی کے لیے) مایۂ ناز، وجہِ افتخار splendid, imposing (sight, building, etc.) شاندار **pride** *n.* (which also see)
prove (proov) *v.t.* & *i.* give proof (*that* something is as stated or give proof of (something) (کو) ثابت کرنا، کا ثبوت دینا ascertain (something) by trial کو پرکھ کر دیکھنا turn out (*to be*) نکلنا **proof** *n.* (which also see)
proverb (*prov*- b) *n.* adage ; saw ; wise saying کہاوت، ضرب المثل، مَثَل **proverbial** (-*ve**-) *adj.* of or like proverbs کہاوتوں کا (سا) widely known (saying, etc.) ہر کسی کو معلوم ہو، زبان زدِ خاص و عام **proverbially** (pro-*vě**-bi-a-li) *adv.* quite commonly بالعموم
provide (pro-*vid*) *v.t.* & *i.* supply the need مُہیّا کرنا، بہم پہنچانا *provide (someone with)* کو دینا *provide for one's family* گھر کا خرچ چلانا make arrangements *for* or *against* future needs, eventualities, etc. کا سوچنا، کے لیے تیار رہنا، کا اہتمام کرنا **provided, providing** *conj.* on condition (or sometimes *that*) بشرطیکہ
providence (*prov*-i-dens) *n.* (old use) thrift کفایت شعاری (*Providence*), God's care for His creatures رُبُوبیت، خدا کی قدرت یا رحمت، قدرت، رحمت (*Providence*), God اللہ تعالیٰ، خدا تعالیٰ خُدا کا فضل، فضلِ ربّانی
providential (-*densh*-) *adj.* coming from Providence خُدا کے فضل سے result of being provident مستقبل کے لیے پس انداز کرنے سے متعلق **provident** *adj.* foresighted دُور اندیش providing for the future مستقبل کے لیے بچانے والا، آئندہ چل کر کام آنے والا *provident fund*, fund to which one contributes regularly from one's salary to put something by for days after retirement ; (when the post is non-pensionable the employer contributes an equal amount to such savings by the employee) پراویڈنٹ فنڈ
province (*prov*-ins) *n.* large administrative division of a country صُوبہ field (of study, etc.) (کا) میدان *(lie) outside (one's) province*, not (be) his specialized subject کا مضمون نہ ہونا **provincial** (pro-*vinsh*-ĕl) *adj.* of a province صُوبائی *provincial autonomy* صُوبائی خُود مختاری parochial تنگ نظری پر مبنی، تنگ دلانہ *n.* one belonging to province (کسی) صُوبے کا فرد **provincialism** *n.* such narrow outlook صُوبائی عصبیّت
provision (pro-*vizh*-ĕn) *n.* providing بہم رسانی preparation (*for* an eventuality) مستقبل کے اہتمام (*for* old age) بڑھاپے کے لیے پس انداز کرنا (usu. *pl.*) foodstuffs اشیائے خوردنی *provision store* پرچون کی دکان *provision merchant* کرانہ فروش، پرچون فروش condition شرط *with the provision that* اس شرط پر کہ، بشرطیکہ **provisional** *adj.* as a temporary arrangement ; interim عارضی طور پر، عارضی، عبوری **provisionally** *adv.* عبوری طور پر **proviso** (pro-*vī*-zoh) *n.* (pl. *provisos*) (in law) limiting clause شرط *with the proviso that* بشرطیکہ **provisory** (pro-*vī*-zĕ-ri) *adj.* conditional مشروط
provoke (pro-*vohk*) *v.t.* enrage غصّہ دلانا، طیش میں لانا، اشتعال دلانا call forth criticism, laughter, etc.) کا باعث بننا impel (someone *to* or *to do* or *into doing* something) کی ترغیب دینا **provoking** *adj.* vexing تکلیف دہ **provocative** (pro-*vok*-a-tiv) *adj.* intentionally enraging or rousing اشتعال انگیز **provocation** (-*kay*-) *n.* act of provoking or thing that provokes ترغیب، اشتعال انگیزی، اشتعال انگیز بات *under provocation* اشتعال میں آ کر
provost (*prov*-ost, or in military use *prov*-oh) *n.* (member) of military police فوجی پولیس کا فرد **provost marshal** (prov-oh-mah*-shĕl) *n.* head of military police فوجی کوتوال

prow (prou) *n.* front of a ship, etc. جہاز وغیرہ کا اگلا حصہ
prowess (*prou*-es) *n.* great bravery، بہادری، دلیری، شجاعت skill in fighting نبرد آزمائی
prowl (prowl) *v.i.* move about stealthily (for preying or stealing) شکار (یا چوری کے موقع) کی تلاش میں دبے پاؤں پھرنا *on the prowl* شکار وغیرہ کی تلاش میں دبے پاؤں پھرتا ہوا
proximity (prok-*sim*-i-ti) *n.* nearness قرب، نزدیکی kinship قرابت
proxy (*prok*-si) *n.* authorized agent مختار agency of substitute مختار کا ذریعہ *by proxy* (vote, etc.) through the agency of one's substitute مختار کے ذریعے، بذریعہ مختار
prude (prood) *n.* woman too squeamish about sexual relations بناوٹی شرم و حیا والی عورت **prudish** (*prood*-ish) *adj.* such (person or manners) بناوٹی شرم و حیا والا **prudery** (*prood*-è-ri) *adj.* being a prude بناوٹی شرم و حیا
prudent (*proo*-dent) acting after careful thought· ہوشیار، ہوشمند، اندھا دھند قدم نہ اٹھانے والا **prudence** *n.* being prudent ہوشمندی
prune (proon) *v.t.* cut off unwanted branches etc., of چھانٹنا
prussic acid *n.* a very deadly poison (also called *hydrocyanic acid*) پروسی تیزاب
pry (pri) *v.t.* & *i.* look too inquisitively (*into* others' affairs) راز جوئی کرنا، کی ٹوہ میں لگے رہنا force open with a lever بیرم سے کھولنا *pry a secret out of* سے کوئی راز لے اڑنا، ٹوہ میں لگا رہنے **prying** *adj.* who pries والا *n.* looking thus رازجوئی، ٹوہ میں لگا رہنا
psalm (sahm) *n.* hymn ترانۂ محمد *the Psalms*, a part of the *Bible* زبور
pseudo- (*sew*-do) *pref.* sham نقلی، جعلی
pseudonym (*sew*-do-nim) *n.* 'nom-de-plume' قلمی نام، تخلص
pshaw (shaw, or shah) *int.* (exclamation of contemptuous impatience) ہونہہ
psychic *adj.*, **psychiatry** *n.*, **psycho analysis** *n.*, **psycho-analytical** *adj.* (see under **psychology**)
psychology (si-*kol*-o-ji) *n.* science of the mind نفسیات **psychologist** *n.* expert in psychology ماہر نفسیات **psychological** (-*loj*-) *adj.* pertaining to psychology نفسیاتی *psychological moment* (for), psychologically suited to the spread of strong influence نفسیاتی لمحہ **psychic** (*sī*-kik) *adj.* of the mind نفسیاتی *n.* (pl) (*psychics*), psycho-analytical research تحلیل نفسیات کی تحقیقات **psychiatry** (si-*kī*-at-ri) *n.* treatment of mental diseases نفسیاتی امراض کا علاج **psychiatrist** *n.* نفسیاتی امراض کا معالج **psycho-analysis** (sī-ko-*an*-al-is-is) *n.* theory of the Austrian Jew, Sigmund Freud (1856-1939), about the division of mind into the conscious and the unconscious نظریۂ لاشعور system of psychology based on it تحلیلی نفسیات **psycho-analytical** (-lit-i) *adj.* pertaining to psycho-analysis تحلیلی نفسیات سے متعلق
pub *n.* (see under **public**)
puberty (*pew*-bĕ*ti) *n.* sexual maturity سن بلوغ، بلوغت، جوان ہونا **pubescent** (-*bes*-ent) *adj.* reaching puberty جوان ہونے والا، بالغ
public (*pub*-lik) *n.* people at large لوگ a section of the public والا طبقہ، والے لوگ، والے *the reading public* کتابیں پڑھنے والا طبقہ *in public*, openly کھلم کھلا، علی الاعلان *adj.* pertaining to the people in general (opp. of *private*) عام، عوامی *a matter of public knowledge* جو بات ہر کسی کے علم میں ہو، کھلی ہوئی بات **public opinion** *n.* general opinion of the people on a sociological issue رائے عامہ *mobilize public opinion* (*on*) (کسی مسئلے پر) رائے عامہ کو منظم (یا بیدار) کرنا **public house**, (or colloq. **pub**) (*pub*) *n.* new and popular kind of tavern in Britain where only alcoholic drinks are sold and consumed شراب خانہ، کلال خانہ **public man** *n.* voluntary social worker ; leader قومی خادم، لیڈر **public relations** *n.* & *adj.* (officer or department) promoting knowledge of official or other policies among the people تعلقات عامہ (کا) **public school** *n.* a kind of very expensive boarding school supposed to provide good education پبلک سکول **public spirit** *n.* readiness to advance public interests عوامی خدمت کا جذبہ **publicly** *adv.* in public ; کھلم کھلا، علی الاعلان **publican** (*pub*-) *n.* keeper of a public house شراب فروش، شراب خانے والا
publicist (-*pub*-li-sist) *n.* freelance journalist writing on topical issues عوامی دلچسپی کے موضوعوں پر قلم اٹھانے والا اصحافی **publicity** (-*lis*-i-ti) *n.* propaganda نشرواشاعت advertising اشتہار بازی *publicity agent*, (same as *Press agent*, which see) **publicize** (-siz) *v.t.* give publicity to کی نشرو اشاعت کرنا
publication *n.* (see under **publish**).
publish (*pub*-lish) *v.t.* make known public کی نشرو اشاعت کرنا print (a boo[k] ... cal, etc.) and put it on sale شائع کرنا **pu[blisher]** one who publishes ناشر **publication** publishing اشاعت (book, peri[odical]) published شائع شدہ کتاب رسالہ وغیرہ
puck (puk) *n.* a mischievous fairy ...
pucker (*puk*-ĕ*) *v.t.* & *i.* gather (lips, ...) wrinkles سکیڑنا، سکڑنا *puckered lips* ... ہونٹ *n.* a small fold شکن

pudding (*pud*-ing) *n.* a kind of soft, sweet dish made of bread, milk, eggs پُڈنگ . پوڈین
puddle (*pud*-el) *n.* small pool of dirty rainwater (on a road, etc.) (سڑک وغیرہ پر) بارش کے گدلے پانی کا گڑھا
puerile (*pew*-è-ril) *adj.* childish طفلانہ silly بچپن، احمقانہ **puerility** (-*ril*-) *n.* being peurile بچپن، پچھورپن
puff (puf) *n.* sudden rush of air ہُوا کا جھونکا steam, smoke, etc., rushed out once جھونکا، ایک بار نکالی ہُوئی بھاپ وغیرہ (also *powder-puff*), piece of fluffy material for applying powder غازہ ملنے کی گدی *v.t.* & *i.* send or come out in puffs جھونکوں سے خارج ہونا، یا کرنا *puff out of*, (of train) move out of the railway station with (the sound of) puffing پھک پھک کرتے ہوئے جانا gasp ہانپنا، سانس پھُولنا blow (*at*) پھونکیں مارنا *puff at* (*one's*) *cigarette* سگرٹ پھونک مار کر موم بتی *puff out the candle* جلدی جلدی پھُونکنا بجھانا swell (*with*) پھُلانا *puffed up*, proud مغرور، متکبر **puffy** (puf-i) *adj.* swollen پھُولا ہوا short-winded جس کی سانس جلدی پھُول جائے
puffin (*puf*-in) *n.* sea-bird with a short, thick beak پفن
pug (pug) *n.* a snub-nosed breed of dog چپٹی ناک والا کُتّا **pug-nosed** *adj.* snub-nosed چپٹی ناک والا
pugilist (*pewj*-i-list) *n.* boxer مُکّے باز **pugilistic** (-*lis*-) *adj.* of boxing مُکّے بازانہ **pugilism** *n.* boxing مُکّے بازی
pugnacious (pug-*nay*-shus) *adj.* quarrelsome لڑاکا، جھگڑالو **pugnacity** *n.* لڑائی جھگڑے کی عادت، جھگڑالو پن
puisne (*pew*-ni) *adj.* (of judge) inferior one in a High Court, etc. چھوٹا جج، قاضی اصغر
pull (pul) *n.* pulling کھینچنا tug کش، جھٹکا، کھینچ *give a pull to* (*someone's*) *sleeve* کی آستین سے جھٹکا دینا تانی rowing for pleasure تھوڑی دیر کے لیے تفریحی کشتی رانی *v. t.* & *i* draw towards oneself کھینچنا *pull* (*something*) *out* نکالنا *pull* (*someone* or *something*) *about*, pull (him, it, etc.) in different directions (کو) اپنی اپنی طرف کھینچنا، کھینچا تانی کرنا treat roughly سختی کرنا *pull* (*something*) *down* (*a*) demolish گرانا، ڈھانا (*b*) dismantle پرزہ پرزہ الگ کر دینا *pull* (*someone*) *down* مرض کا کسی کو کمزور کر دینا *pull it off* کامیاب ہونا *pull out* سے باہر جانا *pull round* صحت پانا *pull through* (*difficulty, illness, etc.*) سے بچ نکلنا *pull together*, work harmoniously میں خوب نباہ ہونا *pull* (*oneself*) *together* ضبط سے کام لینا *pull up*, (*a*) rebuke آڑے ہاتھوں لینا (*b*) stop رُکنا یا روکنا (*c*) gain ground in race آگے نکل جانا *pull up* (*one's*) *socks* آستینیں چڑھانا، زور لگانے کے لیے تیار ہونا *pull to pieces* کڑی نکتہ چینی کرنا *pull a* (*long*) *face* منہ بنانا *pull* (*one's*) *weight* (کوئی کام کرنے میں) پورا حصہ لینا

pull-over *n.* sweater pulled on over the head پل اوور ؛ بالاکش
pulley (*pul*-i) *n.* grooved wheel with rope, etc., for lifting heavy weight چرخی، گھرنی **pulley-block** *n.* block housing a pulley چرخی کا خانہ
pulmonary (*pul*-mo-na-ri) *adj.* pertaining to the lungs پھیپھڑوں کا
pulp (pulp) *n.* fleshy part of fruit گُودا any soft mass ملیدا، گودا *v.t.* & *i.* make into or become pulp ملیدا یا گودا بننا یا بنانا take the pulp out of کا گودا نکالنا
pulpit (*pul*-pit) small platform from which a sermon is delivered منبر
pulse (puls) *n.* throbbing of the arteries felt at the wrist نبض *feel* (*someone's*) *pulse*, (*a*) feel it (کسی کی) نبض دیکھنا (*b*) sound his intentions (کسی سے) عزائم کا پتہ لینا *regular*, (*irregular*, *quick*, or *slow*) *pulse* نبض کی باقاعدہ، بے قاعدہ، تیز یا دھیمی رفتار thrill, throb (of life, etc.) دھڑکن edible seed of plants such as lentils, beans, etc. دال *pulses*, various types of such seeds دالیں *v.i.* throb دھڑکنا
pulverize (*pul*-ve-riz) *v.t.* & *i.* grind to or become powder سفوف بنانا یا بن جانا crush down کچل ڈالنا
pumice (*pum*-is), **pumice-stone** *n.* light spongy lava for cleaning جھانوا
pummel (*pum*-el) *v. t.* (-ll-) punch repeatedly پے در پے گھونسے رسید کرنا
pump (pump) *n.* instrument for forcing fluid in or out پمپ light dancing shoe of patent leather پمپ شو *v. t.* & *i.* force (fluid *out*) نکالنا force fluid (*into* or *up*) بھرنا *pump up a tyre*, inflate it ٹائر میں ہوا بھرنا work a pump پمپ چلانا ask (someone) artfully (*about* his plans, etc.) ڈھنگ سے پوچھنا
pumpkin (*pump*-kin) *n.* a large, yellow, fleshy vegetable کدو، گھیا، توری
pun (pun) *n.* humorous play upon words صنعتِ ایہام کا مزاحیہ استعمال، مزاحیہ ایہام *v.i.* (-nn-) make puns مزاحیہ ایہام کرنا make a pun (*on* or *upon* a word) کسی لفظ کے دو معنی لینا **punster** (*pun*-stĕ*) *n.* one given to punning ایہام کا شائق
punch (punch) *n.* blow with the fist گھونسا، مُکّا instrument for making holes (in paper, etc.) چھیدنے کا آلہ ، پنچ intoxicant mixture of five things (*viz.*, wine, water, lemon, sugar and spice) drunk hot پنچ میلی شراب *punch-bowl* پنچ میلی شراب کا پیالہ *v. t.* strike hard with the fist زور سے گھونسا رسید کرنا make (a hole) with a punch چھیدنا، سوراخ کرنا **punch card** *n.* (see *Addenda*)

a punch

punctilious (punk-*til*-i-us) *adj.* careful in duty فرض شناس very particular in details of etiquette تکلفات کا بہت پابند **punctilio** (punk-til-yoh) *n* (pl *punctilios*) nice point of etiquette تکلف **punctiliousness** *n* تکلفات کی بڑی پابندی

punctual (*punk*-tew-ĕl) *adj.* observing the appointed time وقت کا پابند quite on time بالکل بروقت **punctually** *adv* پابندیٔ وقت کے ساتھ **punctuality** (-*al*-) *n* being punctual وقت کی پابندی

punctuate (*punk*-tew-ayt) *v. t.* insert punctuation marks in (a passage) میں رُمُوزِ اَوقاف اِستعمال کرنا، اَوقاف لگانا emphasize پرزور دینا interrupt every now and then with (cheers, etc.) اس کے دَوران میں (داد وغیرہ) دیتے رہنا **punctuation** (-ay-) *n.* act of punctuating اَوقاف کا اِستعمال، رُمُوزِ اَوقاف کا اِستعمال *punctuation marks*, marks (like comma, full-stop, etc.) used for this purpose اَوقاف، رُمُوزِ اَوقاف *Punctuation mark*, one of such marks وقف، رَمزِ اَوقاف

puncture (*punk*-chĕ*) *n.* minute hole in a (car or bicycle) tube پنکچر any small hole سُوراخ *v. t.* & *i.* get or make a puncture in پنکچر ہونا یا کرنا، سُوراخ ہونا یا کرنا

pungent (*punj*-ent) *adj.* sharp (smell or taste) تیز، کَڑوا sarcastic (remark, etc.) چُبھتا ہُوا **pungency** (punj-ens-i) *n.* quality of being pungent تیزی، چبھن

punish (*pun*-ish) *v.t.* inflict on (someone) penalty for offence سزا دینا **punishable** *adj.* that which can be punished لائقِ تعزیر **punishment** *n.* act of punishing or being punished سزا penalty سزا **punitive** (*pewn*-i-tiv) *adj.* designed to punish تعزیری *punitive action* تعزیری کارروائی *punitive police*, police force posted at a place as a punitive measure تعزیری فوج

punster *n.* (see under **pun**)

punt (punt) *n.* small flat bottomed boat propelled by pushing a long pole against the river-bed بلّی سے کھینچنے والی سیدھی ناؤ *v. t.* & *i.* go in or move a punt سیدھی ناؤ کھینا یا سیدھی ناؤ میں بیٹھنا bet on a horse (in a race) گھوڑدوڑ میں گھوڑے پر شرط بدنا یا لگانا kick a dropped football before it touches the ground ہاتھ سے چھوڑے ہوئے فٹ بال کو زمین پر گرنے سے پہلے ٹھوکر لگانا، پنٹ کرنا **punter** *n.* regular gambler (esp. in races) جواری، گھوڑوں پر شرطیں لگانے والا *It was a punters' day*; the punters were winning well on that day قسمت شرطیں لگانے والوں کا ساتھ دے رہی تھی

a punt being propelled with a pole

puny (*pew*-ni) *adj* undersized weakling پست قامت مُنحنی

pup (pup) *n.* (abbr. of) puppy پلا

pupil (*pew*-pil) *n.* once who is taught (*in* a school, etc.) طالبِ علم، طالبہ، شاگرد dark centre (of the eye) آنکھ کی پُتلی، مَردُمک، مردُمکِ دیدہ

puppet (*pup*-et) *n.* doll, etc., worked by string پُتلی *a puppet show* کٹھ پُتلی، کٹ پُتلی پُتلیوں کا تماشا stooge

a puppet

puppy (*pup*-i) *n.* (pl. *puppies*) young dog پلا haughty youth ; vain coxcomb مغرور نوجوان، اکڑباز، چھیلا

purblind (*pĕ**-blind) *adj.* dim-sighted چُندھا dull کودن، کند ذہن

purchase (*pĕ**-chas) *v. t.* buy خریدنا *purchase* (*something*) *with*, obtain (it) in return for کی قیمت دے کر حاصل کرنا *n.* buying خریدنا *make a purchase* خریدنا *at* (*so many*) *year's purchase*, (of a house, etc.) at a price equivalent to (so many) year's rent, etc. اِتنے برس کے کرائے (یا کی آمدنی) کے برابر قیمت کا something bought خرید

pure (*pew*-ĕ*) *adj.* clean صاف chaste پاک unadulterated خالص *pure and simple*, simply خالص، محض clear (sound) واضح complete (nonsense, etc.) بالکل، محض *a pure accident* محض اِتفاق، امرِ اِتفاق theoretical and not applied (mathematics, science, etc.) خالص، نظریاتی **purely** *adv.* with purity خالص طور پر utterly بالکل، محض **pureness** *n.* being pure خالص ہونا **purity** *n.* being pure پاکیزگی، خالص ہونا **purify** *v. t.* make pure صاف کرنا، پاک کرنا، خالص بنانا **purification** (-*kay*-) *n.* صاف کرنا، پاک کرنا، خالص بنانا **purist** *n.* person too scrupulous about the use of words اَلفاظ کے اِستعمال میں بہت ہی محتاط

purge (pĕ*j) *v. t.* free (*of* or *from* sin, evil, impurities, etc.) پاک کرنا clear (oneself *of* charge) سے بَری ثابت کرنا empty (*the bowels*) by a purgative جلاب دینا، مسہل دینا rid (party, army, etc.) of undesirable elements (پارٹی، فوج وغیرہ) میں سے ناپسندیدہ عناصر کو نکال ڈالنا *n.* ridding thus (پارٹی) سے ناپسندیدہ عناصر کا اخراج purging صاف کرنا، پاک ہونا

purgative (pĕ*g-a-tiv) *n.* & *adj.* (drug) emptying the bowels جلاب، مسہل **purgatory** (*pĕ*g*-a-to-ri) *n.* place of temporary suffering between Heaven and Hell عُرفات this state عُرفات میں ہونا

puritan (*pew*-ri-tan) *n.* one who is very strict and narrow-minded in morals, etc. اخلاقی طور پر تنگ نظر اور سخت گیر (*Puritan*), 16th century Protestant of excessive type پیوریٹن *adj.* اخلاقی تنگ نظری پر مبنی **puritanical** (-*tan*-) *adj.* اخلاقی معاملات میں سخت گیرانہ تنگ نظری پر مبنی

purl (pě*l) *v.i.* (of a brook) flow with a murmuring sound سَرسَر بہنا *n.* this sound سَرسَر
purloin (pě*-loin) *v.t.* pilfer, steal چُرانا
purple (pě-pěl) *n.* & *adj.* mixture of red and blue (اُودا رنگ) ارغوانی (رنگ)
purport *n.* (pě*po*t) sense (*of* a passage, etc.) مفہوم intention behind an act منشا، نیّت *v.t.* (pě*po*t) seem (*to* mean) کا مفہوم نظر آنا seem (*to* be) معلوم ہونا
purpose (pe*-pus) *n.* intention غرض، غایت determination قصد، ارادہ، عزم *on purpose*, intentionally قصداً، جان بوجھ کر *to little purpose, to no purpose* بیکار، بے اثر، بے نتیجہ *serve (one's) purpose* کے لیے مفید مطلب ہونا *to the purpose* مفید مطلب *(be) to the point* بس کام کی بات *v.i.* have as a purpose غرض ہونا، مقصد ہونا **purposeful** *adj.* (one's action) of whose purpose one is conscious بامقصد، واضح مقصد والا **purposely** *adv.* intentionally قصداً، جان بوجھ کر
purr (pě*) *n.* low murmuring sound (of a cat) to show affection خرخر similar sound of a telephone ٹیلیفون کی خرخر *v.i.* (of a cat or telephone) make this sound خرخر کرنا
purse (pě*s) *n.* wallet for money بٹوا bag (containing money) offered as a prize or present تھیلی *v.t.* pucker (lips) ہونٹ سکیڑنا **purser** *n.* accounts and stores officer on a ship جہاز کا افسرِ حسابات (also see **pursy**)
pursuance *n.* (see under **pursue**)
pursue (pě*-sew) *v.t.* chase کا تعاقب کرنا continue with (one's work, etc.) کرتے رہنا، میں لگے رہنا seek; aim at (pleasure, etc.) کے حصول کے پیچھے لگے رہنا، کو حاصل کرنے کے لیے جدوجہد کرنا
pursuit (pě*-sewt) *n.* pursuing جستجو، تعاقب *in pursuit of*, (a) during کے دوران میں (b) pursuing کے حصول کی کوشش میں، کو حاصل کرنے کی کوشش میں job, vocation کام، پیشہ (usu. *pl.*) that which is pursued مشغلہ، مشاغل
pursy (pě*-si) *adj.* purse-proud دولت پر گھمنڈ کرنے والا corpulent موٹا، کپا، پھپس short-winded جس کی سانس جلد پھول جائے، جسے جلدی دم چڑھ جائے (of mouth, eyes, etc.) puckered سُوجی ہوئی (تھوتھنی یا آنکھیں)
purvey (pě*-vay) *v.t.* & *i.* provide (food-stuffs) as a trader (اشیائے خوردنی) بہم پہنچانا (یا پہنچانے کا ٹھیکہ ہونا)
purveyer *n.* one who purveys (اشیائے خوردنی) بہم پہنچانے والا ٹھیکیدار
purview (pě*-vew) *n.* scope حد، دائرہ *not fall within the purview of*, be outside the scope of کے دائرے میں نہ آنا

pus (pus) *n.* matter discharging from festering wound, etc. پیپ، ریم
push (pūsh) *v.t.* & *i.* press away from دھکیلنا، ڈھکیلنا، ریلنا urge (someone *to do* something) (پر) اُبھارنا exert (oneself) to excel others زور لگانا thrust (*up* or *out*) نکلنا یا نکالنا drive (someone *back*) پیچھے دھکیلنا force (one's wares) on the attention of (اپنے مال) کی طرف توجّہ دلانا push (*on, along* or *forward*) one's work, etc. کرتے یا چلتے جانا *be pushed for time* کے پاس بہت مقوڑا وقت ہونا *n.* thrust دھکا، ریلا *at a push*, forced by circumstances ناچار، حالات سے مجبور ہو کر *give (someone) a push* کو دھکا دینا resolve to go ahead with one's work (بڑھنے وغیرہ) کا عزم، ارادہ enterprise ہمّت (slang) dismissal برخاستگی *get the push*, be dismissed برخاست ہونا *give (someone) the push*, dismiss (him) برخاست کرنا **pushing** *adj.* one forging ahead آگے بڑھنے کی جدوجہد کرنے والا، گھس بیٹھ کرنے والا **pushover** *n.* (see *Addenda*)
pusillanimous (pew-si-*lan*-i-mus) *adj.* faint-hearted ڈرپوک، دل کا بودا
puss (poos) *n.* cat بلی **pussy** (*poo*-si) *n.* (child's word for) cat مانو
put (put) *v.t.* (*put, put, put*) place رکھنا set in (a specified position) لگانا cause to be (*in* or *to* a specified state) کی حالت میں لانا express in words میں بیان کرنا propose, state (resolution, question) پیش کرنا backstair influence مخفی اثر ہونا *have a put* اندر خانے دباؤ ڈال سکنا (*Phrases*:) *be much put about*, be treated roughly سے سختی سے سلوک ہونا، سے بدسلوکی ہونا *put (an idea, etc.) across*, present (it), suggest (it) (کوئی نیا خیال وغیرہ) لوگوں کے سامنے رکھنا *put (something) across*, do it successfully گرد لگانا *put an end to* ختم کر ڈالنا *put a check on* (کو) روکنا *put (someone) a question* سے پوچھنا، سے سوال کرنا *put at*, (a) drink deep of (liquor, etc.) جرعہ کشی کرنا (b) suck (cigar, etc.) کا لمبا کش لگانا *put (something) at (some amount)* کی (اتنی) قیمت لگانا *put a spoke in (someone's) wheel* کی راہ میں روڑا اٹکانا *put back (the hands of a clock)*, (a) actually do so گھڑی کی سوئیاں پیچھے کرنا (b) do so metaphorically وقت یا ترقی کی رفتار سست کرنا *put the clock on* گھڑی کی سوئیاں آگے کرنا *put (something) before (someone) as*, present (it to him) to create such an impression (کو) اس رنگ میں پیش کرنا *put aside, put by*, save (for the future) مستقبل کے لیے پس انداز کرنا *put (something) down*, note (it) down لکھنا، لکھ لینا *put down a rebellion (etc.)* curb it (بغاوت وغیرہ) کچل ڈالنا *put (someone) down (as or for)*, take him to be کو سمجھ چھوڑنا *put forth buds (etc.)* کی کلیاں پھوٹنا *put forth (one's) strength* پورا زور لگانا *put forward a theory (etc.)* (نظریہ وغیرہ) پیش کرنا *put forward* آگے بڑھنا، نمایاں ہونا

put (one's) hands in (or *into*) *(one's) pocket* روپیہ خرچ کرنا یا دینا *put (one's) hands in (one's) pockets* مزے سے ہاتھ پر ہاتھ دھرے بیٹھے رہنا ، کام دوسروں پر چھوڑ دینا *put one's hand (to)* (کام) کرنے لگنا ، (کام) میں ہاتھ ڈالنا *let us put our heads together* آؤ باہم سر جوڑ کر بیٹھیں ، آؤ مل کر کام کریں *be hard put to it*, be in a fix بڑی مشکل میں پھنس جانا *put (someone) in mind of* کو یاد دلانا *have the put of*, have an undue advantage over کی بہ نسبت ناجائز طور پر فائدے میں ہونا *put (someone) in the wrong* کسی کو یوں محسوس کرانا جیسے وہ غلطی پر ہو *put in order* ترتیب سے لگانا *put in (a claim, document, etc.)* پیش کرنا *put in at a port*, (of a ship) stop there (جہاز کا) کسی بندرگاہ پر رکنا *put (someone) in fear* ڈرا دینا *put in for a post*, (colloq.) be a candidate for it کسی اسامی کا امیدوار ہونا *put (someone) in prison* جیل میں ڈالنا ، قید کرنا *put (someone) in rage* (or *good humour*) کسی کو ناراض (یا خوش) کرنا *put into (someone's) head*, suggest to someone کے دل میں خیال ڈالنا *put into (a language)*, render into (it) میں ترجمہ کرنا *put into (someone's) mouth*, ascribe to (him) (کوئی بات) کسی سے منسوب کرنا *put into words*, couch (idea, etc.) in words لفظوں کا جامہ پہنانا *put into shape* ترتیب دینا *put it to (someone) that*, challenge him to disprove یہ کہنا کہ کیا آپ اس کو غلط ثابت کر سکتے ہیں ؟ *put life into* میں جان ڈال دینا *put money into*, invest money in (*business etc.*) (کاروبار) میں روپیہ لگانا *put money on a horse*, bet on a horse (گھوڑ دوڑ میں) گھوڑے پر روپیہ لگانا *put (something) off*, postpone (it) ملتوی کرنا *put (someone) off with an excuse* کوئی عذر پیش کر کے ٹال جانا *put (someone) off his guard*, make (him) unwary by a false assurance کو جھوٹا اطمینان دلا کر غافل کر دینا *put (someone) on (his) guard* کسی کو متنبہ کر کے چوکنا کرنا *put (someone) off (his) food* کسی کی بھوک اڑا دینا *put on clothes (etc.)* پہننا *put on speed* رفتار تیز کرنا *put on airs* بننا ، یونہی اکڑتے پھرنا *put on flesh* (or *weight*) موٹا ہونا *put (someone) on (his) honour (not) to do (something)* (کسی کو) اس کی عزت کا واسطہ دے کر کوئی کام کرنے (یا نہ کرنے) کو کہنا *put (someone) on his mettle* (کو) اپنی صلاحیتیں بروئے کار ، جوش دلانا *put (something) on the market*, market it منڈی میں لانا *put (something) on paper*, reduce (it) to writing لکھ لینا ، قلمبند کرنا *put over*, secure appreciation for (film, policy, etc.) کی تعریف کرانا *put out a fire (etc.)* extinguish (it) (آگ) بجھانا *put (someone)* تکلیف دینا ، کو دق کرنا *put out of harbour*, (of a ship) come out of it جہاز کا بندرگاہ سے باہر آنا *put (someone) out of countenance* کو شرمسار کرنا *[p]ut (something) out of (one's) head*, forget all [abou]t (it) (کا) خیال دل سے نکال دینا *put (someone) [out of] temper*, enrage (him) کو ناراض (یا برہم) کر دینا *put [s]omeone) out of the way* کو قتل یا قید کر کے ، راہ سے ہٹانا *put (something) right* کو ٹھیک کرنا *put (something) through* (کوئی کام) مکمل کرنا *put (oneself) in (another's) hands* اپنے کو کسی کے ہاتھ دے دینا (یا کٹھ پتلی بنا لینا) *put (someone) through by telephone* کسی کو دوسرے نمبر سے ملانا *put someone to death* کو قتل کرنا *put (a matter) to* کی خدمت میں پیش کرنا *put up a prayer* دعا کرنا *put up (goods) for sale* (مال) بکری کے لیے پیش کرنا *put up (things) in boxes (etc.)* بکسوں وغیرہ میں (چیزیں) باندھنا *put up (someone's) name* (کا) نام تجویز کرنا *put up a fight* مقابلہ کرنا *put (someone) up to (something)* (کچھ کرنے) کا خیال (کسی کے) ذہن میں ڈالنا *put up with (someone)* (کسی کو) برداشت کرنا *put up (at a place, with a person, for a time)* کے پاس رہنا ، کے یہاں رہنا

putrefy (*pewt*-ri-fī) *v.t.* & *i.* (cause to) rot سڑنا
putrescent (-*res*-ent) *adj.* becoming putrid جو سڑ گل رہا ہو **putrefaction** (-*fak*-) *n.* rotting سڑاند

putrid (*pewt*-rid) *adj.* rotten سڑا گلا (slang) highly distasteful سخت گندا ، سخت خراب

putsch (pooch) *n.* 'coup de main'; bid to seize political power by force انقلاب برپا کرنے کی کوشش

puttee, puttie (put-i) *n.* legging made of cloth strip wound round leg from ankle to knee پٹی *a pair of putties* دونوں پنڈلیوں کی پٹی

a pair of puttees

putty (*put*-i) *n.* cement of lime, etc., for fixing panes in frames شیشہ جمانے کا مسالا ، پوٹین *v. t.* fix with putty پوٹین سے شیشہ کہیں جمانا

puzzle (*puz*-ĕl) *n.* bewilderment حیرانی ، الجھن *in a puzzle* حیران ، الجھن میں پڑا ہوا perplexing question designed to test ingenuity, etc. معما ، [illegible] *jigsaw puzzle*, (see under *jigsaw*) *v. t.* & *i.* cause perplexity to کو حیران کرنا ، کو الجھن میں ڈالنا *puzzle over a problem*, کسی مشکلے پر غور و فکر کرنا *puzzle (something) out*, discover (its) meaning by persevering mental effort کو سخت کوشش سے حل کرنا

pye dog (*pī*-dog) *n.* ownerless Eastern dog of a low mixed breed بازاری کتا

pygmy, pigmy (*pig*-mi) *n.* (pl. *pygmies*) dwarf (esp. one of an African race of pygmies) بونا

pyjamas (pi-*jah*-maz) *n. pl.* sleeping-suit comprising a loose jacket and trousers لباس شب خوابی

pylon (*pī*-lon) *n.* tower to support electric cables and built as a steel framework لوہے کا منارہ

pyorrhoea (pī-o-*ree*-a) *n.* disease causing pus discharge from gums مسوڑھوں کی پیپ ، پائیوریا

pyramid (*pi* ra-mid) *n.* structure with triangular sides meeting at the top ہرم (*Pyramid*), one of such structures built as royal mausoleums in ancient Egypt ہرم (ج: اہرام) **pyramidal** (pi-*ram*-i-dĕl), **pyramidical** (-*mid*-) *adj.* of or like a pyramid ہرم نما

pyre (*pi*-e*) *n.* pile of wood for cremating a dead body چِتا
pyretic (pi-e-ret-ik) *adj.* of, for or producing fever بُخار والا
pyrites (pi-*ri*-teez) *n.* compound of some mineral with sulphur or arsenic آتشی (مرکب) (also *iron pyrites*), sulphide of iron آتشی فولاد
pyro- (pi-ro) *pref.* of fire آتشی obtaining by heating آتشی
pyrotechnic (pi-ro-*tek*-nik) *adj.* of fireworks آتش بازی کا **pyrotechnics** *n. pl.* art of making and displaying fireworks آتش بازی کا فن
Pyrrhic (*pi*-rik) *adj.* gained at too great a cost ناقابلِ برداشت حد تک قیمتی، سخت مہنگا *Pyrrhic victory* بڑی مہنگی پڑنے والی بات *Pyrrhic dance,* Greek war-dance یونانی جنگی رقص
Pythagorean (pi-thag-o-ree-ĕn) *adj.* pertaining to 6th century B. C. Greek philosopher-mathematician Pythagoras or his philosophy *n.* his follower فیثا غورثی
python (*pi*-thon) *n.* boa-constrictor بہت بڑا سانپ، اژدہا (*Python*), *Cl. myth.* a great snake killed by Apollo at Delphi پاٹیتھن soothsayer کاہن person possessed by a familiar-spirit جادوگر **pythoness** *n.* witch چڑیل، ڈائن، جادوگرنی

a python

Q

q, Q (kew) (pl. *q's* or *qs*) seventeenth letter of the English alphabet (equivalent to Urdu ک but in transliteration regarded as equivalent to ق *mind (one's) P's and Q's* (see under **p**) (*Q.*) (abbr. for) query سُوال، س
qua (kwa) *conj.* in the capacity of بحیثیت، کی حیثیت سے
quack (kwak) *n.* charleton عطائی any ignorant pretender to skill جاہل مدّعی cry of a duck بطخ کی قائیں قائیں، قیں قیں *adj.* (remedies) of a quack عطائی کی دوائیں **quackery** (*kwak*-è-ri) *n.* being a quack عطائی ہونا، جاہل مدّعی ہونا
quadrangle (*kwod*-rang-èl) *n.* plane four-sided figure چوگوشہ quadrangular space surrounded by buildings (esp. in a college) اِحاطہ **quadrangular** (kwod-*rang*-ew-lĕ*) *adj.* in the form of a quadrangle چوکور چوگوشیا
quadrant (*kwod*-rant) *n.* one-fourth of a circle or its circumference رُبع دائرہ instrument for measuring height مزولہ

quadrilaterals

quadratic (kwod-*rat*-ik) *adj.* (esp.) of mathematical equation involving the square and no higher power of the unknown quantity مربّعی *n.* quadratic equation مربّعی مساوات، مساوات درجہ دوم مربع مقدار والی
quadrilateral (kwod-ri-*lat*-è-rĕl) *n.* & *adj.* four-sided (plane-figure) چوگوشہ

a quadrant

quadrille (kad-*ril*) *n.* an old-fashoned square dance کڈریل music for it کڈریل کی گت، کڈریل
quadruped (*kwod*-rew-ped) *n.* four-footed animal چوپایہ
quadruple (kwod-*roop*-èl) *adj.* of four چار کا four-fold چوگنا، چارگنا *v. t.* & *i.* make (something) or become four-fold چوگنا کرنا یا ہونا **quadruplets** *n. pl.* four babies born of one mother at one birth چار جُڑواں بچّے
quaff (kwof) *v. t.* drink (something) in deep draughts غٹ غٹ پی جانا
quag *n.* (same as **quagmire,** which see)
quagmire (*kwag*-mi-è*) **quag** *n.* marsh دلدل
Quai d'Orsay (kay-do*-*say*) *n.* French Foreign Office فرانسیسی دفترِ خارجہ
quail (kwayl) *n.* bird like a small partridge بٹیر *v. i.* flinch with fear (*at* or *before* danger, etc.) دُبک جانا
quaint (kwaynt) *adj.* (of person, custom, etc.) pleasingly unusual or old-fashioned عجیب (یا پرانی) وضع کا، عجیب وغریب، انوکھا **quaintly** *adv.* in a quaint manner عجیب انداز سے **quaintness** *n.* quality of being quaint عجیب وضع کا، انوکھا
quake (kwayk) *v. i.* tremble (*with* cold) کانپنا، کپکپی لگنا، کپکپانا tremble (*with* fear) کانپنا (of the earth) have tremors بھونچال آنا، زلزلہ آنا *n.* earthquake بھونچال، زلزلہ
Quaker (*kway*-kè*) *n.* member of the Christian sect called the Society of Friends founded by George Fox (1624—91) کویکر
qualify (*kwol*-i-fi) *v. t.* & *i.* become or make proficient (*for*) کا اہل ہو جانا یا بنا دینا become entitled (*to do* or *for doing* something) مستحق، مجاز be successful (*in* an examination, etc.) میں کامیاب ہونا modify or tone down (statement *with* a limit, etc.) پر قید لگانا، کو نرم کرنا (of an

adjective) describe the quality of (a noun) کی صفت ہونا **qualified** *adj.* trained مُستنَد entitled (*for*, or *to do* or *for doing* something) اَہل restricted مشروط **qualification** (-fi-*kay*-) *n.* (usu. *pl.*) education and training علمیت، اَہلیت limiting statement قید، شرط moderation تعدیل

quality (*kwol*-i-ti) *n.* excellence خوبی، کمال (good or poor) kind (*of*) (کی اچھی یا بری) قسم characteristic خاص بات being "how" (as opposed to being "how much", or *quantity*) کیفیت، ماہیت *quality surveyor*, person measuring up and evaluating the work of builder(s) معمار کا کام پرکھنے والا **qualitative** (*kwol*-i-tay-tiv) *adj.* of quality کیفیت کا ، کیفیتی ، ماہیتی

qualm (kwahm) *n.* momentary sickness متلی جی متلانا (usu. *pl.*) misgiving شک شبہ *have no qualms of conscience*, have no thought of repentance ضمیر کا بالکل ملامت نہ کرنا **qualmish** *adj.* feeling qualms جس کا جی متلا رہا ہو، جس کی طبیعت مالش کر رہی ہو

quandary (kwon-*day*-è-ri) *n.* riddle پہیلی perplexity گومگو کی حالت، حیرانی، سرگشتگی *be in a quandary* گومگو کی حالت میں ہونا

quantity (*kwont*-i-ti) *n.* amount مقدار، کمیت number تعداد **quantities** *n. pl.* large quantity بڑی مقدار (یا تعداد) *in quantities, in quantity,* in bulk بڑی مقدار (یا تعداد) میں **quantitative** (-*tay*-) *adj.* of quantity کمیتی، کمیت کا **quantum** (*kwont*-um) *n.* amount مقدار، کمیت *quantum theory,* theory in physics trying to explain the discontinuous nature of energy within the atom by holding that radiant energy is discharged in separate amounts مقداری نظریہ ، نظریۂ مقادیر، مُعَیّنہ

quarantine (*kwo*-ran-teen) *n.* segregating (someone) to control the spreading of infection علیحدگی ، قرنطینہ *v. t.* put or keep in quarantine قرنطینہ میں رکھنا

quarrel (*kwo*-rèl) *n.* heated dispute or strong disagreement (*with* someone *about* or over something) جھگڑا، مخاصمت its cause جھگڑا، بنائے مخاصمت *v. i.* (-ll-) have a quarrel (*with*) سے جھگڑنا، سے جھگڑا ہونا **quarrelsome** (-sum) *adj.* in the habit of quarrelling جھگڑالو

quarry (*kwo*-ri) *n.* hole, etc., for digging out structural stones پتھر کی کان (lit.) hunted animal, etc شکار، صید *v. t.* dig (stones) out of a quarry کان سے پتھر نکالنا **quarried** (*kwo*-rid) *adj.* stone dug out thus کان سے نکالا ہوا (پتھر)

quart (kwo*t) *n.* quarter of a gallon چوتھائی گیلن

quarter (*kwo**-tĕ*) *n.* fourth part (*of*) (کا) ربع fifteen minutes (past one, two, three, etc.) (کا) چوتھائی سوا fifteen minutes (*to* one, two, three, etc.) پونے (U.S.) coin worth a quarter of a dollar کوارٹر joint including leg ران (also *pl.*) direction طرف *from all quarters, from every quarter* چاروں طرف سے area (esp. of a city) علاقہ (*pl.*) lodgings کوارٹر *take up quarters with* کے پاس ٹھہرنا (usu. soldiers') barracks or small independent room کوارٹر (10) mercy to a vanquished foe شکست خوردہ دشمن کو پناہ دینا *ask for quarter* پناہ مانگنا، امان چاہنا *receive quarter* امان پانا *give quarter (to)* (کو) پناہ دینا، امان دینا (11) quarter cwt. چوتھائی ہنڈرڈ ویٹ (12) range, distance فاصلہ *at close quarters,* نزدیک سے، v.t. divide into four equal shares each برابر کے چار چار حصے کرنا lodge in quarters کوارٹر دینا، کوارٹروں میں رکھنا، رہائش کے لیے جگہ دینا **quarterback** *v. t. & i.* (see *Addenda*) **quarter-deck** *n.* officer's reserved part of the upper deck (*of* a warship) پچھلا عرشہ، چوتھائی عرشہ، محفوظ ربع عرشہ **quarterly** *adj.* once every three months سہ ماہی *adv.* happening at this interval سہ ماہی، ہر تین ماہ کے بعد، ہر چوتھے مہینے *n.* quarterly periodical سہ ماہی رسالہ، سہ ماہی **quartermaster** *n.* officer in charge of army stores رسد رساں، میر سامان، کوارٹر ماسٹر *Quartermaster-General*, (abbr. Q. M. G.), army General in charge of stores, etc. کوارٹر ماسٹر جنرل، سالارِ رسد ، سالارِ سامان

quarto (kwah*-to) *n.* size of a (foolscap or other) sheet folded twice چوتھائی کاغذ، مربع کاغذ book, etc., on paper of this size کوارٹو ، مربعی کتاب

quartz (kwo*ts) *n.* silica in various mineral forms مُردہ سنگ ، صَوّان

quash (kwash) *v.t.* (of a higher court) make void (a lower court's sentence) فیصلہ کالعدم قرار دینا توڑ دینا

quasi- (*kway*-sī, or *kway*-si) *pref.* semi- *quasi-official* نیم سرکاری seemingly بظاہر

quatrain (*kwot*-rin) *n.* verse form comprising a four-lined stanza رباعی

quaver (*kway*-vĕ*) *v. t. & i.* (of sound) vibrate; tremble تھرتھرانا، کپکپانا speak thus کانپتی ہوئی یا تھرائی ہوئی آواز سے بولنا *n.* quavering sound تھرائی ہوئی آواز **quavery** (-ri) *adj.* trembling voice تھرائی ہوئی آواز

quay (kee) *n.* stone platform for loading and unloading ships, etc. گھاٹ

a quay

queasy (*kwee*-zi) *adj.* (of digestion) liable to qualms جسے جلد قے آ جاتے (of food) causing this state متلی کرنے والی (of conscience or its owner) over-scrupulous and hence easily upset حد سے زیادہ محتاط

queen (kween) *n.* wife of a king ملکہ woman sovereign ملکہ (in cards) card bearing a queen's picture تاش کی بیگم (in chess) the most important piece after the king وزیر، فرزین *queen-bee*, egg-producing bee شہد کی مکھیوں کی ملکہ *queen of cities*, a beautiful city عروس البلاد
queer (*kwee*-è*) *adj.* suspiciously odd (looks, remark, etc.) عجیب *a bit queer*, rather mad پاگل سا (colloq.) giddy, fainting جیسے چکر سا آ رہا ہو *feel queer* کو چکر سا آنا، غش کھا کر گرنے کو ہونا *be in Queer Streets*, (of a businessman) be in financial difficulties مالی مشکلات سے دو چار ہونا *v. t.* (colloq.) upset گڑبڑ کر دینا *queer the pitch for* (*someone*), spoil (his) chances کا کام بگاڑ دینا **queerly** *adv.* strangely عجیب انداز سے **queerness** *n.* oddity ; being queer عجیب ہونا
quell (kwel) *v. t.* subdue (rising, etc.) دبا دینا، فرو کرنا
quench (kwench) *v. t.* slake (one's thirst) (ریاس) بجھانا extinguish (fire, etc.) آگ بجھانا
quern (kwĕ*n) *n.* hand-mill for grinding corn, etc. چکی، ہاتھ سے پیسنے کی چکی
querulous (*kwe*-rew-lus) *adj.* complaining شکوہ شکایت کرنے والا whining رونا پیٹنا، چیخنا، چلانا peevish چڑچڑا
query (*kwee*-ri) *n.* (pl. *queries*) question raising a doubt or demanding elucidation سوال formula for repeating or raising a question سوال یہ ہے کہ question-mark (?) سوالیہ نشان this mark put against a doubtful expression علامت استفہام *v. t.* & *i.* ask (*if* or *whether*) پوچھنا express doubt کے متعلق شک کا اظہار کرنا
quest (kwest) *n.* search (*for*) تلاش، جستجو *in quest of*, کی تلاش میں
question (*kwes*-chèn) *n.* inquiring سوال sentence comprising it سوال، سوالیہ فقرہ something inquired سوال، پوچھی ہوئی بات point at issue مسئلہ، سوال doubt, uncertainty شک *beyond question*, certainly یقیناً *call* (*something*) *in question*, (*a*) object to (it) پر اعتراض کرنا (*b*) raise doubts about (it) کے متعلق شک کا اظہار کرنا *out of the question*, impossible ناممکن *that is not the question*, it is irrelevant غیر متعلق بات ہے *it is only a question of time*, sooner or later it will certainly happen ہو کے تو رہے گا *the person* (*etc.*) *in question*, one being talked about just now مذکورہ شخص (وغیرہ) *v. t.* & *i.* ask a question of (someone *about*) سے (کے متعلق) پوچھنا (دیا)، سوال کرنا feel or express doubt about کے متعلق شک (ظاہر) کرنا **questionable** *adj.* doubtful شکوک، مشتبہ **question mark** *n.* query (?) سوالیہ نشان **questionnaire** (kwes-che-*nay*-è*, or kes-tee-o-*nay*-è*) *n.* list of questions drafted and forwarded to a number of persons to gather information or gauge public opinion on a point سوال نامہ ، سوالنامہ
queue (kew) *n.* people waiting for their turn in single file قطار *v. i.* (*queue up*), form into a queue قطار باندھنا
quibble (*kwib*-èl) *n.* play on words ; merely verbal point لفظی الٹ پھیر resort to this to dodge a question باتیں بنانا، سخن سازی *v. t.* use quibbles لفظی الٹ پھیر سے کام لینا argue about unimportant points بیکار بال کی کھال اتارنا
quick (kwik) *adj.* swift (journey) تیز alert person چست ready (*to do* something) ہوشیار، مستعد prompt (reply) فوری sensitive (ear or eye) تیز *quick-tempered*, easily irritable تنک مزاج، تیز مزاج *quick-witted*, (*a*) understanding quickly ذکی، زود فہم (*b*) quick at making jokes فقرے باز (old use) living زندہ، جیتا جاگتا *n.* living flesh زندہ گوشت، بقید حیات *cut to the quick*, hurt (or be hurt in) one's feeling دل کو ٹھیس لگانا **quickly** *adv.* swiftly جلدی سے **quickness** *n.* swiftness جلدی، تیزی **quicken** *v. t.* & *i.* make or become quicker تیز تر ہونا (یا) کرنا (old use) raise from death زندہ کرنا، جلانا **quicklime** *n.* unslaked lime ان بجھا چونا **quick march** *n.* march in quick time فوجی چال، تیز گام *v. i.* (as imperative) تیز چلو، تیز گام **quicksand** *n.* soft wet sand sucking down those who tread over it دلدل، ریگ رواں **quickset** *adj.* (hedge) formed of living bushes جھاڑیوں کی باڑھ **quicksilver** *n.* mercury پارہ، سیماب **quickstep** *n.* a lively dance تیز رقص **quickie** *n.* (see *Addenda*)
quid (kwid) *n.* (pl. same) (colloq.) pound sterling پونڈ، اشرفی
quid pro quo (*kwid*-proh-kwoh) *n.* cumpensation معاوضہ، عوضانہ، تلافی میں دی ہوئی چیز *must find him a 'quid pro quo'* اس کی تلافی کرنی ہی پڑے گی
quiescent (kwī-*es*-ent) *adj.* dormant ساکت **quiet** (kwi-et) *adj.* with no sound خاموش motionless ساکن calm پرسکون (of colours) not bright مدھم well-behaved (child) شریف *n.* being quiet خاموشی، سکوت peace امن، چین *v.t.* & *i.* make or become quiet چپ کرنا (یا) کرانا، پرسکون ہونا **quietly** *adv.* in a quiet manner خاموشی سے، چپکے سے **quietness, quietude** (kwī-è-tewd) *n.* being quiet خاموشی ، سکوت ، امن **quietism** *n.* passive attitude to life esp. as a form of religious mysticism بےخودی **quietus** (kwī-*ee*-tus) *n.* release from life موت، زندگی سے چھٹکارا *get* (*one's*) *quietus* جان کا جنجال ہونا being got rid of کو نجات دینا *give* (*someone his*) *quietus* کو نجات دینا ، کی جان چھوڑنا

quiff (kwif) curl plastered down on the fore-head ماتھے پر پڑے بال، لام
quill (kwil) *n.* large feather of wing or tail پَر its stem used as pen پَر کا قلم spike (of a porcupine) (سیہ کا) کانٹا fishing float ترِ ونا toothpick خلال *adj.* of quill پر کا
quilt (kwilt) *n.* double cover with a padding for use over (or instead of) blankets لحاف، رضائی
quince (kwins) *n.* a pear-like fruit بِہی its tree بِہی کا دَرخت

quinces

quinine (kwi-*neen*) *n.* malarial drug extracted as a liquid from the cincohna tree کونین
quintessence (kwin-*tes*-ens) *n.* real essence جَوہر perfect embodiment (of a quality) (کا) کامِل نمُونہ **quintessential** (-*sensh*-) *adj.* of the nature of (or pertaining to) the quintessence جَوہَری
quip (kwip) *n.* clever hit پھَبتی
quire (*kwi*-ĕ*) *n.* twenty-four sheets of paper کاغذ کا دَستہ
quintuplets *n. pl.* (abb. **quins** pr. kwinz) five children born together of one mother پانچ جُڑواں بچّے
Quisling (*kwiz*-ling) *n.* traitor غدّار one who agrees to serve his country's conqueror اَپنے مُلک کو غلام بنا لینے والے کا خادِم
quirt (kwĕ*t) *n.* (U.S.) short-handled riding whip چابُک *v.t.* lash with it چابُک مارنا
quit (kuit) *v.t.* & *i.* (-tt-) (*quit, quitted, quitted; or, rarely, quit, quit, quit*) leave (someone or *doing* something) چھوڑ دینا leave (a place) سے چلے جانا، کو چھوڑ دینا *Quit-India Movement*, movement launched against the then British government of the Indo-Pakistan sub-continent in August 1942 برطانیہ کے خلاف "ہندوستان چھوڑ جاؤ" کی مہم *adj.* free (*of*) سے آزاد *be quit of*, get rid of سے جان چھُوٹنا **quits** *adj.* on even terms (*with* someone) by returning a blow or debt سے حساب برابر لینا *be quits with* سے بدلہ لے لینا
quittance *n.* (old use) release from obligation قرض سے سُبکدوشی، قرض سے بَریّت **quitter** (*kwit*-ĕ*) *n.* (U.S. colloq.) shirker کام چور poltroon بے ہمّت، بُزدِل
quite (kwɪt) *adv.* somewhat ایک حد تک، کچھ کافی utterly بالکل یکسر truly ٹھیک (*quite, quite so*) (expressive of agreement or understanding) yes, it is or will be so ہاں، بالکل ٹھیک۔ ایسا ہی ہے (یا ہوگا)

quitter *n.* (see under **quit**)
quiver (*kwiv*-ĕ) *v.t.* & *i* shake slightly آہستہ ہلنا یا ہلانا tremble slightly ہلکی کپکپی طاری ہونا (of voice) be tremulous تھرّانا *n.* bag for arrows ترکش

a quiver

quixotic (kwik-*sot*-ik) *adj.* foolishly chivalrous or philanthropic نیک دل احمق، شیخ چلّی based on impossible ideals ناممکن العمل، خیالی پلاؤ والا
quiz (kwiz) *n.* questions asked to test knowledge پرکھنے والے سُوال one given to quizzing دِل لگی باز (rarely) one whose looks, etc., invite quizzing (وہ جس کی شکل وغیرہ دیکھ کر ہنسی آئے، مضحکہ خیز (یا مضحک) شخص (یا) چیز وغیرہ *v.t.* mock at کا مذاق اُڑانا، کی ہنسی اُڑانا، ہنسی سے دیکھنا regard curiously کو چھیڑنے کے انداز سے تکنا regard critically اعتراض کی نظروں سے دیکھنا **quizzical** *adj.* comical مضحکہ خیز teasing چھیڑنے کے انداز والا
quod (kwod) *n.* (slang) prison جیل، قید خانہ
quoits (kwoits) *n.* game in which a big ring is thrown at a pin کُوئٹس
quoit (kwoit) *n.* ring used in quoits کُوئٹ

a quoit

پہلا، کسی زمانے کا، سابقہ، سابق
quondam (kwond-ĕm) *adj.* onetime former سابق، سابقہ
quorum (*kwoh*-rum) *n.* minimum number of the members (*of* a body) without which its proceedings would not be in order کورَم *The quorum is not complete* کورم پورا نہیں ہے
quota (kwoh-ta) *n.* (someone's) fixed share (of something) (کسی کا کسی چیز کا) کوٹا، حصّہ رَسَد، حصّہ
quote (kwoht) *v.t.* repeat (someone's words) کی بات دُہرانا، (کا) قول پیش کرنا cite (from a book) سے اقتباس پیش کرنا give a reference (*from* someone, etc.) to support one's argument حوالہ دینا یا پیش کرنا state the price of (something at a figure) کی قیمت بتانا **quotes** *n. pl.* quotation marks واوین *single quotes*, ' ' اِکہری واوین *double quotes*, " " دُہری واوین (*put*) *within quotes* واوین میں لکھنا **quotation** *n.* something quoted اقتباس، قول dealer's statement of price قیمت **quotation marks** *n.* quotes or marks used to separate quoted words from the rest of the sentence, etc. واوین
quoth (kwohth) *v.t.* (old use) said (for the third person sing. only) اُس نے کہا، وہ بولا
quotient (*kwoh*-shent) *n.* number of times (leaving out the surd) a figure is contained in another حاصلِ تقسیم، خارج قسمت

R

r, R (ah*) (pl. *r's* or *rs*) the eighteenth letter of the English alphabet (equivalent to Urdu) ر; (in pronunciation it is trilled only when it stands at the head of a syllable; otherwise it is always slurred over) *the three R's*, Reading, Writing and ('Rithmetic) as a basic education پڑھائی لکھائی اور حساب ، بُنیادی تعلیم
rabbi (*rab*-i, or *rab*-i) *n*. Jewish priest ربّی
rabbit (*rab*-it) *n*. small hare-like animal خرگوش
rabble (*rab*-ĕl) *n*. disorderly crowd بھیڑ، ہُجوم lowest classes اراذِل
rabid (*rab*-id) *adj*. (of dogs) affected with rabies too zealous
rabies (*ray*-bi-eez) *n*. fatal madness in dogs باؤلا this disease affecting a person bitten by a rabid dog . بڑا پکّا، کٹّر، جنونی، سر فروش
race (rays) *n*. competition in speed دَوڑ strong swift current of water تیز دھارا root of ginger سونٹھ people of one kind and colour, or of one origin نسل species نَوع *v.t.* & *i.* run a race (with someone) سے دَوڑ کا مُقابلہ کرنا *race against time*, exert oneself to finish work (or be) in time جلدی کرنا ، پُوری کوشش کرنا cause (a horse, etc.) to run (esp. in a race) دَوڑانا **racing** *n*. (also *horse-racing*) causing horses to run usu. with the object of punting گھوڑ دَوڑ، ریس **race-course** *n*. enclosure for racing گھوڑ دَوڑ کا مَیدان، ریس کورس **race-horse** *n*. horse running in a race گھوڑ دوڑ والی نسل کا گھوڑا **racial** (*ray*-shĕl) of a race نسلی **racialism** (*ray*-shè-lizm) *n*. tendency to racial feeling causing antagonizm between various human races نسلی عصبیت **racism** (*ray*-sizm) *n*. racialism نسلی عصبیت belief in racial superiority نسلی برتری کا احساس
rack (rak) *n*. shelf or other framework for holding books, plates, hay, etc. ریک، خانہ (old use) instrument of torture شکنجہ destruction تباہی (only in the phrase :) *go to rack and ruin*, be ruined تباہ و برباد ہو جانا *v.t.* torture with the rack سخت cause severe pain کسی کو شکنجے میں کس دینا تکلیف پہنچانا *rack (one's) brain (for something)*, make great mental efforts (کسی غرض سے) دماغ پر بہت زور دینا
racket (*rak*-et) *n*. loud noise شور و غوغا ، غُل غپاڑا (colloq.) dishonest trade by supplying worthless goods بددیانتی کا کاروبار، خراب مال مُہیّا کرنا (colloq.) blackmail دھمکیوں سے روپیہ وُصُول کرنا (also *racquet*), bat used in tennis, badminton, etc. ریکٹ **racketeer** (rak-è-*tee*-è) *n*. one engaged in a trade racket بددیانتی کا کاروبار کرنے والا **racketeering** (-*tee*-è-) *n*. organized blackmail of traders by intimidation دھمکیاں دے کر تاجروں سے روپیہ وُصُول کرنا **racquet** (*rak*-et) *n*. same as **racket** (sense 4, which see)

a racket (sense 4)

racy (*ray*-si) *adj*. having the characteristics of a soil or country مقامی (یا) نسلی رنگ رکھنے والا vigorous (style) زوردار lively (humour) پھڑکا دینے والا
radar (*ray*-dah*) *n*. (acronym formed from the initial letters of *Radio Angle Detection and Ranging*) apparatus locating objects with reflected radio waves راڈر ، لاسلکی آنکھ
radiate (*ray*-di-ayt) *v.t.* & *i.* come out in (or emit) rays of (light or heat) شعاعیں نکلنا یا ڈالنا brighten up with (delight) خوشی سے چمک اُٹھنا spread out from a centre مرکز سے پھیلنا **radiant** *adj*. emitting light منوّر، تاباں bright چمکدار، روشن full of delight شاداں، مسرور **radiance** (*ray*-di-ans) *n*. act of radiating or being radiant درخشانی، تابانی، تابندگی، تنویر چمک، شادمانی **radiation** (-*ay*-) *n*. radiating تنویر، درخشانی **radiator** (*ray*-di-ay-tĕ*) *n*. heater حرارت زا، گرمالہ (in a motor vehicle) apparatus for cooling down the engine حرارت کش، سرد آلہ

a radiator (sense 2)

radical (rad-i-kĕl) *adj*. *i*. pertaining to the root بُنیادی thorough مکمل based on fundamental changes بُنیادی تبدیلیوں والا advocate of basic changes یکسر تبدیلی (یا) بُنیادی تبدیلیوں کا حامی **radically** *adv*. یکسر، بالکل **radicalism** *n*. radical politics بُنیادی تبدیلیوں کی حمایت پر مبنی سیاست ، انقلابی سیاست
radio *n*. (*ray*-di-oh) wireless بے تار، لاسلکی message, etc., thus transmitted بے تار، لاسلکی پیغام (also *radio-set*, or *set* or *station*), apparatus for receiving broadcast programmes ریڈیو *v.t.* & *i.* broadcast نشر کرنا *adj*. of radio ریڈیائی of X-rays ایکس ریز والا، لاشعاعوں والا **radio-active** *adj*. (of a metal) emitting X-rays تابکار **radio-activity** (-*tiv*-) *n*. being radio-active تابکاری **radiogram** (ray-) *n*. (also *radio-gramophone*), combined wireless receiving set and gramophone ریڈیو پروگرام (also *radio-telegram*), message sent by wireless لاسلکی پیغام، بے تار (also *radiograph*), X-ray photograph لاشعاعی تصویر **radiograph** (*ray*-) *n*. X-ray photograph لاشعاعی عکس، لاشعاعی تصویر **radiolocation** (-*kay*-) *n*. detection of aircraft, etc., by means of

adio echoes ریڈیائی تفتیش **radioscopy** (-os-ko-pi) *n.* examination by X-rays لاشعاعی مُعائنہ **radio-therapy** *n.* treatment with X-rays تابکاری علاج ، بجلی کا علاج ، بجلی لگانا

radish (rad-ish) *n.* small edible root وِلائتی مُولی well-known carrot-like, white pungent root مُولی

radium (*ray*-di-um) *n.* name of a radio active metal ریڈیم

radius (*ray*-di-us) *n.* (pl. *radii*, pr. *ray*-di-ī) straight line from the centre to the circumference of a circle نِصف قطر circular area as measured by its radius حَلقہ *within a radius of four (etc.) miles, in the four (etc.) mile radius* چار (وغیرہ) میل کے حلقے میں

radius (R) of a circle

raffle (*raf*-ĕl) *n.* sale by lottery مال کی لاٹری *v.t.* sell (something) thus لاٹری کے ذریعے مال بیچنا ، مال کی لاٹری نکالنا

raft *n.* logs of wood fastened together to flow downstream لٹھوں کا ٹھاٹھ

rafter (raf-tĕ*) *n.* beam of a sloping roof ٹیڑھی چھت کا شہتیر

rafters

rag *n.* scrap of cloth کپڑے کا چھوٹا سا ٹکڑا (*pl.*) tattered clothes چیتھڑے (*dressed*) *in rags* چیتھڑوں میں (joc.) contemptible newspaper چیتھڑا ، ذلیل اخبار *v.t.* & *i.* play practical jokes on کی دُرگت کرنا ، تختہ مشق بنانا **ragamuffin** *n.* person (esp. child) in rags چیتھڑوں والا **ragged** (*rag*-ed) *adj.* in rags چیتھڑوں میں ، شکستہ حال with rough surface کھُردُرا jagged (rock) ناہموار (of style, rhymes, etc.) lacking finish ناتراشیدہ **ragging** *n.* playing of practical jokes گت ، دُرگت **ragtime** (*rag*-tīm) *n.* popular U.S. negro dance ریگ ٹائم *adj.* farcical (army, etc.) مضحکہ خیز

rage (rayj) *n.* violent anger سخت غُصّہ ، طیش passion (*for* something) (کا) بے پناہ شوق craze بڑا فیشن *v.i.* be in a rage (*against*) کے خلاف طیش میں آنا (of storm, etc.) blow violently بہت زوروں کا ہونا ، سخت تیز ہونا

ragged *adj.*, **ragging** *n.*, **ragtime** *n.* (see under **rag**)

raid (rayd) *n.* sudden attack (*on*) اچانک حملہ ، تاخت *air raid*, air attack ہوائی حملہ *Air Raid Precautions*, (abbr. *A.R.P.*) (organization entrusted with) precautions against possible air attack اے-آر-پی ، ہوائی حملے سے بچاؤ (کا محکمہ یا کی تدبیریں) surprise visit for checking or arresting پولیس کا چھاپا *police raid* چھاپا *v.t.* & *i.* conduct a raid on پر اچانک حملہ کرنا ، پر چھاپا مارنا

raider *n.* one who or that which raids اچانک حملہ کرنے والا ، چھاپا مارنے والا

rail (rayl) *n.* bars or rods placed from end to end جنگلا rod, etc., for hanging things on الگنی ، لٹکانے کا ڈنڈا thick steel bar forming a track پٹری (گاڑی یا ٹرام کا) *go off the rails*, (*a*) leave the track پٹری سے اُتر جانا (*b*) become out of order خراب ہو جانا (*c*) get out of control ہاتھ سے نکل جانا ، قابو سے باہر ہو جانا *v.t.* put rails round (to shut *in* or cut *off*) سلاخیں لگا (کر ادھر یا اُدھر کر) دینا use bitter and reproachful language (*against* fate, *at* oppressor) کوسنے دینا ، بُرا بھلا کہنا **railhead** (*rayl*-hed) *n.* point on railway where road transport begins کسی سفر کے ریلیے ریل کا آخری اسٹیشن farthest point reached by a rail track under construction جہاں تک پٹری بنی ہے

railing *n.* (usu. *pl.*) fence جنگلا balustrade round stairs زینہ کا جنگلا **rail-motor** (*rayl*-moh-tĕ*) ڈبّہ ، ریل موٹر *n.* self-propelled railway coach **railway** (*rayl*-way) *n.* (in U.S. rail-road) rail track پٹری transport system using rail track ریل کا ، ریلوے *adj.* pertaining to this system ریل ، ریلوے **railroad** *n.* (U.S.) railway ریل ، ریلوے rail-track ریل کی پٹری ، پٹری *v.i.* (see *Addenda*)

raillery (*rayl*-ĕ-ri) *n.* good-humoured ridicule ہنسی مذاق ، دل لگی ، چُہل

raiment (*ray*-ment) *n.* (lit.) clothing پوشاک ، لباس

rain (rayn) *n.* drops of water from clouds مینہ ، برسات *the rains*, the rainy season برسات shower بارش (*of* bullets, congratulations, etc.) کی بارش *v.t.* & *i.* fall or send in raindrops بارش ہونا ، مینہ پڑنا ، پانی پڑنا *rain cats and dogs* موسلا دھار بارش ہونا *It never rains but pours*, good fortune or misfortune never comes alone جب ہوتا ہے تو بہت کچھ ہوتا ہے fall or send (*down* or *upon*) like rain ٹپ ٹپ گرنا **rainbow** *n.* spectrum on the horizon قوسِ قزح ، دھنک **raincoat** *n.* waterproof coat برساتی **raindrop** *n.* drop of rain بارش کا قطرہ **rainfall** *n.* fall of rain بارش its amount (in cubic inches) at a place بارش کی مقدار **rain-gauge** *n.* measuring instrument for this purpose باراں پیما **rain-proof** *adj.* impervious to rain جس میں سے پانی نہ گزر سکے **rainy** *adj.* day when it rains بارش کا دن *save for a rainy day*, save for unforeseen needs وقت بے وقت کے لیے بچانا

raise (rayz) *v.t.* & *i.* elevate or make higher (prices, one's voice, one's hat, someone's hopes, etc.) اونچا کرنا ، بلند کرنا build بنانا cause (dust, etc.) to rise اُڑانا produce (crops) اُگانا breed (cattle, etc.) کی نسل کشی کرنا bring up (a family) پرورش کرنا ، پالنا levy (army, tax, etc.) فراہم کرنا

call attention to (question, point, objection, protest, etc.) کرنا end (a siege) اُٹھانا **raised** (rayzd) *adj*. high اُونچا
raisin (*ray*-zin) *n*. (usu. *pl*.) dried grape کِشمِش
raison d'etre (ray-zon-day-tè*) *n*. real purpose ; that which justifies عِلّتِ غائی
rake (rayk) *n*. agricultural implement for gathering hay, etc. جیلی ، licentious man لفنگا، عیّاش، گوبیدنی *v.t.* & *i.* smooth soil with rake جیلی سے کھُرچنا gather (something *together*, *up*, *out*, etc.) with a rake جیلی سے اِکٹھا کرنا gather diligently (evidence, etc.) محنت سے جمع کرنا search (*through* or *over* documents, etc. *for*) کو چھان مارنا *rake* (*something up*), bring some forgotten thing to light گڑے مُردے اُکھیڑنا **rakish** (*rayk*-ish) *adj*. immoral (person) آوارہ، عیّاش light swift (ship) سُبک تیز رَو جہاز

a rake (sense 1)

rally (*ral*-i) *v. t.* & *i.* come or bring together for renewed efforts اَز سرِ نَو جِدّ و جُہد کے لیے جمع ہونا یا کرنا (cause to) recover طاقت پکڑنا یا دینا tease good-humouredly جمع ہونا ؛ چھیڑنا، دِل لگی کرنا *n*. gathering اِجتماع *scout rally*, ceremonial gathering of scouts ریلی، سکاؤٹوں کا اجتماع
ram *n*. male sheep مینڈھا (old use) battering beam قلعہ شکن گُرز ramming instrument ٹھونکنے کا آلہ *v. t.* (-mm-) strike heavily زور سے مارنا force (*into* place) thus ٹھونسنا، ٹھونس ٹھونس کر بھرنا
ramble (ram-bèl) *v. i.* walk for pleasure سَیر گشت کرنا، اِدھر اُدھر پھرنا digress (in one's talk, etc.) بے ربط گفتگو یا تقریر وغیرہ کرنا، اِدھر اُدھر کی ہانکنا *n*. pleasure walk without a destination سَیر گشت **rambler** *n*. one who rambles سَیر گشت کرنے والا، اِدھر اُدھر کی ہانکنے والا
rambling *adj*. (talk) with digressions اِدھر اُدھر کی، بے ربط unplanned (streets, etc.) بے ترتیب بنا ہُوا
ramify (*ram*-i-fı) *v.t* & *i*. produce branches شاخ دَر شاخ ہونا form into branches شاخیں نکالنا
ramification *n*. act of ramifying شاخ دَر شاخ ہونا، تفرّع
ramp *v. i.* leap and bound اُچھلنا کُودنا (of animal) stand on hind-legs پچھلی ٹانگوں پر کھڑے ہونا *n*. upward slope چڑھائی **rampage** (ram-*payj*) *v. i.* rush about in wild rage طیش میں بے تاب ہو کر اِدھر اُدھر نِکل جانا *n*. fit of rage جوشِ جُنون، دیوانگی کا دَورہ *be on the rampage*, (of a river) rampage دریا کا دیوانوں کی طرح کناروں سے باہر نکل جانا **rampant** (*ram*-pant) *adj*. (of crime, disease, etc.) beyond control قابو سے باہر (of animal) on the hind-legs پچھلی ٹانگوں پر کھڑا
rampart (*ram*-pah*t) *n*. mound or wall round a fort قلعہ کا پُشتہ

ramshackle (*ram*-shak-èl) *adj*. rickety گِرنے یا ٹوٹنے کے قریب
ranch *n*. (U.S.) large cattle-raising farm مویشی پال کھیت **ranch house** *n*. (see *Addenda*)
rancid (*rans*-id) *adj*. (of butter, etc.) gone bad بدبُودار، بِساندا
rancour (*rank*-ě*) *n*. deep rooted hatred or enmity دِلوں میں بیٹھا ہُوا کینہ
random (*rand*-um) *adj*. haphazard اٹکل پچّو *at random*, aimlessly یُوں ہی، بے سوچے سمجھے
rang *v*. (*pa. t.* of **ring**, which see)
range (raynj) *n*. scope دائرہ، میدان distance to which a gun will shoot مار *at short range* قریب *at long range* دُور area for firing practice چاند ماری کا میدان difference between limits فاصلہ، فرق upper and lower limit (*of*) کم سے کم اور زیادہ سے زیادہ row or series (*of* mountains, prices, colours, etc.) سلسلہ *a wide range of* کئی قسم کا (also *cooking range*), stove with oven وِلایتی چُولھا *v. t.* & *i*. (*over*, *through*, etc.) میں گھومتے پھرنا vary (*from* one *to* another stage) کے مابین ہونا run in a line سیدھا جانا (*range oneself*), place oneself صف آرا ہونا *range* (*oneself*) *with* (or *against*, or *on the side of someone*), join (him) کی صفوں میں شامل ہونا *men who ranged themselves with* (or *against*, or *on the side of*) *the rebels* جو لوگ باغیوں کی صفوں میں شامل ہو گئے
ranger (*raynj*-ě*) *n*. keeper of forests مُحافظِ جنگلات (U.S.) commando مُنتخب فوجی دستے کا سپاہی، کمانڈو
rank *n*. line of soldiers placed side by side صف *the rank*, the army فوج *other ranks*, *rank and file*, privates سپاہی *the rank and file of*, the lowest stratum of کا سب سے نچلا طبقہ status درجہ، عُہدہ social status مرتبہ، حیثیت *people of rank* بڑی حیثیت کے لوگ *adj* overgrown ; too strong, etc. بہت ہی بڑا bad-smelling بدبُودار definitely bad واقعی بُرا *v. t.* & *i*. arrange in ranks صف بستہ کرنا *rank* (*someone*) *with* (*mother*, *etc*.) give him the same status کو (کسی کے) درجے میں رکھنا، کو (ماں وغیرہ) کے برابر سمجھنا، (ماں وغیرہ) کی جگہ سمجھنا have a rightful place in the list of claimants against a bankrupt (کسی دیوالیہ شخص یا اِدارے کے خلاف) جائز دعویداروں میں سے ہونا
rankle (*rank*-èl) *v.i.* continue to irritate میں کھٹکتے رہنا
ransack (*ran*-sak) *v.t.* plunder لُوٹنا، لُوٹ مار کرنا search (a place, etc.) thoroughly (*for* something) اچھی طرح
ransom (*ran*-sum) *n*. money paid for a captive's release فِدیہ freeing of a captive thus فِدیہ *hold* (*someone*) *to ransom* کسی کو پکڑ کر فِدیہ دے کر چھڑانا

فدیہ کا مطالبہ کرنا *v.t.* free (someone) for ransom رفدیہ دے کر چھڑانا
rant *v.t. & i.* (of an actor, etc.) speak violently چلّانا speak boastfully بڑ ہانکنا
rap *n.* quick, light blow دستک *v. t. & i.* (-*pp*-) strike (*at* door, etc.) thus (دروازے پر) دستک دینا give (someone) a rap (کو) آہستہ سے مارنا
rapacious (ra-*pay*-shus) *adj.* avaricious سخت لالچی ، حریص **rapacity** (ra-*pas*-i-ti) *n.* great greed, avarice سخت لالچ ، حرص و آز
rape (rayp) *v.t.* criminally assault (a woman or girl) کی عصمت دری کرنا take away by force چھین لینا ، زبردستی لے جانا *n.* raping عصمت دری a plant yielding oilseeds سرسوں a plant grown for fodder گارا **rapeseed** *n.* سرسوں کے ریا کا بیج rapeseed oil کڑوا تیل ، سرسوں کا تیل
rapid (*rap*-id) *adj.* swift تیز steep بہت ڈھلوان
rapidity (ra-*pid*-i-ti) *n.* swiftness تیزی ، سُرعت
rapier (*ray*-pi-ĕ*) *n.* a slender sword پنچہ ، کٹاری
rapine (*rap*-ɪn) *n* (lit.) plundering لوٹ مار ، سلب و نہب
rapprochement (ra-*prosh*-mon) *n.* renewal of good relations (between two countries) (دو ملکوں کے مابین) تجدیدِ تعلقات
rapt *adj.* absorbed (*in* thought, book, etc.) میں مستغرق ، میں منہمک *with rapt attention* انہماک کے ساتھ enraptured وجد **rapture** (*rap*-chĕ*) *n.* ecstasy وجد fit of great joy بے حد خوشی expression of extreme delight بے حد خوشی کا اظہار
rare (*ray*-ĕ*) *adj.* thin (atmosphere) لطیف scarce شاذ unusually good غیر معمولی طور پر اچھا
rarely *adv.* seldom کبھی کبھار ، شاذ ہی **rarefied** (ray-ĕ*-ri-fɪd) *adj.* (of air, atmosphere, etc.) made rare لطیف **rarity** (*ra*-ri-ti) *n.* being rare ندرت rare thing نادر شے ، نادرۂ روزگار (ج: نوادر)
rascal (*ras*-kĕl) *n.* rogue بدمعاش (said lovingly of a person or child) mischievous شرارتی
rash *n.* outbreak of tiny red spots on the skin سرخ باد *adj.* very hasty (person or action) جلد باز شخص ، جلد بازی کا (کام) reckless (person) عاقبت نااندیش recklessly done (work) اندھا دھند (کام) **rashness** *n.* recklessness جلد بازی ، عاقبت نااندیشی
rasp *n.* scraping file covered with spikes خار دار ریتی ، سوہن *v. t. & i.* scrape with a rasp سوہن کرنا ، سوہن سے رگڑنا make a rough and grating sound ناگوار آواز نکالنا irritate جھنجھلا دینا

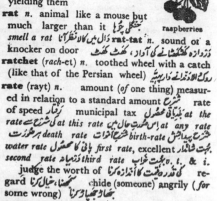

raspberry (*rahz*-be-ri) *n.* sweet (red) berries رس بھری bush yielding them

raspberries

rat *n.* animal like a mouse but much larger than it جنگلی چوہا *smell a rat* دال میں کالا نظر آنا **rat-tat** *n.* sound of a knocker on door دروازہ کھٹکھٹانے کی آواز ، کھٹ کھٹ
ratchet (*rach*-et) *n.* toothed wheel with a catch (like that of the Persian wheel) روک والا دندانے دار پہیہ
rate (rayt) *n.* amount (*of* one thing) measured in relation to a standard amount شرح rate of speed رفتار municipal tax بلدیاتی محصول *at the rate* کی شرح سے *at this rate* اس صورتِ حال میں *at any rate* ہر صورت *death rate* شرحِ اموات *birth-rate* شرحِ پیدائش *water rate* پانی کا محصول *first rate*, excellent بہت شاندار *second rate* درمیانہ *third rate* بہت خراب *v. t. & i.* judge the worth of کی قدر و قیمت کا اندازہ کرنا regard سمجھنا ، خیال کرنا chide (someone) angrily (*for* some wrong) جھاڑ جھپاڑ کرنا
rather (*rah*-dhĕ*) *adv.* somewhat کسی حد تک instead اس کی بجائے more accurately ; better بہتر تو یہ ہے ، بلکہ بہتر تو یہ ہے ، ٹھیک تو یہ ہے more gladly زیادہ خوشی سے (emphatic word for) yes یقیناً ، ضرور
ratify (*rat*-i-fɪ) *v. t.* confirm, endorse (a statement) کی تصدیق کر دینا (of a government) accept (a treaty) signed by its officials, etc. تصدیق کرنا ، کو تسلیم کرنا **ratification** (-*kay*-) *n.* act of ratifying or being ratified تصدیق
rating (*ray*-ting) *n.* categorization کا درجہ متعین کرنا ، درجہ بندی کرنا category (*of* a ship according to tonnage, *of* a student according to examination result) درجہ lowest ranks in the Navy بحریہ کا سپاہی
ratio (*ray*-shi-oh) *n.* (pl. *ratios*), proportion نسبت ، تناسب *in the ratio* 3 : 5 (*i. e.*, three to five) تین اور پانچ کی نسبت سے
ration (*rash*-ĕn) *n.* share (of food) راشن ، راتب share (of anything) حصہ رسدی *v. t.* put (something) on ration کی راشن بندی کرنا put (people) on rations کا راشن مقرر کرنا ، کا حصہ رسدی مقرر کرنا
rational (*rash*-ĕ-nĕl) *adj.* able to reason عاقل ، ذی عقل based on reason معقول ، عقلیت پر مبنی ، مبنی بر عقل that which can be tested by reason عقل کے معیار پر پورا اترنے والا ، معقول **rationally** (*rash*-ĕ-nĕ-li) *adv.* according to reason عقل کے مطابق **rationalism** *n.* belief that everything (esp. religious beliefs) should be tested by reason عقلیت پسندی **rationalist** *n.* one who believes in rationalism عقلیت پسند
rationalistic *adj.* (of methods, etc.) based on

this belief عقلیت پسندانہ **rationalize** (*rash*-na-liz) *v. t.* & *i.* interpret (moral lapse, weakness, etc.) according to supposed reason with a view to presenting it in a good light پُرفریب توجیہ کرنا **rationalization** (-*zay*- *n.* such interpretation پُرفریب توجیہ reorganization of industry on more efficient lines to eliminate waste کارکردگی بڑھانا

ratlin, ratline, ratling (rat-) *n.* (usu. *pl.*) small ropes fixed to the shrouds of a ship بادبان کی چھوٹی رسّی

rattle (*rat*-ĕl) *v. t.* & *i.* (cause to) make a series of quick, short sounds کھڑکھڑ کرنا، جھُن جھُن کرنا move with a rattling noise بڑبڑ کرتے ہوئے جانا (وغیرہ) repeat (*off* something) quickly and thoughtlessly بے سمجھے بغیر فرفر پڑھ دینا *n.* rattling noise کھڑکھڑاہٹ، گڑگڑ، جھُن جھُن *death rattle* نزع کا غرغرہ، گھرا toy producing this noise جھنجھنا **rattle-snake** *n.* venomous American snake making such noise with its tail کھڑکھڑ کرنے والا سانپ

raucous (*rawk*-us) *adj.* hoarse (sound) بھرّائی ہُوئی (آواز) harsh (sound) کرخت

ravage (*rav*-ij) *v. t.* & *i.* destroy تباہ وبرباد کرنا plunder لوٹ مار کرنا، غارتگری کرنا *n.* destruction تباہی، بربادی destroying تباہ کاری *the ravages of* کی تباہ کاری

rave (rayv) *v. i.* shout violently چلا چلا کر بولنا wildly (in delirium, etc.) (ہذیان میں) بکتے جانا speak angrily (*against*) (کے خلاف) جوش سے کہنا (of storm) roar گھن گرج ہونا speak (*of* or *about* something) with (uncalled for) enthusiasm کی تعریفوں کے پُل باندھنا **ravings** *n. pl.* wild talk (*of* a madman) (دیوانے کی) بڑ

ravel (*rav*-el) *v. t.* & *i.* (-ll-) fray (*out*) کناروں کی دھجیاں نکل آنا، گھِسنا *n.* complication پیچیدگی، مشکل

raven (*ray*-ven) *n.* a crow-like large bird پہاڑی کوّا *adj.* glossy black (hair) کالے سیاہ، سیاہ فام *v. t.* plunder غارتگری کرنا eat greedily بھُوکوں کی طرح کھانا **ravenous** (*rav*-e-nus) *adj.* mad for food بھُوک سے بے حال voracious پیٹو

ravine (ra-*veen*) *n.* deep narrow gorge گہری گھاٹی

ravish (*rav*-ish) *v. t.* (of a sight, etc.) enrapture دِل کو لُبھا جانا، بے حد دِل خوش کُن ہونا rape عصمت دری کرنا **ravishment** *n.* ecstatic delight وجد آفریں مسرت

raw *adj.* in its natural state خام *raw materials* خام مال uncooked کچا unskilled; untrained (recruits, hands, etc.) غیر تربیت یافتہ inexperienced (youth) ناپختہ کار، خامکار damp and chilly (weather) سخت سَرد اور مرطوب (of an injured part) stripped of skin جہاں سے گوشت نکل آیا ہو sore (wound) کچا زخم crude (style) بھدا، (اسلوب)

ray *n.* beam (of light, heat, etc.) شعاع rays *of the sun* سُورج کی کرنیں

rayon (*ray*-on) *n.* artificial silk مصنوعی ریشم

raze (rayz) *v. t.* knock (building) down *the ground* (عمارت) گرا دینا، مسمار کرنا destroy (town etc.) م و نشان تک نہ رہنے دینا، تہ و بالا کر دینا

razor (*ray*-zė*) *n.* shaving instrument اُسترا *edge*, its keen edge اُسترے کی دھار *safety razor*, ty designed not to cut the skin سیفٹی ریزر

¹**re** (ree) *prep.* (in Latin phrases) regarding کے متعلق

²**re-** *pref.* again پھر، بار، وا differently دوسرے طور پر، ایک دوسرے mutually اور طریقے سے، اور طرح کو away, back or down پیچھے یا نیچے

reach (reech) *v.t.* & *i.* arrive at پہنچنا get far as پر (یا تک) پہنچنا stretch (*out* one's hand something) (کے لیے) ہاتھ بڑھانا pass (someone som thing) اُٹھا کر دینا، پکڑانا *n.* distance which one hand can reach دسترس distance or circle with which one can move رسائی، پہنچ *within easy rea of* جہاں تک آسانی سے پہنچا جا سکے *out of* (*one's*) *rea* *beyond the reach of* کی دسترس سے باہر straight pa of a river between two bends دریا کے دو موڑوں کے *in the lower reaches of* (*a river*) کے زیریں دریائی حصّہ unbroken stretch of water حصوں میں قطعۂ آب

react (ree-*akt*) *v.t.* act in an opposite wa اثر کرنا act on one another ردِّ عمل ہونا کا اثر ہونا، کا نتیجہ ہونا، کا ردِّ عمل ہونا تعامل کرنا *react to* re *against* ناپسند کرنا **reaction** (ree-*ak*-shĕn) result of action ردِّ عمل، ارتجاع **reactionary** (ree-*ak*-sh na-ri) *n.* & *adj.* diehard رجعت پسند **reactor** *n.* (s *Addenda*)

read (reed) *v.t.* & *i.* (pa. t. and pa. p. *read*, p red) look at the written word and be able make it out پڑھنا understand it after doing پڑھنا utter aloud (*to* oneself or someone) آواز سے پڑھنا، پڑھ کر سُنانا study (some subject a place) پڑھنا (of a play, etc.) give a (*good* *bad*) impression on reading پڑھنے میں (اچھا یا بُرا) لگنا *read between the lines* تحریر کا پنہاں مفہوم پالینا *well-rea* *deeply read* بہت پڑھا لکھا **readable** *adj.* pleasant read دلچسپ کتاب **reader** *n.* one who reads والا، خواندہ، قاری reading-book ریڈر، کتاب teach next to a university professor ریڈر **reading** *n.* to read پڑھنا book knowledge کتابی علم (one نزدیک مفہوم، تعبیر interpretation (*of* something) successive occasions on which a bill brought before a House خواندگی، قرائت recensi قرائت، نسخہ figure *on* dial at a particular m ment شمار، اندراج

ready (*red*-i) *adj*. prepared (*for* or *to do* something) تیار willing (*for* or *to do* something) آمادہ *get ready* تیار ہونا *get (something) ready* تیار رکھنا prompt گھڑا گھڑایا ، تیار *ready with* لیے ہوئے **ready money** *n*. cash نقد **ready-reckoner** *n*. tabulated computations for finding out (for example) a day's salary when a month's is known, حاضر حساب **ready-made** *adj*. (of clothes) already made ; stitched, but not to order سلے سلائے **ready-wit** *n*. repartee حاضر جوابی **readily** *adv*. easily آسانی سے آسانی willingly خوشی سے ، بخوشی **readiness** *n*. being ready تیار ہونا willingness (*for*) پر آمادگی *in readiness for* کے لیے تیار

real (*ree*-èl) *adj*. actually existing حقیقی ، واقعی genuine اصلی *real estate*, land and building غیر منقولہ جائداد **realism** *n*. freedom from sentiment and convention واقعیت پسندی true representation of life (in art and lit.) حقیقت پسندی ، حقیقت نگاری **realist** *n*. one who practises or believes in realism واقعیت پسند ، حقیقت نگار **realistic** *adj*. pertaining to or based on realism واقعیت پسندانہ ، حقیقت پسندانہ ، عملی **reality** (ree-*al*-i-ti) *n*. being real *in reality* در حقیقت something real حقیقت ، واقعہ *the grim, realities of* کے بھیانک واقعات (یا حقائق) **really** (*ree*-è-li) *adv*. in fact واقعی ، درحقیقت **Note : Realism,** as a movement in art or literature, aims at expressing usu. the sordid facts of life as they are in reality **impressionism** was a 19th-century art movement producing general effects through vigorous touches and masses of colour and form ; **post-impressionism** came after this movement with a bid to express the spiritual significance of things ; **expressionism** was still another revolt against impressionism and it tried to give expression to the artist's ideas and emotions through stylized forms.

realize (*ree*-a-liz) *v.t.* be conscious of (one's or someone's position, difficulties, mistakes, etc. so *that*) achieve (hope, ambition, etc.) حاصل کرنا ، پورا کرنا ، جامۂ عمل پہنانا realize one's ambitions پانا get payment (*for*) or profit (*on* something) وصول کرنا **realisation** (-*zay*-) *n*. act of realizing or being realized احساس ، حصول ، تکمیل ، وصولی

realm (relm) *n*. domain قلمرو field (*of* fancy science, etc.) (کا) میدان

realtor (*ree*-al-tē*) *n*. (U.S.) real estate agent دلال جائداد غیر منقولہ ، دلال

ream (reem) *n*. correctly 480, but now usually 500 sheets of paper رم

reap (reep) *v.t.* & *i.* harvest (crop, etc.) فصل کاٹنا **reaper** *n*. one who reaps کٹائی کرنے والا (یا والی) *the solitary reaper* اکیلی کٹائی کرنے والی machine for reaping کاٹنے کی کل درانتی **reaping-hook** *n*. sickle

rear (*ree*-è*) *n*. back پشت ، پیچھا ، عقب *in the rear of* کے پیچھے ، کے عقب میں *in the rear* پیچھے کی طرف last part of a fighting force فوج (وغیرہ) کا عقب *adj*. back پچھلا ، عقبی *v.t.* & *i.* breed (poultry, etc.) کی نسل کشی کرنا bring up (a family) (گھر بار) چلانا raise (the head) اٹھانا ، اونچا کرنا (poet.) build تعمیر کرنا (of a horse) rise on the hind legs (گھوڑے کا) الف ہو جانا

reason (*ree*-zen) *n*. cause of or justification for explanation ; ground (*for*) وجہ ، سبب ، باعث *give no reason for* کی وجہ نہ سمجھانا *(one's) reason for (doing)*, *the reason why (one did it)* کسی کے کچھ کرنے کی وجہ *by reason of*, owing to کی وجہ سے intellectual faculty عقل ، سمجھ *bring (someone) to reason, make (someone) see reason* کو عقل سکھانا *it stands to reason (that)* ظاہر ہے کہ *listen to reason* معقول بات مان بھی لو ، مان بھی جاؤ *anything in reason* ہر معقول بات sanity ہوش *v.t.* & *i.* exercise the power of thinking عقل سے کام لینا ، سوچنا draw logical conclusion استدلال کرنا ، مستنبط کرنا ، منطقی نتیجہ نکالنا argue (*with* someone) to persuade him سے بحث کرنا ، کو قائل کرنے کی کوشش کرنا give as a reason (*that*) وجہ یہ بیان کرنا کہ persuade by reasoning دلائل سے قائل کرنا *reason (someone) into* (or *out of*) *doing (something)* (کسی کو) کوئی کام کرنے (یا نہ کرنے) کے لیے دلائل سے قائل کرنا **reasonable** *adj*. having reason معقول moderate معقول ، مناسب according to reason معقول *n*. logical argument استدلال

reassure (ree-a-*shoo*-è*) *v.t.* dispel the fears or doubts of کے اندیشے دور کرنا **reassuring** *adj*. heartening ہمت افزا

rebate (re-*bayt*) *n*. deduction کٹوتی *get a rebate of* (رقم) کٹوتی ملنا

rebel *v.i.* (re-*bel*) (-ll-) take up arms (*against* the government) بغاوت کرنا ، (حکومت کے خلاف) ہتھیار اٹھانا defy سرکشی کرنا *n*. (*reb*-el) one who rebels باغی *adj*. (*reb*-el) rebelling (army, etc.) باغی **rebellion** (re-*bel*-yěn) *n*. armed rising against the government حکومت کے خلاف ہتھیار اٹھانا ، بغاوت **rebellious** (re-*bel*-yus) *adj*. of or like a rebel باغیانہ participating in a rebellion بغاوت میں حصہ لینے والا wayward منہ زور ، سرکش

rebound *v.i.* (re-*bound*) *v.i.* bounce back after contact اچٹنا *n*. rebounding اچٹنا

rebuff (re-*buf*) *n*. cold or unfriendly refusal to (request, offer, etc.) بے پروایانہ انکار *v.t.* give a rebuff to (کی بات) بے پروائی سے مسترد کر دینا

rebuild (re-*bild*) *v.t.* build anew نئے سرے سے بنانا
rebuke (re-*bewk*) *v.t.* scold (someone *for doing* something) ڈانٹنا، ڈانٹ ڈپٹ کرنا، جھاڑ جھپاڑ کرنا *n.* words used for this purpose ڈانٹ، ڈانٹ ڈپٹ، جھاڑ جھپاڑ
rebut (re-*but*) *v.t.* (-tt-) show (something) to be wrong غلط ثابت کرنا، تردید کرنا، تغلیط کرنا **rebuttal** *n.* act of rebutting تردید، تغلیط
recalcitrant (re-*kal*-si-trant) *adj.* defying the authority سرکش، نافرمان
recall (re-*kawl*) *v.t.* summon back (an envoy, etc.) واپس بلا لینا revoke (a decision or order) منسوخ کرنا recollect کو یاد کرنا *n.* summons to come back واپسی کا حکم possibility of return واپسی کا امکان
recant (re-*kant*) *v.t.* & *i.* renounce (earlier belief, statement, etc.) سے تائب ہونا، سے رجوع کرنا **recantation** (-*tay*-) act of recanting توبہ، رجوع
recapitulate (ree-ka-*pit*-ew-layt) *v.t.* & *i.* go over the main points of (argument, etc.) again کے اہم نکات دہرانا **recapitulation** (-*lay*-) *n.* act of recapitulating اہم نکات کا اعادہ
recapture (ree-*kap*-chĕ*) *v.t.* capture again پھر لے لینا، پر پھر سے قبضہ کرنا recall کو یاد آنا
recast (ree-*kahst*) *v.t.* mould again نئے سرے سے ڈھالنا
recede (ri-*seed*) *v.i.* move back پیچھے ہٹنا withdraw (*from*) سے دستکش ہونا slope backwards پیچھے کی طرف ڈھلوان ہونا decrease in value (کی قدر (قیمت) کم ہونا **receding** *adj.* that recedes پیچھے ہٹنے والا **recession** (re-*sesh*-ĕn) *n.* act of receding (see *Addenda*) پیچھے ہٹنا، دستکش ہونا
receipt (re-*seet*) *n.* receiving or being received پانا، پہنچنا *on receipt of* کے پہنچنے پر *be in receipt of* پانا written acknowledgement of money received رسید (*pl.*) amount of money received وصولی recipe نسخہ *v.t.* write a receipt on a bill بل . رسید بنا دینا
receive (re-*seev*) *v.t.* & *i.* take what is given پانا، کو ملنا welcome استقبال کرنا entertain (visitors) سے ملاقات کرنا (یا) کی خاطر مدارات کرنا be informed of (news, etc.) سننا، پانا admit لے لینا accept as true مسلّمہ ہونا **received** *adj.* that has been taken لیا ہوا، وصول شدہ widely accepted as true مسلّمہ
receiver *n.* person who receives پانے والا receiver of stolen goods چوری کا مال چھپا رکھنے والا official appointed to manage an insolvent's property دیوالیے کا متولّی receptacle ظرف earpiece of a telephone ٹیلی فون کا آواز گیر، گوشہ، گوشی wireless receiving set ریڈیو (یا ٹیلی ویژن سیٹ) **receiving-set** *n.* radio ریڈیو
recension (re-*sen*-shĕn) *n.* revision نظرِ ثانی revised text تصحیح شدہ نسخہ
recent (*ree*-sent) *adj.* new ; of not long ago حال کا، حالیہ **recently** *adv.* حال ہی میں
receptacle (re-*sep*-ta-kĕl) *n.* any sort of container ظرف، جوف
reception (re-*sep*-shĕn) *n.* receiving وصول کرنا manner of receiving وصول یابی *radio reception* ریڈیو کی وصول یابی *poor reception* اچھی وصول یابی نہ ہونا formal party (usu. with drinks and light refreshment) arranged (*in honour of* someone) استقبالیہ welcome (of) خیر مقدم، پزیرائی **receptionist** (re-*sep*-shĕ-nist) *n.* person (usu. some charming young lady) employed by a person or firm to receive clients خیر مقدم کرنے والی (یا والا)، استقبالی **receptive** (re-*sep*-*tiv*) *adj.* (of mind) ready to receive new impressions or ideas اثر پزیر **receptivity** (-*tiv*-) *n.* being receptive اثر پزیری
recess (re-*ses*) *n.* vacation تعطیلات interval, break آدھی چھٹی، وقفہ portion of room with a receding wall گوشہ out of the way place کنج تنہائی secluded and secret part (of) نہاں خانہ
recession *n.* (see under **recede**)
recipe (*res*-i-pi) *n.* (abbr. R/-) statement of the ingredients, etc., of a medicine نسخہ instructions for preparing something (esp. food) ترکیب
recipient (re-*sip*-i-ent) *n.* one who receives وصول کنندہ
reciprocal (re-*sip*-ro-kĕl) *adj.* mutual **reciprocate** (re-*sip*-ro-kayt) *v.t.* & *i.* exchange مبادلہ کرنا express similar (feelings) for the person expressing them first اُنہی جذبات کا اظہار کرنا
recite (re-*sīt*) *v.t.* & *i.* repeat (poem, etc.) aloud from memory زبانی سنانا، انشاد enumerate in order ترتیب وار گننا narrate, recapitulate سنانا
recital (re-*sī*-tĕl) *n.* detailed narration تفصیل، تفصیل سنانا musical entertainment of one composer's work or by one performer (ایک کی) نغمہ سرائی
recitation (res-i-*tay*-shen) *n.* act of reciting زبانی سنانا، سنانا that which is recited نشید
reckless (*rek*-les) *adj.* rash, careless (*of* consequences) اندھا دھند چلانے (وغیرہ) والا، غیر محتاط
reckon (*rek*-ĕn) *v.t.* & *i.* calculate کو شمار کرنا، کا حساب کرنا add (*up*) جمع کرنا، جوڑنا include (*in*) کو حساب میں رکھنا settle accounts (*with*) سے حساب چکانا depend (*on* or *upon*) پر بھروسا کرنا (*that*) خیال کرنا (کہ) look upon (*as*) کو سمجھنا **reckoning** *n.* calculating حساب (*be*) *out in* (*one's*) *reckoning* کے حساب میں غلطی ہونا (hotel) bill (سرائے کا) بل

(*a*) the last judgement یوم حساب (*b*) time when one's misdeeds have to be avenged or atoned for یوم حساب

reclaim (re-*klaym*) *v.t.* request given back واپسی کی درخواست کرنا making (waste land) useful (بنجر زمین کو) قابل کاشت کرنا build dykes to have more (soil) from under water بند باندھ کر سمندر وغیرہ سے زمین خالی کرانا reform (a criminal) (مجرم) کی اصلاح کرنا **reclamation** (-*may*-) *n.* act of reclaiming or being reclaimed واپسی کی درخواست ، (زمین) خالی کرانا ، نکالنا ، زیر کاشت لانا ، اصلاح

recline (re-*klin*) *v.t.* & *i.* lean to rest ٹیک لگانا rest (one's arm, etc., on) (پر) رکھنا ، تکیہ کرنا *in a reclining posture* ٹیک لگائے ہوئے

recluse (re-*kloos*) *n.* & *adj.* solitary (person) گوشہ نشین ، تارک الدنیا ، تنہائی

recognize (*rek*-og-niz) *v.t.* identify پہچاننا know again پہچان لینا accept (claim, government, etc.) کو تسلیم کرنا realize (something or *that*) کچھ لینا ، محسوس کرنا appreciate (one's services, etc.) کی قدر افزائی کرنا **recognition** (-*nish*-) *n.* act of recognizing or being recognized شناخت ، تسلیم کرنا ، احساس ، قدر افزائی *give recognition to* کو تسلیم کرنا

recoil (re-*koil*) *v.i.* (of a gun) rebound دھکا دینا shrink back (*from* something *in* fear, etc.) پیچھے ہٹنا *n.* act of recoiling دھکا ، دبکنا ، دبک کر پیچھے ہٹنا

recollect (rek-o-*lekt*) *v.t.* & *i.* recall یاد پڑنا ، یاد آنا ، ذہن میں لانا **recollection** *n.* recollecting یاد آنا memory یاد that which is recollected یادداشت

recommence (re-ko-*mens*) *v.t.* begin all over again از سر نو شروع کرنا ، پھر سے شروع کرنا

recommend (rek-o-*mend*) *v.t.* make favourable suggestion of (someone, his name or case, to another, *for* job, etc.) کی سفارش کرنا (of a quality) make (someone) acceptable (*to*) قابل قبول بنانا advise مشورہ دینا **recommendation** (-*day*-) *n.* advice مشورہ statement that recommends سفارش

recompense (*rek*-om-pens) *v.t.* require (someone *for* good or bad acts, etc.) بدلہ دینا compensate (someone *for*) کی تلافی کرنا *n.* reward جزا retribution سزا compensation تلافی

reconcile (*rek*-on-sil) *v.t.* make up (quarrel, etc.) جھگڑا چکانا make quarrelled (persons) friends again میں صلح کرنا ، مصالحت کرانا harmonize (two things, or something *with* the facts) ہم آہنگی پیدا کرنا *reconcile (oneself) to something* (اپنے آپ) راضی ہو جانا **reconciliation** *n.* act of reconciling or being reconciled صلح ، مصالحت ، آہنگی

recondite (*rek*-on-dit) *adj.* abstruse (knowledge, author, etc.) مغلق

recondition (ree-kon-*dish*-en) *v.t.* repair and put into good condition again ٹھیک ٹھاک کر دینا **reconditioning** *n.* act of putting into good condition مرمت کر کے ٹھیک ٹھاک کر دینا **reconditioned** *adj.* that has been put into good condition مرمت شدہ

reconnoitre (rek-o-*noi*-tè*) *v.t.* & *i.* inspect (enemy positions, etc.) کی دیکھ بھال کرنا **reconnaissance** (re-*kon*-i-sens) *n.* such inspection دیکھ بھال

reconquer (re-*konk*-è*) *v.t.* conquer again دوبارہ فتح کرنا

reconsider (re-kon-*sid*-è*) *v.t.* consider again پر دوبارہ غور کرنا alter (decision, plan, etc.) بدلنا ، میں ترمیم کرنا

reconstruct (-*strukt*) *v.t.* remodel نئے انداز سے بنانا rebuild از سر نو بنانا

record *v.t.* (rè-*ko*d*) take down for future reference قلمبند کر لینا ، ضبط تحریر میں preserve (sound, form, etc.) for future use (ریکارڈ یا تصویر پر) محفوظ کر لینا indicate دکھانا ، ظاہر کرنا *n.* (*rek*-o*d) document دستاویز written account (*of*) (کا) دستاویزی ثبوت *on record* قلمبند ، مندرج ، اندراج *bear record to* بہم پہنچانا *off the record*, (*a*) (of part of interview, statement, etc.) not meant for publication جسے شائع کرنے کی اجازت نہ ہو ، غیر مجاز (بیان) (*b*) said unofficially غیر رسمی طور پر history-sheet (*of*) ماضی ، ریکارڈ ، سرگزشت ، پہلا کردار *with a good (or bad) record* اچھے (یا برے) ماضی والا limit reached now and never before ریکارڈ *break (or beat or better) the record, set up a new record* ریکارڈ توڑنا ، ریکارڈ قائم کرنا gramophone disc ریکارڈ ، توا *adj.* (of score, crop, attendance, etc.) highest so far آج تک اتنی کبھی نہیں جتنی اب ، انتہائی

recount (re-*kount*) *v.t.* narrate سنانا ، کہنا

recoup (re-*koop*) *v.t.* recover (*oneself*) دوبارہ طاقت بھرنا recompense (someone or oneself for) (کی) کسر پوری کرنا

recourse (re-*ko*s*) resorting رجوع (in the phrase) *have recourse to* سے رجوع کرنا

recover (re-*kuv*-è*) *v.t.* & *i.* regain possession, etc. of (کھوئی ہوئی چیز) دوبارہ پانا become well again صحت پانا *recover oneself*, be oneself again آپے میں آنا

recovery *n.* act of recovering بازیابی ، صحت یابی

recreation (rek-re-*ay*-shen) amusement تفریح

recreate *v.t.* (ree-kre-ayt) create again دوبارہ بنانا (*rek*-re-ayt) refresh (oneself) after toil تفریح کرنا

recriminate (re-*krim*-i-nayt) *v.t.* accuse in return جوابی الزام عائد کرنا ، جوابی الزام **recrimination** *n.* counter charge جوابی الزام

recrudescence (ree-kroo-*des*-ens) *n.* fresh outbreak (*of* disease, trouble, etc.) نیا دَور، دوبارہ ہونا
recruit (re-*kroot*) *n.* new member نیا رُکن newly enlisted soldier رَنگروٹ *v.t.* & *i.* enlist بھرتی کرنا replenish (supplies, etc.) کمی پُوری کرنا
rectangle (rek-*tang*-ĕl) *n.* oblong مستطیل **rectangular** *adj.* of such shape مستطیل
rectify (*rek*-ti-fī) *v.t.* correct تصحیح کرنا **rectification** (-*kay*-) *n.* تصحیح
rectilinear, rectilineal (-*lee*-ni-) *adj.* (of geometrical figure, etc.) bounded by straight lines سیدھی لکیروں میں محیط (شکل)، مستقیمی شکل
rectitude (*rak*-ti-tewd) *n.* integrity ایمان داری، ایمانداری ، دیانت داری، دیانت
rector (*rek*-tĕ*) clergyman of a tithed parish جاگیر والے دیہاتی گرجے کا پادری university or college boss in some places ریکٹر، پرنسپل یا وائس چانسلر **rectory** (*rek*-to-ri) *n.* rector's official residence ریکٹر کی سرکاری قیام گاہ
rectum (*rek*-tum) *n.* last section of the large intestine معائے مستقیم
recumbent (re-*kum*-bent) *adj.* lying down لیٹا ہُوا
recuperate (re-*kewp*-ĕ-rayt) *v.t.* & *i.* recoup oneself صحت یا طاقت بحال ہو جانا **recuperation** (-*ray*-) *n.* act of recuperating بحالیِ صحت، دوبارہ طاقت پکڑنا
recur (re-*kĕ**) *v. i.* (-rr-) occur again پھر ہونا occur again and again بار بار ہونا go back (to a subject) پر واپس جانا **recurrence** *n.* act of recurring اِعادہ، بار بار ہونا **recurrent** *adj.* that recurs بار بار ہونے والا
red *n.* colour of blood سُرخ رنگ یا لال رنگ any colouring matter for this لال رنگ (*Red*) Communist کمیونسٹ *adj.* of the colour of blood سُرخ، لال blushing (*with*) جس کے چہرے پر حیا کی سُرخی دوڑ جائے revolutionary انقلابی enraged غصّے سے لال
red-baiter *n.* (see *Addenda*) **redbreast** (*red*-brest) *n.* (also *robin redbreast*) robin لال چڑی **Red Cross** *n.* world body for the relief of suffering caused by natural disasters, or wars ریڈ کراس ، صلیب احمر St. George's cross as the emblem of England ریڈ کراس ، برطانوی عَلَم (پھریرا) Christian side in the Crusades صلیبی جنگوں کے عیسائی رضاکار **Red Crescent** *n.* Red Cross in certain Muslim countries (excluding Pakistan) ہلالِ احمر **red deer** *n.* stag بارہ سنگھا **red ensign** *n.* (-*sīn*) flag of the British merchant ships برطانوی تجارتی جہازوں کا عَلَم (یا پھریرا) **red flag** *n.* any revolutionary (esp. Soviet) banner انقلابی جھنڈا **red-handed** (-*hand*-) *adj.* while committing crime جُرم کرتا ہُوا، ارتکابِ جُرم کی حالت میں **red herring** (-*he*-) *n.* smoked herring بھُنی ہُوئی ہیرنگ subject raised to distract attention from the po[int] at issue اصل موضوع سے توجہ ہٹانے والی بات (see *Adden*[*da*])
red hot *adj.* heated to redness لال انگارا f[ur]ious غصّے سے لال پیلا **red heat** *n.* سخت گرمی **red-let**[ter] **day** *n.* day of rejoicing جشن کا دن، خوشی کا دن **red ta**[pe] *n.* exercise adherence to form in governm[ent] offices ضابطہ پرستی، سُرخ فیتہ delay caused by غیر ضروری تاخیر methods and mentality of o[ffi]cials دفتری طریقے یا ذہنیت
redeem (re-*deem*) *v. t.* get back (someth[ing] pawned or mortgaged) on repayment of d[ebt] فدیہ دے کر چھڑانا ransom چھڑانا، فک کرنا fu[lfil] (one's promise) قول پُورا کرنا gain (hono[ur]) thus قول پُورا کر کے عزت کو چار چاند لگانا (of Christ) [ab]solve from sins according to Christianity [عیسا]ئیوں کے نزدیک مسیح کا بخشوانا یا نجات دلانا **the Redeemer** Jesus Christ according to Christians [نجات] دہندہ، منجی، مُنجی **redemption** (re-*dem*-shĕn) *n.* act [of] redeeming or being redeemed چھڑانا، فک کرنا *past redemption* ناقابلِ اصلاح **redeeming** *adj.* sav[ing] بچانے والا *the redeeming feature of*, the silver lin[ing] to کی بُرائیوں کے ساتھ یہ اچھا پہلو بھی ہے کہ
redeployment (ree-de-*ploi*-ment) *n.* improv[ed] arrangements in factories to increase out[put] پیداوار بڑھانے کے لیے کارخانے کا بہتر انتظام
redolent (*red*-o-lent) *adj.* fragrant [خوش]بودار suggestive (*of*) کی یاد دلانے والا **redolence** (*red*-o-lens) *n.* fragrance or its suggestion [خوش]بو کا تصور
redouble (re-*dub*-ĕl) *v.t.* & *i.* intensify [شد]ید تر کرنا
redoubt (re-*doubt*) *n.* small fort گڑھی **redoub**[t]**able** *adj.* formidable (opponent) [خوفنا]ک، زبردست
redound (re-*dound*) *v. i.* contribute (*to* o[ne's] credit, advantage, *etc.*) پر منتج ہونا recoil (*up*[on]) (اُسی کی طرف) پلٹ کر آنا
redress (re-*dres*) *v.t.* remedy (the or so[me]one's grievance, etc.) کا ازالہ کرنا compensate [for] (a wrong) کی تلافی کرنا *redress the balance* [حسا]ب برابر کرنا *n.* act of redressing ازالہ compensation
reduce (re-*dews*) *v. t.* & *i.* decrease change (*to*) بنانا *reduce maunds* (*etc.*) *to se*[*ers*] (*etc.*) منوں وغیرہ کے سیر وغیرہ بنانا bring (*to* a sta[te] etc.) کی حالت میں لانا *reduce* (*someone*) *to order* [سرک]ش کو رام کرنا **reduction** (re-*duk*-shĕn) *n.* decrease کمی، تخفیف *at a reduction* قیمت کم کر کے arithmeti[cal] method or sum for changing bigger units i[nto] smaller units تحویل small scale copy [of] picture, etc.) (تصویر یا نقشہ) ہے بنانے پر، مُختصرہ
reductio ad absurdum (re-*duk*-shi-oh-ad-ab-s[ĕ]-dum) *n.* proving something wrong by sho[wing]

ing its logical conclusion to be absurd کسی چیز کو غلط ثابت کرنے کے لیے اُس کے منطقی نتائج کو مہمل ثابت کرنا push-ing something to impractical lengths کسی بات کو غیر معمولی حد تک بڑھا دینا

redundant (re-*dund*-ant) *adj.* superfluous فالتو، **redundancy** (-ans-i) *n.* being redundant بھرتی کا فالتو، غیر ضروری، بیکار یا بھرتی کا ہونا

re-echo (re-*ek*-oh) *v.t.* & *i.* echo again and again بار بار گونجنا

reed *n.* kinds of water plant نرسل its hollow stalk نے musical instrument made of it بانسری، نے *a broken reed*, one who has not proved reliable ناقابلِ اعتبار شخص، بے اعتبار شخص *lean on a reed* ناقابلِ اعتبار شخص کا سہارا لینا **reedy** *adj.* (of sound) shrill تیکھی

reef *n.* rock just below or above the sea-surface سمندر میں سطح کے برابر اُونچی چٹان part of sail that can be rolled up with ropes to control speed بادبانچہ *v. t.* roll up a reef partly or wholly بادبانچہ چھوٹا کرنا **reef-knot** *n.* (also *reefer*), symmetrical double knot برابر کی دوہری گرہ

reek *n.* stench سڑاند *v.i.* stink (*of*) سے سڑاند اٹھ رہی ہونا

reel *v.t.* roll on a reel لپیٹنا stagger in walking ڈگمگا کر چلنا be dizzy چکرانا be shocked چکرا جانا feel (something) to be moving in circles (چیز) چکر کھاتی ہوئی (*reel off a story*), narrate it with ease and speed تیزی سے سُنانا *n.* roller (*of* thread, wire, film, paper, etc.) ریل strip of film about 1,000 feet long فلم کی ریل lively Scottish dance ریل ناچ music for it ریل ، ریل ناچ کی گت یا دُھن

reeve (reev) *n.* (old use) magistrate of town or district مجسٹریٹ علاقہ

refer (re-*fě**) *v. t.* & *i.* (-rr-) allude (*to*) (کا) ذکر کرنا، (کی) طرف اِشارہ کرنا be connected (*to*) سے متعلق ہونا resort (*to* some book or authority *for* information) حوالہ دینا یا دیکھنا send up or hand over (*to*) for decision, etc. کے سپرد کرنا، کے پاس بھیجنا

referee (ref-ě-*ree*) *n.* judge in (certain games) ریفری، پنچ، حکم (also *reference*), one willing to tell about someone's character, etc. جس کا حوالہ دیا جائے *v. i.* be a referee ریفری بننا، حکم بننا **reference** (*ref*-ě-rens) *n.* referring حوالہ note giving reference حوالہ *cross-reference*, reference to another place in the same book اندرونی حوالہ *a reference book*, book falling into the category of encyclopaedias or dictionaries حوالے کی کتاب *reference library*, not a lending library but just a reading-room صرف وہاں بیٹھ کر پڑھنے والا کتب خانہ re-feree جس کا حوالہ دیا جائے statement of one's referee ; testimonial سرٹیفیکیٹ connection تعلق *with reference to*, *in reference to*, about کے متعلق، سلسلہ *without reference to* سے قطعِ نظر **referendum** (ref-e-*rend*-um) *n.* plebiscite ; direct vote of the citizens (*on* an issue) ریفرنڈم، اِستصوابِ رائے عامّہ، اِستصواب

refill (re-*fil*) *v.t.* fill again دوبارہ بھرنا *n.* that with which something is filled again دوبارہ بھرنے کی چیز، لگر

refine (re-*fin*) *v.t.* & *i.* purify خالص بنانا، صاف بنانا make cultured شائستگی سکھانا make elegant شاندار بنانا **refined** (re-*find*) *adj.* cultured شائستہ elegant شاندار **refinement** *n.* purification خالص ہونا یا کرنا politeness شائستگی delicacy نفاست chastity (*of* language, etc.) پاکیزگی **refinery** *n.* factory for refining something صاف سازی کا کارخانہ، صاف سازی

refit (re-*fit*) *v.t.* & *i.* (-tt-) (of a ship) be reconditioned مرمّت سے (جہاز) ٹھیک ٹھاک ہونا recondition (a ship) مرمّت سے (جہاز) ٹھیک ٹھاک ہونا

reflect (re-*flekt*) *v.t.* & *i.* throw back (image, or rays of light or heat) منعکس کرنا express کا اظہار کرنا (*reflect upon*), bring discredit to پر بدنامی کا دھبّا لگانا، کے ماتھے پر کلنک کا ٹیکہ لگانا bring (credit or discredit *upon*) (کی نیک نامی یا بدنامی کا) موجب ہونا meditate (*on*) (پر) غور و فکر کرنا **reflection, reflexion** (re-*flek*-shěn) *n.* reflecting or being reflected منعکس کرنا یا ہونا reflected image, light or heat عکس، انعکاس censure (*upon* or *on* someone or his character) پر بدنامی کا دھبّا، کلنک کا ٹیکہ *cast a reflection on* thought, meditation خیال، غور و فکر *lost in reflection* مستغرق *on reflection*, on second thoughts غور کرنے کے بعد expression (of a thought) اظہار **reflective** (-tiv) *adj.* thoughtful غور و فکر کا عادی **reflector** (re-*flek*-tě*) *n.* device for reflecting light or heat waves عکس انداز

reflex (re-*fleks*) *adj.* automatic, involuntary (action) غیر شعوری، اضطراری *n.* reflex action غیر شعوری فعل **reflexive** (re-*flek*-siv) *adj.* (of pronoun, verb, etc.) implying agent's action on itself راجع الی الفاعل

refloat (refloht) *v. t.* float (a sunken ship) again دوبارہ تیرانا

refold (re-*fohld*) *v.t.* fold once more ایک تہہ اور لگانا

reform *v. t.* & *i.* (re-*fo*m*) improve اِصلاح کرنا یا ہونا (usu. spelt as *re-form* and pr. *ree*-form), form anew اَز سرِ نو بنانا *n.* (re-*fo*m*) improvement اِصلاح (usu. *pl.*) change effected for this purpose اِصلاح، اِصلاحات **reformation** (ref-o*-*may*-shěn) *n.* improvement اِصلاح (*the Reforma-*

tion), the sixteenth-century European movement for reforming Christianity which resulted in Protestantism, etc. مسیحی اِصلاحِ مذہب، تحریکِ اِصلاحِ عیسائیت **reformative** (-tiv) *adj*. tending to reform اِصلاحی **reformatory** (re-*fo**-ma-to-ri) *adj*. reforming اِصلاحی Borstal institution or jail where young culprits are lodged in the hope of reclamation رِیفارمیٹری، اِصلاحی قید خانہ **reformer** *n*. one who works (or usu. leads a movement) for effecting reforms مُصلح **reformist** *n*. reformer مُصلح *adj*. (of zeal, etc.) of a reformer اِصلاحی

refract (re-*fract*) *v.t.* deflect (ray of light) where it enters مُنعطف کرنا *light is refracted when it passes through a prism* نُور منشور میں سے گُزرنے پر مُنعطف ہو جاتا ہے **refraction** *n*. act of refracting or being refracted اِنعطاف **refractory** (re-*frak*-to-ri) *adj*. stubborn ; difficult to control سرکش

refrain (re-*frayn*) *v. i.* hold oneself back (*from* or *from doing* something) سے باز رہنا، سے اِحتراز کرنا *n*. burden of the song ترجیع

refresh (re-*fresh*). *v. t.* quicken (one's memory) (یاد) تازہ کرنا revive (oneself *with* a drink, etc.) تازہ دم ہونا **refresher** *n*. (see *Addenda*) **refreshing** *adj*. تازہ دم کرنے والا، فرحت بخش **refreshment** *n*. (usu. *pl*.) drink, etc., between meals نقل، چائے وغیرہ *refreshment room*, railway restaurant رِیفریشمنٹ رُوم، طعام گاہ

refrigerate (re-*frij*-è-rayt) *v. t.* make cold ٹھنڈا کرنا preserve food thus برودت کے ذریعے اشیائے خوردنی کو محفوظ کرنا **refrigerator** *n*. cupboard fitted with an apparatus for this purpose رِیفریجریٹر، سرد خانہ

refuge (*ref*-ewj) *n*. shelter from danger, etc. پناہ گاہ، ملجا، ماویٰ، جائے پناہ **refugee** (ref-ew-*jee*) *n*. one taking refuge from a natural or man-made calamity پناہ گزیں، پناہ گیر one who takes refuge in another country مہاجر

refulgence (re-*ful*-jens) *n*. glorious radiance تنویر **refulgent** (re-*ful*-jent) *adj*. gloriously shining مُنوّر

refund *v.t.* & *i.* (re-*fund*) pay back (money *to* someone) (کو روپیہ) واپس دینا یا لوٹانا *n*. refunding واپس دی ہوئی رقم، بازدلوائی، بازدہی money refunded

refurbish (-*fĕ**-) *v.t.* polish again دوبارہ چمکانا

refurnish (-*fĕ**-) *v.t.* furnish again نئے سازوسامان سے آراستہ کرنا

refuse *v.t.* & *i.* (re-*fewz*) say 'no' اِنکار کرنا، نہ کرنا decline (*to* accept) (لینے) سے اِنکار کرنا reject مسترد کرنا *n*. (*ref*-yoos) waste material فُضلہ **refusal** (re-*few*-zĕl) *n*. act of refusing اِنکار

refute (re-*fewt*) *v.t.* prove (someone or something) to be wrong کو غلط ثابت کرنا، کی تردید کرنا **refutation** (-*tay*-) *n*. act of refuting تردید، تغلیط

regain (re-*gayn*) *v. t.* recover لے لینا get back to (پر) واپس پہنچنا

regal (*ree*-gèl) *adj*. (of title, office, government, etc.) of or by a king ; royal شاہی، شاہانہ **regally** (*reeg*-è-li) *adv*. in a regal manner شاہانہ انداز سے، شکوہِ خسروانہ کے ساتھ

regale (re-gayl) *v.t.* feast (oneself or someone *with* or *on*) ضیافت کرنا یا اُڑانا (of flowers, beauty, etc.) give delight to کے لیے جنّتِ نگاہ ہونا *n*. choice repast شاندار دعوت، ضیافت delighting thing دِلفریبی

regard (re-*gah***d*) *v.t.* gaze at بغور دیکھنا، ٹکٹکی باندھ کر دیکھنا (usu. but incorrectly) consider (*as*) خیال کرنا، سمجھنا honour (someone or his wishes) کا احترام کرنا **as regards** (az-re-*gah***dz*), **with regard to, in regard to,** as far as this is concerned جہاں تک اِس کا تعلق ہے، کے بارے میں **regarding** *prep*, about کے متعلق *n*. long or steady look ٹکٹکی care (*for*) (کی) پروا *have little regard for* کی پروا نہ کرنا goodwill, affection خیرسگالی esteem اِحترام، لحاظ *hold* (*someone*) *in high regard* کا بڑا اِحترام کرنا (*pl*.) (used toward the close of a letter) good wishes سلام، آداب، تسلیمات *with kind regards* آداب *Please pay my regards to (someone)* کی خدمت میں میرا سلام پہنچا دیجیے گا **regardful** *adj*. thoughtful (*of*) کا خیال کے باب میں رکھنے والا **regardless** *adj*. having no regard بے لحاظ، بے پروا *regardless of* (*something*), leaving (it) aside سے قطع نظر

regatta (re-*gat*-a) *n*. boat or yacht race meet کشتیوں کی دوڑ کے لیے اِجتماع

regenerate (re-*jen*-è-rayt) *v. t.* & *i.* revive spiritually کی رُوح کو بیدار کرنا، اِحیائے اخلاق کرنا give a new lease of life to کو نئی زندگی عطا کرنا **regeneration** (-*ray*-) *n*. revival اِحیا

regency *n*. (see under **regent**)

regent (*ree*-jent) *n*. & *adj*. (person) officiating for a ruler during his or her absence, minority or infirmity شاہ کا قائم مقام **regency** (*ree*-jens-i) *n*. designation (or period of authority) of a regent شاہ کی قائم مقامی (کا منصب یا عرصہ) وغیرہ *regency council*, شاہ کی قائم مقام مجلس

regicide (*rej*-i-sid) *n*. murder of a king بادشاہ (یا ملکہ) کا قتل one committing such murder بادشاہ (یا ملکہ) کا قاتل

regime (ray-*zheem*) *n.* method of ruling طرز حکومت ، نظام حکومت prevailing government موجودہ حکومت **regimen** (*rej*-i-men) *n.* controlled diet پرہیزی کھانا rule حکومت

regiment (*rej*-i-ment) *n.* of army under a colonel's command رجمنٹ ، پلٹن *v.t.* bring under strict (political) discipline پر سخت (سیاسی) نظم وضبط قائم کرنا **regimentation** (-*tay*-) *n.* strict (political) discipline سخت (سیاسی) نظم وضبط bringing people under it سخت (سیاسی) نظم وضبط کے تحت لانا

region (ree-jèn) *n.* large area خطہ area (*of*) (کا) دائرہ **regional** (ree-jè-nĕl) *adj.* of regions علاقائی *West Regional Laboratories*, government industrial research laboratory in West Pakistan مغربی پاکستان کا علاقائی معمل

register (*rej*-is-tĕ*) *n.* book for keeping some record رجسٹر ، بہی mechanical device serving this purpose کلدار بہی ، مشینی بہی *v.t.* & *i.* in the relevant register (کی) رجسٹر کرنا ، تسجیل کرنا ، اندراج کرنا send a letter by registered post رجسٹری بھیجنا ، تسجیل بھیجنا (of a measuring instrument) indicate دکھانا ، بتانا (of someone's face) express (protest, etc.) کے آثار (چہرے پر) دکھائی دینا **registrar** (*rej*-is-trah*) *n.* person in charge of registration رجسٹرار ، ناظم تسجیل ، مسجل **registration** (-*tray*-) *n.* act of registering or being registered رجسٹری کرنا یا کرانا **registry** (*rej*-is-tri) *n.* registration تسجیل office of registration تسجیل خانہ ، دفتر تسجیل

regret (re-*gret*) *n.* sorrow (*for* loss, etc.) افسوس ، رنج disappointment (*at*) تاسف ، مایوسی apology (*for*) معافی *v.t.* (-tt-) look back with sorrow پچھتانا ، متاسف ہونا feel sorry at کا افسوس ہونا apologize (*that*) معافی مانگنا express inability of معذوری کا اظہار کرنا ، معذرت کرنا **regretfully** *adv.* with regret افسوس سے **regrettable** *adj.* sorrowful غمناک undesirable (incident, behaviour, etc.) افسوسناک

regular (*reg*-ew-lĕ*) *adj.* happening at fixed intervals معمول کے مطابق ، باقاعدہ پابندی کے ساتھ methodical (person) بااصول ، باقاعدہ according to procedure or custom باقاعدہ ، باضابطہ professional (player) پیشہ ور fully qualified مستند ، سند یافتہ permanently maintained (army) پکی (یا مستقل) *n.* soldier of the regular army باقاعدہ فوج پکی فوج میں ملازم **regularity** (-*la*-) *n.* being regular باقاعدگی **regularize** (*reg*-ew-la-riz) *v.t.* bring it in conformity with the law قانون کے مطابق بنالینا ، باضابطہ بنالینا **regularly** *adv.* in a regular manner ٹھیک وقت پر ، باقاعدہ ، باقاعدگی سے **regulate** (*reg*-ew-layt) *v.i.* control by rules or system نظام کے تحت لانا ، باقاعدہ بنانا adjust (clock etc.) ٹھیک کرنا **regulation** (reg-ew-*lay*-shĕn) *n.* rule قاعدہ act of regulating باقاعدہ بنانا *adj.* according to rules ٹھیک ، باضابطہ **regulator** (-lay-) *n.* (esp.) pendulum (of a clock) گھڑی کا رقاص ، لنگر

rehabilitate (ree-ha-*bil*-i-tayt) *v.t.* resettle (uprooted person) دوبارہ آباد کرنا ، آبادکاری میں مدد دینا restore (old building) to a good condition ٹھیک ٹھاک کرنا **rehabilitation** (ree-ha-bil-i-*tay*-shĕn) *n.* resettlement آبادکاری

rehash (ree-*hash*) *n.* old material (esp. book or article) put into a new shape پرانی چیز جسے نیا بناکر پیش کیا جائے *v.t.* present (something) thus (پرانی) چیز کو ، تھوڑا سا بدل کر پیش کرنا

rehearse (re-*hĕ*s*) *v.t.* & *i.* practise (a play, etc.) for performance ڈرامے کی مشق کرنا repeat دہرانا narrate سنانا ، بتانا **rehearsal** *n.* practice ریہرسل ، (ڈرامے کی) مشق

reign (rayn) *n.* being a sovereign فرمانروائی its period دور حکومت *v.i.* rule (over) پر حکومت کرنا prevail طاری ہونا

reimburse (ree-im-*bĕ*s*) *v.t.* pay (someone) back (the amount spent) خرچ کی ہوئی رقم ادا کرنا **reimbursement** *n.* act of reimbursing خرچ کی ہوئی رقم کی ادائگی

reins (raynz) *n. pl.* long narrow strap for guiding a horse باگ ، لگام *v.t.* control with reins کی لگام دینا control باگیں ہاتھ میں لینا ، کو قابو میں رکھنا

reindeer (*rayn*-dee-è*) *n.* draught deer of cold regions رینڈیر

reinforce (ree-in-*foh*s*) *v.t.* make stronger (*by* using more material) مضبوط بنانا succour (*by* more men) کمک پہنچانا **reinforcements** *n.* (*pl.*) military succour کمک

reinstate (ree-in-*stayt*) *v.t.* restore (someone) to a former status بحال کرنا **reinstatement** *n.* restoration to former status بحالی

reiterate (ree-*it*-è-rayt) *v.t.* say or do repeatedly بار بار کہنا ، بار بار دہرانا **reiteration** (-ray-) *n.* act of reiterating or being reiterated بار بار دہرانا

reject (re-*jekt*) *v.t.* refuse to accept (offer, etc.) نامنظور کرنا ، مسترد کرنا **rejection** *n.* act of rejecting or being rejected نامنظوری ، استرداد

rejoice (re-*jois*) *v.t.* & *i.* be happy خوش کرنا make merry خوشی منانا be happy (*at*) پر خوش ہونا **rejoicing** (re-*joi*-sing) *n.* happiness (*at* something) خوشی (*pl.*) celebrations جشن

rejoin (re-*join*) *v.t.* & *i.* join again (army, etc.) دوبارہ فوج میں بھرتی ہونا reply جواب دینا **rejoinder**

n. reply to an argument بحث کا جواب statement comprising counter-argument تصنیف پر کے دُو سرے رُخ پر مشتمل بیان counter-charge جوابی الزام
rejuvenate (re-*joov*-e-nayt) *v.t.* & *i.* make or become young again دوبارہ جوان بننا یا بنانا ، اعادۂ شباب کرنا یا ہونا **rejuvenation** *n.* making or becoming young again اِعادۂ شباب
rekindle (ree-*kind*-ĕl) *v.t.* kindle again دوبارہ جلانا ، دوبارہ رَوشن کرنا
relapse (re-*laps*) *v.i.* fall a prey to (*into*) the same disease or evil habit too soon گئی ہُوئی بیماری یا چھوٹی ہُوئی عادت میں فوراً پھر مُبتلا ہو جانا *n.* such falling back عَود
relate (re-*layt*) *v.t.* & *i.* narrate (story, events, etc.) بیان کرنا join (to or with) سے تعلّق (یا واسطہ یا ربط) ہونا یا قائم کرنا **related** *adj.* (*a*) connected (*to*) سے متعلّق (*b*) relation (*to*) رشتہ دار **relation** (re-*lay*-shĕn) *n.* narration بیان connexion (*between* persons or things, or *of* one *to* another) واسطہ ، ربط ، تعلّق family tie رشتہ داری ، رشتہ relative رشتہ دار (*pl.*) dealings روابط ، مَراسم ، تعلّقات business relations کاروباری friendly relations دوستانہ مراسم تعلّقات bear no relation to, be out of all proportion with سے کوئی تناسُب نہ رکھنا in relation to, concerning کی بابت ، کے سلسلے میں **relationship** *n.* relation, connexion تعلّق ، واسطہ family tie رشتہ داری ، رشتہ **relative** (*rel*-a-tiv) *n.* relation رشتہ دار *adj.* connected, relevant (*to*) کے متعلّقہ comparative (advantage, etc.) ایک دوسرے کے مقابلے میں ، اِضافی compared with others نِسبتہً respective اپنا اپنا ، متعلّقہ (of pronoun or adverb) referring a subordinate clause to an antecedent (as who, which, whom, where, when, etc.) اِسم مَوصُول **relatively** *adv.* comparatively نِسبتہً proportionately (*to*) کے متناسب
relax (re-*laks*) *v.t.* & *i.* cease from effort سستانا (of discipline) make or become less tight ڈھیلا کرنا یا ہونا **relaxation** (-*say*-) *n.* making or becoming less tight ڈھیلا کرنا یا ہونا recreation تفریح
relay (re-*lay*) *n.* new shift of couriers, etc. نئی چَوکی *work in relays* باری باری کام کرنا *relay race*, race between two or more teams with each running only a part of the whole distance ریلے رَیس ، چوکی دَوڑ *v.t.* (*ree*-lay) (of a station) broadcast programme received from another station ریلے کرنا ، نشر کرنا
release (re-*lees*) *v.t.* set free رہا کرنا ، چھوڑنا let go چھوڑنا ، جانے دینا deliver (*from*) سے نجات دِلانا send (news item) to paper for publication (خبر) شائع کرنے کے لیے بھیجنا permit (its) publication (خبر) شائع کرنے کی اجازت دینا screen (a film) publicly for the first time (فلم) کی پہلی بار نمائش کرنا ، (فلم) پہلی بار دِکھانا
relegate (*rel*-e-gayt) *v.t.* remove (*to* a lower position, obscurity, etc.) پیچھے کر دینا ، چھوٹی جگہ منتقل کرنا
relegation (-*gay*-) *n.* act of relegating or being relegated درجے میں کمی ، اِنتقال
relent (re-*lent*) *v.i.* become less severe سختی کم کرنا ، نرم کرنا **relentless** *adj.* nyielding بیرحم ، بیدرد
relevant (*rele*-vant) *adj.* pertinent (*to*) مُتعلّقہ ، سے متعلّق
reliable (re-*lī*-a-bĕl) *adj.* trustworthy مُعتبر ، قابلِ اعتماد
reliably *adv.* in a reliable manner مُعتبر طور پر
reliability (re-lī-a-*bil*-i-ti) *n.* trustworthiness اِعتماد ، بھروسہ **reliance** (re-*li*-ans) *n.* trust قابلِ اعتماد ہونا
reliant *adj.* trusting بھروسہ کرنے والا
relic (*rel*-ik) *n.* part of a holy person's body or belongings kept after his death as a revered object تبرّک something (of the past) surviving the ravages of time یادگار
relief (re-*leef*) *n.* alleviation تسکین that which alleviates (pain, etc.) تسکین دینے والی چیز charitable help (like food, clothes, etc.) for those in trouble اِمداد ، اِعانت *relief fund* اِمدادی فنڈ *flood relief committee* مجلسِ امدادِ سیلاب زدگان deliverance نجات new shift for duty نئی ڈیُوٹی reinforcements نیا رستہ freedom from duty کام سے چھُٹی raising of siege محاصرہ اُٹھا لینا interesting change relieving of monotony دِلچسپ تبدیلی design standing out from the surface اُبھرا ہُوا نقش such carving, etc. مُنبّت کاری vivid outline نمایاں ، خدّ و خال ، واضح خاکہ *stand out in sharp relief* بہت واضح ہونا *relief map*, physical map showing the height of the land اِرتفاعی نقشہ **relieve** (re-*leev*) *v.t.* bring relief to کو تسکین ، نجات یا چھُٹی دینا *relieve* (*someone*) *of* (*a load*, *etc.*) (کسی سے بوجھ اُٹھانے کے لیے لے لینا) *relieve* (*someone*) *of* (*his*) *purse* (کسی) کا بٹوہ اُڑا لینا *relieve* (*one's*) *feelings*, vent them
religion (re-*lij*-ĕn) *n.* system of faith and worship دین ، مذہب such system based on belief in Almighty God دین ، مذہب **religious** (re-*lij*-us) *adj.* pertaining to religion دینی ، مذہبی God-fearing (person) خدا ترس conscientious or scrupulous (care, etc.) فرض شناسانہ
relinquish (re-*link*-kwish) *v.t.* let go (one's grip, etc.) چھوڑ دینا give up (hope, etc.) ترک کرنا
relish (*rel*-ish) *n.* appetizing flavour ذائقہ ، مزہ taste (*for*) شوق appetizing thing like sauce, pickles, etc. اچار ، چٹنی وغیرہ *v.t.* & *i.* enjoy (food) مزے سے کھانا have a taste (of) کا مزا آنا
reluctance (re-*luk*-tans) *n.* unwillingness to do ہچکچاہٹ ، تذبذب ، بیدلی ، عدمِ آمادگی **reluctant** (re-*luk*-tant)

dj. unwilling (*to do*) نارضامند، غیر آمادہ، بیدل، ہچکچاہٹ

ly (re-*li*) *v.t.* depend (*on* or *upon*) (پر) بھروسہ کرنا

eliable *adj*., **reliability** *n*., **reliant** *adj*.,

eliance *n*. (see under **reliance**)

main (re-*mayn*) *v.t.* continue (*in* some place or state) (میں) رہنا stay on رہنا be left behind بچنا **remainder** *n*. rest, residue بقیہ (in mathematics) number left over after subtraction باقی **remains** (re-*mayns*) *n. pl.* dead body لاش، نعش ruins کھنڈر what is left (*of* meals) بچا کھچا

emand (re-*mahnd*) *v.t.* (of a court) send (the accused) back to police custody (*for* a period) for completion of evidence پھر حوالات بھیجنا، (پولیس کا) مزید حراست، ریمانڈ ریمانڈ لینا *n*. act of remanding

emark (re-*mah*k*) *v.t.* & *i*. comment (*on* or *about* something, *that*) کہنا، رائے زنی کرنا *n*. comment کہنا، رائے زنی notice دیکھنا *nothing worthy of remark*, not worth looking at دیکھنے کے قابل تو ہے نہیں **re-markable** (re-*mah*k*-a-bĕl) *adj*. extraordinary غیر معمولی **remarkably** *adv*. extraordinarily غیر معمولی طور پر

emedy (*rem*-e-di) *n*. cure (*for* illness, social evil, trouble, etc.) علاج، چارہ *v.t*. provide a remedy for کا علاج کرنا، کا چارہ کار کرنا **remedial** (re-*mee*-di-el) *adj*. (of measures, etc.) providing a remedy; curative علاج (کی تدابیر)

emember (re-*mem*-bĕ*) *v.t.* & *i*. recall یاد آنا keep in mind یاد رکھنا، کو یاد ہونا *remember me* (*to someone*), give my regards to (him) سے میرا سلام کہیے گا **remembrance** *n*. commemoration یاد *in remembrance of* کی یاد میں (*pl.*) kind regards (*of* someone in a letter) (کا) سلام **Remembrance Day** *n*. day (the 11th of November every year or the Sunday immediately preceding it) commemorating those who died in the First and the Second World War دونوں عالمگیر جنگوں میں مرنے والوں کی یاد کا دن

remind (re-*mīnd*) *v.t.* put in mind (*of*, *that* or *to do*) یاد دلانا **reminder** *n*. letter, etc., sent to remind یادداشت

reminiscence (rem-i-*nis*-ens) *n*. recollection (*of*) کی یاد (*pl.*) account of one's past experiences سرگزشت، تذکرہ **reminiscent** (rem-i-*nis*-ent) *adj*. reminding a person (*of* something) کی یاد دلانے والا recalling the past experience بیتے دنوں کو یاد رکھنے والا

remiss (re-*mis*) *adj*. careless; not conscientious (*in*) بے پروا، فرض ناشناس **remissness** *n*. being remiss; carelessness بے پروائی، فرض ناشناسی

remission *n*. (see under **remit**)

remit (re-*mit*) *v.t.* & *i*. (-tt-) (of God) forgive (sins) بخشنا free (someone) from (punishment, fine or debt) معاف کرنا mitigate (pain, effort, etc.) کم کرنا send by money order منی آرڈر کے ذریعے رقم بھیجنا **remittance** (re-*mit*-ans) *n*. sending by money order منی آرڈر کے ذریعے بھیجنا amount remitted منی آرڈر کی ہوئی رقم

remission (re-*mish*-en) *n*. forgiveness (*of* sins, by God) بخشش mitigation (*of* pain, effort, etc.) کمی release from (punishment, fine, debt, etc.) معافی

remnant (*rem*-nant) *n*. remainder بقیہ، بچا کھچا small length of cloth offered cheap after the rest of the piece has been sold ٹکڑا

remonstrate (re-*mons*-trayt) *v.i.* argue in protest (*with* someone *that*) (کسی سے) بطور احتجاج بحث کرنا protest (*against*) کے خلاف احتجاج کرنا، جھگڑنا **remonstrance** *n*. argument in protest احتجاج، احتجاجی بحث

remorse (re-*moh*s*) *n*. deep regret (*for* sin, wrong-doing, etc.) ندامت، پشیمانی **remorseful** *adj*. full of remorse نادم، پشیمان **remorseless** *adj*. without remorse سنگدل، کٹھور

remote (re-*moht*) *adj*. distant; far off دور کا، دیر کا (of place) out of the way, secluded الگ تھلگ (of chance, etc.) slight, faint, meagre, (chance, etc.) ذرا بہت ہی کم *not the remotest idea* ذرا بھی خیال نہیں

remove (re-*moov*) *v.t.* & *i*. take away or off (*from* a place, head, school, etc.) ہٹانا shift (*to* a new house) (نئے گھر) جانا، اٹھ جانا **removal** (re-*moov*-ĕl) *n*. act of removing or being removed ہٹانا، اٹھانا، اٹھ جانا

remunerate (re-*meun*-ĕ-rayt) *v.t.* pay (someone *for*) (کا) معاوضہ دینا **remuneration** (-*ray*-) *n*. payment معاوضہ، اجرت، مشاہرہ **remunerative** (-*ray*-tiv) *adj*. profitable (work, etc.) نفع بخش، منفعت بخش

renaissance (re-*nay*-sans), **ranascence** (re-*nas*-ans) *n*. (*the Renaissance*) revival of humanism in European art and literature یورپ کی نشأۃ ثانیہ revival نشأۃ ثانیہ، یورپ کی نشأۃ ثانیہ کا دور نشأۃ ثانیہ **renascent** (re-*nay*-sent, or re-*nas*-ent) *adj*. coming into new life نئی زندگی پانے والا becoming powerful again پھر ابھرنے والا

rend *v.t.* & *i*. (*rent*, *rent*) tear (*in* two, *off* or *away*) توڑ دینا، کے ٹکڑے ٹکڑے کر دینا **rent** *n*. torn place in a cloth کھونچ gap in hillside شگاف gap in clouds پھٹا ہوا ہونا

render (*rend*-ĕ*) *v.t.* & *i*. give (thanks, service, help, etc., *to*) کرنا give (a perfor-

mance) of پیش کرنا translate (into) ترجمہ کرنا yield up (the dead) نکالنا send in (an account) کرنا make (ill, helpless, etc.) کرنا
rendering *n.* translation ترجمہ **rendition** (ren-dish-ĕn) *n.* translation ترجمہ rendering of dramatic role or musical piece ادائگی surrender حوالگی، شکست خوردگی

rendezvous (*rond*-è-voo) *n.* meeting by appointment وعدہ کی ملاقات place for it وعدہ کی ملاقات کا مقام

rendition *n.* (see under **render**)

renegade (*ren*-e-gayd) *adj.* deserter غدّار

renew (re-*new*) *v.t.* make as good as new نیا بنا دینا make (etc.) again دوبارہ کرنا، (وغیرہ) کی تجدید کرنا **renewal,** (re-*new*-ĕl) *n.* act of renewing or being renewed تجدید ▣ To **renew** is to start something (*e.g.* subscription, acquaintance) again ; to **renovate,** cause to appear new again ; to **restore** as it was ; to **replace** where it was ; to **refresh** one's memory ; to **repair** something partly damaged ; to **refurbish** something by scouring until it shines ; to **regenerate** character : to **recoup** health ; to **revive** interest, etc.

renounce (re-*nouns*) *v.t.* give up (claim, etc.) قطع تعلق کرنا، چھوڑ دینا، سے دستبردار ہونا refuse to own اپنا ماننے سے انکار کردینا **renunciation** (re-nun-si-*ay*-shĕn) *n.* act of renouncing دستبرداری، قطع تعلق

renovate (*ren*-oh-vayt) *v.t.* restore (old building) مرمّت کرکے ٹھیک ٹھاک کرنا **renovation** (-*vay*-) *n.* act of renovating or being renovated مرمّت، درستی

renown (re-*noun*) *n.* fame شہرت **renowned** (re-*nound*) *adj.* well-known مشہور

rent *n.* tenant's periodical payment for the use (of building, machinery, etc.) کرایہ (also called *economic rent*) income from an agricultural piece of land which is over and above that from a worse piece of the same area under cultivation لگان، معاشی لگان *v. t. & i.* pay rent for کرایہ دینا یا ادا کرنا give (*to* or *out to* someone) for rent کرائے پر دینا use in return for rent کرائے پر لینا **rental** (*rent*-ĕl) *n.* amount likely to be received as rent امکانی کرایہ

renunciation *n.* (see under **renounce**)

rep *n.* (school boy's slang) repetition

repair (re-*pay*-è*) *v. t.* recondition مرمّت کرنا set right (mistake, etc.) درست کرنا make amends (*for*) کی تلافی کرنا go frequently or in large numbers (*to*) جانا *n.* act of repairing or being repaired, or the work thus done مرمّت **repairable** *adj.* that can be repaired جس کی مرمّت ہو سکے، مرمّت کے قابل **reparable** (*rep*-a-rab-el) *adj.* (of a loss) that which can be made good قابلِ تلافی

reparation (rep-a-*ray*-shĕn) *n.* compensating تلافی compensation تاوان

repartee (rep-a*-*tee*) *n.* witty retort پھڑکتا ہوا جواب، پھڑکا دینے والا جواب making of such retorts حاضر جوابی

repast (re-*pahst*) *n.* (rich, sumptuous, slight, or some other kind of) meal کھانا

repatriate (ra-*pat*-ri-ayt) *v. t.* send or bring (someone) back to his own country وطن واپس لانا یا بھیجنا **repatriation** (-*ay*-) *n.* act of repatriating or being repatriated وطن کو واپسی

repay (ree-*pay*) *v. t. & i.* pay back چکانا، ادا کرنا make a return to کا معاوضہ دینا **repayment** *n.* act of repaying, or being repaid, or the amount repaid ادائگی، معاوضہ

repeal (re-*peel*) *v.t.* abrogate (a law) (قانون) منسوخ کرنا *n.* act of repealing or being repealed تنسیخ

repeat (re-*peet*) *v. t. & i.* say or do again دہرانا *repeat* (one's) *lesson* سبق کی تکرار کرنا، آموختہ دہرانا *repeat oneself* وہی بات (یا باتیں) دوبارہ کہنا say what has been learnt by heart پڑھی پڑھائی کہنا **repeatedly** (re-*pee*-tid-li) *adv.* time and again باربار **repetition** (rep-e-*tish*-ĕn) (also **rep**) *n.* repeating دہرانا recurrence اعادہ

repel (re-*pel*) *v. t.* (-ll-) push back (the enemy, etc.) دھکیلنا drive away (a temptation) دور کرنا cause dislike گھن لانا، نفرت پیدا کرنا، ناپسند ہونا

repellent (re-*pel*-ent) *adj.* disgusting ; that repels نفرت انگیز، ناپسندیدہ

repent (re-*pent*) *v. t. & i.* wish not to have done it, be filled with remorse (*of*) (پر) پچھتانا، ہاتھ ملنا **repentance** (re-*pent*-ans) *n.* act of repenting پچھتاوا، پشیمانی **repentant** (re-*pent*-ant) *adj.* remorseful پشیمان، نادم، منفعل

repercussion (ree-pĕ*-*kush*-ĕn) *n.* rebounding ردّعمل reverberation گونج، صدائے بازگشت indirect but far-reaching effect بالواسطہ اور دوررس اثرات

repertoire (*rep*-ĕ*-twah*), **repertory** (*rep*-ĕ*-to-ri) *n.* dramatic pieces, etc., which a company is prepared to perform ڈراموں کا تیار ذخیرہ store-house (*of* something) مخزن **repertory company** *n.* (also *rep*), theatrical company with a repertoire of plays ڈراموں کے تیار ذخیرے والی کمپنی

repetition *n.* (see under **repeat**)

repine (re-*pin*) *v. i.* fret (*at* or *against*) کڑھنا، دلگیر ہونا

replace (re-*plays*) *v.t.* take (or put in) the place of کی جگہ لینا (یا کی جگہ پر لگانا) restore واپس اسی جگہ رکھنا provide substitute, etc., in place of the missing original کے بدلے میں دینا (یا رکھنا یا لگانا وغیرہ)

replenish (re-*plen*-ish) *v. t.* again fill (something *with*) the same thing پھر بھرنا **replete** (re-*pleet*) *adj.* well supplied (*with*) سے بھرا بھرا ہونا **repletion** *n.* being or making replete بھرا یا بھرنا **replica** (*rep*-li-ka) *n.* artist's own copy of his work نقش ثانی exact copy ہو بہو نقل **reply** (re-*pli*) *n.* answer (*to*) جواب *v.t.* & *i.* answer (*to* or *that*) جواب make answer in action; react (*to*) کے، جواب میں کرنا **report** (re-*poh**t) *v. t.* & *i.* narrate بیان کرنا bring back information اطلاع دینا، خبر دینا give as news (کی خبر بنانا، (یا مرتب کرنا make a complaint (*to* the authority, police, etc.) about کی رپورٹ کرنا، کی رپٹ لکھوانا give secret information (*to* police) مخبری کرنا go for duty (*at* a place or *to* someone) کام کے لیے حاضر ہونا *n.* account (*of*) اطلاع news خبر rumour افواہ loud noise (*of* firing, explosion, etc.) دھماکا **reporter** *n.* one who reports اطلاع دینے والا one who secretly reports to the police مخبر، مخبری کرنے والا journalist who brings in reports for his paper خبر رساں صحافی **repose** (re-pohz) *v.t.* & *i.* rest آرام کرنا recline (*on*) پر رکھنا put (confidence in someone or his honesty, etc.) (پر) بھروسہ کرنا، (پر) اعتماد کرنا *n.* rest آرام quiet سکون sleep نیند **repository** (re-*poz*-i-tĕ-ri) *n.* safe store (*of*) رکھنے کی محفوظ جگہ، گودام **reprehend** (rep-ri-*hend*) *v. t.* rebuke جھاڑ جھپاڑ کرنا، سرزنش کرنا، تنبیہ کرنا **reprehensible** *adj.* blameworthy لائق ملامت **reprehension** (-*hensh*-) *n.* rebuke ملامت، سرزنش، فہمائش **represent** (rep-re-*zent*) *v. t.* stand for; symbolize کا مظہر ہونا act as an agent to کی نمائندگی کرنا be the elected representative of (constituency, people, etc.) نمائندہ ہونا play the role of کا کردار ادا کرنا profess (oneself *as*) (اپنے کو) بتانا (یا) کہنا explain (one's case or grievances *to*) پیش کرنا (*re-present*, pr. ree-pre-*zent*), present again دوبارہ پیش کرنا **representation** (-*tay*-) *n.* (esp.) explanation of one's case or complaint (*to*) عرضداشت act of representing نمائندگی act of symbolizing کا مظہر ہونا (re-presentation, pr. ree-pre-zent-*ay*-shĕn) act of presenting again دوبارہ پیش کرنا **representative** (rep-re-*zent*-a-tiv) *n.* typical example (*of*) پکا نمونہ agent (*of*) نمائندہ legislator as representing the electorate نمائندہ *adj.* representing نمائندہ duly elected (*government*, etc.) نمائندہ **repress** (re-*pres*) *v. t.* beat back or check (impulse) کو دبا دینا beat down, suppress or subdue (someone) cruelly ظلم سے دبانا، کچل دینا **repressive** *adj.* suppressive ظالمانہ، دبانے والا **repression** *n.* suppression ظلم subduing

reprieve (re-*preev*) *v. t.* cancel (death sentence) سزائے موت معاف کرنا give temporary relief to (someone from trouble, etc.) عارضی مہلت دینا *n.* cancellation of death sentence سزائے موت کی معافی temporary relief عارضی مہلت **reprimand** (*rep*-ri-mahnd) *v.t.* rebuke officially سرکاری طور پر سرزنش کرنا *n.* official rebuke سرکاری سرزنش **reprint** *v. t.* (re-*print*) print more copies دوبارہ چھاپنا *n.* (*ree*-print) book, etc., printed again نئی اشاعت **reprisal** (re-*pri*-zĕl) *n.* revengeful action انتقامی کارروائی **reproach** (re-*proach*) *v.t.* strongly blame (someone *for* or *with*) (پر) ملامت کرنا *n.* words of reproach ملامت disgrace شرمناک بات **reproachful** *adj.* (of looks, words, etc.) expressing reproach ملامت آمیز **reprobate** (*rep*-ro-bayt) *adj.* & *n.* licentious (person) who is hardened in sin بڑا لفنگا، سخت آوارہ **reproduce** (ree-pro-*dews*) *v.t.* & *i.* make a copy of وہی پھر بنانا، کی نقل تیار کرنا cause (music, etc.) to be heard again (*from* a record) کا ریکارڈ بجانا put on (a play) again (کھیل) دوبارہ کرنا bring forth offspring پیدا کرنا **reproduction** (-*duk*-shĕn) *n.* reproducing وہی پھر بنانا bringing forth offspring پیدا کرنا copy (*of*) **reproductive** (-tiv) *adj.* bringing forth offspring پیدا کرنے والا **reproof** *n.* rebuke سرزنش، جھاڑ جھپاڑ **reprove** (re-*proov*) *v. t.* rebuke جھاڑ جھپاڑ کرنا، سرزنش کرنا **reproval** (-*proov*-) *n.* rebuke سرزنش ▣ **Reproof** is a blame expressed personally in firm but kind words; **rebuke** is gentle; **rebuff,** abrupt refusal combined with unflattering reasons; **reprimand** by a superior; **censure** by a moral judge; **stricture** by a law-court; **criticism** purporting to judge impartially, but often construed by the recipient as censure; **reproach** for neglect of duty; **blame** for lack of judgment or courage; **scolding,** noisy fault-finding.

reptile (*rep*-til) *n.* any of the various species of crawling creatures رینگنے والا جانور **republic** (re-*pub*-lik) *n.* democracy جمہوریت democratic country جمہوری ملک، جمہوریہ **republican** (re-*pub*-li-kan) *adj.* of a republic جمہوریہ favouring democracy جمہوریت پسند، جمہوریت کا حامی **repudiate** *v.t.* & *i.* disown (someone) عاق کر دینا، اپنانے سے انکار کر دینا، سے قطع تعلق کر لینا refuse to pay (a debt) ادا کرنے سے انکاری ہونا reject نہ ماننا، مسترد کر دینا

contradict (a statement, etc.) کی تردید کرنا
repudiation (-*ay*-) *n.* act of repudiating or being repudiated قطع تعلق ، عاق کرنا ، انکار ، اِستردَاد
republish *v.t.* publish again دوبارہ شائع کرنا **republication** (-*kay*-) *n.* act of publishing again or being published again دوبارہ اِشاعت
repugnance (re-pug-nans) *n.* aversion (*to*) سے سخت نفرت **repugnant** (re-*pug-nant*) *adj.* disgusting or disagreeable (*to*) (کو) سخت ناپسند
repulse (re-*puls*) *v.t.* & *i.* beat off (the attacking enemy) پسپا کر دینا refuse (offer) انکار کر دینا treat coldly (someone or his friendly gestures) سے سرد مہری کا سلوک کرنا *n.* refusal انکار defeat پسپائی **repulsion** (re-*pul*-shĕn) *n.* strong dislike گھن ، کراہت **repulsive** (-siv) *adj.* causing repulsion کریہہ ، گھناؤنا
reputable *adj.*, **reputation** *n.* (see under **repute**)
repute (re-*pewt*) *v.t.* consider (someone *to be*) جاننا ، سمجھنا ، خیال کرنا *n.* good name fame شہرت **reputation** (rep-ew-*tay*-shĕn) *n.* general (high, low, etc.) opinion of (someone's) character شہرت ، ساکھ *live up to one's reputation*, act as one is expected to جیسا مشہور ہونا ویسا کام کرنا **reputable** (*rep*-ew-tab-ĕl) *adj.* respectable معزز ، محترم
reputed (re-pewt-ed) *adj.* generally supposed (*to be*) مشہور **Reputation** is the opinion held by others as to a person's character; **character**, a person's real value. regardless of the appraisal of others; **fame**, widespread good reputation; **notoriety**, the very opposite of fame.
request (re-*kwest*) *n.* asking for something استدعا petition درخواست thing asked for درخواست demand مانگ ، طلب ، مطالبہ *be in request* کی بڑی مانگ ہونا ، فرمائش *v.t.* make a request (*for*) something or (*that*) کی درخواست (یا) استدعا یا فرمائش کرنا
require (re-kwi-ĕ*) *v.t.* need direct (someone *to do*) حکم دینا demand مطالبہ کرنا **requirement** *n.* (usu. *pl.*) need ضرورت (ج : ضروریات) **requisite** (*rek*-wi-zit) *n.* & *adj.* (thing) needed or required مطلوبہ (شے) **requisition** *n.* official order (*for* supplies) سرکاری مطالبہ command taking over (of the houses) of people for government use (مکانوں وغیرہ پر) زبردستی قبضے کا حکم *v. t.* make demand thus for (supplies, houses, services, etc., *from* a town, etc.) جبری وصولی ، بیشہ
requital *n.* (see under **requite**)
requite (re-*kwit*, or re-kwi-ĕt) *v.t.* make return for (*with*) بدلہ دینا reward (*for*) کا بدلہ دینا avenge کا بدلہ دینا **requital** *n.* reward or revenge بدلہ
rescind (re-*sīnd*) *v. t.* revoke (a decision or law) منسوخ کرنا **recission** (re-*sizh*-ĕn) *n.* act of rescinding or being rescinded تنسیخ
rescue (res-*kew*) *v.t.* deliver (*from*) سے بچانا یا چھڑانا *n.* deliverance *come to the rescue of* کو چھڑانے کے لیے بروقت پہنچنا
research (re-*sĕ*ch*) *n.* careful inquiry (*into*) for discovering new facts (علمی) تحقیق ، تحقیقات *v. i.* make research (*into*) (علمی) تحقیقات کرنا
resemble (re-*zem*-bĕl) *v.t.* be like سے ملنا ، سے ملتا جلتا ہونا ، سے مشابہ ہونا ، سے مشابہت رکھنا **resemblance** *n.* مشابہت
resent (re-*zent*) *v.t.* feel offended about (something or being) برا ماننا **resentful** *adj.* feeling resentment برا ماننے والا **resentment** *n.* indignation, ill-feeling برا ماننا ، آزردگی
reserve (re-*zĕ*v*) *v.t.* set apart (*for*) کے لیے اٹھا رکھنا ، الگ رکھنا keep back for future مخصوص کرنا سنبھال رکھنا *n.* kept for emergency محفوظ (usu. pl.) money kept with this end in view محفوظ سرمایہ (*pl.*) armed forces for use in emergency ریزرو فوج ، فاضل فوج land set apart for a special purpose محفوظ زمین وغیرہ limiting condition شرط قید hesitation جھجک doubt شک *without reserve*, (*a*) without any hesitation کھل کر (*b*) fully ; without any doubt پوری طرح ، تمام و کمال keeping silent ; self-control خاموشی ، ضبط not being sociable الگ تھلگ رہنا ، پیچھے رہنا ، کم آمیزی *break through (someone's) reserve* (کسی کی) کم آمیزی ختم کرنا minimum (price) at an auction, etc. کم سے کم قیمت **reservation** (rez-ĕ*-*vay*-shĕn) *n.* reserving or being reserved (of seat, etc.) in a railway train نشست محفوظ کرانا یا کرنا limiting condition شرط ، قید *without (any mental) reservation* غیر مشروط ، کھلے دل سے
reserved *adj.* set apart (*for*) showing reserve کم آمیز ، پیچھے پیچھے رہنے والا
reservoir (*rez*-ĕ*-vwah*) *n.* large, artificial store of water تالاب ، خزانۂ آب fund (*of* knowledge, etc.) (کا) خزانہ
reside (re-*zīd*) *v.i.* live (*in* or *at*) رہنا ، رہائش رکھنا **residence** (*rez*-i-dens) *n.* (formal word for) house گھر house occupied in an official capacity سرکاری قیام گاہ **resident** (*rez*-i-dent) *adj.* one who resides مقیم *n.* one who resides in a place باشندہ (Resident) Political Agent of the ruling Power posted to a semi-independent State ریذیڈنٹ *n.* **residency** (*rez*-i-dens-i) *n.* Resident's residence ریزیڈنسی **residential** (rez-i-*densh*-ĕl) *adj.* (part of a town) where people live (but do

not work) رہا شدنی

residue (*rez*-i-dew) *n.* remainder بچاکھچا ، بقیّہ

resign (re-*zīn*) *v.t. & i.* tender resignation from (a post or *from* a committee, etc.) مستعفی ہونا give up (claim, etc.) سے دستبردار ہونا *resign oneself to fate,* be ready to endure every misfortune without complaining راضی بہ رضا ہو جانا **re-signed** *adj.* راضی بہ رضا **resignation** (rez-ig-*nay*-shĕn) *n.* resigning مستعفی ہونا intimation of this استعفیٰ being resigned to (something) راضی بہ رضا ہو رہنا

resile (re-*zīl*) *v. i.* go back (*from* one's stand, position, etc.) سے پیچھے ہٹنا ، پر پکا نہ رہنا

resin (*rez*-in) *n.* sticky fluid of pine, etc. گندا بروزہ (also see **rosin**) بروزہ

resist (re-*zist*) *v.t. & i.* use force to prevent advance طاقت سے روکنا strive against کا مقابلہ کرنا ، مدافعت کرنا ، مقاومت کرنا be proof against shock, heat, temptation, etc. سے خراب نہ ہونا **resistance** (re-*zis*-tans) *n.* resisting مقابلہ ، مدافعت ، مقاومت *offer resistance to* کا مقابلہ کرنا *passive resistance,* non-violent non-cooperation with an oppressive political power مقاومت مجہول force retarding motion مزاحمت resisting flow of current or heat برق گزار (یا غیر حر گزار)

resolute (*rez*-o-loot) *adj.* firm of purpose باعزم

resolution (rez-o-*loo*-shĕn) determination عزم ، ارادہ motion (*for* voting at a meeting, or *for* a meeting) قرارداد ، تحریک **resolve** (re-*zolv*) *v.t. & i.* be determined (*that*, or *to do*) عزم ، پکا ارادہ کرنا ، مصمم کرنا solve (a difficulty) حل کرنا set at rest (a doubt) (شک) دور کرنا break up (*into* parts) کا تجزیہ کرنا ، کے اجزا بنانا *n.* determination ارادہ ، پکا قصد ، عزم **resolved** (re-*zolvd*) *adj.* determined ارادہ کیے ہوئے *pa. p.* resolution was carried that قرار پایا کہ

resonance *n.* (see under **resonant**)

resonant (*rez*-o-nant) *adj.* resounding گونجتا ہوا echoing with گونج پیدا کرنے والا **resonance** (*rez*-o-nans) *n.* echo ; resounding گونج ، بانگ ، صدائے بازگشت

resort (re-*zo*t*) *v.i.* have recourse (*to*) سے رجوع کرنا repair (*to*) جایا کرنا *n.* resorting رجوع one who is resorted to جس کے پاس بار بار جایا جائے ، جس سے رجوع کیا جائے beauty-spot visited by many تفریح گاہ recourse کوشش ، دوڑ دھوپ *in the last resort* بالآخر ، آخری کوشش کے طور پر

resound (re-*zound*) *v. t. & i.* echo گونجنا echo (*with*) کی گونج پیدا کرنا be talked about everywhere کا چرچا ہونا (also see **resonant**)

resource (re-*soh*s*) *n.* source of help مدد کا ذریعہ that which helps in escaping trouble بچنے کا ذریعہ device تدبیر skill in devising expedients باتدبیری *a man of resources* باتدبیر آدمی **resources** *n.* wealth, stocks, supplies, etc. (*of* an individual or country) وسائل *natural resources,* land, minerals, power, etc. (of a country) قدرتی وسائل **resourceful** *adj.* skilful in finding expedients باتدبیر **resourceless** *adj.* without any resources بے وسیلہ **resourcefulness** *n.* being resourceful باتدبیری

respect (res-*pekt*) *n.* esteem (of or to) عزت ، احترام ، ادب *show respect to* کا ادب کرنا consideration (*to*) (کا) لحاظ (یا) خیال ، کو بھی پیش نظر *have* (or *pay*) *respect to* کا لحاظ رکھنا ، کا لحاظ کرنا ، کا خیال کرنا *with respect to, in respect of, in respect to,* as regards کی بابت ، کے متعلق *without respect to,* (*a*) paying no heed to کا خیال نہ کرتے ہوئے (*b*) leaving out سے قطع نظر point, particular بات ، معاملہ ، پہلو *in this respect* اس پہلو سے *in some respects* بعض پہلوؤں سے (*pl.*) good wishes, greetings سلام ، آداب ، تسلیمات *v.t.* show respect to کا ادب کرنا ، کا لحاظ کرنا ، کی عزت کرنا be considerate to (someone's feeling, needs, etc.) کا خیال رکھنا ، کا لحاظ کرنا obey (the law) پر عمل کرنا **respectable** *adj.* worthy of respect قابل عزت decent (clothes, manners, etc.) شریفانہ fairly high (amount, income, etc.) کافی **respectably** *adv.* in a respectable manner عزت سے ، باعزت طریق سے **respectability** (-*bil*-i-ti) *n.* being respectable عزت مندی **respectful** *adj.* showing respect (*to*) (کا) احترام کرنے والا **respecting** *pref.* regarding کی بابت ، کے متعلق **respective** (res-*pek*-tiv) *adj.* concerning particular individuals, etc. اپنا اپنا **respectively** *adv.* in the order mentioned علی الترتیب

respiration (-*ray*-) *n.* breathing سانس لینا breath سانس **respirator** (-*ray*-) *n.* artificial breathing mask ہواصاف آلہ iron lung مصنوعی پھیپھڑا ، آلہ تنفس

respite (*res*-pit, or *res*-pɪt) *n.* pause for rest (*from*) آرام کی گھڑی ، آرام کا وقفہ permitted delay in carrying out a sentence سزا میں مہلت *v.t.* give a respite to آرام کا وقفہ دینا delay the punishment سزا میں مہلت دینا

resplendent (res-*plend*-ent) *adj.* splendidly brilliant درخشاں ، تابندہ **resplendence** (-dens) *n.* splendid brilliance شاندار درخشانی

respond (res-*pond*) *v.i.* answer جواب دینا feel the effect of (*to*) کا ردعمل ہونا ، سے متاثر ہونا act in answer to کا معاوضہ دینا **response** (res-*pons*) *n.* answer جواب acting in answer to جوابی اقدام reaction ردعمل ، تاثر ، اثر پذیری **responsive** (res-*pons*-iv) *adj.* quick in responding اثر پذیر

responsible (res-*pons*-i-bèl) *adj.* trustworthy مُعتبر، قابلِ اعتماد (of a job) involving responsibility ذِمّہ دارانہ holding a responsible and high job ذِمّہ دار accountable (*to* someone *for* something) جوابدہ **responsibility** (res-pons-i-*bil*-i-ti) *n.* being responsible ذِمّہ داری being accountable جوابدہی that for which one is responsible ذِمّہ داری، فرض

rest *n.* freedom from work آرام *take rest* آرام کرنا freedom from disturbance سکون *lay to rest,* bury دفن کرنا pause وقفہ support (for something) سہارا، ٹیک (*the rest*), residue باقی، بقیّہ (*the rest*), others دُوسرے، باقی *v. t.* & *i.* stop work or exertion آرام کرنا be free from disturbance آرام پانا give rest to آرام دینا support or recline (*on* or *against*) ٹیک لگانا remain رہنا continue to be ہونا *rest assured* یقین مانیے depend (*on*) پر منحصر ہونا lie (*with*) کے ہاتھ میں ہونا **restful** *adj.* giving rest آرام دِہ calm پُرسکون **restive** (*res*-tiv) *adj.* restless (horse) آرام سے کھڑا نہ ہونے والا impatient بے چین، بیتاب، بیقرار wayward خود سر

restless *adj.* never taking rest آرام نہ کرنے والا، ہر وقت کام میں لگا رہنے والا fidgety چُلبُلا uneasy بے چین، بیتاب، بیقرار، مُضطرِب

restaurant (*res*-to-roṅ) *n.* place where meals are served on payment رَیسٹورانٹ، ریستوران، طعام خانہ

restitution (res-ti-*tew*-shěn) *n.* restoring (*of* stolen thing *to* owner) واپس دینا یا کرنا

restoration *n.* (see under **restore**)

restore (res-*toh**) *v.t.* give back (stolen property *to* owner) واپس دینا reinstate بحال کرنا recondition exactly as before مرمّت سے بالکل پہلا سا بنا دینا bring back (*to* health) صحت یاب کرنا make current (old custom) رائج کرنا **restoration** (-*ray*-) *n.* واپس کرنا، بحالی، مرمّت، تجدید، صحّت یابی، بالکل پہلا سا بنا دینا

restrain (res-*trayn*) *v. t.* check (*from doing*) قابو میں رکھنا **restraint** *n.* restraining پابندی imprisonment قید confinement in a lunatic asylum پاگل خانے میں بند کرنا

restrict (res-*trikt*) *v.t.* keep within bounds حد کے اندر رکھنا impose restrictions on (movement, etc.) پر پابندی لگانا یا عائد کرنا limit تنگ محدود رکھنا

restriction (res-*trik*-shěn) *n.* restricting پابندی (*pl.*) prohibitory limits imposed by the government on the movements, etc. پابندیاں

result (re-*zult*) *n.* issue نتیجہ outcome انجام *v. i.* be a result کا نتیجہ ہونا end (*in*) کا انجام ہونا، کا نتیجہ ہونا

resume (ray-*zew*-may, or *rez*-oo-may) *n.* summary, outline (*of*) خلاصہ، مُلخّص

resume (re-*zewm*) *v.t.* take up or begin after interval or interruption پھر شروع کرنا occupy (one's seat) again پھر بیٹھنا **resumption** (re-*zump*-shěn) *n.* act of resuming or being resumed دوبارہ آغاز، از سرِ نو آغاز، دوبارہ قبضہ

resurrect (rez-è-*rekt*) *v.t.* take up from the grave and bring back to life قبر سے نکالنا، زندہ کرنا، جلانا revive (old custom, etc.) زندہ کرنا **resurrection** *n.* restoration to life زندہ کرنا (*the Ressurrection*), the rising of all the dead on Doomsday حشر، نشر according to the Christians the rising of Christ from the tomb (عیسائیوں کے نزدیک) حضرتِ عیسیٰ کا جی اُٹھنا

resuscitate (re-*sus*-i-tayt) *v.t.* & *i.* revive ; bring back to consciousness (a drowning, etc., person) ہوش میں لانا **resuscitation** *n.* act of resuscitating ہوش میں لانا

retail *n.* (*ree*-tayl) sell in small quantities for consumption and not for resale خوردہ فروشی، پھٹکل *sell by retail* خوردہ فروشی کرنا *retail prices* پھٹکل مال کا بھاؤ *v.t.* & *i.* (*retayl*) sell or be sold by retail (*at* or *for*) پھٹکل بیچنا یا بکنا pass on (gossip) bit by bit بہت سوں کو تھوڑا تھوڑا کرکے بتانا **retailer** (re-*tay*-lě*) *n.* one who sells by retail پرچون فروش، خوردہ فروش

retain (re-*tayn*) *v. t.* keep رکھنا not to part with نہ جانے دینا hold میں رکھنا keep in mind یاد رکھنا engage (a lawyer) so as so obtain his services on payment whenever needed کسی وکیل کو پابند خدمت کر لینا **retainer** *n.* money regularly paid to claim such services whenever needed پابندیٔ خدمت کا عوضانہ (old use) servant or dependent of nobleman (کسی نواب کا) مُصاحب (یا ملازم یا حاشیہ نشین)

retention *n.* act of retaining رکھنا، رہنے دینا، پابند کرنا روکنا، روکے رکھنا **retentive** *adj.* (of memory, grasp etc.) having the power to retain دیردار، قوی روکے رکھنے والا

retaliate (re-*tal*-i-ayt) *v. i.* return evil for evil بدلہ لینا ترکی بہ ترکی جواب دینا **retaliation** (-*ay*-) *n.* act of retaliating بدلہ، انتقام، ترکی بہ ترکی جواب

retard (re-*tah*d*) *v. t.* make slow (someone's speed, etc.) کم کرنا

retention *n.*, **retentive** *adj.* (see under **retain**)

reticence *n.* (see under **reticent**)

reticent (*ret*-i-sent) *adj.* reserved in speech کم گو unwilling to tell (*about*) (کے بارے میں) خاموش **reticence** (ret-i-sens) *n.* being reticent کم گوئی، خاموشی

retina (*ret*-i-na) *n.* sensitive layer at the back of the eyeball آنکھ کا پردہ

retinue (*ret*-i-new) *n*. train of attendants نوکرچاکر، خدم وحشم

retire (re-*tī*-è*) *v.t.* & *i*. (cause to) give up service (at superannuation *on* a pension, etc.) پنشن پر بھیجنا یا پنشن پانا withdraw (*from* or *to* a place) ہٹنا order such withdrawal ہٹنے کا حکم دینا go to bed (*for* the night, etc.) سونے کے لیے جانا

retired (re-*tī*-è*d) *adj*. (of person) having retired (a post) ریٹائرڈ، پنشن یافتہ، سابق (of place) secluded الگ تھلگ **retirement** *n*. state of being retired ملازمت سے سُبکدوش، علیحدگی، تنہائی، آرام *live in retirement*, ہوکر آرام سے رہنا **retiring** (re-*tī*-è-ring) *adj*. reserved کم آمیز

retort (re-*to**t) *v.t.* & *i*. answer back sharply or wittily دنداں شکن جواب دینا، حاضر جوابی سے کام لینا retaliate ترکی بہ ترکی جواب دینا *n*. such an answer حاضر جوابی، دنداں شکن، (یا) ترکی بہ ترکی جواب distilling vessel with a sloping neck قرنبیق، قرع انبیق

retouch (ree-*tuch*) *v.t.* touch up (photograph, etc.) نوک پلک درست کرنا

retrace (ree-*trays*) *v.t.* go back over (one's steps) پر واپس جانا، جس راہ سے آیا ہو اسی راہ پر جانا، رجعت قہقری کرنا recall (past events) کو یاد کرنا، پر دوبارہ غور کرنا

retract (re-*trakt*) *v.t.* & *i*. take back (statement, confession of belief, etc.) واپس لینا، سے پھرنا pull back part of body, undercarriage, etc.) سکیڑنا draw back (skin, etc.) اندر کھینچنا

retreat (re-*treet*) *v.t.* withdraw پسپا ہونا *n*. withdrawal پسپائی *beat a retreat* پسپا ہونا *be in full retreat* بڑی عجلت میں پسپا ہونا *make good (one's) retreat* بحفاظت پسپا ہونا shelter پناہ گاہ secluded place گوشہ تنہائی seclusion, privacy خلوت، تنہائی sunset call on bugle شام کا بگل *sound the retreat* شام کا بگل بجانا signal for withdrawal پسپائی کا بگل (یا نقارہ)

retrench (re-*trench*) *v.t.* & *i*. reduce (staff) کم کرنا، گھٹانا slash (expenses) تخفیف عمل **retrenchment** *n*. act of retrenching or being retrenched تخفیف، کمی

retribution (ret-ri-*bew*-shèn) *n*. punishment for sin بدی کی سزا، گناہوں کا بدلہ revenge بدلہ، انتقام

retrieve (re-*treev*) *v.t.* & *i*. restore (one's loss or fortune) گھاٹا پورا کرنا regain (honour) کھوئی ہوئی عزت دوبارہ پانا

retro- *pref*. back واپس **retrograde** (*ret*-ro-grayd) *adj*. moving backwards پیچھے کی طرف جانے والا، رجعت قہقری کرنے والا become worse رو بہ زوال، روز بروز خراب تر ہونے والا **retrogress** (ret-ro-*gres*) *v.i.* decline, deteriorate پستی کی طرف جانا، زوال پذیر ہونا **retrogression** (ret-ro-*gresh*-èn) *n*. act of retrogressing تنزل، انحطاط، پستی کی طرف میلان **retrogressive** *adj*. declining, deteriorating رو بہ زوال **retrospect** (*ret*-ros-pekt) *n*. view of past events, etc. ماضی پر نظر review of the past گزری ہوئی چیز کا جائزہ *in the retrospect* ماضی کی روشنی میں **retrospection** (-*pek*-) *n*. meditation on the state of feelings which has past گزشتہ جذبات کا جائزہ **retrospective** (-*pek*-tiv) *adj*. of retrospection گزشتہ جذبات کے جائزے سے متعلق (of law, etc.) effective from a past date کسی سابقہ تاریخ سے نافذ *with retrospective effect* (*from*) سابقہ (فلاں تاریخ سے) نافذ

return (re-*tē**n*) *v.t.* & *i*. go back واپس جانا come back لوٹنا، واپس آنا put back واپس رکھنا pay back لوٹانا، واپس کرنا send back لوٹانا، واپس بھیجنا say in reply جواب میں لکھنا elect (someone) as a representative (*to* the Legislature) منتخب *n*. act of returning واپسی *return ticket*, ticket for a return journey واپسی کا ٹکٹ *return journey*, journey to a place and back again آنا جانا، آمد و رفت کا سفر، واپسی والا سفر *on (one's) return home* گھر پہنچ کر repayment حساب چکانا، معاوضہ retaliation بدلہ *in return* (*for*) کے بدلے، کے عوض official report of details باضابطہ اطلاع، کوائف (often *pl*.) profit (*on*) نفع، منافع، آمدنی

returnable *adj*. that which can or is to be returned قابل واپسی، جو واپس کیا جا سکے

reunion (ree-*yew*-ni-èn) gathering of former colleagues, etc., after a long separation بچھڑے ہوؤں کا اجتماع

revalorization (ree-val-o-ri-*zay*-shen) *n*. restoration of the value (of a country's currency) (سکے کی) اصل قیمت بحال کرنا، (سکے کو) پہلی قیمت پر لانا

reveal (re-*veel*) *v.t.* disclose (secret) انکشاف کرنا convey spiritual truth or message وحی بھیجنا، الہام کرنا show دکھانا، ظاہر کرنا **revelation** (-*lay*-) *n*. revealing اظہار، انکشاف، وحی، الہام surprising information نئی بات، انکشاف *It's a revelation to me* میں نے تو کبھی یہ سنا نہیں تھا، میرے لیے تو یہ انکشاف ہے

reveille (re-*vel*-i) *n*. morning call of the bugle صبح کا بگل *sound the reveille* صبح کا بگل بجانا

revel (*rev*-el) *v.i.* (-ll-) make merry رنگ رلیاں منانا take pleasure (*in*) سے لطف اندوز ہونا *n*. merry-making رنگ رلیاں **revelry** (*rev*-el-ri) *n*. noisy merry making خوشی کا ہنگامہ، رنگ رلیاں

revelation (-*lay*-) *n*. (see under **reveal**)

revenge (re-*venj*) *v.t.* retaliate by doing equal harm to (*on someone*) for (oneself, one's friend or insult, etc.) کا بدلہ یا انتقام لینا *be revenged (on someone)* انتقام لینا، بدلہ لینا *n*. revenging بدلہ لینا، انتقام لینا desire to revenge انتقام لینے کی خواہش **revengeful** *adj*. vindictive کینہ جو

revenue (*rev*-e-new) *n.* income آمدنی total annual income of the state (*from* taxes, etc.) مداخل *land revenue*, government income from agricultural land (which in Pakistan goes to the provincial Exchequer) مالیہ *Revenue Assistant*. (in Pakistan) district officer in charge of rural property and land revenue افسرِ مال

reverberate (re-*vĕ**-brayt) *v.t.* & *i.* (of sound) echo گونجنا vibrate backwards واپس مُرتعش ہونا **reverberation** *n.* echo گونج backward vibration باز ارتعاش repercussion دُوررس اثرات

revere (re-*vee*-ĕ*) *v.t.* venerate (saint, sacred things, etc.) کا عقیدت مند ہونا ، کا بے حد احترام کرنا **reverence** (*rev*-ĕ-rens) *n.* feeling of awe and deep respect تعظیم *v.t.* treat with reverence تعظیم کرنا **reverend** (*rev*-ĕ-rend) *adj.* revered محترم ، بزرگ (*the Reverend*) (abbr. *the Rev.* before name and title as *the Rev. Dr. R. M. Ewing*) ریورنڈ مقدس **reverent** *adj.* full of reverence (شخص) مؤدّب محترم **reverential** (rev-ĕ-*rensh*-ĕl) *adj.* full of reverence (انداز) مؤدّبانہ مؤدّبانہ

reverie (*rev*-ĕ-ri) *n.* day-dream محویت ، استغراق ، تصوّر کی دُنیا *lost in reverie* مستغرق ، خیالوں میں کھو جانا . خیالی پلاؤ *indulge in reveries of* اپنے ہی خیالوں میں گم *indulge in reveries* (*of*) (کے) خیالی پلاؤ پکانا

revers (re-*vay*-ĕ*) *n.* (pl. same) turned-back edge of a garment showing its under surface کپڑے کا مُڑا ہوا اُلٹا

reverse (re-*ve**s) *adj.* opposite اُلٹا back دُوسری جانب ، پُشت *n.* defeat شکست *suffer reverses* شکست پر شکست کھانا opposite (of) کا اُلٹ reverse side (*of* cloth, etc.) (کپڑے وغیرہ کا) اُلٹا *v.t.* exchange (positions) ایک دُوسرے سے بدل دینا set aside (a judgment) بالکل بدل دینا move in an opposite position (کار وغیرہ کا) پیچھے کو چلنا (یا) چلانا put in a reverse position اُلٹا کرنا ، اُوندھا کرنا *reverse arms* drill caution to hold rifles downwards رائفل کی نالی نیچے ! **reversal** (re-*ve**-sel) *n.* reversing, or becoming reverse اُلٹا ہونا یا کرنا **reversible** *adj.* (cloth, etc.) which can be used from either side وہ کپڑا یا جامہ جس کا اُلٹا سیدھا کچھ نہ ہو **reversion** *n.* (see under **revert**)

revert (re-*vĕ**t) *v.i.* come back (*to*) former (problem, etc.) (کی طرف) واپس آنا ، (کی طرف) رجوع کرنا demote (someone) to earlier (lower) post پچھلی (چھوٹی) ڈگری پر بھیجنا **reversion** (-*ve**-shen) *n.* act of reverting or being reverted پچھلی (چھوٹی) ڈگری پر واپس آنا

review (re-*vew*) *v.t.* & *i.* consider again جائزہ لینا revise (lesson) کا اعادہ کرنا revise (order, decision, etc.) نظرِ ثانی کرنا ، نگرانی کرنا inspect (troops, etc.) formally کا باقاعدہ مُعائنہ کرنا write a critical account of (a new book, etc.) for the radio or a periodical تبصرہ لکھنا ، کا جائزہ لکھنا *n.* periodical devoted to such matter and to the topics of the day ریویو ، نقاد ، تنقید ، جائزہ reviewing جائزہ ، مُعائنہ ، اعادہ ، نظرِ ثانی ، نگرانی *pass in review* (a) examine مُعائنہ کرنا (b) survey جائزہ لینا

revile (re-*vil*) *v.t.* & *i.* rail at کو گالیاں دینا

revise (re-*viz*) *v.t.* reconsider دوبارہ غور کرنا ، نظرِ ثانی کرنا read through (book, manuscript, etc.) carefully for improvements نظرِ ثانی کرنا ، میں ترمیم کرنا read again for learning more thoroughly نظرِ ثانی کرنا ، اعادہ کرنا ، دوبارہ پڑھنا **revision** *n.* revised version ترمیم شدہ اشاعت reconsideration نظرِ ثانی ، دوبارہ غور extra reading (*of*) نظرِ ثانی ، اعادہ **revisory** (re-*vi*-zo-ri) *adj.* of revision نظرِ ثانی کا

revisit (ree-*viz*-it) *v.t.* visit again دوبارہ ملنے (یا دیکھنے) کو جانا

revival *n.*, **revivalism** *n.*, **revivalist** *n.* (see under **revive**)

revive (re-*viv*) *v.t.* & *i.* come or bring back to consciousness ہوش میں لانا recall (old memories) تازہ کرنا recover or restore from a state of neglect پھر سے پیدا ہونا (یا) کرنا **revival** (re-*vi*-vĕl) *n.* new and deeper interest پہلے سے بھی زیادہ شوق *the Revival of Learning*, the Renaissance یورپ کی نشاۃِ ثانیہ reviving احیا reawakening of interest in religion مذہب سے ازسرِ نو لگاؤ ، احیائے دین (*pl.*) meetings aiming at this مذہب سے لگاؤ پیدا کرنے والے جلسے **revivalist** *n.* earnest preacher devoted to the revival of religion احیائے دین کا کام کرنے والا **revivalism** *n.* such movement تحریکِ احیائے دین **reviver** *n.* esp. (slang) stimulating drink جانفزا جام

revocable *adj.*, **revocation** *n.* (see under **revoke**)

revoke (re-*vohk*) *v.t.* cancel (a law, decision, decree, etc.) منسوخ کرنا **revocation** (-*kay*-) *n.* act of revoking or being revoked تنسیخ **revocable** (*rev*-o-kab-ĕl) *adj.* that can be revoked قابلِ تنسیخ

revolt (re-*vohlt*) *v.t.* & *i.* rise in rebellion بغاوت کرنا (of squalor) disgust (کسی چیز) سے گھن آنا (یا) سے کراہت آنا ، (کسی چیز کا) کراہت پیدا کرنا be disgusted with (squalor) سے گھن آنا (of crime, squalor, etc.) shock, disgust برگشتہ کرنا ، دہشتناک *revolting scene* مکروہ منظر *revolt at* or *against* سے برگشتہ ہونا ، گھن آنا ، برگشتہ کرنے والا منظر ہونا ، سے کراہت آنا

revolute *v.i.* (see under **revolution**)

revolution (rev-o-*lew*-shĕn) *n.* complete change in political or other set-up انقلاب one complete turn of a wheel چکّر revolving round something گردش **revolutionary** *adj.* pertaining to or bringing about a revolution انقلابی *n.* advocate of or worker for a political revolution انقلابی **revolutionize** *v.t.* change (something) thoroughly کو یکسر بدل ڈالنا **revolute** (rev-o-*loot*) *v.i.* (slang) engage in political revolution سیاسی انقلاب میں حصہ لینا (also see **revolve**)

revolve (re-*volv*) *v.t.* & *i.* move round in a circle چکر کھانا یا دینا، گھومنا یا گھمانا turn (some problem) over in the mind to consider it in all its aspects کو ہر پہلو سے سوچنا **revolver** (re-*vol*-vě*) *n.* pistol with revolving bullet chamber for firing more than once without reloading ریوالور، گرداں طپنچہ (also see **revolution**)

a revolver with its trigger (at T)

revue (re-*vew*) *n.* loosely constructed and quite musical play (or series of scenes) satirizing current events حالاتِ حاضرہ پر تلخ تبصرے والا ڈراما

revulsion (re-*vol*-shèn) *n.* sudden and violent change of feeling سخت برگشتگی violent mental reaction ذہنی انقلاب

reward (re-*wo**d*) *n.* recompense for service or merit اِنعام money offered for the return of something lost اِنعام *v.t.* give a reward to (someone *for* something) کو اِنعام دینا

rewrite (ree-*rit*) *v.t.* write again پھر لکھنا، دوبارہ لکھنا write differently نئے انداز سے لکھنا

Rex (reks) *n.* (fem. *Regina*, pr. re-ji-na) (both abb. *R.*) reigning king (or queen) (used after sovereign's name, as: *Charles Rex*; *Elizabeth Regina*) بادشاہ (مؤنث: ملکہ)

Reynard (*ren*-ah*d) *n.* (proper name for) fox لومڑ، روباہ *Reynard the fox* روباہ نامی لومڑ

rhapsodist *n.* **rhapsodize** *v. i.* (see under **rhapsody**)

rhapsody (*rap*-so-di) *n.* highly emotional utterance, poem or music پُرجوش تقریر (یا نظم یا موسیقی) enthusiastic expression of delight in poetry or music شور و آفریں نظم (یا موسیقی) **rhapsodist** *n.* one who rhapsodizes آتش نوا خطیب (یا) شور و آفریں شاعر (یا مُغنّی) **rhapsodize** *v.i.* talk or write rhapsodies پُرجوش تقریر کرنا یا شور و آفریں نظم کہنا یا نغمہ الاپنا

rhetoric (*ret*-o-rik) *n.* impressive use of words فصاحت laws of composition dealing with this بلاغت، معانی، بیان ornamental language مُرصّع زبان **rhetorical** (re-*to*-ri-kèl) *adj.* (of style) emotional جذباتی **rhetorician** (ret-o-*rish*-èn) *n.* one skilled in rhetoric ماہرِ بلاغت one fond of it مُرصّع زبان کا دِلدادہ

rheumatism (*room*-è-tizm) *n.* disease marked by the swelling of joints وجع المفاصل، جوڑوں کا درد **rheumatic** (roo-mat-ik) *adj.* pertaining to rheumatism) وجع المفاصل کا suffering from it وجع المفاصل کا مریض

rhino *n.* (see under **rhinoceros**)

rhinoceros (rī-*nos*-e-rus) *n.* (pl. rhinoceroses, pr. -siz) large thick-skinned African animal with a horny snout گینڈا **rhino** (*rī*-noh) *n.* (slang) rhinoceros گینڈا money روپیہ پیسہ

a rhinoceros

rhomb (rom, or romb), **rhombus** (*rom*-bus) *n.* equilateral parallelogram which is not right-angled شکلِ مُعیّن (یعنی وزد وغیرہ)

rhubarb (*roo*-bah*b) *n.* a plant with juicy stalks ریوند چینی (see *Addenda*)

rhyme (rīm), **rime** (rīm) *n.* words with identical final sound (like *high* and *die*) قافیہ (ج: قوافی) such identity of sound قافیہ verses with rhymed lines مُقفّیٰ نظم *nursery rhymes*, poems for small children بچّوں کے گیت *write in rhyme* قافیہ پیمائی کرنا *v.t.* & *i.* (of words or lines of a poem) end in identical sound ہم قافیہ ہونا use (a word) as rhyming (*with* another) کا قافیہ باندھنا write in rhyme مُقفّیٰ نظم لکھنا، قافیہ پیمائی کرنا **rhymed** (rīmd) *adj.* having rhymes مُقفّیٰ **rhymer** (rī-mě*) *n.* (old use) شاعر **rhymester** (*rīm*-stě*) *n.* versifier; writer of poor verse تُک بند

rhythm (ridhm) *n.* metre وزن، بحر regular ebb and flow of sound in music تال any regular beat باقاعدہ اُتار چڑھاؤ correlated coloured and proportionate shapes in art رنگ و خطوط کا تناسب

rhythmic, rhythmical *adj.* characterized by rhythm موزونیت یا تناسب والا

rib *n.* any one of the curved bones protecting the lungs پسلی thick vein in a leaf پتّے کی رگ **ribbed** (ribd) *adj.* having ribs or such markings پسلی دار

ribald (*rib*-ald) *adj.* (person) using scurrilous and obscene language بدزبان (one) using profane language کفر بکنے والا indecent (talk) گالیوں والی، بدزبان والی profane (talk) کفر کی (باتیں) coarse, vulgar (gesture) گھٹیا، پُشت یا فحش (اشارہ) **ribaldry** (*rib*-ald-ri) *n.* ribald talk or gesture بدزبانی، فحش کلامی، کفر بکنا، فحش اشارہ

riband *n.* (same as **ribbon**, which see)

ribbed *adj.* (see under **rib**)

ribbon (*rib*-ěn), **riband** (*rib*-and) *n.* long narrow ornamental band of silk ربن، فیتہ such a band for tying things فیتہ such a band for some special purpose (like a *typewriter ribbon*) فیتہ *ribbon building, ribbon development*, building of houses along the main road شاہراہ کے کنارے کنارے کی تعمیرات

rice (ris) *n.* white grain widely used as food چاول its plant دھان

rich *adj.* wealthy امیر، دولتمند very costly (jewellery, clothes, etc.) قیمتی، امیرانہ، بڑے ٹھاٹھ کا (of food) containing a lot of fat, etc. مرغن، مچرب fertile (land) زرخیز deep (sound) گونجدار آواز full (colour) گہرا رنگ abounding (*in* something) سے بھرپور، کی بہتات (یا افراط) والا **riches** (*rich-iz*) *n. pl.* wealth دولت abundance کثرت، فراوانی، وفور **richly** *adv.* in a rich manner اچھی طرح سے fully (deserved) پوری طرح **richness** *n.* (of person, things, land, food, etc.) being rich دولت مندی ، مال و دولت، افراط، فراوانی، زرخیزی، مرغن ہونا

rick (rik) *n.* thatched stack of straw, corn, etc. بھوسے وغیرہ کا لپا ہوا بند ڈھیر *v.t.* make (straw, etc.) into a rick ڈھیر لیپ پوت کر رکھنا

a rick

rickets (*rik-ets*) *n.* an infantile disease softening the bones سوکھا، مسان **rickety** (*rik-e-ti*) *adj.* weak-jointed ; shaky (furniture, etc.) کمزور، بودا، گرنے کو، ٹوٹ جانے کو

rickshaw (*rik-shaw*) *n.* light two-wheeled carriage for human beings pulled by a fellow human being رکشا *cycle-rickshaw*, one pedalled by a person instead of being pulled by him سائیکل رکشا *motor-rickshaw, auto-rickshaw*, mechanically propelled one made of a motor-cycle موٹر رکشا

a rickshaw

rid *v.t.* (*rid* ; *rid* or *ridded* ; *rid*) clear (some place *of* a pest) سے پاک کرنا ، سے صاف کرنا *n.* deliverance نجات ، خلاصی (only in the phrase :) *get rid of*, سے نجات حاصل کرنا ، سے جان چھڑانا ، سے پیچھا چھڑانا **riddance** (*rid-ans*) *n.* deliverance نجات ، خلاصی

-ridden (*rid-ĕn*) (pa. p. of *ride* ; used as) *suf.* infested by سے بھرا ہوا oppressed by سے riding ; on پر ، پر پڑا ہوا

riddle (*rid-ĕl*) *n.* puzzling question پہیلی *ask a riddle* پہیلی کہنا یا پوچھنا یا بجھوانا *guess a riddle* پہیلی بوجھنا *speak in riddles* پہیلیاں بجھوانا difficult situation الجھن، مشکل large sieve (for gravel, etc.) چھلنی، چھاج *v.t.* sift in this sieve چھاج میں پھٹکنا make holes in (something) by frying, etc. چھیدنا ، چھید چھید کر ڈالنا

ride (rid) *v.t.* & *i.* (*ride, rode, ridden*) sit on (horse, bicycle, etc.) and manage پر سوار ہونا ، کی سواری کرنا be carried along (*on a camel*) سوار ہونا be carried along (*in* train, bus, carriage, etc.) میں سفر کرنا be carried upon (water or waves) موجوں میں بہے جانا carry (child *on* one's back) کا گھوڑا بننا (of a ship) be moored (*at* anchor) لنگر انداز ہونا be crushed (*by* grief, etc.) کے ریلے آنا، کے منہ میں آنا ، میں گرفتار ہونا (of moon, etc.) seem to float (*in* the sky) تیرتا ہوا لگنا *ride for a fall* behave recklessly اندھا دھند چلنا ، بے سوچے سمجھے کام کرنا *ride out of storm*, tide it over طوفان (یا مصیبت) میں سے بچ نکلنا *n.* journey in a train گاڑی کا سفر journey on horseback سواری riding road سواری کی سڑک distance (of a place, by train or on horseback) in speed-hours (اتنے میل) کا سفر **riding** (*ri-ding*) *n.* گھوڑے کی سواری *adj.* for riding سواری کا **rider** (*ri-dĕ**) *n.* one who rides a horse سوار

ridge (*rij*) *n.* raised strip between furrows on ploughed land (راہن کی) مینڈھ long narrow hill لمبی پہاڑی chain of hills پہاڑیوں کا سلسلہ angle between two downward sloping surfaces (esp. of a roof) (سلامی والی چھت وغیرہ کی) چوٹی *v.t.* form into or mark with ridges مینڈھ بنانا

ridicule (*rid-i-kewl*) *v.t.* deride (person, thing, one's ambitions, fears, etc.) کا مذاق اڑانا ، کا منہ چڑانا *n.* derision مضحکہ، تمسخر **ridiculous** (*ri-dik-ew-lus*) *adj.* absurd مہمل، بیہودہ very silly احمقانہ deserving ridicule مضحکہ خیز

riding *n.* (see under **ride**)

rife (rif) *adj.* (of disease or evil) rampant عام، پھیلا ہوا *rife with*, full of (disease, evil, etc.) سے بھرا ہوا

riff-raff (*rif-raf*) *n.* meanest type of **people** کمینے ، گھٹیا لوگ ، اراذل

rifle (*ri-fĕl*) *v.t.* search and rob ہر چیز لوٹ لینا groove (the barrel of a gun) spirally جھاڑو پھیرنا (بندوق کی نالی) میں جھری ڈالنا *n.* gun with a rifled barrel جھری دار نالی کی بندوق ، جھری دار بندوق ، رائفل ، رفل

rift *n.* (see under **rive**)

rig *v.t.* (-gg-) equip (ship) with rigging, sails, etc. جہاز کے بادبان وغیرہ لگانا **rigging** *n.* ropes, etc., of a ship's sail (بادبان وغیرہ کے) رسے **rigger** (*rig-ĕ**) *n.* one who fits the necessary parts to the frame of an aircraft ہوائی جہاز کا باڈی جوڑنے والا

rigging showing the shrouds (S) and ratlines (R) on yards (Y) and mast (M)

right (rit) *adj.* on the right-hand side (opposite of the *left*) داہنا، دایاں، دہنا *on the right* (*of*), to the right (of) دایاں ہاتھ، سیدھا right hand کی دائیں جانب *the right-hand man* (*of someone*), the chief assistant (*of* someone) کی مونچھ کا بال، دستِ راست (in politics) diehard ; not progressive رجعت پسند، قدامت پسند (کا) دایاں بازو، کے *the Right wing* (*of a party*, etc.) رجعت پسند یا قدامت پسند عناصر (of the side of cloth) meant to be seen کا سیدھا *the right side* (*of*) کی سیدھی طرف (of angle) of 90° قائمہ *right angle* زاویۂ قائمہ correct (answer) ٹھیک، صحیح *put* (or *set something*) *right* (*a*) restore ٹھیک کرنا (*b*) correct تصحیح کرنا proper (person, behaviour, etc.) موزوں، مناسب physically or mentally healthy تندرست، ٹھیک *all right*, (never to be written as *alright*, which is wrong), in perfect health بالکل تندرست *be not right in* (*one's*) *head* دماغ کچھ خراب ہونا just جائز، منصفانہ، صحیح (or *all right*), (form of approval), O. K. ٹھیک، بالکل ٹھیک *adv.* to the right side دہنے ہاتھ *turn right* دائیں، دہنے ہاتھ مڑ جائیے *right and left*, on (or from) all sides چاروں طرف (سے) straight سیدھے exactly ٹھیک completely بالکل justly انصاف سے properly ٹھیک very بہت *Right Honourable*, (form of address to or about a peer below Marquess, a Privy Councillor or a judge of High or Supreme Court والاجناب *n.* the right-hand side دایاں جانب، دہنی طرف that which is proper صحیح اور غلط *right and wrong* ٹھیک، صحیح، مناسب یا جائز بات that which is just or true صحیح، حق یا انصاف کی بات *be in the right* حق پر ہونا، سچا ہونا privilege (کی بات) *by right* حق کے طور پر *by right of*, owing to کی وجہ سے حق *v.t.* put right (wrong, mistake, thing, etc.) ٹھیک کرنا put upright سیدھا کرنا **right turn** *imp.* command for turning to the right! دائیں مڑو، راست گرد *right about turn*, a right turn continued till one faces in the opposite direction دائیں جانب سے اُلٹے **rightful** *adj.* lawful (claimant, owner, holder, etc.) جائز، حق دار just (action) جائز **rightist** *n.* (see *Addenda*) **rightly** *adv.* correctly ٹھیک

righteous (*rī*-chus) *adj.* virtuous ; God-fearing نیک، خدا ترس just (person or action) انصاف پسند، منصفانہ **righteously** *adv.* in a righteous manner نیکی سے، منصفانہ **righteousness** *n.* being righteous نیکی، انصاف

rigid (*rij*-id) hard, unbending (thing) سخت، بے لوچ strict (discipline) سخت inflexible (system, etc.) سخت، جس میں لچک یا گنجائش بالکل نہ ہو **rigidly** *adv.* in a rigid manner سختی سے **rigidity** (ri-*jid*-i-ti) *n.* being rigid سختی، کڑواپن، لچک یا گنجائش نہ ہونا

rigmarole (*rig*-ma-rohl) *n.* long, pointless talk, story or string of words ایسی بات جس کا سر پیر کچھ نہ ہو، بے سر و پا باتیں، بکواس

rigorous *adj.* (see under **rigour**)

rigour (*rig*-ē*) *n.* harshness سختی (*pl.*) extremities (*of* climate, etc.) سختی، بلا کی (گرمی یا سردی) **rigorous** (rig-o-rus) *adj.* harsh سخت، سخت گیر

rill (ril) *n.* (poet.) small brook کول، ندی

rim *n.* thickened or raised edge (*of* bowl, wheel, etc.) (پیالے، پہیے وغیرہ کا) کنارہ *v.t.* (-mm-) be or make a rim for کا کنارہ ہونا یا بنانا

rime (rīm) *n.* (same as **rhyme,** which see)

rind (rīnd) *n.* hard peel (of lemon, melon, etc.) چھلکا

rinderpest (*rind*-ē*-pest) *n.* a kind of dangerous cattle-plague

ring *n.* ornamental circular band for finger انگوٹھی، انگشتری، چھلا any hard hollow circle چھلا *key-ring* کنجیوں کا چھلا circle حلقہ، دائرہ *dance in a ring* حلقہ بنا کر ناچنا enclosure (for circus, cattle show, etc-) احاطہ boxing platform in the form of a raised square مکے بازی کا احاطہ coterie گروہ، ٹولی (وغیرہ) کی ٹولی sound of ringing گھنٹی کی آواز sound of telephone bell ringing ٹیلیفون کی گھنٹی *give a ring to* کو ٹیلیفون کرنا sharp sound of a blow on metal plate ٹن ٹن، ٹن any echoing sound (*of* applause, etc.) اونچی آواز، گونج characteristic quality انداز، خصوصیت، جھلک *ring of sincerity in* (*someone's*) *voice* (کی) آواز میں خلوص کا انداز *v.t.* & *i.* (*ring, ringed, ringed*) (*a*) encircle (round, about) (کے) گرد، گھیرا ڈالنا (*b*) put a ring in the nose of (a bull, etc.) ناتھنا (*ring, rang, rung*) (*a*) (of a bell) sound گھنٹی بجنا، بجنا (*b*) (of a telephone) have its bell ringing or cause it to ring (کو) ٹیلیفون کرنا، فون کرنا *ring* (*someone*) *up* *ring* (*someone*) *off* (سے) ٹیلیفون پر باتیں بند کر دینا (*c*) cause (the bell) to ring گھنٹی بجانا، بجانا *ring for* (*someone*) (کو) بلانے کے لیے گھنٹی بجانا، گھنٹی بجا کر (کسی کو) بلانا *ring the curtain up* (or *down*) (تھیٹر میں) گھنٹی بجا کر پردہ اٹھانا یا گرانا *ring the curtain down* (*on something*), end (it) کا قصہ ختم کرنا (*d*) (of a place) echo (*with* applause, sound, etc.) سے گونج اٹھنا **ringer** *n.* one who rings a bell گھنٹی بجانے والا **ring-finger** *n.* third finger of the left hand انگوٹھی والی انگلی **ringleader** (*ring-*) *n.* leader (*of* a strike, riot, etc.) سرغنہ **ringlet** *n.* small ring چھلا small lock of hair بالوں کی چھوٹی سی لٹ، لٹ **ring-worm** *n.* a skin disease like eczema causing circular patches داد

rink *n.* (also *skating-rink*) level wooden floor

for roller-skating پہیئے والی کھڑاؤں کے ساتھ دَوڑنے کا فرش place meant for this سکیٹنگ کا کلب سکیٹنگ کا فرش

rinse (rins) *v.t.* wash (clothes, utensils, etc.) کھنگالنا، پانی میں سے نکالنا take *out* (the unwanted substance) thus پانی ڈال کر نکالنا، کو خوب دھونا، کو مَل مَل کر *give your hair a good rinsing* سر مَل مَل کر دھوؤ take (*out* the unwanted substance *from*) سے کھنگال کر نکالنا *n.* **rinsing** کھنگالنا *give* (*something*) *a good rinse* اچھی طرح کھنگالنا، خوب کھنگالنا

riot (rī-ot) *n.* violent tumult بلوہ، فساد uncontrolled revelry اُودھم، دھما چوکڑی extravagant display (*of* colour, etc.) (رنگ کا) طوفان *run riot*, (of fancy, etc.) be uncontrolled (تخیل وغیرہ کا) بے روک ہونا *v.i* create tumult بلوہ کرنا، دنگا فساد کرنا (*in*) revel (*in*) رنگ رلیاں منانا، دھما چوکڑی لگانا live wantonly عیاشی کرنا indulge to excess (*in* eating or drinking) اندھا دھند کھانا (یا) بلا نوشی کرنا **riotous** (*rī*-o-tus) *adj.* noisy and disorderly ہنگامہ خیز licentious عیاشانہ، عیاشوں کا (assembly) of persons who are dead-drunk بدمستوں کا

rip *v. t.* & *i.* (-pp-) slash, tear or cut (something) quickly زور سے کاٹنا یا پھاڑنا، چیرنا remove (something *out*, *off*, *open* etc.) کاٹ کر زور سے کھولنا be cleft چِرنا، پھٹنا، شق ہونا *n.* long cut چیر cleft شگاف torn place

ripe (rīp) *adj.* mature (fruit, grain, etc.) پکا، پکا ہوا mature (age, wisdom, judgment, etc.) پختہ prepared (*for* action, mischief, etc.) تیار

ripen (rī-pèn) *v.t.* & *i.* become or make ripe پختہ ہونا یا کرنا، پکنا یا پکانا **ripeness** *n.* being ripe پکنا، پکا ہوا ہونا، پختگی

ripple (*rip*-ĕl) *n.* tiny wave on the surface ہلکی لہر sound (*of* laughter, etc.) with a gentle rise and fall (کی) ہلکے اُتار چڑھاؤ والی آواز (کی) ارتعاش والی آواز *v.t.* & *i.* (cause to) move in ripples (*in*) ہلکورے اٹھنا یا پیدا کرنا produce such sound آواز کا مرتعش ہونا

rise (rīz) *v.i.* (*rise*; *rose* pr. rohz; *risen*, pr. *riz*-ĕn) get up اُٹھنا *rise to* (*one's*) *feet* کھڑے ہو جانا *rise from the dead* جی اُٹھنا get out of bed جاگنا، اُٹھنا، اُٹھ بیٹھنا ascend چڑھنا (of sun) appear above the horizon نکلنا، چڑھنا come to the surface of a liquid (from the bottom, etc.) (پانی وغیرہ سے) باہر نکلنا، اُبھرنا (of dough, etc.) swell up کا خمیر اُٹھنا (of price) increase چڑھنا (of sound) become louder (*to* a sharp pitch, etc.) اُونچی ہونا (of river) have its source (*in* a place) (سے) نکلنا rebel (*against* the government, etc.) (کے خلاف) بغاوت کرنا prosper ترقی کرنا (of a court or committee in session) adjourn (*for the day*) (اس دن کی)

کارروائی ختم کرنا prove equal (*to the occasion*) حالات پر قابو پالینا، موقع کے مناسب ہمت دکھانا fly higher (*in the air*) اُونچا اُڑنا be (*above* petty things, etc.) سے اُونچا ثابت ہونا *n.* increase (*in* price, pay, temperature, etc.) اضافہ going up بڑھنے، اُونچا اُٹھنا amount (*of* increase or ascent) اُونچا ہونے کی مقدار upward slope چڑھائی appearance (of the sun) above horizon طلوع appearance (*of* fish, etc.) above the surface of water پانی میں سے اُبھرنا، سر نکالنا source (*of* a river) منبع **rising** (*rī*-zing) increasing (prices) چڑھتی (یا) بڑھتی، ہوئی قیمتیں (in early youth) approaching the age of (fourteen) (اتنے سال) کی عمر کے قریب (young generation) نئی نسل، نوخیز، نوجوان *n.* ascent چڑھنا coming out prospering ترقی کرنا rebellion, insurrection بغاوت

risk (risk) *n.* danger خطرہ، جوکھوں *at the risk* (*of*) جوکھوں میں ڈال کر *take* (or *run*) *a risk* (or *risks* or *the risk of*) کا خطرہ مول لینا *v. t.* endanger خطرے میں ڈالنا hazard (failure, etc.) کا اِمکان بھی قبول کرنا **risky** (*ris*-ki) *adj.* dangerous خطرناک، جوکھوں کا **riskily** *adv.* while taking a risk خطرے میں پڑ کر

rite (rīt) *n.* solemn religious (etc.) ceremony رسم (جمع: رسوم یا رسومات) *funeral rites* تجہیز و تکفین کی رسومات **ritual** (*rit*-ew-ĕl) *adj.* pertaining to (esp. religious) rites مذہبی رسوم کا *n.* system of rites رسومات this as integral part of religion عبادت کی رسوم، مراسم مذہبی

rival (*rī*-vĕl) *n.* one who vies with another in business or for success حریف one who competes for the hand of the same beloved رقیب equal, peer ثانی، نظیر *be without a rival* بے نظیر ہونا، لاثانی ہونا *adj.* competing مقابلے والا، حریف *v.t.* (-ll-) be a rival of کا حریف یا رقیب ہونا claim equality with or superiority over سے ہمسری (یا برابری) کا دعوے کرنا **rivalry** (*rī*-vĕl-ri) *n.* vying (*with*) حریف ہونا، مدمقابل ہونا، رقابت

rive (rīv) *v.t.* & *i.* cleave چیرنا یا شگاف پڑنا **riven** (*riv*-en) *adj.* cleft چرا ہوا **rift** *n.* split اِفتراق cleft (in clouds) شگاف

river (riv-ĕ*) *n.* large natural stream of water دھارا، ندی، دریا stream (of any fluid) دھارا

rivet (*riv*-et) *n.* bolt with its thin end also hammered on to the fastened plate دوہرے سرے کی کیل، ریٹ

rivets

v.t. fasten (something) with rivets میں دوہرے سرے کی کیل جڑنا، ریٹ لگانا، ریٹیں لگانا fix (the eyes *on* or *upon*) (پر نظریں) گاڑنا یا جمانا absorb (the attention) منہمک کرنا

rivulet (*riv*-ew-let) *n.* small river نالا ، ندی
road (rohd) *n.* prepared track for vehicles, foot-passengers, etc., (*to* some place) سڑک ، رَہ means (*of* doing, etc.) سڑک ، طریقہ *along the road* in the road سڑک پر *on the road*, travelling سفر کرو *clear the road* راستہ صاف *in the road, in (one's) road*, impeding (him) کی راہ میں حائل ہونا *get out of the road*, get out of one's road کی راہ سے ہٹنا **road-metal** *n.* broken stone for macadamizing roads بجری ، روڑا ، کوٹا ہوا پتھر **road-sense** *n.* ability to move safely on the roads on foot or in vehicles سڑک پر چلنے (یا گاڑی چلانے) کا ہوش ، سڑک کی سمجھ ، راستے کا ہوش **road-side** *n.* border of a road سڑک کا کنارہ *adj.* on the roadside سڑک کے کنارے کا **roadster** *n.* (of bicycle, horse, etc.,) (fit) for use on the road سڑک پر چلنے والا ، سڑک پر چلنے کے قابل **readway** *n.* (*the*) metalled part of a road (as distinct from the *pavement*) سڑک کا گولا ، جادہ ، جادۂ راہ ◼ **Road** is the general term ; a **highway** is a main road ; an **avenue**, leads somewhere : a **street**, between buildings or shops ; a **passage**, very narrow way between buildings ; a **boulevard**, broad street planted with trees ; a **pavement** (called a **sidewalk** in the U.S.), path alongside a road for pedestrians.
roam (rohm) *v.t. & i.* wander over (or *about*) مارے مارے پھرنا ، گشت لگانا *n.* rambling walk سیر گشت ، سیر
roan *adj.* mixed with grey بھورا with grey or white patches چتلا ، ابلق *n.* such horse چتلا گھوڑا ، ابلق
roar (roh*, or ro*) *n.* loud and deep sound (of thunder) گرج such cry (of a lion) دھاڑ shout (*of* anger, command or laughter) زور سے بولنا ، دہاڑ ، گرج *v.t. & i.* make such sound بولنا یا ہنسنا (شیر کا) دھاڑنا shout (*out*) a command or in laughter زور سے کہنا یا ہنسنا **roaring** *adj.* stormy طوفانی ، طوفان خیز excellent (health, trade, etc.) شاندار (of night) riotous رنگ رلیوں والی
roast (rohst) *v.t. & i.* parch بھوننا cook or be cooked (*in the oven*) کباب کرنا یا ہونا *n.* roasted meat کباب ، بھنا ہوا گوشت *rule the roast*, be a master of the situation حالات پر قابو پانا ، جاننا ◼ **To roast** is to cook meat before a fire or in oven ; to **broil** a steak on gridiron ; to **grill**, the same as to broil but used exclusively in England.
rob *v.t.* (-bb-) plunder a place, or someone (*of* his belongings) (کو) لوٹنا **robber** *n.* thief using violence ڈاکو **robbery** (*rob*-è-ri) robbing ڈاکہ ◼ A **robber** is one who steals with violence whereas a **thief** is one who does so without violence : a **burglar** is one who enters by night, while a **housebreaker** is one who enters by day.

robe (rohb) *n.* long outer garment چوغہ ، چغہ ، جبا this as award from king, etc. خلعت loose mantle چادر ، ردا **robes** *n. pl.*, garments (of a high office) درباری لباس *robes of state* عبائے شاہی
robin (*rob*-in) *n.* a small red-breasted bird (also called *red-breast* or *robin redbreast*) لال چڑیا ، رابن **Robin Goodfellow** *n.* in *Brit leg.* another name for *Puck* who was a mischievous elf doing people's work when they were asleep نیک پری زاد ، **Robin Hood** *n.* famous English outlaw of the Norman times who is regarded as a hero رابن ہڈ

a robin

robot (*roh*-bot) *n.* automaton کل پرزوں کا آدمی ، کلدار آدمی ، مصنوعی انسان machine-like man مشین کا آدمی traffic signal ٹریفک سگنل ، سڑک کا اشارہ
robust (*roh*-bust) *adj.* (of person or health) vigorous قوی (of mind) sensible ہوشمند ، سمجھدار
rock (rok) *n.* big solid piece of stone چٹان *as firm as a rock* چٹان کی طرح مضبوط reef سمندری چٹان *run on the rocks*, (of a ship) collide with them and be wrecked (جہاز کا) چٹان سے ٹکرا کر پاش پاش ہو جانا *on the rocks*, (*a*) wrecked (ship) تباہ شدہ (جہاز) (*b*) hard-up تباہ حال ، بے زر و مال firm support پکا سہارا *v.t. & i.* (of earth-quake, etc.) shake ہلا دینا sway (cradle, chair, ship, etc.) جھولنا یا جھلانا *rock (a baby) to sleep* بچے کو جھولنا یا جھلا کر سلانا *rocking chair*, chair with two curved sticks (called *rockers*) joining its legs into pairs جھولنے والی کرسی **rock-bottom** *adj.* (of prices) کم سے کم بھاؤ *rock-bottom prices* lowest, floor prices

a rocking-chair with rockers (R)

rocky (*rok*-i) *adj.* full of (or as hard as) rocks پتھریلا ، سنگلاخ **rock 'n roll** *n. & adj.* (U.S.) (music) suggestive of (or accompanied with) a rocking dancing movement "راک اینڈ رول" ، جھومتا راگ ، "جھومو گاؤ" ، جھومنا چو گاؤ
rocket (*rok*-et) *n.* firework shooting high up ہوائی projectile (for launching aircraft or earth satellite) (ہوائی جہاز یا مصنوعی چاند) پرے بھیجنے کا آلہ ، ہوائی ، راکٹ *v.t.* shoot high up quickly (ہوائی کا) چھوٹنا ، تیزی سے اوپر کو اڑنا
rocket-ship *n.* (see *Addenda*)
rod *n.* long straight stick, etc. (for punishing, fishing, or hanging a curtain from) ڈنڈا land measure equivalent to 5½ yards جریب
rode (rohd) *v.* (pa. t. of **ride**, which see)
rodent (*roh*-dent) *n.* any gnawing animal (like a mouse) کترنے والا جانور

rodee (roh-*day*-oh) *n.* rounding up the cattle for branding داغنے کے لیے ڈھور ڈنگر ہنکا کرنا enclosure for this purpose داغنے کا باڑہ، داغ گاہ cowboy's skill in riding unbroken horses نئے گھوڑوں کی سواری، شہسواری exhibition of such skill in riding a motor-cycle موٹر سیکل کی شہسواری کا مظاہرہ
roe (roh) *n.* small kind of deer چکارا mass of eggs in a fish مچھلی کے بیضہ دان میں انڈوں کا گچھا **roe-buck** *n.* male roe نر چکارا، چکارا
rogue (rohg) *n.* rascal بدمعاش swindler, cheat دھوکے باز، ٹھگ (affectionately) mischievous child شریر بچہ، شیطان savage beast (like buffalo, elephant, etc.) living apart from the herd مست جانور، گلے سے الگ رہنے والا جانور *adj.* such savage (elephant, buffalo) مست، گلے سے الگ رہنے والا **roguish** (*roh*-gish) *adj.* (affectionately) mischievous شریر، شیطان dishonest فریب کار، فریب کارانہ **roguishness** *n.* شیطانی، شرارت **roguery** (*rohg*-ĕ-ri) *n.* a rogue's trickery بدمعاشی
roister (*rois*-tĕ*) *v.i.* make merry noisily اُودھم مچانا، دھما چوکڑی لگانا **roisterer** *n.* one who roisters اُودھم مچانے والا، دھما چوکڑی لگانے والا
role (rohl) *n.* actor's depiction (*of* some character *in* a play, etc.) کردار undertaken task کام، کردار
roll (rohl) *v.t.* & *i.* move along by turning over لڑھکنا یا لڑھکانا *rolling-pin*, dough roller بیلن *roll in money*, be very rich پیسے میں کھیلنا *rolling stone*, a person not sticking to any job لڑھکتا پتھر، وہ شخص جو کسی جگہ ٹک کر نہ بیٹھے *a rolling sonte gathers no moss*, no gain accrues to such a person لڑھکتا پتھر کیا حاصل کریگا move along on wheels پہیوں پر چلنا یا چلانا *rolling-stock*, railway engines, coaches, etc. محکمۂ ریل کے انجن ڈبے وغیرہ wrap (or be wrapped) round and round into spherical or cylindrical form لپیٹنا یا لپٹنا rock or be rocked جھولنا یا جھلانا rumble گھڑ گھڑ چلنا move (eyes) to and fro quickly گھمانا، مٹکانا flatten (or *out*) with a roller بیلنا coat with another metal ملمع کرنا (of person or thunder) roar گرجنا (of surfaces) undulate (سطح) لہریا ہونا *roll along*, (*a*) move with a rolling gait جھومتے جھامتے چلنا (*b*) (of a vehicle) rumble گھڑ گھڑ کرتے چلنا *roll in*, come in a large number بڑی تعداد میں آنا *roll (things) into (one)*, join them سب کو ملا کر ایک کر دینا، ملغوبہ بنا دینا *roll up*, increase in number بڑی تعداد بڑھنا *n.* list of names ناموں کی فہرست *call the roll* حاضری لینا *roll-call* حاضری بلانا یا حاضری لینا something rolled into cylindrical or spherical shape گولا یا ڈنڈا *roll of cloth*, its rolled piece کپڑے کا تھان *cream-roll*, cylindrical piece of pastry filled with cream کریم رول *roll of paper*, its reel لپٹا ہوا کاغذ، کاغذوں کی ریل rolling لڑھکنا یا لڑھکانا، جھولنا یا جھلانا rolling sound دھڑ دھڑ، گڑگڑ، ڈھول کی گمک، بادل کی گرج
roller *n.* any cylindrical object for pressing, etc. رولر، رولا، بیلن long swelling wave دور تک جانے والی لمبی لہر، بڑی لہر **steam-roller** *n.* (*a*) mobile roller for road-making سڑک کوٹنے کا انجن، اسٹیم رولر (*b*) any (esp. political) crushing power کچل ڈالنے والی طاقت *v.t.* make level with a steam-roller سڑک کو کوٹنے والے انجن سے ہموار کرنا crush (political) opposition سیاسی مخالفوں کو کچل ڈالنا *roller skate*, wheeled skate پہیے دار کھڑاؤں

a steam-roller

rollick (*rol*-ik) *v.i.* be jovial and boisterous رنگ رلیاں منانا، دھما چوکڑی لگانا **rollicking** (*rol*-i-king) *adj.* boisterous (fun, etc.) اُودھم والا، دھما چوکڑی والا، رنگ رلیوں والا
roly-poly (*roh*-li-*poh*-li) *adj.* (of child) plump موٹا تازہ، گول مٹول، گول گپتہ
Roman (*roh*-man) *n.* citizen of (ancient) Rome (قدیم) روما کا باشندہ *adj.* pertaining to ancient Rome قدیم روما کا، رومی **Roman Catholic** *n.* & *adj.* (follower) of the Christian Church of Rome رومن کیتھولک، کیتھولک **Roman numerals** *n.* the Roman system of notation (as *I* or *i* for 1, *II* or *ii* for 2, *III* or *iii* for 3, *IV* or *iv* for 4, *V* or *v* for 5, *X* or *x* for 10, *L* for 50, *C* for 100, *D* for 500, *M* for, 1,000 and an extra line above symbols for representing them 1,000 times their number as $\overline{X}$ for 10,000) رومی ہندسے **Romanesque** (roh-ma-*nesk*) *adj.* style of architecture prevalent in Europe in the period intervening between classical and Gothic styles رومانی طرز تعمیر *adj.* (of architecture) in this style رومانی
romance (ro-*mans*) *n.* (*Romance*), language of old France رومانس (*Romance*) one of the bastard Latin languages بگڑی لاطینی a verse tale of love and adventure in it مثنوی novel of love and adventure داستان، رومانی داستان، رومانی such incredible nevertheless real experience حیرت انگیز واقعہ love-affair (*between*) (میں) معاشقہ exaggeration of picturesque falsehood مبالغہ آمیز رنگین بیانی imaginative quality تخیل، تخییل، رومانی انداز **romantic** (ro-*mant*-ik) imaginative (person, or tale) رومانی emotional (poetry or other forms of art) subordinating form to subject matter (as distinct from the classic or classical) تخییلی، رومانی، جذباتی *the romantic school of poetry* شاعری میں تخییلی مسلک

Romantic, Romanticist (-sist) *n.* follower of the romantic school (as distinct from a classical writer) رُومانی یا تخییلی شاعر وغیرہ
Romany (rom-a-ny) *n.* gipsy چپسی ، خانہ بدوش gipsy language چپسی شاہی *adj.* gipsy خانہ بدوشانہ جپسیوں کا
romp *v.i.* (of children) run about and play roughly (بچّوں کا) اندھا دُھند بھاگ دوڑ کرنا **rompers** *n. pl.* child's overall (بچّے کے) کھیل کے کپڑے
roof (roof) *n.* (pl. *roofs*) top covering of a house, etc. چھت *roof of the world*, high plateau (esp. of Tibet) بہشت بُلند سطحِ مرتفع *under the roof of*, as the guest of کا مہمان *v.t.* provide a roof چھت ڈالنا یا چھت کا کام دینا
a child in rompers
rook (ruk) *n.* large bird like a crow پہاڑی کوّا رُک (in chess) the piece also called a castle رُخ sharper at dice or cards پتّے باز *v.t.* swindle thus پتّے بازی کرنا charge too high a price from گاہک کو لوٹنا **rookery** (rŭk-ĕ-ri) *n.* place with nests of rooks رُک خانہ cluster of mean houses غریبوں کا محلّہ
rookie (roo-ki) *n.* (army slang) recruit رنگروٹ
room *n.* chamber کمرہ ، کوٹھڑی ، دالان space (*for* standing, etc.) (کی) جگہ *make room, please* ازراہِ کرم راستہ (دیانگر) دیں دیجئے scope (*for* improvement, etc.) (کی) گنجائش **roomed** (roomd) *adj.* having (one, two, etc.) rooms (اتنے) کمروں والا **roomful** *n.* as much (*of* something) as a room will hold کمرہ بھر
rooming-house *n.* (U.S.) lodging-house کرائے پر دیئے جانے والے کمروں والا گھر **roomy** (roo-mi) *adj.* with enough space in it کافی جگہ (یا گنجائش) والا **roominess** *n.* being roomy کافی جگہ (یا گنجائش) رکھنا
roost *n.* perch پرندوں کا رین بسیرا لینا hen-coop مرغیوں کا ڈربہ *v.t.* sleep on a roost بسیرا لینا **rooster** *n.* (U.S.) cock مُرغ ، مُرغا
root *n.* underground part of a plant جڑ *take root, strike root*, (*a*) start growing اُگنے لگنا (*b*) send down a root جڑ پکڑنا (*c*) be firmly planted جم جانا مستحکم ہونا any part (*of* an organ, etc.) which connects it with others جڑ basis, real cause (معاملے) کی تہہ تک پہنچنا *go to the root of* اصل تہہ stem (*of* a word) (لفظ کا) مادّہ (also *root-crop*) any plant (*e.g.*, carrot) whose root is eaten خوردنی جڑ quantity which when made a *square* or raised to the *third*, *fourth*, etc., power yields the given number (indicated by the symbols ∛ ∜ √ etc.) جذر *v.t.* & *i.* take root جڑ پکڑنا *root* (*something*) *out* (or *up*), extirpate it کو جڑ سے اُکھاڑنا
rope (rohp) *n.* thick cord رسّا ، رسّی *rope-dancer*, one who dances on a tight rope بازی گر ، نٹ *rope-trick*, Western idea of an Eastern trick in which the magician hurls the end of rope upward and using it as a pole climbs it to vanish in the air رسّن بازی collection (*of* pearls, turnips, etc.) threaded together on a line (کی) لڑی *v.t.* tie (*up* or *together*) with rope رسّی سے باندھنا lasso رسّا باندھنا mark (*off* with a rope) کی حدبندی رسّی سے کرنا bring (*in* someone) to ensure help from (him) کو پھانسنا
rosary (roh-za-ri) *n.* string of prayer beads تسبیح ، سُبحہ ، مالا rose-garden گلستان ، گلشان rose-bed تختۂ گل
rose (rohz) *n.* a well-known fragrant flower, (usu. pink, though found in various colours) گلاب *gather roses*, seek pleasure عیش اُڑانا *bed of roses*, comfortable circumstances عیش *the rose of* (*a company*), the prettiest girl there میں سے خوبصورت ترین لڑکی pink colour گلابی رنگ *take rose-coloured views, look through with rose coloured spectacles*, be optimistic, etc. بُری چیز کو بھی اچھا سمجھنا **rosette** *n.* rose-shaped ribbon, etc. فیتے کا گلاب ، سجاوٹی گلاب
roseate (roh-zi-ayt) *adj.* rose-coloured گلابی **rosy** (roh zi) *adj.* healthy, (cheeks) گلابی (رخسار) bright (future) پُراُمید مستقبل
rosin (roz-in) *n.* solid left after distilling turpentine from *resin* (which see) گندہ بروزہ
roster (ros-tĕ*) *n.* list of names showing turns of duty (باری باری ڈیوٹی دینے کے لیے) نقشۂ اوقات ، بدلی جدول
rostrum (ros-trum) *n.* public-speaking dais or pulpit (منبر) پلیٹ فارم
rot *v.t.* & *i.* (-tt-) (cause to) decay (کی وجہ سے) سڑنا waste away ضائع جانا ، کو گھن لگنا *n.* decomposition سڑنے کی حالت (colloq.) nonsense فضول بکواس ، فضول *talk rot* بکواس کرنا **rotten** (rot-ĕn) *adj.* decayed (of vegetables, etc.) گلا سڑا (of egg) gone bad گندہ likely to break ٹوٹنے کو ، گرنے کو bad (place, luck, etc.) بُرا ، خراب corrupt (state, etc.) بدعنوانیوں والی
rotary (roh-ta-ri) *adj.* having circular motion محوری گردش والا ، گھومنے والا ، گھماؤ ، گرداں *n.* such printing press چھاپے کی گھماؤ مشین ، گردان مطبع (*the Rotary*), (also *the Rotary Club*), (originally a U.S.) international club supposedly meant to do philanthropic work روٹری کلب **Rotarian** (ro-tay-ri-ĕn) *n.* a member of this club روٹری کلب کا رکن ، روٹیرین
rotate (ro-tayt) *v.t.* & *i.* (cause to) move

round an axis گردش کرنا یا دینا alternate باری باری آنا یا لانا **rotation** (ro-*tay*-shĕn) *n.* rotating زمین کی محوری گردش *the earth's rotation* محوری گردش *in rotation*, by turns باری باری

rote (roht) *n.* (only in the phrase :) *by rote* (*a*) by heart زبانی، حفظ *learn by rote* حفظ کرنا (*b*) mechanically, without thinking سوچے سمجھے بغیر

rotor (*roh*-tĕ*) *n.* vane of helicopter which rotates horizontally ہیلی کوپٹر کا اُفقی گردش والا پنکھ (یا پَر) اُفقی پر

rotund (roh-*tund*) *adj.* (of person) plump and round موٹا تازہ، گول مٹول (of voice) rich and deep گونجدار (آواز) **rotundity** *n.* being rotund گول گپا ہونا

rouble (*roo*-bèl) *n.* Russian unit equivalent to about one rupee رُوبل

roue (*roo*-ay) *n.* rake آوارہ، عیاش شخص

rouge (roozh) *n.* red powder for cheeks سُرخی، گلگونہ گلگونۂ عارض *v.t.* & *i.* apply rouge to سُرخی لگانا

rough (ruf) *adj.* uneven (surface, road, etc.) ناہموار not smooth کھُردرا stormy (weather, sea, etc.) طوفانی، طوفان خیز unruly (child, etc.) دنگے والا harsh (sound) کرخت hard (life) سخت، دُکھی (of draft or work) of first attempt ابتدائی، رف، موٹا موٹا *rough and tumble*, (*a*) disorderly گڈ مڈ (*b*) scuffle لڑائی جھگڑا *rough and ready*, not refined but good for the present purpose کام چلاؤ uncivil (language, manners, etc.) نامعقول، ناشائستہ *rough and ready manner* کام نکالنے والے مگر ناشائستہ طریقے (of treatment) harsh سخت سلوک، (تشدد آمیز سلوک) *n.* ill mannered person بدتمیز hooligan غنڈا uneasy life مشکل، سختی، مصیبت، کڑیاں *have a rough time*, (colloq.) زندگی میں کشمکش ہونا کڑیاں جھیلنا *take the rough with the smooth* تو مصیبت بھی unfinished state ابتدائی، نامکمل صورت، نامکمل حالت *rough-hewn* ایسا ویسا گھڑا ہوا *in the rough* ایسا ویسا *v.t.* ruffle (feathers or hair) (پر یا بال) بے ترتیب کر دینا (*Phrases* :) *rough it (at a place)*, do without usual comforts کسی نہ کسی طرح کاٹ لینا *rough (something) out, rough in (something)*, make a rough copy or sketch of it کو ابتدائی شکل دینا، رف کام کرنا **roughage** (*ruf*-ij) *n.* bran of cereals, etc., eaten as a laxative بھوسی کا دلیا **roughen** (*ruf*-èn) *v.t.* & *i.* make or become rough سخت کرنا کھردرا (یا) (یا ہونا) **rough-house** *n.* free fight لڑائی disturbance ہنگامہ، گڑبڑ *v.t.* & *i.* make a disturbance ہنگامہ کرنا act violently مار پیٹ پر اُتر آنا manhandle (someone) کو مارنا پیٹنا **roughneck** *n.* (U.S.) rowdy person غنڈہ **roughly** (*ruf*-li) *adv.* (also) about تقریباً **roughshod** (*ruf*-shod) *adj.* specially shod (horse) to prevent slipping کھردرے نعل والا *ride roughshod over*, treat unsympathetically سختی کا سلوک کرنا، (سے) برتاؤ میں ہمدردی کو قریب نہ پھٹکنے دینا

roulette (roo-*let*) *n.* revolving disc for gambling جوئے کا گھومنے والا تختہ، چکر

a roulette

round (*adj.*) circular or spherical گول moving in circle حلقہ باندھ کر حلقے میں، دائرے میں complete ; neither more nor less than پُورا، پورے (of numbers) roughly تقریباً، بس کوئی *in round figures*, in tens, hundreds, thousands, etc موٹا حساب، دہائیوں (سینکڑوں یا ہزاروں وغیرہ) میں large (*sum of money*) بڑی (رقم) (game, etc.) in which any (or a large) number can participate کھلا (کھیل) return (journey, trip, ticket, etc.) واپسی کا (سفر)، واپسی (ٹکٹ) *n.* regular succession (*of* duties, etc.) دورہ، چکر، (کام کا) *go the rounds* کام کے چکر پر جانا، دورے پر جانا action in which many participate simultaneously بہت سوں کا ایک ہی وقت میں کام *round of applause* نعرہ ہائے تحسین، سب کی طرف سے واہ واہ round piece گول ٹکڑا single shot ایک بار چلائی ہوئی گولی (وغیرہ) amount of ammunition needed for it گولی، (گولا وغیرہ) single stage in boxing, etc. ایک چکر کا *adv.* in a circle پورا، پورے چکر *all the year round* سال بھر *round about* کے گرد back ; in a half circle پیچھے *look round* پیچھے مُڑ کر دیکھنا encircling کے گرداگرد، کے چاروں طرف not by the direct way چکر کاٹ کر from one to another in rotation باری باری ایک دوسرے کو *bring (someone) round to (one's) view point*, convince him کو قائل کرنا *bring (someone) round*, restore him to consciousness (کو) ہوش میں لانا *come round*, (*a*) regain consciousness ہوش میں آنا (*b*) come from a place in order (*to see someone*) (کی) ملاقات کے لیے آنا *come round to* (*the or someone's view point*), be convinced مان جانا، قائل ہو جانا *prep.* around کے گرد، کے گرداگرد *round-the-world tour* دُنیا بھر کا چکر *v.t.* & *i.* become or make round گول کرنا (یا) ہونا go round (a place) کے گرد جانا negotiate (a bend, etc.) موڑ مڑنا round (something) off, complete it (کو) مکمل کرنا، کو پایۂ تکمیل کو پہنچانا *round up*, finish (speech, etc.) suitably موزوں طریق پر ختم کرنا **roundness** *n.* being round گولائی amount or degree of this curve گولائی **roundabout** *adj.* indirect (way) اِدھر اُدھر سے miscellaneous (papers, etc.) متفرق *n.* merry-go-round چرخ چوں circular enclosure at the crossroads چوک کا چکر

round robin *n.* (also *round Robin*), signatures (on document, etc.) in a circle to avoid the ringleader being spotted out گول دستخطوں والی (عرضداشت)

Round Table *n.* *Brit. leg.* order of knighthood instituted by King Arthur آرتھر کے بنائے ہوئے فوجدار *Brit. leg.* inner circle of his knights who sat at a round table آرتھر کے منتخب فوجدار **round-table** *adj.* (meeting, conference, etc.) on equal terms گول میز، برابری کی سطح کی، جس میں کوئی چھوٹا بڑا نہ ہو **roundly** *adv.* plainly, without mincing matters صاف صاف کھل کر almost تقریباً thoroughly پوری طرح، ٹھیک طرح *go roundly to work.* سیدھی طرح کام پر جاؤ

roundelay (*round*-è-lay) short simple song with refrain ٹیپ کے مصرعے والا ہلکا سا گیت song of a bird زمزمہ

rouse (rouz) *v.t.* & *i.* wake (someone) (or *up from* sleep) جاگنا یا جگانا، بیدار ہونا یا کرنا *wants rousing,* is indolent وہ ڈھیلا سست ہے، اسے تو جھنجھوڑ کر ہی جگایا جائے تو کام کرے stir up (someone's interest, anger, etc.) (کسی کو کام یا غصے پر) ابھارنا، برانگیختہ کرنا stir (someone) up (*to* action, anger, etc.)

rout utter defeat شکست فاش disorderly retreat بھگدڑ *v.t.* put (the enemy) to rout دشمن کو شکست فاش دینا، (یا اس کی) صفوں میں بھگدڑ مچا(نا)

route (root) *n.* course of journey راستہ (pr. rout) formal written marching orders in the army کوچ کا حکم *give* (or *get*) *the route* کوچ کا حکم دینا یا پانا **en-route** *adv.* on the way (*to*) کی طرف جاتے (یا آتے) ہوئے، مازم **route march** *n.* battalion's march during training پلٹن کا مشقی کوچ

routine (roo-*teen*) *n.* customary course of action معمول، ڈھرا، ضابطہ *office routine,* usual procedure عام دفتری ضابطے کی کارروائی *the routine procedure* طریق کار، دفتری ڈھرا

rove *v.i.* ramble without destination ادھر ادھر پھرنا، منہ اٹھائے پھرنا roam (*over* a place) کا چکر لگانا (of eyes) look in various directions (آنکھوں کا) ادھر ادھر دیکھنا **rover** *n.* rambler مٹر گشت کرنے والا، گھومنے والا pirate بحری ڈاکو، سمندری لٹیرا 17-year-old scout روور

row (roh) *n.* horizontal line (*of* persons, seats, houses, etc.) قطار، صف *sitting in the front row* اگلی صف میں بیٹھنا *back row* پچھلی صف outing in a rowing boat کشتی کی سیر *go for a row* چپو والی کشتی کی سیر کو جانا *v.t.* & *i.* (boat) with oars کشتی کھینا *row over* کشتیوں کی دوڑ میں، جیت جانا *row* (*someone*) *down* کشتیوں کی دوڑ میں کسی سے آگے نکل جانا *be rowed out,* (of crew) be exhausted by rowing کشتی کھیتے کھیتے بدحال ہو جانا take (someone) in a boat کشتی میں لے جانا **rower** *n.* oarsman چپو چلانے والا، کھویا **row-lock** *n.* fulcrum for an oar

row (rou) *n.* (colloq.) noisy dispute جھگڑا، رگڑا، جھگڑا، فساد *have a row with* سے جھگڑنا noise شور، ہنگامہ *make a row* طوفان بدتمیزی اٹھانا *What is the row about?* What is the matter, آخر بات کیا ہے؟ being reprimanded گت بننا، جھاڑ پلائی ہونا *get into a row* (*for some mistake*) کسی بات پر گت بننا

rowdy (*rou*-di) *adj.* & *n.* disorderly and noisy (person) جھگڑالو، فسادی، دنگئی **rowdily** *adv.* in a noisy and disorderly manner ہنگامہ برپا کر کے، شور و غل مچا کر **rowdiness, rowdyism** (*rou*-di-ism) *n.* being rowdy دنگا، فساد، ہنگامہ پروری

royal (*roi*-èl) *adj.* pertaining to a sovereign شاہانہ suitable for him شاہانہ of his family شاہی خاندان کا، شاہانہ انداز سے **royalist** (*roi*-è-list) *n.* & *adj.* supporter of monarchy ملوکیت پسند (person) siding with the royalty in a civil war بادشاہ کی پارٹی (کا) ملوکیت پسند (U.S.) any type of diehard رجعت پسند *economic royalist* معاشی رجعت پسند

royalty (*roi*-èl-ti) *n.* position of a sovereign بادشاہی royal power شاہی اقتدار royal family شاہی خاندان members شاہی خاندان کے افراد (pl. *royalties*), part of income (*on* book) paid to the copyright owner حق تصنیف کا معاوضہ sum paid thus for invention حق ایجاد کا معاوضہ sum paid thus to mine-owner (کان کے) حق ملکیت کا معاوضہ

rub (rub) *v. t.* & *i.* (-bb-) subject to friction رگڑنا scrape (*against*) سے رگڑ کھانا scour مانجھنا، صاف کرنا polish صیقل کرنا slide (one's hand, etc.) on ملنا، سہلانا brush (*up* one's English, memory, etc.); refresh one's knowledge of (it) (کی) یاد تازہ کرنا get (*along*) with difficulty مشکل میں گرفتار رہنا reproduce by rubbing چربہ اتارنا *rub* (one's hands, etc.) *with soap* ہاتھوں پر صابن ملنا *rub oil on* پر تیل ملنا پر تیل کی مالش کرنا *rub* (*something*) *off* (or *out* or *away*), remove (stains, shyness, etc) دور کرنا *rub up* (*something*) رگڑ رگڑ کر صاف کرنا *n.* rubbing ملنا، troublesome thing مصیبت (کا) باعث **rubber** *n.* a well-known elastic substance ربڑ، ربڑ eraser ربڑ one who or that which rubs مالشیا، جھانواں وغیرہ (three) successive games مسلسل بازیاں *win the rubber,* (originally used for whist, but now extended to cricket and many other games) win the majority of such games مجموعی بازیاں جیت جانا (pl.) (*rubbers*), galoshes ربڑ کا بالائی بوٹ *adj.* made of rubber ربڑ کا

rubbish (*rub*-ish) *n.* refuse گندگی، میلا، غلاظت nonsense فضول، بکواس

rubble (*rub*-èl) *n.* pieces of brickwork, etc. روڑے

Rubicon (*roob*-i-kon) *n.* name of an Italian river which Julius Caesar crossed in 49 B.C. on his way to power روبیکن *cross the Rubicon,* take an

irrevocable decision or step اٹل فیصلہ کرنا، پیچھے نہ ہٹنے والا قدم اُٹھانا
rubicund (*roob*-i-kund) *adj.* red-faced سُرخ چہرے والا ruddy لال گلال
ruby (*roo*-bi) *n.* (pl. *rubies*) a red precious stone لعل، یاقوت its colour سُرخ رنگ *adj.* of this colour لال سُرخ
ruck (*ruk*) irregular crease (in cloth) سلوٹ *v.t.* & *i.* cause or have rucks سلوٹ ڈالنا یا پڑنا **rucksack** (*ruk*-sak) *n.* knapsack جھولا
rudder (*rud*-e*) *n.* flat steering piece at the stern (*of* ship or aircraft) پتوار guiding principle بنیادی اُصول

a man with a rucksack

ruddy (*rud*-i) *adj.* healthily red (cheeks, face, etc.) سُرخ و سفید
rude (rood) *adj.* disrespectful (person, behaviour, etc.) گستاخ (یا) گستاخانہ uncivilised غیر مہذب crude بھدا، اَن گھڑ violent (shock) سخت **rudeness** *n.* quality of being rude گستاخی، بدتمیزی، غیر مہذب ہونا بھدا پن، اشدت
rudiments (*roo*-di-ments) *n. pl.* elements (of a science, language, etc.) مبادی **rudimentary** (-*ment*-e-ri-) *adj.* elementary اِبتدائی imperfectly developed نامکمل
rue (roo) *v.t.* regret (something past) پر پچھتانا *n.* remorse پچھتاوا، پشیمانی **rueful** *adj.* doleful غمگین
ruff (ruf) *n.* starched neck-frill popular in the 16th century کلف دار گریبان band of colour, etc., round bird's neck طوق، کنٹھا

a ruff

ruffian (*ruf*-i-an) *n.* violent bully غنڈہ بدمعاش
ruffle (*ruf*-èl) *v.t.* & *i.* vex or be vexed پریشان کرنا یا ہونا، مزاج برہم کرنا یا ہونا *easily ruffled* ذرا ذرا سی بات پر جھلّا اُٹھنے والا cause ripples (پانی پر) ہلکی لہریں پیدا کرنا disarrange (hair, feathers, etc.) بے ترتیب کرنا، پریشان کرنا *n.* ornamental frill for clothes چُنّٹ دار جھالر

a girl's dress with ruffles

rug (rug) *n.* thick (woollen) mat نمدہ woollen covering موٹا کمبل
Rugby football (*rug*-bi) *n.* oval football game in which the ball may be handled رگبی، رگر
rugged (*rug*-ed) *adj.* irregular craggy (coast) چٹانوں والا کٹا پھٹا ساحل rough and uneven (surface, terrain, etc.) سخت ناہموار rough کھردرا strongly marked (features) کرخت unpolished but good at heart (manners, honesty, etc.) اکھڑ مگر جِسے قدر لانہ

rugger (*rug*-ĕ*) *n.* (slang for) Rugby football رگبی، رگر
ruin (*roo*-in) destruction (*of* country, crops business, one's hopes) تباہی، خاتمہ *bring to ruin* برباد کرنا *be the ruin of* کی بربادی کا موجب ہونا *ruin seize thee* تیرا بیڑا غرق ہو، تیرا خانہ خراب (often *pl.*) remains (*of* a building or city) کھنڈر (*lie*) *in ruins* کھنڈر ہونا *v.t.* destroy (country, crops, business hopes, etc.) برباد کرنا، تباہ کرنا **ruined** (*roo*-ind) *adj.* destroyed برباد، تباہ in ruins کھنڈر have lost one's property, position, etc. تباہ حال، تباہ حال **ruination** (-*nay*-) *n.* ruining or being ruined تباہی، بربادی **ruinous** (*roo*-i-nus) *adj.* in ruins کھنڈر

▣ A **ruin** is a destruction of hopes or buildings; a **wreck** that which causes misery; a **crash**, sudden and complete; a **destruction,** falling down of a structure; **overthrow,** of a regime, government or other similar institution.

rule (rool) *n.* government حکمرانی، حکومت *rule of the law* قانون کے مطابق حکومت (*under*) *foreign rule* غیر ملکی حکومت *bear rule*, govern حکومت کرنا law or by-law (of an institution, a game, etc.) قاعدہ (ج: قواعد) ضابطہ (ج: ضوابط) (کے ماتحت) *rules of the road*, traffic rules ٹریفک کے قواعد *obey the rules of the game* کھیل کے قواعد پر عمل کرنا norm or standard (*of* behaviour) معیار، دستور principle (*of* science, etc.) اُصول *rule of thumb*, method based on practice and not science عملی اُصول habit; habitual action عادت، دستور *as a rule*, usually عام طور پر، بالعموم *make it a rule* (*to do*) کی عادت ڈال لینا، دستور بنا لینا (also *ruler*), graduated strip for measuring length as well as drawing straight lines چیٹی، رُول، پیمانہ *foot-rule* فٹ رُول، فٹ کا پیمانہ چیٹی *v.t.* & *i.* bear rule (over a country); govern (a country) حکومت کرنا، حکمرانی کرنا give the verdict (*that*) فیصلہ دینا، رکہ *rule* (*something*) *out*, ignore (it) نظر انداز کر دینا *rule* (*the motion, etc.*) *out of order*, refuse to admit (it) for discussion by the House پیش کرنے کی اجازت نہ دینا، خلافِ قاعدہ قرار دینا draw (a line) with a ruler چیٹی سے لکیر کھینچنا *rule* (*something*) *off*, separate it by ruling a line لکیر لگا کر الگ کرنا **ruler** (*rool*-ĕ*) *n.* one who rules حاکم، حکمران، فرمانروا rule for drawing straight lines چیٹی، رُول **ruling** *n.* (*rool*-ing) (esp.) decision (of Judge, Speaker, chairman, etc.) on a point فیصلہ

a rule or ruler

rum (rum) *n.* liquor made from sugar-cane گنے کی شراب *adj.* (slang) queer (person) عجیب
rumba (*rum*-ba) *n.* a kind of dance which

originated among Cuban negroes رُمبا music for it رُمبا کی گت، رُمبا کی دُھن، رَمبا

rumble (*rum*-bèl) low heavy rolling sound (of gunfire, vehicle, thunder, etc.) گرج، گڑگڑاہٹ move with or make such a sound گرجنا، گڑگڑانا گھڑ گھڑ کرنا (slang) detect, see through بھانپ لینا، سمجھ لینا

ruminate (*room*-i-nayt) *v.t.* chew the cud جُگالی کرنا think deeply (*over*) (پر) غور و خوض کرنا

ruminant *n.* & *adj.* ruminating (animal) جُگالی کرنے والا جانور

rummage (*rum*-ij) *v.t.* & *i.* ransack; search (in a place, through papers, etc.) by upsetting everything بُری طرح اُلٹ پلٹ کر دینا **rummage-sale** *n.* sale of old odds and ends for charity خیراتی فنڈ جمع کرنے کے لیے چھوٹی موٹی پرانی چیزوں کی فروخت

rummy (*rum*-i) *n.* popular card game played with two packs in which taking up the cards one by one each player tries to arrange them in consecutive series, etc., before the others رَمی

rumour (*room*-ĕ*) *n.* hearsay اَفواہ *according to rumour* افواہ ہے کہ *The air is full of rumours* افواہیں گرم ہیں *v.t.* spread a rumour further افواہ سُنانا *it is rumoured that* افواہ پھیلی ہوئی ہے کہ **rumoured** (*roo*-mè*d) *adj.* of which there is a rumour جس کی افواہ گرم ہو

rump (rump) *n.* animal's buttock پُٹھا، پُٹھّا

rumple (*rum*-pel) *v.t.* crumple (cloth, hair, paper, etc.) شِکن ڈالنا، مروڑنا

rumpus (*rum*-pus) *n.* (slang) row, brawl جھگڑا uproar شور و غُل، شور و غوغا **rumpus room** *n.* (see *Addenda*)

run (run) *v.t.* & *i.* (-nn-) (*run, ran, run*) (cause to) move with speed دوڑنا یا دوڑانا *run a race* دوڑ میں حصّہ لینا *run a mile (etc.)*, run that distance میل (وغیرہ) بھر دوڑنا (of trains, buses and other vehicles) travel (*to, from* or *between*) (کو، سے یا کے درمیان) چلنا (of roads) have a certain direction (*to, from*) جانا (of machine) keep going چلنا *keep running* چلائے رکھنا manage (organization, club, etc.) چلانا (of an organization, etc.) work چلنا (of liquid, tap, etc.) بہنا، چلنا cause (a liquid, tap, etc.) to flow بہنے دینا، کھلا رکھنا *Who left the tap running?* ٹونٹی کھلی کس نے چھوڑی تھی؟ *His nose is running* اُس کی ناک بہہ رہی ہے (of colour, etc.) spread پھیلنا dash (*against*) (سے) ٹکرانا thrust (*into*) میں چبھونا collide (*into*) سے ٹکرانا get (*through* blockade) (میں سے) نکل جانا smuggle (something *into* a country) (کی) ناجائز درآمد کرنا expose oneself to (the risk of) کا خطرہ مول لینا (of a film, etc.) be still showing چل رہا ہونا become ہو جانا get (*into* debt) مقروض ہو جانا

(of sale of book) reach or get (*into* or *through* so many editions) نکلنا (of agreement) remain in force باقی رہنا cause (one's) eyes, fingers, hand, comb, etc.) to move (*over* or *through*) پھیرنا (of words, verse, musical notes, etc.) stand in a certain order اِس طرح ہونا (colloq.) be a candidate (*for* election, etc.) کا اُمیدوار ہونا (of prices) be (high, low, etc.) ہونا (of knitted material) drop stitches کھل جانا *n.* act of running دوڑ *on the run* (a) running away بھاگ رہا (b) always busy ہمیشہ مصروف (in cricket) unit of score رَن (ج: رَنز) *score 90 runs* نوّے رنز بنانا (of film, etc.) continuous show over (*of* a period) چلنا period (*of* trouble, etc.) عرصہ، مدّت *in the long run*, finally آخر کار، بالآخر، انجام کار type قسم *the common run of men* (or *mankind*) عام لوگ، عوام rapidity of fall گرنے میں تیزی enclosure for poultry مرغی خانہ range of pasture کی چراگاہ permission to make free use (of) مفت استعمال کی اجازت *allow (someone) the run of (one's) books* (or *house*) (کسی کو) اپنی کتابیں (یا گھر) مفت استعمال کرنے کی اجازت دینا sudden demand by many (*on* a commodity) اچانک بڑھ جانے والی مانگ *a run on the bank*, sudden rush (caused by rumours of bankruptcy) for withdrawal of deposits بنک سے روپیہ نکلوانے والوں کا اچانک ہجوم distance travelled by ship in 24 hours (or some other specified time) (جہاز کا) دن بھر میں سفر (*More phrases:*) *run about* (a) (of children) play, etc. کھیلتے پھرنا (b) hurry about (کے لیے) افراتفری میں آنا جانا *run aground* (جہاز کا) خشکی پر چڑھ جانا *let (something) run its course*, allow it to proceed normally to its end دستور یا ضابطے کے مطابق ہونے دینا، اپنا وقت پورا کرنے دینا *run errands*, (also see under *errand*) پیغام لے کر جانا، بازاروں سے سودا سلف لا دینا *run high* (جذبات وغیرہ کا) تیز ہونا *run after* کے عشق میں مارا مارا پھرنا *run across* (or *against* or *into*) *someone* (or *something*) اچانک مل جانا *run after (someone)* سے ملنے کی کوشش کرنا *run away* بھاگ جانا *run away with*, (a) make away with لے کر بھاگ جانا (b) elope with کے ساتھ نکل جانا *The clock (etc.) has run down* چابی نہ لگنے کے باعث گھڑی کھڑی ہو گئی ہے *be run down* مضمحل ہو جانا، بُری طرح تھک جانا *run (someone) down* کی بُرائیاں کرنا *run (one's) head against*, dash against سے سر ٹکرانا *run in*, bring (new automobile or other machine) into good working order by cautious use at first چالو کرنا، رواں کرنا *be run in*, be imprisoned; be sent to the lock-up گرفتار ہو کر حوالات میں بند کر دیا جانا *run in the family* کی خاندانی خصوصیت ہونا *be in the run for* (election) کا اُمیدوار ہونا *run on*, (a) join on to ملانا (b) continue جاری رہنا (c) go on talking incessantly بولتے ہی جانا

run out (*of*) سے خالی ہو جانا *run over*, (*a*) overflow لبالب بہ کر نکلنا (*b*) (of a vehicle) knock down کے نیچے آ جانا *be run over by* کو نیچے لے آنا *run to time*, (of trains, etc.) keep to the schedule وقت پر چلنا *run up* (*a debt, bill, account etc.*), let it increase (قرض وغیرہ) بڑھنے دینا *run up to* (*a place*) مختصر سے قیام کے لیے جانا *run upon*, (*a*) (of thought) recur (خیال) بار بار آنا (*b*) dwell on (a thought) (کسی خیال میں) مستغرق ہونا **run-away** (*run*-a-way) *n.* & *adj.* (person, horse, etc.) that has run away بھاگا ہوا، بھگوڑا، آبق **runner** (*run*-ĕ*) *n.* one who runs دوڑنے والا courier ہرکارہ، قاصد *suf.* (arms-, gun-, etc.) smuggler of (arms, guns, etc.) (اسلحہ وغیرہ) کی ناجائز درآمد کرنے والا *gun-running*, smuggling of contraband arms into a country اسلحہ کی ناجائز درآمد **runner-up** *n.* competitor standing second (*in a game*) دوسرے نمبر پر آنے والا **running** (*run*-ing) *adj.* (*esp.*) continuously لگاتار، مسلسل، پے در پے *running sore*, festering sore رستا ہوا زخم *running commentary on an event* (*etc.*) آنکھوں دیکھا حال، واقعہ کے ساتھ ساتھ تفصیل رواں تبصرہ *be in the running*, having a chance of success (کی) کامیابی کی امید ہونا *be out of the running* (کی) کامیابی کی کوئی امید نہ ہونا **running board** *n.* footboard on either side of car or locomotive فٹ بورڈ **runway** (*run*-way) *n.* paved track for aircraft taking off or landing ہوائی اڈے میں طیارے کی سڑک، ہوائی جہاز کی سڑک

rung (rung) *n.* step of a ladder سیڑھی کا ڈنڈا crosspiece of the legs of a stool, chair, etc. بیچ کا ڈنڈا *v.t.* & *i.* (pa. p. of *ring*, which see)

a ladder with rungs at 'A'

rupee (roo-*pee*) *n.* (abbr. sing. *Re.*; pl. *Rs.*) روپیہ

rupture (*rup*-chĕ*) *n.* end of friendship (*between*) ناچاقی، علیحدگی، افتراق bursting of blood-vessel, etc. فتق، پھٹنا *v.t.* end (a friendship) ناچاقی ہو جانا، لڑ پڑنا، میں لڑائی ہو جانا (of a blood-vessel) burst رگ وغیرہ کا پھٹ جانا، فتق ہونا

rural (*roo*-rĕl) *adj.* pertaining to villages, etc. (opp. of *urban*) دیہی، دیہاتی

ruse (rooz) *n.* deceitful trick چال

rush (rush) *v.t.* & *i.* dash forward (*out, of, to, into*, etc.) تیزی سے جانا یا بھیجنا act quickly but thoughtlessly میں اندھا دھند کود پڑنا force (Bill, etc.) along (*through* the Legislature) hurriedly (بل وغیرہ) جلدی جلدی منظور کرا لینا (of many persons) get (*through, over, across* a place) by pressing forward میں سے زور لگا کر نکل جانا attack (fort, etc.) suddenly and occupy پر اچانک حملہ کر کے قبضہ کر لینا *n.* sweep بہاؤ quick and vigorous onward movement زور great activity کام کا زور *rush-hours* کام کے زور کا وقت strong demand (*for*) (کی) بڑی مانگ trifle ذرہ بھر، ذرا سا، ذری سا، حقیر سی شے *not to care a rush* ذرہ بھر پروا نہ کرنا *not worth a rush* وہ تو دھیلے کا بھی نہیں a reed-like marshy plant سینٹھا

rushes: (left) root; (right) flower

rusk (rusk) *n.* piece of bread baked crisp رسک بسکٹ، رس

rust (rust) *n.* brownish coating formed on iron or steel when exposed to damp زنگ *v.t.* & *i.* (cause to) have rust زنگ لگنا یا لگانا deteriorate in quality for lack of use زنگ آلودہ ہو جانا **rusty** (*rus*-ti) *adj.* covered with rust زنگ آلودہ (of knowledge, ideas, etc.) antiquated زنگ آلودہ

rustic (*rus*-tik) *adj.* rural (person) دیہاتی، گنوار unrefined, crude (manners, speech, etc.) اجڈ، گنوار simple unsophisticated (dress, etc.) سیدھا سادہ *n.* villager with all his simplicity سادہ دیہاتی، گاؤں کا سیدھا سادہ باشندہ **rusticate** (*rus*-ti-kayt) *n.* lead a rural life دیہاتی زندگی بسر کرنا become acclimatized to it دیہاتی زندگی کا عادی ہو جانا expel temporarily (a student *from* the college or university *for* a period) (کالج وغیرہ سے) عارضی طور پر نکال دینا **rustication** (rus-ti *kay*-shĕn) *n.* act of rusticating or being rusticated (کالج وغیرہ سے) عارضی اخراج

rustle (*rus*-ĕl) *n.* whispering sound as of leaves in breeze or silk clothes rubbing against each other سرسراہٹ *v.t.* & *i.* produce this sound سرسر کرنا، سرسرانا (U.S. colloq.) steal (cattle or horses) مال مویشی چرانا، ڈھور ڈنگر کی چوری کرنا **rustler** (*rus*-lĕ*) *n.* person who steals (cattle or horses) ڈھور ڈنگر کی چوری کرنے والا

rut (rut) *n.* wheel-track لیک fixed habit پکی عادت beaten track ڈگر، مبتذل روش *get into a rut*, get on to a beaten track which is profitless and will be difficult to change ڈگر سے باہر نہ نکل سکنا، ڈگر میں پھنس جانا

ruth (rooth) *n.* pity رحم **ruthless** *adj.* pitiless ظالم، بے رحم **ruthlessly** *adv.* pitilessly ظالمانہ طور پر، سختی سے، سنگدلی سے **ruthlessness** *n.* cruelty بے رحمی، سنگدلی، ظلم و ستم

rye (ri) *n.* a well-known fodder grain رائی

ryot (*rī*-ot) *n.* (in Pakistan) landless peasant forced to work as the tenant of some (usu. big) landlord رعیت (ج : رعایا)

rye

S

s, S (es) (pl. *s's* or *ss* pr. *es-iz*) the nineteenth letter of the English alphabet اَیس an S-shaped curve دُہرا خَم any S-shaped object اَیس نُما ، اَیس ('s) (*a*) (abbr. of) *has, is* or *us* دَرگھتا ہے ، رہا ، ہم (*b*) usual mark of the possessive case

Sabbath (*sab*-ath) *n.* day of rest every week which the *Bibble* enjoins on its followers to keep holy سَبَت *Sabbath-breaking,* not observing Sabboth ; profaning it سَبَت کا اِحترام نہ کرنا، سَبَت کی بے حُرمتی کرنا Saturday (as this day of rest for the Jews) ہفتہ Sunday (as this day of rest for the Christians) اِتوار (~~also Sabbat,~~) midnight meeting of witches چڑیلوں کا آدھی رات کا جَلسہ

sable (*say*-bel) *n.* small animal valued for its fur سَمُّور its fur سَمُّور کی کھال ، سَمُّور *adj.* (lit.) dark (clouds, etc.) کالا ، سِیاہ

a sable

sabot (*sab*-oht) *n.* shoe hollowed out from one piece of wood سیبُوٹ ، کھڑاؤں

a sabot

sabotage (*sab*-o-tahzh) *n.* wilful damage to machinery, etc., done in war or as a trade-union weapon توڑ پھوڑ ، تخریب کاری *v.t.* commit sabotage (on) (کی) تخریب کاری کرنا destroy تباہ کرنا ، برباد کرنا **sabotaging** *adj.* (of activities, etc.) of the nature of sabotage تخریبی ، تخریب کارانہ **saboteur** (sab-o-*tē**) *n.* one who sabotages تخریب کار

sabre (*say*-bĕ*) *n.* sword with a curved blade شمشیر ، ٹیڑھی تلوار *the sabre,* (*a*) military force فوجی طاقت (*b*) military rule فوجی حکومت *v.t.* wound or kill with a sabre تلوار سے زخمی یا قتل کرنا

saccharin (*sak*-a-rin) *n.* concentrated sugar prepared from coal-tar سَکرِین

sacerdotal (sa-se*-*doh*-tel) *adj.* priestly مُلّایانہ ، مُلّائی claiming excessive authority for the priesthood مُلّا پرَست

sack (sak) *n.* large bag of strong coarse material بورا plunder لُوٹ مار ، تاخت و تاراج (colloq.) dismissal برطرفی ، برخاستگی *give (someone) the sack,* dismiss (him) برخاست کرنا *get the sack* برخاست ہونا a kind of white Spanish wine شراب *v. t.* put (something) into a sack بوری میں بھرنا plunder لُوٹ مار کرنا ، تاخت و تاراج کرنا (colloq.) dismiss برخاست کرنا **sackcloth** *n.* fabric for making sacks ٹاٹ ، بورِیا (*clothed*) *in sackcloth and ashes,* much aggrieved بالوں میں راکھ ڈالے **sacking** *n.* sackcloth ٹاٹ ، بورِیا

sacrament (*sak*-ra-ment) *n.* any Christian rite عیسائیوں کی مذہبی رسم Holy Communion عشائے رَبّانی **sacramental** (-*ment*-) *adj.* of a sacrament عیسائیوں کی مذہبی رسُوم سے متعلق

sacred (*sayk*-red) *adj.* holy (place, etc.) مُتبرّک solemn (promise, etc.) پکا **sacredly** *adv.* in a sacred manner متبرّک طور پر **sacredness** *n.* being sacred تقدیس ، متبرّک ہونا

sacrifice (*sak*-ri-f is) *n.* offering to God (or a god, etc.) قربانی کا جانور ، قربان thing sacrificed قربانی foregoing of something for the sake of another قربانی thing foregone thus قربانی undergoing trouble or laying down one's life (for a cause, person, etc.) قربانی *at a sacrifice,* (sell) at less than the true value اصل سے کم داموں میں بیچنا *v.t.* & *i.* make a sacrifice قربانی دینا forego as a sacrifice (*to do,* or *for* something) قربانی کرنا **sacrificial** (sak-ri-*fish*-ĕl) *adj.* of sacrifice قربانی کا like a sacrifice قربانی کے انداز کا

sacrilege (*sak*-ri-lej) *n.* disrespect to something sacred مُقدّس چیز کی بے حُرمتی **sacrilegious** (sak-ri-*lee*-jus) *adj.* one who commits a sacrilege (مقدس چیزوں کی) بے حرمتی کرنے والا

sacrosanct *adj.* to be protected for its sacredness مُحترم ، حَرام ، مُقدّس

sad *adj.* sorrowful غمناک ، غمگین ، حزیں causing sorrow غم انگیز ، دردناک **sadden** (*sad*-ĕn) *v. t.* & *i.* make or become sad غم میں مبتلا کرنا یا ہونا **sadly** *adv.* sorrowfully غم سے ، دردناک انداز سے **sadness** *n.* being sad غم ، اَلَم ، غمناکی ، غم انگیزی ، دَردناکی

saddle (*sad*-ĕl) *n.* leather seat on horseback کاٹھی ، زین bicycle or motor-cycle seat گدّی ridge تنگ لمبی پہاڑی *v. t.* put a saddle on horseback زین چڑھانا put a heavy responsibility on (someone) پر بھاری ذمّہ داری ڈالنا *saddled with* (*responsibility, debt, etc.*), burdened with (it) کا بوجھ اُٹھائے ہوئے ، کے بوجھ تلے دبا ہوا **saddlebag** *n.* one of a pair of bags for horseback خُورجین tool bag on a bicycle saddle سائیکل کے سامان کی تھیلی **saddler** (*sad*-lĕ*) *n.* maker of saddles, etc. سازگر ، زین ساز dealer in them ساز فروش ، زین فروش **saddlery** (*sad*-lĕ-ri) *n.* such goods زین ساز (وغیرہ) saddler's business ساز فروشی ، زین فروشی

sadism (*sah*-dizm) *n.* (sexual) perversion resulting in cruelty for joy of it (opp. of *masochism*) سادیت **sadist** *n.* one who practises sadism سادی **sadistic** (sah-*dis*-tik) *adj.* such (acts) سادیانہ

safari (sa-*fah*-ri) *n.* hunting expedition شکار on

safari شکار پر

safe (sayf) *adj.* out of danger خطرے سے باہر protected from it محفوظ، مصئون unhurt بچا ہوا (of person, speed, etc.) not dangerous مامون cautious محتاط جو خطرے والا نہ ہو *to be on the safe-side*, not to take risk خطرہ مول نہ لینا *n.* strong (iron, etc.) chest for keeping valuables in تجوری airy cupboard for food سیف نعمت خانہ **safe-conduct** *n.* permission to move in a dangerous area راہداری document comprising (راہداری) پروانۂ راہداری **safe-deposit** *n.* building with safes let out separately تجوری گھر

a safe (sense 1)

safeguard *n.* protection (*against*) حفاظت (*pl.*, protective measures (*against*) (کے خلاف) حفاظتی اقدامات *v.t.* protect حفاظت کرنا، حفاظتی اقدامات کرنا **safe-keeping** *n.* custody حفاظت، سنبھالنا **safely** *adv.* in a safe manner بحفاظت **safety** (*sayf*-ti) *n.* being safe محفوظ ہونا، حفاظت، سلامتی، بچاؤ *safety first*, have it as the first consideration جان ہے تو جہان ہے *play for safety*, take no risks خطرے سے بچ کر چلنا *in safety*, safely بحفاظت **safety-match** *n.* the ordinary match as distinct from the earlier type which sometimes lighted even without rubbing محفوظ ماچس **safety-pin** *n.* pin with point turned back to fit into a guard سیفٹی پن، محفوظ پن **safety-razor** *n.* razor whose blade does not cut skin حفاظتی اُسترا، سیفٹی ریزر **safety-valve** *n.* valve releasing pressure after danger point حفاظتی کھُل مُنندن harmless outlet for dangerous feelings دل کی بھڑاس نکالنے کا بے خطر ذریعہ

saffron (saf-rĕn) *n.* a well-known flower with purple flowers زعفران، کیسر yellow colour obtained from it کیسری *adj.* bright yellow کیسری، زعفرانی رنگ

sag *v.i.* (-gg-) droop in the middle under weight or pressure دہرا ہونا hang down unevenly جھکنا، خمیدہ ہونا hang sideways *n.* sagging خمیدگی، دہرا ہونا

a saffron flower & bulb

saga (*sah*-ga) *n.* heroic myth (of Scandinavia) (سکینڈے نیویا کا) رزمیہ series of connected books giving the history of a family, etc. کسی خاندان کے حالات پر سلسلۂ کُتب

sagacious (sa-*gay*-shus) *adj.* shrewd, intelligent and quick-witted زیرک، دانشمند **sagacity** *n.* shrewdness زیرکی ، فراست

sage (sayj) *n.* & *adj.* very wise (man) دانا، فرزانہ حکیم، عارف a herb for flavouring food **sagely** *adv.* wisely دانائی سے، حکمت سے ، فرزانگی سے

sago (*say*-goh) *n.* (pl. *sagos*) hard, white grains boiled to make a light starchy food and obtained from a tree (called *sago-palm*) ساگودانہ، سابودانہ

said (sed) *v.* (pa. t. & pa. p. of **say**, which see)

sail (sayl) *n.* canvas sheet spread on a mast to catch the wind and move a ship along بادبان *under sail*, (of ship) with sails spread بادبان لگائے ہوئے *in full sail*, (of ship) with all sails spread پورے بادبان لگائے ہوئے *set sail*, (of ship) begin a voyage سفر کا آغاز کرنا short pleasure excursion in the sea or river سمندر یا دریا کا چھوٹا تفریحی سفر (جہاز یا کشتی میں) *go for a sail* چھوٹے تفریحی سفر پر جانا (always *sing.*) sailing ship بادبانی جہاز *v.t.* & *i.* go on (or begin) a voyage سمندری سفر پر جانا، سمندری سفر شروع کرنا move in a ship, etc., across (a sea, etc.) جہاز وغیرہ میں (کسی سمندر کو) پار کرنا (of ship, etc.) move in water (جہاز وغیرہ کا) چلنا control (a boat or ship) چلانا *n.* sea voyage بحری (یا سمندری) سفر its distance (اتنے دنوں کا) بحری سفر **sailor** (*say* le*) *n.* mariner ملاح، جہازران **sailing** *n.* sea voyage جہاز میں سفر navigating (جہاز) چلانا (of a ship) being navigated (جہاز کا) چلنا *(be) plain sailing*, (be) easy آسان کام (ہونا) **sailings** *n. pl.* ships sailing (from) (سے) روانہ ہونے والے جہاز

saint (saynt) *n.* (abbr. *St.*) holy person ولی (یا ولیہ) a Christian officially recognized by Christians as such مسلّمہ عیسائی ولی (یا ولیہ) *calendar of saints* عیسائی اولیاء کے عرسوں کی فہرست *St. Bernard*, *St. Bernard's dog*, a kind of large dog formerly kept by monks to rescue travellers overtaken by snow سینٹ برنارڈ کا کتا **sainted** (-id) *adj.* canonized (عیسائیت میں) ولی تسلیم کیا ہوا **saintly** (*saynt*-li) *adj.* holy مقدس، متبرک، بزرگی (یا بزرگانہ) like a saint اولیا کا سا **saintliness** *n.* being saintly بزرگی، تقدیس

saith (seth) *v.* (old use ; third person sing. form of *said*, often used as *saith he* or *saith she* in reported speech), says کہتا ہے ، نے کہا

sake (sayk) *n.* (only in the phrases :) *for the sake of* (*someone* or *something*), *for* (*someone's*) *sake*, to please (someone) ; in the interest of (someone or something) کے لیے ، کے واسطے ، کی خاطر

sal *n.* a type of Indian timber سال

salammoniac *n.* ammonium chloride نوشادر

salad (*sal*-ad) *n.* mixture of (green) vegetables used as food سلاد *salad dressing*, mixture of vinegar, oil, etc., put on salad سلاد کا مسالہ cold meat, etc., served with salad سلاد کے ساتھ (مچھلی وغیرہ کا) ٹھنڈا گوشت *fruit salad*, mixed sliced fruits ملے جلے پھلوں کی پھانکیں **salad days** *n. pl.* days of youthful inexperience جوانی کی ناتجربہ کاری، الھڑ جوانی کے دن

salamander (*sal*-a-mand-ĕ*) *n.* a kind of lizard which is believed to live in fire سَمَنْدَر

a salamander

salaried *adj.* (see under **salary**)

salary (*sal*-è-ri) *n.* (pl. *salaries*) pay (*of* so much amount) at monthly or more intervals تنخواہ ، طلب ، مشاہرہ **salaried** (*sal*-a-rid) *adj.* receiving a salary and hence enjoying stability of service, etc. تنخواہ دار ، ملازم ، ملازمت پیشہ *salaried classes*, (as opposed to the *wage-earning classes*) more well-off تنخواہ دار طبقہ ، نسبتہً خوش حال طبقہ **Note : We speak of a *monthly salary of Rs. 200*, but of *Rs. 50 weekly wages* or *Rs. 6 daily wages***

sale (sayl) *n.* selling (*of* something) ; exchanging (it) for money فروخت ، بکری *be on* (or *for*) *sale* فروخت کے لیے ہونا *put on sale* فروخت کے لیے رکھنا the offering (of goods) at low prices for a period سیل ، کم قیمت پر فروخت auction نیلام ، نیلامی ، ہَراج **salable** (*sayl*-a-bel) *adj.* that which can (easily) be sold قابلِ فروخت ، بکاؤ **salesman** *n.* (fem. *saleswoman*) shop assistant دوکان پر مال بیچنے والا ملازم wholesale dealer's travelling agent سیلزمین ، گماشتہ **salesmanship** *n.* art or work of being a salesman گماشتہ گری

salep (*sal*-ep) *n.* a dried medicinal tuber ثعلب مصری

salient (*say*-li-ent) *adj.* prominent or projecting (place, etc.) نمایاں ، اُبھرا ہُوا noticeable (features, points, etc.) اہم ، نمایاں *n.* wedge driven into enemy's front دشمن کی صفِ اوّل میں ڈالا ہُوا شگاف

saline (*say*-lin) *adj.* salty نمکین ، کھاری *n.* saline medical mixture نمکین دوا **salinity** (sa-*lin*-i-ti) *n.* being salty کھاری پن being impregnated with salts شور

saliva (sa-*li*-va) *n.* natural fluid secreted by the mouth لعاب دہن

sallow (*sal*-oh) *adj.* (of skin) unhealthily yellow پیلی ، زرد

sally (*sal*-i) *n.* sortie by surrounded soldiers محاصرے سے نکل کر حملہ *make a sally* محاصرے سے نکل کر حملہ کرنا *sally forth* (or *out*), go out (*on* a journey, or *for* a walk, etc.) نکل پڑنا lively outburst بے ساختہ اظہار joke پھبتی ، لطیفہ ramble بے مقصد سیر

salmon (*sam*-ĕn) *n.* (*pl.* same) a large kind of edible fish سامن its colour orange-pink شرخی مائل ، نارنجی **salmon-trout** *n.* a fish resembling salmon سامن ٹراؤٹ

a salmon

salon (sa-*lon*) *n.* drawing room دیوان خانہ (*the Salon*), famous annual Paris exhibition of the works of living painters, etc. سالون (any place for) exhibition of paintings مصوّری کی نمائش

saloon (sa-*loon*) *n.* large room for social assemblies in a ship, hotel, etc. دیوان خانہ ، ہال dining hall of a ship جہاز کی طعام گاہ *saloon bar*, drinking bar in a hotel ہوٹل وغیرہ کا شراب خانہ (*U.S.*) pub شراب خانہ railway coach not divided into compartments permanently ریل کا سیلون motor-car بغیر چھت والی کار ، سیلون

salt (sawlt) *n.* a well-known white mineral for seasoning food نمک *salt-mine* نمک کی کان ، کانِ نمک *salt-pan*, artificial lake near sea for obtaining salt from sea-water by evaporation طاس نمک *salt-cellar*, small container for salt نمکدان ، نمکدانی *table salt*, purified salt صاف نمک *take* (*story, etc.*) *with a grain of salt*, make allowance for the untrue element in (it), doubt (it) پورا یقین نہ کرنا *not worth* (*one's*) *salt*, not deserving a post and pay, etc. نا اہل ، نا قابل (کے) *eat* (*someone's*) *salt*, be under obligation to (him) کا نمک خوار ہونا *the salt of the earth*, the finest citizens بہترین افراد *an old salt*, a veteran sailor پرانا مانجھی ، تجربہ کار ملاح chemical compound of a metal and an acid نمک *v.t.* put salt on or in (food) میں نمک ڈالنا *adj.* containing (or tasting of) salt نمکین **salty** (*sawl*-ti) *adj.* containing (or tasting of salt) نمکین **saltpetre** (sawlt-*pee*-te*) *n.* a white substance used as an ingredient of gun-powder شورہ ، قلمی شورہ

salubrious (sa-*loob*-ri-us) *adj.* health-giving (climate) صحت بخش **salubrity** *n.* being salubrious صحت بخشی

salutary (*sal*-ew-ta-ri) *adj.* (of advice, exercise) conducive to good results فائدہ بخش ، مفید ، سود مند

salutation (sal-ew-*tay*-shen) *n.* greeting سلام *raise* (*one's*) *hat in salutation* سلام کرنے کے لیے ٹوپی سر سے اٹھانا **salute** (sa-*lewt*) *n.* any symbol of formal salutation (in the army, etc., like the raising of the hand or flag, or the firing of guns, etc.) سلامی *give* (*someone*) *a salute, give a salute to* (*someone*) کو سلامی دینا *v.t.* & *i.* make a salute to (someone) by word of mouth or the raising of hat, etc. کو سلام کرنا give a salute to کو سلامی دینا

salvage (*sal*-vej) *n.* the rescuing of property from loss in shipwreck or by fire, etc. ڈوبتے (یا جلتے) ہوئے سامان میں سے کچھ بچا لینا (یا نکال لانا) things so saved ڈوبنے (یا جلنے) سے بچایا ہوا سامان *salvage depot*, (esp.) place for storing condemned military goods, etc. بچے کھچے سامان کا سٹور payment for it ڈوبنے (یا جلنے) سے بچانے کا معاوضہ *v.t.* save from such loss ڈوبتے (یا جلتے) ہوئے سامان میں سے کچھ بچا لانا یا نکال لانا

salvation (sal-*vay*-shĕn) *n.* saving from sin or (according to Christianity) from its consequences بخشش، نجات rescue *of* رہائی یا نجات، چھٹکارا that which rescues نجات دلانے والی چیز **Salvation Army** *n.* Christian religious organization with military designations for its members (called *salvationists*); (formed by Gen. William Booth in 1865) مکتی فوج **salvationist** *n.* مکتی فوج والا

salve (salv, or sahv) *n.* healing ointment مرہم thing soothing (one's feelings or the conscience, etc.) مرہم (دل کے زخموں پر) پھاہا یا مرہم، (ضمیر کو) تسلی *v.t.* put salve on پھاہا رکھنا، مرہم لگانا be a salve to تسکین پہنچانا

salver (*sal*-ve*) *n.* (usu. round silver) tray for servants to hand things on پیش کرنے کی کشتی یا طشت

salvo (*sal*-voh) *n.* (pl. *salvos*) the firing (or dropping) of a number (*of* guns or bombs) together شلک، (توپوں کی) سلامی، (بموں کی) بوچھاڑ number (*of* bombs) released simultaneously from an (aircraft) ہوائی جہاز سے بیک وقت گرائے جانے والے (بموں کی) تعداد، بوچھاڑ (بموں کی) تعداد spate (of praise, etc.) (تعریف وستائش کی) مار **sal volatile** (sal vo-*lat*-il) *n.* smelling salts ہوش میں لانے کی دوا، تریاق بے ہوشی

Samaritan (sa-*ma*-ri-ten) *n.* of Samria سامری *the Good Samaritan*, one who helps those in distress نیک، فیاض، غریبوں کا مددگار، غریب نواز

Sam *n.* short form for Samuel سموئیل، سموآل *Uncle Sam*, supposed national type of the U.S.A. انکل سام، چچا سام *Sam Browne*, army officer's cross-belt فوجی افسر کی پیٹی

same (saym) *adj.* & *pron.* identical وہی، اسی similar ویسا ہی، ایسا ہی aforesaid یہی، مذکورہ بالا unchanged بالکل اسی طرح، ذرا بھی نہ بدلا ہوا of no difference (*to* one) کے لیے یکساں *be all* (or *just*) *the same to*, make no difference to کے لیے یکساں ہونا *come to the same thing*, make no difference وہی بات ہونا *all the same*, nevertheless, still پھر بھی، تاہم

samovar (sam-o-*vah**) Russian tea-vessel with a shaft for coal to heat سماوار

sampan (*sam*-pan) *n.* small boat of the Chinese type سمپن

sample (*sahm*-pĕl) *n.* specimen نمونہ، بانگی *v. t.* (cause to) test (something) by examining its sample نمونہ دیکھنا یا دکھانا **sampler** (*sahm*-plĕ*) girl's piece of embroidery kept as proof of her skill سوئی سلائی کے کام کا نمونہ، نمونہ

Samson, Sampson *n.* (Bib.) a Jew of great prowess whose strength lay in his hair شمشون any person of great strength بڑا طاقتور شخص، رستم

sanatorium (san-a-*to*-ri-um) *n.* (*pl. sanatoria*) hospital, (esp.) for T.B. patients دق کے مریضوں کا دارالصحت یا دارالشفا، سینی ٹوریم

sanctify (*sank*-ti-fi) *v.t.* regard sacred مقدس قرار دینا **sanctification** (-*key*-) *n.* act of sanctifying or being sanctified مقدس سمجھنا، تقدیس **sanctity** (-ti) *n.* sacredness مقدس ہونا، تقدیس **sanctimonious** (-*moh*-ni-us) *adj.* making a show of sanctity and piety ریاکار، زاہد پر فریب

sanction (*sank*-shĕn) *n.* permission (*for* or *to do* something) اجازت، منظوری being (*of* action, etc.) in line with tradition, general practice, etc. جواز enforcement of respect for law through penalties, etc. قوت نافذہ *sanctions behind the law* قانون کی قوت نافذہ penalty سزا، تعزیر *sanctions against criminals* مجرموں کو سزائیں *v. t.* give sanction of (something) کی منظوری دینا

sanctity (*sank*-ti-ti) *n.* (see under **sanctify**)

sanctuary (*sank*-tew-ĕ-ri) *n.* sacred and protected place مقدس مقام، حرم any place of protection *from* the clutches of law, etc. جائے پناہ، مامن، ملجا *bird sanctuary*, area where it is forbidden to shoot wild birds وہ جگہ جہاں پرندوں کا شکار منع ہو

sand *n.* tiny grains of worn rock ریت، بالو، ریگ *the sands*, expanse of sandy seashore inundated in high tide سمندر کا ریتلا کنارہ *the sands of time*, time; (originally the grains of sand running from one parts of the hour-glass into the other) وقت *footprints on the sands of time*, people who have left their impress on world civilization ریگِ زمانہ پر نقوشِ قدم، مشاہیر، زمانے کے مشہور افراد **sand-bag** *n.* gunny-bag filled with sand ریت کا بورا *v.t.* fortify with sand-bag ریت کے بوروں کی حفاظتی دیوار بنانا fill a gap with sand-bags (میں) ریت کے بورے بھرنا **sand-bank** *n.* one formed by tides ریتا **sandfly** *n.* a kind of fly سینڈ فلائی، مٹر مکھی *sandfly fever*, malaria-like fever caused by it سینڈ فلائی بخار **sand-glass** *n.* hour-glass using sand for indicating time ریت گھڑی **sand-paper** *n.* paper with sand glued to it for smoothing away rough surfaces ریگمال *v.t.* rub with it ریگمال کرنا **sandstone** *n.* rock made mainly of sand بھربھرا پتھر، ریتلا پتھر

a sand-glass

sandy (*sand*-i) *adj.* containing (or covered with) sand ریگ آلود yellowish red (hair, etc.) ریت کے رنگ کا

sandal (*sand*-ĕl) *n.* light shoe with straps on sole چپلی، چپل ladies' light shoes سینڈل **sandalled** (*sand*-ĕld) *adj* **sandalwood** (*sand*-ĕl-wŭd) *n.* a fragrant wood صندل، چندن

sandwich (*san*-wij, or *sand*-wich) *n.* pair of bread slices with meat, etc., between سینڈوچ، روٹی کے دو ٹکڑوں میں گوشت وغیرہ بھرا ہُوا *v.t.* thrust (someone or something) between two others ٹھونسنا *sandwich between* میں ٹھنسا ہُوا ، کے شکنجے میں آیا ہُوا
sane (sayn) *adj.* sensible (person) ہوشمند moderate (views) اِعتدال پسندانہ **sanely** *adv.* wisely, sensibly ہوشمندی سے **sanity** (*san*-i-ti) *n.* being sane ہوشمندی
sang *v.* (pa. t. of **sing**, which see)
sang-froid (sahn-*froh*-a) *n.* coolness in face of danger or difficulty حَواس قائم رکھنا، پریشان نہ ہونا
sanguinary *adj.* (see under **sanguine**)
sanguine (*sang*-gwin) *adj.* confident پُر اِعتماد optimistic پُر اُمّید red-faced سُرخ چہرے والا **sanguinary** (*sang*-gwi-na-ri) *adj.* (of battle, etc.) causing much bloodshed خُونریز، خُوں آشام (of person) cruel and fond of bloodshed سفّاک، خُونریز، خُونی
sanitary (*san*-i-ta-ri) *adj.* hygienic (place, conditions, etc.) صَفائی والا pertaining to cleanliness and protection of health صِحّت اور صَفائی سے مُتعلّق *Sanitary Inspector*, official looking to sanitation داروغۂ صَفائی **sanitation** (san-i-*tay*-shĕn) *n.* prevention of disease through the removal of sewage, etc. صَفائی
sanity *n.* (see under **sane**)
sank *v.* (pa. t. of **sink**, which see)
sans *prep.* (old use) (pr. *sanz*) without کے بغیر، سے محرُوم (in French phrases) (pr. sahn) without کے بغیر، سے خالی *Le belle dame sans merci*, the beautiful lady without mercy بیرحم حسینہ، ستمگر حسینہ
Santa Claus (*sant*-a-klawz) the supposed Father Christmas who fills Christian children's socks with presents on Xmas eve بابا کرسمس
sap *n.* juice in plants serving the same purpose as blood in animals عرق، رس tunnel, etc., dug out to get near the enemy دُشمن تک پہنچنے کی سُرنگ insidious undermining (of resolve, belief, strength, energy, etc.) اَندر ہی اَندر کاٹنا، جڑیں کھوکھلی کرنا (slang) studious person کتابوں کا کیڑا (slang) irksome work محنت طلب کام، سخت اُکتا دینے والا کام (U.S. colloq.) simpleton سادہ لوح *v.t.* drain off the sap of (something) کا عرق نچوڑ لینا destroy (strength, energy, belief, etc.) of ختم کرنا undermine (building, etc.) کی جڑیں کھوکھلی کرنا dig out a tunnel سُرنگ لگانا **sapling** *n.* young tree درخت کا پَودا، نِہال **sapless** *adj.* without sap سُوکھا ہُوا effete ازکار رفتہ **sappy** (*sap*-i) *adj.* full of sap عرق سے بھرا ہُوا young and strong قوی جوان، برناو توانا

sapper *n.* soldier trained to do the work of sapping سُرنگیں وغیرہ کھودنے والا سپاہی *sappers and miners* army corps comprising such soldiers (now called *Pioneer Corps*) سفر مَینا **sapwork** *n.* hard, irksome work for earning one's bread روٹی کمانے کے لیے محنت مشقّت ، محنت مزدُوری
sapid (*sap*-id) *adj.* (lit.) (of talk, etc.) not insipid جو بے لُطف نہ ہو **sapidity**(-*pid*-) being sapid بے لُطف نہ ہونا **sapient** (*say*-pi-ent) *adj.* aping wisdom خواہ مخواہ عقلمندی جتانے والا **sapience** (*say*-pi-ens) خواہ مخواہ عقلمندی جتانے والا
sapphire (*saf*-i-ĕ*) *n.* a blue jewel نیلم *adj.* azure *n.* ہلکا نیلا ، بیسنگوں
sapless *adj.*, **sapling** *n.*, **sapper** *adj.* (see under **sap**)
sappy *adj.*, **sapwork** *n.* (see under **sap**)
Saracen (*sa*-ra-sen) *n.* (old word for) Muslim مُسلمان (from the Arabic شرقیّین meaning the easterners or Orientals)
sarcasm (*sah**-kasm) *n.* sneering remarks طنز، تعریض **sarcastic** (-*kas*-) *adj.* of sarcasm طنز بھرا، طنزیہ طنز آمیز using sarcasm طنز (کرنے) والا **sarcastically** *adv.* in a sarcastic manner طنز سے، طنز بھرے انداز سے
sarcophagus (sah*-*kof*-a-gus) *n.* stone coffin پتھر کا تابوت
sardine (sah*-*deen*) *n.* small fish سارڈین this preserved in oil and tinned سارڈین اَچار
sardonic (sah*-*don*-ik) *adj.* cynical (smile, etc.) تلخ mocking مسخر آمیز بناوٹ والا انداز **sardonically** *adv.* cynically or mockingly تلخی سے، تمسخر آمیز بناوٹ سے
sarong (sah-*rong*) *n.* loose petticoat worn by men and women in Malaya سارونگ
sarsaprilla (sah*-sa-*pril*-a) *n.* a blood-purifying drug عُشبہ its essence جوہر عُشبہ
sartorial (sah*-*to*-ri-ĕl) *adj.* of men's clothes مردانہ پوشاک سے متعلّق of tailors درزیوں سے مُتعلّق
sash *n.* ornamental scarf for waist کمربند such a one for shoulders پٹکا (also *sash window*), frame which holds window-glass and slides up and down اُوپر نیچے کھسکنے والا دریچہ، ساشن کھڑکی
sash-cord *n.* cord for keeping a sash window in a desired position with the help of weights (called *sash-weights*) running over pulleys (called *sash-pulleys*) and hanging in pockets (called *sash-pockets*) *sash-pocket* ساش کی تھیلی *sash-pulley* ساش کی چرخی *sash-weight* ساش کا بوجھ

a girl with a sash

a sash window

sat *v.* (*pa. t.* & *pa. p.* of **sit**, which see)

Satan (*say*-tĕn) *n.* the Devil شیطان، ابلیس **satanic** (sa-*tan*-ik) *adj.* of Satan شیطانی evil, wicked بُرا، شیطنت والا **satanism** (say-ta-nizm) *n.* pursuit of evil for its own sake شیطنت، شوقِ گناہ کے باعث گناہ

satchel (*sach*-el) *n.* young student's bag for schoolbooks بستہ

sate (sayt) *v.t.* gratify fully (کسی خواہش کا) پُورا کرنا surfeit اتنا کھلانا کہ مُنہ بھر جائے *sated with*, cloyed with سے جی بھرا ہُوا

sateen (sa-*teen*) *n.* a shiny cotton or woollen fabric چمکیلا کپڑا، اسٹین

satellite (*sat*-e-lit) *n.* small planet revolving round a larger one تابع سیّارہ (also *earth satellite*), rocket sent up in the sky to revolve round a planet مصنوعی سیّارہ، نقلی چاند *the U.S.* (or *Russian*) *satellite* امریکہ (یا رُوس کا) نقلی چاند hanger-on (of someone) طفیلیا، طفیلی camp-follower (*of* a bigger Power) ماتحت، زیرِ نگیں *satellite States* ماتحت مُلک

satiate (*saysh*-i-ayt) *v.t.* surfeit (with food, pleasure, etc.) (زیادہ دے کر) مُنہ بھر دینا، جی بھر دینا *adj.* (poet.) sated جس کا جی بھرا ہُوا ہو **satiety** (sa-*ti*-è-ti) *n.* feeling of having had too much سے جی بھرا ہُوا ہونا *to satiety*, excessively بہت زیادہ، شکم سیر ہونا، جی بھر کے، بہت زیادہ

satin (*sat*-in) *n.* silk fabric with one side smooth and glossy ساٹن *adj.* like satin ساٹن جیسا

satire (*sat*-i-è*) *n.* (piece of writing in) the literary form which uses irony or ridicule for exposing folly, etc. (of a person, custom, idea, etc.) ہجو **satiric** (sa-*ti*-rik) *adj.* containing satire ہجویہ **satirical** (sa-*ti*-rik-el) *adj.* of (or using) satire ہجو والا، ہجویہ یا ہجو گویانہ **satirically** *adv.* ہجویہ انداز سے **satirist** (*sat*-i-rist) *n.* writer of satires ہجو گو **satirize** (*sat*-i-riz) *v.t.* attack with satire کی ہجو کہنا یا لکھنا

satisfy (*sat*-is-fi) *v.t.* do everything necessary for (someone *in* some case) and leave no room for complaint کی تسلّی کرنا، کی تشفّی کرنا be enough for (one's needs) کے لیے کافی ہونا be equal to (one's expectations) کے لیے تسلّی بخش ہونا، کے مُطابق ہونا convince (someone or oneself *of* something, or *that*) کی تسلّی کرنا کہ، کو یقین دلا دینا کہ، اطمینان کرانا کہ **satisfied** (-fid) *adj.* desiring nothing more مطمئن

satisfaction (sat-is-*fak*-shĕn) *n.* satisfying or being satisfied تسلّی، اطمینان something that satisfies تسلّی بخش feeling of gratification خوشی

satisfactory (sat-is-*fak*-tè-ri) *adj.* giving satisfaction تسلّی بخش good enough (*for* something) کے لیے کافی (اچھا) **satisfactorily** *adv.* تسلّی سے، تسلّی بخش انداز سے

satrap (*sat*-rap) *n.* a provincial governor in ancient Persia قدیم ایرانی صُوبہ دار rich and despotic provincial governor لٹیرا اور جابر صُوبہ دار

saturate (*sat*-ew-rayt) *v. t.* soak بھگونا، بھگو دینا، تر بتر کرنا steep (*in* or *with* learning, prejudice, etc.) سے بھر دینا (science) cause (a fluid) to absorb the greatest possible amount of something سیر کرنا **saturation** (-*ray*-shĕn) *n.* act of saturating or being saturated بھگونا، تر بتر کرنا، سیری، تری *the saturation point*, degree of the saturation of a given amount of fluid after which it cannot absorb the other thing نقطۂ سیری

Saturday (*sat*-ĕ*-day) *n.* the day of the week following Friday ہفتہ، سنیچر

Saturn (*sat*-ĕ*n) *n.* a planet زُحل، کیوان *Cl. myth.* the Roman god of agriculture and civilization ; he is identified with the Greek Cronos whose son, Zeus, had dethroned him سیٹرن **saturnalia** (-*nay*-li-a) *n.* the Roman festival of Saturn in which Christmas festivities originated سیٹرن کا تہوار **saturnine** *adj.* gloomy (like persons born under the supposed influence of Saturn) اُداس، غمناک، بُجھا بُجھا، بُجھا ہُوا سا

satyr (*sat*-ĕ*) *Cl. myth.* one of the lascivious minor forest deities who looked like men in the upper half of their body and like goats in the rest ساطِیر lascivious person بُوالہوس، ہوسناک **satyriasis** (sat-i-*ri*-è-sis) *n.* excessive sexual excitement in males شہوت پرستی

a satyr (sense 1)

sauce (saws) *n.* liquid seasoning for food چٹنی piquancy چٹپٹا پن (colloq.) sauciness گستاخی، شوخ چشمی **saucy** (*saw*-si) *adj.* impudent گستاخ، شوخ چشم **saucily** *adv.* گستاخانہ انداز سے، گستاخی سے، ازرہِ گستاخی **sauceboat** *n.* small tray for sauce چٹنی دانی

saucepan (*saws*-pan) *n.* metal cooking pot (usu. with a lid and a handle) ساس پان، دیگچی

saucer (*saw*-sĕ*) *n.* small dish for a teacup پرچ *cups and saucers* پرچ پیالے *flying saucer*, one of the discs occasionally seen moving in the air during the days of experimentation for earth satellites اُڑن طشتری

saunter (*sawnt*-ĕ*) *v.i.* walk leisurely سیر گشت کرنا، ٹہلنا، ٹہلتے پھرنا، اپنے جی سے پھرنا *n.* leisurely walk سیر گشت

sausage (*sos*-ij) *n.* minced or chopped meat stuffed into a small length of gut or thin membrane and fried

sausage-meat *n.* minced meat put into gut, etc., to make a sausage ساسیج والا قیمہ

savage (*sav*-ej) *adj.* primitive and uncivilized (person, tribe, country, etc.) وحشی wild and fierce (animal) جنگلی رجانور cruel ظالم، جابر *n.* savage person وحشی **savagery** (*sav*-ij-ri) *n.* savage conduct or state وحشی پن، وحشیانہ انداز، جنگلی پن، ظلم، جبر

savanna, savannah (sa-*van*-a) *n.* treeless plain in tropical areas of America امریکی صحرا

savant (sa-*vohn*) *n.* very learned person علامہ، متبحر عالم

save (sayv) *v.t.* & *i.* rescue (*from* danger, loss, etc.) بچانا، محفوظ کرنا *save (someone's) life* کی جان بچانا *save (someone) from (himself)*, save (him) from committing excesses or from their consequences کو اس کی ذات سے بچانا set apart (or *up*) for the future بچا کر رکھنا، بچا بچا کر رکھنا، سینت سینت کر رکھنا، پس انداز کرنا، سنبھال کر رکھنا render unnecessary (*doing* something) سے بچ جانا keep (someone) from the need to undergo (expense, trouble, etc.) سے نجات دلانا، سے بچانا *That will save me a lot of trouble* یوں تو میری مشکل بڑی آسان ہو جائے گی rescue from eternal punishment ابدی عذاب سے نجات دلانا *prep.* except ماسوا، اس کے سوا، کے سوائے *conj.* except (that) سوائے اس کے (کہ) **saving** *adj.* redeeming (feature, etc.) برائی کم کرنے والا، روشن یا امید افزا (پہلو) *the saving grace* (*of some quality*) the redeeming feature of someone with other bad qualities صرف ایک روشن پہلو *n.* rescue نجات amount (*of* time, money, etc.) saved بچت، جمع جتھا، اندوختہ (*pl.*) money saved up بچت

savings bank *n.* department of a bank accepting small savings سیونگ بنک، چھوٹی بچت **saviour** (*sayv*-yĕ*) *n.* one who rescues someone بچانے والا، نجات دینے والا، نجات دہندہ، منجی *The Saviour*, Jesus Christ according to Christians حضرت عیسیٰ، منجی، منجی ▣ **We save** by keeping whole; **preserve** from damage; **conserve** together; **rescue** from harm; **recover** after loss; **snatch** quickly by force; **redeem** by payment after loss; and **salvage** a wreck.

savour (*say*-vĕ*) *n.* taste (*of* something) ذائقہ، مزہ suggestion (*of* a quality) رنگ، کا سا انداز *v.i.* be suggestive (*of* something) کی یاد دلانا، کا سا انداز رکھنا

savoury (*say*-vĕ-ri) *adj.* with a sharp taste چٹ پٹا، چٹپٹا appetizing بھوک لگانے والا، اشتہا انگیز *n.* any kind of savoury dish چٹپٹی

saw *n.* tooth-edged steel blade for cutting آرہ، ارہ wise saying مقولہ، قول، مثل، کہاوت *v.t.* & *i.* (pa. t. of *see*, which look up) دیکھنا (*saw, sawed, sawn*) (*a*) use a saw, آرہ چلانا، آرہ کشی کرنا (*b*) *saw (something) up*, cut it into pieces with a saw چیرنا

sawbones (*saw*-bohnz) *n.* (slang) surgeon جراح

sawdust *n.* particles falling off when something is sawn برادہ **saw-mill** *n.* workshop for sawing wood by machinery لکڑی چیرنے کا کارخانہ **sawyer** (*saw*-yĕ*) *n.* workman who saws timber آرہ کش، ارہ کش

Saxon (*sak*-sun) *n.* member of the Teutonic race which invaded and occupied Britain in the fifth to sixth centuries سیکسن their language سیکسن انگریزی (زبان) Teutonic element in English انگریزی (زبان) میں جرمن عنصر **Anglo-Saxon** *n.* Englishman as distinct from Briton اینگلو سیکسن old English قدیم انگریزی (زبان)، پرانی انگریزی

saxophone (*sak*-so-fohn) *n.* musical wind instrument made of brass سیکسو فون

a saxophone

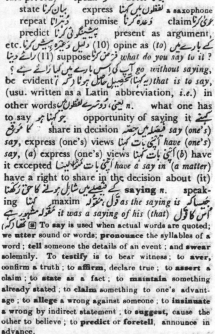

say *v.t.* & *i.* (pr. t. 3rd person sing. *says*, pr. sayz; pa. t. & pa. p. *said* pr. sed) speak کہنا utter بولنا state بیان کرنا express لفظوں میں کہنا repeat دہرانا promise وعدہ کرنا claim دعویٰ کرنا predict پیشنگوئی کرنا present as argument, etc. دلیل وغیرہ پیش کرنا (10) opine as (*to*) کے بارے میں رائے دینا (11) suppose فرض کرنا *what do you say to it?* آپ کی اس بارے میں کیا رائے ہے ؟ *go without saying*, be evident (یہ کہنا) تحصیل حاصل ہونا (کہ) *that is to say*, (usu. written as a Latin abbreviation, *i.e.*) in other words یعنی، دوسرے لفظوں میں *n.* what one has to say جو کہنا ہو opportunity of saying it کہنے کا موقع share in decision فیصلہ میں حصہ *say (one's) say*, express (one's) views اپنی بات کہنا *have (one's) say*, (*a*) express (one's) views اپنی بات کہنا (*b*) have it excepted اپنی بات منوا لینا *have a say in* (*a matter*) have a right to share in the decision about (it) کے فیصلے میں شامل ہونے کا حق رکھنا **saying** *n.* speaking کہنا maxim قول، مقولہ *as the saying is* جیسا کہ قول *it was a saying of his (that)* اس کا مقولہ مشہور ہے (کہ) تھا ▣ **To say** is used when actual words are quoted; we **utter** sound or words; **pronounce** the syllables of a word; **tell** someone the details of an event; and **swear** solemnly. To **testify** is to bear witness; to **aver**, confirm a truth; to **affirm**, declare true; to **assert** a claim; to **state as a fact**; to **maintain** something already stated; to **claim** something to one's advantage; to **allege** a wrong against someone; to **insinuate** a wrong by indirect statement; to **suggest**, cause the other to believe; to **predict** or **foretell**, announce in advance.

scab (skab) *n.* crust over a wound کھرنڈ (slang) blackleg ہڑتال کے فیصلے کی خلاف ورزی کرنے والا مزدور

ہڑتال توڑ مزدور **scabby** (scab-i) *adj.* covered with scabs خارشتی

scabbard (*skab*-ĕ*d) *n.* sheath نیام، میان

scabby *adj.* (see under **scab**)

scabies (*skay*-bi-eez) *n.* itch کھجلی۔ خارش

scaffold (*skaf*-old) *n.* (also *scaffolding*), temporary structure of poles, boards, etc., around a building for workmen to stand on while erecting or repairing the latter پاڑ platform on which criminals are executed پھانسی (وغیرہ) کا تختہ *send (someone) to the scaffold* سزائے موت دینا *go to the scaffold* پھانسی پانا (یا) پھانسی کا حکم ہونا **scaffolding** *n.* materials for a scaffold round a building پاڑ کے لیے بانس تختے وغیرہ scaffold پاڑ

a scaffolding

scald (skawld) *v.t.* burn with hot liquid or steam اُبلتے ہوئے پانی (وغیرہ) سے زخمی کرنا *scald to death* کھولتا ہوا پانی (وغیرہ) ڈال کر مار ڈالنا clean (dishes, etc.) with boiling water گرم پانی سے دھونا boil (milk) (دودھ) اُبالنا (یا کو جوش دینا) *n.* injury from hot liquid, etc. چرکا، پھکا

scale (skayl) *n.* marks at regular intervals for measuring پیمانہ measuring instrument پیمانہ measuring system پیمائش کا نظام *the notation scale* نظامِ اعداد degree درجہ gradation درجہ بندی status رُتبہ، مرتبہ series of musical tones at regular pitch intervals سرگم proportion between the size of a drawing and its original پیمانہ *a map on the scale of one inch to 100 miles* ایک انچ برابر ہے سو میل کے پیمانے پر نقشہ relative size پیمانہ *on a large scale*, big بڑے پیمانے پر *on a small scale*, small, ordinary چھوٹے پیمانے پر، معمولی one of the two pans of a balance (ترازو کا) پلڑا (*pl.*) (*scales*, or *pair of scales*), balance ترازو، میزان *hold the scales even (between two persons, etc.)*, judge between them fairly (کے مابین) انصاف سے فیصلہ کرنا *turn the scale in favour of*, (or *against*), decide a border case in favour of (or against) کے حق میں (یا خلاف) ترازو کا پلڑا جھکانا hard, thin flake on the skin of a fish, etc. چھلکا، فلس any thin hard flake چھلکا، خول chalky crust (on teeth, inside boilers, pipes, etc.) پوشت، چھلکا *v.t.* climb (a wall, cliff, etc.) step by step (or *with* a ladder, etc.) چڑھنا، اوپر چڑھنا، قدم بہ قدم چڑھنا copy according to a certain scale ایک خاص پیمانے پر متناسب شکل کھینچنا change according to certain proportion ایک خاص تناسب سے بدلنا *scale up*, increase by a certain proportion ایک خاص تناسب سے بڑھانا *scale down*, decrease in the same manner ایک خاص تناسب سے گھٹانا take scales from چھلکا، خول، پرت یا پوشت اتارنا come (*off* in flakes پرت اُترنا

scalp (skalp) *n.* skin of the top of the head کھوپڑی کی کھال، چاند، چندیا this skin torn off enemy's head by Red-Indian victor as trophy کھوپڑی کی کھال *v.t.* cut (someone's) scalp off (کی) کھوپڑی کی کھال اُتارنا criticize severely سخت نکتہ چینی کرنا

scalpel (*skal*-pel) *n.* surgeon's light knife نشتر

scamp (skamp) *n.* good-for-nothing person ناکارہ، بیکار آدمی، گیا گزرا *v.t.* do (work, etc.) negligently (کام) دل لگا کر نہ کرنا، (کام) بگاڑنا

scamper (*skamp*-pĕ*) *v.i.* (of playing children or dogs) run swiftly بے تحاشا دوڑنا (of small, frightened animals) run away swiftly out of fear اِدھر اُدھر چھپنے کے لیے بے تحاشا بھاگ اٹھنا *n.* short, swift run (of children or animals) چھوٹی سی تیز دوڑ

scan (skan) *v.t.* & *i.* (-nn-) look at (the horizon, proposal, etc.) attentively کو بڑے غور سے دیکھنا resolve picture into its elements of light and shade for televising it ٹیلی ویژن پر موزونیت دیکھنے کے لیے (تصویر) کا سیاہ و سفید دیکھنا، کی تقطیع کرنا find out the metre of کی تقطیع کرنا (of a line of verse) be metrically correct موزوں ہونا **scanning** *n.* finding out the metre of a line of verse by dividing it into feet تقطیع

scandal (*skand*-ĕl) *n.* event or behaviour شرمناک واقعہ، رسوائی، فضیحت evil gossip meant to injure someone's reputation بدنامی (یا رسوائی) کی باتیں، بدنام کرنے کی باتیں **scandalize** (-līz) *v.t.* indulge in such gossip کسی کو بدنام کرنا shock صدمہ پہنچانا *be scandalized*, be shocked کو صدمہ پہنچنا **scandalous** (skand-ĕ-lus) *adj.* (of rumours, etc.) containing scandal رسوا کُن (of persons) fond of spreading scandal باتیں بنانے والا، بدنام کرنے والا disgraceful شرمناک shocking صدمہ پہنچانے والا۔ دل آزار

scant (skant) *adj.* (old form of *scanty*, used now in certain phrases only, like:) *scant of breath*, out of breath سانس پھولی ہوئی، دم چڑھا ہوا *with scanty courtesy*, impolitely روکھے پن سے **scanty** (*skant*-i) *adj.* barely sufficient بمشکل کچھ insufficient نہ ہونے کے (یا کی) برابر little بہت کم، ناکافی **scantily** *adv.* insufficiently بہت کم۔

scapegoat (*skayp*-goht) *n.* one blamed or punished for another's faults in order to shield the latter جسے دوسروں کی خاطر قربان کیا جائے، دوسروں کی خاطر قربانی کا بکرا بننے والا، قربانی کا بکرا *He has been made a scapegoat* اسے دوسروں کی خاطر قربانی کا بکرا بنایا گیا ہے

scapegrace (*skayp*-grays) *n.* (used playfully of a child) rascal شریر، شیطان کہیں کا
scar (skah*) *n.* mark of a healed wound نشان، داغ *v.t.* (-rr-) mark with scars زخم لگانا (نشان) **scarred** (skah*d) *adj.* marked thus (*by* something) (کے) نشانوں والا، (سے) داغ داغ
scaramouch (*ska*-ra-mouch) *n.* scamp گیا گزرا، بیکار آدمی
scarce (*skay*-ĕ*s) *adj.* having a shortage (*in* the market, etc.) کمیاب rarely met with کم کم ملنے والا *make (oneself) scarce*, go away from a place in order to avoid someone سے بھاگنا، سے رفوچکر ہو جانا **scarcely** *adv.* hardly بمشکل، مشکل سے، ہمیشہ کر کے not at all ہی نہیں، بالکل نہیں just then **scarcity** (*skay*-ĕ*-si-ti) *n.* shortage, dearth کمی، قلت
scare (*skay*-ĕ*) *v.t.* frighten ڈرانا، خائف کرنا *n.* baseless fear بے بنیاد ڈر (یا) خوف alarm among the general public عام اندیشہ، عام خوف و ہراس **scare buying** *n.* (see *Addenda*) **scarecrow** (*skay*-ĕ*-kroh) *n.* dummy man made of sticks and old clothes and put in a field to scare away birds from crops دھوکا **scare-monger** *n.* one who starts a scare ہراس انگیز افواہیں پھیلانے والے، مرجف

a scarecrow

scarf (skah*f) *n.* (pl. *scarves* pr. skah*vz) neck-cloth گلوبند anything like that for the head سر کا رومال small shawl for shoulders, etc. چھوٹا دوپٹہ

a woman with a scarf

scarlet (*skah**-let) *n.* & *adj.* bright red (colour) گلناری (یا) قرمزی رنگ clothes of this colour گلناری لباس *scarlet fever*, infectious fever causing scarlet marks on the skin *scarlet rashes*, measles marks کھسرے کے دانے *scarlet woman, scarlet whore*, (*a*) ancient Rome قدیم روما (*b*) according to Protestants the Church of Rome or Roman Catholicism پراٹسٹنٹوں کے نزدیک عیسائیوں کا رومن کیتھولک فرقہ
scarred *adj.* (see under **scar**)
scathe (skaydh) *v.t.* injure ضرر پہنچانا (used only as :) (*a*) **scathing** (*skay*-dhing) *adj.* severe (criticism, etc.) سخت، شدید (*b*) **unscathed** (un-skaydhd) *adj.* without receiving any injury محفوظ، صاف بچ کر نکلا ہوا (*c*) *without scathe*, unscathed محفوظ، صاف بچ کر نکلا ہوا
scatter (*skat*-ĕ*) *v.t.* & *i.* broadcast (seed, etc.) بکھیرنا go or send in various directions اِدھر اُدھر جانا یا بھیجنا، منتشر ہونا یا کرنا **scattered** (-ĕ*d) *adj.* (of population, bits of information, etc.) not found together کوئی کہیں، کوئی کہیں، منتشر، پراگندہ
scavenge *v.t.* & *i.* (see under **scavenger**)
scavenger (*skav*-enj-ĕ*) *n.* animal (like jackal) or bird (like vulture) living on decaying matter گندگی (یا مُردار) کھانے والا، غلاظت خور، مُردار خور one employed to remove rubbish بھنگی، مہتر، خاکروب، جمعدار **scavenge** (*skav*-enj) *v.t.* & *i.* remove rubbish from گندگی اُٹھانا، میلا اُٹھانا act as scavenger بھنگی کا کام کرنا **scavenging, scavengering** *n.* (doing) scavenger's work بھنگی کا کام (کرنا)
scenario *n.* (see under **scene**)
scene (seen) *n.* place of occurrence (of an event, accident, battle, etc.) جائے وقوع view منظر that which is seen نظارہ، منظر *go for a change of scene* نئی جگہ دیکھنے جانا، نئے مناظر دیکھنے جانا *make a pretty scene* کا منظر بڑا دلکش ہونا (abbr. *sc.*) one of the parts of an act in a play or film سین، منظر *Hamlet Act II, sc. i 5* ہیملٹ کے دوسرے ایکٹ کے پہلے منظر کی پانچویں سطر painted background on the stage تماشا گاہ کا پیچھے کا منقش پردہ *behind the scenes*, (*a*) at the back of the stage پردے کے پیچھے (*b*) underhand (manoeuvring) اندرخانے، اندر ہی اندر (*c*) (person) in the know of such developments رازِ درونِ پردہ جاننے والا noisy argument ; display of bad temper in public دوسروں کے سامنے ہنگامہ برپا *Don't make a scene* دوسروں کے سامنے ہنگامہ برپا مت کرو **scenery** (*seen*-ĕ-ri) *n.* stage scene تماشا گاہ کا منقش پردہ natural beauty منظر، نظارہ **scenic** (*see*-nik) *adj.* pertaining to scenery نظارے سے متعلق *scenic railway*, miniature railway passing through artificial scenery نقلی نظاروں والی کھلونا ریل **scenario** (shay-*nah*-ri-oh or see-nay-ri-oh) *n.* (pl. *scenarios*) details of scenes in a film-story (etc.) منظر نامہ، سینیریو
scent (sent) *n.* fragrance خوشبو perfume عطر، سینٹ *put some scent on* میں عطر لگانا smell of an animal left on its way which helps hounds to track it بو *hunt by scent* بو سے کھوج لگانا *on the scent*, on the right track ٹھیک پیچھا کر رہا *off the scent* پیچھا نہ کر رہا *throw (someone) off the scent*, put him off the track (by wrong suggestions, etc.) پیچھا کرنے والے کو غلط راہ پر ڈال دینا line of investigation تحقیقات کا طریقہ *v.t.* know about (quarry) by scent شکار کی بو پانا، بو سے (شکار) کا پتہ لینا suspect (plot, crime, etc.) کا شبہ ہونا، کا اندازہ ہونا put scent on عطر لگانا
sceptic (*skep*-tic) *n.* philosopher who doubts the possibility of knowledge متشکک one who

doubts the truth of beliefs, traditions, etc. مذہب یا روایات کی صحت کو شک و شبہ کی نظر سے دیکھنے والا **scep-tical** *adj* doubtful (*of*) شکی ، کو شک و شبہ کی نظر سے دیکھنے والا **scepticism** (*skep*-ti-sizm) *n.* feeling of doubt شک ، ارتیاب being a sceptic شک و ارتیاب کی نظر سے دیکھنا

sceptre (*sep*-tě*) *n.* staff serving as a symbol of sovereign's power عصائے شاہی **sceptred** (*sep*-tě*d) *adj.* royal (glory, hand, etc.) شاہانہ ، مُلوکانہ of a sovereign بادشاہ کا

schadenfreude (*shah*-dĕn-froid-è) *n.* malicious enjoyment of others' misfortunes دوسروں کے مصائب پر خوشی ، جنازۂ دشمن پر شادی ، بد طینتی

schedule (*shed*-ewl or U.S. pr. *sked*-ewl) *n.* chart of details جدول (تفصیلات) ، گوشوارہ *according to schedule*, according to the plan منصوبے کے مطابق *v.t.* make a schedule of کا جدول بنانا ، کا گوشوارہ تیار کرنا

scheme (skeem) *n* plan (*for* or *of*) منصوبہ ، تجویز arrangement ترتیب *a colour scheme* رنگوں کی ترتیب plot سازش ، ریشہ دوانی *v.t.* & *i.* plot (*for* or *to do* something) (کی) سازش کرنا **scheming** (*skeem*-ing) *adj.* plotting (person) سازشی *n.* the making of schemes منصوبہ بنانا ، سازش کرنا **schemer** (*skeem*-ě*) *n.* plotter, intriguer سازشی

schism (sizm) *n.* rift in a party (esp. church) owing to differences of opinion پھوٹ ، افتراق **schis-matic** (siz-*mat*-ik) *adj.* (of tendency) causing (or likely to cause) rift افتراق انگیز

schizophrenia (ski-zo-*free*-ni-a) *n.* mental disease marked by lack of connexion between one's thoughts and actions فکر و عمل میں تضاد کی بیماری ، فکر و عمل میں بے تعلقی

scholar (*skol*-ě*) *n.* one with a great knowledge (*of* a branch of learning) (کا) عالم ، فاضل student getting a scholarship owing to good academic record وظیفہ پانے والا (old use) schoolboy (or schoolgirl) طالب علم (یا) طالبعلم (یا طالبہ علم یا طالبہ)

scholarly *adj.* giving evidence of much learning عالموں کا سا ، عالمانہ (as) of scholar(s)

scholarship *n.* great learning علم ، علم و فضل monetary award to an exceptionally good student (given on the basis of an examination result) for continuing his (or her) studies وظیفہ

scholastic (*sko*-las-tic) *adj.* of schools مدرسی ، مکتبی educational تعلیمی of schoolmen who tried to explain religious dogma by logical treatment علم کلام سے متعلق **scholastic philosophy** *n.* such treatment of dogma علم کلام **scholasticism** (sko-*las*-ti-cism) *n.* being scholastic مذہب کی منطقی تشریح کا قائل ہونا ، متکلمین کی پیروی

school (skool) *n.* institution for primary, middle, secondary (or even higher secondary) education سکول ، اسکول ، مدرسہ group (of artists, thinkers, etc.) مکتب و بستان ، مسلک *school of thought* مکتب خیال ، دبستان ، مسلک shoal (of fish) (مچھلیوں کا) غول *v.t.* discipline, train کی تربیت کرنا (of fish) form shoals (مچھلیوں کا) غول بنا کر پھرنا یا رہنا **school-days** *n.* (*pl.*) time when one was at school طالب علمی کا زمانہ **schoolfellow**, **schoolmate** *n.* fellow student at a school سکول کا ساتھی ، ہم مکتب **schooling** *n.* discipline تربیت education at school سکول کی تعلیم **schoolman** *n.* exponent of (or fond of) scholastic philosophy متکلم **school-master** *n.* (fem. *schoolmistress*) school teacher مدرس ، اُستاد ، ماسٹر *The schoolmaster is abroad*, illiteracy or ignorance is being uprooted جہالت کا خاتمہ ہو رہا ہے

schooner (*skoo*-ně*) *n.* sailing vessel with two or more masts دو یا زیادہ مستول کا جہاز

a schooner

science (*sī*-ens) *n.* knowledge (of physical facts) obtained by observation and experiment سائنس a branch of such knowledge سائنس ، تجربی علوم و حکمت ، تجربی علوم expert skill (in boxing or other sports) مہارت ، کُلّی مہارتِ تامّہ **scientific** (sī-en-*tif*-ik) *adj.* pertaining to science سائنسی based on observation and experiment تجربی in accordance with the findings of science سائنس کے اُصولوں کے مطابق ، سائنسی skilful (boxer, etc.) ماہر needing skill مہارت طلب **scientifically** *adv.* in a scientific manner سائنس کے اصولوں کے مطابق ، ماہرانہ مہارت سے **scientist** (*sī*-en-tist) *n.* expert in one of the sciences سائنس دان

scimitar, scimetar, (*sim*-i-tě*) *n.* short Oriental sword with curved blade شمشیر

scintillate (*sint*-i-layt) *v.i.* sparkle چمکنا ، ضو فشاں ہونا radiate (*with* humour, etc.) (ظرافت سے) مملو ہونا **scintillating** *adj.* sparkling ضو فشاں ، ضوبار **scintil-lation** *n.* radiation ; sparkling ضیا باری

scion (*sī*-on) *n.* young member of (an old or noble family) (کا) چشم و چراغ ، (کا) نونہال short cut for grafting (پودے کی) قلم

scissors (*siz*-ě*z) *n. pl.* (also, *pair of scissors*), a common, double-bladed cutting instrument (پودے) چھانٹنے کی قینچی

scoff (skof) *v.i.* mock (*at*) (پر) ہنسنا ، (کا) مذاق اڑانا speak scornfully حقارت آمیز لہجے میں ذکر کرنا *n.* laughing-stock گوشۂ محفل mocking or scornful words تمسخر ، تحقیر آمیز الفاظ **scoffer** *n.* one who

scoffs کا مذاق اڑانے والا، تحقیر آمیز الفاظ برتنے والا one who jibes at religion مذہب کا مذاق اُڑانے والا

scold (skohld) *v.t.* & *i.* find fault noisily جھاڑ جھپاڑ کرنا *n.* woman who scolds جھاڑ جھپاڑ کرنے والی

sconce (skons) *n.* ornamental candlestic with a handle or fixed to the wall آرائشی شمع دان (colloq.) head سر *v. t.* forfeit beer, etc., as punishment for offence against table etiquette آدابِ طعام کی خلاف ورزی پر شراب وغیرہ سے محروم کرنا *be sconced*, (of person or offence) be punished thus آدابِ طعام کی خلاف ورزی کی سزا پانا

a sconce (sense 1)

scone (skohn), **scon** (skon) *n.* (triangular) soft flat cake of wheat or barley تکونی ٹکیہ

scoop (skoop) *n.* deep ladle for taking up flour, etc., or digging up earth کفچہ part of a machine serving that purpose (مشین کا) کفچہ (colloq.) exclusive report for or by a newspaper کسی اخبار کی خاص الخاص خبر، مخصوص خبر *v.t.* lift (*up* or *out*) with a scoop, etc. کفچے سے نکالنا make (a hole or a hollow *in* something) with a scoop کھوکھلا کرنا، جوف پیدا کرنا

scoot (skoot) *v.i.* (colloq.) make off swiftly تیزی سے بھاگ جانا، رفو چکر ہو جانا **scooter** (*skoo-tĕ**) *n.* wheeled footboard for child سکوٹر small motor-cycle looking like a child's scooter چھوٹی موٹر سائیکل، سکوٹر

a scooter (sense 1)

scope (skohp) *n.* range of action دسترس، رسائی capacity گنجائش outlook حدِ نظر range of thought خیال کی وسعت opportunity (*for*) (کا) موقع، اِمکان

scorch (skoh*ch, or sko*ch) *v.t.* & *i.* singe جھلسنا *scorched earth policy*, destroying everything in one's country that might prove useful to the enemy ساڑ پھونک پالیسی، سوخت کاری (colloq.) (of cyclists, etc.) go at high speed سائیکل تیز چلانا

score (skoh*) *n.* scratch or cut نشان، لکیر line drawn for keeping count حساب رکھنے کے لیے لکیر ڈالنا account (esp. of money owing) kept thus (قرض کا) حساب *run up a score*, get into debt قرضدار ہونا *pay off* (or *settle*, or *wipe off*) *old scores*, (*a*) pay off old debts حساب بیباق کرنا (*b*) have revenge بدلہ لینا runs, goals, points, etc. (*of* a team or player) سکور، نمبر cause وجہ، سبب (in the phrases :) *on the score of*, owing to کی وجہ سے، کے باعث *on that score*, for the matter اس وجہ سے، لہٰذا individual directions for the playing or singing of a piece of orchestral music آرکسٹرا کے لیے انفرادی ہدایات good luck خوش قسمتی set of twenty articles کوڑی *v.t.* & *i.* make (cuts, scratches, lines) on (*with* corrections, etc.) لکیریں کھینچنا *score off* (or *out*) *something* قلم زن کرنا keep a record of score in games کھیل میں سکور کا حساب رکھنا make runs, goals or points in a game, etc. سکور کرنا، نمبر لینا، (گول وغیرہ) کرنا، رن بنانا یا کرنا *score a goal*, گول کرنا *fail to score*, fail to win (point, etc.) نہ لے سکنا، نہ بنا سکنا win an advantage (*over* someone) سے اوپر رہنا *score off* (*someone in an argument, etc.*), worst (him) کو ہرانا write music in a score آرکسٹرا کے لیے انفرادی ہدایات قلمبند کرنا **scorer** *n.* one who keeps a score (کھیل وغیرہ کا) سکور رکھنے والا one who scores a tree, etc. نشان لگانے والا سکور والا

scorn (skoh*n) *n.* disdain (*for* someone or something) حقارت *v. t.* disdain (someone or something, or *to do* or *doing* something) because of being evil or unworthy گھٹیا یا بُرا جاننا، حقیر سمجھنا refuse (*to do* or *doing* something) on these considerations بُرا یا گھٹیا سمجھ کر (کرنے) سے انکار کر دینا **scornful** *adj.* showing scorn حقارت آمیز feeling scorn حقیر یا بُرا جاننے والا **scornfully** *adv.* contemptuously حقارت سے

scorpion (sko*-pi-ĕn) *n.* small lobster like animal with a poisonous sting in its tail and once believed to sting itself to death if put in fire بچھو عقرب

Scot (skot) *n.* native of Scotland سکاٹ لینڈ کا باشندہ، اسکاچستانی

Scotch (skoch) *adj.* of Scotland or its people سکاٹ لینڈ، سکاچ *n.* kind of English spoken in Scotland انگریزی کا سکاچ محاورہ *v.t.* wound (snake, etc.) so as to disable without killing زخمی کر دینا، ناکارہ کر دینا

Scottish *n.* & *adj.* (dignified term for) Scot, (person) of Scotland سکاٹ لینڈ کا، اسکاچستانی، سکاچ

scotfree (skot-*free*) *adv.* exempt from municipal tax (formerly called scot) or from any payment محصول سے exempt from punishment سزا سے مستثنیٰ سے آزاد، پاداش سے مستثنیٰ

scoundrel (*skound*-rel) *n.* blackguard ; rascal بدذات unprincipled person بے اصول شخص **scoundrelly** *adj.* wicked بدذاتی والا

scour (skou-ĕ*) *v.t.* clean by rubbing roughly مانجھنا romove (marks, etc., *off*, *out*, or *away*) thus مانجھنا، رگڑ کر اتارنا *n.* scouring رگڑنا

scourge (skĕ*j) *n.* whip for punishment کوڑا تازیانہ، درّہ divine punishment عذاب epidemic, etc., regarded as such وبا *v.t.* castigate کوڑے لگانا punish سزا دینا cause to suffer مصیبت میں مبتلا کرنا

scout (skout) *n.* soldier or ship sent out to

watch the enemy's strength, etc. مخبر یا مخبر جہاز، نگراں سپاہی یا نگران جہاز Boy Scout سکاوٹ *v.t.* & *i.* go out as a scout دشمن کی طاقت کا اندازہ کرنے کے لیے جانا *scout* (or *round for*) (*someone or something that is wanted*) کی مخبری کے لیے پھرنا reject (a proposal or idea) as worthless or ridiculous فضول (یا مضحکہ خیز) سمجھ کر مسترد کر دینا

scowl (skoul) *n.* frown تیوری ill-tempered look بگڑے تیور *v.i.* frown (*on*) کو کڑے تیوروں سے دیکھنا

scram *int.* (U.S. slang) clear out پرے ہٹو، ہٹ جاؤ، دفع ہو جاؤ

scramble (*skram*-bėl) *v.i.* climb or crawl (*up, over, along, into*, etc., a place) on all fours گھٹنوں کے بل چڑھنا یا چڑھانا یا داخل ہونا rush (*for* something) to get it before others can reach there (کے لیے) جد و جہد کرنا یا کد و کاوش کرنا fry beaten (eggs) انڈوں کا حلوہ (یا کھگینہ) بنانا *n.* advance through rough ground, etc. مشکل میں سے ہو کر گزرنا struggle (*for* something) جد و جہد، کد و کاوش

scrap (skrap) *n.* small, unwanted bit ردّی ٹکڑا such a bit of paper پُرزہ unwanted metallic articles for recasting, etc. بالکل ردّی *scrap iron*, iron and steel articles (bought) for melting down ناکارہ لوہا (colloq.) fight, row لڑائی جھگڑا *v. t.* (-pp-) discard as useless ردّی کر دینا، ردّی میں پھینک دینا reject as worthless ردّی کی ٹوکری میں ڈال دینا (colloq.) fight, quarrel لڑنا، جھگڑنا **scrap-book** *n.* book with blank pages for pasting newspaper cuttings, etc., on تراشے لگانے کی کاپی، تراشنامہ **scrap-heap** *n.* heap of waste things, etc. ردّی کا ڈھیر **scrappy** (*skrap*-i) *adj.* (of information, etc.) made up of bits and hence neither complete nor properly arranged ادھر ادھر کا، اکھڑا اکھڑا، بے جوڑ، منتشر

scrape (skrayp) *v.t.* & *i.* rub with a sharp edge to clean کھرچنا remove (mud, etc., *off* a place) thus کھرچ کر اتارنا، یا صاف کرنا rub thus to level or smooth چھیلنا، چھیل کر ہموار یا صاف کرنا damage thus کھرچ کھرچ کر خراب کرنا go (*past, against, through*, etc., something) touching or almost touching it کو چھوتے ہوئے گزرنا *scrape through an examination*, pass at the margin بمشکل کامیاب ہونا، امتحان میں روتے پیٹتے پاس ہونا collect (something) or save (money) (*up* or *together*) with great difficulty بڑی مشکل سے جمع کرنا rub with a grating sound ناگوار آواز سے رگڑنا make (something or a hole, etc.) by scraping چھیل کر بنانا، کھرچ کر بنانا *n.* scraping کھرچنا (یا) چھیلنا its sound کھرچنے کی آواز mark made by scraping کھرچنے کا نشان awkward situation resulting from an escapade بڑی مشکل، بے ڈھب بات *get into a scrape* بڑی مشکل میں پھنس جانا

scraper (*skray*-pė*) *n.* any sharp-edged tool used for scraping کھرچنے یا چھیلنے کا کوئی آلہ

scratch (skrach) *v. t.* & *i* make lines on (something) with sharp edge کریدنا scrape چھیلنا *scratch off* (*paint, etc.*) چھیل کر اتارنا *scratch off* (or *out* or *through*) *a word*, strike it off قلمزن کرنا draw finger-nails across (the skin) to relieve itching کھجانا، خارش کرنا *scratch* (*one's*) *head*, (*a*) do so physically سر کھجانا (*b*) be at one's wit's end کچھ سمجھ میں نہ آنا کہ کیا کرے، سراسیمہ ہونا draw or write carelessly جلدی جلدی لکھنا یا تصویر بنانا produce a harsh noise by rubbing رگڑ کر ناگوار آواز پیدا کرنا، خراش کی آواز دینا *This pen scratches*, یہ قلم خراش کی آواز دیتا ہے withdraw (a horse, a candidate, oneself) from a contest مقابلے سے ہٹا لینا *n.* injury by scratching خراش *escape without even a scratch* صاف بچ جانا harsh noise produced thus خراش کی آواز scratching خراش ڈالنا، کھرچنا، کریدنا starting line in a race وہ لکیر جہاں سے دوڑ شروع ہو، دوڑ کا نقطۂ آغاز *start from scratch*, start from the beginning without any previous assets (کسی کے) کسی پہلی چیز کے بغیر شروع کرنا *come up to scratch* حسب منشا کام کرنے کو تیار ہونا *adj.* got ready with whatever is available جو کچھ مل سکے اس سے بنایا ہوا، یونہی جلدی میں بنایا ہوا *a scratch team* یونہی جلدی میں بنی ہوئی ٹیم *a scratch dinner* جو کچھ موجود ہو اس سے جلدی جلدی تیار کیا ہوا کھانا

scratchy (*skrach*-i) *adj.* (of writing or drawing) done carelessly یونہی سا لکھا (یا کھینچا) ہوا، گھسیٹا ہوا (of a pen) making a scratching noise خراش کی آواز دینے والا

scrawl (skrawl) *v.t.* & *i.* write hurriedly گھسیٹنا، شکستہ لکھنا draw thus یونہی گھسیٹنا *n.* scrawled writing بڑی جلدی میں لکھا ہوا، شکستہ تحریر

scream (skreem) *v.t.* & *i.* cry (*with* fear or pain) in a shrill, loud voice چیخ مارنا *scream with laughter*, laugh very noisily بڑے زور سے قہقہہ لگانا *scream* (*something*), say (it) in a shrill, loud voice اونچی تیکھی آواز سے کہنا *screaming wind* بڑے زور سے سائیں سائیں کرنے والی آندھی *n.* shrill, loud cry زور کی چیخ such noise اونچی تیکھی آواز والا شور

screech (skreech) *v.t.* & *i.* give a low but harsh scream ناگوار آواز سے چیخنا (of owls, monkeys, persons) scream harshly in anger غصے میں چڑچڑ یا چیں چیں کرنا، چیخنا **screech-owl** *n.* barn-owl زور سے چیخنے والا الّو، گھگو one predicting evil برائی کی پیشین گوئی کرنے والا

screen (skreen) *n.* movable, folding framework used as a curtain ٹٹی، چلمن partition for shielding from too much heat, light, or draught اوٹ، پردہ anything for shelter or camouflage آڑ، اوٹ، پردہ *smoke-screen*, clouds of smoke sent up to make ships, aircraft, etc., invisible to the enemy دھوئیں کی اوٹ، دُخانی پردہ frame with wire-gauze to keep out flies, etc. *screen-door* جالی والا دروازہ *screen-window* جالی والا دروازہ (وغیرہ) جالی والی کھڑکی sieve for coal, etc کوئلے (وغیرہ) کی چھلنی white surface for projecting films on to it سکرین، پردۂ فلم، پردہ (*the screen*), moving pictures collectively فلمی دُنیا *adj.* of films فلمی *screen star*, filmstar فلمی ستارہ، اداکار، *screen play* فلم کا (یا کی) فلمی کہانی *v.t.* hide from view with a screen کے آگے پردہ لگا دینا provide a shelter thus کی آڑ میں کر دینا shield from punishment, etc. سے بچانا provide (doors, windows, a house, etc.) with wire-gauze frames (پر یا میں) جالی والے دروازے (وغیرہ) لگانا separate (coal) into different sizes by passing through a screen چھلنی میں سے گزار کر موٹا اور باریک کوئلہ الگ الگ کرنا sift and investigate (person) کے کردار کی چھان بین کرنا *The Martial Law regime set up screening committees and dispensed with the services of a number of high-ranking government officials* مارشل لائی حکومت نے چھان بین کرنے والی کمیٹیاں مقرر کر کے بڑے سرکاری افسروں کو ملازمت سے برطرف کر دیا

two screens

screw (skrew) *n.* threaded metal peg پیچ anything for pressing, etc., twisted like a screw (کوئی سا) شکنجہ *put the screw on* (*someone*), force him (*to do* something) کو شکنجے میں کسنا، شکنجے میں کس کر کام لینا، ستانا، دق کرنا، پریشان کرنا، مروڑی propeller of a ship جہاز کی دھری *air-screw* ہوائی جہاز کی دھری very niggardly person کنجوس، مکھی چوس (colloq.) wages مزدوری، تنخواہ *v. t. & i.* fasten or tighten with screws پیچ لگانا، پیچوں سے کسنا twist round to put (*on* or *off*) مروڑ کر کسنا یا اتارنا exert pressure on (someone *to do* something) پر دباؤ ڈالنا (*Phrases* :) *screw (one's) head round* سر پیچھے کو موڑنا *screw up (one's) eyes* (or *mouth* or *face*), wrinkle the skin round it کو اکٹھا کر کے اس کے گرد جھریاں ڈال لینا *screw up (one's) courage*, banish fear ڈر دور کرنا، ہمت سے کام لینا **screwed** (skrood) *adj.* (also slang) drunk مست، مدہوش، پیے ہوئے **screwdriver** *n.* lever for turning screws پیچ کش **screw-jack** *n.* instrument working with a screw and used for lifting heavy weights جیک

scribble *v.t. & i.* write (*down*) in haste جلدی جلدی گھسیٹنا (of oneself politely) be an author اخبار نویس ہونا، مصنف ہونا make meaningless marks on paper, etc., while thinking or in thoughtless moments بے خیالی میں کاغذ پر یونہی لکیریں مارنا

scribe (skrib) *n.* (Bib.) Jewish jurist یہودی قانون دان، حبر (old use) secretary, clerk کاتب، منشی (old use) professional letter-writer خطوط نویس، منشی author, writer کاتب

scrimmage (*skrim*-ij) *n.* (occasionally *scrummage*) confused struggle دنگا فساد، چھینا جھپٹی *v.i.* take part in it چھینا جھپٹی میں شامل ہونا

script (skript) *n.* handwriting دستی تحریر type imitating handwriting دستی تحریر جیسا ٹائپ (abbr. of) manuscript (*of* radio talk or film play) *script of talk* ریڈیائی تقریر کا مسوّدہ part of a dialogue assigned to an actor ڈرامے میں کسی اداکار کے حصّے کے الفاظ examinee's written answer امتحان میں جواب کا پرچہ، کاپی **scripter** *n.* (see *Addenda*)

scripture (*skrip*-chĕ*) *n.* (*pl.*) (*the Scriptures*) the revealed books الہامی کتابیں (pl.): (*the scripture*), (for Christians), the Bible انجیل study of the Bible انجیل کا مُطالعہ **scriptural** *adj.* of (or based on) the Scriptures الہامی کتابوں کا (یا) الہامی کتابوں پر مبنی

scroll (skrohl) *n.* roll of paper, etc., for writing on لپٹا ہوا کاغذ، طومار، سجل book written on a scroll طومار، سجل

scrub (skrub) *v.t. & i.* (-bb-) clean by rubbing hard رگڑ رگڑ کر صاف کرنا clean (floor, etc.) with soap and water rubbed on it with a stiff brush (called *scrubbing-brush*) (فرش) صابن اور پانی لگا کر صاف کرنا *n.* stunted trees جھاڑ جھنکار land covered with them جھاڑ جھنکاڑ والا علاقہ **scrubby** (*skrub*-i) *adj.* stunted (animal or plant) پست (جانور یا پودا) insignificant (person) بے حیثیت شخص

scrum (skrum), **scrummage** (*skrum*-ij) *n.* (in Rugger) mass of all forwards with ball on the ground in the middle رگبی فٹ بال میں اگلے تمام کھلاڑیوں کا میدان کے وسط میں پڑی ہوئی گیند کے گرد اجتماع

scruple (*skroo*-pĕl) *n.* uneasiness of conscience ضمیر کی خلش hesitation caused by it ضمیر کی خلش کے باعث تذبذب *have no scruples about* (something or *doing* it) (پر) ضمیر کی کوئی خلش نہ ہونا *v.t.* (*scruple to do something*), have scruples about doing it (پر) ضمیر کی خلش ہونا (یا) کے باعث تذبذب ہونا **scrupulous** (*skroop*-ew-lus) *adj.* conscientious even in trifles چھوٹی چھوٹی باتوں میں بھی بڑا محتاط over-attentive to small points of conscience چھوٹی چھوٹی باتوں میں گناہ سے بہت بچنے والا، متشدّد

scrutiny (*skroot*-i-ni) *n.* close examination چھان بین، جانچ پڑتال **scrutinize** (-niz) *v.t.* make a scrutiny of کی جانچ پڑتال کرنا

scuffle (*skuf*-ĕl) *n.* melee دنگا فساد *v.i.* take part in a scuffle دنگا فساد میں حصّہ لینے والا

scull (skull) *n.* oar (as one of a pair) چپّو single oar for propelling کشتی ڈانڈ *v.t.* & *i.* row کشتی کھینا propel کشتی کی سمت متعین کرنا row with one oar at the stern پیچھے بیٹھ کر صرف ایک چپّو سے کشتی چلانا

scullery (*skul*-è-ri) *n.* room for washing kitchen utensils in باورچی خانے کے برتن دھونے کا کمرہ، برتن دھونے کا کمرہ separate place in kitchen for this purpose کھرا **scullion** (*skul*-yĕn) *n.* (old use) cook's boy باورچی خانے کا چھوٹا ملازم

sculpture (*skulp*-chĕ*) *n.* making of statues, etc. سنگ تراشی، سنگتراشی، مجسمہ سازی a piece of such work مجسمہ such work مجسمے *v.t.* & *i.* make a sculpture مجسمہ بنانا decorate with sculpture پر مجسمہ بنانا، مجسّمے سے مزیّن کرنا **sculptor** (*skulp*-tĕ*) *n.* one who makes sculptures سنگ تراش، سنگتراش مجسمہ ساز **sculptural** *adj.* pertaining to sculpture مجسمہ سازی سے متعلق، سنگ تراشانہ

scum (skum) *n.* froth over boiling matter جھاگ worst element (*of* the population, etc.) (کی) گندگی، کی تلچھٹ

scurf (skĕ*f) *n.* flakes of dead skin loosened as new skin grows جلد کی بھوسی these in the head سر کی خشکی، خشکی، بفہ، بفا layer of dirt, etc. (on something) میل (وغیرہ) کی تہہ **scurfy** (*skĕ**-fi) *n.* marked by scurf پپڑی دار، میل کی تہہ والا

scurrilous (*skĕ*-ri-lus) *adj.* obscenely abusive (person or language) گندی (گالیاں)، گندی گالیاں بکنے والا *scurrilous attack on*, violent criticism of پر بڑی سخت نکتہ چینی

scurrility (skĕ-*ril*-i-ti) *n.* scurrilous talk بدزبانی، فحش کلامی scurrilous quality بازاری پن

scurry (*skĕ*-ri) *v.i.* (of children or small animals) run away swiftly چھوٹے چھوٹے قدموں سے تیز بھاگ جانا، جلدی سے کھسک جانا *n.* scurrying تیز روی، جلدی سے کھسک جانا sound of scurrying بھاگ جانے، کھسک جانے، کی آہٹ

scurvy (*skĕ**-vi) *adj.* mean and low (trick, etc.) گھٹیا، کمینگی والا mean and low (fellow) سفلہ، کمینہ *n.* a disease caused by shortage of fresh food فسادِ خون کا ایک مرض، اسقربوط

scuttle (*skut*-èl) *n.* (also (*coal-scuttle*), coal bucket near a fire کوئلوں کی بالٹی opening below water-line (in own ship) to sink it جہاز ڈبونے کے لیے چھید *v.t.* make a hole in (own ship) to sink it for avoiding its capture by the enemy (اپنے جہاز کو) ڈبونے کے لیے اس کے پیندے میں چھید کردینا scurry (*off* or *away*) بھاگ جانا، تیزی سے کھسک جانا، نو دو گیارہ ہو جانا

a coal-scuttle

Scylla (*sil*-a) *n.* name of a rock (lying opposite *Charybdis*) between Italy and Sicily سلّا *between Scylla and Charybdis*, in an awkward situation between dangerous alternatives دوہری مصیبت میں

scythe (sidh) *n.* big sickle-like tool for harvesting بڑی درانتی *v.t.* cut with a scythe بڑی درانتی سے کاٹنا

a peasant with a scythe

sea (see) *n.* expanse of salt water covering the greater part of the earth تری ocean سمندر، بحر a tract of it wholly or partly surrounded by land بحیرہ big wave washing a ship جہاز کے اوپر سے گزرنے والی موج، لہر large amount (*of*) کثرت *a sea* (or *seas*) *of* (*something*), a host of (it) بہت بہت زیادہ *adj.* of the sea بحری، سمندری *on the sea*, (*a*) in ships جہاز پر (*b*) on the seashore ساحل پر *at sea*, (*a*) out of the sight of land خشکی سے دور (*b*) perplexed حیران، سراسیمہ (*c*) astray بھٹکا ہوا *all at sea*, perplexed حیران، پریشان، سراسیمہ *put to sea*, *put out to sea*, (of ship) leave port جہاز کا بندرگاہ سے روانہ ہونا *go to sea*, become a sailor جہازران بننا، جہاز پر نوکری کرلینا *beyond sea, oversea, overseas*, abroad سمندر پار، دوسرے ملکوں میں *the high seas*, beyond the three-mile territorial limit of ملکی پانیوں کی حد سے باہر، کھلا سمندر *the vessel ships a sea*, the ship is washed by a wave لہر جہاز کے اوپر سے ہو کر گزری ہے *seas mountains high* بڑی اونچی لہریں، پہاڑ کی سی لہریں *a heavy* (or *rolling* or *choppy*) *sea* متلاطم، تیز لہریں، طوفانی لہریں *seas of blood* سخت قتل و خون *a sea of upturned faces* اوپر اٹھے ہوئے چہروں کا سمندر **sea air** *n.* healthful seaside air صحت بخش سمندری ہوا **sea-board** *n.* coastal region ساحلی علاقہ **sea-boat** *n.* ship (of good or bad quality) اچھا (یا، برا) جہاز **sea-borne** *adj.* (of trade, etc.) carried in ships جہازوں پر آنے والا مال (وغیرہ) **sea-faring** *adj.* of work or voyages on the sea سمندری، بحری **sea-fight** *n.* sea-battle جہازی، دریا نوردی، بحری لڑائی **sea-front** *n.* part of a town facing the sea شہر کا ساحلی علاقہ **sea-gull** *n.* common seabird with long wings سمندری بگلا، جنگل **sea-legs** *n. pl.* ability to walk on deck of rolling ship ڈولتے جہاز پر چل لینا *get* (*one's*) *sea-legs* ڈولتے جہاز پر چلنے کا عادی ہو جانا **sea-level** *n.* level of the sea surface used as zero-point for reckoning height of land or depth of sea سطح سمندر

sea-lion *n.* large Pacific seal (which see) بحری شیر، بحرِ الکاہل کا بڑا دریائی بچھڑا

a sea-lion

seaman *n.* sailor ملاح navigation expert ماہر جہازران **seamanship** *n.* skill in navigating جہازرانی کی مہارت **sea-port** *n.* town with a harbour بندرگاہ والا شہر **sea-rover** *n.* pirate سمندری لٹیرا، سمندری ڈاکو **seashore** *n.* coast ساحل **seasick** *adj.* sick from the motion of a rolling ship جس کا جی جہاز میں متلائے **sea-side** *adj*. by the sea ساحلی شہر سمندر کے کنارے کا *n*. coastal town, etc. **sea-wall** *n*. embankment for checking encroachment by the sea سمندری پشتہ (وغیرہ) **sea-way** *n*. open water کھلا سمندر **seaweed** *n*. plant growing in the sea or the rocks washed by it سمندری پودا **seaworthy** *adj*. (of ships) fit for a sea-voyage سمندری سفر کے قابل strong مضبوط **sea-worthiness** *n*. سمندری سفر کے قابل ہونا **seaward** *adj*. & *adv*. towards the sea (کی) طرف (کا) سمندر **seawards** *adv*. سمندر کی طرف

seal *n*. piece of wax (on a packet, etc.) stamped with a design (لاکھ کی) مہر piece of lead (usu. thus stamped) on a package سکے کی مہر piece of metal with a design to be stamped on wax or lead مہر guarantee ضمانت *under the seal of* (*something* or *someone*) ضمانت کے ساتھ sea-animal hunted for its fur سیل، دَریائی بچھڑا *v.t.* put a seal on مہر لگانا stamp a seal (یا سکے) پر مہر لگانا لاکھ *sealed pattern*, officially approved pattern (of something) منظور شدہ نمونہ close (a jar, crack, etc.) tightly بند کرنا make (something) airtight میں سے ہوا خارج کر کے بند کر دینا، ہوا روک دینا settle (a bargain) سودا چکانا **sealed** (seeld) *adj*. having a wax seal put on it مہر لگی ہوئی having a lead seal on it سکہ بند (of fate, etc.) decided فیصلہ شدہ *sealed pattern*, approved official pattern of equipment, etc., for supply by contractors فیصلہ شدہ نمونہ، سرکاری نمونہ mysterious سربستہ *It is a sealed book to me*, I do not know anything about this matter میرے لیے یہ ایک سربستہ راز ہے **sealing-wax** *n*. kind of wax used in sealing letters, packets, etc. (مہر لگانے کی) لاکھ

seam (seem) *n*. line where two edges are sewn together سیون any line looking like a seam درز، شگاف comparative thin layer (of something) separating thicker layers of rock, etc. پرت، طبقہ *v.t.* mark (face, etc.) with (scars, wrinkles, etc.) پر جھریاں یا نشان (وغیرہ) ڈالنا *face seamed with wrinkles* جھریوں والا چہرہ mark (something) with fissures میں شگاف ڈالنا **seamstress, sempstress** (*sem*-stres) *n*. woman who earns a living by sewing درزن **seamy** (*see*-mi) *adj*. showing seams جس میں سیون نظر آئے *the seamy side of*, inside of a garment سلا ہوا کپڑا اندر کی طرف سے *the seamy side of life*, miseries and crimes of life or people involved in them زندگی کے تاریک گوشے

seance (*say*-ahns) meeting of spiritualists for the supposed calling up of spirits through the help of a medium رُوحوں سے باتیں کرنے والا حلقہ، حاضرات

sear (*see*-ĕ*) *v.t.* burn the surface with a heated iron داغنا، جھلس دینا make (someone's heart) hard (کا دل) پتھر کر دینا

search (sĕ*ch) *v.t.* & *i.* look (*for* someone) (کو) ڈھونڈنا، (کی) تلاش کرنا explore (a house or someone *for* something) کی تلاشی لینا try to find (*out* the truth, etc.) پانے کی کوشش کرنا probe (one's heart, a problem, etc.) کی گہرائیوں کو ٹٹولنا، کا جائزہ لینا (of wind, etc.) go into every part of کے ہر حصے میں پہنچ جانا *n*. quest (*of*) کی جستجو، کی تلاش *go in search of* کی تلاش میں نکلنا searching تلاشی **searching** *adj*. (of wind, test, look, etc.) going into every part ہر جگہ جانے والا (یا) ہر طرح کا **searchlight** *n*. strong beam of electric light for detecting the enemy, etc. سرچ لائٹ، (برقی روشنی کی) تیز شعاعیں **search-warrant** *n*. official authority to police for searching someone's house, etc. وارنٹ تلاشی

season (*seez*-ĕn) *n*. one of the climatic divisions of the year موسم *the rainy season* برسات suitable period (*of* sale, a game, or something else) (کا) موسم، (کے) دن، (کا) زمانہ، (کا) سیزن *in season*, (of a thing) easily available at ordinary price موسم کا *out of season*, not so بے موسم، بے موسما *in season and out of season*, at all times of the year ہر زمانے میں، ہر موسم میں *for a season*, (old use) for a while تھوڑی دیر کے لیے *close season*, when something may not be hunted (کسی جانور کے) شکار کی بندش کا موسم open season (کسی جانور کے) شکار کی اجازت کا موسم *season ticket*, ticket for repeated journeys over a long period موسمی ٹکٹ period (*in* a town) of social activities (شہر میں) رونق کا زمانہ *v.t.* & *i.* bring (wood, etc.) into a condition suitable for use اچھی حالت میں لانا، پختہ کرنا (of experience, etc.) bring (soldier, etc.) into tip-top condition تجربہ کار بنانا flavour (food) (with salt, spices, etc.) میں مسالا ڈالنا، کو نمک مرچ لگانا **seasonable** *adj*. (of the weather) of the kind usual in that particular season (موسم) مناسب opportune باموقع، برمحل **seasonal** *adj*. happening at certain seasons or changing with them موسمی **seasoning** *n*. salt, spices, condiments, etc., adding flavour to food مسالا

seat (seet) *n*. something to sit on نشست نشست گاہ، نشستگاہ part of a chair, etc., on which one sits سیٹ part of the body resting on it سُرین part of the trousers, etc., covering this portion of the body سیٹ manner of sitting بیٹھنے کا طریقہ، انداز نشست place in which one is entitled to sit (in Parliament, railway train, etc.) نِشَست centre or headquarters (*of*) مَرکز، عِلمی مَرکز *a seat of learning*, university, etc. صَدر مَقام *the seat of government*, capital دَارُالحکُومَت (*one's*) *country seat*, large country-house with landed property حَویلی، دیہاتی حَویلی اور زَمین کے لیے *v.t.* (of a room) have seats for (some number) کے لیے نِشَستیں رَکھنا cause to sit بِٹھانا (in the phrases:) *seat* (*oneself*), *be seated*, sit down بَیٹھنا.

sec (sek) *adj.* (of wine) dry پھیکی (شراب)

secede (si-*seed*) *v.i.* withdraw from membership سے اَلگ ہونا، کی رُکنِیَت چھوڑنا، سے قَطعِ تَعَلُّق کر لینا **secession** (si-*sesh*-en) *n.* act of seceding عَلٰحِدَگی، اِنقِطاع

seclude (si-*klood*) *v.t.* keep (oneself, or someone) aloof اَلگ رَکھنا، تنہائی میں رَکھنا *lead a secluded life* گوشہ گُزینی کی زِندَگی گُزارنا **secluded** *adj.* lonely (spot, life, etc.) اَلگ تھلگ (جگہ)، گوشہ گُزینی یا عُزلَت گُزینی کی (زِندَگی) **seclusion** (sik-*klooh*-en) *n.* act of secluding اَلگ تھلگ کرنا secluded place تنہائی، خَلوَت، اَلگ تھلگ جگہ retirement گوشہ نشینی، گوشہ گُزینی، عُزلَت گُزینی *live in seclusion* گوشہ نشینی اِختیار کرنا

second (*sek*-und) *adj.* next after the first دُوسرا، ثانی، دُوُم *second childhood*, dotage بڑا بُڑھاپا *second class* (*a*) a category of seats for rail journey (abbr. II or 2nd) سیکنڈ، دُوسرا (*b*) (also *second division*), examinee's category of result سیکنڈ ڈِویژن، سیکنڈ کلاس (*c*) inferior گھٹیا *second lieutenant* (abbr. *2nd Lt.* or *2nd Lieut.*, and courteously called a *lieutenant*) سیکنڈ لفٹیننٹ، چھوٹا لفٹین *second nature*, habit عادت، فِطرَتِ ثانیہ *second sight*, faculty of seeing future or distant events as if present غَیب بِینی *Queen Elizabeth II*, (pr. Queen Elizabeth the second) مَلِکہ اِلزَبتھ دُوُم one like دُوسرا، ثانی، جَیسا subordinate or inferior (*to*) سے گھٹیا، سے پَست تَر، سے کَمتَر، سے فَروتَر *n.* one who wins a second place in a competition, etc. دُوسرے دَرَجے پر آنے والا شخص one who supports another in boxing or duel مَدَدگار، حامی (*pl.*) goods below the best quality دُوسرے دَرَجے کا مال sixtieth part of a minute, or a degree سیکنڈ، ثانیہ *the second hand*, (of a watch, etc.) the hand indicating the seconds سیکنڈوں والی سُوئی sixtieth part of a degree of angle ثانیہ، ۱/۶۰ دَرَجہ (colloq.) a short while تھوڑی سی دیر، ذرا *v.t.* support the fighter (in boxing or duel) کی حمایت کرنا speak in support of (someone's motion, etc.) کی تائید کرنا (military use) (pr. si-*kond*) remove (officer) temporarily from his ordinary duty and give him a special post فوجی اَفسر کو عارِضی طَور پر دُوسری جگہ لگانا **second-best** *adj.* next after the best دُوسرے نمبر کا (یا پر) **second-hand** *adj.* resold after use by someone پُرانا، مُستَعمَلہ، سیکنڈ ہینڈ *second-hand books* پُرانی کِتابیں (of news, knowledge, experience, etc.) not first-hand; not based on personal observation, etc. سُنی سُنائی **second-rate** *adj.* inferior گھٹیا

secondary *adj.* following the chief or the first ثانَوی، دُوسرے دَرَجے کا *of secondary importance*, not so important نِسبَتہً کَم اَہَم *secondary education*, education between the primary (the Middle in Pakistan) and the university stages ثانَوی تَعلیم *Board of Secondary Education* مَجلِسِ تَعلیمِ ثانَوی *Secondary examination*, former Matriculation ثانَوی اِمتحان، دَسویں کا اِمتحان *Higher Secondary examination*, the former Intermediate exam. اَعلٰی ثانَوی، اِنٹر **secondly** *adv.*, in the second place دُوسرے، دُوُم، ثانِیاً

secret (*seek*-ret) *adj.* unknown to others خُفیہ hidden پوشیدہ، پِنہاں، مَخفی secluded (place) اَلگ تھلگ، مَخفی secretive (person) اِخفائے راز کا دِلدادہ، کچھ نہ بتانے والا *n.* something secret راز، بھید *keep a secret*, not tell anyone else راز کی بات کسی سے نہ کہنا، مَخفی رَکھنا *in the secret*, among the few who know رازدانوں میں سے *in secret*, secretly خُفیہ real but not widely known cause اَصلی بات، تحقیقی سَبَب، راز *the secret of* (*someone's*) *success* (کی) کامیابی کا راز **secretly** *adv.* in a secret manner پوشیدہ، مَخفی طَور پر **secrecy** (*seek*-re-si) *n.* keeping things secret مَخفی رَکھنا، پِنہاں رَکھنا ability to keep things secret رازداری state of being (kept) secret اِخفا **secretive** (si-*kree*-tiv) *adj.* in the habit of keeping things secret اِخفائے راز کا دِلدادہ reserved کَم گو، دیر آشنا **secretary** (*sek*-re-ta-ri) *n.* employee charged with the duty of entering into correspondence on behalf of his employers سیکریٹری، دَبیر، مُعتَمَد *private secretary*, person (usu. young pretty girl) employed to take dictation, etc., from a boss پرائیویٹ سیکریٹری، مُعتَمَدِ خُصُوصی *honorary secretary*, one doing this work in an honorary capacity آنریری سیکریٹری، مُعتَمَدِ اِعزازی (in the U.K., etc.) (also *Secretary of State*), Minister وَزِیر govt. official in charge of a department مُعتَمَد *Chief Secretary* مُعتَمَدِ اَعلٰی **secretarial** (-*tay*-ri-ĕl) *adj.* of a secretary مُعتَمَد کا pertaining to a secretary's work مُنشِی، مُتَصَدِّی کا (کام) **secretariat, secretariate** (-*tay*-ri-at) *n.* staff of a secretary (or secretaries) مُعتَمَدی، سیکریٹریٹ، لاٹ صاحِب کا دَفتَر

secrete (si-*kreet*) *v.t.* put in a hidden place مَخفی جگہ رَکھنا، چھپا رَکھنا produce by secretion اِفراز کرنا، رُطُوبَت نِکالنا **secretion** (si-*kreesh*-en) *n.* sorting out of some fluid (from blood or sap) by an animal or plant اِفراز fluid secreted اِفراز، ریزِش، رُطُوبَت concealing اِخفا **secretive** (-*ree*-) *adj.*

needlessly reserved کم گو، اِخفائے راز کا دلدادہ

sect (sekt) *n.* unorthodox religious group فرقہ، مذہبی فرقہ، مسلک **sectarian** (sek-*tay*-ri-ĕn) *adj.* pertaining to a sect or sects فرقہ وارانہ *n.* one belonging to a sect (کسی) فرقے کا پیرو

section (*sek*-shĕn) *n.* part (of something) cut off from the rest of it ٹکڑا، قطعہ، قطع component part حصّہ part of a community living separately حصّہ، طبقہ sub-division of a law دفعہ *section 144*, (pr. *sek*-shèn wun-foh*-*foh**) sub-division of a class (or form) of students in a school, etc. فریق division of a piece of writing فصل، حصّہ (also *cross-section*) something represented as if cut straight through تراش، کاٹ **sectional** *adj.* of a section or sections قطعے (یا حصّے یا کاٹ) سے متعلّق communal فرقہ وارانہ made in sections الگ الگ ہو جانے والا، جدا ہو جانے والے ٹکڑوں پر مشتمل

sector (*sek*-tĕ*) *n.* part of a circle, sphere or ellipse قطعہ one of the sub-divisions of an area under military control علاقہ، انتظامی حصّہ *The Martial Law Administration has divided Pakistan into many sectors* مارشل لاء کی حکومت نے پاکستان کو متعدد انتظامی حصّوں میں تقسیم کیا ہے

a sector (sense 1)

secular (*sek*-ew-le*) *adj.* lay (as distinct from *religious*) لادینی، غیر مذہبی **secularism** *n.* doctrine separating politics, etc., from religion غیر مذہبیت، لادینیت

secure (si-*kew*-è*) *adj.* safe (*from* or *against* danger, etc.) محفوظ، بے خطر firmly fixed مضبوطی سے بندھا یا لگا ہوا *v.t.* obtain حاصل کرنا make safe (*from* or *against*) سے محفوظ کرنا make safe (*with*) کے ذریعے مضبوط بنانا make fast مضبوطی سے لگانا keep (prisoner, thing, etc.) so as not to let slip اچھی طرح قابو میں کر لینا **securely** *adv.* مضبوطی سے، حفاظت سے **security** (si-*kew*-ri-ti) *n.* secure state of feeling اطمینان stability پکا ہونا safety حفاظت surety, pledge ضمانت، کفالت *give* (or *offer*) *security for* کی ضمانت دینا document, etc., comprising it وثیقہ certificate of stocks or shares ہنڈی

sedan (se-*dan*) *n.* (also *sedan-chair*), (old use) covered chair carried on poles and formerly used as a vehicle پینس، پالکی closed motor-car بند کار

a sedan-chair

sedate (si-*dayt*) *adj.* calm and composed (person, manners, etc.) سنجیدہ، متین

sedative (*sed*-a-tiv) *adj.* tending to soothe the nerves مسکّن *n.* such a drug مسکّن

sedentary (*sed*-ent-a-ri) *adj.* (of work) done sitting down in a chair, etc. بیٹھے رہنے کا (of a person) not moving about much; sitting down بیٹھا رہنے والا، نشست

sediment (*sed*-i-ment) *n.* dregs تلچھٹ، دُرد mud settling down under water گاد

sedition (si-*dish*-èn) *n.* words or actions inciting to rebellion بغاوت انگیز تقریر (یا اقدام) **seditious** (se-*dish*-us) *adj.* بغاوت انگیز، باغیانہ

seduce (si-*dews*) *v.t.* persuade (someone) to commit sin or crime گمراہ کرنا، ورغلانا، بہکانا، پھسلانا (esp.) persuade a woman to surrender her chastity to one عصمت لٹانے پر آمادہ کرنا **seducer** *n.* گمراہ کرنے والا **seduction** (si-*duk*-shĕn) *n.* جرم (یا گناہ) کی ترغیب **seductive** *adj.* charming and tempting نہایت دل فریب، زہد شکن، توبہ شکن

sedulous (*sed*-ew-lus) *adj.* persevering (person) مستقل، ثابت قدم (something) persisted in deliberately باقاعدگی سے کیا ہوا

see *n.* district under the control of a bishop اسقف کا علاقہ *the Holy see*, the Papacy پاپائی *v.t. & i.* (*see, saw, seen*) look at دیکھنا have the power of sight بصارت رکھنا understand سمجھنا، غور کرنا، کو ادراک ہونا *see the point*, understand it بات سمجھ جانا، نکتہ پا لینا *I see*, I have understood میں سمجھ گیا *you see*, you must have known (or understood) it by now آپ جانتے ہی ہیں (*Phrases* :) *see about* (*something*), arrange to get it done کا انتظام کرنا *see after* (*something*), attend to it کا خیال کرنا *see into* (*something*), inquire into it کی تہہ کو پہنچنا *see* (*someone*) *off*, go to (someone's) starting-point to bid him farewell کو چھوڑنے جانا *see* (*someone*) *out*, go with (him) to the door کسی کو دروازے تک چھوڑنے جانا *see through* (*someone or something*) be not taken in by کو خوب سمجھنا، کے فریب میں نہ آنا، سے دھوکا نہ کھانا *see* (*someone or something*) *through* کے معاملے میں آخر تک کسی کا ساتھ دینا *see to* (*one's*) *business*, mind (one's) business اپنے کام سے کام رکھنا *see to it that*, make sure that دیکھنا تمہیں، خیال رکھنا کہ مبادا *see the back of* (*someone*), *see the last of* (*someone*) سے پیچھا چھوٹنا *see double*, ایک کے دو دو نظر آنا *see red*, be enraged غصّے سے لال پیلا ہونا *see life*, have a wide experience of the world دنیا دیکھنا *see a joke*, enjoy it لطیفے سے لطف اندوز ہونا *to have seen service*, to be a veteran کار آزمودہ ہونا *see eye to eye* (*with someone, in something*), agree with (him on that point) سے متعلّق ہم خیال ہونا *see the light* (*of the day*), come into being عالمِ وجود میں آنا **seeing** *n.* sight بینائی، بصارت exercising this power دیکھنا ■ To see is the general word. To **stare at** is to look hard; to **perceive**, begin to see something unexpected; to **notice**, pay attention to to **remark**, take notice of ; to **gaze** in wonderment at : to **observe** in detail attentively ; to **behold** something worthwhile : to **examine**, study in detail ; to **view** something deliberately : to **distinguish**-between several similar things : to **descry** with displeasure ; to **discern** with effort and judgment : to **espy** suddenly something hidden ; to **note** something already seen ; to **watch**, keep looking at.

seed part of a plant from which a new plant grows بیج، دانہ origin (*of* something) اَصل کی *run* (or *go*) *to seed*, (*a*) (of a plant) begin to produce seed پودے کا بیج دینے لگنا (*b*) grow careless of one's clothes, etc. بہیئت کذائی بنا لینا *v.t.* & *i.* (of plants) stop flowering and begin to produce seed (پودے کا) بیج دینے لگنا take the seed out of (fruit, etc.) سے بیج نکالنا arrange a tournament in such a way that the best players do not meet in its earlier matches بڑے جوڑ آخر میں رکھنا **seeded** (*see*-did) *adj*. (of players, esp. of tennis) of proved worth (and hence left over for playing against an equally strong opponent in the last round) شاندار اور آزمودہ کھلاڑی **seed-corn** *n*. corn preserved as seed بیج کے لیے رکھا ہوا غلہ **seedling** *n*. young plant raised from a seed پنیری، پنیری کا پودا، تخمی پودا **seedsman** *n*. one who deals in seeds بیج بیچنے والا، تخم فروش **seedy** (*see*-di) *adj*. shabby بھدا، ہیئت کذائی والا (colloq.) unwell (person or condition) ناسماز

seek *v.t.* & *i.* (*seek, sought, sought*) look for تلاش کرنا try to find ڈھونڈنا want to have مانگنا چاہنا، اجازت چاہنا *seek for*, look for ڈھونڈنا *seek to do* (*something*), try to do (it) کی کوشش کرنا *be sought after*, (*a*) be wanted مطلوب ہونا (*b*) be much in demand کی بہت مانگ ہونا *play at hide and seek* (*with*) سے آنکھ مچولی کھیلنا

seem *v.i.* create the impression of being محسوس ہونا، لگنا *It seems to me as if* مجھے تو یوں لگتا ہے جیسے appear (*to be*) نظر آنا، معلوم ہونا **seeming** *adj*. apparent though not necessarily real دیکھنے میں تو، بظاہر، بظاہر تو **seemly** (*seem*-li) *adj*. proper and decorous (behaviour) مناسب، موزوں، ٹھیک **seemliness** *n*. being seemly ; propriety مناسب ہونا، موزونیت

seep *v. i.* percolate رسنا، ٹپکنا **seepage** (*seep*-ej) *n*. seeping رسنا amount seeping جو رس کر آئے oozing out of water through land "سیم"

seer (*see*-ĕ*) *n*. one who sees into the future غیب دان، روشن ضمیر Pakistan unit of weight سیر

seesaw (*see*-saw) *n*. rocking plank for children to play on ہنڈولا this as a children's

a seesaw

game جھولا جھولی *v.i.* move up and down on a seesaw جھولا جھولی کھیلنا oscillate جھولنا vascillate متلون مزاج ہونا

seethe (seedh) *v. i.* (of liquids) boil and bubble کھولنا be agitated (*with* anger, discontent, etc.) ہیجان میں آنا، اضطراب کی حالت میں آنا

segment (*seg*-ment) *n*. part cut (or marked) ٹکڑا، قطعہ *segment of a circle* دائرے کا قطعہ part (*of*) کا حصہ

segregate (*seg*-re-gayt) *v. t.* separate الگ کرنا، علیحدہ کر دینا **segregation** (-*gay*-shĕn) *n*. keeping (*of* races, sexes, patients, etc.) separate علیحدگی، ایک دوسرے سے جدا رکھنا

seismic (*sīz*-mik) *adj*. of earthquake زلزلے سے متعلق، زلزلیاتی **seismograph** (*sīz*-) *n*. instrument for recording the intensity and direction of an earthquake زلزلہ پیما، زلزلہ نگار **seismology** (sīz-*mol*-o-ji) *n*. science which studies earthquakes علم زلزلہ، زلزلیات

seize (seez) *v. t.* & *i.* take hold of forcibly or suddenly پر قبضہ کرنا، زبردستی لے لینا attach (property) in payment of debt قرق کرنا، ضبط کرنا grasp *seize (someone) by the collar* کی گردن دبوچنا (of machinery) be jammed by friction or excessive heat جام ہو جانا capture پر قبضہ کرنا take prisoner گرفتار کرنا comprehend and make use of سے فوراً فائدہ اٹھانا، سے استفادہ کرنا *seize an opportunity* موقع سے فوراً فائدہ اٹھانا *seize upon an idea* نئے خیال سے استفادہ کرنا

seizure (*seezh*-ĕ*) *n*. seizing قبضہ، گرفت، گرفتاری ضبطی، قرقی fit of (brain or heart) disease دورہ، (دل کا) دورہ

seldom (*sel*-dum) *adv*. rarely کبھی کبھار، شاذ و نادر

select (si-*lekt*) *v.t.* pick out by preference ; chose چننا، منتخب کرنا *adj*. chosen thus چیدہ، منتخب، عمدہ of or for chosen persons مخصوص **selection** *n*. selecting انتخاب *natural selection*, survival of the fittest بقائے اصلح carefully made collection انتخاب، چنی ہوئی چیزیں number of things from which to select جن میں سے انتخاب کیا جا سکے **selective** (se-*lek*-tiv) *adj*. able to select انتخاب کا اہل characterized by selection خاص چیزوں تک محدود، چیدہ چیدہ **selector** *n*. one who selects (esp., a team) چننے والا ، انتخاب کنندہ

[1]**self** *n*. (pl: *selves* pr. selvz) one's own person نفس، آنا، خود، ذات its dignity خودی ego انا one's special characteristics کردار، شمائل (*one's*) *better self*, انسان کا برتر کردار self-interest ذاتی اغراض *one with no thought of self* بے غرض، بے لوث **selfish** (*sel*-fish) *adj*. self-interested, lacking consideration for others

selfishly *adv.* خودغرضی سے ۔ خود مطلبی، خود غرض، مطلب پرستانہ **selfishness** *n.* خود غرضی، مطلب پرستی **selfless** *adj.* incapable of selfishness بے غرض، بے غرضانہ، بے لوث
[2]**self** *pref.* of its own ; automatic آپ سے آپ، خود بخود *self-taught*, taught without the help of a teacher استاد کی مدد کے بغیر in relation to oneself اپنا، خود **self-accused** *adj.* one who has been accused by himself آپ پھنسا ہوا، خود گرفتہ **self-accusation** *n.* آپ پھنسنا **self-assertion** *n.* asserting one's own point without evidence آپ ہی زور دینا point thus asserted بے دلیل دعوے **self-centred** *adj.* interested mainly in oneself اپنے آپ میں مگن **self-coloured** *adj.* of the same colour all over یکساں رنگ والا، بالکل ہم رنگ **self-command** *n.* control over one's own feelings جذبات پر قابو **self-conceited** *adj.* vain خودبین **self-conscious** *adj.* shy خود آگاہ، شرمیلا **self-consciousness** *n.* خود آگاہی **self-control** *n.* control of (sexual or baser) emotions ضبط نفس **self-contained** (-taynd) *adj.* (of a house) complete for a family and having private entrance بالکل الگ (of a person) reserved اپنے آپ میں مگن **self-denial** *n.* refusal to yield to one's natural impulses نفس کشی **self-determination** *n.* a people's right to decide the type of government they shall have حق خود اختیاری **self-evident** evident without proof صاف ظاہر، بدیہی **self-government** *n.* right to govern oneself independently (in certain matters) حکومت خود اختیاری **self-governing** *adj.* (of territory, etc.) enjoying self-government خود مختار **self-important** *adj.* self-conceited برخود غلط **self-indulgent** *adj.* fond of one's own comfort, etc. خودبین تن پرور **self-interest** *n.* devotion to selfish ends خود غرضی، مطلب پرستی **self-interested** *adj.* خود غرض، مطلب پرست **self-made** *adj.* (person) succeeding by his own efforts, **self-possessed** *adj.* calm and confident ٹھنڈے دل و دماغ کا **self-possession** *n.* ٹھنڈا مزاج **self-preservation** *n.* protecting oneself from extinction, etc. حفظ نفس **self-realization** *n.* self-knowledge as a moral principle خود شناسی، خودی **self-regard** *n.* self-interest خود غرضی، مطلب پرستی **self-reliance** *n.* confidence in own ability خود اعتمادی **self-reliant** *adj.* confident of own ability خود اعتماد **self-respect** *n.* consciousness of living a respectful life خودداری **self-righteous** *adj.* believing in one's own goodness زہد فروشی، تقوے فروشی **self-sacrifice** *n.* sacrificing personal interests for the sake of others قربانی، ایثار **self-same** *adj.* (*the self-same person*) (the) same (person) ہو بہو، بعینہٖ، بجنسہٖ **self-seeking** *n.* selfishness خود غرضی، مطلب پرستانہ خود غرضی **self-sown** *adj.* (of plant) growing by itself without being sown by someone خودرو **self-starter** *n.* part of machine for starting it without turning the crank-handle چال بٹن **self-styled** *adj.* calling oneself such without having a right to do so خود ساختہ **self-sufficient** *adj.* needing no help from others خود کفیل presumptuous برخود غلط **self-supporting** *adj.* earning one's livelihood اپنے پاؤں پر کھڑا **self-taught** *adj.* learning or learnt without a teacher's help خود آموز **self-will** *n.* obstinacy خودسری، خودرائی **self-willed** *adj.* obstinate خودسر، خود رائے، ضدی

sell (sel) *v.t.* & *i.* (sell, sold, sold) dispose of (something) for money بیچنا، فروخت کرنا keep for sale کی تجارت کرنا (of goods) be sold بکنا betray (something) for reward, etc. صلے کی خاطر غداری کرنا *sell (something off)*, sell it at cheap rates بیچ ڈالنا، بیچ کھانا سستا لگانا *sell out*, sell one's share اپنا حصہ بیچ ڈالنا *sell (someone) up*, sell his goods to realise money owed by him کا مال بیچ کر روپیہ وصول کرنا **seller** *n.* one who sells بیچنے والا، فروخت کنندہ (in combinations) فروش *bookseller* کتاب فروش، کتب فروش that which is sold بکاؤ، بکنے والا، فروخت ہونے والا *a best-seller*, a book which is sold in large numbers ہاتھوں ہاتھ بکنے والی کتاب **sellers' market** *n.* market conditions when goods are scarce and sellers can raise the prices of their wares بائع کی منڈی

selvage, selvedge (*sel*-vij) *n.* edge of cloth so firmly woven as not to unravel کنی، کور

selves (selvz) *pron.* (pl. of *self* in *pronouns* ; as *themselves*) خود آپ

semantics (si-*mant*-iks) *n. pl.* (used as sing.) branch of philology dealing with meanings مفہومیات

semaphore (*sem*-a-foh*) *n.* system of signalling by flags, etc. جھنڈی کے ذریعے اشارہ پرچی اشارہ *v.t.* & *i.* send (messages) by semaphore جھنڈی کے ذریعے اشارہ کرنا، پرچی اشارہ

signalling by semaphore

semblance (*sem*-blans) *n.* likeness مشابہت outward appearance ظاہری شکل صورت guise بھیس *put on semblance of* کا بھیس بدل کر، کی سی شکل بنا کر *not even the semblance of*, not even بالکل نہیں، کی صورت تک نہیں

semen (*seem*-en) *n.* germinal fluid of males نطفہ، منی

semester (se-*mes*-tĕ*) *n.* (U.S.) half of an academic year نصف تعلیمی سال، میقات

semi- (*sem*-i) *pref.* half نصف، نیم، آدھا، آدھ *semi-circle* نصف دائرہ only partly نیم، کسی حد تک *semi-civilized* نیم مہذب *semi-official* نیم سرکاری **semicolon** (*sem*-i-

koh-lĕn) *n.* the punctuation mark سیمی کولن، وقفِ ناقص؛
semi-final *n.* (also *pl.*) the last but one match in a competition سیمی فائنل
seminal (*sem*-i-nĕl) *adj.* of semen نطفی pregnant with consequences معنیٰ خیز
seminar (*sem*-i-nah*) *n.* scholars meeting for the discussion of a problem حلقہ، مباحثہ students discussing thus with a teacher, etc. حلقۂ درس، جماعت **seminary** (*sem*-i-na-ri) *n.* Roman Catholic training centre for priests پادریوں کی درسگاہ (old use) school درسگاہ breeding-ground (*of*) کی جڑ کا اڈا
Semite (*see*-mīt) *n.* person descended from Shem سامی **Semitic** (se-*mit*-ik) *adj.* descended from Shem or having to do with his descendants سامی *n.* the Semitic family of languages سامی اَلسنہ
senate (*sen*-ayt) *n.* of a bicameral Parliament (as in the U.S.A.) سینیٹ، ایوان State council of ancient Rome قدیم روما کی مجلس اعیان، سینیٹ، سینات governing body of university سینیٹ، مجلس جامعہ جامعاتی انتظامیہ **senator** (*sen*-a-tĕ*) *n.* member of a senate سینیٹ کا رکن
send *v.t.* & *i.* (*send, sent, sent*) despatch بھیجنا make بنا دینا *send for* (*someone*), ask him or her to come بلا بھیجنا *send for* (*something*), place order for it منگوانا *send forth*, produce (leaves, etc.) نکالنا *send in* (or *up*), (*one's name, work, etc.*) enter کا داخلہ بھیجنا *send forward, send on,* اپنے آپ سے آگے بھیجنا پہلے بھیجنا *send* (*someone*) *word, send word to* (*someone*), send message to (someone) کو پیغام بھیجنا *send off*, despatch بھیجنا **send-off** *n.* gathering (at railway station, etc.) to bid farewell to a traveller الوداع، الوداعی اجتماع، چھوڑنے جانا *give* (*someone*) *a hearty send-off* کسی کو پرتپاک طور پر چھوڑنے جانا
senile (*see*-nīl) *adj.* of old age بڑھاپے کا، ضعیفی کا showing characteristics of old age سٹھیایا ہوا
senility (se-*nil*-i-ti) *n.* feebleness of old age ضعیفی، سٹھیا جانا
senior (*seen*-i-ĕ*) *adj.* older بڑا، بزرگ higher in status, etc. مقدم، سینیئر (after a name) the older person with the same name بڑا *n.* senior person بزرگ، مقدم **seniority** (see-ni-*o*-ri-ti) *n.* being older بزرگی being senior in status, etc. تقدم، اوّلیت
senor (*sen*-yo*) *n.* (fem. *senora*) Spanish title equivalent to Mr. جناب، صاحب
sensation (sens-*ay*-shĕn) *n.* feeling (*of*) احساس ادراک news, etc., causing a stir سنسنی خیز خبر، سنسنی، ہیجان such stir ہیجان انگیز خبر thrill **sensational** *adj.* causing a stir ہیجان انگیز، سنسنی خیز (of periodicals) presenting sensational news سنسنی خیز، جذباتی
sense (sens) *n.* power (*of* sight, hearing, smell, taste or touch) حس، حاسّہ consciousness (*of*) (کا) احساس appreciation (*of* duty, humour, etc.) حس، احساس، ذوق meaning معنیٰ، مطلب، مفہوم *make sense* با معنیٰ ہونا، معنیٰ رکھنا *It makes no sense*; nonsense یہ بیہودہ بات ہے، یہ بے معنیٰ بات ہے (also *commonsense*), practical wisdom سوجھ بوجھ، عقل *a man of sense* سوجھ بوجھ والا، عقلمند *have sense enough to* (*do*) کی عقل رکھنا (*pl.*) normal state of mind ہوش *in* (*one's*) *senses*, sane ہوش میں *out of* (*one's*) *senses* mad پاگل، مدہوش *bring* (*someone*) *to* (*his*) *senses*, cause (him) to behave properly after foolishness کسی کے حواس ٹھکانے لگانا *come to* (*one's*) *senses*, حواس ٹھکانے لگانا *v.t.* perceive by instinct کا احساس ہونا be vaguely aware of (danger, etc.) (خطرہ) سا محسوس کرنا **senseless** *adj.* stupid بیوقوف، احمق unconscious بیہوش *knock* (*someone*) *senseless* اتنا مارنا کہ بیہوش ہو جائے **sensibility** (sens-i-*bil*-i-ti) *n.* capacity to experience delicate emotion احساس ہونا susceptibility (*to*) (کا) احساس **sensible** (*sens*-i-bĕl) *adj.* expressing good sense معقول، ہوشمندانہ wise عقلمند، ہوشمند، زیرک aware (*of*) سے آگاہ appreciable by the senses کافی محسوس، واضح **sensibly** *adv.* معقولیت سے، ہوشمندی سے **sensitive** (*sens*-i-tiv) *adj.* quick to receive impressions زود حس، اثر پذیر، سریع الاثر *sensitive to* (*something*), (*a*) easily affected by it فوراً محسوس کرنے والا (*b*) easily offended by it کو ناپسند کرنے والا easily offended زود رنج، نازک دماغ (of instruments) able to record small changes حساس، سریع الحس (of photographic film, etc.) affected by light عکس پذیر **sensitivity** (sens-i-*tiv*-i-ti) *n.* being sensitive اثر پذیری **sensitise** (sens-i-tīz) *v.t.* make (photographic film, etc.) sensitive عکس پذیر ہونا **sensory** (*sens*-o-ri) **sensorial** (sens-*oh*-ri-ĕl) *adj.* of the senses حسیاتی **sensual** (*sens*-ew-ĕl, or *sensh*-oo-ĕl) *adj.* (fond) of the pleasures of the senses only شہوانی lustful بوالہوس، ہوس پرست **sensualist** *n.* sensual person
sensuous (*sens*-ew-us) *adj.* of the senses حسیاتی، حواسی، حسّی
sent *v.* (pa. t. & pa. p. of **send,** which see)
sentence (*sent*-ens) *n.* complete group of words containing a subject and a predicate (expressed or understood) جملہ، کلام تام punishment given by a law-court سزا، تعزیر judges'

order containing it محکم سزا، حکم فیصلہ *v.t.* state that (someone) is to be punished in a certain manner سزا کا حکم دینا *sentence (someone) to a term of* (so many years', etc.) *imprisonment, etc.* کسی کو اتنے سال وغیرہ کی سزا کا حکم سنانا **sentențious** (sĕn-*tensh*-us) *adj.* pithy (statement) بلیغ، مجمل (of person) سخن ساز، شاندار رسمی باتیں بنانے والا affecting such style pithy and witty فقرے باز

sentient (*sensh*-i-ent) *adj.* capable of feeling ذی حس

sentiment (*sent*-i-ment) *n.* mental feeling خیال، احساس emotional feeling جذبہ tender feeling تاثیر display of emotion (rather than reason) جذباتیت viewpoint نقطۂ نگاہ، نقطۂ نظر **sentimental** (-*ment*-ĕl) *adj.* full of, moved by or exciting tender-feelings جذباتی *have a sentimental value for someone,* (of something) despite being ordinary in itself be valuable to someone owing to emotional attachment (کسی شے کا) معمولی ہونے کے باوجود کسی کے لیے جذباتی طور پر انمول ہونا **sentimentalist** *n.* sentimental person جذباتی **sentimentality** (-*tal*-i-ti) *n.* جذباتیت

sentinel (*sent*-i-nel) *n.* sentry فوجی پہریدار، سنتری

sentry (*sent*-ri) *n.* (pl. *sentries*) soldier keeping guard فوجی پہریدار، سنتری **sentry-box** *n.* duty-cabin for a sentry سنتری خانہ **sentry-go** *n.* sentry's beat گشت *be on sentry-go* پہرہ ہونا سنتری کی گشت

separate (*sep*-ĕ-rit) *adj.* apart الگ، جدا، علیحدہ not together الگ الگ، جدا جدا، علیحدہ علیحدہ not joined منفصل *v.t.* & *i.* (*sep*-ĕ-rayt) make or become separate (*from*) (سے) الگ ہونا یا کرنا go each one his ownway اپنی اپنی راہ لگنا **separable** *adj.* that which can be separated جو الگ ہو سکے، انفصال پذیر

separation (-*ray*-) *n.* separating or being separated جدائی، علیحدگی، فراق، ہجر، ہجر divorce طلاق estrangement علیحدگی period of separation علیحدگی کی مدت، جدائی کی گھڑیاں **separatism** *n.* opposite of unionism علیحدگی پسندی **separatist** *n.* opposite of unionist علیحدگی پسند

sepia (*see*-pi-a) *adj.* & *n.* dark brown (paint or colour) (سرخی مائل رنگ)

sepoy (*see*-poi) *n.* Indian soldier in the former British Indian army دیسی سپاہی

September (sep-*tem*-bĕ*) *n.* the ninth month of the Western calendar ستمبر

septic (*sep*-tik) *adj.* infected جراثیم زدہ، زہر خونی causing infection مفسد خون، سڑنے والا، زہر خونی کرنے والا putrefied بدبودار، متعفن، عفونت دار *septic tank,* tank for causing sewage to disintegrate سڑنے والی حوضی

septicaemia (sep-ti-*see*-mi-a) *n.* blood-poisoning فسادِ خون

Septuagint *n.* Greek version of the *Old Testament* عہد عتیق کا یونانی ترجمہ، ہفتادی ترجمہ، سبعینی

sepulchre (*sep*-ĕl-kĕ*) *n.* tomb قبر، تربت، مرقد، مزار *the Holy Sepulchre,* the tomb thought to be Christ's مرقد مسیح *whited sepulchre,* hypocrite منافق **sepulchral** (-*pul*-) *adj.* of a sepulchre قبر کا، ضریحی of burial تدفین سے متعلق gloomy and dismal تیرہ و تار، بھیانک *sepulchral voice,* deep and gloomy voice بری ہوئی آواز

sequel (*si*-kwel) *n.* result following انجام، نتیجہ *in the sequel,* later on انجام کار، عاقبۃ الامر concluding portion (of a narrative, etc.) (کہانی وغیرہ کا) انجام، تتمہ، تکملہ

sequence (*see*-kwens) *n.* unbroken series سلسلہ succession تعقیب، سلسلہ *in sequence,* one after another سلسلہ وار، ترتیب وار، یکے بعد دیگرے coming next اگلا حصہ counterpart of a 'scene' in a film فلمی منظر

sequester (see-*kwes*-tĕ*) *v.t.* & *i.* separate (someone) from others الگ کرنا، علیحدہ کر دینا withdraw oneself to a quiet place گوشہ نشین ہو جانا، گوشہ نشینی اختیار کرنا، عزلت گزینی اختیار کرنا **sequestered** (-tĕ*d) *adj.* (esp.) secluded (life) گوشہ نشینی کی (زندگی)

seraglio (se-*rah*-li oh) *n.* harem حرم سرا، حرم

seraph (*se*-raf) *n.* (pl. *seraphs,* or *seraphim*) angel of the highest order فرشتہ، ملک **seraphic** (se-*raf*-ik) *adj.* angelic ملکوتی

sere (*see*-ĕ*) *adj.* withered مرجھایا ہوا *sere leaves* مرجھائے ہوئے پتے *sere-age* سخت بڑھاپا

serenade (se-ri-*nayd*) *n.* outdoor evening music sung or played by a lover beneath his beloved's windows فغانِ نیم شبی، نغمۂ شبینہ *v.t.* & *i.* play a serenade (*to* someone) (کی خاطر) نغمۂ شبینہ گانا یا بجانا، فغانِ نیم شبی کرنا **serenader** *n.* player of a serenade نغمہ سرائے شب

serene (se-*reen*) *adj.* placid پرسکون calm سکون، وقار، متانت متین **serenity** (si-*ren*-i-ti) *n.* سکون، وقار، متانت

serf (sĕ*f) *n.* land slave; labourer bound to and transferred with the land زرعی غلام **serfdom, serfhood** *n.* serf's condition زرعی غلامی such system of land tenure زرعی غلامی کا نظام

serge (sĕ*j) *n.* a kind of durable twilled woollen cloth سرج

sergeant, serjeant (*sah**-jent) *n.* non-commissioned officer in the army immediately above a corporal حوالدار، سارجنٹ police official with rank below that of an inspector سارجنٹ **sergeant-major** *n.* highest non-commissioned rank in the army سارجنٹ میجر، حوالدار میجر، حوالدار اسلحہ **sergeant-at-arms**

n. official in a legislature to keep order سارجنٹ ایٹ آرمز
serial (*se*-ri-ĕl) *adj.* of a series سِلسِلے کا، سِلسِلہ وار *serial number* سِلسِلہ وار نمبر *serial order* ترتیب (of a story, film, etc.) appearing in parts سِلسِلہ وار، قسط وار *n.* serial story قسط وار افسانہ **serially** *adv.* in serial order ترتیب وار **seriatim** *adv.* point by point سِلسِلہ وار، ایک ایک کر کے، یکے بعد دِیگرے
sericulture *n.* breeding of silkworms ریشم کے کیڑے پالنا۔ ریشم سازی
series (*see*-reez) *n.* number of similar things, etc., arranged in order سِلسِلہ، زنجیرہ *a series of (something)*, a succession of it مُسَلسَل
serious (*see*-ri-us) *adj.* thoughtful سَنجِیدہ، مَتِین important because dangerous (illness, condition, etc.) اَہَم، تشویشناک، سَخت not slight (matter) قابلِ توجہ not in jest سچ مُچ، واقعی *Are you serious ?* سچ مُچ ؟ **seriously** *adv.* in a serious manner سَنجِیدگی، مَتانت سے، سَخت **seriousness** *n.* being serious تشویشناکی، مَتانت
sermon (*se**-mun) *n.* religious address in a place of worship خُطبہ، وَعظ any moral lecture وَعظ، وَعظ و نصیحت
serpent (*se**-pent) *n.* large snake سانپ base deceiver ناگ **serpentine** *adj.* meandering, tortuous بَل کھاتا ہُوا *v.i.* move thus بَل کھاتے ہُوئے جانا
serrate (se-*rayt*), **serrated** (se-*ray*-tid) *adj.* notched like a saw دَندانہ دار
serried (*se*-rid) *adj.* (of soldiers in ranks) standing or moving closely together shoulder to shoulder شانہ بشانہ
serum (*see*-rum) *n.* watery part of the blood خُوناب، کیلُوس، لِنف such liquid used for inoculation سیرم، کیلُوس، لِنف
servant (*sĕ**-vant) *n.* one who works for another or others for payment مُلازِم *public servant*, government servant سرکاری مُلازِم *civil servant*, member of a civil service سِول حاکم، شہری حاکم، اعلیٰ غیر فوجی مُلازِم *domestic servant* نوکر، خانگی مُلازِم، نِجی نوکر *servant-girl*, woman or girl employed as domestic servant نوکرانی، خادِمہ
serve (*sĕ*v*) *v.t.* & *i.* work for (someone) کا مُلازِم ہونا، کا نوکر ہونا *serve as* (*cook, etc.*) be employed thus کی حیثیت سے کام کرنا *serve for*, work on behalf of کی جانب سے خِدمات انجام دینا *serve* (*one's*) *country* in *serve* (*a year, etc.*) *in the army* (کسی جگہ) کسی کی خِدمات انجام دینا فوجی مُلازمت کرنا *serve on* (*a committee, etc.*) be its member (انجمن وغیرہ) کا رُکن ہونا *serve* (*customers, in a shop, etc.*), attend to them کی خِدمت میں حاضِر رہنا *serve* (*someone*) *with* (*goods, services, etc.*), supply them to him بہم پہنچانا *serve* (*someone, food, etc.*), place (it for him) on the table for a meal کے لیے دسترخوان چُننا pass a period (of imprisonment, apprenticeship, etc.) (اپنی) مُدت گُزارنا *serve a sentence, serve time*, undergo imprisonment قید کاٹنا *serve* (*one's*) *apprenticeship, serve* (*one's*) *time*, pass the usual period of apprenticeship پُوری شاگردی کرنا، سیکھنا *serve* (*one's*) *time*, (also) go through (one's) term of office مُدت مُلازمت پُوری کرنا deal (*out*) پہنچانا، تقسیم کرنا be satisfactory for a purpose جس سے کام چل جائے، کے مُفید مَطلب ہونا *serve* (*someone's*) *turn*, have the effect he desires کے مُفیدِ مَطلب ہونا *serve the purpose of*, be used as کے طور پر استعمال ہونا *serve the purpose of* (*doing, etc.*), have the effect of کی ضرورت پُوری کرنا کا اثر رکھنا *serve* (*one's*) *need* *that will not serve*, that which is not good enough جو نہ چل سکے *serve as* (*something*), be useful as کا کام دینا treat someone *well, shamefully*, etc.) سے (اچھا، شرمناک وغیرہ) سلوک کرنا (یا) پیش آنا *serve right*, retaliate بدلہ لینا *It serves him right* ; it is a suitable punishment for his misdeeds وہ اِسی سزا کا مستحق تھا deliver (a summons, etc. *on* someone) or summon (someone *with*) سے (سمن وغیرہ) کی تعمیل کرانا (in tennis, etc.) take the turn to service سَروِس کرنا، پہلی گیند پھینکنا **service** (*sĕ**-vis) *n.* serving in a beneficial manner خِدمات *meritorious services* قابلِ قدر خِدمات (*one's*) *service to the cause of* (*something*) کے لیے خِدمات *the services of a lawyer* (or *doctor, etc.*) وکیل (یا ڈاکٹر وغیرہ) کی خِدمات being a servant نوکری، مُلازمت position as a servant *go into service*, become a domestic servant نوکری branch of public employment سرکاری مُلازمت کا شعبہ *the Civil Service*, (*a*) highest cadre of government service other than in the armed forces اعلیٰ شہری مُلازمتیں (*b*) its members سِوِل حُکام، شہری حُکام *the services, the fighting services*, the Army, Navy and Air Force فوج، لشکر *on active service*, engaged on military duties in time of war لام پر *service dress* (or *rifle*, etc.), military dress (or rifle, etc.) فوجی وَردی (یا رَائفل وغیرہ) use کام، خِدمت *at your service*, at your disposal ; willing to serve you کی خِدمت کے لیے حاضِر، کی خِدمت پر کمر بستہ system supplying (esp. communication) needs of the public سَروِس *train* (etc.) *service*, trains (etc.) running (to or between) گاڑیاں congregational prayer باجماعت نماز، جماعت religious ceremony for (marriage, burial, etc.) مذہبی تقریب، اجتماع complete set of table-dishes, etc. کھانے کا سیٹ *a tea service of*

21 pieces چائے کا اکیس چیزوں والا سیٹ serving of food and drink (in hotels, etc.) ملازموں کی خدمات work done by domestic servants ٹہل ، نوکروں کا کام *a service flat*, a flat whose rent includes charges for cleaning, etc. وہ فلیٹ جس کے کرائے میں صفائی کی اجرت بھی شامل ہو serving (*of* summons, etc.) تعمیل (in tennis, etc.) throwing of the first ball for a fresh point سروس ، پہلی گیند weariness تھکن ، تھکاوٹ *to have seen service* تھکا ہارا یا گھسا پٹا ، نظر آنا expert repair or maintenance work performed by vendor after sale سروس *service station*, workshop where motor-vehicles are serviced موٹر کاریں وغیرہ درست کرنے کا کارخانہ *v.t.* put (car, etc.) into good order by overhauling it ٹھیک ٹھاک کرنا repair or maintain after service سروس دینا ، مرمت کرنا

serviceable (sĕ*-vi-sab-ĕl) *adj.* durable پائیدار useful کارآمد ، کام کے قابل

serviette (se*-vi-*et*) *n.* table-napkin کھانے کی میز کا رومال ، دسترخوان ، دستمال

servile (*se**-vil) *adj.* of slaves غلاموں کا slave-like غلامانہ mean کمینہ ، ذلیل ، فرومایہ **servility** (*-vil-*) *n.* slavery غلامی meanness کمینگی **servitude** (*-se*-*) *n.* slavery غلامی *penal servitude*, imprisonment involving hard labour قید بامشقت

sesame (*ses*-a-mi) *n.* a species of oil-seed or the plant yielding it تل ، کنجد ، سِم سِم *open sesame*, (from *The Arabian Nights*' story of *Ali Baba and Forty Thieves*) any magic password at which closed doors, etc., fly open کھل جا سم سم ، کھل سم سم ، طلسم کشا

sesqui- *pref.* half again ڈیوڑھا

session (*sesh*-ĕn) *n.* assembly for deliberations اجلاس *in session*, (of Parliament, etc.) sitting کا اجلاس جاری ہونا *be in session* جس کا اجلاس جاری ہو sitting (*of* a court) اجلاس *petty sessions*, court of two or more justices of the peace in the U.K. for the trial of minor local offences برطانوی مقامی عدالت *Sessions Court*, district court in Pakistan whose presiding judge may decide all criminal cases including those involving murder charges سیشن کورٹ *Sessions Judge*, presiding judge of a Sessions Court سیشن جج any period during which meetings or lectures are held میقات *the winter session of a university* جامعاتی سرمائی میقات **sessional** *adj.* pertaining to a session میقاتی

set *n.* number of things belonging to a group سیٹ ، جوڑی group ٹولی ، گروہ ، طائفہ series سلسلہ group of games in tennis counting as a unit for the winning score سیٹ (usu. *pl.*) setting, etc., for a particular scene in a theatre or film-studio مستقل منظر ، سیٹ apparatus آلہ *radio-set* ریڈیو *v.t. & i.* put in a place رکھنا ، جڑنا ، لگانا ، دھرنا ، بٹھانا become stiff اکڑنا ، کھڑے ہونا ، سخت ہو جانا affix چسپاں کرنا ، لگانا fix (hair) by damping it (in *setting-lotion*) so that it dries in waves (بال) گھنگریالے بنانا (بالوں میں) عارضی گھنگر ڈالنا *setting-lotion*, lotion used in setting the hair عارضی گھنگر ڈالنے کا تیل (of the sun, etc.), go out of sight in the evening ڈوبنا ، غروب ہونا become intense بڑھنا ، جوش میں آنا ، زور پکڑنا (of mental qualities) mature پختہ ہو جانا make (question-paper) (پرچہ) بنانا *set a question* امتحان میں سوال پوچھنا *set apart*, (*a*) set aside الگ کرنا (*b*) reserve (*for*) کے لیے مخصوص کرنا *set aside*, (*a*) separate الگ کرنا ، علیحدہ کرنا (*b*) annul (a decision, etc.) منسوخ کرنا ، مسترد کرنا *set by*, reserve for future use اٹھا رکھنا ، رکھ چھوڑنا *set sail*, start travelling by a sailing-vessel جہاز پر روانہ ہونا *set the razor*, sharpen it استرے کی دھار بنانا *set (one's) teeth*, clench them as a sign of firm resolve دانت بھینچنا *set (something) at naught*, (*a*) nullify کالعدم کرنا (*b*) not to heed it کی بالکل پروا نہ کرنا *set at ease, set at rest*, relieve person of (his) anxieties, etc. کو تسلی دینا ، کے خدشات دور کرنا *set at defiance*, defy کی خلاف ورزی کرنا *set (someone) free* (or *at liberty*), free (him) کو چھوڑ دینا ، کو رہا کرنا *set on fire*, ignite کو جلا دینا ، کو آگ لگا دینا *set on foot*, begin کو شروع کرنا *set right*, put right سیدھا کر دینا *set pen to paper*, begin to write لکھنے لگنا *set spurs to (horse)* (گھوڑے کو) ایڑ لگانا *set to*, begin quarrel جھگڑنے لگنا *set to (something)*, start doing (it) کرنے لگنا *set (someone) over (another)*, put (someone) in authority over (another) کے سر پر مسلط ہونا *set out*, (*a*) begin a journey روانہ ہونا (*b*) display لگانا *set out on a journey (etc.)* سفر پر روانہ ہونا *set off*, (*a*) adorn کی زینت بڑھانا (*b*) set it right ٹھیک کرنا *set down*, write down لکھ لینا *set (something) down to*, attribute it to کا باعث قرار دینا *set against*, (*a*) to poison (one) against کا مخالف بنانا (*b*) reckon as counterbalancing کا توڑ قرار دینا *set in order*, put in order سلیقے سے رکھنا ، ترتیب سے رکھنا *set in*, come in vogue رائج ہونا *set foot on* پر قدم رکھنا *set before*, expound to سے عرض کرنا ، کو پیش کرنا *set eyes on*, see کو دیکھنا *set (one's) face against (doing something)*, oppose it resolutely کی سخت مخالفت کرنا *set (one's) cap at (someone)*, (of a woman) try to attract (him) as suitor پر ڈورے ڈالنا *set (something) going*, put (it) in motion کو حرکت میں لانا *set back*, impede کی راہ میں روڑے اٹکانا *set forth*, (*a*) start on journey روانہ ہونا (*b*) expound پیش کرنا *set much by, set store by*, depend on; value highly پر انحصار کرنا ، کو بہت ضروری سمجھنا *set little* by سیٹ بیک کو بالکل غیر ضروری سمجھنا **setback** *n.* impediment رکاوٹ relapse دوسرا دھچکا *to receive a serious setback* کو سخت دھچکا لگنا **set-down** *n.* rebuff گٹ پاسنگ **set-off** *n.* counter-balance جھاڑ جھپاڑ thing set off against another for adornment آرائش، زیبائش **set-out** *n.* display پیشکش، نمائش **set-square** *n.* right-angled triangular appliance (with 30°, 60° or 45°, 49° as the other two angles) for drawing lines سیٹ سکوئر، گنیا **set-up** *n.* (colloq.) organization اِدارہ its establishment عملہ arrangement of machinery, etc. (سامان وغیرہ کی) ترتیب order, arrangement نظام، انتظام، بندوبست *under the new set-up* نئے نظام کے تحت

settee (se-*tee*) *n.* long seat with a back accommodating two or more for conversation صوفہ

setting (*set*-ing) *n.* background پس منظر environment ماحول frame for setting jewels جس میں جڑت ہو any frame فریم، چوکھٹا music set to certain words طرز، دھن putting in place لگانا، رکھنا، جڑنا

settle (*set*-èl) *v.t.* & *i.* come to rest آرام سے بیٹھ جانا established in an abode رہنے لگنا، آباد ہونا be established (in a particular walk of life) پر لگ جانا، ہو جانا، خاص طریق زندگی اختیار کرنا sink to the bottom تہ نشین ہو جانا، بیٹھ جانا repay (debt, etc.) چکانا، ادا کرنا pay ادا کرنا decide (a case) نبٹانا، بنٹانا، کا فیصلہ کرنا **settler** *n.* colonist آبادکار **settlement** *n.* colony نوآبادی terms on which something is settled تصفیہ، شرائط تصفیہ deed containing them تصفیہ کی دستاویز، تصفیہ social reformers of a district on intimate terms with the working-class people there (رفاہی کارکنوں کی) انجمن

seven (*sev*-en) *n.* & *adj.* 7 سات **seventh** *adj.* 7th ساتواں، ساتویں **seventhly** *adv.* in the seventh place *in the seventh heaven*, very happy بہت خوش **sevenfold** *adj.* & *adv.* seven times سات گنا **seventeen** *n.* & *adj.* 17 سترہ *sweet seventeen*, bloom of a woman's youth برس پندرہ یا کہ سولہ کا سن ہے جوانی کی راتیں مرادوں کے دن، عنفوانِ شباب **seventeenth** *adj.* 17th سترھواں **seventy** (*sev*-) *n.* & *adj.* 70 ستر **seventieth** *adj.* 70th سترواں

sever (*sev*-ē*) *v.t.* & *i.* disjoin الگ کرنا، جدا کرنا divide in two دو ٹکڑے کرنا cut asunder ایک علیحدہ کرنا دوسرے سے کاٹ ڈالنا come asunder الگ کرنا، جدا کرنا **severance** (*sev*-ē-rans) *n.* severing الگ کرنا، جدا کرنا severed state چھدائی، علیحدگی سے کاٹ کر الگ کر دینا **several** (*sev*-rēl) *adj.* many متعدد a few کئی various مختلف **severally** *adv.* individually الگ الگ *severally and collectively* فرداً فرداً بھی، مجموعی طور فرداً فرداً بھی

severe (se-*vee*-è*) *adj.* strict سخت گیر، سخت harsh سخت violent سخت، شدید، جابرانہ plain سادہ، سیدھا سادہ **severity** (se-*ve*-ri-ti) *n.* strictness سخت گیری violence شدت plainness سادگی ill-treatment سختی، بدسلوکی، برا برتاؤ **severely** *adv.* strictly or harshly سختی سے Ⓢ **Severe** signifies lacking in gentleness. Again, we speak of a **stern** parent or command; **strict** orders which leave no latitude; **rigorous** punishment which is well enforced; **austere** attitude, which is marked by self-restraint; **grim** determination which is merciless; **rigid** rule which cannot be relaxed to suit individual needs.

sew (soh) *v.t.* & *i.* (*sew*; *sewed*; *sewn* or *sewed*) stitch with hand or sewing-machine سینا *sew up a hole* (کپڑے کی) پھٹی ہوئی جگہ سی دینا *sew on a button* بٹن لگانا *sew money into (one's) belt* پیٹی میں روپیہ سی کر محفوظ کر لینا **sewing-machine** *n.* machine for this purpose worked with hand or treadle مشین، سلائی کی مشین

a sewing-machine worked with a treadle (T)

sewage (*sew*-ij) *n.* water conveyed to sewers گندے نالے کا پانی، بدرو کا پانی *sewage farm*, one irrigated with sewage وہ کھیت جس میں گندے پانی سے کاشت ہو **sewer** (*sew*-e*) *n.* drain (usu. covered in underground) گندہ نالہ، بدرو **sewerage** (*sew*-è-rij) *n.* drainage system in a city شہر کی بدرروئیں

sewn (sohn) *v.* (pa. p. of **sew**, which see)

sex (seks) *n.* being male or female جنس، صنف (*the sex*), women عورتیں، عورت sexual emotions جنسی جذبات *the sterner sex*, men مرد، صنفِ کرخت، جنسِ ذکور *the fair* (or *gentle*, or *softer*, or *weaker*) *sex*, women عورت، صنفِ نازک *sex appeal*, attraction for the opposite sex جنسی کشش *the opposite sex*, males (for females) and vice-versa جنسِ مخالف *sex urge*, passions incited by sex جنسی جذبہ **sexual** (*sek*-sew-èl) *adj.* pertaining to sex جنسی **sexy** (*sek*-si) *adj.* (of books, thought, etc.) full of or inciting sexual urge جنسیاتی، جنسی

sextant (*seks*-tant) *n.* instrument (with a graduated 60° arc standing upright) for measuring vertical angles and employed by sailors to find out the latitude and longitude of a place زاویہ پیما، سُدس فلکی

sailor with a sextant

sexton (*seks*-tun) *n.* caretaker of a church or churchyard محافظ گرجا grave-digger گورکن

shabby (*shab*-i) *adj.* worn-out پھٹا پرانا، فرسودہ

in worn-out clothes پھٹے پُرانے کپڑے پہنے unkind, mean or undignified (treatment) بُرا، ذلت آمیز، رُسوا کُن
shabbily *adv.* in worn-out clothes پھٹے پُرانے کپڑوں میں *shabbily dressed* پھٹے پُرانے کپڑوں میں in an undignified manner رُسوا کُن طور پر **shabbiness** *n.* in tatters پھٹے پُرانے کپڑوں میں ہونا unkindness, undignified treatment رُسوا کُن سلوک

shack (shak) *n.* rough hut جھونپڑی، جھونپڑا

shackle (*shak*-ël) *n.* (usu. *pl.*) hand-cuff ہتھکڑی iron-band put round the ankle بیڑی *in shackles* بیڑیاں پہن لینا (*pl.*) curbs پابندیاں، بندشیں *v.t.* put shackles round the ankles of کے بیڑی ڈالنا curb پر پابندی لگانا

shade (shayd) *n.* place screened from strong light چھاؤں، سایہ depth of colour گہرا رنگ darker part of a picture, etc. تصویر کا تاریک حصہ very small amount of کچھ، قدرے، تھوڑا سا screen for dimming light آڑ، سرپوش *v.t. & i.* put in shade چھاؤں کرنا، سایہ کرنا put a screen on پر سرپوش لگانا make (parts of a picture, etc.) darker than the rest تاریک کرنا change gradually from one (into another colour) ایک رنگ سے دوسرے رنگ میں بتدریج بدلنا

shady (*shay*-di) *adj.* (*shady, shadier, shadiest*) screened from light گھنا، سایہ دار (of deal, bargain, etc.) not quite honest مشتبہ

shadow (*shad*-oh) *n.* patch of shade سایہ dark figure projected by a body intercepting the rays of light پرچھائیں، سایہ this as the body's appendage ہمزاد reflection in mirror, etc. عکس constant companion سائے کی طرح ساتھ پھرنے والا، ہمزاد reminder (*of*) رکا، سایہ unreal thing بے حقیقت شے وہم slightest trace ہلکا سا نشان، نام و نشان *not even the shadow of* کا نام و نشان تک نہیں dark part of a room کمرے کا تاریک حصہ obscurity گمنامی shelter پناہ outline نقشہ *coming events cast their shadow before*, ہونہار بروا کے چکنے چکنے پات یا آنے والی مصیبت کا نقشہ پہلے ہی نظر آجاتا ہے (poet.) portrait تصویر *v.t.* (poet.) overspread with shadow پر صورت سایہ ڈالنا watch secretly خفیہ نگرانی کے لیے پیچھے پیچھے پھرنا *shadowed by the C.I.D.* خفیہ پولیس جس کے پیچھے لگی ہوتی ہو vaguely set *forth* in a prophetic manner کی مبہم سی پیشگوئی کرنا *adj.* imaginary, unreal نقلی، فرضی *shadow boxing*, boxing against imaginary opponent for pratice نقلی مکے بازی *shadow cabinet*, one formed by the opposition and comprising potential ministers حزب اختلاف کی کابینہ، فرضی کابینہ *shadow factory*, one built for reserve capacity in emergencies فالتو کارخانہ **shadowy** (*shad*-oh-i) *adj.* casting a shadow سایہ دار unreal بے اصل، وہمی

shady *adj.* (see under **shade**)

shaft (shahft) *n.* thin cylinder چھڑ، نلی arrow تیر stem of a column ستون trunk bar of a vehicle with which a horse is harnessed بم passage for escape of smoke, etc. انگیٹھی hole leading into a mine کان کا راستہ shank (of a machine) دھرا

shag *n.* rough growth of coarse hair بھرے بال **shaggy** (*shag*-i) *adj.* having shags لمبے موٹے بالوں والا، جھبرا

shake (shayk) *v.t.* & *i.* (*shake, shook, shaken*) move to and fro violently and quickly زور زور سے ہلانا tremble کانپنا shock (someone); upset (his) composure متزلزل کرنا، کپکپا دینا، پریشان کر دینا weaken کم کرنا، زور گھٹانا *shake down*, bring down violently جھٹکے کر نیچے گرا دینا *shake hands (with)*, *shake (someone) by the hand* ہاتھ ملانا، مصافحہ کرنا *shake (one's) fist*, threaten thus مکا دکھانا *shake a leg*, dance ناچنا، رقص کرنا *shake (one's) head*, nod refusal سر ہلا کر انکار کرنا *shake in (one's) shoes*, tremble with fear ڈر کے مارے کانپنا *shake the house*, tidy it up گھر کو جھاڑ دینا، گھر کی صفائی کرنا *n.* shaking جھٹکا anything shaken (esp. a beverage) مخلول (U.S.) glass of milk with or without egg (انڈے والے) دودھ کا گلاس
hand-shake *n.* shaking of their right hands by two persons ہاتھ ملانا، مصافحہ **shake-down** *n.* bedding laid on floor فرش پر بستر، فرشی بچھونا improvised straw-bed پرالی بچھال **shakeout** *n* (see *Addenda*)

Skakespearian, Shakesperian (shayks-*pee*-ri-an) *adj.* (as) of Shakespeare شیکسپیئر کا، دیسا

shaky (*shay*-ki) *adj.* insecure غیر محفوظ trembling لرزاں tottering ڈگمگانے کو unreliable بے اعتبار، غیر معتبر wavering متذبذب، متذبذب

shall (shal) *auxiliary v.* (*shalt* with thou; pa. t. and conditional *should*; and *shouldst* with thou; negative *shall not* or *shan't*, *should not* or *shouldn't*) (with 1st person) in future گا، گے، گی (with 2nd & 3rd persons) certainly in future ضرور (کرے وغیرہ) گا، گے، گی

shale (shayl) *n.* a slate-like stone شیل

shallow (*sha*-loh) *adj.* not deep (water) کم گہرا، اتھلا superficial اوپری with superficial knowledge سطحی mean کم ظرف *n.* shallow place پایاب مقام *v.t. & i.* decrease in depth گہرائی میں کم ہوتے جانا

shalt *auxiliary v.* the form of **shall** (which see) used with *thou*. کے ساتھ مستعمل شکل thou کی shall

sham *v.t.* & *i.* (-mm-) pretend to be جھوٹ موٹ بناوٹی، مصنوعی کرنا، کا بہانہ کرنا *adj.* pretended, counterfeit *n.* pretence بناوٹ، دکھاوا pretending to be what he is not بناوٹی، نقلی، بناشیتی

shamble (*sham*-bĕl) *v. i.* move in a shuffling manner لڑکھڑا کے چلنا *n.* such walk لڑکھڑاہٹ (*pl.* used as *sing.*) (*a*) slaughterhouse بوچڑخانہ، مذبح (*b*) hence scene of bloodshed قتل گاہ، مقتل، جہاں خون کی ندیاں بہہ جائیں

shame (shaym) *n.* feeling of being guilty, ridiculed or disgraced شرم، شرمندگی restraint for avoiding this شرم، لاج، حیا ignominy بے عزتی رسوائی، فضیحت *put to shame* شرمندہ کرنا *without shame, past shame, lost to shame,* shameless ڈھیٹ، بے شرم، بیحیا *what a shame !* very unjust ! بڑی شرمناک بات ہے، بڑی بے انصافی ہو *think shame to* (do, etc.) disdain to (do, etc.) سے عار آنا، میں شرم محسوس کرنا *shame !, for shame !, fie for shame !, shame on (someone) !* shameful (for him) شرم شرم *v.t.* & *i.* make ashamed and force (*into* or *out of* something) شرم دلا کر کرنے یا نہ کرنے پر مجبور کرنا **shamefaced** (*shaym*-fayst) *adj.* shy, bashful بے شرم، بیحیا **shameless** *adj.* without shame شرمیلا **shameful** *adj.* causing shame شرمناک flagrant شرمناک

shampoo (sham-*poo*) *v.t.* lather and rub (the head) (سر) صابن سے مل مل کر دھونا، کا شیمپو کرنا، (سر کو) صابن لگا کر ملنا treat (someone) thus in the head کے سر کو صابن لگا کر ملنا، کا سر صابن سے مل مل کر دھونا، کا شیمپو کرنا *n.* shampooing (سر) صابن سے مل مل کر دھونا، شیمپو *dry shampoo*, powder or alcohol for this purpose خشک شیمپو

shank *n.* part of the leg between knee and ankle پنڈلی، ساق stem ڈنڈی *Shank's mare*, one's own legs اپنی ٹانگیں، ٹانگ سوار، سڑک سوار

shan't (shahnt) *auxiliary v.* shall not ; spoken negative of **shall** (which see)

shanty (*shant*-i) *n.* hut, hovel, cabin جھونپڑی (also spelt **chanty**, pr. *shahnt*-i) sailor's song ماہی گیر کا گیت، ملاح کا نغمہ، ملاحی

shape (shayp) *n.* figure شکل، صورت orderly arrangement ترتیب، صورت *in any shape or form,* (*a*) in any way کسی بھی صورت میں (*b*) of any sort کیسا ہی *get (one's) ideas into shape*, put them into orderly form کو ٹھیک صورت دینا *take shape*, (*a*) be realized عمل میں آنا (*b*) become definite کسی کروٹ بیٹھنا *v. t.* & *i.* form بنانا give signs of future آئندہ کی صورت بننا *be shaping well* کچھ بنتا ہی نظر آنا **shapeless** *adj.* lacking definite shape غیر متشکل not well shaped بیڈول **shapely** *adj.* well-shaped خوبصورت، خوش شکل

share (*shay*-ĕ*) *n.* portion حصہ، بخرہ (also *ploughshare*), blade of a plough پھالی، ہل کا پھل *v.t.* & *i.* divide into parts بانٹنا، تقسیم کرنا have a share (in) میں اشتریک ہونا، (میں) حصہ دار ہونا receive a share of کا حصہ پانا **share-cropper** *n.* (U.S.) farmer who pays his rent with an agreed portion of the crop بٹائی دینے والا

shark (shah*k) *n.* a species of large voracious fish شارک swindler پتے باز extortioner غصب و نہب کرنے والا usurer سود خوار *v. i.* practise usury سود کھانا، سود خوار ہونا be an extortioner غصب و نہب کرنا swindle پتے بازی کرنا

a shark

sharp (shah*p) *adj.* fine-edged (opp. of blunt) تیز keen تیز shrill تیز، تیکھی steep تیز angular یکدم مڑنے والا سخت ڈھلوان pungent تیز acid کھٹا، تیزابی harsh سخت dishonest بد دیانت above normal pitch بہت اونچا (see *Addenda*) ; hence *look sharp*, (also) be dressed, etc., in the latest fashion بن ٹھن کر نکلنا، خوب فیشنیبل ہونا *n.* (in music) a semitone above the named note (opp. of *flat* which is semitone below the normal) ڈیوڑھا سُر *sharps and flats*, black notes on a piano پیانو کے کالے پردے *sharp's the word !, look sharp !,* hurry up جلدی کرو *sharp work*, (*a*) quick action فوری کارروائی (*b*) hard fighting سخت لڑائی **sharpen** *v. t.* & *i.* make sharp تیز کرنا **sharper** *n.* one who lives by cheating (esp. at cards) پتے باز **sharpest** *adj.* hungry بھوکا **sharpshooter** *n.* marksman بڑا نشانہ باز

shatter (*shat*-ĕ*) *v.t.* & *i.* break suddenly into many pieces پاش پاش کر دینا dissipate (health, nerves) کو سخت صدمہ پہنچانا end (hopes, etc.) پر پانی پھیر دینا، کو ختم کر دینا

shave (shayv) *v. t.* & *i.* remove hair with a razor پھیلنا، تراشنا pare (wood, etc.) چھیلنا، تراشنا pass closely without touching کے بالکل پاس سے ہو کر گزرنا *n.* being shaved by oneself or another حجامت، شیو *clean shave* ڈاڑھی مونچھ کا صفایا *close shave* خوب گھٹا *comfortable shave* اچھے اُسترے سے حجامت مٹوا ہونا **shaving brush** *n.* brush for lathering the hair شیونگ برش، شیو کا برش **shavings** *n. pl.* refuse of planing **shaver** *n.* youngster نوجوان

shavian (*shay*-vi-an) *adj.* as or in the style of the English dramatist, George Bernard Shaw (1856-1950) مشہور انگریز ڈرامہ نویس شا کے طرز کا، بہ اُسلوب شا

shavings *n. pl.* (see under **shave**)

shawl *n.* shoulder-wrap شال

she (shee) *pron. 3rd person sing.* nominative *case, fem. gender* (objective : *her* ; possessive : *her* or *hers* ; *pl., they, them, their, theirs*) وُہ *n.* woman عَورَت *the not impossible she*, a woman one may meet and love with favourable response مُمکِن الحصُول عَورَت *Is it a he or a she ?* مرد ہے یا عَورَت؟ *adj.* female مادہ (as in *she-goat* بَکری *she-devil*, malignant woman عذاب جان عَورَت

sheaf (sheef) *n.* (*pl.* *sheaves* pr. sheevz) bundle of corn-stalks bound after reaping مُٹھا پُولی، مُٹھا bundle (of arrows, paper, etc.)

shear (*shee*-ĕ*) *v.t.* & *i.* (*shear, sheared, shorn*) cut with shears مُونڈنا، کاٹنا، تراشنا **shears** (*shee*-ĕ*z) *n.* large pair of scissors for clipping sheep's wool, etc. بڑی قینچی **shorn** (shoh*n) *adj.* sheared مُنڈا ہُوا (*shorn of*), without سے عاری سے محرُوم

sheath (sheeth) *n.* (pl. *sheaths*, pr. *sheedhz*) close-fitting cover for blade of a sharp or pointed weapon, etc. نیام، مِیان **sheathe** (sheedh) *v.t.* put (the sword) into a sheath نیام میں ڈالنا، نیام کے اَندر کرلینا

shebang (shi-*bang*) *n.* (U. S. slang) anything of present interest بات، چیز *the whole shebang* house گھر store ذخیرہ گاہ

shed *n.* roofed shelter without walls and used as a workshop or for storing things or for keeping cattle, etc. چھپّر، شیڈ *loco-shed*, shed for locomotives or railway engines *v.t.* (of blood, tears, etc.) cause to flow بہانا *shed the blood of* (*someone*), kill him کو قتل کرنا، کا خُون کرنا، (یا بہانا) *shed one's blood for* (*something*), lay down one's life in its defence کی خاطر جان دینا، پر قُربان ہو جانا (of a tree, etc.) let fall its (leaves) گرانا، کے (پتّے) جھڑنا

a shed

shedding *n.* بہانا، گرانا

sheen *n.* brightness, gloss چمک، چمک دمک *adj.* (poet.) bright چمکیلا، تاباں

sheep *n.* (masc. or fem.) (*pl.* the same) a well-known wool-covered animal بھیڑ (یا) مینڈھا **sheepish** *adj.* stupidly shy جھینپُو **sheep-cote** (*sheep*-koht), **sheep-cot** (-kot), **sheep-fold** *n.* shelter for sheep بھیڑوں کا باڑا

sheer (*shee*-ĕ*) *adj.* mere بالکُل، محض، نِرا، سراسر *a sheer waste of time* محض تضیِیع اَوقات *adv.* perpendicularly عمُوداً، سیدھا directly سیدھا clean صَاف *v. i.* take oneself (*off*) اَلگ ہو جانا، جُدا ہو جانا

sheet *n.* complete piece of paper as made پُورا کاغذ، کاغذ کا تختہ، تاؤ large thin piece (*of* iron, glass, paper, cloth, etc.) چادر، تختہ any flat surface تختہ

sheetanchor *n.* large anchor used in an emergency بڑا لنگر last dependence آخری سہارا

shelf *n.* (*pl.,* *shelves*) board projecting from a wall or forming one tier of a bookcase, etc., used for placing things تختہ sand-bank ریتی projecting part of cliff چٹان کا نِکلا ہُوا حِصّہ *on the shelf*, (*a*) laid aside زینتِ طاقِ نِسیان (*b*) past work ناکارہ **shelve** (shelv) *v.t.* & *i.* fit (cupboard, etc., with shelves) میں تختے لگانا place on a shelf تختے پر دھرنا defer (plan, etc.) کھٹائی میں ڈالنا، زینتِ طاقِ نِسیان بنانا (of a surface) slope gently ڈھلوان ہونا

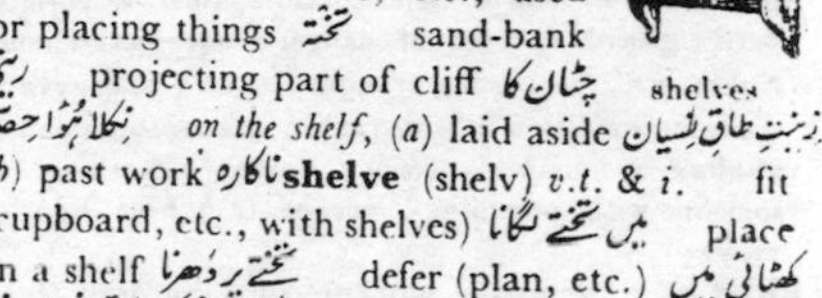
shelves

shell (shel) *n.* hard outer covering خول، کھپرا، چھلکا پوشت large explosive bullet *v. t.* & *i* remove the shell from چھلکا اُتارنا، خول اُتارنا take out of shell خول میں سے نِکالنا، دانے نِکالنا bombard گولہ باری کرنا **shell-fish** *n.* any kind of shelled fish, etc. کھپرے دار مچھلی، صَدَفی مچھلی، صَدَفہ **shelling** *n.* bombardment گولہ باری **shell-less** *adj.* without a shell بے خول، بے پوشت **shelly** (*shel*-i) *adj.* having a shell خول دار، پوشت دار

shellac (she-*lak*) *n.* lac melted into thin plates for making varnish چپڑا لاکھ، چپڑا *v.t.* (-ack-) varnish with shellac چپڑا لاکھ پھیرنا

shelter (*shel*-tĕ*) *n.* protection پناہ place giving protection پناہ گاہ، ملجا place providing covering محفُوظ جگہ *v.t.* serve as shelter to کے لیے پناہ دینا، کی حِفاظت کرنا shield کو پناہ گاہ کا کام دینا give (oneself) shelter (*under, in, from*, etc.) کی آڑ لینا، (کے) زیرِ حفاظت آنا، (کی) پناہ لینا **sheltered trade** *n.* trade enjoying protection against foreign competition تامینی تجارت

shelve *v.t.*, **shelves** *n. pl.* (see under **shelf**,

shepherd (*shep*-ĕ*d) *n.* one who tends sheep گڈریا، چرواہا، رَاعی pastor نگہبان، مُحافظ، رَاعی *the good Shepherd*, a Christian name for Christ حضرت عیسیٰؑ

shepherdess *n. fem.* female shepherd گڈرنی، رَاعیہ

sheriff (*she*-rif) *n.* chief officer of law in a British county or shire شیرِف، شائر دار

sherry (*she*-ri) *n.* a white Spanish wine شیری **sherry-glass** *n.* small glass with a capacity of about four table-spoonfuls جام شیری

shew (shoh) *v.* **shewd** (shohd) *v.* **shewn** (shohn) *v.* (old spelling of **show,** which see)

shibboleth (*shib*-o-leth) *n.* party catchword کسی جتھے کا خاص لفظ

shield (sheeld) *n.* plate of armour carried in front of the body ڈھال، سپر similar thing used as a trophy شیلڈ، سپر its representation شیلڈ کی تصویر، سپرنُما، شیلڈ کا مارکہ one who protects حمایتی v.t. shelter کی حفاظت کرنا، کو بچانا، کو پناہ دینا ▣ We **shield** someone by exposing ourselves instead ; **protect** someone or something against a possible peril ; **guard** in case of danger ; **safeguard** one's rights, etc., from being trampled upon ; **preserve** in the same condition in which it is ; **champion** a cause; **shelter** a homeless person ; **cover** something or someone with something ; **screen** from heat, light or view.

shift *n.* group of workmen taking over from another شِفٹ، بَدل چوکی its duty hours بَدل چوکی change تبدیلی expedient حکمتِ عملی، مصلحت contrivance نئی ترکیب dodge ٹال مٹول، گول مول بات *make shift, make a shift,* manage somehow کسی نہ کسی طرح کام چلا ہی لینا *shift with* (or *without*) *something* سے ریا کے بغیر) کام چلا ہی لینا *v.t.* & *i.* change بدلنا *shift* (*one's*) *ground*, change (one's) stand in an argument دلیل کی بات بدلنا *shift the scene* منظر بدلنا *the scene shifts* منظر بدل جانا use expedients کسی نہ کسی طرح کام چلا ہی لینا، حکمتِ عملی سے کام لینا *must shift as* (*he*) *can, must shift for* (*himself*), must manage somehow or other ; must use expedients کسی نہ کسی طرح کام چلانا ہی ہوگا، اسے ہاتھ پاؤں مارنے ہی ہوں گے، اسے کوئی ترکیب لڑانی ہی پڑے گی۔ **shiftless** *adj.* incapable of using expedients ناکارہ، بے تدبیر **shifty** *adj.* ((rarely) not shiftless حکمتِ عملی سے کام لینے والا (usu.) addicted to deceit چالباز، عیار، چالاک

shilling (*shil*-ing) *n.* British silver coin worth 12 pence شلنگ

shilly-shally (*shil*-i-shal-i) *n.* vacillation تذبذب *adj.* vacillating تذبذب میں، ڈانوا ڈول *v.i.* vacillate دبدھے میں ہونا، ڈانوا ڈول ہونا، تذبذب میں پڑنا

shimmer (*shim*-ĕ*) *n.* faint trembling light ٹمٹماہٹ *v.i.* shine thus ٹمٹمانا

shimmy (shim-i) *n.* (nursery word for) chemise شمیز

shin, shin-bone *n.* bone front of the leg below the knee پنڈلی کا اگلا حصہ *v.t.* & *i.* climb (*up* wall, ladder, tree, etc.) (پر) چڑھ جانا

shine (shin) *v.i.* & *i.* (*shine, shined, shone*) emit a steady light چمکنا، روشن ہونا be admirable (*in* something) چمکنا، نمایاں ہونا، ممتاز ہونا (also *shine, shined, shined*) (usu. *shine up*), give a shine to (boots, plate, etc.) پالش ہونا *n.* sunshine دھوپ، اُجالا lustre on surface of (boot, plate, etc.) چمک *put a good shine on* کو چمکانا *Give your boots a shine, sir* بوٹ پالش، بوٹ پالش کرالو *take the shine out of,* (*a*) impair the brilliance of چمک دمک ختم کر دینا (*b*) throw into shade کو مات کر دینا **shiny** (*shī*-ni) *adj.* shining روشن، چمکیلا

shingle (*shing*-èl) *n.* loose pebbles on the seashore سمندر کے کنارے چھوٹے گول پتھر wooden roof-tile چوبی کھپرا hair cropped very short خشخشی (U.S.) small wooden signboard نام کی چھوٹی چوبی تختی *hang out* (*one's*) *shingle,* (of lawyer or doctor) open own office or clinic اپنا کاروبار شروع کرنا، دفتر (یا مطب) کھولنا *v.t.* make a roof with shingles چوبی کھپرے کی چھت ڈالنا crop the hair thus خشخشی کرنا (یا کرانا)

Shinto (*shin*-toh) *n.* the prevalent Japanese faith meaning "the way of the gods" شنتو، جاپانی مذہب، دیوتا دھرم

shiny (*shī*-ni) *adj.* (see under **shine**)

[1]**ship** *n.* sea-going vessel جہاز، سفینہ *v.t.* & *i.* (-pp-) put, take or send (goods, etc.) in a ship جہاز کے ذریعے بھیجنا agree to serve in a ship for a voyage کرائے کے عوض جہاز میں نوکری کر لینا *on board the ship, on shipboard,* in a ship جہاز میں **shipmate** *n.* fellow sailor in a ship جہاز میں ہم سفر **shipment** *n.* amount of goods shipped at one time جہاز کے ذریعے بھیجا ہُوا مال **shipper** *n.* one arranging for goods to be shipped جہاز کے ذریعے مال بھیجنے کا انتظام **shipping** *n.* ships (*of* a country, port, etc.) (کے) جہاز loading in a ship جہاز میں لادنا **shipshape** *adj.* well-arranged ٹھیک ٹھاک **shipwreck** *n.* destruction of a ship جہاز کی تباہی *v.t.* (cause to) suffer shipwreck جہاز کی تباہی کا شکار ہونا یا کرنا **shipwright** *n.* shipbuilder جہاز ساز **shipyard** *n.* place where ships are built مرکزِ جہاز سازی

[2]**-ship** *suf.* for making nouns which denote the office held by someone, his status as holding it or his tenure of it ی، یت (as, *ownership* (ملکیت)

shire (*shī*-è* ; in combinations shĕ*) *n.* British country شائر، برطانوی ضلع

shirk (shĕ*k) *v.t.* & *i.* avoid (something or *doing* it) سے پہلو تہی کرنا، سے کنی کترانا، سے گریز کرنا **shirker** *n.* one who shirks work کام چور ▣ We **shirk** an unpleasant task by pretending we have no time or ability to do it ; **avoid** a person or place where unpleasantness is expected by keeping away from it ; **dodge** trickily or skilfully a creditor or peril ; **escape** from harm's way by running.

shirt (shĕ*t) *n.* loose-fitting undergarment for men قمیص *in* (*one's*) *shirt sleeves* کوٹ کے بغیر

shiver (*shiv-ĕ**) *n.* trembling from fear or cold کپکپی، لرزہ، تھرتھری one of many small broken pieces (of glass, etc.) ریزہ *v.t.* & *i.* tremble کانپنا، لرزہ براندام ہونا break into shivers ریزہ ریزہ ہونا

▣ We **shiver** with cold or fear ; **shudder** at the thought of peril ; **tremble** all over with fear ; **shake** suddenly and violently. Again things **quiver** when they tremble along the length of a cord or muscle ; **quake,** when they move in a mass ; **vibrate,** when they return an imparted motion.

shoal (shohl) *n.* part of the sea with submerged sandbanks سمندر کا آبدوز والا حصّہ shallow place in it اتھلا سمندر large number (*of* fish) swimming together جھنڈ (مچھلیوں کا) multitude بڑی تعداد، ہجوم *in shoals*, in large number بڑی تعداد میں *v.i.* (of fish) from shoals (مچھلیوں کا) جھنڈ بننا *adj.* shallow (water) پایاب، اتھلا **shoaly** (shoh-li) *adj.* such part of the sea as dangerous for ships پُرخطر

shock *n.* sheaves of grain stood propping one another for drying in the field اناج کا جا بجا گٹھا untidy mass of hair (on the head) اُلجھے موٹے بال *shock-headed*, with such hair ژولیدہ مو violent blow caused by collision, etc. ٹکر، تصادم its effect صدمہ (also *electric shock*) such effect of the passage of electric current through the body بجلی کا جھٹکا، جھٹکا، شاک sudden nervous tension صدمہ، ذہنی یا قلبی صدمہ condition caused thus صدمہ *v.t.* cause shock صدمہ پہنچانا، دھچکا لگانا، دل پر اثر کرنا disgust سخت نفرت پیدا کرنا **shocking** *adj.* evil سخت بُرا **shock troops** *n. pl.* selected troops trained to make violent attacks

shod *v.* (*pa. t.* & *pa. p.* of **shoe,** which see)

shoddy (*shod*-i) *adj.* below standard گھٹیا counterfeit مصنوعی ، بناوٹی

shoe (shoe) *n.* covering for the foot not reaching above the ankles بوٹ، جوتا، شو (also *horse-shoe*), iron-piece nailed into the foot of the horse نعل *v.t.* (*shoe, shod, shod ; shoeing*) put shoes on (a horse) کا نعل لگانا **shod** *adj.* having shoes بوٹ والا **shoe-black** *n.* shoe-shine boy بوٹ پالش کرنے والا **shoe-horn** *n.* device for getting the heel easily into a tight-fitting shoe بوٹ چڑھانے کا آلہ **shoe-maker** *n.* cobbler موچی، کفش دوز **shoe-lace, shoe-string** *n.* lace to tie shoes تسمہ

shone (shon) *v.* (pa. t. & pa. p. of **shine,** which see)

shoo *int.* cry used for frightening away birds etc. شو، چھو *v.t.* frighten (birds, etc., *off* or *away*) thus شو شو کر کے اڑانا، چھو کرنا

shook (shŭk) *v.* (*pa. t.*) of **shake,** (which see)

shoot *v.t.* & *i.* (*shoot, shot, shot*) come, go, send or dart, (*out, in, up*, etc.) suddenly or swiftly تیزی سے آنا یا جانا یا چلنا یا چلانا ، *shoot an arrow* تیر چلانا (of pain) go thus (*along* a part of the body) ٹیس اُٹھنا *shooting pain* ٹیس fire (gun, etc.) چلانا fire a gun (etc.) بندوق (وغیرہ) چلانا aim (*at* someone) thus نشانہ کرنا hit (someone) کو گولی مارنا (of prices, etc.) go *up* suddenly یکایک چڑھ جانا grow اُگنا، بڑھنا take a cinema picture of (a scene) کی شوٹنگ کرنا، کو فلمانا *n.* young plant کونپل hunting party شکاریوں کی ٹولی **shooting** *n.* shooting of a gun, etc. بندوق چلانا *shooting-range*, rifle-range چاند ماری کا میدان *shooting war*, (see *Addenda*) *adj.* that which moves swiftly بڑی تیزی سے گزرنے والا *shooting-star*, meteor شہابِ ثاقب (also see **shot**)

shop *n.* place where goods can be bought دکان *shop assistant* دکان کا نوکر (also *workshop*), place where machines, etc., are manufactured or repaired کارخانہ، ورکشاپ *v.t.* (-pp-) go to various shops to buy things خرید و فروخت کے لیے جانا، سودا سلف لینے جانا **shopping** *n.* buying from a shop ; خریداری، خرید و فروخت *go shopping*, go down to market, etc., to make purchases for home خرید و فروخت کے لیے جانا *have some shopping to do* خرید و فروخت کے لیے جانا پڑنا **shopkeeper** *n.* owner of a retail shop دکاندار، خردہ فروش **shoplifter** *n.* one who steals from shop while pretending to go there as a customer اٹھائی گیرا **shop-soiled, shop-worn** *adj.* damaged not by use but by handling in the shop دکان زدہ **shopwalker** *n.* shop assistant in a big establishment showing customers round the place or directing them to the right department بڑی دکان میں رہنما ملازم

shore (shoh*) *n.* coast کنارا، ساحل *on shore, on land* کنارے پر، ساحل پر

shorn *v.* (pa. p. of **shear,** which see)

short (sho*t) *adj.* not long or tall چھوٹا، کوتاہ less than the standard (weight, amount, distance, etc.) کم، ناقص *give short weight* کم تولنا *a short cut*, quicker than usual way (*to* or *to do* something) کا چھوٹا راستہ *short of*, (*a*) without having enough کے بغیر، ناکافی ہونے کی وجہ سے (*b*) if not نہ ہو سکے تو *short of breath*, quickly becoming breathless جس کی سانس جلد پھول جائے expressed in few words مختصر expressing in a few words مختصر بات کہنے والا curt (reply) تیکھا expressing annoyance جھلا اٹھنے والا *for short*, as a shorter form of name مختصر *in short*, in a few words مختصر، قصّہ کوتاہ (of biscuits), crisp خستہ *adv.* abruptly یکایک، یکدم، یک لخت *fall short of*, fail to reach سے کم رہ جانا، پورا نہ اُترنا *n.* (usu. *short*-circuit), electric circuit of short resistance usu. causing bulb, etc., to fuse شارٹ *v.t.* (usu. *short-circuit*), be fused thus شارٹ ہونا **shortage** *n.* scarcity, dearth کمی، قلّت، کمیابی **shortcoming** *n.* weak point خامی، کمزوری **shorten** *v.t.* & *i.* make or become shorter چھوٹا کرنا یا ہونا **shortfall** *n.* (see *Addenda*) **shorthand** *n.* system of rapid writing using special symbols مختصر نویسی **shorthanded** *adj.* not having enough workers جس کے پاس کافی مزدور (یا کارکن) نہ ہوں **short-lived** *adj.* brief مختصر **shortly** *adj.* briefly مختصراً soon not long (سے) تھوڑی ہی دیر پہلے، تھوڑی ہی دیر جلدی *after* (کے) تھوڑی ہی دیر بعد curtly رُوکھے پن سے، ٹکا سا **shortness** *n.* being short اختصار، چھوٹا ہونا، کوتاہ ہونا **shorts** *n.* short trousers نکر رُوکھا پن، جھلاہٹ **short-sighted** *adj.* myopic نزدیک بیں not far-sighted عاقبت نااندیش، کوتاہ بیں **short-tempered** *adj.* easily made angry گرم مزاج، زُود رنج **short wave** *adj.* (wireless) with a wave length of 10 to 100 metres شارٹ ویو **short-winded** *adj.* breathless جس کی سانس جلد پھول جائے

shot *n.* firing of a gun, etc. فائر، گولی چلنا یا چلانا *do (something) like a shot*, do (it) at once فوراً کرنا *off like a shot* گولی کی طرح، تیر کی طرح، بڑی تیزی سے sound of shooting بندوق کی آواز، گولی کا تڑاخا attempt to do something کوشش کرنا *have a shot* کوشش (*sing.* used for *pl.*) tiny balls in a cartridge چھرّے (*good* or *poor*) marksman نشانچی **shotgun** *n.* sporting gun (as distinct from a *rifle*) بندوق

should (shŭd) *auxiliary v.* past form of **shall** (which see) used in indirect narration where the principal verb is in the past tense گا ought to کو چاہیے **shouldn't** (*shud*-ĕnt) *auxiliary v.* (negative spoken form of *should*) ought not to کو نہیں چاہیے

shoulder (*shohl*-dĕ*) *n.* place where the arm joins the body کندھا، شانہ (*pl.*) the upper part of the back کندھے *take (something) on (one's) shoulders*, assume responsibility for کی ذمّہ داری لینا animal's foreleg as meat شانہ، پُٹھا shoulder-like part (*of* something) شانہ *v.t.* take on (one's) shoulder کی ذمّہ داری لینا push with the shoulder کندھے سے دھکیلنا *shoulder (one's) way through a crowd*, گھس بیٹھ کر آگے بڑھنا **shoulder-blade** *n.* flat bone of the shoulder مونڈھا

shout *n.* loud call اُونچی آواز *v.t.* & *i.* give a shout چلّانا speak in a loud voice چلّا کر کہنا

shove (shuv) *v.t.* & *i.* (colloq.) push دھکیلنا، ٹھیلنا *n.* push دھکّا

shovel (shuv-ĕl) *n.* spadelike tool بیلچہ، کرچھا *v.t.* (-ll-) take (*up*) with a shovel کرچھے سے اُٹھانا (clear a path, etc.) with a shovel بیلچے سے راستہ ہموار کرنا

show (shoh) *v.t.* & *i.* (*show, showed, shown*; old spelling: *shew, shewed, shewn*) cause to see دکھانا lead لانا *show (someone) in* کسی کو کمرے کے اندر لے جانا *show (someone) out* گھر سے باہر نکالنا *show off*, make a display of (one's accomplishments, etc.) کی شان دکھاتے پھرنا، بَنْنا *show (something) off*, make noticeable by contrast نمایاں کرنا یا ہونا *show up*. (colloq.) be present (*at* a meeting, etc.) جانا *show (someone or something) up*, make the truth about (him or it) known to others کی اصلیت بتانا، کی حقیقت سے آگاہ کرنا *show fight*, give signs of being ready to fight لڑنے مرنے پر تیار ہونا *show (one's) hand*, disclose (one's) plans اپنے منصوبے ظاہر کرنا *show the way to*, set an example for کے لیے مثال قائم کرنا *n.* showing اظہار *a show of hands*, raising of hands for or against a proposal in voting کے حق میں یا خلاف ہاتھ کھڑے کرکے رائے دینا exhibition نمائش *to be on show* کی نمائش ہونا display for impressing others ٹیپ ٹاپ، دکھاوا *for show* محض دکھاوے کے لیے، نمود، نمائش public entertainment in cinema or theatre کھیل، شو، تماشا *put up a good show*, do well قابلِ داد کام کرنا *show-business*, business of providing dramatic or other entertainments کھیل تماشے، تھیٹر کا کام یا فلم لائن (colloq.) anything that is going on جو کچھ ہو رہا ہو *give the whole show away* کی تفصیلات منظرِ عام پر لانا **showdown** *n.* (slang) declaration of one's intention, etc. کھل کر میدان میں آنا *have a showdown with (someone)*, bring lurking hatred for (someone) to a climax and fight it out with him (کسی سے) آر ج حد کر دینا **showing** *n.* causing to see دکھانا *on (one's) own showing*, as admitted by (oneself) خود اپنے لفظوں میں (یا عمل سے) *make a poor showing*, give a poor impression اچھا اثر نہ ڈالنا **showman** *n.* organizer of public entertainments تماشے کا منتظم **showmanship** *n.* art of attracting customers for one's wares گاہک کھینچنے کا فن **showy** (*shoh*-i) too gaudy بھڑکیلا **showily** *adv.* for show دکھاوے کے لیے

shower (shou-ĕ*) *n.* short fall of rain, etc. چھینٹا، بوچھاڑ large number (of things) arriving together جھڑی، بوچھاڑ، ریل، بھرمار (also *shower bath*), bath in which the bather receives sprinkling water from overhead فوّارے دار غسل خانہ bath there نو ذرے کے نیچے نکلنا

shrank *v.* (pa. t. of **shrink,** which see)

shrapnel *shrap*-nel, *n.* bullets in a shell which explodes to scatter them گولی دار ، گولی دار گولہ

a shrapnel

shred *n.* rag چیتھڑا ! *torn to shreds,* tattered جس کے چیتھڑے ہو گئے ہوں fragment ٹکڑا ! *not a shred of,* none at all ذرہ بھر بھی نہیں become or make into shreds چیتھڑے ہو جانا یا کرنا

shrew (*shroo*) *n.* scolding woman لڑاکا عورت **shrewish** (*shroo*-ish) *adj.* sharp-tongued لڑاکا

shrewd (shrood) *adj.* sharp-witted and sensible سمجھدار، ہوشمند، زیرک (of a guess) near the truth کچھ ٹھیک ٹھیک ہی ٹھیک سا **shrewdness** *n.* being shrewd سمجھ ، ہوشمندی ، زیرکی

shriek (shreek) *n.* scream چیخ *v.t.* & *i.* scream چیخنا

shrift *n.* (only in the phrase) *short shrift,* little time between announcement and execution of a punishment سزا کے اعلان اور تکمیل میں بہت کم وقفہ *give* (*someone*) *a short shrift* کو بچ نکلنے کی مہلت نہ پانا *get a short shrift* بچ نکلنے کی مہلت نہ پانا

shrill (shril) *adj.* piercing (sound, voice, etc.) باریک اور تیز ، تیکھی

shrimp *n.* a kind of shellfish ایک قسم کی مچھلی ، شرمپ very small person ٹھنگنا

shrine (shrin) *n.* tomb مزار ، روضہ casket containing sacred relics تبرکات دان place associated with some revered person or object مقدس یادگار

shrink *v.t.* & *i.* (*shrink, shrank, shrunk*) make or become smaller (of cloth through soaking) سکڑنا ، سکیڑنا ، شرنک ہونا یا کرنا move back (*from* something) in terror, etc. دبکنا **shrunken** *adj.* flinching دبکا ہوا ، سکڑا ہوا **shrinkage** *n.* shrinking سکڑن its degree سکڑن

shrive (shriv) *v.t.* (*shrive, shrove, shriven*) (old use) (*of* a penitent) confess توبہ کرنا ، اعتراف گناہ کرنا (of a priest) absolve (a penitent) بخشنا ، توبہ قبول کرنا

shrivel (*shriv*-el) *v.t.* & *i.* (-ll-) (cause to) become curled up (through heat, frost, old age, etc.) مُرمُر ہو جانا

shroud *n.* cloth wrapped round a corpse کفن cover (of mist, etc.) (کا) پردہ (*pl.*) ropes supporting a ship's mast مستول بردار رسے *v.t.* wrap in a shroud کفنانا ، تکفین cover (*in* mystery, etc.) (میں) چھپانا ، کا پردہ ڈالنا

shrub shrub *n.* a small bush چھوٹی جھاڑی **shrubbery** *shrub*-ĕ-ri *n.* place planted with shrubs جہاں چھوٹی جھاڑیاں بہت ہوں

shrug (shrug) *v.t.* & *i.* (-gg-) lift slightly (*one's shoulders,* to express doubt, indifference, etc. کندھے اچکانا *n.* such a movement کندھے اچکانا ، دوش برداری

shrunk, shrunken *v.* (pa. t. & pa. p. of **shrink,** which see)

shudder (*shud*-ĕ*) *v.i.* shiver with horror (*at* the sight of, etc.) کانپنا ، رونگٹے کھڑے ہونا *n.* such uncontrollable trembling کپکپی ، تھرتھری ، لرزہ

shuffle (*shuf*-ĕl) *v.t.* & *i.* drag one's feet (*along*) گھسٹ کر چلنا ، پیر رگڑ رگڑ کر چلنا mix (playing cards) before dealing تاش پھینٹنا put (papers, etc.) into disorder گڈمڈ کر دینا do (something) carelessly یونہی سا کرنا juggle with words سخن سازی کرنا **shuffler** *n.* one who juggles with words سخن ساز

shun (shun) *v.t.* (-nn-) avoid سے بچنا ، سے حذر کرنا

shunt (shunt) *v.t.* & *i.* divert (a railway engine or electric current) from one line to another لائن بدلنا (of a railway engine) be shunted to a siding بند لائن پر چلے جانا put off ملتوی کرنا ، کھٹائی میں ڈالنا

shut (shut) *v.t.* & *i.* (*shut, shut, shut*) close بند ہونا یا بند کرنا *shut down,* (of a factory, etc.) stop work بند کرنا یا بند ہونا *be shut in,* (of a building, etc.) be cut off (from a view or from easy access) گھر جانا *shut off,* (*a*) stop the supply of بند کر دینا (*b*) switch off (a wireless set, etc.) بند کرنا *be shut off,* be segregated from (society, etc.) سے کٹ جانا *shut up,* fasten doors, etc., well اچھی طرح بند کرنا *shut up !* be quiet خاموش ، بس چپ رہو *shut* (*someone*) *up,* make (someone) stop talking چپ کرا دینا

shutter (*shut*-ĕ*) *n.* movable cover for a door or window تختہ ، کواڑ ، چھلی *put up the shutters,* (*a*) close a shop دوکان بند کرنا ، یا بڑھانا (*b*) stop doing business کاروبار بند کر دینا (in a camera) cover of lens for admitting and shutting off light عدسہ پوش

shutters

shuttle (*shut*-ĕl) *n.* part of weaving machine that carries the thread from side to side جلاہے کی نال similar part in sewing machine پھرکی ، شٹل *v.t.* & *i.* move to and fro thus ادھر سے ادھر جانا

shuttlecock *n.* feathered cork tossed to and fro in badminton شٹل کاک ، چڑی **shuttle train** *n.* train running to and fro between a short distance کم سفر گاڑی ، شٹل

[1]shy (shi) *adj.* timid (person or behaviour) کترانے والا ، کنیانے والا bashful (person or behaviour) شرمیلا ، لجیلا ، حیا دار easily frightened (animal) بدکنے

fight shy of, evade سے کنی کترانا، سے بچنا، سے جھجکنا (slang) short of (or of some money) having lost it سے محروم *v.t.* (*shied, shied*) (*shy at*), (of a horse) turn aside from in fear سے بھڑکنا، سے بدکنا

shyly (*shī*-li) *adv.* bashfully

shyness *n.* being shy شرم، حیا، لاج

[2]**shy** (shī) *suf.* showing fear or distaste of سے بھاگنے والا، سے روکنے والا *work-shy* کام سے بھاگنے والا، کام چور

shyster (*shīs*-tě*) *n.* tricky lawyer (or other professional man) چلتا پرزہ

Sibyl (*sib*-il) *n.* pagan prophetess کاہنہ

(sic) (sik) assertion in parentheses guaranteeing the accuracy of a quotation apparently wrong بعینہٖ

sick (sik) *adj.* ill بیمار (after the verb *to be*) vomiting or disposed to vomit جسے قے آئی ہو، جسے متلی ہو رہی ہے *be sick* قے کرنا *feel sick*, متلی ہونا *go sick*, report for medical treatment علاج کے لیے جانا *sick of*, tired of سے بیزار *sick at (or about something)*, regretting پُرتاسف *sick for*, filled with a longing for کے لیے بیتاب

sicken (*sik*-ěn) *v.t.* & *i.* fall ill بیمار ہونا make or become tired (*of*) سے بیزار ہونا

sickening *adj.* disgusting بیزار کن

sickly (*sik*-li) *adj.* (taste, etc.) causing a sick feeling متلی frequently ill روگی، سدا روگی، دائم المرض weak کمزور suggesting illness مریضانہ، بیماروں کا سا

sicklily (*sik*-li-li) *adv.* in a sickly manner بیماروں کی طرح

sickness *n.* illness بیماری vomiting متلی، قے (یا)

sickle (*sick*-ěl) *n.* well-known small tool with a curved blade for harvesting درانتی *hammer and sickle*, these as symbols of Soviet or Communist supremacy درانتی اور ہتھوڑا (also see **scythe**)

a sickle

side (sīd) *n.* one of the surfaces of an object پہلو، رخ، طرف *on all sides*, everywhere چاروں طرف *by the side of*, compared with کے مقابلے میں *side by side* (*with*), touching or close together پہلو بہ پہلو *put (something) on one side*, (*a*) put it away, پرے کرنا (*b*) save it for future use آڑے وقت کے لیے بچانا team of players ٹیم، فریق *take sides*, support one party in a dispute لڑائی جھگڑے میں کسی ایک فریق کا ساتھ دینا، طرفداری کرنا، جانبداری کرنا *adj.* not the main, subsidiary ضمنی *v. i.* (side with), support (in a dispute) کی حمایت کرنا **side-arms** *n.* swords or bayonets تلواریں، سنگینیں **side-board** *n.* table, usually with drawers and cupboards in a dining-room نعمت خانہ **side-car** *n.* small one-wheeled car fastened at the side of a motor-cycle سائیڈ کار، بغلی کار

a motor-cycle with a side-car

side issue *n.* subsidiary question (in relation to the main one) ضمنی بات، علیحدہ مسئلہ **side-light** *n.* something throwing extra light on a problem جداگانہ بات، مزید روشنی *throw an interesting side-light on* پر مزید دلچسپ ضمنی تشریح، روشنی ڈالنا **sideline** *n.* occupation which is not one's main work ضمنی کاروبار **side-long** *adj.* & *adv.* from the side پہلو کی طرف سے **side-saddle** *n.* lady's saddle for keeping the feet on the same side of the horse یکرخی زین *adv.* on a side-saddle یکرخی زین پر **side-show** *n.* small show at a fair, etc. ضمنی تماشا comparatively less important ضمنی کام **side-track** *n.* branch road ذیلی راستہ *v. t.* evade discussion of (an issue, etc.) ٹال دینا، گول کر جانا turn (someone) away from his main purpose کو غلط راہ پر ڈالنا **side-walk** *n.* (U.S.) pavement فٹ پاتھ، پٹڑی

sideward *adj.* **sidewards** *adv.* towards a side پہلو کی جانب **sideways** *adv.* to or from the side پہلو کی جانب سے with the side first پہلو کے بل

siding (*sī*-ding) *n.* short railway track at the side of the main line for shunting سائیڈ لنگ، بغلی پٹڑی، کھڈرا، کھڈرلائن

sidereal (sī-dee-ri-ěl) *adj.* (of day, year, time, etc.) determined or measured by means of stars نجومی، فلکی (دن، سال یا وقت)

siding *n.*, **sideward** *adj.*, **sidewards** *adv.*, **sideways** *adv.* (see under **side**)

sidle (*sī*-děl) *v.i.* walk (*up to* or *away from* someone) gradually sidewards in nervous way ڈبک کر چلنا، گھبراتے ہوئے چلنا

siege (seej) *n.* beleaguring (*of* a town, etc). محاصرہ *lay siege to*, besiege کا محاصرہ کرنا

siesta (see-*es*-ta) *n.* afternoon nap قیلولہ

sieve (siv) *n.* utensil with holes in the bottom for sifting چھلنی (also see **sift**)

a sieve

siffleur (*sif*-lě*) *n.* (*fem. siffleuse* pr. *sif*-lěz) whistling artist سیٹی میں گانے والا یا والی، صفیرباز

sift *v.t.* & *i.* separate (one thing *from* another) by putting through a sieve چھاننا examine (evidence) carefully کی چھان بین کرنا shake (*on something*) through a sift چھلنی میں سے ڈالنا

sigh (*sī*) *v.i.* take a deep whispering breath آہ بھرنا، ٹھنڈی سانس لینا (of the wind) make such a sound سائیں سائیں کرنا feel longing (*for*) کے لیے آہیں بھرنا *n.* act of sighing آہ

sight (sīt) *n.* (faculty of) seeing بصارت *lose (one's) sight*, become blind اندھا ہو جانا *have short* *sight, have near sight*, suffer from myopia نزدیک بیں نگاہ رکھنا *have long sight*, see something only at a long distance دُور بیں نگاہ رکھنا *know (someone) only by sight*, know him by appearance and not as an acquaintance محض صُورت آشنا ہونا *lose sight of*, (*a*) see no longer کا نظروں سے اوجھل ہو جانا (*b*) be out of touch with سے ناآشنا ہونا (*c*) fail to keep in mind کا ذہن سے نکل جانا *catch sight of*, succeed in seeing دیکھ لینا *at sight, on sight*, as soon as it is seen دیکھتے ہی *in sight*, that which can be seen سامنے جو نظر آسکے *out of sight*, نظروں سے اوجھل *out of sight out of mind* آنکھ اوجھل پہاڑ اوجھل opinion رائے، خیال anything seen منظر، نظارہ (*pl.*) noteworthy places worth visiting قابلِ دید مقامات *see the sights (of an area)* (کے) قابلِ دید مقامات کی سیر کرنا (colloq.) ridiculous thing عجیب نمونہ device helping to take aim when using a gun or telescope مکھی thing thus observed نشانہ *v.t.* catch sight of دیکھنا see (something) by coming near it قریب آ کر دیکھنا، کی زیارت کرنا observe (a star, etc.) by using sights مشاہدہ کرنا **sightseeing** *n.* visit to the sights of a place قابلِ دید مقامات کی سیر **sightseer** *n.* one who goes about sightseeing قابلِ دید مقامات کی سیر کرنے والا (کسی شہر) کے دیکھنے کے لائق جگہوں کی سیر کرنے والا

sign (sīn) *n.* symbol علامت، رمز *mathematical signs*, symbols used in mathematics ریاضی کی علامات، علاماتِ ریاضی (also *signboard*), words, etc., on a board or plate سائن بورڈ *traffic signs* ٹریفک کے نشانات، علامات (usu. *pl.*) evidence (*of*) کے آثار آمد و رفت movement of the hands or the head as expressive of words اشارہ *v.t. & i.* write one's name on (document, etc.) دستخط کرنا *sign (something) away*, surrender (it) by signing a deed اپنے دستخطوں سے بیچ ڈالنا *sign (someone) up*, employ him by signing a contract کو معاہدے پر نوکر رکھنا signify (*to* or *for* someone *to do* something) کرنے کا اشارہ کرنا **sign-board** *n.* board with one's name or advertisement on it سائن بورڈ **sign-post** *n.* upright post (on cross-roads) with arms, showing directions of roads رہنما کھمبا

a sign or signboard

signal (*sig*-nĕl) *v.t. & i.* (-ll-) send a message (*to* someone) by means of signs (*that* or *to do* something) سگنل کرنا اشارات سے اطلاع دینا use signals *n.* sign اشارہ (also *railway-signal*), post with arms to warn drivers سگنل، ریل کا اشارہ starting point *for* a series نقطۂ آغاز *adj.* remarkable (service, event, etc.) نمایاں، ممتاز **signalize** *v.t.* make (event, etc.) signal کو نمایاں بنانا **signal-box** *n.* cabin from where railway signals are worked سگنل خانہ **signaller** *n.* one who sends or receives messages by signals سگنلیئر **signalman** *n.* one who works railway or naval signals سگنلیئر

signatory (*sig*-na-tè-ri) *n. & adj.* (person, country) that has signed an agreement معاہدے پر دستخط کرنے والا، فریقِ معاہدہ (also see *signature*)

signature (*sig*-na-chĕ*) *n.* (usu. *pl.*) person's name signed by himself دستخط (also *signature tune*), (see *Addenda*)

signify (*sig*-ni-fī) *v.t. & i.* show by a sign اشارہ کرنا make known (one's approval, etc.) کا اظہار کرنا be a sign of کا مظہر ہونا mean کے معنی ہونا *signify much* (or *little*), be of much (or little) importance اہمیت رکھنا (یا نہ رکھنا) **significance** (sig-*nif*-i-kans) *n.* meaning معنی، مطلب، مفہوم importance اہمیت **significant** (sig-*nif*-i-kant) *adj.* important اہم having a suggestive meaning معنی خیز **signification** (sig-ni-fi-*kay*-shĕn) *n.* exact meaning (*of* a word) کا ٹھیک مفہوم

silence (*sī*-lens) *n.* being quiet خاموشی، سکوت *listen to (someone) in silence* کی بات خاموشی سے سُننا *v.t.* make (someone quiet) چُپ کرا دینا، خاموش کرا دینا cause (something) to be quiet شور رکوا دینا make (someone) unable to reply کو لاجواب کر دینا **silencer** (*sī*-lens-ĕ*) *n.* device for reducing the noise of a machine آواز روک، شور روک (also see **silent**)

silent (*sī*-lent) *adj.* quiet چُپ، خاموش without sound بے آواز، ساکت saying little or nothing کم گو giving no news (*on an issue*, etc.) (کے بارے میں) خاموش **silently** *adv.* quietly خاموشی سے

silhouette (sil-oo-*et*) *n.* outline of something or (usu. side-view) of someone seen against a light background سیاہ خاکہ *v.t.* show or make a silhouette of (someone or something *against*) کا سیاہ خاکہ ہونا

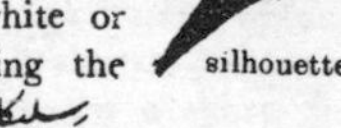

silhouette

silica (*sil*-i-ka) *n.* hard white or colourless substance forming the chief ingredient of sand سِلیکا

silk *n.* thin soft thread prepared by silkworms ریشم، ابریشم *artificial silk, artsilk*, (now usu. called) rayon مصنوعی ریشم، نقلی ریشم fabrics made from this ریشمی کپڑا، ریشم *adj.* made of silk ریشمی **silken** *adj.* (lit.) sleek (hair, etc.) نرم، ملائم pleasantly soft (voice) ملائم **silkworm** (*silk*-wĕ*m) *n.*

there

shrank v. (pa. t. of **shrink**, which see)

shrapnel (*shrap-nel*) n. bullets in a shell which explodes to scatter them

a shrapnel

shred n. rag *torn to shreds*, tattered fragment *not a shred of*, none at all become or make into shreds

shrew (*shroo*) n. scolding woman **shrewish** (*shroo-ish*) adj. sharp-tongued

shrewd (*shrood*) adj. sharp-witted and sensible (of a guess) near the truth **shrewdness** n. being shrewd

shriek (*shreek*) n. scream v.t. & i. scream

shrift n. (only in the phrase) *short shrift*, little time between announcement and execution of a punishment *give (someone) a short shrift* *get a short shrift*

shrill (*shril*) adj. piercing (sound, voice, etc.)

shrimp n. a kind of shellfish very small person

shrine (*shrin*) n. tomb casket containing sacred relics place associated with some revered person or object

shrink v.t. & i. (*shrink, shrank, shrunk*) make or become smaller (of cloth through soaking) move back (*from something*) in terror, etc. **shrunken** adj. flinching **shrinkage** n. shrinking its degree

shrive (*shriv*) v.t. (*shrive, shrove, shriven*) (old use) (of a penitent) confess (of a priest) absolve (a penitent)

shrivel (*shriv-el*) v.t. & i. (-ll-) (cause to) become curled up (through heat, frost, old age, etc.)

shroud n. cloth wrapped round a corpse cover (of mist, etc.) (*pl.*) ropes supporting a ship's mast v.t. wrap in a shroud cover (in mystery, etc.)

shrub (*shrub*) n. a small bush **shrubbery** (*shrub-e-ri*) n. place planted with shrubs

shrug (*shrug*) v.t. & i. (-gg-) lift slightly (*one's shoulders*), to express doubt, indifference, etc. n. such a movement

shrunk, shrunken v. (pa. t. & pa. p. of **shrink**, which see)

shudder (*shud-e**) v.i. shiver with horror (at the sight of, etc.) n. such uncontrollable trembling

shuffle (*shuf-el*) v.t. & i. drag one's feet (*along*) mix (playing-cards) before dealing put (papers, etc.) into disorder do (something) carelessly juggle with words **shuffler** n. one who juggles with words

shun (*shun*) v.t. (-nn-) avoid

shunt (*shunt*) v.t. & i. divert (a railway engine or electric current) from one line to another (of a railway engine) be shunted to a siding put off

shut (*shut*) v.t. & i. (*shut, shut, shut*) close *shut down*, (of a factory, etc.) stop work *be shut in*, (of a building, etc.) be cut off (from a view or from easy access) *shut off*, (a) stop the supply of (b) switch off (a wireless set, etc.) *be shut off*, be segregated from (society, etc.) *shut up*, fasten doors, etc., well *shut up!* be quiet *shut (someone) up*, make (someone) stop talking

shutter (*shut-e**) n. movable cover for a door or window *put up the shutters*, (a) close a shop (b) stop doing business (in a camera) cover of lens for admitting and shutting off light

shutters

shuttle (*shut-el*) n. part of weaving machine that carries the thread from side to side similar part in sewing machine v.t. & i. move to and fro thus **shuttlecock** n. feathered cork tossed to and fro in badminton **shuttle train** n. train running to and fro between a short distance

shy (*shi*) adj. timid (person or behaviour) bashful (person or behaviour) easily frightened (animal)

of) celebrate in poetry **singsong** (*sing-song*) *n.* (*in a*) tone of monotonous regularity

singe (*sinj*) *v.t.* & *i.* burn off the tips or ends (esp. of hair) blacken the surface of (cloth, etc.) by burning burn feathers, etc., of (poultry, etc.) after killing **single** (*sing-èl*) *adj.* one only of one side *single ticket*, ticket for a single (and not return) journey for the use of one only unmarried *v.t.* choose (*out*) from others (*for* something) **single-handed** *adj.* alone *adv.* without help from others **single-minded** *adj.* unselfishly devoted to one cause **singly** *adv.* one by one by oneself **singleton** *n.* one person, etc., (as opposed to a *pair*)

singular (*sing*-ew-lĕ*) *adj.* uncommon غیر معمولی strange عجیب، نرالا، انوکھا very outstanding (action) یکتا، عدیم المثال (grammar) of the form used in speaking of one person or thing واحد، مفرد *n.* singular form (of a word) واحد، مفرد **singularity** (sing-ew-*la*-ri-ti) *n.* the quality of being singular انوکھا پن، یکتائی **sinister** (*sin-is-tĕ**) *adj.* of evil omen منحوس of malignant aspect منحوس، بُرا سا بنا ہوا wicked شر انگیز (of the) left بایاں **sink** *v.t.* & *i.* (*sink, sank, sunk*) go down or under ڈوبنا، غرق کرنا (cause a ship) to sink ڈبونا (of heart, foundation, etc.) become weaker or lower بیٹھنا *His heart sank at the news* یہ خبر سن کر اس کا دل بیٹھ گیا make (well, etc.) by digging کھودنا (of liquids) penetrate (*into*) میں سرایت کرنا affect deeply پر اثر کرنا، میں گھر کرنا put (money) permanently into an undertaking میں رقم ہمیشہ کے لیے لگا دینا *n.* fixed basin in the kitchen with a drain for taking off water, used for washing dishes, etc. اَوْنچا کھرا، باورچی خانے کا بیسن **sinking** *adj.* that which goes down ڈوبنے والا *sinking feelings*, feeling in the stomach caused by hunger or fear دل بیٹھا جانا *sinking fund*, part of income put aside for gradual repayment of a debt ذخیرۂ ادائگی **Sino-** (si-noh) *pref.* Chinese چینی، چین **sinuous** (*sin*-ew-us) *adj.* full of curves پیچدار، پُر پیچ و تاب **sip** *v.t.* & *i.* (-pp-) drink (something) taking it in a very small quantity at a time کی چسکی لگانا *n.* sipping چسکی **siphon** (*sī*-fun) *n.* V-shaped pipe for drawing liquid from a container سیفن، نخدار نلکی، سارِقہ bottle from which soda-water, etc., can be forced out by pressure of gas in it سیفن *v.t.* & *i.* (cause to) draw (*out, off*) through a siphon سیفن کے ذریعے نکلنا یا نکالنا **sir** (sĕ*) *n.* title of a knight or baronet سَر title of respect جناب، جناب والا **sire** (*sī*-è*) *n.* (old use) father of male ancestor باپ، دادا وغیرہ، مورثِ اعلیٰ title of respect used when addressing a king or emperor جہاں پناہ، وَلی نعمت the male parent (of horse or other beast) (as opposed to *dam*) باپ **siren** (*sī*-ren) *n.* *Cl. myth.* one of a number of winged women whose songs charmed sailors and caused their destruction سائرن، سیرن woman who attracts and is dangerous to men قاتل حسینہ woman who sings with a sweet voice خوش آواز مُغنّیہ whistle for sending warnings, etc. سائرن، بھونپو **sirloin** (*sĕ**-loin) *n.* best part of loin of beef گائے کے گوشت میں پٹھے کا بہترین حصہ **sissy** (*sis*-i) *n.* & *adj.* (also *cissy* pr. *sis*-i) (U.S. slang) effeminate person **sister** (*sis*-tĕ*) *n.* daughter of the same parents as one بہن، سگی بہن *half-sister*, daughter of one of the same parents as one سوتیلی بہن senior hospital nurse سسٹر، بڑی نرس nun *adj.* of the same design, etc. جوڑی، جیسا، جیسے **sisterhood** *n.* society of nuns living together in a religious order راہبات کی جماعت religious body of women خواتین کی مذہبی انجمن **sister-in-law** *n.* sister of one's wife سالی sister of one's husband نند wife of one's brother بھابی **sisterly** *adj.* of or like a sister خواہرانہ **sit** *v.t.* & *i.* (*sit, sat, sat*) (-tt-) be seated بیٹھنا be in session کا اجلاس ہونا (of birds) rest for the night بسیرا لینا (of birds) hatch انڈوں پر بیٹھنا، آنا، بیٹھنا (of clothing, etc.) fit انڈے سینا keep one's seat on (a horse) (گھوڑے) پر آسن جمائے رہنا *sit down under* (*an insult, etc.*), suffer (it) without complaint پی جانا، برداشت کر لینا *sit for* (*a place in Parliament*), represent (it) کی نمائندگی کرنا *sit for* (*an examination*), take it میں بیٹھنا، دینا *sit for* (*one's portrait*), have (one's portrait) painted while sitting before an artist بیٹھ کر کھچوانا *sit on* (*a committee, etc.*), be a member of (it) رکن ہونا *sit* (*or sit up*) *on* (*a question*), (of a jury, etc.), inquire into it کی تحقیقات کرنا *sit* (or *sit up*) *on* (someone), (colloq.) snub (him) کو جھاڑ جھپاڑ کرنا *sit out (a play)*, remain to witness (it) to the end بیرع آخر تک بیٹھنا *sit up*, take an upright position after lying flat اٹھ بیٹھنا *sit up till (late in the night, etc.)*, keep awake till then دیر تک جاگتے رہنا *make (someone) sit up*, shock or surprise him کو سخت حیران کر دینا **sitting** *n*. time for which person, assembly or court sits continuously نشست *finish a book at one sitting* ایک ہی نشست میں کتاب ختم کر دینا **sitter** *n*. (esp.) one who sits for a portrait تصویر کھچوانے والا *baby-sitter*, person employed to sit with and look after a small baby while its parents are away بچے کے پاس بیٹھنے والا، بچہ نشین *baby-sitting*, attending a baby thus بچہ نشینی **sit-down strike** *n*. strike in which workers remain in their workhouse till the dispute is settled کام پر جاکر کام نہ کرنے والی ہڑتال، کارخانہ نشینی

site (sit) *n*. place (*of* something past or present, or *for* something to be) (کا) موقع (کی) جگہ *v.t*. locate, place کا مقام متعین کرنا، کا پتہ کرنا

situated (*si*-tew-ay-tid) *adj*. (older form ; *situate*) of a town, building, etc.) placed واقع (of a person) in (certain) situation اس حالت میں، آندریں **situation** (*-ay-*) *n*. position (*of* a town, building, etc.) موقع حالات state of affairs at a certain time صورتِ حال employment نوکری

six (siks) *n*. & *adj*. 6 *at sixes and sevens*, in confusion پریشان **sixth** *adj*. 6th چھٹا **six-fold** *adj*. six times چھ گنا **sixer** *n*. (in cricket) hit for six runs چھکا **sixteen** (*siks-teen*) *n*. & *adj*. 16 سولہ **sixteenth** *adj*. 16th سولھواں **sixty** (*siks-ti*) *n*. & *adj*. 60 ساٹھ **sixtieth** *adj*. 60th ساٹھواں

size (sIz) *n*. degree of largeness or smallness جسامت، قد، قامت، تقطیع، ناپ *about the size of*, about as large as جتنا، تقریباً، اتنا جتنا *of some size*, fairly large کافی بڑا one of the standard sizes in which articles are made سائز *size nine (etc.) shoes* نو (وغیرہ) نمبر کا جوتا *v.t*. arrange in sizes جسامت کی ترتیب سے لگانا *size up* (a situation, etc.) form an opinion of کے متعلق رائے قائم کرنا، کا اندازہ کرنا **sizable** *adj*. of a fairly large size کافی بڑا

sizzle (*siz-èl*) *n*. hissing sound as of something cooking in fat سوں سوں *v.i*. make such a sound سوں سوں کرنا

skate (skayt) *n*. one of a pair of sharp-edged steel blades to be fastened to a boot for moving smoothly over ice برفانی کھڑاؤں (also *roller-skate*), one of a pair of implements with a set of castors attached to shoes for gliding over level floor کفشی پہیے، سکیٹ a species of flat-bodied fish مرمچھ مچھلی *v.i*. go on skates برفانی کھڑاؤں سے برفانی کھڑاؤں (یا کفشی پہیوں) پھسلنا **skating** *n*. act of skating برپھسلنا، سکیٹ کرنا **skating-rink** *n*. piece of ice or floor for skating سکیٹ گاہ

skein (skayn) *n*. length of silk or wool yarn coiled into a bundle لچھا

skeleton (*skel*-e-tun) *n*. bones of an animal body arranged (as) when living ڈھانچا، ڈھانچ framework (of building or of an organization, etc.) ڈھانچا، ڈھانچ outline (*of* plan, etc.) خاکہ، منصوبہ *adj*. basic بنیادی *skeleton key*, master key ہر قفلی کنجی *skeleton staff*, the minimum necessary staff بنیادی عملہ

a skeleton

sketch (skech) *n*. rough and quickly made drawing خاکہ short account or description مختصر بیان short, humorous play, etc. خاکہ، سکیچ، خاکہ *v.t*. & *i*. make a sketch of کا خاکہ بنانا *sketch (something) out*, give a rough plan of کا خاکہ بیان کرنا

sketchy (*skech-i*) *adj*. lacking detail or finish مختصراً، سرسری، یونہی سا، سرسری **sketchily** *adv*. سرسری طور پر

skewer (*skew-ě**) *n*. pointed stick for holding meat together while cooking سیخ، کباب کی سیخ *v.t*. fasten with a skewer سیخ میں پرونا

ski (shee or skee) *n*. one of a pair of long, narrow strips of wood, strapped to the boots for moving over snow لمبا برفانی جوتا، شی، سکی *v.i*. (*ski, ski'd, ski'd*) move over snow on skis شی (یا سکی) پر پھسلنا

skid *n*. piece of wood or metal fixed under the wheel of a cart, etc., to prevent it from turning پہیے کی روک slipping movement (of the wheels of a car, etc.) on a slippery road موٹر کا پھسلنا *v.i*. (-dd-) (of a car, etc.) slip (sideways) (موٹر کا) پھسلنا

skiff (skif) *n*. small light boat, moved by a single rower ہلکی کشتی

skill (skil) *n*. ability to do something well and expertly مشق، مہارت، ہنر مندی **skilled** (skild) *adj*. trained تربیت یافتہ، کاریگر *skilled workman* کاریگر needing skill مہارت طلب experienced تجربہ کار

skilful *adj*. having or showing skill ماہر، کاریگر

skim *v.t*. & *i*. (-mm-) remove cream or scum from the surface of (a liquid) ملائی اتارنا، پپڑی اتارنا *skim the cream off* دودھ میں سے مکھن نکالنا *skim the milk* ملائی اتار لینا move lightly (*over* a surface) not or lightly touching it ساتھ سے گزر جانا، چھوتے ہوئے گزر جانا read through something quickly سرسری طور پر دیکھ لینا، پر سرسری نظر ڈال لینا

skim-milk (*skim*-milk) *n*. (also popularly called

skimmed milk), milk from which the cream has been skimmed ملائی اُترا دُودھ

skimp (skimp) *v.t.* & *i.* supply or use less than enough کم دینا (یا) کم اِستعمال کرنا *skimp cloth in making a suit* سُوٹ میں کپڑے کی نا روا بچت کرنا **skimpy** *adj.* less than enough کم (of a dress, etc.) too small or too tight بہت چھوٹا (یا) بڑا تنگ

skin *n.* outer covering of animal body کھال، چمڑی، چمڑا، جلد outer covering of a fruit چھلکا container made of skin for holding liquids, etc. مشک *v.t.* & *i.* (-nn-) take the skin off کھال اُتارنا (slang) swindle, fleece کی کھال اُدھیڑنا، کا سر (یا) اُدھیڑنا مُونڈنا **skin-deep** *adj.* superficial سطحی **skinflint** *n.* miser کنجوس skinny (*skin*-i) *adj.* very thin پتلا، دُبلا

skip *v.t.* & *i.* (-pp-) jump lightly and quickly اُچھلنا، کُودنا jump over a rope (called a *skipping-rope*) which is turned over the head and under the feet as one jumps رسّی پھلانگنا go from one thing to another ایک چیز کو چھوڑ کر دُوسری کی طرف جانا read (a book) thus disjointedly (کتاب) جستہ جستہ دیکھنا *n.* skipping movement پھلانگ، جست *n.* cage bucket in which men or materials are lowered into a mine نیچے اُتارنے کی ٹوکری **skipper** (skip-ĕ*) *n.* captain (of a small merchant ship or of a playing team) کپتان **skip stop** *n.* (see *Addenda*)

a girl is skipping

skirmish (skĕ*-mish) *n.* unplanned fight between small parties جھڑپ *v. i.* have a skirmish کی جھڑپ ہونا

skirt (skĕ*t) *n.* woman's garment that hangs from the waist سایا، لہنگا part of a dress, etc., below the waist دامن (*pl.*) outskirts (of town, etc.) کنارہ، مضافات *v.t.* be on the skirts of کے کنارے واقع ہونا pass along the outskirts of کے کنارے کنارے جانا

skit *n.* short humorous play, copying and making fun (*of* something) سکیٹ (colloq.) crowd ہجوم (pl.) (*skits*), lots or heaps of بہت، ڈھیروں کے ڈھیر **skittish** *adj.* lively (person) شوخ، چنچل excitable (horse) بھڑکنے والا، بدکنے والا

skittles (*skit*-elz) *n.* game in which a ball is bowled at nine wooden pins (each called a *skittle*) سکیٹلز

skivvy (*skiv*-i) *n.* (colloq.) (contemptuous term for) female domestic servant نوکرانی، ماما

skulk (skulk) *v.i.* hide چھپنا move secretly through cowardice چھپتے پھرنا avoid (work or duty) پہلو بچانا move secretly with an evil purpose داؤں لگانا

skull (skul) *n.* bony case of the head کھوپڑی، کاسۂ سر **skull-cap** *n.* close-fitting cap worn by old men تنگ ٹوپی

skunk *n.* furry animal which gives off a bad smell when attacked سکنک its fur سکنک کی سمور

sky (skī) (pl. *skies*) the heavens آسمان **skyhigh** *adj.* & *adv.* up in (to) the sky آسمان تک بہت ہی اُونچا **skylark** *n.* small bird that sings as it flies high into the sky اُونچا چنڈول **skylight** *n.* window in a roof شمسی روشندان **skyline** *n.* outline of things seen against the sky خطِ فلکی **sky-scraper** *n.* very tall building بڑی اُونچی عمارت **skytyping** *n.*, **skywriting** *n.* (see *Addenda*)

a skylark

a skylight

slab *n.* thick flat piece of stone or other solid substance سِل

slack (slack) *adj.* very careless سُست، کاہل، لاپروا not doing the work carefully کام میں سست with not much business جب کاروبار نہ ہو loose ڈھیلا ڈھالا *n.* (*the slack*), that part of a rope, etc., which hangs loosely (رسّے وغیرہ کا) کھلا کنارہ coal dust کوئلے کا چُورا (*pl.*) trousers پتلون *v.i.* be lazy or careless in one's work کام میں سست ہونا *slack off* (or *up*), reduce speed, (of work) (کام کی) رفتار کم کر دینا **slacken** (*slak*-en) *v.t.* & *i.* make or become slower سُست ہو جانا **slacker** *n.* (colloq.) person who tries to avoid his proper share of work کام چور **slackly** *adv.* lazily, carelessly or loosely سُستی سے، بے پروائی سے، ڈھیلے ڈھالے انداز سے **slackness** *n.* سُستی، کاہلی، ڈھیلا پن

slag *n.* waste matter remaining when metal has been extracted from ore دھات کا میل

slain (slayn) *v.* (pa. p. of **slay**, which see)

slake (slayk) *v.t.* satisfy (thirst) (پیاس وغیرہ) بجھانا *slake lime* چونا پانی میں بجھانا، چونا بجھانا *slaked lime* بجھا ہوا چُونا satisfy (desire for revenge, etc.) خواہش پوری کرنا

slam *v. t.* & *i.* (-mm-) shut (door, etc.) violently زور سے بند ہونا (یا کرنا) put (*down*), etc. with force زور سے پھینکنا (یا پٹخنا) *n.* noise of (a door, window, etc.) being slammed (دروازہ وغیرہ) زور سے بند کرنے کی آواز

slander (*sland*-ĕ*) *n.* false statement damaging a person's reputation بہتان، تہمت، اتہام make such a statement بہتان باندھنا **slanderous** *adj.* making such statements افترا پرداز containing slanders بہتان آمیز

slang *n.* popular words or phrases not suitable for good writing عامیانہ تلفظ kind of slang used by a special class *adj.* such popular words) عامیانہ *v.t.* use abusive language to کو گالی دینا

slangy (*slang*-i) *adj.* fond of using slang عامیانہ الفاظ استعمال کرنے والا full of slang عامیانہ

slant (slahnt) *n.* slope ڈھلان، ڈھال *on the slant,* slanting ترچھا (U.S.) viewpoint نقطۂ نگاہ، زاویۂ نظر *give a new slant to (news item, etc.)* (خبر وغیرہ) کو مخصوص زاویۂ نگاہ سے پیش کرنا *v.i.* slope

slap *n.* quick blow with the open hand چپت، تھپڑ تھپڑ لگانا، طمانچہ مارنا *v.t.* (-pp-) hit with a slap کھلا پنجہ put (something *down*) with a slapping noise چپت رسید کرنا ٹھپ کر کے رکھنا **slapdash** (*slap*-) *adj.* reckless بے پرواہ *adv.* recklessly بے پروایانہ، بے پروائی سے

slapstick (*slap*-stik) *n.* & *adj.* boisterous low (comedy) of the roughest kind (طربیہ) مار دھاڑ والا گھٹیا

slash *v.t.* & *i.* make long cuts in (or *at* something) with a sweeping stroke کاٹ ڈالنا strike hard with a whip چابک زور سے مارنا *n.* act of slashing کاٹ such cut چیر

slat *n.* long, thin narrow piece of wood, etc. (esp. one of a set in venetian blinds) چپٹی

slate (slayt) *n.* rock splitting into thin, smooth layers سلیٹ usu. oblong piece of this used for roofs سلیٹ sheet of slate in a wooden frame for writing on سلیٹ *slate-pencil,* pencil used for writing on a slate سلیٹی *clean slate,* (*a*) impressionable mind اثر پذیر ذہن (*b*) good record اچھا ماضی *clean the slate, start with a clean slate,* begin afresh without commitments از سر نو شروع کرنا *v.t.* roof with slates سلیٹ کی چھت ڈالنا (colloq.) scold لتاڑنا **slaty** *adj.* like or containing slate سلیٹ کا سا blue-grey (colour) سلیٹی

slattern (*slat*-ĕ*n) *n.* untidy woman گندی عورت پھوہڑ **slatternly** *adj.* untidy or slovenly (woman) گندی، پھوہڑ

slaughter (*slaw*-tĕ*) *v.t.* kill (an animal) for food حلال کرنا، ذبح کرنا kill (people) in great numbers کا قتل عام ہونا *n.* killing of animals for food حلال کرنا، ذبح کرنا killing of many people (in war) قتل عام **slaughter-house** *n.* place where animals are killed for food بوچڑ خانہ، مذبح، مسلخ

slave (slayv) *n.* one who is the property of another and bound to serve him غلام one compelled to work very hard for someone else جس سے سخت کام لیا جائے *be a slave to* (or *of something*) be in the habit کا عادی ہونا، کی عادت میں مبتلا ہونا *be a slave of* (someone), be in (his) power کا غلام ہونا *v.t.* work hard (*at* something *for* a living, etc.) بڑا سخت محنت کرنا **slave-driver** *n.* man in charge of slaves غلاموں کا نگران hard task-master ظالم آقا، جابر آقا

slavery (*slayv*-ĕ-ri) *n.* being a slave غلامی custom of having slaves غلامی hard and ill-paid employment سخت نوکری **slavish** *adj.* (of habits, character, etc.) like that of slaves غلامانہ weak and submissive (person) ذلیل without originality غلامانہ

slaver (*slayv*-ĕ*) *v.i.* let spittle flow from the mouth رال بہنے دینا، رال ٹپکانا *n.* saliva رال، لعاب دہن gross flattery سخت خوشامد person or ship engaged in slave-trade بردہ فروش

slay *v.t.* (*slay, slew, slain*) murder مار ڈالنا، قتل کرنا

sled (sled) *n.* (same as [1]**sledge,** which see)

[1]**sledge** (slej) *n.* (also *sleigh* pr. slay, or *sled*) vehicle with long narrow strips instead of wheels used for moving on snow برف گاڑی *v.t.* & *i.* travel by sledge برف گاڑی میں جانا carry in it برف گاڑی میں لے جانا

a sledge, sled or sleigh

[2]**sledge, sledge-hammer** *n.* heavy hammer used by blacksmiths لوہاروں کا بڑا ہتھوڑا، ہتوڑا *sledge-hammer blow,* (*a*) violent blow سخت ضرب (*b*) violent attack سخت حملہ

sleek *adj.* soft and smooth (hair or fur) نرم، ملائم، چکنا، چپڑا having sleek hair or fur ملائم بالوں والا (of a person, his behaviour) specious چکنی چپڑی باتوں والا *v.t.* make sleek ملائم بنانا smooth with the hand ہاتھ سے صاف کرنا

sleep *n.* rest in a state of natural unconsciousness سونا، نیند، خواب *v.t.* & *i.* (slept) take rest thus سونا، آرام کرنا *sleep (one's headache, etc.) off,* recover from (it) by sleeping سے سو کر آرام کرنا (of a hotel, etc.), have enough beds for (اتنے لوگوں کی) میں خوابگاہیں ہونا **sleeper** *n.* one who sleeps سونے والا heavy log of wood on which railway lines are laid سلیپر، پٹڑیوں کا کندا sleeping car bed in it سونے والے ڈبے میں بستر

sleepers under a rail track

sleeping-car, sleeping-carriage *n.* railway carriage with berths used as beds سونے والا ڈبہ

sleeping-draught *n.* medicine inducing sleep خواب آور دوا **sleeping-pill** *n.* pill for this purpose خواب آور گولی **sleeping partner** *n.* person who puts money into a business but plays no active part in it وہ ساجھی جو انتظام میں شریک نہ ہو، غیر دخیل شریک **sleepless** *adj* without sleep بے خواب unable to get sleep جسے نیند نہ آئے **sleeplessness** *n.* being without sleep بے خوابی **sleep-walker** *n.* somnambulist خواب خرام **sleep-walking** *n.* somnambulism خواب خرامی **sleepy** *adj.* about to sleep ; dozing جیسے نیند ہو needing sleep خواب آلودہ، نیم خوابیدہ، نیم خواب کی ضرورت ہو quiet خاموش inactive پُرسکون *sleepy sickness*, inflammation of the brain accompanied by lethargy نیم خوابی کا مرض، دماغی ورم کی بیماری کی ہوئی نیم خوابی **sleepily** *adj.* drowsily ; as if in sleep نیم خوابیدہ انداز سے **sleepiness** *n.* being sleepy نیم خوابی، نیند سی S To **sleep** is the general term : to **nod** is to drop the head sleepily ; to **doze,** go off into light sleep ; to **drowze,** do so heavily while trying to keep awake ; to **slumber,** sleep long and peacefully ; to **snooze,** between duties ; to **repose,** relax ; to **rest,** do so without sleeping ; take a **siesta,** sleep for a short while after lunch.

sleet *n.* partly frozen rain برف و باراں *v.i.* برف و باراں کا پڑنا

sleeve (sleev) *n.* part of a garment covering the arm آستین *turn up (one's) sleeves,* (a) prepare for fighting لڑائی کے لیے تیار ہونا (b) prepare for work کمر بستہ ہونا *laugh in (one's) sleeve*, be secretly amused منہ ہی منہ میں ہنسنا *have (something) up (one's) sleeve*, have a secret plan, etc., for future use آڑے وقت کے لیے تیار رکھنا

sleigh (slay) *n.* (also *sled*, or *sledge* pr. slej) sledge, esp. one drawn by a horse برفانی گاڑی **sleigh-bell** *n.* bell attached to the harness of a horse گھوڑے کے ساز کی گھنٹی

sleight (slit) *n.* (used only in the phrase :) *sleight of hand*, skill in the use of one's hands for performing juggling tricks ہاتھ کی صفائی شعبدہ بازی

slender (*slend-ĕ**) *adj.* tall and thin (column, stalk, etc.) پتلا اور لمبا not fat دُبلا پتلا graceful چھریرا small تھوڑا slight بہت کم *a slender chance of success* کامیابی کا بہت کم امکان

slept *v.* (pa. t. & pa. p. of **sleep,** which see)

sleuth (slooth) *n.* (also *sleuth-hound*) bloodhound following a scent کھوجی کتا (colloq.) detective سُراغ رساں، جاسوس

slew (sloo) *v.* (pa. t. of **slay,** which see) *v.t.* & *i.* (also *slue*, pr. sloo) turn (*round*) into a new direction زبردستی موڑنا

slice (slis) *n.* thin flat piece cut off something (esp., bread or meat) ٹکڑا *v.t.* cut into slices ٹکڑے کاٹنا cut (a piece) off (something) سے ٹکڑا کاٹنا

slick (slik) *adj.* (colloq.) smooth صاف، ملائم tricky (person or manners) چکنی چپڑی باتوں والا *n.* (see *Addenda*)

slide (sl.d) *v.t.* & *i.* (*slide, slid, slid*) (cause to) slip along over a polished surface پھسلنا، رپٹنا (of things) move easily and smoothly سرکنا *let things slide,* be remiss سے غافل ہونا pass gradually without being aware (*into* a condition) دھیرے دھیرے ہو جانا *n.* sliding پھسلنا smooth slope down which things or persons can slide پھسلن، پھسلواں ڈھلوان such smooth sliding board with stairs on the opposite side for children to slide down پھسلن، پھسلنی mass of rock or snow sliding downhill پھسلنے والا تودہ picture slid into a projector and shown on a screen سلائیڈ فلم glass plate on which is placed something to be examined under a miscroscope خوردبین کا شیشہ part of a machine, etc., that slides مشین کا پھسلواں حصہ

a slide (definition 3)

slide rule *n.* rule with a sliding part, used for mathematical calculations سرکنے والا پیمانہ، سرکنا پیمانہ **sliding-scale** *n.* scale according to which one thing goes up or down in relation to changes in something else (as for example, wages in proportion to prices) متغیر شرح

slight (slit) *adj.* slender پتلا small چھوٹا، تھوڑا، معمولی not serious ; unimportant غیر اہم *n.* lack of proper respect سبکی، تذلیل، اہانت *v.t.* treat (someone) thus کی سبکی کرنا **slightly** *adv.* a little کچھ، کسی قدر سے *slightly better* بہتر حد تک، قدرے

slim *adj.* slender پتلا، دُبلا small چھوٹا، تھوڑا، معمولی inadequate ناکافی *v.i.* (-mm-) eat less to become slim ; dieting and exercises for this purpose دُبلا ہونے کے لیے کم خوری اور ورزش

slime (slım) *n.* fine oozy mud پتلی کیچڑ any similar substance شیرہ کا سا **slimy** (*slī-mi*) *adj.* slippery پھسلنا hard to hold because too soft لجلجانا covered with slime کیچڑ میں لت پت repulsively servile ذلیل خوشامدی

sling *n.* band looped round (broken arm) to support it گلے کی پٹی، گل پٹی band round anything to lift, throw or support it فلاخن، پھندا *v.t.* & *i.* (*sling, slung, slung*) throw (something) with force (*at*) زور سے پھینکنا suspend (something) so that it can swing or be lifted لٹکانا

slink *v.i.* (*slink, slunk, slunk*) sneak (*about, away, by, off*) in a secret, guilty or ashamed manner کھسک جانا، سرک جانا

slip *v.t.* & *i.* (-pp-) slide سرکنا *slip into (a dress) slip (it) on,* put it on quickly جلدی سے پہننا *slip out of (a dress), slip (it) off,* take it off quickly جلدی سے

آتا رنا fall or almost fall thus پھسل پڑنا sneak away پیچھے سے نکل جانا، کھسک جانا *It slipped my memory* I forgot it یہ بات میرے ذہن سے نکل گئی *The years slipped by* وقت گزر گیا get away by not being held firmly سرک جانا، نکل جانا make a small mistake (*in* something) through carelessness میں چوک جانا
n. slipping پھسلنا، رپٹنا، لغزش *give* (*someone*) *the slip* get away from (him) سے کھسک جانا، بچ کر نکل جانا minor mistake سہو، غلطی *slip of the pen*, error in writing سہو قلم *slip of the tongue*, error in speaking زبان کی لغزش loose cover for a pillow, etc. غلاف narrow strip of paper کاغذ کا لمبا پرزہ، تراشہ (*pl.*) bathing-drawers تیراکی کا جانگیا

slipper (*slip-ĕ**) *n.* loose-fitting light shoe worn indoors سلیپر، زیرپائی **slippery** (*slip-ĕ-ri*) *adj.* (surface, etc.) on which one may slip پھسلنی، رپٹنی **slipshod** (*slip-shod*) *adj.* slovenly پھوہڑ، بدسلیقہ careless بے پروا

slipslop (*slip-*) *n.* sloppy food پتلی غذا sloppy work چلاؤ کام sloppy sentiments بلاسبب رقت آمیز جذبات

slit *n.* long, narrow tear, etc. چاک، شگاف *v.t.* & *i.* (-tt-) (*slit, slit, slit*) make a slit in چیرنا، چاک کرنا، شگاف کرنا tear into narrow pieces پھاڑنا، پتلے لمبے ٹکڑے کرنا open by slitting چاک کرنا

slither (*slidh-ĕ**) *v.i.* (slang) go sliding and bumping (*down* slope) نیچے اچھلتے ہوئے کھسکتے جانا

slobber (*slob-ĕ**) *v.t.* & *i.* let spit run from the mouth رال بہنے دینا، رال بہانا do slovenly پھوہڑپن سے کرنا display foolish emotion of love بیجا محبت کرنا. *slobber over* (*someone* or *something*) have foolishly excessive love or admiration for بیجا محبت یا تعریف کرنا

slogan (*sloh-gun*) *n.* Scottish war-cry نعرۂ جنگ popular phrase used to advertise something or to make clear the aim of a party نعرہ any party-cry نعرہ *raise slogans* نعرے لگانا

sloop *n.* small one-masted ship یک مستولی جہاز، ایک مستول والا جہاز small warship used as escort حفاظتی جہاز

a sloop

slop *v.t.* & *i.* (-pp-) spill چھلکنا *n.* (slang) policeman سپاہی، پلسیا **slops** *n.pl.* dirty, waste water from the kitchen, etc. گندا پانی liquid food for people پتلی غذا، آش **sloppy** *adj.* (of road, etc.) wet and dirty with rain or slops گندے پانی کے گڑھوں اور کیچڑ والی (سڑک) dirty dining table (of food) consisting of slops پتلی غذا foolishly sentimental (person or behaviour) جذباتی، رقت آمیز (colloq.) careless بے پروا (colloq.) untidy گندا

sloppy *adj.* (of road) wet with rain-pools جس پر گڑھوں میں پانی کھڑا ہو (of food) liquid پتلی (of drink) non-alcoholic غیر نشہ آور (of work) slipshod چلاؤ، خراب (of sentiment) maudlin بلاسبب رقت آمیز

slope (*slohp*) *n.* inclined plane as seen looking downwards ڈھلان piece of rising or falling ground نشیب *v.t.* & *i.* have a slope ڈھلوان ہونا give a slope to ڈھلوان بنانا، ٹیڑھا کرنا، ترچھا کرنا *slope arms*, (*a*) place and hold rifle in a sloping position on the left shoulders کندھے پر بندوق ترچھی لگانا (*b*) drill caution for this purpose بندوقیں ترچھی

slosh *v.t.* (colloq.) beat, thrash مارنا، پیٹنا

slot *n.* narrow opening through which a coin, etc., is to be put شگاف، درز *v.t.* (-tt-) make a slot in شگاف ڈالنا **slot-machine** *n.* one from which something (like tickets, etc.) may be obtained by putting a coin through a slot سکہ ڈال کر ٹکٹ (وغیرہ) نکالنے والی مشین، سلاٹ کل، شگاف کل

sloth (sloth) *n.* a South American animal clinging upside down to branches of trees سلاتھ laziness سستی، کاہلی **slothful** *adj.* indolent سست، کاہل، احدی

slouch (slouch) *v.i.* be in a lazy, tired posture بے ہنگم طریق سے چلنا (یا بیٹھنا یا کھڑے ہونا)

slough *n.* (pr. slou) marsh دلدل (pr. sluf) *n.* cast off skin of a snake کینچلی *v.t.* & *i.* (pr. sluf) (-ff-) cast off (or *away* or *off*) like slough کینچلی اتارنا

▣ A **slough** (pr. slou) is a mud-hole ; a **bog** is a place filled with wet decaying ma. a **marsh,** flooded lowlands ; a **swamp,** land satura with water ; a **quagmire,** soft wet land yielding under the feet.

sloven (*sluv-en*) *n.* careless and untidy person (in dress, habits or work) میلا کچیلا، پھوہڑ، بے سلیقہ **slovenly** *adj.* careless in dress, habits or work پھوہڑ، بے سلیقہ

slow (sloh) *adj.* taking a long time to do آہستہ، سست، دھیما *slow-motion film*, film with an abnormally large number of exposures per second سست رو فلم (of a clock) showing a time earlier than the correct time پیچھے (of surface) slowing down the movement دھیما کرنے والی، ہلکا کرنے والی *v.t.* & *i.* (cause to) go (*down* or *up*) at slower speed than before آہستہ ہونا یا کرنا **slow-coach** *n.* dull of wit موٹی عقل والا behind times پرانے خیال کا acting slowly سست رو، کاہل الوجود **slow-motion** *adj.* moving at slower than normal speed کم رفتار **slowly** *adv.* not fast آہستہ **slowness**

n. being slow آہستگی **slow-witted** *adj*. dull of wits موٹی عقل والا
sludge (sluj) *n*. thick mud گاڑھی کیچڑ sediments in a drain موری کی کیچڑ thick dirty grease, etc. تیل کا میل
slug (slug) *n*. kinds of shell-less snails destroying gardens باغ دشمن کیڑا a slug
sluggard (*slug-ĕ*d*) *n*. lazy person سست، کاہل الوجود **sluggish** (*slug*-ish) *adj*. inactive بے ہمت، بے ذوق، سُست، بند slow-moving منٹھا، سست
sluice (sloos) *n*. (also *sluice-gate* or *sluice-valve*), sliding door regulating the level of water by controlling its flow بند کا دروازہ current of water through a sluice بند کے دروازے میں سے پانی کا دھارا thorough washing with a stream of water *v.t.* & *i.* send a stream of water over پانی کا دھارا چھوڑنا wash with a stream of water پانی کے دھارے سے دھونا (of water) come out in a stream پانی کا دھارا بہنا provide with sluice-gates بند کے دروازے لگانا
slum (-slum) *n*. street overcrowded with dirty houses گندی تاریک گلی (*pl*.) part of a town where there are slums شہر کا گندی گلیوں والا حصہ gum-like non-lubricating residue of crude oil, etc. غیر دہنی تلچھٹ
slumber (*slum-bĕ**) (lit.) *n*. sleep نیند، خواب *v.i.* sleep محو خواب ہونا، سونا
slump (slump) *v.i.* drop or fall (*down* or *into*) heavily گر پڑنا، دھڑام سے گرنا (of prices, trade, activity) fall steeply بالکل مندا ہونا *n*. general drop in prices, trade activity, etc. تنزل بازاری، کساد بازاری
slung (slung) *v*. (pa. t. & pa. p. of **sling**, which see)
slunk (slunk) *v*. (pa. t. & pa. p. of **stink**, which see)
slur (slĕ*) *v.t.* & *i.* (-rr-) run sound of one word or phrase into another so as to make them indistinguishable مدغم کرنا merge musical notes thus مر غول بھرنا، گٹکری بھرنا minimise (point or fact) نظر انداز کرنا، چشم پوشی کرنا *slur over (someone's) faults* (کسی کی) خطاؤں سے چشم پوشی کرنا *n*. reproach ملامت something that damages one's reputation act of slurring sounds ادغام
slush (slush) *n*. soft melting snow پگھلتی ہوئی برف slime پتلی کیچڑ
slut (slut) *n*. slovenly woman پھوہڑ عورت
sly (slı) *adj*. deceitful عیار، مکار، چلتا ہوا secretive کائیاں *on the sly*, secretly چپکے چپکے، خفیہ طور پر

playfully mischievous شرارت بھرا
smack (smak) *n*. blow given with the open hand چپت، چانٹا its sound چٹاخ، چانٹے کی آواز sound of the parting of lips چٹخارا small sailing-boat for fishing ماہی گیر جہاز، مچھیروں کا جہاز slight flavour (*of*) شائبہ، (کا) *v.t.* & *i.* part lips audibly ہونٹ چٹخانا *smack (one's) lips*, make a smacking sound with the lips to show pleasure ہونٹ چاٹنا taste مزا دینا be suggestive of کا شائبہ ہونا *adv*. suddenly and violently چٹاخ سے، دھڑسے
smacker *n*. (slang) sounding blow زناٹے دار چپت (وغیرہ) loud kiss چٹاخ سے لیا ہوا بوسہ large specimen بڑا نمونہ
small (smawl) *adj*. not large چھوٹا partly معمولی mean ذلیل *look* (or *feel*) *small*, look (or feel) foolish or ashamed کھسیانا ہونا *small change*, coins of small value ریزگاری *the small hours (of the morning)*, the early hours (1 A.M. to 4 A.M.) رات کا پچھلا پہر *small talk*, talk about unimportant things غیر اہم باتیں *on the small side*, a little too small کچھ چھوٹا *the still small voice*, conscience ضمیر، ضمیر کی آواز
smalls (smawlz) *n. pl*. (colloq.) small articles of laundry دھلائی کے چھوٹے چھوٹے کپڑے **small-arms** *n. pl*. weapons light enough to be carried in the hand چھوٹے آتشیں اسلحہ، بندوق، پستول وغیرہ **small-pox** *n*. a dangerous disease leaving permanent marks on the skin چیچک **small fry** *n*. young fish in a shoal چھوٹی مچھلیاں youngsters of any group چھوٹے **smallholding** *n*. piece of agricultural land not more than 50 acres دو مربعہ تک کا قطعہ اراضی
smallholder *n*. person owning only that much چھوٹا زمیندار
smart (smah*t) *adj*. bright and fresh ترو تازہ clean صاف ستھرا well-dressed خوش پوش quick-witted طباع، حاضر جواب skilful ہوشیار، ہشیار (U.S.) promising ہونہار fashionable ٹھاٹ کا، سجا سجایا *smart set*, ultra-fashionable people بڑے ہی فیشنیبل لوگ brisk (walk) تیز severe (pain, blow, punishment, etc.) سخت، شدید *v. i.* feel pain (*under* blow, wound, insult, etc.) کے باعث درد ہونا (of insult, wound, etc.) be painful میں درد ہونا، درد کرنا *n*. stinging pain **smarten** *v. t.* & *i.* (*smarten up*), make or become smart چست و چالاک ہونا یا بنانا **smartness** *n*. being smart تیزی، شوخی، تیز طبعی، بانکپن **smart-money** *n*. money paid as penalty or compensation ڈنڈ، تاوان
smash *v.t.* & *i.* break or be broken into pieces توڑ پھوڑ، پاش پاش ہونا یا کرنا *smash up*, break violently ملیا میٹ کرنا، تہس نہس کرنا force a way, violently (*into*

or *through*) میں سے زور سے گزرنا defeat utterly شکست فاش دینا پاش پاش ہونا یا کرنا *n.* smashing collision ٹکر، تصادم *smash-and-grab raid*, raid in which a thief smashes a shop window and makes away with valuables دکان کا شیشہ توڑ کر مال اڑالے جانے والا accident حادثہ sudden disaster اچانک بربادی bankruptcy دیوالیہ پن *adv.* with a smash پرزے پرزے ہوتے
smasher *n.* (slang) heavy blow زور کی مار heavy fall دھم سے گرنا telling argument زوردار دلیل *smashing adj.* unusually good غیر معمولی (طور پر) اچھا بہایت شاندار
smattering *n.* slight knowledge (*of* something) شُد بُد **smatterer** *n.* one with a smattering of (esp. many subjects) کئی باتوں کی شُد بُد رکھنے والا
smaze *n.* (see *Addenda*)
smear (*smee-ĕ**) *v.t.* & *i* cover or mark *with* something oily or sticky لینا، ملنا make dirty greasy marks on کے دھبے ڈالنا (of ink) spread and make dirty marks, etc. پھیل کر دھبہ بنانا *n.* mark made by smearing داغ، دھبا (see *Addenda*) *smear campaign*, (see *Addenda*) **smeary** (-ri) *adj.* smeared داغدار
smeech (smeech), **smitch** (smich) *n.* smell of burning (کسی شے کے) جلنے کی بو، سلگنے کی بو
smell (smel) *n.* perfume or odour as it is detected by the nose بو *v.t.* & *i.* (*smell, smelt, smelt*) perceive by smell سونگھنا have or emit a particular smell کی بو ہونا یا دینا stink بدبودار ہونا، کی سڑاند اٹھنا be suggestive (*of*) کی بو آنا *smell out*, (*a*) dicover by the sense of smell سونگھ کر جان لینا (*b*) discover (a secret, etc.) by careful inquiry تفتیش سے معلوم کرنا **smeller** *n.* (slang) nose ناک blow on the nose ناک پر گھونسا **smelling-salts** *n. pl.* sharp-smelling substance used to relieve headache or cure faintness لخلخہ **smelling-bottle** *n.* bottle for sniffing smelling-salts from لخلخے کی شیشی **smelly** *adj.* emitting a bad smell بدبودار

■ A **smell** is the general term for that which is perceived by the nose; **odour,** used poetically or of unpleasant smells; **perfume,** thing giving pleasant smell by chemical action; **tang,** a peculiar smell; **scent,** of an animal as perceived by another animal; **trail,** line along which scent travels and which is followed by hunters.

smelt *v. t.* melt (ore) (خام دھات) کو پگھلانا separate (metal) from ore by doing this خام دھات کو پگھلا کر صاف کرنا (pa. t. & pa. p. of **smell,** which see)
smile (smil) *n.* joyful expression on the face مسکراہٹ، تبسم *v.t.* & *i.* have this expression مسکرانا *smile on* (at *upon*) *something*, approve of it کو پسند کرنا **smilingly** *adv.* with a smile مسکراتے ہوئے مسکراہٹ کے ساتھ
smirch (smĕ*ch) *n.* (lit) stain (*on* one's reputation) کلنک کا ٹیکہ، داغ، دھبا *v. t.* dishonour کے ماتھے پر کلنک کا ٹیکہ لگانا stain دھبا لگانا، داغدار کرنا
smirk (smĕ*k) *n.* habitual, foolish smile مستقل احمقانہ مسکراہٹ put on smile بناوٹی مسکراہٹ *v.i.* smile thus احمقانہ انداز سے مسکراتے رہنا، بناوٹی انداز سے مسکرانا
smite (sm.te) *v.t.* & *i.* (*smite, smote, smitten*) (lit. or jocular) hit hard کو سخت ضرب لگانا defeat utterly کو شکست فاش دینا *smitten by* (or *with*), (*a*) deeply attracted by کو دل ہار دینے والا (*b*) attacked by (an illness) کا شکار
smitch (smich) *n.* (same as **smeech,** which see)
smith (smith) *n.* worker in metals دھات کا کام کرنے والا (also *blacksmith*) worker in iron لوہار، آہنگر
smithy (*smidh*-i) *n.* black smith's workshop لوہار کی دکان، لہارخانہ forge لوہار کی بھٹی
smithereens (smidh-è-*reenz*) *n. pl.* small fragments چھوٹے چھوٹے ٹکڑے *break* (or *blow*) *into smithereens, smash to smithereens* ریزہ ریزہ کر دینا
smithy *n.* (see under **smith**)
smitten *v.* (pa. p. of **smite,** which see)
smock (smok) *n.* overall like a long shirt لبادہ
smocking *n.* gathers کڑھائی کی چنٹیں
smoke (smohk) cloud rising from fire دھواں، دود *end in smoke*, have no satisfying result ملیامیٹ ہونا، فش ہونا act of smoking tobacco تمباکو نوشی، سگرٹ (یا سگار یا حقہ وغیرہ) پینا (colloq.) cigarette, cigar, etc. سگرٹ، سگار *v.t.* & *i.* give out smoke دھواں چھوڑنا، سے دھواں نکلنا breathe in and out the smoke of burning tobacco تمباکو پینا، سگرٹ (وغیرہ) پینا dry and preserve (meat, etc.) with smoke دھوئیں سے سکھا کر رکھنا stain or darken with smoke دھوئیں سے کالا کرنا drive out with smoke دھوئیں سے نکالنا **smoker** *n.* person who smokes tobacco تمباکو نوش، سگرٹ (وغیرہ) پینے والا **smoky** (*smoh*-ki) *adj.* full of smoke دھوئیں سے بھرا پڑا like smoke in taste, appearance, etc. دھوئیں جیسا **smokeless** *adj.* (burning) without smoke دھواں دیئے بغیر (جلنے والا)، بے دُود free from smoke صاف **smokescreen** *n.* cloud of smoke intended to hide military or naval operations دھوئیں کے بادل **smoke-stack** *n.* outlet for smoke and steam from a steamship, railway engine or factory چمنی
smooth (smoodh) *adj.* having a surface like that of glass صاف، ہموار (of the sea) without waves ساکن (of movement) free from shaking, bumping, etc. ہچکولوں کے بغیر of even consistence

یکساں easily flowing (sound or speech) رَوانی والا flattering (person or manners) خوشامد والا pleasant but insincere چکنی چپڑی باتوں ٹالا، چکنی چپڑی باتیں *v.t.* & *i.* make smooth (*down* or *out*) ہموار کرنا free from difficulties آسان کرنا، سُلجھانا *smooth away (someone's) objections* اعتراضات دور کرنا **smoothly** *adj.* without any trouble ٹھیک سے، اچھی طرح **smoothness** *n.* نرمی، ہمواری، رَوانی، خوشامد **smooth bore** *n.* unrifled gun بندوق، سیدھی نالی کی بندوق **smooth-faced** *adj.* pleasant but insincere دل کا کھوٹا، تن کا اُجلا، من کا میلا **smooth-spoken, smooth-tongued** *adj.* using smooth words چکنی چپڑی باتیں کرنے والا

smote (smoht) *v.* (pa. t. of **smite,** which see)

smother (*smudh-ĕ**) *v.t.* & *i.* kill by stifling گلا گھونٹنا، دم گھونٹ کر مار ڈالنا cover completely (*in* or *with*) (سے) ڈھانپ لینا overwhelm (*with* caresses, etc.) (سے) ناک میں دم کرنا suppress (yawn, anger, affair, etc.) ظاہر نہ ہونے دینا، دبا دینا put out (a fire) بجھا دینا cause (a fire) to burn slowly by covering it with ashes, etc. راکھ تلے دبا دینا

smoulder (*smohl*-dĕ*) *v.i.* burn slowly without flames سُلگنا، اندر ہی اندر جلنا (of passions) burn thus اندر ہی اندر بھڑکتے رہنا *n.* smouldering fire دبی ہوئی آگ چنگاریاں، سُلگنے والی آگ ardent but unexpressed passions سوزِ دروں

smudge (smuj) *n.* dirty mark as of ink which has been rubbed دھبّا، داغ *v.t.* & *i.* make a smudge on پر دھبّا ڈالنا **smudgy** (*smuj*-i) *adj.* stained داغدار، مسخ شدہ

smug (smug) *adj.* self-satisfied برخود غلط too fond of comfort and respectability (عام فہم کا) تنگ نظر خوشحال (university slang) unsocial person lacking athletic interests کھیلوں سے بھاگنے والا، غیر ملنسار، آدم بیزار

smuggle (*smug*-èl) *v.t.* & *i.* get (goods) illegally (*into* or *out of* a country or *through* the customs, etc.) سمگل کرنا، غیر قانونی درآمد یا برآمد کرنا take (something or someone) secretly (into, etc.) خفیہ طور پر **smuggler** (*smug*-le*) *n.* one who smuggles سمگلر، غیر قانونی درآمد یا برآمد کرنے والا

smut (smut) *n.* soot from burning coal کلونس mark made by it کالک کا دھبّا obscene talk (or words, etc.) فحش باب **smutty** *adj.* dirty with smuts کالک کے دھبّوں والا obscene فحش *smutty story* فحش کہانی

snack (snak) *n.* light and hasty meal میں کھایا ہوا معمولی کھانا share حصّہ (only in the phrase :) *go snacks*, take each a share حصّے کرنا، اپنا اپنا حصّہ لینا *snack-bar n.* restaurant, etc., where light hasty meals are served جلدی کھائے جانے والے معمولی کھانوں کی دکان

snaffle (*snaf*-èl) *v. t.* (slang) steal چرانا appropriate ہتھیانا، اُڑانا

snag *n.* jagged stump کُنٹھ dangerous, sharp rock in the sea سمندر میں کھڑی چٹان unsuspected hindrance غیر متوقع رُکاوٹ

snail (snayl) *n.* kinds of small slimy animal with shells گھونگا

snake (snayk) *n.* slender crawling reptile without limbs سانپ **snaky** (*snay*-ki) *adj.* of or like a snake سانپ کا سا infested with snakes سانپوں سے بھرا ہوا

snap *v.t.* & *i.* (-pp-) bite suddenly (and often noisily) (*at*) دانت کٹکٹا کر کاٹ کھانا snatch (*at* something) جھپٹا مارنا *snap (someone's) head off*, interrupt someone suddenly and impatiently بات کاٹنا break with a sharp noise ٹوٹ جانا open or close thus تڑاقے سے کھلنا، یا کھولنا یا بند ہونا یا بند کرنا *snap (one's) fingers* انگلیاں چٹخانا fire (pistol, etc.) سے داغنا take a snapshot of تصویر اُتارنا، فوٹو اُتارنا *n.* snapping تڑاق سے ٹوٹنا (یا توڑنا) یا کھلنا یا کھولنا، یا بند ہونا یا بند کرنا sound of snapping تڑاقا، چٹاخا *a cold snap*, a sudden and short period of cold weather سردی کی لہر، ٹھر snapshot تصویر، ترتری تصویر، ترتری فوٹو، سنیپ شاپ *adj.* done quickly and without much warning اچانک، فوری suddenly اچانک، یکا یک *adv.* with a snap تڑاقے سے

snappy *adj.* clever, bright and lively تیز، طرار *adv.* (colloq.) quickly فوراً، جلدی *make it snappy*, do it quickly جلدی کرو **snapshot** *n.* photograph taken quickly with a hand ترتری تصویر، ترتری فوٹو، سنیپ شاٹ

snare (*snay*-ĕ*) *n.* noose for catching small animals and birds پھندا any trap جال، دام، پھندا *v.t.* catch in a snare کو پھندے میں پھانسنا، کو دام میں لانا، پر جال ڈالنا

snarl (snah*l) *v.t.* & *i.* (of dogs) growl angrily showing the teeth غرّانا speak (*out*) ill-temperedly expressing dissent جلی کٹی سنانا *n.* act of snarling غرّانا its sound غرّاہٹ

snatch (snach) *v.t.* & *i.* put out the hand suddenly and take (*up, down, away, off, from,* etc.) چھیننا، جھپٹنا، جھپٹا مارنا، ہاتھ مارنا *snatch at* (*something*), try to get it by snatching چھیننے کی کوشش کرنا get (an hour of sleep, etc.) when the chance occurs لینا، پانا *n.* sudden stretching out of the hand to get something جھپٹا (usu. *pl.*) short pieces (*of* song, speech, etc.) متفرق ٹکڑے

sneak (sneek) *v.t.* & *i.* (go away, in, off, etc.) secretly or quietly کھسک جانا، چپکے سے چل دینا (colloq.) steal (someone's property) thus چرا لے جانا *n.* cowardly underhand person بزدل، سازشی، چغل خور

sneer (*snee*-ĕ*) *n.* scornful smile حقارت آمیز مسکراہٹ such words طنز *v.t.* & *i.* (sneer *at* someone or something), treat him, etc., thus ہنسی اُڑانا

▣ **A sneer** is a scornful grimace or a verbal expression of amused contempt ; **sarcasm,** series of such scornful expressions ; **satire,** such expression in biting words ; **gibe,** refined and concealed expression of such contempt ; **quip,** remark with such contempt : **jeer,** rude words of contempt spoken direct to the person ; **irony,** the sarcastic method as usu. used in literature.

sneeze (sneez) *n.* sudden uncontrollable outburst of air through the nose and mouth چھینک *v.i.* make a sneeze چھینکنا *not to be sneezed at,* not bad, quite good بُرا نہیں، اچھا ہے

sniff (snif) *v.t.* & *i.* draw air in through the nose so that there is a sound سانس اَندر کھینچنا، ناک سے سُوں سُوں کرنا (*sniff at*), do so to show disapproval or contempt ناک بھوں چڑھانا draw (*up* something) in the nose as one breathes ناس لینا (*sniff at*), smell by doing this سُونگھنا، سُونگھ کر دیکھنا *n.* sniffing سانس اَندر کھینچنا its sound سُوں سُوں، سُڑ سُڑ a breath (*of* air, etc.) جھونکا **sniffle** *v.i.* speak with a very nasal twang ناک میں بولنا speak thus to affect piety منمنانا speak as if suffering from cold زُکام سے ناک میں بولنا

snigger (*snig-ĕ**) *n.* suppressed laugh (at some indecency) چپکے چپکے ہنسنا *v.t.* laugh thus (*at* or *over* something) چپکے چپکے ہنسنا

snip *v.t.* & *i.* (-pp-) cut (*off*) with scissors کترنا، قینچی سے کاٹنا *n.* cut made by snipping تراش something snipped off کترن (slang) certainty پکّی بات، یقینی بات

snipe (snip) *n.* a gamebird with long bill چہا *v.t.* & *i.* shoot (*at* someone) from a hiding-place (esp. in darkness) رات کو چھپ کر گولی مارنا attack at night شبخون مارنا **sniper** *n.* soldier who snipes شبخون مارنے والا

a snipe

snippet (*snip*-et) *n.* small piece cut off تراشہ (*pl.*) small bits of news, etc. مختصر خبریں، چھوٹی چھوٹی خبریں، متفرق خبریں

snivel (*sniv*-el) *v.i.* (-ll-) cry with affected grief, sorrow, or fear, بناوٹی طور پر بسورنا whine کی ناک بہنا *n.* affected grief in talk, etc. بناوٹی رِقّت

snob *n.* one who pays too much respect to social position or wealth امارت پرست، غریبوں کو حقیر جاننے والا **snobbish** *adj.* snob-like امارت پرستانہ somewhat of a snob امارت پرست سا **snobbery, snobbishness** *n.* being a snob امارت پرستی

snollygoster *n.* (see *Addenda*)

snooker (*snook-ĕ**) *n.* a kind of billiards played with coloured balls on a table (called *snooker's table*) سنوکر **snooker's table** *n.* table for snooker سنوکر کی میز

snoop *v.i.* pry خواہ مخواہ تجسّس کرنا sneak *about* کے پیچھے دَبے پاؤں لگے رہنا **snooper** *n.* one who pries خواہ مخواہ تجسّس کرنے والا، دَبے پاؤں پیچھے لگا رہنے والا

snooze (snooz) (colloq.) *n.* short sleep between duties تھوڑی سی نیند nap قیلولہ *v.i.* take a nap قیلولہ کرنا sleep a while esp. between duties ذرا سی دیر کو سونا، کام کے وَقفے میں سونا

snore (snoh*) *v.i.* breathe roughly and noisily while sleeping خراٹے لینا *n.* sound of snoring خراٹا **snorer** *n.* one who snores خراٹے لینے والا

snort (sno*t) *v.t.* & *i.* (of a horse) force air violently out through the nose نتھنوں سے آواز نکالنا، نتھنے پھلانا (of an angry or incredulous person) do this to show contempt, impatience, etc. نتھنے پھلانا *n.* snorting نتھنے پھلانا its sound نتھنوں کی آواز device for submarines to take in air for engines when fully submerged آبدوزوں کی بادکشی

snout *n.* projecting nose and mouth of an animal like that of a pig تھوتھنی similar pointed front of anything تھوتھنی (contemptuously) human nose and mouth

snow (snoh) *n.* frozen vapour falling or fallen from the sky in flakes برف (slang) cocaine کوکین *v.t.* & *i.* (-*ed*, -*ing*) (of snow) come down from the sky برف گرنا، برف پڑنا، برفباری ہونا *it snows* برف پڑتی ہے، برفباری ہوتی ہے *be snowed up* (*in a place*), be prevented by snow from going out برفباری کے باعث نکل نہ سکنا come or send (*down*) in showers کی بوچھاڑ ہونا یا کرنا **snowball** *n.* lump of snow pressed together for throwing in play برف کا گولہ anything that increases quickly in size as it moves forward بڑھتی رہنے والی چیز **snow-bound** *adj.* snowed up during travels برفباری کے باعث رُکا ہوا **snow-drift** *n.* bank of snow heaped up by wind برفانی ڈھیر **snow-drop** *n.* a kind of small white flower or the plant yielding it برف پھول **snowflake** *n.* feather-like piece of falling snow برف کا گالا **snow-plough** *n.* device for clearing roads, etc., of snow برف روب، برفکش **snow-shoe** *n.* shoe-like frame for walking on soft snow برفانی بُوٹ **snowy** (*snoh*-i) *adj.* of snow برفانی like snow برف کا سا snow-clad برف پوش، برفپوش

snub (snub) *v.t.* (-bb-) scold (a junior) جھاڑ جھپاڑ کرنا hurt (someone's) feelings دِل توڑنا reject (an offer) thus مسترد کرنا *n.* snubbing words جھاڑ جھپاڑ such behaviour دِل شکنی *adj.* (of nose) short, thick and slightly turned مُڑی ہوئی ناک

snuff (snuf) *v.t.* & *i.* (lit.) sniff سانس اَندر کھینچنا take snuff ناس لینا trim the charred part of a wick گل تراشنا، گل جھاڑنا put out (a candle) thus گُل جھاڑ کر بتی بجھانا *n.* powdered tobacco for taking up in the nose نسوار، ناس، ہُلاس charred part of a wick گُل **snuff-colour** *n.* dark-brown colour نسواری

snuffle (*snuf*-ĕl) *v.i.* make sniffing sounds سُوں سُوں کرنا breathe noisily because of inhaling through obstructed nose سُڑ سُڑ کرنا talk with a nasal accent esp. owing to cold سُوں سُوں کرنا *n.* زُکام کے باعث ناک میں بولنا snuffing its sound سُوں سُوں کرنا

snug (snug) *adj.* warm and comfortable خُوب گرم اور آرام سے sheltered محفوظ tidy صاف ستھرا

snuggle draw (*close to* someone) in affection پیچھے کر بیٹھنا، پیار سے ساتھ لگنا nestle (*up* or *in* bed) for warmth (بستر میں) گرم ہو کر لیٹنا

so (soh) *adv.* in this or that way ایسے، اِس طرح in the same way اِسی طرح *just so, quite so,* (forms of agreement) ہاں ہاں، ٹھیک *not so,* (form of dissent) نہیں تو *if so,* if it be like that ایسا ہو تو *and so forth, and so on,* continuing thus وغیرہ وغیرہ، وَقِس عَلیٰ ہٰذا، اِلخ *as* (*good etc.*) *as,* (for positive forms) اِتنا، جتنا (*not*) *so* (*good, etc.*) *as,* (for negative forms) اِتنا نہیں جتنا *so that,* on the condition that تاکہ، اِس طرح کہ very, very much بہت، بہت ہی *int.* (denoting approval) ہاں ہاں، ٹھیک *conj.* therefore اِس لیے، لہٰذا، پس (old use) provided that اگر، بشرطیکہ *pron.* that very thing یہی *I told you so,* (form of reproach) میں نے پہلے ہی کہا تھا، کہا تھا ناں میں نے؟ *You don't say so?* (form of surprise) یہ آپ کہتے ہیں؟ *so he says,* (assertion to end anticipated surprise, etc.) وہ تو یہی کہتا ہے، کہتا تو وہ یہی ہے *or so,* about *an hour or so* تقریباً ایک گھنٹہ، تقریباً *so far,* (a) to that extent یہاں تک، اِتنی دُور (b) to that point وہاں تک *so-called,* undeservedly called نام نہاد *so far as,* to the extent to which جہاں تک *so far so good,* it is well up to that point یہاں تک تو ٹھیک ہے *so long as,* till جب تک *so long,* farewell till we meet again خُدا حافظ *so much for,* no more need be said about اِس کے متعلق مزید کہنے کی ضرورت نہیں *so-and-so,* substitute for name فلاں *so to say,* (apology for new or exaggerated statement) یُوں کہیے *so so,* (colloq.) not very good ایسا ویسا *so that's that,* (colloq.) (for winding up discussion) اچھا تو یہ بات ہے!

soak (sohk) *v.t.* & *i.* become or make wet through بھیگنا یا بھگونا، تر بتر ہونا یا کرنا absorb جذب کرنا، سوکھنا، پی لینا (of rain, etc.) pass (*through, into,* etc.) جذب کرنا، تر بتر *n.* soaking بہت گیلا کر دینا heavy rainfall زور کی بارش، چھاجوں پانی (برسنا) کرنا یا ہونا

soap (sohp) *n.* fatty substance to make lather for washing صابن، صابُون *soft-soap,* (esp.) flattery خوشامد، چاپلوسی *v.t.* rub soap on صابن لگانا، صابن ملنا wash with soap صابن سے دھونا **soap bubble** *n.* bubble of soapy water صابن کا بُلبلا **soap opera** *n.* (see *Addenda*) **soap-suds** *n. pl.* mass of lather صابن کا جھاگ، صابن کا پھین **soapy** *adj.* of or like soap صابن کا سا flatterer خوشامدی، چاپلوس

soar (sohr) *v.i.* fly higher and higher اُوپر کو اُڑنا، اور اُوپر کو اُڑنا (of prices, etc.) increase too much بہت بڑھ جانا

sob *v.t.* & *i.* (-bb-) catch the breath while weeping سسکیاں بھرنا، سسکیاں لینا *n.* such catching of the breath or its sound سسکی، سُبکی ▣ To **sob** is to catch the breath while weeping or in grief; **weep,** shed tears; **cry,** make a vocal noise with or without tears; **wail,** utter long, plaintive cries; **whine,** complain in a nasal drawl; **whimper,** complain in whining tones; **groan** in prolonged, low tones as in great pain.

sober (*soh*-bĕ*) *adj.* calm and serious سنجیدہ، متین not drunk جو مست نہ ہو، ہوشیار avoiding drunkenness جو شراب نہ پیے، صُوفی temperate اعتدال پسند (of colours) not bright صُوفیانہ *v.t.* & *i.* make or become sober نشہ اُترنا یا اُتارنا **sobriety** *n.* being sober سنجیدگی، متانت

sobriquet (*soh*-ri-kay), **soubriquet** (*soob*-) *n.* nickname عرف، فرضی نام

soccer (*sok*-ĕ*) *n.* (slang) (not quite good spelling of **socker**), association football فٹ بال

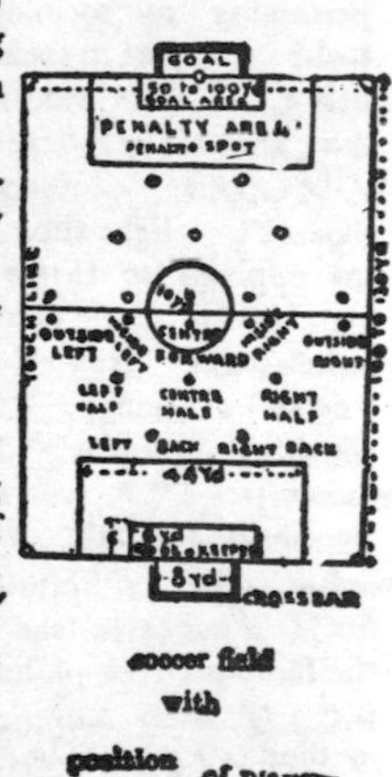

soccer field with position of players

sociable (*soh*-sha-bĕl) *adj.* fond of company ملنسار، یار باش، صحبت پسند friendly دوستانہ **sociability** (-*bil*-) *n.* being sociable ملنساری، یار باشی، صحبت

social (*soh*-shĕl) *adj.* (of animals, etc.) living in groups گروہ پسند (of people) living in communities تمدنی، منظم، عمرانی (of relations, customs etc.) معاشرتی، معاشی، اجتماعی *social welfare* معاشی بہبود، رفاہِ عامہ *social security,* (esp.) freedom from want and unemployment معاشرتی اطمینان، محتاجی اور بیکاری سے رستگاری in society درجہ میں (*one's*) *social equals* کے ہم مرتبہ of joint entertainment *social gathering* تفریحی اجتماع *n.* gathering arranged in a club, etc., for talk and entertainment تفریحی اجتماع

sociality *n.* being-social گروہ پسندی، مدنیت، طبع، عمرانیت **social contract** *n.* theory that mankind agreed to impose restrictions on individual liberty in order to establish State معاہدۂ عمرانی، عمرانی معاہدہ **socialism** *n.* principle that individual liberty should be surrendered to the State which should own and manage all the resources in the interest of the community as a whole اشتراکی، اشتراکیت **socialist** *n.* advocate of socialism **socialistic** (*-lis-*) *adj.* tending towards socialism مائل بہ اشتراکیت، اشتراکیت پسند، اشتراکی **socialize** (*-liz*) *v.t.* make socialistic اشتراکی بنانا nationalize قومی ملکیت بنانا، قومیانا

societal *adj.* (see under **society**)
society (soh-*si*-e-ti) *n.* social community معاشرہ، سماج، سوسائٹی customs, etc., of such a group معاشرتی رسم و رواج the rich and fashionable classes اونچا طبقہ company (of friends) حلقہ association (*for* a purpose) انجمن *debating society*, organization for conducting practice or other debates انجمن مباحثہ **societal** (soh-*si*-e-tĕl) *adj.* pertaining to society عمرانی، معاشرتی
sociology (soh-shi-*ol*-o-ji ; or *U.S.*, soh-si-*ol*-o-ji) *n.* study of the nature and history of human Society عمرانیات **sociological** (*-loj-*) *adj.* pertaining to sociology عمرانیاتی **sociologist** (*-ol-*) *n.* expert in sociology ماہر عمرانیات
sock *n.* short stocking not reaching the knee جراب، موزہ *a pair of socks, socks* جرابوں کا جوڑا، جرابیں loose sole used inside a shoe پاتابہ light shoe of comic actors (as opposed to *buskin* which was the high boot of tragic actors) موزہ، ہلکا جوتا a sock
sockdologer (sok-*dol*-o-gĕ*), **sockdolager** (*-dol*-a-) *n.* (slang) decisive blow فیصلہ کن ضرب clinching argument ساکت دلیل، برہان قاطع
socker (*sok*-ĕ*) *n.* (correct spelling of **soccer**) association football فٹ بال
socket (*sok*-et) *n.* hollow into which something fits گھر، خانہ **socratic** (sok-*rat*-ik) *adj.* like that of the famous Greek philosopher *Socrates* (469-399 B.C.) سقراطی *the Socratic method*, the dialectical method سقراطی طریقہ، جدلیاتی طریقہ *Socratic irony*, ignorance feigned to entice others into giving hollow arguments سقراطی طنز
sod *n.* grass-covered (usu. oblong or square) piece of land سبزے کا تختہ (poet.) surface of the earth سطح زمین، روئے گیتی *under the sod*, in the grave قبر میں، زیر زمین، مدفون (swear-word) sodomite لونڈے باز *v.t.* (-dd-) cover (land) with sods سبزے کا تختہ لگانا
soda (*soh*-da) *n.* one of the common chemical compounds of sodium (esp. its carbonate or bicarbonate) *washing soda, sodium carbonate* a sodium compound used for washing clothes کھاری سوڈا *sodium bicarbonate*, another sodium compound used for leavening bread میٹھا سوڈا *soda water*, aerated water سوڈا، بوتل **soda-fountain** *n.* counter from which soda water, etc., is served سوڈا فونٹین، شربتی چشمہ
sodden (*sod*-ĕn) *adj.* wet through (*with* rain, etc.) شرابور، تربتر stupid through too much drinking سخت بہکا ہوا (of bread, etc., heavy and dough-like کچی (ڈبل روٹی)
sodium (*soh*-di-um) *n.* a soft, silver-white alkaline metal which is one of the elements سوڈیم
sodomy (sod-o-mi) *n.* homosexuality esp. between males غیر فطری تعلق، اغلام، لونڈے بازی **sodomite** *n.* one guilty of it in active capacity لونڈے باز (*opp.* of catamite)
sofa (*soh*-fa) *n.* chair-like seat for more than one person صوفہ، کوچ **Note :** The word *sofa* is the English form of the Arabic word صُفّہ (suffa) meaning 'platform.' It first denoted the open-air platform in the mosque of the Holy Prophet (Peace be on him !) at Medina. The word for this *platform* (which incidentally was the first university set up under Islam) came to be adopted, owing to this sacred association, by the Abbasids for comfortable seats in their palaces and was later borrowed from them by the English-speaking people.
soft *adj.* not hard نرم smooth (skin, hair, cloth, etc.) ملائم (of light) not glaring دھیمی (of colour, eyes, etc.) not bright مدھم (sound) low دھیمی mild (words, etc.) نرم، دھیمے (of words) intended to please خوشامدانہ (of heart) easily touched نرم *soft drinks, soft water*, water easy to wash with ہلکا پانی *soft drinks*, cold drinks which are non-alcoholic (like fruit-juices, etc.) غیر نشہ آور شربت **soften** (*sof*-ĕn) *v.t.* & *i.* make or become soft نرم کرنا یا ہونا **softly** *adv.* in a soft manner نرمی سے، تحمل سے، دھیمے پن سے، آہستہ
soggy (*sog*-i) *adj.* (of ground) heavy with water سیلی
soigne (*swahn*-yay) *adj.* (of a woman's toilet) exquisite in detail نوک پلک نکلا ہوا، خوب شاندار
soil *n.* ground زمین earth مٹی the earth in which plants grow مٹی (*one's*) *native soil*, (one's) mother-land اپنا وطن dirty mark داغ، دھبا *v.t.* & *i.* become or make dirty گندا ہونا یا کرنا، دھبا پڑنا یا ڈالنا

soiree (*swah*-ray) *n.* evening party for talk or discussion محفلِ شب، رات کی محفل
sojourn (*suj*-ĕ*n, *soh*-jĕ*n) *n.* temporary stay (*with* someone, *at* or *in* a place, *for* a time) عارضی قیام *make a sojourn* عارضی قیام کرنا *v.i.* stay temporarily (*with, at, in,* or *for*) عارضی قیام کرنا
sola *n.* (see under **solar**)
solace (*sol*-es) *n.* comfort (*to* someone *in* trouble or pain) (دُکھ میں) تسلّی، (درد سے) تسکین *v.t.* give solace to تسلّی دینا، تسکین پہنچانا
solar (*soh*-lĕ*) *adj.* of the sun سُورج کا، شمسی *solar eclipse*, eclipse of the sun سُورج گرہن، کسوف *solar system*, the sun and the planets نظامِ شمسی **sola** (*soh*-la), **sola topi** *n.* (corruption of) solar topi; pith helmet سولا ہیٹ
sold (sohld) *v.* (pa. t. & pa. p. of **sell**, which see)
solder (*sohl*-dĕ*) *n.* easily melted metal for joining edges of harder metal ٹانکا *v.t.* join with solder ٹانکا لگانا، جھالنا **soldering** *n.* joining with solder ٹانکا لگانا **soldering-iron** *n.* tool used for soldering کاویہ

a soldering-iron

soldier (sohl-jĕ*) *n.* one who serves in the army فوجی، سپاہی *v.i.* (usu. as gerund) serve as soldier سپاہی کی حیثیت سے کام کرنا *go soldiering* سپاہی بننا **soldierly, soldier-like** *adj.* like a soldier سپاہیانہ smart چُست، پھرتیلا brave بہادر، بہادرانہ ▣ A **soldier** is one engaged in military service; **warrior** is the poetic word for him; a **recruit** is one recently enlisted; a **conscript** is one compulsorily enrolled.
sole (sohl) *n.* underpart of the foot تلوا underpart of shoe, sock, etc. تلا any kind of flat sea fish چپٹی مچھلی *adj.* one and only ایک ہی single تنہا، اکیلا (of rights, agency, etc.) restricted to one واحد، بلا شرکتِ غیرے **solely** *adv.* alone تنہا only صرف، محض

a sole (sense 3)

solecism (*sol*-e-sizm) *n.* grammatical or idiomatic قواعد یا محاورے کی غلطی offence against etiquette بدتہذیبی، بدتمیزی
solemn (*sol*-em) *adj.* performed with religious ceremony مذہبی رسوم والا performed with ceremony باضابطہ moving the feelings دِل پر اثر causing deep respect شاندار، پُر رعب، احترام پیدا کرنے والا grave سنجیدہ important سنجیدہ **solemnly** *adv.* سنجیدگی سے، دل سے **solemnity** (so-*lem*-ni-ti) *n.* being solemn سنجیدگی، باضابطگی solemn ceremony سنجیدہ تقریب **solemnise** (*sol*-em-niz) *v.t.* perform (wedding, etc.) with the usual rites کے (لوازمے) مراسم بجالانا celebrate (festival) منانا
solicit (so-*lis*-it) *v.t.* & *i.* ask (someone) earnestly (*for* something) درخواست کرنا ask repeatedly (*for*) اصرار کرنا **solicitor** (so-*lis*-i-tĕ*) *n.* lawyer who prepares legal documents (as opposed to a *barrister* who is the lawyer pleading a client's case at the court) سالِسٹر
solicitous (so-*lis*-i-tus) *adj.* anxious (*about*) کا خواہاں، پر دل سے آمادہ eager (to do something) مُتمنّی، مُتردد considerate (*for*) بڑا خیال رکھنے والا **solicitude** (so-*lis*-i-tewd) *n.* anxiety (*for*) پریشانی، تشویش
solid (*sol*-id) *adj.* not fluid ٹھوس three-dimensional ٹھوس not hollow ٹھوس strong (building, argument, unity, etc.) مضبوط، قوی *solid in defence of (one's) country* حبّ الوطنی میں چٹان کی طرح of the same substance throughout ٹھوس، خالص، یکسر continuous مسلسل، لگاتار *solid gold* خالص سونا، زرِ ناب *n.* body or substance which is solid and not fluid ٹھوس شئے **solidly** *adv.* firmly مضبوطی سے، چٹان کی طرح **solidarity** (-*da*-ri-ti) *n.* unity bred by common interests اتحاد **solidify** (so-*lid*-i-fi) *v.t.* & *i.* make or become solid ٹھوس بنانا یا بننا، جمانا یا جمنا **solidity** (so-*lid*-i-ti) *n.* quality of being solid ٹھوس پن **soliloquy** (so-*lil*-o-kwi) *n.* speaking out one's thoughts to oneself aloud when no one else is about خود کلامی **soliloquize** *v.i.* talk to oneself دل سے باتیں کرنا، خود کلامی کرنا
solitary (*sol*-i-tĕ-ri) *adj.* lonely تنہا، یکہ و تنہا only one یگانہ، یکہ و تنہا living alone اکیلا رہنے والا *solitary confinement*, imprisonment in a separate cell قیدِ تنہائی living the life of a recluse گوشہ نشین (of place) seldom visited سُونا، اُجاڑ، سنسان *n.* recluse گوشہ نشین، خلوت گزین **solitude** (*sol*-i-tewd) *n.* solitary state تنہائی، خلوت گزینی، گوشہ نشینی solitary place تنہائی، سُونا مقام، سنسان جگہ
solo (*soh*-loh) *n.* piece of music for a single person's performance سولو، اکیلے کا گیت (یا نغمہ) *adv.* alone اکیلے **soloist** (*soh*-loh-ist) *n.* person who gives a solo سولو گر، تنہا نغمہ سرا
solstice (*sol*-stis) *n.* time at which the sun is farthest north or south of the equator نقطۂ انقلاب *summer solstice*, such time occurring about June 21 صیفی نقطۂ انقلاب *winter solstice*, such time occurring about December 22 شتوی نقطۂ انقلاب **soluble** *adj.*, **solubility** *n.*, **solution** *n.*, (see under **solve**)
solve (solv) *v.t.* find the answer to (a problem, etc.) حل کرنا find a way out of (a

difficulty, etc.) حل کرنا **solution** *n.* (so-*loo*-shĕn) *n.* answer (to a question, etc.) جواب، حل way of dealing with a difficulty, etc. حل process of dissolving تحلیل liquid that results مَحلُول *a solution of sugar in water,* پانی میں شکر کا محلول **soluble** (sol-ew-bèl) *adj.* that can be dis ved حل پزیر **solubility** (-*bil*-) *n.* being soluble **solutionist** (so-*loo*-shè-nist) *n.* regula r of newspaper puzzles اخباری معمّے کا دِلدادہ

solvent (*sol*-vent) *adj.* (of a liquid) able to dissolve other substances مُحلّل having money enough to pay off one's debts قرض ادا کرنے پر قادر، صاحب مقدرت *n.* solvent substance مُحلّل **solvency** *n.* ability to pay off one's debts مقدرت

sombre (*som*-bè*) *adj.* dark تیرہ و تار dismal اداس، غمناک

sombrero (som-*bree*-roh) *n.* Mexican hat with a broad brim سمبریرو

some (sum) *adj.* unspecified (person, thing, amount, etc.) کچھ، کوئی *pron.* some (person, etc.) کچھ، ایک حد تک کسی *somewhat,* in some degree کچھ، کوئی حد تک *someone somebody,* (*a*) someone کوئی، کوئی شخص (*b*) an important person اہم شخص *something* کچھ *sometimes* کبھی کبھی، کبھی کبھار *sometime,* (with designations) former *somewhere* کہیں نہ کہیں *somehow, somehow or other,* in one way (or for some reason) or other کسی نہ کسی طرح

somersault (*sum*-ĕ*-sawlt), **somerset** (*sum*-ĕ*-set) *n.* leap in which one turns head over heels landing on one's feet قلابازی *v.i.* turn a somersault قلابازی لگانا یا کھانا

somnambulism (som-*nam*-bew-lizm) *n.* sleepwalking خواب خرامی **somnambulist** (-ist) sleepwalker خواب خرام

somniferous (som-nif-e-rus) *adj.* sleep-inducing (drug) خواب آور

somnolent (*som*-no-lent) *adj.* almost asleep نیم خوابیدہ، نیم خواب، اونگھتا ہوا causing sleep خواب آور **somnolence** *n.* drowsiness غنودگی

son (sun) *n.* a person's male child بیٹا، لڑکا one of the progeny (*of*) فرزند one of the spiritual descendants or devotees (*of*) فرزند *my son!,* (form of address to younger persons) بیٹا، بیٹے، میاں *the Son of God, the son of Man,* Christ according to Christianity, ابن آدم *the sons of men,* mankind بنی آدم، نوعِ انسانی *Son of the soil,* (*a*) countryman دیہاتی (*b*) person recognizable as native of a district مخصوص علاقائی شکل والا **sonless** *n.* one without a male issue جس سے بیٹا نہ ہو **son-in-law** *n.* husband of one's daughter داماد، جنوائی

sonny (*sun*-i) *n.* (as vocative) term of endearment for son بیٹا، بیٹے small boy بیٹے، میاں

sonant (*soh*-nant) *adj.* (of a letter) that which is sounded ملفوظ

sonata (soh-*nah*-ta) *n.* musical composition (for one instrument) in three or four connected parts سوناتا

song *n.* vocal music گانا words for vocal music گیت bird's song زمزمہ *for a song,* very cheaply مفت، بہت سستا **songster** *n.* male singer گویّا song-bird چہچہانے والا پرندہ **songstress** *n.* female singer گویّا، گانے والی، مُغنیّہ Ⓢ **Song** is the general word. We speak of a church **hymn**, a Christmas **carol**, a funeral **dirge**, and a national **anthem**.

sonnet (*son*-et) *n.* kind of poem containing only 14 lines of 10 syllables each سانیٹ، چہار دہی **sonneteer** (-*tee*-è*) *n.* composer of sonnets سانیٹ نویس *v.t.* & *i.* compose sonnets سانیٹ کہنا address sonnets to (a lady) or celebrate (her) in sonnets کی شان میں سانیٹ کہنا

sonny *n.* (see under **son**)

sonorous (so-*no*-rus) *adj.* having a rich sound گونجنے والا with a resounding voice پُرآواز، بلند آواز (of language, etc.) impressive پُراثر، اثر آفریں

sonority (-*no*-), **sonorousness** *n.* being sonorous بلند آوازی، گونج، پُرآوازی

soon *adv.* early سویرے in a short time جلدی، جلد، تھوڑی دیر میں willingly بخوشی، خوشی سے *would as soon,* (*would sooner*), would (more) willingly زیادہ خوشی سے *sooner or later,* at some time کبھی نہ کبھی، دیر سویر *as sooner as, no sooner than,* immediately as جلد یا بدیر جونہی، جونہی کہ، جیسے ہی *no sooner said than done,* done immediately بات ادھر منہ سے نکلی ادھر پوری ہوئی

soot (sŭt) *n.* black powder in smoke or deposited by it کالک، کلونس **sooty** (sŭti) *adj.* full of soot دھوئیں سے کالا blackish کالا سا

sooth (sooth) *n.* (old use) truth سچ، صداقت *in sooth,* truly سچ، سچ مچ، درحقیقت **soothsayer** *n.* fortune-teller قسمت کا حال بتانے والا، کاہن

soothe (soodh) *v.t.* calm (someone) تسلی دینا alleviate (pain, etc.) کو تسکین پہنچانا tone down (anger, etc.) دھیما کرنا **soother** (*soo*-dhĕ*) *n.* (esp.) rubber nipple used for quieting infants by making them suck it چوسنی

sooty *adj.* (see under **soot**)

sop *n.* piece of bread, etc., soaked in milk, soup, etc. شوربے یا دودھ میں بھیگی ہوئی روٹی، ثرید something offered to someone as temporary relief عارضی تسلی *v.t.* (-pp-) dip (bread, etc.) into milk, soup, etc. دودھ وغیرہ میں بھگونا absorb liquid, etc. جذب کرنا، میں تر بتر ہونا **sopping** *adj.* & *adv.* wet through شرابور، بھیگا ہوا *sopping wet*, wet all through شرابور **soppy** *adj.* wet through شرابور full of maudlin sentiment بلا سبب رقت والا

sophism (*sof*-izm) *n.* clever but false reasoning intended to deceive مغالطہ، غلط دلیل، باطل استدلال، سفسطہ **sophistry** (*sof*-is-tri) *n.* habitual use of such false reasoning سفسطہ، سوفسطائیت، مغالطہ آمیزی **sophist** (*sof*-ist) *n.* one who uses sophistry غلط دلیلوں سے دھوکا دینے والا، سوفسطائی **sophisticate** (so-*fis*-ti-kayt) *v.t.* & *i.* argue thus غلط استدلال کرنا، مغالطہ دینا، تدلیس کرنا spoil the naturalness میں تصنع پیدا کرنا غلط دلیلوں سے دھوکا دینا adulterate (wine, etc.) میں ملاوٹ کرنا **sophisticated** *adj.* not simple and natural تصنع والا **sophistication** (-*kay*-) *n.* lack of simplicity تصنع، بناوٹ

sophomore (*sof*-o-moh*) *n.* (U.S.) second-year student of college or university (امریکی جامعات کا) دوسرے سال کا طالب علم

soporific (soh-po-*rif*-ik) *adj.* sleep inducing خواب آور *n.* such drug خواب آور دوا

soprano (so-*prah*-noh) *adj.* with the highest female singing voice پنچم میں بلند ترین زنانہ آواز میں *n.* such voice پنچم woman or boy with such voice پنچم میں گانے والی (یا والا)

sorcerer (*so**-se-rě*) *n.* magician pretending to call up evil spirits جادوگر، ساحر **sorceress** *n.* woman sorcerer جادوگرنی، ساحرہ **sorcery** (*so**-sè-ri) *n.* witchcraft جادو، جادوگری، سحر، افسوں، فسوں طرازی

sordid (*so**-did) *adj.* wretched (conditions) خستہ (of behaviour) mean ; prompted by self-interest تنگدلانہ dirty گندا

sore (soh*) *adj.* (of a part of the body) tender and painful دکھتا ہوا aggrieved (heart) چوٹ کھایا ہوا، دکھا ہوا، زخمی hurting (the feelings) دل خراش annoying تکلیف دہ (old use) great (need, etc.) اشد، سخت *n.* sore place on the body دکھتی ہوئی جگہ inflammation پھوڑا **sorely** *adv* greatly (oppressed, tempted, etc.) بہت، سخت

sorrow (*so*-roh) *n.* grief دکھ، رنج، غم، الم، ملال، اندوہ its cause غم کا باعث regret افسوس *v.i.* feel sorrow (*at*, *over* or *for* something) (پر) افسوس کرنا (کا) غم ہونا **sorrowful** *adj.* feeling sorrow غمگین، غمزدہ، ملول causing sorrow غمناک، اندوہگین

sorry (*so*-ri) *adj.* feeling sadness غمگین feeling regret (*for*, *about* or *to do* something) (پر) متاسف، جسے (کسی بات کا) افسوس ہو *sorry !* please excuse me معاف کیجیے pitiful (state) قابل رحم worthless (excuse) بے معنی

sort (*so**t) *n.* kind قسم *what sort of*, of what type کس قسم کا *a good sort*, likable اچھا، پسندیدہ *be out of sorts* (colloq.) be rather unwell علالت ہونا، بیمار سا ہونا، مضمحل ہونا *v.t.* & *i.* arrange in various groups الگ الگ ڈھیریاں بنانا *sort letters*, arrange them in groups according to their destination خط الگ الگ کرنا (*sort out*), separate (good things from bad ones, etc.) چھانٹ کر الگ کرنا **sorter** *n.* (esp.) post-office worker who sorts letters سارٹر، چھانٹنے والا

sortie (*so**-ti) *n.* sally of besieged soldiers to attack besiegers محصور فوج کا حملہ آوروں پر ہلہ combat mission of aircraft ہوائی دستے کی مہم

S O S (*es*-oh-es) *n.* wireless message for help from a ship, etc., in danger خطرے میں فریاد کا لاسلکی پیغام، فریاد any urgent call for help فریاد

sot *n.* one constantly stupid with drinks ہمیشہ بدمست رہنے والا، پکا شرابی

sou (soo) *n.* French half-penny صفر دو پیسہ *not a sou*, no money کچھ بھی نہیں

sough (soo, or sow, or suf) *n.* sighing sound of wind in trees, etc. سائیں سائیں *v.i.* (of wind) make such a sound سائیں سائیں کرنا

sought (sot) *v.* (pa. t. & pa. p. of **seek**, which see)

soul (sohl) *n.* spirit ; immaterial part of a human being روح، جان conscience باطن، ضمیر human being شخص، متنفس personification (*of* some quality) مجسم **soulful** *adj.* having or showing deep feeling احساس والا **soulless** *adj.* lacking higher or deep feelings بے حس، بے حس، بیدرد

sound *n.* that which can be heard صوت، آواز *the sound of* (*one's*) *voice* کسی کے بولنے کی آواز *within sound of*, near enough to hear جہاں سے (کسی چیز کو) سن سکیں an element of speech آواز، حرف inlet of the sea خلیج، کھاڑی narrow strip of water joining two larger areas of it آبنائے *adj.* healthy صحیح سالم، تندرست in good condition اچھی حالت میں cogent (reason, etc.) درست، قوی، مضبوط dependable قابل اعتماد wise (step, decision, etc.) دانشمندانہ ہوشمندانہ thorough (sleep, etc.) پورا *adv.* thoroughly (asleep) گہرا sound asleep گہری نیند میں *v.t.* & *i.* (cause to) produce sound بجنا، آواز نکالنا، بجانا *sound an alarm* خطرے کی گھنٹی بجانا، آگاہ کرنا give the impression of being (reasonable, etc.) معلوم ہونا، لگنا test by listening ٹھونک بجا کر دیکھنا test and measure the depth (of the sea, etc.) with a lead weight on a rope (called a *sounding-line*) کی گہرائی ناپنا try to learn

a sound-box

views of (*someone on* a subject) (کسی کے بارے میں) کسی کے خیالات کی ٹوہ لینا، کا اندازہ کرنا **sound-box** *n.* part of gramophone for reproducing sound ساؤنڈ بکس، صدا گاہ **sound-film** *n.* talkie ٹاکی، گویا فلم **sound-proof** *adj.* that which the sounds cannot penetrate جس سے باہر آواز نہ جا سکے، آواز روک **soundly** *adv.* with good judgment ہوشمندی سے، دانشمندانہ thoroughly پوری طرح **soundness** *n.* گہرائی، صحت مندی، فرزانگی، اچھی حالت **soundings** *n. pl.* depth of sea as taken with lead سمندر کی گہرائی part of sea not too deep for ordinary soundings (*i.e.*, 100 fathoms) سمندر کا کم گہرا حصہ

soup (soop) *n.* liquid food made by boiling meat, vegetables, etc. یخنی، آش *be in the soup*, (colloq.) be in trouble مشکل میں، مصیبت میں

sour (*sou*-ĕ*) *adj.* having a sharp, acid taste کھٹا، ترش (of milk, etc.) spoilt by fermentation پھٹا ہوا ill-tempered چڑچڑا پن، بدمزاج sharp-tongued بدزبان *v.t.* & *i.* make or become sour کھٹا ہو جانا یا کر دینا **sourly** *adv.* with ill-temper بدمزاجی سے **sourness** *n.* being sour کھٹائی، ترشی **sour-dough** (*sou*-ĕ*-doh) *n.* (U.S.) old-timer پرانا، اگلے وقتوں کا

source (soh*s) *n.* starting point (of a river) منبع origin سرچشمہ، اصل book or person whence some information was or can be obtained ماخذ

souse (sous) *v.t.* put in pickle کا اچار ڈالنا throw liquid (*over* or *into*, etc.) ڈالنا send or go with a plunge (into water, etc.) میں غوطہ دینا یا لگانا

south (south) *n.* point or direction opposite the north جنوب، دکھن *adj.* of or in the south جنوبی *adv.* towards the south جنوب کی طرف **southerly** (sudh-ĕ*-li) *adv.* & *adj.* (of winds) from the south جنوب سے (آنیوالی) towards the south جنوبی، جنوب کی طرف، سمت جنوب **southern** (*sudh*-ĕ*n) *adj.* in or of the south **southward, southwards** *adv.* towards the south جنوب کی طرف، سمت جنوب **South Pole** *n.* point of earth opposite the North Pole قطب جنوبی **South Sea** *n.* the Pacific Ocean بحر الکاہل **sou'wester** *n.* strong southwestern wind جنوب مغربی جھکڑ waterproof hat with a wide flap to protect the neck برساتی ٹوپی

a sou'wester

souvenir (*soo*-ve-nee-ĕ*) *n.* thing given, taken, or kept in memory (of person, place or event) یادگار، نشانی

sovereign (sov-rin) *adj.* highest (authority) اعلیٰ unlimited لا محدود (of a ruler) having sovereign power مطلق العنان independent (State) خود مختار، آزاد efficacious (remedy) : of proved value مجرب، حتمی، حتمی *n.* ruler فرمانروا £1 British gold coin (now replaced by the pound note) سونے کا پونڈ، طلائی پونڈ **sovereignty** (*sov*-rin-ti) *n.* sovereign power حاکمیت، اقتدار اعلیٰ

soviet (*soh*-vi-et) *n.* council of workers constituting the government of the Centre or in the part of the U.S.S.R. سوویٹ Communist کمیونسٹ، کمیونسٹ، اشتمالی (غلط مگر عموماً) اشتراکی *Soviet Russia*, the U.S.S.R. (*i.e.*, the Union of the Soviet Socialist Republics) روس، اشتراکی روس Russian روسی *Soviet propaganda* روسی پراپیگنڈا

sow (soh) *v.t.* & *i.* (*sow, sowed, sown,* or *sow, sowed, sawed*) put (seed) in the land بونا put seed (in the land) بیج بونا *n.* (*Sou*) female pig سؤرنی *have the wrong sow by the ear*, (*a*) fix on the wrong person غلط شخص کو پکڑنا (*b*) have the wrong notion غلط خیال پر ہونا

soya (*soh*-ya), **soya-bean** (*soh*-ya-been) *n.* a well-known edible plant yielding oilseed سویا بین

spa (spah) *n.* spring of mineral water with medicinal properties معدنی چشمہ place with such a spring معدنی چشمے والا مقام

space (spays) *n.* that in which everything exists فضا، بسیط place جگہ *an open space*, place not built on کھلی جگہ unoccupied place خالی جگہ، گنجائش distance (*between* two or more objects) فاصلہ interval (*of* time) وقفہ، مدت، عرصہ (see *Addenda*) *v.t.* (in printing) place (words or letters) with regular spaces between یکساں فاصلے پر لگانا *space out* (*words or letters*) (الفاظ یا حروف) کھلے کھلے لگانا **space ship** *n.* (see *Addenda*) **space travel** *n.* (see *Addenda*) **spacious** (*spay*-shus) *adj.* roomy کھلا، کشادہ، وسیع، فراخ **spatial** *adj.* of, relating to or existing in space (as opposed to *temporal*) مکانی

spade (spayd) *n.* tool for digging بیلچہ، پھاوڑا *call a spade a spade*, speak out plainly لگی لپٹی رکھے بغیر کہہ دینا playing-card with black design حکم (تاش میں) *v.t.* dig (also *up*) with a spade بیلچے سے کھودنا، کھودنا **spadework** *n.* careful, hard work in the initial stages (*of*) ابتدائی کام، ابتدائی مراحل persistent attention to details تفصیلات پر مسلسل نظر

a spade

spadeful *n.* as much as will be lifted by a spade بیلچہ بھر

spaghetti (spa-*get*-i) *n. pl.* kind of macaroni پتوڑی سویاں

spake (spayk) *v.* (old use) (pa. t. of *speak*)

spalpeen (*spal*-peen) *n.* mischievous fellow ; rascal شرارتی ، بدمعاش
spam (spam) *n.* sausage meat which is tinned and spiced ولایتی کبابوں کا ڈبوں میں بند مسالے دار قیمہ ، سپام
span *n.* distance (about 9 inches) between the tips of a grown-up man's thumb and his little finger when stretched out بالشت ، نو اِنچ part between the supports of an arch محراب کا خلا distance between two consecutive supports of a bridge پل کی دو کھمبوں کا درمیانی فاصلہ *a bridge crossing the river in a single span* درمیانی کھمبوں کے بغیر بنا ہُوا پُل interval (*of* time) وقفہ ، مدّت ، عرصہ *v.t.* (-nn-) (of a bridge) extend across (a space) ایک کنارے سے دوسرے کنارے تک پھیلا ہُوا ہونا ، بنا ہُوا ہونا make a bridge across پر پُل بنانا encompass کو محیط ہونا ، کا احاطہ کرنا measure by hand spans بالشت سے ماپنا
spangle (*spang*-ĕl) *n.* tiny ornamental disc of shining metal stitched on to dress ستارہ ، سلمہ ستارہ *v.t.* cover with spangles ستارے ٹانکنا ، سلمہ ستارہ لگانا cover as with spangles جگہ جگہ جڑنا *star-spangled sky*, sky spangled with stars تاروں بھری رات
spaniel (*span*-yel) *n.* species of dog with long silky hair and large drooping ears پنیئر کُتّا ، پنیئر sycophant خوشامدی
spank *v.t.* punish by slapping (on the buttocks) with the open hand چوتڑوں پر مارنا (of a horse or ship) move swiftly تیزی سے چلنا **spanking** *adj.* (colloq.) excellent شاندار ، عُمدہ fresh and strong (breeze) تازہ ، تیز
spanner (*span*-ĕ*) *n.* wrench for nuts نٹ کسنے والا رِنچ

a spanner

spar (spah*) *n.* strong pole for supporting sails بڑی بلّی *v. t.* (-rr-) (of gamecock) attack with spurs (مُرغ کا) خار سے حملہ کرنا use one's fists for attack and defence in boxing مُکّے مارنا ، گھونسے بازی کرنا argue بحث کرنا *sparring partner*, boxer's partner during training گھونسے بازی کی تربیت میں ساتھی
spare (*spay*-ĕ*) *v.t.* & *i.* refrain from damaging کو چھوڑ دینا show mercy to پر رحم کرنا *spare (someone's) life*, not kill him کو قتل نہ کرنا ، کی جاں بخشی کرنا leave (no pains, no expense, etc.) سے دریغ نہ کرنا *not spare (oneself)*, use all (one's) energy پُوری کوشش کرنا find (the time, the money, etc., *for*) by being careful کے لیے فالتو ہونا *spare (someone, something)* کو دینا *enough and to spare*, quite enough بہُت کافی use in small quantities تھوڑا تھوڑا برتنا ، کے اِستعمال میں کفایت شعاری سے کام لینا *be sparing with* (something) کم کم اِستعمال کرنا ، سمجھ کر برتنا تھوڑا تھوڑا برتنا *adj.* extra ; beyond one's need فالتو kept in reserve for فالتو *spare parts (of a machine)*, parts needed to replace broken ones (مشین کے) فالتو پرزے *a spare room*, one kept for guests مہمانوں کے لیے کمرہ ، مہمان خانہ lean (person) پتلا دُبلا ، دھان پان (of meals, diet, etc.) small in quantity کم ، مختصر *n.* spare part of a machine, etc. فالتو پُرزہ **sparing** *adj.* economical (*of*) (میں) کفایت شعار **sparingly** *adv.* very little بہُت تھوڑا ، بہُت کم
spark (spah*k) *n.* small burning piece present in ashes or thrown off چنگاری ، شرارہ flash of light produced by breaking of an electric current بِرقی شرارہ sign (*of* life, energy, etc.) چنگاری ، جوت flash (*of* wit) چمک ، دِلکشی *v.i.* give out sparks سے چنگاریاں نکلنا **sparking-plug** *n.* device for firing the gas in a petrol engine, etc. انجن میں گیس بھڑکانے والا پُرزہ ، آتش زن ، آتشزن
sparkle *n.* flashes of light چمک دمک ، تابانی *v.i.* send out flashes of light چمکنا ، دمکنا
sparrow (*spa*-roh) *n.* common brownish bird چڑیا ، گوریّا ، گنجشک
sparse (spah*s) *adj.* (of population, beard, etc.) not dense چھدرا ، پھیلا ہُوا **sparsely** *adv.* چھدرا **sparsity** *n.* being sparse چھدرا ہونا
Spartan (*spah**-tĕn) *n.* & *adj.* (citizen) of Sparta سپارٹا کا رہاشندہ (person) unafraid of hardship سختیوں کا عادی ، سادہ زندگی کا عادی ، سخت کوش (of living conditions) hard because very simple سادہ ، سخت کوش
spasm (spazm, or spasm) *n.* convulsive tightening of muscles ، کھچاوٹ sudden fit (*of* pain, grief, etc.) دَورہ **spasmodic** (spaz-*mod*-ik) *adj.* occurring or done at irregular intervals کبھی کبھی caused by spasms دَوروں کی طرح affected by spasms جیسے دَورہ پڑتا ہو
spat *v.* (pa. t. & pa. p. of **spit**, which see) *n.* (usu. pl.) cloth cover worn over the upper part of a shoe and round the ankle ساق پوش spawn of shellfish گھونگھا مچھلی کے انڈے

spats

spate (spayt) *n.* flood سیلاب ، طُوفان *in spate* طغیانی پر ، جس میں سیلاب آیا ہُوا ہو sudden rush (*of* business, etc.) زور
spatial (*spay*-shĕl) *adj.* (see under **space**)
spatter (*spat*-ĕ*) *v.t.* & *i.* (of mud) fly or send in drops in all directions کیچڑ کے چھینٹے پڑنا یا ڈالنا *n.* spattering کیچڑ کا چھینٹا ، چھینٹیں
spatula (*spat*-ew-la) *n.* instrument like a blunt

table-knife for mixing or spreading plaster, etc. ملانے کی چھری

spawn *n. pl.* eggs of fish, frogs, etc. مچھلی (یا مینڈک وغیرہ) کے انڈے (contemptuously) too many children بچّوں کا جھول thread-like matter from which fungi grow سماروغی مادّہ *v.i.* produce spawn (مچھلی وغیرہ کا) انڈے دینا، انڈے بچّے دینا

speak (speek) *v.t.* & *i.* (*speak, spoke, spoken* ; old pa. t. : *spake*) say ; utter words کہنا، بولنا *speak out*, express one's views openly کھُل کر کہنا *speak (one's) mind*, say plainly true (even if unpleasant) things صاف صاف کہہ دینا، کھری کھری سُنانا *speak up*, speak loudly اُونچی آواز سے کہنا *nothing to speak of*, (a) nothing worth mentioning قابلِ ذکر بات نہیں (b) not much کچھ بھی نہیں، زیادہ نہیں *be not on speaking terms with*, having quarrelled with سے بول چال بند ہونا *speak well for*, be evidence in favour of کے حق میں دلیل ہونا *have a speaking likeness*, (of a portrait, etc.) be lifelike منہ بولتی (تصویر) ہونا، ہو بہو ہونا **speaker** *n.* one who speaks بولنے والا one who speaks in public تقریر کرنے والا، مقرّر، خطیب (*the Speaker*), the President of a legislature صدر مقننہ، سپیکر **speaking** *n.* act of speaking بولنا *public speaking*, art of speaking in public فنِ تقریر، خطابت **speak-easy** *n.* (U.S. slang) illicit liquor shop ناجائز شراب کی دُکان، شراب کی غیر قانونی دُکان

spear (*spee*-ĕ*) *n.* long-handled weapon with sharp metal point نیزہ، برچھا، برچھی، بلم *v.t.* wound with a spear نیزہ مارنا، برچھی مارنا **spearhead** *n.* pointed part of a spear نیزے کی انی، انی person or group chosen to head a thrust or lead an attack ہراوُل دستہ، ہراوُل

special (*spesh*-ĕl) *adj.* uncommon خاص، غیر معمولی particular خاص، مخصوص *special train*, extra train for a special purpose سپیشل، فالتو گاڑی *special police*, additional police force to help the regular police force in emergencies ایڈیشنل پولیس *special representative* (or *correspondent*), person representing a periodical to cover a special occasion نمائندہ خصوصی، نامہ نگار خصوصی (also *special*), exceptional in degree امتیازی، غیر معمولی **specialist** (*spesh*-ĕ-list) *n.* expert (*in* special branch of a field) متخصص، سپیشلسٹ **speciality** (*spesh*-i-al-i-ti), **specialty** (*spesh*-ĕl-ti) *n.* special characteristic (*of*) امتیازی خصوصیت thing for which a person or place is well-known خاص شے، خاص الخاص تحفہ **specialize** (*spesh*-ĕ-lɪz) *v.t.* & *i.* be or become a specialist (*in* something) (کا) متخصص بننا (کا) ماہر ہونا give special or particular attention to کا خاص خیال رکھنا، کی طرف خصوصی توجّہ دینا **specialization** (-*zay*-) *n.* specializing (*in*) میں تخصّص پیدا کرنا، (کا) ماہر بننا، (میں) تخصّص، (میں) مہارت

specie (*spee*-shi, or *spee*-shi-ĕ) *n.* money in the form of coins (as distinct from currency notes) سکّے *adj.* in coins سکّوں میں

species (*spee*-sheez, or *spee*-shi-eez) *n.* (*pl.* the same) division of a genus نوع *the species, our species*, mankind نوعِ انسان (colloq.) sort قسم

specific (*spes*-i-fik) *adj.* definite (orders, etc.) قطعی، واضح، صاف not general ; concerning a particular thing خصوصی، مخصوص *specific gravity*, the weight of any substance relative to that of an equal volume of water ثقلِ نوعی، کثافتِ نوعی tried, efficacious (remedy) مجرّب، حکمی، خصوصی *n.* specific remedy مجرّب دوا، حکمی دوا **specify** (*spes*-i-fi) *v.t.* mention definitely صراحت کرنا give the name and details of کی تعیین کرنا، کی تفصیلات دینا **specification** (-*kay*-) *n.* (esp. in *pl.*) detailed instructions for design, materials, etc. (*of* something) تفصیل، تشریح (ج : تفصیلات، تشریحات)

specimen (*spes*-i-men) *n.* sample (*of*) نمونہ example (*of*) مثال part taken to represent the whole بانگی، نمونہ

specious (*spee*-shus) *adj.* seemingly (though not really) true بظاہر صحیح، مغالطہ آمیز

speck (spek) *n.* small spot داغ، دھبّا tiny bit (*of* dust, etc.) ذرّہ *v.t.* mark with specks دھبّے ڈالنا، داغ دھبّے ڈالنا **specked** *adj.* marked with specks دھبّوں والا **speckle** (spek-ĕl) *n.* one of the distinct natural colour spots on the skin, feathers, etc. دھبّا، داغ، چتّی *v.t.* mark with speckles دھبّے ڈالنا، چتّی ڈالنا **speckled** *adj.* having speckles چتلا

specs (speks) *n. pl.* (see under **spectacle**)

spectacle (*spek*-ta-kĕl) *n.* noteworthy sight نظارہ public display with ceremony تقریب کا نظارہ (*pl.*) (also *pair of spectacles*), plastic or metal frame for glasses to adjust eyesight عینک، چشمہ *see everything through rose-coloured spectacles* ساون کے اندھے کو ہرا ہی ہرا سوجھتا ہے *make a spectacle of (oneself)*, behave or dress ridiculously مضحکہ خیز صورت بنانا (یا بات کرنا) **specs** (speks) *n. pl.* (colloq.) spectacles عینک، چشمہ **spectacular** (spek-*tak*-ew-le*) *adj.* making a fine spectacle قابلِ دید، دلکش، شاندار

spectator (spek-*tay*-tĕ*) *n.* onlooker تماشائی، ناظر

▣ **A spectator** is one who sees, particularly one who attends a spectacle or arranged show ; **a beholder,** one who watches attentively ; an **onlooker,** one who happens to look without much interest ; **a witness,** one who is present and sees or hears ; an **eye-witness,** one who sees all the details with his own eyes ; an **observer**, one who carefully studies all the details,

spectre (spek-tè*) *n.* ghost بھوت، مُردے کی رُوح جو پیکرِ خیالی illusory figure طیف مُجسّم نظر آئے haunting fear of expected trouble اندیشہ، خوف **spectral** *adj.* like a spectre بھوت کا سا of or like a spectrum طیفی *spectral analysis*, analysis of light with a spectroscope into the colours comprising it تحلیلِ طیفی *spectral colours* طیفی الوان، طیفی **spectrum** (spek-trum) (pl. *spectra*) rainbow-like band of colours formed by rays of light which have passed through a prism or shower of rain قوسِ قزح طیف **spectroscope, spectrometer** *n.* instrument for measuring a spectrum طیف پیما

speculate (*spek*-ew-layt) *v.i.* guess (*how to do* or *about* something) قیاس سے کام لینا (also *speculate in* something) deal in financial transactions of a risky kind (esp. in hope of large future profits) کا سٹا کرنا **speculator** *n.* one who speculates سٹے باز **speculation** (-*lay*-) *n.* entering into such transactions سٹا، سٹے بازی، سٹا کرنا، سٹے بازی کرنا guesswork قیاس، اٹکل

sped *v.* (pa. t. & pa. p. of **speed**, which see)

speech *n.* power of speaking قوّتِ گویائی، تکلّم talk given in public تقریر *make a speech* تقریر کرنا (rarely) language زبان، بولی **speech-day** *n.* annual ceremonial day at school with speeches and prize distribution جلسۂ تقسیمِ انعامات **speechless** *adj.* struck dumb with deep emotions وفورِ جذبات سے ساکت **speechify** *v. i.* (contemptuously) make boring or uncalled for speech تقریر بازی کرنا

speed *n.* rate of moving رفتار، شرحِ رفتار *high speed* تیز رفتار *slow speed* آہستہ رفتار، نرم رفتار، ہلکی رفتار *at full speed* پُوری رفتار سے *at a speed of 30 m.p.h.* تیس میل فی گھنٹہ کی رفتار سے *speed limit*, maximum speed permissible زیادہ سے زیادہ رفتار، انتہائی مُعیّنہ رفتار، انتہائی رفتار *exceed the speed limit* مُعیّنہ رفتار سے تیز چلانا *attain a high speed* بہت تیز جا سکنا، تیز رفتار حاصل کرنا swiftness تیزی، پھرتی *more haste less speed*, mere scurry slows down speed جلدی کا نتیجہ پشیمانی، پھرتی کا انجام بُرا *v.t.* & *i.* (*sped*) (cause to) go (*up*) quickly تیز ہونا یا کرنا، تیز جانا یا لے جانا، تیز چلنا یا چلانا *speed past (something)* کے پاس سے تیزی سے گزر جانا *God speed you !* (old use) May God prosper you ! خدا بھلا کرے *god speed*, such expressed wish دُعائے خیر *wish (someone) god speed* (کو) دُعائے خیر دینا **speedometer** *n.* instrument for recording the speed رفتار پیما **speedy** (*spee*-di) *adj.* quick تیز رفتار immediate فوری **speedily** *adv.* quickly جلد، جلدی **speed cop** *n.* police motor-cyclist detailed to check motorists' speed موٹروں کی رفتار کا جائزہ لینے والا، موٹر سائیکل سوار سپاہی، رفتاری سپاہی **speedway** *n.* road for fast motor traffic موٹروں کی تیز آمد و رفت کے لیے سڑک track for motor-cycle racing موٹر سائیکلوں کی دوڑ کا میدان (یا راستہ)

spell (spel) *v.t.* & *i.* (*spell, spelt, spelled* ; or *spell, spelled, spelled*) write or speak the letters that make (a word) کے ہجے کرنا result in (disaster, etc., *to* someone) کا انجام (کسی کے لیے) ہونا، کا نتیجہ (کسی کے لیے) نکلنا *n.* period (*of* time) وقفہ، تھوڑی دیر *a spell of cold weather*, cold wave سردی کی لہر *leave (someone or something) alone for a spell* کو کچھ دیر کے لیے چھوڑ دینا turn باری words used as a charm سحر، جادو، افسون، منتر، ٹونا، ٹوٹکا *under a spell*, mastered or controlled by, or as by, a spell سحر زدہ، مسحور extreme attraction کشش، جذب **spelling** *n.* way a word is spelt ہجے **spellbound** *adj.* with the attention held (as) by a spell مسحور *hold (someone) spellbound* کو مسحور (یا مبہوت) کر دینا

spend *v.t.* & *i.* (*spend, spent, spent*) pay out (money, on goods, services, etc.) (پر) خرچ کرنا، (پر) صرف کرنا use up (energy, time, material, etc.) ختم کرنا، خرچ کرنا **spendthrift** *n.* one who wastes money فضول خرچ **spent** *adj.* tired, exhausted تھکا ہوا، تھکا ماندہ

sperm *n.* fertilizing fluid of a male نر کا مادہ تولید، منی **spermatic** (-*mat*-) *adj.* pertaining to sperm منوی **spermatism** *n.* ejection of sperm انزال **sperm-whale** *n.* whale yielding a white fat used for candles, etc. سپرم ویل

a sperm-whale

spew, spue (spew) *v.t.* & *i.* (old use) vomit قے کرنا، اُگلنا

sphere (*sfee*-è*) *n.* any kind of globe کُرہ any of the concentric revolving spheres enclosing the earth according to Ptolemy کُرہ، فلک *the sphere of the moon, the lunar sphere* فلکِ قمر *music of the spheres*, their musical sounds نغمۂ افلاک star ستارہ planet ستارہ field (*of* activity, interest, etc.) دائرہ، حلقہ *distinguished in many spheres* متعدّد معاملات میں ممتاز *a country's sphere of influence*, foreign area where it has or claims special right کسی بیرونی طاقت کا حلقۂ اقتدار **spherical** (*sfe*-ri-kèl) *adj.* shaped like a sphere کُروی **spheroid** (*sfe*-roid) *n.* body almost spherical کُرہ نما ▣ We speak of the **sphere** of one's activity ; **scope** of one's ability ; **field,** wherein one labours ; **province,** wherein one is competent ; **domain,** where one is master ; **realm,** wherein one is king ; **range,** up to which one can reach.

sphinx (sfinks) *n.* (*the Sphinx*), stone Egyptian statue with a lion's body and a woman's head ابُوالہَول (the *Sphinx*), monster in Greek mythology, with the head of a woman, body of a lioness and wings who proposed a riddle to travellers and strangled them to death if they could not solve it; Oedipus solved her riddle whereupon she plunged into water and died سِفنکس person keeping his thoughts and intentions secret دِل کا بھید نہ کھولنے والا ، گھُنّا

the sphinx

spice (spɪs) *n.* any of the seeds or roots (like pepper, etc.) used as a flavouring گرم مَسالا suggestion (*of* humour, etc.) (کی) چاشنی trace (*of* danger, etc.) (کے) آثار **spicy** (*spī*-si) *adj.* having much spice مسالے دار aromatic خوشبودار ، مُعَطّر (of story) with indecent details فحش *v.t.* add flavour to (something) with spice میں گرم مسالا ڈالنا ، کو چٹپٹا بنانا

spick (spik) *adj.* (used only in the phrase:) *spick and span*, quite trim and smart بَنا ٹھَنا

spicy *adj.* (see under **spice**)

spider (*spī*-dĕ*) *n.* kinds of eight-legged creature well-known for spinning webs to entrap small insects مکڑی ، مکڑا

spied (spɪd) *v.* (pa. t. & pa. p. of **spy**, which see)

spike (spɪk) *n.* sharp point تیز نوک pointed piece of metal (like the one worn in running shoes) باہر کو نکلی ہوئی کِیل ، تیز نوک والی کِیل large sharp nail میخ ear of grain بال ، بالی spiked bar نوکدار سلاخ *v.t.* put spikes on (shoes, etc.) کھُرّی کیلیں لگانا fasten with spikes میخیں جَڑنا pierce or injure with spikes میخوں سے زخمی کرنا plug vent of (gun, etc.) to make it useless (بندوق وغیرہ) کا مُنہ کیل ٹھونک کر بند کرنا

spill (spil) *v.t.* & *i.* (*spill, spilled, spilled*; or *spill, spilt, spilt*) (of liquid or powder) (allow to) run over the side of the container گِرنا ، گرانا ، بہنا یا بہانا *It is no use crying over spilt milk* اب پچھتائے کیا ہوت جب چڑیاں چُگ گئیں کھیت upset (horse, carriage, etc.) or cause (the rider, a passenger, etc.) to fall (گھوڑے گاڑی وغیرہ) کو یا سے گرانا *n.* fall from a horse, carriage, etc. (گھوڑے یا گاڑی) سے پٹخنی کھا کر گرنا *n.* thin strip of wood or a rolled or twisted piece of paper for lighting candles, etc. فلیتہ ، کاغذ کی بتّی

spin *v.t.* & *i.* (*spin*; *spun*, or *span*; *spun*) (*-nn-*) make thread or make (cotton, etc.) into thread کاتنا ، دھاگا کاتنا form (web, etc.) by means of threads (جالا) تانَنا *spin* (*something*) *out*, make it last long دیر تک چلانا (also *spin round*), (cause to) whirl round گھومنا ، گھمانا compose (story, poem, etc.) کہانی کہنا ، قصّہ سُنانا ، کہنا ، لکھنا *spin a yarn*, tell a story *n.* spinning motion given to a ball in cricket, etc. سپین ، گھوم ، چکّر short drive in a motor-car, ride on a cycle, etc. چکّر ، سَیر *go for a spin* چکّر لگانے جانا diving descent of aircraft combined with its rotation ہوائی جہاز کا چکّر کھاتے ہوئے نیچے آنا **spinning-wheel** *n.* a simple kind of hand propelled machine for spinning چرخہ **spinner** *n.* (esp.) ball sent with a spin in cricket چکّر کھاتی ہوئی گیند ، گھوم گیند

spinach (*spin*-ij) *n.* a well-known vegetable پالک

spindle (*spind*-ĕl) thin rod used for twisting and winding thread (ہاتھ سے کاتنے کی) تکلی (چرخے کا) تکلا (یا) سلائی axle; bar on which something turns دُھرا ، چرخی **spindly** *adj.* long and thin تکلے جیسا لمبا اور پتلا ، تکلا سا **spindle-shanks** *n.* person with long, thin legs لمبی پتلی ٹانگوں والا

spinal *adj.* (see under **spine**)

spine (spɪn) *n.* backbone ریڑھ ، فقرات one of the sharp needle-like parts on some plants and animals سُوئی ، خار ، اُبھار **spinal** (*spī*-nĕl) *adj.* of the spine ریڑھ کا ، ریڑھ کی ہڈی کا ، فقراتی *the spinal column*, the backbone ریڑھ ، ریڑھ کی ہڈی ، فقرات ، سِلسِلۂ الظّہر *the spinal cord*, nerve-fibres in the spine حرام مغز ، کار شتہ **spineless** *adj.* having no spine جس کی ریڑھ کی ہڈی نہ ہو cowardly; lacking character بزدل ، بے ہمّت ، غیر مستقل مزاج **spiny** *adj.* having spines (*i.e.*, needle-like parts) سُوؤں والا ، خاردار

spinster (*spins*-tĕ*) *n.* woman who has never married ناکتخدا عورت legal term for such woman تارکہ **spinsterhood** *n.* state of being a spinster تارکہ ہونا ، ناکتخدائی

spiny *adj.* (see under **spine**)

spiral *adj.* rising or advancing in a cone-like continuous curve round a pivot چکّردار *n.* such coil مخروطی چکّر *v.i.* (-ll-) move in a spiral چکّر دار ہونا

spire (*spī*-ĕ*) *n.* slender conic structure on a tower کلس

spirit (*spi*-rit) *n.* soul رُوح ، جان this part of a human-being regarded as something separate رُوح ، بھوت ، پریت ، ہمزاد fairly; supernatural being پری ، جن ، بھوت *the spirits*, (*a*) the supernatural beings, (*b*) the souls of the dead اَرواح *the abode of spirits*, place where the souls of the dead live عالمِ اَرواح guts, courage ہمّت ، حوصلہ ، جوش وَلوَلہ (often *pl.*) cheerfulness خوشدلی. زندہ دلی *in high spirits*, happy, hopeful بہشت خوش *in low spirits, in poor spirits, out of spirits*, sad, hopeless افسردہ، پژمردہ، بجھا بجھا mood انداز، طور *in a spirit of* (service, mischief, etc.) بطور سا central figure (*of*) رُوح و رَواں real purpose underlying a law etc. (as opposed to its *letters* or mere wording) رُوح، اصلی مقصد، منشا *the spirit in letter and spirit* الفاظ اور منشا دونوں کے پیش نظر *and not the letter of the law* قانون کے الفاظ نہیں بلکہ منشا (*pl.*) strong liquors تیز شرابیں (*pl.*) alcohol الکحل، سپرٹ *spirit lamp*, one in which alcohol is burned سپرٹ لمپ *spirit level*, simple instrument for testing whether a surface is level سپرٹ لیول essence (*of*) ست، جوہر، رُوح *v.t.* take (someone or something *away* or *off*) secretly or mysteriously اُڑا لے جانا، چپکے سے اُڑا لے جانا، چپکے سے کھسکا دینا **spirited** *adj.* courageous بہادر lively زندہ دل، خوش باش (of horse) full of life جاندار، تیز طرّار vigorous (attack, etc.) پُرجوش، زوردار **spiritless** *adj.* without energy بے ہمّت depressed افسردہ، پژمردہ، مضمحل **spiritual** (*spi*-ri-tew-ĕl) *adj.* of the soul رُوحانی of or caring for religion دینی، مذہبی *Lords spiritual*, Bishops, etc., in the House of Lords (as distinct from the *Lords Temporal*) برطانوی دارالامرا کے پادری ارکان pertaining to spirits ارواح سے متعلق *n.* religious song of American negroes کالے امریکنوں کا دینی نغمہ **spiritualism** *n.* belief in the possibility of receiving messages from the spirits of the dead اَرواحیّت metaphysical belief in the independent existence of soul رُوحانیت **spiritualist** *n.* believer in the possibility of calling up of the souls of the dead by living persons اَرواحیّت پرست **spirituous** (*spi*-ri-tew-us) *adj.* (of liquids) containing alcohol نشہ آور، الکحل ▣ A spirited person is one who is not easily downed, enterprising, who goes out to conquer new fields, energetic, who does quickly and nicely whatever comes to his hand.

spirt (spĕ*t) *n.* & *v.t.* & *i.* (same as **spurt**, which see)

spit *v.t* & *i* (*spit, spat, spat*) (-tt-) send (*out* liquid) from the mouth تھوکنا (of a cat, etc.) make an angry spitting noise پھنکارنا utter (words) angrily غضبناک ہو کر منہ سے (الفاظ) نکالنا put (meat, etc.) on a bar for roasting (کباب) سیخ پر چڑھانا *n.* spitting تھوکنا angry spitting noise (*of* a cat, etc.) پھنکارا spittle تھوک bar on which meat is roasted سیخ **spitfire** *n.* hot-tempered person تند خو، تیز مزاج a kind of fighting plane سپٹ فائر، شعلہ فشاں **spittle** (*spit*-el) *n*, liquid of the mouth تھوک **spittoon** (spi-*toon*) *n.* pan for spitting into اُگالدان

spittoons

spite (spit) *n.* malice کینہ، بغض، عناد desire (*against* someone) to hurt ضرر رسانی، شر *out of spite, done from spite* محض ضرر پہنچانے کی نیت سے *in spite of, despite*, (a) notwithstanding کے باوجود (b) not prevented by (*it, all*, etc.) باوجود یکہ، بایں ہمہ *v.t.* injure or annoy out of spite کینہ جوئی کرنا، کینہ سے نقصان پہنچانا **spiteful** *adj.* having or showing spite کینہ پرور **spitefully** *adv.* کینہ پروری سے *cut off (one's) nose to spite (one's) face*, indulge (one's) ill temper to (one's) own hurt ضد میں آکر مونچھیں منڈوا لینا

spiv (spiv) *n.* (slang) person living by petty exploitation of people by indulging in black-market, etc. چوربازاری کرنے والا، قومی جونک

splash *v.t.* & *i.* cause (a liquid) to fly about in drops کے چھینٹے اُڑانا، چھپ چھپ کرنا (of a liquid) fly about and fall in drops کے چھینٹے اُڑانا make wet by splashing کے چھینٹے ڈالنا stain by splashing میں لت پت کرنا move, fall, etc. (*into* something) so that there is splashing سے لتھیڑنا چھپ چھپ کر کے چلنا، غڑپ سے گرنا *splash (one's) way across the stream* میں چھپ چھپ کر کے گزرنا print (news, etc.) in bold headline (across a page, etc.) بڑی بڑی سُرخیوں سے چھاپنا *n.* splashing چھینٹا، چھپکا its sound چھپ چھپ، غڑپ stain داغ، دھبّا *make a splash*, attract attention by making a show of one's wealth شان جتانا flash ; news item printed, or for printing, with bold headline اہم خبر

splay *v.t.* & *i.* (of an opening) slope outwards (موکھے کا) باہر کو نکلے ہوئے ہونا *adj.* (of feet) broad and turned outwards چوڑے چوڑے، باہر کو نکلے ہوئے

spleen *n.* part of the abdomen which the seat of the red corpuscles of blood تلی، طحال peevishness بدمزاجی، تنک مزاجی، غصہ، چڑچڑاپن *vent (one's) spleen on (someone)* کسی پر اپنا غصہ جھاڑنا، غصہ نکالنا *in a fit of spleen* غصے سے **splenetic** (sple-*net*-ik) ill-tempered تند خو، بدمزاج pertaining to the inflammation of the spleen ورم طحال سے متعلق *n.* one suffering from it تلی کا مریض

splendid (*splen*-did) *adj.* magnificent grand (thing, place, quality, etc.) شاندار، عالیشان excellent (idea, etc.) عمدہ، شاندار (colloq.) satisfactory اچھا، ٹھیک

splendour (*splen*-dĕ*) *n.* magnificence

brightness چمک شان و شوکت، شان و شکوہ دمک، آب و تاب
splenetic *adj.* (see under **spleen**)
splice (splis) *v.t.* join (strings, etc.) by weaving the strands of one into those of the other (رسی وغیرہ) کو گوندھ کر جوڑنا join (two pieces of wood) by fastening them so that they overlap (لکڑی) کے سروں کو ایک دوسرے پر رکھ کر جوڑنا join (persons) in wedlock کا عقد کرنا *n.* join made by splicing گوندھ کر یا ایک دوسرے پر رکھ کر لگایا ہوا جوڑ
splint *n.* strip of wood, etc., bound to a broken bone to keep it in the right position ٹوٹی ہوئی ہڈی پر باندھی ہوئی کھپچی، کھپچی
splinter (*splin-tě**) *n.* sharp-edged bit *of* wood) split off a larger piece چھپٹی sharp pointed piece (of grass, bomb, etc.) flying from the main thing کرچ کرچ *v.t.* & *i.* (cause to) come off as a splinter چھپٹی ہونا (یا) کرنا، کرچ کرچ اُڑنا (یا) رگڑنا *splinter group n.* (see *Addenda.*)
split *v.t.* & *i.* (*split, split, split*) (-tt-) (cause to) break or be broken into two or more parts, esp. from end to end along the line of natural division لمبائی کے رُخ پھٹنا یا پھاڑنا divide into parts بانٹنا، تقسیم کرنا، ٹکڑیوں میں بانٹنا *be split up* (*on or over an issue*), have a rift (on it) (پر) پھوٹ پڑ جانا (پر) کھنڈت پڑ جانا (پر) سخت اختلاف ہونا *split open, break open by bursting* پھٹ پڑنا *split (one's) sides*, laugh violently لوٹ پوٹ ہونا *a splitting headache*, a very severe one سخت سر درد، سر میں سخت درد *split hairs, make* very fine distinctions (in an argument, etc.) as to cloud the real issue بال کی کھال نکالنا، مین میخ نکالنا *hair-splitting*, making such distinctions بال کی کھال نکالنا *split on (someone)*, (colloq.) (*a*) give away (his) secret کا راز افشا کرنا give information about him کے متعلق بتانا *split the difference*, agree upon a price, etc., between the figures suggested by the two sides درمیان درمیان مصالحت کرنا *n.* crack made by splitting شگاف، درز division (*in* a group, etc.) caused by difference of opinion اختلاف، پھوٹ، کھنڈت *adj.* divided into small parts بٹا ہوا *in a split second*, in a very brief instant of time پلک جھپکتے میں
splutter (*splut-ě**), **sputter** (*sput-ě**) *v.t.* & *i.* speak quickly and confusedly (*from* excitement, etc.) جوش یا گھبراہٹ میں کہنا یا بڑبڑانا sound as in spitting تھو تھو کرنا *spit out* (*words*) تھو تھو کرکے بولنا
spoil *v.t.* & *i.* (*spoilt* or *spoiled*) become or make useless (*by* something) (سے) خراب ہونا یا کرنا harm the character of (children, persons, etc.) by wrong upbringing and paying too much attention to their comforts and wishes عادتیں خراب کرنا، کو بگاڑنا (of food, etc.) become unfit for use خراب ہو جانا، سڑ جانا *be spoiling for* (a fight, etc.), be eager for (it) پر تلا بیٹھا ہونا deprive (someone) by stealth or plunder (*of* something) کا مال چرانا، کو لوٹنا *n.* (*pl.*) plunder لوٹ مار stolen goods چوری کا مال profits (*of* political power, etc.) لوٹ کھسوٹ
spoke (spokh) *n.* any one of the bars or wires connecting the hub of a wheel with its rim (outer edge) (پہیے کا) تار (یا) آرا *v.t.* & *i.* (pa. t. of **speak**, which see)
spokesman (*spokhs*-man) *n.* person deputed to voice the feelings (*of* another or *of* a group) ترجمان، نمائندہ
spondee (*spond*-i) *n.* metrical foot comprising two long syllables سپونڈی، فعلن **spondaic** (spon-*day*-ik) verse of solemn rhythm comprising these سپونڈی ارکان میں
spoliation (spoh-li-*ay*-shen) *n.* plunder لوٹ مار
sponge (spunj) *n.* species of simple sea animal or (something like) its light structure of soft elastic material full of holes and able to absorb water easily سپنج، اسفنج *throw up the sponge, chuck up the sponge*, admit one's defeat or failure شکست تسلیم کرنا *v.t.* & *i.* wash, wipe or clean with a sponge سپنج سے دھونا، پونچھنا (یا) صاف کرنا *sponge up* (liquid), take it up with a sponge سپنج سے پانی سوکھنا *sponge on (someone)*, (colloq.) live on him without giving anything in return پر بوجھ بننا، طفیلی ہونا **sponge-cake** *n.* a kind of soft yellow cake سپنج کیک **sponge cloth** *n.* soft fabric with wrinkled surface سپنجی بافت کا کپڑا، سپنجی کپڑا
sponger *n.* (old form : *sponge*) one who sponges on others طفیلی، مفت خورا **spongy** (*spunj-i*) *adj.* porous and elastic like a sponge سپنج کا سا، اسفنجی
sponsor (*spons-ě**) *n.* person who first puts forward a proposal کا پیش کرنے والا one who takes upon oneself the responsibility (*of*) ذمے دار، ضامن، کفیل person taking upon himself the responsibility (of a radio programme, etc.) پیشکار، پیشکش کرنے والا advertiser who pays for a radio programme in which his advertisements' wares also appear مشتہر پیشکار godfather or godmother دینی کی ذمے دار، باپ (یا) دینی ماں *v.t.* act as a sponsor for اپنے سر لینا present (programme, etc.) پیشکش کرنا sponsor radio programme for own advertise-

ments اشتہاری پیشکاری کرنا act as godfather, etc. دینی باپ (یا ماں) بننا

spontaneous (spon-*tay*-ne-us) *adj.* done or occurring freely and naturally without any suggestion from outside آپ سے آپ، اپنے آپ، خود بخود، بے ساختہ **spontaneity** (spon-ta-*nee*-i-ti) *n.* being spontaneous بے ساختگی lack of conscious artistic effort آمد، بے ساختگی

spool *n.* reel ; cylinder for holding a wound thread, film, etc., on ریل

a spool of film

spoon *n.* very small bowl on a long handle for taking up food چمچہ، چمچی، چمچ *tea spoon* چائے کی چمچی *dessert spoon* پھل چاول کھانے کا چمچہ *table-spoon* کھانے کا چمچہ، چھوٹا چمچہ، بڑا چمچہ *be born with silver spoon in mouth,* (*a*) be born in rich family پرتکلوں کا (b) be extremely lucky قسمت کا دھنی ہونا، امیر ہونا similar but bigger thing used for stirring کفگیر (colloq.) one making love, درد عشق میں مبتلا، کبھو، شیدائی *v.t.* take (*up* or *out*) with a spoon چمچے سے نکالنا **spoonfed** *adj.* (of person) looked after too carefully جس کی بہت ناز برداری ہو (of industry) much subsidized ; artificially encouraged by the government بہت زیادہ امداد پانے والی **spoonful** *n.* as much (*of* something) as a spoon will contain چمچہ بھر

spoonerism (*spoo*-nē-rizm) *n.* confusion of two or more words by wrong placing of initial sounds (as *dear queen* and *queer dean, crushing blow* and *blushing crow*) ابتدائی حروف کا ادل بدل، تجنیس

spoor (*spoo*-ē*) *n.* track (*of* quarry) کھوج its scent بو

sporadic (spo-*rad*-ik) *adj.* rare ; occurring occasionally here and there نادر الوقوع، شاذ، کبھی کبھی **sporadically** *adv.* in a sporadic manner کبھی کبھار کا، کبھی کبھی، کبھی کبھار، کہیں کہیں

spore (spoh*) *n.* seed-like stage in the life of a fern, etc. تخم، بزری

sporran (*spo*-rĕn) *n.* large fur-covered pouch which scottish Highlanders wear in front of their kilt سکاچستانی کمربند کا تھیلا، کمر بندی کیسہ، کیسۂ کمر

a sporran

sport (spo*t) *n.* activity engaged in for amusement تفریح، دل بہلاوا، کھیل کود، کھیل تماشا، لہو و لعب ❷ an outdoor activity like games, swimming, wrestling or fishing کھیل hunting شکار ❸ (*pl.*) athletic meet دوڑ کود کے مقابلے jest ٹھٹھا، مذاق، دل لگی *make sport of,* ridicule him کا مذاق اڑانا (*say something*) *in sport,* (say it) just in fun and not seriously ہنسی سے کہنا، محض دل لگی سے کہنا (colloq.) sportsman کھلاڑی، شکاری، معقول شخص *v.t.* & *i.* amuse oneself by playing about اچھلتے کودتے پھرنا، کدکڑے مارنا (colloq.) have or wear (dress, beard, etc.) for proud display اتراتے پھرنا، کی نمود و نمائش کرنا، بن ٹھن کے نکلنا **sporting** *adj.* of sport تفریحی، کھیل کا، کھیلوں کے متعلق fond of sport کھیل کود کا شائق، لہو و لعب کا دلدادہ with a gladly accepted risk of losing جوکھوں بھرا *a sporting chance* شاذ امکان sportsmanlike معقولیت پسندانہ، معقول *sporting offer* خوش طبع، چہل باز معقولیت پسندانہ پیشکش **sportive** *adj.* playful خوش طبعانہ، چہل سے **sportively** *adv.* **sportsman** *n.* one who takes part in sports کھلاڑی one fond of sports سیر شکار، کھیل کود یا تفریح کا دلدادہ، لہو و لعب کا شائق one regarding life as a game in which others have to be given a fair chance کھلنڈرا، کھیل کے آئین پر چلنے والا one who is cheerful even in defeat باہمت، نہ رونے والا one who plays a bold game حوصلہ مند **sportsmanlike** *adj.* ready to obey the rules کھیل کے آئین کے پابند fair جائز، معقول honourable باعزت، آبرومندانہ **sportsmanship** *n.* being a sportsman کھلاڑی (یا کھیل کا شائق) ہونا reasonableness معقولیت پسندی

spot *n.* small mark داغ، نشان stain دھبا، داغ pimple مہاسا blemish (*on* character) (کردار پر) داغ، (دامن پر) دھبا particular place جگہ، موقع، محل، جائے وقوع (*do something*) *on the spot,* (do it) there and then وہیں (کرنا)، اسی وقت (کرنا)، اسی دم کرنا (*the men*) *on the spot,* (the men) present at the place موقع پر موجود لوگ *the man on the spot,* one who knows واقف کار، باخبر، جاننے والا *spot cash,* payment on delivery وصولی پر قیمت، نقد، نقد عند الوصول *spot prices,* prices quoted for such payment نقد، عند الوصول بھاؤ (colloq.) small quantity (*of* something) ذرا سا a drink جام مے *v.t.* & *i.* (-tt-) mark or become marked thus (*with* something) پر (کسی چیز کے) دھبے پڑنا یا ڈالنا recognize (someone *in* a crowd, etc.) کو پہچان لینا، کی نشاندہی کرنا pick out; make a correct guess کو تاڑ لینا (U.S. slang) decide on the assassination of (someone) کے قتل کا فیصلہ کرنا **spotless** *adj.* quite clean صاف ستھرا، بے داغ unblemished بے عیب، بے داغ **spotlight** *n.* beam of strong light directed (*on* someone or something) مرتکز روشنی lamp projecting it مرتکز روشنی کا لیمپ prominence شہرت *v.t.* bring (an evil, etc.) to public notice with a view to eradicating it (برائی وغیرہ) پر روشنی ڈالنا **spotty** (*spot*-i) *adj.* marked with spots داغدار، داغ داغ، دھبوں والا

spouse (spouz*) *n.* (poet. or pedantic) husband or wife شریک زندگی

spout *n.* pipe of a vessel for the outflow of liquid ٹونٹی lip for this purpose مُنہ pipe for carrying off rain-water from a roof پرنالہ mouth of a fountain فوارے کا مُنہ، فوارہ stream of liquid coming out with great force دھار *up the spout*, in pawn رہن، گرو، گِروی *v.t. & i.* (of liquid) come or send out with force (*from*) دھار بن کر نکلنا، پھوٹ بہنا (colloq.) declaim دُھواں دھار تقریر کرنا (colloq.) recite (poem) rhetorically پُرتکلف انداز سے پڑھنا

sprain (sprayn) *v.t.* have pain and swelling in one's muscle by getting (a joint) twisted (کے جوڑ) میں موچ آنا *be* (or *get*) *sprained*, (of joint) be swollen thus میں موچ آ جانا *n.* such injury موچ

sprang *v.* (pa. t. of **spring**, which see)

sprat *n.* a kind of small sea-fish سپریٹ small child ننھا سا بچہ thin person پتلا دُبلا شخص، دھان پان شخص

sprawl *v.i.* sit or lie with the arms and legs loosely spread out پاؤں پسار کر بیٹھنا یا لیٹنا fall in such a way as to come down thus یوں گرنا کہ ٹانگیں پھیل جائیں *send (someone) sprawling*, knock (him) down کسی کو مار گرانا (of handwriting) be of loose, irregular form لمبے لمبے حرفوں میں لکھنا (of plant) spread thus بے قاعدہ پھیلنا *n.* sprawling position پاؤں پسار کر لیٹنا، بیٹھنا یا گرنا، بے قاعدہ پھیلنا

spray *n.* tiny drops (of liquid) sent through air پھوار (rarely) sprig, of leaves or flowers پتّوں (یا پھولوں) بھری ٹہنی (often) similar piece of jewellery قلم، آرائشی شاخ *v.t.* send out (paint, etc.) in a spray کی پھوار ڈالنا scatter liquid, etc. on (something) thus پر پھوار ڈالنا **sprayer** *n.* well-known syringe-like device for spraying فوارہ، پچکاری

spread (spred) *v.t. & i.* (*spread, spread, spread*) (also *spread out*), unfold ; extend پھیلانا put (something *on* another) thus (پر) بچھانا cover (something *with* another) پر بچھانا put (something *on* another) or cover (something *with* another) لگانا *spread the table*, put food, dishes, etc., on the dining-table for a meal میز لگانا، دسترخوان بچھانا (of rumour, disease, liquid, etc.) (cause to) become widely extended پھیلنا، پھیلانا *n.* spreading پھیلنا *the spread of a disease* بیماری کا پھیلنا extent پھیلاؤ، وسعت، کشادگی *the spread of an arch* محراب کی کشادگی *the spread of a bird's wings* پرندے کے پروں کا پھیلاؤ extension اشاعت، ترویج *the spread of education* ترویجِ تعلیم، اشاعتِ تعلیم anything spread چادر (وغیرہ) *bedspread*, coverlet چادر، پلنگ پوش (slang) meal provided ; feast کھانا، دعوت

spree *n.* lively frolic رنگ رلیاں holidaying with a view to breaking away from routine کام سے چھٹیاں، سیر و تفریح period of carousing ; idle drunken days عیش و نشاط *be on the spree, have a spree*, be having a spree عیش کرنا، مزے اُڑا رہا ہونا

sprig *n.* small shoot with its flowers, leaves, etc. پتّوں (یا پھولوں) بھری ٹہنی، ڈالی scion (*of*) کا، کے چشم و چراغ pattern of a sprig printed on cloth ڈال کا ٹھپا

sprightly (*sprit*-li) *adj.* lively زندہ دل، خوش طبع، شگفتہ خاطر brisk تیز، چُست **sprightliness** *n.* liveliness زندہ دلی، شگفتہ مزاجی

spring *v.t. & i.* (*spring, sprang, sprung*) jump suddenly اُچھل پڑنا، کودنا move suddenly (*up, down, out*, etc.) from rest یکایک اُٹھ بیٹھنا *spring to (one's) feet* اُچھل پڑنا *spring out of bed* بستر سے یکدم باہر نکل آنا come (*out*) thus from concealment اچانک نکل آنا (also *spring up*), shoot out from the ground, etc. اُگ پڑنا، پھوٹنا arise (*from*) (سے) نکلنا come from (سے) اچانک آ جانا bring (a surprise on someone) (کسی کو) بھونچکا کر دینا cause (mine, trap, etc.) to go off چلا دینا، کو حرکت میں لانا (of wood) crack میں شگاف پڑ جانا *spring a leak*, (of barrel, ship, etc.) leak by developing crack ٹپکنے لگنا *n.* springing اُچھلنا، کودنا، اچانک آنا، نکلنا یا اُٹھنا elasticity لچک springing movement زقند، چھلانگ natural fountain چشمہ، سوتا origin ; cause اصل، سرچشمہ، منبع elastic metal coil کمانی *spring balance*, device with a spring to measure weight سپرنگ بیلنس، کمانی دار ترازو *springboard*, board with a loose end for diving from it with a spring چھلانگ مارنے کا تختہ، چھلانگ تختہ، زقند تختہ *the spring of a vehicle*, devices for lessening the effects of bumping کمانیاں flowering season بہار، ربیع *the spring of*, the best period of کا بہترین حصہ *the spring of life*, youth جوانی، شباب (*pl.*) (springs), period of spring tides مدِّ کامل کا وقت **spring-tide** *n.* very high fortnightly tide after full and new moons (as opposed to *neap-tide*) مدِّ کامل **springy** (*sprinj*-i) *adj.* elastic لچکدار **springless** *adj.* without springs کمانیوں کے بغیر، بے کمانی **springtide** (lit.), **springtime** *n.* the spring season موسمِ بہار، فصلِ بہار

springe (sprinj) *n.* (old use) snare, noose پھندا، لاسا

springy *adj.* (see under **spring**)

sprinkle (*sprink*-ĕl) *v. t. & i.* scatter drops or bits of water, sand, flour, etc., (*on* a surface or a surface *with* something) (پر) چھڑکنا *n.* small shower چھڑکنا **sprinkler** *n.* one who sprinkles چھڑکنے والا appliance for sprinkling water چھڑکاؤ کی کل

sprinkling *n.* small quantity or number (*of* people, etc. at a place) ; a few, here and

there چند ، چند ایک
sprint *v.i.* run at full speed for a short while تھوڑی دیر کو بگٹٹ دوڑنا *n.* such a run چھوٹی بگٹٹ دوڑ **sprinter** *n.* runner of short races چھوٹی بگٹٹ دوڑوں میں حصہ لینے والا
sprite (sprit) *n.* fairy پری ، جن
sprout *v.t.* & *i.* put forth shoots کی کونپل پھوٹنا ، put forth hair مسیں بھیگنا (of shoots) spring پھوٹنا ، (of rain, etc.) cause (plants) to grow *n.* shoot of a plant کونپل
spruce (sproos) *n.* (also *Spruce fir*) a kind of fir جرمن صنوبر *adj.* trim and smart in dress or appearance بنا ٹھنا *v.t.* & *i.* (*spruce oneself up*), make oneself spruce بناؤ سنگار کرنا
sprung *v.* (pa. p. of **spring,** which see)
spry (spri) *adj.* lively خوش مزاج ، زندہ دل quick-witted زود فہم ، ذہین active پھرتیلا ، چست ، مستعد
spud (spud) *n.* (slang) potato آلو
spue (spew) (another spelling of **spew,** which see)
spume (spewm) *n.* (lit.) foam جھاگ ، پھین
spun (spun) *v.* (pa. p. of **spin,** which see)
spur (spě*) *n.* sharp-toothed wheel fitted to the heel of a rider's boot for urging the horse forward مہمیز کی پھرکی ، مہمیز *put spur to, set spur to,* urge forward thus ایڑ لگانا *spur a willing horse,* incite unnecessarily خواہ مخواہ اکسانا *win (one's) spurs,* earn by bravery the gold spurs of knighthood بہادری سے اعزاز پانا any impetus (*to*) کے لیے تحریک ، محرک (یا) ، ہیجان *on the spur of the moment,* on a sudden impulse وہیں ، جھٹ ، وقتی جذبے کے تحت sharp point at the back of a cock's leg مرغے کی ٹانگ کا خار ridge, literary extending from a hill ایک طرف کو نکلی ہوئی پہاڑی *v.t.* (-rr-) urge on (as) with spurs (کو) ایڑ لگانا ، (کو) مہمیز کرنا
spurious (*spew*-ri-us) *adj.* (of coin, claim, quality, etc.) not genuine جعلی
spurn (spě*n) *v.t.* kick away with contempt ٹھکرانا ، پرلات مارنا reject (offer, etc.) مسترد کرنا
spurt, spirt (spě*t) *v.t.* & *i.* (usu. *spirt*) (of liquid, flame, etc.) (cause to) burst forth (*up, out, down,* etc.) in a jet پھوٹ نکلنا ، بیک نکلنا یا نکالنا ، شعلے کا بھڑک اٹھنا (usu. *spurt* of a runner) increase the pace towards the end of a race رفتار یکدم تیز کر دینا *n.* sudden bursting forth (*of* liquid, flame, energy, etc.) زور ، جوش
sputnik (*spoot*-nik) *n.* (Russian) satellite moon (originally a Russian word meaning *fellow-traveller*) سپوتنک ، مصنوعی چاند ، ہمسفر
spy (spī) *n.* one trying to get secret information in a foreign country جاسوس one who keeps a secret watch (*on* the activities of others) خفیہ طور پر کڑی نظر رکھنے والا ، مخبر *v.t.* & *i.* (spy *on* or *upon*), watch secretly خفیہ طور پر کڑی نظر رکھنے والا ، بغور دیکھنا act as a spy (*on*) (کی) مخبری کرنا observe دیکھنا discover دیکھنا **spy-glass** *n.* small telescope چھوٹی دوربین [S] A **spy** is one sent to watch from an unsuspected position in enemy territory ; a **scout**, one sent ahead to reconnoitre ; a **traitor,** one who delivers one's friends' side to their enemies ; an **informer,** one who secretly gives inside information ; an **eavesdropper**, one who listens at keyholes, in corridors and when people are not on their guard ; a **detective**, one who investigates crimes or mysteries ; an **intelligence man** is the name a country gives to her own spy.
squab (skwab) *n.* short fat person موٹا اور ناٹا cushion گدی *adj.* short and fat موٹا اور ناٹا thick گدگدا
squabble (*skwob*-ěl) *n.* noisy quarrel (*about* an unimportant matter) فضول جھگڑا *v.i.* quarrel noisily (*about*) بے معنی بات پر جھگڑنا
squad (skwod) *n.* small group of persons working or being trained together ٹکڑی ، دستہ
squadron (*skwod*-rěn) *n.* division of a cavalry regiment comprising 120 to 200 men سواروں کا دستہ number of warships forming a unit جنگی جہازوں کا دستہ unit of aircraft comprising 10 to 18 machines (فوجی طیاروں کا) پرہ
squalid (*skwo*-lid) *adj.* dirty گندا ، گھناؤنا wretched خستہ حال **squalidness, squalor** *n.* squalid condition گندگی ، غلاظت ، خستگی ، زبوں حالی
squall (skwal) *n.* child's scream of fear or pain بچے کی چیخ sudden sharp wind-storm with rain or snow *v.i.* give squalls چیخ مارنا ، چیخ اٹھنا
squander (*skwond*-ė*) *v.t.* waste (time, money, etc.) گنوانا ، ضائع کرنا
square (*skway*-ě*) *n.* plane right angled figure with four equal sides مربع **square** space in a town enclosed with buildings چوک result obtained when a number is multiplied by itself مربع *adj.* having the shape of a square مربع (of corner, shoulder, etc.) having or forming a right angle زاویہ قائمہ والا ، سیدھا level or parallel (*with*) کے متوازی perpendicular (*to*) کے عمودی honest (dealings) دیانتدارانہ ، منصفانہ *a square deal, a square argument,* one in which everyone is treated fairly منصفانہ سلوک settled (account) صاف *get square with* (*someone*), (*a*) pay debts or settle accounts سے حساب صاف کرنا (*b*) have one's revenge on (him) سے بدلہ لینا *square*

meal, enough and satisfying meal پیٹ بھر روٹی *square inch* (*etc.*) area equal to that of a square with sides of one inch (etc.) مربع انچ (وغیرہ) *two* (*etc.*) *square inches*, area double (etc.) that دو (وغیرہ) مربع انچ *two* (*etc.*) *inch square*, area equal to that of a square with sides of two (etc.) inches (=4 square inches) دو انچ مربع *square root* (*of a number*), another number whose square would give this number (کا) جذر *v.t.* & *i.* make square مربع بنانا cause one line, surface, etc., to be at right angles to another زاویۂ قائمہ پر رکھنا make level ہموار کرنا، سیدھا کرنا get the square of (a number) کا مربع کرنا mark (*off*) in squares کے مربعے بنانا make or be consistent (*with*) سے ہم آہنگ ہونا یا بنانا (colloq.) bribe رشوت *square up*, (*a*) settle accounts with سے حساب صاف کرنا (*b*) threaten by assuming boxing attitude آستینیں چڑھانا (c) put (confusion, etc.) right درست کرنا

squash (skwosh) *v.t.* & *i.* crush (flat or into a small space) گودا نکالنا، نچوڑنا snub جھاڑ جھپاڑ کرنا suppress (person, proposal, etc.) دبا دینا get out of crowd by pressing one's way through ہجوم میں گھس پیٹھ کر راستہ نکالنا، دھکم دھکا کر کے نکلنا *n.* number of persons squashed together بھیڑ، ہجوم drink made from juice of crushed fruit used as a cold drink رس، سکواش a game played with soft ball and rackets سکواش a kind of edible gourd ایک قسم کا کدو، سکواش

squat (skwot) *v.i.* (-tt-) sit on one's heels with knees drawn up گھٹنے اٹھا کر بیٹھنا (colloq.) sit (*down*) بیٹھنا *adj.* dumpy (person) ناٹا اور موٹا very low in comparison with breadth پست

squatter *n.* one who occupies public land or building without legal right زبردستی قبضہ کرنے والا، دھرنا مار کر بیٹھنے والا

squawk (skwawk) *n.* (of ducks, hens, etc.) loud, harsh cry قیں قیں، کڑ کڑ *v.i.* utter this cry قیں قیں کرنا، کڑ کڑانا

squeak (skweek) *n.* short, shrill cry (of a mouse, etc.) چیں such sound (of an unoiled hinge, etc.) چیں چیں، چوں چوں *a narrow squeak*, (*a*) a narrow escape from danger بمشکل بچنا (*b*) a narrow escape from failure روتے پیٹتے کامیاب ہونا *v.t.* & *i.* make a squeak چیں چیں کرنا، چوں چوں کرنا say in a squeaking voice چیں چیں کرنا **squeaky** *adj.* squeaking چیں چیں کرنے والا **squeaker** *n.* (also) young bird پرندے کا بچہ

squeal (skweel) *n.* longer squeak indicating pain, fear تیکھی چیخ *v.t.* & *i.* give a squeal تیکھی آواز سے چیخنا say in a squealing voice چیں چیں کر کے بولنا

squeamish (*skwee*-mish) *adj.* with a stomach easily made sick نازک معدے والا، جسے بات بات پر قے آئے easily disgusted or offended نازک مزاج too critical بڑا نکتہ چیں too scrupulous ضرورت سے زیادہ محتاط

squeegee (*skwee*-jee) *n.* rubber-edged cleaner for wiping moisture off smooth surface آب صاف

squeeze (skweez) *v.t.* & *i.* press tightly بھینچنا reduce size thus بھینچنا، چھوٹا کرنا force (*into* a new shape) بھینچ کر نئی شکل میں لانا extort (money or information *from*, *out of*) سے زبردستی وصول کرنا get thus juice, etc. (*out of*) رس نکالنا *squeeze a lemon*, *squeeze juice out of a lemon* لیموں نچوڑنا *squeeze* (*one's*) *way through* (*a crowd*) (بھیڑ) میں سے دھکم دھکا کر کے نکلنا *squeeze one's* (*way*) *into* (*a place*) گھس پیٹھ کر بیٹھ جانا *squeeze* (*someone's*) *hand*, press it to show sympathy, etc. (کسی) کا ہاتھ دبانا *n.* squeezing بھینچنا، زور سے دبانا crowded place بھیڑ close fit پھنسا ہوا pressure دباؤ

squelch (skwelch) *v.t.* & *i.* suppress (person, proposal, etc.) دبا دینا (of mud, etc.) make a sucking sound when feet are lifted from it پچ پچ کرنا

squib (skwib) *n.* a small firework thrown by hand پھچھوندر (یا) ہوائی lampoon ہجو، ہجویہ نظم

squint (skwint) *v.i.* be cross-eyed بھینگا ہونا look sideways (*at*) کنکھیوں سے دیکھنا look with half-shut eyes نیم وا آنکھوں سے دیکھنا *n.* squinting position of the eyeballs بھینگا پن (colloq.) glance (*at*) اچٹتی ہوئی نظر

squire (skwɪ-ĕ*) *n.* chief landowner in a British parish گاؤں کا بڑا زمیندار (old use) knight's attendant نائٹ کا ہمرکاب (old use) man escorting a lady خاتون کا ہمرکاب

squirm (skwĕ*m) *v.i.* wriggle from discomfort بیچینی (یا بدحواسی یا پریشانی) ظاہر کرنا wriggle from shame پیچ و تاب کھانا، شرم سے سمٹتے جانا

squirrel (*skwi*-rĕl) *n.* small bushy-tailed animal living in trees گلہری

squirt (skwe*t) *v.t.* & *i.* (of liquid or powder) force (or be forced) out in a thin steam فوارہ چھوڑنا یا چھوٹنا *n.* instrument for squirting پچکاری jet دھار

squish (shwish) *n.* (colloq.) marmalade مارملیڈ، نارنگی کا مربہ

stab *v.t.* & *i.* (-bb-) wound with a pointed weapon چھرے سے زخمی کرنا push (a knife, etc.) into گھونپنا، بھونکنا (of pain, etc.) produce a sensation as of being stabbed ٹیس اٹھنا *n.* stabbing

blow چھرے کا گھاؤ
stable (stay-bèl) *n.* building in which horses are kept طویلہ ، اصطبل *v.t.* put or keep (horses) in a stable طویلے میں باندھنا race horses (*of* a particular stable, club or person) دَوڑ والے گھوڑے اصطبل *adj.* firm مستحکم ، مضبوط balanced متوازن not likely to change غیر تغیّر پذیر ، نہ بدلنے والا **stability** (sta-*bil*-i-ti) *n.* being stable مضبوطی ، استحکام غیر تغیّر پذیری **stabilize** (*stab*-i-l-z) *v.t.* make stable مضبوط کرنا ، مستحکم کرنا ، استحکام عطا کرنا **stabilization** (-zay-) *n.* act of stabilizing or being stabilized استحکام maintenance of the purchasing power of a country's currency by fixing its value in terms of gold سکے کی قیمت سونے میں متعیّن کر دینا ، سکے کا استحکام
staccato (sta-*kah*-toh) *adj.* (of music) played with breaks between the successive notes وقفوں والا ، غیر مسلسل *adv.* (music played) thus وقفے دے کر
stack (stak) *n.* large thatched pile of stored straw, etc. بھوسے وغیرہ کا لپا ہوا ڈھیر ، کُپ neatly arranged pile (*of* wood) (لکڑیوں کی) ٹال neatly arranged pile (*of* books) (کتابوں کی) قطار (also *chimney-stack*) (*a*) tall factory chimneys (کارخانے کی) چمنی ، دُود کش number of chimneys side by side on a roof (چھت پر) چمنیوں (یا دُود کشوں) کی قطار *stacks of* (*something*), (colloq.) many of them, large quantities of them بہت سا *v.t.* make into a stack لپا ہوا ڈھیر لگانا pile up انبار لگانا instruct (aircraft waiting to land) to fly at different levels اُترنے والے طیاروں کو جدا جدا بلندیوں پر اُڑنے کی ہدایت دینا
stadium (*stay*-di-um) *n.* enclosed area for games, etc., with stands for spectators سٹیڈیم foot-race course in ancient Greece پیدل دوڑ کا میدان
staff (stahf) *n.* strong walking-stick ڈنڈا ، سونٹا ، لاٹھی ، عصا pole serving as a support ڈنڈا ، کھمبا *flag staff* جھنڈے کا ڈنڈا rod as symbol of sovereignty عصائے شاہی group of assitants under a head عملہ ، اہلکار (also *staff officers*), senior military officers helping the commander in organizing a campaign سالارِ جنگ کا عملہ (pl. *staves*) set of five parallel lines and the spaces between them on which musical notes are written موسیقی لکھنے کی پانچ سطریں ، پنج سطر *v.t.* act as a staff کے اہلکار بننا provide staff کو عملہ مہیّا کرنا
stag *n.* male deer ہرن **stag-party** *n.* party for men only صِرف مردوں کا اجتماع ، مردانہ محفل
stage (stayj) *n.* any raised platform چبوترہ part of a theatre on which actors appear سٹیج theatrical work ڈراموں میں کام ، ناٹک کا فن *stage-craft* ناٹک کا فن ، تمثیل پیش کرنے کا فن the profession of acting اداکاری *go on the stage*, become an actor اداکار بننا *stage-manager*, one conducting a play ناٹک کا مہتمم *stage-effect*, effect as that of a play گہرا اثر ، اثر آفرینی *stage fright*, nervousness felt on facing an audience لوگوں کے سامنے آنے سے گھبراہٹ scene (*of* action) موقع ، جائے وُقوع ، میدانِ عمل step *in* the development of (something) مرحلہ ، مقام *at an early stage* (*in*) (کے) شروع ہی میں distance between two stopping places on a route مرحلہ ، منزل *v.t.* & *i.* put (a play) on the stage (ڈراما) سٹیج پر لانا ، (ڈراما) کرنا arrange effectively for (an event) (کو) شاندار طریقے سے کرنا **stage-coach** *n.* (old use) public horse-drawn vehicle plying by stages on a regular route سٹیج کوچ **stager** *n.* (only in the phrase) *old stager*, very experienced person بڑا تجربہ کار ، گھاگ ، خرّانٹ *staging post* *n.* regular stop on air route ہوائی راستے میں مستقل جائے نزول
stagger (*stag*-ĕ*) *v.t.* & *i.* walk unsteadily (from weakness or drunkenness) لڑکھڑانا ، ڈگمگانا لڑکھڑاتے ہوئے چلنا (of a blow) make (someone) unsteady لڑکھڑا دینا shake (conviction of) متزلزل کر دینا shock deeply چکرا دینا ، بوکھلا دینا (کا ایمان) *staggered by* (*something*) سے دینا ، بدحواس کر دینا چکرایا ہوا time (holidays, events, shifts, duties, etc.) differently to avoid their occurring together الگ الگ وقت پر رکھنا ، پھیلا دینا *n.* staggering movement چکر ، چال ، لغزش ، لڑکھڑاہٹ ، ڈگمگاہٹ **staggerer** *n.* (esp.) event that staggers on بوکھلا دینے والا واقعہ
stagirite (stag-i-rit) *n.* (*the Stagirite*), Aristotle اَرسطو
stagnant (*stag*-nant) *adj.* still and stale (water) بند unchanging ساکن ، جامد inactive سُست ، مندا **stagnate** *v.i.* be stagnant بند ہونا ، ساکن ہونا ، مندا ہونا be dull through disuse, etc. ناکارہ ہونا **stagnation** (-*nay*-) *n.* being stagnant جمود
staid (stayd) *adj.* quiet and serious (person, behaviour, etc.) متین ، سنجیدہ ، باوقار
stain (stayn) *v.t.* & *i.* (of liquids) change the colour of بدرنگ کر دینا change in colour بدرنگ ہونا make dirty or coloured marks on کے دھبے ڈالنا *stained with gravy* (*etc.*) سالن کے دھبے لگے ہوئے *blood-stained* خون آلودہ colour with a penetrating substance رنگ چڑھانا colour (glass) with milky or other translucent colours دُودھیا کرنا *stained glass windows* دُودھیا شیشوں والی کھڑکیاں blemish (character, reputation, person, etc.) کو بٹّہ لگانا ، داغ لگانا colour (wall paper) دیواری کاغذ کو رنگنا ، رنگ بنانا

n. liquid used for staining wood, etc. سرایت کرنے والا رنگ stained place داغدار جگہ dirty mark دھبا، داغ blemish (*on*) دھبا، داغ

stainless *adj.* (of surface, character, etc.) without بے داغ، بیداغ non-rusting جسے زنگ نہ لگے، بیداغ *stainless steel,* alloy of chromium and steel بیداغ فولاد، زنگ نہ لگنے والا فولاد

stair (*stay-ě**) *n.* (*pl., stairs, also flight of stairs*) series of fixed steps leading from one floor of a building to another زینہ، سیڑھیاں any one of these سیڑھی کا پایہ، قدمچہ، سیڑھی

staircase *n.* portable or fixed series of stairs inside or outside the walls of a building زینہ، سیڑھیاں سیڑھی **upstairs** *adj.* & *adv.* (on) the upper floor اوپر کی منزل (میں)، اوپر **downstairs** *adj.* & *adv.* نچلی منزل (میں)، نیچے

stake (stayk) *n.* strong pointed post نوکدار کھمبا نوکدار بلّی (old use) such a post to which a heretic was tied for being burnt to death کھمبا جس سے کافر کو جلاتے وقت باندھیں، کافر سوز کھمبا *condemned to the stake,* condemned to such death زندہ جلا دیے جانے کی سزا money risked in gambling, horse-race, etc. شرط کا روپیہ بدی ہوئی رقم *at stake,* risked thus بدا ہوا *be at stake,* be risked خطرے میں ہونا *v.t.* support with a stake کھمبے سے سہارا دینا mark (*out, off,* or *in*) with stakes کھمبوں کی باڑ لگا کر الگ کرنا pin (money, one's hopes, etc. *on*) پر لگانا

stalactite (*stal*-ak-tit) *n.* hanging lime deposit in a cave (چونے کا) سقفی قلم

stalagmite (stal-ag-mit) *n.* projecting lime deposit on the floor of a cave (چونے کا) فرشی قلم

stalactites (top) & stalagmites (bottom)

stale (stayl) *adj.* (of food) not fresh باسی (of story, joke, news, etc.) uninteresting because heard before پرانا، باسی، بے لطف **staleness** *n.* not being fresh باسی ہونا

stalemate (stayl-*mayt,* or *stal*-mayt) *n.* (in chess) position of chessmen in which no further move is possible زچ impasse, deadlock تعطّل *v.t.* reduce (opponent) to standstill without defeating him کو زچ کرنا

stalk (stawk) *v.t.* & *i.* approach (quarry) cautiously and stealthily شکار کو دبے پاؤں جا دبوچنا stride grimly آہستہ آہستہ وقار سے چلنا stride proudly بانکی چال چلنا *n.* non-woody stem of a plant ڈنٹھل، ڈنڈی

stall (strawl) *n.* compartment for one animal in a stable, etc. تھان table, etc., used as a shop خوانچہ small open-fronted shop ہاٹ، سٹال *tea-stall* چائے کا ہاٹ *book-stall* بُک سٹال، بکسٹال (in theatre) expensive seats nearest the stage سٹال (in cinema) expensive seats farthest from the screen سٹال seat in a chair of the church سماع خانہ کی نشست *v.t.* & *i.* keep (animal) in a stall تھان پر باندھنا (of a motor car engine) (cause to) fail owing to insufficient power (موٹر کے انجن کا) نہ چلنا (of aircraft) (cause to) go out of control through loss of speed (ہوائی جہاز کے انجن کا) نہ اُڑنا obstruct and delay میں رکاوٹ ڈالنا evade ٹالنا

stallion (*stal*-yěn) *n.* uncastrated male horse for breeding نسل کشی والا گھوڑا، بیج کا گھوڑا، اسپِ نر

stalwart (*stawl*-wě*t) *adj.* tall and strong لمبا تڑنگا brave بہادر resolved باعزم firm (supporter) پکا، مضبوط

stamen (*stay*-men) *n.* pollen-bearing part of a flower پھول کا نر حصہ، زردار حصہ، زیرہ

stamina (*stam*-i-na) *n.* staying-power قوتِ برداشت، سکت

stammer (*stam*-ě*) *v.t.* & *i.* stutter, speak haltingly ہکلانا speak (*out*-something) thus ہکلا کر کہنا *n.* stammering رک رک کر کہنا، ہکلاہٹ

stammerer *n.* one who stammers ہکلا

stamp *v.t.* & i. put (in anger one's foot) down with force غصے میں (پاؤں) زمین پر زور سے مارنا put down one's foot with force (*on* something) پر پاؤں زور سے مارنا *stamp* (*something*) *down,* suppress it (کسی چیز) کو بزور دبا دینا *stamp out,* put an end to by strong measures کا خاتمہ کر دینا، کو مٹا ڈالنا put (lettering) on (something) by pressing a stamp on it مہر لگانا print (design, etc.) thus نقش ابھارنا put a postage stamp on پر ٹکٹ لگانا put a judicial or other stamp on پر سٹامپ لگانا، اسٹام لگانا (of action, etc.) distinguish (someone *as*) (کی حیثیت سے) نمایاں کرنا، ممتاز کرنا *n.* stamping in anger with the foot غصے میں زمین پر زور سے پاؤں مارنا thing used for the printing of lettering مہر thing used for printing design, etc. چھاپ، مہر *rubber-stamp* ربڑ کی مہر *rubber-stamp,* (esp. in bad sense) give official sanction to something decided elsewhere پر صاد کرنا lettering or design stamped مہر، چھاپ، نقش sign (of something) (کے) آثار، (کی) چھاپ kind, type نمونے، قسم (also *postage stamp*), piece of paper with design, etc., printed on it stuck or as a proof of pre-payment ٹکٹ (also judicial stamp), similar piece as proof of the payment of court fees, etc., etc. اِسٹامپ ، اسٹامپ *revenue stamp* رسیدی ٹکٹ

stampede (stam-*peed*) *n.* sudden rush (of people, horses, cattle, etc.) owing to fright بھاگڑ، ہڑ بڑی. *v.t.* & *i.* rush thus بھاگڑ پڑنا، ہڑبڑی مچنا cause to stampede بھاگڑ ڈالنا، ہڑبڑی مچانا

stanch (stanch, or stansh) *v. t.* (same as **staunch,** which see)

stand *v.t.* & *i.*(*stand, stood, stood*) be in a stationary upright position کھڑا ہونا rise or raise to this position کھڑا ہونا، کھڑا ہو جانا، کھڑا کرنا *stand the ladder against the wall* سیڑھی کو دیوار پر لگانا یا ٹیکنا be of (a certain height) when standing اونچا ہونا، لمبا ہونا (of persons, words, etc.) remain without change وضع پر قائم رہنا، قائم رہنا endure (hardship, etc.) برداشت کرنا، جھیلنا put up with (insult, etc.) برداشت کرنا undergo (one's trial *for* an offence) پر مقدمہ چلانا be in a certain situation ہونا، کی حالت میں ہونا *stand in need of*, need کی ضرورت ہونا *stand well with one's boss*), be in his good books آقا وغیرہ کی نظروں میں اچھا ہونا *stand to win*, have a chance of winning کے جیتنے کا امکان *stand to lose*, be likely to lose کے ہارنے کا امکان ہونا (colloq.) provide (*someone* tea, etc., in a restaurant, etc., and pay for it کے پیسے دینا، کو پلانا (یا کھلانا) *stand away* (*from*), stand back (from) or move away (from an advanced position) سے پیچھے ہٹنا *stand by*, (*a*) be an inactive spectator پاس کھڑے ہو جانا (*b*) be ready (for action, help, etc.) (کے لیے) تیار رہنا (*c*) support (someone) کی مدد کرنا (*d*) be faithful to کا ساتھ نہ چھوڑنا *stand for* (*a*) be a symbol of کی علامت ہونا (*b*) comprise پر مشتمل ہونا (*c*) be a candidate for (legislature, etc., in an election) کا اُمیدوار (*d*) support (a cause, principle, etc.) کی تائید کرنا، کا حامی ہونا (*e*) tolerate, endure برداشت کرنا *stand (one's) ground*, not to give in اپنی بات پر ڈٹے رہنا، نہ جھکنا *stand a good chance (of doing)*, be likely to (do) کا بہت امکان ہونا *stand a poor chance of (doing)*, be unlikely to (do) کا کوئی امکان نہ ہونا *stand on ceremony*, pay too much attention to formalities رسوم کی پابندی کرنا، تکلف سے کام لینا *stand on end*, (of hair) be pricked with fear (رونگٹے) کھڑے ہونا *stand off*, remain at a distance پرے رہنا *stand out*, (*a*) be prominent (*among*) میں نمایاں ہونا

(*b*) continue to resist (*against*) کے خلاف ڈٹے رہنا continue firm (*for*) (کا) آخر تک قائم رہنا، آخر تک حامی رہنا (پر) *it stands to reason (that)*, it is reasonable (that) سمجھ میں آنے کی بات ہے، بڑی معقول بات ہے *stand up for*, (*a cause etc.*), fight for it کے لیے جدّوجہد کرنا *stand up to*, face boldly کا ڈٹ کر مقابلہ کرنا *n.* stationary position کھڑے ہونا *come to a stand*, stop رُکنا *bring to a stand*, stop (someone or something) کو روکنا resistance مقابلہ، مقاومت، مدافعت *make a stand*, fight (*for* or *against*) (کے لیے یا کا) مقابلہ کرنا basis *take (one's) stand* (*on* or *upon* a point, etc.), base one's argument (on it) (پر) اپنے دلائل کی بُنیاد رکھنا position ; point of view موقف، نقطۂ نگاہ small piece of furniture, for placing a thing on اڈا، پلیمنڈا shed اڈا بسوں کا اڈا *bus stand* کرائے کی کاروں کا اڈا، اڈا ٹیکسی *taxi stand* کرائے کی گاڑیوں کا اڈا *cab stand*, stand for taxis, etc. اڈا *news stand*, small stall for the sale of newspapers, etc. اخباروں کی چھوٹی دُکان (U.S.) witness-box عدالت میں گواہوں کا کٹہرا **stand at ease** *v.i.* (of soldiers, etc.) stand in a prescribed manner which is less stiff than attention آرام سے کھڑے رہنا، کھڑے آرام *n.* (*stand-at-ease*), this position کھڑے آرام **stand-by** *n.* reliable support in time of need پکا سہارا **standing** *n.* continuance (دیر) طوالت *of long standing*, continuing since long (کو) دیر کا، دیر سے چلا آ رہا established position or reputation حیثیت، مسلّمہ حیثیت *of standing, of high standing* بڑی حیثیت کا *of no standing* بے حیثیت، کم حیثیت regular باقاعدہ *standing army* باقاعدہ فوج *standing order*, order for something to be done regularly استمراری حکم، جاری حکم **stand-offish** (*of-*) *adj.* cold and distant in manner رُوکھا، خشک

standpoint *n.* view point نقطۂ نگاہ، نقطۂ نظر، زاویۂ نگاہ، زاویہ

standstill *n.* stop رُکنا، ٹھہراؤ، قیام *be at a standstill*, be stationary ساکن ہونا *a standstill*, stop dead بالکل رُک جانا *bring to a standstill*, stop روک لینا، روک دینا *standstill agreement*, agreement on 'status quo' pending final decision معاہدۂ قائمہ

standard (*stand*-ĕ*d) *n.* flag (of royalty, regiment) to which loyalty is given or asked since it is regarded as a symbol of certain principles جھنڈا، پرچم class in a primary school (پرائمری کی) پانچویں measure (*of* weights, lengths, qualities, etc.) پیمانہ، معیار (*be* or *come*) *up to the standard*, معیاری ہونا (*high* or *low*) *standard of living* معیارِ زندگی *adj.* coming up to the standard معیاری *standard authors*, authors accepted as good models معیاری مصنّف (*West Pakistan, etc.*) *standard time*, reckoning of time (in relation to Greenwich time) as officially adopted for West Pakistan (or any other country or part thereof)

معیاری وقت، سٹینڈرڈ ٹائم upright support کھمبا *standard lamp*, lamp on a tall standard with base on floor فرشی لیمپ، فرشی شمع **standardize** *v.t.* make according to fixed standards ایک معیار کے بنانا، ہم معیار بنانا **standardized** *adj.* made according to fixed standards ہم معیار، ہم معیاری **standardizing, standardization** (*-zay-*) *n.* ہم معیاری، ہم معیاریت

stank *v.* (pa. t. of **stink,** which see)

stanza (*stanz*-a) *n.* group of lines forming a division of a poem بند

staple (*stay*-pèl) *n.* U-shaped nail hammered into a wall کنڈا piece of wire for stitching sheets of paper together کاغذ سینے کا تار chief produce (*of* a country) خاص پیداوار chief export (*of* a country) خاص درساوری جنس chief element (*of* something) جزوِ خاص *adj.* chief, main (food, product, export, etc. *of*) اصلی، بڑا

star (stah*) *n.* (also *fixed star*), any heavenly body (apart from planets) seen as a fixed point ستارہ، تارا figure (★) regarded as representing a star ستارہ، تارا medal of this design تمغہ famous actor, actress, singer, author, etc. نامی شخص، ستارہ *filmstars*, chief actors and actresses of the screen فلمی ستارے heavenly body regarded as influencing a person's fate ستارہ hence fate, luck قسمت، نصیب، بھاگ *be born under a lucky star*, be lucky in life خوش نصیب ہونا *curse (one's) stars* قسمت کو رونا *v.t.* & *i.* (-rr-) mark or decorate with a star or stars ستارے ڈالنا، ستارے کا نشان be a star actress or actor (*in* a film or play) بڑا اداکار ہونا، بڑی اداکارہ ہونا **starry** *adj.* (of sky or night) full of stars تاروں بھرا bright like stars ستاروں کی طرح چمکتا ہوا **starfish** *n.* star-shaped fish تارا مچھلی **starlight** *n.* light of stars تاروں کی چھاؤں **stars and stripes** *n.* U.S. flag امریکی جھنڈا تارے دھاریاں **star-turn** *n.* principal item in some entertainment تماشے کا بہترین حصہ، کھیل (وغیرہ) کی جان

a starfish

starboard (*stah**-be*d) *n.* right-hand side of a ship or aircraft from the point of view of a person facing forward (as opposed to *larboard* or *port*) (جہاز یا ہوائی جہاز کی) داہنی سمت

starch (stah*ch) *n.* white tasteless substance forming part of wheat, potatoes, etc. نشاستہ this substance separated for stiffening collars کلف، ماوا، مانڈی *v.t.* make (collars, etc.) stiff with starch کو کلف لگانا **starchy** *adj.* having starch نشاستے والا

stare (*stay*-è*) *v.t.* & *i.* look fixedly تکنا، گھورنا ٹکٹکی باندھ کے دیکھنا *stare at (someone's) face, stare (someone) in the face* کو ٹکٹکی باندھ کر دیکھنا (of eye) be wide open کھلا ہونا، مرٹ مرٹ دیکھنا (of an object) be right in front of (someone) کے بالکل سامنے آنا **staring** *adj.* too conspicuous (colours) بہت شوخ wide open (eyes) کھلی کی کھلی looking fixedly گھورتی ہوئی

starfish *n.* (see under **star**)

stark (stah*k) *adj.* stiff owing to death اکڑا ہوا، سخت quite, entirely بالکل، یکسر *stark naked* بالکل ننگا، مادر زاد برہنہ *adv.* entirely بالکل، یکسر

starlight *n.* (see under **star**)

starling (*stah**-ling) *n.* a kind of small bird noted for its imitation, chattery and stealing habits شارک، گرسل

a starling

starry *adj.* (see under **star**)

start (stah*t) *v.t.* & *i.* begin (a journey) چلنے لگنا، نکلنا set out شروع کرنا، پر روانہ ہونا begin (business) چلانا، شروع کرنا begin (work, etc.) شروع کرنا *it started to rain, it started raining* بارش ہونے لگی (cause to) come into existence شروع کرنا، لگانا، شروع ہونا یا کرنا make a sudden movement (from one's seat, etc.) owing to fear or surprise چونک اٹھنا دھک سے رہ جانا (of a horse) shy بدکنا، بھڑکنا *start back* (or *forward, aside,* etc.) بدک کر پیچھے (یا آگے یا ایک طرف وغیرہ) ہونا *n.* starting آغاز، ابتدا setting out روانگی *make an early start*, set out early جلدی چل پڑنا sudden movement caused by sudden fear or surprise چونک اٹھنا shying بدکنا، بھڑکنا starting point مقام روانگی، نقطہ آغاز amount (*of* time or distance) by which a runner starts in front of (others) دوڑ میں (فاصلے یا وقت کی) رعایت، رعایت *give (someone) a start* کو (کسی کو اتنے وقت یا فاصلہ) کی رعایت دینا *by fits and starts*, irregularly پابندی سے نہیں، بیقاعدگی سے

startle (*stah*t-èl*) *v.t.* cause to start owing to sudden fear or surprise چونکا دینا، گھبرا دینا، حواس باختہ کر دینا **startler** *n.* event which startles چونکا دینے والا واقعہ

starve (stah*v) *v.t.* & *i.* (cause to) suffer from hunger فاقے کرنا (یا) دینا، بھوکوں مرنا (یا مارنا) *starve (someone) into (something or doing something)*, force (him to do it) by denying (him) food فاقے دے دے کر مجبور کرنا *be starving (for food)*, be extremely hungry پر فاقے گزرنا، سخت بھوکا ہونا *starve to death*, cause death thus فاقے دے دے کر مارنا *be starved to death*, die thus فاقوں سے مر جانا **starvation** (*-vay-*) *n.* act of starving or being starved فاقہ زدگی، فاقہ *starvation level* فاقوں کی حد تک

state (stayt) *n.* condition (*of* place, thing, person, mind, health, etc.) حالت *in a poor state of health* بیمار، بیمار سا status رتبہ، مرتبہ، منصب (the

State), self-governing country or such part of it ریاست pomp and show ; ceremonial formality شان وشوکت، شان وشکوہ *drive in state* (*through* the streets, *to* a place), (بادشاہ کا) شان وشکوہ سے جانا *the state coach*, the sovereign's coach for driving in state شاہی گاڑی *lie in state*. (of a dead person) be placed where the public may pay respect before burial (نعش کا) آخری رُونمائی کے لیے رکھا جانا *v.t.* express (one's views, reasons, etc.) carefully in words وضاحت سے کہنا، بیان کرنا، کا اظہار کرنا *state that* کہنا کہ *state why* (or *how* or *who*, etc.) بتانا کہ کیوں (یا کِس طرح یا کون وغیرہ) **stated** (*stay*-tid) *adj*. made known (time, etc.) مذکورہ، بنائے ہوئے alleged مبیّنہ **stately** *adj*. dignified, impressive شان وشوکت والا، پُرشکوہ **statecraft** *n*. art of government آئینِ جہانبانی **statesman** (*stayts*-man) *n*. (pl. *statesmen*) influential or highly-placed politician سیاستدان، مدبّر **statesmanlike** *adj*. showing a statesman's wisdom مدبّرانہ **statesmanship** *n*. مدبّری **stateroom** *n*. splendid room in a large house reserved for special occasions خاص کمرہ passenger's private cabin in a ship or private compartment in a train خاص کمرہ **statement** *n*. presentation in considered words and with implied correction of facts, views, a problem, etc. بیان *make a statement* بیان دینا *issue a statement* بیان جاری کرنا

static (*stat*-ik) *adj*. balanced, not moving ساکن *static water*, local water supply which needs pumping in as it is not under pressure دباؤ کے بغیر پانی، پمپ کا محتاج پانی **statics** (*stat*-iks) *n. pl.* (used with *sing*. verb) branch of physics dealing with balanced forces or things at rest سکونیات

station (*stay*-shěn) *n*. position (of someone, *of* or *in* life) رُتبہ، حیثیت، منصب place where something is جگہ، مقام local office of some organization مقامی، دفتر، شاخ duty post (of police, fire service, etc.) اڈا، مقام، مرکز، مستقر *police station* تھانہ *Station House Officer*, (abbr. as *S.H.O.*), official in charge of a police station تھانیدار، ایس ایچ او *fire-station*, place where the engines and local staff of a fire brigade stand ready for being called in emergencies فائر سٹیشن، آگ بجھانے کا مرکز (also *railway station*), stopping-place for railway trains (along with the buildings, etc., connected with it) سٹیشن، ریل کا سٹیشن، ریل کا مستقر، ریل گاہ *v.t.* put (someone or oneself) at a certain station لگانا، مقرر کرنا **station-master** *n*. man in charge of a railway station سٹیشن ماسٹر، ریلگاہ دار **station wagon** *n*. (see *Addenda*)

stationary (*staysh*-ě-ně-ri) *adj*. unchanging غیر تغیر پذیر not moving ساکن **stationery** (*staysh*-ě-ně-ri) *n*. writing materials, etc. سامانِ کتابت، کاغذ، قلم، دوات وغیرہ **stationer** *n*. dealer in stationery سامانِ کتابت بیچنے والا

Statism *n*. (see *Addenda*)

statistics (sta-*tis*-tiks) *n. pl.* facts and figures collected and arranged for information and comparison اعداد و شمار (used with a *sing*. verb) the science of statistics فنِ اعداد و شمار، شماریات **statist** (*stay*-tist), **statistician** (sta-tis-*tish*-ěn) *n*. expert in statistics ماہرِ شماریات **statistical** (-*tis*-) *adj*. pertaining to statistics شماریاتی

statue (*stat*-ew) *n*. sculpture (*of* person, animal, etc.) بُت، مجسمہ *equestrian statue*, human figure on horseback سوار کا مجسمہ **statuette** (stat-ew-*et*) *n*. small statue چھوٹا سا مجسمہ **statuesque** (sta-tew-*esk*) *adj*. like a statue in pose, immobility or clearness of outline مجسمہ آسا

stature (*stach*-ě*) *n*. height (of a person) قد، قامت

status (*stay*-tus) *n*. rank ; relative position (of a person, community, etc.) درجہ، رُتبہ، مرتبہ، حیثیت **status quo** (stay-tus-koh) *n*. existing position of affairs, etc. حالتِ موجودہ، موجودہ حالت *adv*. in the existing position بدستور، بحالتِ موجودہ **status quo ante** (*stay*- tus-kwoh-*ant*-i) *n*. position before a recent change پہلی حالت *adv*. (also, '*status quo*'), in the earlier position پہلی حالت میں، بدستور

statute (*stat*-ewt) *n*. written law ; enactment ; law passed by a Legislature تحریری قانون **statutory** (stat-ew-tě-ri) *adj*. required by a statute قانونی، قانون کے مطابق، مطابقِ قانون

staunch (stawnch) **stanch** (stahnch) *v.t.* (usu. spelt as *stanch*) stop the flow of blood from (a wound) (زخم) سے خون کا بہاؤ بند کرنا، سے خون روکنا *adj*. (usu. spelt *staunch*) firm, trustworthy (friend, supporter) پکا، مخلص، سرگرم، پُرجوش

stave (stayv) *n*. one of the curved strips of the side of a barrel (لکڑی کے پیپے کی) پٹی، پچھیٹی fragment of song or verse گانے یا نظم کا ٹکڑا *v.t.* (*stave ; staved* or *stove ; staved*) make a hole by smashing planks (*in* a door, *in* the side of a ship, etc.) سوراخ کرنا، چھید کرنا (*stave off*), ward (*off* danger, disaster, etc.) روکنا

stay *v.t.* & *i*. remain (*at* a place, *in the house*, etc.) رہنا *stay where* (*one*) *is*, جہاں کا تہاں، وہیں رُک جانا، رُک جانا *stay put*, (U.S.) (of person or thing) remain where he, it, etc. is اپنی جگہ پر رہنا *stay for* (*something*) کسی کام کے لیے ذرا رُک جانا *stay away* (*from*) keep away (from) سے پرے رہنا، نہ جانا *stay out*, not to come home گھر نہ آنا *stay up late*, not go to bed

until late in the night دیر تک جاگتے رہنا *has come to stay*, (colloq.) has become an accepted fact ; must now be regarded as permanent مسلّم ہو گیا، پکا ہو گیا
  live for a time (*with* someone, or *at* a hotel, etc.) ٹھہرنا، رہنا، قیام کرنا postpone (proceedings, etc.) ملتوی کرنا، روکنا check (the progress of) روک دینا be able to continue (work, etc.) (کام) میں آخر تک جاری رکھنا، (کام) میں لگے رہنا *stay to the end* آخر تک لگے رہنا *staying power*, endurance قوت برداشت *n.* staying (*at*) رہنا، قیام period of staying قیام کی مدت support *the stay of* (*one's*) *old age* بڑھاپے کا سہارا rope or wire supporting a mast مستول کا رستا (*pl.*) corset چولی، محرم، انگیا، سینہ بند stopping (of case, proceedings, etc.) التوا

stead (sted) *n.* (only in the following phrases :) *in* (*someone's*) *stead*, instead of (someone), in lieu of (him) کے بدلے، کی (یا کے) بجائے *stand* (*someone*) *in good stead*, prove useful to (him) in time of need کے لیے مفید ثابت ہونا، کی مدد کرنا

steadfast (*sted*-fast) *adj.* firm and unchanging (پر) پکا، (پر) قائم، پکا، ثابت قدم، مستقل keeping firm (*to*) ثابت قدم، استوار

steadfastness *n.* firmness استقلال، ثابت قدمی

steady (*sted*-i) *adj.* standing firm پکا، مضبوط، مستحکم well-balanced متوازن regular, unceasing لگاتار، مسلسل، متواتر unchanging in movement, speed, direction, etc. ایک جیسا، یکساں، برابر *a steady wind* یکساں رفتار سے چلنے والی ہوا *steady rate of* کی یکساں رفتار (of person) regular (in behaviour, habits, etc.) باقاعدگی والا، ثابت قدم constant (faith, aim, etc.) پکا، راسخ، نہ بدلنے والا *v.t.* & *i.* become steady مضبوط ہونا، پکا ہونا keep steady نہ ہلنا، ڈٹ کر رہنا make steady پکا کرنا، مضبوط کرنا **steadily** *adj.* ثابت قدمی سے **steadiness** *n.* being steady استقلال، ثابت قدمی، یکسانی، تسلسل، باقاعدگی

steak (stayk) *n.* thick slice (of meat or fish) قتلہ *beef-steak* گائے کے گوشت کا قتلہ

steal (steel) *v.t.* & *i.* (*steal, stole, stolen*) take away (another's property) secretly and unlawfully چرانا move (*in, out, away,* etc.) secretly and quietly چپ چاپ گھس آنا (یا، چلتے آنا)، دبے پاؤں چلنا secure unawares or by a trick اچانک یا دھوکے سے لے لینا *steal a march on* (*someone*), do something before (him) and so win an advantage over him سے پہلے کر کے بازی لے جانا **stealth** (*stelth*) *n.* stealing, theft چوری، دزدی evasion of notice چوری، پوشیدہ کام *do* (*something*) *by stealth*, *do it secretly*, چوری چھپے کرنا، چپ چاپ کرنا **stealthy** (*stel*-thi) *adj.* done quietly چوری، چوری چھپے doing (something) secretly چوری چھپے کرنے والا **stealthily** *adv.* چوری چھپے، چھپے چوری ▣ To **steal** is to take away something unlawfully and secretly for one's own use ; **purloin** an article by carrying it away ; **swindle** someone out of something by clever tricks ; **rob** someone or some place with violence ; **pilfer** something by plundering it pettily ; **filch** small articles from a place ; **embezzle** or **defalcate,** misappropriate money put in trust.

steam (steem) *n.* vapour rising from boiling water بھاپ *steam engine*, engine propelled by steam بھاپ کے زور سے چلنے والا انجن، بھاپ انجن *like a steam-engine*, with great energy بڑے زور سے *steamship* دخانی کشتی *get up steam*, (*a*) heat boilers ready for working engine انجن گرم کرنا (*b*) gather one's energies کمر باندھنا، کمربستہ ہونا *let off steam*, (*a*) relieve steam بھاپ نکالنا (*b*) relieve one's suppressed feelings (by denouncing, etc.) دل کا غبار نکالنا، جوش ٹھنڈا کرنا *v.t.* & *i.* give out steam سے بھاپ نکلنا، بھاپ بن کر اڑنا *steaming hot*, very hot سخت گرم، ابلتا ہوا cook with steam-heat بھاپ سے پکانا move (*up, away, off* a place, or *at* a speed of) بھاپ کے زور سے چلنا **steamer** *n.* steamship دخانی کشتی، جہاز vessel in which food is cooked by being steamed دخانی دیگچی **steam roller, steamroller** *n.* steam engine for macadamizing roads سٹیم رولر *v.i.* (*steamroller*), (see *Addenda*) **steamy** *adj.* full of steam بھاپ سے بھرا ہوا of or like steam بھاپ کا سا

steed *n.* (poetical) horse گھوڑا، اسپ، شبدیز (esp.) war-horse جنگی گھوڑا

steel *n.* hard alloy of iron with carbon or other elements فولاد، اسپات *cold steel*, swords, etc. (as opposed to fire-arms) تیر تلوار *a heart of steel*, (*a*) strong heart قوی دل (*b*) hard heart پتھر کا دل *foe worthy of* (*one's*) *steel*, one worth fighting with لڑائی کے شایاں، ٹکر کا حریف *steel-clad*, wearing armour زرہ پوش، بکتر بند *steel-grey*, dark grey سیاہی مائل، کالا سا *v.t.* harden (oneself, one's heart *to do* something or *against* something) (دل) کو سخت کر لینا، دل کڑا کرنا *adj.* of steel فولاد **steely** *adj.* like steel in hardness, polish, etc. فولاد کا سا **steelyard** *n.* weighing-machine with a graduated arm along which a weight slides سٹیل یارڈ، جھپل کانٹا

a steelyard

steep *adj.* sloping sharply سیدھا، ڈھلان *n.* (poet.) steep hill ; cliff کھڑی چٹان، کراڑا *v.t.* soak بھگونا، شرابور کرنا، تربتر کرنا *steeped in* (*knowledge, etc.*) میں ڈوبا ہوا

steepen *v.t.* & *i.* be or make steep ڈھلوان ہونا یا بنانا

steeple (*stee*-pĕl) *n.* high church-tower with a spire گرجے کا منارہ any such high and conspicuous building اونچی عمارت **steeple-chase** *n.* cross-country horse-race with obstacles like ditches and hedges کھائی باڑ گھڑ دوڑ such foot-

race کھائی، باڑ دوڑ **steeple-jack** *n.* workman who climbs and repairs steeples, chimneys or other high buildings اونچی عمارتوں کی مرمت کرنے والا
steer (*stee-ĕ**) *n.* young bullock بچھڑا *v.t.* & *i.* direct (the course, or a ship, boat, motor-car, etc.) خاص سمت چلنا یا چلانا **steering-wheel** *n.* wheel by which the driver guides a motor-car or the steersman controls the rudder of the boat رُخ ٹھیک رکھنے کا پہیہ، سمت دار **steersman** *n.* man who steers a ship جہاز کا رُخ ٹھیک رکھنے والا، سمت بین **steerage** (*stee-è-rej*) *n.* part of a ship for passengers paying the lowest fares جہاز میں سستے مسافروں کا حصّہ
stellar (stel-ĕ*) *adj.* of the stars ستاروں سے متعلق، نجمی، کوکبی
stem *n.* part of a plant coming up from the roots تنہ part of a leaf, flower, fruit, that joins it to the stalk, branch, etc. ڈنڈی slender shaft which joins spreading extremities ڈنڈی main part of a word to which prefixes or suffixes are affixed for making new words (as *man* is the stem of *men*, *man's*, *manly*, *unmanly*, *manned* etc.) لفظ کا جزوِ اصلی، اصل، مادہ stock نسل، اصل، خاندان main upright timber at bow of a ship جہاز کے پیش کا شہتیر hence, front part of a ship *from stem to stern,* جہاز کے پیش سے لیکر پشت تک *v.t.* & *i.* (-mm-) originate (*from* or *in*) سے نکلنا check, stop (a current of water, etc.) روکنا، کے آگے بند باندھنا resist or make headway against (the current, waves, tide, etc., or the tide of) سے مقابلہ کرنا
stench *n.* bad smell بدبو، سڑاند، عفونت (also see **stink**)
stencil (*stens-il*) *n.* thin sheet with designs, or letters cut through it for printing them نقش ساز تختی something printed thus تختی کا نقش *v.t.* (-ll-) print by means of a stencil نقش ساز تختی سے چھاپنا یا نقش کرنا
Sten-gun (*sten*-gun) *n.* light-weight machine-gun سٹین گن
stenography (sten-*nog*-ra-fi) *n.* shorthand مختصر نویسی **stenographer** (ste-*nog*-ra-fĕ*) *n.* typist able to take dictation in shorthand مختصر نویس، نقل نگار
Stentor (*sten*-tĕ*) *Cl. myth.* loud-voiced herald celebrated by Homer اِسٹنٹور، سٹنٹر **stentorian** (-*to*-) *adj.* loud and strong (voice) بلند آواز، بہت اونچی آواز *n.* loud-voiced person بلند آواز شخص
[1]**step** *v.t.* & *i.* (-pp-) move one foot (after the other) in a direction چلنا، قدم اٹھانا، قدم رکھنا step into (car, train, boat, etc.) میں سوار ہونا، قدم بڑھانا *step on to* (*a raised place, etc.*), get on to it پر قدم رکھنا، پر چڑھنا *step off* (*it*), come down from (it) سے اُترنا، سے نیچے آنا *step down* (a carriage, etc.), get down from it سے اُترنا *step in* (or *into a room*), (dignified word for) enter it میں داخل ہونا *step forward* قدم آگے رکھنا، بڑھنا *step back* پیچھے ہٹنا *step up to,* approach کے پاس آنا، کے نزدیک ہونا *step up* (production), raise (it) بڑھانا، میں اضافہ کرنا *step across* (*a stream, etc.*) کو پھلانگنا *step aside,* (*a*) get to a side پرے ہٹ جانا (*b*) withdraw oneself پیچھے ہٹ جانا *step aside* let someone else take one's place پرے ہو جانا، کسی کے لیے اپنی جگہ چھوڑ دینا، الگ ہو جانا *step out,* walk quickly by long steps لمبے لمبے قدم اٹھانا، تیزی سے چلنا *step this way please* ادھر تشریف لائیے، قدم رنجہ فرمائیے *n.* stepping once قدم رکھنا، ایک قدم، قدم اٹھانا distance covered thus قدم *walking with slow steps* آہستہ قدم اٹھانا، دھیرے دھیرے چلنا *step by step*, gradually رفتہ رفتہ، دھیرے دھیرے (also *foot-step*), sound made by walking آہٹ، قدموں کی چاپ (also *footstep*), mark made by a step نقشِ قدم، نقشِ پا *in (someone's) step*, following his example کے نقشِ قدم پر way of walking چال، چال ڈھال *recognize (someone's) step* کی چال پہچاننا *in step*, (in walking or dancing) putting the right foot to the ground at the same time as others قدم ملانا place for the foot when going up or down قدمچہ، سیڑھی، پایہ *mind the steps* سیڑھیوں پر قدم سوچ کر رکھنا (*pl.*) *steps, a pair of steps, step-ladder*, folding ladder with flat steps instead of rungs چوڑے قدموں کی تہ ہونے والی سیڑھی one action as part of series (*towards* or *to do* something) قدم، اقدام *the first step towards* کی طرف پہلا قدم *a step forward* ترقی کی طرف قدم *one step forward two steps backward* تھوڑی سی ترقی زیادہ تنزل *take steps (to do something)* کے لیے قدم اٹھانا، کا اقدام کرنا rise to higher rank ترقی *get one's step* ترقی پانا
stepping-stone *n.* stone, etc., placed in water or mud to enable crossing it without getting wet گزر پتھر means (*to* something) وسیلہ، ذریعہ
[2]**step-** *pref.* by remarriage سوتیلا *stepfather* سوتیلا باپ *stepmother* سوتیلی ماں *stepchild* سوتیلا بچہ *stepson* سوتیلا لڑکا *stepdaughter* سوتیلی لڑکی *stepbrother* سوتیلا بھائی *step-sister* سوتیلی بہن **stepmotherly** *adj.* unkind like the treatment meted out by a stepmother سوتیلی ماں کا سا، ظالمانہ *stepmotherly treatment* سوتیلی ماں کا سا سلوک، ظالمانہ سلوک
stepney (*step*-ni) *n.* (*pl.* stepneys) extra rim with tube and tyre carried on a motor vehicle, etc. فالتو پہیہ

steppe (step) *n.* level treeless plain, esp. in Russia دسائبیریا کا) لق ودق صحرا، سٹیپ کا میدان، سَرزِ صحرا

stereoscope (*ste*-ri-ès-kohp) *n.* apparatus by which two photographs of the same thing, taken from slightly different angles, are seen as a single representation with the effect of solidity مُجسّم بین **stereoscopic** (-*kop*-ik) *adj.* (of view) giving solid effect ٹھوس

a stereoscope

stereotype (*ste*-ri-o-tip) *n.* printing plate made from a mould of set-up type or matrix طباعتی تختی *v.t.* mould stereotypes طباعتی تختی ڈھالنا fix the form of (something) permanently رَسمی بنا دینا **stereotyped** *adj.* conventional, unoriginal (ideas, phrases, etc.) گھسے پٹے

sterile (*ste*-ril) *adj.* barren (land) بنجر، اُوسر (of woman, animal) not reproductive بانجھ، اُوسر (of plant) producing no seed بے ثمر futile free from microbes جراثیم سے پاک

sterility (ste-*ril*-i-ti) *n.* being sterile بنجر ہونا، بانجھ پن

sterilize *v.t.* free from germs کے جراثیم مارنا render incapable of reproduction تولید کے ناقابل بنانا **sterilization** (-*zay*-) *n.* freeing from microbes by boiling in water جراثیم کُشی، اِتلافِ جراثیم rendering (or being rendered) incapable of reproduction ناقابلِ تولید کر دینا

sterling (*stĕ**-ling) *adj.* (of gold and silver) of the standard quality fixed by the government کھرا، خالص، کامل عیار، معیاری (after figures mentioning pounds only) (abbreviated as *s.* or *tg.*) exact پورے نوّے پونڈ £90 صرف، پورے sound (character, worth, etc.) قابلِ قدر excellent نہایت شاندار *n.* British currency برطانوی سکّے *payable in sterling* ادا کئی برطانوی سکّے میں *sterling area*, countries accepting sterling سٹرلنگ کا علاقہ *pound sterling* برطانوی پونڈ

stern (stĕ*n) *adj.* severe سخت گیر، سخت harsh سخت، سخت گیرانہ *n.* back end of a ship or boat جہاز کی پشت، دُنبالہ **sternness** *n.* strictness سختی، سخت گیری

stet *v.* instruction to the printer to let a deleted word, etc., stand تصحیح، مَنسُوخ، صاد

stethoscope (*steth*-os-kohp) *n.* doctor's instrument for listening to the beating of he heart, etc. صدر بین

stevedore (*steev*-è-doh*) *n.* man p the oading or unloading of ships بندرگاہ کا قُلی

stew *i.* cook or be cooked slowly in water or ov juice in a closed dish دَم پخت اِسٹو بنانا *n.* dish of stewed meat, vegeta es, etc. سالن، دَم پخت، اِسٹو *in a stew* (colloq.) in an anxious condition پریشان

steward (*stew*-ĕ*d) *n.* manager of food-suppliers in a club, college, etc. مُنتظمِ رَسَد servant who attends to the needs of passengers in a ship or aircraft (ہوائی جہاز) میں مسافروں کا نگران خادم، نگران خادم such a one at a public gathering نگران man responsible for organizing details of a public entertainment or meeting مُہتمم manager of another's property (esp., an estate or large house) داروغہ جائداد **stewardess** *n.* woman steward in a ship نگران خادِمہ

stick (stik) *n.* thin branch of a tree or bush ٹہنی، شاخ slender piece of wood, cane, etc. چھڑی، بید، قمچی also (*walking-stick*), stick held in hand while walking چھڑی، لکڑی stick-like piece (*of* shaving-soap, chalk, sealing wax, etc.) بتّی number (*of bombs*) released from an aircraft in rapid succession (ہوائی جہاز سے گرائے ہوئے بموں کی) دھار *v.t.* & *i.* (*a*) (*stick, sticked, sticked*) support (a tender plant, etc.) with sticks (*b*) چھڑیاں لگانا (*stick, stuck, stuck*) thrust point of needle, weapon, etc. (*into, through*, etc.) چبھونا impale (*on*) کے چھرا گھونپنا، پر چڑھانا سے بندھنا (colloq.) stab چبھنا، کے خنجر بھونکنا remain stuck (*in* something) چبھا رہنا، لگا ہونا place (person or thing) in specified position رکھنا، لگانا (cause to) stand (*up* or *out*) کھڑا ہونا (یا) کرنا، نکلنا، تانتا attach (*to, on, down, in, together*, etc.) with an adhesive چپکانا remain (*together*) مُتحد رہنا چسپاں کرنا be constant (*to*) سے وفاداری کرنا fail to progress owing to difficulty اٹکنا، اٹک جانا *I am stuck* میں تو پھنس جانا، چل نہ سکنا وہ نام جو چپک *nickname that will stick* مشکل میں پھنس گیا جاتے *stick at*, hesitate at جھجکنا، اٹکنا *stick at nothing*, (of someone) be reckless or unscrupulous سے کچھ بعید نہ ہونا *stick bills* اِشتہار چسپاں کرنا *bill-sticking prohibited* یہاں اِشتہار چسپاں کرنا منع ہے *stick fast*, get stuck اٹکنا *sticking in* (*one's*) *gizzard*, (of injustice) unbearable ناقابلِ برداشت *stick out for* (*better terms etc.*), refuse to give way until پر اڑ جانا *stick it out*, (colloq.) endure (hardships, etc.) to the end مشکلات کا مردانہ وار مُقابلہ کرنا *stick up for*, defend, support کی حمایت کرنا **stuck up** *adj.* arrogant مغرور conceited خود بین exclusive خلوت پسند *stick-in-the-mu* (*a*) unprogressive مُتشدّد، غبی (*b*) so-and-so (as *Mr. Stick-in-the-mud*) فلاں **sticking-plaster** *n.* adhesive plaster put on wound, etc. to h ld dressing چپکنے والی پٹّی **sti er** *n.* adhesive el چپکنے **sticky** (*stik*-i) *adj.* (of mud, liqu surface, fingers, etc.) tending to stick to anything that touches it چپکنے والا، چپچپا (of weather) muggy (موسم) چپچپا (slang) very unpleasant سخت ناگوار *come to a sticky end* کا بُرا انجام ہونا (colloq.) unyielding نہ ماننے والا، ہٹیلا، ضدی **stickiness** *n.* being sticky چپکنا، چپچپا ہونا

stickler (stik-lĕ*) *n.* (*a stickler for*), one who insists upon the importance of formality, discipline, etc. (پر) مُصِر

sticky *adj.* (see under **stick**)

stiff (stif) *adj.* not easily changed in shape سخت *stiff collar*, starched collar کلف والا کالر، کلف دار کالر not easily bent اکڑا ہوا *feel stiff in the joints* جوڑ جوڑ درد کرنا، جسم اکڑا ہوا ہونا (of a paste) hard to stir سخت difficulty سخت formal (manners) تصنع بھرا، سرد مہرانہ stern سخت، دُرست strong (breeze, liquor, etc.) **stiffen** (*stif*-èn) *v.t.* & *i.* make or become stiff سخت کرنا یا ہونا، اکڑ جانا **stiffness** *n.* being stiff سختی، تصنع (یا) کڑا ہونا **stiff-necked** *adj.* stubborn سرکش، ضدی

stifle (*stī*-fèl) *v.t.* & *i.* smother گلا گھونٹنا suppress (yawn) دبا دینا gag زبان بندی کرنا *stifle all opposition*, suppress it by gagging it زبان بندی کر کے مخالفت ختم کر دینا (of heat, conditions, etc.) be oppressive بہت تکلیف دِہ ہونا **stifling** *adj.* oppressive تکلیف دِہ، ظالمانہ، گلا گھونٹنے والا *n.* smothering زبان بندی gagging

stigma (*stig*-ma) *n.* mark of shame or disgrace رُسوائی، بدنامی، کلنک کا ٹیکہ، دامن پر داغ **stigmatize** (*stig*-ma-tīz) *v.t.* describe (someone) scornfully (*as* a traitor, etc.) (غدار وغیرہ) کہہ کر بدنام کرنا

stile (stīl) *n.* set of steps or posts for climbing over a fence or wall so arranged that only human beings and no animal will cross it جانور روک سیڑھی *help a lame dog over a stile* بُرے وقت میں کام آنا upright post (of a door, etc.) دروازے وغیرہ (کی) کھڑی سلاخ

still (stil) *adj.* motionless ساکن، بے حِس و حرکت *still life*, picture of fruit, flower, etc. پھولوں پھلوں کی تصویر *still waters run deep*, great emotions, etc., underlie calm طوفان سے پہلے خاموشی ہوتی ہے *still small voice*, promptings of conscience or God ضمیر کی آواز not effervescent, not sparkling جس میں اُبال نہ آئے hushed, quiet خاموش، ساکت of gentle sound دھیمی آواز والا *adv.* nevertheless پھر بھی، تاہم still now اب تک even to this time ابھی تک still then تب تک for the future جب تک *n.* hushed state خاموشی، سکوت (*in*) *the still of night* رات کی خاموشی (میں) سکوتِ شب (میں) apparatus for distilling alcohol شراب کشید کرنے کا آلہ، بھبکا، انبیق (in film industry) ordinary photograph (as distinct from a moving picture); just one shot as a photograph of a part of a film ساکن تصویر *v.t.* make (crying child, appetite, conscience, fear, noise, etc.) چپ کرانا، تسکین دینا **stillborn** *adj.* (child) dead when born (بچہ) مُردہ پیدا ہونا *still birth* مُردہ بچہ پیدا ہونا **stilly** (*stil*-i) *adv.* quietly چپ چاپ، خاموشی سے in the heart دل ہی دل میں *adj.* (poet.) soundless (night) خاموش، پُرسکوت

stilt *n.* one of a pair of poles with raised footsteps پاؤں والا بانس، پایا بانسا **stilted** (*stil*-ted) *adj.* stiff and unnatural (speech, writing, manners, etc.) تصنع والا

a boy on stilts

stimulant (*stim*-ew-lant) *n.* drug or drink making one energetic چستی پیدا کرنے والا، نشاط انگیز، محرک، مہیج

stimulate (*stim*-ew-layt) *v.t.* excite اُبھارنا، تحریک پیدا کرنا، ہیجان پیدا کرنا urge (someone) on (*to*, or *to do* something) پر آمادہ کرنا، پر اُبھارنا **stimulating** *adj.* rousing پُرجوش thought-provoking خیال آفریں **stimulus** (*stim*-ew-lus) *n.* (pl. *stimuli* pr. *stim*-ew-lī) that which stimulates محرک، مہیج

sting *n.* sharp and poisonous pointed organ (*of* wasps, etc.) ڈنک، نیش such pointed part (of plants like nettle, etc.) سوئی، کانٹا pain caused by this جلن، ٹیس any mental or physical pain اذیت *v.t.* & *i.* (*sting, stung, stung*) prick with a sting ڈنک مارنا have the power to sting ڈنک مارنے والا ہونا (of chillies) cause burning sensation in the mouth منہ جلا دینا cause sharp pain to سخت اذیت پہنچانا (of the body) feel sharp pain سخت اذیت محسوس کرنا، میں ٹیس اٹھنا (slang) involve (someone) in expense کا خرچ ہونا، لٹ جانا *be stung*, (*a*) be involved in expense کا خرچ کرانا (*b*) be swindled (*for* an amount) کی اتنی رقم ہتیالی جانا، (کی اتنی رقم) لٹ جانا یا جانی *He was stung for a tenner* اس کے دس روپے (یا پونڈ) لُٹ گئے

stingy (*stinj*-ĕ) *adj.* niggardly (person, etc.) کنجوس *stingy with the sugar*, (of tea etc.) having little of it میں چینی کم ہے scanty (allowance, etc.) بہت تھوڑا، کم، ذرا سا ▣ A **stingy** person is one who is not generous; **mean,** who acts in an unfriendly way; **avaricious,** who keeps his money closely; **miserly,** who has money yet lives in discomfort; **penurious,** afraid of a shortage in the supplies; **parsimonious,** who hands out supplies sparingly.

stink *v.i.* (*stink; stank* or *stunk; stunk*) have a nasty smell بدبودار ہونا، متعفن ہونا، سے بدبو نکلنا *n.* nasty smell بدبو، عفونت، تعفن

stint *v.t.* & *i.* be sparing (*of* something) میں کنجوسی کرنا، بہت تھوڑا خرچ کرنا keep (someone) on a small allowance (*of* something in order to spare for others) کو تھوڑا دینا *n.* limitation of effort or supply کی *without stint*, (*a*) without limit بے حد (*b*) freely آزادانہ allotted amount of work, etc. مقررہ مقدار

stipend (*sti*-pend) *n.* clergyman's salary پادری کی تنخواہ subsistence allowance وظیفہ، گزارہ الاؤنس **stipendiary** (*-pend*-i-) *adj.* salaried تنخواہ

stipple (*stip*-èl) *v.t.* draw or paint with dots instead of lines, etc. لکیروں کی بجائے نقطوں سے تصویر بنانا

stipulate (*stip*-ew-layt) *v.t.* & *i.* put forward as a necessary condition (*that*) صاف صاف شرط کرنا کہ (*stipulate for*), require (as part of an agreement) کی شرط مقرر کرنا **stipulation** (*-lay-*) *n.* condition شرط، معاہدہ

stir (stě*) *v.t.* & *i.* (-rr-) move ہلنا (یا) ہلانا، حرکت کرنا (یا) حرکت دینا go on moving a spoon, etc., in a liquid, in order to mix it thoroughly ہلانا، چلانا چمچے چلا کر گاڑھا کرنا *stir* (*a liquid*) *into* (*a paste*) سے ہلاتے جانا (usu. *stir up*), excite (emotions, blood, etc.) جوش میں لانا، بھڑکانا *n.* stirring حرکت دینا، ہلانا bustle, disturbance ہلچل، اضطراب *make quite a stir* ہلچل پیدا کرنا (slang) prison قید خانہ، جیل **stirring** *adj.* exciting ہیجان خیز moving پُر جوش

stirrup (*sti*-rup) *n.* foot-rest hanging down from a saddle رکاب **stirrup-pump** *n.* pump worked with a foot-rest and discharging water through a nozzle to extinguish small fires سٹرپ پمپ، پاؤں والا پمپ

a stirrup

stitch (stich) *n.* single movement of a needle and thread in and out of cloth, etc., in sewing ٹانکا، بخیہ complete turn of the wool, etc., over the needle in knitting سلائی the thread, etc., seen between two holes made by a needle بخیہ *take the stitches out* (*of*) کے بخیے اُدھیڑنا (never used in the plural) sharp pain in the side caused by running, etc. چبھن، ہوک *v.t* & *i.* put stitches سینا، ٹانکے لگانا، بخیہ کرنا

stoat (stoht) *n.* ermine in its brown summer coat *v.t.* sew up (edges of cloth or a tear in cloth) with invisible stitches باریک سینا

stock (stok) *n.* lower part of a tree trunk تنہ، تنے کا نچلا حصہ base (of a rifle, etc.) کندا *lock, stock and barrel*, completely بالکل، پوری طرح سے handle (of a tool, etc.) دستہ line of ancestry اصل، نسل *come of a* (*particular*) *stock* (کسی) نسل سے ہونا goods kept by a shopkeeper سامان، مال *be in stock* موجود ہونا *be out of stock* موجود نہ ہونا، مل نہ سکنا *take stock*, list goods in stock مال کی فہرست بنانا *take stock of* (*situation, someone's ability*, etc.), review کا جائزہ لینا *stock-taking*, listing or review جائزہ (also *live-stock*), farm animals مال مویشی، ڈھور ڈنگر *stock-farmer*, one who breeds live-stock مال مویشی پالنے والا *stock-breeding*, مال مویشی پالنا liquid in which (meat, etc.) has been stewed (گوشت وغیرہ کا) پانی (یا) رس money lent to a government on interest تمسک shares in the capital of a business company حصص *the Stock Exchange*, market for the sale of stocks and shares سٹاک ایکسچینج، بازارِ حصص (*pl.*) (*the stocks*) (old use) framework with holes for the feet in which criminals were placed کاٹھ (*pl.*) framework for supporting a ship during repairs or construction جہاز ران *adj.* usual (phrase, joke, argument, size) عام broad band of leather or some stiffened material worn round (چرمی یا کلف دار) گردن بند *v.t.* (of a ship, etc.) keep in stock رکھنا، میں ہونا equip (a place *with*) میں فراہم کرنا put (someone) in the stocks کے پاؤں میں کاٹھ ٹھونکنا **stock-broker** *n.* one conducting the sale of stocks and shares for others on commission دلالِ حصص **stock company** *n.* theatrical company putting on its plays almost permanently at a particular theatre زیادہ تر کسی ایک تھیٹر میں کام کرنے والی ناٹک کمپنی، سٹاک کمپنی **stock-in-trade** *n.* things needed for one's trade or activity ضروری سامان **stock-jobber** *n.* speculator in stocks حصص کا سٹے باز **live-stock** *n.* (same as *stock* 6 above) مال مویشی **dead-stock** *n.* capital earning no profit غیر سود مند سرمایہ **stockist** *n.* one who stocks goods for wholesale تھوک فروش **stock-pile** *v.t.* accumulate stocks of (commodity) (تجارتی مال کا) ذخیرہ کرنا *n.* جمع کیا ہوا تجارتی مال (ضروریات کے) ذخائر accumulated stocks **stock-piling** *n.* act of accumulating stocks of (commodity) (تجارتی مال) جمع کرنا **stock-still** *adv.* motionless بے حس و حرکت **stockyard** *n.* place where farm animals are kept before being killed or marketed مویشی خانہ **laughing-stock** *n.* butt of ridicule نشانۂ تضحیک، گرُوئے محفل

a culprit in the stocks

stockade (sto-*kayd*, or *stok*-ayd) *n.* defensive wall of upright stakes دھس، لکڑیوں کا مورچہ *v.t.* put stockade round ...س لگانا، لکڑی کا مورچہ بنانا

stocking (*stok*-ing) *n.* foot-covering reaching to or above the knee لمبی جراب *stockings, a pair of stockings* لمبی جرابیں *blue-stocking*, woman having or affecting literary taste ادبی ذوق والی (یا ادبی مدعی) عورت

stocky (*stok*-i) *adj.* short, strong, and thick (person, animal, plant) گٹھیلا، چھوٹا اور موٹا، ناٹا اور موٹا

stodgy (*stoj*-i) *adj.* heavy and solid (food)

بھاری، ثقیل (of books, etc.) uninteresting because overfull of facts or details حد درجہ ثقیل کے باعث بے لطف

stoic (*stoh*-ik) *n.* (*Stoic*), philosopher following Zeno (late 4th century B.C.) of Cyprus who insisted on the control of passions, (the word is derived from the name of his school at Athens) رُواقی person with austerity and fortitude زاہد one bearing hardships without complaining صابر، مُتوکّل *adj.* stoical زاہدانہ، صابرانہ

stoical *adj.* of or like a stoic زاہدانہ ، صابرانہ

stoicism *n.* زُہد، رُواقیت ، صبر

stoke (stohk) *v.t.* & *i.* put (coal, etc.) on (a fire, or the fire of a furnace, etc.) میں کوئلہ ڈالنا **stoke-hole, stokehold** *n.* place where a ship's furnaces are stoked کوئلہ دان، زُغال دان **stoker** *n.* workman who stokes کوئلہ دان ، زُغال دان

stole (stohl) *v.* (pa. t. of **steal,** which see) *n.* Christian priest's strip of cloth worn پادریوں کا گلوبند، پٹکا woman's wrap with the ends hanging down in front شال

stolen (*stoh*-lèn) *v.* (pa. p. of **steal,** which see) *adj.* pilfered چوری کا ، چرایا ہُوا

stolid (*stol*-id) *adj.* not easily moved بےحس slow to display emotions جذبات ظاہر نہ کرنے والا

stomach (*stum*-èk) *n.* part of the body in which food is digested معدہ (polite word for) belly پیٹ، شکم appetite بھوک inclination میلان wish خواہش، اُمنگ رغبت guts ہمّت *have no stomach for (doing something)*, (*a*) not be inclined to (do) پر آمادہ نہ ہونا، کی خواہش نہ ہونا (*b*) lack the courage to (do) کی ہمّت نہ ہونا *v.i.* find (a food) palatable خوراک، کا گوارا ہونا (in negative or interrogative sentences only) brook (an insult, etc.) برداشت کرنا

stone (stohn) *n.* piece of rock پتھر *throw stones at*, (*a*) cast them at پر پتھر پھینکنا (*b*) make aspersions against کے خلاف باتیں بنانا *break stones*, (*a*) make road-metal پتھر کوٹنا (*b*) do it as a bad means of earning a living محنت مزدوری کرنا *leave no stone unturned (to do)*, do one's best (to do) پوری کوشش کرنا *give (someone) a stone for bread*, mock (him) with pretence of help مدد کا نام کر کے مذاق اُڑانا *precious stones*, gems جواہرات *meteoric stone*, stony meteorite حجر شہابی thing made of this پتھر کی چیز *millstone* چکّی کا پاٹ disease technically known as calculus پتھری unit of weight equivalent to 14 lb., (abbreviated as *st.*) سٹون، ساڑھے سات سیر hard seed in certain fruits گٹھلی *v.t.* throw stones at پر پتھر پھینکنا take stones from (fruit) کی گٹھلیاں نکالنا *adj.* of stone پتھر کا utterly

(blind, deaf, dead, etc.) بالکل *stone-cold*, cold like a stone پتھر کی طرح بےجان **Stone Age** *n.* period of history when men made weapons of stone پتھر کا زمانہ

stone-mason *n.* man who cuts stone and builds with it پتھر کا کام کرنے والا *stone-pit*, quarry پتھر کی کان

stone's cast, stone's throw *n.* short distance 50 to 150 yards پچاس سے ڈیڑھ سو گز کا فاصلہ **stone-waller** cautious batsman محتاط بلّے باز **stoneware** *n.* pottery made of flinty clay پتھر کے برتن **stonework** *n.* masonry پتھر کی تعمیر **stony** (*stoh*-ni) *adj.* having many stones پتھریلا hard (heart, etc.) پتھر کا سا، سخت

stood (stŭd) *v.* (pa. t. & pa. p. of **stand,** which see)

stooge (stooj) *n.* comedian's assistant and foil چھوٹا بھانڈ، جمورا minion and scapegoat of a gangster ڈاکو کا چیلا henchman of a political leader, etc. پٹھو (U.S.) person learning to fly ہوا بازی سیکھنے والا، اناڑی ہوا باز *v.i.* be a stooge جمورا ہونا پٹھو ہونا fly (*around, about*) پرواز کرنا

stool *n.* small backless seat سٹول، تپائی *fall between two stools*, succeed in neither plan دونوں منصوبوں میں ناکام ہونا (usu. *footstool*), low support on which to rest the feet قدمچہ (*pl.*) evacuation of bowels حاجت (*pl.*) stool-like accommodation for it کھڈی (*pl.*) matter thus evacuated مٹی، پاخانہ، پخانہ

stoop *v.t.* & *i.* bend (or bend *the body*) forward (*with* old age, or *to do* something) جھکنا، جھکانا walk thus سر اور کندھے جھکا کر چلنا debase (oneself) جھکنا، (اپنے کو) ذلیل کرنا *she stoops to conquer* وہ دل کے جیتنے کو جھکتی ہے come down (*to* cheating, etc.) کسی ذلیل حرکت پر اتر آنا *n.* position of the body with the shoulders curved and the head bent forward سر اور کندھے جھکانا *walk with a stoop* سر اور کندھے جھکا کر چلنا

stop *v.t.* & *i.* (-pp-) come or bring to a standstill رُکنا، رُکنا یا روکنا fill up (leak, hole, etc.) بند کرنا *stop (one's) ears*, cover them with the hands and refuse to listen کان بند کر لینا، کانوں پر ہاتھ دھرنا، کانوں میں اُنگلیاں ٹھونس لینا discontinue payment of (wages, cheque, etc.) کی ادائگی روک لینا stay (*at* home, *in* bed, etc.) میں ہی رہنا *n.* stopping or being stopped رُکنا، روکنا *came to a sudden stop* یکدم ختم کرنا، کا خاتمہ کرنا *put a stop to*, end رُک جانا interval وقفہ place where buses, etc., stop regularly بس کے رُکنے کی جگہ، بس سٹاپ، بس مقام *bus-stop* مقام *the nearest bus-stop*, the one nearest a place قریب ترین بس سٹاپ device for altering the tone of a musical

instrument ہرنا، ہرنالگو (in writing, printing) punctuation mark کامل وقفہ، ختمہ وقف *full stop*, period
stopcock *n.* valve for controlling the flow of fluid through a pipe ڈاٹ **stopgap** *n.* thing or person filling the place of another for a time رکنا، رکاؤ، دفع الوقتی **stoppage** *n.* being stopped up obstruction رکاوٹ interruption مداخلت **stop press** *n.* latest news added to a newspaper on the printing-machine سٹاپ پریس، چھپتے چھپتے **stopper** *n.* plug for closing the mouth of a bottle, etc. ڈاٹ، کاگ *v.t.* close with a stopper کی ڈاٹ لگانا **stop-volley** *n.* (in Tennis) stroke close to net dropping the ball dead on the other side نہ اٹھنے والی ضرب، سٹاپ والی **stop-watch** *n.* watch with a hand that can be started and stopped at will for exactly timing events سٹاپ واچ، روک گھڑی
storage *n.* (see under **store**)
store (stoh*) *n.* supply of something kept for future use ذخیرہ *in store*, kept ready for future use تیار، آئندہ کے لیے محفوظ، آئندہ کے لیے ذخیرہ *be in store for (someone)* (of trouble, etc.) be about to befall (him) کی شامت آئی *in store for* کے مقدر میں (*pl.*) goods, etc., of a particular kind or for a special purpose ذخیرہ، سٹور *military stores*, food, clothing, arms and ammunition for the army فوجی ذخائر گودام، ذخیرہ place where goods are kept (*pl.*) shop selling many varieties of goods سٹور دکان، (*U.S., sing.*) any kind of shop سٹور *set store by (something), set great store on (something)*, value (it) highly کی بڑی قدر کرنا، کو اہم سمجھنا، کو سہارا لیجانا *set no great store by (it)* کی قدر نہ کرنا، کو کچھ نہ سمجھنا *v.t.* (also *store up*), keep or collect for future use مستقبل کے لیے جمع کرنا put in a warehouse for safe keeping حفاظت کے لیے رکھنا stock (a place, one's mind, etc. *with*) میں جمع کرنا (of place) accommodate کی گنجائش رکھنا **storage** *n.* storing جمع کرنا، ذخیرہ کرنا *storage battery*, accumulater; apparatus for storing electric energy برقی مخزن، مخزن برق برقی ذخیرہ space used for it گودام *cold storage*. storage with refrigeration سرد گودام، سرد خانہ charges for it گودام میں رکھنے کی اجرت، گودام کا کرایہ **storehouse** *n.* place for storing گودام، ذخیرہ
storey (*stoh*-ri) (pl. *storeys*), **story** (pl. *stories*) *n.* floor or level in a building منزل *first storey*, ground floor پہلی منزل *second storey*, first floor دوسری منزل
storied (*stoh*-rid) *adj.* having (one, two, etc.) storeys منزلہ *three-storied* سہ منزلہ، تین منزلہ

stork (sto*k) *n.* a large, long-legged bird بگلا، لق لق، لقلق

a stork

storm (sto*m) *n.* violent weather-disturbance طوفان *sand-storm* ریت کا جھکڑ *snow-storm* طوفان برف و باراں (also *dust-storm*), very strong wind آندھی، جھکڑ commotion (in the mind) طوفان commotion in human relations طوفان، ہلچل، ہنگامہ شورش، ہنگامہ، فساد *storm in a tea-cup*. excitement over trifles فضول سی بات پر ہنگامہ violent outburst (*of* protest, hisses, cheers, applause, etc.) بوچھاڑ rush of troops into the enemy's fortifications محاصرہ فوج کا دھاوا *take (a place) by storm*, capture (*it*) by a sudden and violent attack ایک دم سے دھاوا کرکے قبضہ کرلینا *v.t. & i.* shout angrily (*at*) (پر) برس پڑنا force (a way *into* a place) (میں) دھم سے کودنا (میں)، دیوانہ وار گھس آنا take (a place) by storm ایک دم سے دھاوا کرکے قبضہ کرلینا
stormy (*sto**-mi) *adj.* boisterous (wind, sea, etc.) طوفانی، طوفان خیز (of area) having storms طوفانی quarrelsome. violent (meeting, interview, periodical, etc.) ہنگامہ خیز ▣ **A storm** is a high wind about 80 miles an hour; a **gale** is less than that; a **hurricane**, more than that and also accompained by rain and thunder; a **blizzard** is a storm with cold, wind and snow; **tempest** is the poet. word; a **cyclone** is a wind travelling in a very large circle; a **tornado** is a funnel-shaped cloud; a **typhoon** is a heavy oriental storm.
story (*stoh*-ri) *n.* account of past events بیان، سرگزشت tale کہانی *short story* مختصر افسانہ، افسانہ plot (*of* novel, play, etc.) کہانی، قصہ، پلاٹ (esp. in children's language) lie جھوٹ، گپ storey منزل
stout *adj.* (of person) fat خاصا موٹا، جسیم، بھیم و شحیم undaunted and resolute (companions, heart, etc.) مضبوط، پکا، مضبوط *stout-hearted* مضبوط دل والا (of shoes and other things) strong and thick مضبوط اور موٹے *n.* a kind of strong dark beer جو کی کالی شراب
stove (stohv) *n.* cooker ولایتی چولھا، سٹوو closed fire-place بند چولھا، بند انگیٹھی
stow (stoh) *v.t.* pack carefully and closely (*away* or *in* a ship's hold, etc.) قرینے سے رکھنا، سنگوانا fill (a trunk, etc., *with* things) میں قرینے سے رکھنا، میں سنگوانا
stowaway *n.* one who hides oneself in a ship or aircraft in order to make a journey without passport and ticket چوری سفر کرنے والا **stowage** *n.* stowing سنگوانا stowed things سنگوایا ہوا سامان its charges سنگوائی
strabismus (stra-*biz*-mus) *n.* squint بھینگاپن **strabismal, strabismic** *adj.* squint-eyed بھینگاپن، بھینگے پن والا

straddle (*strad*-ĕl) *v.t.* & *i.* stand with the legs wide apart ٹانگیں پھیلا کر کھڑا ہونا sit or stand across (a seat, a horse) with the legs widely separated ٹانگیں پھیلا کر کھڑا ہونا یا بیٹھنا ، پر drop bombs from side to side across (target) (ہدف) کے دونوں طرف بم گراتے جانا *n.* straddling ٹانگیں پھیلا کر کھڑا ہونا یا بیٹھنا this posture ٹانگیں پھیلانا

straggle (*strag*-ĕl) *v.i.* wander here and there اِدھر اُدھر مارے مارے پھرنا (of a locality) have sprung up without a design اِدھر اُدھر پھیلا ہوا ہونا (of creepers, things, etc.) lie thus untidily اِدھر اُدھر بکھرا ہوا ہونا drop behind while on the march چلتے میں ساتھیوں سے پیچھے رہ جانا **straggler** *n.* one who straggles پیچھے رہ جانے والا

straight (strayt) *adj.* without a bend سیدھا، راست، مستقیم *straight line*, line which is not curved سیدھی لکیر، خطِ مستقیم parallel to the horizon, etc.) کے متوازی neat ; in good order ترتیب سے، قرینے سے *put (something) straight*, tidy (it) up کو صاف کرنا honest (person, behaviour, etc.) دیانتدار، دیانتدارانہ frank (reply, etc.) صاف صاف، سیدھا *a straight fight* (*etc.*), contest (etc.) between persons or (usu. political) parties doing their best to win سخت مقابلہ *keep a straight face*, refrain from smiling or laughing ہنسی ضبط کرنا (U. S.) (of whisky) undiluted خالص، بے آمیزش *a whisky straight* خالص وسکی *adv.* in a straight line سیدھا، سیدھے by or in the shortest way سیدھے، ناک کی سیدھ میں without delay بلا تاخیر direct سیدھے، براہِ راست *come straight home*, سیدھے گھر چلے آنا *straight away, straight off*, immediately, at once, فوراً، اسی وقت، بلا تاخیر directly (*across, in, on, out*, etc.) بالکل *say (something) straight out*, say (it) openly or without hesitation کھل کر کہنا، بے جھجک کہنا

straighten (*stray*-tĕn) *v.t.* & *i.* make or become straight سیدھا کرنا یا ہونا **straightforward** *adj.* honest upright (person) دیانتدار honest (behaviour, etc.) دیانتدارانہ simple (problem, work, etc.) آسان، سہل، سادہ

strain (strayn) *v.t.* & *i.* stretch tightly (*at* something) کھینچنا، تاننا cause (someone or oneself) to make the maximum effort پر بہت زیادہ بوجھ ڈالنا make the maximum possible use of (powers, muscles, etc.) سے پورا کام لینا tire or injure (something, etc.) thus زیادہ کام لے کر تکلیف پہنچانا *strain every nerve to do (something)* انتہائی کوشش کرنا sprain (ankle, etc.) میں موچ لانا twist (word, fact, etc.) from its true meaning کی غلط تاویل کرنا hold (someone) tightly (*to* oneself or *in* one's arms) کو گلے سے لگانا، کو سینے سے چمٹانا pass (liquid) through piece of cloth or a strainer etc. چھاننا *n.* being stretched کھچاؤ، تناؤ force exerted کھچاؤ، تناؤ severe demand (*of* something on one's strength, etc. حد سے زیادہ بوجھ injury caused thus حد سے زیادہ کوشش کا نقصان (*pl.*) verse (*of* some kind) شعر (*pl.*) music نغمات، موسیقی mode of speech, writing, behaviour, etc. طرز، انداز، اسلوب inherited trait of character خاندانی خصوصیت *The strain runs in the family*, یہ خصوصیت سارے خاندان میں ہے

strained (straynd) *adj.* forced, unnatural (feelings and behaviour) بناوٹی، مصنوعی، تکلف unfriendly کشیدہ، غیر دوستانہ *strained relations* کشیدگی، کشیدہ تعلقات **strainer** *n.* vessel with small holes for straining liquids چھنی، چھلنی

a strainer

strait (strayt) *n.* (usu. pl. *straits*, pr. *strayts*) channel of water connecting two seas آبنائے (*pl.*) (financial, etc.) difficulties مشکلات *(be) in great straits* سخت مشکلات میں گھرا ہونا *adj.* (old use) narrow تنگ **straiten** *v.t.* reduce to straits مشکل میں ڈالنا، مصیبت میں مبتلا کرنا *straitened circumstances*, hard up مشکلات میں مبتلا

strand *n.* (lit.) sandy shore (of river or sea) ریتیلا کنارہ، ریتیلا ساحل any of the strings, etc. of a rope or cable رسی کی لڑ single hair بال *v.t.* & *i.* (of a ship) run aground (جہاز کا) ساحل پر چڑھ جانا (used only in the passive) (*be stranded*), be left alone and without any resources (*in* a place) بے یار و مددگار رہ جانا **stranded** (*stran*-did) *adj.* left alone, resourceless یکّہ و تنہا، بے یار و مددگار

strands of a rope

strange (straynj) *adj.* queer انوکھا، نرالا surprisingly unusual عجیب not familiar ناواقف، نامعلوم foreign پردیسی، غیر ملکی، اجنبی *adj.* unaccustomed (*to*) سے ناواقف، کا عادی نہیں **strangely** *adv.* in a strange manner حیرت سے *strangely enough*, it is strange that حیرانی کی بات ہے، حیرت انگیز بات ہے کہ **stranger** *n.* person in a place or in company that he does not know ناواقف **strangeness** *n.* being strange ناواقفیت، اجنبیت، انوکھاپن

strangle (*strang*-ĕl) *v.t.* kill by throttling گلا گھونٹ کر مار ڈالنا hinder the breathing of کا گلا گھونٹنا، کی سانس بند کرنا **stranglehold** *n.* (in the figurative sense) deadly grip شکنجہ، سخت گرفت

strangulate (*strang*-ew-layt) *v. t.* prevent circulation of blood, bowels, etc., by compression دبا کر خون یا پاخانہ روک دینا، حبس (یا) اختناق کرنا

strangulation (*-lay-*) *n.* such prevention of circulation حبس یا اختناق
strap *n.* leather band with a buckle for fastening things together چمڑے کی پٹی ، فیتہ ، تسمہ band to keep wrist-watch, etc. in place فیتہ *v.t.* (-pp-) fasten with a strap تسمے سے باندھنا hold in place thus تسمے سے کسنا beat with a strap کوڑے لگانا **strapping** *n.* beating with a strap کوڑے لگانا tall and strong (person) لمبا تڑنگا
stratagem (*strat*-a-jem) *n.* clever device to deceive the enemy in war جنگی چال any trick چال ، داؤں **strategy** (*strat*-e-ji) *n.* art of directing the movement of armed forces فن لشکر کشی **strategist** *n.* expert in strategy لشکر کشی کا ماہر **strategic** (stra-*tee*-jik), **strategical** (*-tee-*) *adj.* pertaining to strategy لشکر کشی سے متعلق ، جنگی ، حربی **stratocracy** (*-tok-*) *n.* military government فوجی حکومت
stratosphere (*strat*-us-fee-ĕ*) *n.* high layer of atmosphere having a constant temperature, part of atmosphere lying above troposphere (which see) بالائی کرۂ ہوائی ، بالائی فضا
stratum (*stray*-tum) *n.* (pl. *strata*) layer in earth's crust طبقہ ، پرت social class طبقہ **stratify** (*strat*-i-fī) *v.t.* & *i.* form or arrange into layers تہیں جمنا یا جمانا **stratification** (*-kay-*) *n.* stratifying تہیں جمنا
straw *n.* cut stalks of dried grain plants بھوسا ، پیال one such stalk تنکا straw hat تنکوں کی ٹوپی *roof thatched with straw,* تنکوں کی چھت *the last straw (on the camel's back)*, addition to a burden, etc., which, though small, makes the whole burden unbearable (اونٹ کی پیٹھ پر) آخری تنکا *straw vote,* (U.S.) bid to gauge public opinion on an issue by an unofficial vote غیر سرکاری استصواب ، غیر رسمی استصواب *man of straw,* (a) poor person غریب ، نادار ، مفلس (b) imaginary person set up to be quoted فرضی شخصیت *catch at a straw, snatch at a straw,* try to seize any hopeless chance in desperation تنکوں کا سہارا لینا *make bricks without straw,* attempt impossible task سعیِ لاحاصل کرنا *not to care a straw* (or *two straws*) *for,* not to care at all for کی بالکل پروا نہ کرنا **straw colour** *n.* pale yellow ہلکا ، زرد یا پیلا رنگ **straw-coloured** *adj.* pale-yellow ہلکا زرد ، پیلا **strawy** (*straw*-ĕ) *adj.* of the flavour of cheap tea or cheap eggs بدمزہ ، بھوسے کا سا
strawberry (*straw*-be-ri) *n.* a small, soft red juicy fruit سٹابری ، اسٹابری its plant سٹابری ، اسٹابری
stray *v.i.* wander (*from* the right path), بھٹکنا ، بھٹکتے پھرنا lose the path راستہ بھول جانا wander away (*from* companions) بچھڑ جانا *adj.* having strayed بھٹکا ہوا rare, isolated اکا دکا *n.* strayed child or beast بھٹکا ہوا بچہ یا جانور **strays** (strayz) *n. pl.*, (esp.) homeless children بے گھر بچے ، یتیم *waifs and strays* (a) homeless or neglected children یتیم ، بے سہارا بچے (b) odds and ends متفرقات

■ We **stray** when we wander from a set place; **deviate** from the right course or straight path; **roam** aimlessly; **rove** habitually; **ramble** in search of unknown amusement; **emigrate** from one's country and **immigrate** to another country to settle permanently.

streak (streek) *n.* irregular band (esp. distinguishable by colour) in anything (رنگدار) دھاری *like a streak of lightning,* very fast بہت تیز ، برق صفت trace (*of* bad quality) اثر ، شائبہ *v.t.* mark with streak(s) دھاریدار بنانا **streaky** (*stree*-ki) *adj.* having streaks دھاریدار
stream (streem) *n.* river دریا brook ندی ، نالا ، نالہ *upstream,* moving or situated upwards of a river, etc. دریا کے اوپر کی طرف ، بہاؤ کا رخ *downstream* دریا کے نیچے کی طرف current (*of* something) دھارا *stream of consciousness,* individual mental experience comprising a succession of clear as well as vague thoughts emotions, etc. سلسلۂ خیال *go with the stream,* (also) fall in with the general tendency زمانے کا ساتھ دینا ، عوام کے ساتھ چلنا *go against the stream,* (also) not to do so زمانے کا ساتھ نہ دینا *v.i.* (of object) run with liquid پانی کی دھار گرنا ، بہانے لگنا (of blood, people, etc.) flow as a current دریا کا بہنا **streamer** *n.* pennon لمبا تکونا جھنڈا ، علم long narrow ribbon of paper, etc. جھنڈی banner (headline) پورے صفحے کی سرخی **streamlet** *n.* small stream نالا ، نالہ **streamline** *n.* line followed by a streaming fluid بہاؤ کا رخ ، دریا یا ہوا کا رخ *v.t.* shape so as to reduce resistance to air, water or difficulties کی رکاوٹیں دور کرنا ، ٹھیک کر دینا **streamlined** *adj.* (of car, boat, administration, etc.) shaped thus صاف ، بے رکاوٹ
street *n.* road in town or village with houses along it بازار ، گلی ، محلہ ، کوچہ *street cries,* cries of hawkers خوانچے والوں کی آوازیں *not in the same street* (*with* or *as*), not nearly so good (as) اتنا اچھا نہیں جتنا *on the streets,* living by prostitution طوائف ، کسبی *street arab,* homeless child بے گھر بچہ
strength (strength) *n.* being strong مضبوطی ، قوت power طاقت ، قوت *strength of mind,* resolute temper مستقل مزاجی *on the strength of,* (a) incited by کے باعث (b) relying on کی سند سے ، بسند number تعداد ، نفری *in strength, in great strength,* in a large number بڑی تعداد میں *What is your strength?* How

many of you are there? تم کل کتنے ہو؟ *on the strength*, on the muster-roll of the regiment, etc. پلٹن کی نفری میں **strengthen** *v.t.* & *i.* grow stronger طاقتور ہو جانا، طاقت پکڑنا grow powerful زور پکڑنا reinforce مضبوط کرنا، بڑھانا *strengthen (someone's) hand*, enable (him) to take further action کے ہاتھ مضبوط کرنا (also see **strong**)

strenuous (*stren*-ew-us) *adj.* very hard working and energetic (person) سخت محنتی، جفاکش (of work) needing a great effort محنت طلب، جانفشانی کا

stress (stres) *n.* emphasis (on syllable, meaning, etc.) زور *lay stress on*, emphasize پر زور دینا *under the stress of (something)* کے دباؤ تلے *driven by stress of (something)* کے دباؤ تلے آکر difficulty, trouble مشکل، تکلیف times of stress مشکلات کا زمانہ tension کھچاؤ، دباؤ *v.t.* put stress on پر دباؤ ڈالنا emphasize پر زور دینا

stretch (strech) *v.t.* & *i.* make wider by pulling کھینچنا، تاننا، پھیلانا make taut کھینچ کر کسنا *stretch (something) tight* کھینچ کر سیدھا کرنا extend (*for* a distance) تک پھیلا ہوا ہونا reach out بڑھانا *stretch (one's) arms*, (*a*) extend them ہاتھ پھیلانا (یا) کھولنا (*b*) extend them after getting up from bed اٹھ کر جماہی (یا جمائی) لیتے ہوئے ہاتھ پھیلانا *stretch one's legs*, go for a short walk سیر کو جانا *stretch out (one's) arm for (something)* ہاتھ بڑھا کر اٹھا لینا become wider پھیلنا، چوڑا ہونا *stretch oneself out (on), lie at full length (on)* پاؤں پسار کر لیٹنا، دراز ہونا misrepresent (point, word, etc.), by exaggerating or twisting it کی غلط تاویل کرنا *stretch a point in (someone's) favour*, treat (him) more favourably than is right (کسی کی) ناجائز طرفداری کرنا، (یا) بیجا حمایت کرنا (slang) hang (criminal, etc.) پھانسی دینا *n.* stretching کھینچنا، تاننا being stretched کھنچ جانا، پھینچنا unbroken extent (*of* land) مسلسل ٹکڑا continuous period (*of* time) عرصہ، مدّت *at a stretch*, consecutively مسلسل، لگاتار **stretcher** *n.* light canvas-covered frame for carrying a sick or injured person سٹریچر، بیمار ڈولی **stretcher-bearer** *n.* one of the two persons carrying a patient, etc. on a stretcher سٹریچر بردار

strew (stroo) *v.t.* (*strew*; *strewed*; *strewed* or *strewn*) scatter (flowers, etc., *on* a surface) پھیلانا spread (a surface *with* sand, etc.) پھیلانا

stricken (*strik*-ĕn) (old use) *v.* (pa. p. of *strike*, which see) *adj.* affected (*with*) سے متاثر، زدہ *terror-stricken* خوفزدہ advanced (*in years*) بہت بوڑھا

strict (strikt) *adj.* stern سخت گیر، سخت severe سخت، کڑا exact ٹھیک، صحیح clearly defined (truth, sense, etc.) بالکل واضح، صریح requiring exact observance پورا، بالکل *in strict* (or *strictest*) *confidence*, provided there is absolutely no betrayal راز کی بات، اس شرط پر کہ راز افشا نہ ہو **strictly** (*strikt*-li) *adv.* severely سختی سے exactly ٹھیک ٹھیک *strictly speaking*, speaking the exact truth سچی بات تو یہ ہے، درحقیقت، لگی لپٹی رکھے بغیر

stricture (*strik*-chĕ*) *n.* (*pl.*) censorious comments (*of* a revising judge *on* or *upon* the lower court's verdict) سخت نکتہ چینی، ہدف ملامت بنانے والا تبصرہ، توبیخی اعتراض (medicine) constriction تضییق

stride (strɪd) *v.t.* & *i.* (*stride*, *strode*, *stridden*) walk with long steps ڈگ بھرنا pass (*over* or *across* something) with one step پر سے پھلانگنا (کو) پھاندنا stand with legs apart پاؤں پھیلا کر کھڑا ہونا get on horseback سوار ہونا *n.* one step قدم distance covered in one stride قدم، جست *take (obstacle) in (one's) stride*, (*a*) cross (it) without special effort آسانی سے پھلانگ جانا (*b*) overcome (a difficulty) easily مشکل مرحلہ آسانی سے طے کر لینا *make great strides*, make rapid progress بڑی تیز رفتاری سے ترقی کرنا

strident (*strī*-dent) *adj.* loud and harsh (sound) کرخت، سخت with such sound کرخت آواز والا

strife (strɪf) *n.* (lit.) quarrels جھگڑا، فساد (also see **strive**)

strike (strɪk) *v.t.* & *i.* (*strike, struck, struck*) hit مارنا، لگانا، وار کرنا aim a blow (*at*) کو گھونسا لگانا *strike home*, give a hard blow کاری ضرب لگانا *strike (someone) on the chin (etc.)* (کی) ٹھوڑی (وغیرہ) پر مارنا *strike back*, retaliate بدلہ لینا *strike a blow for* (some purpose) کے لیے ضرب لگانا *strike at the root of (something)*, end (it) کی جڑوں پر کلہاڑا چلانا *strike off, strike out*, cross out (a word, etc.) کاٹنا، قلمزن کرنا *strike out (for a place)*, begin to swim towards (it) کی طرف تیرنے والا *strike out for (oneself)*, (*a*) begin a new activity نیا کام شروع کرنا (*b*) start own business اپنا کاروبار شروع کرنا *strike up (friendship with someone)* شروع کرنا (cause to) sound by striking سے آواز نکالنا، بجنا، بجانا *the clock struck twelve* گھڑی نے بارہ بجائے make (a coin, medal, etc.), by stamping out (سکہ وغیرہ) ڈھالنا light (a match) by rubbing it ماچس جلانا discover پانا، معلوم کرنا، دریافت کرنا، پرکھنا *strike an average (between)* کا اوسط دریافت کرنا (یا) نکالنا *strike a balance*, (*a*) balance accounts آمد و خرچ برابر کرنا (*b*) find a middle course (*between*), compromise (*between*) میں توازن قائم کرنا *strike the right path (through a place)* میں سیدھی راہ نکالنا *strike oil* (or *gold*) زمین سے تیل (یا سونا) نکالنا remove (flag, sail tent) (جھنڈا یا بادبان) اتارنا، خیمہ اکھاڑنا (also *strike out*) mov (*across, towards*, etc., a place) جانا، راہ اختیار کرنا cause (fear, terror, etc., *into*) (خوفزدہ کرنا، خوف) پیدا کرنا suddenly cause to be (dumb, blind, etc.) اچانک کر دینا be struck (dumb, blind, etc.) اچانک ہو جانا have a strong effect upon the mind پر اثر کرنا، کو لگنا (of an idea) occur to (someone) suddenly کو اچانک (خیال) آنا، کو سوجھنا (of something) suddenly occur (as an idea) to کو سوجھنا، کو خیال آنا stop working, etc., to press demands ہڑتال کرنا strike (a theme) پر گفتگو چھیڑنا enter into (bargain) سودا کرنا (also *strike root*), (of plant) grow root جڑ پکڑنا *strike out*, (also) become firmly planted جڑ پکڑنا، جم جانا *n.* striking work ہڑتال *go on strike* ہڑتال کرنا *be on strike* ہڑتال کر رہا ہونا *sympathetic strike*, strike by workers of other places in sympathy ہمدردانہ ہڑتال *token strike*, small strike undertaken only as a token of protest علامتی ہڑتال *sit down strike*, دھرنا مار کر بیٹھے رہنا، کام نہ کرنا *pen down strike*, keep sitting in office doing nothing under protest حاضر ہڑتال striking (oil, etc.) in the earth (تیل وغیرہ) نکالنا **strikebound** (*strik*-bound) *adj*. (of industry, etc.) paralysed or crippled by strike ہڑتال سے شل، ہڑتال کے باعث بالکل چوپٹ یا دھرے کا دھرا **strike-breaker** *n.* new worker employed to replace strikers ہڑتال توڑنے والا، ہڑتال توڑ **striking** (*strik*-ing) *adj*. attracting attention جاذبِ توجہ extraordinary غیر معمولی prominent نمایاں

string *n.* fine cord ڈوری، رسی، سُتلی *pull the strings*, control the actions of others as if they were puppets کے تار ہلانا thin ribbon ڈوری، پتلا فیتہ tightly stretched wire, stisng, etc. (in *stringed* musical instruments) تار series of things threaded together لڑی large number (of things or persons) in a line or as if in a line سلسلہ (*pl.*) (*the strings*), musical instruments played with a bow سارنگی جیسے ساز (*pl.*) (*strings*), (colloq.) (usu. secret and unpleasant) conditions attached to offer, aid, etc. شرطیں، شرائط *without strings, without strings attached to it*, بلا شرط، غیر مشروط *v.t.* & *i.* (*string, strung, strung*) put string(s) on (a stringed instrument) کا تار لگانا tie or hang on strings, etc. تار پر لٹکانا *string lamps on a tree* درختوں پر قمقمے تاروں سے لگانا put facts, etc.) together جوڑنا، پھیلانا *strung up, high-strung, highly strung*, (of nerves or person) بہت بے چین، بے حد حساس **stringed** (stringd) *adj*. (of musical instruments) producing sound when their strings are pulled or struck against (ستار، سارنگی وغیرہ جیسے) تار والے آلاتِ طرب **stringy** (*string*-i) *adj*. like string ڈوری کا سا having strings ڈوری دار *stringy meat*, meat full of tough fibres سخت ریشے دار گوشت

stringency *n.* (see under **stringent**)

stringent *adj*. (of rules, measures, etc.) leaving no loop-hole بہت سخت **stringency** (-*ens*-) *n.* being stringent سختی

stringy *adj*. (see under **string**)

strip *v.t.* & *i.* (-pp-) (also *strip off*), take off (clothes, covering, bark, etc.) (کپڑے، غلاف، چھال وغیرہ) اُتارنا deprive (someone *of* his belongings) سے محروم کر دینا undress کپڑے اُتارنا *n.* long, narrow piece (of land, paper, cloth, wood, etc.) لمبا ٹکڑا، چوڑی پٹی

stripe (strɪp) *n.* long, narrow band of distinct colour, etc. on cloth, etc. دھاری V-shaped mark showing rank of a soldier, etc. فیتی *stripes* (usu. *pl.*) a blow with a whip کوڑے کی ضرب رفیتیاں

stripling *n.* growing young man ; one whose figure has not yet filled out نوخیز لڑکا، امرد

strive (strɪv) *v.i.* (*strive, strove, striven*) struggle (*with* someone, *against* something) مقابلہ کرنا make great efforts (for or *to do* something) سخت کوشش کرنا، جدّ و جہد (یا جدّ و جہد) کرنا **striven** (*striv*-ėn) pa. p. of *strive* (above) (also see **strife**)

strode (strohd) *v.i.* pa. t. of **stride, which** see)

stroke (strohk) *n.* hard blow چوٹ، ضرب one of a series of regularly repeated movements in games (swimming, rowing, etc.) ہاتھ mark made with single movement of pen or brush جنبش، کشش *with one stroke of the pen*, بیک جنبشِ قلم single effort کچھ بھی *not to do a stroke of work* کچھ بھی کام نہ کرنا piece (of luck, etc.) کا ایک واقعہ *stroke of luck* حسنِ اتفاق (سے)، خوبیِ تقدیر ہے sound made by a bell striking the hourse گھنٹہ بجنے کی آواز *the stroke of five*, at five o'clock پانچ بجے sudden unconsciousness بیہوشی، غشی، غش *sun stroke* سن سٹروک، دھوپ سے بیہوشی fondling ہاتھ پھیرنا، سہلانا

stroll (strohl) *n.* quiet leisurely walk چہل قدمی، ہوا خوری *v.i.* go for a stroll چہل قدمی کرنا، ہوا خوری کرنا، ٹہلنا، سیر کرنا

strong *adj*. not weak زور آور، قوی، طاقتور، مضبوط large in number بڑا، کثیر التعداد (of building, faith, etc.) not to be shaken پکا، مضبوط، طاقتور (of wind, etc.) forceful, vigorous, violent سخت، زوردار، تیز، پُرزور (of situation, etc.) having a powerful effect زوردار، مؤثر، اثر آفریں (of solution) having much of the dissolved substance تیز *a strong solution* تیز محلول *strong drink*, alcoholic drink شراب **strength** *n.* (see separate entry) **strong verb** *n.* verb forming its past tense and past participle by a vowel change (like, *see, saw, seen*), as opposed to *weak verbs* (like *kill*, etc., which add *ed, d* or *t* for this purpose) تعلیل والافعل، مُتعلّل **strong-room** *n.* one that is strongly built for keeping valuables مضبوط کمرہ **strong-box** *n.* safe تجوری **stronghold** *n.* fort قلعہ any fortified building قلعہ، بلند مقام، گڑھی powerful centre (*of* a cause) مضبوط مرکز، گڑھ، مرکز

strop *n.* leather strap for sharpening a razor or blade اُسترا لگانے کا چمڑا *v.t.* (-pp-) sharpen on a strop اُسترا، پٹے (یا چمڑے) پر لگانا

a strop

strove (strohv) *v.* (pa. t. of **strive,** which see)

struck (struk) *v.* (pa. t. & pa. p. of **strike,** which see)

structure (*struk*-chĕ*) *n.* way in which something is built or organized ساخت، بناوٹ building عمارت any complex whole پیچیدہ چیز framework (of a building, etc.) ڈھانچہ، ڈھانچ

structural *adj.* pertaining to the structure ساخت سے متعلق pertaining to the framework ڈھانچ کا

struggle (*strug*-ĕl) *v.i.* make violent efforts (*for* or *to do* something) سخت کوشش کرنا، جدوجہد کرنا، ہاتھ پاؤں مارنا *n.* struggling کشمکش، کشاکش great efforts سخت کوشش، جدوجہد *the struggle for existence,* the struggle of living things resulting in the survival of the fittest individual or species جہد للبقا، جہد للبقا (یا تنازع للبقا)، جہد حیات

strum (strum) *v.t.* & *i.* (-mm-) play music carelessly or without skill (ساز کو) اناڑی پن سے چھیڑنا

strung (strung) *v.* (pa. t. & pa. p. of **string,** which see)

strut (strut) *v.t.* & *i.* (-tt-) walk (*about, around,* etc.) in a stiff self-satisfied way اترا کے چلنا، اکڑ کے چلنا support with a transverse beam اڑ وار *n.* stiff way of walking اترا کے چلنا transverse beam, etc. used as a support in a framework آڑ، اڑ واڑ

stub (stub) *n.* short remaining end (of a cigarette, pencil, etc.) بچا کھچا ٹکڑا stump of a tree ٹھنٹھ *v.t.* (-bb-) uproot the stump of a tree ٹھنٹھ کو جڑ سے اکھاڑنا injure (one's toe) by striking it against something ٹھوکر سے پیر کی انگلی کا زخمی ہونا **stubby** *adj.* short and thick (fingers, etc.) موٹا اور چھوٹا

stubble (*stub*-ĕl) *n.* ends of grain plants left in the ground after harvest پودوں کے ٹھنٹھ short stiff growth of beard ٹھنٹھی ڈاڑھی

stubborn (*stub*-ĕ*n) *adj.* obstinate ضدی، سرکش، ہٹ دھرم، ہٹیلا، ہٹ کا پکا، منہ زور **stubbornness** *n.* obstinacy ضد، ہٹ دھرمی، سرکشی، منہ زوری ◙ A **stubborn** person is one who is not moved by reason ; **obstinate,** who persists in his own course despite warnings ; **opinionated,** who will not yield to the judgment of others ; **perverse,** who goes contrary to accepted notions of morality or to commonsense.

stubby *adj.* (see under **stub** above)

stucco (*stuk*-oh) *n.* a kind of wall plaster سٹکو، سٹکو سے استرکاری کا مسالہ *v.t.* plaster with it استرکاری کرنا

stuck (stuk) *v.* (pa. t. & pa. p. of *stuk,* which see) ; **stuck up** *adj.* (see under **stick**).

stud (stud) *n.* double-headed button put through two buttonholes to fasten a shirt front, etc. سٹڈ، دہرا بٹن ornamental knob on the surface of a gate, etc. گل میخ number of horses, kept by one owner for racing or breeding ایک مالک کے گھوڑے، نسل کشی یا گھوڑ *stud-horse* اسپ نر، سانڈ گھوڑا *stud-farm* farm for breeding horses گھوڑی پال مرکز *v.t.* (-dd-) set (as) *with* studs جڑنا *studded with stars,* (of sky) starry تاروں بھرا *studded with jewels* جڑت کا

studio (*stew*-di-oh) *n.* workroom of a painter, sculptor, photographer, etc. سٹوڈیو، نگار خانہ room from which radio programmes are broadcast سٹوڈیو، صداخانہ، نگار خانہ (*pl.*) complete establishment where screen plays are filmed سٹوڈیو، نگار خانہ *The National Studios* نیشنل سٹوڈیو، نگار خانہ قومی

study (*stud*-i) *v.t.* & *i.* learn or discover (something) by reading, observation, etc. مطالعہ کرنا، پڑھنا، بغور پڑھنا *study medicine, study to be a doctor* ڈاکٹری پڑھنا give great consideration to (someone's wishes, feelings etc.) کا پورا خیال رکھنا *n.* studying پڑھائی، مطالعہ *make a study of* کا مطالعہ کرنا *begin (one's) studies* پڑھائی شروع کرنا *prosecute (one's) studies* تحصیل علم میں مصروف ہونا (someone's) room for studying and writing مطالعہ کا کمرہ، دفتر reading the books (*of* a subject) مطالعہ sketch, etc., made for practice or experiment نقشہ، خاکہ، تصویر thing, etc., that deserves to be the object of thought غور طلب بات، قابل غور مسئلہ especial object of endeavour پیش نظر معاملہ، زیر غور بات **student** *n.* one who is studying طالب علم، طالب **studious** (*stew*-di-us) *adj.* having or showing the habit of studying مطالعہ کا شائق painstaking محنتی، کوشاں، سرگرم

stuff (stuf) *n.* material مال *It is not a good stuff.* یہ مال اچھا نہیں any unimportant and hence unspecified thing چیز، شے material of poor quality گھٹیا مال، معمولی nonsense فضول، بکواس (old use) woollen cloth اُونی کپڑا *v.t.* press (something) tightly into کو بھرنا، میں ٹھونسنا fill (something) tightly (*with* another) ٹھونسنا، سے بھرنا stuff (fowl, etc.) with spices (مُرغے میں) مسالہ بھرنا *stuffed fowl* مسالہ بھرا مُسَلّم مُرغ fill the skin of (a dead bird or animal) with material کھال بھر کر زندہ جانور کی شکل بنا دینا **stuffing** *n.* material for stuffing (furniture, etc.) جو چیز اَندر بھری جائے، بھرتی seasoning stuffed in fowl, etc. بھرا ہُوا مسالہ **stuffy** (*stuf*-i) *adj.* (of room) lacking fresh air, badly ventilated بَند بَند، جہاں دَم گھٹتا ہو

stultify (*stul*-ti-fɪ) *v.t.* cause to seem foolish or ridiculous مضحکہ خیز بنانا، نشانۂ تضحیک بنانا make meaningless بے معنیٰ بنانا، بیہُودہ بنانا undo the effect of (oneself, one's action) by later inconsistent action کا اثر باطل کرنا، کا ابطال کرنا، کی خُود تردید کرنا **stultification** *n.* act of stultifying or being stultified تضحیک، تردید

stumble (*stum*-bèl) *v.i.* strike the foot against something and almost fall ٹھوکر کھانا *stumble on* (or *upon*) *something*, find it by chance اتفاق سے پا جانا *stumble at* (*something*), feel doubts or scruples about کے بارے میں مُشتبہ ہونا، تامّل ہونا hesitate پس و پیش کرنا fumble for words موزوں لفظ نہ ملنے کے باعث اٹک اٹک کر بولنا *n.* stumbling ٹھوکر walk thus قدم قدم پر ٹھوکریں کھاتے ہُوئے جانا **stumbling-block** *n.* something causing difficulty رُکاوٹ، تنگ راہ

stump (stump) *n.* short part of a tree remaining just above the ground when the trunk has been cut down ٹُھنٹھ remaining part of a limb which has been cut off ٹُنڈ anything remaining after the main part has been cut or broken or has worn off بچا ہُوا ٹکڑا، بقیہ ٹکڑا (cricket) one of the three upright sticks (called *the wicket*) at which the ball is bowled وِکٹ *v.t.* & *i.* walk (*along*, *about*, etc.), with stiff movements اکڑی ہُوئی ٹانگوں سے کھٹ پٹ کرتے جانا (colloq.) (of a question) baffle (سُوال وغیرہ کا انسان کو) چکرا دینا، چکر میں ڈالنا، اُلجھن میں ڈالنا (cricket) end the innings of (batsman) by touching the stumps with the ball while he is out of position وِکٹ پر گیند مار کر (کسی کو) آؤٹ کر دینا (slang) pay up ادا کر دینا، چکا دینا (slang) (*stump up*), produce (requisite sum) (مطلوبہ رقم) ادا کر دینا **stumpy** (*stum*-pi) *adj.* short and thick چھوٹا اور موٹا، موٹا ناٹا

stun (stun) *v.t.* (-nn-) make unconscious (by a blow on the head, etc.) (سر پر مار کر) بیہوش کر دینا shock ذہنی صدمہ پہنچانا، ہوش اُڑا دینا

stung (stung) *v.* (pa. t. & pa. p. of **sting**, which see)

stunk (stunk) *v.*, pa. p. of **stink**, which see)

stunt (stunt) *n.* (colloq.) something done to attract attention اشتہاری حرکت، خاص کرتب *v.t.* stop or check the growth of نشو و نما کو روکنا (یا کم کرنا) **stunted** (*stunt*-id) *adj.* ill-developed, undersized جس کی نشو و نما رُک گئی ہو، جو چھوٹا سا رہ گیا ہو

stupefy (*stewp*-i-fɪ) *v.t.* (of drink, toil, amazement) dull the wits or senses of (someone) کے حواس باختہ کرنا، کو مدہوش کرنا *be stupefied with* سے حواس باختہ ہونا **stupefaction** (-*fak*-) *n.* act of stupefying or being stupefied بدحواسی، حواس باختگی

stupendous (stew-*pend*-us) *adj.* amazingly tremendous حیرت انگیز، عظیم الشان

stupid (*stew*-pid) *adj.* slow-witted کند ذہن، غبی foolish بیوقوف، احمق uninteresting (game, mistake, answer) بے لطف، پھیکا **stupidity** (stew-*pid*-i-ti) *n.* being stupid حماقت، کند ذہنی، بے لطفی

stupor (*stew*-pĕ*) *n.* dazed state caused by drugs, drink, etc. مدہوشی utter amazement سخت حیرت

sturdy (*stĕ**-di) *adj.* robust موٹا تازہ، ہٹا کٹا، قوی ہیکل

sturgeon (*stĕ**-jèn) *n.* a kind of edible fish سٹرجن مچھلی

stutter (*stut*-ĕ*) *v.t.* & *i.* stammer ہکلانا

sty (stɪ) *n.* (pl. *sties*, pr. stɪz) (also *stye*), inflammed swelling on the edge of eyelid گوہانجنی *A sty in the eye* گوہانجنی نکل آئی (now usu. *pig-sty*), enclosure for pigs سؤر خانہ dirty room (or house) گندا کمرہ (یا گندا گھر)

Stygian *adj.* (see under **Styx**)

style (stɪl) *n.* manner of writing or speaking اُسلوب، طرز، انداز characteristic manner of doing anything طرز، خاص رنگ *style of life* رہن سہن کا طریق، طرزِ زندگی distinctive quality which makes something superior شان، امتیازی شان *do things in style* شان سے کام کرنا fashion فیشن، طرز *the latest style in dress* لباس کا جدید ترین فیشن design, sort نمونہ، قسم، طریق right title used when addressing some خاص القاب *v.t.* describe by a certain title, etc. القاب سے یاد کرنا **stylish** (*stɪ*-lish) *adj.* having style صاحبِ طرز fashionable شاندار، فیشنیبل **stylist** (*stɪ*-list) *n.* writer paying much attention to style انشا پرداز، لفاظ writer with a characteristic style صاحبِ طرز ادیب **stylistic** (stɪ-*lis*-tik) *adj.* of style in writing اُسلوب سے متعلق، اُسلوبی

Styx (stiks) *Cl. myth.* the river encompassing Hades دوزخ کا دریا، سٹکس *cross the Styx*, die مرنا، مر جانا **Stygian** *adj.* of the Styx, of Hades دوزخی murky تاریک، تیرہ و تار

stylo (*stɪ*-loh) *n.* (pl. *stylos*) fountain-pen writing

like a pencil سٹائلو، سیاہی پنسل
suave (swayv) *adj.* cultured, agreeably polite شائستہ ، خوش خلق
[1]**sub** (sub) *v.t.* & *i.* (-bb-) put news in a form suited to the needs of the periodical for which it is being prepored سَب کرنا
[2]**sub-** (sub) *pref.* (with names of officials) junior نائب چھوٹا *sub-division*, *sub-inspector* سَب اِنسپکٹر *Sub-Inspector of Police*, نائب نگراں، چھوٹا داروغہ (abb. *S.I.*) تھانیدار، داروغہ *Assistant Sub-Inspector of Police*, (abb. *A.S.I.*) چھوٹا داروغہ، چھوٹا تھانیدار *Sub-Lieutenant*, (in Navy) counterpart of army lieutenant چھوٹا لفٹین، نائب لفٹیننٹ (with names of organizations) branch *sub-committee* ذیلی کمیٹی، ذیلی مجلس almost *sub-human* نیم وحشی ، نیم کم و بیش، قریب قریب، تقریباً ، نیم *sub-tropical* نیم استوائی نیم متمدن forming of a division between two others ذیلی *sub-group* ذیلی گروہ *sub-species* ذیلی نوع under زیر، تحت *subcutaneous*, (of injections) just under the skin زیر جلدی ، جلدی
subaltern (*sub*-al-tē*n) *n.* 1st or 2nd Lieutenant سبالٹرن ، لفٹین ، لفٹیننٹ
sub-committee *n.* (see under **sub-**)
subconscious (sub-*kon*-shus) *adj.* of those mental activities of which we are unaware or only partly aware تحت الشعوری نیم شعوری **subconsciousness** *n.* part of the mind dealing with these تحت الشعور ، نیم شعور
sub-continent *n.* a large indepent part of a continent برِّ عظیم **subcutaneous** *adj.* (see under [2]**sub-**)
subdivide (-id) *v.t.* & *i.* divide further تقسیم در تقسیم کرنا، آگے بانٹنا **subdivision** *n.* subdividing تقسیم در تقسیم further division (*of*) اور چھوٹا حصہ further division of an administrative or other division سَب ڈویژن ، زیر قسمت **Sub-Divisional Officer** *n.* (abb. *S.D.O.*) officer in charge of an administrative or other sub-division ایس۔ڈی۔او، سَب ڈویژن افسر
subdue (sub-*dew*) *v.t.* overcome کو زیر کرنا ، کو مغلوب کرنا bring under control کو قابو میں کرنا tone down, soften دبانا ، ہلکا کرنا ، دھیما کرنا **subdued** *adj.* مغلوب ، دھیما ، ہلکا

We **subdue** a rebel group or uncontrollable passion, **overcome** an obstacle, **overpower** one who resists, **subjugate** our passions or enemies by bringing them under conrtol, **vanquish** an enemy in battle, **conquer** an enemy's stronghold or territory, **enslave** a population, **tame** a wild animal and **master**, a person who thought himself an equal.

sub-editor (-*ed*-) *n.* editor 'subbing' the news سَب ایڈیٹر، نائب مدیر **sub-group** *n.* (see under [2]**sub-**)
subhead (*sub*-hed) *n.* subdivision (of an article, legislation, etc.) مشق **sub-heading** *n.* words showing contents of part of an article ذیلی عنوان
sub-human *adj.* (see under [2]**sub-**)
subject *n.* (*sub*-jekt) (usu. *pl.*) any member of a state except the supreme ruler شہری، باشندہ، رعیت something talked about, written about, or dealt with موضوع *change the subject*, talk of something else موضوع بدلنا something studied at school or university مضمون title, as, indicative of the contents (*of* essay, etc.) موضوع، عنوان noun, etc., bringing the verb (*of* a sentence) into action مُسنَد الیہ، مُبتدا ، فاعل *adj.* (*sub*-jekt) (of nations, peoples, etc.) under foreign government or protection محکوم liable (*to*) کا امکان رکھنے والا *adj.* & *adv.* (*subject to*), conditional on (someone's approval, etc.) کی شرط پر، بشرط ، بہ اُمید *v.t.* (sub-*ject*) bring, (country or nation) under control کو محکوم بنانا ، کو زیر نگیں کرنا bring (someone) under control کو قابو میں کرنا cause (oneself or someone) to undergo (criticism, pain, etc.) کا ہدف بنانا **subjection** (-*jek*-) *n.* subjecting or being subjected زیر کرنا یا ہونا
subjective (sub-*jek*-tiv) *adj.* pertaining to the conscious subject rather than to the external world داخلی، موضوعی (of art or artist) not realistic but expressing the artist's own thought غیر حقیقت پسندانہ ، داخلی nominative (case) حالتِ فاعلی، رَفع **subjectivity** (-*tiv*-i-ti) *n.* being subjective داخلیت
subjectivism *n.* doctrine that knowledge is incapable of objective proof because it is subjective داخلیت **subject-matter** *n.* contents (as distinct from *style*) of a piece of writing موضوع
subjoin *v.t.* add as an appendix (*to*) آخر میں لگادینا، آخر میں جوڑ دینا
sub-judice (sub-*jew*-di-si) *adj.* (of a law-suit) being heard by the court زیر سماعت *This case is 'sub-judice.* یہ مقدمہ ابھی زیر سماعت ہے
subjugate (*sub*-joo-gayt) *v.t.* subdue کو زیر کرنا ، کو مغلوب کرنا ، کو زیر نگیں کرنا **subjugation** (-*gay*-) *n.* act of subduing زیر نگیں کرنا ، تسلط قائم کرنا being subdued محکومی ، غلامی **subjugator** *n.* conqueror فاتح ، غالب آنے والا
subjunctive (-*junk*-) *n.* mood of the verb expressing wish, condition, etc. اِنشائیہ *adj.* of this mood اِنشائیہ
sub-inspector *n.* (see under [2]**sub-**)
sublet (sub-*let*) *v.t.* & *i.* rent (*place* of which one is a tenant *to* someone else) آگے کرایے پر دینا
sub-lieutenant *n.* (see under [1]**sub-**)
sublimate (*sub*-li-mayt) *v.t.* convert into

vapour and then solidify جوہر اُڑانا، تصعید کرنا regard or present base desire as the product of a higher motive اِرتفاع کرنا، مرتفع کرنا n. product of sublimating تصعید شدہ شے **sublimation** (-*may*-) *n*. act of sublimating or being sublimated تصعید، اِرتفاع، تہذیب

sublime (sub-*līm*) *adj*. best, highest برتر، بہترین inspiring awe and wonder پُرجلال *the sublime and the beautiful* جلال وجمال، پُرجلال اور باجمال **sublimity** (sub-*lim*-i-ti) *n*. being sublime جلال

sub-machine gun *n*. large automatic pistol بڑا خودکار طمنچہ، ننھی مشین گن

submarine (*sub*-ma-reen) *adj*. under the surface of the sea آب دوز، آبدوز *n*. under-water ship or boat

submerge (-*mĕ*j*) *v.t.* & *i*. put or go under water غرق کرنا، زیر آب کرنا، غرق ہونا (of water) inundate غرقاب کرنا (of grief, misfortune, etc.) overwhelm ڈبونا **submerged** *adj*. inundated or overwhelmed ڈوبا ہوا (of submarines) go down under water غوطہ لگانا، زیر آب جانا (*Cf.* surface) sink out of sight ڈوب کر آنکھوں سے اوجھل ہو جانا

submission *n*., **submissive** *adj*. (see under **submit**)

submit (sub-*mit*) *v.t.* & *i*. (-tt-) yield (to insult, authority, etc.) اطاعت اختیار کرنا، فرمانبرداری کرنا surrender (oneself or something *to*) کے حوالے کرنا put forward (plan, report, application, etc., *to* someone *for* decision, orders, etc.) وغیرہ کے لیے کسی کے غرضی وغیرہ) پیش کرنا suggest (*that*) عرض کرنا، گزارش کرنا **submission** *n*. submitting فرمانبرداری، اطاعت suggestion گزارش، معروضہ submissiveness تسلیم ورضا plan, etc. submitted پیشکش **submissive** *adj*. obedient فرمانبردار، اطاعت شعار meek tractable اطاعت پزیر، انقیاد پزیر، منقاد resigned تسلیم ورضا کو شیوہ بنانے والا

subnormal *adj*. below normal اوسط سے کم درجے کا

subordinate (sub-*o*d*-i-net) *adj*. inferior in rank (*to*) (کا) ماتحت *n*. (sub-*o*d*-i-net) person in a subordinate position ماتحت عہدیدار person working under another ماتحت *v. t.* (sub-*o*d*-i-nayt) treat as subordinate (*to*) سے کمتر قرار دینا make subordinate (*to*) (کا) ماتحت بنانا

suborn (sew-*bo*n*) *v.t.* bribe someone *to* commit perjury or crime رشوت دے کر جھوٹی شہادت دلانا (یا جرم کرانا)

subpoena (sub-*pee*-na) *n*. writ ordering someone to appear in court عدالت کا بلاوا، سمن، سفینہ *v. t.* (*subpoena*, *subpoena'd*, *subpoena'd*) serve subpoena on سمن جاری کرنا، سمن کی تعمیل کرانا

subscribe (sub-*skrīb*) *v. t.* & *i*. donate (amount) in common with others (*to* a cause, or *for* something) میں چندہ دینا *subscribe to a periodical, etc*.), (agree to) pay its subscription کا چندہ دینا، کا خریدار بننا *subscribe to* (*views, opinions etc.*) share (them) کی تائید کرنا، پرصاد کرنا sign (one's name or document) (پر) دستخط کرنا **subscriber** *n*. one who pays subscription چندہ دینے والا one who signs دستخط کرنے والا **subscription** (-*skrip*-) *n*. donation چندہ price (*of* newspaper) for regular delivery چندہ signature دستخط

subsequent (*sub*-si-kwent) *adj*. later بعد کا following اگلا **subsequently** *adv*. later on بعد میں، بعد ازاں

subserve (sub-*se*v*) *v.t.* serve as means to (an end) کا ذریعہ ہونا، کا معاون ہونا **subservient** (sub-*sĕ**-vi-ent) *adj*. giving too much respect تابع فرمان conducive as means (*to*) (کا ذریعہ، (میں) معاون **subservience** (-*sĕ**-) *n*. being subservient

subside (sub-*sīd*) *v.i.* (of flood water) sink to the normal level عام سطح پر آجانا (of suspended thing) settle, come down بیٹھ جانا (storm, passion, etc.) die away فرو ہو جانا (of ground) cave in دھنس جانا (of buildings) settle lower down in the ground بیٹھ جانا (of person) sink down into chair or on ground گر پڑنا **subsidence** (*sub*-si-dens) *n*. بیٹھ جانا، فرو ہونا، عام سطح پر آجانا، گر پڑنا

subsidiary (sub-*sid*-yĕ-ri) *adj*. not of primary importance but serving as a support (*to*) ذیلی *subsidiary industries*, industries supporting others ذیلی صنعتیں (of company, etc.) controlled by other (company, etc.) ذیلی، ماتحت

subsidize *v.t.* (see under **subsidy**)

subsidy (*sub*-si-di) *n*. grant by one government (*to* another) in return (*for* military alliance, etc.) (فوجی تعاون کے بدلے) امداد grant (*by* government *to* an industry) for keeping prices low قیمتیں کم کرنے کے لیے امداد، امداد **subsidize** (*sub*-si-dīz) *v.t.* give a subsidy to امداد دینا **subsidized** (-*dīzd*) *adj*. getting such grant امداد پانے والا

subsist (-*sist*) *v.i.* exist وجود رکھنا live or be kept alive (*on* some food, *by* some occupation) کو خوراک (پر یا سے) زندہ رکھنا provide sustenance for بہم پہنچانا **subsistence** (sub-*sis*-tens) *n*. existence زندگی، وجود، بقا، ہستی what one lives on or, by (one's) *means of subsistence*, how (one) earns one's living روزی معاش، روزی کا ذریعہ *subsistence allowance, subsistence money*, money given as merest pittance to defray food expenses مصارف خورد و نوش کا وظیفہ، گزارہ الاؤنس

sub-species *n.* (see under ²**sub-**)
substance (*sub*-stans) *n.* material, thing چیز، شَے basic part (*of* something) اَصل، اَصلی جُزو، اَصلیت essence (of speech, argument, etc.) حقیقت جوہر، لُبّ لُباب summary خُلاصہ firmness مضبُوطی solidity ٹھوس پن property مال و دَولت، روپیہ پیسہ *a man of substance*, روپے پیسے والا، صاحبِ حیثیت **substantial** (sub-*stansh*-ĕl) *adj.* strongly or solidly built or made ٹھوس، مَضبُوط real اَصلی، حقیقی having physical existence مادّی considerable کافی wealthy دولتمند، روپے پیسے والا، حیثیت والا practically تقریباً پُورا، تقریباً پُوری طرح *be in substantial agreement with*, agree on all important points سے پُوری طرح مُتفِق ہونا **substantiate** (sub-*stansh*-i-ayt) *v.t.* prove (claim, statement, etc.) by adducing facts in support of it کا ثبُوت مُہیّا کرنا، کے لیے جس کے ثبُوت میں حقائق پیش کرنا *unsubstantiated* حقائق نہ ملیں
substantive (sub-*stant*-iv) *adj.* not subsidiary ; basic بُنیادی having independent existence مُستقِل expressing existence وُجُود ظاہر کرنے والا *the substantive verb*, the verb 'to be' فعلِ وُجُودی (یعنی ہونا) *noun substantive*, noun as distinct from adjective اِسمِ ذات (of one's rank) permanent ; original اَصلی *n.* noun substantive اِسمِ ذات
subtend (sub-*tend*) *v.i.* (of a line) be opposite an angle زاویے کے سامنے ہونا، زاویے کے مُقابل ہونا
subterfuge (*sub*-tĕ*-fewj) *n.* trick for escaping trouble or something unpleasant حیلہ، بہانہ، ٹالنے کی ترکیب dodging excuse سُخن سازی
subterranean (sub-te-*ray*-ni-an) *adj.* underground زیرِ زمین
substitute (*sub*-sti-tewt) *n.* person or thing taking the place of another بَدَل one acting for another قائم مقام *v.t.* put or use as a substitute, (*for*) قائم مقام بنانا، کی جگہ رکھنا **substitution** (-*tew*-shun) *n.* act of substituting or being substituted *n.* قائم مقام بنانا، (کسی کی) جگہ رکھنا *substitution table*, a table in which a word of the same, meaning or function is put in as the given word

subtle (*sut*-ĕl) *adj.* (older spelling *subtil*) too fine to be easily perceived or described رقیق، باریک mysterious (humour, smile, charm, etc.) لطیف quick and clever at perceiving گہرا، ناقابلِ بیان (of critic, etc.) making delicate differences باریک بیں sensitive حسّاس elaborate دقیقہ سنج (design, argument, etc.) پیچیدہ **subtilize** (*sut*-i-liz) *v.t.* & *i.* make fine distinctions باریکیاں پیدا کرنا **subtlety** (*sut*-ĕl-ti) *n.* (older spelling *subtilty*) being subtle باریکی، لطافت، نُکتہ سنجی، باریک بینی، نکتہ، بات، نُکتہ سنجی a subtle point
subtract (sub-*trakt*) *v.t.* take (a number or quantity away (*from* another number etc.) تفریق کرنا، منفی کرنا، گھٹانا، نکالنا **subtraction** (-trak-) *n.* act of subtracting تفریق
subtropical *adj.* (see under ²**sub-**)
suburb (*sub*-ĕ*b) *n.* outlying area (*of* a city نَواحی بستی **suburbs** (sub-ĕ*bz) *n. pl.* outlying areas (*of* a town) مُضافات، نَواحی بستیاں، نَواحی آبادی، گِرد و نَواح *in the suburbs*, away from the centres of business and fashion شہر کی رونق سے دُور **suburban** (sub-ĕ*b-ĕn) *adj.* of or in a suburb قصباتی *suburban railway*, railway connecting the suburbs of a town with it
subvert (sub-*vĕ*t*) *v. t.* overthrow (religion, government, principles, etc.) by weakening people's morale (مذہب) تخریب کرنا، عوام کا حوصلہ پست کرکے حکُومت یا اَخلاق کی جڑوں پر کلہاڑا چلانا **subversive** (-vĕ*-) *adj.* tending to subvert تخریبی **subversion** (sub-*ve**-shun) *n.* subverting تخریب
subway (*sub*-way) *n.* underground passage or tunnel to cross a street or railway زیریں راہ، پائیں راہ (U.S.) tube زمین دوز ریل
succeed (suk-*seed*) *v.t.* & *i.* accomplish what one has been trying to do کامیاب ہونا be successful (*in*, or *in doing* something) میں کامیاب ہونا *succeed in the examination, succeed in passing the examination* اِمتحان میں کامیاب ہونا، اِمتحان پاس کرنا (of a plan, etc.) have a good result کامیاب ہونا follow (someone) and take his place (*as*) کی جگہ (کچھ) بننا، کا جانشین ہونا، کے بعد آنا (*succeed to*), inherit کا وارث ہونا *succeed to the throne*, succeed as the sovereign تخت و تاج کا وارث بننا (بادشاہ بننا) **success** (suk-*ses*) *n.* succeeding کامیابی، کامرانی doing well ترقّی، فروغ good fortune خوش قسمتی person or thing that succeeds کامیاب، کامران، فائز المرام **successful** *adj.* having success (*in*) کامیاب **successfully** *adv.* in a successful manner کامیابی سے **succession** (suk-*sesh*-ĕn) *n.* the coming of one thing after another in time or order کے بعد ہونا، کے بعد آنا *the succession of day and night* دِن رات کا ایک دُوسرے کے بعد آنا *in succession*, one after the other ایک دُوسرے کے بعد، پے بعد دیگرے series (of things) سلسلہ *a succession of*, continuous لگاتار، مُسلسل، پے در پے succeeding to a title, to property, etc. جانشینی right of succeeding to someone حقِ جانشینی persons having this right (کی) جانشینی کا حقدار *first in succession to (something)* جانشینی کا اوّلین حقدار **successive** (suk-*ses*-iv) *adj.* consecutive لگاتار، مُسلسل، پے در پے **successor** (suk-*ses*-ĕ*) *n.* person or thing that succeeds another (as opposed to *predecessor*) جانشین، بعد میں آنے والا

succes fou (sook-say-foo) *n.* success marked or celebrated by wild enthusiasm پُرجوش خوشی والی کامیابی ، کامیابی کا جوش
success *n.*, **successful** *adj.*, **successfully** *adv.* **succession** *n.*, **successive** *adj.*, **successor** *n.* (see under **success**)
succinct (suk-*sinkt*) *adj.* terse, brief (style) مختصر اور جامع ، مُوجز **succinctly** *adj.* briefly مختصراً **succinctness** *n.* brevity ایجاز ، اختصار
successor *n.* (see under **success**)
succour (*suk*-ĕ*) *n.* help given in time of need اَڑے (یا آڑے) وقت پر (یا میں) مدد ، اِمداد ، اِعانت *v.t.* give succour to اَڑے (یا آڑے) وقت پر (یا میں) مدد دینا ، اِمداد و اِعانت
succulence *n.* (see under **succulent**)
succulent (*suk*-ew-lent) *adj.* juicy (fruit) رَس بھرا ، رسیلا thick and fleshy (leaves, trunk, etc.) موٹا **succulence** *n.* being succulent رَس بھرا ہونا ، رسیلا پن ، موٹا ہونا
succumb (su-*kum*) *v.i.* yield (*to* a temptation, etc.) (کا) شکار ہونا *succumb* (*to one's wounds*, etc.), die (of them) زخموں کی تاب نہ لا کر چل بسنا
such (such) *pron.* that یہ *as such*, in the state named earlier in the sentence اسی حیثیت سے *all such*, all such persons ایسے تمام لوگ *and such*, etc. وغیرہ them وہ ، اُن کو ، اُنہیں *adj.* of the same kind or degree (*as* or *that*) ایسا ، اِس طرح کا ، اِتنا ، اِس قدر *such a*, (*never a such*) ایسا ، اِتنا extremely (good, bad, etc.) بہت ہی (اچھا ، بُرا وغیرہ) *such a big* (*etc.*), (colloq. for) so big (etc.) اِتنا بڑا (وغیرہ) **suchlike** *adj.* such (things, etc.) اِس قسم کی چیزیں
suck (suk) *v.t.* draw (liquid) into the mouth by the use of lip muscles (*from*) چُوسنا *suck* (*something*) *dry*, بالکل چُوس لینا ، (کا) سارا رَس چُوس لینا squeeze, (toffee, gum, one's thumb or something else) in the mouth چُوسنا absorb (liquid) (*in* or *up*, *from*) چُوسنا ، جذب کرنا ، سوکھنا draw into mind (*out of*) (سے) حاصل کرنا *suck* (*someone's*) *brains*, get information, etc., from (him) for one's own use کا دماغ چاٹنا ، کا سر کھانا *n.* sucking چُوسنا (of whirlpool, marsh, etc.,) engulf غرق کر دینا (*suck up*, or *suck in*), (school slang) play the toady (*to*) کی خُوشامد درآمد کرنا *suck-up*, toady خُوشامدی **sucker** (*suk*-ĕ*) *n.* pump-piston فشارہ pipe for sucking through چُوسنے کی نلی plant's shoot springing beside its stem زیر بچہ **suckle** (*suk*-ĕl) *v.t.* feed with milk from the breast or udder دُودھ پلانا ، چُسانا
suckling (*suk*-ling) *n.* infant or young animal being suckled دُودھ پیتا بچہ ، شیر خوار **suction** (*suk*-shun) *n.* sucking چُوسنا ، جذب کرنا production of partial vacuum thus to draw something or hold two things together خلا پیدا کر کے کھینچنا یا ملانا ، کشش *suction pump*, pump working in this principle
sudden (*sud*-ĕn) *adj.* *n.* quick or unexpected اچانک ناگہانی *all of sudden*, suddenly اچانک ، یکایک ، یکا یکی ، دفعتہً **suddenly** *adv.* unexpectedly, all of a sudden اچانک ، یکایک ، یکا یکی ، دفعتہً
suds (sudz) *n. pl.* (also *soap-suds*) soap-froth صابن کا جھاگ ، صابن کا پھین
sue (sew) *v.t.* & *i.* go to law against (someone *for* something) (کسی پر کسی چیز کی) نالش کرنا request (someone *for* mercy, peace, etc.) درخواست کرنا ، اِستِدعا کرنا
suede (swayd) *n.* undressed kid-skin for gloves, etc. میشہ ، سُوئید
suet (*sew*-et) *n.* hard fat of kidneys and loins used as cooking medium پیٹھ کی چربی
suffer (*suf*-ĕ*) *v.t.* & *i.* feel (pain, etc.) اُٹھانا ، جھیلنا ، برداشت کرنا ، کو ہونا *suffer from fever* کو بخار ہونا incur loss نقصان اُٹھانا ، گھاٹے میں رہنا incur (loss, etc.) (نقصان) اُٹھانا be in trouble مصیبت میں پڑنا ، مصیبت اُٹھانا brook برداشت کرنا ، گوارا کرنا (old use) permit, allow to come, etc. اجازت دینا ، آنے دینا **sufferance** *n.* implied permission; tacit consent اعتراض نہ ہونے کے باعث مفروضہ اجازت *on sufferance*, by virtue of tacit consent اعتراض نہ ہونے کے باعث رُخصت **suffering** *n.* (esp. in *pl.*) what one has to endure تکلیف ، مصیبت ▣ To **suffer** is to submit reluctantly to pain, illness, etc., to **endure** something lasting; to **stand** something without wincing; to **brook**, tolerate.
suffice (su-*fis*) *v.t.* & *i.* be enough (someone, *for* someone, or *to someone's needs*) (کے لیے) کافی ہونا **sufficient** (su-*fish*-ent) *adj.* enough کافی **sufficiency** (su-*fish*-en-si) *n.* sufficient quantity (*of*) کافی مقدار
suffix (*suf*-iks) *n.* letter or syllable added at the end of a word لاحقہ *v.t.* (su-*fiks*) to add (letter or syllable *to* a word) at end of it لاحق کرنا ، لاحقہ لگانا
suffocate (*suf*-o-kayt) *v.t.* & *i.* choke گلا گھونٹنا kill thus گلا گھونٹ کر مار دینا (cause to) have difficulty in breathing دَم گھٹنا (یا) گھونٹنا **suffocating** *adj.* close حبس والا ، گھٹن والا ، اُمس والا **suffocation** (-*kay*-) *n.* act of suffocating or being suffocated گلا گھونٹنا ، حبس ، گھٹن ، اُمس
suffrage (*suf*-rij) *n.* vote for a member of the Legislature پارلیمانی انتخاب میں رائے ، ووٹ right to vote thus حق رائے دہندگی ، حق رائے دہی **suffragist** *n.* advocate of giving women the right to vote عورتوں کے حق رائے دہی کا حامی **suffragette** (-*jet*-) *n.* woman suffragist حق رائے دہی کی حامی (یا) طالب

suffuse (su-*fewz*) *v.t.* (of colour, blush, hue, etc.) spread slowly over the surface of (something) as from within دوڑ جانا ، چھا جانا ، چڑھ جانا *suffused with (colours)* کے (رنگ) میں رنگا ہوا (of tears) spread thus پھیل جانا

sugar (*shoo*-gĕ*) *n.* sweet substance made from the juice of beet-root or sugar-cane کھانڈ ، شکر ، چینی *brown-sugar* شکر device for making harsh words or unsavoury thing palatable ناگوار شے کو گوارا بنانے والی چیز *sugar-coat* ناگوار کو گوارا بنانا *sugar-coated (pills)* گولی بنائی ہوئی (تلخ بات یا شے) شکر لپٹا ہوا sweet words چکنی چپڑی باتیں flattery خوشامد درآمد ، خوشامد *v.t.* sweeten with sugar چینی ڈالنا ، شکر ڈالنا **sugary** (*shoo*-gĕ-ri) *adj.* tasting of sugar چینی والا ، میٹھا flattering خوشامد والا ، چاپلوسی کا **sugar-cane** *n.* cane yielding sugar گنا ، اوکھ ، ایکھ *cane-sugar* گنے کی چینی **sugar-beet** *n.* beet yielding sugar میٹھا ، چقندر *beet-sugar* چقندر کی چینی **sugar-mill, sugar-refinery** *n.* mill manufacturing sugar کھانڈ کا کارخانہ ، کارخانہ شکر سازی **sugar-crystals** *n. pl.* grains of sugar چینی کے دانے *crystal sugar* دانہ دار چینی **sugar-cube** *n.* sugar made into cubes equal to a tea-spoonful each چینی کی ڈلی ، شکر کی ڈلی **sugar-tongs** *n.* pair of tongs for lifting sugar-cubes شکر گیر

suggest (su-*jest*) *v.t.* propose (کی) تجویز پیش کرنا cause to understand سمجھانا bring (an idea, etc.) into the mind کا خیال دلانا ، ایما betray; express ظاہر کرنا **suggestion** (su-*jes*-chĕn) *n.* that which is suggested تصور ، خیال mysteriously thought-provoking idea اشارہ ، ایہام ، ایما *auto-suggestion, self-suggestion* خود ایمائی slight indication (*of*) اثر **suggestive** (su-*jes*-tiv) *adj.* bringer (*of* idea, etc.) to the mind کا خیال دلانے والا smacking (*of*) (کا) اثر رکھنے والا thought-provoking خیال آفریں replete with suggestions معنیٰ خیز

suicide (*sew*-i-sīd) *n.* deliberately killing oneself خودکشی *commit suicide* خودکشی کرنا one who does so خودکشی کرنے والا **suicidal** (sew-i-*sī*-dĕl) *adj.* very harmful to one's own interests خودکشی کے مترادف

suit (soot, sewt) *n.* set of outer clothing made of the same meterial سوٹ ، جوڑا *a man's suit*, jacket, waistcoat and trousers سوٹ *a two-piece suit* دو چیزوں والا سوٹ ، کوٹ اور پتلون *a woman's suit*, coat and skirt زنانہ سوٹ ، کوٹ اور گھوٹ *a suit of armour* زرہ بکتر request made to a ruler, superior, etc. عرضی ، معروضہ (also *law-suit*), case in a court of law مقدمہ ، نالش ، دعویٰ any of the four sets of cards (تاش میں) ایک رنگ کے تمام پتے *suit of spades* (or *clubs*, or *hearts*, or *diamonds*) حکم (یا چڑیا یا پان یا اینٹ) کے سارے پتے *follow suit*, (*a*) throw card of the same suit اسی رنگ کا پتا ڈالنا (*b*) do what someone else does کسی کے نقش قدم پر چلنا ، وہی کرنا جو دوسرا کرے proposal for marriage شادی کی درخواست یا پیشکش *v.t.* satisfy the needs of (someone) کی ضرورتوں کے لیے کافی ہونا be convenient or right for (someone) کے لیے موزوں ہونا (of climate) be good for (someone) کو راس ہونا (esp. of clothes) look well when worn پھبنا ، سجنا ، اچھا لگنا (*suit something to*), wake fit or appropriate (*to*) (کے) مطابق بنانا **suited** (*sewt*-id) *adj.* fit (*to do* or *for doing*) کے لیے موزوں ، کے مناسب **suitable** (*sewt*-a-bĕl) *adj.* right (*for* something) کے لیے موزوں ، کے شایاں **suitably** *adv.* in a suitable manner موزوں طور پر **suitability** (-*bil*-) *n.* being suitable مناسبت ، موزونیت

suitcase *n.* small case for carrying one's clothes, etc. in a journey سوٹ کیس **suitor** (*sewt*-ĕ*) *n.* person filing a law-suit دعویٰ دائر کرنے والا ، نالش کرنے والا ، مدعی man courting a woman شادی کی درخواست کرنے والا ■ **Suitable** is that which is right for a person or the occasion; **proper**, recognized as right; **appropriate**, in good taste; **worthy**, of one's efforts or of one's good name; **applicable**, to a case.

a suitcase

suite (sweet) *n.* personal attendants of a sovereign or other important personage خدم و حشم (also *suite of rooms*), flat فلیٹ complete set of articles of furniture (of a room) (کسی کمرے کا) پورا سازو سامان ، سیٹ set of dance tunes ناچ کی مکمل دھن ، ناچ گت

sulfa *n.*, [2]**sulfa-** *pref.* (see *Addenda*)

sulk (sulk) *v.i.* refuse to speak owing to being in a bad temper روٹھا ہوا ہونا *n. pl.* (*the sulks*), condition of sulking روٹھا ہوا ہونا ، آزردگی *in the sulks* روٹھا ہوا ، روٹھا ہوا **sulky** *adj.* sulking روٹھا ہوا ، آزردہ having a tendency to sulk اکل کھرا ، جلا بھنا **sulkily** *adv.* in a sulky manner جل بھن کر ، روٹھ کر

sullage (*sul*-ej) *n.* sewage بدررو کا پانی ، گندے نالے کا پانی filth, refuse میلا ، غلاظت ، گندگی

sullen (*sul*-en) *adj.* silently bad-tempered خفا ، بیزار ، روٹھا ہوا unforgiving معاف نہ کرنے والا (of sky, weather, etc.) dark and gloomy تیرہ و تار ، اداس

sullied *adj.* (see under **sully**)

sully (*sul*-i) *v.t.* stain (someone's goods name) دھبا لگانا ، داغ لگانا ، کلنک کا ٹیکا لگانا **sullied** (*sul*-id) *adj.* stained (name, character, etc.) داغدار

sulphur (*sul*-fĕ*) *n.* light yellow non-metallic element burning with a blue flame and a stifling smell گندھک، ہڑتال، کبریت **sulphuric** (sul-*few*-rik) *n.* containing sulphur گندھک کا *sulphuric acid* گندھک کا تیزاب **sulphate** (-fayt) *adj.* salt of sulphuric acid سلفیٹ **sulphite** (-fɪt-) *n.* salt of sulphurous acid سلفائٹ **sulphurous, sulphureous** *adj.* containing sulphur in its lower combining proportion تھوڑی گندھک والا

sultry (*sul*-tri) *adj.* (of the weather) hot and close حبس والا، اُمس والا، ہمس والا

sum (sum) *n.* total obtained by adding together numbers or amounts میزان amount of money مبلغ رقم amount of (rupees, etc.) amount of (annas) موازی problem in arithmetic حساب کا سوال، سوال resume خلاصہ *in sum*, brief resume towards the end of speech, etc. خلاصۂ مطالب *v.t.* & *i.* (-mm-) (*sum up*) give the total of (some figures) جمع کرنا، میزان لگانا express briefly (the chief points of what has been said, etc.) آخر میں خلاصۂ مطالب بیان کرنا **summary** (*sum*-a-ri) *n.* (pl. *summaries*) precis ; short restatement of chief points (*of*) خلاصہ، ملخص، تلخیص *adj.* (of trial, justice, etc.) done or given without delay or attention to small matters سرسری

summarize (*sum*-a-rɪz) *v.t.* make a summary of کا خلاصہ کرنا، کی تلخیص کرنا be a summary of کا خلاصہ ہونا

summer (*sum*-ĕ*) *n.* the warm season of the year گرمیاں، گرمی کا موسم، موسمِ گرما *v.i.* spend the summer (*at*, *in*, etc.) **summertime** *n.* snmmer گرمیاں (also *daylight-saving*), time substituted for real time in summer to save daylight گرمیوں کا وقت **summer-house** *n.* garden shelter with seats ; bower کنج **summer-school** *n.* series of university lectures specially arranged during the summer vacation گرمائی دروس، گرمائی اسباق **summer vacation** *n.* long period of holidays during summer گرمیوں کی چھٹیاں، تعطیلاتِ گرما

summersault *n.*, **summerset** *n.* (same as **somersault**, which see)

summit (*sum*-it) *n.* top (*of* hill, etc.) چوٹی acme (*of* ambition, etc.) انتہا، حد، منتہا، کمال *adj.* (of conference, talks, etc.) of the heads of the four big powers of the mid-20th century world (*viz.*, U.S.S.R., U.S.A., U.K. & France) سربراہوں کی، اعلیٰ *Khrushchev and Eisenhower are accusing each other of wrecking the Summit Conference.* سربراہوں کی کانفرنس کی ناکامی کی ذمہ داری کا الزام خروشیف اور آئزن ہاور ایک دوسرے کو دے رہے ہیں (یا ایک دوسرے کے سر تھوپ رہے ہیں) *enlarged summit*, conference of big powers for settling world issues سربراہوں کی بڑی کانفرنس

summon (*sum*-un) *v.t.* issue orders to (someone) to appear in a court of law عدالت میں طلب کرنا، بلانا، بلوانا call (people) together for a meeting, etc. پروانہ طلبی جاری کرنا، کے نام سمن جاری کرنا call (meeting) بلا بھیجنا کا اجلاس بلانا، کا اجلاس کی دعوت دینا muster or call (*up* one's energy, courage, *for* or *to do* something) طلب کرنا ہمت باندھنا، حوصلہ کرنا

summons (*sum*-unz) *n.* (pl. *summonses*, pr. *sum*·un-ziz) order to appear before a judge پروانہ طلبی، سمن orders (*to do* something) کرنے کا حکم orders to appear (somewhere) حاضری کا حکم *v.t.* serve a summons on سمن کی تعمیل کرانا

summum bonum (*sum*-um-*boh*-num) *n.* maximum good سب سے زیادہ بھلائی، خیرِ کثیر، خیرِ اکثر

sump (sump) *n.* container for petrol in a petrol-engine پٹرول دان pit into which waste liquid drains گندے پانی کی حوضی

sumptuary (*sump*-tew-ĕ-ri) *adj.* (of legislation against luxury) regulating expenditure اخراجات پر پابندی عاید کرنے والا، خرچ پر پابندی لگانے والا، اخراجات گھٹانے والا

sumptuous (*sum*-tew-us) *adj.* magnificient (feast, dinner, etc.) پرتکلف، شاندار of costly richness بیش بہا

sun (sun) *n.* the heavenly body which is the centre of our solar system سورج، آفتاب (also *sunlight*), the light or warmth of the sun دھوپ *sit in the sun* دھوپ میں بیٹھنا *have the sun in (one's) eyes* دھوپ آنکھوں میں پڑنا *rise with the sun* تڑکے اٹھنا *(someone's) sun is set*, (his) time of prosperity is over اس کے اقبال کا آفتاب ڈوب گیا *hail the rising sun*, curry favour with the new party چڑھتے سورج کی پوجا کرنا *under the sun*, in the world دنیا میں *a place in the sun*, favourable position or conditions اچھی جگہ، ساز گار ماحول میں، خوش نصیب *with the sun*, clockwise ساعت دار *against the sun*, anti-clock-wise غیر ساعت دار *take the sun*, sit in it دھوپ کھانا *make hay while the sun shines*, make the best of the opportunities چڑھتے دریا میں ہاتھ دھونا *on which the sun never sets*, worldwide عالمگیر *Let not the sun go down upon your wrath* صبح کا غصہ شام تک بھول جاؤ (یا بھلا دینا چاہیئے) *Nothing is new under the sun* دنیا میں کوئی شے نئی نہیں ہوتی *v.t.* (nn-) put in the rays of the sun دھوپ میں رکھنا (*sun oneself*), sit in the sun دھوپ کھانا **sunbath** *n.* basking دھوپ کھانا **sun-beam** *n.* ray of the sun سورج کی کرن **sun-blind** *n.* external shade of a window کھڑکی کا سائبان **sunburn** *n.* darkening of the skin caused by the sun دھوپ میں سنولانا *sun-burned*, *sunburnt* دھوپ میں سنولایا ہوا **sun-dial** *n.* apparatus for showing the time by the shadow of a rod, etc., on a scaled dial دھوپ گھڑی **sundown** *n.* sunset

عروبِ آفتاب ، غروب **sundowner** *n.* (colloq.) drink at sunset جامِ شام tramp timing his arrival at a station in the evening شام کو پہنچنے والا ، طارق **sun-dried** *adj.* dried in the sun دُھوپ میں سُکھایا ہُوا **sunflower** *n.* tall plant with yellow flowers سُورج مُکھی **sunlight** *n.* light of the sun سُورج کی رَوشنی ، دُھوپ **sunlit** *adj.* lighted by the sun جہاں سُورج کی رَوشنی پہنچے ، دُھوپ والا **sunny** (*sun*-i) *adj.* bright with sunlight دُھوپ سے رَوشن bright like the sun چہرہ رَوشن ، آفتابی ، مُنوّر ، تاباں ، تابندہ cheerful (smile, etc.) شگفتہ ، دِلکش **sunrise** (*sun*-rīz) *n.* sun's appearance above the horizon طلُوع time when it appears طلُوعِ آفتاب ، فجر ، سَویرا colours seen in the horizon then شفق کی لالی ، شفق کی سُرخی ، شفق **sunset** *n.* setting of the sun غروب its time شام colours seen in the horizon then شفق کی لالی یا سُرخی ، شفق **sunshade** *n.* parasol زنانہ چھاتا shade of tarpaulin, etc., outside a shop دُکان کا سائبان **sunshine** *n.* bright sunlight دُھوپ fair weather شاندار دُھوپ area illuminated by sunlight دُھوپ والا حِصّہ *sunshine roof,* sliding part of the roof of a saloon motor-car بند کار کی چھت کا کھُلا حِصّہ ، دُھوپ چھت cheerfulness خوش دِلی ، شگفتگی **sun-spot** *n.* dark patch seen on the sun at times سُورج پر داغ ، داغِ آفتاب **sunstroke** *n.* sudden unconsciousness, etc., caused by exposure to excessive heat of the sun لُو کا اَثر **sun-worship** *n.* worship of the sun سُورج کی پرستش **sun worshipper** *n.* سُورج کی پُوجا کرنے والا **sunward** *adj.* & *adv.* **sunwards** *adv.* towards the sun سُورج کی طرف **sunwise** *adv.* clockwise ساعت وار

a sunflower

sundae (*sun*-dī) *n.* (U.S.) portion of ice-cream served with fruit or nuts in it میوہ دار قلفی ، پھل والی ملائی برف

Sunday (*sun*-di) *n.* first day of the week اِتوار *Sunday best,* (one's) best clothes بہترین لباس *Sunday school,* classes held on Sunday for religious instruction اِتوار کو دینی دَرس **Note: Sunday** is the day sacred to the *sun* ; **Monday,** to the *moon* ; **Wednesday,** to the chief Scandinavian god, *Woden* (or Mercury) ; **Thursday**, to the Scandinavian god *Thor* who was Woden's son (or Jove) ; **Friday,** to the Scandinavian goddess *Frigg* or *Frigga* who was Woden's wife (or Juno or Venus) ; **Saturday,** to *Saturn*, the Roman god of agriculture.

sunder (*sun*-dĕ*) *v.t.* sever, separate جُدا کرنا ، کاٹ ڈالنا

sundry (*sund*-ri) *adj.* (old use or in jest) various سبھی ، ہر ایک ، متفرق *all and sundry,* each and all

sundries (*sund*-riz) *n. pl.* oddments ; various small items that need not separately be named متفرّقات

sung (sung) *v.* (pa. p. of **sing,** which see)

sunk (sunk) *v.* (pa. p. & old. pa. t. of **sink,** which see) **sunken** (*sunk*-ĕn) *adj.* hollow (eyes) دھنسی ہُوئی آنکھیں fallen in (face) پچکے ہُوئے گال

sup (sup) *v.t.* & *i.* (-pp-) drink by sips گھونٹ گھونٹ کر کے حلق سے اُتارنا *He needs a long spoon that sups with the devil* ; speaking with a tempter is fraught with risks بُروں کی صحبت میں بیٹھنا خطرے سے خالی نہیں take supper شام کا کھانا کھانا make one's supper (*off* or *on* something) (میں سے) شام کو کھانا *n.* mouthful (*of* a liquid) پُورا گھونٹ ، جُرعہ

super (*sewp*-ĕ*) *adj.* (shopkeepers' slang) superfine بہت بڑھیا *n.* (slang) supernumerary actor; extra فالتو اداکار unwanted interrupter خواہ مخواہ مخل صحبت ہونے والا ، غیر شخص unnecessary or extra item بدِ فاضِل any Tom, Dick or Harry نتھو خیرا

²**super-** (sewp-ĕ*) *pref.* more or greater than ; beyond what is (human, etc.) فوق ، مافوق ، ماوَرا (heated, abundant, etc.) to an unusually high degree بیحد ، اَز حد ، بے اِنتہا ، حد درجہ put on the top of (something) کے اُوپر ، پَر ، بالائے

superannuate (sewp-ĕ*-*an*-ew-ayt) *v.t.* retire and give old age pension to (someone) پیرانہ سالی کے باعث سُبکدوش کر کے وظیفہ دینا dismiss (someone) because of age or weakness پیرانہ سالی کے باعث برطرف کرنا *adj.* (-et) past work or use از کار رفتہ ، گیا گزرا

superannuated (-tid) *adj.* very old پیرانہ سال sent on old-age pension پیرانہ سالی کے باعث سُبکدوش **superannuation** (-*ay*-) *n.* پیرانہ سالی کے باعث برطرفی یا پنشن دے کر الگ کرنا ، پیرانہ سالی کی پنشن

superb (sew-*pĕ**b) *adj.* magnificent نہایت شاندار

supercharger (*sew*-pĕ*-chah*-jĕ*) *n.* device for forming additional quantity of explosive mixture in an internal-combustion engine بڑا دھماکا دینے والا ، سُپرچارجر

superciliary *adj.* (see under **supercilious**)

supercilious (sew-pĕ*-*sil*-i-us) *adj.* showing contemptuous indifference نخوت پسند ، متکبّر ، حقارت سے دیکھنے والا ، ناک چڑھا insolently indifferent گستاخانہ بے پروائی والا **superciliary** *adj.* over the eyes آنکھوں کے اُوپر of the brows بھوؤں کا **superciliousness** *n.* being supercilious نخوت ، ناک چڑھا پن

supererogation (sew-pĕ*-e-ro-*gay*-shĕn) *n.* the doing of more work than duty requires فرض منصبی (مذہبی ، اُدا ارفل) سے زیادہ کام کرنا *work of supererogation*

supererogatory (sew-pe*-e-*rog*-a-to-ri) *adj.*

(of work, etc.), more than what duty requires to be done نفلی، فرضِ منصبی سے بھی زیادہ

superficial (sew-pĕ*-*fish*-ĕl) *adj*. on or of the surface سطحی lacking depth سطحی، اوپری **superficially** *adv*. سطحی طور پر

superfine (*sewp*-è*-f̲n) *adj*. very fine بیحد نفیس، بہت بڑھیا

superfluous (soop-ĕ*-*floo*-us) *adj*. more than is needed فالتو، زائد، فاضل، زائد از ضرورت **superfluity** (sewp-ĕ*-*floo*-i-ti) *n*. being superfluous فالتو ہونا، زائد از ضرورت ہونا، فاضل ہونا superfluous amount فالتو، فاضل، زائد از ضرورت

superheat (sew-pĕ*-*heet*) *v.t*. heat (steam) to above boiling point بیحد گرم کرنا، (بھاپ) پانی کے درجہ کھولاؤ سے زیادہ گرم کرنا

superhighway *n*. (see *Addenda*)

superhuman (sew-pĕ*-*hew*-man) *adj*. more than human مافوق البشر

superincumbent (sew-pĕ*-in-*kum*-bent) *adj*. placed or resting on something پر قائم، پر رکھا ہوا

superinduce (sew-pĕ*-in-*dews*) *v.t*. bring on (sleep, etc.) by external influence خارجی اثر سے (نیند وغیرہ) لانا

superintend (sewp-ĕ*-in-*tend*) *v.t*. & *i*. arrange and direct (work, etc. of) نگرانی کرنا، انتظام کرنا **superintendence** *n*. نگرانی، انتظام **superintendent** *n*. official manager ناظم، نگران head of the clerical establishment of some branch of the Secretariat, etc.

superior (soo-*pee*-ri-è*) *adj*. (of things) better than the average بڑھیا، اوّل درجے کا، اعلیٰ درجے کا better, higher برتر preponderable (number force, etc.) بڑا، زیادہ، عظیم تر preferable in quality (to) بہتر، بڑھیا (سے) senior in rank, etc., (to) بڑا، بالادست priggish (person, air, manners, etc.) خود پسند، خود پسندانہ not influenced by flattery, temptation, etc.) میں نہ آنے والا *n*. one's better in rank, authority, status, etc. بزرگ، برتر better etc., than another (*in* something) بہتر، برتر، فائق (*Superior*), head of a monastery or convent سربراہ **superiority** (soo-pee-ri-*o*-ri-ti) *n*. being better برتری، تفوّق

superlative (soo-*pĕ**-la-tiv) *adj*. best اعلیٰ، بہترین (also *superlative degree*), form of adjectives or adverbs expressing the highest or a very high degree (as *bravest*, *most wisely*, etc.) تفضیلِ کل، افضل full of superlatives, expressed in too strong terms مبالغہ آمیز، اغراق و غلو سے پُر التفضیل

superman (sew-pĕ*-*man*) *n*. (pl. *supermen*) ideal man in the philosophy of Nietzsche's (1844-1900) who is above mortals فوق البشر

supermarket *n*. (see *Addenda*)

supermundane (sew-pĕ*-*mund*-ayn) *adj*. superior to earthly things غیر ارضی، عالمِ بالا کا

supernal (sew-*pĕ**-nĕl) *adj*. (poet.) divine ملکوتی of the skies آسمانی

supernatural (sewp-ĕ*-*nach*-è-rĕl) *adj*. that which is not controlled by physical laws خارقِ عادت، خارق العادت، مافوق الفطرت **supernaturalism** *n*. belief in the existence of the supernatural مافوق الفطرت باتوں پر یقین، مافوقیت **supernaturalist** *n*. person who believes in or faith that involves belief in the supernatural مافوقیت پرست

supernumerary (sew-pĕ*-*newm*-è-ra-ri) *adj*. in excess of the normal number معمول سے زیادہ، فالتو *n*. extra person فالتو شخص

supersede (sew-pĕ*-*seed*) *v.t*. , oust کی جگہ لینا cancel کو منسوخ کرنا، کو منسوخ کرنا put someone or something in the place of کی جگہ رکھنا یا مقرر کرنا، کی جگہ دینا **supersession** (sew-pĕ*-*sesh*-èn) *n*. act of superseding or being superseded ترک، تنسیخ دوسرے کی جگہ لینا

supersonic (sew-pĕ*-*son*-ik) *adj*. (of speed) faster than that of sound آواز سے بھی تیز، ماورائے الصّوت، فوق الصّوت (of aircraft) travelling at such speed آواز سے تیز، بالائے صوت

superstition (sew-pĕ*-*stish*-un) *n*. unreasoning belief in, or fear of, something mysterious ضعیف الاعتقادی، اوہام پرستی، توہّم (ج : توہّمات) idea or practice based on such belief or fear توہّم، اوہام **superstitious** (-*stish*-us) *adj*. pertaining to superstition اوہام پرستانہ having superstition اوہام پرست، ضعیف الاعتقاد

superstructure (*sew*-pĕ*-struk-chĕ*) *n*. part of the buildings which rests above the foundation بالائی عمارت (of a ship) parts above the main deck بڑے عرشے سے اوپر کا حصّہ، جہاز کا بالائی حصّہ discussions (of a system or philosophy) based on its principles مباحث

supertax (*sew*-pĕ*-taks) *n*. additional income-tax on higher incomes سوپرٹیکس، مزید محصول، زائد محصول

supervene (sew-pĕ*-*veen*) *v.i*. occur as an interruption in حائل ہونا، بیچ میں آجانا

supervise (sew-pĕ*-*viz*) *v.i*. oversee (workers, organization, etc.) نگرانی کرنا **supervizor** *n*. (sew-pĕ*-vi-zĕ*) overseer, superintendent نگران، منتظم **supervision** (-*vizh*-un) *n*. overseeing نگرانی

supine (sew-*pin*) *adj*. lying face upwards (opp. of *prone*) پیٹھ کے بل، چت inactive کاہل slow to act سست

supper (*sup-ĕ**) *n.* last meal of the day رات کا کھانا، شام کا کھانا
supplant (sup-*lahnt*) *v.t.* supersede کی جگہ لینا oust (someone) by unfair means and replace him کو چالاکی سے نکال کر اس کی جگہ لینا، کو اُکھاڑ کر اس کی جگہ جم جانا
supple (*sup*-èl) *adj.* of a child's limbs, etc.) not stiff, flexible نرم، لچکدار (of mind) responsive قبولیت کے مادے والا، اثر پذیر adaptable اثر پذیر artfully compliant کو پٹو کرنے والا، دب کر کام نکالنے والا
supplement *n.* (*sup*-li-ment) *n.* something added later to complete ضمیمہ، تکملہ angle forming 180° along with another تکملہ opp. of *complement* extra part of a periodical containing a particular type of additional material ضمیمہ extra issue (*of* a periodical) ضمیمہ *v.t.* (sup-li-*ment*) add *to* (information, stock, etc.) میں اضافہ کرنا، کو بڑھانا **supplementary** (sup-li-*ment*-è-ri) *adj.* additional مزید extra فالتو (of budget, examination) in addition to the regular one سپلیمنٹری، ضمنی (of two angles) together making up 180° (as distinguished from *complementary angles*) تکمیلی زاویے i.e. those that together make up half that much اضافی زاویے
suppliant *n.* & *adj.* (see under **supplicate**)
supplicate (*sup*-li-kayt) *v.t.* & *i.* ask humbly and earnestly (*for* something) کی اِلتجا کرنا **supplication** (-*kay*-) *n.* supplicating اِلتجا **suppliant** (*sup*-li-ant) *n.* one supplicating; one begging for some boon or mercy ملتجی، رحم کا طالب *adj.* expressing supplication ملتجیانہ
supply (sup-*lī*) *v.t.* provide (something) بہم پہنچانا، مہیا کرنا provide something needed by someone) کی ضرورت پوری کرنا provide (someone *with* something) کو مہیا کرنا، کو دینا meet (the need *for* something) کی ضرورت پوری کرنا meet (a deficiency, etc.) پورا کرنا، کی تلافی کرنا fill (place, etc.) as substitute (جگہ) پر کرنا *n.* supplying بہم رسانی that which is supplied رسد، بہم پہنچائی ہوئی چیز available stock, etc., (of something) رسد، ذخیرہ *supply and demand*, stocks available and demanded طلب و رسد، رسد و طلب *the law of supply and demand* the principle of economics that prices of commodities are determined by the ratio of their supply in the market to a demand for them by the consumers قانونِ طلب و رسد (*pl.*) stores necessary for some public need رسد
support (su-*poh*t*) *v.t.* prop up; bear the weight of کا بوجھ اٹھانا، کو اٹھائے رکھنا، کا سہارا ہونا endure, tolerate (fatigue, life, etc.) برداشت کرنا، سہنا (someone) to go on کی ہمت بڑھانا، کی حوصلہ افزائی کرنا give strength to (claim, view, organization, etc.), by adherence, etc. کی تائید کرنا، کی حمایت کرنا provide (a person, one's family) with necessities برداشت کرنا، کی کفالت کرنا، کا کفیل ہونا، کا سہارا ہونا (in drama) play a role opposite the leading character *n.* supporting or being supported سہارا، پشت پناہ، سہارا، کفیل what supports تائید، حمایت، کفالت *in support of*, in order to promote معاون، کے حق میں
supporter *n.* one who supports حامی، مددگار، سہارا، کفیل
suppose (su-*pohz*) *v.t.* assume فرض کرنا (used as a suggestion) let آؤ، آو تو *Suppose we go for a walk* آؤ سیر کو چلیں believe; reckon likely خیال کرنا، سمجھنا guess کا خیال ہونا imply the existence of کے وجود پر دلالت کرنا، پر دلالت کرنا **supposed** (su-*pohzd*) *adj.* assumed مفروضہ expected (*to do*, etc.) (سے کسی کام کے کرنے) کی توقع ہونا *be supposed to*, should; have the duty to کو چاہیے کہ، کے لیے ضروری ہے کہ *He is supposed to know that.* اس سے کا فرض ہے کہ *He* یہ جانتے کی توقع کی جاتی ہے، اس کا فرض ہے کہ جانے *is not supposed to do it*; it is not his duty to do it یہ کام کرنا تو اس کا فرض نہیں reputed or alleged (character, quality, etc.) مبینہ **supposedly** (su-*poh*-zid-li) *adv.* according to general belief مبینہ طور پر **supposing** (-*pohz*-) *conj.* if اگر assuming فرض کیجیے، فرض **supposition** (sup-o-*zish*-un) *n.* supposing قیاس آرائی، خیال assumption مفروضہ، قیاس idea خیال، رائے **supposititious** (su-poz-i-*tish*-us) *adj.* spurious جعلی، فرضی
suppository (su-*poz*-i-tè-ri) *n.* medicine rolled like a cylinder to put into some cavity to dissolve there بتی، رشیافہ
suppress (sup-*res*) *v.t.* put down (rebellion, opposition etc.), with a heavy hand کچل دینا، دبا دینا put an end to ختم کرنا، خاتمہ کرنا avoid giving vent to (yawn, groan, smile, etc.) ضبط کرنا، روکنا withhold (name, evidence, fact, etc.) نہ بتانا، پوشیدہ رکھنا ban (circulation of; book, etc.) ممنوع قرار دینا، کی اشاعت روک دینا **suppressed** *adj.* banned (book, news, etc.) ممنوعہ (of illness) checked outwardly but not cured دبا ہوا withhold نہ بتایا ہوا، پوشیدہ رکھا ہوا (of people, emotions, etc.), curbed دبا ہوا **suppressor** *n.* one who suppresses دبانے والا **suppression** (-*resh*-un) *n.* suppressing اِمتناع، اِخفا، خاتمہ ▣ We **suppress** something undesirable; **do away** with something established; **eliminate** something unnecessary; **subdue** an emotion; **quell** a revolt; **quench** a thrist; **repress** a legitimate feeling; **smother** something under something; **allay** a fear.

suppurate (*sup*-ew-rayt) *v.i.* form pus ، پکنا میں پیپ پڑنا

supreme (soop-*reem*) *adj.* highest in rank or authority ہستی برتر، برتر ، اعلیٰ *the Supreme Being*, God خُدا تعالیٰ، خدائے برتر *the Supreme Court* سب سے بڑی عدالت عدالتِ عالیہ **supremely** *adv.* extremely ، بیحد ، نہایت ، نہایت اہم **supremacy** (soop-*rem*-è-si) *n.* being supreme سب سے بڑا ہونا، برتری، تفوّق ، اقتدارِ اعلیٰ highest authority حاکمِ مطلق ، حاکمِ اعلیٰ

sur- (sĕ*) sub ماتحت، چھوٹا، ذیلی super برتر، بالا، بڑا

surcease (sĕ*-*sees*) (old use) *v.t.* cease رُک جانا ، بند ہو جانا *n.* cessation رُک جانا

surcharge (*sĕ**-chah*j) *n.* additional charge لیجگی کی، فاضل رَد، مزید بار extra load, مزید بار fine for underpayment of stamps or false property-returns جُرمانہ marked printed on stamp changing its value نئی قیمت *v.t.* (sĕ*-*chah*j*) overload مزید بار ڈالنا exact as surcharge جُرمانہ ڈالنا supersaturate بہت زیادہ بھر دینا

surd (sĕ*d) *n.* (also *surd number*, or *surd root*), irrational number or quantity مجذورِ اصم silent letter غیر ملفوظ

sure (*shoo*-ĕ*) *adj.* certain, confident (*of* or that) (کے بارے میں) یقین رکھنے والا، غیر متذبذب، شک نہ رکھنے والا (*feel*) *sure of oneself*, (feel) self-confident خود اعتمادی والا (ہونا) definite پکا، بالضرور، ضرور *be sure to* (*do, etc.*), not to fail to (do, etc.) ضرور کرنا *make sure*, (*a*) satisfy oneself اپنی تسلّی کر لینا (*b*) do the needful to feel certain (of something) کا پورا بندوبست کر لینا safe and reliable پکّا، یقینی، حتمی *a sure remedy*, حکمی عِلاج *to be sure*, is it really true واقعی سچ *sure enough*, (*a*) certainly یقیناً (*b*) as expected اُمید کا مل ہے کہ **surely** (*shoo*-ĕ*-li) *adv.* (*a*) certainly یقیناً، لازماً (*b*) as expected اُمید کامل ہے کہ

surety (*shoo*-ĕ*-ti) *n.* guarantee ضمانت guarantor for someone's debts or duties ذمّے دار *stand surety for someone* کا ضامن بننا، کی ضامن، کفیل ضمانت دینا

surf (sĕ*f) *n.* foam of waves breaking on the shore لہروں کا جھاگ ، کفِ دریا breaking of waves on the shore (ساحل پر) تلاطمِ امواج **surf-riding,** sea-sport in which one balances oneself on a long and narrow board which is being drawn by a motor-boat تختوں پر کفِ دریا کے ساتھ بہنا **surf-board** board used for this purpose کفِ دریا پر بہانے والا تختہ **surfy** *adj.* full of surfs پُر کف like surf کفِ دریا کا سا

surface (sĕ*-fis) *n.* exposed [side(s) of anything سطح the outward appearance شکل صورت ظاہری شکل و صورت ، ظاہری پہلو ، ظاہر *v.i.* (of a submarine) rise to the surface of the sea (آبدوز کا) سطح پر آنا اُوپر آنا (*cf.* submurge)

surfiet (*sè**fit) *n.* overeating, etc., which results in satiety پُرخوری feeling of heaviness caused by overeating پُرخوری کے باعث گرانی excess (*of* anything) کی کثرت سے زیادتی being fed up with اُکتا جانا *v.t.* overeat (*oneself on* something) سے منہ پھر جانا بہت زیادہ کھا جانا be satiated (*with*)

surge (se*j) *v.i.* move forward in or like billowing waves (*out of, over*, etc., a place) اُمنڈ آنا *n.* forward rush of waves اُٹھتی ہوئی موج *the surge of the ocean* سمندر کی اُٹھتی ہوئی موج onrush (of passion, people, etc.) طوفان، بحرِ متلاطم

surgeon (*se**-jen) *n.* doctor who performs operations جرّاح ، ماہرِ جراحت **surgery** (*se**-jè-ri) *n.* treatment of ailments by operations فنِ جرّاحی ، جرّاحی surgeon's consulting room جرّاح کا مشورہ خانہ جراحت doctor's dispensary مطب، طبیب کا دوا خانہ جرّاح کی دُکان **surgical** *adj*. pertaining to surgery جرّاحی کا، جرّاحی کے متعلق ، جراحتی

surly (*sĕ**li) *adj.* rude, sour-tempered and unfriendly اکھڑ، بدمزاج، اکل کھرا **surlily** *adv.* in surly manner اکھڑپن سے **surliness** *n.* being surly اکھڑپن ، بدمزاجی ، اکل کھرا پن

surmise (sĕ*-*mīz*) *n.* conjecture as to the nature or existence of something اندازہ، قیاس *v.t.* & *i.* infer doubtful conjecture thus اندازہ لگانا، قیاس آرائی کرنا

surmount (se*-*mount*) *v.t.* overcome (difficulties, etc.) دُور کرنا get over (obstacles پر غلبہ پانا ، پر قابو پانا (passive) (*be surmounted by* or *with*), be crowned with, have (something) on the top کے اُوپر ہونا ، کے اُوپر لگا ہوا ہونا

surname (*sĕ**-naym) *n.* family name خاندانی نام

surpass (sĕ*-*pahs*) *v.t.* outdo, excel, exceed سے بڑھ جانا، سے بازی لے جانا، پر سبقت لے جانا، سبقت لے جانا **surpassing** *adj*. unmatched بے نظیر ، بے مثال

surplice (*sĕ**-plis) *n.* clergymen and choristers' white gown with wide sleeves (پادریوں وغیرہ کا) سفید جُبّہ

surplus (*sè**-plus) *n.* something left over بچا ہوا ، زائد (opp. of *deficit*), excess of public revenue over expenditure بجٹ توفیر (of population) number besides that whose needs can be supplied زائد **surplusage** (sĕ*-plu-sej) *n.* wasteful excess تضییع آمیز زیادتی ، بیکار توفیر

surprise (sĕ*-*prīz*) *n.* unexpected thing خلافِ توقع بات، اچنبھا feeling caused by it اچنبھا، تعجب، حیرت catching unawares or unprepared اچانک جا لینا *v. t.* بے خبری میں جا لینا capture (place enemy, etc.) by sudden attack اچانک حملہ کر کے قابو میں کر لینا

come upon (someone) suddenly and unexpectedly اچانک جالینا (یا پہنچنا) astonish حیران کر دینا، بھونچکا کر دینا be surprised by (or at) (سے یا پر) بھونچکا رہ جانا hasten (someone into doing something) جلدی جلدی کرنے پر مجبور کر دینا **surprising** (-*prīz*-) *adj.* astonishing because sudden and expected عجیب، حیرت انگیز

surprisal (-*prīz*-) *n.* come upon suddenly بے خبری میں آ لینا astonishment حیرانی، حیرت

surrender (su-*rend*-ĕ*) *v.t.* & *i.* give up (town, etc., *to*) کے حوالے کرنا lay down (arms) سپر انداز ہونا، ہتھیار ڈال دینا stop fighting and yield ہتھیار ڈال دینا، اطاعت قبول کرنا give up (claim, freedom, سے دستبردار ہونا *surrender* (*oneself*) *to*, yield (oneself) to (habit or emotion) سے مغلوب ہو جانا *n.* surrendering حوالے کر دینا، سپر اندازی، دستبرداری، قبول اطاعت

surreptitious (su-rep-*tish*-us) *adj.* (of actions) done secretly or stealthily خفیہ، پوشیدہ **surreptitiously** *adv.* stealthily چھپ چھپا کر، چوری چھپے، چپکے چوری

surround (su-*round*) *v.t.* enclose کے گرد گھیرا ڈال لینا، کو گھیر لینا، کو گھیرے میں لے لینا کا محاصرہ کرنا، **surroundings** *n. pl.* everything around and about a place گرد و پیش، گرد و نواح environment ماحول

surtax (*sĕ**-taks) *n.* additional tax on very high incomes بڑی آمدنیوں پر مزید ٹیکس، سر ٹیکس *v. t.* impose surtax on بڑی آمدنیوں پر مزید ٹیکس لگانا

surveillance (sĕ*-*vayl*-yans) *n.* watch kept over workers or suspects نگرانی *under surveillance*, watched زیر نگرانی *keep* (*someone*) *under surveillance*, keep watch over (him) کو زیر نگرانی رکھنا

survey *v.t.* (sĕ**vey*) take a general view of پر طائرانہ نظر ڈالنا examine the general state of کا جائزہ لینا measure up (land, etc.) for mapmaking کی مساحت کرنا *n.* (*se**-vay) general view طائرانہ نظر land surveying مساحت map, etc. of landsurveying نقشہ *Survey of Pakistan* محکمۂ مساحتِ پاکستان **surveyor** (sĕ*-*vey*-ĕ*) *n.* one who surveys land or buildings ناظر مساحت *Surveyor-General* ناظرِ مساحتِ اعلیٰ

survival *n.* (see under **survive**)

survive (sĕ**viv*) *v.t.* & *i.* continue to be کا وجود قائم رہنا، عالم ہست و بود میں رہنا remain alive after (someone) کے بعد تک زندہ رہنا escape and live till after illness, calamity, etc. سے بچ جانا **survival** (-*viv*-) *n.* surviving بقا، باقی رہنا، بچ جانا *survival of the fittest*, survival of the best (individual or species) in the evolutionary struggle for existene بقائے اصلح that which has survived ancient times یادگارِ ماضی **survivor** *n.* person who has safely come out (*of* a calamity, etc.) باقیماندہ، پسماندہ (*pl.*) relatives of the deceased پسماندگان

susceptible (su-*sep*-ti-bĕl) *adj.* easily influenced by feelings حساس (*susceptible to*), easily affected by, open to اثر پذیر capable (*of* proof, etc.) کے قابل **susceptibility** (-*bil*-) *n.* sensitiveness حساس ہونا (*pl.*) beliefs, etc., which become one's weakness and about which one is very sensitive دکھتی ہوئی رگ بنے ہوئے احساسات، مجروح ہو سکنے والے جذبات

susceptive (su-*sep*-tiv) *adj.* concerned with the receiving of emotional impression تاثری

suspect *v.t.* (sus-*pekt*) be inclined to believe کا خیال ہونا، کو گمان ہونا have misgivings about (the truth, etc., of something) پر شبہ ہونا، کو مشکوک سمجھنا feel that (someone) is guilty کو مشتبہ سمجھنا feel that (someone) is guilty (*of* something or *of doing* something) (کسی پر کسی بات کا) شبہ کرنا *n.* (*sus*-pekt) one suspected of crime مشتبہ شخص، مشتبہ *adj.* of doubtful character مشکوک چال چلن کا suspected مشتبہ

suspend (sus-*pend*) *v.t.* & *i.* remain floating (*in* air or liquid) معلق رہنا hang up (*from* a place) لٹکانا postpone (meeting, etc.) ملتوی کرنا stop (constitution, law, employee, etc.) from duty or working for the time being معطل کرنا stop (payment, etc.) for a time عارضی طور پر روک دینا delay (judgement, etc.) میں تاخیر کرنا **suspenders** *n. pl.* pair of supports for socks, etc. گیلس، جرابوں کے رفیتے pair of braces گیلس **suspension** (sus-*pensh*-ĕn) *n.* suspending or being suspended لٹکانا، تعلیق، التوا، تعویق، تاخیر، تعطل، معطلی *suspension bridge*, bridge suspended on steel cables لٹکتا پل، معلق پل

suspense (sus-*pens*) *n.* uncertainty (about something) (انتظار کی) پریشانی، تشویش، امید و بیم کی حالت، کیفیتِ بیم و رجا *keep* (*someone*) *in suspense* کو تشویش میں ڈالے رکھنا

suspension *n.* (see under **suspend**

suspicion (sus-*pish*-un) *n.* being suspected شبہ feeling that something is wrong شک و شبہ، بدگمانی (*be*) *above suspicion*, (be) so good that suspicion is out of the question شک و شبہ سے بالا ہونا، بدگمانی سے بالا ہونا suggestion (*of*) کا شائبہ، کا شبہ **suspicious** (sus-*pish*-us) *adj.* causing suspicion مشتبہ having suspicion شکی

suspire (sus-*pı*-e*) *v. i.* (poet.) sigh آہ بھرنا

sustain (sus-*tayn*) *v.t.* hold up ; keep from falling, etc. کو اٹھائے رکھنا، کا بوجھ اٹھانا، کو سہارا دینا، کو سنبھالے رکھنا (of food) give strength enough to pull along زندہ رکھنا keep up (an argument or attempt) (کوشش) جاری رکھنا، (استدلال) کو اچھی طرح نبھانا suffer (loss or defeat) اٹھانا (of law) uphold (a case, argument, etc.) کو حق بجانب قرار دینا

sustained (sus-*taynd*) *adj*. continued over a long time اچھی طرح نبھایا ہوا ، دیر تک جاری رکھا ہوا **sustenance** (*sus*-te-nans) *n*. food غذا food-value ; nutrition غذائیت

suzerain (*sewz*-ĕ-rayn) *n*. feudal lord نظام جاگیرداری (رئیس)، سردار State or ruler in relation to a semi-independent country over which a general or nominal control is enjoyed حکمران ریاست (کا فرمانروا)

suzerainty (*sewz*-ĕ-rayn-ti) *n*. such control محدود فرمانروا

svelte (svelt) *adj*. (esp. of female figure) slender and graceful نازک ، نازک اندام

swab (swob) *n*. mop, etc. for cleaning floor, tables, etc. by wetting it کوچی ball of cotton-wool, etc. for washing wounds, etc. گدی، جاذب گدی، سوکھ گدی (slang) clumsy fellow بھدا آدمی *v.t.* (-bb-) clean with a swab گدی (یا کوچی) سے صاف کرنا take (*up* liquid) with a swab گدی (یا کوچی) سے (رطوبت) خشک کرنا

swag (swag) *n*. (slang) stolen goods چوری کا مال money got by corrupt means بدعنوانی کی کمائی

swagger (*swag*-ĕ*) *v.i.* strut اینٹھ کر چلنا be boastful رعب جمانا behave in a self-important manner تحکمانہ انداز اختیار کرنا *n*. such manner دھونس such gait اکڑ ، اینٹھ کر چلنا ہیکڑی

swain (swayn) *n*. (poet.) young rustic دیہاتی نوجوان bucolic lover دہقانی عاشق ، دیہاتی عاشق

swallow (*swol*-oh) *v.t.* & *i*. allow (food, etc.) to go down one's throat نگلنا *swallow a camel and strain at a gnat*, have scruples about small gains but accept big ones without qualms of conscience چھوٹی چھوٹی باتوں میں دیانتداری کا اظہار اور بڑی باتوں میں بے ایمانی eat up quickly جلدی جلدی کھانا، ہڑپ کرنا (of expenses, etc.) use up (earnings, etc.) کھا جانا believe (something) credulously ناقابل یقین یا انہونی بات پر یقین کر لینا stomach (insult) چپ چاپ برداشت کرنا not to give vent to (one's anger, etc.) پی جانا take (one's words) back expressing regret اپنے الفاظ واپس لینا، اپنے کیے پر اظہار افسوس کرنا (of water, etc.) engulf غرق کر دینا *n*. swallowing نگلنا، ہڑپ کرنا small, swift flying summer bird with long wings and forked tail ابابیل

a swallow

swallow-tail *n*. (also *swallow-tailed coat*), men's evening-dress coat گاؤدم دامن والا کوٹ

swam *v*. (pa. t. of **swim**, which see)

swamp (swomp) *n*. bog, marsh دلدل *v.t.* (of water) soak (boat with what it holds) شرابور کر دینا overwhelm (with work, customers, applications, etc.) کی بھرمار سے ناک میں دم کر دینا (of something) absorb (another) by its superior numbers اپنے اندر گم کر دینا

swampy (*swamp*-i) *adj*. with or growing in swamps دلدلی

swan (swon) *n*. a large, graceful, ducklike water-bird of usually white colour reputed to sing melodiously ہنس، راج ہنس *the Swan of Avon*, Shakespeare بلبل ایوان، شیکسپیر **swan's-down** *n*. its soft under-feathers used as powder-puff ہنس کے نرم پر **swan-song** *n*. fabled song of swan before its death ہنس کا آخری نغمہ one's last achievement آخری شاہکار

swank (swank) (colloq.) *v.i.* swagger دھونس جمانا talk boastfully ڈینگ مارنا *n*. showing off نمود ، نام و نمود

swap (swop) *v.t.* & *i*. (-pp-) (same as **swop**, which see)

sward (swo*d) *n*. (lit.) turf ; expanse of short grass سبزہ زار ، دوب کا تختہ

swarm (swo*m) *n*. large number of birds, insects, shooters, etc. moving about together (esp. round prey or enemy) جھنڈ cluster of emigrating bees شہد کی مکھیوں کی فوج *n. pl*. large numbers (*of* children, etc.) ہجوم ، بھیڑ *v.t.* & *i*. move about in large number جھنڈ میں اڑنا (of places, roads, beds, etc.) be crowded or infested with (visitors, travellers, tramps, fleas, etc.) سے بھرے ہونا climb (*up* rope, pole, tree, etc.) by gripping with the knees and hands ہاتھ پاؤں سے چمٹ کر چڑھنا

swarthy (*swo*dh*-i) *adj*. dark (complexion) کالا، کالا کلوٹا ، سیاہ فام

swash (swosh) *v.t.* & *i*. make the sound of water washing about چھپ چھپ کرنا (old use) strike violently سخت زور سے مارنا، اندھا دھند لگانا *n*. sound of swashing water چھپ چھپ **swashing blow** *n*. violent blow زور کا گھونسا، ضرب کاری **swash-buckler** *n*. bully دھونس دینے والا mercenary swordsman بھاڑے کا بانکا

swat (swot) *v.t*, (-tt-) (colloq.) hit (a fly) with a sharp blow of the hand, etc. (مکھی) زور سے مارنا (یا) کچل دینا

swath (swoth) (pl. *swaths* pr. swodhz), **swathe** (swaydh) *n*. band of cleared ground left after one passage of mower ایک بار گھاس چھلنے کے بعد والی جگہ (only *swathe*), wrapping, bandage

swathe (swaydh) *v.t.* wrap (limb or person) tightly in bandages or wraps پر پٹیاں باندھنا

sway *v.t.* & *i*. move or be moved to and fro unsteadily ہلنا جلنا، جھولنا، ہلانا جلانا direct مرضی کے مطابق چلانا rule over پر حکمرانی کرنا (of speech, etc.) influence کو متاثر کرنا be controlled by (impulse, etc.) پر چلنا *n*. swaying movement جھولنا (یا) جھلانا rule حکمرانی influence, control اثر

be under the sway of, (a) be influenced by کے زیرِ اثر ہونا (b) be ruled by کے تابع فرمان ہونا
swear (*sway-ë**) *v.t.* & *i.* (*swear, swore, sworn*) take oath قسم اُٹھانا، حلف اُٹھانا administer oath قسم دینا، حلف دینا cause to take oath قسم کھلانا *swear (someone) to secrecy (etc.)* (کسی) کو رازداری (وغیرہ) کی قسم دینا promise on oath (*to do* or *that*) کی قسم کھانا، کا عہد کرنا *swear to* (or *by* or *before*), appeal to (someone or something) as witness and guarantee of oath کی قسم کھانا *swear (something) off*, swear to give it up کے ترک کی قسم کھانا *swear (someone) in (Minister, etc.)*, administer oath (of office to him) کو عہدے پر فائز ہوتے وقت حلف دینا *swear by (something)*, have great confidence in the efficacy of (medicine, etc.) پر پُورا یقین ہونا use curses and bad words گالی دینا *swear at (someone)* کو گالیاں دینا **swear-word** *n.* curse; profane oath گالی **sworn evidence** *n.* evidence given on oath حلفیہ بیان **sworn brothers, sworn friends** *n.* very intimate friends گہرے دوست، جگری دوست
sweat (swet) *n.* perspiration *in a sweat*, perspiring heavily پسینے میں شرابور *by* (or *in*) *the sweat of (one's) brow*, by dint of hard work خون پسینہ ایک کر کے (colloq.) hard work سخت محنت sweating state پسینے کی حالت sweat-like moisture on the surface پسینے کی طرح رِسنے والی نمی *v.t.* & *i.* perspire کو پسینہ آنا work hard خون پسینہ ایک کرنا سخت محنت کرنا drive (someone) to work very hard at extremely low wages (مزدوروں وغیرہ کا) خون چوسنا، عرق نکالنا *sweated labour*,
sweater *n.* thick jersy سویٹر **sweaty** *adj.* (of clothes) wet with sweat پسینے میں تر بتر smelling of sweat جس میں سے پسینے کی بُو آئے
swede (sweed) *n.* Swedish turnip سویڈن کا شلغم (*Swede*), native of Sweden سویڈن کا باشندہ
sweep *v.t.* & *i.* (*sweep, swept, swept*) brush away (place, dust, dirt, etc.) جھاڑنا، جھاڑو سے صاف کرنا brush جھاڑو دینا move quickly (*over* or *along*) removing things coming in the way اُڑائے جانا *sweep (someone) off (his) feet*, cause (him) to fall down گرا دینا *sweep the board*, (a) win all the money in gambling سارا روپیہ جیت لینا (b) win completely پوری طرح جیت لینا *sweep the seas*, drive away all enemies from there دشمن کو سمندر سے مار بھگانا glide (along) swiftly تیزی سے گزر جانا، تیز چلنا stretch (in some direction) in a large curve خطِ ہلالی میں مڑنا، بڑا موڑ مڑنا move (*in* or *out of* a place) in a stately manner شان سے گزرنا row with a sweep لمبے چپّو سے (کشتی) کھینا *n* sweeping (as) with a brush, or broom جھاڑو دینا sweeping movement تیز حالت *make a clean sweep (of)*, get rid of old customs, prevalent order, etc.) at one stroke ایک ہی ضرب میں ختم کرنا long unbroken curve (of road, river, sloping land, etc.) لمبا موڑ range of something moved thus پھیلاؤ (also *chimney-sweep*) man whose work is sweeping soot from chimneys دود کش کی صفائی کرنے والا، دُود روب long oar worked by standing rower لمبا چپّو **sweeper** *n.* person who sweeps جاروب کش *street sweepers* جاروب کش، جارب بھنگی، مہتر machine for sweeping جارب *carpet-sweeper*, machine for sweeping carpets etc. قالین روب (in Pakistan) member of the depressed classes who adopts scavenging as a profession بھنگی، مہتر **sweeping** *adj.* far-reaching (change, etc.) دُور رس too generalized (statement) ignoring important exceptions بہت عام
sweepstake, sweepstakes *n.* gambling on a horse-race گھڑ دوڑ کا جُوا
sweet *adj.* tasting like sugar میٹھا، شیریں *taste sweet*, (of some eatable) be sweet میٹھا ہونا perfumed; pleasant to smell خوشبودار fresh pleasant to hear سُریلا، خوش اِلحان attractive (person, temper, etc.) دلکش just as one pleases پسندیدہ، مرضی کے مطابق *at (one's) sweet will* اپنی مرضی کے مطابق gentle شریفانہ (in women's words) very pretty (thing) بہت خوبصورت (slang) *a sweet one*, a painful blow with the fist زور کا گھونسا *n.* (also *sweet-dish*), dish of sweet food as part of a meal میٹھا (*pl.*) (also *sweetmeat*), very sweet sugared eatable مٹھائی، شیرینی (*pl.*) delights (*of* office, etc.) (اقتدار وغیرہ کی) خوشیاں (یا) فوائد (vocative) darling پیارے، پیاری، جانِ من، جانی **sweeten** (*sweet-ën*) *v.t.* & *i.* make or become sweet میٹھا ہونا یا بنانا **sweetening** *n* substance which sweeetens میٹھا بنانے والی چیز، میٹھا **sweetheart** *n.* lover شیدائی، محبوب، محبوبہ **sweetmeat** *n.* (usu. *pl.*) sweets, esp., bonbons or plum, etc. preserved in sugar مٹھائی، شیرینی **sweet stuff** *n.* sweets مٹھائی، شیرینی **sweety** *n.* (pl. *sweeties* pr. *swee-tiz*) (child's word for) confection or sweetmeat مٹھائی **sweet tooth** *n.* taste for sweet foods مٹھائی کا شوق **sweet-toothed** مٹھائی کا شائق **sweet-potato** *n.* well-known twining plant with sweet tubers شکر قندی **sweet oil** *n.* oil without a bitter taste میٹھا تیل **sweet-root** liquorice ملٹھی، اَصل السُّوس **sweet seventeen** *n.* this year of one's life میٹھا برس، برس پندرہ یا کہ سولہ کا سن **sweet brier** *n.* a king of sweet-smelling wild rose جنگلی گلاب
swell (swel) *v.t.* & *i.* (*swell; swelled, swelled, swollen*) (cause to) grow in volume پھیلنا یا پھیلانا

(cause, to) become louder بُلند ہونا یا کرنا raise سُوجنا، آماس ہونا (up) اُبھارنا have inflammation سُوجنا، آماس ہونا curve (up or out) باہر کو نکلنا (یا)، نکالنا، اُبھرنا، اُبھارنا *swell with pride*, feel very proud بہت اترانا، بڑا فخر محسوس (suffering from) کرنا *swelled head*, (suffering from) conceit پُر غرور، غرور، مغرور *n.* gradual increase of sound (of) چڑھاؤ، بتدریج بلندی slow rise and fall of the sea's surface after a storm اُتار چڑھاؤ (colloq.) well-dressed or important person بڑے ٹھاٹھ والا، چھیلا *adj.* (colloq.) smartly dressed خوش پوش distinguished ممتاز، نمایاں **swelling** *n.* inflammation سُوجن، وَرَم، آماس

swelter (*swel-tĕ**) *v.i,* be uncomfortably hot سخت گرمی ہونا be oppressed with heat (or *with* heat) مارے گرمی کے بُرا حال ہونا

swept *v.* (pa. t. & pa. p. of **sweep,** which see)

swerve (*swĕ*v*) *v.t.* & *i.* (cause to) turn aside suddenly اچانک مُڑنا (یا)، موڑنا، جھوک کھانا (یا) کھلانا deviate (*from* the right path, etc.) منحرف ہونا cause (ball) to swerve in air جھوک کھلانا *n.* swerving movement جھوک، انحراف

swift *adj.* (lit.) speedy, (reply, retribution, etc.) فوری quick (runner, *to do,* etc.) تیز *adv.* (poet.) swiftly تیزی سے، تیز *n.* (long-winged) insect-eating bird (e.g., a swallow) ایک قسم کا ابابیل تیز پرواز ابابیل **swiftly** *adv.* quickly جلدی سے، تیزی سے

swig (slang) *n.* draught of liquor شراب کا گھونٹ، چسکی *v.t.* & *i.* take draughts (of) چسکی لگانا

swill (swil) *v.t.* & *i.* (*swill out*), pour water over تریڑا دینا، کھنگالنا drink greedily ڈکوسنا *n.* inferior liquor ٹھرّا liquid food for pigs سُؤر کی مائع خوراک

swim *v.t.* & *i.* (*swim, swam, swum*) move oneself along in water تیرنا، پیرنا cause to do so تیرانا، پیرانا move swiftly سُبک رفتاری سے چلنا float (in) تیرنا be flooded (with water, tears, etc.) سے بھر جانا overflow (*with*) چھلک جانا (of head) be dizzy (سر) چکرانا (of something) seem to go round and round (*before* one's eyes) چکر کھانا، چکر کھاتا لگنا *n.* swimming تیرنا، پیرنا *go for a swim* تیرنے کے لیے جانا *be in the swim,* be participating in social functions تقریبات میں حصّہ لینا *be out of the swim* تقریبات وغیرہ سے الگ رہنا *swim suit,* (see *Addenda*) **swimming** *n.* تیراکی، پیراکی **swimmingly** *adv.* (of things or person) (go, get along, etc.) easily, with a swing بڑے مزے سے، آرام سے **swimmer** *n.* one who swims تیراک، پیراک

swindle (*swind-ĕl*) *v.t.* & *i.* cheat (someone *out of money,* etc.); get (money, etc., *out of* someone) fraudulently دھوکے سے لینا، ٹھگ لینا *n.* fraud ٹھگی، فریب، دھوکا inexpensive thing sold as a valuable دھوکے سے بیچا ہوا گھٹیا مال **swindler** *n.* one who swindles ٹھگ، دھوکے باز، عیّار، فریبی

swine (swɪn) *n.* (*pl.* the same) (lit.) pig سُؤر، خنزیر lover of filth گندگی کا شائق degraded person بے غیرت آدمی bestial person بہیمانہ خصلتوں والا

swing *v.t.* & *i.* (*swing, swung, swung*) (of something fixed at one end or side) move to and fro in a curve جھولنا (یا) جھلانا walk or run with a free, easy movement لپک کر چلنا turn in a curve مُڑنا (یا) موڑنا، گھومنا (یا) گھمانا *n.* swinging movement جھوٹا، جھونٹا (go) *with a swing,* easily, swimmingly آرام سے (ہونا)، بڑے مزے سے (ہونا) (be) *in full swing,* (be) in full operation پورے زور شور سے جاری ہونا seat held by ropes, etc., for swinging on پینگ **swing-shift** *n.* (see *Addenda*)

swipe (swɪp) *n.* (in cricket) reckless hard hit زور کی ہِٹ *v.t.* (in cricket) hit hard thus زور کی ہِٹ لگانا (slang) steal چرانا، چوری کرنا

swirl (*swĕ*l*) *v.t.* & *i.* (of liquid, air, dust, etc.) whirl, eddy, (*about* a place) (میں) چکر کھانا *n.* eddy چکّر

swish *v.t.* & *i.* swing (stick, whip, etc.) through the air with a hissing sound سڑاک سے مارنا، پھٹکارنا make such sound سڑاکا (of clothes, wind, etc.) move with a rustling sound سرسر کرنا (of heavy rain) fall with such sound چھم چھم پڑنا *n.* sound of heavy rain چھم چھم (یا) برسنا rustling سرسراہٹ sound of (or suggesting) a cane or wip being swished سڑاکا *adj.* (of clothes, etc.) fashionable, smart فیشن ایبل

switch (swich) *n.* device for making or breaking a connexion between railway points کینچی device for changing an electric circuit سُوئچ، بجلی کا بٹن thin twig or stick for whipping a horse, etc. چھڑی، قمچی، چابک *v.t.* & *i.* turn (electric current) بجلی کا بٹن دبانا **switch on** electric light, fan, radio, etc.. (بتی) جلانا، پنکھا وغیرہ چلانا *switch off* (بتی وغیرہ) بند کرنا move (train or tram) to another track کینچی بدلنا، کی پٹڑی بدلنا turn (one's thoughts or a conversation) from one subject to another بدلنا whip with a switch چابک لگانا (of a horse) swing (its tail, etc.) with a jerk دُم وغیرہ جھٹکے سے ہلانا (of tail, etc.) swing with a jerk جھٹکے سے ہلنا **switchback** *n.* railway that twists and turns up and down steep slopes ریل کی لہریا پٹڑی **swicthboard** *n.* apparatus with numerous switches, esp. for making (electric or telephone) connexions سُوئچ بورڈ، سُوئچ تختہ، بٹن تختہ.

swivel (*swiv*-el) *n.* freely moving joint consisting of a ring and pivot چول کَندا جس میں گھومنے والا، متحرک جوڑ، چول چھلّا *v.t.* & *i.* (-ll-) turn (as) on a swivel چول پر گھومنے **swivel-eyed** *adj.* squint-eyed بھینگا، گھومتا یا گھماتا

swollen (*swol*-ĕn) *v.* (pa. p. of **swell,** which see)

swoon *v.t.* & *i.* faint غش کھانا، کو غش آنا، غش کھا کر گرنا *n.* fainting fit غش، غشی، غشی کا دورہ

swoop *v.i.* (of a bird of prey) come (*down, on* or *upon* something) with a rush پر جھپٹنا، پر ٹوٹ پڑنا (colloq.) snatch away چھین لینا *n.* plunge (*of* a bird of prey) جھپٹ، جھپٹنا sudden hostile descent اچانک حملہ *with a swoop, at one fell swoop,* with a sudden hostile, descent ; swooping down جھپٹا مار کر

swop, swap (swop) (colloq.) *v.t.* & *i.* (-pp-) exchange (one thing *for* another) (سے) بدلنا *n.* such exchange ادلا بدلی

sword (sohd) *n.* long steel-bladed weapon of war تلوار (military slang) bayonet سنگین *put to the sword,* kill مار ڈالنا، قتل کرنا *cross* (or *measure*) *swords with,* (*a*) fight a sword-battle with سے تیغ آزمائی کرنا (*b*) dispute with سے بحث کرنا *draw the sword,* begin war تلوار نیام میں، لڑائی چھیڑنا *sheathe the sword,* cease war لڑائی ختم کرنا *throw* (*one's*) *sword into the scale,* back (one's) claim with big arms تلوار کے ذریعے فیصلہ (*the sword*), military power فوجی طاقت (*the sword*), arbitrament of war جنگ سے فیصلہ **swordfish** *n.* large sword-like fish کٹار مچھلی، تیغ ماہی **sword-law** *n.* military domination فوجی اقتدار **sword of justice,** judicial authority عدالت، انصاف **sword of the spirit,** word of God خدا کا کلام کی تلوار **sword-play** *n.* fencing شمشیر بازی repartee حاضر جوابی cut-and-thrust argument چوٹیں **swordsman** *n.* one having specified skill with the sword تیغ زن، شمشیر باز **swordsmanship** *n.* تیغ زنی، شمشیر بازی

swore, sworn *v.* (pa. t. & pa. p. respectively of **swear,** which see)

swot (swot) *v.i.* (slang) study hard پڑھائی میں محنت کرنا، سخت محنت سے پڑھنا *swot up* (*a subject, etc.*) سخت محنت سے یاد کرنا *n.* student interested in books rather than sports ; bookworm کتاب کا کیڑا hard study مطالعے میں سخت محنت effort needed for it پڑھائی کی محنت

swum (swum) *v.* (pa. t. & pa. p. of **swim,** which see)

sybarite (*sib*-a-rɪt) *n.* luxurious effeminate person عیش پرست، آرام طلب، بے ہمت عیاش **sybaritic** (-*rit*-) *adj.* عیش پرستانہ

sybil, sibyl (*sib*-il) *n.* pagan prophetess کاہنہ sorceress جادوگرنی fortune-teller فال کھولنے والی hag بدصورت بڑھیا، چڑیل

sycamore (*sik*-a-moh*) *n.* large fig-like Egyptian tree yielding hard wood سِکامُر shady tree (of the same species as maple) or its hard wood جمیز

a sycamore (sense 2)

sycophant (*sik*-o-fant) *n.* flatterer; toady بیجد خوشامدی، چاپلوس، لوڈی **sycophantic** (-*fant*-) *adj.* بیحد خوشامدی

sycophansy (sik-o-fan-si) *n.* flattery خوشامد، چاپلوسی، تملّق

syllabic *adj.*, **syllabication** *n.*, **syllabification** *n.*, **syllabize** *n.* (see under **syllable**)

syllable (*sil*-a-bĕl) *n.* word or division of word regarded as a unit of pronunciation and containing one vowel sound رکن تہجی، بول *not a syllable* ایک بول بھی نہیں، کوئی آواز نہیں *v.t.* (poet.) utter (word, name) منہ سے نکالنا **syllabry** (-ri) *n.* syllables used (as in Chinese) as characters بولوں والی الف بے **syllabic** (si-*lab*-ik) *adj.* of or in syllables رکن تہجی کا **syllabize** *v.t.* divide into syllables ارکان تہجی پر بانٹنا **syllabication, syllabification** *n.* division into syllables ارکان تہجی پر تقسیم uttering thus ایک ایک بول کرکے بولنا **syllabled** *adj.* having (one, two, etc.) syllables (اتنے) ارکان تہجی والا **mono-syllabic** *adj.* having one syllable ایک بول والا، ایک رکنی **di-syllabellic** *adj.* having two syllables دو بولوں والا، دو رکنی **tri-syllabic** *adj.* having three syllables تین بولوں والا، سہ رکنی **quadri-syllabic** *adj.* having four syllables چار بولوں والا، چہار رکنی **multi-syllabic,** *adj.* having many syllables کثیر الارکان

syllabus (*sil*-a-bus) *n.* outline of a prescribed course of studies نصاب outline or programme of college lectures, etc. خاکہ، نصاب

syllogism (*sil*-o-jizm) *n.* (logic) form of reasoning in which a *conclusion* is reached from two given or assumed propositions (called *major* and *minor premises*) and having a common thing (called the *middle term*) (صغریٰ اور کبریٰ سے) نتیجہ نکالنا، قیاس **syllogize** (*sil*-o-jiz) *v.t.* & *i.* put into this form قیاس کی صورت دینا

sylph (silf) *n.* elemental spirit of the ai[r] روح ہوا، ہوا پری slender, graceful young woman نازک اندام حسینہ

sylvan, silvan (*sil*-vĕn) *adj.* of woods دشتی، جنگل کا having woods جنگلوں والا

symbol (*sim*-bĕl) *n.* thing, etc., commonly regarded as typifying something نشان، نشانی،

symbolic (sim-*bol*-ik), **symbolical** (sim-*bol*-i-kĕl) *adj*. pertaining to, used as or using symbol(s) علامتی، اشارتی، رمزی اشاری، رمزی *be symbolic of*, be suggestive of کی علامت ہونا **symbolically** *adv*. اشارۃً، کنایۃً **symbolize** *v.t.* be a symbol of کی علامت ہونا treat (story, picture, etc.) not literally but allegorically کی تاویل کرنا use a symbol for کی علامت بنانا **symbolist** *n*. member of the mystic school of French poets of the late 19th and early 20th century who reacted against the drabness of realism and tried to write more subtle and musical verse اِشاری any writer or artist following these ideas in his field اِشاری **symbolism** *n*. theory or practice of symbolists اِشاریت system of symbols اِشارات، رموز representation by symbols اِشاریت، رمزیت study of the Christian creed علم عقائد مسیحی

symmetry (*sim*-et-ri) *n*. pleasant and balanced relation of parts, etc. تناسُب، موزونیت having two exactly similar things, etc., on either side توازُن، تشاکُل harmony ہم آہنگی **symmetrical** (-*met*-) *adj*. having symmetry متناسِب، متوازن، ہم آہنگ **symmetrically** *adv*. تناسُب (یا توازُن، تشاکُل، ہم آہنگی) لیے ہوئے

sympathetic *adj*., **sympathize** *v.i.* (see under **sympathy**)

sympathy (*sim*-pa-thi) *n*. sharing the feelings of others ہمدردی compassion (*for*) غمخواری، ہمدردی، دِلسوزی *feel sympathy for* سے ہمدردی رکھنا (یا) کرنا *in sympathy, with*, agreeing with (a proposal, etc.) سے متفق *universal sympathy* (*for*) سے ہر ایک کی ہمدردی **sympathetic** *adj*. having sympathy ہمدرد showing sympathy اِظہارِ ہمدردی کرنے والا caused by sympathy ہمدردانہ، متعلق *sympathetic ailment* (*etc.*), subsidiary disease (etc.) as a reaction to one already existing مرض بالاشتراک، ذیلی بیماری **sympathize** *v.i.* feel or express sympathy (*with*) سے ہمدردی رکھنا، سے اظہارِ ہمدردی کرنا **sympathizing** *adj*. compassionate اظہارِ ہمدردی والا *n*. compassion اظہارِ ہمدردی

symphony (*sim*-fo-ni) *n*. elaborate instrumental composition in three (or usu. four) parts for full orchestra سمفنی، کئی گتوں کا سازینہ (poet.) harmonious sounds ہم آہنگ آوازیں

symposium (sim-*poh*-zi-um) *n*. set of articles on one subject from various writers and viewpoints presented at one meeting مجلسِ مذاکرہ after-dinner drinking-party in ancient Greece محفل رقص و سرود، بزمِ مے

symptom (*simp*-tum, or *sim*-tum) *n*. change in the body's condition indicating illness بیماری کی علامت، عرض sign of the existence (of something) (کی) علامت **symptomatic** (-*mat*-) *adj*. serving as a symptom (*of*) (کی) علامت، عرضی

syn- (sin), **syl**- (sil), **sym**- (sim), **sys**- (sis), **sy**- (si), *pref*. with مع، با، بہ، ہم

synagogue (*sin*-a-gog) *n*. Jewish assembly for religious teaching and worship یہودیوں کی دینی مجلس Jewish house of worship یہودی معبد، صلات **synagogical** (-*gog*- or -*goj*-) *adj*. pertaining to a synagogue صلاتی

synchronize (*sink*-ro-nīz) *v.t.* & *i*. (cause to) happen simultaneously بیک وقت ہونا (یا) کرنا، توافق agree in time (*with*) کے ساتھ واقع ہونا (of clocks, watches, etc.,) make them show exactly the same time کا وقت ملانا **synchronization** *n*. ہم وقت ہونا (یا) کرنا یا ثابت کرنا، وقت ملانا

syncopate (*sink*-o-payt) *v.t.* shorten (word) by omitting letters حذف کرنا invert accents in music سُروں کا زور اُلٹنا **syncopation** *n*. حذف، سُروں کا زور اُلٹنا **syncope** (*sink*-o-pi) *n*. syncopation حذف؛ غش، غشی، غشی کا دورہ fainting fit سُروں کا زور اُلٹنا

syndicate (*sind*-i-kayt) *n*. committee of delegates (called *syndics*) (of associations of individuals or firms) set up for promoting common interests سنڈیکیٹ، تعاونی انجمن special committee of the Senate of some universities سنڈیکیٹ، مجلسِ خصوصی organization controlling a number of newspapers شرکتِ اخبارات organization providing articles, etc., to periodicals مقالہ رسان ادارہ *v.t.* form into a syndicate تعاونی انجمن بنانا publish (article, picture, etc.,) in numerous newspapers, etc., through a syndicate مقالہ رسان ادارے کے واسطے سے متعدد جرائد میں شائع کرنا **syndic** *n*. member of a syndicate سنڈیکیٹ کا رکن **syndicalism** *n*. late 19th century trade unionism of France aiming at the transfer of economic and political power into the workers' hands through general strikes فرانس کی اشتراکی مزدور تحریک، ہڑتالی اشتراکیت **syndacalist** *n*. advocate of syndicalism ہڑتالی اشتراکیت

syne (sīn) *adv*. (Scottish word for) since (used in the phrase :) *auld lang syne*, days of long ago اگلے وقت، بھلے زمانے

synecdoche (si-*nek*-do-ki) *n*. part used to represent whole in names, used as a figure of speech بدل، لزوم مالا یلزم

synod (*sin*-od) *n*. special assembly of the representatives of a Church to discuss matters of policy and creed کلیسائی مجلس

synodal, synodic, synodical *adj*. pertaining to a synod کلیسائی مجلس کا

synonym (*sin*-o-nim) *n.* word with the same meaning as another in the same language مُترادِف، ہم معنیٰ **synonymous** (si-*non*-i-mus) *adj.* of the same meaning (*with*) کے مُترادِف **synonymity** (-*nim*-) *n.* being synonyms مُترادِف ہونا **synonymy** *n.* synonymity مُترادِف ہونا use of redundant synonyms (as *unless* and *until*) ضرُوری مُترادِفات کا اِستِعمال
synopsis (si-*nop*-sis) *n.* (pl. *synopses*) outline (of a book, etc.), given at its opening or separately خاکہ
syntax (*sint*-aks) *n.* structure of phrases or sentences ترکیبِ کلام body of such rules نحو **syntactic, syntactical** *adj.* of syntax نحوی
synthesis (*sinth*-e-sis) *n.* (pl. *syntheses*) combining of separate parts, substances, sentences, etc., into a whole (as opposed to their *analysis*) ترکیب result of this process مُرکّب **synthetic** (sin-*thet*-ik) *adj.* (natural produce) prepared artificially ترکیبی، مصنوعی brought into being by synthesis
syphilis (*sif*-i-lis) *n.* a infectious venereal disease آتشک، گرمی
syphon, siphon (*si*-fon) *n.* pipe with unequal legs for conveying liquid سیفن، سارقہ tapped bottle for aerated water سوڈے کی ٹونٹی دار بوتل *v.t.* & *i.* (cause to) flow through syphon سیفن میں سے گزرنا یا گزارنا
syringe (*si*-rinj) *n.* any kind of pump for squirting or injecting liquids پچکاری *v.t.* clean with syringe پچکاری سے دھونا inject with a syringe پچکاری لگانا
syrup, sirup (*si*-rup) *n.* thick sugary liquid often containing some drug or flavour شربت refined molasses راب
system (*sis*-tĕm) *n.* orderly arrangement (of words, ideas, theories, things, etc.), working together to form a co-ordinated whole نظام methods or principles (*of*) نظام، اُصُول، طریق، طرز classification تقسیم، اِصطِفاف (*the system*), the human body جسمِ انسانی، بدن **systematic** (-*mat*-) *adj.* methodical باقاعدہ not unprincipled مُنظّم، بااُصُول according to a plan سوچا سمجھا not casual intentional پکّا **systematically** *adv.* methodically باقاعدہ، بااُصُول طور پر
systole (*sis*-toh-li) *n.* contraction of the heart or other organ اِنقباض (opp. of *diastole* which means dilation) اِنبساط

T

t, T (tee) (pl. *t's* or *ts*) the 20th letter of the English alphabet ٹی *to a t*, precisely بالکل ٹھیک *dot the i's and cross the t's*, make the details or meanings quite clear پُوری طرح واضح کرنا
ta (tah) (children's or jocular word for) thank you *ta muchly for it* شکریہ بڑی مہربانی
tab *n.* small piece fixed to a garment, etc., as a badge, handle or ornament تکمہ، گھنڈی، پٹی red tab worn over senior army officer's collar لال پٹی (colloq.) check حساب *keep tab* (or *tabs*) *on*, (*a*) keep an account of کا حساب رکھنا (*b*) have under observation پر نظر رکھنا
tabard (*tab*-ĕ*d) *n.* garment worn over armour زرہ بکتر کے اُوپر کا لبادہ
tabby (*tab*-i) *n.* coarse wavy silk ہلکا لہریا ریشم دریائی (also *tabby-cat*), female cat, esp. grey or brownish with dark stripes دھاری دار بلی spiteful female gossip (esp. a spinster) بدطینت اور بکی کنواری بڑھیا
tabernacle (*tab*-e*-na-kĕl) *n.* tent used by the Israelies as sanctuary in their wandering مظلّہ temporary house عارضی گھر body so regarded فانی جسم **tabernacled** *adj.* with ornamental canopy مظلّہ دار **feast of the Tabernacles** name a Jewish festival عیدِ المظال
table (*tab*-ĕl) *n.* flat piece of wood raised on legs for sitting at it میز person sitting at a table میز کے گرد بیٹھے ہُوئے لوگ (also *dining-table*), table for dining at کھانے کی میز، دسترخوان *lay the table* دسترخوان چُننا *keep a good table*, provide good meals اچھا کھانا دینا chart, list, catalogue, etc., (of information, etc.) نقشہ، جدول *multiplication table* پہاڑے *time-table* اوقات نامہ *time and fare table* اوقات و کرایہ نامہ *v.t.* make a chart جدول میں درج کرنا، کا نقشہ بنانا present (motion) for discussion بحث کے لیے پیش کرنا put (motion or bill) on the speaker's table to put it off ملتوی کرنا **tabular** (*tab*-ew-lĕ*) *adj.* arranged in tables جدولی **tabulate** (*tab*-ew-layt) *v.t.* arranged in tables کا جدول بنانا، کا نقشہ بنانا **tabulator** (-*lay*-) *n.* one calculating and making tables جدول ساز machine for doing

so جدوَل ساز **tabula rasa** (*tab*-ew-la-*ray*-sa) *n.* surface ready to be written صاف سلیٹ infant's consciousness بچّے کا اثر پزیر ذہن material for one to fashion according to will مرضی کے مطابق ڈھالنے کی چیز **table-cloth** *n.* cloth for spreading over a table میز پوش **table-land** *n.* plateau سطحِ مرتفع **table-knife** non-folding knife چھری **table-spoon** *n.* large spoon for serving food بڑا چمچہ **table-tennis** *n.* ping-pong پنگ پانگ **table d'hote** *n.* (also *table dinner*), meals served at a hotel at a fixed price مقرّرہ قیمت کا کھانا

tableau (*tab*-loh) *n.* (pl. *tableaux* pr. -lohz) picture تصویر dramatic situation regarding a story at the end of it مؤثر ڈرامائی واقعہ sudden effective scene ڈرامائی منظر **tableau vivant** (-vi-vohn) *n.* group of motionless persons representing a person or scene خاموش نظارہ، تصویر آسا منظر

tablet (*tab*-let) *n.* flat sheet (of wood, etc.) for writing تختی such inscribed sheet of stone, bronze, etc., fixed to or built in a wall لوح، تختی cake (of soap) (صابن) ٹکیہ thin disc of compressed medicine ٹکیہ، قرص flat hard sweet مٹھائی کی ٹکیہ **tabloid** *n.* small table of medicine چھوٹی ٹکیہ (U.S.) small-sized sensational pictorial newspaper that gives its news in an easily readable form چھوٹا سنسنی خیز مصوّر اخبار *adj.* sensational (journalism) سنسنی خیز

taboo, tabu (ta-*boo*) *n.* act or thing forbidden or held sacred by primitive religion مقدّس، حرام rules or beliefs forbidding it by its sanctification رسمِ تحریم *put under a taboo*, forbid ممنوع قرار دینا *adj.* (used only at the end) prohibited ممنوع *that is taboo* یہ ممنوع ہے **taboo** *v.t.* (*taboo*, *tabooed*, *tabooed*) forbid, put under a taboo ممنوع قرار دینا **tabooed** (ta-*bood*) *adj.* forbidden ممنوع avoided by tacit consent جائز سمجھا جانا

tabor, tabour (*tay*-bě*) small drum طنبورہ

tabular *adj.*, **tabulate** *v.t.*, **tabulator** *n.* **tabula rasa** *n.* (see under **table**)

tacit (*tas*-it) *adj.* implicit, understood without being put into words بن کہے، خاموش *tacit consent* خاموش رضامندی، الخاموشی نیم رضا **taciturn** (*tas*-i-tě*n) *adj.* in the habit of talking little کم گو، کم سخن

taciturnity (tas-i-*tě*n*-i-ti) *n.* being taciturn چپ کی عادت، کم گوئی، کم سخنی

tack (*tak*) *n.* small, flat-head nail کیل، پِن، چوڑا کوکا، میخ long loose stitch for temporary, etc., fastening لمبا ٹانکا، نگندا sailing vessel's obliquely windward course as determined by the position of sails سمتِ جہاز *on the starboard tack*, with the wind on the right داہنی جانب course of action راہِ عمل، راستہ *on the right* (or *wrong*) *tack* صحیح (یا غلط) راہ پر *try another tack* نئی راہ آزمانا rope, etc., for securing sail-corner in a particular position بادبانی رسّا substance چیز food کھانا *hard-tack*, ship's hard biscuit سخت جہازی بسکٹ *v.t.* & *i.* fasten (or *down*) with tacks میخوں سے لگانا put large stitches لمبے لمبے ٹانکے لگانا، نگندے لگانا attach منسلک کرنا sail in a zig-zag course ٹیڑھا میڑھا چلنا change course of action طرزِ عمل بدلنا، مسلک بدلنا

tackle (*tak*-ěl) *n.* set of ropes and pulleys for lifting weights or sails جرِّ ثقیل equipment (for fishing, etc.) سامان seizing (opposite player in rugger, thief, etc.) پکڑنا *v.t.* & *i.* seize (opposite player in rugger, thief, etc.) گتھم گتھا ہونا، پکڑنا do (a piece of work) کرنا deal with (a problem, etc.) پر غور کرنا، کو سلجھانا deal with (a person) tactfully سے نبٹنا

a tackle (sense 1)

tact (takt) *n.* skill in handling persons and situations successfully without causing offence موقع شناسی، ہوشیاری، سلیقہ، عقل **tactful** *adj.* (of person) full of tact موقع شناس، ہوشیار (of action) marked by tact موقع شناسی کا **tactless** *adj.* lacking tact بے عقل، موقع ناشناس، بے تکا، زبان کا پھوہڑ **tactfully** *adv.* in a tactful manner موقع شناسی سے **tactlessly** *adv.* displaying lack of tact بے عقلی سے، موقع ناشناسی سے

tactics (*tak*-tiks) *n.* *pl.* (usu. used with *sing.* verb) art of disposing ships or armed forces for or during battle ترتیبِ فوج کا فن، مصافیات schemes, etc., for carrying out a policy تدبیر، حکمتِ عملی **tactical** *adj.* of tactics شاطرانہ، ترتیبِ فوج سے متعلّق، مصافیاتی **tactician** (tak-*tish*-ěn) *n.* expert in tactics ماہرِ مصافیات

tactile (*tak*-til, or *tak*-tIl), **tactual** (*tak*-tew-ěl) *adj.* of the sense of touch لمسی having this sense لمس پذیر

tadpole (*tad*-pohl) *n.* partly developed frog or toad مینڈک کا بچہ

taffeta (*taf*-ě-ta) *n.* thin and glossy but stiff silk material تافتہ، دریائی

taffrail, tafferel *n.* railing round ship's stern جہاز کا عقبی کٹہرا

tag *n.* loose, ragged end ناہموار سرا metal end on a lace دھات کا سرا lace with transverse metal-ends ٹیگ label on luggage or article for showing price or address چٹ trite quotation پامال مقولہ *v.t.* (-gg-) join (a piece of writing, etc., *to* or *on to* another) جوڑنا، جوڑ دینا

follow (someone or *after* someone) closely دُم چھلّا ہونا، دُم چھلّا بنا ہوا ہونا fasten a tag to دھات کا سرا لگانا put a tag through ٹیگ لگانا

tail (tayl) *n.* long hanging part at the back of an animal دُم، پونچھ *turn tail,* run away, back out دُم دبا کر بھاگنا *with the tail between the legs,* subdued ہار کر، مار کھا کر *tails up,* (of person) in fighting form لڑنے مرنے پر تیار anything like a tail دُنبالہ back or lower part of anything پچھلا حصّہ، دُنبالہ the worst (*of* the group) سب سے خراب دُم (often *pl.*) (in tossing) side of a coin opposite the one with the head زنجیر *head or tail?* which of these sides you choose for yourself? تصویر یا کہ زنجیر *Heads we win tails you lose;* we win in either case چت بھی میری پٹ بھی میری entail وہ جائداد جو صرف صُلبی اولاد کو مِلے، مشروط ملکیّت *adj.* entailed مشروط، مشروط بہ شادی *v.t.* & *i.* having a tail دُمدار join (*to*) سے جوڑنا (*tail off*), become smaller (towards the end) آخر کی طرف چھوٹا ہوتا جانا **tail-coat** *n.* men's evening dress or its coat دُمدار سُوٹ یا کوٹ، دو پاکھا کوٹ **tail-light** *n.* lamp at the back (*of* car, train, etc.) عقبی بتّی **tail-spin** *n.* spinning-drive of aircraft چکّر غوطہ، چکّر کُھنبی

tailor (*tay-lĕ**) *n.* maker of men's clothing درزی (as opposed to a *dressmaker* or زنانہ درزی who stitches women's clothes) *v.t.* cut out and stitch سینا *well-tailored,* (*a*) with well-made clothes on نفیس لباس پہنے (*b*) well-stitched نفیس سِلا ہُوا **tailoring** *n.* stitching of clothes or its charges سِلائی **tailor-made** *adj.* women's well-fitting clothes stitched by a tailor درزی سے سِلے ہُوئے (زنانہ کپڑے)

taint (taynt) *n.* trace of (bad quality, infection, etc.) داغ، شائبہ *v.t.* & *i.* make or become infected خراب ہونا (یا کرنا)، غلیظ ہونا (یا کرنا) (of meat) begin to putrefy خراب ہونے لگنا have or impute some bad quality داغدار ہونا، (یا بنانا)

take (tayk) *v.t.* & *i.* (*take; took* pr. tŭk; *taken* pr. *tayk*-ĕn) grasp with the hand or grasp with an instrument, etc. پکڑنا، لینا *take (someone's) hand* کا ہاتھ پکڑنا *take (something) up with (one's) fingers* انگلیوں سے پکڑنا *take hold of (something)* پکڑنا capture قبضہ کرنا surprise آلینا catch by pursuit جا پکڑنا، جا لینا win (prize) پانا fall ill with a (disease) کو (بیماری) ہونا *be taken ill* بیمار ہونا *catch cold* زکام ہونا be set ablaze by (fire) کو (آگ) لگنا، جلنے لگنا attract (the fancy, etc.) کو اچھا لگنا *be not much taken with the idea* کو یہ خیال کچھ اچھا نہ لگنا carry (something *to* a place) لے جانا accompany (someone *to* a place) لے جانا convey (someone *in* car, etc.) چھوڑ آنا، لے جانا eat (something) کھانا drink (something) پینا inhale (breath) (سانس) لینا avail oneself of or get permission for (a holiday) لینا enjoy (bath) کرنا charge or receive (money) وصول کرنا، لینا envince (interest *in* something) (سے دلچسپی) لینا feel (pride, pleasure *in* something) (پر فخر) محسوس کرنا rent (a house, etc.) کرائے پر لینا hire (a tonga, taxi, etc.) کرائے کرنا، کرائے پر لینا get (newspaper, etc.) لینا make (*notes of*) (نوٹ) لینا یا لکھنا، (یادداشت) قلمبند کرنا (*of* work) spread over (a period of time) (اتنا وقت) لینا، میں (اتنا وقت) لگنا require کی ضرورت ہونا *It takes two to make a quarrel* دونوں ہاتھ سے بجتی ہے suppose, presume خیال کرنا، سمجھنا *take (something) for granted* کو تسلیم شدہ بات جاننا، کو طے شدہ امر سمجھنا *take (someone) to be (good, etc.),* mistake (him) for a (good, etc., person) کو غلطی سے (اچھا وغیرہ) سمجھ بیٹھنا (of a vaccine, etc.) have effect اثر کرنا (of plant) strike root لگ جانا، جڑ پکڑنا (of photographic subject) turn out (well or badly) اُترنا، نکلنا (of thing, exhibition, etc.), prove attractive مقبول ہونا choose and make one's own (wife) سے شادی کرنا go on board (ship, train, bus, etc.) پر سوار ہونا، پکڑنا secure (photograph) اُتارنا have (aim) (نشانہ) باندھنا ascertain (measurement, etc.) (پیمائش وغیرہ) لینا have recourse to (thought, measure, steps, flight, etc.) اختیار کرنا enter upon (journey) کرنا exert (care, heed, etc.) کرنا accept (pupils, lodgers, responsibility, view, etc.) قبول کرنا be allowed (precedence, degree) کو ملنا submit to (orders, consequences, insult, punishment, advice, hint) قبول کرنا conceive (alarm, comfort, pity, fright offence, umbrage, etc.) محسوس کرنا muster up (courage, resolution) کرنا understand (meaning, speaker) سمجھنا allow oneself (time) لینا hold (catch) کیچ کرنا catch out (batsman) کیچ آؤٹ کرنا habitually consume استعمال کرنا *take orders,* be ordained پادری بننا become popular ہر دلعزیز ہونا، مقبول عام ہونا *n.* amount taken جو کچھ لیا ہو، لیا ہُوا (*Phrases:*) *take after (a relation),* resemble (him) in looks کی شکل پر ہونا *take back (one's words, take (them) back,* withdraw (them) واپس لینا *take (something) back* واپس لے لینا *take (something) down* (*a*) lower it نیچے کرنا (*b*) write down (notes, etc.) لکھنا، قلمبند کرنا *take (someone) down,* lower (his) pride کا غرور توڑنا، کا دماغ ٹھکانے لگانا *take (someone)* in, (*a*) receive (him) as a guest, etc. کا میزبان بننا (*b*) deceive, cheat کو فریب دینا **take** (*something*) **in** (*a*) understand (it) سمجھ لینا ، سمجھ جانا (*b*) see at a glance ایک نظر میں دیکھ لینا (*c*) receive (newspaper, etc.), regularly باقاعدگی سے منگوانا (*d*) reduce the area, width, etc., of (*e.g.*, a garment) کا گھیرا (وغیرہ) چھوٹا کرنا ، کو چھوٹا کرنا (*e*) include کو شامل کرنا *take* (*someone*) *in charge*, arrest (him) کو گرفتار کرنا *take* (*someone*) *into* (*one's*) *confidence*, trust (him) with a secret کو راز کی بات بتانا *take it into* (*one's*) *head to* (*do*), conceive the idea of (doing) کا خیال سر میں سمانا *take it easy*, not to hurry or exert oneself آرام سے کام کرنا *Take it easy* ' آرام سے ، دھیرج سے ' *take* (*someone*) *in the act of*, catch (him) red-handed کرتے ہوئے جا پکڑنا *take it that*, assume سمجھنا *Take it*, suffer punishment سزا بھگتنا *take liberties* (*with*), disregard etiquette کھل کھیلنا (یا) ، زیادتی کرنا *take* (*one's*) *life in* (*one's*) *hand*, go alone in danger خطرے میں تنہا جانا *take notice of*, (*a*) show somehow that one has noticed سے آگاہی کا اظہار کرنا (*b*) comment on it پر تبصرہ کرنا *take no*, accept a refusal ناں سن لینا ، انکار قبول کر لینا *take-off*, *n*. (*a*) mimicry نقل (*b*) place from where one jumps جہاں سے کودا جائے (*c*) (of aircraft) ground to run along and take off پرواز گاہ (*d*) (in films) scene that has been photographed فلمایا ہوا منظر ، شاٹ *take off* (*a*) remove (clothes, hat, shoes, etc.) اتارنا (*b*) deduct وضع کرنا ، کاٹنا *take* (*report, etc.*) *as read*, include without being read پڑھے گئے بغیر کارروائی میں شامل کر لینا *take on*, (*a*) undertake (work) کام کا ذمہ لینا ، اپنے سر لینا (*b*) engage (workers) (مزدور) رکھنا (*c*) assume (some quality or appearance) اختیار کرنا *take out*, (*a*) obtain (licence, etc.) لینا (*b*) obtain (insurance policy) بیمہ کرانا (*c*) remove (stain) دور کرنا *take* (*something*) *over*, take charge of or succeed to the management or ownership of کام سنبھالنا ، قبضہ ہونا *take place*, occur واقع ہونا ، وقوع پذیر ہونا *take rise* (*in*), come into being from (سے) شروع ہونا *take sides*, declare one's sympathies in a dispute طرفداری کرنا *take stock*, *take stock of* (see under *stock*) یا جائزہ لینا *take* (*someone's*) *temperature* کو تھرمامیٹر لگانا *take the cake* (or *biscuit*), (slang) surpass all سب سے بازی لے جانا *take the chair*, become the chairman and start proceedings as such کرسیٔ صدارت پر بیٹھنا ، کارروائی شروع کرنا *take the lead* (*in*), assume leadership (in) کی قیادت کرنا ، میں بڑھ چڑھ کر حصہ لینا ، میں نمایاں حصہ لینا *take the liberty* (*of doing*), presume (to do) کرنے کی جرأت کرنا *take the offensive*, begin the attack (جھگڑے یا حملے میں) پہل کرنا ، جارحیت پر اترنا *take the wind out of* (*one's*) *sails*, frustrate (him) by telling (him) something کے پیروں تلے سے زمین نکال لینا *take* (*something*) *to heart*, be grieved by دل کو لگنا *take to* (*one's*) *heels*, run away بھاگ جانا *take to flight* بھاگ جانا *take to* (*someone*, or *something*), form a liking for کو پسند آنا *take to* (*something* or *doing it*), adopt it اختیار کرنا *take* (*someone*) *to wife*, marry (her) سے شادی کرنا *take up*, (*a*) lift اٹھانا (*b*) absorb جذب کرنا (*c*) occupy (time or space) لینا (*d*) attract (attention) ملتفت کرنا (*e*) arrest (person) گرفتار کرنا (*f*) proceed to deal with کی طرف توجہ کرنا (*g*) interrupt (speaker) کی تقریر میں بول اٹھنا (*h*) correct (speaker) کی غلطی کی طرف اشارہ کرنا *take upon* (*oneself*), assume (burden or responsibility) اٹھانا *take upon* (*oneself*) *to do*, presume to do کرنے کی جسارت کرنا *take up the cudgels* (*on behalf of*), fight (it) out کی زور شور سے حمایت شروع کرنا *take wind*, become known مشہور ہونا *take* (*one's*) *audience with* (*one*), convince (them) as (one) proceeds کو ہمنوا بنا لینا **taking** *adj*. contagious متعدی attractive دلکش *n*. agitated condition اضطراب (*pl*.) amount of money received by a shop, etc., during a given period کل آمدنی ، مجموعی یافت **take-home pay** *n*. (see *Addenda*)

tale (tayl) *n*. story قصہ ، کہانی *fairy tales* پریوں کی کہانیاں account ماجرا ، سرگزشت scandal رسوا کن قصہ *tell tales* (*about someone*) کی بدگوئی کرتے پھرنا **tale-bearer** *n*. informer چغلخور (یا چغل) بدگو

talent (*tal*-ent) *n*. natural skill (*for*) طباعی ، جوہر persons with talent جوہر قابل ، صلاحیت ، ذہانت *there is no dearth of talent in Pakistan* پاکستان میں جوہر قابل کی کمی نہیں ancient weight 56 lb. and above ایک قدیمی وزن ، ٹیلنٹ ancient money worth £ 200 and above ایک قدیمی سکہ ، ٹیلنٹ **talented** (-id) *adj* having talent ذہین ، طباع ، جوہر قابل

talisman (*tal*-iz-man) *n*. charm supposed to bring good luck تعویذ

talk (tawk) *v.t.* & *i*. speak بولنا speak (*to*) سے بات کرنا give utterance to کہنا spread reports افواہیں پھیلانا persuade (someone *into*, *out of*) (کے حق میں یا کے خلاف) قائل کرنا *talk* (*something*) *over*, *talk* (*something*) *over with* (*someone*), discuss (it) to set (his) doubts at rest بحث کرکے سمجھانا ، بحث کرکے شکوک دور کرنا *talk* (*someone*) *out of doing* (*something*), persuade (him) not to do it کو خیال ترک کرنے پر آمادہ کرنا *talk* (*someone*) *round*, make him agree to something thus کو قائل کرنا *n*. talking بولنا ، بات کرنا informal lecture (*on the radio or otherwise*) تقریر conversation گفتگو ، بات چیت ، باتیں *small talk*, conversation on unimportant subjects بیکار

باتیں، ادھر اُدھر کی باتیں **tall talk**, boastful exaggeration شیخی (*become*) *talk of the town*, (become) someone or something) everyone is talking about ہر ایک کی زبان پر ہونا، کا گھر گھر چرچا ہونا **talkee-talkee** (tawk-) *n.* lingo غیر ملکی زبان جو سمجھ میں نہ آئے **talkative** (*tawk*-a-tive) *adj.* talking a lot باتونی، بکّو، بکواسی **talkies** (*tawk*-iz) *n. pl.* (colloq.) sound films (opp. *movies*) ٹاکی، بولتے فلم، متکلّم فلم

tall (tawl) *adj.* (of persons) of more than ordinary height لمبا *six-foot tall, six feet tall* چھ فٹ لمبا *How tall are you?* تمہارا قد کتنا ہے higher than surrounding زیادہ اونچا hard to believe; exaggerated (talk, story) شیخی، شیخی کی باتیں، شیخیاں ناقابلِ تسلیم excessive; unreasonable (request) *adv.* with exaggeration شیخیاں بگھار کر *talk tall* شیخیاں بگھارتے ہوئے کہنا **tallness** *n.* being tall لمبا ہونا

tallow (*tal*-oh) *n.* hard fat (used for making candles, etc.) سخت چربی *adj.* made of tallow سخت چربی کا

tally (*tal*-i) *v.t.* & *i.* cause (accounts) to agree حساب ملانا (of stories, accounts or amounts) correspond (or *with*) آپس میں ملنا، (کے) مطابق ہونا *n.* score حساب، گنتی، لیکھا، کھاتا piece of wood divided into halves retained by parties and having equal notches of score on them گنتی کے نشان والی لکڑی

tally-ho (*tal*-i-hoh) *int.* huntsman's cry on catching sight of the quarry لش لش *n.* this cry للکار، لہکار *v.t.* & *i.* urge on (hounds) thus للکارنا

Talmud (*tal*-mud) *n.* fundamental code of Jewish law comprising written law, traditions and comments تالمد، تالمود

talons (*tal*-unz) *n. pl.* claws of a bird of prey پنجہ، چنگل

tamarind (*tam*-a-rind) *n.* (very sour fruit of) a tropical tree املی، تمرِ ہندی

tambour (*tam*-boo*) *n.* small drum طنبورہ، دف round frame for embroidery گول اڈّا، کارچوبی اڈّا

tambourine (tam-*boo*-reen) shallow drum with one skin and jingles طنبورہ، دف

tame *adj.* not wild; pet (animal) پالتو، اہلی dull (scenery, etc.) بے تکلف، بے کیف of weak character کمزور، ودّو *v.t.* make tame پالتو بنانا، رام کرنا curb دبانا humble کچل دینا، بل نکال دینا **tamer** *n.* one who tames wild animals پالتو بنانے والا

tam-o'-shanter (-*shant*-) **tammy** *n.* well-known round woollen cap fitting the head closely but bulging out at the top to provide a sort of brim

tamper (*tam*-pě*) *v.i.* meddle (*with* document, etc.) میں تحریف کرنا **tampering** *n.* تحریف

tan *adj.* yellowish-brown *n.* yellowish-brown colour of کتھئی رنگ sun-burnt skin سانولا پن *v.t.* & *i.* (-nn-) make (an animal's skin) into leather (چمڑا) کمانا، دباغت کرنا، کھال رنگنا make or become brown with sunburn سنولا، سانولا ہونا یا کرنا (slang) thrash خوب پیٹنا، گندی کرنا **tanner** *n.* workman who tans skins چمڑا کمانے والا، کھالیں رنگنے والا، دباغت کرنے والا **tannery** (*tan*-ě-ri) *n.* place where skins are tanned کھالیں رنگنے کا کارخانہ، کارخانۂ دباغت **tanning** *n.* چمڑا کمانا، کھالیں رنگنا، دباغت

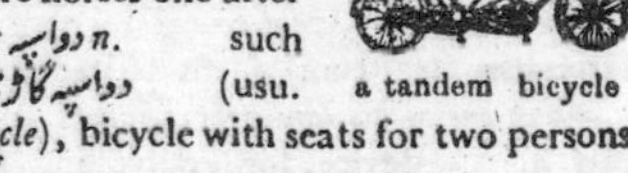
a tandem bicycle

tandem (*tand*-em) *adv.* with two or more horses one after the other *n.* دو اسپہ such carriage دو اسپہ گاڑی (usu. *tandem bicycle*), bicycle with seats for two persons دُہری سیکل

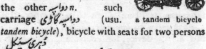

tang *n.* sharp smell تیز بو characteristic taste (*of*) خاص مزہ part of tool fitting into the handle دستے کے اندر والی نوک *v.t.* & *i.* (cause to) make sharp sound (of a string, etc.) ٹن کرنا، ٹن کی آواز نکالنا

tangent (*tanj*-ent) *n.* straight line touching a curve but unable to cut it even if drawn longer مماس *common tangent* مماس مشترک *tangent of an angle*, (in mathematics) ratio of the perpendicular to the base قدر مماسی *go* (or *fly*) *off at a tangent*, change suddenly from one line of thought to another یکایک بات بدل لینا

tangerine (tanj-ě-*reen*) *n.* small loose-skinned orange سنترہ، سنگترہ (*Tangerine*), a native of Tangiers طنجہ کا باشندہ

tangible (*tanj*-i-bel) *adj.* that which can be touched محسوس clear and definite (proof, etc.) واضح، قطعی

tangle (*tang*-el) *n.* confused mass (of string hair, etc.) گچھا *v.t.* & *i.* make or become confused, disordered اُلجھانا (یا) اُلجھنا، اُلجھن میں ڈالنا

tango (*tang*-oh) *n.* slow South American dance for two persons ٹانگو (ناچ)

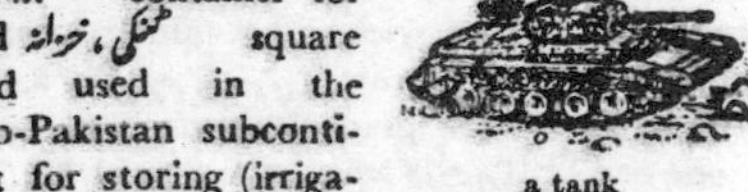
a tank

tank *n.* container for fluid ٹنکی، خزانہ square pond used in the Indo-Pakistan subcontinent for storing (irrigation or other) تالاب armoured fighting vehicle moving on caterpiller track ٹینک، عرّابہ **tanker** *n.* ship with tanks for carrying oil نفت بردار جہاز **tankage** *n.* amount that a tank will hold ٹنکی کی گنجائش

tankard (*tank*-ĕ*d) *n.* tall metal mug (usu. with a hinged lid) for beer بیئر کا جَسام ، جام بُوزہ
tantalization *n.*, **tantalize** *v.t.* (see under **Tantalus**)
Tantalus (*tant*-a-lus) *Cl. myth.* a son of the Greek god of gods, Zeus, who divulged his father's secrets and was punished by being made to stand in water up to his chin, the water receded whenever he wanted to drink it تنٹلس **tantalize** (*tant*-a-liz) *v.t.* tease someone by raising hopes which will not be realized ترسانا کلپانا **tantalizing** *adj.* ترسانے والا **tantalization** *n.* ترسانا
tantamount (*tant*-a-mount) *adj.* equivalent (*to* something) کے مُترادف
tantrum (*tan*-trum) *n.* fit of bad temper بدمزاجی کا غلبہ *in one of his tantrums* جھلّایا ہُوا
tap *n.* device for controlling flow from a container, etc. ٹونٹی *on tap*, (of beer, etc.) ready for consumption as lying in a barrel with a tap تیار light blow تھپکی ، دستک *v.t.* let (fluid) out of something through a tap کی ٹونٹی کھولنا draw sap from (tree) by incising the bark چھید کر رَس نکالنا try someone *for* loan or information سے لینے کی کوشش کرنا try to obtain (loan or information *from*) سے لینا make a connexion of (the telephone) for listening secretly to the conversation of another ٹیلیفون ٹیپ کرنا ، ٹیلیفون پر دُوسروں کی باتیں خفیہ طور پر سُننا *v.t.* & *i.* (-pp-) give a tap (*at* the door) دستک دینا strike (someone) gently (*on* the shoulder, etc.) کو تھپکی دینا strike (one's foot, etc.) lightly (*on* something) پر مارنا **tap-dancing** *n.* dancing characterized by the tapping of the feet پاؤں کی تال والا ناچ
tape (tayp) *n.* long narrow strip فیتہ magnetized ribbon for recording sounds صَدائی فیتہ **tapemeasure** *n.* flexible tape of cloth, etc., marked for measuring کپڑے (وغیرہ) کا گز **tape-recorder** *n.* machine for recording sound on a sensitized magnetic ribbon (called a *tape*) and replaying it (فیتہ دار) صدا بند ، ٹیپ ریکارڈر
taper (tay-pe*) *n.* wick with a thin wax coating, burnt to give light پتلی موم بتّی ، مومی بتّی *v.t.* & *i.* make or become gradually narrower towards one end گاؤدُم ہونا یا بنانا *tapers off to a point* گاؤدم ہو کر بانکل باریک ہو جانا
tapestry (*tap*-es-tri) *n.* fabric with designs or pictures woven into it, used for decorating walls مُشجّر ، قالی بافت cloth made in its imitation for curtains, cushions etc. ٹیپسٹری پردوں والا کپڑا ، مُشجّر
tapioca (tap-i-*oh*-ka) *n.* a starchy food prepared in the form of grains from the tree called cassara کسارا سُوجی
tapster *n.* attendant serving liquor ساقی
tar (tah*) *n.* (also *coal-tar*), black, thick and sticky substance obtained from coal کولتار ، لُک *v.t.* (-rr-) cover with tar کولتار بچھانا **tarmac** *n* (also *tar-macadam*) mixture of tar and crushed stone used for road surfaces, etc. بجری اور کولتار کا مُرکّبا ، تارنگ tarred road for an aircraft to taxi
tarantula (ta-*rant*-ew-la) *n.* a large poisonous spider ترن تلا **tarantism** (-*rant*-) *n.* hysterical impulse to dance caused by its poison ترن تلا جُنُون **tarantella** (-*tel*-) *n.* dance supposed to cure it ترن تلا ناچ
taratantara (ta-ra-*tant*-a-ra) *n.* sound of a trumpet ترئی کی آواز
tarboosh *n.* tasselled Muslim cap ترکی ٹوپی
tardy (*tah**-di) *adj.* late دیر کرنے والا ، دیرباز slow سُست **tardily** *adv.* سُستی سے **tardiness** *n.* being tardy سُستی
tare (*tay*-ĕ*) *n.* a kind of weed ایک قسم کا خودرو چارہ allowance for wrapping, etc., deducted from gross weight ٹیر دھڑا ، کٹوتی *tare and let*, rule for such deduction صحیح وزن نکالنے کا گُر (یا اُصول) weight of motor-vehicle without load and fuel خالی موٹر کا وزن
target (*tah**-get) *n.* mark to aim at with arrow, gun, bomb, etc. نشانہ ، ہدف butt for scorn and criticism ہدف ، نشانہ ultimate figure, level, quantity, etc., aimed at in something (*e.g.*, savings, export, production, etc.) نصب العین ، منصوبہ ، پروگرام *adj.* (of area) that is the objective of bombing, etc. نشانہ ، ہدف
Targum (*tah**-gum) *n.* any of the ancient Aramaic versions of *the Bible* ترگم ، ترگوم ، ترجمہ
tariff (*ta*-rif) *n.* list of fixed charges for board and lodging at a hotel نرخ نامہ list of taxes on imports and exports محصول نامہ درآمد و برآمد customs duty on a particular category of imports for protecting home industry تامینی محصول
tarmac *n.*, **tar-macadam** *n.* (see under **tar**)
tarnation (tah*-*nay*-shen) (U. S. slang) (substitute for) damnation, damnable or damnably لعنت ، لعنتی ، ملعون
tarnish (*tah**-nish) *v.t.* & *i.* (of metal surfaces) (cause to) lose brightness چمک جاتی رہنا ، چمک ختم کر دینا sully (reputation, fair name, etc.) داغدار کرنا ، پر دھبہ لگانا

tarpaulin (tah*-*paw*-lin) *n.* sheet of canvas made water-proof with tar ترپال
tarry (*ta*-ri) *v.i.* (lit.) wait (for) رکا، اِنتظار کرنا، کی defer (going, coming, etc.) دیر راہ تکنا (یا دیکھنا) be tardy سُستی کرنا stay (*at, in*, etc., a place) کو لگنا رو والا ٹھہرنا، قیام کرنا *adj.* smeared with tar
tart (tah*t) *adj.* of acid taste ترش، کھٹا bitter (reply, etc.) ترش، تلخ *n.* fruit pie پھلوں والا سموسہ pastry with jam on or in it مربّے والی پیسٹری (slang) prostitute a tart (sense 1 & 2
tartan (*tah**těn) *n.* Scottish woollen fabric with brightly coloured stripes crossing one another at right angles چارخانہ اونی کپڑا، چوخانہ اونی کپڑا soldier of a Scottish regiment گھاگرا پلٹن کا سپاہی
tartar (tah*-te*) *n.* incrustation forming on the teeth دانت پر جمی ہوئی زردی، دانت کا میل (Tartar), native of Tartary تاتاری *adj.* (*Tartar*) intractable person وحشی، ناماٗنس *catch a Tartar*, find intended victim more formidable than oneself سیر کو سوا سیر ملنا *young Tartar*, ill-tempered child بدمزاج بچّہ
Tartarus (*tah***t*-a-rus) *n.* place of torture in Hades ترترس hell دوزخ
task (tahsk) *n.* assignment, set piece of work دیا ہوا کام، مفوّضہ کام *home-task*, homework گھر پر کرنے کے لیے دیا ہوا اسکول کا کام، گھر کا کام *take* (*someone*) *to task*, scold (him *for* or *about* something) سے سختی سے باز پرس کرنا *task. force*, unit of armed forces sent out on a special mission کارِ خاص پر بھیجی ہوئی فوج *v.t.* impose task on کو کام تفویض کرنا، پر کام کا بوجھ ڈالنا (of a task) put a strain on (someone's powers) پر زیادہ بوجھ ڈالنا **task force** *n.* part of land, sea and air forces separately or combined which is entrusted a special operation in a war مہم جو دستہ **task-master** *n.* one who imposes hard tasks on others کام کا بوجھ ڈالنے والا
tassel (*tas*-ěl) *n.* ornamental tuft of hanging threads, etc. پھندنا (یا) جھالر **tasselled** *adj.* having tassels پھندنے والا، جھالر دار
taste (tayst) *n.* sense of the tongue and mouth by which flavour is known ذائقہ *sweet to the taste*, مزیدار quality (*of* something) made known by this sense مزہ small quantity (*of* food) ذرا سا liking (*for*) ذوق (کا) *have a taste for* کا ذوق رکھنا *not to* (*one's*) *taste* کو ناپسند، کو ناگوار ability to enjoy beauty in art and literature ذوق ability to chose and use the best kind of behaviour, etc. ذوقِ سلیم، عقل *in good taste*, pleasing اچھا، پسندیدہ *in bad taste* برا، ناپسندیدہ، ناگوار *v.t.* & *i.* be aware of the taste of (something) چکھنا، (کا) مزہ چکھنا (of food, etc.) have a taste of (or *of*) کا مزہ ہونا (یا رکھنا) be suggestive of کی چاشنی رکھنا experience سے لطف اندوز ہونا **tasteful** *adj.* (of person) showing good taste باذوق، صاحبِ ذوق پسندیدہ، اچھا in good taste اچھی طرح، خوش **tastefully** *adv.* nicely, artistically ذوق سے **tasteless** *adj.* (of food) having little or no flavour بے مزہ، پھیکا in bad taste بدمزگی کا، ناگوار **tastelessly** *adv.* بدمزگی سے **tasty** *adj.* pleasing to the taste مزیدار، لذیذ **taster** *n.* one employed to test by tasting مزہ چکھ
tat *v.t.* & *i.* embroider edges by netting thread کنارے کے دھاگوں کی جالی بنانا، جالی دار، حاشیہ بنانا **tatting** *n.* such edgings کنارے کی دھاگوں کی جالی
ta-ta (ta-*tah*) *int.* (child's word for) good-bye خدا حافظ
Tate-Gallery *n.* permanent exhibition of pictures and sculptures in London ٹیٹ گیلری، لندن کا تصویر خانہ
tatter (*tat*-è*) *n.* (usu. *pl.*) rag چیتھڑا torn or loosely hanging piece of cloth, etc. دھجی، پھٹا ہوا ٹکڑا، پرزہ *in tatters*, (*a*) in rags چیتھڑوں میں (*b*) in torn strips پرزے پرزے، پھٹا پرانا **tattered** *adj.* ragged
tattle (*tat*-ěl) *v.i.* gossip ill-naturedly فضول بکواس کرنا *n.* ill-natured gossip بکواس، واہی تباہی باتیں
tattoo (ta-*too*) *v.t.* mark (someone's skin) with permanent patterns گودنا *n.* such marks گودنے کے نقوش beating of the drum to call soldiers back to quarters at night رات کی نوبت military fete at night فوج کا شبینہ مظاہرہ any such fete شبینہ مظاہرہ
taught (tawt) *v.* (pa. t. & pa. p. of **teach**, which see)
taunt (tawnt) *n.* jeering remark طعنہ *v.t.* jeer at (someone *with* something) (کا) طعنہ دینا **tauntingly** *adv.* jeeringly طعنہ دیتے ہوئے
Taurus (*taw*-rus) *n.* name of a sign of the zodiac بُرجِ ثور
taut (tawt) *adj.* tightly stretched (string, nerves, etc.) تنا ہوا (nautical) fit for use ٹھیک ٹھاک
tautology *n.* use of redundant words مترادفات کی بھرتی the saying of the same thing again in different words معنوی تکرار **tautological** (-*loj*-) *adj.* معنوی تکرار والا
tavern (*tav*-è*n) *n.* (old use) inn سرائے pub شراب خانہ
taw *n.* playing marble گولی، انٹا play with them گولیاں کھیلنا dividing line in this game گولی انٹے کا پالا

tawdry (*tawd*-ri) *adj*. showy but cheap and common بھڑکیلا اور بھونڈا ، بھڑکدار اور بھدا

tawny (*taw*-ni) *adj*. orange-brown (complexion, etc.) پکا ، گندمی

tax (taks) *n*. share of income or expenses paid by citizens to the public exchequer ٹیکس ، محصول (be) *a tax on* (*something*), (be) a burden on (it) پر بوجھ ہونا *v.t.* put a tax on (person, thing, etc.) پر ٹیکس لگانا ، پر ٹیکس عائد کرنا *tax* (*someone*) *with*, accuse (him) of کا الزام لگانا be a tax on پر بوجھ ہونا **taxable** *adj*. that which is or can be taxed ٹیکس کی زد میں آنے والا **taxation** *n*. taxes محاصل system of raising money by taxes تحصیل محاصل decision about levying tax from persons, etc. تشخیص محاصل **tax-free** *adj*. (of goods) not taxed محصول معاف (of dividends, etc.) after tax has been paid by the company محصول ادا شدہ

taxi (tak-si) *n*. (also a *taxi-cab*) motor-car for hire ٹیکسی ، کرائے کی موٹر *v.i.* go in a taxi ٹیکسی میں جانا (of aircraft) move on wheels before taking off or stopping ہوائی جہاز کا زمین پر چلنا **taximeter** *n*. (also *meter*), apparatus for indicating the fare for a journey in a taxi کرایہ نما

taxidermy (*tak*-si-dě*-mi) *n*. art of stuffing the skins of animals with lifelike effect جانوروں کی کھال میں بھس بھرنے کا فن ، پوست انبازی **taxidermist** *n*. one who does that پوست انباز

tea (tee) *n*. popular drink made from the dried leaves of an evergreen shrub چائے this shrub چائے کا پودا its dried leaves چائے ، چائے کی پتی (also afternoon tea) time in the late afternoon for tea سہ پہر کی چائے کا وقت *high tea*, meal taken with afternoon tea سہ پہر کی چائے کے ساتھ کھانا **tea-cloth** *n*. small cloth for a tea-table چھوٹا میزپوش cloth for drying dishes, etc. صافی **tea-cosy** *n*. padded cover for the tea-pot چائے پوش **tea-cup** *n*. cup for tea چائے کی پیالی amount contained by it پیالی بھر **tea-pot** *n*. kettle-like pot for tea چائے دانی **tea-set, tea-service** *n*. number of cups, saucers, plates, tea pot, milk jug, etc., of the same pattern for use at tea چائے کا سیٹ **tea-spoon** *n*. spoon for taking tea چائے کا چمچہ ، چمچی as much as will be contained by it چمچی بھر **tea-things** *n. pl*. (colloq.) cups, plates, etc., needed for tea پرچ پیالیاں ، چائے کا سیٹ

teach (teech) *v. t. & i*. (*teach, taught, taught*) give a lesson پڑھانا ، تعلیم دینا give a lesson in (کرنا) سکھانا explain (*how to do*) کا سبق دینا ، سکھانا drive it home to کے ذہن نشین کرنا **teaching** *n*. that which is taught تعلیم instructing پڑھانا ، سکھانا (usu. *pl*.) philosophy or system of morals (*of* someone) تعلیمات ، ارشادات ، افادات **teacher** *n*. one who teaches استاد ، معلم ، مدرس reformer مصلح

teak (teek) *n*. a kind of hard wood used in ship-building ساگوان tree yielding it ساگوان

teal (teel) *n*. (collective *sing*. used for *pl*.) small fresh-water duck چھوٹی ٹیلیں ، پن کُکڑی

team (teem) *n*. two or more draught animals pulling together جوڑی ، جوٹ number of persons playing together and forming one side in certain games ٹیم any group working together ایک ساتھ کام کرنے والے *adj*. co-operative (spirit, work, etc.) مشترکہ **teamster** *n*. one who drives a team of draught animals جوڑی چلانے والا **teapoy** *n*. small three-legged table تپائی

[1]**tear** (*tay*-ě*) *v.t. & i*. (*tear, tore, torn*) pull sharply apart or to pieces پھاڑنا ، چیرنا *tear to pieces, tear to bits*, ٹکڑے ٹکڑے کرنا ، پرزے پرزے کرنا *tear* (*a thing*) *in two* دو ٹکڑے کر دینا make (a hole in something) by pulling sharply میں شگاف ڈالنا ، کو چاک کرنا *tear* (*a piece of clothing*) *on a nail, etc*. کا کھونٹی سے پھٹنا ، میں الجھ کر پھٹنا cause (something) to be (*down, away, off, out of*, etc.) by pulling sharply پھاڑ لینا become torn پھٹنا go speedily in great excitement (*in* or *out of*) جلدی جلدی کرنا act thus جھپٹنا (usu. passive) destroy the peace of کا امن خاکستر کرنا *n*. torn place (in something) چاک **tearing** *n*. pulling sharply apart پھاڑنا ، چیرنا ، چاک کرنا *adj*. vehement (speed, pace, rage, propaganda) سخت ، شدید

[2]**tear** (*tee*-ě*) *n*. drop of salty water coming from the eye آنسو ، اشک (be) *in tears*, (be) weeping روتا ہوا ، روتا ہوا ، بسورتا ہوا **tearful** *adj*. weeping بسورتا ہوا (of eyes, etc.) wet with tears اشکبار **tearfully** *adv*. with tears in eyes روتے ہوئے

tease (teez) *v.t*. worry or annoy (someone *with* jokes, questions, etc.) playfully or unkindly چھیڑنا ، دق کرنا ، تنگ کرنا ، کے سر ہو جانا pick (wool) into separate fibres (اون) تُنّنا dress (cloth) with teasels کپڑے کا رُواں اٹھانا *n*. one who teases others چھیڑ چھاڑ کرنے والا **teaser** *n*. (slang) very confusing question پیچیدہ سوال difficult task مشکل کام **teasingly** *adv*. چھیڑتے ہوئے ، شرارت سے ، چھیڑ خانی کے طور پر **teasel, teazle** (*tee*-zěl) *n*. a flower-head used for raising nap on cloth ولایتی گوکھرو

teat (teet) *n*. nipple (عورتوں کا) سر پستان ، (جانوروں کا) تھن ، بھٹنی ، چوچی

technical (*tek*-ni-kěl) *adj*. of or pertaining to mechanical or industrial arts صنعتی ، پیشہ ورانہ ، فنی

technical terms, (of something) words used in it in a special sense اِصطلاحات ، فنی اصطلاحات pertaining to the methods used by experts ماہرانہ ، ہنرورانہ ، تکنیکی *technical skill* ہنرورانہ مہارت **technicality** (-*kal*-) *n.* technical word, etc. اِصطلاح fine technical point فنی نکتہ **technician** (tak-*nish*-èn) *n.* person skilled in the technique of some craft فنی ماہر ، مستری **technique** (tek-*neek*) *n.* method of doing something expertly کاریگر ، تکنیک ، صنعت گری any method آداب فن ، اُصول principles of an art, etc. طریقِ کار ، فن expert handling of an art فنی قابلیت **technics** *n. pl.* principles of an art آداب فن ، حرفیات **technocracy** (tek-*nok*-ra-si) *n.* hierarchy of technical experts organizing a nation's industrial resources کاریگر شاہی **technology** (-*nol*-) *n.* science of industrial arts (as opposed to *engineering* which is their practice) فنی مہارت ، پیشہ ورانہ مہارت **technological** (-*loj*-) *adj.* حرفیاتی **technologist** (-*nol*-) *n.* پیشہ ورانہ ماہر ، ماہر حرفیات

Teddy bear (*ted*-i-bay-è*) *n.* child's toy bear کھلونے کا ریچھ

Teddy boy *n.* teen-aged boy who is a hooligan نوجوان غنڈا

Te Deum name of a hymn ٹی ڈیئم

tedious (*tee*-di-us) *adj.* tiresome ; slow, long and boring اُکتا دینے والا ، تھکا دینے والا **tedium** *n.* boredom اُکتاہٹ ، بے کیفی monotony بے لطفی

tee *n.* golfer's starting place ٹی *v.t.* & *i.* place (ball) on tee (گیند) ٹی پر رکھنا *tee off*, (*a*) commence golf گالف شروع کرنا (*b*) begin (discussion, etc., *with* remarks, proposals, etc.) (اسے) شروع کرنا

teem *v.i.* be present in numbers بہت بڑی تعداد میں (teem with) have in large numbers میں بہت پڑا ہونا *rivers teeming with fish* مچھلیوں سے بھرے ہوئے دریا **teeming** *adj.* present in large numbers بہت بڑی تعداد میں *teeming millions* لاکھوں ، کروڑوں

teen-age (*teen*-ayj) *n.* (U.S.) age from 13 to 19 نئی جوانی ، عنفوانِ شباب **teen-aged** (-ayjd) *adj.* (of boy or girl) of this age نئی جوانی والا (یا والی) **teen-ager** *n.* boy (or girl) of this age نئی جوانی والا (یا والی)

teens (teenz) *n. pl.* the numbers 13 to 19 تیرہ سے اُنیس تک کے اعداد such years of one's life تیرہ سے اُنیس سال کی عمر کی *(be) in (one's) teens*, (be) of 13 to 19 years of age تیرہ سے اُنیس سال کی عمر کا (ہونا) ، عنفوانِ شباب میں (ہونا)

teeth *n.* (*pl.* of **tooth,** which see)

teethe (teedh) *v.i.* (of a baby) be getting its first teeth (شیرخوار بچے) کے دانت نکلنا ، کے دودھ کے دانت نکلنا

teetotal (tee-*toh*-těl) *adj.* of or advocating total abstinence مخالفِ منشیات **teetotaller** (-toh-) *n.* total abstainer تارکِ منشیات ، صوفی **teetotalism** مخالفِ منشیات

tele- (*tel*-i) *pref.* long distance دور **telecamera** *n.* (see *Addenda*) **telecast** *n.* (see *Addenda*) **telecommunication** *n.* (usu. *pl.*) electrically operated communication through wires or wireless like telegraph, telephone, teleprinter, television, etc. ٹیلی کمیونیکشن ، دور رسانی **telegram** (-gram) *n.* message sent by telegraph تار ، برقیہ **telegraph** (-grahf) *n.* electrical apparatus for transmitting messages along wires or by wireless تار برقی ، تار ، برقی پیغام رسانی *post and telegraph department*, *posts and telegraphs depart* محکمہ ڈاک و تار *wireless telegraphy* بے تار کی پیغام رسانی ، تار برقی ، لاسلکی ، بے تار *v.t.* & *i.* send (news, etc.), by telegraph تار کے ذریعے بھیجنا ، کا تار بھیجنا **telegraphic** (-*graf*-) *adj.* of or by telegraphy تار کا (یا) کے ذریعے very brief (phraseology) بیحد مختصر ، بہت کم لفظوں میں **telegraphist** (te-*lig*-ra-fist) *n.* person trained to send and receive message by telegraph تار بابو **telegraphy** (te-*lig*-ra-fi) *n.* use or science of the telegraph تار ، تار کا فن ، تار سازی **telepathy** (te-lep-a-thi) *n.* mental communication اِشراق **telephone** (*tel*-i-fohn) *n.* apparatus for talking to someone at a distance through wires or by wireless ٹیلیفون ، فون *v.t.* & *i.* use the telephone فون کرنا دور گو convey by telephone فون پر کہنا **telephonic** (-*fon*-) *adj.* by or of a telephone ٹیلیفون پر (یا) کا **telephonist** *n.* telephone-operator فون کار ، ٹیلیفون میں کام کرنے والا **telephony** *n.* use or science of the telephone ٹیلیفون کا فن یا اِستعمال its manufacture فون سازی **teleprinter** (-*tel*-) *n.* (also *creed*) telegraphically operated typewriter ٹیلی پرنٹر ، کریڈ ، دور نویس **telescope** (*tel*-i-skohp) *n.* tube or set of tubes with lenses for making distant objects appear nearer and large (a set of double tubes being called *binoculars*) دوربین *v.t.* & *i.* make or become shorter by means of sections that slide one within the other ایک دوسرے میں گھس جانا (of a collision of trains) thrust one (bogey) into the other ایک دوسرے میں گھسا دینا *adj.* able to be seen with a telescope دوربین ہی سے دیکھا جا سکنے والا of or containing a telescope دوربین والا having sections which slide one within the other ایسے حصوں والا جو ایک دوسرے میں گھس جائیں **telescopy** (-pi) *n.* use of telescopes دوربین کا اِستعمال manufacture of telescopes دوربین سازی **television** (*tel*-i-*vizh*-èn) *n.* (abbr. *T.V.*) process of transmitting a view of events, plays, etc. (while these are taking place) by radio to a distant television receiving set (called a *T.V. set*) ٹیلی ویژن ، دُور نُمائی *television set* دُور نُما **televise** (*tel*-e-vIz) *v.t.* & *i.* transmit by television ٹیلی ویژن پر نشر کرنا ، دُور نمائی کرنا **televisor** (*tel*-i-vI-zĕ*) *n.* apparatus for televising دُور نُما **televiewer** (*tel*-i-vew-ĕ*) *n.* one who uses a television set to see things دُور بِین ، دُور نظر

Telemachus (te-*lem*-a-kus) *Cl. myth.* the son of the legendary Greek hero *Odysseus* and his wife, *Penelope* تیلیمکس

tell (tel) *v.t.* & *i.* (*tell, told, told*) speak to کو کہنا سے کہنا state بیان کرنا state before کو بتانا (with *can* or *be able to*), know apart, distinguish (one from the other, or the difference between) میں فرق کرنا (یا) بتانا foretell, predict پیش گوئی کرنا ، پیشینگوئی کرنا *is no telling what will happen* مستقبل کے متعلق کوئی پیشگوئی نہیں کی جا سکتی have a marked effect (*upon*) پر اثر رکھنا ، پر نمایاں اثر کرنا badly influence the health of (someone) کی صحت پر بُرا اثر ڈالنا (old use) count گِننا ، شمار کرنا *tell* (*one's*) *beads*, say (one's) prayers with a rosary تسبیح پڑھنا *all told*, altogether مجموعی طور پر ، بحیثیت مجموعی *tell off*, count one by one and give orders (*for* a task, or *to do* something) ایک ایک کر کے حکم دینا (colloq.) scold جھاڑ جھپاڑ کرنا ask (someone *to do* something) کو کہنا ، کی ہدایت کرنا ، کا حکم دینا **teller** (*tel*-ĕ*) *n.* one who is employed for receiving and paying out money over a bank counter زر شمار person in the Legislature who counts votes رائے شمار one who tells کہنے والا ، بیان کرنے والا **telling** *adj.* effective کارگر ، اثر آفرین **telltale** *n.* & *adj.* (person or thing that) makes known a secret or someone's feelings, etc. چغل خور (یا) چغل ، راز افشا کرنے والا

temerity (te-*me*-ri-ti) *n.* rashness بیباکی ، جانبازی ، تہوّر

temper (*tem*-pĕ*) *n.* degree of hardness or elasticity (of steel, etc.) پختگی اور لچک disposition, mood مزاج *be in a temper, show temper*, be angry غصے میں ہونا *in a good temper*, in a pleasant mood خوش ، خوش خوش *in a bad temper*, annoyed or angry بگڑا بیٹھا ، جلا بُھنا *keep (one's) temper*, keep (one's) anger under control غصہ قابو میں رکھنا *lose (one's) temper* غصے سے لال پیلا ہو جانا ، آپے سے باہر ہو جانا *out of temper* (*with someone*), angry (*with him*) سے (یا) پر سخت بگڑا ہوا ، (سے) سخت ناراض *v.t.* & *i.* give the required temper to (steel, etc.) by heating and cooling, etc. تیار کرنا ، پختہ کرنا mollify ; moderate severity of (justice, wind, etc., *with*) اعتدال پر لانا ، کی سختی کم کرنا ، (کی) آمیزش سے نرم کرنا **tempera** (*tem*-pĕ-ra) *n.* distemper, painting پکا پلستری رنگ ، ڈسٹمپر

tempered *adj.* (in compounds) having a specific kind of temper مزاج والا ، مزاج ، خُو *sweet-tempered* شگفتہ مزاج *ill-tempered* بد مزاج ، تُند خُو **temperament** (-*tem*-) *n.* nature ; disposition ; mental tendencies as determined by physical constitution فطرت ، مزاج ، طبیعت اُفتادِ طبع **temperamental** (-*ment*-) *adj.* caused by temperament فطرتی ، قدرتی capricious, whimsical مُتلوّن مزاج having a neurotic temperament عصباتی ، زود حِس ، زود رنج

temperance (*tem*-) *n.* moderation in drinking شراب نوشی میں اعتدال teetotalism شراب سے پرہیز self-control in behaviour, etc. اعتدال ، ضبطِ نفس ، ضبط **temperate** (*tem*-) *adj.* showing temperance اعتدال پسند (of climate, region, etc.), free from extremes of heat and cold مُعتدل **temperature** (tem-pe-ra-che*) *n.* degree of heat or cold درجۂ حرارت ، ٹمپریچر *take (someone's) temperature*, measure it with a thermometer کا درجۂ حرارت دیکھنا *be running temperature, have a temperature*, have fever کو بخار ہونا

tempest (*tem*-pest) *n.* violent storm طوفان ، طوفانِ باد و باراں **tempestuous** (tem-*pes*-tew-us) *adj.* stormy (weather) طوفانی ، طوفان خیز turbulent (times etc.) ہنگامہ خیز ، پُر آشوب (زمانہ)

temple (*tem*-pĕl) *n.* place of worship معبد ، مندر *Inns of the Temple, Inner Temple, Middle Temple*, inns of the court in London formerly occupied by Knights Templar اِنر ٹمپل ، مڈل ٹمپل flat part between the ear and the forehead کنپٹی **Templar** *n.* (also *Knight Templar*), military religious order of the Christians of the Middle Ages aimed against Muslims عیسائی دینی فوجدار

tempo (*tem*-poh) *n.* speed at which a piece of music is played رفتار speed of any work, etc. رفتار

temporal (*tem*-po-rĕl) *adj.* pertaining to time زمانی not spiritual, pertaining to earthly life above دُنیوی of the temple کنپٹی کا ، صُدغی *n.* temple-bone صُدغی ہڈی **temporal augment** *n.* device for lengthening vowel-sound مدّ

temporary (*tem*-po-ra-ri) *adj.* lasting for a short time only عارضی ، وقتی ، ہنگامی **temporarily** (*tem*-) *adv.* just for the time-being عارضی طور پر ، عارضی

temporize (*tem*-po-riz) *v.i.* delay decisions فیصلے میں تاخیر کرنا act so as to gain time دفع الوقتی کرنا conceal one's ulterior motives تقیّہ کرنا ، دِل کی بات چھپا جانا get work down somehow or other کسی نہ کسی طرح کام چلا لینا

tempt *v.t.* try to persuade (someone *to do* something) پر اُکسانا ، ترغیب دینا allure (someone

into doing something) میں پھنسانا
temptation (-*tay*-) *n.* tempting or being tempted ترغیب، تحریص something that tempts لالچ ترغیب **tempter** (*temp*-tě*) one who tempts ترغیب دینے والا، اکسانے والا (*the Tempter*), Satan شیطان **temptingly** *adv.* اکساتے ہوئے
ten *n.* & *adj.* 10 دس **tenth** *adj.* 10th دسواں **tenfold** *adj.* & *adv.* ten times (a given amount or quantity) دس گنا
tenable (*ten*-a-bèl) *adj.* (of stipend, pension, etc.) that can be held or drawn (*by* someone *for* a period) مؤقت (of stand, position, etc.), that can be defended or maintained (of place, position, argument, etc.), that which can successfully be defended قابلِ مدافعت **tenability** (-*bil*-) *n.* قابلِ ادائگی ہونا ، قابلِ مدافعت ہونا
tenacious (te-*nay*-shus) *adj.* holding tightly; adhesive پکا، مُحکم، مضبوط slow to relinquish (one's or its) hold (*of* possession, purpose, principle, habit, etc.) آسانی سے نہ چھوڑنے والا، (پر) سختی سے قائم **tenacity** (te-*nas*-i-ti) *n.* being tenacious مضبوطی، اِستحکام، اِستقلال
tenant (*ten*-ant) *n.* one who pays rent for the use of land مُزارع، لگان دار، اَسامی one who pays rent for the use of a building, etc. کرائے دار، کرایہ دار *v.t.* use as a tenant مُزارع (یا اَسامی یا لگان دار یا کرایہ دار) ہونا **tenancy** (*ten*-ans-i) *n.* use of land as a tenant لگان داری، مُزارع ہونا، اَسامی ہونا use of building as a tenant کرایہ داری length of time during which a tenant uses land or building اَسامی یا کرایہ دار ہونے کی مُدت
tend *v.t.* & *i.* take care of (the sick) کی تیمارداری کرنا، کی خبرگیری کرنا look after (machine, cattle, etc.) کی دیکھ بھال کرنا have a tendency (*upwards*, *downwards*, *towards*, or *to* something, or *to do* something) کی طرف مَیلان ہونا (of steps, etc.) move or be directed *towards*, etc.) (کی طرف) رُخ ہونا **tendency** (*tend*-ens-i) *n.* inclination (*to do*, *to* or *towards*, something) مَیلان، رُجحان **tendentious** (ten-*densh*-us) *adj.* designed to promote a cause مبنی بر مقصد
tender (*tend*-ě*) *n.* separate part of railway engine for fuel and water اِنجن کا آب بردار حصہ، اِنجن کا small ship attending a larger one to carry stores and put on or take off passengers, etc. ہرکاری کشتی one who looks after (something) مُحافظ، نگران *n.* statement of the sum for which one will contract to do something ٹینڈر، ٹھیکے کا تخمینہ، پیشنہاد پیشنہاد *adj* soft (meat) نرم ملائم، نرم و نازک delicate نازک loving محبت آمیز painful when touched دُکھتا ہُوا requiring tact نازک young and frail نوزائیدہ، کمزور of love, pity, etc. محبت weak کمزور، نااُستوار *tender of*, careful not to hurt ہمدردی کا میں بہت مُحتاط *v.t.* & *i.* offer (payment of debt, or *for* or *to do* something) کی پیشکش کرنا present for acceptance (one's) services, resignation, **tenderfoot** *n.* (slang) greenhorn ناتجربہ کار شخص، نَوارِد **legal tender** *n.* form of money or currency for a country which cannot be legally rejected in any payment زرِ قانونی **tenderness** *n.* نرمی، مُلائمت نزاکت دُکھتا ہُوا ہونا، رَحمدِلی، شَفقت، مُحتاط ہونا
tendon (*tend*-un) *n.* tough cord that joins muscle to bone وَتر
tendril (*tend*-ril) *n.* thread-like shoot of a climbing plant which twists round a support بیل کی شاخ
tenement (*ten*-e-ment) *n.* separate flat in a building جُدا فلیٹ **tenement house** *n.* large house with a number of flats at low rents سستے فلیٹوں والی عمارت
tenet (*ten*-et, or *teen*-et) *n.* doctrine (of a religion) عقیدہ principle (of a party, etc.) اُصول
tenner (*ten*-ě*) *n.* (colloq.) £10 note دس پونڈ کا نوٹ any currency note worth 10 (rupees, etc.) دس کا نوٹ
tennis (*ten*-is) *n.* (also *lawn-tennis*) well-known game for two or four players who hit a soft ball over a low net with a cat-gutted bat (called a *racket*) ٹینس **tennis-court** *n.* ground on which tennis is played ٹینس کورٹ **table-tennis** *n.* ping-pong; kind of tennis played on table پنگ پانگ
tenon (*ten*-un) *n.* end of a piece of wood shaped to go into a mortise to make a join چُول
tenor (*ten*-ě*) *n.* prevailing course (*of* one's life) رَوِش، رفتار general meaning (*of* a speech, etc.) مَنشا، مُدّعا highest kind of normal adult male voice (موسیقی میں) بلند ترین مردانہ آواز person with such voice بلند ترین آواز موسیقار
tense (tens) *n.* verb-form showing time فعل کا زمانہ، فعل *adj.* tightly stretched تنا ہُوا excited; highly strung (nerves, emotions, etc.) کشاکش کی حالت میں strained (relations) between two persons, etc. کشیدہ **tenseness, tensity** *n.* being tightly stretched کھچاؤ، تناؤ **tensile** (*tens*-il) *adj.* of tension کھچاؤ والا capable of being stretched کھچاؤ کے قابل **tension** (*tensh*-un) *n.* state or degree of being tense کھچاؤ highly-strung state کشاکش strained state of relations کشیدگی hostility kept in check but likely to break out دبی ہوئی مخالفت maintenance of high degree of exertion مُسلسل جانکاہ محنت

tent *n*. canvas shelter on poles تنبو ، خیمہ *pitch a tent* خیمہ لگانا *strike a tent* خیمہ اکھاڑنا **tent-peg** *n*. one of the pegs to which tent-poles are tied with tent-ropes خیمہ کی میخ **tent-pegging** *n*. riding with lance past a tent peg trying to take it off میخ اکھاڑنا **tent-pole** *n*. pole of a tent تنبو کی بلّی
tent rope *n*. rope of a tent طناب
tentacle (*tent*-a-kèl) *n*. slender boneless part of certain animals used by them as a hand or feeler ریشۂ حاسّہ ، گیرہ
tentative (*tent*-a-tiv) *adj*. not final but experimental (suggestion, etc.) آزمائشی ، تجربی **tentatively** *adv*. experimentally آزمائشی طور پر ، تجربے کے طور پر
tenterhooks (*tent*-ĕ*-hŭks) *n. pl*. (only in the phrase :) (*be*) *on* (*the*) *tenterhooks*, (be) in a state of anxious suspense خلجان میں ہونا ، مخمصے میں (ہونا)
tenth (tenth) *adj*. (see under **ten**).
tenuous (*ten*-ew-us) *adj*. thin پتلا ، مہین باریک meagre (income, etc.) کم ، معمولی delicate (difference, distinction, etc.) نازک **tenuity** (-*new*-) *n*. باریکی ، نزاکت ، کمی
tenure (*ten*-yĕ*) *n*. holding or use (*of* land) حقِ لگان داری its period or conditions لگان داری ، حقِ قبضہ کی مدّت یا شرائط occupation, period or conditions (*of* office) عہدے پر فائض رہنا ، عہدے کی مدّت یا میعاد ، عہدے کی شرائط *security of tenure* عہدے یا لگان داری کا پکا ہونا *feudal tenure*, land held under feudalism جاگیرداری ، جاگیر *military tenure* فوجی خدمت سے مشروط جاگیر ، منصب
tepee (*tee*-pee) *n*. conical tent of the American Red Indians سُرخ ہندیوں کی راوٹی ، ٹپیی
tepid (*tep*-id) *adj*. lukewarm شیر گرم
teratology (-*tol*-) *n*. study or narration of miracles, etc. معجزیات ، مطالعۂ خوارق
tercentenary (tĕ*-*sent*-e-na-ri) *n*. 300th anniversary سہ صد سالہ برسی ، سہ صد سالہ جشن
tercel, terciel *n*. male hawk باز ، شاہین
terebenth (te-re-binth) *n*. turpentine-yielding tree بُطم ، تارپین کا درخت **terebene** *n*. disinfectant got from it ترپینیاب **terebenthine** *adj*. of terebinth تارپینی
tergiversate (*tĕ**-ji-vĕ*-sayt) *v.i*. go back on one's words, principles, etc. سے منحرف ہونا ، سے پھر جانا **tergiversation** *n*. going back on one's words, principles, etc. انحراف ، ارتداد
term (tĕ*m) *n*. fixed period (*of* office, imprisonment, etc.) میعاد period during which law courts, universities, etc., are open میقات (*pl*.) conditions (*of* something offered to, or agreed to by, someone) شرائط *make* (or *come to*) *terms* (*with* someone), reach an agreement (with him) (سے) سمجھوتہ کرنا *inquire about terms* (*for something*), ask about charges, etc. شرائط (یا کرایہ وغیرہ) دریافت کرنا *be on good terms with* (*someone*) friendly with (him) سے دوستانہ تعلّقات (ہونا) (also *technical term*), word conveying a definite idea, etc., in a branch of study اِصطلاح (pl.) words *in terms of high praise* بڑے تعریفی کلمات کے الفاظ ، کلمات *in abuse terms*, گالیوں کے ساتھ *v.t.* name کا نام دینا ، سے موسوم کرنا
terminable (*tĕ*m*-i-nay-bèl) *adj*. that which can be ended اختتام پذیر for a specific period میعادی **terminal** (*tĕ*m*-i-nĕl) *adj*. of or taking place each term میقاتی *terminal examinations* میقاتی امتحانات forming the last point (*of* a railway, etc.) آخری ، آخر کا ، سرے کا final دھرکا ، سرے کا *n*. terminal point of electric circuit, etc. دھرکا سرا
terminate (*tĕ*m*-i-nayt) *v.t. & i*. come to an end ختم کرنا put an end to ختم کرنا end (*in*) پر ختم ہونا **termination** (-*nay*-) *n*. final part (*of* word, etc.) آخری حصّہ ending اختتام
terminology (-*nol*-) *n*. system of terms (*of* a branch of study) اصطلاحات ، مصطلحات
terminus (tĕ*m-i-nus) *n*. (pl. *terminuses, termini*) station at the end of a railway ریل کا آخری سٹیشن ، ٹرمینس end (of a tram, bus, or air route) (کا) آخری اڈّا (*Terminus*), *Cl. myth*. the god who guarded boundaries ٹرمینس
termite (*tĕ**-mit) *n*. white ant دیمک
terpsichore (tĕ*p-*sik*-o-ree) *Cl. myth*. the Muse of dancing ترپسکری
terra (*te*-ra) *n*. earth مٹی ، زمین
terrace (*te*-ris) *n*. flat piece of ground on a slope ڈھلان کے اُوپر کا چبوترہ ، چبوترہ raised walk round house or in garden روش continuous row of uniform houses on or along a slope اونچی جگہ یکساں مکانوں کی قطار **terraced** (te-risd) *adj*. having terraces or raised walks روشوں والا (of roof) flat and not sloping as is almost everywhere built in Pakistan plains رسیدھی چھت
terra-cotta (te-ra-*kot*-a) *n*. hard, reddish-brown earth پکائی ہوئی مٹی ، سُرخی مائل مٹی works of art in it پکائی ہوئی مٹی کی مورتیاں یا برتن ، ٹیراکوٹا
terra-firma (te-ra-*fe**-ma) *n*. dry land خشکی solid ground ٹھوس جگہ (*be*) *on terra firma* قدم جمے ہوئے ہونا
terrain (te-*rayn*) *n*. tract of land regarded by a geographer or a tactician from the view point of its physical features خطّہ ، قطعۂ زمین
terrestrial (te-*res*-tri-el) *adj*. of the earth

کُرۂ زمین کا، کُرۂ اَرض کا earthly دُنیاوی، دُنیوی، اَرضی of land (as opposed to *marine* which means of the sea) بَرّی، خُشکی کا **terrene** (te-*reen*) *adj.* terrestrial مٹی کا، اَرضی

terrible (*te*-ri-bèl) *adj.* dreadful ہولناک، خوفناک grievous (mistake, etc.) افسوسناک (colloq.) very great بہت بڑا، بہت **terribly** *adv.* (colloq.) very much بہت

terrier (*te*-ri-ĕ*) *n.* species of small dog bred for digging rabbits (etc.) from their burrows ٹیریئر member of the Territorial Force (used as a nickname) ٹیریئر

terrific (te-*rif*-ik) *adj.* dreadful, terrible خوفناک، ہولناک، دہشتناک (colloq.) extremely great (speed, etc.) انتہائی، قیامت کا

terrify (te-ri-fi) *v.t.* strike with terror : frighten سخت ڈرا دینا، ہولا دینا، دہشت پیدا کرنا

territorial *adj.* (see under **territory**)

territory (*te*-ri-to-ri) *n.* land forming part of a State or under the domination of a ruler عملداری، قلمرو، علاقہ extent of land over which one's work spreads رقبہ، علاقہ **territorial** (te-ri-*to*-ri-ĕl) *adj.* of territory قلمرو کا، حاکم کی محروسہ کا، علاقائی *territorial waters*, the three-mile width of the sea stretching along the coast (of a country) علاقائی سمندر *the Territorial Army*, irregular army (of Britain) comprising civilians trained for home-defence in their spare time علاقائی فوج، وطنی فوج، داخلی فوج

terror (*te*-rĕ*) *n.* great fear سخت خوف، دہشت، ہیبت person or thing causing it ہوّا، خوفزدہ کرنے والا مُردنی

terrorism *n.* use of violence to terrorize people for political purposes دہشت پسندی **terrorist** *n.* one who believes in or has recourse to terrorism as a method of securing political power دہشت پسندی **terroristic** (-*ris*-) *adj.* (of methods, etc.) of terrorism دہشت پسندانہ

terse (tĕ*s) *adj.* brief, to the point and forcible (speech, style, speaker, etc.) مختصر اور جامع، جارح بات کہنے والا، اختصار پسند، تھوڑے لفظوں میں پوری بات کہنے والا . **tersely** *adv.* تھوڑے سے لفظوں میں، مختصراً **terseness** *n.* ایجاز، اختصار اور جامعیت

tertiary (*te**-shè-ri) *adj.* of the third degree (compare *primary* & *secondary*) تیسرے درجے کا، ثالث *n.* (*the Tertiary*), third formation (in geology) (اَرضیات کا) دورِ ثالث

terza rima (tah*t-sa-*ree*-ma) *n.* rhyme-scheme and metre of Dante's *Divine Comedy* رسہ قافیہ، مثلث

test *n.* examination امتحان trial (*of* something) آزمائش standard (*of* or *for* something) fixed for knowing its value, etc. معیار examination (*of* something for knowing its composition or quality) جانچ، جائزہ، امتحان، پھٹکانا *put* (*something*) *to the test*, make trial (of it) کو جانچنا، کی آزمائش کرنا، کا تجربہ کرنا *stand the test*, not fail امتحان میں پورا اترنا *a test pilot*, pilot taking aircraft on test flights آزمائش کرنے والا ہوا باز hard shell of some animals کڑا، سخت خول، صدفہ، قشر *v.t.* put to the test کو جانچنا، کا تجربہ کرنا *test* (*a thing*) *for* (*something*), examine something to see if it is or contains something دیکھنے کے لیے تجربہ کرنا کہ ہے یا نہیں be a test of کی تصدیق کرنا، کا شاہد ہونا

test-match *n.* one of the matches of a cricket tour that will count towards the result شماری مقابلہ، بڑا مقابلہ، ٹیسٹ میچ **test-tube** *n.* thin glass tube with one end closed used in chemical tests تجرباتی نلکی، تجربہ نلکی

test-tubes

testaceous (tes-*tay*-shus) *adj.* (of animal) with a test صدف دار، قشری **testacean** *n.* mollusc, etc., with a test صدفہ، قشری جانور

testacy *n.* (see under **testament**)

testament (*tes*-ta-ment) *n.* will وصیت (used in the phrases) *the last will and testament* آخری وصیت، وصیت نامہ one of two main divisions of the Bible عہد نامہ، عہد *the Old Testament* پرانا عہد نامہ، عہدِ عتیق *the New Testament* عہدِ جدید، نیا عہد نامہ، عہد نامہ covenant of God with men معاہدہ، عہد نامہ **testator** (tes-*tay*-tĕ*) *n.* (fem. *testatrix*) one who has left a particular will موصی، موصیہ، خاص وصیت چھوڑنے والا (یا والی)

testate (*tes*-tayt) *adj.* & *n.* leaving a will وصیت کر جانے والا *die testate* مرنے سے قبل وصیت کر جانا **testamentary** *adj.* of, by, or according to a will وصیتی، وصیت کا، (یں)، یا کے مطابق **testacy** (*tes*-ta-si) *n.* being testate وصیت چھوڑ جانا

testicle (*tes*-ti-kel) *n.* the semen-secreting gland خصیہ، فوطہ، بیضہ

testify (*tes*-ti-fi) *v.t.* & *i.* give evidence in a law-court, etc. (*against*, *on behalf of*, or *that*) شہادت دینا *testify to*, be a proof or evidence of پر دلالت کرنا، کا ثبوت ہونا، کی شہادت دینا solemnly declare (*that*) حلفیہ بیان دینا، ایمان سے کہنا indicate (assent, grief, etc.), by words or action کا اظہار کرنا declare one's faith openly اپنے عقائد کا کھل کر اعلان کرنا **testimonial** (-*moh*-) *n.* written statement testifying to a person's merits, etc. سند، تصدیق، صداقت نامہ given to someone to show appreciation of services سندِ خوشنودی memento given to someone by several persons collectively خوشنودی کی یادگار **testimony** (*tes*-ti-mo-ni) *n.*

statement in a law-court, etc., testifying to the truth of something شہادت، تصدیقی بیان proof or sign of something ثبوت، دلیل open declaration of one's religious beliefs اپنے عقائد کا کھلم کھلا اعلان
testy (*tes*-ti) *adj.* short-tempered (person), چڑچڑا، جھلّا، زُود رنج، تنک مزاج
tetchy (*tech*-i) *adj.* touchy (temper, person, subject, horse, etc.) چڑچڑا nervous عصبانی، جلد گھبرا جانے والا
tetanus (*tet*-a-nus) *n.* disease causing continuous contraction of some or all voluntary muscles تشنج، کزاز **tetanic** *adj.* of, like, or causing tetanus کزازی
tete-a-tete (tayt-a-*tayt*) *n.* private meeting between two persons تخلیہ، خلوت their talk تخلیے میں بات چیت private talk not overheard by anyone کی باتیں
tether (*tedh*-ĕ*) *n.* rope, etc., by which an animal is fastened while grazing to prevent it from straying چرنے کے وقت باندھی ہوئی رسّی limit, bounds حد، انتہا (be) *at the end of* (one's) *tether*, (be) at the end of (one's) resources, etc. اس سے آگے بس نہ چلنا *beyond* (*one's*) *tether*, not within (one's) knowledge or power کی بساط سے باہر *v.t.* fasten with a tether (جانور کو) چرنے کے وقت رسّی باندھنا
tetra- (*tet*-ra) *pref.* four چار، چہار، چہارگانہ **tetrahedron** (-hed-) *n.* (pl. *-rons*, or *-ra*) solid figure in four plane sides چار سطحی مجسّم **tetragon** *n.* plane straightlined figure with four angles, چوگوشہ شکل، ذوالاربعۃ الزوایا
text (tekst) *n.* author's own words (*of* a book, article, etc.), apart from notes, etc. متن passage, etc., from the Scripture as the subject of a sermon or discussion آیت *stick to* (*one's*) *text*, avoid irrelevance صرف کام کی بات کرنا، اِدھر اُدھر کی باتیں نہ کرنا
text-book *n.* book prescribed for pupils for the study (*of* a subject) نصاب، نصاب کی کتاب، مقرّرہ کتاب، درسی کتاب
textile (*teks*-tɪl) *adj.* pertaining to the manufacture of cloth پارچہ بافی (یا سے متعلق) *textile industry* صنعتِ پارچہ بافی suitable for weaving, etc. بُننے کے قابل *n.* fabric کپڑا، پارچہ **texture** (*teks*-chĕ*) *n.* arrangement of threads in a fabric, esp. their degree of closeness, etc. بافت، بناوٹ structure (*of* skin, wood, etc.) when felt or looked at ساخت بناوٹ، ریشہ
Thalia (tha-*li*-a) *Cl. myth.* the Muse of comedy ثلائیہ one of the Graces ثلائیہ
than (dhan) *prep.* (introducing second member of a comparison, properly used only before *whom*) as compared with *conj.* in comparison with سے، کی بہ نسبت *He is taller than I* وُہ مجھ سے لمبا ہے (Note that "*He is taller than me*" is a grammatically wrong colloquial form ; so you should avoid it and instead say : "*He is taller than I*") *rather than* (do, etc.) کی بجائے *other than* (*someone*), but, except کے سِوا
thank (thank) *v.t.* express gratitude to (someone *for* something or doing something) کا شکریہ ادا کرنا، کا شکرگزار ہونا *Thank you, I thank you* مہربانی، شکریہ express gratitude to (God *for* something) کا شکر کرنا، کا شکریہ ادا کرنا *Thank God! God be thanked* خدا کا شکر ہے **thanks** (thanks) *n. pl.* expression of gratitude شکریہ، مہربانی (*give, send, receive, get, owe, etc.*) thanks to someone کا شکریہ (ادا کرنا وغیرہ) *thanks to*, owing to کی بدولت، کے باعث *give thanks*, say grace کھانے پر دُعا کرنا *Much thanks I got for it*, (ironically) it was a thankless task خوب قدردانی ہوئی
thankful *adj.* grateful (*to*) شکر گزار، ممنون، احسانمند **thankfully** *adv.* with thanks شکریے کے ساتھ **thankless** *adj.* (of task, etc.) for which there are no thanks (وہ کام) جس کی قدر نہ ہو یا صلہ نہ ملے (of person) not thankful ناشکرا، احسان ناشناس **thankfulness** *n.* gratitude احسانمندی، شکرگزاری **thanklessness** *n.* ingratitude ناشکرگزاری، احسان ناشناسی، احسان فراموشی
thanksgiving *n.* expression of thanks to God خدا کا شکر a special form of Christian prayer عیسوی دُعائے شکر *thank you* (polite form of acceptance) شکریہ، مہربانی *No thank you*, (polite form of refusal) معافی چاہتا ہوں، شکریہ *I will thank you to* (*something*), (reproachful demand) شرم کرو، دو بھی *you* (*etc.*) *may thanks yourself* (*etc.*) *for that*, you (etc.) owe it to no one else یہ سب تمہارے (وغیرہ) طفیل ہے *Thanking you in anticipation, I* (*etc.*) *am*, (closing formula for application, etc.) منظوری کی توقع میں (یا پیشگی) شکریہ ادا کرتے ہوئے میں ہوں *Thank you for nothing*, (expression of scornful rejection) جی بس، معاف کیجئے
that (dhat) (pl. *those* dhohz.) *adj.* & *demonstrative pron.* the more distant (thing or person) وُہ *So that's that*, (formula for closing talk or discussion) اچھا تو یہ بات ہے! not this but the other (thing or person) the former (thing or person) وہ، پہلا *relative pron.* who جو، جس which جو، جس، جو کچھ *conj.* because کہ، کیونکہ in order that تاکہ *so that*, that as result یوں کہ، تاکہ *such that*, such as a result ایسے کہ، ایسا کہ، یوں کہ like that ایسا (antecedent to an omitted relative)

ﻫ Note That as a *relative pronoun*, is generally omitted when it refers to the *object*; as: *This is all I care about.*

thatch (thatch) *n.* dried straw, reeds, etc. گھاس پھونس roof made with it چھپّر، پھونس کی چھت، گھاس پھونس *v.t.* cover (a roof, etc.) with thatch چھپّر چھانا، چھپّر ڈالنا *thatched cottage*, cottage or house with such roof چھپّر کا گھر

thaw *v.t.* & *i.* (of a frozen thing) پگھلنا cause (a frozen thing) to melt پگھلا دینا (of mist, frost, etc.) ختم ہو جانا *It thaws*, the frost has ceased پالا جاتا رہا (of person or behaviour) become less formal کھلنا (cause to) become less formal سرد مہری دور کرنا *n.* thawing برف پگھلنا season or weather conditions causing thawing برف پگھلنے کا موسم

the (pr. dhè before consonants; dhi before vowels; and *dhee* when emphasized) *demonstrative adj.* (also called *the definite article*) (description of speoies) (اس کا اردو میں کوئی ترجمہ نہیں کیا جاتا) particularizing a thing, etc., which needs no identification یہ، وہ (preceding definition by a relative clause) وہ (for distribution) ایک *one pice in the rupee*, one pice per rupee ایک روپیہ، فی روپیہ (conversion of adjective into a plural noun; as, *the rich*) (اردو میں اس کے ساتھ فعل جمع آتا ہے) (before a proper noun for suggesting uniqueness) (before a proper noun, for mentioning thing or person of his, her or its qualities in another age or region as; *President Ayyub is the Abraham Lincoln of Pakistan* (اردو میں اس کا کوئی ترجمہ نہیں کیا جاتا) *adv. preceding comparatives* by as much as (as in: *the more the better*) جتنا، اتنا equivalent of, or in addition to, a phrase introduced by *for, on that account, so much*, etc.) بھی

theatre (*thi*-e-tě*) *n* building where plays are acted تماشا گاہ *the theatre*, plays and acting ڈرامے، ڈرامے کا فن، تمثیلی ادب، اداکاری *go to the theatre*, go to see a play ڈراما دیکھنے جانا lecture hall with rising seats in rows لیکچر گاہ ﻫ (also *operation theatre* or *operating theatre*), room in a hospital where surgical operations are performed اپریشن کا کمرہ، جراحت خانہ

a theatre

theatrical *adj.* of or for the theatre تھیٹر کا (یا کے لیے) designed for exaggerated effect مبالغہ آمیز، اثر جمانے کے ڈھب کا unnatural (behaviour, etc.) بناوٹی، تصنع آمیز، اداکارانہ **theatricals** *n. pl.* dramatic performances by amateurs (also called *private theatricals*) غیر پیشہ ورانہ ڈرامے **theatric** *adj.* of theatre تھیٹر کا of actors or acting اداکارانہ

thee (dhee) *pron.* accusative case of *thou* تجھے، تجھ کو (یا سے وغیرہ)

theft (theft) *n.* stealing (*of*) چرانا act of stealing چوری، سرقہ، دزدی

their (*dhay*-è*) *possessive adj.* (pl. of *his*, *her* and *its* ان کا، اُن کا **theirs** (*dhey*-è*z) *possessive pron.* (pl. of *his*, *hers* and *its*) اُن کا، ان کا

theism (*thee*-izm) *n.* belief in the existence of God and revelation (as distinct from *deism* which denies revelation) دینیت

them (dhem) *pron.* (accusative case of *they*) اُنھیں، اُن، اِن کو (یا سے وغیرہ) **themselves** (dhem-*selvz*, *pron.* (pl. of *himself*, and *itself*) اپنے آپ کو، خود کو *they themselves* (emphatic form) آپ خود، خود آپ

theme (theem) *n.* idea which has elaborately been worked out in a piece of writing, etc. مرکزی خیال subject on topic (*of* talk) موضوع school exercise on a set theme مضمون، جواب مضمون short tune which is repeated or expanded (in a piece of music) موضوع نغمہ *theme song*, the leading song in a melody ترجیعی نغمہ، ترجیعہ گیت

then (dhen) *adj.* at that time تب، اس وقت a another time پھر afterwards اس کے بعد، بعد ازاں immediately وہیں، فوراً *there and then* وہیں *conj* therefore لہٰذا، اس لیے in that case اس صورت میں ایسی صورت میں *n.* that time تب، وہ وقت، وہ زمانہ *adj.* (*the then*), of that time اس وقت کا، اس زمانے کا، تب کا (old use or formal) from there وہاں سے (formal) from that اس سے from that time onwards اس وقت سے

theocracy (the-*ok*-ra-si) *n.* government in which God is the sovereign and religion the law دینی حکومت priestly government ملائیت **theocratic** (*krat*-) *adj.* based on theocracy دینی

theodolite *n.* land-survey instrument زاویہ پیما

theogony (the-*og*-o-ni) *n.* theory of the genesis of gods دیو مالا

theologian *n.*, **theological** *adj.*, **theologize** *v.t.* & *i.* (see under **theology**)

theology (the-*ol*-o-ji) *n.* science of the nature of religious belief دینیات any particular philosophical system of it علم کلام **theologian**

(thee-o-*loh-ji-en*) *n.* expert in theology عالمِ دین، ماہرِ دینیات کا عالم **theological** (thee-o-*loj*-i-kel) *adj.* pertaining to theology دینیاتی **theologize** *v.t.* & *i.* express in terms of theology دینیاتی انداز سے بیان کرنا

theorem (*thee*-o-rem) *n.* statement which though not self-evident, can convincingly be proved by argument نظری حقیقت mathematical statement for which a reasoned proof is required کُلیّہ geometrical proposition to be proved شکلِ ہندسی

theoretic *adj.*, **theoretical** *adj.*, **theoretics** *n. pl.* **theorist** *n.* **theorize** *v. i.* (see under **theory**)

theory (*the*-o-ri) *n.* general principles of an art or science (as distinct from its *practice*) اصول reasoned supposition put forward to explain facts or events نظریّہ **theoretic, theoretical,** (thee-o-*ret*-) *adj.* based on theory and not on practice or experience نظری، نظریاتی **theoretics** *n. pl.* قیاسیّات **theorize** (*thee*-o-riz) *v.i.* make theories (*about*) نظریات قائم کرنا **theorist** (*thee*-o-rist) *n.* inventor of a theory نظریّہ پیش کرنے والا holder of a theory نظریے کا حامی person fond of theoretics نظریات پسند، نظریاتی، نظری

theosophy (the-*os*-o-fi) *n.* religious system basing knowledge on intuitional and mystical concept of God thus making it possible for everyone to have this knowledge فلسفیانہ دین، تھیوسوفی **theosophist** (-os-) تھیوسوفیٹ، فلسفی دین کا پیرو

therapeutics (the-ra-*pew*-tiks) *n. pl.* (used with sing. verb) curative branch of medicine معالجات **therapeutic** *adj.* tending to the cure of disease دافعِ مرض of therapeutics معالجاتی، علاجی

-therapy *suf.* medical treatment as indicated by (the taking on this suffix) علاج (کا یا والا)

there (*thay*-è*) *adv.* in that place وہاں at that point اس جگہ in that respect اس حیثیت سے، یوں in that matter اس سلسلے میں، اس بارے میں *n.* that place or point وہ جگہ *inter.* (to draw attention) اے لو، اَیلو *particle* (pr. *dhe*-è*) (used with *to be*, *to come*, etc., and all passives in questions and inverted statements ; as, *there was a boy ; there comes a girl ; there were seen*) اردو میں اس کا کوئی ترجمہ نہیں کیا جاتا **thereabouts** near that place وہیں، کہیں near that number, quantity, degree, etc. اس کے قریب **thereafter** afterwards بعد ازاں **thereat** (old use) at this اس پر **thereby** by that means اس ذریعے سے in that way اس طرح، یوں **therefore** *adv.* for that reason لہٰذا، اس لیے **therein** *adv.* in that (place) اس میں، اس جگہ **thereinafter** *adv.* after that in the same document آگے چل کر **therein-before** اس سے پہلے **thereof** (old use) of it اس کا **thereon** on it **there's** there is ہے **thereto** to it اس پر **thereupon** then اس کے بعد، پھر owing to that اس وجہ سے، اس لیے، چنانچہ immediately فوراً ہی **therewith** (old use) besides اس کے ساتھ (ہی)

therm (thĕ*m) *n.* unit of heat حرارہ **thermal** *adj.* pertaining to heat حرارت کا **thermal springs** (also called *thermae*), springs of warm or hot water گرم پانی کے چشمے

thermometer (thĕ*-*mom*-e-tĕ*) *n.* instrument for measuring temperature مقیاس الحرارت، تھرمامیٹر حرارت پیما، تپش پیما

thermos (the*-mos) (also called *flask* or *thermos flask*), vacuum flask تھرماس

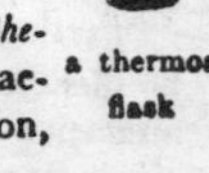
a thermos flask

Thersites (the*-*si*-tes) *Cl. myth.* a Greek notorious for his ugliness ; he was killed by Achilles ترسیٹس

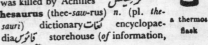

thesaurus (thee-*saw*-rus) *n.* (pl. *thesauri*) dictionary لُغات encyclopaedia قاموس storehouse (*of* information, etc.) مخزن

these (dheez) *demonstrative pron. & adj.* (*pl.* of *this*) یہ (جمع)

theta (*thee*-ta) *n.* letter of the Greek alphabet as a mathematical symbol (θ) تھیٹا

thesis (*thee*-sis) *n.* (pl. *theses*) theory put forward and supported by arguments دعویٰ، نظریّہ such essay written and submitted for a university degree مقالہ

thews (thewz) *n. pl.* one's muscular strength بدنی قوّت *thews and sinews*, bodily strength جسمانی قوّت muscles پٹھے، عضلات

they (dhay) *pron.* (nominative case) (accusative case, *them* ; genitive case, *theirs* or *their*) (*pl.* of *he, she, it*) those persons or things وہ *they who, they that,* those persons who جو، جنھوں نے *they say,* it is generally said کہنے میں، کہا جاتا ہے **they'll** they will وہ (کریں) گے they shall وہ ضرور (کریں) گے **they're** they are وہ ہیں **they've** (*dhay*-ev) they have ان کے پاس ہے، وہ رکھتے ہیں، انھوں نے (کہا) ہے

thick (thık) *adj.* having a depth موٹا (of a line) wide چوڑا bold (letter, etc.) جلی، موٹا dense (forest, hair, etc.) گھنا، گنجان (of liquid) flowing stiffly گاڑھا cloudy or foggy (atmosphere) ابر آلود، کہر آلود (*thick with*), full of سے بھرا ہوا much بہت سا dunce, stupid غبی، کُند ذہن

(10) continuous لگاتار، مسلسل (11) (of voice) hoarse owing to cold, etc. بیٹھی ہوئی (12) (colloq.) very friendly (*with*) گاڑھی دوستی رکھنے والا *n.* thickest part سب سے دبیز حصّہ part where activity is greatest سب سے گنجان یا ہنگامے والا حصّہ *in the thick of the battle* گھمسان کے رن میں *through thick and thin*, whatever the conditions may be ہر حال میں *adv.* continuously لگاتار، مسلسل، پے در پے، تابڑ توڑ *come thick and fast*, come quickly and in large numbers لگاتار، تابڑ توڑ

thicken (*thik*-ĕn) *v.t.* & *i.* make or become thick موٹا کرنا یا ہونا، گاڑھا کرنا یا ہونا **thickheaded** *adj.* stupid احمق، غبی، ٹھس **thickness** *n.* (also) layer تہہ موٹاپا، دبازت **thickest** *adj.* short and stout (person) موٹا اور ناٹا closely massed گنجان **thick-skinned** *adj.* with a thick skin موٹی کھال والا insensitive to insults, reproaches, etc. ڈھیٹ، جس پر بات کا اثر نہ ہو without delicate feelings بے حس، احساس سے عاری **thick-skulled, thick-witted** *adj.* stupid, slow to understand کم فہم، کند ذہن **thickening** *n.* making or becoming thick گاڑھا کرنا یا ہونا، موٹا کرنا یا ہونا thickened part موٹا ہو جانے والا حصّہ thing with which gravy, etc., is thickened شوربا گاڑھا کرنے کی چیز

thicket (*thik*-et) *n.* thick growth of shrubs, etc. گنجان جھاڑیوں کا سلسلہ، جھاڑی، بن

thief (theef) *n.* (pl. *thieves* pr. theevz) person who steals secretly and sometimes with violence چور **thieve** (theev) *v.t.* & *i.* steal چوری کرنا، چرانا **thievery** (*theev*-ĕ-ri) *n.* stealing چوری **thievish** *adj.* given to thieving چوٹّا

thigh (thi) *n.* part of leg above knee ران، جانگھ

thimble (*thim*-bĕl) *n.* metal-cap for protecting the finger end when pushing a needle through cloth, etc. انگشتانہ **thimbleful** *n.* (colloq.) sip of liquor جرعہ، شراب کا گھونٹ sip (*of* any liquid) ذرا کا گھونٹ

thin (thin) *adj.* not thick پتلا، باریک not fat چھریرا، دبلا، پتلا feeble (voice, sound) کمزور (of type) not bold خفی، باریک watery (soup, etc.) پتلا not close set (hair, etc.) چھدرا without many people خالی خالی *a thin house*, scanty audience بہت تھوڑے حاضرین (colloquial) flimsy (excuse) بے بنیاد، ناقابل قبول *have a thin time*, have a dull or uncomfortable time وقت بے لطف گزرنا *v.t.* & *i.* (-nn-) make or become thin کم ہونا یا کرنا، گھٹنا یا گھٹانا *thin out a plant* پودے کی افزائش کے لیے پرانی شاخیں کاٹنا *thin the plants out* مزید پیداوار کے لیے کچھ پودے نکال دینا **thinness** *n.* دبلاپن **thin-skinned** (*thin*-skind) *adj.* sensitive to criticism. etc. زودحس easily offended نفور، زود رنج

thine (dhine) possessive *pron.* (old use or poet.) yours تیرا

thing (thing) *n.* object چیز، شے *a dear old thing*, dear person or thing پیارا یا پیاری *poor thing*, one deserving pity غریب، دکھیا (*pl.*) general conditions or cicumstances حالات، معاملات *Ever since General Ayyub has taken over as President things are getting better and better every day in this country* جب سے جنرل ایوب نے زمام صدارت سنبھالی ہے اس ملک کے حالات روز بروز بہتر ہوتے جا رہے ہیں (*pl.*) (colloq.) (*one's*) belongings, esp. clothes سامان، کپڑا لتا *the very things, the things*, what is right, just what is needed جو چاہیے وہی، اصل چیز، اصل بات *(be) not quite the thing today (etc.)*, be unwell that day اس روز طبیعت کچھ ناسازسی ہونا **thingamy, thingumajig, thingumbob, thingummy** (*thing*-) *n.* person or thing whose name one forgets; what's-his-name; what-d'y-call-it وہ دیکھو بھلا سا نام ہے اس کا

think (think) *v.t.* & *i.* (*think, thought, thought* pr. thawt) use one's mind سوچنا، خیال کرنا، تصوّر کرنا have in mind as a result of سمجھنا hold the opinion کی رائے ہونا *think highly* (or *well*) *of* (*someone* or *something*), have a high (or good) opinion of (him, her or it) کے متعلق بڑی اچھی (یا اچھی) رائے رکھنا *think little of* کے متعلق بری رائے رکھنا *think nothing of*, (*a*) not to have a good opinion of کے متعلق بری رائے رکھنا (*b*) not to consider remarkable کو کچھ نہ جاننا، کو معمولی سمجھنا *think better of* (*doing something*), reconsider it and better give it up کے متعلق پھر غور کرنا، کو چھوڑنے کی سوچنا *think* (*something*) *out*, consider carefully and plan پر غور کر کے انتظام کرنا پر بہ پوری طرح غور کرنا *think* (*something*) *over*, consider further before deciding it پر نظر ثانی کرنا، کو پھر سے سوچنا **methinks** (mi-*thinks*), **methinketh** *v.* it seems to me مجھے یوں لگتا ہے جیسے **methought** (mi-*thawt*) *v.* it seemed to me مجھے یوں لگا (یا لگتا تھا) جیسے **thought** (thawt) *n.* (see separate entry)

third (thĕ*d) *adj.* & *n.* 3rd تیسرا **thirdly** *adv.* in the third place تیسری بات یہ ہے کہ، تیسرے، سوم، ثالثاً **third-rate** *adj.* of poor quality گھٹیا، گیا گزرا **third person** *n.* (grammar) one not present غائب person present at a meeting besides the principals تیسرا شخص **third man** *n.* (in cricket) fielder between point and short slip تھرڈ مین **third party** *n.* party in a law-suit other than the principal parties مزید فریق، اور لوگ *third party risks*, insurance risks involving persons other than the assured person مزید خطرات، دوسروں کے نقصانات **third degree** *n.* police torture of criminals for getting confessions تشدد، مار پیٹ *third degree methods* تشدد

thirst (thĕ*st) *n.* feeling caused by the need to drink پیاس strong desire (*for*) (کی) پیاس ، (کی) لگن *v.i.* have thirst پیاسا ہونا be eager (*for*) (کے لیے) بیتاب ہونا **thirsty** *adj.* (of person or animal) having thirst پیاسا (of land, etc.), needing irrigation ; dry خشک ، پیاسا (of work) causing thirst پیاس لگانے والا **thirstily** *adv.* پیاس سے

thirteen (*the**-teen*) *adj.* & *n.* 13 تیرہ **thirteenth** *adj.* 13th تیرھواں **thirteen-fold** *adj.* 13 times تیرہ گنا

thirty *adj.* & *n.* 30 تیس **thirtieth** *adj.* تیسواں **thirty-fold** *adj.* 30 times تیس گنا

this (dhis) *demonstrative adj.* & *pron.* (pl. *these* pr. dheez) person or thing near, just mentioned or about to be mentioned یہ (م) ، اِس

thistle (*this*-ĕl) *n.* wild flowery plant with prickly leaves گوکھرو this as the national symbol of Scotland گوکھرو **thistly** *adj.* full of thistles گوکھرو بھرا prickly, thorny خار دار **thistledown** *n.* thistle seeds with hair enabling them to float on the wind گوکھرو کے بیج *as light as thistledown*, very light ہلکا پھلکا

a thistle

thither (*dhi*-dhĕ*) *adv.* (old use) to that place اُس جگہ ، اُس جا in that direction اِدھر اُدھر کو

Thomas the Rhymer (*Tom*-us-dhĕ-*ri*-mĕ*) *Scottish leg.* (also called *Thomas Rhymer*, *Thomas of Ercildoune* or *Thomas of Earlston*) Scottish poet, prophet and magician ٹامس رائمر

thong (thong) *n.* narrow strip of leather چمڑے کا تسمہ ، تسمہ

Thor (tho*) *Scandinavian myth.* the son of *Woden* and himself the god of thunder and war ; famous for his mighty hammer and for his belt which doubled his strength تھور

thorax (*tho*-raks) *n.* part of the body between neck and abdomen چھاتی ، سینہ ، صدر (in insects) middle section of the body وسطی حصہ

thorium (*tho*-ri-um) *n.* name of a radio-active metallic element تھوریم

a thorax

thorn (tho*n) *n.* sharp-pointed growth on the stem of a plant کانٹا ، خار shrub with thorns خار دار جھاڑی **thorny** *adj.* abounding in thorns خار دار difficult (question) ٹیڑھا ، مشکل of subject hard to handle without offence پُرخار ، نازک

thorough (*thĕ*-ru) *adj.* complete in every way پورا ، مکمل ، پوری چھان بین *a thorough probe* مکمل تحقیقات detailed مفصل **thoroughly** *adv.* پوری طرح **thoroughness** *n.* being thorough مکمل ہونا **thoroughbred** *adj.* (of animal) of pure breed نسلی ، نسل دار *n.* such horse نسلی گھوڑا **thoroughfare** *n.* road much used by traffic شاہراہ road which is not private شارعِ عام ، عام گزرگاہ *No thoroughfare*, (*a*) warning that this road is private یہ شارعِ عام نہیں (*b*) warning that this road is closed at the other end پرلی طرف راستہ بند **thorough-going** *adj.* complete پورا ، پورا پورا ، مکمل through and through پکا ، کٹر ، سخت

thou (dhou) *pron.* (accusative case, *thee* ; genitive *thine* or *thy* ; plurals : nominative, *ye* ; accusative *you* ; genitive, *yours* or *your* ; now only *you*, *yours* and *your* are in use for all forms) (old use or poet. for *sing.*) you تو

though (dhoh) *conj.* although اگرچہ (Note that in modern English, *yet*, which is used after *although*, is strictly avoided after *though*) as if جیسے ، گویا *what though*, it matters little that کیا ہوا ، گو *adv.* (never used in the beginning and usu. coming separately at the end) all the same یوں تو

thought (thawt) *n.* idea خیال power of thinking اِدراک ، قوتِ خیال process of thinking غور و فکر worry اُلجھن ، پریشانی philosophy, theories etc. خیالات ، نظریات ، فلسفہ opinion رائے ، خیال intention (*of doing* something) (کا) خیال ، (کا) اِرادہ ، (کی) نیت **thoughtful**. *adj.* considerate (*of* others) (کا) خیال رکھنے والا ، بامروت full of thought صاحب فکر showing thought ہوشمند **thoughtfully** *adv.* ہوشمندی سے ، مروت سے **thoughtfulness** *n.* quality of being thoughtful ہوشمندی ، مروت **thoughtless** *adj.* inconsiderate (*of* others) (کا) خیال نہ کرنے والا ، بے مروت unthinking بے سوچے سمجھے careless بے پروا ، غافل خود غرض **thoughtlessly** *adv.* بے سوچے سمجھے ، بے پروائی سے ، غفلت **thoughtlessness** بے پروائی ، خود غرضی ، بے مروتی **thought control** *n.* (see *Addenda*)

thousand (thou-zĕnd) *n.* & *adj.* 1,000 ہزار **thousandth** *adj.* 1,000th ہزارواں **thousand-fold** *adj.* 1,000 times ہزار گنا

thrall (thrawl) *n.* slave غلام in bondage to (a habit, etc.) (کے) پنجے میں گرفتار ، جکڑا ہوا bondage غلامی ، گرفتاری *have (someone) in thrall* کو اپنا غلام بنائے ہوئے ہونا **thraldom** *n.* slavery, bondage غلامی ، گرفتاری

thrash (thrash) *v.t.* & *i.* beat with stick or

whip پیٹنا، کوڑے لگانا defeat ہرانا، شکست دینا thrash گاہنا (*thrash out*), thoroughly discuss (a problem) کی چھان بین کرنا، ہر پہلو پر غور کرنا **thrashing** *n.* beating مار پٹائی، ٹھکائی، ٹھکس، مرمت *give (someone) a good thrashing* کی خوب مرمت کرنا *get a good thrashing* کی خوب مرمت کرنا

thread (thred) *n.* length of spun fibres دھاگا، تاگا chain (*of* thought, an argument, etc.) (کا) سلسلہ (کی) لڑی spiral ridge round a screw پیچ *v.t.* put thread through (a needle) میں دھاگا ڈالنا put (beads, etc.) on a thread میں پرونا make (*one's way*), through (a crowd, etc.), by going in and out among them ادھر ادھر سے نکل کر ہجوم میں سے اپنا راستہ بنانا **threadbare** *adj.* (of cloth) worn thin تار تار old and much used (argument, etc.) پامال، فرسودہ، گھسا پٹا

threat (thret) *n.* warning given (to someone) to punish or hurt (him) if he does not do what he is expected to دھمکی sign of coming trouble, etc. اندیشہ، خطرہ **threaten** (*thret*-en) *v.t.* & *i.* intimidate (someone *with* something) دھمکی دینا use threats (*to do* something) کی دھمکی دینا (of clouds etc.), give warning of (danger, trouble, etc.) کے خطرے کی اطلاع دینا (of something unpleasant) seem likely to come کا خطرہ پیدا ہونا **threateningly** *adv.* with threats دھمکاتے ہوئے

three (three) *n.* & *adj.* 3 تین **three-fold** *adj.* three times (a number) تین گنا **three-score,** ساٹھ ٦٠ **three-quarter** *adj.* (of portrait) presenting face between full and profile بغلی چہرے والی (of portrait) including body to below hips کمر سے نیچے تک کی amounting to three quarters پون، تین بٹے چار **three-ply** *n.* & *adj.* (wood) with three layers سہ تہی (لکڑی) **three-lane** *adj.* (of road) wide enough for three lines of traffic on either side (سڑک) تہراہی *three-dimensional adj.* (see Addenda) **three-penny bit** *n.* 3d. coin تین پنس کا سکہ **threepence** (*threp*-ens) *n.* 3d تین پنس **the three R's** *n.* reading (w)riting and (a)rithmetic ابتدائی تعلیم، لکھنا، پڑھنا اور حساب **three cheers** *n.* hip-hip-hip-hurrah thrice repeated (*for* someone) (کے لیے) تین نعرے **three times three** *n.* nine cheers نو نعرے **three-legged race** *n.* race of couples with a right and a left leg of the two tied together تین ٹانگی دوڑ **Three in One** *n.* Trinity عیسائیوں کا عقیدہ، تثلیث

threnetic *adj.*, **threnodic** *adj.* (see under **threnody**)

threnody (*threen*-o-di) *n.* dirge ماتمی گیت، مرثیہ

threnetic, threnodic *adj.* مرثیہ کے متعلق، سوز خواں، ماتمی

thresh (thresh) *v.i.* & *i.* beat the grain out of (wheat, etc.) گاہنا beat wheat, etc., for this purpose دانے گاہنا

threshold (*thresh*-ohld) *n.* plank, etc., under a doorway چوکھٹ، دہلیز beginning (*of*) آغاز *on the threshold of (one's) career as (something)* کی حیثیت سے زندگی کے آغاز ہی میں

threw (threw *v.* pa. t. of **throw,** which see)

thrice (thrıs) *adv.* three times تین بار

thrift (thrift) *n.* habit of economy کفایت شعاری **thrift** *adj.* economical کفایت شعار

thrill (thril) *n.* excited feeling passing like a wave along the nerves جذبات کی لہر، جھرجھری، پھریری، اہتزاز experience causing it ہیجان خیز بات *v.t.* & *i.* feel a thrill (*with*) (کے باعث) جذبات کی لہر سی دوڑ جانا cause a thrill in جذبات کی لہر دوڑا دینا **thriller** *n.* (esp.) exciting novel سنسنی خیز ناول، ہیجان خیز ناول such film ہیجان خیز فلم

thrive (thrīv) *v.i.* (*thrive, throve, thriven*) (of business, etc.) خوب کامیابی سے چلنا succeed پنپنا grow strong or healthy (*on* a food, etc.) سے پھلنا پھولنا **thriving** *adj.* flourishing کامیاب، پنپتا، اٹھتا

throat (throht) *n.* front part of the neck گلا gullet حلق، گلا **throaty** (*throh*-ti) *adj.* thick (voice) بیٹھی ہوئی

throb (throb) *v.t.* (-bb-) (of the heart, pulse, etc.) beat دھڑکنا beat more rapidly than usual (*with* excitement, etc.) (کے باعث) زور زور سے حرکت کرنے لگنا (of wound) have the beat of the pulse felt in it پھڑکنا *n.* a throbbing or vibration دھڑکن، ارتعاش

throes (throhz) *n. pl.* pangs (of childbirth) دردِ زہ sharp pains شدید درد *in the throes of,* struggling with کی کشمکش میں

thrombosis (throm-*bos*-is) *n.* clotting of blood in blood-vessel انجمادِ خون *coronary thrombosis,* such clotting in brain دماغ میں انجمادِ خون

throne (throhn) *n.* ceremonial seat of a sovereign, etc. تخت، سریرِ سلطنت royal authority شاہی اقتدار (*the Throne*), the sovereign فرمانروا، بادشاہ

throng (throng) *n.* crowd بھیڑ، ہجوم، انبوہ، ازدحام، ریلا، اژدہام *v.t.* & *i.* crowd round کی بھیڑ لگ جانا

throttle (throt-el) *v.t.* strangle کا گلا گھونٹنا check the utterance of (words) زبان سے نکالنے کی اجازت نہ دینا control the flow of steam, etc., to an engine انجن میں بھاپ وغیرہ کی آمد کو کم یا زیادہ کرنا *n.* (also *throttle-valve*), valve controlling the flow of steam, etc., into an engine انجن کی بھاپ نکالنے کے لیے کھلا منفذ، مخارہ

through (throo), **thro'** (throo) *prep.* into and

then out of میں سے from end to end or side to side of ایک سرے سے دُوسرے سرے تک over the whole extent of پر from beginning to end of اوّل سے آخر تک by means of کے ذریعے in consequence of کے باعث، کے نتیجے میں *adv.* from one end, etc., to another ایک سرے سے دُوسرے سرے تک from beginning to end اوّل سے آخر تک *adj.* clear صاف، واضح unobstructed بلامزاحمت (of passenger or train) going from one point to another without break or change سیدھا، براہِ راست **through and through** complete(ly) thoroughly پُورا، مکمل، کٹّر **throughout** *adv.* & *prep.* in every part (of) (کے) ہر حصّے میں، (میں) ہر جگہ from end to end (of) ایک سرے سے دُوسرے سرے تک، سراسر from beginning to end (of) (کے) اوّل سے آخر تک، سراسر

throve (throhv) *v.* (pa. t. of **thrive,** which see)

throw (throh) *v.t.* & *i.* (*throw, threw, thrown*) hurl, fling پھینکنا put (clothes *on, off, over,* etc.) carelessly (کپڑے) جلدی جلدی یا بے پروائی سے اُتارنا یا پھینکنا move (one's arms, legs, etc., *out, up, down, about,* etc.) violently سختی سے ہلانا *throw (one's) chest* سینہ تان کر کھڑے ہو جانا (of a horse) cause the rider to fall to the ground گرانا، گرا دینا (of a wrestler) force an opponent to the floor پچھاڑنا (at dice) cast پھینکنا، اُچھالنا shape (pottery) on potter's wheel چاک پر بنانا (*Phrases* :) *throw away,* (one's advantages, chance, etc.), lose by foolishness or neglect اپنی حماقت یا غفلت سے کھو دینا *throw (something) in* میں گھسیڑنا *throw (something) in, throw (something) into the bargain,* give something extra, without addition to the price اُوپر سے الگ دینا، گھاتے میں دینا، روکن میں دینا، روکن جھوکن میں دینا، جھوکن میں دینا، رُونگا دینا *throw in (one's) lot with,* decide to share the fortune of کسی کے ساتھ اپنی قسمت وابستہ کر لینا *throw (oneself) into (an activity,* etc.), participate in (it) vigorously and enthusiastically میں جوش سے حصّہ لینا *throw a party,* (colloq.) give a party دعوت دینا *throw a kiss,* kiss one's hand to mean a kiss to someone اپنا ہاتھ چوم کر کسی کی طرف اشارہ کرنا *throw off,* (*a*) get rid of سے نجات حاصل کرنا (*b*) cast off اُتار دینا *throw open (entry,* etc.), make it open to all persons عام کر دینا، کی عام اجازت دینا *throw out,* (*a*) make (a suggestion) (تجویز) پیش کرنا (*b*) give (a hint) in a casual way (اشارہ) کرنا (*c*) reject (a Bill) نامنظور کرنا، مسترد کرنا (*d*) put (batsman) out by throwing at the wicket وکٹ میں گیند مار کر آؤٹ کر دینا (*e*) confuse (speaker) by interruption دخل دے کر ہراساں کر دینا *throw over,* abandon (a plan, friend) ترک کر دینا، چھوڑ دینا *throw up,* (*a*) vomit (food) اُگلنا، کی قے کر دینا (*b*) resign from (a position) سے مستعفی ہو جانا

n. throwing or being thrown from horseback گھوڑے پر سے گرنا یا گرانا throwing or being thrown in wrestling پچھاڑنا یا پچھڑنا distance to which something can be thrown اتنی دُور جہاں تک (کچھ) پھینکا جا سکے *within a stone's throw (of a place),* quite near (it) (کے) بالکل قریب **throw-off** *n.* start of race, hunting, etc. دَوڑ، شکار وغیرہ کا آغاز

thrum (thrum) *v.t.* & *i.* (-mm-) pluck at (strings, harp, etc.), playing on (it) carelessly (کے تار) یونہی چھیڑنا، تن تن کرنا strike fingers on table, etc., thus طبلہ سا بجانا *n.* loose ends of warp thread left unfinished جھالر any short loose thread left کوئی ٹوٹا ہوا تار sound of thrumming طبلہ سا بجانے یا تن تن کرنے کی آواز، تن تن *thread and thrum,* (*a*) all together سب ایک ساتھ (*b*) good and bad all together اچھا بُرا سب **thrummy** *adj.* having a thrum جھالردار

thrush (thrush) *n.* a kind of song-bird ترغ throat disease in children قلاع such disease in hooved animals قلاع

thrust (thrust) *v.t.* & *i.* push suddenly or violently زور سے دھکیلنا stuff (*into* something) ٹھونسنا make a forward stroke with (a sword, etc.) گھونپنا، بھونکنا *thrust oneself,* (or *one's nose*) *in,* interrupt ; get involved خواہ مخواہ ٹانگ اڑانا *be thrust from,* deprived of سے محرُوم کر دیا جانا *n.* thrusting دھکا، جھٹکا، گھائی، وار strong attempt to push forward into the enemy's lines, etc. دُشمن کی صفیں چیرنے کی کوشش

thud (thud) (-dd-) dull sound as of a blow on something soft گدکا، بھدکا *v.i.* fall or strike with this sound بھد سے گرنا (یا)، بھد سے مارنا

thug (thug) *n.* professional Indian robber of early 19th century ٹھگ one who lives by violence غنڈہ، خونی، بدمعاش

thumb (thumb) *n.* short, thick finger set apart from the other four ہاتھ کا انگوٹھا، انگوٹھا *under (someone's) thumb,* under (his or her) influence and control کے زیرِ اثر، کے تابع فرمان *rule of thumb,* rough and ready method based on experience or practice موٹا اصُول *v.t.* turn over (leaves of a book) ورق پلٹنا make dirty by doing this (کتاب کو) ہاتھوں سے میلا کرنا **thumb-nail** *n.* nail of the thumb انگوٹھے کا ناخن **thumb-nail sketch** *n.* thumb-nail sized portrait ناخن جتنی تصویر hasty word-picture سرسری تذکرہ **thumb-print, thumb-impression** *n.* this as identification mark نشان انگوٹھا **thumbscrew** *n.* ancient instrument of torture انگوٹھے کا شکنجہ

thump (thump) *v.t.* & *i.* strike heavily with the fist or hand زور سے ہاتھ مارنا، زور سے مُکا مارنا (of the heart) beat fast دھک دھک کرنا، زور سے دھڑکنا *n.* heavy **blow** with the fist or hand مُکّا، گھونسا، تھپّڑ **thumping** *adj.* (slang) very big (majority, lie, etc.) بہُت بڑا **thumper** *n.* (slang) outrageous lie سفید جھوٹ big specimen بڑا

thunder (*thund*-ĕ*) *n.* loud noise of clouds (with or without lightning) (بادل کی) گرج، گھن گرج، (بجلی کی) کڑک loud noise (of guns, etc.) گرج *v.t.* & *i.* emit thunder (بادل کا) گرجنا، (بجلی کا) کڑکنا make a loud noise like thunder کڑکنا، بڑی اونچی آواز سے بولنا speak (*out* something) loudly گرج کر کہنا، کڑک کر بولنا *thunder against* (*someone*), denounce (him) vehemently کے خلاف سخت اعتراضات کرنا، سختی سے ڈانٹنا **thunderbolt** *n.* flash of lightning بجلی، کوندے کی لپک sudden and unforeseen disaster ناگہانی اُفتاد، غیبی گولا **thunderclap** *n.* sound of lightning بجلی کی کڑک، کڑک sudden and unforeseen disaster ناگہانی اُفتاد، غیبی گولا such sad news قیامت کی خبر **thunderstorm** *n.* storm and lightning بجلی آندھی اور بارش، طوفانِ برق و باراں **thunderstruck** *adj.* struck by lightning جس پر بجلی گرے amazed ہکّا بکّا، بھونچکّا، حیران، سرگشتہ **thundry** (thund-ri) *adj.* (of weather) giving signs of thunder گھن گرج کی آمد والا **thunderous** *adj.* as loud as thunder گرجدار، کڑک والا

Thursday (*thĕ*s*-day) *n.* the fifth day of the week (originally regarded as being sacred to *Thor* or the god of thunder who was the conuterpart of the Roman Jove or Jupiter and the Greek Zeus) جمعرات، پنجشنبہ

thus (dhus) *adv.* in this (or that) way اِس طرح، یُوں to this (or that) point or degree اِس حد تک، اِتنا *thus much* اِتنا *thus far* یہاں تک *thus and thus*, in such and such a way اِس اِس طرح

thwack (thwak) *v.t.* hit with a stick پیٹنا، ٹھونکنا *n.* such hit ٹھکائی، ڈنڈے کا وار

thwart (thwo*t) *v.t.* frustrate (someone) کی راہ میں حائل ہونا، میں مزاحم ہونا foil (someone's) plans ناکام بنا دینا *n.* rower's seat کشتی کھینے والے کی نشست

thy (dhı) *possessive adj.* (old use or poet.) yours (*sing.*) تیرا **thine** (dhın) *possessive pron.* (old use or poet.) yours (*sing.*) تیرا **thyself** (dhı-*self*) *reflexive pron.* (old use or poet.) yourself (*sing.*) تو خود، اپنے آپ (کو وغیرہ)

thyme (tīm) *n.* plant with fragrant leaves for flavouring food صعتر **thymol** (*tı*-mol) *n.* a strong disinfectant made from it ٹائمول **thymy** (*ti*-mı) *adj.* scent (as) of thyme صعتری

thyroid (*thı*-roid) *adj.* in the form of a shield ڈھال کا سا *thyroid gland*, (*a*) ductless gland in the throat greatly influencing growth and development تھائی رائڈ گلانڈ، سپری غدہ، سپر نما غدہ (*b*) drug made from animals' thyroid gland تھائی رائڈ گلانڈ

thyrsus (*thĕ**-sus) *Cl. myth.* staff borne by Bacchus and his train

tiara (ti-*a*-ra) *n.* coronet for a woman نکٹ Pope's crown پاپائے روما کا تاج conical cap of ancient Persians کلاہ **tiara'd** (ti-*a*-rad) *adj.* having a tiara کجکلاہ

tick (tik) *n.* light regular sound (of a clock, watch, etc.) ٹک ٹک، کھٹ کھٹ، کھٹکا small mark (✓) put against names, figures, etc., in a list to show that something is correct or that it has been accounted for جائزے کی علامت، ٹک مارک، ٹک *on tick*, (slang) on credit اُدھار a small blood-sucking insect چیچڑ *v.t.* & *i.* (of a clock, etc.) make ticks ٹک ٹک کرنا، کھٹ کھٹ کرنا put a tick against ٹک کرنا، ٹک مارک لگانا *tick* (or *tick off*) *the items in a list* (*etc.*) فہرست میں مختلف رقموں وغیرہ پر ٹک کرنا *tick* (*someone*) *off*, (slang) rebuke (him) جھاڑ جھپاڑ کرنا، لعن طعن کرنا (*tick over*), (of an internal combustion engine) run slowly with gears disconnected (انجن کا) بند ہو کر کھٹ کھٹ کرنا

ticket (*tik*-et) *n.* small card, etc., giving the holder the right to travel by train, bus, etc., or to a seat in a theatre, etc. ٹکٹ label or chit on an article indicating its price قیمت کی پرچی *v.t.* put a ticket on (esp. something to be sold) پر قیمت کی پرچی لگانا

tickle (*tick*-èl) *v.t.* & *i.* touch the nerves of the sensitive part of the skin so as to excite laughter گدگدانا، گدگدی کرنا *It tickles* اِس سے مجھے گدگدی ہوتی ہے *tickle* (*someone*) *in the ribs* کی پسلیوں میں گدگدی کرنا have an itching feeling گدگدی ہونا please (one's sense of humour or of taste) سے ہنسی آنا، سے محظوظ ہونا، محظوظ کرنا *n.* tickling or the sensation caused by it گدگدی **ticklish** *adj.* (of person) easily made to laugh or wriggle when tickled جس کے گدگدی بہُت جلد اُٹھتی ہو (of person) much too sensitive زود حس (of problem, etc.) requiring tact to handle ٹیڑھا (of piece of work, etc.) apt to go wrong پیچیدہ، مشکل

tidal *adj.* (see under **tide**)

tide (tid) *n.* regular rise and fall in the level of the sea, caused by the attraction of the moon جوار بھاٹا، مد و جزر (*at*) *high tide* کامل مد (کے وقت) (*at*) *low tide* کامل جزر (کے وقت) *neap-tide*, tide on the 7th and 21st nights of the lunar month مد و جزرِ اصغر *spring-tide*, tide on the 1st and 14th of the lunar month مد و جزرِ کامل *flood-tide* مد *ebb-tide* جزر *tide-way*, part of river affected by tide جوار بھاٹے والا حصہ

work double tide, work day and night دن رات کام کرنا tendency (of public opinion, etc.) رُجحان ، زور ، سیلاب *v.t.* (*tide over*), get over or enable (someone) to get over (a period of difficulty, etc.) مُشکلات پر قابو پانا ، پر غالب آنا **tidal** (*tī*-dĕl) *adj.* of the tide جوار بھاٹے کا ، مَدّ و جزر *a tidal wave*, a huge wave accompanying an earthquake بہُت بڑی لہر

tidings (*tī*-dingz) *n. pl.* (used with a sing. verb) news received خبر ، اِطلاع

tidy (*tī*-di) *adj.* neat and clean صاف سُتھرا orderly باترتیب ، سلیقے کا *n.* antimacassar کُرسی کی پُشت کا غلاف bag for odds and ends مُتفرّقات کا تھیلا *v.t.* (also *tidy up*) make tidy (oneself, room, etc.) صاف کرنا put in order (table, paper, etc.) سلیقے سے رکھنا **tidily** (*ti*-di-li) *adv.* صاف ، سلیقے سے

tie (tī) *v.t. & i.* (*tie, tied, tied ; tying*) fasten (*with* string, rope, etc.) باندھنا *tie (someone's) feet together* پیر ایک دُوسرے کے ساتھ باندھ دینا *tie up a parcel* بنڈل باندھنا make (a knot) (گرہ) باندھنا (یا) لگانا (یا) دینا (*be tied up*), be held up (*by*) میں رُکاوٹ پڑ جانا ، رُک جانا (of conditions in an agreement, etc.) restrict the freedom of کو پابند کر دینا (also *tie with*), (of players or teams) make the same score (as) ٹائی پڑ جانا ، برابر رہنا *n.* that which holds people together رِشتہ ، تعلّق *family ties* خاندانی تعلّقات (*a tie on someone*), that which takes up one's attention and limits freedom of action کو پابند کر دینا ، کا پابند بن جانا equal position (between persons, teams, etc.) in matches, competitions, etc. ٹائی ، برابری *end in a tie*, (of a match, etc.) ٹائی پڑ جانا ، برابر رہ جانا necktie نکٹائی

tier (*ti*-ĕ*) *n.* one of a number of rows (in a picture-house, etc.) parallel to and rising above one another مُتوازی اور بُلند ہونے والی نشستوں کی قطار ، مُتوازی قطار *v.t.* put in tiers مُتوازی قطاروں میں رکھنا (یا) کھڑا کرنا

tiff (tif) *n.* slight quarrel ذرا سا جھگڑا ، خفگی sip of liquor شراب کا گھونٹ ، چُسکی

tiffin (*tif*-in) *n.* (Anglo-Pakistani word for) lunch ٹفن

tiger (*ti*-gĕ*) *n.* well-known fierce animal with black stripes on yellow skin شیر (slang) formidable rival in a game (opp. *rabbit*) سخت ٹکر کا حریف **tigress** (*tig*-res) *n. fem.* female tiger شیرنی **tigon** (*tī*-gon) *n.* offspring of tiger and lioness شیر اور ببر شیرنی کا دوغلا بچّہ

tight (tīt) *adj.* fitting closely تنگ ، کسا ہُوا fixed closely مضبوطی سے لگا ہُوا (of knots, etc.) not easily unfastened سخت ، مضبوط fully stretched (rope, etc.) تنا ہُوا ، کسا ہُوا closely or firmly put together or packed so as to occupy the smallest possible space پُوری طرح بھرا ہُوا (of money) not easily available کمیاب produced by pressure داب میں آیا ہُوا needing pressure جسے داب کی ضرورت ہو *a tight squeeze* زور کا داب (*be*) *in a tight corner*, (be) in a situation from which escape is difficult مُشکل میں گرفتار ہونا ، پھنسا ہُوا ہونا *a tight fit*, no room for any more things, etc. کوئی گنجائش نہ ہونا ، پہلے ہی ٹھُنسا ہُوا ہونا made so that nothing (of the specified thing) can escape or enter it بند *air-tight* ہوا روک ، ہوا بند *water tight* پانی روک ، آب بند *in water-tight compartments* ایک دُوسرے سے بالکل الگ تھلگ *adv.* tightly پُوری طرح کسا ہُوا ، مضبوطی سے ، بالکل بند **tighten** (*tit*-ĕn) *v.t. & i.* (also *tighten up*), make or become tight (not loose) کسنا ، کس کر لگانا (یا) باندھنا *tighten up the (loose) screws* ڈھیلے پیچوں کو کسنا ، پیچ کسنا *tighten (one's) belt*, economize کفایت شعاری شروع کرنا ، پیٹ پر پتھر باندھ لینا **tight-fisted** *adj.* mean کمینہ miserly کنجوس **tights** *n. pl.* acrobat's skin-tight garment covering the legs and body نٹوں کا بدن سے چپکا ہُوا لباس **tightly** *adv.* پُوری طرح کسا ہونا ، بالکل بند **tightness** *n.* کسا ہُوا ، مضبوطی سے ، بالکل بند ہونا ، ٹھُنسا ہُوا ہونا

tigon *n.*, **tigress** *n.* (see under **tiger**)

tile (tīl) *n.* plate of baked clay, for covering roofs چکنی مٹّی کا کھپرا ، کھپرا ، کھپریل *pantile*, curved roof-tile چھت کا کھپرا ، کھپریل *glazed tile*, decorative tile for walls, etc. روغنی ٹائل

till (til) *conj.* until جب تک ، تاوقتیکہ ، یہاں تک کہ *prep.* until تک ، تا *n.* money-drawer in a shop counter دُکان میں روپیہ رکھنے کی دراز ، تختے کے نیچے کی غلّک *v.t.* cultivate (land) کاشت کرنا **tiller** (*til*-ĕ*) *n.* one who tills land ; peasant, cultivator کاشتکار ، کسان handle fixed to the rudder of a small boat پتوار کا دستہ **tillage** (*til*-ej) *n.* tilling کاشتکاری

tilt *v.t. & i.* (cause to) come into a sloping position ایک طرف جھکنا یا جھکانا (*tilt at*) (old use) (of person on horseback) ride at (someone) with lance سوار کا نیزہ لے کر کسی پر پل پڑنا ، با نیزے کا وار کرنا (*tilt at*), attack (someone) in speech or writing پر سخت اعتراضات کرنا *n.* tilting جھکنا ، جھکانا sloping position جھکاؤ tilting with lances نیزے کا وار کرنا (*at*) *full tilt*, at full speed and with great force پُورے زور اور تیزی سے ، تند و تیز ، تندی و تیزی سے

timber (*tim*-bĕ*) *n.* wood prepared for use in building, etc. عمارتی لکڑی beam forming a support (in a roof, ship, etc.) شہتیر ، کڑی trees large enough for use as timber عمارتی لکڑی والے درخت **timbered** *adj.* made with (a framework) of timber لکڑی کا (یا) لکڑی کے ڈھانچے والا **timbertoes** *n.*

(slang) person with a wooden leg لکڑی کی ٹانگ والا heavy-treading person بھاری بھاری قدموں سے چلنے والا
timbre (*tim*-bĕ*) *n.* characteristic quality of a musical voice or sound apart from its pitch and intensity آواز کی کیفیت
timbrel (*tim*-brel) *n.* (old use) tambourine طنبورہ، دَف
time (tīm) *n.* the hour of the day وقت • point at, or period during, which things happen وقت، مُدّت، زمانہ *in time,* early enough (*for* or *to do* something) (کے لیے)، بَروَقت، سے پہلے *on time,* exactly on time بَروَقت *after a period of time, in the future* جَلدی، وَقت سے پہلے ہی، آگے چل کر، آئندہ *in good time,* early *in no time,* (colloq.) very soon, or very quickly بہت جلد، فوراً، آناً فاناً *the time is up,* the time allowed is over وَقت ختم (ہو گیا) *at one time,* during a certain period of time in the past ایک زمانہ میں *at the same time,* (*a*) simultaneously ایک ہی وَقت، بیک وَقت (*b*) nevertheless تاہم *from time to time,* occasionally وقتاً فوقتاً *time and again, time and time again,* (*a*) repeatedly بار بار (*b*) often اکثر *for the time being,* for the present فی الحال *time out of mind,* period of time further back than memory can go مُدّتوں *(work) against time,* (work) fast because time is limited پہلے وَقت پر ختم کرنے کے لیے سخت جلدی (کرنا) appropriate season موزوں وَقت، مُناسب موقع opportunity موقع interval وَقفہ، مُدّت occasion وَقت، موقع (one's) life عمر، زمانہ hour of death آخری وَقت hour of travail مُصیبت کا وَقت، آڑا وَقت، اڑا وقت (*pl.*) multiplied by ضرب *two times four is eight,* (English way of repeating the multiplication tables) چار دُونی آٹھ (*pl.*) (*a*) fold گُنا *four times,* four-fold چار گُنا (*b*) on (so many occasions) بار، مرتبہ، دفعہ (usu. *pl.*) period of time associated with something or someone زمانہ، عہد، دَور *in ancient times,* پرانے زمانے میں *the time of, the times of,* دَور system of measuring time وقت *Greenwich time,* گرینیچ کا وَقت *summer time,* گرمیوں کا وَقت length of musical note تال، گَت *in time,* (in music) تال کے ساتھ، گت کے مُطابِق *out of time,* (in music) بے سُرا، بے سُر، تال کے بغیر *beat time,* show the time of music by movements of the hand, etc. تال دینا *v.t.* choose or arrange the time for (something to happen) (کسی کام کے لیے) وَقت مُقرّر کرنا do (something) on time وَقت پر کرنا measure the time taken by (someone) or by (something) کا وَقت لینا
time-bomb *n.* bomb timed to explode after being put in position مُؤقّت بَم **time-honoured** *adj.* respected because old قدیم اور مُقدّس **time-lag** [n]al between cause and effect عِلّت و معلول میں وقفہ، مُدت **timeless** *adj.* unending غیر مُختتم، ختم نہ ہونے والا **timely** (*tīm*-li) *adj.* coming or occurring at the right time بروقت **time-server** *n.* selfish opportunist ابنُ الوَقت **time-table** *n.* schedule of times at which things are to be done ٹائم ٹیبل، اَوقات نامہ **time-work** *n.* work for which payment is by the hour or day وَقت کے مُطابِق اُجرت والا کام
timid (*tim*-id) *adj.* cowardly, easily frightened بُزدِل، ڈرپوک، بودا **timidly** *adv.* with timidity بُزدلی سے، بُزدلانہ **timidity** (-*mid*-) *n.* quality of being timid بُزدلی **timorous** (*tim*-o-rus) *adj.* timid بُزدِل، ڈرپوک، بودا **timorously** *adv.* بُزدلی سے، بُزدِلانہ
tin *n.* soft white metal used for coating iron sheets قلعی، رانگا، ٹین tin-plated container ٹین کا ڈبہ، کنستر، ٹین *v.i.* coat with tin پر ٹین چڑھانا، کو قلعی کرنا pack in tins ٹین کے ڈبّے (یا ڈبّوں) میں بند کرنا **tin lizzie** *n.* (slang) Ford (or any other) motor-car (فورڈ) کار **tinplate** *n.* sheet-iron coated with tin ٹین **tinsmith** *n.* tinman, tinker ٹین ساز **tinware** *n.* tin vessels, etc. ٹین کا سامان
tincture (*tink*-chĕ*) *n.* medical substance dissolved in alcohol الکحلی مُرکّب، (دوا کا) رُوح شراب میں محلول اَنگلچر trace or suggestion (*of*) (کی) جھلک، (کا) شائبہ small amount (*of*) ذرا سا (کی) اپٹ *v.t.* colour slightly کو ہلکا سا رنگ دینا slightly modify (something with) کی پُٹ دینا
tinder (*tind*-ĕ*) *n.* any dry material easily catching fire from a spark آگ پکڑنے والی کوئی سُوکھی چیز، سوختہ
tinge (tinj) *v.t.* colour slightly (with red, etc.) (کا) ہلکا سا رنگ دینا affect slightly (*with*) ہلکی سی جھلک پیدا کرنا *n.* slight colouring (*of*) ہلکا سا رنگ slight trace (*of*) جھلک، شائبہ
tingle (*ting*-ĕl) *n.* stinging feeling in the skin جھنجھناہٹ، جھرجھری any sort of excitement بےچینی، اضطراب *v. i.* have a stinging feeling کو جھنجھناہٹ ہونا feel excitement (*with*) بےچین ہونا، جھرجھری لینا
tinker (tink-ĕ*) *n.* tinplate worker who travels from place to place and repairs kettles, pans, etc. سفری ٹین ساز، قلعی گر *v. i.* (*tinker with*), do repairs without expert knowledge بے ڈھنگے پن سے مرمّت کرنا (*tinker away at*), do (something) clumsily بے ڈھنگے پن سے کام لینا (*tinker away at*), fiddle with (something) دفعِ الوقتی کے لیے کام کرنا
tinkle (*tink*-ĕl) *v.t.* & *i.* (cause to) make a succession of sounds as of the ringing of small bells ٹن ٹن بجنا (یا) بجانا، کی جھنکار ہونا (یا) دیکھنا *n.* such sounds جھنکار

tinsel (*tin*-sel) *n.* glittering metallic strips, etc., for cheap decoration گوٹا، کناری، لچکا such thin sheets سستی دھات کے چمکدار ورق cheap, showy brilliance اوپری چمک *adj.* tawdry بھڑکدار

tint *n.* light shade of a colour (کسی رنگ کا) ہلکا سا روپ *v.t.* give a tint to ہلکا سا رنگ دینا

tintinnabulation (tin-tin-ab-ew-*lay*-shun) *n.* tinkling جھنکار

tiny (*tī*-ni) *adj.* very small بہت چھوٹا سا، ننھا سا

-tion (shun) *suf.* (for forming nouns that denote :) state of being ٹ،ن،ت،ی (as : *exhaustion* تھکاوٹ، تھکن، درماندگی) act of doing (etc.) ت، ی (as : *opposition* مخالفت

¹tip *n.* tapered end نوک *the tips of* (*one's*) *fingers* انگلیوں کی پوریں (*have* or *be*) *on the tips of* (*one's*) *fingers*, (of facts, details, etc.) well-remembered برنوکِ زبان، مستحضر small piece put on end of something سرا **tiptoes** *n. pl.* tip of the toes پیر کی انگلیوں کا اگلا حصہ *on tiptoes*, (walking) on toes for quietness پنجوں کے بل (چلنا) دبے پاؤں (چلنا) **tiptoe** *v.i.* (*tiptoed* ; *tiptoeing*) walk quietly or be on the toes پنجوں کے بل چلنا یا کھڑا ہونا **tiptop** *adj.* exceedingly good (condition) بڑی اچھی (حالت) **tip-up** *adj.* (of seat) hinged so that it can be raised for passing freely تہہ ہو جانے والی

²tip *v.t.* & *i.* (-pp-) (also *tip up* or *tip over*), (cause to) rise on one side or at one end ایک طرف سے اونچا ہونا (یا) کرنا، ترچھا ہونا (یا) کرنا، جھکنا (یا) جھکانا overturn دھکیل دینا (یا) الٹ دینا empty (contents of something) (*out of* or *into*) by tipping میں سے گرانا (یا) اوندھا *n.* place where rubbish, etc., may be tipped کوڑا کرکٹ پھینکنے کی جگہ

tip *v.t.* (-pp-) touch or strike lightly چھونا، ہلکا سا لگنا، آہستہ سے لگنا give (money, etc., to someone) in an informal way بخشش دینا، انعام دینا *give a tip to* (*someone*), *tip* (*someone some money*) کو بخشش دینا (also *tip off*), give secret information to (someone) about the winning horse, the future value of shares, etc. اطلاع دینا *n.* light blow ہلکی سی ضرب extra money paid to a waiter, etc., for personal services بخشش، انعام secret information about the winning horse or the future value of shares, etc. خفیہ پیشگی اطلاع practical advice on the method (*for* something) (کی) غمزہ ترکیب **tipster** *n.* one who gives tips about races گھڑ دوڑ کے متعلق خفیہ پیشگی اطلاع دینے والا

Tipperary (tip-è-*ray*-ri) *n.* a song popular among British soldiers of World War I ٹپریری

tippet (*tip*-et) *n.* fur cloak for the shoulders worn by women بے آستین کی پوستینی قبا

tipple (*tip*-èl) *v.t.* & *i.* be given to taking much liquor بہت شرابی ہونا drink (wine, etc.) چڑھا جانا *n.* liquor شراب **tippler** *n.* one who tipples بڑا شرابی، بلا نوش

tipsy (*tip*-si) *adj.* intoxicated نشے میں چور متوالا، مدہوش

tiptoe *v.i.*, **tiptoes** *n. pl.* (see under ¹**tip**)

tirade (*tī*-rayd) *n.* scolding rant (*against*) پرجوش ملامتی تقریر such poem پرجوش ملامتی نظم

tire (*tī*-è*) *n.* (same as *tyre*, which see) *v.t.* & *i.* make or become weary تھکنا یا تھکا دینا bore or be bored اکتا دینا (یا) اکتا جانا *tire of*, lose interest in سے دلچسپی نہ رہنا، سے اکتا جانا **tired** (*tī*-ĕ*d) *adj.* weary تھکا ہوا *tired out*, exhausted سخت تھکا ہوا ہونا bored اکتایا ہوا، تنگ آیا ہوا **tireless** *adj.* not easily tired (person, energy, etc.) انتھک، ان تھک ceaseless (worker) لگاتار (کام کرنے) والا **tiresome** *adj.* troublesome تکلیف دہ tiring تھکا دینے والا very difficult کٹھن

tiro (*tī*-roh), **tyro** (*tī*-roh) *n.* novice مبتدی، نو آموز، اناڑی **tirocinium** (ti-ro-*sin*-i-um) *n.* apprenticeship, training سکھلائی

'tis (tiz) (abbr. of) it is یہ ہے

tissue (*tis*-ew, or *tish*-ew) *n.* any fine fabric باریک بنی ہوئی چیز skin, muscles, nerves, cells, etc., of an animal or plant نسیج، خلیوں کا سلسلہ web or network (*of* lies, etc.) (کا) پوٹ، (جھوٹ کی) طومار **tissue-paper** *n.* thin soft paper put on pictures, etc. مومی کاغذ

tit *n.* kinds of small bird (like the *titlark*) چڑیا (also *titmouse*), a kind of small bird پھدکی (old use) small horse ٹٹو (old use) girl لڑکی، چھوکری (only the phrase :) *tit for tat*, blow in return for blow ترکی بہ ترکی جواب اینٹ کا جواب پتھر *it is only tit for tat* یہ تو صرف ادلے کا بدلہ ہے *give* (*him*) *tit for tat* اسے ترکی بہ ترکی جواب دو

Titan (*tī*-tĕn) *Cl. myth.* one of the children of Uranus (Heaven) and Gaea (Earth), who were the parents or uncles and aunts of the gods (called the Olympians) ٹائٹن، تیتن the sun سورج huge person, animal or thing بہت بڑا person of remarkable genius غیر معمولی ذہانت والا

titanic (tī-*tan*-ik) *adj.* huge بہت بڑا، عظیم

titbit (tit-*bit*) *n.* choice morsel مزیدار لقمہ، نوالہ choice bit (*of* news, etc.) دلچسپ، مزیدار چٹکلا

tithe (tīdh) *n.* one-tenth عشر، دسواں حصہ tax amounting to one-tenth of produce, etc. عشر such tax for the support of English priest *v. t.* subject (property or owner) to tithe پر عشر لگانا

titillate (*tit*-) *v.t.* stimulate imagination as by

tickling تصوّر کو گدگدانا titillation (*-lay-*) *n.* تصوّر میں گدگدی ہونا یا کرنا

title (*ti*-tèl) *n.* name (of a book) نام name (*of* a poem, essay, short story, picture, etc.) عنوان word used to show a person's rank or occupation لقب ، القاب (also title of honour), title bestowed as honour خطاب legal right (*to* or *to do* something) حق استحقاق right (*to* property) حقِ ملکیت **titled** (*ti*-tèld) *adj.* having a title of honour خطاب یافتہ **title-deed** *n.* document proving a title to property دستاویزِ ملکیت **titlepage** *n.* page at front of book giving the title, author's name, etc. سرورق **title-role** *n.* role of a character after whom a play is named عنوانی کردار **titular** (*tit*-ew-lĕ*) *adj.* existing in name at least, though not necessarily wielding authority رسمی ، نمائشی nominal برائے نام giving a name to جس کے نام پر نام رکھا ہو

titmouse *n.* (see **tit** sense 2)

titter (*tit*-ĕ*) silly half-suppressed laugh کھسیانی ہنسی *v.i.* laugh thus کھسیانی ہنسی ہنسنا

tittle (*tit*-èl) *n.* least quantity ذرہ بھر ، ایک شوشہ **not one jot or tittle**, not at all, not in the least بالکل نہیں

tittle-tattle (*tit*-èl-*tat*-èl) *n.* gossip گپ شپ *v.t.* gossip گپ شپ کرنا ، گپ بازی کرنا

titular *adj.* (see under **title**)

to (pr. tu ; emphatic : too ; still more emphatic : *too*) *prep.* in the direction of کو ، کی طرف as far as تک far کو ، کی غرض سے sign of the indirect object کو (sign of the infinitive by prefixing it to the imperative as *to*+see=to see) (دیکھو + نا) with reference to ; towards کا in comparison with بمقابلہ ، کے مقابلے میں (sign of the complement ; as, *I have the honour to be*) (ہوا) نے کا involved or included in کا ، میں *That's all there's to it* ; there is nothing more in this connexion بس یہ تو اتنا ہی ہے ، اس کی تو فقط اتنی سی بات ہے *adv.* (pr. *too*) to or in the normal position واپس *come to*, revive ہوش میں آنا to a standstill, etc. بس *Is the door to?* کیا دروازہ بند ہے؟ *heave to*, cease motion رک جانا *to all appearance*, apparently بظاہر *to all eternity*, for ever ہمیشہ ہمیشہ *to arms*, take up arms مسلح ہو جاؤ *to come*, future آنے والا *to a t*, precisely بالکل ٹھیک *to hand*, (a) within reach قریب (b) (of letter) arrived موصول ہو گیا *to let*, offered at lease کرایے کے لیے خالی *to my knowledge*, as far as I know جہاں تک مجھے معلوم ہے ، جہاں تک میرا علم ہے *not to my knowledge*, not so far as I know میرے علم کے مطابق ، میرے علم میں *to my mind*, (a) in my opinion میرے خیال میں (b) that I like میری پسند کا *to my thinking*, in my opinion میرے خیال میں *to no purpose*, useless بیکار ، لاحاصل *to perfection*, perfectly بالکل ٹھیک *to scale*, according to the scale تناسب سے *to taste*, according to it حسبِ ذائقہ *to the life*, (of portrait, etc.) lifelike منہ بولتی *to the point*, *to the purpose*, relevant, relevantly متعلقہ ، جو غیر متعلق نہ ہو *to wit*, viz., namely یعنی *to and fro*, (froh) (a) backwards and forwards دو مقامات کے درمیان ، آگے پیچھے (b) here and there ادھر ادھر

toad (tohd) *n.* frog-like animal that lives chiefly on land ایک بہت بڑا مینڈک جسم کا مینڈک ، مکروہ repulsive person مکروہ شخص **toad-eating** *n.* toadyism ٹوڈی پن ، خوشامد **toadstool** *n.* kind of umbrella-shaped fungus سانپ کی چھتری **toady** (*toh*-di) *n.* one who flatters someone in the hope of gain خوشامدی ، کاسہ لیس ، ٹوڈی *v.t.* & *i.* flatter (someone) thus کی خوشامد کرنا ، کی کاسہ لیسی کرنا **toadyism** (toh-di-izm) *n.* sycophancy کاسہ لیسی

a toad

toast (tohst) *n.* sliced bread made brown and crisp by being heated ڈبل روٹی کا سینکا ہوا ٹکڑا ، توس wish for the good health and happiness of (someone) expressed while raising a glass of wine کا جام صحت نوش کرنا ، جام صحت person who is toasted جس کا جام صحت نوش کیا جائے *v.t.* & *i.* make (sliced bread, etc.) brown before a fire, etc. (ڈبل روٹی وغیرہ) سینکنا make or become warm before a fire آگ کے قریب رکھ کر گرم کرنا ، آگ تاپنا wish good health and happiness to (*someone*) by raising a glass of wine کا جام صحت نوش کرنا

tobacco (to-*bak*-oh) *n.* (pl. *tobaccos*) leaves used for smoking تمباکو plant bearing these leaves تمباکو **tobacconist** (to-*bak*-o-nist) *n.* shopkeeper selling tobacco تمباکو فروش

toboggan (to-*bog*-an) *n.* long and narrow hand-sledge دستی برف گاڑی *v.i.* go down a snow-covered slope on a toboggan چھوٹی برف گاڑی میں برفانی ڈھلان پر سے پھسلنا ، دستی برف گاڑی چلانا

toco (*toh*-koh) *n.* (corruption of the Urdu word ٹھوکو) thrashing ٹھکائی

tocsin (*tok*-sin) *n.* alarm signal on bell خطرے کی گھنٹی

today, to-day (to-*day*) *n.* this day آج the present times آج ، آجکل *adv.* in the day آج in the present times آج ، آجکل

toddle (*tod*-èl) *v.i.* walk with short uncertain steps like a baby (*to a place*, or *one's way*) بچے کی طرح ڈگمگا کر چلنا *n.* such walk بچوں کی سی ڈگمگاتی ہوئی چال **toddler** *n.* baby who can toddle پاؤں پاؤں چلنے والا بچہ ، ننھا منا

toddy (*tod*-i) *n.* sweetened drink prepared by adding water to alcoholic spirits سپرٹ کا گرم شربت palm-tree sap or fermented liquor made from it تاڑی

to-do (tū-doo) *n.* (colloq.) commotion ہلچل، کھڑبڑ، افراتفری fuss مصیبت، دردِ سر lot of excitement and talk شور و غوغا

toe (toh) *n.* one of the five jointed ends of the foot پاؤں کی انگلی *from top to toe*, from head to bottom, completely بالکل، سرتاسر *tread on (someone's) toes*, offend (him) کو ناراض کرنا part of a sock, shoe, etc., covering the toes (جراب یا جوتے کا) پنجہ *v.t.* touch with the toes پنجے سے چھونا، کو پنجہ لگانا *toe the line*, (*a*) stand with toes on the starting-line ready for a race دوڑ کے آغاز کی لکیر پر پنجوں کے بل کھڑا ہونا obey the party's orders even if not to one's liking چار و ناچار پارٹی کا ساتھ دینا، پارٹی کے حکم کی تعمیل کرنا **toe-nail** *n.* nail of the toe پیر کا ناخن **big toe, great toe** *n.* inner toe پاؤں کا انگوٹھا **little toe** *n.* outer toe پاؤں کی چھوٹی انگلی

toff (tof) *n.* (slang) gentleman or one passing as such (اصلی یا نقلی) شریف آدمی *the toffs*, upper classes بالائی طبقہ

toffee, toffy (*tof*-i) *n.* hard sticky sweet made of sugar and butter ٹافی

tog *v.t.* (slang) dress کپڑے پہنانا equip with clothes کپڑے دینا **togs** (togz) *n. pl.* (slang) clothes کپڑے، پوشاک

toga (*toh*-ga) *n.* civil dress of the ancient Romans comprising a piece of plain cloth wrapped round the body ٹوگا، رومی ٹوپی **toga'd** (*toh*-gad) *adj.* wearing a toga ٹوگا پہنے ہوئے، رومی دھوتی میں

a Roman in a toga

together (to-*gedh*-ĕ*) *adj.* in company اکٹھے in juxtaposition ایک دوسرے سے simultaneously ایک ساتھ، بیک وقت *together with*, (*a*) along with مع، بمعیت (*b*) as well as اور بھی on end ; continuously کئی کئی، مسلسل، کئی

toil *v.i.* work hard (*at* something) (پر) سخت محنت کرنا move with difficulty (*through, up*, etc.) مشکل سے جانا *n.* hard work سخت محنت، مشقت، جانفشانی (*toils*) *n. pl.* snare پھندا، دام machinations کے پھندے میں *caught in the toils* (*of something*) چالبازیاں پھنسا ہوا، کی چالبازیوں کا شکار **toiler** *n.* one who toils جان مارنے والا **toil worn** *adj.* (of person, face, limb, etc.) very tired سخت تھکا ہوا **toilsome** (*toil*-sŭm) *adj.* (of work) involving toil مشقت طلب

toilet (*toi*-let) *n.* process of doing the hair, etc., make-up ہار سنگھار process of dressing پوشاک، لباس style dress, etc. کپڑے بدلنا، لباس تبدیل کرنا of dress لباس کی وضع قطع place for easing nature پاخانہ، بیت الخلا *toilet paper*, paper used in toilet or privy پاخانہ پونچھنے کا کاغذ، مستنجبرا *toilet articles*, things needed for the make-up سنگھار کا سامان *toilet set*, brush, comb, hand-mirror, etc. سنگھاردان *toilet-table*, dressing table سنگھار کی میز

token (*tohk*-en) *n.* sign or mark (*of* something) کی نشانی، نشان، نشانی، ثبوت *in token of*, as a mark of کی نشانی کے طور پر piece of metal stamped for use as a ticket or temporary receipt for something due ٹوکن *adj.* serving only as a symbol علامتی *token payment*, payment (by individuals or States) of a small part of what is owed made to show that the debt is recognized برائے نام (یا نام کی) ادائگی، علامتی ادائگی *token strike*, strike for a short time resorted to only as a symbol of dissatisfaction, etc. علامتی ہڑتال

told (tohld) *v.* (pa. t. & pa. p. of **tell,** which see)

tolerate (*tol*-ĕ-rayt) *v.t.* brook, bear, put up with برداشت کرنا، گوارا کرنا allow without protest جائز رکھنا **tolerable** *adj.* that which can be tolerated گوارا، قابلِ برداشت fairly good اچھا خاصا **tolerance** *n.* act of tolerating برداشت temper which tolerates بُردباری، نرم مزاجی **tolerant** *adj.* having or showing tolerance بُردبار، متحمل showing toleration روادار **toleration** (-*ray*-) *n.* tolerating religious freedom رواداری

toll (tol) *n* tax on the use of a road, bridge, harbour, etc., in travelling چُنگی tax on the use of a part of a road for private business تہہ بازاری proportion of grain kept by miller for grinding پسائی، پسائی کی کٹوتی *take a toll of*, (*a*) پسائی کی کٹوتی کرنا (*b*) cause abstract a portion of میں سے بڑوں کی جان (heavy, etc.) deaths in a group لینا **toll-bar, toll-gate** *n.* one at which a toll must be paid چُنگی کی چوکی (یا پھاٹک)، چُنگی زدک

²toll (tol) *v.t.* & *i.* (of a bell) ring with slow regular strokes (گھنٹی یا گھنٹہ) بجنا ring thus (*for* someone, *for* his death) (کی وفات پر) ماتمی گجر بجنا cause (a bell) to ring in this way گجر (یا ماتمی گجر) بجانا، گھنٹہ بجانا *n.* sound made by the tolling of a bell گھنٹے کی چوٹ، ٹن ٹن

Tom *n.* abbr. of the English name Thomas ٹوم، ٹام *Tom, Dick and Harry*, (*a*) any person taken at random ہر ایک، کوئی بھی (*b*) man in-the street نتھو خیرا *Tom Thumb*, (*a*) a brave little character from fairy tales ٹام تھم (*b*) diminutive person ننھا سا، بالشتیا

tomahawk (*tom*-è-hawk) *n.* light axe used by Red Indians as a tool and weapon ٹوماہاک *v.t.* strike with a tomahawk ٹوماہاک کا وار کرنا kill with it ٹوماہاک مار مار کر مار ڈالنا criticize (book or author) severely پر سخت تنقید کرنا

a tomahawk

tomato (to-*mah*-toh) *n.* (pl. *tomatoes*) *n.* well-known soft, juicy red or yellow fruit usually cooked with meat or eaten raw in salads ٹماٹر، ولائتی بینگن

tomb (toom) *n.* a grave with a monument over it مقبرہ (poet. or rhetorical) any grave قبر **tomb-stone** *n.* stone set up on a tomb قبر کا کتبہ، سنگِ مزار، لوحِ مزار، کتبہ

tomboy (*tom*-boi) *n.* romping girl who likes rough noisy games ہڑدنگی شوخ لڑکی، چنچل

tomcat *n.* fully grown male cat جوان بِلا، بلا

tome (tohm) *n.* large and heavy book or volume ضخیم کتاب

tomfool (tom-*fool*) *n.* one who cannot be serious غیر سنجیدہ given to talking stupidly حماقت کی باتیں کرنے والا fool احمق، بیوقوف **toomfoolery** *n.* stupid talk بیوقوفی کی بات stupid behaviour لغو حرکتیں ludicrously inadequate measures مضحکہ خیز حد تک ناکافی اقدام

tomnoddy (tom-*nod*-i) *n.* simpleton بیوقوف، سادہ لوح

~~**Tommy** (*tom*-i) *n* (also *Tommy Atkins*),~~ private of the British army ٹامی، گورا **tommy-gun** *n.* small machine-gun ٹامی گن **tommy-gunner** ٹامی گن والا **tommy-rot** *n.* (slang) folly حماقت non-sense لغویات، بکواس mismanagement بدانتظامی

tomorrow (to-*mo*-roh) *n.* the day after today کل

tomtom (*tom*-tom) *n.* drum used in the Indo-Pakistan subcontinent ڈھول، ڈھولک *v. t.* beat a tomtom ڈھول بجانا

ton (tun) *n.* measure of weight equivalent to 2,240 lb. in the U.K. or 2,000 lb. in the U.S., about 28 maunds (often used as sing. after numbers ; as *four ton*) ٹن (colloq.) (*tons of*), much, many بہت، بہت *tons of (money, thanks, etc.)* بہت (سا روپیہ، بہت شکریہ وغیرہ)

tone (tohn) *n.* sound with reference to its quality آواز *speak in sweet* (or *angry, entreating, etc.*) *tone* (رشیریں (یا غصیلی یا لجاجت بھری) آواز میں کہنا rise or fall of the voice in speaking بات کرتے کا لہجہ، آواز کا انداز، آواز کا اُتار چڑھاؤ، گمک (in music) any of the five large intervals between one note and the next which together with two semi-tones make up an octave (سرگم کا) سُر general spirit (of a community, institution, etc.) رنگ، انداز shade (of colour) رنگ کی گہرائی degree (of light) (روشنی کا) زور *v.t.* & *i.* give a particular tone of colour to مناسب رنگ دینا، ہلکا رنگ بھرنا (of colours) be in harmony *with* سے ملنا make the sound high or low (آواز میں) ٹھیک، گمک پیدا کرنا *tone down*, make or become less intense ہلکا کرنا یا ہونا، نرم کرنا یا ہونا *tone up*, (*a*) make or become higher in sound اونچا کرنا یا ہونا (*b*) make or become brighter روشن کرنا (یا ہونا) **toned** (tohnd) *adj.* with particular kind of tone ایک خاص انداز کا **toneless** *adj.* dull بے لطف، بے کیف lifeless (voice, etc.) بے جان

tonga (*tong*-a) *n.* (English spelling of the Urdu word meaning) two-wheeled horse-driven vehicle ٹانگہ، تانگا، تانگہ

tongs (tongz) *n. pl.* (also *a pair of tongs*), tool for taking up and holding (coal, sugar, ice, etc.) چمٹا، چمٹی *Not to touch (someone or something) with a pair of toys*

tongue (tung) *n.* movable organ of the body with a loose end in the mouth, used for talking and tasting زبان، بازبان *have (one's) tongue in (one's) cheek*, say (something) that (one) does not mean to be taken seriously شرارت سے (کچھ) کہنا *hold (one's) tongue*, be silent چپ رہنا، خاموش ہو جانا language زبان *(one's) mother tongue* مادری زبان anything like a tongue زبان، گاؤدم چیز burning part (of a flame) (شعلے کی) لَو **tongue-tied** *adj.* unable to speak (through fear or shyness) جس کی زبان کو تالا لگ گیا ہو، ڈر یا حیا سے خاموش

tonic (*ton*-ik) *adj.* strength-giving drug, etc. مقوی دوا (in music) keynote بنیادی سُر، اصلی سُر *adj.* strength-giving مقوی **tonic sol-fa** *n.* musical notation taught in teaching singing سا رے گا ما

tonight, to-night (to-*nit*) *n.* the coming nigh[t] آج رات، آج کی رات *adv.* in or during the coming night آج رات، آج کی رات

tonnage (*tun*-ej) *n.* cargo carrying capacity of a ship stated in tons (100 cubic feet having one ton capacity) جہاز کی ضخامت ٹنوں میں total tonnage of a country's merchant shipping کسی ملک کے تجارتی بیڑے کی مجموعی ضخامت capacity of a ship to carry goods, passengers, etc. جہازی باربرداری کی گنجائش charge per ton on cargo, etc., for transport جہاز میں مال کا فی ٹن کرایہ، فی ٹن کرایہ

tonsil (*tons*-il) *n.* either of the two small [illegible] the

glands in the back of the throat گلے کی گلٹی **ton-sillitis** (tons-i-*lī*-tis) *n.* inflammation of the tonsils گلے کی گلٹیوں کا وَرَم
tonsure (*tonsh*-ĕ*) *n.* shaving of the top of the head (of one about to become a priest or monk) سر مُونڈنا، چندیا مُونڈنا the part of the head so shaved مُنڈی ہُوئی چندیا

man with a tonsure

too *adv.* also بھی more than enough ضُرورت سے زیادہ incredibly ناقابلِ یقین حد تک *too (good, etc.), to be (true, etc.)*, incredibly so ناقابلِ یقین حد تک
took (tŭk) *v.* (pa. t. of **take,** which see)
tool any hand-implement used by workmen اَوزار، ہتھیار *machine tools,* (*a*) tools operated by power مشینی اَوزار (*b*) (tools, etc.), used in the manufacture of machinery کلیں بنانے کے اَوزار used by another for dishonest purposes آلۂ کار *a tool of (someone), a tool in the hands of* (*someone*) کا آلۂ کار
toot *n.* sound of trumpet, etc. تُرم تُرم *v.t.* & *i.* (cause to) give out a toot تُرم تُرم کرنا یا نکالنا
tooth (tūth) (pl. *teeth*, pr. teeth) one of the 32 bone-like growths in jaws دانت *fight* (*someone or something*) *tooth and nail,* fight (against it) with all one's force پُورے زور سے لڑنا، کاٹ کر مُقابلہ کرنا *in the teeth of* (*opposition, etc.*), against the full force of (opposition, etc.) کے مُقابلے میں tooth-like part (of saw, comb, etc.) دندانہ cut to make teeth in (something) میں دندانے بنانا، میں دانتے ڈالنا **tooth-ache** *n.* pain in the tooth or teeth دانتوں کا دَرد، دانت کا دَرد **tooth-brush** (*tuth*-brush) *n.* brush for cleaning the teeth دانتوں کا بُرش **tooth-paste** (-payst) *n.* cream for applying to the tooth-brush for cleaning the teeth ٹُوتھ پیسٹ، دانتوں کا خمیرہ، خمیرہ **tooth-powder** *n.* for this purpose منجن **toothpick** *n.* quill, etc., for picking the teeth خلال **toothless** *adj.* without teeth جس کے دانت نہ ہوں، دانتوں کے بغیر (of comb, etc.), with teeth دندانے دار **toothsome** (tūth-sum) *adj.* tasty (food) مزیدار
top *n.* upper part (of anything) اُوپر کا حصّہ، اُوپر peak چوٹی utmost degree (of something) بہت *at the top of* (*one's*) *voice,* as loudly as possible پُورے زور سے بولتے ہُوئے، بہت اُونچی آواز سے a well-known spinning toy لٹّو *sleep like a top,* sleep soundly مزے کی نیند سونا *adj.* of or at the top اُوپر کا، اُوپر والا highest in degree سب سے اُونچا انتہائی people in high position چوٹی کے لوگ *v.t.* (-pp-) provide a top for کا بالائی حصّہ لگانا، چوٹی لگانا ڈھکنا لگانا be a top to کا بالائی حصّہ ہونا reach the top of (کی) چوٹی پر پہنچنا come or be at the top of cut off the top of (plant, etc.) کی پُھننگ کاٹنا **topcoat** *n.* overcoat اوورکوٹ **top-drawer** *adj.* (see *Addenda*) **top-hat** *n.* men's tall silk hat اُونچا ہیٹ، اُونچی ریشمی ٹوپی، ٹاپ ہیٹ

a top-hat

top-heavy *adj.* too heavy at the top جس کا اُوپر کا حصّہ نیچے کی بہ نسبت زیادہ بھاری ہو ill-balanced غیر مُتوازن (of a department) having too many highly paid officers (محکمہ) جس میں بیش قرار تنخواہ پانے والے افسر ضُرورت سے زیادہ ہوں **topmast** *n.* upper part of a mast مستول کا بالائی حصّہ **topmost** *adj.* highest سب سے اُونچا
topping *adj.* (colloq.) excellent شاندار **top sawyer** *n.* distinguished personality اہم شخصیت the one of the pair who has an upper hand بالادست
topaz (*toh*-paz) *n.* a yellow (etc.) gem پکھراج
tope (toph) *v.i.* be a heavy drunkard بڑا شرابی ہونا، بلانوش ہونا **toper** (*tohp*-e*) *n.* heavy drunkard بڑا شرابی، بلانوش
topee, topi (*tohp*-ee) *n.* sola topee ; pith hat سولا ہیٹ، ٹوپ
topic (*top*-ik) *n.* subject for discussion موضوعِ بحث
topical *adj.* (of news, etc.) of current interest مسائلِ حاضرہ کے متعلّق regarding a topic کسی موضوع سے متعلّق
topography (to-*pog*-ra-fi) *n.* geographical features of an area جُغرافیائی خصوصیات their description جُغرافیائی خصوصیات کا تذکرہ drawing a map (*of an area*) نقشہ سازی، نقشہ نویسی **topographical** (top-o-*graf*-i-kĕl) *adj.* جُغرافیائی خصوصیات کے متعلّق
topple (*top*-ĕl) *v.t.* & *i.* (cause to) be unsteady and overturn ڈگمگا کر گرنا (یا) گرانا
topsyturvy (top-si-*tē**-vi) *adj.* upside down اُلٹا، اوندھا in confusion اُلٹ پلٹ، درہم برہم *n.* state of confusion ابتری، افراتفری
torch (to*ch) *n.* piece of wood treated with oil, etc., at one end and used as a flaming light مشعل anything that enlightens مشعل (یا) مشعلِ (راہ) electric hand-light بیٹری
tore (toh*) *v.* (pa. t. of **tear,** which see)
torment *n.* (*to**-ment) *n.* severe bodily or mental suffering جسمانی یا رُوحانی اذیت، دَرد و کرب its cause اذیت، مُوجبِ اذیت *v.t.* (to*-*ment*) cause severe suffering to کو سخت اذیت دینا، کو سخت کوفت پہنچانا annoy تنگ کرنا، دِق کرنا **tormentor** *n.* one who torments اذیت پہنچانے والا
torn (toh*n) *v.* (pa. p. of **tear,** which see)
tornado (to*-*nay*-doh) *n.* (pl. *tornadoes*) hur-

ricane طوفان violent whirlwind سخت آندھی، زور کی آندھی

torpedo (to*-pee-doh) *n.* (pl. *torpedoes*) cigar-shaped self-propelling explosive shell travelling water level تارپیڈو، آبدوز گولہ *v.t.* strike with a torpedo پر تارپیڈو چھوڑنا، تارپیڈو کا نشانہ بنانا *v.i.* strike, sink with a torpedo تارپیڈو سے اُڑانا **torpedo-boat** *n.* small warship from which torpedoes are fired تارپیڈو کشتی

a torpedo

torpid (to*-pid) *adj.* (of hibernating animals) not moving or feeling بے حس و حرکت benumbed سُن، بے حس sluggish سُست apathetic دلچسپی نہ لینے والا **torpidity** (-pid-), **torpor** (to*-pë*) *n.* torpid condition بے حسی، سُن ہونا، سُستی، دلچسپی نہ لینا

torrent (to-rent) *n.* violent rushing stream (of water, etc.) تیز دھارا *rain falling in torrents* موسلا دھار بارش ہونا violent outburst (*of* questions, swear words, etc.) (کی) بوچھاڑ **torrential** (to-rensh-ĕl) *adj.* (of rain, etc.) like a torrent سخت of a torrent تیز دھارے کا، تند و پُر شور

torrid (to-rid) *adj.* very hot (region, weather, etc.) بہایت گرم، حار *the Torrid Zone* the tropics منطقہ حارہ

torsion (to*-shĕn) *n.* twisting مروڑنا، مروڑی *torsion balance*, instrument for measuring minute forces by the torsion of a fine wire تفتیلی ترازو

torso (to*-soh) *n.* (pl. *torso*) human trunk ٹانگوں اور بازوؤں کے بغیر دھڑ statue of this part of the human body ٹانگوں اور بازوؤں کے بغیر دھڑ کا مجسمہ

tortoise (to*-tus) *n.* slow-moving four-legged reptile enclosed in two shells کچھوا **tortoise-shell** *n.* its shell *adj.* clouded dark brown and yellow of the colour of tortoise-shell کچھوے کے خول کے رنگ کا

a tortoise

tortuous (to*-tew-us) *adj.* sinuous ; undulating ; full of bends پیچ در پیچ involved (style, etc.) پیچیدہ، مغلق

torture (to*-chĕ*) severe physical or mental suffering شدید (جسمانی یا روحانی) اذیت *v.t.* cause torture to کو سخت اذیت پہنچانا *torture (someone) to make (him) confess*, use third degree methods for extorting a confession from (him) اقبالِ جرم کرانے کے لیے تشدد کرنا **torturer** *n.* one who tortures سخت اذیت پہنچانے والا

Tory (toh-ri) *n.* member or sympathiser of the British Conservative Party برطانوی قدامت پسند جماعت کا رکن یا ہمدرد، قدامت پسند، رجعت پسند **Toryism** *n.* being a Tory قدامت پسندی، رجعت پسندی

tosh *n.* (slang) nonsense بکواس

toss (tos) *v.t.* & *i.* (cause to) move (*about*) from side to side جھولنا یا جھولانا (cause to) move up and down اُچھلنا یا اُچھالنا throw away carelessly بے پروائی سے پھینکنا throw up through the air (*to* someone) (کی طرف) پھینکنا *toss up a coin*, spin a coin up into the air and guess whether head or tail will be on top when it falls ٹاس کرنا، سکہ اُچھالنا *toss for it*, decide something thus ٹاس سے فیصلہ کرنا، سکہ اُچھال کر فیصلہ کرنا jerk (*one's head*) up and back to suggest contempt or indifference move restlessly from one side to another کروٹیں بدلنا *toss (something) off*, drink (it) straight down ایک ہی گھونٹ میں پی جانا *n.* tossing movement اُچھلنا، اُچھالنا، جھولنا، جھلانا، پھینکنا، سر کا جھٹکا، زور کی کروٹ throwing of the coin or decision taken thus ٹاس *win the toss*, guess rightly when a coin is tossed up ٹاس جیتنا *lose the toss* ٹاس ہارنا **toss-up** *n.* something whose outcome depends on chance اتفاق کی بات، قسمت کی بات

tot *n.* very small child ننھا منا، ننھا، منا small quantity of liquor شراب کا گھونٹ، تھوڑی سی *v.t.* & *i.* (-tt-) (colloq.) add (*up to*) کی میزان ہونا

total (tohtĕl) *n.* entire amount رقم added up amount میزان *adj.* (of amount, etc.), entire مجموعی complete مکمل، ہمہ گیر، کُل *total war*, war in which every available resource of a nation neglected کُلی جنگ، ہمہ گیر جنگ *v.t.* (-ll-) add up جمع کرنا amount to کی میزان ہونا **totally** *adv.* entirely بالکل، سراسر **totality** *n.* being total میزان، مجموعیت

totalitarian (toh-tal-i-tay-ri-ĕn, *adj.* (of a State) in which only one political party is allowed and all persons are entirely under the authority of a one-party government اجتماعی (ریاست) **tatalitarianism** *n.* being totalitarian ریاست کی اجتماعیت

totalizator (toh-ta-lı-zay-tĕ*) *n.* tote ; machine for registering bets on horse-race, etc. میزانی مشین، میزانی کل، میزانی **totalize** (toh-ta-liz) *v.t.* combine into a total کی میزان لگانا

tote (toht) *n.* (colloq.) totalizator میزانی مشین، میزانی کل، میزانی *v.t.* (U.S.) transport (supplies, timber, etc.) پہنچانا، منتقل کرنا

totem (toh-tem) *n.* animal or other natural object considered by the primitive people to have a close connexion with a family group توتم، خاندانی نشان، توتم (also *totem-pole*), carved pole representing this object توتم، خاندانی نشان کا عصا، توتم **totemistic** (-mis-) *adj.* characterized by totem توتمی **totemism** (toh-te-miz-) *n.* stage of civilization characterized by totem توتمی دور، توتمیت

totter (*tot-ē**) *v.i.* walk with weak, unsteady steps لڑکھڑاتے ہوئے چلنا، کے پاؤں لڑکھڑانا be almost falling گرنے کو ہونا **tottery** (*tot-è-ri*) *adj.* unsteady لڑکھڑاتا ہوا

touch (tuch) *v.t.* & *i.* be, come or bring into contact with (something) through one's skin چھونا، کو ہاتھ لگانا be adjacent to کے متصل ہونا affect (someone or his feelings) کے دل پر اثر کرنا پر اثر کرنا (usu. in the negative) be equal to (someone *as*) کو پہنچنا، کے برابر ہونا *touch at* (*port*), (of a ship) visit (it) for a short stay میں تھوڑی دیر کو لنگر انداز ہونا *touch on, touch upon*, briefly say something about (a subject, etc.) کے متعلق کچھ کہنا *touch up* (*picture, piece of writing, etc.*), make small changes in (it) to improve (it) کے خط و خال بنانا *touch* (*someone*) *for* (*a sum of money*), get (it) out of (him) سے اڑانا، سے ہتیانا *n.* touching چھونا، لمس *soft to the touch* چھونے میں ملائم، ملائم (usu. *pl.*) stroke made with a pen, brush, etc. قلم (یا برش وغیرہ) کی کی نوک پلک *give* (or *add*) *finishing touches to* جنبش درست کرنا slight trace (*of* something) ہلکا سا اثر، چاشنی connexion رابطہ، واسطہ، تعلق *be in touch* (*with something*), be in regular communication (with it) سے مستقل رابطہ ہونا، سے باخبر ہونا *be out of touch* (*with*), have no information (about) سے بالکل بے خبر ہونا *lose touch* (*with*), become out of touch (with) سے رابطہ نہ رہنا، سے بے خبر ہو جانا style of doing an artistic work, etc. فنکاری، کاریگری، (فنکار یا کاریگر کا) ہاتھ *the touch of a master*, masterly style ماہر کا ہاتھ، فنکار کا ہاتھ **touch-and-go** *adj.* hanging in the balance ; uncertain مشتبہ، مشکوک، شک والا *be touch-and-go whether* مشکوک ہونا کہ **touched** (tuchd) *adj.* (colloq.) mentally deranged سودائی، پاگل **touching** *adj.* pitiable دردناک arousing sympathy ہمدردی کا موجب affecting the heart رقت انگیز **touchstone** *n.* piece of stone on which gold is rubbed to test its purity کسوٹی anything serving to test the purity or standard (*of*) (کی) کسوٹی **touchy** (*tuch-i*) *adj.* easily offended زود رنج، زود حس **touchiness** *n.* being touchy زود رنجی، زود حسی

tough (tuf) *adj.* not easily cut, broken, or worn out سخت *tough meat* سخت گوشت hardy (soldier) جفاکش، جھیل سکنے والا difficult (work or problem) مشکل rough and violent (person) مار پیٹ پر اتر آنے والا، غنڈہ *n.* tough man غنڈہ **toughen** (*tuf-èn*) *v.t.* & *i.* make or become tough سخت کرنا یا ہونا

tour (*too-è**) *n.* journey out and home again during which several or many places are visited سیاحت such journey undertaken as a part of one's duty دورہ *v.t.* & *i.* make a tour of کی سیاحت کرنا **tourist** (*too-è-rist*) *n.* person on holiday making a tour for pleasure سیاح، چھٹیوں میں سیر کرنے والا **tourism** (*too-è-rizm*) *n.* (also *tourist trade*), travels by tourists, esp. as a source of income to the country visited سیاحت، سیاحی

tour de force *n.* (pl. *tours de force*) action calling for great skill مہارت کا کام

tourism *n.*, **tourist** *n.* (see under **tour**)

tournament (*too*-è-na-ment*) *n.* series of matches between a number of teams or players عام مقابلہ، کھیلوں کا عام مقابلہ، ٹورنامنٹ *a cricket tournament* کرکٹ ٹورنامنٹ، کرکٹ کا عام مقابلہ (old use) (also called *tourney*), tilting match between armed knights on horseback نائٹوں کا نیزہ بازی کا مقابلہ، نائٹوں کی نیزہ بازی

tourney (*too*-è-ni*) tournament (sense 2) نائٹوں کا نیزہ بازی کا مقابلہ، نائٹوں کی نیزہ بازی

tourniquet (*too*-è-ni-ket*) *n.* device for stopping bleeding by twisting something tightly against an artery لہو روک

tousle (*touz-èl*) *v.t.* make (hair or person) untidy بکھیرنا (یا نوچنا)، خراب کرنا

tout *n.* person who pesters others to use his establishment's services, etc., or buy something through him, etc. پیچھے پڑنے والا، دلال such an agent of a lawyer منشی، ٹاؤٹ person who sells information about race-horses گھڑ دوڑ کا دلال، ٹاؤٹ *v.i.* act as a tout (*for* custom, or *for* some commodity) دلالی کرنا employ touts دلال رکھنا

tout court (too-koo*) *adj.* merely ; only صرف *He called me William 'tout court'* ; he called me just William without having the courtesy to add Mr., etc. اس نے مجھے صرف ولیم کہہ کر خطاب کیا

tout ensemble (toot-on-*sonb*-èl) *n.* combined general effect as viewed in a glance مجموعی تاثر، مجموعی اثر

tow (toh) *v.t.* pull (another vehicle or boat)

along by a rope رستے سے کھینچنا (of a horse) move along the bank pulling a boat in water (گھوڑے کا) (گھوڑے کا) کشتی کو رستے کشتی کھینچنا *have* (or *take*) *boat in tow* سے کھینچنا (of persons) be in attendance on کی دیکھ بھال کرنا **tow-path, towing-path** *n*. path along the side of a river or canal for use in towing رستے سے کشتی کھینچنے والے گھوڑے کیلئے دریا یا نہر کے کنارے پٹڑی *n*. fibres of jute or flax for making a rope پٹ سن کا ریشہ **towage** (*toh*-ej) *n*. towing رسے سے کھینچنا charges for it کھنچائی

towards (to-*wo**dz, or toh*dz) *prep*. in the direction of کی طرف، کی جانب، کی سمت near کے قریب for کے متعلق regarding کے لیے، کی غرض سے، بغرض

toward *adj*. (used only at the end) near نزدیک *prep*. (the less usual form of *towards* in all senses of the latter) قریب

towel (*tou*-el) *n*. piece of cloth for drying oneself تولیہ piece of cloth for drying dishes etc. صافی

tower (*tou*-è*) *n*. tall, slender building مینارہ، منار، مینار *clock-tower*, tower with a clock fixed in it گھنٹہ گھر tall part of a building منارہ، برج، برجی *v.i.* be very tall in relation to the height of the surroundings بہت اونچا ہونا (*tower above*), be above others in ability, etc. سے کہیں بلند ہونا **towering** *adj*. great بہت

town (toun) *n*. city شہر small city قصبہ the people of a town شہر کے لوگ، شہر والے *talk of the town* جس کا سارے شہر میں چرچا ہو **town-hall** *n*. building housing the local government offices ٹاؤن ہال، بلدیاتی دفاتر کی عمارت، ایوانِ بلدیہ its big hall which is used as the venue of public events ایوانِ بلدیہ

toxic (*tok*-sik) *adj*. of poison زہر کا poisonous زہریلا caused by poison زہر کے باعث

toy (toy) *n*. child's plaything کھلونا *v.i.* (*toy with*) handle (something) absent-mindedly بے پروائی سے ہاتھ لگانا touch with the fingers انگلیوں سے چھونا not to think very seriously about (something) کے متعلق سنجیدگی سے نہ سوچنا while away time by busying oneself with دفع الوقتی کے لیے (کسی چیز) سے دل بہلانا

trace (trays) *v.t.* mark (*out*) the outline (*of* a place) کا خاکہ کھینچنا copy (something) by placing a transparent paper, etc., on it and drawing the visible lines, etc. ٹریس کرنا، چربہ اتارنا follow or discover (someone or something) by observing traces and bits of evidence کا کھوج لگانا، کا سراغ لگانا *trace (something) to its source* کی اصل کا پتہ لگانا *n*. sign, etc., of the earlier existence of an extant (species, culture, etc.) آثار extremely small quantity (*of* something) بہت کم مقدار، شائبہ، جھلک either of the straps by which a poled vehicle is drawn by a horse, etc. راس **tracing** *n*. copy (of something) made by tracing ٹریسنگ، چربہ، عکس **traceable** (*trays*-a-bèl) *adj*. that which can be traced جس کا سراغ مل سکے *The counsel submitted that the original document was not traceable* وکیل (یا وکیلوں) نے گزارش کی کہ اصل دستاویز کا کوئی سراغ نہیں ملتا

tracery (*trays*-è-ri) *n*. natural arrangement (of frost, etc.) in a decorative way قدرتی آرائش ornamental stonework پتھر کے کٹاؤ کا آرائشی کام

track (trak) *n*. left by a cart, etc., in passing along لیک (*pl*.) series of footmarks left by a person or animal in moving along قدموں کے نشان، کھوج *on the track of*, in pursuit of کے تعاقب میں *in track of*, following the example of کے نقشِ قدم پر *make track for*, (colloq.) go towards کی طرف جانا path made by frequent use پگڈنڈی *off the track*, on a wrong path غلط راہ پر course (*of* something) راہ set of rails of trains, etc. (ریل کی) پٹڑی، لائن *single track*, one pair of rails اکہری پٹڑی *double track* دوہری پٹڑی endless belt used instead of wheels on tanks, etc. زنجیری پہیہ *tracked vehicles* زنجیری پہیئے والی گاڑیاں prepared course for racing دوڑ کے مقابلے کی راہ *track events*, athletic races (as distinct from jumping, etc.) دوڑیں *v.t.* follow (an animal, etc., *down*) along its tracks کا کھوج لگانا **trackless** *adj*. having no track بے سراغ

tract (trakt) *n*. stretch (*of* agricultural land, water, etc.) قطعہ short printed essay on some topic رسالہ **tractable** *adj*. amenable اثر پذیر، تاثر پذیر، تربیت پذیر easily controlled قابو میں آ جانے والا، قابو کا

a tractor

traction (*trak*-shun) *n*. pulling of something over a surface کھینچنا، بارکشی power used for this

purpose بارکش توانائی **tractor** (*trak-të**) *n.* motor vehicle used for pulling ploughs, etc. ٹریکٹر
trade (trayd) *n.* buying and selling of goods بیوپار، کاروبار، تجارت *trade price*, price for retailers تاجرانہ نرخ *only to trade*, (for sale) only to retailers of that article صرف خوردہ فروشوں کے لیے *drive a roaring trade*, have a good business کاکاروبار خوب چلنا handicraft or other such occupation پیشہ، دستکاری *a baker (etc.) by trade* پیشے کے لحاظ سے نانبائی (وغیرہ) *jack of-all-trades*, one who can turn his hand to anything ہرفن مولا workers engaged in a trade پیشہ فند *v. t. & i.* engage in trade تجارت کرنا، کاروبار (کی)، تجارت کرنا *trade in (something)* بیوپار کرنا *trade (one thing) for another* کا مبادلہ کرنا، ایک کے بدلے دوسری دنیا *trade on* (or *upon*) (*something*), take undue advantage of it سے ناجائز فائدہ اٹھانا **trader** *n.* merchant تاجر **tradesman** *n.* shopkeeper دکاندار **trade cycle** *n.* alternating succession of good and bad trade condition تجارتی چکر، تجارتی دور، تجارتی اتار چڑھاؤ **trade mark** design, lettering, etc., used by a manufacturer as a distinctive mark for his products ٹریڈ مارک، مارکہ، چھاپ، تجارتی نشان **trade union, trades union** *n.* workmen's organization to fight for their rights انجمن پیشہ وراں، ٹریڈ یونین **trade-unionism** *n.* advocacy of the principles of trade unions انجمنائے پیشہ وراں کے اصولوں کی حمایت **trade-unionist** *n.* انجمنائے پیشہ وراں کے اصولوں کا حامی **trade winds** *n.* pl. strong winds blowing constantly towards the equator from the north-east and the south-west تجارتی ہوا، بادِ مراد، بادِ شرطہ
tradition (tra-*dish*-un) *n.* opinion, belief, principles of art, etc., handed down from the past روایت **traditional** *adj.* that which has been accepted by tradition روایتی، روایت کے مطابق **traditionary** *adj.* of the nature or status of tradition روایتی
traduce (tra-*dews*) *v.t.* slander کو بدنام کرنا، پر بہتان باندھنا
traffic (*traf*-ik) *n.* people and vehicles along road and streets سڑکوں پر آنے جانے والے لوگ اور گاڑیاں، ٹریفک such movement آمد و رفت، ٹریفک *traffic lights*, red and green signals for controlling traffic آمد و رفت کو باقاعدہ بنانے والی بتیاں، ٹریفک لائٹ transport business done by a railway, steamship line, etc. ریلوں جہازوں وغیرہ کی آمد و رفت trading (usu. *in* contraband goods) تجارت، ناجائز تجارت *v.i.* trade (usu. *in* contraband goods. etc.) (کی) خرید و فروخت کرنا، (کی) ناجائز تجارت کرنا
tragedy (*traj*-e-di) *n.* drama of a serious and solemn kind with elevated diction and sad ending حزنیہ، المیہ، ٹریجڈی an extremely sad event of real life شدید حادثہ **tragedian** (tra-*jee*-di-an) *n.* writer of tragedy المیہ نگار actor in tragedy المیہ اداکار **tragedienne** (-*en*) actress in tragedy المیہ اداکارہ **tragic** (*traj*-ik) *adj.* of tragedy المیہ سے متعلق، المیہ نگاری سے متعلق، المیہ calamitous
trail (trayl) *n.* mark (*of* distinction, smoke, etc.), left by someone or something that has passed by and caused it نشان، منظر track or scent followed in hunting شکار کا کھوج (یا) نشان (کی) بو *hot on the trail*, close behind the quarry کے پیچھے پیچھے path through rough country پگڈنڈی *v.t. & i.* pull or be pulled along behind پیچھے پیچھے گھسیٹنا یا گھسٹتے آنا persue ; follow the track of کا پیچھا کرنا (of creeping plants) grow along the ground پر پھیلنا walk wearily (*along*) رینگ رینگ کر چلنا، گھسٹتے ہوئے چلنا **trailer** *n.* vehicle drawn by another پیچھے لگی ہوئی گاڑی، پیوستہ گاڑی trailing plant زمین پر پھیلنے والا پودا set of short extracts from a film shown as its advertisement ٹریلر، فلم کا نمونہ، نمونہ
train (trayn) *v.t. & i.* give teaching and practice to (someone *for* or *to be* something) (کی) تربیت دینا aim (gun, etc., *on* or *upon* something) (بندوق وغیرہ) کا نشانہ (کسی چیز کی طرف کرنا) cause (a plant, etc.), to grow in a particular direction (پودے وغیرہ) کا رخ کسی طرف کرنا، کسی خاص شکل میں اگانا *n.* line of railway carriages drawn together by an engine گاڑی، ریل، ٹرین، ریل گاڑی number (*of* persons, or animals, etc.), moving in a line چلتی ہوئی قطار series (*of* thoughts, ideas, events) سلسلہ group of attendants travelling with a king, etc. خدم و حشم part of a long dress or robe that lies on the ground لٹکتا ہوا دامن، دنبالہ line of gunpowder leading to a mine, etc. بارود کا سلسلہ *in train*, ready تیار **trainer** *n.* one who trains

(horses, etc.) سدھانے والا one who trains (athletes, etc.) سکھلانے والا ، وَرزش کا اُستاد ، وَرزش اُستاد **training** *n.* act of teaching and giving practice تربیت ، سکھلائی *training college,* college for training teachers ٹریننگ کالج ، تربیتِ اساتذہ کا ادارہ *(be) in training (for some athletic activity),* (be) in good physical condition (for it) تیار (کے لیے) *not in training (for)* کے لیے تیار نہیں

trait (tray) *n.* distinguishing quality (*of* character) خصوصیت ، اِمتیازی وَصف ، طُرّۂ اِمتیاز

traitor (*tray*-tě*) *n.* one who betrays a friend بیوفا ، نمک حرام one who is false *to* a cause or *to* one's country, etc. **traitorous** *adj.* of or like that of a traitor غدّارانہ **traitress** *n.* woman traitor بیوفا ، نمک حرام ، غدّار

trajectory (*traj*-ek-to-ri) *n.* curved path described by a bullet, etc. خطِ حرکت ، خطِ منحنی curved line or surface cutting others at regular angles مُستَدِیر

tram *n.* (also *tramcar*), electric railway or carriage running along it on public roads ٹریم ، ٹرام **tramline, tramway** *n.* line of rails for trams ٹریم کی پٹڑی ، ٹرام کی پٹڑی **tram-lines** *n. pl.* (colloq.) either pair of parallel boundary-lines of a tennis-court ٹینس کورٹ کی حد بندی کے مُتوازی خط

trammel (*tram*-el) *v.t.* (-ll-) hamper, impede کی راہ میں روڑا اٹکانا ، کے کام میں رکاوٹیں ڈالنا *n.* (*pl.*) impediments (*of* routine, etc.) رکاوٹیں ، پابندیاں something put round the feet of a horse to hamper its movement (گھوڑے کے پاؤں کی) زنجیر ، کڑا

tramp *v.t.* & *i.* walk with heavy steps گھسٹتے ہوئے چلنا ، بھاری قدموں سے چلنا walk for a long distance (a place, or *through* or *over* it) (کا) پیدل چکر لگانا roam about aimlessly or because of having no home آوارہ گردی کرتے پھرنا *n.* sound of heavy footsteps دھپ دھپ ، اونچی چاپ long walk لمبا پیدل سفر homeless person doing no regular work and roaming about from place to place آوارہ گرد ، بیکار cargo vessel going to ports in search of cargo مزدوری ڈھونڈنے والا بار بردار جہاز

trample (*tramp*-ěl) *v.t.* & *i.* tread heavily (*on*) (کو) روندنا crush (something *down*) under the feet کو پاؤں کے تلے کچلنا

trance (trahns) *n.* abnormal, unconscious and dreamy condition with visions وَجد be in a trance حالتِ وَجد میں ہونا ، کو وَجد آنا

tranquil (*trank*-wil) *adj.* calm and quiet پُرسکون **tranquilly** *adv.* پُرسکون انداز سے **tranquillity** (tran-*kwil*-i-ti) *n.* calmness سکون ، خاموشی

trans- *pref.* on or to the other side of کے پار ، کے دُوسری طرف beyond ماورا

transact (*tranz*-akt) *v.t.* do, conduct (business, deal, etc., *with* someone) انجام دینا ، (سودا وغیرہ) کرنا

transaction (tranz-*ak*-shěn) *n.* piece of business سودا ، کاروبار ، مُعاملہ transacting it (سودا وغیرہ) کرنا ، انجام دینا (*pl.*) proceedings of a society کارروائی (*pl.*) record of such proceedings رُوئیداد ، رُوداد

transcend (trans-*end*) *v.t.* be or go beyond or outside the range of (experience, imagination) سے ماورا ہونا ، سے بلند تر ہونا *adj.* surpassing برتر ، اَعلیٰ ، ماورا (of God) absolute مُطلق beyond imagination ماورائے اِدراک **transcendental** (-ent-) *adj.* (esp.) beyond experience, etc. ماورائی **transcendentalism** *n.* belief in transcendental philosophy ماورائیت ، مَوصُوعیت

transcribe (trans-*krīb*) *v.t.* copy in writing (*from* something, or in full *from* shorthand notes) (تحریر کی) نقل کرنا **transcript** (*trans*-cript) *n.* something transcribed نقل **transcription** (-*krip*-) *n.* transcribing نقل something transcribed (*into* a special form of writing) (میں یا کے مطابق) نقل *phonetic transcription of word* تلفظ کے مطابق الفاظ کی نقل

transept (*trans*-ept) *n.* either (*north* or *south* end of the shorter part of a cross-shaped church چلیپا نما گرجے کا عرضی حصّہ

transfer *v.t.* & *i.* (*trans*-fě*) (-rr-) shift (someone or something *from* one place, etc., *to* another) بدلنا ، منتقل کرنا ، کی تبدیلی کرنا hand over (property, etc.) to somebody کے نام کرنا ، کو منتقل کرنا *n.* (*trans*-fě*) transferring تبدیلی (esp.) transferring (*of* property) اِنتقال document embodying this change دستاویز ، اِنتقال جائداد *transfer-paper,* paper for taking impressions or print etc. چربے کا کاغذ *transfer-ink,* ink used for this purpose چربے کی سیاہی **transferable** *adj.* that which can be transferred اِنتقال پذیر **transference** *n.* transferring from one job or station to another تبدیلی **transferee** (-*ree*) *n.* one to whom property, etc., is transferred منتقل اِلیہ

transfigure (trans-*fig*-ě*) *v.t.* change the shape or appearance of (something or someone) to make it glorious (as opposed to *disfigure* and as distinct from the general term *transform*) بدل کر شاندار بنا دینا ، کی کایا پلٹ دینا ، کا یا پلٹ کر دینا **transfiguration** (-*ray*-) *n.* such change شاندار تبدیلی ، کایا پلٹ ، تبدیلِ ہیئت *the Transfiguration,* the miraculous transfiguration of Jesus Christ مسیح کی معجزانہ تبدیلِ ہیئت

transfix (trans-*fiks*) *v.t.* pirece (*with* a pointed weapon, etc.) چھیدنا cause (someone) to be unable to move, think, etc., (*with* fear, surprise, etc.) کو مبہوت کر دینا ، پر سکتہ طاری کر دینا

transform (trans-*fo*m*) *v.t.* change the shape or appearance, of (someone or something) کایا پلٹنا، کایا پلٹ کر دینا change the nature or quality of قلب ماہیت کرنا **transformation** *n.* تبدیلی، کایا پلٹ ، قلب ماہیت **tranformer** *n.* (esp.) device for transforming electric current from A.C. to D.C. or from one voltage to another ٹرانسفارمر، مُبَدِّل

transfuse (tras-*fewz*) *v. t.* transfer (something esp., blood *from* one living person *to* another) مُنتقل کرنا **transfusion** *n.* transfusing اِنتِقال transfusing of blood اِنتقال خُون

transgress (tranz-*gres*) *v.t.* & *i.* go beyond (a limit) (حد) سے بڑھنا break (a law, treaty, agreement) کی خِلاف ورزی کرنا do wrong ظلم کرنا، تعدّی کرنا sin گناہ کرنا، گنہگار ہونا **transgression** (*-gresh-*) *n.* حد سے بڑھنا، خِلاف ورزی کرنا ، **transgressor** *n.* wrongdoer مُجرِم، خطا کار sinner گنہگار، عاصی

transient (*tranz*-i-ent) *adj.* lasting for a short time only ناپائدار، آنی جانی disappearing too soon گزرنیا ، برق پا

transit (*tranz-it*) *n.* passing (across, over through or *from* one place *to* another) گزرنا، عبور crossing (*of* a heavenly body) over the observatory (سیارے وغیرہ کا) رصدگاہ پر سے گزرنا being conveyed اِنتقال *be lost* (*etc.*) *in transit* سفر میں کھو جانا (وغیرہ)

transition (*tranz*-ish-en) *n.* change (*from* one condition to another) تبدیلی، تغیُّر *transition period*, interim period عبوری دور **transitional** (*-zish-*) *adj.* pertaining to transition عبوری

transitive (*tranz*-i-tiv) *adj.* (of a verb) taking a direct object which is expressed in the sentence (فعل) متعدّی

transitory (*tranz*-i-to-ri) *adj.* transient ناپائدار، آنی جانی، گزرنیا، برق پا temporary عارضی، وقتی

translate (tranz-*layt* or trans-*layt*) *v.t.* render (something said or written *into* another language) ترجمہ کرنا put (view, idea, etc. *into* action) (کو عمل میں) لانا **translation** (tranz-*lay*-shen or trans-lay-shĕn) *n.* translating ترجمہ translated piece, rendering ترجمہ **translator** *n.* one who translates مُترجِم

transliterate (tranz-*lit*-è-rayt) write (a word or words) in the corresponding letters of another script دوسرے رسم الخط میں لکھنا **transliteration** (*-ray-*) *n.* دوسرے رسم الخط میں لکھنا، دوسرے رسم الخط میں لکھا ہوا

translucence, translucency *n.* (see under **translucent**)

translucent (tranz-*loo*-sent) *adj.* allowing light to pass through but not clearly (as opposed to *transparent*) نیم شفاف **translucence** *n.*, **translucency** *n.* being transluscent نیم شفاف ہونا

transmigrate (*tranz*-mig-rayt) *v. t.* (of a soul) go into another body کا تناسخ ہونا **transmigration** (*-ray-*) *n.* act of transmigrating or belief in it as part of religions creed

transmission *n.* (see under **transmit**)

transmit *v.i.* (-tt-) pass on (message, news etc. *by* something) بھیجنا، پہنچانا، اِرسال کرنا، مُنتقِل کرنا pass on (a disease) لگانا let (heat, current, etc.) through or along پہنچانا، مُنتقِل کرنا **transmitter** (*-mit-*) *n.* apparatus for broadcasting radio messages, etc. ٹرانسمٹر، مُنشر apparatus for sending out telegrams, etc. پیام رساں **transmission** (tranz-*mish*-èn) *n.* sending out, conveying پہنچانا، ترسیل، اِبلاغ broadcast message نشریہ period over which a programme is broadcast at a stretch مجلس

transmutation *n.* (see under **transmute**)

transmute (tanz-*mewt*) *v.t.* change the form or nature of تبدیلِ ہیئت کرنا، قلبِ ماہیت کرنا، اِستحالہ کرنا change (base metal *into* gold) (سے سونا) بنانا **transmutation** (*-tay-*) *n.* اِستحالہ ، قلب ماہیت

transom (trans-ĕm) *n.* (also *transom-window*) small window above a door or window کھلنے والا روشن دان ، ہوادان

transparence *n.*, **transparency** *n.* (see under **transparent**)

transparent (trans-*pay*-è-rent) *adj.* that which can be seen through like clearglass شفاف unmistakably clear, apparent واضح، ظاہر، بیِّن **transparence, transparency transparentness** *n.* شفاف ہونا، شفافی ، کھلا ہوا ہونا، واضح ہونا

transpire (trans-*pi*-è*) *v.t.* & *i.* (of an event a secret) come to light ظاہر ہو جانا emit (moisture, vapour, etc.) خارج کرنا (in vulgar use) happen (سوقیانہ اِستعمال) ہونا

transplant *v.t.* take up (plants, etc.) with their roots and plant them in another place (پودے کو) ایک جگہ سے اکھاڑ کر دوسری جگہ لگانا change (person or thing) thus مُنتقِل کرنا، دوسری جگہ لے جا کر آباد کرنا **transplantation** (*-tay-*) *n.* مُنتقلی

transport *v.t.* (trans-*po*t*) convey (persons,

goods) from one place to another (مسافر یا اسباب) لے جانا، کی نقل و حمل کا انتظام کرنا send (a criminal) to a distant colony as punishment کالے پانی لے جانا، عبور دریائے شور لے جانا (passive) be carried away by (strong emotion: usu. joy ; rarely anger) (خوشی سے) پھولے نہ سمانا، غصے میں آپے سے باہر ہونا *n.* (*trans*-po*t) transporting ذریعہ نقل و حمل، نقل و حمل means of transport سواری، گاڑی وغیرہ *motor transport*, (abb. *M.T.*), motor vehicles used as transport نقل و حمل کے لیے موٹر گاڑیاں (*pl.*) ecstasy وجد، کیف (*pl.*) extreme rage طیش *in transports* حالت وجد میں، طیش میں *in transports of delight* وجد میں *in transports of rage* طیش میں *adj.* of or transporting نقل و حمل کا، یا کے متعلق **transportation** (-*tay*-) *n.* transporting or being transported نقل و حمل sending to a distant colony (*for* life, etc.) as a punishment کالے پانی کی سزا، عبور دریائے شور

transpose *v.t.* cause (two or more things) to change places کی ترتیب بدلنا، کو ادل بدل کرنا، کی ادلا بدلی کرنا **transposition** (-*zish*-) *n.* such change تبدیلی، ادل بدل changed position بدلی ہوئی ترتیب

trans-ship (transh-*ip*) *v.t.* shift (*from* or *to*) a ship or other conveyance سے یا میں منتقل کرنا **transshipment** (مسافروں یا سامان کی دوسری گاڑی جہاز وغیرہ میں) منتقلی

transubstantiate (-tansh-i-) *v.t.* change into another substance (esp. used of Eucharist) استحالہ

transverse (*trans*-vě*s, or tranz-vě*z) *adj.* lying across, crosswise چوڑے رخ قاطع پڑا ہوا، معترض **transversely** *adv.* چوڑے رخ، قطع کرتا ہوا

trap *n.* device for catching animals, etc. گڑھا، پھندا *mouse-trap* چوہے کا پھندا، پھانسی trick for making (someone) do or something he does not wish to do or say جال، دام *lay* (or *set*) *a trap* (*for* someone or *to do* something) کے لیے جال بچھانا *fall into a trap*, be caught by a trick جال میں پھنسنا light, two-wheeled carriage pulled by a horse or pony یکہ، ٹانگہ، ٹم ٹم (*pl.*) baggage, belongings سامان *v.t.* (-pp-) take in a trap پھندے میں پھانسنا capture by a trick دام میں لانا furnish (horse) with trappings (گھوڑے) کو سجانا، پر ساز ڈالنا، پھانسنا **trapdoor** *n.* door in floor فرشی دروازہ **trapper** *n.* one who traps animals for their skins کھال کی خاطر پکڑنے والا **trappings** *n.* (see separate entry)

a mouse-trap

trapes (trayps) *v.t.* (of skirt) trail دامن کا گھسٹنا (esp. of women) go about wearily (usu. on errands) سودا سلف کے لیے گھسٹتے پھرنا

trapeze (tra-*peez*) *n.* horizontal bar or rod supported by two ropes for use by acrobats or athletes ورزشی پینگ، ورزشی جھولا

a gymnast on a trapeze

trappings (trap-ings) *n. pl.* ornamental cloths or fittings (*of* a horse, etc.) گھوڑے کا آرائشی ساز (یا) جھول decorations (*of* a public office, etc.) ساز و سامان

Trappist (trap-ist) *n.* monk of an order noted for silence خاموش راہب، چپ شاہ

trash *n.* worthless material ردی چیز، فضول شے worthless piece of writing معمولی **trashy** (*trash*-i) *adj.* worthless فضول، بیکار، بیہودہ

travail (*trav*-ayl, or *trav*-il) *n.* pangs of childbirth دردِ زہ hard work, toil سخت محنت *v. i.* (rhetorical) laborious effort جد و جہد کرنا (old use) be in labour دردِ زہ میں مبتلا ہونا

travel (*trav*-el) *v.t.* & *i.* (-ll-) journey سفر کرنا make long journeys سیاحت کرنا (of light, sound, etc.) حرکت کرنا *n.* travelling سفر (*pl.*) long journey abroad سیاحت *tales of travel* سیاحت نامے، سیاحت کے قصے **traveller** (*trav*-e-le*) *n.* one who travels مسافر، سیاح *commercial traveller*, travelling salesman سفری ایجنٹ *traveller's tale*, concocted story من گھڑت قصہ **travelled** (*trav*-ĕld) *adj.* (also *well-travelled*), one who has been about the world جہاں گرد **travelogue** (*trav*-e-log or -lohg) *n.* illustrated lecture-narrative on expedition سیاحی کی مہم کا تصویری لکچر such article, etc. سیاحی کی مہم کا تصویری تذکرہ

traverse (*trav*-ĕ*s) *v.t.* go across کے پار جانا، میں سے گزرنا travel across کے مشرق سے مغرب تک سفر کرنا lie across کو قطع کرنا کے عرضاً واقع (یا پڑے) ہونا to cross oppose, contradict کا ابطال کرنا، کی مخالفت کرنا، کی تردید کرنا *adj.* crossing across قاطع *n.* contradiction (of opponent's statement) تردید، ابطال movement or structure across something قاطع (حرکت، خط، چیز وغیرہ)

travesty (*trav*-es-ti) *n.* wilfully disfigured version, etc., (*of* something) بگڑی ہوئی صورت، بگاڑی ہوئی شکل bad and ridiculous or painful rendering (*of* justice, truth, etc.) (کا) مذاق اڑانا، (کا) منہ چڑانا *It is a travesty of justice* یہ انصاف کا منہ چڑانا ہے، یہ انصاف کا مذاق ہے *v.t.* make or be a travesty of کا منہ چڑانا، کا مذاق کرنا

trawl *n.* large wide-mouthed fishing net بڑا جال، مہا جال **trawler** *v.t.* & *i.* go fishing with a trawl مہا جال ڈالنا، مچھلی پکڑنے کی کشتی *n.* boat used for trawling مہا جال والی کشتی، مہا جال کشتی، دام کشتی

tray *n.* large flat plate or board with raised edges سینی، کشتی، ٹرے *tea-tray* چائے کی کشتی، ٹرے

treacherous (*trech*-ē-rus) *adj*. false or disloyal (*to* a cause friend etc.) بیوفا، غدّار، دغاباز unreliable (memory, ground, etc.) دھوکے باز **treachery** (*trech*-ē-ri) *n*. violation of faith by desertion دغا، بیوفائی، غدّاری

treacle (*treek*-ēl) *n*. thick, dark syrup produced while sugar is being refined شیرہ ، راب

tread (tred) *v.t.* & *i*. (*tread, trod, trodden*) put one's foot or feet down (*on*) چلنا، قدم رکھنا *tread on (someone's) toes* (or *corns*) annoy (him) by saying غصّہ دلانے والی بات کہنا (*seem to*) *tread on air*, be very happy خوشی سے پھولا نہ سمانا *tread in (someone's) footsteps*, follow (his) example کے نقشِ قدم پر چلنا *tread on the heels of (someone)*, (*a*) follow (him) to a place کے پیچھے پیچھے جانا (*b*) (of an event) follow another کے فوراً بعد ہونا tread a path to (a place) چل چل کر (کسی جگہ) تک پگڈنڈی بنانا *tread the stage* (or *boards*), act in play سٹیج پر آنا crush (down, in, etc.) with the feet پاؤں سے کچل دینا *tread out (fire, etc.)* پیر سے بجھا دینا *tread out (rebellion, etc.)* سختی سے دبا دینا *tread under foot* کچل دینا *n*. manner of walking چال sound of footsteps چاپ part of a step or stair on which the foot is placed (as opposed to a *riser* which is the vertical piececonnecting two treads (زینہ کا یا بانس کی سیڑھی کا ڈنڈا) سیڑھی، قدمچہ part of a tyre, sole, etc. which touches the ground ٹائر یا جوتے وغیرہ کا زمین پر ٹکا ہوا حصّہ **treadmill** *n*. cylinder set to turn by man's feet پاؤں چکی، پیر چکی monotonous toil اکتا دینے والا کام، چکی

treadle (*tred*-ēl) *n*. the driving part of machine which is worked by the pressure of the foot ٹریڈل، پائدان، پاؤں سے چلنے والا ہتھا *v.i.* work a treadle ٹریڈل چلانا **treadle-machine, treadle-press** *n*. printing press worked thus ٹریڈل مشین، پائدانی مطبع **treason** (*tree*-zen) *n*. disloyalty to one's country, king or government بغاوت، غدّاری **treasonable, treasonous** *adj*. punishable because of being of the nature of treason باغیانہ

treasure (*trezh*-ē*) *n*. great riches بہت مال و دولت gold, silver and jewels, etc. زر و جواہر store of gold, silver and jewels, etc. خزانہ highly valued object بیش بہا چیز very talented person نہایت قابل شخص very useful person بڑا کام کا آدمی *The girl is a perfect treasure* یہ لڑکی لاکھ روپے میں بھی سستی ہے *art treasures* شاندار تصویریں مجسّمے وغیرہ *v.t.* & *i*. store up for future use سینت سینت کر رکھنا، سنبھال کر رکھنا store (*up*) in memory or otherwise as dear or valuable عزیز رکھنا، جان سے عزیز رکھنا، کلیجہ سے لگائے رکھنا، جان سے لگانے رکھنا **treasurer** *n*. one in charge of money, etc., belonging to a bank, etc. خزانچی one in similar capacity to an organization ; financial secretary خزانچی، خازن، مُہتممِ مال **treasury** (*trezh*-ē-ri) place where treasure is kept خزانہ government department in charge of public money خزانہ، خزانۂ عامرہ *the Treasury* برطانوی وزارتِ خزانہ *treasury note*, currency note (of £1 or 10 s. in Britain) نوٹ *treasury bench*, front-bench of the British Parliament برطانوی پارلیمنٹ کی صفِ اوّل، صفِ وُزرا *treasury benches*, government party in a Legislature حزبِ مُوافق **treasurehouse** *n*. museum, art gallery, etc. تصویر خانہ store (*of* information, etc.) خزانہ **treasure trove** *n*. treasure found hidden, of which a large part goes to the State دفینہ

treat (treet) *v.i.* & *i*. act or behave towards سے سلوک کرنا، سے برتاؤ کرنا *treat (someone) kindly* سے نرمی کا سلوک کرنا *treat (someone) as* (or *as if he were*) *a subordinate* سے ماتحتوں کا سا سلوک کرنا consider (something lightly, as a joke, etc.) سمجھنا present (a subject, etc.) پر کہنا، پر لکھنا، پیش کرنا *treat of*, (of a book, etc.) be about کے متعلق ہونا، پر ہونا (*treat someone to*), provide (him) with something pleasant free ; provide (him) with free food, etc. کی دعوت کرنا *treat (someone) to dinner* رات کا کھانا کرنا give medical or surgical care to (a person, disease) کا علاج کرنا improve, etc. (a substance *with* something) for final manufacture سے ٹھیک کرنا، کر لگانا discuss or arrange terms (*with* someone) سے شرائط طے کرنا *n*. rare delight نعمت **treatment** *n*. way of treating someone برتاؤ، سلوک *the treatment meted out to (someone)* سے کیا ہوا برتاؤ، سے سلوک medical or surgical cure (of someone or something) علاج *undergo (someone's) treatment* کے زیرِ علاج کرنا

treatise (*tree*-tis, or *tree*-tiz) *n*. essay, book, etc., of a serious kind (*on* a subject) رسالہ ، مقالہ

treaty (*tree*-ti) *n*. formally signed agreement (between nations) مُعاہدہ negotiations (between persons) گفت و شنید (only in the phrase :) *be in treaty with* سے گفت و شنید ہونا

treble (*treb*-ēl) *n*. highest of the four principal parts in singing ; soprano پنچم threefold amount تین گنا رقم *adj*. threefold تگنا triple تگنا of or for the treble تین گنا *v.t.* & *i*. multiply or be multiplied by three تگنا کرنا یا ہونا

tree *n*. large plant with a single, self-supporting woody stem (called the *trunk*) and branches درخت، پیڑ *family tree*, list showing or giving famil descent ; genealogical table شجرہ

efoil (*tref*-oil, or *tree*-foil) *n.* any plant with three-lobed leaves تپتیا پودا similar ornamental design in architecture, etc. تپتیا کام **trefoiled** *adj.* تپتیا کام والا، تپتیا پھول

rek *n.* (-kk-) long journey by ox-wagon as a South African custom بیل گاڑی پر لمبا سفر (slang) departing چل پڑنا migration of body of persons thus بہت سوں کا ترکِ وطن *v.i.* undertake long journey by ox-wagon بیل گاڑی پر لمبا سفر کرنا migrate ترکِ وطن کرنا drive (wagons or goods thus) بیل گاڑی (پر) ہانکنا

trellis (*trel*-is) *n.* strips of wood, etc., crossing one another used as a support for climbing plants جعفری *v.t.* put a climbing plant on a trellis (بیل) جعفری پر چڑھانا

a trellis

tremble (*trem*-bĕl) *v.i.* shake (*with* fear, anger, cold, etc.) کانپنا، لرزنا، تھرانا *n.* trembling کپکپی، لرزہ

tremendous (tre-*mend*-us) *adj.* terrific ہولناک، مہیب (colloq.) astonishingly great بہت ہی بڑا (slang) very skilful (*on* something) بہت لائق

tremolo (*trem*-o-loh) *n.* tremulous effect in singing or playing لرزتی ہوئی آواز، لرزاں آواز

tremor (*trem*-ĕ*) *n.* trembling کپکپی، لرزہ thrill (*of* excitement, fear or other emotion) لہر، جسم میں دوڑ جانے والی (خوشی، خوف وغیرہ کی) لہر

trem lous (*trem*-ew-lus) *adj.* trembling کانپتا ہوا timid گھبرایا ہوا nervous جھجکنے والا، ڈرپوک

trench *n.* protective ditch for soldiers مورچہ ditch for draining off water گہری نالی خندق *v.t.* & *i.* advance by making trenches مورچے کھودتے ہوئے آگے بڑھنا make trenches in گہری نالی کھودنا

trencher *n.* wooden platter for cutting bread on کٹھوتی

trenchant (*trench*-ant) *adj.* sharp (sword) تیز biting, terse and outspoken (language, criticism) تلخ اور صاف گویانہ (اسلوب)، کڑی تنقید **trenchancy** *n.* being trenchant تیزی، تلخی، سختی

trend *n.* tendency رجحان، میلان general direction رخ، سمت *v. i.* have a certain trend or have a trend (*towards*) کی طرف مائل ہونا

trepan (tre-*pan*) *v.t.* (-nn-) inveigle (into) پھانسنا، ورغلانا، بہکا کر (کوئی کام) کرانا

trepidation (trep-i-*day*-shĕn) *n.* fear and trembling خوف اور لرزہ flurry بےچینی، اضطراب

trespass (*tres*-pas) *v.i.* go (*on* or *upon* private land) without permission (میں) مداخلتِ بیجا کرنا، (میں) مجرمانہ مداخلت کرنا، (میں) بلا اجازت داخل ہونا encroach (*upon* someone's time, etc.) خارج ہونا، مخل ہونا (old use) do wrong (against) کا قصور کرنا trample (someone's rights, etc.) (حقوق) پامال کرنا make unwarrantable demands (*on* someone's hospitality, etc.) سے ناجائز فائدہ اٹھانا meddle بیجا مداخلت کرنا trespass on (someone's) preserves (کسی کے) مخصوص معاملات میں بیجا مداخلت کرنا *n.* trespassing مداخلتِ بیجا، پامالی، قصور **trespasser** *n.* بیجا مداخلت کرنے والا

tress (tres) *n.* portion or lock of hair on the head بالوں کی لٹ، زلف، گیسو، کاکل (*pl.*) long flowing hair (of women or children) (عورتوں بچوں کے) لمبے بال

trestle (*tres*-ĕl) *n.* one of the movable wooden supports for a workman's bench, etc. قینچی دار گھوڑی **trestle-bridge** *n.* bridge supported on such framework قینچی دار پل

tri- (trī) *pref.* three تین، سہ، ثلث (as : *tripod* تپائی

triad (*trī*-ad) *n.* group or union of three تین کا جوڑا (یا) مجموعہ (Cf. dyad)

trial (*trī*-al) *n.* test آزمائش، تجربہ *a trial of strength* (*between*) مقابلہ *give* (*something*) *a trial*, use (it) to see if it is any good کی آزمائش کرنا *a trial flight*, flight (of a new aircraft) for testing it آزمائشی پرواز *trial match*, match for the selection of players for an important team آزمائشی میچ، انتخابی میچ *on trial*, for testing تجربے کے لیے، بطور آزمائش something or someone troublesome or annoying (*to*) (کے لیے) بلائے جان، کی شامتِ اعمال، تکلیف دہ شے یا شخص examination (*of* an accused) in a lawcourt (*for* an offence) کا مقدمہ (کے الزام میں کسی کی) سماعت (also see **try**)

triangle (*tri*-ang-ĕl) *n.* plane figure with three straight sides مثلث any three points not in a straight line تکون any triangular instrument تکونا اوزار triangular steel bar struck with a steel rod to serve as a musical instrument تکونا باجا، تکون (also the *eternal triangle*), emotional situation in which a couple and another man or woman are involved جذباتی مثلث، ابدی مثلث

triangular (tri-*ang*-ew-lĕ*) *adj.* in the shape of a triangle مثلث، تکونا in which three persons, etc., take part تین والا، سہ گانہ

tribal *adj.* (see under **tribe**)

tribe (trīb) *n.* racial group living as a community under one or more chiefs قبیلہ **tribal** (*trī*-bĕl) *adj.* of or pertaining to a tribe قبائلی *tribal territory*, (in Pakistan) area inhabited by Pathan tribes قبائلی علاقہ، آزاد علاقہ **tribesman** *n.* member of a tribe قبائلی

tribulation (trib-ew-*lay*-shĕn) *n.* great trouble مصیبت grief رنج، دکھ cause of grief رنج، دکھ

tribunal (tri-*bew*-nĕl) *n.* place of judgment عدالت judges appointed for special duty خصوصی عدالت، ٹریبیونل

tribune (*trib*-ewn) *n.* (also *tribune of the people*), one of the high civil officers elected annually from among the common people in ancient Rome ٹریبیون dais پلیٹ فارم rostrum منبر popular leader رلیڈر

tribute (*trib*-ewt) *n.* tax paid by one government or ruler to another خراج، باج something done, said, or given as a compliment (*to*) خراج تحسین **tributary** (*trib*-ew-ta-ri) *adj.* paying tribute to another باجگزار flowing into another معاون *n.* river flowing into another معاون دریا

tricar (*trī*-kah*) *n.* three-wheeled motor-car تین پہیئے کی موٹر، سہ چرخی موٹر

trice (tris) *v.t.* pull (*up*) and tie (a sail) in place (بادبان) کس کر باندھنا *n.* (only in the phrase) *in a trice*, at once فوراً، فی الفور

trick (trik) *n.* fraud فریب، دھوکا، چال *tricks of the trade*, prevalent petty dishonesties of a profession کسی پیشے کے گر *play a trick on (someone)* سے چال چلنا out of the way feat (by a juggler, trained dog, etc.) کرتب، کھیل *conjuring tricks* مداری کے کھیل habit (*of doing* something) (کی) عادت the right way of doing something which is learnt by practice ڈھب، کرنے کا طریقہ، صحیح طریقہ *shall soon learn* (or *get*) *the trick of it* اس کا ڈھب جلد ہی سیکھ جائے گا practical joke شرارت (cards played in) one round (of bridge, etc.) (تاش کا) ہاتھ *take a trick, win a trick*, win one round ایک ہی ہاتھ جیت جانا *v.t.* deceive (someone *out of* something or *into doing* something) by a trick کو دھوکا دے کر لینا یا کرانا **trickery** *n.* fraud دھوکا، فریب، دغا **trickster** *n.* one who is in the habit of tricking others دھوکے باز، فریبی، عیار **tricky** (*trik*-i) *adj.* crafty چالاک، کائیاں، دغاباز ticklish مشکل full of pitfalls پیچیدار requiring skill ہوشیاری کا طالب، احتیاط طلب

trickle (*trik*-ĕl) *v.t.* & *i.* (cause to) flow in drops or in a small stream ٹپکنا، رسنا، ٹپکانا *n.* stream of drops ٹپکا weak flow پتلی دھار *shrink to a trickle* کم ہوتے ہوتے پتلی دھار رہ جانا (یا) کم ہوتے ہوتے ٹپکنے پر آ رہنا

tricolour (*tri*-kul-ĕ*) *n.* flag with three stripes of different colours ترنگا جھنڈا *adj.* having three colours ترنگا، سہ رنگا

tricycle (*tri*-sik-ĕl) *n.* (abbr. *trike*), three-wheeled cycle ٹرائیسکل، تین پہیوں کی سائیکل، سہ چرخہ

a child's tricycle

trident (*tri*-dent) *n.* spear with three points سہ شاخہ برچھا

tried (trid) *v.* (pa. t. & pa. p. of try, which see)

triennial (tri-*en*-i-ĕl) *adj.* lasting for three years تین سال تک رہنے والا، سہ سالہ happening, etc., every three years ہر تیسرے سال ہونے والا، سہ سالہ *n.* triennial event سہ سالہ تقریب، سہ سالہ واقعہ

trifle (*tri*-fĕl) *n.* unimportant thing معمولی سی چیز unimportant event, etc. ادنیٰ سی بات، معمولی سی بات waste time on trifles بیکار باتوں میں وقت کھونا small amount تھوڑی سی مقدار small amount of money تھوڑا سا پیسہ sweet dish of cake, jam, cream, etc. رنش کیک *adv.* (*a trifle*), a little ذرا، ذرا سا، تھوڑا *seems a trifle annoyed* وہ کچھ برہم سا نظر آتا ہے *v.t.* & *i.* talk lightly without serious purpose فضول باتیں کرنا play act thus lightly کھیل سمجھنا play idly (*with* the fingers, etc.) کھیلنا، شغل کرنا waste (*away* time, etc.) گنوانا، ضائع کرنا، کھونا **trifling** *adj.* unimportant معمولی سا، یونہی سا، غیر اہم

trig *n.* brake پہیہ روک، روک *adj.* smart, trim سجا سجایا، آراستہ پیراستہ *v.t.* apply the brakes to روکنا، روک لگانا prop (*up*) سہارا دے کر کھڑا کرنا deck (*up* or *out*) سجانا، بنانا سنوارنا

trigger (*trig*-ĕ*) *n.* lever for releasing a catch (esp. of a fire-arm لبلبی، (بندوق کا) گھوڑا *pull the trigger* (بندوق کا) گھوڑا چلانا

triglyph (*trig*-lif) *n.* tablet of a frieze with three vertical grooves آرائشی گلگری کی چھنٹ دار تختی

trigonometry (trig-o-*nom*-et-ri) *n.* branch of mathematics dealing with the relations between sides and angles of triangles علم مثلث

trike (trik) *n.* (abbr. of **tricycle**, which see) (*Cf.* Like)

trilateral (tri-*lat*-ĕ-rĕl) *adj.* three-sided تین اطراف والا، سہ طرفہ (of agreement, etc.) having three parties to it سہ طرفہ، سہ گانہ

trilingual (trī-*ling*-wĕl) *adj.* of or in three languages تین زبانوں کا (یا) میں speaking three languages سہ زبان، تین زبانوں کا ماہر، تین زبانیں جاننے والا

trill (tril) *n.* vibrating sound of the voice کھنکتی گٹکری کے ہوئی آواز، گٹکری *v.t.* & *i.* sing with trill کھنکتی ہوئی آواز سے گانا utter speak thus ساتھ گانا the sound of (*one's r*, or *one's r's*) with a trill کھنکتی ہوئی آواز سے نکالنا، پر کر کے نکالنا **trilling** *n.* (also) triplet تین جڑواں بچوں میں سے ایک

trillion (*tril*-yĕn) *n.* & *adj.* (*U. K.*) a million million million دس سنکھ (*U. S.*) a million million دس کھرب

trilogy (*tril*-o-ji) *n.* group of three tragedies each complete in itself but with a common subject سہ المیہ such group of any three books سہ نثریا سہ نظم

trim *adj.* in good order خوش ترتیب neat and tidy صاف ستھرا *v.t.* & *i.* (-mm-) make (hedge, etc.) trim by cutting away uneven parts کانٹ چھانٹ کرنا، کانٹ چھانٹ کرکے دُرُست کرنا set right (wick of a lamp) thus (رگل) کاٹنا set right (beard) thus (داڑھی) کو تراش کر دُرُست کرنا، (داڑھی) تراشنا cut out undesirable parts چھانٹنا، چھانٹ دینا decorate (a hat, dress, etc. with lace, etc.) لیس لگانا، (فیتہ) لگانا make (a boat, ship) steady by arranging of cargo, passengers, etc. evenly کا بوجھ برابر کرنا arrange (sails) to suit the wind (بادبان) ٹھیک لگانا *n.* being prepared (*for* something) تیاری، تیار ہونا *get into trim for the athletic meet* ورزشی مقابلوں کے لیے تیار ہونا *out of trim* خراب حالت میں، بے ترتیبی **trimness** *n.* being trim، خوش ترتیبی، آراستگی، ستھرا پن **trimming** *n.* lace, ribbon, etc., for trimming dresses or hats گوٹ، لیس، فیتہ، کناری وغیرہ (pl.) accessories served (with a dish) (کھانے کی چیز کے) لوازمات **tri-nitro-toluol** (trī-nit-ro-*tol*-ew-ol) *n.* (abb. *T.N.T.*, or *trotyl*) a high explosive ٹی این ٹی

trinity (*trin*-i-ti) *n.* being three تین ہونا group of three تین کا مجموعہ، تین میں ایک *the Trinity*, the union of God the Father, God the Son, and God the Holy Ghost according to Christianity تثلیث، توحید فی التثلیث

trinket (*trink*-et) *n.* small and cheap ornament چھوٹا سا سستا زیور

trio (*trī*-oh, or *trī*-oh) *n.* group of three تین کی جوڑی، تِکڑم in music group of three singers or players تین کا طائفہ، تین کی چوکی یا ٹکڑی musical composition for them تین کا راگ

trip *v.t.* & *i.* (-pp-) go along (esp. on tiptoes) with quick, light steps نزاکت سے تیز چلنا (cause to) stumble (*over* something) ٹھوکر کھانا، ٹھوکر لگنا، ٹھوکر لگانا، اڑنگا لگانا *trip up*, (a) fall ٹھوکر کھا کر گرنا (b) cause to fall ٹھوکر سے گرنے کا باعث بننا، اڑنگا لگانا (c) err غلطی کرنا (d) cause to err غلطی کا موجب بننا *n.* pleasure excursion سیر، تفریحی سفر ship's voyage جہاز کا سفر stumble ٹھوکر، لغزش error غلطی، ٹھوکر، لغزش **tripper** *n.* one who makes short excursions for pleasure تفریحی سفر کرنے والا

tripartite (tri-*pah**-tit) *adj.* (of an agreement) to which there are three parties سہ طرفہ، سہ گانہ having three parts تین حصّوں والا

tripe (trip) *n.* part of the stomach of an ox, etc., used as food اوجھڑی (slang) inferior stuff گھٹیا مال (in cricket) easy bowling ہلکی گیند (slang) worthless talk, writing, ideas etc. فضول بکواس

triple (*trip*-ĕl) *adj.* made up of three (parts or parties) تہرا، سہ گانہ، تگنا *triple five*, with three fives, 555, پانسو پچپن *triple M.A.*, one who is an M.A. in three subjects ٹرپل ایم اے، تہرا ایم۔اے *v.t.* & *i.* make, become or be three times as much or as many تگنا کرنا (یا) ہونا (یا) ہو جانا

triplet (*trip*-let) *n.* (colloq.) trilling بچوں میں سے ایک (pl.) three such children جڑواں بچے set of three تین کی جوڑی three successive lines rhyming together ہم قافیہ مثلث

triplex (*trip*-leks) *adj.* of three parts تین پرت کا *triplex glass*, unsplinterable glass comprising two sheets which sandwich a sheet of transparent plastic material تین پرت کا شیشہ، ریزہ ریزہ نہ ہونے والا شیشہ

triplicate (*trip*-li-ket) *adj.* that of which three copies are made تہرا، جس کے تین نسخے ہوں *n.* one of the three similar documents, etc. تین نسخوں میں سے ایک copy forming the third document etc. تیسرا نسخہ *in triplicate*, original with two copies تین نسخے، اصل اور دو نقلیں *v.t.* (*trip*-li-kayt) make in triplicate تین نسخے تیار کرنا، تین ایک جیسی چیزیں بنانا

tripod (*trī*-pod, or *trip*-od) *n.* three-legged stool or three-legged support for a camera, etc. تپائی

a tripod

tripos (*trī*-pos) *n.* honours degree at Cambridge University، ٹرائپوس، کیمبرج کا بی۔اے آنرز list of successful candidates کامیاب طلبہ کی فہرست

trisect (trī-*sect*) *v.t.* divide (line, angle, etc.) into three equal parts تین برابر حصّوں میں بانٹنا، کی تثلیث کرنا divide into any three parts تین حصّوں میں بانٹنا

tristful (*trist*-ful) *adj.* (poet.) sad حزیں، غم والا

trite (trit) *adj.* hackneyed (quotation, ideas, feelings, etc.) فرسودہ، پامال

Triton (*trī*-ton) *Cl. myth.* son of the Greek sea-god Poseidon ٹرٹین

triturate (*tri*-tew-rayt) *v.t.* grind to powder or paste سفوف بنانا، مالیدہ کرنا

triumph (*tri*-umf) *n.* victory (*order*) فتح remarkable success شاندار کامیابی *a shout of triumph*, نعرۂ کامرانی *achieve great triumphs* شاندار کامیابی حاصل کرنا joy of success فتح و کامرانی کی خوشی supreme example (*of* something) کی شاندار مثال procession entry into Rome of victorious Roman general جشنِ فتح، رومی سپہ سالار کا فتوحات کے بعد جشن *v.t.* win a victory (*over*) پر فتح حاصل کرنا exult (*over*) پر خوش ہونا، پر فخر کرنا be happy owing to victory, success, etc. خوش ہونا **triumphal** (tri-*um*-fal) *adj.* of or for a triumph جشنِ فتح کا (یا) کے متعلق expressing triumph فاتحانہ **triumphant**

(trī-*um*-fant) *adj.* victorious فاتح، فتحمند successful کامیاب، بامُراد happy over successful victory نازاں

triumvirate (trī-um-vi-rayt) *n.* coalition government in ancient Rome روماکی سہ شخصی حکومت any party of three persons تین افراد کی پارٹی، تین کی ٹولی **triumvir** (*-um-*) *n.* member of a triumvirate سہ شخصی حکومت کا رُکن

triune (*trī*-yewn) *adj.* three in one (used of the Christian concept of God) تین میں کا ایک

trivial (*triv*-i-al) *adj.* ordinary معمولی unimportant غیر اہم worthless ناکارہ، نکما **triviality** (*-al-*) *n.* trivial thing, etc. معمولی سی چیز trivial idea, etc. فضول بات

trod, trodden *v.* (pa. t. & pa. p. of **tread**, which see)

troche (*troh*-ki) *n.* metrical foot consisting of a short foot followed by a long one دوال رُکن، ٹراکی **trochaic** (tro-*kay*-ik) *adj.* of or in trochees ٹراکی رُکنوں کی نظم (pl.) such verse ٹراکی رُکنوں میں دوال نظم

troglodyte (*trog*-lo-dīt) cave-dweller of ancient times غار نشیں

trois-temps (troh-a-ton) *adj.* & *n.* in ordinary time (waltz) عام رفتار کا (والس ناچ)

Trojan (*troh*-jan) *adj.* & *n.* (native) of Troy ٹرائے کا (باشندہ) (colloq.) first class worker or fighter اعلےٰ درجے کا کارکن یا نبرد آزما

troll (trohl) *v.t.* & *i.* sing (*out*) song in snatches or during other occupation کام کے دوران میں ریا ٹھوڑا ٹھوڑا گانا

trolley (*trol*-i) *n.* (pl. *trolleys*) low truck pushed by workmen on railway ٹرالی contact wheel between a tramcar worked by an overhead electric cable ٹرالی، بالائی چسگر، چکّر

trollop (*trol*-op) *n.* disreputable woman فاحشہ slut پھوہڑ عورت

trombone (*trom*-bohn) *n.* large trumpet-like musical instrument with a sliding tube بڑا بگل، پھسلواں بگل

troop (troop) *n.* group of persons or animals, esp., when moving or about to move or just arrived سفر پر جانے والا (یا سے آیا ہُوا) گروہ، اُڑتا ہُوا جھنڈ، مائل بپرواز جھنڈ، ابھی آکر بیٹھا ہُوا جھنڈ any group, etc., گروہ cavalry unit رسالہ (*pl.*) soldiers فوجی *v. i.* come or go together in a group (*in, into, out of,* etc., a place) جمگھٹے آنا یا جانا **trooper** *n.* cavalry private رسالہ کا سپاہی *swear like a trooper*, swear vehemently سخت گالیاں دینا **troop-carrier** *n.* large aircraft for transporting troops فوج بردار طیّارہ **troop-ship** *n.* ship (for) transporting soldiers فوجی نقل وحمل کا جہاز

trope (trohp) *n.* deviation from the normal way of saying something, used as a rhetorical device مجاز

trophy (*trof*-i) *n.* memento of a victory or success فتح (یا کامیابی کی) نشانی، ٹرافی *annex a trophy*, win it ٹرافی حاصل کرنا group of things arranged for display نمائش کے لیے رکھی ہُوئی چیزیں pile of the spoils of war مالِ غنیمت کا ڈھیر

tropic (*trop*-ik) *n.* line of latitude 23° 27' North (called the *tropic of Cancer*) or South (called the *tropic of Capricorn*) خطِ سرطان (یا خطِ جدی) (*pl.*) *the tropics*, the part of the world between these lines منطقۂ حارّہ، خطِ سرطان اور خطِ جدی کا درمیانی علاقہ **tropical** *adj.* (as) of the tropics منطقۂ حارّہ کا (سا) گرم سیر

troposphere (*trop*-os-fee-è*) *n.* lower part of atmosphere (as distinct from stratosphere) extending about seven miles upwards from the surface of the earth پائیں کُرۂ ہوائی

trot *v.t.* & *i.* (-tt-) (of horses, etc.) run with legs at diagonal pace ; run at medium pace ڈُلکی چلنا cause (a horse) to run thus ڈُلکی چلانا *trot out*, (*a*) trot a horse for show ڈُلکی چلا کر دکھانا (*b*) display (something) for appreciation کے لیے اہتمام سے پیش کرنا (of a person) run with short steps ناز نخرے سے آہستہ آہستہ دوڑنا go fussily (*about*) کرتے پھرنا *n.* trotting pace ڈُلکی چال، ڈُلکی *go off at a trot* دوڑ دُھوپ *go for a trot*, go out on horseback for pleasure سواری کے لیے جانا constant effort or duty محنت اور مستعدی کا کام، دوڑ دُھوپ *keep* (*someone*) *on the trot*, give (him) no rest کو بھگائے پھرنا toddling child ڈگمگا کر چلنے والا چھوٹا بچہ **trotter** *n.* horse trained for trotting ڈُلکی چلنے والا گھوڑا (*pl.*) animal's feet as food پائے (slang) human feet پاؤں، پَیر

troubadour (*troob*-a-doo*) *n.* travelling love-poet and singer in Mediaeval France قرونِ وسطیٰ کا غزل گو، مُطرب شاعر، طرب دار

trouble (*trub*-èl) *v.t.* & *i.* inconvenience تکلیف دینا، زحمت دینا *trouble* (*someone for* or *to do something*) کو تکلیف کرنا کی زحمت دینا *trouble about* *be troubled with* (*a disease*) سے تکلیف اُٹھانا worry پریشان کرنا یا ہونا *be troubled by* کے باعث پریشان ہونا ruffle (water, etc.) میں تلاطم برپا کرنا disturb (peace) امن تباہ کرنا *n* inconvenience تکلیف، بے آرامی، زحمت worry پریشانی calamity مصیبت *be in trouble* مصیبت میں ہونا

get into trouble مشکل میں پھنسنا difficulty *have trouble with* کو مشکل پانا extra effort زحمت *it will be no trouble* اس میں کیا زحمت ہوگی *take trouble (to do something)* کی زحمت اٹھانا *trouble with* (or *over*) (*something*), (*a*) use great care میں بڑی احتیاط کرنا (*b*) take pains over it پر جان کھپانا، میں بڑی محنت کرنا **troublesome** (*trub*-èl-sum) *adj.* causing trouble تکلیف دہ needing much care احتیاط طلب pestering (person) دق کرنے والا **troublous** (*troub*-lus) *adj.* (of times) full of insecurity and confusion پر آشوب (دور)

trough (trawf) *n.* long, open container of food or drink for animals ناند any channel like it in shape پنالی large hollow vessel لگن hollow between two waves انخفاض

trounce (trouns) *v.t.* beat thoroughly بری طرح مارنا، کندی کرنا defeat ہرانا، شکست دینا

troupe (troop) *n.* company of actors or artistes set of acrobats, performing animals, etc. طائفہ جوڑی، ٹولی **trouper** *n.* member of a troupe of actors, etc. طائفے والی (یا والا)، طائفے کا رکن

trousers (*trou*-ze*z) *n. pl.* (also *pair of trousers*), men's two-legged, outer garment reaching from waist to ankles پتلون *two pairs of trousers* دو پتلونیں **trouser-pocket** *n.* پتلون کی جیب **trouserbutton** *n.* پتلون کا بٹن **trousering** *n.* cloth for trousers پتلون کا کپڑا **troused** (-zĕ*d) *adj.* پتلون پہنے ہوئے

trousseau (*troo*-soh) *n.* bride's outfit دلہن کا جوڑا، لباس عروسی

trout *n.* (pl. same, but even the pl. is used with *sing.* verb) a kind of fresh-water fish ٹراؤٹ، گھینٹی

trouvaille *n.* windfall چھپر پھاڑ کر ملی ہوئی چیز

trouvere (troo-*vay*-è*) *n.* an epic poet of Mediaeval France مطرب، رزم گو

trover (*troh*-vĕ*) suit to recover value of lost or detained goods دعویٰ بابت جائداد منقولہ

trove *n.* (see **treasure-trove**)

trow (troh) *v.t.* (old use) believe خیال کرنا wonder کو حیرت ہونا

trowel (*trou*-el) *n.* flat-bladed tool for spreading mortar on bricks کرنی *lay it on with a trowel*, lavish praise حد سے زیادہ تعریف کرنا، مسکہ لگانا gardener's tool with a curved blade for lifting plants کھرپا *v.t.* lay mortar with a trowel گارا پھیلانا، گارے کا ردا چڑھانا

a trowel

troy (troi) *n.* (also *troy weight*), British system of weights used for gold and silver in which 1 lb. is equivalent to 12 oz., 1 oz. to 20 dwt. (called *pennyweight*) and 1 dwt. to 24 grams ٹرائے وزن، ٹرائے

truant (*troo*-ant) *n.* student, etc., who is absent without permission سکول (وغیرہ) سے بھاگا ہوا، گریز پا *play truant*, (*a*) be absent from school, etc., without permission سکول (وغیرہ) سے بھاگ جانا، بلا اجازت غیر حاضر رہنا، گریز پائی کرنا (*b*) roving (thoughts, etc.) گریز پا (of time) spent in truancy کام سے بھاگ کر گزارا ہوا **truancy** (*troo*-ans-i) *n.* playing truant (وقت) کام سے بھاگنا، بلا اجازت غیر حاضر رہنا

truce (troos) *n.* stopping of fighting for the time-being التوائے جنگ، عارضی صلح، متارکہ agreement to this effect جنگ کا معاہدہ **trucial** (*troosh*-ĕl) *adj.* about or with which there has been a truce treaty معاہداتی

truck (truk) *n.* open motor vehicle for heavy goods ٹرک، چھکڑا any other such vehicle for the road چھکڑا open wagon in a goods train (مال گاڑی کا) چھکڑا railway porter's barrow ٹھیلا barter مبادلہ، ادل بدل، اَدلا بدلی *truck system*, paying the workmen in goods instead of money مزدوری میں جنس دینا *have no truck with*, have nothing to do with سے کوئی واسطہ نہ رکھنا *stand no truck*, waste no time in bargaining سودے بازی میں وقت ضائع نہ کرنا *v. t. & i.* barter (something *for* another) کے عوض بیچنا، کا مبادلہ کرنا **truckage** *n.* conveyance in truck چھکڑے میں مال لے جانا charges for it کرایہ، باربرداری practise of bartering مبادلہ کا رواج

truckle (*truk*-èl) *v.i.* slavishly (*to*) سے بالکل دب جانا *n.* low bed of servant or pupil (also *truckle-bed*), that could be pushed in below the master's کھٹیا، چھوٹی چارپائی

truculence *n.* (see under **truculent**)

truculent (*truk*-ew-lant) *adj.* desirous of fighting جنگجو of agressive temper تند خو **truculence** (*truk*-ew-lens) *n.* being truculent جنگجوئی، تند خوئی

trudge (truj) *v.i.* walk heavily or wearily (*through* snow, mud, etc.) گرتے پڑتے چلنا *n.* long tiring walk طویل تکلیف دہ سفر، لمبا تھکا دینے والا پیدل سفر

trudgen (*truj*-èn) *adj.* (of *stroke* in swimming) with alternate right and left arm (تیرنے میں) باری باری کا (ہاتھ)

true (troo) *adj.* in accordance with fact or reality سچ، سچا *come true*, (of a hope or dream) become fact ; happen پورا ہونا، سچ ثابت ہونا correct درست، صحیح *true copy*, copy according to the original صحیح نقل، اصلی نقل ge[nuine] faithful (or faithful to someo[ne]) وفادار، مخلص

true blue, (*a*) (of person) thoroughgoing پکّا (*b*) (of party) consistent بااُصُول **truism** (*troo*-izm) *n*. an obviously true statement which need not have been made پیش پا اُفتادہ حقیقت **true-bill** *n*. grand jury's verdict بڑی جیوری کی رائے **truly** (*troo*-li) *adj*. sincerely خلوص سے *Yours truly*, formula for closing a letter نیازمند، مخلص truthfully سچ، سچ مچ certainly یقیناً really واقعی، درحقیقت

trump (trump) *v. t.* (*trump up*), fabricate (excuse, charge, etc.) wrongly جھوٹا بنانا defeat (*card or player*) مارنا، کو جیتنا *n*. (in whist) (card of, a) suit ranking above other suits ترپ کا پتہ، ترپ *play a trump*, (*a*) play this card ترپ کھیلنا، ترپ لگانا (*b*) take a surprisingly advantageous step ترپ کی چال چلنا *trump card*, (*a*) this card ترپ کا پتہ (*b*) master-stroke حکمتی تدبیر

trumpery (*trum*-pe-ri) *n*. worthless finery سستے زیور *adj*. such showy but worthless (ornaments, furniture, arguments, etc.) جھوٹے زیور، ٹیپ ٹاپ پلشت، گھٹیا

trumpet (trum-pet) *n*. musical wind instrument of brass ترم، بگل *blow (one's) own trumpet*, praise oneself اپنا ڈھول پیٹنا something shaped like a trumpet ترم نما *v.t. & i.* play a trumpet ترم بجانا (of an elephant) emit a trumpet such a cry چنگھاڑنا *trumpet-call*, (*a*) sound of trumpet ترم کی آواز (*b*) urgent call to action فوری عمل کی دعوت **trumpeter** *n*. cavalryman giving signals on trumpet رسالہ کا ترمچی **trumpet-major** *n*. chief trumpeter رسالہ کا بڑا ترمچی

truncate (trunk-*ayt*) *v.t.* cut off the tip or end of (something) سرا کاٹنا **truncated** (trunk-*ayt*-id) *adj*. cut off at the top جس کا سر کٹا ہوا ہو، مقطوع incomplete نامکمل **truncation** (-*kay*-) *n*. cutting off the top سرا کاٹنا

truncheon (*trunch*-ěn) *n*. policeman's short club سپاہی کا ڈنڈا baton as symbol of authority عصائے اِقتدار، عصائے منصبی

trundle (*trund*-ěl) *v.t. & i.* draw (wheel-barrow) گڑھکانا roll (child's hoop) along پہیہ چلانا bowl (cricket ball) along گڑھکانا (of ball, hoop, or some awkwardly heavy person or vehicle) roll along لڑھکنا *n*. small wheel fixed to the leg of a chair, etc. پائے کا چھوٹا پہیہ

trunk (trunk) *n*. main stem of a tree تنہ body without head and limbs دھڑ main body of structure مرکزی حصہ، بنیادی حصہ long nose of elephant سونڈ large travelling box for clothes, etc. ٹرنک، بکس، بکسا *adj*. direct and main سیدھا اور بڑا *trunk-road*, main road connecting towns بڑی سڑک، شاہراہ *grand trunk road*, (abbreviated as *G. T. Road*) بڑی شاہراہ، جرنیلی سڑک *trunk-line*, (*a*) such telephone line ٹرنک لائن (*b*) main railway مین لائن *trunk-call*, telephone call beyond the local area ٹرنک کال

truss (trus) *n*. bundle (*of* hay or straw) گھاس کا گٹھا compact cluster of fruit or flowers گچھا framework supporting a roof, bridge, etc. پیل پایہ، کھم *truss bridge*, bridge with trusses پیل پائے دار پل belt for a patient of hernia فتق کی پیٹی *v.t.* support with truss کھم لگاکر سہارا دینا tie with arms to sides کی مشکیں کسنا *truss up* (*a chicken*), pin its wings to the body before cooking it پکاتے کے لیے مرغ کے بازو باندھ دینا

trust (trust) *n*. faith (*in* someone or something) as being reliable (پر) اعتماد، (پر) اعتبار، بھروسا *take on trust* accept as true without testing کے متعلق حسنِ ظن پر اعتبار کر لینا، کے متعلق حسنِ ظن سے کام لینا *on trust*, (*a*) without proof اعتبار کر کے، حسنِ ظن سے کام لیتے ہوئے (*b*) on credit اُدھار، اعتبار پر person or thing confided in معتمد، بھروسے کا responsibility ذمّہ داری property held and managed by persons (called *trustees*) for another's benefit ٹرسٹ، تولیت، وقف *the improvement trust*, one for improving the look of a town, etc. امپروومنٹ ٹرسٹ، تولیتِ ترقی، ترقیاتی وقف *the port trust*, body managing a port تولیتِ بندرگاہ legal relation between the trustees and the property تولیت such property وقف جائداد، جائداد زیرِ تولیت association of business firms for a special purpose ٹرسٹ، اتحادِ تجار، اشتراک *v.t. & i.* have trust in (or *in*) پر اعتماد کرنا، (پر) یقین کرنا give into the care of کی تحویل میں دینا، کے سپرد کرنا، کی امانت میں دینا allow credit, to a customer, etc. اُدھار دینا believe کا خیال ہونا، کو اُمید ہونا let (someone) have his own way پر چھوڑنا **trust-deed** *n*. deed executing a trust تولیت نامہ، وثیقۂ تولیت **trustee** (trus-*tee*) *n*. one who is in charge of property or business held in trust متولّی **trusteeship** *n*. being a trustee تولیت responsibility for a territory granted by the United Nations تولیت **trusting, trustful** *adj*. relying, not suspicious اعتبار کرنے والا **trustworthy** *adj*. reliable بھروسے کا، قابلِ اعتبار، لائقِ اعتماد **trusty** (*trust*-i) *adj*. (old use) loyal وفادار doing behests faithfully فرض شناس

truth (trooth) *n*. (pl. *truths* pr. troodhz) *n*. being true سچائی، صداقت، راستی that which is true سچ، سچائی، صداقت fact حقیقت، واقعہ true statement or belief سچائی، صداقت، حقیقت **truthful**

adj. habitually true (person) سچا، راستباز true سچا ⓢ We speak of a **truthful** person or statement. **Frank** means not concealing ; **guileless**, one not aware of the dangers of being frank ; **candid**, impartial and frank ; **artless** or **unsophisticated**, one who does not disguise; **naive**, one expecting no evil because of being amusingly simple.

try (tri) *v. t.* & *i.* (*try, tried, tried ; trying*) attempt (or *to do*, or *for* something) کی کوشش کرنا *try for a job*, become a candidate for it ملازمت کے لیے درخواست دینا، ملازمت کا امیدوار بننا test (something) to see if it is satisfactory کا تجربہ کرنا، آزمانا، آزما کر دیکھنا *try (clothes, hat, shoe, etc.) on*, put on to see if it fits or suits پہن کر دیکھنا *try (one's) hand at (something)*, make an attempt to work (it) کو استعمال کرنے کی کوشش کرنا *try (something) out*, use it for testing it کو تجربۃً استعمال کرنا، کو دیکھنا *try and (do something)*, (colloq. for) *try to (do something)*, (کرنے) کی کوشش کرنا (of judge) examine (*accused* or *case for* an offence) کی سماعت کرنا *be tried (for an offence)* (کسی پر اُس کے جرم میں مقدمہ چلنا) strain (eyes, etc., etc.) پر حد سے زیادہ بوجھ ڈالنا *try (someone's) patience (etc.)* کے صبر (وغیرہ) کو حد سے زیادہ آزمانا *n.* attempt کوشش *have a try*, کوشش کر کے (یا پہن کر) دیکھنا **trying** (*tri*-ing) *adj.* difficult to endure صبر آزما exasperating تکلیف دہ **try-on** *n.* (colloq.) bid to deceive فریب دہی کی کوشش **try-out** *n.* experimental trial آزمائشی معائنہ test of popularity (etc.) ہر دلعزیزی (وغیرہ) دیکھنے کا تجربہ

tryst (trist) *n.* (old use) meeting between lovers وصل its promise وعدۂ وصل time and place for it وعدۂ وصل کی جگہ یا وقت، موعدِ وصل meeting of any other persons or the promise, time and place of it ملاقات (کا وعدہ) (یا وقت یا مقام) *keep tryst* ملاقات کا وعدہ پورا کرنا *break tryst* ملاقات کا وعدہ پورا نہ کرنا

tsar, tzar *n.* (same as **czar**, which see)

tsetse (*tset*-si), **tzetse** (*tzet*-zi) *n.* African fly causing fatal disease in cattle with its bite سی سی مکھی، تسیٹ سی

tuan (too-*ahn*) *n.* (Malayan title signifying) master, lord آقا *Tuan Jim, Lord Jim* جم آقا

tub (tub) *n.* large, open topped round cask ناند، کونڈ (also *bath-tub*), large vessel for bathing ٹب، ٹپ (colloq.) bath غسل *have a cold tub* ٹھنڈے پانی کے ٹب میں بیٹھ کر نہانا

tubby (*tub*-i) *adj.* short and fat (person) ٹھگنا، گول مٹول، موٹا اور ناٹا

tube (tewb) *n.* pipe (esp. of glass or rubber) نلکی، نلی soft metal container the contents of which are taken out by pressing it ٹیوب *tooth-paste tube* دانتوں کے منجن کی ٹیوب *tube bridge*, covered bridge shaped like a hollow rectangle بند پل underground railway زمین دوز ریل، ٹیوب (U.S.) radio valve ریڈیو کا والو fluorescent light نلکی کی، ٹیوب، ڈنڈا بتی **tubing** *n.* length (*of* tube) نلکی کی لمبائی **tubular** *adj.* tube-shaped نلکی کا سا، نلکی نما having tubes نلکیوں والا **tube-well** *n.* shaft sunk deep into earth from which water is pumped out with a machine نل کنواں، ٹیوب ویل

tuber (*tew*-bĕ*) *n.* swollen underground stem (like potato) which is capable of yielding new plants گٹھا، بصلہ **tubercle** (*tewb*-ĕ*-kĕl) *n.* tumour formed in the lungs, etc., in consumption دق کا دانہ small knob, etc. چھوٹی سی گانٹھ **tuberculosis** (tew-bĕ*-kew-*loh*-sis) *n.* (abbr. *T.B.*) consumption of the lungs سل، دق، ٹی بی **tubercular** (tew-*bĕ*k*-ew-lĕ*) *adj.* of tuberculosis دق (کے دانے) کا سا **tuberculous, tuberculose** *adj.* suffering from tuberculosis دق کا مارا ہوا، دق میں مبتلا

tuck (tuk) *n.* flat fold stitched in a garment for ornament or shortening پلیٹ (slang) sweets and other eatables مٹھائی، چائے وغیرہ *v.t.* & *i.* roll or push (*up* one's sleeves, etc.) into a securer position (آستین وغیرہ) چڑھانا یا اڑسنا *tuck* oneself or someone *up, in* something, cover warmly by pulling bed clothes over, round, etc. میں لپیٹنا *tuck in*, eat heartily خوب سیر ہو کر کھانا **tuck-shop** *n.* shop in a school, college, hostel, etc., selling tea, sweets, pastries, etc. ٹک شاپ، مٹھائی کی دکان

Tuesday (*tewz*-day) *n.* the day following Monday (regarded as being sacred to *Tiw* or *Mars*) منگل، سہ شنبہ

tuft (tuft) *n.* bunch (of hair, feathers, grass etc.) held together firmly at one end or growing closely thus گچھا bunch (of threads, etc.) similarly arranged پھندا **tuft-hunter** *n.* one seeking the society of titled persons خطاب یافتہ لوگوں کے پیچھے پیچھے پھرنے والا

tug (tug) *v.t.* & *i.* (-gg-) pull violently with a jerk زور سے جھٹکا دینا (*tug at*) pull at (something) زور سے کھینچنا *n.* sudden or violent pull جھٹکا، زور کا جھٹکا strenuous effort سخت کوشش mental shock صدمہ (also *tug-boat*), small steamboat for towing ships ٹگ، جہاز کھینچنے والی کشتی **tug-of-war** *n.* competition in which two teams pull against each other on a long, thick rope رسّا کشی

a tug-of-war

tuition (tew-*ish*-ŏn) teaching تعلیم private

coaching ٹیوشن ، اتالیقی (also *tuition-fees*), fee for teaching فیس
tulip (*tew*-lip) *n*. bell shaped spring flower growing on a tall stem لالہ **tulip-tree** *n*. an American flowering tree شقائق ٹیوولیپ

a tulip

tulle (tul) *n*. soft fine material for veils, etc. نقاب وغیرہ کے لیے نرم جالی کا کپڑا
tumble (*tum*-bėl) *v. t.* & *i.* (cause to) fall suddenly and violently (*down, off, out of*, etc.) اُلٹ کر گرنا ، بُری طرح گرانا *n.* such fall اُلٹ کر گرنا ، بُری طرح گرانا (colloq.) untidy state درہم برہم ہونا ، گڑبڑ *all in a tumble* سب کچھ درہم برہم ہے **tumbledown** *adj*. (of building) in bad repair ; likely to collapse ٹوٹا پھوٹا ، خراب خستہ ، بُری حالت میں *v.t.* (slang) fall in with (proposal, etc.) مان جانا grasp the meaning of سمجھ جانا
tumbler (*tum*-ble*) *n*. stemless drinking glass لوٹن کبوتر acrobat بازیگر such pigeon گلاس **tumblerful** *n*. (pl. *tumblerfuls*) as much as a tumbler will hold گلاس بھر
tumbrel, tumbril (*tum*-bril) *n*. cart for carrying prisoners to the guillotine during the French Revolution تمبرل ammunition cart گولی بارود والا ٹھیلا dung-cart which can be tipped at one end گندگی کا چھکڑا
tumour (*tew*-mě*) *n*. diseased growth in some part of the body رسولی
tum-tum *n*. light one-horse carriage ٹم ٹم
tumult (*tew*-mult) *n*. uproar and commotion ہنگامہ ، کہرام mental excitement اضطراب ، بےچینی ، بیقراری (*be*) *in a tumult*, (of someone or his mind) be in an excited state بےچین ہونا **tumultuous** (tew-*mul*-tew-us) *adj*. noisy and violent ہنگامہ خیز in a state of confusion درہم برہم
tun (tun) *n*. large cask for wine شراب کا بڑا پیپا fermenting cask شراب کا خمیر اٹھانے کا پیپا
tundra (*tund*-ra, or *toond*-ra) *n*. treeless marshy plain in the arctic regions ٹنڈرا partially frozen desert برف پوش صحرا ، برفانی صحرا
tune (tewn) *n*. series of notes forming the music (*of* a song) دُھن ، طرز *sing* (or *play*) *a tune* طرز نکالنا ، کسی دھن میں گانا ، کوئی دھن بجانا *sing another tune*, (esp.) change one's tone from arrogance to humility اکڑ چھوڑ کر عاجزانہ انداز اختیار کرنا correct pitch ٹھیک سُر agreement between pitches of notes ملے ہوئے سُر آہنگ ، ہم آہنگی *sing* (or *play*) *in tune* سُر ملا کر گانا (یا بجانا) *in tune* سُر ملے ہوئے *out of tune* بےسُرا harmony, concord ہم آہنگی ، توافق *out of tune with* (*someone* or *something*), not happy with, clashing with میں گھل مل نہ سکنا ، سے میل نہ کھانا *in tune with*, getting on well with سے پوری طرح گھلا ملا ، سے ہم آہنگ *v.t.* & *i.* adjust (a musical instrument) to the right pitch کا سُر ٹھیک کرنا *tune up*, (of an orchestra) put the instruments in tune (آرکیسٹرا میں) سب باجوں کے سُر ٹھیک کرنا *tune in*, adjust a radio so as to receive the programme from (a particular station) (ریڈیو) پر (کوئی) جگہ لگانا **tuneful** *adj*. having a pleasing tune سُریلا
tuner (*tewn*-ě*) *n*. (esp.) one who tunes pianos, etc. پیانو (وغیرہ) ٹھیک کرنے والا **tuning-fork** *n*. two-pronged fork struck against something to produce a standard note سُر ملانے کا دوشاخہ ، سُر دوشاخہ

a tuning fork

tungsten (*tungs*-tėn) *n*. a grey metal used in making steel ٹنگسٹن
tunic (*tewn*-ik) *n*. military coat with belt پیٹی دار کوٹ Roman coat رُومی چغہ
tunnel (*tun*-el) *n*. underground passage through a hill (esp.) one for a railway سُرنگ *v. t.* & *i.* make a tunnel through (hill, etc.) سُرنگ بنانا make (one's *way through*) (میں سے) راستہ نکالنا
tuppence (*tup*-ens) *n*. (colloq.) two-pence دو پنس
tu quoque (tew-*kohk*-e) *n*. identical retort ترکی بہ ترکی الزام ، (یہ کہنا ،) ایں گناہیست کہ در شہر شما نیز کنند
turban (*tě**-ban) *n*. a well-known kind of head-dress پگڑی ، صافہ ، عمامہ women's brimless hat زنانہ ٹوپی turban-like tape(s) on a hat ہیٹ کا سجاوٹی فیتہ
turbid (*tě**bid) *adj*. muddy (liquid) گدلا (of colour) not clear مَیلا (of style) not lucid اُلجھا ہوا ، مبہم
turbine (*tě**bin) *n*. engine whose driving-wheel is spun by a strong current of (water, steam or air) چرخ *water turbine* آبی چرخ *steam-turbine* بھاپ چرخ ، چرخ خاب *air turbine* ہوا چرخ ، چرخ ہوا **turbo-jet** *n*. & *adj*. (with) jet-propelled gas turbine چرخ ہوا دھارا (یا دھکے) والا
turbot (*tě**-bot) *n*. large and flat edible sea-fish ٹربٹ مچھلی
turbulent (*te**b-ew-lent) *adj*. riotous (mob, assembly) ہنگامہ خیز given to making disturbances شورش پسند ، ہنگامہ پرور insubordinate بےادب ، گستاخ ، سرکش furious (wind, waves, passions, etc.) طوفانی ، طوفان خیز ، متلاطم **turbulence** *n*. being turbulent سرکشی ، مفسدہ پردازی ، شورش پسندی ، تلاطم خیزی
Turco (*tě**-koh) *n*. (pl. *Turkos*) member of French Algerian troops فرانس کا الجزائری فوجی

²Turco-, Turko (*tĕ**-koh) *pref.* of Turkey ترکی
tureen (tew-*reen*) *n.* deep covered dish from which soup, curry, vegetables, etc., are served at table یخنی یا سالن وغیرہ کا، ڈونگا

a turren

turf (tĕ*f) *n.* (piece cut from) soil surface with grass roots growing in it دوب تختہ (*the turf*), horse-racing گھڑدوڑ *on the turf*, (engaged) in it regularly گھڑدوڑ کا مشغلہ (*the turf*), race-course گھڑدوڑ کا میدان، ریس کورس *v. t.* lay ground with turf دوب لگانا (colloq.) turn (someone) *out* نکال دینا
turfite (*te***f*-it) *n.* person on the turf گھڑدوڑ کا شائق
turgid (tĕ*-jid) *adj.* (rarely used) swollen by disease سوجا ہوا، متورم bombastic (style or language) لفاظی والا، لفاظانہ
Turk (tĕ*k) *n.* member of the Ottoman race ترک (also *young Turk, regular Turk*), unmanageable child قابو میں نہ آنے والا بچہ، لڑاکا بچہ **turkey** (tĕ*-ki) *n.* a large fowl used as food ترکی مرغ، ٹرکی *turkey-cock*, male turkey noted for its strut and for its reddening in excitement ترکی مرغ، نر ترکی **Turkish** (*tĕ*-kish) *n.* the Turkish language ترکی *adj.* in the Turkish language or of Turkey or the Turks ترکی **Turkish bath** *n.* hot-air bath followed by massage بھاپ کا غسل اور مالش (*pl.*) establishment providing this حمّام **Turkish towel** *n.* long-napped towel لمبے رُوئیں کا تولیہ **Turkish delight** *n.* a kind of sweetmeat dissolving in the mouth راحت لُکم

a turkey

turmeric (*tĕm*-ĕ-rik) *n.* a yellow root used as a condiment (also in powder form) پسی ہوئی (ہلدی)
turmoil (tĕ*-moil) *n.* uproar and confusion افراتفری، ہنگامہ، ہل چل
turn (tĕ*n) *v. t. & i.* move partly or completely or several times round گھومنا (یا) گھمانا move so as to face in a different direction پلٹنا (یا) پلٹنا، مڑنا (یا) موڑنا change in nature, quality, etc. ہوجانا (یا) کردینا *His hair turned grey.* اُس کے بال سفید ہو گئے *The milk turned sour.* دُودھ پھٹ گیا shape (something) while it is being turned on lathe خراد پر چڑھنا be shaped thus خراد پر چڑھنا stitch (a garment) again by making its inner surface the outer one اُلٹنا reach and pass (an age, time, corner, etc.) سے گزرنا، ہوجانا *Has he turned twenty-five?* کیا وہ پچیس سال کا ہو گیا ہے *It had just turned eight.* بس آٹھ بجے ہی ہیں *turn away*, dismiss (visitor, employee) نکال دینا، سے جان چھڑانا *turn against*, begin to dislike or become an enemy of کا مخالف ہوجانا *turn adrift*, give no further support to کو مزید مدد نہ دینا *turn about*, turn so as to face in the opposite direction مڑنا، پلٹنا *about turn!* military caution to turn and face rear مڑو، بازگرد *right turn!* دائیں مڑو *left turn!* بائیں مڑو *right about turn, turn and turn about*, go on turning about چکر کھاتے جانا، مڑتے جانا *turn down*, (a) reduce (the flame of a lamp, etc.) by turning دھیما کرنا (b) reject (an offer, the person making it) مسترد کرنا *turn in*, (a) go into a place in passing چلتے چلتے ہو آنا (b) (colloq.) go to bed سو جانا *turn into*, translate into (a language) میں ترجمہ کرنا *turn on*, start the flow of (water, electric current, etc.) by turning a tap, switch, etc. رواں کرنا، (ٹونٹی) کھولنا، (بجلی) جلانا یا کھولنا *turn off*, (a) stop the flow of (water, electric current, etc.) بند کرنا (b) dismiss (servant) نکال دینا *turn out*, (a) stop the flow of (gas) by turning a tap کھولنا (b) put out by force دبا دینا (c) expel نکال دینا (d) produce (goods) بنانا، تیار کرنا (e) empty (one's pockets, place, etc.) for cleaning or in search of something خالی کرنا، اُلٹ پلٹ کرنا، اُگلنا دینا (f) come, go, bring or send out for a purpose کسی مقصد کے لیے آنا (یا) جانا (یا) لانا یا بھیجنا (g) ultimately be آخر کار ہونا (h) prove to be نکلنا، ثابت ہونا *turn over*, transfer the control of (a business, etc., *to* someone) کو سونپنا، کے ہاتھوں میں دینا *turn to*, (a) go to (someone something, *for* help, comfort, etc.) کا سہارا لینا، کا رُخ کرنا (b) begin work کام شروع کرنا (c) attend to کی طرف توجہ کرنا *turn up* (a) (of persons) arrive پہنچنا، آپہنچنا (b) (of objects) be found by chance اتفاق سے مِلنا (یا) مِل جانا، ہاتھ آنا (c) (of a chance, etc.) appear (موقع) ملنا *turn a deaf ear to*, refuse to listen to سننے سے انکار کردینا، سے کان بند کرلینا *without turning a hair*, without being exhausted, etc. تھکے یا گھبرائے بغیر *turn and rend*, assail (friend) with abuse پر گالیوں کی بوچھاڑ *turn an honest penny*, contrive to make money by some odd job کام کاج کرکے روپیہ کمانا *turn back*, begin to retrace one's steps اُلٹے پھر آنا، لوٹنے لگنا *turn one's coat*, change sides اپنی وفاداری کا رُخ بدلنا *turn inside out*, reverse (garment) (کپڑا) اُلٹا کرلینا *turn on* (*one's*) *heels*, go abruptly away in displeasure ناراض ہوکر اُٹھ جانا *turn over a new leaf*, mend one's ways نئی زندگی شروع کرنا، راہِ راست پر آجانا *turn round*, (a) turn about مڑنا (b) reserve one's policy اپنا طرزِ عمل بالکل بدل لینا *turn* (*someone*) *round* (*one's*) *finger*, have complete mastery over (him) کو کٹھ پتلی کا ناچ نچانا *turn tail*, (slang) run away دُم دبا کر بھاگنا *turn the page*, turn over a leaf ورق پلٹنا *turn the scale*, (a) change a situation by one's

presence or influence صورتِ حال بدل دینا، فیصلے پر اثر انداز ہونا، رُخ بدل دینا *turn the tables* (on), convert losing into winning game بازی کا رُخ بدل جانا، ہاری ہوئی بازی جیت جانا *turn turtle*, capsize اُلٹ جانا *turn to account* profit by, make serviceable سے فائدہ اُٹھانا *turn down*, invert, اُلٹ دینا *turn* (*one's*) *back on*, desert, abandon چھوڑ دینا *turn* (*someone's*) *brain*, madden him کو پاگل کر دینا *turn the corner*, (*a*) go round it موڑ مڑنا (*b*) pass a crisis successfully خیریت سے بیچ نکلنا *turn* (*someone's*) *head*, fill (him) with vanity کا دماغ خراب کر دینا *turn* (*one's*) *hand to*, engage temporarily in وقتی طور پر لگنا *can turn* (*his*) *hand to anything*, is versatile ہر فن مولا ہے *turn* (*one's*) *stomach*, make one (want to) vomit سے قے آنے لگنا *n.* turning movement چکر change of direction (in the road, etc.) موڑ *give a new turn to*, change the course (of thought, events, etc.) کا رُخ بدلنا change of state پلٹنا *take a turn for the better*, become better بہتر ہونا rotation *wait* (*until it is*) (*one's*) *turn* اپنی باری کا انتظار کرنا *in turn, by turn*, first one then the other باری باری *out of turn*, before or after the regular time اپنی باری سے پہلے یا بعد *take turns at* (*something*), do (it) in turn باری باری کرنا spell of activity or duty اپنی باری کا *take a turn at* (*something*) کے متعلق اپنی باری کا کام کرنا کام walk, stroll سیر *take* (or *go for*) *a turn* (*in a place*) (میں یا کو) سیر کے لیے جانا any of series of musical performances as a part of a single entertainment باری، چیز action عمل (*do someone*) *a good turn* (سے) نیکی (کرنا) (*do someone*) *a bad* (or *evil*) *turn* (سے) برائی (کرنا) *one good turn deserves another*, kindness should be repaid نیکی کا بدلہ نیکی special aptitude (*for*) رُجحان، میلان *have a literary turn* ادبی رُجحان ہونا *give* (*someone*) *a turn*, (*a*) shock (him) کو صدمہ پہنچانا (*b*) give (him) a thrill of terror پر کپکپی طاری کر دینا *serve* (*one's*) *turn*, be satisfactory for (one's) purpose کے لیے کافی (یا ٹھیک) ہونا *done to a turn*, (of meat, etc.) cooked exactly to the extent needed بالکل ٹھیک پکانا **turncoat** *n.* time-server ابن الوقت **turncock** *n.* person whose duty it is to regulate water-supply پانی کی مقدار کم و بیش کرنے والا **turner** *n.* one who works a lathe خراد کرنے والا، خرادیا **turnery** *n.* turner's workshop خراد کی دکان wooden articles made on lathe خراد پر بنا ہوا لکڑی کا سامان **turning** *n.* place where a road branches off from another موڑ such a branch road شاہراہ سے نکلنے والی سڑک **turning-point** *n.* point at which one turns مُڑنے کی جگہ crisis نقطۂ انقلاب **turnkey** *n.* gaoler جیلر، داروغہ **turn-out** *n.* output (of a factory) کارگزاری attendance of people (*at* a meeting etc.) حاضری، حاضری کی تعداد general appearance of one's equipment بناؤ emptying (of room etc.) کی سب چیزیں نکال دینا، خالی کر دینا things moved in emptying a place, etc. باہر نکالی ہوئی چیزیں **turnover** *n.* amount of money received in a business within a specified period مقررہ وقت کی بکری **turnpipe** *n.* bar or gate across private road for toll-collecting; (orig. it used to be in the form of a revolving spiked bar) روک پھاٹک **turn-round** *n.* (of ship) process of entering, a port, unloading and reloading and leaving port جہاز کا بندرگاہ کا چکر دروازہ **turn-screw** *n.* screw-driver **turnstile** *n.* revolving gate چکر دروازہ revolving barrier چکر **turn-table** *n.* revolving platform for turning locomotives انجن موڑنے والا چکر، انجن موڑ

a turnstile

turnip (*tĕ**-nip) *n.* a well-known edible root or the plant yielding it شلغم، شلجم

turpentine (*tĕ**-pen-tīn) *n.* (abbr. *turps*) spirit made from the resin of pine trees تارپین، تارپین کا تیل

turpitude (*tĕ**-pi-tewd) *n.* wickedness خباثت، خبث، خبثِ نفس

turps *n.* (see under **turpentine**)

turquoise (*tĕ**-kwoiz, or *tu**-koiz) *n.* a greenish-blue gem فیروزہ (also *turquoise green*) its colour فیروزہ کا رنگ

turret (*te*-ret) *n.* small tower, at the corner of a building چھوٹا برج، برجی revolving steel structure round a gun to protect gunners توپچی کی حفاظت کے لیے متحرک آڑ

turtle (*tĕ*-tel) *n.* sea-tortoise سمندری کچھوا، بحری سنگ پشت *turn turtle*, capsize اُلٹ جانا (usu. *turtle-dove*), a kind of cooing dove جنگلی فاختہ

tusk (tusk) *n.* long tooth (of an elephant, etc.) ہاتھی کا دکھانے کا دانت، ہاتھی کا دانت

tussle (*tus*-el) *n.* (colloq) struggle (*with* someone, *over* something) کشمکش، کشاکش scuffle کشتی، ہاتھا پائی *v.i.* struggle کھینچا تانی کرنا wrestle (*with*) ہاتھا پائی کرنا

tussore (*tus*-oh*), **tusser** (*tus*-ĕ*) a kind of silk the silkworm producing it ٹسر

tut (tut) *inter.* (usu. *tut tut* !), expression of impatience ہٹ، ہٹ ہٹ، ہونہہ، اُونہہ ہونہہ

tutelage *n.* **tutelary** *adj.* (see under **tutor**)

tutor (*tew*-tĕ*) *n.* private teacher خانگی معلم guide to whom a young man is entrusted اتالیق university teacher who guides the studies of a number of students ٹیوٹر، نگراں اُستاد ۔ طلبہ کے مُطالعہ کا نگران *v.t.* & *i.* act as tutor (*to someone*) اتالیقی پیشہ کرنا adopt this as a profession کا اتالیق ہونا exercise restraint over (someone, oneself, or one's passions) کو قابو میں رکھنا instruct (witness to give false evidence) لکھانا، پڑھانا، سکھانا **tutorial** (tew-*to*-i-al) *adj*. of tutor or his work اتالیقی، ٹیوٹر کا *n*. (also *tutorial class*), work under a tutor ٹیوٹر کی نگرانی میں مطالعہ، ٹیوٹوریل **tutelage** (*tewt*-è-lej) *n*. guardianship سرپرستی restraint exercised over another's conduct پابندی **tutelary** *adj*. giving protection سرپرستانہ **tutoress** *n*. woman tutor اُستانی، آتون **tutorship** *n*. being a tutor اتالیقی

tutti (*too*-ti) *adj*. (in music) all voices and instruments playing together یک آواز *n*. such piece of music یک آواز گانا (یا) بجنا

tutu (*too*-too) *n*. ballet dancer's short, stiff and spreading skirt اونچی پشواز

tuwhit tuwhoo (tu-*hwit*-tu-*hwoo*) *n*. owl's cry اُلّو کی آواز *v.i.* (of owl) cry اُلّو کا بولنا

tuxedo (tuk-*see*-doh) *n*. (U. S.) dinner jacket ڈنر کا کوٹ

twaddle (*twod*-èl) *n*. silly talk بکواس *v.t.* utter twaddle

twain (twayn) *n*. (old use) two دو couple, pair جوڑی *in twain*, asunder دو ٹکڑے

twang *n*. sound of tight string being pulled and released تن تن، تن تن کی آواز *v.t.* & *i.* (cause to) make this sound بجنا ، بجانا

'twas (twoz) (abbr. of) it was تھا

tweak (tweek) *v.t.* pinch and twist نوچ کھسوٹ کرنا، نوچنا، کھسوٹنا *n*. sharp pinch and twist نوچ کھسوٹ

tweed (tweed) *n*. thick soft woollen cloth of various patterns (for coats, etc.) کوٹ کا گرم کپڑا، ٹوئیڈ

tweedledum and tweedledee (tweed-el-*dum*-and-tweed-el-*dee*) *n*. pair neither easily distinguishable nor worth distinguishing ; differing in name only وہ چیزیں جن میں محض نام کا فرق ہو

'tween (tween) *prep*. (abbr. of **between**, which see)

tweeny *n*. maid-servant helping two others درمیانی ملازمہ

tweezers (*twee*-zě*z) *n. pl*. (also *pair of tweezers*), small pincers for pulling out hair, etc. موچنا

twelfth *adj*. (see under **twelve**)

twelve (twelv) *n*. & *adj*. 12 **twelfth** (twelfth) *adj*. 12th بارھواں *n*. (*the twelfth*), August 12 as the opening of grouse-shooting بارھویں **twelfthly** *adv*. in the 12th place دوازدہم **Twelfth-night** *n*. January 5 (as the twelfth night after Xmas) formerly celebrated with games, drinking and feasting to mark the end of Xmas festivities بارھویں رات **twelvemonth** *n*. period equal in length to a year's time بارہ ماہ کی مدّت

twenty (*twen*-ti) *n*. & *adj*. 20 بیس **twentieth** *adj*. 20th بیسواں **twenty-one** (...**nine**) 21 (...29) اکیس (...انتیس) **twenty-first** (...**ninth**) 21st(...29th) اکیسواں (...انتیسواں) **twenty-five** *n*. 25 پچیس line drawn in hockey-ground 25 yards from either goal پچیس ground between this and goal-line پچیس

'twere (abbreviated form of) it were ہوتا

twerp (twě*p) *n*. cheerfully or noisily ill-bred person ہڑبونگی

twice (twis) *adv*. double دگنا، دوہرا two times دو بار

twiddle (*twid*-èl) *v.t.* & *i*. turn (thumbs) over each other idly انگوٹھے ایک دوسرے پر گھمانا **twiddle** (*one's*) *thumbs*, be idle کو کوئی کام نہ ہونا، مکھیاں مارنا

twig *n*. small shoot at the end of a branch ٹہنی، ڈالی، چھوٹی سی شاخ

twilight (*twi*-lit) *n*. faint half-light before sunrise or after sunset جھٹپٹا

twill (twil) *n*. cloth so woven as to have a surface of oblique ridges parallel to one another دو سوتی بُننا ، ٹوِل بنانا *v.t.* weave thus ٹوِل

twin *n*. either of the two children born together of the same mother جڑواں بچّہ *adj* born together جڑواں identical and associated with each other ایک سے دو یکساں **twinship** *n* being twins جڑواں ہونا ، یکساں ہونا

twine (twin) *n*. thin string ڈوری، سُتلی *v.t.* & *i*. twist بٹ کر بنانا، بٹنا، گوندھنا (*into*) wind (*round*) کے گرد لپیٹنا

twinge (twinj) *n*. sudden, sharp pain (*of* mind or body) ٹیس ، جُبھن

twinkle (*twink*-èl) *v.i.* shine with a dim, unsteady light ٹمٹمانا، جگمگانا (of eyes) shine (*with* fun, etc.) میں چمک آنا (of flag, or feet in dancing) be in rapid wavering motion تیز غیر متوازی حرکت کرنا *n*. twinkling light جگمگاہٹ، چمک **twinkling** *n*. closing and opening of the eye پلک جھپکنا *in a twinkling, in the twinkling of an eye*, instantaneously پلک جھپکتے میں

twirl (twě*l) *v.t.* & *i*. rotate quickly تیزی سے گھومنا cause (dance-partner, umbrella, etc.) to rotate quickly کو تیزی سے گھمانا twist (moustache) quickly تیزی سے مروڑتے جانا *n*. twirling

motion تیز چکر rapid twists تیزی سے مروڑنا pen flourish قلم کی کشش
twist *v.t.* & *i* wind (a number of strands, etc.) one around another بٹنا، بلا کر بل دینا rotate one end only مروڑنا *twist (someone's) arm,* do this as torture مروڑ کر تاڑنا بازو مروڑنا *twist off* (of road, river, etc.) take curved course بل کھانے مُڑتے جانا، میں پیچ و خم ہونا force (someone's words, etc.) out of their true meaning مروڑ تروڑ کر غلط معنی بٹنا، مروڑنا، بل کھانا *n.* پہنانا twisting or being twisted بل کھانا twisted place پیچ، بل anything made by twisting بٹی ہوئی چیز rہا، دینا turn given to ball before bowling چکر predilection رجحان، افتادِ طبع *n.* dishonest person بے ایمان، بد دیانت (in cricket) ball bowled with a twist چکر والی گیند
twit *v.t.* (-tt-) taunt (someone *with* fault, or *with* having done something wrong) (کا) طعنہ دینا
twitch (twich) *n.* sudden uncontrollable movement (of eye, etc.) پھڑکنا sudden, quick pull جھٹکا *v.t.* & *i.* make a twitch پھڑکنا (also *twitch at*), jerk جھٹکا دینا pull (*off, out of,* etc.) with a jerk جھٹکا دے کر کھینچنا
twitter (*twit*-ĕ*) *v.i.* (of birds) chirp چہچہانا (of person) speak with a shrill feeble voice چیں چیں کرنا *n.* such sounds *in a twitter,* (*a*) excited بے چین (*b*) nervous owing to fear ڈر کے مارے گھبرایا ہوا
two (too) *n.* & *adj.* 2 *in two,* asunder دو ٹکڑے *two can play at that game,* (threat of retaliation) ہم بھی منہ میں زبان رکھتے ہیں (مجھے) بھی جواب دینا آتا ہے *two of a trade,* rival experts حریف پیشہ ور *two-handed,* (*a*) (of game) for two دو کا کھیل (*b*) (of sword) wielded with both hands دو ہاتھوں سے چلائی جانے والی **twopence** (*tup*-ens) *n.* 2d. دو پنس **twopenny** (*tup*-ĕ-ni) costing 2 d. دو پنس **twosome** (*too*-sum) *n.* tete-a-tete رازکی باتیں
tycoon (ti-*koon*) *n.* (U.S.) (colloq.) business magnate (from the Japanese word for *lord*) سیٹھ
tying (*tī*-ing) *v.* (pr. p. of **tie**, which see)
type (tip) *n.* example (*of* a quality) مثال specimen (*of* something) نمونہ *true to type,* having the normal attributes ٹھیک نمونے کا *deviate from the type,* مختلف نمونے کا ہونا class with regard to its common characteristics قسم thing serving as a symbolic foreshadowing مثال، علامت، اشارہ letters, etc., cast in lead ٹائپ *in large type* جلی *in small type,* باریک حروف میں خفی حروف میں *v.t.* & *i.* write (something ; or well) with a typewriter ٹائپ کرنا
typesetter (-set-) *n.* machine or worker that sets type for printing حروف کرنے والا کاریگر یا مشین
typewriter (tip-*rī*-tĕ*) *n.* machine with a keyboard on which one presses one's fingers to write out ٹائپ رائٹر، نقل نگار **type-founder** (-*found*-) *n.* one who casts (or *founds*) type ٹائپ ساز **typewrite** (*tīp*-r.t) *v.t.* & *i.* write with a typewriter ٹائپ کرنا

a typewriter

type-written (*tīp*-rit-ĕn) *adj.* written with a typewriter ٹائپ کیا ہوا، ٹائپ شدہ **typical** (*tip*-i-kĕl) *adj.* serving as a type مثالی، اشارتی characteristic نمونے کا، امتیازی، مخصوص **typically** (*tip*-i-ka-li) *adv.* مخصوص، مثالی طور پر **typify** (*tip*-i-fī) *v. t.* be symbolic of کی علامت ہونا، کا نشان ہونا، کا مجسمہ ہونا represent the type of کا نمونہ ہونا، کی مثال ہونا foreshadow (آنے والے واقعے) کی خبر دینا **typification** (-*kay*-) *n.* نمونہ، علامت، مثال، مجسمہ، علامت یا مثال ہونا یا بنانا **typist** (*tip*-ist) *n.* one who types in order to earn a living ٹائپسٹ نقل نگار، کام کرنے والا، نقل نویس، نقل ساز، نقل پرداز **typography** (ti-*pog*-ra-fi) *n.* art of printing ٹائپ میں چھاپنے کا فن، فنِ طباعت kinds of type used in a printed matter ٹائپ کا انداز، طباعت، چھپائی **typographical** *adj.* of typogrophy طباعتی *typographical errors,* misprints کتابت کی غلطیاں، سہوِ کتابت
typhoid (*tī*-foid) *n.* (also *typhoid fever*), disease affecting the intestines میعادی بخار *adj.* like typhus ٹائیفس کا سا **typhus** (*tī*-fus) *n.* contagious fever causing red spots on the body and producing great weakness ٹائیفس، پھول ماتا
typhoon (tī-*foon*) *n.* violent hurricane of the China seas چین کے سمندروں میں چلنے والی طوفانی ہوا ❷ any violent windstorm طوفان
typhus *n.* (see under **typhoid**)
typical *adj.*, **typically** *adv.*, **typify** *v.t.*, **typification** *n.* (see under **type**)
typist *n.* (see under **type**)
Tyr (tē*) Norse *myth.* the god of war ; (he was a son of Woden) ٹر، تیر
tyrant (*tī*-ĕ-rant) *n.* oppressive dictator or sovereign جابر فرمانروا، ظالم آمر (Greek history) oppressive dictator who has usurped power ظالم any oppressive master ظالم حاکم، غاصب حکمران **tyr-**

annical (ti-*ran*-i-kel, or *ti-ran*-i-kel) *adj.* **tyrannous** (*ti*-ra-nus) *adj.* like a tyrant جابر حاکم کا سا of a tyrant جابرانہ مستبدانہ **tyrannize** (*ti*-ra-niz) *v.i.* exercise tyranny (*over*) ظلم کرنا، تشدد کرنا، جابرانہ حکومت کرنا **tyranny** (*ti*-ra-ni) *n.* cruel and unjust use of power استبداد، جور و استبداد، جابرانہ حکومت (Greek history) government by tyrant ظالم غاصب فرمانروا کی حکومت
tyre, tire (*ti*-è*) *n.* band of metal or rubber round the rim of **a wheel** ہال (also *pneumatic tyre*), tyre of a motor vehicle etc. (filled with an inflated tube) ٹائر
tyro (*ti*-roh) *n.* (same as **tiro, which see**)
Tyrtaeus (*tĕ**-*tee*-us) *Cl. myth.* the lam Athenian schoolmaster who was sent to Sparta where his orations inspired the Spartans to victory ترتیئس
tzar (zah*) *n.* (same as **Czar, which see**)

U

u'u (yew) (pl. *u's* or *us*) the twenty-first letter of the English alphabet یو
U.P. (yew-pee) *v.i.* (slang) up ; get up اٹھو بھی اٹھو
ubiquitous (yew-*bik*-wi-tus) *adj.* omnipresent ہر جگہ موجود ہونا **ubiquity** *n.* omnipresence ہر جگہ موجود، حاضر
U-boat (*yew*-boht) *n.* German submarine (called in German *untersee*) جرمن آبدوز
udder (*ud*-ĕ*) *n.* milk-bag of milch-cattle, etc. تھن **uddered** *adj.* having udders تھنوں والی
ugh (uh) *int.* (expressive of horror or disgust) اف، ہے (عورتوں کی زبان پر)، اوئی
ugly (*ug*-li) *adj.* بدصورت scowling (sky, etc.) طوفان کے آثار والا threatening ڈراؤنا، خطرناک، مہیب **an ugly customer**, a dangerous person خطرناک شخص
ukulele (yew-koo-*lay*-li) *n.* four-stringed guitar popular in Hawaii اکلیلی ستار، ہوائی ستار
a ukulele
ulcer (*ul*-sĕ*) *n.* festering sore ناسور corrupting influence (اخلاقی، سیاسی وغیرہ) ناسور
ulna (*ul*-na) *n.* (pl. *ulnae* pr. *ul*-nee) inner bone of the forearm ہاتھ کی اندرونی ہڈی، زند اسفل **ulnar** *adj.* of or pertaining to ulna زند اسفل کا، یا کے متعلق
ulterior (ul-*tee*-ri-ĕ*) *adj.* lying beyond پرلا، پرے کا secret ; besides that which is admitted خفیہ، دزدیدہ **ulterior motives**, secret and usu. bad motives دزدیدہ مقاصد
ultimate (*ul*-ti-mayt) *adj.* final آخری basic (truths, principle, etc.) بنیادی **ultimately** *adv.* finally بالآخر، انجام کار
ultimatum (*ul*-ti-*may*-tum) *n.* final offer or demand (before resort to drastic measures like strike, war, etc.) آخری بات، الٹی میٹم **give an ultimatum (to)** دینا، آخری بات کہہ دینا، کو الٹی میٹم دے دینا
ultimo (*ul*-ti-moh) (abbr. *ult.*) of the last month ماہِ گزشتہ، گزشتہ
[1]**ultra-** (*ul*-tra) *pref.* beyond ماورا (سے) **ultra-short wave**, (wireless) with a wave-length below 10 metres الٹرا شارٹ ویو too much of ; beyond what is reasonable or usual غیر معمولی حد تک، حد سے زیادہ **ultra-modern** بہت ہی نئے فیشن کا
[2]**ultra** (*ul*-tra) *n.* person advocating extreme steps or views انتہا پسند
ultra violet *adj.* invisible rays beyond the spectrum ماورائے بنفشی
ultra vires (*ul*-tra-*vi*-reez) beyond authority ; hence unlawful ماورائے اختیار، غیر آئینی
Ulysses (yew-*lis*-eez) *Cl. myth.* Roman name of the Greek hero, Odysseus, famous for his wanderings یولیسیز
umbrage (*um*-brayj) *n.* offence ناراضگی، خفگی (usu. in the phrase :) **take umbrage (at)**, take offence سے خفا ہونا، پر اظہار ناراضگی کرنا
umbrella (um-*brel*-a) *n.* parachute-like shelter from the sun (or rain) چھتری، چھاتا (also *umbrella barrage*, or *air umbrella*), screen of fire or fighter aircraft put up as protection against air attack چھاتا بند
umpire (*um*-pi-è*) *n.* person acting as judge in a game or dispute امپائر، فیصلہ دینے والا، قاضی *v.t.* & *i.* act as umpire (*in*) کا منصف ہونا، کی امپائری کرنا
umpteen *adj.* (slang) several, numerous کئی، متعدد **for the umpteenth time** کئی بار کے بعد پھر
un- (un) *pref.* (before *adj. adv.*) not (as unfaithful) غیر وفادار (before nouns) lacking (as *unwillingness* غیر رضامندی) غیر (before verbs) (for expressing the reversal or the opposite of idea of the verb) اصل فعل کے متضاد کا ترجمہ کیا جاتا ہے (as *uncover* دکھولنا)
unabashed (un-a-*basht*) *adj.* without a feeling

بے شرم، بے حجاب، بے حیا of shame
unabated (-*bay*-) *adj*. (of a storm, etc.) in full strength اس زور سے، پورے زور سے
unable (un-*ayb*-ĕl) *adj*. not able (*to do*) کے ناقابل
inability *n*. (see separate entry)
unabridged *adj*. not abridged مکمل، بلا اختصار
unaccompanied *adj*. alone اکیلا، تنہا
unaccomplished *adj*. incomplete ادھورا، نامکمل ناتمام not refined (in manners) ناشائستہ
unaccountable *adj*. not answerable کے لیے جواب نہیں inexplicable جس کی وجہ سمجھ میں نہ آ سکے
unaccustomed *adj*. not accustomed جو عادی نہ ہو unusual غیر معمولی
unacknowledge *adj*. not confessed جسے تسلیم نہ کیا گیا ہو not acknowledged or noticed جسے دیکھا نہ گیا ہو (یا) جس کی رسید نہ دی جائے
unadopted *adj*. not adopted اختیار نہ کیا ہوا (esp., of new roads, etc.) not maintained by the local bodies لاوارث
unadvised *adj*. imprudent غیر دانشمندانہ without advice from anyone کسی کے کہے بغیر
unaffected *adj*. untouched or uninfluenced (*by*) جس پر کسی چیز کا کوئی اثر نہ ہو، جو (کسی کی) زد میں نہ آئے without affection بلا تصنع
unalloyed *adj*. pure خالص
unanimity *n*. (see under **unanimous**)
unanimous (yew-*nan*-i-mus) *adj*. (of persons), agreeing (*in* opinion for something) متفق، یکدل، (of vote or decision) with full accord یک آواز اتفاق رائے سے، بالاتفاق **unanimity** (yew-na-*nim*-i-ti) *n*. full accord
unanswerable *adj*. incontrovertible ناقابل تردید
unarm *v.t*. deprive of arms اسلحہ چھین لینا **unarmed** *adj*. without weapons اسلحہ کے بغیر، خالی ہاتھ، خالی ہاتھوں defenceless بے بس
unashamed *adj*. not ashamed بے شرم
unassailable *adj*. (position, argument, etc.) that cannot be attacked زوردار، مستحکم
unassisted *adj*. without assistance امداد کے بغیر، بلا استعانت
unassuming *adj*. not pushing oneself forward پیچھے پیچھے رہنے والا modest بڑھ بڑھ کے باتیں نہ بنانے والا unattractive سیدھا سادہ
unattached *adj*. separate جدا، الگ (property) not seized for debt جسے قرق نہ کیا گیا ہو، جس کی قرقی نہ ہوئی ہو
unauthorized *adj*. not supported by any authoritative source غیر مستند not authorized; unlawful ناجائز، غیر قانونی
unavailable *adj* not available جو دستیاب نہ ہو سکے
unavailing *adj*. in vain لاحاصل، بے فائدہ
unavoidable *adj*. that cannot be avoided مجبوری (کی بات)، ناگزیر **unavoidably** *adv*. ناچار، مجبوراً
unaware *adj*. ignorant (*of*) سے بے خبر **unawares** *adv*. by surprise اچانک *be taken* (or *caught*) *unawares* (*by something*), be caught at a disadvantage (by it) سے بے خبری کے عالم میں مارا جانا، (کو) بے خبری میں آ لینا
unbalance *v.t*. unhinge (mind) پاگل کر دینا، سے پاگل سا ہو جانا **unbalanced** *adj*. not quite sane (person or mind) پاگل سا
unbar *v.t*. undo the bar (of a door) to open (it) کھولنا **unbarred** *adj*. open کھلا
unbearable *adj*. not bearable ناقابل برداشت
unbeaten *adj*. not surpassed جس سے ابھی تک کوئی بڑھا نہ ہو (of a century of scores, etc., in cricket) completed without being bowled out آؤٹ ہوئے بغیر
unbecoming *adj*. improper (*of* someone *to do*) ناموزوں، نامناسب not suitable to one's appearance نہ سجنے والا، میل نہ کھانے والا
unbelief (un-be-*leef*) *n*. lack of faith کفر، بے اعتقادی
unbeliever *n*. one who does not believe in God or matters of creed کافر **unbelievable** *adj*. ناقابل یقین **unbelievably** *adv*. extremely بہت ہی، حد درجہ ناقابل یقین حد تک
unbend (un-*bend*) *v.t*. & *i*. make straight سیدھا کرنا relax (the mind, etc.) from strain کو آرام دینا become less formal in behaviour (*to*) سے بے تکلف ہونا **unbending** *adj*. unyielding (person) سخت، نہ مڑنے والا rigid (steel, etc.) نہ ماننے والا
unbiased, unbiassed *adj*. impartial، غیر متعصب، غیر جانبدارانہ
unbidden *adj*. uninvited بن بلایا
unbind *v.t*. set (a prisoner) free رہا کرنا make loose کھولنا
unblemished *adj*. spotless (character, etc.) بے داغ
unbolt *v.t*. open (a door, etc.) by drawing back the bolt کھولنا، چٹخنی کھولنا
unbosom *v.t*. (*unbosom oneself to someone*), tell him freely one's anxieties, etc. پریشانیاں سنانا، دل کا حال کہنا
unbounded *adj*. unlimited (space, freedom, pleasure, etc.) بے حد، بے پایاں
unbridled *adj* uncontrolled (*by* violent fury, etc.) قابو میں نہ آنے والا (of horse) without bridle بے لگام
unbroken *adj*. not broken ثابت، صحیح سالم uninterrupted لگاتار unbeaten جس سے کوئی بڑھا نہ ہو
unburden *v.t*. take a load off بوجھ اتارنا *unburden oneself of* (*secret, etc., to someone*), reveal or confess it to کو سنا کر اپنے دل کا بار ہلکا کرنا
unbutton *v.t*. unfasten the buttons of (some

garment) کے بٹن کھولنا
uncalled-for (-*kawld*-) *adj*. unnecessary غیر ضروری نامُناسب، نامَوزُوں inadvisable
uncanny *adj*. mysterious پُراسرار unearthly غیرارضی
unceremonious *adj*. familiar بے تکلفانہ discourteous اکھڑ، اکھڑپن سے
uncertain *adj*. doubtful مُشتبہ، غیریقینی not decided (*as to*) (کے بارے میں) ابھی فیصلہ نہ کیا ہُوا **uncertainty** *n*. hesitation مذبذب suspense غیریقینی حالت
unchain *v.t*. unfasten the chain of (dog, etc.) زنجیر کھول دینا
uncharitable *adj*. severe or even unfair in criticising نہ بخشنے والا not kind and generous to the poor کنجُوس، سخاوت نہ کرنے والا **uncharitableness** *n*. کِسی کو نہ بخشنا، کنجُوسی
uncharted *adj*. not marked on a map جو ابھی نقشے پر نہ آیا ہو so far undiscovered نامَعلوم
uncircumcised *adj*. not circumcised غیرمختون
uncivil *adj*. rude اکھڑ، بدتہذیب
uncivilized *adj*. not civilized; uncultured غیرمتمدّن غیرمُہذّب
unclasp *v.t*. open the clasp of کھولنا
uncle (*unk*-ĕl) *n*. brother of one's mother ماموں husband of one's maternal aunt خالو husband of one's paternal aunt پھوپھا elder brother of one's father تایا younger brother of one's father چچا any elderly person who is friendly to one چچا
unclean *adj*. soiled مَیلا evil (spirit) بُرا (بھوت پریت) obscene فحش
unclothe *v.t*. & *i*. undress کپڑے اُتارنا strip (someone) naked (کِسی کے) کپڑے اُتار لینا
uncoil *v.t*. & *i*. unwind کے بل کھولنا be unwound کھُلنا
uncomfortable *adj*. causing discomfort تکلیف دِہ not at ease بے آرام
uncommon *adj*. extraordinary غیرمعمُولی rare شاذ **uncommonly** *adv*. extraordinarily، بہُت غیرمعمُولی طور پر
uncommunicative *adj*. incommunicative، چُپ خاموش، نہ بتلانے والا
uncompromising *adj*. not yielding نہ ماننے والا not giving in on any point to bring about a compromise غیرمُصالحانہ
unconcern *n*. lack of concern بے پروائی **unconcerned** *adj*. not concerned بے پروا، مُطمئن
unconditional *adj*. absolute (surrender, etc.) غیرمشرُوط **unconditioned** *adj*. not conditioned: hence instinctive غیرمحصر، جبلّی، فطری **unconditioned reflex**, (in) psychology) instinctive response to a stimulus (opp. of *conditioned reflex*) فطری ردِّعمل، جبلّی ردِّعمل
unconscionable (un-*kon*-shè-na-bèl) *adj*. unreasonably long (delay, time, etc.) بہُت ہی زیادہ، غیرمعمُولی
unconscious *n*. (the unconscious) the sub-conscious mind تحت الشعور، لاشعور *adj*. senseless بیہوش unintentional نادانستہ، غیرارادی not conscious (*of* ridicule, etc.)
unconstitutional *adj*. not according to the constitution غیرآئینی
uncork *v.t*. open cork of (bottle) بوتل کھولنا
uncouth (un-*kooth*) *adj*. boorish (manners) گنواروں کا سا clumsy (person) unfamiliar (place) عجیب (جگہ) انجان (جگہ)
uncover *v.t*. & *i*. remove the cover of ڈھکنا اُٹھانا take off one's hat (on entering a room) سر سے ٹوپی اُتارنا expose (plot, etc.) (راز) فاش کر دینا
uncritical *adj*. not able to judge تنقید کی قابلیّت نہ رکھنے والا not critical غیرمُعترضانہ، غیرمعترض against the rules of criticism اُصُولِ تنقید کے خلاف
unction (*unk*-shĕn) *n*. soothing ointment تسکین دینے والا مرہم pretended suavity کھوکھلی نرمی، مُنافقانہ نرمی
unctuous (*unk*-tew-us) *adj*. pretentiously suave مُنافقانہ نرمی والا
uncultivated *adj*. not refined ناشائستہ not tilled غیرمزرُوعہ
undaunted *adj*. fearless نڈر، بیخوف undismayed مایُوس نہ ہونے والا
undeceive *v.t*. remove (someone's) wrong belief کی غلط فہمی دُور کرنا
undecided *adj*. not decided غیرفیصلہ شُدہ (of person) hesitant دُبدھے میں، مُذبذب، مُتذبذب
undefiled *adj*. not defiled پاک
undeniable *adj*. incontrovertible ناقابلِ اِنکار
[1]**under** (*und*-ĕ*) *prep*. below تلے، کے نیچے less than سے کم subject to کے تحت included in میں according to کے مُطابق in a state of کی حالت میں *adj*. lower سے نیچا lower in rank کم تر *adv*. in (or to) a lower place نیچے کی طرف *under repair* جس کی مرمّت ہو رہی ہو *under discussion* زیرِبحث *under protest*, after recording protest احتجاج سمیت *under orders* (*of*), having been ordered (by someone to) کے حکم پر
[2]**under-** *pref*. (before nouns) below کے نیچے، کے ماتحت، سے کم (before verbs) below نیچے سے کم (before verbs) incompletely نامکمل
underact *v.t*. not do the work as one could do (کام) کا حق ادا کرنا

underbred *adj.* not well-bred نا شائستہ ، کمینہ
under-carriage *n.* landing gear of an aircraft ہوائی جہاز کا زیریں حصہ
undercharge *v.t.* charge less than the proper price کم قیمت لینا *n.* doing as a form of bribe کم قیمت لینا reduced price کم قیمت
underclothes, underclothing *n.* clothes worn under the outer dress (like vest, etc.) زیر جامہ
undercurrent *n.* current flowing below the surface سطح سے نیچے بہنے والا دھارا ، اندرونی دھارا ، مخفی دھارا underlying tendency (of rebellion, etc.) بغاوت کا مخفی یا اندرونی دھارا
undercut *v.t.* (-kut) sell (goods) or offer (services) at lower rates to oust competitors دوسروں کو نکالنے کے لیے کم معاوضہ لینا *n.* (und-) upward blow in boxing اوپر کو گھونسا
underdog (und-) *n.* poor and helpless person as representing the lowest social stratum بیچارہ ، غریب
underdone *adj.* (esp. of meat) not completely cooked throughout پوری طرح نہ پکا ہوا ، کہیں کہیں سے کچا (گوشت)
underestimate *v.t.* belittle کو بالکل حقیر جاننا ، کے متعلق غلط اندازہ کرنا
undergarment *n.* underclothing زیر جامہ
undergo (-goh) *v.t.* experience (hardship, etc.) مشکلات میں سے گزرنا ، تکلیفیں برداشت کرنا ، کڑیاں جھیلنا go through (a process) پر (کوئی) عمل ہونا
undergraduate (-grad) *n.* student working for his or her first degree بی-اے (یا بی-ایس سی) کا طالب علم (یا کی طالبہ)
underground (-ground) *adj.* & *adv.* below the ground زمین کے نیچے ، زیر زمین secret (or secretly) مخفی ، خفیہ ، کھل کر سامنے نہ آنے والا go *underground* چھپ جانا ، کھل کر سامنے نہ آنا *n.* (*the underground*), the tube, underground railway زمین دوز ریل
undergrown *adj.* stunted جس کی بالیدگی پوری طرح نہ ہوئی ہو
undergrowth (und-) *n.* bushes, etc., growing under taller trees بڑے درختوں کے سایے میں اُگی ہوئی جھاڑیاں
underhand *adj.* secretly causing damage اندر ہی اندر نقصان پہنچانے والا dishonest بے ایمانی کا (bowling in cricket) with the hand kept below the shoulder نیچے ہاتھ کی (گیند پھینکنا) *adv.* damaging secretly اندر ہی اندر نقصان پہنچاتے ہوئے dishonesty بے ایمانی سے ، بد دیانتی سے
underlay *n.* waterproof paper, sheet, etc., for laying under carpet, etc. زیر انداز **underlie** (-li) *v.t.* lie beneath کے نیچے ہونا be the basis of (theory, etc.) کی بنیاد ہونا be at the bottom of (an affair) کی تہہ میں ہونا ، کی اصل وجہ ہونا
underline (-lin) *v.t.* draw a line under (a word, etc.) کے نیچے خط کھینچنا stress پر زور دینا ، کی اہمیت کی طرف اشارہ کرنا *n.* descriptive caption under an illustration تصویر (یا نقشے وغیرہ) کے نیچے تشریحی عبارت
underling (und-) *n.* (contemptuously) person in an unimportant position under (esp., an oppressive person or regime) (کا) گماشتہ ، (کا) کارندہ
undermentioned *adj.* mentioned below, following مندرجہ ذیل ، درج ذیل ، ذیل کا
undermine (-min) *v.t.* hollow out at the base نیچے سے کاٹنا weaken (someone's) health or authority secretly and gradually اندر ہی اندر جڑیں کھوکھلی کرنا
undermost *adj.* lowest سب سے نیچا
underneath *adv.* below نیچے *prep.* below کے نیچے
underpaid *adj.* low-paid ; getting less than called for by the nature of the task کام سے کم تنخواہ پانے والا ، ناکافی اُجرت (یا تنخواہ) پانے والا **underpay** *v.t.* ناکافی اُجرت (یا تنخواہ) دینا
underrate *v.t.* belittle کا اُس سے بہت کم اندازہ لگانا جتنا وہ ہے
underscore *v.t.* underline کے نیچے خط کھینچنا
undersell (-sel) *v.t.* sell (goods) at a lower price than (competitors) in order to oust them مقابلے میں دوسروں سے کم قیمت پر بیچنا
undershot *adj.* with the lower teeth protruding beyond the upper جس کا نچلا جبڑا باہر کو نکلا ہوا ہو
undersigned (-sind) *adj.* (the undersigned), the person(s) who sign under this document or advertisement راقم ، دستخط نگار ، زیر دستخطی
understand (und-è*-stand) *v.t.* & *i.* (*understand, understood, understood* pr. und-è*-stŭd) comprehend سمجھنا make (oneself) understood (by) پر اپنا مطلب واضح کرنا be conversant with (a language, one's business, etc.) سے خوب واقف ہونا realize محسوس کرنا ، سمجھنا learn or believe (or that) کو معلوم ہونا ، کا خیال ہونا supply mentally (a word which has not been used) مقدر کرنا ، محذوف جاننا **understood** *adj.* such (word) محذوف ، مقدر **understandable** *adj.* that can be understood جو سمجھ میں آ سکے ، قابل فہم
understanding *n.* knowledge علم intelligence ذہانت ، علم agreement (between) (میں) مفاہمت *come to* (or *reach*) *an understanding* (میں) مفاہمت ہو جانا ، میں سمجھوتہ ہو جانا condition واضح شرط *on understanding* اس واضح شرط پر *adj.* intelligent ذہین ، فہیم considerate دوسروں کے جذبات (وغیرہ) کا پاس کرنے والا
understate (-stayt) *v.t.* state too weakly اصل سے بہت کم بیان کرنا tell less than the full truth گھٹا کر سچی بات پوری پوری نہ کہنا **understatement** *n.* [illegible] بیان

n. disturbed state of mind گھبراہٹ ، پریشانی
uneconomic *adj*. against the principles of economics معاشی اُصولوں کے خلاف unprofitable غیر منفعت بخش ، بے منافع
uneducated *adj*. illiterate اَن پڑھ ، ناخواندہ not well-educated ایسا ویسا پڑھا ہُوا
unedifying *adj*. not edifying روحانی افادے سے خالی immoral مُخرّبِ اخلاق ، مُخرّبِ اَخلاق
unedited *adj*. (of book) not edited غیر مُرتّب ، unpublished غیر شائع شُدہ
unelected *adj*. not elected غیر مُنتخب
unembarrassed *adj*. calm in the face of danger جو گھبرا یا ہُوا یا تنگ نہ ہو
unemotional *adj*. not emotional غیر جذباتی
unemotionally *adv*. غیر جذباتی انداز سے ، ٹھنڈے دِل سے
unemployed *adj*. jobless بیکار ، بیروزگار **the unemployed** all those (of an area) who are jobless بیروزگار
unemployment *n*. being jobless بیروزگاری **un-employment benefit**, payment made to an unemployed person by his trade union or under his terms of insurance وظیفۂ بیروزگاری
unending *adj*. not ending جاری رہنے والا ، غیر مُختتم
unengaged *adj*. not busy غیر مصروف
un-English *adj* not English in characteristics colour, etc. غیر انگریزی against the genius or principles of the English language انگریزی کے مزاج کے خلاف ، غیر انگریزی
unenlightened *adj*. not enlightened تاریک خیال
unenrolled *adj*. not enlisted جو بھرتی نہ ہُوا ہو not enrolled جس کا نام درج رجسٹر نہ ہُوا ہو
unenterprising *adj*. lacking enterprise جس میں بڑے کاموں میں ہاتھ ڈالنے کا حوصلہ نہ ہو
unentertaining *adj*. uninteresting غیر دِلچسپ ، خشک ، بے لُطف
unenthusiastic *adj*. not enthusiastic بے جوش ، جوش سے خالی
unenumerated *adj*. not enumerated جس کی ابھی گنتی نہ ہُوئی ہو
unequal *adj*. not equal غیر مُساوی unjust غیر مُساویانہ (*unequal to*), not capable of nor strong enough for (the task) کے ناقابل
unequivocal *adj*. clear ; not equivocal واضح ، غیر مُبہم
unerring *adj*. accurate (aim, etc.) بے خطا (نشانہ)
unessential *adj*. not essential غیر ضروری ، غیر اہم
uneven *adj*. not even اُونچا نیچا ، ناہموار
uneventful *adj*. with no important event in it معمُولی ، غیر ہنگامہ خیز
unexampled *adj* unprecedented فقیدُ المثال
unexceptionable *adj*. so good that no exception can be taken to it بے عیب
unexpected *adj*. sudden اچانک not expected غیر مُتوقّع **unexpectedly** *adv*. نامُتوقّع ، غیر مُتوقّع طور پر ، اچانک
unexpired *adj*. (of term, agreement, etc.) stil current قائم ، جاری ، جو ختم نہ ہُوا ہو
unexposed *adj*. not exposed بند (of sensitive film or plate) not used غیر مُستعملہ
unfailing *adj*. reliable قابلِ اعتماد constant مُسلسل
unfair *adj*. unjust جانبدار ، غیر مُنصف not impartial جانبدارانہ ، غیر مُنصفانہ unlawful ناجائز **use of unfair means in the examination**, copying, etc. امتحان میں ناجائز ذرائع کا استعمال
unfaithful *adj*. infidel ; non-Muslim غیر مُسلم treacherous; not faithful (friend, servant, etc.) غیر وفادار of (husband or wife) adulterous ناجائز تعلق رکھنے والا (یا والی) شادی شُدہ not reliable ; inaccurate غیر مُعتبر ، غلط ، ٹھیک کام نہ دینے والا
unfaltering *adj*. not faltering نہ رُکنے والا یا والی (آواز یا قدم) ، نہ ڈگمگانے
unfamiliar *adj*. strange اجنبی ، غیر مانُوس ، اَن جانا not acquainted (*with*) (سے) ناآشنا
unfashionable *adj*. not fashionable جو رواج کے مُطابق نہ ہو ، غیر مُروّجہ ، جو رواج کے خلاف ہو **unfashioned** *adj*. rough اَن گھڑ
unfasten *v.t*. undo a knot, etc. کھولنا
unfathomable, unfathomed *adj*. excessively deep بے پایاں ، اتھاہ
unfavourable *adj*. adverse مُخالفانہ not suitable (*for*) ناموزُوں **unfavourably** *adj*. adversely کے خلاف ، مُخالفانہ
unfeasible *adj*. impracticable ناقابلِ عمل
unfeeling *adj*. lacking feeling or sympathy بےحس
unfeigned *adj*. not feigned حقیقی ، بے تصنّع
unfeminine *adj*. against the nature of women ناموزُوں غیر نسائی ، غیر نسوانی **unfit** *adj*. not suitable ناموزُوں
unfitting *adj*. loose fitting ڈِھیلا
unflagging *adj*. untiring (energy, zeal, etc.) اَن تھک
unfledged *adj*. (of bird) yet without feathers بے پَر و بال immature ناتجربہ کار ، خام کار
unflinching *adj*. (of courage, resolve, etc.), not shrinking پُختہ ، پکّا
unfold *v.t*. & *i*. spread open کھولنا ، کُھل جانا disclose کا انکشاف کرنا
unformed *adj*. not yet formed or developed کچّا ، اَدھورا
unfortunate *n*. & *adj*. unlucky (person) بدنصیب ، بدقسمت ill-timed (remark, etc.) بے سوچا سمجھا ، بے موقع **unfortunately** *adv*. unluckily بدقسمتی سے regrettably افسوس ہے کہ

understood *v*. (pa. t., pa. p.) & *adj*. (see under **understand**)

understudy (*und-*) *n*. one undergoing training to replace another (esp. actor) دوسرے کی جگہ لینے کے لیے کام سیکھنے والا (اداکار)

undertake (*-tayk*) *v.t.* (*undertake, undertook, undertaken*) taken upon oneself (*that* something or *to do* it) اپنے سر لینا، کی ذمہ داری لینا، کا بیڑا اٹھانا begin (some work) شروع کرنا **undertaking** *n*. acceptance of responsibility by one ذمہ داری promise وعدہ task کام **undertaker** *n*. one whose business is to manage funerals تجہیز و تکفین کرنے والا (یعنی غسال، کفن دوز، تابوت بردار، گورکن وغیرہ)

undertone (*und-*) *n*. subdued tone دبی ہوئی (دھیمی یا ہلکی) آواز *talk in undertones* بڑی دھیمی آواز سے باتیں کرنا

undertook *v*. (pa. t. & pa. p. of **undertake**, which see)

undervalue (*-val-*) *v.t.* underrate (کو) حقیر جاننا، (کی) صحیح قدر و قیمت کا اندازہ نہ کر سکنا

underwear (*und-*) *n*. underclothing (including vest, etc.) زیر جامہ

underwood *n*. bushes, etc., growing in the shade of trees in a forest چھوٹے پودے، تل جھاڑی

underworld (*und-*) *n*. people (*of* society, a city, etc.) living by vice and lawbreaking چور اچکے، بدمعاش lowest social stratum معاشرے کا سب سے نچلا طبقہ Hades : land of the dead پاتال

underwrite (*-rit*) *v.t.* insure against (esp. marine) loss (جہازوں وغیرہ کا) بیمہ کرنا undertake to buy all unsold (shares) by a certain date غیر فروخت شدہ (حصص) خریدنے کا معاہدہ کرنا **underwriter** (*und-*) *n*. (marine) insurer بحری بیمہ کرنے والا one undertaking to buy unsold shares غیر فروخت شدہ حصص خریدنے کا معاہدہ کرنے والا

undersigned (*-zind*) *adj*. unintentional نادانستہ

undesirable (*-de-zi-è-*) *adj*. unseemly (act) ناپسندیدہ unwanted and inconvenient (person) ناگوار، ناپسندیدہ، تکلیف دہ *n*. (*pl*.) undesirable persons ناپسندیدہ افراد

undetermined *adj*. not defined غیر واضح not settled غیر فیصل شدہ not fixed غیر معین

undeviating *adj*. unchanging (policy, course, etc.) نہ بدلنے والا

undiscernible *adj*. that which cannot be seen جو نظر نہ آسکے **undiscerning** *adj*. not seeing clearly کم نظر not understanding clearly بے بصیرت، کم فہم

undisciplined *adj*. unruly بدتمیز، غیر تربیت یافتہ

undiscovered *adj*. that which has not been discovered غیر دریافت شدہ

undisguised (*-gizd*) *adj*. open, not disguised کھلا، صریح

undisturbed *adj*. not disturbed پرسکون

undivided *adj*. not divided غیر منقسم، غیر تقسیم شدہ، نہ بٹا ہوا، سالم **undivided India** متحدہ ہندوستان

undo (un-*doo*) *v.t.* (*undo, undid, undone*) do away with the results of کا اُلٹ کرنا، کا اثر باطل کرنا unfasten (a knot) کھولنا be the ruin of کو برباد کرنا **undone** *adj*. ruined تباہ، برباد **undoing** *n*. downfall زوال ruin تباہی reversal of something done بالکل اُلٹ کر دینا

undoubted *adj*. not be doubted غیر مشتبہ **undoubtedly** *adj*. certainly بے شک، یقیناً **undoubting** *adj*. not doubting شبہ نہ کرنے والا

undreamed (un-*dreemd*), **undreamt** (un-*dremt*) *adj*. not even dreamt (of) جس کا خواب تک میں خیال نہ آیا ہو exquisite نہایت شاندار، جو خواب میں بھی نہ دیکھا ہو

undress (*un*-dres) *n*. informal dress بے تکلفانہ لباس *v.t.* & *i*. take off the dress کے کپڑے اُتارنا **undressed** *adj*. naked ننگا، برہنہ، عریاں in night clothes شب خوابی کے لباس میں in informal dress بے تکلفانہ لباس میں

undrinkable *n*. nor fit for drinking جو پینے کے قابل نہ ہو، غیر نوشیدنی

undue *adj*. undesirable, unlawful ناواجب، ناروا، ناجائز *show undue favour to* کی ناجائز حمایت کرنا excessive بہت زیادہ، غیر معمولی **unduly** *adv*. بہت زیادہ، ناجائز طور پر

undulate (*un-*dew-layt) *v.t.* (of surface) be wavy لہریا ہونا have a wavy motion لہرانا **undulating** *adj*. wavy لہریا **undulatory theory** *n*. theory that light travels in waves نور کا نظریۂ تموج

unduly *adv*. (see under **undue**)

undying *adj*. immortal (fame, etc.) لازوال، دائمی، جاودانی، زندۂ جاوید

unearned *adj*. not earned by effort بے محنت کمایا ہوا *unearned income*, income from land, property, etc. بے محنت کمائی

unearth *v.t.* dig out کھود کر نکالنا discover (hidden facts) and bring them to light بڑی جستجو سے معلوم کر کے لوگوں کو پیش کرنا **unearthly** *adj*. supernatural مافوق الفطرت weird پراسرار ghastly بھیانک (colloq.) (of hour, time, etc.) absurdly early بہت سویرے *unearthly hour* بہت ہی سویرا

uneasiness *n*. (see under **uneasy**)

uneasy *adj*. disturbed, anxious پریشان feeling awkward گھبرایا ہوا، پریشان not very comfortable or stable (peace, etc.) غیر یقینی، مخدوش **uneasiness**

uninitiated *adj*. not initiated متعارف سے نا آشنا
uninjured *adj*. without injury صحیح سالم
uninspired *adj*. commonplace (speech) معمولی (تقریر)
uninsured *adj*. not insured غیر بیمہ شدہ
unintelligible *adj*. not intelligible ناقابلِ فہم
unintentional *adj*. not intentional غیر ارادی
uninteresting *adj*. not interesting غیر دلچسپ، بے لطف
uninterrupted *adj*. not interrupted لگاتار
union (*yew*-ni-un) *n*. (of firms) join or be joined متحد ہونا، مل کر ایک ہو جانا joining or being joined in marriage شادی concord اتفاق، مُوافقت، *in perfect union* پوری طرح ہم آہنگ ہم آہنگی، اتحاد (also *trade union*) combination of workmen مزدور یونین league or confederation وحدت، وفاق، اتحاد *the Union of Soviet Socialist Republics*, (abb. *U.S.S.R*) روس، اتحادِ جماہیرِ اشتراکیۂ روس **unionist** *n*. (in Britain) member of a trade union مزدور یونین کا رکن **Union Jack** *n*. flag of the United Kingdom یونین جیک، برطانوی پرچم
unique (yew-*neek*) *adj*. the only one of its kind منفرد unparalleled بےمثال، فقیدالمثال **uniquely** *adv*. منفرد دیا، بےمثل انداز سے **uniqueness** *n*. بےمثل ہونا
unison (*yew*-ni-sun) *n*. tune in which all sing the same note ; concord (as distinct from *harmony*) مل کر (یا باہم آہنگی سے) ہم آہنگی *act in unison* کام کرنا
unit (*yew*-nit) *n*. individual person or thing, or their group regarded as a single entity وحدت *One-Unit* (or *Unit*), (in Pakistan) integrated West Pakistan وحدتِ مغربی پاکستان any standard of measurement اکائی the smallest whole number ; one ایک
unite (yew-*nit*) *v.t. & i*. join together متحد ہونا، ایک ہو جانا associate closely (*in* something or *in doing* something) متحد ہو کر کام کرنا **united** *adj*. consolidated متحدہ *the United States of America*, (abbr. *U.S.* or *U.S.A.*) امریکہ، ریاستہائے متحدۂ امریکہ *the United States of Indonesia*, (abbr. *U.S.I.*) انڈونیشیا، ریاستہائے متحدۂ انڈونیشیا *the United Arab Republic*, (abbr. *U.A.R.*) union of Egypt and Syria جمہوریۂ متحدۂ عربیہ *the United Kingdom*, (abb. *U.K.*) England, Scotland and Northen Ireland برطانیہ
(the) unities *n. pl*. (see under **unity**)
unity (*yew*-ni-ti) *n*. being united اتحاد oneness وحدت **the unities** *n. pl*. (also *the dramatic unities* or *the unities of place, time and action*) supposed limitations on drama originating from its Greek form تمثیلی وحدتیں
universal *adj*., **universalize** *v.t*., **universally** *adv*. (see under **universe**)
universe (*yew*-ni-vē*s) *n*. (*the Universe*), the whole creation کائنات، کون و مکان **universal** *adj*. of or pertaining to all ہمہ گیر، عالمگیر without any exception ہمہ گیر، بلا استثنا *universal rule* ہمہ گیر قانون (یا اصول) (of electrical machinery) working on both A.C. and D.C. ہر دو برقی لہروں والا، یونیورسل **universally** *adv*. everywhere ہر جگہ by all سب کا
universalize *v.t*. make (or treat as) a general rule ہمہ گیر اصول بنا لینا (یا سمجھنا)
university (yew-ni-*ve**sity) *n*. highest seat of learning یونیورسٹی، دانشگاہ، جامعہ *adj*. of a university جامعاتی *university examination*, one held by it جامعاتی امتحان *university degree*, degree awarded by it جامعاتی سند
uninvited *adj*. not invited (guest) بن بلایا، ناخواندہ
uninviting *adj*. unattractive غیر دلکش repellent گھناؤنا، کریہ، مکروہ
unjust *adj*. unfair (person or action) بے انصاف (یا) غیر منصفانہ
unjustifiable *adj*. not justifiable جس کا جواز پیش نہ کیا جا سکے، جس کا کوئی جواز نہ ہو
unkempt *adj*. not combed (hair) پریشان، الجھے ہوئے untidy (person) گندہ slovenly پراگندہ حال
unkind *adj*. harsh (person, words, deeds, etc.) سخت، نا ملائم
unknowing *adj*. not knowing نادانستہ **unknowingly** *adv*. نادانستہ **unknown** *adj*. not known نامعلوم unidentified گمنام *the Unknown Warrior*, *the Unknown Soldier*, (tomb of) unidentified warrior as symbolizing the country's sacrifice گمنام سپاہی *n*. unknown person or thing نامعلوم شخص یا شے *adv*. (*unknown to*), without the knowledge کے علم میں آئے بغیر
unlaboured *adj*. spontaneous (style) بیساختہ، آمد والا
unladylike *adj*. not as expected of a lady اچھی خواتین کی شان کے منافی
unlawful *adj*. illegal غیر قانونی not permissible ناروا، ناجائز
unlearn (un-*lē*n*) *v. t*. forget what one has learnt or come to believe بھلانا **unlearned** (-*lē*nd*) **unlearnt** (un-*lē*nt*) *adj*. (of lesson) not learnt جو یاد نہ ہو **unlearned** (-nid) *adj*. not well-educated کم پڑھا لکھا
unless (un-*les*) *conj*. if not اگر نہ except when جب تک نہ
unlettered *adj*. illiterate ان پڑھ، ناخواندہ
unlicensed *adj*. not licensed لائسنس کے بغیر، بلا اجازت
unlicked *adj*. unshaped ان گھڑ

unlike *adj*. different مختلف *be quite unlike (something)* نئے انداز کا ہونا، سے بالکل مختلف ہونا **unlikely** *adj*. improbable (*to do*) بعید از قیاس
unlimited *adj*. not limited غیر محدود too much بہت ہی، بہت زیادہ
unload *v.t.* remove the load, cargo, etc., from سے مال اتارنا
unlooked-for *adj*. unexpected نامتوقع، غیر متوقع
unlucky *adj*. unfortunate بدقسمت، بدقسمتی سے
unmade *adj*. (see under **unmake**)
unmake *v.t.* undo بگاڑ دینا **unmade** *adj*. not yet made جو ابھی بنا نہ ہو
unman *v.t.* deprive of courage, unnerve کے اوسان خطا کر دینا **unmanly** *adj*. without courage غیر مردانہ وار، بے ہمت
unmanageable *adj*. not easy to manipulate مشکل، قابو میں نہ آنے والا
unmannerly *adj*. ill-mannered بدتمیز، بدتہذیب ill-bred بے ترتیب
unmarked *adj*. not marked جس پر نشان نہ ہو unnoticed جو نظروں میں نہ آیا ہو
unmarketable *adj*. not marketable ناقابل فروخت
unmarriageable *adj*. (of age) below puberty جو شادی کی عمر کا (یا کی) نہ ہو **unmarried** *adj*. not married مجرد، غیر شادی شدہ
unmask *v.t.* & *i.* take the mask off نقاب اٹھانا show up (plot, etc.) نقلی چہرہ اتارنا
unmatched *adj*. peerless بے نظیر
unmeaning *adj*. senseless بے معنی unintentional نادانستہ، غیر ارادی
unmeant *adj*. not meant جس کا مطلب یہ نہ ہو
unmeasured *adj*. not measured بغیر اندازہ کے unmeasurable بے انتہا
unmentionable *adj*. too bad to be mentioned ناگفتہ بہ، ناقابل ذکر
unmerciful *adj*. cruel (treatment) سخت، ظالمانہ
unmerited *adj*. undeserved بلا وجہ
unmethodical *adj*. without proper method ڈھیلی
unmistakable *adj*. clear واضح about which no mistake is possible جس کے متعلق غلطی نہ ہو سکے **unmistakably** *adv*. certainly یقیناً
unmitigated *adj*. absolute (lie, scoundrel, etc.) پکا
unmodified *adj*. without modification اسی طرح، بلا ترمیم
unmotherly *adj*. not as expected of a mother غیر مادرانہ، ماںتا کے بغیر
unmounted *adj*. not on horseback گھوڑے پر نہیں not mounted (picture, etc.) جڑی ہوئی نہیں
unmourned *adj*. whose death nobody mourns جس کا کوئی ماتم نہ کرے
unmoved *adj*. firm in purpose پکا not affected by emotion جس پر جذبات کا اثر نہ ہو not moved اپنی جگہ پر پڑا ہوا
unmusical *adj*. not musical بےسرا without an ear for music موسیقی کے معاملے میں بے ذوق
unnamed *adj*. not named جس کا نام قصداً نہ لیا گیا ہو
unnatural *adj*. artificial مصنوعی lacking natural feelings فطری جذبات سے محروم (of crime, etc.) contrary to nature غیر فطری، خلاف فطرت، خلاف وضع فطرت *unnatural offence*, abnormal sexual relations (esp. homosexuality) فعل خلاف وضع فطرت، غیر فطری جنسی تعلق
unnecessary *adj*. not necessary غیر ضروری، لاطائل **unnecessarily** *adv*. کچھ زیادہ ہی، ضرورت سے زیادہ
unnerve *v.t.* unman ; cause to lose self-control اوسان خطا کر دینا
unnumbered *adj*. not counted جو گنے نہ گئے ہوں innumerable ان گنت، بیشمار، لاتعداد
unobjectionable *adj*. not objectionable ناقابل اعتراض
unobtainable *adj*. not obtainable جو مل نہ سکے، ناپید، نایاب
unoccuped *adj*. not occupied خالی
unoffending harmless بے ضرر innocent (words) معصومانہ
unofficial *adj*. (of news) not officially confirmed غیر سرکاری، غیر مصدقہ not of official nature غیر سرکاری
unopened *adj*. not opened بند کا بند
unopposed *adj*. without opposition بلا اختلاف
unorthodox *adj*. original نئے، اپنے
unowned *adj*. without owner لاوارث
unpaid *adj*. (of bill) not paid واجب الادا
unpalatable *adj*. offensive ناپسندیدہ
unparalleled *adj*. matchless بے نظیر
unpardonable *adj*. (of offence, etc.) that cannot be pardoned ناقابل معافی
unparliamentary *adj*. contrary to parliamentary usage غیر پارلیمانی *unparliamentary language* (*or conduct*), (humorously), indecent ناشائستہ
unpatriotic *adj*. not patriotic جو وطن دوستی پر مبنی نہ ہو
unpeopled *adj*. uninhabited غیر آباد
unperceived *adj*. unnoticed جو نظر نہ آیا ہو
unpleasant disagreeable ناگوار، ناخوشگوار **unpleasantness** *n*. bad feeling (*between*) ناخوشگوار تعلقات
unpoetical *adj*. not poetical, prosaic غیر شاعرانہ
unpolled *adj*. (of votes) not polled نہ ڈالے گئے
unpopular *adj*. not popular غیر ہردلعزیز
unpractical *adj*. not practical غیر عملی

unpractised *adj*. without practice جسے مشق نہ ہو
unprecedented *adj*. without precedent بےنظیر
unprejudiced *adj*. impartial غیر جانبدارانہ، بالانصاف، منصفانہ
unpremeditated *adj*. not deliberately planned بے سوچا سمجھا
unprepared *adj*. not prepared تیاری کے بغیر
unpresentable *adj*. ugly بدنما not fit to be presented جو پیش کرنے کے قابل نہ ہو
unpretending *adj*., **unpretentious** *adj*. making little show سیدھا سادہ، منکسر المزاج
unprincipled *adj*. without good moral principles بے اصول
unprivileged *adj*. not privileged جسے مراعات حاصل نہ ہوں
unproductive *adj*. not productive غیر پیدا آور
unprofessional *adj*. not professional غیر پیشہ ورانہ (of conduct, etc.) against professional ethics, etc. پیشے کے اصول کے خلاف
unprofitable *adj*. profitless غیر نفع بخش (of servant) content to do no more than his duty بس صرف اپنا کام کرنے والا
unprogressive *adj*. not progressive غیر ترقی پسند، backward پسماندہ غیر ترقی پذیر
unprotected *adj*. not protected غیر محفوظ، بلا حفاظت
unprovided *adj*. not provided (*with* esp. money) جس کا پاس نہ ہو
unprovoked *adj*. without any provocation کسی اشتعال کے بغیر
unpublished *adj*. not published or made public غیر شائع شدہ
unpunctual *adj*. not punctual جو وقت کا پابند نہ ہو
unqualified *adj*. without any conditions غیر مشروط not qualified غیر سند یافتہ *unqualified practitioner*, quack عطائی
unquestionable *adj*. that which cannot be doubted یقینی، مسلّمہ **unquestioning** *adj*. yielding without question بے چون و چرا
unquiet *adj*. restless بے چین، مضطر
unquotable *adj*. not fit to be quoted ناگفتہ بہ
unravel *v.t.* & *i*. (-ll-) separate the threads of کھولنا become separate کھل جانا solve (mystery) پالینا، حل کرنا، دریافت کرنا
unread *adj*. not read جسے پڑھا نہ گیا ہو **unreadable** *adj*. too dull to be read بے لطف
unreal *adj*. not real غیر حقیقی، موہوم
unreasonable *adj*. not reasonable نامعقول **unreasonably** *adv*. نامعقولیت کی حد تک
unreasoning *adj*. not using reason عقل سے کام نہ لینے والا
unreceipted *adj*. for which a receipt has not been issued بے رسید
unreciprocated *adj*. (of love, etc.) which is not reciprocated جس کا جواب (محبّت وغیرہ) سے نہ دیا گیا ہو
unreclaimed *adj*. (of soil) not brought under the plough جو قابل کاشت نہ بنائی گئی ہو not reformed غیر اصلاح شدہ
unrecorded *adj*. جو اندراج میں نہ آیا ہو، غیر مندرج
unredeemed *adj*. (of pawn, etc.) not taken out جسے چھڑایا نہ گیا ہو، غیر منفک not paid واجب الادا (of promise) not fulfilled تشنۂ تکمیل
unrefined *adj*. not refined کثیف uncultured ناشائستہ
unreflecting *adj*. thoughtless نہ سوچنے والا
unreformed *adj*. not reformed غیر اصلاح شدہ
unregenerate *adj*. having had no moral awakening غیر ہدایت یافتہ
unrelenting *adj*. relentless بے رحم، بے رحمانہ
unreliable *adj*. not reliable ناقابل اعتماد، غیر معتبر
unrelieved *adj*. lacking relief بے مدد not relieved of monotony بے تنوّع
unremitting *adj*. incessant (care) کم نہ ہونے والا، مسلسل
unremunerative *adj*. (of work, etc.) that has no remuneration غیر فائدہ بخش، جس کا معاوضہ نہ ملے
unrepresentative نمائندہ
unrequited *adj*. (of love, etc.) not returned or rewarded جس کا صلہ نہ ملے
unreservedly (-id-) *adj*. frankly کھل کر
unresolved *adj*. not solved حل طلب not resolved گومگو کی حالت میں، مذبذب
unresponsive *adj*. not responsive بے حس، غیر ہمدرد
unrest *n*. disturbed condition عام بے چینی، گڑبڑ **unresting** *adj*. working continuously مسلسل کام کرتے جانے والا
unrestrained *adj*. not restrained جسے روکا نہ گیا ہو
unrestricted *adj*. without any restrictions بلا پابندی
unrighteous *adj*. unjust بے انصاف، غیر منصفانہ wicked بدکار، برا
unripe *adj*. not ripe کچّا، خام
unrivalled *adj*. peerless بے نظیر
unromantic *adj*. not romantic غیر رومانی
unruffled *adj*. unperturbed پرسکون
unruled *adj*. not ruled غیر محکوم not lined سادہ، لکیروں کے بغیر **unruly** *adj*. not easily controlled آسانی سے قابو میں نہ آنے والا disorderly (child) اودھم مچانے والا
unsafe *adj*. not safe غیر محفوظ
unsatisfactory *adj*. not satisfactory ناتسلی بخش **unsatisfying** *adj*. ناتسلی بخش **unsatisfied** *adj*. غیر مطمئن

unsavoury *adj*. disgusting (scandal) طبیعت مُنغّص کرنے والا
unscathed (un-*skaydhd*) *adj*. without injury or suffering صاف، محفوظ، بغیر چشم زخم کے
unscientific *adj*. transgressing the principles of science غیر سائنسی
unscrupulous *adj*. having no scruples بے ایمان، بَدْ دِیانت
unsearchable *adj*. beyond the reach of search جس کی تلاش ممکن نہ ہو
unreasonable *adj*. not apt بے موقع، بے محل
unseat *v.t.* remove from saddle زین سے اُتار پھینکنا remove from parliamentary seat ممبری سے ہٹانا
unseaworthy *adj*. (of ship, etc.) not fit to sail سمندر میں جانے کے ناقابل
unsectarian *adj*. not sectarian غیر فرقہ وارانہ
unseemly *adj*. & *adv*. (old use) improper(ly) نامناسب (طور پر)
unseen *n*. & *adj*. unseen (passage, translation, etc.) set in the examination اَن دیکھا، غیر دَرسی
unserviceable *adj*. not serviceable جو کام نہ دے سکے، ناکارہ
unsettle *v.t.* make anxious تشویش ڈالنا (of bill, account, etc.) not paid واجب الادا make uncertain غیر یقینی بنانا *unsettled weather*, uncertain weather غیر یقینی (یا تغیر پذیر) موسم not to colonize آباد نہ کرنا uproot (population) بے خانماں کرنا make full of disturbances ہنگامے کرنا **unsettled times** period of unrest ہنگامہ خیز دَور، ہنگاموں کا زمانہ
unshakable, unshaken *adj*. firm (resolved) غیر متزلزل
unshapely *adj*. unhewn بدنما، ان گھڑ
unshrinking *adj*. fearless بے جھجک، نڈر
unsighted *adj*. not yet seen جو ابھی دیکھا نہ گیا ہو (of gun) without sights مکھی کے بغیر (of umpire) precluded from seeing جو آڑ کے باعث دیکھ نہ سکا ہو
unsightly *adj*. repulsive گھناؤنا
unsigned *adj*. not signed بے نام، بے دستخط
unskilful *adj*. not skilful بے مشق، اناڑی **unskilled** *adj*. untrained for a technical job غیر کاریگر *unskilled labour* غیر کاریگر مزدور
unsociable *adj*. not sociable کم آمیز
unsocial *adj*. not social غیر معاشری unsociable کم آمیز
unsoiled *adj*. not clear جو میلا نہ ہوا ہو، بالکل صاف
unsold *adj*. not sold out غیر فروخت شدہ
unsolicited *adj*. not asked for بے طلب، بِلا بُلایا
unsophisticated *adj*. artless بے تصنع، بناوٹ سے خالی
unsought *adj*. not sought بے طلب

unsound *adj*. unbalanced (mind) کم دماغ کے فعل fallacious غلط، مبالغہ آمیز diseased غیر صحت مند، بیمار والا
unsounded *adj*. unfathomed (depth) اتھاہ، بے پایاں
unsparing *adj*. lavish (or *in*. praise, efforts etc.) بے دریغ merciless بیدردانہ، بیدرد
unspeakable *adj*. beyond description (good or bad) ناقابلِ بیان
unspecified *adj*. not specified غیر معیّن
unspoiled, unspoilt *adj*. not spoiled جو بگڑا نہ ہو
unspoken *adj*. not spoken اَن کہی
unsporting *adj*. (same as **unsportsmanlike**, which see)
unsportsmanlike *adj*. **unsporting** *adj*. lacking sportsman spirit مردانگی کی شان کے خلاف
unstable *adj*. not stable غیر یقینی، متلوّن، بدلتا رہنے والا
unstained *adj*. immaculate بیداغ
unstamped *adj*. not stamped جس پر مہر نہ لگی ہو جس پر ٹکٹ نہ لگا ہو، بیرنگ
unstatesmanlike *adj*. not as expected of a statesman غیر مدبرانہ
unsteady *adj*. fluctuating تغیّر پذیر not steady ڈانواں ڈول
unstinted *adj*. unsparing (support, etc.) بیدریغ
unstressed *adj*. (of syllable) unaccented جس پر زور نہ دیا گیا ہو
unstrung *adj*. unnerved بدحواس
unstudied *adj*. spontaneous بیساختہ
unsubstantial *adj*. unreal غیر مادی، موہوم lacking solidity بودا، کمزور
unsubstantiated *adj*. not proved جو ثابت نہ ہو سکا ہو
unsuccessful *adj*. not successful ناکام
unsuitable, unsuited *adj*. unfit ناموزوں
unsullied *adj*. spotless بیداغ
unsurpassable *adj*. whom none can surpass جس پر کوئی سبقت نہ لے جا سکے
unsuseptible *adj*. not susceptible غیر اثر پذیر
unsuspecting *adj*. not suspecting شبہ نہ کرنے والا
unsweetened *adj*. not made sweet (by) جسے میٹھا نہ بنایا گیا ہو
unswept *adj*. not swept جہاں جھاڑو نہ دی گئی ہو
unswerving *adj*. firm پکا، ثابت قدم
unsworn not sworn غیر حلفی
unsymbolic, unsymbolical *adj*. not symbolic (of) جس میں کسی چیز کا اشارہ نہ ہو، غیر اشاری
unsymmetrical *adj*. without symmetry بے تناسُب
unsympathetic *adj*. lacking sympathy غیر ہمدردانہ

unsystematic *adj*. lacking system بے طریقہ، بے اُصول
untainted *adj*. not tainted (character) غیر آلودہ، غیر مُلوَّث
untalented *adj*. lacking talent جس میں کوئی جوہر نہ ہو
untasted *adj*. not tasted جو چکھا نہ گیا ہو
untaught *adj*. not taught جو پڑھایا نہ گیا ہو
unteachable *adj* جسے پڑھایا نہ جا سکے
untenable *adj*. not tenable بودا، کمزور، غیر مُستحکم
untended *adj*. not tended جس کی خبر گیری نہ کی گئی ہو
untested *adj*. not tested جانچا نہ ہُوا
unthankful *adj*. ungrateful ناشکرا، ناشکر گُزار
unthinkable *adj*. unimaginable ناقابلِ تصوّر unlikely بعید از قیاس **unthinking** *adj*. نہ سوچنے والا **unthought of** *adj*. not thought of بے سان گمان **unthoughtful** *adj*. careless بے پروا unthinking غور نہ کرنے والا، نہ سوچنے والا
untidy *adj*. not tidy بے سلیقہ، گندا
untie (un-*ti*) *v.t*. unbind کھولنا، کی گرہ کھولنا **untied** *adj*. not tied کھلا ہُوا (یا) کھولا ہُوا
until *prep*. & *adv*. till تک except when جب تک as long as and more جب تک
untilled *adj*. not tilled غیر مزروعہ، غیر کاشت شدہ
untimely *adj*. inopportune (remark) بے موقع، بے محل premature (death) قبل از وقت
untiring *adj*. not tiring ان تھک
unto (*un*-too) *prep*. (old use) to کی طرف
untold *adj*. not told ان کہی countless بے شمار، ان گنت، بے حد، بے حد و حساب، ناگفتہ بہ
untouchable *adj*. pariah; low caste or non caste person with whom caste Hindus avoid contact اچھوت **untouchability** *n*. this is as a Hindu institution اچھوت ہونا، (یا) اچھوت سمجھنے کا مُعاشرتی نظام **untouched** *adj*. not touched (by hand, etc.) جسے چھُوا نہ گیا ہو، جسے مَس نہ کیا گیا ہو
untoward (un-*tew*-è*d) *adj*. (old use) hindering تکلیف دہ inopportune بے موقع، بے محل refractory سرکش، ضدی unlucky بد قسمتی والا
untraceable *adj*. not traceable جس کا سراغ نہ ملے
untrained *adj*. not trained غیر تربیت یافتہ
untrammelled *adj*. unhampered آزاد، بے روک ٹوک
untransferable *adj*. not transferable ناقابلِ انتقال، جسے منتقل نہ کیا جائے
untranslatable *adj*. not such as can be translated ناقابلِ ترجمہ
untravelled *adj*. who has not travelled جس نے سیاحت نہ کی ہو
untried *adj*. untested آزمایا نہ ہُوا، غیر آزمودہ inexperienced ناتجربہ کار
untrodden *adj*. not trodden upon بے آمد و رفت
untroubled *adj*. calm پُرسکون not troubled غیر مضطرب
untrue *adj*. false جھوٹ، غلط unfaithful (*to*) بے وفا **untruthful** *adj*. liar جھوٹا
untrustworthy *adj*. unreliable غیر معتبر، ناقابلِ اعتبار
unturned *adj*. not turned نہ ہلایا ہُوا *leave no stone unturned* ہر طرح سے کوشش کر دیکھنا
untutored *adj*. not schooled ایسا ویسا پڑھا ہُوا not tutored جو سکھایا ہُوا نہ ہو
unused *adj*. not used, new نیا، غیر مستعمل
unusual *adj*. extraordinary غیر معمولی
unutterable *adj*. inexpressible ناقابلِ بیان
unvaccinated *adj*. not vaccinated جسے چیچک کا ٹیکہ نہ لگا ہو
unvalued *adj*. not yet valued جس کی قیمت لگائی گئی ہو not esteemed جس کی قیمت نہ پڑی ہو
unvaried, unvarying *adj*. unchanging غیر متغیر monotonous تنوع سے خالی
unvarnished *adj*. not varnished بے وارنش unembellished کسی رنگ آمیزی کے بغیر
unvarying *adj*. (same as **unvaried**, which see)
unveil *v.t*. remove the covering from (statue, etc.) at public ceremony نقاب کشائی کرنا *unveil oneself*, (of a woman, etc.) throw off the veil بُرقع اُتارنا reveal (plot, etc.) بے نقاب کرنا *unveiling ceremony* رسمِ نقاب کشائی
unverified *adj*. not verified غیر مصدّقہ
unversed *adj*. unskilled (*in*) کسی فن میں دخل نہ رکھنے والا
unwarrantable *adj*. unauthorized بلا اجازت، غیر مستند unwarranted بے ضمانت، ناجائز **unwarranted** *adj*. not guaranteed بے ضمانت unlawful ناجائز
unwary *adj*. not cautious, off the guard غافل، غیر محتاط
unwatchful *adj*. not watchful (of) جو چوکس نہ ہو
unwatered *adj*. not watered جسے پانی نہ دیا گیا ہُوا without water بے آب not adulterated with water جس میں پانی نہ ملایا گیا ہُوا، خالص
unwavering *adj*. unchanging غیر متزلزل
unweaned *adj*. not yet weaned شیر خوار، جس کا دودھ ابھی چھڑایا یا بڑھایا نہ گیا ہو
unwearying *adj*. untiring (efforts) ان تھک
unwelcome *adj*. not welcome جس کی آمد پسند نہ ہو
unwell *adj*. indisposed کچھ بیمار، علیل
unwept *adj*. not wept for جس پر کوئی نہ رویا ہو
unwholesome *adj*. injurious to health مُضرِ صحت with bad moral effect مخربِ اخلاق
unwieldy *adj*. so big, etc. as to be awkward to move or control جس کو اٹھانا وغیرہ مشکل ہو
unwilling *adj*. not willing (*that*) *for* or *to do*

something) نارضامندی، نارضامندانہ *adv*. not willingly سے، بدلی سے

unwise *adj*. imprudent غیر دانشمند، غیر دانشمندانہ

unwished *adj*. not wished (*for*) غیر مطلوب، ناخواستہ

unwitting *adj*. unintentional نادانستہ

unwomanly *adj*. against what is expected of woman غیر نسوانی، غیر نسائی

unwonted *adj*. unusual غیر متوقع

unworkable *adj*. unpracticable ناقابلِ عمل

unworldly *adj*. not worldly غیر دُنیوی، رُوحانی

unworn *adj*. not worn غیر مستعمل

unworthy *adj*. not worthy (*of*) جو شایانِ شان نہ ہو unfit غیر مستحق، نااہل

unwrap *v.t.* remove the wrapper from کو کھولنا

unwritten *adj*. (of a statute, convention, etc.) not written but universally accepted غیر نوشتہ، غیر تحریری *unwritten law*, (*a*) law based on conventions or customs غیر تحریری قانون (*b*) supposed right to kill, etc., in defence of self-honour (esp. by murdering the abductor of one's wife) بیوی کے اغوا کرنے والے کو قتل کا حق، جوشِ غیرت میں آکر انتقام

unyielding *adj*. firm نہ جھکنے والا

unyoke *v.t.* loosen from the yoke جُوئے سے الگ کرنا، کے کندھوں سے جُوا اتارنا

[1]**up** (up) *adv*. & *prep*. to a higher place اُوپر، اُوپر کو، اُوپر تک on the place mentioned پر completely پُوری طرح، پُورا straight سیدھا out of bed جاگ اُٹھا dressed and ready اُٹھ کر تیار *go up*, (*a*) go upstairs or to a higher place اُوپر جانا (*b*) (of price) rise چڑھنا *be up*, جاگ اُٹھنا، اُٹھ کر تیار ہونا *be up to*, (*a*) busy with میں مصروف (*b*) equal to (a task, *doing* something) کے قابل (*c*) doing (some mischief, etc.) شرارت میں لگا ہُوا *it is up to us* (*to do*) یہ اب ہمارا کام ہے، یہ کرنا ہمارا فرض ہے *be up to much*, be useful مفید ہونا *get up* کو جالینا *bring up as issue* مسئلہ اُٹھانا *catch up with* get up (*out of bed*) جاگ اُٹھنا *keep up with* کا ساتھ دینا *up in arms* لڑنے کو تیار (*his*) *blood is up* وہ بڑے طیش میں ہے *be up in* (*a subject*) (کسی مضمون) میں خُوب تیز ہونا *the sun is up* سُورج نکل آیا ہے، (دن) چڑھ آیا ہے *the game is up*, *it is all up with us*, we are defeated beyond hope of recovery ہم بُری طرح مارے گئے *n*. rise عُروج، بلندی *the up and downs of life* زندگی کے نشیب و فراز (*be*) *on the up-and-up* (U.S. colloq.) (*a*) (be) improving بہتر بنتا ہُوا (ہونا) (*b*) (be) honest دیانتدار ہونا *v.i.* (colloq.) abruptly begin doing something یکایک (کرنے) لگنا *he ups and says* وہ اُٹھ کر کہتا ہے pick up (something *with* stick, one's fist, etc.) اُٹھانا، (ہاتھ بڑھا کر) سے اُٹھانا

[2]**up-** (up) *pref*. اُوپر *pray with upraised hands* ہاتھ اُٹھا کر دُعا کرنا *upturned nose* اُوپر کو مڑی ہُوئی ناک

upbraid (up-*brayd*) *v.t.* reprove جھاڑ جھپاڑ کرنا

upbringing (-*bring*-) *n*. home training (*of* child) (بچے کی) تربیت

upcast *n*. upward throw اُوپر پھینکنا *adj*. of the inland area اندرونِ مُلک کا

upgrade *v.t.* put in a higher category اُونچے درجے میں لانا

upheaval (-*heev*-) *n*. heaving up with force زور سے اُٹھانا great disturbance انقلاب great change

uphill *adv*. (up-*hil*) up a slope اُوپر کی طرف *adj*. (*up*-hil) sloping upward اُوپر کی طرف arduous (task, etc.) سخت مشکل، بڑا کٹھن، دُشوار

uphold (up-*hold*) *v.t.* (uphold) confirm (a judgment, etc.) برقرار رکھنا defend (a cause) کی تائید کرنا hold up

upholster (-*hohl*-) *v.t.* cover furniture with padding, etc. پوشش لگانا provide (a room) with curtains, carpets, etc. (کمرے میں) پردے وغیرہ لگانا **upholsterer** *n*. one who upholsters furniture, etc. پوشش والا **upholstery** *n*. upholstering پوشش material used in it پوشش (کا سامان)

upkeep (*up*-keep) *n*. keeping (of something) in good order نگہداشت، اچھی حالت میں رکھنا، سنبھالنا its cost نگہداشت کا خرچ

upland (*up*-land) *n*. (often *pl*.) high land اُونچا علاقہ *adj*. situated at a high altitude اُونچی سطح کا

uplift *v.t.* (up-*lift*) lift up اُٹھانا، بلند کرنا raise to higher moral or social plane اُونچا کرنا، کی بہبود کا کام کرنا *n*. (*up*-lift) raising of social (etc.) status بہبود rise in level بلندی، اُونچا ہونا، اُٹھنا upheaval ہلچل، گڑبڑ (U. S.) edifying influence ذہنی (یا رُوحانی) سربلندی عطا کرنے والا اثر

upon (u-*pon*) *prep*. on پر، کے اوپر against (wall) پر of the moment of کے موقع پر *come upon* (*someone*) (کو) پالینا *put upon* (*someone*) پر حد سے زیادہ بوجھ ڈالنا

upper (*up*-e*) *adj*. higher اُوپر کا، بالائی *the upper ten*, *the upper ten thousand*, the aristocracy اُونچا، بلند *n*. upper part of shoe جُوتے کا اُوپر کا حصّہ **uppermost**, **upmost** *adj*. & *adv*. highest سب سے اُوپر کا، بلند، بلندترین on or to the top اُوپر (کا) **upperhand** *n*. superiority, advantage (*of* someone) تفوّق، بالادستی *have the upperhand of* پر تفوّق رکھنا، سے بالادست ہونا control (*over someone*) قابُو *get the upperhand* (*over someone*) کو قابُو میں کرلینا

uppish (*up*-ish) *adj*. proud ; presumptuous مغرور اپنے کو خُدا جانے کیا سمجھنے والا

upright *adj*. erect بالکل سیدھا، کھڑا honest دیانتدار *adv*. erect سیدھے honestly دیانتداری سے

uprightly *adv.* دیانتداری سے **uprightness** *n.* integrity دیانتداری
uprising (-*riz*-) *n.* getting out of bed اُٹھنا، جاگنا بیداری rebellion بغاوت
uproar (*up*-roh*) *n.* noisy confusion ہنگامہ، گڑبڑ شور و غوغا **end in (an) uproar,** (of a meeting) end thus گڑبڑ میں ختم ہونا **uproarious** *adj.* (of laughter, high spirits, etc.) بہت اُونچا (of meeting) with noisy confusion گڑبڑ والا
uproot (up-*root*) *v.t.* extirpate جڑ سے اُکھاڑنا root out (evil, etc.) خاتمہ کرنا، جڑ سے اُکھاڑنا
upset *v.t.* & *i.* (up-*set*) (-tt-) disturb, annoy برہم کردینا، پریشان کردینا throw into disorder درہم برہم کردینا . میں گڑبڑ مچادینا upturn اُلٹ دینا (of boat, etc.) capsize اُلٹ جانا bring (someone's plans) to nought (تدبیریں) اُلٹی کردینا *n.* (*up*-set) upsetting اُلٹ دینا یا اُلٹ جانا، برہمی، پریشانی، گڑبڑ، اُلٹی
upshot (*up*-shot) *n.* outcome (*of*) کا نتیجہ
upside (*up*-sid) *n.* upper side (*of*) اُوپری طرف، بالائی منزل **upside-down** (*up*-sid-*down*) *adv.* with the top at the bottom and *vice versa* بالکل اُلٹا، اوندھا in a state of confusion درہم برہم **upstage** (*up*-stayj) *adj.* supercilious, disdainful بدمزاج، تنک مزاج، تند خو
upstairs (up-*stay*-ĕ*z) *adj.* on an upper storey اُوپر کی منزل کا (یا والا) *adv.* to or on an upper storey اُوپر، اُوپر کی منزل پر (یا کو) *n.* upper storey بالائی منزل؛ اُوپر کی منزل
upstart (*up*-stah*t) *n.* & *adj.* (one) who has suddenly risen to wealth, etc. نیا نواب، نوخاستہ
upstream (up-*streem*) *adv.* against the current بہاؤ کے اُلٹے رُخ، دھارے کے مخالف **uptake** (*up*-tayk) *n.* grasping the point *quick in the uptake* تیز فہم، زُود فہم
up-to-date (*up*-to-*dayt*) *adj.* of up to now اب تک کا latest (information, fashion, etc.) تازہ ترین
upturned *adj.* capsized اُلٹ گیا ہُوا
upward *adj.* moving or directed up اُونچا *upward trend of prices* قیمتوں میں اضافے کا رُجحان *adv.* towards a higher level اُوپر **upwards** (*up*-wĕ*dz) *adv.* upward اُوپر *upwards of,* more than سے اُوپر، سے زیادہ
Urania (yew-*ray*-ni-a) *Cl. myth.* the Muse of astronomy یُورینیہ
uranium (yew-*ran*-i-um) *n.* a radio-active metal yielding atomic energy یُورینیم
Uranus (*yew*-ra-nus) *n.* name of a planet یُورانس *Cl. myth.* the heavens regarded as the grandfather of *Zeus* یُورانس

urban (ĕ*-*ban*) *adj.* of or in a town (as opposed to rural) شہری *urban area, urban district* شہری علاقہ
urbanize *v.t.* change to urban character شہری بنانا change the rural character of (district) and make it (look like) a city شہر (کا سا) بنانا، میں شہر آباد کرنا **urbanization** *n.* شہری بنانا، شہر (کا سا) بنانا، میں شہر آباد کرنا
urbane (ĕ*-*bayn*) *adj.* refined (manners, person, etc.) تہذیب یافتہ، شائستہ، بااخلاق **urbanely** *adv.* تہذیب و شائستگی سے
urbanity (-*ban*-) *n.* تہذیب، شرافت، شائستگی
urbanize *v.t.* (see under **urban**)
urchin (ĕ*-chin) *n.* naughty kid شریر لڑکا *street-urchins,* urchins بازاری بچے، بازاروں میں کھیلتے پھرنے والے شریر بچے
urge (ĕ*j) *v.t.* press or drive (person, horse, etc., *on* or *onward*) آگے بڑھانا press (someone *to do* something) (کسی شخص پر کسی کام کے لیے) زور دینا press (*upon* someone the need, etc., *for* or *of*) کے ذہن نشین کرنا *n.* (lit.) yearning (*to do* or *for doing* something) خواہش، شوق، لگن **urgent** (ĕ*-jent) *adj.* calling for immediate attention اہم، تاکیدی، فوری importunate (person, his voice, request etc.) تعجیل طلب، اصرار والا، مُصِر **urgently** *adv.* immediately فوراً **urgency** *n.* need for immediate action سختی، اہمیت، فوری توجہ کی ضرورت importunity سخت اِصرار
urgency *n.,* **urgent** *adj.,* **urgently** *adv.* (see under **urge**)
uric *adj.,* **urinal** *n.,* **urinate** *v.i.* (see under **urine**)
urine (*yew*-rin) *n.* waste fluid discharged from the bladder پیشاب، قارورہ، بول *pass urine* پیشاب کرنا **urinate** *v.i.* pass urine پیشاب کرنا **urinal** *n.* specified place for urinating پیشاب خانہ **uric** *adj.* of or pertaining to urine بولی، پیشاب کا *uric acid* بولی تیزاب، پیشاب کا تیزابی مادہ
urn (ĕ*n) *n.* a kind of (decorated) vase (منقش) سامان such container for storing the ashes of the dead خاکدان large metal container in a restaurant for keeping tea, etc., hot اُرن، سماوار

an urn

us (us) *pron.* (abbr. *'s*) (1st person, *pl.* objective case of I, which see) ہمیں، ہم کو، ہمارے (پاس وغیرہ)
usage (*yewz*-ij) *n.* custom, practice رواج، دستور (رائج دستور) treatment سلوک *He met with rough usage* اُس سے بُری ہوئی mode of using طریقِ استعمال (esp.) mode of using words محاورہ، الفاظ کا استعمال *modern English usage* نیا انگریزی محاورہ، موجودہ طریقِ استعمال (also see **use**)
use *v.t.* (yewz) *use, used, used*; pr. yewzd)

put to some purpose برتنا ، اِستعمال کرنا treat سے سلوک کرنا use (*something*) *up*, *use up* (*something*), consume the whole of سارا اِستعمال کرلینا، ختم کر ڈالنا *Use others as you would like them to use you* دُوسروں سے جیسا سلوک کرو n. (yews) سے چاہتے ہو ، ویسا ہی اُن سے کرو بھی using or being used اِستعمال advantage فائدہ manner of using اِستعمال practise مشق ، اِستعمال custom رواج ، دستور right to the use (*of*) (کا) حق power of the use (*of*) کے اِستعمال کی طاقت اِستعمال *be in use* اِستعمال میں ہونا ، زیرِ اِستعمال ہونا *come into use*, (a) begin to be used اِستعمال ہونے لگنا (b) come into vogue کا رواج چلنے رہنا *go out of use*, *fall out of use* کا رواج ہونا *lose the use of* (*one's*) *arm* (*etc.*) ہاتھ (وغیرہ) نہ ہلا سکنا

used (yewst) *adj.* accustomed (*to* some hardship etc.) (کا) عادی ، (کا) خوگر *be used to* (something) کا عادی ہونا کا خوگر ہونا *auxiliary v.* (only in the past) (expressing habituation) was (or were) accustomed (*to do, go, see, etc.*) کیا ، جایا ، دیکھا وغیرہ کرتا تھا **useful** (*yews*-ful) *adj.* of use مُفید ، کارآمد **usefully** *adv.* کارآمد طریق پر ، مُفید طور پر ، فائدہ بخش انداز سے **usefulness** *n.* مُفید ہونا ، افادیت **useless** *adj.* worthless فضول ، ناکارہ ، بیکار **uselessly** *adv.* بیکار ، یُونہی **uselessness** *n.* ناکارہ ہونا

user (*yew*-zĕ*) *n.* one who uses اِستعمال ہونے والا ، برتنے والا ، اِستعمال کنندہ continued use of a right کسی حق کا مُسلسل اِستعمال (also see **usage**)

usher (*ush*-ĕ*) *n.* steward (in a theatre, etc.) for showing people to their seats نقیب door-keeper in a law-court calling persons when needed عدالت کا چپڑاسی *v.t.* show (someone *in*) اندر لے جانا ، اندر کا راستہ دکھانا take (someone *into*) اندر لے جانا کے آگے آگے چلنا . کا نقیب (*usher in*), herald ہونا ، کی آمد کی خبر دینا **usherette** (ush-ĕ-*ret*) *n.* female usher نقیبہ

usual (*yew*-zhoo-al) *adj.* habitual معمُول کے مُطابق customary حسبِ عادت regular پہلا ، زور والا ، معمُولاً ، عام *as usual* حسبِ معمُول ٹھیک **usually** *adv.* generally عام طور پر ، عمُوماً

usurp (yew-*zĕ*p*) *v.t.* take unlawful and unmerited possession of (the throne, someone's position or power, etc.) غصب کرنا **usurper** *n.* one who usurps غاصب **usurpation** *n.* act of usurping غصب

usury (*yew*-zhu-ri) *n.* exorbitant rate of interest بھاری سُود business of lending money at such rates سُود خواری **usurer** (*yew*-zhu-rĕ*) *n.* one who runs this business سُود خوار ، سُود خور ، بنیا ، مہاجن

utensil (yew-*tens*-il) *n.* container in everyday use عام اِستعمال کا برتن ، ماعُون such instrument in household (esp., kitchen) use عام اِستعمال کی چیزیں ، ماعُون *household utensils* گھر کے اِستعمال کی عام چیزیں

Uther (*yew*-thĕ*) *Brit. leg.* father of King Arthur یُوتھر

utilitarian *n.*, **utilitarianism** *n.*, **utilities** *n. pl.*, **utilization** *n.*, **utilize** *v.t.* (see under **utility**)

utility (yew-*til*-i-ti) *n.* usefulness افادیت *adj.* (of furniture, clothes, etc.), made in austere and usu. standardized styles (as opposed to *luxurious*) سیدھا سادہ ، محض ضرُورت پُوری کرنے والا **utilities** *n. pl.* useful services like water supply, etc. ضرُوری خدمات *public utilities*, such public services رفاہِ عامّہ کے کام ، شہری (یا عوامی) خدمات **utilitarianism** (-*tay*-) *n.* ethical doctrine testing the moral value of an action by its utility in creating the greatest happiness of the greatest number of people افادیت **utilitarian** *n.* one who believes in it افادی *adj.* for use rather than for show or decoration افادی ، ضرُورت کی

utilize (*yew*-ti-liz) *v.t.* use برتنا ، اِستعمال کرنا ، (کو) کام میں لانا find a use for کا مَصرف ڈھونڈنا **utilization** (-*zay*-) *n.* اِستعمال ، اِستفادہ

utmost (*ut*-mohst) *adj.* farthest دُور ترین ، اِنتہائی greatest زیادہ سے زیادہ ، اِنتہائی *n.* the most that can be حتی المقدُور ، پُوری طرح ، زیادہ سے زیادہ جتنا زیادہ ہو سکے *to the utmost* خُوب عیش کرنا ، پُوری طرح زیادہ *enjoy* (*oneself*) *to the utmost* حتی المقدُور لُطف اُٹھانا ، دادِ عیش دینا *do* (*one's*) *utmost* (*to*) کوشش کرنا ، اپنے والی پُوری کوشش کرنا ، (میں) کوئی کسر اُٹھا نہ رکھنا

Utopia (yew-*toh*-pi-a) *n.* any ideally perfect place مثالی پروگرام perfect sociological system مثالی مُعاشرت خیالی دُنیا ، خوابوں کی دُنیا ، لامکاں imaginary place

utopian *n.* visionary خیالی دُنیا میں رہنے والا *adj.* fascinating but impracticable (scheme, etc.) خیالی ، ناقابلِ عمل

utter (*ut*-ĕ*) *adj.* absolute, entire, complete بالکُل ، پُورا ، کامل *v.t.* emit audibly with the mouth (a word, a sigh, a groan, a sound, etc.) زبان سے نکالنا ، کی آواز نکالنا speak, say کہنا ، بولنا circulate (base coins, etc.) (جعلی سکے وغیرہ) چلانا **utterance** (*ut*-e-rans) *n.* something said جو کہا جائے (often *pl.*) speech تقریر expression اِظہار *give utterance to* (*one's*) *feelings* اظہارِ جذبات کرنا manner of speaking بولنے کا طریق ، اندازِ گفتگو **utterly** *adv.* entirely بالکل ، قطعاً ، سراسر **uttermost** *adj.* greatest, utmost زیادہ سے زیادہ ، اِنتہائی farthest, utmost دُور ترین

uvula (*yewv*-ew-la) *n.* (*pl.*, *uvulae*) small pendent part of the palate towards the neck حلق کا کوا ، لہات

uxorious (uk-*so*-ri-us, or -*soh*-) *adj.* so fond of one's wife as to appear to be foolish زن مُرید

V

v, V (vee) (pl. *v's* or *vs*) the twentysecond letter of the English alphabet (pr. like the و in Urdu) وی (as Roman numeral) five پانچ any V-shaped thing, joint, etc. وی the symbol of the much-hoped-for British victory popularized by (Sir) Winston Churchill during World War II "وی" برائے وکٹری، فتح کی علامت

vacant (*vay*-kant) *adj.* unoccupied (house, room, place, seat, post, etc.) خالی empty (space, mind) خالی stupid (looks, eyes, etc.) احمقانہ **vacantly** *adv.* stupidly احمقانہ انداز سے، حماقت سے without any signs of thought or interest جیسے خلا میں، بے معنی طور پر **vacancy** (*vay*-kans-i) *n.* being vacant خلا، خالی ہونا **post**, etc., for which an incumbent is needed اسامی، خالی جگہ *vacancy caused by the death of* کی موت سے خالی ہونے والی جگہ *advertise a vacancy for* (a post, etc.) کی اسامی کے لیے اشتہار دینا

vacate (va-*kayt*) *v.t.* give up (house, seat, etc. *for* someone) خالی کرنا، چھوڑنا، چھوڑ دینا **vacation** (-*kay*-) *n.* vacating (*of*) خالی کرنا long recess in schools, colleges, universities and law-courts) تعطیلات *summer vacation* گرمیوں کی چھٹیاں، تعطیلات گرما (U.S.) any stretch of holidays چھٹیاں

vaccinate (*vak*-si-nayt) *v. t.* inoculate with vaccine to develop immunity from smallpox, etc. چیچک (وغیرہ) کا ٹیکہ لگانا **vaccinator** *n.* one who vaccinates ٹیکہ لگانے والا **vaccination** *n.* vaccinating چیچک (وغیرہ) کا ٹیکہ لگانا one dose of it چیچک (وغیرہ) کا ٹیکہ **vaccine** (*vak*-sin, or -seen) *n.* virus of cowpox چیچک کے ٹیکے کی دوا virus of other diseases similarly prepared ویکسین

vacillate (*vas*-i-layt) *v.t.* waver ڈگمگانا، جھولتے پھرنا hesitate (*between* different opinions, etc.) پس و پیش کرنا، مذبذب ہونا **vacillation** (-*lay*-) *n.* تذبذب، پس و پیش

vacuity (va-*kew*-i-ti) *n.* emptiness خالی ہونا empty space خلا mental emptiness ذہنی خلا lack of intelligence in looks, etc. احمقانہ انداز

vacuous (*vak*-ew-us) *adj.* unintelligent, blank (looks) احمقانہ unmeaning (remark) یونہی سا

vacuum (*vak*-yew-um) *n.* (pl. *vacuums*, or *vacuua*) empty space out of which even air has been pumped out خلا lacuna ; lack of some necessary thing خلا *talk in vacuum*, speak in absolute terms without taking the existing conditions into consideration خلا میں باتیں کرنا **vacuum-brake** *n.* train-brake worked by exhausting air خلا بریک **vacuum cleaner** *n.* broom sucking dust in to sweep it away گرد کش **vacuum flask** *n.* thermos flask تھرماس، خلا بوتل

vade-mecum (vay-di-*mee*-kum) *n.* handbook to which constant reference is made حوالہ کی کتاب، رفیق کتاب

vagabond (*vag*-a-bond) *adj.* tramp بے خانماں، مارا مارا پھرنے والا (of life, etc.) given to wandering بے گھر، بے دَر، مارا مارا پھرنے والا، آوارہ گرد، خانہ بدوش tramp آوارہ گرد، مارا مارا پھرنے والا **vagabondage, vagabondism** *n.* state of being a vagabond بے خانماں ہونا، آوارگی

A vagabond is a worthless, homeless person ; **vagrant** is a legal term for one who has no apparent means of support ; a **tramp** is one who goes from place to place ; a **wanderer,** without any bad sense attached to it, is one who travels from one place to another.

vagary (va-*gay*-ri) *n.* (pl. *vagaries*) whim, caprice من کی ترنگ (*pl.*) sudden changes (of fortune, weather, fashion, etc.) آئے دن کی تبدیلیاں

vagina (va-*gi*-na) *n.* sexual passage to the womb اندام نہانی leaf-base surrounding the stem غلاف

vagrant (*vayg*-rant) *adj.* roving (tribes, etc.) خانہ بدوش **vagrancy** (*vayg*-) *n.* being a vagrant خانہ بدوشی کی زندگی، آوارہ گردی

vague (vayg) *adj.* not distinct مبہم، غیر واضح *be vague about* (*something*) کے متعلق گول مول بات کہہ جانا (person, looks, etc.) of uncertain character مشتبہ، مشکوک **vaguely** *adv.* غیر واضح طور پر، مشکوک انداز سے **vagueness** *n.* being vague ابہام

vain (vayn) *adj.* useless بیکار unsuccessful (attempt, etc.) ناکام، لاحاصل too proud (*of* one's beauty, talent, wealth, etc.) (دولت، علم، عقل، حسن وغیرہ) کا گھمنڈ کرنے والا، خود بین، خود نما، خود پسند *in vain*, to no effect بیکار، لاحاصل **vainly** *adv.* غرور سے، فضول **vainglory** *n.* boastfulness شیخی، لاف زنی **vainglorious** *adj.* boastful شیخی خورا، لاف زن

vale (vayl) *n.* (poet.) valley وادی، گھاٹی

valediction (val-e-*dik*-shun) *n.* farewell الوداع **valedictory** (-dik-) *adj.* (of speech, etc.) bidding farewell الوداعی

valency (*vay*-lens-i), **valence** (*vay*-lens) *n.* (in chemistry) combining power of an atom or group of atoms in terms of hydrogen atoms or their equivalent گرفت
valentine (*val*-en-t.n) *n.* sweetheart chosen on St. Valentine's day یوم ویلنٹائن پر چنا ہوا محبوب ، ولنٹینی محبوب letter, verses, etc., sent to one's valentine محبوب کے نام رقعہ caricature, etc., sent on the occasion یوم ویلنٹائن پر بھیجی ہوئی مزاحیہ چیز
St. Valentine's Day *n.* February 14 as the day when one may make love to anyone (the custom originating in the belief that birds mate on that day of the year یوم ویلنٹائن ، ولنٹینی تہوار
valet (*val*-et, or *val*-ay) *n.* manservant looking after his master's clothes and other bodily needs خاص خدمتگار ، بیرا
valetudinarian *adj.* infirm دائم المرض ، کمزور too anxious about one's health اپنی صحت کی حد سے زیادہ فکر کرنے والا
valetudinarianism *n.* اپنی صحت کے متعلق ہر وقت کی تشویش
Valhalla (val-*hal*-a) *Norse myth.* banquet-hall of the chief god, Woden, where the heroes slain in battle lived and were feted
valiant (*val*-yant) *adj.* (lit.) brave دلیر ، بہادر ، شجاع
valiantly *adv.* بہادری سے **valour** *n.* (see below)
valid (*val*-id) *adj.* acceptable according to law قانونی sound (reasons, arguments, etc.) معقول ، قوی **validate** (*val*-) *v.t.* make valid قانونی شکل دینا **validity** (-*lid*-) *n.* being valid قانونی طور پر جائز ہونا ، معقول ہونا
valise (va-*lees*) *n.* small travelling-bag سفری بیگ ، سفری تھیلا

a valise

valley (*val*-i) *n.* low-lying land between hills often with a river, etc. flowing through it وادی ، گھاٹی ▣ A **valley** is a level country between hills ; a **hollow**, small depression in the landscape ; a **basin** is of a river and its tributaries ; **dale** is a poetic word ; a **glen** is a secluded, narrow valley between low hills.
valorize (*val*-o-riz) *v. t.* (of the government) stabilize or raise the value of (something) حکومت کا کسی شے کی قیمت برقرار رکھنے یا بڑھانے کے لیے اقدام ، کی قدر داری کرنا
valorization (-*zay*-) *n.* قدر داری
valour (*val*-*ĕ**) *n.* prowess in war بہادری ، مرد میدان ہونا
valorous *adj.* brave مرد میدان (Also see **valiant**)
value (*val*-yew) *n.* intrinsic worth قدر و قیمت (in economics) amount of labour, etc., that has gone into the production (*of* something) قدر *money value* (*of*) the price it will fetch دکا مول (usu. pl.) standard of conduct, art, etc. قدر ، (ج : اقدار) *v. t.* put a price on قیمت لگانا ، آنکنا esteem (something) highly کی قدر کرنا **valuable** *adj.* of much value قیمتی **valuables** *n. pl.* jewellery, gold plate, valuable clothes, etc. مال و دولت ، قیمتی چیزیں
valuation *n.* estimated price قیمت کا اندازہ evaluating کی قیمت کا اندازہ کرنا **valueless** *adj.* having almost no value جس کی کوئی قدر و قیمت نہ ہو ، بے وقعت
invaluable *adj.* extremely valuable انمول
valve (valv) *n.* arrangement for controlling the flow of fluids والو ، کھل منڈن (in U.S. called a *tube*), bulb-like apparatus for strengthening electro-magnetic waves والو ، مجسّر

a valve or tube

vamp *n.* upper leather of front of shoe جوتے کے پنجے کا بالائی چمڑا (colloq.) seductive woman who exploits men دلالہ ، عیار حسینہ *v.t.* & *i.* improvise (something) out of used material پرانے مال سے بنا لینا make (it) presentable by patching پیوند لگا کے کچھ شکل نکال لینا improvise accompaniment to music سنگت کے لیے ساز کا کچھ انتظام کرنا (colloq.) (of women) exploit (men) by alluring them دام حسن میں پھانس کر چھل دینا
vampire (*vam*-pi-ĕ*) *n.* ghost supposed to suck the blood of human beings in sleep سوتوں کا خون چوسنے والی بلا ، ویمپائر person preying on another ویمپائر (also *vampire bat*), a kind of bat which sucks blood ویمپائر ، خون آشام چمگادڑ
van *n.* covered (motor) vehicle for delivery of goods بند چھکڑا railway carriage for luggage or guard ریل میں مال یا گارڈ کا ڈبہ foremost part of army or fleet in battle ہراول ، مقدمہ leaders (of a movement) (تحریک) کا ہراول دستہ ، کی صف اول persons heading a procession جلوس کا ہراول دستہ **van-guard** *n.* guard marching in front (*of* army, fleet, procession, etc.) محافظ دستہ
Vandal (*vand*-al) *n.* ignorant wilful destroyer of beauty, art, etc. تہذیب سوز ، غارتگر حسن تہذیب **vandalism** تہذیب سوزی
vandyke (van-*dik*) *n.* & *adj.* a process of printing, much like off-set *vandyke brown*, deep rich brown چوبخ ، نسواری *vandyke beard*, pointed beard فرنچ کٹ (ڈاڑھی)
vanish (*van*-ish) *v.t.* disappear suddenly دفعۃً غائب ہو جانا fade away فضا میں تحلیل ہو جانا (of hopes, etc.) cease to exist ختم ہو جانا ، جاتا رہنا ، معدوم ہو جانا *vanishing cream*, face cream leaving no trace when rubbed well وینیشنگ کریم ، معلوم نہ ہونے والی کریم
vanity (*van*-i-ti) *n.* silly pride about one's beauty, talent, wealth, etc. جھوٹا ناز ، بیجا غرور

empty show جھوٹی شان unsubstantial thing مایا، سراب، غیر حقیقی شے، بے اصل بات *Vanity of vanities, all is 'vanity* مایا ہی مایا ہے سب کچھ مایا، دنیا ایک سراب ہے اور بس
vanquish (*vank*-wish) *v.t.* overcome (someone) پر غالب آنا، کو نیچا دکھانا **vanquished** *adj.* fallen (foe)
vapid (*vap*-id) *adj.* insipid پھیکا، بے لطف **vapidity** (*-pid-*) *n.* insipidity پھیکا پن، بے لطف ہونا
vaporize *v.t.* & *i.*, **vaporization** *n.* (see under **vapor**)
vapour (*vay*-pĕ*) *n.* liquid or solid substance changed into gas (بخار (ج: بخارات یا ابخرہ **vaporize** *vao*-po-riz) *v.t.* & *i.*, (cause to) become vapours بخارات بننا یا بنانا، تبخیر ہونا یا کرنا **vaporization** *n.* act of vaporizing تبخیر، عمل تبخیر
variable *adj.*, **variance** *n.*, **variation** *n.*, **varied** *adj.*, **variegated** *adj.*, **variety** *n.*, **various** *adj.* (see under **vary**)
varnish (*vah**-nish) *n.* (resinous liquid giving) a a shiny coating وارنش *v. t.* coat with varnish وارنش کرنا
varsity (*vah**-si-ti) *n.* (usu. *'varsity*) (colloq.) university یونیورسٹی، جامعہ
vary (*vay*-ri) *v. t.* & *i.* (*vary, varied ; varying*) change بدلنا یا بدلانا، مختلف ہونا (یا کرنا) differ اختلاف رکھنا **variable** *adj.* changeable تغیر پزیر inconstant متلون *n.* (in Maths) indeterminate quality which may be given any numerical متغیر
variability *n.* being variable تغیر پزیری، تلون
variance *n.* varying تغیر، تبدیلی difference of opinion اختلاف رائے difference فرق، اختلاف *be at variance with* سے مختلف ہونا *n.* & *adj.* alternative متبادل **variation** (vay-ri-*ay*-shun) *n.* change تبدیلی، تغیر degree of change فرق، تبدیلی
varied (*vay*-rid) *adj.* (of career, etc.) often changed کئی بار بدلا ہوا (of opinion, things, etc.) of different sorts قسم قسم کا، مختلف قسموں کا **variegated** (*vay*-ri-gay-ted) *adj.* having irregular patches of various colours بوقلموں **variety** (va-*ri*-ĕ-ti) *n.* (pl. *varieties*) diversity رنگارنگی something to relieve of monotony تبدیلی collection (*of* different goods, reasons, etc.) کئی، متعدد *variety show, variety entertainment*, songs, dances, skits, etc., arranged for one show رنگارنگ کھیل **various** (*vay*-ri-us) *adj.* different مختلف several متعدد
vase (vahz, or vayz) *n.* any ornamental jar منقش مرتبان such a jar used for holding flowers inside a building on mantelpiece or outside it on gate posts, etc. گلدان

a vase

vaseline (*vas*-ĕ-lin) *n.* an ointment and lubricant prepared from petroleum وسلین، ویزلین
vassal (*vas*-ĕl) *n.* holder of land in return for military help to his master منصبدار faithful servant وفادار خادم، حلقہ بگوش **vassalage** *n.* being a vassal اسامی ہونا، منصبداری
vast (vahst) *adj.* extensive بہت بڑا، وسیع
vat *n.* big vessel for holding liquids ناند (یا)، کڑھاؤ
vaudeville (*vohd*-vil) *n.* variety show رنگارنگ کھیل
vault (vawlt) *n.* series of arches forming a roof محراب دار چھت، قوسی چھت cellar (for storing valuables, wine, etc.) تہ خانہ burial cellar تابوت خانہ *v.t.* & *i.* leap over (or *over* **something**) with the hands resting on it پر ہاتھ رکھ کر کودنا *n.* leaping thus جست **pole-vault** *n.* vault over a pole with the hands resting on it بانس کی چھلانگ
vaulted *adj.* (of roof, etc.) having vaults قوسی، محراب دار **vaulting-horse** *n.* oblong wooden stool with padded top used for practice in vaulting کودنے کا گھوڑا، گھوڑا، گھوڑی

a vaulting-horse

vaunt (vawnt) *v.t.* boast, brag بڑ ہانکنا، ڈینگ کی لینا
veal (veel) *n.* calf-flesh as food بچھڑے کا گوشت
veer (*vee*-ĕ*) *v.t.*&*i.* (of wind or public opinion) change (*round to* some point) بدلنا، رخ بدل کر جانا let out (rope) رسی کو ڈھیلا کرنا
vegetable (*vej*-e-tab-ĕl) *n.* food plant سبزی، ترکاری *adj.* of or obtained from plants نباتی **vegetarian** (*-tay-*) *n.* one who does not eat meat گوشت سے پرہیز کرنے والا، نبات خور *adj.* comprising vegetables only نباتی **vegetate** *v.i.* grow as a plant اگنا rot ; have no chance to do the talented work one can پڑے سڑنا، بیکاری کے دن گزارنا، کچھ نہ کرنا **vegetation** (*-tay-*) *n.* plants in general نباتات plants of an area کے پھل پودے growing as plants روئیدگی، بالیدگی
vehement (*vee*-ĕ-ment) *adj.* vigorous شدید، قوی impassioned پرجوش **vehemence** (*vee*-i-mens) *n.* شدت، جوش، سختی
vehicle (*vee*-i-kĕl) *n.* any wheeled conveyance گاڑی medium of expression (*for* thoughts, feelings, etc.) ذریعۂ اظہار **vehicular** (vee-*ik*-ew-lĕ*) *adj.* of vehicles گاڑیوں کا *vehicular traffic*, vehicles on the move گاڑیاں
veil (vayl) *n.* covering for the face نقاب، برقع، پردہ *take the veil*, become a nun راہبہ بن جانا *under the veil of* کے پردے میں *v.t.* put a veil over نقاب اوڑھانا conceal (one's intentions, etc.) چھپانا
vein (vayn) *n.* tube in the body carrying

blood back to the heart line in a leaf line of different colour in a piece of stone دھاری thin layer of ore, etc., sandwiched between layers of rocks (چٹان میں) معدنی پَرت mood مزاج ، انداز

velocity (ve-*los*-i-ti) *n.* rate of motion in a given direction رَفتار *accelerated velocity* مُسرِع رَفتار *constant* (or *uniform*) *velocity* یکساں رَفتار *resultant velocity* مُنتَجِہ (یا مُتبدِّل) رَفتار *variable velocity* حاصِل رَفتار

velvet (*vel*-vet) *n.* silk cloth with a thick nap on one side مخمل *be on velvet*, be in an advantageous position کا ہاتھ اُوپر ہونا *adj.* made of (or soft like) velvet مخملی **velveteen** (*-teen-*) *n.* similar cotton cloth نقلی مخمل **velvety** *adj.* soft as velvet مخملی

venal (*vee*-nal) *adj.* who may be bought over to do wrong ضمیر فروش done for monetary gain only ضمیر فروشانہ

vend *v.t.* sell, carry on the sale of (goods) بیچنا ، فروخت کرنا **vendor** *n.* one who vends دُکاندار ، بیچنے والا **vendee** (ven-*dee*) *n.* customer ; one to whom things are sold گاہک ، خریدار

vendetta (ven-*det*-a) *n.* blood feud قتل پر خاندانوں کی لڑائیاں

veneer (ve-*nee*-è*) *n.* thin layer of fine quality wood glued to the surface of cheaper wood (in furniture, etc.) عمدہ لکڑی کی باریک پَرت mask (of politeness, etc.) نقاب ، پَرت ، آڑ *v.t.* put a veneer on ملمع چڑھانا ، آڑ لینا

venerable (*ven*-e-rab-èl) *adj.* highly respectable (owing to age or qualities) محترم ، مُقدّس **venerate** *v. t.* respect deeply بڑا احترام کرنا **veneration** *n.* deep respect احترام ، اجلال و احترام

vengeance (*venj*-ens) *n.* revenge انتقام ، بدلہ **vengeful** *adj*. vindictive کینہ جُو ، انتقام پرور

venial (*vee*-ni-al) *adj.* (of sin, crime or error) not serious, far from being unpardonable معمولی سا قابلِ مُعافی ، صغیرہ **veniality** (vee-ni-*al*-i-ti) *n.* triviality (*of* offence, etc.) قابلِ مُعافی ہونا ، معمولی سا ہونا

venison (*ven*-zèn) *n.* deer meat ہرن کا گوشت

venom (ven-) *n.* poison of snake سانپ کا زہر ، بس spite بُغض ، کینہ **venomous** *adj*. deadly مُہلک spiteful کینہ جُو ، کینہ پرور

vent *n.* small hole for passage of air روزن such passage for any other fluid موری *make a vent, find a vent* روزن (یا موری) میں سے نکلنا outlet for pent-up feeling *give vent to (one's anger, etc.)* express (it) ذریعۂ اظہار کا اظہار کرنا *find vent*, be uttered کا اظہار ہونا *v.t.* provide an outlet for زبان پر آنا

ventilate (*vent*-i-layt) *v.t.* make arrangements for the supply of fresh air ہوادار بنانا bring (issue, etc.) before the public (مسئلہ) عوام کے سامنے لانا **ventilation** *n.* ہوادار بنانا **ventilator** (*vent-*) *n.* outlet for used air روشندان

ventriloquism (ven-*tril*-o-kwizm) *n.* art of producing voice sounds which deceive the hearers about their source or origin طرح طرح کی آوازیں نکالنا ، انتقالِ صوت **ventriloquist** *n.* one skilled in ventriloquism طرح طرح کی آوازیں نکالنے والا

venture (*vench*-è*) *n.* risky undertaking جوکھوں کا کام *at a venture*, at random یونہی ، علی التّخت *v.t.* & *i.* risk danger or loss جان جوکھوں میں ڈالنا ، خطرناک کام کا بیڑا اُٹھانا take the courage (*to do*) کی جُرأت کرنا put forward (suggestion, opinion, etc.) پیش کرنا **venturesome** (*vench*-è*-sum) *adj.* daredevil بےخطرے خطرناک مُعاملہ ، جان جوکھوں کا کام risky (act) میں کُود جانے والا

venue (*ven*-ew) *n.* rendezvous, place (*of* the meeting) مقام ، مُلاقات کا مقام place of occurrence (*of* a crime, etc.) جائے وُقوعہ ، مَوقع

Venus (*vee*-nus) *Cl. myth.* the Roman goddess of love and beauty (identified with the Greek goddess *Aphrodite*) وینس ، زُہرہ the evening star زُہرہ sexual love personified جِنسی مَحبّت ، افرودائتی sexual desire جنسی خواہش sexual influences

veracious (ve-*rash*-us) *adj.* truthful سچا ، راستباز true (statement, etc.) سچا ، صحیح **veracity** (ve-*ras*-i-ti) *n.* راستبازی ، صداقت **veranda, verandah** (ve-*rand*-a) *n.* floored portico along the sides of a building برآمدہ

verb (vè*b) *n.* part of speech expressing state or action فعل **verbal** (vě*-bal) *adj.* pertaining to words لفظ بہ لفظ ، لفظی oral زبانی verbatim pertaining to verbs فعلی **verbally** (vě*-ba-li) orally زبانی **verbatim** (vě*-*bay*-tim) *adj.* & *adv.* (of report, etc.) word for word لفظ بہ لفظ (of translation) literal لفظی ، تحت اللفظ **verbiage** (vě*-bi-aj) *n.* pompous array of words لفاظی **verbose** (vě*-*bohs*) *adj.* wordy لفاظی والا **verbosity** (vě*-*bos*-i-ti) *n.* لفاظی

verdant (vě*-dant) *adj.* fresh and green (vegetation, etc.) ہرا بھرا (of landscape, etc.) covered with it سرسبز **verdancy** *n.* being fresh and green ہرا بھرا ہونا ، شادابی ، تر و تازگی **verdure** (vě*d-yè*) *n.* being verdant ہرا بھرا ہونا ، تازگی ، طراوت ، شادابی verdant growth سبزہ ، ہریالی

verdict (vè*-dikt) *n.* decision of jury جیوری کا فیصلہ ، ارکانِ جیوری کی رائے *The jury brought in a verdict of 'not guilty'.* جیوری نے بریّت کا فیصلہ دیا ، ارکانِ جیوری کی رائے میں مُلزم ملزموں کی بے گناہی عیاں تھی opinion (of someone on something) given

after a test فیصلہ
verge (ve*j) *n.* brink *be on the verge of* (disaster, etc.) کے قریب ہونا *be on the verge of (doing something)* کرنے ہی کو ہونا *v. i.* incline (*towards*) (کی طرف) مائل ہونا یا جھک رہا ہونا (*verge upon*), be on the verge of کے قریب ہونا
veridical (ve-*rid*-i-kĕl) *adj.* veracious سچا (of something supernatural, etc.) coinciding with reality حقیقت سے ہم آہنگ، حقیقت آسا
verifiable *adj.*, **verification** *n.* (see under **verify**)
verify (*ve*-ri-fi) *v.t.* check up or establish the truth of کی تصدیق کرنا **verifiable** (ve-ri-*fi*-a-bĕl) *adj.* قابل تصدیق **verification** (ve-ri-fi-*kay*-shun) *n.* act of verifying or being verified تصدیق **verily** (*ve*-ri-li) *adv.* (old use) really سچ، واقعی **verisimilitude** (ve-ri-si-*mil*-i-tewd) *n.* air of being true سچ لگنا، حقیقت آسا ہونا **verity** (*ve*-ri-ti) *n.* reality حقیقت true statement سچی بات truth (*of*) (کا) سچ **veritable** (ve-ri-*tab*-ĕl) *adj.* real اصلی in fact, rightly named اسم بامسمّیٰ
verily *adv.*, **verisimilitude** *n.*, **veritable** *adj.*, **verity** *n.* (see under **verify**)
vermicelli (vĕ*-mi-*chel*-i, or vĕ*-mi-*sel*-i) wheat paste made into threads for cooking سِوَیّاں
vermicide (*vĕ**-mi-sid) *n.* drug for killing worms کیڑے مار دوا، کرم کش
vermilion (vĕ*-*mil*-yĕn) *n.* & *adj.* bright red colour obtained from *cinnabar* (which see) شنگرفی رنگ
vermin (*vĕ**-min) *n.* (collective ; usu. with *pl.* verb) small animals (like rats) or insects (like fleas) that are pests چھوٹے ضرر رساں جانور یا کیڑے مکوڑے **verminous** *adj.* caused by or infested with vermin کیڑوں بھرا، کیڑوں کا پیدا کیا ہوا
vernacular (vĕ*nak-ew-lĕ*) *adj.* of the home-born slave خانہ زاد کا (of a language) of one's own country ملکی، مقامی (of a word) of dialect کھڑی بولی کا *n.* language (*of* a country) ملکی زبان dialect بولی
vernal (*vĕ**-nĕl) *n. adj.* of or as in spring بہار کا، بہار سا
vernier (*vĕ**-ni-ĕ*) *n.* small sliding scale used for obtaining fractions of the sub-divisions of the original scale متحرک پیمانہ
veronal (*ve*-ro-nĕl) *n.* sleep-inducing drug خواب آور دوا
versatile (*vĕ**-sa-til) *adj.* (of mind, genius, etc.) clever at many things ہمہ گیر **versatility** (-*til*-) *n.* ذہنی ہمہ گیری، ذہن و دماغ وغیرہ کی ہمہ گیری
verse (vĕ*s) *n.* poetical form نظم، منظوم چیز، موزوں کلام piece of poetry نظم، نظم کا ایک حصہ one line of verse مصرع، مصرعہ a numbered sentence, etc., of the Scriptures آیت **versification** (-*kay*-) *n.* making of verses نظم کرنا being in verse-form نظم کی صورت **versed** (ve*sd) *adj.* (also *well-versed*) experienced (*in* something).; with masterly knowledge (*in* some subject) (کا) ماہر
version (*vĕ**-shun) *n.* translation ترجمہ *Authorized Version*, (abbr. *A.V.*), the English translation of *the Bible* completed in 1611 بائبل کا مستند ترجمہ recension قرأت یا قراءت (*one's*) account (*of* an event, etc.) روایت، بیان *What is your version of the event* آپ کے خیال میں یہ واقعہ کیونکر ہوا
vers libre (vay-ĕ*-*leeb*-rĕ) *n.* verse in varied rhythm آزاد نظم، نظم آزاد **verslibrist** (vay-ĕ*-*leeb*-rist) *n.* آزاد نظم لکھنے والا
versus (*vĕ**-sus) *prep.* (abbr. *v.*, or *vs.*) (in a law-case) against بنام (in games) opposed by اور، کا جوڑ، کے مقابلے میں
vertebra (*vĕ**-*teb*-ra) *n.* single segment of the spine فقرہ **vertebrate** *n.* & *adj.* (animal, bird, etc.) having a spine ریڑھ کی ہڈی والا، ذوالفقرات، ذوالفقار
vertex (*vĕ**-teks) (pl. *vertices*, or *vertexes*) highest point (of triangle, cone, etc.) راس
vertical (*vĕ**-ti-kel) *adj.* upright عمودی
vertigo (*vĕ**-ti-goh) *n.* dizziness چکّر
verve (ve*v) *n.* enthusiasm and spirit (*in* writing, arts, etc.) زور، جوش
very (*ve*-ri) (*very, verier, veriest*) *adv.* in a high degree بہت، بڑے *adj.* absolute, complete نرا، بالکل mere ہی same وہی، بالکل وہی
Very light (*ve*-ri-lit) *n.* small coloured flare fired from a pistol for signalling (named after its inventor Samuel Very) شیخ ویری، ویری
vesper (*ves*-pĕ*) *n.* (*Vesper*), the evening star; Venus ستارۂ شام (*pl.*) evening service in the church گرجے میں شام کی نماز (*pl.*) evening song شام کا گیت
vessel (*ves*-ĕl) *n.* container for liquids برتن، ظروف vein رگ tube, etc. نلی، نالی **ship** جہاز (divine, etc.), instrument مظہر، پیکر
vest *n.* undergarment for the upper part of the body بنیان (U.S.) waistcoat واسکٹ، صدری **vest-pocket** *n.* pocket of waistcoat واسکٹ کی جیب *adj.* so small as may be carried in the vest-pocket واسکٹ کی جیب میں آنے والا
Vesta (*ves*-ta) *Cl. myth.* Roman goddess of hearth and home whose priestesses took the oath of virginity and had to keep the sacred fire burning وستا، وِستا (*vesta*), a kind of match مومی دیا سلائی **vestal** *adj.* vowed to chastity پاکدامن

virgin کنواری old maid کنواری بڑھیا

vestige (*ves*-tij) *n.* trace (*of* something) (کا) نام و نشان

vet *n.* (colloq.) veterinary surgeon سلوتری *v.t.* (-tt-) (colloq.) examine (someone) medically (کا) ڈاکٹری معائنہ کرنا scrutinise and correct (piece of writing, report, etc.) کو ٹھیک کرنا، پر نظرِ ثانی کرنا

veteran (*vet*-è-ran) *n.* & *adj* very experienced (soldier, etc.) بڑا تجربہ کار

veterinary (*vet*-è-ri-na-ri) *adj.* pertaining to the diseases of animals بیطاری *n* veterinary surgeon سلوتری، بیطار

veto (*vee*-toh) *n.* (pl. *vetoes*) right to reject or prohibit حقِ استرداد statement comprising it استرداد *put* (or *exercise*) *a veto on* (*something*), *put* (*one's*) *veto on* (*something*), (کے بارے میں حقِ استرداد استعمال کرنا *v.t.* (*veto, vetoed, vetoed*) use a veto against کے بارے میں حقِ استرداد استعمال کرنا

vex (veks) *v.t.* irritate, annoy تنگ کرنا، پریشان کرنا، دِق کرنا *How vexing!* پریشان کن بات ہے agitate about کے بارے میں ہلچل مچانا *vexed question*, (esp. political) issue brewing public unrest ہنگامہ خیز مسئلہ، ہلچل پیدا کرنے والا معاملہ **vexation** (-*say*-) *n.* پریشانی، تشویش انگیز معاملہ، تشویش **vexatious** (vek-*say*-shus) *adj.* annoying پریشان کن بات، پریشان کن، تکلیف دِہ (of law-suit) initiated for harassment پریشان کن

via (*vi*-a, or *vee*-a) *prep.* by way of براہ، کے راستے میں *via* **media** (*vi*-a-*mee*-di-a) *n.* middle course (*between* extremes) درمیانی راہ

viable (*vi*-a-bèl) *adj.* capable of existing زندہ رہ سکنے والا، قائم رہ سکنے والا capable of developing نشوونما پا سکنے والا، ترقی کر سکنے والا

viaduct (*vi*-a-dukt) *n.* arched bridge for rail or road across low ground نشیب کا پُل

vial (*vi*-al) *n.* small bottle شیشی

viands (*vi*-andz) *n. pl.* (lit.) excellent food with a variety شاندار کھانے

vibrate (vi-*brayt*) *v.t.* & *i.* (of structure, strings, voice, etc.) quiver مرتعش ہونا cause to quiver میں ارتعاش پیدا کرنا، کو مرتعش کرنا

vibrant (*vib*-rant) *adj.* vibrating مرتعش resonant (*with*) سے گونجنے والا thrilling (*with joy*, etc.) (جس میں خوشی وغیرہ کی) لہر دوڑ رہی ہو **vibration** (-*ray*-) *n.* ارتعاش **vibrator** *n.* vibrating part مرتعش **vibratory** *n.* of or pertaining to vibration ارتعاشی

vicar (*vik*-ĕ*) *n.* parish clergyman not in receipt of tithes وِکر **vicarage** *n.* vicar's official residence وِکر گاہ vicar's office وِکر کا عہدہ **vicarious** (vi-*kay*-ri-us) *adj.* done or deputed as substitute for someone نیابتی (of pleasure, suffering, etc.) felt in place of another بالواسطہ، نیابتی

[1]**vice** (vis) *n.* sin, immorality گناہ very bad habit بری عادت، خدا کی مار، خدا کی سنوار، مار bench-clamp شکنجہ، اڈے پر لگا ہوا شکنجہ *as firm as a vice*, firmly fixed مضبوط لگا ہوا **vicious** (*vish*-us) *adj.* wicked (person, life, etc.) آوارہ، برا faulty, unsound غلط، ناقص spiteful نفرت بھرا، کینہ پرور kicking (horse) دولتیاں جھاڑنے والا **vicious circle** *n.* fallacy of proving something from that which depends on it for its own proof دور، استدلالِ دوری pair (or series) of (usu. bad) things that intensify each other by reaction چکر، بندھا ہوا چکر، برائی کا چکر

a vice (sense 3)

[2]*vice* (vis) *prep.* in succession to; in place of. کی جگہ، کی بجائے، کے بجائے

[3]**vice-** (vis) *pref.* officiating for برائے deputy نائب، وائس *Vice-Principal* وائس پرنسپل، نائب صدر مدرس *Vice-Admiral* نائب امیر البحر *Vice-Chairman* نائب صدر *Vice-Consul* نائب قنصل *Vice-Chancellor*, resident administrative head of a university وائس چانسلر، نائب شیخ الجامعہ *vice-regent*, deputy to the regent بادشاہ کے قائم مقام کا نائب

viceroy (*vis*-roi) *n.* British sovereign's representative governing a colony, etc. وائسرائے، نائب شاہ **vicerein** (*vis*-rayn) *n.* viceroy's wife وائسرائے کی بیگم **viceregal** (-*ree*-) *adj.* of a viceroy وائسرائے کا **viceroyalty** (-vis-) *n.* office of a viceroy نائب شاہ کا منصب

vicegerent (vis-*je*-rent) *n.* holder of delegated power خلیفہ، نائب *God's vicegerent* خلیفۃ اللہ

vice versa (*vi*-sè-*vĕ*-sa) *adv.* the other way round اور یونہی اس کے برعکس

vicinity (vi-*sin*-i-ti) *n.* neighbourhood (*of*) گرد و نواح، قرب و جوار، نواح

vicious *adj.* (see under [1]vice)

vicissitude (vi-*sis*-i-tewd) *n.* (usu. *pl.*) change; تغیر، ups and downs (*of* life, etc.) نشیب و فراز

victim *n.* animal (to be) sacrificed in religious ceremony قربانی کا جانور، بَلی casualty حادثے میں مرنے یا زخمی ہونے والا one who suffers because (*of* someone's cruelty, own folly, circumstances, etc.) (کا) تختۂ مشق، (کا) نشانہ بننے والا، (کا) ہدف بننے والا، (کا) ستم رسیدہ one who is duped پھنسنے والا، شکار **victimize** *v.t.* persecute ایذائیں پہنچانا، تختۂ مشقِ ستم بنانا cheat پھانسی دینا dismiss or punish (someone, usu. the ringleader) for fomenting trouble کے خلاف انتقامی کارروائی کرنا، برخاست کرنا **victimization** *n.* انتقامی کارروائی، ظلم و ستم، برخاستگی

victor (*vik*-tĕ*) *n.* conqueror فاتح winner جیتنے والا **victory** (*vik*-tè-ri) *n.* success (in battle, game, etc.) فتح، جیت **victorious** (vik-*to*-ri-us) *adj.* having gained victory فاتح، جیتنے والا **Victoria Cross** *n.* highest British military award for bravery وکٹوریا کراس، صلیبِ وکٹوریا

victual (*vit*-ĕl) *n.* (usu. *pl.*) provisions کھانے پینے کا سامان *v.t.* & *i.* supply or stock with victuals کھانے پینے کا سامان بہم پہنچانا یا بھر لینا

vicuna (vi-*koo*-na), **vicugna** (vi-*koon* ya) *n.* an American animal valued for its silky wool ویکونا (also *vicuna cloth*), cloth (like the one) made from its wool ویکونا

vide (*vid*-è) *v.* (abbr. *v.*) see (certain page of book, etc.) دیکھیے (صفحہ فلاں وغیرہ)، د ک۔ یہاں (اٹھوع گنبد بہ آں)

vidilicet (vi-*dee*-li-set, but usu. pr. *naym*-li) *adv.* (abbr. *viz.*) (usu. spoken as) *namely* یعنی **vide supra** *v.* see above ملاحظہ ہو اوپر **vide infra** *v.* see below ملاحظہ ہو نیچے

video- *pref.* (see *Addenda*)

videocast *n.* (see *Addenda*)

vie (vi) *v.i.* (*vie, vied, vied ; vying*) compete (*with* someone *for* something) مقابلہ کرنا

view (vew) *n.* sight (*of*) منظر، نظارہ that which is seen منظر، نظارہ opinion خیال، رائے **point of view** نقطۂ نگاہ، نقطۂ نظر، زاویۂ نگاہ، زاویۂ نظر intention ارادہ wish مرضی landscape منظر، نظارہ *be in view* نظر آنے لگنا *come into view* نظر آنا، دکھائی دینا *be on view*, be exhibited کو نمائش میں رکھنا، کی نمائش ہونا *take a light view of* کو معمولی سمجھنا، سے درگزر کرنا *take a serious view of* کو معمولی نہ سمجھنا، سے درگزر نہ کرنا *in view of* (something) کے پیشِ نظر *with a view to* (doing something) کے خیال سے، کرنے *fall in with* (someone's) *views*, *meet* (*someone's*) *views* کی بات مان جانا، کی خوشی کرنا *a house with a view* بڑے اچھے منظر والا گھر *v.t.* see دیکھنا، پر نظر ڈالنا consider پر غور کرنا **viewer** (*vew*-ĕ*) *n.* (also *televiewer*), (esp.) one who uses a T.V. receiving set ٹیلی وِژن دیکھنے والا، دُور ناظر **viewpoint** *n.* point of view نقطۂ نگاہ، نقطۂ نظر، زاویۂ نگاہ، زاویۂ نظر **viewy** (*vew*-i) *adj.* (colloq.) having some fad جس کے سر پر کسی شے کی دُھن سوار ہو، خبطی، سرپھرا **viewless** *adj.* (poet.) invisible نظر نہ آنے والا، جنبر مرئی

vigil (*vij*-il) *n* staying awake to pray شب بیداری doing so to keep watch (رات کو) پہرہ دینا **vigilance** *n.* keeping watch پہرہ watchfulness چوکسی *vigilance committee*, self-organized body for maintaining order in trouble spots or troublous times امن کمیٹی، محلہ کمیٹی **vigilant** *adj.* watchful چوکنا، چوکس

vigilante (vij-i-*lant*-i) *n.* member of a vigilance committee محلہ کمیٹی کا رُکن

vignette (veen-*yet*) *n.* portrait, design, picture, etc., with background shaded off and without a border نیم تصویر تلمی چہرہ

vigour (*vig*-ĕ*) *n.* strength قوت، طاقت، کس بل، دم خم energy جان force (of style, etc.) زور، جوش **vigorous** *adj.* forceful, vehement طاقتور، جان دار چاق چوبند، زوردار، جاندار ▣ **Vigour** is the naturally available muscular energy of living objects, or the force of style, **strength**, of a person or thing ; **activity**, fondness for purposeful movements , **intensity**, of an emotion **virility**, manhood ; **stamina**, innate endurance

vile (vil) *adj.* shameful (habit, etc.) شرمناک (colloq.) bad (weather, etc.) خراب، گندا **vilify** (*vil*-i-fi) *v.t.* slander (someone) کو بدنام کرتے پھرنا **vilification** (vil-i-fi-*kay*-shun) *n.* slandering بدنام کرنا، رُسوا کرنا

villa (*vil*-a) *n.* big country bungalow with its own garden, etc. کوٹھی

village (*vil*-ej) *n.* group of houses, etc., far smaller than a town گاؤں، دیہہ، دیہات *adj.* of village دیہاتی، گنوار **villager** (*vil*-i-jĕ*) *n.* rustic دیہاتی، دیہی

Village-AID *n.*, **V -AID** *n.* village *a*gricultural and *i*ndustrial *d*evelopment ; (name of the new fangled Pakistan Department which has been rechristened *B.N.R.* or the *Bureau of National Reconstruction* قومی تعمیر کا شعبہ، ترقیِ دیہات، دیہی امداد

villain (vil-en) *n.* wicked man بدمعاش one who wrongs the hero (in a play) ولن *villain of piece* ڈرامے کا ولین، اس معاملے میں خرابی برپا کرنے والا

villainous *adj.* evil بہت بُرا **villainy** *n.* (*vil*-è-ni) (*vil*-è-nus) evil conduct بُرائی

villein (*vil*-in) *n.* feudal tenant holding by menial service کمیرا، کمین (rarely) villain ولن

vim *n.* (colloq.) energy ہمت، کس بل، دم خم

vindicate (*vind*-i-kayt) *v.t.* disprove the allegations against کی برائت کرنا، کو بیگناہ ثابت کرنا **vindication** (*-kay-*) *n.* بیگناہی کا ثبوت، برائت

vindictive (vin-*dik*-tiv) *adj.* evincing a desire for revenge کینہ جو، کینہ پرور، انتقام پرور

vine (vin) *n.* climbing plant bearing grapes انگور کی بیل، تاک، رز **vineyard** *n.* area planted with it انگور کا باغ، تاکستان **vinery** (*vin*-ri) *n.* hothouse for vine تاک خانہ **vinegar** (*vin*-e-gĕ*) *n.* a sour liquid for pickling, etc سرکہ **vintage** (*vin*-tij) *n.* grape harvest (of any one season) انگور کی فصل wine from one season's harvest کسی فصل کی شراب **vintner** (*vint*-nĕ*) *n.* (old use) wine-seller شراب فروش

violate (*vī*-o-layt) *v.t.* break (the law, oath, pact, etc.) کی خلاف ورزی کرنا desecrate کی بے ادبی کرنا، کی بے حرمتی کرنا break in upon (someone's privacy) (کی تنہائی وغیرہ میں) مخل ہونا (also *violate the chastity of*), rape کی عصمت دری کرنا **violation** (*-lay-*) *n.* act of violating or being violated خلاف ورزی، بے حرمتی، خلل اندازی، عصمت دری **violable** *adj.* (of pact, etc.) which can be cancelled قابل تنسیخ

violent (*vī*-o-lent) *adj.* severe شدید، سخت vehement (passions, etc.) پرجوش، بے قابو marked by violence تشدد آمیز **violently** *adv.* سختی، شدید، بے قابو ہو کر، شدت، سختی تشدد سے **violence** *n.* being violent violent conduct تشدد *an outbreak of violence* عام دنگا فساد

violet (*vī*-o-let) *n.* a fragrant, bluish-purple flower بنفشہ its colour بنفشی (یا بنفشئی) *adj.* of this colour بنفشی *ultra-violet rays*, invisible rays of the spectrum beyond its violet end ماورائے بنفشی شعاعیں

violin (*vī*-o-*lin*, or *vī*-o-lin) *n.* fiddle وائلن، ولایتی سارنگی، چوتارہ **viol** (*vī*-ol) *n.* old form of violin سارنگی **viola** (*vī*-o-la) *n.* large violin بڑی وائلن **violinist** (*-lin-*) *n.* player of iolin وائلن نواز **violincello** (vī-o-lin-*chel*-oh) (or *cello*) *n.* a large-sized violin چیلو

a violin

viper (*vī-pě**) *n.* small kinds of very poisonous snake treacherous person مار آستین، غدار malignant person بدطینت

virago (vi-*ray*-goh) *n.* (pl. *viragos*), fierce and abusive woman لڑاکا عورت

virgin (*vě**-jin) *n.* chaste maiden کنواری دوشیزہ *adj.* pure and untouched (snow, etc.) صاف، پاکیزہ (of soil) never tilled so far جو کبھی زیر کاشت نہ آئی ہو unused غیر مستعمل **virginity** (*-jin-*) *n.* modesty پاکدامنی، عصمت، عفت being absolutely new or untouched پاکیزگی

Virginia (vě*-*jin*-i-a) *n.* tobacco from Virginia ورجینیا تمباکو

virginibus puerisque (vě*-*jin*-i-bus-pew-è-*risk*-è) *adj.* (suitable for or addressed to) girls and boys لڑکیوں اور لڑکوں کے لیے، بچوں بچیوں کے لیے

virile (*vi*-ril, or *vī*-è-ril) *adj.* (of person) with masculine sexual power قوت مردمی والا، مرد manly (person) بہادر، مردانگی والا vigorous (style) زوردار

virility *n.* quality of being virile قوت مردمی، مردانگی، بہادری، زور، جوش

virtu (*vě**-tew, or vě*-*too*) taste for fine arts فنون لطیفہ کا ذوق artistic quality حسن curio نادر شئے **virtuoso** (vě*-tew-*oh*-soh) *adj.* (pl. *virtuosi*; pr. -see) art connoisseur باذوق، صاحب ذوق one skilled in its mechanical side ماہر فن accomplished performer of music شاندار موسیقار **virtuosity** (vě*-tew-*os*-i-ti) *n.* extraordinary technical skill in one of the fine arts صاحب ذوق ہونا، فن سے واقف ہونا، شاندار موسیقار ہونا، فنون لطیفہ میں سے کسی میں غیر معمولی مہارت، شاندار فنکاری

virtual (*vě**-tew-al) *adj.* in fact though not in name عملی، درحقیقت **virtually** *adv.* عملاً، درحقیقت

virtue (*vě**-tew) *n.* moral excellence پارسائی goodness نیکی، خیر پاکدامنی *by virtue of*, owing to کی وجہ سے *in virtue of*, exercizing کو بروئے کار لاتے ہوئے، کو استعمال کرتے ہوئے **virtuous** (*vě**-tew-us) *adj.* chaste (woman) باعصمت (خاتون) good (person) نیک **virtuously** *adv.* نیکی سے، پارسائی سے

virtuosity *n.*, **virtuoso** *adj.* (see under **virtu**)

virulent (*vi*-roo-lent) *adj.* deadly (poison) مہلک (زہر)، (مرض) قاتل poisonous (disease, etc.) زہریلا bitter (hatred, words, etc.) سخت زہرناک **virulence** *n.* ہلاکت آفرینی، سختی، زہرناکی **virus** (*vī*-è-rus) *n.* poison of a contagious disease (کسی) متعدی مرض کا زہر bitter hatred سخت منافرت poisonous effect (*of* something) on morals, etc. (کا) زہریلا اثر

visa (*vee*-zah), **vise** (*vee*-zay) *n.* endorsement on passport by the officials of the country which it is intended to visit or leave ویزا، راہداری پر غیر ملکی تصدیق *v.t.* put a visa on ویزا دینا

visage (*viz*-ij) *n.* (lit.) face چہرہ **visard** *n.* (same as **visor,** which see)

vis-a-vis (vee-za-*vee*) *adv.* facing (one another) آمنے سامنے *prep.* about, concerning کی بابت، کے متعلق، کے بارے میں

viscid (*vis*-id), **viscous** (*vis*-kus) *adj.* sticky; semi-fluid (like treacle) لیس دار، نیم سیال **viscosity** (vis-*kos*-i-ti) *n.* being viscous نیم سیال ہونا، لیس دار ہونا، پیچپچاہٹ **viscose** (*vis*-kohs) *n.* celluloid in a fluid state ready for the manufacture of rayon, etc. وسکوس، سیال، سیلولائیڈ

viscount (*vī*-kount) *n.* British nobleman above a baron and below an earl in rank وائی کاؤنٹ a kind of jet aircraft وائکونٹ

visible (*viz*-i-bel) *adj.* that which can be seen جو آنکھوں کے سامنے ہو، جو دیکھا جا سکے، مرئی *be visible, be in sight* دکھائی دینا **visibility** (*-bil-*) *n.* being visible مرئی ہونا clearness of atmosphere for this purpose صفائی its range جہاں تک دکھائی دے سکے دکھائی دینا، ہوا کا صاف ہونا

vision (*vizh*-èn) *n.* something seen in a dream خواب something seen in imagination تصور، خواب power of imagining تصور (always used without any article) political foresight or sagacity سیاسی دُور اندیشی (یا) سیاسی فراست (always used without any article) imaginative insight دُور بیں فراست

visionary (*vizh*-è-nè-ri) *adj.* imaginary خیالی unrealistic (person, scheme, etc.) ناقابلِ عمل بات *n.* visionary person خیال پرست کرنے والا

visit (*viz*-it) *v.t.* & *i.* go to (a place) for a short while جانا call on (someone) سے مُلاقات کرآنا (یا جانا) (old use) punish (someone *for* a sin) سزا کے طور پر نازل ہونا *n.* visiting مُلاقات *pay a visit (to someone), pay (someone) a visit* کی مُلاقات کو آنا (یا جانا) period of visiting مُلاقات وغیرہ کا عرصہ، دیر *on a short visit* تھوڑی دیر کا چکر **visitor** *n.* caller مُلاقاتی one who visits a place کسی جگہ آنے والا **visitation** (viz-i-*tay*-shun) *n.* divine punishment for sins عذاب، شامتِ اعمال

visor, vizor (*vi*-zē*), **visard, vizard** (*vi*-zah*d) *n.* movable face-piece of a helmet مِغفر

a helmet with a visor (×)

vista (vis-ta) *n.* view through long, narrow rows of trees تنگ و دراز منظر، درختوں کی تنگ دو رویہ قطاروں سے منظر a continuous view مسلسل منظر series of future or past events viewed thus ماضی یا مستقبل کا سلسلۂ واقعات

visual (*viz*-ew-al) *adj.* pertaining to sight مرئی *visual aids in teaching*, maps, charts, diagrams, films, etc., used for teaching purposes تعلیم کے مرئی وسائل **visualize** *v.t.* picture (something) mentally کی ذہن میں تصویر لانا **visualization** *n.* mental picture (*of* details, thing, etc.) ذہنی نقشہ

vital (*vi*-tèl) *adj.* of life زندگی کا affecting life زندگی پر اثر انداز ہونے والا *vital parts*, organs injury to which may affect the whole life اعضائے رئیسہ fatal (wound, etc.) مُہلک supreme (importance, etc.) بے حد *n.* (*pl.*) (*the vitals*) vital organs اعضائے رئیسہ the very life (*of*) جان، زندگی **vitality** (vi-*tal*-i-ti, or vi-) *n.* vital power قوّتِ حیات virility قوّتِ مردمی endurance حوصلہ، برداشت energy ہمّت، طاقت، کس بل، دم خم **vitalize** (*vi*-ta-liz) *v.t.* energize میں جان ڈالنا

vitamin (*vit*-a-min) *n.* sorts of healthgiving substance present in foodstuffs or administered medically حیاتین، وٹامن *Vitamin* A^1, B^2,...*C*,*D* حیاتین الف، ب، بٓ، ... ج، د

vitiate (*vish*-i-ayt) *v.t.* impair the quality of کو خراب کر دینا make ineffective بے اثر بنا دینا

vitriol (*vit*-ri-ol) *n.* sulphuric acid گندھک کا تیزاب any of its salts گندھک کے تیزاب کا کوئی نمک **vitriolic** (-*ol*-) *adj.* concerning sulphuric acid گندھک کے تیزاب کا (یا والا) trenchant دِل پاش پاش کرنے والا

vituperate (vi-*tew*-pè-rayt) *v.t.* revile, abuse گالیاں دینا **vituperation** (-*ray*-) *n.* abusive words گالیاں، سب و شتم **vituperative** *adj.* full of abusive words

vivacious (vi-*vaysh*-us) *adj.* lively زندہ دِل **vivacity** (vi-*vas*-i-ti) *n.* زندہ دِلی

viva (*vee*-va) *int.* long live زندہ باد

viva voce (*vi*-va-*voh*-se) *adj.* oral زبانی orally زبانی *n.* oral examination ; interview as a part of the examination زبانی امتحان، انٹرویو

vivid (*viv*-id) *adj.* clear (description) صاف، واضح intense (colour) گہرا، تیز bright (light) تیز vigorous (imagination) قوی، زوردار **vividly** *adv.* clearly صاف، وضاحت سے

vivisect (*viv*-i-sekt) *v.t.* dissect living animal زندہ جانور کی چیر پھاڑ کرنا **vivisection** (-*sek*-) *n.* such dissection زندہ جانور کی چیر پھاڑ

vixen (*vik*-sen) *n.* female fox لومڑی spiteful woman کینہ پرور عورت

viz. (*naym*-li, or viz) (abb. of *videlicit*) namely یعنی

vizard *n.* **vizor** *n* (same as **visor,** which see)

vocabulary (vo-*kab*-ew-la-ri) *n.* list of terms or difficult words of a book appended to it (with explanations) فرہنگ، فہرستِ الفاظ words known to ذخیرۂ الفاظ terms, etc., used in a profession (کسی پیشے کی) اصطلاحات range of such words (*of*) کا ذخیرۂ الفاظ *have a good vocabulary* کا ذخیرۂ الفاظ کافی بڑا ہونا *build up (one's) vocabulary* اپنا ذخیرۂ الفاظ بڑھانا

vocal (*voh*-kel) *adj.* pertaining to voice نطقی، صوتی *vocal cords, vocal chords*, voice-producing part of the throat صوتی اوتار، اوتارِ صوت **vocalist** *n.* singer گویّا، مُغنّی *the vocal organs* صوتی اعضا *vocal music*, music sung گانا، غنائی موسیقی

vocation (vo-*kay*-shun) *n.* trade پیشہ *adj.* professional پیشہ ورانہ *vocational guidance*, expert advice on the choice of a profession پیشے کے انتخاب کے متعلق ماہرانہ مشورہ

vocative (*vok*-a-tiv) *adj.* & *n.* (case) of addressing حالتِ ندا، مُنادیٰ

vociferate (vo-*sif*-è-rayt) *v.t.* clamour ; utter (words) noisily and persistently چیخ چیخ کر کہنا، گلا پھاڑ پھاڑ کر کہنا **vociferation** *n* act of vociferating گلا پھاڑ پھاڑ کر کہنا **vociferous** *adj.* clamorous ; insisting noisily گلا پھاڑ پھاڑ کر کہنے والا، پُر شور انداز سے اصرار کرنے والا

vodka (*vod*-ka) *n.* popular Russian liquor واڈکہ، واڈکا

vogue (vohg) *n.* fashion رواج *be in vogue be all the vogue, have a great vogue*, be popular

voice (vois) *n.* sound given out in speaking

or singing آواز power of making such sounds نُطق، قوّتِ گویائی *lose (one's) voice*, (*a*) be unable to speak قوّتِ گویائی سے محروم ہونا (*b*) be unable to sing well گلا بیٹھا ہونا right to assert one's opinion آواز، شنوائی *have no voice (in a matter)* کی کوئی شنوائی نہ ہونا، کوئی آواز نہ ہونا *v.t.* express (the feelings or grievances *of*) کا اظہار کرنا (in grammar) (active or passive) form of verb (فعل کا) طور *active voice* طورِ معروف، معروف *passive voice* طورِ مجہول، مجہول **voiceless** *adj.* بے آواز

void *n.* vacuum خلا *adj.* empty (*of*) (سے) خالی (also *null and void*) not binding کالعدم

voile (voil) *n.* a well-known thin cotton fabric (used *plain* or *printed*) وائل، وَیل

volatile (*vol*-a-til) *adj.* rapidly evaporating طیّار، اُڑ جانے والا changeable متلوّن gay (person) خوش باش، زندہ دِل

volcano (vol-*kay*-noh) *n.* (pl. *volcanoes*) hill emitting molten rock (called *lava*) through its opening (called a *crater*) آتش فشاں پہاڑ، جوالا مُکھی *active volcano* بھڑکتا آتش فشاں *dormant volcano* دَبا آتش فشاں *extinct volcano* بُجھا یا ٹھنڈا آتش فشاں **volcanic** (vol-*kan*-ik) *adj.* pertaining to a volcano آتش فشانی

volition (vo-*lish*-ĕn) *n.* (in psychology) willing ارادہ

volley (*vol*-i) *n.* shower of missiles hurled together باڑھ barrage (*of* questions, etc.) بوچھاڑ (in tennis) return of ball before it touches the ground والی *v.t.* return ball thus والی مارنا fire a volley (بندوقوں وغیرہ کی) باڑھ مارنا **volley-ball** *n.* a well-known ball-game والی بال ball used in it والی بال

volt (vohlt) *n.* unit of electromotive force حرکی برق کی اکائی، وولٹ sudden leap in fencing to avoid a thrust وار خالی دینا *v.t.* move thus وار خالی دینا

voltage (*vol*-tej) *n.* total electromotive energy (*of* something) in volts وولٹیج **voltmeter** *n.* instrument for measuring voltage وولٹ پیما

voluble (*vol*-ew-bĕl) *adj.* fluent (person or speech) فصیح **volubly** *adv.* fluently بڑی رَوانی سے **volubility** (-*bil*-) *n.* fluency رَوانی، فصاحت

volume (*vol*-ewm) *n.* book کتاب one of a set of books جِلد swell (*of* sound) (آواز کا) حجم (یا) گُونج space occupied by something حجم، جسامت large amount, etc. (*of*) (کا) ڈھیر (*pl.*) moving masses (of steam, smoke, etc.) بادَل

voluminous (vo-*lew*-mi-nus) *adj.* very lengthy (writing); running into many volumes طُول طَویل prolific (writer, etc.) پُرگو، پُرنویس of considerable volume ضخیم

volunteer (vol-un-*tee*-ĕ*) *n.* one who willingly offers to do something رضاکار one offering his services thus to a cause والنٹیئر، رضاکار *v.t.* offer (services, help, or *to do* something) کی رضاکارانہ پیشکش کرنا state in a court without being asked to do so اپنی خوشی سے (بیان) دینا **voluntary** (*vol*-unt-a-ri) *adj.* done of one's own free will رضاکارانہ **voluntarily** (*vol*-) *adv.* رضاکارانہ، اپنی خوشی سے

voluptuous (vo-*lup*-tew-us) *adj.* for or of the gratification of senses ظاہری حواس کی تسکین کا (یا کے لیے) easy-going, licentious (person) عشرت پسند **voluptuousness** *n.* ظاہری حواس کی تسکین **voluptuary** (-*lup*-) *n.* licentious person عیّاش، عیش و عشرت میں اُڑانے والا

vomit (*vom*-it) *v.t.* & *i.* be sick قے کرنا، اُلٹی کرنا disgorge (smoke, etc.) in large quantities بہُت باہر نکالنا *n.* vomited food قے

voodo (*voo*-doo) *n.* U.S. negroes' belief in witchcraft جادو پر یقین، جادو their use of it جادوگری

voracious (vo-*ra*-*shus*) *adj.* very hungry بہت بُھوکا ravenous نَدیدہ avid (reader) بہت شائق **voracity** (-*ras*-) *n.* being voracious بہت بھوکا ہونا، نَدیدہ ہونا، بہت شائق ہونا

vortex (*vo**-teks) *n.* (pl. *vortices*, pr. -seez) whirlpool بھنور، گرداب whirlwind بگولا، گردباد any whirling mass چکّر

votaress *n.* (fem. of **votary, which see**)

votary (*voht*-ĕ-ri) *n.* (fem. *votaress*) devotee (*of*) (کا) پرستار one bound by vow to the service (*of*) (کے لیے) زندگی وقف کرنے والا

vote (voht) *n.* right to express one's choice (*for*) رائے دہندگی (یا رائے دہی) کا حق such formal choice (by ballot, show of hands, etc.) رائے، ووٹ *put (something) to the vote*, decide it thus پر رائے شماری کرنا total number of votes polled کُل آرا resolution (*of confidence*, or *no confidence*) carried by majority (اعتماد یا عدم اعتماد کی) قرارداد resolution (*of thanks*) (تشکر کی) قرارداد *v.t.* & *i.* give a vote (*for* or *against*) (کے حق میں یا کے خلاف) ووٹ دینا *vote (someone) in*, elect (him) منتخب کرنا propose (or *that*) (کہ) تجویز پیش کرنا jointly express the opinion (کہ) مشترکہ طور پر خیال ظاہر کرنا grant (a sum of money) by vote or accept (a Bill) thus مشترکہ رائے سے منظور کرنا **voter** *n.* (esp.) one having the right to vote at election رائے دہندہ **voting** (*voh*-ting) *n.* casting of votes رائے دہندگی counting of votes رائے شماری

votive (*voh*-tiv) *adj.* (offering) given in fulfilment of a vow منّت کا، نذر کا

vouch (vouch) *v.i.* make oneself responsible

(*for* someone or the truth, etc., of something) کا ذمّے دار ہونا **voucher** (*vou*-chĕ*) receipt of money paid رقم ادا کرنے کی رسید، رقم کی رسید **vouchsafe** (vouch-*sayf*) *v.t.* be kind enough to give (reply, etc.) از راہِ کرم (کچھ) کرنا be kind enough (*to do*) عنایت کرنا
vow (vow) *n.* solemn promise (*of*) (کا) عہد such promise in the form of oath (کی) قسم *make a vow* (*to do* something, or *that*) عہد کرنا *break a vow* قسم توڑنا، عہد توڑنا (*be*) *under a vow of*, (be) pledged to کا عہد کیے ہوئے ہونا
vowel (*vou*-èl) *n.* sound of voice without audible friction or stoppage of breath حرفِ علّت کی آواز (in English) anyone of the symbols (viz., *a, e, i, o, u,*) representing such sounds حرفِ علّت
voyage (*voi*-ij) *n.* long journey by water سمندر کا سفر، بحری سفر، جہاز کا سفر *v.i.* journey thus جہاز کا سفر کرنا
Vulcan (*vul*-kan) *Cl. myth.* the lame Roman god of fire who was a skilled smith ; (he is identified with the Greek *Hephaestus*) وَلکن **vulcanize** (*vul*-ka-nīz) *v.t.* treat rubber with sulphur for hardening it گندھک ملا کر ربڑ کو سخت کرنا repair tyres, etc., thus ربڑ کی چیزوں کی مرمّت کرنا، وَلکنائیز کرنا **vulcanite** *n.* vulcanized rubber سخت ربڑ، وَلکنائٹ
vulgar (*vul*-gĕ*) *adj.* unrefined (taste, language, habits, manner, etc.) بازاری، سُوقیانہ **vulgarity** (-*ga*-) *n.* being vulgar سُوقیانہ پن
vulnerable (*vul*-nè-rab-èl) *adj.* open to attack, etc. ہدف بننے والا، غیر محفوظ
vulpine (*vul*-pīn) *adj.* (as) of the fox crafty عیّاری، عیّارانہ
vulture (*vul*-chĕ*) *n.* hawk-like large bird living on carrion گِدھ، کرگس greedy extortionate person taking undue advantage of the misfortunes of others مُردار خور، ظالم، کرگس صفت انسان
vying (*vī*-ing) *v.* (pr. p. of **vie,** which see)

W

w, W (*dub*-lè-yoo, or *dub*-èl-yoo) (pl. *w's* or *ws*) the twenty-third letter of the English alphabet ڈبلیو **Note :** While **v** is pronounced like و in Urdu, **w** is pronounced like و in Arabic. The difference may further be explained in this way that in uttering the **v** sound we force out our breath through the upper teeth while they are resting against the lower lip ; but in producing the **w** sound we just breath out through pouted lips. It may also be noted that words beginning with **wh** are all pronounced as if they began with **hw** instead.
wack (wak) *n.* (slang) eccentric person سنکی، خبطی **wacky** (*wak*-è) *adj.* eccentric سنکی، خبطی
wad (wod) *n.* pad for stopping up a hole نرم ڈاٹ packet (*of* papers or currency notes) گڈّی *v.t.* (-dd-) stuff with a wad (سوراخ وغیرہ میں) کپڑا ٹھونسنا **wadding** *n.* padding گدّی
waddle (*wod*-èl) *v.i.* walk with short steps rolling sideways (موٹے شخص یا جانور کا) جھومتے جھامتے چلنا *n.* such walk جھومتے جھامتے چلنا
wade (wayd) *v.t.* & *i.* walk (*through* water, mud, etc., or **across** a stream, etc.) میں سے ہو کر گزرنا *wade through slaughter to throne* بڑے قتل و خونریزی کے بعد تخت حاصل کرنا ford on foot پایاب جانا *wade through* (*a dull book*, etc.) بڑی مشکل سے پڑھنا
waft (wahft) *v.t.* carry along gently through the air or on the water نرمی سے اُڑا کر (یا بہا کر) لے جانا *n.* breath of air ہوا کا جھونکا whiff (of perfume, etc.) (خوشبو کی) لپٹ
wag (wag) *v.t.* & *i.* (-gg-) swing (tongue, head, tail, etc.) ہلنا (یا) ہلانا *wag one's head*, strike it in decision تمسخر سے سر ہلانا *n.* wagging movement جنبش merry joker مسخرا **waggish** *adj.* fond of tricks and jokes مذاق والی طبیعت کا done in sport ہنسی ہنسی میں، دِل لگی میں **waggery** (*wag*-e-ri) *n.* facetiousness دِل لگی، ہنسی، ٹھٹھول
wage (wayj) *n.* (usu. pl.) (usu. regular payment) for services rendered اُجرت *living wages* اُجرت جو گزارے کے لیے کافی ہو *v.t.* carry on (war, campaign, etc.) (لڑائی) کرنا، (مہم) چلانا
wager (*way*-jĕ*) (lit.) *n.* bet شرط *lay a wager on* شرط بدنا (یا) باندھنا (یا) لگانا *v.t.* & *i.* پر شرط لگانا
waggle (*wag*-èl) *v.t.* & *i.* (colloq.) wag
wagon, waggon (*wag*-un) *n.* four-wheeled vehicle for heavy loads چوپہیہ چھکڑا open railway truck (مال گاڑی کا) چھکڑا
waif (wayf) *n.* stray child گم گشتہ بھولا بھٹکا بچّہ، بھٹکا ہوا بچّہ، بے گھر بے در homeless and helpless person شخص، بے خانماں مُفلس ownerless animal or object لاوارث مال (یا جانور) **waifs and strays** *n.* homeless and neglected children بے خانماں یا لاوارث بچّے odds and ends متفرّقات
wail (wayl) *n.* long sorrowful cry کراہ، لمبی دردناک چیخ such sound (*of* wind) (طوفانی ہوا کی) بھیانک آواز

lamentation in words *(over)* مُتر ادّاری cries of grief (*for*) کا ماتم، اپر، گریہ وزاری sorrowful complaint دردناک شکوہ *v.t.* & *i.* lament (*for* or *over*) پرگریہ وزاری کرنا utter wail کراہنا complain sorrowfully پُردرد شکوہ کرنا (of wind) sound mournfully (ہوا کا) بھیانک آواز سے چلنا

wain (wayn) *n.* (poet.) wagon گاڑی

wainscot (*wayn*-skot) *n.* wooden panelling on the walls of a room دیوار پر لکڑی کا حاشیہ، تختہ بندی *v.t.* (*wainscot, wainscoted, wainscoted*) line (a wall) thus تختہ بندی کرنا

waist (wayst) *n.* part of the body between the ribs and hips کمر garments covering it کمر

waistcoat (*ways*-kot, or *wes*-kot ; or U.S. wayst-koht) *n.* men's close-fitting sleeveless garment worn between shirt and jacket واسکٹ، صدری

wait (wayt) *v.t.* & *i.* tarry (for) رکنا، انتظار کرنا linger (*to do, till* or *until*) رکنا، انتظار کرنا delay (something) میں دیر کرنا *wait up*, keep awake (*for* something to happen) کے لیے جاگتے رہنا *wait upon* (*someone*) serve, attend کی خدمت کرنا *wait at table*, serve food, etc. ویٹر کی خدمت انجام دینا، کھانا حاضر کرنا *n.* waiting انتظار period of waiting انتظار *lie in wait* (*for a quarry*, etc.) (کی) گھات میں بیٹھنا **waiter**, *n.* (fem. *waitress*) one who waits at table in restaurant, etc. ویٹر، کھانا لانے والا

waive (wayv) *v.t.* forego (right or claim) چھوڑ دینا، سے دستکش ہونا

wake (wayk) *n.* track left by ship آبی لیک *in the wake of*, (*a*) after کے بعد (*b*) following کے نقش قدم پر *v.t.* & *i.* (pa. t. *woke* or *waked* ; pa. p. *waked*, *woke*, or *woken*) (*wake*, or *wake up*), rouse جاگنا یا جگانا rouse (*up*) from lethargy کو غفلت سے بیدار کرنا stir (*up* memories, etc.) تروتازہ become or make conscious of (*to* dangers, etc.) کا احساس کرنا **wakeful** *adj.* unable to sleep جاگ رہا (of night) giving little sleep آنکھوں میں کٹنے والی watchful چوکنا، چوکس، ہوشیار **waken** (*wayk*-en) *v.t.* & *i.* wake جاگنا، جگانا، ہوش میں آنا یا لانا، خبردار کرنا

walk (wawk) *v.t.* & *i.* go on foot چلنا، پیدل چلنا cause to walk چلانا، چلا کر لے جانا *walk away* (or *off*) *with*, steal چرا لے جانا *n.* going on foot پیدل چلنا doing so for enjoyment سیر، چہل قدمی path for walking روش، پٹری، پگڈنڈی، راستہ *walk of life*, profession, status, etc. زندگی کا شعبہ *in every walk of life* زندگی کے ہر شعبہ میں manner of walking چال **walkover** *n.* (colloq.) easy victory because of weak or no opposition مفت کی جیت *get a walkover* مفت میں جیت جانا **walkie-lookie** *n.* (see *Addenda*) **walkie-talkie** *n.* (see *Addenda*)

wall (wawl) *n.* upright structure serving as the side of a building دیوار such structure round a city, etc., for defence شہر پناہ، فصیل *fight with* (*one's*) *back to the wall*, fight under extremely hard conditions جان سے ہاتھ دھو کر لڑنا، تخت یا تختہ سمجھ کر لڑنا *go to the wall*, (*a*) be defeated شکست کھا جانا (*b*) be pushed aside as weak or helpless پس منظر میں ہٹا دیا جانا *v.t.* close up (an opening) with a wall بند کرنا، اینٹیں چن دینا **walled** *adj.* surrounded by a (defensive) wall فصیل والا **wall-less** *adj.* without (walls) بے دیوار **wallet** (*wol*-et) *n.* pocket case for currency notes, etc. بٹوا (old use) provision bag for journey توشہ دان

wallow (wol-oh) *v.i.* roll about (*in* mud, etc.) (کیچڑ وغیرہ میں) لوٹنا *wallow in money*, be rich پیسے میں کھیلنا take delight (*in*) کے مزے لینا، سے لطف اندوز ہونا

walnut (*wawl*-nut) *n.* (well-known tree bearing) an edible nut اخروٹ *adj.* (furniture) made from it اخروٹ کی لکڑی کا

walrus (wol-rus) *n.* a large sea-animal سمندری گھوڑا، والرس

waltz (wawls, or wawlts) *n.* kind of graceful dance (or music for it) in triple time والس (ناچ) والس کی دھن *v.i.* dance a waltz والس کی دھن پر ناچنا

wan (won) *adj.* pale and weak (person) پیلا، کمزور، نقیہ jaded (looks) تھکی ہوئی، بے رونق pr (light, etc.) کمزوری سے، مدھم، ماند، مدھم، پھیکی **wanly** *adv.*

wand (wond) *n.* long slender stick used by magicians or fairies جادو کی چھڑی conductor's baton تال دینے کی چھڑی، طائفے قوال کی چھڑی symbol of authority عصائے اقتدار

wander (*wond*-ě*) *v.i.* roam (*about*) ادھر ادھر پھرنا مارا مارا پھرنا stray (*from* the right path, etc.) گمراہ ہو جانا، گم کردہ راہ ہو جانا، بھٹک جانا be delirious (*in* the mind) بہکنا **wanderer** *n.* سیلانی **wanderings** *n. pl.* ramblings سیر و سیاحت **wanderlust** (*vahnd*-ě*-loost) *n.* great fondness for travelling پاؤں میں چکر آوارگی شوق رہ نوردی *have a wanderlust* کے پاؤں میں چکر ہونا

We **wander** aimlessly ; **ramble**, looking for novelty; **tramp** in order to cover a long distance ; **hike** for pleasure ; **stroll** contentedly ; **saunter** purposelessly ; **promenade** sociably; **plod** dejectedly; **trudge** tiredly; and **migrate** from one's country to a new one.

wane (wayn) *v.i.* (of the moon) show a smaller area after full moon (as opposed to *wax*) چاند کا گھٹنا weaken گھٹ جانا، کم ہو جانا *n.* waning زوال، کمی، زوال، انحطاط *be on the wane* زوال پذیر ہونا، رو بہ انحطاط ہونا

want (wont, or wahnt) *n.* need (*of*) ضرورت، احتیاج *be in want of* کا ضرورتمند ہونا lack (*of*) کمی *v.t.* & *i.*

wish for چاہنا need کا ضرورتمند ہونا، کی ضرورت رکھنا lack (or *in*) (میں کسی چیز کی) کمی ہونا *be wanting, be missing* غائب ہونا *be wanting (in manners, etc.)* (میں تمیز وغیرہ) نہ ہو *want for nothing*, have everything that one needs کے پاس سب کچھ ہونا، کے پاس اللہ کا دیا سب کچھ ہونا کے پاس کسی چیز کی کمی نہ ہونا **wanting** *prep.* without کے بغیر *adj.* missing غائب lacking (*in*) سے خالی، سے محروم not up to the required standard ہلکا، گھٹیا *weighed and found wanting* میزانِ عمل میں پورا نہ اُترنا

wanton (wont-un) *adj.* wildly playful اٹکھیلیاں کرنے والا، کلیلیں کرنے والا capricious چنچل، من موجی unruly بے قابو luxuriant and disorderly (growth, etc.) بے اندازہ gratuitous (insult, etc.) بلاوجہ، خواہ مخواہ کا (of destruction, etc.) without any purpose یونہی، بلامقصد، اندھا دھند lewd آوارہ، اوباش unchaste (woman) فاحشہ immoral (thoughts) گندے خیالات *n.* wanton woman چھنال، فاحشہ *v. i.* be wanton in behaviour شوخ یا چنچل ہونا **wantonly** *adv.* in a wanton manner شوخی سے، بلاوجہ، یونہی، بے اندازہ، اندھا دھند

war (wo*) *n.* armed fight between nations, etc. جنگ *declare war on or upon* کے خلاف اعلانِ جنگ کرنا *make war (upon)* (سے) جنگ کرنا *be at war (with), go to war (against)* کے خلاف جنگ کرنا *sinews of war*, money for war جنگ کے لیے روپیہ، سرمایہ *war of nerves*, bid to bring the enemy to his knees by gradually destroying his morale اعصابی جنگ *civil war*, war between rival groups of a country for capturing political power خانہ جنگی *man-of-war*, warship جنگی جہاز *be on the warpath*, (*a*) be fighting مصروف رہا ہونا (*b*) be bellicose آمادۂ جنگ ہونا، جنگ کے لیے تیار ہونا *war to the knife*, war with both parties inflicting the greatest damage گھمسان کا رن *v.i.* (-*rr*-) (old use) make war جنگ کرنا **warring** *adj.* rival (creed, etc.) حریف **war-cry** *n.* phrase shouted in war نعرۂ جنگ party slogan (جماعت کا) نعرہ **war-dance** *n.* dance of the savages before they go to battle جنگی ناچ **warfare** *n.* war جنگ actual fighting لڑائی **warhead** *n.* explosive head of missile, etc. رسائیل کا منہ، سرِ انداختہ **warlike** *adj.* fond (or suggestive) of war جنگجو، جنگجویانہ **warrior** *n.* (lit.) soldier جنگجو، نبرد آزما **warship** *n.* man-of-war جنگی جہاز **war-worn** *adj.* (of country, etc.) ruined by war جنگ میں تباہ ہو جانے والا (of person) exhausted by war لڑائی میں تھکا ہوا war veteran نبرد آزما، کار آزمودہ

warble (*wo**-bèl) *v.t. & i.* (of birds) sing melodiously چہچہانا make a musical sound سُریلی آواز نکالنا، گانا *n.* (bird's) song (پرندے کا) چہچہانا، نغمۂ طائر such musical sound سُریلی آواز

ward (wo*d) *n.* minor under the care of a guardian or court of wards زیرِ ولایت guarding نگہداشت *keep watch and ward* دیکھ بھال، حفاظت، نگہداشت کرنا administrative division or electoral district of a town حلقہ division of a hospital or prison وارڈ، کمرہ *v.t.* (*ward off*), avert (blow, danger, disease, etc.) کو روکنا، سے بچنا **warden** (*wo**-den) *n.* controller of a prison or hostel وارڈن، نگران A.R.P. controller in an area وارڈن *warden post*, his office وارڈن پوسٹ، اے آر پی کی چوکی **wardenship** *n.* being a warden نگراں کا عہدہ، نگراں ہونا **warder** *n.* (fem. *wardress*), jailor وارڈر، داروغۂ جیل

wardrobe (*wo*d*-rohb) *n.* cupboard for hanging up and storing clothes وارڈروب، کپڑوں کی الماری، جامہ دان *wardrobe trunk*, trunk so made as to serve as wardrobe when stood on end وارڈروب ٹرنک، جامدانی (one's) stock of clothes (کسی کے) کپڑے لتے *wardrobe dealer*, dealer in second-hand clothing پرانے کپڑوں کا بیوپاری، سیکنڈ ہینڈ کپڑوں والا

ware (way-e*) *n.* (*pl.*) articles placed for a sale دکان کا مال (usu. in compounds) manufactured goods مصنوعات، مال **warehouse** *n.* godown گودام big shop بڑی دکان *v.t.* store in a warehouse گودام میں رکھنا

warily *adv.* (see under **wary**)

warm (wo*m) *adj.* rather hot گرم *make things warm for (someone)*, (*a*) punish (him) کو سزا دینا (*b*) create trouble for him کے لیے حالات خراب کرنا (of clothes, weather, climate, etc.) keeping hot گرم sincere (welcome) پُرجوش، گرمجوشانہ *warm disposition* تپاک، مہر و محبت heated (discussion) گرما گرم (of colour) suggesting warmth گرم *v.t. & i.* (also *warm up*) make warm گرم کرنا become warm گرم ہونا، کو گرمی پہنچنا become enthusiastic جوش میں آنا excite گرمانا (*warm to or towards*) feel sympathy or affection for پر رحم (یا پیار) آنا *n.* warming or being warmed گرمی *have a warm* سردی دور کرنا **warmly** *adj.* enthusiastically گرمجوشی سے **warmblooded** *adj.* (of animals) having warm blood گرم خون easily excited گرم مزاج (یا) جذباتی **warm-hearted** *adj.* of warm disposition پُرتپاک **warmth** *n.* not cold; being warm گرمی excitement جوش warm disposition تپاک، مہر و محبت

warn (wo*n) *v.t.* inform (someone of danger, etc.) متنبہ کرنا، سے آگاہ کرنا give a warning to (someone) for improving his behaviour, etc. تنبیہ کرنا (polite or journalistic word for saying :) protest strongly خبردار کرنا، متنبہ کرنا، آگاہ کرنا **warning** *n.* notice تنبیہ، آگاہی notice to mend one's

ways تنبیہ administer a warning (to) (کو) تنبیہ کرنا words or events, etc., that warn تنبیہ
warp (wo*p) *v.t.* & *i.* twist out of shape موڑنا یا مُڑنا، ٹیڑھا میڑھا ہونا (یا کرنا)، اینٹھنا (یا) اینٹھ جانا lead (disposition, etc.), astray; make perverted غلط راہ پر ڈالنا، گمراہ کرنا، خراب کرنا haul (a ship) by rope to fixed point (جہاز) کو کھینچنا *n.* warped part ٹیڑھا میڑھا یا اینٹھا ہوا حصّہ، کجروی going astray long threads forming the basic structure of a piece of cloth (as opposed to the *weft*) تانا، تار rope for warping a ship جہاز کھینچنے کا رسّا
warrant (wo-rant) *n.* justification جواز official authority (*for* or *of*) (کے لیے) اجازت نامہ (often *pl.*) written order to arrest someone وارنٹ گرفتاری sign (*one's*) *death warrant*, take a suicidal step خود اپنی موت کے وارنٹ پر دستخط کرنا certificate appointing a man as a warrant-officer وارنٹ *v.t.* guarantee کی ذمے داری لینا، کی ضمانت دینا justify کا جواز پیش کرنا **warrantable** *adj.* legitimate جائز، قانونی، قاعدے کے مطابق (of stag, etc.) of an age when it can lawfully be hunted شکار کے قابل، شکار کی عمر کا، جائز **warrant-officer** *n.* (in armed forces) holder of the highest rank below commissioned and junior commissioned officers وارنٹ افسر **warrantor** *n.* guarantor ضامن، گارنٹی دینے والا **warrantee** (-*tee*) *n.* one receiving a guarantee جسے یقین دلایا جائے **warranty** *n.* authority or justification (*for* doing something) اختیار (یا) جواز
wary (*way*-è-ri) *adj.* cautious of danger چوکس، چوکنا، ہوشیار *wary of* (*doing something wrong*), too cautious to do it میں بہت محتاط **warily** *adv.* چوکسی سے، احتیاط سے
wash (wash) *v.t.* & *i.* clean with water دھونا *wash dirty linen in public*, give publicity to own domestic quarrel گھر کے جھگڑے باہر کہتے پھرنا، اپنے گھر کی برائیاں باہر بیان کرنا *wash* (*one's*) *hands of something*, refuse to accept responsibility for کی ذمّے داری لینے سے انکار کرنا clean (*with* something) دھونا (of a material) be capable of being washed without damage دُھل سکنا (of streams, sea, etc.) flow past کے ساتھ بہنا (یا) ہونا *wash up*, (*a*) wash dishes, etc. برتن صاف کرنا (*b*) wash دھونا *wash* (something) *off* (or *out*) دھو ڈالنا، پانی سے چھڑانا *wash* (*something*) *away, off, overboard, etc.* بہالے جانا (of rain) cause (an outdoor sporting event) to be cancelled کے باعث منسوخ ہو جانا *be washed out*, (*a*) (of batsman) score nil and be out کوئی رن بنائے بغیر آؤٹ ہو جانا (*b*) (of the match) be cancelled منسوخ ہو جانا (*c*) be enfeebled or demoralized کمزور ہو جانا (یا)، ہمّت ہار بیٹھنا *n.* washing دھونا being washed دُھلنا (*the wash*), clothes, etc., that are to be (or are being or have been) washed دُھلائی place where clothes are washed گھاٹ (یا) دھونے کی جگہ lotion زخم دھونے کی دوا، لوشن، زخم شو any liquid prepared thus محلول *whitewash* (دیوار پر پھیرنے کی) سفیدی wake پن لیک **washing** *n.* دھونا *washing soda*, sodium carbonate dissolved in water for washing, etc. سوڈا، کپڑے دھونے کا کپڑا **washerman** *n.* launderer دھوبی **washerwoman** *n.* laundress دھوبن **washer** *n.* machine for washing clothes کپڑے دھونے کی کل soft, flat ring for making a screw, etc., tight واشل
wash-stand (*wosh*-stand), **wash-hand-stand** (*wosh*-ha-stand) *n.* washing table with basin, jug, etc. آفتابہ، سلفچی، سلپچی **wash-basin** *n.* basin for washing hands, etc. سلفچی، بیسن **wash-out** *n.* sudden soil erosion مٹی وغیرہ کا بہہ جانا (colloq.) worthless فضول، ناکارہ complete failure to hit the target گولی کا نشانے سے دور جانا، نشانے پر بالکل نہ لگنا
washy (*wash*-i) *adj.* pale (colour) ہلکا، پھیکا thin, watery (solution) ہلکا
wasp (wosp) *n.* a flying insect with a sharp sting بھڑ **waspish** *adj.* petulant, irritable (person or temper) چڑچڑا، جھلّا
wast (wost) *v.* (old form of *was* used with *thou*) تھا
waste (wayst) *adj.* barren (land) بنجر (of paper, cotton, etc.), useless and thrown away ردّی *v.t.* & *i.* make no (good) use of سے فائدہ نہ اُٹھانا (of time, energy, etc.) use more than is necessary ضائع کرنا، گنوانا، کھونا (of money) squander اُجاڑ دینا، اُجاڑ کرنا، برباد کرنا (land) waste اُجاڑنا، اُڑانا (cause to) lose (*away*) strength gradually (کو) ویرانہ بنانا، گھلنا، گھل گھل کر مرنا، گھلانا *n.* wasting or being wasted ضائع کرنا یا ہونا، تضییع *go to waste*, *run to waste*, be wasted ضائع جانا useless and unwanted things ردّی (usu. *pl.*) waste land بیابان، اُجاڑ
wastage (*ways*-tej) *n.* loss by waste ضائع جانا، تضییع amount wasted جو کچھ (یا) جتنا کچھ ضائع جائے **wasteful** *adj.* causing waste ضائع کرنے والا **waste-pipe** *n.* pipe for carrying away waste water گندے پانی کی نالی، پرنالہ **waste-paper basket** *n.* (abbr. *w. p. b.*) ردّی کی ٹوکری **wastrel** (*ways*-trel) *n.* good for-nothing wasteful person نکما، فضول خرچ، نکھٹو **waster** *n.* wastrel نکھٹو، نکما، فضول خرچ thing spoilt in the process of manufacture ساخت کے دوران میں خراب ہو جانے والی چیز، بد ساختہ
watch (woch) *v.t.* & *i.* observe, keep looking at (show, match, etc.) دیکھنا guard پہرہ داری کرنا، نگہبانی کرنا look out for کا انتظار کرنا wait for (one's

turn, opportunity, etc.) کا انتظار کرنا beware of بچنا Watch the wire! سے بچنا کہیں تار میں پاؤں نہ اُلجھ جائے (old use) remain awake at night جاگتے رہنا، رات آنکھوں میں کٹنا n. vigil; keeping watch پہرہ داری watch and ward پہریداری keep watch (over) پر پہرہ دینا، کی نگہبانی کرنا in the watches of the night, while one lies awake جاگتے کٹنے والی راتوں میں wait (for) کا انتظار کرنا be alert چوکنا رہنا be on the watch (for), be alert lest چوکنا رہنا مبادا watchman or body of watchmen پہریدار، چوکیدار watch committee, body of officials looking after policing and lighting in an area پاسبان انجمن، واچ کمیٹی (on board a ship) four-hour period of duty for one shift of the crew نوکری کی باری crew on this shift جہاز پر نوکری کی باری دینے والے ملاح small time-piece for wrist or pocket گھڑی pocket-watch جیبی گھڑی wrist-watch کلائی کی گھڑی **watchful** *adj.* alert چوکس، چوکنا، ہوشیار **watchman** *n.* watch چوکیدار، پہریدار **watchword** *n.* password (*for* the night) پہرے کا لفظ slogan (*of* a party, etc.) نعرہ

water (*wau*-tĕ*) *n.* the liquid which we drink every d y پانی *under water*, inundated زیرِ آب *spend money like water*, spend it lavishly روپیہ پانی کی طرح بہانا *shed blood like water*, shed it recklessly اندھا دھند خونریزی کرنا *be in* (or *get into*) *hot water*, foolishly get into trouble مصیبت مول لینا *in deep water* (or *waters*), in trouble مصیبت میں گرفتار *throw cold water on*, discourage (plan, etc.) کے ناممکن العمل ہونے کا خیال ظاہر کرنا، کو ٹھنڈے پانی میں بٹھا دینا *hold water*, prove to be sound ٹھیک ثابت ہونا state of flood or tide سیلاب *at high water* انتہائی جزر (یا) اونچے درجے کا سیلاب *at low water* انتہائی مد (یا) جزر *in low water*, hard up مالی مشکلات میں گرفتار *keep* (*one's*) *head above water*, avoid financial difficulties مالی مشکلات سے بمشکل بچے رہنا (usu. *pl.*) mass of water (like the sea, lake, etc.) سمندر، جھیل وغیرہ *cross the waters* سمندر پار جانا *on the water*, in a boat جہاز میں، کشتی پر solution in water آبی محلول *soda-water*, aerated water بوتل، سوڈا *v.t.* & *i.* put water on پر پانی ڈالنا give water to (garden) کو پانی دینا give water to (domestic animal) کو پانی پلانا (of the eyes) fill with water بھر آنا (of the mouth) fill with saliva میں پانی بھر آنا quality of jewel, etc. آب *pearl of the first water* اول درجے کی آب کا *of the first water*, excellent نہایت آبدار، اعلیٰ درجے کا urine پیشاب (in phrases:) *make water, pass water* پیشاب کرنا add water میں پانی ڈالنا (یا ملانا) *water scheme* (*etc.*) *down*, tone (it) down نرم کرنا *water down the details* diminish their horror, etc. تفصیلات کے برے اثرات کم کرنا

water-buffalo *n.* (correct word for the) common domestic buffalo بھینس، بھینسا **water-carrier** *n.* one who supplies drinking water in skins, etc. بہشتی، سقہ **water-cart** *n.* (also *water-waggon*), (esp.) cart for watering roads, etc. چھڑکاؤ کی گاڑی **water-closet** *n.* (abbr. *W.C.*) stool for evacuation of bowels from which waste matter is drained down by pulling down the chain of a cistern and releasing water طہارت خانہ، فلش *E. & W.C. laid*, (of house) having electricity and water-closet بجلی اور فلش لگا ہوا

Water-closet (or W.C.)

water-colour *n.* (*pl.*) paints mixed with water آبی رنگ picture painted with them آبی رنگ کی تصویر **water-course** *n.* (channel of) small stream (esp., one which is not perennial) نالہ **watercress** *n.* a salad plant آبی سلاد **waterfall** *n.* cascade آبشار **waterfowl** *n.* any (game-) bird living near water دریائی پرندہ، کوئی مرغابی **waterfront** *n.* part of a town beside the sea, etc. شہر کا سمندر (وغیرہ) کی طرف کا رخ **watering-place** *n.* holiday resort on the sea-side ساحلی سیرگاہ spa معدنی پانی کا چشمہ pool whither animals go for water جوہڑ **water-lily** *n.* kinds of waterplant with floating leaves کنول، نیلوفر (وغیرہ) **water-line** *n.* line where the waters touch a boat or ship پانی کی لکیر **waterlogged** *adj.* marshy (ground): through which too much of water seeps سیم زدہ (of boat) too heavy to float owing to water that has seeped into it سخت گیلی جو ڈوب جائے (of wood) wet گیلی **waterlogging** *n.* (of an area) being waterlogged سیم زدہ ہونا، سیم زدگی **water-melon** *n.* a well-known large kind of melon تربوز **water-mill** *n.* mill worked by water current پن چکی **water-nymph** *n.* minor goddess living in water پن دیوی **water of life** *n.* the water supposed to bestow eternal life آبِ حیات، امرت **water-pipe** *n.* water supply pipe (usu. connected with the mains) پائپ، نل **waterpolo** *n.* handball game played by swimmers چوگانِ آبی، پانی پولو **water-power** *n.* mechanical power obtained from a current of water آبی قوت **water-proof** *adj.* impervious to water جس میں پانی سرایت نہ کرے، پن روک، نمی روک، غیر نمدار *n.* raincoat برساتی *v.t.* make (something) waterproof ایسا بنانا کہ پانی اس میں سرایت نہ کرے، پن روک (یا نمی روک) بنانا، غیر نمدار بنانا **water-rate** *n.* charges for

the use of public water supply نل کا کرایہ، نل کا بل
watershed *n.* mountain, etc., separating river basins پن دھارا، فاصل آب **water-skin** *n.* skin for carrying water مشک، مشکیزہ **waterspout** *n.* column of sea-water raised by whirlwind to meet a whirling cloud گمنڈی فوارہ **water-supply** *n.* supply of water پانی کی بہم رسانی its amount پانی کی مقدار **water-tight** *adj.* such that water cannot get into or out of it پن روک *watertight compartments,* (a) such parts پن روک خانے (b) hard-and-fast artificial divisions مصنوعی حصے fool proof (rule, accd etc) جس میں بچنے کی کوئی گنجائش نہ نکل سکے **water-tower** *n.* tower supporting a tank پن منار **water-waggon** *n.* water-cart چھڑکاؤ کی گاڑی *be on the water-waggon,* (slang) be a teetotaller شرابی نہ ہونا، صوفی ہونا **water-wave** *n.* wave in hair produced by water (بالوں کی) آبی لہر **water-waving** *n.* producing water-waves (بالوں میں) آبی لہریں ڈالنا **waterway** *n.* navigable channel کشتی رانی یا جہاز رانی کے قابل گزرگاہ **water-wheel** *n.* power wheel worked by water پن پہیہ **water-wings** *n. pl.* floats attached to shoulders of persons learning to swim آبی بازو **waterworks** *n. pl.* establishment for public water-supply کارخانۂ آب رسانی **watery** *adj.* of (or like) water پانی کا (سا) pale (colour) پھیکا very weak (solution) بڑا پتلا

watt *n.* (abbr. *W.*) unit of electrical power واٹ، برقی قوت کی اکائی *a 60 W. bulb* ساٹھ واٹ کا بلب

wattle (*wot*-ĕl) *n.* structure of plaited twigs woven over for use as wall or roof چھپر *wattle and daub,* wattle covered with clay لپائی والا چھپر

wave (wayv) *v.t. & i.* (cause to) undulate or flutter to and fro لہرانا، لہلہانا، حرکت دینا make a signal thus (*to* or *at* someone *to do* something, *or on, away,* etc.) (ہاتھ وغیرہ) ہلا کر اشارہ کرنا *wave someone away* ہاتھ کے اشارے سے پرے جانے کو کہنا say good-bye (*to*) الوداع کہنے کے لیے ہاتھ ہلانا (cause to) undulate لہرانا *n.* billow لہر، موج *be tossed by the waves* موجوں کے تھپیڑے کھانا anything like a wave موج، لہر، گھونگر (وغیرہ) *light-waves* امواج نور sudden fit (*of* enthusiasm, etc.) (کی) لہر sudden increase in کی لہریں یکدم اضافہ *a heat wave* گرمی کی لہر *a cold wave* سردی کی لہر *a crime wave* جرائم کی لہر **wavy** *adj.* undulating لہریا **wave-length** *n.* distance between a wave's highest point (called *crest*) and its lowest (called *trough*) لہر کی لمبائی، طول موج

waver (*way*-ver) *v.i.* (of things, shadows, etc.), move to and fro unsteadily ادھر ادھر ہلنا (یا) flicker جھلملانا hesitate (*between*) تھرتھرانا

begin to give way in fighting پس و پیش کرنا کے قدم (یا پاؤں) اکھڑنا

wax *v.i.* (of the moon) grow larger (as opposed to *wane*) بڑھنا grow (*in* power, etc.) (میں) اضافہ ہونا (old use) become (merry, indignant, etc.) ہونا *n.* sticky substance made by bees for their honeycombs and used by human beings for candles, etc. موم anything similar موم جیسی (نقلی) موم *ear-wax* کان کا میل *paraffin-wax* کوئی چیز *sealing-wax* لاکھ (slang) fit of anger غصہ، طیش، جوش **waxen** *adj.* of or like wax مومی **waxwork** *n.* figure modelled in wax مومی پتلا (*pl.*) place (like *Madam Tussaud's* in London) where they are on show مومی پتلوں کی نمائش گاہ

way *n.* road, street, path, etc. راستہ، راہ *highway,* trunk road شاہراہ *by-way* چھوٹا راستہ *over the way, across the way,* on the other side of the road سامنے بالمقابل، سڑک کے پرلی طرف *pave the way for* کے لیے راہ ہموار کرنا *be in (someone's) way,* obstruct (his) path (کی) راہ میں حائل ہونا *get out of the way* کے راستے سے ہٹ جانا *out of the way,* extraordinary غیر معمولی *make way (for)* کے لیے راستہ چھوڑنا *be on the way* راستے میں ہونا، آ رہا ہونا *lead the way,* act as guide آگے آگے چلنا *go a little way with* کے ساتھ تھوڑی دور چل کر راستہ دکھانا track سڑک (یا) پٹڑی *tramway* ٹرام کی پٹڑی *railway* ریل کی پٹڑی route (*from* one place *to* another) راستہ *lose (one's) way* راستہ بھول جانا *find (one's) way* راستہ تلاش کرنا *the quickest* (or *shortest*) *way* سب سے چھوٹا راستہ *on the way home* گھر جاتے ہوئے direction طرف *look this way* ادھر (یا اس طرف) دیکھیے *go that way* اُدھر (یا اُس طرف) جائیے *the wrong way round,* in the direction opposite to the one needed اُلٹی طرف *a long way from* سے دُور method (*of doing* or *to do* something) طریقہ *ways and means,* (esp. financial) resources وسائل behaviour, habit عادت، دستور *have winning ways* کی عادت دلنشیں ہونا طریقہ، طرز (usu. *pl.*) customs رواج، دستور، طور طریقے aspect, point پہلو، بات *in some ways* بعض پہلوؤں سے *in no way* کسی بات میں بھی نہیں progress, advance ترقی، راستہ *make (one's) way in the world,* carve out a successful career for oneself دنیا میں ترقی کرنا، اپنا راستہ بنانا *be under way,* (primarily of ship) be moving چل رہا ہونا (10) condition حالت *be in bad way* بری حالت میں ہونا (*More phrases* :) anyway, at any rate بہر صورت *be in the family way,* be pregnant کے پاؤں بھاری ہونا *in a family way,* without ceremony گھر کی طرح، اپنا گھر سمجھ کر، بے تکلفی سے *by the way,* by the by, incidentally ضمناً، برسبیل تذکرہ *by way of,* (a) as بطور (b) for کے لیے (c) during کے دوران میں

in a way, to some exten ایک طرح سے، ایک حد تک *in a small way, in (one's) own small way*, on a small scale چھوٹے پیمانے پر *go (one's) own way*, go according to own habit اپنے دستور کے مطابق چلنا *get (one's) own way*, have what one wants or do as one wants to اپنی مرضی کرنا، اپنی بات پوری کرا لینا *give way*, (a) yield (to or under pressure, etc.) ٹوٹ جانا، دب جانا، مان جانا (b) break, bend sink, etc. بیٹھ جانا، جھکنا، غرق ہو جانا (وغیرہ) *lie in (someone's) way*, be (his) vocation کے پیشے سے متعلق ہونا، کا پیشہ ہونا، کا کام ہونا *gather way*, (of ships) gain speed کی رفتار تیز ہو جانا *lose way* کی رفتار سست ہو جانا **wayfarer** (*way*-fay-ĕ-rĕ*) *n.* (lit.) traveller (esp. on foot) پیدل چلنے والا، راہی *n.* side of the road سڑک کا کنارہ، پیادہ رو، راہگیر *adj.* of or at the wayside سڑک کے کنارے (کا یا پر)، بر لب راہ، بر لب سڑک **waylay** (way-*lay*) *v.t.* (*waylay, waylaid, waylaid*) lie in wait for (someone) to rob (or attack him) راستے میں روکنا، (کی) رہزنی کرنا **wayward** (*way*-w*ĕd) *adj.* wilful خودسر، خودرائے، ضدی، سرکش

we (wee, or wi) *pron.* (nominative *pl.* form of *I*) ہم

weak (week) *adj.* feeble (person, sight, hearing, thing, etc.) کمزور *the weaker sex*, women صنف نازک (of argument, promise, etc.) کمزور، بودا، کچا (of style) lacking vigour پھسپھسا (of a solution) not strong ہلکا، پتلا (in grammar) (verbs) forming past and past participle by the addition of *ed t* (or even *d*) یکساں خاتمے والے فعل **weaken** *v.t.* & *i.* become or make weak کمزور ہو جانا (یا) کر دینا **weak-kneed** *adj.* lacking a strong will کمزور، بودا **weakling** *n.* very weak creature مریل **weakly** *adj.* sickly بیمار سا *adv.* in a a weak manner کمزوری سے **weak-minded** *adj.* mentally unsound جس کا دماغ کچھ خراب ہو، ضعیف دماغ والا easily influenced دوسروں کے کہنے میں آجانے والا **weakness** *n.* being weak کمزوری (one's) weak point عیب، کمزوری *be (one's) weakness* کی کمزوری ہونا a special or foolish liking (*for*) شوق، رغبت inability to resist temptation کمزوری

weal (weel) *n.* welfare بہبودی، بہبود (also *wale*), mark of blow or whip on the skin مار کا نشان، رنبیل

wealth (welth) *n.* riches lot (*of* detail colour, etc.) (کی) کثرت *have a wealth of* میں بہتات ہونا **wealthy** (*wel*-thi) *adj.* rich امیر

wean (ween) *v.t.* cause to give up suckling دودھ چھڑانا cause (someone) to turn (*away from* bad habit, etc.) (کی عادت) چھڑانا

weapon (*wep*-un) *n.* something to fight with ذریعہ، ہتھیار any means of ending resistance ہتھیار

wear (*way*-ĕ*) *v.t.* & *i.* (wore, worn) put on (clothes, ornaments, shoes, etc.) پہننا (put on headgear, spectacles, etc.) لگانا grow (hair, beard, moustaches, etc.) رکھنا، کے ہونا put on (an expression on the face, looks, etc.) پر ہونا، کے آثار ہونا (cause to) waste (*away*, thin, *into* holes, etc. خراب ہو جانا، گھس جانا (promise to) endure (*for* a period) چلنا (یا) چلنے والا ہونا (*Phrases*:) *wear off*, (of a feeling) pass away خود بخود جانا، رہنا *wear on*, (of time) pass away gradually آہستہ آہستہ گزر جانا *wear out*, (a) tire or be tired تھکا دینا (یا) تھک جانا (b) (of patience, etc.) end ختم ہو جانا *n.* clothing کپڑے، لباس use as such پہننا، استعمال damage by use استعمال سے نقصان *show (signs of) wear* معلوم ہونا کہ پرانا، پہن پہن کر خراب *the worse for wear* استعمال شدہ ہے *wear and tear*, depreciation in value owing to normal use گھس پس جانا (in combination with something) for wearing پوش *footwear*, shoes, etc. جوتا، جوتے، پاپوش *underwear*, undergarment (esp., for lower part of the body) زیر جامہ

weary (*way*-ĕ-ri) *adj.* tired تھکا ہوا، تھکا ماندہ tiresome تھکا دینے والا *v.t.* & *i.* become or make weary تھک جانا (یا) تھکا دینا **wearily** *adv.* تھک کر **weariness** *n.* being weary تھکاوٹ **wearisome** (*way*-ĕ-ri-sum) *adj.* tiresome تھکا دینے والا tedious اکتا دینے والا

weasel (*wee*-zel) *n.* a kind of mongoose ایک قسم کا نیولا، راسو

weather (*wedh*-ĕ*) *n.* state of atmosphere at a particular time and place موسم *v.t.* & *i.* tide over (the crisis, storm, etc.) مشکلات میں سے ہو کر نکلنا، (مشکلات) کا مقابلہ کر کے نکلنا (of wood) be seasoned ٹھیک ہونا erode (موسمی تغیرات کا) گھس ڈالنا

weather-beaten *adj.* (of face) showing traces of exposure to the rigours of climate موسم کی سختیوں کا اثر نظر آنا (of person) having been through thick and thin سرد و گرم چشیدہ **weather-bound** *adj.* (of ship, traveller, etc.) unable to proceed owing to bad weather موسم کی خرابی کے باعث رکا پڑا **weathercock** *n.* (often cock-shaped) device showing the direction of the wind مرغ باد نما person suiting his principles to changed circumstances ابن الوقت، مرغ باد نما

weathercock

weave (weev) *v.t.* & *i.* (*weave, wove, woven*) make (threads) into cloth, etc., or (clothe, etc.) form threads بننا ❷ spin (web) (جالا) بُننا(یا) تَننا contrive (plot) from incidents (قصّہ یا کہانی) گھڑنا (of stream) meander (its ways through). (میں سے) چکّر کاٹتی ہُوئی یا بَل کھاتی ہُوئی گزرنا n. (coarse, fine, plain, etc.) style of weaving بناوٹ، نسیج **weaver** n. one whose trade is to weave cloth on handloom, etc. جُولاہا، کوری، نُور باف

web n. net spun by a spider جالا network (of lies, etc.) جال skin joining the toes of certain birds پنجوں کے درمیان کی جھلّی **webbed, web-footed** adj. (of birds) with space between toes filled with web-like growth جھلّی دار پنجوں والا **webbing** n. coarse woven belt used for girths, etc. وَیبنگ، موٹی نِواڑ strong edging to finer fabric کنّی

wed v.t. & i. (wed, wedded, wedded) marry سے شادی کرنا (be wedded to), hold or be devoted to پر قائم ہونا، کا دِل و جان سے پیرو ہونا **wedding** n. marriage ceremony شادی، تقریبِ شادی *wedding-ring*, ring given to the woman on wedding or engagement شادی کی انگوٹھی **wedlock** n. married state شادی شُدہ ہونا تاہّل *born out of wedlock*, (of children) illegitimate ناجائز (اولاد)

wedge (wej) n. V-shaped piece (*driven into* something) for splitting it خانہ such a piece for securing something پچّر *the thin end of the wedge*, small change, etc., leading to bigger changes, etc. اہم نتائج پیدا کرنے والا چھوٹا کام v.t. keep (something) open with a wedge میں پانہ لگانا secure (it) with a wedge پچّر لگانا

W

a wedge (W)

Wednesday (*wenz*-day, or -di, or *wed*-nez-) n. the day of the week immediately following Tuesday (sacred to the Scandinavian god *Woden*) بُدھ

wee (wee) adj. (Scottish) very small چھوٹا سا *wee bit* ذرا سا، ننّھا سا

weed (weed) n. wild plant growing unwanted among useful plants گھاس پھُوس، رزنی، اڑاہا (pl.) (also *widow's weeds*), a new widow's black mourning dress نئی بیوہ کا ماتمی جوڑا v.t. & i. take weeds out of (the ground) نلائی کرنا، نرانا (*weed out*), root out valueless things (*from* valuable ones) دُور کرنا **weedy** adj. full of weeds رزنی والا weak, lank, (young person) لمبا اور نحیف، لاغر

week n. seven-day period from Saturday midnight to Saturday midnight ہفتہ *this day week* آج ہی کے دِن *Wednesday week* ایک بُدھ چھوڑ کر اگلے بُدھ *week before last* دو ہفتے پہلے any consecutive period of seven days ہفتہ، سات دِن working days of the week ہفتہ، ہفتہ کار **weekday** n. any day of the week except Sunday کام کا دِن، ہفتہ کار کا دِن **week-end** n. Sunday with Saturday as half or full day as one's period off-duty ہفتہ اتوار **weekly** adj. & adv. once a week ہفتے میں ایک بار per week فی ہفتہ n. weekly periodical ہفتہ وار اخبار، ہفت روزہ

weep v.t. & i. (*weep, wept, wept*) shed tears (*for* or *over* something or someone رونا *weep for joy* خوشی کے مارے رونا **weeping** adj. shedding tears روتا ہُوا (of tree) with hanging branches لٹکتی ہُوئی شاخوں والا

weft n. woof بانا، پود

weigh (way) v.t. & i. find the heaviness of (something) in scales, etc. تولنا، وزن کرنا be thus found (so much) heavy (کا اتنا) وزن ہونا gauge the importance or value of کی اہمیّت (یا قدر و قیمت) کا اندازہ کرنا *weigh the consequences* (*of*) (کا) انجام سوچنا *weigh (one's) words*, choose them carefully بات کو تولنا compare (two things, or one thing *with* or *against* another) موازنہ کرنا (*Phrases* :) *weigh anchor*, (of ship) set out on voyage چل پڑنا، لنگر اٹھانا *weigh with*, (a) seem important to کو اہم معلوم ہونا (b) carry weight with پر اثر انداز ہونا *weigh* (*someone* or *something*) *down*, crush (him or it) under (his, etc.) weight or pull it down بوجھ تلے پیس ڈالنا (یا سے گرا دینا) *weigh upon* (of something) hang heavy on (one's mind) (کا) دِل پر بوجھ ہونا **weigh** n. heaviness, owing to gravitational pull وزن *sell by weight* تل کر بکنا (یا) بیچنا piece of metal for weighing things against it on scale باٹ importance اہمیّت، وزن، وقعت load بوجھ، وزن v.t. make heavy by putting weight on وزن رکھ کر بھاری کر دینا (*weigh down*), burden (*with* something) کے بوجھ تلے دبانا **weighty** (*wayt*-i) adj. very heavy بوجھل، بہت بھاری important (argument, etc.) اہم

weir, wear (*way*-e*) n. dam بند

weird (*wee*-è*d) adj. uncanny پُراسرار supernatural مافوق الفطرت (colloq.) abstruse ناقابلِ فہم، عجیب **weirdly** adv. پُراسرار انداز سے

welcome (*wel*-kum) adj. (of guest, news, etc.) received gladly and with warmth of affection مُبارک، خوش آئند *make (someone) welcome*, make (him) feel that he is welcome کو اپنی آمد ناگوار محسوس نہ ہونے دینا *You are welcome (to do it)*; with pleasure بڑے شوق سے n. kindly greetings, etc. (*to* someone) on his arrival خوش آمدید، خیر مقدم، اہلاً و سہلاً و مرحبا *give a warm welcome to* پُرجوش خیر مقدم کرنا *have a cold welcome* (*from* or at) بڑا سَرد مِہرانہ برتاؤ ہونا *give a cold welcome to it* سے رُکھائی سے پیش آنا *v.t.* greet with pleasure خوش آمدید کہنا receive with pleasure کا خیر مقدم کرنا *welcome (suggestion, etc.) warmly,* (تجویز وغیرہ) بہت پسند کرنا *welcome (suggestion, etc.) coldly* (تجویز وغیرہ) ناپسند کرنا، نظر انداز کر دینا

weld *v.t.* & *i.* join (pieces of metal) together by heat and pressure کی وَیلڈنگ کرنا، تپا کر جوڑنا (of iron, etc.) be capable of being welded تپ کر جُڑ سکنا، کی وَیلڈنگ ہو سکنا unite closely (*into* one, etc.) جُڑ جانا، ایک ہو جانا *n.* welded joint وَیلڈنگ کا جوڑ، جوڑ **welder** *n.* one who adopts welding as his profession وَیلڈنگ کرنے والا، جوڑنے والا

welfare (*wel*-fay-ĕ*) *n.* good health صحت prosperity خوشحالی well-being بہبود، بہبودی *Welfare State*, State looking to the welfare of all its citizens (esp. through national health insurance, old age pensions or unemployment grants, etc.) رفاہی ریاست، بہبودی ریاست

well (wel) *n.* (old use) spring چشمہ، باؤلی deep brick-lined), shaft for water-supply کنواں *sink a well* کنواں کھودنا *draw water from a well* کنوئیں سے پانی نکالنا *tube-well*, pipes sunk into the earth for drawing large supplies of water with a machine pump ٹیوب وَیل، نل کنواں hole for mineral oil تیل کا کنواں، تیل کا چشمہ central shaft from the roof to the basement of a building for staircase or lift زینے کا گرد (یا لفٹ کا گھر) (large) inkpot دوات source of river منبع، سرچشمہ source for the supply (*of* information, etc.) سرچشمہ good اچھائی satisfactory state تسلّی بخش حالت *adj.* (*well, better, best*) in good health اچھا، خیریت سے in a satisfactory state اچھا، ٹھیک *it would be well to (do)* بہتر یہ ہو گا کہ *well and good*, I have no objection بہت اچھا، بجا، درست، ٹھیک، بالکل ٹھیک، مجھے کوئی اعتراض نہیں *adv.* in a nice place اچھی جگہ in a good condition اچھی طرح in a good style or manner بہت خوب، بہت اچھا، بڑی اچھی طرح intimately اچھی طرح، خوب definitely پوری طرح considerably کافی، کہیں in a praiseworthy manner قابلِ تعریف انداز سے، اچھی طرح *well done!* شاباش! with good reason بجا طور پر *you may well be surprised to know that* تم یہ سن کر بجا طور پر حیران رہ جاؤ گے کہ *int.* (expressing surprise, etc.) اچھا (expressing relief) شکر ہے (expressing resignation) ہاں! *as well*, also (used at the end) بھی *as well as*, in addition to (used with a *sing.* verb) کے علاوہ، مزید برآں *(be) well out of (something)* سے نجات پانا اچھا ہی (ہے) *wish (someone) well* کی کامیابی کی دعا کرنا *come off well* خوش نصیب ثابت ہونا، کامیاب ہونا *speak well of* کی تعریف کرنا *treat (someone) well* سے اچھا برتاؤ کرنا *well past (an age)* (اپنی عمر) سے کافی بڑا *you may as well (do)* ہاں تم بھی کیوں نہیں (کرتے) *you may well ask that* تم بجا طور پر سوال کر سکتے ہو کہ *be (or feel) well* خیریت سے ہونا *the sick and the well* بیمار اور صحتمند

[2]**well-** (wel) *pref.* good خوب، بہ، بہتر، اچھا **well-advised** *adj.* practically wise عقل کے تقاضے کے مطابق *He would be well-advised (to do)* عقل ہو تو بھی (کرے وغیرہ) **well-appointed, well-found** *adj.* well-equipped ہر لیس کانٹے سے لیس **well-balanced** *adj.* sane ہوشمند **well-behaved** *adj.* orderly باتمیز، باسلیقہ **well-being** *n.* welfare بہبود health صحت prosperity خوشحالی **well-born** *n.* of a rich, etc., family اونچے گھرانے کا، عالی خاندان **well-bred** *adj.* brought up well اچھی تربیت والا **well-chosen** *adj.* opportunely selected ٹھیک انتخاب کیا ہوا **well-connected** *adj.* well-born عالی خاندان having connexions with persons of high social status اونچے لوگوں سے میل جول والا **well-disposed** *adj.* favourable (*to* or *towards*) (پر) مہربان **well-doing** *n.* virtuous deeds نیک اعمال **well-done** *adj.* (of meat) done to a turn بڑی اچھی طرح پکا ہوا **well done!** *int.* (expressing praise) شاباش **well-enough** *adj.* fairly good. کافی اچھا **well-edited** *adj.* nicely edited (book) اچھی ترتیب کی ہوئی **well-favoured** *adj.* handsome خوبصورت، خوش شکل، خوش گل **well-founded, well-grounded** *adj.* well-trained (*in* the rudiments of a subject, etc.) مضبوط بنیادوں والا **well-informed, well-posted** *adj.* having much knowledge بڑا باخبر **well-judged** *adj.* opportunely done عقل سے کیا ہوا، بالکل ٹھیک کیا ہوا **well-knit** *adj.* compact (body, structure, etc.) گٹھا ہوا **wellknown** *adj.* famous مشہور **well-meaning, well-intentioned** *adj.* with good intentions نیک نیت، نیک نیتی پر مبنی **well-meant** *adj.* (of action) well-meaning نیک نیتی پر مبنی **well-made** *adj.* shapely خوشنما **well-met** *int.* (old form of greeting) خوب ملے یار! **well-nigh** *adv.* almost قریب قریب، تقریباً **well-timed** *adj.* برِ وقت، ٹھیک وقت پر کیا ہوا **well-to-do** *adj.* rich امیر، خوشحال **well-on** *adj.* at an advanced stage کافی کچھ ہو گیا ہوا **well out of** *adj.* safely rid of سے بخیریت چھٹکارا پایا ہوا **well-pleased** *adj.* (سے) خوش **well-pleasing** *adj.* (کے لیے) تسلّی بخش **well-proportioned** *adj.* متناسب **well-read** *adj.* بڑا پڑھا لکھا **well-regulated** *adj.* orderly بہت باقاعدہ **well-reputed** *adj.* well-known مشہور **well-seeming** *adj.* specious جھوٹا، ریاکارانہ **well-set, well-set-up** *adj.* (of person or body) well-knit گٹھا ہوا **well-spoken** *adj.* refined in speech خوش گفتار **well-tried** *adj.* tested آزمودہ **well-trodden** *adj.* much frequented (path) جس پر بہت آمد و رفت ہو **well-turned** *adj.* well-expressed (remark, etc.) بڑا اچھا **well up**

quite good ; not far from the top (*in*) (میں) بڑا اچھا
well-wisher *n.* خیر خواہ **well-worn** *adj.* worn out پھٹا ہوا trite (expression) فرسودہ
welladay *int.* (old use) alas ! ہائے افسوس، افسوس
welt *n.* leather strip sown between the shoe-upper and the sole جوتے کی مغزی
welter (*wel*-tĕ*) *v.i.* wallow (*in*) لتھڑنا، لوٹنا be steeped (*in*) لتھڑنا *n.* confusion گڑبڑ، افراتفری medley (*of*) گڈمڈ
wench (wench) *n.* (old use) healthy (esp. rustic) lass (گاؤں کی) صحتمند کنواری servant girl جوان نوکرانی
wend *v.t.* make (*one's way* home, etc.) جانا، کی راہ لینا
went *v.* (pa. t. of **go,** which see)
wept *v.* (pa. t. & pa. p. of **weep,** which see)
wert (wĕ*t) (conditional form of *was* for use with *thou*) (اگر تو) تھا
west *n.* one of the four points of the compass مغرب، پچھم *the west wind*, wind blowing from the west پچھوا (*the West*), the European and American nations or their civilisation مغرب، مغربی (اقوام) (یا) مغربی تہذیب *adj.* of the west مغربی *West End*, fashionable quarter of London لندن کا امیرانہ علاقہ *adv.* westwards مغرب کی طرف *travel west* مغرب کے سفر پر جانا، *go west*, (*a*) die مر جانا (*b*) be killed مارا جانا مغرب کی طرف جانا
western *adj.* pertaining to the west مغربی *n.* film, play or novel based on the life of the U.S. cattle districts امریکی چراگاہوں کی زندگی کے متعلق فلم یا ناول **westerner** *n.* native of the West مغربی ملکوں کا باشندہ native of the western U.S. مغربی امریکہ کا باشندہ
westernize *v.t.* introduce western civilization in (a country or person) مغربی رنگ میں رنگ لینا **westerly** *adj.* & *n.* (*n.* pl. *the westerlies*) (wind) blowing from the west پچھوا (of direction) towards the west مغربی **westernmost** *adj.* farthest west مغرب کی طرف بہت دور
wet *adj.* moist نم soaked بھیگا ہوا rainy (day) بارش کا (یا والا) thin (mud, etc.) پتلی (کیچڑ) (of country) without prohibition جہاں شراب بندی نہ ہو *v.t.* (-tt-) make wet بھگو دینا *n.* rain مینہ، بارش moisture **wet nurse** *n.* woman who suckles another's baby انّا، دایہ **wet blanket** *n.* person who damps conversation گفتگو کو بے لطف بنانے والا یا ختم کرانے والا **wet dock** *n.* dock for ships to float پانی والی گودی **wetting** *n.* becoming wet بھیگنا، بھیگ جانا **wet war** *n.* see *Addenda*)
wh- (On the pronunciation of words beginning with *wh*, the famous English lexicographers, Fowler brothers, make this observation : "Most speakers sound the *w* alone except on the rare occasions when confusion between one word and the other, as *whet* and *wet*, may be obviated by the *h* sound ; *wh* is then sounded as *hw*." The compiler of this dictionary, however, dares to add that most good speakers pronounce all the words beginning with *wh* as beginning with *hw*. This is the pronunciation followed in this dictionary)
whack (hwak) *v.t.* hit with a stick or whip so as to produce a sharp sound زناٹے کی رسید کرنا *n.* sharp hit زور کی مار its sound زناٹا
whale (hwayl) *n.* kinds of the largest sea-animal وہیل مچھلی، وہیل (colloq.) tremendous, thing, etc. بہت زیادہ چیز (وغیرہ) *a whale of* (*something*), no end of (it) بے حد، بے انتہا، بے اندازہ *be a whale on* (or *at*, or *for something*), (*a*) be very good at (it) میں بہت اچھا ہونا (*b*) be keen on (it) پر بہت راغب ہونا **whalebone** *n.* bone from its upper jaw وہیل (کے جبڑے) کی ہڈی **whaler** *n.* ship or person hunting whales وہیل پکڑنے والا جہاز (یا) وہیل کا شکاری

a whale

whammy *n.* (see *Addenda*)
wharf (hwo*f) *n.* (pl. *wharfs* or *wharves*) mooring pier for the loading and unloading of ships مال گودی **wharfage** (*hwo**f-ij) *n.* series of wharfs مال گودیاں payment made for the use of a wharf مال گودی کا کرایہ **wharfinger** (*wo**-finj-e*) *n.* one in charge of a wharf مال گودی کا ناظم
what (hwot) *pron.* (*interrogative*) which thing *What is he?* What is his profession, status, etc. ? وہ کرتا کیا ہے؟ وہ ہے کیا؟ (*cf.* who?) *pron.* (*relative*) that which جو *adj.* which کونسا how much کتنا all that جو کچھ *adv.* partly کچھ تو *what* (*with*) کچھ تو (سے) *conj.* that کہ *int.* (expressive of surprise) کیا! ہائیں! *what about* (*something, etc.*) کا کیا حال ہے *what for*, why کیوں *what next* آگے آگے دیکھئے ہوتا ہے کیا *come what will* کچھ ہی کیوں نہ ہو، دیکھا جائیگا *know what is what*, discriminate between right and wrong, etc. میں فرق کر سکنا **whatever, whatsoever** (-*ev*-) *adj.* at all بالکل، کچھ بھی *pron.* all that جو بھی، جو کچھ بھی no matter what کچھ بھی کیوں نہ ہو (emphatic form of the interrogative) what کیا، آخر کیا **whatnot** *n.* a knick-knack cabinet متفرق چیزوں کی الماری hat rack ٹوپی وغیرہ لٹکانے کا کھلا شیشہ دار خانہ many things besides وغیرہ وغیرہ
wheal (hweel) *n.* mine کان (esp.) tin-mine قلعی کی کان

wheat (hweet) *n.* the well-known foodgrain گندم ، گیہوں its plant گندم کا بوٹا **wheaten** *adj.* of coarse wheat flour موٹے آٹے کا

wheedle (*hweed*-ĕl) *v.t.* (usu. of children) get by cajoling (money, etc. *out of* parents, etc.) خوشامد کر کے سے نکلوانا persuade (parents, etc.) by flattery (*into doing* something) سے خوشامد سے کام لینا (of children, etc.) cajole خوشامد کرنا

wheel (hweel) *n.* circular frame turning on axle پہیہ *be at wheel*, drive a (car, etc.) موٹر (وغیرہ) چلانا *v.t.* & *i.* push or pull (something on wheels) while one moves on foot ہاتھ سے لیے جانا ، ٹھیلنا *wheel a bicycle* پیدل چلتے ہوئے سائیکل ساتھ لیے جانا convey (something *to* a place) in a wheelbarrow, etc. ہتھ گاڑی وغیرہ میں لے جانا (cause to) negotiate a bend مڑنا یا موڑنا *right* (or *left*) *wheel*, drill caution to turn right (or left) in marching (دائیں یا بائیں) طرف

wheeled *adj.* having wheels پہیئے دار vehicular (traffic) گاڑیوں کا **wheelbarrow** *n.* small one-wheeled vehicle for small loads ہتھ گاڑی **wheelwright** *n.* one who makes wheels and coaches, etc. تانگے یا ٹھیلے بنانے والا

a wheelbarrow

whelp (hwelp) *n.* puppy پلّا cub شیر کا بچہ unmannered boy or youth بدتمیز لڑکا *v.i.* (of animal) reproduce بیانا

when (hwen) *n.* the time کب ، ہونے کا وقت *pron.* what time کب that time جب *adv.* (*interrogative*) at what time کب (relative) at the time جب while, whereas حالانکہ **whenever** (hwen-*ev*-ĕ*) *adv.* at every time when جب بھی *conj.* as often as جب بھی

whence (hwens) *adv.* from where کہاں سے why کیسے ، کیوں to the place from where جہاں سے ..... وہیں

where (*hway*-ĕ*) *n.* place of occurrence موقع ، مقام *pron.* (*interrogative*) (in) which place کہاں (relative) (in) which place جہاں *adv.* (interrogative) in, to or from which place کہاں (سے) (relative) in, to or at which place جہاں whatever place جہاں بھی ، جہاں **whereabouts** *adv.* in or near what place جہاں ، کہاں *n.* place where someone or something is اتا پتہ *someone's whereabouts* کسی کا اتا پتہ **whereas** (-az) *conj.* although حالانکہ (mostly in legal use) since ہرگاہ **whereat** *adv.* upon which جس پر ، جس کے باعث **whereby** *adv.* by which کس سے ، جس سے **wherefore** *adv.* (old use) why, what for کس لیے **wherein** *adv.* in what کسی بات میں in which جہاں ، کہاں **whereof** *adv.* of which or what جس کا ، کس کا **whereon, whereupon** *adv.* on what or which کس پر ، جس پر as the result of which جس پر ، جس کے باعث **wherever, wheresoever** *adv.* in, to or at, whatever place جہاں ، کہاں (emphatic form of) where جہاں بھی ، کہیں بھی **wherewith** *adv.* with which جس سے **wherewithal** *n.* (*the*) money with which (*to do* something) کرنے کے لیے روپیہ **anywhere** *adv* at any place کہیں **everywhere** *adv.* at all places ہر جگہ **somewhere** *adv.* at some unnamed or unknown place کہیں نہ کہیں

whet (hwet) *v.t.* (-tt-) sharpen (a knife, etc.) on a whetstone, etc. سان پر لگانا ، لگانا make (the appetite) keen تیز کرنا ، زور کی (بھوک) لگانا **whetstone** *n.* stone for whetting سان ، سنگِ فسان

whether (*hwedh*-ĕ*) *conj.* if آیا no matter if خواہ *whether......or* خواہ ... خواہ *whether or not* ہو یا نہ ہو

whew (hwew) *int.* (expressing astonishment) ہونہہ

whey (hway) *n.* watery part of sour milk دودھ (یا دہی) کا پانی ، ماءُ الجبن

which (hwich) *adj.* (interrogative) what کونسا (relative) what جو ، جونسا *pron.* (interrogative) what one (or ones) کونسا (یا کونسے) (relative) that, the one that, any that جو ، جونسا **whichever** *pron.* any one (or ones) of the two (or more) that جو بھی *adj.* any ; no matter which of the two (or more) کوئی سا ، جو بھی

whiff (hwif) *n.* puff (*of* air, etc.) ہلکا سا جھونکا puff (of smoke) ہلکا سا کش smell (*of* cigar, etc.) مہک small cigar چھوٹا چرٹ

Whig (hwig) *n.* earlier name of the British Liberal Party وگ (*Whig*), member of that party وگ ، آزاد خیال

while (hwil) *conj.* during کے دوران میں although حالانکہ *n.* period دیر ، وقت ، عرصہ *once in a while*, occasionally کبھی کبھار time or pains taken in doing something وقت ، محنت وغیرہ *worthwhile* (*to do*), *worth* (*one's*) *while* (*to do*), worth the time or effort spent on it مفید ، کارآمد *v.t.* pass (*away the time*) (pleasantly) وقت (ہنسی خوشی) میں کاٹ دینا

whilom (*hwi*-lom) (old use) *adj.* former پہلا ، سابق *adv.* formerly پہلے

whim (hwim) *n.* caprice من کی موج ، ترنگ ، لہر (also see **whimsy**)

whimper (*hwim*-pĕ*) *n.* weak cry of pain or fear (by a child) ریں ریں *v.i.* cry thus ریں ریں کرنا ، بسورنا

whimsical *adj.* (see under **whimsy**)

whimsy (*hwim*-zi) *n.* (pl. *whimsies*) ❶ whim من کی موج ، ترنگ fancy خبط **whimsical** *adj.* ❶ full of whimsies خبطی capricious موجی ❸ often changing متلون مزاج odd عجیب (Also see **whim**)

whine (hwīn) *n.* long plaintive cry of a dog رِجھینکنا *v.t. & i.* cry thus جھینکنا complain of something thus رورو کر شکایت کرنا کہ ask (*for* help) by debasing oneself گڑگڑا کر مدد مانگنا

whinny (*hwin*-i) *n.* gentle neigh of horse expressing pleasure خوشی کی ہنہناہٹ *v.i.* (of a horse) neigh thus خوشی سے آہستہ آہستہ ہنہنانا

whip (hwip) *n.* handle with a lash کوڑا ، چابک member of a parliamentary party responsible for the attendance of others when a division is forced پارٹی وہپ ، جماعتی چابک دار *v.t. & i.* strike with a whip کوڑے لگانا ، چابک مارنا beat (eggs, cream, etc.) انڈے وغیرہ پھینٹنا take (*out* a knife, etc.) suddenly جھٹ سے نکال لینا take (*off* one's coat, etc.) suddenly جلدی سے اُتارنا **whipping** *n.* castigation سزا کے طور پر کوڑے لگنا یا لگانا **whipcord** *n.* tightly twisted thin cord سخت ڈوری **whip-round** *n.* charitable appeal made to members of a club or friends, etc. دوستوں (یا کلب کے ممبروں) سے چندے کی اپیل ، چندے کے لیے یار یاری

Ⓢ To **whip** is to hit on the flesh with a stinging thing like a thong or thin rope; to **punish**, in general; to **chastise**, formal; to **castigate** and to **scourge** are poetic words; to **lash** is to hit with a flat surface; to spank is to strike (esp. someone's bottom) with a flat surface.

whipper-snapper (*hwip*-è*-snap-ĕ*) *n.* small child ننھا مُنّا insignificant person who happens to be presumptuous بزخودِ غلط شخص ، اپنے کو نہ جانے کیا سمجھنے والا

whire, whirr (hwĕ*) *n.* sound of a swiftly moving wheel گھر گھر sound of a fast-flying bird's wings کٹ کٹ *v.t.* make such sounds گھر گھر (یا) کٹ کٹ کرنا

whirl (hwe*l) *v.t. & i.* revolve rapidly تیز گھومنا یا گھمانا be giddy (of car, train, driver, etc.) move or convey (off, away, etc.) swiftly (گاڑی یا موٹر کا) تیزی سے چلنا ، (گاڑی یا موٹر میں) تیزی سے لے جانا *n.* whirling movement تیز چکر **whirligig** (*hwĕ**-li-gig) *n.* merry-go-round چکر جھولا child's toy like a merry-go-round چکر جھولا کھلونا **whirlpool** *n.* eddy بھنور ، گرداب **whirlwind** *n.* whirl of dust, etc. بگولا ، گردباد

whirr (hwĕ*) *n. & v.t.* (same as **whir**, which see)

whisht (hwisht) *int.* (demanding silence) چپ ، خاموش ، شو

whisk (hwisk) *n.* small light brush for flies or dust چھوٹا مورچھل instrument for beating up cream or eggs چھوٹی متھنی light movement (of tail, etc.) جانور کی دُم کی) حرکت یا بلونی *v.t. & i.* brush (*off*, *away, etc.*) lightly مورچھل سے جھاڑنا take or go (*off, away*) swiftly (*to* a place) تیزی سے جانا یا لے جانا (of animal) move (its tail) swiftly (دُم) جلدی جلدی پھیرنا

a whisk

whisker (*hwis*-kĕ*) *n.* (usu. *pl.*) hair growing on the sides of the face گل مچھے ، گل مُوچھیں stiff hair near the mouth of a cat, etc. بلی (وغیرہ) کی مونچھ

whisky (*hwis*-ki) *n.* strong liquor made from barley, etc. وِسکی glass of it وِسکی کا جام

whisper (*hwis*-pĕ*) *v.i.* say (something) in undertones (*to*) سرگوشیوں میں کہنا ، کانا پھوسی کرنا (of wind, leaves, etc.) rustle سرسر کرنا *n.* (something said in) a whispering sound سرگوشی ، کانا پھوسی ، راز کی بات rumour اُڑتی ہوئی خبر ، افواہ **whisperingly** *adv.* سرگوشیوں کے انداز میں

whist (hwist) *n.* a well-known card-game for four players کوٹ پیس (یا) ترپ

whistle (*hwis*-èl) *n.* shrill note made by blowing سیٹی ، صفیر instrument for producing this sound سیٹی *blow a whistle*, use this instrument for producing the note سیٹی بجانا musical sound made by birds پرندوں کی سیٹی ، صفیر *v.t. & i.* make whistle by blowing through the lips سیٹیاں بجانا ، سیٹی بجانا *whistle a tune*, produce music thus سیٹی میں کوئی دُھن گانا signal (*to* someone) thus or by blowing a whistle سیٹی کا اشارہ کرنا

white (hwīt) *adj.* of colour of milk or snow سفید (یا) سفید یا سپید hoary (hair) بانگل سفید fair-skinned گورا pale زرد ، پیلا spotless بے عیب ، بے داغ innocent (soul) معصوم *n.* the colour of milk or snow سفید رنگ fair-skinned person گورا (یا) گوری anything white کوئی سفید چیز *dressed in white* سفید پوشاک میں *the whites of the eye* آنکھ کی پتلی کی سفیدی *white of an egg* انڈے کی سفیدی **white ant** *n.* termite دیمک **whitecaps** *pl.* foam covering a surge لہر کا جھاگ والی بلندی ، لہر کا جھاگ **white coffee** *n.* coffee with milk دودھ والی کافی ، شیر دار قہوہ **white elephant** *n.* rare but too burdensome possession سفید ہاتھی **whiting** (*wīt*-ing) *n.* powdered (and then solidified) white chalk, etc., for cleaning (صفائی وغیرہ کے لیے) کھریا *a white lie* a harmless, excusable lie told for the sake of politeness قابلِ معافی جھوٹ **Note:** The English *white lie* is quite *different* from the Urdu سفید جھوٹ **white feather** *n.* cowardice بزدلی *show the white feather* بزدلی دکھانا **white flag** *n.* symbol of surrender or truce سفید جھنڈا ، شکست یا عارضی صلح کا جھنڈا **white paper** *n.* British Government's report (*on*) قرطاسِ ابیض **white man** *n.* (member of) European race گوری نسل (کا) *white man's burden*, Western nations' self-styled duty of civilizing the coloured races used as a cloak for their imperialistic tactics اقوامِ مغرب کی ذمہ داری **white sale** *n.* sale of household or body linen لٹھے کے کپڑوں چادروں وغیرہ کی فروخت

white scourge *n.* T. B. تپ دق، دق، دق سل **white slave**, European girl kidnapped for prostitution بیسوا بنانے کے لیے پکڑی ہوئی ولایتی گوری **whitesmith**, tinman قلعی گر **white war** *n.* war without bloodshed سفید جنگ، خونریزی کے بغیر جنگ (esp.) economic war معاشی جنگ **whitewash** *n.* thin slaked lime for coating walls, etc. سفیدی means of whitewashing character (کی) بریت میں کچھ کہنا، لیپا پوتی *v.t.* coat (something) with whitewash (پر) سفیدی کرنا bid to clear (someone) of accusations, etc. لیپا پوتی کرنا، (کی) بریت میں کچھ کہنا

whiten (*hwīt*-ĕn) *v.t.* & *i.* make or become white

whiteness *n.* quably or state of being white

whither (*hwidh*-e*) *adv.* (old use) where کدھر

Whitsun (*hwit*-sun), **Whitsunday** *n.* seventh Sunday after Easter ایسٹر کے بعد کا ساتواں اتوار، سفید اتوار

Whitsuntide *n.* Whitsun and the following week سفید اتوار والا ہفتہ

whittle (*hwit*-el) *v.t.* & *i.* cut thin strips of چھیلنا cut (*down* or *away*) gradually آہستہ آہستہ بڑی کمی کرنا

whiz, whizz (hwiz) *n.* sound of something rushing through the air سن سے نکلنے کی آواز، سن کی سی آواز *v.i.* fly past with this sound سن کی سی آواز کے ساتھ نکل جانا

who (hoo) *pron.* (objective case : *whom* possessive case : *whose*) (interrogative) what (sort of) person (or persons) کون، کونسا (relative) (the one) that جو، جس نے anyone who جو بھی، جس نے بھی (emphatic form of who) آخر کون، آخر کس نے، آخر جو، آخر جس نے

whole (hohl) *adj.* entire پورا، سارا، تمام unbroken, not cracked صحیح سالم، ثابت undivided پورا، تمام (old use) healthy تندرست، صحت مند *n.* total (*of*) کل something complete مکمل چیز، ساری چیز *on the whole* بحیثیت مجموعی *the whole of* سارے کا سارا unbroken ثابت، سالم *a whole number*, integer صحیح (عدد) *escape with a whole skin* صحیح سلامت بچ نکلنا

whole-hearted *adj.* unhesitating (support, etc.) مکمل، پورا، مخلصانہ **whole-hogger** *n.* extremist انتہا پسند *go the whole hog* (*for something*), (*a*) do it thoroughly پوری طرح کرنا (*b*) go to the extreme پر پہنچنا **whole-sale** *n.* selling of goods for resale (as opposed to *retail*) تھوک *sell* (*by*) *wholesale* تھوک بیچنا *wholesale dealer* تھوک فروش complete (massacre, etc.) پورا، عام **wholesome** *adj.* (of air, food or place) conducive to health صحت بخش

wholly *adv.* entirely پوری طرح، سارا

whom (hoom) *pron.* objective case of *who* (which see) جسے، جنہیں، جس کو (وغیرہ)، جن کو (وغیرہ)

whoop (hwoop), **hoop** (hoop) *n.* loud and eager cry (*of* joy, etc.) قہقہہ gasping sound after cough کھوں کھوں، کھڑ کھڑ **whooping-cough, hooping-cough** *n.* (children's) disease marked by spasms of coughing without the discharge of phlegm کالی کھانسی **whoopee** (hwoop-ee) *n.* (U.S. colloq.) noisy rejoicings خوشی کا ہنگامہ (esp. in the phrase :) *make whoopee*, rejoice noisily خوشی سے ہنگامہ برپا کرنا

whooping-cough *n.* (see under **whoop**)

whop (hwop) *v.i.* (-pp-) (slang) defeat ہرانا thrash مارنا، پیٹنا **whopper** *n.* (slang) big lie سفید جھوٹ any big specimen بڑا، بڑا نمونہ **whopping** *adj.* (slang) very big بہت بڑا

whore (hwoh*) *n.* (indecent word for) prostitute رنڈی، کسبی *v.i.* (old use) go to whores زناکاری کرنا **whoredom** *n.* زناکاری

whose (hwooz) *pron.* (possessive case of **who,** which see) کس کا، کن کا

why (hwī) *adv.* (interrogative) for what reason کیوں، کس لیے (relative) the reason for which جس لیے، جس وجہ سے *int.* (expressive of surprise) ہیں، ہائیں *n.* (pl. *whys*, pr. whīz) cause وجہ، سبب

wick (wik) *n.* thread or tape feeding the flame (*of* a candle, lantern or stove) بتی *trim the wick* بتی کاٹنا

wicked (*wik*-ĕd) *adj.* sinful گنہگار، عاصی، بد اعمال bad بُرا، بد طینت، شیطان spiteful, ضرر رساں، بُرا immoral (act) بدکاری کا، بُرا roguish شوخ، شرارت بھرا **wickedly** *adv.* بد طینتی سے **wickedness** *n.* بد اعمالی، برائی، فسق و فجور، بد طینتی، ضرر رسانی، شرارت

wicker (*wik*-ĕ*) *n.* plaited twigs, etc. گندھی ہوئی شاخیں (یا ڈالیاں یا ٹہنیاں) **wickerwork** *n.* wicker furniture, etc. گندھی ہوئی ٹہنیوں کا سامان

wicket (*wik*-et) *n.* (also *wicket-door* or *wicket-gate*) small door or window in a gate بڑے پھاٹک میں لگی ہوئی کھڑکی، چور کھڑکی turnstile entrance پھرکی دروازہ small opening for selling tickets, etc. ذرا سی کھڑکی three cricket stumps with bails on top وکٹ member of the batting team بلے باز، اندر کھیلنے والی (یا بیٹنگ کرنے والی) ٹیم کا کھلاڑی stretch of grass between the two wickets دونوں وکٹوں کا درمیانی فاصلہ، وکٹ *take a wicket*, ایک بلے باز کو نکال باہر کرنا، ایک کھلاڑی آوٹ کرنا *two* (*etc.*) *wickets down* دو (وغیرہ) کھلاڑی آوٹ، دو بلے باز باہر *keep* (*one's*) *wicket up*, آوٹ نہ ہونے کی کوشش کرنا *win by four* (*etc.*) *wickets*, with only six batsmen out چار (وغیرہ) وکٹوں سے جیت لینا **wicket-keeper** *n.* member of the fielding team standing behind the wicket وکٹ کیپر

wide (wīd) *adj.* broad چوڑا، عریض manifold بہت، کئی، متعدد *a man of wide interests*, one versed or interested in many subjects کئی مضامین میں دلچسپی رکھنے والا

give wide berth to (*someone*), avoid (him) سے بچنا، سے دُور دُور رہنا *be wide of the mark*, be far from what is aimed at نشانہ خطا ہونا، تیر نشانے پر نہ بیٹھنا *wide ball*, wide of the mark ball in cricket دُور ہٹ کر گرنے والی گیند *adv.* in various directions کئی طرف، ہر طرف *search far and wide* دُور دُور تک ہر طرف تلاش کرنا completely پُوری طرح *with (one'e) eyes wide open*, *with (one's) eyes wide awake* پُوری طرح چوکس، چوکنّا *wide apart* کے بیچ میں بڑا فاصلہ *widespread*, (a) found over a large area دُور تک پھیلا ہُوا (b) current everywhere عام **widen** (*wid*-èn) *v.t.* & *i.* make or become wider چوڑا یا وسیع ہونا یا کرنا **widely** over a large area دُور تک considerably بہُت at long intervals دیر دیر بعد **width** (width) *n.* breadth چوڑائی، عرض *Fifteen feet in width, 15-foot-wide, 15 feet wide* پندرہ فٹ چوڑا being wide چوڑا ہونا

widow (*wid*-oh) *n.* woman whose (last) husband has died and who has not married since بیوہ

widower (*wid*-oh-è*) *n.* man whose wife has died and who has not married since رنڈوا

widowed (*wid*-ohd) *adj.* made into a widow or widower بیوہ (یا رنڈوا) کر دینا **widowhood** *n.* state of being a widow بیوگی، رنڈاپا

width *n.* (see under **wide**)

wield (weeld) *v.t.* hold (sceptre, sway, power, authority, control. influence) رکھنا، والا ہونا، کا مالک ہونا hold and use (sword, axe, etc.) چلانا، گھُمانا employ (power, sword, etc.) کو کام میں لانا، کو استعمال کرنا

wife (wif) *n.* (pl. *wives*, pr. wivz) married woman (in relation to her husband) بیوی، جورُو، زوجہ *old wives' tale*, silly tradition توہّم، احمقانہ روایت **wifehood** *n.* being a wife بیوی ہونا **wifelike, wifely** *adv.* like a good wife نیک بیویوں کی طرح، اچھی بیوی کے شایاں

wig *n.* head-covering of false hair worn by judges etc. وِگ، مصنوعی بالوں کا کنٹوپ *v.t.* rebuke sharply سخت سخت ڈانٹ ڈپٹ جھاڑ جھپاڑ کرنا **wigging** *n.* sharp rebuke

wiggle (*wig*-èl) *n.* scull ; row (boat) with single oar at the stern پیچھے بیٹھ کر صرف ایک چپّو سے ناؤ کھینا

wight (wit) *n.* (old use or jocular) man or person آدمی، شخص

wigwam (*wig*-wam) *n.* Red Indian hut or tent ریڈ انڈین کا جھونپڑا (یا خیمہ)

wild (wild) *adj.* untamed (animal) جنگلی، وحشی *wild-boar* جنگلی سُور *wild goose* جنگلی بطخ *wild-goose chase*, running after impossibilities; vain attempts ناممکن بات کے پیچھے دَوڑنا، فضُول کوشش، سعیِ لاحاصل *wild-cat* جنگلی بِلّا *wild-cat schemes*, reckless financial schemes اندھا دُھند مالی منصُوبے (of plants) growing in natural state خود رَو *run wild* (of plants) grow on their own خُود رَو ہونا uninhabited and uncultivated (place) اجاڑ، غیر آباد stormy (seas, weather, wind, night, etc.) طُوفانی، طُوفان خیز frantic (with rage, anxiety, etc.) آپے سے باہر، بیتاب *wild with joy*, خوشی سے بیتاب، جامے میں پھُولا نہ سمانے والا *drive wild with* سے پاگل ہو رہا *wild about* (or *to do*) (*something*) کے لیے بیتاب *wild about* (*someone*), wildly in love with کے پیچھے دیوانہ (of youth) leading a recklessly immoral life سخت عیّاش (of children, etc.) without restraint بے قابو، شتر بے مہار *allow (child) to run wild* کو شتر بے مہار نکلنے دینا *wild work*, unlawful activities غیر قانُونی حرکات (of times, etc.) troublous پُر آشوب (of hair, dress, etc.) disorderly پریشان *adv.* without control بے قابُو without care بے حفاظت *n.* (pl. *the wilds*), uncultivated areas غیر آباد علاقے **wildly** *adv.* rashly جلدبازی، بیتابی، اندھا دُھند، بے سوچے سمجھے **wildness** *n.* وحشت، جنگلی ہونا، خُود رَو ہونا **wildfire** *n.* Greek fire آتش گیر سیّال *spread like wildfire*, (of news) spread rapidly تیزی سے پھیلنا **wilderness** (*wild*-dě*-nes) *n.* desert صحرا *a voice in the wilderness*, moralist to whom none would listen مُصلح جس کی آواز کوئی نہ سُنے، صدا بصحرا

wile (wil) *n.* crafty words meant to deceive پُرفریب الفاظ trick چال، فریب، مکر، دھوکا *the wiles of the devil* شیطان کے فریب *v.t.* trick (someone *away*, or *into doing* something) دھوکے سے گمراہ کرنا **wily** (*wi*-li) *adj.* cunning مکّار، فریبی، چالباز

wilful *adj.*, **wilfully** *adv.*, **wilfulness** *n.* (see under **will**)

will (wil) *n.* mental power to choose own way اختیار، ارادہ what is liked by one مرضی، منشا، رضا *have (one's) will* اپنی مرضی کرنا *God's will be done* رضائے الٰہی پُوری ہو *be married against (one's) will* خلافِ مرضی شادی ہونا *at will*, as one pleases حسبِ مرضی، جب چاہے *a tenant at will*, one who can be turned out without notice تابعِ مرضی مُزارع (یا اسامی) (also *will-power*), control over one's impulses قوّتِ ارادی resolve عزم، پکّا ارادہ testament وصیّت *v.* (abbr. *'ll*; negative *will not* or *wont*; pa. t. & conditional *would* or *'d*; negative *wouldn't* or *'d not*; with *thou* the present form is *wilt* or *'lt*; pa. t. and conditional *wouldst, wouldest*, or *'dst*) (*auxiliary*) (forming compound future or conditional tenses) ہوگا، ہُوا ہوگا وغیرہ (expressing insistence) ضرُور ہی (request) کیا آپ، ازراہِ کرم (habit) ہی *v.t.* (same forms) wish چاہنا be willing پر راضی ہونا promise وعدہ کرنا be determined to ضرُور، لازماً (ہونا) *v.t.* (*will, willed, willed*) leave (property) by will to کے نام وصیّت کر جانا **willing** *adj.* ready (*to do*) the needful, etc. (پر) راضی، رضامند، آمادہ، تیار cheerfully ready خوش، آمادہ voluntarily رضاکارانہ، خوشی سے **willingly** *adv.* خوشی سے **willingness** *n.* آمادگی **wilful** *adj.* self-willed خودسر obstinate ضدی، ہٹیلا deliberate (action) دیدہ دانستہ، قصداً کیا ہوا **wilfully** *adv.* عمداً قصداً، ضد سے، خودسری سے **wilfulness** *n.* ضد، خود رائی، خودسری، سرکشی

will o'-the-wisp (wil-o-the-*wisp*) *n.* jack-o'-lantern) غول بیابانی elusive person جو شخص ہمیشہ کبھی ہاتھ نہ آئے something pursued in vain طرح دے جانے والی چیز

willow (*wil*-oh) *n.* a waterside tree with pliable branches بید its wood بید مجنوں، بید cricket bat کرکٹ کا بلّا **willowy** *adj.* slender (person) with graceful movements نازک اور لچکدار having a large number of willows بکثرت بیدوں والا

a willow-tree

willy nilly (*wil*-i-*nil*-i) *adv.* willingly, خواہی نخواہی، مرضی ہو یا نہ ہو

wilt *v.t.* & *i.* wither مرجھا جانا *v.* (*auxiliary*) (second person sing. form of **will,** which see) گا

wily *adj.* (see under **wile**)

Wimbledon (*wimb*-ĕl-dun) *n.* & *adj.* (pertaining to the) international lawn-tennis championship meeting at Wimbledon ومبلڈن

win *v.t.* & *i.* (-nn-) (*win, won, won*) gain a victory جیتنا، فتح حاصل کرنا be successful in getting (victory, prize, promotion, fame, etc.) پانا، حاصل کرنا be victorious in (battle, competition, race, etc.) میں reach (the shore, etc.) by effort کوشش سے پہنچنا، میں جیتنا persuade (someone) to come (*over to* one's side or views) (کو) ساتھ ملا لینا، (کو) ہمنوا بنا لینا *n.* success in competition, etc. جیت **winner** *n.* one who (or the team which) wins جیتنے والا victor فاتح، فتح مند **winning** *adj.* attractive (ways, looks, smile, etc.) and likely to win favour دلکش pertaining to a win جیت *winning post*, post marking the end of the race-track (گھوڑ دوڑ میں) جیتنے کا پالا، جیت پالا **winnings** *n. pl.* money made by gambling جوئے کی جیت

wince (wins) *v.i.* start back (*under* the knife, *at* the insult, etc.) جھرجھری لینا، کو جھرجھری آنا *n.* starting back جھرجھری لینا

wincey (*wins*-i) *n.* (pl. *winseys*) pure or mixed woollen material for dresses ونسی **winceytte** (wins-i-*et*) *n.* such material with less wool ونسیٹیٹ

winch (winch) *n.* windlass چرخی

wind *n.* (pr. wind, except in poetry where it is often pr. wınd) current of air ہوا، چلتی ہوا *fair wind*, wind helping the ships بادِ موافق، بادِ مُرطہ، بادِ شرط *contrary wind* بادِ مخالف *windbound*, (of ship) held up by contrary wind بادِ مخالف کی وجہ سے رُکا ہوا (also *strong wind*), strong current of air آندھی *in the wind* being secretly planned اندر ہی اندر ہو رہا ہونا، اندر خانے ہو رہا ہونا *see* (or *find out*) *how the wind blows*, (*a*) wait for the future developments دیکھیں اونٹ کس کروٹ بیٹھتا ہے (*b*) try to gauge public opinion دیکھیں لوگ کیا کہتے ہیں *fling to the winds, cast to the winds*, give up چھوڑ دینا، ترک کر دینا *take the wind out of* (*someone's*) *sails*, forestall (him) in speech or action سے پہلے کہہ (یا کر) دینا long senseless talk فضول بکواس breath needed for running, etc. دم، سانس *lose* (*one's*) *wind* سانس پھول جانا *short-winded* جس کی سانس جلدی پھول جائے *long-winded*, (*a*) (one) who is not short-winded جس کی سانس جلدی نہ پھولے (*b*) long (speech) طویل (*c*) (person) who goes on talking باتونی scent (of something) carried by wind بُو *get wind of*, (*a*) scent کی بُو پا لینا (*b*) suspect کا شبہ ہونا (*c*) come to know of secretly (کی) سُن گُن پا لینا gas in the stomach ریح **winds** *n. pl.* strong, seasonal air currents over wide zones ہوائیں musical wind-instruments in an orchestra ہوا باجے، پُون باجے *v.t.* (with various pronunciations) (A) (*wind* pr. wind ; *winded* ; *winded* pr. *wind*-id) give rest to (an out-of-breath horse) دم دینا cause to be out of breath دم چڑھا دینا follow or detect by scent بُو سونگھ کر ڈھونڈ لینا یا پیچھا کرنا (B) (*wind* pr. wınd ; *wound* ; *wound*, pr. wound) coil (watch, etc.) چابی دینا *wind up*, (*a*) coil completely پوری طرح چابی دینا (*b*) end ختم ہونا یا کرنا (*c*) work up بھڑکانا *wound up* بھرا ہوا، برافروختہ meander (دریا کا) بل کھاتے ہوئے جانا spiral چکر بن کر اٹھنا *winding staircase* چکر دار زینہ turn the handle of (a windlass, etc.) (چرخی) گھمانا haul (or *up* something thus) چرخی سے اوپر کھینچنا insinuate (one's way *into*) خوشامد در آمد سے گھس جانا (10) cover (part of body *with* bandages, etc.) (پر) باندھنا (11) pursue (one's way or course) windingly (*up* or *down* a place) چکر کاٹ کر جانا (یا آنا) (C) (*wind* pr. wınd ; winded, winded pr. wınd-id ; or less correctly *wound*, *wound* pr. wound) (12) blow (horn, bugle, etc.) بجانا، پھونکنا **windfall** *n.* fruit blown down by the wind آندھی سے گرا ہوا پھل unexpected piece of good fortune نعمتِ غیر مترقبہ such monetary gift چھپّر پھاڑ کر ملی ہوئی دولت **wind-gauge** *n.* instrument for measuring intensity of wind بادپیما **wind**

instrument *n.* any musical instrument played by blowing through it ہَوا باجا ، پَوَن باجا **winding-sheet** (*wind-*) *n.* shroud کفن **wind-jammer** *n.* (slang) merchant sailing-vessel تجارتی بادبانی جہاز

windmill *n.* grinding mill with large wooden sails worked by wind پَوَن چکّی **windpipe** *n.* air passage from the throat to the lungs نرخرا ، سانس کی نالی **wind-screen** *n.* (U.S. *wind shield*) *n.* sheet of glass in front of a motor vehicle's front seat ہَوا روک شیشہ ، ہَوا روک **wind-sock** *n.* canvas cone (in aerodrome etc.) flying from a mast-head to indicate the wind-direction بادنما جراب ، بادنما **wind-tunnel** *n.* device for producing artificial air current for testing aircraft models, etc. بادزن **windward** *adj.* (of the side) lying in that direction ہَوا کے رُخ کا *adv.* towards the wind ہَوا کے رُخ **windy** (*wind-*i) *adj.* (place) with much wind ہَوادار (day, etc.) with much wind بڑی ہَوا والا wordy بِزی لفاظی والا **windless** (*wind-*les) *n.* without wind جس میں ہَوا نہ چلے

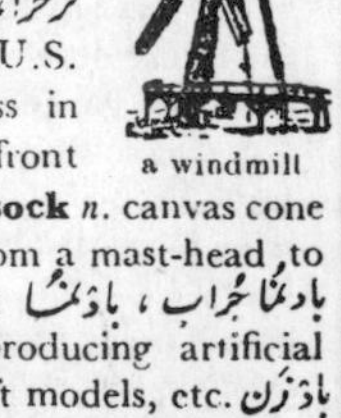
a windmill

windlass (*wind-*las) *n.* winch ; device for hauling with a rope rolling on an axle turned by a handle چرخی

window (*wind-*oh) *n.* opening in a wall for fresh air and light کھڑکی ، دَریچہ **window-dressing** *n.* arranging wares attractively in a shop window دُکان کی بیرونی الماری میں چیزیں لگانا skilful presentation of something actually not so good لیپا پوتی ، پُرفریب نمائش

windy (*wind-*i) *adj.* (see under **wind**)

wine (win) *n.* liquor made from grape-juice خمر ، انگور کی شراب *Adam's wine*, water پانی *new wine in old bottles*, new principle(s) in an old form نیا اُصُول پُرانے انداز سے after-dinner wine-party دعوتِ مے نوشی **winebibber** (*win*-bib-ĕ*) *n.* tippler پکا شرابی **wine-glass** *n.* small glass for wine جام ، ساغر ، ساتگیں **wine-press** *n.* press for squeezing juice out of grapes انگور کا عرق نکالنے کی کل ، انگور افشار **wine vault** *n.* wine-cellar شراب رکھنے کا تہ خانہ

wing *n.* limb used by a bird for flying پرندے کا بازو ، پَر ، بال ، شہپر *on the wing*, flying اُڑ رہا *under (someone's) wing*, under (his) protection کے زیرِ حمایت part (*of* or *to* a building, army, etc.) stretching out at the side بازو ، پہلو ، نکلا ہُوا حصہ Air Force formation of two or more squadrons وِنگ ، ہَوائی بیڑہ *Wing Commander*, a high rank in the Air Force وِنگ کمانڈر ، بیڑہ دار (*pl.*) hidden sides of the stage سٹیج کے بازو badge of qualified member of aircrew ہَوا بازی کی سند *wings*, badge of qualified pilot ہَوا بازی کی سند *get the wings* پکّے ہَوا باز کی سند پانا out of the broad support surfaces of an aircraft (ہَوائی جہاز کا) بازو mud-guard of motor-vehicle موٹر (وغیرہ) کا مڈگارڈ ، کیچ روک *v.t.* equip *with* wings بازو پر لگانا shoot (a bird) in the wing زخم لگانا travel by flying (*its way* across some place, etc.) اُڑ کر جانا **winged** (wingd) *adj.* having wings پَروں والا **wingless** *adj.* without wings بے پَر

wink *v.t.* & *i.* blink (one's eye or eyes) (آنکھ یا پلک یا پلکیں) جھپکنا *wink at (someone)*, give (him) a hint by winking آنکھ سے (یا کا) اشارہ کرنا ، آنکھ مارنا *wink at (a or someone's) mistake*, overlook it کو نظر انداز کر دینا *n.* winking آنکھ جھپکنا *forty winks*, nap قیلولہ *not to sleep a wink, not to have a wink of sleep* رات آنکھوں میں کاٹنا (یا کٹنا) ، بالکل آنکھ نہ لگنا signalling thus آنکھ کا اشارہ *tip (someone) the wink*, give (him) a hint privately کو آنکھ سے اشارہ کر دینا

winning *adj.*, **winner** *n.* (see under **win**)

winnow (*win*-oh) *v.t.* separate chaff from grain by tossing and letting fall in air current پھٹکنا separate (something *from* another which is less useful) الگ کرنا ، علیحدہ کرنا

winsome (*win*-sum) *adj.* attractive (personality, child, smile, etc.) دِلکش

winter (*wint*-ĕ*) *n.* coldest season of the year (from December to March in N. hemisphere) سردی کا موسم ، سردیاں ، موسمِ سرما ، سرما any gloomy period (*of*) رنج ، اُداسی *adj.* pertaining to winter سرمائی ، سردی کا ، سردیوں کا *long winter nights* سردیوں کی طویل راتیں *winter clothing* گرم کپڑے *v.t.* & *i.* pass the winter (*in* warm place, etc.) (میں) سردیاں کاٹنا یا گزارنا feed (cattle, etc.) during winter سردیوں میں کھانے کو دینا **wintry** (*wint*-ri) *adj.* of or like winter سرمائی ، سردیوں کا (سا)

wipe (wip) *v.t.* clean or dry (something) by rubbing (*with* or *on* a cloth, etc.) پونچھنا *wipe (one's) tears away* آنسو پونچھنا *wipe the dishes* پلیٹیں پونچھنا *wipe (something) dry* پونچھ کر خشک کرنا *wipe (one's) hands on a towel* ہاتھ تولیے سے پونچھنا *wipe up (a liquid)*, dry (it) by soaking a piece of cloth in it خشک کرنا *wipe (out or off vessel, etc.)*, clean (it) دھو ڈالنا *wipe off (disgrace, insult, etc.)*, remove (it) دُور کرنا *wipe off (or out something)*, destroy (it) completely (کا) نام و نشان مٹا ڈالنا ، حرفِ غلط کی طرح مٹانا *n.* wiping پونچھنا ، خشک کرنا

wire (*wi*-è*) *n.* metal drawn out like thread تار a length of it تار *telegraph wires* تار *telephone wires* ٹیلیفون کے تار (colloq.) telegram تار ، برقیہ *pull the wires*, (*a*) control puppets thus تار ہلا کر پتلیوں کو نچانا (*b*) control (trend of events, persons, etc.) thus پیچھے بیٹھ کر تار ہلانا *wire-pulling* پیچھے بیٹھ کر تار ہلانا *wire-puller* پیچھے بیٹھ کر تار ہلانے والا *wiredraw*, (*a*) draw a wire تار کھینچنا (*b*) draw too fine distinctions in arguments, etc. حد سے زیادہ بال کی کھال نکالنا ، باریکی سے کام لینا *v.t.* & *i.* fasten (something) with wire تار سے باندھنا install insulated wires (*for* electric current) بجلی لگانا send a telegram to کو تار بھیجنا **wiry** (wī-ri) *adj.* stiff like wire تار کی طرح سخت thin but strong (person) دُبلا مگر زور والا **wire netting** *n.* wire-gauze تار کی جالی

wireless (*wī*-è*-les) *adj.* without the use of wires بے تار، لاسلکی *wireless telephony* لاسلکی، دُور گوئی *wireless telegraphy* بے تار، لاسلکی پیغام رسانی pertaining to wireless ریڈیو *wireless station*, broadcasting house ریڈیو سٹیشن، نشرگاہ *wireless-set*, wireless receiving set ریڈیو *wireless licence*, radio licence, licence for keeping wireless set(s) at a particular place ریڈیو لائسنس *n.* wireless telephony or telegraphy لاسلکی نشریات نشریات radio ریڈیو، منتشر *listen to* (*something*) *on* (or *over*) *the wireless* ریڈیو پر سُننا

wisdom (*wiz*-dum) *n.* being wise عقلمندی، دانشمندی *all the wit and wisdom of* (*a place*), all (its) wise men کسی جگہ کے تمام دانشمند philosophical thoughts فلسفیانہ افکار sententious sayings اقوالِ زرّیں، جوامعُ الکلم *the wisdom of our ancestors* اسلاف کے اقوالِ زرّیں **wisdom-tooth** *n.* (pl. *wisdom-teeth*) one of the four cut usu. after one is 20 عقل ڈاڑھ *cut* (*one's*) *wisdom-teeth* (*a*) cut these teeth کی عقل ڈاڑھیں نکلنا (*b*) gain discretion جوانی کی ہوشمندی کو پہنچنا

wise (wīz) *adj.* discreet دانشمند having a knowledge and knowing how to use it علم و عقل والا prudent (act) عقلمندی کا، دانشمندانہ suggestive of being wise عقلمندوں کی طرح، دانشمندانہ انداز سے *n.* (old use) manner طرح، طریق (now in the phrases :) *any wise* کسی طرح بھی نہیں *in no wise* کسی نہ کسی طرح *in this wise* اس طرح، یوں **wiseacre** (*wīz*-ay-kè*) *n.* sententious person trying to appear wiser than he is حکمت بگھارنے والا **wise crack** *n.* smart pithy remark ; quip چٹکنے والی بات، چُست فقرہ ، پھبتی **wise-crack** *v.i.* make wise cracks فقرے کسنا، فقرے بازی کرنا، پھبتی کہنا **wisely** *adv.* عقل سے، دانشمندی سے **wise-saw** *n.* proverb ضرب المثل، کہاوت **wise-woman** *n.* midwife دایہ witch چڑیل، جادوگرنی fortune-teller فال رَمل کھولنے والی

-wise (wīz) *suf.* (added to nouns to mean) like کی طرح، کا سا، کے مطابق ، کے رُخ *clockwise* گھڑی کی سوئیوں کے رُخ *anti-clockwise* گھڑی کی سوئیوں کے اُلٹے رُخ

wish *v.t.* & *i.* long for آرزو کرنا، تمنا رکھنا express a desire کی تمنا ظاہر کرنا say words of greeting to سلام (یا خدا حافظ وغیرہ) کہنا pray (*for*) (کی) دُعا کرنا pray for (something) for (someone) (کے لیے) کی دُعا کرنا want چاہنا *n.* desire خواہش، مرضی *in deference to* (*someone's*) *wishes* کی خواہش پر عمل کرتے ہوئے *with all good wishes* آپ کی بہبود کا متمنی، دُعائے خیر کے ساتھ **wishful** having a desire آرزومندانہ based on vain hopes خوش فہمی پر مبنی *wishful thinking*, belief founded on wishes rather than facts ; believing that something will turn out in accordance with one's wishes خوش فہمی میں مبتلا ہونا ، خوش فہمی کا شکار ہونا **wisher** *n.* one who wishes خواہاں، طالب *well-wisher* خیر خواہ

wish-wash, wishy-washy *n.* watery (soup, etc.) پانی پتلا، پتلا پانی سا

wistful (*wist*-ful) *adj.* pensive حسرت بھرا *give* (*someone*) *a wistful look* (کو) حسرت بھرے انداز سے دیکھنا showing a vague, unsatisfied desire مشتاق، آرزومند *wistful eyes* مشتاق نگاہیں **wistfully** *adv.* حسرت سے ، آرزومندی سے

wit *n.* (*sing.* or *pl.*) intelligence سمجھ quick grasp of the situation, etc. زیرکی، ہوشمندی *have* (*one's*) *wits about* (*one*), (*a*) understand quickly بھانپ جانا (*b*) not be unnerved حواس قائم رکھنا *out of* (*one's*) *wits* بد حواس *be at* (*one's*) *wit's end* سمجھ میں نہ آنا کہ کیا کرے یا کہے ، بد حواس ہو جانا *live by* (*one's*) *wits* ٹھگی کو پیشہ بنانا clever and humurous talk بذلہ سنجی ، لطیفہ ، پھبتی person skilled in it بذلہ سنج **witticism** (*wit*-i-sizm) *n.* piece of wit پھبتی، لطیفہ **witty** (*wit*-i) *adj.* humourous (person) بذلہ سنج humourous (talk) پُر لطف ، ظرافت بھری **wittily** *adv.* بذلہ سنجی سے ، ظرافت سے

witch (wich) *n.* ugly woman using magic with evil intentions چڑیل، ڈائن woman magician جادوگرنی ، ساحرہ charming young woman ساحرہ ، دلربا، عشوہ طراز old hag بدصورت بڑھیا، ڈھڈو، مائی ڈلہ **witchcraft** *n.* use of such magic جادو **witchdoctor** *n.* male witch جادوگر **witchery** (*wich*-è-ri) *n.* witchcraft جادوگر، کالا علم great charm (*of* beauty, etc.) جادوگری، دلکشی، دلربائی، عشوہ طرازی، سحر آفرینی، سحر انگیزی **witch hunt** *n.* (see *Addenda*)

with (widh) *prep.* in the company of کے ساتھ beside کے پاس in the care of کے پاس in the possession of کے پاس by means of سے، کے ساتھ in the state of سے، میں as a consequence of کی وجہ سے ، کے سبب ، کے باعث despite کے باوجود from سے (10) against کے مقابلے میں (11) having as partner at other end سے، کے ساتھ (12) favourable to کے موافق (13) having والا (14) at the same time کے ساتھ *lie with the lamb and rise with the sun* سرِ شام سو جانا اور صبح سویرے اُٹھ بیٹھنا

withal (wi-*dhawl*) *adv.* (old use) moreover مزید برآں ، نیز ، بھی
withdraw (widh-*draw*) *v.t.* & *i.* (*withdraw, withdrew, withdrawn*) draw back پیچھے ہٹنا یا ہٹانا (of the army) retreat پسپا ہونا take back (money *from* bank) نکلوانا take out (child *from* school) اُٹھانا recant (statement, offer etc.) واپس لینا یا ہونا ، واپس لینا **withdrawal** (widh-*draw*-ĕl) نکلوانا ، اُٹھانا ، پسپائی ، پیچھے ہٹنا یا ہٹانا
wither (*widh*-ĕ*) *v.t.* & *i.* (of plant) dry *away with* blight, etc.) مرجھانا dry (*up* a plant, etc.) مرجھا دینا ، پژمردہ (of hope, etc.) be shattered ٹوٹ جانا cover (someone) with shame شرم سے (کسی کو) پانی پانی کر دینا *give a withering look* (*to*) (کو) یوں دیکھنا کہ وہ شرم سے پانی پانی ہو جائے ، (پر) جانکاہ نظر ڈالنا **withering** *adv.* withered پژمردہ blighting جانکاہ
withhold (widh-*hold*) *v.t.* (*withhold, withheld, withheld*) refuse to give money, etc.) روک لینا restrain (someone *from*) سے روکنا
within (wi-*dhin*) *adv.* (old use) inside اندر *prep.* inside کے اندر *within* گھر کی چار دیواری کے اندر not beyond کے اندر اندر *live within* (*one's*) *means* (or *income*) آمدنی سے بڑھ کر خرچ نہ کرنا *within reach* جہاں تک رسائی *within hearing* جہاں تک آواز پہنچ سکے ہو سکے *within a mile* (*etc.*) *of* (a place) (کسی جگہ) سے میل (وغیرہ) بھر کے اندر
without (wi-*dhout*) *prep.* outside of کے باہر not having (doubt, home, etc.) کے بغیر ، بلا *adv.* out-of-doors باہر ہی ، گھر سے باہر from the outside باہر سے (old use) outside باہر *go without* (*something*), do without (it) کے بغیر گزر جانا *It goes without saying* ; it is too well-known and doubtlessly true مشہور بات ہے
withstand (widh-*stand*) *v.t.* (*withstand, withstood, withstood*) hold out against (attack, pressure, etc.) کا ڈٹ کر مقابلہ کرنا ، کے مقابلے میں جمے رہنا
witness (*wit*-nes) *n.* one who deposes in a court of law گواہ *the witness was sworn in* گواہ کو حلف دیا گیا (also *eye-witness*), one who has a first-hand knowledge of چشم دید گواہ ، عینی شاہد one who attests (a deed, etc.) گواہ one who bears testimony (*to* someone's character, etc.) (کی) تصدیق کرنے والا one who or that which is an instance (*of* or *to* someone's cruelty, etc.) کا ثبوت ، کا آئینہ دار *v.t.* & *i.* be a witness to (deed, etc.) گواہی ڈالنا be an eye-witness of (something) کا چشم دید گواہ ہونا see (an event) دیکھنا
witticism *n.*, **witty** *adj.* (see under **wit**)
wittingly (*wit*-ing-li) *adv.* intentionally قصداً knowingly جان بوجھ کر

wives *n.* (*pl.* of **wife**, which see)
wizard (*wiz*-ĕ*d) *n.* magician جادوگر great genius حیرت انگیز قابلیت کا مالک ، ساحر ، جادوگر **wizardry** *n.* جادوگری
wizen (*wī*-zĕn), **wizened** (*wiz*-ĕnd), **weazen** (*wee*-zĕn) *adj.* shrivelled (face, features, etc.) سوکھا اور جھرّیوں والا
wobble, wabble (*wob*-ĕl) *v.t.* rock اِدھر اُدھر کھڑے جھولنا move unsteadily ڈگمگاتے ہوئے چلنا vacillate مذبذب ہونا *n.* rocking اِدھر اُدھر جھولنا move unsteadily ڈگمگانا
Woden (*woh*-den), **Odin** (*oh*-din) *Norse myth*. the king of gods and men ; he was the husband of Frigga and held his court in *Valhalla* (or Paradise), his courtiers being the persons who were killed in battles اودن
woe (woh) *n.* grief غم ، الم misery دکھ ، مصیبت ، تکلیف *a tale of woe* دکھ بھری کہانی cause of woe شامت اعمال ، جان کا روگ *Bad children are a woe to their parents* بُرے بچے ماں باپ کی شامت اعمال ہوتے ہیں **woes** (wohz) *n. pl.* cause of woes دکھ ، آلام و مصائب ، باعث رنج و غم **woeful** *adj.* full of or causing woe دردناک ، دکھ بھرا ، درد انگیز
woke (wohk), **woken** (*wohk*-en) *v.* (see under **wake**)
wolf (wŭlf) *n.* (pl. *wolves* pr. wulvz) a dog-like wild animal بھیڑیا ، گرگ (*earn enough to*) *keep the wolf from the door*, earn about the minimum needed to) maintain one's family, etc. بمشکل گزر بسر کے لیے کمانا *wolf in sheep's clothing*, dangerous but innocent-looking person فرشتہ صورت ، شیطان سیرت **wolfish** (*wŭlf*-ish) *adj.* such (person) گرگ سیرت

a wolf

woman (*wum*-an) *n.* (pl. *women*, pr. *wim*-in) grown-up female of the human race عورت female human sex عورت ، طبقۂ نسواں ، صنف نازک *play the woman*, (*a*) weep عورتوں کی طرح آنسو بہانا (*b*) *give way to fear* عورتوں کی طرح ڈر جانا *There is a woman in it* ; the incident is due to love, etc., for a woman اس میں ضرور عورت کا ہاتھ ہے *stir the woman in her* کسی عورت کی نسوانی ہمدردی (وغیرہ) کو بیدار کرنا **womanhood** *n.* women in general طبقۂ نسواں ، صنف نازک being a woman عورت ہونا ، نسائیت ، نسوانیت puberty of a woman عورت کی جوانی *reach womanhood* لڑکی کا جوان ہو کر عورت بننا **womanish** *adj.* effeminate (person, habits, etc.) نسوانیت والا ، نسائیت والا ، زنانہ (of things) more suitable for women than men عورتوں کے لیے ٹھیک **womanly** *adj.* (of modesty, etc.) proper to a woman نسوانی (حیا وغیرہ) **womanise**

v.t. & i. (of a man) lead a licentious life عیاشی کرنا make effeminate مردوں میں نسائیت پیدا کرنا

womb (woom) *n.* uterus ; female mammal's organ holding the offspring before its birth بچہ دانی ، رَحِم any deep cavity (*of*) گہرائی *in the womb of time* مستقبل کی گہرائیوں میں ، مستقبل کے پردے میں

women (*wim*-in) *n.* (pl. of **woman,** which see)

won (wun) *v.* (pa. t. & pa. p. of **win,** which see)

wonder (*wund*-ĕ*) *n.* amazement حیرت ، حیرانی that which amazes اُعجوبہ marvel کرامات ، تعجب remarkable example (*of*) پُر اعجاز شئے (کا) حیرت انگیز نمونہ *look at (something) in wonder* کو حیرت سے تکنا *be filled with wonder (at)* (سے) بہت حیران ہونا ، (سے) ششدر رہ جانا *no wonder that* پھر عجب کیا ہے کہ *for a wonder* حیرت ہے کہ (یا جو) *work wonders*, produce remarkable results معجزہ اثر ہونا ، حیرت انگیز اثر ہونا *wonder-worker*, one who works wonders حیرت انگیز کام کرنے والا *wonder-working*, that which works wonders اعجاز آفریں *wonder-struck*, greatly amazed حیرت زدہ ؛ ہکا بکا ، بھونچکا *v.t. & i.* be amazed (*at*) (سے) حیرت زدہ ہونا feel a desire to know (*about* something, *who, what, why, whether*, etc.) جاننے کی خواہش ہونا کہ **wonderful** *adj.* remarkable حیرت انگیز **wonderment** *n.* surprize حیرت **wondrous** (*wund*-rus) *adj.* (lit.) wonderful حیرت انگیز

wonky (*wonk*-i) *adj.* (slang) shaky, unsteady لڑکھڑاتا ہُوا unreliable بے اعتبار ، غیر معتمد

[1]**wont** (wohnt) *n.* (one's) habit or routine (کی) عادت *adj.* used (*to*) کا عادی *he is wont to* کا عادی ہے ، کا دستور ہے کہ ، کا معمول ہے کہ **wonted** (*wohnt*-id) *adj.* usual حسب معمول ، حسب عادت

[2]**won't** (wohnt) *v.* (abb. of *will not*) (see under **will**)

woo (woo) *v.t. & i.* court (a woman) سے (شادی کی نیت سے) معاشقہ کرنا ask (her) hand in marriage کو شادی کا پیام دینا coax کی خوشامد کرنا try to win (fame, wealth, etc.) حاصل کرنے کے لیے جدوجہد make a bid to (sleep) کی کوشش کرنا

wood (wŭd) *n.* hard part of a tree under its bark لکڑی ، چوب *firewood* ایندھن ، ہیزم (also *pl.* with the same meaning) small forest جھاڑ جھنکل ، چھوٹا جنگل *out of the wood*, rid of difficulties مصیبت سے چھوٹنا بن نکل آیا **woodbine, woodbind** *n.* honey-suckle ووڈبائن a cheap brand of cigarettes very popular in Britain ووڈبائن **woodnymph** *n.* minor goddess living in (a tree) in the forest بن دیوی **wood-pulp** *n.* wood crushed into pulp لکڑی کا گودا **woodcraft** *n.* knowledge of forest conditions جنگلات سے واقفیت

woodcut *n.* print from a wooden block لکڑی کے ٹھپے سے بنی ہوئی تصویر **woodcutter** *n.* person who lives by selling wood he has cut لکڑہارا **wooded** (*wŭd*-id) *adj.* covered with woods جنگل والا ، بنوں والا covered with trees درختوں سے لدا ہُوا **wooden** *adj.* made of wood لکڑی کا ، چوبی *wooden spoon*, last place in a competition آخری درجہ stiff سخت stupid احمق **woodland** *n.* (usu. *pl.*) tree-covered land درختوں سے بھرا ہُوا علاقہ *adj.* tree-covered درختوں سے بھرا ہُوا **woodman** *n.* forester داروغۂ جنگل woodcutter لکڑہارا **woodpecker** *n.* kinds of bird clinging to tree-stems کٹھ پھوڑا ، ہُدہُد (وغیرہ) **woodwork** *n.* carpentry بڑھئی کا کام ، کھاتی کا کام articles made of wood لکڑی کی چیزیں wooden parts of a building عمارت میں لکڑی کا کام **woody** (*wŭd*-i) *adj.* of or like wood لکڑی کا (سا) covered with trees or woods درختوں سے بھرا ہُوا ، جنگل پوش

a woodpecker

woof *n.* (also called *weft*), threads running along the breadth of a piece of cloth بانا ، پود

woof or weft (horizontal) running across the warp (vertical)

wool (wŭl) *n.* fine hair such as found on sheep, etc. اُون ، پشم *much cry and little wool*, disappointing result کھودا پہاڑ نکلا چوہا yarn made from it اُونی دھاگا *knitting wool* بُننے کی اُون *dyed in the wool*, (*a*) dyed before spinning or weaving بٹنے یا بُننے سے پہلے رنگا ہُوا (*b*) thorough-going پُورا پکا ، کٹر woollen cloth اُونی کپڑا anything like carded wool پشم جیسا *cotton wool* دُھنی ہُوئی رُوئی **woollen** (*wŭl*-en) *adj.* made of wool اُونی *n.* (*pl.*) woollen clothes اُونی کپڑے **wool-gathering** *adj.* absent-minded اپنے ہی خیالوں میں ڈوبا ہُوا *n.* absent-mindedness اپنے ہی خیالوں میں ڈوبا (یا غرق) *be or go wool-gathering*, اپنے ہی خیالوں میں غرق ہو جانا (یا رہنا) **wool-sack** *n.* Lord Chancellor's seat in the British House of Lords دارالامرا میں جائے صدر **wool-work** *n.* woollen embroidery اُونی کشیدہ کاری **woolly** (*wŭl*-i) *adj.* made of wool اُونی looking like wool پشم جیسا with wool جس پر خوب اُون ہو vague involved ideas, (picture, brain, etc.) مبہم ، اُلجھا ہُوا husky (voice) بیٹھی ہُوئی ، بھاری *n.* (*pl.* *woollies*) sweater سوئیٹر

woozy (*wooz*-i) *adj.* (slang) confused جس کا اپنا ذہن صاف نہ ہو shaky جس کے پاؤں لڑکھڑا رہے ہوں

word (wĕ*d) *n.* meaningful single spoken sound or its written symbol لفظ ، کلمہ talk بات *have a word with (someone)*, talk to (him) سے بات کرنا *have words with (someone)*, quarrel with him سے جھگڑنا *by word of mouth*, verbally زبانی promise

وعدہ *word of honour* پکا وعدہ *give (someone one's) word of honour* کو قول دینا *take (someone) at (his) word* سے وعدہ کرنا *give (someone one's) word* کسی کی بات کا اعتبار کرنا *keep (one's) word* قول نبھانا *break (one's) word* قول نہ نبھانا *be as good as (one's) word* اپنا قول پوری طرح نبھانا remark بات command حکم *give the word (to do)* (کا) حکم دینا news خبر message پیغام *send (someone) word* کو پیغام بھیجنا *leave word for (someone)* کے نام پیغام دے جانا *God's word*, the scriptures کلام الہٰی، کتابِ الہٰی *word for word*, verbatim لفظ بہ لفظ، من و عن *word play*, puns, etc. ضلع جگت *v. t.* couch in words لفظوں میں ادا کرنا *well-worded* اچھے لفظوں میں لکھا ہوا **wording** *n.* choice of words to express meaning اظہارِ مفہوم کے لیے الفاظ کا استعمال، انتخابِ الفاظ **word-perfect** *adj.* able to repeat the words perfectly well فرفر سنا دینے والا **wordy** (*wě*d*-i) *adj.* verbose ضرورت سے زیادہ الفاظ پر مشتمل، ضرورت سے زیادہ الفاظ استعمال کرنے والا in or of (esp. written) words لفظوں میں (یا کا)

wore (woh*) *v.* (pa. t. of **wear**, which see)

work (wo*k) *n.* physical or mental labour کام doing (as opposed to *play*) کام (of machine) making something کام something done or to be done; undertaking کام *piece of work* کام what is done کام *set to work*, begin to do it کام شروع کرنا *have a lot of work to do*, have much on hand بڑا کام ہونا *make short work of*, (*a*) finish (something) quickly جلدی کر لینا (*b*) get rid of (someone) سے جان چھڑانا (*c*) destroy ضائع کر دینا job نوکری، کام، ملازمت *be out of work*, be unemployed بیکار ہونا *at work*, (*a*) at one's office, etc. نوکری پر (*b*) busy with work کام میں لگا ہوا instruments, etc. of work جن چیزوں سے کام کیا جائے embroidery aids سوئی سلائی product (*of* **author, artist musician**, etc.) تخلیقی کام، کی کاوشِ فکر کے نتائج *a work of art* فنکاری کا نمونہ تخلیقی چیز the complete books (*of* an author) کلیات، تحریریں (*pl.*) factory کارخانہ *the Public Works Department*, (abbr. *P. W. D.*) محکمۂ تعمیرات عامہ (*pl.*) moving parts of a machine (esp. of a clock) متحرک پرزے *v.t.* & *i.* (*work, worked*: old pa. t. & pa. p. *wrought* which also see) do work کام کرنا manage (machine, etc.) چلانا implement (a scheme) or keep (it) going چلانا perform (wonders) (معجزے) کرنا (of machine) operate چلنا *in working order* چالو (of a plan, method, etc.) be successful کامیاب ہونا، ٹھیک طرح چلنا cause (oneself, person, animal, machine, etc.) cause to work سے کام لینا set in motion چلانا *This machine is worked by electricity* یہ مشین بجلی سے چلتی ہے have influence (*upon* someone's feelings, etc.) پر اثر انداز ہونا shape (metal) by hammering (لوہا وغیرہ) کوٹ (یا پیٹ) کر کچھ بنانا shape (clay, etc.) by kneading گوندھنا chalk (*out* plan, etc.) بنانا، تیار کرنا (*work out*), solve a sum, etc. (سوال) حل کرنا embroider (design, etc., on something) by stitching کاڑھنا (cause to) move or go slowly or laboriously (or *in out, through*, or *into* some condition) دھیرے دھیرے (کھل) جانا، (میں) لگانا، محنت سے کرنا (*Phrases*:) *work (one's) way through (difficulties)* مشکلات کے باوجود بڑھتے جانا *work (a few jokes) into a lecture* تقریر میں کچھ لطیفے شامل کر دینا *work off*, spend (extra energy, etc.) میں لگانا *work off (one's) temper (on)* (پر) اپنا غصہ نکالنا *work up*, (*a*) build gradually (business, etc.) آہستہ آہستہ بنانا (*b*) excite (revolt, someone's feelings, etc.) پیدا کرنا، ابھارنا، ہیجان میں لانا **workable** *adj.* practicable قابلِ عمل **workability** *n.* being workable قابلِ عمل ہونا *the workability af a plan* کسی منصوبے کا قابلِ عمل ہونا **working** *adj.* of work کام کا *working day*, not a holiday کام پر جانے کا دن، چھٹی کے علاوہ کوئی بھی دن (of model) showing action بالکل ٹھیک چھوٹا نمونہ (of person) engaged in manual work مزدوری کرنے والا *working man*, manual labour مزدور executive (committee) عاملہ، مجلسِ عاملہ needed for carrying on the work کام چلانے کا *working capital* کام چلانے کا سرمایہ *working expenses* کاروباری اخراجات *working vocabulary* زیرِ استعمال ذخیرۂ الفاظ (opp. *recognition vocabulary*, **worker** *n.* one who works کام کرنے والا active member (*of* a party) کارکن humdrum (life, existence etc.) معمولی، یونہی، بس گزر رہی ہے **work-a-day** *adj.* matter-of-fact عملی commonplace معمولی، عام **work-bag, workbasket, workbox** *n.* women's portable container for needlework سوئی سلائی کی ٹوکری (یا کا تھیلا) **workbook** *n.* U.S. version of the much-maligned Pakistani 'Bazaar notes' نوٹ drill book مشق کی کاپی **workhouse** *n.* poor house in Britain محتاج خانہ **workman** *n.* factory worker مزدور **workman-like** *adj.* of or like a good workman, اچھے مزدور کی طرح skilful ماہرانہ **workmanship** *n.* skill in making کاریگری، مہارت **workout** *n.* performance for practice مشق (colloq.) trying experience سخت تجربہ، تلخ تجربہ **work party** *n.* group of women social workers meeting to do some knitting or embroidery with a view to helping the poor directly or by selling the products and donating the proceeds to them ورک پارٹی **working party** *n.* committee, etc. appointed to investigate and report on some issue تحقیقاتی کمیٹی such party set up to secure efficiency in industry, etc. انتظام بہتر بنانے والی

work-people *n.* working men (or women) مزدور، مزدوری پیشہ لوگ کمیٹی

workshop *n.* factory کارخانہ place for repairing machinery ورکشاپ، مرمت خانہ

work-shy *adj.* (of person) shirking work کام چور

world (wĕ*ld) *n.* the earth and everything on earth دنیا *the Old World*, Europe, Asia and Africa پرانی دنیا *the New World*, N. & S. America امریکہ *citizen of the world*, one travelling abroad so often as to be left with little allegiance to any one country پردیسی people living on the earth لوگ، دنیا والے any other planet کوئی اور ستارہ world-wide field (of something) دنیا *the world of sports* کھیلوں کی دنیا *the film world* فلمی دنیا (one's) environment (کی) دنیا، (کا) ماحول stratum of society طبقہ material affairs, life, etc. دنیوی زندگی وغیرہ *a man of the world*, (a) one interested in material life دنیا دار (b) experienced تجربہ کار *make the best of both worlds* دنیا و دین دونوں کے کام کا ہونا *a world of (something)*, very much or very many (of it) ایک دنیا، بہت *for all the world alike*, perfectly resembling ایک دوسرے سے بالکل مشابہ *make a noise in the world*, win fame مشہور رہنا

worldling *n.* worldly person دنیا دار شخص

worldly *adj.* material مادی *worldly goods* جائداد، مال و دولت، مال و منال mundane opp. (of *spiritual*) دنیوی، مادی

world power *n.* vast state عظیم سلطنت، دولت عظمیٰ

worldwide *adj.* embracing the whole world عالمگیر، عالمی

worm (we*m) *n.* kinds of boneless small crawling animals کیڑا mean or base person ذلیل شخص *a worm will turn*, even a weak person will on occasions retaliate ایک وقت آتا ہے کہ چیونٹی بھی کاٹتی ہے *v.t.* work (*one's* way *through* or *into*) چپکے چپکے خوشامد یا چالاکی سے پہنچ جانا find (secret, etc. *out of* someone) (کسی سے) چالاکی سے راز معلوم کر لینا

worm-eaten *adj.* (of wood, etc.) rotten جسے گھن (یا کیڑا) لگا ہوا ہے

wormwood *n.* a well-known little herb افسنتین (also *gall and wormwood*), cause of bitterness (*to*) (کے لیے) تلخی کا موجب، (کی) زندگی تلخ کرنے والا، (کے لیے) سوہان روح

worn (woh*n) *v.* (pa. p. of **wear**, which see)

worry (*wu*-ri) *v.t.* & *i.* trouble (someone); pester (someone *with* questions, etc.) دق کرنا، تنگ کرنا، پریشان کرنا inconvenience (someone *to do* something) (کے لیے) تنگ کرنا، (کے لیے) پیچھے پڑ جانا (of a dog) bite and shake the teeth be anxious or uneasy (*about*) کے متعلق سخت پریشان (یا فکر مند) ہونا *worry about trifles* چھوٹی چھوٹی باتوں پر خواہ مخواہ پریشان ہونا *n.* anxiety پریشانی

worse (wĕ*s) (the comparative degree of *bad*) *adj.* more bad زیادہ برا more ill زیادہ بیمار *adv.* more badly زیادہ بری طرح *worse off*, (a) more maltreated جس سے اور بھی برا سلوک ہو (b) poorer زیادہ غریب in a worse condition زیادہ بری حالت میں

worsen (wĕ*-sĕn) become or make worse بدتر ہونا یا کرنا، زیادہ خراب ہونا یا کرنا

worship (wĕ*-ship) *n.* adoration (*of* some deity) عبادت، پرستش such ritual reverence عبادت، پوجا *public worship*, congregational prayer معبد میں عبادت، نماز با جماعت *place of worship*, place set apart for this purpose عبادت گاہ، معبد admiration (*of* someone else) حد سے زیادہ عقیدت، پرستش *hero-worship*, extreme admiration for a hero بطل پرستی *Your* (or *His*) *Worship*, form of address to or about a mayor or magistrate حضور والا، جناب والا، والا جناب، بندہ پرور *v.t.* & *i.* adore کی عبادت (یا پرستش) کرنا، کو پوجنا

worshipper *n.* one who worships (as a usu. practice) عبادت گزار، عابد

worshipful *adj.* honourable محترم title of respect for magistrate, etc. محترم

worst (wĕ*st) (the superlative degree of *bad*) *adj.* most bad بدترین، سب سے زیادہ خراب *be prepared for the worst*, be ready to endure it or accept its challenge بدترین صورت حال کے لیے بھی تیار رہنا *if the worst comes to the worst*; even in the worst circumstances بدترین صورت حال میں بھی *get the worst of it*, suffer defeat ہارنا، ہار جانا، شکست کھانا *adv.* most badly بدترین انداز سے *v.t.* defeat ہرانا، شکست دینا *worst (the enemy) in battle*, defeated him کو شکست دینا

worsted *adj.* (wĕs-ted) defeated شکست خوردہ، ہارا ہوا *n.* (*woos*-ted) twisted wollen yarn بٹا ہوا اونی دھاگا cloth manufactured from it (mostly used for trousers بٹے ہوئے اونی دھاگے کا) ورسٹڈ *adj.* made of worsted

worth (wĕ*th) *n.* money value قیمت، مول، (کا) (a *rupee's*) *worth of* (*something*), as many (or as much) as a rupee will buy ایک روپیہ کا جتنا آئے merit, excellence خوبی *adj.* value equal to ہزار روپے کا مال *worth Rs. 1,000* کا مال، کی قیمت کا، کی مالیت کا well-rewarding the money, time, energy, etc. spent on it (*of something*) کا، کے عوض سستا، کا حقدار، کا مستحق *be worth its value in gold* سونے کے تول بھی سستا *it is worth it* کے عوض سستا ہے (*be*) *well worth doing* (*etc.*) (of something) (be) amply smited to it *worth our while*, (*to do*), worth the time, etc. spent on (کے) لائق، (کا) مستحق

worthless *adj.* useless بیکار، ناکارہ، فضول

worth-while *adj.* useful; worth the time, or money spent on it مفید، سود مند، کار آمد، کے عوض ٹھیک

worthy (wĕ*-dhi) *adj.* deserving حقدار، مستحق able; deserving respect قابل احترام deserving (*of* respect) (کے) لائق، (کے) قابل، (کے) شایاں of good character having worth or value قدر و قیمت والا بُلند اخلاق (as *suf.*) fit for کے قابل *seaworthy* سمندری سفر کے قابل *n.* (old use) worthy person قابلِ احترام شخصیت، سربرآوردہ شخص **worthily** *adv.* قابلیت ▣ The **worth** of a thing is in itself; its **value** is as judged by people; its **price**, what the owner wants for it; its **cost**, what the owner gave for it; its **merit**, worth not measured in terms of money; its **excellence**, superior goodness.

would (wūd) *v.* (conditional mood of **will,** which see) **would-be** *adj.* & *adv.* vainly aspiring to be کا زبردستی خواہشمند *would-be gentleman* خواہ مخواہ کا شریف زبردستی (یا بغیر مستحق طور پر) شریف کہلانے کا خواہاں trying to be ہونے کے لیے کوشاں

wound (woond) *n.* cut or opening in the flesh زخم، گھاؤ injury (*to* one's feelings, prestige, pride, etc.) صدمہ، ٹھیس *v.t.* injure زخمی کرنا، گھائل کرنا hurt the feelings of کو صدمہ پہنچانا، کو ٹھیس لگانا **wounded** *adj.* injured زخمی *the wounded*, soldiers wounded in battle زخمی

wove (wohv), **woven** (*woh*-vĕn) *v.* (*pa. t.* & *pa. p.* of **weave,** which see)

wow (wou) *n.* (U. S. slang) (of drama etc.) sensational hit بہت کامیاب (ڈراما)

wrack (rak) *n.* wreck تباہی، بربادی (only in the phrase :) *wrack and ruin* تباہی و بربادی

wraith (rayth) *n.* ghost بھوت (one's) double seen shortly before or after one's death ہمزاد

wrangle (*rang*-ĕl) *n.* noisy dispute جھگڑا، تو تو میں میں *v.i.* dispute thus تو تو میں میں، شور مچا مچا کر جھگڑنا **wrangler** *n.* one who wrangles تو تو میں میں کرنے والا (*Wrangler*) first-class tripos in Mathematics from Cambridge رینگلر *Senior Wrangler*, Wrangler standing first سینیئر رینگلر

wrap (rap) *v.t.* & *i.* (-pp-) cover (someone) or oneself *up* in blanket, etc.) میں لپیٹنا roll (blanket, etc. *round* someone) (پر) لپیٹنا، (پر) اچھی طرح لپیٹنا hide (*up* one's meaning, etc., *in*) میں چھپا لینا (*be*) *wrapped up in* (*something* or *someone*), (*a*) (be) absorbed in پر توجہ میں مستغرق، میں ڈوبا ہوا ہونا (*b*) (be) devoted to پر سو جان سے فدا ہونا *n.* covering (like shawl, etc.) چادر، شال، کھیس وغیرہ **wrapper** *n.* paper cover for something ریپر، لپٹا ہوا کاغذ **wrapping** *n.* material for a wrapper لپیٹنے کا کاغذ wrapper لپٹا ہوا کاغذ

wrath (wroth) *n.* (lit.) rage سخت غصہ، غضب، طیش، قہر *Flee from the wrath to come* قہرِ خداوندی سے بچو **wrathful** *adj.* (poet.) very angry (person, looks, etc.) غضبناک، قہر آلود

wreak (reek) inflict (vengeance *on* or *upon*) (سے) انتقام لینا give rein to (one's fury *on* or *upon*) (پر اپنا غصہ) نکالنا

wreath (reeth) *n.* (pl. *wreaths* pr. reedhz) chaplet پھولوں کا مکٹ large ring of flowers for placing on a grave, etc. پھولوں کا بڑا مکٹ، پھول *He placed a wreath on Iqbal's grave* اس نے اقبال کے مزار پر پھول چڑھائے ring or spiral (of smoke, etc.) مرغولہ، لچھا

weeathe (reedh) *v.t.* & *i.* cover (*in* mist, smiles, etc.) سے ڈھانپنا

wreck (rek) *n.* ruined ship شکستہ جہاز sunken ship ڈوبا ہوا جہاز anything else badly damaged ٹوٹی پھوٹی چیز building lying in ruins کھنڈر ruin تباہی، بربادی *v.t.* cause the wreck of (ship, building, hopes, etc.) تباہ کرنا *wrecking amendment*, amendment to a Bill, etc. proposed to defeat its very purpose

wreckage (*rek*-ij) *n.* fragments of something wrecked تباہ شدہ چیز کے حصے، ٹوٹے پھوٹے حصے، شکستہ حصے **wrecked** *adj.* (of ship) ruined or sunken تباہ شدہ (یا) ڈوبا ہوا (also *shipwrecked*), (of sailors, etc.) having suffered shipwreck تباہ شدہ جہاز کے ملاح، مسافر وغیرہ

wren (ren) *n.* a very small song-bird رین چڑیا Royal Naval Service in Britain رین، بحری چڑیا

wrench (rench) *n.* violent pull (or twist) زور کا جھٹکا (یا مروڑ) tool for twisting nuts, etc. رینچ، ڈھبری کش distress caused by parting فراق کا صدمہ *v.t.* pull (or twist) violently زور کا جھٹکا دینا، زور سے مروڑ دینا *wrench* (*something off, away, round, from, out, of, open*, etc.) زور کا جھٹکا دے کر (کھولنا وغیرہ) sprain (someone's ankle) by twisting ٹخنا مروڑ کر موچ ڈالنا distort (facts, meaning, etc.) to suit a theory, etc. مسخ کرنا، موڑ توڑ کر (یا مروڑ تروڑ کر) بیان کرنا

wrest (rest) *v.t.* snatch (something) violently (*from* someone or *out of* his hands) جھٹکا دے کر چھین لینا distort (meaning of a passage, etc.) to suit own ends اپنی مرضی کے معنی پہنانا

wrestle (*res*-ĕl) *v.t.* & *i.* grapple with (someone) and try to throw him down کشتی کرنا fight (*against* temptation, etc.) کا مقابلہ کرنا struggle (*with* a problem) سوال حل کرنے کے لیے دماغ لڑانا *n.* wrestling match کشتی، دنگل hard struggle سخت کشمکش

wrestler *n.* one who wrestles پہلوان

wretch (rech) *n.* very pitiable person بیچارہ، بدنصیب very mean person سخت کمینہ، ذلیل شخص

wretched (*rech*-id) *adj.* miserable بدنصیب، بدبخت، مصیبت زدہ mean; very bad (place, etc.) گھٹیا، بہت خراب (of weather, etc.) causing inconvenience تکلیف دہ، خراب

wriggle (*rig*-ĕl) *v.t.* & *i.* twist and turn the body as or like a worm بل کھانا twist and turn (body or a part of it) thus کو بل دینا (*wriggle*

out of), escape from (something or doing something) with great effort سے تڑپ کر نکل جانا
-wright (rit) *suf.* maker بنانے والا، ساز *shipwright*, maker of ships جہاز ساز *playwright*, dramatist تمثیل نگار
wring (ring) *v.t.* (*wrung*) squeeze (or *out*) by twisting hard مروڑنا، نچوڑنا *wring water out of (cloth)* کپڑے سے پانی نچوڑنا *wring (or wring out) wet clothes* بھیگے کپڑے نچوڑنا *wring (a chicken's) neck* (کی) گردن مروڑنا *wringing wet*, (of clothes) very wet بہت گیلا *wring money out of (someone)* سے جبراً روپیہ وصول کرنا *wring a confession out of (someone)* سے جبراً اقبال جرم کروانا
wrinkle (*rink*-èl) *n.* furrow in the skin جھری crease in cloth, etc., (esp. one caused by folding) شکن چنٹ (colloq.) useful tip ضروری نصیحت *v.t.* & *i.* make or get (or *up*) wrinkles in (something) پر جھریاں ڈالنا، (میں) شکن ڈالنا
wrist (rist) *n.* joint connecting the hand with the forearm کلائی **wristlet** (*rist*-let) *n.* ornament for the wrist بند anything worn round the wrist کلائی پر باندھنے کی کوئی چیز **wristband** (*rist*-band) *n.* detachable and starched double-cuff علیحدہ، کلف دار، کف
writ (rit) *n.* written command from High Court, etc., restraining someone from action حکم امتناعی *writ petition* درخواست برائے حکم امتناعی *serve writ on* deliver it officially to the person against whom it is issued حکم امتناعی پہنچانا anything written نوشتہ، لکھی ہوئی چیز *the Holy Writ*, the Christian Scriptures (according to the Christians) انجیل
write (rIt) *v.t.* & *i.* (*write, wrote, written*) form words on paper, etc., with pen, etc. لکھنا write (someone a letter, or a letter to someone) کو خط لکھنا express (confession, etc.) in words تحریر کرنا compose (book, article, etc.) لکھنا، تحریر کرنا tell (*about* something) in writing کے متعلق لکھنا note (*down*) لکھ لینا disparage (someone *down*) in writing کی بد تعریفی کرنا *have (something) written on one's face*, see its traces there کے آثار چہرے پر ہونا (*write up*), (*a*) write about something describing it کی تفصیلات لکھنا (*b*) write thus in praise کی تعریف میں قلم اٹھانا (10) *write (something) off*, (*a*) cancel (bad debt, etc.) قلمزن کر دینا (*b*) compose at writing pace قلم برداشتہ لکھ دینا **writer** (*rIt*-ĕ*) *n.* one who writes لکھنے والا (old use) clerk کلرک، منشی author مصنف **writing** (*rīt*-ing) *n.* handwriting خط that which is written لکھا ہوا art of producing literature تصنیف و تالیف (*pl*) literary productions ; (usu. prose) words تصنیفات
writing-desk, writing-table *n.* table for resting paper on while writing لکھنے کی میز **writing-paper** *n.* paper for writing (and not printing) on لکھنے کا کاغذ **writing-ink** *n.* similar ink لکھنے کی سیاہی **writing-master** *n.* composition tutor انشاپردازی سکھانے والا، معلم انشاپردازی، منشی **writing-case** *n.* portable case for writing material قلمدان
writhe (rīdh) *v.i.* twist the body in pain تشنج ہونا، اینٹھن ہونا roll about in pain درد سے لوٹ پوٹ ہونا be stung (*with* shame, or *at* or *under* insults, etc.) سے سخت اذیت ہونا
wrong (rong) *adj.* incorrect غلط not morally right برا unjust (decision) غیر منصفانہ not the proper غلط illegal غیر قانونی side of cloth, etc., which is not right الٹی طرف، الٹا *adv.* incorrectly غلط in a manner not morally right برے انداز سے *n.* wrong act غلطی something morally wrong غلطی (usu. *pl.*) injustice(s) ناانصافیاں *be in the wrong* غلطی پر ہونا *put (someone) in the wrong*, make (him) feel as if he is to blame کسی کو زبردستی سے قصوروار بنا دینا، کسی کو یہ خیال دلانا کہ خطا اسی کی ہے *on the wrong side of (an age)*, be above (that age) (داشتنے سے) زیادہ عمر کا ہونا *be in the wrong box*, be in awkward *position* بڑی الجھن میں گرفتار ہونا *go wrong*, (*a*) (of machine, etc.) get out of order خراب ہو جانا (*b*) fall into evil habits کے اخلاق بگڑ جانا *v.t.* do wrong to پر ظلم کرنا treat or judge unfairly پر سختی کرنا impute bad motives to سے غلط نیت منسوب کرنا **wrongdoing** *n.* crime جرم sin گناہ
wrongful *adj.* unlawful ناجائز، غیر قانونی unfair نامناسب، ناروا **wrongfully** *adv.* ناروا طور پر **wrongly** *adv.* mistakenly غلطی سے
wrote (roht) *v.* (pa. t. of **write,** which see)
wroth (rohth, or roth) *adj.* (poet.) angry ناراض
wrought (rawt) *v.* (old pa. t. & pa. p. of *work* ; now used only as an adjective) *adj.* hammered کوٹا ہوا *wrought iron*, one which is not cast کوٹا ہوا لوہا (of feelings, etc.) worked *up* بھڑکایا ہوا، بھڑکا ہوا *in a wrought up state* بہت گرم، بھڑکا ہوا
wrung (rung) *v.* (pa. t. & pa. p. of **wring,** which see)
wry (rI) *adj.* twisted to one side ٹیڑھا، ترچھا (of face) twisted out of shape as an expression of disgust, etc. بنا ہوا *make a wry mouth, make a wry face* برا منہ بنانا، منہ بنانا

X

x, X (eks) (pl. *x's* or *xs*) the twenty-fourth letter of the English alphabet ; (akin to the Sanskrit letter representing *ksh*, it is variously pronounced as *ks* and *gz*) ایکس (as Roman numeral) ten دس (in Algebra) the first unknown quantity لا unknown influence پُراَسرار اَثر
xebec (*zee*-bek) *n.* small three-masted Mediterranean ship of old days زیبق
xenophobia (zen-o-*foh*-bi-a) *n.* morbid dislike of foreigners اجانب بیزاری ، بدیسی بھڑک
Xmas (*kris*-mas) *n.* (abbr. for) Christmas کرسمس ، میلادِ مسیح ، بڑا دن
X-rays (*eks*-rayz) *n. pl.* (also *Rontgen rays*) electric rays which can penetrate solids (discovered by Rontgen in 1895) لاشعاعیں apparatus for using them لاشعاعی آلہ photograph (of human bones, etc.) taken by this means لاشعاعی عکس *v.t.* treat, examine, or photograph (something) thus لاشعاعی عکس لینا ، یا لاشعاعی علاج ، (یا معائنہ) کرنا
xylo- (*zī*-loh) *pref.* wood ; wooden لکڑی (کا) ، چوبی
xyloid (*zī*-loid) *adj.* resembling wood لکڑی کا سا ، چوب نما
xylonite (*zī*-lo-nit) *n.* celluloid سیلولائٹ ، سیلولیٹ
xylophone (*zī*-lo-fohn) *n.* old-fashioned musical instrument consisting of wooden bars and played with two small sticks چوبی باجا

a xylophone

Y

y, Y (wi) (pl. *y's* or *ys*) twenty-fifth letter of the English alphabet وائی (in Algebra) the second unknown quantity 'ء'
yacht (yot) *n.* light sailing-boat or steam vessel fitted up for racing or pleasurecruising بجرا ، دوڑ (یا سیر) کے لیے کشتی *v.i.* sail in a yacht بجرے کی سیر کرنا
yachting *n.* racing or sailing in a yacht بجرا چلانا **yachtsman** *n.* one who keeps or sails a yacht بجرے والا

a yacht

yah *int.* (expressing derision) ہونہہ
yahoo (*yah*-hoo) *n.* uncouth person ; (derived from the name given by Swift in *Gulliver's Travels* to degenerate human beings) گنوار ، اُجڈ ، یاہو
Yahweh (*yah*-we) *n.* another form of Jehovah اللہ ، خدا ، یہوواہ
yak *n.* long-haired Tibetan ox بتی بیل ، یاک
yam *n.* a tropical creaper کچالو its edible root کچالو (یا رتالو) کی بیل رتالو

a yak

yank (yank) *v. t.* (slang) pull with a jerk (*back, out*, etc.) (جھٹکے کے ساتھ) کھینچنا *People said that he had yanked back Pakistan from the edge of dissolution* لوگوں کا کہنا تھا کہ اُس نے پاکستان کو انتشار کے غار کے کنارے سے جھٹکے کے ساتھ کھینچ لیا ہے *n.* sudden jerk جھٹکا
Yankee (*yank*-i) (*U.S.*) *n.* a U.S. citizen امریکی *adj.* American امریکی ، یانکی **Yankee-Doodle** *n.* name of a U.S. national song ایک امریکی ترانہ ، یانکی ڈوڈل
yap *n.* shrill bark (پلّے کی) ٹوں ٹوں *v.i.* yelp shrilly like a puppy (پلّے کا) ٹوں ٹوں کرنا talk rot بک بک کرنا
yapp *n.* limp leather binding of a book overlapping its edges مڑے ہوئے کناروں کی نرم جلد ، یاپ جلد
yard (yah*d) *n.* measure of three-foot-length گز three-foot-long measuring rod گز spar slung crosswise to a mast to support a sail (مستول پر بادبان کے سہارے کی) بلّی enclosure round a building احاطہ enclosure for a special purpose یارڈ *churchyard* قبرستان *marshalling yard*, railway yard where trains are made up یارڈ *shipyard*, ship-building establishment جہاز سازی کا مرکز *the school yard*, its playground مدرسے کا میدان *backyard*, yard at back of the house پچھلا صحن *brickyard*, kiln and its surroundings بھٹہ (یا بھٹے کا) پزاوہ
yarn (yah*n) *n.* any thread spun for knitting and weaving سوت وغیرہ (colloq.) story (esp. a long and impossible one) بنائی ہوئی لمبی چوڑی بات ، من گھڑت قصہ ، رام کہانی *v.i.* tell tales رام کہانی سنانا *spin a yarn* (or *yarns*), tell traveller's tales رام کہانی سنانا *spin us a yarn* اچھا کوئی قصہ تو سنایئے ، اچھا کوئی کہانی کہئے
yawn *v.t.* & *i.* open the mouth sleepily جمائی (یا جمائیاں) لینا ، جماہی (یا جماہیاں) لینا (of cave, gulf, etc.) be wide open ; gape منہ پھاڑے کھڑا ہونا utter or say with a yawn جمائی لیتے ہوئے کہنا *n.* act of yawning جمائی (یا جماہی) **yawner** *n.* one who yawns جمائیاں لینے والا
yaws (yawz) *n.* contagious skin disease marked

by raspberry like swellings یاز
yclept, ycleped (i-*klept*) *adj.* called ; named نامی (مشتق)، مشتقات (مشتقاة)
ye (yee, or *yi*) *def. article* (old form of) the (before a vowel) THE (انگریزی کے حرف) کی قدیم صورت *pron.* (old form of) you تم (abbr. of) you تم *How d'ye do?* how do you do? کیا حال چال ہے؟ مزاج شریف، مزاج عالی، مزاج گرامی، مزاج اقدس، مزاج معلی
yea (yay) *adv.* & *int.* (old use) yes ہاں، ہاں جی *Let your yea be yea and your nay nay* ہاں کرو خواہ ناں اس پر بہرصورت پکے رہنا *n.* yes ہاں، جی ہاں affirmative vote ہاں **yeas** (yayz) *n. pl.* persons voting for a motion قرارداد کے حق میں ووٹ دینے والے
yean (yeen) *v.t.* & *i.* (of yew or she-goat) bring forth (بھیڑ یا بکری کا) بیانا **yeanling** *n.* young lamb or kid بره (یا) میمنا
year (*yee-ĕ**) *n.* length of time taken by the earth to revolve round the sun (about 365¼ days) برس، سال period of 12 months from any date سال *calendar year*, Jan. 1 to Dec. 31 تقویمی سال *financial year*, *fiscal year*, (now in this country and the U.S.A.) from July 1 to June 30 مالی سال *academic year*, (in this country) April 1 to March 31 تعلیمی سال **years** *n. pl.* several years کئی سال، سالہا سال age عمر old age بڑھاپا، ضعیفی *be in years*, be elderly بوڑھا ہونا، ضعیف ہونا *year by year*, each year سال بہ سال *year in year out*, continuously, irrespective of seasons سدا، ہمیشہ، برابر *yearlong*, lasting a whole year سال بھر کا *year of grace*, year of the Christian era سنِ عیسوی *the year 1984*, the year nineteen eighty-four of the Christian era ۱۹۸۴ء سن ۱۹۸۴ء **yearling** *n.* animal between one and two years old یکسالہ **yearly** *adj.* occurring every year ہر سال، سال کے سالانہ، ہر سال کا، سال کے سال کا *adv.* every year سال once a year برس دن کے دن، سال میں ایک بار *yearly statement*, statement submitted in an establishment soon after, or towards, the end of every financial year ; also called a (*yearly*) *return* نقشہ سالانہ، سالانہ نقشہ، سالانہ کوائف
yearn (yĕ*n) *v.i.* be filled with longing (*for* or *after* or *to do* a desired thing, or *to* or *towards* a person) کا مشتاق (یا آرزومند) ہونا، کی آرزو ہونا، کی آرزو میں مرنا be filled with compassion (*over*) (پر)، رحم آجانا
yearning *n.* longing آرزو، تمنا **yearningly** *adv.* longingly آرزومندانہ
yeast (yeest) *n.* leaven خمیر *yeast power*, power used for leavening سفوف خمیر
yegg (yeg) *n.* (slang) robber ...ing open his victims' safes سیف توڑنے والا، تجوری توڑ ڈاکو
yell (yel) *v.t.* & *i.* scream چیخنا، بلبلا ...m) shout (something) out بلبلا اٹھنا shout (*at*) پکارنا shout (*with laughter*) (قہقہہ) بلند کرنا (U. S.) such a cry چیخ، قہقہہ، اونچی آواز، شور buck up! شاباش
yellow (*yel*-oh) *n.* & *adj.* (of) the colour of gold زرد، پیلا یا، بسنتی (رنگ) *yellow back*, cheap novel (formerly in yellow covers) گھٹیا ناول *yellow fever*, a tropical fever turning the skin yellow ایک قسم کا یرقان، زرد بخار *yellow jaundice*, jaundice یرقان *the yellow men*, Mongolian race زرد نسل *yellow peril*, danger of the yellow men becoming more powerful than the white man زرد خطرہ *yellow press*, sensational chauvinistic papers سنسنی خیز خبریں شائع کرنے والے قوم پرست اخبار (colloq.) cowardly بزدل، ڈرپوک *v.t.* & *i.* (cause to) become yellow پیلا پڑنا یا کردینا، زرد ہونا (یا) کردینا
yelp *v.i.* crying (of a dog) in pain or excitement (کتے کا) بھونکنا *n.* such a cry بھونک
yen *n.* Japanese unit of currency almost equivalent to one rupee ین
yeoman (*yoh*-man) *n.* (pl. *yeomen*) (old use) small-holder چھوٹا زمیندار، مالک کاشتکار *do yeoman's service*, (*to*) *do yeoman service* (*to*), help (someone) in his dire need کی مصیبت میں مدد کرنا *yeoman of the guard*, member of the British sovereign's bodyguard برطانوی فرمانروا کے محافظ دستے کا فرد **yeomanry** (-ri) *n.* volunteer cavalry force raised from yeomen زمینداروں کا رضاکار رسالہ
yes *int.* it is so (affirmative answer to a question) ہاں، ٹھیک ہے furthermore اور ہاں، مزید *n.* the word "yes" ہاں *say yes* (*to*) consent بر آں
yesman *n.* weak characterless person who always 'says' yes to whatever his superiors may say جی حضور یا
Y.M.C.A., *n.*, **Y.W.C.A.**, *n.* (see under **young**)
yesterday (*yes*-tĕ*-day) *n.* the day before today (گزشتہ) کل ابھی کل ہی، ابھی اگلے روز a recent day the time past ماضی *adj.* of the day before today کل کا *yesterday morning* کل صبح *adv.* on the before today کل
yet *adv.* till now, till then اب تک، اس وقت تک still, even now ابھی تک even more ابھی اور، اور بھی sooner or later جلد یا بدیر *conj.* nevertheless, however پھر بھی، تاہم
yew *n.* an evergreen tree often planted in graveyards ایک سدابہار درخت، بیؤ its wood formerly used for making bows for archery and even now for furniture بیؤ کی لکڑی

yield (yeeld) *v.t.* & *i.* produce دینا give (profit) (نفع) دینا produce result پر منتج ہونا concede assent ہاں کہہ دینا comply with or submit (*to*) کی بات مان لینا، کی خواہش کے آگے جھک جانا surrender (something *to*) کے حوالے کر دینا *yield the palm to*, be surpassed by (سے) کسی اور کا بازی لے جانا *yield up the ghost*, die مرجانا refuse to admit one's inferiority (*in* something *to none*) اپنے کو (کسی سے) کمتر نہ سمجھنا *n*. crop; agricultural produce پیداوار *the yield per acre* فی ایکڑ پیداوار output, return پیداوار **yielding** *adj*. compliant (person or nature) مان جانے والا (of clay, etc.) pliable آسانی سے مڑ تڑ جانے والا ▣ To **yield** is to give in to a superior force ; to **capitulate** on certain conditions ; to **cave in** under a great weight ; to **submit** to the inevitable ; to **resign** oneself ; **give up** something which one held.

yo-ho, yo-heave ho *int*. sailors' cry in heaving ھیّا ہو! ھیّا! ھیا ہو ھیّا!

yoke (yohk) *n*. wooden frame for coupling oxen drawing a plough, etc. جوا pair of draught oxen بیلوں کی جوڑی *a yoke of oxen*, a pair of draught oxen بیلوں کی جوڑی *come under the yoke* (*of*), *endure the yoke* (*of*), *pass under the yoke* (of), *submit to* (*someone's*) *yoke*, acknowlege defeat and submit to (someone) کسی سے ہار مان کر اس کا حلقہ بگوش ہو جانا *throw off the yoke* (*of*), rebel (against) سے بغاوت کرنا balancelike wooden frame for carrying a pair of pails on human shoulders بہنگی separately made shoulder piece of a shirt, etc. یوک، شانہ *v.t*. put a yoke on (oxen) جوا رکھنا *yoke to*, couple with, join to جوڑنا **yoke-fellow** *n*. associate in work جوڑی دار husband میاں wife بیوی

a yoke of oxen

yokel (*yohk*-el) *n*. rustic سادہ دیہاتی

yolk (yohk) *n*. the yellow of an egg (انڈے کی) زردی

yon (yon), **yonder** (*yond*-ĕ*) *adj*. & *adv*. at a distance, but in sight over there پرلا، سامنے کا، سامنے، آگے، پرے، وہ پرے

yore (yoh*) *n*. (poet.) time long past اگلے وقت، پرانا زمانہ، سلف، ایامِ ماضی *of yore*, of olden days اگلے وقتوں کا، پرانے زمانے کا *in the days of yore*, in ancient times پرانے زمانے میں، اگلے وقتوں میں

you (yoo, yew, or yè) *pron*. (second person *sing*. or *pl*. but always taking a verb in the pl.) person or persons spoken to تم، آپ، تو every-one آپ، ہر ایک anyone, one آپ، کوئی، انسان *You never can tell* کوئی نہیں کہہ سکتا *It is difficult at first, but you soon get used to it* شروع شروع میں تو مشکل ہے مگر انسان جلد ہی اس کا خوگر ہو جاتا ہے **you'd** (abbr. for) you would تم (ہو) گے، آپ (ہوں) گے، تو (ہو) گا **you'll** (abbr. for) you will تم (ہو) گے، آپ (ہوں) گے، تو (ہو) گا **you're** (*yoo*-ĕ*) (abbr. for) you are تم ہو، آپ ہیں، تو ہے

your (*yoo*-ĕ*) belonging to or coming from you تمہارا، آپ کا، تیرا *your most obedient servant*, (subscription of official letters, sometimes written as : *yours etc.*) آپ کا نہایت فرمانبردار خادم **yours** (*yoo*-ĕ*z) (form of *your* used without the qualified noun or predicatively) تمہارا، آپ کا، تیرا *I have lost my pen ; may I have yours ?* میرا قلم کھو گیا ہے کیا آپ کا قلم لے لوں؟ *Yours sincerely, sincerely yours*, (subscription of a private or nowadays even a business latter) مخلص *Yours affectionately*, (subscription of letter to a relative), (*a*) (from an elder) تمہارے لیے دعا گو (*b*) (to an elder) آپ کا پیارا، طالبِ دعا *Yours obedientlly*, (subscription of official letter or application) آپ کا فرمانبردار *Yours truly, Yours faithfully*, (subscription of a business or formal letter) نیاز مند **yourself** (yoo-è*-*self*) (pl. *yourselves*) (reflexive form of *you*) (تم، آپ یا تو) خود، آپ (with *you* to make it emphatic) *you yourself*, تم خود، تم آپ، آپ خود، تو خود، تو آپ، تم ہی، تمہیں، آپ ہی، تو ہی

young (young) *adj*. in the early part of life جوان still near its beginning نوجوان in the very early part of چھوٹا، کم سن، کمسن fresh, vigorous, strong صحتمند، زوردار، قوی inexperienced ناتجربہ کار *n*. (of birds or animals) young offspring (جانور یا پرندے کا) بچہ those who are young نوعمر **young man** *n*. (*pl*., youngmen) youth *Young Men's Christian Association*, (abbr. *Y.M.C.A.*) (*a*) world organization of Christian youth نوجوان عیسائیوں کی انجمن، وائی۔ایم۔سی۔اے (*b*) its offices or one of its branches وائی۔ایم۔سی۔اے *Young Women's Christian Association*, (abbr. *Y.W.C.A.*), its counterpart for women وائی۔ڈبلیو۔سی۔اے **youngster** (*yong*-ste*) *n* (esp. male) child بچہ **youngish** *adj*. somewhat young نوعمر، کم سن، کمسن

youth (yewth) *n*. being young جوانی young man نوجوان *the youth*, young persons نوجوان *the youth of the nation is degenerate* نوجوانانِ قوم کا اخلاق بگڑ چکا ہے **youths** (pr. yewdhz) *n*. *pl*. young men نوجوان *youths and maidens* نوجوان مرد اور عورتیں **youthful** *adj*. young نوجوان having the qualities of youth جوانی کا، جوان **youthfulness** *n*. جوانی، شباب **youth hostel** *n*. any one of the cheap hostels set up (by *the youth-hostelling movement*) for the benefit of hikers یوتھ ہوسٹل

yowl (youl) *n*. long wailing cry چیخ، لمبی دردناک چیخ *v.i*. utter such cry چیخنا، لمبی دردناک چیخ مارنا

Yule (yewl) *n*. Christmas میلادِ مسیح، کرسمس Christmas festival کرسمس، کرسمس کا تہوار، بڑا دن **yule-tide** (*yewl*-tid) *n*. Christmas time or season کرسمس کے ایام، کرسمس *yule-log*, big log of wood for an open fire indoors on Christmas eve کرسمس پر جلانے کی کیلی

Z

z, Z (zed) (*pl*., *z's* or *zs*) the twenty-sixth letter of the English alphabet (in algebra) the third unknown quantity

zany (*zay*-ni) *n*. (old use) buffoon who mimicked the clown on the stage تھیٹر کے بڑے مسخرے کا بھدا نقال foolish jester بیوقوف مسخرا simpleton

احمق، سادہ لوح، بیوقوف

zeal (*zeel*) *n.* ardour (*for* something, *for* a cause, etc.) شوق، سرگرمی، جوش *work with zeal* جانفشانی سے کام کرنا **zealous** (*zel*-us) *adj.* enthusiastic (worker, supporter, etc.) پُرجوش، سرگرم **zealously** *adv.* جوش سے، سرگرمی سے **zealot** (*zel*-ot) *n.* fanatic supporter of cause جوشیلا حامی، مجنونانہ جوش والا ہیرو **zealotry** (-ri) *n.* fanatic support of a cause نہایت پُرجوش حمایت، مجنونانہ جوش والی سرگرمی

zebra (*zeeb*-ra) *n.* horse-like wild animal with dark stripes on a tawny body گورخر *adj.* having such stripes کالی دھاریوں والا، زیبرا

a zebra

zeit-gist (tsit-gist) *n.* spirit of the times ; trend of thought in a particular period رُوحِ عصر، رُوحِ زمان

zenith (*zen*-ith) *n.* point of the sky directly overhead (as opposed to *nadir*) سمت الرّاس acme (*of* fame, etc.) پُورا عُروج، اَوجِ کمال، منتہائے کمال *be at the zenith, be at (one's) zenith* پُورے عُروج پر ہونا، اَوجِ کمال پر ہونا

zephyr (*zef*-ĕ*) *n.* west wind پچھوا gentle breeze نسیم **Zephyr** *n.* (poet.) the West Wind personified زیفر **Zephyrus** (*zef*-i-rus) *Cl. myth.* the West Wind personified زیفرس

zero (*zee*-roh) *n.* (pl. *zeros*) cipher صِفر the symbol 0 • nothing کچھ بھی نہیں، ہیچ lowest point صِفر point between + and − on a scale for reckoning positive and negative quantity صِفر (also *zero-hour*) point of time in a military operational movement from which other intervals are reckoned وَقتِ آغاز *the zero-hour for,* the time to start work on کام کے آغاز کا وَقت

zest *n.* relish, appetizing flavour, piquancy مزا، چٹخارا، چٹپٹا پن *add a zest to* کو چٹپٹا بنانا keen interest ذوق وشوق، شوق *enter into (something) with zest* بڑے شوق سے شروع کرنا

zeugma (*zeug*-ma) *n.* such use (for homorous effect) of two words in relation to a third that although it is correct yet the relation sounds incongruous in one case صَنعَتِ اِجتماعِ ضِدّین

Zeus (*zee*-us) *Cl. myth.* the Greek god of gods (identified with the Roman *Jupiter*, or *Jove*) زِیُوس

zigzag (*zig*-zag) *n.* line, path, etc., consisting of straight lines with sharp-angled turns in alternate directions پُرپیچ وخم راستہ (لکیر وغیرہ) *adj.* with such turns ٹیڑھا میڑھا، پُرپیچ وخم *adv.* in a zigzag course ٹیڑھا میڑھا *v.i.* (-gg-) move or be in a zigzag course پیچ و خم کھاتے ہوئے چلنا یا ہونا، ٹیڑھا میڑھا چلنا یا ہونا

zinc (zink) *n.* a non-rusting bluish white metal جست

Zingaro (*zing*-a-roh) *n.* (pl. *zingari*, pr. -ri) Italian name for a gipsy خانہ بدوش، جپسی

Zion (zi-on) *n.* Jerusalem صیہون، بیت المقدس، القدس بیت المقدس یروشلم its Holy Hill صیہون God's kingdom آسمانی بادشاہت **Zionism** *n.* movement culminating in the formation of the so-called Jewish state of *Israel* صیہونیت **Zionist** *n.* its supporter صیہونی

zip *n.* sharp whispering sound (as of a bullet going through the air) سنسناہٹ، سَن کی سی آواز **zipper, zip-fastener** *n.* fastener for clothes, bags, etc., worked by a catch on metal edges زِپ

zither (*zith*-ĕ*), **zithern** (*zith*-ĕ*n) *n.* flat, six-stringed musical instrument چھ تارا

zodiac (*zoh*-di-ak) *n.* imaginary belt of the sky divided into twelve equal parts (called the *signs of the zodiac*) through each of which the sun, moon and planets appear to pass in turn once a year منطقۃ البروج *sign of the zodiac* بُرج **Note :** The twelve *signs of the zodiac* are : *Aries* (or Ram) حمل (یا میکھ) *Taurus* (or Bull) ثور (یا برکھ) *Gemini* (or Twins) جوزا (یا متھن) *Cancer* (or Crab) سرطان (یا کرک) *Leo* (or Lion) اسد (یا سنگھ) *Virgo* (or Virgin) سنبلہ (یا کنیا) *Libra* (or Balance) میزان (یا تلا) *Scorpio* (or Scorpion) عقرب (یا برسچک) *Sagittarius* (or Archer) قوس (یا دھن) *Capricornus* (or Capricorn or Goat) جدی (یا مکر) *Aquarius* (or Water-carrier) دلو (یا کنبھ) *Pisces* (or Fishes) حوت (یا مین)

zonal *adj.* (see under **zone**)

zone (zohn) *n.* (old use) girdle پیٹی، کمربند any band of distinctive colour پٹی، دھاری، حلقہ area with distinctive features or special purpose عِلاقہ *war zone* جنگی عِلاقہ any one of the five divisions of the earth through imaginary longitudes منطقہ *arctic zone, frigid zone* منطقۂ باردہ *temperate zone* منطقۂ معتدلہ *torrid zone* منطقۂ حارّہ **zonal** (*zoh*-nel) *adj.* pertaining to zones عِلاقائی arranged in zones عِلاقہ وار

zoo (zoo) *n.* (short form for) zoological gardens enclosure where wild, living animals are kept for scientific study and public exhibition چڑیا گھر

zoology (zoh-*ol*-o-ji) *n.* branch of science studying the natural history of animals حیوانیات **zoological** (zoh-o-*loj*-i-kĕl) *adj.* of zoology حیوانیاتی *zoological gardens,* zoo چڑیا گھر **zoologist** (zoh-*ol*-o-jist) *n.* expert in zoology ماہرِ حیوانیات

zoom *n.* humming sound زناٹا *v.t.* & *i.* (of aircraft, bees, etc.) move with such sound زناتے سے گزر جانا (slang) force (aircraft) to ascend swiftly at a very steep angle ہوائی جہاز، تیزی سے سیدھا اُوپر لے جانا

zoophyte (*zoh*-o-fit) *n.* any kind of plant sea-animal (like sponge) نباتی حیوان

zounds (zoundz) *int.* (old use) (short form of God's wounds) لاحول ولاقوۃ

zymosis (zi-*moh*-sis) *n.* formentation of ge cause of disease تخمیر جراثیم ؛ جراثیمی **zymot** *mot*-ik) *adj.* (of disease) developing by zyn